P9-CDX-105

International Directory of

COMPANY
HISTORIES

International Directory of

COMPANY

HISTORIES

VOLUME 49

Editor

Jay P. Pederson

ST. JAMES
PRESS®

Detroit • New York • San Diego • San Francisco • Cleveland • New Haven, Conn. • Waterville, Maine • London • Munich

International Directory of Company Histories, Volume 49

Jay P. Pederson, Editor

Project Editor
Miranda H. Ferrara

Editorial
Erin Bealmear, Joann Cerrito, Jim Craddock,
Stephen Cusack, Peter M. Gareffa,
Kristin Hart, Melissa Hill,
Margaret Mazurkiewicz, Carol A. Schwartz,
Christine Tomassini, Michael J. Tyrkus

Imaging and Multimedia
Randy Bassett, Robert Duncan, Lezlie Light

Manufacturing
Rhonda Williams

LIBRARY OF CONGRESS CATALOG NUMBER 89-190943

ISBN: 1-55862-475-9

BRITISH LIBRARY CATALOGUING IN PUBLICATION DATA

International directory of company histories. Vol. 49
I. Jay P. Pederson
33.87409

Printed in the United States of America
10 9 8 7 6 5 4 3 2 1

CONTENTS _____

Preface . . . . page vii
List of Abbreviations ix

Company Histories

A. Schulman, Inc. 3
A.T. Cross Company 8
Adolf Würth GmbH & Co. KG 13
Alldays plc 16
Allied Worldwide, Inc. 20
Apartment Investment and Management
    Company 24
Archstone-Smith Trust 27
Autogrill SpA 31
Avery Dennison Corporation 34
AXA Colonia Konzern AG 41
Bayard SA 46
Benchmark Capital 50
Berkshire Realty Holdings, L.P. 53
Big Idea Productions, Inc. 56
Blimpie International, Inc. 60
British Energy Plc 65
BT Group plc 69
Cadbury Schweppes PLC 75
Cargolux Airlines International S.A. 80
Chanel SA 83
ChartHouse International Learning
    Corporation 87
Christian Dior S.A. 90
Computer Associates International, Inc. 94
Corus Group plc 98
Cybex International, Inc. 106
Dixons Group plc 110
Donaldson Company, Inc. 114
Dynegy Inc. 119
E.piphany, Inc. 123
Elior SA 126
Equity Residential 129
Equus Computer Systems, Inc. 133

Falconbridge Limited 136
First Aviation Services Inc. 140
FPL Group, Inc. 143
Gables Residential Trust 147
Gallaher Group Plc 150
Gambro AB 155
Gardner Denver, Inc. 158
Geberit AG 161
GFI Informatique SA 165
GfK Aktiengesellschaft 169
Global Outdoors, Inc. 173
Guangzhou Pearl River Piano Group Ltd. . . . 177
GulfMark Offshore, Inc. 180
Handspring Inc. 183
Hanna Andersson Corp. 187
Hilton Group plc 191
Hines Horticulture, Inc. 196
Hutchison Whampoa Limited 199
IAWS Group plc 205
Iberdrola, S.A. 209
Idemitsu Kosan Co., Ltd. 213
Ingram Industries, Inc. 217
ISS A/S 221
Jefferson Smurfit Group plc 224
Johnson Matthey PLC 230
Jones Lang LaSalle Incorporated 236
JPI 239
Karl Kani Infinity, Inc. 242
Land Securities PLC 246
Libbey Inc. 251
Madeira Wine Company, S.A. 255
Matalan PLC 258
Midwest Grain Products, Inc. 261
MPS Group, Inc. 264

National Starch and Chemical Company . . . 268
National Wine & Spirits, Inc. 271
Natrol, Inc. 275
Natural Alternatives International, Inc. 279
The Neiman Marcus Group, Inc. 283
Nolo.com, Inc. 288
Novar plc 292
Oakley, Inc. 297
OAO Siberian Oil Company (Sibneft) 303
Omnicare, Inc. 307
Opsware Inc. 311
Oregon Chai, Inc. 315
Penauille Polyservices SA 318
Phat Fashions LLC 322
Phillips, de Pury & Luxembourg 325
Pilot Corporation 328
The PMI Group, Inc. 331
R.C. Bigelow, Inc. 334
Ronson PLC 337
Royal Dutch/Shell Group 340
Sandia National Laboratories 345
The Sanofi-Synthélabo Group 349
Sappi Limited 352
Schering-Plough Corporation 356

Scottish Power plc 363
Shoppers Drug Mart Corporation 367
Société Tunisienne de l'Air-Tunisair 371
Sophus Berendsen A/S 374
SSL International plc 378
Steria SA 382
Tanger Factory Outlet Centers, Inc. 386
TDK Corporation 390
The Toronto-Dominion Bank 395
Transport Corporation of America, Inc. 400
Trinity Mirror plc 404
Triple Five Group Ltd. 411
Tsingtao Brewery Group 416
24/7 Real Media, Inc. 421
Uny Co., Ltd. 425
VA TECH ELIN EBG GmbH 429
ValueClick, Inc. 432
Vebego International BV 435
Velocity Express Corporation 438
Vought Aircraft Industries, Inc. 442
W.P. Carey & Co. LLC 446
William Hill Organization Limited 449
Woodward Governor Company 453
Yamato Transport Co. Ltd. 458

Index to Companies 463
Index to Industries 659
Geographic Index 695
Notes on Contributors 727

PREFACE

The St. James Press series *The International Directory of Company Histories (IDCH)* is intended for reference use by students, business people, librarians, historians, economists, investors, job candidates, and others who seek to learn more about the historical development of the world's most important companies. To date, *IDCH* has covered over 5,700 companies in 49 volumes.

Inclusion Criteria

Most companies chosen for inclusion in *IDCH* have achieved a minimum of US$25 million in annual sales and are leading influences in their industries or geographical locations. Companies may be publicly held, private, or nonprofit. State-owned companies that are important in their industries and that may operate much like public or private companies also are included. Wholly owned subsidiaries and divisions are profiled if they meet the requirements for inclusion. Entries on companies that have had major changes since they were last profiled may be selected for updating.

The *IDCH* series highlights 10% private and nonprofit companies, and features updated entries on approximately 45 companies per volume.

Entry Format

Each entry begins with the company's legal name, the address of its headquarters, its telephone, toll-free, and fax numbers, and its web site. A statement of public, private, state, or parent ownership follows. A company with a legal name in both English and the language of its headquarters country is listed by the English name, with the native-language name in parentheses.

The company's founding or earliest incorporation date, the number of employees, and the most recent available sales figures follow. Sales figures are given in local currencies with equivalents in U.S. dollars. For some private companies, sales figures are estimates and indicated by the abbreviation *est.* The entry lists the exchanges on which a company's stock is traded and its ticker symbol, as well as the company's NAIC codes.

Entries generally contain a *Company Perspectives* box which provides a short summary of the company's mission, goals, and ideals, a *Key Dates* box highlighting milestones in the company's history, lists of *Principal Subsidiaries, Principal Divisions, Principal Operating Units, Principal Competitors,* and articles for *Further Reading.*

American spelling is used throughout *IDCH,* and the word ''billion'' is used in its U.S. sense of one thousand million.

Sources

Entries have been compiled from publicly accessible sources both in print and on the Internet such as general and academic periodicals, books, annual reports, and material supplied by the companies themselves.

Cumulative Indexes

IDCH contains three indexes: the **Index to Companies**, which provides an alphabetical index to companies discussed in the text as well as to companies profiled, the **Index to Industries**, which allows researchers to locate companies by their principal industry, and the **Geographic Index**, which lists companies alphabetically by the country of their headquarters. The indexes are cumulative and specific instructions for using them are found immediately preceding each index.

Suggestions Welcome

Comments and suggestions from users of *IDCH* on any aspect of the product as well as suggestions for companies to be included or updated are cordially invited. Please write:

The Editor
International Directory of Company Histories
St. James Press
27500 Drake Rd.
Farmington Hills, Michigan 48331-3535

ABBREVIATIONS FOR FORMS OF COMPANY INCORPORATION

A.B.	Aktiebolaget (Sweden)
A.G.	Aktiengesellschaft (Germany, Switzerland)
A.S.	Aksjeselskap (Denmark, Norway)
A.S.	Atieselskab (Denmark)
A.Ş.	Anomin Şirket (Turkey)
B.V.	Besloten Vennootschap met beperkte, Aansprakelijkheid (The Netherlands)
Co.	Company (United Kingdom, United States)
Corp.	Corporation (United States)
G.I.E.	Groupement d'Intérêt Economique (France)
GmbH	Gesellschaft mit beschränkter Haftung (Germany)
H.B.	Handelsbolaget (Sweden)
Inc.	Incorporated (United States)
KGaA	Kommanditgesellschaft auf Aktien (Germany)
K.K.	Kabushiki Kaisha (Japan)
LLC	Limited Liability Company (Middle East)
Ltd.	Limited (Canada, Japan, United Kingdom, United States)
N.V.	Naamloze Vennootschap (The Netherlands)
OY	Osakeyhtiöt (Finland)
OAO	Otkrytoe Aktsionernoe Obshchestve (Russia)
OOO	Obshchestvo s Ogranichennoi Otvetstvennostiu (Russia)
PLC	Public Limited Company (United Kingdom)
PTY.	Proprietary (Australia, Hong Kong, South Africa)
S.A.	Société Anonyme (Belgium, France, Switzerland)
SpA	Società per Azioni (Italy)
ZAO	Zakrytoe Aktsionernoe Obshchestve (Russia)

ABBREVIATIONS FOR CURRENCY

$	United States dollar	KD	Kuwaiti dinar
£	United Kingdom pound	L	Italian lira
¥	Japanese yen	LuxFr	Luxembourgian franc
A$	Australian dollar	M$	Malaysian ringgit
AED	United Arab Emirates dirham	N	Nigerian naira
		Nfl	Netherlands florin
B	Thai baht	NIS	Israeli new shekel
B	Venezuelan bolivar	NKr	Norwegian krone
BFr	Belgian franc	NT$	Taiwanese dollar
C$	Canadian dollar	NZ$	New Zealand dollar
CHF	Switzerland franc	P	Philippine peso
COL	Colombian peso	PLN	Polish zloty
Cr	Brazilian cruzado	PkR	Pakistan rupee
CZK	Czech Republic koruny	Pta	Spanish peseta
DA	Algerian dinar	R	Brazilian real
Dfl	Netherlands florin	R	South African rand
DKr	Danish krone	RMB	Chinese renminbi
DM	German mark	RO	Omani rial
E£	Egyptian pound	Rp	Indonesian rupiah
Esc	Portuguese escudo	Rs	Indian rupee
EUR	Euro	Ru	Russian ruble
FFr	French franc	S$	Singapore dollar
Fmk	Finnish markka	Sch	Austrian schilling
GRD	Greek drachma	SFr	Swiss franc
HK$	Hong Kong dollar	SKr	Swedish krona
HUF	Hungarian forint	SRls	Saudi Arabian riyal
IR£	Irish pound	TD	Tunisian dinar
K	Zambian kwacha	W	Korean won

International Directory of
COMPANY
HISTORIES

✦. A. Schulman

A. Schulman, Inc.

3550 West Market Street
Akron, Ohio 44333-2699
U.S.A.
Telephone: (330) 666-3751
Toll Free: (800) 662-3751
Fax: (330) 668-7204
Web site: http://www.aschulman.com

Public Company
Incorporated: 1928
Employees: 2,331
Sales: $975.2 million (2001)
Stock Exchanges: NASDAQ
Ticker Symbol: SHLM
NAIC: 325211 Plastics Material and Resin
    Manufacturing; 325991 Custom Compounding of
    Purchased Resins; 326199 All Other Plastics Product
    Manufacturing

A relatively small plastics manufacturer, A. Schulman, Inc. is something of an anomaly in an industry dominated by huge diversified companies. The company concentrates on producing special plastic resins and compounds, color concentrates, and various specialty additives. Unlike its larger competitors, which derive profit from small margins on massive production runs of common plastics, A. Schulman produces high margin, special use plastics that demand the employment of special technologies and production methods. The company's plastic compounds are used in a variety of applications, including plastic bags and packaging materials for household products; automotive parts, such as steering wheels and bumper guards; consumer items, such as pens, soft drink coolers, and skateboards; office equipment, such as computer cases and trim for office chair arms; and agricultural products, such as greenhouse coverings and plastic mulch. A. Schulman also acts as a merchant, purchasing production overruns and surplus stocks of plastic materials and reselling them directly to customers through its marketing operations as a broker. Finally, as a distributor, A. Schulman, mainly through its European operations, sells plastic products of other companies, including ATOFINA, BASF Aktiengesellschaft, BP p.l.c., Exxon Chemical Ltd., Solvay S.A., and Vestolit GmbH & Co. KG. A. Schulman has very extensive operations in Europe, and 59 percent of its sales originated on that continent during fiscal 2001.

Roots in Rubber

The company was founded by Alex Schulman, who established a rubber brokerage in Akron, Ohio, in 1928. Working out of a small shop, Schulman purchased and resold wholesale and scrap rubber, which his customers would refashion into a variety of rubber products. While Schulman cultivated a clientele, the business remained small. The largest consumers of rubber were tire makers, automobile companies, and hose manufacturers. These companies purchased raw virgin rubber on a huge scale, providing few large sales opportunities for Schulman's enterprise.

In 1930, just as Schulman's business became stable, the nation was plunged into the Great Depression. Demand for most products, including rubber, fell precipitously. Before rubber stocks were depleted, prices nosedived, eliminating demand for used rubber. A few years later, when rubber became scarce, this demand recovered, providing some support to Schulman's business and enabling him to realize a small margin on his sales. The A. Schulman Company recovered from the Depression slowly, as Alex Schulman's business depended almost entirely on the successes and resources of his customers. Fortunately, Schulman was not crushed by fluctuations in the broader rubber market or larger final markets, as were many tire, automobile, and hose manufacturers.

By the late 1930s and early 1940s, the onset of war in Europe and then in the Pacific caused industrial demand for rubber to increase. Rubber was an important war commodity, and sources of rubber were limited. As a result, a premium was placed on companies that could recycle scrap rubber, producing a useful product from waste. A. Schulman and several other companies in the scrap rubber business were placed under the authority of a war production board that had responsibility for coordinating efficient production of essential commodities and setting prices. Often Schulman did not know who his customers ultimately were. While it took a few months to gain footing, Schulman's company went into full production, supplying mulched rubber for recasting into tires, window seals, and numerous other products.

1940s and 1950s: Expanding into Scrap Plastic and Then Plastics Manufacturing

The scarcity of rubber during the war helped to accelerate the development of substitute and synthetic rubber products. The most important of these is what we know today as plastic, which was extremely useful in small castings, exhibiting many of the same resilient and durable qualities as rubber. Although the primary ingredient in plastic was petroleum, also a crucial and limited war commodity, plastic like rubber could be recycled. As the war progressed, A. Schulman began to accept scrap plastic for chipping and shipment to casting mills. By the end of the war, A. Schulman had doubled its product line to include scrap rubber and scrap plastic. In 1950, having heard some convincing arguments from a young salesman named William Zekan, Schulman realized he stood on the threshold of a new industry.

Schulman hired Zekan in 1937 after meeting him on the golf course of the Rosemont Country Club, where the 18-year-old Zekan worked as a caddie. Although Zekan started at A. Schulman as an office boy, earning less than he could as a caddie, he stayed with the business and was promoted to salesman just before he enlisted in the army at the outbreak of the war. Zekan returned to the company after his tour, and in 1947 he was tapped by Schulman to head his New York sales office. Here the shy and reserved Zekan learned the art of sales. He honed his skills of persuasion, and later told *Chemical Week,* "The customer is going to buy, everything being equal, from the guy that he likes the best." Zekan performed exceptionally well in New York, and when he was called back to Akron in 1953, it was to take the number two position under Alex Schulman.

Schulman and Zekan developed a new strategy during this period to abandon the scrap markets and move the company into the plastics manufacturing business. Rather than molding its own products, A. Schulman would draw on its substantial reputation as a raw product supplier and concentrate on making plastic compounds. This product is manufactured in the form of pellets, smaller than peanuts. By applying heat, these pellets could be extruded or molded into many types of finished products.

The company grew considerably during the 1950s, mostly on the strength of cheap oil as well as the increasing number of applications for plastic. For the first time, automobile manufac-

turers began molding plastic parts for cars, including dashboards, interior side panel trim, and window insulation.

Searching for new growth markets, Schulman established a network of small plants in Britain, France, and Germany. There he hoped to get in on the ground floor of emerging industries in postwar Europe. The company later established a plant in Canada that served various plastics consumers in that country, including the automotive industry.

1960s Through 1980s: The Zekan Era

Alex Schulman died in 1962, and his will specified that Zekan should succeed him as president of the company. For his part, Zekan had become so deeply involved with executive decisions under Schulman that, despite the founder's sudden death, the transition to new leadership was smooth.

The 1960s were a period of strong growth for A. Schulman. It was during the decade after Schulman's death that the company began to really define its place in the industry. The company began to produce plastics, albeit in smaller quantities than competitors, with special characteristics. Often the tolerances of these products were specified in advance of manufacture by the customer. The company then instructed its laboratories to design a plastic to meet those specifications. Thus, with the employment of technology, A. Schulman was able to offer a limited quantity of plastics that could outperform other plastics.

As a major player in this vital niche market, A. Schulman was somewhat insulated from the competition elsewhere in the industry. Because A. Schulman dealt in a unique family of products, it was able to sell on quality and not price. This produced a new sales philosophy which, Zekan later told *Forbes,* was "We don't talk price, we talk quality."

The company's ability to build such a strong position in the market led Zekan to consider expansion. Rather than just the addition of production facilities, Zekan was concerned with innovations in his product line. Unable to adequately fund technological research internally, he went forward with plans to take the company public in 1972.

In 1973 an Arab-Israeli war triggered an oil embargo against the United States that caused the price of petroleum to skyrocket. For plastics producers like A. Schulman, this meant temporary shortages of raw materials and necessary price increases. While these price increases were ultimately passed along to the consumer, the net effect was a serious recession that forced many companies in the plastics industry to go out of business. A. Schulman remained insulated from much of this activity because it produced a product defined by quality and technology rather than simply by price. Nonetheless, the company did suffer some reverses because of the onset of recession.

By 1977 inflationary pressure had stabilized, but a second oil crisis two years later caused additional price shocks that continued to cut into demand. By 1982, automobile manufacturers had entered a prolonged period of serious financial trouble. Because they were large consumers of specialty plastics, A. Schulman's growth continued to lag. Hoping to tie its products to growing companies in the automotive industry, A. Schulman began cultivating relationships with Japanese plastics manufacturers,

Key Dates:

1928: Alex Schulman founds A. Schulman as a rubber brokerage in Akron, Ohio.
Mid-1940s: A. Schulman expands into scrap plastic.
1950s: Company begins manufacturing plastic compounds.
1962: Alex Schulman dies; William Zekan assumes company leadership.
1972: Company goes public.
1991: Zekan dies; Terry Haines takes over as CEO.
1998: Company opens its Product Technology Center in Akron, Ohio, and its Color Technology Center in Sharon Center, Ohio.
2000: Company ends production at its Akron plant.

with the intention of gaining supply contracts with Japanese car makers.

The timing was perfect. Several companies, including Honda and Toyota, began building large production facilities in the United States during this time. In 1988, A. Schulman established a joint venture with Japan's largest chemical company, the Mitsubishi Kasei Vinyl Company, and set up a new plastics plant at Bellevue, Ohio. With the help of Mitsubishi Kasei, A. Schulman concluded numerous supply contracts with Honda, Nissan, and Toyota.

The addition of new customers forced A. Schulman to modernize and expand its production facilities. The company spent $33 million to increase worldwide capacity by 25 percent. Still, the company avoided becoming overly reliant on only a few customers in a single industry. The company's five largest accounts comprised less than 10 percent of sales.

More Acquisitive Under Haines in the 1990s

Zekan had a hands-on leadership style and a genuine love of selling. He kept the reins of the company tightly in his hands, prompting some critics to fear that this concentration of power could leave a void in management. But A. Schulman had a highly capable second tier of management that would be put to the test and would ultimately rise to the challenge in 1989, when Zekan, aged 69, underwent surgery for treatment of cancer. It was at this juncture that Zekan promoted three senior managers in preparation for his retirement. One of these was Terry Haines, who was named president, while Zekan remained chairperson and CEO.

Retirement, however, never came. Zekan remained in charge of the company until his death in January 1991. Haines remained president and took on the duties of CEO as well. Robert Stefanko, who ran the finance department, was elected chairperson. With the death of Bill Zekan, A. Schulman, Inc. lost the last link to its founder. But it also marked the beginning of a new era.

While the company had shunned growth by acquisition for nearly its entire existence, A. Schulman took over the French plastics company Diffusion Plastique in August 1991. Initial integration of the business was difficult but ultimately success-

ful. In addition, the company's joint venture with Mitsubishi Kasei posted its first profit in 1992. That year A. Schulman posted its tenth consecutive record for annual net income and was ranked 12th on the *Fortune* 500 list of companies with highest total return over ten years, averaging 37.2 percent.

The run of earnings increases ended in 1993, however, as economic weakness in Europe and unfavorable exchange rates led to declines in both sales and earnings, the latter falling by 12 percent. Seeking new markets for growth, A. Schulman had earlier in the decade earmarked Mexico as a key market, opening an office in Mexico City in 1990. Around the same time of the passage of the North American Free Trade Agreement (NAFTA) in late 1993, A. Schulman announced plans to build a $15 million plant in Mexico. In September 1995 the compounding plant, located in San Luis Potosi, began operation, with a focus on serving the automotive and packaging sectors in Mexico. This was A. Schulman's 11th plant worldwide and its first in Latin America.

Domestically, A. Schulman turned to acquisitions to fuel growth in the mid-1990s. In 1994 the company acquired Nashville, Tennessee-based ComAlloy International Corp., an affiliate of Exxon Corporation's Exxon Chemical Company. Generating about $30 million in annual revenue, ComAlloy specialized in thermoplastics used in high-strength applications for the electrical, appliance, and automotive sectors. During 1995 Eastman Chemical Company sold its compound polypropylene business to A. Schulman. This unit produced colored and filled polypropylene and foam products that were used primarily in the manufacturing of injection-molded plastic automotive parts. A second acquisition in 1995 was that of Texas Polymer Service Inc., a division of J.M. Huber Corporation with annual revenues of $15 million. Based in Orange, Texas, the division supplied custom compounding, tolling services, and engineered plastics compounding. In November 1996 A. Schulman acquired the business and assets of a manufacturing plant in Sharon Center, Ohio, which became the location of the company's new Specialty Compounding Division. Both revenues and profits fell during fiscal 1996—with the latter tumbling by 21 percent—because of a steep drop in plastic resin prices, which led customers to reduce inventories, and also due to high start-up costs associated with the company's new initiatives in Mexico and elsewhere. Despite major auto strikes, the company recovered during fiscal 1997 thanks to improving market conditions, as profits increased from $42.2 million to $50.7 million.

Continuing its overseas expansion in the last years of the century, A. Schulman acquired the assets of a distributor and merchant in Warsaw, Poland, in August 1997; this business became the basis for a new Polish subsidiary. Later that year, the company acquired Isopolymer, Inc., which had been the distributor of A. Schulman products in Italy and which had annual sales of about $30 million. In January 1998, production began at a new plastics compounding plant in Surabaya, Indonesia, that had been built through a joint venture to serve the Asia-Pacific region. This was the firm's seventh plant located outside the United States. Also during 1998 the company opened an office in Hungary. Back home, the firm opened its Product Technology Center in Akron, Ohio, and its Color Technology Center in Sharon Center, Ohio, that same year. At the Product Technology Center, A. Schulman employees could work with customers to formulate custom compounds and, at the center's laboratories, create trial runs of customized products both to test the manufacturing process and to evaluate the end product. Similarly, the Color Technology Center was designed to provide customers with a full range of color services, aided by the staff and by a variety of equipment for analysis, color formulation, and testing. Similar technology centers were opened in Europe as well.

Partly in reaction to the company's difficulties during 1996, a powerful activist pension fund, the California Public Employees' Retirement System (CALPERS), identified A. Schulman as one of several "underperforming" public companies in a report issued in early 1998. CALPERS accused the company of speculating on resin prices, a criticism firmly denied by the company, and of failing to articulate a strategic plan for the company. The pension fund also called on the company to add more independent directors to the company board and to change the way the board was elected so that the entire board had to stand for election each year—the latter being one way to make a company takeover easier. Although A. Schulman refused to change the election rules, the firm did reduce the size of the board from 13 to 10, with the three departing members being company insiders; this gave a bigger percentage of seats to outsiders. The company also announced that it was working on a strategic plan and said that neither of the moves was in response to the pressure from CALPERS. Later in 1998, during the firm's annual meeting, shareholders approved a nonbinding resolution asking the board to consider adopting the annual election of all board members, but shareholders rejected a resolution that urged the board to "arrange for the prompt sale of A. Schulman, Inc. to the highest bidder." Such pressure from shareholders was inevitable given the poor performance of the company's stock over most of the bullish 1990s; one response of the company's board was to initiate an aggressive stock repurchasing plan to improve per share earnings.

A. Schulman continued an ongoing program of renovating and upgrading its manufacturing facilities, spending $35 million on capital expenditures in 1999, $32 million in 2000, and $33.4 million in 2001. During this period new manufacturing lines were added to the firm's plants in Givet, France; Nashville, Tennessee; and San Luis Potosi, Mexico. Additional capacity was gained through the purchase of a plant in Gorla Maggiore, Italy, in July 2000.

Early 21st-Century Struggles

After achieving record per share earnings of $1.51 in 1999, A. Schulman began faltering. The company recorded per share earnings of $1.25 and $0.43 in 2000 and 2001, respectively. Demand was down because of slowdowns in the world's economies, particularly the U.S. economy; profit margins were affected by the higher cost of plastic feedstocks; and A. Schulman, with its extensive European operations, was also being hit hard by the weakness of the euro. The company responded with an effort to save $15 million a year by cutting jobs, manufacturing lines (at least temporarily), and other operations. In December 2000 production was ended at the plant in Akron, Ohio, although the facility continued to be used for other functions, including warehousing, logistics, and the Product Technology

Center. This was the biggest cost-cutting move, and it involved the elimination of 129 jobs. The company also closed six district sales offices, centralizing such operations at the company headquarters. Also during 2001, product innovation continued at A. Schulman with the introduction of Invision, which the company called "a lightweight, soft-to-the-touch, environmentally friendly alternative to polyvinyl chloride."

With the more uncertain economic and political climate that followed in the wake of the events of September 11, 2001, the challenges facing A. Schulman were on the increase. Despite this, early encouraging results from fiscal 2002 led the company to make plans for renewed growth. Thus, in early 2002, the firm announced that it was in the early stages of planning for the establishment of manufacturing plants in Poland and China. With its history of innovation, a unique line of products, and a diversified customer base, A. Schulman was well positioned to begin a new era of steady growth.

Principal Subsidiaries

N.V. A. Schulman, Plastics, S.A. (Belgium); N.V. A. Schulman, S.A. (Belgium); A. Schulman, S.A. (France); A. Schulman Plastics, S.A. (France); Diffusion Plastique (France); A. Schulman GmbH (Germany); A. Schulman, Inc., Limited (U.K.); A. Schulman Canada Ltd.; A. Schulman Foreign Sales Corporation (U.S. Virgin Islands); Master Grip, Inc.; Gulf Coast Plastics, Inc.; A. Schulman AG (Switzerland); ASI Investments Holding Co.; ASI Akron Land Co.; A. Schulman International, Inc.; A. Schulman de Mexico, S.A. de C.V.; ASI Employment, S.A. de C.V. (Mexico); AS Mex Hold, S.A. de C.V. (Mexico); Texas Polymer Services, Inc.; Polyvin GmbH (Germany); A. Schulman Aschersleben GmbH (Germany); A. Schulman Polska Sp. z o.o. (Poland); A. Schulman Plastics S.p.A. (Italy); A. Schulman International Services N.V. (Belgium); A. Schulman Hungary Kft. (Hungary); PT A. Schulman Plastics, Indonesia (65%); The Sunprene Company (70%); A. Schulman Plastics S.L. (Spain); A. Schulman Europe GmbH (Germany).

Principal Competitors

Cabot Corporation; Ampacet Corporation; BASF Aktiengesellschaft; Imperial Chemical Industries PLC; ATOFINA; Hercules Incorporated; Rohm and Haas Company.

Further Reading

Brammer, Rhonda, "Ready to Roll?," *Barron's,* October 13, 1997, pp. 21–22.

Brockinton, Langdon, "Zekan's Rise from Office Boy to Chief Executive," *Chemical Week,* July 13, 1988, pp. 29+.

Byrne, Harlan S., "A. Schulman Inc.: Plastics Supplier Profits from Foreign Affairs," *Barron's,* November 19, 1990, pp. 53+.

Flint, Troy, "Schulman Sale Idea Gets Cool Response," *Cleveland Plain Dealer,* December 11, 1998, p. 1C.

Gleisser, Marcus, "A. Schulman Denies Calpers Charge of Underperformance," *Cleveland Plain Dealer,* February 25, 1998, p. 1C.

Higgs, Richard, "Mexican Market Keeps A. Schulman Growing," *Crain's Cleveland Business,* October 23, 1995, p. 14.

Lappen, Alyssa A., "You Just Work Your Heart Out," *Forbes,* March 5, 1990, pp. 74+.

Maturi, Richard J., ''Pssst! Plastics Is the Word for Growth at A. Schulman, Where Profits Are Compounding,'' *Barron's,* April 7, 1986, pp. 50+.

McFadden, Michael, ''A Plastics Play on the Dollar's Dip,'' *Fortune,* November 11, 1985, pp. 158+.

Slakter, Ann, and Homer Starr, ''Schulman: A Timely Switch to Plastics,'' *Chemical Week,* July 9, 1986, pp. 34+.

Yerak, Rebecca, ''A. Schulman Inc.'s Worst Days Passed, Bullish Analysts Say,'' *Cleveland Plain Dealer,* June 9, 1996, p. 3I.

——, ''Akron Firm Eyes Major Acquisition,'' *Cleveland Plain Dealer,* December 10, 1993, p. 1E.

——, ''Schulman Planning to Revamp Its Board,'' *Cleveland Plain Dealer,* April 15, 1998, p. 1C.

—John Simley
—update: David E. Salamie

A.T. Cross Company

One Albion Road
Lincoln, Rhode Island 02865-3700
U.S.A.
Telephone: (401) 333-1200
Fax: (401) 334-2861
Web site: http://www.cross.com

Public Company
Incorporated: 1916
Employees: 840
Sales: $123.5 million (2001)
Stock Exchanges: American
Ticker Symbol: ATX
NAIC: 339941 Pen and Mechanical Pencil
   Manufacturing; 422120 Stationery and Office Supplies
   Wholesalers

The largest and oldest manufacturer of fine writing instruments in the United States, A.T. Cross Company produces a broad line of high-quality pens, pencils, and other gift items and markets them in more than 140 countries worldwide. For decades a much-coveted status symbol, Cross writing instruments were first made in 1846, when Alonzo Townsend Cross founded the company. Over the ensuing century and a half, the Cross brand developed into one of the strongest names in U.S. business, becoming a fixture in homes and offices everywhere. A.T. Cross encountered rough sledding in the 1990s as sales of pens dramatically slowed, and the company hoped to return to its past glory in the early 21st century through the introduction of "hipper" new products and by diversifying outside its core area in order to evolve into a personal accessories firm.

Early History

Two generations of the Cross family directed the fortunes of A.T. Cross during its first six decades of business. The most famous of the Crosses and the man who lent his name to the enterprise was the company's founder, Alonzo Townsend Cross, a 19th-century English inventor who steered his family into pen manufacture in 1846 in the state of Rhode Island—the birthplace and headquarters of A.T. Cross Company. Though the formative efforts of Alonzo Townsend Cross and his descendants gave the company its name and a stable foundation upon which to build, another family—the Bosses—exerted greater influence over the history of A.T. Cross's development and controlled the company for a longer period of time. During most of the 1990s, the third generation of the Boss family, led by Bradford R. Boss and Russell A. Boss, superintended A.T. Cross's operation, having gained their executive positions atop the A.T. Cross corporate ladder by virtue of Walter Boss's acquisition of the company from the Cross family in 1916. From 1916 forward and from Walter Boss downward, the Boss family built Cross into one of the most recognizable brands in the history of American business.

For all intents and purposes, A.T. Cross, while under the stewardship of the Boss family, created the market for high-priced, prestigious pens in the United States, emerging as the first U.S. manufacturer of fine writing instruments with any appreciable might to compete in an arena dominated by foreign manufacturers. Before A.T. Cross's rise in the fine writing instrument field, the overwhelming majority of pens accorded any prestige were fountain pens manufactured more often than not in Europe; A.T. Cross changed all that with its slender, high-quality ballpoint pens, throwing aside consumer tastes of the past and creating a new trend that consumers wholly embraced.

In the years following the conclusion of World War II, ballpoint pens eclipsed fountain pens as the writing instrument of choice for those seeking the rarified air an elegant writing instrument could impart to its owner. It was a trend sparked by and benefited from by A.T. Cross, whose silver and gold metal pens and their lifetime warranty of superior performance were the rage for decades. The company was meticulous in its approach to the manufacture of mechanical pens and pencils, dictating exacting standards that A.T. Cross employees adhered to throughout the roughly 150 assembly steps involved in producing Cross writing instruments. Much of this assembly work was done by hand at the company's headquarters in Lincoln, Rhode Island, where skilled employees, each functioning as a quality-control expert, closely monitored the complicated pro-

Company Perspectives:

Cross is a rapidly evolving company, poised to ignite its business and be the innovative leader. We understand the importance of making our products relevant to today's consumer. We will provide consumers with distinctive and inspiring products to help them express their thoughts, feelings and style.

cess of making one of the world's most esteemed products. If a Cross writing instrument did not conform to manufacturing tolerances that were as precise as ensuring that engraved grooves were within one ten-thousandth of an inch of perfection, or if a Cross writing instrument demonstrated the slightest hint that its ink ball might clot, the product was summarily discarded. As a result, fewer than 2 percent of A.T. Cross's writing instruments were returned to the company's headquarters under its much publicized lifetime warranty.

Equally as important as A.T. Cross's emphasis on manufacturing a flawless product was the image associated with the company's writing instruments, which during the 20th century became synonymous with achievement, class, and sophistication. Cross writing instruments stood as ubiquitous symbols of distinction, prized gifts given to graduates, ascending corporate executives, and anyone else upon whom honor could be bestowed. The emergence of the Cross name as one of the most prestigious brand names in the business world was predicated on the company's renowned attention to the quality of its products and then successfully articulated by effective marketing.

Initial Public Offering in 1971

Underpinned by product quality and global name recognition, A.T. Cross evolved into the preeminent, stalwart force in its industry, dominating competitors and holding a tight grip on the market for fine writing instruments. Perennially, the company controlled 40 percent of the market for fine writing instruments, a market share that gave other writing instrument manufacturers little hope of ever mounting a successful attack on the industry leader. As the decades of Boss leadership progressed, A.T. Cross became increasingly stronger, entrenching itself as a manufacturer and marketer without rival. It was this powerful business force that converted to public ownership in 1971, ending its 125-year existence as a privately held company. In the wake of the company's first public stock offering, A.T. Cross succeeded as it never had before, posting record sales and record profits during the decade that followed its entry into the public spotlight. Between 1971 and 1981, A.T. Cross recorded an annually compounded growth rate of 19.6 percent in sales and an even more prodigious 21.6 percent in net income.

During the early 1980s, a national economic recession caused A.T. Cross's annual sales to dip nearly 10 percent and earnings more than 20 percent in 1982, but despite the temporary stain on the company's otherwise exemplary financial record since the 1971 initial public offering, Bradford and Russell Boss were sitting atop the largest and oldest maker of high-priced pens and pencils. Their company was the reigning cham-

pion in a $500-million-a-year market, but changes in A.T. Cross's structure and corporate strategy were being orchestrated by the two brothers that would alter the future course taken by their long-held family business.

1980s Diversification

The corporate strategy implemented during the early 1980s was born during the late 1970s, when the two Boss brothers were cruising Narragansett Bay in a chartered yacht after watching the America's Cup trials. It was the summer of 1977, and the two brothers were discussing A.T. Cross's business. At the time, their company derived 70 percent of its total sales from purchases of Cross products as gifts, which led the two Boss brothers to think about expanding and diversifying into other gift products. As the implications of their discussion on Narragansett Bay set in, the two brothers began to reshape their product lines to reflect and tap into the gift merchandising expertise acquired during the more than century-long existence of A.T. Cross, but six years would pass before Bradford and Russell Boss made their decisive move.

After years of contemplating what the appropriate acquisition for A.T. Cross to execute might be, the two brothers finally made their move in 1983. In October of that year, A.T. Cross acquired Mark Cross, Inc., a privately held company that coincidentally shared the Cross name with its new parent company. A.T. Cross paid $5.5 million for Mark Cross, a store-chain and mail-order retailer of high-priced luggage, handbags, briefcases, other leather goods, and assorted gifts. The bid to acknowledge its gift-business expertise gave A.T. Cross a chain of 17 company-and-licensee-owned retail stores and a mail-order business that added more revenue muscle to an enterprise already posting record financial results.

The acquisition of Mark Cross was followed by the purchase of a similarly oriented company, Manetti-Farrow, Inc., in 1987. During the years bridging these two acquisitions and the company's evolution into a business focused on the gift-giving market, A.T. Cross continued to flourish, becoming what one writing instrument retailer referred to as "a cleverly disguised gift manufacturer." Annual sales marched upward with each passing year, with the company's roughly 50 gold and sterling silver ballpoints, felt tips, desk sets, leather merchandise, and other gift products continuing to attract consumers. Known as a conservative company, Cross was methodically moving forward, yet recording financial growth that belied the staid and steady approach the nearly century-and-a-half-old business was pursuing. A.T. Cross confidently moved forward through the 1980s, reaching $247 million in sales and $36 million in net income by the end of the decade. As the 1990s neared, the road ahead appeared to lead toward continued success, prompting A.T. Cross's manager of product marketing to note in *Adweek's Marketing Week,* "We do not just catch on to a trend. We may not have the most timely approach, but we'll have the best-researched product."

Changes in the Early 1990s

The dynamics of the fine writing instrument market were changing, however, as A.T. Cross headed into the 1990s, and the changes underway would catch the venerable giant without a timely response to an emerging trend. Competition had begun

---

Key Dates:

1846: Alonzo Townsend Cross founds the company in Rhode Island.
1916: Walter Boss acquires the company from the Cross family.
1971: A.T. Cross Company goes public.
1983: Mark Cross, Inc., a leather goods retailer, is acquired.
1993: Mark Cross is sold to Sara Lee Corporation.
1996: Pen Computing Group is formed.
1998: Pen Computing Group introduces the CrossPad electronic notepad.
1999: Losses from the CrossPad total $24.3 million, leading to a $20.1 million loss for A.T. Cross; David G. Whalen is named president and CEO, becoming the first person outside the Boss family to head up the company in 83 years.
2000: Major restructuring is launched that includes the closing down of the firm's manufacturing and distribution facility in Ireland.
2001: Company shuts down the Pen Computing Group.

---

to intensify during the mid-1980s, with Germany's Mont Blanc, France's Waterman, and other European pen manufacturers such as Lamy, Aurora, and Ferrari gaining momentum. Pushing these companies forward was the reemergence of the fountain pen as a status symbol and widely desired writing instrument, the same type of pen that A.T. Cross had helped to vanquish from the marketplace three decades earlier. In the hearts and minds of consumers, the fountain pen was back, driving the wholesale sales of the once-obsolete product upward, as people across the country turned back the clock to purchase a product that possessed what one industry observer termed ''a beguiling combination of homespun utility, quiet glamour, and fashionable nostalgia.''

Wholesale sales of fountain pens doubled between 1986 and 1991, but A.T. Cross, a company that prided itself on its slow and sure strategy, did not flesh out its collection of slender ballpoints with fatter fountain pens until 1990, years after the surge in demand had begun. ''Cross had the market locked for so long they took it for granted,'' remarked one writing instrument retailer to a *Forbes* reporter several years after A.T. Cross introduced its ''Signature'' line of fountain pens. Financially, the company faltered, as annual sales and earnings fell from their record highs in 1989. By 1993, the $247 million in sales recorded in 1989 had fallen to $165 million, and net income had plunged from $36 million to $8 million, precipitous drops that caused widespread concern among A.T. Cross's executive management.

For a recovery, the fate of the company fell to the hands of Russell Boss, who began to reshape A.T. Cross during the early 1990s. Manufacturing processes were streamlined, parts inventories were reduced, and A.T. Cross employees were encouraged to take early retirement, all in the hope that the company's profitability could be restored. The changes effected saved A.T. Cross roughly $5 million annually, giving it a leaner look for the years ahead. Further changes were soon to follow, including the

divestiture of its Mark Cross subsidiary in 1993. Sold 10 years after it was acquired, Mark Cross was purchased by Sara Lee Corporation, a transaction that gave A.T. Cross $7 million, and occurred at the same time the company brought to market in record time the Cross ''Townsend'' line. Sporting the middle name of A.T. Cross's founder, the Townsend line featured fatter and heavier pens, both in ballpoint and fountain pen models, that were decorated in several shades of lacquer as well as gold and silver metal.

On the heels of these developments, A.T. Cross formed a new products division called the Pen Computing Group in 1996 to develop merchandise complementary to its core business. During his announcement to the press about the formation of the new division, Russell Boss explained his intentions to those in attendance, saying, ''In conjunction with leading high-technology companies, we will develop products that combine the functionality and beauty of our distinctive writing instrument products with state-of-the-art technology to meet the needs of this fast-growing market.'' With this new facet of its business providing an opportunity for growth in the future, A.T. Cross moved forward, past its 150th year of business and toward the late 1990s, still ranking as the dominant leader in its field.

Red Ink Flowing in the Late 1990s

Unfortunately, continued fierce competition and a significant slowdown in premium pen sales—sparked in part by the shift to computers—unleashed a dark period of declining sales and red ink in the late 1990s. Sales dropped steadily from the mid-1990s high of $191.1 million in 1995 to $127 million in 1999. The year 1997 brought the first of four straight years of net losses for A.T. Cross. Among a number of late 1990s cost-cutting moves was the closing down of the Manetti-Farrow subsidiary in 1997. The company also ventured unsuccessfully into the watch business in the late 1990s.

During this period, the much-ballyhooed Pen Computing Group had some initial success with its new product offerings but then the initiative fizzled out. Late in 1996 the division launched its first product, the Cross DigitalWriter, which was an inkless ''pen'' designed for writing on the screens of personal digital assistants (PDAs), such as the PalmPilot. During 1997 the Cross iPen debuted, generating $1 million in revenue that year. The iPen could be used to mark up and edit electronic documents on a Windows 95 PC, while at the same time performing all of the functions of a mouse. The most-hyped product that came out of the Pen Computing Group—and ultimately the biggest disappointment—was the CrossPad, an electronic notepad initially priced at $399 that enabled the user to capture electronic copies of handwritten notes and then transfer them to a PC for storing, organizing, and converting into computer text files. Developed in partnership with IBM and introduced in March 1998, the CrossPad enabled the pen Computing Group to achieve 1998 revenues of $25 million, or about 16 percent of overall company revenues. A.T. Cross's chief operating officer, John Buckley, told *Barron's* in June 1998 that the CrossPad had the potential to triple the company's revenues, comparing the product to the PalmPilot. Significant problems with the product's handwriting recognition software were one factor in a precipitous drop in sales in 1999, however, and the CrossPad racked up $24.3 million in losses that year, leading the company to post an overall net loss of $20.1

million. Late in 1999 production of the CrossPad was drastically reduced, and eventually, in 2001, the plug was pulled on the Pen Computing Group.

New Leadership for the New Century

In November 1999 David G. Whalen was named president and CEO of A.T. Cross. Whalen, who had been head of the North American unit of upscale sunglasses maker Ray-Ban Sun Optics, became the first person outside the Boss family to head up the company in 83 years. At the same time, Russell Boss became company chairman, and Ronald Boss was named chairman emeritus. Despite the passing of the leadership baton, Boss family interests remained in firm ownership control of the firm through their 25 percent stake in the company and their power to elect two-thirds of the board as a result of their full control of the Class B shares.

The new leader moved quickly in an attempt to turn around the company's fortunes. Early in 2000 A.T. Cross launched a restructuring of its writing instruments operations. The company's plant in Ballinasloe, Ireland, which had been in operation since 1972, was closed, and writing instrument manufacturing and distribution was consolidated at the company headquarters in Lincoln, Rhode Island. Approximately 160 jobs were cut from the payroll, and the company took a $19.9 million restructuring charge. For the year, A.T. Cross posted a net loss of $8.1 million on revenues of $130.5 million. Other developments during the year included the introduction of a new corporate logo to be used worldwide, replacing several variations that had been in use, and a renewed emphasis on new product development. New products accounted for 20 percent of revenues in 2000, a doubling from the 10 percent level of the previous year. Among the introductions was a new pen line called Morph, which featured adjustable grips. Also on the increase were sales through the company's website, cross.com, with online revenues tripling from 1999 to 2000.

Results for 2001 were something of a mixed bag. Revenues declined 5.4 percent as a result of difficult economic conditions, particularly during the second half of the year and in the wake of the events of September 11. Declines in corporate gift giving, which generally accounted for more than 20 percent of the company's business, had a significant effect on revenues. On the bright side, A.T. Cross eked out a profit, reporting net earnings of $980,000. A hip new ad campaign and slick new packaging supported a slew of new product offerings, and revenue from new products reached 30 percent. Introduced during 2001 were the Ion, a futuristic-looking chrome-plated pen that was about two inches long and used gel ink; and the MicroPen, which combined a ballpoint pen with a stylus tip that could used with most PDA models.

The 57 percent decline in profits that A.T. Cross suffered during the first quarter of 2002 showed that the firm's turnaround was far from complete. New products continued to be rolled out, however, including an innovative new multifunctional pen called the Cross Matrix that was aimed at the Generation X crowd. As part of an attempt to evolve into a personal accessories company, A.T. Cross returned to the watch field in January 2002 with the debut of a new line of Cross watches for the corporate gift-giving market. A.T. Cross was also seeking new distribution channels for its products. Among new retail channels in the United States were Franklin Covey and CompUSA outlets, and the company was also investigating a return to department stores, a retail sector it had previously had difficulty with.

Principal Subsidiaries

ATX Marketing Company; ATX International, Inc.; A.T. Cross Export Company Limited (Virgin Islands); A.T. Cross Limited (Ireland); A.T. Cross (Canada), Inc.; A.T. Cross (Europe), Limited (U.K.); A.T. Cross Espana, S.A. (Spain); A.T. Cross Deutschland GmbH (Germany); Cross Company of Japan, Ltd.

Principal Competitors

Société BIC; Compagnie Financière Richemont AG; The Gillette Company; Newell Rubbermaid Inc.; S.T. Dupont S.A.; Faber-Castell AG.

Further Reading

Arditi, Lynn, "Cross Closes Leather Seller," *Providence Journal-Bulletin,* July 11, 1997, p. F1.

Barmann, Timothy C., "A.T. Cross Drops Prices on Electronic Cross-Pads," *Providence Journal,* February 4, 1999, p. G1.

——, "A.T. Cross Is Crossing Over: It Has Devised a Writing Instrument for Computer Use," *Providence Journal-Bulletin,* December 5, 1996, p. G1.

——, "Prophet and Loss," *Providence Journal,* April 27, 2001, p. G1.

DeMaio, Don, "Cross Points to New Line of Pens for Turnaround," *Providence Business News,* May 9, 1994, p. 3.

Henderson, Barry, "Mightier Than the Pen," *Barron's,* June 8, 1998, pp. 24, 26.

"High-Class Recession: A.T. Cross Sales and Profits Dip," *Fortune,* March 7, 1983, p. 8.

Leibowitz, David S., "Dream Holdings Redux," *Financial World,* February 18, 1992, p. 87.

——, "Will What Went Down Go Back Up Again?," *Financial World,* February 16, 1993, p. 82.

Levine, Joshua, "Pen Wars," *Forbes,* January 6, 1992, pp. 88 +.

Love, Martin, "Two Bosses, Two Crosses," *Forbes,* December 5, 1983, p. 66.

Maremont, Mark, "Kazarian Presses Cross's Owners amid Red Ink at Pen Maker," *Wall Street Journal,* November 16, 1999, p. C1.

Merrick, Barbara Lambert, *Writing History: The A.T. Cross Company and the Making of a New England Industry,* Boston: D.R. Godine, 1996.

Michals, Debra, "How Cross Pens Keep the Black Ink Flowing," *Business Week,* August 18, 1986, p. 58.

Oliver, Brian, "The Penpushers," *Marketing,* October 10, 1991, p. 29.

Pare, Michael, "Russell A. Boss: A.T. Cross Drawing Fine Line to Future Gains," *Providence Business News,* May 22, 1995, p. 2.

"Pen Maker to Post Drop in Net Income and Sales," *Wall Street Journal,* July 12, 1996, p. 2.

Schuman, Michael, "Thin Is Out, Fat Is In," *Forbes,* May 9, 1994, pp. 92 +.

Tooher, Nora Lockwood, "We've Been Going the Wrong Way for Three and One-Half Years," *Providence Journal-Bulletin,* June 21, 1994, p. 1.

Toth, Deborah, "A.T. Cross Gets the Lead Out and Expands into Fine-Point Mechanical Pens," *Adweek's Marketing Week,* May 29, 1989, p. 32.

Trachtenberg, Jeffrey A., "The Not-So-Ugly Americans," *Forbes,* December 1, 1986, p. 212.

Wyss, Bob, "A.T. Cross Appoints Ray-Ban Executive New Boss," *Providence Journal,* November 9, 1999, p. E1.

——, "A.T. Cross Slashes CrossPad," *Providence Journal,* October 22, 1999, p. F1.

——, "Court Ordered to Take Second Look at Fraud Suit," *Providence Journal,* April 16, 2002, p. E1.

——, "Cross Lays Off Workers in Ireland," *Providence Journal,* February 19, 2000, p. B.

——, "Cross Sketches Its Future," *Providence Journal-Bulletin,* April 24, 1998, p. F1.

——, "Cross Words No Puzzle: Kazarian May Have a Takeover in Mind," *Providence Journal,* January 24, 2001, p. E1.

——, "New CEO Hopes to Put His Brand on A.T. Cross," *Providence Journal,* November 16, 1999, p. E1.

——, "Seeking a New Boss: Cross Will Pen a New Chapter When It Hires Its New CEO," *Providence Journal,* April 23, 1999, p. H1.

——, "Straight to the Point: A.T. Cross Changes Logo," *Providence Journal,* September 9, 2000, p. B1.

——, "Underperforming A.T. Cross Pummeled by Market," *Providence Journal,* September 11, 1998, p. F1.

—Jeffrey L. Covell
—update: David E. Salamie

DER MONTAGEPROFI

Adolf Würth GmbH & Co. KG

Reinhold-Würth-Str. 12-16
D-74653 Künzelsau-Gaisbach
Germany
Telephone: (+49) 79-40-15-0
Fax: (+49) 79-40-15-10-00
Web site: http://www.wurth.com

Private Company
Incorporated: 1945
Employees: 37,398
Sales: EUR 5.28 billion (2001)
NAIC: 332722 Bolt, Nut, Screw, Rivet, and Washer
Manufacturing

Adolf Würth GmbH & Co. KG is the world's leading distribution group specialized in the fasteners market—that is, screws, nuts, and bolts, and other accessories—which is also the company's original product line. Yet Würth offers a far-ranging, diversified line of more than 50,000 products, many of which are marketed under the company's and its subsidiaries' brand names. These products include hand tools and power tools and machines; automotive products, including aftermarket parts and fittings; paints and related products; fittings for the furniture and construction industries; as well as water and heating pipes and systems and heating and air conditioning systems. The company also owns a publishing house and distributes work clothing. Würth typically targets the professional crafts market, but also supplies to mid- and large-scale businesses. Since the late 1990s the company has been branching out to supply the OEM and DIY markets. The Würth Group is composed of more than 265 companies—about half of which operate under their own names as part of the company's Allied Companies division. Würth is present on five continents and 80 countries, with more than 37,000 employees and sales of EUR 5.28 billion. After nearly 60 years in business, Würth remains a privately held company owned by the founding Würth family, represented by Reinhold Würth, son of the company founder and the chief architect of its growth into one of the largest distribution companies in Germany. While Würth remains ac-

tive in the company, it is now run by Chairman Dr. Walter Jaeger and CEO Harald Unkelbach.

Fastening Success in the 1950s

In the aftermath of World War II, Adolf Würth, who had spent some 20 years as a screws and fasteners salesman, set up his own wholesale business, in the town of Künzelsau. Würth's business remained a small one, although he was joined by son Reinhold, who, at the age of 14 became the company's first apprentice. At the age of 17, Reinhold Würth received his wholesale and retail trade license. By then, however, the younger Würth was already somewhat of a veteran traveling salesman for the company.

The early 1950s was a time of vast reconstruction in Germany and the Würth business was one of many similar businesses. Adolf Würth's management of the business was described as "conservative." Indeed, by the early 1950s, the business was posting annual sales of just DM 170,000, the equivalent of approximately $80,000.

Adolf Würth died in 1954, leaving Reinhold Würth, then 19 years old, to take over the family business. The younger Würth proved a more dynamic businessman and quickly expanded the business's operations beyond the Künzelsau region. By 1955, the company had boosted its sales to DM 176,000, a rise of more than 20 percent in just one year. From then on, Würth set a goal for his business of achieving double-digit sales growth each year—a record the company was to maintain, for the most part, throughout its history.

The extraordinary growth of the German economy and the success of its industry in the postwar decades created a booming demand for Würth's core fasteners—the screws, nuts, and bolts that were literally required to rebuild the country. Würth quickly spread throughout Western Germany, eventually opening more than 80 branch offices.

The economic boom, meanwhile, had spread throughout Western Europe, and by the early 1960s, Würth determined to expand the company internationally. The company made its first foreign expansion move in 1962, when it launched a subsidiary

---

Company Perspectives:

"Visions set unexpected energy free." Würth Trading Group wants to massively extend its share in the world market of assembly technology.

---

in The Netherlands. That first operation was quickly followed in other countries throughout Europe, including Italy, Switzerland, Austria, and Belgium. In 1965, Würth restructured the company into a limited partnership, wholly owned by the Würth family.

Having expanded throughout Europe in the 1960s, the company next began preparing to enter farther-flung markets. In 1969, the company entered the United States—the world's single largest fasteners market—with the launch of The Würth Screw and Fastener Corporation. Based in Monsey, New York, the subsidiary initially limited its sales area to New York, Connecticut, New Jersey, and Massachusetts, but quickly grew to cover much of the northeastern region. One year later, Würth opened a subsidiary in South Africa as well. By then the company had grown beyond its original headquarters, and in 1969 Würth moved into a new facility in the Gaisbach area of Künzelsau.

Würth entered the 1970s with sales of DM 53 million. Despite a setback in 1975—the only year the company saw negative sales growth—by the end of the decade, Würth's revenues had leapt to DM 330 million. Reinhold Würth continued to set ambitious goals for the company, announcing his determination to raise revenues to more than DM 1 billion by the middle of the 1980s. Aiding the company's growth was its steady international expansion, including the establishment of its first subsidiary operation in Australia in 1981. Acquisitions of existing businesses played a key role in Würth's development, such as the purchase of Winzer Industrial in 1986 and Monks and Crane, a leading engineering distributor, in 1990, both in the United Kingdom. By 1985, Würth had reached its DM 1 billion goal. Two years later, after the company's sales had climbed to DM 1.3 billion, Würth announced a new company goal—that of reaching the DM 10 billion mark by the year 2000.

To fulfill that goal, Würth completed its first bond issue, raising a loan of CHF 75 million. The company continued its international expansion, notably in Asia, where it acquired a Japanese company to establish itself in that market in 1987, and in Malaysia, where the company launched a new subsidiary the same year. Closer to home, the company expanded into the former Eastern Germany only months after the country's reunification in 1990.

Global Leader for the 21st Century

The 1990s were to be an era of strong growth for Würth as it worked toward Reinhold Würth's "Vision 2000." In 1992, the company moved to a new, DM 60 million headquarters in Gaisbach-Künzelsau. That building also featured an art museum, the Museum of Modern Art of the 20th Century, open to the public and featuring Reinhold Würth's extensive art collection—numbering more than 5,500 works, including the works of Picasso, Christo, Hrdlicka, and others.

Reinhold Würth retired from active management in 1994, saying: "I didn't want to destroy through a possible obstinacy of old age what I had been building up by then." Nonetheless, Würth remained an active advisor to and ambassador for the company as it continued its worldwide expansion. Beginning the decade with the equivalent of EUR 1.5 billion (about DM 3 billion) in sales, Würth's sales had jumped to EUR 2.2 billion by 1995.

Much of the company's growth during the period came through an aggressive acquisition campaign, helping the company build up its market position in the highly fragmented market. Many of the company's acquisitions enabled it to enter and reinforce its position in new markets, beyond its traditional fasteners business, such as the 1989 purchase of Sartorius, a tools manufacturer originally founded in Dusseldorf in 1879. Würth added production capacity to its distribution business with the purchase of L & C Arnold, based in Ernsbach, in 1994.

A feature of many of Würth's acquisitions was the company's willingness to keep existing management in place, often allowing the new subsidiary to continue to trade under its own name. In this way, Würth encouraged its subsidiaries, most of which had been founded and remained managed by entrepreneurs like Reinhold Würth, to maintain their entrepreneurial culture. This feature helped attract a number of the company's acquisitions, particularly at the turn of the century as the beginnings of a consolidation phase began to take hold in the fasteners industry. Because Würth remained a steadfastly private company, acquisitions were always paid for in cash—another attractive feature for many of the company's acquisition targets. The company's cash-purchase policy led Würth to complete several more bond offerings through the decade. Yet the company's private status meant that it was able to plow profits back into the business.

Würth opened an enlarged distribution facility in 1996, with 52,000 meters of floor space, at a cost of DM 60 million. That facility helped to support the company's strong growth over the following year, in which the company added more than DM 1 billion in sales. By then, the United States represented a rapidly growing share of the company's business, as Würth adopted a new strategy of focusing growth on that market. In 1996, the company acquired Revcar Fasteners, based in Roanoke, Virginia, signaling the start of Würth's intention to take part in the consolidation of the U.S. fastener market.

The Revcar acquisition was to be the first of a flurry of U.S. purchases extending through the end of the decade. In 1997, Würth's acquisitions included Eastern Fastener Corporation, founded in 1962, as a distributor of marine hardware, and the Baer Supply Company, founded in Chicago in 1950, as a distributor of cabinet and furniture fasteners and fittings. Adams Nut & Bolt and Snider Bolt & Screw also were added that year. Other notable U.S. acquisitions included the purchases of Service Supply Co., based in Indiana, and Action Bolt & Tool, based in Florida, in 1999.

A number of acquisitions had not only enabled Würth to consolidate its position in its domestic market, but also helped it grow into one of that country's largest distribution firms. Among the company's acquisitions of the period were the addi-

Key Dates:

1945: Adolf Würth founds a small screw and bolt distribution business in Künzelsau, Germany.
1954: Reinhold Würth takes over Adolf Würth GmbH & Co. after his father's death.
1962: Company establishes its first international subsidiaries in The Netherlands and Switzerland before extending throughout Europe.
1969: Company establishes its first business in the United States, The Würth Screw and Fastener Corporation.
1970: Würth launches a subsidiary in South Africa.
1981: A subsidiary is opened in Australia.
1985: Company tops sales of DM 1 billion for the first time, and sets the goal of reaching DM 10 billion (EUR 5 billion) by 2000.
1987: Company expands into Asia with the purchase of a business in Japan and establishment of a subsidiary in Malaysia.
1992: Company moves into new corporate headquarters that also houses an art museum.
1994: Reinhold Würth retires from active management of the company.
1996: Company begins an acquisition drive in the United States with the purchase of Revcar Fasteners.
2000: Würth tops EUR 5 billion in sales; now forecasts rise in sales to up to EUR 15 billion by 2010.

tion of L & C Arnold in 1994, a manufacturer of furniture-grade and other fasteners, founded in 1898. In 1995, Würth acquired Hahn + Kolb GMBH, which also was preparing to celebrate its 100th anniversary. In 1996, Würth added Fega, or Fränkische Elektrogrosshandlung Ansbach, founded in 1978; the following year, the company acquired Mepla-Werka, a specialist in furniture fittings and inventor of the concealed hinge, and Conmetall, based in Celle, founded in 1976.

Helping to finance these acquisitions was the completion of the company's largest ever bond issue, worth EUR 150 million. The influx of capital enabled the company to continue its acquisition drive in 2000, buying up Schossmetall Gruppe, founded in 1953 in Salzburg, and Uni Elektro, founded in 1970

through the merger of three existing businesses. These purchases, along with others—the company had acquired nearly 100 companies worldwide since 1998—helped the company match its Vision 2000 goal, as it topped the EUR 5 billion mark that year.

Würth was not prepared to rest on its laurels, however. Already the world's leading distributor of fasteners and related products, with a 4 percent share of the global market, Reinhold Würth announced his latest "Vision 2001," calling for the company to increase its market share by as much as 16 percent and its sales to as high as EUR 15 billion by the year 2010.

Principal Subsidiaries

Wuerth Israel Ltd; Würth á Islandi ehf (Iceland); Würth Albania Ltd. (Albania); Würth Argentina S.A.; Würth Armenia; Würth Australia Pty. Ltd.; Würth Aztur Ltd.Sti. (Azerbaijan); Würth Belarus Ltd.; Würth Belux N.V. (Belgium); Würth Bulgaria Ltd.; Würth Canada Ltd.; Würth Chile Ltda.; Würth Danmark Montageteknik A/S; Würth do Brasil Peças de Fixaçao Ltda; Würth Estonia A.S.; Würth France S.A.; Würth Guangzhou (China); Würth International Trading Co. Ltd. (Shanghai); Würth Oy, Riihimäki (Finland); Würth Tehran Ldt. (Iran); Würth-Hrvatska d.o.o. (Croatia).

Principal Competitors

Daniel Measurement and Control Inc.; Textron Inc. (TXT); Illinois Tool Works Inc.; Nucor Corporation; Kanthal AB; Textron Fastening Systems; Metaldyne Corp.; Hilti AG; Textron Fastening Systems Inc.; TT Electronics plc; ACCO Brands Inc.; SPS Technologies Inc.; Fastenal Company; Premier Farnell plc; Harbour Group Ltd.; McKechnie Group; Fairchild Corp.; Gunnebo AB; Stanley-Bostitch Inc.

Further Reading

Ball, Robert, "Unsung Champions," *Time International,* September 30, 1996, p. 3.
Fraza, Victoria, "The Würth of North America," *Industrial Distribution,* March 1999, p. 96.
Keough, Jack, "Merger Activity Is Finally Slowing Down," *Industrial Distribution,* March 2000.

—M. L. Cohen

Alldays plc

Alldays House
Chestnut Ave
Chandlers Ford
Eastleigh, Hampshire SO53 3HJ
United Kingdom
Telephone: (+44) 23-8064-5000
Fax: (+44) 23-8064-5111
Web site: http://www.alldays.co.uk

Public Company
Incorporated: 1998
Employees: 10,196
Sales: 524.9 million ($839.8 million) (2001)
Stock Exchanges: London
Ticker Symbol: ALD
NAIC: 445120 Convenience Stores

Alldays plc is one of the United Kingdom's leading operators of convenience stores. The company's network includes more than 630 stores—at least 600 of which are owned directly by the company. Alldays has positioned itself as a "top-up" marketer, that is, the place for customers to come in order to buy items forgotten during a supermarket shopping trip. As such, the company's stores feature a relatively wide range of products, but most product categories are limited to a single brand name. The company also features various convenience amenities, such as in-store ATM machines; postal services; bakeries, featuring L'Art du Pain bakeoff facilities; and "Movie Nights" video and DVD rental outlets. Alldays also owns and operates eight gasoline stations. Average store size in the Alldays network is 1,750 square feet. Confectionery, tobacco, and newsstand sales make up the largest percentage of the company's revenues, at 60 percent. Yet Alldays has begun stepping up its presentation of fresh and chilled foods, both of which deliver higher-margin sales. Alldays stumbled hard after an aggressive expansion drive in the 1990s, which saw the company's retail network swell to nearly 1,100 stores. A restructuring effort permitted the company to return to operational profits in 2001, yet a heavy debt burden, the result of a store buyback and

disposal program begun in the late 1990s, left the company with continued net losses. Alldays aborted a plan to sell off the company at the end of 2001, and instead has focused on renewed growth, including attracting new franchise outlets, as well as a redesigned store format and product offering. Alldays is led by CEO Stuart Lawson and non-executive Chairman Alan Cole. The company is traded on the London stock exchange.

Wholesale to Retail Group in the 1990s

Alldays' origins lie in the wholesale food trade in Scotland. The company was originally formed as Watson & Philip in the late 1960s and became one of the principal wholesale food suppliers to the VG and Spar supermarket chains, distributing to nearly 200 stores throughout Scotland. The company also developed its own network of wholesale trade cash and carry stores under the Trademarket name. After going public, Watson & Philip branched out into two additional directions, catering services and convenience stores, the latter operated under the VG and Spar banners. By the late 1980s, Watson & Philip had built up its own network of 37 convenience stores. The company's total sales reached £250 million.

In 1991, Watson & Philip merged with another food wholesaler, Amalgamated Foods. That company had built up a complementary business to Watson & Philip, supplying the VG and Spar supermarket network in England, and specifically in the Midlands, East Anglia, and southeast regions. Amalgamated reached some 900 stores in all, and had also developed its own retail network of about 30 convenience stores, with sales of around £175 million by the beginning of the 1990s. While both merger parties initially kept their own names and management, the deal was in fact a takeover of Amalgamated by Watson & Philip, then led by Chairman Ian Macpherson.

Watson & Philip placed its name across the whole of its operations. The company's convenience store network, which now neared 70 stores, maintained the Spar and VG banners for the time being. But the acquisition of Amalgamated had also brought the company a new banner, "All-day," developed by Amalgamated as a sub-brand for its retail store network. Soon after the acquisition Watson & Philip decided to adopt the

Alldays banner for all of its stores. The company meanwhile continued to build on its wholesale side, particularly with the opening of a new depot in Aberdeen in 1991 that gave the company frozen and chilled food capacity.

The Amalgamated acquisition signaled the start of a transition away from Watson & Philip's wholesale operations, hard hit by the long recession in the United Kingdom at the beginning of the 1990s. Instead, the company placed its growth prospects on its retail division, and determined to expand its network of convenience stores. Since the Amalgamated acquisition, Watson & Philip had continued adding to its network, topping 100 stores in 1993. That year, however, saw the company make a big step toward achieving its goal of creating a nationwide chain of convenience stores when it paid £21 million to acquire the U.K. Circle K convenience store chain operations.

Circle K added more than 200 stores to the Watson & Philip network, bringing the company's total store numbers over 300, some 80 of which were franchised stores. The company maintained the Circle K banner for a time as it tested new store formats for both Alldays and Circle K in an effort to determine which had the greatest appeal for the U.K. consumer public.

Convenient Focus in the 21st Century

The acquisition of Circle K brought Watson & Philip in conflict with the Spar/VG buying network, as Circle K belonged to the rival Nisa Today buying network. Despite the company's denials that it would leave Spar/VG, the breakup appeared inevitable, and by the end of 1993, the company had severed its ties with Spar/VG, subcontracting its distribution activities to a group of third-party distributors. Soon after, Watson & Philip pulled out of the Nisa Today buying network as well, a move that underlined its determination to redevelop itself as a focused retail store group. After Macpherson became ill, David Bremner took over as company CEO.

By 1994, Watson & Philip had decided to rebrand all of its stores—which included a number of Spar and VG stores—as Alldays. The company not only rolled out the new banner across the network, it also launched a new store design, placing more of an emphasis on fresh foods. The company's departure from its former buying groups also enabled it to change its product range—which had been built around Spar and Nisa private labels—to feature more prominently the major brand names.

With nearly 350 Alldays stores by the middle of 1994, Watson & Philip had created the United Kingdom's first nationally operating convenience store chain. By then, the company had begun to dispose of the remaining parts of its former wholesale business, pulling its Trademarket cash and carry arm out of England (that division was sold to Booker in 1999),

focusing that business around six stores in Scotland and a single store in northern England.

The company now turned its major focus on its retailing arm, promising an aggressive growth policy—indeed, by the end of that year the company had added more than 50 new stores, and promised up to 70 new stores per year, with a goal of topping 1,000 stores throughout the United Kingdom. As Bremner told *Grocer*: "We think there are about 7,000 perfect locations for c-stores. If we get 1,000 over a sensible period of time, that gives us a 15% share of the market."

In order to fuel this expansion, Watson & Philip developed its own—controversial—franchising concept. Instead of a more standard franchise network, the company created a series of so-called Regional Development Companies (RDC). Each RDC operated as an independent company, capable of borrowing capital to pursue its expansion. Each RDC was initially created around a hub of four to six stores "loaned" by Watson & Philip; an individual RDC was encouraged to grow, however, to a maximum of 40 stores. Bank loans arranged by an RDC were backed by Watson & Philip, while new constructions were carried out as joint ventures with construction companies.

Watson & Philip's foodservice distribution wing continued to grow through the mid-1990s, and that division became one of the United Kingdom's main players in the sector. The company also began foodservice distribution onto the European continent, although international operations remained a small part of the division's business. Instead, Watson & Philip heightened its focus on its convenience store network, which, under the RDC plan, began to grow strongly. By the end of the year, the company had opened more than 100 new stores—of which 77 were franchised stores. During this time, the company closed 22 existing stores as it shuffled its geographic mix, bringing its total at the end of the year to 450 stores. Aiding the growing network was the launch of the British National Lottery. Alldays was quick to place ticket terminals in its stores, boosting revenues with the accompanying license fees, but also increasing traffic into the stores.

The company began 1996 with the announcement of opening an additional 100 stores—a figure reached by the end of the year. Yet in October of that year the company was forced to post a quarterly profit warning—largely due to expansion efforts in its foodservice division. While the company quickly recovered, the profit warning suggested growing trouble for the company. Aggressive growth had begun to drain its resources; meanwhile, despite the aggressive expansion of the convenience store network, like-for-like sales were growing more slowly, by just 1 percent.

New CEO Colin Glass, who took over after Bremner joined supermarket group Sainsburys, managed to revive the company's like-for-like sales growth, which climbed to a respectable 6 percent by 1997. The company was also boosted by a deal made with Total Oil placing Alldays convenience shops in up to 250 Total gasoline stations across the United Kingdom. Under Glass, the company stepped up its franchise campaign. By the end of 1997, the company's franchise network featured 31 RDCs, which operated 300 stores, out of a company total of 759 stores. The company itself owned only 252 stores, with the rest operated by non-RDC franchises. Yet by then, stock market

Key Dates:

1991: Wholesale foodservices group Watson & Philip merges with another food wholesaler, Amalgamated Foods; all of the company's stores are placed under the ''Alldays'' banner.

1993: Company acquires 200 Circle K stores for £21 million as it begins its transition into a retail convenience store group.

1994: All of company's stores are rebranded as Alldays stores; company sells most of its Trademarket wholesale cash-and-carry operations.

1995: Company begins aggressive expansion through Regional Development Company (RDC) franchise concept, with goal to top 1,000 stores by 2000.

1998: Company sells off Watson & Philip foodservice division and changes name to Alldays plc; acquires 48-store Walter Wilson chain.

1999: As operating losses deepen, Alldays announces its intention to buy out its RDCs.

2000: Alldays announces it is up for sale, but finds no suitable buyer.

2002: Alldays returns to operating profitability and prepares to launch a new store design.

analysts were already beginning to raise questions over the plan, which took operational control of a large part of the company's store network away from Watson & Philip, while burdening the company with a great deal of financial responsibility.

Despite these concerns, Watson & Philip continued its aggressive growth—by the end of 1998, the company had reached 959 stores, nearly half of which were operated by its RDC network. In 1998, Watson & Philip decided to concentrate fully on convenience stores, selling the Watson & Philip foodservice division to catering group Brake Brothers for £38 million. With that sale went the Watson & Philip name as well—and the company now renamed itself Alldays Plc.

By then, Alldays had grown through the acquisition of a rival convenience store chain, Walter Willson's, based in Gateshead and operating in the English northeast and Scottish border region. That acquisition brought the company 48 new stores, boosting Alldays' total to some 200 new stores for the year.

Yet Alldays' expansion proved too rapid. By 1999, the company resembled, as the *Daily Telegraph* described it, ''one of those elaborate pyramids of fruit built by bored grocers.'' After a slip in profits in 1998, the company's pyramid was revealed to be resting on a shaky base. The company faced mounting competition from the United Kingdom's large supermarket groups, which were turning to small-store formats to counter resistance to further ''superstore'' openings. At the same time, Alldays had moved beyond its traditional product mix to add items such as books, videos, compact discs, and even home electronics equipment, none of which found a ready market from Alldays' customers. Attempts to introduce such ''Americanisms'' as fast-food and being open 24-hours a day were also unsuccessful.

Most importantly, however, all but seven of the company's 32 RDCs were losing money and becoming an increasing financial burden for Alldays. The poor condition of a number of RDC-owned stores also tarnished the Alldays' brand itself. Even Alldays' company-owned stores were posting negative sales growth, as the company's debts climbed to a crushing £170 million and its operating profits slumped.

By mid-1999, the company had worked out a £200 million financial rescue package, the primary component of which required it to buy out the owners of its RDCs and take back control of its convenience store network. Buybacks began in August 1999, but quickly ran into trouble as the owners of the company's few profitable RDCs refused to sell their businesses. An agreement was worked out by the end of October—the buybacks proceeded, although without CEO Glass, who tendered his resignation. The company also sold off the last of its Trademarket operation, becoming a pure-play convenience store group.

Glass was replaced by David Chapman, an industry veteran coming from a 25-year career at Sainsburys. Chapman set to work restoring the Alldays concept as well, refitting its stores—and particularly the former RDC-operated stores—with a return to the basic convenience store products that had built the company. Meanwhile, a price-cutting initiative was put in place in order to attract customers back into Alldays stores. The number of these continued to be pared, with the closing of poorly performing locations set up by its more aggressive RDCs and the sales of 32 stores to rival Costcutter. By the end of 2000, Alldays owned more than 675 stores outright; another 70 stores were held under the four remaining, profitable RDCs.

Yet Alldays continued to suffer through 2000, particularly with the end of its agreement with Total, and the resulting loss of some 200 Total-owned stores. The company's share price collapsed to just a fraction of its former value and by the end of the year Alldays' acknowledged that it was up for sale. Yet no suitable bidders stepped up, and in 2001, Alldays decided to ''trade its way'' out of its financial troubles.

Clapham was forced to resign at the beginning of 2001. New CEO Stuart Lawson ended the price-cutting operation—which had not succeeded in returning customers to the stores, while further depressing the company's operating profits. Instead, Alldays returned to revitalizing the Alldays store concept. The company began working on a new store design, and also began adding new amenities, such as in-store bakeries, video and DVD rentals, and in-store post offices, to attract the motoring public.

Alldays returned to operating profitability by the end of 2001—although interest payments on its huge debt continued to depress net profits. By 2002, the company prepared to test its new store design. At the same time, the company hoped to renew expansion of the store network, once again seeking new franchises. This time, however, the company intended to remain in control of the Alldays brand. Despite its difficulties at the turn of the century, Alldays had grown into the United Kingdom's leading convenience store group with 630 stores flying the Alldays banner.

Principal Subsidiaries

Aire Convenience Stores Limited; Alldays Stores Limited; Alldays Franchising Limited 100 licensing; Beds & Bucks Convenience Stores Limited; Central Convenience Stores Limited; Central & Fife Convenience Stores Limited; Cymru Convenience Stores Limited; Hereward Convenience Stores Limited; Home Counties Convenience Stores Limited; Kennet & Avon Convenience Stores Limited; Kent Convenience Stores Limited; Lancashire Convenience Stores Limited; Lothian and Borders Convenience Stores Limited; Merlin Convenience Stores Limited; Norcam Convenience Stores Limited; North Scotland Convenience Stores Limited; North West Convenience Stores Limited; Northumbria Convenience Stores Limited; Perihelion Convenience Stores Limited; Saxon Convenience Stores Limited; South East Convenience Stores Limited; Southern Convenience Stores Limited; Strathtay Retail Limited; Surrey Convenience Stores Limited; Tees and Wear Convenience Stores Limited; Thames Valley Convenience Stores Limited; Trent Convenience Stores Limited; Walter Willson Limited; West Mercia Convenience Stores Limited; West Scotland Convenience Stores Limited.

Principal Competitors

Booker Cash and Carry Ltd.; T&S Stores PLC; C J Lang and Son Ltd.; Bestway Holdings Ltd.

Further Reading

''Battered Alldays Vows to Get Back to the Basics,'' *Grocer*, January 23, 1999, p. 6.

Eggleston, Sheila, ''Alldays Turns up the Instore Heat,'' *Grocer*, August 4, 2001, p. 6.

Gregory, Helen, ''Alldays Loses but Promises to Bounce Back,'' *Super Marketing*, June 23, 2000, p. 3.

Hunt, Julian, ''Time to Motor,'' *Grocer*, March 4, 2000, p. 36.

——, ''What Next for Alldays?,'' *Grocer*, March 4, 2000, p. 33.

''Merger Boosts Alldays Chain,'' *Super Marketing*, May 3, 1991, p. 14.

Palmer, Camilla, ''Glass Pledges to Stay the Course,'' *Grocer*, October 9, 1999 p. 5.

—M. L. Cohen

ALLIED ☾ WORLDWIDE.

Allied Worldwide, Inc.

**5001 U.S. Hwy. 30 West
Ft. Wayne, Indiana 46818
U.S.A.
Telephone: (219) 429-2511
Toll Free: (800) 234-2788
Fax: (219) 429-1853
Web sites: http://www.alliedvan.com
http://www.navl.com
http://www.global.com**

Private Company
Employees: 7,000
Sales: $2.37 billion (2000)
NAIC: 484210 Used Household and Office Goods
Moving; 484230 Specialized Freight (Except Used
Goods) Trucking, Long Distance

Allied Worldwide, Inc. is the largest provider of relocation services in the world and one of the largest providers of high value freight transportation. Through its four brands of service—North American Van Lines, Allied Van Lines, Global Van Lines, and Pickfords—Allied Worldwide provides transportation services in North America, Europe, Asia, Australia, and New Zealand. In addition to residential, corporate, and government relocation services, Allied Worldwide provides domestic and international shipments of high value goods, such as delicate electronics, communications, and medical equipment and fine art. Services at North American Logistics include warehousing, parts distribution, less-than-load transport, and emergency shipments of replacement parts; these services are offered in domestic and international markets.

The Early Decades of North American and Allied Van: 1920s–60s

Allied Worldwide formed in 1999 when North American Van Lines acquired Allied Van Lines. The transaction merged two of the oldest and largest moving companies in the United States. Both companies emerged from the increased mobility of

Americans during the 1920s and 1930s when highway development and road improvements eased family relocations over longer distances.

A group of independent movers formed Allied Van Lines (AVL), the first national moving company, in 1928 in Mackinaw, Michigan. Prompted by the National Furniture Warehousemen's Association, the group banded together to create more efficient operations, primarily to limit the number of empty miles as trucks often returned empty from a long distance delivery. Allied Van Lines provided dispatch and information services from a central office in Chicago, allowing for coordination of outbound and return deliveries. The network of agents grew quickly along the East Coast, the Midwest, and the South. In 1929 AVL transported more than 5,700 shipments and recorded $850,000 in revenues. By 1931 the company counted 261 truck owner-agents, an additional 113 sales agents, 234 vans, and 13 dispatch offices, attaining a reputation as "the careful movers." The company expanded to the West Coast in 1934, providing coast-to-coast service. Allied Sea Van Company provided international shipping services beginning in 1958, finding many of its customers among military personnel stationed abroad. In 1965 AVL revenues surpassed $100 million. Although AVL had been originally established as a nonprofit company, stockholders approved conversion to for-profit status in 1968, allowing excess funds to be retained for capital improvements. AVL became a private company in 1981 when the operator-shareholders purchased publicly owned stock.

North American Van Lines (NAVL) had similar origins, being founded in 1933 by a group of 12 independent movers associated with United Van Services. They were dissatisfied with the quality of that company's operations and the lack of an extensive agent network. In addition to opening a central dispatch office in Cleveland, NAVL issued the moving industry's first pricing tariff, by county, to simplify agent sales. By 1938 the founders built a network of 120 agents. In 1940 the company started to provide household moving with company-owned vehicles driven by company employees. NAVL entered commercial freight trucking services in the late 1940s, transporting furniture and appliances. The company relocated to New Haven, Indiana, in 1947. Overland and water transportation ser-

---

Key Dates:

1928: Allied Van Lines is founded in Mackinaw, Michigan; office established in Chicago.

1933: North American Van Lines is founded in Cleveland.

1952: North American Van Lines begins international shipments.

1958: Allied Van Lines establishes Allied Sea Van Company for international shipments.

1965: North American Van Lines establishes its High Value Products division.

1968: Pepsico purchases North American Van Lines.

1975: Allied Van Lines launches Special Products Division.

1980: Motor Carrier Act and Household Goods Transportation Act deregulates moving industry.

1985: Norfolk Southern purchases North American Van Lines.

1992: Both Allied Van Lines and North American Van Lines initiate quality service programs.

1998: Investment firm acquires North American Van Lines.

1999: Allied Worldwide is formed with the merger of Allied Van Lines and North American Van Lines.

2000: Allied Worldwide purchases Global Van Lines.

---

vices to Alaska began in 1952, and expanded into van-sea-van service to Europe in 1956.

During the 1960s NAVL sought to improve the quality of its moving services. The company initiated a quality assurance program to enhance estimation, packing, storage, and transportation performance. The company later extended the program to agent warehouses and facilities. Also, in 1965 NAVL began to provide transportation for sensitive high technology and electronic equipment and other special needs with the formation of the High Value Products division. Trucks for the division were equipped with air-ride suspension for a smoother ride. Equipment on some vehicles included lifts, cranes, or climate control, the latter for art and medical research. The company owned the trucks which transported delicate goods and manned them with highly skilled drivers. During the early 1970s NAVL's reputation for quality played a role in retaining a contract to transport the renowned King Tutankhamen exhibit of ancient Egyptian treasures.

Pepsico purchased NAVL in 1968. Initial changes involved adding the red, white, and blue colors to the logo and relocating its headquarters to Fort Wayne, Indiana, in 1978. During its tenure as a subsidiary of Pepsico, NAVL thrived despite a difficult economy and industry deregulation.

Economic and Legal Developments
Leading to Changes in Operations: 1970s–80s

During the 1970s the demand for moving household goods declined as high mortgage rates deterred people from purchasing and moving to new homes. Corporate relocation slowed as middle-management employees often shunned relocation. Both NAVL and AVL responded to the situation by expansion in other

areas of service. In 1975 AVL launched its Special Products Division, to handle delicate, high technology equipment, art exhibits, and other special needs. NAVL sought new national accounts for its High Value Products and Commercial Transport Divisions and improved its on-time record. The company based promotions for its Household Goods Group on having "moved the treasure of a King," referring to its handling of the King Tut exhibit. The resiliency of the Household Goods Group came from military and government accounts and new agent locations, with 832 in 1981, the largest network in the country.

The Motor Carrier Act and the Household Goods Transportation Act, both passed into law in 1980, deregulated household goods moving, creating a very competitive environment. Prior to the change the Household Goods Bureau fixed prices used industry-wide, based on weight by mile, and competition among van lines occurred mainly over service quality. Deregulation allowed carriers to increase or decrease rates by 10 percent without approval by the Interstate Commerce Commission. After deregulation carriers lowered prices, offering discounts up to 60 percent off previous rates, and new companies entered the business. The price to haul household goods decreased from $1.28 per mile in 1980 to $1.14 per mile in 1990. AVL responded to the "price wars" with a 9 percent rate discount in early 1983. Meanwhile the whole system of determining prices became more complicated with regional pricing, including within a metropolitan area. Whereas AVL's mainframe computer had been used primarily to track shipments and equipment, deregulation made strategic pricing imperative. In 1987 AVL invested in a system of personal computers, allowing employees to determine profitable but competitive prices more quickly.

NAVL had already implemented internal cost controls and responded to deregulation with volume incentives, guaranteed pricing, and replacement cost protection. The company gained federal approval in 1982 to transport almost any general commodity. NAVL changed its commercial fleet to accommodate larger, heavier loads, adding 48-foot trailers and converting single axle tractors to tandem axle. Also, NAVL introduced the Customized Logistics and Distribution Services to provide just-in-time delivery. For instance, newly produced automotive parts were shipped to assembly plants as needed, saving customers inventory expense by storing freight at intermediate warehouse facilities. By 1983 general freight accounted for 60 percent of total revenues of $560 million; NAVL recorded net income of $25 million in 1983. Despite difficulties in the moving industry during the 1970s and the early 1980s, NAVL recorded a compound annual growth rate of 13.6 percent from 1975 to 1984.

Pepsico decided to focus operations on its core food and beverage business in 1984 and sold NAVL to Norfolk Southern Corporation, the holding company for Norfolk Southern Railroad. Norfolk Southern purchased NAVL for $315 million, plus accrued interest for deferred payment, finalizing the sale in June 1985 for a total of $375.7 million in cash. Norfolk Southern allowed NAVL to continue to operate as before, though it did integrate NAVL into a network of intermodal transportation with Norfolk Southern Railroad.

Triple Crown Service, introduced in 1986, offered customers the convenience of the van line's door-to-door service and the cost benefits of less expensive rail service. "Road-railer cars," outfitted with both rail and truck wheels, were connected to a tractor or placed directly on the railroad for ease of transfer. Also, the road-railer cars were connected to lighter and faster lines of transportation. In 1993, Conrail purchased a stake in Triple Crown, initially adding four rail terminals to the existing system of 12 terminals.

In the late 1980s emphasis on NAVL's International Group increased, providing relocation services and commodities freight forwarding through 250 overseas agents and sales representatives. The 1987 acquisition of Midi Data Transport Speditions GmbH, in Frankfurt, provided a foundation for expansion into Europe. In 1992 NAVL formed a joint venture with 60 European moving companies in 15 countries. With a 40 percent stake in UTS Europe, NAVL shared its operational technology and expertise to coordinate shipments for fully loaded trucks and fewer empty miles.

AVL experienced similar changes during the late 1980s. In 1988 AVL initiated VanRail service using shipping containers easily transferred from truck to railcar. The same year National Freight Consortium (NFC) of London purchased AVL for $100 million and AVL became part of the largest international network of movers, as Allied Pickfords. In 1993 NFC acquired Allied Canada and opened Allied International offices in Beijing, Bangkok, Moscow, Saigon, and Manila.

Business-to-business service became a more important aspect for moving companies. The business of moving household goods was a mature and seasonal market, with most moves occurring during the summer, while commercial accounts provided year-round stability. Logistical parts distribution and temporary warehousing of goods became more important aspects for competing for corporate clients in domestic and international markets. AVL instituted "Express One" less-than-load transportation service for commercial customers, consolidating freight with household goods to make a full load. Both NAVL and Allied Pickfords offered international service which streamlined the transport of a client's retail goods by offering a single-source of distribution, rather than a number of carriers, transporting goods from the factory to port of departure, and from destination port to warehouse.

Another economic downturn in the late 1980s, and increased competition from railroads led to a decline in demand for van line movers. NAVL revenues declined from a peak of $844 million in 1988 to $797.3 million in 1991. Business slumped in all areas, with the biggest decline in Relocations Services, at 9 percent in 1991; NAVL fared well compared to the 10 percent decline nationwide. NAVL recorded losses beginning in 1989 when the company began to convert the Commercial Transport Division from owner-operator carriers to company-owned trucks driven by employees. Though business remained steady in the division, losses prompted Norfolk Southern to put that business up for sale. Without a buyer, however, NAVL discontinued service and dismantled the division in 1993.

NAVL continued to provide special logistical services, order fulfillment, and parts distribution to commercial customers as part of the High Value Products division. NAVL invested in trailers with special equipment for moving delicate goods, and satellite communications, for moment-by-moment location. To

accommodate expansion into this area of shipping, NAVL opened logistics centers in Sacramento; San Diego; and Billings, Montana. The company obtained lucrative contracts for parts distribution with Wang, Hewlett-Packard, and GE Medical and a contract renewal with IBM.

Quality service became an important means of competition in the moving industry during the early 1990s. Both NAVL and AVL initiated programs to improve service. AVL's standards, under "The Quality Alliance," sought to improve customer service with its agents, drivers, and corporate personnel. AVL formed Allied University, a training facility which provided courses on safety, equipment standards, and customer service. Also, AVL developed the Special Products Division by launching its Showcase Fleet with drivers specially trained to handle exhibits. In 1995 AVL became the official carrier of the Imperial Tombs of China exhibit, featuring art and treasures from 500 B.C.

NAVL took the initiative to provide quality service as well. In 1992 the company introduced the first mobile driving simulator, taking driver education classes directly to drivers nationwide. NAVL launched its proprietary Home Touch! software, allowing agents to perform estimates on laptop computers in the customer's home. The company became the first van line to receive ISO certification for the movement of certain electronic equipment. In 1996 NAVL recorded revenues of $930 million.

Merging to Form Largest Carrier of Household Goods: 1999

The formation of Allied Worldwide began in 1998 when the investment firm Clayton, Dubilier & Rice (CDR) purchased NAVL from Norfolk Southern for $200 million. A year later CDR arranged a merger of AVL and NAVL, forming the world's largest relocation company. CDR paid NFC $400 million in cash and $25 million in stock. The merger also involved Pickfords Removals, a moving and storage service, whose history has been traced to the 1630s, with operations in the United Kingdom. NFC acquired Pickfords in 1969 and sold the company along with AVL. Allied Pickfords operated through agents, representatives, and company-owned branches in Europe, Australia, New Zealand, and Asia.

The list of Allied Worldwide brands expanded further in April 2000 with the acquisition of Global Van Lines for $4.2 million. The predecessor company was founded in 1933 and Global grew to become one of the largest van lines in the country, offering domestic and international relocation services and special handling transportation services. Global established industry standards for equipment, including air-ride suspension, climate control, donut wheel trailers, high cube trailers, logistic-track cargo systems, and aluminum cargo beams. It was the first moving company to develop separate divisions for electronics and exhibits. Global gained renown by becoming a major carrier of NASA equipment, such as lunar rovers and manned spacecraft. Allied Worldwide integrated Global into the NAVL network of agents, but retained the brand name.

At the start of the new century Allied Worldwide placed the emphasis for future growth on customized logistics and parts distribution for commercial customers. Activities included restructuring the division and several executive appointments. An alliance with Jardine Logistics expanded parts distribution opportunities in the Asia-Pacific region. In Europe, North American Logistics initiated a system of "parts banks," decentralized warehouses that stored replacement parts for electronic equipment. These warehouses were located strategically so mobile repair engineers had easy access to replacement parts. Warehouse computers were linked to client systems for inventory availability and stock management. The company completed implementation of the system in October 2000.

Principal Subsidiaries

Allied Van Lines, Inc.; Allied Pickfords; Global Van Lines; North American Van Lines, Inc.; Transguard Insurance Company; VanGuard Insurance Agency, Inc.

Principal Divisions

Van Lines Network Services; Moving and Storage Services; Logistics Services.

Principal Competitors

AMERCO; Atlas World Group, Inc.; UniGroup, Inc.

Further Reading

"Allied Van Board Votes Stock Plan," *New York Times*, September 19, 1981, p. 30.

Bowman, Robert, "Van Lines Seek New Profit Opportunities; with the Traditional Household Goods Market Slumping, Van Lines Are Diversifying to Remain Competitive," *Chilton's Distribution*, March 1989, p. 50.

Coia, Anthony, "Going Global in Europe," *Warehousing Management*, June 2001, p. 26.

Curtis, Carol E., "No Moves Is Bad News," *Forbes*, June 7, 1982, p. 158.

Deming, Brian, "Hauler Looks Forward; North American Sets Quality As Its Goal," *Fort Wayne News-Sentinel*, March 22, 1993, p. 1B.

——, "N. American Seeks Buyer for Division," *Fort Wayne News-Sentinel*, June 26, 1993, p. 1A.

——, "NAVL Downshifts on Plans to Expand Business in Mexico; Hauling Mostly One-Way—North to South—Is Inefficient," *Fort Wayne News-Sentinel*, May 24, 1993, p. 3B.

——, "Triple Crown to Join Rail Transport Venture; The Company Expects to Double Its Local Employment," *Fort Wayne News-Sentinel*, March 31, 1993, p. 1A.

"Investment Firm Buys North American Van Lines," *Fort Wayne News-Sentinel*, January 12, 1998, p. 1A.

LeDuc, Doug, "Mover Speeds Up Estimates," *Fort Wayne News-Sentinel*, May 19, 1997, p. 8B.

——, "NAVL Changes the Way It Charges," *Fort Wayne News-Sentinel*, October 23, 1995, p. 7B.

——, "NAVL Unit Shutdown Goes Forward; The Company Is Offering Commercial Transport Employees Job-Hunting Help," *Fort Wayne News-Sentinel*, September 6, 1993, p. 1B.

——, "North American Out of the Red," *Fort Wayne News-Sentinel*, March 2, 1992, p. 10B.

——, "North American Van Lines Joins Forces with Overseas Companies to Develop a European Moving Operation," *Fort Wayne News-Sentinel*, April 27, 1992, p. 1B.

——, "North American Van Lines Uses Special Trailers to Keep Fragile Loads from Getting Rattled," *Fort Wayne News-Sentinel*, July 27, 1992, p. 1A.

——, "North American Van Lines Will Be Part of the Largest Mover," *Fort Wayne News-Sentinel*, September 14, 1999, p. 1A.

——, "190 Jobs Cut at North American," *Fort Wayne News-Sentinel*, November 9, 1990, p. 1A.

McDonald, Mitchell, E., "It's Not Just a Van Line Anymore," *Traffic Management*, February 1991, p. 47.

McKenna Frazier, Lynne, "NAVL Parent Gets Global," *Fort Wayne News-Sentinel*, April 12, 2000, p. 1B

Moskal, Brian S., "Eastern Skirmish; CSX, Norfolk Southern Playing Monopoly," *Industry Week*, May 14, 1984, p. 22.

"North American Van Growth Set," *Richmond Times-Dispatch*, January 21, 1992, p. A9.

"Rates Reduced 9% By Allied Van Lines," *New York Times*, February 3, 1983, p. D5.

Schafer, Laurie, "Moving Toward Brighter Horizons, and in New Directions," *Handling & Shipping Management*, April 1983, p. 68.

Zarley, Craig, "PCs Ease Allied Van Line's Move into Newly Competitive Environment," *PC Week*, July 21, 1987, p. 45.

—Mary Tradii

Apartment Investment and Management Company

2000 S. Colorado Boulevard, Suite 2-1000
Denver, Colorado 80222-7900
U.S.A.
Telephone: (303) 757-8101
Toll Free: (888) 789-8600
Fax: (303) 759-3226
Web site: http://www.aimco.com

Public Company
Incorporated: 1994
Employees: 7,800
Sales: $1.55 billion (2001)
Stock Exchanges: New York
Ticker Symbol: AIV
NAIC: 525930 Real Estate Investment Trusts

Apartment Investment and Management Company (AIMCO) is the largest U.S. real estate investment trust (REIT) in terms of apartment units—owning or managing more than 360,000. The Denver, Colorado, business is second to Equity Residential when it comes to sales, a function of the REIT's strategy of concentrating on second tier properties. Altogether it owns more than 1,500 properties, located in 46 states, Puerto Rico, and the District of Columbia.

Launching a Real Estate Business: 1975

One of AIMCO's founders, and its longtime chairman and CEO, was Terry Considine, who was also well known for his political activities. He was born in San Diego to a well-off family and was educated at Groton and Harvard University before he received a J.D. from Harvard Law School in 1971. He became involved in real estate while at Harvard, acquiring and operating apartment and commercial properties. He also syndicated apartment properties, selling limited partnerships to others while serving as general partner. Still a law student, he established a REIT under the sponsorship of the prestigious Boston real estate firm of Cabot, Cabot, and Forbes. Upon graduation Considine remained in Boston, becoming a member of the Massachusetts Bar. Following a real estate crash in 1974, he established a new venture he named The Considine Company, later known as The Cairn Company, which he built into one of the country's largest property management firms. In 1981 he moved to Colorado and became involved in politics through his father-in-law, Howard "Bo" Callaway, the state chairman of the Republican Party. In 1986 Considine attempted to win the U.S. Senate seat vacated by Gary Hart but was unable to secure the Republican nomination, despite a well-financed campaign. A year later he became a state senator, appointed to a vacancy after his district's state senator resigned. He would win the Republican nomination for the U.S. Senate in 1992, Gary Hart's old seat once again vacant, but Considine ultimately lost out to Democrat Ben Nighthorse Campbell (who, in an ironic twist, soon changed his party affiliation to Republican).

Considine met one of the future founders of AIMCO, Steve Ira, in 1987, when he acquired a 75 percent interest in McDermott, Stein and Ira Marketing Management (MSI), Denver's largest fee-operated apartment management company. Ira had become involved in real estate in an unusual manner. He was originally a police officer who moonlighted as a security guard at his own apartment community. He eventually quit the police department and in 1982 went to work with Arthur McDermott and Chuck Stein, who had been partners in apartment management since 1979. Considine assumed the MSI name, then in 1988 he expanded the business geographically with the acquisition of a Florida-based property management company, Property Asset Management (PAM). Two years later MSI changed its name to Property Asset Management.

Because Considine was busy serving as a state senator he asked Ira to take an active role in running the growing property management business. Considine was impressed by Ira's hands-on management style, embodied in his "one-hour rule," which maintained that his top people had to live within one hour travel of a property they managed, by all available means of transportation. Together, Considine and Ira, who served as president, grew PAM into the 12th largest fee management com-

Company Perspectives:

AIMCO succeeds by providing quality services to residents and third-party management clients, good jobs to employees, and attractive returns to shareholders.

pany in the country. By 1994 they decided to form their own apartment REIT.

Establishment of REITs: 1960

REITs were established by Congress in 1960 as a way for small investors to become involved in real estate in a manner similar to mutual funds. REITs could be taken public and their shares traded just like stock. They were also subject to regulation by the Securities and Exchange Commission. Unlike stocks, however, REITs were required by law to pay out at least 95 percent of their taxable income to shareholders each year, a provision that severely limited the ability of REITs to raise funds internally. During the first 25 years of existence, REITs were only allowed to own real estate, a situation which hindered their growth. Third parties had to be contracted to manage the properties. Not until the Tax Reform Act of 1986 began to change the nature of real estate investment did REITs begin to gain widespread usage. Tax shelter schemes that had drained potential investments were shut down: Interest and depreciation deductions were greatly reduced so that taxpayers could not generate paper losses in order to lower their tax liabilities. The 1986 Act also permitted REITs to provide customary services for property, in effect allowing the trusts to operate and manage the properties they owned. Despite these major changes in law, REITs were still not fully utilized. In the latter half of the 1980s banks, insurance companies, pension funds, and foreign investors (in particular, the Japanese) provided the lion's share of real estate investment funds. That period also witnessed overbuilding and a glutted marketplace, leading to a shakeout in the industry. With real estate available at distressed prices in the early 1990s REITs finally became an attractive mainstream investment option.

To help in forming a REIT, Considine and Ira turned to their largest client, PDI, Inc., a Los Angeles asset management firm run by Peter Kompaniez and Robert Lacy. The four men became the founding partners of AIMCO. A lawyer, Kompaniez had helped to create four REITs while a senior partner at a Los Angeles law firm. In 1986 one of his clients hired him to serve as president of a company, which among other holdings included some 6,000 apartments. He left in 1992 to form PDI with Lacy, and they hired PAM to serve as their fee manager. When Kompaniez and Lacy agreed to team up with Considine and Ira, they added the PDI business to the mix of AIMCO, which also included properties controlled by Considine.

With Considine named president and CEO, AIMCO completed an initial public offering of shares in July 1994, raising almost $170 million. The REIT quickly moved to use some of the funds to buy 37 apartment properties, totaling nearly 10,000 units, spread across Colorado, Utah, New Mexico, Nevada,

Georgia, Florida, and Arizona. From the outset AIMCO focused on Class B properties, where management believed a greater increase in rent could be achieved in the coming years. By contrast, tenants of Class A properties might opt to buy homes if rents reached a certain threshold.

Aimco grew at a steady clip during its first two years, but became especially aggressive in 1997. In little more than a year the REIT's market capitalization increased from $1 billion to nearly $3 billion, and shareholder's equity expanded from $216 million to $1 billion. The most important acquisition of this period was the $296 million purchase of NHP Inc., the nation's second largest apartment management company, with 133,000 units under its purview. NHP was established in 1970 as The National Housing Partnership, a private-for-profit business created as a result of Title IX of the Housing and Urban Development Act of 1968 and dedicated to the promotion of private investment in the building of low and moderate income housing. Over the next 15 years NHP developed more than 300 affordable housing projects, which it also managed. In the early 1980s the corporation began to offer property management services to third-party multifamily properties. NHP went public in 1995. It had a significant presence in the Atlantic states and the Midwest, which complimented AIMCO's strengths in California and the Southwest and provided solid geographic diversification. As part of the NHP transaction, AIMCO gained an interest in Foxchase Apartments, which later in the year it bought outright for $69 million. Foxchase was a 200-building community of more than 2,100 apartments located in Alexandria, Virginia, some ten miles south of Washington, D.C. Also in 1997 AIMCO acquired 8,175 units in 35 apartment communities from Winthrop Financial Associates for an aggregate price of approximately $253.5 million. The garden-style apartment communities were located in Arizona, Texas, Florida, Michigan, Georgia, Illinois, and North Carolina.

Because of proposed changes in the laws that governed REITs, AIMCO created a spinoff, CK Services Inc., which contained non-core business services, such as food services, assisted living, and home health. The new company was named after Considine and Kompaniez, who jointly owned it. AIMCO, in the meantime, continued to focus on growing its property management business and ownership of apartment properties. In May 1998 it acquired Ambassador Apartments, Inc., a Chicago REIT, at a cost of $713.6 million in stock, cash, and assumed debt. The Ambassador deal brought with it ownership and management of some 16,000 units in 52 apartment communities, located in Arizona, Colorado, Florida, Georgia, Illinois, Tennessee, and Texas. An even larger acquisition was completed in October 1998 when AIMCO purchased Insignia Financial Group, Inc., a floundering South Carolina-based REIT controlled by its founder Andrew Farkas, who according to the *Wall Street Journal* was involved in the "controversial business of taking control of real-estate partnerships and buying out limited partners at steep discounts. Separately, Mr. Farkas will spin off what is left of Insignia's rapidly growing commercial-property services business." AIMCO paid $350 million in stock and $460 million in assumed debt to acquire ownership of 122,000 apartment units and third party management of another 69,000. As a result AIMCO became the country's largest land-

<table>
<tr><td colspan="2">

Key Dates:

</td></tr>
<tr><td>1975:</td><td>Terry Considine forms The Considine Company, later renamed The Cairn Company.</td></tr>
<tr><td>1987:</td><td>Cairn acquires McDermott, Stein & Ira, becoming MSI.</td></tr>
<tr><td>1988:</td><td>MSI acquires Property Asset Management and becomes PAM.</td></tr>
<tr><td>1994:</td><td>PAM converts to REIT status and is taken public.</td></tr>
<tr><td>1997:</td><td>NHP, Inc. is acquired.</td></tr>
<tr><td>1998:</td><td>Property management division of Insignia Financial Group is acquired.</td></tr>
<tr><td>2001:</td><td>Casden Properties is acquired.</td></tr>
</table>

lord with 390,000 apartment units in 2,100 communities under its ownership and/or management.

In 1999 AIMCO made adjustments to its portfolio, acquiring 28 apartment communities in a series of transactions at an aggregate cost of $494 million, while selling 63 properties at an aggregate cost of $426 million. In addition the REIT initiated a major development project in south Florida on the former site of Miami Beach's legendary Flamingo Hotel. The new project was to be called The Grand Flamingo and projected to become the largest apartment community in south Florida. At a cost of $121 million, AIMCO planned to renovate existing structures on a 17 acre site as well as build a new 32-story apartment tower, resulting in a 1,690 apartment unit community.

HUD Lawsuit: 1999

With much of its portfolio devoted to the affordable housing sector, AIMCO found itself coming under fire from housing activists and the government, related in large part to its NHP-acquired properties. Many of AIMCO's tenants took advantage of a federal housing subsidiary program, Section 8, which was introduced in 1974. Landlords who signed up for the program received subsidies for low-income tenants, who in turn were guaranteed to pay no more than 30 percent of their income for housing. Not only did AIMCO opt out of the Section 8 program, it announced its intention to sell the Section 8 properties it had acquired from NHP. The REIT was also accused of buying HUD properties on the cheap and then developing them in order to raise rents to a higher level than Section 8 participants could bear, resulting in low-income and older tenants losing their housing. In 1999 HUD sued AIMCO, alleging mismanagement of HUD-assisted or insured apartment properties. The matter would not be settled until August 2001 when the two parties reached a $4.2 million settlement in which AIMCO was absolved of any wrongdoing.

With REITs undergoing a period of consolidation in reaction to investor pressure in the late 1990s, AIMCO was one of the most aggressive companies in the apartment sector. In 2000 it acquired Oxford Realty Financial Group, Inc. in a cash, stock, and assumption of debt transaction valued at nearly $1.2 billion. AIMCO gained 167 apartment communities located in 18 states, nearly 37,000 units in total. Individual acquisitions in 2000 also resulted in AIMCO adding 12 apartment properties at a cost of $136.5 million. At the same time, the REIT sold off 64 apartment properties, as well as some parcels of land and commercial properties, realizing an aggregate sales price of $573.5 million. By now AIMCO was very much dedicated to reducing its holdings in the affordable housing market.

Continuing to adjust the mix in its portfolio, in 2001 AIMCO bought five apartment properties in separate transactions, paying $120 million, while also selling 72 apartment properties, a commercial property, and land for nearly $410 million. Despite soft economic conditions, exacerbated by the terrorist attacks of September 11, 2001, AIMCO surprised industry analysts when in December 2001 it announced the $1.5 billion acquisition of Casden Properties, a Los Angeles-based REIT with over 17,000 apartments. Almost two-thirds of the units, some 11,000, were conventional apartments and did not fit in with AIMCO's stated strategy of mitigating its exposure to affordable housing. According to management, however, the REIT intended to redevelop many of the properties and sell off others. Also as a part of the Casden purchase, AIMCO acquired a subsidiary, National Partnership Investment Corp. (NAPICO), which as a general partner controlled over 40,000 apartments in 400 properties. As a result AIMCO entered 2002 with more than 360,000 apartments that it owned and/or managed, an asset base of some $15 billion, making it the largest apartment owner and operator in the United States.

Principal Competitors

Archstone-Smith Trust; Equity Residential; Lend Lease Corporation Limited.

Further Reading

Burrough, D.J., "Denver Firm Buys 7 Valley Complexes," *Business Journal—Serving Phoenix & the Valley of the Sun,* August 26, 1994, p. 1.

Enkoji, M.S., "Denver-Based Company Grows into Nation's Largest Owner of Apartments," *Sacramento Bee,* January 27, 2002.

Griswold, Dan, "Man on a Mission," *National Review,* October 5, 1992, p. 26.

Moore, Paula, "HUD, AIMCO Clash Over Housing," *Denver Business Journal,* May 8, 1992, p. 3A.

Pacelle, Mitchell, "Insignia Sells Apartment Business to AIMCO for $350 Million in Stock," *Wall Street Journal,* March 18, 1998, p. B14.

Rogers, Beth, "The Evolution of AIMCO," *National Apartment Association,* July 1, 1998.

—Ed Dinger

Archstone-Smith Trust

9200 E. Panorama Circle, Suite 400
Englewood, Colorado 80112
U.S.A.
Telephone: (303) 708-5959
Fax: (303) 708-5999
Web site: http://www.archstonesmith.com

Public Company
Incorporated: 1963 as El Paso Real Estate Investment
    Trust
Employees: 3,300
Sales: $829.2 million (2001)
Stock Exchanges: New York
Ticker Symbol: ASN
NAIC: 525930 Real Estate Investment Trusts

Archstone-Smith Trust, with headquarters in Englewood, Colorado, is the third largest apartment real estate investment trust (REIT) in the United States. The REIT owns nearly 80,000 apartments, representing a total market capitalization of approximately $10 billion. Its Archstone Communities brand operates garden-style units, and the Charles E. Smith brand is dedicated to high-rise properties. The core markets for Archstone-Smith are California, southeast Florida, Boston, Chicago, Seattle, and Washington, D.C. More recently it has staked a claim in the highly competitive New York City market, becoming the first multifamily REIT to purchase an operating apartment property in Manhattan.

Origins of Archstone-Smith Dating Back to 1963

The lineage of Archstone-Smith can be traced back to the 1963 formation of a Texas REIT named El Paso Real Estate Investment Trust. REITs were a new creation, established by Congress in 1960 as a way for small investors to become involved in real estate in a manner similar to mutual funds. REITs could be taken public and their shares traded just like stock. They were also subject to regulation by the Securities and Exchange Commission. Unlike stocks, however, REITs were required by law to pay out at least 95 percent of their taxable income to shareholders each year, a provision that severely limited the ability of REITs to raise funds internally. During the first 25 years of existence, REITs were allowed only to own real estate, a situation that hindered their growth. Third parties had to be contracted to manage the properties. Not until the Tax Reform Act of 1986 changed the nature of real estate investment did REITs begin to gain widespread usage. Tax shelter schemes that had drained potential investments were shut down: Interest and depreciation deductions were greatly reduced so that taxpayers could not generate paper losses in order to lower their tax liabilities. The Act also permitted REITs to provide customary services for property, in effect allowing the trusts to operate and manage the properties they owned. Despite these major changes in law, REITs were still not fully utilized. In the latter half of the 1980s the banks, insurance companies, pension funds, and foreign investors (in particular, the Japanese) provided the lion's share of real estate investment funds. That period also witnessed overbuilding and a glutted marketplace, leading to a shakeout in the marketplace. With real estate available at distressed prices in the early 1990s REITs finally became an attractive mainstream investment option.

El Paso Real Estate changed its name to Property Trust of America in 1970. It became involved in a wide range of real estate investments, in the 1980s investing in everything from shopping malls to a Holiday Inn located in San Francisco's Fisherman's Wharf. Although the REIT was diversified, it also was difficult for investors to evaluate, since its assets were spread across various sectors performing at different levels. Property Trust would attain focus, namely the apartment market in the Southwest, when it became involved with real estate mogul William D. Sanders. Beginning in July 1989 the REIT became the target of a solicited takeover by Sizeler Property Investors Inc., a Kenner, Louisiana, REIT that owned nearly 10 percent of Property Trust. Over the next several months Sizeler sweetened its tender offer in a bid to gain a controlling 55 percent stake, but was rebuffed. The matter finally came to a close in February 1990 when Sizeler gave up and sold off its shares of Property Trust to SWRT Inc., a company created by Sanders for the purpose. At the same time, Sanders reached an agreement with Property Trust on an option to purchase 600,000 new nonvoting, convertible preferred shares. He further agreed to acquire no more than 32

Company Perspectives:

Our mission is to leverage the talents and resources of our organization to reinvent our industry and create value for our shareholders, customers and associates. Our innovative approach to the apartment business is what sets Archstone-Smith apart from the competition.

percent of the REIT over the next two years, during which time he would vote his shares with management.

Sanders, a Texas native with a B.S. degree in agriculture from Cornell University, made his fortune in Chicago. In 1968, at the age of 28, he founded LaSalle Partners, today one of the largest asset managers in the country, building it into a prominent real estate advisory and asset-management firm that catered to institutional investors. LaSalle attained global reach and the prestige of a Wall Street financial house despite its Midwest locale. In the late 1980s, at the height of the real estate boom, he sold his partnership stake for an estimated $65 million to the Japanese firm of Dai-ichi Mutual Life Insurance Co. Critics have charged over the years that he sensed the market was about to collapse and that he left the Japanese holding the bag. Sanders maintained that he simply wanted to become involved in the development side of real estate. Retiring to Santa Fe, New Mexico, he pursued a grand strategy of building a vast real estate empire, a one-stop shopping approach that would not only encompass REITs devoted to individual sectors but also a services group, real estate investment banking, consulting, and research. In 1990, with the financial backing of several institutional investors and an assembled team of top real estate talent, he created Security Capital Group to fulfill his vision. His first investment was in Property Trust of America, the first phase in the creation of a family of REITs, each devoted to a different sector.

Focusing on Apartments in the 1990s

A year after Sanders bought into Property Trust, the REIT hired a Sanders-controlled company, Southwest Realty Advisors Inc., to serve as its advisor. It also announced that it planned to acquire and develop multifamily housing in the Southwestern markets, thereby beginning the REIT's emphasis on apartments, especially on the low-income market. Property Trust began making public offerings to fund expansion, in June 1991 raising $22 million. Also in that month C. Ronald Blankenship was elected chairman of the REIT, replacing Tad R. Smith, who had resigned in the wake of his indictment regarding alleged securities fraud involving El Paso Electric Co. Blankenship had been managing director of Southwest Capital Group Inc., part of the Sanders Security Capital group of companies. Fueled by additional offerings, Property Trust over the next three years aggressively acquired and developed properties in Arizona, Colorado, New Mexico, Oklahoma, and Texas. The focus on apartments proved lucrative for its investors, as reflected by the REIT's 20 percent annual growth in funds from operations over the period 1992–94.

In 1994 R. Scot Sellers became Managing Director, responsible for the REIT's investment strategy and implementation.

Only a few months later, in December 1994, Property Trust agreed to acquire another Sanders-controlled REIT, Security Capital Pacific Inc., for $139 million in stock and the assumption of $128 million in debt. Security Capital Pacific concentrated on apartment projects generally located in the Northwest, including markets in California, Washington, Oregon, Utah, Colorado, Nevada, and Idaho. Because of the Sanders connection to both REITs, the deal generated some controversy, with critics charging that Property Trust shareholders were getting a better deal than Security Capital Pacific shareholders. Properties owned by Security Capital Pacific were considered of higher quality and located in markets that were about to enter an economic upswing. Moreover, analysts noted that because the Pacific Northwest market was lagging some two years behind the Southwest, which was likely to cool, Property Trust would be in a position to sell off properties at the height of the market in the Southwest, the proceeds of which could be used to buy properties in the Northwest at the bottom of the cycle. The transaction was completed in March 1995 and Property Trust changed its name to Security Capital Pacific Trust. The REIT then raised $217.2 million in a new offering, the money earmarked to pay down $203 million in debt.

In 1995 Sellers initiated a strategy to reposition the REIT's portfolio in an effort to concentrate on protected markets, areas with limited land and more difficult to develop because of strict regulations and other factors. In such markets the REIT could benefit from a tight housing situation. At this point in its development of Security Capital Pacific Trust, almost 70 percent of its portfolio was concentrated in the states of Texas, Arizona, and New Mexico. To achieve Sellers's goal the REIT would have to sell off almost all of its assets and then reinvest in new communities. The wise selection of markets to enter led to robust growth for Security Capital Pacific Trust. It began to invest in the San Francisco Bay area in 1995, then in 1996 made a major push into the southern California apartment market, altogether investing more than $400 million in the state just as it entered into a period of record growth. Sellers was named chairman and CEO in June 1997, and then in 1998 took the REIT into the Boston market just as it was beginning to enjoy strong growth, again to the benefit of the bottom line.

Sanders, in the meantime, took the parent corporation, Security Capital, public in September 1997, but his dreams of a multifaceted real estate empire were already beginning to dissipate. The offering raised almost $600 million at $28 a share, but almost immediately the price began to erode, a situation that would only be exacerbated by an industrywide slump in the price of REITs over the next two years. Security Capital dropped below $12 by September 1999, which forced Sanders to make significant changes to his real estate interests, perceived by many investors as too complicated.

While some of Sanders's REITs struggled, Security Capital Pacific Trust continued to grow. A general slump in REIT share prices led to a period of consolidation in the industry, as pressure mounted on smaller companies to join with larger rivals in order to compete. For Security Capital Pacific Trust, greater size provided an efficient way to create a national platform through which it could execute a capital recycling strategy. In 1998 it merged with Atlanta-based Security Capital Atlantic Inc. in a $1.1 billion stock swap. Again, it was a deal

<table>
<tr><td colspan="2">

Key Dates:
</td></tr>
</table>

Key Dates:

1963: El Paso Real Estate Investment Trust is formed.
1970: The name is changed to Property Trust of America.
1990: William D. Sanders buys into the REIT.
1995: Following the acquisition of Security Capital Pacific Inc., the REIT becomes Security Capital Pacific Trust.
1998: The name Archstone Communities is assumed after the acquisition of Security Capital Atlantic Inc.
2001: The acquisition of Charles E. Smith Residential Realty Inc. results in Archstone-Smith Trust.

between two Sanders-dominated REITs that engendered some criticism. Unlike the thriving Security Capital Pacific Trust, Security Capital Atlantic had failed to perform up to expectations since its initial public offering in 1996, yet both were equally valued in the merger. Although Sellers had long eclipsed Sanders in the running of Security Capital Pacific Trust, the latter remained a focus of media attention in the deal. According to *Business Week,* for instance, "Pacific shareholders griped that Sanders bailed out a loser with a winner at their expense. Sanders, who defends the deal, claims he had nothing to do with the pricing because it was decided by the individual boards." Once the transaction was completed, the resulting REIT assumed the name of Archstone Communities. The Archstone name was coined by Lippincott & Margulies, one of the nation's leading branding firms involved in the naming of numerous new products, including Starbucks. Armed with a new name, the company was ready to create the industry's first national brand in apartments. If Archstone was able to develop brand loyalty among tenants, it stood to realize a number of benefits, including high occupancy rates, reduced turnover, and more referrals, as well as the ability to charge higher rentals. With more than 90,000 apartments in 19 states and Washington, D.C., the REIT was well on its way to achieving nationwide penetration.

In 1999 Archstone continued to look to revamp its portfolio and expand into new areas of the country. Archstone acquired two Chicago-area apartment communities, the 460-unit Garden Glen Apartments located in Schaumburg, Illinois, and the 125-unit Prairie Court located in Oak Park, Illinois. In addition, the REIT gained a toehold in the Minneapolis market with the purchase of the 196-unit complex in Eden Prairie, Minnesota, situated less than 15 miles from downtown Minneapolis. The cost of these Midwest purchases totaled $72.4 million. At the same time that Archstone was shedding noncore assets, it was selling apartment properties in Birmingham, Alabama; Columbus, Ohio; and Jacksonville, Florida. Archstone also made strides in establishing its brand identity in 1999, launching a number of initiatives, including SafeRent, an Internet application that reduced the approval of new tenants from the industry standard of one or two days to just 30 seconds. Archstone then implemented an instant refund program, providing tenants with refunds on their security deposits on the day they moved out, in contrast with the 30 days industry standard. The REIT also took advantage of computer programs in revenue management, employing forecasting algorithms to help in calculating future

demands. In 2001 Archstone launched its Lease Rent Optimizer, a program that individual properties could use to help determine the optimum price of its apartments.

Becoming Archstone-Smith Trust in the Early 21st Century

Sanders finally cut his ties to Archstone in 2001, a development that was welcomed by the REIT's management, which believed that having a single shareholder controlling almost 40 percent of its equity had held down the price of its stock. This disconnect between the stock price and the underlying value of Archstone's assets led management to spend more than $550 million in just two years to repurchase about 18 percent of its common shares. For different reasons, Sanders, under pressure from the board of Security Capital Group and outside investors, had begun to buy up shares of the parent company's stock in order to bolster its sagging price. To simplify Security Capital's complex structure he took private some of the REITs he had founded. Others, like Archstone, had simply grown much too large to acquire, and he began to sell off his interests. He unloaded the last of his $787 million stake in Archstone in February 2001, which he then used to pay off a $530 million loan. Less than a year later, Sanders's grand dream for a real estate empire came to a muted conclusion. On Friday, December 14, at the unusual hour of 9 p.m., it was announced that GE Capital Corp. had agreed to buy Security Capital at $26 per common share in a $4 billion deal.

Sellers led Archstone to an even higher level when in May 2001 he brokered an agreement to acquire Charles E. Smith Residential Realty Inc. for $2.2 billion in stock and the assumption of $1.4 billion in debt. Smith Residential was the apartment business REIT of the 50-year-old, family-founded Charles E. Smith Cos. Focusing on the high-rise market, it owned interests in more than 50 apartment buildings, as well as two shopping centers, located in Washington, D.C., Boston, Chicago, and southeastern Florida, totaling around 24,000 units. In addition, the REIT managed another dozen apartment complexes. An affiliate, Smith Corporate Living, offered upscale temporary accommodations for business travelers. Once the acquisition was complete, the resulting Archstone-Smith Trust owned almost 87,500 apartment units, with nearly 5,000 more under construction, and a total market capitalization of more than $9 billion. At the time, it became America's fourth largest REIT and the second largest multifamily housing REIT. The acquisition was also a major step in shifting the concentration of Archstone-Smith's portfolio to the top protected markets, with downtown high-rise properties being considered the ultimate in protected assets.

With the business now organized into three sections—the east division, the west division, and the Charles E. Smith division—Archstone-Smith completed the year 2001 posting revenues of $829.2 million and net income of $257.9 million. In the process of turning over its portfolio, the REIT had sold off some $3.6 billion in noncore assets while spending $2.5 billion to acquire apartments, aside from mergers, and another $2 billion on development. Unlike many public companies, it maintained healthy growth into 2002, despite difficult economic conditions.

In May 2002 Archstone-Smith announced that it was entering the highly competitive New York City market by acquiring a 506-unit upscale, twin-tower, high-rise apartment property located in Manhattan's Upper West Side near Lincoln Center at a cost of $210 million. The building, completed in May 2000, featured three levels of parking and first floor retail space. It offered studio and one- and two-bedroom luxury apartments with monthly rents ranging from $2,350 to $8,590. With the financial services industry hard hit by a weak economy and a new supply of apartments about to become available in the surrounding area, some questioned the wisdom of Archstone-Smith entering the New York market at this time. Nevertheless, the REIT achieved one of its major goals and management insisted that time would prove the wisdom of the deal.

Principal Subsidiaries

Archstone Communities Incorporated; Archstone Financial Services, Inc.; Charles E. Smith Residential Realty Inc.

Principal Competitors

Apartment Investment and Management Company; Equity Residential; United Dominion Realty Trust, Inc.

Further Reading

Faris, Mark, ''Wall Street Cautiously Gives Nod to Merger of Archstone-Smith,'' *Multi-Housing News,* July 2001, p. 1.

Kirkpatrick, David D., ''REIT Interest: William Sanders Raises Shareholders' Ire,'' *Wall Street Journal,* April 15, 1998, p. B12.

Nickel, Karen, ''A REIT with the Right Idea,'' *Fortune,* August 26, 1991, p. 26.

Opdyke, Jeff D., ''Property Trust's Planned Merger Could Hold Benefits for Investors,'' *Wall Street Journal,* February 1, 1995, p. T2.

Pacelle, Mitchell, ''REITs Plan Merger Aimed at National Branding,'' *Wall Street Journal,* April 2, 1998, p. A4.

''A REIT Mogul in a Fine Mess,'' *Business Week,* March 1, 1999, p. 96.

Rudnitsky, Howard, ''Reinventing Bill Sanders,'' *Institutional Investor,* April 2001, p. 114.

Ursery, Stephen, ''Timing Is Everything,'' *National Real Estate Investor,* June 2002, p. 12.

Vinocur, Barry, ''High Respected Property Firm Draws Fire for Plans to Merge,'' *Barron's,* December 19, 1994, p. 40.

—Ed Dinger

Autogrill SpA

Palazzo Z
Strada 5
20089 Rozzano
Milano
Italy
Telephone: (+39) 02-48-26-32-24
Fax: (+39) 02-48-26-36-14
Web site: http://www.autogrill.com

Public Company
Incorporated: 1977
Employees: 41,000
Sales: EUR 3.38 billion ($2.7 billion) (2001)
Stock Exchanges: Italian
Ticker Symbol: AGL
NAIC: 722110 Full-Service Restaurants; 722410 Drinking
    Places (Alcoholic Beverages)

Autogrill SpA is the world's leading operator of travel restaurant facilities. Based in Milan, Italy, and more than 57 percent owned by the Benetton clothing family, Autogrill operates some 4,300 restaurants, cafés, and other catering facilities in highway service areas, airports, train stations, city centers, and shopping malls. The company's sales come primarily in Italy (30 percent of sales) and North America (52 percent of sales), where the company has been market dominator since its acquisition of HMSHost, acquired in 1999 for $929 million. The rest of Europe, including France, Spain, Germany, Austria, Greece, Portugal, Switzerland, and the Benelux countries, adds nearly 18 percent of sales, and represents the company's main expansion focus. Through HMSHost, Autogrill has operations in Australia and New Zealand and plans to expand into other Asian Pacific markets. Autogrill has developed a number of restaurant brands and concepts. Spizzico is the company's fast-food pizza format, with 160 restaurants. The 140 restaurants in the Ciao chain offer a free-flow cafeteria dining concept. Acafe is the company's coffee bar formula introduced at the beginning of the 2000s. Snack Bar, with 404 outlets, is usually combined with the company's Market format, with 363 locations, offering

fast-food and convenience grocery. The company also operates traditional restaurants under the La Galleria brands. Internationally, Autogrill operates additional brands, such as Passaggio in Switzerland, while rolling out its core brands in those markets as well. In addition to its own brands, Autogrill operates a variety of concessions, including an agreement to open up to 500 Burger Kings in Italy; and, largely through HMSHost, franchises for Starbucks, TCBY, CPK ASAP, Sbarro, Chili's Too, Chocolate Factory, Dunkin' Donuts, Cinnabon, Pizza Hut, and KFC Express. Formerly a part of Italian government-owned Società Meridionale Finanziaria (SME), Autogrill has been traded on the Italian stock exchange since 1996.

Birth of an Italian Fast-Food Leader in the 1970s

Autogrill's history traces back to the development of Italy's roadway network in the postwar years. As more Italians took to the road, the need arose for service areas and restaurants to serve the increasingly mobile public. Many of these restaurants were simple affairs, such as a small roadside stand opened along the highway between Milan and Novara in 1947. By the 1960s, traffic had increased to the point where the stand was transformed into a major service station and restaurant, called the Autogrill Pavesi. That restaurant was to provide the model for the future Autogrill chain, with the restaurant housed on a bridge across the highway. Pavesi itself was to grow into one of Italy's most prominent roadside restaurant chains.

By the 1970s, Italy's highways and freeways were dotted with restaurants, many of which were operated as parts of large-scale chains. Yet vehicle use plummeted with the Arab oil embargo and the ensuing financial crisis, which saw drastic increases in gasoline prices throughout Europe. Many of the countries roadside service restaurant chains were struggling financially. In 1997, the Italian government, through Società Meridionale Finanziaria (SME), took over three chains, Motta, originally founded in 1928 as a bar in Milan, restaurant chain Alemagna, and Autogrill Pavesi, and reformed the operation as Autogrill SpA.

At its debut, Autogrill operated some 270 restaurants along the country's highways. The company soon adopted the Autogrill brand as its primary roadside brand, replacing the Motta, Pavesi, and Alemagna names. Autogrill also began developing its new brands and restaurants, as well as targeting other operating locations. In 1982, the company moved into Italy's city centers, launching the Ciao restaurant chain, a self-service cafeteria style concept featuring Italian cuisine. Ciao was to develop into what the company called a ''free-flow'' concept, which caught on well with the Italian diner. By the end of the century, Autogrill operated nearly 140 Ciao restaurants.

During the late 1980s, Autogrill began developing a new restaurant concept, based on the fast-food experience then beginning to take hold in Europe. While many observers remained skeptical about the chances of success of the fast-food concept in a nation devoted to its cuisine—indeed, McDonald's initial attempt to enter Italy met with less than spectacular results—Autogrill's fast-food concept was built around pizza. Dubbed Spizzico, the new restaurant concept was launched in 1989, with a first restaurant in Piemonte. Spizzico proved appealing to the Italian consumer, and by the end of the century Autogrill operated some 150 Spizzicos in Italy.

Autogrill had come to dominate the Italian roadside market by the early 1990s. In addition to seeking new operating sectors, the company now began to eye the international market for its future expansion. In 1993, Autogrill took its first step beyond Italy, forming a 50–50 joint venture with Spain's Cepsa in order to take over that country's Propace roadside restaurant chain. That same year, Autogrill entered France as well, a market that was to grow to become Autogrill's second largest international market. The company continued to invest in its Spanish subsidiary, acquiring the Hermesa y Arhos restaurant group in 1995. Through the mid-1990s, however, the company's international presence remained minor, representing just 5 percent of its sales in 1996.

International Leader in the 21st Century

The privatization of much of Italy's nationalized companies began in 1993 and stepped up in the mid-1990s. Autogrill, then operated from within the larger GS Supermarkets group, came up for sale in 1995. The Benetton family, which had already built up one of Italy's most successful retail empires, had become one of the most prominent purchasers of former government-run businesses. Through its private holding company, Edizioni, the Benetton family began amassing a diversified portfolio of service industry operations, worth more than EUR 7 billion by the end of the decade. Edizioni was awarded its bid for GS and Autogrill, and the restaurant group was promptly spun off as an independent company, and placed under the leadership of CEO Paolo Prota Giurleo.

Autogrill went public in 1996—although Edizioni maintained a 57 percent controlling share of the group. With limited

growth prospects in Italy—the company already operated nearly 400 restaurants and other catering outlets, the company now turned in earnest to its international growth. Autogrill's initial aim was to create a pan-European empire of roadside restaurants by expanding beyond its existing French and Spanish operations. An early triumph for the company came with the award for a highway concession along the Athens-Lamia-Thessaloniki highway in Greece. By 1997, the company had launched its restaurant, elaborating on its long-held bridge-like structure, and incorporating not only a Ciao restaurant, but its Spizzico, Market, and Snack Bar formats as well.

The year 1997 was to become a turning point for Autogrill's international growth as it rapidly expanded into nearly all of the major European markets. Most of the company's foreign expansion came through acquisitions of existing roadside operators. Such was the case in Germany and Austria, which the company entered after it bought up some 14 restaurants from the Wienerwald group. That year, also, Autogrill acquired Sogerba from British group Granada, which had acquired 70 restaurants, including the 43-restaurant Côte France chain, one of the largest operators of roadside restaurants in France, with its acquisition of Forte.

Autogrill's acquisition drive continued in 1998. The company acquired AC Restaurants & Hotels, a group based in the Netherlands that operated 38 AC branded roadside restaurants together with 12 hotels in the Benelux market, as well as seven Le Chesnoye restaurants in Luxembourg. Later that year, Autogrill reinforced its position in France when it acquired Frantour Restauration, the 50-strong chain of railway restaurants, bars, snack bars, and cafes owned by French national railway body SNCF. These acquisitions helped the company claim the European leadership of the highway and freeway restaurant sector, with nearly 650 restaurants and catering outlets. By the end of 1998 more than 25 percent of the company's sales, which topped L 2.3 trillion ($1.24 billion), came from outside France.

In 1999, Autogrill continued to consolidate its European position. After finalizing the Frantour acquisition, the company turned to Spain, where it bought out Cepsa and took full control of the Procace joint venture. The company also negotiated an exclusive 20-year master franchise agreement with the Burger King Corporation to introduce as many as 500 Burger King restaurants into the Italian market.

Yet Autogrill's biggest triumph came in August 1999, when it reached an agreement to acquire Host Marriott Services, the catering division of the Host Marriott Group, in a cash and debt deal worth $929 million. Renamed HMSHost under Autogrill, the acquisition doubled the company's revenues and established it as the world's leading highway restaurant group, and one of the world's top three commercial restaurant groups. HMSHost also gave the company a strong position in the North American airport concessions market, with restaurants in some 60 airports, as well as concessions for such noted landmarks as the Empire State Building, and franchises including Sbarros, Starbucks, Burger King, TCBY, and Pizza Hut.

The HMSHost acquisition not only gave Autogrill a position in a number of new markets, such as Canada, Australia, and New Zealand, it also gave it an opportunity to expand into the

Key Dates:

1947: First Pavesi roadside stand is established along Milan-Novara highway.
1962: Pavesi restaurant is rebuilt as bridge structure.
1977: SME, owned by Italian government, bails out Pavesi and bundles it with two other roadside restaurant operators, Motta and Alemagna, into a new structure called Autogrill.
1982: Autogrill launches its Ciao restaurants concept.
1989: Spizzico fast-food pizza restaurant format debuts.
1993: Autogrill expands into Spain and France.
1995: SME sells Autogrill to Edizioni, the holding company of the Benetton family.
1996: Autogrill floats on Italian stock exchange, but remains majority controlled by Benetton.
1997: Autogrill begins its international expansion in earnest, acquiring 14 restaurants from the Wienerwald group to enter Germany and Austria, and Sogerba, with 70 restaurants, in France.
1998: Company acquires AC Restaurants & Hotels in the Netherlands and Frantour Restauration in France.
1999: Autogrill acquires Host Marriott Services, renamed HMSHost, to become the world's leading travel restaurants group.
2000: Company acquires Passaggio, the Swiss travel restaurants leader.
2001: Company acquires Flughafen-Restaurant, gaining concession for the Zurich airport; acquires 25 percent of Anton Airfood of the United States.
2002: Autogrill acquires 70 percent of Receco in Spain, 22 pecent of Pastarito in Italy, and full control of SMSI Travel Centres Inc. in Canada.

European airports sector as well, on the basis of HMSHost's strong reputation in that market. In 2000, for example, Autogrill gained restaurant concessions for the Bologna Airport and for Athens International Airport, the former directly, the latter through HMSHost. Other airport concessions awarded at that time were for the Los Angeles International Airport and the Salt Lake City airport. Meanwhile, HMSHost became Autogrill's launch pad for entry into the United States—the company opened its first Spizzico restaurant in New York in 2000.

At the beginning of 2000, Autogrill began rolling out the first Italian Burger Kings, a number of which were combined with Spizzico restaurants in a new dual-brand restaurant concept. At the end of that year, the company continued its international expansion with an entry into Switzerland, buying up Passaggio, the country's leading operator of restaurants in highway service areas, railroad stations, and airports. The company consolidated its Swiss position the following year when it acquired Flughafen-Restaurant, the concession holder for the Zurich airport.

Autogrill began exporting its brands at the turn of the century, rolling out the Autogrill, Spizzico, Ciao, and Acafe formats in selected foreign markets. The company was also developing new amenities, such as the Toilette Lounge, an extended restroom format. The company also planned to roll out a package of services geared toward the business traveler. Autogrill also moved into the retail sector with the launch of a drugstore at the Fiumicino airport in Rome.

In June 2001, HMSHost reached an agreement to acquire a 25 percent stake in Anton Airfood, Inc., one of the leading refreshment services companies for the airport sector in the United States with operations at 11 airports. That year, Autogrill restructured its operations under a new CEO, Livio Buttignol, formerly with the GS Supermarkets group. With a flattened management structure, Autogrill prepared to continue its worldwide expansion, eyeing growth into new markets in Asia, such as in Malaysia and China.

Autogrill showed no signs of slowing down in 2002. The company reached an agreement to acquire Ristop, an Italian motorway restaurants company with 26 concessions, then purchased a nearly 22 percent stake in Pastarito, the leading Italian restaurant chain with 70 city center-based restaurants. In the foreign market, the company increased its position in Spain with the purchase of 70 percent of Receco, which operated food concessions along the Spanish high-speed rail network. In North America, the company acquired SMSI Travel Centers Inc., a major highway catering provider in Ontario. By then, Autogrill was approaching an empire of nearly 5,000 restaurants and other catering outlets—with no sign of slowing down in the near future.

Principal Subsidiaries

HMSHost Corporation.

Principal Competitors

McDonald's Corporation; Compass Group Plc; Sodexho Alliance SA; Whitbread PLC; Elior SA; Accor SA; Aramark Corporation.

Further Reading

"Autogrill to Grow Italy's No. 1 Full-Service Chain," *Nation's Restaurant News*, April 1, 2002, p. 43.
Clark, Jennifer, "Autogrill Expanding into Train Stations," *Reuters*, June 21, 1999.
Larner, Monica, "The McDonald's of Pizza?," *Business Week*, January 11, 1999, p. 17.
McGeary, Jennifer, "Hitting the Highway," *Restaurants & Institutions*, September 1, 1999, p. 28.
"Restaurant Chain Autogrill to Expand in US," *Eurofood*, March 28, 2002, p. 8.

—M. L. Cohen

Avery Dennison Corporation

150 North Orange Grove Boulevard
Pasadena, California 91103
U.S.A.
Telephone: (626) 304-2000
Fax: (626) 792-7312
Web site: http://www.averydennison.com

Public Company
Incorporated: 1977 as Avery International Corporation
Employees: 17,300
Sales: $3.8 billion (2001)
Stock Exchanges: New York Pacific
Ticker Symbol: AVY
NAIC: 322222 Coated and Laminated Paper
     Manufacturing; 322233 Stationery, Tablet, and
     Related Product Manufacturing; 339941 Pen and
     Mechanical Pencil Manufacturing

Avery Dennison Corporation was formed in the fall of 1990 by the merger of two *Fortune* 500 companies, Avery International Corporation, based in Pasadena, California, and Dennison Manufacturing Company, headquartered in Framingham, Massachusetts. Best known for its office labels, the merged firm also manufactures consumer packaging labels, self-adhesive stamps, Marks-A-Lot and HI-LITER markers, automotive films and labels, tapes, specialty chemicals, battery-testing labels, notebooks and three-ring binders, and stationery. Increasingly active internationally, Avery Dennison generated 40 percent of its revenues in 2001 outside of the United States.

The two companies had a relationship that dated to 1941, when, following the resolution of a patent dispute involving a dispenser for self-adhesive labels, Dennison became Avery's customer. Avery supplied labels to Dennison that the Massachusetts company sold under the brand name Pres-a-ply, competing with Avery products. By formally joining their two companies Avery and Dennison now share a history dating back more than 155 years.

Dennison Manufacturing Company: 19th-Century Origins

Dennison Manufacturing began in 1844 when Aaron Dennison, a Boston jeweler, returned to his family home in Brunswick, Maine, and with his father, Andrew Dennison, and his sisters began making paper boxes. The father and son soon created a machine to facilitate the making of cardboard boxes. At the time most jewel boxes were imported semiannually; the new Dennison business had a ready-made domestic market.

Andrew Dennison presided over the manufacturing of the boxes while Aaron continued working at his jewelry business. As a sideline he purchased materials for the boxes and sold the finished product. In 1849 Aaron Dennison became a full-time manufacturer of the machine-made watch, turning the sales end of the box business over to his younger brother, Eliphalet Whorf (E. W.) Dennison.

Fourteen years later, the family business was a partnership, Dennison and Company, between E.W. Dennison and three nonfamily members. Working out of a small factory in Boston, the company produced jewelry tags, display cards, and shipping tags, while the boxes continued to be made in Maine. The development of the shipping tag represented Dennison's continuing attempt to diversify, to provide a better product than was currently available, and to create new markets. In 1863 Dennison patented the placement of a paper washer on each side of the hole in a shipping tag, thus providing a more durable tag. Dennison and Company sold ten million tags that first year.

By 1878 the company had a large factory in Roxbury, Massachusetts, the box plant in Brunswick, Maine, and stores in New York, Philadelphia, and Chicago. The company incorporated, becoming the Dennison Manufacturing Company, headed by E.W. Dennison. Henry B. Dennison, E.W.'s son, became president in 1886, the year of his father's death. He served until 1892, when a conflict between the production end, which was Henry's responsibility, and the sales management led to his resignation. Henry K. Dyer, based in New York, became president.

The company returned to family leadership in 1909 when Charles Dennison, another son of E.W., became president. He had previously held positions as vice-president and treasurer. In 1911 Charles Dennison presided over the reincorporation of the company under the same name. When the company originally incorporated in 1878, the managers held all of the stock. Under the terms of E.W. Dennison's will, however, employees participated in profit sharing, receiving stock and the privilege of purchasing additional stock under favorable terms. Over time, people not directly involved in manufacturing acquired on the basis of stock ownership substantial influence on the board and were able to direct policy in ways that Dennison family members found undesirable. The reincorporation plan, spearheaded by Charles Dennison and his nephew Henry Sturgis Dennison, a director of the company, returned control to the managers of production through creation of different categories of stock.

In 1898 under Dyer's direction all of the company's manufacturing operations had been centralized in Framingham, Massachusetts. Under the reincorporation plan, sales operations as well moved to Framingham. By 1911 Dennison Manufacturing's line included tags, gummed labels, paper boxes, greeting cards, sealing wax, and crepe paper. The firm supplied a variety of stationery and paper goods. There were Dennison stores in Boston, New York, Philadelphia, Chicago, St. Louis, and in London, England.

Crepe paper eventually became a major sales item for Dennison Manufacturing Company. In the 1870s the firm began to import tissue paper from England to sell to retail jewelers. Its supplier also provided it with colored paper, which was sold to novelty companies. Crinkling the paper expanded its uses; by 1914 Dennison manufactured its own crepe paper.

The production of crepe paper led to the creation of a line of holiday supplies, including Christmas tags and seals. Eventually the company manufactured items for all of the major holidays including Halloween, St. Valentine's Day, Easter, and St. Patrick's Day. Dennison also had a thriving side business selling pamphlets about parties, crafts, and holidays, highlighting the many uses of Dennison products, particularly crepe paper. The holiday line folded because of declining profits in 1967.

Progressive Management in Early 20th Century

In 1917 Henry Sturgis Dennison, grandson of E.W. Dennison, became president of the company; he held the position for 35 years. As a believer in the scientific management theories of Frederick W. Taylor, Dennison initiated many reforms, including reduction in working hours, establishment of health services and personnel departments, creation of an unemployment fund, and nonmanagerial profit sharing.

Although Henry Dennison served as president of Dennison Manufacturing Company until his death in 1952, he made a significant mark on the world outside the family business. Dennison served as a member of the Commercial Economy Board of the National Defense Council during World War I and, following the war, served as a member of President Warren G. Harding's unemployment conference. He was the author of several books, including *Profit Sharing: Its Principles and Practice,* 1918, written with Arthur W. Burritt and others; *Toward Full Employment,* 1938, written with Lincoln Filene and other industrialists; and *Modern Competition and Business Policy,* 1938, coauthored with John Kenneth Galbraith.

Many businessmen did not support President Franklin Roosevelt and the New Deal; Dennison did, chairing the Industrial Advisory Board of the National Recovery Administration (NRA). This body examined all NRA codes while they were being developed. When the U.S. Supreme Court declared many of the NRA's codes unconstitutional, Dennison became an adviser to the National Resources Planning Board.

During the Great Depression, Dennison Manufacturing suffered, along with the rest of the nation, recording net losses in both 1931 and 1932. The following year the company recovered, once again showing a profit. Profits, however, did not return to pre-Depression levels, making recapitalization necessary and rendering inoperative the profit sharing plan of 1911.

The war economy of the 1940s helped put Dennison back on its feet, and in 1942 sales passed the level of 1929. By 1951 sales were $37.3 million and net earnings were $2.1 million.

Henry S. Dennison suffered a heart attack in 1937 and turned over the active management of the company to John S. Keir, vice-president. Dennison's death in 1952 ended more than 100 years of Dennison family leadership of the Dennison Manufacturing Company.

Attempts at Diversification in the 1960s and 1970s

During the 1960s Dennison experienced further change when, in 1962, it incorporated in Nevada, in a move to decrease taxes. In 1966 Nelson S. Gifford became a director of the company.

By the 1960s analysts considered Dennison Manufacturing Company as part of the label, or marking, industry. Its major operations focused on paper and tag conversion and the production of imprinting and price-ticketing machines.

In 1964 Dennison became the majority shareholder in Paul Williams Copier Corporation. This step was part of its strategy for producing a copier to challenge Xerox. The plan originated

Key Dates:

1844: Aaron Dennison and his father, Andrew Dennison, begin manufacturing paper jewelry boxes in Brunswick, Maine.

1863: The business is now a partnership, Dennison and Company, between Eliphalet Whorf (E. W.) Dennison, younger brother of Aaron, and three nonfamily members; in addition to boxes, the firm has begun making jewelry tags, display cards, and shipping tags at a factory in Boston.

1878: Company is incorporated as Dennison Manufacturing Company.

1898: Dennison's manufacturing operations are centralized in Framingham, Massachusetts.

1917: Henry Sturgis Dennison, grandson of E.W. Dennison, begins 35-year stint as company president.

1935: R. Stanton Avery forms Los Angeles-based Kum-Kleen Adhesive Products Co. to produce self-adhesive labels.

1938: Kum-Kleen is renamed Avery Adhesives.

1941: Avery begins supplying labels to Dennison, which the latter sells under the brand name Pres-a-ply.

1946: Avery Adhesives incorporates as the Avery Adhesive Label Corporation.

1952: Henry S. Dennison dies, ending more than 100 years of Dennison family leadership of Dennison Manufacturing.

1954: Avery creates a division called Avery Paper Company (later called Fasson), which specializes in producing and selling self-adhesive base materials, often to competing label makers.

1961: Avery goes public.

1964: Avery Adhesive is renamed Avery Products Corporation.

1990: Avery International and Dennison Manufacturing merge to form Avery Dennison Corporation.

1999: European office products joint venture is created with Zweckform Büro-Produkte G.m.b.H.

2002: Jackstädt GmbH, privately held maker of self-adhesive materials based in Germany, is acquired.

in 1957, when, under license from RCA, Dennison began work on a dry copier that differed in several important technological ways from Xerox machines.

Dennison also produced print-punch machines for generating price tags in a relationship with Cummins, the maker of Data Read Machines. Dennison in the 1960s was a high-tech firm, particularly in the arena of packaging. The company could, through an instantaneous heat process, transfer a graphic design to plastic. The process, therimage, was cheaper than more conventional methods.

Building on this technological base, Dennison continued to invest heavily in research and development. In 1979 Dennison formed a joint partnership with Canada Development Corporation (CDC)—Delphax—to develop high-speed, nonimpact printers. Using proprietary technology, the company sought to

create products to compete with laser printers. Xerox subsequently bought CDC's 50 percent interest in Delphax.

Late 1980s Retrenchment

In the 1980s Dennison's other technological ventures took it further afield. The company held the majority interest in Biological Technology Corporation, which was working on diagnostic products, using researchers from Massachusetts Institute of Technology and Harvard University. Potential products included pregnancy test supplies.

Returning to its office products base, Dennison stayed abreast of computer technology, producing floppy discs as well as office furniture. In the 1980s Dennison's stationery division accounted for almost half of sales and profits. The attempt to develop a copier to challenge Xerox, begun in 1957, had not succeeded.

In 1985 Dennison experienced a significant economic downturn, which prompted a five-year restructuring plan. A large source of Dennison's problems came from heavy investments in research and development. Streamlining for the next two years, Dennison sold seven businesses and shut down four others. This process left the company with three key businesses: stationery, systems, and packaging. The stationery division, actually two units, Dennison National and Dennison Carter, remained the major contributor to profits. Systems was divided into retail and industrial units, produced bar-code printing machines, and was the world's leading manufacturer of plastic price-tag threads. The ongoing restructuring plan involved the consolidation of Dennison National and Dennison Carter, and the integration of systems was scheduled for completion in 1990.

Because of the company's commitment to this program, the news in the spring of 1990 of a merger between Dennison and Avery caught industry observers by surprise. Both companies, however, had been suffering depressed earnings and sought strength in union.

Avery International Corporation: Founded 1935

R. Stanton Avery founded the company that would eventually become part of Avery Dennison Corporation in 1935 with capital of less than $100 from his future wife, Dorothy Durfee. Avery created Kum-Kleen Adhesive Products Co. to produce self-adhesive labels using machinery he had developed while working at the Adhere Paper Company.

Based in Los Angeles, Kum-Kleen first marketed its labels to gift shops and antique stores and then expanded to other retail establishments, including furniture, hardware, and drugstores. In 1938, Avery Adhesives, the company's new name, suffered a fire that destroyed all of its equipment except a stock of labels. While rebuilding, Avery implemented changes in the die-cutting machinery; the technology Stan Avery developed remained the standard for the industry.

Before the development of self-adhesives, labels were either pregummed or applied with glue. Initially self-adhesive labels did not have a coating that would facilitate removal of the label from its backing and, therefore, they were difficult to use. Early labels were punched rather than cut. The innovation of Avery

Adhesives occurred on two levels: technological, improving and streamlining the manufacturing process; and product definition, creating a market.

World War II and the total economic mobilization it necessitated created problems for Avery Adhesives as well as for other industries. The raw materials necessary to produce the adhesive for the labels, natural and synthetic rubber and solvents derived from petroleum, were required by the military. Avery Adhesives, needing permission from the federal government to continue production and to obtain materials, focused on manufacturing industrial items rather than the labels for consumer goods it had previously produced. Among the products were waterproof labels bearing ''S.O.S.'' in Morse code that were stuck on rescue radios. When the war ended, this focus on labels for industrial and commercial uses persisted. The war economy hastened market acceptance of pressure-sensitive labels.

Postwar Incorporation

In 1946 Avery Adhesives incorporated, becoming the Avery Adhesive Label Corporation. At the time of incorporation, more than 80 percent of the company's output consisted of industrial labels that were sold to manufacturers who placed them on their own products, usually consumer items, using automatic label-dispensing machines. The original retail base of Avery Adhesives persisted, providing 10 percent of output. The company sold unprinted labels in dispenser flat-pack boxes to stationery stores and other retail establishments through a distribution network. The final aspect of the new corporation's business consisted of selling pressure-sensitive material to printers and others who used them in other products, such as masking tape. Tape rolls produced by Avery were used in the manufacturing of department store price labels. This aspect of Avery's business, which contributed 10 percent to output, was known as converting. These industrial categories were the forerunners of Avery's divisions in the 1960s and 1970s.

In the 1940s Avery perceived itself as the only company in the self-adhesive label industry to offer a full line of products. Competition did exist for transparent mending tape, not part of Avery's line. Minnesota Mining and Manufacturing was the leader in that field.

A challenge to Avery occurred in the 1950s in the form of a patent suit. Avery had taken out a patent for its method of producing self-adhesive labels. Because other self-adhesive products predated Stan Avery's technological innovations, the label itself could not be patented. In 1950 Avery Adhesive brought suit against Ever Ready Label Corporation, then the leader in the industry, alleging infringement on Avery's basic patent. In 1952 a New Jersey court ruled against Avery, stating that there was ''not an invention'' and that the patent was only a method, not a unique product.

Meeting the Challenge: The 1960s

The loss of the patent had serious consequences for Avery, ultimately changing the nature of its business, and had a ripple effect on the self-adhesive and label industry. The short-term outcome of the patent decision of 1952 was the creation, in 1954, of a new division, the Avery Paper Company. The division produced and sold self-adhesive base materials, often to competing label companies. Eventually this division dominated manufacturing at Avery, eclipsing label sales.

In the 1960s four different branches made up the loosely defined label industry. There were manufacturers of various rubber stamps for paperwork, metal labelers including engravers and stencilers, adhesive label manufacturers, and producers of specialized marking devices. The total volume of this diverse industry was approximately $150 million with annual growth of 3 percent. In the adhesive label category the leading manufacturers were Avery Products Corporation (the name was changed in 1964), 3M, the Simon Adhesive Products and Eureka Specialty Printing divisions of Litton Industries, and the Kleen-Stik products division of National Starch and Chemical Corporation.

Avery had four divisions in the marking or identification aspect of the industry. Fasson, the new name of Avery Paper Company, was a supplier of raw materials. A second division used these raw materials to manufacture Avery labels. Another division, Rote, manufactured hand-embossing machines, and Metal-Cal, acquired in 1964, made anodized and etched aluminum foil for nameplates. Another aspect of Avery's business in the 1960s was machines that embossed vinyl tape. Avery's main product continued to be self-adhesive labels used in a range of products, including automobiles and airplanes.

The 1960s represented a period of much growth for Avery and U.S. industry in general. The period witnessed the rise in mergers and the development of the diversified corporation, culminating in the emergence of the conglomerate.

In 1961 Avery became publicly owned; it was listed on the New York Stock Exchange in 1967. That year, the company had 2,500 workers and two major components. Label products included the domestic Avery Label division and four wholly owned foreign subsidiaries. The other component was base materials, predominantly Fasson and Fasson Europe. The major buyers of base materials were industrial firms, including the graphic arts trade. In 1968 Avery's share of the industry's $200 million in sales was $63 million. The late 1960s were good years for Avery, as it developed specific units to target specific markets.

In 1974 Avery made the *Fortune* 500 list for the first time. Avery was last on the list, and its competitor 3M was 50th. The 1970s presented Avery with the first major impediment to growth since World War II. Once again the company faced problems caused by a situation outside its immediate control. The oil crisis of 1975 heavily affected Avery, a company dependent on petrochemicals. Avery faced increased costs, oversupply, and declining demand. The price per share of Avery's stock dropped to $22, from a high of $44 the previous year.

Diversification in the 1980s

By 1980 Avery had reversed its downward slide by diversifying and by controlling costs, prices, and employment levels. The materials units included raw materials, Fasson, and specialty materials, such as Thermark. Thermark produced hot stamping materials for automobiles and appliances. Fasson continued to be the bread-and-butter unit of Avery; its self-adhesives were now being used on disposable diapers. The converting unit had moved into the production of labels for data processing and home and office use. Avery continued to maintain foreign operations, centered in Western Europe and located as well in Canada, Mexico, and Australia.

Seven years later Avery International was the nation's leading producer of self-adhesive materials and labels. The company's revenues were three times greater than ten years previously. In the late 1980s, however, profits flattened. The main reasons were Avery's involvement in the disposable diaper market and its ongoing competition with 3M. Avery first began producing tape for diapers in 1977 and by 1984 was the sole supplier to Kimberly-Clark Corporation, manufacturers of Huggies. 3M did the same for Pampers, which were made by the Procter & Gamble Company. 3M's tape was one piece while Avery's contained a tiny piece of plastic that could fall off and perhaps be swallowed. Kimberly-Clark turned to 3M. In 1986 Avery developed its own one-piece tape in an attempt to win back Kimberly-Clark's business. Avery also attempted to challenge 3M in two other areas—transparent tape and self-sticking notes. Avery later abandoned this effort.

In a thorough restructuring, beginning in 1987, Avery closed some manufacturing facilities, domestic and overseas, and announced plans to cut the number of employees by 8 percent. Avery was, however, succeeding in its attempt to strengthen its share of the diaper tape market.

1990 Merger of Avery and Dennison Capping Decade of Competition

Avery's merger with Dennison was the culmination of 50 years of infrequent negotiations between the two companies. Dennison had made the first overture in 1941, but balked at the $200,000 price demanded by founder Stan Avery. That figure increased considerably in the ensuing five decades. Charles ("Chuck") Miller, who had advanced to Avery's chief executive office in 1977, turned the tables on Dennison, embarking on more than a decade of negotiations. He hoped that Dennison would cap a string of acquisitions in the early 1980s, but the 1987 talks failed once again.

Success came in 1990, when Dennison employees and officers, who controlled more than 20 percent of the company's stock, accepted Avery's $287 million bid. But Miller, who retained the top spots at the merged firm, soon realized that his was a Pyrrhic victory. Dennison lacked proper controls, its overseas operations were losing money, and its domestic businesses were fraught with inefficiencies. To make matters worse, a mild economic recession worsened shortly after the union was completed.

Miller moved quickly to reorganize Dennison while rationalizing it with Avery. He hired a consultancy to evaluate Dennison's subsidiaries and spun off or liquidated about $350 million (sales) unprofitable divisions and product lines by 1995, eliminating about 900 employees in the process. Miller cut another 900 workers outright in the meantime. The adoption of time-based management principles helped the merged companies increase efficiency via inventory reduction and expedited ordering, among other strategies.

Avery Dennison also sharpened its focus on research and development in the early 1990s. By 1996, products developed after the merger contributed one-third of its annual sales. Innovations included the nation's first self-adhesive postage stamp, PowerCheck on-battery tester (created in cooperation with Duracell Inc.), new Band-Aid adhesives, and Translar recyclable label stock. Perhaps more important, the company instituted a customer-oriented new product development process.

The year in which Avery Dennison became a reality, 1990, was not a good one for the new company. Sales increased only 1 percent, from $2.4 billion to $2.6 billion, and net income declined from $114.2 million to a scanty $5.9 million. But as CEO Miller's reorganization began to take effect, Avery Dennison's bottom line improved. By 1995, revenues had increased to more than $3 billion, and profits burgeoned to $143.7 million.

Late 1990s and Beyond: Economic Espionage Lawsuit, Joint Ventures, and Acquisitions

In 1997 Avery Dennison filed a lawsuit against Four Pillars Enterprises Ltd., accusing the Taiwanese firm of fraud and espionage. The lawsuit came after two top executives of Four Pillars were arrested in the United States and charged with economic espionage, money laundering, and mail fraud. The case involved a former Avery Dennison researcher, Victor Lee, who testified during the trial that he had passed on trade secrets to Four Pillars while working as a paid "consultant" for the firm (and while still working for Avery Dennison). Among the secrets involved were chemical formulations for Avery's diaper tape, self-stick postage stamps, and battery labels. In 1999 both the company and the executives were convicted, although the judge in the case threw out 18 of the 21 charges brought against Four Pillars and the executives. In early 2000 Four Pillars was fined $5 million, one of the executives received six months of home confinement and 18 months of probation, and the other was placed on one year of probation. Also in 2000 the jury in Avery Dennison's civil suit awarded the company $40 million in damages. On a broader level, the case was significant because it was the first case tried under the Economic Espionage Act of 1996.

In May 1998 Philip M. Neal was promoted from president and COO to president and CEO. Miller remained chairman, having ended his 21-year stint as chief executive. Under Neal's leadership in the late 1990s and early 2000s, Avery Dennison continued to aggressively seek overseas growth. Early in 1999 the company contributed the bulk of its office product businesses in Europe to a new joint venture with Zweckform Büro-Produkte G.m.b.H., a leading German office products supplier. Avery Dennison held a majority stake in the new company, which was called Avery Dennison Zweckform Office Products Europe G.m.b.H. Another joint venture was formed in Japan with Hitachi Maxell, this one too involving office products. Back home, Avery Dennison paid about $150 million to acquire Stimsonite Corporation, a Niles, Illinois-based maker of reflective safety products for the transportation and highway safety markets (such as reflective coatings on highway signs). Seeking to counter a growth slowdown that began in late 1998 and continued into 1999, Avery Dennison launched a restructuring program early in 1999 involving the closure of eight manufacturing and distribution facilities, the elimination of 1,500 jobs, and a $65 million pretax charge. The goal was to achieve about $60 million in annual cost savings by 2001.

The overseas growth drive continued in 2000. Early that year the company announced that it would spend $40 million to expand its manufacturing operation in China. Avery Dennison was already the largest manufacturer of pressure-sensitive label stock in that country. In Europe the firm acquired the Adespan pressure-sensitive materials operation of Panini S.p.A. of Italy. Adespan, whose products included bar code and beverage labels, had sales of about $75 million in 1999 from its base of customers in Europe, Latin America, and Australia. The Adespan business became part of Avery Dennison's Fasson Roll Europe Division, which was based in the Netherlands. Also in 2000 Miller retired from his position as chairman, although he remained on the company board. Neal became chairman and CEO, while Dean A. Scarborough was named president and COO. Scarborough had previously held the title of group vice-president, Fasson Roll Worldwide.

With the U.S. economy falling into recession in 2001, Avery Dennison saw both its revenues and profits decline. Seeking to reduce costs, the firm announced midyear that it would cut an additional 450 jobs from its workforce. Acquisitions in 2001 included the purchase from Costa Mesa, California-based Stomp Inc. of the CD Stomper line of compact disc and DVD labels as well as the purchase of Dunsirn Industries, Inc. of Neenah, Wisconsin, a maker of nonadhesive label materials. In September 2001 Avery Dennison announced that it would acquire Jackstädt GmbH of Germany for approximately $295 million. The acquisition, which was delayed by a German regulatory review, was finalized in May 2002. With $400 million in 2001 revenues, Jackstädt was the world's largest privately held maker of self-adhesive materials. Following completion of the deal, the headquarters of Avery Dennison's European pressure-sensitive materials operation were relocated to Jackstädt's site in Wuppertal, Germany. Avery Dennison also announced that the merger would result in the elimination of 800 to 1,000 jobs from the combined workforce over a two-year period. The reorganization was expected to cost from $60 million to $70 million.

Principal Subsidiaries

A.V. Chemie AG (Switzerland); ADC Philippines, Inc. (Philippines); ADESPAN S.R.L. (Italy); ADESPAN U.K. Limited; AEAC, Inc.; Avery (China) Company Limited; Avery Automotive Limited (U.K.); Avery Corp.; Avery de Mexico S.A. de C.V.; Avery Dennison (Fiji) Limited; Avery Dennison (Guangzhou) Co. Ltd. (China); Avery Dennison (Guangzhou) Converted Products Limited (China); Avery Dennison (Hong Kong) Limited; Avery Dennison (India) Private Limited; Avery Dennison (Ireland) Limited; Avery Dennison (Kunshan) Limited (China); Avery Dennison (Malaysia) SDN. BHD.; Avery Dennison (Shanghai) International Trading Limited (China); Avery Dennison (Thailand) Ltd.; Avery Dennison Australia Group Holdings Pty Limited; Avery Dennison Belgie B.V. B.A. (Belgium); Avery Dennison C.A. (Venezuela); Avery Dennison Canada Inc.; Avery Dennison Chile S.A.; Avery Dennison Colombia S.A.,; Avery Dennison Converted Products de Mexico, S.A. de C.V.; Avery Dennison Coordination Center B.V.B.A. (Belgium); Avery Dennison Danmark Holding ApS (Den-

mark); Avery Dennison Deutschland G.m.b.H. (Germany); Avery Dennison do Brasil Ltda. (Brazil); Avery Dennison Dover S.A. (Argentina); Avery Dennison Etiket Ticaret Limited Sirketi (Turkey); Avery Dennison Europe Holding (Deutschland) G.m.b.H & Co KG (Germany); Avery Dennison Finance Danmark A.p. S. (Denmark); Avery Dennison Finance France S.A.S.; Avery Dennison Finance Germany G.m.b.H.; Avery Dennison Finance Luxembourg S.A.R.L.; Avery Dennison Foreign Sales Corporation (Barbados); Avery Dennison France S.A.; Avery Dennison Group Danmark A.p.S. (Denmark); Avery Dennison Health Management Corporation; Avery Dennison Holding & Finance The Netherlands B.V.; Avery Dennison Holding AG (Switzerland); Avery Dennison Holding G.m.b.H. (Germany); Avery Dennison Holding Luxembourg S.A.R.L.; Avery Dennison Holdings Limited (Australia); Avery Dennison Hong Kong B.V. (Netherlands); Avery Dennison Hungary Limited; Avery Dennison Iberica, S.A. (Spain); Avery Dennison Investments The Netherlands B.V.; Avery Dennison Italia S.p.A. (Italy); Avery Dennison Korea Limited; Avery Dennison Luxembourg S.A.; Avery Dennison Materials France S.A.R.L.; Avery Dennison Materials G.m.b.H. (Germany); Avery Dennison Materials Ireland Limited; Avery Dennison Materials Nederland B.V. (Netherlands); Avery Dennison Materials Pty Limited (Australia); Avery Dennison Materials U.K. Limited; Avery Dennison Mexico S.A. de C.V.; Avery Dennison Nordic A/S (Denmark); Avery Dennison Norge A/S (Norway); Avery Dennison Office Products (NZ) Limited (New Zealand); Avery Dennison Office Products (PTY.) Ltd. (South Africa); Avery Dennison Office Products Company; Avery Dennison Office Products De Mexico, S.A. de C.V.; Avery Dennison Office Products France S.A.S.; Avery Dennison Office Products Italia S.r.l. (Italy); Avery Dennison Office Products Manufacturing & Trading Limited Liability Company (Avery Dennison Ltd.) (Hungary); Avery Dennison Office Products PTY Limited (Australia); Avery Dennison Office Products U.K. Limited; Avery Dennison Osterreich G.m.b.H. (Austria); Avery Dennison Overseas Corporation; Avery Dennison Pension Trustee Limited (U.K.); Avery Dennison Peru S.A.; Avery Dennison Polska Sp. Z O.O. (Poland); Avery Dennison Scandinavia A/S (Denmark); Avery Dennison Schweiz AG (Switzerland); Avery Dennison Security Printing Europe A/S (Denmark); Avery Dennison Shared Services, Inc.; Avery Dennison Singapore (PTE) Ltd; Avery Dennison South Africa (Proprietary) Limited; Avery Dennison Suomi OY (Finland); Avery Dennison Sverige AB (Sweden); Avery Dennison Systemes d'etiquetage France S.A.S.; Avery Dennison U.K. Limited; Avery Dennison Verwaltungs G.m.b.H. (Germany); Avery Dennison Zweckform Austria G.m.b.H.; Avery Dennison Zweckform Office Products Europe G.m.b.H. (Germany); Avery Dennison Zweckform Unterstutzungskasse G.m.b.H. (Germany); Avery Dennison, S.A. de C.V. (Mexico); Avery Dennison-Maxell K.K. (Japan); Avery Etiketsystemer A/S (Denmark); Avery Etiketten B.V. (Netherlands); Avery Etiketsystem Svenska AB (Sweden); Avery Graphic Systems, Inc.; Avery Guidex Limited (U.K.); Avery Holding B.V. (Netherlands); Avery Holding Limited (U.K.); Avery Holding S.A. (France); Avery Maschinen G.m.b.H. (Germany); Avery Pacific Corporation; Avery Properties PTY. Limited (Australia); Avery Research Center, Inc.; Avery, Inc.; BOA/IWACO Offset A/S (Denmark); Dennison Comercio, Importacas E Exportacao Ltda. (Brazil); Dennison Development Associates; Dennison

International Company; Dennison International Holding B.V. (Netherlands); Dennison Ireland Limited; Dennison Manufacturing (Trading) Ltd. (Channel Islands); Dennison Manufacturing Company; Dennison Office Products Limited (Ireland); DMC Development Corporation; Dunsirn Industries, Inc.; Etikettrykkeriet A/S (Denmark); Fasson Canada Inc.; Fasson Portugal Produtos Auto-Adesivos LDA. (Portugal); IWACO A/S (Denmark); IWACO Labels & Labelling Systems OY (Finland); Iwaco Norge AS (Norway); LAC Retail Systems Limited (U.K.); Monarch Industries, Inc.; Ocawi Sverige AB (Sweden); PT Avery Dennison Indonesia; Retail Products Limited (Ireland); Security Printing Division, Inc.; Spartan International, Inc.; Spartan Plastics Canada, Ltd; Steinbeis Office Products Beteiligungs G.m.b.H. (Germany); Stimsonite Australia PTY Limited; Stimsonite Corporation; Stimsonite do Brasil Ltda (Brazil); Stimsonite Europa Limited (U.K.); Stimsonite International, Inc.; Tiadeco Participacoes, Ltda. (Brazil); Zweckform U.K. Ltd.

Principal Divisions

Converting Americas; Converting Asia; Fasson Roll Europe; Fasson Roll North America; Graphics Europe; InfoChain Express; Materials Asia Pacific; Materials South America; Office Products Europe; Office Products North America; Retail Information Services; Reflective Products Division; Specialty Tape Division Europe; Specialty Tape Division U.S.; Worldwide Specialty Tapes.

Principal Competitors

3M Company; Bemis Company, Inc.; Wallace Computer Services, Inc.; Fortune Brands, Inc.; Moore Corporation Limited; Brady Corporation.

Further Reading

Avery, R. Stanton, and Charles D. Miller, *Avery International: Fifty Years of Progress,* New York: Newcomen Society of the United States, 1986, 28 p.

Barrett, Amy, "The Loved One," *Financial World,* February 18, 1992, pp. 26–27.

Beauchamp, Marc, "A Sticky Business," *Forbes,* January 26, 1987, p. 61.

Biddle, Frederic M., "Avery Dennison Wins $40 Million in Secrets Case," *Wall Street Journal,* February 7, 2000, p. B18.

Chuang, Tamara, "A New Spin on Avery," *Orange County Register,* March 9, 2002.

Clark, David L., *Avery International Corporation 50-Year History, 1935–1985,* Pasadena, Calif.: Avery International Corporation, 1988, 195 p.

Darlin, Damon, "Thank You, 3M," *Forbes,* September 25, pp. 86–87.

Dennison Beginnings, 1840–1878, Framingham, Mass.: Dennison Manufacturing Company.

Dennison, James T., *Henry S. Dennison, 1877–1952, New England Industrialist Who Served America,* New York: Newcomen Society in North America, 1955, 32 p.

"Earning a Comeback Label," *Financial World,* March 1, 1980, pp. 28+.

Gellene, Denise, "Avery Scotches Unprofitable Tape Business, to Pare Work Force by 8 Percent," *Los Angeles Times,* November 10, 1987.

Hamilton, Denise, "Avery Dennison and the Public's Big Stamp of Approval," *Los Angeles Times,* May 4, 1995, p. J12.

John S. Keir, Portland, Ore.: The Dennison Manufacturing Company, 1960.

Meagher, James P., "Avery International Co.: A Restructuring Has Improved Avery," *Barron's,* April 18, 1988, pp. 57+.

Miller, Charles D., "Seeking the Service Grail," *Financial Executive,* July-August 1993, pp. 14–16.

Nguyen, Hang, "Avery Acquires Stomp's Line of CD, DVD Labels," *Los Angeles Times,* February 14, 2001, p. C2.

Oliver, Myrna, "R. Stanton Avery: Label Firm Founder," *Los Angeles Times,* December 13, 1997, p. A20.

Paley, Norton, "A Sticky Situation," *Sales and Marketing Management,* May 1996, pp. 40–41.

Peltz, James F., "Avery Dennison Sticks by Slow, Steady Growth," *Los Angeles Times,* July 22, 1998, p. D1.

Penenberg, Adam L., and Marc Barry, *Spooked: Espionage in Corporate America,* Cambridge, Mass.: Perseus, 2000, 188 p.

Pettersson, Edvard, "Wall Street Labels Avery a Good Buy, As Earnings Rise," *Los Angeles Business Journal,* November 8, 1999, p. 42.

Rublin, Lauren R., "New Wrapping and Trim: Dennison Fashions a Handsome Recovery," *Barron's,* November 14, 1988, pp. 18+.

Rundle, Rhonda L., and Joseph Pereira, "Avery, Dennison Plan to Merge in Stock Swap," *Wall Street Journal,* May 29, 1990, p. A6.

Seventy-Five Years, 1844–1919, Framingham, Mass.: Dennison Manufacturing Company.

Slater, Eric, "Industrial Spying Case Winds Down," *Los Angeles Times,* April 24, 1999, p. A19.

Starkman, Dean, "Two Taiwanese Are Convicted for Espionage," *Wall Street Journal,* April 29, 1999, p. B16.

Vollmers, Gloria, "Industrial Home Work of the Dennison Manufacturing Company of Framingham, Massachusetts, 1912–1935," *Business History Review,* Autumn 1997, pp. 444–70.

Walters, Donna K.H., "Hello, Our Name Is ... Pasadena's Avery Dennison Has Turned Label Making into an Art," *Los Angeles Times,* May 31, 1993, p. D1.

"Why Avery International and Dennison Joined Forces," *Mergers and Acquisitions,* January/February 1991, pp. 49+.

Yang, Eleanor, "Avery Dennison Plans Job, Factory Cuts," *Los Angeles Times,* January 27, 1999, p. C2.

—Amy Mittelman
—updates: April Dougal Gasbarre, David E. Salamie

AXA Colonia Konzern AG

Gereonsdriesch 9-11
50670 Köln
Germany
Telephone: (49) (221) 148-101
Fax: (49) (221) 1482-1704
Web site: http://www.axa.de

Public Company
Incorporated: 1839 as Kölnische Feuer-Versicherungs-
   Gesellschaft
Employees: 14,622
Sales: $8.51 billion (2000)
Stock Exchanges: Frankfurt
Ticker Symbol: COL
NAIC: 524113 Direct Life Insurance Carriers; 524114
   Direct Health and Medical Insurance Carriers (pt);
   524118 Other Direct Insurance (Except Life, Health,
   and Medical) Carriers (pt); 524126 Direct Property
   and Casualty Insurance Carriers (pt); 524127 Direct
   Title Insurance Carriers; 524292 Third Party
   Administration of Insurance and Pension Funds (pt)

AXA Colonia Konzern AG is Germany's fourth largest primary insurer based in Cologne. Through its operative subsidiary, Colonia Versicherung Aktiengesellschaft, the group provides a broad variety of personal and property insurance services such as general and professional liability, accident, fire, auto, transportation, life, and health coverage to private and corporate clients. Major brand names are Colonia, Nordstern, Darag, and Deutsche ärzteversicherung.

AXA Colonia is part of the world's largest insurance holding company, the AXA Group, which holds about 80 percent of AXA Colonia shares. As part of AXA, AXA Colonia offers international coverage concepts for multinational companies. The AXA Colonia group also offers several financial services including asset management, construction financing, bond funds, and real estate funds.

Early Years As Fire Insurer: 1839–1902

AXA Colonia's origins go back to a law enacted in 1837, banishing most foreign—mainly French—insurers from the German state of Prussia. This was the chance for the two brothers Abraham and Simon Oppenheim, of the Cologne-based Oppenheim bank, to pursue their plans for a fire insurance business in the form of a joint stock company within the thriving heart of the Rhineland. On June 22, 1839, five founders gave birth to Colonia by signing the company agreement after they had received a concession from the Prussian emperor Kaiser Wilhelm III: the Cologne bankers Simon Oppenheim, Heinrich Ziegler, Wilhelm Ludwig Deichmann, and Carl-Eduard Schnitzler, and Cologne's Chamber of Commerce President Peter Heinrich Merkens who became chair of the board. They were joined by other Cologne businessmen to constitute the first executive board of the Kölnische Feuer-Versicherungs-Gesellschaft (Fire Insurance Company of Cologne). The company's first fire insurance plan covered buildings and furniture consumed or damaged by fire and lightning. Documents, money, precious gemstones, and gunpowder mills, however, as well as fire resulting from earthquakes or acts of war, were not covered.

Johann Heinrich Daniel Kamp, an experienced banker and entrepreneur residing in Cologne, became the company's first director and took the first steps to get the business going, which meant to create a close network of representatives as soon as possible. By 1843, 59 general agencies in 57 towns, including more than 260 subsidiaries, represented the newly licensed firm. Because the name Kölnische Feuer-Versicherungs-Gesellschaft was not easy to remember by potential customers, the name "Colonia" was used instead, referring to the female allegorical figure that gave the city of Cologne its name. In 1841, the company's first brand name was approved by the Ministry for the Interior as a prefix to the company name.

Colonia's initial business concession allowed the company to do business in the German state of Prussia only. In the years after its founding, however, it modestly expanded into a few small German states as well as into The Netherlands and Denmark. A devastating fire in the German harbor town of Hamburg in 1842 was Colonia's first big challenge. Because of the company's high share capital basis, all claims—amounting to

41

Company Perspectives:

We offer a comprehensive line of coverage in all areas of personal and property insurance, focused on the needs of private, commercial and industrial clients. We promote a solid foundation for assets and the financial security of our clients by means of an extensive variety of financial services: construction financing, bond funds, real estate funds, and other financial instruments. Our strengths are the close relationship of our representatives to clients, the continuous work on new types of insurance and financial services and the development of innovative special products. Our staff is characterized by their competent counsel, their comprehensive understanding of customer service and their acknowledged reliability. We are aware of our responsibility for the life-planning, health care, and secure livelihood of our clients. We understand that our job as an insurance company is an ethical and social one as well. In our work we take into account the latest findings of science, technology and environmental studies. We observe in advance economic and social changes and do our business in harmony with environmental needs.

more than one-third of Colonia's annual premium income—were settled through cash payments within five weeks. Resulting from this experience, the board of directors decided to establish Colonia's own reinsurance company. After the first European economic crisis had delayed this project for several years, the Rückversicherungs-Aktien-Gesellschaft Colonia was set up under Colonia's third managing director, Jakob Gilbert, who served the company in this position between 1868 and 1883. Until the end of the 19th century, Colonia offered fire insurance only. In 1853, Concordia, Cölnische Lebensversicherungs-Gesellschaft, a life insurance provider, was opened and closely linked to Colonia through Abraham Oppenheim as a member of both companies' boards of directors.

New Products, Alliances, and Crises: 1903–45

Since its founding, Colonia had been a driving force in setting up alliances to promote the mutual interests of insurance companies. In the late 19th century, it joined five other insurance companies in founding the ''Federation of German Private Fire Insurers,'' an organization that provided statistics linked with their business. While it was not a price cartel, minimum rates for fire insurance were set beginning around 1900. Between 1903 and 1917, Colonia added new insurance products to its business: a burglary and theft insurance; an insurance against loss of rent caused by fire, lightning, or explosion; a burst pipes insurance; a consequential loss insurance; a price difference insurance (i.e., for the sugar trade); and a marine insurance. By 1914, Colonia employed more than 70 people.

Beginning in 1919, Colonia entered two decades of new alliances through mergers and acquisitions to compete in the consolidating insurance sector. In December 1919, the company agreed to merge with the Kölnische Unfall-Versicherungs-Aktiengesellschaft (K.U.), another Cologne-based insurer active in the industrial liability as well as in individual accident, collec-

tive, passenger, sea voyage, and glass and valuables insurance, in which Colonia had been holding a substantial share since 1880. Colonia took over all of K.U.'s assets and insurance contracts—and its full name. The new Colonia Kölnische Feuer- und Kölnische Unfall-Versicherungs-Aktiengesellschaft, however, entered troubled times.

First of all, the merger went anything but smoothly. K.U.'s workforce could not get used to the more bureaucratic Colonia culture and none of the parties was willing to give up its independence. In addition, Germany's economy went through difficult times after World War I, including dwindling markets through lost territories and a collapse of the German currency due to inflation in 1920. Colonia, as a fire insurer, was not allowed by law to do business in foreign currency—a fact that put Colonia's reinsurance subsidiary, which had to pay back loans in foreign currency, into deep debt. Thanks to the brisk intervention of Colonia's supervisory board in the spring of 1923, the company was able to survive the turmoil. In October, Dr. Christian Oertel, a highly respected German insurance manager, was elected as chairman of Colonia's board. He successfully reorganized and streamlined management, sales, and administration, replaced bureaucracy by a more participatory culture to motivate Colonia's and former K.U.'s employees, increased Colonia's share capital, and rearranged its holdings.

In response to rapidly increasing competitive pressure, Colonia entered an agreement with the two other main insurance companies of the Rhineland to support each other if needed in 1921, sealed by a mutual exchange of shares. The agreement was hit hard in 1929, however, when one of the partners went bankrupt. In the years after 1924, Colonia bought holdings in several companies, many of which were sold again over the next ten years, when the company retained shares in ten companies, among them a 35 percent share in the Berlin-based Nordstern Allgemeine, and a 40 percent share in the Cologne-based reinsurer Kölnische Rückversicherungsgesellschaft. In 1938, the company was renamed Colonia Kölnische Versicherungs-AG. Before World War II began, Colonia was Germany's third largest private insurance company, with a workforce of about 880.

Postwar Boom and Major Mergers: 1946–72

In Colonia's first balance sheet after the war, the company's assets displayed were worth less than 60 percent of the prewar value. About a third of Colonia's buildings in the western part of Germany were destroyed. In the ''Soviet Zone,'' Colonia's property was expropriated: ten branch offices and about 40 percent of the company's business volume were lost. Dr. Robert Pferdmenges, a close acquaintance of West Germany's new president, Konrad Adenauer, who had rescued the Oppenheim bank during the Nazi years and succeeded Simon Alfred von Oppenheim as a partner, led Colonia's reconstruction efforts as chair of the supervisory board. Colonia's chairman of the management board was Karl Haus, another representative of the Oppenheim bank in charge of its insurance holdings, who became the first president of the Association of German Insurers. While Colonia mainly focused on reconstruction in the early 1950s, the first signs of the postwar boom were seen when Colonia's traditional branches made profits again. Colonia's premium income increased by 15 percent from 1954 to 1955 to a total of DM 76.6

Key Dates:

1839: Kölnische Feuer-Versicherungs-Gesellschaft is incorporated.
1919: Colonia merges with Kölnische Unfall-Versicherungs-Aktiengesellschaft.
1923: Dr. Christian Oertel is named chairman of the board of Colonia.
1975: Colonia Insurance Company (UK) Ltd. is formed.
1990: Colonia opens a branch office in Dresden.
1991: Colonia is restructured under the name Colonia Konzern AG.
1996: Compagnie Union des Assurances de Paris (UAP) becomes the parent company of Colonia.
1997: Compagnie Union des Assurances de Paris (UAP) merges with AXA SA; CKAG Colonia Konzern AG becomes AXA Colonia Konzern AG.

million. The company especially participated in the postwar boom of auto insurance, and new products such as livestock and textiles insurance were offered. Otto Vossen, an experienced insurance manager who had joined Colonia in 1946, took over chairmanship of the management board in 1963. An engineer with a creative mind, he pioneered Colonia's product management by introducing machinery, contract works, warranty, and building contractors' insurance for businesses, as well as an early version of renter's insurance and a new-value insurance for houses, among other offerings. A brand new office building in Cologne built in 1968 included a ''drive-in station'' for the fast settlement of claims. By 1969, Colonia's workforce reached 2,160, up from about 1,000 in 1953.

In 1967, Dr. Nikolaus Graf Strasoldo, former assistant of Dr. Robert Pferdmenges and successor of Karl Haus as a personally liable partner of the Oppenheim bank, became Colonia's chairman of the supervisory board himself. Together with Otto Vossen, he created a new corporate structure in one of the biggest merger deals in the history of Germany's insurance market. In a first major step, Colonia merged with the Lübeck-based National Versicherung, with which it was already closely connected through majority shareholdings of the Kölnische Verwaltungs-AG and the Oppenheim bank, as well as through a community of interests. All of National's assets and obligations were transferred to Colonia and the new company was renamed Colonia National Versicherungs-Aktiengesellschaft. In a second step, Colonia merged with two other major insurers, the Gladbacher Feuerversicherungs-Gesellschaft and the Schlesische Feuer, after it received major holdings in those companies from its ''Rhineland Group'' partner Aachener and Münchener in a share exchange transaction. Colonia also integrated the Westdeutsche Schlachtvieh-Versicherungsgesellschaft, a wholly owned subsidiary since 1959. Including those major deals, a total of 12 well established German insurers were merged with Colonia, making it one of the largest insurance companies in Germany with DM 685 million in premium income. Internally, Vossen and Strasoldo energetically pushed Colonia through a rapid restructuring program eliminating 24 of the former 30 executive board members of the merged companies after 1972. The 79 divisional offices of those companies were managed by Cologne headquarters while sales and claims settlement divisions were decentralized. At the end of the legal part of Colonia's major coup, it was given the new name Colonia Versicherung Aktiengesellschaft in 1971.

A New Leader and a New Identity: 1973–88

While legal matters were settled and Colonia's turnover tripled through the merger to about DM 3 billion, the new giant had to be merged internally—an even more challenging task. Dieter Wendelstadt, a 45-year-old dynamic leader and outsider, not at all familiar with the insurance business, was chosen by Graf Strasoldo as representative of Colonia's major shareholder, the Oppenheim bank, to accomplish that task. Strasoldo became chairman of the supervisory board and Wendelstadt took over as CEO. Soon after, he presented his fresh and unconventional concept for Colonia to increase service efficiency, expand internationally, and substantially improve internal communication among the different company divisions. To increase service quality, separate sales offices were established for corporate clients to better serve their special needs. To get closer to customers, new local offices were set up. To improve service quality, a new training center was opened in 1976. Claas Kleybold, Colonia's new marketing and sales executive, concentrated on the reorganization of the sales channels and the introduction of a comprehensive electronic data processing system. By 1979, Colonia's service network was one of the largest in Germany's insurance landscape, including 80 local offices, 1,700 full-time agents, and 13,000 part-time agents.

Colonia's decision to expand internationally was driven mainly by the ongoing internationalization of its corporate clients. To provide insurance services for its subsidiaries abroad, but also to further distribute Colonia's own risks, the company started working with experienced local partners through minority holdings. Colonia's first foreign subsidiary—Colonia Insurance Company (UK) Ltd.—was established in London in 1975. One year later, Colonia was the first German insurer to receive a license for conducting business in the United States, namely in New York. In the following years, Colonia gradually expanded into most of the other states as well as in Europe, Canada, Brazil, and Saudi Arabia.

After the big merger Colonia's headquarters were spread over 13 different locations in Cologne, making internal communication quite complicated. A symbol of the new concept of ''live communication'' (open and participatory management style), a DM 250 million office complex was erected for Colonia employees in December 1983. At the end of the 1980s, Colonia was one of Germany's leading insurance groups, including its main subsidiaries, Colonia Lebensversicherung AG (life insurance), Colonia Krankenversicherung AG (health insurance), the Colonia Bausparkasse (construction financing), and its majority shareholdings Nordstern Allgemeine Versicherungs-AG, Kölnische Rückversicherungsgesellschaft (reinsurance), and Rheinisch-Westfälische Boden-Credit-Bank (real estate financing). Private policies, auto and life insurance in particular, contributed about one-third of Colonia's premium income, and fire insurance and industrial liability insurance were its most important products for businesses. Some 1,300 independent agents exclusively offering Colonia policies were supported by 85 local sales offices, 16 divisional and branch offices, traveling salespeople, part-time agents, and brokers.

International Expansion with New Partners: 1989–99

Between 1989 and 1991, major changes in the marketplace as well as from the side of its shareholders forced Colonia to adapt quickly. In its 150th anniversary year, Colonia's quiet financial backer, the Oppenheim bank, sold its majority share to the second biggest private French insurance firm, Compagnie Financiere du Groupe Victoire. Together with two other Victoire subsidiaries, the Danish Baltica and the Dutch Nieuw Rotterdam, Colonia belonged to the newly created Vinci B.V. headquartered in Utrecht, The Netherlands, which ranked fifth in Europe's insurance market with about DM 19 billion.

After the two German countries were reunited, Colonia expanded into the new East German market. The first branch office was opened in Dresden in 1990 and expanded to a network of 19 branch offices, 180 sales managers, and 12 general agents by the mid-1990s. In 1990 Colonia acquired a 40 percent share in DARAG, the reinsurer for East German firms involved in international trade, refocusing the business toward insuring operational risks for large and middle-sized clients. New offices were also opened in Poland and Hungary.

A new group structure became effective in 1991. The Colonia Versicherung AG transferred its business to its wholly owned subsidiary Wikinger Lloyd Versicherungs-AG, Köln, which was renamed Colonia Versicherung AG and took over operations. The "old" Colonia Versicherung AG became the new Colonia Konzern AG and functioned as a management holding company for the whole group. Claas Kleybold succeeded Dieter Wendelstadt, the man who had freed the marketing and sales position on the management board for Kleybold in 1973, as CEO in 1991. A passionate art collector, Kleybold later developed a Colonia specialty—art insurance.

The first consolidated result of the new Colonia group was a gross premium income of DM 7.6 billion. In 1994, the abbreviation CKAG was added to Colonia's name. In the same year, the U.S. firm General Re, the world's fourth largest reinsurance firm, acquired a majority share in Colonia's reinsurance subsidiary Cologne Re in a $630 million deal, creating the world's third largest reinsurance company and strengthening Cologne Re's capital backup. In 1996, premium income of the Colonia group amounted to DM 10.8 billion, the third largest among Germany's insurers. After several changes of majority shareholders in the mid-1990s, the French Compagnie Union des Assurances de Paris (UAP) finally became Colonia's parent company in 1996 and then merged with the French AXA SA—with DM 100 billion in world sales and DM 770 billion of managed assets—in a $9 billion deal in 1997. The AXA group now held about 69 percent of Colonia's equity capital and, consequently, CKAG Colonia Konzern AG became AXA Colonia Konzern AG in 1997. As a part of one of the world's leading insurance groups, Colonia was enabled to offer its business clients comprehensive international coverage. In 1997, AXA's net profit was DM 260 million, a 10 percent growth over 1996 profits.

In 1998, the AXA Colonia group founded AXA Colonia KAG and AXA Colonia Asset Management GmbH, two asset management subsidiaries with assets worth DM 35 billion, and launched a 24-hour-customer service center with about 100 employees. One of Colonia's major cases in that year was the tragic accident of the International City Express train near the German town of Eschede in June 1998. With total premium income slightly lower than in 1997, AXA Colonia predicted total sales of about 10.4 billion and an 8 percent decrease of its workforce down to about 8,580 for 1998. In early 1999, AXA Colonia was working on new products, such as private pension funds combined with life insurance, and planning to merge the Nordstern companies with AXA Colonia. It also was planning to take over the Hamburg-based competitor Albingia for DM 1.66 billion, depending on the approval of Albingia's British parent company Guardian Royal Exchange Plc. Albingia, the world market leader for insuring sports events with a mass audience, generated a premium income of approximately DM 2 billion in 1997. AXA Colonia also announced that Dieter Wendelstadt would retire after the annual meeting in 1999 while Claas Kleybold would resign as CEO and succeed retiring Dieter Wendelstadt as chairman of AXA Colonia's supervisory board.

Insuring the 21st Century

The beginning of the 21st century proved a challenging period for the big European insurance companies, and AXA Colonia was no exception. A significant decline in revenues in the industrial insurance sector, which forced Colonia to take an underwriting loss of $192 million in its commercial businesses in 2000, forced the company to increase prices for corporate insurance by approximately 60 percent, while simultaneously cutting back on the range of coverage offered. At the same time, the company was compelled to transfer its multinational industrial insurance holdings to AXA Corporate Solutions in Paris, the international business insurance branch of its parent company, the AXA Group. Under the terms of the reorganization, AXA Colonia retained control over businesses in Germany, Switzerland, Scandinavia, and Austria.

This period also saw a shift in Colonia's overall business strategy. While the company's emphasis had traditionally been placed on its accident and damage insurance segments, which accounted for more than 50 percent of Colonia's total business in 2000, it was becoming increasingly clear that the profit margins afforded by these products were small relative to the more lucrative life and health insurance sectors. Toward this end, the company set itself the goal of increasing the overall premium income afforded by its life and health products, to account for 66 percent of its total business by 2005. An even more dramatic development came in the spring of 2001, when Colonia entered into preliminary talks with Deutsche Bank AG over the possibility of forging a "bancassurance" partnership. Bancassurance, the practice of using the traditional banking branch system as a distribution channel for insurance products, had become common in a number of European countries in the 1990s, but had yet to establish a firm foothold in Germany. The takeover of Dresdner Bank by Colonia rival Allianz AG, however, which resulted in the implementation of a bancassurance program, prompted the company to explore bancassurance as a viable means of expanding its business. Although Colonia's ambitions fell shy of an acquisition of Deutsche Bank, it did seek to join forces with Deutsche Herold, the insurance division of the banking giant. In addition to creating a range of new avenues for the sale of the company's products, as well as increasing the scope of its marketing efforts, the proposed venture would allow Colonia to begin selling the insurance offerings of other companies, a practice that was becoming prevalent in the highly competitive German insurance market. In light of the fact that Deutsche Herold ranked fourth among German insurers, while Colonia ranked sixth, the proposed merger had the potential to help the combined company compete with industry leaders Allianz, AMB, and Ergo.

During this time, Colonia also began exploring the possibility of expanding its product line. One sector that seemed to offer enormous potential was art insurance. In September 1999 the company's AXA Nordstern Art Versicherung AG division established AXA Nordstern Art, with the aim of offering both private and corporate art insurance products worldwide, with an emphasis on the Canadian and Asian markets. The company also shored up its presence in the Eastern European mortgage market, most notably in Hungary, where it launched a network of franchise agencies in July 2000. Amidst this flurry of activity, by the end of 2000 AXA Colonia was able to boast its ninth consecutive year of increased profits and could likely look forward to an even more substantial increase in its business in the near future.

Principal Subsidiaries

AXA Versicherung AG (99.8%); AXA Lebensversicherung AG (99.1%); AXA Krankenversicherung AG; Deutsche Ärzteversicherung (97.9%); AXA Art Versicherung AG; AXA Bank AG; AXA Bausparkasse AG; "die Alternative" Versicherungs-AG; DARAG Deutsche Versicherungs- und Rückversicherungs-AG; AXA Konzern AG, Vienna; Roland Rechtsschutz-Versicherungs-AG (39.9%); General Re-CKAG Reinsurance and Investment S.a.r.l. (Luxembourg; 49.9%).

Principal Competitors

Allianz AG; ING Groep N.V. (Netherlands); Zurich Financial Services (Switzerland).

Further Reading

"Der Audsenseiter," *Capital,* October 1975.

"AXA-Colonia Sees Deutsche 24 As Ideal Partner Bancassurance," *Global News Wire,* April 17, 2001.

"AXA Colonia to Build Up Global Position in Art Insurance," *AFX European Focus,* September 20, 1999.

Brennan, Eilis, "Insurance Sector Spree Reaches $9bn," *European,* October 21, 1994, p. 25.

"Claas Kleybold 60," *Börsen-Zeitung,* September 3, 1997.

"Claas Kleybold 60 Jahre," *Frankfurter Allgemeine Zeitung,* September 3, 1997.

"Company Profile," Cologne: AXA Colonia Konzern AG, 1998.

Die Colonia von 1989 bis 1992, Cologne: Colonia Konzern AG, 1992.

"Dieter Wendelstadt 60 Jahre," *Börsen-Zeitung,* December 12, 1989.

"France's Axa SA to Take Over UAP in Stock Swap," *Minneapolis Star Tribune,* November 13, 1996, p. 3D.

"Gen Re Deal with Colonia a 'Home Run'," *National Underwriter,* July 11, 1994, p. 3.

"Der harte Graf," *Capital,* June 1976.

"The Insurance Industry Is in Trouble," *Economist,* January 16–22, 1999.

Looking Back to the Future—150 Years of Colonia Versicherung AG, Cologne: Colonia Versicherung AG, 1989.

Schlingensiepen, Ilse, "AXA Colonia Squeeze," *Lloyd's List,* December 13, 2000.

—Evelyn Hauser
—update: Steve Meyer

Bayard SA

3, rue Bayard
75008 Paris
France
Telephone: + 33 1 44 35 60 60
Fax: 01 44 35 61 61
Web site: http://www.bayardpresse.com

Private Company
Incorporated: 1873 as Maison de la Bonne Presse
Employees: 1,500
Sales: EUR 390 million ($380 million) (2001 est)
NAIC: 511120 Periodical Publishers; 511130 Book
   Publishers

One of France's oldest publishing groups, Bayard SA is also one of the country's largest, particularly in its three target markets of the youth, senior citizen, and Christian sectors. Bayard is active in the newspaper market, with the daily *La Croix,* published since 1883, and in the book publishing and magazine publishing sector. The company publishes more than 100 magazine titles worldwide, including 39 in France alone, reaching more than 50 countries and an estimated readership of 30 million. The company's flagship titles include *Pomme d'Api,* the leading French magazine for the two- to seven-year-old age group, also published in 11 countries under varying names; *Notre Temps,* a lifestyle magazine for senior citizens that has also found success in the Dutch, Belgian, and German markets; the *J'aime Lire* series, said to be read by one of every two French youth; *Pèlerin,* the company's first publication, launched in 1873; and other titles including *Choice, Enfant, D Lire; Panorama,* and *Le Monde de la Bible.* In book publishing, Bayard has captured the leading share of the French youth market, with a list of more than 900 titles and sales of some nine million books per year. Bayard is also building a presence in the multimedia market, with a range of CD-ROM and music titles; the company has also launched Bayardweb, a web site production company in association with Suez and Médéric, as a vehicle for the development of web sites for the company's magazine titles. Bayard is a private company owned by the

Assumptionist religious order. The company is led by President Alain Cordier.

19th-Century Religious Roots

In 1845, Emmanuel D'Alzon founded a new religious order in Nîmes, the Augustins de l'Assomption, in part as a reaction against the French revolution and a looming secularization of French society. The Assumptionists, adherents of the Roman Catholic Church, were officially recognized by Pope Pius IX in 1864. In the early 1870s, the group began organizing its first pilgrimages. In order to lend support to its pilgrims, the Assumptionists began producing a newsletter in 1872 named *Pèlerin.* A year later, the newsletter became a weekly publication, and enjoyed continuous publication into the beginning of the 21st century.

The publication of *Pèlerin* awakened a new vocation for the Assumptionists, who quickly adopted the use of the press for spreading their religious and social vision. The congregation created its own publishing house, Maison de la Bonne Press, which was to remain the group's imprint until the 1950s. *Pèlerin* remained the group's sole imprint during the 1870s, becoming an illustrated journal in 1877.

The 1880s marked a new era in the Assumptionist's publishing arm. In 1880, the group debuted *La Vie des Saints,* a publication which remained in print until the dawn of World War I. The group produced a number of other long-lived titles, such as *Echos de Notre Dame de France à Jérusalem,* launched in 1889 and remaining in publication until 1938, and *Mon Almanach,* launched in 1893 and ending publication only in 1940. Yet the group's most successful publication remained its daily newspaper, *La Croix,* launched in 1883 and which quickly became the country's most influential Catholic newspaper.

In the 1890s, La Croix became notorious for its vehement anti-Dreyfus, and anti-Jewish editorial policy. Proudly proclaiming itself "the most anti-Jewish newspaper in France," *La Croix* through its scurrilous attacks became, in part, responsible for the expulsion of the Assumptionist order from France at the beginning of the 20th century and the enacting of legislation guaranteeing the official separation of church and state in France.

Company Perspectives:

Bayard is a market leader in children's educational press, religious publications, and seniors press.

Despite its—temporary—expulsion from France in 1900, the Assumptionist order and the Maison de la Bonne Press continued producing new titles, in addition to its existing catalog, including *La Croix* and *Pèlerin.* World War I was to provide a new rupture for the publishing house, which saw many of its journals, magazines and newspapers shut down for the duration.

Following the war and especially in the years leading to World War II, Maison de la Bonne Presse, and particularly *La Croix* and *Pèlerin,* adopted a more moderate, pro-Republican tone. The group continued its focus on religious publications, launching notably *La Documentation Catholique* in 1919, which, together with *La Croix* and *Pèlerin,* was to be the only other group publication from before World War II to survive into the 21st century. In the 1930s, however, Maison de la Bonne Presse ventured into what was later to become a group specialty, that of youth-oriented magazines. One of the first of these was *Bayard,* introduced in 1936 and remaining in production into the 1960s.

Worldwide Publisher in the New Century

The 1950s marked an era of change for Maison de la Bonne Presse, as the publishing house emphasized a stronger separation between its editorial policy and the Assumptionist congregation. While members of the Assumptionist order maintained key positions in the publishing house's hierarchy, the company took on more and more laypersons to design and produce its publications. This change was underlined by the adoption of a new name for the publishing house, that of Bayard Presse. Although owned by the Assumptionist order, Bayard was technically independent. Run on a nonprofit basis—the Assumptionist order did not take any of Bayard's profits—the company enjoyed the return of all profits as capital for future investment.

Bayard launched a number of new titles in the 1950s, such as *Bible et Terre Sainte, Rallye Jeunesse,* and *Images Lumineuses.* Most of these titles were shortlived, although some, such as *Catéchiste d'Aujourd'hui* and *Presse Actualité,* remained in publication into the 1970s and 1980s. At the beginning of the 1960s, the company found more lasting success with the newsmagazine *Panorama.* Launched in 1962, *Panorama* remained a part of the company's catalog at the turn of the century.

The year 1966 marked a new and significant moment for Bayard. In that year, the company published a new magazine called *Pomme d'Api.* Targeting the children's market—and specifically the pre-reader market, *Pomme d'Api* presented an innovative format for the time, utilizing primarily images and easy to read text. The magazine quickly became the most popular children's magazine in France, and continued to attract as many as half of the country's young readers at the beginning of the 21st century. Already the country's leading Catholic press publisher, Bayard with *Pomme d'Api* signaled the start of

its effort to become the premier publishing group for the French children's market.

By 1968, however, the company had readied the launch of the third pillar of its publishing catalog, that of the senior's market. In that year, the company debuted a new magazine targeted specifically at the over-50 set, called *Notre Temps* (Our Times). The new magazine proved an instant success and later became one of the company's flagship publications in its drive to internationalize its publishing operations.

In the 1970s, Bayard extended its children's publishing activities with the launch of several successful magazines, each targeting specific age groups and interests, including *Okapi* in 1971, *Les Belles Histoires de Pomme d'Api, Astrapi,* and especially the *J'aime Lire* series, all of which were to enjoy continuous publication into the next century. The period marked the first of Bayard's title acquisitions, including *Jardin Magazine,* acquired in 1975, and *Karaté, Onze,* and *Première,* all of which were acquired in 1979. These titles also marked an attempt to diversify further the company's publishing operations. The company had not neglected its Christian publishing side, however, launching several new magazines and journals, including *Points de Repère* in 1973, *Vivante Eglise* in 1974, *Le Monde de la Bible* and *La Foi Aujourd'hui* in 1977, and *Les Pages de l'Evénement* in 1978.

Bayard Presse began its move into the international publishing arena at the beginning of the 1980s. Already in 1978 the company had found success with an English language version of *Pomme d'Api,* called *Little Red Apple,* and launched in Hong Kong. Among the markets entered during the 1980s were Spain, mainland China, Italy, Belgium, and Turkey. The company's entry into these markets typically involved the introduction of a local language edition of one of the company's titles, such as *Notre Temps* in Belgium, which was issued in a Flemish-language version, *Onze Tijd,* in 1988. A year later, the company published a Canadian version, *Le Bel Age.*

A partnership agreement made in 1987 with U.K. media group Emap brought the company into the United Kingdom with titles including *Choice* and *Yours,* both introduced in 1989. Together with Emap, the company acquired one of France's most successful magazines, *Le Chasseur Français,* dedicated to hunting, in 1990. That magazine was placed into a joint holding, Medianature, which began acquiring more titles targeting the nature audience.

Bayard stepped up its international activity in the 1990s, entering the Netherlands with, among others, *Plus,* a Dutch-language edition of *Notre Temps,* in 1990. By then the company had also entered Germany, Finland, Sweden, Poland, Greece, and Korea in the early 1990s, while making a first step into the United States with the publication of an English-language version of *Pomme d'Api,* entitled *Ladybug.*

Pomme d'Api proved a particularly successful foreign ambassador for the group. By 1996, the company celebrated the 30th anniversary of the children's magazine with editions in 11 languages, including *Caracola,* a Spanish version launched in 1988; *Hoppla,* launched in Germany in 1989; a Catalan-language edition, *Cucafera,* in 1991, followed by *Leppis* (Finland) and an

Key Dates:

1845: Emmanuel d'Alzon founds Augustinians of the Assumption (Assumptionists).

1872: *Pèlerin* is published as a newsletter.

1873: Assumptionists create publishing arm Maison de la Bonne Presse and *Pèlerin* begins weekly publication.

1877: *Pèlerin* becomes an illustrated weekly.

1883: Bonne Presse launches daily newspaper *La Croix*.

1900: Assumptionist congregation is expelled from France.

1936: *Bayard* is launched as a youth magazine.

1950: Bonne Presse becomes Bayard Presse.

1966: *Pomme d'Api*, a magazine for pre-reading children, appears.

1968: *Notre Temps*, a magazine targeting the senior citizen market, is introduced.

1978: The first foreign publication, the English-language *Red Apple*, is published.

1987: Company forms joint-publishing partnership agreement with Emap of the United Kingdom for titles including *Choice* and *Yours*.

1990: Bayard forms Medianature in partnership with Emap to acquire *Le Chasseur Français*, a popular French hunting magazine.

1992: Company acquires *Enfant* magazine.

1994: Company acquires *Ami des Jardins, La Chasse,* and *Pêche et Poissons,* becoming leading ''nature'' publisher in France.

1999: Bayard acquires Twenty-third Publications and Catholic Digest in the United States to become the leading North American Catholic press publisher.

2000: Company acquires Novedis (Novalis), a leading Canadian Catholic press publisher.

edition for Quebec, Canada, that same year. By 1996, *Pomme d'Api* had also entered Poland, as *Bec!* and Korea as *Te Ne Ne.*

Bayard continued to tack onto its titles list with a number of acquisitions, such as *Enfant* magazine, geared toward parents of young children, acquired in 1992. The company also built up its ''nature'' selection, adding to *Le Chasseur Français* with the acquisition of titles including *La Chasse* and *La Pêche et les Poissons,* both acquired in 1994, and *Terre Sauvage,* acquired in 1996, which helped boost Bayard to the leadership in the French hunting and fishing market.

In order to revive the sagging sales of the *La Croix* newspaper, Bayard took the bold step of converting that evening paper into a morning daily to better serve its primarily subscriber-based readership. At the same time, La Croix's design was overhauled, presenting a more modern look in order to attract a larger share of newsstand purchases. The changeover, accomplished in January 1998, proved a success, and *La Croix* once again enjoyed climbing sales.

The 1999 acquisition by Emap of *Pleine Vie* magazine, Bayard's main competitor in the senior's market, led to the breakup of the two companies' longstanding partnership. Bayard was able to console itself with a new partnership, formed in 1998, with publishing house Gallimard. The new partnership, called Gallimard-Bayard Jeunesse, was formed in order to consolidate both companies' positions in the French youth market, giving it an undisputed lead in children's publications.

The company also began looking to North America for its future growth. Already in 1997 Bayard had acquired a series of children's titles, including *Owl, Chickadee,* and *Chirp,* with strong readership bases in Canada and the United States. In 1999, Bayard made two significant acquisitions in that country, buying first Twenty-third Publications, and then Catholic Digest. These acquisitions helped make the company the leading Catholic press publisher in North America, a position solidified with the purchase of Canada's Novedis in 2000.

Losses in 1999, however, had by then forced a shakeup in Bayard's operations, including the ouster of longtime president Bernard Porte, who had been responsible for the company's internationalization and, in the eyes of the company's Assumptionist owners, its increasing secularization. Porte's place was taken by Alain Cordier. The changeover was accompanied by a shakeup in the group's titles, as the group dropped a number of its money-losing titles, including *Le Bel Age,* an attempt to reach the over-70 market.

Bayard nonetheless continued to build on its successful operations, such as its youth-oriented pocket books publishing division, which had gained the top position in the French market and particularly with its successful franchise of the Harry Potter series. The company had also expanded into multimedia, producing CD-ROMs and music CDs, as well as creating, in partnership with Suez and Médéric, its Bayardweb Internet portal, launched in 2001. That year marked the release of the latest Pomme d'Api edition, in Holland, under the name Pompoen, as well as a German edition of Notre Temps, entitled Lenz.

By then, Bayard had returned to profits, and, with sales topping EUR 390 million, had gained the number five position among French publishing groups. The company had also refocused its press publishing operations around its three core target markets of youths, Christians, and seniors, selling off its Medianature holdings to Emap. The company expected to continue its successful extension of its titles into international markets—already by 2002 Bayard's *Notre Temps* seniors magazine had found new markets in Belgium (as *Plus*) and Denmark (as *Vi over 60*).

Principal Subsidiaries

Bayard Presse International SA; Bayard Presse Publicité SARL; Société Centrale de Presse et de Publicité SA; Soderel SA; Unijep SA; Diana SA; Canope SA; Gallimard Bayard Jeunesse SA (50%); Bayard Web SNC; Bayard Hachette Routage SA (50%); Bayard Presse Benelux SA (Belgium); Senior Publications Nederland BV (Netherlands); Grieg Media AS (Norway; 25%); Bayard Presse UK Ltd; Bayard Press Espagne SA (Spain); Publications Senior Inc. (Canada); Bayard Press Canada Inc.; Bayard Inc. (U.S.A.); Bayard Presse Asie (Hong Kong); Senior Publications Deutschland (Germany).

Principal Competitors

AOL Time Warner Inc.; Bertelsmann AG; Sunset Publishing Corp.; Roularta Media Group NV; Quebecor Inc.; R.R. Donnelley and Sons Co.; McGraw-Hill Companies Inc.; Advance Publications Inc.; Orkla ASA; Wolters Kluwer NV; Reed Elsevier Inc.; VNU NV; Gruner + Jahr AG und Co.; Axel Springer Verlag AG; Hachette Filipacchi Medias; Verlagsgruppe Georg von Holtzbrinck GmbH; EMAP plc; Hubert Burda Media Holding GmbH und Co KG; Sanoma WSOY Group; Independent News and Media plc; Timon SA; Emmis Communications Corp.

Further Reading

Claude-François, Jullien, ''Grandes manoevres autour de la presse catho,'' *Nouvel Observateur*, March 27, 1997.

Cordier, Alain, ''Que se passe-t-il à Bayard Presse?'' *La Croix*, October 27, 2000.

Groussard, Véronique, ''A Bayard Presse, l'actionnaire, c'est Dieu,'' *Challenges*, June 1, 2000.

La Porte, Arnaud, ''La Croix proche de l'equilibre,'' *La Croix*, June 5, 2002, p. 22.

''Le riposte de Bayard à Emap,'' *Challenges*, October 1, 1999.

—M. L. Cohen

Benchmark Capital

Suite 200, 2480 Sand Hill Road
Menlo Park, California 94025
U.S.A.
Telephone: (650) 854-8180
Fax: (650) 854-8183
Web site: http://www.benchmark.com

Private Company
Incorporated: 1995
Employees: 35
NAIC: 523910 Venture Capital Companies

Venture capital firm Benchmark Capital stresses a team approach, and the team has shared in some spectacular results. Benchmark's 1997 investment of $6.7 million in online auctioneer eBay holds the record for best-performing Silicon Valley investment ever: by the spring of 1999, this stake was worth $5 billion. Benchmark's clients are managers of pension funds and college endowments, as well as wealthy individuals, and the firm prides itself on its service to the entrepreneurs behind its portfolio companies.

An Ambitious Start in 1995

Benchmark Capital was set up in 1995 by four ambitious young men. Robert C. Kagle was a consumer marketing expert who had spent the previous dozen years with Technology Venture Investors. A native of Flint, Michigan, Kagle had a keen interest in the Depression era and loved to regale his colleagues with tales of speculative pitfalls. Bruce Dunlevie also had prior venture capital experience, at Merrill Pickard Anderson & Eyre, and had worked earlier at Arthur Andersen and Goldman Sachs. A New York native who grew up in Dallas, Dunlevie was a former football player with a secret penchant for literature. Kevin Harvey, Benchmark's resident techie, had gone to Rice University like Dunlevie, and had invested in a database software company while still at Merrill Pickard. Andrew Rachleff, with a background in network equipment and telecommunications, rounded out the founding four.

Uniquely, profits would be distributed equally among the partners, a practice said to eliminate infighting. The partners were not tagged with ranks such as ''senior'' or ''associate.'' The group set for itself the goal of becoming the number one venture capital firm within ten years, hence the ambitious Benchmark name. The group expressed a preference for high-tech ventures with the potential for creating or capturing huge consumer markets; Benchmark provided seed capital for entrepreneurs at the very earliest stages of a venture.

The group raised $85 million for its first fund, Benchmark I. They turned it into $7.8 billion, an extraordinary return of 92 times the original investment. Kagle believed the success of ventures depended mostly on finding and backing extraordinary people. Most of the entrepreneurs who obtained financing from Benchmark were referred by business colleagues.

Soon, the firm developed its own pipeline for finding the great commercial ideas of the near future. Benchmark named Keith Krach its first ''entrepreneur-in-residence'' (EIR) in 1996. Earlier in his career, Krach had run a robotics joint venture for GM; he became the carmaker's youngest vice-president at the age of 26. Krach then built up a mechanical engineering software company, Rasna, which he sold for $200 million, recorded *Fortune*. Krach teamed up with fellow Benchmark EIR Paul Hegarty to develop Ariba Technologies, which would supply a Java-based system for enabling employees of corporations to order office supplies online.

Within a couple of years, half of Benchmark's investments were in EIR-created companies. ''There's much less risk,'' partner Andrew Rachleff told *Fortune*. In addition, Benchmark benefited by being able to invest in a company in the very earliest stages of financing, when shares were cheapest.

According to Silicon Valley business writer Randall Stross, venture capitalists like the partners at Benchmark saw themselves as company-builders, rather than mere investors. They were intimately involved with the companies they helped develop, serving on boards and consulting informally with their CEOs.

David Beirne became a partner in May 1997. Before joining Benchmark, he had established a successful executive recruiting firm, Ramsey Beirne.

Raising the Stakes in 1997

In 1997, Benchmark made what would be considered the best-performing venture investment of all time. It put $5 million from the Benchmark I fund into eBay Inc., the online auction service, obtaining a 22 percent share in the company. The 1998 IPO of eBay was extraordinarily successful; Benchmark's stake would be worth $2.5 billion by early 1999, according to *Business Week*—an unbelievable return of nearly 50,000 percent. After a secondary offering, eBay's valuation peaked at $26 billion.

In April 1999, Benchmark's share was worth more than $5 billion when it made a partial distribution in April 1999. Its $4 million investment in Ariba would be worth nearly $1 billion. This tale and others were chronicled in the book *eBoys* by Randell E. Stross, a Menlo Park native who had the very unique position of writer-in-residence at Benchmark from the fall of 1997 to the fall of 1999.

The group raised $125 million for its Benchmark II fund in 1997. Some of the companies in this portfolio were Scient, Critical Path, Red Hat, and Handspring, a PDA (personal digital assistant) maker formed by the founders of Palm, Inc. This fund was another winner, eventually worth $2.5 billion.

Benchmark also backed a few companies that did not perform, and when this happened, they tended to fail on a grand scale. TriStrata, developer of encryption software for corporate networks, was one such investment. David Beirne brought it to the attention of his group, which in July 1998 invested $6.5 million in it, suggesting a valuation of $97.4 million. TriStrata would not show any revenues at all for at least another two years. By this time its CEO Paul Wahl had resigned, as had its board of directors, who felt unable to work with founder John Atalla (pioneer of ATM PIN codes). Benchmark's investment was left in place, but the group suffered a significant drain on its resources and reputation—Beirne had spent considerable time persuading Wohl to leave his position as CEO of SAP America to head the venture.

Late 1990s E-tailers

The firm raised $175 million for its Benchmark III fund in 1998. This fund was heavy on e-tailers such as Living.com, a furniture site. The optimism surrounding e-commerce was beginning to wear off. 1-800-Flowers.com went public in August 1999 at $21 a share; by the end of the year, it had fallen to $13. Another Benchmark III company, web furniture store Living .com, would fold by the beginning of 2001.

Approximately $1 billion was raised for Benchmark IV. Given Benchmark's historical preference for working on relatively small deals of $5 million or less, this raised questions about the ability of the investing partners, which numbered seven in 2000, to efficiently invest larger amounts of money in each company. Benchmark IV included an $18 million investment in MVP.com, a celebrity-backed sporting goods site, and a $20 million stake in Juniper Financial Corp.

Benchmark investments Ashford.com (watch sales), Webvan (Internet-based groceries delivery), PlanetRx.com Inc., and E-Loan were all hit hard in the mass e-commerce sell-off of May 2000. The IPO market had shifted to optical networking, noted *Business Week*. Benchmark named Alex Balkanski, former C-Cube Microsystems Inc. CEO, a partner to boost its expertise in semiconductors and networking.

Venturing Abroad in 2000

Benchmark always thought big and in 2000, this meant thinking globally. The group established an office in London in 2000, led by partner George Coelho, who was eager to bankroll Europe's talented, underfunded entrepreneurs. In 2002, the $750 million Benchmark Europe I Fund was reduced to $500 million due to the perception that companies were requiring less financing to break even than in previous years. Benchmark also had a $220 million fund for investments in Israel.

Benchmark's interest in consumer-oriented start-ups was somewhat against the prevailing fashion among venture capitalists in 2002. One of Benchmark's biggest bets, so to speak, was the European person-to-person gambling site Flutter.com. Other investments included Keen.com, where users could purchase advice from experts in various fields, and Orchestria Corporation, a provider of Internet security software for the corporate market.

Webvan, the ambitious Internet grocer start-up, went bankrupt in the summer of 2001. It had been conceived by Louis Borders, founder of the bookstore chain, and had attracted premium management talent and investors. Though Benchmark was an early backer, the VC firm only lost its $3.5 million initial investment. The *San Francisco Chronicle* noted that the value of Benchmark's stake had peaked at $1.2 billion on Webvan's first day as a public company.

Principal Operating Units

Silicon Valley; Europe; Israel.

Principal Competitors

Hummer Winblad Venture Partners; Kleiner Perkins Caufield & Byers; Menlo Ventures; Sequoia Capital.

Further Reading

Beauprez, Jennifer, ''The Fine Art of Venture Financing'' (interview with Robert Kagle), *Denver Post,* March 12, 2000, p. L4.

Bransten, Lisa, ''Benchmark Capital Sues Company It Nurtured,'' *Wall Street Journal,* July 11, 2002, p. C5.

Bushrod, Lisa, ''Benchmark Reduces European Fund,'' *European Venture Capital Journal,* June 1, 2002, p. 15.

Creswell, Julie, ''Benchmark and Goldman: An IPO Pipeline? Venture Capitalists and the Bankers Who Love Them,'' *Fortune,* January 10, 2000, p. 168.

Davis, Glynn, ''A Benchmark for Investment?,'' *New Media Age,* April 18, 2002, pp. 28+.

Emert, Carol, ''Venture Lessons in Webvan Collapse,'' *San Francisco Chronicle,* July 15, 2001, p. E1.

Fletcher, Richard, ''Over Funded and Over Here; Silicon Valley's Venture Capitalists Are Heading to London with Fat Wallets,'' *Sunday Telegraph,* November 19, 2000, p. 12.

Himelstein, Linda, ''Robert C. Kagle,'' *Business Week,* September 27, 1999, p. EB38.

——, ''Taking the Valley by Storm: Benchmark Aims to Out-Venture Kleiner Perkins,'' *Business Week,* February 15, 1999, p. 90.

Kroll, Luisa, ''Valley of the Mudslingers,'' *Forbes,* January 8, 2000, p. 60.

McGee, Suzanne, ''Deals & Deal Makers: Sky Is No Longer the Limit for Venture-Capital Firms,'' *Wall Street Journal,* May 9, 2000, p. C1.

Mullaney, Timothy J., ''Still the Benchmark to Bet On?,'' *Business Week,* August 7, 2000, pp. 68–73.

Stross, Randall E., *eBoys: The True Story of the Six Tall Men Who Backed eBay and Other Billion-Dollar Start-Ups,* New York: Ballantine Books, 2000.

——, ''When the Money Goes Down the Drain,'' *Fortune,* April 17, 2000, pp. 535–48.

Taber, George M., ''Life Inside a Silicon Valley Venture Firm'' (review of *eBoys* by Randall E. Stross), *Business News New Jersey,* August 8, 2000, p. 27.

Warner, Melanie, ''The New Way to Start Up in Silicon Valley,'' *Fortune,* March 2, 1998, pp. 168–74.

Wiegers, Alex, ''Once Bitten...,'' *San Jose and Silicon Valley Business Journal,* July 10–16, 1995, p. 12.

Wilmsen, Steven, ''Loan to On-Line Firm Gets Out-of-Sight Returns; Venture Capitalists' Collection from eBay: 160,000 Percent,'' *Boston Globe,* April 9, 1999, p. C1.

—Frederick C. Ingram

Berkshire Realty Holdings, L.P.

1 Beacon Street, Suite 1550
Boston, Massachusetts 02108
U.S.A.
Telephone: (617) 646-2300
Toll Free: (888) 867-0100
Fax: (617) 646-2375
Web site: http://www.berkshireapartments.com

Private Company
Incorporated: 1990 as Berkshire Realty Company
Employees: 956
Sales: $210 million (2000 est.)
NAIC: 531110 Lessors of Residential Buildings and
    Dwellings

Berkshire Realty Holdings, L.P. is a private real estate investment firm located in Boston, although it is not involved in the New England market. Rather, it acquires, develops, and operates multifamily apartment properties in select cities located in the states of Florida, Georgia, Maryland, New York, North Carolina, South Carolina, and Texas, as well as Washington, D.C. The company's portfolio includes some 80 properties and more than 26,000 apartment units.

Launch of Real Estate Business
by the Krupp Brothers in 1969

Brothers Douglas and George Krupp formed a Boston real estate business in 1969 called Krupp Companies. Its activities grew beyond the buying and sell of real estate to include property and asset management services, mortgage banking, and healthcare facilities. Eventually, the businesses were placed under a holding company, The Berkshire Group. The Krupps launched dozens of real estate limited partnerships, including the Krupp Cash Plus I through IV series, which were offered to the public from 1985 to 1988. Because of changes in the tax laws in 1986, as well as a sagging real estate market, the partnerships struggled through the remainder of the decade. While investors fared poorly, the Krupps as general partners were collecting management fees and were doing much better.

In November 1990 the Krupps announced their intention to "roll up," or combine, the four Cash Plus partnerships into a publicly traded real estate investment firm (REIT), Berkshire Realty Company, which had been formed in April 1990. It was intended to own 30 properties located in 15 states, including 16 apartment buildings with nearly 4,400 apartments and 13 shopping centers with 2.5 million square feet of retail rental space. By converting the partnerships into a REIT investors would gain immediate liquidity.

REITs were a little-used investment structure originally established by Congress in 1960 as a way for small investors to become involved in real estate in a manner similar to mutual funds. REITs could be taken public and their shares traded just like stock. They also were subject to regulation by the Securities and Exchange Commission. Unlike stocks, however, REITs were required by law to pay out at least 95 percent of their taxable income to shareholders each year, a provision that severely limited the ability of REITs to raise funds internally. During the first 25 years of existence, REITs were allowed only to own real estate, a situation that hindered their growth. Third parties had to be contracted to manage the properties. Not until the Tax Reform Act of 1986 began to change the nature of real estate investment did REITs begin to gain widespread usage. Tax shelter schemes that had drained potential investments were shut down. Interest and depreciation deductions were greatly reduced so that taxpayers could not generate paper losses in order to lower their tax liabilities. The Act also permitted REITs to provide customary services for properties, in effect allowing the trusts to operate and manage the properties they owned. Despite these major changes in law, REITs were still not fully utilized. In the latter half of the 1980s the banks, insurance companies, pension funds, and foreign investors (in particular, the Japanese) provided the lion's share of real estate investment funds. That period also witnessed overbuilding and a glutted marketplace, leading to a shakeout in the marketplace. With real estate available at distressed prices in the early 1990s, REITs finally became an attractive mainstream investment option.

The terms of the Krupps' plan to combine the four Cash Plus partnerships and exchange investors' interests for shares of the Berkshire REIT caused an immediate adverse reaction from investors, and initiated one of the most contentious roll-ups the industry had witnessed in many years. Despite the attraction of gaining liquidity, many investors were upset by the investment philosophy espoused by Berkshire, which they felt was not consistent with the original Cash Plus prospectuses, which promised a low-risk approach that had eschewed borrowing and had attracted them to the investment in the first place. Moreover, the partnerships were intended as finite investments, set to be liquidated at specified dates; the REIT would have an infinite life. The Krupps maintained that the previous investment strategy had not worked and now planned to borrow money in order to take advantage of attractive properties that might become available. Investors were further angered by the high fees that the Krupps were in line to receive during every stage of the roll-up process. According to Barry Vinocur, writing in *Barron's,* "In most other roll-ups, sponsors have emphasized that consolidating partnerships would result in cost savings. But in Krupp's roll-up, instead of dropping, the fees going to the company would actually soar by roughly 40%." In addition, investors questioned the estimated value of the partnership's properties, alleging that the numbers were inflated. Also causing some concern were the provisions of the Krupp management contract, a four-year term that could only be terminated for "cause," as well as a clause that called for the REIT to pay the managers an amount equal to 18 months worth of management should the Krupps be removed at "any time" for "any reason." Such a removal was unlikely, however, because another provision required a supermajority of shareholders to vote out Berkshire's directors. Investors also feared that the Krupps had an incentive to sell off existing properties in order to earn an asset management fee for buying new properties.

Opposition of Major Investors to 1991 Roll-Up

It was many of the same investment firms that had sold the original investments who were the most vocal in their criticism of the roll-up, including PaineWebber, Smith Barney, Legg Mason, First of Michigan, A.G. Edwards, Royal Alliance Associates, and Kavanaugh Securities. All of them recommended that investors reject the proposal. As a result, the Krupps were forced to make changes, three times revising the terms, as well as extending the deadline for investors to vote on the roll-up. In the end, the proposal cut the transaction fees, and the Krupps agreed not to use more than 15 percent leverage and not to charge asset management fees when proceeds from the sale of an existing property were reinvested. One of the most important concessions was a change in the charter that mandated a review of Berkshire's portfolio at the end of 1998, at which point a liquidation plan had to be submitted to shareholders.

Even with these changes to the offer, the vote on the roll-up continued to generate controversy and the deadline on the vote was pushed back four times. Some investors had requested the names and addresses of other investors in the Cash Plus partner-

ships, with the expressed purpose of making contact to discuss the roll-up vote. Not only did the general partners not send the lists as required by provisions in the 1934 Securities and Exchange Act, they asked for additional information from the requestors. A number of complaints were made to the SEC, which eventually leveled charges against the general partners. Investors did finally receive the lists, but according to the SEC suit it took an average of 13 weeks after the initial requests were made for the appropriate lists to be delivered. Even then, the investors who received the lists considered them to be unusable. They were some 5,000 pages long, the names printed in tiny black print set against a dark maroon page that not only caused eyestrain but prevented the list from being photocopied. The resulting SEC suit would linger for more than a year before the general partners agreed to cease and desist from future proxy violations. By this time, of course, the roll-up vote had been long since completed. In the end, in June 1991, investors in only two of the partnerships agreed to the proposal. Investors in the two partnerships that represented some 70 percent of the total assets, however, agreed to exchange their partnership units for shares in Berkshire Realty.

With access to the capital markets, Berkshire experienced a period of steady growth. Revenues improved from $39.6 million in 1992 to nearly $68.5 million in 1994, although net income fell from $7.3 million to $5.8 million in the same period. In 1995 Berkshire underwent some changes. It was restructured as an umbrella partnership real estate investment trust (UPREIT), and then it shifted its business strategy. Because Berkshire lacked the resources to effectively operate in all of its historical markets, management elected to exit the Midwest market and began selling off all of its properties in the region. The REIT now focused on Washington, D.C., and 12 other cities located in six target markets: the Carolinas, Georgia, Tennessee, Florida, and Texas. Although Berkshire would develop A properties, they were deemed too expensive to acquire. Purchases, therefore, were generally limited to B and C assets. Boston continued to be the headquarters of the REIT and where management strategy and corporate finance functions were conducted, but Atlanta also became an important hub for company operations. With most of Berkshire's development activities taking place in the Southeast, Atlanta housed the development group, as well as the property management company, because of its proximity to most of Berkshire's properties.

As a result of Berkshire's strategy, the REIT saw revenues improve to more than $70 million in 1995 while posting a $14.8 million net profit. In 1996 revenues almost reached $90 million, but Berkshire lost $14.3 million. At the end of the year, the REIT's assets included 35 apartment communities, totaling 12,435 units, and investments in six retail centers. Management now decided to sell off its retail portfolio and reinvest the proceeds in the development of apartment communities. In 1997 Berkshire lost an additional $8.4 million as it continued adjustments to its portfolio. By year's end it had investments in 68 properties located in the Mid-Atlantic states, the Southeast, Florida, and Texas: 18,773 apartment units in total.

Reaching a Crossroads in 1998

In 1998 Berkshire reached a crossroads, required by the terms of its roll-up agreement to evaluate its current state and determine whether the REIT should be sold, merged, or liqui-

Key Dates:

1969: Krupp Companies is formed.
1985: The first Krupp Cash Plus real estate partnership is launched.
1990: Berkshire Realty is formed as a REIT.
1991: Two Cash Plus partnerships are rolled up into Berkshire.
1998: As required by roll-up provisions, the directors consider strategic alternatives for Berkshire.
1999: Berkshire is taken private by its management group.

dated. Moreover, a general slump in REIT share prices put pressure on companies the size of Berkshire to join up with larger rivals in order to compete. Accordingly, in May 1998 a committee of outside directors engaged Lazard Freres & Co. and Lehman Brothers for assistance in exploring its strategic alternatives and preparing a plan to be considered by shareholders by the end of the year, as required by the roll-up provisions. There was no shortage of suitors for Berkshire, which boasted a market capitalization of nearly $450 million and owned real estate valued at $769 million. Finalists included Chicago's Equity Residential and the New Jersey private apartment developer Charles Kushner. Douglas Krupp also led a management buyout effort, which included Blackman Group Inc. and Goldman, Sachs & Company.

The sale of Berkshire now assumed overtones of the earlier roll-up flap. As reported by the *Boston Globe* in March 1999: "Just this week, as the bidding process seemed to be winding up, Krupp dropped one new item into the public record: His offer was contingent on Berkshire Realty showing that certain services provided to apartment tenants did violate REIT laws. A problem with Berkshire's legal status would have huge tax consequences and temper all bids for the company. The nature of those services that gave Krupp a late case of the willies? Berkshire had discounted rents to five tenants who ran aerobics classes for their neighbors. . . . The company confirmed yesterday that the Internal Revenue Service had already determined that such an arrangement was acceptable. Even if there was a problem, the worst-case tax fine would have been about $25,000.''

Krupp's first buyout offer of $11.05 a share, a $1.15 billion deal, was deemed by the committee of outside directors to be insufficient. After Equity Residential dropped out of the running it appeared that Kushner had won the bidding with an offer of $12.50 a share, but in the end Kushner balked and failed to present the required letter of credit or the financing commitments. Instead Berkshire was sold to the Krupp group at $12.25 per share, or $660 million in cash and the assumption of some $600 million in debt. Having taken Berkshire private, with the new entity becoming Berkshire Realty Holdings, L.P., Krupp's management team kept the company's finances and activities closely guarded.

Principal Competitors

Equity Residential; JPI; Lincoln Property.

Further Reading

"General Partners Settle SEC Charges They Violated Proxy Rules in Roll-Up," *Tax Management Financial Planning Journal,* August 18, 1992, p. 289.

Pacelle, Mitchell, "Faced with Opposition, Krupp Corp. Revises Plan to 'Roll Up' Partnerships," *Wall Street Journal,* December 3, 1990, p. C5.

Pereira, Joseph, "Investors Approve Roll-Up of Just Two of Four Partnerships Managed by Krupp," *Wall Street Journal,* June 6, 1991, p. A11.

Syre, Steven, and Charles Stein, "Curious Case of Berkshire Realty: Would You Play Poker with Douglas Krupp?," *Boston Globe,* March 24, 1999, p. D1.

Vinocur, Barry, "A Sponsor Takes Heat on Plan to Merge Program," *Barron's,* November 26, 1990, p. 20.

——, "Votes for Sale . . . Krupp's Latest," *Barron's,* February 11, 1991, p. 49.

—Ed Dinger

Big Idea Productions, Inc.

206 Yorktown Center
Lombard, Illinois 60148
U.S.A.
Telephone: (630) 652-6000
Fax: (630) 652-6001
Web site: http://www.bigidea.com

Private Company
Incorporated: 1993
Employees: 200
Sales: $40 million (2000 est.)
NAIC: 512110 Video Production

Big Idea Productions, Inc. is one of the fastest growing film production companies in the United States, having quickly succeeded in becoming the largest animation studio in the Midwest. Big Idea with its VeggieTales and 3-2-1 Penguins video series has sold record numbers of children's videos through both Christian product retailers and national retail discount stores, including Target, Wal-Mart, Kmart, and Walgreens. VeggieTales characters are now among the most widely recognized icons of the preschool set. Founder and Chairman Phil Vischer, a devout Christian, sees Big Idea's mission as enhancing the moral and spiritual fabric of society through the use of creative media. The Big Idea vision is to ''become the most trusted family media brand in the world.''

The Dream Stage: Childhood Through the 1980s

Vischer began making movies when he was nine years old using his grandfather's 8mm camera. Vischer's interest in moviemaking became a sideline when his educational pursuits took him not to film school but to St. Paul Bible College (now Crown College) in St. Bonifacius, Minnesota.

Vischer pursued a Bible degree for several years but decided to leave the college to follow a vocation in computer animation, an area in which he had hoped to combine his passion of things biblical with a lively interest in storytelling and computer graphics. While at St. Paul Bible College, Vischer met close

friend and puppeteer Mike Nawrocki. Nawrocki shared a vision with Vischer of creating quality, humorous, animated videos for children, videos that would bring positive messages to what the two saw as a values-starved industry. Nawrocki, Vischer, and Vischer's wife, Lisa, began collaborating on story ideas and producing character sketches that the fledgling company now referred to as ''Sunday morning values, Saturday morning fun!'' Previously created Christian children's videos were often serious, and somber, or had sickly sweet messages without a lot of universal appeal. The work the Vischers and Nawrocki began was refreshingly different.

Vischer attempted to make a go of it in his Chicago area home, but needed a good deal of funding in order to produce movies of the caliber he wished to make. Taking on computer design work for other enterprises was one way he tried to bankroll an animated film of his creation. Eventually Vischer compiled a few short films and many hours of homespun animation that were compelling enough for his family and friends to take a significant risk. Jeopardizing their financial security in order to establish the production company in earnest, Vischer's parents took out a second mortgage on their home while friends cashed in their modest retirement funds, and Big Idea Productions was born.

Producer or Producer at Last

Working out of a spare bedroom on an SGI Indigo computer system, Vischer experimented with his first computer-animated, three-dimensional snippet, ''Mr. Cuke's Screen Test,'' a forerunner of the full-length VeggieTales videos. Vischer realized his artistic limitations early and settled on vegetable characters so he would not have to work with the detailed animation that body limbs and hair would require. According to Visher, his use of veggies was almost thwarted by a strong interest in animated candy bars. Much to the relief of many sugar-conscious parents, Vischer decided that vegetables would promote a healthier lifestyle to today's youth.

Larry the Cucumber, developed in 1991and voiced by partner Mike Nawrocki, was Big Idea's first character. Larry's sidekick, Bob the Tomato (Larry's Abbott to Bob's Costello),

Company Perspectives:

Most major media companies today name shareholder value or profitability as their top priority. At Big Idea, our priorities are: people first, products second, profits third. Profiting is like breathing. As humans, we must breathe to live, but we do not live to breathe. As a company, Big Idea must profit to exist, but we will not exist merely to profit. Achieving our goal of building a top four family media brand takes a tremendous amount of capital, but we will never sacrifice the needs of kids or of our employees simply to increase our wealth. The world is full of media companies that are out to make a buck. The world desperately needs a media company that is out to make a difference.

made his debut with Vischer himself providing his voice. With backing from Vischer's friends and family, Big Idea hired two part-time art students as assistants and embarked in 1993 on its first major production, *Where is God When I'm S-Scared?*

The video represented the first full-length, fully computer-animated children's video ever produced, and made use of humorous songs, entertaining characters, and a Christian faith-based message.

At first, the videos released by Big Idea were selling at a normal pace for previously unknown works, and marketing was initially restricted to Christian booksellers throughout the United States. Soon, however, the videos took on an almost cult following among college students at Christian colleges nationwide. Word spread and *Where Is God When I'm S-Scared?* and new releases from Big Idea were soon pouring off the shelves. By 1995, four separate videos were in the marketplace and with very little promotion 40,000 videos had sold that calendar year. It was soon believed that the Christian/values-driven consumer of children's videos had been greatly underestimated, but nothing even remotely similar to VeggieTales had been done before and the quality and humor behind the message had attracted a larger demographic than had ever been believed possible.

The appeal to college students would prove indicative of Big Idea's success. Parents and children alike could appreciate Vischer and company's innocent take on Monty Pythonesque humor. More sanctimonious Christians took comfort in the promise that Big Idea had never and would never portray Jesus in vegetable form.

The messages Vischer and his ever expanding staff chose to focus on often usurped biblical themes and with a little creative license and contemporary story lines presented the message in new packaging. For instance, in 1997 Big Idea released its eighth original title, *Josh and the Big Wall!* The story echoed the biblical story of Jericho but placed the scene in contemporary times with catchy tunes and interesting animated vegetable characters.

In 1998, Big Idea hit the big time. Discount giants Wal-Mart, Target, Kmart, and Walgreens began merchandising VeggieTales videos and products. Wal-Mart and restaurant chain Chuck E. Cheese added promotions based on Veggie-Tales characters to their offerings. Capitalizing on the popular-ity of VeggieTales mania, Chuck E. Cheese family restaurants added VeggieTales movies and songs to the entertainment menu at its 330 restaurants in 44 states.

In December 1998, Big Idea produced its first national television special based on its VeggieTales series. *The VeggieTales Christmas Spectacular* helped bring about sales of more than six million videos.

Keeping up with demand, Big Idea released one of its most popular films in the summer of 1999, *Larry Boy and the Rumor Weed*. The film was shown in theaters nationwide on a limited release. In a single day more than 350,000 people turned out to view the film. The film featured the popular Larry the Cucumber and his alter ego, Larry Boy, a cucumber superhero who helps save the metropolis of Bumblyburg from a nasty rumor weed and teaches children the lesson that spreading gossip can be harmful.

Larry Boy and the Rumor Weed continued the craze for home video purchase and by the end of 1999 sales hit eight million videos.

The biblical stories that Big Idea recreated included stories from both the Old and New Testament. *Rack, Shack & Benny,* a remake of the story of Shadrach, Meshach, and Abednego from the Old Testament book of Daniel included Nebby K. Neezer, a villainous zucchini; likewise, *David and the Giant Pickle* and *The Gourds Must Be Crazy,* were remakes, respectively, of the Old Testament story of David and Goliath and the New Testament story of Zaccheus the tax collector.

Big Idea was credited with starting a resurgence in Bible and Bible-story related consumer spending. According to an article in *Newsweek* magazine, "a new parental emphasis on spirituality has coincided with a boom in reading-age kids." In addition, Christian Booksellers Association President Bill Anderson claimed that, "VeggieTales are so strong that they are pulling up the rest of the market."

Big Idea's sales figures were also of epic proportion. According to VideoScan Inc., a national market research firm, four VeggieTales videos ranked in the top 30 among all children's videos in terms of sales. This was particularly noteworthy since the ranking was not only among videos with religious content, a feat never before matched by a faith-based production company.

Big Idea Growing Bigger

Quickly outgrowing its corporate office and studio space, Big Idea made plans in 1999 to relocate to downtown Lombard, Illinois. The city had courted the company to take over an historic downtown theater in dire need of renovation. The plan originally called for a $17 million corporate headquarters. Big Idea set up temporary offices in Lombard's Yorktown Shopping Center while moving ahead with design plans, but in a decision that strongly disappointed Lombard's community leaders Big Idea backed out of the theater location, maintaining that the company's rapid growth had unfortunately made the 2.5 acre theater project inadequate for future projected company growth.

When assessing its needs for a new location, the company made plans to include some sort of entertainment complex

Key Dates:

1989: Phil Vischer starts his own computer production company.
1991: Vischer creates Larry the Cucumber and the 12-second film "Mr. Cuke's Screen Test."
1992: Vischer produces "Veggie Tales-Take 38," introducing Bob the Tomato.
1993: Vischer and friend Mike Nawrocki raise money from friends and family and launch Big Idea Productions; *Where's God When I'm S-Scared?*, the first full-length, entirely computer-animated film, is released in December.
1994: Big Idea sells 40,000 VeggieTales videos through Christian bookstores around the country.
1995: Video sales total 100,000.
1996: With several releases available in the VeggieTales series, sales near 500,000.
1997: Eight videos are now available and sales reach 1.5 million for the year.
1998: National discount chains begin selling VeggieTales videos; *The VeggieTales Christmas Spectacular* is telecast on national TV.
1999: Number of videos sold reaches eight million.
2000: VeggieTales 13, *King George and the Ducky*, receives *Parenting* magazine's Video Magic Award.

onsite. Big Idea envisioned a gift shop, studio tours, a theme restaurant (where of course kids would eat their "veggies"), and perhaps a small hotel.

By late 1999 the company settled on another Lombard site that was better suited to the company's growing needs: a 30-acre parcel of land that the company planned to develop over time.

In large marketing events, Big Idea began coupling new video releases with limited big screen premiers in major U.S. cities. In March 2000, King George and the Ducky played to sold-out crowds in Atlanta, Dallas, and Los Angeles at a Saturday matinee. Christian bookstores and churches also held screenings helping to promote VeggieTales and its "Sunday morning values, Saturday morning fun."

With the expansion of the company, Big Idea began to take its self-promotion more seriously. The company brought on Cornelius Lee, a former Motorola executive, and hired Carmichael Lynch of Minneapolis, Minnesota, to launch Big Idea's first real advertising campaign. The company had secured licensing agreements with Fisher Price, Hallmark, Hadaad Clothing, and Spring Industries. Merchandise with the recognizable VeggieTales logo was offered nationally by large scale retailers.

The appeal of VeggieTales was captured in a *Seattle Times* article dated August 5, 2000. The *Times* noted that Seattle's Family Christian Store sold 100 or more advance sales before the videos even came out. Manager John Stapp explained the mass appeal: "The reason they're so popular is they work on several levels of humor. The kids like them because they're cartoons, and they're funny and there's a lot of action, but the dialogue gets in things that are lost on the kids. There are zingers only adults pick up, they're just charming."

The Big Idea Production's web site was often frequented by VeggieTales fans. The family friendly site offered children's shockwave games, information on new releases, and places to post artwork and letters. The site was created using a variety of Macromedia web authoring products and provided entertainment in typical Big Idea fashion.

A New Cast of Characters

In November 2000, Big Idea promoted its new video property, 3-2-1 Penguins! Utilizing the Kennedy Space Center's Visitor Complex in Cape Canaveral, Florida, Big Idea introduced four new space bound penguins into its cast of characters: Zidgel, Midgel, Fidgel, and Kevin. Like the company's VeggieTales releases, the Penguins! movies had a lesson to teach. The four space explorers experienced *Trouble on Planet Wait-Your-Turn*. The Penguins! series, like VeggieTales would be direct-to-video products sold through both Christian retail stores and other discounters.

Unlike the other movies, however, Penguins! made use of graphically more complex characters and was more sophisticated in its writing. The production costs associated with making 3-2-1 Penguins! were also significantly higher. While the VeggieTales classic *Where Is God When I'm S-Scared?* cost a mere $60,000 to produce, Penguins! cost in the range of $700,000 to $1 million.

Many viewers have likened Penguins! to a combination of Monty Python meets Chuck Jones, the classic Warner Bros. animator. The Penguins! series was meant to target boys from 9 to 12 years old who had outgrown VeggieTales on their most basic level, yet were still too young to understand the humor in the films that appealed to adults.

The next big enterprise for Big Idea was well underway for release in 2002. The first full-length big screen VeggieTales movie, *Jonah: A VeggieTales Movie,* was scheduled to appear in theaters nationwide sometime in 2002.

By that year Big Idea had already captured a huge new market of video entertainment, a market that it had pioneered and helped to shape. It appeared well positioned to attain its 20-year goal of becoming perhaps the "most trusted family media brand in the world." As they say in Lombard, "now that's a big idea."

Principal Competitors

Walt Disney Company; Warner Bros.; EBI Video (Treetop Studios); Tommy Nelson; Billy Young Productions.

Further Reading

"Big Idea Productions Announces Its First DVD Title," *DVD News,* January 29, 2001, p. 3.
Heffley, Lynne, "Children; Look and Listen; Easy-to-Swallow Veggie; Boy's Best Friend," *Los Angeles Times,* April 20, 2000, p. F31.
Knapp, Kevin, "Big Idea Bows out of Lombard Theater: Downtown Rehab Anchor up in Air," *Crain's Chicago Business,* October 11, 1999, p. 6.

Langmaid, Wilfred, Rev., ''Veggie Tunes, Veggie Tales: Larry Boy Soundtrack,'' *Canadian Business and Current Affairs Anglican Journal,* April 2000, p. 13.

''New Products,'' *Drug Store News,* June 26, 2000, p. 202.

''VeggieTales Video Brings Moral Fiber to Big Screen,'' *USA Today,* March 27, 2000, p. 9D.

''Videos; Family,'' *Star Tribune,* June 30, 2000, p. 3E.

Webster, Nancy Coltun, ''VeggieTales; Cornelius Lee,'' *Advertising Age,* June 26, 2000, p. S18.

—Susan B. Culligan

Blimpie International, Inc.

1775 The Exchange
Suite 600
Atlanta, Georgia 30339
U.S.A.
Telephone: (770) 984-2707
Toll Free: (800) 447-6256
Fax: (770) 933-6098
Web site: http://www.blimpie.com

Private Company
Incorporated: 1977 as International Blimpie Corporation
Employees: 109
Sales: $30.7 million (2001)
NAIC: 722211 Limited-Service Restaurants; 533110
　　Lessors of Nonfinancial Intangible Assets (Except
　　Copyrighted Works)

Blimpie International, Inc. is the franchiser for Blimpie restaurants, the second largest submarine sandwich chain in the United States, trailing Subway. By mid-2002, there were about 2,000 Blimpie outlets in operation, located in 47 U.S. states and in 15 other countries. Unlike many restaurant chains, Blimpie does not generally operate ''company stores.'' Virtually all of its income is derived from the various fees associated with franchise arrangements. In addition to freestanding outlets and locations in malls and store clusters, Blimpies can be found in a variety of nontraditional sites, such as inside convenience stores, gasoline station food marts, schools, office complexes, hospitals, and sports arenas. A key area of growth is in the development or acquisition of other brands. In 1999 the company launched Pasta Central, a franchised chain within the ''home meal replacement'' category featuring Italian-style pasta and pizza; the concept was exclusively a vehicle for cobranded Blimpie/Pasta Central outlets. Two years earlier, Blimpie International acquired majority control of Maui Tacos, a Mexican quick-service restaurant with a Hawaiian flavor. Maui Tacos in 1998 launched Smoothie Island, a chain offering blended fruit-based beverages.

Early History

The first Blimpie sub shop was opened in Hoboken, New Jersey, in 1964 by Tony Conza, Peter DeCarlo, and Angelo Bandassare, a trio of former high school buddies. Inspired by a successful Point Pleasant, New Jersey, operation called Mike's Submarines, Conza, DeCarlo, and Bandassare speculated that a similar restaurant would do well in Hoboken. They raised $2,500 in seed capital by borrowing from friends and began serving essentially the same sandwich for which people were lining up at Mike's. The original Blimpie was an instant hit, and, before long, customers began asking about starting up franchises. The first franchise was sold to a friend in western New York for $600 during the company's first year of operation.

In 1965 Bandassare left the company to start his own food service supply firm. Conza and DeCarlo decided to expand into New York City, beginning with a store on 55th Street in Manhattan, near Carnegie Hall. By 1967 there were ten Blimpies in the chain, four of which were owned by the company's two remaining founders. Unfortunately, Conza and DeCarlo were not experienced businessmen, and, in spite of the chain's rapid growth and good sales volume, profits were difficult to make. To keep the company afloat, the partners sold the four stores they owned and began to concentrate primarily on franchising.

By the mid-1970s, Conza felt the time was ripe to introduce Blimpie subs to the South. Partner DeCarlo, however, was against the move. This disagreement eventually led to a split between the two men. In 1976 Blimpie was divided into two separate entities, with both retaining rights to the Blimpie trademark. DeCarlo became head of a new, completely independent company, Metropolitan Blimpie (later renamed Blimpie's of New York, Inc.), which controlled franchising rights in New York, New Jersey, and other parts of the East Coast. Conza retained control of the original company, which was incorporated in 1977 as International Blimpie Corporation. Conza, a college dropout with no business credentials other than his experience with Blimpie, remained chairman and CEO of Blimpie through January 2002.

During the late 1970s, Conza was willing to sell franchises anywhere there was an interested franchisee. Blimpie began

Company Perspectives:

Blimpie International, Inc. is dedicated to increasing stake-holder value through developing, franchising, and supporting a portfolio of world-class brands.

Stakeholders (franchisees, subfranchisers, master licensees, employees, suppliers, and shareholders) recognize that "increasing value" is dependent upon providing consumers with superior products and services.

selling franchises both for individual stores and for whole territories. Unfortunately, many of these new franchises were rather isolated from the rest of the chain, and some of the benefits of franchise arrangements—chainwide advertising, for example—had little effect in those locations. Although the chain was growing rapidly, several of the newer stores failed. By 1983, International Blimpie's annual revenues were approaching $1 million, and Blimpie's franchises totaled 150. Conza took the company public that year, with a modest initial over-the-counter offering of 90 cents per share.

Mid-1980s: Ill-Fated Diversification Program

Over the next few years, Blimpie embarked on a diversification program that failed miserably. Conza began to feel that there was no future in submarine sandwiches. At the same time, he longed for the kind of respect that comes only to real restaurateurs, not fast-food moguls. In 1984 Conza opened the Border Café, a tablecloth restaurant serving southwestern cuisine on Manhattan's swanky Upper East Side. Although the Border Café did reasonably well at first, this shift in focus proved to be a major blunder. While Conza was turning his attention away from the subs that had gotten him where he was, competitor Subway—which was founded in 1965, just a year after the first Blimpie's was opened—was beginning an expansion drive that would push it far ahead of Blimpie as the world's foremost submarine sandwich chain.

To reflect his increasing concentration on non-Blimpie activities, Conza changed the name of the company to Astor Restaurant Group, Inc. in October 1986. Meanwhile, the Blimpie's chain was stagnating. The number of outlets was stalled at about 200. In Manhattan, the company's birthplace, the Blimpie name suffered severe image problems. In the early days, the company had not been particularly selective as to who could get a franchise. In addition, its early franchise contracts allowed operators quite a bit of latitude in how the restaurants were to be run. This led to a degree of uniformity among stores far below that of other national fast-food chains, not to mention a reputation for questionable sanitation standards.

After the Border Café's initial success, Conza opened two more of them in 1986, one in Woodstock, New York, and the other—with New York Yankee Dave Winfield as a partner—on the Upper West Side of Manhattan. Unfortunately, the Border Café idea turned out to be a big money loser. Although Astor brought in $4.5 million in revenues for 1987 (its largest total yet), the company showed a net loss of $347,800 for the year. That year, only 30 new Blimpie restaurants were opened,

and company stock was in free fall, bottoming out as low as 15 cents per share. Gradually, Conza's interest in his core business began to return. Over the next couple of years, Atlanta became the company's biggest target for new Blimpie's franchises. In 1987, the company celebrated the opening of the 50th Blimpie's store in the Atlanta area by giving away 25,000 free sandwiches to customers there.

Late 1980s and Early 1990s: Revitalizing Blimpie

By 1988 Conza had realized the error of his ways, and he quickly got out of the Tex-Mex business. Seeing the tremendous success of Subway, Conza decided to redouble his efforts in the hoagie arena. He began to address the Blimpie problem with renewed vigor and a more systematic approach than he had used before. The first step in Conza's revitalization program was to identify four fundamental problems plaguing the business: a lack of goals, poor use of financial resources, low employee morale, and procrastination. He then got together with a group of managers and drew up a list of "101 Small Improvements." Delegating to his senior staff much of the day-to-day managing he had always done himself, Conza went on the road in an attempt to open up the long-closed channels of communication between Blimpie and its franchisees.

Next, Blimpie launched a quality-control program aimed at cleaning up its 140 New York restaurants, which had long been sources of embarrassment to the chain. At the same time, Conza continued in his efforts to improve relations with franchisees, many of whom had become disgruntled over the last decade. In addition to flying to dozens of cities to meet restaurant owners, Conza formed a franchisee advisory council to keep him apprised of important issues; he launched a newsletter called *No Baloney News* and a toll-free hotline to get important information out to franchisees; and he gave franchisees more control over advertising through the formation of regional advertising co-ops.

In 1989 Blimpie began testing a new low-calorie menu in the hope of attracting a bigger share of the increasingly fat-conscious American public. The new menu, called Blimpie Lite, included a variety of tuna-, crab-, chicken-, and turkey-based items, in both salad and pita-bread sandwich form. The following year, the company launched another test: gourmet salads sold under the name Blimpie Fresherie. Blimpie also began tinkering with its prototype restaurant design around this time, incorporating the company's signature lime-green and yellow colors into a sleeker look for new outlets. By 1990 the Blimpie turnaround was well underway, with systemwide sales reaching $120 million per year.

The Blimpie chain continued to grow steadily through the early 1990s. Much of this growth was fueled by the company's area developer program, in which franchise rights were sold for an entire area to a developer, who then subfranchised those rights to individual operators. The company continued testing new products throughout this period. In 1991 Blimpie unveiled its Quick Bite menu in response to the appearance of value menus in many fast-food establishments, including arch-rival Subway. Items on the Quick Bite menu included three-inch hero sandwiches for 99 cents, a six-inch bacon, lettuce, and tomato sandwich for $1.59, and a veggie pocket pita sandwich, also priced at $1.59. The company also began testing pizza at a

Key Dates:

1964: First Blimpie sub shop is opened in Hoboken, New Jersey, by Tony Conza, Peter DeCarlo, and Angelo Bandassare.

1965: Bandassare leaves the company.

1976: Conza and DeCarlo divide Blimpie into two separate entities, with DeCarlo keeping the locations in the Northeast and forming a new company called Metropolitan Blimpie (later Blimpie's of New York, Inc.) and Conza retaining control of the original company and the rights to the Blimpie name everywhere else.

1977: Conza incorporates the original company as International Blimpie Corporation.

1983: Company goes public.

1984: Blimpie diversifies by launching Border Café, a sit-down restaurant chain.

1986: Company name is changed to Astor Restaurant Group, Inc.

1992: Following the divestment of Border Café, company changes its name to Blimpie International, Inc.

1995: The 1,000th Blimpie outlet opens; first overseas unit opens in Stockholm, Sweden.

1997: Blimpie acquires a 75 percent stake in Maui Tacos.

1998: Smoothie Island chain is launched through Maui Tacos.

1999: Pasta Central is launched as a concept to be co-branded with the Blimpie sub shops.

2002: A private investor group led by Jeffrey K. Endervelt, a Blimpie subfranchisee, agrees to take Blimpie International private in a $25.7 million transaction; Endervelt replaces Conza as chairman and CEO of the firm.

handful of locations in an effort to breathe some life into its dinner business. Conza's attempts to improve franchisee relations continued as well. The company's first annual franchisee convention was held in 1991.

By the beginning of 1992, there were Blimpie restaurants in 27 states. That year, the chain passed the 500-unit mark and the company changed its name to Blimpie International, Inc., reflecting the renewed focus on the sub brand. In the spring of 1993, Blimpie began trading its stock on the up-and-coming NASDAQ exchange. Around this time, the company began to sink more resources into advertising than it had in the past, doubling its marketing budget to about $2 million per year. A new advertising campaign was launched, encompassing just about every medium available, including television, radio, print, and point-of-purchase. This campaign marked the introduction of the chain's new tag line: "Simply Blimpie for fresh-sliced subs." Some of the television spots featured people on the street struggling to repeat the tongue-twisting phrase, "Simply Blimpie."

Sales throughout the Blimpie system reached $132 million by 1993, and Blimpie International earned $1 million on $12 million in revenue. By autumn of that year, the chain had grown to 670 outlets. Improved marketing support from the parent

company helped reduce the rate of franchise failures from 10 percent to 3 percent. In some cases, such as in the brutally competitive Chicago market, Conza allowed franchisees to divert their 6 percent annual franchise fee to advertising.

As the 1990s continued, Blimpie came up with a new concept that accelerated the chain's growth even further. Blimpie's franchises began appearing in a variety of nontraditional locations. First it was convenience stores. As convenience store proprietors began to seek out new ways to compensate for declining cigarette sales, they started turning to fast food. Blimpie's was the natural choice for many, for two main reasons: a real kitchen was not required, and startup costs were relatively low (as little as $35,000) compared with other fast-food operations. Among the early nontraditional sites for Blimpie's outlets were the Des Moines, Iowa-based Kum & Go convenience store chain; Texaco Food Marts in Mississippi; and the food court at the University of Texas. Blimpie's also became part of the first Home Depot superstore restaurant section, located in Atlanta.

In 1994, the 800th Blimpie, in Iron City, Michigan, was opened. That year, the company launched several new concepts to further its drive for nontraditional venues. The Blimpie kiosk was a movable, condensed restaurant that could fit into a 100-square-foot area. The kiosk, which could serve four types of sandwiches, drinks, and side orders, was designed for use at stadiums, fairs, and other special events. Another new idea was the movable display cart, suitable for high-traffic areas such as airports, college campuses, and concerts. Other new wrinkles included a special refrigerated case for convenience stores (Blimpie's fastest-growing market), and the Blimpie Bakery, offering a variety of baked goods aimed at boosting early morning business.

Blimpie reached two major milestones in 1995. Largely on the strength of its nontraditional location push, the chain passed the 1,000-outlet mark that year. Blimpie International also lived up to the second word in its name for the first time in company history, with the opening of a location in Stockholm, Sweden. As the 1990s continued, the company looked for more new ways to sell Blimpie sandwiches, including vending machines, outlets in supermarkets, and new types of carts and other mobile product delivery systems.

Late 1990s and Beyond: Seeking Growth Through New Concepts

With the opening of new outlets in the United States slowing and with overseas growth occurring only at a very slow pace (there were only 61 overseas locations in 15 countries by 2001), Blimpie launched a new diversification effort in the late 1990s. The first such initiative came late in 1997 when the company acquired a 75 percent stake in Maui Tacos, a fast-food chain with six units in Hawaii. This concept featured traditional quick-service Mexican food, such as burritos, tacos, and quesadillas, but with a Hawaiian twist, such as meat marinated in pineapple, lime, and other Hawaiian flavorings. Under Blimpie's majority ownership, Maui Tacos was soon introduced to the mainland, and by 2001 there were 15 such units in nine states and the District of Columbia.

After almost two years of in-house development, Blimpie launched Pasta Central in 1999. Unlike Maui Tacos, Pasta Central was not a standalone concept but was created as a co-branding vehicle that would be coupled with Blimpie Subs & Salads. Cobranding emerged as a hot growth vehicle in the late 1990s and involved the placement of two (or more) restaurant brands within a single unit. There were a number of rationales behind cobranded units, including the idea that the additional choices that they offered customers made them more attractive to groups of people, but for Blimpie International it was the desire to increase dinner revenues that propelled the creation of Pasta Central. Because sandwiches were largely considered lunch fare, Blimpie Subs outlets made the bulk of their sales from 11 a.m. to 2 p.m. Pasta Central, by contrast, with its Italian-style pasta dishes and its pizza offerings, was designed to generate a lot of traffic during dinner, thereby making it complementary to Blimpie. In addition, Pasta Central was also created with a home meal replacement component built in—a selection of prepared refrigerated and frozen entrees and pre-packed foods for preparation at home. By mid-2001 there were eight units cobranded with Blimpie and Pasta Central, with the units located in Puerto Rico, Georgia, South Carolina, Texas, and Wyoming.

A third new concept was Smoothie Island, which was launched through Maui Tacos in 1998. Smoothie Island's menu featured beverages blended with frozen yogurt and fruit. In addition to opening standalone units, including such nontraditional locations as airports, health clubs, and grocery stores, Blimpie also planned to cobrand Smoothie Island with both the Maui Tacos and Blimpie concepts—both in dual-branding and tribranding formats. By mid-2001 there were 80 Smoothie Island units located in the United States, Puerto Rico, and four other countries.

By the turn of the millennium, Blimpie International was struggling. Net income had fallen steadily throughout the second half of the 1990s—dropping from the high of $4 million in fiscal 1995 to just $1.1 million in fiscal 2000. A main factor in this decline was that the subfranchiser rights to the Blimpie Subs chain had largely been sold by the mid-1990s, thus bringing a halt to what had been a steady stream of income. Another factor was that the drive to open nontraditional outlets was far from a winning strategy. Many of these units proved unprofitable, and a number of them were subsequently closed. During one 12-month period from mid-2000 to mid-2001 the company closed 155 underperforming Blimpie outlets, 70 percent of which were in nontraditional locations. The company also announced plans to close seven unprofitable company-owned Maui Tacos and Smoothie Island outlets, a move that would leave the firm with just five company-owned stores out of its nearly 2,000 sites. Also during 2001, the Blimpie chain began receiving a revamping that involved menu upgrades, more extensive point-of-sale merchandising, and an overhaul of the decor. One of the key changes to the menu was the addition of a line of hot grilled sandwiches that proved quite popular in market testing.

As Blimpie's struggles continued—net income having fallen below $100,000 for the fiscal year ending in June 2001—investors showed little interest in the company, and the price of the company's stock sagged. Seeing little benefit in being a publicly traded firm, Blimpie joined the growing ranks of restaurant companies fleeing the public market. In October 2001 a private investor group led by Jeffrey K. Endervelt, owner of the 44-unit Blimpie of California subfranchise, agreed to buy Blimpie International for $25.7 million. The transaction was completed in January 2002, whereupon Endervelt took over as chairman, president, and CEO, and Conza, who was a partner in the investor group, remained involved at the company but in an advisory capacity. Although Blimpie remained far behind Subway in the battle for hoagie supremacy, the new ownership and leadership perhaps signaled the beginning of a brighter era for Blimpie.

Principal Subsidiaries

B I Concept Systems, Inc.; Maui Tacos International, Inc. (73%).

Principal Operating Units

Blimpie Subs & Salads; Pasta Central; Smoothie Island.

Principal Competitors

Doctor's Associates Inc. (Subway); The Quizno's Corporation; Schlotzsky's, Inc.; Triarc Companies, Inc.; Panera Bread Company.

Further Reading

Bird, Laura, "Building a Lighter, Fresher Blimpie," *Adweek's Marketing Week,* August 6, 1990, p. 23.

"Blimpie Program Helps BUILD Neighborhoods," *Nation's Restaurant News,* November 13, 2000, p. 122.

"Blimpie Seeks Financial Health in Cutting Back Company Units," *Nation's Restaurant News,* May 18, 2001, pp. 18, 40.

"Blimpie's Starts Quality Drive in Manhattan," *Nation's Restaurant News,* April 4, 1988, p. 63.

Cohen, Andrew, " 'Blimpie' and 'Lite' May No Longer Be Contradictory Terms," *Wall Street Journal,* April 27, 1989, p. B5.

Conza, Tony, "My Biggest Mistake," *Inc.,* April 1999, p. 105.

——, *Success: It's a Beautiful Thing: Lessons on Life and Business from the Founder of Blimpie International,* New York: Wiley, 2000, 242 p.

Dugan, I. Jeanne, "Half a Loaf at Blimpie," *Business Week,* August 10, 1998, pp. 43–44.

Edwards, Joe, "Astor Puts Blimpie in a Growth Mode," *Nation's Restaurant News,* November 9, 1987, p. F25.

Frumkin, Paul, "Blimpie Sets Course with Concept Revamp," *Nation's Restaurant News,* August 27, 2001, pp. 1, 132.

——, "Private Investor Group Set to Buy Blimpie for $26M," *Nation's Restaurant News,* October 22, 2001, pp. 1, 11, 71.

Gabriel, Frederick, "A Divided Blimpie Charts New Course," *Crain's New York Business,* September 15, 1997, p. 4.

Grimm, Matthew, "Blimpie Plans Winter Image Push," *Adweek's Marketing Week,* September 2, 1991, p. 7.

Hamstra, Mark, "Blimpie Goes Hawaiian, Buys Mexican Chain," *Nation's Restaurant News,* November 10, 1997, pp. 1, 143.

——, "Hawaiian-Style Mexican Hits the Mainland with Maui Tacos," *Nation's Restaurant News,* November 23, 1998, pp. 1, 108.

Howard, Theresa, "Now on Deck for Blimpie: NASDAQ, New Ad Campaign," *Nation's Restaurant News,* February 22, 1993, p. 16.

Keegan, Peter O., "Under New VP, Blimpie Int'l. Eyes Nontraditional Growth," *Nation's Restaurant News,* September 5, 1994, p. 7.

Kleinfield, N.R., "Trying to Build a Bigger Blimpie," *New York Times,* December 13, 1987, p. F4.

O'Dwyer, Gerard, ''Blimpie Develops a Swede Tooth,'' *Crain's New York Business,* December 11, 1995, p. 17.

Richman, Louis S., ''Rekindling the Entrepreneurial Fire,'' *Fortune,* February 21, 1994, p. 112.

Rigg, Cynthia, ''Blimpie's Cuts Mustard with Convenience Stores,'' *Crain's New York Business,* October 11, 1993, p. 3.

Touby, Laurel, ''Blimpie Is Trying to Be a Hero to Franchisees Again,'' *Business Week,* March 22, 1993, p. 70.

Vranica, Suzanne, ''Can Blimpie Heroes Defeat a Giant?,'' *Wall Street Journal,* May 8, 2002, p. B8.

Zuber, Amy, ''Blimpie Eyes Higher-End QSR, Opens Pasta Central,'' *Nation's Restaurant News,* April 19, 1999, pp. 1, 6.

—Robert R. Jacobson
—update: David E. Salamie

British Energy

British Energy Plc

3 Redwood Crescent
East Kilbride
Strathclyde G74 5PR
United Kingdom
Telephone: (+44) 135-526-2000
Fax: (+44) 135-556-5656
Web site: http://www.british-energy.com

Public Company
Incorporated: 1996
Employees: 5,310
Sales: ($3.01 billion) (2001)
Stock Exchanges: London New York
Ticker Symbol: BGY
NAIC: 221113 Nuclear Electric Power Generation;
        221119 Other Electric Power Generation

British Energy Plc, in addition to being the United Kingdom's largest power generator (by producing more than 20 percent of the country's power supply through a network of eight nuclear power stations and several non-nuclear stations), is also a fast-growing energy producer in the North American market. Through AmerGen, its 50 percent joint venture with Exelon (formerly PECO and Unicom), the company owns three U.S. nuclear plants, including Three Mile Island's Unit I (which, unlike sister Unit II, has never posed a direct public health risk). AmerGen's other U.S. holdings include Clinton Power Station in Illinois and Oyster Creek in New Jersey. These stations add nearly 2,500 megawatts (MW) capacity to the company's 9,600 MW in the United Kingdom. The company also holds a purchase agreement for the Vermont Yankee station, which is pending government approval. Meanwhile, British Energy also has expanded strongly into Canada, where it controls an 82 percent share of Bruce Power. That company has signed a 17-year lease with Ontario Power Generation for the operation of up to eight "Candu" (Canada Deuterium Uranium) reactors in southwestern Ontario. Four of those reactors are already operational, totaling 6,200 MW in capacity; the company expects to bring two more reactors online by 2003.

British Energy also has been taking steps to diversify beyond nuclear power. The company owns a coal-fired power plant in Yorkshire. On a more progressive front, British Energy has been investing in renewable power sources, particularly wind farms. The company has formed the Huron Wind 50–50 joint venture with Ontario Power Generation, and it expects to launch a wind farm, of yet undetermined capacity, on Lake Huron in 2002. In the United Kingdom, British Energy has partnered with Amec for a planned 600 MW wind farm in the Hebrides Islands off of the west coast of Scotland. These moves have come in response to new British government legislation barring new nuclear plant development while raising the percentage of renewable energy to 20 percent of the country's total power supply. British Energy, privatized in 1996, trades on the London and New York stock exchanges.

Inheriting the United Kingdom's Nuclear Power Industry in the 1980s

Electrical power generation and supply in the United Kingdom remained a sporadic and mostly local and regional concern until the 1920s, when the British government began to take steps to ensure the distribution of electrical power throughout the country. In 1926, the government formed the Central Electricity Board, which in turn began building a national power grid system linking up the various power stations already in operation. The existence of the grid, which meant that electrical power could be transmitted all over the country, encouraged the creation of an extensive network of privately held power stations.

By the middle of the 1940s, the United Kingdom counted more than 600 power stations. Yet voltages and pricing varied widely from one place to another, while many of the country's more remote locations continued to lack electricity. In 1947, the British government set up new regulations governing the power generation industry. A government-owned coordinating board was created with the mission to bring the power generation industry under control, ensuring complete national coverage, while standardizing voltages and pricing. At the same time, a network of regional electricity boards was created to act as retailers for the nation's power output. These boards took responsibility for converting energy for end-consumer use.

Company Perspectives:

British Energy's vision statement is "to be the world's leading nuclear energy company."

By the 1950s, the United Kingdom was caught up in a wave of nationalization efforts that saw the government take control of many of its most essential industries. The electrical power industry was nationalized in its turn in 1957, when the newly established Central Electricity Generating Board took over responsibility for the nation's power generation and transmission. At that time, the United Kingdom was inaugurating its own nuclear power industry, with the first British prototype nuclear plant going online in 1956. Located at Calder Hall, it was also the first plant in the world to provide electricity for the commercial market.

Nuclear power in the United Kingdom was almost doomed from the start. In 1957, fire broke out at the nuclear plant at Windscale (later known as Sellafield), which produced plutonium for nuclear weapons, leaking radioactive waste in what was the world's worst civil nuclear disaster at the time. Nonetheless, the British government pushed ahead with its nuclear power project. Following the successful launch of the Calder Hall plant, the government built two more prototype plants before beginning the construction of full-scale power plants. By the mid-1960s, the United Kingdom featured nine full-scale plants, in addition to the three prototypes, all of the Magnox gas-cooled reactor type.

By the mid-1960s, the British government had decided to switch to newer Advanced Gas-Cooled Reactor (AGR) technology for its next series of reactors, constructing five power stations in England and two more in Scotland. The first of these plants began operations in 1976, and the last was brought online in 1988. In the late 1970s, however, the government began exploring the next generation of nuclear power types, and in 1978 the government adopted the Pressurized Water Reactor (PWR) model, which had by then become the most widely used reactor type in the world. Yet England was to see the construction of only one PWR plant, the Sizewell B in Suffolk, which finally began construction after nearly ten years of public debate. Three more PWR plants were also in the planning stages. In the meantime, the infamous accident at the Three Mile Island nuclear power plant in 1979 and the more devastating disaster at Chernobyl in 1986 had cooled public enthusiasm for nuclear power. The Sizewell project went through, however, and at last was commissioned in 1995.

Privatized Nuclear Power Company in the 1990s

In the late 1980s, the British government, led by Margaret Thatcher, sought to extend its privatization drive begun earlier in the decade to the nation's electrical power industry. A government White Paper released in 1988 led to the Electricity Act of 1989, which broke up the Central Electricity Generating Board into four companies, including Nuclear Electric. This company, however, remained controlled by the British government, following the 1988 White Paper's recommendation. At

that time, the nuclear power industry was considered too expensive—at least in comparison with its fossil fuel-based rivals—to be spun off as a private concern. In addition, the government was still pursuing plans to construct the three additional PWR-based power stations.

These power stations were put permanently on hold in 1994, as the British government enacted legislation barring development of any new nuclear power plants for the foreseeable future, although the proposed PWR stations remained on the drawing board. Nonetheless, the government remained committed to nuclear power as a diversified—and virtually emissions-free—source of power, which by then had come to represent more than 25 percent of the country's total power supply. As part of the 1994 legislation, the government began making plans to privatize Nuclear Electric, marking the end of the country's long privatization effort.

The privatization began to take shape by mid-1995, as plans were revealed to split up Nuclear Electric into two bodies, the first controlling the country's older Magnox-based reactors, which were deemed too old and too close to decommissioning—an expensive, lengthy process—to be placed in the private sector. The second company was to be named British Energy, which in turn was to serve as a holding company for two subsidiary operations, Nuclear Electric, which took over nuclear power operations in England and Wales, and Scotland Nuclear, which took over the nuclear power plants in Scotland. By the end of 1995, the as yet unofficial British Energy had already canceled plans to build two of the proposed new PWR stations.

British Energy's privatization nearly derailed before it was even formalized, however. By the beginning of 1996, British Energy had begun insisting that the British government shoulder part of the hefty decommissioning burden that British Energy was expected to pay—as part of the privatization, British Energy pledged to contribute to a long-term fund to provide for future plant decommissioning costs (decommissioning a nuclear power plant was a process that stretched over 100 years). In March, the company revealed that it had been losing between £50 million and £550 million per year during the previous five years. This revelation sparked the British government to put up £230 million toward British Energy's decommissioning fund, as well as slash its debt back to £700 million from £1.5 billion. These moves did indeed put the privatization back on track; yet, when the newly privatized company finally launched its IPO, it found itself valued at far less than had been originally hoped.

International Power Generator in the 21st Century

British Energy's first move was to begin to plot a diversification of its operations. For this, the company looked in two directions: the first, taking the company into power generation from non-nuclear fuel sources; the second was to take the company overseas. At the end of 1996, the company announced, but then abandoned, plans to build a gas-fired power plant near Lancaster. Instead, British Energy bought a 12.5 percent stake in Humber Power, an operator of a gas-fired power plant in South Humber (British Energy sold these shares in 2001). The company also entered an agreement with Southern Electric to build a series of small gas-fired power plants.

Key Dates:

1956: The first British nuclear power plant is inaugurated, at Calder Hall, and becomes the first such plant in the world to provide electricity for the commercial market.

1957: The Central Electricity Generation Board (CEGB) is created and takes over control of power generation in the United Kingdom.

1964: CEGB begins planning next generation, AGR-based (Advanced Gas-Cooled Reactor-based) nuclear power plants.

1976: Construction of the first AGR-based power plant is completed.

1978: CEGB begins planning new generation of PWR-based (Pressurized Water Reactor-based) nuclear power plants.

1988: A government White Paper recommends privatization of British electrical generation industry, except for nuclear power.

1987: CEGB is broken up into four components, including Nuclear Electric, which groups nuclear power plants and remains government controlled.

1994: The British government announces its intention to privatize Nuclear Electric.

1995: British Energy is established as a holding company for Nuclear Electric and Scottish Nuclear.

1996: British Energy, listed on the London and New York stock exchanges, is privatized.

1997: British Energy forms AmerGen 50–50 joint venture with PECO (later Exelon) in order to acquire nuclear power plants in the United States.

1998: Nuclear Electric and Scottish Nuclear are combined to form British Energy Generation.

1999: AmerGen acquires Three Mile Island, Clinton, and Oyster Beach nuclear power plants in the United States; the company begins a diversification drive into non-nuclear-based power sources.

2000: The company buys a coal-fired power plant in Yorkshire for £340 million.

2001: The company acquires a 17-year lease for eight nuclear power plants at Bruce Power facilities in Lake Huron, Ontario; the company announces plans to build a 600 megawatt wind farm in a joint venture with Amec in the Hebrides Islands, off of Scotland.

Meanwhile, British Energy had been holding talks with Philadelphia-based PECO, which resulted in the creation of the 50–50 joint venture AmerGen Energy. This new company had as its mission to acquire and operate nuclear power plants in the United States, where deregulation, and the eagerness of utility companies to shed their plants, opened a series of affordable acquisition targets. By the end of 1998, the company had identified some 100 nuclear power plants in the United States as possible acquisition targets. At that time, the company streamlined its structure, fusing Nuclear Electric and Scottish Nuclear into a single subsidiary, British Energy Generation.

AmerGen made headlines in 1998 when it became the first company to purchase a nuclear power plant. In October 1998, the company reached an agreement to pay $100 million to acquire the now infamous Three Mile Island plant. At that time, British Energy announced a goal of matching its U.K. generating capacity of 9,600 MW in the United States. The Three Mile Island acquisition was completed at the end of 1999. At the same time, AmerGen announced its acquisition of two more nuclear plants, at Clinton, Illinois, for US $20 million, and at Oyster Beach, New Jersey, for US $10 million. Meanwhile, the joint venture also was negotiating an agreement to purchase the Vermont Yankee power plant.

By then, British Energy was attempting to extend into the power distribution field, paying £105 million to acquire Hyder's South Wales Electricity (SWALEC) retail energy supply division in 1999. That attempt, which included a failed bid to acquire London Electricity, was swiftly abandoned, however, and in 2000 the company sold off SWALEC for £210 million.

Unable to build new nuclear plants in the United Kingdom, British Energy nonetheless had begun a drive to extend the lives of a number of its existing plants. In July 2000, the company succeeded in gaining ten-year extensions on two of its plants, in Torness and Heysham. By then, British Energy had stepped up its efforts to diversify its fuel sources, including the £640 million purchase of the coal-fired Eggborough power station in 1999.

Throughout this time, British Energy had been negotiating with Ontario Power Generation, which was under orders to reduce its grip on the province's power supply to 35 percent, to lease its Bruce Power nuclear facilities at Lake Huron. That agreement was signed in 2001, giving British Energy an additional eight nuclear plants—four of which were operational—with 6,200 MW of generating capacity, for a price of £1 billion. The company announced its intention to bring the four shuttered Bruce reactors back online, with the first two expected to be operational in 2002.

As the British government began a new energy review in 2001, British Energy announced its interest in constructing a new nuclear power plant in Hunterston, while urging the government to commit some £10 billion to the nation's nuclear power program—or see the company target the overseas markets for its future investments. Yet British Energy continued to hedge its bet, seeking a further diversification into alternative fuel sources. At the beginning of 2001, British Energy announced that it had formed a joint venture with Renewable Energy Systems to construct an offshore wind farm. This effort joined the company's construction of a 10 MW wind farm on Lake Huron, expected to be commissioned in 2002. At the end of 2001, however, British Energy pledged to step up the pace, announcing its agreement with Amec to build a 600 MW wind farm in the Hebrides Islands, off of Scotland, which, if completed, was to become the largest wind farm in Europe. In just a few years since its privatization, British Energy had successfully negotiated a diversification, becoming an international, multi-source power generation giant.

Principal Subsidiaries

AmerGen Energy LLC (U.S.A.; 50%); British Energy Generation Limited; British Energy Generation (U.K.) Limited; British Energy Power & Energy Trading Limited; British Energy (U.S.) Holdings Inc; Bruce Power LP (Canada; 85%); Eggborough Power Limited; Huron Wind (Canada; 50%); Lochside Insurance Limited; Offshore Wind Power Limited (50%); United Kingdom Nirex Limited (11%).

Principal Competitors

The AES Corporation; American Electric Power Company, Inc.; Canadian Utilities Limited; Duke Energy Corporation; Electricité de France; Exelon Corporation; International Power plc; PowerGen plc; PPL Corporation; Scottish and Southern Energy plc; Scottish Power plc; Southern Company; Tractebel s.a.; TXU Europe Group plc; Aquila, Inc.

Further Reading

Arthur, Charles, "They're Selling Off the Family Plutonium," *Independent on Sunday,* May 26, 1996, p. B1.

Foley, Stephen, "Brit Energy—One to Store Away," *Independent,* September 26, 2001, p. 21.

Gribben, Roland, "British Energy Aims to Double Capacity," *Daily Telegraph,* November 12, 1998.

Harrison, Michael, ed., "British Energy and Amec Plan Giant Wind Farm in Hebrides," *Independent,* December 14, 2001, p. 19.

Harrison, Michael, "British Energy Warns It May Shift Investment Abroad," *Independent,* November 8, 2001, p. 21.

Spears, John, "British Energy Keen on Province," *Toronto Star,* June 13, 2001.

"The State of the Atom," *Economist,* July 20, 1996, p. 58.

Ward, Olivia, "New Operator at Bruce Drawing Heat Elsewhere," *Toronto Star,* June 30, 2000.

—M. L. Cohen

BT Group plc

BT Centre
81 Newgate Street
London EC1A 7AJ
United Kingdom
Telephone: (44) 20-7356-5000
Fax: (44) 20-7356-5520
Web site: http://www.groupbt.com

Public Company
Incorporated: 1984 as British Telecommunications plc
Employees: 137,500
Sales: $28.95 billion (2001)
Stock Exchanges: London New York
Ticker Symbols: BTA (London); BTY (New York)
NAIC: 513310 Wired Telecommunications Carriers;
513322 Cellular and Other Wireless
Telecommunications; 513330 Telecommunications
Resellers; 514191 On-Line Information Services;
551112 Offices of Other Holding Companies

BT Group plc was formed in 2001 to serve as the holding company for British Telecommunications plc. British Telecommunications came into being in early 1984 through the transformation of a former state utility, at a turning point in the development of U.K. and European telecommunications. Since being privatized, BT has maintained its position as the dominant provider of local and long-distance telephone service in the United Kingdom, but has faced increasing competition and seen its market share fall as the English government continues to deregulate the market. BT has subsequently looked abroad for its future growth and is in the process of developing a global telecommunications network for multinational companies.

The Birth and Growth of the Telephone Industry in England: 1869–1969

British Telecommunications' administrative and technological roots are mingled with those of the U.K. Post Office and reach back into the second half of the 19th century, when inventors at home and abroad, such as Alexander Graham Bell, Thomas Edison, and Guglielmo Marconi, were applying electromagnetic principles to the development of practicable forms of telecommunications. Out of this the modern telegraph, followed by the telephone, was born. In 1850 the first submarine telegraph cable was laid across the English Channel. In 1878 Bell demonstrated his newly patented telephone to Queen Victoria, and in 1879 England's first telephone exchange opened in London. It was in the United Kingdom, too, that the first international telephone call was made, in 1891, between England and France. The telegraph and telephone were at first exploited by private enterprises, but they were gradually taken over by a U.K. government department, the General Post Office. The reversal of that nationalization process was completed in the early 1990s.

In 1869 the Postmaster General was granted the exclusive right to transmit telegrams within the United Kingdom. At first the telephone was slow to catch on and was not regarded by the Post Office as a serious threat to its telegraphic network. The first independent U.K. telephone service provider, Telephone Company Ltd., was set up in 1879 and in 1880 merged with its competitor, Edison Telephone Company, to form United Telephone Company. Seeing that the telephone was beginning to take customers away from its telegraph service, the Post Office embarked on a series of protective measures, and in 1880 the government brought an action against the recently formed United Telephone Company, claiming that it was operating in contravention of the Telegraph Act of 1869. The High Court subsequently decided that the telephone was a form of telegraph. The merger was revoked, and telephone companies were required to be licensed by the telegraph monopoly holder, the Post Office.

The next stage in the process of squeezing out competition and establishing a state telephone monopoly was the building up of the Post Office's own system. In 1896 the Post Office completed its improved telephone network by taking over the trunk lines of National Telephone Company, the largest of its licensees, and started to set up its own local telephone exchanges. It was then decided that more national licenses would be granted. National Telephone Company continued to operate a local service until its license expired in 1911, but in 1912 the

Post Office was granted a monopoly on the supply of telephone services throughout the United Kingdom. It took over all of National Telephone Company's exchanges and opened an automatic exchange in Epsom, south of London.

Since 1899 several of the larger towns and cities, including Glasgow, Brighton, Swansea, Portsmouth, and Kingston upon Hull (Hull), had each been operating an independent local telephone service, but their number gradually dwindled as they were bought out by National Telephone Company or the Post Office. In 1913 only Hull was left. By cooperating with successive competitors—National Telephone Company and the Post Office—it survived, first as the Hull Corporation Telephone Department, a municipal enterprise run by the Hull City Council, and since 1987, as a limited company, Kingston Communications (Hull) PLC, wholly owned by Hull City Council and a licensed public telecommunications operator (PTO), with interconnection agreements with BT and BT's competitor, Mercury Telecommunications Limited.

The Move Toward Privatization: 1969–90

A landmark in the prehistory of BT was the Post Office Act of 1969, which changed the status of the Post Office. This former government department became a state public corporation under the Secretary of State for Industry. The telecommunications services remained in the Post Office but were divided from the postal services into Post Office Telecommunications.

Three further events marked the telephone industry's move toward an environment of free competition. First came the passage of the 1981 British Telecommunications Act, which took Post Office Telecommunications out of the Post Office, turning it into an autonomous, though still state-owned, body known as British Telecommunications Corporation or, more familiarly, British Telecom. Second was the 1984 Telecommunications Act, by which BT was privatized, the telecommunications market was further liberalized, and a regulatory body was set up. Third, the Duopoly Review in 1990 resulted in the government's 1991 decision to further increase telecommunications competition. The government also decided to sell off its remaining shares in BT, although this decision was not influenced by the Duopoly Review.

In July 1981 the British Telecommunications Act, which separated telecommunications from the Post Office and set up a new state public corporation to supply them, also gave the government powers to license competitors in the operation of the domestic telephone network. As well as modifying the state company's statutory monopoly of the telephone network, this act took away its monopoly in the provision of telecommunication equipment, leaving it only with the right to supply and install a subscriber's first telephone. The act not only opened the market to competition in value-added services, such as data processing and storage, but also allowed other providers to use BT's lines.

In October 1981 Mercury Telecommunications Limited was chosen to receive a 25-year renewable license to operate a national and international digital network—a system that encodes information as a series of on-off signals—to compete with BT's trunk traffic. Mercury had been set up early in 1981 by British Petroleum, Barclay's Merchant Bank, and Cable and Wireless plc (C&W) to enter the business of long-distance communications, offering a customized service to companies. The license allowed it to interconnect with the BT network and to enter the European and U.S. sectors. In 1983 the government undertook for seven years not to license any company but BT and Mercury to carry telecommunications services over fixed links. Under this duopoly policy, Mercury, which began operating in 1986, was to be BT's single serious network competitor until the early 1990s. Less than a year after the 1981 act, the government announced its intention to privatize the British Telecommunications Corporation.

At the end of 1982 the first telecommunications bill had reached the committee stage, when the general election of May 1983 was called. The bill immediately died, but was presented again in the new Parliament and finally became law in its second form, the Telecommunications Act of April 12, 1984. It had undergone 320 hours of debate and discussion, during which BT itself had briefed members of Parliament on its views and interests. By the act, BT lost its exclusive right to run telecommunications systems, and all PTOs had to be licensed. The new company was to be sold as an integrated organization. Fragmentation, similar to the breakup of American Telephone and Telegraph Company (AT&T) in the United States, would have left the resultant entities too small to defend the home market from foreign competition, to stand up to multinationals in the world markets, and to command the technology and the financial strength for adequate research and development. In November 1984, 3.01 billion ordinary shares of 25 pence were offered for sale at 130 pence per share, the first figure being the nominal or face value of the share, and the second its sale price, or market value, at the time of sale. The government retained a 48.6 percent stake in the new company, valued at the time of sale at £7.8 billion. All the offered shares were bought.

Under the terms of the 1984 act, BT's main activity was to supply telecommunications services in the U.K. market of 55 million people in accordance with a 25-year operating license from the Department of Trade and Industry. Starting in 1984, BT's performance and development were conditioned by an official regulatory body, the semi-independent Office of Telecommunications (Oftel), set up in August 1984 under the Secretary of State for Trade and Industry and headed by the Director General of Telecommunications (Bryan Carsberg being the first to hold the post). A major role of this body was, by simulating the effects of real competition, to prevent BT from abusing its inherited dominance of the U.K. telecommunications market during the process of deregulation. Nevertheless, the fairness of the competition was often disputed by interested parties. In its severely regulated environment, BT had lost the security of being a state monopoly, without gaining the freedom of action of a wholly autonomous business. Oftel monitored BT's pricing, accounting, investment policies, and quality of services;

Key Dates:

1880: Telephone Company Ltd. merges with Edison Telephone Company to form United Telephone Company.
1969: Post Office Telecommunications is formed.
1981: The British Telecommunications Act is passed.
1984: British Telecommunications plc becomes privatized.
1994: British Telecom enters strategic alliance with MCI Communications to form Concert Communications Company.
2001: BT Group plc is formed as a holding company.

issued licenses to additional competitors; and continued to facilitate the interconnection of rival services to the BT network. Competitors, for their part, tended to feel that BT was favored by the regulator. The new British Telecommunications plc created by the 1984 act then shared its monopoly in telecommunications systems with Mercury as well as Kingston Communications, plus some general licensees.

When BT became a separate state corporation in 1981, before its rebirth in 1984 as a privatized company, it inherited from its Post Office days an evolved network. This network had to be brought up to date at the same time BT was taking on competition from operators starting from scratch. These competitors were using the latest technology, without public service obligations, and were able, for example, to go straight to digital systems and cheaper and more efficient fiber-optic cable, while BT still had copper wire circuits to be amortized. BT kept technology in the forefront, however, and spent 2 percent of its turnover on research and development to keep it there. The domestic telephone services sector was by far BT's largest operating division in terms of assets, revenue, and number of employees. In 1990 it accounted for nearly 75 percent of turnover. Its core business was the public switched telephone network (PSTN). The 20 millionth U.K. telephone was installed in 1975, the system became fully automatic in 1976, and in the early 1990s BT, with more than 25 million lines, operated the world's sixth largest telephone network, with nearly 100,000 public pay phones. In 1990 BTUK—the product of the 1987 merger of BT's local communications services and national networks divisions—was operating more than 7,000 local exchange units, of which nearly half were already digital.

Meanwhile, Mercury's market share in the early 1990s was variously estimated between 3.7 and 5 percent, but was increasing markedly. An efficiency and investment effort was BT management's response to this new competition and to growing demands and service expectations from its customers. Waiting times for connections and repairs were reduced, and new digital equipment was introduced into the network, including exchanges that use microchip technology to integrate the switching and transmission elements of the network, resulting in a higher quality of service and improved voice transmission. All trunk exchange units were digital since June 1990. BT aimed to have a fully digital network by the year 2000. In addition, new

products, such as microwave radio transmission in the city of London, were offered.

Another area within which BT faced stiff competition was the capricious mobile communications market. BT's Mobile Telephone System 4, a noncellular service introduced in 1981, with 7,000 subscribers at the beginning of 1990, had capacity problems at peak periods and was being replaced by a cellular network, Cellnet, shared by BT's 60 percent and Securicor Communications. Its rival, using another network, was Racal-Vodafone. In February 1989 BT bought, for £907 million, a 20 percent interest in McCaw Cellular Communications, Inc., a U.S. mobile cellular telephone and broadcasting systems provider and operator.

In the late 1980s, BT offered a wide range of VANS—value-added network services, including such electronic mailbox services as Telecom Gold and Message Handling Service—in the United Kingdom. In November 1989, to further its strategies in the home and international VANS market, BT bought, for £231 million, the U.S. company Tymnet, one of the largest VANS companies in the world, and consolidated some of its own international services under a new company, BT Tymnet Inc. BT started setting up an ISDN—integrated services digital network—that could eventually replace the other networks by offering all data, voice, text, and image network services at high speed, with circuit-switched digital connections from a single access point. Although ISDN was of primary importance in BT's plans for the future, like other telecommunications firms, BT had to move slowly in this area, needing to await definition of international standards and to raise the consciousness of potential customers. A pilot service was launched by BT in June 1985 that by the end of 1989 was available to 75 percent of business users.

Adapting to a New Competitive Market: 1991–96

In the early 1990s BT faced major changes. The duopoly policy was reviewed in 1990, and a report issued in January 1991 was followed two months later by a government recommendation that both BT and Mercury should face greater competition in local, trunk, and international services. BT was still barred from offering entertainment services on cable television, but after some hard bargaining, Bryan Carsberg, director of telecommunications; Peter Lilley, secretary of state for trade and industry; and Iain Vallance, BT's chairman, agreed on amendments to BT's 25-year license. BT was then allowed to proceed with further rebalancing between telephone rentals and call charges and with customized tariffs. It was announced that the sale of a slice of the government's residual share in BT would take place in November 1991.

In the face of increasing competition, BT engaged in a rationalizing and restructuring operation. In the year ending March 31, 1990, a slimming-down and cost-control operation began, covered by an exceptional charge of £390 million. In the following year, 18,800 jobs were shed and overtime work was cut, while another 10,000 terminations were planned for 1991–92. In April 1991 the reshaped company announced that the three former operating divisions, BTUK, comprising Local Communications Services and National Networks; BTI, British Telecom International; and CSD, Communication Services Division, would be replaced. In their stead were placed two major divisions that dealt directly with customers: Personal Communications and Business Communications, both supported by a Products and Services Division. BT's international and U.K. networks were brought together into a new Worldwide Networks Division, and some business activities best managed separately, such as mobile communications and operator services, comprised a new Special Business Division.

Early in 1991 BT's intensified drive to consolidate its image as a smart, market-oriented world organization with a human face was signaled by its integration of the current BT acronym into a new blue and red logo, representing a dancing piper apparently delivering a sound message. A new designer image was commissioned for the group and was widely publicized; public telephones were replaced by newly designed models; and the bright yellow of BT vehicles began to be replaced, in a notoriously expensive replace-or-respray operation, by a stylish gray.

As the 1990s continued, BT's challenges became more intense. While at least 98 percent of its revenues and profits continued to come from its home market, the additional competition allowed under the 1991 review of the duopoly policy combined with continued moves by Oftel to reduce BT's monopoly began to seriously erode BT's position in the U.K. market. From 1991 to early 1996, some 150 firms started operations in the United Kingdom that were competitive with BT, several of the most important of which were cable firms owned by U.S. Baby Bell companies. As a result, BT's share of the U.K. telephone market tumbled, with its residential customer market share falling from 99 percent in 1991 to 93 percent in 1995 and its business customer market share falling from 94 percent in 1991 to 83 percent in 1995. Some analysts were predicting that by 2000 BT's share of the U.K. residential market would fall to as low as 65 percent.

In response, BT continued the cost-cutting program it began in 1990. More than 100,000 jobs had been eliminated by 1995, reducing the BT workforce from 239,000 in 1990 to 137,500 in 1995. The program was to be continued into the late 1990s, moving toward a goal of a 100,000-employee workforce with productivity levels in line with the Baby Bells. BT's upstart competitors also forced the company to upgrade its service and lower its prices since they were luring away BT customers by offering low prices and better service. In fiscal 1995 BT reduced prices on both domestic and international long-distance calls, adding up to more than £800 million in savings for its customers for the year. That same year, BT increased capital expenditures 23 percent in order to improve customer service and upgrade its network.

Meanwhile, the often cantankerous relationship between BT and Oftel grew more confrontational in the mid-1990s. Perhaps not coincidentally, these BT-Oftel battles took place after 1993, the year in which the British government sold nearly all of its remaining stake in BT for $7.43 billion. In 1995, BT expressed support for the development of number portability—the ability of customers to keep the same phone number even if they changed telephone suppliers—but objected to a plan that the company felt would place a disproportionate share of the costs on BT. In response to BT's rejection of the plan, Oftel referred the matter to the Monopolies and Mergers Commission, the first

time BT had been subjected to such a referral. Later in 1995, the regulator announced that it wanted to reduce BT's return on capital from the 15.6 percent of 1995 to as low as 8 percent. If forced to accept this, the company's ability to invest for future growth might be seriously damaged. Such a possibility sent BT stock plunging throughout 1995.

The overall impact of the competition and regulation showed clearly in BT's revenues and profits. The company revenue growth had stagnated, with the £13.15 billion figure of 1991 only increasing to £13.89 billion in 1995. Profits fell in three of the four years from 1992 to 1995, and fell overall from £2.04 billion to £1.74 billion.

Embattled at home and certainly facing more and more pressure there for the foreseeable future, BT almost had no choice but to look overseas for its long-term survival. Early attempts at international expansion had failed, including the 1986 purchase of Mitel Corp., a Canadian phone equipment manufacturer that BT sold in 1992 at a loss of £120 million ($200 million); and the company's stake in McCaw Cellular, which it sold in 1992 to AT&T (which had just purchased a larger stake in McCaw) at a profit exceeding £200 million ($333 million). According to Vallance, these investments no longer fit into the company's international plans, which now centered around building a global telecommunications network offering comprehensive services to multinational corporations. Vallance's first attempt at this failed, however. In 1991 the company set up a subsidiary, Syncordia Corp., in Atlanta, Georgia, to start such a network on its own, but had little success attracting either customers or the telecommunications partners it needed around the world to make the venture succeed.

Syncordia was shut down three years later, after BT realized it had erred attempting to go it alone. In mid-1993, BT's second attempt to go global began with the announcement of an alliance with the major U.S. telecommunications firm MCI Communications Corp. The alliance, which received final approval in mid-1994, involved BT purchasing a 20 percent stake in MCI for £2.86 billion ($4.2 billion). The two firms set up a joint venture called Concert Communications Company, based in England, which was 75 percent owned by BT and 25 percent by MCI. Syncordia was folded into the new venture, which would inherit Syncordia's charge of providing telecommunications services for multinational corporations.

To make Concert work, however, BT needed additional partners in other areas of the world. Over the next few years, BT set up alliances with several European companies including Norwegian Telecom, Tele Denmark, Telecom Finland, and Banco Santander of Spain. A foothold in the important German market also was secured in a 1995 alliance with the German conglomerate Viag AG, in which the partners planned to start a joint venture that would offer Concert services. BT now had a solid network of partners in Europe and North America, but remained weak in the critical Asian market, having allied only with International Telecom Japan Inc., a small international carrier. Meanwhile, AT&T was working furiously to set up its own system of global alliances through its WorldPartners program. By 1995, while AT&T had had more success than BT in Asia, having established partnerships with KDD of Japan and with Singapore Telecom, the U.S. giant was having difficulties making inroads in Europe.

In the midst of the difficult 1995 BT endured, two top executives left the company, one retiring and one resigning. Vallance decided to step aside as CEO, while remaining chairman, and turned to an outsider, Peter L. Bonfield. Taking over as CEO in early 1996, Bonfield had been the chief executive of ICL PLC, a British computer company owned by Fujitsu Ltd. Observers noted that Bonfield's experience with Japanese business practices might help BT in its effort to enhance its alliances in Asia.

Heading into the new century, British Telecommunications was certainly being squeezed in its still all-important home market. Its international activities were still very much in a start-up phase and needed time to turn the company's huge investments in them into profits. The question was whether its cash would be drained faster at home than its payoff abroad. Perhaps, therefore, needing to move faster than AT&T to secure a global network, it appeared in early 1996 that BT might try effecting a major merger to gain its missing Asian link. The most significant possibility was that BT would merge with Cable and Wireless plc (C&W), which owned 80 percent of the main home market competitor of BT, Mercury. Merger talks between C&W and BT began in late 1995. If it happened, the merged firm would have to sell off Mercury, but more important, BT would have gained C&W's 57.5 percent stake in Hong Kong Telecommunications Ltd. and its telecommunications businesses in Japan and Australia. BT might finally break free of its dependence on the U.K. market.

The Challenges of Globalization: 1997–2002

As the 21st century loomed, British Telecom found itself under increasing pressure to look abroad for new opportunities to expand its business. A number of factors contributed to the urgency of BT's position. By mid-1996 the Office of Telecommunications, wary of the near-stranglehold BT held on the domestic market—the company was still providing phone service to nearly 90 percent of all English households—was already beginning to implement measures that would help reduce consumer telephone rates by up to 40 percent within a five-year span. At the same time, the regulatory agency introduced procedures that greatly simplified the process by which customers were able to transfer phone numbers to new accounts. The new rules delivered a significant blow to BT; by the end of 1997, the company was losing close to 60,000 domestic customers a month. Finally, the imminent unification of Europe, along with the broader trend toward globalization, threatened to make the British phone industry too competitive for BT to retain its position as the United Kingdom's telephone powerhouse.

In the information age, it was becoming clear that corporations needed to be able to provide a full range of phone, Internet, and wireless services in order to remain competitive. Believing that the Internet would soon account for a higher volume of communications traffic than the telephone, BT began searching for a high-powered merger, with the aim of establishing itself as an international corporation with the capacity to meet the technological needs of the new century. Although C&W seemed in many ways a perfect fit, the companies were ultimately unable to work out a deal, and BT was forced to look into other options. One possibility was to join forces with MCI, a company in which BT already owned a 20 percent stake. The two corporations entered negotiations in the summer of 1996, and by the

following summer were on the verge of inking a $22 billion agreement. The deal stalled in August 1997, however, with MCI's announcement that it expected to suffer losses of up to $800 million for the previous year. The news struck trepidation in the hearts of BT's majority shareholders, and the two companies entered renegotiations. Unfortunately for BT, the merger was suddenly blindsided in October 1997, when Worldcom Inc., a fast-rising U.S. telecommunications firm, made an offer for MCI that exceeded BT's by nearly $13 billion. BT once again found itself without a partner.

The company immediately began searching for other possibilities. In July 1998 it entered into a promising new partnership with AT&T, wherein the companies merged their international operations into a single entity. The combined businesses had the potential to generate more than $10 billion in revenue annually, and to place the two industry giants in a position to gain a foothold in newly deregulated telecommunications markets worldwide. One particularly attractive target was Japan; in March 1999, the companies acquired a combined 30 percent stake in Japan Telecom, the country's fourth largest telephone company. Encouraged by the initial promise of the joint venture, the companies pooled their global wireless phone operations in September 1999. The new company, called Advance, boasted more than 41 million customers across the world, and promised to generate more than $12 billion a year.

In the end, however, BT's international expansion strategy proved to be hastily conceived. For one, Advance took longer than expected to generate a substantial product line. Worse, BT's efforts to achieve a wide global reach over a short period ultimately spread its resources far too thin, and by May 2001 the company had accumulated $43 billion in debt and was reporting its first fiscal year loss since becoming privatized. Under siege by investors, Chairman Sir Iain Vaillance resigned, and BT was forced to dump several of its minority holdings in overseas telecommunications companies, including its shares in Japan Telecom. By October the joint venture with AT&T was defunct, and the company had undertaken a massive restructuring. The result was the formation of the BT Group, which became the holding company for British Telecom. Although the divestitures and the streamlining of its business operations had helped BT get a handle on its debt, it was clear that the company needed to seriously rethink its ambitions for the future.

Principal Subsidiaries

BT Australasia Pty Limited (Australia); BT Cableships Limited; BT Cellnet Limited; BT Communications Management Limited; BT (Hong Kong) Limited; BT Ignite GmbH (Germany); BT Ignite GmbH & Co. (Germany); BT Ignite Nederland BV (Netherlands); BT North America Inc. (U.S.); BT Property Limited; BT Subsea Cables Limited; BT Telecomunicaciones SA (Spain); BT (Worldwide) Limited; BT Wireless Limited; Clear Communications Limited; Esat Digifone Limited (Ireland; 50.5%); Esat Group Limited (Ireland); Farland BV: Manx Telecom Limited; Syntegra Groep BV (Netherlands); Syntegra SA (France); Syntegra (USA) Inc.; Telfort Mobiel BV (Netherlands); Viag Interkom GmbH & Co.; Tell Limited; Yellow Book USA Inc.; Yellow Pages Sales Limited.

74   **BT Group plc**

Principal Operating Units

BT Ignite; BTopenworld; BT Retail; BT Wholesale; BTexact Technologies.

Further Reading

Competition and Choice: Telecommunications Policy for the 1990s, London: HMSO, March 1991.

Cowell, Alan, "British Telecom Chairman Quits amid Stockholder Anger," *New York Times,* April 27, 2001, p. C2.

Dwyer, Paula, "The Sun Never Sets on British Telecom," *Business Week,* December 7, 1992, pp. 54–55.

Eglin, Roger, "BT Prepares to Beat the World," *Management Today,* July 1993, pp. 9–10.

"Europe" and "The United Kingdom," *DATAPRO Reports on International Telecommunications 1990–91,* Delran, N.J.: McGraw-Hill, 1990–91.

Flynn, Julia, and Mark Lewyn, "Why Telecom's Odd Couple Is Trying So Hard," *Business Week,* September 20, 1993, pp. 96, 98.

Flynn, Julia, Catherine Arnst, and Gail Edmondson, "Who'll Be the First Global Phone Company?," *Business Week,* March 27, 1995, pp. 176–80.

Flynn, Julia, Mark Lewyn, and Gail Edmondson, "What a Time to Take Over at British Telecom," *Business Week,* January 29, 1996.

Hass, Nancy, "The Whipping Boy: Meet British Telecom's Iain Vallance, the Rodney Dangerfield of Telecommunications," *Financial World,* September 15, 1992, pp. 48–49.

Hudson, Richard L., "BT Faces a Line of Potential International Competitors," *Wall Street Journal,* April 29, 1993, p. B4.

Lewis, Peter H., "MCI and British Telecom to Join Networks for Internet Market," *New York Times,* June 11, 1996, p. D5.

"Major Telecommunications Companies in Europe," *Profile of the Worldwide Telecommunications Industry,* Oxford: Elsevier Advanced Technology, 1990.

Newman, Karin, *The Selling of British Telecom,* London: Holt, Rinehart and Winston, 1986.

Purton, Peter, "Is BT Lost in the Fog of World Events?," *Telephony,* December 7, 1992, pp. 7-8.

Schiesel, Seth, "AT&T and British Telecom Merge Overseas Operations," *New York Times,* July 27, 1998, p. A1.

"Shooting a Line," *Economist,* July 10, 1993, pp. 62–63.

—Olive Classe
—updates: David E. Salamie, Steve Meyer

Cadbury Schweppes

Cadbury Schweppes PLC

25 Berkeley Square
London W1J 6HB
United Kingdom
Telephone: (44) 20-7409-1313
Fax: (44) 20-7830-5200
Web site: http://www.cadburyschweppes.com

Public Company
Incorporated: 1969
Employees: 36,460
Sales: $6.84 billion (2000)
Stock Exchanges: London New York
Ticker Symbols: CBRY (London); CSG (NYSE)
NAIC: 311320 Chocolate and Confectionery
 Manufacturing from Cacao Beans; 311330
 Confectionery Manufacturing from Purchased
 Chocolate; 311340 Nonchocolate Confectionery
 Manufacturing; 312111 Soft Drink Manufacturing;
 422450 Confectionery Wholesalers

Cadbury Schweppes PLC is one of the oldest and largest family-run businesses in the world today. Although confectioner Cadbury Limited merged with the carbonated drinks company Schweppes Limited in 1969, Cadbury Schweppes is still run by members of the Cadbury family, which has been represented in Cadbury's top management for almost 180 years. The company is currently the world's third leading producer of soft drinks and fourth leading confectionery manufacturer.

The Birth of a Chocolate Giant: 1824–68

The history of Cadbury dates back to 1824, when John Cadbury opened his grocery business in Birmingham. From the start, drinking-cocoa and chocolate were his most popular products, and in 1831 he moved to larger quarters and began manufacturing his own cocoa products. In 1847 he took on his brother Benjamin as a partner. Two years later the Cadbury brothers spun off their retail operations to Richard Cadbury Barrow, a nephew, and concentrated on manufacture and wholesale distri-

bution. In 1853 Cadbury Brothers received a royal warrant as manufacturers to Queen Victoria; the company still holds the distinction of being confectioner to the Crown.

Shortly thereafter, however, business began to decline. The two Cadbury brothers dissolved their partnership in 1860 when Benjamin left the company, and John also retired the very next year. He left the business to his sons Richard and George, who continued to struggle for several years. But in 1866, the new Cadbury brothers introduced an improved process for pressing cocoa butter out of the cocoa bean to produce cocoa essence. This resulted in purer drinking-cocoa and plentiful cocoa butter that could be made into eating chocolate. In 1868, Cadbury Brothers began marketing its own lines of chocolate candy, reviving its fortunes and breaking the stranglehold that French confectioners had on the British market.

Innovation and Expansion: 1879–1964

Renewed success brought with it renewed expansion. In 1879 Cadbury Brothers began constructing a new factory outside Birmingham. In 1881 the firm received its first export order from a representative in Australia, and by the middle of the decade its overseas business had expanded to New Zealand, South Africa, India, the West Indies, and both North and South America. In 1899 it incorporated as Cadbury Brothers Limited, with George Cadbury as chairman.

In 1906 Cadbury Brothers introduced a new recipe for milk chocolate, marketed under the name Cadbury Dairy Milk, which has remained a mainstay of its product line ever since. After World War I, innovations in industrial technology made the manufacture of chocolate cheap enough to price chocolate candy for a wider market, and the company accordingly re-tooled its factory for mass production in the late 1920s. Cadbury Brothers opened its first overseas plant in Australia in 1922, and more foreign production ventures followed from its 1919 acquisition of J.S. Fry & Sons. In 1932 Fry's Canadian plant began to manufacture Cadbury products, and the next year Cadbury Fry, now a subsidiary of Cadbury Brothers, opened a factory in Ireland. Cadbury Brothers also began to manufacture in South Africa in 1939 and India in 1947.

Company Perspectives:

As a major global beverage and confectionery company, we are dedicated to the manufacturing, marketing and distribution of our branded products around the world. Today, Cadbury Schweppes employs over 36,000 people and our products are available in almost 200 countries across the world.

Throughout the postwar years, Cadbury maintained its position as the leading chocolate manufacturer in the world's leading per-capita candy-consuming nation. (''They chew through plays and they chew through films and they chew in trains,'' a theater critic for the *London Daily Mail* once lamented. ''They suck lollies through *Macbeth* and *Hamlet*, and they while away Tennessee Williams with the chocolates with the scrumptious centers.'') In 1962 Cadbury and Cadbury Fry, along with their competitor Rowntree, accounted for 51 percent of British candy sales.

In 1964 Cadbury entered the sugar-candy business when it acquired confectioner Pascall Murray. All the while, the company remained a family business. At the time of the merger with Schweppes, its chairman had always been a direct descendant of John Cadbury and the vast majority of its stock belonged to family members or trusts.

Testing the Waters: The Early Years of Schweppes Limited, 1790–1851

The same cannot be said, however, for Schweppes Limited, which has not felt the guiding hand of a Schweppe for almost 200 years. The company bears the name of Jacob Schweppe, a German-born jeweler and amateur chemist who entered into a joint venture in 1790 with pharmacist Henry Gosse, engineer Jacques Paul, and his son Nicholas. Together, they formed Schweppe, Paul & Gosse, which devoted itself to producing artificial mineral water. Schweppe moved to London in 1792 to establish the company's English operations, and when the partnership dissolved the next year he retained the business for himself.

In those days, aerated water was believed to have medicinal value, and Schweppe's brand was popular because it contained a higher degree of carbonation than its competitors. In 1799 Schweppe sold a 75 percent interest in his business to three men from the island of Jersey and retired. The company, however, continued to use the Schweppe name.

In 1834 Schweppes, as it was now named, was bought by William Evill and John Kemp-Welch, whose descendants would remain associated with the company until 1950. In 1836 the company received its first royal warrant, from the Duchess of Kent and Princess Victoria, soon to become Queen Victoria. Schweppes also gained substantial prestige when it was granted a catering concession for the Great Exhibition of 1851.

Diversification and International Growth: 1870–1969

The company began to introduce new product lines in the second half of the century. Schweppes started marketing ginger ale in the 1870s. Tonic water, now its most famous product, also appeared at about this time in response to a demand from Britons returning from India who had developed a taste for the solution of quinine, sugar, and water they had drunk there as a malaria preventative. In 1885, Schweppes introduced a carbonated lemonade. Such was the company's success during the Victorian era that it went public in 1897.

In 1923 Schweppes consolidated its overseas operations into a single British-based subsidiary. This move was intended to facilitate further international expansion. During the interwar years and through World War II, however, the company's fortunes began to wane as sales went soft. It was not until Sir Frederick Hooper took over as managing director in 1948 that Schweppes regained its strength through shrewd marketing and a renewed focus on its overseas business. An integral part of that campaign for two decades was the use of Commander Edward Whitehead, who became chairman of Schweppes USA in 1952, as the company's U.S. advertising spokesman. From the early 1950s through the early 1970s, Commander Whitehead, whom *Time* once described as an ''engaging walrus,'' ingratiated himself with Americans as he espoused his products' unique ''Schweppervescence.'' By 1962, foreign operations accounted for one-fifth of the company's net sales.

Schweppes was forced to diversify as the demand for soft drinks and mixers at home leveled off. In 1960 it acquired three makers of jams and jellies: Hartley's, Moorhouse, and Chivers. These acquisitions required substantial reorganization, however, and did not work out very well; by 1964 only Hartley's was turning a profit for its parent company. Nonetheless, Schweppes prospered under Sir Frederick Hooper's guidance. Its annual profits increased nearly sevenfold between 1953 and 1962, from $756,000 to $4.8 million. Hooper retired in 1964 and was succeeded by Harold Watkinson, a former Conservative defense minister.

Joining Forces: 1969–90

In 1968 Schweppes acquired Typhoo Tea to further diversify its product line and strengthen its ties to grocery retailers. But with no growth in its domestic markets, Lord Watkinson realized that overseas expansion was the key to Schweppes's future. Unfortunately, its capital base was tiny compared with that of the American conglomerates with which it would have to compete. That fall, Watkinson met with Cadbury Chairman Adrian Cadbury at a trade show and found that Cadbury had similar concerns about his own company. Schweppes and Cadbury began merger talks soon thereafter and reached an agreement in January 1969.

Technically, Schweppes came out of the merger as the surviving company. It bought out Cadbury stockholders by replacing their shares with $290 million worth of its own stock. Watkinson became chairman in the new chain of command, with Adrian Cadbury assuming the titles of deputy chairman and co-managing director. But the new company bore the Cadbury name in front of Schweppes's, and the candy business was clearly not to be neglected. Although the two companies consolidated some of their operations, they maintained autonomy in the matter of distribution, since bottling franchisees controlled local distribution in the soft drink business.

The 1970s were marked by further diversification and attempts to capture international markets. In 1973 Cadbury

Key Dates:

1790: Jacob Schweppe, Jacques Paul, and Henry Gosse join to form Schweppe, Paul & Gosse.

1792: Jacob Schweppe moves to London.

1824: John Cadbury begins selling cocoa and chocolate in Birmingham, England.

1834: William Evill and John Kemp-Welch acquire Schweppes, as the company is now known.

1853: Cadbury Brothers receives royal warrant to manufacture chocolate for Queen Victoria.

1868: Cadbury Brothers introduces its first line of chocolate candy.

1897: Schweppes Limited goes public.

1899: Cadbury Brothers Limited is incorporated.

1906: Cadbury Brothers begins marketing Cadbury Dairy Milk.

1922: Cadbury Brothers opens a plant in Australia.

1969: Cadbury Limited merges with Schweppes Limited to form Cadbury Schweppes PLC.

1974: Adrian Cadbury becomes chairman of Cadbury Schweppes.

1982: Cadbury Schweppes acquires Duffy-Mott.

1986: Cadbury Schweppes acquires Canada Dry and Sunkist soft drink lines from RJR Nabisco.

1995: Cadbury Schweppes acquires Dr Pepper/Seven Up.

1999: Cadbury Schweppes sells non-U.S. soft drink business to Coca-Cola.

Schweppes ventured into alcoholic beverages when it acquired Courtney Wines International from LRL International. Also in 1973, Schweppes South Africa merged with Groovy Beverages. A year later, it acquired Pepsi Cola South Africa. But most of Cadbury Schweppes's moves in the early 1970s were small in scale and generally unsuccessful. It also spread itself thin at home by introducing a large number of unprofitable new products.

Adrian Cadbury succeeded Watkinson as chairman in 1974, and under his direction Cadbury Schweppes focused its efforts on gaining a greater share of the lucrative U.S. market. In 1978, aided by a strong pound, it acquired Peter Paul, a Connecticut-based confectioner, for $58 million. This gave Cadbury Schweppes a 10 percent share of the U.S. candy market in one swoop. In 1982 it bought Duffy-Mott, a producer of fruit juices and other fruit products, from American Brands for $60 million.

Cadbury Schweppes made several other overseas acquisitions in the early 1980s. In 1980 it increased its stake in its French subsidiary, Schweppes France, to 100 percent. In 1982 it purchased a two-thirds interest in Rioblanco, a Spanish soft drink company that owned the Schweppes franchise in Spain. In 1984 it acquired Cottees General Foods, General Foods' Australian subsidiary and a producer of coffee products, jams, jellies, and fruit juice cordials. In Britain it ended its 32-year-old franchising agreement with PepsiCo in 1985 to become Coca-Cola's British franchisee, noting Coke's dominant position in the British market.

But Cadbury Schweppes remained focused on the U.S. market throughout the 1980s. In 1985 it acquired Sodastream Hold-

ings, a British company that produced equipment for making carbonated drinks at home, as a way of trying to capture U.S. customers without competing head-on with Coke and Pepsi—Cadbury Schweppes held only 1 percent of the U.S. market in 1986, while the two native giants controlled roughly three-quarters between them.

But Cadbury Schweppes began to take on Coke and Pepsi with increasing vigor. In 1986 it bought the Canada Dry and Sunkist soft drink lines from RJR Nabisco for $230 million. RJR Nabisco was anxious to leave the soft drink business in the face of increased competition from Coca-Cola and Pepsi, which were growing ever larger. Pepsi had just acquired Seven Up, and Coca-Cola had agreed to buy Dr Pepper, a deal that would later fall apart. Sunkist was in danger of losing market share to Coca-Cola's new Minute Maid line and Pepsi's Slice. But while RJR Nabisco was ready to get out, Cadbury Schweppes was desperate to get into the market. Buying Canada Dry and Sunkist increased its share of U.S. soft drink sales to 5.3 percent, making it the fourth largest soft drink company in the nation.

Cadbury Schweppes then spun off Canada Dry's Canadian operations to Coca-Cola for $90 million. It needed the cash to acquire 30 percent of Dr Pepper as part of a consortium that included the brokerage house Shearson Lehman Brothers and Dallas-based investment group Hicks & Haas. This group bought the soft drink company from Forstmann Little & Company for $416 million.

Cadbury Schweppes became the subject of takeover speculation in 1987 after General Cinema announced that it had acquired an 8.3 percent interest in the company. General Cinema, a soft drink bottler that also owned the Neiman Marcus department stores and operated a large movie theater chain, said that it had bought the Cadbury Schweppes shares purely as an investment. But speculation increased later that year when General Cinema raised its stake to 18.2 percent. The next year, rumors circulated that Swiss giant Nestlé would try to acquire Cadbury Schweppes. With stock prices depressed in the wake of the October 1987 stock market crash and Cadbury Schweppes's strong financial performance, it was an attractive takeover candidate.

Amid all this uncertainty, however, Cadbury Schweppes continued to go about its business. In 1987 it acquired Chocolat Poulain, a French confectioner, from Midial for $173.1 million. In 1988 it sold its U.S. confectionery operations to Hershey Foods as a franchise, deciding that its products would benefit from Hershey's superior distribution network in the United States. In 1989 it bought out the British confectioner Bassett Foods to rescue it from a hostile takeover by the Swedish consumer products concern Procordia. It also continued its pursuit of the U.S. soft drink market by acquiring Crush International from Procter & Gamble for $220 million. At that point, Cadbury Schweppes controlled a 4.7 percent market share in the United States and a 15.1 percent share in Canada.

In a sense, the takeover speculation surrounding Cadbury Schweppes was a tribute to its success over the last decade. In 1979 the company announced that it would refocus on its core businesses and devote itself to cracking the U.S. marketplace. In 1986 it sold off its domestic beverage and foods division, which included the tea and jam businesses that Schweppes had acquired in the 1960s and Cadbury's popular Smash instant mashed potato product. All of its other important actions in the 1980s related to confectionery and soft drinks. These moves paid off. Cadbury Schweppes increased its share of U.S. soft drink sales almost fivefold and improved its financial situation significantly.

But perhaps the most interesting aspect of Cadbury Schweppes was the fact that it remained a family-run business even though it had also become a major corporation. Sir Adrian Cadbury (he was knighted in 1977), the great grandson of John Cadbury, was still chairman in 1990. His brother Dominic was appointed CEO in 1983.

Competing in the Global Marketplace: 1990–2002

In the early 1990s, with European unification looming on the horizon, Cadbury Schweppes began to develop a new business strategy, one that would give it a chance to establish leading positions in a variety of highly competitive foreign markets. In spite of its global reach, Cadbury Schweppes still had only a niche presence in the majority of the countries where it did business; although the company had operations in numerous countries worldwide, none of its overseas holdings were substantial enough to dominate any one region. Chairman Dominic Cadbury summed up the company's dilemma in June 1993: "If you are more than national, but less than global, you are an uncomfortable animal to describe." In short, Cadbury Schweppes needed to boost its international profile.

Each of the company's core businesses presented its own unique challenges. Expanding the company's soft drink line in Europe was, in many respects, fairly straightforward. To attain the sales volume necessary to justify building a new network of bottling plants, the company needed to find a way to increase distribution of its products in Europe. Although a number of its brands, notably Schweppes and Canada Dry, had name recognition overseas, they did not claim a commanding share of any one marketplace. The company considered establishing new operations in individual countries, but joint ventures, with which the company already had a lot of experience, seemed much more appealing in the long term. One such pact, with Apollinaris Brunnen in Germany, was forged in 1991, and showed strong sales after only its first year of operation.

In the United States, however, the company's strategy was radically different. Since the cola market was clearly dominated by Coke and Pepsi, Cadbury Schweppes looked for opportunity in the fruit juice and non-cola marketplaces. A number of crucial acquisitions helped put the company on the map. In August 1993 Cadbury Schweppes obtained a 20.2 percent stake in Dr Pepper/Seven Up; the following month, the company acquired A&W, the largest root beer producer in the United States, for $334 million. Although small steps, these deals helped set the stage for further growth. In 1995 the company paid $1.6 billion for the remaining stake in Dr Pepper/Seven Up, giving it a 17 percent share of the overall U.S. soft drink market. On one hand, this number was still small compared with the shares commanded by Coke and Pepsi. It also gave Cadbury Schweppes a full 50 percent, however, of the non-cola drink sector, a segment that was growing far more

rapidly than the cola business, accounting for 35 percent of the $49 billion U.S. soft drink industry in 1995.

There were still obstacles to overcome, however. Coke and Pepsi controlled much of the U.S. distribution and bottling systems that Cadbury Schweppes had been using for years, and for the most part the arrangement had been stable. Now that Cadbury Schweppes was jockeying for market share, however, the relationships between the companies were in danger of becoming less friendly. Less than eager to remain at the mercy of its competitors, Cadbury Schweppes began looking into the possibility of establishing its own network by striking deals with independent bottlers. Unfortunately, the independents were notoriously disorganized in the United States, and any worthwhile system would take several years, and a substantial investment, to set in place. In February 1998 the company took a preliminary step toward creating its own network when it formed American Bottling, a joint venture with two independent bottlers in the U.S. Midwest. Perhaps most significant, in mid-1999 Cadbury Schweppes sold all of its non-U.S. soft drink holdings to Coca-Cola for $700 million, signaling its intention to devote itself full-time to the U.S. market.

The sale also infused the company with a large dose of investment capital, putting it in a position to strengthen its European confectionery business through acquisition. In the late 1990s the company also began playing with the idea of further diversification. Although the company ultimately failed in its bid to acquire Nabisco in July 2000, it would not rule out future attempts to try to enter the snack food business. By the dawn of the new century, however, the company's most pressing concern was clearly the U.S. beverage market. Although building the necessary infrastructure would require time and resources, the company's ambitions in this sector remained high.

Principal Subsidiaries

Schweppes France; Schweppes Spain; Schweppes Belgium; Schweppes Portugal; Cadbury Aguas Minerales (Mexico); Cadbury TreborBasset; Cafe Cadbury; Cadbury France; Hollywood (France); Cadbury Dulciora (Spain); Cadbury Portugal Productors de Confeitaria LSA; Piasten Schokoladenfabrik Hofmann (Germany); Cadbury Wedel (Poland); Cadbury O.O.O. (Russia); Cadbury Netherlands BV; Cadbury Ireland; Dr Pepper/Seven Up, Inc. (U.S.A.); Mott's (U.S.A.); Snapple Beverages Group (U.S.A.); Cadbury Trebor Allan (Canada); Jaret International (U.S.A.); Cadbury Stani (U.S.A.); Cadbury Schweppes Pty Ltd. (Australia); Cadbury Food Co. Ltd. China; Cadbury Food Co. Beijing (China); Trebor Wuxi Confectionery Co. (China); Cadbury Four Seas Co. Ltd. (Hong Kong); PT Cadbury Indonesia; Cadbury Japan Ltd.; Cadbury Confectionery Malaysia Sdn Bhd; Cadbury Confectionery Limited (New Zealand); Cadbury Philippines; Cadbury Singapore PTE Limited; Cadbury Schweppes (South Africa); Bromor Foods (South Africa); Cadbury Kenya; Cadbury Ghana; Cadbury Nigeria; Cadbury Egypt; Cadbury India Ltd.

Principal Competitors

The Coca-Cola Company (U.S.A.); Mars, Incorporated (U.S.A.); PepsiCo, Inc. (U.S.A.).

Further Reading

de Jonquieres, Guy, "An Uncomfortable Animal Seeks Big Game Status," *Financial Times* (London), June 8, 1993, p. 21.

Denton, Nicholas, and Roderick Oram, "Cadbury Schweppes Set to Pay Pounds 1bn for US Drinks Group," *Financial Times* (London), January 23, 1995, p. 1.

Williams, Iolo A., *The Firm of Cadbury 1831–1931,* London: Constable and Co., 1931.

Willman, John, "Cadbury Schweppes Nears $700m Deal with Coca-Cola," *Financial Times* (London), July 29, 1999, p. 27.

—update: Steve Meyer

Cargolux Airlines International S.A.

Luxembourg Airport
L-2990 Luxembourg
Luxembourg
Telephone: (+352) 4211-1
Fax: (+352) 43 54 46
Web site: http://www.cargolux.com

Private Company
Incorporated: 1970
Employees: 1,333
Sales: $739 million (2000 est.)
NAIC: 481112 Scheduled Freight Air Transportation

Luxembourg's Cargolux Airlines International S.A. is Europe's largest cargo-only airline, ranking in the top five of this category worldwide. Cargolux operates a fleet of more than 12 Boeing 747-400F freight aircraft—the largest fleet of this type of aircraft in the world—flying to 49 locations; the company also coordinates a network of 15 trucking subcontractors to expand its total reach by an additional 42 truck route destinations. Billing itself as the "freight-forwarders airline," Cargolux sells freight carrying capacity to logistics companies and freight forwarding companies, which in turn coordinate the shipping needs of manufacturers, distributors, and other customers. Cargolux and other all-cargo carriers play a key role in the development of international trade, delivering cargo to destinations, including manufacturing centers, not served by passenger airlines. Cargolux has achieved strong growth since the late 1990s, in part because the company has adopted a policy of using only a single type of aircraft, which enables it to cut down on fuel, operating, and maintenance costs. The company's 747-400Fs each allow a maximum payload of 129 tons; the company's planes average nearly 16 hours of flight time daily, for an annual combined carrying capacity of nearly 450,000 metric tons and nearly four million ton-kilometers flown. The company also operates one of Europe's largest modern cargocenters, with a capacity of more than 500,000 tons, located at its Findel, Luxembourg airport home base. Since former CEO Heiner Wilkens's surprise resignation in 2001, the company has been led by chairman and founder Roger Sietzen, who has taken on the added role of acting CEO. Cargolux is a privately held company, although the company may have plans to go public in the early years of the new century. Principal shareholders include Luxair (34.9 percent); Swissair, through SAirLogistics (33.7 percent); and a consortium of Luxembourg-based financial institutions.

Freight Carrying Cooperative in the 1970s

During the 1960s, Loftleidir, the Icelandic national airline, began looking for a means to dispose of its aging fleet of Canadair CL-44 aircraft. Originally operated as passenger airliners (Icelandic's later CL-44 models, which carried 214 passengers, were then the world's largest), the CL-44 had never successfully imposed itself on the airline market, and by the end of the decade Icelandic sought to shift its fleet to newer, more fuel-efficient aircraft. Yet the company found no buyers for its planes. Instead, the company met up with the head of a logistics company, Salen Shipping (which changed its name to Cool Carriers in 1984), who proposed that the two companies convert the CL-44s to a cargo fleet and set up an airfreight joint venture.

The two partners decided to set up the new company in Luxembourg. The location gave the company a base in a centrally situated European hub, while enabling the proposed cargo-only airline to avoid the traffic at the continent's larger airports, where passenger planes received priority treatment. Salen and Icelandic then began looking for local partners for the new venture, bringing in Luxair, the Luxembourg national airline, and a consortium of Luxembourg financial institutions. In 1970, Cargolux, a Luxembourg registered company, was founded. The Luxembourg airport became the company's home and site of its maintenance facilities.

Cargolux made its first flight, to Hong Kong, in September of that year. The company's CL-44 was capable of a maximum payload of 24 tons. At the start, the company did not operate on a fixed, scheduled route basis, but instead flew to destinations on a per-order basis. Cargolux also flew a number of humanitarian missions.

By 1972, however, Cargolux's flights to Asia were running on a more regular basis, and the company set up its first

Company Perspectives:

Mission—Our mission is to secure the profitability of our company by providing freight forwarders unrivaled competitive advantage in their operations worldwide.

Values—We are a dynamic, multinational, customer-focused organization. We stand for integrity, tolerance and teamwork. We set ourselves the highest standards and we deliver on our promises. We succeed through the quality of our relationships. We value every contribution made by our employees to securing the profitability of our company. We abide by the laws and regulations governing our activities. We respect the environments and communities within which we operate.

scheduled flights, using Hong Kong as a hub. Supporting the company's operations was an expanding fleet of planes. By 1973, the company operated five CL-44s, all of which came from Icelandic. The company also added a second aircraft type, the DC-8, which had a maximum payload of 46 tons. Soon after, Cargolux adopted its slogan, "You name it, we fly it."

In 1974, Icelandic Air turned over its maintenance and engineering department to Cargolux, which then opened a two-hangar facility in Luxembourg, as well as a new headquarters in 1975. The facility, which also handled maintenance on the company's DC-8s, became especially noteworthy not only for the high level of its CL-44 maintenance program, but also for its development of safety modifications for the CL-44. As production on the CL-44 ended in the mid-1970s, Cargolux's maintenance program became solely responsible for the safety of its fleet.

Nonetheless, the CL-44's small size meant that the aircraft type's future was nearing an end with Cargolux as well. The company began phasing out its CL-44 fleet. At first the DC-8 took over as the company's flagship aircraft. But by the late 1970s, Cargolux already had begun to seek expanded cargo capacity.

Cargolux ordered the first of its new class of aircraft in 1977, purchasing a Boeing 747-200F, which featured a maximum payload of 119 tons. While the company awaited delivery of the new plane, it continued expanding its routes using the DC-8. By the end of the 1970s, Cargolux had set up a strong network of destinations throughout Asia, as well as to the Middle East and Africa.

The DC-8's days were soon numbered at Cargolux, when the company took delivery of its first 747 in 1979. A second 747 was added in 1980; by then Cargolux began planning the phase-out of its DC-8 fleet. Meanwhile, Cargolux's Asian operations extended into China, when the company signed a joint venture agreement with China Airlines in 1982. The company began working with another major and long-term customer when Swiss-based freight forwarder Panalpina began subcontracting aircraft in Cargolux's fleet. Featuring Cargolux crews as well, the flights, operated under Panalpina subsidiary Air Sea Broker, guaranteed Cargolux filled capacity on its aircraft. Over the course of the decade to follow, the relationship between the two companies continued to develop as Panalpina established a number of fixed international cargo routes—to the point where

the company was rivaling many of the world's largest airlines in terms of flown tonnage.

Gaining World Leadership in the 21st Century

In 1983, Cargolux inaugurated its CHAMP (Cargo Handling and Management Planning) computer system, which was to receive regular updates over the following two decades. Soon after its implementation, CHAMP began attracting interest from other airlines, and Cargolux began selling CHAMP to other carriers. In that year, also, Cargolux moved into passenger services, offering flights to pilgrims traveling to Mecca. These flights proved successful enough for the company to begin leasing additional 747s to service its Hajj passengers.

Cargolux sold off the last of its DC-8 fleet in 1984 and ordered a third 747-200F. That airplane arrived in 1986. The following year, Cargolux gained a new shareholder, Lufthansa, which acquired a 24.5 percent share, taking over Icelandic's shareholding. At the same time, Luxair reinforced its own shareholding, boosting its stake to 24.53 percent.

Cargolux's relationship with Luxair tightened in 1988 when the two airlines set up a joint venture passenger airline, Lionair, flying on B747-100 aircraft. That venture lasted only a couple of years, however, ending in 1990. By then, Cargolux had joined the top ranks of world cargo airlines and had become one of the largest cargo-only carriers.

The year 1990 marked a turning point for the now 20-year-old company. Cargolux ordered three new 747-400Fs with a maximum payload of 129 tons. At the same time, Cargolux held an option for the purchase of an additional three 747-400F craft. The company also updated its CHAMP system, which was now used not only by Cargolux, but by eight other cargo carriers as well. Meanwhile, Panalpina's expansion had enabled Cargolux to increase its route network as the two companies cooperated closely on establishing new lines—often using Cargolux crews on leased aircraft, with capacity guaranteed by Panalpina.

This activity helped boost Cargolux's sales to new highs, nearing $300 million in revenues by the end of 1991. Then in 1993, the company took delivery on the first two of its new 747 series—Cargolux became the first in the world to operate flights on the new state-of-the-art cargo aircraft and was to remain the only European operator flying the 400F class of 747s. These planes were flown alongside the company's existing fleet of 747-200s.

The third 747-400F was added to Cargolux's fleet in 1995. In that year, also, the company took on a new CEO and president, Heiner Wilkins, when Roger Sietzen, who had been among the company's founders, stepped up to the chairman's position. Wilkens led Cargolux into a new expansion phase. In 1996, the company opened its new cargo center at Luxembourg Airport, which, at 500,000 tons capacity, was among the largest and most modern in Europe. That year, Lufthansa sold its shares in the company to SAirLogistics, subsidiary of Switzerland's Swissair. This led to the signing of a cooperation agreement between Cargolux and another Swissair subsidiary, SwissCargo. At the same time, Luxair strengthened its own position in the company, building its shareholding to nearly 35 percent. Swissair later increased its own shareholding to 33 percent in 1998.

Key Dates:

1970:   Cargolux is founded as a partnership between Loftleidir Icelandic and Salen Shipping; joined by Luxair and others, using Icelandic's fleet of CL-44 planes, Cargolux begins operations in Luxembourg.

1973:   With a fleet of five CL-44 planes, Cargolux adds the first of a series of DC-8 aircraft.

1979:   Cargolux takes delivery on the first 747-200F and begins phaseout of the CL-44, and then the DC-8.

1983:   Cargolux introduces the CHAMP computerized cargo handling system.

1984:   Cargolux phases out the last of its DC-8 fleet.

1988:   Cargolux forms short-lived Lionair passenger airline joint venture with Luxair (closes in 1990).

1993:   Cargolux takes delivery on its first 747-400F aircraft.

1996:   Cargolux inaugurates a new 500,000-ton capacity cargo center at Luxembourg airport.

1998:   Cargolux begins phaseout of the 747-200F in favor of developing a fleet based on a single type of aircraft (the 747-400F).

2000:   The company continues to expand its route network, reaching more than 90 destinations, including 49 air destinations and 42 trucking destinations.

2001:   Cargolux takes delivery of its 11th 747-400F.

2002:   Delivery of its 12th 747-400F is slated for September, giving Cargolux the world's largest fleet of this type of aircraft.

Cargolux continued to expand its network of destinations, reaching 31 international destinations by 1997, supported by nearly 70 offices in 40 countries. Cargolux also exercised its option to purchase additional 747-400Fs, adding two more in 1997, then placing an order for an additional five aircraft, as well as options on two more, in 1998. By then, Cargolux made the strategic decision to phase out its fleet of 747-200s. Instead, the company adopted the model established by highly successful airline Southwest, which operated a fleet based on a single aircraft model. By reducing its fleet to a single model of aircraft, Cargolux expected to achieve greater economies, both in maintenance and in fuel costs.

The last of the company's 747-200F aircraft was sold off in 1998. By the end of 1999, Cargolux had increased its 400F series fleet to ten aircraft. The company also continued opening up new air routes, including to Shanghai, China, and to Montevideo, Uruguay. The company completed its coverage of all of the world's continents when it opened scheduled routes to Australia and New Zealand at the end of that year. In that year, also, Cargolux's relationship with Panalpina took on a new closeness when the Swiss-based freight forwarder formed the SwissGlobalCargo joint venture with SAirLogistics (Panalpina took full control of SwissGlobalCargo in 2001).

By the end of 1999, Cargolux's revenues neared $650 million, and the company had succeeded in capturing not only the lead position among European cargo carriers, but also a spot in the top five of the world's leading cargo-only carriers. In that year, the company continued adding new routes, including regular flights to Seoul, Korea, and expanding its flights, in partnership with China Eastern, to Shanghai. At the end of that year, Cargolux added a new route in South America, to Ecuador's Latacunga. By then, the company's list of destinations had topped 90 cities, including 49 by air and an additional 42 connected through subcontracts with local trucking companies.

CEO Wilkens resigned abruptly in April 2001, despite the company's strong annual results—sales had neared $740 million for the year 2000. Yet Wilkens, who favored stepping up Cargolux's 747-400F purchases—at $150 million per aircraft—came into conflict with the company's board of directors, which shied away from such a large-scale financial commitment during a time of widespread economic uncertainty. With the United States entering an apparent recession in 2001, Cargolux was forced to brace itself for diminishing business. Chairman Roger Sietzen took back the CEO seat while the company began looking for Wilkens's successor.

Nonetheless, the company took delivery on an 11th 747-400F in August 2001, with a 12th aircraft expected for delivery in September 2002. Although Cargolux appeared to be placing further fleet expansion on hold, that position was expected to be temporary and most likely short-lived. A number of financial analysts had begun to forecast the United States' emergence from its recession; many others began to question whether the country had entered a recession at all. Whichever proved correct, the return to growth of the U.S. economy promised to give a new boost to the demand for international air cargo services—and new business for Cargolux.

Principal Subsidiaries

Geraldine Aircraft Leasing Co. Ltd. (Cayman Islands); Elena Aircraft Leasing Co. Ltd. (Cayman Islands); Lionair SA (45%); Luxfuel SA (30%).

Principal Competitors

Air Cargo, Inc.; Atlas Air Worldwide Holdings, Inc; Air T, Inc.; Airborne, Inc.; BAX Global Inc.; CargoLifter AG; Fine Air Services Corp.; Pilot Air Freight Inc.

Further Reading

"Cargolux Expands B747-400F Fleet to 10 Planes," *World Airport Week,* December 9, 1999.

"Cargolux on Steady Expansion," *Shippers Today,* April 16, 2001.

Chandler, Patricia M., "Globalization Drives Expansion of All-Cargo Carriers," *Transportation & Distribution,* June 1, 1997, p. 61.

Krause, Kristin S., "Southwest As Role Model," *Traffic World,* October 16, 2000.

Page, Paul, "Cargolux Chief Wilkens Resigns Abruptly," *Air Cargo World,* April 24, 2001.

Siweck, Jean-Lou, "Cargolux: No Cash, No Ticket," *d'Land,* April 21, 2000.

—M. L. Cohen

Chanel SA

135, Avenue Charles de Gaulle
92521 Neuilly-sur-Seine Cedex
France
Telephone: (+33) 1-46-43-40-00
Fax: (+33) 1-47-47-60-34
Web site: http://www.chanel.com

Private Company
Incorporated: 1924 as Parfums Chanel
Employees: 912
Sales: $2.5 billion (2001 est.)
NAIC: 325620 Toilet Preparation Manufacturing

Chanel SA is one of the legendary names in perfumes. The company has parlayed its prestigious brand name into a world-leading retail empire. In addition to its flagship perfume brand Chanel No. 5—which has long been the world's top-selling perfume—Chanel has expanded its line to include women's fashions, jewelry and accessories, handbags, leather goods, and other products. While its products are sold through third parties, Chanel also operates its own network of more than 80 company-owned retail stores worldwide. There are also more than 120 Chanel shop-in-shop boutiques in leading department stores around the world. Chanel has also begun building up a portfolio of luxury brands, including gunsmith Holland & Holland and high-end French bathing suit maker Eres, bought in 1997. In 2002, rumors began circulating of a possible marriage with the famed house of Hermès. During the new millennium, Chanel has stepped up its purchases in the luxury sector, acquiring A. Michel et Cie, exclusive hat maker for the haute couture set and the famed Les broderies Lesage, which provides embroidery for the haute couture industry. These acquisitions complement the company's existing fashion industry holdings, such as the Lemarie, a flowers and feathers craftsman and Desrue, producer of buttons. Meanwhile, Chanel has been attempting to break into the skin care segment, launching its own line under the Precision brand. Chanel SA is a private company wholly owned by the Wertheimer family. The company's revenues are estimated to top EUR 2 billion per year.

Launching Perfume History in the 1920s

Chanel SA traces its roots back to 1870, when Ernest Wertheimer moved from Alsace, France, to Paris during the Franco-Prussian War. Shortly after his arrival he purchased an interest in a French theatrical makeup company called Bourjois. Bourjois successfully introduced dry rouge to the European market in the 1890s. The company grew rapidly, and by the early 1920s, Bourjois had begun making and distributing skin creams from his Rochester, New York, plant for cosmetic industry giant Helena Rubenstien. By the 1920s, Bourjois had become the largest cosmetics and fragrance manufacturer in France.

Though the Wertheimer family would control the finances of Chanel from its inception, the impetus and creative vision for the company came from Coco Chanel. Theophile Bader, founder of the successful French department store chain Galeries Lafayette, introduced Coco Chanel to Ernest Wertheimer's son, Pierre, in 1922. Coco Chanel sought financial help from Pierre Wertheimer to market a fragrance she had developed in 1921. An admirer of Coco Chanel, Pierre Wertheimer wanted to help her succeed and, two years after their introduction, he founded Parfums Chanel to make and sell her upscale perfume, named Chanel No. 5. Pierre Wertheimer funded the venture and retained a 70 percent ownership share in the company. Coco Chanel got a modest 10 percent of the company and Bader received 20 percent.

During the 1920s and 1930s Parfums Chanel thrived. In addition to selling the famous Chanel No. 5 perfume, the company eventually introduced other fragrances. In 1929, Pierre Wertheimer introduced Soir de Paris, a fragrance aimed at the general public and marketed through the Bourjois company. Meanwhile, Coco Chanel operated a successful fashion studio near the Louvre museum in Paris. Under an agreement with the Wertheimers, she operated her design business as a separate company, but sold the clothes under the Chanel name. Although Parfums Chanel and Coco Chanel's design business flourished, the personal relationship between Coco Chanel and Pierre Wertheimer deteriorated.

The friction between Coco Chanel and the Wertheimer family stemmed from Coco Chanel's dissatisfaction with the terms of

Key Dates:

1922: Pierre Wertheimer agrees to back new perfume developed by Coco Chanel, and founds Parfums Chanel.
1929: Company launches new fragrance, Soir de Paris.
1954: Coco Chanel makes Parisian comeback after fleeing to Switzerland following World War II.
1974: Alain Wertheimer takes control of company.
1983: Karl Lagerfeld is hired as Chanel designer.
1996: Chanel acquires gun maker Holland & Holland.
1997: Chanel acquires high-end swimwear designer Eres.
2001: Chanel acquires stake in luxury watchmaker Bell & Ross.
2002: Chanel acquires milliner A. Michel et Cie. and embroidery house Lesage.

their original agreement. Coco Chanel resented what she viewed as an attempt by the Wertheimers to exploit her talents for their own gain. She felt she should have a larger than 10 percent portion of the company, and she argued that she had unwittingly signed away the rights to her own name. The Wertheimers countered her grievances with an argument that reminded Coco Chanel that the Wertheimers had funded her venture in the first place, giving her the chance to take her creations to market, and had made her a relatively wealthy woman.

In 1935 Chanel hired a Parisian attorney, René de Chambrun, to renegotiate her agreement with the Wertheimers. But the Wertheimers successfully quashed those attempts. Furthermore, her fashion business sputtered during the late 1930s and at 56 years of age Coco Chanel closed it when the Nazis invaded France. Coco Chanel found a new way to fight the Wertheimers during World War II. In fact, the Wertheimers fled the country in 1940, eventually landing in the United States. With the powerful Wertheimer family gone, Coco Chanel went to work trying to use new occupation regulations to take control of the Parfums Chanel partnership. But the savvy Wertheimers stymied that move, too. In their absence, they found an Aryan proxy to run their businesses and keep Coco Chanel at bay.

During World War II, Coco Chanel stayed in Paris, moving into the Hotel Ritz with her new paramour, Hans Gunther von Dincklage, a Nazi officer. According to one of Coco Chanel's biographers, Edmonde Charles-Roux, she played a role in a secret peace mission near the end of the war. Charles-Roux contends that German intelligence sent Coco Chanel to visit Winston Churchill as part of a secret peace mission. Coco Chanel was arrested immediately after the liberation of France and charged with abetting the Germans, but Churchill intervened on her behalf and she was released.

Postwar Comeback

After her release, Coco Chanel immediately fled France for Switzerland. Meanwhile, Pierre Wertheimer returned to Paris to resume control of his family's holdings. Despite her absence, Coco Chanel continued her assault on her former admirer and began manufacturing her own line of perfumes. Feeling that

Coco Chanel was infringing on Parfums Chanel's business, Pierre Wertheimer wanted to protect his legal rights, but wished to avoid a court battle, and so, in 1947, he settled the dispute with Coco Chanel, giving her $400,000 and agreeing to pay her a 2 percent royalty on all Chanel products. He also gave her limited rights to sell her own perfumes from Switzerland.

Coco Chanel never made any more perfume after the agreement. She gave up the rights to her name in exchange for a monthly stipend from the Wertheimers. The settlement paid all of her monthly bills and kept Coco Chanel and her former lover, von Dincklage, living in relatively high style. It appeared as though aging Coco Chanel would drop out of the Chanel company saga.

At 70 years of age in 1954, Coco Chanel returned to Paris with the intent of restarting her fashion studio. She went to Pierre Wertheimer for advice and money, and he agreed to finance her plan. In return for his help, Wertheimer secured the rights to the Chanel name for all products that bore it, not just perfumes. Once more, Wertheimer's decision paid off from a business standpoint. Coco Chanel's fashion lines succeeded in their own right and had the net effect of boosting the perfume's image. In the late 1950s Wertheimer bought back the 20 percent of the company owned by Bader. Thus, when Coco Chanel died in 1971 at the age of 87, the Wertheimers owned the entire Parfums Chanel operation, including all rights to the Chanel name.

Pierre Wertheimer died six years before Coco Chanel passed away, putting an end to an intriguing and curious relationship of which Parfums Chanel was just one, albeit pivotal, dynamic. Coco Chanel's attorney, Rene de Chambrun, described the relationship as one based on a businessman's passion for a woman who felt exploited by him. ''Pierre returned to Paris full of pride and excitement [after one of his horses won the 1956 English Derby],'' Chambrun recalled in *Forbes.* ''He rushed to Coco, expecting congratulations and praise. But she refused to kiss him. She resented him, you see, all her life.''

Pierre Wertheimer's son, Jacques, took control of the Chanel operation in 1965. The 55-year-old Jacques was perhaps best known for his management of the family's racing stables and horse breeding operations; Pierre Wertheimer had established one of the finest racing stables in the world in 1910, and Jacques became a renowned horse breeder. According to some critics, however, he did not direct as much attention on the operation of Chanel.

New Management in the 1970s

In 1974, Jacques's 25-year-old son Alain Wertheimer gained control of the company. While the press suggested that the move to new management involved animosity and family feuds, Chanel management maintained that control was ceded in a friendly and peaceable manner.

Chanel No. 5 was still a global perfume leader when Alain Wertheimer took the helm. But, with only 4 percent of the pivotal $875 million U.S. market, its dominance was fading. After years of mismanagement, Chanel had become viewed by many Americans as a second-rate fragrance that appealed to out-of-style women. Alain Wertheimer succeeded in turning Chanel around in the United States. He removed the perfume from drugstore shelves in an effort to create a greater sense of scarcity and exclusivity. As the number of U.S. outlets carrying Chanel No. 5 plummeted from 18,000 to 12,000, Alain Wertheimer pumped millions into advertising Chanel's fragrances and cosmetics. His efforts increased profits.

In 1980, Alain Wertheimer stepped up efforts in Chanel's U.S. fashion operations. Attempts to parlay the Chanel fashion division into a profit center and promotional device for Chanel's fragrances succeeded. A large part of the company's success could be credited to its hiring of famed designer Karl Lagerfeld in 1983, who revitalized the company's clothing fashions and remained its chief visionary into the next century.

During the 1980s Chanel opened up more than 40 Chanel boutiques worldwide. By the late 1980s those shops sold everything from $200-per-ounce perfume and $225 ballerina slippers to $11,000 dresses and $2,000 leather handbags. Importantly, Alain Wertheimer refused to relinquish control of anything related to the family's Chanel operations. In fact, Chanel remains one of the few companies in the cosmetic and apparel industry that does not license its fragrances, cosmetics, or apparel to other producers or distributors.

While Lagerveld revamped the company's clothing designs, the rest of the company's designers and marketers carefully maintained a conservative, proven image so as not to tamper with the Chanel legend. Although other perfumes had changed to follow short-term trends, the Chanel fragrance remained classic and unchanged. Even the Chanel No. 5 bottle, with its traditional black-and-white label and simple lines, was considered a work of art by the company. "We introduce a new fragrance every 10 years, not every three minutes like many competitors," explained Chanel marketer Jean Hoehn Zimmerman in *Marketing News*. "We don't confuse the consumer. With Chanel, people know what to expect. And they keep coming back to us, at all ages, as they enter and leave the market." Indeed, the launch of a new fragrance, Coco, in the 1980s, was to provide the company with another strong perfume success.

Luxury Goods Conglomerate for the 21st Century

As a result of Alain Wertheimer's efforts during the 1980s and early 1990s, Chanel's performance improved significantly. Going into the 1990s, in fact, Chanel was considered a global leader in the fragrance industry and a top innovator in fragrance advertising and marketing. Chanel continued to spend more on advertising than almost any other perfume company and, as a result, was reaping the fattest profit margins in the industry. In addition, the company had continued to expand into new product lines, including Chanel watches retailing for as much as $7,000; additions to its popular shoe line; and other high-priced clothes, cosmetics, and accessories.

The Wertheimers would have been wealthy without their Chanel business. However, Chanel's success in the 1980s was credited with boosting the Wertheimer family's wealth to a new level, and by the late 1990s the Wertheimer family's fortune was estimated to top $5 billion. Alain Wertheimer moved his offices to New York in the late 1980s, reflecting Chanel's emphasis on the U.S. market. Although sales of high-end goods were hurt by the global recession of the early 1990s, demand

began recovering in the mid-1990s and Chanel continued to expand its boutique chain and product line.

Wertheimer remained chairman of the company while Françoise Montenay, the company's CEO and president, was charged with bringing it into the next century. In the 1990s Chanel began expanding its holdings, acquiring Lemarié, one of the most renowned feather and flower crafts houses for the Parisian fashion industry. The company continued in this trend with the acquisition of milliner A. Michel et Cie. and embroidery house Lesage. Chanel was rumored to be interested in acquiring another famed supplier to the haute couture set, boot- and shoemaker Massaro.

In 1996, Chanel acquired exclusive gun maker Holland & Holland. The company's attempt to extend that brand name to a wider range of fashions met with a lukewarm reception, forcing Chanel to scale back and realign Holland & Holland to its original concept. A more promising acquisition came in 1997, when Chanel bought high-end swimsuit maker Eres. In 2001, the company acquired a stake in up-and-coming watchmaker Bell & Ross.

Chanel continued to expand its retail holdings at the beginning of the century. In 2001 the company's U.S. subsidiary launched a new retail concept, featuring only accessories bearing the Chanel name. In July 2002 the company rolled out a new jewelry and watch flagship store on New York's Madison Avenue, and expected to build up these sales with the expansion of its network of independent retailers. Shortly after, the company opened a new, 1,500-square-foot handbag and shoe flagship store next door to its jewelry and watch store in New York, bringing the total number of Chanel stores in the United States to 25. The company also targeted the Far East, opening a new 2,400-square-foot boutique in Hong Kong, and paying nearly $50 million to acquire a building in Japan's Ginza shopping district. After 80 years, the Chanel name continued to attract customers from around the world.

Principal Subsidiaries

Chanel Inc. (USA); Chanel KK (Japan); Chanel Hong Kong; Paraffection.

Principal Competitors

Bulgari S.p.A.; Cartier SA; Chanel S.A.; Christian Dior SA; Gianfranco Ferre SpA; Gianni Versace SpA; Gucci Group N.V.; Hermès International; I Pellettieri d'Italia S.p.A.; LVMH Inc. (U.S.); LVMH Moët Hennessy Louis Vuitton SA; Montres Rolex S.A.; Puig Beauty & Fashion Group; Compagnie Financière Richemont AG; S.T. Dupont S.A.; Tiffany & Co.

Further Reading

Berkowitz, Harry, "Not Everyone Shared Caged Fantasy: Does New Chanel Ad Evoke Freedom or the Same Old Constraining Attitudes?," *Newsday*, August 30, 1992, sec. 1, p. 72.

Berman, Phyllis, and Zina Sawaya, "The Billionaires Behind Chanel," *Forbes*, April 3, 1989, p. 104.

"Chanel rachète les somptueuses broderies Lesage," *Agence France Presse*, June 29, 2002.

Hunter, Catherine E., "Scientist, Inventor, Futurist," *Drug & Cosmetic Industry,* May 1993, p. 20.

Johnson, Rebecca, "Scent of a Woman," *ADWEEK Eastern Edition,* November 29, 1993, p. 30.

Kamen, Robin, "Exec Suiting Up for Growth: Chanel to Open New Boutiques, Cater to Buyers," *Crain's New York Business,* August 15, 1994, sec. 1, p. 13.

Oliver, Joyce Ann, "She Innovates Without Destroying a Legend," *Marketing News,* December 10, 1990, p. 10.

Peyrani, Béatrice, "Chanel, le luxe et le secret," *L'Expansion,* August 29, 1996.

Strandberg, Keith W., "Chanel Expands Independent Retailer Base," *National Jeweler,* July 1, 2002, p. 26.

Swisher, Kara, "Chanel Bucks the Trend Toward Tysons Corner," *Washington Post,* May 7, 1990, p. E31.

Treacy, Karl, "Chanel Goes On Specialty House Spending Spree," *Fashion World*, July 2, 2002.

—Dave Mote
—update: M.L. Cohen

ChartHouse International Learning Corporation

221 River Ridge Circle
Burnsville, Minnesota 55337
U.S.A.
Telephone: (952) 890-1800
Toll Free: (800) 328-3789
Fax: (952) 890-0505
Web site: http://www.charthouse.com

Private Company
Incorporated: 1955 as Ray Christensen and Associates
Employees: 42
Sales: $10 million (2001 est.)
NAIC: 512110 Motion Picture and Video Production;
512120 Motion Picture and Video Distribution

ChartHouse International Learning Corporation's series of *Fish!* business training films and books have become well-known in corporate America, inspiring companies to transform their work atmosphere and revitalize customer service by applying the fun-loving Fish! Philosophy. ChartHouse Learning prefers to call its products educational films, since the principles embodied in aphorisms such as "Choose Your Attitude" and "Be There" can be applied in almost any life situation. From its headquarters in Burnsville, Minnesota, the company distributes the *Fish!* films in close to 20 different languages to more than 50,000 customers worldwide. Fans of *Fish!* can also buy a related book, while "Idea Agents" at company headquarters act as consultants who help adapt the philosophy to an individual company's needs. The success of the *Fish!* series was preceded by nearly 50 years of filmmaking experience at ChartHouse. Company founder Ray Christensen made many documentary films and a highly regarded safety film. The company is also credited with introducing the business world to the concept of paradigms through a series of business films that came out in the 1980s. John Christensen has since taken over the firm from his father, acting as chief executive officer, or, as ChartHouse Learning styles it, "Playground Director."

Safety Films and Business Paradigms: 1955–96

Ray Christensen began making films in Omaha, Nebraska, in 1955. His one-man freelance firm, Ray Christensen and Associates, started out filming television commercials. But soon Christensen was drawn to making documentary films, and he traveled widely in pursuit of a range of projects. His work documented the efforts of an African tribe trying to preserve water resources and a group of developmentally challenged people in Nebraska working to fulfill their individual potential. According to ChartHouse, Christensen's films "had a way of inspiring people to see the usual in unexpected and unusual ways."

In 1968 Christensen moved his operation to Minneapolis, hoping to find more opportunity in the Twin Cities area. He pitched his services door-to-door in search of a business that wanted to make a documentary about itself. In the early 1970s the young firm took on the name Filmedia Inc. Shortly thereafter Filmedia was hired to film a safety documentary for Federated Insurance, a business insurance company. Christensen threw his energies into learning about the subject, attending safety seminars and memorizing statistics on workplace injuries. A friend and past client, football commentator Pat Summerall, hosted the film. When it came out in 1977, the film set a new tone for safety training by emphasizing overall attitude as a crucial injury prevention technique. The film was endorsed by the head of the Minnesota Safety Council and became a bestseller. Christensen eventually made four films as part of the series. Federated Insurance requested a distribution deal, but Christensen declined at first. He acquiesced to a second offer, and Filmedia branched out into the distribution sector of the film industry.

Other projects from Filmedia's early years included documentaries for the Lutheran Church, the Catholic Church, and World Missions. But the firm's next big breakthrough came from a dinner party introduction that brought Christensen together with Joel Barker, a "futurist" with a knack for bringing innovative thinking to the business world. Barker was working as a consultant for Northern States Power at the time, and an NSP executive who happened to be a friend of Christensen's decided the two should meet. Out of the ensuing partnership came *The Business of*

Paradigms, a 35-minute film that appeared in 1982. The film developed the ideas of Thomas Kuhn, author of *The Structure of Scientific Revolutions.* Kuhn examined how the greatest scientific discoveries usually came from those who broke with established thought. Barker and Christensen, on the other hand, looked at how the business world was hindered by an adherence to traditional rules and management patterns. By recognizing and changing the "paradigms" that dictated action in the business world, according to the film, managers would be more successful in thinking about the future. The Japanese watch industry, for example, was one of the "Galileos" of the business world: when the well-established Swiss watchmakers remained tied to spring-wound mechanisms, the Japanese conquered the market with quartz-movement watches. *The Business of Paradigms* became one of the best-selling business films of all time, and made the concept of paradigms familiar in corporate and pop culture. ChartHouse CEO John Christensen said he knew the term had entered common usage when it was used by UPS in a commercial in the mid-1980s.

Later that decade Filmedia changed its name to ChartHouse, a reference to the place on a sailing vessel that holds navigational tools such as the compass, sextant, and maps. Like the navigational instruments, ChartHouse's mission was not to tell its clients where to go, but to give them the tools to set their course. In 1991 the firm followed up on the success of Barker's film by adding a second video, "The Power of Vision," to the "Paradigms" series. In the film, Barker explained vision as "the result of dreams in action," and traveled the world trying to make this concept applicable for his audience. From the Parthenon in Greece to a public school in Harlem, he showed how people had turned their dreams into real accomplishments through the power of vision.

An Inspiring Message from Seattle Fishmongers: 1997–2000

The connections and expertise that ChartHouse acquired in the making of the paradigms films prepared the firm to capitalize on an even bigger business training phenomenon. This time it was Ray Christensen's son John who would lead the project. John Christensen had started working in ChartHouse's shipping department as a teenager in 1985. At first he had no particular inclination to follow his father into the film industry, and instead got a degree in Park and Recreation Studies from the University of Minnesota. After college, while working with

kids as a summer camp director, he saw the value of artistry and teaching. He went back to ChartHouse and worked his way up to the higher ranks of the company.

Inspiration hit during a visit to Seattle in 1997. John Christensen heard from the concierge at his hotel that the Pike Place Market was worth a visit. Strolling through the market, Christensen noticed quite a bit of commotion centered around a fish vendor. Workers were tossing fish around, customers were ducking and screaming, and cashiers were picking on regular customers who had been away too long. The whole atmosphere was charged with fun and energy. Christensen, as he related the story to *Minnesota Business,* approached one of the cashiers to find out what was happening. The employee said, "Did you have lunch today? Chances are your waiter or waitress took your order, brought your food without a smile or a hello, and then you paid your bill and left a tip." The cashier paused, looked Christensen in the eye, and said emphatically, "This is our time, yours and mine. How can I help you?"

The fish vendors' attitude impressed Christensen as the ideal of customer service. The experience in Seattle stood out even more strongly when compared to less-than-satisfying interactions back home. Christensen took his three-year-old daughter to the pediatrician, where the receptionist typed in her name without even looking at them, the nurse did her job mechanically in cold, sterile surroundings, and there was no sense of human connection during the whole visit. It seemed that the rest of the world could benefit from a little of the fishmongers' refreshing attitude.

So Christensen put together a video with Steve Lundin, then a filmmaker, writer, public speaker and business school professor, and soon to become known as the "Big Tuna Ph.D." at ChartHouse. Harry Paul, a professional speaker and consulting partner with motivational firm Ken Blanchard Companies, also took part in the project. *Fish! Catch the Energy, Release the Potential* was released in 1998. The 17-minute film profiled the Pike Place fishmongers, showing how they had succeeded in improving working morale and customer service. The video highlighted four principles that could be applied at any company: Play, Make Their Day, Be There, and Choose Your Attitude. According to the Fish! Philosophy, a lighthearted approach improves productivity and creativity, while small acts of kindness "make their day" by turning routine encounters into special memories. The film encouraged viewers to be fully present and wholehearted in their daily tasks, and, finally, pointed out that individuals could choose to concentrate on the good and let go of negative things that cannot be changed. John Christensen summed up the film's approach in a company-produced biography: "The ChartHouse vision is an invitation to people to become fully immersed in their lives, using these four seemingly simplistic ideas. In many ways the Fish! Philosophy is really ancient wisdom for modern times, a lifestyle choice to engage in life-long learning and self-improvement. The products we offer are really learning tools, from some of the best mentors one could have—real-life experiences that ultimately speak to the human spirit."

Fish! was fun to watch, and it became a bestselling video that spurred record growth at ChartHouse. The firm grew at a rate of 25 percent annually over the next few years, and the

Key Dates:

1955: Ray Christensen begins making commercials and documentaries in Omaha.
1968: Christensen moves to Minnesota and renames his firm Filmedia Inc.
1977: Christensen's safety documentary for Federated Insurance wins acclaim.
1982: *The Business of Paradigms,* made with Joel Barker, is introduced.
1991: A second Joel Barker film, *The Power of Vision,* comes out.
1997: John Christensen visits Seattle and is inspired by the Pike Place fishmongers.
1998: The first *Fish!* film appears.
2000: A *Fish!* book and Fish! Camps are introduced.

workforce doubled to 42 employees by 2002. Meanwhile, the video was being translated into numerous languages and a sequel film was in the works. The second film in the series, *Fish! Sticks,* appeared in 1999. While the same length as the original, the sequel told the Pike Place fishmongers' story in greater depth. Shop owner Johnny explains how he used to hate his job, but by applying a few attitude-changing concepts, his business became famous, fun, and profitable.

Fish! *Growth: 2000–2002*

John Christensen's success with the *Fish!* series built on and surpassed his father's success with the ''paradigms'' videos. At midnight on December 31, 1999, control of ChartHouse was officially transferred to a new generation. In a symbolic ''passing of the torch,'' Ray Christensen handed his son a director's viewfinder during a New Year's dinner with the Seattle fishmongers. Under the younger Christensen's leadership, the *Fish!* line of learning tools expanded. A book authored by *Fish!* collaborator Steve Lundin came out in March 2000. Titled *Fish! A Remarkable Way to Boost Morale and Improve Results!*, the book told the story of a workplace so cold and disconnected that it was known as the ''Toxic Energy Dump.'' After two years, the book had been translated into 11 languages and was distributed in 27 countries.

As interest grew in the Fish! philosophy, ChartHouse began hosting live learning events to give managers direct experience with the Fish! principles. These events, known as Fish! Camps, attracted leaders from companies such as Barnes & Noble, Target, and Musicland Stores. Steve Lundin acted as counselor at many of the events, which drew participants to Minnesota from as far away as California and South Africa.

A second book, *Fish! Tales*, was published in April 2002. Senior ChartHouse writer Philip Strand joined Steve Lundin in producing the book, which portrayed four real-life workplaces that had improved results and morale with the help of the Fish! materials. The book also included numerous shorter profiles of

companies that had successfully applied the Fish! philosophy. Christensen estimated that 15,000 companies were using the series in 2002, including the majority of *Fortune* 100 companies. Fish! committees had even sprung up at some firms, and the Fish! philosophy was leaving its idiosyncratic track at workplaces across the nation. Employees at Liberty Diversified Industries in New Hope, Minnesota, for example, put image-distorting mirrors in their bathrooms, while managers at Sprint were inspired to perform disco dances in bunny slippers. In four years, Fish! had developed from a mere training video into a corporate subculture. ChartHouse customers included such companies as Southwest Airlines, 3M, Hewlett Packard, and Ford Motor.

But the Fish! principles had implications beyond the business realm. ChartHouse heard of the philosophy being used to save marriages and turn despondent people away from a suicidal path. Christensen subsequently began adapting the series for special audiences such as schools and hospitals, using the same storytelling style to show how various organizations had successfully applied the Fish! philosophy. ''We measure our growth not by revenue numbers but by the stories of transformation that come back to us, the numbers of lives we help change,'' Christensen said in a ChartHouse company profile. ''ChartHouse is truly finding the deeper layers of where the Fish! Philosophy can go into the culture.'' The company was also rounding out the Fish! series with a video version of *Fish! Tales* and a book version of *Fish! Sticks*. In addition, ChartHouse pursued projects outside the *Fish!* series, such as a film underway in the summer of 2002 on how to bring innovation alive. The company saw its products as educational tools that, rather than promoting a company-mandated policy, encouraged viewers to adopt a genuine attitude change that had consequences for all areas of their lives.

Principal Competitors

Robbins Research International, Inc.

Further Reading

Brouillard, Sarah, ''All the Buzz: ChartHouse Learning Created the Fish! Phenom—and Spawned a Subculture,'' *Minnesota Business,* June 2002, pp. 24–26.

Brown, Tom, ''Of Paradigms . . . and Visions: Joel Barker Says They Can Tell You a Lot About Business Success—and Failure,'' *Industry Week,* March 4, 1991, p. 11.

Cruz, Sherri, ''The Philosophy of Fish,'' *Star Tribune,* October 12, 2000, p. 1D.

Ellet, Bill, ''Team Spirit,'' *Training & Development,* May 2000, p. 108.

Emerson, Dan, ''Tossing Fish Hooks Training Devotees,'' *CityBusiness* (Minneapolis), January 19, 2001, p. 19.

Lelyveld, Nita, ''Pike Place Fishmongers Showing Up As Example of Fun at Work,'' *Knight-Ridder/Tribune News Service,* August 4, 2000.

Selix, Casey, ''Fish! Reels in Followers,'' *St. Paul Pioneer Press,* Tuesday, April 30, 2000, p. 1C.

—Sarah Ruth Lorenz

Christian Dior S.A.

30, avenue Montaigne
75008 Paris
France
Telephone: (+33) 1-44-13-24-98
Fax: (+33)-1-44-13-27-86
Web site: http://www.dior.com

Public Company
Incorporated: 1946 as Christian Dior Ltd.
Employees: 55,179
Sales: EUR 12.56 billion ($11.47 billion) (2001)
Stock Exchanges: Euronext Paris
Ticker Symbol: CDI
NAIC: 315232 Women's and Girls' Cut and Sew Blouse
    and Shirt Manufacturing; 315233 Women's and Girls'
    Cut and Sew Dress Manufacturing; 315234 Women's
    and Girls' Cut and Sew Suit, Coat, Tailored Jacket
    and Skirt Manufacturing; 315999 Other Apparel
    Accessories and Other Apparel Manufacturing;
    316991 Luggage Manufacturing; 325620 Toilet
    Preparation Manufacturing; 551112 Offices of Other
    Holding Companies

Christian Dior S.A. remains a leader in the world of fashion after more than 50 years. Yet Christian Dior has grown far beyond its high fashion origins to become one of the world's leading luxury goods holding companies, through LVMH Moët Hennessy Louis Vuitton, led by Bernard Arnault. While Christian Dior continues to lend its name and prestige as the parent company to Arnault's luxury goods empire, it remains a tiny part of the company's overall sales. With EUR 350 million in sales, Christian Dior Couture represents just 2 percent of the company's total sales of more than EUR 12 billion in 2001. Christian Dior S.A. is organized into two main divisions: Christian Dior Couture and LVMH. The latter includes holdings in Wine & Spirits (Moët & Chandon, Dom Pérignon, Veuve Clicquot, Krug, etc.); Watches & Jewelry (TAG Heuer; Ebel; Zenith); Fashion & Leather Goods (Louis Vuitton, Givenchy, Donna Karan, Christian Lacroix, Kenzo); Selective Retailing (DFS; Sephora; Le Bon Marché; La Samaritaine); and Perfumes & Cosmetics (Parfums Christian Dior; Guerlain; Parfums Givenchy; Kenzo Parfums). Other LVMH interests include Art & Auction magazine and the Tajan art auction house. Yet Christian Dior Couture remains the company's flagship—and icon of the worldwide fashion industry—and the primary subject of this profile. John Galiano has served as the fashion house's artistic director since 1996 and is credited with revitalizing the company's image. Since 2001, Galiano has been seconded by Hedi Slimane, in charge of creating a new men's line for the house. In addition to its haute couture apparel, Christian Dior operates a network of 130 boutiques around the world.

A Winding Path to Fashion

Christian Dior was born in 1905. As heir to a family fortune built on fertilizer and chemicals, Dior had little ambition to finish college, instead whiling away his 20s in Paris bars in the company of poets and artists. Dior dabbled in art, and in 1928, launched a gallery financed with a large gift from his father. But when heavy borrowing and the Great Depression combined to bankrupt the family business in the early 1930s, Dior's family was forced to sell homes, furniture, jewelry, and other heirlooms.

Dior moved in with a friend in Paris and decided to utilize his artistic talents in the fashion industry. Beginning in the mid-1930s, he designed on a freelance basis, selling drawings of hats and gowns to magazines and couture houses. He snared a full-time position with Robert Piguet's fashion design house in 1938, but was soon drafted into service for World War II. Assigned to "farm duty"—helping farmers' wives and other short-handed agriculturists tend their land—Dior was fortunate to be in unoccupied Provence when the German Army advanced in June 1940 and was subsequently discharged from the service. He returned to Paris in 1941 and found work as a design assistant with the couture house of Lucien Lélong, designing custom-made dresses, suits, and ball gowns for some of the wealthiest women in the world.

Postwar Origins of the House of Dior

In 1946, French fabric maven Marcel Boussac—then the nation's wealthiest man—offered to back Dior's launch of his own maison de couture. Though the new house of fashion became part of a vertically integrated textile business, it was initially a vanity property for Boussac, comparable to his world renowned stable of racehorses. Christian Dior Ltd. started out that year with 85 employees, capital of FFr 6 million, and "unlimited credit." In exchange for his creative genius, Dior negotiated a generous salary; a significant, though not controlling, stake in the firm; legal status as its leader; and one-third of pretax profits. It was quite an unusual arrangement, given Boussac's legendary—and eventually self-defeating—appetite for control. The company was a majority-owned affiliate of Boussac Saint-Freres S.A.

The designer introduced his first and most famous line—dubbed the "New Look" by Carmel Snow of *Harper's Bazaar*—in 1947. The collection was a striking refutation of the war's deprivation: whereas rationing restricted the amount of fabric used in a dress or skirt, Dior used an extravagant 20 yards of only the finest fabrics in his long, wide skirts. With help from elaborate undergarments, the dresses emphasized the feminine figure, from the tiniest of waists to peplum- or tulle-enhanced hips and tight-fitting bodices, often with deep décolletage.

The line was an immediate and nearly complete success, garnering a clientele ranging from European royalty to Hollywood starlets and generating sales of FFr 12.7 million by 1949. Dior opened a New York outlet before the year was out and established London operations in 1952. From the outset, fully half of the company's sales were made in the United States. By the end of 1953, the company had operations in Mexico, Canada, Cuba, and Italy. Women who could not afford the haute couture copied it at home. Soon enough—and to Dior's chagrin—knock-off artists did the "dirty work" for them. Eventually, the maison fought fire with fire, establishing a prêt à porter (ready to wear, abbreviated in the trade as "rtw") line of somewhat less expensive versions of the couture line. The designer stayed with the "New Look" for seven years, becoming a virtual dictator of hem lines and lengths in the process.

Diversification, Licensing Speed Growth in the Late 1940s

Again backed by the Boussac fortune, Dior launched Christian Dior Perfumes Ltd. in 1948. The namesake owned one-fourth of the new venture, a childhood friend who managed France's Coty perfumery held another 35 percent, and patron Boussac owned the remaining stake. By 1950, a licensing program devised by Dior General Manager Jacques Rouët put the now famous name on dozens of accessories, including ties, hosiery, furs, hats, gloves, handbags, jewelry, lingerie, and scarves. While denounced by Dior's colleagues in the French Chamber of Couture as a cheapening of the high-fashion industry's image, this licensing scheme would become a cornerstone

of the company's long-term success and a trend that would only grow stronger in the decades to come.

By the mid-1950s, the Dior empire included eight companies and 16 affiliates, and employed 1,700 people on five continents. In 1949 alone, Christian Dior fashions constituted 75 percent of Paris fashion exports, and 5 percent of all French export revenues. Though Christian Dior launched several successful lines—including the "A," "Y," "Arrow," and "Magnet"—from 1954 to 1957, none would surpass the initial introduction of the "New Look" in impact. By the time the house celebrated its tenth anniversary in 1957, it had sold 100,000 garments. Though in his early 50s, Dior was by this time preparing for his retirement, having suffered two heart attacks. A third seizure took his life that same year, ironically while he was on a recuperative trip to Italy. Though his couture career spanned scarcely a decade, he had established himself as one of the modern era's best known fashion designers. Writing for *Contemporary Fashion*, Kevin Almond asserted that "By the time Dior died his name had become synonymous with taste and luxury."

New Generations of Design Leadership After Dior's Death in 1957

The founder's death left the house in chaos. Jacques Rouët considered shuttering the worldwide operations, but neither Dior's licensees nor the French fashion industry—which owed 50 percent of its export volume to the House of Dior—would consider it. Instead, Rouët—who would continue to guide the company's day-to-day operations into the 1980s—promoted 22-year-old Yves Saint Laurent, whom Dior had hired just two years previous, as lead designer. Launched in 1958, the young designer's trapeze line was successful, but his 1960 "bohemian" look met heavy criticism from the press, especially the influential fashion industry magazine *Women's Wear Daily*. When Saint Laurent was drafted into the armed service that year (he went on to found his own house in 1962), he was succeeded by Marc Bohan, another protégé of Dior hired to head the London outlet shortly before the founder's death. Bohan would go on to serve Dior until 1989, far longer than the founder. *Contemporary Fashion*'s Rebecca Arnold credited Bohan with keeping the House of Dior "at the forefront of fashion while still producing wearable, elegant clothes," and *Women's Wear Daily*, not surprisingly, claimed that he "rescued the firm."

Troubles at Dior's parent company, Boussac, would visit drastic change on the maison de couture in the 1980s. The roots of the problems reached back to the 1970s. Still owned and led by its octogenarian founder (known as "King Cotton" in his home nation), Group Boussac had by this time grown to encompass 65 textile mills and 17,000 employees. Despite its size, several imperatives of the maturing industry—consolidation, competition from imports, the shift to synthetics—had knocked Boussac from the top of France's fabric heap to a struggling number five by 1971. Reluctant to close money-losing plants and lay off workers, King Cotton did little to prevent his textile operations from suffering heavy losses in the 1970s. Money generated by his remaining one-third share of Dior helped to prop up the Boussac group for several years, and the parent company raised millions by selling its stake in Dior Perfumes. In 1981, the government-owned Institute de Development Industriel took control of the insolvent company, infusing FFr 1 billion (almost $200 million) in the company from 1982 to

Key Dates:

1941: Christian Dior becomes design assistant for Lucien Lélong.
1946: Backed by Marcel Boussac, Dior launches his own fashion house.
1947: Debut of Dior's "New Look" line revolutionizes women's fashion.
1948: Company launches Christian Dior Perfumes.
1949: Dior opens first boutique in New York.
1950: Company begins licensing Dior name.
1952: Company opens London boutique.
1957: Christian Dior dies of a heart attack.
1958: Yves Saint Laurent becomes lead designer for Dior, launching his own career.
1984: Bernard Arnault acquires failed Boussac group—including control of Christian Dior—for one franc.
1990: Christian Dior acquires controlling share of Moët Hennessy Louis Vuitton, founding the LVMH luxury goods empire; begins cutting back number of Dior licenses.
1996: Arnault names John Galliano as lead designer in order to revive Christian Dior image.
1997: Dior buys back control of its ready-to-wear line and retail chain, including 13 stores in Japan.
2001: Hedi Slimane is named to create new men's fashion line; company launches new retail concept, Christian Dior Haute Joaillerie.

1985. When Boussac finally went bankrupt, a group of investors led by Bernard Arnault acquired it for "one symbolic franc" in December 1984. The 34-year-old Arnault divested the textile group's industrial operations, focusing on its Bon Marché department store and Christian Dior.

Evolution into a Luxury Powerhouse in the 1980s

Under Arnault, Dior became the cornerstone of one of the world's largest and most important fashion companies. The new leader formed Christian Dior S.A. as a holding company for the fashion house, then used the holding company as a vehicle to purchase a controlling stake in Moët Hennessy Louis Vuitton (LVMH) in 1990. (His Au Bon Marché and Financière Agache companies were also involved in the complex acquisitions.) Before long, Arnault had woven an intricate web of high-end brands, including the Christian Lacroix and Celine fashion houses; the Hubert de Givenchy fashion and fragrance operations; and the Dior fragrance business. By 1991, when Arnault sold a minority stake in Dior on the public market, LVMH had grown to become France's top luxury goods group and its second largest publicly traded firm.

Dubbed "king of luxury goods" by *Time,* Arnault took part in the supervision of Dior's design direction as well as its operations. Though the couture division was by this time an unprofitable operation, Arnault considered it a fundamental element of the Dior brand cachet. In 1989, he hired Italian designer Gianfranco Ferré to succeed Marc Bohan as the maison's artistic director. In keeping with his standing as the first non-Frenchman to guide the house, Ferré broke from the romantic and flirtatious traditions set by Dior and Bohan, respectively, opting instead to continue in his own well-established vein with a collection described by Kevin Almond in *Contemporary Fashion* as "refined, sober and strict."

Arnault even served as managing director of Dior from the December 1990 firing of Beatrice Bongibault to September 1991, when he hired former Au Bon Marché President Philippe Vindry. Vindry's strategies included a 10 percent average reduction in the retail price of Dior prêt à porter. (A wool suit still cost more than $1,500.) The change helped increase sales at Dior's headquarters store by 50 percent from 1990 to 1991. Vindry also reorganized Dior into three divisions: women's ready-to-wear (also encompassing lingerie and childrenswear), accessories and jewelry, and menswear. Management also strove to rein in internal management of the Dior brand and image by reducing licensees and franchised boutiques. Arnault and Vindry nearly halved the number of Dior licensees from 280 in 1989 to less than 150 by 1992, opting for quality and exclusivity over quantity and accessibility. By mid-decade, Christian Dior S.A. had added company-owned stores in Hong Kong, Singapore, Kuala Lumpur, Cannes, and Waikiki to its core shops in New York, Hawaii, Paris, and Geneva. This strategy held out the potential to increase direct sales and profit margins while maintaining high-profile locations. François Baufume, who succeeded Vindry as managing director of Dior Couture in 1993, continued to reduce licensees, which numbered around 120 by mid-decade.

Christian Dior Couture's sales increased from FFr 673 million ($129.3 million) in 1990 to just over FFr 1 billion ($177 million) in 1995, while net income grew from FFr 115 million ($22 million) to FFr 156 million ($26.9 million).

New Designer to Lead House in the Late 1990s

In 1996, Arnault "ruffled some French feathers" by appointing British designer John Galliano to succeed Gianfranco Ferré as Dior's head. Arnault noted that while he "would have preferred Frenchmen," he chose a Briton "for a very simple reason: talent has no nationality." The CEO even compared maison Dior's newest designer to the founder in a December 1996 *Women's Wear Daily* article, noting that "Galliano has a creative talent very close to that of Christian Dior. He has the same extraordinary mixture of romanticism, feminism, and modernity that symbolizes Mr. Dior. In all of his creations—his suits, his dresses—one finds similarities to the Dior style."

Galliano was instrumental in reviving Dior's image— stirring up continued controversy with such events as a "homeless show," featuring models dressed in newspapers and paper bags, and an "S&M show." The resulting controversy helped stimulate sales of Dior clothing, as well as accessories and perfumes. Meanwhile, President and CEO Sidney Toledano continued trimming away at the company's list of licensees, taking control of the ready-to-wear clothing and accessories bearing the Christian Dior brand name. Dior also adopted a policy of taking control of the Dior franchise- and licensed retail network, buying up 13 stores from Japan's Kanebo in 1997, and acquiring its Spanish distributor in 1998, among others. The company began opening new stores, boosting its chain of retail boutiques to 130 by 2002.

Christian Dior Couture had built its fame on women's fashions. But in 2001 the company gambled that it could become equally famous for its men's fashion. In that year the company hired Hedi Slimane, who, at age 32, had already gained famed as a designer for Yves Saint Laurent. Slimane's first show in January 2001 was an instant success and the company quickly noted among its customers such luminaries as Mick Jagger and Brad Pitt. In that year, also, the company launched a new retail concept, Christian Dior Haute Joaillerie, under the artistic direction of Victoire de Castellane, in an effort to lend the Christian Dior prestige to its luxury jewelry market. These efforts helped the division's sales begin to climb, nearing EUR 300 million in 2000 and topping EUR 350 million by 2001. By then, Christian Dior Couture had beat the odds, reviving its image and reclaiming its place as one of the world's most innovative fashion houses.

Principal Subsidiaries

Christian Dior S.A. has more than 600 subsidiaries worldwide.

Principal Competitors

Bulgari S.p.A.; Cartier SA; Chanel S.A.; Gianfranco Ferre SpA; Gianni Versace SpA; Gucci Group N.V.; Hermès International; I Pellettieri d'Italia S.p.A.; LVMH Inc. (U.S.); Montres Rolex S.A.; Puig Beauty & Fashion Group; Compagnie Financière Richemont AG; S.T. Dupont S.A.; Tiffany & Co.

Further Reading

Adler, Jerry, "The Riches of Rags," *Newsweek,* December 16, 1996, p. 77.

Cattani, Jane, "Dior Lives," *Harper's Bazaar,* December 1996, pp. 195–98.

Deeny, Godfrey, "François Baufume: Directing Dior," *Women's Wear Daily,* February 28, 1995, pp. 6–7.

——, "A New Dior Taking Shape Under Vindry," *Women's Wear Daily,* October 28, 1992, pp. 1–3.

Duffy, Martha, "The Pope of Fashion," *Time,* April 21, 1997, pp. 112–13.

Goldstein Lauren, "Born Again Christians: Is There Room in the House of Dior for Two Very Strong Yet Vastly Dissimilar Fashion Designers?," *Time International,* February 19, 2001, pp. 54 + .

Jacobs, Laura, "Dior's Couture D'Etat," *Vanity Fair,* November 1996, pp. 92–97.

Kurzwell, Allen, "Dior: 40 Years of Triumph," *Harper's Bazaar,* September 1987, pp. 152–53.

Lichfield, John, "Half Man, Half Label," *Independent,* December 6, 2000, p. 1.

Lowthorpe, Rebecca, "Deconstructing Galliano: The Man Behind Dior Puts His Work On," *Independent,* July 27, 2001, p. 9.

Middleton, William, and Kevin West, "In Arnault's Worlds, Luxury and the Future Are Keys to Empire," *Women's Wear Daily,* December 9, 1996, pp. 1–4.

Pochna, Marie-France, *Christian Dior: The Man Who Made the World Look New,* New York: Arcade Publishing, 1996.

de Réthy, Esmeralda, and Perreau, Jean-Louis, *Christian Dior: The Early Years 1947–1957,* Vendome Press: New York: 2002

—April Dougal Gasbarre
—update: M.L. Cohen

Computer Associates International, Inc.

One Computer Associates Plaza
Islandia, New York 11788-7000
U.S.A.
Telephone: (516) 342-6000
Toll Free: (800) 225-5224
Fax: (516) 342-6800
Web site: http://www.ca.com

Public Company
Incorporated: 1976
Employees: 17,000
Sales: $4.19 billion (2001)
Stock Exchanges: New York
Ticker Symbol: CA
NAIC: 511210 Software Publishers

Computer Associates International, Inc. (CA) is one of the largest computer software vendors in the world. The company sells over 1,200 different products, most of which are designed for businesses rather than home computer users. Because the majority of its products are behind-the-scenes workhorses designed to help big computer networks function, CA's specialty is often called ''plumbing'' in the software industry. Approximately half of the company's revenue derives from products associated with mainframe computers. CA is the market leader in designing software for managing corporate networks. The company also has a large share of the market for data security and data storage. Other products manage data for wireless networks and run Internet applications. Over 95 percent of *Fortune* 500 companies use CA software. The company grew enormously through acquisitions, buying up some 60 companies in its first 20 years. Founder Charles Wang gave up the chief executive position in 2000, but remains chairman of the board.

Software's Potential in the 1970s

Computer Associates was founded in 1976 by Charles Wang. Born in Shanghai, Wang moved with his family to the United States in 1952 when he was eight years old. His father had been educated at Harvard and was a supreme court justice

in Shanghai, but had to start over in the United States. The family settled in Queens in New York City, and the elder Wang eventually became a law professor. Two of the sons also studied law, while Charles studied math and physics at Queens College. After his graduation in 1967, Wang took a job as a trainee computer programmer. Though he had little background in the field, Wang took an instant liking to programming. At this time, large, expensive mainframes were the most important computers, and the software industry barely existed. IBM, which sold most mainframes, included basic software in their price, and all customized programming was done in-house. In 1969, the U.S. government began requiring that software be sold separately, allowing individual entrepreneurs to offer competition.

After his first trainee job, Wang worked for a small computer service bureau in New York City that marketed software for the Swiss company Computer Associates (CA). When CA decided to establish its own business in the United States, Wang saw an opportunity and in 1976 began Computer Associates International as a joint venture with the Swiss company. With only two partners and a tiny Manhattan office, Wang limited himself to marketing software by telephone. The company was at first funded only by Wang's various credit cards. After an initial failure, he succeeded with CA-SORT, a program enabling computers to sort through data quickly and economically. Wang's SORT offered competition to a similar IBM program, and Wang convinced many businesses with IBM hardware to change over to CA's product. Mainframe software was licensed rather than sold, and the recurring revenue from the licenses of the SORT software was a great boost to Computer Associates.

Computer Associates began expanding, hiring salespeople and programmers, and in 1978 Wang's brother Tony, a lawyer, joined the firm. Sales of SORT generated enough money for Wang to buy new programs from smaller firms and market them to customers who already owned SORT. Wang's success allowed him to buy out the original Swiss company in 1980. The company went public in 1981.

Expansion Through Acquisitions in the 1980s

Computer Associates grew rapidly through acquisitions, buying Capex in 1982 for $22 million in a stock swap. Capex, which was half of CA's size, sold support software for programmers. In 1983, Wang purchased Stewart P. Orr Associates for $2 million and Information Unlimited Software for $10 million. He continued two years later, acquiring Sorcim for $27 million, Johnson Systems for $16 million, and Arkay Computer for an undisclosed amount. With these purchases, Computer Associates became the top independent vendor of system utilities, with a continuing specialization in data compression. In 1985, CA paid CGA Computer $25 million for Top Secret, a computer-security program. Although critics maintained that Wang had paid too much for the program, which had sales of $10 million a year, Wang saw great potential in the product, and sold $36 million worth of Top Secret in the first year after the acquisition. His purchases also brought some software for personal computers, which was the fastest-growing segment of the computer market.

CA's main focus at this time was on products designed to improve the performance of IBM equipment. Each time IBM upgraded its computers, it kept portions of old designs so customers could continue to run their older programs; as a result, IBM mainframes were powerful but inefficient. This market presented a particular opportunity for CA because IBM did not make an effort to market products that pointed out defects in its computers; therefore Computer Associates did not have to compete against IBM's larger resources.

The firm also continued to attempt to break into applications software, which was earning firms like Microsoft Corporation and Lotus Development Corporation huge sums of money in the personal computer market. It made an important move into applications in 1986 with the $67 million purchase of Integrated System Software Corp., which specialized in graphics software. It also purchased Software International, a maker of financial applications, for $24 million. Despite this new applications strength, system utilities still accounted for 70 percent of Computer Associates' revenues in 1986.

In 1987, Computer Associates made its largest purchase yet, acquiring rival Uccel for about $830 million in stock. Uccel had been a competitor in the market for systems utilities software, so the purchase strengthened Computer Associates' already strong systems utilities sector, adding 7,500 customers to CA's base of 26,000 while eliminating a rival company. The purchase temporarily made CA the largest independent software company, ahead of Microsoft, whose strengths lay in software for personal computers. CA also had far more products, marketing about 200 kinds of software to Microsoft's 26 and Lotus's 15.

Uccel software filled in several gaps in CA's systems utility product line, but excessive product overlap required a growth strategy involving relentless cost-cutting to maximize profits. CA dismissed 25 percent of Uccel's staff of 1,200 within five days of receiving approval for the deal from the Justice Department. Although some analysts criticized CA throughout its history for focusing on acquisitions at the expense of developing its own programs, Wang's continued pursuit of market share through acquisitions increased his firm's sales from $450 million in 1986 to $628.8 million in 1987. Most of the 13 percent of sales it spent on research and development went to improving its newly acquired software.

By 1988, Computer Associates employed 4,500 people in 22 countries and reported $842.1 million in sales. To service its 30,000 customers, which included most *Fortune* 500 companies, CA had a worldwide sales force of 1,200, with an additional 1,400 in sales support. This high salesperson-to-customer ratio allowed salespeople to concentrate on a few clients; nevertheless, the company received poor ratings for customer satisfaction. Customers brought in by the acquisitions complained of difficulty in finding the right person at CA to answer questions and of CA representatives who appeared to be more interested in making sales than providing support.

CA's acquisitions had brought it financial strength and a broad range of software. Its SuperCalc spreadsheet application, bought in 1984, led the company into competition with Lotus and its 1-2-3 spreadsheet, which had become the best-selling software in the personal computer market. Easywriter, a word-processing program bought in 1983, also brought CA strength in the personal computer market. Due to rapid technical advances that made them increasingly powerful, sales of smaller computers grew more quickly than those of mainframes, an aid to Computer Associates. The firm's utilities helped customers squeeze more efficiency from their existing mainframes, and system software such as utilities still accounted for about 75 percent of company revenue. Hoping to lessen its dependency on systems software, CA announced that it would expand applications software to about one-third of its business.

Computer Associates acquired another maker of database management software in late 1988, buying Applied Data Research, Inc. for $170 million from Ameritech. CA temporarily ceased its acquisitions in 1989 following the purchase of Cullinet Software Inc. for $289 million. Cullinet sold database management systems, and CA hoped to use the firm's products to help its applications run on IBM, Digital Equipment, and Unix systems. But some of Cullinet's software competed with software Computer Associates already offered, forcing some customers to delay purchasing decisions until CA made it clear which software it would be continuing to offer.

Soon after the purchase, CA terminated about 900 Cullinet positions. The absorption of Cullinet, along with need for internal streamlining (the assignments of CA's 600 U.S. salespeople had begun to overlap, with up to four representatives servicing one account), necessitated a corporate reorganization. Simultaneously, mainframe and minicomputer sales slacked off, hurting the market for programs. With the acquisition of Uccel and Cullinet, Computer Associates became the first software firm to top $1 billion in sales, in 1989. As a result of its mounting

Key Dates:

1976: Charles Wang and partners start CA International as a joint venture with the Swiss firm Computer Associates (CA).
1980: Wang and partners buy the Swiss parent company.
1981: The firm goes public.
1987: CA International acquires rival Uccel for $830 million.
1995: CA International acquires Virginia-based competitor Legent for $1.78 billion.
2000: Founder Wang resigns as CEO.

problems, however, CA's growth dropped from 45 percent in 1989 to 6 percent in 1990, and its stock price dropped 50 percent.

Computer Associates was again sharply criticized for a lack of focus after the Cullinet deal. CA responded by unveiling Computing Architecture 1990s in April 1990, a software strategy intended to bring some order to the group of software products it had acquired during the past decade. The plan had three major components: database management, systems management, and applications. The firm vowed to make all of its programs work together and "talk" to each other across different types of computer hardware and operating systems. This type of networking was increasingly important in the computer industry, with networks of smaller computers displacing mainframes. The Computing Architecture 1990s system, which used software intermediaries to connect different types of computer systems, applying them like telephone switches, was made possible in part by CA Datacom/DB, a widely installed database management system the firm acquired with Applied Data Research in 1988. To help the plan along, Computer Associates spent $190 million on research and development in 1990.

In combination with the Computing Architecture 1990s plan, Wang spent 1990 refocusing his 7,000 employees on product development and customer service. Programmers worked overtime to update older programs and boost customer confidence. Supercalc 5, released in 1990, included graphics and database management, making it competitive with Lotus 1-2-3 and Microsoft Excel. CA-Cricket Presents was a desktop presentation package that sold for half the price of competitors like Aldus Persuasion and Microsoft PowerPoint. CA-Textor, released in 1992, was an entry-level word processor designed to work with Microsoft's Windows graphic interface. Despite numerous programs for personal computers, Computer Associates suffered from anonymity in the personal computer market, with Supercalc attaining only about a 5 percent share of the spreadsheet market.

New Products and Markets in the 1990s

Computer Associates pushed aggressively into foreign markets, notably Canada and Japan, and overseas sales accounted for 40 to 45 percent of annual revenues. CA became more flexible in pricing its annual maintenance fees for updating and troubleshooting software. These fees comprised 33 percent of revenues, up from 20 percent four years earlier. Despite this

increased flexibility, the firm's pricing policies were controversial, angering some because of the tough stand taken on prices when a client changed the way it used CA software.

Continuing its push to work with different computer platforms, CA agreed in 1991 to make many of its products work with Hewlett-Packard's Unix-based computers and reached a licensing agreement with Apple Computer to allow its databases to be accessed through Apple's Macintosh computers. It also bought a number of software vendors including Access Technology, whose software worked on Vax systems made by Digital Equipment. Computer Associates acquired On-Line Software International Inc. for about $120 million and Pansophic Systems Inc. for about $290 million, both mainframe software manufacturers. Sales for 1991 came to $1.35 billion.

Computer Associates' ambitious restructuring was hindered in a legal dispute with rival Electronic Data Systems Corporation (EDS) beginning in 1991. EDS accused Computer Associates of unfair business practices including monopoly and licensing fraud, breach of contract, and misuse of copyright. In early 1992, CA countersued, accusing EDS of pirating its software and wide-scale fraud. The dispute was not settled until 1996.

Bitter feelings toward CA were evidently common among its customers, yet the company had a vast array of extremely useful products, and so the company was hard to avoid. In 1995, the company announced a deal worth $1.78 billion to acquire its competitor Legent Corporation, a Virginia-based software maker. This was at the time the biggest takeover deal ever in the software industry. Legent's strength was in so-called client-server computer software, where instead of a large, powerful mainframe, a network of computers interacted through software stored in a central server computer. CA had made a move toward client-server computing two years earlier, bringing out a new product called CA-Unicenter. CA had also bought another client-server software specialist in 1994, the ASK Group. It also acquired Cheyenne Software Inc. in 1996, a company that specialized in data storage software on network computers. By the mid-1990s, about one-third of CA's sales were in client-server software products. The company's revenue grew to over $3.5 billion in 1996, and earnings and CA's stock price also rose year by year through the first half of the decade.

By the late 1990s, the company was still growing, yet it faced new problems. One was that it was more difficult for CA to keep acquiring smaller companies. The Justice Department had put conditions on the company's further takeovers after the huge Legent deal. In addition, CA's stock price tended to yo-yo, fueled in part by Wall Street analysts' concerns that the company bought up firms with mature products and then squeezed money out of them, rather than looking for emerging products from young competitors. Moreover, though CA made a major effort beginning in the mid-1990s to turn around its reputation for poor customer service, a survey in 2001 showed only 10 percent of large customers were satisfied with CA. CA had a 25 percent share of the mainframe computer software market by the late 1990s, only one point behind market leader IBM, yet the mainframe market was expanding only very slowly. The company relaunched its premier client-server software in 1997, Unicenter TNG, hoping for more of the booming network market.

Despite growing revenue, CA continued to hit bumps in the late 1990s and into the new millennium. A slowdown in its European markets and the economic slump in Asia affected company earnings. Charles Wang, second-in-command Sanjay Kumar, and another top executive were given huge bonuses in 1998, for which the company had to take a $675 million charge against earnings to pay. In 2000, a court order required the executives to pay back about half the bonus, some $550 million. CA had made two additional large acquisitions in 1999 and 2000, shelling out for software maker Platinum and then Sterling Software. The company now had a huge amount of debt, almost three times earnings. In August 2000, Charles Wang agreed to step out of the CEO role and not handle the day-to-day business of the company. He remained chairman, and the CEO job went to former President Sanjay Kumar. Kumar vowed to grow the company without more acquisitions, though this seemed difficult to do. He was perhaps more popular than the gruff Wang, and he personally intervened in 2001 when Wal-Mart Stores declared it would stop using CA software. Nevertheless, investors seemed dissatisfied with CA's prospects, and the board faced a proxy battle in the summer of 2001. Management's picks remained on the board, but the company faced further criticism. It had changed its accounting method in October 2000 in order to even out profit and revenue from long-term contracts. The company ended up with two sets of numbers, which was confusing, and in 2002 the Securities and Exchange Commission was prompted to investigate CA's book-keeping. CA planned a $1 billion bond offering in February 2002 that would have refinanced some of the company's $3.5 billion debt to a more favorable rate. But the day before the bond offering, the investor's service Moody's declared it was considering downgrading CA's debt rating, citing a tightening cash flow, and CA canceled the offering. By 2002, the company had over 1,200 software products, and was still the leader in several key markets.

Principal Subsidiaries

interBiz; iCanSP; ACCPac; CA Federal; MultiGen-Paradigm.

Principal Competitors

International Business Machines Corporation; Microsoft Corporation; BMC Software Inc.

Further Reading

Barry, Dan, "Computer Mogul Refines His Game," *New York Times*, February 4, 1997, pp. B1, B6.

Byrne, John, "How Executive Greed Cost Shareholders $675 Million," *Business Week*, August 10, 1998, p. 29.

Carroll, Paul B., "Computer Associates to Unveil Strategy to Bring Order to Its Software Products," *Wall Street Journal*, April 30, 1990.

Cortese, Amy, "Sexy? No. Profitable? You Bet," *Business Week*, November 11, 1996, pp. 88–98.

Feder, Barnaby J., "The Migrations of Behemoth's Soul and Software," *New York Times*, August 16, 1992.

Field, Anne R., "Computer Associates Buys Its Way to the Top," *Business Week*, June 15, 1987.

Guidera, Jerry, "As Computer Associates Kills $1 Billion Deal, It Jabs Moody's," *Wall Street Journal*, February 8, 2002, pp. C1, C4.

——, "Computer Associates Won't Alter Methods," *Wall Street Journal*, February 25, 2002, pp. A3, A6.

Hafner, Katherine M., "How Computer Associates Climbed to No. 1 in Software," *Business Week*, July 11, 1988.

Hamm, Steve, "A Long Climb Out of a Deep Rut," *Business Week*, February 25, 2002, p. 124.

——, "No Way to Run a Software Giant," *Business Week*, July 17, 2000, p. 46.

——, "You Call That Change?," *Business Week*, August 21–August 28, 2000, p. 52.

Lubove, Seth, "A Pain in the Posterior?," *Forbes*, May 18, 1998, p. 98.

Markoff, John, "Ruling May Restrict Copyrights for Software," *New York Times*, June 24, 1992.

Miller, Michael W., "Computer Associates Disarms Its Critics," *Wall Street Journal*, April 28, 1989.

Schwartz, Evan I., "Computer Associates Gets User-Friendly," *Business Week*, January 21, 1991.

——, "Faulty Vision," *Business Week*, July 30, 1990.

Slutsker, Gary, "Charles Wang and His Thundering Nerds," *Forbes*, July 11, 1988.

Teitelbaum, Richard, "Tough Guys Finish First," *Fortune*, July 21, 1997, p. 82.

Zuckerman, Laurence, "$1.78 Billion Legent Deal Will Create Software Giant," *New York Times*, May 26, 1995, pp. D1, D3.

—Scott M. Lewis
—update: A. Woodward

Corus Group plc

30 Millbank
London SW1P 4WY
United Kingdom
Telephone: (+44) 20-7717-4444
Fax: (+44) 20-7717-4455
Web site: http://www.corusgroup.com

Public Company
Incorporated: 1967 as the British Steel Corporation
Employees: 64,900
Sales: $17.49 billion (2000)
Stock Exchanges: London New York Amsterdam
Ticker Symbols: CS (London, Amsterdam); CGA (New York)
NAIC: 331111 Iron and Steel Mills

Corus Group plc, one of the largest steel companies in Europe, came into being in 1999 with the merger of British Steel plc and Dutch steelmaker Koninklijke Nederlandsche Hoogovens en Staalfabrieken NV. The company manufactures, processes, and distributes metals products to the construction, automotive, mechanical engineering, packaging, and other markets—primarily in Europe. The bulk of its production facilities are in the United Kingdom, but it also has a presence in The Netherlands, Germany, France, Belgium, the United States, and Canada. The company's products include coated and uncoated steel strip products, sections and plates, tubular products, engineering steels, wire rods, stainless steel, and carbon steel products. Corus also operates a significant aluminum business; as of early 2002, however, the company was planning to sell its aluminum-related units.

Early History and Development

The company is the successor, by way of the state-owned British Steel Corporation (BSC), of the leading private steel companies that survived the Depression of the 1920s and 1930s and World War II. Under the Labour government of 1945 to 1951 these companies first profited from the large compensation payments they received for giving up their coal mining interests to the state and then were nationalized themselves, on the grounds that they formed an oligopoly with the power to restrict output, raise prices, and prevent technical progress. The Iron and Steel Corporation of Great Britain was established in 1950 as a state holding company for their shares, but the steelmasters retained the initiative, mainly through a boycott organized by the British Iron and Steel Federation (BISF), the industry's trade association, which they controlled.

In the autumn of 1951 a new Conservative government suspended the corporation's activities after eight months of mostly ineffective existence. Between 1953 and 1963 an Iron and Steel Holding and Realisation Agency sold off 16 of the 17 nationalized firms, mostly to the former shareholders. At the same time an Iron Steel Board was given the negative powers of fixing maximum prices for products sold in the United Kingdom and approving or rejecting any investment of more than £100,000. Price control was nothing new, having begun on a more modest scale in 1932, with the result by the 1950s that losses during low points of the economic cycle could not be offset by higher profits in more prosperous times. The companies' reluctance to invest intensified, and the Iron and Steel Board—or rather the taxpayers who financed it—became the major source of new investment funds.

During the 1950s and 1960s the British steel industry lost its historic advantages of cheap coal and plentiful iron ore, the industry's basic raw materials. Coal prices rose by 134 percent between 1950 and 1967, and the domestic iron ore industry was neglected in favor of ore from new fields overseas. Rearmament, from 1950 onward, caused the company to retain old plants, instead of investing in costly new plants, in the attempt to keep up with demand. Between 1945 and 1960 total crude steel production in the United Kingdom doubled in volume, an increase attributable in large part to such technical innovations as oxygen-based production and continuous casting. The claim that the industry had now been taken out of politics was belied by the events of 1958 and 1959, when the Conservative prime minister, Harold Macmillan, sanctioned not the single extra strip mill the industry wanted, but two, one at Llanwern in Wales and another at Ravenscraig in Scotland, both subsidized from public funds and neither able to operate at full capacity.

The British steel industry's problems, however, were not all due to the government or the companies. It faced new rivals,

Company Perspectives:

Corus aims to be an innovative company with a strong customer focus, providing metal solutions to an increasingly sophisticated marketplace. The Corus strategy is targeted at creating shareholder value by achieving world class competitiveness through operating excellence and technological advance. The emphasis is on achieving leading positions in attractive market sectors where sustainable growth can be achieved.

especially in Japan, as well as old ones, in France, West Germany, Belgium, and Luxembourg, which were now protected by the European Coal and Steel Community and some of which were blessed with deep-water harbors taking in high-grade ores. In addition, there was a general fall in the rate of growth of world demand for steel from about 1960, leading to declining prices and profits for the steel industry worldwide, a scramble to dispose of surplus output at the lowest sustainable prices, and a worldwide steel glut that lasted until 1969. The British industry in particular continued to be marked by a cautious attitude learned in the 1920s and never shaken off and by the refusal of the individual firms to cooperate with one another in anything that might threaten their own identities. The steel industry faced the 1960s with a fragmented structure based on investment decisions that, apart from the establishment of the Ravenscraig mill, had been made in the 1930s.

Re-Nationalization Under Labour in the Mid-1960s

In 1964 the Labour Party returned to office with a commitment to re-nationalize steel. The BISF's response was the Benson report, which concluded that the industry needed to go over entirely to the basic oxygen process, to build extra capacity in much larger plants, to site them near the coasts (for raw materials supplies), and to shed 65 percent of existing plant space and 100,000 workers. These proposals gave the government new ammunition, since in spite of the companies' claims that they could provide most of the necessary capital from their falling profits, it was clear that the industry alone could not hope to finance these developments. The nationalized British Steel Corporation (BSC) began operations on July 28, 1967, just when new orders were at their lowest level in five years, and in a period of mergers among companies in France, Germany, and Japan. At its inception BSC was the second largest steel company in the non-communist world, endowed with the assets of the 14 crude steel companies, whose output exceeded 475,000 tons. They employed 268,500 people and included Richard Thomas & Baldwins, a company that had remained in state ownership since 1951.

BSC faced some formidable problems. First, since compensation to the former owners was based on stock market values, and not—as in private mergers and acquisitions—on net assets or future profitability, the shareholders received about £350 million more than the assets were worth. A later Conservative government recognized the loss to BSC and wrote off that amount of its debt in 1972. In addition, the 14 companies' return on capital had fallen from 15 percent in 1956 to 3.7 percent, making them unable to carry out the Benson plan they had commissioned, and the sorry state of their assets was bound to

damage BSC's profitability for some time to come. In addition, 10 percent of crude steel production and about 30 percent of finished steel production remained in the private sector, leaving BSC with the generally less profitable bulk steel and lower-quality finished steel business. As the private firms were effectively subsidized through the controls on BSC's pricing of crude steel sold to them, they could concentrate resources on technical advances that allowed higher productivity, giving them about a third of the market for finished steel, with only a quarter of total capacity, by the late 1970s. In this respect BSC was unlike its major rivals abroad, which were diversified within steel and across other sectors. Finally, BSC's capital consisted of £834 million, to be repaid to the Treasury at a fixed rate of interest, regardless of its profit cycle. Between 1967 and 1980 BSC's interest payments were equivalent to 73 percent of its losses. A private sector company in the same situation would not have been burdened with interest payments.

Unlike other public corporations BSC had been given the freedom to decide organizational questions for itself. Its structure was regionally based until 1970, divided into six product divisions until 1976, configured on a different geographical basis until 1980, and then redivided into different product divisions with numerous profit centers within them and linked to a new system of mostly self-financing local bonus schemes for the workers.

One unique aspect of BSC's organization was the presence of worker-directors, first on the boards of the regional groups, then on the boards of the product divisions, and last, after 1976, on the main board. The steel industry long had enjoyed a comparably good record in industrial relations. The relatively few strikes in the industry's history had usually been over demarcation among the trade unions, of which there were 17 in the industry in 1967, and among which the Iron and Steel Trades Confederation (ISTC) was dominant, containing half of the 80 percent of the workforce that belonged to unions. It was the ISTC that felt most threatened by change, since it would tend to cut into the union's base among the less skilled workers. The part-time worker-directors were appointed after consultations with these unions and with the Trades Union Congress (TUC), the national labor federation. Since the management retained its monopoly of information and authority, the influence of these unelected representatives was minimal, ceasing altogether with their abolition in 1983, three years after the defeat of the national steelworkers' strike had signaled the end of the trade unions' influence in the company. In 1970 and 1971 the new Conservative government at first considered various ways of breaking up or partially privatizing BSC, then decided to continue with the status quo while raising the corporation's borrowing limits and giving some flexibility on pricing. BSC later announced that with British steel prices held below European Community levels from 1967 to 1975 the losses amounted to about £780 million, representing another indirect subsidy to the private sector, in this case to steel consumers.

BSC in the 1970s

The corporation initiated its "heritage program" in 1971 and 1972 to develop the strengths and overcome the weaknesses of the assets inherited from the private companies, in particular the low productivity of blast furnaces, which was due to inefficient cooling and the use of such low-grade material as coking

Key Dates:

1918: A group of manufacturers in The Netherlands establish a national iron and steel business, Koninklijke Nederlandsche Hoogovens en Staalfabrieken NV.

1924: Hoogovens first begins producing pig iron.

1928: Hoogovens launches a fertilizer factory, Mekog.

1930: Hoogovens establishes a cement factory.

1939: Hoogovens begins producing steel.

1950: Hoogovens establishes Breedband NV, a subsidiary that produced hot strip, cold band, and tinning materials; The Iron and Steel Corporation of Great Britain is established as a state-owned holding company for newly nationalized steel companies that had formerly been in the private sector.

1953: Great Britain begins re-privatizing its steel companies, selling them off primarily to former shareholders.

1958: Hoogovens opens its oxysteel factory, which employed a new production method.

1967: Great Britain again nationalizes its steel industry, forming the British Steel Corporation.

1972: Hoogovens joins with German steelmaker Hoesch Dortmund to form Estel, the fourth largest steel company in Europe.

Early 1980s: Hoogovens dissolves its joint venture with Hoesch Dortmund.

1987: Hoogovens expands its aluminum division; the British government announces plans to privatize British Steel Corporation.

1988: Hoogovens sells off all businesses but those pertaining to aluminum and steel; British Steel Corporation is privatized as British Steel plc.

1995: British Steel announces plans to expand in Latin America, central Europe, and Asia.

1997: British Steel builds its first steelmaking facility outside the United Kingdom, in Alabama; it begins a program of job reductions to keep costs down.

1999: British Steel and Hoogovens merge, forming Corus Group.

2000: Corus merges its stainless steel subsidiary with a Finnish stainless producer to form AvestaPolarit.

2001: Faced with heavy losses and a weak market, Corus announces massive cuts in production and jobs.

2002: Corus announces that it plans to sell its aluminum businesses.

coal with a high sulfur content. By 1973 BSC had invested £764 million in this program and in such new projects as Anchor III, the construction of a new plant at the Appleby-Frodingham complex in Scunthorpe, Lincolnshire, on the site of abandoned ironstone workings. At the nearby port of Immingham, a terminal was built to accommodate 100,000-ton vessels bringing foreign ore for the furnaces. The opening of the plant only three years after the scheme was authorized seemed to bode well for BSC's increased efficiency, and helped accelerate the trend whereby imported ores rose from 55 percent of the total used in the United Kingdom in 1967 to 85 percent in 1974.

By 1973 British steel consumption had exceeded 18 million tons a year. The ten-year development strategy started in 1973 envisaged concentration of resources on five inherited sites, and on a new sixth complex in Teesside. Some £3 billion—half from BSC, half from the taxpayers—were to be spent on raising capacity and on shutting down older plants, with the loss of at least 50,000 jobs—in other words, a slightly revised version of the BISF's Benson report. BSC also did something that the steelmasters had never done; it created a subsidiary, BSC (Industry) Ltd. in 1975, to invest in new nonsteel ventures in areas where its closure program would hit hardest.

The development strategy committed the government, BSC, and the country to the largest capital investment program in British history. Also in 1973, the United Kingdom joined the European Community, where excess capacity in steel was already at the highest level in the world and where BSC could no longer rely on an 8 percent tariff to keep European imports out. Then came a worldwide slump, caused by the Arab oil embargo and the ensuing energy crisis. The collapse of demand for steel during 1975 caused BSC to accelerate its closure program, after a public fight over the issue with the Labour government and, in

1977, to give up the ten-year strategy in favor of aiming for 30 million tons by 1982.

Operating Under Conservative Policies in the 1980s

The Conservative government elected in 1979 at first announced that no more money would be available for BSC. Then in 1980, when BSC's losses rose to £545 million, the government increased its borrowing limit once again, while the board announced that 60,000 jobs would be cut within 12 months. The 13-week national strike that followed, the first in the steel industry since 1926, cut deeper into BSC's profits as imports rose to fill the gap it caused.

In 1980 and 1981 the Conservative government abolished the BSC's statutory duties to promote the supply of iron and steel and to further the public interest, took new powers to direct BSC's use of its assets, and wrote off a total of £5 billion of debts. In the next few years BSC regained some lost ground and beat European records for closing plants and making cuts in the workforce, but by 1982 British customers' demand for steel was down to slightly more than 12 million tons, and BSC's share of this market went below 50 percent for the first time. The majority of the private steelmakers also sought state aid and received about £50 million in 1982—more in later years. They benefited as well from the ''Phoenix'' series of joint ventures with BSC, starting in 1981, since they were financed mainly out of public funds.

British Steel plc: Late 1980s and 1990s

In 1986 the chairmanship of BSC passed to Robert Scholey, who had spent his entire career in the industry and whose father was a director of one of the pre-1967 private steel firms. In 1987, with Scholey's full support, the government announced its intention to privatize BSC and the company became British Steel plc in 1988, just before demand for steel began to fall. The new company undertook to keep all five of its main plants open until the end of 1994, subject to market conditions.

British Steel plc's first 18 months were certainly eventful. The company carried out the fourth overhaul of its production structure since 1967, ending up with five divisions—general steels, strip products, stainless steels, distribution, and diversified activities. The company then won the contract to supply rails for the Channel Tunnel, was fined by the European Commission—along with five other steel companies—for participating in an illegal cartel to fix stainless steel prices, acquired the Mannstädt division of the German steel firm Klöckner-Werke, and announced that the hot strip mill at Ravenscraig would be shut down in 1991. It replaced national pay bargaining with divisional and local talks to reinforce the emphasis on productivity and increased total payments to the directors of the company by 78 percent.

The pendulum of ownership of British Steel often led to discussions of its management, yet the act of nationalizing the company seemed to have made little difference to its operations. Even BSC's huge investment program might have been carried out by a public board aiding private firms, as in the 1960s, although BSC's second chairman, Sir Monty Finniston, told the House of Commons Select Committee on Nationalized Industries in 1977: "We would have done nothing if we were in the private sector, absolutely nothing." At the same time the company's history revealed that the act of privatizing did not automatically improve its efficiency or contribute to its economic growth.

Steel production was repeatedly affected by changes in the world economy. Supplies of coal and iron ore were subject to enormous fluctuations in price and volume. The industry had fixed capital costs. Steel was a raw material, with construction accounting for 18.5 percent of British Steel's sales in 1989 and 1990; the motor industry accounting for 14.6 percent of sales; and other manufacturers providing further sales. Fluctuations in the steel industry's economic conditions depended on the demand for its customers' products, not for steel itself. Government intervention, to control prices, protect jobs, promote regional development, and secure self-sufficiency, had been pervasive but inconsistent. Steel production displayed long-term tendencies toward alternating crises of under- and over-production, in what had generally been a four-year cycle. The postwar history of the British steel industry displayed all of these features, and apparently would have done so regardless of ownership.

The company's improved results in the late 1980s, both in and out of state ownership, were due—at least in part—to the growth of the British economy, to the global fall in the prices of raw materials, and to favorable movements on the foreign exchange markets since 1985. Post-tax profit, declared in June 1990 after BSC's first full year in the private sector, was £565 million.

In 1990 iron ore and coal prices moved upward again, while sales of steel in the United Kingdom fell by approximately 10 percent, and the company's own pretax profits fell by 27 percent. The company decided to shut down the Clydesdale seamless tube works, and the chairman stated that running five big integrated plants put the company at a competitive disadvantage.

Foreign Expansion Signaling Growth in the 1990s

In 1992, British Steel merged its stainless steel division with Avesta AB, of Sweden. The following year, the economy in the United Kingdom began to advance and so did demand for steel. By 1994, the company had returned to profitability after two years of heavy losses. In 1995, British Steel announced plans to expand its operations in Latin America, central Europe, and Asia, in the expectation that demand for steel from these emerging markets would persist into the next century. For example, the British Steel Track Products Ltd. unit, which supplied rails and railway infrastructure, was involved in projects in several countries in Latin America, including Brazil, Colombia, and Paraguay. In 1996, the company sold 6,000 tons of rails to Latin America, chiefly in fulfillment of a $3 million contract to supply rails to Peru's state-owned Empresa Nacional de Ferrocarriles. Plans for 1997 included selling 10,000 to 15,000 tons of rails for Brazil's Sao Paulo subway.

In 1997, British Steel built its first steelmaking facility outside the United Kingdom, in Tuscaloosa, Alabama. The unit, Tuscaloosa Steel, was located on the banks of the Black Warrior River and produces plate in coil and cut length form used in the construction, transportation, and energy industries. Some 800,000 tons were expected to be produced annually. In nearby Mobile, British Steel invested in two Direct Reduction Iron units that would produce feedstock for the Tuscaloosa plant and another company unit, Trico Steel, based in Decatur. Trico was British Steel's first steelmaking joint venture in the United States. Its 25 percent stake was part of a $450 million project that produced high quality, light-gauge, hot rolled coil.

In addition to expanding in overseas markets and investing in joint ventures, British Steel sought to maintain profitability by selling units. In 1997, the company sold British Steel Forgings, the unit that supplied forged and machined components to the automotive and aerospace industries, to United Engineering Forgings Ltd. It also began streamlining operations, eliminating redundancies. Between 1997 and mid-1999, the company cut some 7,000 jobs.

At the end of the 1990s, the European steel industry underwent a wave of mergers and acquisitions. This was spurred in part by overcapacity across the industry, which drove steel prices down and made cost efficiencies a prerequisite for profits. The consolidation also was influenced by the advent of the Euro, which served to level the playing field by reducing variations in pricing across country and currency lines.

British Steel, like other steelmakers, had been adversely affected by the soft market. Despite its efforts to cut costs in 1997 and 1998, the company was unable to stay profitable, posting a net loss in 1999. With steel companies across Europe consolidating to stay afloat, it began to appear that British Steel would have to follow suit. In 1999, the company entered merger talks with Koninklijke Hoogovens, a smaller steelmaker based in The Netherlands.

Hoogovens's Early History

Koninklijke Nederlandsche Hoogovens en Staalfabrieken NV (Hoogovens) first came into existence just after World War I and gradually developed into a business specializing in steel and aluminum raw materials and products. As part of the trend in The Netherlands toward self-sufficiency in vitally important products, the idea proposed by a group of prominent manufacturers, led by H.J.E. Wenckebach from 1918 to 1924, took increasingly firm hold. They set out to establish a fully integrated national iron and steel industry capable of converting pig iron into steel products and semi-finished products. It was Wenckebach's vision, reinforced by his wide business experience, that sustained the project.

With the support of major industrialists such as the brothers Stork, owners of a machine factory; J. Muysken, transport; H. Colijn, Royal Dutch/Shell; F.H. Fentener van Vlissingen, Steenkolen Handelsvereniging (SHV); and A.F. Philips, in the incandescent lamps industry, a large part of the capital needed was acquired by subscription. The national interest and considerations of business prestige marked the nexus of personal relations between government officials and financiers. Without the contribution of Dfl 7.5 million from the Dutch state and of Dfl 5 million from the municipality of Amsterdam, the Dfl 30 million required could not have been raised. Participation by the state proved to be of crucial importance in enabling the company to stand up to the powerful competition in Europe. The execution of the major project, a blast furnace, steel, and rolling-mill works, was spread over a lengthy period because of the rapidly rising costs. Not until 1953 was it put into full effect.

Aside from financing, finding a suitable location was a significant strategic problem. The choice fell on the city of Ijmuiden, owing to its favorable seaboard location, symbolized in the emblem of the enterprise, the starfish. In The Netherlands, poor in raw materials, a ready supply of imported iron ore and pit-coal was of vital importance, as was the possibility of easy export. Other locations—near Rotterdam and Moerdijk—were ruled out because of the poor structure of the local soil. The construction of the first blast furnaces, however, still had to wait.

The first step was taken in 1918 in collaboration with the steel manufacturing firm of Demka at Utrecht. In 1920 a contract was concluded with the German steel business of Phoenix in Dortmund, enabling Hoogovens to convert its own pig iron into steel products at another factory. At this stage, Hoogovens was to confine itself to building two blast furnaces. A minority interest in Phoenix ensured a permanent place for Hoogovens within the European steel industry. This interest ran counter to the original plan for an independent basic industry, a conflict mitigated, however, by the resulting transfer of expertise. This dichotomy was to be Hoogovens's persisting paradox.

The production of pig iron in the first furnace began on January 24, 1924, under the control of the technical manager, A.H. Ingen Housz. The director from 1920 to 1945, G.A. Kessler, was faced with the task of placing the business on a sound economic footing. Hoogovens secured a foothold in the pig iron export market by maintaining direct contact with its customers. It could deliver a high-quality product at a low price. On the domestic market, growth in turnover was explosive. The volume of business rose from a quarter of the domestic pig iron market in the first year of production to three-quarters in 1934.

Production costs were kept under control by the utilization of various byproducts. In 1928, the fertilizer factory, Mekog, was launched, in conjunction with Royal Dutch/Shell, for the consumption of coking-oven gas. In 1930 the cement subsidiary Cemij was formed in collaboration with ENCI, to produce blast furnace sealants. By this means a competitive war between the Dutch cement producers Hoogovens and ENCI was prevented, and independence from foreign competition was achieved. Compared with pig iron turnover, sales of byproducts were stable, and were sufficient to cover Hoogovens's fixed expenses.

To strengthen Hoogovens's position on the domestic market, a steel study center was set up, in cooperation with the Dutch authorities, which resulted in a steel plan. The steel plan had become necessary in view of the recession affecting—in the first instance—participation in the Vereinigte Stahlwerke (German Consolidated Steelworks). Demand for pig iron declined. Meanwhile, from 1936 onward, demand for raw steel and steel semi-finished products was very much on the increase, making it feasible to start building a steel factory. In 1939 steel production began at the Siemens-Martin factory. The age of iron was over. Consequently, the twin-headed directorate was expanded to include a doctor of economics, M.W. Holtrop, later to become director of De Nederlandse Bank. In 1940 the turnover of pig iron amounted to Dfl 10.2 million, of byproducts Dfl 3.1 million, of steel Dfl 7.1 million, and of tubing Dfl 1 million.

A dividend was paid to shareholders for the first time in 1939. The large scale of investments, along with the devaluation of the monetary value of the part-holding in Vereinigte Stahlwerke necessitated a strict internal policy regarding costs. Thanks to considerable credits from the Nederlandse Handel Maatschappij (Dutch Trading Company) and Royal Dutch/ Shell, the crisis of the 1930s was surmounted. Yet up to 1940 Hoogovens was still no more than a moderate-sized enterprise compared with the steel giants of Europe.

1940s–60s: New Facilities, Methods, and Products at Hoogovens

During World War II, more than 50 percent of Hoogovens's shares were assigned to an Office of Administration in order to enable Hoogovens as a group of interested parties to resist excessive German infiltration. It worked. During the war, Hoogovens took over B. Van Leer's roller business. Until then Hoogovens had had its semi-finished products made in the rolling-mills of Demka and Van Leer.

Social responsibilities were a primary concern for Hoogovens's board, and a social department was established. After a difficult start, accompanied by strikes, good labor relations were important to the employers' association. There was no strict hierarchy. The cooperation of a flexible, informed, and dedicated workforce determined the free and easy organizational structure. Team spirit was reinforced by the technical character of the business and the hard physical work. Staff associations were encouraged and training, both general and technical, was carried out within the factory. In 1926 a social fund, the Wenckebach Fund, was created for the benefit of the staff. Pension funds followed, in 1929 for executives, and in 1938 for the workforce.

Foremost during the early postwar years was the Breedband project, which included the construction of a hot strip mill, cold band, and tinning installations. The tinplate surface inspectors in the tinning mills were the first women production assistants in a traditionally male occupation. The Breedband rolling-mills were financed by a contribution of Dfl 150 million from the state, within the framework of its industrial policy, Dfl 23.5 million of which came from Marshall Plan aid. The subsidiary, set up in 1950 as Breedband NV, in which Hoogovens itself invested Dfl 60 million, was fully incorporated in the blast furnace business in 1964 when Hoogovens purchased the state's shares. To put into effect the integration of furnaces, steel factory, and rolling-mills, management was from the outset in the hands of Hoogovens. During this period engineer Ingen Housz was in charge.

Hoogovens's share of output in the European Coal and Steel Community rose from 1.1 percent in 1952 to 3.4 percent in 1967. New production methods followed in rapid succession. In 1958 the oxysteel factory went into production. The process entailed blowing oxygen into liquid pig iron, by which process the carbon was burned off and steel obtained. From the beginning in 1924 it had been necessary to operate, whatever the state of the market, in a factory in a constant state of reconstruction; technical innovation was of crucial importance. In 1980 the continuous casting machine was introduced, realizing a continuous output of steel for slabs.

Hoogovens has been managed since 1961 by a five-member directorate. The directorate, known since 1965 as the board of directors, had proceeded on the policy of previous directors. Company programs included profit-sharing for personnel in 1949, the introduction of an industrial council in 1957, uniform conditions of labor for workers and salaried staff in 1966, and a comprehensive program of training, accommodation, and recreation. As a rule, half the personnel had been involved in in-house training schemes. Without well-trained steel workers, Hoogovens could not have kept pace with technological developments.

1970s–Early 1980s: Merger and Dissolution

By 1971 Hoogovens's activities were no longer restricted to steel production. The Hoogovens concern had established its present structure with the acquisition of subsidiaries in the aluminum, oil and gas, and coal sectors. In 1966 the board voted in favor of collaborating with the German steel firm of Hoesch in Dortmund, in the belief that this cooperation would take the companies into joint position among the top ten steel enterprises in Europe. Hoogovens had a 15 percent share in Hoesch. According to the chairman of the board of directors, P.L. Justman Jacob, this collaboration was a good thing for Hoogovens. All the same, mergers across the frontiers struck him, in 1968, as ''damned difficult.'' In 1972 Hoogovens Ijmuiden and Hoesch Dortmund, the main industrial plants of the respective companies, amalgamated to form the steel firm of Estel, taking them to fourth place in Europe. Yet only 25 percent of turnover was achieved on the domestic market. The shipment of raw materials and products to and from its own port, the largest in The Netherlands after Rotterdam and Amsterdam, made Hoogovens a desirable partner in a merger.

After the worldwide economic crisis of 1973 came the 1975 European steel crisis. Schemes for curbing the overproduction of steel in Europe made it essential that Hoogovens keep abreast

of technology. Only modern businesses that could provide a high-quality product at a low price would survive. The much criticized Maasvlakte project—involving the establishment of a second blast furnace concern in Rotterdam—was then abandoned. By May 25, 1983, Hoogovens had produced 100 million tons of steel since 1939. The one million frontier had been crossed in 1958.

After seven years of crisis in the steel industry and handicapped by governmental financial support given to its European competitors, Estel was no longer strong enough financially to carry out independently a restructuring of—in particular—the steel business in Dortmund. Among the last steel enterprises in the European Economic Community (EEC) to ask for assistance from a government, Estel requested help from the German and Dutch authorities. The conditions laid down by the German authorities meant that the merger between Hoesch Dortmund and Hoogovens would have to be terminated. What Justman Jacob had anticipated in 1968 came to pass. The crisis in steel and the government subsidies of other European steelworks, as well as differences in national industrial policies, made a binational undertaking unworkable.

In 1981 the European Commission ruled that any offer of support must be dependent on a commitment to reduction in capacity and a program of restructuring. This would result in a recovery of earning power. Production and pricing agreements, imposed by Brussels, controlled the European steel industry since 1980. Through the closure of Demka and curtailment of hot strip mill production, Hoogovens contributed more than its share toward putting the EEC steel industry on a sound footing. As a result, in 1982 Hoogovens developed a strategy for the years 1982 to 1985.

The strategy was then focused on diversifying activities in steel manufacture, maintaining low price levels, and raising productivity. An extensive investment program, centered on the steel business, was intended to be one-third financed by the Dutch government. The viability of the Hoogovens business was evident from the fact that other European steel concerns received considerably greater government support. Again, the company had no trouble obtaining money from the capital market, owing to the soundness of its planning and support from the Dutch government.

Over the period 1974 to 1985, as one of the few large integrated steel businesses in the EEC, Hoogovens was able to limit cuts in staffing to 22 percent. This took place without forced dismissals, through natural attrition and retraining. The industrial council had from the start opposed any loss of jobs. The management made it a point of policy. Hoogovens's commitment to reducing job cuts, as far as possible, corresponded to the government's wishes. The state with 14 percent and the city of Amsterdam with 6 percent initially had owned a fifth of Hoogovens's shares.

Late 1980s–Late 1990s: A Two-Metal Company

After 1984 the state of the steel market improved, enabling Hoogovens as one of the primary European steel concerns to become profitable again. Hoogovens diversified in an attempt to become less dependent on the cyclical movement in steel. The aluminum division was expanded substantially in 1987 by the takeover of several German firms. All the same, Hoogovens remained a medium-sized business in which 4.5 percent of EEC steel production was concentrated. Liberalizing of the steel market could lead to a rise in production for export-oriented business. In 1988 the Noordwinning Group, involved in natural gas, was sold off, followed in 1989 with the divestments of the cement factory and the cable factory. As a result, Hoogovens became a two-metal concern, with the aluminum sector accounting for 30 percent of the turnover. Growing environmental and technical requirements had resulted in Hoogovens's developing into a supplier of flue-gas desulfurizing installations. On his retirement in 1988 the departing director, J.D. Hooglandt, summed up the current strategy: ''Not more steel, but doing more with it.''

Although Hoogovens was profitable when it entered the 1990s, its fortunes suffered a sudden reversal in the early years of the decade. The company posted losses of 51 million guilders ($27 million) in 1991, due to both depressed metal prices and weak demand, especially in Western Europe. The losses in 1992 and 1993 were much worse: 595 million guilders and 234 million guilders, respectively. Hoogovens responded with deep cuts, scaling back capital spending and curbing both steel and aluminum production, reducing its workforce by some 2,300.

The company returned to profitability in 1994, and remained profitable throughout the next few years. During that time, it expanded its aluminum business, acquiring the extrusion business of VAW Aluminum AG in Germany, a producer of large aluminum sections; Afal, an aluminum panels and sidings division of the French company, Pechiney-Batiment. Hoogovens also added to its steel operations, building a new thin strip caster plant at its Ijmuiden facility, opening a new hot-dip galvanizing line in Belgium, and increasing its holdings from 50 to 100 percent in the German company Hille and Muller.

In 1999, when Hoogovens approached British Steel about the possibility of a merger, it was profitable and healthy, but still a relatively small presence in the world steel market. All that changed just a few months later; when the merger was complete, Hoogovens became part of the largest steel company in Europe and the third largest in the world.

Late 1990s: Corus Group

On October 6, 1999, British Steel and Hoogovens merged, forming Corus Group plc. The CEOs of the two former companies, John Bryant and Fokko van Duyne, became joint chief executives. The new company, which located its headquarters in London, had 66,000 employees and annual sales of $14.8 billion.

Not only did the merger make Corus the largest steelmaker in Europe, it also made it a multi-metals company—with Hoogovens's strong aluminum units added to the business mix. This positioned the new company to provide a wider range of products and services. Corus believed that such diversification was increasingly important, because many of its major customers—such as automobile makers and construction companies—were themselves consolidating. As their businesses expanded and diversified, they needed suppliers with both a wide range of products and a broad international presence.

Within a few months Corus took another step to reinforce its position as a multi-metals player, merging its 51 percent owned stainless steel subsidiary, Avesta Sheffield, with a Finnish stainless producer, Outokumpu Oyj. Joined, the two companies—renamed AvestaPolarit—became the second largest stainless steel company in the world. The company also acquired a majority interest in Reycan, a division of Canada's Reynolds Metals Co. Reycan was a producer of aluminum heat exchanger material, with the North American auto industry as its main market.

Corus also wasted little time in taking advantage of the potential efficiencies inherent in a merger. Within its first year of operation, the steel giant had cut production deeply, eliminating more than 4,000 jobs. But even with such drastic cuts, Corus was unable to compensate for external problems in the market. Demand for steel was weak, and an oversupply on the world market, consequently, had pushed prices down. The company's earnings also were affected adversely by the strength of the pound relative to the Euro, which made it less competitive than its counterparts in the markets to which it exported. As a result of these adverse factors, Corus posted a £1.05 billion loss for 2000.

Faced with widespread criticism and pressure from company directors, Corus's joint CEOs, John Bryant and Fokko van Duyne, resigned from their posts in December 2000, having led the new company for little more than a year. An interim leader was appointed while directors looked for a new CEO. Meanwhile, the company went into self-preservation mode, making radical reductions in its production. It announced plant and/or line closings at Llanwern, Ebbw Vale, Bryngwyn, and Shotton facilities, in Wales, and at Teesside in England. It also announced plans to streamline functions across other U.K. businesses, resulting in further staff reductions. Together, the cutbacks were to eliminate some 6,000 jobs.

The layoffs drew criticism from both the labor unions and the British government. Union representatives accused Corus of taking a short-term approach to a long-term problem and offered their own alternative to the cuts—a government-backed ''rescue package'' that would pay for half of the wages of the employees identified for layoff if Corus would wait a year before restructuring. Both Britain's Prime Minister and Trade Secretary also urged the company to consider the union plan, but Corus rejected the offer and moved forward with its cuts.

It was into this maelstrom of restructuring that the company's new CEO, Tony Pedder, stepped in September 2001. Pedder had joined British Steel in 1992 and had headed up the company's Strip Products division.

Looking Ahead: Shedding Aluminum

Corus continued to lose money in the early part of the new century, posting a net loss of £385 million in 2001. In March 2002, the company announced that it was looking for a buyer for its three aluminum businesses. Pedder indicated that, as the aluminum industry continued to consolidate, Corus was finding it harder to compete against ever larger players. Selling its aluminum business indicated that the company had given up its stated goal of being a multi-metals supplier and, instead, was planning a return to a single focus on steel.

Principal Operating Units

Corus Building Systems; Corus Colors; Corus Construction & Industrial; Corus Consulting; Corus Engineering Steels; Corus Metal Services Europe; Corus Metal Service International; Corus Metal Service North America; Corus Packaging Plus; Corus Rail; Corus Research, Development & Technology; Corus Special Profiles; Corus Special Strip; Corus Strip Products Ijmuiden; Corus Strip Products UK; Corus Tubes; Corus Tuscaloosa; Cogent Power Ltd (75%); Corus Aluminum Extrusions; Corus Aluminum Rolled Products; Corus Primary Aluminum.

Principal Competitors

Arcelor; ThyssenKrupp AG; USX Corporation.

Further Reading

Abromeit, Heidrun, *British Steel,* Leamington Spa: Berg Publishers, 1986.

Bryer, R.A., et al., *Accounting for British Steel,* Aldershot: Gower Publishing, 1982.

de Vries, Joh., "From Keystone to Cornerstone. Hoogovens Ijmuiden 1918–1968. The Birth and Development of a Basic Industry in the Netherlands," in *Acta Historiae Neerlandicae,* The Hague: Brill Academic Publishers, 1973.

——, *Hoogovens Ijmuiden, 1918–1968. Ontstaan en groei van een basisindustrie,* Amsterdam: KNHS, 1968.

Heal, David W., *The Steel Industry in Post-War Britain,* London: David & Charles, 1974.

Heerding, A., *Cement in Nederland,* Amsterdam: CEMIJ, 1971.

Moffit, Brian, "Corus Takes Crucial Steps for Its Future," *Steel Times,* June 2001, p. 190.

Ovenden, Keith, *The Politics of Steel,* London: Macmillan, 1978.

Vaizey, John, *The History of British Steel,* London: Weidenfeld & Nicolson, 1974.

van Elteren, Mel C.M., *Staal en Arbeid. Een sociaal-historische studie naar industriële accomodatieprocessen onder arbeiders en het desbetreffende bedrijfsbeleid bij Hoogovens 1924–1966,* Leiden: Brill, 1986.

—Patrick Heenan, Henk Muntjewerff,
and Joachim F.E. Bläsing
(translated from the Dutch by Hubert Hoskins)
—updates: Dorothy Kroll, Shawna Brynildssen

Cybex International, Inc.

10 Trotter Drive
Medway, Massachusetts 02053
U.S.A.
Telephone: (508) 533-4300
Fax: (508) 533-5500
Web site: http://www.ecybex.com

Public Company
Incorporated: 1953 as Lumex, Inc.
Employees: 451
Sales: $85.2 million (2001)
Stock Exchanges: American
Ticker Symbol: CYB
NAIC: 421910 Sporting and Recreational Goods and
    Supplies Wholesalers

Cybex International, Inc. designs, manufactures, and markets premium quality fitness equipment for commercial, professional, and home use. The company's products are designed to provide biomechanically correct movements with minimal impact and maximum ease of use. Cardiovascular fitness products include stationary bicycles in upright and recumbent riding positions, steppers, and treadmills. Cardiovascular equipment utilizes computer electronics to control speed, resistance, and other factors; most models are available with a heart rate monitor. Strength training equipment includes individual components or multi-station units that exercise all muscle groups. The equipment is available with selectorized or manually loaded weights designed for constant resistance in the full range of physical motion or with free weights. The personal gym for home use and the multi-gym for small fitness centers, use selectorized weights and provide over 30 biomechanically correct exercises in a compact unit. The company's products are sold under the Cybex, Trotter, and Eagle brands.

Building the Cybex Brand

Cybex International took its name from the Cybex brand of physical therapy and fitness equipment. Lumex, Inc., a thera-

peutic health and hospital products company founded in 1947, acquired the patent for the first Cybex product, the Cybex Dynamometer, in 1969. A physical rehabilitation device, the Cybex Dynamometer assessed the strength of isolated joints. The equipment provided isokinetic resistance which accurately accommodated for the variable exertion applied by a body joint or muscle group as it progressed through its full range of motion. This resistance allowed for a constant rate of pressure so that the joint would not be overburdened or underchallenged at any point of its movement. The combination of resistance and speed control (isokinetic means ''constant velocity'') provided rapid, effective results in rehabilitation and exercise.

Lumex sold the Cybex Dynamometer along with other physical rehabilitation and exercise products, such as the Fitron stationary bicycle, updated for variable speeds, and the Kinitron progressive weight-bearing machine. The Orthotron assessed ankle, knee, hip, and shoulder movements. Physical therapy equipment generated $600,000 in revenues in 1974 and Lumex created the Cybex division the following year.

Lumex developed into a major designer and manufacturer of performance measurement and rehabilitation systems, with the Cybex brand becoming known nationally and internationally. Sports teams, such as the Dallas Cowboys, and individual athletes, including boxer Muhammad Ali and baseball pitcher Tom Seaver, used Cybex equipment in their athletic training programs. Lumex sponsored seminars nationwide to educate physicians, physical therapists, orthopedic surgeons, and athletic trainers in the proper use of isokinetic equipment. In 1982 the company expanded its sales team and formed a field service group to set up and calibrate the equipment. A referral service provided information about clinics that used Cybex equipment. Cybex products gained international exposure in 1982 at the World Physical Therapy Congress in Sweden. The company held its first training seminars for European agents, with sales representatives in over 20 countries.

In 1981 Lumex relocated Cybex division operations and manufacturing to Ronkonkoma, New York, as the company prepared to expand the Cybex product line. New factory construction provided manufacturing space in Ronkonkoma, adding 60,000 square feet to the existing 40,000-square-foot factory and office facility. New products in 1982 included the Orthotron KT1 and KT2 designed specifically for knee rehabilitation in sports medicine. The Cybex Data Reduction Computer (CDRC) provided instant calculation and analysis of data for the Cybex II Dynamometer; the CDRC provided more accurate as well as different kinds of measurements. Lumex entered the fitness equipment industry in 1983 with the acquisition of Eagle Performance Systems, Inc., manufacturer of strength training equipment for health clubs and fitness centers. The acquisition included a large manufacturing facility in Owatonna, Minnesota.

Lumex applied Cybex system technology to the development of back rehabilitation systems, the company's largest product development project to date. After several years of research and development, the company began to ship product in November 1985. The three products in the Cybex Back Systems line utilized proprietary software to calculate, analyze, store, and print information as they precisely tested and measured specific aspects of back function. Lumex promoted Cybex Back Systems through an extensive marketing and public relations campaign to inform physicians, physical therapists, hospitals, insurance providers, and consumers. Clinical Educators provided full day training sessions with actual patients. By 1988 the back rehabilitation systems were fully developed with updated software and hardware, allowing the company to divert research and development funds to new products.

Preparing for Growth in Fitness and Medical Markets: 1980s

Lumex began to reorganize and streamline in 1988, preparing to evolve the company in both the medical and fitness equipment markets. Lumex created separate medical and fitness subdivisions within the Cybex division in 1988, each with its own marketing and product development programs. In addition, Lumex created a new customer relations department; reorganized the factory floor to allow for more efficient movement of materials and finished product; and implemented similar computer platforms on its products.

New products in 1988 included a stationary bicycle, a rower, and an upper-body ergometer for the measurement of upper body performance. That year Lumex introduced the MET series, a line of video-based, computer-controlled exercise machines. The company also launched Cybex Strength Systems, a line of free weight exercise machines.

Cybex brand's international presence expanded and developed in the late 1980s. With sales agents in more than 40 countries, the company saw international sales increase 70

percent in 1988, exceeding projections. That year Lumex expanded its product offerings to international clients to include Cybex Back Systems and Cybex Fitness Systems. In September the company's fitness equipment and rehabilitation systems were highlighted at the Seoul Olympic Scientific Congress.

Lumex initiated advisory boards of medical and fitness professionals to help improve existing equipment designs as well as originate new designs. New products included the fourth generation of the Cybex Extremity Testing and Rehabilitation System, introduced in 1991. At the prompting of the medical advisory board, the system provided both powered and non-powered options and continuous passive motion. The fitness advisory board assisted the development of Cybex Modular Strength Systems, a revolutionary line for the exercise of individual muscle groups that offered high performance with minimal space requirements. Lumex developed two new stationary bicycles, "The Bike," set in an upright position, and "The Semi," in a semi-recumbent, or leaning position, introduced in 1992 and 1993, respectively. Two home strength-training systems were introduced as well. The year 1994 saw the introduction of the Plate Loaded Series of weight training equipment which allowed for both the controlled resistance of state-of-the art strength training equipment and the feel of a free weight workout. Lumex opened a facility dedicated to research and development in Colorado Springs, Colorado, in 1994. The location was chosen due to a concentration of athletics-oriented organizations in the area, including the Olympic Training Center.

The company's marketing efforts involved audiovisual presentations, public service booklets, participation in trade shows, advertisements in trade and professional journals, and cooperative advertising with authorized dealers. Lumex marketed its products through 19 sales representatives and five independent sales agents in the United States. Customers included hospital physical therapy departments, physical therapists in private practice, medical research laboratories, sports medicine clinics, professional sports organizations, fitness centers, and individual consumers. Cybex Financial Corporation, formed in 1992, provided capital equipment financing to customers within the United States. International distribution involved an in-house staff of 13 people to handle the activities of 60 distributors worldwide. Lumex opened offices in Belgium and Germany in 1992 and 1993, respectively. Asia and Pacific Rim distribution was handled through a new office in Japan.

In 1995 Lumex introduced its first treadmill, "The Mill," featuring the Cybex Controlled Impact System with nine settings to accommodate for level of stringency in relation to the user's stride, weight, and fitness. The Eagle Performance's new line of premium variable resistance strength training equipment, the VR2, incorporated the patented Dual Axis technology for free movement, rather than machine-defined movement.

Specializing in Fitness Equipment: 1995

In 1995, under the leadership of Ray Elliot as CEO, Lumex decided to restructure operations to concentrate activities on the design and manufacturing of fitness equipment. The company finalized the sale of the Lumex division of health and medical equipment to Fuqua Enterprises in April 1996 and received $40.75 million in cash. Lumex then adopted the name Cybex

Key Dates:

1969: Lumex, Inc., purchases the patent for the Cybex Dynamometer, used for assessing joint strength.
1975: Lumex creates the Cybex division of isokinetic physical rehabilitation equipment.
1983: Company enters the fitness equipment market with the acquisition of Eagle Performance Systems.
1985: Shipment of products in the Cybex Back Systems line begins.
1988: International sales increase 70 percent; Cybex products are showcased at Seoul Olympic Scientific Congress.
1992: Cybex Financial Corporation is formed to provide capital equipment financing.
1995: Lumex begins to restructure company to focus on fitness equipment and therapeutic healthcare products.
1997: Cybex merger with Trotter, Inc. is completed.
1998: Cybex acquires Tectrix Fitness Equipment, Inc.
2000: Cybex reorganizes due to losses.

International. In 1996 Cybex formed a 50/50 joint venture with its distributor in the United Kingdom, The Forza Group. The new venture, CYBEX Forza International, distributed fitness products in the Middle East, Africa, and Russia. Forza handled sales, marketing, and administration, and Cybex provided products on a cost-plus basis. CYBEX Forza also offered other fitness equipment from The Step Company, Cross Conditioning, Reebok, Tectrix, and Quinton.

Cybex International announced its pending merger with Trotter, Inc. in late 1996. A subsidiary of UM Holdings (formerly United Medical Corporation), Trotter brought its own distinguished history to Cybex International. Engineer Edward Trotter constructed a motorized treadmill in 1970 out of concern for his own cardiovascular health. He formally started his company in 1973, providing customized treadmills for the consumer market in Boston, later expanding to other cities. Trotter operated the business from his basement in Holliston, Massachusetts, until 1979 when he relocated to a 5,000-square-foot industrial space. He hired Peter Haines to manage sales and marketing two years later. In 1983 sales reached $2 million and the company relocated to a 25,000-square-foot manufacturing plant. Edward Trotter retired that year and sold the company to UM Holdings, which retained Haines as president. Trotter, Inc. relocated again in 1987, to a 70,000-square-foot facility. With 65 employees and 150 sales agents nationwide, the company initiated its first national advertising campaign. By 1990, Trotter treadmills were rated best in class in a market research survey. International sales extended to Europe, the Middle East, Africa, Asia, Australia, and South America.

Trotter reached two important milestones in 1992. The company introduced its tenth generation of treadmills, the 500 series for home use, and moved to its current location in Medway, Massachusetts, to a 100,000-square-foot facility which housed the company's headquarters and manufacturing plant. The facility allowed Trotter to expand its product offerings. In 1993

Trotter introduced its first climber exercise equipment and a new series of treadmills for commercial use. With the purchase of Pyramid Fitness, Trotter entered the strength training market, with free-weight and "selectorized" equipment (whereby users selected the weight by inserting a pin under the heaviest weight desired). Trotter gained a manufacturing plant in Pennsylvania as well as a base line of products that it developed into Galileo Strength Equipment, launched in 1995. Sales at Trotter reached $48 million in 1996.

Completion of the merger between Cybex and Trotter occurred in May 1997. John Spratt and Ray Elliot stepped down from their positions as Cybex board chair and CEO, respectively. Haines took the position of CEO at the newly formed company, the first global, publicly owned company in the fitness equipment industry. The merger made Cybex the only company with a comprehensive line of cardiovascular and strength training fitness equipment needed to fully outfit a fitness center. It also combined Cybex's reputation in the commercial market with Trotter's name recognition in the consumer market.

The process of integration began with the elimination of almost 200 jobs as plants closed in Pennsylvania, New York, and Washington, and the research and development facility closed in Colorado. Consolidation of operations at Medway created 70 new jobs, however. Cybex retained Eagle's Owatonna facility. Cybex dissolved the joint venture agreement with the Forza Group in June. A new distribution agreement gave London-based Forza Fitness Equipment exclusive rights for markets in the United Kingdom, Austria, Germany, Switzerland, Russia, and the former Soviet block countries. Cybex took over sales and distribution to other international locations, combining it with Trotter's sales and distribution network.

Choosing to focus business operations in the fitness industry, Cybex sold its line of isokinetics testing and physical rehabilitation equipment, which accounted for approximately 16 percent of revenues. Henley Healthcare purchased the product line and licensed the Cybex brand for the equipment. Also, Henley secured limited distribution of other Cybex products to the healthcare industry in North America. Some physical rehabilitation clinics continued to purchase Cybex fitness equipment.

Cybex confronted many challenges as a newly integrated company. The first year after the merger, Cybex reported a net loss of $5.2 million on consolidated sales of $90.2 million. In 1998 sales increased to $132.4 million, and net income to $1 million, on the strength of a new product and the acquisition of Tectrix Fitness Equipment. Formed in 1988, Tectrix was known for the stair climber ClimbMax, a revolutionary fitness product introduced in 1989, and the BikeMax line of stationary exercise bicycles, launched in 1993. Tectrix added approximately $30 million to Cybex revenues. New products in 1998, including The Hiker, offset slower sales. Cybex launched the PG400 Personal Gym, a compact workout unit for the home market. The equipment provided over 30 biomechanically correct exercises with the full range of motion for all muscle groups.

Faltering amid Successes As New Century Begins

In early 2000 Cybex launched its web site for online shopping and customer support. In addition to providing product information, the site offered training tips, and news and articles on the science of human performance. At "Ask Tracy," Cybex Education and Training Manager Tracy Morgan answered questions about health and fitness. The site featured a calculator to determine body mass and target heart rate based on personal information. Customer support included order tracking and spare parts ordering in real time, features that benefited overseas distributors as well.

To promote the web site, Cybex offered an online contest, "Who Wants to Feel Like a Millionaire?" When visitors correctly answered a health or fitness question, posted every week for eight weeks, they were entered in a prize drawing. For the grand prize Cybex offered a spa vacation at one of four Destination Spa Group locations. For second prize the company offered a 300T home treadmill, and for third prize a custom workout designed by Tracy Morgan.

After an absence of new products in 1999, in early 2000 the company launched three commercial products. The Cybex 600T Treadmill featured a heart rate monitor and new shock absorption technology. The MG500 Multi-Gym provided movement flexibility in a compact design for corporate and hotel fitness centers. The FT360 Functional Trainer featured flexible exercise options and creative programming. By July the company experienced a backlog of orders for new products. The FT 360 Functional Trainer won the award for Best Product Design and Innovation by *Health and Fitness Business* magazine, at the magazines trade show, the first award given for commercial products.

Despite the success of these new products, the year 2000 closed with a 30 percent decline in sales during the last quarter, prompting sudden adjustments at the executive level. Haines retired as CEO, being replaced by John Aglialoro, chairman of UM Holdings, while three executive officers resigned, including the CFO. Cybex restructured its executive offices as it replaced these executives and cut its overall workforce by 26 percent. Other action included revision of the warranty program, discount policies, credit standards, and leasing and service operations. In December Cybex closed its Irvine, California, facility, and moved cardiovascular equipment production to a new facility in Medway.

The company's sales staff was restructured along with standards for dealer authorization. The 108 active dealers in North America were given a defined sales territory, requirements for sales goals, and standards for personnel training in sales techniques as well as product usage. Cybex sales staff served the dealers while 17 territory managers and two regional sales

directors and a new vice-president directed the department's operations. Three national account managers served large commercial customers under a new vice-president. In February 2001 Cybex terminated its distribution agreement with Forza and transferred European sales and distribution into a new subsidiary, Cybex International UK Ltd. Cybex planned to attend more closely to its 58 independent distributors worldwide.

Organizational change impacted sales and earnings in 2000 and 2001. In 2000 the company recorded $25.4 million in charges, including costs for relocation of Irvine operations and $16.9 million in Tectrix goodwill. The year finished with $125.3 million in sales, and a net loss of $20.6 million. Rumors of pending dissolution of the company prompted Aglialoro to issue public letters in November 2000 and February 2001, reassuring customers of the company's stability, and to replace its auto-attendant telephone system with a live receptionist. Changes in company credit policies as well as general economic conditions impacted sales in 2001, which declined 32 percent to $85.2 million; the company reported a net loss of $0.7 million. Problems with replacement parts ordering motivated a new warranty program providing free annual preventive maintenance during the warranty period. Cybex expected the introduction of new products in 2002 to improve sales.

Principal Subsidiaries

Cybex Financial Corporation; Cybex International UK, Ltd.; Eagle Performance Systems, Inc.: Tectrix Fitness Equipment, Inc.; Trotter, Inc.

Principal Competitors

Guthy-Renker Corporation; ICON Health & Fitness, Inc.; Soloflex.

Further Reading

Agoglia, Joh, "Cybex Acquires Tectrix; VR Line Virtually Saved," *Sporting Goods Business*, June 10, 1998, p. 22.

"Cybex to Cut 200 Positions," *Boston Herald*, August 9, 1997, p. 14.

Gatlin, Greg, "Cybex International Cutting 160 Employees," *Boston Herald*, December 30, 2000, p. 18.

Harrison, Joan, "A Merged Fitness Firm Reaches Its Season; a Partnering of CYBEX and Trotter Ripens Their Growth Prospects," *Mergers & Acquisitions*, November-December 1997, p. 38.

Pare, Michael, "Cybex Focuses on Quality in All Ways," *Providence Business News*, June 28, 1999, p. 1B.

—Mary Tradii

Dixons Group plc

Dixons Group plc

Dixons House
Maylands Avenue
Hemel Hempstead
Hertfordshire HP2 7TG
United Kingdom
Telephone: (44) 14-4235-3000
Fax: (44) 14-4223-3218
Web site: http://www.dixons-group-plc.co.uk

Public Company
Incorporated: 1937 as Dixon Studios Ltd.
Employees: 31,223
Sales: $6.75 billion (2001)
Stock Exchanges: London
Ticker Symbol: DXNS
NAIC: 443111 Household Appliance Stores; 443112
   Radio, Television, and Other Electronics Stores;
   443120 Computer and Software Stores; 443130
   Camera and Photographic Supplies Stores

Dixons Group plc is the largest specialized retailer of consumer electronics in Europe and controls more than 1,250 retail outlets in the United Kingdom, Ireland, Scandinavia, Spain, Portugal, and Hungary. The driving force behind the company's expansion from one small portrait studio was Stanley Kalms. Dixons' chairman achieved this stunning growth by entering two fast-growing markets at an early stage in their development: photographic goods in the 1950s and consumer electronics in the 1970s. In both cases, Dixons helped to build these markets in the United Kingdom and grew with them. Also credited with bringing the superstore concept to Britain, Kalms was knighted for ''services to electrical retailing'' in 1996.

1930s Origins

The retail powerhouse's origins can be traced to the 1930s, when Charles Kalms, a Jewish immigrant from Eastern Europe, founded a portrait photography studio in London. In 1937 he and a friend decided to set up a photographic studio at Southend-on-Sea, not far from London. They incorporated the business as Dixon

Studios Ltd., choosing the name Dixon out of a telephone directory in preference to their own. Kalms's friend gave up his share in the business within two years, and Kalms took full control, while continuing to run another business at the same time.

During World War II, when so many men and women were separated from their families, there was a great demand for portrait photographs, and the business flourished. By the end of the war the company had expanded to a chain of seven studios in the London area. After 1945, however, the market contracted as fast as it had grown, and Dixon was reduced to a single studio in the North London suburb of Edgware.

Postwar Expansion into Retailing

In an effort to boost sales, Charles Kalms began to sell cameras and other photographic equipment, and the studio gradually turned into a shop. This changeover gathered pace when Charles Kalms's son Stanley joined the business in 1948. Although only 17, he proved to be a natural salesman with remarkable ambitions. A onetime colleague recalled that Stanley Kalms sold some cameras with great success even before he had discovered how to load the film. The retail side of the business grew quickly, and father and son agreed to concentrate on developing it. By 1953 the company was able to start opening branches again, this time under the name Dixon Camera Centre.

In those early postwar years, few people in Britain could afford to spend much on their hobbies, but interest in photography grew fast. Dixon met this situation by selling new and used goods at attractive prices and by offering credit terms. At an early stage it started advertising, at first in photographic magazines and local papers, then in national newspapers. In this way it built up a large mail-order business as well as retail sales. By 1958 it had 60,000 mail-order customers, and the shop business had grown to six branches. In that year Dixon moved its head office to larger premises, still in Edgware. The company then employed almost 100 people.

The company showed unusual enterprise in buying as well as selling. In the 1950s the photographic market in the United Kingdom was dominated by British, U.S., and German manufacturers, and the law at that time allowed manufacturers to dictate the prices at which their products were retailed. This did

Company Perspectives:

Through all our brands we aim to provide unrivaled value to our customers by the range and quality of our products, our competitive prices and our high standards of service.

Our objective is to create value for our shareholders, career opportunities for our employees and the best possible value and service for our customers.

not suit Dixon's competitive style, and Stanley Kalms began to look elsewhere for manufacturers who would supply him directly at low prices. He began regular buying trips to the Far East and by hard bargaining and bulk buying was able to import goods at prices that enabled Dixon to offer unbeatable value to its customers. In Japan he found manufacturers willing to supply products made to Dixon's specifications. At that time Japanese goods were not highly regarded in Europe, so Dixon marketed the goods under the German-sounding name of Prinz.

Dramatic Growth in the 1950s Culminating in 1962 IPO

By the end of the 1950s incomes in Britain were rising sharply, and the market for photographic goods doubled in value between 1958 and 1963. Camera design was improving, color film prices were falling, and a craze for home-movie kits—camera, projector, and screen—swelled demand. Dixon, having established a reputation for good value and quality, was one of the chief beneficiaries. Its profits rocketed from £6,800 in 1958 to £160,000 in 1962, and in that year the company went public under the new name of Dixons Photographic Ltd. The Kalms family retained voting control, with more than three-quarters of the shares in their hands at this time, but the shares released to the market proved highly popular.

At the time of the stock offering Dixons had only 16 shops, five of them in London, and with the help of the offering it acquired more. Two chains of camera shops, Ascotts, with 13 stores, and Bennetts, Dixons' largest specialty competitor, with 29 branches, were bought in the next two years. Dixons also opened more shops from scratch, including one on a prime site near Marble Arch, London. By the end of 1964 the company had 70 shops and by 1969 it had more than 100.

Growth in profits was more erratic. Retail sales were depressed in some years by government action to restrict credit, and some of the company's expansionary moves lost money in the short term. In 1967 a large color film processing plant at Stevenage was purchased, the most up-to-date one in Europe at the time; it operated at a loss for a while before making a profit. Dixons also began to manufacture photographic accessories and display material and made substantial losses on this business before abandoning it in 1970.

Increase in Profitability and Forays into Foreign Markets in the 1970s

The key to Dixons' next leap in profits, in the early 1970s, was its move into electronics retailing. This began very cautiously in 1967, when some audio and hi-fidelity units were put on sale in

six branches as an experiment. They sold well and were soon introduced into all branches. By 1970 Dixons had introduced its own Prinzsound brand. The next year, television sets were sold experimentally in 25 stores. They, too, were a great success, in part because the recent arrival of color television had created a large television replacement market. After that, Dixons introduced a host of new products in quick succession, including electronic calculators, radio/cassette recorders, music centers, and digital clock/radios. To make room for all these new products, the company had to enlarge its stores. In two consecutive years its total selling space was increased by 30 percent or more.

The effect of these developments on profits was dramatic. From £226,000 in 1970—a bad year—profits soared to £828,000 in 1971, £2.3 million in 1972, and £4.9 million in 1973. The company had established itself in a new market with tremendous growth potential, and its reputation with the investing public, who by this time held the majority of its shares, stood high.

In fact, its next few years proved to be an unhappy period. This was partly because the economic climate changed for the worse in 1974, but chiefly because the company tried to buy its way into other new markets with less positive results.

Dixons started to expand abroad in the early 1970s, at first with success. Through small marketing companies in Sweden and Switzerland, it found valuable new outlets for its own brand of products throughout Europe. In 1972 it bought a large Dutch photographic and optical retail business, G.H. Rinck NV, a company with nearly 60 stores in The Netherlands, compared with Dixons' 150 stores in the United Kingdom at that time. As in Britain, Dixons opened more branches and introduced more products, but the Dutch business never approached the U.K. stores in profitability and for two consecutive years incurred losses.

This experience deterred Dixons from further expansion in foreign markets for some years. Instead, it embarked in 1976 on a new form of expansion in the United Kingdom. With the hope of achieving a large increase in outlets for its goods at one stroke, it bought Weston Pharmaceuticals, a chain of 200 drugstores, for £11 million, together with a wholesale business supplying independent druggists. The idea was to widen Weston's range to include Dixons products, in the same way that Boots, originally a pharmaceutical company, had so successfully broadened its range to include other consumer goods. "Boots must be our model," said Peter Kalms in the *Investors Chronicle* of January 30, 1976, soon after the takeover.

These hopes were never realized. It became apparent within a short time that Weston had serious problems within its existing business and that any major expansion was out of the question. Its profits declined, then turned to losses. Dixons wrestled with Weston's financial problems for four years in an effort to turn it around, but in 1980 decided to recoup what it could of its investment by selling all the drugstores. The wholesale business was kept for some years longer, but seldom produced a substantial profit.

Meanwhile, the struggle to save Weston's retail business had left Dixons with a shortage of working capital, and this had led the company to sell G.H. Rinck in 1978. Thus by 1980 two major investments had come to nothing, and the company's reputation as a growth stock was tarnished. The recession of 1981–82

Key Dates:

1937: Charles Kalms opens Dixon Studios Ltd. in Southend-on-Sea, England.
1953: The Dixon Camera Centre chain is launched.
1972: Dixons acquires G.H. Rinck NV.
1984: Dixons acquires Currys Group PLC.
1991: The first PC World Superstore opens.
1998: Dixons launches Freeserve Internet services.
1999: Dixons acquires Norwegian electronics retailer Elkjop.

delayed Dixons' recovery, with the result that its profits, after discounting inflation, showed no real growth for six years.

Reemphasis on Electronics Business in the 1980s

Dixons' main electronics retailing business, however, continued to expand throughout this period. By 1982 the company had raised the number of its stores to 260 and increased their average size. New electronic products were introduced as they were manufactured, including home computers, video recorders, and digital watches. By competitive pricing policies, Dixons won a sizable share of all these new markets. It launched a new house brand, this time with a Japanese name, Saisho. The photographic side of the business also continued to grow; its processing capacity was increased, and a property development unit was established successfully.

All of these investments paid off handsomely once Weston's problems had been left behind and the recession ended. In 1984 Dixons' profits jumped by 46 percent. On the strength of this fresh spurt of growth, the company made its biggest-ever takeover in December of that year. This time it chose a British company with a business closely complementary to its own. Currys Group PLC (Currys) was a chain of 570 shops, selling refrigerators, freezers, washing machines, and electronics, including a television rental business. Although it owned twice as many shops as Dixons, Currys' turnover was no greater, and its recent performance had been less dynamic. Nevertheless, it was a sound business with a good name, and Dixons had to pay £248 million for it. Kalms would later reflect that it was ''one of the deals of the century.''

Currys was a much older business than Dixons. It began in Leicester in 1888 as a bicycle shop and, in the cycling boom of the 1890s, manufactured and sold bicycles. When its founder, Henry Curry, retired in 1910, his sons carried on the business—a partnership formed in 1897 as H Curry & Sons—and expanded it greatly. It ceased to manufacture, but developed into a nationwide chain of shops selling cycles, radios, baby carriages, toys, and sporting goods, and became a public company in 1927. The second and third generations of the Curry family continued to manage it, however, until the Dixons takeover. By that time the company had ceased to deal in cycles and sporting goods, but had become one of the leading retailers of domestic electric appliances of all kinds. The acquisition included Currys' Mastercare service division and the Bridgers chain of discount electronics and appliance stores.

The merger of Dixons and Currys, under the name of Dixons Group, put the company into the top echelon of British retailers. Even after selling the television rental shops, the new company had more than 800 stores in the United Kingdom and its staff had grown to 11,000. Currys retained its separate identity within the company, but its business methods were brought more into line with Dixons'. In the boom conditions of the mid-1980s, the combination brought further large increases in profits.

Flurry of Acquisitions in the Late 1980s

Stanley Kalms, however, was not content even with this empire. In 1986 he launched a bid for Woolworth Holdings, the British branch of Woolworth. The U.S. parent had sold its 52 percent controlling stake in this to a consortium of British investors in 1982, and Woolworth Holdings was still struggling to raise its profits after a long period of stagnation. Kalms believed that Dixons could do the job better, as well as obtain new outlets for its own merchandise. In the end, Dixons' £1.8 billion bid was turned down by the institutional investors who controlled most of Woolworth Holdings' shares.

Thwarted in this plan, Dixons looked around for other investment opportunities. In 1986 it acquired the 340-shop Supersnaps chain, the leading U.K. specialist in retail film processing. Then, in 1987, it made two major acquisitions in the United States, the Silo and Tipton electrical and appliance retailing chains. Silo Inc., with 119 stores and 2,000 employees, was the third largest electrical retailer in the United States and was strong in the East and Midwest. Tipton Centers Inc. was based in St. Louis and had 24 other stores.

With these acquisitions Dixons controlled more than 1,300 stores worldwide, with 3.5 million square feet of selling space. By 1991 it doubled the number of its U.S. outlets, gaining a presence on the West Coast as well, and the worldwide store total had risen to nearly 1,450.

But size did not necessarily equate with success. Dixons' pretax profits peaked at £103 million in 1988, and when recession softened the consumer electronics market, profits started to decline. As a result, Dixons found itself at the receiving end of a takeover bid in 1989. The bidder was none other than Woolworth, by then renamed Kingfisher, a company that had made a strong recovery since its 1986 financial difficulties. Dixons was saved from this threat by the Monopolies and Mergers Commission, which ruled that Dixons and Kingfisher as a unit would have an excessive share of the electrical goods market. Kalms later estimated that the two companies wasted £40 million in fees on the bid and counterbid.

The 1990s and Beyond

The Silo acquisition proved, as one analyst put it, ''disastrous,'' racking up millions in losses under Dixons' management. In 1993, the U.K. parent sold the chain to America's Fretter Inc. in exchange for a 30 percent stake in the acquiring company. Dixons also divested its Supersnaps subsidiary to Britain's Sketchley plc during this period.

Hoping that it had stanched the flow of red ink, Dixons refocused on the domestic market, acquiring Vision Technology Group Ltd. (VST) in 1993. VST had been formed just two years prior via the amalgamation of several mail-order computer companies in 1991. The merged firms opened their first retail outlet, PC World Superstore, that same year, offering computers, peripherals, software, and accessories. Following the acquisition, Dixons divested VST's mail-order operation and concentrated on a dramatic expansion of the four-store chain. By the end of 1996, there were 25 PC World outlets throughout the United Kingdom. Dixons also hatched a new member of the retail family in 1994, launching The Link stores, specializing in retail communications services and products. By the end of 1995, this new chain boasted 48 outlets throughout the United Kingdom.

After four decades at the helm, sexagenarian Stanley Kalms began to relinquish many of the day-to-day operations of his retail empire to a new CEO, John Clare, in the late 1980s and early 1990s. Remaining as chairman, Kalms continued to oversee strategy. Although earnings remained fairly flat at £1.9 billion in the early 1990s, pretax profit rose from £76.7 million in fiscal 1992–93 to a record £135.2 million in fiscal 1994–95.

Keeping Pace with the Digital Age: 1996–2002

Having solidified its market position on the domestic front, Dixons was once again able to turn its attention to building its presence abroad. In January 1997, not long after opening the first Dixons store in Ireland, the company acquired the retail arm of Dublin-based Harry Moore Ltd. In addition to giving Dixons an additional six outlets in Ireland, the deal lent some critical momentum to its overall expansion strategy, enabling it to permeate the Irish market in a very short span of time. A more significant acquisition came in December 1999, when Dixons successfully outbid rival Kingfisher plc for Norwegian electronics retailer Elkjop. Elkjop, which owned 154 stores throughout Scandinavia and in Iceland and claimed a 12 percent share of the overall Nordic market, in addition to 30 percent of the market in Norway, was clearly a highly coveted prize, and signified a substantial victory for Dixons. Whereas Kingfisher was already well established in a number of European countries—it owned the Darty and But chains in France, and the German computer supplier Promarkt—the purchase of Elkjop marked Dixons' official entry into continental Europe. As part of the company's broader European strategy, Dixons planned to follow up this deal by introducing two of its other retail concepts, PC World and the Link, into the Scandinavian marketplace. By July 2001, Dixons had established a retail presence in Hungary, Spain, and Portugal, in addition to acquiring a 15 percent stake in Kotsovolos, the largest electronics seller in Greece.

Amidst this flurry of activity overseas, Dixons continued to strengthen its domestic business, buying the Byte Computer Stores chain from Specialist Computer Holdings in April 1998. The acquisition gave Dixons an additional 16 retail outlets in the United Kingdom. At the same time, Dixons was forging a number of important partnerships with manufacturers. In October 1998 the company reached an agreement with Apple to carry iMac computers in its PC World stores, as well as in select Dixons and Currys locations. The following year Dixons reached an agreement with 01 Communique Laboratories Inc., a communication software company based in Canada, to distribute the company's unified messaging software in Europe.

During this period the company also made its first foray into the Internet industry. In February 1998 the company launched Freeserve, the first nonsubscription Internet provider in the United Kingdom. The company's innovative billing system rates—comparable to local telephone charges, based on per-minute use, with no monthly fee—proved very popular in Britain, and by July 1999 Freeserve had become the largest Internet service provider in the country, with more than 1.25 million subscribers. That same month, the provider joined with World Telecom plc to create a web-based email service. By January 2000, Freeserve's subscriber base had increased to 1.57 million. In the end, however, Dixons decided that its Internet business was leading it too far away from its core interests, and by mid-2000 it sold its stake in Freeserve. Once again devoting all its energy toward its consumer electronics business, by July 2001 Dixons was enjoying pretax profits of $647.1 million, compared with $472.1 million the previous year. With sales of cell phones and digital cameras booming, the company had every reason to feel confident about further increased profits in the future.

Principal Subsidiaries

Elkjop ASA (Norway); UniEuro (Italy; 24%); Kotsovolos S.A. (Greece; 15%).

Principal Divisions

PC World Business; PC ServiceCall; Mastercare; Partmaster Direct; Dixons Group Business Services; European Property.

Principal Operating Units

Dixons; Currys; PC World; The Link; PC City (Spain).

Principal Competitors

ASDA Group Limited; Box Clever Technology; Kingfisher plc.

Further Reading

Cope, Nigel, "The Vogue for Looking Good," *Management Today,* October 1993, pp. 68–71.
Davidson, Andrew, "Stanley Kalms," *Management Today,* January 1995, pp. 38–41.
"Dixons a Powerhouse in U.K. & U.S.," *Discount Store News,* May 6, 1991, p. 96.
"Dixons Group to Buy Elkjop of Norway," *European Report,* December 8, 1999.
Fallon, James, "Dixons Fights Takeover Bid: Silo Pretax Net Dives 86.4 Percent," *HFD-The Weekly Home Furnishings Newspaper,* January 29, 1990, pp. 105–06.
Hisey, Pete, "Silo Decides Its Future Is Better with Fretter," *Discount Store News,* October 4, 1993, pp. 1–2.
Meares, Richard, "Dixons Group Considers Getting Rid of Freeserve Stake," *National Post,* May 9, 2000, p. C14.
"Silo's $326 Million Loss Drags Dixons Down," *Television Digest,* July 13, 1992, pp. 13–14.

—John Swan
—updates: April Dougal Gasbarre, Steve Meyer

Donaldson Company, Inc.

1400 West 94th Street
Minneapolis, Minnesota 55431-2370
U.S.A.
Telephone: (952) 887-3131
Fax: (952) 887-3155
Web site: http://www.donaldson.com

Public Company
Incorporated: 1918
Employees: 8,230
Sales: $1.14 billion (2001)
Stock Exchanges: New York
Ticker Symbol: DCI
NAIC: 336399 All Other Motor Vehicle Part
Manufacturing; 333411 Air Purification Equipment
Manufacturing; 333999 All Other Miscellaneous
General Purpose Machinery Manufacturing

With operations in North and South America, Europe, South Africa, and Asia, Donaldson Company, Inc. is one of the world's largest manufacturers of specialty air and liquid filters. Donaldson's products are used in applications ranging from whole factory air filters to tractors and construction equipment, to computer disk drives. After suffering its first and only net loss in 1983, the company that *Money* magazine once characterized as a "baby blue chip" made a long, difficult comeback. Having accomplished the shift from its mature, cyclical core business, Donaldson chalked up 12 consecutive years of double-digit increases in earnings per share from 1990 to 2001.

Pre-World War I Foundation

Founder and company namesake Frank Donaldson was born and raised in southern Minnesota. After earning a degree in engineering from the University of Minnesota in 1912, he went to work as the western U.S. sales representative of Bull Tractor Company in Minneapolis. Donaldson found that one unhappy customer in Utah was having a great deal of difficulty keeping his new Bull tractor running. Donaldson had the dust-choked vehicle completely refurbished, but within a few days it was again out of commission. Taking matters into his own hands, Donaldson improvised a filter from a wire cage, eiderdown cloth, and an eight-foot-long pipe. When the enterprising young salesman proudly told his supervisors of his "modification," he was promptly fired for pointing up Bull's flaws.

Donaldson realized that although he was out of a job, he had something better: an invention that could be sold to tractor companies throughout the farm belt. With some help from his father, W.H.L. Donaldson, who owned a St. Paul hardware store, and his brother Bob, a sheet-metal fabricator, Frank designed a filter he called the "Twister." The conical device used centrifugal force to spin dirt out of the air before it passed into the engine. In 1916, Frank and his father each made an initial $200 investment in the new enterprise and named it Donaldson Engineering Company. Frank began demonstrating prototypes to former employer Bull Tractor, as well as other major midwestern equipment manufacturers.

External and internal pressures made Donaldson's early years a bumpy roller-coaster ride. Sales were rather slow that first year, but in 1917 the company won a contract to manufacture air cleaners for artillery tractors used in World War I. Before the year was through, Frank was drafted into the Army Corps of Engineers, leaving his father to run the fast-growing business. Overwhelmed, W.H.L. brought Bob into the firm at a salary of $150 per month and 25 percent of the company's profits (or half of W.H.L.'s stake). But when a competing filter company, Wilcox-Bennet, brought a potentially expensive patent infringement suit against Donaldson later that same year, the patriarch went back on his employment agreement with Bob, applying the funds he saved to the company's legal defense. Bob withheld access to his machine shop in retribution, throwing the business further into chaos. Worse yet, W.H.L. began claiming sole ownership of the busy company that Frank had founded.

Interwar Reorganization and Early Growth

Months of infighting followed Frank's postwar homecoming. In the fall of 1918, the family settled its disagreement by incorporating the business as Donaldson Company, Inc. Frank owned 45 percent of the new corporate entity, Bob got 25 percent, their sisters Amanda and Mae each owned 12.5 percent, and mother Lottie held 5 percent. W.H.L. relinquished corporate ownership, settling instead for a royalty on any air filter he invented. Since he never came up with a product for Donaldson, the company's incorporation marked his final formal involvement in the firm. (Lottie gave Frank her shares upon W.H.L.'s death in 1926.) The lawsuit that precipitated this ownership crisis remained unsettled until 1919, when Donaldson agreed to purchase a U.S. license for Wilcox-Bennet air filters for $15,000 and a royalty on each unit.

The 1920s brought stability, new products, and increased prosperity. In 1920 Donaldson launched a second type and brand of filter, the Simplex. This air cleaner used oil-soaked moss to trap dust before it could enter a motor or engine and cause damage. The company combined characteristics of both its filters with the introduction of the patented Duplex that same year. Donaldson also forged its first contract with the John Deere Tractor Company during the 1920s. John Deere would become a major customer, accounting for one-third of annual sales by the end of the decade. After suffering a $4,000 loss in 1921, the company saw its sales multiply from $19,554 in 1924 to $204,667 by 1928. By 1929, Donaldson was selling 200,000 units per year.

In addition to new product development, Donaldson sought close involvement with its customers' design processes so that their filters would work as well as possible in each manufacturer's tractors. In fact, the company began producing oil-bath type air cleaners in response to customer demand. In 1929 the corporation hired William Lowther to design a proprietary oil-washed air cleaner. His N.S. Filter was patented in 1932, but by that time the company would be scrambling to come up with the funds needed to begin manufacturing the new product.

Donaldson also diversified into tractor seats and spark-arresting mufflers in the late 1920s. The company had hoped to use a stock offering to fund the launch of an aftermarket car heater during this period as well, but the stock market's 1929 crash postponed that first public equity flotation.

Nature conspired with the worsening economy, wreaking havoc on America's farmers and the industries that served them. A five-year drought and grasshopper plagues denuded the midwestern landscape, turning the heartland into a dust bowl. When farmers hurt, tractor companies hurt and so did Donaldson. During the 1930s, the Minnesota manufacturer slashed its payroll by 70 percent, from 40 to 12, and its chief executives halved their own salaries and borrowed against life insurance policies to keep their business afloat. In 1934 Donaldson defaulted on payments to several suppliers.

It was then that Frank Donaldson and corporate attorney Ken Owen devised a plan to get the company's new oil-washed air cleaner into production and revive its cash flow. They sold the device's patent for $4,000 to a group of investors composed primarily of Donaldson stockholders. In exchange for a small royalty on each unit sold, the new owners licensed rights to produce the filter back to the company. Ford Motor Company started testing the filter mid-year and soon found that the device served its purpose well without sacrificing speed or efficiency. The contract that resulted took Donaldson from famine back to feast within months. Sales to Caterpillar, John Deere, Cummins Engine, and many other manufacturers of heavy vehicles boosted sales to $465,000 and profits to $88,000 by 1935.

By the end of this traumatic decade, annual sales hovered near $1 million, and the company's 200 employees manufactured 300,000 air cleaners each year. With a dominant 90 percent share of the market for farm and construction engine air cleaners, Donaldson sought growth through exports to Great Britain, Sweden, New Zealand, and Australia.

World War II and Beyond

During World War II, Donaldson manufactured bomber gun sights, bayonet holders, crankcase valves for tanks, and, most important, air cleaners for tanks used in the difficult and dusty conditions of the North African desert.

The early 1940s brought a management shakeup as well. After Frank Donaldson suffered a stroke in 1942, brother Bob retired from day-to-day oversight of the company to become chairman. While Frank Donaldson continued as president, John Enblom was promoted from acting general manager to executive vice-president with effective control. This administrative arrangement lasted only two years. When Frank died of heart failure in 1945, John Enblom advanced to the presidency. Upon his return from World War II service, Frank Donaldson, Jr., assumed the title of vice-president.

In spite of this unexpected leadership transition and a month-long strike, Donaldson did well during the early 1940s. Having established its first branch office in Milwaukee, Wisconsin, in 1938, the company added satellite offices in Cleveland, Chicago, and Detroit, and launched its first international production facility in Canada. Sales multiplied from less than $1 million in 1939 to $3.5 million by 1947, with profits topping $359,000.

But in the late 1940s, the Internal Revenue Service began to question the royalty plan that had saved Donaldson from bankruptcy during the Great Depression. The government agency charged that the royalties were "dividends in disguise," and that the company owed back and current taxes on these diverted profits. The IRS contended that royalties are paid before taxes and, therefore, are considered a tax-deductible business expense and that dividends are paid out of after-tax profits. By paying "royalties" to what was essentially a group of shareholders, the company had avoided $1.3 million in taxes in the process. Donaldson, which was worth only $1.27 million at the time, struggled to reach a lower settlement with the IRS over the next two years, but finally had to go to court.

Key Dates:

1916: Frank Donaldson and his father, W.H.L. Donaldson, found Donaldson Engineering Company to market an air filter that the son has designed.

1918: The business is incorporated as Donaldson Company, Inc.

1951: Three senior executives quit to form Crenlo Corp.; Frank Donaldson, Jr., becomes company president at age 31.

1955: Company goes public.

Early 1970s: Company diversifies through the acquisitions of Torit Corp., Majac, Inc., and Kittell Muffler and Engineering.

1973: Frank Donaldson, Jr., becomes chairman and CEO; William Hodder is named president.

1983: Severe early 1980s recession leads to the company's first-ever annual loss, a major reorganization, and a more thorough program of diversification.

1996: Hodder retires and is replaced as CEO by company veteran William Van Dyke.

1999: AirMaze Corporation is acquired.

2000: Donaldson acquires the DCE dust control business of Invensys plc; revenues surpass the $1 billion mark for the first time during the year ending in July.

2002: Ultrafilter International AG of Germany is acquired.

The legal crisis brought on a mutiny of sorts at Donaldson. President John Enblom, along with pivotal employees Bill Lowther and Roger Cresswell, all members of the executive committee, issued an ultimatum: either Frank, Jr., sold them 51 percent of the company for $200,000, or they would all quit and start a competing company. Frank, Jr., marshaled the Donaldson family—which still owned the vast majority of the company's equity—and they agreed not to sell.

True to their word, the three executives quit to form Crenlo Corp. in 1951. At the age of 31, Frank, Jr., became president of a company with $5.5 million in annual sales. Although he had a degree in engineering from Harvard, where he minored in economics and graduated cum laude, his lack of day-to-day experience made the early 1950s a difficult period of transition for the business.

Frank, Jr.'s first order of business was to replenish the "brain trust." He sought management help from his cousin, Dick Donaldson, who became vice-president of sales and engineering. The new president established the company's first formal research and development department in 1951 and brought in consultants from the Stanford Research Institute the following year. Seven years of research and testing resulted in the 1959 launch of the "Donaclone," the first heavy-duty air cleaner to use a paper filter. The brand name combined Donaldson and cyclone, and the device harked back to the company's original Twister brand filter. It used a series of "cyclone tubes" to spin dirt out of the air. The Duralife paper filter served as a final dirt trap. The new product was such a success

that, during its first year, it accounted for 20 percent of Donaldson's annual sales.

In the meantime, Donaldson had gone public in 1955 with a modest $124,000 offering. Frank, Jr.'s first decade in office was incredibly successful. Sales nearly doubled, from $5.5 million in 1950 to a record $10.1 million in 1959, and profits more than doubled, from $315,000 to $669,000 during the same period.

But this was only the beginning of what a company history dubbed "the age of the Donaclone." Sales tripled over the course of the 1960s, to $35.9 million in 1969, as clients ranging from Caterpillar to the U.S. Army adopted the new filter for their heavy-duty machinery. Geographic expansion also contributed to this growth, as Donaldson established joint ventures and licensing agreements with businesses in Britain, France, Germany, Brazil, and Australia. By the end of the decade, it had wholly owned subsidiaries in Germany, Belgium, and South Africa as well. Formalized in 1963, the International Division grew 30-fold from 1963 to 1970.

Frank Donaldson, Jr., advanced to chairman and CEO in 1973. In a departure from the traditional promotion from within, Donaldson hired William Hodder, formerly president of Target Stores and a director of Donaldson for just four years, to succeed the founder's son. Hodder took the company on something of an acquisition spree, merging with St. Paul, Minnesota's Torit Corp. and acquiring Majac, Inc. and Kittell Muffler and Engineering in rapid succession. The new affiliates helped diversify Donaldson from its core. Torit added dust collectors that could clear the air in whole factories, while Majac specialized in making dust (it disintegrated materials to specifically sized bits) and Kittell produced heavy-duty sound controllers. Donaldson also diversified from within, establishing a hydraulic fluid filter division in 1975.

In spite of inflation and the energy crunch, Donaldson's strategy of "focused diversification" kept the company's sales and earnings on a countercyclical rise throughout the decade. Sales broke both the $100 million and $200 million thresholds over the course of the decade, and net income more than doubled from $6 million to $14.2 million. In 1979 the company was listed on the New York Stock Exchange.

Reorganization and Retrenchment in the 1980s

After this stellar decade, however, "stagflation" hit Donaldson's core constituencies hard in the early 1980s. Two prominent examples of the recession in the heavy machinery industry were International Harvester, which lost $3 billion, and John Deere, whose plants came to a standstill for two months during the early 1980s. Donaldson's sales skidded from $264 million in 1981 to $203 million by 1983, when the company suffered its first-ever annual loss, a $3.5 million shortfall. Blaming its difficulties in part on overexpansion in the late 1970s, the company closed two plants and scaled back the remaining U.S. production to 50 percent of capacity. Employment was reduced by more than 25 percent from 1980 to 1985. Administrative personnel accepted mandatory unpaid leave and a salary freeze. Sales and profits began to recover in 1984, the same year that Frank Donaldson, Jr., announced his retirement.

But perhaps most important, the early 1980s crisis highlighted Donaldson's dependence on a mature market and precipitated a more thorough diversification. From 1984 to 1990, the company poured $40 million into acquisitions and joint ventures and plowed another $50 million into research and development. Hoping to eliminate duplication of effort and gain efficiencies, top executives reorganized the company into five groups: Industrial, International, Original Equipment, Aftermarket, and Worldwide Support. Having focused almost exclusively on the original equipment market throughout its history, the company began to target the filter aftermarket. Research and development efforts paid off in the form of new products for industries ranging from computers to passenger autos to pharmaceuticals. Sales in nontraditional markets grew to $129.5 million by 1990, almost one-third of annual sales.

It took most of the 1980s for these new strategies to come to full fruition, but the geographic, product, and market diversification helped even out Donaldson's cyclical performance. The budding conglomerate began to realize its goal of steady growth in profitability in the early 1990s, when rising net sales combined with an annual return on sales of more than 5 percent. Revenues increased from $422.9 million in 1990 to $704 million in 1995, and net income jumped from $21 million to $38.5 million.

Building Toward $1 Billion in Sales in the 1990s

With Chairman and CEO Hodder nearing mandatory retirement, Donaldson settled the question of succession. In 1994 William Van Dyke capped a more than 20-year career at the company with his appointment to the positions of president and chief operating officer. He advanced to the chief executive office in August 1996. Also during that year Donaldson continued its overseas expansion by acquiring Tecnov S.A., a maker of heavy-duty exhaust mufflers based in France. The company also sold off the operations of its subsidiary in Brazil.

Growth in emerging markets in Asia was a high priority during this period. In 1996 Donaldson formed a joint venture to manufacture Torit industrial-filtration products in Guilin, China. The following year the company established a subsidiary in South Korea called Donaldson Korea Co., Ltd. During 1999 Donaldson opened a new facility in Wuxi, China, for the manufacture of computer disk drive filtration products. This facility and a sister facility in Hong Kong generated more than $50 million in revenue during 1999, which represented nearly 5 percent of the company total.

There were a number of acquisitions in the late 1990s that helped to keep Donaldson's revenue figures soaring ever upward, with two being particularly noteworthy. In April 1997 the company acquired the Armada Tube Group, a manufacturer of exhaust products, for $11.3 million. Old Saybrook, Connecticut-based Aercology Incorporated, maker of industrial air filtration products, was acquired for $9.8 million in July of that same year. During fiscal 1999, the pace of acquisition slowed as deteriorating market conditions led Donaldson to focus on cost containment. A number of efficiency measures were put into place, including a $20 million inventory reduction, and the company also announced plans to close its Oelwein, Iowa, manufacturing plant, a move that involved the elimination of 125 jobs. As a result, Donaldson managed to increase its net

earnings by 9.5 percent to $62.4 million on revenues of $944.1 million. Helping to propel sales forward was the introduction of the next-generation PowerCore air-intake filtration system for heavy-duty on-road and off-road vehicles.

As Donaldson grew in size, its appetite for acquisitions grew as well, resulting in more expensive deals. In November 1999 the company acquired AirMaze Corporation for $31.9 million. AirMaze, which had manufacturing facilities in Stow, Ohio, and Greenville, Tennessee, was a supplier of heavy-duty air and liquid filters, air/oil separators, and high-purity air filter products. In February 2000 Donaldson acquired the DCE dust control business of Invensys plc for $56.4 million. Based in Leicester, England, DCE fit in very well alongside Donaldson's Torit business and provided Donaldson with a major presence in the industrial dust collection sector outside North America with its strong presence in the European market, where it generated 70 percent of its sales, and with its assembly operations in South Africa, Australia, and Japan. In mid-2002 Donaldson paid about $68 million for Ultrafilter International AG, a Haan, Germany-based firm specializing in compressed-air filtration systems and related parts and equipment. Like DCE, Ultrafilter fit the three criteria that Donaldson had been emphasizing in its diversification; namely, according to Van Dyke, ''it expands our presence in industrial markets; it focuses on replacement parts; and the majority of its revenues are outside of the U.S.''

By the early 21st century, Donaldson Company had delivered a remarkably consistent level of achievement over a period of more than a decade. By fiscal 2001, revenues had increased for 18 consecutive years, and they surpassed the $1 billion mark for the first time during fiscal 2000. From 1989 to 2001, revenues had increased nearly threefold. Earnings nearly quintupled during that same period. The company had also achieved double-digit annual earnings per share increases for 12 consecutive years, spanning from 1990 to 2001. Barring a severe economic meltdown, there did not appear to be any reason why the extremely well-run company could not continue along this same path of achievement.

Principal Subsidiaries

Torit Australia Pty. Ltd.; Donaldson Australasia Pty. Limited; Donaldson Sales, Inc. (Barbados); Donaldson Coordination Center, B.V.B.A. (Belgium); Donaldson Europe, B.V.B.A. (Belgium); DCE Scandinavia APS (Denmark); Donaldson France, S.A.S. (France); Tecnov Donaldson, S.A.S. (France); DCE S.A. (France); DCE Neotechnik GmbH (Germany); Donaldson Gesellschaft m.b.H. (Germany); Donaldson India Filter Systems Pvt. Ltd.; PT Donaldson Systems Indonesia; Donaldson Italia s.r.l. (Italy); Nippon Donaldson Limited (Japan); Donaldson Luxembourg S.a.r.l. (Luxembourg); Donaldson, S.A. de C.V. (Mexico); Diemo S.A. de C.V. (Mexico); Donaldson Filtration Industrial S. de R.L. de C.V. (Mexico); Donaldson Torit, B.V. (Netherlands); DCE Benelux B.V. (Netherlands); Air Master China Ltd.; Donaldson Far East Limited (China); Guilin Air King Enterprises Ltd. (China); Donaldson (Wuxi) Filters Co., Ltd. (China); Donaldson Filtration (Asia Pacific) Pte. Ltd. (Singapore); Donaldson Filtration Systems (Proprietary) Ltd. (South Africa); Donaldson Korea Co., Ltd.; DCE Donaldson Sistemas de Filtracion, S.L. (Spain); Donaldson Filtros Iberica S.L. (Spain); Donaldson Filter Components

118 Donaldson Company, Inc.

Limited (U.K.); DCE Donaldson Ltd. (U.K.); Tetratec Europe Limited (U.K.).

Principal Operating Units

Industrial Products; Engine Products.

Principal Competitors

Cummins, Inc.; Pall Corporation; ESCO Technologies Inc.; BHA Group Holdings, Inc.; MFRI, Inc.

Further Reading

Abelson, Reed, "Exhausting the Possibilities," *Forbes,* May 25, 1992, p. 260.

Croghan, Lore, "Don't Look Back," *Financial World,* July 18, 1995, p. 50.

Goodman, Jordan E., "These Baby Blue Chips Promise to Become Grown-up Champs," *Money,* May 1991, p. 65.

Jaffe, Thomas, "Cleaner Air Company," *Forbes,* September 14, 1992, p. 562.

Keenan, Tim, "Let's Clear the Air: Donaldson, Hoechst Celanese Develop New Filter," *Ward's Auto World,* September 1995, p. 85.

Martin, Norman, Christopher A. Sawyer, and Marjorie Sorge, "The Ultimate in Air Fresheners," *Automotive Industries,* February 1996, p. 173.

Morais, Richard C., "Hong Kong Is Just Around the Corner," *Forbes,* October 12, 1992, p. 50.

Peterson, Susan E., "Donaldson Buys Filter Company," *Minneapolis Star Tribune,* June 14, 2002, p. 1D.

——, "Hodder's Legacy: Donaldson CEO Leaves Company on Solid Ground After Years of Growth," *Minneapolis Star Tribune,* July 29, 1996, p. 1D.

——, "Van Dyke Heir Apparent to Take Over Donaldson," *Minneapolis Star Tribune,* August 11, 1994, p. 3D.

——, "Visible Success: Filter Maker Donaldson Co. Was in a Highly Cyclical Business, but Since Broadening Its Customer Base It Has Consistently Had Double-Digit Growth," *Minneapolis Star Tribune,* December 10, 2001, p. 1D.

"Salesman's Solution to Tractor-Choking Dust Leads to Founding of Filter Manufacturing Company," *Hydraulics and Pneumatics,* May 1983, p. 80.

Toward a Cleaner, Quieter World: History of the Donaldson Company, 1915–1985, Minneapolis, Minn.: Donaldson Co., Inc., 1985.

Youngblood, Dick, "Diversified Firm Yields Dividends," *Minneapolis Star Tribune,* February 4, 1991, p. 1D.

—April Dougal Gasbarre
—update: David E. Salamie

Dynegy Inc.

1000 Louisiana, Suite 5800
Houston, Texas 77002
U.S.A.
Telephone: (713) 507-6400
Toll free: (877) 439-6349
Fax: (713) 507-3871
Web site: http://www.dynegy.com

Public Company
Incorporated: 1984 as Natural Gas Clearinghouse
Employees: 6,700
Sales: $42.24 billion (2001)
Stock Exchanges: New York
Ticker Symbol: DYN
NAIC: 211112 Natural Gas Liquids (e.g., Ethane, Isobutane, Natural Gasoline, Propane) Recovered from Oil and Gas Field Gases; 221210 Natural Gas Distribution; 221112 Electric Power Distribution Systems

Dynegy Inc. is one of the world's leading energy commodity and service providers, offering "one-stop" gathering, processing, marketing, and transportation of natural gas, natural gas liquids, crude oil, and electricity. Led almost since its formation by Chairman and CEO Charles L. (Chuck) Watson, Dynegy achieved its market dominance through several mergers and acquisitions in the middle and late 1990s. By the early 2000s, subsidiary Dynegy Midstream Services had become a top producer and marketer of natural gas liquids in North America, with an interest in about 14,000 miles of pipelines and more than 33 gas processing facilities. Dynegy Marketing and Trade was a leading producer of electricity, with 19,000 megawatts (MW) of generating capacity, and a top marketer and trader of natural gas and power. Dynegy's subsidiary Illinois Power served 650,000 electricity and natural gas customers in 2001, and Dynegy Global Communications moved its parent company into the broadband market, with a 5,100-mile fiber optic network.

Dynegy's marketing arm essentially acts as an energy services middleman. Dynegy has arranged for the purchase of natural gas supplies from as many as 600 different suppliers ranging from major natural gas producers to small independents. The company has purchased or negotiated for the purchase of specific volumes of natural gas through fixed short-term and long-term contracts and arranged for their transmission or transportation through company-owned and third-party pipeline systems. Supplies purchased have been aggregated by the company and resold to the company's customers, including local distribution companies, energy utility companies, power plants, and retail and industrial end-users. Dynegy complements its marketing activities with the gathering, processing, fractionation (that is, separation into component parts), and transmission of natural gas liquids, crude oil, and other petroleum and gas-based products, such as butane.

Negotiating the Deregulation of the 1980s

The natural gas industry was tightly regulated until the late 1970s, with the gathering, transportation, and marketing of natural gas dominated by a few companies and pricing restrictions that kept gas prices below market value. Prior to deregulation, natural gas typically was sold on a flat-rate, long-term contract basis. Gas producers sold to interstate pipeline companies, which sold the gas to distributors, which in turn marketed the gas to end-users. The National Gas Policy Act (NGPA) of 1978 began the process of deregulation, loosening restrictions on the transmission, marketing, and production of natural gas, and establishing new pricing layers, which removed price controls from new gas production. Over the next decade and a half the NGPA would be implemented by a series of orders promulgated by the Federal Energy Regulatory Commission (FERC), beginning with Order 380, introduced in 1984, which allowed third-party marketers to sell gas at prices competitive with the gas producers. This was followed by Order 436, which allowed transportation of natural gas over interstate pipelines and opened the way for market-responsive pricing.

The immediate effect of the NGPA was to increase drilling activities, as producers sought to develop gas resources that could be sold without pricing restrictions. But, in 1982, with the onset of a national recession, demand for natural gas collapsed. This situation opened the way for a new method of selling gas,

---

Company Perspectives:

We Believe in People: People are the foundation of our success and the key to achieving our vision. We are committed to an environment in which all individuals have the opportunity and responsibility to achieve a high degree of personal and professional satisfaction and growth. We will recognize, reward and promote those who live our value.

---

spot pricing, and, with the deregulation of the industry, gave rise to an industry of third-party marketers. The Natural Gas Clearinghouse was set up in June 1984 as a broker for negotiating spot market transactions between producers and end-users. The Clearinghouse itself would not take title to the gas it brokered. The Clearinghouse was formed as a joint venture by investment banker Morgan Stanley, New York law firm Akin, Gump, Strauss, Hauer & Feld, and Transco Energy Company, an interstate natural gas pipeline company with a 10,000-mile system reaching an 11-state market. By October 1984, the Clearinghouse was in business, arranging its first spot market sale of 200 million daily cubic feet of natural gas. The company also negotiated with other pipeline systems to link up with the Clearinghouse.

The venture struggled in its first year. Then Transco and other pipeline companies defected, believing they could negotiate better pricing on their own. Morgan Stanley bought out Transco and Akin, Gump in 1985 for $24 million and recruited Chuck Watson to head up the company. Watson, then 35 years old, had gained 13 years of experience in the energy industry at Conoco Oil. Born at the Great Lakes Naval Academy in Illinois, Watson graduated with a business degree from Oklahoma State University and went to work for Conoco. Considered a rising star at the company, Watson received a series of promotions around the company, giving him a wide range of exposure to pipeline transportation and operations and to the marketing of natural gas and natural gas liquids. When Morgan Stanley hired him as president and CEO of the Natural Gas Clearinghouse, Watson set out to change the company's focus. Instead of merely acting as a broker, Watson used Morgan Stanley's financial backing to buy and then resell gas, while also beginning to build the company's own transmission, distribution, and processing infrastructure through a series of acquisitions. Meanwhile, new orders promulgated by FERC began to increase the volumes of gas the independent marketers were allowed to handle. The Clearinghouse quickly gained a leadership position in the gas marketing field, seeing sales rise to 1.3 billion daily cubic feet by 1988 and then top two billion daily cubic feet the following year, making the Clearinghouse the country's largest independent natural gas marketer.

The Bill Gates of Gas in the 1990s

Watson sought further growth for the company. In 1989, he arranged to sell the Clearinghouse to two oil and gas exploration and production companies, Apache Corporation and Noble Affiliates, Inc., gaining those companies' financial backing to fuel expansion. Watson remained as president, CEO, and ultimately chairman of the Clearinghouse. At the end of 1989, he

arranged for the Clearinghouse to acquire Apache's Nagasco, Inc. gas gathering system, boosting the Clearinghouse's natural gas volume to 2.55 billion daily cubic feet. The following year, the Clearinghouse, which had been developing natural gas futures, began trading gas futures at the New York Mercantile Exchange. By 1990, the Clearinghouse was posting annual revenues of $1.7 billion.

By the beginning of the 1990s, however, margins on sales of natural gas were dropping from a high of 25 cents per 1,000 cubic feet to the single-digit range in the 1990s, reaching a low of two to three cents per 1,000 cubic feet in the 1990s. Watson responded by expanding the Clearinghouse beyond natural gas marketing into gathering, processing, and marketing natural gas, as well as other fuel oils, building the Clearinghouse into a "one-stop energy store." The company formed its NGC Oil Trading and Transportation subsidiary and began expanding its gathering and processing capacity through acquisitions and contracts of facilities. Between 1990 and early 1994 the company spent some $150 million buying gathering systems and processing and storage facilities. Financing the company's expansion came from selling it, adding Dekalb Energy Company to the list of owners. Then, in 1992, the company, which had revenues of nearly $2.1 billion in 1991, with an operating profit of $78.5 million, was sold to Louisville Gas & Electric Company and British Gas, each of which controlled a one-third share of the company; management retained control of the remaining one-third. In that year, FERC Order 636 took away the last of the regulatory restrictions on the natural gas industry. In response, the Clearinghouse, through a new subsidiary, Hub Services, Inc., joined with three gas utility companies to form Enerchange LLC, which would own and operate three natural gas marketing hubs. The hubs, which were located at the intersection of interstate pipelines, offered various transaction services to customers, including taking deliveries from multiple suppliers and arranging sales to a range of distributors and end-users.

The company's revenues, aided by growing sales of natural gas liquids and crude oil, neared $2.5 billion in 1992 and $2.8 billion in 1993. The company's operating profit, a key industry indicator, also remained strong, at $96.8 million in 1992 and $92 million in 1993. Net profits for these years were $44 and $46 million, respectively, highlighting the tight margins available in the industry. These margins were also leading to an industry shakeout, as the field of marketers began to narrow, and mergers and acquisitions among industry giants marked the industry's consolidation. Canada's Nova Corporation entered the U.S. field in 1994, paying $170 million for Louisville Gas & Electric's share in the Clearinghouse; ownership was now split at 36.5 percent held by both Nova and British Gas and 17 percent held by Clearinghouse management. Terms of the Nova acquisition also brought the Clearinghouse into Canada, through a 50 percent joint venture in Novagas Clearinghouse Ltd., based in Calgary. Also in 1994, the Clearinghouse moved to enter the European market, then beginning its own deregulation, forming the Accord Energy joint venture with British Gas.

Watson, however, continued to steer the Clearinghouse toward his "energy store" concept. In 1995, the company took an important step toward increasing its capacity in products other than natural gas when it merged with publicly held Trident NGL Holdings Inc. The deal, worth more than $750 million in

Key Dates:

1984: Natural Gas Clearinghouse is established as a natural gas broker.
1989: Company acquires Apache's Nagasco, Inc.
1992: Company is bought by Louisville Gas & Electric Company, British Gas, and management, each owning a third.
1995: Company merges with Trident NGL Holdings Inc.
1996: Company merges with most of Chevron Corporation's natural gas and gas liquids businesses, including Warren Petroleum.
1997: Company acquires Destec Energy.
1998: NGC changes its name to Dynegy Inc.
2000: Company purchases Illinova, including subsidiary Illinois Power.
2001: Company backs out of a deal to purchase troubled rival Enron.

cash, stock, and the assumption of Trident's debt, more than doubled the company's natural gas liquids capacity. The merger also took the company public. The company's name was changed to NGC Corporation, reflecting the company's diversification from its natural gas marketing base. By 1995, natural gas marketing contributed only 65 percent of the company's $3.7 billion in revenues. By then, Watson was already preparing to complete the company's energy store concept, bringing NGC into selling electricity. Setting up its Electric Clearinghouse subsidiary in 1994, NGC was poised to take advantage of the coming deregulation of the electricity marketing industry, which, at an estimated $200 billion per year, was some three times larger than the natural gas market.

The energy store concept was not unique to NGC. The importance of being able to offer customers a full range of energy services was recognized throughout the industry. A new wave of mergers and acquisitions swept the industry. With the Trident merger, NGC's share of the market had grown to 8 percent, and the company began to forecast capturing as much as 12 percent during the second half of the decade. By the end of 1996, however, the company had easily surpassed its own forecast. In January 1996, NGC entered talks with industry giant Chevron Corporation to merge Chevron's gas gathering, processing, and marketing operations with NGC. By June of that year the companies had reached agreement and, by September 1996, the merger was completed. NGC acquired Chevron's Natural Gas Business unit and parts of its Warren Petroleum subsidiary; Chevron joined British Gas and Nova as owners of NGC, with each controlling approximately 25 percent of the company. NGC's Trident subsidiary was renamed Warren Petroleum, and Chevron's natural gas marketing activities were merged under the Natural Gas Clearinghouse subsidiary. The Chevron merger also added to the company's electricity capacity, making NGC the country's third largest independent power marketer.

With the merger, NGC also became the industry's largest gas marketer, with daily volumes of ten billion cubic feet and daily sales of some 470,000 barrels of natural gas liquids taking a 14 percent share of the market. Analysts began comparing

Watson, who had steered NGC to become one of the top 150 businesses in the country, with Microsoft's Bill Gates. Watson stepped down as president in November 1996, but retained his chairman and CEO titles, promising to continue controlling day-to-day activities.

1997–2001: Further Growth Through Acquisitions

In January 1997, the company announced its intention to spend $650 million on capital improvements, investments, and acquisitions. The company's efforts to purchase more electric power plants and gas processing plants was thwarted by a lack of cash. Only 12 percent of NGC was traded publicly; the rest was owned by employees and three companies. Watson arranged to buy out Nova and British Gas and float their shares on the market, raising the publicly traded portion of the company to 60 percent. The resulting funds helped NGC purchase Destec Energy, an independent power producer. NGC sold Destec's foreign operations, its Tiger Bay cogeneration plant, and its lignite reserves, but hung on to its U.S. power plants.

Also in 1997, NGC formed several alliances with regional power companies, including NICOR, All Energy, and Canada's Consumersfirst. The company continued that strategy in 1998, joining forces in the Southeast with Piedmont Natural Gas and AGL Resources to create SouthStar Energy. These joint ventures gave NGC an entrée into local retail markets. That same year, NGC changed its name to Dynegy Inc.

With revenues of $15.4 billion in 1999, Dynegy had more than doubled its 1997 take of $7.3 billion. Although net income, $152 million, was only 1 percent of revenues, it represented a respectable margin for a wholesaler. The company's retail energy business proved unprofitable in 1999, losing the company $3.5 million. Dynegy, however, was not willing to abandon the electricity retail market. Following its successful strategy in the gas market of purchasing gas processing plants and large producers, Dynegy sought to acquire its own electric power producer, eventually settling on Illinova. Financial difficulties at Illinova helped Dynegy negotiate the bargain basement price of $2 billion. In 2000, Dynegy finalized its purchase of Illinova, acquiring in the process 75-year-old Illinois Power, five power plants, and more than 600,000 retail customers.

Focusing more resources on retail electricity meant Dynegy had to pull back in other areas. In 1999, the company's midstream business sold four gas processing plants, thus reducing operating expenses by $50 million. The following year, ONEOK bought more of Dynegy's natural gas assets for $308 million.

With a plan to trade bandwidth online, Dynegy purchased two fiber-optic network providers in 2000: Taxis in Britain, and Extant in the United States. The company also began selling electricity and natural gas online in 2000 through Dynegydirect.

Enron Angst in 2001

Having long stood in the shadow of its rival Enron, Dynegy jumped at the chance to play the white knight when Enron faced possible financial ruin in 2001. As the preeminent energy trader in the world, Enron was valued at $70 billion early in the year.

Several high-level resignations and revelations about suspect accounting practices that may have inflated the company's bottom line sent Enron's stock plummeting. In November, Dynegy announced that it would save Enron by purchasing it for only $9 billion in Dynegy stock. Further nasty revelations about Enron's financial position kept its stock falling, until, only two weeks after Dynegy's offer, Enron's market capitalization was $270 million. Dynegy pulled out of the deal, sealing Enron's fate: its stock fell to below $1 a share and bankruptcy was inevitable.

The failed deal was not entirely a fiasco for Dynegy, however. Dynegy had invested $1.5 billion in Enron as part of the merger terms, in return for the right to acquire Enron's subsidiary Northern Natural Gas (NNG) if the merger fell through. The U.S. natural gas pipeline was valued at $2.25 billion before the deal, making it a nice consolation prize. Although Enron fought the transfer of the subsidiary, at the end of January 2002 Dynegy announced that it had completed its acquisition of NNG.

The spectacular collapse of Enron led to a closer scrutiny of its fellow energy traders, who seemed tainted by association. Although energy trading accounted for only 20 percent of Dynegy's revenues, compared with 80 percent at Enron, Dynegy saw its stock drop to $20 a share by January 2002. Falling oil and gas prices also hurt Dynegy's prospects early in 2002. CEO Watson promised to improve the company's liquidity and bolster its bottom line with a $1.25 billion restructuring plan. Asset sales and capital expense reductions would bring in about $750 million, and a stock offering was expected to raise another $500 million. Whether these measures would be enough to reassure nervous investors remained to be seen.

Principal Subsidiaries

Dynegy Canada; Dynegy Customer Care; Dynegy Europe Energy; Dynegy Europe Communications; Dynegy Global Communications; Dynegy Operating Company; Dynegy Midwest Generation; Dynegy Midstream Services; Dynegy Northeast Generation; Dynegy Storage Limited; Dynegy Technology Strategy & Ventures; Illinois Power Company; Northern Natural Gas Company; Wholesale Energy Network.

Principal Competitors

American Electric Power, Inc.; Aquila, Inc.; Duke Energy; Exxon Mobil Corporation; Reliant Energy.

Further Reading

Ackman, Dan, "Dynegy Catches Enron's Flu," *Forbes,* December 18, 2001.

Boitano, Margaret, "Is Dynegy the Next Enron? Probably Not. It's More Like the Anti-Enron," *Fortune,* December 18, 2000, p. 166.

"Central Unit Set Up for Spot Sales," *Oil & Gas Journal,* June 25, 1984, p. 32.

"The Deal Not Taken," *Forbes,* November 28, 2001.

Durgin, Hillary, "Energy Firms See Future Role As Multi-Service 'Stores,' " *Houston Chronicle,* September 5, 1995, Bus. Sec., p. 1.

Grugal, Robin M., "NGC Corp.," *Investor's Business Daily,* August 5, 1996, p. A4.

Hotz, Lindsay K., "Dynegy Completes Merger," *Houston Business Journal,* June 9, 2000, p. 11B.

McWilliams, Gary, "Chuck Watson's Power Play," *Business Week,* April 8, 1996, p. 98.

Palmeri, Christopher, "Power Base," *Forbes,* February 21, 2000, p. 88.

——, "Power Broker," *Forbes,* November 6, 1995, p. 60.

Toal, Brian A., "Not So Fanciful Pipe Dreams," *Oil & Gas Investor,* October 1995, p. 59.

Weinberg, Neil, and Daniel Fisher, "Power Player," *Forbes,* December 24, 2001, p. 52.

Williams, John, "Business Powers Locked in Feud Over Summit: Watson's Laid-Back Style Hides Intensity," *Houston Chronicle,* December 22, 1996, p. A1.

—M. L. Cohen
—update: Susan Windisch Brown

E. E.PIPHANY™

E.piphany, Inc.

1900 South Norfolk Street, Suite 310
San Mateo, California 94403
U.S.A.
Telephone: (650) 356-3800
Fax: (650) 496-2431
Web site: http://www.epiphany.com

Public Company
Incorporated: 1996 as E.piphany Marketing Software
Employees: 700
Sales: $125.7 million (2001)
Stock Exchanges: NASDAQ
Ticker Symbol: EPNY
NAIC: 511210 Software Publishers

E.piphany, Inc. is one of the leading developers and vendors of customer relationship management (CRM) software. Its flagship CRM software suite includes sales, marketing, service, and analytic applications. When the company went public in 1999, investors pushed its stock price to dizzying heights. With the recession of 2001, demand for CRM software slowed considerably. E.piphany's stock lost much of its value, and the company reported larger than expected losses. It introduced version E.6 of its CRM software suite in the first quarter of 2002, hoping that its new generation of CRM software would spark an increase in CRM spending.

Developing Customer Relationship Management Software: 1996–98

E.piphany, Inc. was founded in November 1996 as E.piphany Marketing Software. The company secured its first round of venture capital funding in March 1997 and a second round in January 1998. During this period the company was developing software for marketers that would capture and analyze customer data for enhanced marketing campaigns. This type of software would come to be known as customer relationship management (CRM) software. For 1998 E.piphany reported revenue of $3.4 million, with services contributing $1.2 million.

In May 1998 Roger Siboni joined E.piphany as president and CEO. Siboni, a graduate of the University of California at Berkeley, was formerly the deputy chairman and chief operating officer (COO) of the accounting and consulting firm KPMG Peat Marwick LLP. Siboni had a 20-year career at KPMG before joining E.piphany. At KPMG he helped numerous technology startups become major public companies, and he was centrally involved in driving the growth of KPMG's consulting and high technology practices.

Releasing Commercial Version of CRM Software and Going Public: 1999

At the beginning of 1999 E.piphany released the first commercially available version of its E.4 CRM software system. The web-based software suite was designed for organizations that wanted to use their customer data to create one-to-one marketing initiatives. According to Martha Rogers of the Peppers and Rogers Group, a consulting firm that specialized in one-to-one marketing, E.piphany's software made it easier for companies to adopt a customer-centric approach to marketing. The entire E.4 suite consisted of 16 modules, of which eight were released in January 1999 and eight later in the year. The modules enabled the analysis and integration of customer-related data in the areas of finance, sales, marketing, electronic commerce, and support services. A typical deployment of E.piphany's E.4 system cost about $500,000, with individual modules beginning at $200,000. Early adopters of E.4 included Charles Schwab & Co., Capital BlueCross, Visio Corp., and Hewlett-Packard Co.

E.piphany went public later in 1999 and held its initial public offering (IPO) on September 22. There was strong demand for the firm's stock, with 4.15 million shares offered at $16 a share. From the start E.piphany's stock price was extremely volatile. By the beginning of November it was trading at higher than $80 a share, having received a boost when the firm gained Amazon.com as a customer for its E.4 CRM system. The firm also released new and updated product modules for its E.4 suite, including modules for analyzing and reporting on customer behavior, for managing e-mail and web marketing campaigns, and others.

E.piphany made its first post-IPO acquisition in November when it announced that it would acquire RightPoint, Inc. for about $392 million in stock. RightPoint developed software that supported real-time, interactive communications with customers. Its software enabled call center representatives to make specific offers to customers on the basis of information retrieved from the company's database of customer information. The day after the announcement, E.piphany's stock surged 40 percent to an all-time high of $157.75.

Expanding Through Acquisitions and Releasing E.5 for E-Commerce: 2000

E.piphany's next acquisition gave analysts cause to question the fundamental valuations of Internet companies. In March 2000 E.piphany announced that it would acquire privately held Octane Software for $3.2 billion in stock. Octane specialized in software for multichannel customer interaction applications and infrastructure software for sales, service, and support. Octane had revenue of $3 million in 1999 and was expected to generate about $35 million in 2000. E.piphany's stock had recently peaked at $317 a share. With the acquisition of Octane, E.phipany would have more than 125 customers, including American Express, Compaq Computer Co., GTE, and Procter & Gamble.

In early April E.piphany announced two acquisitions: iLeverage, a marketing software provider, for about $28.5 million in stock, and eClass Direct, Inc., a direct-mail marketing company that specialized in e-mail marketing services, for nearly $60 million in stock. Following the announcement regarding eClass Direct, E.piphany's stock lost 32 percent of its value, reducing the value of the eClass acquisition to $35.6 million. During the month E.piphany's stock traded in a range from about $45 a share to $125 a share.

E.piphany introduced version E.5 of its CRM software suite in July 2000. The new version incorporated applications from recently acquired Octane Software, merging E.piphany's analytics, campaign management, e-mail marketing, and real-time personalization software with Octane's applications that automated sales, service, and support functions. Thus version E.5 merged CRM's operational and analytical capabilities. E.5 was capable of managing inbound and outbound customer interaction via the web. It had a base price of about $200,000. Through a three-way agreement with LoudCloud Inc. and Interelate, E.piphany's E.5 software was made available as a hosted service, which made it accessible to companies that could not afford to purchase it. Later in the year E.piphany released a version of E.5 for business-to-business electronic commerce.

In October E.piphany and Sun Microsystems entered into a strategic marketing agreement, with both companies joining forces on product development, sales, and marketing. Under the agreement E.piphany's CRM software would be integrated into the Sun Solaris operating system and be marketed as a CRM solution to both firms' customers.

Slowdown of Spending on CRM Software: 2001

By the beginning of 2001 E.piphany had about 300 customers in a wide range of vertical industries, including airlines, automotive, e-commerce, financial services, hospitality, and telecommunications. The company's revenue went from $19.2 million in 1999 to $127.3 million in 2000. It had formed alliances with the Big 5 consulting firms and partnerships with manufacturers such as Hewlett-Packard, Cisco Systems, and Sun Microsystems. Its principal competitors were Siebel Systems, PeopleSoft, and Kana Communications.

E.piphany added sales force automation software to its offerings with the acquisition of Moss Software Inc. in February 2001. Moss had more than 100 customers, many of them in financial services and high-tech. E.piphany also acquired the intellectual property of Radnet Inc., a Cambridge, Massachusetts-based developer of portal technology and groupware applications.

By the start of the second quarter of 2001 it was clear that demand for CRM software was softening. Analysts began lowering 2001 revenue estimates for E.piphany and other companies in the CRM sector. E.piphany's stock, which began the year around $53 a share, fell below $10 a share in April. The company announced that its first quarter revenue would not meet expectations. Losses continued to mount throughout the year, with E.piphany recording a $1.98 billion loss for the third quarter, which the company attributed primarily to the declining stock value of several companies it had acquired.

During the first half of 2001 E.piphany entered into partnerships with ChannelWave and Comergent to offer a platform for building a customer-driven demand chain. The platform would facilitate collaborative marketing, sales, and service efforts for manufacturers, resellers, retailers, and other channel partners. Later in the year E.piphany released its E.5 System Demand Chain Solutions package, which allowed manufacturers, channel distribution partners, and retailers to share customer information across the demand chain. Other modules added to the E.5 system in 2001 included an upgraded sales force automation module.

Introducing E.6, a New Generation of CRM Software: 2002

Although 2001 was a difficult year for E.piphany, the company hoped its next generation of CRM software would put it within striking distance of the top CRM vendors. The E.6 suite was introduced in March 2002 and offered more than 100 new features. The new suite supported a rich interaction with customers and included a set of designer tools to help configure applications. E.6 was built on top of a web-based system, Java2 Enterprise Edition (J2EE), and melded many of the technologies E.piphany had acquired from other companies. With E.piphany continuing to receive industry recognition for its CRM software in 2002, the company hoped that its new genera-

Key Dates:

1996: The company is founded as E.piphany Marketing Software.
1998: Roger Siboni joins E.piphany as president and CEO.
1999: E.piphany launches the first commercially available version of its E.4 software system and goes public later in the year.
2000: The company acquires Octane Software for $3.2 billion; the company releases E.5 CRM software suite.
2001: Sales and earnings slow as CRM spending softens.
2002: The company introduces E.6 software suite.

tion of CRM software would spark more spending on CRM software in the year to come.

Principal Competitors

Kana Software, Inc.; Oracle Systems Corporation; PeopleSoft, Inc.; SAP Aktiengesellschaft; Siebel Systems, Inc.

Further Reading

"Analysis Does Business," *PC Week,* February 1, 1999, p. 52.

Ashman, Anastasia, "Roger Siboni," *Internet World,* March 1, 2001, p. 28.

Borden, Susan, "E.piphany Partners to Polish Demand Chain," *CRM Daily,* March 19, 2001.

"B2B: Fast Facts," *Inter@ctive Week,* April 3, 2000, p. 38.

Callaghan, Dennis, "Bearish Market Chews up CRM Firms' Profits," *eWeek,* April 16, 2001, p. 37.

——, "Clustering Customer Data," *eWeek,* July 31, 2000, p. 30.

——, "E-Market Intelligence: Broadbase, E.piphany Target Marketplaces with Analytics Offerings," *eWeek,* October 2, 2000, p. 48.

——, "E.piphany Extends Its CRM Line," *eWeek,* February 26, 2001, p. 1.

——, "Sun, E.piphany Join Forces," *eWeek,* October 9, 2000, p. 28.

Clancy, Heather, "Datamart Included," *Computer Reseller News,* August 21, 2000, p. 115.

"Customer Focus: Marketing Automation," *Software Magazine,* August 2001, p. 71.

Darrow, Barbara, "E.piphany Builds New CRM App Around J2EE," *Computer Reseller News,* March 18, 2002, p. 4.

——, "E.piphany Preps Sales Component for E.5," *Computer Reseller News,* May 14, 2001, p. 90.

Dembeck, Chet, "E.piphany Makes First Post-IPO Acquisition," *E-Commerce Times,* November 16, 1999, http://www.ecommerce times.com.

"E.piphany Delivers CRM for B2B, B2C," *Customer Interface,* September 2000, p. 65.

"E.piphany: Everything You Need to Know About Your Client," *Business Week,* July 26, 1999, p. EB20.

"E.piphany Posts Big Loss," *InfoWorld,* October 29, 2001, p. 22.

George, Tischelle, "Sun and E.piphany Unveil CRM Deal," *InformationWeek,* October 9, 2000, p. 48.

Grygo, Eugene, "E.piphany, Octane Wed Analysis and Content," *InfoWorld,* March 20, 2000, p. 14.

Harreld, Heather, "CRM Vendors Unfold Architecture Plans," *InfoWorld,* March 18, 2002, p. 44.

Holt, Stannie, and Dylan Tweney, "Vendors Hone Business Decision-Support Tools," *InfoWorld,* January 18, 1999, p. 18.

Karpinski, Richard, "E-Marketing Gains Measures of Integration, Sophistication," *InternetWeek,* November 1, 1999, p. 23.

Macaluso, Nora, "Stock Watch: EClass Buy Hurts E.piphany," *E-Commerce Times,* April 17, 2000, http://www.ecommerce times.com.

Maselli, Jennifer, " 'How May I Help You?' Could Mean So Much More," *InformationWeek,* March 18, 2002, p. 30.

Morphy, Erika, and Kimberly Hill, "Analyst: Launch Puts E.piphany 'in Striking Distance' of Siebel," *CRM Daily,* March 20, 2002.

Russell, Joy D., "E.piphany Aims at Siebel's Market," *VARbusiness,* January 7, 2002, p. 26.

Sweat, Jeff, "Analysis Turns to Action," *InformationWeek,* July 24, 2000, p. 22.

Taylor, Dennis, "E.piphany Price Soared Before Announcement," *Business Journal,* November 19, 1999, p. 1.

——, "Two Firms Beat Crowded Path to Market," *Business Journal,* November 5, 1999, p. 1.

Temple, James, "No Longer Recession Proof," *San Francisco Business Times,* March 9, 2001, p. 19.

Tillett, L. Scott, "CRM Tools Adapt to E-Marketplaces," *InternetWeek,* September 25, 2000, p. 30.

Trott, Bob, "Growing the Demand Chain," *InfoWorld,* March 19, 2001, p. 10.

——, "Sun, CA Take CRM Plunge," *InfoWorld,* October 9, 2000, p. 8.

Wang, Andy, "Internet Stock Sell-Off Continues, But Investors Keep Cool," *E-Commerce Times,* October 19, 1999, http://www .ecommercetimes.com.

——, "Stock Watch: E.piphany IPO Also Set for Big Opening," *E-Commerce Times,* September 22, 1999, http://www.ecommerce times.com.

——, "Stock Watch: E.piphany Surges After Acquisition," *E-Commerce Times,* November 17, 1999, http://www.ecommerce times.com.

Whiting, Rick, "Sales Decline Abroad Hits E.piphany, *InformationWeek,* July 9, 2001, p. 32.

—David P. Bianco

Elior SA

61-69 rue de Bercy
75589 Paris Cedex 12
France
Telephone: (+33) 1-40-19-47-88
Fax: (+33) 1-40-19-47-12
Web site: http://www.elior.com

Public Company
Incorporated: 1991 as Bercy Management
Employees: 45,072
Sales: EUR 2.07 billion ($2.0 billion) (2001)
Stock Exchanges: Euronext Paris
Ticker Symbol: ELR
NAIC: 722110 Full-Service Restaurants; 722211 Limited-
    Service Restaurants; 722320 Caterers

Elior SA is one of the top three contract catering groups in Europe—and number one in France and Spain. The company focuses on two primary catering categories: Institutional Catering, which includes service to schools, hospitals, and businesses; and Commercial Catering, including the ownership and management of restaurants along freeways, in railway stations and airports, fast-food restaurants, and in museums and other public facilities, including Paris's Louvre and the Eiffel Tower. Institutional Catering remains the company's largest division, with nearly 70 percent of the company's revenues. The company's operations are carried out under a variety of brand names, including Eliance, the umbrella name for its commercial catering activities; Avenance, the company's contract catering brand; British brands Nelson Hind, High Table, and Brian Smith; Spanish brands, including Areas and Serunion; autoroute (freeway) concessions l'Arche in France and Ars in Spain; and franchised and other restaurant brands including Pomme de Pain, Quick, Station Sandwich, TJs, Opus, and Buffalo Grill. The company also owns a number of prestigious restaurants, including the Jules Verne at the Eiffel Tower, Le Drouant, the Le Ciel de Paris at the top of the Montparnasse Tower, the Restaurant du Musée d'Orsay, and Le Grand Louvre. Since consolidating its position in the French market, Elior has been actively expanding its interna-

tional presence, notably in the United Kingdom and Spain, but also in the Netherlands, Belgium, Luxembourg, and Italy, as well as a presence in the Latin American market. In 2001, international operations accounted for nearly 40 percent of the company's total revenues of nearly EUR 2.1 billion. Listed on the Euronext Paris stock exchange, Elior is led by Co-Chairmen Francis Markus and Robert Zolade, who founded the company in 1991.

Launching a French Catering Leader in the 1990s

Francis Markus and Robert Zolade began their careers in the collective catering business in the 1970s, working for Jacques Borel International. Both men gained top level positions with Jacques Borel—Marjus became the president of the company's collective catering subsidiary Générale de Restauration, while Zolade was named general manager of Jacques Borel's collective catering division.

Jacques Borel had started his business in the mid-1950s with a single restaurant. By the middle of the 1970s, Borel had become the leading restaurant group in Europe, while subsidiary Générale de Restauration had become the leading European collective catering company. Borel also ran a thriving franchise catering operation under insignias including Café Route and L'Arche. The company had also developed the world's largest luncheon voucher network, issuing more than 165 million vouchers per year through much of Western Europe.

Borel's attempt to enter the hotel business began in the mid-1970s, notably with the takeover of Sofitel, a chain of some 45 four-star hotels in France and Belgium and elsewhere in Europe. Yet Sofitel ran into trouble toward the end of a decade marked by a long worldwide recession. In 1980, Borel sold the Sofitel group to fast-rising SIEH, the owner of the highly successful mid-priced hotel brand Novotel, and other hotel brands including Ibis and Mercury. Three years later, Novotel SIEH acquired the rest of the Borel group, including its Générale de Restauration subsidiary. The merged group then took on a new name, Accor, becoming one of the world's largest hotel and restaurant groups.

Both Markus and Zolade remained with Accor, building up its new collective catering and restaurants operation. Accor

Company Perspectives:

Strategy: To meet the demands of a constantly changing market, and to strengthen its position as a major player in the European restaurant industry, Elior is deploying an ambitious development strategy articulated around five key objectives: capitalize on our leading position in France to support international growth; promote grow through partnerships with local operators; improve operating margins; increase sales and market share through innovative marketing; build synergies between businesses and geographic regions.

Our values: A commitment to quality, guest satisfaction, vendor loyalty. . . . The success of Elior brands in inventing new dining pleasures over the last ten years is due to the group's core values. We value: friendliness, creativity, commitment to quality.

continued expanding its hotel business, launching the Formula 1 brand in the mid-1980s and moving into the United States at the beginning of the 1990s with the acquisitions of the Motel 6 and Regal Inns hotel groups. By the end of the 1980s, Accor, which had begun preparing the contested takeover of Belgian hotel and tourism group Wagons-Lits, completed in 1991, decided to dismantle its collective catering business.

In 1991, Markus and Zolade left Accor and set up a new company, Bercy Management, for the express purpose of buying up a controlling stake in the Générale de Restauration subsidiary. Together with 300 of the subsidiary's managers, Markus and Zolade completed the buyout, gaining 35 percent and management control of the business. Accor maintained a 50 percent equity interest in its former subsidiary, while the remaining shares were picked up by investor Générale des Eaux, which was later to form the basis of Vivendi.

Markus and Zolade became co-presidents and co-chairmen of the company, and set out to build Bercy Management into France's leading collective catering group. Yet from the start, Bercy Management also set its sights beyond France—one of the new company's first moves was to take a minority shareholding in England's High Table, a high-end executive dining and catering company based in London.

In 1993, Bercy Management expanded in France, acquiring a stake in catering group Elitair. Another acquisition made that year, of Orly Restauration, gave the company an opening into the airport concessions sector with that company's Orly airport-based operations. The following year, Bercy Management bought out Accor's shares in the Générale de Restauration company, raising its stake to 85 percent. The company next turned to the Spanish market, where it launched a new subsidiary targeting the airport catering sector, Elite Aeropuertos. In 1995, the company strengthened its French operations with the acquisition of French-style fast-food chain Pomme de Pain.

Meanwhile, Bercy Management's relationship with High Table attracted the interest of another London-based catering group, Catering & Allied. Established in 1975, Catering & Allied had grown into an important player in the U.K. collective catering market and had also built up a solid position in the

Netherlands. As that company's founders faced retirement, they turned to Bercy Management. In 1995 the two companies created a 50–50 partnership called Eurocater, which took over Catering & Allied's Dutch holdings and gave Bercy Management a 27 percent share in Catering & Allied.

Bercy Management continued to develop its international holdings, including stepping up its presence in the United Kingdom through the acquisition of catering group Drummond Thompson in 1996. The company by then had also completed its acquisition of High Table. In France, the company had rapidly built up its position in that country's institutional catering market. Yet Bercy Management's operations in the commercial catering side, grouped under its Elitair subsidiary, had lagged behind in growth.

European Catering Leader in the 21st Century

The solution to this problem came in 1997, when one of France's leading commercial catering groups, Holding de Restauration Concédée (HRC), became available. Unable to finance an acquisition of HRC by itself, Bercy Management turned to capital investment group Advent International, with whom Zolade already had a personal working relationship. Bercy Management and Avent International then created a joint venture, Eliance, held at 51 percent by Bercy Management, which contributed its existing Elitair concessions catering arm. Grouped with the HRC operations, Eliance became France's leading commercial and concessions catering company.

Meanwhile, Bercy Management moved to gain complete control of its Générale de Restauration holding, buying out both Générale des Eaux and its manager shareholders in 1997. The following year, Bercy Management restructured its holdings, changing its name to Elior and regrouping its activities around two primary cores: Avenance, which became the umbrella for the company's contract catering operations; and Eliance, its commercial and concessions catering arm. As result of the restructuring, Advent exchanged its 49 percent share in Eliance for a 25 percent share in the new unified Elior. These changes were made in order for Elior to beginning preparing its public offering.

In the meantime, Elior increased its international expansion effort. In 1999, the company took over Midlands, England-based Brian Smith. That acquisition not only doubled Elior's U.K. presence, but also gave it a 50 percent share of that country's high-end executive catering market. Soon after that acquisition, Elior completed its partnership with Catering & Allied when Elior stepped up its participation in Eurocater to 80 percent; Eurocater also took over all of Catering & Allied's U.K. and Netherlands operations, as well as Elior's Dutch holdings. The acquisitions of Brian Smith and Catering & Allied boosted Elior to the fifth-place position in the U.K. catering market.

In France, Elior acquired full control of autoroute concessions group SRPMC. The company also acquired hospitals and healthcare specialist GHS Exploitation, and Société Hôtelière de l'Aéroport International de Brest, which operated restaurant concessions at the Brest airport. The company then entered Italy, acquiring a minority stake in that country's Ristochef; the following year, Elior increased its holding in that company to

Key Dates:

1991: Francis Markus and Robert Zolade found Bercy Management and buy out 35 percent stake in Générale de Restauration from Accor; Bercy acquires minority stake in High Table.

1993: Company acquires stake in Elitair and Orly Restauration.

1994: Bercy establishes subsidiary Elite Aeropuertos in Spain.

1995: Company acquires Pomme de Pain and begins partnership with Catering & Allied.

1997: Company acquires 100 percent control of Générale de Restauration; in partnership with Advent, company purchases HRC, which is placed under Eliance joint venture.

1998: Company restructures operations and changes its name to Elior; Advent takes direct stake of 25 percent.

1999: Elior acquires Brian Smith of the United Kingdom, Osesa in Spain, and Aerocomidas in Mexico.

2000: Company acquires 50 percent of Ristochef in Italy; goes public on Euronext Paris stock exchange; acquires Scotland-based Nelson Hind.

2001: Elior concludes strategic partnership agreements with Areas and Serunion, both in Spain.

50 percent. In Spain, meanwhile, the company acquired contract caterer Osesa. That purchase led the company to Latin America the following year, with the purchase of a 51 percent share of Mexican airport catering concessions group Aerocomidas.

Elior went public in April 2000 in order to fuel its continued international expansion. At that time the company acknowledged its interest in entering the U.S. market. In the meantime, the company continued building on its rise to European leadership, acquiring, in June 2000, Scotland's Nelson Hind. That purchase made Elior the number three contract catering group in the United Kingdom.

The company's expansion drive continued through 2001, with Elior reaching a strategic alliance with Spanish companies Areas and Serunion, helping to lift Elior to the position of the number one contract catering company in Spain. The company also expanded into new markets, notably Portugal and Morocco. Other acquisitions made by Elior in 2001 included a 38 percent share in France's Services & Santé, and a 34 percent share in that country's LRP. The company also completed a new public offering, selling an additional 19 percent of its stock. Following that offering, some 57 percent of Elior's stock was listed on the market.

By 2002, Elior had transformed itself from a largely France-oriented company into a leading European contract catering firm. Some 40 percent of the company's revenues were now generated outside of France. Despite difficult market conditions following the attack on the World Trade Center in September 2001, Elior managed to record continued revenue growth, while a tight control on costs enabled it to boast stronger gains in profits. The company was then able to look forward to continued expansion, applying its formula of acquisitions and partnerships to build a collective catering powerhouse.

Principal Subsidiaries

Gourmet Club; HRC; Océane de Restauration; PDP Centres Commerciaux; PDP Drouot; PDP International; PDP Lafayette; PDP les Terrasses; PDP Montparnasse; PDP Paris Centre; PDP Paris Halles; PDP Rive Gauche; Personnal; Pomme de Pain; Resapro; Restaurants et Sites; Resteurop; Rosell; Sogeccir; S2R Ile-de-France; S2R Province; Sagrec; Sahpra; Saresp; SBSO; SC2R; SRB; SSR; Soferest; Sopresthel; Sorebor; Soregis; Sorenolif; Soresco; Sorreg; SPAB; SPAC; SRAB; SRBE; SRNA; STS Alsace; STS Lorraine; Suite et Faim; Académie Elitair; Actair; Ancienne Douane; Aprest; Arpège; Avenance; Avenance Enseignement; Avenance Entreprises; Avenance Santé-Résidences; Avenance Services; Bercy Services I; Bercy Services IV; Buffet Dijon; Buffet Marseille; Buffet Montparnasse; C Bobbia Restauration Moderne; C2L; C3L; Coservices; Cores; Drouant; Drouant Exploitation; EGSR; Eliance; Eliance au Printemps; Eliance Centre Pompidou; Eliance Développement; Eliance Exploitation; Eliance Expo; Eliance Gestion; Eliance Marseille Provence; Eliance Montpellier; Eliance Rail; Eliance Roissy 2F; Eliance Services; Eliance Tolbiac; Eliance Tour Eiffel; Elior Gestion; Elior Services; Eurobar; Expresself; FCF; GSR Ciel de Paris; Avenance Group Catering (U.K.); Catering & Allied (U.K.; 80%); Drummond Thompson (U.K.; 80%); Elior UK; Eurocater (U.K.; 80%); Hallmark (U.K.; 80%); High Table (U.K.; 80%); Renard Services (U.K.; 40%); Avenance Catering Ltd (U.K.); Eliance UK; Nelson Hind Cat. Management Plc (U.K.); Nelson Hind Holdings Ltd (U.K.); Elior Nederland (Netherlands; 80%); Holland Catering Specialisten (HCS) (Netherlands; 80%); Le Grand Bernard (Netherlands; 80%); Restoplan (Netherlands; 80%); Elior Catering BV (Netherlands; 80%); Elite Aeropuertos (Spain); Mediterranea de Restaurantes (Spain); Raesa (Spain; 51%); Recyg (Spain); Grupo Osesa SA (Spain); Osesa Aeropuertos (Spain); Gerelux (Luxembourg); Ristochef EC (Italy; 50%); Elibel (Belgium).

Principal Competitors

Compass Group Plc; Sodexho Alliance SA; Accor, Aramark Corporation,; Autogrill SpA.

Further Reading

Bozec, Louise, "Elior Cites Control of UK Margins As International Earnings Soar," *Caterer & Hotelkeeper*, June 27, 2002, p. 5.

"Elior Makes Plans for Global Expansion," *Caterer & Hotelkeeper*, January 18, 2001.

"Elior Spreads Its Wings Abroad," *Eurofood*, December 16, 1999.

"Elior Will Test Markets with EUR 380m Combined Offering," *Euroweek*, May 18, 2001, p. 24.

Iskander, Samer, "Elior Expands Its UK Side," *Financial Times*, June 14, 2000, p. 29.

—M. L. Cohen

Equity Residential

2 North Riverside Plaza
Chicago, Illinois 60606
U.S.A.
Telephone: (312) 474-1300
Fax: (312) 454-8703
Web site: http://www.eqr.com

Public Company
Incorporated: 1993 as Equity Residential Properties Trust
Employees: 6,400
Sales: $2.3 billion (2001)
Stock Exchanges: New York
Ticker Symbol: EQR
NAIC: 525930 Real Estate Investment Trusts

Equity Residential is part of the farflung business empire of Chicago billionaire Samuel Zell, known as the "Grave Dancer" for his penchant of buying and turning around distressed businesses. Equity Residential is a real estate investment trust that acquires, owns, and operates apartment properties, the largest publicly traded REIT of its kind in the United States. It owns more than 1,000 properties in all parts of the country, totaling nearly 225,000 units. Zell serves as chairman of the board, but day-to-day responsibilities are handled by CEO Douglas Crocker II, who in late 2001 announced his intention to step down as soon as a suitable replacement could be found.

Fleeing Poland at Outbreak of World War II

Samuel Zell was the only son of a Polish Jewish couple who fled their native country only hours before it was invaded by German forces in 1939, the final step in the buildup to World War II. The couple immigrated to Chicago where Zell was born in 1941. The family was supported by the selling abilities of Zell's father, who was known to peddle flour and jewelry as well as real estate. By 12 years of age Zell displayed his own entrepreneurial bent. Sent to Hebrew class in the suburbs each afternoon, he noticed at the train station a new Chicago-based magazine named *Playboy,* which was not generally available in his neighborhood. According to Zell, he began to buy issues for 50 cents at the train station, then resold them for $1.50 in the schoolyard.

After graduating from high school in 1959, Zell went to college as a political science major at the University of Michigan where he met his future long-term partner, Robert Lurie, who was a fraternity brother. As an undergraduate Zell began to manage some off-campus housing property and was able to accumulate enough of a stake for him and Lurie to go into the real estate business together. The two men were almost polar opposites in personality but complemented one another. Zell was the outspoken, often abrasive, visionary—the rainmaker—while Lurie was the retiring numbers man who minded the store. Both men continued to run their fledgling real estate business in Ann Arbor when they went on to law school at the University of Michigan. By the time they graduated in 1966, they owned a city block of student housing, all resulting from a $1,500 down payment.

Zell intended to practice law, however, and accepted a position with the Chicago firm of Yates Holleb and Michelson at a salary of $116 a week, with the possibility of earning more by bringing in new business. According to Zell he suffered through his first week drafting a contract, then over the weekend took advantage of real estate contacts to cobble together an apartment project in Toledo, Ohio, which he presented to the firm's partners on Monday morning. All of them were impressed enough to invest in the deal. During the first year at Yates Holleb, he earned $93,000 in commissions, compared with $7,000 in salary, for a total compensation that eclipsed the firm's senior partners. Zell stayed on until 1968, then decided to quit the practice of law and again joined forces with Lurie to pursue real estate ventures.

Zell and Lurie formed Equity Finance and Management Company in 1968. They became involved in two small development projects but quickly decided that there were too many uncontrollable elements and that the risks simply outweighed the rewards. Zell concluded that much of a developer's compensation was psychological, the ability to point to a structure and declare that he had built it: "Look how big it is!" Instead Zell and Lurie elected to concentrate on acquiring existing properties at below replacement cost from distressed developers, a practice that would lead to Zell's "Grave Dancer" moniker. One of their first deals of this kind involved a 1,000-unit apartment and office complex in downtown Cleveland. The property was in such poor shape that it was mostly inhabited by squatters. The partners renovated the complex and turned it into a fully rented facility worth many times more than the nominal amount they paid to acquire it.

Zell and Lurie were well positioned to take advantage of the collapse of the real estate market in 1974, buying numerous properties on the cheap. With high inflation during the decade those properties then experienced a tremendous increase in value. They concentrated on buying apartment buildings in fast-growing cities, primarily located in Sunbelt states. It was also a time of many dubious real estate tax shelter schemes, and in 1976 Zell became caught up in a federal investigation that nearly devastated the partnership. He and three Chicago tax attorneys, one of whom was his brother-in-law Roger Baskes, were indicted for their part in transferring some assets to an offshore bank to avoid paying taxes. Zell was not the target of the investigation and received immunity in exchange for his testimony. Although he attempted to exculpate Baskes, his brother-in-law was still sentenced to two years in a federal penitentiary. The incident would haunt Zell for years to come, as competitors strategically reopened the wound, despite the fact that Baskes and Zell maintained warm relations.

Acquiring American Management & Investment Inc. in 1981

Zell and Lurie gained national attention in 1981 when they acquired a controlling 68 percent stake in Great American Management & Investment Inc., an Atlanta-based REIT with some $500 million in assets. It had been one of the largest REITs in the United States before going bankrupt in 1977. The partners sold much of Great American's assets, restructured its debt, and returned it to fiscal health. Zell and Lurie then moved beyond residential and commercial real estate, applying the same principles of buying properties at distressed prices to the corporate world. Moreover, with real estate values spiraling out of control, Zell sensed that a crash was coming, making it a good time to diversify into other areas. The partners bought stakes in Consolidated Fibers, Commodore Corp., and Itel Corp. They became involved in a wide range of businesses, including radio stations, fertilizer companies, dredging equipment, drugstores, mattresses, and rail cars. An investment in bicycle maker Schwinn was a notable failure, but the bulk of their turnaround activity proved lucrative.

Many real estate operators who had engaged in dubious tax shelter schemes during the 1970s faced a day of reckoning when the Tax Reform Act of 1986 undercut their activities, resulting

in the crash that Zell had anticipated. As in an earlier time, he and Lurie were able to take advantage of other people's problems and acquire properties at a steep discount. In 1987 they began to set up real estate "vulture funds" with Merrill Lynch & Co. and acquired the bulk of the properties that would form the basis of Equity Residential. By the end of the decade, however, commercial banking money dried up and severely hampered Equity Finance. More important, Lurie was diagnosed with cancer during this period and the final years of his life were difficult for both men. Unable to accept the inevitable, the partners reportedly stopped seeing each other to conduct business, instead talking by telephone on an hourly basis. Lurie died in 1990 and much of his day-to-day duties were taken over by Sheli Rosenberg, also an attorney with a flair for deal-making. She had done some work for Equity Finance during the 1970s while a partner at the Chicago firm of Schiff Hardin & Waite. She went to work for Zell and Lurie in 1980 to start an in-house law firm and became their top lawyer, involved in the structuring of all their major deals.

Zell was able to scrape by during the recession of the early 1990s but his deal-making activity was curtailed. When real estate began to recover, he and others rediscovered the value of REITs. REITs originally were created by Congress in 1960 as a way for small investors to become involved in real estate in much the same way a mutual fund allowed them to pool resources to buy stocks. REITs could be taken public and their shares traded like any other stock, but they were required by law to pay out at least 95 percent of their taxable income to shareholders each year, thus severely limiting the ability of REITs to raise funds internally. REITs also were hindered because they were only allowed to own real estate. Third parties had to be engaged to operate or manage the properties. Moreover, the tax code made direct real estate investments an attractive tax shelter for many individuals, thereby absorbing funds that might have been invested in REITs. The Tax Reform Act of 1986 not only eliminated these tax shelters, it also permitted REITs to provide customary services for property, in effect allowing the trusts to operate and manage the properties they owned. Nevertheless, REITs were still not embraced as an investment option because banks, insurance companies, pension funds, and foreign investors (in particular the Japanese) were investing heavily in real estate. Overbuilding and a glutted marketplace, however, resulted in falling property values in the early 1990s, and lending institutions, as a result of the recent savings and loan debacle, were forced by regulators to be more circumspect about their investments. Capital essentially dried up and REITs finally became an attractive way for many private real estate companies to raise funds. Moreover, property owners like Zell realized that by converting their holdings into REIT shares they could postpone paying capital gains taxes.

The Formation of Equity Residential As a REIT in 1993

Zell converted three of the Merrill investment funds into REITs, one of which was Equity Residential Property Trust, formed in Maryland in March 1993. To handle the day-to-day operations of the new REIT, which started out with 22,000 apartment units, he hired Douglas Crocker, who established an executive team well before the REIT was formed and spent six

Key Dates:

1969: Samuel Zell and Robert Lurie form Equity Finance and Management Company.
1987: Co-managed funds with Merrill Lynch form basis of Equity Residential.
1990: Lurie dies of cancer.
1993: Equity Residential Properties Trust is formed as a REIT.
1997: Merry Land & Investment Co. is acquired.
2002: The company shortens its name to Equity Residential.

months analyzing the apartment market in 30 U.S. cities. They targeted communities that had vibrant economies yet were strict on issuing zoning permits, thus limiting the supply on housing. Crocker was also thorough in the management structure of the REIT, following a corporate model that was unusual for real estate. He instituted a profit-sharing plan for all employees and extended stock options down to the regional manager level. He even set up a training program, known as Equity University, for promising young executives. Unlike many real estate operators, Crocker made certain that Equity Residential paid attention to the kind of details that are often neglected but prove crucial in the long run: making sure that painting is done on a regular basis, the hedges trimmed, the pool cleaned. A major part of Equity Residential's strategy was to take advantage of size to buy equipment and services in bulk. From the outset the REIT was aggressive in acquiring new properties, focusing on B-plus and A-grade apartment complexes built before 1985. In little more than a year, it added nearly 11,000 apartments at a cost of $478 million. The areas of the country initially targeted included Seattle, Portland, southern California, Las Vegas, Dallas, the research triangle in North Carolina, Atlanta, and Florida.

Equity Residential soon graduated from purchasing small portfolios to acquiring entire real estate companies, due in large part to institutional investors shying away from smaller REITs. Larger players such as Equity Residential now vied with one another to achieve the kind of size that would make them more attractive investments. Early in 1997 Zell's REIT acquired New York-based Wellsford Residential Property Trust for $620 million in stock and the assumption of $332 million in debt. The Wellsford portfolio totaled some 19,000 apartments located mostly in Colorado, Utah, Texas, Arizona, Nevada, New Mexico, Washington, and Oklahoma. In August 1997 Equity Residential paid $625 million in stock and assumed $432 million in debt to acquire Arizona-based Evans Withycomb Residential Inc. and its nearly 16,000 apartment units. Equity Residential also continued to pursue smaller deals and by the end of 1997 had nearly doubled in size over the course of the year. In March 1998 the National MultiHousing Council announced that the REIT was now the largest single owner of apartments, with a total of 138,923 units. At the beginning of 1997 Equity Residential had ranked only sixth.

The REIT continued its buying spree in 1998, spurred by a general slump in REIT share prices that put pressure on smaller companies to join up with larger rivals to compete. Equity

Residential established a major presence in Silicon Valley by acquiring approximately 1,000 apartments from Lincoln Property Co. It then acquired Merry Land & Investment Co., a major apartment owner in the Southeast based in Augusta, Georgia. At a cost of $1.54 billion in stock and the assumption of $656 million in debt, Equity Residential added nearly 35,000 apartment units spread across nine states. A year later it paid $730 million for Lexford Residential Trust, gaining 36,609 apartment units, located in 16 states. The Lexford deal was a departure from previous transactions because it involved lesser grade assets, apartments that were geared toward the "cost-conscious renter." Crocker explained that although the company would continue to focus on multistory garden apartments it also planned to pursue niche opportunities such as Lexford's, as well as housing for students and the elderly.

During the depressed real estate market of the late 1990s the price of Equity Residential shares languished, but conditions improved by early 2001. Housing shortages in major cities allowed the REIT to raise rental rates. Moreover, the company was able to take advantage of falling interest rates to refinance debt. Several months later, however, terrorist attacks on U.S. soil had a debilitating effect on an already troubled economy and Equity Residential began to feel the effects. In October 2001 management announced that it expected earnings to be adversely affected for the remainder of 2001 and into the next few years, with leasing of some units proving more difficult and rents likely to fall in some cities. In fact, rising unemployment in 2002 had an impact on vacancy rates while at the same time low interest rates encouraged some renters to buy homes. To help maintain occupancy, the company slashed rents and even instituted rent-free months. Equity Residential, which also dropped Properties Trust from its name in 2002, even began to sell off more apartments than it acquired. Although profits were down by 13.6 percent in 2001, the company continued to be very profitable and looked to rebound with the economy. Of more concern for the REIT was recruiting new leadership. Crocker, 61, announced in October 2001 his intention to retire, and although he planned to stay at the helm for the next three years he initiated a search for his replacement and also put in place a future senior management team.

Principal Subsidiaries

ERP Operating Limited Partnership; Equity Residential Properties Management Corp.

Principal Competitors

Apartment Investment and Management Company; Archstone-Smith Trust; Lincoln Property Company; Security Capital Group; Walden.

Further Reading

Barboza, David, "Visions of a Brand-Name Office Empire," *New York Times,* December 16, 2001, p. 1.
Barsky, Neil, "Buying Low: Sam Zell Was Right About Real Estate—and Still Overbought," *Wall Street Journal,* July 9, 1992, p. A1.
Gray, Patricia Bellew, "Unlikely Mogul: Breezy and Irreverent, Raider Sam Zell Runs a $2.5 Billion Empire," *Wall Street Journal,* November 7, 1985, p. 1.

Henkoff, Ronald, ''Property to the People,'' *Fortune,* October 13, 1997, pp. 98–100.

Kirkpatrick, David D., ''Big Apartment Firm Is to Buy Merry Land,'' *Wall Street Journal,* July 9, 1998, p. A4.

Laing, Jonathan R., ''The Vulture Capitalist,'' *Barron's,* July 30, 1990, p. 8.

Pacelle, Mitchell, ''Zell-Controlled REIT Will Buy Rival in $620 Million Swap in Push to Be No. 1,'' *Wall Street Journal,* January 17, 1997, p. A3.

——, ''Zell's Residential Agrees to Buy Rival Apartment Firm for $625 Million,'' *Wall Street Journal,* August 28, 1997, p. A2.

—Ed Dinger

Equus Computer Systems, Inc.

719 Kasota Avenue
Minneapolis, Minnesota 55414
U.S.A.
Telephone: (612) 617-6200
Toll Free: (866) 378-8727
Fax: (612) 617-6298
Web site: http://www.equus.com

Private Company
Incorporated: 1991
Employees: 350
Sales: $161 million (2001 est.)
NAIC: 541512 Computer Systems Integration Design
Consulting Services; 334111 Electronic Computer
Manufacturing

Equus Computer Systems, Inc., is one of the largest of the "tier two" computer system builders in the United States. Begun in 1989 by computer engineer Andy Juang, Equus provides computer resources to Value Added Resellers (VARs) and Systems Integrators (SIs) through ten regional satellite offices strategically placed throughout the country. The company provides engineering, manufacturing, and customer service at its locations in Minnesota, Kansas, Illinois, California, Michigan, Missouri, Ohio, Texas, Colorado, and Washington state. Competing with such giants as Dell and Gateway, Equus has built its reputation by providing unmatched customer service and computer systems that are custom configured to meet even the smallest of business needs.

The Late 1980s and 1990s:
The White Box Revolution

In 1989, Andy Juang, a Taiwanese immigrant, had been working for Cray Research in St. Paul, Minnesota, for several years. Juang had come to the United States in 1993 to enroll at the University of Houston's computer science master's program, and had been offered a position at Cray Supercomputer after completing his degree. Juang had spent his four-year term at Cray working on two different projects in its research and development sector, and was disillusioned when both of his projects were scrapped before reaching the final production stage. This sense of futility, coupled with a desire to set his own course, led him to rethink his employment future. Considering both a second master's degree—this time in business administration—or investing the money in a small start-up company and doing some risky experiential learning along the way, Juang chose the path less traveled.

Juang decided to invest in his own build-to-order personal computer company after meeting with an acquaintance, Joseph Chou. Chou had succeeded in starting Pony Computer in Ohio, one of many such small build-to-order PC suppliers cropping up in the United States at the time. It was determined that Juang would open a similar franchise in the Minneapolis/St. Paul area, otherwise referred to as the Twin Cities. With $30,000 investment money of his own and another $30,000 from Chou, the two built a partnership and Juang founded a small retail storefront computer store.

Juang was optimistic from the start. He placed an advertisement in a regional technology magazine, hired five employees, and waited for the orders to roll in. Juang's optimism was rewarded when demand for the company's PCs nearly overwhelmed the small start-up. In its first month the company had $100,000 in orders and by year's end Juang and his Minneapolis-based Pony Computer franchise had done $3 million in sales.

With the franchise's success, a rift developed in the partnership. Chou wanted to take control of the new operation while Juang wanted to maintain his ownership. A legal battle ensued which Juang won in a court's decision. The ruling allowed Juang to buy out Chou's interest in the company.

Following the legal fight, Juang renamed his company Equus Computer Systems and continued to build and grow the company at a remarkable rate. This was an era when many recent computer science graduates were putting together computer packages for profit. Personal computers were making their way into businesses and homes at an astounding pace and the availability of hardware and software in the marketplace allowed industrious individuals to control a small piece of the market.

There were many fundamental business practices that Equus did well in order to maintain its competitive edge. One trick was to keep inventory control very tight. Though inexperienced, Juang knew that stocking technology-related inventory translated into lost revenue and there were times the company stayed ahead of the competition by ordering equipment on a daily or weekly basis. In the computer industry, products were ever changing and technology rapidly improving; older components meant lower prices.

With the PC business booming during the 1990s, Equus was poised to capture its share of the market. Its Nobilis brand of computer made use of Microsoft and Intel components and remained competitive with other build-to-order operations.

The 1990s: Redirection

The 1990s rise in demand for PCs also brought competition from computer superstores. When Equus was faced with the volume sales and liberal return policies of the superstores, the company's leadership studied the situation and redirected the company to compete by serving a niche in the market the superstore could not reach. Equus took itself out of the retail market and focused its work on Value Added Resellers (VARs)—those smaller computer suppliers who were building computer systems and networks for companies who needed computer systems configured to work in their unique corporate settings. Equus provided services to VARs at a fraction of the cost that the VARs would have had to charge to maintain the necessary laboratory equipment and personnel themselves. This process, known as ''outsourcing,'' actually saved VARs money in repair costs.

From 1992 to 1996 Juang attempted to replicate the success he had in Equus when he started ten other similar companies in Texas, Illinois, Missouri, Colorado, California, Ohio, Michigan, Kansas, and Washington state. In a November 2001 article in *Minnesota Business,* Juang described the overwhelming responsibility he faced when trying to control and manage ten separate corporations in ten U.S. cities. He stated, ''Physically, I couldn't take it. I was pretty much on the phone as much as eight to ten hours a day. I was almost breathless. My management style back then was 'I have to manage everything, I have to talk with everybody.' ''

It was not long before Juang realized that managing the business of ten independent franchises would prove too difficult for even the most skilled business owner, and in 1997 he brought the companies under the Equus corporate structure and worked on establishing a management team equal to the task of centralizing control while maintaining a quality local presence at each of the satellites. The company continued to offer full engineering, manufacturing, and customer service at each of it ten operations sites.

Looking Forward: 2000 and Beyond

In another attempt to stay one step ahead of the competition and find a new direction for the company, Equus turned its attention to Systems Integrators (SIs) in the late 1990s. Working with SIs seemed a logical extension of the company's business. SIs like VARs were better served by using Equus's labor force and expertise than by hiring their own. The company anticipated this and moved in to establish relationships with a wide network of Systems Integrators.

In another attempt to continue to grow in an ever changing and highly competitive industry, Equus adapted when the market for desktop PCs began to decline in the late 1990s. Equus began producing computer notebooks and servers and was able to keep its production from falling off significantly. Though still not at the 1998 revenue high of $185 million, the company maintained considerable sales levels. In over six years, Equus managed to exceed 6,000 percent growth, and was able to achieve that ratio without incurring any long-term debt.

In March 1998, Equus hired Mary Jo Farell as its corporate marketing manager. Farell was just one of several experienced managers Equus brought in to revamp the corporate structure and create a workable and strong management team.

In February 1999, Equus created a sister company, Exelus, to meet another industry need. Forecasting the increased market for repair and warranty services, Juang and the leadership team including Kevin Porter, vice-president for business development, established Exelus to provide services to businesses wanting to save time and money by utilizing one ''point of contact'' when it came to their company's information technology. Exelus was created to expedite project management services, aid with installation, repair work and support, and accelerate hardware and software package configuration for the company's network. Porter was named president at Exelus in 1999.

With an Equus presence distributed over a good portion of the country, the East Coast and southeastern United States were the only areas where Equus did not have satellite offices. Despite the absence of representation in these regions, Equus together with Exelus made it clear that it ''provided on-site service to every zip code in the continental United States through an extensive network of more than 4,000 technology professionals.''

Its prominence in the Midwest was clear by May 2000 when Equus Computer Systems topped *Minneapolis-St. Paul City Business*'s chart of minority-owned businesses. The ranking by revenue was an indicator of how far Juang and Equus had come from the founder's initial investment of $30,000. Andy Juang, a recent immigrant and just over 40 years old, had built a

Key Dates:

1989: Andy Juang partners with Joseph Chou to start a Pony Computer franchise in Minneapolis; revenues exceed $3 million.

1991: Juang goes to court for control of the company, wining legal battle and renaming the enterprise Equus Computer Systems.

1992: Experiencing competition from computer superstores, Equus changes direction from direct consumer retail sales to providing sales and service to other businesses.

1994–96: Equus opens satellite locations throughout the United States.

1997: Equus reorganizes its management structure.

1998: Sales revenue hits new high mark at $185 million.

1999: Equus founds sister company Exelus.

2000: Experiencing decline in sales of PCs, Equus expands its services to include sales and service to Systems Integrators and companies manufacturing components using embedded computer technology.

company worthy of first honors among other multimillion-dollar corporations in the Twin Cities.

In 2000 Equus took notice of the increased demand for microcomputers in all sorts of differing industries. Computers were included in many industrial components from children's toys and games, to appliances, medical devices, audio/video displays, and manufacturing parts.

Embedded technology and the increasing demand for its maintenance and repair appeared good prospects for yet another area of the competitive computer market. Thus it created a Custom Solutions Division in 2000 to address original equipment manufacturer (OEM) business needs in this area.

A large measure of Equus's success and growth in its industry was its adaptability. The company had been compelled by industry competition and changes to look for new directions at every turn and bump in the market. The company's ability to adapt to such pressures directly contributed to its stability and

growth in an industry that had been hard hit by softening markets in the late 1990s and early part of 2000. Equus appeared focused on its mission with one eye kept on market trends in order to keep afloat and stay one step ahead of the competition.

Principal Subsidiaries

Equus Computer Systems of Minnesota, Inc.; Equus Computer Systems of Kansas, Inc; Equus Computer Systems of Illinois, Inc; Equus Computer Systems of CA, Inc.; Equus Computer Systems of Michigan, Inc.; Equus Computer Systems of Missouri, Inc.; Equus Computer Systems of Ohio, Inc.; Equus Computer Systems of Texas, Inc; Equus Computer Systems of Washington, Inc.; Equus Computer Systems of Colorado, Inc.

Principal Divisions

Custom Solutions Division.

Principal Competitors

Gateway, Inc.; Dell Computer Corporation; International Business Machines Corporation; Hewlett-Packard Company.

Further Reading

Boyer, Theron, ''Minority-Owned Businesses,'' *Minneapolis-St. Paul City Business,* May 12, 2000, p. 24.

Druskoff, Mark, ''Warhorse,'' *Minnesota Business,* November 2001, p. 54.

''Equus Computer Systems Introduces the Nobilis Pro Series of Desktops,'' *Business Wire,* September 22, 1998.

''Equus Computer Systems Names New Chief Financial Officer,'' *PR Newswire,* July 30, 1998.

''Equus Computer Systems Names New Corporate Marketing Manager,'' *Business Wire,* March 11, 1998.

''PC Manufacturers Roll Out Windows XP Ready PCS,'' *PC Business Products,* August 2001.

Terdoslavich, William, ''From Drawing Board to Reality,'' *Computer Reseller News,* September 30, 1996, p 29.

''Top'-sy Turvy,'' *VAR Business,* June 7, 1999.

—Susan B. Culligan

Falconbridge Limited

95 Wellington Street, Suite 1200
Toronto, Ontario M5J 2V4
Canada
Telephone: (416) 956-5700
Fax: (416) 956-5757
Web site: http://www.falconbridge.com

Public Subsidiary of Noranda Inc.
Incorporated: 1989
Employees: 6,234
Sales: $1.74 billion (2000)
Stock Exchanges: Toronto
Ticker Symbol: FL
NAIC: 212234 Copper Ore and Nickel Ore Mining;
  212299 All Other Metal Ore Mining; 327992 Ground
  or Treated Mineral and Earth Manufacturing

Falconbridge Limited is a leading base metals mining company operating out of Toronto, Canada. Its primary commodity is nickel, which is instrumental in the manufacture of stainless steel, followed by copper, cobalt, and platinum group metals. Falconbridge owns nickel mines in Canada and the Dominican Republic, and ever since 1930 has maintained a refinery in Norway. The company is majority owned by Noranda, a Canadian natural resources company that controls more than 50 percent of its stock. Falconbridge shares trade on the Toronto Stock Exchange.

Founding of Falconbridge: 1928

Falconbridge took its name from the township of Falconbridge, Ontario, an area possessing large deposits of nickel. In 1928, businessman Thayer Lindsley paid $2.5 million for mining claims in the area and created Falconbridge Nickel Mines Limited. The new company took immediate steps to work the claims, and despite the stock market crash of 1929 it was able to sink a shaft and begin to develop the mine, as well as build a smelter. Falconbridge still had to refine the ore, however, and the International Nickel Company of Canada (INCO)

retained the North American rights to refining technologies. As a result the company turned to Kristiansand, Norway, where it purchased an operating refinery, renaming it Nikkelverk. The inconvenience of working on two continents was offset by the low cost of Norwegian electricity, a major expense in the electrolytic refining process for nickel. Moreover, Falconbridge was now positioned to take advantage of a growing European market for nickel that commanded higher prices than in the United States. The company engaged a London firm, Brandeis, Goldschmidt & Co., to market the product to the Continent.

Falconbridge completed its first full year of production in 1931, and business was adversely affected by the depressed world economy. Conditions improved somewhat the following year and the company was able to expand its operations, constructing a precious metals plant at Nikkelverk and sinking a second mine shaft in Canada. The company benefited from higher metal prices in the late 1930s, but it also became concerned about the political climate in Europe, as Germany became increasingly more militant. Even after the Continent became embroiled in war, Nikkelverk continued to operate. In addition to producing gold, silver, platinum, and palladium, the plant began to refine iridium, rhodium, and ruthenium. In 1940, Germany occupied Norway, and Falconbridge lost its refining capacity.

Because nickel was an important metal in Canada's war effort, INCO now provided refining services to Falconbridge. Despite the loss of manpower to the Army, the company stepped up production, with all of its metal either sold directly to the government or allocated to industry for military use. It was not until 1945, with the end of war in Europe, that Falconbridge regained Nikkelverk. Despite shortages of coke, coal, and electricity, the plant renewed its operations, and the company was able to take advantage of improving nickel and copper prices. By 1947, in the midst of a postwar boom, Falconbridge recorded its highest profits since 1939. Nikkelverk was modernized and the company looked forward to a promising future, encouraged by the emerging new uses for nickel.

While demand for nickel began a steady rise in the 1950s, production in the free world was limited to the Canadians and the French with its operations in New Caledonia. The advent of the Korean War then created an even greater need for the metal.

The U.S. government began a program of stockpiling nickel and negotiated an incentive-laden contract with Falconbridge to buy nickel through 1961 at a price above market value. As a result, commercial customers were only able to acquire nickel on a quota basis and pent-up demand drove the price even higher. Falconbridge used its newfound prosperity to upgrade facilities and sink additional mines. By the middle of the decade the company had five mines in operation and four others in development. Throughout the 1950s, Falconbridge established production records each year. Commodity prices eroded somewhat as demand declined in 1957, yet profits continued to be healthy. Efforts were also initiated to explore a 300-square-mile concession in the Dominican Republic. By the end of the 1950s, despite a strike in the U.S. steel industry, the demand for nickel remained quite high.

In 1961, Falconbridge acquired some major assets from Ventures Limited, another company controlled by Thayer Lindsley. These acquisitions included controlling interests in gold mining firms Giant Yellowknife Mines Limited and Kiena Gold Mines Limited; copper producer Kilembe Mines Limited; the undeveloped copper and zinc deposits of Lake Default Mines Limited; and the silver, lead, and zinc mining operations of United Keno Hill Mines Limited. As part of this transaction, a large stake of Falconbridge stock would pass to McIntyre Porcupine Mines Limited.

Superior Oil Gaining Control in the 1970s

Falconbridge experienced a small slump in the early 1960s when its contracts with the U.S. government expired, but the company quickly recovered as nickel consumption reached new heights and copper prices escalated because of political unrest in some copper-producing countries. Prices remained strong until a recession in 1971. By now the company saw a shift in ownership control. Superior Oil Co. of Houston, Texas, and its Canadian subsidiary acquired a 40 percent interest in McIntyre Porcupine, thereby gaining a 37 percent stake in Falconbridge, which it then increased to about 43 percent. Superior Oil would eventually gain control of the board and effectively run the company.

No longer operating with limited competition in the world, Falconbridge expanded internationally in the 1970s. To better market its products, the company established Falconbridge International Limited, as well as Falconbridge Europe S.A. to cater specifically to European customers. Later in the decade, Falconbridge U.S. Inc. was established to improve marketing to the United States. Moreover, South Africa properties began to produce platinum, and the Dominican concessions finally bore nickel. Overall, however, the 1970s featured unsteady business

conditions and uneven financial results. Inflation hurt earnings in 1974, and weak demand in 1977 caused Falconbridge to post its first loss. But when conditions improved, the company achieved record earnings in 1979.

In 1980, D. Broward Craig was named president and chief executive officer of Falconbridge, reported to be handpicked by Superior Oil and lured away from St. Joe Minerals Corp., where Craig had served as president. After only five months at Falconbridge, however, he resigned. Although a company press release cited "disagreements over matters of policy" without providing elaboration, the press speculated that Craig was frustrated by the conflicting desires of privately held Superior Oil and the responsibilities of publicly traded Falconbridge. In particular, Craig was said to be upset when the Superior Oil-dominated board voted to suspend dividend payments for the third quarter, citing falling nickel prices. Although analysts derided the decision as being arbitrary, the board's assessment of the situation was borne out by subsequent events. Commodity prices continued to decline, reaching their lowest level in decades and resulting in Falconbridge posting a loss in 1981, only the second in its history.

Craig's successor, H.T. Perry, was replaced in 1982 by William James, who would have a major impact on Falconbridge. James earned a Ph.D. in geology from Montreal's McGill University in 1957 and worked several years with his father's well-respected mining consulting company before being hired by Noranda in 1973 to run a subsidiary. Although a scientist by training, he revealed a natural business acumen, and also gained a reputation for being brash. He was recruited by Superior Oil to rescue Falconbridge, and he quickly set about the task. He slashed the workforce, including the main Toronto office staff, by about 40 percent. He leased one of the two floors the company occupied in an office tower, gave up his corner office for a much smaller one, and even shared a secretary with the president of a subsidiary. Operations were briefly suspended at Canadian and Dominican mines, as well as in Norway. James turned to the equity markets to raise money for capital purposes, and in the process changed the company's name to Falconbridge Limited. Nevertheless, Falconbridge still lost $81 million in 1982. It was not until the fourth quarter of 1983 that the company returned to profitability, and not until 1984 did the company post a profit for an entire year.

In 1985, Mobil purchased Superior Oil, then sold its Falconbridge interests to Dome Mines. More importantly that year, James outmaneuvered his ex-boss and mentor at Noranda, Alfred Powis, to acquire Kidd Creek Mines, a major silver, copper, zinc, and gold producer. The ore body, located near Timmons, Ontario, was discovered in 1964 by Texasgulf. It was so abundant in natural riches that it instantly made Texasgulf into a major diversified mining company. The Canada Development Corp. (CDC) forced a sale in 1981 in order to retain national control over the resources. Canada then experienced a movement towards privatization and CDC put Kidd Creek on the block. Noranda, cash-strapped because of a cost-reduction program, negotiated a joint venture with CDC, but James swept in with a $1.3 billion offer to acquire the property outright. His willingness to pay a premium of 66 percent over book value, some $245 million, won the day. Noranda and Falconbridge operated out of the same office building, and Powis visited his

Key Dates:

1928: Thayer Lindsley acquires mining claims in Falconbridge, Ontario.
1929: Norwegian refining facility, Nikkelverk, is acquired.
1931: Company completes its first year of full production.
1940: Nikkelverk is lost to occupying German forces.
1945: Company regains Nikkelverk.
1961: Company diversifies operations with acquisition of major mining interests.
1982: Company name is changed to Falconbridge Limited.
1985: Kidd Creek Mines Limited is acquired.
1989: Falconbridge is acquired by Noranda Inc. and Trelleborg AB and taken private.
1994: Stock offering returns Falconbridge to public company status.

rival's lobby to share in the champagne celebration, but his desire to gain Kidd Creek remained unabated.

Depressed metal prices, which persisted despite a recovering economy in 1986, prevented Falconbridge from enjoying immediate benefits of the Kidd Creek acquisition. James cut costs, in the process selling off a number of assets, but the purchase had been predicated on rising metal prices, and it was simply impossible to make money on Kidd Creek at current levels. While a short-term mistake, the property continued to hold long-term promise, and by 1988 it was a major contributor to Falconbridge's record earnings for the year. Powis, in the meantime, was hatching a plan to acquire Kidd Creek. Noranda began to buy up shares of Falconbridge stock, and by 1988 it became apparent that it intended to acquire a controlling interest and in effect purchase the company without paying a premium. James responded by agreeing to sell the company to Amax Inc., a Greenwich, Connecticut, aluminum, coal, and gold mining company, for $2.42 billion. He also instituted a ''poison pill,'' a shareholder rights plan that prevented Noranda from adding to its Falconbridge holdings. James put Powis into a bind: Noranda would benefit from the Amax deal as a major shareholder, yet he still coveted Kidd Creek. Clearly, James was not going to let him take over Falconbridge without paying a premium, and not just for a controlling interest but in a purchase for the entire company. The struggle would last more than a year, but in the end Noranda would pay $31.50 each for the shares it did not control, instead of the $23 it had paid earlier. In order to finance the $1.8 billion deal, however, Powis had to take on an equal partner, Sweden's Trelleborg AB. In the process, Falconbridge was taken private. James knew that he would not stay on as CEO, quipping to reporters, ''I just cost them too g—damned much money.'' He was replaced in the near-term by Alex Balogh, and in 1990 by Franklin Pickard, who had worked part-time at Falconbridge since the age of 16 and during his summers in college trained to become a metallurgical engineer.

Returning to Public Status: 1994

Nickel prices entered the downside of a cycle in the early 1990s, caused in large part by exports to the West from the Soviet Union. Falconbridge, which was forced to temporarily shut down some mines and production facilities, recorded a loss for 1993 when the price of nickel bottomed out. To raise capital, Falconbridge went public again, taking advantage of rising nickel prices to raise close to $600 million. Over the course of the next year, Trelleborg also took the opportunity to sell off its shares as part of a plan to cut debt and focus on its wholly owned businesses. Falconbridge proved to be a wise investment for the Swedish company, which realized a $600 million return on its money in only a few years.

The conservative Trelleborg influence on the Falconbridge board was replaced by more aggressive directors. Pickard took advantage of that situation in 1996 to make an aggressive bid for Diamond Fields Resources and its nickel deposits in Voisey's Bay, discovered in 1994 and believed to be the highest-grade nickel find in the world. Longtime rival Inco already owned a 25 percent stake in Voisey's Bay. It was unlikely from the start that Inco would allow Falconbridge to buy the assets, and in the end it outbid its smaller rival. Nevertheless, Falconbridge was able to take away more than $50 million in a non-completion fee.

Under Pickard, Falconbridge initiated a growth plan in 1996 that would double nickel production over the next 15 years, with an emphasis on expansion into the South Pacific nickel-rich island of New Caledonia. With the use of nickel in high-alloy steel steadily increasing, he chose to position Falconbridge to take advantage of the trend, rather than be overly concerned about near-term price fluctuations. In addition, he oversaw the company's development of a Raglan, Quebec, nickel and copper property, as well as the Collahuasi copper mine in Chile. Pickard was visiting the mine in September 1996 when he suffered a heart attack and died. Although shaken by the sudden turn of events, interim CEO Alex Balough vowed that the company would carry on with Pickard's agenda. Several weeks later a permanent replacement was named: Oyvind Hushovd, who had been born in Norway, started out at Nikkelverk, and worked for Falconbridge for more than 20 years. He had served as an executive in the company in both Norway and Toronto.

Financial results in the late 1990s were mixed at Falconbridge. Profitable years in 1996 ($250 million) and 1997 ($137 million) were followed by a $36.4 million loss in 1998, caused by depressed metal prices that were due in large part to an Asian economic slump and Russian overproduction. When prices recovered, Falconbridge recouped its losses, posting a $153.1 million profit in 1999. The company followed with record results in 2000, earning $245.7 million on revenues of $1.75 billion. Weak metal prices in 2001, as well as a lingering strike at one of its facilities, dampened profits and caused the company to cut back on production. Despite the cyclical nature of commodity prices, however, Falconbridge remained a strong company with a healthy long-term outlook.

Principal Subsidiaries

Falconbridge Europe S.A.; Falconbridge U.S. Inc.; Falconbridge International S.A.; Falconbridge Nikkelverk A/S; Falconbridge Dominicana, C. por A.; Société Minière Raglan du Québec Itée; Compania Minera Dona Ines de Collahuasi S.C.M.; Falconbridge Nouvelle Caledonie SAS.

Principal Competitors

Inco Limited; Norilsk Nickel.

Further Reading

Berman, Phyllis, ''Stiff Upper Lip,'' *Forbes,* July 1, 1985, p. 50.

Chisholm, Patricia, ''Mr. Perpetual Motion,'' *MacLean's,* August 14, 1989, p. 37.

Cook, James, ''Wait and See,'' *Forbes,* June 30, 1986, p. 50.

Daly, John, ''The Final Victory,'' *MacLean's,* October 2, 1989, pp. 40–41.

DeMont, John, with John Daly, ''Getting the Best Price,'' *MacLean's,* August 14, 1989, pp. 34–36.

Lamphier, Gary, ''Falconbridge's Chief Is Used to Comebacks,'' *Wall Street Journal,* August 4, 1989, p. 1.

Schacter, Mark, ''Falconbridge's James Faces Big Task Trying to Make Kidd Creek Pay Off,'' *Wall Street Journal,* May 5, 1986, p. 1.

——, ''Falconbridge's Plan to Buy Mining Company Is Rock-Solid Strategy, Many Analysts Believe'' *Wall Street Journal,* December 26, 1985, p. 1.

Wells, Jennifer, ''Striking It Rich,'' *MacLean's,* February 26, 1996, p. 36.

—Ed Dinger

First Aviation Services Inc.

15 Riverside Avenue
Westport, Connecticut 06880-4214
U.S.A.
Telephone: (203) 291-3300
Fax: (203) 291-3330
Web site: http://www.firstaviation.com

Public Company
Incorporated: 1995
Employees: 183
Sales: $105.7 million (2002)
Stock Exchanges: NASDAQ
Ticker Symbol: FAVS
NAIC: 336412 Aircraft Engine and Engine Parts
Manufacturing; 488510 Freight Transportation
Arrangement; 493190 Other Warehousing and
Storage; 551112 Offices of Other Holding Companies

First Aviation Services Inc. (FAvS) is the holding company for Aerospace Products International (API). FAvS was created in 1995 to acquire National Airmotive Corporation, a leading repair and overhaul specialist for Allison turbine engines, but sold this unit in late 1999 to concentrate on the distribution and logistics businesses. API supplies a number of components to companies in the aerospace industry, manufactures custom hose assemblies, and provides third-party logistics services. Another majority-owned subsidiary of FAvS, AeroV Inc., manages a business-to-business e-commerce service.

NAC's Origins

Oakland, California's National Airmotive Corporation (NAC) was founded in 1960. It became an authorized maintenance center for the Allison Engine Company (later a division of General Motors) in 1970. NAC specialized in gas turbine engines such as the Allison T56/501, used in military turboprop aircraft such as the Lockheed Martin C-130 Hercules and the P3C Orion; the Allison 250, which dominated the light helicopter market; and the Pratt & Whitney PT6, used in planes and choppers.

In late 1990, Intermark Inc., NAC's corporate parent at the time, put NAC up for sale. It was acquired by Triton Group Ltd., a San Diego-based investment group.

In February 1992, NAC moved its Allison 250 overhaul and repair operation from Van Nuys to a new 9,600-square-foot facility at Brackett Field in La Verne, California. NAC also had a satellite operation in Salt Lake City.

NAC acquired Heli-Turbine International and Heli-Dyne, Inc., both helicopter service centers, from Long Beach-based California Airmotive in April 1994. In late 1994, Sabreliner Corp. forged a deal to buy NAC from Triton. Sabreliner overhauled a wide range of engines, though the Allisons serviced by NAC were missing from its lineup. The price was reported to be $12 million to $15 million plus the assumption of another $15 million in debt. However, the deal was called off in February 1995. A month later, First Aviation Services emerged as the buyer. FAvS paid Triton $13 million in cash and assumed NAC's debt.

Creation of First Aviation: 1995

First Aviation Services Inc., headquartered in Westport, Connecticut, was created by First Equity Group in March 1995 as a holding company for National Airmotive Corporation (NAC), which it acquired from Triton Group, Ltd. on June 1, 1995. FAvS paid $30.36 million for NAC, including assumed debt of $17.96 million. NAC had net sales of $83.09 million in the fiscal year ending March 31, 1995. It had 350 employees at the time of its acquisition by FAvS.

Michael C. Culver was CEO of FAvS. He had cofounded First Equity ten years earlier along with Aaron P. Hollander, who served as chairman of First Aviation's board.

First Aviation's headquarters were relocated from Stamford to Westport, Connecticut, in March 1997. The company had reported sales of $104.24 million for the fiscal year ending January 31, 1997.

IPO and API in 1997

FAvS completed an initial public offering on April 4, 1997, simultaneously acquiring Aircraft Parts International Combs

Key Dates:

1995: First Equity Group buys National Airmotive from Triton Group, creating First Aviation as a holding company.

1997: First Aviation goes public, acquires API from AMR Combs.

1999: Rolls-Royce North America buys NAC; API expands into Canada.

2000: API establishes Asia/Pacific base in the Philippines.

its Aero Repair and Overhaul business, reported *Aero Safety and Maintenance.*

Expanding in Asia/Pacific and Cyberspace in 2000

API set up a hub in the Philippines in the spring of 2000 in order to improve service to customers in Asia and the Pacific. (Besides its original Memphis warehouse, API also had distribution centers in Calgary, Alberta, and Montreal.) API Asia Pacific Inc. set up toll-free telephone service throughout the region, and also used e-commerce and mainframe-to-mainframe data interchange. The hub was located at Clark International Airport, a former U.S. Air Force Base convenient to FedEx Corp.'s Subic Bay hub. The previous fall, FedEx Global Logistics chose API as the sole aerospace service provider in its Integrated Solutions Group. Several other contracts with major air freight carriers followed in the next two years.

Another important venture was soon launched to bring EDI access to small aviation parts suppliers—which made up 80 percent of the market, according to the trade publication *Overhaul & Maintenance.* EDI, or electronic data interchange, had traditionally only been available to original equipment manufacturers (OEMs) and their affiliates. However, AeroV, which began as a subsidiary of FAvS, made EDI standards accessible over the Internet, giving small parts suppliers more direct access to airlines. In June 2000, FAvS gave ARINC a 25 percent equity stake in AeroV in exchange for a direct link to ARINC's global EDI network.

API acquired five distribution centers from Superior Air Parts, Inc. in July 2001, paying $4.6 million in cash. Superior also hired API to provide third-party logistics services. FAvS revenues passed the $100 million mark for the first time in the fiscal year ended January 31, 2002. Net sales were $105.7 million, producing a gross profit of $22 million.

(API Combs) from AMR Services. "API Combs was conceived from ground zero in 1988 to be the aviation products supplier of the future," noted FAvS's 1997 annual report. Originally called Aircraft Parts International, the company built its service on advanced communications technology and next-day delivery from its warehouse in Memphis—also home to overnight shipping giant Federal Express.

In 1992, API parent company AMR Combs had consolidated its corporate jet support unit with API, which until then had focused on regional airlines and fixed-base operators (FBOs). The two divisions together had sales of $45 million at the time.

After the IPO, which listed FAvS on the NASDAQ, First Equity's (indirect) holding in First Aviation was reduced from 75 percent to 41 percent, but it remained the controlling shareholder. FAvS was aiming to provide "total aftermarket support to its customers" by capitalizing on consolidation in the aerospace parts industry; the IPO gave it more flexibility in pursuing future acquisitions by paying down debt. FAvS was interested in companies whose customer base, product line, or technology complemented or expanded its existing operations, according to a company press release.

G.E. "Jerry" Schlesinger was named president of API in October 1997, three months after joining FAvS. Feeling some effects of the Asian financial crisis, FAvS launched a cost-cutting effort at NAC in April 1998, hoping to save $3 million a year. Eighty jobs were cut and the light turbine engine operations were consolidated at the Long Beach, California facility.

Sale of NAC: 1999

A year later, FAvS announced it was considering selling off NAC as the parent company reported a $1.7 million loss for the fiscal year ended January 31, 1999. The company had a total of 510 employees at the time; 380 of these were with NAC. FAvS sales were $153.7 million, up just $100,000. The NAC unit, though, was posting record sales—$94 million. However, the FAvS board had developed a strategic plan to invest in the growing logistics business. In September 1999, Rolls-Royce agreed to buy NAC for $73 million. Rolls-Royce was growing

Principal Subsidiaries

Aerospace Products International, Inc.; AeroV Inc. (75%).

Principal Divisions

Distribution; Logistics.

Principal Competitors

AAR Corp.; Aviall; Aviation Distributors.

Further Reading

"Aircraft Services Co. Goes Public to Pay Off Acquisitions," *Corporate Financing Week,* March 10, 1994, p. 12.

"AMR Combs Consolidates Parts Distribution Operations," *Weekly of Business Aviation,* June 29, 1992, p. 269.

Bangsberg, P.T., "US Aerospace Firm Expands in the Philippines," *Journal of Commerce,* March 13, 2000, p. 26.

"First Aviation Explores Possible Sale of National Airmotive," *Weekly of Business Aviation,* May 3, 1999, p. 200.

"First Aviation Services Announces an Acquisition, a Distribution Agreement and a Third Party Logistics Contract with Superior Air Parts," *Equities,* July 2001, p. 24.

"First Aviation Services Completes IPO, Looks to Expand," *Aerospace Daily,* April 9, 1997, p. 54.

"First Aviation Services, Inc. (FAVS)," interview of CFO John A. Marsalisi, *Wall Street Transcript,* June 18, 2001, pp. 48+.

"First Aviation Services Is Parent Company of National Airmotive, API," *Weekly of Business Aviation,* April 7, 1997, p. 152.

"First Aviation to Cut Jobs at NAC Unit," *Los Angeles Times,* April 7, 1998, p. D2.

Goodman, Adam, "Sabreliner Acquisition Falls Through," *St. Louis Post-Dispatch,* February 11, 1995, p. 9A.

——, "Sabreliner Zooms in Size with California Purchase," *St. Louis Post-Dispatch,* December 9, 1994, p. 1C.

Proulx, Jim, "AeroV Wants to Let Little Guys Rule," *Overhaul & Maintenance,* September 2000, p. 73.

"Rolls-Royce Will Purchase Engine Services Company NAC," *Aero Safety and Maintenance,* September 17, 1999, p. 5.

Velocci, Anthony L., Jr., "Engine Makers Target Greater MRO Share," *Aviation Week & Space Technology,* September 27, 1999, pp. 27–28.

—Frederick C. Ingram

FPL Group, Inc.

700 Universe Boulevard
Juno Beach, Florida 33408-0420
U.S.A.
Telephone: (561) 694-4000
Fax: (561) 694-4620
Web site: http://www.fplgroup.com

Public Company
Incorporated: 1925 as Florida Power & Light Company
Employees: 10,992
Sales: $8.47 billion (2001)
Stock Exchanges: New York Tokyo London Philadelphia
Ticker Symbol: FPL
NAIC: 221122 Electric Power Distribution; 221112 Fossil
Fuel Electric Power Generation; 221113 Nuclear
Electric Power Generation; 221119 Other Electric
Power Generation

FPL Group, Inc. is a holding company that provides electricity to 7.3 million people in Miami, southern Florida, and 14 other states through its subsidiaries Florida Power & Light and FPL Energy. Its oil, natural gas, and nuclear power plants provide energy for residential, industrial, and commercial customers. The company is also the largest wind power owner in the nation. Its power rates are lower than national averages, and it has been praised for protecting the environment. In addition to producing and distributing electricity, FPL Group through its subsidiary FPL FiberNet provides fiberoptic cable and services to Florida telecommunications companies. FPL Group ranks as number 226 in the 2002 *Fortune* 500 list of the United States' largest companies and the 13th largest company in the utilities (gas and electric) industry.

Origins and Early History

During a massive real estate boom and population increase in 1925 Florida Power & Light Company (FP&L) was formed when a number of local electric and gas companies were consolidated by American Power & Light Company, a large utility holding company. FP&L included properties formerly owned

and operated by Miami Electric Light & Power Company, Miami Gas Company, Miami Beach Electric Company, Southern Utilities Company, Daytona Public Service Company, Ormond Supply Company, Lakeland Gas Company, St. Johns Electric Company, and Southern Holding Company. By 1930 company profits were $2.7 million on revenue of $11.4 million.

In 1941 the city of Miami bought the company's water operations for $5.1 million, and FP&L sold its Miami Beach bus transportation system. In 1946 FP&L sold its water distribution system in Coral Gables, Florida. In 1950 American Power & Light, carrying out the provisions of a Congressional act limiting utility holding companies, spun off FP&L as an independent company. In 1951 FP&L sold its electric properties in the Florida towns of Perry, Madison, and Monticello to Florida Power Corporation.

Post-World War II Growth

FP&L had weathered the Great Depression with the help of increasing demand for home electricity. During World War II, the U.S. economy recovered, and industrial demand for electricity increased sharply. Southern Florida's population and economy grew quickly after World War II, as soldiers who had been stationed in the area returned with their families to live there or to vacation. From 1949 to 1954 the customers in FP&L's territory increased from 295,000 to 463,000, while company revenue doubled from $38.7 million to $77.5 million. In 1952 FP&L announced a ten-year, $332 million construction program designed to triple the firm's electricity production capacity. The plan included construction of ten major power stations throughout FP&L's territory. Florida was growing so fast that in 1954 FP&L increased its ten-year plan to $410 million. By 1955 FP&L supplied electric power to 1.54 million people in 448 communities in the central and northern parts of Florida. Its gas system included 300 miles of gas mains, and gas plants in Miami, Daytona Beach, Lakeland, and Palatka, Florida. In 1958 the company sold its three gas plants and distribution systems to the Houston Corporation.

As Florida grew from the 20th most populous state in 1950 to the tenth largest state in 1960, FP&L grew along with it. By 1964 FP&L served 2.7 million people in 555 communities, its

143

Company Perspectives:

A strong culture of continuous improvement is perhaps the greatest advantage we have. Our people share the strong belief that no matter how well we may be performing now, we can always get better.

---

revenue reaching $235 million in 1964. In 1965 the company signed 20-year contracts to buy natural gas from Pan-American Petroleum Corporation and Florida Gas Transmission Company. FP&L also decided to develop the use of nuclear power. Its two nuclear plants, south of Miami at Turkey Point, however, did not come on line until 1973, and did so at a cost of $120 million each.

FP&L has suffered many power shortages due in part to the heat, humidity, and salt from the ocean, which make generating and delivery equipment difficult to maintain. On August 5, 1969, an explosion and fire at the firm's Cutler Ridge power plant caused a blackout along 50 miles of Florida's east coast, including Miami and Fort Lauderdale. Much of the power returned within 90 minutes for the nearly two million people affected. In April 1973 power failed twice in two days, affecting three million residents, some for as long as seven hours. The cause was defective equipment at the Turkey Point nuclear plants and at the oil-fueled plant at Port Everglades. The failures hurt the company's image, especially since they occurred the day after the company was awarded a $40 million rate increase.

Despite problems at Turkey Point, FP&L's fuel diversification proved important when the energy crisis hit in 1973 and oil prices skyrocketed. Natural gas and nuclear energy supplied about half of the firm's fuel needs, but the remainder of FP&L's fuel needs were filled by oil. Therefore, FP&L was granted a rate increase to offset the large increase in oil prices. The rate increases angered consumers.

In 1973 the company formed Fuel Supply Service, Inc. to secure fuel supplies. In 1974 Florida's attorney general ruled that utilities could not automatically pass along rises in fuel costs to customers. The ruling came just as FP&L was preparing a large stock and bond offering, which had to be canceled. The incident caused a lowering of the company's bond rating that management estimated would cost $300 million in higher interest rates. FP&L also was hurt in a recession that caught Florida with rows of unsold condominiums, and the state's growth slowed for the first time since World War II. Within a few years, however, Florida again was growing rapidly, and FP&L launched a massive building program to keep up, building seven new generating plants.

Another blackout left three million customers without electricity for several hours in 1977. It was FP&L's seventh major blackout in eight years, giving the company the worst power-failure record of U.S. electric utilities. The company was particularly vulnerable to power failures because it was isolated from the rest of the U.S. power grid. FP&L could draw some power from other Florida utilities when failures hit, but not enough to meet demand. The other utilities often did not have enough surplus power to offer, and FP&L's connections with them were

inadequate. In 1979 FP&L began a $335 million transmission expansion project, building two high-capacity power lines from Miami to the Georgia border to increase its access to other utilities. In 1981 FP&L won a major rate increase of $256 million, followed by increases of $101 million in 1982 and $238 million in 1983.

By 1977, the company's two Turkey Point nuclear power plants, damaged by corrosion, needed to be rebuilt, at a cost of about $500 million each. The Nuclear Regulatory Commission fined the company on several occasions for safety violations at the plants. FP&L also had to make extensive repairs to its nuclear plant at St. Lucie, north of Palm Beach. Nonetheless, FP&L pushed ahead with a second nuclear power plant at St. Lucie. FP&L finished the plant nearly on time in 1983, a rarity in nuclear power plant construction.

In part because of the problems with power failures and its nuclear power plants, FP&L moved to a Japanese-inspired style of management during the early 1980s. FP&L began stressing quality control, creating special quality-control teams, and keeping detailed records of the causes of power failures and other problems. The new management style initially faced opposition from middle managers. By 1989 the company had 1,900 quality-control teams, with most of its workforce participating. Each team worked to solve specific problems that prevented the company from achieving its goals. Results were impressive. Service outages dropped from 100 minutes per customer per year to 43 minutes per year, far below the U.S. average of 90 minutes per year. Employee injuries decreased, as did customer complaints. The company was adding 130,000 customers a year, but requested no rate increases to pay for additional equipment. Government officials and managers from other U.S. companies attended FP&L seminars on adapting these management techniques, and FP&L was widely praised as one of the best-managed U.S. corporations.

In 1984 FPL Group, Inc. was formed as a holding company with FP&L as the primary subsidiary. Through a stock offering, the company raised $75 million for diversification. In 1985 John J. Hudiburg became chairman and CEO of FPL Group's Florida Power & Light subsidiary. He and FPL Group Chairman Marshall McDonald pushed quality control even harder. FPL Group made its first major move to diversify in 1985 when it bought the Philadelphia, Pennsylvania-based Colonial Penn Life Insurance Company for $565 million. The same year FPL Group also set up ESI Energy Inc. to participate in nonutility energy projects, such as converting waste to energy and finding other alternative energy sources. Additional FPL Group ventures included cable television, commercial and industrial real estate, and the maintenance of citrus groves.

By 1985 FP&L was the fourth largest electric utility in the United States, and one of the fastest growing. It supplied service to 700 communities in 35 counties of Florida, including most of the territory along the east and lower west coasts of the state. With the addition of the second nuclear plant at St. Lucie, only 13 percent of the company's power was oil-generated. FP&L was working on ways to increase off-peak sales and reduce peak demand. In 1987 the utility raised the price of electricity during peak hours and lowered it during off-peak hours.

Key Dates:

1925: Florida Power & Light (FP&L) Company is formed as part of the American Power & Light Company.

1950: FP&L becomes independent of American Power & Light Company and is listed on the New York Stock Exchange.

1952: FP&L begins a major expansion to deal with post-war growth.

1958: Three gas plants and distribution systems are sold to the Houston Corporation.

1964: The company begins constructing the Cape Canaveral plant.

1965: FP&L contracts to buy natural gas for 20 years from Pan-American Petroleum Corporation and Florida Gas Transmission Company.

1972: Turkey Point Unit 3 nuclear plant comes on line.

1973: Fuel Supply Service, Inc. is organized and Turkey Point Unit 4 nuclear plant is brought on line.

1976: St. Lucie Unit 1 nuclear plant comes on line.

1977: FP&L has its seventh major blackout in eight years.

Early 1980s: FP&L begins new management style inspired by Japanese practices.

1983: The company finishes work on its second nuclear plant at St. Lucie.

1984: FPL Group, Inc. is organized as a holding company.

1985: FPL Group buys Colonial Penn Life Insurance Company and sets up ESI Energy Inc.

1989: FPL Group is honored as the first non-Japanese company to receive the coveted Deming Prize for quality control.

1990: The company returns to U.S.-style management and buys 76 percent of Georgia Power Company's plant near Atlanta.

1991: Colonial Penn is sold after losing money.

1994: The Martin Power Plant Units 3 and 4 are completed.

2001: Jim Broadhead retires after 13 years as chairman and CEO, replaced by Lewis Hay III.

In 1989 James Broadhead replaced McDonald as chairman of FPL Group. Also that year, FPL Group became the first non-Japanese company to receive the Deming Prize, the prestigious Japanese quality-control award named for W. Edwards Deming, the American business consultant who helped Japanese companies modernize after World War II. Hudiburg, however, who, with McDonald, led the company's drive to win the award, had resigned several months earlier in the wake of Broadhead's appointment. Broadhead had made clear his intention of discontinuing FPL Group's new direction in management. In 1990 Broadhead moved the company back toward decentralized U.S. management. The Japanese-based system had become unpopular among large segments of the company's workforce because of the long hours and paperwork involved. A subsidiary, Qualtec, Inc., continued to advise outside clients on certain aspects of quality improvement. Broadhead also was displeased with continuing maintenance problems at Turkey Point. Broadhead felt that Hudiburg had not adequately addressed operating deficiencies at Turkey Point.

Meanwhile, FPL Group's diversification efforts had proven disastrous. Colonial Penn Life Insurance was losing money, as was FPL's Telesat cable television service. FPL Group took a $72 million write-off in 1986 when it discontinued several unprofitable insurance lines. In 1989, with the U.S. insurance industry in recession, FPL Group took a $689 million write-off for Colonial Penn's losses and a $62 million write-off related to its cable television and real estate businesses. Because of the write-offs, income for 1990 came to only $6 million on sales of $6.3 billion.

The 1990s and Beyond

FPL Group decided to sell its troubled insurer, as well as its real estate and cable television businesses, and to focus its attention on energy-related businesses. It sold Colonial Penn in August 1991, but the real estate and cable television businesses remained on the market. In addition, predictions that Florida's population growth would slow in the 1980s proved wrong. A cold spell in late 1989 led to rotating blackouts. When two plants failed in July 1990, FP&L asked customers to use less air conditioning to prevent brownouts. In 1990 the company announced a plan to spend $6.6 billion by 1999 to increase its capacity by 5,400 megawatts, or about 36 percent. FPL Group raised $677 million for the project in 1990 through two stock offerings. To ease its power squeeze, the utility bought its first out-of-state property, purchasing 76 percent of Georgia Power Company's 846-megawatt, modern, coal-fired plant near Atlanta for $614 million. The company also planned to build a 100-mile transmission line, further connecting its electrical grid with that of Florida Power Corporation.

In 1990 nuclear power made up 24 percent of FP&L's energy mix, oil 23 percent, natural gas 17 percent, coal 3 percent, and purchased power 33 percent. In late 1990 the company had to shut down its Turkey Point nuclear plant for 11 months to refuel it and install a backup generator, cutting FP&L's generating capacity by 10 percent. The Turkey Point plant had run at only 49 percent capacity since 1987, suffering from poor maintenance and equipment failures that led to $700 million in repair bills between 1983 and 1990.

FPL Group faced a difficult rebuilding program in the 1990s, following its mostly failed diversification program. It faced a profitable future, however, supplying electricity to one of the fastest growing regions of the United States. It had to keep up with that growth but also become more efficient in order to compete in an era of energy deregulation.

New plants were built in the 1990s to meet energy demands. In 1994 the company put into service its Martin Power Plant Units 3 and 4. According to the company's web site, these units became operational ahead of schedule and ''more than $100 million below budget.'' The company's Lauderdale Plant was redone to triple its energy generating capability.

In 2000 FPL produced 26 percent of its electricity in nuclear power plants, 25 percent in oil plants, and 25 percent in natural gas plants. The company purchased 17 percent of its power and got just 7 percent from coal plants. Most of its power went to residential customers (50.4 percent of kilowatt hours) and commercial customers (40.2 percent), with the remainder used by industrial customers, public power agencies, railways, and energy wholesalers.

FPL Group reported increased operating revenues and net income for the year ending on December 31, 2001. Its operating revenues reached $8.47 billion, compared with $7.08 billion in 2000. That boosted the company's ranking on the *Fortune* 500 list from number 264 in 2001 to number 226 in the April 15, 2002 issue of *Fortune.* Its net income increased from $745 million or $4.38 per share in 2000 to $792 million or $4.69 per share in 2001. "Despite a rather tumultuous year for the electric industry," said FPL Group Chairman and CEO Lew Hay in a press release, "FPL Group produced solid results largely driven by an increasing number of customers at Florida Power & Light and a growing power plant portfolio at FPL Energy."

Florida Power & Light, the main subsidiary, in 2001 added almost 87,000 new customers and accounted for $695 million of the parent FPL Group's net 2001 income of $792 million. Subsidiary FPL Energy in 2001 increased its net income to $105 million from $83 million the year before.

The net income of FPL FiberNet, LLC, the smallest subsidiary, was exceeded by corporate expenses. It expanded its fiber-optic networks, however, in the Miami, Orlando, Tampa, St. Petersburg, Jacksonville, Fort Lauderdale, Boca Raton, and West Palm Beach areas. At the end of 2001 FPL FiberNet had about 2,500 miles of fiber.

In 2002 FPL looked forward to completely converting its Sanford Plant from oil to natural gas. By January 2003 the repowered plant was expected to double its generating capacity. Likewise, the company anticipated tripling the power of its Fort Myers Plant by using less polluting natural gas. It also planned to complete two new natural gas units at Fort Myers to provide reserve power for peak demand times.

The company planned to increase its energy production using wind turbines, a still small but rapidly growing part of the energy industry. In 2001 subsidiary FPL Energy doubled its previous wind capacity by adding 844 megawatts of new wind energy capability in Kansas, Texas, Wisconsin, Washington, and Oregon. This relatively new source of electricity produced no pollution but was erratic due to wind fluctuations. Many farmers and other land owners liked this new option, for they were paid an annual lease without having any operating responsibilities.

Meanwhile, FPL Group enjoyed some very positive developments in the commercial nuclear power industry. In 1999 nuclear power was the cheapest form of energy in the nation, averaging 1.83 cents per kilowatt-hour, compared with 2.07,

3.24, and 3.52 cents for coal, oil, and natural gas production. Nuclear plants also operated 90 percent of the time, compared with 69, 40, and 30 percent operating times for coal, hydroelectric, and oil/natural gas plants, respectively. Problems with nuclear plant wastes remained, but the industry had come a long way from the dismal past of poor management and nuclear accidents like Three Mile Island.

After more than 75 years in business, FPL Group seemed proud of its past accomplishments and confident in its future. In 2002 it pointed out on its web site that the average residential power rates were 23 percent higher than its own and that, adjusted for inflation, FPL's rates were the lowest in the 75-year history of the company.

Lewis Hay III, FPL Group's chairman, president, and CEO, reported in a March 22, 2002 letter to his firm's shareholders that the company's earnings per share had grown consistently from $3.33 in 1996 to $4.69 in 2001. The following month the company announced that it had agreed to buy 88.2 percent of the Seabrook Nuclear Generating Station in New Hampshire for a total of $836.6 million. Such acquisitions of new power plants, along with increased output from its existing plants and sound financial performance, prepared FPL Group for future challenges.

Principal Subsidiaries

Florida Power & Light Company; Qualtec, Inc.; FPL Energy LLC; FPL FiberNet, LLC; FPL Group Capital Inc.

Principal Competitors

MidAmerican Energy Holdings Company; Progress Energy, Inc.; TECO Energy, Inc.

Further Reading

Fins, Antonio N., "Feeling the Heat at a Florida Utility," *Business Week,* November 12, 1990.

Gabor, Andrea, "How a Florida Utility Became an Unlikely Contender for Samurai Success," in *The Man Who Discovered Quality: How W. Edwards Deming Brought the Quality Revolution to America— The Stories of Ford, Xerox, and GM,* New York: Penguin Books, 1990, pp. 162–87.

Jacobson, Gary, and John Hillkirk, "Crazy About Quality," *Business Month,* June 1989.

Tucker, William, "More Nukes, Please," *Weekly Standard,* April 2, 2001, pp. 26–29.

—Scott M. Lewis
—update: David M. Walden

Gables Residential Trust

2859 Paces Ferry Road, Suite 1450
Atlanta, Georgia 30339
U.S.A.
Telephone: (770) 436-4600
Fax: (770) 435-7434
Web site: http://www.gables.com

Public Company
Incorporated: 1993
Employees: 1,210
Sales: $282.5 million (2001)
Stock Exchanges: New York
Ticker Symbol: GBP
NAIC: 525930 Real Estate Investment Trusts

Based in Atlanta, Georgia, Gables Residential Trust is an umbrella partnership real estate investment trust (UPREIT). It is one of the largest owners and operators of upscale apartment complexes in select cities in the southeastern and southwestern United States, focusing on the ''infill'' areas that separate the suburbs from the urban center. In addition to Atlanta, the company maintains offices in Boca Raton, Houston, Dallas, and Washington, D.C., all of which essentially operate as independent enterprises. The main office provides finance, accounting, and other administrative functions. Altogether, Gables owns or has interests in approximately 27,000 apartments, and also manages some 80 properties for third parties, totaling nearly 24,000 units.

Trammell Crow: Becoming a Real Estate Legend After World War II

Gables grew out of real estate ventures launched by legendary Dallas real estate man Trammell Crow. He was born in Dallas in 1916, the fifth of eight children, and following his graduation from high school went to work for the Mercantile Bank in Dallas while studying law and accounting in evening classes at Southern Methodist University, ultimately becoming a Certified Public Accountant. In 1941, nine months before Pearl Harbor, he joined the Navy as an ensign and was assigned to finance. Through the war years he rose to the rank of Commander. Years later, he expressed the importance of his time in the service: ''I think those years in the Navy were worth a couple of M.B.A. programs to me.'' After being discharged he established Trammell Crow Company and soon became a major force in real estate. In 1948 he completed his first development project, a warehouse in downtown Dallas. He developed the Dallas Market Center in 1957, a structure that would influence subsequent marts around the world. Crow also was credited with originating the atrium concept for modern buildings. In the late 1960s his company opened its first offices outside of Dallas and a few years later opened its first international office. By 1971 *Forbes* recognized Crow as the largest private real estate operator in the United States. In the 1980s his company, which encompassed a number of industries, sought to become a truly national real estate enterprise. As part of this effort Trammell Crow Residential was established to do business in the apartment sector. It was a decentralized operation with a large number of divisions run independently by local management.

In 1993 executives from three of Trammell Crow Residential's most profitable divisions—Atlanta, Dallas, and Houston—began to discuss among themselves ways to raise new capital to grow their businesses. Talk of selling properties to existing real estate investment trusts (REITs) was abandoned soon in favor of combining the divisions to create their own trust. REITs had been originally created by Congress in 1960 as a way for small investors to become involved in real estate in a manner similar to mutual funds. REITs could be taken public and their shares traded just like stock and were also subject to regulation by the Securities and Exchange Commission. Unlike stocks, however, REITs were required by law to pay out at least 95 percent of their taxable income to shareholders each year, a provision that severely limited the ability of REITs to raise funds internally. During the first 25 years of existence, REITs were allowed only to own real estate, a situation that hindered their growth. Third parties had to be contracted to manage the properties. Not until the Tax Reform Act of 1986 began to change the nature of real estate investment did REITs begin to gain widespread usage. Tax shelter schemes that had drained potential investments were shut down: Interest and depreciation deductions were greatly reduced so that taxpayers could not generate paper losses in order to lower their tax liabilities. The act also permitted REITs to provide customary services for property, in effect allowing the trusts to operate and manage the properties they owned. Despite these major changes in law, REITs still were not fully utilized. In the latter half of the 1980s the banks, insurance companies, pension funds, and foreign investors (in particular, the Japanese) provided the lion's share of real estate investment funds. That period also witnessed overbuilding and a glutted marketplace, leading to a shakeout in the marketplace. With real estate available at distressed prices in the early 1990s REITs finally became an attractive mainstream investment option.

1993 Meeting Leading to the Creation of Gables

On July 3, 1993, four of the principle executives of the three Trammell Crow Residential divisions met in Atlanta, with two others participating by conference call from Texas. They were Marcus Bromley, Atlanta divisional partner; John Rippel, Houston divisional partner; Peter Parrott, Dallas divisional partner; Bill Hammond, COO of Residential Services Group, south central region; Marvin Banks, CFO, Atlanta and Dallas division; and Jordan Clark, Atlanta divisional partner of development and acquisitions. The six men that day agreed to form an umbrella partnership REIT, which would be called Gables Residential Trust. Some of the divisions' properties already bore the Gables brand, making the name worth exploiting. Bromley and Rippel took lead positions in the new organization, with Bromley slated to assume the role of CEO and chairman of the board and Rippel as president and COO. Both men had been with Trammell Crow since 1982. Because two of the divisional partners had to relinquish some authority to Bromley in the new structure, the founders of the REIT felt it was important to retain as much as possible the corporate structure that allowed the divisions to thrive under Trammell Crow. As a result the three chief field offices were given a major degree of autonomy, and only certain administrative functions, such as accounting, investor relations, and human resources, were slated to be centralized in a headquarters operation that would share space with the Atlanta office. There was some reduction in headcount, but each location retained its staff for property development, acquisition, construction, and property management.

To make these plans a reality and launch an initial public offering (IPO) of shares the founders agreed that a timetable had to be set. According to Bromley, "We had learned from the past that if you put a timetable on a project, you have a better chance of getting it done efficiently. If you put a year-end timetable on it, you have an even better chance of getting it done, so we said: 'Year end!'" Given that they had only allowed themselves six months to accomplish a diverse number of complicated tasks it was a highly ambitious schedule. They quickly decided to retain Arthur Andersen and Company, which was already familiar with the Trammell Crow Residential operations, to do the REIT's audits and due diligence work. Despite already having

much of the necessary paperwork in their files, the founders knew that Wall Street would want a thorough review of the properties that would form the basis of Gables. It proved to be a difficult, time-consuming task.

Gables then chose the Boston firm of Goodwin, Procter & Hoar to serve as its "issuer counsel" and help structure the IPO and negotiate with investment bankers. Goodwin had just completed the creation of the Avalon REIT, which was comprised of Trammell Crow entities in the Northeast. In August, negotiations were initiated to buy or transfer assets that would be part of the new REIT. It was a complicated endeavor to determine the interests of the various investors. Almost every property involved a joint venture with an institution and required a separate negotiation. This work would actually continue until the day the REIT made its offering. Gables next chose an investment banker, interviewing six of the country's top firms before settling on Merrill Lynch & Company in mid-September. Of less importance, but still crucial, was the hiring of a reliable printer to produce the voluminous amount of paperwork that would have to be generated, including a prospectus and various other legal and financial documents. Printing costs alone in creating the REIT totaled some $450,000.

Gables filed its registration statement in late October in order to meet its self-imposed deadline, but because the market was soft in the days following Thanksgiving, management elected to move back its offering from December to January. In the meantime, a credit line of $175 million was established and a week before Christmas several of the REIT's top executives launched a month-long road show to promote the upcoming offering. They even took the Concorde to London for a day trip, but found little support from European investors. Enthusiasm was much greater in the United States, and when the IPO was completed on January 26, 1994, it was oversubscribed. The company sold some 9.4 million common shares at a price to the public of $22.50 per share, netting Gables approximately $190 million, much of which was earmarked to retire debt.

Day-to-day operations continued on much as before, but now executives became more concerned with meeting the 8 percent dividend projected during the offering, creating pressure to make the quarterly numbers. Gables also felt the need to maintain a strong image for both prospective investors and residents. The company created a training program for the property management group, dubbed "The Gables University." With some of the money raised from the IPO, Gables launched a $200 million development plan for six cities: Dallas, Houston, Austin, Atlanta, Memphis, and Nashville. The first part of the effort was a $35 million investment in the Dallas area that featured three new projects totaling some 900 apartments.

Adding the South Florida Operation in 1990

To reach its goal of becoming a "super regional owner," Gables shifted its emphasis from growth by development to growth through acquisition starting in 1996. The company was especially active in 1998. In February of that year Gables acquired the Greystone Communities in the Houston area, adding some 913 units. A month later Gables acquired an Austin property with 308 units. A much larger transaction, however, was completed in April 1998 when Trammell Crow Residen-

Key Dates:

1993: Gables Residential Trust is incorporated.
1994: The REIT's initial public offering is launched.
1998: Trammell Crow Residential South Florida is acquired.
1999: John Rippel resigns.
2000: Bromley resigns as CEO in favor of Chris Wheeler.

tial's South Florida Division was brought into the fold, firmly establishing a presence in the highly desirable South Florida markets for Gables while immediately adding 4,200 upscale apartments. Gables paid $155 million in cash and assumed debt of more than $135 million. Altogether the REIT now owned 81 apartment communities with nearly 24,000 units located in nine southeastern cities, and an additional 1,800 units were either under development or lease-up. The company's holdings grew to $1.5 billion. As a result of these developments, revenues grew and the price of Gables stock kept pace. In June the REIT placed 3.3 million common shares with five institutional investors, its market capitalization now totaling $1.8 billion.

After the South Florida acquisition, Gables's management elected to return its focus to the development of its own apartment complexes. It moved forward, however, without one of its principle founders, John Rippel, who in March 1999 announced he was resigning as president and COO. He explained that because he continued to live in Houston and did not wish to relocate his family to Atlanta, he was simply weary of the constant travel required of his position. A short time later Bromley relinquished the CEO position to become executive chairman, leading some in the media to suspect a "palace coup," a notion dispelled by all the parties involved. Rippel was replaced by Michael Hefley and Bromley, by Chris D. Wheeler, who had joined the REIT as part of the Trammell Crow Residential's South Florida transaction. In the meantime, the company raised funds for development, drawing $56 million from Fleet Financial Group for three projects located in Atlanta; Weston, Florida; and West Palm Beach, Florida. Gables also entered into a joint venture with J.P. Morgan Investment to develop and manage seven apartment communities located in four of the REIT's nine markets, budgeted at more than $200 million. Moreover, in 1999 Gables tested a new sector, offering single-family units, aimed at an older demographic, people who might sell their homes for investment purposes but wanted to rent something more substantial than an apartment. The venture was called Palma Vista, a 189-unit development located in Palm Beach County.

At the same time that Gables was spending money on new projects in 1999 it was selling off properties. Although a large portion of the money raised was earmarked for development, almost as much was used to buy back company stock in an effort to reduce the availability of shares. The plan continued into 2000, with Gables beginning to exit some of its previous markets: San Antonio, Memphis, and Nashville. In addition to raising money to buy back stock, management adopted a strat-

egy of concentrating the REIT's portfolio on six to eight economically diversified markets. Although the company would enjoy less geographic diversity, it still hoped to find a blend of markets that would provide some protection from the vagaries of real estate values. Moreover, it elected to concentrate even more of its resources on infill areas.

In 2000 Bromley resigned as executive chairman and Wheeler assumed the additional post of chairman of the board. He instituted a novel bonus plan that year, one that attempted to link executive compensation with the performance of Gables compared with other REITs. Only if the company outperformed 75 percent of its rivals would executives receive 100 percent of their bonuses. On the other hand, if 75 percent outperformed Gables, then executives received no bonus at all. Although management was confident that Gables would enjoy a strong year, in the end the REIT finished in the middle of the pack, slightly below the sector average. As a result, managers received only half of their bonus. Nevertheless, management believed the plan was worth keeping.

In 2001 Gables continued to sell off properties while acquiring others in order to reposition the portfolio for what it hoped would be optimal performance. All told, the company sold $94 million in real estate assets while spending $117 million to acquire others. Of major importance was Gables's entry into a new and promising market for its operation, that of Washington, D.C. In September 2001 the company paid $24.2 million for an 82-unit high-rise in the Dupont Circle neighborhood, which was then renamed Gables Dupont Circle. Wheeler's attempts to reshape the REIT continued in 2002 when he initiated a major shakeup, resulting in the resignation of several top executives. Instead of three regions, the company was now divided into two, East and West.

Principal Subsidiaries

Gables Realty Limited Partnership; Gables Residential Services, Inc.; Gables Central Construction, Inc.; Gables East Construction, Inc.

Principal Competitors

Equity Residential; Post Properties, Inc.; United Dominion Realty Trust, Inc.

Further Reading

Bromley, Marcus E., "Thoughts on Going Public," *National Real Estate Investor,* September 1994, p. 24.
"Gables Puts Focus on Growth Market," *National Mortgage News,* August 28, 2000, p. 12.
"Gables Residential Trust," *Wall Street Transcript,* January 2, 1995.
Silver, Jeff, "Gables' Ability to Shift Gears Propels Its Growth," *Atlanta Business Chronicle,* August 7, 1998.
Taylor, Terry, "The Making of a REIT," *Journal of Property Management,* September–October 1994, p. 59.
Wilbert, Tony, "Major Shake-Up at Gables Was No 'Palace Coup,'" *Atlanta Business Chronicle,* May 17, 1999.

—Ed Dinger

Gallaher Group Plc

Members Hill
Brooklands Road
Weybridge
Surrey KT13 OQU
United Kingdom
Telephone: (44) 1932-859-777
Fax: (44) 1932-849-119
Web site: http://www.gallaher-group.com

Public Company
Incorporated: 1896 as Gallaher Limited
Employees: 3,519
Sales: $7.94 billion (2001)
Stock Exchanges: London New York
Ticker Symbol: GLH
NAIC: 312221 Cigarette Manufacturing; 312229 Other
  Tobacco Product Manufacturing (pt)

Gallaher Group Plc is the second largest tobacco company in the United Kingdom, with manufacturing operations throughout the world. Its best known premium brands of cigarettes include Benson & Hedges and Silk Cut. Until 1997, Gallaher was a wholly owned subsidiary of American Brands, Inc., of Old Greenwich, Connecticut, in the United States. Since being divested from American Brands in 1996, Gallaher has undertaken a substantial overseas expansion program, acquiring cigarette manufacturers in Russia and Austria, and entering a strategic partnership with Shanghai Tobacco in China.

The Early Years

Gallaher was founded by Tom Gallaher, who in 1857 started his own business in Londonderry, making and selling pipe tobaccos. Within 16 years, he had prospered enough to move to larger premises in Belfast. Toward the end of the 1870s, Tom Gallaher crossed the Atlantic for the first time in order to personally supervise the buying of his company's tobacco leaves. He visited Kentucky, North Carolina, Virginia, and Missouri, and following his first trip the expedition became an

annual event. Gallaher rose to become a notable figure in trade on both sides of the Atlantic.

During the first half of the 19th century, the pipe had gradually given way in popularity to the cigar. The military was credited in large part with this shift, as British soldiers returning from the Crimea campaign of 1854–56 introduced an item they had adopted from their French and Turkish allies—the cigarette. Smoking fashions in Britain underwent a change that Gallaher was astute enough to exploit. Soon other tobacco manufacturers also began to cater to this change in tastes. By 1888, he was producing flake tobaccos and cigarettes, which, included in the full range of Gallaher products, were displayed at the Irish exhibition in London during that same year. The expedition also saw the opening of Gallaher's first London premises, just inside the famous "square mile" of the city, at 60 Holborn Viaduct.

The first London factory was opened the following year at Clerkenwell Road to increase production, and in 1896 the Belfast factory moved into larger quarters. That same year, the company was incorporated as Gallaher Limited. An important development two years later was the discovery of a yellow and white burley leaf. Gallaher started to use it immediately, and in 1908 completed a transaction important to the history of the industry by purchasing the entire Irish tobacco crop.

The social history of smoking in the late Victorian and Edwardian ages was marked by the triumph of the cigarette. To that point in time, tobacco manufacturers had employed manual labor to make cigarettes as required, but soon cigarette-making machinery sped up production and thus satisfied the rising demand. It became acceptable for women to smoke, and new types of cigarettes were created to serve that market as well. By the outbreak of World War I in 1914, the cigarette had established its dominance over all other forms of smoking; it was considered vital to the welfare and morale of the armed forces and a valuable means of exchange.

Production increased significantly, and Tom Gallaher was the master of a thriving business when he died in 1927 at the age of 87. He had maintained an active interest in the company until the time of his death and had achieved great civic respectability

Company Perspectives:

The Group's strategy is to maintain and develop strong market positions, capitalising on its proven ability to build brand equity.

In the key UK cigarette market, Gallaher aims to defend vigorously its leading position in the high margin premium sector and to continue to increase its share of the growing low price sector.

Gallaher's international strategy is to continue to develop a balanced portfolio of interests in established and emerging markets with growth prospects—either independently or through strategic alliances or acquisitions. The Group's core international sales concentrate on building brands for local smokers.

Innovative advertising and creative marketing initiatives have built up brand recognition and loyalty with Gallaher's consumers over many years. This brand equity and superior marketing skills enable the Group to meet, and anticipate, changing trends, and to continue to develop new markets, with new brands and line extensions.

as a governor of the Royal Victoria Hospital in Belfast. He also was credited with being the first person in the tobacco industry to introduce a 47-hour working week and annual paid holiday.

The Mid-1900s: Gallaher's Expansion Efforts

Smoking, and cigarette smoking in particular, enjoyed a continuous popularity throughout the 1930s and 1940s. The anxieties of World War II were a further stimulus to tobacco consumption. In the 1950s, however, evidence was produced that not only linked smoking to lung cancer and heart disease, but also suggested that long-term cigarette smokers might be more susceptible to lung cancer than pipe or cigar users, or nonsmokers. These findings seemed to do no harm to Gallaher Limited, however, which was looking to expand in 1955 and succeeded in acquiring the U.K. and Irish interests of the prestigious Benson & Hedges company.

Benson & Hedges had enjoyed development and success parallel to Gallaher Limited, though in a more elevated style. Richard Benson and William Hedges began their business in 1873. Benson & Hedges notably departed from the custom of dispensing tobacco by weight. Their tobacco was prepared as a blend or mixture and packed in a sealed tin. This assured the customer that his goods would reach him in the freshest possible condition and also had experienced no tampering. The business also benefited from the patronage of the *bon vivant* Prince of Wales, later King Edward VII, who asked Benson & Hedges to prepare and make into cigarettes a parcel of Egyptian tobacco leaf that he had acquired. They did this, and adapted the style to market "Cairo Citadel," one of the first Egyptian-type cigarettes to be made in Britain.

When smoking became popular with women during Edward's reign, Benson & Hedges produced variations of the cigarette designed to appeal to women, tipped with rose leaves or violets, for example, or on a miniature scale. Increasing demand led to the

establishment of a separate factory, although the original shop remained at its location on Old Bond Street. During World War II, the shop was bombed and practically destroyed, but was rebuilt with the return of peace. When Benson & Hedges joined Gallaher, it brought not only its best-selling cigarettes, but also its Royal Warrant, which was first bestowed by Queen Victoria "to purvey cigarettes and cigars for use in her household," and later renewed by subsequent monarchs.

In 1962, Gallaher acquired J. Wix and Sons Ltd. of London, the makers of Kensitas, a well-known cigarette. The company's vendor was The American Tobacco Company, which made the transaction in exchange for a stake in Gallaher's stock. By 1968, American Tobacco had increased its holdings in Gallaher shares to 67 percent. American Tobacco had been a relative failure in its native tobacco market, but was now using a steady cash flow wisely to buy and diversify. In 1969, in recognition of its changing profile, it was renamed American Brands, Inc.

An American Brands Subsidiary: 1970s–80s

Meanwhile, Gallaher itself began to broaden its scope. An interesting and substantial acquisition in 1970 was the Dollond & Aitchison Group, whose main specialty was the supply of optical services and advice, spectacles, contact lenses, and accessories. Dollond & Aitchison possessed an extensive branch network throughout the United Kingdom. Also acquired was a small ophthalmic instruments manufacturing and distributing operation, called Keeler Limited.

Gallaher continued this diversification phase by making its first foray into retail distribution. In 1971 it established the Marshell Group, a retail franchise operation that sold mainly tobacco products and confectionery through concessions within major retail stores across the United Kingdom. Within 20 years the concessions numbered around 635, and the company also had more than 50 of its own retail outlets.

Two similar acquisitions followed in 1973. The TM Group, previously called Mayfair, was a company operating vending machines that dispensed cigarettes, drinks, and snacks in licensed and industrial catering outlets. Perhaps TM's best known manifestation in the United Kingdom was the ubiquitous Vendepac machine. Another purchase was that of Forbuoys plc, a chain of shops selling tobacco, confectionery, newspapers, and magazines, again with branches throughout the United Kingdom.

Using its standing as a subsidiary of a giant conglomerate, Gallaher was able to continue its expansion and diversification without severely troubling its balance sheet. Dollond & Aitchison's overseas expansion began in 1974 with the acquisition of the Italian company Salmoiraghi Vigano, which added the retailing of optical and medical instruments to the group's interests. The following year, American Brands finally controlled 100 percent of Gallaher's shares. It was arranged that the chairman and chief executive of Gallaher Limited would sit on the board of American Brands, while American Brands would have non-executive directors on the Gallaher board.

Gallaher continued to make acquisitions. In 1984, it purchased Prestige Group plc. Under the "Prestige" brand name, the company produced stainless steel cookware, pressure cook-

Key Dates:

1857: Tom Gallaher begins making and selling pipe tobaccos.
1873: Benson & Hedges is founded.
1896: Gallaher Limited is incorporated.
1955: Gallaher acquires the U.K. and Irish interests of Benson & Hedges.
1962: Gallaher acquires J. Wix and Sons Ltd.
1969: The American Tobacco Company is renamed American Brands, Inc.
1996: American Brands spins off Gallaher Limited.
2000: Gallaher acquires Russian cigarette manufacturer Liggett-Ducat.

ers, bakeware, and kitchen tools and accessories. Under another brand name, Ewbank, it also marketed carpet sweepers. Established in 1937, Prestige was the leading non-electrical housewares manufacturer in the United Kingdom. Following the Prestige acquisition in 1984, Dollond & Aitchison opened the first fast-service optical department store in Europe at Yardley near Birmingham, England. Additional stores, called ''Eyeland Express,'' have followed since then.

In 1988, along with other companies in Northern Ireland, Gallaher was approached by the former Fair Employment Agency for Northern Ireland, which sought cooperation in a study to ascertain to what degree equality of opportunity was being afforded to Protestants and Roman Catholics. The agency had been advised of Gallaher's longstanding interest in the question, and the report concluded: ''The efforts made by the company and the local Trade Union officials to introduce locally meaningful equal opportunity measures are positive and encouraging and the Agency is satisfied that the action taken is indicative of real commitment to provide equality of opportunity.''

The following year, the section of Gallaher's business represented by Dollond & Aitchison suffered a setback when the British government abolished free vision tests for the majority of people, and spectacles and contact lenses for retail became liable for value-added tax. In fact, this severely affected the entire industry in the United Kingdom, but Gallaher remained confident, and continued as planned with the expansion of the Eyeland Express chain. Within two years, Dollond & Aitchison had virtually completed a major restructuring of its retail and service facilities. It became the largest optical group in Europe, with more than 500 outlets in the United Kingdom alone and strong and profitable overseas business.

The 1990s and Beyond

Gallaher Limited began the 1990s with a strategy based on diversification. Further strategic development of Gallaher's nontobacco interests continued with the acquisition of Whyte & Mackay Distillers Ltd., in February 1990. The company, as well as its three Scottish distilleries, was headquartered in Glasgow. One of those distilleries was a bottling company, William Muir (Bond 9) Limited, based in Leith, near Edinburgh. Its products were the blended whiskeys Whyte & Mackay Special Reserve

and The Claymore, as well as the single malts The Dalmore, Tomintoul-Glenlivet, and Old Fettercairn. In April 1990, Whyte & Mackay reinforced its branded business and acquired the worldwide trademark rights to Vladivar vodka, the United Kingdom's second largest vodka brand. Other than scotch whiskey, vodka was the most popular distilled spirit in the United Kingdom.

Meanwhile, the tobacco business, managed by Gallaher Tobacco, remained a strong performer. In the declining U.K. cigarette market, Gallaher had increased its volume of sales and was making the three leading brands: Benson and Hedges Special Filter, Silk Cut, and Berkeley Superkings. Gallaher also manufactured the leading U.K. pipe tobacco, the leading cigar, and the second largest brand of hand-rolling tobacco in the United Kingdom. Gallaher International, the export arm, also was undergoing increased development in the early 1990s, and was well placed to take advantage of the trend toward low-tar cigarettes, pushing for markets in France, Spain, and Greece.

Since its inception, Gallaher had maintained considerable holdings in Northern Ireland, and by the 1990s was one of the largest manufacturing employers there. Operations included a warehouse complex for tobacco leaf at Connswater, East Belfast, and a sales distribution center on the outskirts of the city. Production took place at Lisnafillan, near Ballymena, County Antrim, in a modern factory complex handling cigarettes, pipe tobacco, and hand-rolling tobacco. Also at Lisnafillan was the company's research and development division, which was a particularly vital establishment to Gallaher's drive to keep its position as market leader in low-tar cigarettes.

Gallaher also continued to operate in the Republic of Ireland, where it was the second largest tobacco company. Cigarettes, pipe tobacco, and hand-rolling tobacco were manufactured in a factory just outside Dublin. On the British mainland, three top-selling cigarette brands and a wide range of smaller brands were made at the famous Senior Service factory at Hyde, east of Manchester, and cigars were produced at Cardiff and Port Talbot in south Wales.

In the mid-1990s, Gallaher continued to increase recognition of its name in its home market, through various types of sponsorship. Although it had withdrawn patronage of the Silk Cut Tennis Championship in 1990, the Benson & Hedges Cup at Lord's remained an important sponsorship. This cricket competition was vital to the Test and County Cricket Board during those years, as the sponsorship arrangement guaranteed the organization £3 million over a five-year period. Other sponsorships within the Benson & Hedges portfolio were the International Open Golf Championship at St. Mellion, Cornwall; the Masters Snooker Tournament at Wembley; the Silk Cut Showjumping Derby; and the Silk Cut Nautical Awards. In Northern Ireland, small business development was encouraged by the Gallaher Business Challenge Award Scheme, and the company was also the major private sponsor of the Ulster Orchestra.

As Gallaher entered the last few years of the century, the strength of its tobacco industry holdings was tested when the European Community (EC) banned all advertising of tobacco products on U.K. television. At the time the ban was instituted, Gallaher owned the United Kingdom's biggest cigar brand,

Hamlet, but was fighting for continued market share dominance with Imperial's Castella brand. During the weeks preceding the ban, Gallaher ran most of its old and new advertisements on U.K. television in a last-ditch effort to maintain its edge. For years, the Hamlet television advertisements had been wildly popular with the U.K. public and had won 15 Lion awards at the International Advertising Film Festival at Cannes. Gallaher also produced a 30-minute video showcase of the best of the Hamlet advertisements over the years, which was then sold to the public to keep the spirit of the 27-year Hamlet campaign alive.

Within a year of the tobacco advertising ban, Gallaher introduced a new entry in the budget-priced sector of the cigarette market. The brand Mayfair was introduced, and it joined Gallaher's Berkeley Superkings brand, which was currently the best-selling brand in the budget-priced market. Mayfair was immediately given a poster advertisement campaign, which focused mainly on the low price of the product. Furthermore, Gallaher attempted to appeal to potential customers by lowering the cost of Mayfair by the same amount that the government had just added as duty to the cost of the cigarettes. Soon thereafter, Gallaher also introduced its Eclipse brand, which was classified as a "super luxury length" product and joined other cigarettes at the opposite end of the spectrum from Mayfair. At that time, Gallaher was producing the top three cigarette brands in the United Kingdom.

Gallaher continued to reap success, even despite criticisms and raised eyebrows from industry analysts regarding marketing and pricing decisions made by the company. By 1996, Gallaher had grown to account for more than 50 percent of American Brands' yearly sales figures. The following year, American Brands made the decision to spin off Gallaher. Prior to the spinoff, Gallaher had helped American Brands achieve $6.9 million in 1996 tobacco sales alone. Following the divestiture, American Brands changed its name to Fortune Brands, Inc. The new name more accurately reflected that corporation's holdings—ironically, "American" Brands had been responsible for numerous international holdings for years, including Gallaher.

Back in Business: Gallaher in the 21st Century

The years immediately following its spinoff from American Brands were an extremely busy time for Gallaher. Although the tobacco industry in Britain was in the midst of making a small comeback in the late 1990s, with companies like Gallaher and Imperial Tobacco gaining listings on the London stock market, an increasingly complicated marketplace posed a number of challenges to Gallaher. For one, high taxes on cigarettes in the United Kingdom were pushing many consumers toward cheaper brands. Although Gallaher's Benson & Hedges still dominated the market for premium cigarettes in Britain, the company had minimal background with cut-rate brands, making it vulnerable to Imperial in this rapidly growing sector. The challenge was to establish an inexpensive cigarette that could compete with Imperial's Lambert & Butler, which in itself claimed more than 10 percent of the overall cigarette market in the United Kingdom. Although Gallaher had introduced its own cut-rate brand, Mayfair, in 1992, it still accounted for only 2.1 percent of the total market as late as May 1997. Recognizing the need to become more aggressive, the company launched a second cut-rate brand, Sovereign, in late 1996. Bolstered by a huge

marketing campaign, the move soon paid off, and by late 1997 Sovereign and Mayfair could boast sales growth of 89 percent over the course of only six months. By September 2000, Mayfair had become the third leading cigarette in the overall market.

Another problem confronting Gallaher during this period involved the alarming rise in sales of "bootleg" cigarettes in England. High duties were an invitation for smugglers to try to seize a portion of the U.K. market, and 1998 saw the share of overall cigarette sales commanded by bootleggers rise from 2 percent to 3 percent in only six months. In light of the price differentials between legitimate and contraband cigarettes—a pouch of Golden Virginia hand-rolled tobacco could be sold by smuggler for around £3, compared with £7.95 in a tobacco shop—it was not difficult to understand Gallaher's concern. Heavy lobbying for government intervention did begin to show results by the year 2000, when increased vigilance by customs agencies caused the rate of decline in duty-paid cigarette sales to go down from 12 percent to slightly more than 2 percent. The bootlegging situation, however, also prompted Gallaher to look elsewhere for ways to offset the decline in profits. Although a strong British pound during the late 1990s had already cut into Gallaher's overseas revenues, the company continued to view international expansion as critical to its sustained growth. Toward this end, Gallaher set out on an acquisition spree in the five years after it was divested from American Brands, a strategy that raised its operating profits by 20 percent over a two-year span and expanded its overall annual cigarette production from 33 billion to 60 billion. Gallaher's purchase of Moscow-based Liggett-Ducat in June 2000 gave the company control of nearly 17 percent of the Russian cigarette market. More significant, the deal nearly doubled the company's production capacity, while simultaneously placing it in an ideal position to begin marketing cigarettes in Eastern Europe and Central Asia. The Liggett-Ducat acquisition was followed by a joint venture with state-run Shanghai Tobacco in China in February 2001, and in June 2001 Gallaher successfully outbid rival Imperial for Austrian Tabak, paying $2 billion for a company responsible for 90 percent of cigarette sales in Austria. By 2002 the company was competing for control of German cigarette manufacturer Reemtsa, the largest private tobacco company in the world, while also eyeing possible entries into cigarette markets in the Middle East and Africa. With U.K. profits diminishing, Gallaher was clearly looking abroad to build the foundation for its future success.

Principal Subsidiaries

Airton Cigar Sales Limited; Benson & Hedges, Ltd.; Benson & Hedges (Dublin) Ltd.; Cope & Lloyd (Overseas) Ltd.; Cope Brothers & Co., Ltd.; Gallaher (Dublin) Limited; Gallaher (Ukraine) Limited; Gallaher Asia Limited; Gallaher Asset Finance 1998 Limited; Gallaher Asset Finance 2000 Limited; Gallaher Austria (Holdings) Limited; Gallaher Austria Limited; Gallaher Benelux Limited; Gallaher Canarias SA; Gallaher Finance and Distribution Limited; Gallaher Finance Limited; Gallaher Finance Overseas Limited; Gallaher France EURL; Gallaher Group plc; Gallaher Hellas SA; Gallaher International Limited; Gallaher Kazakhstan LLC; Gallaher Limited; Gallaher Overseas (Holdings) Limited; Gallaher Overseas Limited; Gallaher Pensions Holdings Limited; Gallaher Pensions Limited;

Gallaher Quest Trustees Limited; Gallaher Services Limited; Gallaher Spain S.A.; J.R.F. Realty, Inc.; Roughburn Forestry Limited; S.N. Farms Limited; S.N. Woodlands Limited; Silk Cut (Dublin) Limited; Silk Cut SA; The Galleon Insurance Company Limited; The Schooner Insurance Company Limited.

Principal Competitors

British American Tobacco p.l.c.; Imperial Tobacco Group PLC; Philip Morris International Inc. (U.S.A.).

Further Reading

Blackwell, David, ''Gallaher Attacks Bootleggers,'' *Financial Times* (London), March 13, 1998, p. 26.
——, ''Gallaher Looks Abroad for Growth Opportunities,'' *Financial Times* (London), February 28, 2001, p. 28.
Bowes, Elena, ''Hamlet Cigars Skirt TV Ban,'' *Advertising Age,* July 1, 1991, p. 28.
Johnson, Mike, ''Last Big Puff for Cigars As EC Snuffs Out Use of TV,'' *Marketing,* September 12, 1991, p. 8.
Meller, Paul, ''Gallaher Brand Bumps Up Budget Sector,'' *Marketing,* February 20, 1992, p. 4.
——, ''Gallaher Cost Freeze Heightens Price War,'' *Marketing,* March 19, 1992, p. 7.
——, ''Hamlet Enters Post-TV Era,'' *Marketing,* April 2, 1992, p. 14.
——, ''Silk Cut Lowers Kingsize Tar Levels,'' *Marketing,* April 2, 1992, p. 8.
Ross, Sarah, ''Gallaher and Imperial Move on Austrian Tabak,'' *Financial Times* (London), February 19, 2001, p. 28.

—Paul Stevens
—updates: Laura E. Whiteley, Steve Meyer

Gambro AB

Hamngatan 2
PO Box 7373
SE-103 91 Stockholm
Sweden
Telephone: (+46) 8-613-65-00
Fax: (+46) 8-611-28-30
Web site: http://www.gambro.com

Public Company
Incorporated: 1964 as Gamla Brogatans Sjukvårdsaffär
Employees: 17,999
Sales: SKr 26.72 billion ($2.7 billion) (2001)
Stock Exchanges: Stockholm New York
Ticker Symbol: GAMBB
NAIC: 621492 Kidney Dialysis Centers; 334510
    Electromedical and Electrotherapeutic Apparatus
    Manufacturing

Sweden's Gambro AB specializes in renal care products, services, and equipment. With sales of nearly SKr 27 billion ($2.7 billion) per year, Gambro has captured the position as the world's second largest dialysis services company, behind Germany's Fresenius AG. Gambro operates through three primary business units. Gambro Healthcare, its largest division accounting for nearly 60 percent of sales, operates an extensive network of dialysis treatment facilities, with more than 670 clinics worldwide. More than 520 of the company's clinics are located in the United States. Gambro Renal Products, the next largest division representing more than 35 percent of sales, makes and distributes products for hemodialysis, peritoneal dialysis, and renal intensive care treatments under the Gambro and Hospal brand names. The company has long been a leader in pioneering technology for dialysis treatments and operates several research and development laboratories in Sweden, the United States, France, Germany, Japan, and elsewhere. The last and smallest of the Gambro divisions is Gambro BCT—for Blood Component Technology—which produces products for apheresis (blood separation), blood component collection, and blood component purification. The United States represents Gambro's largest market, at more than

60 percent of sales. Europe contributes more than 10 percent of annual sales. Asia is also a significant market for the company's products and services. Gambro was formerly known as the manufacturing division of Incentive AB, run by Sweden's Wallenberg family. The company trades on both the Stockholm and New York stock exchanges.

Dialysis Pioneer in the 1960s

Nils Alwall, a Lund, Sweden-based professor, invented the world's first single-use artificial kidney in the early 1960s. In 1964, Swedish industrialist Holger Crafoord became determined to introduce Alwall's breakthrough invention to the medical world, forming a new company, known as Gamla Brogatans Sjukvårdsaffär (translated as Old Bridge Street Medical Supplies Company). The company quickly became known as Gambro and began developing the single-use artificial kidney into a marketable product. In 1967, Gambro debuted its parallel plate dialyzer and began mass production.

With the success of its first dialysis machine, Gambro was able to step up its research and development efforts. By the beginning of the 1970s, the company had readied a new product, the AK-3, which became the world's first automatic dialysis machine. The success of this product led the company to expand its manufacturing base, with the opening of a production facility in Germany, the leading European market for dialysis products. The company also moved into France, establishing its subsidiary Gambro SA in 1972.

Gambro scored another first in 1977 when it introduced the successor to the AK-3, the AK-10, which incorporated new microcomputer technology to become the first computer-controlled dialysis machine. In 1980, the company debuted a new polyamide membrane. Then in 1983, Gambro went public, listing simultaneously on the Stockholm and New York stock exchanges and becoming Gambro AB.

Gambro continued to expand its operations, introducing dialysis services—including opening its own treatment centers—in addition to manufacturing dialysis machines and equipment. The company's growth hit a glitch during the 1980s, however, when healthcare cuts in the United States carved out a share of

155

Company Perspectives:

VISION: To be the globally preferred partner among patients and healthcare providers by delivering world class blood- and cell-based solutions and services.

  CORE PURPOSE: To save lives and improve the quality of life for the people we serve.

Gambro's single largest market. By the mid-1980s, however, Gambro was preparing to continue its expansion and began searching for acquisitions.

In 1987, Gambro paid the equivalent of $187 million to acquire France-based Hospal, one of its main European rivals and itself the developer of a breakthrough dialysis membrane. Hospal had been formed in 1977 when Rhone-Poulenc and Sandoz merged their artificial kidney divisions. Hospal then acquired control of the high-flux AN69 membrane—considered the world's most advanced membrane technology of the time—as well as other patents, which enabled it to gain a significant market position. Hospal went on to develop its own dialysis system, which it launched in 1985 as the Filtral dialyzer.

After acquiring Hospal, Gambro launched a new breakthrough product, the BiCart Cartridge, using a dry bicarbonate cartridge for bicarbonate-based dialysis systems. In 1988, Gambro found itself a new owner, when Swedish investment company Cardo bought out the Crafoord family and other Gambro shareholders.

Building a Leadership Position in the 1990s

At the start of the 1990s, Gambro began a new expansion drive. In 1990 the company acquired its U.S.-based rival Cobe, for $253 million. Like Gambro, Cobe had been founded in 1964 as a maker of dialysis machines. A year after its founding, Cobe released its first significant product, a plastic extracorporeal blood set for use in chronic hemodialysis treatment regimes. The product, an industry first, formed the basis for the company's strong growth in the 1970s.

The 1970s began for Cobe with the release of a new generation of dialysis, the first in the world to offer servo-controlled dialysate proportioning. That machine also included an electronic monitoring and alarm system. In 1975, Cobe launched a new product line, the Centry 2, billed as the world's first fully integrated dialysis machine. At the beginning of the 1980s, Cobe began its own expansion drive, diversifying into Blood Component Technology (BCT) products with the acquisition of IBM Biomedical Products in 1984. The following year, Cobe introduced its new generation of dialysis machines, the Centrysystem 3, an integrated, computer-driven hemodialysis machine. Cobe meanwhile began to develop a range of blood separation, cleansing, storage, and related products for blood banks and other research companies. This resulted in the launch of Cobe's Spectra Apheresis System in 1988.

Gambro kept the Cobe brand name following the acquisition, as it targeted the United States for its 1990s growth. Gambro had already begun opening its own dialysis clinics in the United States; in 1992, the company began building toward critical mass in that operation with the acquisition of majority control of REN Corporation, then the leading operator of dialysis clinics in the United States (Gambro acquired 100 percent control of REN in 1995). In that year as well the company introduced its Centrynet data acquisition system.

Gambro's dialysis line included hemodialysis systems, which purified blood using external artificial kidneys, and intensive care systems. In 1994, the company entered a new dialysis category with the launch of its first peritoneal dialysis system, which enabled blood-cleansing treatment in the patient's own body. That year also marked a new turning point, when Incentive AB, an investment company held by Sweden's Wallenberg family, acquired the Cardo stake in Gambro. Incentive took full control of Gambro in 1996. Incentive maintained the company's Gambro, Cobe, Hospal, and other brand names.

With its new financial backing, the Gambro division continued its acquisition spree, acquiring nearly 100 companies and dialysis clinics during the decade to build up its network of manufacturing and treatment facilities. The company also began to concentrate on its core renal care businesses, selling off a number of Cobe's diversified operations. In this way, the company sold off operations in intensive care and anesthesia in 1994.

By then, Gambro's treatment clinic operations had taken a new step forward. In 1996, the company acquired American Outpatient Services Corporation and its 16 dialysis treatment clinics. That purchase brought Gambro's total clinics to 125. Yet the company targeted its clinics operation for still stronger growth. In 1997, the company acquired Vivra, another leading network of dialysis treatment clinics based in the United States. Its renal care division was boosted by the launch of its new renal intensive care system, Prisma, that same year.

By 1998, Incentive, which had been operating as a widely diversified industrial holding company with businesses including the Vikto Hasselblad camera company and the Hagglunds military vehicle business, had succeeded in streamlining itself into a focused healthcare company targeting the renal care market. In that year, Incentive changed its name to Gambro AB. That year, Gambro continued its own streamlining, selling off its Cobe cardiopulmonary business to Italy's Sorin Biomedica. At that time, the company discontinued use of the Cobe brand name.

Gambro's nearly decade-long growth drive had left the company burdened with debt. By 1999, the company was forced to restructure its operations, at a cost of more than SKr 1 billion. The reorganization also included the elimination of the company's multiple brand names. The company's product lines and operations were now brought under either the Gambro (and Gambro BCT) or the Hospal names, while the company was reformed into three primary business units—Gambro Healthcare, which took over operation of the company's more than 600 dialysis clinics; Gambro Renal Products, which provided the umbrella for its dialysis systems; and Gambro BCT. At the same time, the company also closed down two of its U.S. production sites, moving manufacturing to its facilities in France, Italy, and Mexico.

The restructuring hit Gambro's share price. By 2000, rumors began to circulate that Gambro had entered talks with Fresenius,

Key Dates:

1964: Gambro is founded in order to develop and market an artificial kidney invented by Nils Alwall, of Lund, Sweden; Cobe, based in Colorado in the United States, is founded to develop and market dialysis systems.

1965: Cobe launches its first product, a plastic extracorporeal blood set for use in chronic hemodialysis treatment regimes.

1967: Gambro begins production of the first commercial dialysis system.

1971: Gambro launches the AK-3 dialysis machine.

1975: Cobe launches the Centry 2, the world's first fully integrated dialysis machine.

1977: Rhône-Poulenc and Sanofi combine their artificial kidney divisions to create Hospal SA.

1983: Gambro goes public on the Stockholm and New York stock exchanges.

1984: Cobe acquires IBM Biomedical Products.

1987: Gambro acquires Hospal.

1990: Gambro acquires Cobe.

1992: Gambro acquires a stake in REN Corporation in the United States and begins building a network of dialysis treatment facilities in that country.

1994: Gambro is acquired by Incentive AB, owned by the Wallenberg family of Sweden, which then streamlines its industrial holdings to focus on healthcare.

1996: Gambro acquires American Outpatient Services Corporation and its 16 dialysis treatment clinics.

1997: Gambro acquires Vivra, boosting its dialysis clinics network in the United States.

1998: Gambro sells off the Cobe brand name and noncore cardiopulminary division; Incentive changes its name to Gambro AB.

1999: Gambro undergoes $135 million restructuring drive.

2000: Gambro launches the Polyflux filter-based dialysis system.

2001: Gambro acquires Renal Management Inc., based in the United States.

Gambro continued to launch new products at the turn of the century, including the latest generations of its AK series of dialyzers. In 2000, the company released its new Polyflux synthetic hemodialysis filters, considered the most advanced of its type on the market at the time. The following year, Gambro announced that it had acquired Renal Management Inc., based in the United States. That purchase added 21 new clinics to Gambro's network, as well as acute dialysis services in 16 hospitals and related facilities. With more than 670 clinics, including 520 in the United States, Gambro then announced that it had reached "critical mass" and intended to slow down its acquisitions beginning in 2002.

Principal Subsidiaries

Parkdialysen AB; Scandinavian Heart Center AB; Örekron Holding AB; Örekron Service AB; Gambro Fastighet AB; Incentive Aircraft TWO AB; Incentive Grosshandel AB; Gambro NV/SA (Belgium); Hospal SA/NV (Belgium); Gambro BCT-Europe SA (Belgium); Gambro do Brasil Lda (Brazil); Gambro BCT Ltd. (U.K.); Gambro S.A. (France); Scandinavian Incentive Holding B.V. (Netherlands); Gambro Dasco SpA (Italy); Gambro China Ltd.; Gambro Medical Products Co. Ltd. (China); Gambro Medical Sales (Shanghai) Co. Ltd. (China); Gambro Korea Ltd. (South Korea); Gambro Poland Spzoo; Gambro Healthcare Poland Spzoo; Gambro Investimentos SGPS Lda (Portugal); Gambro Lda (Portugal); Sopamed AG (Switzerland); Gambro Taiwan, Ltd.; Gambro GmbH (Germany); Gambro Kft (Hungary); Gambro Inc. (U.S.A.); Gambro Reinsurance SA (Luxembourg).

Principal Divisions

Gambro Healthcare; Gambro Renal Products; Gambro BCT.

Principal Competitors

Aksys, Ltd.; American Healthways, Inc.; Baxter International Inc.; DaVita Inc.; Dialysis Corporation of America; Fresenius Medical Care Aktiengesellschaft; Haemonetics Corporation; Minntech Corporation; Renal Care Group, Inc.; Rockwell Medical Technologies, Inc.; Terumo Corporation.

Further Reading

"Fresenius Denies Plans for Gambro Merger," *Reuters,* June 7, 2000.
"Gambro Buys 21 Clinics in the United States," *Reuters,* April 3, 2001.
"Gambro Makes Major Expansion in Dialyzer Production," *Biotech Equipment Update,* March 1, 2000.
Heller, Richard, "Gambro Up for Grabs?," *Forbes,* July 24, 2000.

—M. L. Cohen

its larger German rival, to merge the two companies' operations. Both sides, however, denied the rumors. Similar rumors followed the launch of a joint venture with another rival, Baxter International, for the development of dialysis equipment and products. Yet as Gambro's stock once again began to grow, the company's continued independence seemed more certain.

Gardner Denver, Inc.

1800 Gardner Expy.
Quincy, Illinois 62301
U.S.A.
Telephone: (217) 222-5400
Fax: (217) 228-8247
Web site: http://www.gardnerdenver.com

Public Company
Incorporated: 1993
Employees: 2,000
Sales: $419.82 million (2001)
Stock Exchanges: New York
Ticker Symbol: GDI
NAIC: 333912 Air and Gas Compressor Manufacturing;
333412 Industrial and Commercial Fan and Blower
Manufacturing; 333911 Pump and Pumping
Equipment Manufacturing

Gardner Denver, Inc. is a manufacturer of stationary air compressors, blowers, and pumps. Roughly three-quarters of the company's sales are derived from the sale of stationary air compressors. Stationary air compressors are used in a variety of industrial applications, including manufacturing, materials handling, and as a source of power for air tools and equipment. Gardner Denver's blowers are used in engineered vacuum systems, wastewater aeration, and in pneumatic conveying. The company's pumps are used in the oil and gas industry and in water jetting systems.

19th-Century Origins

Gardner Denver's lengthy involvement in the industrial equipment industry began in 1859, when the company's founder, Robert W. Gardner, started Gardner Company. The company's first product was derived from Gardner's efforts to redesign an existing product, the "fly-ball" governor, which provided speed control for steam engines. Gardner's creation found a receptive audience among oil drillers, whose rigs and hoisting mechanisms relied on steam for power. Governors

provided the means for Gardner Company to establish itself as a financially viable enterprise, serving as the company's sole source of income for its first two decades of business. Equally as important, Gardner's revamped steam-engine governors introduced the company to the industry—oil and gas production—that would provide the bulk of its customers for more than the ensuing century-and-a-half.

Gardner Company began to take on its 20th-century characteristics through diversification. The company's first foray beyond steam-engine governors occurred when Gardner again re-engineered an existing product. Seeking to find additional sources of income from the oil and gas industry upon which he relied, Gardner began tinkering with steam pumps. Steam pumps were originally designed to provide water for pressurized boilers, but Gardner discovered the pumps could be easily converted to mud pumps, the type of pumps used in drilling for oil and natural gas. He began making mud pumps in 1890, which added a second product line that bolstered the company's recognition among the country's fortune-seeking explorers and drillers. The demand for Gardner Company's mud pumps increased exponentially roughly a decade later when a major oil strike at the Spindletop Oil Field in 1901 triggered a surge in business throughout Texas. Perhaps more important than the spike in sales realized in the months after the Spindletop discovery was Gardner Company's third attempt at diversification, also completed at this time. Concern regarding the anticipated decline in demand for steam power prompted Gardner to develop a product line that could sustain his company in a post-steam-power era. His solution was the manufacture of vertical, high-speed air compressors. A century later, the manufacture of compressors constituted a major business area of Gardner Denver.

1927 Merger

The adoption of the Gardner Denver name occurred nearly three decades after the company began manufacturing air compressors. By this point in the company's development, Gardner's son, J. Willis Gardner, was in charge of the firm. In 1927, J. Willis Gardner orchestrated the merger of his father's company with its largest customer, Denver Rock Drill Manufacturing Company, a manufacturer of equipment for oil wells, mining, and construction. The merger greatly broadened the scope of Gardner Company's business, creating Gardner-Denver Company. In its new guise, the company supplied equipment for oil wells, pipeline trenching, mining, dam and tunnel projects, and highway construction.

For the next half-century, Gardner-Denver developed its diversified business interests, recording steady growth as an independent company. The expertise and customer base developed by the company attracted the attention of a larger suitor, as celebrations marked the 120th anniversary of Robert Gardner's fly-ball governor. In 1979, Cooper Industries, Inc. acquired Gardner-Denver, ending the company's existence as an independent entity.

Founded in 1833, Cooper Industries began as a manufacturer of power and compression equipment for the natural gas industry. By the time its path crossed with Gardner-Denver, Cooper Industries was diversifying into a number of different business areas. Beginning in the 1960s, the company broadened its product lines to include automotive products, electrical power equipment, tools and hardware, and petroleum and industrial equipment. Gardner-Denver, along with other acquisitions, helped Cooper Industries establish a presence in petroleum and industrial equipment markets.

Once acquired by Cooper Industries, Gardner-Denver was split into ten unincorporated divisions, its identity subsumed by its new parent company. Of the ten divisions that previously composed Gardner-Denver, two remained pertinent to the future of the Gardner Denver name. The Gardner-Denver Air Compressor Division and the Petroleum Equipment Division, whose roots traced back to the beginning of the 20th century, formed the foundation of the new Gardner Denver that would emerge in the 1990s. In 1985, the two divisions were consolidated by Cooper Industries, forming the Gardner-Denver Industrial Machinery Division. During the next several years, the size of the division was expanded, its product lines increased by acquisitions completed by Cooper Industries. In 1987, Cooper Industries acquired the Sutorbilt and DuroFlow blower product lines, as well as a line of industrial compressors marketed under the name Joy. These assets were absorbed by the Gardner-Denver Industrial Machinery Division.

Independence in the 1990s

During the early 1990s, Cooper Industries' corporate strategy underwent significant change. Roughly 30 years of diversification had created a multibillion-dollar conglomerate with a

broad range of business interests, but, in the eyes of company executives, the economic climate of the 1990s dictated a change in philosophy. The company decided to focus on its two most profitable business segments, electrical products and tools and hardware, a decision that led to the divestiture of many of the companies Cooper Industries had acquired, the Gardner-Denver Industrial Machinery Division included. To rid itself of the division, Cooper Industries formed a wholly owned subsidiary named Gardner Denver, Inc., which absorbed the assets and liabilities of the Gardner-Denver Industrial Machinery Division, effective on the last day of 1993. Several months later, on April 15, 1994, Cooper Industries spun off Gardner Denver, Inc. as a separate, independent company.

Its ties to Cooper Industries severed, Gardner Denver began its second era of independence as a manufacturer of industrial air compressors, blowers, and pumps used in the petroleum industry. As the company moved forward as an independent entity, growth was achieved in large part through acquisitions, a strategy espoused by its leader, Ross J. Centanni. Centanni had joined Cooper Industries in 1980, as the director of its corporate planning and development group. In 1985, Centanni was named director of marketing for the Gardner Denver Industrial Machinery Division, before being appointed vice-president and general manager of the division in 1990. When the spinoff was completed Centanni was named president and chief executive officer, posts he would occupy for the remainder of the 1990s. Under his stewardship, Gardner Denver embarked on a vigorous acquisition campaign that extended the company's product lines, added new product technology, and increased its overseas business.

Gardner Denver's acquisition campaign began in 1996. The company acquired NORAMPTCO, Inc., which was renamed Gardner Denver Holdings Inc., and its primary operating subsidiary, Lamson Corporation. Lamson designed and manufactured centrifugal blowers and exhausters used in various industrial and wastewater applications. The acquisition enabled Gardner Denver to enter the market for centrifugal blowers, which operated at reduced noise levels mandated in select niche markets previously inaccessible to Gardner Denver. The second acquisition in 1996 was a Tulsa, Oklahoma-based oilfield pump manufacturer named TCM Investments, Inc. Aside from giving the company a physical presence in the oilfield market, the addition of TCM allowed Gardner Denver to become the sole supplier of repair parts and re-manufacturing services to some of its customers.

With acquisition targets on the horizon, Centanni reorganized Gardner Denver in 1997. He opted for a decentralized structure that, in his opinion, could better support the growth engendered by the company's ongoing acquisition campaign. In August, the company was separated into two divisions: the Gardner Denver Blower Division and the Gardner Denver Compressor and Pump Division. The latter business segment was enriched by the company's only acquisition of 1997, the purchase of Tampere, Finland-based Oy Tamrotor AB, a manufacturer of lubricated rotary screw compressor air ends. When Gardner Denver was spun off from Cooper Industries, international business accounted for only 15 percent of sales, derived almost entirely from the sale of pumps. Centanni wanted to increase the company's involvement in overseas markets, and the addition of Tamrotor represented a significant move in this direction, providing Gardner Denver with

Key Dates:

1859: Robert W. Gardner founds the company.
1890: Gardner Company begins manufacturing mud pumps.
1927: A merger with Denver Rock Drill Manufacturing Company creates Gardner-Denver Company.
1979: Cooper Industries acquires the company.
1985: Gardner-Denver Industrial Machinery Division is formed.
1994: Gardner Denver, Inc. is spun off by Cooper Industries.
1996: A domestic and international acquisition campaign begins.

a manufacturing base in Europe and access to European compressor markets. Although Tamrotor was liquidated in 1999, Gardner Denver continued to operate in Finland under the name Gardner Denver OY.

After completing only one acquisition in 1997, Gardner Denver displayed more aggressive acquisitive energy in 1998. In January, the company acquired two companies, Champion Pneumatic Machinery Company, Inc. and Geological Equipment Corporation. Princeton, Illinois-based Champion manufactured low horsepower reciprocating compressors, a new market for Gardner Denver. Geological Equipment, based in Fort Worth, Texas, manufactured and repaired pumps, providing Gardner Denver with entry into the water jetting market. The company also bolstered its presence in Europe in 1998, acquiring the Wittig Division controlled by Mannesmann Demag AG. Completed in March, the deal added to Gardner Denver's manufacturing presence in Europe and opened distribution channels for its blower products.

By the end of 1998, Gardner Denver had achieved its fourth consecutive year of double-digit sales growth, in large part derived from its acquisition campaign. Revenues reached $385 million, 30 percent more than the total recorded the previous year, and net income increased 33 percent from 1997's total, climbing to $36.8 million. Encouraged by these figures, Centanni, elected chairman of the board in 1998, pressed ahead with acquisitions in 1999, purchasing the $14-million-in-sales Allen-Stuart Equipment Company in April. A maker of custom packages for blower and compressor equipment, Allen-Stuart served customers in the petrochemical, power generation, oil and gas production, and refining industries. The company's entry into the water jet market was strengthened the same month Allen-Stuart joined the fold, when Butterworth Jetting Systems, Inc., a $12 million-in-sales company based in Houston, Texas, was acquired. In October, the company accelerated its penetration of the centrifugal compressor market by acquiring $11 million-in-sales, Kentucky-based Air Relief, Inc.

The acquisition spree continued in 2000, as Gardner Denver fleshed out its capabilities in centrifugal blowers and water jetting. The company acquired Invincible Airflow Systems in January, broadening its centrifugal blower product offerings. Later in the year, Gardner Denver added to its involvement in the water jetting market by acquiring two Houston, Texas-based companies, Jetting Systems and Accessories and CRS Power Flow, Inc., which supplied aftermarket parts and accessories.

In 2001, Gardner Denver expanded abroad and domestically. The company established a presence in England by acquiring the Hamworthy Belliss & Morcom compressor business controlled by Powell Duffryn Ltd. With nearly $60 million in annual revenue, the Gloucester-based compressor operation was expected to strengthen Gardner Denver's distribution and service networks in Europe, North America, and South America. At home, the company recorded another sizable increase to its revenue volume by acquiring $41 million-in-sales Hoffman Air and Filtration Systems. Based in Syracuse, New York, Hoffman supplied centrifugal blowers and vacuum systems for wastewater treatment and industrial applications.

By the end of 2001, a five-year acquisition campaign had delivered substantial increases to the scope and size of Gardner Denver's business, promising a continuation of the campaign in the future. The 14 acquisitions completed between 1996 and 2001 drove sales up to $420 million and shaped the company into a more internationally oriented enterprise. By the beginning of the 21st century, roughly 30 percent of the company's sales came from business abroad, double the percentage recorded when it was spun off from Cooper Industries. As Gardner Denver entered the new millennium, further acquisitions were anticipated.

Principal Subsidiaries

Air Relief, Inc.; Allen-Stuart Equipment Company; CRS Power Flow; Hamworthy Belliss & Morcom; Hoffman Air and Filtration Systems; Invincible Air Flow Systems; Jetting Systems & Accessories; Lamson Corporation; TCM Investments, Inc.; Wittig Division.

Principal Divisions

Compressor Division; Blower Division; Pump Division.

Principal Competitors

Atlas Copco AB; Ingersoll-Rand Company Limited; National-Oilwell, Inc.

Further Reading

"Gardner Denver Forms New Pump Division," *Modern Bulk Transporter,* October 1, 2001, p. 24.
"Gardner Denver, Inc.," *Industrial Distribution,* November 2001, p. 14.
"Invensys Has Sold Its Hoffman Business to Gardner Denver Inc. for $45m Cash," *Engineer,* September 7, 2001, p. 7.

—Jeffrey L. Covell

GEBERIT

Geberit AG

Schachenstrasse 77
CH-8645 Jona
Switzerland
Telephone: (+41) 55 221 6300
Fax: (+41) 55 221 6747
Web site: http://www.geberit.com

Public Company
Founded: 1874
Employees: 4,144
Sales: SFr 1.16 billion (2001)
Stock Exchanges: Swiss
NAIC: 327111 Vitreous China Plumbing Fixture and
China and Earthenware Fittings and Bathroom
Accessories Manufacturing; 332913 Plumbing Fixture
Fitting and Trim Manufacturing; 332998 Enameled
Iron and Metal Sanitary Ware Manufacturing

Geberit AG is Europe's leading manufacturer of sanitary technology. The Jona, Switzerland-based company covers every aspect of sanitation systems and components, with products covering the entire range of building sanitation needs, from water supply to wastewater drainage. The company's products are developed along eight primary groups, divided into two major sectors. Under Sanitary Systems, which accounts for nearly 62 percent of Geberit's sales, the company's products include: Installation Systems; Flushing Systems, including water-saving technologies such as dual-volume and flush/stop systems; Public products and systems for public restroom facilities; Waste Fittings and Traps, for restrooms, bathrooms, and kitchens; Sanitary Products, including the company's "shower toilets," outfitted with bidet-like spray systems. Installation Systems represents the largest single Sanitary Systems market, with more than 37 percent of the company's total sales. Under the Piping Systems category Geberit includes: Building Drainage Systems, with complete piping and fittings assemblies for new construction and building renovations, which represents 20 percent of total group sales; Water Supply Systems; and Underground Piping Systems, which include products and systems for

water and gas supply, sewage, drainage, and irrigation. Geberit operates in more than 70 countries worldwide, with eight manufacturing plants in Switzerland, Germany, the United States, Austria, Liechtenstein, Italy, Portugal, and China. Germany represents Geberit's single largest market, at 35.5 percent of sales in 2001. Italy, at 16.4 percent, and Switzerland, at 13 percent, are also major markets for the company, while the United Kingdom, Austria, the Benelux countries, and France account for nearly 24 percent of sales. Other markets, including North America, Asia, and the Middle East, added 11.5 percent to the company's sales of SFr 1.16 billion in 2001. In 2002, however, Geberit stepped up its presence in the United States, with the acquisition of The Chicago Faucet Company. Geberit's decentralized management structure typically places operational responsibility on the managers of its subsidiaries, which enables the company to remain reactive to local markets. Geberit also maintains a strong portfolio of brand names, including Hansgrohe, Balena, Geberit, Prosan, and others. Long a family-owned company, Geberit went public in 1999 on the Swiss Stock Exchange.

Sanitary Technology Pioneer at the Dawn of the 20th Century

Caspar Melchior Gebert started out as a plumber in Rapperswil, Switzerland, receiving a trade permit in 1874. Through the end of the century, Gebert built up his plumbing business. At the dawn of the 20th century, however, Gebert decided to enter manufacturing as well, and in 1905 began producing toilet tanks. Gebert's first tank, called the "Phoenix," was built of wood and lined with lead, and also featured a lead flush mechanism. The tank system represented somewhat of a breakthrough in the development of modern sanitary systems and the company was awarded a patent on the design in 1912. Gebert himself was not to live to see that event; upon his death in 1909, the company was taken over by his sons Albert and Leo.

By the end of that decade, Gebert had developed markets for the company's tanks across Switzerland, as well as throughout much of the region. Gebert set up a number of production workshops in order to supply these foreign markets. Production levels began to grow again as World War I drew to a close, prompting the company to build a new production plant in Rapperswil, in 1917. The new facility included the company's own foundry. The following year, the company added a new range of products, including u-bend pipes and taps and valves, which also were used by the chemicals industry.

In 1921, the company centralized all of its manufacturing activity into the single facility in Rapperswil. The company continued to develop its foreign markets, particularly in the German-speaking countries. By the end of the 1920s, however, the Gebert family extended the company's reach into France, with the opening of a sales office in Paris in 1929.

The company continued to develop its product lines and in the mid-1930s the company once again placed itself at the forefront of sanitary technology. The development of plastic was to take its place among the most significant events of the 20th century, transforming nearly every aspect of people's lives. In 1935, the Gebert family company became one of the first to begin adapting the new plastic material to its toilet tank and piping systems. The noncorroding nature of the new material made it ideally suited for use in producing certain components for toilet systems, particularly in the concealed systems being developed for public facilities.

World War II placed a halt on the company's growth. By the 1950s, however, with much of Europe undergoing a vast reconstruction and a corresponding economic boom, the company returned to its position as innovators in sanitary technology. In 1952, the company debuted its first all-plastic Geberit toilet tank. That product, produced with the newly developed polyethylene plastic, marked a new success for the company.

International Growth in the 1950s

The next generation of Geberts, brothers Heinrich and Klaus, took over management of the family-owned company in 1953. At that time, the company registered the Geberit trademark and adopted the slightly modified word as the new company name. Geberit then began to expand its European interests, creating a new international distribution subsidiary and opening new foreign offices offering sales and technical services.

Germany represented the market with the largest growth potential, particularly given the vast rebuilding effort needed in the postwar years. In order to position itself in the German market, Geberit created its first foreign subsidiary in 1955 in Pfullendorf, which constructed its own production plant and began developing a dedicated network of sales and technical service offices across Germany.

In addition to pursuing the foreign market, Geberit eyed an expansion of its product line. The flexibility of the new generation of plastics enabled the company to begin developing complementary product ranges, starting with Geberit's first drainage

systems products, including u-bends and odor traps and related components, in 1956.

Geberit launched a new foreign subsidiary in France in 1959, which was followed by the establishment of a subsidiary in Vienna, Austria, in 1965. By then the company had moved to a larger plant in Rapperswil-Jona, constructed in 1962 to meet the growing demand. In 1964, the company marked a new successful product launch when it introduced its first concealed tank system that year.

Geberit's growth was particularly strong in Germany, and in 1967 the company built a new manufacturing facility for its Pfullendorf subsidiary. The company expanded its Jona plant and, in particular, added blow-molding production technology, reducing the cost of its toilet tank production. In 1972 Geberit added a third production plant, in Potterbrunn outside of Vienna. In that year, Geberit moved into a new market with the addition of a subsidiary in Belgium. A subsidiary was formed in The Netherlands in 1973.

During the 1970s, Geberit continued to add new product categories, extending its product range to include full drainage systems, flush-mounted systems, and introducing new components for the hygiene sector. The company remained wholly focused on Europe until the mid-1970s. In 1976, however, Geberit made its first attempt to enter the U.S. market, launching a subsidiary and production plant in Michigan City, Indiana, in 1976. The United States was to remain a relatively minor market for Geberit, however.

Sanitary Technology Leader in the New Century

A more significant event for the company came with its move into the installation systems market in 1977. That product market became the company's single largest, accounting for more than one-third of its sales at the dawn of the 21st century. At the same time, Geberit began developing a range of other products, such as the so-called "shower toilet," which featured a bidet-like spray attachment for standard and custom-built toilets.

The 1980s saw continued growth for the company. Geberit expanded its Pfullendorf plant again in 1980, while opening a warehouse facility at its Rapperswil-Jona site that same year. In 1984, Geberit moved into the Scandinavian market with the opening of a subsidiary in Denmark. A major step forward in the company's growing installation systems business came with the acquisition of Sanbloc GmbH, a producer of components for installation systems based in Weilheim, Germany.

The company automated its production process in 1987. In 1989, Geberit moved into new product territories, specifically with an entry into the fresh water supply systems sector, a move accomplished in part by the acquisition of a shareholding in FAE Fluid Air Energy, which gave the company the exclusive license for marketing FAE's products.

The company built a new, larger factory in Potterbrunn, which opened in 1990. Another production plant, placed under the company's Pretec subsidiary, was added in Liechtenstein in 1994, in order to take advantage of the newly opening markets in the eastern region of the reunified Germany as well as other Eastern European markets. By then, the company had begun to

Key Dates:

1874: Caspar Gebert opens a plumbing shop in Rapperswil, Switzerland.

1905: Gebert develops a wooden toilet tank, the Phoenix, which is patented in 1912.

1935: Gebert begins developing components using plastics, one of the first in the market to adopt the new material.

1952: Company debuts the first all-plastic toilet tank.

1953: Company adopts the name and trademark of Geberit.

1955: Company launches its first foreign subsidiary and product facility in Pfullendorf, Germany.

1956: Company begins producing components for wastewater systems.

1959: Company establishes a subsidiary in France.

1964: Company launches the first concealed toilet tank.

1965: Company forms a subsidiary in Austria.

1972: Company starts up a subsidiary in Belgium.

1973: A subsidiary is formed in The Netherlands.

1977: Company enters the installation systems market.

1985: Company acquires Sanbloc GmbH, a manufacturer of components for installation systems based in Germany.

1991: The Gebert family retires from active management and the first nonfamily member, Gunter Kelms, is named CEO.

1997: Geberit is acquired by investment firm Doughty Hanson.

1999: Geberit goes public on the Swiss stock exchange; the company acquires Caradon Terrain in England and 70 percent of FAE Fluid Air Systems.

2002: The company acquires a controlling stake in Huter Vorfertigung GmbH, based in Austria; the company acquires The Chicago Faucet Company, based in the United States.

prepare its transition to a public company. In 1991, the company hired its first CEO from outside the Gebert family. Under Gunter F. Kelm, the company redeveloped its management structure, adopting a decentralized structure that gave its subsidiary greater operation control and responsibility. By 1992, the company's sales had topped SFr 785 million—a near-doubling of the company's revenues in just four years.

Geberit continued to invest heavily, at an average rate of some SFr 80 million per year. The company opened a new production plant in its Rapperswil-Jona headquarters, and then constructed a plant for its Mepla product range in Givisiez, Switzerland. At the same time, Geberit acquired additional production capacity in Italy and Portugal. In 1994, Geberit launched a new subsidiary, Balena, as the brand for its line of toilet-showers. The company successfully developed the brand and its product line, topping 100,000 customers by the end of the decade.

In the mid-1990s, Geberit began investigating its options for the future, and in 1995 the company announced that it was considering a public offering to enable the founding family to

cash out of the business. Instead, Geberit was sold to British investment house Doughty Handson, manager of the largest private equity investment fund in Europe, in 1995. Gunter Kelm and the rest of Geberit's management team remained in place, acquiring a minority share in the company, which projected a public offering for later in the decade.

With stronger financial backing, Geberit began a series of acquisitions, such as that of Italian PVC-pipe manufacturer Deriplast, acquired in 1995. The following year the company, through Deriplast, acquired another Italian company, Walking Pipe Italiana. In 1996, also, Geberit acquired Buchler Werkzeugbau AG, of Germany. Then, at the beginning of 1999, the company moved into the United Kingdom with the purchase of Caradon Terrain Ltd., a maker of drainage systems and other products under the Terrain brand name. Not all of the company's expansion moves came through acquisition, however; in 1998, the company prepared its drive into the Asian markets with the opening of a production plant in China.

By the end of 1998, with sales topping SFr 1 billion for the first time, Doughty Hanson announced its intention to launch Geberit—now named Geberit AG—as a public company in 1999. That listing was accomplished in June 1999.

The successful initial public offering gave Geberit the funds to pursue new acquisitions. In July 1999, the company acquired a further stake in FAE Fluid Air Energy, raising its shareholding position to 70 percent, with an agreement to take full control of FAE by 2001.

Geberit was hit hard by a slumping German building sector in 2001, which saw the company's sales drop slightly. Yet Geberit hit back the following year with two key acquisitions. The first, made on January 1, 2002, gave the company a controlling stake of Austria's Firma Huter Vorfertigung GmbH, a company established in the 1970s specializing in installation systems. Then, in July 2002, Geberit strengthened its position in the North American market with the acquisition of The Chicago Faucet Company. The purchase of that company extended Geberit's product range to include commercial faucets and fittings, as well as four new production plants in the United States. Long established as a European sanitary technologies leader, Geberit prepared to extend its leadership to a global level in the new century.

Principal Subsidiaries

Afluxo S.A.; Balena DoucheWC AG; Buechler Werkzeugbau AG; Deriplast S.p.a; FAE Fluid Air Energy SA; Geberit B.V.; Geberit Beteilgungs GmbH & Co. KG; Geberit Deutschland GmbH & Co.; Geberit Finance Ltd. (Channel Islands); Geberit Flushing Technology Co. Ltd.; Geberit GmbH & Co. KG; Geberit Holding AG; Geberit Holding B.V.; Geberit International AG; Geberit Ltd.; Geberit Management GmbH; Geberit Manufacturing Inc.; Geberit Marketing e Distribuzion SA; Geberit N.V.; Geberit Plumbing Technology Co. Ltd.; Geberit Produktions AG; Geberit Produktions GmbH; Geberit S.A.; Geberit S.a.r.l.; Geberit South East Asia Pte. Ltd.; Geberit Sp.z.o.o.; Geberit Technik, AG; Geberit UK Ltd.; Geberit Vertriebs AG; Geberit Verwaltungs AG; Geberit kft; Geberit spol s.r.o.; Geberit spol.s.r.o.; Gemax Gebaeudetechnik GmbH;

Gerberit A/S; Gerberit Vetriebs GmbH; Hansgrohe Geberit S.A.S.; Mutra Investments B.V.; Plastek S.r.l.; Pretec Sanitaertechnik Produktions GmbH; Prosan GmbH; Prosan d.o.o.; Sanbloc GmbH; Sanplas Handels GmbH.

Principal Competitors

Tostem Inax Holding Corp; TOTO Ltd.; Kohler Co.; Air Water Inc; Takara Standard Co Ltd.; Eagle Industries Inc.; Uralita SA; USI Plumbing Products; Villeroy und Boch AG; Cleanup Corp.; Sanitec Corp.; Compania Roca Radiadores SA; Keramik Holding AG; Elkay Manufacturing Co.; E I D Parry India Ltd.;

Coop Costruttori Scarl; Homeform Group Manchester; Ideal Standard SpA.

Further Reading

"Geberit Buys FAE Fluid Air Energy," *Reuters,* July 7, 1999.

Lenius, Pat, "Geberit Celebrates 25 Years in North America," *Supply House Times,* December 2001, p. 14.

"Swiss Company Nabs Pipe Extruder Terrain," *Plastics News,* March 15, 1999, p. 12.

Wicks, John, "Royal Flush: Geberit Makes the Water Flow," *Swiss Business,* January-February 1994, p. 9.

—M. L. Cohen

GFI Informatique SA

199 rue Championnet
75018 Paris
France
Telephone: (+33) 1 44-85-88-88
Fax: (+33) 1-44-85-88-89
Web site: http://www.gfi.fr

Public Company
Incorporated: 1970
Employees: 12,583
Sales: EUR 1.1 billion ($1.3 billion) (2001 pro forma)
Stock Exchanges: Euronext Paris
Ticker Symbol: GFI
NAIC: 541512 Computer Systems Design Services;
541511 Custom Computer Programming Services;
541330 Engineering Services

GFI Informatique SA is one of the fastest-rising information technology (IT) services companies in France, with its sights set on becoming one of the top companies in the European IT services market. GFI concentrates on the information systems sector and operates in four key areas—Consulting; IT Systems Engineering and Integration; Enterprise Software Development and Implementation; and Outsourcing, including operational services and maintenance—enabling it to bill itself as a total solutions partner. The company has long focused on such core IT areas as intranet, Internet, and the fast-developing telecommunications sector, particularly mobile communications networks. Systems integration, the company's historic core, remains its largest revenue source, at nearly 60 percent of revenues. The company has been making inroads in stepping up its Outsourcing operations, a growing market offering the added attraction of medium- and long-term contracts, and that division accounted for 18 percent of the company's 2001 sales of EUR 600 million. At the turn of the century, GFI has been transforming itself from a focus on the French market to a truly international company, with operations throughout western Europe, as well as bridgeheads in Africa and North America. France remains the company's single largest market, however, at 58 percent of sales; the rest of Europe

accounts for 41 percent of the company's sales. GFI has long grown through acquisitions, and in June 2002, the company made its most significant acquisition yet when it agreed to buy up the Thales IS information systems subsidiary of Thales. The newly merged company claimed the number four spot in the French IT market, and one of the top spots in all of Europe, with combined revenues of more than EUR 1 billion. GFI, led by Chairman and CEO Jacques Tordjman, expects to double and even triple its revenues by 2005.

French IT Pioneer in the 1970s

GFI Informatique's origins lay in the first wave of the information technology industry in the late 1960s. With the advent of relatively powerful, smaller, and more affordable computer systems, the implementation of information systems quickly became a corporate necessity. GFI Informatique was created in 1970 in order to meet the new demand for developing and maintaining computer systems. One of the earliest entrants in the French IT industry, GFI was bought by Scicon International, a rapidly expanding British software and information systems company, in 1985.

By then, GFI had hired industry veteran Jacques Tordjman to lead the company's engineering division. Tordjman had started out in the late 1960s as a computer engineer with Philips. In 1971, Tordjman left Philips for a management position at Honeywell-Bull. During the 1970s, Tordjman launched two businesses on his own, before taking on his new position at GFI in 1984. Tordjman brought GFI's focus to bear especially on the industrial, distribution, and services sectors. By 1985, Tordjman had been named president of GFI Techniques Bull, a division focused on the Bull computer system. That division quickly rose to the top of the market for Bull computer-based systems throughout Europe.

Tordjman's performance was recognized in 1990, when he was named CEO of the entire Groupe GFI Informatique. Tordjman quickly led GFI on a strong expansion program, making a series of acquisitions, including the information systems division of Carbonnages de France as well as CORI, Infosys, and Proget. By 1991, GFI had more than doubled its revenues.

In 1991, however, GFI's parent company, then named SD-Scicon, was bought up by the United States' EDS, at the time a subsidiary of General Motors and also the world's leading IT services company. EDS's French assets were combined with GFI's, creating a new subsidiary, EDS-GFI. Tordjman's role in GFI's success was recognized with his appointment as CEO of the newly enlarged company.

By the mid-1990s, EDS-GFI had risen to the number three spot in France's IT market. Yet EDS, which was regaining its independence from General Motors at the time, had begun to restructure its operations and was preparing to withdraw from the French market. This turn of events gave GFI, and Tordjman, an opportunity. In 1994, GFI formally acquired all of EDS's intellectual property in France. The following year, Tordjman led a management buyout of EDS-GFI. The company then relaunched itself as GFI Informatique.

Backed by his management team and by a strong portfolio of financial investors, Tordjman drafted the first of a number of three-year plans for GFI, adopting as its core strategy the strengthening of the company's domestic network to place GFI on a national scale. At the time of the management buyout, GFI had just 900 employees and revenues of FFr 400 million (approximately EUR 60 million) and the entirety of its business was focused on the French market. In its first years as a newly independent company, GFI now began to expand its core competencies into a wider variety of business sectors, boosting its position in the banking, finance, and insurance sectors, as well as the public sector, while adding capabilities for the transportation and logistics markets, and, especially, positioning itself in the soon-to-boom telecommunications sector.

Acquisitions made up a key element in GFI's strategy. Between 1995 and 1997, GFI picked up a string of companies. The addition of Medianet, Vigiscan, Magellan, Yole, Cotre, and others enabled GFI to boost its share of the enterprise software market. The company strengthened its position in the new technologies arena with the purchases of companies including Promind, Netstar, Antarès, and DE3I, an IT services joint venture between Dassault and IBM. In all, GFI made some 30 acquisitions during this period. Accompanying these acquisitions were GFI's first international growth moves, notably through the establishment of subsidiaries in Luxembourg and Switzerland, and the purchase of the Belgian operations of U.K.-based IT group Sema. International growth was especially important to help the company gain a stronger share of large-scale corporate companies.

International IT Player in the 21st Century

By the end of its first three-year plan, GFI had succeeded in tripling its revenues, nearing the equivalent of EUR 140 million in 1997 and well exceeding its initial target. In 1998, GFI launched a new three-year plan, aimed at boosting the company's revenues past FFr 2 billion (approximately EUR 300 million) by extending the company's international reach, while also solidifying its position in France. That position took on new scale in January 1998 when the company acquired AT&T Electronic Commerce and AT&T Istel, the French operations of the U.S. telecommunications giant. These acquisitions were bundled into a new subsidiary, GFI NT, and enabled GFI to gain a position among the top five of France's nascent e-business market.

GFI went public in May 1998, floating 11 percent of its shares on the Paris Bourse's secondary market. The company's stock was quickly added to a number of the Paris exchange's main indices, and the company won added recognition by being named France's top IT services company for the year. The stock listing enabled GFI to continue its expansion, backed by a war chest of more than FFr 500 million. The company now targeted southern Europe, notably with an entry into Spain with the purchases of Arcissa, Arcitel, and Advanced Vision Technologies, as well as the acquisition of Atel, a specialist in IT systems and network administration. The company also strengthened its operations in Switzerland that year, with the purchase of IT services company Planet, based in Nyon. Meanwhile, the company gained entry into a new business area, that of consulting, bringing the company closer to its goal of becoming a total IT services solutions provider. The company's initial foray into the segment came through the acquisition of French company SME Conseil, which had built up expertise particularly in the banking and credit card sectors.

In 1999, GFI's acquisitions continued, including the purchases of Ceacti and Groupe Gallius, both in France, and the acquisition of a majority share of Atel Group, based in Milan, Italy, giving the company its first operations in that country. The company added to its southern European holdings with an entry into Portugal, while also establishing subsidiary operations in Morocco, from which it expected to base its expansion into the African continent.

In April 1999, the company expanded into the United Kingdom with the purchase of a 60 percent share of ECS Ltd., a company specializing in LAN/WAN systems integration and the leading independent company in the United Kingdom in that market sector. ECS, later renamed GFI Informatics, became the basis of GFI's expansion into the U.K. market. In France, meanwhile, the company purchased SINORG, which was focused on the public sector, particularly in the integration of systems for local communities.

These latest acquisitions enabled GFI to complete its second three-year plan some 14 months ahead of schedule—indeed, by the end of 1999, the company's revenues topped the equivalent of EUR 375 million. In order to finance these acquisitions and to continue its expansion, the company moved its listing to

Key Dates:

1970: GFI, one of the earliest French IT services companies, is founded in Paris.

1985: GFI is acquired by Scicon International, based in the United Kingdom.

1990: Jacques Tordjman is appointed CEO of GFI and leads the company on a series of acquisitions that double the company's sales.

1991: EDS acquires Scicon in a hostile takeover and combines GFI with its French operations to form EDS-GFI.

1995: Tordjman leads a management buyout of GFI, including all of EDS's intellectual property, and relaunches the company as GFI Informatique; GFI goes on an acquisition drive, acquiring 30 companies by 1997 and entering Belgium, Luxembourg, and Switzerland.

1998: GFI lists on the Paris stock exchange's secondary market; GFI enters the Spanish market through several acquisitions; GFI begins consulting services.

1999: GFI acquires SINORG, Ceacti, and Groupe Gallius in France; GFI enters Italy with the acquisition of Atel Group; GFI enters Africa with the purchase of two companies in Morocco; GFI acquires ECS in England.

2000: GFI acquires Olivetti Information Systems in Italy; GFI enters North America with the purchase of Proben, in Canada; GFI enters Germany with the acquisition of SPS; GFI acquires Multizoom in Switzerland and ASN in The Netherlands.

2001: GFI acquires SKR in Germany and IXI in France.

2002: GFI acquires Thales IS to become one of the top three IT services companies in France and one of the top ten IT services companies in Europe.

the Parisian main board, completing a successful secondary offering.

GFI now launched its third three-year plan. The company's new objectives called for it to take a place among the top European IT services companies with revenues of more than EUR 1 billion. To achieve this goal, the company, which had built up a solid position in southern Europe, turned its expansion interest to northern Europe. At the beginning of 2000, GFI made three significant acquisitions, entering Germany with the purchase of SPS, an e-business and intranet specialist; buying ASN in The Netherlands, a network engineering company; and reinforcing its position in Switzerland with Multizoom, which helped the company to become the leading IT services company in the French-speaking region of that country.

GFI also strengthened its holdings in Italy, with the acquisition of Olivetti Information Systems, in 2000. The company then turned its sights toward the North American market. In 2000, the company acquired Proben, based in Canada, as a bridgehead for its eventual expansion into that region, particularly into the important U.S. market.

Yet Europe remained the company's immediate focus. In 2001, the company reinforced its position in Germany with the acquisition of SKR GmbH, a company with offices in Bremen, Hamburg, and Hanover that focused on the supply chain management sector. The company also acquired IXI Group, based in France, boosting its consulting business. Meanwhile, the addition of Calléo, based in Zurich, gave the company e-business consulting operations in Switzerland, the United Kingdom, and Germany. These and other acquisitions helped the company's revenues top EUR 600 million by the end of the year.

In July 2002, GFI took a major step in achieving its goal of positioning itself among the top European IT services companies when it reached an agreement to acquire Thales IS, the IT services wing of Thales SA, eager to refocus itself on its core defense electronics business. For a purchase price of EUR 150 million, as well as the transfer of 25 percent of GFI's stock to Thales—in a deal worth a total of EUR 350 million—GFI's pro forma revenues now neared EUR 1.1 billion. The Thales IS addition strengthened GFI's European presence—giving it a ranking in the top ten, and the number three spot in France behind leaders Cap Gemini and Atos Origin. Through Thales, GFI also gained operations in Latin America and Asia.

With more than 40 percent of its sales now achieved outside of France, GFI had become a truly international IT services company. The company now began preparing the launch of its fourth three-year plan, to go into effect in 2003. Among the features of the new plan was a focus on developing the company's outsourcing operations, that is, the development of long-term and recurring services and maintenance contracts. Already in 2001, the company had succeeded in boosting the share of outsourcing operations in its overall revenues to 18 percent, enabling the company to gain greater mid- and long-term visibility over its business. The thrust into outsourcing, combined with the company's history of strategic operations, suggested that GFI was well placed to achieve its newest growth goals, that of doubling, and perhaps tripling, its revenues by 2005.

Principal Subsidiaries

GFI Informatique; GFI ISS GFI NT; GFI New Business; Informatique et Services; Tekhne; SCI Gifimo; Financière Sinorg; GFI Progiciels; GIE Anis; SME Conseil; Némausic; SCI Via Domitia; Acteam; Image & Promotion; Eccla; GFI Consulting; SCBF; CIPM; SNCI; IXI Group; GFI Benelux (Belgium); GFI NB Belgium; GFI Luxembourg; ASN (Netherlands); ASN West (Netherlands); GFI International (Switzerland); Groupe Calleo (Switzerland; 52%); Grupo Corporativo GFI Informatica (Spain); Arcisa Levante (Spain); Arcitel (Spain); GFI Web Espagne (Spain); Docutex (Spain); Euskalsoft (Spain); Gastinfo (Spain); 3B Norte (Spain); GFI IT (U.K.); GFI Informatics (U.K.); GFI Informatica (Italy); GFI Technology (Italy); GFI Consulting Italy; Integra (Italy); Datability (Italy); GFI Consulting 2000 (Italy); GFI OIS (Italy); Engisanità (Italy; 50%); Soluzioni (Italy; 60%); Compuquali (Portugal); GFI Holding GmbH (Germany); GFI SPS AG (Germany); SPS UB Kom (Germany); SPS PB GmbH (Germany); UBS (Germany); IT Media (Germany); SKR System (Germany); SKR & Co (Germany); Professional System (Morocco); Archos (Morocco); GFI Africa (Ivory Coast); GFI Canada Inc.; La Gestion Proben (Canada).

Principal Competitors

Cap Gemini Ernst & Young; Atos Origin PF; Getronics NV; Logica plc; CMG; WIM Data; Tieto Enator; Steria SA; Unilog SA; Sopra SA; Transiciel SA; Sylis SA.

Further Reading

"Acquisition Fever in French IT Services," *Computergram International,* February 19, 1999.

Dalongeville, Fabrice, "GFI Informatique prépare sereinement 2002," *Distributique,* May 2001.

Moreh, Michael, " 'Une fusion d'envergure courant 2002,' Jacques Tordjman, président-directeur général de GFI Informatique," *Newsbourse,* January 13, 2002.

Morel, François, "INTERVIEW: Jacques Tordjman PDG GFI Informatique," *Journal du Net,* February 9, 2000.

Ruello, Alain, "Jacques Tordjman, PDG de GFI Informatique: 'Il n'y aura pas de restructuration,' " *Les Echos,* June 19, 2002, p. 16.

Tillier, Alan, and Renee Cordes, "GFI Wins Thales Bidding," *Daily Deal,* June 19, 2002.

—M. L. Cohen

GfK Aktiengesellschaft

Nordwestring 101
90319 Nuremberg
Germany
Telephone: (+49) 911-395-2685
Fax: (+49) 911-395-4041
Web site: http://www.gfk.com

Public Company
Incorporated: 1935 as Gesellschaft für Konsum-, Markt-
   und Absatzforschung
Employees: 4,750
Sales: EUR 531.67 million ($520 million) (2001)
Stock Exchanges: Frankfurt
Ticker Symbol: BBFGFK
NAIC: 541910 Marketing Research and Public Opinion
   Polling

Nuremberg-based GfK Aktiengesellschaft is one of the leading European market research companies with a growing worldwide presence. The company ranks number one in Germany and has claimed the number seven spot worldwide. GfK, which originally stood for "Gesellschaft für Konsum-, Markt- und Absatzforschung" (Consumer Market and Distribution Research Company), has since adopted the more modern motto of "Growth from Knowledge." The company is organized into four primary business divisions: Consumer Tracking, which accounts for more than 16 percent of sales, and operates in 24 European countries; Non-Food Tracking, through continuous retail sales surveys in 44 countries, which generates 23.6 percent of sales; Media, which includes media usage measurements for television and radio audiences, as well as online usage and other non-traditional media forms, adding slightly more than 12 percent; and the company's largest division, Ad-hoc Research, which provides various information services for developing strategic, operational, and marketing policies. With operations, including partnerships, in nearly 90 countries, GfK's Ad-hoc Research activities are the company's largest, generating 41.5 percent of shares. GfK's geographic breakdown remains largely focused on Europe. Germany alone accounts for nearly 40 per-

cent of sales, while the rest of Western Europe adds more than 45 percent to the company's revenues. Asia and America play a more minor role for the company, at 5.5 and 6.5 percent of sales, respectively. GfK has been growing rapidly since the late 1990s, more than doubling its sales in just five years to reach EUR 531 million in 2001. Much of this growth has come through acquisition, such as the purchase of majority control of the United Kingdom's Martin Hamblin Group in 2001, which gave the company a spot in the top ten of that country's market research sector—the second largest market research market in the world. The acquisition joins GfK's international network of more or less independently operating subsidiaries. In 2002, the company's network included more than 110 subsidiaries, offices, and equity "partnerships" in 51 countries. The company is forecasting sales growth to more than EUR 1 billion by 2005. GfK is listed on the Frankfurt stock exchange and is led by CEO Klaus Wübbenhorst.

Market Research Pioneer in the 1930s

Professor Wilhelm Vershofen was already considered the founder of German market research by the 1930s. Vershofen had published his first paper on the subject, entitled "Menschen im Markt" (Markets and People), in 1925. Putting theory into practice, Vershofen set up the "Instituts für Wirtschaftsbeobachtung der Deutschen Fertigware" (The German Branded Goods Market Observation Institute) that same year. Working under the auspices of the University of Nuremberg, the Institute launched one of the world's first market research fieldwork operations, generating the first available data tracking consumer purchasing and behavior patterns.

Vershofen's work inspired a number of others, including Ludwig Erhard, later the German Minister of Foreign Affairs who led the German "Wirtschaftwunder" of the 1950s and became known as the father of the deutschemark. In the 1920s Erhard joined Vershofen as an assistant, and became one of the founding members of GfK.

Another founding member of the GfK club was Erich Schäfer, who, as a professor at the University of Nuremberg, had developed his "Theorie der Absatzlehre und Marktorschung'' (The Theory of Retail and Distribution), before publishing the groundbreaking work ''Grundlagen der Marketforschung'' (Principles of Market Research) in 1928. Schäfer's emphasis on tracking not only consumer behavior but distribution patterns as well was to encourage GfK to include both areas in its own development.

By 1934 Vershofen's work on market research, and particularly on developing the basic principles of conducting consumer research through field interviews, resulted in the drafting of an important monograph, ''Konsumentenbefragung auf breiter Basis'' (Broadly Based Consumer Interviewing). Presented before an audience of German industrialists, including Wilhelm Mann of IG Farben, who had developed the famed Bayer ''Cross'' logo, Vershofen's ideas called for replacing the more or less haphazard market research initiatives of German businesses—which often relied on informal, and often biased reports from salesmen and others returning from travels around Germany. Instead, Vershofen proposed the creation of a dedicated network of correspondents, unaffiliated with any single industry or business, be trained to conduct consumer-based interviews. This network was to be put into service as part of a cooperative formed by various member companies, which could call on the cooperative's services.

Vershofen's paper was positively received, and in 1935 Vershofen, together with Erhard, Schäfer, and Dr. Georg Bergler, founded Gesellschaft für Konsum-, Markt- und Absatzforschung, or GfK, in Nuremberg. Wilhelm Mann, who had also been a student of Vershofen, became a company patron, one of the founding members of the cooperative, and ultimately its president. The backing of Mann helped win over other major manufacturers in the country.

GfK set about building its interviewer network, a process conducted in large part by Georg Bergler, who traveled throughout Germany locating and training ''correspondents.'' Bergler also sought a cross-section of German society in order to form a representative pool. By the end of 1935, GfK had gathered several hundred correspondents, and had developed a purchasing power ''map'' of Germany. The completion of this first correspondents network enabled the company to begin its first market research study in 1936, commissioned under the title ''Die Bekanntheit von Warenzeichen'' (The Awareness of Trademarks).

That study was followed by some 70 more in the years up to the end of World War II. The company treated a large variety of consumer issues, products, and categories, ranging from personal care products and soap use to bread consumption and automobile purchases to advertisement campaign effectiveness measurements. GfK's work attracted growing numbers of businesses into the cooperative—by the end of the war, the GfK cooperative included nearly 150 member companies. While a number of studies were commissioned by and for single clients, much of GfK's early work benefited multiple clients, forming a pool of market research and consumer behavior statistics.

After the German capitulation in 1945, Bergler took over leadership of GfK, which was required to apply for a business license from the Allied authorities. Because GfK was relatively untainted by any direct relationship with the Nazi party—it had never conducted research for the party, and indeed had established close ties with members of the German resistance—the license was duly granted and the cooperative resumed operations in 1945, now backed by 70 member companies. The devastation of Nuremberg had destroyed much of GfK's archives as well; nonetheless, the group was able to begin reconstructing its correspondents network.

The institution of the new deutschemark gave the group one of its first major government contracts, when, in 1950, it was awarded a contract for measuring the purchasing strength of the new currency. By 1955, GfK had released its first Purchasing Power Map of the Federal Republic. GfK was active in promoting the cause of market research in general, joining in the establishment of the Nuremberg Institute of Marketing Economics in 1950. In 1956, GfK and its partner founded a new journal, *Absatzwirtschaft* (Marketing Economics), that went on to become the country's leading marketing economics publication.

The strong German economy led to boom years for GfK, which branched out into other specialty market research, particularly advertisement effectiveness measurements and television and radio audience ratings. In the mid-1950s, the group began its longstanding relationship with consumer products group Henkel, developing a Household Panel for that company in 1956. GfK's foundation membership continued to grow, topping 600 member companies by the end of the 1950s. Meanwhile, the group began developing new, more sophisticated measurement tools. In 1957, GfK created its Household Panel, boasting more than 1,000 households. These were outfitted with the new GfK Household Calendar, a 53-page weekly diary tracking correspondent families' household purchases. Tracking was also extended across a larger range of consumer products.

Growing Through Innovation and Expansion: 1950s–90s

By the end of the 1950s, the influx of new data led GfK to begin automating its data processing. The group took another step toward modernizing its operations in 1967 when it took part in the founding of Europanel, an association of European market research companies, one of the earliest attempts to share consumer panel findings across European borders. By then, GfK had already begun its own international development, opening a subsidiary, GfK Austria, and developing a Household Panel for that country. GfK's German Household Panel continued to develop as well, topping 5,000 households in 1961.

Key Dates:

1935: Market research pioneer Wilhelm Vershofen and others found Gesellschaft für Konsum-, Markt- und Absatzforschung (GfK) in Nuremberg.

1936: First consumer tracking study, "Die Bekanntheit von Warenzeichen," is completed.

1945: Following World War II, GfK is granted a business license and begins rebuilding its operations.

1956: Company forms its first Household Panel featuring 1,000 member households.

1960: Company establishes GfK Austria.

1972: Company forms G&I Forschungsgemeinschaft für Marketing joint venture (fully acquired by GfK in 1983).

1978: GfK establishes subsidiary in the Netherlands.

1981: Company establishes subsidiary in France.

1982: GfK introduces company-operated panel stores, featuring EPOS cash register tracking system.

1984: Company establishes GfK Fernsehforschung in order to monitor television viewing patterns.

1990: GfK joins in formation of the European Market Measurement Database, a consortium capable of providing household panel data from nearly 60,000 households across Europe; establishes subsidiary in Russia.

1997: Company forms Romtec-GfK joint venture in United Kingdom, acquiring full control in 2001.

1999: GfK goes public with listing on the Frankfurt Stock Exchange.

2002: Company acquires Informark Pty (Australia) and 35 percent of M2A (France).

GfK also responded to the increasingly sophisticated and varied consumer market by setting up more targeted consumer research operations. Such was the case with the creation of a new 1,000-strong Individual Panel in 1963. In 1966, GfK launched a new subsidiary operation, GfK Store Tests, as part of an analysis of the German retail trade market. By the end of that decade, the company's Household Panel had topped 10,000 households, while its increasingly international operations enabled it to launch a new European Purchasing Power Map in 1968.

In 1970, GfK launched a new business unit, GfK Retail Research, dedicated to research on retail markets. As part of this operation, the company set up new panels, the Basic Panel and the Leader Panel, with data covering some 60 different retail product groups.

At the beginning of the 1970s, also, the group began instituting new panels dedicated to products in the non-food category, starting specifically with photographic products. By 1971, this panel had attracted ten major photography products manufacturers in Germany; that panel was later extended to measure not only the photographic market, but the electrical product and consumer electronics product markets as well. GfK's early diversification in this area enabled the company to become the world leader in this market research category. The company's willingness to innovate continued in the 1970s with the launch

of the GfK ERIM Panel, a project which consisted of outfitting consumers with personal identity numbers, which could then be entered by participating retailers, enabling a more detailed tracking of household purchases.

GfK expanded in other ways in the 1970s, beginning a series of joint ventures and equity partnerships with the founding of G&I Forschungsgemeinschaft für Marketing in conjunction with Munich-based Infratest. That partnership became 100 percent controlled by GfK in 1983. A similar joint venture, S&G France, was founded in partnership with French market researcher Secodip in 1979, while I&G Retail Research, formed in partnership with IHA, brought the group into Switzerland that same year.

GfK continued its international expansion, setting up GfK Niederlande in Amsterdam in 1978, and GfK Great Britain in 1980 to enter those foreign markets. The group also began a series of acquisitions, particularly in Germany, including the Institut für Markt und Preis, based in Mainz, in 1980. The group set up a dedicated subsidiary in France the following year, and made its first entry into the United States through a partnership with New York-based NGA. Meanwhile, GfK extended its retail panel research operations into Scandinavia, beginning with Sweden in 1981. The following year, in partnership with TRC in Japan, GfK began conducting its first Electrical Product Leader panel in that country.

The ERIM panel gave way to still more sophisticated retail measurement instruments in the 1980s, starting with the roll-out, in 1982, of a series of group-operated panel stores, which were equipped with EPOS cash registers to generate computer data on consumer shopping and spending habits. In 1984 the company stepped up its position in the television viewing monitoring sector with the establishment of subsidiary GfK Fernsehforschung. By the middle of the decade, GfK had become a market research leader in Germany, operating six subsidiaries in that country, with 11 other subsidiary operations, including joint ventures and partnerships, in 11 countries.

The 1990s marked an era of vast change for the market research community. With the increasing internationalization of the consumer market—as manufacturers began operating on a global scale and brand names became recognized by and marketed to a worldwide consumer audience—the need arose to generate cross-border market research data. Meanwhile, the need for market research itself had reached a new level of acceptance as manufacturers, leery of committing to a huge product development and marketing process, sought more accurate and targeted testing of consumer markets. Market researchers themselves began shifting more and more to an international scale, gaining size through a thorough industry consolidation. By the end of a decade-long shakeout, the market research pool had shrunk to just 11 truly major players—including GfK.

The relaxation of trade barriers across Europe in the early 1990s also led GfK to join with AGB, Secodip, and a number of other European market research companies to form the European Market Measurement Database, a consortium capable of providing household panel data from nearly 60,000 households across Europe. GfK continued to develop internationally on its own as well, setting up a joint venture with AGB in England in

1990, which was taken over by GfK entirely in 1992 and renamed GfK Marketing Services Ltd. in 1992. By then, GfK had established a subsidiary in Russia and opened a branch office in the Czech Republic as it began preparing to expand its operations into the new, liberated Eastern bloc countries, which it did in 1991 with the formation of a subsidiary in Slovakia.

By the mid-1990s, GfK's revenues had topped the equivalent of EUR 250 million as the company stepped up its international expansion. By 1998, the company's international operations accounted for more than half of its total revenues, although Germany remained its single largest market. Continued acquisitions were to enable GfK to double its sales by 2001, topping the EUR 500 million mark. Among the company's growth moves made during the period was the setting up of a joint venture with UK IT market specialist Romtec in 1997, and the purchase of a majority share in Switzerland's IHA Institut für Marktanalysen in 1998. That year, the company acquired the Netherlands' Intomart Benelux and France's ISL (Institute de Sondages Lavialle), further boosting its international media measurement operations.

Bright Future

Fueled by a public listing on the Frankfurt Stock Exchange in 1999, GfK's acquisition drive continued into the new century. By 2001, the company operations included more than 100 subsidiaries, branch offices, and joint venture and equity partnerships in more than 50 countries worldwide. Purchases included a 65 percent share of Orange Interactive Research in Sweden; 20 percent of software developer Caribou Lake in the United States; a 51 percent stake in Germany's Enigma; a 51 percent share of the Martin Hamblin Group, which boosted GfK's position to number seven in the U.K. market; and a 20 percent share of Indicator, of Brazil, giving GfK an entry into the South American market. Another important purchase that year was the acquisition of full control of Switzerland's Tele-control, a developer of television and radio measurement technologies and hardware.

GfK showed no signs of slowing down as the new century got underway. Indeed, the company began forecasting a new doubling of its revenues, to EUR 1 billion by 2005. Already in 2002, and despite the poor economic climate, GfK continued its

growth moves, acquiring Informark of Australia as well as a 35 percent stake in French veterinary medicine specialist M2A. One of the world's oldest market research companies, GfK had proven itself a shrewd competitor within its own market—claiming a solid position in the world's top ten market research companies.

Principal Subsidiaries

Contest-Census Gesellschaft für Markt- und Meinungsforschung; mit beschränkter Haftung; dm-plus Direktmarketing GmbH; ENCODEX International GmbH; ENIGMA Institut für Markt- und Sozialforschung Jürgen Ignaczak GmbH; Ernst und GfK Grundstücksgesellschaft; GfK CEE Finance GmbH; GfK Data Services GmbH; GfK Fernsehforschung GmbH; GfK Marketing Services GmbH & Co. KG; GfK PRISMA Institut für Handels-, Stadt- und Regionalforschung GmbH & Co. KG; Media Markt Analysen GmbH & Co. KG; Modata GmbH. GfK has international subsidiaries in The Netherlands, France, Belgium, Spain, Singapore, Austria, Sweden, Denmark, Hungary, United States, China, Australia, Japan, Korea, Hong Kong, Malaysia, United Kingdom, Croatia, Italy, Greece, Cyprus, Poland, Portugal, Brazil, Romania, Russia, Czech Republic, Slovakia, Ukraine, Switzerland, and Thailand.

Principal Divisions

Consumer Tracking; Non-Food Tracking; Media; Ad-hoc Research.

Principal Competitors

ACNielsen Corp.; IMS Health Inc.; The Kantar Group; Taylor Nelson Sofres; Information Resources; NFO Worldwide Inc.; Nielsen Media Research; United Information Group Ltd.; Ipsos Group SA.

Further Reading

"GfK Achieves Best Results Ever in the History of the Company," *Ad Hoc News*, February 28, 2001.
Reilly, Mark, "German Firm Purchases Caribou Lakes," *City Business*, January 26, 2001, p. 2.

—M. L. Cohen

Global Outdoors, Inc.

43445 Business Park Drive
Temecula, California 92590
U.S.A.
Telephone: (909) 699-4749
Fax: (909) 699-4062
Web site: http://www.globaloutdoors.com

Public Company
Incorporated: 1984 as Global Resources, Inc.
Employees: 70
Sales: $17.2 million (2001)
Stock Exchanges: NASDAQ OTC
Ticker Symbol: GLRS.OB
NAIC: 513210 Cable Networks; 561599 All Other Travel
    Arrangement and Reservation Services; 721211
    Recreational and Vacation Camps

Global Outdoors, Inc.—known as Global Resources, Inc. from 1984 to 1996—owns and operates The Outdoor Channel and related businesses that appeal to outdoor enthusiasts, especially to amateur gold prospectors. These related businesses include the Gold Prospectors' Association of America (GPAA) and LDMA-AU, Inc. (Lost Dutchman's Mining Association).

The Outdoor Channel (not to be confused with the more widely distributed Outdoor Life Network) was launched in 1993 and began full-time broadcasting in 1994. As of March 1, 2002, it was carried on some 3,800 cable systems representing a potential audience of 33 million households. Of those, The Outdoor Channel had approximately 11.7 million subscribers. It also was seen on various satellite systems.

Gold Prospectors' Association of America (GPAA) is the largest recreational gold prospecting club in the world with some 34,000 members. It sponsors an annual gold prospecting trip to Alaska, as well as other prospecting trips. It also sells products and services related to recreational gold prospecting and publishes the magazine *Gold Prospector*. The Lost Dutchman's Mining Association (LDMA) is a national gold prospecting campground club with about 6,000 members.

LDMA owns campground properties in California, Oregon, Nevada, Arizona, Colorado, Georgia, and North and South Carolina. The Trips Division of Global Outdoors sponsors annual recreational prospecting trips to the gold mining region of California and to the company's 2,300-acre gold mining camp located near Nome, Alaska.

Diverse Businesses Focusing on the Outdoors: 1984–96

Global Resources, Inc. was incorporated in Alaska on October 22, 1984. At the same time Gold Prospectors' Association of America (GPAA) was incorporated as an affiliated company of Global Resources, which began selling memberships in GPAA. Prior to that, from 1968 to 1984, memberships in GPAA were sold by a proprietorship operated by Global Resources' founders, including George Massie. Global Resources and GPAA were incorporated when Massie raised $500,000 in a blind-pool public offering to fund trips to Alaska for GPAA members.

In 1990 Global Resources began producing the *Gold Prospector Show,* a long-form infomercial designed to sell memberships in GPAA. In 1992 the show was broadcast on a wider range of broadcast and cable television channels, with Global Resources purchasing the air time. Wider airing of the *Gold Prospector Show* resulted in a boost in GPAA memberships.

GPAA launched The Outdoor Channel in 1993. Global Resources intended The Outdoor Channel to be a primary vehicle for promoting its products and services, including memberships in GPAA. The Outdoor Channel also would promote the Lost Dutchman's Mining Association (LDMA) and its Trips Division. A long-term contract between Global Resources and The Outdoor Channel gave Global Resources the rights to ten hours of programming time and 30 60-second advertising spots per week. In February 1995 Global Resources acquired 100 percent of GPAA's stock for 2.5 million shares of stock valued at $8.75 million.

From 1990 to 1995 Global Resources financed its activities with cash flows from operations. In January 1996 a private placement of common stock raised gross proceeds of more than $832,000, with net proceeds to the company of about $700,000. In August 1995 Global Resources officially changed its name to Global Outdoors, Inc. The name change became effective July 23, 1996.

In 1994 George Massie's sons, Perry T. Massie and Thomas H. Massie, took over their father's executive roles. Perry Massie, who was CEO of Global Resources since 1986, assumed the additional roles of president and chairman. His brother, Thomas Massie, became executive vice-president of Global Resources and president of GPAA.

As of 1995, the LDMA, a national recreational gold prospecting campground club, had more than 4,700 members. Exposure over The Outdoor Channel resulted in 3,500 new members joining the club between January 1993 and the end of 1995. As a result of a major marketing campaign, approximately 1,600 new members joined the LDMA in 1995. Membership in LDMA cost up to $4,500, with significant discounts available to those who purchased memberships at gold trade shows or outings sponsored by Global Outdoors. Members were entitled to use any of the 14 campgrounds owned by the company or by affiliated organizations. Members were allowed to keep all gold found while prospecting on any of the company's properties. By mid-1996 LDMA had more than 6,000 members, but membership leveled off at more than 5,000 for the latter part of the 1990s.

Global Resources' Trips Division sponsored unique recreational prospecting trips to Australia and to the company's 2,300-acre campground near Nome, Alaska. Its principal trip was the annual trip to Alaska. Participation in the Alaska trip grew from 100 people in 1982 to 369 in 1995; in some years more than 500 people participated in the Alaska trip. The Trips Division introduced a trip to Australia in 1995, which went to the Western Australia gold fields. For 1996 the Trips Division offered six two-week and six four-week excursions to Australia. Global Resources also owned a 51 percent interest in American Prospecting Equipment Co., which marketed products for the recreational prospector.

The Outdoor Channel: 1993–2002

The Outdoor Channel was the first national television network devoted primarily to traditional outdoor activities, including hunting, fishing, shooting sports, rodeo, and recreational gold prospecting. Launched in 1993 as a part-time network, it began broadcasting full-time in April 1994. Its owner was originally the GPAA, a separate company affiliated with Global Resources. Global Resources became the owner of The Outdoor Channel in February 1995, when it acquired 100 percent of GPAA's stock.

GPAA was headed by George Massie and his son Perry. GPAA began buying infomercial time on broadcast stations in

the mid-1980s for its gold prospecting show. The infomercials sold GPAA memberships. As the price of infomercial time increased, GPAA purchased an hour of cheaper satellite time. It began acquiring related outdoors programming on a barter basis and eventually filled a 24-hour channel. When GPAA purchased a transponder, The Outdoor Channel was born.

Before it obtained cable distribution, The Outdoor Channel was available to C-band satellite subscribers. The company focused its efforts on obtaining wider distribution primarily in areas where there was the greatest number of outdoor enthusiasts, which meant cable systems in rural areas. In 1995 The Outdoor Channel's signal became available via a satellite that was easier for multi-system operators (MSOs) to pick up. By the end of 1995 The Outdoor Channel had national carriage agreements in place with several MSOs, including TCA Cable, the 21st largest MSO in the United States with more than 600,000 subscribers; Fanch Communications (250,000 subscribers); Service Electric Cable (250,000 subscribers); Bresnan Communications (200,000 subscribers); and the National Cable Television Cooperative, whose unaffiliated members had more than 4.5 million subscribers. The Outdoor Channel also was broadcast via direct broadcast satellite (DBS). Its satellite signal was unscrambled, so viewers did not have to purchase subscriptions.

In 1995 The Outdoor Channel produced about 15 percent of its programming and acquired the rest from other sources. Its programming was aimed at the outdoor enthusiast and included shows devoted to hunting, fishing, recreational gold prospecting, rodeo, and scuba diving. Programming also included talk shows emphasizing issues related to the outdoors. The company's strategy was to produce and acquire higher quality programming over time, such as the Bass Champions Team Tournament Trail, which The Outdoor Channel began broadcasting in 1998.

In February 1996 Global Outdoors hired Christopher B. Forgy as president and CEO of The Outdoor Channel. Forgy was formerly senior vice-president of marketing, sales, and programming for Times Mirror Cable Television and was the immediate past chairman of the Cable Television Administration and Marketing Society. When Forgy was hired, The Outdoor Channel had only 400,000 cable subscribers out of the five million homes it was reaching. About 1.5 million homes were receiving The Outdoor Channel via syndicated distribution on low-power broadcast stations, and the rest came from backyard satellite dish owners.

When Forgy left The Outdoor Channel at the end of 1997, he was replaced by Andy Dale, formerly senior vice-president of operations, who became president and chief operating officer (COO). Chairman Perry Massie assumed the position of CEO until September 1998, when Dale was named CEO and co-president. The Outdoor Channel was in the process of trying to sell a minority stake in the network and raise up to $4 million. At the time the network was operating with a staff of 15 people. Since it was founded in 1993, The Outdoor Channel had lost about $5 million, a relatively small amount for a start-up cable network.

In 1999 The Outdoor Channel was launched as an a la carte or stand-alone channel on Dish Network for $1.99 per month. In

Key Dates:

1984: Global Resources, Inc. and Gold Prospectors' Association of America (GPAA) are incorporated as affiliated companies in Alaska.
1990: Global Resources begins producing the *Gold Prospector Show,* an infomercial designed to sell memberships in GPAA.
1993: GPAA launches The Outdoor Channel as a part-time network.
1995: Global Resources acquires 100 percent of GPAA's stock.
1996: Global Resources changes its name to Global Outdoors, Inc.
2001: The Outdoor Channel celebrates its ten millionth subscriber.

2000, it became part of Dish Network's Top 150 package. By March 2002, The Outdoor Channel had 2.4 million subscribers on Dish Network.

Toward the end of 1999 The Outdoor Channel launched a $3 million marketing campaign designed to increase consumer awareness and demand. The bulk of the campaign consisted of print ads in outdoor-sports-oriented magazines that ran during the first half of 2000. Radio and television ads were scheduled for the second half of the year. During 1999 The Outdoor Channel reported an increase in subscribers from 4.5 million to 6.2 million.

During 2000 The Outdoor Channel added several new series, including *ATV Television, Motorcycle Digest, Motorcycle Adventures,* and *Classic Car Garage.* The channel also added *Raceline,* a weekly show about NASCAR racing, and *Roadfaring,* a show designed for RV fans. The Outdoor Channel also was broadcasting more than 50 different weekly programs devoted to hunting and fishing, including 14 different programs focused on bowhunting. It tried to distinguish its programming from that of the Outdoor Life Network by not showing any programs about mountain biking, skiing, or rock climbing.

Toward the end of 2000 Global Outdoors, which owned 84 percent of The Outdoor Channel, announced that it was exploring alternatives, such as a strategic investment partner or equity financing. Chairman Perry Massie made it clear that The Outdoor Channel had a substantial cash reserve and no significant debt and was under no financial pressure to seek outside funding.

For 2000 Global Outdoors reported revenue of $13.98 million, nearly 55 percent more than 1999. Net income grew 9.1 percent to $2.1 million, up from $1.9 million in 1999. During the year The Outdoor Channel added 2.8 million cable and DBS subscribers and was broadcast in nearly 12 million homes, not all of which had to subscribe to the channel to receive it. In the first quarter of 2001 The Outdoor Channel celebrated its ten millionth subscriber.

In August 2001 Global Outdoors hired investment banker Bear Stearns & Co. to support the growth of The Outdoor Channel. At the time Global Outdoors noted that although it was cash-flow positive, the company felt the right partner could help increase The Outdoor Channel's market penetration. Analysts speculated that competition was heating up between The Outdoor Channel and Outdoor Life Network (OLN), after Comcast Corp. bought out the other owners of OLN in May 2001.

For 2001 revenue increased 24 percent to $17.2 million, but earnings declined to $810,888. Lower income for 2001 was attributed to the addition of employees during the year as well as to increased technical expenses and paring down some debt. The company also was stuck with more than $1 million in bad debt from a company that provided The Outdoor Channel with infomercial clients. As a result, The Outdoor Channel began handling its own infomercial bookings, a less costly arrangement.

In January 2002 The Outdoor Channel signed a national affiliation agreement with Comcast Corp., the third largest MSO with eight million subscribers. It also renewed its affiliation agreement with the National Cable Television Cooperative, an association of small and mid-sized cable operators representing 13 million households. As of March 1, 2002, The Outdoor Channel was carried on some 3,800 cable systems representing a potential audience of 33 million households. Of those, The Outdoor Channel had approximately 11.7 million subscribers.

Principal Subsidiaries

The Outdoor Channel, Inc.; Gold Prospectors' Association of America, Inc.; LDMA-AU, Inc.

Principal Competitors

ESPN2; The Outdoor Life Network; The National Network.

Further Reading

Brown, Rich, "NCTC Taps Four New Nets," *Broadcasting & Cable,* February 3, 1997, p. 70.

——, "Outdoor Signups," *Broadcasting & Cable,* November 27, 1995, p. 88.

"The Business Press, Ontario, Calif., Company Earnings Column," *Knight-Ridder/Tribune Business News,* April 9, 2001.

Gold Prospectors' Association of America, "What Is the GPAA?," June 26, 2002, http://www.goldprospectors.org.

"Hunting Seven Days a Week," *Bowhunting,* July 2000, p. 26.

Katz, Richard, "Battle of the Outdoor Channels," *Multichannel News,* April 29, 1996, p. 64.

——, "Times Mirror's Forgy Scales a New Mountain," *Multichannel News,* May 20, 1996, p. 3.

Moss, Linda, "Forgy Exits Outdoor Channel," *Multichannel News,* December 8, 1997, p. 150.

——, "Outdoor Channel Gets Comcast Deal," *Multichannel News,* January 28, 2002, p. 10.

"Must-See TV," *Sport Truck,* April 2000, p. 22.

"New Networks: Our List So Far," *Multichannel News,* November 28, 1994, p. 88.

"Outdoor Channel Breaks $3M Marketing Effort," *Multichannel News,* December 6, 1999, p. 112.

"Outdoor Channel Explores Options," *Multichannel News,* October 30, 2000, p. 2.

''Outdoor Channel Reports 24 Percent Jump in 2001 Revenues,'' *Knight-Ridder/Tribune Business News,* April 6, 2002.

''Outdoor Channel Weighs Options,'' *Multichannel News,* August 20, 2001, p. 6.

Pomerantz, Dorothy, ''Call of the Wild,'' *Forbes,* May 27, 2002, p. 152.

''Temecula, Calif.,'' *Multichannel News,* November 9, 1998, p. 44.

''Temecula, Calif.-Based Cable Channel's Subscriber List Tops 10 Million,'' *Knight-Ridder/Tribune Business News,* May 16, 2001.

''Temecula, Calif.-Based Outdoors Channel Hopes to Woo Media Partner,'' *Knight-Ridder/Tribune Business News,* August 24, 2001.

—David P. Bianco

Guangzhou Pearl River Piano Group Ltd.

<table>
<tr><td>

Yu Wei Xi Road
South Hua Di Da Dao
Fang Cun
Guangzhou
China
Telephone: +020 81503507
Fax: +020 81502649
Web site: http://www.pearlriverpiano.com

Pearl River Piano Group America Ltd.
1521 S. Carlos Avenue
Ontario, California 91761
U.S.A.
Telephone: (909) 673-9155
Toll Free: (800) 435-5086
Fax: (909) 673-9165

State-Owned Company
Incorporated: 1956 as Guangzhou Piano Factory
Employees: 4,500
Sales: $80 million (2001 est.)
NAIC: 339992 Musical Instrument Manufacturing

</td></tr>
</table>

Guangzhou Pearl River Piano Group Ltd. emerged in the 1990s as a leading manufacturer of upright and grand pianos under the Pearl River brand name. The state-owned company operates a massive 3.1 million-square-foot factory, the world's largest, that stretches along the banks of the Pearl River in the southern Chinese city of Guangzhou. In the center of the complex is a huge lumberyard and wood processing center; surrounding buildings contain the machinery necessary to fashion raw materials into soundboards, key actions, and cabinets. Although founded in 1956, Pearl River began to grow quickly only in the mid-1980s, after social and economic reforms in China created an environment more conducive to free enterprise. The company benefited from a surge in domestic piano purchases in the early 1990s, and began to focus heavily on Western markets by the end of the decade. Of the 85,000 pianos produced in Guangzhou in 2001, about 20 percent have been sold overseas. In addition to

pianos, the company owns factories that make guitars, violins, and traditional Chinese percussion instruments. Pearl River President Tong Zhi Cheng has been instrumental in implementing the changes that gained the company a reputation for well-made pianos. His openness to advice from outside experts and willingness to invest heavily in up-to-date machinery has won the respect of the music industry. The company's combination of value and quality make it a formidable competitor for more established Japanese and Korean manufacturers.

Economic Reform and the Beginning of Growth: 1956–92

When founded in 1956, the Guangzhou Piano Factory consisted of six shops and about 100 employees. The company was organized by a group of reed organ dealers who decided to try their hand at producing pianos. After many tests and trials, the group put together a model that was purchased by a customer in Hong Kong. About 13 more pianos carrying the Pearl River brand name were sold over the next year. The Pearl River group was breaking new ground in China with the manufacture of pianos. Aside from a Shanghai company that had been started decades earlier by an English businessman, the country had no experience with the instrument. Consequently, Pearl River's early products were fairly rough in design and quality. In its first ten years of business, the factory imported components such as plates, actions, keyboards, and hardware from overseas companies. Production stood at about four units a month. The Chinese Cultural Revolution, beginning in 1966, prevented any substantial development at Pearl River, and production remained at less than 1,000 units per year into the mid-1970s.

In 1978 China initiated a series of economic reforms that paved the way for rapid sales growth at the Guangzhou factory. Production grew to 800 units per month in 1985. Meanwhile, interest in pianos was growing among the populace. As a result of China's one-child policy, parents tended to invest considerable resources in their child's cultural and personal development. Piano lessons seemed to be a good way to raise a cultivated, well-behaved child, and as China's relaxed export policy generated more disposable income in some families, national sales of pianos grew from 20,000 a year in the early 1980s to 60,000 a year in 1992.

Company Perspectives:

Our mission is to pursue development at the highest quality in the industry. Our promise is to deliver to you, our customer, an heirloom quality instrument for you and for the generations to follow. You will find that our fine pianos, orchestra instruments, guitars and percussion instruments, from entry-level to professional, are of the best value for the dollar. If you wish to invest in a world class musical instrument, we sincerely hope you will consider a quality product from the Pearl River Piano Group!

Responding to growing demand, the Pearl River factory began to gear up for higher production levels. The construction of a new five-story, one million-square-foot factory in 1987 marked the beginning of a period of intensive capital investment. Tong Zhi Cheng, who took over as general manager in 1992, was a key figure in turning Pearl River from a mediocre domestic supplier to a respected manufacturer capable of winning customers in competitive Western markets. Tong had decades of experience with the company. He had joined Pearl River in 1959 on the recommendation of his father, who was one of the company's first employees. Now in the head management position, Tong made it clear that quality, up-to-date production would be Pearl River's number one goal. As he told *Music Trades* magazine in February 2001, "Fifteen years ago, dealers would come to the NAMM (National Association of Music Merchants) show, sit down and play our pianos, and then leave. Rather than continue in our ways, we took these criticisms to heart and set out to build a piano that could compete with other fine pianos of the world."

Pursuing Quality Production: 1992–98

A hallmark of Tong's approach was a willingness to learn from outside experts. He engaged Bud Corey, a onetime production manager for Wurlitzer piano, to evaluate Pearl River's production methods. Corey's suggestions prompted large investments in automated equipment and climate control systems. The entire department in charge of key and action production, for example, needed to be air conditioned in order to regulate humidity and eliminate the warping of keys. Numerically controlled machines were installed to cut keys, jacks, and hammers. Other foreign experts, brought in from Japan and Germany, evaluated Pearl River's cabinet finishing process. They recommended installing an Italian-built polyester finishing line, in which a computer-controlled machine applied the correct amount of polyester finish, which was then sanded and buffed by machine to a smooth glossy shine.

Such extensive investment in automated equipment was unusual for a company in China, where the price of labor was relatively low. Although Pearl River offered its workers such benefits as transportation to the factory, subsidized housing, free lunch, and medical and retirement payments, individual salaries were small, keeping the cost of labor much lower than in the United States or Japan. The company could have relied on more labor-intensive production methods, but Tong's goal was to implement the best production methods regardless of cost.

When a job was best done by a machine, the machine was bought; those jobs best done by hand were left to workers. The final finishing and sanding of the piano plate, for example, was still done by hand by a team of dozens of workers.

Pearl River's capital investment programs paid off in numbers of pianos produced. Production quintupled to 4,000 units a month between 1985 and 1995. In addition, a 1995 joint venture agreement with Yamaha Corporation of Japan bolstered Pearl River's status as one of the world's major piano manufacturers. Under the agreement, the two factories would build a 200,000-square-foot piano factory in Guangzhou. The factory would be, in large part, an assembly plant, using parts supplied by both Yamaha and Pearl River. Pearl River would get 40 percent of the plant's output, with the remainder going to Yamaha. The venture was an opportunity for Yamaha to gain a foothold in the Chinese market, while also helping it make more competitively priced pianos for export around the world. In addition, it allowed Pearl River to observe firsthand the management techniques of a more experienced competitor. By 2000, the factory employed 250 people and was making 9,000 upright pianos a year. Each unit was labeled as a product of Guangzhou Yamaha Pearl River Piano Inc.

An event of ceremonial significance for Pearl River was a celebration of Hong Kong's return to China on July 11, 1997. In an event organized jointly with the municipal Party Committee, 97 Pearl River grand pianos were played together, accompanied by a 1,997-person chorus. The ensemble performed national favorites and newly commissioned songs for live broadcast. The event won widespread recognition for Pearl River pianos. The company declared that the advancement of Chinese culture would remain one of its most important goals.

The Chinese government recognized Pearl River as a valuable part of the evolving national economy and urged that several smaller city-owned instrument manufacturers, which had been losing money in the mid-1990s, become part of the successful piano manufacturer. Later in 1997, a guitar factory, a percussion factory, and a violin factory fell under Pearl River management. The companies returned to profitability after improvements in organization and productivity.

Another milestone for international credibility was reached in 1998. That year Pearl River was granted International Standard Organization ISO 9001 certification for its complete line of upright and grand pianos. The certificate was awarded after an independent audit team examined and approved all aspects of production, assembly, and service at the company.

Winning Over Western Markets: 1999–2002

The ISO approval would be helpful in marketing pianos abroad. Although domestic consumption of pianos was up to about 100,000 units a year, total production in China was around 130,000 in 1997. Smaller enterprises were struggling in the oversupplied market, but Pearl River hoped to retain solid profits through exports. In October 1999 the company opened its first foreign subsidiary in Ontario, California, ending about ten years of selling abroad solely through independent distributors. The Ontario, California facility consisted of a showroom and a distribution center. Once again, Tong followed his policy

Key Dates:

1956: Guangzhou Piano Factory produces its first Pearl River piano.
1978: China implements economic reforms, and sales at Pearl River begin to grow.
1987: A new one million-square-foot factory is completed.
1992: Tong Zhi Cheng takes over as general manager.
1995: A joint venture agreement is formed to build a factory with Yamaha of Japan.
1999: Pearl River opens its first foreign subsidiary in Ontario, California.

of seeking outside expertise to conquer unfamiliar territory. He hired Al Rich, an American with long experience in the piano industry, to manage the U.S. subsidiary. After two years, Rich succeeded in getting Pearl River pianos into about one-third of specialized U.S. piano retail shops. Sales in the United States increased every month for the next two years, despite an overall downturn in the U.S. piano market.

Also in 1999, Pearl River bought the German brand name Ritmüller. Pearl River planned to use scale designs based on earlier Ritmüller models to produce the pianos in a special section of the Guangzhou factory. Tong pledged that his company would use only the finest materials to produce world-class pianos that would preserve the European heritage of the brand, which had been founded in Germany in 1795.

The demand for pianos in China remained strong despite the Asian economic crisis. Some dealers reported that they hardly had to advertise or train sales people, since passersby would come in and buy an instrument for their children. Pearl River set a record of 64,000 domestic shipments in 2001, representing about a 60 percent market share in China. Nevertheless, domestic competition confirmed the company in a longer-term orientation toward export sales. Pearl River's U.S. market share, at 5 percent in 2001, was small but growing. The company exported 13,000 pianos that year, amounting to about 20 percent of company sales.

The vast majority of the pianos sold at home and abroad were uprights, but Pearl River hoped to increase its sales of grand pianos with the completion of a 500,000-square-foot addition to the grand piano production area. The new facility was designed based on ambition estimates for future expansion. Only 2,000 grand pianos were produced in 2001, with double that amount planned for 2002. The new facility, however, was designed to accommodate the production of 30,000 grands per year.

An increased focus on research and development activities was expected to support expansion. The R&D team grew from a staff of three in 1999 to 25 in 2001, and worked on designing new pianos as well as ensuring quality procedures for existing models. In addition, David R. Campbell, an American with decades of experience in executive positions at U.S. piano manufacturers, came to Pearl River as Director of Technical Services in September 2001. His task was to improve quality standards and production methods, particularly with respect to the planned export of grand pianos to the United States. Campbell evaluated Pearl River's existing grand pianos and came up with 22 points for improvement, all of which were implemented in less than six months in an effort to bring the company's grands up to world-class standards.

U.S. Sales Manager Al Rich explained Pearl River's dual focus on quality and value to *Music Trades* in April 2002: "We are very cognizant that our pricing provides a strong incentive to buy. But $6,000 for a grand is still a lot of money, and when you ask someone to part with that kind of money, the quality has to be there. A good selling price isn't enough." President Tong Zhi Cheng continued to be extremely responsive to the demands of the market and the requirements of quality production. He oversaw expenditures of $6 million in 2001 for new polyester finishing equipment, an automated cutting machine for soundboard ribs, and other woodworking machinery. Tong foresaw a continuance of Pearl River's rapid growth. He set the goal of being the world's number one producer of acoustic pianos by 2005, with 100,000 vertical pianos and 20,000 grands to be made each year.

Principal Subsidiaries

Pearl River Piano Group America Ltd.; Guangzhou Yamaha Pearl River Piano Inc.

Principal Competitors

Yamaha Corporation; Young Chang; Samick Musical Instruments; Baldwin Piano & Organ Company.

Further Reading

Flannery, Russel, "Piano Man," *Forbes Global*, March 13, 2002.
Harding, James, "Tickling the Ivories Until They Come Up Shining with Quality," *Financial Times (London)*, October 23, 1998, p. 31.
"Inside Pearl River Piano," *Music Trades*, February 2001, p. 178.
"Pearl River Hires Veteran Campbell to Raise Quality Standards," *Music Trades*, September 2001, p. 98.
"Pearl River Launches Ritmüller Piano," *Music Trades*, January 2000, p. 50.
"Top Growth Stories of 2001: Pearl River Piano," *Music Trades*, April 2002.
"Yamaha Opens in China," *Music Trades*, April 1995, p. 33.

—Sarah Ruth Lorenz

GulfMark Offshore, Inc.

4400 Post Park Parkway, Suite 1170
Houston, Texas 77027
U.S.A.
Telephone: (713) (963-9522
Fax: (713) 963-9796
Web site: http://www.gulfmark.com

Public Company
Incorporated: 1997
Employees: 1,053
Sales: $114.1 million (2001)
Stock Exchanges: NASDAQ
Ticker Symbol: GMRK
NAIC: 333132 Oil and Gas Field Machinery and
   Equipment Manufacturing

GulfMark Offshore, Inc. is a Houston-based firm that has found a niche providing support vessels and related services to companies involved in offshore exploration and drilling of oil and natural gas. Although most of GulfMark's activity is conducted in the North Sea, some of its 53-vessel fleet also operates in southeast Asia, Brazil, and west Africa. The company uses six types of vessels to support its customers. Platform supply vessels are large-capacity cargo ships used to carry fuel, water, drilling equipment, and other supplies in support of offshore construction and maintenance work. Anchor handling, towing, and supply vessels are used primarily to set anchors for drilling rigs, but also serve to tow mobile drilling rigs and perform limited supply duty. Construction support vessels are designed for specific tasks, such as pipe carriers or pipe-laying barges. Standby rescue vessels are required for use in the harsh conditions of the North Sea and serve as a safety patrol for offshore facilities. They carry rescue personnel and specialized equipment and are capable of providing first aid as well as shelter. Finally, GulfMark operates crewboats, high-speed personnel and cargo transports.

GulfMark's Lineage Dating Back to 1953

GulfMark grew out of Gulf Interstate Co., which was organized in 1953 as a pipeline engineering firm. By 1959, when it

began operating as a public company, the firm had a net worth of less than $500,000. Gulf Interstate was involved in the construction of the $200 million Transwestern Pipeline, which extended from west Texas to California and was completed in 1960. The company continued to flourish in engineering, gaining a reputation as an innovator in this field. Gulf Interstate engineers designed and oversaw the construction of the world's first long-distance ammonia pipeline, the Gulf Central Pipeline, which was completed in 1970. Now a $7 million company, Gulf Interstate looked to diversify. Operating pipelines was a natural offshoot of its expertise, but as early as 1960 the company's management had begun investing in real estate, becoming especially interested in high-rise Houston office buildings. It owned the Americana Building, a ten-story building that also housed its headquarters, located in the heart of Houston's business center. Across the street was the Houston Natural Gas Building, a 28-story structure in which Gulf Interstate held a 40 percent interest. The company also owned the Gulf Credit Card Center, which it leased to the Gulf Oil Company for its credit card operations. Moreover, Gulf Interstate acquired a 10 percent stake in some 3,300 undeveloped acres near Houston International Airport, as well as some property in Buffalo, New York. Gulf Interstate became involved in the marine terminal business, operating a ''tank farm'' in South Shield, England. The facility included 26 tanks to store gas and oil, as well as docking facilities.

Entering the Support Vessels Business: 1970s

It was also in the early 1970s during Gulf Interstate's diversification efforts that it became involved in the support vessel business that would one day evolve into GulfMark. The company acquired a 49 percent interest in a Louisiana company called Gulf Overseas Marine Corporation. The remaining stock was owned by a single individual. Gulf Overseas provided utility boats that supplied the 100 drilling rigs that operated in the Gulf of Mexico. In addition it supplied crews for anchor handling duties. With each rig in the Gulf requiring at least two support boats, the company recognized a growing opportunity. Gulf Interstate also took a 50 percent ownership position in a subsidiary formed in 1973, Gulf Overseas Shipbuilding Corporation, to build two deep sea tug boats, with the possibility of additional future construction.

Gulf Overseas would be in need of these new vessels because in 1974 it accepted an attractive offer from a foreign company and sold its three-vessel fleet, generating an after-tax profit of nearly $1 million. Also in that year, Gulf Interstate sold the Americana Building and its Buffalo properties. Although still primarily an engineering company, it continued to cast about for business opportunities. Gulf Interstate bought a stake in Northwest Pipeline Corporation. It undertook oil and gas exploration in Texas and Oklahoma through a subsidiary, Gulf Interstate Exploration, Inc.

The promise of Gulf Overseas failed to materialize and in 1976 the business was forced to file for bankruptcy, resulting in Gulf Interstate reducing its ownership position. In the meantime, the company became involved in other fields almost by accident. In its efforts to protect underwater pipeline crossings, Gulf Interstate entered the erosion-control business through two subsidiaries: Hold That River and Ercon Corp. It soon emerged as a leader in the field, offering expertise in the building and maintenance of sea walls and other means to protect beachfront properties. Gulf Interstate's work on underground pipeline detection also led the company into the development of radar systems.

Management of Gulf Interstate anticipated that a severe downturn in the oil and gas industry was on the horizon and in the early 1980s took steps that would ensure the company's survival in an economic climate that proved to be the ruin of much larger firms. The company reduced staff and overhead expenses, as well as cut back on investments in research and development. Moreover, it ceased its involvement in drilling and seismic studies and raised cash by selling off assets not crucial to its core operations. In October 1983 the company changed its name to Gulf Applied Technologies, a year in which it generated revenues of $16.7 million and reported a net loss of $3.2 million. With a strong cash position the company was prepared to survive, but the prospects for its traditional pipeline business in the United States were ''practically nonexistent,'' according to its annual report. Although Gulf Applied lost another $9 million over the next two years, it was able to return to the black in 1986, posting a profit just short of the $1 million mark. The company focused its efforts on four operating segments: engineering, pipeline and terminals, radar systems, and erosion control. By the end of the decade, however, it would undergo a thorough restructuring.

In 1989 Shearson Lehman Hutton Group gained control of the company after acquiring a 30.5 percent stake in Gulf Applied. Much of Gulf Applied's operations were disposed of, with the exception of erosion control services. Moreover, new management decided to expand the offshore marine services business in which the company had become involved through Gulf Overseas Marine Corporation in the 1970s. A major step in making this transition occurred in October 1990 when the company pur-

chased the marine division of Offshore Logistics, Inc. for $17.8 million in cash. The assets acquired included 12 offshore support vessels, as well as support facilities, spare parts, and ongoing contracts. Three inactive crewboats were sold at book value, while five continued to operate in Southeast Asia, three in the North Sea, and one in the waters of Brazil. The new assets were folded into the Gulf Offshore Marine Division, which included a warehouse and servicing center in Louisiana held over from the company's earlier business in support vessels.

Early in 1991 Gulf Applied changed its name to GulfMark International, Inc. It now operated in two industry segments: offshore marine services and erosion control services through its Ercon subsidiary. Ercon also owned a 21 percent stake in Energy Ventures, Inc., which was involved in drilling and workover services, drill pipe and premium tubulars, and the manufacture of artificial lift systems. Over the next two years GulfMark was especially active in building up its marine service division, adding four support vessels, three of which were wholly owned and the other 55 percent owned by a subsidiary. The division added to its fleet over the next few years, contracting with Norwegian shipyards to build new ships for deployment in the North Sea. In addition it acquired assets from BP Shipping in July 1993, so that by 1994 Gulf Offshore had 20 support vessels at its disposal. As these ships entered service, revenues began to grow for the corporate parent at a pace that the erosion control division could not match. After posting total revenues of $7.5 million in 1990 and $17.2 million in 1991, GulfMark reached $27.9 million two years later. Of this amount, erosion control contributed $5.3 million. In 1994 corporate revenues totaled nearly $34.5 million, but Ercon's business increased to just $6.8 million. GulfMark's momentum stalled somewhat in 1995, due to poor results in Southeast Asia. Revenue improved only slightly to just more than $36 million, and the company posted a $1.9 million loss on the year. In 1996, with three more support vessels in operation, total sales improved to $41.7 million and GulfMark returned to black ink, generating an $8.4 million net profit. Revenues from Ercon, however, dipped by nearly 21 percent.

GulfMark Offshore a 1997 Spinoff

In December 1996, GulfMark announced that it would spin off its Gulf Offshore division to shareholders as a new publicly traded company. In April 1997 shareholders approved the transaction and the company's offshore marine services assets were transferred to a new wholly owned subsidiary called GulfMark Offshore, Inc. It was then spun off and shareholders of ''Old GulfMark'' received equal shares in ''New GulfMark.'' The remaining assets, Ercon and a stake in Energy Ventures Inc., were then acquired by Energy Ventures in a tax-free merger that distributed 2.2 million shares of Energy Ventures stock to GulfMark shareholders. For legal and tax reasons, the deal was structured as a spinoff but in practical terms New Gulfmark was the old company without the erosion control business. It retained the same board of directors, the same headquarters, and essentially the same management team. GulfMark was now more of a pure play offshore marine services company with no secondary line of business to distract investors. Later in 1997 the company made a public offering of stock, netting $33.4 million, which was earmarked for upgrading the fleet and building new vessels, as well as repaying debt.

Key Dates:

1953: Gulf Interstate Co. is formed as a pipeline engineering firm.
1959: Gulf Interstate goes public.
1983: The company changes its name to Gulf Applied Technologies.
1989: Shearson Lehman Hutton acquires a 30.5 percent stake.
1990: The marine division of Offshore Logistics is acquired.
1991: The company is renamed GulfMark International.
1997: The marine services division is spun off as GulfMark Offshore, Inc.

In November 1997 GulfMark announced that it would add six support vessels to its fleet, three of which were already under construction, and three others to be built. A few months later, in February 1998, the company expanded its fleet through acquisition, paying $73 million in cash and the assumption of debt to purchase Brovig Supply, a Norwegian ship-owning company. As a result GulfMark added five more support vessels to its North Sea area of operation, and by the end of 1998 the total number of vessels in the fleet grew to 42. These additional ships had a dramatic impact on the balance sheet. In 1997 GulfMark recorded modest improvements over the previous year, with revenues increasing to $46 million, while turning a $6.1 million net profit. In 1998, however, the company saw sales almost double, topping $86.1 million, and net income totaled $20.8 million, despite a downturn in the price of oil and gas. To fund further growth, GulfMark completed a private placement of $130 million in notes in June 1998.

Continued volatility in oil and gas prices hampered GulfMark's growth in 1999. The company expanded the fleet, with four new vessels entering service, three of which were owned and one chartered. Nevertheless, poor economic conditions led to revenues falling to $72.3 million and net income to $1.86 million. As the energy market recovered in 2000, GulfMark regained its momentum and initiated an aggressive new construction program to prepare for continued growth. It signed contracts worth approximately $148 million with Norwegian shipbuilder Aken Brattvaag for four new supply vessels

and three anchor handling tug supply vessels. All seven were scheduled to be completed in time to replace vessels under charter. Revenues for the year improved to $77.7 million and net income grew to $7.9 million.

An increase in day rates for its vessels as well as expansion of the fleet through acquisitions set the stage for record results in 2001. The most significant acquisition was the $61.8 million deal for Sea Truck Holding, a Norwegian support vessel company, adding five platform supply vessels to the GulfMark fleet, which would reach 50 in number by the end of the year. Revenues increased to more than $114 million and net income to nearly $38 million in 2001. Despite a downturn in the stockmarket, shares of GulfMark displayed strong growth, improving from $23 in early October to more than $41 in late April. The company had no difficulty in selling $1.5 million shares of common stock in a March 2002 secondary offering, netting $50.3 million, which management intended primarily to pay down debt. GulfMark stock was so strong that in May 2002 management announced a two-for-one split. Clearly, GulfMark was attracting the attention of Wall Street, and some analysts speculated that the company was still undervalued and might very well attract a large bidder.

Principal Subsidiaries

GulfMark North Sea Ltd.; GulfMark Norge AS; Sea Truck AS.

Principal Competitors

SEACOR SMIT; Tidewater Inc.; Trico Marine.

Further Reading

"Edward Guthrie—GulfMark Offshore Inc.," *Wall Street Transcript,* April 30, 2001.
"Gulf Applied Asserts It Won't Have Profit from Operations in '84," *Wall Street Journal,* May 7, 1984, p. 1.
Marcial, Gene G., "GulfMark Is a Gusher," *BusinessWeek,* May 6, 2002, p. 111.
Osler, David, "GulfMark Offshore Snaps Up Sea Truck Support Ship Firm," *Lloyd's List International,* May 31, 2001, p. 3.
Rublin, Lauren R., "How to Survive in the Oil Patch: Gulf Applied Technologies Does That and More," *Barron's National Business and Financial Weekly,* March 2, 1987, p. 15.

—Ed Dinger

Handspring Inc.

189 Bernardo Avenue
San Francisco, California 94043
U.S.A.
Telephone: (650) 230-5000
Toll Free: (888) 565-9393
Fax: (650) 230-2100
Web site: http://www.handspring.com

Public Company
Incorporated: 1998
Employees: 425
Sales: $370.9 million (2001)
Stock Exchanges: NASDAQ
Ticker Symbol: HAND
NAIC: 334111 Electronic Computer Manufacturing

Handspring Inc. is a leading innovator in the handheld computing industry. The company develops, manufactures, and markets a family of expandable handheld computers for a broad range of markets and customers. Handspring's flagship technology is the Springboard platform, which provides a simple and easy method for hardware and software expansion. Handspring sells its Visor line of handheld computers, along with a line of Springboard expansion modules and accessories, via its web site and through select Internet and retail partners in Asia, Canada, Europe, Japan, and the United States.

Computers and the Human Brain: 1979–92

In 1979, Jeff Hawkins graduated from Cornell University with an undergraduate degree in electrical engineering. He then went to work at Intel in Oregon, and then in Boston. Hawkins worked for Intel for three years before moving on to GRiD Computer Systems Corp., a small Silicon Valley-based company, in 1982.

GRiD was founded in 1979 in Mountain View, California, by Glenn T. Edens and others. The company was exploring the possibilities of mobile computing, in part to fulfill a growing need within the U.S. and NATO military forces for a rugged portable

computer system. The year Hawkins joined the small company, they released the GRiD 1100 Compass, a revolutionary Clamshell-style laptop computer. This innovation was followed by the GRiDCASE 12xx series, the world's first Intel 8088-based MS-DOS IBM PC-compatible portable personal computer in 1984. A 286-XT version, called the GRiDCASE 1520, came out in 1986, followed by the 1530, a 386DX version, in 1988.

But Jeff Hawkins was interested in more than just creating a mobile computer. He wanted a machine that would respond to the true needs of its users. By day, he worked at GRiD; by night, he studied the human brain. "My ultimate goal is to build a new industry around silicon-based, temporal, auto-associative memories. Products that incorporate these memories will understand the world much as you and I do," he said in a 1988 interview in *Fast Company.* In 1986, Hawkins's wife suggested he go to school to learn more about the brain. Consequently, he enrolled in the Ph.D. program in Biophysics at the University of California at Berkeley, where he studied information processing in biological systems, also known as "computational neuroscience."

Frustrated with the environment, Hawkins left academia in 1988 with no degree, but with a lot of information on neural networks and pattern recognition. About this time, Hawkins created an algorithm for handwriting recognition, which he called PalmPrint. Hawkins licensed PalmPrint to GRiD, his former employer, and became their vice-president of research. His goal was to develop pen-based hardware and software. The following year, in 1989, Hawkins was successful in his goal, as the company released the GRiDPad 1900, the world's first Pen-and-Display IBM PC-compatible PC Tablet. Also that year, Fort Worth, Texas-based Tandy Corporation bought GRiD Computer Systems Corp. GRiD was subsequently sold to AST Research Inc. in 1993. That company survived as late as 2002 as London-based GRiD Defence Systems Ltd., which bought out GRiD Computer Systems UK Ltd., and as GSCS Inc. (formerly GRiD Government Systems).

Hands-Down Leader: Palm Computing Inc., 1992–98

Wanting to change the world, Hawkins set off from GRiD/Tandy on his own in January 1992. With funding from Tandy,

Company Perspectives:

The Big Idea: To fundamentally change the way people organize, manage and communicate. The Grand Plan: To be the leading provider of handheld computing products. And just how do we plan on doing that? By inventing solutions that enable truly simple organization and that provide easy access to the Web so people can really communicate with each other—from shirt pockets rather than their desktops. To that end we will: 1). Build a world-class team. It's a given, but you can't succeed without one. 2). Battle complexity. Simplicity is what it's all about. Because if it's not simple no one will use it. 3). Think about the future. Build a platform that provides for unique functionality, expands possibilities, offers flexibility and personalization for consumers and developers alike. 4). Never rest on our laurels. Innovate, innovate, innovate. The Daily Mantra: Keep it small, simple, affordable and connected. Those are the principles that inspired the creation of the Visor, and they will continue to drive every future Handspring product innovation.

Merrill Pickard Anderson & Eyre (MPAE), and Sutter Hill Ventures, combined with partnerships involving Geoworks, Tandy, and Casio, Hawkins founded Palm Computing Inc. to create a new type of handheld computing product. He immediately hired Donna Dubinsky to run the company. Dubinsky had previously risen through the ranks at Apple Computer, and then went on to become vice-president of international sales at Claris, before joining Palm. In June 1993, the company hired Ed Colligan, previously vice-president of strategic and product marketing at Radius Corporation, as its marketing manager, and the company's executive team had formed the triumvirate that would go on to lead both Palm and Handspring to resounding success. Bruce Dunlevie, a venture capitalist at MPAE and a member of the board of directors at Geoworks, also would play a prominent role in Palm and Handspring.

Meanwhile, Hawkins improved on his earlier creation, PalmPrint, when he invented the Graffiti text entry method in 1994. This was a neural network-based handwriting recognition system, which solved the handwriting recognition problem (where such products as the Apple Newton had failed) by asking users to learn a simple method for making letters recognizable by software. That same year, Hawkins defined a short list of design goals for what would become the first PalmPilot, then called "Touchdown." In addition to incorporating Graffiti, the new device should, according to Hawkins, fit in a shirt pocket, be designed for desktop synchronization, deliver instant performance, and be easily affordable.

By late 1994, Palm Computing was in search of financing to bring the Touchdown vision to fruition. But with the handheld computing industry awash in failed attempts, few investors were eager to jump in. In September 1995, Dubinsky contacted U.S. Robotics to see about investing the $5 million they needed. Recognizing the device's potential, U.S. Robotics purchased Palm Computing instead, for $44 million in stock, and the name "Pilot" was born.

The race to handheld computing was now finally engaged in earnest. Of course the journey really had its start in the mid-1980s, when a host of companies began investigating the idea of a truly mobile computer that could offer real functionality yet be carried around in a jacket pocket. Over the next decade, both large companies and start-ups had attempted and repeatedly failed to create successful handheld computing devices.

Atari was first, in 1989, with the Portfolio handheld computer, followed by a Hewlett-Packard (HP) calculator with some agenda functions, then the Casio BOSS and the Sharp Wizard series. In 1991, HP introduced the HP 95 LX, a small microcomputer operating on MS-DOS, with a full version of Lotus 1-2-3 embedded in the architecture. Psion, a British company, introduced the Psion 3, which was almost a sub-notebook computer. In January 1992, Apple CEO John Sculley coined the term "personal digital assistant" (PDA), launching a whole new frenzy for handheld computers.

The second wave of handhelds began in 1993. That June, Palm Computing announced that it would be releasing the Zoomer later that year. Apple beat the tiny company to the punch, releasing the Newton that August. The Newton featured handwriting recognition. The use of a touchscreen that allowed a user to scribble on its surface with a pen or stylus changed the paradigm of computing from traditional desktop or laptop computing to "notebook" computing. Zoomer came out in October and was followed by a wave of less-than-inspired offerings from other companies, including AT&T's EO, IBM's Simon, Motorola's Marco, and the Psion 3a, among others. Sharp continued developing its Wizard series while, at the same time, teaming with Apple on the Newton. Casio continued development on its BOSS series, and worked with Tandy and Palm on the Zoomer.

By 1995, approximately $1 billion had been spent and lost in this pursuit, including $75 million by Kleiner Perkins Caufield & Byers at GO Corporation and $500 million by Apple. Companies struggled along with tiny improvements and tweaks here and there and no clear industry segment leader emerged. The next developments would not come until 1996, but some of the pioneers would not be around to see them. GO Computing went under in 1994; Apple's Newton hung on until 1997.

Palm led the pack of new innovations. The first Pilots were shipped in April 1996, about the same time Microsoft announced Windows CE, a "compact edition" of its popular operating system designed for laptops and handhelds. Due to the failure of earlier handheld computers, sales for the Palm Pilot were slow at the start. But sales took off over the 1996 holiday season, and the company grew at an extraordinary rate. Had Palm Computing been an independent company, it would have been one of the fastest-growing companies in history. The PalmPilot itself became the most rapidly adopted new computing product ever introduced, with more than 12 million units sold by mid-2001. The company also spawned its own software and accessories industry, including the Palm Operating System (PalmOS), which has become the standard for palm-based computers.

In June 1997, 3Com Corporation acquired U.S. Robotics, and with it, Palm Computing. U.S. Robotics had let Palm operate independently; 3Com began incorporating the acquisi-

Key Dates:

1992: Jeff Hawkins founds Palm Computing Inc.
1995: U.S. Robotics purchases Palm for $44 million in stock.
1998: Jeff Hawkins and Donna Dubinsky found Handspring Inc.
1999: Company ships Visor and the first Springboard modules.
2000: Company establishes European and Japanese headquarters; the company launches its successful IPO on NASDAQ; the one millionth Visor and the first VisorPhone are shipped; Bluelark Systems Inc. is acquired.
2001: First third-generation Visor is shipped.
2002: Company ships the first Treo, a combination mobile phone, personal digital assistant, and wireless data transmitter.

tion into its corporate structure, and the autonomy was over. In July 1998, the core team that created the original PalmPilot left 3Com Corporation. Ironically, 3Com spun Palm out again as an independent, publicly traded subsidiary on March 2, 2000.

Springing Forth in New Directions: Handspring Inc., 1998

When Jeff Hawkins, Donna Dubinsky, and Ed Colligan, the core team that developed and marketed the PalmPilot, left Palm/3Com, it was not to retire. The trio, in 1998, formed Handspring Inc., a company dedicated to developing the next generation of handheld computers. The new company secured initial funding from leading venture capital firms such as Kleiner Perkins Caufield & Byers (KPCB) and Benchmark Capital in August of that year, with subsequent funding from QUALCOMM, Inc. in July 1999.

The Visor, Handspring's first product, was the next step in the evolution of the handheld computer. It first shipped in late 1999. Just as the PalmPilot established an open software architecture for handheld computing, the Visor introduced a new hardware and software platform with its Springboard expansion slot, designed to hold plug-and-play expansion modules. With the slot, the Visor was able to extend its functionality to wireless communications, MP3 players, paging, digital photography, global positioning, or anything developers decided to put into a Springboard module. Handspring garnered the support of numerous third-party Springboard module developers and began selling its own line of expansion modules. Handspring's third-party developers included Arkon, Card Access, Datastick Systems Inc., EA Sports, Franklin Covey, Franklin Electronics, Geo Discovery, Global Access, Go America, IDEO, Imagiworks, Infinity Softworks, Innogear, Landware, Karrier Communications, Magellan, Margi Systems, Nexian, Novatel, Omnisky, Pacific Neo-Tek, Peanut Press, Pocket Express, Shinei, Sierra Wireless, Sprint, Sycom, Symbol, Targus, Texas Instruments, Widcomm, Xircom, and many others.

The Visor used the industry-leading PalmOS software, licensed from its number one competitor, making it compatible

with thousands of applications. The Visor also offered several added advantages, including USB support, enhanced applications, and built-in Macintosh compatibility. With the Visor family of handhelds (which would include a wide range of designs, screen displays, prices, and functionality), Handspring went on to uphold the basic tenets of the original PalmPilot philosophy, while using Springboard to create an open platform with limitless potential.

The year 2000 was a great one for Handspring. It was during this year that the company established regional headquarters in both Tokyo and Geneva. The company had a successful IPO in June, raising approximately $200 million. The company also began its philanthropic work in earnest when it sold the one millionth Visor and the first VisorPhone—a combination dual-band world phone and wireless modem that allowed the user to make phone calls, surf the web, check email, chat online, and more, wirelessly—on eBay. The final accomplishment of 2000 was acquiring Mountain View, California-based Bluelark Systems Inc., developers of Blazer and BlueSky, a PalmOS web browser and proxy server that enabled fast, seamless Internet access from handheld computers.

During 2001, the company established the Handspring Foundation, a fund established to support organizations and programs dedicated to creating positive change in their communities. Ed Colligan was promoted from senior vice-president of marketing and sales to chief operating officer.

Also that year, Handspring announced that it would be releasing a new line of wireless communicator products called the Treo, a device that combines a mobile phone; wireless data applications such as email, short messaging, and Internet browsing; and a Palm OS organizer into one compact device. The first units to be offered for sale anywhere in the world were up for bid on eBay as part of a larger charity initiative by eBay and the Consumer Electronics Association called "Bids to Help Kids," which featured donated consumer electronics items for bid on eBay. Proceeds went to Big Brothers Big Sisters of America, the nation's largest youth mentoring program.

By the end of 2001, some analysts predicted that the market for handheld computers would grow exponentially in the next few years, with worldwide shipments expected to reach 63 million units by 2004. Some companies, such as the already established Xybernaut Corporation and InfoCharms, as well as various start-ups, began attempting to bring even the next step—wearable computers. With the technological expertise of the team leading Handspring, the company remained poised to benefit from the upsurge in interest in mobile computing technology.

Principal Competitors

Palm, Inc.; Hewlett-Packard Company; Compaq Computer Corporation; Psion; Acer Inc.; Casio Computer Co., Ltd.; Ericsson; Kyocera Corporation; Microsoft Corporation; Motorola, Inc.; Nokia Corporation; Research in Motion; Samsung Electronics Co., Ltd.; Sharp Corporation; Siemens AG; Sony Corporation; Symbian Ltd.; Symbol Technologies, Inc.; Xybernaut Corporation.

Further Reading

DiCarlo, Lisa, ''Top Tech Execs: Hawkins, Dubinsky,'' *Forbes,* December 15, 2000.

Dillon, Pat, ''The Next Small Thing,'' *Fast Company,* June 1998, p. 97.

——, ''The Right Way to Make Mistakes,'' *Fast Company,* June 1998, p. 108.

——, ''This Is Jeff Hawkins on Brains,'' *Fast Company,* June 1998, p. 104.

Fishman, Charles, ''Face Time: Donna Dubinsky,'' *Fast Company,* January 2001, p. 74.

Tobias, Arlyn, ''The Parents of the Pilot Try for an Encore with Handspring—Q&A: A Talk with the Palm Pioneers,'' *Fortune,* November 1999.

—Daryl F. Mallett

hanna Andersson®

Hanna Andersson Corp.

1010 NW Flanders Boulevard
Portland, Oregon 97209
U.S.A.
Telephone: (503) 321-5275
Toll Free: (800) 222-0544
Fax: (503) 321-5289
Web site: http://www.hannaandersson.com

Private Company
Incorporated: 1983
Employees: 250
Sales: $50 million (2001 est.)
NAIC: 454110 Electronic Shopping and Mail-Order
   Houses; 448140 Family Clothing Stores

Hanna Andersson Corp. specializes in all-cotton children's clothing of the sort found in Scandinavia. The catalog company, which began marketing all-cotton children's clothing imported from Sweden and Denmark throughout the United States in 1984, has developed over the years to manufacture 60 percent of its product line domestically. Throughout the 1980s, Hanna was known for being socially, environmentally, and philanthropically progressive, but hard times in the 1990s led to cost-cutting reforms. In the early part of the new century, Hanna was branching out overseas and into the women's clothing and children's bedding and home goods markets.

1983–89: Immediate Success As a Catalog Retailer of Children's Clothes

When Gun Denhart's second son, Christian, was born in 1980, she searched fruitlessly in New York for the sort of soft, durable, all-cotton clothes she had been used to in Sweden. Reasoning that there was an untapped market for colorful, well-made, natural-fiber clothing in the United States, Gun and her husband, Tom, went to Sweden "and brought back a couple of hundred dollars worth of clothing which [they] gave away to friends." "Everybody loved the clothes," according to Tom Denhart in the _Portland Business Journal_ in 1986. "That was our market research."

Tom Denhart was then a vice-president and creative director for Ogilvy & Mather, a top advertising agency in New York, and yearning for a change. Gun, with a degree in business from the university in Lund, Sweden, was the financial manager of an international chain of language schools. Trusting they would find a niche for their product, the couple left their jobs, packed up their two sons, and moved to Tom's native Portland for a "simpler life." There, according to a November 1989 article in _Working Woman_ magazine, using every penny of the $250,000 they had made on the sale of the Greenwich, Connecticut house, they set up business in 1983 "with a telephone, a card file and inventory spread throughout the house." The new Hanna Andersson Corp. was jointly owned by the couple and by a Swedish apparel manufacturer.

The Denharts returned to Sweden to select manufacturers and produced their first catalog in 14 days; it featured the children of friends wearing Hanna outfits photographed at Gun's parents' house in Sweden. It contained inch-square cloth swatches, which the two entrepreneurs cut and glued into it by hand. Advertised in _Parents_ magazine for $1 under the header, "Why Are Swedish Babies So Happy?," the first Hanna catalog went out to 75,000 addresses. The clothes it featured were moderate to upper range in price, functional, everyday, never gimmicky—"quality, cute, and not too expensive for people who are sick of all of the 'frou-frou' in children's clothes," according to Denhart in a 1986 _Portland Business Journal_ article. "[I]f it's hard to wash, no matter how cute it is we'll never carry it."

According to observers, the couple made a good business team. Tom handled the graphics, creating "the personality of the catalog, but he couldn't have done it if she weren't such a great merchant," according to the head of Muldoon Direct, Inc. in a 1986 _Working Women_ article. "She's very methodical and organized, but at the same time she's warm and caring about the organization," according to David Smith of _Smith & Hawken_ and _SelfCare_ catalogs in the same _Working Women_ selection. From the start, the Denharts strove to convey a lifestyle image as well as sell children's clothes; they named their catalog company after Gun's grandmother, Hanna Andersson, who loved children, "equated waste with sin," and whose name was "pleasant and Swedish-sounding," according to a 1994 *Direct Marketing* article.

The company grossed $300,000 its first year and doubled its sales every year throughout the rest of the 1980s. Business was so good that Hanna moved out of the Denharts' house in 1986 and into a 9,000-square-foot warehouse that also served as the business's office and store. Within nine months of this move, Hanna moved again to a facility seven times larger than the last. In 1989, the company bought the adjoining building to create a 100,000-square-foot headquarters for Hanna Andersson Corp. In the summer of 1989, the business doubled its staff from 50 to 100 and mailed 3.5 million catalogs throughout the United States. By November, Hanna had added another 50 workers.

In the early days at Hanna, orders were filled manually by number and date. But the company's swift growth soon convinced Gun of the need to computerize. By the second half of the 1980s, computer software enabled Hanna to print out completed order forms and shipping tickets while simultaneously keeping track of how many of a specific item had been sold and how many remained in stock. Working with small factories in Sweden and Denmark that airshipped goods weekly, the company maintained a just-in-time inventory system, stocking just enough items to satisfy predicted demand. If something proved popular, these suppliers would immediately make more.

Still, back orders proved to be a constant customer complaint. In an attempt to rectify this situation, Hanna helped her major supplier set up a small factory in Portland where workers stitched together precut garments shipped in bulk from Europe. In 1986, Hanna Andersson also made a foray into wholesaling to retailers, but a lot of stores soon dropped the clothes because their wholesale price was so close to the catalog price. By 1990, the retail store had expanded threefold, and in July the company opened its first discount outlet store. The company also began to manufacture a private-label product line for Bendel's department store.

Hanna's wave of growth coincided with a U.S. switch to natural fibers and the parenting years of affluent baby boomers, who could afford to spend a little more on their children's clothes. Having entered the specialty catalog business just before it took off, the company by 1990 had become a $23 million dollar business with 200 employees. It sold 1.5 million items at prices averaging $20 and took as many as 5,000 calls a day. Recognizing the need for experienced management, the Denharts hired Hanna's first chief operating officer, Mary Roberts, in 1988. By 1990, Hanna was selling its lifestyle and clothes to its 300,000 customers, drawing in revenues of about $30 million.

The company also established a "Hanna way" in terms of its employee relations and open management style. Unusual benefits included stipends for child care (half the bills up to $3,000 per child), extended parental leave, a "wellness" program of yoga classes, a gourmet cafeteria, and deep discounts on clothes. In fact, as the recession of the early 1990s set in, Hanna continued to expand workplace benefits, leading *Working Mother* to name it one of the 85 best companies for working parents in 1991. Wages were average, but when sales were good so were bonuses. Even the phone clerks took part in a profit-sharing plan, which paid up to 5 percent of wages. Accommodating the large number of working mothers (approximately 80 percent of its workforce were women), Hanna offered a wide range of part-time schedules, and anyone who worked at least 30 hours per week qualified for benefits. Even those who worked only 20 hours per week received full medical and dental insurance plus sick and vacation leave.

The company also distinguished itself for its charitable donations. The Hannadowns program, instituted in 1985, allowed customers to send back used, outgrown clothing for a 20 percent discount on their next order. Returned items—an average 3,000 items per month—were donated to more than 125 charities nationwide. By 1994, Hanna had issued more than $700,000 in credit on nearly 150,000 pieces of clothing. Hanna also matched any employee donation up to $500 per charity and chose three charities in 1993 where it donated time, clothing, and money. HannaShare, the employee matching program, donated 5 percent of the company's pretax profits to charities. Beginning in 1994, the firm gave everyone the opportunity to spend eight volunteer hours per year for their favorite charity.

Environmentally, too, Hanna stood apart from other businesses. Gun, concerned about the fact that Hanna's catalogs used up 500 trees a year, started a reforestation program in the national park near Zigzag, Oregon. To offset the negative environmental consequences of cotton growing and processing, the company purchased its cotton from Peru where fewer chemicals were used and dyed its materials in a Danish mill with unusually strict wastewater controls.

The Early 1990s: Questioning the "Hanna Way"

Through the recession of the early 1990s, the company continued to enjoy double-digit growth: approximately $40 million in sales in 1992, up from $34 million in 1991. The increasingly poor economic climate, however, coupled with changes in the company's day-to-day management in 1992, led to a situation that called into question the "Hanna way" of doing business.

The Denharts had tired of the everyday aspects of running a large business. Gun Denhart had begun to lecture on socially responsible entrepreneurship and wanted to devote more time to her philanthropic interests. Tom Denhart took a sabbatical to restore boats and spend time with his son, handing over creative management of the catalog to a new director who attempted to put her stamp on it. The innovation proved disastrous. When the revamped catalog appeared, sales took a nosedive. They rebounded once the redesign was shelved, but 1993 revenues were only 8 percent more than those for 1992. Profit margins, too, began to erode in the face of the increased costs of employee health insurance and postage and a market that was increasingly competitive.

Key Dates:

1983: Gun and Tom Denhart move to Portland, Oregon, and set up Hanna Andersson Corp.

1984: The company mails out its first catalog.

1986: Hanna moves into a 9,000-square-foot warehouse that also serves as the business's office and store, then within a year to a much larger facility.

1988: Mary Roberts becomes chief operating officer.

1989: The company buys the adjoining building to create a 100,000-square-foot headquarters.

1992: The catalog is revamped after Tom Denhart takes a year's sabbatical.

1993: The company moves its distribution center to Kentucky and cuts its workforce by 10 percent; Roberts becomes president of Hanna.

1994: The company targets the Japanese market.

1995: Phil Iosca replaces Roberts as president.

1996: Hanna reduces its annual mailing by about 25 percent and eliminates 15 percent of its workforce.

1999: Hanna opens two more full-price stores, in White Plains, New York, and Minneapolis, Minnesota.

2001: A management-led investment group joined by Dorset Capital and Weston Presidio buys Hanna.

Hanna had always calculated a "double bottom line," tallying both profits and good works. In 1993, however, the company's benefits and payroll taxes equaled the company's net earnings. "We became so introspective that we lost sight of what was happening outside the company," Gun Denhart was quoted in *Inc.* in 1994.

The company responded by moving the manufacture of 50 percent of its clothes to 15 factories on the West Coast and in North Carolina in 1992. It also moved its distribution center to Kentucky to cut down on shipping times and charges to its East Coast customers and those around the Great Lakes in 1993, the same year Hanna cut its workforce by 10 percent, or 20 employees, 90 percent of whom were eventually rehired.

The Denharts knew they had to cut costs and improve efficiencies further, but they did not want to be the ones to do it. Instead, they placed the company under the control of a committee of four managers. When this committee's rapport disintegrated in the face of hard-to-decide issues, Gun established the position of Hanna president and Roberts took the job in 1993.

Tom returned to his role as creative director while Gun focused her energies on long-range growth through international sales and retail expansions. It would take Hanna several years to find the balance between social and fiscal responsibility, but the company eventually trimmed its child care subsidy to 40 percent, eliminated reimbursement for parking costs, and closed its gourmet cafeteria. A team of managers designed Hanna's first three-year plan, which emphasized more rigorous marketing and planning. They contracted with new manufacturers so that 60 percent of Hanna's clothing was made in the United States, 30 percent in Europe, and 10 percent in the Far East.

The Mid-1990s–2001: New Strategies for Growth

Hanna's strategy for pursuing growth focused on broadening its domestic retail market and increasing its Japanese mail-order business simultaneously. In 1994, the company targeted its Japanese market, in which it had been dabbling since 1989, when it realized that the average Japanese customer spent twice as much as Americans. It introduced Japanese language catalogs and opened a Japanese-language call center in Tokyo with direct access to an online inventory and order system. As a direct result, Japanese sales tripled to 6.5 percent of overall revenues. Hanna also opened two more full-price stores in New York and Minnesota in 1999, bringing its total number of stores to five, with its original full-price store at its headquarters and two outlet stores in Portland and New Hampshire.

Roberts resigned in 1995 and was replaced by Phil Iosca, former group president of Lands' End. The company was still struggling with increased postal rates and paper costs, softening demand, and greater competition. That year, the company did not reach its profit target and did not contribute to employees' retirement accounts. But management's cost-cutting measures had begun to turn things around. In 1994, sales stood at $47 million, up only $3 million from the year before. By 1995, Hanna had total sales of $52 million on an annual circulation of 14 million catalogs.

Still, in 1996, the company reduced its annual mailing by about 25 percent and instituted other cost-cutting measures. It eliminated three senior managers and 60 jobs (or 15 percent of its workforce) and scaled back on less popular clothing items. In 1998, the Hannadowns program discontinued issuing credit for returned items and the child care subsidy was diminished to 40 percent.

Hanna still looked overseas for the solution to its weakened revenues despite the fact that the percent of total sales to Japanese customers went from 20 percent in 1997 to around 15 percent in 2000. This slackening was attributed to the decline of the yen and fading popularity of ordering from Western catalogs. In 2000, Hanna set its sights on the United Kingdom and Germany as its first European targets through the Internet. In 1998, it introduced bedding and other home goods for children. In 1999, it focused increased attention on selling to women after women's clothes accounted for 20 percent of sales, double the level of previous years.

In 2001, a management-led investment group joined by San Francisco-based Dorset Capital and Weston Presidio bought Hanna, which had reached $65 million in revenue for 2000. Gun stayed on with the company as a member of its new board of directors and part owner; however, she also assumed control of the Hanna Andersson Charitable Foundation, a new nonprofit that funded groups directly benefiting children and women. Management's short-term goal was to continue to develop new products for Hanna and to concentrate on its e-commerce efforts, which in 2001 accounted for 25 percent of sales.

Principal Competitors

Biobottoms; Childcraft; The Gap, Inc.; Gymboree Corporation; Lands' End, Inc.; L.L. Bean, Inc.; OshKosh B'Gosh, Inc.; The Walt Disney Company.

Further Reading

Cyr, Diane, ''Working Woman Finds Out How Hanna Andersson Toughened,'' *Working Woman,* June 1998, p. 28.

Goldfield, Robert, ''If at First You Don't Succeed,'' *Portland Business Journal,* January 28, 2000, p. 13.

''Gun Denhart: Hanna Andersson Corp.,'' *Chain Store Age Executive,* December 1, 1993, p. 24.

Inskeep, Martha, ''Couple Finds Swedish Look Is Hot for Tots,'' *Portland Business Journal,* August 11, 1986, p. 1.

Marks, Anita, ''Children's Clothing Designer Finds Niche at Hanna Andersson,'' *Portland Business Journal,* November 16, 1992, p. 12.

Murphy, Anne, ''Too Good to Be True,'' *Inc.,* July 1994, p. 34.

Oppenheimer, Todd, ''Hanna Andersson: Swedish Socialism Is Good Business,'' *Willamette Week,* February 21–27, 1991, p. 10.

Raphel, Murray, ''How Swede It Is,'' *Direct Marketing,* March 1994, p. 16.

Updike, Robin, ''Kids, Clogs, and Cotton—Hanna Andersson Is One of the Hottest Children's Wear Companies in the U.S.,'' *Seattle Times,* October 28, 1992, p. C1.

Wilkinson, Stephan, ''The Bold New Force in Kids' Wear,'' *Working Woman,* November 1989, p. 54.

—Carrie Rothburd

Hilton Group plc

Hilton Group plc

Hilton Group plc

Maple Court
Central Park
Reeds Crescent
Watford WD24 4QQ
United Kingdom
Telephone: (020) 7856-8000
Fax: (020) 7856-8001
Web site: http://www.hiltongroup.com

Public Company
Incorporated: 1967 as Ladbroke Group PLC
Employees: 55,413
Sales: £4.16 billion ($6.04 billion) (2001)
Stock Exchanges: London
Ticker Symbol: HG
NAIC: 713210 Casinos (Except Casino Hotels); 713290
    Other Gambling Industries; 713940 Fitness and
    Recreational Sports Centers; 721110 Hotels (Except
    Casino Hotels) and Motels

Since Hilton Group plc was founded more than 115 years ago as a small agency to handle the horseracing bets of England's high society, it has grown from a simple partnership between a local horse trainer (Arthur Bendir) and a friend to become one of the world's leading companies in the hotel and leisure industries. The partnership, originally known as Ladbroke and Co., was named for the village in the county of Warwickshire, England, where it was first established; it became Ladbroke Group PLC in 1967 and then Hilton Group plc in 1999. In the new millennium, Hilton Group consisted of two divisions: Hilton International and Ladbroke Betting and Gaming. During 2001, the former generated only about 37 percent of the revenues of Hilton Group but was responsible for more than 60 percent of the profits.

Hilton International holds the rights to the Hilton name outside of the United States, and it operates more than 380 hotels—under the Hilton and Scandic brands—in 70 countries worldwide. Since early 1997 Hilton International and Hilton Hotels Corporation (the owner of the Hilton brand in the United States) have cooperated, through a worldwide marketing alliance, on such matters as sales and marketing, the Hilton HHonors loyalty program, and a central reservation system. Hilton International also operates more than 90 LivingWell health clubs.

Ladbroke Betting and Gaming is the world's leading bookmaker, with 2,500 betting shops in the United Kingdom, Ireland, and Belgium. In addition to these in-person betting outlets, Ladbroke also offers telephone and Internet gambling opportunities, with the latter including sports betting, numbers games, and an online casino featuring poker, blackjack, roulette, baccarat, craps, and slot machines. Ladbroke also owns Vernons Pools Limited, which is one of the two major soccer betting pools in the United Kingdom.

Acquisition by Cyril Stein-Led Group of Investors: 1957

Because its betting activities were illegal under British law but permitted on an unofficial basis, Ladbroke maintained a very low profile for almost 70 years after its founding in 1886. After relocating to London's West End around 1900, it quickly became the country's quality credit betting business. In 1957 Ladbroke was acquired by a group of investors led by Cyril Stein, who served as chairman until the end of 1993. Spurred by the legalization of off-track betting in 1963, the size of Ladbroke's racing subsidiary increased significantly in order to reach beyond the upper classes to all who wanted to try their luck at picking a winner. In 1967 the company went public as Ladbroke Group PLC, offering its shares for sale on the London Stock Exchange, and by 1971 the company owned and operated 660 licensed betting shops in the United Kingdom.

Although its betting operations assured Ladbroke of a fairly steady cash flow, Stein knew that Ladbroke also needed to build strong assets as a base for future growth. Applying the expertise they had gained in the racing business, Stein and his management team embarked upon a diversification strategy that took the company beyond horse betting into the property development and hotel industries.

Company Perspectives:

Hilton Group is a global company operating in the hospitality and gaming markets with the leading brand names of Hilton and Ladbrokes. The group intends to enhance shareholder value by exploiting its prime position in these international markets, both of which are expected to experience significant long-term growth.

Diversifying Beyond Horse Betting in the 1970s

Through its 1972 acquisition of the London & Leeds Development Corporation, Ladbroke aggressively entered the real estate market with office projects in the eastern United States as well as in Paris, Amsterdam, and Brussels. Property development activities in the United Kingdom led to the formation of four other subsidiaries: Ladbroke Group Properties, handling commercial and residential projects in and around London; Ladbroke City & County Land Company, to oversee local and out-of-town retail projects; Gable House Properties, the largest operator of retirement and nursing homes in the country, acquired in 1986 to develop commercial, residential, and retail properties; and Ladbroke Retail Parks, for the construction of retailing centers outside of London.

Ladbroke entered the lodging business in 1973, when it opened three moderately priced hotels which quickly grew into a profitable chain throughout the country. The success of this venture and the continuing health of Ladbroke's betting and real estate operations helped the company weather the severe losses it incurred during a short-lived entry into the casino business. Casinos, which Ladbroke had hoped might be a lucrative adjunct to its hotel business, were abandoned in 1979 after the company lost its license in a highly publicized case in which it was found guilty of violating government gaming regulations.

Expanding Internationally in the 1980s

Five years later, Ladbroke capitalized on an opportunity to expand its racing operations into Belgium. With the 1984 acquisition of Le Tiercé S.A., a chain of Belgian betting shops, Ladbroke rapidly established itself as a leading force in that country's racing industry. Although a plan to purchase the Arizona-based Turf Paradise racetrack fell through in that same year due to problems with obtaining state regulatory approval, Ladbroke successfully acquired the Detroit Race Course at the beginning of 1985 and took the first step toward making its presence felt in U.S. horseracing.

Further expansion in the European racing market occurred in April 1986 when Ladbroke was awarded exclusive rights to open off-track betting shops throughout The Netherlands. That year also saw the company pursue a new avenue for growth in the retailing area by purchasing Home Charm Group PLC, a leading chain of over 100 do-it-yourself stores operating throughout the United Kingdom under the Texas Homecare name, for £200 million.

The company's growth was marked by expansion and acquisition in some areas balanced by consolidation and divestitures in others. As part of a strategy intended to eliminate involvement in markets in which Ladbroke did not hold a major position, the company sold a number of businesses grouped under its entertainment division in 1986, including Lasky's, a chain of consumer-electronics stores, as well as amusement arcades, bingo halls, and local newspaper-publishing operations, while retaining more profitable ventures in magazine publishing and cable television.

That accomplished, the company turned its attention to establishing a more contemporary and stable image. Ladbroke instituted several measures intended to upgrade the public's perception of off-track betting parlors, such as adding snack bars and live television. Ladbroke also joined with three other major bookmakers in 1986 to form Satellite Information Services (SIS), a television communications company set up to transmit horse and greyhound racing directly to Britain's off-track betting shops.

The bookmakers' involvement in SIS prompted an investigation by the government's Office of Fair Trading (OFT) into possible conflicts of interest. The government was particularly concerned about the bookmakers' influence on the SIS system and their potential for creating a monopoly, but also about their power to shift attendance away from the racecourses to off-track shops and thus affect the odds determining payouts for winning bets. A second investigation resulted from similar concerns over the bookmakers' power expressed by the National Greyhound Racing Club. Ladbroke's share in SIS, which was larger than those of the other investors, made it a primary target of the investigation.

At the same time, Ladbroke brought a suit before the High Court in which it accused the Extel communications group of starting a series of false rumors about the company that had caused a run on Ladbroke shares, reducing the company's value by £200 million in only two days. Ladbroke argued that Extel, which operated a competitive sports-information service, had sought to sabotage the first public offering of SIS stock by simultaneously releasing several damaging reports, including a rumor that Cyril Stein had resigned and implications of improper relationships between prominent racing individuals. The rumors were never substantiated, and the OFT investigations ultimately yielded no evidence of wrongdoing on Ladbroke's part.

Acquiring Hilton International in 1987

Although Ladbroke had become the second largest operator of hotels within its own country by the late 1980s, it had not yet achieved a worldwide reputation in the lodging industry. If anything, its sale of the Parkmount Hospitality Corporation and the Dallas-based Rodeway Inn organization to Ramada, Inc. had reduced the company's reach and influence outside the United Kingdom. That all changed in 1987 when Ladbroke successfully acquired the 91-hotel Hilton International chain for £645 million (more than $1 billion) from Allegis Corporation. Ladbroke's bid for Hilton, which beat out several other heavyweight bidders, represented its second attempt in two years to purchase the hotel chain. The first had fallen short when Hilton's previous owner, Transworld Corporation, turned Ladbroke down in favor of an Allegis bid of higher value. This time, however, Stein used a three-week time limit to pressure Allegis

Key Dates:

1886: A local horse trainer in the village of Ladbroke named Arthur Bendir and a friend establish Ladbroke and Co. to take horseracing bets.

c. 1900: Company is relocated to London's West End.

1957: Ladbroke is acquired by a group of investors led by Cyril Stein, who begins a long stint as chairman.

1967: Company goes public as Ladbroke Group PLC, with a listing on the London Stock Exchange.

1973: Company enters the lodging business with the opening of three mid-priced U.K. hotels.

1979: Short-lived entry into the casino business ends when the firm is found guilty of violating government gaming regulations.

1984: Le Tiercé S.A., a chain of Belgian betting shops, is acquired.

1986: Company acquires the Texas Homecare chain of do-it-yourself stores.

1987: Ladbroke acquires Hilton International from Allegis Corporation for more than $1 billion.

1989: The Vernons football pools operation is acquired.

1994: Stein retires; John Jackson is named chairman and Peter George, chief executive; strategic reviews are conducted, leading to a decision to refocus the company on hotels and gaming; company reenters the casino business with the purchase of three London casinos.

1995: Texas Homecare is sold to J Sainsbury.

1997: Hilton International and Hilton Hotels Corporation enter into a worldwide marketing alliance; Ladbroke's property division is shut down.

1998: Regulators rule Ladbroke's purchase of the Coral chain of betting shops to be anticompetitive and force the company to sell the chain.

1999: The company acquires Stakis plc for £1.2 billion, gaining 54 hotels and 22 casinos in the United Kingdom and Ireland, as well as the 68-unit LivingWell chain of health clubs; Ladbroke changes its name to Hilton Group plc.

2001: The company acquires Scandic Hotels AB, the leading operator of hotels in the Nordic region, for £620.2 million.

to accept the Ladbroke offer immediately instead of waiting for the other bidders to receive approval from their respective governments.

The Hilton International purchase made Ladbroke one of the largest hotel operators in the world, with a presence in 44 countries, including the United States where Hilton's six Vista International hotels joined the Ladbroke fold. (In 1964 Hilton International had been spun off from Hilton Hotels Corporation, which held the rights to the Hilton name in the United States.) It also gave the company a 50 percent share in Hilton's advanced reservation system, which Ladbroke viewed as an important link to travelers around the world. One year later, Ladbroke upgraded and renamed most of its original hotels in the United Kingdom, reintroducing them as part of the Hilton National chain.

Meanwhile, technological enhancements such as a full-color electronic showboard and new Gold Star shops, with services appealing to a wider range of customers, were introduced to maintain Ladbroke's position as a leader in racing and off-track betting. Its presence as the only British betting company operating in the United States expanded, too: Ladbroke obtained licenses to conduct off-track betting in Wyoming and Pennsylvania, acquired The Meadows racetrack in Pittsburgh in 1988, and purchased San Francisco's Golden Gate Fields in 1989. Ladbroke also acquired a major competitor in the United Kingdom, Thomson T-Line and its Vernons football pools operation (which involved gambling on British professional soccer games), that same year, increasing its share of the betting business in the United Kingdom.

By the end of the 1980s, Ladbroke's hotels accounted for the largest share of the company's business activity. Since the Hilton acquisition, Ladbroke had opened more than 13 new, four-star hotels around the globe and had many others under development. It also operated numerous holiday villages and health and leisure clubs within the United Kingdom, and the Comfort Hotel chain throughout Europe. In the late 1980s, more than 50 new outlets were added to the Texas Homecare operation, which was the second largest do-it-yourself retailer in the United Kingdom with 200 stores. Meanwhile, Ladbroke's racing business continued strong with 1,800 retail betting shops throughout the United Kingdom.

Refocusing on Hotels and Betting and Gaming in the 1990s

The early 1990s were difficult years for Ladbroke as Hilton International suffered from the recession in various parts of the world, Texas Homecare's profits fell because of fierce competition in the do-it-yourself sector, and the company's already troubled U.K. gambling operations were hurt further with the November 1994 debut of a national lottery in the United Kingdom, which particularly affected the Vernons football pools business. The company's reaction to the last of these difficulties was to increasingly look overseas for opportunities to expand its gambling business. In 1993 Ladbroke announced a plan to develop an off-track betting business in Argentina over the next five years. In January 1995 Ladbroke moved into the bingo hall business in Argentina, when it took over the operation of a bingo hall in Buenos Aires. The company then began to build new bingo halls in Posadas and Salta. Bingo halls were also opened in Sao Paulo, Brazil, during this period.

The turning point for the company's fortunes, however, came at the beginning of 1994, when John Jackson was named nonexecutive chairman and Peter George group chief executive, together taking over the leadership of Ladbroke from the retiring Stein. For 37 years, Stein had run the company in a fairly autocratic manner, and, despite Ladbroke's status as a public company, had instilled an aura of secrecy around it. Jackson and George not only promised a new era of collective management and openness—backed up in March 1994 when the two men participated in the company's first-ever press conference—but also moved quickly to refocus the company's operations. They ordered a series of strategic reviews, which were conducted in 1994 and which concluded that Ladbroke should refocus on hotels and gaming and divest its commercial property and retailing divisions. Subsequently, Ladbroke in March 1995 sold Texas Homecare to J Sainsbury plc for £290 million. Then, from 1995 to early 1997, Ladbroke gradually disposed of nearly all of the assets of its property division, finally closing the division down in March 1997.

A byproduct of the company's new focus was its return to casino gambling more than 14 years after its ignominious exit from the sector in 1979. In September 1994 Ladbroke established a new gaming subsidiary called Ladbroke Clubs Limited and purchased three London casinos—Maxims, Chesters, and the Golden Horseshoe—from City Clubs Limited for £50 million ($75 million). Ladbroke then made additional moves toward its goal of establishing a broadly based international gaming operation. In April 1996 the Barracuda Casino, another London casino, was bought from Stakis plc. In July 1997 Ladbroke signed a letter of intent to acquire Colorado Gaming & Entertainment Co., which owned three casinos in the Colorado gambling towns of Black Hawk and Central City. The $87 million deal, completed in August 1998, marked Ladbroke's first foray into casinos in the United States. In August 1997 Ladbroke was awarded a London casino license, which would bring its number of London casinos to five. At the same time, the company was in the process of bidding for three casino licenses in South Africa.

In late 1995 and early 1996 Ladbroke became the subject of takeover rumors as its stock continued to perform miserably. The depressed stock was in part caused by the troubles in the company's U.K. betting operations, which continued to take a heavy hit from the national lottery, and by the failure of Ladbroke and Hilton Hotels Corporation to reunite the Hilton brand, which Hilton Hotels was reluctant to do. In fact, Hilton Hotels, which like Ladbroke was also involved in gaming, was one of the companies said to be interested in acquiring Ladbroke. All of this was resolved, however, with the August 1996 announcement that Hilton International and Hilton Hotels had entered into an alliance that would reunite the Hilton brand, 32 years after it was split apart. The alliance agreement was signed in January 1997, with Hilton International and Hilton Hotels agreeing to cooperate on sales and marketing, loyalty programs, hotel development, and other operational areas. Ladbroke and Hilton Hotels also gained the opportunity to purchase up to 20 percent of each other. In February the first major initiative of the new alliance, the Hilton Honors Worldwide loyalty program (later known as Hilton HHonors), was launched.

Also in February 1997, Ladbroke Racing acquired the A.R. Dennis chain of 114 betting shops in London and southeastern England for £31.3 million. The purchase boosted the number of Ladbroke Racing betting outlets in the United Kingdom to 1,925. By the end of 1997 the revamping of the group's operations initiated by the new managers was clearly taking hold, with Ladbroke posting healthy pretax profits of £226.3 million ($327.6 million), an increase of 39 percent over the previous year.

At the very end of 1997 Ladbroke acquired the Coral group of companies from Bass plc for £375.5 million ($543.6 million). Coral was the number three operator of betting shops in the United Kingdom, with more than 800 outlets. The takeover, however, was referred to the Monopolies and Mergers Commission in April 1998, and the commission ruled in September that the merger was anticompetitive and ordered Ladbroke to sell the bulk of the acquired assets within six months. In February 1999 Ladbroke sold the U.K. businesses of Coral to Morgan Grenfall Private Equity Limited, a subsidiary of Deutsche Bank AG, for £390 million. Ladbroke did retain Coral's 50 betting shops in Ireland and eight betting shops in Jersey, which were rebranded under the Ladbrokes name.

Major Hotel Acquisitions and a New Name Around the Turn of the Millennium

During 1998 discussions of a possible merger of Hilton International and Hilton Hotels Corporation went nowhere, and Ladbroke was outbid in the battle to buy the Inter-Continental Hotels and Resorts chain by none other than Bass. Following these setbacks, Ladbroke completed a major hotel acquisition in March 1999, purchasing Stakis plc for £1.2 billion ($1.9 billion). Gained in the deal were 54 hotels and 22 casinos in the United Kingdom and Ireland, as well as the 68-unit LivingWell chain of health clubs. The Stakis hotels were subsequently rebranded under the Hilton name, and their addition made Ladbroke the number two hotelier in the United Kingdom, trailing only Granada Group PLC. Stakis's chief executive, David Michels, who had worked at Hilton International before joining Stakis, became head of the division following the takeover.

In May 1999, shortly after completion of the Stakis acquisition, Ladbroke changed its name to Hilton Group plc. By doing so, the company adopted the more widely recognized of its two main brands, and the move also reflected the increasing importance of the hotel operations, which now generated two-thirds of the overall profits and represented more than 80 percent of the group's assets. The group's two divisions were now called Hilton International and Ladbroke Betting and Gaming. Also in the immediate aftermath of the Stakis takeover, and following a review of the combined Hilton and Stakis portfolios, Hilton Group sold ten of its U.K. hotels.

After 37 years at the company, George stepped down from his position as chief executive in June 2000, and Michels succeeded him. In November of that year, Hilton Group and Hilton Hotels Corporation formed a joint venture to lead a worldwide expansion of the Conrad brand of luxury hotels. One month later, Hilton Group sold the bulk of its casino operations, including its 27 casinos in the United Kingdom, to Gala Group Holdings Plc for £235.3 million. Seeking to pare back on the large portfolio of hotels that it owned in the United Kingdom—a property portfolio worth £1.9 billion—Hilton Group sold 11 U.K. hotels to the Royal Bank of Scotland Group plc for £312 million; it then leased back the properties so that it continued to run the hotels but no longer had to contend with the burdens of ownership.

The funds raised through these divestments enabled Hilton Group to complete another major hotel acquisition. In June 2001 the company completed a £620.2 million ($883 million) purchase of Stockholm-based Scandic Hotels AB, the leading operator of hotels in the Nordic region. Most of Scandic's 154 properties were mid-priced hotels and were under either the Scandic or Holiday Inn brand. All of the Holiday Inns and some of the Scandics would be rebranded under the Hilton name, but about 130 Scandic hotels in the Nordic region would retain their name because it was well-known in the region. With the acquisition of Scandic and the opening of 15 new Hilton hotels during 2001, Hilton Group ended the year with 384 hotel properties and nearly 100,000 rooms.

Like most hoteliers, Hilton Group's hospitality operations were quite negatively affected by the global travel slowdown that came in the wake of the events of September 11, 2001. Profits for the year were flat compared to the previous year, while revenues increased only 2.4 percent. Making up for Hilton International's poor showing was the Ladbroke Betting and Gaming division, which reported an increase in profits of 23 percent. One factor in this increase was Ladbroke's rapidly growing online gambling business, which turned a profit for the first time that year. Looking to the future, Hilton Group was certain to continue to expand its ever more important hotel operations, and from 2002 through mid-2004 it planned to open 41 new Hiltons. There was also continued speculation on two fronts: that the company would divest its Ladbroke division in order to concentrate solely on the hospitality industry; and that the company would merge with, acquire, or be acquired by Hilton Hotels Corporation.

Principal Subsidiaries

Hilton International Co. (U.S.A.); Hilton UK Hotels Limited; Inter-National Hotel Services Limited; LivingWell Health & Leisure Limited; Metropole Hotels (Holdings) Limited; Scandic Hotels AB (Sweden); Stakis Limited; Ladbrokes Limited; Ladbroke (Ireland) Limited; Ladbrokes International Limited (Gibraltar); Tiercé Ladbroke SA (Belgium); Vernons Pools Limited; Hilton Group Finance plc.

Principal Divisions

Hilton International; Ladbroke Betting and Gaming.

Principal Competitors

Marriott International, Inc.; Hyatt International Corporation; Starwood Hotels & Resorts Worldwide, Inc.; Six Continents Hotels, Inc.; Whitbread PLC; Thistle Hotels Plc; Accor; SAS AB; Millennium & Copthorne Hotels plc; William Hill Organization Limited; Coral Eurobet plc; Stanley Leisure PLC; Camelot Group Plc; The Rank Group PLC.

Further Reading

Andorka, Frank H., Jr., "Ladbroke Deal Throws Open U.K. Market," *Hotel and Motel Management,* March 15, 1999, pp. 3, 21.

Banta, Ken, "Better Going at Ladbrokes?," *Management Today,* November 1995, pp. 54–58.
Benady, David, "Pools Gold," *Marketing Week,* September 25, 1997, pp. 46–49.
Blackwell, David, "Gamblers Shun Ladbroke," *Financial Times,* September 2, 1995, p. WFT5.
Burt, Tim, "Ladbroke Goes Back to Casinos After 14 Years," *Financial Times,* March 7, 1994, p. 22.
Coleman, Zach, "Hilton Group Finds Business Steady in Asia," *Wall Street Journal,* August 20, 2001.
Daneshkhu, Scheherazade, "The Big Bet Goes on Team Work," *Financial Times,* March 13, 1995, p. 10.
——, "Bookmaker Racing to Meet Deadline," *Financial Times,* September 26, 1998, p. 20.
——, "Hilton Hotels to Take 5% of Ladbroke," *Financial Times,* January 14, 1997, p. 20.
——, "Ladbroke's Check-In Time Still Looks Undecided," *Financial Times,* October 25, 1997, p. 19.
——, "More Rooms with a View in Expansionary Mood," *Financial Times,* January 16, 2001, p. 26.
——, "A Takeover Gamble That Looks Far from Being a Safe Bet," *Financial Times,* July 25, 1998, p. 7.
——, "Weighing the Odds on a Change of Luck," *Financial Times,* February 2, 1996, p. 18.
Hannon, Kerry, "Long Shot," *Forbes,* April 16, 1990, pp. 92–93.
Killgren, Lucy, "Name Stake," *Marketing Week,* April 22, 1999, pp. 35–36.
Merss, Marcia, "Gentlemen, Your Wagers," *Forbes,* November 21, 1983, p. 328.
Orwall, Bruce, "Hilton Unveils Marketing Deal with Ladbroke," *Wall Street Journal,* August 30, 1996, p. B2.
Prada, Paulo, "Hilton Group CEO, George, to Leave the Hotel Concern," *Wall Street Journal,* May 8, 2000, p. B14.
Robinson, Elizabeth, "Ladbroke Leaves Less Room at the Inn for Small Operators," *Financial Times,* February 9, 1999, p. 28.
Rudnitsky, Howard, "Second Time Around," *Forbes,* November 14, 1988, p. 47.
Skapinker, Michael, "Ladbroke Plans to Reduce Staff in Reorganisation," *Financial Times,* November 11, 1994, p. 20.
——, "Names Change Problems Remain," *Financial Times,* March 4, 1994, p. 22.
——, "Self-Reliant Streak to Jack of All Trades," *Financial Times,* January 19, 1994, p. 18.
——, "Stein Dismounts but Remains in Trading," *Financial Times,* September 3, 1993, p. 18.
Walsh, Dominic, "Corporate Profile: Ladbroke," *Times* (London), July 27, 1998, p. 43.
——, "Hilton Acquires Scandic in £668m Deal," *Times* (London), April 24, 2001, p. 21.
——, "Recovering Hilton Looks on the Bright Side," *Times* (London), March 1, 2002, p. 31.

—Sandy Schusteff
—update: David E. Salamie

Hines Horticulture, Inc.

12621 Jeffrey Road
Irvine, California 92620
U.S.A.
Telephone: (949) 559-4444
Fax: (949)786-0986
Web site: http://www.hineshorticulture.com

Public Company
Incorporated: 1976 as Hines Holding Company
Employees: 5,525
Sales: $423.3 million (2000)
Stock Exchanges: NASDAQ
Ticker Symbol: HORT
NAIC: 444220 Nursery and Garden Centers Without Tree
      Production

Hines Horticulture, Inc. is a leading operator of commercial nurseries in North America, producing approximately 4,100 varieties of ornamental, container-grown plants primarily for outdoor use. It has 13 nurseries in the United States and Canada and is the largest North American producer of ornamental container and field-grown plants. It is also one of the largest North American producers of sphagnum peat moss and peat-based potting and growing mixes, with 16 peat-harvesting sites. It produces and distributes horticultural products through its two operating divisions: Hines Nurseries and Hines Color. The company sells its nursery products primarily to the retail segment, which includes premium independent garden centers, as well as leading home centers and mass merchandisers, such as Home Depot, Lowe's, Wal-Mart, Kmart, and Target.

1920–76: From Family-Owned Business to Weyerhauser Subsidiary

James W. (Bud) Hines, Sr., a forestry graduate of Cornell University, founded Hines Horticulture in 1920 in Altadena, California. From his father, Hines had learned as a boy to love plants, propagation techniques, and nursery procedures. The nursery remained a family-owned business and moved to the ten-acre Irvine Ranch in Irvine almost 40 years later in 1958. James W. Hines, Jr., who had studied business administration at the University of California in Los Angeles, and Cecil Shirar joined Hines, Sr., as joint owners of the nursery that year.

By 1976, the nursery had grown to 320 acres and incorporated as Hines Holding Company. It was acquired by the Weyerhauser Company of Tacoma, Washington. Weyerhauser, a timber company whose leadership wanted to increase its offerings in the growing industry, expanded the Irvine nursery by another 100 acres and started two new Hines facilities in Houston, Texas, and Vacaville, northern California.

With the Hines family no longer heading up its nursery, however, the company came upon hard times in the early 1980s. Despite revenues of $27 million in 1983, the company lost $3 million. Then, in 1984, Douglas D. Allen joined the business as its president, and with new management, he steered the company to firmer ground. Allen built key elements of the company's infrastructure and designed much of its methodology. By 1989, the company had made $10 million on revenues of $47 million. In 1990, Weyerhauser sold its portion of the business to several of Hines's managers and a private investment group, the Macluan Capital Corporation of Vancouver, British Columbia. In 1992, company sales were approximately $50 million.

1993–2000: Growth Through Acquisition

Under new management, the company embarked upon expansion through the purchase of other nurseries and related companies. An aggressive acquisition campaign led to the addition of 12 companies between 1993 and 2000. The purpose of this strategy was to generate growth by diversifying product offerings and increasing Hines's geographic presence. The first of its acquisitions was Sun Gro Horticulture Inc., a leading national producer of premium growing media and mixes, sphagnum peat moss, and peat products. Sphagnum peat moss is partially decomposed sphagnum moss, a plant whose unique cellular structure makes it highly air- and water-absorbent and ideal for root development. Two years later, the company acquired Oregon Garden Products (OGP), a producer of ornamental, cold-tolerant, container-grown plants and flowering color

Company Perspectives:

More than a company, we are a diverse community of dedicated people working together to realize our full potential and the potential of our company, our customers and the many businesses that are touched by Hines Horticulture everyday. Unified by our deeply held values and shared vision, we provide the leadership that sets the standards and shapes the future for our industry. We believe that there is no greater way to dignify ourselves and our customers than to consistently provide outstanding quality in everything that we do. Never satisfied, we strive to break through the boundaries between yesterday's achievements and tomorrow's possibilities. But it is our heart, our passion and our caring that drives our performance and makes us who we are.

Key Dates:

1920: James W. Hines, Sr., founds Hines.
1957: Company buys Irvine Ranch; Hines, Jr., and Cecil Shirar join as part owners.
1976: After incorporating as Hines Holding Company, business is acquired by Weyerhauser Company.
1990: Macluan Capital Corporation and certain managers buy out the company.
1993: Company acquires Sun Gro Horticulture Inc.
1995: Company is acquired by Madison Dearborn Capital Partners, L.P.
1998: Company completes its initial public offering and acquires Lakeland Peat Moss, Ltd.
2000: *Greenhouse Grower* magazine names Hines number one.
2002: Company sells Sun Gro Horticulture Canada Ltd. and Sun Gro Horticulture Inc.

plants. This acquisition further broadened Hines Nurseries' product mix and brought with it undeveloped acreage for future expansion.

Another significant development in the company's history occurred in 1995 when Hines was itself acquired by Madison Dearborn Capital Partners, L.P. Under Madison Dearborn, Steve Thigpen, who had a B.S. in plant and soil science and a Ph.D. in plant physiology, assumed the role of Hines's chief executive officer. Thigpen, like Allen, had joined the company in 1984, having headed up Weyerhauser's research efforts after it purchased Hines. He also spent ten years as general manager of Hines's Vacaville operation.

As the big box retailers, such as Lowe's, Home Depot, Wal-Mart, and Kmart, continued to grow, spurring consolidation among growers to keep up with their demand for product, Hines's list of acquisitions lengthened. In 1996, it acquired the assets of Iverson Perennial Gardens, Inc. and Flynn Nurseries, Inc. Iverson, located in South Carolina, produced perennial flowers and plants, which it sold primarily to home centers and mass merchandisers in the eastern, southeastern, and midwestern regions of the United States. Flynn produced ornamental plants, flowering color plants, and perennials and was located in southern California.

In 1997, Hines, with yearly revenues of $201 million, acquired certain assets of Pacific Color Nurseries, which produced color bedding plants, and Bryfogle's Wholesale, Inc. Bryfogle's, too, produced color bedding plants, which it sold primarily to home centers and mass merchandisers in California. With the 1998 acquisition of Lakeland Peat Moss, Ltd., Hines gained facilities for the production of peat moss and peat-based potting and growing mixes in Canada and Oregon. Lakeland's products were sold primarily to retail customers and, to a lesser extent, greenhouse growers, vegetable farmers, and golf course developers in the western United States.

The company's revenues for 1998 were almost $235 million. It went public in 1998, raising $56 million with its initial public offering and becoming the only public commercial grower. Unfortunately for Hines, however, the growing industries did not command much attention among investors in the late 1990s, and the company's price per share declined steadily. By Decem-

ber 2000, it had dipped below the $5 required minimum for continued listing on the NASDAQ and was for a time at risk of being removed from the stock exchange.

Hines made three more acquisitions in 1999, Atlantic, Pro Gro, and Strong Lite, and two more, Lovell Farms and Willow Creek Greenhouses, in 2000. Atlantic further added to the company's capacity as a producer of flowering potted plants and annual bedding plants, while Pro Gro and Strong Lite, producers of composted, bark-based growing mixes, added to Hines's other product lines. The company's revenues continued to increase, reaching $277.7 million with profits of $15.4 million, in 1999.

By the year 2000, there were only a handful of companies in the $20 billion growers market that could compete with Hines. The company had more than ten nursery and greenhouse locations and almost 20 peat moss and potting mix sites and covered more than 4,300 acres throughout North America. With the acquisition of Lovell Farms in Florida and Willow Creek Greenhouses in Arizona, both of which specialized in color bedding and holiday plants, the company had significantly enhanced its geographic scope. According to Thigpen in a 2000 *GrowerTalks* article, Hines had reached "critical mass" and set about to reorganize itself internally.

2000–2002: Reorganization and Economic Slowdown

To accommodate the differences between the color business, with its growing period of a matter of months, and the nursery business, with a growing period of years, Hines split its operations into three functional divisions: nursery, color, and growing media. Despite obvious differences, the three divisions had a great deal in common: Thigpen cited the company's reliance on grower teams—"not weeders and waterers and such, but teams who grow the crop and are responsible for crops from start to finish"—in the *GrowerTalks* article.

Hines's revenues for 2000 were $423 million with profits of $12.4 million, 40 percent of total sales from the nursery division, 30 percent from peat moss, and 28 percent from flowering color operations. It was ranked number one by *Greenhouse Grower*.

Yet, although the company was enjoying increasing profitability, its prolonged growth spurt had left it heavily leveraged. After a fire in November destroyed a significant portion of a peat harvesting production facility in Canada, the company made the decision to sell its Sun Gro business, consisting of Sun Gro Horticulture Canada Ltd. and Sun Gro Horticulture Inc. After searching for a year and a half, in March 2002 it found a buyer.

To compound matters, the economic slowdown and energy crisis of 2001 introduced additional difficulties for Hines. It caused a slowdown in sales across the board that led Hines and its competitors to raise prices, switch fuels, and explore alternative energy sources. Hines, still ranked the largest grower nationally for the second year in a row, decided to forego acquisitions in 2001 in order to make debt reduction and financial liquidity its primary objectives. Having abandoned its role as producer of growing media, the company was now focused on its two remaining markets, greens and color.

Principal Subsidiaries

Hines Nurseries, Inc.; Enviro-Safe Laboratories, Inc.

Principal Competitors

Color Spot Nurseries; Monrovia Nurseries; Premier CDN Enterprises.

Further Reading

Ballon, Michael, "Hines Looks to Shed Sun Gro Peat Moss Unit," *Los Angeles Times,* August 14, 2001, p. 2.

Beytes, Chris, "Critical Mass: Hines Horticulture CEO Speaks Out on Industry Consolidation, Big Box Retailers, and the Company's Plans for Expansion," *GrowerTalks Magazine,* July 2000, p. 38.

Henne, Laura, "Top 100 Growers on Red Alert," *Greenhouse Grower,* May 2001, p. 17.

Johnson, Eric, "Growing Gains," *Irvine Spectrum News,* January 22–26, 2002, p. 1.

McCabe, Diana, "California Horticulture Firm Has Growing Sales, Lacks Wall Street Backing," *Orange County Register,* September 13, 1998.

——, "Vine and Dandy," *Orange County Register,* September 13, 1998.

—Carrie Rothburd

Hutchison Whampoa Limited

Hutchison Whampoa Limited

Hutchison House, 22nd Floor
10 Harcourt Road
Hong Kong
Telephone: (852) 2128 1188
Fax: (852) 2128 1705
Web site: http://www.hutchison-whampoa.com

Public Company, 49.9-Percent Owned by Cheung Kong
(Holdings) Limited
Incorporated: 1977
Employees: 100,000
Sales: HK$61.46 billion ($7.88 billion) (2001)
Stock Exchanges: Hong Kong
NAIC: 551112 Offices of Other Holding Companies;
233110 Land Subdivision and Land Development;
233200 Residential Building Construction; 233310
Manufacturing and Industrial Building Construction;
445110 Supermarkets and Other Grocery (Except
Convenience) Stores; 488310 Port and Harbor
Operations; 513320 Wireless Telecommunications
Carriers (Except Satellite); 721110 Hotels (Except
Casino Hotels) and Motels

Hutchison Whampoa Limited, a vast conglomerate based in Hong Kong, has become a force to be reckoned with in real estate, ports, retailing, manufacturing, telecommunications, infrastructure, and energy. As one of Hong Kong's most venerable *hongs* (colonial trading houses), Hutchison began as an importer and wholesaler before diversifying in the 1960s. Bloated and unwieldy in the 1970s, the company (then known as Hutchison International) unloaded dozens of companies, strengthened its bottom line, and merged with Hongkong and Whampoa Dock (in 1977) to form Hutchison Whampoa Limited. Taken over by Li Ka-shing's Cheung Kong (Holdings) Limited in 1979, Hutchison Whampoa soon dominated the world's second busiest East-West trading and shipment ports system; owned substantial property in Hong Kong's pricey real estate market; and held major shares of top performing infrastructure, energy, investment, retailing, and telecommunica-

tions companies. With Hong Kong's return to Chinese ownership in July 1997, Hutchison Whampoa, along with other colony companies, began a new era of corporate life.

Colonial Roots, 1800s to Mid-1900s

Hutchison Whampoa's immense success was in great part due to the Opium Wars between the British and the Chinese. The first round, fought from 1839 to 1842 and easily won by the British, secured the use of Hong Kong and five ports for open trade through the Treaty of Nanking. The second round, from 1856 to 1858, was resolved through the Tientsin treaties that gave Great Britain, France, Russia, and the United States further access to Asian trade through 11 additional ports. Although the resolution of opium conflicts spawned many companies responding to free trade, the two companies that later became Hutchison Whampoa Limited were directly influenced by the Second Opium War and its consequences.

Hutchison Whampoa's roots lay in two of Hong Kong's earliest colonial trading companies. The first, Hutchison International, was established as an importer and wholesaler of consumer products by John Hutchison in 1880. The second company, Hongkong and Whampoa Dock, preceded Hutchison by nearly two decades. Founded in 1861, a year after the Kowloon peninsula was added to China's Treaty of Nanking secessions of 1842, Hongkong and Whampoa Dock was the crown colony's first registered company. In the beginning the company's future was somewhat uncertain; its owner, John Couper, had disappeared during the second opium conflict and was presumed kidnapped and dead.

Whampoa carried on, under new management, with its dry dock operations located on the deepwater port of Canton, one of China's largest and busiest cities and the first Chinese port frequented by Europeans. Four years after its charter, Whampoa purchased its first Hong Kong docks. Linked by the Canton-Kowloon railroad, Whampoa expanded its prominence as a transshipment gateway between Hong Kong, China, and the world. By 1898 when the New Territories (the mainland area joining Kowloon, along with Deep Bay, Mirs Bay, and well over 200 offshore islands) were leased to the British for the next

99 years, both Whampoa and Hutchison International were well established in the area.

Hong Kong, though separated from its erstwhile parent country both geographically and politically, was affected by China's upheavals over the next several decades. The Boxer Uprising (1898–90), the end of the Manchu dynasty in 1912, and the advent of World War I sent ripples through Hong Kong's trading, yet World War II did by far the most damage when the Japanese occupied the colony. Throughout these tumultuous years, both Hutchison International and Whampoa continued their businesses and managed to grow.

A Jewel of the Crown: 1950–79

In the 1950s Hutchison International and Hongkong and Whampoa Dock thrived independently. Hong Kong became an increasingly busy worldwide port despite its small land mass (just shy of 399 square miles). By the mid-1960s Hutchison International was being run by Sir Douglas Clague, who had big plans for the 85-year-old company. Clague began a far-flung diversification program by buying controlling interest in A.S. Watson and Hongkong and Whampoa Dock. The former retailed soft drinks, drugs, and food through supermarkets and drugstores, while Whampoa's dry dock operations had expanded throughout the Hong Kong area. After Watson and Whampoa, Clague caught acquisition fever and gobbled up a myriad of companies in the following years. In 1969 Hutchison entered the property development sector, and in 1973 the firm acquired Park 'N Shop supermarkets.

By the mid-1970s most of Clague's kingdom was crumbling around him, which forced the Hongkong & Shanghai Bank to step in and rescue Hutchison. Pouring money into the company (for what amounted to more than a 20 percent stake), the Bank sent Clague packing and brought in Australian spinmaster "Dollar" Bill Wyllie to turn Hutchison around.

Wyllie lived up to his name and reputation during his tenure and markedly reduced expenses in a few short years. In 1976 he sold off 103 companies; a year later he acquired the remaining interest of Hongkong and Whampoa Dock and merged it with Hutchison. The rechristened company, Hutchison Whampoa

Limited, was in good financial shape and controlled much of Hong Kong's dock activity through its shipyards and container terminals. In 1978 the company went public, listing on the Hong Kong stock exchange under the ticker symbol HUTH. To Wyllie and Hutchison Whampoa's management, the sky was the limit for the revitalized company. Yet despite his profound impact, Wyllie would have a short tenure at Hutchison.

A mere two years after the merger and one year after going public, Hongkong & Shanghai Bank unexpectedly sold its 22.8 percent interest in Hutchison Whampoa for half of its worth. The new owner, Cheung Kong (Holdings) Limited, was run by the legendary Li Ka-shing, one of Hong Kong's richest men.

New Ownership, New Directions, 1980–89

Hutchison Whampoa's acquisition thwarted any plans Wyllie may have had of his own and he left the company in 1981, with Li becoming chairman. Li Ka-shing came to his power and prominence the hard way. Soon after fleeing China in 1940, Li's father died and the 13-year-old was faced with supporting his family. Working for a manufacturer of plastics and watchbands, Li sold plastic flowers on the street. By the time he was 23, he had saved a few thousand dollars, which he invested in his own plastics company. This company, eventually named Cheung Kong (Holdings), became the colony's largest private property developer and was responsible for building about 25 percent of Hong Kong's new apartments annually.

As the 1980s progressed and the Hong Kong-China reunification drew closer (in July 1997), many residents and businesses began to fret about the changes of reverting to Beijing's control. When the Chinese government remained adamant about their sovereignty rights, leaving little room for negotiation, the resulting economic slump affected both Hong Kong and the mainland. To all appearances, however, Hutchison Whampoa was doing exceedingly well, with revenue reaching just over $671 million (HK$5.2 billion) in 1984. That same year China and Great Britain announced a new agreement over the colony's status to quell mounting uneasiness and stop the flight of some 50,000 business professionals per year. Although Hong Kong would be allowed to keep its own legal system and capitalist economy, China, nevertheless, would retain ultimate control of the land mass and its surrounding bays and islands.

Another mitigating factor of the 1980s was the ongoing problem of losing precious land to the sea, making Hong Kong real estate increasingly valuable. In response to the shrinking marketplace, Whampoa's former dockyards at Hung Hom were razed to make way for the Whampoa Garden complex. Mid-decade brought Simon Murray, a former French paratrooper and Foreign Legionnaire, to Hutchison Whampoa's helm as managing director. By the time Murray arrived, the company's Hongkong International Terminals (HIT) unit had become the world's largest privately-owned container terminal operator, helping pump turnover to nearly $705.4 million and income to $154 million in 1985 into the company.

Hutchison began diversifying again in the mid- to late 1980s, this time into utilities (Hongkong Electric, with a complete monopoly on Hong Kong's electric service), mining (the United Kingdom's Cluff Resources), oil (Canada's Husky Oil),

Key Dates:

1861: Hongkong and Whampoa Dock is founded.

1880: John Hutchison founds Hutchison International as an importer and wholesaler of consumer products.

1960s: Hutchison gains controlling interests in A.S. Watson, operator of drugstores and supermarkets, and Hongkong and Whampoa Dock.

Mid-1970s: Hongkong & Shanghai Bank steps in to rescue the faltering Hutchison, taking a stake in excess of 20 percent.

1977: Hutchison acquires remaining stake in Hongkong and Whampoa Dock and merges it with Hutchison to form Hutchison Whampoa Limited.

1978: Company goes public with a listing on the Hong Kong stock exchange.

1979: Hongkong & Shanghai Bank sells its 22.8 percent interest in Hutchison Whampoa to Cheung Kong (Holdings) Limited; Cheung Kong's founder, Li Ka-shing, takes over as chairman of Hutchison Whampoa two years later.

1985: Company diversifies into energy by buying a controlling interest in Hongkong Electric, sole supplier of electricity to Hong Kong, and into telecommunications with the establishment of Hutchison Telephone Company Limited.

1991: Hutchison Whampoa purchases 75 percent stake in Felixstowe Ltd., the leading container port in the United Kingdom.

1994: Telecommunications unit launches digital mobile phone service in the United Kingdom under the brand name "Orange."

1996: U.K. telecommunications operations are reorganized under Orange plc, which is then floated on the London and New York stock exchanges, leaving Hutchison with a 48.2 percent stake.

1997: Li's business empire undergoes a major restructuring, with a major component involving Cheung Kong Infrastructure Holdings Limited becoming a majority-owned subsidiary of Hutchison Whampoa; Hutchison purchases stake in a company that is soon known as VoiceStream Wireless Corporation.

1999: Hutchison sells its stake in Orange plc to Mannesmann AG for $14.6 billion, including a 10 percent interest in Mannesmann.

2000: Vodafone AirTouch PLC acquires Mannesmann, leaving Hutchison with a 5 percent stake in Vodafone; Hutchison sells part of this stake for $5 billion.

2001: Deutsche Telekom (DT) acquires VoiceStream, with Hutchison exchanging its stake for $885 million in cash and a 4.9 percent stake in DT, representing a $3.8 billion profit.

and telecommunications (in Hong Kong, the United Kingdom, and Australia). Involvement in the latter began in 1985 with the establishment of Hutchison Telephone Company Limited, which was formed to launch Hong Kong's first cellular telephone system. In two short years from 1985 to 1987, revenue had almost doubled from $705 million to $1.36 billion and income rose from $154 million to $240 million. By 1989 income had grown to $391 million on turnover of $2.3 billion.

A World Leader: 1990–96

Hutchison Whampoa extended its telecommunications network through a three-way joint venture with Cable & Wireless and the China International Trust & Investment Corporation (CITIC) in 1990, sending the AsiaSat I (a 2,750-pound refurbished Hughes satellite), into space. The next year Hutchison Whampoa was on a roll: the AsiaSat I was put to use for STAR TV, broadcasting to 38 Asian countries (or roughly 52 percent of the world's population) through another three-way joint venture between Hutchison (18 percent), News Corp. (63 percent), and Li (19 percent); Millicom, a U.K. cellular phone company, was added to Hutchison's telecommunications unit (making it the largest cellular provider in the United Kingdom); and nearly all of Whampoa Garden had been sold by year's end.

The company's HIT unit augmented its operations with 75 percent of Felixstowe Ltd., the U.K.'s leading container port, in 1991 and a half-interest in Shanghai's container port in 1992, furthering its dominance as the world's largest privately owned container terminal operator with 65 percent of Hong Kong's container traffic (over 200 container trucks passed through its gates every hour). On the heels of these accomplishments came 1992 figures of $2.7 billion in turnover and an income dip from 1991's $428 million to just under $393.6 million because of a weak year for Husky Oil (whose shares the company had unsuccessfully tried to sell) and continuing setup costs for telecommunications expansion.

With Hong Kong's 99-year lease nearly over and Communist rule looming on the horizon, Hutchison Whampoa, like many companies based in the colony, hoped a solid footing with Beijing would ensure a smooth transition. To this end Hutchison continued to develop joint ventures for mutual advantage, because, as Li diplomatically told *Financial World,* "economic pluses outweigh political minuses." In 1993, amidst a flurry of new agreements with the mainland, Simon Murray left Hutchison because of disagreement over the company's future. Yet it was business as usual, when Chinese officials announced their intention to build the country's largest commercial store ever, with the bulk of its financing (95 percent) coming from Hutchison. When year-end figures were released, the company had ample reason to celebrate: income rose 107 percent from 1992's $393.6 million to $813 million on turnover of $3.2 billion. A good portion of these profits were attributable to the sale of Hutchison's and the Li family's interests in STAR TV to News Corp. for $525 million, a figure that was six times the amount originally invested.

The next year, 1994, Hutchison bought the remaining interest in Felixstowe Ltd., after paying Orient Overseas a reported $75 million for its 25 percent share. The firm's telecommunications unit launched a digital mobile phone service in the United

Kingdom under the brand name "Orange." Additionally, Hutchison entered into another deal involving several Hong Kong and Chinese partners investing $120 million in Shanghai property. As Hong Kong real estate reached a critically limited state, Hutchison increasingly turned to China for lucrative property transactions. Hutchison finished the year with slightly less than $3.9 billion in revenue and broke the $1-billion-mark for income, the majority coming from Hong Kong businesses, 5 percent from Asia, 2 percent from the United States, and a loss from the European group due to the costs of setting up its new telecommunications ventures.

The telecommunications unit got a boost in 1995 with the coming expiration of Hongkong Telecom's monopoly on domestic fixed service networks. Along with two other competitors, Hutchison received approval to develop its own services. In real estate, Hutchison paid $125 million to buy out the Hong Kong Hilton's lease to tear down the hotel in favor of more marketable developments. Though the recently refurbished hotel was quite profitable, the value of its land parcel far exceeded its worth. Hutchison turnover for 1995 was $4.5 billion, up 16 percent from 1994, and income rose 19 percent to $1.2 billion.

In 1996 Hutchison announced plans for a new company, Hutchison Telecommunications (Hong Kong) Limited, to consolidate its telecommunications interests, which included mobile phones, fixed lines, and paging systems. The company formed Orange plc as a holding company for its U.K. telecommunications operations and then sold 30 percent of Orange on the London and New York stock exchanges, reducing the company's effective stake to 48.2 percent. Hutchison also bought back a 25 percent share of its domestic paging business from Motorola. As the company's last year under British rule, 1996 brought downturns in both Hutchison's container terminals and real estate units. Yet by the end of the year ports and real estate were recovering and expected to post satisfactory gains. Hutchison's 168-year-old retailing and manufacturing division, A.S. Watson & Company, continued to thrive in 1996 with a virtual monopoly of supermarket and drugstores in Hong Kong and more in China, Taiwan, and Singapore; and Orange, Hutchison's European telecommunications gamble, was taking hold in its market while a similar service in Hong Kong was expected to rival Hongkong Telecom.

Dealmaking Par Excellence, Late 1990s and Beyond

In March 1997 Li engineered a major restructuring and streamlining of his Hong Kong business empire. During the previous year Li had spun out of Cheung Kong and taken public a new entity called Cheung Kong Infrastructure Holdings Limited (CKI), which held the infrastructure investments in China and Hong Kong of the Li family. Initially, Hutchison Whampoa held a 4 percent stake in CKI, but this stake was increased to 85 percent as part of the March 1997 restructuring. Hutchison Whampoa also transferred its 35 percent stake in Hongkong Electric Holdings Limited to CKI, thereby reducing its stake in Hongkong Electric to 30 percent. Finally, Cheung Kong's stake in Hutchison Whampoa was increased from 45.4 percent to nearly 49 percent. These moves greatly simplified Li's holdings. Cheung Kong remained at the top and retained control of Hutchison Whampoa, which now served as the umbrella holding company for Li's wide-ranging interests in ports, real estate,

supermarkets, telecommunications, and other businesses, including infrastructure. The latter operations were now amalgamated within CKI, which had become a majority-owned subsidiary of Hutchison Whampoa, and CKI was now positioned, just in advance of the return of Hong Kong to Chinese rule, to focus on infrastructure projects in China, where it was already involved in toll roads, toll bridges, and power plants. Among other developments in 1997, Hutchison Telecommunications Limited moved into the U.S. wireless telephone market for the first time with the purchase of a 19.9 percent stake in Western PCS Corporation, which was soon renamed VoiceStream Wireless Corporation.

The diverse nature of Hutchison's operations and the breadth of their geographic reach helped mitigate the effects of the Asian financial crisis of 1997–98, although Hutchison saw its net income fall 31 percent in 1998, declining from $1.63 billion to $1.12 billion. Developments in 1998 included the formation of Harbour Plaza Hotel Management (International) Limited, a joint venture between Hutchison and Cheung Kong (Holdings) that was formed to manage the group's hotels in Hong Kong, mainland China, and the Bahamas and to develop hotel operations in other markets.

Li Ka-shing's reputation as a consummate dealmaker was greatly enhanced by a series of blockbuster deals that began in 1999. In October of that year Hutchison sold its 45 percent stake in Orange plc to Germany's Mannesmann AG for $14.6 billion, part in cash and part in the form of a 10 percent interest in Mannesmann. Then in February 2000 Vodafone AirTouch PLC acquired Mannesmann, leaving Hutchison with a 5 percent stake in Vodafone. Hutchison promptly sold 30 percent of this stake, raising about $5 billion in the process and swelling the company's horde of cash to more than $13 billion.

In the meantime, Hutchison Whampoa in 1999 made a further investment of $957 million in VoiceStream Wireless, in support of that firm's acquisition of Omnipoint Corporation. This increased Hutchison's stake to more than 30 percent. In May 2001 Deutsche Telekom acquired VoiceStream, and as part of the transaction Hutchison exchanged its stake for $885 million in cash and a 4.9 percent stake in the German company, representing a profit of about $3.8 billion on an investment that lasted less than four years.

There were still other developments on the telecommunications front during this period. In November 1999 Hutchison Whampoa entered into a $1.2 billion joint venture with Global Crossing Ltd. to develop a fiber-optic telecommunications network in Hong Kong. By January 2002, however, the debt-strapped Global Crossing had filed for Chapter 11 bankruptcy protection, and after discussions of a possible Hutchison takeover of the U.S. fiber-optic company collapsed, Hutchison bought out Global Crossing's shares in the joint venture. In April 2000 Hutchison used some of its huge stockpile of cash to invest in the next-generation wireless telephone system, known as 3G, which would incorporate high-speed Internet connections and video. That month the firm acquired a 3G license in the United Kingdom for $6.7 billion. Later in the year Hutchison sold 20 percent and 15 percent stakes in the license to NTT DoCoMo of Japan and KPN Mobile of the Netherlands, respectively, for a total of $3.15 billion. Subsequently,

Hutchison purchased 3G licenses in Italy, Austria, Denmark, Hong Kong, Australia, and New Zealand.

Outside of telecommunications, Husky Oil, the Canadian energy concern 49 percent owned by Hutchison Whampoa, merged in August 2000 with Renaissance Energy to form Husky Energy Inc. The new company, one of the largest integrated oil and gas companies in Canada, was then taken public, reducing Hutchison's stake to 35 percent and giving Hutchison a profit of $540 million in the process. In December 1999 Hutchison entered the media field through the establishment of Tom.com Limited, which was initially owned 40 percent by Hutchison and 20 percent by Cheung Kong (Holdings), with the remainder held by other investors. Launched as an Internet portal and taken public in February 2000, Tom.com morphed into a media conglomerate through a series of acquisitions. By early 2002, Tom.com had become the largest publisher of print media in Taiwan, the largest outdoor advertising firm in China, and the dominant player in the sports marketing industry on the mainland. There were other purely e-commerce ventures as well. In January 2000 Hutchison joined forces with Priceline.com Inc. to expand Priceline's name-your-own-price Internet model into Asia through a new venture called Hutchison-Priceline Limited. During 2001 Hutchison and Cheung Kong (Holdings) each purchased approximately 15 percent of the stock of Priceline itself. Then in April 2002 the Hutchison-Priceline venture launched a Priceline-model Internet travel service for Asia.

Despite difficult economic conditions around the world in 2001, Hutchison Whampoa posted a healthy net income figure of $1.55 billion on revenues of $7.88 billion. Having parlayed his investments in Orange, VoiceStream, and other businesses into a huge pile of cash estimated at $7 billion in mid-2001, the 72-year-old Li Ka-shing continued to head up Hutchison and its parent company and to take big gambles. It appeared that Li's son Victor was the heir apparent, but it was far from apparent when the heir might take over from Li, who had often said that he would retire after Hong Kong reverted to Beijing's control. Li was gambling on the Internet and the 3G high-speed wireless system, just when those sectors had grown out of favor, the former because of the bursting of the dotcom bubble and the latter because of delays in the technology's development. It nevertheless seemed foolhardy to bet against Li, who had often confounded the skeptics on his way to building a global powerhouse.

Principal Subsidiaries

PORTS AND RELATED SERVICES: Buenos Aires Container Terminal Services S.A. (Argentina; 64%); Ensenada International Terminal, S.A. de C.V. (Mexico; 64%); Europe Container Terminals B.V. (Netherlands; 76%); Freeport Container Port Limited (Bahamas; 95%); Harwich International Port Limited (U.K.; 90%); Hongkong International Terminals Limited (87%); Hutchison Delta Ports Limited (Cayman Islands); Hutchison International Port Holdings Limited (British Virgin Islands); Hutchison Ports (UK) Finance Plc (90%); Hutchison Westports Limited (U.K.; 90%); Internacional de Contenedores Asociados de Veracruz, S.A. de C.V. (Mexico; 82%); Karachi International Container Terminal Limited (Pakistan; 82%); Logistics Information Network Enterprise Limited (Cayman Islands); Mid-Stream Holdings Limited (British Virgin Islands);

Myanmar International Terminals Thilawa Limited (85%); Panama Ports Company, S.A. (82%); Port of Felixstowe Limited (U.K.; 90%); PT Ocean Terminal Petikemas (Indonesia); PT Jakarta International Container Terminal (Indonesia; 51%); Thai Laemchabang Terminal Co., Limited (Thailand; 56%); Tanzania International Container Terminal Services Limited (63%); Thamesport (London) Limited (U.K.; 90%). TELECOMMUNICATIONS: H3G S.p.A. (Italy; 88%); Celltel Limited (Ghana; 80%); HI3G Access Aktiebolag (Sweden; 60%); Hutchison 3G Austria GmbH; Hutchison 3G UK Limited (65%); Hutchison Telecommunications Argentina S.A. (90%); Hutchison E-Commerce International Limited (British Virgin Islands); Hutchison Paging Services Limited; Hutchison Telecommunications (Hong Kong) Limited; Hutchison Telecommunications PCS (USA) Limited (British Virgin Islands); Hutchison Telecommunications Limited; Hutchison Telecommunications (Australia) Limited (58%); Hutchison Telecommunications Paraguay S.A.; Hutchison Telephone Company Limited (75%); Lanka Cellular Services (Private) Limited (Sri Lanka). PROPERTY AND HOTELS: Aberdeen Commercial Investments Limited; Cavendish Hotels (Holdings) Limited (51%); Elbe Office Investments Limited; Foxton Investments Limited; Glenfuir Investments Limited; Grafton Properties Limited; Harley Development Inc. (Panama); Hongville Limited; Hutchison Estate Agents Limited; Hutchison Hotel Hong Kong Limited; Hutchison International Hotels Limited; Hutchison Lucaya Limited (Bahamas); Hutchison Properties Limited; Hutchison Whampoa Properties Limited; Hutchison Whampoa Properties (Management & Agency) Limited; Hybonia Limited; Mossburn Investments Limited; Omaha Investments Limited (88%); Palliser Investments Limited; Provident Commercial Investments Limited; Rhine Office Investments Limited; Trillium Investment Limited (Bahamas); Turbo Top Limited; Vember Lord Limited. RETAIL AND MANUFACTURING: A.S. Watson & Company, Limited; A.S. Watson European Investments S.a.r.l. (Luxembourg); A.S. Watson Group (Europe) Holdings Limited (British Virgin Islands); A.S. Watson Group (HK) Limited (British Virgin Islands); Fortress Limited; Hutchison Harbour Ring Limited (Bermuda; 50.5%); Hutchison Whampoa (China) Limited; Park 'N Shop Limited; Powwow Limited (U.K.); Savers Health and Beauty Limited (U.K.); Watson Park'N Shop Limited (Taiwan); Watson's Personal Care Stores Pte. Ltd. (Singapore); Watson's The Chemist Limited. ENERGY AND INFRASTRUCTURE: Anderson Asia (Holdings) Limited (85%); Cheung Kong China Infrastructure Limited (85%); Cheung Kong Infrastructure Holdings Limited (Bermuda; 85%); Green Island Cement (Holdings) Limited (85%). FINANCE AND INVESTMENTS: Binion Investment Holdings Limited (Cayman Islands); Cavendish International Holdings Limited; Hongkong and Whampoa Dock Company, Limited; Hornington Limited (British Virgin Islands); Hutchison International Finance (BVI) Limited (British Virgin Islands); Hutchison International Limited; Hutchison OMF Limited (British Virgin Islands); Hutchison Whampoa (Europe) Limited (U.K.); Hutchison Whampoa Finance (00/03) Limited (Cayman Islands); Hutchison Whampoa Finance (CI) Limited (Cayman Islands); Hutchison Whampoa Hongville Finance Limited (Cayman Islands); Hutchison Whampoa International (01/11) Limited (British Virgin Islands); Ottershaw Limited (British Virgin Islands); Strategic Investments International Limited (British Virgin Islands; 87%); Hutchison Whampoa

Europe Investments S.a.r.l. (Luxembourg); Willesden Limited (British Virgin Islands); Zeedane Investments Limited (British Virgin Islands).

Principal Operating Units

Ports and Related Services; Telecommunications; Property and Hotels; Retail and Manufacturing; Energy and Infrastructure.

Principal Competitors

Jardine Matheson Holdings Limited; Swire Pacific Limited; The Wharf (Holdings) Limited; New World Development Company Limited; Sime Darby Berhad; HSBC Holdings plc.

Further Reading

Canna, Elizabeth, ''Deal Links Hong Kong Giants,'' *American Shipper,* April 1992, p. 67.

Chan, Anthony B., *Li Ka-shing: Hong Kong's Elusive Billionaire,* Toronto: Macmillan Canada, 1996, 251 p.

Chowdhury, Neel, ''Hong Kong's Looking Good,'' *Fortune,* December 9, 1996.

Clifford, Mark L., Hugh Filman, and Stanley Reed, ''Li Ka-shing Sneaks Back into the Wireless Game,'' *Business Week,* May 15, 2000, p. 66.

DuBashi, Jagannath, ''Changing the Guard,'' *Financial World,* April 2, 1991, p. 56.

Einhorn, Bruce, and Mark L. Clifford, ''Bottom-Fishing in the Tech Swamp,'' *Business Week,* July 2, 2001, p. 52.

Gilley, Bruce, ''Colour of Money: Hutchison's Sale of British Mobile-Phone Firm Orange Casts Doubt on the Hong Kong Group's Global Strategy,'' *Far Eastern Economic Review,* November 11, 1999, p. 48.

——, ''Deep Water: Beijing Moves to Curb Li Ka-shing's Influence over China's Ports in Favour of Other Players,'' *Far Eastern Economic Review,* November 2, 2000, p. 26.

Goldstein, Carl, ''Stranglehold Loosens,'' *Far Eastern Economic Review,* October 15, 1992, p. 60.

Knecht, G. Bruce, ''Hong Kong Billionaire Li Ka-shing Marshals His Fortune in a Search for Greener Pastures,'' *Wall Street Journal,* October 15, 1998, p. A17.

Landler, Mark, ''European Report Says Hong Kong Tycoon Is Too Influential,'' *New York Times,* October 27, 2000, p. C4.

——, ''For Billion-Dollar Risks, Just Dial Hutchison,'' *New York Times,* July 22, 2000, p. C1.

——, ''Wheeler-Dealer, Tycoon, Trader,'' *New York Times,* August 25, 2000, p. C1.

Mitchell, Mark R., ''Uncle's Tom China,'' *Time International,* March 4, 2002, pp. 30+.

Morton, Peter, ''Husky Oil Put on Sale Block,'' *Oil Daily,* April 4, 1991, p. 1.

''Preparing for China,'' *Economist,* January 11, 1997, pp. 58–59.

Reyes, Alejandro, ''The Superman of Hong Kong,'' *Asiaweek,* August 15, 1997.

Sender, Henny, ''Boardroom Tangle: Hong Kong's Hutchison in Disarray Over Strategy,'' *Far Eastern Review,* November 5, 1992, p. 63.

——, ''Hey Big Spender,'' *Far Eastern Economic Review,* August 14, 1997, p. 60.

Tanzer, Andrew, ''Li Breaks Out,'' *Forbes,* November 25, 1991, p. 100.

Wonacott, Peter, ''Hong Kong's Li Ponders European Push: Deal with Mannesmann Could Spark Telecom Giant,'' *Wall Street Journal,* October 27, 1999, p. B13D.

——, ''Hutchison's New-Economy Bets Pay Off Handsomely for Chief,'' *Wall Street Journal,* July 25, 2000, p. C18.

—Taryn Benbow-Pfalzgraf
—update: David E. Salamie

IAWS Group plc

151 Thomas Street
Dublin 8
Ireland
Telephone: 353 (0)16121200
Fax: 353 (0)16121321
Web site: http://www.iaws.ie

Public Company
Incorporated: 1897 as the Irish Co-Operative
    Agricultural Agency Society Ltd.
Employees: 1,100
Sales: EUR 1.10 billion (2001)
Stock Exchanges: Irish London
Ticker Symbol: IAW
NAIC: 111140 Wheat Farming; 311119 Other Animal
    Food Manufacturing; 311211 Flour Milling; 311313
    Beet Sugar Manufacturing; 311330 Confectionery
    Manufacturing from Purchased Chocolate; 311340
    Nonchocolate Confectionery Manufacturing; 311611
    Animal (Except Poultry) Slaughtering; 311712 Fresh
    and Frozen Seafood Processing; 311812 Commercial
    Bakeries; 311821 Cookie and Cracker Manufacturing;
    311919 Other Snack Food Manufacturing; 311991
    Perishable Prepared Food Manufacturing; 311999 All
    Other Miscellaneous Food Manufacturing; 325314
    Fertilizer (Mixing Only) Manufacturing; 325320
    Pesticide and Other Agricultural Chemical
    Manufacturing; 422510 Grain and Field Bean
    Wholesalers; 422690 Other Chemical and Allied
    Products Wholesalers

From its late 19th-century origins in Ireland's cooperative movement, IAWS Group plc has grown into a leading food group. IAWS has bakery, confectionary, and other food operations in Ireland, the United Kingdom, continental Europe, and the United States. It is the largest fishmeal producer and largest blended fertilizer producer in the British Isles. The group's relatively new packaged foods business, built largely through a series of acquisitions, has been its fastest growing area.

Origins

According to the official centennial history of IAWS, the cooperative movement in Ireland began in the late 1880s with dairy farms, whose products were being displaced by new European methods of making butter. At the same time, the short shelf life of dairy products gave farmers little leverage with commercial creameries. There soon evolved federations of individual cooperatives, which were concerned with both obtaining the best prices for their members' wares and with securing adequate supplies.

Horace Plunkett, considered the founder of the co-op movement, and others created an administrative body in 1894 called The Irish Agricultural Organisation Society (IAOC; renamed the Irish Co-Operative Organisational Society in 1979). The IAOC convinced the Irish Co-Operative Agency Society Ltd. (IACSL), founded in 1893, to focus on marketing butter and dairy equipment. A new organization, the Irish Co-Operative Agricultural Agency Society Ltd. (ICAAS), was formed in Dublin on January 15, 1897, to address the problem of procuring quality supplies, particularly seeds and fertilizers. Plunkett was chairman for its first two years. He was assisted, at first, by three employees. Lieutenant Colonel Loftus A. Bryan succeeded Plunkett in 1899.

ICAAS was renamed the Irish Agricultural Wholesale Society Ltd. (IAWS) in December 1897. Turnover was £14,500 in the first year, and the agency showed a modest profit. Soon, IAWS had expanded its offerings to include hardware, flour, and insecticides, much to the ire of existing local traders. IAWS opened two additional stores, in Galway and Thurles, in 1899. An early venture into cattle trading proved disastrous, and by December 1900 IAWS was insolvent. Plunkett personally bailed out the agency with £2,000. An anonymous donor provided another £3,500 in 1903. By 1905, IAWS was again posting a profit.

In 1907, IAWS allowed its member societies to sell groceries. Irish Producers Ltd., an association of egg and honey producers, joined with IAWS in 1908. The group soon established facilities in Sligo and Enniskillen to package eggs under the brand name ''Karka.'' IAWS established a banking department in November 1910 to give the co-ops access to credit. The group also bought an interest in a ship to transport goods in late 1909, though the venture closed three years later.

A 1913 libel case against the head of the Department of Agriculture, T.W. Russell, who had claimed IAWS was insolvent, won the group no damages but garnered much positive press coverage. During World War I, IAWS worked to ensure a stable supply of food and kept bread prices in its stores at prewar levels. Otherwise, the group's business activities continued to grow, and IAWS set up a number of new departments. Harold Barbour, chairman between 1910 and 1922, helped guarantee the group's finances during this period of unrest and provided funds for a new warehouse. Turnover exceeded £1 million in 1919.

The 1920 creation of Northern Ireland necessitated the formation of separate organizations in Ulster for both IAWS and its sister society, IAOS. In 1922, Barbour resigned IAWS to lead the newly created Ulster Agricultural Organisation Society (UAOS); his place as chairman was taken by Dermod O'Brien, who was also designing the Irish Free State's new currency. By this time, IAWS was losing money as turnover slipped to £700,000. Refinancing was obtained, pay cuts were instituted at all levels of the organization, and preference shareholders agreed to waive interest payments due them in 1924 and 1925. Alongside these setbacks, IAWS benefited from two government initiatives in the late 1920s: new regulation of the creamery industry and the establishment of a factory to make sugar from beets, for which IAWS supplied the seed.

Striving for Self-Reliance: 1930–70

In the 1930s, the Great Depression and the Economic War with Britain curtailed the business of IAWS, its member co-ops, and their individual member farms. After coming to power in 1932, the Fianna Fáil party suspended annuity payments to the British throne, resulting in the Crown hammering Irish agricultural imports with huge duties. Fianna Fáil also placed a high priority on making Ireland self-sufficient, which tended to benefit IAWS. In 1934, IAWS was able to post a tiny profit for the first time in 14 years. In 1939, IAWS began importing Swedish wheat for growing and milling, replacing that previously imported from Canada.

The need for self-reliance was increased by World War II, which cut off sources of many agricultural inputs, such as machinery, fertilizers, and twine. During the war, IAWS re-

searched the domestic production of seeds for a variety of vegetables, and in 1941 formed Associated Seedgrowers Ltd. (ASG) with a consortium of seed companies. Dermott O'Brien died in 1945 and was succeeded as chairman by Thomas Westropp Bennett.

IAWS achieved total sales of £2.25 million in 1950, though it represented just a quarter of the total business of its member co-ops. There were a number of interesting new ventures launched during the decade. In 1956, IAWS began importing sugar into Northern Ireland for Comhlucht Siucre Eireann Teo (the Irish Sugar Company). This venture was broken up in the early 1970s after the latter company took a share in a competing distributor. After the introduction of a 50 percent import duty on stainless steel churns in 1959, IAWS began manufacturing its own. IAWS began operating a fishmeal factory in 1967. The group also started marketing a series of new high nitrogen compound fertilizers for Richardsons of Belfast, which soon proved successful. Beginning in the late 1970s, IAWS produced its own blended fertilizers.

In 1962, IAWS Chairman Thomas Westropp Bennett died. His successor, Owen Binchy, died three years later and was replaced by Ned Wall. Patrick I. Meagher was chairman from 1971 to 1991.

New Challenges in the 1970s and 1980s

The 1970s saw many changes, some good, some not. The Troubles, of course, made living and working dangerous at times. Ireland's entry into the European Economic Community (EEC) in 1973 opened up new markets for the country's agriculture and eventually resulted in IAWS receiving grants to develop, for example, grain handling facilities.

A new competitor, Co-Operative Agricultural Purchases Ltd., had been set up in 1966. However, in 1974 it collapsed under the pressure of a global oil crisis and a bad year for cattle. IAWS turnover was about £25 million at the time, and, thanks largely to rampant inflation, reached £60 million in 1979. However, the organization was losing money again. To help rectify the situation, the board appointed Philip Lynch, formerly of R. & H. Hall, as managing director. The management structure was also streamlined. These changes were led by Philip Lynch, former managing director of Power Seeds, who became CEO of IAWS in mid-1983. IAWS returned to profitability during the year.

Flour producer Boland Mills and the business of Townsend Flahavan, both in receivership, were acquired in 1984. IAWS also started a new venture to trade and export barley. The next year, IAWS bolstered its fertilizer manufacturing base by acquiring a 30 percent holding in Gouldings. It acquired the remaining shares in 1986. Boland Mills was merged with three similar firms—Dock Milling Company, Davis Mosse, and Howard Brothers—in 1987. IAWS was divided into three divisions: Fertilisers, Food Products, and IAWS-Agri Ltd., which focused on producing and sourcing agricultural inputs.

Going Public in 1988

In the fall of 1988, a subsidiary company, IAWS Group plc, was created for listing on the Dublin Stock Exchange. The

Key Dates:

1897: Irish Co-Operative Agricultural Agency Society Ltd. is founded in Dublin.
1907: Member societies are allowed to sell groceries.
1908: Egg and honey producers society joins IAWS.
1919: The company's revenues exceed £1 million.
1934: IAWS posts first profit in 14 years.
1941: Associated Seedgrowers consortium is formed.
1956: IAWS begins importing sugar into Northern Ireland.
1967: First IAWS fishmeal factory opens.
1984: Flour producer Boland Mills is acquired.
1988: IAWS Group plc goes public.
1989: Shamrock Foods is acquired.
1990: IAWS acquires R&H Hall.
1997: Groupe Ikem and Cuisine de France are acquired.
1999: Catering food company Delice de France is bought.
2001: U.S.-based La Brea Bakery is acquired.

recapitalized entity continued to acquire companies. The group bought a 90 percent share in Sheriff & Sons Ltd., an English trader of grain, fertilizer, and chemicals. Shamrock Foods, a market leader in cooking and baking supplies in Ireland, was acquired in 1989. A subsequent investment in the First National Bakery Company (FNCB) involved IAWS in all phases of wheat production and consumption. FNBC launched its Irish Pride brand in 1990.

In the same year, 1990, IAWS took over the R & H Hall Group plc, a leading importer of ingredients for animal feed and a major producer of wheat. Acquiring Hall, which had been publicly traded since 1967, doubled IAWS' size. The purchase was worth IR£42 million. Other acquisitions followed soon after. The group bought another English fertilizer producer, Independent Fertilisers, and later acquired three other makers: John Parsons, Pertwee, and Malton. IAWS diversified by buying Suttons Ltd. and Suttons Oil Ltd., distributors of coal and oil. In May 1990, IAWS made a hostile takeover bid for rival R&H Hall. However, the offer, worth IR£42.5 million, had to surmount regulatory scrutiny, since the combined company would have controlled 62 percent of Ireland's imported livestock grain and feed ingredients.

IAWS Group continued to grow. It acquired the Pertwee and Parson fertilizer business in 1992, and the Nordos fishmeal company in early 1994. The Malting Company of Ireland was added in July. Pretax profits rose from IR£10.1 million to IR£12.8 million (£12.6 million) in fiscal 1994. In 1995, IAWS acquired Scotland's United Fish Products for about IR£12 million. It also completed some important domestic acquisitions: the Malting Company of Ireland, Unifood, and Premier Proteins.

The Irish Agricultural Wholesale Society owned 64 percent of IAWS Group plc in the mid-1990s. Turnover in 1995 exceeded IR£510 million; nearly a third of revenues were coming from the United Kingdom. In the spring of 1996, the Society reduced its ownership in the Group to less than 51 percent, giving the Group better access to capital markets.

IAWS Group bought Master Foods, a distributor of Mars candy bars, in September 1996. The next January, it acquired a stake in its first European producer, buying Groupe Ikem, a French fertilizer company with a 15 percent market share in France. At the time of its centenary in 1997, IAWS had 1,850 employees and continued to grow. Turnover for the fiscal year ending July 31 was £581 million, producing a pretax profit of £21 million. In October 1997, the group made its largest purchase yet, acquiring the specialty bread maker Cuisine de France, which had 2,300 retail stores in the United Kingdom and Ireland, for IR£51 million. IAWS soon announced plans to increase its milling capacity to supply dough for its new acquisition, which was contracting out between 60 and 70 percent of its bread making.

Beyond 2000

Catering food company Delice de France was bought for £35 million in 1999. The investments in convenience foods were paying off; IAWS Group's food division accounted for 40 percent of revenues (EUR 982.2 million) and 50 percent of profits (£30.2 million or EUR 49.8 million) in 2000. The Cuisine de France line was developing a presence in North America, starting with 200 outlets in Chicago. To supply its Cuisine de France line, IAWS formed a bakery joint venture with Tim Horton's, a Canadian doughnut shop chain (and a subsidiary of Wendy's International) that also had a large par-baked bagels business. IAWS hoped the new bakery, built in Brantford, Ontario, would generate IR£108 million in sales in its first year. In July 2000, IAWS bought Pierre, the Irish specialty baking operations of its rival Northern Foods plc.

IAWS' expansion into the United States accelerated with the acquisition of 80 percent of La Brea Bakery, a $20 million Los Angeles specialty baker, in the last half of 2001. The $55 million purchase gave La Brea the means to expand to the U.S. East Coast. Construction soon began on a $50 million plant near Philadelphia.

Managing Director Philip Lynch described 2001 as ''a superb year, our best.'' Turnover rose 12 percent to EUR 1.10 billion while pretax profits (excluding exceptionals) of EUR 59.8 million were 20 percent higher than in 2000.

Principal Subsidiaries

Alba Proteins Ltd. (U.K.; 82%); Boland Mills Ltd.; Coppermore Ltd.; Cuisine de France Ltd.; Cuisine de France Ltd. (U.K.); Delice de France plc (U.K.); Goulding Chemicals Ltd.; Hall Silos Ltd. (U.K.); IAWS Fertilisers (UK) Limited; IAWS Management Services Ltd.; IAWS-Agri Society Ltd.; Irish Pride Bakeries; La Brea Bakery (U.S.A.; 80%); P.B. Kent & Co. Ltd. (U.K.); Pierre's Foodservice Limited; Power Seeds Ltd.; Premier Proteins Ltd.; R&H Hall Ltd.; R & H (Holdings) Ltd. (U.K.); Roma Foods; Shamrock Foods Ltd.; Shamrock Distribution Ltd.; SFP (Shetland Fish Products) Ltd. (50%); Soil Fertility Dunns (U.K.); Unifood Ltd.; United Fish Products Ltd. (U.K.); United Fish Industries Ltd.; United Fish Industries (UK) Ltd.

Principal Divisions

Agri-Business; Food; Proteins and Oils.

Principal Competitors

Associated British Foods plc; Cargill, Incorporated; Kerry Group plc; Northern Foods plc.

Further Reading

Aughney, Jim, ''IAWS Pre-Tax Jumps 20% in 'Superb Year','' *Irish Independent,* September 19, 2001.

Brown, John Murray, ''IAWS in £51 Million Cuisine de France Purchase,'' *Financial Times* (London), Companies & Finance: U.K. and Ireland, October 7, 1997, p. 24.

——, ''IAWS Invests in Canadian Bakery Venture,'' *Financial Times* (London), Companies & Finance: U.K. and Ireland, March 7, 2001, p. 28.

——, ''IAWS Lifted by Growing Appetite for Convenience,'' *Financial Times* (London), Companies & Finance: U.K. and Ireland, September 21, 2000, p. 30.

——, ''IAWS to Raise Capacity for Making Dough,'' *Financial Times* (London), Companies & Finance: U.K. and Ireland, October 17, 1997, p. 22.

——, ''Ready-to-Bake Product Range Fattens IAWS,'' *Financial Times* (London), Companies & Finance: U.K. and Ireland, September 19, 2001, p. 28.

Fulmer, Melinda, ''La Brea Bakery to Be Sold,'' *Los Angeles Times,* Bus. Sec., July 21, 2001, p. 1.

Gill, Joe, ''New Rules Will Fuel Food Companies' Corporate Plans,'' *Irish Times,* Bus. Sec., May 27, 1996, p. 17.

IAWS Group plc, *History of IAWS & the Co-Operative Movement,* Dublin: IAWS Group plc, 1997, http://www.iaws.ie/history/history.htm.

McGrath, Brendan, ''Co-Ops to Cut Stake in IAWS from 56% to 44% in Historic Move,'' *Irish Times,* Bus. Sec., May 4, 1996, p. 14.

——, ''IAWS Chooses Calgary for Site of Next Bakery,'' *Irish Times,* Bus. Sec., January 17, 2001, p. 19.

——, ''IAWS Seeks £100 Million in Sales from Canadian Bakery,'' *Irish Times,* Bus. Sec., March 7, 2001, p. 20.

McManus, John, ''IAWS Exceeds Expectations,'' *Financial Times* (London), October 26, 1994, p. 26.

O'Sullivan, Jane, ''Award Recognizes IAWS's Excellence,'' *Irish Times,* May 1, 1998.

Shanahan, Ella, ''IAWS Seeks US Supplier for Food Brands,'' *Irish Times,* Bus. Sec., January 6, 2001, p. 17.

Shepherd, John, ''IAWS Offers Pounds 42.5m for Rival R&H Hall,'' *Independent* (London), May 9, 1990, p. 25.

Watkins, Steve, ''And Now It's Time to Dish Off Your Firm: Building a Company Is One Thing; Selling It at the Right Point Is Quite Another,'' *Investor's Business Daily,* October 25, p. A8.

—Frederick C. Ingram

IBERDROLA

Iberdrola, S.A.

Cardenal Gardoqui, 8
48008 Bilbao
Spain
Telephone: (+34) 944 151 411
Fax: (+34) 944 154 579
Web site: http://www.iberdrola.es

Public Company
Incorporated: 1901 as Hidroeléctrica Ibérica
Employees: 12,800
Sales: EUR 8.11 billion (2001)
Stock Exchanges: Madrid Mercado Continuo
Ticker Symbol: IBE
NAIC: 221122 Electric Power Generation, Transmission and Distribution; 531210 Offices of Real Estate Agents and Brokers; 541330 Engineering Services; 541512 Computer Systems Design Services; 551112 Offices of Other Holding Companies

Bilbao-based Iberdrola, S.A., with more than nine million customers worldwide, is the second largest electric utility in Spain behind ENDESA. The company was formed after the 1992 merger of two smaller private utilities to create an entity that would be able to hold its own in the coming liberalization of the European Union's power industry. Of Iberdrola's 16,000-megawatt generating capacity, more than half is supplied by hydroelectric installations, while thermal plants, powered by coal, oil, gas and nuclear reactors, make up the remaining capacity. Domestic activities account for most of Iberdrola's revenue, but the company also has established a significant presence in Latin America, particularly in Mexico and northeastern Brazil. In addition, the company is active in electricity distribution in Bolivia and Guatemala and water distribution in Chile and Uruguay. Subsidiary company Iberdrola Diversificación has extended the company's reach by acquiring stakes in multimedia, Internet, and real estate firms; the subsidiary Iberdrola Ingeniería y Consultoría serves outside clients as well as Iberdrola with construction and energy engineering. The company's latest strategic plan, however, calls for growth based on core activities in the power sector.

Early Electrification and Growth: 1901–92

The utilities that eventually united in Iberdrola trace their roots back to some of the earliest applications of electricity in Spain. In July 1901, mining engineer Juan Urrutia led a group of entrepreneurs in forming Hidroeléctrica Ibérica in Bilbao. The company had substantial financial backing from the newly created Banco de Vizcaya and was constituted to exploit the hydroelectric capacity of several rivers in the industrialized north of Spain. Three years later the Martín Galíndez power station, at Quintana on the river Ebro, began supplying electricity to Bilbao. Meanwhile, civil engineer José Orbegozo, at the head of another group of Bilbao-based entrepreneurs, set up the Sociedad General de Transportes Eléctricos with the intention of developing power installations along the international stretch of the river Duero. A third company, Hidroeléctrica Española (Hidrola), was founded in May 1907 to electrify Madrid and Valencia. The new company had close ties to Hidroeléctrica Ibérica, which contributed concessions on three central Spanish rivers and owned 44 percent of Hidrola's capital. Two years later Hidrola's Salto de Molinar power station was operating on the river Júcar and was connected to Madrid by one of the largest power lines of its type in Europe at the time.

After 1918 the Sociedad General de Transportes Eléctricos went through a name change, merged with the Consorcio de Saltos de Duero, and eventually became known as Saltos de Duero. Saltos de Duero continued producing power along the river Duero, as well as opening Spain's first major hydroelectric station, Salto de Ricobayo, on the Esla river in 1935. The other utilities also increased their generating capacity gradually in the 1920s. Growth in the power sector was suspended for close to two decades, however, after the start of the Spanish Civil War. General Francisco Franco began his reign at the end of the war in 1939, marking the beginning of a period of economic isolationism and social instability that lasted through the end of World War II. Against this backdrop, Saltos de Duero and Hidroeléctrica Ibérica merged in 1944, forming Iberduero.

In the 1950s, foreign aid was sent to Spain, industrial production increased, and the demand for electricity grew substantially. Both Iberduero and Hidrola completed several large hydroelectric and thermal power plants between 1957 and 1969, including Aldeadávila, Valdecañas, José María Oriol, and

Villarino. When nuclear technology became available, Iberduero cooperated with another small utility to open the Santa María de Garoña nuclear plant in 1971. The oil crisis in the mid-1970s soon spurred increased nuclear development as Spain tried to lessen its dependence on imported fuel oil. In 1975, the government's first National Energy Plan promoted nuclear energy, prompting Hidrola and Iberduero to invest heavily in new plants. Two second-generation nuclear power stations opened in 1981 at Almaraz and Cofrentes. The Spanish government, however, reappraised its energy needs a few years later and made the decision in 1984 to freeze all nuclear construction due to overcapacity, high building costs, and inflation. The decree left private utilities with a large debt burden.

As the energy sector matured, the existing utilities went through an asset exchange process in an effort to balance their positions in the market. Hidrola took over Hidroelèctrica de Cataluña, a company with a significant presence in Catalonia. In addition, the Red Eléctrica de España was created in 1985 as the owner of a unified national electric system, with the participation of all of Spain's utilities.

Merger and Consolidation: 1992–96

In the early 1990s, the state utility ENDESA, created by the Franco regime in the 1940s, drew attention to itself with a series of acquisitions. The Spanish government, worried that the nation's smaller private utilities would be unable to compete in the coming Europe-wide market, was encouraging ENDESA to swallow one small utility after another. To counterbalance ENDESA's growing influence, Hidrola and Iberduero made the decision to merge. A 50–50 joint venture, HI Holding, was established in 1991 to manage the merger. On November 1, 1992, the union of the two companies became official, and the new entity took the name Iberdrola. Madrid businessman Inigo de Oriol became chairman of the company, and Iberduero's former Chairman Manual Gomez de Pablos became honorary chairman of Iberdrola. The former managing director of Iberduero, Jose Antonio Garrido, maintained his position in the new company. As the European community discussed a restructuring of the energy sector, Garrido tried to ready Iberdrola for a time when large firms would be free to choose among competing power suppliers. He emphasized service and quality, implementing a new incentive-based pay system and a reorganization of the company structure.

After the merger, Iberdrola and ENDESA each controlled about 40 percent of Spain's generating capacity. Iberdrola's capacity was, in large part, made up of hydroelectric and nuclear-powered stations, which gave the company an edge in environmental compliance but also saddled it with a debt burden left over from the 1984 suspension of nuclear plant con-

struction. The company had about Pta 516 billion tied up in unfinished plants. In addition, although the company's generating costs were about 20 percent below the national average, government regulations forced Iberdrola to buy some of its electricity from ENDESA at greater cost. The Electric Sector Planning Bill, or LOSEN, approved in 1994, began the process of introducing competition into the energy industry. An energy sector reorganization helped the two companies balance their positions relative to each other. Among other exchanges, Iberdrola sold Hidroeléctrica de Cataluña to ENDESA in 1993 to consolidate ENDESA's presence in Catalonia. After the first full year of joint operation, Iberdrola reported an almost 12 percent increase in pretax profit to Pta 91.1 billion. At the same time, the company's debt peaked at Pta 1,800 billion near the end of 1993.

Iberdrola became involved with the international power sector shortly after the merger. In 1992 the company entered Latin America with the purchase of Litoral Gas and the Güemes Thermal Power Station in Argentina. Three years later Iberdrola acquired controlling stakes in the Bolivian electricity distributors Electropaz and Elfeo. The subsidiary Iberdrola Energía, or Iberener, was created in 1995 to manage Latin American holdings. In 1996 two Chilean utilities were added to Iberdrola's international portfolio.

Meanwhile, there were positive developments at home. A five-year drought in Spain finally ended in 1996, improving the performance of hydroelectric plants and having positive ramifications throughout the economy. In the spring of that year Iberdrola's debt problem was addressed with a government-backed plan to convert debt into securities through an international bond issue. The move immediately erased Pta 539 billion of debt from the company's balance sheet, and company Chairman Oriol announced plans to continue debt reduction at a rate of Pta 70 to Pta 80 billion per year.

Deregulation and International Investment: 1996–2002

Late in 1996 an "Electrical Protocol" was drawn up that pushed Spain further down the road to an open market. In about ten years, consumers would be free to choose the cheapest power provider. Reforms for the first few years, however, centered around a gradual decrease in electricity rates. The government's policy had been to fix prices based on investment cost rather than on actual production cost. To the base price were added surcharges for distribution, external costs, and a levy to pay for servicing the debt securities related to the stalled nuclear plants. The government now decreed a rate reduction of three percent for 1997 and 2 percent the following year.

Faced with a drop in revenue, Iberdrola cut its staff to around 11,500 from 15,080 in 1992 and reorganized its departments to force them to work more efficiently. Debt servicing costs were also down, since the company's 1997 debt, at Pta 850 billion, was only half of the 1993 peak figure. The cost-cutting measures led to a 4.9 percent increase in consolidated profits for 1997, despite a 14 percent drop in revenue.

Iberdrola also planned to boost profits by entering into a more ambitious international investment program. In July 1997

Key Dates:

1901: Hidroeléctrica Ibérica is founded in Bilbao.
1907: Hidroeléctrica Española (Hidrola) is founded to electrify Madrid and Valencia.
1944: Saltos de Duero and Hidroeléctrica Ibérica merge, forming Iberduero.
1975: The First National Energy Plan promotes nuclear energy.
1984: The Spanish government suspends construction on nuclear plants.
1992: Hidrola and Iberduero merge, forming Iberdrola.
1996: The Electrical Protocol outlines policies for creating an open energy market.
1997: Iberdrola begins heavy investment in Latin America.
2001: CEO Ignacio Sánchez Galán introduces his Strategic Plan for doubling Iberdrola's size.

Iberdrola led a consortium that paid $1.6 billion for a 52 percent stake in the Brazilian distributor Companhia de Electricidade da Bahia, or Coelba. Through Coelba, Iberdrola then took over the energy distributor COSERN. These were the first electricity privatizations in the underdeveloped northeast region of Brazil. Although the region was poorer than the industrialized south, it also had more potential for growth. Iberdrola further increased its global reach in 1998, when the company acquired 80 percent of Empresa Eléctrica de Guatemala S.A. (EEGSA) in an alliance with the Portuguese utility Electricidade de Portugal, S.A. (EDP). In 1999 Iberdrola gained control of Essal, a water company in Chile, and Energy Works, a U.S. company that obtained power for large industrial customers. While it was expanding into other countries, Iberdrola also diversified its operations. Involvement in the gas sector was desirable since the company had plans to build gas-fired plants with combined cycle generators. Accordingly, in 1997 Iberdrola allied with the Spanish companies Repsol, an oil company, and Gas Natural, a gas distributor partially owned by Repsol, to take over two Rio de Janeiro-based gas companies and two more gas companies in Colombia. Other diversification included the formation of a telecom joint venture with Telefonica, the national telecom operator, and the founding of the data management firm Iberdrola Sistemas in 1997.

As Iberdrola branched out abroad, the deregulation process was gaining momentum at home. Beginning in 1998, about 400 large industrial customers were allowed to choose their power suppliers for the first time. Later that year the government determined that the liberalization process laid out in the Electrical Protocol was too gradual and set a new schedule with the effect that by October 1999 about 8,000 companies, constituting 44 percent of Spain's energy consumption, would have their pick of providers. The electricity rate reduction for 1999 also was bumped up from 1 to 2.5 percent. Iberdrola, used to having its customers assigned to it, recognized that marketing and customer service would have to become more important elements of company culture. The company implemented a 24-hour helpline for small consumers and designated teams of employees to draft tailor-made energy plans for large consumers.

As the various entities of Spain's power sector jockeyed for power, rumors of merger negotiations emerged. Late in 1999 the oil company Repsol, which had already cooperated with Iberdrola in some gas-related acquisitions, was reported to be holding merger talks with Iberdrola. Banco Bilbao Vizcaya, the largest shareholder in both companies, backed the merger, but an opposing faction, made up of ENDESA and the bank la Caixa, used their holdings in Repsol to successfully resist the merger.

Iberdrola carried on with its acquisitive strategy. Early in 2000 the firm partnered with the Italian energy group Eni and the Portuguese utility EDP in a deal that won it about 4 percent of Galp, Portugal's oil and gas utility. That deal was followed by the $1 billion purchase of Brazilian electric distributor CELPE, which built on Iberdrola's existing presence in the northeast part of that country. In other advances, the company closed a deal to provide drinking water and sewage services in Uruguay and made an agreement with its Portuguese neighbor EDP to share a fiber optic network on the Iberian peninsula. The planned acquisition of the U.S. company FPL Group Inc., the parent of Florida Power & Light, fell through, however. The deal, which would have pushed Iberdrola into the ranks of the most prominent global utilities, was rejected by the board. More promising developments were seen in Iberdrola's efforts to enter the gas market. In the fall of 2000, the company struck a deal with Eni under which the Italian company would provide gas to Iberdrola over a 15-year period, while the two would work together to create an alternative gas trading company in Spain.

By the end of 2000 a proposed merger, this time with ENDESA, was once again a hot topic. Iberdrola had rejected a more lucrative bid from Gas Natural in favor of a union with ENDESA. Repsol, a major stockholder in Gas Natural, considered launching a hostile bid but dropped the idea due to worries about political repercussions. As talks with ENDESA advanced, analysts calculated that the combined company would control about 80 percent of Spain's electricity market. The government was drawn to the idea of a national energy powerhouse, but nevertheless had to protect the competitive ideal. Government conditions proved to be too restrictive, and in February 2001 the two companies dropped the merger plan at the last minute, unwilling to accept rules that would limit them to 42 percent of national generating capacity. Observers speculated about which other major European companies might be interested in bidding for Iberdrola.

In the spring of 2001, however, a new chief executive came to Iberdrola with ambitious plans for the company to expand on its own. Ignacio Sánchez Galán set the goal of doubling Iberdrola's size over the next five years with investment in core power and gas activities both at home and abroad. Soon after taking the reins, he began bidding for control of Italian, Czech, and Polish energy companies. Galán's "Strategic Plan" for 2002–06 was approved in the fall of the year. It called for extensive construction of combined cycle facilities powered by gas, with a particular focus on increasing generating capacity in Mexico and northeast Brazil. The plan also committed Iberdrola to investment in renewable energy, including wind power, and set the goal of gaining 20 percent of the Spanish gas market by the end of the five-year period. A new Gas Unit was created in 2001 to manage all activity in the sector, and Iberdrola's first eight gas supply contracts were signed that year. By the end of the first quarter of 2002, Iberdrola had achieved a 4.1 percent share of the national gas market and commissioned the first combined-cycle plant in Mexico ahead of schedule. In Spain, the company's construction program for combined-cycle facilities was given a boost with the purchase of an unfinished plant from Enron, the failed U.S. energy broker. Diversification outside the energy sector was receiving less attention as Iberdrola focused on widening its global influence in a range of energy-related activities.

Principal Subsidiaries

Iberdrola Generación, S.A.U.; Iberdrola Redes, S.A.U.; Iberdrola Distribución Eléctrica, S.A.U.; Iberdrola Diversificación; Iberdrola International, B.V. (Netherlands); Iberdrola Energía, S.A.U.; Iberdrola Sistemas, S.A.U.; Iberdrola Ingeniería y Consultoría, S.A.; Iberdrola México S.A. de C.V. (Mexico); Iberdrola Gas, S.A.; Empresa Eléctrica de Guatemala, S.A. (Guatemala; 39.57%); Companhia Electricidade do Bahia, S.A. (Brazil; 42.76%); Apex 2000, S.A.U.; Elfeo, S.A. (Bolivia; 59%); Electropaz (Bolivia; 57%); URAGUA, S.A. (Uruguay; 49%).

Principal Divisions

Generation; Distribution; Retailing; Gas; Renewable Energy; International (South American Platform, Mexico/Guatemala Platform); Engineering & Consultancy; Non-Energy Related Business.

Principal Competitors

ENDESA S.A.; Gas Natural; Hidrocántabrico; Unión Fenosa.

Further Reading

Bollen, Brian, "The Mains in Spain," *Mergers & Acquisitions International,* August 1, 1991.

Burns, Tom, "Repsol and Iberdrola in Venture Talks," *Financial Times,* July 19, 1996, p. 24.

———, "Rivals Thwart Repsol-YPF Takeover Plan," *Financial Times,* November 15, 1999, p. 32.

———, "You Can Please More People in Less of the Time: Spain," *Financial Times,* November 6, 1998, p. 4.

Burns, Tom, and Leslie Crawford, "Iberdrola Agrees to Bid from Endesa," *Financial Times,* October 18, 2000, p. 36.

Deogun, Nikhil, and Carlta Vitzthum, "Effort by Iberdrola to Buy FPL in U.S. Runs Afoul of Spanish Firm," *Wall Street Journal,* April 19, 2000, p. A6.

Dyer, Geoff, "Brazil Power Stake Sold for R$1.73bn," *Financial Times,* August 1, 1997, p. 25.

Johnson, Keith, "Spanish Electricity Providers Call Off Big Merger," *Wall Street Journal,* February 6, 2001, p. A15.

Jones, Matthew, "Iberdrola Takes Aim at a Clear Growth Target," *Financial Times,* October 26, 2001, p. 27.

"Liberty in Theory: Iberdrola," *Economist (U.S.),* August 29, 1992, p. 62.

Nicholson, Mark, "Spanish Electricity Utilities Reach Agreement to Reduce Nuclear Debt," *Financial Times,* June 7, 1993, p. 17.

Taylor, Andrew, "Iberdrola in Enron Purchase," *Financial Times,* April 11, 2002, p. 27.

"Turned Off: Spain's Failed Power Merger," *Economist (U.S.),* February 10, 2001, p. 6.

Vitzthum, Carlta, "As Spain Liberalizes Electricity Market, Utilities Such As Iberdrola Aim to Please," *Wall Street Journal,* May 15, 1998, p. B7D.

White, David, "Electricity Industry: Radical Reforms Ahead," *Financial Times,* May 27, 1997, p. 3.

———, "Iberdrola in Plan to Halve Debt," *Financial Times,* May 23, 1996, p. 34.

White, David, and Peter Wise, "Iberdrola Climbs 12% Despite Weak Peseta," *Financial Times,* March 1, 1994, p. 30.

—Sarah Ruth Lorenz

Idemitsu Kosan Co., Ltd.

1-1, Marunouchi 3-chome
Chiyoda-ku, Tokyo
Japan
Telephone: (3) 3213-3115
Fax: (3) 3213-9354
Web site: http://www.idemitsu.co.jp

Private Company
Incorporated: 1911 as Idemitsu & Co.
Employees: 3,872
Sales: ¥2.56 trillion ($19.38 billion) (2001)
NAIC: 324110 Petroleum Refineries

Idemitsu Kosan Co., Ltd., Japan's second largest oil refiner, is named after its founder, Sazou Idemitsu. The company has a nationwide network of 23 overseas offices, 22 domestic offices, and 7,000 service stations. The Idemitsu group's primary activities are the securing of oil resources, crude oil refining, and petroleum product marketing. The group also has interests in alternative energy sources such as coal, uranium, and geothermal generating, as well as petrochemicals and related fields. The group operates nine tankers and five refineries, which produce oil, gasoline, kerosene, lubricants, and liquefied petroleum gas. Idemitsu Kosan is one of the most growth-oriented companies in Japan. The company is organized as a joint stock company, with all shares held by the Idemitsu family and by the employees.

Company Origins in the Early 20th Century

Sazou Idemitsu began his career selling lubricants in the northern part of Kyushu in Japan, as an agent for the Nippon Sekiyu (Oil) Co. Ltd., and established Idemitsu & Co. in 1911. In 1913, he began selling fuel oil for fishing boats at Shimonoseki port; this business opened up nationwide marketing opportunities. He studied fuel combustion efficiency and promoted fuel conversion from expensive paraffin oil—kerosene—to cheaper raw light oil. In 1923, he became a pioneer of retailing methods by introducing small tanker vessels equipped with fuel meters, thus replacing canned fuel distribution for fishing boats. After his marketing success in Japan, he extended his sales activities to Manchuria. In 1914 he began to sell lubricants to the South Manchuria Railroad Co. Ltd., a Japanese-owned national railroad company that was central to Japan's imperialistic plans for China, and to an expanding market in northeast China. At the time, the supply of lubricants to China was dominated by foreign companies such as Standard Oil, Royal Dutch/Shell group, through its Japanese subsidiary, Asiatic Petroleum Company. Idemitsu & Co. attempted to open up the market for Japanese companies by demonstrating the competitive quality and price of its goods. In 1916, Idemitsu opened the Dairen branch, competing with large foreign companies, and sold lubricants, fuel oil, cement, volcanic ash, and machine tools.

During the winters of 1916 to 1918, accidents frequently occurred on the South Manchuria railroad, as lubricants froze and axles often overheated. In 1919, the railroad company systematically tested the efficiency of every lubricant available and concluded that Idemitsu's product was among the best. It granted exclusive agency to Idemitsu & Co. From 1919 to 1922 Idemitsu established further sales branches in Qindao in China, Taipei and Chilung in Taiwan, and Seoul in Korea. In 1929, Nippon Sekiyu (Oil) Co. established Taiwanese and Korean branches and began direct sales. Consequently, the sales activities of Idemitsu, as an agent of Nippon Sekiyu (Oil), had to be restricted in those areas.

Idemitsu expanded his business between 1920 and 1923 in spite of the postwar recession in the Japanese economy. After 1924 he experienced financial difficulties and closed several foreign branches quickly to protect his business. After 1931, he expanded again into the Manchurian market but with more careful strategic planning.

In 1932, after the Japanese established a puppet government in Manchuria, the Japanese government controlled major commodities and industries. As a result, the functions of Idemitsu were limited to those of a distributor under the controlled economy. By 1939 oil distribution in Japan was tightly controlled by the government and the sales divisions—wholesale and retail—of each oil company were organized into regional distribution associations. Sazou Idemitsu was forced to reduce sales activities. To ensure the safety of his business, he decided to diversify beyond oil sales into transportation by tanker with his first oil tanker, *Nisshomaru*, launched in 1938; oil refining through investment in Kyushu Oil Refinery Co. Ltd.; and other products.

Company Perspectives:

Our corporate mission is to provide stable energy supplies. For the future, we intend to further strengthen our capabilities in manufacturing and distribution, to fulfill our mission to society as an energy corporation.

In 1940, Idemitsu & Co. moved its domestic headquarters from Moji City in Kyushu to Tokyo and established a new joint stock company, Idemitsu Kosan K.K., with a capital of ¥4 million. The Chinese and Manchurian interests were reorganized into separate regional subsidiaries. In 1939, Idemitsu began to build a 100,000-tonnage scale oil tank in Shanghai and imported paraffin oil (kerosene) and volatile oil, including benzine and naphtha, from the United States. After the outbreak of the Pacific War in 1941, however, almost all industries came under the control of the military government, and the activities of the company were limited to distribution.

Changes in the Petroleum Industry: 1940s–60s

After World War II, the Japanese petroleum industry was controlled by the Supreme Commander for the Allied Powers (SCAP). In reality expatriate managers from Standard Oil, Shell, Caltex, Tidewater, and Union Oil constituted a Petroleum Advisory Group that decided Japanese petroleum policies. After the abolition in 1949 of the Oil Distribution Public Corporation, which had been set up during the war by the Japanese government to ration scarce oil, ten companies, including Standard Oil, Shell, and Caltex, were selected as petroleum products suppliers by the Ministry of International Trade and Industry (MITI). Idemitsu Kosan was included in the ten, and it dissolved its longstanding ties with Nippon Sekiyu (Oil) Co. Ltd.

In 1952, according to the peace treaty that became effective that year, the Japanese government abolished price controls on petroleum products and permitted a foreign exchange quota for importing naphtha. In 1951 Idemitsu Kosan was permitted by MITI to build a new tanker, which was launched in the same year. Using his new tanker, Idemitsu imported high-octane gasoline from California and sold it in the Japanese domestic market. Soon, however, the major U.S. oil companies decided that there were profits to be made from selling naphtha directly to Japan, and they began to restrict sales of naphtha to Idemitsu in California. Idemitsu changed its sourcing to Houston, Texas, but soon sales were restricted there also. Eventually, Idemitsu found a supplier in Venezuela. As naphtha sales in Japan by foreign companies increased, MITI felt the necessity for import restrictions to protect the domestic oil industry. MITI, therefore, passed the Oil Industry Law, which restricted the number of oil importers. As a result, only a few foreign companies could continue to import oil to Japan, and those that could were forced to do so through joint ventures with Japanese companies. Soon Japan saw the rapid establishment of its own petrochemical industry.

As Idemitsu was at that time only an importer and distributor of naphtha, his company was unable to import oil because of the domination of major foreign oil companies. It became essential, therefore, for Idemitsu to establish a reputation as an oil importer. The nationalization in 1953 of Anglo-Iranian Oil by the Iranian

government and the resulting friction between the Iranian and British governments were fortuitous for Idemitsu. The Iranian government was unable to find a customer because of the dangerous wartime conditions, until Idemitsu decided to send his large tanker *Nisshomaru* to procure Iranian oil. He managed to secure a price 30 percent lower than the standard market price of the time. The British government was displeased by Idemitsu's behavior, however, and lodged a complaint with MITI. Although Idemitsu's action was applauded by the Iranians and the Japanese public, MITI felt that it had been put in a difficult position and Idemitsu fell out of favor with MITI officials. To protect his company against repercussions, Idemitsu tightened the closed ownership policy of his company still further.

Both the restriction of naphtha exports and the Japanese government's alteration of its policy to favor domestic refineries posed a serious threat to Idemitsu Kosan. Refineries had to be constructed quickly. In May 1956 Idemitsu began construction of Tokuyama oil refinery, which went into operation in March 1957. In 1960, after the addition of a second refinery facility, Tokuyama refinery's production capacity amounted to 140,000 barrels per day.

By the following decade, Idemitsu was concentrating its efforts on constructing refinery facilities. In 1963 the Chiba oil refinery was built, producing 100,000 barrels per day. This was followed by the Hyogo oil refinery in 1970, the Hokkaido oil refinery in 1973, and the Aichi oil refinery in 1975. Idemitsu began to pursue a vertical integration strategy, from crude oil importing to refinery and sales of products. In July 1962 the world's largest tanker, *Nisshomaru III,* was completed, and Idemitsu established the Idemitsu Tanker Co. Ltd. to manage the oil transportation division. From 1962 to 1981, Idemitsu completed ten mammoth tankers—with a tonnage of more than 200,000—and established a worldwide network for petroleum transportation.

In 1963, Idemitsu's petrochemical facility in the Tokuyama refinery went into operation, and the company entered new fields of production. In 1964 Idemitsu established Idemitsu Petrochemical Co. Ltd., which became the center of the Tokuyama refinery complex. In 1962, MITI introduced the Oil Industry Law to control excess production and price competition between petroleum companies. Idemitsu opposed the law because it restricted competition and obstructed freedom of business. In the second half of 1962, Sekiyu Renmei—the Oil Producers' Federation—was organized at the instigation of MITI and began to restrict production. The federation failed to prevent overproduction, however, and price competition resulted in spite of the cartel agreement. Idemitsu stood against such curbing of production, and it withdrew from the federation. In November 1965, the seamen's union struck, the first such strike in Japanese history. The result was a major shortage of petroleum products. Idemitsu disregarded the quota and went into full production. The Oil Producers' Federation and MITI criticized the decision, but Idemitsu continued to ignore the restriction until the strike ended.

In February 1966 price control of petroleum products was abolished, and in August the production quota was repealed. In September 1966, MITI asked Idemitsu to return to the federation. The company did so in October. Sazou Idemitsu became the chairman of the board, although he retained effective control

Key Dates:

1911: Sazou Idemitsu establishes Idemitsu & Co. as an agent for Nippon Sekiyu, a Japanese oil company.
1914: Idemitsu opens Dairen branch.
1919: Idemitsu begins to open sales branches in China, Taiwan, and Korea.
1938: Idemitsu launches its first oil tanker.
1940: Company relocates its headquarters to Tokyo and establishes new joint stock company, Idemitsu Kosan K.K.
1949: Idemitsu is chosen as one of ten companies to be petroleum suppliers to the Ministry of International Trade and Industry; the company dissolves its ties with Nippon.
1951: Company launches a new tanker and begins importing high-octane gasoline from California; company launches Apollo brand gasoline in Japan.
1953: Company begins importing oil from Iran.
1957: Idemitsu completes construction of Tokuyama Refinery.
1962: Company incorporates Idemitsu Tanker Co.; company completes construction of world's largest tanker.
1963: Idemitsu completes its Chiba Refinery; company begins petrochemical operations at Tokuyama refinery.
1964: Company establishes Idemitsu Petrochemical Co., Ltd.
1970: Hyogo Refinery is completed.
1973: Hokkaido Refinery is completed.
1975: Aichi Refinery is completed.
1984: Idemitsu begins producing oil in the offshore field of Niigata Prefecture.
1986: Company begins to acquire coal mining interests in Australia.
1989: Idemitsu acquires partial exploration rights in the Snorre Oil Field in the North Sea and in the continental shelf concession in Australia.
1991: Company opens service stations in Portugal.
1992: Company opens service stations in Puerto Rico.
1996: Japan's oil industry is deregulated.
1998: Idemitsu opens Tokyo's first self-service gasoline station.

of the company, and his younger brother Keisuke Idemitsu took his place as president. This was a necessary step if the reconciliation with MITI was to take place.

Diversification and Reorganization: 1970s–80s

Under the leadership of Keisuke Idemitsu, the company and its subsidiaries internalized such production functions as mining, refinery, and transportation of raw materials, and diversified the product range. In 1976, Idemitsu Japan Sea Oil Development Co. Ltd., established in 1961, was reorganized as Idemitsu Oil Development Co. Ltd. Idemitsu Oil & Gas Co. Ltd. started oil and gas drilling in the offshore field of Niigata Prefecture, beginning commercial production in 1984. In 1987 Idemitsu began to develop an oil field in southeast Turkey with

the Finnish company Neste Oy. In 1989 Idemitsu acquired 10 percent ownership of two concessions of the Snorre oil field in the Norwegian sector of the North Sea. In the same year, Idemitsu acquired 25 percent ownership of the northwest continental shelf concession in Australia and participated in oil drilling operations in various places around the world, including the United Kingdom, Egypt, Gabon, Pakistan, Myanmar, Australia, and Brazil.

In 1977 the company set up a new energy department to promote alternative sources of energy. In 1980, imports of coal from Australia began and the Coal Cartridge System (CCS) was developed to supply coal for small users. The Chiba Bulk Terminal was built in 1986. From this period, Idemitsu started to acquire coal mining interests in Australia, including the Ebenezer mine in Queensland (225 million tons reserve) and the Muswellbrook mine in New South Wales (594 million tons reserve). By 1990 the company had acquired another four foreign coal mining operations—with an estimated total of 2.5 billion tons of deposits—and had become the largest Japanese coal mining company.

In 1979 the Idemitsu Geothermal Development Co. Ltd. was established, and research drilling for geothermal generating plants began in the Hokkaido, Tohoku, and Kyushu concessions. In the Oita project in Kyushu a pilot plant was built. This was an experimental factory plant to examine technological capability and economic feasibility for starting up a master plant.

In the area of uranium exploration, Idemitsu took a 12.87 percent stake in the predevelopment work at the Cigar Lake Project in Saskatchewan, Canada, entering into partnership with CAMECO and COGEMA Canada. As the result of trial bowling—test drilling to estimate the total amount of deposits available—the uranium deposits at Cigar Lake were estimated at 192,500 tons, and mining operations were to begin in 1991.

After 1985, as a result of the "reverse oil shock," the price of oil declined rapidly, and some of Idemitsu's alternative energy resources development projects lost their economic effectiveness. Meanwhile, a debate was brewing as to whether Japan should allow imports of petroleum products. While most of the oil industry argued against inviting outside competition, Idemitsu argued in favor of doing so, as a means of stimulating competition and benefiting the consumer. This pro-competition stance was in keeping with the position it took in 1962, when it resigned from the Oil Producers Federation in protest of industry regulation.

Ultimately, the Japanese government settled on a compromise, which laid the foundation for free importation but placed conditions on it for at least a ten-year period. Passed in 1986, this was the Special Petroleum Law. Further relaxing of oil industry regulations followed through the end of the 1980s, with the government removing gasoline production quotas and making it easier for oil refineries to get capacity upgrade permits.

Deregulation and Industry Restructuring: 1990s

Idemitsu kicked off the 1990s by expanding its service station network outside Japan's borders for the first time. In 1991, the company opened its first stations in Portugal. The following year saw further expansion, with service stations opening in Puerto Rico.

Idemitsu also stepped up its production and refining capabilities in the early 1990s. Between 1992 and 1994, the company began production in its Snorre oil field in the North Sea and its Ensham coal mine in Australia. It also completed construction of a lubricating oil plant in the United States and initiated construction of a new residue-cracking unit at its Hokkaido refinery.

Although the Japanese government had been relaxing its regulatory holds since the middle of the 1980s, its biggest step toward deregulation came in 1996. In March of that year, Japan's Ministry of International Trade and Industry abolished the Special Petroleum Law, thereby opening the door for free importation and intensifying competition, particularly in the gasoline markets. As the industry began to rethink its structure, further governmental regulations were altered. For example, in April 1998, the prohibition of self-service pumps at gasoline stations was lifted. Idemitsu took rapid advantage of this regulatory easing, opening Tokyo's first self-service gas station that same month. The company's second and third self-service stations opened in June and July 1998, in Fujisawa and Chiba City.

Idemitsu proved to be aggressive and forward-thinking in environmental issues as well. The company had already introduced a gasoline brand that reduced benzene content to less than 1 percent in 1993—three years before Japan even passed regulations restricting Benzene. In the spring of 1998, the company also introduced a low energy-consumption engine oil, ZEPRO Mile-Stage SJ.

Near the end of the 1990s, Japan's oil consumption began to decline, as the country felt the effects of a prolonged economic crisis. As consumption slumped, it became apparent that the oil industry was too large, with a total daily capacity that well exceeded domestic demand. This intense domestic competition, coupled with increasing pressures from international competitors, led to consolidation within the industry. In 1999, Nippon Oil Co. and Mitsubishi Oil Co., Japan's second and sixth largest oil companies, agreed to merge. The new entity, Nippon Mitsubishi Oil Corporation, became the largest oil company in the country, supplanting Idemitsu Kosan. Other industry mergers included Showa Shell and Japan Energy in 1999, and Tonen and General Sekiyu in 2000.

Looking Ahead

As the 21st century got underway, Idemitsu Kosan was the only major Japanese refiner to remain unmerged. According to the U.S. Energy Information Administration's April 2001 Japan Analysis Brief, Idemitsu's debt load made it an unattractive partner for a merger. Relief from that debt might ultimately take the form of a public offering, according to the May 25, 2000 *Asia Times Online*. The *Asia Times* quoted Idemitsu's president as saying, ''In order to pursue stable management, we want to be able to tap the capital markets directly instead of being completely reliant on bank borrowing.''

While no further news of an IPO surfaced, Idemitsu continued to pursue expansion opportunities. In March 2002, the company acquired the rights to develop offshore oil fields in Norway's North Sea. It planned to begin production in 2003.

Principal Subsidiaries

Apollo Service Co. Ltd; Apollo (Thailand) Co., Ltd.; Apollo America Corporation; Idemitsu Apollo Corporation (U.S.A.); Apollo Resources Co., Ltd. (Australia); Kuo Horng Co., Ltd. (Taiwan); Idemitsu Petrochemical Co., Ltd.; Idemitsu Oil Exploration Co., Ltd.; Niigata Oil Exploration Co., Ltd.; Idemitsu Naoestu Oil Exploration Co., Ltd.; Idemitsu Petroleum Norge, a.s.; Idemitsu Snorre Oil Exploration Co., Ltd.; Idemitsu Norway Oil Exploration Co., Ltd.; Shigemune Sea Transportation Co. Ltd.; Idemitsu Tanker Co. Ltd.; Idemitsu Oil Development Co. Ltd.; Idemitsu Oil & Gas Co. Ltd; Idemitsu Queensland Pty., Ltd.; Petrochemicals Malaysia Sdn. Bhd.; Calbu Industry Co. Ltd.; Shiroyama Kosan Co. Ltd.; Polycarbonados do Brazil Co. Ltd.; Idemitsu Uranium Exploration Canada, Ltd.; Idemitsu Oita Chinetsu Co., Ltd.; Idemitsu Engineering Co. Ltd.; Uni Chemical Industry Co. Ltd.; Idemitsu Dupont Co. Ltd.; Idemitsu Credit Co. Ltd.; Idemitsu Chemicals U.S.A. Incorporated; Idemitsu China Co., Ltd.; Dalian Idemitsu Chinaoil Co., Ltd.; Idemitsu International (Asia) Pte., Ltd. (Singapore); Idemitsu International (Europe) P.L.C. (U.K.); Idemitsu International-America Latina Industria e Comercio Ltda. (Brazil); Gasolinas de Puerto Rico Corporation; Idemitsu Chemicals Co. Ltd.; Idemitsu D.S.M. Co. Ltd.; Okinawa Sekiyu Seisei Co., Ltd.; Toho Oil Co., Ltd.; Koshin Oil Co., Ltd.; Munakata Shipping Co., Ltd.

Principal Competitors

Cosmo Oil Company, Limited; Japan Energy Corporation; Nippon Mitsubishi Oil Corporation.

Further Reading

Fifty Years of Idemitsu, Tokyo: Idemitsu Kosan K.K., 1970.
The History of Nippon Sekiyu, Tokyo: Nippon Sekiyu K.K., 1990.
''Japan Country Analysis Brief,'' Energy Information Administration, U.S. Department of Energy, April 2001, http://www.eia.doe.gov/emeu/cabs/japan2.html.
Kimoto, Seiji, *Story of Idemitsu Sazou,* Tokyo: Nikkan Shobo, 1982.
Okabe, Akira, *History of Industries in the Showa Era* (Vol. III), Tokyo: Nippon Hyoron Sha, 1986.
A Short History of Idemitsu, Tokyo: Idemitsu Kosan K.K., 1960.
Takakura Shuji, *A Biography of Idemitsu Sazou,* Tokyo: President Publishing Co., 1990.
''Terminal Condition: Japan's Troubled Oil Firms,'' *Economist,* October 26, 1996.

—Kenichi Yasumuro
—update: Shawna Brynildssen

Ingram Industries, Inc.

One Belle Meade Place
4400 Harding Road
Nashville, Tennessee 37205
U.S.A.
Telephone: (615) 298-8200
Fax: (615) 298-8242
Web site: http://www.ingram.com

Private Company
Incorporated: 1938 as Wood River Oil and Refining
   Company
Employees: 6,500
Sales: $2.07 billion (2000)
NAIC: 483211 Inland Water Freight Transportation;
   493190 Other Warehousing and Storage; 524210
   Insurance Agencies and Brokerages

Ingram Industries, Inc. is a privately held Nashville-based company with a broad array of activities. The company is the leading distributor of books in the United States, through its Ingram Book group. Ingram Book's subsidiaries also wholesale videocassettes, magazines, and other materials. Ingram Marine is the third largest player in the inland waterway transportation industry, owning and operating more than 1,800 barges. Ingram also operates insurer Permanent General Co., which specializes in auto insurance for high-risk drivers. The company spun off its computer distribution company, Ingram Micro Inc., in 1996. This is now a separate publicly owned company, though Ingram family members control a majority of the stock.

Roots in Timber and Oil

Ingram got its start in the energy industry, which dominated company activities until the 1980s. Ingram's genesis was an outgrowth of another great fortune. The Ingram family first derived their money from the Weyerhaeuser timber company, which was founded in part by O. H. Ingram's grandfather. With the proceeds from the block of stock in Weyerhaeuser that he inherited, O.H. Ingram established himself as a successful oil refiner in the 1930s. In 1938, he and a partner formed the Wood River Oil and Refining Company, which operated a refinery near St. Louis. Although the refinery was later sold to the Sinclair company, Ingram used this base to branch out into other related areas. In 1946, the company began operating barges to bring crude oil to its St. Louis refinery.

In the 1950s, Ingram formed the Ingram Oil & Refining Company. In 1963, O.H. Ingram died, and the family business was taken over by his two sons, Frederic and Bronson, who changed the company's name to Ingram Corporation. Under the stewardship of Frederic and Bronson, the Ingram holdings grew dramatically over the next three decades. The brothers began by focusing their efforts on the company's inland barge company, which at that time was losing $2 million a year.

To finance expansion, the company borrowed money from bankers who were impressed by the Ingrams' reputations. The Ingrams bought properties that related to their father's legacy of barging and petroleum activities and also acquired a number of other companies based in Tennessee. A year after their father's death, for instance, the Ingrams bought the Tennessee Book Company. This company was a textbook depository for the public school systems of Tennessee.

Also in the mid-1960s, Ingram moved into the insurance industry for the first time, buying the Tennessee Insurance Company. This company, which had been established in 1930, was purchased as an adjunct of the company's other businesses. The Ingram brothers had realized that the extensive physical assets of their holdings and their marine operations required substantial outlays for property, liability, and marine insurance. Rather than give that money to an outsider, they decided to buy a company that would then provide cost-effective insurance for other Ingram properties. Tennessee Insurance not only sold insurance directly to Ingram affiliates, it also reinsured those risks with Lloyds of London and other insurance brokers around the world.

Throughout the 1960s, Ingram continued to expand its holdings in petroleum and related fields. The company acquired assets in oil and chemical trading and transporting, oil refining, pipeline construction, and barging. Ingram relied on its status as a private company to move quickly and decisively in sealing

Key Dates:

1938: Wood River Oil and Refining Company is founded.
1946: The company enters the barge business.
1963: Founder O.H. Ingram dies.
1970: Ingram Book Co. is formed.
1978: Overall name is changed to Ingram Industries.
1985: The company acquires computer distributor Micro D.
1995: Bronson Ingram dies; his widow Martha leads company.
1996: The company is reorganized; Ingram Micro is spun off as a publicly traded company.

pacts. These strengths assisted the Ingram brothers in making a number of important deals with foreign companies. By the end of the 1960s, these activities had allowed Ingram to build the world's third largest offshore company, which it subsequently sold to McDermott, Inc.

New Directions in the 1970s and 1980s

Although Ingram's primary focus throughout the 1960s lay in the energy industry, at the end of the decade, the company's book distribution unit began to demonstrate unexpected growth. After the arrival of a new company president in 1969, the distributor, which had been making about $3 million in trade sales, began a series of innovative programs.

In 1970, Ingram formed the Ingram Book Company to handle the company's trade book distribution operations. Taking advantage of new technologies, Ingram introduced personalized ordering, rapid shipments, toll-free telephone lines, and deep wholesaler discounts. The company took as its slogan, "Remember . . . with Ingram . . . the bookseller comes first," and soon won a host of satisfied customers. In 1972, Ingram Book built on these gains by developing a microfiche system that provided weekly inventory updates to booksellers. In addition, the company later rolled out co-op advertising programs with its clients; a separate catalogue showcasing mass paperback titles, called Paperback Advance; and special procedures for supplying inventory to stores that were just starting.

Throughout that time, Ingram's other divisions were also growing. Early in 1970, the company made tentative plans to sell stock to the public in order to finance further expansion, but those plans were dropped in June. With this decision, Ingram also withdrew from arrangements to merge with a pipeline company. However, in 1973, Ingram did form a joint venture to build an oil refinery in Louisiana with Northeast Petroleum Industries, Inc. This project, which became the largest refinery ever constructed from scratch in the United States, was eventually sold to Marathon Oil.

In 1974, Ingram acquired Tampimex Oil, a London-based petroleum broker with revenues of $680 million. Two years later, Ingram's aggressive pursuit of revenue growth dropped the company into hot water, when the brothers were accused of participating in a $1.3 million kickback scheme to win a sludge-hauling contract from the city of Chicago for its barge line. Chicago had awarded Ingram a $43 million contract for the job

in 1971, which was renewed in 1973, and the indictment charged that these awards had not been subject to a competitive bidding process. In 1977, the Chicago Metropolitan Sanitary District also sued the company for illegal operations.

Despite these legal entanglements, the Ingrams forged ahead with their program of expansion. In 1975, the company formed a joint venture to develop petroleum in Iran. In the following year, Ingram entered negotiations to buy the U.S. Lines shipping company and also began a move into the coal market. Eventually, Ingram came to broker over two million tons of coal annually, most of it to a large Ohio utility. Ingram also became a leading transporter of coal, particularly on the lower Ohio river.

By the end of 1976, Ingram's book distribution unit had also become the predominant American wholesaler of trade books after revolutionizing the book distribution industry. Company sales had risen to exceed $60 million a year, as Ingram pushed ahead with further technological developments and geographic expansion. From its base in Nashville, the company had added an East Coast distribution center in Jessup, Maryland, and had also purchased the Raymar Book Corporation, giving it two West Coast centers. In October 1976, gross monthly orders reached $1 million for the first time.

Ingram Book followed up on these advances by forming the Ingram Retail Advisory Council, made up of independent booksellers, at the 1977 convention of the American Booksellers Association. With the advice of this group, the company set out to develop a computer system for bookstore management, which was unveiled two years later under the name INVOY.

In 1978, the Ingrams rearranged the corporate structure of their holdings, and changed the name of their company from Ingram Corporation to Ingram Industries, Inc. This change better conveyed the increasingly diverse nature of the company's activities. In 1981, Ingram Book branched out from wholesaling to purchase the John Yokley Company, a commercial printer. Despite the success of this division, the Ingram Barge Company remained the largest subsidiary of the company. In 1984, Ingram moved to double the size of this operation when it purchased two U.S. Steel Corporation barge lines. In December, Ingram announced that it would pay $81 million for Ohio Barge Lines, Inc., and the Mon-Valley Transportation Company. In this way, the company expanded its inland waterways operation from Pittsburgh to Houston. In addition, Ingram added the capacity to carry coal, steel, and chemicals to its other barge operations, which moved stone, grain, and petroleum.

At this time, Ingram was rebuffed in its effort to take over the Corroon & Black company. Ingram had offered $253 million to buy the 92.2 percent of Corroon & Black's stock which it did not already own, but this offer was rejected by the company's board. In 1985, however, Ingram announced a substantial investment in its petroleum wellhead equipment manufacturer and supplier. The company changed its subsidiary's name from Gulco Industries, Inc., to Ingram Petroleum Services, Inc., and spent over $10 million to move the company from its position as a mid-sized onshore Oklahoma City firm, serving the middle region of the United States, to an international offshore supplier.

Four years later, Ingram also augmented its barge operations when it bought the marine assets of the American Barge and Towing Company of St. Louis. The company purchased 319 barges and eight tugboats from American Barge, expanding its own fleet by 30 percent. Ingram planned to operate these barges, designed to carry wheat, on the upper Mississippi river. Ingram also announced that it would buy 23 barges and 5 tugboats from System Fuels, Inc. These properties were customized for the transport of liquids.

Despite these moves and Ingram's prominent place in the inland transportation industry, by the end of the 1980s rapid growth in the company's distribution activities meant that they had begun to contribute the lion's share of Ingram's revenues. Over the course of that decade, the balance of earning power within the conglomerate had gradually shifted away from heavy industrial activities toward the distribution of consumer products. The company had expanded its book distribution arm to include magazines and videotapes. In addition, Ingram Computer had been established to distribute computers and peripheral supplies from a warehouse in Buffalo, New York.

Rising As a Distributor in the 1990s

Ingram's move toward distribution got a significant boost when Ingram took over Micro D, Inc., a southern California personal computer distributor in which Ingram had owned a majority interest for three years. Micro D had been the leading player in the personal computer distribution industry, which had grown dramatically in size during the 1980s, from $1.6 billion in sales in 1985 to $4.8 billion in 1989. Micro D's revenues during that time had shot up to $553 million in 1988. Ingram combined Micro D with Ingram Computer and called the new company Ingram Micro D, which was later shortened to Ingram Micro. It held 20 percent of the computer distribution market, twice as much as its nearest competitor. However, the consolidation of the two companies proved somewhat rocky, as the southern California ethos clashed with that of its new eastern owner. A number of key executives left Micro D, and the company lost two major accounts in the two months after the merger.

In July 1989, Ingram made another acquisition in the consumer goods field when it purchased Permanent General Companies, Inc. and made it a subsidiary of the Tennessee Insurance Company. This enterprise provided auto insurance to high-risk drivers in Tennessee and financing services to help customers pay premiums. With more than 40 percent of the Tennessee market for high-risk auto policies, the company planned to expand further into other southeastern markets.

Despite the early management difficulties at Ingram Micro, the company continued to dominate the computer distribution field, and by the start of the 1990s, Ingram could boast that it owned the largest player in both this field and in book distribution. One computer publication reported that 90 percent of Ingram's total income of more than $2.5 billion came from its distribution activities. By 1991, Ingram executives were predicting that the company's biggest arena for growth in the 1990s would be global expansion of the microcomputer market. The company made efforts to establish a beachhead in Europe, starting up operations in the United Kingdom to prepare for broader activities as Europe unified its markets.

In March 1992, Ingram strengthened its distribution operations further when the company purchased the Commtron Corporation, a videocassette wholesaler, and merged it with its Ingram Entertainment, Inc. subsidiary, which also distributed videocassettes. After this merger, the two companies controlled an estimated one-third of the market.

By the end of 1993, Ingram Entertainment's fellow distributor, Ingram Micro, was still contributing a substantial portion of the company's revenues. Overall, the Ingram conglomerate encompassed 54 different units, spanning industries from petroleum refining to book distribution. The complex corporation was held together by the surviving Ingram heir, Bronson Ingram, who was chairman, and the company's CEO, Chip Lacy. Lacy was credited with having pushed the company to invest in state-of-the-art computers and automation. He also argued for taking Ingram public. Bronson Ingram had declared that he would retire from the company when he was 65, which would have been in 1997. But he was diagnosed with cancer and died six months later, in June 1995, at the age of 63. The company had revenues of $9 billion at the time of his death. Ingram's widow, Martha, then took his place as chair of the company. She had previously been involved in Ingram Industries as director of public affairs and was concerned principally with the firm's charitable giving. Yet Martha Ingram clearly understood the company's operations thoroughly, and she proved herself a formidable new leader. She and her four children controlled some 60 percent of Ingram's stock. CEO Lacy asked her to put the family stock in a trust and let him run things. But that was not the way Martha Ingram wanted it. Instead, Lacy resigned in May 1996, and the company split up into three parts. Ingram Entertainment, which comprised the firm's video distribution business, was spun off into a private firm owned 95 percent by Ingram's son David. The two older sons, Orrin and John, became co-presidents of Ingram Industries. This company continued to operate Ingram Marine, the barge unit; Ingram Book Group, the book wholesaler; and Ingram Insurance, including Permanent General. Then Ingram Micro, which was by far the biggest portion of the company, was spun off to the public, though the family retained 75 percent of its shares. CEO Lacy had overseen the growth of this unit, and his resignation before the initial public offering seemed like it could have been bad news. But Ingram Micro got a new CEO, Jerre Stead, formerly of AT&T, in August 1996, and the public offering went off successfully in November. The company's surge of growth over the early 1990s had gone almost unnoticed, as it was in the unglamorous behind-the-scenes business of computer distribution. Ingram Micro also had a very low profit margin, which was typical of the distribution industry. But the newly public company did well. Its stock rose about 15 percent in its first two months on the New York Stock Exchange. By 1997, it was found at number 113 on the *Fortune* 500 list.

Ingram Industries was a much smaller company after the spinoff of its computer distribution business. Its revenue in the mid-1990s stood at about $1.5 billion, compared to $12 billion for Ingram Micro. Most of its sales came from the book distribution arm, which handled about 25 percent of U.S. book distribution by 1997. By that time the company had seven warehouses and was able to offer next-day service to almost the entire country. By 2000, Ingram Industries had seen its sales grow to over $2 billion. The book division alone had almost a dozen subsidiaries, including an international distribution company, and Ingram seemed firmly entrenched as the leading wholesale book distributor.

Principal Subsidiaries

Ingram Barge Co.; Ingram Book Co.; Ingram Distribution Group Inc.; Lightning Source Inc.; Permanent General Co.; Spring Arbor Distributors Inc.; Ingram Library Services Inc.; Ingram Customer Systems Inc.; Ingram International Inc.; Ingram Periodicals Inc.; Publisher Resources Inc.; Retailer Services Inc.; Tennessee Book Co.

Principal Competitors

American Commercial Lines LLC; Baker & Taylor Corp.; Follett Corp.

Further Reading

Carey, Christopher, "Firm Here Sells Fleet of Barges," *St. Louis Post Dispatch,* February 23, 1989.

Cruz, Mike, "Ingram Micro Consolidates," *Computer Reseller News,* November 15, 2001, p. 30.

Faircloth, Anne, "Minding Martha's Business," *Fortune,* September 29, 1997, p. 173.

"The Hungry Millionaires," *Forbes,* November 1, 1976.

"Ingram Continues to Expand Its Services," *Publishers Weekly,* November 15, 1976.

"Ingram: Divide and Conquer," *Electronic Buyers' News*, October 2, 1995, p. 94.

Longwell, John, and Pedro Pereira, "All Eyes on Ingram IPO," *Computer Reseller News,* April 29, 1996, p. 3.

Milliot, Jim, " 'No Ties Between Ingram Entertainment and Book Co.'," *Publishers Weekly,* May 25, 1998, p. 11.

Moltzen, Edward F., "Proxy Reveals Ingrams Hold the Reins," *Computer Reseller News,* April 14, 1997, p. 42.

Olmos, David, "Verdict Still Out on Micro D," *Los Angeles Times,* May 30, 1989.

Pereira, Pedro, "Bronson Ingram," *Computer Reseller News,* November 15, 1998, p. 39.

Redlond, Kristen, "Q & A: The Elusive Man at the Helm of Ingram Micro Parent," *Computer Reseller News,* September 9, 1991.

Snow, Nick, "Despite Down Market, Ingram Will Expand," *Oil Daily,* November 18, 1985.

—Elizabeth Rourke
—update: A. Woodward

ISS A/S

Bredgade 30
DK-1260
Copenhagen K
Denmark
Telephone: (+45) 38 17 00 00
Fax: (+45) 38 17 00 11
Web site: http://www.iss-group.com

Public Company
Incorporated: 1901
Employees: 270,000
Sales: EUR 4.68 billion (DKr 34.85 million) (2001)
Stock Exchanges: Copenhagen London
Ticker Symbol: ISS
NAIC: 551112 Offices of Other Holding Companies;
561210 Facilities Support Services; 561330 Employee
Leasing Services; 561720 Janitorial Services; 621610
Home Health Care Services

ISS A/S runs the largest cleaning business in the world. It has more than 270,000 employees in 36 countries in Europe, Asia, and Latin America. ISS is unusual among cleaning companies in that it maintains friendly relationships with trade unions, and offers its blue collar employees something of a career ladder. The group claimed to reap such rewards as low turnover and better quality service through these progressive practices. ISS looks to specialized areas such as cleaning hospitals and semiconductor assembly facilities for its fastest growth; the group also has a few auxiliary enterprises such as caring for the aged.

Company Origins

ISS grew out of a small security firm established in Copenhagen in 1901. The company created an important new subsidiary, Det Danske Rengorings Selskab A/S (The Danish Cleaning Company, or DRS), in 1934. At first, DRS had 43 employees and just two customers. Then, in 1943, the company ventured out of Denmark and established offices in Sweden. Soon, the group had 2,000 employees. A Norwegian subsidiary, Norsk Rengjorings Selskap a.s., was established in 1952.

In 1963, a cleaning supplies company, Darenas, was formed. The group expanded into Germany in 1965 and Switzerland in 1967. The next year saw the acquisition of cleaning companies in the United Kingdom as well as the Netherlands. The cleaning services business continued its geographic expansion, reaching Austria and Spain in 1971. The same year, ISS acquired part of Servi Systems Oy, Finland's largest cleaning and environmental services group. Soon afterward, ISS began doing business in Brazil.

A Global Group in 1973

The scale of the international holdings of ISS led to a restructuring of the company in 1973. The parent company was renamed ISS-International Service System A/S, and the firm took on a new corporate identity.

The growth of ISS was more than a matter of simple corporate expansion. The company had begun changing the entire cleaning industry, which before had been highly fragmented, carried out by hundreds of undifferentiated businesses and thousands of underappreciated workers. ISS prided itself on its wages and training, according to the *Financial Times*. Moreover, the *Economist* noted that the company's policy with respect to its labor force was designed to enhance motivation: ISS typically sent cleaners out in mobile groups of two or three rather than isolating them at specific sites, thus promoting a sense of pride and teamwork among their employees.

ISS Group achieved consolidated turnover of DKr 1 billion in 1975. The group set up a catering subsidiary in Norway in the same year. In 1976, the ISS Center for Service Management was established near Copenhagen. In 1977, ISS Group shares debuted on the Copenhagen Stock Exchange. The company was also expanding its cleaning operations to Greece.

ISS took a major stake in a New York facilities management firm, the Prudential Building Maintenance Corp., in 1979. This was soon renamed ISS Inc., and by 1987 it had operations across the United States. ISS Group bought out the remaining shares of this company in 1990.

ISS launched an employee stock ownership plan in 1986. A number of cleaning companies in Scandinavia, West Germany,

Company Perspectives:

Since the early years of the ISS Group, our corporate behavior has been guided by ethical values which today are deeply embedded in our corporate culture. ISS does not measure its success simply in financial terms, but in equal measure by how much we fulfil our responsibilities to our employees, customers, shareholders and society in general. ISS was formed in Denmark 100 years ago on the basis of core Scandinavian values—equality, fairness, and openness—in our dealings with people inside and outside the organization. A profound commitment to training and education is another fundamental element of the Group's Danish inheritance.

and the United States were acquired in the late 1980s, bringing total group employment to more than 100,000. At the same time, a number of the diversified enterprises that ISS had entered in the 1970s were sold off. ISS wanted to be the ''Rolls Royce of cleaning,'' Waldemar Schmidt later told *Director* after becoming CEO.

Expansion Continues in the 1990s

ISS entered the Hungarian cleaning market in 1990 via a joint venture. Slovenia followed in 1991. ISS acquired control of Sweden's ASAB Group in 1991, as well as Evon Beheer B.V., a Dutch hospital services company. Expansion continued to the south in 1992 with the addition of cleaning operations in Portugal. ISS also acquired control of the largest private cleaning services business in Finland, Servi Systems Oy.

ISS acquired the U.S.-based National Cleaning Group in 1993 for $93.5 million. This made ISS North America's largest cleaning business, with annual sales of $950 million. With more than 120,000 employees, ISS was also the world's largest industrial cleaning firm. Also in 1993, ISS launched its ISS University to implement new initiatives for staff training.

ISS began trading on the New York Stock Exchange in 1994, five years after its shares were listed on London's International Stock Exchange. The group expanded by acquisition in France and Switzerland, acquiring control of Net Inter and SHT/Hasco, which specialized in the health care segment of the Swiss cleaning market.

ISS acquired ESGO B.V., a large and fast growing support services group active in Asia, in 1995. ESGO had 10,000 employees and turnover of $50 million a year. ISS CarePartner was formed in 1995 to provide services for senior citizens in a variety of settings. This segment of the company experienced its greatest success in Nordic countries.

ISS continued to play a progressive role in labor relations in the mid-1990s. The group supported minimum wage increases in the United Kingdom and showed an unusual willingness to cooperate with trade unions. In 1995, ISS set out to form a consultative works council for its employees, borrowing a practice from the world of manufacturing (and anticipating a European Union directive to do so by September 1996). Such gestures were made in the name of ultimately producing a greater number of clients

and increasing shareholder value via higher employee morale and lower turnover. They also eased resistance from labor unions in the United Kingdom when the group sought public sector cleaning contracts, observed the *Financial Times*.

Waldemar Schmidt, company veteran of 20 years (mostly outside Denmark), took over as chief executive in late September 1995. His predecessor, Poul Andreassen, was credited with building ISS into the world's largest cleaning business in his 33 years leading the company. Schmidt took over towards the end of a trying year. The company had lost contracts in the United States, renegotiated ones in Germany, and pulled out of the bidding to renew a cleaning contract at London's Heathrow Airport when a competitor undercut the £5 per hour wages it paid its cleaning staff by 30 percent. The group risked becoming classified as a subcontractor as full service facility management companies increased in popularity. ISS now hoped to maintain its margins by focusing on specialized cleaning services.

Mid-1990s Scandal and Recovery

ISS's foreign subsidiaries were allowed a great deal of independence, due to the numbers of contracts they had to manage and the localized nature of the business. In at least one case, this freedom was abused. A scandal emerged in mid-1995 involving false accounting practices over a ten-year period at ISS's U.S. subsidiary. This ''great earthquake'' resulted in a DKr 2 billion (£220 million) loss in the first half of 1996.

ISS Inc., the U.S. branch of the business, had to be sold, though it was ISS's largest unit, accounting for 40 percent of group sales. Aaxis Limited acquired it in 1997, while ISS Group took a 19.5 percent holding in Aaxis, which was listed on the Montreal exchange. The same year, ISS Group took its own shares off the New York Stock Exchange and sold off assets such as its headquarters building and the ISS University Hotel. Its Darenas supply operations were also sold off.

ISS Group acquired Germany's NWG Holding, Europe's largest hospital cleaning specialist, in 1998. NWG's annual revenues were about DKr 1.4 billion and the firm employed 17,000 workers. ISS Group's presence in Asia was also bolstered as the group acquired Reliance Environmental Services, a 7,000-employee business based in Hong Kong. Both these additions were dwarfed by the 1999 acquisition of Abilis, Europe's second largest cleaning and specialized services provider, for DKr 3.6 billion. Abilis added 50,000 employees and turnover of more than DKr 5 billion to ISS Group. An incredible recovery had been achieved in just three years. After the Abilis acquisition, ISS had a total of 195,000 employees in more than 70 companies in 32 countries and was a market leader in Europe and Asia.

Eric S. Rylberg was named CEO in an August 2000 restructuring. ISS continued to expand rapidly, acquiring 53 companies in 2000 alone. Larger acquisitions included Klinos SA in France and RCO Holdings PLC in the United Kingdom. ISS also announced a pending merger with Jydsk Rengoring a/s in Denmark and the planned acquisition of Lavold Groep in the Netherlands. Turnover for the year rose 45 percent to DKr 28.72 billion (EUR 3.85 billion). Operating profit rose 42 percent to DKr 1.45 billion (EUR 195 million).

Key Dates:

1901: ISS is founded as a Copenhagen security firm.
1934: Danish Cleaning Company is formed.
1943: ISS establishes its first transnational operation in Sweden.
1973: The Group restructures after global expansion.
1977: ISS shares are listed on the Copenhagen Stock Exchange.
1979: Holdings in U.S.-based facilities management firm are acquired.
1993: The acquisition of the National Cleaning Group makes ISS the market leader in the United States.
1995: The discovery of accounting irregularities leads to the sale of the U.S.-based arm of the company.
2000: Revenues and income rise sharply as company expands and restructures.

100 in 2001

Between 1998 and 2001, the group added 150,000 employees to its existing 115,000 as it acquired more than 100 new companies. The group entered a new market—Japan—in 2001. It was another strong year as turnover and operating profit rose to EUR 4.68 billion (DKr 34.85 million) and EUR 219 million (DKr 1.63 billion), respectively.

Principal Subsidiaries

ISS Europe A/S; ISS Finans A/S; ISS Nordic A/S; ISS Overseas A/S.

Principal Divisions

CarePartner; Damage Control; Facility Services; Food Services; ISS Aviation.

Principal Competitors

Rentokil Initial plc; The ServiceMaster Company.

Further Reading

Baker, Bob, "Most Century City Janitors Decide to Walk Off the Job," *Los Angeles Times,* May 31, 1990, p. B3.

——, "Tentative Accord OKd to End Janitors' Strike," *Los Angeles Times,* June 26, 1990, p. B1.

Barnes, Hilary, "Danish Group to Issue 3m Shares in New York," *Financial Times* (London), September 5, 1994, p. 21.

——, "Danish Group's Clean Start: Hilary Barnes Looks at How ISS Outsourced Its Management Training," *Financial Times* (London), Bus. Education, October 27, 1997, p. 15.

——, "International People: Schmidt Wastes No Time at ISS," *Financial Times* (London), October 3, 1995, p. 22.

——, "A New Broom with the Know-How," *Financial Times* (London), October 31, 1995, p. 23.

——, "Shares in ISS Plunge After US Profits Were Overstated," *Financial Times* (London), May 31, 1996, p. 19.

Carnegy, Hugh, "At a Loss to Explain 10-Year Scandal: Revelations of False Accounting Have Badly Shaken ISS," *Financial Times* (London), August 16, 1996, p. 19.

——, "Cleaning Group Loses £220m After US Accounting Scandal," *Financial Times* (London), August 16, 1996, p. 1.

"Cleaning Up Around the World," *Director* (London), July 1996, p. 17.

Donkin, Richard, "Cleaner Service—Richard Donkin on How One Company Recruits and Motivates Employees in a Low-Wage Industry," *Financial Times* (London), February 22, 1995, p. 13.

"EWC Agreement at ISS," *European Industrial Relations Review* (London), November 1995, pp. SS13 +.

Gavison, Yoram, "Sweeping into New Corners; Until Now, Foreigners Have Focused on High-Tech. But This Week, ISS Bought 50% of Ashmoret—A Janitorial Services Firm," *Ha'aretz* (Tel Aviv), August 19, 1999.

Johnson, Mike, "Unloading Unnecessary Operations," *Management Review* (New York), January 1997, p. 6.

MacCarthy, Clare, "A Sweeping Success at Cleaning Up," *Financial Times* (London), June 8, 1999, p. 15.

Mahoney, Kevin, "A Clean Start," *People Management,* June 11, 1998, p. 31.

Maitland, Alison, "From Dead-End Job to Bright Career," *Financial Times* (London), September 3, 2001, p. 7.

Marsh, David, "Can Europe Compete? Cleaning Up Continental Competitors—Case Study, ISS; High-Quality Cleaning Can Be a Pan-European Business, According to the Danish Company That Leads the World in This Field," *Financial Times* (London), March 1, 1994, p. 14.

Pike, Alan, "A Stronger Emphasis Now on Partnership," *Financial Times* (London), November 18, 1999, p. 1.

"Service with a Smile," *Economist,* April 25, 1998, pp. 63–64.

Taylor, Robert, "Works Councils Go Commercial," *Financial Times* (London), July 26, 1995, p. 12.

—Frederick C. Ingram

Jefferson Smurfit Group plc

Beech Hill
Clonskeagh
Dublin 4
Ireland
Telephone: (1) 202-7000
Fax: (1) 269-4481
Web site: http://www.smurfit-group.com

Public Company
Incorporated: 1934 as James Magee & Sons Ltd.
Employees: 26,751
Sales: EUR 4.51 billion ($4.04 billion) (2001)
Stock Exchanges: Dublin London New York
Ticker Symbols: SMFT; JS (New York)
NAIC: 322121 Paper (Except Newsprint) Mills; 322130
    Paperboard Mills; 322210 Paperboard Container
    Manufacturing; 322224 Uncoated Paper and Multiwall
    Bag Manufacturing; 551112 Offices of Other Holding
    Companies

Jefferson Smurfit Group plc has expanded from its origins in
the Irish packaging industry to become one of the world's
largest makers of paper-based packaging products, including
containerboard, corrugated containers, and folding cartons. In
addition to packaging, the group also has significant operations
in paper bags and décor base paper, which is a specialty paper
used in such products as wallpaper. As of mid-2002, Jefferson
Smurfit and its subsidiaries and associated companies—
including the U.S.-based Smurfit-Stone Container Corporation,
which was 29 percent owned by the group—had operations in
30 countries in Europe, Latin America, and North America,
including 23 paper mills, 135 converting units, and eight wastepaper reclamation facilities. The group is believed to be the
world's largest collector of wastepaper for recycling, with much
of the collected material going into the production of paper and
paperboard at the group's various plants. During fiscal 2001,
about two-thirds of group sales were generated in Europe, 18
percent in Latin America, and 15 percent in the United States.

In August 2002 Jefferson Smurfit shareholders approved a
EUR 3.7 billion ($3.61 billion) takeover of the company by
Madison Dearborn Partners, a private equity investment firm
based in Chicago. If approved by regulators, the deal would also
end the relationship between Jefferson Smurfit and Smurfit-Stone
Container as the ownership interest in the latter was slated to be
spun off to shareholders as part of the terms of the takeover.

Early History

The history of the company began with a young man from
England making good in Ireland. Jefferson Smurfit, the son of a
shipyard worker, was born in Sunderland, in northeast England,
in 1909. His father died when he was ten years old. He became
an apprentice salesman in a large department store at 14; he
once said that life had made him into a little old man by that age.

In 1926 he accepted his uncle's offer of work in the tailoring
business in St. Helens, Lancashire. Eight years later he moved
to Belfast and opened his own tailoring business, James Magee
& Sons Ltd., after marrying a local woman. The priest who
conducted his wedding introduced him to the box-making business in Dublin. The priest had become involved with a factory
there through one of his parishioners. The priest noticed
Smurfit's keen business sense and asked the young man to act as
an advisor. Smurfit saw the potential of the business and turned
his attention to learning more about the technology of box-
making. Meanwhile the tailoring business was expanding rapidly, and soon Smurfit owned four shops. He acquired full
control of the Dublin box-making factory in 1938 and poured
more of his energies into that business, giving up his tailor's
shops and moving permanently to Dublin.

After 1939, when World War II broke out in Europe, the
materials for box-making became much harder to find. Smurfit
was able to keep his business going because he adapted the
technology and his products to meet the demands of wartime.
An example of this adaptation was the production of thick paper
with straw in it for use in Irish schools. Because of the scarcity
of paper and packaging during the war, Smurfit was able to
capitalize on the overwhelming demand. The company concentrated on corrugated box production and had two papermaking

<table>
</table>

Company Perspectives:

Our objective is to sell to our customers products that conform to their requirements, on time, at a competitive price. We will do this by providing the encouragement and means for continuous improvement in our process, technology, products and services. In this endeavour, we are committed to working with the highest standards of ethics in a team-like manner, bringing credit to ourselves, our shareholders and our community.

machines working at full capacity. He had good relations with the trade unions and was proud that there were no strikes. By 1950, his Dublin factory was five times its initial size and producing eight times the original turnover. By this time, the company was known as Jefferson Smurfit & Sons Limited, a name adopted in 1942.

Smurfit's sons, Michael and Jefferson, Jr., were soon brought into the business. Michael, the eldest of Jefferson Smurfit's four sons, started on the factory floor (in 1952), as Jefferson, Jr., did later. Their father insisted that they join the appropriate union. Both went on to specialize, Jefferson, Jr., in sales, Michael in company administration. Michael then took the opportunity to continue studying management techniques in Canada and the United States. After completing his training he ran a corrugated box factory with another brother, Alan, in his father's hometown, St. Helen's, returning to his father's company in 1966 as joint managing director with Jefferson, Jr.

Rapid Expansion Through Acquisitions in the 1960s and 1970s

The 1960s were a period of considerable expansion for the company. In 1964 Jefferson Smurfit & Sons became a public company quoted on the Dublin Stock Exchange. Smurfit acquired Temple Press Ltd., a manufacturer of cartons and boxes, in 1968, and then took its first steps outside its original area of business when, in 1969, it acquired Browne & Nolan Ltd., a printing, packaging, publishing, and educational supply company. The parent company was now large enough to be quoted on the International Stock Exchange in London. Jefferson, Sr., realized that his son Michael should be given more incentive to stay with the company and not become a potential rival. In 1969 he was appointed deputy chairman just as the company began to look seriously at acquisitions beyond the United Kingdom. In 1970 the company doubled its size with the purchase of the Hely Group of companies, which were involved in radio and television distribution, educational and office supplies, and packaging. Also that year, the continuing expansion of the Smurfit businesses was symbolized in a change of name, to Jefferson Smurfit Group Limited. Michael Smurfit brought the corrugated box factory in St. Helen's into the new group. The group concentrated a great deal of effort on its overseas expansion plans. It acquired the British carton making and printing company W.J. Noble and Sons in 1972. A year later its purchase of the print and packaging division of the U.K. firm Tremletts Ltd. brought plants in the United Kingdom and in Nigeria into the group. But the American market proved to be the most

lucrative of its overseas ventures. Its 40 percent investment in the paper and plastic manufacturing firm Time Industries Inc. of Chicago, in 1974, gave it a foothold in the United States. It increased this initial investment to 100 percent in 1977.

Jefferson Smurfit, Sr., died in 1977, at the age of 68. Michael succeeded him as chairman and Jefferson, Jr., took over as deputy chairman. Their younger brothers moved up too, Alan to head U.K. sales and Dermot Smurfit to become managing director of the paper and board division. Their father left them a company that was beginning to diversify and internationalize itself in earnest yet continuing to lay stress on its base in Jefferson, Sr.'s adopted homeland.

In 1968 Jefferson, Sr., had seen the acquisition of Temple Press as an act of faith in the future of the Irish economy. The new chairman did not abandon this faith. The group carried on investing in Ireland, by acquiring, for example, Irish Paper Sacks Ltd.; Goulding Industries Ltd., maker of plastic film and sacks; and half the equity of the Eagle Printing Company Ltd. The more companies Jefferson Smurfit acquired, the more raw materials it needed. It decided to sell 49 percent of its corrugated box interests in Ireland and the United Kingdom to the Swedish paper company Svenska Cellulosa Aktiebolaget in return for a guaranteed supply of kraftliner. The sale also provided cash for further expansion abroad. Jefferson Smurfit acquired 51 percent of the Australian company Mistral Plastics Pty Ltd. in 1978. In 1979, it paid $13 million for a 27 percent share of the Alton Box Board Company. At the time this was the largest investment by an Irish company in the U.S. economy. It increased to 51 percent five months later.

U.S. Investments Highlighting 1980s Acquisitions

The Jefferson Smurfit Group established itself as a major supplier of print and packaging in the United States in the 1980s. In Ireland it bought a small stake in the Woodfab group, the largest user of native timber and a significant presence in the Irish forestry sector. But Smurfit saw its greatest potential in the U.S. market, where there have never been tight restrictions on foreign ownership or investment. Smurfit's method, a relatively cautious one, was to purchase a minority holding of a U.S. company, observe its profits rising, and then move to 100 percent ownership. Thus the 27 percent holding in the Alton Box Board Company, acquired in 1979, formed the bridgehead for complete acquisition in 1981. In a variation on the same technique, in 1982 Smurfit formed a 50–50 joint venture to take over the packaging and graphic arts divisions of Diamond International, then bought out the partner's shares to gain full control in 1983.

Clearly, the group's long-term strategy of becoming an international competitor was coming closer to realization, and Michael Smurfit was earning his reputation as a canny businessman. In 1983 shares in the U.S. wing of the group, the Jefferson Smurfit Corporation, were floated on the market, generating $46 million for further investment. The group then decided to expand into a new area of business, setting up a joint venture with Banque Paribas, known as Smurfit Paribas Bank Ltd. Jefferson Smurfit, Jr., left the group in 1984, because of ill health, and his two younger brothers were appointed joint deputy chairmen. The following year, the 50th since the company's founding, was

Key Dates:

1934: Jefferson Smurfit opens a tailoring business, James Magee & Sons Ltd., and soon becomes involved in a box-making factory in Dublin.
1938: Smurfit gains control of the box-making factory and exits from tailoring.
1942: Company name is changed to Jefferson Smurfit & Sons Limited.
1964: Company goes public with a listing on the Dublin Stock Exchange.
1968: Temple Press Ltd. is acquired.
1969: Company acquires Browne & Nolan Ltd.
1970: Size of company doubles with purchase of the Hely Group of companies; company is renamed Jefferson Smurfit Group Limited.
1974: Company ventures into the U.S. market for the first time with the purchase of a 40 percent stake in Chicago-based Time Industries.
1977: Smurfit dies and is succeeded by his eldest son, Michael.
1981: Company completes its takeover of U.S.-based Alton Box Board Company.
1983: Bulk of U.S. interests are reorganized within Jefferson Smurfit Corporation (JSC).

1985: Jefferson Smurfit Group is re-registered as a public limited company.
1986: In a joint venture with Morgan Stanley Leveraged Equity Fund, the firm acquires Container Corporation of America (CCA).
1987: The manufacturing operations of CCA on the European continent and in Venezuela are acquired.
1994: JSC is taken public, with the group retaining a 46.5 percent stake; company acquires Cellulose du Pin, the paper and packaging unit of France's Compagnie de Saint-Gobain.
1998: JSC and Stone Container Corporation merge to form Smurfit-Stone Container Corporation; following the merger, Jefferson Smurfit Group holds a 33 percent interest in Smurfit-Stone.
2000: Smurfit-Stone acquires St. Laurent Paperboard Inc., reducing Jefferson Smurfit's stake in Smurfit-Stone to 29.5 percent.
2002: Jefferson Smurfit agrees to be taken over by Madison Dearborn Partners, with the deal including the spinoff of the stake in Smurfit-Stone to shareholders.

marked by re-registration as a public limited company. After achieving considerable success in its purchases of packaging companies, Smurfit acquired the Publishers Paper Company, based in Oregon, in 1986. This company supplied newsprint to such well-known papers as the *Los Angeles Times.* It was renamed Smurfit Newsprint Corporation and continued to supply several newspapers. The same year, in its largest deal yet, Smurfit set up a joint venture with Morgan Stanley Leveraged Equity Fund to pay Mobil $1.2 billion for its subsidiary, Container Corporation of America (CCA), which produced paperboard and packaging, and in 1987 it purchased outright the manufacturing operations of CCA on the European continent and in Venezuela. The group thus more than doubled the value of its U.S. holdings and moved into manufacturing in mainland Europe for the first time.

The second half of 1987 was a difficult time for the Smurfit family. First, Jefferson Smurfit, Jr., died at the age of 50. He had contributed a great deal to the group's expansion through his expertise in sales and marketing. Then, like many other companies, Smurfit lost an enormous amount of value in the stock market crash in October. The value of its shares fell by more than half, but since demand for paper products remained steady it was just a question of riding out the storm.

In 1988, Dublin marked its millennium as a city, and Jefferson Smurfit Group, with its strong ties to the Irish capital, played a part in the celebrations by donating the Anna Livia Fountain in memory of Jefferson Smurfit, Sr. Anna Livia, symbolizing the River Liffey flowing through the city to the sea, is a leading character in James Joyce's novel *Finnegan's Wake.* The group also contributed to the restoration of the Mansion House, the residence of the lord mayor of Dublin, and sponsored a Millennium Science Scholarship, to be awarded to a doctoral

student specializing in high technology. Other Smurfit activities in 1988 included the establishment of Smurfit Natural Resources to continue its own private afforestation program in Ireland and the purchase of the Spanish packaging firm Industrial Cartonera, as well as 30 percent of Papelera Navarra, also based in Spain. Adding to these a 35 percent stake in Inpacsa, in 1989, gave the group interests in four paper mills, eight corrugated box plants, and 20 percent of the paper and packaging market in Spain.

In 1989 the group's publishing division grew with the launch of a new weekly newspaper, the *Irish Voice,* in the United States, where it also had an interest in the magazine *Irish America.* The *Irish Post* in the United Kingdom increased its circulation and Smurfit Print in Ireland produced more computer manuals. In the United States, an industrial dispute at Smurfit Newsprint Corporation lasted more than seven months and cost the company about $25 million in profits. The group was also affected by lengthy strikes in the packaging industry in Italy. Latin American operations were slowly expanding. Smurfit Carton de Colombia and Smurfit de Venezuela put much effort into researching and developing the genetic enhancement of eucalyptus trees. Researchers believed that eucalyptus trees could be harvested in five years rather than the normal eight years. This was done by clonal reproduction, producing the fastest growing commercial trees in the world, from which a good quality uniform pulp can be manufactured. The Colombian company also produced writing paper, using a mix of different species of hardwood found in the tropical forests. By 1989, Smurfit Latin America had substantially more than 20 percent of the paper and board market in Venezuela and Colombia. The Latin American companies in the group provided opportunities for further education to their employees. In Colombia, for example, the company offered training in farm and forest tending as well as elementary schooling for children in the country areas near Smurfit timberland.

In 1989 the group made heavy use of junk bonds to restructure its U.S. operations, which had accounted for about 65 percent of its profits in 1988. A 50–50 joint venture between the Smurfit group and the Morgan Stanley Leveraged Equity Fund created a new private holding company, SIBV/MS Holdings, for most of the group's subsidiaries in the United States. The reorganization, which included the repurchasing of the minority stake in Jefferson Smurfit Corporation that had been publicly held, generated $1.25 billion and boosted the value of the group's shares by 50 percent. The group next decided to continue to expand north of the U.S. border, and it purchased 30 percent of PCL Industries Ltd., a Canadian company specializing in the conversion of plastics, with its own interests in the United States. The group also formed a partnership with the Canadian firm Tembec, Inc. to build a bleached lightweight coated mill in Quebec. Meanwhile, Smurfit International, the European division of the group, added to its operations the German company C.D. Haupt, a major paper-recycling mill, placing Smurfit in a strong position to profit from new opportunities in reunited Germany and in Eastern Europe. More Italian firms such as Ondulato Imolese, an integrated corrugated manufacturer, and Euronda, producer of corrugated cases and sheets, also joined the group.

By 1990 Jefferson Smurfit Group had established itself as the largest gatherer and consumer of wastepaper in the world, and it completed the purchase of Golden State Newsprint Co. Inc., which was renamed Smurfit Newsprint Corporation of California, and Pacific Recycling Co. Inc. As environmental awareness became commercially viable the group began to build up its recycling division by acquiring several existing units and announcing its intention to invest in a newsprint production unit, using scrap paper, in New York state.

In the United States, as in Latin America, Smurfit tried to involve itself within the community. It provided special programs for its employees, such as training at the Smurfit Technical Institute, and sponsored young children in Fernandina Beach's Literacy Program. In Ireland, too, some of the Irish universities were endowed with chairs and financial support for academic projects, of which the leading example was the Michael Smurfit School of Business at University College, Dublin.

By the beginning of the 1990s the Smurfit Group was producing a diversity of goods, from presentation boxes for Waterford crystal to takeout pizza boxes, and it continued to diversify further. It formed Nokia Smurfit Ltd. in a joint venture with Nokia Consumer Electronics, which distributes television, video recorders, and satellite equipment in Ireland and is a division of the Finnish company Oy Nokia Ab. It bought back its 49 percent interest in Smurfit Corrugated Ireland from Svenska Cellulosa and bought another 24.5 percent of U.K. Corrugated, boosting its ownership to 50 percent. One of its subsidiaries in the United Kingdom bought Texboard, a manufacturer of paper tubes. The group aimed to extend its already diversified board manufacturing and conversion business. It also purchased another U.K. firm, Townsend Hook, a leading producer of corrugated paper cases and coated papers, which gave Smurfit more than 20 percent of the corrugated case industry in Britain.

In 1991 Jefferson Smurfit added to its recycling business with the acquisition of several French companies, such as Centre de Dechets Industriels Group (CDI), the second largest wastepaper company in France, and the Compagnie Generale de Cartons Ondules, an integrated mill and converting operation. In addition, it bought the Lestrem Group, which specialized in manufacturing solid board, accounting for about 20 percent of the market in France. It also set up a new subsidiary, Smurfit France.

The Smurfit Group carried diversification still further by deciding to invest in the leisure business in Ireland. Its activity in this area included the RiverView Racquet and Fitness Club, Waterford Castle Golf and Country Club, and the new development of the Kildare Hotel and Country Club.

Major Mid-1990s Acquisitions in Europe

In the mid-1990s Jefferson Smurfit turned to Continental Europe for acquisitions, beginning with France. In a deal that doubled the company's European operations, Jefferson Smurfit in late 1994 purchased the paper and packaging unit, Cellulose du Pin, of France's Compagnie de Saint-Gobain for IR£682 million ($1.02 billion). Cellulose du Pin brought with it operations in France, Italy, Spain, and Belgium and manufactured recycled paper, corrugated boxes, coated wood-free paper, and paper bags. Following the acquisition, Jefferson Smurfit assumed the top position in the European corrugated industry.

To help fund the purchase, the company turned to its U.S. operation, taking it public once again, with Jefferson Smurfit Corporation (JSC) reemerging as a public company. About IR£155 million ($248 million) was raised through the offering, after which the Jefferson Smurfit Group retained a 46.5 percent stake in JSC.

Additional European acquisitions quickly followed that of Cellulose du Pin. In May 1995 Jefferson Smurfit paid FFr 452 million for Les Papeteries du Limousin of France, an independent corrugated packaging firm with capacity of 220,000 metric tons of recycled containerboard. The purchase enabled Jefferson Smurfit to cancel plans to build a new mill in France. The following month saw the company make its first move into Scandinavia, with the IR£68 million ($109 million) purchase of a 29 percent stake in Munksjö AB, a Swedish producer of bleached pulp, specialty papers, and board. Also acquired in 1995 was a 27.5 percent stake in Austria-based Nettingsdorfer Beteilgungs AG, a producer of paper and board, with interests in corrugated container operations.

These 1995 moves, coupled with the 1994 acquisition of Cellulose du Pin, meant that Jefferson Smurfit had quadrupled its Continental European operations in less than two years. Further, Continental Europe had become the Jefferson Smurfit Group region generating the most revenue, surpassing the Ireland/U.K. region for the first time.

Always looking for new opportunities, Jefferson Smurfit made a few inroads into Asia in 1995. In May Jefferson Smurfit Corporation formed a joint venture in China, which soon thereafter bought a controlling interest in a linerboard mill near Shanghai. In December Jefferson Smurfit Group formed a joint venture, called Smurfit Toyo, with the New Toyo Group of Singapore. Smurfit Toyo planned initially to manufacture folding cartons in Singapore, Hong Kong, and China. Jefferson Smurfit's approach to Asia was clearly a cautious one, though the company had a long-term goal of being an important player in the region.

Jefferson Smurfit's pace of acquisition slowed in 1996 and 1997 as the industry entered another of its cyclical downturns complete with overcapacity and the concomitant depressed prices. Revenues and profits fell significantly both years. During 1997 the company did complete some smaller deals. It purchased majority ownership of two Argentinean companies—Celulosa de Coronel Suarez, S.A., maker of paperboard, and Asindus, S.A., producer of corrugated cases—and acquired outright two German producers of corrugated boxes and board: Wellit GmbH Wellpapenfabrik and Schneverdinger Wellpappenwerk GmbH & Co. KG.

Late 1990s Creation of Smurfit-Stone Container

During 1998 Jefferson Smurfit engineered the merger of Jefferson Smurfit Corporation and Stone Container Corporation, creating Smurfit-Stone Container Corporation. The $1.3 billion deal was completed in November 1998, with Smurfit-Stone emerging as the largest producer of containerboard in the United States. Just prior to the transaction's completion, Jefferson Smurfit Group purchased an additional 18 percent interest in JSC for $516 million. The group's overall interest in JSC translated into a 33 percent stake in Smurfit-Stone. Two months before this merger closed, Jefferson Smurfit Group purchased from JSC 50 percent of Canadian corrugated container maker MacMillan-Bathurst, which was renamed Smurfit MBI. Also in 1998 Jefferson Smurfit increased its shareholding in Nettingsdorfer to 75 percent and divested Smurfit Condat, which operated a coated paper mill in France.

Integration issues related to Smurfit-Stone Container dominated 1999. A key rationale behind the merger had been the opportunity to reduce capacity in the containerboard sector and thereby boost prices. By late 1999 Smurfit-Stone had shut down four of its plants and laid off about 1,700 workers, reducing the company's containerboard capacity by about 20 percent; this had the desired effect of boosting prices by early 2000. Smurfit-Stone also began selling off noncore assets in order to reduce a heavy debt burden it had inherited from Stone Container. Overall, Smurfit-Stone was aiming to slash annual operating costs by $350 million. Jefferson Smurfit was also busy paring noncore assets during 1999, divesting Smurfit Finance and, together with its partner Banque Paribas, selling Smurfit Paribas Bank to Anglo Irish Bank Corporation plc.

In May 2000 Smurfit-Stone Container spent $1.4 billion to acquire St. Laurent Paperboard Inc., a Canadian producer of specialty containerboard and graphics packaging. This reduced Jefferson Smurfit's stake in Smurfit-Stone to about 29.5 percent. From 2000 to early 2002 Jefferson Smurfit completed a number of acquisitions, most of which were centered in Europe and involved the company's core containerboard and corrugated container businesses. During 2000 the company acquired U.K.-based Norcor Holdings plc; Neopac A/S, which increased its market share in Denmark to 17 percent; and Fabrica Argentina de Carton Corrugado, which doubled its market share in Argentina, to 13 percent. In December 2000 the company in-

creased its holding in Nettingsdorfer to 100 percent. In February 2001 a 25 percent interest in Leefung-Asco Printers Limited was acquired, with this investment in a Hong Kong company viewed as an initial step toward securing a meaningful position in Asia. In the early months of 2002 Jefferson Smurfit also gained full control of Munksjö AB.

In February 2002 Michael Smurfit announced that he would step down as chief executive of the group at the end of October 2002 but would remain chairman. Smurfit by this time was a controversial figure. He was praised in some quarters—particularly overseas—as a paper industry visionary, focusing for years on the need to prevent or eliminate industry overcapacity and thereby prop up prices. But in his home country (or rather, former home country, given that he officially resided in Monaco for tax reasons), his image was that of an overpaid executive unresponsive to the shareholders in his public company, who considered the firm to be perpetually underperforming. Everyone would agree, however, that it was Michael Smurfit who had created the Jefferson Smurfit of the early 21st century, be that good or bad. Moreover, since he intended to remain chairman, there were doubts about who would be calling the shots starting in November 2002. That month, Gary McGann would be promoted from president and chief operations officer to chief executive of the group. McGann had joined Jefferson Smurfit only in 1998, having previously been the chief executive of Aer Lingus Limited, an airline owned by the Irish state. Taking over McGann's previous position would be Michael's son Tony, who had headed Smurfit Europe.

Takeover by Madison Dearborn in Early 2000s

One of Jefferson Smurfit's persistent problems was that the minority stake it held in Smurfit-Stone Container made it difficult for investors to determine the actual worth of the company, which tended to depress the share price of the company's stock. By early 2002 it appeared that the company was on the verge of selling the stake. But then Madison Dearborn Partners, a Chicago-based private equity investment firm that had previously made several investments in the paper and packaging industry, approached Jefferson Smurfit about a possible takeover. In June, Jefferson Smurfit accepted a EUR 3.7 billion ($3.61 billion) takeover bid from Madison Dearborn, and two months later Jefferson Smurfit shareholders voted in favor of the bid. As a key part of the deal the stake in Smurfit-Stone Container would be spun off to Jefferson Smurfit shareholders, who would receive one Smurfit-Stone share for every 16 shares of Jefferson Smurfit that they owned; for the Jefferson Smurfit shares themselves, the holders would receive EUR 2.15. Under the terms of the deal, the top executives of the company, including Michael Smurfit and McGann, would remain with the newly privatized Jefferson Smurfit. As a group these managers owned about 10 percent of the company, and from the proceeds they would receive from the takeover, they would then repurchase about a 7 percent stake in the new company.

Principal Competitors

Svenska Cellulosa Aktiebolaget SCA; Kappa Packaging Group; DS Smith Plc; Stora Enso Oyj; UPM-Kymmene Corporation; International Paper Company; Georgia-Pacific Corporation; Amcor Limited; Weyerhaeuser Company.

Further Reading

Barrington, Kathleen, "Michael Smurfit: He Hasn't Gone Away, You Know," *Sunday Business Post* (Ireland), February 10, 2002.

Brown, John Murray, "Boxing Clever," *Financial Times,* December 7, 1998.

——, "High Prices and French Input Boost Smurfit," *Financial Times,* August 24, 1995, p. 20.

——, "New Man Leads Smurfit's Paper Chase," *Financial Times,* February 19, 2002, p. 24.

——, "Topsy-Turvy Ride Has Soft Landing," *Financial Times,* June 18, 2002, p. 27.

Byrne, Harlan S., "Jefferson Smurfit Corp.: The Paperboard Producer Plans More Acquisitions," *Barron's,* March 27, 1989, p. 39.

——, "Paper De-Cycler," *Barron's,* August 7, 1995, p. 21.

Canniffe, Mary, "Wright to Run Group Day to Day," *Irish Times,* May 3, 1996.

Cordell, Valerie, *The First Fifty Years,* Dublin: Jefferson Smurfit Group, 1984.

DeKing, Noel, "Smurfit Moves to the Top Through Acquisitions, Skilled Management," *Pulp & Paper,* December 1988, p. 110.

Du Bois, Peter C., "Irish Alchemy: The Acquisitive Smurfit Group Turns Paper into Sizzling Profits," *Barron's,* August 28, 1995, pp. MW7–MW8.

Ford, Jonathan, "Consolidation Likely to Follow a Paper Celebration," *Financial Times,* May 12, 1998, p. 27.

Hargreaves, Deborah, "US Flotation Boosts Jefferson Smurfit," *Financial Times,* September 29, 1994, p. 22.

Hollinger, Peggy, and David Buchan, "Smurfit to Double European Operations," *Financial Times,* August 3, 1994, p. 17.

Klebnikow, Paul, "Who Needs Trees?: There's Always the Sunday New York Times," *Forbes,* June 26, 1989, pp. 108, 110, 114.

Lavery, Brian, "Chicago Firm Plans to Acquire an Irish Conglomerate," *New York Times,* June 18, 2002, p. W1.

——, "Trying to Fit a Family into a Sale," *New York Times,* May 17, 2002, p. W1.

Loeffelholz, Suzanne, "Equity Is Blood: Why Michael Smurfit's Bedroom Walls Are Lined with Spreadsheets," *Financial World,* April 3, 1990, pp. 96, 98.

McGrath, Brendan, "The Wright Stuff," *Irish Times,* July 5, 1996.

Miller, James P., "Stone Container Agrees to a Merger with Jefferson Smurfit in Stock Deal," *Wall Street Journal,* May 11, 1998, p. B4.

Murray, Michael, "Smurfit Faces Ruthless Future If Madison Dearborn Takes Over," *Sunday Business Post* (Ireland), May 12, 2002.

O'Sullivan, Jane, "Smurfit Investors Overwhelmingly Back Madison Bid," *Irish Times,* August 8, 2002, p. 16.

Palmeri, Christopher, "Psst! Let's Raise Prices!," *Forbes,* October 4, 1999, pp. 60+.

Quinn, Eamon, "Packing It in at Smurfit," *Sunday Business Post* (Ireland), May 5, 2002.

Ratner, Juliana, "Irish Eyes Smile for Madison," *Financial Times,* May 4, 2002, p. 14.

Sesit, Michael R., Erik Portanger, and Debra Marks, "Madison Group Bids $3.5 Billion for Paper Maker," *Wall Street Journal,* June 18, 2002, pp. A12, A13.

"Smurfit Defends Logic of the Stone Merger," *Sunday Business Post* (Ireland), October 11, 1998, p. 29.

"Succession Race Hots Up at Smurfit Group," *Irish Independent,* August 26, 2001.

Urry, Maggie, "A Story of Success That Turned to Excess," *Financial Times,* May 3, 2002, p. 23.

—Monique Lamontagne
—update: David E. Salamie

JM

Johnson Matthey

Johnson Matthey PLC

2-4 Cockspur Street
Trafalgar Square
London SW1Y 5BQ
United Kingdom
Telephone: (44) 20-7269-8400
Fax: (44) 20-7269-8433
Web site: http://www.matthey.com

Public Company
Incorporated: 1891 as Johnson, Matthey & Co. Limited
Employees: 6,637
Sales: $8.36 billion (2001)
Stock Exchanges: OTC London
Ticker Symbols: JMPLY (OTC); JMAT (London)
NAIC: 325188 All Other Basic Inorganic Chemical
Manufacturing (pt); 325411 Pharmaceutical
Preparation Manufacturing (pt); 325510 Paint and
Coating Manufacturing; 325131 Inorganic Dye and
Pigment Manufacturing; 325132 Synthetic Organic
Dye and Pigment Manufacturing; 331491 Nonferrous
Metal (Except Copper and Aluminum) Rolling,
Drawing, and Extruding (pt); 331492 Secondary
Smelting, Refining, and Alloying of Nonferrous Metal
(Except Copper and Aluminum) (pt); 333999 All
Other Miscellaneous General Purpose Machinery
Manufacturing (pt); 334413 Semiconductor and
Related Device Manufacturing; 335999 All Other
Miscellaneous Electrical Equipment and Component
Manufacturing; 336399 All Other Motor Vehicle Parts
Manufacturing: 334419 Other Electronic Component
Manufacturing; 421940 Jewelry, Watch, Precious
Stone, and Precious Metal Wholesalers; 422950 Paint,
Varnish, and Supplies Wholesalers

Johnson Matthey PLC has been involved in the processing
and marketing of precious metals since its founding in 1817.
Although it is most widely known for its activities in platinum—it is a world leader in the refining, marketing, and

technological development of the metal—Johnson Matthey has
been increasingly positioning itself as a leader in advanced
materials technology, including catalysts and pollution control
systems, electronic materials, specialty chemicals, and pharmaceutical compounds. Johnson Matthey also manufactures decorative and specialized materials for the ceramics, plastics, paint,
ink, and construction industries. In 2001 the company acquired
British pharmaceutical firm Meconic, becoming the only company in the United Kingdom legally authorized to sell medical
heroin and cocaine. Johnson Matthey has an extensive international presence, with operations in 34 countries.

Building a Precious Metals Firm in the 19th Century

The founder of Johnson Matthey was Percival Johnson, who
in 1817 set himself up at 79 Hatton Garden in Holborn, London,
as an "Assayer and Practical Mineralogist." As such, he valued
gold by applying chemical and physical tests to determine the
exact quantity of gold in a bar. Johnson's business rapidly
gained distinction when he began offering to buy back the bars
of gold that he assayed, thereby becoming the first London
assayer to issue a guarantee of quality. In the early 1830s a
small gold refinery was built at the Hatton Garden premises for
the refining and assaying of gold bars that were then coming
into London from Brazil. These were complex gold bars, containing impurities that were not easy to remove. Having successfully extracted platinum group metals from the bars and
proven his technical prowess, Johnson established the firm at
the forefront of the London bullion market. The firm took full
advantage of the gold rushes of California, from 1848, and of
Australia, from 1851, while supplies of silver arrived throughout the 1850s and 1860s in the form of demonetized silver
coinage—coinage that had gone out of circulation—from European states. A large-scale silver refinery was built at adjacent
premises in Hatton Garden.

Johnson's interest in metallurgy had already brought him
into contact with platinum, which had been the subject of considerable scientific interest throughout the early 19th century
because of its strength and resistance to corrosive acids. He set
up a small-scale refinery for the metal at Hatton Garden, with
limited supplies coming from Colombia.

In 1838 George Matthey joined the company as an apprentice. Matthey's scientific talents, coupled with a shrewd business sense, were the driving force behind the company's development in the platinum industry during the second half of the 19th century. When the Great Exhibition was first proposed, Matthey persuaded Johnson to exhibit a number of platinum articles, together with specimens of other platinum group metals: palladium, iridium, and rhodium. The display was a success, and Matthey became determined to make the company preeminent in the platinum business. He succeeded in gaining a more assured supply of the metal through direct arrangements with owners of a mine in the Ural mountains in Russia, then a newly discovered source. In the 1867 International Exhibition in Paris, the company displayed a wide variety of platinum-manufactured goods on a scale never seen before. The exhibit was awarded a gold medal ''for perfection and improvement in the working of platinum.'' Under Matthey's direction, platinum refining and fabricating grew from about 15,000 ounces in 1860 to about 75,000 ounces a year in the 1880s. The manufacturing of sulfuric acid boilers was the largest single use of platinum until the early 1900s.

The diversity of the company had actually been established from the beginning by Johnson. From the chemical refining of gold, Johnson produced a range of vitreous colors for the glass and pottery industries. He became the first refiner of nickel in Britain, with ''nickel silver,'' popular as a silver plate. In 1833 production of silver nitrate began, its use being primarily for medical purposes in the form of lunar caustic. Over the following decades the development of photography generated considerable demand for silver nitrate.

By 1860, the year of Johnson's retirement, many of the company's present-day activities had been established: assaying and refining of bullion, platinum refining and marketing, the production of vitreous colors for glass and pottery manufacturers, and a constant experimentation and development of niche markets for other rare and precious metals. Hatton Garden remained the rather compact home of the refining, assaying, and experimental work so vital to the firm's future. There was, in addition, a small workshop in Clerkenwell, used for the manufacture of platinum dishes, crucibles, and other laboratory instruments. A total of 25 people were employed in 1860, with a

trio of partners who dominated the firm's development over the next four decades: George Matthey, his younger brother Edward Matthey, and John Sellon—Percival Johnson's nephew. It was this trio, and their descendants, who were to dominate the company's development until the mid-20th century.

Over the next 50 years, technological and marketing progress coincided with a securing of supplies. Gold-refining facilities were improved and expanded at Hatton Garden in response to the arrival of African gold, and the silver refinery received constant supplies of demonetized coin from across Europe. The reputation of the assaying and chemical laboratories grew, and in the mid-1880s Johnson Matthey succeeded in establishing itself as the ultimate referee of assayers and, as a certifier of ore quality, of South African Rand gold. Platinum supplies were secured from Russia through the cooperation of the metals houses of Quennessen of France and Heraeus of Germany; together the three European companies dominated the world platinum trade through control of this source, and ignored demands from the tzar for a refinery to be built within Russia. In 1894 the cartel was formalized through the creation of an association named The Allied Houses. In 1911 Johnson Matthey signed an agreement with the Nicolai Pavdinsky Company in the Urals, which gave Johnson Matthey the rights to mine a substantial body of platinum-bearing ore in return for Johnson Matthey building a local refinery. Despite World War I, and the chaos caused by the overthrow of the tzar, the plant was in full operation by 1918. No platinum ever reached London, however. During this period Johnson Matthey promoted the use of platinum as a corrosive-resistant electric conductor, and when platinum prices rose above gold for the first time in the 1900s the company encouraged the interest of jewelers. When the market for sulfuric acid boilers died at the turn of the century, fresh demand had been built up in other sectors.

In 1898 the company expanded its service to jewelers by purchasing new rolling mills in nearby Hop Gardens; here silver and gold alloys were formed into sheet, wire, and tube semimanufactured goods. The company's interest in colors had been boosted in the late 1870s when it gained the British and Empire marketing rights to a variety of industrial glazes, stains, and enamels, including so-called rolled gold, from the Roessler company of Frankfurt. Roessler soon was renamed Degussa; the two companies had a history of close association dating back to the 1860s. After initial skepticism, the Staffordshire potters took to the advanced colors and Johnson Matthey became an established supplier in that area. Meanwhile, the company's interest in the rare and often novel metals was given a strong commercial footing with the 1870 acquisition of the Manchester-based Magnesium Metal Company. During the 40 years that followed, the Magnesium Metal Company's plant at Patricroft produced magnesium for flash photography and laboratory work, antimony for hardening bullet heads, vanadium for black dye and ink, and electrolytically-produced aluminum. It is thought that the statue of Eros in London's Piccadilly Circus—dedicated to the philanthropist seventh Earl of Shaftesbury—was made of aluminum from the Patricroft works.

In 1891 the company became Johnson, Matthey & Co. Limited, a private limited company, and during the 1890s and 1910s an increasing amount of departmentalism took place as the sons and nephews of the ruling trio took over the responsibilities and increasingly delegated power to trusted clerks and technical

Key Dates:

1817: Percival Johnson begins work as a mineralogist in London.
1838: George Matthey joins Johnson's office as an apprentice.
1860: Percival Johnson retires.
1870: Johnson Matthey acquires the Magnesium Metal Company.
1891: Johnson Matthey is incorporated as Johnson, Matthey & Co. Ltd.
1919: London Gold Market is founded.
1931: Rustenburg Platinum Company is formed.
1969: Johnson Matthey enters into joint venture with Tanaka Kikinzoku Kogyo KK of Japan to form Tanaka Matthey KK.
1981: Johnson Matthey & Co. Ltd. becomes Johnson Matthey Public Limited Company.
1994: Johnson Matthey joins Cookson Group PLC to form Cookson Matthey Ceramics plc.
1998: Johnson Matthey acquires Cookson's stake in Cookson Matthey Ceramics.
2001: Johnson Matthey acquires Meconic.

experts. It was at this point that a corporate policy was adopted that remains at the heart of the company still: only to take part in activities in which the company could dominate. When a product's development fell out of the control of the company, Johnson Matthey's interests in it would be sold off.

World War I Through World War II Era

During World War I Johnson Matthey established itself as an innovative developer of strategic materials, despite significant supply disruptions affecting most of the metals with which the company dealt. The company was able to satisfy the Allied demand for products such as platinum catalysts, used to make sulfuric acid for explosives manufacturing, and magnesium powder, used to make incendiary bombs for dropping on German airships. In 1916 the company was brought under the direct control of the government, and platinum catalysts and electrical and magneto contacts for cars, airplanes, and tanks were manufactured in a modernized platinum workshop. The company expanded its production of silver nitrate to meet the demands of the photographic industry, and in 1916 began manufacturing its own liquid gold. In 1918 the colors division was given a firm production base through acquisition of the Sneyd color works at Burslem. A Birmingham branch of Johnson Matthey was established in the same year to supply the city's jewelry trade, and the Sheffield silversmith E.W. Oakes & Co. Ltd. was purchased. Despite difficulties in obtaining supplies, demands of industry were met and at the end of the war the air ministry gave an official message of thanks to the company for its supplies of high-precision equipment.

In 1918 John Sellon died. In order to secure a closer working relationship with the two South African mining houses that were of most significance to the company's gold activities, his shares in the company were offered in equal parts to Consolidated Gold

Fields of South Africa Ltd. and to the Johannesburg Consolidated Investment Company. This is the origin of the controlling stake held by the Anglo American Corporation today.

During the early 1920s the company faced considerable problems due to continued disruptions in the supply of precious metals. From 1922 the South Africans refined their own gold, while regular supplies of platinum from the Urals had failed to resume after the war despite the ingenious attempts of Arthur Coussmaker. Coussmaker was a platinum expert with Johnson Matthey whose attempts to gain a secure supply of Russian platinum had involved deals with White Russian military forces and impromptu meetings with Soviet officials in western European cities. The difficulties of supply led to the early 1920s being a low point in the fortunes of Johnson Matthey. In 1924, however, Dr. Hans Merensky discovered the huge platinum-laden reef in the South African Transvaal that bears his name today. Coussmaker, by then a board member, made an immediate trip to the Transvaal where he identified the Rustenburg area as the most promising part of the reef. Consolidated Goldfields of South Africa and Johannesburg Consolidated Investments had mines in the Rustenburg district, and after an initial platinum mine boom in the mid-1920s those were the only mines operating in the slump that followed. Coussmaker persuaded the two mining houses to merge their platinum interests, and in 1931 the Rustenburg Platinum Company was formed. Johnson Matthey became a refiner and distributor for what was, and remains, the world's largest platinum mine. A smelting works and an electrolytic refinery were built at Brimsdown, in Essex, to extract the platinum metals according to a refining method established by Ernest Deering and Alan Powell of the Hatton Garden staff.

In 1919 Johnson Matthey joined N.M. Rothschild's bank and four other leading bullion brokers to form the London Gold Market, where a daily price-fixing still sets the price of gold. When gold supplies from South Africa ended, the sulfuric acid refinery at Hatton Garden was kept in operation through a constant stream of demonetized silver from central and Eastern Europe. Much of this came via the Silberfeld brothers, initially based in Riga, who throughout the interwar period supplied Johnson Matthey with Russian Imperial coins and gold rubles, and with silver Maria Theresa coins from an office in Vienna. The company established branches in Warsaw and Prague and came to own 75 percent of the Bank Powszechny Depozytowy in Poland.

Johnson Matthey's manufacturing capacity in this period was boosted by the acquisition in the early 1920s of the metal fabricating firm of R. Buckland & Son Ltd. In 1925 Johnson and Sons Smelting Works Ltd. of Brimsdown, Middlesex, was acquired. This was a sweeps, scrap, and residue refinery business that had been set up originally in the mid-19th century by a brother of Percival Johnson. During the 1930s the bullion refining and smelting operations were rationalized, the colors section was strengthened by a full-time research department, and a team of enterprising salesmen crossed Europe in motor cars.

At the outbreak of World War II Johnson Matthey was appointed government agent for the control and handling of platinum stocks, and manufactured items of the material grew in response to the rising demand. Products included electrical fine wires, electrodes, aircraft spark plugs, laboratory crucibles, and wire gauze catalysts for the preparation of nitric acid. Demand for platinum with a high iridium content led to Coussmaker's establishment of a refinery in Pennsylvania, where concentrates from Alaskan deposits were turned into contact tips for automagnets.

While bullion trade was severely limited by Bank of England supervision, and jewelry sales were almost forbidden, industrial demand—especially from photographic related industries—was strong for silver-based products. Some special uses of silver compounds included the manufacture of silver ball bearings for airplane engines, and desalination packs that enabled ditched airmen, or shipwrecked sailors, to survive on sea water. Bomb damage during the blitz of autumn 1940 resulted in the Brimsdown smelting works being put out of action temporarily, and the entire contents of the company museum and archive collection were destroyed.

Postwar Expansion

With the end of the war came a period of rapid overseas growth for the company, much of it having been prepared from the early 1940s in expectation of a postwar boom. Representatives were sent around the world to study competitors, examine suppliers, and to establish new markets. Operations in North America, South Africa, Australia, and India were expanded as a result, with growth in Europe taking place later with the establishment of subsidiaries in France and The Netherlands in 1956, Italy in 1959, Sweden in 1960, Belgium in 1961, and Austria in 1962. Developments at home moved at an equally rapid pace: two colors factories in Staffordshire were opened immediately after the war, and in 1951 the colors section acquired Universal Transfers Co. Ltd. Johnson Matthey was now a market leader in the manufacture of color pigments and screen-printed transfers for the pottery and glass industries. In 1953 Harlow Metal Co. Ltd. was formed to merge the company's mechanical production interests, and in 1957 a new platinum refinery was built at Royston that brought together the company's refining operations. In 1954 Universal Matthey Products Ltd. was formed, to produce platinum catalysts for U.S. manufacturers of high-octane petrol. Enthusiasm by the North American auto industry for catalytic converters encouraged Johnson Matthey to conduct extensive research on the auto catalyst during the late 1950s and early 1960s. In 1962 L.B. Hunt was appointed director of research at new purpose-built laboratories at Wembley.

In 1963 Blythe Colours, based in Stoke-on-Trent, was acquired. This brought to Johnson Matthey an extended range of industrial colors, a worldwide network of agents, and a strong north European section based in The Netherlands. A consolidation of bullion activity took place during the 1950s and 1960s, culminating in the formation of Johnson Matthey Bankers Ltd. (JMB). Representing Johnson Matthey on the London gold market, JMB traded in the gold, silver, and precious metals produced by Johnson Matthey subsidiaries around the world.

A major reorganization of the company took place in 1966 and 1967, with the establishment of four divisions within which all of the company's activities and subsidiaries were placed. These were the Jewelry and Allied Traders Division (JAT); the Chemical Division; the Industrial Division; and the Ceramic Division. A mechanical production unit was established to cater to the production needs of the four divisions. In 1969 expansion

into Asia culminated with the establishment of Tanaka Matthey KK, a joint venture company with Tanaka Kikinzoku Kogyo KK of Japan. Japan was a major consumer of platinum jewelry, and the joint venture enabled Johnson Matthey to dominate the market there.

1970s and 1980s

The 1970s were a decade of organic growth, with few acquisitions taking place. In 1980, however, a significant move into the U.S. jewelry trade—a business that was unfamiliar to the company—led to losses estimated at more than £60 million and in 1981 the board looked to JMB to help make up the loss. JMB had done well from the spectacular rise in bullion activity that had accompanied the Soviet invasion of Afghanistan in 1980, and pressure was placed on the subsidiary to expand out of bullion-related loans and into high-risk lending in areas with which it was unfamiliar. The bank's loan book expanded, from £50 million at the end of 1981 to some £500 million by March 1984, with its contribution to group profits going from just under 25 percent in 1981 to more than 60 percent in 1983. By late 1983, however, the Bank of England had begun to suspect the quality of some of the loans. In the summer of 1984 their suspicions extended to cover the accounting practices of Arthur Young. In September 1984 the full extent of the bad loans taken on by JMB became apparent, and the Bank of England organized a bailout by JMB's creditors, shareholders, and U.K. clearing and merchant banks. The Bank of England purchased JMB for a token £1. The collapse of JMB was a disaster: in the words of the *Economist,* October 6, 1984, ''The Johnson Matthey Parent Company lost its shirt, [and] its shareholders a lot of money.'' Meanwhile, in 1981 Johnson, Matthey & Co. Limited officially changed its name to Johnson Matthey Public Limited Company.

Charter Consolidated, effectively the holding company for Anglo American's interests in Johnson Matthey, found itself with a 38.3 percent stake in the group as a result of its assistance in the bailout of JMB, and sent in its own man, Neil Clarke, to become Johnson Matthey's chairman. In June 1985 Clarke appointed Gene Anderson as chief executive. Over the next five years the company was transformed, with £70 million of disposals made over the next two years, including an interest acquired in Wembley Stadium. The workforce was cut significantly while profits doubled to £64 million between 1986 and 1989. A total of 74 semiautonomous companies, loosely grouped into divisions, but many legally distinct and with their own boards, were reorganized into four operating divisions. These were the Catalytic Systems Division, which includes automotive exhaust and industrial air pollution control systems; the Materials Technology Division, which combines the group's rare-earth, pharmaceutical, and special materials interests; the Precious Metals Division, which acts as the sole marketing agency for Rustenburg Platinum and controls the group's gold and silver marketing and refining businesses; and the Colour and Print Division that ties together the group's industrial colors and printing businesses. Investment in new plant and research was expanded, and in 1990 a new autocatalyst production plant was opened in Belgium to meet anticipated European demand. Research into the medical possibilities of platinum-based drugs was boosted, with cancer and HIV-fighting drugs developed.

In December 1989 Anderson resigned after failing to persuade the board to expand into nonplatinum areas. The proposed move would have diluted Anglo American's shareholding in Johnson Matthey through a share issue, and moved Johnson Matthey away from an increasing reliance on the Rustenburg mine. In testing the resolve of the South Africans, Anderson confirmed their control over the group. Almost immediately after Anderson resigned, Clarke also resigned. David J. Davies, Charter's deputy chairman, was transferred to become Johnson Matthey's chairman.

1990s and Beyond

Johnson Matthey's operating results in the early 1990s were generally positive, as the company began to see results from its late 1980s restructuring. Sales increased steadily from £1.73 billion in 1991 to £1.96 billion in 1994. Before-tax profits also increased steadily to a record £73.8 million in 1993 before declining in 1994 to £65.3 million thanks in part to the loss of a catalytic converter contract with General Motors toward the end of the year. Throughout this period, the company continued to restructure its operations, in particular in its Materials Technology Division. On the down side, the Precious Metals Division continued to provide more than 60 percent of Johnson Matthey's sales, while contributing only about one-quarter of the operating profit.

There were signs, however, that the company would be able to lessen the impact that precious metals had on its overall performance. The clearest signal came in 1993 when Charter Consolidated sold its 38.3 percent stake in Johnson Matthey for £342 million ($492 million). About 20 percent would remain in the indirect control of Anglo American since it was sold to Garrick Investment Holdings Ltd., a firm jointly held by Johannesburg Consolidated Investment Co. and Minorco of South Africa, both of which in turn were in the indirect control of Anglo American. The other 18.3 percent was sold to two British brokerage firms, Barclays de Zoete Wedd Ltd. and UBS Phillips & Drew Ltd., who were to sell the shares to investors, thus somewhat diluting Anglo American's control.

Anglo American remained in charge of Johnson Matthey through Chairman Davies, but the next few years would see the company make its most aggressive expansion moves in years, all of which fell outside the precious metals area. In March 1994, Johnson Matthey and Cookson Group PLC, a U.K.-based metals fabrication firm, combined their respective ceramics businesses into a 50–50 joint venture called Cookson Matthey Ceramics plc. This venture absorbed Johnson Matthey's Colour and Print Division, leaving the firm with the remaining three divisions and its share of the Cookson joint venture. Later in 1994, Johnson Matthey and Cookson entered into merger talks that would have created a global precious metals/industrial materials giant, but discussions were discontinued in November after the two sides could not come to an agreement on terms. The joint venture was not affected, however, and it subsequently posted positive results during its first two years in existence.

The Materials Technology Division was the next area to be targeted for growth with the 1995 acquisition of Advance Circuits Inc. (ACI) for £106.4 million ($170.2 million). ACI was a U.S.-based electronics industry supplier of multilayer printed circuit boards and plastic laminate packaging for semiconductors, the latter an emerging industry. The deal extended Johnson Matthey's range of products within the area of electronic materials, so much so that following the acquisition the company's divisions were restructured once more. The Materials Technology Division had two components—electronic materials and chemicals. The former, including the newly acquired ACI, would become a new Electronic Materials Division, a move that highlighted the importance of this area to the company's future. The latter was merged into an enlarged Precious Metals Division, which then consisted of platinum marketing and fabrication businesses, precious metal chemicals and platinum refining businesses, and worldwide gold and silver businesses. The new Electronic Materials Division soon was bolstered further through the early 1996 purchase from Cray Research Inc. of printed circuit board manufacturing facilities in Wisconsin. The company also planned to invest $200 million in capital expenditures from 1996 through 1998 in its newest division.

A New Focus for the 21st Century

Johnson Matthey had its best year ever in 1995, with total sales of £2.27 billion and before-tax profits of £95.4 million. However, the company began to experience a bit of a slump in 1996, particularly in its precious metals and ceramics divisions. Profits for both businesses saw little growth over the course of the year, due primarily to decreased demand for ceramic tiles in Europe, as well as a significant price drop for platinum, rhodium, and palladium. Although the company expected both of these segments to recover eventually, it also began to explore ways to increase sales over the short term. One solution to the slowdown in the ceramics business was further expansion overseas, particularly in South America and Asia.

At the same time, promising developments in Johnson Matthey's other segments, which included electronics materials and catalytic systems, helped offset the lackluster results in precious metals and ceramics. By mid-1997 two of the company's biggest customers, Volkswagen and Chrysler, were increasing their orders for catalytic converters, lifting profits in the division to £34.1 million for the year. The company also was exceeding expectations with its semiconductor packaging operations in the United States, where production levels stood at one million units a month by November 1997 and had the potential to increase to 1.6 million by March 1998. The boost was due in large part to increased sales of the Intel Pentium II computer chip, which provided Johnson Matthey with its principal source of business.

During this period the company also saw promising results in its pharmaceutical materials segment. Profits grew by 51 percent over the course of 1997, giving Johnson Matthey reason to believe that it could seize a 25 percent share of the U.S. market for methylphenidate, a compound used in treating attention deficit disorder, before the end of the decade. The company also continued to enjoy high margins from sales of Carboplatin, an anti-cancer treatment derived from platinum, which the company marketed in the United States through a joint venture with Bristol-Myers Squibb.

Adverse developments in two of Johnson Matthey's other segments the following year, however, led to dramatic changes in the company's portfolio. Continued poor results in the ceramics division, due primarily to declining prices for zircon, a key whitening agent, led to the collapse of Cookson Matthey Ceramics. The company purchased Cookson's stake in the joint venture for £65 million in January 1998, allowing it to consolidate its ceramics holdings and cut operating costs by £4 million, mainly through consolidation. At the same time, decline in demand for Intel processors had a major impact on the company's electronics material business, prompting the company to consider selling the division. The announcement of this proposal received strong approval from shareholders, who were generally wary of the relative weakness of the division's overall market share. The company finally found a buyer in mid-1999, giving it more than £500 million to spend on expanding its other core businesses.

By the year 2000 the company had decided to focus more intently on expanding its pharmaceutical and catalytic segments. In June 2001 Johnson Matthey purchased Meconic, a British pharmaceuticals firm and the largest opiates supplier in the world, for £147.1 million. With the acquisition Johnson Matthey became the only company in the United Kingdom with the right to legally distribute medical heroin and cocaine; considering the fact that the painkiller market was growing at a rate of 6 percent a year by 2001, the deal had great potential for the company. Meanwhile, progressively stricter emissions laws in the world's most substantial automobile markets produced continued demand for the company's catalytic converters. With an eye toward environmental concerns heading into the 21st century, the company also was beginning to invest in the development of fuel cell technology, establishing a separate division for the new business in June 2001. Although precious metal prices were still flat by 2002, and the company's ceramics business continued to flounder, Johnson Matthey clearly had strengthened its holdings in other key sectors and was poised to maintain its leading market share in key businesses for the foreseeable future.

Principal Subsidiaries

HEA (Hydrogen Engineering Applications) Ltd.; Johnson Matthey Ceramica Lda (Portugal); Matthey-Beyrand & Cie SA (France); Johnson Matthey Poland; Johnson Matthey Limited (Australia); Johnson Matthey (New Zealand) Limited; Johnson Matthey Ceramics (Thailand) Ltd; Johnson Matthey BV (Netherlands); The Argent Insurance Co Ltd (Bermudas); Johnson Matthey Inc. (U.S.A.); Johnson Matthey Sdn Bld (Malaysia); Johnson Matthey BV (France); Australian Bullion Company; Johnson Matthey Limited (Canada); Johnson Matthey & Brandenberger AG (Switzerland); Johnson Matthey Italia Spa; SA Johnson Matthey NV (Belgium); Johnson Matthey Moscow Office (Russia); Johnson Matthey Services Ltd (India); Johnson Matthey Argentina SA; Arora Matthey Limited (India; 40%);

Johnson Matthey S.A. (France); Johnson Matthey Pharmaceutical Materials Inc. (U.S.A.); Johnson Matthey (Czech Republic); Johnson Matthey de Mexico SA de C.V.; Johnson Matthey Fuel Cells; Johnson Matthey Ceramics SA (Spain); J.M. Select; Johnson Matthey Medical Products (U.S.A.); Johnson Matthey A/S (Denmark); Shape Memory Applications Inc. (U.S.A.); Johnson Matthey Brazil Ltda; Johnson Matthey Vehicle Testing & Dev. LLC (U.S.A.); Johnson Matthey Ceramics Sdn Bhd (Malaysia); Johnson Matthey Ceramics (Asia) Pte Ltd (China); Johnson Matthey Ltd (Ireland); Johnson Matthey (Shanghai) Chemical Ltd. (China); Johnson Matthey Ltd. (China); Johnson Matthey Macfarlan Smith (Scotland); Johnson Matthey Ceramica Ltda (Brazil); Johnson Matthey (Singapore) Pte Ltd; Johnson Matthey (Pty) Ltd (South Africa); Svenska Emissionsteknik AB (Sweden); Johnson Matthey GmbH (Germany); Johnson Matthey (Sweden); Johnson Matthey India Private Ltd (CSD); Johnson Matthey Ceramics India Ltd; Johnson Matthey Hong Kong Ltd; Johnson Matthey Japan Inc; Johnson Matthey Structural Ceramics (U.S.A.); Johnson Matthey Ceramics South Africa (Pty); Almiberia SA (Spain); Johnson Matthey GmbH Alfa Products (Germany).

Principal Divisions

Catalysts & Chemicals Division; Pharmaceutical Materials Division; Precious Metals Division; Colours & Coatings Division.

Further Reading

Andrews, Walter, ''Johnson Matthey Planning Three Acquisitions,'' *Electronic News,* July 4, 1994, p. 50.

Batchelor, Charles, ''Johnson Matthey Captures Meconic,'' *Financial Times* (London), June 22, 2001, p. 23.

''Cookson, Johnson Matthey Discontinue Merger Talks,'' *Wall Street Journal,* November 23, 1994, p. A9.

Dawkins, William, ''Principles of a Profitable Alliance,'' *Financial Times,* November 6, 1995, p. 14.

Gooding, Kenneth, ''Ceramics Superstars Aim High,'' *Financial Times,* August 18, 1995, p. 16.

''How Johnson Matthey Kept Bankers Up from Dusk to Dawn,'' *Economist,* October 6, 1984.

Hunt, L.B., ''George Matthey and the Building of the Platinum Industry,'' *Platinum Metals Review,* April 1979.

''Johnson Matthey,'' *Investors Chronicle,* December 2, 1994, p. 70.

McDonald, Donald, ''The Rise of Johnson, Matthey & Co. Ltd.,'' in *A History of Platinum,* London: Johnson Matthey, 1961.

Minton, Anna, ''Johnson Matthey Shifts to Catalysts and Drugs,'' *Financial Times* (London), December 3, 1999, p. 22.

Pretznik, Charles, ''Johnson Matthey May Spin Off Division,'' *Financial Times* (London), November 26, 1998, p. 24.

—Tom C.B. Elliott
—updates: David E. Salamie, Steve Meyer

Jones Lang LaSalle Incorporated

200 East Randolph Drive
Chicago, Illinois 60601
U.S.A.
Telephone: (312) 782-5800
Toll Free: (800) 527-2553
Fax: (312) 782-4339
Web site: http://www.joneslanglasalle.com

Public Company
Incorporated: 1997
Employees: 13,700
Sales: $881.67 million (2001)
Stock Exchanges: New York
Ticker Symbol: JLL
NAIC: 531210 Offices of Real Estate Agents and Brokers

Jones Lang LaSalle Incorporated (JLL) is a global real estate services and investment management company with offices in 32 countries spread across five continents. JLL assists institutions, corporations, and wealthy investors in buying, selling, and managing real estate assets. Services provided by the company include investment banking, real estate finance, and corporate finance, as well as property development, property management, project management, and tenant representation. The company has more than $23 billion of public and private assets under management.

Origins

Although not created in name until 1999, JLL enjoyed a rich history stretching back to the 18th century. The corporate title JLL first appeared when Chicago-based LaSalle Partners Incorporated merged with London-based Jones Lang Wootton, creating a global real estate services and investment management company with nearly $1 billion in annual revenue. Of the two companies, LaSalle Partners could be considered the upstart, although the breadth and depth of clients and experience brought to the corporate marriage by the Chicago-based company were considerable. In terms of length of existence, however, the U.S. half of JLL paled when compared with the storied past of its British counterpart. Jones Lang Wootton was founded nearly 200 years before LaSalle Partners, providing an extensive prelude to the birth of JLL on the eve of the 21st century.

The enterprise that became known as Jones Lang Wootton began operating in 1783. That year, Richard Winstanley established himself as an auctioneer in London's Paternoster Row, where the business would remain for more than 70 years. Richard Winstanley's son, James, joined the Paternoster Row business in 1806, working as an auctioneer alongside his father. James Winstanley eventually inherited full control over the business, operating it as a sole proprietor until he formed a partnership with James Jones in 1840. Together, the pair presided over the company until Jones gained sole control over the company. In 1860, he moved the company to King Street, home to the business for more than a century. Like the Winstanleys, Jones's son, Frederick Jones, joined his father in business, renaming the company Frederick Jones and Co. after his father's retirement. Further replicating the evolution of the Winstanley era, Frederick Jones struck up a partnership after his father's departure. When Frederick Jones retired in 1872, his partner, C.A. Lang, became sole proprietor of the business, renaming it Jones Lang and Co. C.A. Lang's son inherited control of the company before passing it on to his son. Three generations of stewardship by the Lang family carried the company into the modern era.

The start of World War II in 1939 also marked the year Jones Lang and Co. merged with a 47-year-old company named Wootton and Son. The union created Jones Lang Wootton, a company whose growth would benefit significantly from the destruction caused by a world at war. By the end of the war in Europe, London bore the marks of German air raids. The destruction of property by bombing and fires was exacerbated by the destruction of documents that delineated boundaries and ownership of the property destroyed. Amid the confusion, Jones Lang Wootton stepped into the breach. The company searched for the owners of small land parcels, combined the properties, and secured contracts for either leasing or purchasing the amalgamated land parcels. By so doing, Jones Lang Wootton was able to secure licenses for development, which put the company in an enviable position for growth when the massive task of rebuilding London began in earnest in 1954. The company forged agreements entitling it to engage in development and leasing activities during the city's reconstruction, registering its first notable success with the development of Barrington House in Gresham Street. A slew of projects followed, including much of the new speculative development in the city and in prime locations in the city's West End.

Post-World War II Expansion

Jones Lang Wootton's participation in post-World War II development and reconstruction delivered powerful growth, providing the financial means and the confidence to expand internationally. The company established its first major overseas presence in Australia. In 1957, a British expatriate residing in Australia, Ronald Collier, approached Jones Lang Wootton officers in London, seeking their support. Although there was no investment market in Australia, company officials foresaw significant potential in the country. In 1958, the company established offices in Sydney and Melbourne, embarking on its involvement in buying, selling, and in the investment management of real estate assets. By the mid-1960s, the company's presence in Australia had become entrenched, developing into an operation consisting of nearly two dozen partners and a staff of 300. Jones Lang Wootton's success in Australia served as a springboard for expansion throughout the Pacific Rim. Offices were established in New Zealand, Singapore, Kuala Lumpur, Hong Kong, and Tokyo. As the company fleshed out its presence in the Southeast Asia and Pacific regions, it also broadened the scope of its operations closer to home. Jones Lang Wootton expanded into Scotland in 1962 and into Ireland in 1965, followed by a push into continental Europe. An office was opened in Brussels in 1965, paving the way for expansion into Holland, France, and Germany. Mindful of opportunities to the east, the company opened offices in Budapest, Prague, and Warsaw.

The Late 1960s Birth of LaSalle Partners

As Jones Lang Wootton was orchestrating its European expansion, LaSalle Partners was beginning its corporate life. The company was founded in 1968 as IDC Real Estate, a small El Paso, Texas-based firm that grew quickly. The company soon exhausted the opportunities available to it in commercial real estate and investment transactions in El Paso, prompting its founders to relocate to Chicago in 1972. The change in headquarters helped fuel robust growth during the 1970s, as the company focused on identifying client needs, providing superior service, and cultivating initial client contacts into long-term business relationships. In 1977, the company changed its name to LaSalle Partners.

The establishment of the LaSalle Partners name in the Midwest coincided with extension of the Jones Lang Wootton empire to the east. The expansion of the latter company's operations throughout Europe in the 1960s was followed by its first foray into the United States in the 1970s. Jones Lang Wootton opened an office in New York City in 1975, marking

the birth of Jones Lang Wootton USA. Initially, the small satellite office focused on real estate and investment opportunities in midtown and downtown New York City, using thorough market analysis to compensate for its relatively diminutive stature. During the early 1980s, the scope of Jones Lang Wootton USA widened, as the operation benefited from the increasing influx of British, Asian, and Middle Eastern money into the United States. Attuned to the needs of these foreign clients, the company found itself ushering in substantial capital into the property markets, as well as providing a range of services that included project management, property management, and leasing. Between 1980 and 1982, the growth of the U.S. operation reflected the surge in business, as its staff swelled from roughly a dozen employees to more than 40 employees.

By the beginning of the 1990s, Jones Lang Wootton's presence in the United States, as well as its presence overseas, had grown considerably. In the United States, through Jones Lang Wootton USA, the company operated in eight cities, employing more than 500 employees. Elsewhere, Jones Lang Wootton offices fanned across the globe, comprising a network of 56 offices located in 19 countries. Worldwide, the company performed $14 billion worth of debt and equity transactions, generating roughly $4 billion in sales by marketing its expertise in managing, leasing, financing, and selling real estate. Through its global ties, the company drew upon the resources of pension funds, commercial banks, savings institutions, private investors, property companies, and insurance companies, using the resources to provide debt and equity financing.

For its part, LaSalle Partners entered the 1990s with ambitious plans to expand its operations. In the last years leading up to its merger with Jones Lang Wootton, the company embarked on an acquisition campaign that added significantly to the might of the soon-to-be created JLL. In 1994, LaSalle Partners acquired a real estate investment advisor named Alex Brown Kleinwort Benson Realty Advisors Corporation. A London-based investment advisor, CIN Property Management Limited, was added two years later, followed by the acquisition of a property and development management company named Galbreath Company in 1997. After completing its initial public offering of stock in July 1997, LaSalle Partners purchased the project management business belonging to Satulah Group in January 1998. Later in the year, the company purchased the fourth largest management services firm in the United States, COMPASS Management and Leasing, Inc. In its last major transaction before its merger with Jones Lang Wootton, LaSalle Partners acquired the U.S. retail property management business of Lend Lease Real Estate Investments, Inc., completing the deal in October 1998.

In the months leading up to the merger with LaSalle Partners, Jones Lang Wootton focused on reorganizing its worldwide operations, seeking to create an integrated, single holding company. Worldwide, the company generated $482.5 million in revenue in 1998, with approximately three-quarters of the total derived from its activities in Europe and North America. The globalization of the property business, according to Jones Lang Wootton officials, necessitated the integration of the company's operations, producing business synergies that coordinated research, marketing, information technology, and human resources departments. The globalization of the property business also prompted the company to make another decision, the effect

Key Dates:

1783: Richard Winstanley forms the predecessor to Jones Lang Wootton.

1860: The London business moves from Paternoster Row to King Street and eventually becomes known as Frederick Jones and Co.

1872: Company is renamed Jones Lang and Co.

1939: Jones Lang and Co. merges with Wootton and Son to form Jones Lang Wooton.

1968: IDC Real Estate, the predecessor to LaSalle Partners, is formed.

1999: LaSalle Partners and Jones Lang Wootton merge, creating Jones Lang LaSalle Incorporated.

of which would be far more profound than integrating operations. In the company's 1998 annual report, Christopher Peacock, Jones Lang Wootton's president and deputy chief executive officer, stated that there was a need "to consider mergers and acquisitions as a means of accelerating our growth, particularly in North America." Peacock's wish list grew longer, leading him to add that the "consequent need for increased access to external capital would require us to weigh several options carefully, including remaining an integrated private company, taking a capital partner, or becoming a publicly quoted company." Based in Chicago and operating as a publicly held company, LaSalle Partners represented the answer to both of Peacock's needs.

Creating Jones Lang LaSalle Through 1999 Merger

Jones Lang Wootton and LaSalle Partners merged on March 1999, creating JLL, a truly global real estate services firm and investment manager with pro forma revenue of $814 million. Although both companies professed similar corporate values, promising to ease the union of their corporate cultures, the merger proved to be more complex than anticipated. The process of integrating operations and creating the appropriately sized infrastructure to support the new concern consumed time and resources, leading to an actual net loss of $94.8 million in 1999—far more than expected. Under the stewardship of Stuart L. Scott, JLL's chairman and chief executive officer, the company resolved its difficulties, developing a cost-reduction program at the end of 1999 that promised to realize $15 million in savings in 2000 and $20 million in savings the following year.

After moving past the difficulties of the merger, JLL emerged as a powerful force. The company touted itself as the largest property management concern in the world, overseeing more than 680 million square feet of real estate, and as the first fully integrated, global hotel investment services firm. Follow-

ing the merger, the two business segments were operated as LaSalle Investment Management and Jones Lang LaSalle Hotels. LaSalle Investment, with $22 billion of assets under management by 2002, assisted customers in buying, selling, and managing property, offering services such as property development, property management, project management, leasing, and tenant representation. Jones Lang LaSalle Hotels provided advisory, transaction, financial, and management services.

As JLL plotted its course for the 21st century, the process of integrating LaSalle Partners and Jones Lang Wootton continued. The early years of the new century saw the company reduce its debt and achieve financial growth, despite the constraints of a difficult global economy. Between 1999 and 2001, JLL reduced its debt by $100 million, eclipsing the company's original two-year projection of $40 million. In 2001, the company posted $40.5 million in net income and generated $881.7 million in revenue, compensating for the lackluster results of 1999. In January 2002, Christopher Peacock succeeded Scott as chief executive officer, leaving Scott to concentrate exclusively on his role as JLL's chairman. Under their leadership, JLL pressed forward, well positioned to continue the legacy of success established by generations of company executives.

Principal Subsidiaries

LaSalle Investment Limited Partnership; LaSalle Investment Management, Inc.; Jones Lang LaSalle International, Inc.; LaSalle Investment Management Securities, Inc.; Jones Lang LaSalle Americas, Inc.; Jones Lang LaSalle (Europe) Ltd. (U.K.); LaSalle Partners International (U.K.); Jones Lang Wootton (U.K.); Jones Lang LaSalle Australia Pty. Limited.

Principal Competitors

CBRE Holding, Inc.; Cushman & Wakefield, Inc.; Grubb & Ellis Company.

Further Reading

Derven, Ronald, "Jones Lang Wootton Offers Global Services; Diverse Real Estate Firm Is Ready for the 1990s," *National Real Estate Investor,* March 1990, p. 94.

King, Carrie, "At JLW, the Greatest Opportunities Are Still Ahead," *National Real Estate Investor,* October 1997, p. 50.

Kosseff, Jeffrey, "Property Manager: Bigger's Better Even for Local Clients," *Crain's Detroit Business,* March 12, 2001, p. 13.

Richardson, Patricia, "Profile: Selling Real Estate Firm's Lesser-Known Turf to Wall Street," *Crain's Chicago Business,* March 18, 2002, p. 15.

Selwitz, Robert, "Jones Lang/LaSalle Merger Results in Stronger Capabilities," *Hotel & Motel Management,* June 14, 1999, p. 82.

Sheridan, Mike, "Full-Service Firms Entering Bold, Challenging New Era," *National Real Estate Investor,* July 1999, p. 40.

—Jeffrey L. Covell

JPI

600 E. Los Colinas Boulevard, Suite 1800
Irving, Texas 75039
U.S.A.
Telephone: (972) 556-1700
Fax: (972) 556-3784
Web site: http://www.jpi.com

Private Company
Incorporated: 1976 as Jefferson Properties, Inc.
Employees: 1,500
Sales: $1 billion (2000 est.)
NAIC: 531110 Lessors of Residential Buildings and
Dwellings

JPI is the largest U.S. developer of luxury apartments, many of which are a cross between an upscale house and a fine hotel, offering amenities including garages, "urban vegetable gardens," marble entryways, high ceilings and spacious rooms, fitness centers, 24-hour concierge services, and high-tech gadgetry such as broadband Internet access, theater-quality sound in living rooms, and closed circuit television that allows tenants to monitor gates, swimming pools, and play areas. Based in Irving, Texas, the company also manages some 24,000 apartments located in 12 states and is involved in building student housing, both on campus and off. Hunt Realty Corporation is a major investor in JPI, as is GE Capital Services.

Founding Family Made 19th-Century Fortune in Cattle

JPI was originally formed in 1976 as Jefferson Properties, Inc., a subsidiary of Southland Financial, a business founded by the Carpenter family of Dallas, Texas, one of the city's original business dynasties. A hundred years earlier the family had become involved in the cattle business, then in 1927 John Carpenter, Sr., moved into the insurance industry, establishing Southland Life Insurance Co. His real estate activities included the 1928 purchase of 200 acres in Irving for a family estate, which Carpenter named Hackberry Creek Ranch. His son, Ben H. Carpenter, became an executive at Texas Power and Light

Company, then assumed the chairmanship of Southland in 1959 when John Carpenter died. In addition to insurance and cattle, Ben Carpenter, along with his brother-in-law Dan C. Williams, pursued the real estate business through Southland Financial Company and added significant acreage to Hackberry. In 1971 they merged the insurance operation with Southland Financial and took the company public.

In the early 1970s the family ranch struggled because of high taxes, and Carpenter found it difficult to continue in the cattle business. In a stroke of good fortune, the new Dallas-Fort Worth International Airport was built nearby, opening in 1973. Carpenter decided that he either had to sell Hackberry Creek or develop it. He chose the latter course, telling the *New York Times* in 1990, "When I thought about it, I realized, here was an opportunity from scratch to plan the best possible use of a piece of property on a large scale." The result was a development that his mother dubbed "El Ranchito de las Colinas," or the little ranch of the hills, which became simply known as Las Colinas. Carpenter bought additional land until Las Colinas encompassed 12,000 acres. His planned community, also dubbed the Emerald City of the north Texas plains, was grand and sweeping. Although it might take as many as 20 years to fulfill his dream, Carpenter wanted to make Las Colinas America's premier corporate address, a self-contained, well regulated community built around a core of business parks, complete with Venetian canals and an overhead monorail, as well as luxury homes and apartment communities where business leaders could rub shoulders with their peers. It was a Disneyland for the executive class, combining Old World charm with the advances of tomorrow. Jefferson Properties was one of a number of real estate companies Carpenter created to develop Las Colinas, providing JPI with deep roots in serving the luxury market.

Formation of JPI Inc. in 1989

Las Colinas proved to be a prohibitively expensive undertaking, and the company, despite landing such tenants as Kimberly-Clark, was unable to generate the necessary capital. In 1983 ever profitable Southland Life Insurance was sold for $352 million and still Carpenter had to borrow heavily. By 1984 Southland Financial owed nearly $500 million, and to relieve shareholder pressure he attempted to take the company private but other investors, including Ivan Boesky, sensed an opportunity and entered the picture, driving up the price of Southland's stock and effectively scuttling Carpenter's deal. His health failing, Carpenter ultimately underwent several heart bypass operations. His son, John Carpenter III, succeeded him as CEO of Southland. They twice turned to Michael Milken to raise $200 million in junk bonds, but with the crash of the Dallas real estate market in 1986, Los Colinas was saddled with excessive debt and Southland came close to losing the development. Finally in 1988 Teachers Insurance and Annuity Association and JMB Realty, a Chicago-based real estate corporation, saved the Carpenters from bankruptcy. In a restructuring that followed, Southland Financial was liquidated and in 1989 Jefferson Properties split off, changing its name to JPI Inc., with the younger Carpenter serving as chairman.

Actively involved in both apartment development and management as well as commercial properties in the Dallas-Fort Worth area, JPI, based in Las Colinas, received a major boost when Hunt Consolidated Inc. (parent of Hunt Realty) agreed to acquire a major stake in the business and provide significant equity capital to fund ongoing multifamily developments. Under terms of the agreement, JPI would construct and manage the communities and Hunt would share ownership and income. Hunt Consolidated was run by Ray Hunt, one of the many offspring of famed Texas oil billionaire H.L. Hunt. Born in Illinois, H.L. Hunt was the son of a banker and left home at the age of 16, supporting himself to a large degree by playing cards. In the 1920s he ran a gambling hall in Arkansas during an oil boom and became involved in the petroleum business. After moving to east Texas in the early 1930s he ultimately established the Hunt Oil Company and became, for a time, the richest man in the United States. In addition to money Hunt also acquired wives and produced a wealth of children. The mother of Ray Hunt, who was born in 1943, was Ruth Ray, a secretary at Hunt Oil Company. It was not until 1957 that H.L. Hunt married her and legally adopted Ray and his three siblings.

JPI moved beyond the Dallas-Fort Worth area, developing multifamily communities in Florida, Virginia, Georgia, and Colorado. In 1994, in order to focus on apartment construction and management, it merged its commercial property operations, a portfolio of some three million square feet, with Texas-based Fuller-Macfarlan Real Estate Services. With all classes of apartment development thriving in the mid-1990s, particularly in Sunbelt markets, JPI focused on the luxury sector. The driving force was the generation of aging, affluent baby boomers who no longer cared for the responsibilities of homeownership. They wanted the space of a house and the convenience of a garage, but also the security and other amenities associated with a hotel.

JPI developed a concept for the luxury market it called Project 2000, the prototype of which, Jefferson Estates, was unveiled in January 1996 at the National Association of Home Builders Convention. The community was being built in Richardson, Texas, a complex of 528 units located in the heart of the area's telecom corridor. JPI hoped to attract a tenant base from the 100,000 high-tech employees working at some 500 firms in the North Dallas area. The company also formed partnerships with firms to supply many of the extras that these tenants would find attractive. For instance, Xencom Communication provided intelligent thermostats, which allowed residents to monitor and adjust their heating and air conditioning by telephone. Southwestern Bell equipped the units with high-speed Internet access, in addition to surround sound and video-on-demand.

By the end of 1996 JPI reached $1 billion in assets, with 20,000 apartment units in ten states. In addition to the luxury apartment market it became involved in another niche, student housing. Colleges across the country were facing an extreme shortage: With the number of available on-campus beds at less than four million, some 4.4 million students had to seek alternate housing, either staying at home or other off-campus facilities. In certain markets the opportunity for developers was even greater. California public colleges and universities, for instance, could only accommodate 125,000 of the state's 700,000 full-time undergraduates. Texas public institutions, with 140,000 beds, were unable to house more than two-thirds of its students, and New York, with 145,000 beds, was only slightly better off. Moreover, college enrollment was expected to rise by nearly 20 percent over the next decade. Privately financed and run student housing was also a highly fragmented industry, offering an excellent opportunity to an experienced, well-regarded developer such as JPI. School administrators, strapped for funding, were more than receptive to private companies who offered a no-cost, no-risk way to house an increasing number of students. In 1996 JPI developed or acquired five student on-campus housing projects, mostly in Texas, for a total of nearly 3,400 beds. JPI then moved into building on-campus apartment buildings, which were operated very much like dormitories, including the presence of resident assistants to iron out problems. Unlike dorms, privately built accommodations included such amenities as a private phone line and cable-TV hookup in each room, as well as individual computer connections—added values that were in keeping with JPI's reputation.

The idea of privately built and operated on-campus housing began with Texas A&M earlier in the 1990s. According to a 1998 *Wall Street Journal* article, "The first on-campus privatized housing deals were structured as ground leases, where the developer got the lion's share of the cash flow but the university continued to own the land and generally took title of the apartment buildings after 30 or 40 years. Lately, however, the trend has been for colleges to use not-for-profit foundations to own the apartment complex, while the developer received a fee for building and operating the complex.''

Joint Venture with GE Capital: 1997

Jefferson Estates was completed and opened in the spring of 1997, launching JPI's Project 2000 initiative. Later in the year the company formed a joint venture, JPI Partners, with GE Capital Services to build luxury apartment and student housing

Key Dates:

1971: Southland Financial goes public.
1976: Southland Financial forms Jefferson Properties, Inc.
1989: Jefferson Properties splits off as JPI when Southland Financial is dissolved.
1991: Hunt Consolidated buys a 50 percent stake in JPI.
1997: GE Capital Service forms joint venture with JPI.

communities across the country. GE Capital had already participated as an investor in over 40 JPI projects in Texas, Colorado, Florida, and the Northeast. Under terms of the agreement GE Capital would supply the bulk of funding, its initial commitment totaling $470 million. Hunt Realty would also own a stake in the venture. In addition to its cash, GE Capital carried clout and opened new doors for JPI. Because GE Capital Real Estate was already located in Canada, JPI began exploring the Canadian market in 1998, looking to take advantage of recent modifications in the country's rent control legislation. JPI Partners opened an office in Toronto but GE Capital's help was invaluable in helping the newcomers become familiar with Canadian regulation and practices.

JPI was actively building through much of 1998, but a downturn in the economy forced the company to cut back on development late in the year and into 1999. JPI soon regained its momentum, starting construction of 28 new projects that comprised 10,500 units. The company also sold 35 communities, some 13,500 units, to institutional investors. After devoting considerable attention to its core markets of Washington, Philadelphia, and North Carolina, JPI became increasingly interested in other markets. By the spring of 2000, JPI had 24,000 apartments under management and another 17,300 under development, spread across 22 states, including a presence in Arizona, California, Colorado, Nevada, New Hampshire, and Virginia.

JPI moved into the Columbus, Ohio, area in 2000, breaking ground on a 395-unit complex. It also began construction in downtown Toronto, a city with a 1 percent vacancy rate that had gone years without a new luxury high-rise rental building. With 424 units, the building featured such luxuries as a Hollywood viewing theater, teaching kitchen, fitness center, virtual golf facility, and business center, as well as a party room, barbecue areas, hot tub, spa, and sun decks on the roof. It was scheduled to open in the fall of 2002.

In 2001 JPI continued to enter new markets, including the outskirts of New York City. It began construction of a new gated community, Jefferson at Aberdeen, to be located in New Jersey's Aberdeen Township. The complex was to be comprised of six four-story Victorian-style buildings, some 290 luxury apartments in all. It was also located near a New Jersey Transit train station, providing a 45-minute commute to Manhattan. Also in 2001 JPI looked to New York's Westchester County, and after a lengthy negotiation with White Plains city officials was able to work out a deal on a site that for more than 20 years other builders had tried and failed to develop. Jefferson at White Plains called for an eight-story building housing 251 luxury apartments, as well as 30 separate townhouses.

In the aftermath of the terrorist attacks of September 11, 2001, and a troubled economy, coupled with overbuilding in some areas, JPI like other landlords had to contend with a sharp downturn in the apartment rental market. It was forced to lower rents in some cases and even offer inducements to prospective tenants, including digital cameras, 25-inch televisions, or $200 gift certificates. Nevertheless, JPI remained well positioned for the long run, and set its sights on international markets, where it again hoped to leverage GE Capital's presence and expertise, with plans to enter Mexico and Western Europe in 2003.

Principal Subsidiaries

JPI Partners.

Principal Competitors

Castle & Cooke, Inc.; Gables Residential Trust; Trammell Crow Company.

Further Reading

Blumenthal, Karen, "Luxury-Apartment Rentals Are Booming," *Wall Street Journal,* September 22, 1995, p. B1.

Brown, Steve, "Ray Hunt to Invest in JPI Program," *Dallas Morning News,* April 19, 1991, p. 1D.

Chuang, Tamara, "JPI Thriving Despite Recent Snags," *Arlington Morning News,* December 20, 1996, p. 6A.

Garbarine, Rachelle, "Apartments Planned Near Aberdeen Train Station," *New York Times,* January 14, 2001, p. 11.

Holt, Nancy D., "Development: Luring Renters with Exotic Amenities," *Wall Street Journal,* February 25, 1998, p. B12.

Kleinfield, N.R., "To the Brink and Back in Real Estate," *New York Times,* January 7, 1990, Section 3, p. 1.

Page, Robert D., " 'Partnerships for the Future' May Hold Key to Apartment Success," *National Real Estate Investor,* January 1997, p. 30.

Rudnitsky, Howard, "Billion-Dollar Fire Sale," *Forbes,* November 17, 1986, p. 44.

Templin, Neal, "Apartments Replace the Dorm," *Wall Street Journal,* October 28, 1998, p. B18.

Totty, Michael, "Southland Financial May Have a Rescuer," *Wall Street Journal,* May 16, 1988, p. 1.

—Ed Dinger

Karl Kani Infinity, Inc.

500 S. Molino Street, Suite 215
Los Angeles, California 90013
U.S.A.
Telephone: (213) 626-6076
Fax: (213) 626-88434
Web site: http://www.karlkani.com

Private Company
Incorporated: 1994
Employees: 34
Sales: $82 million (2000 est.)
NAIC: 422320 Men's and Boys' Clothing and
Furnishings Wholesalers; 422330 Women's,
Children's, and Infants' Clothing and Accessories
Wholesalers

Karl Kani Infinity, Inc. designs and markets clothing intended for African American tastes and physiology. Fashion designer Karl Kani made his name as a pioneer of baggy designer jeans and colorful shirts for black male youth in the early 1990s. Since then Kani has expanded his clothing line to include business casual, under the Karl Kani label; tailored clothing, using the Kani label; and sportswear, under Karl Kani Black Label. Casual and athletic styles are labeled as Kani Endurance. Karl Kani Infinity designs and markets clothing for African American women, children, and infants as well. Karl Kani Life is a line of denim clothing available in men's and women's fashions. The company's clothing is sold in upscale department stores and specialty clothing stores worldwide.

Karl Kani: From Local Hit to National Force in Fashion

Carl Williams changed his name to Karl Kani—pronounced, "Can I?"—to reflect the mantra that he awoke with every morning: Can I do it? Can I become the "Ralph Lauren of the streets?" Kani began to make clothing for himself in the mid-1980s while attending high school and working as a newspaper carrier. Kani disliked many of the designer clothes available in stores, particularly the slender jean styles that required African Americans to purchase large waist sizes so that the jeans fit their hips. Kani began to design his own jeans, with loose-fitting legs and hips and a proper fit at the waist; a tailor then constructed them. Kani's friends and neighbors in the Flatbush area of Brooklyn liked the styles, casual knit shirts as well as the baggy jeans, and requested such clothing for themselves. A hands-on business course at his high school helped Kani develop his hobby into a business. Through word-of-mouth Kani's designs attained local popularity and soon Kani began selling jeans and shirts at local basketball tournaments and outside Manhattan nightclubs. Thus Kani helped to start a revolution in fashion with a black urban style that would attract young suburban males as well.

In 1988, at the age of 19, Kani decided to move to Los Angeles, the manufacturing center of the clothing industry. With $1,000 and a few clothing samples, he opened Seasons Sportswear in the Crenshaw district of south central Los Angeles, living and working at the store, producing clothing in the back. Three months later, however, a burglar stole his samples. Kani closed the shop and began making clothing in his one-bedroom apartment in Hollywood. He promoted the clothing line by selling catalogs for $2 each for mail-order sales that kept him in business. He also sold his clothing on the streets. Kani designed a new line of clothing to prepare for MAGIC, a fashion industry trade show held every February in Las Vegas. Kani did not have funds to pay for a booth, so he circulated his business cards and invited buyers to view the clothing at his hotel room. In addition to baggy jeans and casual shirts, Kani offered heavyweight fleece "hoodies" (hooded jackets), color denim jackets, and jean and velour sweatsuits in bright colors. Shirts, hoodies, and certain other pieces featured the Karl Kani logo in huge letters.

The hip hop style of clothing designed for the African American physique gained in popularity and Karl Kani obtained sales from clothing stores that catered to urban blacks. His first wholesale orders came from specialty stores, such as Simon's in Brooklyn and Up Against the Wall in Washington, D.C. Other customers included Strictly Sportswear in Detroit; Tuckers Department Store in St. Louis; Cavaliers in Washington, D.C.;

Montego Bay in Queens; and Puffer Red in Ypsilanti, Michigan. Karl Kani clothing became popular with several black rappers and athletes, including Dr. Dre, Kool G Rap, Ed Lover, Mike Tyson, Heavy D, and Big Daddy Kane.

Kani's breakthrough to national sales occurred when he joined Threads for Life. In 1990, at a party at The Paladium Club in Los Angeles, Kani met Carl Jones, who had developed the Cross Colours line of multi-ethnic clothing. Impressed with Kani's designs and sales potential, Jones invited Kani to join his company as his own division and offered to provide contacts and financial support. The following year Kani joined Cross Colours and moved into a 50,000-square-foot warehouse. His first week there Kani received a $3 million order from Merry-Go-Round, a chain of retail stores. Soon Karl Kani clothing was available in national and regional chains, including Oak Tree, one of the country's largest chains of men's clothing stores. His big breakthrough came in 1992, when Macy's Department Stores began to buy Karl Kani designs for urban locations. Karl Kani pants and shirts sold for $65 to $70 retail, T-shirts for $36, and jackets for $80 to $90.

With Karl Kani and Cross Colours at the forefront of a fashion revolution, Threads for Life revenues increased from $15 million in 1991 to $89 million in 1993. The Karl Kani division accounted for 40 percent of revenues, approximately $36 million in 1993. The popularity of Cross Colours and Karl Kani clothing presented several problems for the company. The backlog of orders and the attendant problem of order fulfillment required the company to seek licensing partnerships for clothing production in 1993. The transfer to licensed manufacturing occurred so quickly, however, that many orders went unfilled. Also, the company overextended itself financially in its attempts to accommodate rapid growth.

Despite these difficulties Kani introduced his first line of footwear in stores in November 1993. The footwear, including high-top boots for $130 and sneakers for $70, was an immediate success. A $500,000 television advertising campaign involved spots on MTV, BET, and network television.

Reclaiming Control in the Mid-1990s

The difficulties at Threads for Life, including his own unhappiness at having to obtain final approval for his designs, prompted Kani to separate from the company and start anew. He learned much about the clothing industry from Jones, such as trendsetting, how to make contacts, and about the marketplace in general. Kani decided to use this experience and $500,000 in profits to start Karl Kani Infinity, purchasing his trademarked name from Jones in 1994.

As CEO of his own company, Kani hired experts in the clothing industry to handle sales and administration while he focused on clothing design. From Threads for Life he brought in Jeffery Tweedy as vice-president of sales and marketing and A.Z. Johnson as West Coast account executive. For president Kani hired Derek Tucker, former president of Oaktree, who was responsible for bringing urban streetwear to that chain.

As problems from Threads For Life followed Kani to his new company, he sought to rebuild trust with former customers. He promised to fulfill purchase orders, with customers cautiously placing small orders at first. Kani formed licensing partnerships carefully, choosing those that provided control over how much merchandise was sold, when, and where. Karl Kani staff were situated at offices of licensees, foregoing the customary minimum sales guarantee in exchange for staff involvement in the daily business of manufacturing. Karl Kani received royalties of 8 percent to 14 percent, higher than the industry average. Karl Kani Infinity recorded $43 million in revenues in 1994, its first year, despite a problem with counterfeit Karl Kani clothing.

Karl Kani began to diversify the line of clothing options to attract a broader customer base. New products included a line of clothing for big and tall men, prompted by Kani's conversations with professional basketball players too tall for his clothing. In February 1995 Karl Kani launched a line of boys sportswear, sizes 4–20, including jeans, T-shirts, sweatshirts, jackets, and leather vests and jackets. A line of men's leather goods and outerwear was introduced the following August.

Karl Kani licensees distributed clothing to department and clothing stores worldwide, but for Kani the big coup came with the opening of concept shops specifically for Karl Kani fashions. In November 1995 A&S in Brooklyn opened a 1,200-square-foot concept shop for Karl Kani designs and Macy's 34th Street store in New York offered 1,000 square feet of space. Kani appeared at Macy's on his 27th birthday that November to launch the shop. The event involved a fashion show of men's and boys' wear as well as a preview of the new women's collection. The spring collection included lycra dresses, linen skirts and jackets, stretch denim jeans, and terry sweatsuits.

By the end of 1995 Karl Kani clothing sold in over 300 stores nationwide, including Nordstrom, Dayton Hudson, Belk's, and Maison Blanche, while overseas sales originated in England, Germany, and Australia. The company opened offices in Taiwan and Hong Kong to oversee offshore production and distribution, including manufacturing activities in the Philippines, China, and Macao. Footwear sold in 14 countries, including Japan, Switzerland, Belgium, France, and the Czech Republic.

Karl Kani Infinity reported $69 million in revenues in 1995. The distribution of sales covered jeans at 45 percent of revenues, footwear at 30 percent; children's clothing accounted for 15 percent, and outerwear covered the balance at 10 percent. Of domestic sales, 40 percent originated along the East Coast with New York and Atlanta being the largest markets for Karl Kani designs. Chicago accounted for 15 percent of sales in the Midwest. In 1996 Karl Kani Infinity was listed number 25 on *Black Enterprise* magazine's list of the top 100 black-owned businesses based on 1995 sales.

Karl Kani fashions continued to find new outlets in urban as well as suburban stores in 1996. Marshall Fields in Chicago

Key Dates:

1989: Fashion designer Karl Kani opens Seasons Sportswear in south central Los Angeles.
1991: Karl Kani joins Threads for Life with his own division.
1994: Kani severs relationship with Threads for Life and forms Karl Kani Infinity.
1995: Karl Kani concept shops open in New York, Chicago, and Atlanta.
1999: Karl Kani forms new divisions for diverse lines of clothing.
2001: Karl Kani Life is launched with a record label and major advertising campaign.
2002: Kani receives the Urban Fashion Pioneer Award.

opened a 500-square-foot concept shop and Macy's at Fulton Street in Brooklyn and Atlanta's Lenox Square accommodated Kani shops as well. Karl Kani's reach extended to some suburban and mainstream retail outlets, though the company encountered resistance to a stereotype of the Karl Kani customer in reference to the rapper lifestyle. To reach potential patrons in these markets Karl Kani advertised in *Rolling Stone* and *GQ* magazines, as well as *Ebony Man*. Rappers Tupac Shakur and Aaron Hall were featured in some of the ads.

Kani felt that promotion of the company required his personal involvement, in addition to clothing design, so that his audience knew the man behind the designs. He attended fashion events at department store concept shops as well as at other public events. He attended trade shows to stay abreast of buyers' preferences. Also, he visited friends and neighbors in Brooklyn every few months to maintain contact with the clothing styles they liked and to spot potential trends.

Developing New Styles, New Clothing Lines: Late 1990s

Karl Kani offered a variety of designs as it expanded the number of clothing lines. Fall 1996 designs included racing, rugby, and university themes. Racing styles included casual tops with several zippers. Rugby styles bore vertical or horizontal stripes, flags, patchwork, and rubber buttons. Under the promotional line "Kani State," university designs involved cardigans with stripes or crests. A new line of outerwear included reversible bubble jackets with detachable arms, available in bright primary colors.

Recognizing that his customer base had matured beyond baggy jeans, Kani introduced lines of dress clothing and business casual clothing. Incorporating sophisticated designs, the couture line, manufactured in Italy, offered suits, slacks, blazers, and shirts in gabardine, worsted wool, silk, cashmere, and linen. Retail prices ranged from $1,200 to $1,500. In 1997 Karl Kani introduced the new Black Label line of sportswear. The collection included Eisenhower jackets, cotton or wool pants, knits, and shirts. Maintaining his sense of style, Kani designed traditional oxford shirts, but in a fuller cut and with bright colored stripes. Price points ranged form $80 to $120 for

shirts, and $150 for pants. The line included lower price points for jeans, at $40 to $60, down from $75 to $110. To display the wider variety of Karl Kani clothing, the company opened a 4,600-square-foot showroom in New York.

In 1999 Karl Kani formed new divisions by label to differentiate the various lines of clothing. Casual and athletic styles were placed under Kani Endurance, tailored clothing under the Kani label, business casual under Karl Kani Label, and sportswear under Karl Kani Black Label.

Karl Kani hoped to maintain his original customer base and still attract younger fashion buyers. To celebrate the ten-year anniversary of Kani's business, the company launched Karl Kani Limited Edition, a collection of the original designs that made Karl Kani popular with young, urban men. With production limited to 50,000 pieces, Kani's first customers were given sales preference.

Kani continued to create new clothing designs, seeking to create and promote new trends. For 1999 new additions to the Black Label collection included merino wool sweaters and sweater vests, Pima cotton shirts, leather-front shirts with wool sleeves, and unconstructed jackets. Jean styles for spring included color washes in orange, green, red, purple, and sky blue, as well as a dirty denim wash that made blue jeans look like they had been dipped in petroleum. At the February 2000 MAGIC trade show, Kani's new collection came together under the theme "Minks & Jeans," featuring outerwear and jeans. The line included denim pieces with mink trim. Mink, rabbit, fox, or beaver parkas were available in three-quarter or full lengths. Karl Kani designs were distinct from other clothing lines in that fur was available dyed in burgundy, electric blue, baby blue, and black.

Kani explored a variety of options in expanding and promoting his clothing business. Kani considered license options for underwear, loungewear, eyewear, home furnishings, and fragrances. The company looked at possible cooperative opportunities in different media, such as the Black Entertainment Network (BET) and movie and music production. In a reverse of popular rap stars starting clothing lines, Karl Kani decided to start a record label. Called Kani Life, the label signed promising rappers, such as Stacks and Pulle Black, and used them as models to advertise Karl Kani clothing. The company planned to cross market the clothing with music samples in the pockets of blue jeans and offering free CDs with a clothing purchase.

In August 2001 the company launched a new clothing design concept, Karl Kani Life, a collection of denim clothing. The line featured slim silhouettes with futuristic washes, such as bleached and color sandblasted. Karl Kani offered both men's and women's lines, the latter introduced in November for the winter holidays. The $3 million advertising campaign involved hand-drawn sketches of denim urban apparel. Advertising venues included a billboard in New York's Times Square and spreads in *Vibe, Galmour, Honey, XXL, Maxim,* and *Essence* magazines. Karl Kani continued with the line with similar styles for 2002.

Often referred to as the "godfather" or "grandfather" of urban street clothing, Kani received recognition for his contribution to fashion in 2002. The Urban Fashion Community recognized Kani with the Urban Fashion Pioneer Award, presented at a gala event along with other fashion awards in June.

Principal Competitors

FUBU; Maurice Malone Designs; Phat Fashions LLC; Tommy Hillfiger Corporation.

Further Reading

Bynum, Chris, "Kani Can; The 'Ralph Lauren of the Streets' Realizes His Dream," *New Orleans Times-Picayune,* June 20, 1998, p. E1.

Chance, Julie, "Karl Kani: Urban Design," *Essence*, November 1, 1995, p. 27.

Dolbrow, Sandra, "Kani's 'Life' Goes on with Print, Outdoor," *Brandweek*, November 26, 2001, p. 8.

"Faces of the Nineties: Mean Jeans," *Daily News Record*, August 11, 1992, p. 6.

Hayes, Cassandra, "From Mainstream to Urban Scene," *Black Enterprise*, October 1995, p. 64.

Ingrassia, Michele, "The Rebirth of Kani Kool," *Newsweek*, October 31, 1994, p. 53.

"Kani Gets into Shape," *Women's Wear Daily*, May 18, 1995, p. 7.

Lloyd, Fonda Maria, "Kani Hip Hops to His Own Company: Karl Kani Infinity Is Set to Compete with Cross Colors," *Black Enterprise*, July 1994, p. 16.

McAllister, Robert, "Kani Can Do," *Footwear News*, January 16, 1995, p. 5.

Muhammad, Tariq K. "From Her to Infinity: Karl Kani," *Black Enterprise*, June 1996, p. 140.

Murray, Stanley H., "A Can-Do Attitude," *Success*, April 1996, p. 17.

Quintanilla, Michael, "Stylemaker Karl Kani: New School," *Los Angeles Times*, September 10, 1999, p. 1.

Romero, Elena, "Color Brightens up Denim for Spring 2000; Young Men's Jeans Makers Use Tinted Washes to Give Denim a Fresh New Look," *Daily News Record*, August 16, 1999, p. 58.

——, "Animal Attraction," *Daily News Record*, February 11, 2000, p. 18.

——, "Hip-Hop Designers Gaining Recognition in Mainstream Market; Maturing into Important Young Men's Vendors," *Daily News Record*, April 16, 1996, p. 5.

——, "Karl Kani Close to Signing Tailored Clothing License," *Daily News Record*, August 30, 1999, p. 56.

——, "Karl Kani Infinity, BET May Be Near Joint Venture: Young Men's Maker, Media Company Reportedly Have Been in Long-Term Negotiations," *Daily News Record*, October 12, 1998, p. 4.

——, "Karl Kani Shows New Sign of Life," *Daily News Record*, August 27, 2001, p. 18.

——, "Second Round Proves Success Wasn't a Fluke for the Urban Sportswear Karl Kani," *Dallas Morning News*, July 14, 1999, p. 5E.

——, "Urban Sportswear Pioneer Karl Kani Celebrates 10 Years: Sets Eyes on Fragrance, Loungewear, Home Furnishings, and Feature Films for the Year 2000," *Daily News Record*, February 15, 1999.

Royal, Leslie E., "Hip-Hop on Top," *Black Enterprise*, July 2000, p. 92.

Thompson, Kevin D. "The Freshman Class of '95," *Black Enterprise*, June 1995, p. 144.

—Mary Tradii

Land Securities PLC

5 Strand
London, WC2N 5AF
United Kingdom
Telephone: (44) 20-7413-9000
Fax: (44) 20-7321-0302
Web site: http://www.landsecurities.co.uk

Public Company
Incorporated: 1905 as Land Securities Assets Co. Ltd.
Employees: 1,096
Sales: $916.6 million (2001)
Stock Exchanges: London
Ticker Symbol: LAND
NAIC: 531110 Lessors of Residential Buildings and
    Dwellings; 531120 Lessors of Nonresidential
    Buildings (Except Miniwarehouses); 531190 Lessors
    of Other Real Estate Property; 531210 Offices of Real
    Estate Agents and Brokers; 531312 Nonresidential
    Property Managers; 531311 Residential Property
    Managers; 531390 Other Activities Relating to Real
    Estate

Unlike most of its competitors, Land Securities PLC has achieved and maintained its position as the United Kingdom's largest property company by concentrating on the home market rather than expanding overseas. Apart from an unsuccessful venture into the Canadian market, via its subsidiary Ravenseft Properties Ltd. in the 1950s, no attempts have been made to expand abroad. Rapid growth since the 1940s has been based on specialization in the highest quality London offices and, through Ravenseft, the redevelopment of provincial shopping centers. Diversification into industrial property and retail warehouses has made an increasing contribution to growth.

The Birth of a Real Estate Empire: 1944–50

Land Securities originated in 1944, when in the spring of that year Harold Samuel bought a tiny property company, Land Securities Investment Trust Ltd. (originally incorporated in 1905 as Land Securities Assets Co. Ltd.), with assets of three houses and government securities valued at about £19,000. By March 1952 assets had rocketed to £11.1 million due to Samuel's skillful property market dealing.

Harold Samuel was born in 1912. After leaving school in 1929 he began work in the estate agency firm of Johnston Evans & Co., in London. A childhood acquaintance was Louis Freedman, whose provincial shop development activities were to complement Samuel's London office acquisitions and developments following World War II.

One of the most talented of all property tycoons, Harold Samuel understood the ways in which flaws and imperfections in the property market could be exploited, and he introduced many of the techniques that were to make fortunes for the new breed of property developers in the early postwar years. One of the factors behind his remarkable success as a property entrepreneur was his use of borrowed funds to expand holdings, a technique that he put to good effect in the unsophisticated property market of the 1940s. In his book *The Property Boom*, Oliver Marriott recounts how the fledgling Land Securities was able to obtain its first properties without committing too much of its own capital. Properties in Hatch End were bought in 1944 for £15,213: £9,477 being paid by bank loan, while other properties were bought at Neasden for £4,847; £3,335 being raised by mortgaging. Insurance companies generally were happy to provide mortgage finance, given the shortage of investment outlets other than gilts (high-grade securities) in the late 1940s. Interest rates were low, due to the Attlee government's cheap money policy, while a shortage of new properties, fostered by government building controls and materials shortages, ensured that rising property prices more than covered interest payments. The early accounts for Land Securities illustrated the importance of borrowed funds; in March 1948 the company's equity stood at £70,000, while mortgages and loans amounted to £1.3 million.

Another area in which Samuel showed considerable skill involved circumventing or taking advantage of the complex legal framework that regulated the property market in the early postwar years. Until 1947, borrowing was limited to £10,000 unless permission to exceed this sum was given by a government body known as the Capital Issues Committee. For some

Company Perspectives:

For over fifty years we have remained at the forefront of our industry. In 1944, when Harold Samuel, later to become Lord Samuel, acquired Land Securities Investment Trust, the company owned three houses in Kensington together with some government stocks. His strategy was to enter into partnership with many of the UK's local authorities and work with them to rebuild towns and cities after the war. His vision was enduring: by 1969, through a series of property and corporate acquisitions, we had become the largest UK quoted property company—a position we still hold today.

In leading the market, we continue to innovate by developing and implementing new strategies. We have focused our portfolio, acquired Trillium and continue to bring new skills and people into the group.

years after 1947 money could not be borrowed without the consent of this body. Samuel overcame these problems by establishing subsidiaries, each of which could borrow up to the limit, and by taking over property companies that already had agreed borrowings.

He also took advantage of a lucrative provision of the Town and Country Planning Act of 1947, under which a block of flats that had been requisitioned for office use could remain as office property without the payment of any development charge. He acquired a number of former flats that could now be used as offices; often their owners did not know of this provision and he obtained them at very attractive prices. Yet another of Samuel's innovations was his early institution of the full repairing and insuring lease, which, by placing responsibility for repairs and insurance with the tenant, lowered property management costs.

Harold Samuel had definite views about the types of properties that were likely to prove the most profitable long-term investments. He concentrated almost exclusively on London offices with first class specifications and locations. If a new property did not come up to his standards it likely was refurbished to bring it up to the highest quality. This often entailed heavy expenditure and a temporary loss of income, but resulted in higher rents and property values in the long run.

Postwar Expansion: The 1950s

From the end of World War II until 1954, severe restrictions governed property development, prohibiting any development that was not granted a government building license. As a result Land Securities dealt chiefly in the purchase, rather than development, of properties, concentrating on the west end of London. The company was able to do some development, however, prior to the removal of controls by taking on projects in the one area for which licenses could be obtained, offices for government occupation. Samuel preferred government and other large tenants because of the security of their tenure and the fact that they could take on an entire building, thereby lowering management costs. In the case of one building, Regent Arcade House, Land Securities waited for more than a year to find a single prestigious tenant; one that suited its requirements, the Bank of

England, finally was found. This was a time of rapid growth for the company; its assets, which amounted to only £19,321 in 1944, had grown to £11 million by 1952.

A number of early takeovers increased assets and drew public attention to Samuel's entrepreneurial skills. These takeovers included United City Property Trust in 1948 and the much more important acquisition of Associated London Properties (ALP) for £2.1 million in 1951, which almost doubled the book value of Land Securities' assets. Associated London Properties' assets included a number of office blocks let at prewar rents, with leases that were due to expire between 1958 and 1961, at which time they could be re-let for substantially higher rents. Although ALP's directors were well aware of the value of these properties, they were unable to raise dividends since this value would not be reflected in increased income until the leases expired. Samuel was able, therefore, to acquire the company at a price that reflected its current, rather than potential, income value. He also received other benefits from the acquisition. Cash was raised from the sale of Associated London Properties' residential and factory assets and, more important, the remaining assets included a large number of properties with no mortgage commitments, which could be used to raise further mortgage finance.

Two years later, Land Securities launched another takeover bid, this time for the Savoy Group. The bid sparked controversy and ended in failure, but had some positive results. It was wrongly claimed that Samuel intended to convert the Savoy Group's hotels into offices and the resulting hostile press reaction contributed to the failure of the bid. This adverse publicity left Samuel feeling that he had been unjustly treated by the press, and thereafter he kept as far out of the public eye as possible. By earning him a reputation as a skilled corporate predator, however, this episode enhanced his reputation in the city and made it easier for Land Securities to raise development finance on attractive terms.

In the ten years after 1954, when building license restrictions were lifted, Land Securities greatly expanded development activities, becoming one of the most prominent developers in London. The property market experienced a boom as the demand for property raced ahead of supply, which had been held back by wartime bombing and postwar shortages and development controls. Its rapidly expanding development program allowed the company to take full advantage of the large profit margins that were available to developers during these boom years, resulting in rising profits and rapid growth.

While Samuel concentrated on the London office market, Land Securities also was able to obtain a stake in the lucrative provincial shop market from 1946 via Ravenseft, a subsidiary that became fully owned in 1955. Ravenseft was set up by Louis Freedman and Frederick Maynard. Both Freedman and Maynard had begun their careers in estate agency in London during the 1930s. Here they learned, along with many others who were to become successful developers in the postwar years, the art of property dealing.

With the help of Samuel, who provided valuable contacts, Freedman set up Ravensfield Investment Trust Ltd., as it was then called, in 1946. Ravensfield's strategy was to operate in the provincial markets, where competition was less fierce than in

London. By 1949 Freedman realized that to cover all of the provincial markets he needed a partner, and he was able to attract Fred Maynard from the estate agents Healey & Baker. From 1949 to 1966 their company, under the new name Ravenseft Properties Ltd., was to invest £60 million in new shops comprising more than 400 developments in 150 U.K. towns and cities. It pioneered the redevelopment of bombed-out town and city centers in cooperation with the municipal authorities. A virtual lack of competition in these markets and the prestige value of its association with Land Securities were important factors behind Ravenseft's rapid early growth. The very nature of the type of developments that Ravenseft had chosen to undertake also contributed to success. Building licenses were obtained easily for this type of development, and as the local authorities were eager to see such projects go ahead they were prepared to use their powers of compulsory purchase to acquire the necessary land.

Once the supply of blitzed city sites began to run down, Ravenseft turned to the "New Towns," which were then largely at the planning stage. It took the gamble that these towns would become successful commercial centers, a gamble that proved to be highly rewarding. It also attempted, unsuccessfully, to enter the Canadian property market in 1956, its failure being in large part due to its unwillingness to take on a Canadian partner with detailed knowledge of the local market. Ravenseft pulled out of Canada in 1962 and Land Securities since avoided dealings in overseas property, even going so far as selling a stake in the valuable Pan Am building in New York when subsequently taking over the stake's owner, City Centre Properties Ltd., in 1968. In 1955, when Samuel bought up the remaining 50 percent of Ravenseft's shares, the deal valued the company at £2.1 million.

During 1955, Samuel also consolidated Land Securities' debts and capital structure. Due to the high regard in which the company was held by the city at this time he was able to issue £20 million of debentures, which were taken up by Legal & General, Norwich Union, and the church commissioners, with an interest rate of only 4.5 percent, virtually no higher than that which was available for gilt-edged stocks to government bonds.

By the late 1950s the credit squeeze made fundraising much more difficult for property developers, as the Bank of England instructed the banking sector to reduce lending. These restrictions shifted the balance of power in favor of the financial institutions when making funding agreements with developers. The institutions began to ask for a percentage of the profits from developments, while being careful not to take on too much of the risk. In the spring of 1959, Legal & General and Land Securities entered into the industry's first convertible debenture agreement. A total of £6 million was to be lent to Land Securities for expansion, on the security of a debenture. What made this deal unusual was that £1 million of this was convertible into Land Securities' ordinary shares at a price equivalent to 22 shillings 6 pence per share. Legal & General thereby secured a stake in any profits that might result from the funding. The arrangement drew a negative reaction from the press, as it led to a dilution of Land Securities' equity. Such deals, however, were to become standard over the next few years.

Shifting Strategies: Growth Through Acquisitions, 1964–89

The imposition of the "Brown Ban" on office development in and around London in November 1964 reduced the scope for Land Securities' expansion through further developments. Therefore, the company turned to takeovers as a source of growth. In the late 1960s, two very important takeover bids were launched. The first of these involved the acquisition of City Centre Properties Ltd. in 1968. City Centre, the former vehicle of one of the United Kingdom's most famous property developers, Jack Cotton, and latterly Charles Clore, had a number of valuable assets, including the stake in the aforementioned Pan Am Building, and raised the value of Land Securities' assets to £325 million. In April 1969 another successful takeover bid was launched, for The City of London Real Property Company Ltd. (CLRP), one of the U.K.'s oldest and most prestigious property companies. Established in 1864, it had concentrated its activities on City of London office property and owned what was probably the highest quality property portfolio of any institution. This acquisition swelled Land Securities' portfolio to more than £600 million and made Harold Samuel the largest property owner in the world. In 1971, Westminster Trust Ltd. was added to Land Securities' portfolio, with its £20 million of assets including New Scotland Yard.

By the early 1970s, Land Securities was regarded by many commentators as a sleeping giant. In fact, it had one of the largest development programs of all U.K. property companies. Land Securities was, however, more skeptical than most that the property boom would go on forever and did not borrow beyond its current ability to repay its debts, unlike many of its competitors. It emerged from the 1974 property crash in better shape than many of its rivals, although not completely unscathed, as shown by its share value, which had topped a price of 279 pence in 1973 and fell to 100 pence in 1974.

In the late 1970s, Land Securities made some adjustments. Property and land were sold, development projects were curtailed, and funds were raised by rights issues rather than borrowing, in order to avoid debts at a time of high interest rates. During these years, a time of rising prices for development land as institutional investment forced property prices up, Land Securities concentrated on developing its own property portfolio by redevelopment, refurbishment, and lease reconstruction, rather than buying land at what it considered to be expensive prices.

In 1983, the value of the company's property assets topped £2 billion. Unlike many of the United Kingdom's other large property companies, Land Securities still refrained from overseas expansion, concentrating instead on improving its U.K. portfolio. Assets were concentrated in the most conventional types of investment property; in 1985 60 percent of the portfolio was made up of offices, with shops accounting for 37 percent. During the mid-1980s, however, the company began to develop and acquire a number of out-of-town retail warehouses and food superstores. By 1988, after four years of activity, it had acquired a potential area of four million square feet of these types of buildings, spread over 50 locations throughout the country. Land Securities undertook some shop developments during the 1980s, but still concentrated activities in the central London office sector. During the summer of 1984, developments in progress included more than one million square feet of central London offices.

Harold Samuel died on August 28, 1987, having remained chairman of Land Securities until his death. In 1963 he had been the first developer to receive a knighthood and had been made a life peer in 1972. P.J. Hunt, the company's managing director, became both chairman and managing director. During 1987 Land Securities became the United Kingdom's first property company with more than £3 billion in assets. The rise in asset value was matched by an increase in borrowing, which rose from £231 million in March 1985 to £837 million in May 1987. New borrowing was arranged entirely on a long-term basis at a fixed rate of interest. Rising interest rates at the end of the decade, therefore, had little effect on development finance.

A key factor behind Land Securities' success was the inherent strength of the portfolio, built up by its founder, Lord Samuel. He was credited with inventing the maxim, "There are three things you need in property, these are: location, location, and location."

The Changing Face of London Real Estate in the 1990s

Entering the new decade, Land Securities remained as firmly wedded to its business strategy as ever, and in 1990 the company was continuing to forge long-term rental agreements with its clients. Since many of these agreements were in place through the year 2000, Land Securities was able to maintain good profit margins throughout the decade, in spite of sharp declines in rental prices and the adverse effects of England's recession on the city's business environment. Although the economic slowdown kept many corporations from expanding during this period, thus cutting demand for office space, Land Securities remained active in expanding its portfolio during the early 1990s, spending more than £600 million on new properties from 1991 to 1994.

Land Securities also became involved with a number of new construction projects in the middle to late 1990s, many of them outside of London. In 1996 the company was busy developing two shopping centers in the city of Birmingham. One, Caxton Gate, was completed that same year, while a second shopping complex, backed by investment capital exceeding £250 million,

was already in the works by May. At the same time, improvements to the transportation infrastructure in London, most notably the upgrading of commuter rail routes and the development of a central terminal for Channel Tunnel traffic, created a wave of new construction along the outskirts of the city and in the suburbs, a trend that prompted the company to look beyond the city center for new opportunities.

In the late 1990s, however, the real estate market shifted, and demand for prime rentals in central London once again rose. Anticipating that this trend would last for some time, Land Securities committed £650 million in 1998 to creating or refurbishing nearly 4.5 million square feet of property in the city. The following year, in response to the steady influx of businesses back into town, the company increased its development budget to £1.75 billion over the next five-year period. Land Securities also entered into negotiations with tenants and telecom companies in May 2000 to discuss the possibility of creating a telecommunications infrastructure for its central London properties.

There were other, more subtle shifts in the London real estate industry during this period, however, forcing the company to reevaluate its core strategy. The trend toward securing long-term leases was evolving gradually into a more tenant-friendly business strategy among the major London realtors. With many of the leases on Land Securities' primary properties set to expire, and with greater competition for tenants, the company's traditional philosophy—that the key to steady growth lay in the breadth of a realtor's holdings—was gradually making way to a more strictly profit-oriented mentality, with a focus on enhancing returns for investors. In response to this trend, Land Securities purchased Trillium, a property outsourcing group specializing in high-volume buying and selling of real estate, in November 2000. The move signaled a definitive, and crucial, break from tradition for Land Securities, who hoped to retain its dominant position in London real estate by paying close heed to the changing face of the market. Although the company was confronting a management crisis in the early 21st century, caused in part by this radical shift in business strategy, by 2002 it was clear that Land Securities had made a successful transition to remain competitive in the new investment-driven real estate climate.

Principal Subsidiaries

Land Securities Properties Limited; Ravenseft Properties Ltd.; The City of London Real Property Company Ltd.; Ravenside Investments Ltd.; Ravenseft Industrial Estates Ltd.; Land Securities Trillium Limited.

Principal Operating Units

Portfolio Management; Development; LS Trillium.

Principal Competitors

The British Land Company PLC; Canary Wharf Group plc; MEPC Limited.

Further Reading

Aris, Stephen, *The Jews in Business,* London: Jonathan Cape, 1970.

''Balance Sheet Strength at Land Securities,'' *Investors Chronicle,* June 7, 1985.

Bull, George, and Anthony Vice, *Bid For Power,* London: Elek Books, 1958.

Cohen, Norma, ''Land Securities Abandons the Traditional Way,'' *Financial Times* (London), November 3, 2000, p. 25.

Erdman, Edward, *People and Property,* London: Batsford, 1982.

Foster, Michael, ''Company File: Land Securities,'' *Estates Gazette,* June 20, 1981.

Gordon, Charles, *The Two Tycoons: A Personal Memoir of Jack Cotton and Charles Clore,* London: Hamish Hamilton, 1985.

''Land Securities: Topping £3 Billion,'' *Investors Chronicle,* May 22, 1987.

London, Simon, ''Land Securities Spies Upturn,'' *Financial Times* (London), November 14, 1996, p. 22.

Marriott, Oliver, *The Property Boom,* London: Hamish Hamilton Ltd., 1967.

''Obituary—Lord Samuel: Developer,'' *Financial Times,* September 1, 1987.

Smyth, Hedley, ''The Historical Growth of Property Companies and the Construction Industry in Britain Between 1939 and 1979'' (unpublished Ph.D thesis), University of Bristol: 1982.

Suzman, Mark, ''Land Securities Underlines Rental Recovery,'' *Financial Times* (London), May 22, 1997.

Whitehouse, Brian, *Partners in Property,* London: Birn, Shaw, 1964.

—Peter Scott
—update: Steve Meyer

Libbey Inc.

300 Madison Avenue
Toledo, Ohio 43604
U.S.A.
Telephone: (419) 325-2100
Fax: (419) 325-2117
Web site: http://www.libbey.com

Public Company
Incorporated: 1993
Employees: 3,200
Sales: $421.7 million (2001)
Stock Exchanges: New York
Ticker Symbol: LBY
NAIC: 327213 Glass Container Manufacturing

Libbey Inc. of Toledo, Ohio, is North America's top producer of glass tableware. In existence for nearly 200 years, the company bills itself as "America's Glassmaker." Since going public in 1993 and gaining its independence after many years operating as a subsidiary or division of Owens-Illinois, Libbey has expanded into new tableware products. Through acquisitions it has grown into a major provider of ceramic and metal flatware to America's foodservice industry. Subsidiary Syracuse China produces dinnerware and World Tableware makes metal flatware and hollowware. In addition, a joint venture with Mexican glassware manufacturer Vitrocrisa has allowed Libbey to further its efforts to market its products internationally.

Origins of Libbey Reaching Back to Late 1700s

Glassmaking was one of the earliest industry start-ups attempted in the New World, dating as far back as 1608 to the London Company's Jamestown, Virginia, settlement. The venture failed, but over the next 150 years other businessmen followed, so that by the time of the American Revolution the Colonies had an established, although unsteady, glass industry. New England became a natural location for glassmakers, the forests offering a cheap and readily available source of fuel, a dependable workforce, and access to world markets through Boston harbor. Libbey's most distant ancestor is the Boston

Crown Glass Company, which was chartered in the late 1700s to produce crude window glass, so-called crown glass, and is credited with introducing lead glass to the North Atlantic states. In 1814 some of its employees struck out on their own, forming the Boston Porcelain and Glass Company to produce fine glass at a plant located in East Cambridge. Within three years, however, the business failed, and in November 1817 its assets were auctioned off to a group of four investors. In February 1818 the new company, Libbey's direct ancestor, became known as the New England Glass Company, a name it would retain for the next 60 years.

The most influential man of the investment group was Deming Jarvis, the son of a wealthy Boston businessman who had worked at Boston Porcelain as a clerk. He now became the first agent, or general manager, for New England Glass, a position he held until 1826. Perhaps of more importance to the company's future prosperity was his exclusive holding of the American rights to the production of red lead, which was required in the making of fine tablewares. Most of the country's other 40 glasshouses continued to produce crown window glass, but Jarvis's monopoly permitted New England Glass to compete with European glassmakers on an even playing field. In its first year of operation, with a workforce of 40, the company produced goods valued at $40,000. By 1849 New England Glass became the largest glassmaker in the world, employing 500, with the value of goods produced growing to $500,000.

New England Glass was well known for its high quality glass products. Not only did it produce blown pieces in both clear glass and a range of colors, it also pioneered the process of pressed glass. Technical advances in the industry and other factors, however, would mitigate the advantages of an excellent reputation for quality craftsmanship. In 1864 a former employee, William Leighton, developed a soda lime formula to replace lead in the making of glass. It was cheaper and safer, lessening the risks of lead poisoning to workers, and also produced glass that was thin and hard, easy to cool, and ideal for pressing. While most glassmakers soon switched over to the new mix, New England Glass refused, its management firmly believing the new lime-based glass to be of inferior quality. The company suffered a further economic disadvantage because of the distances it had to ship coal to serve as its fuel, now that the pine forests of New England were depleted.

Libbey Family Becoming Involved with New England Glass: 1870s

As New England Glass struggled to compete in the 1870s, barely managing to survive the depression of 1873, the Libbey family became involved with the company. William L. Libbey joined New England Glass as agent in 1870. He had been part owner of Mount Washington Glass and shared New England Glass's commitment to quality. In fact, when the business began to operate at a loss and the directors voted in 1874 to close the company, Libbey convinced them to continue. Despite cutbacks, New England Glass continued to post losses, and in 1878 the directors elected to lease the properties to Libbey. Until 1880 the company continued to operate as New England Glass, then changed its name to W.L. Libbey and Son, Proprietors. The son was Edward Drummond Libbey, who had gone to work for his father at New England Glass in 1872 as a chore boy, apparently as a way for the father to convince the son to enroll at Harvard University, which young Libbey had refused to do. Eventually Edward enrolled at Maine's Kent Hill Academy with the intent of becoming a Methodist minister. A throat infection, however, permanently impaired his voice and destroyed his ability as a public speaker. As a result, he returned to New England Glass in 1874, taking a position as a clerk and learning firsthand the financial difficulties that the company now faced. By 1880 he was made a partner, precipitating the change in the name of the business, and when his father died in 1883 Edward, at the age of 29, assumed control.

Over the next five years Edward Libbey managed to keep the company afloat despite chronic fuel shortages and labor difficulties. With the discovery of natural gas fields in the Midwest, Libbey began to search the area for a suitable place to relocate the business. In February 1888 he signed a generous contract to transfer his glass works to Toledo, Ohio. The city fathers agreed to provide a four-acre factory and 50 lots for workers' homes. Moreover, Toledo was ideally situated, close to natural gas fields, a major railroad center, as well as Lake Erie. As part of the move, the business was incorporated in Ohio as W.L. Libbey & Son Company, then renamed in 1892 as Libbey Glass Company.

In August 1888 a special train arrived in Toledo from Boston containing 50 carloads of machinery and 250 workers. Perhaps the most valuable asset of all was a young glassblower named Michael J. Owens. Born to poor immigrant parents in West Virginia he had gone to work in a glass factory at the age of ten. Ambitious and eager to further his own education, Owens developed his talent for public speaking and became a union

organizer. Libbey quickly recognized Owens's leadership abilities and put the 29-year-old glassblower in charge of the new Toledo plant. Despite the advantages of the Toledo location and Owens's talents, however, the company continued to lose money. A turning point came in 1892 when the Corning Glass Works was shut down by a strike and Libbey Glass was able to secure a contract from Edison General Electric to produce handblown light bulbs. In that same year Libbey made a decision, opposed by some directors, that would result in transforming the struggling business into the most important cut glass manufacturer in the world: He secured the exclusive rights to build and exhibit a fully operating glass factory at Chicago's 1893 Columbian Exposition.

Well positioned on the Midway Plaisance of the Exposition, the Libbey Pavilion was designed to look like a palace. Visitors for the price of 10¢ (later increased to 25¢) could observe the craft of handblowing and cutting glass. The price of admission could then be applied toward the purchase of a glass souvenir, such as a slipper, hatchet, paperweight, or cup and saucer. More expensive cut glass items were also offered for sale. The highlight of the Libbey exhibits was a spun glass dress. With over two million people visiting its pavilion and garnering considerable press attention, Libbey Glass was now able to place its fine cut glass wares at some of the most prestigious stores in the country, including New York's Tiffany's. Cut glass now entered its "Brilliant Period," a run of popularity that lasted for 25 years.

With Libbey Glass enjoying the fruits of prosperity, Edward Libbey was able to back the pioneering work of Michael Owens. After designing machines to produce light bulbs, tumblers, and lamp chimneys, Owens in 1903 invented the automatic bottle blowing machine, one of the most important advances in the history of glassmaking, resulting in a variety of glass products that now became affordable to the masses. Owens also perfected the first automatic flat glass making machine. Several new companies grew out of Owens's inventions: the Toledo Glass Company to make tumblers and lamp chimneys; the Owens Bottle Company; and Libbey-Owens Sheet Glass Company. Libbey Glass, meanwhile, continued to focus on the fine cut glass market. Although Edward Libbey remained the company's largest stockholder, he withdrew from active participation in its affairs in 1896, choosing instead to devote most of his time to the businesses created to exploit Owens's inventions.

The "Brilliant Period" for cut glass began to wind down during World War I, when not only did consumers' tastes begin to change, but wartime restrictions limited necessary chemicals. Libbey attempted to maintain the business by introducing "Lightware," a less expensive product because the walls were thinner and required less cutting time, but the effort was poorly promoted and proved to be a disappointment for the company. Edward Libbey continued to hold a controlling interest in Libbey Glass until 1920, three years before his death, when the business was reorganized as the Libbey Glass Manufacturing Company.

Libbey Glass enjoyed something of a resurgence in the 1920s with the introduction of the "safedge" tumbler, the rim of which was chip resistant. The company was especially successful in selling this line to the restaurant market. With the

Key Dates:

1818: New England Glass Company is formed.
1872: William Libbey joins New England Glass.
1880: Company is renamed W.L. Libbey and Son, Proprietors.
1888: Company moves to Toledo, Ohio.
1893: Libbey Pavilion at Chicago's Columbian Exposition leads to period of strong growth.
1933: Business is sold to Owens-Illinois.
1993: Libbey Inc. is spun off from Owens-Illinois.
1995: Syracuse China is acquired.

repeal of prohibition in 1933, the demand for glassware products from restaurants and bars grew even greater. Unfortunately, a poor decision in 1931 to attempt to reestablish the Libbey name in the fine art glass market more than offset these positive developments. A. Douglas Nash, who had been more of a sales executive than a designer for Tiffany, was hired to create a new line of luxury stemware. Despite the friction Nash caused with longtime Libbey craftsmen, he did produce some beautiful work, which received considerable attention when it debuted in 1933. Given the wide-reaching effects of the Depression, however, the timing could not have been worse and the line proved to be a disaster for the company. In 1935 Owens-Illinois bought Libbey Glass for $5 million. Owens-Illinois was the result of the 1929 merger of the Owens Bottle Machine Company and the Illinois Glass Company.

Libbey Glass became a wholly owned subsidiary of Owens-Illinois and with better management in place was able to regain its equilibrium and prosper during the remainder of the Depression. Of note during this period was a promotional tie-in with Walt Disney's highly successful animated film *Snow White and the Seven Dwarfs*. Countless tumblers featuring characters from the movie were filled by dairies with cottage cheese and sold across the country. Now on a better financial footing, Libbey was able to make a successful return to the fine glass market, launching a new line of crystal called Modern American. The series ended with the advent of World War II, as the company turned its attention to producing tubes for radar, x-ray machines, and other electronic equipment. In 1944 the company was folded into Owens-Illinois and began operating as the Libbey Glass Division of the parent corporation.

Post–World War II Focus on Household Market

Shortly after the United States entered World War II, Libbey Glass began making plans to focus on the household market for glassware in the postwar world. This strategy, coupled with the Baby Boom, resulted in a period of robust sales growth. Pre-packed sets of eight tumblers, ''Hostess Sets,'' introduced in 1945, were especially successful, and by offering a variety of changing styles and designs, Libbey Glass became a major force in popular-priced glassware. Annual sales, which totaled $7 million in 1943, grew to $40 million by 1968.

Although Libbey Glass was a profitable business while a part of Owens-Illinois, by the 1990s it was becoming stagnant,

prevented from pursuing acquisitions or expanding into new areas. Owens-Illinois, burdened with debt, decided to spin off the Libbey Glass Division as Libbey Inc. in a public offering, completed in June 1993. At the same time, the new company also acquired Libbey-St.Clair, Canada's top producer of glass tableware. According to a *Barron's* profile of Libbey written several months after the IPO, ''Owens-Illinois had drained Libbey of $310 million of dividends the prior three years, leaving Libbey with a negative net worth of $95 million at 1993 year-end. Fortunately, the freeing of Libbey occurred as the company's earnings were hitting a record pace, and cash flow was accelerating.''

Leading the independent company as chairman and CEO was John Meier, a man with 24 years of experience with the Libbey Glass Division. He set an ambitious goal of becoming a $500 million company within five years, to be achieved by expanding into department stores with more upscale products while at the same time growing the mass merchandise side of the business by pursuing new glassware categories. There was also a willingness to move beyond glassware to other complementary tabletop items. In October 1995 Libbey paid $40.7 million in cash to acquire Syracuse China, a major maker of ceramic dinnerware to the foodservice industry. It was originally founded in 1871 as The Onondaga Pottery and over the course of its history earned a strong reputation for its high quality dinnerware and ability to adjust to changing tastes in American dining. The addition of Syracuse China contributed to record results for Libbey in 1995, the company posting sales of $357.5 million, a 7.1 percent increase over the previous year's $334 million. Net income reach $30 million, a 12.5 percent bump over 1994's 26.7 million.

In 1997 Libbey expanded its international presence and broadened its product lines when it agreed to purchase a 49 percent interest in Mexico's top glass tableware supplier, Vitrocrisa, a subsidiary of Grupo Vitro S.A., the country's largest glassmaker. Libbey also acquired World Tableware from Vitro S.A., a supplier of dinnerware, metal flatware, and serveware to the foodservice market. For Libbey, World Tableware provided a way to enter the flatware business, part of a strategy to coordinate the colors and patterns of the company's glassware with dinnerware and flatware. Although these transactions bode well for the long-term health of Libbey, in the short run the company experienced some sluggish quarters in the late 1990s, necessitating some restructuring measures. Nevertheless, the company attempted to acquire its main rival in the tabletop business, Oneida Ltd., a move vigorously opposed by Oneida's board. Libbey ultimately backed away from the takeover bid.

In 2001 Libbey agreed to buy the Anchor Hocking glass business from Newell Rubbermaid Inc. for more than $330 million. In addition to beverageware, Anchor Hocking produced bakeware and ovenware. Although Libbey's management maintained that the primary purpose of the acquisition was to bolster its bakeware and serveware business, the Federal Trade Commission opposed the deal because it believed that competition in foodservice glassware would be adversely impacted. In June 2002 Libbey was forced to abandon this deal as well. Despite these setbacks, Libbey was clearly a company eager to continue its expansion beyond glassware into all aspects of the tabletop market.

Principal Subsidiaries

Syracuse China; World Tableware.

Principal Competitors

Lancaster Colony Corporation; Newell Rubbermaid Inc.; Oneida Ltd.

Further Reading

Bernard, Ann-Margaret Keho Sharyn, ''Smashing Success,'' *HFD,* October 24, 1994, p. 46.

Byrne, Harlan S., ''A Glass Act,'' *Barron's,* April 11, 1994, p. 20.

Fauster, Carl U., *Libbey Glass Since 1818: Pictorial History & Collector's Guide,* Toledo, Ohio: Len Beach Press, 1979, 415 p.

Goldbogen, Jessica, ''Extending Its Reach Libbey Unwraps First Dinnerware, Flatware,'' *HFN,* January 12, 1998, p. 41.

Keefe, John Webster, *Libbey Glass; A Tradition of 150 Years, 1818–1968,* Toledo, Ohio: Toledo Museum of Art, 1968, 69 p.

—Ed Dinger

Madeira Wine Company, S.A.

Rua dos Ferreiros, 191
P.O. Box 295
9003 Funchal
Madeira
Telephone: 351-91-740100
Fax: 351-91-740101
Web site: http://www.madeirawinecompany.com

Private Company
Incorporated: 1913 as Madeira Wine Association
NAIC: 312130 Wineries

Madeira Wine Company, S.A. is the leading producer and exporter of madeira wine, which is produced on the island of Madeira, a Portuguese possession located 400 miles off the coast of Morocco in the Atlantic Ocean. Madeira wine is a fortified alcoholic beverage, similar to port, which is made by combining wine with brandy and other ingredients such as grape juice and heating it for an extended period of time. Much madeira is sold in bulk to France and Germany, where it is used as a cooking ingredient, while the rest is bottled and sold to tourists or exported. The company has been controlled since 1989 by the Symington family, Scottish immigrants who began producing port wine in Oporto, Portugal, in the late 1800s. The Blandy family of Madeira, which controlled the company from 1925 to 1989, continues to own a minority stake. The leading brands produced by the Madeira Wine Company are Blandy, Cossart Gordon, and Leacock. The company also operates the Old Blandy Wine Lodge in Funchal, Madeira, which is a major tourist attraction on the island.

Origins

The production of wine on Madeira dates to the 15th century, when the island was discovered by the Portuguese mariner Joao Concalves Zarco, who gave it its name (meaning ''woods'') when he landed there in 1420. He found that it was covered with a dense rainforest which was virtually impenetrable, and according to legend Zarco set it afire, after which it burned for seven years until the entire island was covered with a thick blanket of ashes. Zarco was appointed governor and ordered by Portugal's Prince Henry to plant sugar cane, grains, and grapes, for which the nutrient-laden ashes were perfectly suited. Export of wine was minimal until the late 1600s, when the King ordered ships heading across the Atlantic to Portugal's colonies in South America to take on wine at the island. This coincided with the wine shipping business becoming dominated by British immigrants to Madeira, a situation which would remain constant for years to come. Over the next century madeira wine became popular both in South America and in the British colonies of North America, where it was used to toast the Declaration of Independence in 1776. George Washington was also said to enjoy a daily pint of madeira at dinner.

Madeira wine was fortified, which typically consisted of adding brandy to the basic wine produced from fermented grapes. This addition increased the wine's alcohol content and acted as a preservative. The fortification process was introduced in the mid-1700s when the island's wine shippers began using it to help keep the wine from going bad during its long ocean voyage to the Americas. Unlike fortified port wine, which was aged in cool, quiet cellars, madeira achieved its distinctive flavor through stress—a combination of the jostling it got traveling across the Atlantic and the heating it took from the hot ocean sun. The benefits of this process were discovered when an unsold shipment of fortified madeira was returned to the island after traveling across the ocean and back. Henceforth madeira producers asked ships stopping at the island to add barrels of the wine to their holds as ballast so it could travel the seas and gain its distinctive flavor.

In later years the same effect was achieved by heating the wine as part of its production process, typically to a temperature of 120 degrees for a period of three months. A longer heating period at a slightly lower temperature, with a more gradual cooling process, would produce the best grade of wine, and the better types were allowed to age in attics for four or five years. A minimum of 18 months was required for a wine to reach maturity, but the best madeiras were aged for decades. Over time, four main types of madeira came to be produced. These included the dry, lighter Rainwater style, originally developed for export to antebellum southern U.S. plantations; the less dry

Sercial and Verdelho; and the darker, richer Bual and Malmsey (all but Rainwater were named for the grape the wine was made from). The quality of the end product was dependent upon the type of grapes used, the kind of fortification, and the aging and heating process.

Banding Together to Cut Costs

Over the years a number of different firms came to produce madeira on the island. In 1913 several leading exporters, Wm. Hinton & Sons, Welsh & Cunha, and Henriques, Camara, & Cia, formed the Madeira Wine Association, which was designed to help its members reduce overhead by pooling costs. The three founding partners became shareholders in the new company, which took full ownership of the assets of each, who remained distinct entities in name only.

In 1925 Blandy Brothers & Co., Thomas Mullins, and Leacock & Co. became additional shareholders in the Association and John Ernest Blandy was named its head. The well-respected Mullins, who was not a wine shipper, became the company's manager. Production was at a low point during this era, with many firms hurt by the impact of American prohibition and the Russian revolution (madeira was extremely popular with the Russian aristocracy), as well as the lingering aftereffects of several vine diseases that had devastated production in the late 19th century. The 1930s and 1940s were also a difficult period, with sales continuing to be dampened by a worldwide economic slowdown and World War II. Following the war the situation improved only marginally as drinking habits changed and fortified wines such as madeira and port fell out of general favor. Madeira wine did find a new market in the Scandinavian countries of Sweden, Denmark, and Finland, however, while the French began to import increasing amounts of a lower-quality madeira made from Tinta Negro Mole grapes for use as a cooking wine. By the 1950s this grape comprised more than three-fourths of the crop produced on the island, and wine produced for bulk imports to France became the primary form of madeira manufactured.

Other companies became partners in the Association between 1925 and the postwar period, including Luiz Gomes da Conceicao & Filhos, T.T. da Camara Lomelino, and Cossart Gordon & Co. Ltd., which came on board in 1953. By this time more than two dozen companies had combined forces in the firm, including all of the island's British shippers and many of its Portuguese ones. The Association continued to be headed by members of the Blandy family, who had lived on Madeira since 1811 and had developed a number of other business interests including shipping, real estate, newspaper publishing, hotel man-

agement, banking, and orchid growing. Though different brands were produced using the various shareholders' individual names, in actuality they were bottled from common stocks of wine and blended to fit established styles by the Association's chief blender. The maintenance of separate names was a fiction that the company's sales agents, then numbering more than 70, kept up by use of different business cards for the various brand names, which sometimes caused embarrassment when a single agent pretended to work exclusively for multiple companies.

Beginning in the early 1970s the madeira wine producers' fortunes began looking up after the government took steps to help upgrade the quality of the island's wines. Free grafting of ''classical'' varieties of grapes was offered for growers who wished to switch to them from Tinta Negro Mole or other forms of produce such as bananas. Some vineyards were lost, however, following the 1974 revolution in Portugal, when democracy was restored to the formerly fascist country. The new government allowed tenant farmers the chance to take control of their land and resell it, and many did, leading to the conversion of many vineyards into housing developments and other uses.

The 1974 revolution also affected the company directly when its bank was nationalized. The bank's new leadership stopped making loans to many businesses, including the Association, which led to problems such as difficulties with its workforce. The older Association directors were soon overwhelmed by the situation and left the company, leaving it in the control of the Blandy and Leacock families. A disagreement about the future direction of the firm led to the Blandy family taking over the Leacocks' shares several years later, which finally helped bring needed stability to the company. During the first few years after the revolution the Association had gone through five managing directors, four financial directors, and four production directors.

In 1979 the Madeira Wine Institute was formed by the Portuguese government, which had the power to regulate most aspects of the industry. The Institute established a set of rules including one requiring that wines contain at least 85 percent of the type of grape shown on the label. The Institute later helped negotiate the standards for wine which were adopted when Portugal entered the European Union in 1986. During this period, the Madeira Wine Association—which changed its name to the Madeira Wine Company (MWC) in 1981— reduced the number of names it used on bottles to about nine from the more than two dozen of earlier years, which greatly simplified the task of the company's chief wine blender.

A New Partner: Late 1980s

Toward the end of the 1980s the Blandys decided to seek outside help in improving worldwide distribution and brand awareness. They approached the Symington family, which they had known for many years, for assistance. In 1988 the Symingtons invested in the company and the following year gained controlling interest when the remaining minority shareholders sold out. The Blandys retained just over 40 percent ownership. The Symingtons manufactured port wine, had an international distribution network, and had developed expertise in high quality manufacturing techniques. The family had come from Scotland in 1882 to Oporto, Portugal, and over the years

Key Dates:

1913: Madeira Wine Association is formed by three export companies.
1925: Blandy and Leacock firms join Association.
1953: Cossart Gordon becomes a shareholder.
1974: Following Portuguese revolution, Blandy and Leacock families take control of firm.
1981: Madeira Wine Association changes name to Madeira Wine Company.
1989: Symington family takes a majority stake in company.
2000: Major renovation of wine production facilities is completed.

had developed their business into a leading port winery through the acquisition of several large companies including Warre's, Graham's, Dow's, and Smith Woodhouse. The Symingtons were well regarded within the wine industry for their sharp focus on the business. Though living for more than a century in Portugal, the family remained proud of their U.K. heritage, retaining membership in the Oporto Cricket and Lawn Tennis Club. The Blandys also maintained strong ties to their ancestral homeland.

At this time most of the madeira produced was still being sold in bulk to France and Germany for use as cooking wine. A quarter of this lesser-grade wine was shipped by MWC, which also produced more than half the island's bottled varieties. Much bottled madeira was in fact consumed by tourists to the island, who bought it at a winery tour or to take home, rather than by the inhabitants of Madeira itself. Leading foreign consumers of the company's bottled wines were Britain, the United States, France, Japan, the Scandinavian countries, and Canada.

MWC also operated the Old Blandy Wine Lodge in the center of Madeira's capital of Funchal, which was visited by more than 200,000 people per year. The beautiful and historic lodge showcased the finest wines of the island, and featured a tasting room devoted to vintage madeiras. Wine was produced on the site, and the company also maintained a separate, more functional facility for production of the remainder of its output.

Following the takeover by the Symingtons, efforts were made to increase the prestige of the company's product and broaden its distribution. The three principal brands, Blandy, Leacock, and Cossart Gordon, were promoted, and further efforts were made to induce growers to plant more of the traditional, "noble" types of grapes in place of the lesser varieties that were used to produce bulk-shipment madeira. The Symingtons met some initial resistance when they attempted to change the flavor characteristics of their madeira, making a more "fruity" wine and relying less on the heating process. The Madeira Wine Institute took a dim view of the changes, with its tasting panel continually rejecting samples of Symington-produced madeira. Eventually a workable compromise was reached between the traditional styles and the newer one. Despite the controversy among purists, the company's products became popular with consumers, and MWC's fortunes began to look up under its new ownership.

In the 1990s the Symingtons began a major renovation project at the company's winemaking facility in Funchal, which was completed in 2000. The equipment used for blending and storage of the firm's finer wines was upgraded in anticipation of a growth in interest in bottled madeira, which the Symingtons continued to work diligently to create.

Under the guidance of the Symington family, the Madeira Wine Company was in the best shape it had been in years. The company's improved production facilities and its focus on increasing brand awareness and expanded bottled madeira sales were likely to continue to bring in steady revenues for the firm.

Principal Competitors

H.M. Borges, Sucrs, Lda.; Henriques & Henriques, Lda.; Vinhos Justino Henriques, Filhos, Lda.; Pereira d'Oliveira (Vinhos), Lda.; Vinhos Barbeito (Madeira), Lda.; Silva Vinhos.

Further Reading

Liddell, Alex, *Madeira,* London: Faber and Faber, 1998.
"A Lot of Bottle," *Economist,* December 20, 1986, p. 102.
Maitland, Alison, "Survey of Madeira," *Financial Times (London),* June 17, 1992, p. 35.
White, David, "Family Keeps Winning Blend," *Financial Times (London),* November 21, 1996, p. 4.
——, "Survey—Madeira: An After-Dinner Curiosity," *Financial Times (London),* May 28, 1996, p. 3.
——, "Survey—Madeira: Part of the Landscape," *Financial Times (London),* May 28, 1996, p. 3.
Wise, Peter, "Survey of Madeira," *Financial Times (London),* May 6, 1994, p. 111.

—Frank Uhle

Matalan PLC

Gillibrands Road
Skelmersdale, Lancashire WN8 9TB
United Kingdom
Telephone: +44-1695-552-400
Fax: +44-1695-552-401
Web site: http://www.matalan.co.uk

Public Company
Incorporated: 1985
Employees: 8,039
Sales: $845.4 million (2001)
Stock Exchanges: London
Ticker Symbol: MTN
NAIC: 448140 Family Clothing Stores; 452910
   Warehouse Clubs and Superstores

Matalan PLC is the fastest growing retailer in the United Kingdom with more than 120 stores that market High Street fashion at bargain prices. Like the U.S.-based Sam's Club, Matalan PLC is located outside of larger cities and offers a club warehouse concept in savings. Each store boasts an average of 30,000 square feet of clothing for the whole family. The company has been rapidly expanding since its founding in 1985.

1985–95: U.S. Trip Sparks Business Idea

John Hargreaves was the son of a Liverpool docker who had worked himself into the successful position of market trader in the 1970s. But in the early 1980s, he took a trip that changed his life. While on vacation in the United States, he became fascinated with the retail concept of club warehouses—located outside of towns and with deep discounts. Hargreaves was determined to try the concept in the United Kingdom; in 1985, he opened the first Matalan Discount Club in Preston.

The idea was a success and, by 1995, Matalan had expanded to 50 stores across the country. It introduced a new concept to the United Kingdom and offered consumers a choice of better prices and good selection.

1995–99: Growing and Going Public

John Hargreaves gave up the chief executive seat in 1996 to Angus Monro but remained as chairman of the board. In 1997, the company, which had outgrown its Preston location, moved its headquarters to Skelmersdale and added a distribution center there. By early 1998, Matalan boasted 75 stores and record financial results for 1997, including a 24 percent increase in sales and an 87 percent increase in profit. In May 1998, the company listed 23.4 million shares on the London Stock Exchange to "reduce indebtedness and provide (the company) with increased flexibility to pursue expansion plans," according to a company press release.

By the end of 1998, Matalan had added 12 new stores and 210,000 square feet of selling space. The company also diversified its product line to include housewares and other non-clothing wares. "I am pleased to report that the consistent application of our strategy and delivery of our outstanding value for money proposition has produced a record set of results," said Hargreaves. Earnings per share were up 64 percent, yielding a final dividend of 5.5 pence per share.

Same-store sales grew 18.5 percent in the first nine weeks of 1999. However, the company cautioned investors not to expect that type of sustained return. "I'd like to look forward to 18.5 percent for the rest of the year, but clearly we're not planning for that," said Ian Smith, finance director in an interview with the *Extel Examiner*. "We're planning for much more modest growth than that—probably in line with last year, maybe slightly behind last year would be my sentiment at the moment." In 1999, Matalan bought the rights to Falmer, the second largest ladies' casualwear brand in the United Kingdom.

In June 1999, Matalan experienced its first major downturn in stock trading as U.S. retailer Wal-Mart announced its foray into the U.K. market. Wal-Mart, part of the inspiration for the birth of Matalan, purchased ASDA Group PLC and was expected to drive prices and margins down across the country. The news, however, did not stop profits from rising in Matalan's stores. Profits were up 169 percent in the first half of 1999, prompting stocks and confidences to rise. "The business continued to grow strongly in the first half of 1999, driven by like-for-

Company Perspectives:

Matalan is a totally unique out of town retailer, committed to providing outstanding value for money. We offer up to the minute fashion and home wares at prices up to 50 percent below the equivalent High Street price. More value: By buying direct from the manufacturer, by being situated at low cost, convenient out of town locations, keeping overhead costs low and operating on lower margins, Matalan is able to offer unbeatable value! More style: With all the latest key looks for the season, from modern basics to classic styles, and with a great selection of top brands including, Falmer, Playtex, and Wrangler, Matalan offers fantastic values for all the family. You will also find clothes from top designers like Valentino, Calvin Klein, Ralph Lauren. More choice: Nobody else offers such fantastic value and great ranges. So it's no wonder we're the fastest growing fashion retailer.

like sales growth of 15.4 percent from our core estate as well as new space contribution,'' said Hargreaves.

By October 1999, demand for Matalan stock was high but a limited amount was available for trading on the London Stock Exchange since Hargreaves and his family held 60 percent of the stock in the company. The weeks prior to the Christmas shopping season were successful, with total sales up 43.9 percent over 1998 figures.

2000 and Beyond: Bumps in the Road for Matalan

By early 2000, the effects of U.S. retailer Wal-Mart's purchase of George at ASDA stores were obvious in the United Kingdom and caused a weakening demand for middle market clothing stores. However, Matalan, also a discount retailer, had felt little effect from the entry of Wal-Mart. The trend was seen across the United Kingdom, where retail consultant Verdict predicted that discount retailers' share of the market would increase from 8.9 percent in 1999 to 13.9 percent by 2004.

In the first ten weeks of 2000, the trading price of Matalan stock was up 31.2 percent, a strong indication of investor confidence in the company due to increases in revenue. However, Matalan Chief Executive Angus Monro cautioned, ''Probably in the second half of the year there will be some slowing down of those rates of like-for-like sales growth.''

The company announced in 2000 that it was continuing with its aggressive growth—increasing floor space in its stores, opening larger stores, and relocating those stores that were now deemed too small at under 10,000 square feet. The company was also identifying up to 220 new locations for the stores as well as preparing to launch a Matalan credit card.

Founder and Chairman John Hargreaves and his family decided to place 45.4 million shares on the market in 2000, reducing their stake in the company from 64 percent to 52 percent. The news was welcomed at the London Stock Exchange.

Matalan's credit card was launched in October 2000 and offered a competitive low rate of 11.9 percent, lower than other

department store cards in the United Kingdom. When used for Matalan shopping, the card's annual rate dropped to 5 percent.

During 2000, Matalan's share in the U.K. clothing market rose from 1.9 percent to 2.4 percent. The number of employees rose 42 percent from 5,660 to 8,039 and active membership in the Matalan Discount Club grew 43 percent, from 4.4 million to 6.3 million. Total retail space increased 50 percent. Despite these positive numbers, Christmas 2000 was disappointing and resulted in a stock plunge in January 2001. While the company's like-for-like sales were higher than the previous year, the forecasts had been higher still and the market reacted negatively to the underperformance. Matalan lost half its market value in the half hour after the announcement that it had slower growth than expected as well as remaining inventory to sell at a discount.

In April 2001, the company and its stock were hit once again as Angus Monro resigned suddenly amid rumors of a disagreement about the company's future. The company released a brief statement that read, ''Angus has established a platform for the business to grow and will leave the business in a sound financial and strong trading position. During the five years of his tenure, he has made an outstanding contribution. However, given his stated intention to leave the business in two to three years' time and the Board's desire to develop aggressively its strategic options, it has been agreed with him that it is more appropriate that he leaves at this time.''

The mutual nature of the decision seemed debatable. Monro had just the week before told the *London Times* of his plans for the future of the company. After his resignation, the *Sunday Times* quoted unnamed friends of Monro as saying he was ''ambushed'' and ''astonished.'' The company's board announced that founder and Chairman John Hargreaves would assume the chief executive duties until a replacement could be found.

As the search for a replacement began, market watchers reported in an *AFX News* article in May 2001 that some analysts wondered if a disagreement between Monro and the Hargreaves family had caused his departure and, if so, what that would mean for recruiting a replacement. Since the family owned 52 percent of the company, some believed that their influence might be overwhelming to the board and to a new chief executive. However, Finance Director Ian Smith said, ''I'm sure that anybody that aspires to chief executive status will have the gumption to talk to John and will fully understand the sort of person that John is and that he is not a dictatorial owner.''

In July 2001, the company purchased Lee Cooper Group Ltd., a maker of branded jeans and casual clothing. As Europe's second largest jean company, Lee Cooper employed 1,100 people and had operations in Europe, the Middle East, Asia, and Latin America. Matalan announced that Lee Cooper's management would continue and that it would act as a stand-alone division of Matalan.

Matalan recruited Paul Mason, age 41, as its new chief executive in August 2001, luring him away from his position as president and managing director of competitor ASDA Wal-Mart U.K. Mason had 20 years of retail experience and had been at ASDA for six years, playing an instrumental role in Wal-Mart's purchase of the business. ''I am extremely pleased

Key Dates:

1985: Company is founded by John Hargreaves.
1996: John Hargreaves resigns as chief executive and is replaced by Angus Monro.
1997: Matalan moves headquarters to Skelmersdale.
1998: The company lists on the London Stock Exchange under the symbol MTN.
2000: Matalan launches credit card.
2001: Matalan announces purchase of the second largest European jeans maker, Lee Cooper Group; CEO Angus Monro resigns and is replaced by Paul Mason.

to have been offered what is one of the most exciting and prestigious roles in U.K. retailing. I look forward very much to helping build on Matalan's unique strengths and market positioning," said Mason.

Retail analysts applauded the move, and the future looked bright for Matalan. However, in October Matalan reported a sharp downturn in sales that resulted in a 16 percent drop in its stock price. The company reported that the slowdown was due to several factors, including the September 11 terrorist attacks in the United States. For 2001, Matalan's stock was down considerably and was grouped among the worst performing retail stocks in Britain. The news was not all bad, however, as Matalan's market share among clothing retailers increased and the recent purchase of Lee Cooper jeans. The company also announced plans to move into continental Europe to further expand its growth.

Principal Competitors

ASDA Wal-Mart U.K.; Marks and Spencer p.l.c.; Arcadia Group plc.

Further Reading

Carter, Helen, "Disgraced Pathologist to Lose Job," *Guardian*, February 2, 2001.

"Children's Clothing Market on Brink of 'Major Developmental Phase'—Verdict," *Extel Examiner*, October 19, 1998.

Davey, James, "Matalan Appoints Headhunters to Search for Monro Replacement," *AFX News*, May 9, 2001.

Griffiths, Ben, "Retailers Hit by Poor Christmas Sales," *Business a.m.*, January 12, 2001.

Hardcastle, Elaine, "Slowdown at UK's Matalan Sends Shares Tumbling," *Yahoo Finance*, October 31, 2001.

"Landowner One of the Richest in the World," *Northern Echo*, June 16, 1000.

"Matalan Buys Rights to Falmer Brand," *Extel Examiner*, May 21, 1999.

"Matalan Cautions Current Trading Figures not Sustainable," *Extel Examiner*, March 10, 1999.

"Matalan Issues Pathfinder Prospectus for LSE Float," *Extel Examiner*, April 20, 1998.

"Matalan Poised for FTSE Promotion," *BBC News*, August 24, 2001.

"Matalan Sees Further Sales Growth in 1999, Margin Growth Slower," *Extel Examiner*, March 19, 1999.

"Matalan's Hargreaves Unlikely to Reduce 60 Percent Share Before March," *Extel Examiner*, October 15, 1999.

"Matalan Surges on Buoyant Current Trading News," *Extel Examiner*, October 15, 1999.

"Matalan to List on LSE by Placing 23.4 mln Shares at 235 p/shr," *Extel Examiner*, May 7, 1998.

"Matalan Tops List of FTSE 250 Fallers on Wal-Mart Impact Fears," *Extel Examiner*, June 15, 1999.

"Matalan Up As Merrill Lynch Lifts Target Price and Forecast," *Extel Examiner*, October 19, 1999.

Mills, Lauren, "Card to Shake Up British Shopping," October 3, 2000, http:www.theage.com.au.

Walsh, Fiona, and Robert Lea, "Top Trio Plunge on High Street Shock," *Evening Standard*, January 11, 2001.

—Melissa Rigney Baxter

Midwest Grain Products, Inc.
Creating Better Solutions, Naturally

Midwest Grain Products, Inc.

1300 Main Street
Atchison, Kansas 66002
U.S.A.
Telephone: (913) 367-1480
Fax: (913) 367-0192
Web site: http://www.midwestgrain.com

Public Company
Incorporated: 1957
Employees: 416
Sales: $229.2 million (2001)
Stock Exchanges: NASDAQ
Ticker Symbol: MWGP
NAIC: 311119 Other Animal Food Manufacturing;
    311822 Flour Mixes and Dough Manufacturing from
    Purchased Flour; 312140 Distilleries

Based in Atchison, Kansas, Midwest Grain Products, Inc. produces a variety of natural ingredients derived from wheat. Taking advantage of its location in the heart of the nation's farm belt, the company buys wheat from area farms and grain elevators and processes it at facilities located in Atchison as well as in Pekin, Illinois. The wheat is milled into flour, and water is added to extract vital wheat gluten, which is then dried into powder and sold in bulk. It is an important ingredient in bread, improving texture as well as making dough pliable and helping it to rise. Some of the company's wheat gluten is set aside to produce specialty wheat products. The leftover starch slurry is further processed to extracted premium wheat starch, which also is sold as a bulk powder. What is left of the slurry is then mixed with corn or milo and fermented and distilled into alcohol. The remains of the distilling process are used to produce a high protein additive for animal feed, and even the carbon dioxide emitted during fermentation is tapped and sold. In all, Midwest Wheat makes use of nearly 95 percent of the grain it processes. In recent years the company has aggressively sought niche markets for its wheat products, both food- and nonfood-related. Food products include Wheatex, a meat, fish, and poultry substitute, as well as Pasta Power, an egg replacement that is especially useful in the canning of spaghetti and other pasta products. The company's wheat proteins also have found applications in cosmetics and personal care products. Its biodegradable gluten/starch resins are an environmentally friendly alternative to plastic and have been used to produce disposable eating utensils, food containers, and even golf tees. Much of Midwest Grain's value-added ingredients are produced by its wholly owned subsidiary, Kansas City Ingredient Technologies, located in Kansas City, Kansas.

Founding of the Company by Cloud L. Cray, Sr., in 1941

The history of Midwest Grain is very much the legacy of the Cray family. The company's founder, Cloud L. Cray, Sr., was a Detroit investment banker who had no intentions of going into business in a remote town in Kansas. He traveled to Atchison in September 1941 to look at a non-operational grain-based ethanol plant. After arranging to purchase the facility he planned to dismantle the equipment and build a plant closer to home in Michigan. According to company lore, however, he was won over by local boosters and agreed to keep the operation in Atchison. A seasoned businessman, Cray was further swayed by the proximity of the town to the company's primary raw ingredient: wheat. The original business was named Midwest Solvents, employed 40, and devoted its initial activities to producing industrial alcohol for wartime use during World War II.

At the conclusion of the war, the company turned its attention to distilling drinking alcohol, in the beginning only selling in bulk to very large customers, but ultimately supplying smaller companies as well. In 1950 the company became directly involved in the spirits industry when it purchased one of the oldest whiskey brewers in the United States, the McCormick Distilling Company of Weston, Missouri, which had been established in 1856 by Ben Halladay, who is better remembered as a part-owner of the Overland Stage and the Pony Express. In addition to whiskey, the distillery also produced popular varieties of rum, gin, and vodka, and perhaps became best known for its commemorative ceramic whiskey decanters that celebrated Revolutionary War heroes, gunslingers, trains, and Elvis Presley. Not only did Midwest Grain find a steady outlet for its beverage alcohol in McCormick Distilling, Atchison and Weston were separated by only 20 miles, which provided a further competitive advantage.

In 1947 Cray's son, Cloud L. Cray, Jr., better known as "Bud," became an officer and director in the company. During the 1950s he grew increasingly more involved in the running of the business and was named president. It was during this decade that Midwest Grain made a concerted effort to diversify its product mix, broaden its customer base, and make fuller use of the grain it was processing. The expansion of the company began in 1953 when the Atchison plant added the equipment needed to recover vital wheat gluten, which at first was used only in the making of monosodium glutamate. The emphasis soon shifted to the production of vital wheat gluten for use in bakery products. By the end of the decade the demand was so high for vital wheat gluten that more equipment was added and a separate gluten division was formed.

In 1965 Midwest Grains added a wheat starch division. The initial product was to serve as an ingredient for wallpaper paste, which was produced by separating wheat paste from wheat slurry and then drying it into a powder form. In addition to other industrial applications, the company also found a wide variety of uses in baking and other food needs. Wheat starch could act as a baking agent similar to corn starch and found uses in pastries as well as glazes, soups, and sauces. In the 1970s, as Americans began looking for alternative fuels, Midwest Grain found a new market for its industrial alcohol and began producing ethanol.

New Leadership Beginning in 1980

Cloud L. Cray, Sr., died in 1979. A year later Bud Cray became chief executive officer and chairman of the board. He was replaced as president by his son-in-law, Ladd Seaberg, who earned a degree in chemical engineering from Texas Tech University in 1969 and began his tenure with the company in the same year. After a brief stint as distillery production manager, he became vice-president and manager of the starch division, then became plant manager in 1972, and served as general manager in the year prior to becoming president of the company. By 1988 he would rise to the CEO position, although Bud Cray remained a very active chairman of the board. Also in 1980 the company took an important step when it purchased the Pekin, Illinois facility, a gamble that revealed how optimistic management felt about the company's prospects. Looking back a dozen years later, Bud Cray noted to a reporter that for a while the Pekin plant "looked like a millstone around our necks that might indeed drag us under water."

During this period of expansion the company was organized as a network of strategic business units, in essence mini-companies. The system was more a matter of convenience than a thought-out plan, and although it was an efficient way to integrate new activities, there were long-term drawbacks in not fully integrating all of the company's operations. A seamless approach to doing business clearly made sense because a waste product of one unit became the raw material of another.

Much of the growth potential in the 1980s involved food-related products, which led the company to change its name to Midwest Grain Products in 1985. To maintain a steady supply of wheat flour to feed its operations, the company purchased an Atchison flour mill in 1987 from The Pillsbury Company. Vital wheat gluten looked especially promising for the company, with few competitors in North America. European Union suppliers accounted for just 2 percent of gluten imports to the United States in 1985, according to statistics from Kansas State University. That amount would soon show a dramatic increase that severely impacted Midwest Grain. Because of Europe's government-supported starch industry, gluten became a cheap byproduct that was dumped in the U.S. market. This situation was not anticipated by Midwest Grain when it acquired the Pekin plant in the beginning of the decade, nor when the company went public in October 1988. In fact, earlier in the year European suppliers, backed by an export subsidy from the European Community, were unable to make a serious dent in the U.S. market. Midwest Grain was believed to hold a strong advantage over imports because it could provide a steady supply of gluten to its customers as well as consistent quality. Investors concurred with management's thinking. The initial public offering was priced at $14 a share, with 1.1 million shares sold, half by stockholders and the rest by the company. A major portion of the money raised was then used to upgrade facilities. The price of Midwest Grain stock then rose steadily over its offering price, and judging from the company's financial results, investor confidence appeared well placed. For fiscal 1988 the company reported net income of $10.1 million, or $1.73 per share, on sales of $164.1 million. The following year saw revenues grow to $191.7 million and net income improve by 30 percent, topping $13.1 million, or $2.09 per share.

In the early 1990s Midwest Grain continued to be undaunted by European competition in the wheat gluten business. Both of its plants were operating at full capacity, the investment in the Pekin plant now seemingly justified. In 1991 the company invested $6 million to expand its production capacity to keep pace with an anticipated increase in demand for its gluten. In addition, the market for ethanol also appeared to be improving. Management was dissatisfied, however, with the loose organization of the company. There was too much duplication of effort between the business units, and as a result Midwest Grain underwent a major restructuring in 1992, becoming organized in a more traditional manner. The company was now divided into three marketing divisions, headed by three managers responsible for distillery, starch, and gluten products. Because of this shift, the McCormick Distilling Company no longer fit in. It was involved in selling spirits at the wholesale and retail level, whereas its parent company was more interested in serving major customers in bulk. In late 1992 McCormick Distilling was sold to a group of private investors, but Midwest Grain continued to supply the operation with beverage alcohol.

To support its continued growth, Midwest Grain launched a $75 million expansion program in 1993 to double its production capacity over the course of the next three years. Much of this increase was in anticipation of a growing demand for ethanol, which appeared likely to become an approved gasoline additive. It was a calculated risk for the company, but one with which investors agreed. In the first few months of 1993 the price of Midwest Grain stock rose 24 percent, more than four times higher than the Dow Jones industrial average. Although the gamble on

Key Dates:

1941: Cloud L. Cray, Sr., founds the business after buying Atchison, Kansas, ethanol plant.
1947: Cloud L. Cray, Jr., becomes a company officer.
1950: McCormick Distilling Company is acquired.
1953: The company begins to produce wheat gluten.
1957: The business is incorporated in Kansas.
1965: The wheat starch division is launched.
1979: Cloud L. Cray, Sr., dies.
1988: The company goes public.
1998: Quotas on subsidized European imports of gluten are imposed.

ethanol would pay off, cheap European wheat gluten finally had an adverse impact on Midwest Grains in the mid-1990s.

Cheap European Wheat Gluten Adversely Affecting Sales in the Mid-1990s

European wheat gluten imports tripled from 1994 to 1996, resulting in Midwest Grain's sale of the commodity falling from $70.1 million to $39.5 million. As a consequence, the company's net income fell from $15.8 million in 1994 to a loss of $3.4 million in 1996. A drop in gluten sales also had a ripple effect on Midwest Grain, its product lines so interconnected that cutting back on the manufacture of gluten forced a reduction in other commodities that depended on gluten byproducts. Much of the added capacity gained in the expansion launched earlier in the decade remained unused. Also during this period, Bud Cray, at the age of 73, retired from active management of the company, although he retained his title as chairman of the board.

Midwest Grains and its chief competitor, the U.S. division of Australian giant Manildra Group, lobbied Washington for relief on cheap European wheat gluten and were successful in achieving a three-year quota on the imports, beginning June 1, 1998. In the interim, Midwest Grain launched an effort to develop value-added products, through the application of wheat chemistry, to replace the eroding revenue stream of vital wheat gluten. Moreover, investors had begun to view the company as subject to the vagaries of commodity price swings, with the result that the price of Midwest Grain stock suffered. By adding specialty wheat protein products that exploited niche opportunities the company hoped to change that perception and improve its position in equity markets.

Much of Midwest Grain's specialty products remained food-related. The company developed Wheatex, a solid food product that served as a replacement for meat, poultry, and fish, either for vegetarian applications or to simply extend meat. It was also pliable and could be made into patties, links, or whatever shape a customer might require. Wheatex also featured a neutral taste that did not contend with added flavors, and because of its water-binding properties it was able to retain natural meat juices. Midwest Grains also developed an egg replacement product it called Pasta Power, which was especially useful in enhancing pasta products, thereby making them more suitable for canning.

Midwest Grains also sought nontraditional uses for wheat protein, amino acids, and starch, in particular cosmetics and personal care products, for which it served as an excellent alternative to animal proteins and other vegetable-based proteins. Product applications included mascara, body washes, facial cleansers, skin creams, hair sprays, and shampoos. Midwest Grains also developed biodegradable wheat gluten and starch resins that could be molded like plastic to make environmentally friendly items. They also could be used to make pet treats and chews. Management was aggressive in pursuing these new opportunities. In 1997 specialty products replaced just 1 percent of the company's gluten sales, a number that increased to 5 percent a year later. For fiscal 2001 these products accounted for 23 percent of Midwest Grain's total revenues.

In February 2001, Midwest Grain purchased a facility in Kansas City, Kansas, to produce Wheatex. The company also received financial help in the form of a $26 million federal grant as part of an effort to help the gluten industry cope with the effects of subsidized European imports. To support the growth of specialty products, the company's board in October 2001 approved an expansion project for the Atchison plant, taking advantage of an $8.3 million grant from the U.S. Department of Agriculture. Midwest Grains' researchers continued to develop new applications for wheat starch and wheat protein. In 2002 the company introduced Arise, a wheat protein product for use in frozen dough and fresh baked goods. Whatever short-term harm Midwest Grains may have suffered from the dumping of cheap European white gluten, it was becoming increasingly more evident that the company, by making a virtue out of necessity, was now much better positioned for future growth.

Principal Subsidiaries

Midwest Grain Pipeline, Inc., Midwest Grain Products of Illinois, Inc.; Kansas City Ingredient Technologies, Inc.

Principal Competitors

Archer-Daniels-Midland Co.; Cargill, Incorporated; High Plains.

Further Reading

Bouyea, Bob, "Midwest Grain Takes a Risk with Expansion," *Peoria Journal Star,* September 16, 1993, p. A11.
——, "Midwest Grain to Expand in Pekin Production," *Peoria Journal Star,* January 5, 1993, p. A1.
Fruehling, Douglas, "Trade Pact Hurting Grain Processors," *Peoria Journal Star,* November 7, 1995, p. C1.
Jaffe, Thomas, "Going with the Grain," *Forbes,* April 12, 1993, p. 145.
Meyer, Gene, "Kansas Grain Processor Refines Its Structure," *Kansas City Star,* September 22, 1992, p. E16.
——, "Private Investors to Buy McCormick Distilling Co.," *Kansas City Star,* December 8, 1992, p. D3.
"Midwest Grain Products Inc.," *Wall Street Transcript,* June 14, 1993.
"Midwest Grain Scores Solid Gains in First Year As Publicly Held Company," *Milling & Baking News,* October 24, 1989, p. 18.
Nicolova, Rossitsa, "Feds Make Midwest Grain's Year More Bountiful," *Kansas City Business Journal,* August 11, 2000, p. 8.

—Ed Dinger

MPS Group, Inc.

1 Independent Drive
Jacksonville, Florida 32202-5060
U.S.A.
Telephone: (904) 360-2000
Toll Free: (800) 852-2281
Fax: (904) 360-2814
Web site: http://www.modispro.com

Public Company
Incorporated: 1992 as AccuStaff Inc.
Employees: 185,000
Sales: $1.55 billion (2001)
Stock Exchanges: New York
Ticker Symbol: MPS
NAIC: 561330 Employment Leasing Services

MPS Group, Inc. is a Jacksonville, Florida company that provides consulting and staffing services in the areas of information technology, finance and accounting, law, e-business, human capital automation, engineering, executive search, and workforce management. After becoming a regional power in the early 1990s, the company has engaged in an aggressive acquisition campaign, rolling up scores of temp agencies across the country and transforming itself into a national staffing firm large enough to rival much better known Manpower and Kelly Services. MPS has sold off its clerical staffing business, the traditional base of the temp industry, in favor of higher margin professional and technical placement. Aside from its extensive North America operation, MPS also operates in the United Kingdom and continental Europe.

Refusing the Limitations of the Glass Ceiling: 1970s

The origin of MPS is very much the personal success story of a woman named Delores Kesler. Born Delores Mercer, she grew up in Jacksonville on a poultry farm. Her father's primary source of income was his job at Southern Bell, and poultry was just one of a number of side ventures in which he would engage over the years. None of them proved successful, however, due

in some measure to his alcoholism. He died when Kesler was just 19. Despite his disease and mounting debts, she was very close to her father. As a teenager she began to manage his checkbook, in the process gaining valuable practical business experience. He was also instrumental in setting high expectations for her and instilling a belief in Kesler that she was capable of accomplishing anything that she set her mind to. Coming of age in the early 1960s, she graduated from high school with expectations that did not extend beyond getting married and starting a family, and by the age of 22 Kesler was divorced and a single parent. Because of her father's death she also was helping to support her mother and younger brother. She went to work at an International Harvester dealership as a secretary and was promoted to various positions in personnel and sales. At one point she was training salespeople, but was herself denied the opportunity to become a salesperson. She watched the men she trained quickly pass her in salary. Hoping to enter their ranks by gaining a college degree, she tried to take advantage of a tuition reimbursement program only to learn that it was limited to male employees. A sympathetic supervisor named Bob Walls found a way around the rules by submitting her application using an initial instead of her first name. With tuition aid, Kesler went to school at night while working full-time and raising a family, although she had to drop out eventually and never did complete her college education. She then left International Harvester to spend eight years managing a nurses registry business. In 1977 she decided to start her own business, after concluding that she was already running a business for someone else and could do it better if she had control.

After conducting some research Kesler resolved to start a temporary medical staffing agency. While working in the personnel department at International Harvester, she became familiar with the temp business, setting up training seminars for International Harvester around the country and hiring local temporary employees to assist her. Kesler wrote a business plan for her proposed venture, which she then shared with banks in an effort to secure a $50,000 start-up loan. Unable to grasp the potential of her idea, because the industry was very much limited to clerical workers and far from mature, or they were dissuaded by her gender, nine different banks turned her down. Kesler then applied to a high school classmate who served as a loan officer at the tenth bank she targeted. He confided that no bank would lend her that amount of money. Rather than be discouraged, however, Kesler simply asked how much he was authorized to lend without additional approval. Told $10,000, she immediately pressed for that amount of money, which her ex-classmate reluctantly agreed to provide. Kesler set up a bare bones operation—little more than a card table, folding chair, and telephone—and within six months of starting Conval-Aide Medical Staff in 1977, she was able to repay the $10,000 loan.

Establishing Associated Temporary Staffing in 1978

In 1978 Kesler started a second staffing agency, Associated Temporary Staffing, which became known as ATS Services Inc., supplying clerical and industrial workers. In retrospect, it was perfect timing to enter the temp business. Annual payroll in the industry grew from $4 billion in 1983 to nearly $20 billion a decade later. In 1987 ATS was named one of the 500 fastest growing companies in the United States by *Inc.* magazine, and Kesler also was gaining her share of recognition as one of the country's top female entrepreneurs. Generating $35 million a year in revenues, ATS dominated its local market. Kesler entered new territories and eventually decided that she could take her business national and challenge the only three staffing companies operating nationwide. Growing larger also was becoming a necessity to stay competitive in the industry. In 1992 she engineered the merger of ATS with three other companies: Abacus Services Inc., BSI Temporaries, and Metrotech Inc. The new company was named AccuStaff. As part of the deal, the medical staffing business of ATS was pulled out and passed into the hands of Kesler's son and daughter, who would operate the business under the ATS name.

Terms of the merger also called for Kesler to serve as president and chief executive officer for one year while a new top executive was recruited and hired, at which point she would become chairman of AccuStaff. The national search for a new CEO lasted almost two years. Ultimately Kesler tabbed Derek Dewan, who had been instrumental in structuring the AccuStaff merger while working as a managing partner with Coopers & Lybrand. The son of Christian Lebanese immigrants, Dewan's father became an accountant and moved his family to Jacksonville in 1968. Dewan graduated from an area high school and then studied accounting at the University of South Florida. He returned home to Jacksonville, taking a job with Price Waterhouse before joining the Jacksonville office of Coopers & Lybrand in 1982. Talented and hardworking, Dewan made partner at the age of 29. He took on the ATS account and began to work closely with Kesler, eventually serving as both her accountant and business adviser in the complicated transaction that resulted in the creation of AccuStaff. One reason why

Kesler's executive search dragged on so long was her courting of Dewan. He rejected an initial offer because a retirement at Coopers allowed him to become a managing partner at the Jacksonville office. AccuStaff, on the other hand, was far from the national operation that Kesler envisioned, with operations only in a handful of states and revenues of just $89.1 million in 1993. Kesler offered Dewan a job a second time, and after some reflection he decided that AccuStaff offered the best possibility for taking the next step in his career without leaving the Jacksonville area. He accepted and took over as CEO of the company in January 1994.

Dewan's first priority was to take AccuStaff public in order to amass a war chest for an aggressive expansion campaign. Even before the offering, AccuStaff began acquiring staffing companies, primarily in the Southwest and Midwest where the use of temp services was growing at an accelerated clip. Revenues grew to $137.1 million in 1994, and net income increased to $3 million, a significant improvement over the $700,000 in earnings posted in 1993. In 1995 AccuStaff would add another ten companies to the fold, including agencies that supplied attorneys and computer technicians. As a result, revenues in 1995 almost doubled, topping $267 million, and net income improved to $8.7 million. It was an impressive showing, but only a harbinger of what was to come.

Kesler turned over the chairmanship of AccuStaff to Dewan in 1996, and a year later she retired from the board to pursue her charitable interests. Dewan now stepped up the pace of acquisitions, rolling up 39 more staffing companies during the course of 1996, in particular strengthening the company's professional services: accountants, lawyers, engineers, and information technology (IT) specialists. Karen L. Tippet in a 1996 *Wall Street Journal* article described Dewan's method: ''Once he identifies a target, he makes a generous offer that sometimes involves equity in AccuStaff; promises to make a place at AccuStaff for executives who want to stay on, even allowing the target company to keep its name.'' Moreover, Dewan was persistent, refusing to accept rejection easily. By far the most significant acquisition of the year was the $900 million stock purchase of Career Horizons Inc., to that point the largest acquisition of an American staffing company. In one stroke, Dewan transformed AccuStaff into the nation's fourth largest staffing company, trailing only Manpower, Kelly Services, and Olsten Corp. Focusing on healthcare, financial services, and IT, Career Horizons was formed in 1990 and spun off by Manpower. Career Horizons also had been engaged in an expansion program, having itself added nine acquisitions since leaving Manpower. Not only did the Career Horizons acquisition extend the reach of AccuStaff to more than 750 offices in 43 states, it promised to have a significant impact on the company's bottom line. To attract the business of major corporations, it was important that AccuStaff have the capability to service all regions of the country. Simply put, national companies did business with other national companies. Aside from taking AccuStaff to that level, Dewan hoped to achieve $1 billion in annual revenues by 2000. That mark would be easily achieved in fiscal 1996, when the company booked sales of nearly $1.45 billion, while also realizing a $27.9 million net profit.

Dewan was a relentless empire builder, known to sleep only four hours a day and maintain a dedicated telephone line in his

Key Dates:
1978: Delores Kesler forms ATS Services.
1992: ATS merges with three staffing companies to create AccuStaff.
1994: Derek Dewan is named CEO and takes the company public.
1996: Career Horizons acquisition makes AccuStaff a billion-dollar company.
1997: Kesler retires from the board.
1998: AccuStaff changes its name to Modis Professional Services following the sale of Strategix subsidiary.
2001: The company assumes the name of MPS Group.

home to continue his never-ending string of negotiations. His aggressive style, however, sometimes caused friction both within and outside the ranks of AccuStaff, but few could question his success. In 1997 he continued to roll up staffing companies at a tremendous clip, adding 28 acquisitions during the course of the year. The company moved into career development and outplacement services, assisting clients in placing laid-off employees, by acquiring Manchester Inc., a Philadelphia, Pennsylvania firm. AccuStaff also engaged in some reorganization in 1997, grouping its information technology businesses under a new division named Modis, as well as creating MindSharp Learning Centers to offer training services. Moreover, Dewan began to look beyond the U.S. borders, opening offices in Toronto and London, and making plans to enter Europe. In 1997 AccuStaff continued a string of impressive results, generating $102 million in net profits on more than $2.4 billion in sales.

Selling a Strategic Unit in 1998

In 1998 AccuStaff backed off its consolidation efforts, opting instead to focus on the higher margin business of its information technology and professional divisions. In March the company sold off its healthcare division for $116 million. It next announced that its commercial staffing businesses would be spun off as a separate company, Strategix, which was to be taken public later in the year. What remained of AccuStaff would then be renamed Modis Professional Services. Wall Street investors received the idea with little enthusiasm, and they responded harshly to the report of Dewan's arrest for solicitation in late July 1998. He was charged with offering $40 to a police prostitution decoy, which he adamantly denied. Nevertheless, the price of AccuStaff stock plummeted, resulting in a loss of $500 million in the company's market value. Dewan's vow to prove his innocence in court failed to rally the price of AccuStaff shares, which was due in some measure to Wall Street's increasing disinterest in the stock of temp firms. With an IPO for Strategix looking less promising, Dewan decided instead to sell the subsidiary to Ranstad Holding NV, a Dutch international staffing company, for $850 million. Dewan earmarked approximately $420 million to pay off the company's debt and the balance reserved for further acquisitions, especially in the IT area. Upon the completion of the transaction AccuStaff officially changed its name to Modis Professional Services.

Despite his arrest, Dewan maintained the support of his board. He continued to express his intention to fight the solicitation charges, but his attorney never sought discovery of the prosecution's evidence, a move that according to Florida public records laws would have made an audiotape between Dewan and the police decoy available to the media. In May 1999 he finally pleaded no contest to the misdemeanor charge, agreeing to pay a fine of $150 while not admitting or denying the charge. Although Dewan said he did not think he violated the law, he decided that it was in the best interests of everyone involved simply to settle the matter.

The price of Modis stock continued to languish in 1999, prompting Dewan to announce a further reorganization of the company, which was intended to unlock the hidden value of Modis. The plan was to split professional business staffing services and the information technology unit. The IT business would be further divided by spinning off the e-business division. The result would be three separate companies and three separate IPOs. It would also mean that top executives would be promoted to serve as the CEOs of the new entities. Because of poor market conditions, especially in the technology sector, the plan never came to fruition and a year later, in November 2000, it was abandoned. As a result, Dewan also decided to step down as CEO in favor of Timothy D. Payne, who had been tabbed to head one of the separate companies. Payne joined the company in 1997 when AccuStaff acquired Openware Technologies Inc., a company he was running. Dewan remained as chairman of the board, giving up day-to-day responsibilities but continuing to plot Modis's overall strategy. In addition, the company bolstered its board, adding such national figures as former U.S. Senate Majority Leader George J. Mitchell.

With the U.S. economy slipping into recession in 2001, Modis cut debt and positioned itself to take advantage of an eventual recovery. It also directed increasing attention to expanding its European presence. Although revenues were down in 2001, the company remained profitable, posting net income of $8.3 million. Because the company used the Modis brand of its information technology business, the board voted to change the name of the parent corporation to MPS Group to avoid confusion and enhance Modis brand recognition. In February 2002 Payne announced his intention of adding four specialized business areas over the next two years, achieved either through start-ups or by acquisition. He also suggested that nurse staffing services might be a possible new business. If so, it would link MPS to its roots, when a single mother entered the medical staffing business with nothing more than a card table, folding chair, a telephone, and a belief in herself.

Principal Subsidiaries

Idea Integration Corporation; Modis Inc.; Prolianz Corporation.

Principal Competitors

Adecco S.A.; Cambridge Technology Partners, Inc.; Computer Horizon; Kelly Services, Inc.; Manpower, Inc.; Robert Half International Inc.

Further Reading

Basch, Mark, "Breaking Down the Modis Name," *Florida Times-Union,* July 23, 2001.

Bryant-Friedland, Bruce, "CEO Adds Humility to Price of Success," *Florida Times-Union,* October 4, 1998.

Cristy, Matt, "The Rise and Rise of AccuStaff," *Business Journal of Jacksonville,* January 31, 1997.

Deogun, Nikhil, "AccuStaff to Acquire Career Horizons in a $900 Million Stock Transaction," *Wall Street Journal,* August 27, 1996, p. A3.

Johnson, Anne M., "No Toke at the Top," *Florida Trend,* October 1994, p. 58.

Rather, Dan, *The American Dream: Stories from the Heart of Our Nation,* New York: William Morrow, 2001.

Tippet, Karen L., "Chairman's Energy Fuels AccuStaff's Speedy Rise," *Wall Street Journal,* December 11, 1996, p. F1.

—Ed Dinger

National Starch and Chemical Company

10 Finderne Avenue
Bridgewater, New Jersey 08807-3300
U.S.A.
Telephone: (908) 685-5000
Toll Free: (800) 797-4992
Fax: (609) 409-5699
Web site: http://www.nationalstarch.com

Wholly Owned Subsidiary of Imperial Chemical
*   Industries PLC*
Incorporated: 1895 as National Gum and Mica Company
Employees: 10,100
Sales: $2.69 billion (2001)
NAIC: 325520 Adhesive Manufacturing

A subsidiary of U.K. giant Imperial Chemical Industries PLC, National Starch and Chemical Company is a major manufacturer of adhesives; sealants; specialty synthetic polymers; electronic and engineering materials; and specialty food, healthcare, and industrial starches. Its products are used in a wide range of applications, including packaging, foods and beverages, paper, textiles, electronics, furniture, skin lotions, and hair care products. With its headquarters in Bridgewater, New Jersey, National Starch has a global reach, employing more than 10,000 people at 158 facilities located in 36 countries spread across six continents.

Founding the Company in 1895

National Starch was established in 1895 by a 25-year-old New Yorker with the unusual name of Alexander Alexander. Responding to an advertisement in a local newspaper for a business for sale at 11th Avenue and 45th Street in Manhattan, he was able to purchase the National Gum and Mica Company for $1,200. The company used corn, potatoes, tapioca, and other vegetable starches to produce adhesives, used in preparing paper and textiles for printing. It also produced related products such as mica pulp and gold gums. By 1912 the business was successful enough to relocate to new facilities on 59th Street as well as purchase a small pigment company, Crescent Color Pigment, located south

of New York City in Dunellen, New Jersey. This acquisition allowed National Gum to become involved in the manufacture of pigments for coated paper and wallpaper. It was a highly profitable sideline for decades, because only after World War II did wallpaper companies decide to mix their own colors.

Most of National Gum's business came from fast-drying adhesives, the need for which grew rapidly during the early decades of the 1900s, primarily because of the rising demand for packaged goods. In addition, the company supplied its adhesives to the paper and leather goods industries. When National Gum began to compound adhesives for the box industry in 1920, it ushered in a period of tremendous growth, as revenues tripled by 1926, reaching $1 million. At the same time, Alexander abandoned Manhattan, moving to Dunellen to be close to his production base. It was also in 1920 that Alexander's son-in-law, Frank K. Greenwall, joined the company. He would ultimately head the business and be involved with the company for more than 60 years, providing continuity in management that extended into the next century.

In 1928 National Gum changed its name to National Adhesives Corporation after merging with two smaller adhesives companies located in upstate New York and Ohio. To support its growing business the company constructed a dextrin refinery in Plainfield, New Jersey, which opened in 1934. Demand for starch-based adhesives continued to grow despite the Depression, necessitating the acquisition of a corn starch company to insure a steady supply of starch and consistent pricing. In 1939 National Adhesives became even more involved in the starch business when it acquired Piel Brothers Starch Co., located in Indianapolis, and as a result changed its name once more, this time to National Starch Products.

Continued Prosperity Following Alexander's Death in 1940

In 1940 Alexander died but the company he founded continue to prosper. Military needs during World War II open up new areas for National Starch. Its scientists found new uses for starches in such areas as textile and food products. The company developed synthetic adhesives suitable for any climate, which proved extremely useful in wartime applications. During the 1940s National Starch also created polyvinyl acetate for use in high-speed packaging. By the end of the decade, annual sales reached $16 million, as the company began to transform itself from a modest adhesives company into a large specialty company. Over the course of the 1950s, revenues rose significantly as National Starch made an even greater commitment to research and development. Greenwall was named chairman in 1958 and was instrumental in integrating marketing and research functions. He also was aggressive in merchandising new products and growing the business through acquisitions. To reflect the new breadth of its operations, in 1959 the company changed its name to National Starch and Chemical Company.

By 1961 annual revenues grew to $60 million, and the company continued to grow by both internal and external means, domestically and internationally. To improve distribution, National Starch began building regional manufacturing facilities in 1963. It also settled on a product mix that would remain consistent for many years to come: 40 percent adhesives, 40 percent starches, and 20 percent specialty chemicals. As a result, the company created new divisions in 1968: Adhesives, Resins and Specialty Chemicals, and Starch. National Starch took an important step in expanding beyond the United States in the late 1960s when it acquired Le Page's Ltd., Canada's largest maker of consumer glues, and Australia's Adhesives & Resins Pty Ltd. Over the ensuing years, National Starch also acquired major stakes, if not 100 percent, of adhesive, starch, and seasoning companies in Britain, France, Holland, Mexico, Japan, and South Africa.

Sound business practices were aided by good luck to some extent in the 1970s. The company's researchers developed a modified starch that had properties of gum arabic, resulting in a product called Capsul. When the largest supplier of natural gum arabic, the Sudan, cut its output, National Starch was ready to take advantage. In a similar way, when the Environmental Protection Agency banned solvent-based adhesives, the company was well positioned with its lines of hot-melt adhesives and water-based emulsions. Also during the 1970s National Starch used acquisitions to help gain market share in the automotive, machinery, and appliance industries. The 1974 purchase of California-based Ablestik Laboratories opened the door to selling high-performance epoxy-based adhesives to the microelectronics industry. The following year National Starch acquired Permabond International Corp., which produced cyanoacrylate and anaerobic instant adhesives used in the automotive, electronics, and consumer markets.

Despite having the ability to use its corn mills to produce high volume commodities like corn syrup, laundry starch, or ureaformaldehyde for plywood, the company remained com-

mitted to manufacturing and marketing specialty items that carried a much higher margin and avoided the volatile price swings suffered by so many companies that sold commodities. Management was conservative, as evidenced by its 1975 purchase of a used laboratory building to serve as the company's new headquarters, but there was no arguing that it was highly successful. National Starch reached a turning point in the late 1970s, however, when Greenwall reportedly feared a hostile takeover of the company. In 1978 he was approached by the AngloDutch food and detergent giant Unilever about a possible buyout. Unilever had been formed in 1930 when Brothers Lever of England merged with the Dutch Margarine Union. Because of tax implications, and a bit of corporate pride, the new entity became a two-headed multinational, with both a British and Dutch component that managed to function as a single company. Unilever was not averse to spending money on acquisitions, but it was reluctant to stray too far from the industries it knew well. National Starch, which sold raw materials used by many Unilever units, was a company that fit into that mold. Unilever offered more than double the book value to acquire the stock of National Starch, much of which was owned by insiders and officers, for a deal totaling $484 million. It was a generous offer that Greenwall, who owned a 15 percent stake in the company, maintained he had to accept for the sake of shareholders. Although he freely admitted that he personally profited from the transaction, his contention that he would have faced lawsuits from angry shareholders if he had not accepted the offer was probably more than just a jest.

In reality, life with Unilever as a corporate parent brought virtually no change to the day-to-day affairs of National Starch. Unilever did not even install one of its officers on the company's board. Moreover, National Starch continued to do business with Unilever's biggest competitors, Colgate-Palmolive and Procter & Gamble. For that matter, the company also did business with its own direct competitors, such as selling specialty starches to Heinz and Borden, which also had adhesives divisions. National Starch continued to operate with the same respect for customer confidentiality as it had before the Unilever purchase.

In 1980 National Starch ranked 449 on the *Fortune* 500 and a year later jumped to 405, with consolidated sales of $668 million and net income of $41.4 million. Following Greenwall's tenure, other longtime executives of the company stepped up to assume leadership positions. In fact, every president and CEO of National Starch throughout its history had risen through the ranks of the company. In 1986 National Starch topped $1 billion in annual sales. James A. Kennedy, who had joined the company in 1962, became president and CEO in 1990, and under his leadership National Starch continued to expand its global reach and breadth of products, which now totaled more than 2,000 in number. He was instrumental in an early entry into Asia, which proved to be a major source of growth. The company also produced record results each year, an unbroken string that stretched back to the early 1970s. In 1994 National Starch surpassed $2 billion in revenues.

The 1997 Sale of National Starch

Unilever continued to be a hands-off corporate parent, and because National Starch was very much a cash cow in Unilever's four-company specialty chemical unit, there was no

Key Dates:

1895: Alexander Alexander founds the business through the acquisition of National Gum and Mica Company.
1928: Company changes its name to National Adhesives Corporation.
1939: Following the acquisition of The Piel Brothers Starch Company, the company's name changes to National Starch Products, Inc.
1940: Alexander dies.
1959: The company's name changes to National Starch and Chemical Company.
1978: Unilever acquires the company.
1997: Unilever sells National to Imperial Chemical Industries PLC.

reason to interfere. By 1997 Unilever decided, however, to concentrate on consumer products and put the four specialty chemical businesses on the block. In addition to National Starch they included the British firm of Crosfields and Dutch companies Quest International and Unichema International. A year earlier Imperial Chemical Industries (ICI) had attempted to buy the unit but had been rebuffed. ICI's new CEO, Charles Miller Smith, had previously worked for Unilever and was familiar with the specialty chemical companies. He inherited a business in ICI that was exposed to the price swings of the commodity chemical industry, with shares that lagged behind the London stock market by some 25 percent. As Smith searched for possible acquisitions that could help lift ICI out of the mire, he kept coming back to the four Unilever specialty businesses. When Unilever announced that it was ready to unload the unit, either piecemeal or whole, Smith was ready to make a preemptive offer to purchase the entire package. Major competitors of National Starch, including Henkel, H.B. Fuller, and Elf Atochem, also appeared ready to weigh in with bids. Although Unilever could have conceivably realized more money by selling the businesses separately, it proved to be a willing seller and quickly came to terms with ICI, which in the end agreed to a debt-free price of $8 billion for all four specialty businesses.

In conjunction with the sale to ICI, Kennedy was appointed chairman and CEO of the subsidiary, and elected an executive director of the parent company. As with Unilever, National Starch was allowed to operate with no interference and continued to produce record results. In May 1999 Kennedy announced that after 37 years with National Starch he was retiring. As was the tradition of the company that stretched back more than a century, senior posts were filled from within. William H. Powell, the executive vice-president of the Industrial Starch and Food Products Division, was named the new chairman and CEO. Walter F. Schlauch, the company's chief operating officer, also assumed the role of president. In the final year of the

century, National Starch produced its 30th consecutive year of growth in operating profits. At the same time new management prepared for a new century, instituting a restructuring effort that closed eight older factories in favor of more modern plants. Likewise, two R&D centers in Europe were scheduled to be relocated to newer, state-of-the art facilities.

Although more stable than commodity chemical companies, National Starch was still dependent on the well-being of the global economy. In 2000 the company's three-decade stretch of record growth was interrupted, although it still remained a profitable business. Not only did National Starch face an unprecedented increase in the price of raw materials, as well as spikes in the cost of energy and freighting, it had to contend with a significant downturn in its North American sales. Attempts to increase prices in keeping with these conditions were too late to have significant impact for the year.

With the U.S. economy slipping, coupled with the lingering effects of the terrorists attacks of September 11th, National Starch faced even greater challenges in 2001. Demand for its products fell while the cost of energy and raw materials continued to rise. Management initiated cost reduction measures, which included a 9 percent reduction in headcount. Revenues fell by 7.1 percent over the previous year and operating income was off by 17.5 percent. Nevertheless, National Starch still generated revenues of $2.56 billion and posted operating income of $336 million, a performance in extremely adverse economic conditions that was a testament to the company's underlying strength.

Principal Operating Units

Specialty Polymers and Adhesives/Europes; Specialty Polymers and Adhesives/Americas; Natural Polymers; Advanced Ingredients; Electronic and Engineering Materials.

Principal Competitors

Akzo Nobel N.V.; BASF Aktiengesellschaft; Dow Chemical Co.; Henkel KGaA; H.B. Fuller Company; Elf Atochem.

Further Reading

"National Starch and Chemical Corp.: Expanding into High Technology," *Business Journal of New Jersey,* February 1990, p. S46.
"National Starch Does It the Old Way," *Chemical Week,* October 13, 1982, p. 33.
"The Rebound of ICI," *Economist,* May 10, 1997, p. 63.
Robinson, Jeffrey, "Ubiquitous Unilever: The Giant Company Moves to Cash in on Its Global Reach," *Barron's,* January 17, 1983, p. 60.
"Unilever to Divest National Starch, Quest Operations," *Milling & Baking News,* February 18, 1997, p. 1.
Young, Ian, "ICI Snaps Up Unilever Units for $8 Billion," *Chemical Week,* May 14, 1997, p. 8.

—Ed Dinger

National Wine & Spirits Inc.

National Wine & Spirits, Inc.

700 W. Morris Street
Indianapolis, Indiana 46206
U.S.A.
Telephone: (317) 636-6092
Fax: (317) 685-8810
Web site: http://www.nwscorp.com

Private Company
Incorporated: 1934 as National Liquor Company
Employees: 1,618
Sales: $681.6 million (2002)
NAIC: 422820 Wine and Distilled Alcoholic Beverage
   Wholesalers

With corporate headquarters in Indianapolis, National Wine & Spirits, Inc. (NWS) is a privately owned distributor of wine and spirits, one of the largest in the United States. Serving the Midwest, it is the largest distributor of spirits in Indiana, with a 54 percent market share, and in Michigan, with a 52 percent market share. The company's 30 percent market share in Illinois makes it one of the largest distributors in that state as well. NWS also owns a 25 percent stake in Commonwealth Wine & Spirits, a Kentucky distributor with a 36 percent market share for wine and spirits. NWS is a holding company, its operations conducted through several wholly owned subsidiaries, including National Wine & Spirits Corp. in Indiana; Union Beverage Company, Hamburg Distributing Company and Chicago Wine Merchants in Illinois; and NWS Michigan, Inc. in Michigan. NWS also owns United States Beverage, a national broker of malt-based products. To service its markets, NWS maintains seven distribution centers, five cross-docking facilities, and a fleet of more than 300 delivery trucks. Customers are categorized as either off-premise or on-premise, according to where the products are consumed. Off-premise customers are package liquor stores, grocery stores, mass merchandisers, and drugstores, while on-premise customers include bars, restaurants, and hotels. NWS features many well known brands of spirits, such as Absolut, Chivas Regal, Jim Beam, and Smirnoff. Depending on the market state, the company is the exclusive

distributor of spirits for suppliers such as Diageo (Guinness/UDV), Fortune Brands (in all four states), Allied Domecq, and Pernod Ricard. In Indiana and Illinois NWS is the exclusive distributor of such top wineries as Kendall Jackson and Banfi Vintners, as well as many offerings from Canandaigua Wine Company (Constellation Brands), the country's second largest wine supplier. In certain markets NWS also distributes premium cigars to augment its fine wines and spirits business.

Repeal of Prohibition: 1933

The great experiment of banning alcoholic beverages in the United States, Prohibition, began in 1919 but lasted little more than a decade. Americans drank just as much, if not more in some cases, and outlawing alcohol resulted in well-funded organized crime rather than greater sobriety. In 1933 President Franklin Roosevelt repealed Prohibition, and a year later the National Liquor Company, predecessor to NWS, was issued Permit #7 from the Indiana Alcoholic Beverage Commission to distribute spirits in the central Indiana area. Designed to keep organized crime out of the industry, as well as to facilitate the collection of taxes, a new three-tier regulatory framework was erected at both the federal and state levels. Spirit, wine, and beer manufacturers were effectively banned from selling directly to retailers or consumers, making distributors like National Liquor a necessary part of the new system. A number of states, however, kept out private industry entirely, the government acting as the exclusive distributor and/or retailer of alcoholic beverages.

Original stock certificates for National Liquor Company were issued on April 9, 1935, to George Galm, Laura Galm, and Jules Fansler. The Galms relinquished their shares on December 12 of that year, when John J. Ohleyer was issued shares. For the remainder of the decade, Fansler served as president with Mr. Galm as secretary. Although Fansler continued his involvement with the company until 1948, he began selling his shares on March 1, 1940, when Frank M. McHale, lead partner of McHale and Douglass law firm (now McHale Cook & Welch), acquired a 20 percent interest in the company, registered shares in his wife's name, Mabel E. McHale, and held them until September 1955.

On August 15, 1941, Ohleyer sold his shares to businessman and politician Frank E. McKinney. The shares were registered

Company Perspectives:

National Wine & Spirits is the largest distributor of wine and spirits in the Midwest and one of the largest in the country. Our market leadership is a result of nearly 30 years of superior service to our supplier and retail partners.

in the name of his wife, Margaret W. McKinney, and their children. McKinney, by this time president of American Fletcher National Bank (AFNB), and McHale, were the two most prominent leaders of the state Democratic Party. From 1941 until the McKinneys and McHales redeemed their shares in 1955, the majority of the shares were female-owned, at one point 78 percent. The McKinney children later stated they never knew of their ownership; in reality, Frank E. McKinney and Frank M. McHale controlled the company.

McKinney was born and raised in Indianapolis, the son of a fireman who rose to the rank of chief of the department. A high school dropout, he went to work in 1919 at an Indianapolis bank as a messenger. He moved to another bank three years later to work as a bookkeeper, eventually becoming a cashier in 1933. In the meantime McKinney became acquainted with the man who proved pivotal in his future endeavors, Donie Bush, a local sports hero who had played 16 years in Major League Baseball before coming home to manage the Indianapolis Indians minor league team. Bush turned over his finances to McKinney and was not only influential in helping McKinney to one day become a baseball owner, he provided entrée into the Indiana Democratic Party. In 1934 McKinney was elected as Marion County treasurer, a post that helped make his fortune. During the Depression the treasurer was given a percentage of the back taxes he collected, an incentive that provided enough earnings to secure a $100,000 loan to purchase the Fidelity Trust Company, thus making him at the age of 30 the youngest president of a financial institution in the United States. With Fidelity Trust as a foundation, McKinney was able to acquire other banks and branch into other businesses, such as National Liquor.

By 1944, he had acquired a controlling interest in National Liquor, but shares were held by family members because of his increasing involvement in politics. In 1940 he was named vice-chairman of the Democratic National Committee, and in 1951 was appointed its chairman. During the time of the McHale-McKinney ownership, politicians in many states played an active role in the beverage alcohol business. Many of the state laws regulating the industry today were crafted during this period.

National Liquor acquired Capitol Hill Distributing in 1952 and issued shares to owner Marven M. Lasky and family members in 1952, 1953, and 1954, eventually giving them a 30 percent interest. This acquisition was the first of many that enabled National to become a key distributor in the Midwest. Up until this point, National had primarily represented the Schenley product line of spirits in central Indiana. The Capitol Hill acquisition brought Seagram and Hiram Walker spirits into the portfolio. Along with Capitol Hill, Lasky owned Melody Hill, a line of products made from wine brought in and bottled for sale to retailers. This line, later sold to Gallo, was also added to the

National portfolio. At this time, distributors were not pursuing the wine side of the alcoholic beverage business. By entering the wine market, National took its first step toward becoming a dominant wine distributor, especially in the expanding grocery market. The Capitol Hill and Melody Hill deals set the stage for company growth that would continue the rest of the century.

The Lasky ownership was short-lived, as virtually all shares of the McHale, McKinney, and Lasky families were redeemed on September 26, 1955, when National Liquor's sales manager, Charles E. Johnson, Jr., acquired the company. The change of ownership at this time was motivated by Frank McKinney's desire to become Secretary of Treasury under Adlai Stevenson, a presidential candidate during McKinney's tenure as chairman of the National Democratic Party. Although Johnson did not have the financing for the purchase, McKinney arranged credits from Schenley, loans from Bankers Trust, and eventually a loan from AFNB.

Ownership Change in 1973

Ownership of National Liquor did not change again until 1973, when the current chairman and CEO of NWS, James LaCrosse, first became involved with the business. A Harvard M.B.A., LaCrosse and brothers William and Cameron Johnston bought National Liquor from Charles Johnson, Jr., intending to hold onto the business just long enough to turn it around and resell it. At the time National Liquor remained very much a local distributor, booking just over $14 million in 1973. Because business showed such dramatic improvement in just six months, the partners decided to hold onto the company. A year later William Johnston died and his interest passed to his widow, Norma Johnston, who in 2002 still controlled a 17 percent stake. In 1995 Cameron Johnston sold out to LaCrosse, who now owned 83 percent of National Liquor.

Under LaCrosse's leadership, National Liquor saw its revenues improve steadily through the 1980s. On December 30, 1982, the company changed its name to National Wine & Spirits Corporation. Also in that decade the company completed several significant acquisitions including those of Kiefer Stewart, Conard Liquors, Allen Products, Midwest Liquors, Stadium Liquor, Liquors Inc., General Liquors, Fort Wayne Liquor, and Standard Liquors. NWS also absorbed some product lines and personnel from competitors forced to close their doors, such as Lake Shore Liquors and Fred Beck. Additional distribution hubs were located in South Bend and Evansville, with sales offices in Fort Wayne and Merrillville, later moved to Crown Point. As a result of this external growth, NWS's annual revenues, well below $50 million in 1980, topped $150 million by 1990.

By the 1990s NWS was poised for diversification. In 1991 the company launched a bottled water business, Cameron Springs Co., to take advantage of Americans' increasing thirst for so-called designer water. The Cameron name had deep roots in Indiana, dating back to the 1800s when a man named William Cameron bought a property near Attica, Indiana, which featured a spring that had a reputation for restorative properties. According to lore, a farmer named Samuel Story, who suffered from rheumatism, engaged in a drainage project at the springs. After weeks of wading around in hip-deep mud and drinking liberally from the spring, he discovered that his rheumatism was cured.

William Cameron opened a small hotel near the springs and sold products he dubbed Magno-Mud and Lithia Water. A businessman named Henry Kramer then purchased the property and in 1885 opened a posh health resort and spa, Mudlavia Hotel. In 1920 it was destroyed by fire, never rebuilt, and the miracle springs became neglected. In its search for a source of water many decades later, NWS learned of Cameron Springs and tests revealed it was a suitable product. In the summer of 1991 Cameron Springs Co. began marketing its water, which also included processed Indianapolis municipal water, to grocery stores and restaurants, as well as to home and office coolers. The label also offered distilled water. To support the venture, work was begun on a 31,000-square-foot bottling plant in Indianapolis.

Furthermore, in 1991 NWS acquired the Chicago distributor Union Liquor Company, another family-owned business that grew out of the repeal of Prohibition. Established by the Leavitt family it started out distributing beer, but when it branched into wine and spirits changed its name to Consolidated Distilled Products, Inc. (CDP). Expanding into the rectifying business (the blending and filtration of spirits already distilled), the company launched Consolidated Rectifying, Inc. (CRI). Union Liquor Company was also established to serve as a distributor in the Chicago area, becoming especially influential in the restaurant fine-wine market. The company moved into the super premium beer market in the 1980s. Shortly after NWS acquired Union Liquor (which changed its name to Union Beverage Company in 1996) it added CRI. To solidify its presence in Illinois, NWS subsequently acquired Hamburg Distributing Company and two other wholesalers downstate, then in 1993 purchased Chicago-based Federated Industries, Inc., along with three outstate and downstate distributors. Supporting these units were distribution hubs located in Chicago, Champaign, Peoria, and Springfield, and sales offices in Rockford and Belleville, later moved to Collinsville. The closing of Continental Distributing Company in Chicago in 1996 provided further opportunity for Union Beverage to add product lines and personnel.

In 1996, U.S. Beverage was founded as a national broker of increasingly popular microbrewed, craft beers, as well as imports and specialty malt products. In March 1997 it commenced operations as a division of NWS. In the ensuing years U.S. Beverage obtained the exclusive U.S. distribution rights to Hooper's Hooch, a flavored malt beverage produced by Bass PLC; the beers of Goose Island Brewing Company; the products of Grolsch International; and Seagram's Coolers and Rick's Lemonade.

NWS moved into new territories in the late 1990s. When Michigan elected to privatize the distribution of spirits in 1997, NWS began doing business in the state through its newly formed subsidiary, NWS Michigan, Inc., quickly lining up exclusive deals with Michigan's major spirits suppliers. To expand its operation, in 1999 NWS Michigan acquired broker R.M. Gilligan, Inc., making the company the largest distributor in the state. It gained a 52 percent market share, serving some 11,500 customers from its main warehouse in Brownstown and distribution hubs in Grand Rapids and Escanaba. NWS also moved into nearby Kentucky when in 1998 it acquired a 25 percent interest in Commonwealth Wine & Spirits, a joint venture with two other distributors, Vertner Smith Company and Kentucky Wine & Spirits.

Reorganization Creates Corporate Holding Company in 1998

In the late 1990s the industry underwent a period of consolidation. With annual revenues of more than $540 million NWS was one of the country's top ten distributors but in this new, highly competitive environment it was essentially forced to grow larger, to either be the acquirer or the acquired. In keeping with this reality, in December 1998 the company underwent a reorganization and the present NWS holding company was formed. LaCrosse (or a family trust) and Mrs. Johnston owned virtually all of the stock of the Indiana and Michigan subsidiaries, and along with Martin H. Bart owned the Illinois subsidiary. A longtime Seagram's executive, Bart joined the Illinois operation as vice-chairman in 1995. LaCrosse and Mrs. Johnston exchanged their shares for stock in the new holding company, while Bart exchanged his shares in the old Illinois entity for shares in the new Illinois entity. The reorganization complete, the stage was set for a major bond offering in January 1999 to fund future expansion. NWS raised $110 million through the sale of high yield or "junk" bonds, a first for wholesale distributors, which typically relied on their own funds or traditional bank lending. Much of the proceeds, in fact, were used to pay down bank debt, freeing up a large line of credit and allowing NWS access to the debt market if it needed to.

In 2000 NWS decided to sell Cameron Springs to Perrier Group for $10.4 million in cash. Focused on its core business—spirits and wines—NWS enjoyed steady growth following its reorganization in 1998. Revenues topped $600 million in fiscal 2000 and improved to $681.5 million for fiscal 2002, despite difficult economic conditions. There was every reason to believe that trend would continue in the foreseeable future, especially in light of the alcoholic beverage industry's traditional immunity to recessions. By mid-2002, the National Wine & Spirits family prepared itself for more changes and challenges as consolidation in the industry continued to unfold.

Principal Subsidiaries

NWS-Illinois, LLC; NWS, Inc.; NWS Michigan, Inc.; United States Beverage, LLC (50%); National Wine & Spirits Corp.; Union Beverage Company; Hamburg Distributing Company; Chicago Wine Merchants.

Principal Competitors

Glazer's Wholesale Drug; Johnson Brothers; Southern Wine & Spirits.

Further Reading

Berman, Phyllis, ''Smoke Alarm,'' *Forbes,* July 17, 2000, p. 82.

Dalesio, Emery P., ''National Wine Turns to Water,'' *Indianapolis Business Journal,* July 22, 1991, p. 1.

''Indiana's Own Designer Water,'' *Indiana Business Magazine,* September 1991, p. 84.

Pletz, John, ''Bond Sale Turns Heads,'' *Indianapolis Business Journal,* March 1, 1999, p. 1.

''Wine Goes Online,'' *Indianapolis Business Journal,* September 20, 1999, p. 1.

—Ed Dinger

Natrol, Inc.

21411 Prairie Street
Chatsworth, California 91311
U.S.A.
Telephone: (818) 739-6000
Fax: (818) 739-6001
Web site: http://www.natrol.com

Public Company
Incorporated: 1997
Employees: 283
Sales: $87.1 million (2000)
Stock Exchanges: NASDAQ
Ticker Symbol: NTOL
NAIC: 325411 Medicinal and Botanical Manufacturing;
    325412 Pharmaceutical Preparation Manufacturing

Natrol, Inc. manufactures and distributes a variety of nutritional and herbal supplements through supermarkets, drugstores, health food stores, and mass-market retailers nationwide. In addition to providing vitamin, mineral, and herbal supplements for general health, Natrol offers a variety of products for specific health needs, such as men's, women's, and children's health, joint health, weight loss, energy enhancement, sleep enhancement, and brain function. Natrol's subsidiary ProLab Nutrition, Inc. produces sports nutrition products and Laci Le Beau Tea offers a variety of herbal tea products. Essentially Pure Ingredients sells bulk ingredients to other supplement makers.

Origins As a Cosmetics Firm in the Early 1980s

Founded in 1980 by Elliot Balbert, Natrol originated as a cosmetics company. In 1982 the company began to market nutritionally based weight loss products, hence the name Natrol, for "natural control." Natrol expanded organically in the area of nutritional supplements, using manufacturing contractors to produce the company's vitamins, minerals, herbs, and specialty formulations, such as Natural High, an energy enhancer, and Oat Bran Fiber Caplets. In 1986 the company introduced its first major product, Ester-C, a form of vitamin C absorbed into the bloodstream rapidly. Although FDA rules did not allow Natrol to promote Ester-C as a cure for the cold or treatment for symptoms of a cold, common knowledge of the benefits of vitamin C supported sales of the product. Natrol advertised Ester-C in magazines directed to health-conscious consumers, such as *Delicious, Better Nutrition, Great Life, Prevention,* and *Health,* and in mainstream magazines, such as *TV Guide, McCall's, Family Circle,* and *Women's Day.* In 1990 Natrol began to advertise on the radio show "Larry King Live." Another long-term success, Calms Kids, provided parents with a natural alternative to treating hyperactivity in children. Natrol reported sales of $2.5 million in 1989 and nearly doubled sales in 1990, with profits at approximately 8 percent of sales.

Natrol distributed its products to health food stores through wholesale distributors Tree of Life and United Natural Foods and direct to General Nutrition Centers. The company expanded distribution of its products through independent mail-order catalogues; through mass-market drugstores, such as Walgreen's, American Drug Stores' Osco, and Sav-On stores; through mass-market merchandisers Wal-Mart and Target; and through grocery store chains, including Von's and Ralph's. Other outlets included resort hotels, salons, airport shops, and on the Internet via such sites as MotherEarth.com. Natrol began to vertically integrate the company, first packaging supplements purchased in bulk, then acquiring encapsulating and tableting equipment to manufacture its nutritional supplements. By 1993 Natrol revenues increased to $9.5 million, garnering net income of $279,000.

Benefits of Federal Law for Natrol and the Supplements Industry in the Mid-1990s

The Dietary Supplements Health and Education Act of 1994 had a profound impact on Natrol and the nutritional supplements industry. The law allowed supplement marketers to state claims as to the health benefits of nutritional products on merchandise labels, without claiming that they treated or cured disease. In addition, several new studies helped to promote the benefits of certain herbs and substances, attracting the attention of aging baby boomers. High-profile products that drew strong consumer response included Melatonin, a hormone that acts as an antioxidant and sleep aid; DHEA, an anti-aging substance; kava kava, an herbal relaxant; and St. John's Wort, shown to relieve depression.

While the supplements industry reported 20 percent to 40 percent growth between 1994 and 1998, Natrol exceeded those growth rates. Revenues increased 95 percent in 1995, to $23.6 million on the strength of Melatonin sales, which accounted for $6.7 million or 28 percent of total revenues. In 1996 Natrol experienced a 73 percent increase in revenues to $40.8 million. Sales of Melatonin and DHEA, introduced in March, accounted for more than half of total revenues, with $22.9 million in sales. In addition to publicity from clinical studies on health supplements, Natrol's national advertising campaign served to increase sales as well.

Increased public interest in health supplements benefited Natrol, but the company's ability to maintain sales growth relied on the introduction of new products. In 1997 Natrol experienced a 57 percent decline in sales of DHEA and Melatonin, or $13.1 million. Sales from new products offset the decline, accounting for $8.9 million in sales. Natrol introduced 30 new supplements in 1997, a total of 58 stock keeping units, including different quantities and tablet and capsule forms. Two popular supplements, Kavatrol, made with kava kava root, and Mood Support, made with St. John's Wort, sold well due to publicity surrounding clinical studies about the herbs.

Natrol took several steps to support and continue swift growth. In the spring of 1997 the company opened a new, 90,000-square-foot manufacturing facility, quadrupling the company's manufacturing capacity to produce 100,000 million tablets and capsules and to fill 20 million bottles per year. Natrol increased its advertising budget incrementally from 10.5 percent of sales in 1995 to 16.2 percent in 1997, stabilizing at 15 percent of sales, and launched its first television campaign to promote Kavatrol in 1997. On high-profile national radio shows, such as Rush Limbaugh's and Dr. Laura Schlesinger's programs, Natrol provided nutritional supplement information on the "National Health Minute." A new sales team enhanced relationships with health food store customers, leading to $6.8 million in growth from existing customers. Natrol reported total revenues of $42.9 million in 1997.

Expansion Through Acquisitions and Initial Public Offering of Stock in the Late 1990s

Natrol diversified its product offerings through vertical integration. The company acquired Pure-Gar, Inc. for $11 million in February 1998. Pure-Gar manufactured and distributed garlic supplements under two brand names, Quintessence and Highgar Farms. In addition, the company sold bulk nutritional ingredients to other nutritional supplement makers. Pure-Gar supplied garlic, primarily, as well as vegetable, fruit, and herbal and other botanical powders. In November Natrol purchased Laci La Beau, maker of a line of herb teas for weight loss. Natrol paid $7.5 million for the company, which recorded $7.2 million in revenues for the fiscal year ending June 1998. Laci La Beau added nine new teas in 1997. The July 1998 initial public offering of stock supported expansion. At $15 per share, the stock offering garnered $59.1 million and netted $44.64 million.

Sustaining a line of 145 products and continually adding new products required Natrol to seek additional shelf space with existing customers. During 1998 several major retailers added new products to their existing lines of Natrol products. American Drug Stores added 16 products to its offerings at more than 1,500 locations, including Lucky grocery stores. Fedco, a high-volume mass-market merchandiser in California, added 49 products and Rite-Aid drugstores added 20 products to its current line of five products at nearly 4,000 stores nationwide. Other retailers that accommodated new Natrol products included Schnuck's, with 170 grocery and superstores in the Midwest, BJ's Wholesale Club in the Northeast, and The Caldor Corporation, a mass merchandiser with 130 stores in the Northeast. Sales reached $68.2 million in 1998, garnering $7.5 million in net earnings.

In February 1999 Natrol acquired Essentially Pure Ingredients (EPI), a provider of raw materials to supplement manufacturers. Natrol combined EPI with Pure-Gar and retained the EPI name for that division. In March 1999 Pure-Gar obtained exclusive rights to distribute MelaPure, pharmaceutical grade Melatonin by VitaPure Ltd. in the United Kingdom.

New products in 1999 included several herbal products, such as hawthorne berry, licorice root, damiana leaf, gotu kola, and ginger root supplements. In June Laci Le Beau repackaged and relaunched its line of herb teas and extended the line of Super Dieter's and Green Tea, adding decaffeinated and flavored products, such as cherry, peppermint, and tropical fruit. Natrol introduced specialty herbal tea products under the Laci Le Beau name, including Throat Care, Heavenly Nights, and Tummy Care. New products for women involved Cran Support for urinary tract health, Woman's Multiple, and a calcium supplement with magnesium and vitamin D.

A new media campaign in 1999 featured television advertisements with Balbert talking about Natrol's mission to provide high quality products and services. Outlets included "CNN Headline News" and "Larry King Live," TBS, TNT, and network TV game shows. A print campaign supported the television spots. Natrol redesigned its logo as well, to attract consumer attention.

Natrol continued to attain additional shelf space with its customers. Eckerd Drug Stores, with 2,900 stores in 20 states, added 60 stock keeping units to its line of eight Natrol products. Target stores added 29 new Natrol products. With 4,000 stores in 24 states, CVS drugstores added 32 products to its line of Natrol products and Pharmor added 43 products for distribution at its 130 drugstores. Albertson's and other grocery stores expanded their lines as well.

Natrol sought to expand its product line with the acquisition of ProLab Nutrition, Inc. for $29 million cash and stock. ProLab specialized in sports nutritional products for body builders, athletes, and other physically active customers. ProLab produced powdered supplements for weight gain, weight loss, meal replacement, and performance enhancement. With $30 million in annual revenues, ProLab sold its products through gyms and health food stores nationwide as well as in Canada, Germany, and the United Kingdom. The acquisition benefited each company, as Natrol planned to facilitate improvements in manufacturing, product development, and marketing at ProLab, and ProLab planned to assist in the international distribution of Natrol products and in domestic distribution in the sports fitness market. ProLab operated a 32,000-square-foot distribution center in Bloomfield, Connecticut, which Natrol expanded to 52,000 square feet.

In 2000 ProLab introduced the Solutions line of nutritional supplements for women, primarily nutritional powders and power bars under the Awesome brand. Cory Everson, six-time Ms. Olympia winner and renowned fitness expert, represented the brand. To promote the product line, Natrol sponsored a sweepstakes offering a four-day stay at Everson's Fitness Adventure Camp, held twice a year in Malibu; second prize was $250 worth of Solutions products. Other women's products introduced by Natrol, under the Natrol for Women line, included soy protein bars and nutritional powders with ingredients beneficial to women, particularly for hormone balance during menopause.

Natrol redesigned and expanded its line of children's products, the Kids Companion line. The new trade dress involved two cartoon characters, Nate and Kate, dragons designed specifically for Natrol. New nutritional products included multiple vitamins, a supplement to enhance memory in chewable or liquid form, and nutritional bars in peanut butter, blueberry, and other kid-friendly flavors. Natrol targeted the Kids Companion line to upscale, health-conscious parents. Promotional products included tattoos, lunch boxes, and a growth chart, all featuring Nate and Kate.

Dramatic Decline in Interest in Nutritional Supplements at the Beginning of the New Century

The boom in popularity of nutritional supplements during the mid-1990s subsided by 2000, affecting Natrol and the supplements industry as a whole. New studies questioned the validity of health claims of nutritional supplements, particularly St. John's Wort and Vitamin C. Balbert attributed some of the decline to poor quality products on the market. As new competitors sought to capitalize on public demand for nutritional products, less knowledgeable buyers used lower quality ingredients. For instance, Balbert declined to purchase thousands of kilos of St. John's Wort when the stock did not meet Natrol's standards for quality. It was likely that the seller found a buyer in another nutritional supplement manufacturer and that consumers found the products to be ineffective.

Other factors that affected Natrol included a slower consumer market, leading to a high level of product returns from retail stores, triple the norm, and a related write-down of losses. The supplements market matured quickly during the 1990s, with market saturation expanding the availability of nutritional supplements to a wider array of retail stores. Furthermore, a spectacular new product did not appear and draw extraordinary sales as in previous years. In addition, Natrol lost a private-label manufacturing contract.

The fickle nature of consumer trends dissuaded investors; in August 2000 Natrol's stock dropped to between $2.00 and $2.25 per share, despite the company's strong reputation in the industry. Natrol reported an increase in sales in 2000, at $87.1 million; much of that increase was attributed to ProLab revenues after its first full year of operation as a Natrol subsidiary. Without ProLab sales of $21.2 million in 2000, Natrol revenues actually declined from $76.8 million in 1999 to $65.9 million in 2000. Natrol recorded a net loss of $5.2 million in 2000 in contrast to a net income of $9.2 million in 1999.

By January 2001, Natrol decided to reorganize the executive offices and to institute budget cuts and several marketing initiatives to improve sales. To reduce excess inventory Natrol initiated a buy-one-get-one-free offer, reduced prices to retailers, issued coupons, and provided value-added purchases.

Natrol continued to launch new products and to seek new outlets for them in 2001. The company introduced GlucoChews for joint health, which replaced glucosamine and chondroitin in the body, as the body makes less of these substances as it ages. Natrol relaunched the Quintessence brand of garlic products. New multiple vitamins under the My Favorite Multiple line included a Complete Care supplement with antioxidants; 50-Plus, specially formulated for joint, vision, and heart health; and My Favorite Energizer. Other products included REMEDIEF for pain management; Dry Mouth Relief; Natrol Complete Balance AM/PM Menopause Formula; and Natrol My Defense, containing patented Immune Enhancer AG. A significant new product, FlexAnew for joint health, became available at more than 25,000 retail stores nationwide within three months of its introduction in June. GNC agreed to carry ProLab sports nutrition products at more than 4,500 stores. In September Natrol initiated a multimillion-dollar advertising campaign to support the sale of new products; the campaign included television and print advertising, as well as public relations activities and special promotions.

Difficulties in the supplements industry were reflected in Natrol's financial results for 2001. The company recorded revenues of $76.2 million and a net loss of $20.3 million. The loss included a $20 million write-down on goodwill on ProLab as the product line did not produce the financial results anticipated when Natrol purchased the company. The company reduced its debt and improved operating costs, however. In March Natrol launched Natrol Stress Complex, a premium quality sleep aid, a combination of Melatonin, valerian root, the amino acid glutamine, and vitamin E; the company initiated a national campaign for the product in September 2002.

Principal Subsidiaries

Essentially Pure Ingredients; Laci Le Beau Tea; ProLab Nutrition, Inc.

Principal Competitors

Hauser, Inc.; Herbalife International; Twinlab Corporation; Weider Nutrition International; Wyeth Laboratories.

Further Reading

Adamson, Deborah, ''Man Finds Success with Nutritive Pills,'' *Daily News of Los Angeles,* June 20, 1997, p. B1.

Dougherty, Conor, ''Cost Cutting a Remedy for Dietary Supplement Maker,'' *Los Angeles Business Journal,* August 20, 2001, p. 32.

Medearis, John, ''Vitamin Firms Must Tread Lightly in Ad; Nutrition: A Chatsworth Supplement Company Must Adhere to Strict FDA Rules in Its Product Claims,'' *Los Angeles Times,* May 3, 1990, p. D4.

''Natrol Adopts Nate the Dragon,'' *Chain Drug Review,* August 14, 2000, p. 31.

''Natrol Extends Vitamin Line,'' *Drug Store News,* May 21, 2001, p. 95.

''Natrol in Midst of Relaunching Its Herbal Tea Business,'' *Chain Drug Review,* June 7, 1999, p. 293.

''Natrol Is in an Expansion Mode,'' *Chain Drug Review,* June 19, 2000, p. 156.

Netherby, Jennifer, ''Fortunes of Vitamin Maker Weaken in Troubled Sector,'' *Los Angeles Business Journal,* August 29, 2000, p. 25.

''Popular Garlic Remedy Enjoys Comeback,'' *Drug Store News,* February 19, 2001, p. 35.

Sommer, Constance, ''Natrol Seeks the Right Elixir to Energize Sales,'' *Los Angeles Times,* September 26, 2000, p. B9.

Tenerelli, Mary Jane, ''Herbal Decay: Natrol CEO Elliot Balbert Talks About the Decline of the Herbal Market and Possible Remedies,'' *Global Cosmetic Industry,* February 2001, p. 50.

—Mary Tradii

Natural Alternatives International, Inc.

1185 Linda Vista Drive
San Marcos, California 92069
U.S.A.
Telephone: (760) 744-7340
Fax: (760) 744-9589
Web site: http://www.nai-online.com

Public Company
Incorporated: 1985
Employees: 114
Sales: $42.2 million (2001)
Stock Exchanges: NASDAQ
Ticker Symbol: NAII
NAIC: 325411 Medicinal and Botanical Manufacturing;
  325412 Pharmaceutical Preparation Manufacturing

Natural Alternatives International, Inc. (NAI) formulates and manufactures nutritional supplements, including vitamins, minerals, herbs, and specialty formulas, for private-label distributors as well as for its proprietary product lines. NAI-branded products include Green Farm and Natural Alternatives nutritional supplements and ProLean weight loss products. NAI services to the private-label market include custom formulation, clinical studies of nutritional products, regulatory assistance, packaging design, and product marketing.

Providing Nutritional Alternatives to Pharmaceutical Drugs in 1980

Mark Le Doux founded Natural Alternatives International (NAI) in 1980 to produce proprietary vitamins and other nutritional supplements as healthy alternatives to drugs. Le Doux wanted to provide nutritional products that heal the causes of disease, rather than alleviate symptoms, as drugs tend to do. Le Doux's guiding philosophy followed that of Hippocrates, who said, "Let food be your medicine." The company's employees included Elinor Le Doux as director of research, and Bruce Le Doux as director of medical sales. Marie Le Doux, Mark's mother and a major investor, took the position of chairwoman.

NAI's first line of vitamin and nutritional products eased the maladies of substance abuse during recovery from addiction; these products sold under private labels through physicians.

The company developed and produced nutritional products sold through various marketing and distribution channels. "Fitness Builder," a line of products designed to promote physical fitness, found customers among athletes, body builders, and military personnel. NAI distributed Fitness Builder products through health food stores, wholesale distributors, consumer direct distributors, and military Post Exchanges in southern California. Products for the mass market included Med-Cap vitamin supplements, a line of all-capsule vitamins sold through large regional chains, and brand-name Natural Alternatives products, sold through large discount retail chains.

Contract manufacturing involved production of nutritional supplements for private-label brands. NAI manufactured and sold in bulk form tablet and capsule nutritional supplements for private label distribution to KAL brand vitamins and AMCON Industries, a division of Amway Corporation. In addition to manufacturing vitamins, NAI provided bottling and labeling of NAI-made products under private-label brands for Pharmavite Corporation; Filmore Foods; Prime Natural Products; Redken Laboratories; Simpak Corporation; and Ultra Drug Corporation. Over time NAI added label design, brochures, and other marketing services to enhance its private-label business.

After six years in operation NAI recorded $2.64 million in revenue and net income of $100,076 for the fiscal year ended June 30, 1986. Contract manufacturing accounted for 60 percent of revenues. Sales to health food stores accounted for 25 percent of NAI revenues, down from 50 percent the previous year as NAI streamlined its customer list to select chains, finding it too costly to develop products for each health food store. The upfront expenditure in bottles, labels, and product inventory involved a high level of risk because the investment did not always reap a return and many of the small companies proved to be a high credit risk.

In 1986 American Acquisitions, Inc. purchased NAI and then changed its name to NAI and dissolved the subsidiary, the original NAI. Just prior to the acquisition, the two companies

---

Company Perspectives:

Founded in 1980, NAI prides itself on a strong commitment to health, scientific integrity and quality. We provide comprehensive solutions that include custom formulations based on scientific research, the highest manufacturing standards, supervision of international regulatory compliance, and marketing support. We have established partnerships and work to develop tailored solutions for our clients' nutritional product needs.

With state-of-the-art manufacturing facilities in San Marcos, California and Lugano Switzerland, and a sales presence in Yokohama, Japan, NAI is able to fulfill the needs of our customers around the world.

---

integrated the board of directors and management. Le Doux remained CEO and William P. Spencer joined as COO and executive vice-president. The new company traded on the National Association of Securities Dealers exchange.

Under the new ownership arrangement, NAI began to expand its customer base, including international markets. Growth of the business originated primarily from new clients in the medical and contract manufacturing divisions. In 1988 the company experienced a sudden burst of growth with two major manufacturing contracts. An agreement with S.A. International involved a line of 22 proprietary nutritional supplements produced for export to Pacific Rim countries, including Taiwan, Singapore, and Malaysia. For Jenny Craig Weight Loss Centers NAI began to manufacture supplements used in that company's weight loss programs. The five-year, $12 million contract covered distribution to half of Jenny Craig's 300 clinics. Other significant contracts included Weider Health & Fitness, for sports nutrition supplements, and Neuro-genesis, for substance abuse recovery supplements. NAI invested in high-speed, state-of-the-art manufacturing and bottling equipment to keep pace with the influx of new business. New clients boosted NAI sales by 72.4 percent in fiscal 1989, to $7.3 million, and garnered net income of $439,000. (A recall of the controversial amino acid supplement L-Tryptophan had negligible impact on sales and earnings.) In April 1990, NAI shifted to the NASDAQ Additional List following a 1-to-50 reverse stock split, which allowed NAI to enter the exchange at $2 per share.

Seeking Diversified Market Base As Public Interest in Nutritional Supplements Grows During the 1990s

NAI secured its reputation in the area of health sciences with the introduction of revolutionary new products for immunity, metabolic fitness, substance abuse treatment, premature aging, and other consumer health concerns. During the early 1990s scientific studies increased demand for nutritional supplements and NAI capitalized on this interest by creating a radio program to inform the public about nutrition in general and NAI products in particular. Mark Le Doux hosted the 15-minute show ''The Natural Alternative, Recipes for Healthier Living,'' which aired Monday through Friday at 6:45 p.m. and on Sunday at 12:45 p.m. Radio stations carried the show in central and southern California and into Mexico.

In May 1990 NAI acquired the trademark and net assets of DBA Laboratories, makers of 115 nutritional products sold under the Sonergy brand. Customers included retail drug stores and grocery stores, primarily in southern California. NAI planned to expand distribution to all of California and later to other western states. NAI adopted the brand name for the new subsidiary, renamed Sonergy, Inc.

By 1991 NAI utilized more than 15,000 formulations for vitamin and nutritional supplements, produced for private-label businesses and its proprietary lines. The company's manufacturing capacity reached 11 million capsules per day. In fiscal 1991, NAI reported $10.4 million in revenues, actually a 13 percent decline from the previous year, at $11.9 million. Along with an industrywide decline in sales, the company experienced a decline in demand as several clients reduced inventories and one client, who previously accounted for 7 percent of revenues, discontinued operations. Higher sales at Sonergy offset the decline, which would have been at 23 percent; Sonergy accounted for 1 percent of sales in 1990, but increased to 14 percent of sales in 1991. Net income declined from $1.13 million in 1990, to $252,394 in fiscal 1991.

NAI sought diverse opportunities for business expansion. In March 1992 NAI became an ''Official Supplier'' of nutritional supplements to the U.S. Olympic Committee. NAI produced a multivitamin-mineral supplement, a multisourced Vitamin C supplement, and a Calcium/Magnesium/Vitamin D supplement. Jameson Pharmaceuticals, Inc. distributed the products to drug, grocery, and mass merchant retailers. NAI acquired CellLife International for $412,500, including $255,000 in cash and the balance in stock. CellLife marketed raw materials to pharmaceutical companies in Europe. NAI planned to expand CellLife into markets in the United States and worldwide.

In fiscal 1992 and 1993, NAI experienced tremendous growth, with revenues increasing 39 percent and 34 percent, respectively. In fiscal 1992, NAI reported revenues of $14.5 million and net earnings of $753,837. Jenny Craig, NuSkin International, and Weider Health and Fitness accounted for 64 percent of revenues in 1992. In addition, NAI began to test market its Green Farm and Natural Alternatives proprietary lines of vitamins in Europe and Asia. In November 1992 NAI opened a manufacturing facility in Mexico, forming Natural Alternatives al de Mexico, SA de C.V.

NAI continued to find new manufacturing clients. When deciding whether to engage in manufacturing contracts, NAI looked for companies that fit certain standards. NAI sought clients on a financially sound footing, not high-risk, capital-intensive ventures. The client's business needed to be large enough to create economies of scale and to be diversified in its product line. In addition, new clients had to be interested in global distribution.

The pattern of growth continued during fiscal 1993, when NAI recorded revenues of $19.4 million, including a 50 percent increase in the fourth quarter to $6 million. Net income increased 28 percent to just less than $1 million. To improve profit margins NAI streamlined operations at CellLife and Sonergy. At Sonergy NAI eliminated some products and product lines,

Key Dates:

1980: Company is founded by Mark Le Doux.
1986: New investment and ownership arrangement funds company growth.
1988: NAI signs agreements to manufacture supplements for S.A. International and Jenny Craig Weight Loss Centers.
1992: NAI enters raw materials distribution with acquisition of CellLife International.
1995: *Forbes* lists NAI on its list of the World's Best Small Companies.
1998: Revenues peak at $67.9 million before a decline in sales for the company and industry.
2000: NAI implements cost-cutting program to maintain profitability.

and maintained the high-profit weight loss products, changing the brand and subsidiary name to ProLean.

During the mid-1990s, public interest in nutritional supplements continued to rise, attracting the interest of related businesses, such as NordicTrack. In February 1995 NAI signed a supply agreement with NordicTrack to develop and manufacture a line of nutritional supplements and snacks and fitness programs to be distributed through the company's retail locations and direct response call centers. The products were developed to be complementary to the fitness requirements of cross-country ski exercisers, treadmills, and other NordicTrack fitness equipment.

The company's growth culminated in a five-year annual compound growth rate of 38 percent from 1991 to 1995 and earned NAI a place on *Forbes* magazine's list of the World's Best Small Companies in 1995. That year NAI reported record sales of $37.4 million and net income of $2 million. At the end of fiscal 1995 the company reported an order backlog valued at $13.6 million, compared with $3.8 million in 1994. In addition to growth through new business, NAI saw a dramatic increase in sales due to an expected increase in the price of raw materials. NAI's success with the Jenny Craig line of nutritional supplements continued with the introduction of two new supplements in April 1996. Daily Success provided vitamins and minerals, including calcium and iron, and Protect Plus provided antioxidant nutrition.

A clinical study at the University of Texas in 1997 affirmed the health benefits of certain weight loss nutritional supplements co-designed by NAI and NSA, Inc. The eight-week test looked at the effectiveness of JuicePlus, made with extracts of fruits, such as apple, orange, pineapple, papaya, and other fruits, or vegetables, including carrots, parsley, beets, spinach, and tomatoes; Thins, a chewable wafer; and AbsorbaLean, a proprietary product made with plant fibers that absorb dietary fat from the bloodstream and body. Members of the test group saw an improvement in body composition, having lost fat and maintained muscle mass, as compared with the control group. Following the study, NAI obtained exclusive rights for Glucatrol, the fiber compound used in AbsorbaLean. The Shimizer Chemical Corporation had been processing the fiber, made from the

Japanese Konjoc plant, for seven generations. Konjoc fiber absorbs water, fat, and cholesterol and stabilizes blood sugar.

As global demand for herbal and nutritional supplements grew dramatically, NAI sought to expand its manufacturing capacity. The company installed a tablet manufacturing operation to handle increased demand and planned to open a new manufacturing facility in Carlsbad in 1999. Sales increased to $67.9 million in fiscal 1998, including $14.9 million in international sales, garnering net income of $5.9 million. NAI reported an order backlog of $24 million.

In the spring of 1999 NAI entered into a joint venture with FitnessAge, Inc. to sell a line of customized natural supplements via the Internet. The site would include a fitness assessment program to be used with professional assistance at FitnessAge centers, health clubs, spas, weight loss centers, and other similar locations. The program determined individual needs through algorithms that calculated physiological age based on standard tests of fitness: cardio/respiratory; flexibility; strength/endurance; and body composition.

In a new venture with Jenny Craig, NAI began to manufacture Advanced Nutrients by Jenny Craig, developed by Dr. Art Ulene. Dr. Ulene appeared on the *Today* show for 20 years, becoming known nationally as "America's Wellness Doctor." The line of 22 products included five vitamin and mineral supplements, nine herbal supplements, and eight nutritional supplements. The line was sold exclusively through a new Jenny Craig web site.

For Classic Beauty Supplements, Inc. NAI formulated and manufactured a proprietary line of nine products for distribution through spas and beauty salons. Designed specifically for women, the line included products for hair and nail strength, skin radiance, energy, diet and weight loss, PMS, menopause, and general well being. Classic Beauty launched the line at the International Esthetics, Cosmetics and Spa Conference and distribution began June 1, 1999.

NAI completed a collaborative study with the Naval Health Research Center in San Diego to evaluate the effectiveness of supplements designed to reduce "oxidative stress" caused by the body's use of oxygen during strenuous activity. The study took place at the Marine Corps Mountain Warfare Training Center in Bridgeport, California; 50 volunteers tested the supplements in cold-weather, mountain training.

Rapid growth led NAI to open two new facilities in September 1999. NAI consolidated several small, raw materials warehouses into one large, state-of-the-art facility in Vista, California. The company also tested and quarantined raw materials at that facility. A manufacturing facility in Lugano, Switzerland, handled encapsulation, tablet compression, and packaging for products distributed in Europe. In addition, NAI opened a sales office in Yokohama, Japan.

Many Factors Leading to Decline in Sales Between 1999 and 2001

NAI experienced a dramatic shift in its financial situation when NuSkin Enterprises, one of the company's largest customers, did not renew its manufacturing contract with NAI and began the process of transferring to another manufacturer. Sales declined 15.5 percent from $67.9 million in 1998, with a net profit of $5.9 million, to $57.4 million in 1999, with a net loss of $2.9 million. Other factors contributing to the decline in sales included a slower economy and a sudden drop in public interest in certain herbal and anti-aging supplements that became explosively popular during the mid-1990s.

NAI implemented a number of measures to reduce expenses, including discontinuation of low-profit products and the layoff of 95 people, or 47 percent of the company's workforce, between January and June 2000. The company halted use of temporary production personnel and reduced executive compensation and benefits. CEO Mark LeDoux reduced his annual salary by 31 percent. NAI also began to restructure its executive management, culminating in Mark Le Doux stepping down as CEO and taking the position of chairman of the board. In addition, NAI found new tenants for the Carlsbad facility, freeing the company from its lease commitment and saving unnecessary overhead expenses.

The company implemented in-house packaging capabilities to reduce operating expenses. NAI diversified distribution by establishing a Direct-to-Customer sales operation through television, direct mail, and e-commerce distribution. In addition, NAI redesigned its web site for easier consumer navigation. ASD Systems, Inc. installed new software to improve the efficiency of call center services, order fulfillment, customer services, and Internet order processing; ASD handled these distribution services as well.

Although NAI attained new clients, the company's revenues continued to decline as the company lost two additional contract manufacturing customers. In fiscal 2001 NAI reported $42.2 million in revenues, including $5.7 million from the new consumer direct business. The company reported a loss of $4.9 million due to noncash charges, such as equipment depreciation, which were not operations related. On the brighter side, product sales in Europe more than doubled, from $3.4 million in 2000 to $7.5 million in 2001. NSA, distributor of the popular Juice Plus line and other products, renewed its exclusive contract with NAI in January 2001. NAI continued to seek new opportunities for nutritionally enhanced products through an October 2001 agreement with Bon Coeur, Inc. to use that company's proprietary bio-food technology and formulas.

Principal Subsidiaries

CellLife International, Inc.; Natural Alternatives International Europe SA; ProLean, Inc.

Principal Competitors

GNC, Inc.; Perrigo Company; Rexall Sundown, Inc.

Further Reading

Hardie, Mary, "Natural Alternatives Plans Acquisition for Growth; Two Years After Buying Stake in Biotech Venture, San Marcos Company Seeks Deal with Health Firm," *San Diego Business Journal,* February 12, 1990, p. 8.
"Plant Extracts Fight Disease," *Chain Drug Review,* February 1, 1999, p. 28.

—Mary Tradii

Neiman Marcus

The Neiman Marcus Group, Inc.

1618 Main Street
Dallas, Texas 75201
U.S.A.
Telephone: (214) 741-6911
Fax: (214) 573-6142
Web site: http://www.neimanmarcusgroup.com

Public Company
Incorporated: 1987
Employees: 15,400
Sales: $3.02 billion (2001)
Stock Exchanges: New York
Ticker Symbol: NMG
NAIC: 452110 Department Stores; 454110 Electronic
   Shopping and Mail-Order Houses

The name Neiman Marcus is practically synonymous with upscale retailing in the United States. In the early 21st century, The Neiman Marcus Group, Inc. operated through two main segments. The specialty retail stores segment included the 33 stores bearing the famous Neiman Marcus name and Bergdorf Goodman, another high-end retailer with two stores in Manhattan. The Neiman Marcus Direct segment included the Neiman Marcus catalog as well as two other catalog operations—Horchow and Chef's Catalog—and e-commerce web sites for all three brands. In addition, the group held majority control of Kate Spade LLC, maker of upscale designer handbags and accessories, and Gurwitch Bristow Products, LLC, maker of Laura Mercier cosmetics. Throughout much of its nearly 100-year history, Neiman Marcus has been the clothing store of choice for many of the nation's most fashion-conscious people.

Early History: The First Neiman Marcus Store

From the very beginning, the founders of Neiman Marcus aimed high. The original store was opened in Dallas in 1907. Its proprietors were Herbert Marcus, his sister Carrie, and Carrie Neiman's husband, Al Neiman. All three were working in various retail positions in the Dallas area around 1900. Frustrated by their dead-end jobs, Marcus and Neiman decided to strike out on their own. The pair moved to Atlanta in 1905 to start a sales promotion and advertising business. The venture was quite successful, and they were offered a lucrative buyout deal after only two years of operation. Given the choice between $25,000 cash or the Missouri franchise for Coca-Cola and some stock in that young company, they opted for the cash. In retrospect, that decision cost them a fortune, as Coke went on to become the Real Thing. In taking the cash, however, they acquired the seed money to launch the first Neiman Marcus store.

Neiman and Marcus returned triumphantly to Dallas in 1907 and immediately set out to open a store that sold the finest women's clothing money could buy. The store was lavishly furnished and stocked with clothing of a quality that was not commonly found in Texas. Within a few weeks, the store's initial inventory, mostly acquired on a buying trip to New York made by Carrie, was completely sold out. Oil-rich Texans, welcoming the opportunity to flaunt their wealth in more sophisticated fashion than was previously possible, flocked to the new store. In spite of a nationwide financial panic set off only a few weeks after its opening, Neiman Marcus was instantly successful, and its first several years of operation were quite profitable.

In 1913 the original Neiman Marcus store, and most of its merchandise, was destroyed by a fire, the first of several in the company's history. Within about two weeks, however, the store reopened at a temporary site nearby, and construction was quickly begun on a new permanent location. With capital raised through the sale of stock to a handful of manufacturing companies, the new building was ready for business by the autumn of 1914. In its first year at the new building, Neiman Marcus recorded a profit of $40,000 on sales of $700,000, nearly twice the totals reached in its last year at the original location.

Business at Neiman Marcus got better and better over the next several years, as money from oil, cattle, and cotton continued to flow into Texas. Throughout this period, the store maintained its commitment to extravagance, lining the aisles with the fanciest merchandise that could be found. Gradually, the store's reputation expanded beyond the borders of Texas, and soon glamorous types from Hollywood, New York, and even Europe were making special trips to Dallas to shop at Neiman Marcus.

Company Perspectives:

Our mission is to be the leading specialty retailer of fine merchandise to discerning, fashion-conscious consumers from around the world. We will strive to exceed customer expectations for service, quality and value as we build upon our longstanding tradition of excellence.

As we pursue this mission, we are guided by the following important values. We will maintain an uncompromising commitment to quality and the highest levels of customer service in all of our businesses and endeavors. We will adhere to the highest levels of integrity and ethical standards in dealing with all constituencies, including customers, suppliers and employees. We will aspire to achieve a leadership position in every one of our operating businesses. Our management decisions will emphasize long-term benefits to the value of our businesses, not short-term gains. We will employ capable, motivated people; follow sound management practices; utilize new technology efficiently; and reinvest earnings and additional capital as required to grow our businesses and maintain the corporation's financial health. We will strive to maximize the potential of all employees and maintain a professionally challenging work environment. We will be socially and environmentally responsible and support worthwhile causes, especially in those communities in which we operate.

In 1926 Al and Carrie Neiman were divorced, and Neiman's interest in the store was bought out by the Marcus family. The Marcuses remained at the top of the company's management for the next 60 years. Stanley and Edward Marcus, two of Herbert's sons, joined the company in 1926. A big expansion project at the store was completed in 1927, following the acquisition of some property next door. As a result, the store's capacity was nearly doubled. Neiman Marcus added men's clothing to its offerings with the 1928 opening of the Man's Shop. By 1929, the store's net sales had reached $3.6 million.

Adding Lower-Priced Merchandise in the 1930s and 1940s

The onset of the Great Depression forced Neiman Marcus to shift its strategy. During the 1930s, the company began to include less expensive clothing lines in its inventory in hopes of keeping customers whose fortunes had taken a turn for the worse. At the same time, the store continued to stock the pricier, high-end items that made it famous, and it continued to attract wealthy Texans. Company lore from this era tells of a barefoot teenage girl walking confidently into the store and ordering thousands of dollars worth of merchandise. Her father had just struck oil, and her first impulse was to head straight for Neiman Marcus. By striking a balance between upper-crust fashions and more moderate ones, Neiman Marcus was able to maintain its elite reputation while also broadening its customer base. This successful transition to a more democratic clientele enabled the company to sustain its impressive growth rate, and by 1938 annual sales had broken the $5 million mark. Along the way, the store's Man's Shop was expanded, first in 1934 and again in 1941.

The move to include lower-priced merchandise accelerated during the 1940s. World War II brought hundreds of high-paying defense manufacturing jobs to the Dallas area. To the female workers and the wives of their male counterparts, shopping at Neiman Marcus was like a dream come true. The Marcuses were quick to stock their store with merchandise that was affordable to this new wave of middle-class customers. Between 1942 and 1944, sales at Neiman Marcus grew from $6 million to $11 million. Still, the company was able to cultivate its special relationship with the super-rich, and the store took on a sort of split personality. This trend increased even further at the war's end, as more companies opened offices in Dallas, and young families with junior executive salaries settled in.

The immediate postwar years saw many changes at Neiman Marcus. Shortly after the war's end Marcus's two other sons, Herbert, Jr., and Lawrence, joined the company. In 1946 Neiman Marcus suffered the second major fire in its history. Despite substantial damage to both the building and its merchandise, the store was closed for only five days. Even with the loss of those peak Christmas shopping days, the store recorded its best season to date that year. Herbert Marcus, Sr., died in 1950, and Carrie Neiman died just two years later, leaving Stanley Marcus in charge of the company's operations.

Postwar Expansion

Stanley Marcus led the company through a period of rapid expansion during the 1950s. In 1951 a second store was opened at Preston Center in the suburbs of Dallas. In 1952 a new service building was opened to handle merchandise for both stores. The following year a major renovation project added a fifth and a sixth floor to the Dallas store. In 1955 Neiman Marcus made its move into the Houston market. Rather than take on the expense of a new building, the company merged an existing store, Ben Wolfman's, into its operation. The company's reputation for lavish display grew along with its stores, as the company inaugurated the annual Neiman Marcus Fortnight in 1957. The Fortnight was a presentation of fashions and culture from a particular country, held in late October and early November of each year. Another popular annual publicity stunt was launched in 1960. Beginning that year, an extraordinary His and Hers gift selection was included in each Neiman Marcus Christmas catalog. His and Hers gifts over the years have included such spectacular items as submarines, dirigibles, and robots.

Another generation of Marcuses came on board in 1963, when Stanley's son Richard Marcus joined the company as a buyer. The following year, fire devastated the main Dallas store, again during the peak Christmas shopping season. Once again, the store was reopened quickly, and the repair work included improvements to the store's appearance. In 1965, with the population of suburban Dallas growing by leaps and bounds, the Preston Center store was closed, and a new store, more than twice as big, was opened at NorthPark Center, also in the Dallas suburbs. Another branch was opened in nearby Fort Worth around that time as well. By 1967 the four Neiman Marcus stores in operation were generating annual sales of $58.5 million, and the company's profit for that year was in excess of $2 million.

Neiman Marcus ceased being a family business in 1968, when the company was merged into Broadway-Hale Stores, Inc., a

Key Dates:

1907: First Neiman Marcus store, specializing in upscale women's clothing, is opened in Dallas by Herbert Marcus, his sister Carrie, and her husband, Al Neiman.

1928: Men's clothing is added to the store's offerings with the opening of the Man's Shop.

1951: Second Neiman Marcus store is opened in a Dallas suburb.

1955: Expansion outside Dallas begins with the opening of a store in Houston.

1968: Company merges into Broadway-Hale Stores, Inc. (later Carter Hawley Hale Stores, Inc.), aiding further expansion.

1984: The Limited attempts a hostile takeover of Carter Hawley; General Cinema Corporation steps in as white knight, acquiring a 38.6 percent stake in Carter Hawley.

1987: Second hostile takeover attempt leads to spinoff of Carter Hawley's specialty store division as a publicly traded firm called The Neiman Marcus Group, Inc.; General Cinema (later Harcourt General, Inc.) holds a 60 percent stake in the new firm, which includes the Neiman Marcus stores, Bergdorf Goodman, and the Contempo Casuals chain.

1988: Neiman Marcus Group acquires the Horchow catalog operation.

1995: Contempo Casuals chain is sold to Wet Seal, Inc.

1998: Chef's Catalog is acquired; first Galleries of Neiman Marcus stores open; Neiman Marcus Group acquires a 51 percent stake in Gurwitch Bristow Products, LLC, maker and marketer of the Laura Mercier cosmetic line.

1999: A 56 percent interest in designer handbag maker Kate Spade LLC is acquired; Harcourt General ends its majority control of The Neiman Marcus Group, reducing its stake to 10 percent.

West Coast retail chain with 46 stores and revenue of $457 million. The merger enabled Neiman Marcus to expand at a much faster pace than would have been possible as an independent entity. Over the next decade-and-a-half, the chain grew at a rate of about one store a year. With the opening of stores in California, Florida, and several other states during the 1970s, Neiman Marcus became a coast-to-coast operation. Atlanta; St. Louis; Northbrook, Illinois; Washington, D.C.; and White Plains, New York, were among the other places to receive new Neiman Marcus stores during this period. Although this quick proliferation lessened Neiman Marcus's exclusive image in the eyes of some customers, the major loss of luster that some feared would accompany its marriage to a less ritzy chain did not occur.

Meanwhile, changes and expansion were taking place at Neiman Marcus's Texas strongholds, too. The Dallas service center was dramatically enlarged in 1973, and in 1977 a new store at Ridgmar Mall replaced the previous Fort Worth location. In 1975 Stanley Marcus became executive vice-president of Carter Hawley Hale Stores, Inc. (formerly Broadway-Hale),

in charge of its specialty store division, which included Neiman Marcus. Son Richard was named chairman and CEO of Neiman Marcus in 1979. By 1980, the year the company opened its first store in the Northeast, annual sales were in the neighborhood of $350 million.

Emergence of The Neiman Marcus Group in the 1980s

The nationwide expansion of Neiman Marcus proceeded most quickly between 1979 and 1984, when the chain doubled in size to 21 stores. By 1984, however, it was clear that not all of the new stores were performing as well as expected against such rivals as Bloomingdale's and Saks Fifth Avenue. At that point parent Carter Hawley Hale pulled in the reins on the chain's growth. In 1984 a hostile takeover bid for Carter Hawley was launched by retail chain The Limited, which offered to buy the company for $1.1 billion. In battling against the takeover, Carter Hawley found a white knight in General Cinema Corporation, a company whose $1 billion in revenue came from soft drink bottling and movie theaters. General Cinema bailed Carter Hawley out by purchasing 38.6 percent of the company's voting stock.

Two years later, The Limited teamed up with shopping center magnate Edward DeBartolo to launch a second attempt at Carter Hawley. This time, the defense involved a corporate restructuring (completed in 1987) that included spinning off Carter Hawley's specialty store division into an independent, publicly traded entity called The Neiman Marcus Group, Inc. In exchange for its Carter Hawley stock, General Cinema was awarded 60 percent interest in the new company, which consisted of not only the Neiman Marcus stores, but also of exclusive New York retailer Bergdorf Goodman and the 200-store Contempo Casuals chain. Neiman Marcus stores contributed about three-fourths of the group's sales power. The Neiman Marcus Group expanded further in 1988 with the purchase of Dallas-based Horchow Mail Order, a cataloger specializing in upscale home furnishings, linens, and tabletop decorative items.

As General Cinema sought to return Neiman Marcus to its dominant position among upper-end specialty retailers, Allen Questrom was named president and CEO of Neiman Marcus Stores, replacing Richard Marcus and drawing the final curtain on the Marcus dynasty. By 1990, The Neiman Marcus Group, led by Neiman Marcus Stores, was General Cinema's most important money-maker, contributing about 90 percent of General Cinema's $92 million in operating profit. Questrom resigned his position in February of that year and was succeeded as president and CEO of Neiman Marcus stores by Terry Lundgren.

A new round of expansion began at Neiman Marcus under Lundgren. New stores were opened in Denver in 1990; Minneapolis and Scottsdale, Arizona, in 1991; and Troy, Michigan (a Detroit suburb), in 1992. In 1993 Lundgren was given the title of chairman, while remaining CEO. Gerald Sampson, formerly with The May Department Stores Company, was named president and chief operating officer of Neiman Marcus Stores. For that year, the company recorded revenues of $1.45 billion, a 12.7 percent jump over the previous year. Part of this success during a tough retail climate resulted from an increased emphasis on big-name designer labels, such as Calvin Klein, Georgio

Armani, and Donna Karan. General Cinema, meantime, was renamed Harcourt General, Inc. in 1993.

As the 1990s rolled on, Neiman Marcus continued its attempts to attract new, younger customers, while maintaining its commitment to meet the needs of its core, upscale clientele. Toward this end, NM Workshop boutiques that focused on career wardrobes were added at several Neiman Marcus locations. In addition, construction was begun on a new Neiman Marcus store in Short Hills, New Jersey, in 1994, and other stores in New Jersey and Pennsylvania were planned. The year 1994 also brought another reshuffling among executives. Lundgren left the company for a position at Federated Department Stores, Inc. in February. The vacated chairman and CEO spots at Neiman Marcus stores were filled by Burton Tansky, who formerly held those titles at Bergdorf Goodman. Continuing as CEO of the parent company, Neiman Marcus Group, was Robert J. Tarr, who assumed the CEO position in 1991 and was also the CEO of Harcourt General.

In July 1995, in a move designed to enable the group to focus more fully on the upscale Neiman Marcus and Bergdorf Goodman businesses, the money-losing Contempo Casuals chain was sold to Wet Seal, Inc. for $1 million in Wet Seal stock. By mid-1996 the number of Neiman Marcus stores had grown to 29, and the chain had its best year ever during fiscal 1996, posting record operating earnings of $134 million on record sales of $1.6 billion, the latter being a 12 percent increase over the previous year. Also in 1996 came the debut of the Book, a so-called magalog that combined the selling features of a catalog with the editorial content of a magazine; by mid-1997 monthly circulation of the book had ranged from 675,000 to 1.2 million. Late in 1996, Tarr resigned unexpectedly from his positions at both Neiman Marcus Group and Harcourt General. Richard A. Smith, the chairman of both companies, was named CEO of The Neiman Marcus Group. Smith's son, Robert A. Smith, was named president and COO of Neiman Marcus Group.

Late 1990s and Beyond: Expanding, Gaining Independence from Harcourt

Expansion was on the agenda in the final years of the 1990s. In early 1998 the group's direct mail operation, Neiman Marcus Direct, was bolstered through the acquisition of the Chef's Catalog for $31 million in cash. Founded in 1979, the Chef's Catalog offered gourmet cookware and high-end kitchenware. Running out of the types of large markets that are able to support a Neiman Marcus store, the group developed a concept extension that could be introduced into smaller markets. Dubbed The Galleries of Neiman Marcus, these stores initially ranged in size from 9,000 to 12,000 square feet (the average size of a Neiman Marcus store was 141,000 square feet) and featured precious and designer jewelry, gifts, and decorative home accessories. To test the new concept, three Galleries stores were opened, in Cleveland, Ohio, in November 1998; in Phoenix, Arizona, in December 1998; and in Seattle, Washington, in October 1999. The third avenue of expansion in the late 1990s stemmed from a trend in the industry in which top designers, such as Ralph Lauren, Gucci, and Prada, were opening up their own retail outlets and thereby beginning to compete with Neiman Marcus, Bergdorf Goodman, and others (although the brands continued to be sold in these and other upscale retailers).

In late 1998, Neiman Marcus Group launched a plan to spend as much as $200 million over the succeeding few years taking stakes in up-and-coming brands sold at the group's retail stores. In November 1998 the group spent $6.7 million for a 51 percent stake in Gurwitch Bristow Products, LLC, maker and marketer of the Laura Mercier cosmetic line. Launched in 1996 by Janet Gurwitch, a former executive vice-president of merchandising at Neiman Marcus, the Laura Mercier line was generating about $9 million in annual revenues at the time of the purchase. Then in February 1999, Neiman Marcus Group paid $33.6 million for a 56 percent interest in Kate Spade LLC, a maker of high-end designer handbags and accessories with 1998 revenues of about $27 million. Finally, in October 1999, neimanmarcus.com was launched as the chain's e-commerce web site.

Also in October 1999, Harcourt General ended its majority control of The Neiman Marcus Group by spinning off the bulk of its stake to its shareholders. Following the transaction, Harcourt held a 10 percent interest in the group. On the store development front, the 31st Neiman Marcus opened in Honolulu, Hawaii, in 1998. Florida was the next expansion area, with a store opening in Palm Beach in 2000 and one in Tampa in 2001. Two more—in Coral Gables and Orlando—were slated to begin operating in 2002. In addition, a replacement store was opened in Plano, Texas, in 2001, and there were plans for new Neiman Marcuses in San Antonio, Texas, and Atlanta, Georgia, as well.

In May 2001 Tansky was named CEO of Neiman Marcus Group. He also remained head of Neiman Marcus stores as well, at least on an interim basis, following the departure in January 2001 of Hugh Mullins, who had headed up the chain for only ten months. The group posted record revenues of $3.02 billion for the fiscal year ending in July 2001, but sales flagged during the first half of the following year as high-end retailers were hit particularly hard, first by a stumbling economy and then by the severe cutback in consumer spending that came in the wake of the events of September 11, 2001. The Harcourt General era of Neiman Marcus's history came to an end in April 2002 with the former company's announcement that it had liquidated its entire remaining stake in Neiman Marcus Group.

Stanley Marcus, another important link to the company's past, died in January 2002 at the age of 96, having served as chairman emeritus since 1975. In his 1974 book *Minding the Store,* Marcus asserted that a company's quality standards inevitably decrease as its number of branches increases. Since that time, Neiman Marcus has managed to thwart its longtime leader's axiom through both good and bad economic periods. Despite its geographic spread and the more populist range of its merchandise, Neiman Marcus's reputation as the store of choice for the elite remained more or less intact.

Principal Subsidiaries

Bergdorf Goodman, Inc.; Bergdorf Graphics, Inc.; Chef's Catalog, Inc.; Ermine Trading Corporation; Gurwitch Bristow Products, LLC (51%); Kate Spade LLC (56%); NEMA Beverage Corporation; NEMA Beverage Holding Corporation; NEMA Beverage Parent Corporation; NM Direct de Mexico, S.A. de C.V.; NM Financial Services, Inc.; NM Nevada Trust; NM Office, Inc.; NM Visual, Inc.; Neiman Marcus Funding Corporation; Neiman Marcus Holdings, Inc.; Neiman Marcus Special Events, Inc.; Quality Call Care Solutions, Inc. (Canada); Pastille by Mail, Inc.; Worth Avenue Leasing Company.

Principal Competitors

Federated Department Stores, Inc.; Saks Incorporated; The May Department Stores Company; Dillard's, Inc.; Nordstrom, Inc.

Further Reading

"Big Deal in Big D," *Newsweek,* November 4, 1968, p. 94.

Bird, Laura, "Haute Brands: Neiman Marcus, Saks Wage Expensive Battle for Upscale Shoppers," *Wall Street Journal,* November 21, 1996, pp. A1+.

Deutsch, Claudia H., "Neiman-Marcus Minds the Store," *New York Times,* September 4, 1988, p. F4.

Edelson, Sharon, "NMG's Tarr Mulling Bergdorf Expansion, Growth for Neiman's," *Women's Wear Daily,* August 19, 1996, pp. 1, 12.

Ferry, John William, *A History of the Department Store,* New York: MacMillan, 1960, pp. 161–68.

Haber, Holly, "Deep in the Heart of Texans," *Women's Wear Daily,* July 21, 1997, pp. 8+.

——, "Neiman's New Chief: Maximizing Growth for a 'Mature' Company," *Women's Wear Daily,* March 20, 2000, p. 1.

——, "Winning Big in Designer," *Women's Wear Daily,* October 27, 1993, pp. 8–9.

Harris, Roy J., and David Stipp, "Carter Hawley Blocks Takeover Attempt with Plan to Spin Off Its Specialty Stores," *Wall Street Journal,* December 9, 1986, p. 3.

Hessen, Wendy, "Neiman's Bold Move: Freestanding Stores for Fine Jewelry, Gifts," *Women's Wear Daily,* October 8, 1997, pp. 1+.

"History of Neiman Marcus," Dallas: Neiman Marcus Co., 1992.

Johannes, Laura, "Harcourt General to Spin Off Stake in Neiman Marcus," *Wall Street Journal,* May 18, 1999, p. C11.

Kaufman, Leslie, "Luxury's Old Guard, Battered by New Realities," *New York Times,* December 16, 2001, sec. 3, p. 1.

Lohr, Steve, "Neiman-Marcus Testing Northeast," *New York Times,* September 4, 1980, p. D1.

Marcus, Stanley, *Minding the Store: A Memoir,* Boston: Little Brown, 1974, 383 p.

——, *Quest for the Best,* New York: Viking Press, 1979, 227 p.

Mason, Todd, "That Neiman-Marcus Mystique Isn't Traveling Well," *Business Week,* July 8, 1985, pp. 44–45.

"The Merchant Prince of Dallas," *Business Week,* October 21, 1967, pp. 115–18.

Moin, David, "NM Acquires 56% of Kate Spade," *Women's Wear Daily,* February 5, 1999, p. 2.

——, "NM Expecting Minimal Fallout from Tarr's Abrupt Resignation," *Women's Wear Daily,* December 19, 1996, pp. 2+.

——, "NM Group Puts Vendors at Top of Shopping List," *Women's Wear Daily,* December 3, 1998, p. 1.

——, "The NMG Problem: Finding the Successor to CEO Burt Tansky," *Women's Wear Daily,* January 30, 2002, p. 1.

Moin, David, and Sharon Edelson, "Neiman's Gold Rush: An Intensified Effort to Promote Luxe Life," *Women's Wear Daily,* April 10, 1996, pp. 1+.

Montgomery, Leland, "General Cinema: The Value of Camouflage," *Financial World,* September 1, 1992, p. 17.

"Neiman Doesn't Shop Around for Leadership," *Chain Store Age,* March 1997, pp. 48, 50.

Pace, Eric, "Stanley Marcus, the Retailer from Dallas, Is Dead at 96," *New York Times,* January 23, 2002, p. A16.

Palmeri, Christopher, "Retailer's Revenge," *Forbes,* May 3, 1999, pp. 62+.

Pereira, Joseph, "Neiman-Marcus Names Questrom to Head Chain," *Wall Street Journal,* August 15, 1988, p. 21.

Seckler, Valerie, "NM Dumps Contempo for $1 Million in Stock," *Women's Wear Daily,* April 4, 1995, p. 2.

"A Store That Serves Two Markets," *Business Week,* September 19, 1953, p. 136.

Strom, Stephanie, "New Neiman Marcus Head Is Named," *New York Times,* April 22, 1994, p. D4.

Tolbert, Frank X., *Neiman-Marcus, Texas,* New York: Henry Holt and Co., 1953.

Vargo, Julie, "Neiman's at 90: Kicking Up Its Heels Texas-Style," *Daily News Record,* August 25, 1997, pp. 24+.

Williamson, Rusty, "Tansky at the Top: Named Chief Executive of Neiman's Group," *Women's Wear Daily,* February 21, 2001, p. 1.

—Robert R. Jacobson
—update: David E. Salamie

Nolo.com, Inc.

950 Parker Street
Berkeley, California 94710-2524
U.S.A.
Telephone: (510) 549-1976
Toll Free: (800) 728-3555
Fax: (800) 645-0895
Web site: http://www.nolo.com

Private Company
Founded: 1971 as Nolo Press
Employees: 79
NAIC: 511130 Book Publishers; 511210 Computer
    Software Publishing, Including Design and
    Development, Packaged

Nolo.com, Inc. is the leading publisher of self-help books and software that help individuals understand and gain access to the legal system without using lawyers. In 1971 it founded this new publishing specialty in the early years of the Information Age. It publishes more than 250 titles that help its customers deal with divorce, bankruptcy, real estate, running a small business, estate planning, and a wide variety of other common concerns. It offers legal reference information, forms to complete, and links to related web sites. Begun as a book publisher, Nolo increasingly relies on electronic commerce as more individuals gain access to the Internet. In the 1990s other companies and organizations followed Nolo's lead by making print and web-based legal information available. Of course, Nolo admits that it is no substitute for a lawyer when one is really needed. Nonetheless, it continues to play a major role in helping consumers deal with an increasingly complex legal system.

Origin and Early History

In 1971 lawyers Ralph Warner and Charles Sherman did their best to answer the legal questions from poor individuals who came to their storefront Legal Aid Office in Richmond, a few miles from Berkeley, California. Many sought advice for divorce, bankruptcy, wills, and other common legal problems. Warner and Sherman became frustrated, however, over not being able to serve thousands who made too much money to qualify for their government-subsidized service and yet could not afford to hire a lawyer.

Warner and Sherman then decided to put together two books: *How to Do Your Own Divorce in California* and *The California Tenants' Handbook.* At first several New York publishers rejected their work. "I kept getting blank stares," recalled Warner in the January 31, 2000 *Business Week.* "One guy thought his brother-in-law was playing a practical joke."

The two founders thus started Nolo Press out of Warner's attic to publish legal self-help books in plain English as a way to avoid the expensive services of a lawyer. Their company name was derived from the Latin phrase "nolo contendre," or "I choose not to contest." They simply extended that idea to mean "I choose not to publish." Nolo Press "rented a space (for the books) in the Berkeley co-op produce department between the broccoli and celery," said Janet Portman, the company's publisher, in the September 15, 2000 *San Francisco Chronicle.*

Due to little advertising, only a few hundred copies of the California divorce book were sold initially. Sales exploded, however, after the head of the Sacramento County Bar held a news conference to condemn the book, while a photo of him denouncing the book was published statewide. The proverbial law of unintended consequences thus helped Nolo Press get started.

When Nolo published its California divorce book in 1971, less than 1 percent of filed divorces were done without an attorney. The company reported that by 2001, after it had published more than 800,000 copies of its book, more than 60 percent of uncontested California divorce cases were handled without the help of a lawyer.

Nolo authors kept writing new self-help books and initiating other projects to bring the law to the masses. For example, in 1973 they started the Wave Project, which trained 18 nonlawyers to type up divorce forms for those who did not want or need a lawyer. Soon project trainees all over California provided their services for just $45, a fraction of lawyer-aided divorces. In 1975 Nolo moved to a separate office in a former Berkeley

Company Perspectives:

Nolo's mission is to make the legal system work for everyone—not just lawyers.

clock factory. It had already published 15 books, so running an office in Ralph Warner's attic was no longer feasible.

Nolo Press was just one of several small independent presses started in or near Berkeley at about the same time. Others included Heyday Books founded in 1974, Ten Speed Press in 1970, and Ulysses Press in 1983. Some failed, but between 30 and 50 still were operating in 2000, the highest concentration except for Manhattan. Small publishers flourished in the area due to the free speech emphasis in the center of the counterculture, proximity to the University of California Press, many eager writers and editors, and a Berkeley ordinance protecting small low-tech businesses.

Nolo Press took advantage of such local conditions, as well as a general cultural shift from institutional help to self-help. John Naisbitt in his number one bestseller *Megatrends* described this trend. "For decades, institutions such as the government, the medical establishment, the corporation, and the school system were America's buffers against life's hard realities . . . During the 1970s, Americans began to disengage from the institutions that had disillusioned them and to relearn the ability to take action on their own. In a sense, we have come full circle. We are reclaiming America's traditional sense of self-reliance."

Naisbitt also pointed out, however, that the number of lawyers was rapidly increasing as part of the growing Information Age. The total number of lawyers in the United States went from 250,000 lawyers in 1960 to 622,000 in 1983. Big law firms rapidly expanded in the 1980s and 1990s as the economy boomed. The fact that both self-help and professionals were growing simultaneously was part of the trend to have more options and diversity, instead of the either-or orientation of the past.

Early legal self-help advocates like those at Nolo Press were aided by criticism of the legal profession. For example, the 1969 book *The Trouble with Lawyers* described "how the American middle class is victimized by inept, lazy, and corrupt lawyers," according to the paperback version's cover. The high cost of lawyers was of course a major problem, which led to other companies like Pre-Paid Legal Services offering prepaid legal insurance and the rise of paralegals or legal assistants who could conduct legal research and do some other tasks for much less per hour than lawyers.

Developments in the 1980s

Nolo Press in 1980 published its first issue of the *Nolo News*. The first editorial in the small eight-page publication urged California to increase the limit at small claims courts to $5,000, which became a reality 11 years later. Soon, newly elected President Ronald Reagan reduced spending for legal aid by $100 million, which increased the need for legal self-help even

more. Meanwhile, Stanford University law professor Deborah Rhode concluded that the claim was worthless that nonlawyers were dangerous because they provided limited legal services.

In 1985 Nolo Press introduced its WillMaker software, which became its bestseller. In 2000 the company came out with its eighth version of WillMaker, which could be used to produce a will, a living will with medical provisions, a financial power of attorney, and burial and other final instructions. WillMaker did not cover all possibilities, though, such as joint wills for spouses. In any case, Nolo reported in 2001 that WillMaker "had over a million satisfied users, making Nolo responsible for more wills than any law firm in history."

By the mid-1980s Nolo's books had become very popular. Libraries even reported that Nolo titles were among their most stolen books, so the company began replacing for free one Nolo title each year in libraries across the nation.

The 1990s and Beyond

As the self-help legal movement grew, many Americans continued to give the legal profession little respect. When Nolo launched its first web site in 1994, it included lawyer jokes that poked fun at greedy and crooked lawyers—for example, "What do you get when you cross a lawyer with a demon from hell? Another lawyer."

In 1997 the Texas Supreme Court's Unauthorized Practice of Law Committee began investigating the work of Nolo Press and other self-help legal publishers. Attorney Steve Elias, who authored some of Nolo's works, said in the June 16, 1998 *Washington Times* that no other states had claimed that Nolo's publications violated their rules concerning the unauthorized practice of law.

Nolo founder Ralph Warner said in the same article, "If the Texas legal establishment can successfully ban law books written for ordinary citizens, who is to say Texas doctors can't ban self-help medical publications and Texas accountants self-help tax books and software?"

In January 1999 U.S. District Court Judge Barefoot Sanders ruled that self-help legal software could not be sold under the 1939 Texas statute defining what constituted the practice of law. He also noted that the state legislature instead of the courts might be the proper place to clarify this issue. Within a few months the Texas House approved House Bill 1507 by a 138–2 vote, and the Texas Senate voted 26–4 to do likewise. As signed into law by Texas Governor George W. Bush, the new law asserted that written materials, books, forms, and software programs were not an unauthorized practice of law if they clearly stated that they were not substitutes for an attorney.

That effectively ended the Texas Supreme Court's investigation of legal self-help publishers such as Nolo Press, although the court's attorney in this matter argued that the courts, not the legislature, were the place to define what could be done. In any case, on its web site Nolo.com reported that its victory was due to the work of the Austin, Texas law firm of George and Donaldson and supporting efforts by the American Association of Law Libraries, the Texas Library Association, and five indi-

Key Dates:

1971: Two former Legal Aid lawyers begin Nolo Press by publishing two self-help law books.

1975: The company moves to its new office in Berkeley, California.

1980: *Everybody's Guide to Small Claims Court* is first published.

1985: The company introduces the first version of its WillMaker software.

1994: Nolo launches its web site.

1999: Nolo Press changes its name to Nolo.com, Inc.; Texas's approval of a new law allowing publication of legal self-help materials leads to a Texas State Supreme Court committee ending its investigation of Nolo.com.

viduals who cooperated in filing a lawsuit that helped lead to the passage of H.B. 1507.

In 1999 Nolo Press changed its name to Nolo.com, Inc. "Less and less will we be making our money in the traditional book markets," said Steve Elias, the company's associate publisher, in the July 12, 1999 *Publishers Weekly.* "Increasingly, we're going to be making it on the Web." In addition to online legal assistance, there also was an online advice column called Ask Auntie Nolo written by Barbara Kate Repa, a lawyer who specialized in work-related issues.

Nolo.com in the new millennium used various alliances and joint operations to serve the public. For example, in 2000 it signed a content distribution agreement with ThirdAge.com, a leading media and marketing site for those older than 45. Nolo.com's information about legal issues concerning retirement, estate planning, and family law were welcomed by ThirdAge.com, a private company based in San Francisco. Also in 2000, Nolo.com signed a content and licensing partnership with San Francisco's eHow.com, an online company providing solutions on how to get things done. A third agreement in 2000 was with CBS.MarketWatch.com, a San Francisco-based provider of financial and business news.

In January 2001 a strategic alliance with the United Kingdom's Epoch Software, Plc gave Nolo.com users the capability to use Epoch's Rapidocs software to create complicated legal documents over the Internet without consulting an attorney. Nolo.com also partnered with ImageTag Inc., based in Chandler, Arizona. ImageTag's KwikTag E technology was used to organize and use paper as digital documents. Nolo.com signed an agreement with Property Automation Software Corporation to let the latter's TenantLawCenter.com have access to Nolo's real estate articles, a benefit to property managers, real estate professionals, and others. Other Nolo.com partners included AllBusiness.com, books24X7.com, garage.com, homestore.com, netlibrary, Rentals.com, and Vault.com.

Such partnerships and web sites were just part of the exploding legal self-help movement. A search engine in 2000 located about 330,000 web sites when a search asked for "free legal advice." Some thus argued that state regulation of lawyers

was obsolete and that the solo law practice was going the way of the dinosaur. "The licensing of the legal profession, primarily by states, seems increasingly archaic in a global community," said Frederick J. Krebs, president of the American Corporate Counsel Association, in the *Washington Times* on July 21, 2000. President William H. Mellor III of the Institute for Justice argued that lawyers would be eliminated as middlemen when potential clients instead relied on the Internet, self-help software, and paralegals. To promote such changes, a group called HALT, or Help Abolish Legal Tyranny, was organized.

The issues involved in the conflict between the organized bar and the legal self-help movement were described by the Progressive Policy Institute (PPI), part of the Democratic Leadership Conference. In response, Bill Litant, the Massachusetts Bar Association's communications director, said in the *Boston Herald,* "The issue that bar associations need to tackle is not how to prevent people from accessing do-it-yourself legal information, but how to make professional legal help affordable for many people, because for many it certainly isn't."

The bar in fact participated in the legal self-help movement, at least to some extent. The American Bar Association provided some online information, although most of that was intended for lawyers.

As Nolo.com headed into the 21st century, it was proud of its several awards and honors. For example, *PC Magazine* on February 14, 2001 honored Nolo in its "Top 100" list. On March 12, 1998 Nolo received the Webby "1998 People's Voice Award" for having the best information in the business and money category. Based on this excellent performance, Nolo appeared well prepared to meet its future challenges as a niche player in the information technology field.

Principal Competitors

Made E-Z Products, Inc.

Further Reading

Bloom, Murray Teigh, *The Trouble with Lawyers,* New York: Simon and Schuster, 1969.

Clewley, Robin, "The Independent Type/Since the 1960s, Small Presses Have Found a Way to Publish and Flourish in Berkeley," *San Francisco Chronicle,* September 15, 2000, p. 1.

Emmons, Natasha, "Texas Investigates Nolo Press," *Legal Assistant Today,* May/June 1998, p. 22.

Goldberg, Stephanie B., and Gary Poole, "Success at Nolo Press," *Business Week,* January 31, 2000, p. F24.

Holt, Patricia, "Do-It-Yourself Law," *San Francisco Chronicle,* May 19, 1996, p. 2.

Hughes, Polly Ross, "Bill to Lay Down the Law on Self-Help Software/Controversial Measure Reversing Statewide Ban Is Awaiting Gov. Bush's Signature," *Houston Chronicle,* June 13, 1999, p. 1.

Mitchell, Barbara, "Willmaker 8," *Library Journal,* December 2000, p. 204.

Mulvihill, Maggie, "At the Bar; On-line Law Services Now Face Their Own Legal Threat," *Boston Herald,* July 11, 2000, p. 28.

Murray, Frank J., "Internet Age Shakes the Legal Profession, Bars Must Rethink Regulations," *Washington Times,* July 21, 2000, p. A1.

Naisbitt, John, *Megatrends: Ten New Directions Transforming Our Lives,* New York: Warner Books, 1982.

''Nolo.com and Epoch, the Leading U.S. & British Consumer Law Sites, Form Strategic Alliance to Improve Legal Access,'' *Business Wire,* January 8, 2001, p. 1.

''Nolo.com, Nation's Leading Self-help Legal Provider, Teams with Top Financial Site, CBS.MarketWatch.com,'' *Business Wire,* February 16, 2000.

''Property Automation Software's TenantLawCenter.com to Add Content from Nolo.com,'' *Business Wire,* January 23, 2001.

Schmitt, Richard B., ''E-Commerce (A Special Report): On the Battlefield—Lawyers vs. the Internet: For Some Nonlawyers, the Web Is a Cure for What Ails the Legal Profession; Many Attorneys Object,'' *Wall Street Journal,* July 17, 2000, p. R36.

Veigle, Anne, ''Texas Court May Lasso Self-Help Law Publisher,'' *Washington Times,* June 16, 1998, p. E4.

Wessel, Harry, ''Book Explains Using Small-Claims Court,'' *Charleston Gazette* (Charleston, W.V.), November 12, 2000, p. 5F.

Zeitchik, Steven M., ''Nolo Press Changes Name, Web Site,'' *Publishers Weekly,* July 12, 1999, p. 14.

—David M. Walden

Novar plc

Novar House
24 Queens Road
Weybridge
Surrey KT13 9UX
United Kingdom
Telephone: (44) 1932-850-850
Fax: (44) 1932-823-328
Web site: http://www.novar.com

Public Company
Incorporated: 1985 as Caradon plc
Employees: 14,733
Sales: $2.15 billion (2001)
Stock Exchanges: London
Ticker Symbol: NVR
NAIC: 323116 Manifold Business Forms Printing (pt);
331316 Aluminum Extruded Product Manufacturing;
334290 Other Communications Equipment
Manufacturing; 335931 Current-Carrying Wiring
Device Manufacturing; 421610 Electrical Apparatus
and Equipment, Wiring Supplies, and Construction
Material Wholesalers; 551114 Corporate, Subsidiary,
and Regional Managing Offices; 561621 Security
Systems Services (Except Locksmiths)

Novar plc is a U.K.-based corporation consisting of three primary business segments: security systems, aluminum product manufacturing, and secure check printing services. Although the company was founded only in 1985, as a result of a complex series of mergers, acquisitions, and divestments, it actually traces its origins to those of Metal Box plc, a pioneer in the British tinning industry and eventually a giant in packaging in general. In 1989 MB Group (the former Metal Box) merged with Caradon (which was formed in 1985 as a spinoff from Reed International) to create MB-Caradon PLC. Then in 1993 MB-Caradon divested itself of its packaging roots and soon underwent another name change, becoming Caradon plc. Another name change came in 2001, when the company became

known as Novar plc. The beginning of the 21st century found Novar searching for ways to divest itself of a number of its holdings, in the hope of streamlining its image and committing to a single core business.

Early Roots of the Tinning Industry

The canning of foods, or "tinning" as it is often called in Britain, has been a common method for preserving food for about a century. Before that time, all foods had to be purchased fresh, salted, or dried. The industry that developed to produce these cans, or "tins," in Britain was controlled originally by numerous family firms, each with a small tin can making factory in which workers could turn out 200 cans in an hour. These family concerns were small, profitable, and only mildly competitive in such a large market.

One of the family canmakers was initially a printing business established in 1855 by Robert Barclay, a Quaker. His main customer was Barclay's Bank (owned by distant relatives), for whom he printed checks. Barclay's brother-in-law, John Fry, joined him as a partner in 1867, and their company, Barclay & Fry, became Britain's largest check printer. With the help of some technical information sold to him by an early industrial spy in France, Barclay developed the process of offset lithography and tried to sell it to many other firms. He died of a stroke in 1876 before any sale could be finalized.

The new printing process ended up being leased to Huntley, Boorne & Stevens, tin box makers for the biscuit company Huntley & Palmer (the two Huntleys also were related). Huntley & Palmer was the first manufacturer to use the offset process to print designs on their own tins; prior to that their tins had been hand-painted. Soon, Carr's Biscuits also were using printed tins; these were manufactured by their Quaker relatives, Hudson Scott & Sons. Sometime during the 1890s, Barclay & Fry decided to use their offset process themselves, but they remained primarily stationery printers.

Decorated biscuit tins were very popular throughout Great Britain and many homes had quite large collections of them. There were Alice in Wonderland designs, tins to commemorate every grand occasion, and tins resembling miniature cottages or

Company Perspectives:

Novar plc is an international group whose core activities are: Intelligent Building Systems; Indalex Aluminum Solutions; Security Printing Services. Our new name for the group, Novar plc, signifies our continued transformation from low growth industrial businesses into higher growth markets. We believe Novar has the positive connotations we want for our businesses going forward providing enhanced customer solutions and increasing technology in the markets we share.

featuring birds, books, or beauty spots. The tin making industry grew and since labor costs were low, profits were high. Soon, the Trade Boards Act required tin manufacturers to improve worker conditions and wages, and this caused some of the employers to form the British Tin Box Manufacturers Federation to protect their interests.

Founding Metal Box in 1921

World War I brought more business to the industry; a new product had to be manufactured—the ration tin used by British troops. Due to government restrictions on tin, many of the companies in the Federation cooperated closely, and after the war, in 1921, four of these tin box makers, Hudson Scott, F. Atkins & Co., Henry Grant & Co., and Barclay & Fry, formed the Allied Tin Box Makers, Ltd. A year later they changed their name to Metal Box & Printing Industries. From the beginning it was understood that each of the member companies would remain private, but that all would cooperate in controlling the market and making acquisitions.

Before long, however, the group's comfortable control of their market was threatened by the importation of an American method of semiautomatic can making that could produce 200 cans every minute. G.E. Williamson's family firm, which had refused to join the manufacturers' group, purchased the new American machinery in 1927 and began to produce cans for the government's Fruit & Vegetable Research Station in Gloucestershire. The research organization was interested in advanced canning methods in order to increase the markets for British farm produce.

Inevitably, with its superior technology, the U.S. canning industry quickly became interested in the British market. American Can moved in first by purchasing a small independent company and renaming it the British Can Company, Ltd. It then attempted to acquire Metal Box & Printing Industries. In its determination to resist a takeover, however, Metal Box arranged a partnership that not only kept it independent, but defined and nurtured its growth. The company signed an agreement with American Can's U.S. rival, Continental Can. The two firms exchanged stock shares and Metal Box was given the exclusive right in Great Britain to purchase canning machinery, technical advice, training, and patent licenses from Continental Can. This effectively eliminated the competition, as no other British company was able to purchase the technology. In little more than a year, British Can was in disarray. Metal Box agreed to buy it out on the condition that American Can stayed out of Great Britain and Ireland for the next 21 years.

These deals, illegal under the business laws of later decades, had been arranged by Metal Box's Robert Barlow. Still under 40, Barlow was now the head of Britain's canning monopoly and determined to make it even larger. But his aggressive managerial style alienated most of the old family leaders of the group's companies, and many resigned from the board of directors. Barlow wanted to bring all member companies under one authority and ignored those on the board who opposed him. He set up an executive committee with two others, Hepworth and Crabtree, to make policy decisions and, essentially, to circumvent the board.

In 1931 Barlow's committee instituted a single accounting system for all member companies in an attempt to force some kind of uniformity on them under a newly created head office. The managing director of Barclay & Fry tried to have Barlow fired, but Barlow called a meeting of the entire board and convinced them that his plan would make the company stronger still. As Barlow consolidated his position he banished some of his detractors to plants in South Africa and demanded the resignations of others. By 1935 he was in complete control of Metal Box and had, in large part, succeeded in centralizing sales and supplies, and rationalizing production functions, for all of the company's plants.

Succeeding in Spite of the Great Depression

Metal Box experienced nothing but success during the Great Depression. As smaller canmakers collapsed, the company purchased them, and by 1937, Metal Box was selling 335 million cans a year. Following the American example, Metal Box had begun to manufacture the equipment needed to seal the cans onsite and sold this machinery to its customers. Metal Box was not interested in expanding into the field of food production, but it did open a publicity department to increase interest in canned foods. Whenever there were difficulties, either with suppliers or customers, Metal Box considered a takeover. For example, inefficient management at a tin plate supplier in South Wales led Metal Box, with the help of Continental Can, to purchase the company.

Surprisingly, Metal Box's income from security check printing combined with turnover from machine manufacturing and interests in mining, and so on, was double that of its income from the cans themselves. Profits rose dramatically for Metal Box in the 1930s—from £103,480 in 1931 to £316,368 in 1939.

Throughout the decade Barlow had maintained a strong interest in foreign markets. Partnerships or subsidiaries had been formed in France, The Netherlands, Belgium, India, and South Africa. Continental Can was still Metal Box's mentor and main partner and the two essentially divided up the world markets between themselves. Metal Box was to expand within Europe and the British colonies, while Continental Can would develop interests in the rest of the world.

In the late 1930s, the innovative company planned to produce new forms of packaging such as card containers with metal ends and cans with wax lining for beer. The onslaught of World War II, however, curtailed new production in favor of equipment for the troops. Containers for gas masks were easy to make in tin box factories, and Metal Box produced 140 million of them for the government. The paint tin production lines were adapted to pro-

Key Dates:

1921: Allied Tin Box Makers, Ltd. is formed.
1922: Allied Tin Box Makers, Ltd. becomes Metal Box & Printing Industries.
1985: Caradon plc is incorporated.
1989: Caradon merges with MB Group (formerly Metal Box) to create MB-Caradon PLC.
1993: MB-Caradon PLC is renamed Caradon plc.
1996: Caradon divests itself of the majority of its European engineering and distribution operations.
2000: Caradon sells off its plumbing unit.
2001: Caradon becomes Novar plc.

duce casings for antitank mines. Shell casings and ration tins also were produced by the millions. Even so, due to strict government controls, company profits fell to £242,428 in 1945.

Expanding into Other Forms of Packaging Following World War II

In 1943, as the war turned in the Allies' favor, Barlow established a committee to plan new forms of packaging that could be exploited as soon as the war was over. Consequently, Metal Box was an innovator in the field, quickly moving toward paper, foil, and plastic container products as the postwar economy began to improve. But Metal Box still dominated the British can and carton market. Between 1941 and 1961, eight new factories were built or purchased, and by the 1960s, Metal Box was the leading packaging supplier to some of the largest companies in the world, including Unilever, Nestlé, Heinz, Imperial Tobacco, BAT, ICI, Hoechst, and Shell.

After the war, Metal Box was more than ready for further organizational changes. The accounting department was restructured and a financial comptroller was appointed. In addition, administrative functions were more clearly defined and brought under central control, and subsidiaries were made more accountable to central management. Barlow retained his position as executive chairman, but in 1946, he brought in D.W. Brough as his managing director. Brough had been in charge of operations in South Africa; nevertheless, he lasted less than two years. Barlow replaced him with two executives, G.S. Samways and D. Ducat, and these two men served as joint managing directors until Samways's resignation in 1954; Ducat then served alone, but Barlow still maintained overall control until his retirement in 1961.

In the late 1940s, the U.S. Department of Justice filed an antitrust suit against Continental Can and began to investigate its arrangements with Metal Box. The two companies hastily modified their agreement in 1950 and cooperation between them was restricted to machinery and technical information; all mutual ventures and attempts at market controls were dropped. The modified agreement was renewed and slightly expanded in 1970 and was slated to continue until 1990.

Up to 1970, Metal Box had continued to expand both at home and abroad. In Britain, Wallis Tin Stamping Co., Brown Bibby & Gregory, and Flexible Packaging were all acquired,

widening Metal Box's product line to include plastic film, aerosols, central heating, and engineering. The company established facilities or subsidiaries in Italy, Malaysia, Tanzania, Japan, and Iran, and upgraded the older plants in India, France, and South Africa. Even so, Metal Box still conducted three-quarters of its business in the United Kingdom.

In 1967 the Board of Trade referred the British can industry to the Monopolies Commission, which ruled that Metal Box was operating a monopoly—supplying 77 percent of all metal containers, 63 percent of aerosols, and 80 percent of open-top cans. Nevertheless, the Commission concluded that the company's monopoly did not harm the public interest and did not find Metal Box lacking in efficiency, innovations, or service. Its report even praised Metal Box for passing on savings to its customers. But the company was instructed to terminate all of its exclusive arrangements, both with customers and with suppliers. Thus, in one stroke, Barlow's market control procedures were ended.

Diversifying Beyond Packaging in the 1970s

The 1970s were a decade of significant changes for Metal Box. Under the direction of Chairman and Chief Executive Alex Page, the company began to make serious moves to diversify outside of packaging, a mature industry unable to support long-term growth. The company's diversification was a measured one, however, and the areas targeted—although seemingly far removed from packaging—were nonetheless considered similar in terms of the manufacturing technology involved. Thus the company had by the mid-1970s begun to build—primarily through acquisitions—significant operations in the manufacturing of radiators used in central heating systems as well as a machinery building group. In late 1975 a company reorganization highlighted the importance of these new ventures when they were placed into a new diversified products group, alongside a packaging group that included Metal Box's traditional businesses. Also in 1975 the company moved its headquarters from central London to Reading. Sales reached the $1 billion mark in 1976.

As the 1970s progressed, Metal Box's packaging unit faced a climate of increasing competition at home and abroad. The company opened itself to further competition in 1978 when it abandoned its licensing deal with Continental Can, which immediately began to build a plant in Wales to make two-piece aluminum cans. By this time, two-piece cans were considered state of the art because they used 40 percent fewer raw materials in their manufacture. Metal Box had moved to set up its factories to make two-piece cans, but was initially thwarted by its workforce, which balked at the continuous production process needed for the manufacturing to be most efficient. Eventually, in 1982, Metal Box had to abandon two-piece manufacturing at one of its plants and decided to close another one, but did manage to initiate two-piece production at other plants.

While dealing with these troubles at home, the company increasingly looked overseas for opportunities for growth. In 1979 Metal Box opened a two-piece can plant in Carson, California, that eventually would supply Pepsi-Cola with 625 million cans a year. The company also acquired Risdon Manufacturing, a maker of cosmetics packaging based in Connecticut. In Europe Metal Box sought to build on its existing operations in southern Europe (which were primarily in Italy, Greece, and Portugal), by entering into a licensing agreement with France's Carnaud, whereby Metal Box provided equipment and expertise for a two-piece can plant near Brussels to be built by Carnaud. Cans from the plant were to be sold in the Benelux countries and parts of France and West Germany. As a result of these overseas moves, the portion of Metal Box profits derived outside the United Kingdom increased from 41.4 percent in 1977 to 55.5 percent in 1980. By the end of the 1970s revenues had reached $2.7 billion.

Blockbuster Deals in the 1980s

Metal Box barely survived through a difficult period in the early 1980s, ravaged by a recession and hampered by a management team that lacked the kind of forward thinkers needed in an environment marked by increasing competition. By the mid-1980s Dr. Brian Smith had been brought in as chairman; previously, he had helped to turn around ICI. In January 1988 Murray Stuart became chief executive of the newly named MB Group, after having joined the company as finance director in 1981. Smith and Stuart would by the end of the decade engineer deals that completely transformed the company.

The name change reflected a desire to deemphasize the company's tinning roots. By the late 1980s MB Group had steadily built up its nonpackaging operations to the point where it was Europe's largest manufacturer of central heating radiators, through its Stelrad unit; it had developed a bathroom products business with the Stelrad Doulton brand; and its Clarke Checks subsidiary—built through a series of small acquisitions—had become the fourth largest printer of checks in the United States. Stelrad was boosted further in 1988 with the acquisition of the leading producer of radiators in continental Europe, Henrad Beheer of Belgium.

Smith and Stuart next surprised many observers when they agreed in October 1988 to merge MB's packaging operations with those of Carnaud to form CMB Packaging SA, based in Brussels. CMB, of which MB initially held a 25.5 percent stake, immediately became the third largest packaging company in the world and was better able to compete on the global stage than MB packaging could on its own. Carnaud gained management control of the new company, but more important to MB was the £240 million in cash it received from the merger, money it could use to further bolster its nonpackaging units. MB did just that in September 1989 when it acquired American Bank Stationery Co. for £193.7 million, beefing up its U.S. security printing operations.

Another blockbuster deal for Smith and Stuart came only one month later. After a year of negotiations, MB acquired Caradon plc in a £337.6 million reverse takeover, with half the amount in cash and half in Caradon shares converted to those of MB. Caradon had been founded in 1985 through a £61 million management buyout of the U.K. building products division of Reed International, the U.K. publishing giant. Caradon, which had gone public in 1987, was a perfect fit with MB's central heating and bathroom products since its top brands were Twyfords bathroom and sanitary products, Mira showers, Terrain plastic pipes, and Celuform plastic timber. Following the acquisition, Smith retired and the newly named MB-Caradon PLC was headed by

Stuart as chairman and Peter Jansen, Caradon's chief, as chief executive and in charge of day-to-day operations.

1990s and Beyond

Not surprisingly, MB-Caradon next sold its stake in CMB (at the time known as Carnaud MetalBox), and thus divested itself of its Metal Box roots. The £467.5 million ($700 million) generated by the April 1993 sale was used almost immediately when MB-Caradon paid £800 million ($1.2 billion) for RTZ Corp.'s RTZ Pillar industrial products group in August of that same year. Pillar brought with it construction, general engineering, automotive, and aviation operations. Yet another name change followed on the heels of this acquisition when MB-Caradon became Caradon plc.

By 1994, through these and other deals, Caradon had established itself as a leader in doors and windows, with its other operations being plumbing products, electrical products, structural and engineering operations, and security printing. That year, sales nearly doubled, having reached £1.61 billion, while operating profits were a record £205.4 million.

The following year Caradon acquired a 43 percent stake in Weru Aktiengesellschaft, a German leader in doors and windows. Later in the year, however, profits suffered as sales of doors and windows in the United States fell sharply, the cost of raw materials used to make plastic products rose, and the U.K. building industry suffered a general depression. Operating profits fell as a result, to £127.1 million, and sales increased only 6.4 percent.

In response Jansen launched a restructuring late in 1995: 1,600 jobs were eliminated, a layer of management was jettisoned so that the directors of the five divisions reported directly to Jansen, and noncore businesses began to be divested. In December 1996 Caradon sold off 18 businesses for a total of £220 million ($360 million), including most of its European engineering and distribution operations. Meanwhile, the company spent £48.2 million ($75 million) for another 30 percent of Weru, bringing its total stake to almost 80 percent.

The 1996 divestments were in many cases long overdue (some dated back to the merger of MB Group and the original Caradon; others came with RTZ Pillar) and were a key to a possible company turnaround. More divestments were certainly possible, and the North American engineering and security printing units were the leading candidates. Caradon was also likely to make further acquisitions in the late 1990s to beef up its already considerable building products operations, which accounted for 80 percent of overall company sales in 1996.

New Challenges in the 21st Century

By late 1997, after suffering heavy losses in its windows and doors business both at home and in the United States, Caradon decided it was time for the company to begin heading in a new direction. In November, Jurgen Hintz, former head of Carnaud MetalBox, was appointed new chief executive officer. At first glance it appeared as if his primary task would be to devise a business strategy that would establish the company as a leader in the building products industry. Caradon's root problem, however, actually had more to do with the diversity of its holdings. Because the company was unable to boast a leading market position in any single enterprise, a sudden downturn in a particular business sector often had a significantly negative impact on investor confidence. Upon taking control, Hintz recognized right away that it would be extremely difficult to build a solid profile, along with brand recognition, for a corporation with such a wide range of unrelated interests. In the wake of the recent slump in the building supplies industry, the new CEO felt compelled to consider other ways to bolster Caradon's corporate identity.

The first step involved selling off some of the company's less promising businesses. Not long after Hintz assumed command, Caradon dumped its door and window businesses. The company's interests in plastic pipes and garage doors soon followed, and in October 2000 it sold its plumbing business to HSBC Private Equity for £442 million. On the one hand, the most logical new focus for the company lay in its intelligent building systems unit. The company had been building some momentum in this market for some time; it was already the sole supplier of sprinkler systems to the Wal-Mart chain, as well as the lighting and temperature control units for Sainsbury's, a major British supermarket chain. At the same time, Hintz clearly remained open to the possibility of further diversification, assuming the right opportunity came along. His goal was not necessarily to streamline the conglomerate completely, but to reinvest the capital from its recent divestments into business segments that would offer long-term profitability.

Such a radical transformation could hardly be expected to reap dividends overnight, and the late 1990s proved to be a time of great uncertainty for the company. As late as October 2000 Hintz was still forced to admit that "in essence, Caradon has no real core business." Unfortunately, a number of the company's investors agreed with this assessment. In December 2000 the UK Active Value Fund, an investment group that owned a 10 percent stake in Caradon, called for an emergency shareholder meeting to reevaluate the company's strategy. The group's main goal was to force the company to commit to a single core business, put a freeze on acquisitions of more than £10 million, and buy back £130 million of its own shares. Hintz was able to repel this action, at least temporarily, by promising to undertake a thorough restructuring. One immediate result of the reorganization was the adoption of the company's new name, Novar plc, in early 2001. While the UK Active group remained skeptical of the direction the company was taking, it was clear that Hintz had brought an aggressiveness to Novar's business strategy that had been lacking. What was still unclear by the year 2002 was which of Novar's three primary businesses would serve as the foundation of the company's future.

Principal Subsidiaries

MK Electric Limited; Friedland Limited; Esser Security Systems GmbH (Germany); Esser-effeff Alarm GmbH (Germany); Gent Limited; Eltek Fire and Safety Systems AS (Norway); Trend Control Systems Limited; Novar Controls Corporation (U.S.A.); Innovex Controls Inc. (U.S.A.); Brand-Rex Limited; Albert Ackermann GmbH & Co. KG (Germany); Indalex (U.S.A./Canada); Mideast Aluminum (U.S.A.); Indal Technologies Inc. (Canada); Indalloy (Canada); Brampton Foundries Limited (Canada); Clarke American Checks, Inc. (U.S.A.); Checks in the Mail, Inc. (U.S.A.)

Principal Divisions

Doors & Windows; Electrical; Structural & Engineering; Security Printing.

Principal Competitors

Alcoa Inc. (U.S.A.); Deluxe Corporation (U.S.A.); Tyco International Ltd. (U.S.A.)

Further Reading

Bowditch, Gillian, "Caradon Agrees £337m Deal with MB Group," *Times* (London), October 4, 1989, p. 31.
Campbell, Colin, "MB Ties Up Packaging Interests with Carnaud," *Times* (London), October 27, 1988, p. 25.
Felsted, Andrea, "Caradon Defends Acquisition Strategy," *Financial Times* (London), December 29, 2000, p. 18.
Foster, Geoffrey, "The Remaking of Metal Box," *Management Today,* January 1985, pp. 43–51.
"Metal Box Aims to Kick Continental Can," *World Business Weekly,* September 1, 1980, pp. 10–11.
Oates, David, "Metal Box Re-Packages Its Operations," *International Management,* May 1976, pp. 10–13.
Reader, W.J., *Metal Box: A History,* London: Heinemann, 1976.
Taylor, Andrew, "Caradon Signals Boardroom Shake-up: Building Products Group Poised to Name New Chief Executive," *Financial Times* (London), November 14, 1997, p. 17.
Urry, Maggie, "Bold Deal Soothes Anxious Onlookers," *Financial Times,* August 26, 1993, p. 19.

—updates: David E. Salamie, Steve Meyer

Oakley, Inc.

One Icon
Foothill Ranch, California 92610
U.S.A.
Telephone: (949) 951-0991
Toll Free: (800) 403-7499
Fax: (949) 454-1071
Web site: http://www.oakley.com

Public Company
Incorporated: 1975
Employees: 1,685
Sales: $429.3 million (2001)
Stock Exchanges: New York
Ticker Symbol: OO
NAIC: 339115 Ophthalmic Goods Manufacturing;
    316219 Other Footwear Manufacturing; 334518
    Watch, Clock, and Part Manufacturing; 339920
    Sporting and Athletic Goods Manufacturing; 446130
    Optical Goods Stores

Oakley, Inc. is an innovation-driven designer, manufacturer, and distributor of high-performance eyewear, including sunglasses and goggles. Oakley sunglasses sell for anywhere from $65 to $335 a pair. Although known best for its sunglasses, Oakley has also expanded into footwear, watches, apparel, and accessories. Key aspects of the company's success include celebrity endorsements, especially by athletes, together with high-tech designs that include interchangeable lenses, high optical clarity, and damage resistance, and selective distribution through high-end retailers and specialty stores, including the Oakley-owned O Stores, Oakley Vaults, Sunglass Designs, Sporting Eyes, and Occhiali da Sole. These elements of Oakley's brand-building strategy work together to increase the perceived value of the company's products. Its products are not available from mass-market retailers, and Oakley vigorously litigates any unauthorized distribution of its products as well as patent infringements to keep competitors out of its lucrative business.

Beginnings: Moving from Handgrips to Goggles to Sunglasses

Oakley was founded by Jim Jannard in 1975 when he began selling handgrips for motocross motorcycles from the back of his car. Something of a motorcycle enthusiast, Jannard attended the University of Southern California in 1970. The long-haired student dropped out, reportedly because the Irish setter he brought to class irritated his professors. He spent about a year driving around the Southwest on his motorcycle. When he returned to Los Angeles, he traded in his motorcycle for a small Honda and began selling motorcycle parts out of his trunk to shops that serviced motorcycles. In 1975 he designed a rubber grip for off-road motorcycles and began selling it along with the motorcycle parts. That was the beginning of Oakley, a company he named after one of his dogs.

Jannard was in his mid-30s when he began Oakley. Toward the end of the decade he began selling motocross goggles. Featuring his own designs, the goggles were made of high-impact plastic that was lighter and stronger than the glass goggles then in use. With the help of some young salespeople, Jannard began handing them out at motocross competitions and selling them through Oakley's motorcycle parts accounts.

When the motorcycle goggles became a hot item, Jannard began developing eyewear that was part goggles and part sunglasses for skiers and bicyclists. In 1983 Oakley began selling ski goggles. Next year the company moved into the sunglasses market. Cyclist Greg Le Mond wore Oakley sunglasses in 1986 on his way to winning the Tour de France, becoming the first of many star athletes to be associated with marketing Oakley sunglasses. Jannard was encouraged to develop new sunglass models. One was the company's trademark Blades model, which featured interchangeable wraparound lenses that slipped into a simple carbon-fibre frame.

To market his new sunglasses, Jannard and his salespeople handed out many pairs to top athletes in the late 1980s and early 1990s. At one golf tournament, they gave a pair to basketball star (and golfer) Michael Jordan, who became a regular wearer of Oakley sunglasses. Other celebrities who have been associated with Oakley sunglasses include Nike chief Philip Knight, tennis star Andre Agassi, skater Bonnie Blair, and baseball great Cal Ripken, Jr.

A key element of Oakley's distinctive marketing approach has been the use of influential athletes. Relying primarily on the "editorial" endorsement of influential athletes, Oakley was able to increase consumer awareness of the company's product performance and overall brand image. Oakley believed serious athletes were quick to recognize the superior technology and performance of its products.

Many of Oakley's endorsements were obtained at little or no cost. In 1994 Oakley paid about $4 million to its endorsers, or about three cents per sales dollar. Andre Agassi, for example, did not charge his friend Jannard for his endorsement, even though he used to have an endorsement contract with Bausch & Lomb's Ray-Ban brand of sunglasses. By comparison, it cost Phil Knight of Nike $10 million per year to sign Agassi to an endorsement contract for ten years. Michael Jordan, who first wore Oakley sunglasses while playing golf, then while playing baseball for the Birmingham Barons, negotiated a stock package with Jannard when Oakley went public in 1995 that included a position on the company's board of directors.

The use of influential athletes to endorse its products helped make Oakley the acknowledged leader in the sports sunglasses market. Its high-performance sunglasses and goggles were worn by professional baseball and basketball players, skaters, skiers, cyclists, golfers, tennis players, and others. In 1990 the company had net income of $7.7 million on sales of $68.6 million. Sales were off slightly in 1991, then rebounded in 1992 to $76.4 million, with net income increasing to $9.1 million.

In the early 1990s Oakley's products were becoming popular in the nonsports fashion segment of the market. Sales and net income rose significantly in 1993 and 1994, to $92.7 million and then $124 million. By the end of 1994, the company made eight lines of sunglasses and three lines of goggles, accounting for a 13 percent market share of the U.S. premium (over $30 retail) sunglasses business. Its products were distributed in more than 60 countries.

Throughout its history Oakley has been selective about introducing new products. Starting with the basic Blades brand, which retailed for around $110 plus $60 for each additional coated lens in 1995, the company developed other product lines. The least expensive was the Frogskins line, which sold for $40 a pair. Agassi wore Oakley's Eye Jackets brand, which were introduced in December 1994. The M-Frame, a high-impact line that featured superhard polycarbonate lenses, could withstand a blast from a 12-gauge shotgun at 15 yards, or the force of a one-pound pointed weight dropped from a height of four feet. They sold for about $130 a pair in 1995. Trenchcoats, a line of camouflage eyewear, were introduced in October 1995, followed by Straight Jackets in May 1996. The much anticipated X-Frames were introduced in February 1997. Oakley also made three lines of goggles: H2O, Motocross, and Ski.

Going Public in 1995

As Oakley prepared to go public in 1995, Jannard gave himself a $21 million bonus at the end of 1994. He owned 64.8 percent of the company, and his net worth was estimated to be $750 million. His chief executive officer, Mike Parnell, who was 42 in 1995, received about $4.8 million in 1994. They each owned jet planes that they leased back to the company after it went public. Parnell owned about 7 percent of Oakley. Overall, the company was valued at about $820 million.

The year 1995 began well. Sales for the first half were 37 percent above sales for the first half of 1994. In August, 10 million shares were offered to the public at $23 per share, some $4 to $6 higher than the range of $17 to $19 per share originally envisioned by the underwriters. The initial public offering (IPO) raised $230 million, with $154 million going to insiders. Jannard made nearly $139 million. His holdings in the company were valued at $627 million after the stock rose to $27.125 a share on the day after the IPO, making him the second richest Orange County resident behind billionaire Donald Bren. The remaining $76 million for Oakley was earmarked to build a new corporate headquarters and pay off debt.

Litigating Infringements and Unauthorized Distribution in the 1990s

In December 1995, Oakley won two patent infringement suits against Bausch & Lomb Inc. and Lombardie Booster. The Court of Commerce in Paris ruled that some models of Bausch & Lomb's Killer Loop sunglasses infringed on two of Oakley's design patents. In a separate judgment, the same court ruled that Lombardie Booster's Infrared and Morpho sunglasses infringed on three of Oakley's design patents. Although Oakley was awarded less than $50,000 in damages in each case, the rulings served to help Oakley keep its competitors from copying its trendy glasses. Earlier in the year, the company was able to halt the sale of fake Oakleys delivered to Big 5 Sporting Goods, which the retailer had heavily advertised. The retailer agreed to cooperate with Oakley in tracking down the distributor of the fake sunglasses, all of which were ordered destroyed by the court. In April 1996 Oakley filed suit against The Clubhouse, a sporting goods store located in Thousand Oaks, California, charging that it resold Oakley sunglasses to an unfashionable discount warehouse. The discounter, Price/Costco, apparently offered Oakley's e Wire brand sunglasses in its mail-order catalog.

Key Dates:

1975: Jim Jannard founds Oakley when he begins selling handgrips for motocross motorcycles.
1984: Company enters the sunglass market.
1986: Cyclist Greg Le Mond sports Oakley sunglasses while winning the Tour de France.
1995: Oakley goes public through an IPO that raises $230 million.
1998: Company introduces its first athletic shoe.
2001: Company acquires Iacon, Inc., operator of mall-based sunglass specialty stores Sunglass Designs, Sporting Eyes, and Occhiali da Sole.

Historically, Oakley vigorously litigated any unauthorized distribution of its products as well as patent infringements. This helped keep competitors out of such a lucrative business. One attorney told *Forbes* that Oakley "uses litigation as a marketing tool." He estimated he had spent 2,000 hours helping ten sunglass makers fight Oakley in court in the early 1990s.

Oakley had some 320 patents issued or pending worldwide, plus 249 registered trademarks, as of 1995. Jannard's chief legal advisor, boyhood friend Gregory Weeks, spent much of his career enforcing Oakley's patents and trademarks, starting with Jannard's first motorcycle handlebar grip. Oakley exhibited zero tolerance for counterfeiters and used its sales force, concerned consumers, and private investigators to seek out counterfeiters and sue them.

New Headquarters, New Competition, and a Sales Setback: 1996–97

In January 1996 Oakley unveiled plans for its new "interplanetary corporate headquarters," to be located on 40 acres in Foothill Ranch in Orange County. The $35 million facility had "the look and feel of a post-industrial age gone awry," according to the *Orange County Register*. "Steel beams, oversized rivets, and galvanized metallic surfaces give the structure—dubbed 'Technical Center'—a dark, intimidating presence." Jannard reportedly wanted the facility to "look as if it were the sole survivor in a 'post-nuclear kill zone.'"

A sense of privacy was achieved by setting the facility back from the main entrance, where a winding road took visitors past rock formations. The dark-shaded, two-story building came into view only after the final turn of the road.

Over the main doorway, plans called for a 40-foot high metal ring with a convex stainless steel center, similar to Oakley's trademark ellipsis. Inside were the corporate offices, an auditorium, a boutique, and a museum. The adjacent warehouse was the size of four football fields and contained a basketball court. Other features of the Oakley campus included a helicopter landing pad, a small park for employees, a jogging track that circled the area, and an amphitheater. Much of the corporate campus appeared to reflect Jannard's personal style and took into account the youth of the company's workforce, whose average age was under 30.

As for landscaping, an architect who had done work for Great Britain's royal family designed prehistoric-looking rockwork to surround the campus. Native plants and trees were to be used around the grounds instead of manicured lawns, and the parking lot would be lighted by heavy-duty airport landing discs instead of traditional parking-lot lights.

Oakley held its first-ever annual meeting for shareholders at El Toro, California, in June 1996. Jannard presided over the meeting, which was attended by basketball star Dennis Rodman and was held at the Command Museum at El Toro Marine Corps Air Station. Soldiers wearing Oakley camouflage Trenchcoat sunglasses directed shareholders at the base. Jannard, refusing as usual to allow his photograph to be taken, was wearing black M-Frames sunglasses during the meeting.

The company reported to shareholders on 1995 earnings, which grew 49 percent to $39.6 million. Sales rose nearly 40 percent to $173 million. The company's stock had nearly doubled to $45.25 per share since its IPO in August of the previous year. Jannard gave a speech to the shareholders in which he emphasized Oakley's high-tech abilities and competitive strength. "We solve problems with inventions and then we wrap those inventions in art," he said about the company's products. The next line of sunglasses that Oakley planned to introduce were X Metals. The company also planned to introduce sunglasses especially for cricket players in the international market.

A secondary offering of stock, underwritten by Merrill Lynch & Co. and Alex Brown & Sons Inc., also took place in June. Jannard and Parnell were planning to sell about five million shares, worth about $220 million at current market prices. After the sale, Jannard would still own at least 45 percent of the company. Jannard's compensation for 1995 consisted of a $380,697 salary and a $9.3 million bonus, earned in part for exceeding financial performance targets.

In August Oakley entered into an agreement with Essilor International and its U.S. subsidiary Gentex Optics, makers of prescription lenses. The deal gave Oakley access to prescription lens laboratories and lens-making capabilities. Oakley planned to make its e Wire frames ($130) available in prescription sunglasses within a month. Previously, prescription lenses had accounted for less than 1 percent of the company's sales and were limited to only two of its sports sunglasses. Oakley's agreement with Essilor International and Gentex Optics was expected to cut the time for obtaining prescription lenses for Oakley sunglasses from three weeks to just one week.

In addition, Oakley was granted an option to purchase Essilor and Gentex's nonprescription-lens unit within four years. At the time Gentex was the world's leading producer of advanced-technology polycarbonate lenses and was Oakley's sole supplier of polycarbonate lenses. As part of the deal, Oakley also obtained an exclusive right to purchase a new scratch-resistant coating and decentered sunglass lens blanks, which would enable it to create optically superior dual lens sunglasses.

In October, Nike announced it would enter the $1.5 billion premium sunglasses market. It planned to focus on sports performance sunglasses, the same niche occupied by Oakley. Nike began with two styles of sunglasses designed specifically for track and field, the V12 ($160) and the V8 ($145). Nike also announced it would introduce the Magneto brand of glasses in the winter of 1996–97. The unusually designed Magnetos had no temples; they adhered to the face of the wearer with two small, semi-sticky round discs called AMPs that were placed on the wearer's temples. The AMPs held the sunglasses to the face with tiny magnets. The advantage, according to Nike: the glasses were lighter and would not bounce when you ran.

After effecting a two-for-one stock split in early October, Oakley experienced problems with one of its principal distributors. Sunglass Hut International, Inc. reported lower than expected sales for September, causing Oakley's stock price to drop by 16.9 percent. Sales to Sunglass Hut accounted for approximately one-third of Oakley's total volume in the first half of 1996. On December 5, Oakley announced that Sunglass Hut had cancelled all purchase orders through January 1997. Oakley delayed the launch of its new X Metal brand of sunglasses, and its stock lost 33 percent of its value, falling to $10.625 a share.

In November Oakley announced it had reached an agreement to acquire Serval Marketing, its exclusive distributor in the United Kingdom and Ireland. The distributor would be renamed Oakley U.K. Based outside London, England, Serval Marketing had been Oakley's exclusive U.K. and Irish distributor for 15 years, since 1981. It employed about 35 individuals, and its chairman, Carl Ward, and managing director, Ray Tilbrook, were signed to five-year employment contracts to ensure they would continue in the same roles for Oakley U.K.

Closing out a very eventful year, three shareholders filed a class-action suit in December against Jannard and Michael Parnell, Oakley's two top executives, charging they misrepresented the state of the company's operations to take advantage of Oakley's secondary stock offering in June 1996. The two underwriting firms and Oakley were also named in the suit. According to the suit, Jannard sold nine million shares at $23.81 per share (adjusted for October's stock split) for $205.2 million, and Parnell sold 1 million shares for $22.8 million. Six weeks later, Oakley's stock dropped to $15.375 on news that Sunglass Hut was experiencing weak sales. The lawsuit charged that company executives artificially inflated Oakley's stock by claiming that business with Sunglass Hut was strong and that the X Metal line would be introduced by the end of 1996. Several other similar class-action lawsuits were soon filed.

Sales in the fourth quarter of 1996 declined sharply, because of the loss of orders from Sunglass Hut and sluggish European sales. For the year, sales were up 27 percent to $218.6 million from $172.5 million in 1995. Net income for the fourth quarter was only $3.6 million versus $9.2 million the previous year. For the year, net income increased 16 percent to $46 million from $39.6 million a year ago.

Oakley moved into its new Foothill Ranch headquarters in early 1997 while still struggling from the aftermath of the Sunglass Hut debacle. Revenues for the first quarter of 1997 fell 29 percent, and earnings plunged from $11 million the previous year to $550,000. The full-year results for 1997 were no better: net income fell to $19.6 million while revenues declined to $194 million. During the year Oakley took a number of steps to

lay the ground for a turnaround, including a renewed focus on product innovation and a ramping up of new product introduction. After belatedly introducing the X Metal line in February, Oakley in April launched Fives, a frame designed specifically for the heads of women, which are typically smaller than those of men. In August the Eye Jackets line was extended with the introduction of a frame called Topcoat. Pursuing an aggressive strategy to achieve direct distribution in its international markets, Oakley began such an operation in Japan in May 1997. One month later, the company acquired One Xcel, Inc., maker of distortion-free face shields used with the sports helmets of athletes in the National Football League and the National Hockey League. Also accomplished was the addition of about 400 new retail accounts in order to lessen the company's reliance on the still struggling Sunglass Hut. By 1999 sales to Sunglass Hut would account for only about 23 percent of Oakley's sales. Continuing its litigious ways, Oakley filed the first of several suits against Nike in July 1997, alleging that the shoe company had infringed a patent covering several Oakley sunglass designs. Nike later countersued, and Knight and Jannard's relationship turned acrimonious. In September 1997 Link Newcomb, who had been the company's COO, was promoted to CEO, replacing Parnell, who was named vice-chairman. Because of the company's poor performance, Jannard took the unusual step of foregoing any compensation for the year, receiving neither a salary nor any stock options.

Rebounding and Diversifying in the Late 1990s and Early 2000s

Soon after suing Nike, Oakley took on the company in the heart of its market—that of footwear. Oakley announced in August 1997 that it planned to enter the athletic shoe market, and in June 1998 the O Shoe made its debut, priced at $125. Despite sporting a funky design and the company's usual high-tech materials, the shoe was perhaps most noteworthy for being manufactured entirely in the United States, at the Orange County plant. This was a direct challenge to the contention of Nike and other shoemakers that they had to manufacture overseas in order to make a profit. A further diversification of the product line came in December 1998 when Oakley introduced its first wristwatch, the Time Bomb, which retailed for between $1,300 and $1,500. The company was also by this time offering a line of apparel and accessories. Other 1998 moves included the purchase of the Oakley division of its Canadian distributor. This drive to directly market and sell its products in foreign markets continued in succeeding years. In November 1999 Oakley's Australian distributor was acquired; in June 2000 the company took over the distribution of Oakley products in Austria and also opened a new office in Munich, Germany.

The year 1999 turned out to be a turbulent one for Oakley as the shoe line, which was not yet profitable, proved to be a drag on earnings. Although revenues increased 11 percent for the year, profits fell 18 percent, to $19.8 million. There was also turmoil in the management ranks, as Oakley hired William D. Schmidt, a former Olympic javelin thrower and former Gatorade executive, as CEO in April, with Newcomb returning to the COO position. In October, with the stock price down to around $6 per share and Wall Street pressing the company to drop the troubled shoe line, Schmidt left the company, having apparently sided with the Wall Street analysts. Jannard refused to back down from his challenge to Nike, and even assumed the CEO position for the first time, vowing to take a greater hands-on role at the firm.

To turn the shoe line around, Jannard reversed course and outsourced manufacturing to a South Korean contractor. Plans were also formulated to significantly expand the shoe line to offer a broader line that would be more appealing to major retailers such as Foot Locker and REI. Oakley had introduced two lower-priced models in 1999, ShoeTwo at $90 and ShoeThree at $99, but then eight more styles debuted during 2000, ranging in price from $75 to $120. By late 2000 the shoe line was in the black, aided by much wider distribution into about 2,700 stores worldwide. Also helping Oakley's shoe sales—as well as the sales of its other products—was the decision in mid-1999 to hire the company's first outside ad agency, which led to a new print campaign that debuted in early 2000. In July 1999 Oakley established its first retail outlet, opening the first O Store in Irvine, California. In October, Oakley made its entire product line available through the company web site, and direct Internet sales totaled $1 million for the final quarter of 1999. Also aiding sales of sunglasses in 2000 were the exploding pair of X Metals that Tom Cruise wore in the opening scenes of the motion picture blockbuster *Mission: Impossible 2*. Revenues for 2000 increased 41 percent, hitting $363.5 million, and profits skyrocketed 83 percent, to a record $51.1 million. By late 2000, meanwhile, the good news coming out of the Foothill Ranch headquarters sent the company stock soaring; it tripled in value from its level of a year earlier.

Another important development in 2000 was the settlement of the various class-action lawsuits that had been filed in 1996 and 1997 accusing the company's executives of misleading investors. To the chagrin of Jannard, who continued to insist he had done nothing wrong, the company's insurance carrier elected to settle the lawsuits rather than keep fighting them, agreeing to pay the plaintiffs $17.5 million.

In March 2001 Oakley expanded its retail operations by opening its first outlet store, which it located in Milpitas, California. Dubbed Oakley Vault, the store featured mostly products from the previous season and discontinued styles, along with selected first-run merchandise. By the end of 2001 there were two Oakley Vaults along with four O Store locations, with plans in place to expand these concepts primarily in the California, Texas, and Florida markets. Oakley's retail operations gained added importance in April 2001 when Luxottica Group S.p.A. acquired Sunglass Hut. Luxottica had purchased the Ray-Ban brand from Bausch & Lomb in 1999 and was therefore Oakley's main sunglasses competitor. Fears that the new ownership of Sunglass Hut would lead to reduced stocking of Oakley products soon proved justified as Luxottica told Oakley in early August 2001 that Sunglass Hut would order only about one-sixth of what Oakley had been expecting. Responding quickly and aggressively, Oakley expanded its distribution network by partnering with several sporting goods retailers, including Champs, the Finish Line, and Foot Locker. In October 2001 Oakley acquired Iacon, Inc., which was based in Scottsdale, Arizona, and which operated 40 sunglass specialty stores in malls under the names Sunglass Designs, Sporting Eyes, and Occhiali da Sole. During its most recent fiscal year, Iacon had

reported revenues of $15 million. In December 2001 Oakley signed a three-year agreement with Luxottica that would return Oakley products to the shelves of Sunglass Hut, although not to the level seen prior to the acquisition.

Oakley had had a strong first half of the year during 2001, but the Sunglass Hut feud combined with the downturn in the U.S. economy and the effects of the events of September 11 sent both sales and profits plunging. For the year, revenues increased 18 percent, aided in large measure by a significant jump in international sales—an increase large enough that non-U.S. sales accounted for more than one-half of overall revenues for the first time. Another key trend was the increasing importance of sales of non-sunglasses products, which accounted for 33 percent of overall sales in 2001 (compared to just 18 percent in 1997). The net income figure of $50.4 million was a slight decrease over the preceding year.

In February 2002 Oakley established an office in Brazil to facilitate the shipping of products to that nation. Oakley further broadened its distribution channels in early 2002 when it began opening ''concept shops'' in Macy's West and Parisian department stores featuring Oakley products from all of the company's product categories. In May of that year, Oakley and Nike ended their nearly five-year-long court battle, reaching an undisclosed settlement with neither of the two sides admitting wrongdoing and with the companies agreeing to ''compete in the marketplace.'' A new battle between the two rivals was soon underway, however, as a result of Oakley's foray into the basketball shoe market that was dominated by Nike. Oakley was clearly a fierce competitor, with an ever-widening product line and an expanding distribution network, and there seemed to be no reason to doubt that Oakley would remain one of the hottest consumer brands.

Principal Subsidiaries

Bazooka, Inc.; Oakley SARL.

Principal Competitors

Luxottica Group S.p.A.; Marchon Eyewear, Inc.; Safilo SpA; Signature Eyewear, Inc.; NIKE, Inc.; Reebok International Ltd.; adidas-Salomon AG.

Further Reading

Ballon, Marc, ''Oakley to Resume Sales Through Sunglass Hut,'' *Los Angeles Times,* December 13, 2001, p. C2.

Barron, Kelly, ''Day in the Sun: Oakley's Reclusive Chairman Jim Jannard Presides Over the Company's First Annual Meeting in a Very Unconventional Place,'' *Orange County (Calif.) Register,* June 29, 1996, p. C1.

———, ''Oakley Pairs Up with Prescription-Lens Firm,'' *Orange County (Calif.) Register,* August 28, 1996, p. C1.

Bellantonio, Jennifer, ''Oakley Takes Aim at Nike's Basketball Shoe Dominance,'' *Orange County (Calif.) Business Journal,* June 24, 2002, p. 1.

Earnest, Leslie, ''Oakley Proves Sales Mission Possible,'' *Los Angeles Times,* July 20, 2000, p. C1.

———, ''Oakley Sets Aside CEO in Favor of Gatorade Veteran,'' *Los Angeles Times,* April 22, 1999, p. C1.

Ellerton, Delbert, ''Oakley Has Gray Day As Sunglass Hut Orders Fade,'' *Los Angeles Times,* August 3, 2001, p. C1.

Fulmer, Melinda, "Taking the Shades Off Oakley," *Orange County (Calif.) Business Journal,* September 2, 1996, p. 1.

Griffin, Cara, "Making a Quantum Leap," *Sporting Goods Business,* December 2001, pp. 44–45.

Johnson, Greg, "Oakley Races to Enter Athletic Shoe Industry," *Los Angeles Times,* August 14, 1997, p. D1.

——, "A Pair in the Glare: Oakley's Legal Attack on Nike Illustrates the Competitiveness of the Sunglasses Industry," *Los Angeles Times,* July 18, 1997, p. D1.

Kravetz, Stacy, "Sunglass Maker Hopes to Get a Lift from Athletic Shoes," *Wall Street Journal,* October 16, 1997, p. B1.

Leibowitz, Ed, "A Trip to Planet Oakley," *Los Angeles Times Magazine,* March 16, 1997, p. 22.

McHugh, Josh, "Who's Hiding Behind Those Shades?," *Forbes,* October 23, 1995, pp. 66+.

Mehta, Stephanie N., "For Everything Under the Sun, Specialized Sunglasses," *Wall Street Journal,* February 5, 1996, p. B1.

Montgomery, Tiffany, "Broadening the Oakley Horizon," *Orange County (Calif.) Register,* April 27, 2002, p. 1.

"Oakley Says Sales Strong After Stock Price Drops," *Women's Wear Daily,* October 14, 1996.

Reeves, Scott, "Sharper Focus: Hurt by Missteps, Sunglass Maker Oakley Is Down, but Not Out," *Barron's,* June 30, 1997, pp. 20–21.

Sanders, Edmund, "Way Out Work Site: Oakley Is Building What It Describes As an 'Interplanetary' Headquarters in Foothill Ranch," *Orange County (Calif.) Register,* January 18, 1996, p. C1.

Schaben, Susan, "A New Focus," *Orange County (Calif.) Business Journal,* June 12, 2000, p. 1.

——, "Oakley: What a Difference a Year Makes," *Orange County (Calif.) Business Journal,* January 1, 2001, p. 8.

Starr, Mark, and Leslie Kaufman, "It's Not Just About Shoes," *Newsweek,* May 18, 1998, pp. 50–51.

"Sunglasses Maker Oakley Scores Two More Victories Against Design Copycats," *Knight-Ridder/Tribune Business News,* December 14, 1995.

"Three Oakley Holders File Suit Against Two Executives; Class Action Charges Insider Trading," *Daily News Record,* December 31, 1996.

Woodyard, Chris, "Oakley's Founder Looks Like a Million—and Then Some," *Los Angeles Times,* August 10, 1995, p. D1.

—David P. Bianco
—update: David E. Salamie

OAO Siberian Oil Company (Sibneft)

Sadovnicheskaya St. 4
113035 Moscow
Russia
Telephone: (+7) 95 777 3152
Fax: (+7) 95 777 3114
Web site: http://www.sibneft.ru

Public Company
Incorporated: 1995
Employees: 47,000
Sales: $3.57 billion (2001)
Stock Exchanges: OTC
Ticker Symbol: SBKUY
NAIC: 211111 Crude Petroleum and Natural Gas
Extraction; 213112 Support Activities for Oil and Gas
Field Operations; 324110 Petroleum Refineries

Moscow-based OAO Siberian Oil Company, known as Sibneft, is one of Russia's top vertically integrated oil concerns. The company is active in exploration, production, refining, and wholesale marketing. Sibneft's production activities are centered around the western Siberian city of Noyabrsk, where there are proven crude reserves of 4.6 billion barrels. The company's refinery in the southern Siberian city of Omsk produces about 500,000 barrels a day and is the country's number one producer of high-octane gas. Sibneft also holds a 36 percent stake in a refinery in Moscow. The company's retail operations encompass more than 1,000 gas stations in western and central Siberia. Sibneft is closely held, with only about 12 percent of shares belonging to minority investors. Russian tycoon Boris Berezovsky has played a central, although never fully publicized, role in the company. More recently, Roman Abramovich has emerged as the figure in control of Sibneft. The company is nominally held, however, by several European banks, including ING Barings (23 percent), ABN AMRO (20 percent), and Deutsche Bank (17 percent). Eugene Shvidler has been president of Sibneft since 1998. Although the political entanglements and opaque dealings of Russia's ''oligarchs'' have occasionally made investors uneasy about Sibneft, the company also has garnered attention for its moves to improve corporate governance. In particular, the company was the first in Russia to publish financial accounts according to U.S. generally accepted accounting principles.

Soviet-Era Development

The first oil discoveries in western Siberia came in the early 1960s. At that time, the Volga-Urals region, together with older developments in the Caspian and North Caucasus, accounted for the majority of Soviet oil production. Production in the Volga-Urals region began to drop, however, after 1975 as fields matured. The government hoped to offset this loss with production gains in western Siberia, and began pushing for more exploration there. In 1975 an engineering group was formed to explore the upper reaches of the Ob River. The group developed the Kholmogorskoye oilfield, the northernmost development at the time, and constructed the Kholmy pioneer settlement. The field began producing in 1976.

With production declines becoming more urgent, in 1981 the Soviet government adopted resolution 241, ''On urgent steps to accelerate construction in the West Siberian oil and gas complex.'' The resolution set out an ambitious oil production plan and directed the Kholmogorneft company to construct the settlement of Noyabrsk. On April 15, 1981, Noyabrskneftegas (''neft'' is the Russian word for oil) was officially established. Housing and construction workers were brought in from far and wide to promote rapid development of the new complex. The Sutorminskoye, Muravlenkovskoye, and Vyngapurovskoye fields started producing in 1982. By 1985, a substantial industrial infrastructure had been built, and growth averaged about five million tons of crude a year.

The oil production methods applied at Noyabrsk, however, were unsustainable in the long run. Through the mid-1980s, the Soviet government had been pouring money into increased drilling in order to fend off declines in production. But most of the new developments, including those at Noyabrsk, were managed to maximize short-term recovery with little attention paid to prudent reservoir management practices. A decline in production was inevitable. After a 1988 peak, when the Soviet Union produced more crude than any other country, production began a decade-long fall to about half the peak level. Between 1991 and 1992 production fell 16.8 percent at Noyabrsk's largest fields.

The Battle for Control: 1991–98

The Soviet Union was dissolved in 1991. Soon state-held enterprises were being transformed into private entities, as the powerful battled for control of Russia's lucrative resources. The first privatizations came in 1992, when three vertically integrated oil companies were formed. Sibneft was created three years later in a second wave of privatization. On August 24, 1995, a presidential decree united the Noyabrskneftegas production association with the Omsk oil refinery to form the backbone of the new company. The Omsk refinery, constructed in 1955, was the largest and most up-to-date in the country, and had a history of processing oil from the Noyabrsk fields. Also rolled into Sibneft were the exploration unit Noyabrskneftegasgeophysica and the distributor Omsknefteproduct. The initial terms of the privatization process stipulated that the government was to retain control of 51 percent of the company for three years, and foreign ownership was limited to 15 percent. In January 1996, auctions turned over 49 percent of Sibneft to private investors.

The new company hired Miller and Lents, a Houston oil and gas consulting firm, to conduct independent audits of crude reserves at Noyabrsk. Audits were carried out annually from 1996 onward. The greatest challenge facing Sibneft was to stabilize production, which had been falling steadily through the early

1990s from 506 barrels per day in 1993 to 367 barrels per day in 1996. After 1996, yearly declines were smaller, but annual drops of 3 to 5 percent continued until the end of the decade.

Although Sibneft was supposed to remain under state control for three years, the cash-strapped government soon began looking for a loophole in that rule. Under the notorious ''shares for loans'' program, private investors provided loans to the government in exchange for the right to manage state holdings. Since the government never allocated funds to repay the loans, holdings in major enterprises were in effect transferred to business tycoons in a series of closed deals. In December 1995 the Finance Oil Corp. (FNK) gained control of Sibneft, then valued at about $600 million, in exchange for a $100 million loan. FNK was widely assumed to be controlled by business tycoon Boris Berezovsky, although Sibneft consistently denied any formal ties to Berezovsky. In May 1997 FNK officially gained control of Sibneft, managing to fend off a challenge from Oneximbank, owner of rival oil company Sidanco. Sibneft's holdings were in jeopardy again that December when a government commission threatened to seize control of the Omsk refinery if Sibneft failed to pay a tax bill estimated at $88 million. On Christmas Day, however, Sibneft agreed to make a substantial payment, averting the asset seizure.

As the post-Soviet oil industry matured, it began looking abroad for capital support. In late summer 1997 Sibneft became the first Russian company to issue a Eurobond. The $150 million bond was the first in a series of Russian corporate debt issues. Later that year industry consolidation became a hot topic. In January 1998 Sibneft signed a letter of intent to merge with Yukos, another large West Siberian oil company controlled by financier Mikhail Khodorkovsky. Prime Minister Viktor Chernomyrdin was present as the signing ceremony, expressing the government's desire to see the country's approximately 16 firms consolidated into four or five. The merged company, to be known as Yuksi, would be the largest private sector oil company in the world in terms of reserves. The merger would certainly bring benefits related to efficiency, as Sibneft's surplus refining capacity would balance out Yukos's excess crude extraction. Nevertheless, minority shareholders worried that the merger had more to do with accumulating political clout than with improved management. As the business press marvelled at the potential clout of such a giant oil concern, falling crude prices and disagreements over strategy cast doubt on the deal. Merger plans were conclusively abandoned in May 1998.

Low crude prices continued to put a squeeze on Russian oil, and industry leaders asked for tax breaks from the government. Oil company taxes, however, were by far the government's largest source of revenue. The drop in revenues associated with low oil profits led to the August 1998 financial crisis, when the ruble was severely devalued and the government defaulted on its loans. Sibneft weathered the crisis more easily than some, managing to meet all of its loan obligations. One casualty of the crisis was a deal with Elf Aquitaine SA, in which the French company called off plans to pay $528 million for a 5 percent stake in Yuksi/Sibneft. Sibneft went looking for an alternative partner to develop its Sugmut field, which had reserves estimated at 672 million barrels.

Key Dates:

1955: A refinery is opened in Omsk.
1975: An engineering group begins drilling on the upper Ob River.
1981: Noyabrskneftegas, an oil production association, is officially established.
1988: Soviet oil production peaks and begins to decline.
1995: A presidential decree forms Sibneft, uniting Noyabrskneftegas and the Omsk refinery.
1997: Boris Berezovsky's Finance Oil Corp. gains control of Sibneft.
1998: A planned merger with Yukos is called off amid falling oil prices.
1999: Roman Abramovich emerges as a major stakeholder in Sibneft.
2000: Crude production at Sibneft rises for the first time.

Advances in Efficiency and Transparency: 1998–2000

In the wake of the failed merger and the financial crisis, Sibneft began to focus on improving its own efficiency and transparency. In July 1998 the company had published a corporate governance charter, which provided for adding non-executives to the board. In September of that year Sibneft moved to consolidate its various units into a single share. Newly issued shares in the parent company were exchanged for equity held by outside investors in Sibneft's subsidiaries. A new contract with Schlumberger, the U.S. oil services firm, also boded well for the future. In a pilot project, Schlumberger had significantly improved flow rates at 150 wells by applying hydro-fracturing techniques. Sibneft also was moving ahead with exploration despite low oil prices, having brought 209 new wells into production in 1998.

A new president, Eugene Shvidler, took the helm at Sibneft that year, moving up from his former position as chief financial officer. With more experience in the industry than many of the businessmen at the head of Sibneft, Shvidler had the potential to improve on the company's mixed results and falling production. Things got off to a rough start in 1999, when commandos raided Sibneft's Moscow headquarters and federal investigators seized equipment allegedly used to eavesdrop on President Boris Yeltsin. Observers speculated that the raid was ordered by Prime Minister Yevgeni Primakov, who hoped to improve his chances at winning the presidency by targeting the company supposedly controlled by Yeltsin's friend Berezovsky.

Developments later in the year, however, showed more promise. Sibneft launched a level one ADR (American Depositary Receipt) program in April, allowing its shares to be sold over the counter in Frankfurt, Berlin, and the United States. That spring an issue of 300 million new shares facilitated the consolidation of the Noyabrskneftegas production subsidiary into its parent company. The maneuver increased Sibneft's free float in 1999 from less than 3 percent to 12 percent. In the fall Sibneft solidified its connection with Schlumberger in an alliance that would allow the oilfield services firm to make broad improvements on oil and gas extraction without having to negotiate specific contracts. In addi-

tion, Sibneft drew on the expertise of other services firms, such as BJ Services of Canada. The firm also broke ground in 1999 by hiring accounting firm Arthur Andersen to publish its accounts according to U.S. generally accepted accounting principles. The accounts showed a profit of $315.1 million on revenues of $1.74 billion in 1999. Although revenues were down slightly from the previous year, net income was up nearly nine times due in part to a fall in production costs related to the devalued ruble. Some observers, however, put a more negative spin on the year, noting that the company spent a modest $59 million on capital investment, and crude production had reached an all-time low of 322 barrels per day.

Late in 1999 Roman Abramovich, a 33-year-old close friend of the Yeltsin family, emerged as an executive and major shareholder at Sibneft. In a well publicized visit to Noyabrsk, he said he controlled about 40 percent of the company and announced plans to run for the governorship of Chukotka province in the Russian Far East. In a *New York Times* article, Michael Wines wrote that Russia's oil companies seemed to be leaving their "murky" past behind them: "Russia's oil tycoons largely founded their empires through dark-of-night political deals and squeezing out competitors, and until lately they have run their companies pretty much the same way. But now, if the barons themselves are to be believed, the era of wildcatter capitalism is over." Wines noted that Sibneft had recently touted itself as "Russia's most progressive company" in a local newspaper, a statement backed up by its publishing of GAAP-audited accounts and a corporate governance charter. Management also was improving under Shvidler. The company was close to paying off three quarters of its debt and planned to open 1,000 retail gas stations in Siberia.

Nevertheless, concerns lingered about possible conflicts of interest in the relations between Sibneft and its subsidiaries and customers. The true ownership of the company also remained unclear. Almost 90 percent of the company was controlled by an insider group, but the actual holdings of individuals could not be verified. The potentially destabilizing political ties of the company's management were another worry. Such pessimistic views seemed corroborated when, in August 2000, Sibneft's Moscow headquarters were raided by the tax police. Russia's new president, Vladimir Putin, had been taking a hard line with many Yeltsin-era "oligarchs," but had been criticized for favoring Abramovich, who had close ties to the Yeltsin-Putin circle. Soon, however, Sibneft was singled out and accused of paying lower taxes than any of the competitors. Sibneft claimed the government's figures were inaccurate and cooperated in supplying the tax police with documents. Much of this political maneuvering was related to the battle to gain control of newly privatized oil concerns. Sibneft was bidding in partnership with Yukos for the Onaco oil company. The two companies lost the bid to Tyumen Oil Co., but Sibneft did manage to gain control of 40 percent of Orenburgneft, Onaco's main producing subsidiary.

Rising Revenues and Increased Investment: 2000–02

In spite of a few negative incidents, the year 2000 as a whole marked a turnaround. Sibneft saw its first rise in crude production—a 5 percent gain to 338 barrels per day—since the founding of the company. Net revenues for the year soared to $2.4 billion, and net profit more than doubled to $674.8 million as the oil industry revelled in high crude prices. Sibneft also brought four new fields into production in 2000, bought two refined products retailers in the Urals region, and invested over $50 million in an upgrade of the Omsk refinery. In November the company entered into a joint venture with Yugraneft, the Russian subsidiary of U.K.-based Sibir Energy. The partnership would work on developing sections of the Priobskoye field and the Palyanovskoye deposit, where reserves were estimated at about 2.1 billion barrels. With a rosy financial outlook, Sibneft was able to pour money into several more development projects. The company planned to triple capital investment in 2001 to $595 million, with $120 million targeted at the one-billion-barrel Sugmut deposit.

In 2001 Sibneft burnished its reputation for corporate governance. The company won a $175 million syndicated loan from Western banks that spring, a sign of rising confidence on the part of Western financiers. Then in August Sibneft announced that it would pay an unprecedented dividend of $612 million, a move that gained the company even more credibility in the eyes of shareholders. More cynical observers, on the other hand, speculated that there was likely to be an ulterior motive to the large payout. Sibneft's reputation did in fact suffer a blow when the details were revealed about a certain deal in December 2000. The *Russia Journal* reported that Sibneft had bought a 27 percent stake from core shareholders, including Abramovich, then sold the shares back just before the dividend payout. The deal apparently functioned as an interest-free loan to company insiders, and minority shareholders protested that they should have had a chance to buy some of the 27 percent stake. Sibneft responded that there was no requirement that shares be offered for wider sale, asserting that the transactions were merely a matter of dealing with extra cash on the one hand and a need for debt reduction later.

Net revenue rose again in 2001 to $3.57 billion and profits reached $1.3 billion. Sibneft acquired 36 percent of a refinery in Moscow that year and, in a joint venture with Yukos, began exploring for oil in the Chukotka autonomous district, where Abramovich had recently been elected governor. Company President Eugene Shvidler told Sabrina Tavernise of the *New York Times* that the oil industry was focusing more and more on good management rather than battles for control. "The industry has consolidated and gotten a lot smarter," he said. "Owners are leaving management roles, and professionals are taking their place. Owners are people who like to do deals. But after that, you need to just sit and make money. That's a totally different type of work—more boring."

For the time being, however, the "boring" details of management continued to vie with ownership maneuvers as Sibneft entered 2002. The company opened its first gas station in

Moscow early that year and planned a $61 million program to expand its retail operations with 200 more outlets. At the same time, oil companies were vying for control of the state-owned Slavneft, which was scheduled to be partially privatized in October. Sibneft's continuing ties to inside Kremlin circles gave the company an edge. Former Sibneft executive Yuri Sukhanov was appointed president of Slavneft in May, putting Sibneft in a good position to acquire the 20 percent stake that was expected to be auctioned.

Principal Subsidiaries

OAO Moscow Oil Refinery (36%); OAO Omsknefteproduct (94%); OAO Sibneft-Noyabrskneftegas (97%); OAO Sibneft-Noyabrskneftegasgeophysica (81%); OAO Sibneft-Omsk Oil Refinery (87%).

Principal Competitors

OAO LUKOIL; OAO NK YUKOS; OAO Gazprom; OAO Surgutneftegas; OAO Tatneft.

Further Reading

Caryl, Christian, "Going for the Jugular," *U.S. News & World Report,* February 15, 1999, p. 41.

Fairlamb, David, "Petroleum Realpolitik," *Institutional Investor,* April 1998, pp. 21–22.

Freeland, Chrystia, and Norma Cohen, "Sibneft Prevents Refinery Seizure," *Financial Times* (London), December 29, 1997, p. 11.

Heath, Michael, "Sibneft Slammed over Murky Deal," *Russia Journal,* October 26, 2001, p. 3.

Jack, Andrew, "Oil Chief Steps into Light," *Financial Times* (London), November 5, 1999, p. 10.

——, "Russian Tax Police Raid Oil Company," *Financial Times* (London), August 11, 2000, p. 6.

Jones, Matthew, "Sibir Agreement to Develop Oil Fields in Siberia," *Financial Times* (London), November 21, 2000, p. 36.

"The Plot Thickens: The Fight for Slavneft Is Starting to Heat Up," *FSU Energy,* May 17, 2002, p. 1.

"Russia: Sibneft Goes for Growth," *Petroleum Economist,* August 2001, p. 36.

"Russian Oil. Look See, It's Yuksi," *Economist,* January 24, 1998, p. 62.

"Sibneft to Bid for Ina," *NEFTE Compass,* June 20, 2002, p. 4.

"Small Might Be Beautiful," *Petroleum Economist,* January 1999, p. 36.

Tavernise, Sabrina, "Investors in Russian Oil Are Lured with Dividends," *New York Times,* September 5, 2001, p. W1.

Wines, Michael, "Russia's Oil Barons Say Wildcatter Capitalism Era Is Over," *New York Times,* December 29, 1999, p. 1.

"Yukos and Sibneft Team Up in Chukotka," *NEFTE Compass,* August 16, 2001, p. 4.

—Sarah Ruth Lorenz

Omnicare, Inc.

<table>
<tr><td>

1600 RiverCenter II
100 East RiverCenter Boulevard
Covington, Kentucky 41011
U.S.A.
Telephone: (859) 392-3300
Fax: (859) 392-3333
Web site: http://www.omnicare.com

Public Company
Incorporated: 1981
Employees: 9,300
Sales: $2.15 billion (2001)
Stock Exchanges: New York
Ticker Symbol: OCR
NAIC: 422210 Drugs and Druggists' Sundries
    Wholesalers

</td></tr>
</table>

Omnicare, Inc. is the nation's major provider of pharmaceutical products and services to nursing homes, assisted living institutions, and other long-term care facilities. Its pharmacies usually provide prescription drugs and pharmaceutical consulting services to geriatric institutions located within a 150-mile radius. It buys many of its drugs from wholesale distributor McKesson Corporation, but increasingly purchases drugs directly from manufacturers. Related services include infusion therapy, computerized billing and drug monitoring, and dialysis services. Omnicare also uses its relationships with nursing homes to serve as a contract research organization (CRO) that conducts a wide variety of clinical trials in 27 countries for pharmaceutical and biotechnology companies.

Origins and Changing Directions in the 1980s

On May 19, 1981, Omnicare, Inc. was incorporated under the laws of Delaware. The company was started to operate healthcare services that it had gained from W.R. Grace & Company and Chemed Corporation. On May 20, 1981, the company chose Edward L. Hutton, a longtime W.R. Grace officer, as chairman and Joel F. Gemunder as president; they continued to lead the

company for many years. Two months later, in July 1981, Omnicare began publicly trading its common stock.

Omnicare and Chemed remained closely entwined for several years. Chemed had started as a W.R. Grace subsidiary in 1971 with Edward L. Hutton as its president and CEO. In 1982 Chemed became totally independent as a public entity. Other Omnicare officers or directors, such as Jon D. Krahulik and Kevin J. McNamara, also served as Chemed leaders, while Chemed owned a great deal of Omnicare common stock. In addition, Omnicare for many years subleased its corporate headquarters from Chemed in Cincinnati.

In its early years Omnicare ran a variety of businesses that generally provided products and services to hospitals. In 1984 Omnicare acquired Labtronics, Inc. for an initial payment of $3 million in cash and stock. Based in Palo Alto, California, Labtronics served hospitals by maintaining and repairing their medical equipment.

Several general and specific problems made Omnicare's hospital focus problematic. The average patient spent less time in the hospital, and hospital occupancy rates declined rapidly in the 1980s to only about 50 percent. At the same time outpatient and home-based care increased. Reflecting those trends, in 1982 Omnicare lost 14 contracts with American Medical International Inc., which owned and operated hospitals. Another 12 hospital and pharmacy contracts ended with American Medical in 1984, and ten more such contracts expired in 1986.

In 1984 Omnicare President Joel F. Gemunder also mentioned that the federal government's restrictions on hospital costs reimbursements hurt Omnicare's business. Thus the company tried to shift to serving home-care patients, which grew to about 25 percent of Omnicare's revenue in 1984. Omnicare left the home-care field, however. Meanwhile, it reduced its hospital business.

In 1983 Omnicare reported revenue of $200.4 million and net income of $17.7 million. Revenue rose in 1984 to $211.8 million. Almost half (44 percent) of Omnicare's 1984 revenue came from its Los Angeles subsidiary, called HPI Health Care Services, which provided 125 hospitals in the United States with pharmacy and other medical management services.

Company Perspectives:

Omnicare has a direct impact on the health of senior citizens. We have leveraged our pharmaceutical expertise to create unique databases and proprietary clinical information services, all focused on providing the safest, most appropriate, most cost-effective drug therapies for the elderly. Our programs and services encourage early diagnosis and treatment, since this usually provides the best quality of life at a lower cost.

In 1985 Omnicare began a series of major changes, including both divestitures and acquisitions, that reoriented the company to focus on providing pharmacy services to nursing homes and other institutional customers. It tried to sell HPI Health Care Services to Hospital Corporation of America, the nation's first multihospital corporation, but those negotiations fell apart in 1985.

In 1986 Omnicare sold two businesses. Early in the year it sold the hospital products division of its Inspiron Corp. to Intertech Resources Inc. for $13.3 million. That division manufactured and distributed disposable respiratory products for hospitals. In the fall of 1986 Omnicare sold Reliacare Inc., a subsidiary chain of home healthcare dealerships, to National Medical Care Inc. of Waltham, Massachusetts.

In 1988 it completed the first of many acquisitions of companies that provided pharmacy products and services to geriatric institutions. Then in 1989 it sold HPI Health Care Services to Diagnostek Inc. for about $27 million. That was a major step, since it marked Omnicare's departure from the hospital pharmacy business.

Growth in the 1990s and Beyond

In 1990 the 1987 Omnibus Budget Reconciliation Act was implemented. The act strengthened the federal government's regulations that required nursing homes to hire pharmacy consultants to ensure better patient care. Omnicare provided such services by monthly reviewing each patient's drug program, monitoring adverse reactions, advising better therapies, and checking each facility's record keeping and drug administration policies.

In the early 1990s Omnicare abandoned more businesses as a way to focus on its institutional pharmacy sector. Thus in 1990 the Bunn/Xorbox Group was divested, and in December 1992 it sold the Veratex Group of businesses, except for Labtronics, Inc., to Chemed Corporation for $62 million cash. At the time Chemed held 27 percent of Omnicare's stock. In 1993 Omnicare divested Labtronics, which was the last step in eliminating its medical and dental products businesses.

At the same time Omnicare continued to acquire companies that provided pharmacy services to nursing homes. In 1992 it acquired seven midwestern companies: Westhaven Services Co. in Toledo, Ohio; Pharmacare, Inc. and an affiliated firm in Louisville, Kentucky; PRN Pharmaceutical Services, Inc. in Indianapolis; Home Pharmacy Services, Inc. in Belleville, Illi-

nois; Crystal Care Corporation in Ashland, Kentucky; Interlock Pharmacy Systems in St. Louis; and Tulsa's Ross Drug, Inc.

Whereas Omnicare in the early 1990s still was in the early stages of building its pharmaceutical business, its sales were much less than before all of its divestitures. In 1991 sales were just $38.3 million and net income from continuing operations was $1.2 million. In 1992 the company reported a 169 percent increase in sales to $102.99 million and net income from continuing operations of $3.4 million.

Four more acquisitions were done in 1993, again all in the Midwest. They included Freed's Pharmacy, Inc. in Overland Park, Kansas; Kansas City Nursing Services in Kansas City, Kansas; Enloe Drugs, Inc. in Decatur, Illinois; and Dover, Ohio-based Anderson Medical Services, Inc.

Seven Omnicare acquisitions followed in 1994: Griffith, Indiana's Care Pharmaceutical Services, Inc.; Schaufler Prescription Pharmacy in Belleville, Illinois; Weber Medical Systems in Skokie, Illinois; Wadsworth, Ohio's Lo-Med Prescription Services, Inc.; Unicare, Inc. in Montgomery, Alabama; Lawrence Medical Supply, Inc. in Deerfield, Illinois; and Kirkland, Washington's Evergreen (including Evergreen Pharmaceutical, Inc. and Evergreen Pharmaceutical East, Inc.). Omnicare thus extended its consolidation strategy from the Midwest into parts of the South and West.

Omnicare spent $87 million for its seven 1994 acquisitions, which brought its total number of acquisitions up to 24 for an investment of about $213 million. To finance these acquisitions, in November 1994 Omnicare raised a net of $59.2 million through a public offering of its common stock. In February 1995 it signed an agreement with a six-bank consortium to replace its $50 million credit facility with a new five-year revolving credit facility of $135 million. By the end of 1994 Omnicare served about 147,600 individuals living in 1,725 institutions in 13 states: Alabama, Indiana, Illinois, Kentucky, Kansas, Michigan, Missouri, Montana, Ohio, Oregon, Oklahoma, West Virginia, and Washington.

To assist its institutional customers, in June 1994 Omnicare came out with its trademarked "Geriatric Pharmaceutical Care Guidelines," which it believed was "the first clinically-based formulary for the elderly residing in long-term care institutions," according to its 1994 10-K annual report. Developed just for Omnicare by the Philadelphia College of Pharmacy and Science, the Guidelines considered patients' health conditions, cost comparisons, and other factors.

The company's growth led to new offices. In late 1996 it had too many employees for its Chemed Center headquarters in Cincinnati, so it moved ten employees to a small office in Covington, Kentucky's RiverCenter office tower. This initial move came after the Kentucky Economic Development Finance Authority in November 1996 authorized tax incentives to get Omnicare to cross the Ohio River to nearby Covington. In 1997 Omnicare decided to move its headquarters to the newly built second RiverCenter tower, where it remained after the turn of the century.

In 1997 Omnicare purchased West-Val Care, the long-term care segment of Encino, California's West-Val Pharmacy Inc.

Key Dates:

1981: Omnicare is incorporated and its common stock begins to be publicly traded.
1985: The company begins emphasizing pharmacy services for long-term care facilities.
1989: Diagnostek in August acquires HPI Health Care Services, Inc. from Omnicare.
1990: Omnicare divests the Bunn/Xorbox Group.
1992: Selling the Veratex Group completes the transition to a geriatric pharmaceutical firm; seven acquisitions are completed.
1993: Omnicare acquires four companies.
1994: The Omnicare Guidelines is introduced to help clients provide better services; seven institutional pharmacies are acquired; Heartland Healthcare Services is started as a 50/50 partnership with Health Care and Retirement Corporation.
1996: Seventeen more institutional pharmacies are acquired.
1997: Coromed Inc. acquisition begins Omnicare's contract pharmaceutical research business.
1998: Omnicare acquires 11 more companies.
1999: Omnicare acquires Life Care Pharmacy Services and Pharmacy Care Associates.
2002: In January Omnicare completes its acquisition of American Pharmaceutical Services.

With annual revenue of $3.5 million, West-Val Care furnished long-term patients with pharmaceuticals and related products and services. In September 1997 Omnicare acquired Brookside Park Pharmacy Inc. Based in West Seneca, New York, Brookside served about 8,000 nursing home patients from its pharmacies in West Seneca, New York; Dunlap, Illinois; and Abilene and Tyler, Texas. The Brookside acquisition marked Omnicare's first operations in Texas.

Another 1997 acquisition was Pharm-Corp of Maine Inc., whose pharmacies served 40 Maine nursing homes and similar institutions. This marked Omnicare's entry into the nuclear pharmacy industry in which nuclear isotopes were given to patients to help doctors diagnose internal ailments.

Omnicare announced in August 1997 that it was moving ahead on its largest acquisition to date. It said that it would pay $222.6 million and assume $11.6 million in debt to acquire American Mediserve Corporation, a Naperville, Illinois pharmacy services firm that served 51,400 persons in 11 states. In addition, American Mediserve served another 27,000 individuals through a joint venture. It had annual revenues of $144 million.

In December 1997 Omnicare completed its acquisition of Coromed Inc. of Troy, New York, a company that contracted with pharmaceutical and biotechnology firms to provide research services. This was Omnicare's first acquisition of a contract research organization (CRO), which took advantage of Omnicare's already existing relationships with numerous nursing homes and other long-term healthcare institutions. This was a major turning point for Omnicare, for now it was involved in the testing of new drugs, not just the distribution of drugs.

At the end of 1997 Omnicare provided its pharmacy services to about 443,100 individuals in 5,500 nursing homes, retirement centers, and other long-term care facilities in 37 states. Some 7,450 workers, including 1,796 part-time, were employed at the end of the year. In its 1997 10-K annual report to the Securities and Exchange Commission, Omnicare said that it was "the largest independent institutional pharmacy company in the U.S."

The company's sales grew steadily from $223.1 million in 1993 to $307.7 million in 1994, $399.6 million in 1995, $536.6 million in 1996, and $895.7 million in 1997. Meanwhile, Omnicare reported its net income rising from $11.25 million in 1993 to $13.5 million in 1994, $24.8 million in 1995, $43.45 million in 1996, and $55.7 million in 1997.

In 1998 Omnicare grew rapidly by acquiring 11 other companies, including IBAH, Inc. of Blue Bell, Pennsylvania, a product research and development company with annual sales of $88.1 million and 22 offices in 16 nations. Acquired for $63.3 million in stock, CompScript Inc. provided mostly pharmacy management services to about 20,000 patients in 137 nursing homes and long-term care facilities. Other 1998 acquisitions included Premiere Institutional Pharmacy Inc. based in Van Nuys, California; Med World Pharmacy Inc. in Valley Cottage, New York; and Inpatient Pharmacy in Hauppauge, New York.

Omnicare continued to grow by acquisitions in 1999. It gained Life Care Pharmacy Services Inc., a subsidiary of Cleveland's Life Care Services of America Inc. and Cedar Rapids, Iowa's Pharmacy Care Associates to build up its geriatric pharmacy distribution business, while strengthening its contract research capabilities by acquiring Institut für numerische Statistik Dr. Hasse GmbH in Cologne, Germany.

Omnicare Inc. in 2001 increased its revenues to $2.15 billion from $1.97 billion the year before. Its 2001 revenues earned it a ranking as the nation's 657th largest company, according to *Fortune* on April 15, 2002. In the healthcare industry, Omnicare was listed as the 26th largest company. In 2001 Omnicare also had profits of $74 million, a healthy 52 percent annual increase, and 9,000 employees, down 3 percent from 2000.

In January 2002 the company completed a major acquisition by buying most assets of American Pharmaceutical Services Inc., which served patients through its 32 pharmacies in 15 states. Once again Omnicare continued its role as a major consolidator of the geriatric pharmaceutical distribution and consulting industry.

Omnicare proved to be a great example of a company that changed directions to take advantage of healthcare and demographic trends beginning in the 1980s. Since hospital occupancy rates fell and numerous community hospitals closed their doors, Omnicare quit providing products and services for such large institutions. Second, it shifted to serving the rapidly aging American population by providing pharmacy services to nursing homes, assisted living facilities, and other geriatric institutions. Omnicare's focus on such smaller facilities was part of a general decentralization trend in the postindustrial Information Age.

Principal Subsidiaries

Omnicare Pharmacy and Supply Services, Inc.; Omnicare Pharmaceutics, Inc.; Omnicare Management Company; Omnicare Holding Company; Omnicare Clinical Research; Quebec, Inc.; ComScript, Inc.

Principal Competitors

NCS HealthCare, Inc.; PharMerica, Inc.

Further Reading

"Business Brief—Omnicare Inc.: Agreement Reached to Buy CompScript for $63.3 Million," *Wall Street Journal,* February 24, 1998.

Goel, Vindu P., "Chemed Corp. Metamorphosis Name of the Game," *Plain Dealer* (Cleveland), June 23, 1995, p. 7E.

Hodges, Cheryl D., "Omnicare Completes Sale of Hospital Pharmacy Business," *Business Wire,* August 17, 1989.

——, "Omnicare Reports Strong Increase in 1992 Earnings," *Business Wire,* February 4, 1993.

"IBAH, Inc.," *Pharmaceutical Executive* (Corporate Close-Up Supplement), December 1998, p. 38.

Lazarus, Ian, "CROs: Cross Over Now," *Pharmaceutical Executive,* July 2001, pp. 66–72.

Lenzner, Robert, Christopher Helman, and Daniel Kruger, "Streetwalker," *Forbes,* December 10, 2001, p. 206.

Miller, Nick, "Omnicare Buys Pharmacy, Gains 8,000 Patients," *Cincinnati Post,* September 17, 1997, p. 6B.

——, "Omnicare's Reach Grows into Maine," *Cincinnati Post,* October 2, 1997, p. 6B.

——, "$144M Omnicare Acquisition Its Biggest Buy Ever," *Cincinnati Post,* August 8, 1997, p. 7C.

"Omnicare Acquires Coromed," *Wall Street Journal,* December 31, 1997, p. C20.

"Omnicare Acquires Med World," *Wall Street Journal,* March 11, 1998, p. B8.

"Omnicare Buys Labtronics in Cash, Stock Transaction," *Wall Street Journal,* February 2, 1984, p. 1.

"Omnicare Buys Pharmacy Care," *Wall Street Journal,* February 8, 1999, p. B9H.

"Omnicare Inc. Acquisition," *Wall Street Journal,* April 8, 1998, p. B6.

"Omnicare Inc. Sells Assets of Its Home Health Chain," *Wall Street Journal,* October 2, 1986, p. 1.

"Omnicare Purchases a Business," *Wall Street Journal,* December 23, 1997, p. A7.

"Omnicare Says Profit May Be 'Flattish' in 1984; Stock Falls 20% to $21," *Wall Street Journal,* May 22, 1984, p. 1.

"Omnicare Sells Division to Unit of Chicago Firm," *Wall Street Journal,* April 3, 1986, p. 1.

"Omnicare to Buy Life Care Unit," *Wall Street Journal,* June 4, 1999, p. B5A.

"Omnicare's German Acquisition," *Wall Street Journal,* January 6, 1999, p. B10D.

O'Toole, Timothy S., "Chemed Completes Acquisition of Veratex Group from Omnicare," *Business Wire,* December 21, 1992.

——, "Chemed Names Hutton Chairman and Chief Executive, Krahulik Becomes President and Chief Operating Officer," *Business Wire,* November 4, 1993.

Peale, Cliff, "Omnicare Edges Toward Ky. Move," *Cincinnati Post,* January 30, 1997, p. B8.

—David M. Walden

Opsware Inc.

599 N. Mathilda Avenue
Sunnyvale, California 94085
U.S.A.
Telephone: (408) 744-7300
Fax: (408) 744-7379
Web site: http://www.opsware.com

Public Company
Incorporated: 1999 as Loudcloud, Inc.
Employees: 368
Sales: $56.0 million (2002)
Stock Exchanges: NASDAQ
Ticker Symbol: LDCL
NAIC: 511210 Software Publishers

For approximately two and one-half years, from early 2000 through mid-2002, Opsware Inc., formerly Loudcloud, provided a hosted software solution to companies engaged in electronic commerce. The company's hosted software service featured its proprietary technology, Opsware, which was unavailable as a separate software product. Opsware's most notable feature is its ability to automate many of the manual tasks associated with web site maintenance and management. In June 2002 the company announced that it was selling its hosting and managed services business to EDS for $63.5 million in cash. The sale provided the company, which officially changed its name to Opsware, Inc. in late summer 2002, with much needed cash and enables the company to focus on developing and selling enterprise-level software for electronic commerce.

Providing Web Hosting and Managed Services for Electronic Commerce: 1999–2000

The formation of Loudcloud, Inc. was announced in September 1999. The company's founders included some of the Internet's best-known innovators, including Netscape Communications Corporation cofounder Marc Andreessen and former Netscape and America Online (AOL) executive Ben Horowitz. At AOL Horowitz was the executive in charge of the company's e-commerce platform division and oversaw the development of Shop@AOL, the Internet's largest shopping destination.

Loudcloud's other cofounders were Tim Howes, co-inventor of the Lightweight Directory Access Protocol (LDAP), which became the Internet standard for directories, and Sik Rhee, designer of the Kiva application server. All four cofounders worked together at Netscape and then at AOL after Netscape was acquired by AOL and Sun Microsystems.

Details about Loudcloud's products and services were not made public until February 2000. At the industry conference Demo 2000, the company announced that it would offer a packaged solution to help companies put up speedy and reliable Internet sites primarily for business-to-business e-commerce. Loudcloud's service combined hosting, storage, hardware, and software development into a single package. It utilized the company's proprietary software, known as Opsware, to automate the configuration, bandwidth provisioning, and other tasks required to configure and manage a web site. Loudcloud claimed that Opsware provided unprecedented levels of scalability and reliability. The company's service was offered as a package, and its software was not sold separately.

Loudcloud began business with seven customers and $68 million in venture capital funding from Benchmark Capital and Morgan Stanley Dean Witter. Its initial group of customers included HomeGain, Skills Village, Acteva Inc., Wish.com, CFOWeb, Dreamlot, and Catapulse. At first, the company's target market consisted of dot-com companies that had already received venture capital funding, but Loudcloud soon added more substantial enterprises to its customer list.

Loudcloud's management team consisted of Marc Andreessen as chairman, Ben Horowitz as CEO, Tim Howes as chief technology officer (CTO), and Sik Rhee as vice-president of research. Under a strategic partnership with Hewlett-Packard (HP), the two companies would work together to develop systems and processes to deliver portals and web sites for dot-com companies, with HP providing Intel-based NT and Linux servers. Similar partnerships were announced with Sun Microsystems, EMC, Oracle, and iPlanet. Loudcloud's initial hosting partners were GlobalCenter Inc. and Exodus Communications Inc.

In May 2000 the company launched myLoudcloud, a portal that offered customized services for Loudcloud customers. The site made it easy for client companies to obtain performance statistics about their sites, including number of impressions and unique visitors to their sites. After moving into a 75,000-plus-square-foot building—more than five times its previous space—in June, Loudcloud announced in July that it had received an additional $120 million in venture capital financing from a group of investors led by Capital Research and Management. Loudcloud's staff had grown to 250 employees, and the company had more than 20 customers. That same month, when Microsoft announced its new Microsoft.Net strategy, it was noted that Loudcloud was included on the team that would help Microsoft pursue its Internet strategy.

Loudcloud added an Internet services portal to its home page in August 2000. The eServices Directory, as it was called, was open to the public and provided a guide to the various Internet services offered by Loudcloud as well as a directory of the company's strategic partners. It also included a list of companies that Loudcloud endorsed, either because they used Loudcloud products and services or they warranted a ''best practices'' rating.

Toward the end of 2000 Loudcloud introduced two new services aimed at growing customer segments. Instant ASP, aimed at Loudcloud's growing base of ASP (application service provider) customers, was a package of billing, scheduling, and failover services. For customers whose e-commerce business was rapidly expanding, Loudcloud offered the Global Connect service, which included load balancing and disaster recovery. As Loudcloud celebrated its first anniversary in September 2000, its list of customers had grown to about 30 and included Nike Corp., Britannica.com Inc., and Interelate Inc. The company's staff had grown to 370 employees. The company also announced that it was expanding internationally, opening offices in London, Paris, and Munich, Germany. Perhaps more significant, Loudcloud filed papers with the Securities and Exchange Commission (SEC) for its initial public offering (IPO).

Going Public in an Unfavorable Business Climate: 2001

Loudcloud introduced some software and service upgrades at the beginning of 2001. They included Global Response Smart Cloud, a service enhancement that allowed customers to measure and compare the real-time response rates of their sites with their competition. In February the company introduced Opsware 2.0, an upgrade that included new tools for content deployment, disaster recovery, and operations auditing. Loudcloud also announced a partnership with America Online to host and manage AOL's merchant e-commerce services, including its QuickCheckout wallet technology.

Loudcloud held its IPO on March 9, 2001. The unfavorable investment climate for Internet companies caused the company

to reduce its proposed offering. Initially, the company planned to offer ten million shares, then 10 percent of the company, at $10 to $12 a share, giving Loudcloud a market value of about $1.1 billion. By February the company said it would offer 20 million shares, or 30 percent of the company, at $8 to $10 a share, giving Loudcloud a market value of only $600 million. Then, just before the IPO, Loudcloud priced its shares at $6 and offered 25 million shares, raising $150 million for the company. Investors were wary of Internet companies that had yet to turn a profit, and Loudcloud posted an operating loss of $164.8 million on revenue of $15.5 million for its fiscal year ending January 31, 2001. As a result of the IPO, Andreessen's stake in Loudcloud was reduced from 18 percent to 12 percent.

As part of an effort to attract larger enterprises, especially those with in-house corporate data centers that were operated without the help of a third-party co-location facility, Loudcloud introduced Opsware 2i, a subscription-based service that would plug customers and their web site operations into Loudcloud's Network Operations Center. Opsware 2i marked the first time that Loudcloud offered its services to a corporate in-house data center. To better serve enterprise customers, Loudcloud later in the year unbundled its managed service offerings to allow customers the option of purchasing only one of its application-management services or to mix and match them.

Loudcloud's financial problems continued to mount during the rest of 2001. In May the company laid off 19 percent of its staff, or 133 workers. It was an attempt to cut costs in the face of declining demand. By June Loudcloud's stock was trading around $2.50 a share, less than half of its offering price. Its stock fell another 25 percent to below $2 a share, when the company reported a wider-than-expected net loss of $60.3 million on revenue of $11.7 million for the quarter ending April 30, 2001. During the quarter Loudcloud gained $42 million in contracts from Ford Motor Co., Network Appliance, and USA Today. The company said its $205 million in cash was enough to fund its business plan. Losses for the next quarter, however, reached $76 million on revenue of $14.1 million, including a $30.2 million restructuring charge.

A five-year partnership with Qwest Communications International that was announced in September 2001 helped validate Loudcloud and boost its stock price 42 percent in one day. The partnership gave Loudcloud access to Qwest's sales force as well as to its infrastructure and data center space. Under the partnership Qwest would leverage its existing data center and bandwidth assets and use Loudcloud's managed services expertise to offer enterprise customers a managed solution. In addition, Loudcloud would manage Qwest.com, the company's corporate Internet site.

Loudcloud gained another important customer in November 2001 when it won the contract to design, host, and manage the British government's public portal UK Online (www.ukonline.gov.uk). Loudcloud won the contract when British Telecom, the site's former manager, was forced to re-bid for the contract after the original one expired.

New and existing customers provided Loudcloud with enough orders during the quarter ending October 31, 2001, for the company to post a significant gain in revenue while reducing its losses.

Key Dates:

1999: The formation of Loudcloud, Inc. is announced.
2000: Loudcloud's mission as a software infrastructure service provider for an enterprise's Internet operations is clarified.
2001: Loudcloud goes public in a business climate unfavorable to Internet companies.
2002: Loudcloud sells its managed services and hosting business to EDS for $63.5 million; the company is renamed Opsware, Inc.

For the quarter Loudcloud reported revenue of $14.3 million and a loss of $40.7 million, compared with revenue of $4.6 million and a loss of $58.2 million for the same quarter in 2000.

Selling Hosting Business to Focus on Software Development: 2002

During the first half of 2002 Loudcloud introduced new services to improve customer relations, upgraded its customer management portal, and released Managed Services 3.0. An upgraded version of its Code Deployment System made it easier for customers to manage web site changes and included stronger security and on-demand backup features. Among the new features added to its customer management portal—where customers could manage, report on, and change their web infrastructure—was the ability to break out costs by business units. The company also reduced the base price of Managed Services 3.0, which included deployment and launch services, application and infrastructure services, and client services, to $10,000 per month. Among the new features found in Managed Services 3.0, which automated manual functions associated with web site maintenance, was a Patch Management System that automatically detected and deployed security patches. The software also automated a 40-point security inspection.

In June 2002 Loudcloud announced that it would sell its core managed services and hosting business to EDS for $63.5 million in cash. In addition, EDS agreed to pay Loudcloud $52 million over the next three years to license the company's software for its own managed hosting operations. The sale also included Loudcloud's customer base of about 50 web hosting clients.

The sale of its hosting business marked a significant change in Loudcloud's business model. Instead of providing and hosting electronic commerce software solutions, the company would focus exclusively on developing and selling software to corporate customers. As part of the change, the company adopted the name Opsware, Inc. later in the year, in order to more closely identify itself with the name of its flagship software product. The company announced that it would immediately launch an enterprise version of Opsware 3.0, which was previously available only as a hosted service.

Principal Competitors

International Business Machines Corporation; NOCpulse Inc.; Changepoint Corporation; Evolve Software, Inc.; Niku Corporation.

Further Reading

"Andreessen Is Ready to Host," *PC Week,* February 28, 2000, p. 39.

"Andreessen Launches Loudcloud," *Business Journal,* February 11, 2000, p. 30.

Braunschweig, Carolina, "VCs Rain $120M Down on Loudcloud," *Private Equity Week,* July 3, 2000, p. 3.

Burt, Jeffrey, "Service Gauges Response Rates," *eWeek,* January 15, 2001, p. 39.

"The Cabinet Office," *Marketing,* November 22, 2001, p. 11.

"Cloudy Day at Loudcloud," *San Francisco Business Times,* May 4, 2001, p. 58.

Cohen, David, "Andreessen Plays Host to New Era in Web Site Management," *New Media Age,* May 31, 2001, p. 44.

Corcoran, Elizabeth, "Growing Up Is Hard to Do," *Forbes,* April 29, 2002, p. 36.

Darrow, Barbara, and Amy Rogers, "Loudcloud—The Secret Is Out—Goal: Become Infrastructure Provider to B2B Stars," *Computer Reseller News,* February 7, 2000, p. 7.

Doyle, Eric, "Loudcloud Adds Automatic Protection for E-Business," *Computer Weekly,* June 6, 2002, p. 34.

Fonseca, Brian, "Loudcloud Makes MSP Bid for Enterprise-Class Customers," *InfoWorld,* April 23, 2001, p. 24.

——, "MSPs Forge Software Trail," *InfoWorld,* June 24, 2002, p. 41.

——, "MSPs Stress Customer Needs," *InfoWorld,* January 21, 2002, p. 24.

Gilbert, Alorie, "Loudcloud Sees Better Days Ahead," *InformationWeek,* September 3, 2001, p. 26.

Gillmor, Dan, "Foe? Partner? No Big Deal; It's Just Business," *Computerworld,* July 10, 2000, p. 26.

Graebner, Lynn, "Loudcloud Increases Space by Factor of Five with Move," *Business Journal,* June 9, 2000, p. 4.

Greenemeier, Larry, "Loudcloud Has a Stormy Quarter," *InformationWeek,* June 18, 2001, p. 36.

Holland, Roberta, "Loudcloud Portal Clears Up Site Stats," *PC Week,* May 8, 2000, p. 56.

"HP and Loudcloud Partner to Provide Software Services to Internet Businesses," *EDP Weekly's IT Monitor,* February 14, 2000, p. 7.

Koblentz, Evan, "Host with the Most," *eWeek,* September 18, 2000, p. 18.

——, "Loudcloud Portal Opens Up Expertise," *eWeek,* August 14, 2000, p. 38.

——, "Opsware 2.0 Speeds Code Deployment," *eWeek,* February 19, 2001, p. 44.

"Loudcloud, AOL Partner," *eWeek,* March 5, 2001, p. 3.

"Loudcloud Issues IPO," *InfoWorld,* March 12, 2001, p. 5.

"Loudcloud Makes Stand-Alone Opsware Tools Available," *InternetWeek,* June 26, 2002.

"Loudcloud Stock Drops Under $2 Marker," *IPO Reporter,* June 25, 2001.

"Loudcloud Updates Customer Management Portal," *InternetWeek,* April 3, 2002.

"Marc Andreessen's New Company," *Content Factory,* October 27, 1999.

Mardesich, Jodi, "Andreessen Starts It Up," *Fortune,* November 22, 1999, p. 51.

Moozakis, Chuck, "Platforms Centralize Mgm't of Hosted Apps," *InternetWeek,* February 14, 2000, p. 10.

Musero, Frank, "The Unlucky Seven: New Issue Busts of 2001," *IPO Reporter,* June 18, 2001.

Nelson, Matthew G., "Loudcloud Looks to IPO for Sunnier Skies," *InformationWeek,* October 9, 2000, p. 18.

O'Connor, Colleen, "IPOs Show Signs of Life, But Still Weak," *IPO Reporter,* March 12, 2001.

——, "Loudcloud Rains on Late-Stage Buyers, But IPO Shines on Initial VC Supporters," *Private Equity Week,* March 19, 2001, p. 11.

Opsware, Inc., ''Founders Story,'' July 3, 2002, http://www.opsware .com.

''A Pioneer Once More,'' *Business Week,* February 28, 2000, p. 41.

''The Poster-Child Who Grew Up,'' *Economist (U.S.),* March 9, 2002.

''Qwest Validates Loudcloud's Viability,'' *Telephony,* September 3, 2001, p. 14.

Regan, Keith, ''Loudcloud Sells Hosting Biz to EDS for $63.5M,'' *E-Commerce Times,* June 17, 2002, http://www.ecommerce times.com.

Roberts-Witt, Sarah L., ''Loudcloud,'' *Internet World,* July 1, 2000, p. 54.

Rogers, Amy, ''Loudcloud's New Services Target ASPs, E-Business,'' *TechWeb,* September 15, 2000.

Rogers, Amy, and Barbara Darrow, ''Start-Ups Have Heads in Loudcloud,'' *Computer Reseller News,* February 21, 2000, p. 41.

Rogers, James, ''Loudcloud to Host UK Online,'' *Computer Weekly,* November 22, 2001, p. 6.

Sliwa, Carol, ''Andreessen Targets Web Outsource Model,'' *Computerworld,* September 25, 2000, p. 32.

Smetannikov, Max, ''Loudcloud: Coming Out with a Whimper,'' *Interactive Week,* March 12, 2001, p. 20.

Smith, Tom, ''EDS Buys Loudcloud Hosting Business for $63.5 Million,'' *InternetWeek,* June 17, 2002.

——, ''Latest Loudcloud Service Starts at $10,000 Per Month,'' *InternetWeek,* May 8, 2002.

''These Days, Even Stars Can Fizzle on the Launchpad,'' *Business Week,* March 5, 2001, p. 40.

Torode, Christina, ''Loudcloud Gets a Lift,'' *Computer Reseller News,* November 26, 2001, p. 22.

——, ''Loudcloud Unbundles Managed Services Offerings,'' *Computer Reseller News,* August 13, 2001, p. 10.

Vijayan, Jaikumar, ''Loudcloud Expands Outsourcing Services,'' *Computerworld,* April 23, 2001, p. 25.

—David P. Bianco

Oregon Chai, Inc.

1745 NW Marshall Street
Portland, Oregon 97209
U.S.A.
Telephone: (503) 221-2424
Toll Free: (888) 874-2424
Fax: (503) 796-0980
Web site: http://www.oregonchai.com

Private Company
Incorporated: 1994
Employees: 31
Sales: $15 million (2000 est.)
NAIC: 311920 Coffee and Tea Manufacturing

Oregon Chai, Inc. offers a line of aseptically packaged chai concentrates and latte mixes in foodservice and consumer sizes and ready-to-drink soy-based chai lattes. The company's products, which have captured a greater than 60 percent share of the chai market, are distributed throughout the United States, Canada, the United Kingdom, and Guam through foodservice, natural foods, and grocery channels.

Catching the Wave of the
Coffeehouse Movement: 1994–95

In 1989, Heather Howitt, a native of Portland, Oregon, and then a student of anthropology at the University of California in Santa Cruz, was trekking in India's Himalayas. Yearning for a latte, she instead purchased a cup of hot *masala chai,* a sweet mix of black tea, spices (including pepper), and milk, from a local peddler. Although she did not immediately enjoy the taste, Howitt, a veteran coffee drinker, soon became a "chai" aficionado.

"Chai" is the generic word for tea throughout parts of the Middle East, Asia, and Africa. As a mixture of black tea and spices, it first appeared in the United States during the 1960s, brought back by young counterculture travelers. There it thrived in alternative circles, at ashrams and communes. Back at school in California, Howitt went looking for chai and noticed it for

sale at coffee houses near campus. But once she had completed her undergraduate degree in 1992 and moved back to Portland, Howitt could no longer purchase the drink she had come to love.

"I decided to figure it out for myself and it was a total pain," Howitt said of learning to brew her own chai in a 1997 issue of the *Portland Business Journal.* "I looked at tons and tons of Asian chai recipes." After three years of experimenting, from 1990 to 1993, she was satisfied that she had developed a drink concentrate that would please the American palate, a mixture that included vanilla, cinnamon, ginger, and honey—slightly sweeter than the chai she had first tasted—"more dessert-y" than traditional chai. Howitt's concentrate, when mixed with an equal portion of steamed milk or soy milk, was a cross between Indian chai and the increasingly popular designer lattes served in coffee houses, an alternative to espresso drinks. "Ours is more of a vanilla, dessert, honey drink as opposed to a serious cup of spice tea," said Howitt of her drink in a 1995 *Baltimore Sun* article.

In 1994, at age 25, Howitt put her graduate coursework in urban studies at Portland State University on hold, and with the help of her mother, Tedde McMillan, and a $3,000 loan, she applied for a business license to sell her tea concentrate. The mother-daughter team manufactured their product in the basement of a Portland church, running the business from Howitt's old bedroom in her parents' home. Joined by high school friend Lori Spencer, Howitt went around Portland, selling the liquid chai concentrate, packaged in plastic bottles with hand-designed labels, to local coffee shops and natural food retailers from the trunk of her car. By the end of that year, the new business, called Oregon Chai, had annual sales of $20,000.

Revenues for Oregon Chai's first full year of business in 1995 were about $200,000. In early 1995, nine months after its introduction, Oregon Chai had met with such success that the company branched out with an eight-ounce milk and chai blend in a juice-box type container. Certainly the success was in part due to the company's product being in the right place at the right time. Chai had remained mostly a West Coast phenomenon since its introduction stateside in the 1960s. But during the 1990s, catching the wave of the burgeoning coffeehouse movement, the drink became more widespread. By the mid-1990s, chai had made it to the midwestern states. Seattle-based Starbucks started selling dry chai in teabags and serving it hot and cold in early 1995. Two years later, the Lipton Teahouse in Pasadena, California, was serving a chai product of its own.

"It's catching on. The demand for the product is tremendous," announced Rex Bird, veteran restaurant executive and the company's new president, in the *Oregonian* in 1996. "As tea and other new-age beverages become more popular, this one has tremendous potential as an alternative to coffee espresso latte." Advertisements for chai claimed that it was low in calories, with little or no caffeine or refined sugars, and no preservatives. Many chai manufacturers further boasted using only natural ingredients and recyclable containers, and hailed medicinal properties of the spices it contained, appealing to both the New Age and environmental crowds.

Putting Together a Business Plan for Success: 1996–97

With Oregon Chai growing by leaps and bounds, Howitt and her team, aware of their own lack of business acumen, sought out the advice of experts. They put together a board of directors that included Joel Lewis, an advertising executive, and Dwight Sinclair, a broker. "These guys," according to J.B. Groh of Crown Point Group Ltd. in a 1997 *Inc.* article, "are more aggressive from a marketing standpoint than their competitors, many of whom seem content to remain backwoods mom-and-pops selling chai out of the back of a VW bus." Both board members had prior experience in the food industry.

The company's management took the advice of its board. Using contact-management software and schooled in distribution practices by one board member, Oregon Chai saw its distribution list swell from six to 130. Distributors and retailers also had suggestions that the start-up jumped on; when Sunshine Dairy Foods, a Portland distributor, advised that company representatives show up in the wee hours of the morning to pass out samples of chai to truckers, they did so. The chai was popular and, as a result, Oregon Chai's distribution network became a source of free marketing and advertising. Nature's Fresh Northwest, a chain of natural food stores in Portland, came up with the suggestion that the company put its chai in a retail package. With point-of-purchase materials designed by another board member, the company introduced aseptic packaging in 1995 that had the advantage of affording a one-year shelf life.

By 1996, the company's second full year in business, it had turned its first profit. Oregon Chai had become the premier-selling natural foods product nationally in the black tea category, with 120 distributors (including Sysco, Associated

Grocers, United Grocers, Sunshine Dairies, Northwest Dairies, Pike Place Creamery, Food Services of America, Mountain People NW, and Peterson & Co.) and 3,500 accounts ranging from Portland-area dairies to clients in Saudi Arabia. The company's sales grew some 450 percent to just more than $1 million, while the entire domestic chai market amounted to only $7.5 million in sales.

As the business grew, the company obtained a Small Business Administration loan and arranged for a financing package of $500,000 from Crown Point Ventures, a Portland investment firm. By 1997, Crown Point had helped Oregon Chai raise $450,000. Pouring every penny back into the business, that year Oregon Chai pulled in more than $2.7 million in revenue. Oregon Chai products were sold in all 50 states through natural food channels, and the company was nearing national distribution in foodservice and mass retail.

Continuing Consumer Demand in the Late 1990s and Beyond

By 1998, the company's sales had increased to $6.8 million, which amounted to a 1,277 percent increase since 1995, and the company had 200 distributors. Howitt credited the company's swift success to several factors. In addition to the press coverage that spurred and accompanied growing interest in chai, the staff put in thousands of hours each year on the floor of food marketing trade shows. "We see that as our grass roots promotion," Howitt explained in the *Portland Business Journal* in 1998.

Howitt also credited the time Oregon Chai had spent in building its distribution channels and the company's switch to aseptic packaging. "Really our customer base has forced the distribution," said Howitt in the 1998 *Portland Business Journal* article. "We'll get a college in New York and they only use three of the top distributors; so they'll force it down their distributor's throat. Then the distributor is calling us to get it." In 1998, Oregon Chai ranked number one in both the natural foods chai and tea categories with its original drink mix, and the company introduced two new flavors, Kashmir Green Tea and Herbal Bliss.

In 1999, the company continued to expand its product offerings with the launch of its naturally caffeinated Chai Charger and its first certified organic product, Organic Chai. It also introduced a new product line, ready-to-drink soy tea lattes. After five years in business, Oregon Chai enjoyed $8.5 million in annualized sales and a 64 percent share of the natural foods chai category. To accommodate such growth, the company relocated its headquarters to a trendy neighborhood in the northwest quarter of Portland.

Chai sales nationally amounted to about $30 million in 2000. Of this figure, Oregon Chai controlled about $11 million, a sum that landed it on *Inc.*'s Top 500 list. "Chai [had become] to the emerging U.S. tea market what cappuccino and latte were to the specialty coffee market when it arose a few years ago," according to Brian Keating, founder and president of Sage Group International LLC, a tea market-research company in Seattle, in an *Inc.* article in 2001. Industry watchers continued to debate whether the chai phenomenon was a trend or here to stay. In the meantime, Oregon Chai continued to respond to consumer demand with the introduction of a smaller package and the launch of a new line of powdered instant chai tea latte mixes.

Principal Competitors

Bodhi Chai; LiveChai; Mountain Chai; Pacific Chai; Sattwa Chai; Yogi Tea Company.

Further Reading

Bianchi, Alessandra, "Anatomy of a Start-Up," *Inc.,* September 1997, p. 67.

Cirillo, Joan, "Chai Becomes More People's Cup of Tea," *Baltimore Sun,* August 16, 1995, p. 1E.

Dondero, Tony, "Oregon Chai Brews Growth Plan," *Portland Business Journal,* March 28, 1997, p. 19.

Grund, John, "Chai Rhymes with Bull's-Eye," *Oregon Business,* April 1997, p. 19.

Hill, Jim, "Oregon Chai Hopes Rex Bird Can Work His Magic Again," *Oregonian,* September 24, 1996, p. B16.

Raths, David, "Oregon Chai Steeps in Profits, Recognition," *Portland Business Journal,* June 26, 1998, p. S17.

Sen, Colleen Taylor, "Chai: Tea That's Hot (or Cool) and Hip," *Chicago-Sun Times,* April 15, 1998, p. 1.

—Carrie Rothburd

Penauille Polyservices SA

6, Allee des Conquelicots
94478 Boissy Saint Léger Cedex
France
Telephone: (+33) 1-45-10-64-00
Fax: (+33) 1-45-10-64-10
Web site: http://www.penauille.com

Public Company
Incorporated: 1970 as Etablissements Penauille
Employees: 58,144
Sales: EUR 1.27 billion ($1.12 billion) (2001)
Stock Exchanges: Euronext Paris
Ticker Symbol: PPS
NAIC: 561720 Janitorial Services; 561790 Other Services
    to Buildings and Dwellings; 488119 Other Airport
    Operations; 561612 Security Guards and Patrol
    Services; 488190 Other Support Activities for Air
    Transportation

Fast-rising Penauille Polyservices SA is one of the world's leading commercial services companies, operating through two primary divisions: Business Services, including cleaning, security, maintenance and engineering, call center and switchboard management, luxury printing and packaging, temporary personnel, and other services, and which accounts for about 46 percent of the company's annual revenues; and Airport Services, operated through subsidiaries Servisair and Globeground, which is the world's leading provider of ground-handling services to major and mid-sized airports, which represented 54 percent of the company's sales of nearly EUR 1.27 billion in 2001. While Penauille's Business Services division remains highly focused on France, where it is market leader, its Airport Services component has made it an internationally operating company, with a presence in more than 200 airports in 40 countries worldwide, and providing services to some 850 airlines. Europe remains the company's single largest market, representing more than 85 percent of sales; the company has been building a presence in the United States, which contributed about 13 percent of sales. Penauille's positioning in Airport Services—built largely on the

acquisitions of Servisair in 1999 and Globeground in 2001—has given the company a strategic position in the upcoming deregulation of the European airline industry, slated for 2003. Penauille is led by founder and majority shareholder Jean-Claude Penauille and is quoted on the Euronext Paris stock exchange.

Cleaning Up France in the 1970s

Jean-Claude Penauille founded Etablissements Penauille in 1970 as a cleaning operation targeting the commercial business market. Penauille's company grew throughout the 1970s, remaining focused on the Paris region. Toward the end of the decade, however, Penauille sought to expand his business into other areas of France. At the same time, Penauille wanted to try out a number of management theories he had been developing, particularly that of building up a network of largely autonomous business units.

In 1979, Penauille made its first acquisition, purchasing another cleaning operation in the center of France. Penauille was later to make it a practice of leaving in place existing managers, who were given responsibility for the subsidiaries' day-to-day decisions. In this way, Penauille was able to remain responsive to its growing number of local markets.

The company's success in integrating this first subsidiary encouraged it to expand its network, and in 1981 the company began opening a series of branch offices. Once again, local managers were given a great deal of independence—and responsibility. While Penauille expanded into new geographic markets, it also began looking to expand into new business areas. In 1985, the company added a new cleaning segment, that of the hospital market, when it acquired two companies, both based in the Paris region.

Penauille continued to develop its cleaning services operations through the end of the 1980s. Yet the company was already preparing to expand its base of operations and to redefine itself as a ''business services'' company. In 1989, Penauille took its first step toward achieving this expansion when it acquired a company that specialized in providing luxury printing and packaging services to the business market. At the same time, Penauille continued its geographic expansion, adding branch offices in Toulouse, Pau, and Lyons. Then, in 1990, the company launched a new subsidiary in Monaco.

Business Services Group in the 1990s

Penauille was to undergo a dramatic transformation during the 1990s, developing from a relatively minor cleaning company into one of the French market's largest business services providers, before leaping onto the world stage as a major player in the airport services sector. Geographic expansion played a primary role in the company's growth, as it continued to build up its French network with new branch office openings, including eight new offices created in 1991 and five more added in 1992.

Yet much of the company's growth during the period was fueled by a steady series of acquisitions. The first of these came in 1991, when Penauille acquired six smaller companies. These acquisitions also brought the company into a new business area, that of security services. The following year, Penauille continued its acquisition drive, buying up four new cleaning services companies, and adding a new security services company as well. In 1992, also, Penauille took its first step into a promising new market: airport services. Yet this sector was to remain a minor one for the company, in part because of the highly regulated airport industry, which had assured virtual monopoly control over the services segments of the country's airports, barring Penauille from entry.

Penauille continued growing in 1993, adding a new company in the south of France. In that year, also, the company began preparing its public offering, rolling out a new IT system, adding its own training facility, redeveloping its maintenance operations—including building up an engineering component—while continuing to expand its national branch network with the opening of three new offices. The company also instituted a quality program.

The year 1994 represented a turning point for Penauille. The company's national network expanded again, into the Corrèze region, with the purchase of a cleaning services operation located there. Penauille's efforts to achieve higher quality levels were rewarded in 1994 by the granting of ISO 9002 certification to its Boissy-Saint-Léger branch facility. That certification was to become just the first in a series of ISO 9002 and other quality certifications.

By then, Penauille had grown to a company with more than 9,000 employees across a network of more than 60 branches and subsidiaries, which combined to post more than the equivalent of EUR 100 million in annual revenues, giving it the fifth-

place position in the French cleaning and business services sector. That market remained highly fragmented, with more than 9,000 companies, most of which were comprised of less than 50 employees, sharing a market that was already estimated at more than EUR 5 billion at the time.

Penauille recognized the opportunities to be had in consolidating the sector. At the same time, gaining in size was to help it attract a new class of large-scale corporations. The lingering recession of the early 1990s forced more and more companies to seek cost-cutting initiatives, and numbers of corporations now turned toward outsourcing many of the services, including cleaning and maintenance, that had formerly been handled in-house. For this reason, the services sector was to witness strong growth through the 1990s.

Penauille was committed to gaining a primary place in the business services market. The company took a big step toward achieving its growth objectives with the acquisition of cleaning services firm Groupe C in late 1994. Founded in 1975 and boasting annual revenues of more than EUR 30 million, Groupe C helped boost Penauille to within reach of its closest rivals, which at the time included GSF and Abilis.

Global Airport Services Leader in the New Century

In order to finance the Groupe C acquisition and to provide capital for future acquisitions, Penauille went public, selling 16 percent of its shares on the Paris Stock Exchange's secondary market in December 1994. Jean-Claude Penauille was the company's primary shareholder, while much of the remaining stock was held by a solid base of institutional investors. The public offering also led the company to change its name, to Penauille Polyservices, to highlight its diversified services offerings.

The company continued its acquisition drive in 1995, buying up four more companies, all of which were located beyond the company's Paris region headquarters. Penauille continued adding to its quality certifications as well, adding 14 new ISO 9002 certifications in that year, and 12 ISO 9002 certifications in the following year. In 1996, also, Penauille acquired two new cleaning services companies, once again located outside of its Paris home, strengthening the company's national reach. In that year, Penauille diversified into a new services sector, that of industrial services, acquiring a company named Peco.

The following year, Penauille extended its cleaning services operations with the purchase of Net Expansion, a company that specialized in offering cleaning services for nuclear energy facilities. The company also boosted its security component, opening three new branch offices for that operation. In 1998, Penauille acquired RMTI, which gave it climate control and electrical engineering capabilities, bringing Penauille closer to becoming a full-range provider of business services.

Penauille's airport services wing had remained modest throughout the 1990s. That position began to change in 1998, however, when Penauille acquired GSA from French airline AOM. GSA operated ground services, including passenger services, and aircraft handling services, in airports throughout France. The addition of GSA gave Penauille operations in eight of France's airports, including the country's two largest airports, Roissy and Orly.

Key Dates:

1970: Company is founded by Jean-Claude Penauille as Etablissements Penauille, offering cleaning services to the Paris region.

1979: Penauille makes its first acquisition, institutes policy of creating autonomous subsidiary and branch office operations.

1985: Company enters hospital cleaning specialty through acquisition of two companies in Paris region.

1991: Company enters security services; acquires a total of six companies during the year.

1992: Penauille begins airports services operations.

1994: Company acquires Groupe C and takes a listing on the Paris Stock Exchange's secondary market.

1996: Company acquires Peco, adding industrial services capacity.

1997: Company acquires Net Expansion, which specializes in cleaning services for nuclear facilities.

1998: Penauille acquires AOM subsidiary GSA, an airport services provider; acquires RMTI, which adds electrical engineering services to the business services portfolio.

1999: Company acquires Servisair, the leading airport services company in the United Kingdom.

2000: Company acquires ICS, the leading U.K. airplane cleaning company; acquires Global and Tri-Star Aviation, both airport services providers in the United States.

2001: Penauille purchases 51 percent of Globeground, the ground handling and airport services subsidiary of Lufthansa.

2002: Penauille completes acquisition of Globeground, becoming the world's leading airport services group.

Penauille had been making strong growth gains, nearing EUR 200 million in 1996, topping EUR 300 million in 1997, and soaring past EUR 400 million in 1998. Yet airport services remained the smallest part of the company's operation, at about 25 percent of sales. Meanwhile, Penauille remained wholly focused on the French market, despite the increasing internationalization of its core businesses and its major clients. The decision by the European Community to deregulate the region's airports, which, for the most part remained monopoly controlled, also promised a new era of international competition.

In 1999, Penauille played the white knight to England's Servisair Plc, which was fighting off a hostile takeover attempt by construction-turned-services group Amey Plc. Servisair accepted Penauille's buyout offer, which not only topped Amey's bid, but also promised to leave Servisair's management in place. Indeed, Servisair was quickly to become Penauille's international airport services brand.

Servisair had been founded in 1954 by the British and Commonwealth Shipping Company, taking on the name Servisair in 1967. Dedicated to ground handling and airport services such as passenger ticketing and check-in services from the start, Servisair benefited when the United Kingdom became one of the first European countries to abolish services monopolies in many of its airports. Servisair grew strongly, and by the 1990s had become the largest independent airport services group in the United Kingdom.

Servisair had not limited itself to the United Kingdom; the company had begun expanding internationally in the mid-1980s, acquiring operations in the Netherlands and establishing offices in Spain and Portugal, before expanding to the Republic of Ireland at the end of the decade. Servisair went public in 1994, listing on the London Stock Exchange, then continued its expansion, with operations in Sweden, Norway, and Denmark.

Penauille's £94 million offer transformed the company into an international operation and one of the largest airport services companies in Europe, with revenues of more than EUR 920 million by 2000. In that year, Penauille entered the U.S. market, acquiring two ground handling services businesses, Global, based in Cleveland, and Tri-Star Aviation, based in Dallas/Ft. Worth. Placed under its Servisair subsidiary, the acquisitions gave Penauille operations in airports in 18 cities in the United States. These acquisitions also helped complete the internationalization of Penauille's sales—with 50 percent of the company's revenues now coming from outside of France.

Penauille's operations were now more or less evenly divided between its airport services and business services divisions. If the former was to become the company's largest revenue generator, at 56 percent of 2001 sales, Penauille was not neglecting the latter's growth. Already in 1999, the company had continued to strengthen its French presence, buying a company in Angers, which also gave it offices in the north of France. In that year, also, Penauille took its first steps in internationalizing its business services operation, launching subsidiaries in Italy and Portugal. Then, in 2000, Penauille brought its business services division into Spain, with the acquisition of that country's Selmarsa, a cleaning company.

Penauille continued to build on its two divisions through 2001, notably with the acquisitions of Groupe Capricorne, which gave it cleaning services operations in the Brittany region, and GEC, which operated in the country's southeastern region. At the same time, Penauille moved to expand its business services divisions on the international scene, acquiring Knights, based in the Republic of Ireland.

Yet airport services remained the company's most dynamic division. In April 2000, Penauille acquired ICS, the leading airplane cleaning services provider in the United Kingdom, which operated in 17 airports in England and Ireland. Then, in May 2001, Penauille announced that it had reached an agreement with Germany's Lufthansa to acquire that company's airport services wing, Globeground. The purchase, which was to take place in a two-step process to be completed in July 2002 for a total cost of more than EUR 350 million, transformed Penauille into the world's leading airport services company, adding operations in more than 115 airports worldwide—bringing Penauille's operations to a total of 200 airports in 40 countries and on four continents, and pro forma revenues of more than EUR 1.5 billion.

The deregulation of Europe's airports was slated for 2003, giving Penauille the prospect of large new markets for its future expansion. At the same time, the company was able to look forward to a continued boom in the business services sector, as the trend toward outsourcing was expected to remain strong in the new century. Penauille intended to remain a leading player, looking forward to the coming consolidation of the as yet highly fragmented business services market.

Principal Subsidiaries

Penauille: Globeground: Globeground Holding (Germany; 51%); Etablissements Penauille; Protecnet; Penauille Ingenierie; Sarema; Sam Sarema; Generale de Prestations; Nef Entreprises; Penauille Polysecurite; TAT; KMI; C'Vert; Miroir 2000; Rev; Aubnet; Polyurbaine; Trocme; Proclean; GEC; Capricorne Proprete; GES; Selmar (Spain); Penauille Italia; Safira (Portugal; 49%); Knights (Ireland; 75%); Polyassistance Aeroportuaire Servisair: Servisair Plc (U.K.); Servisair Holding BV (Netherlands); Servisair Greece; Servisair Asia Ltd (Hong Kong); Servisair Norge Ltd (Norway); Servisair Ireland Ltd; Servisair Denmark A/S; Servisair Deutschland GmbH; Servisair Itali Spa; Servisair Espana SA; Servisair Portugal Lda; Servisair France SA; Heathrow Cargo Handling Ltd (U.K.; 50%); Global Ground Services Inc. (U.S.A.); Servisair Inc. (U.S.A.).

Principal Divisions

Business Services; Airport Services.

Principal Competitors

ISS A/S; Jacobs Engineering Group Inc.; Rentokil Initial plc; ServiceMaster Co. (SVM); Grupo Ferrovial SA; Ecolab Inc.; All Star Maintenance Inc.; Societe d'Amenagement Urbain et Rural; Toyo Construction Co Ltd.; ABM Industries Inc.; SOGEA; Kier Group plc; Sanitors Southwest Inc.; Vorwerk und Co.; P Dussmann GmbH und Co KG; Austin Industries Inc.; Covanta Energy Corp.; Spotless Group Ltd.; One Source; Tokyu Community Corp.; Sho-Bond Corp.; MITIE Group PLC; Asea Brown Boveri NV/SA; Pedus Services Inc.; O.C.S Group Ltd.; ISS France SA; Japan Maintenance Co Ltd.; VA TECH ELIN EGB GmbH; Unicco Service Co.; Eulen SA.

Further Reading

Cori, Nicholas, and Hubert Tassin, "Un entretien avec Jean-Claude Penauille," *Journal des Finances*, August 23, 1999.

Fainsilber, Denis, "Penauille devrait acquerir le britannique Servisair," *Les Echos*, March 15, 1999, p. 24.

Mason, Jeff, "Lufthansa to Sell Ground Services to Penauille," *Reuters*, May 30, 2001.

"Penauille Plans Share Sale to Finance Acquisition," *Reuters*, May 31, 2001.

Secondi, Jacques, "Peanuaille s'occupe de tout," *Nouvel Economiste*, May 3, 2002.

—M. L. Cohen

Phat Fashions LLC

512 7th Avenue
New York, New York 10018
U.S.A.
Telephone: (212) 391-9443
Fax: (212) 391-9448
Web site: http://www.phatfarm.com

Division of Rush Communications
Founded: 1992
Employees: 30
Sales: $150 million (2001 est.)
NAIC: 315223 Men's and Boys' Cut and Sew Shirt (Except Work Shirt) Manufacturing; 315224 Men's and Boys' Cut and Sew Trouser, Slack, and Jean Manufacturing; 315232 Women's and Girls' Cut and Sew Blouse and Shirt Manufacturing; 315239 Women's and Girls' Cut and Sew Other Outerwear Manufacturing; 315999 Other Apparel Accessories and Other Apparel Manufacturing

Phat Fashions LLC, using the Phat Farm and Baby Phat labels, is the apparel segment of Rush Communications, one of the most successful African American-owned media companies in the United States. "Phat" is street slang for "the ultimate," and according to some is an acronym for "pretty hot and tempting." For almost 20 years founder and CEO Russell Simmons has successfully marketed rap and hip-hop music and culture to a mass audience. Phat Fashions since its inception in 1992 has moved beyond the design and marketing of urban hip-hop male clothing to include fashions for women and children. In more recent years, Simmons's wife, former model Kimora Lee, has assumed a large measure of responsibility for growing the business, helping to transform Phat Fashions into a true lifestyle brand, including the introduction of perfume and jewelry, and plans for cosmetics, bedding, and other non-fashion items. Not only is the merchandise sold in two company-owned Phat Farm stores in New York and Montreal and on the company's web site, its clothing lines are carried by some 3,000 U.S. retail locations, including distribution through Federated Department Stores, Macy's, and Bloomingdale's.

Russell Simmons and Rap Music: Late 1970s

Russell Simmons grew up in a lower-middle-class neighborhood of Queens, New York, a short distance from a well-known drug-dealing area. As the age of 13 he entered the drug trade, was arrested twice, but managed to avoid serving any jail time and by 1975 enrolled in college at New York's City College, studying sociology. Around this time rap music was beginning to emerge from the streets of Harlem and the Bronx. He not only became enamored with the music and its lifestyle, he recognized a business opportunity. He made friends with party promoters and began to put together his own shows on campus and even at an area roller rink. He also turned to managing some of the acts he promoted, creating Rush Management, drawing on his childhood nickname of "Rush" for the name of his new venture. He quickly proved that he had a knack for knowing how to sell rap, and eventually dropped out of school to run the business full-time.

Simmons first gained widespread attention as the founder of Def Jam Records, which he established with Rick Rubin in 1983. On the surface they were an incongruous pair. Rubin, white and wealthy, grew up in Long Island listening to progressive punk music of the 1970s, dismayed that most of the students at his high school were far more interested in the rock sounds of such groups as the Doors, Led Zeppelin, and Pink Floyd. Rubin then discovered rap music, years later telling *Rolling Stone*, "I liked rap but might not have been as interested if people had accepted the Ramones and the Talking Heads at first." Rubin began to attend rap shows at New York University, where he began his studies in 1981, but in addition attended clubs where he realized the importance of the DJ in rap and the technique of scratching on records. He planned to attend law school, but as a hobby began to produce rap records employing scratching on his own independent label that he called Def Jam, running the enterprise, funded by his family, out of his dorm room. By now Simmons was also involved in producing some records, essentially as a way to promote his acts. When Simmons met Rubin, he was surprised that the

Key Dates:

1983: Russell Simmons helps found Def Jam Records.
1991: Simmons begins operating on a number of fronts through an umbrella company named Rush Communications.
1992: Phat Fashions is created.
1993: Baby Phat is launched.
1998: Phat Fashions turns to licensing strategy.
2001: Baby Phat does first solo fashion show.

young producer was white, but very much respected his work and the two became friends.

It was Rubin who suggested in 1982 that he and Simmons form their own record company using the Def Jam name. Simmons was reluctant at first because he wanted to sign many of his artists to a production deal with a major label. According to a *Rolling Stone* interview with Rubin, he convinced Simmons by saying, ''Look, you already think this record is a hit. Here's what we're going to do—I'll produce all the records. I'll do the business. I'll run the company.'' Simmons signed on and by 1985 Def Jam had achieved enough success to gain the attention of CBS Records, which offered a generous distribution deal that took the label to a much higher level. A year later, Def Jam debuted one of the most influential artists in rap, 17-year-old LL Cool J. The label followed that success with the unlikely act of The Beastie Boys, three white Jewish boys from the Bronx.

Despite their success together, Rubin and Simmons eventually began to grow apart, and by 1990 dissolved their partnership, with Simmons and CBS retaining Def Jam. Simmons also began to launch a number of other ventures, which he organized under an umbrella company he called Rush Communications. In 1991 he teamed with top Hollywood producers Bernie Brillstein and Brad Grey to develop ''Def Comedy Jam,'' featuring emerging African American comedians. The show proved to be an immediate hit for HBO, further establishing Simmons's reputation in the entertainment industry. His move into fashion was not surprising, given the importance of clothing to hip-hop culture, the fans imitating the looks that their favorite artists assumed on stage and in their videos, but his admitted motivation was more basic: He liked to date models.

Launch of Phat Fashions: 1992

Simmons created Phat Fashions in 1992 and began selling his Phat Farm line of clothing at a small shop located on Prince street in Manhattan's trendy SoHo district. To help him in an unfamiliar business he teamed with Marc Bagutta, who owned his own Soho boutique. The line's designers, neither formally trained, were a pair of 22-year-old former skateboarding graffiti artists named Alyasha Jibtil Owerka-Moore and Eli Morgan Gesner, who grew up together in New York. Perhaps Simmons's most important contribution to the venture was his ability to put prominent rap artists in Phat clothes. Nevertheless, both he and the designers shied away from the hip-hop tag or being pigeonholed simply as makers of clothes for urban teens. Rather, they suggested the line offered classic clothes, and in truth the designers were clearly

influenced by Ralph Lauren, Timberland, and Tommy Hilfiger. This connection was not surprising, however, because these were the clothes, albeit sized too large, that teenagers from Brooklyn and the Bronx were wearing when the hip-hop style evolved. Phat Fashions, no matter what its philosophy, was successful from the outset, generating some $2 million in sales during its first year of operation, and subsequently was picked up by specialty stores across the country.

The initial clothing for Phat Fashions was geared towards the urban male, but in 1993 a women's line, Baby Phat, was launched. A fitted T-shirt line not only proved popular, it also helped in building brand awareness. To help grow the burgeoning apparel company, Simmons brought in Martin Kace in 1996 to reorganize the business and serve as the first independent president and CEO of a Rush Communications' division. Kace had considerable experience in the industry, his latest post before joining Phat being the chairmanship of Joe Boxer Corp. Kace oversaw the design of a 4,500-square-foot showroom and office, but otherwise results did not meet Simmons's expectations and in 1998 he elected to again restructure the company, which he felt had been plagued by sourcing and production problems.

Simmons now chose to follow a licensing strategy for Phat Fashions, and after meeting with a number of potential partners, decided to form a joint venture with Turbo Sportswear, a 20-year-old Perth Amboy, New Jersey, active outerwear manufacturer known for producing such brands as First Down, Triple F.A.T. Goose, and Phenom. The partners formed a new company, American Design Group (ADG), which would be awarded the master license for Phat Farm apparel. Simmons retained ownership of Phat Fashions and became president of ADG. Through the new venture, the partners hoped to achieve the kind of upscale distribution that Simmons had originally envisioned for Phat, expanding beyond urban ethnic to compete more evenly with the likes of Tommy Hilfiger, Calvin Klein, and Ralph Lauren. As part of the deal, a sub-brand called All-City Athletique was formed under ADG to produce more athletic-styled looks at a lower price point to complement the Phat Farm label. In addition, ADG would relaunch the Baby Phat line through a licensing agreement. ADG signed a number of initial licensing agreements for Phat Fashions, including outerwear to Turbo Sportswear, underwear to Ruby Azark, children's to Parigi, a casual walking shoe to Vida, and leather to Comet International.

Also in 1998 Simmons married Kimora Lee, who would soon have a major impact on Phat Fashions through her designs for the Baby Phat line. Lee, half-Japanese and half-African American, grew up in St. Louis. By the age of ten she stood 5'8'' and reached her adult height of six feet as a teenager. Because Lee was the object of childhood taunts, her mother enrolled her in a modeling workshop at the early age of 11. Her exotic look did not go unnoticed for long: By age 13 she was appearing on Paris runways, ultimately becoming the face of Chanel. She first met Simmons in 1992 when he was 35 and she was just 17. They later became better acquainted when Lee served as the host of Simmons's magazine-format television show, *Oneworld,* devoted to urban youth culture.

In 1999 worldwide licensing rights to Baby Phat were awarded to Aris Industries, renewable for up to 25 years. Aris's

CEO, Arnold Simon, brought with him nearly 30 years of experience in the apparel industry and involvement in the licensing of such recognizable brands as Calvin Klein Sportswear, Perry Ellis, Members Only, and FUBU. Both Phat Fashions and Aris expressed a desire to grow Baby Phat into a global brand. Later in 1999 Aris also received a license to design a line of junior sportswear under Baby Phat. Unlike the male Phat Farm line, the new junior clothes were intended to be less street influenced.

Phat Fashions continued to broaden its horizons in the year 2000. It launched a lingerie line, licensed to International Intimates, and designed and inspired by Lee. The first collection targeted the 18- to 34-year-old woman and was intended to be sold in department stores and specialty boutiques, as well as Phat Farm stores. Also in 2000 plans for a Harlem flagship megastore were announced. In addition to Phat clothing, the 14,000-square-foot outlet planned to carry other lines such as ''Puff Daddy'' Combs, Polo, and Versace, plus merchandise that ranged from home furnishings to jewelry and even pagers. According to Simmons, the Harlem operation was a lifestyle store, ''the first of what should be many, many stores.'' He took another step in transforming Phat into a lifestyle brand later in 2000 when he signed a licensing agreement with Stern Fragrances to produce a fragrance collection for the Phat Farm and Baby Phat labels. The first offering, named Premium, a Phat Farm product, debuted in 2001. It was supported by the launch of a small clothing collection called Premium, which was also positioned as part of Phat Fashion's ten-year anniversary.

First Solo Show for Baby Phat: 2001

Highlighting 2001 was Kimora Lee and Baby Phat's first solo show of its sportswear collection, presented at the prestigious ''7th on Sixth'' annual event in Manhattan's Bryant Park. Although everything produced under the Baby Phat label was made under licenses, Lee's influence was considerable, ranging from design aspects to advertising. In only two years since the relaunch of Baby Phat, the line reached $30 million in annual sales, a mark that Phat Farm took six years to accomplish. Also debuting at the show was Baby Phat's new costume jewelry line, produced by Lee Angel. In the spring of 2001 Baby Phat, under a licensing agreement with Noho Leather, did a test launch of leather outerwear and sportswear, which received a major rollout later in the year. Baby Phat also made plans to open its first freestanding shop, to be located near the Phat Farm store in Soho. Moreover, Phat Fashions prepared to relocate to a larger showroom at 512 Seventh Avenue, a move finally accomplished in August 2002.

In 2001 Phat Fashions looked to improve its footwear business. Phat Farm, attempting to find a niche not dominated by the likes of Nike, launched a new athletic footwear line that combined casual uppers with athletic outsoles, as well as attempted to reflect an attitude shared by the company and its customers. Baby Phat, as well, made plans to launch its own footwear line. By now the Baby Phat line under Lee's guidance was the driving force behind Phat Fashions and was very much the spearhead for making Phat into a lifestyle brand. Unlike other fashion companies influenced by the hip-hop culture that burned brightly for a brief moment of time, Phat Fashion after ten years in existence appeared to have established itself as a business poised for growth beyond the fate of the music scene that originally inspired it.

Principal Divisions

Phat Farm; Baby Fat.

Principal Competitors

FUBU; Karl Kani Infinity, Inc.; Tommy Hilfiger Corporation.

Further Reading

Espinoza, Galina, ''Phat Cats,'' *People Weekly,* July 1, 2001, p. 97.

Gault, Yolanda, ''Hip-Hop Fashions Phatter Than Ever,'' *Crain's New York Business,* August 17, 1998, p. 3.

Greenberg, Julee, ''Baby Phat Takes a Big Step,'' *WWD,* January 31, 2002, p. 10.

Hughes, Alan, ''Phat Profits,'' *Black Enterprise,* June 2002, pp. 148–56.

Romero, Elena, ''Phat Farm Grazing in New Pasture,'' *Daily News Record,''* June 22, 1998, p. 6.

Seliger, M., and A. Light, ''Kings of Rap,'' *Rolling Stone,* November 15, 1990, p. 106.

Simpson, Janice, ''The Impresario of Rap,'' *Time,* May 4, 1992, p. 69.

Vaughn, Christopher, *Black Enterprise,* December 1992, p. 66.

Wadyka, Sally, ''Style with a Street Beat,'' *Mademoiselle,* March 1993, p. 54.

—Ed Dinger

Phillips, de Pury & Luxembourg

3 West 57th Street
New York, New York 10019
U.S.A.
Telephone: (212) 940-1200
Fax: (212) 688-1647
Web site: http://www.phillips-auctions.com

Private Company
Founded: 1796
Employees: 500
Sales: $223.9 million (2000)
NAIC: 453998 Auction Houses; 453920 Art Dealers

Phillips, de Pury & Luxembourg is the world's third largest auction house, but lags well behind the much better known Sotheby's and Christie's. Established in England more than 200 years ago, Phillips has been based in New York since 2001 and continues to maintain offices in London and other major cities around the world, as well as a salesroom in Geneva, and a gallery and salesroom in Zurich. With Sotheby's and Christie's reeling from a price-fixing scandal, Phillips has attempted in recent years to take advantage of the situation to move aggressively into the high-profile art market and transcend its reputation as an essentially British rural concern that handles the contents of country estates and second-tier art works. After some initial success Phillips has stepped back from its aggressive play in the fine arts market.

Birth of an Auction House: 1796

The great auction houses of the world were established in England in the 1700s. Sotheby's, founded by a Mr. Baker, held its first sale in 1745, auctioning off a collection of books. The house focused on books for many years, gaining prestige for handling the sale of books that belonged to such notable people as Napoleon and Telleyrand. Former midshipman James Christie established his auction house in 1766 and developed a reputation for art sales. It was not until World War I that Sotheby's set out to challenge Christie's dominance in art, resulting in today's well-known rivalry between the two concerns. Phillips was established in 1796 by Harry Phillips, Chris-

tie's former head clerk, a man of ambition as well as flamboyance. Despite lacking the funds to hire a staff or lease his own premises, he was still able to conduct a dozen sales during his first year in business. He also showed a willingness to handle a wide variety of items, from tea services to a saddle mare. Phillips focused on the aristocracy, especially the auctioning off of the contents of their country estates, and became the house of choice in these matters. In fact, Phillips was the only auction house ever to hold a sale in Buckingham Palace. Among the famous estates Phillips handled were Beau Brummel, Marie Antoinette, and Napoleon.

Phillips's business began to prosper in short order and he was able to open a salesroom on New Bond Street in London's West End. He displayed an innovative spirit, establishing practices still followed today. To promote important auctions he held them at night following a lavish reception. Harry Phillips ran the auction house until his death in 1840, leaving a highly successful business to his son, William Augustus Phillips. For many years the second generation Phillips ran the business as the sole proprietor, then in 1879 brought in his son as a partner, changing the name of the company to "Messrs Phillips & Son." Three years later his son-in-law Frederick Neale joined the company and the name was amended to "Phillips, Son & Neale." Control of the auction house passed out of the hands of the Phillips's family in the 1930s when Edwin and Robert Hawkins took over. In 1939 the Phillips' home of more than 100 years on New Bond Street was destroyed by fire and a new headquarters was established across the street.

Christopher Weston bought the business in the early 1970s. Also in that decade the company returned to its "Phillips" name, while at the same time it finally began to broaden its reach after nearly 200 years of a staid existence. Not only was a regional network established in Britain, Phillips opened offices in New York City, Sydney, and Zurich. Despite these advances under Weston the auction house finally began to garner widespread attention only after he sold his 96 percent stake in Phillips in January 1998 as part of a merger with Foster & Cranfield, another venerable British auctioneer. Established in 1843, Foster & Cranfield specialized in life assurance policies, interests in trusts, and the sale of other financial assets. The resulting enterprise was named Phillips Auction Group and under new management the British provincial network was cut back.

Acquisition of Phillips by LVMH: 1998

Less than two years later ownership of Phillips changed once again, at a time when the major auction houses drew the attention of arch-rival French luxury goods purveyors François Pinault and Bernard Arnault. First, Pinault, who controlled Pinault-Printemps-Redoute, acquired Christie's in May 1998. Arnault, who controlled LVMH Moët Hennessy Louis Vuitton, responded by attempting to acquire Sotheby's. When that effort failed, he turned to Phillips a year later and in November 1999 purchased the business for approximately $110 million. His intention of creating a luxury conglomerate and building up the reputation of Phillips in the art world was given a boost a few months later when in February 2000 it was revealed that Christie's and Sotheby's were the subjects of a New York grand jury investigation, which was looking into whether the world's two largest auction houses had colluded on an increase in commission charges in 1992 and 1995. The scandal quickly forced Sotheby's chairman, Alfred Taubman, to resign. Seven months later Christie's agreed to pay $256 million to settle the matter, and Sotheby's and Taubman agreed to pay $326 million.

With trust in Christie's and Sotheby's severely shaken, Arnault attempted to take advantage of the opening to compete in the fine art market with Phillips. According to the *Wall Street Journal*, ''Arnault announced that he would cherry-pick only the best art and leave the dross to online auction sites or his rivals. He began spending freely on star paintings, lavish parties and celebrity appearances. At Phillips' first major sale, actress Sharon Stone strolled the aisles in a red dress, stroking sculptures during the bidding. People close to the company put the amount he is willing to lose to establish the Phillips brand at $250 million.'' Despite Arnault's willingness to spend money, Phillips' spring sale in New York was not a success. Nevertheless, the perennially third ranked auction house was causing a stir and changing the traditional way the auction world operated. Phillips not only made lavish guarantees of a minimum sale price in order to lure major works of art, it began to buy collections outright. Instead of acting as a middleman between buyers and sellers, it was taking on inventory. Many sellers continued to rely on Christie's and Sotheby's, but others, especially estate attorneys with no ties to tradition, were won over by Phillips' generous terms. The *Wall Street Journal* reported that ''some Sotheby's executives fret that Mr. Arnault's real plan is to depress Sotheby's stock and try again to buy the company. Mr. Arnault has said that's not his goal.''

With Phillips struggling to reach its targets at its major evening sales, in December 2000 Arnault merged the auction house with de Pury & Luxembourg, a private dealership based in Geneva operated by two former Sotheby's executives who left in 1997 to start their own business. They advised some of the world's wealthiest art collectors, including Ronald Lauder, Monique Barbier-Muller, Sammy Ofer, and Rolf and Margit Weinberg. Simon de Pury had been chairman of Sotheby's Europe and was a trilingual auctioneer, while his partner Daniella Luxembourgh was the former deputy chairman of Sotheby's Switzerland. The new entity resulting from the merger was named Phillips, de Pury & Luxembourg, with the Geneva dealership continuing its operations as a subsidiary. In addition, the expanded Phillips prepared to open an 8,600-square-foot gallery in Zurich, which was slated to hold four shows a year. The main business of Phillips, according to top management, would be focused on paintings, jewelry, and furniture, the most profitable areas in the auction world. Electing to remain relatively small, the company eschewed the less profitable businesses of Christie's and Sotheby's, including books, wines, and even collectibles such as paperweights. While its rivals maintained some 70 expert departments, Phillips chose to operate with about 10 specialties, concentrating on the high end of the auction business, in particular Impressionist and modern paintings, and fine jewelry.

De Pury was named chairman of Phillips and moved quickly to bring in another former Sotheby's executive to serve as chief executive of a revitalized North American operation in New York. In January 2001 he chose John Block, a senior Sotheby's auctioneer, who had been vice-chairman of Sotheby's North America as well as co-chairman of its worldwide jewelry department. In addition to day-to-day responsibilities for the running of Phillips North America, Block was also slated to head the firm's jewelry department worldwide. To assist him in this endeavor, he raided Sotheby's, taking several jewelry experts with him to Phillips. The New York operation was later strengthened in 2001 with the opening of a new headquarters at 3 West 57th Street in midtown Manhattan, after Phillips had spent almost 20 years at an Upper East Side address. The new home of the auction house, which was conveniently located close to the 57th Street headquarters of LVMH, was a 54-year-old, 12-story limestone building, for which Phillips would be the sole tenant. Because the ground floor had been formerly occupied by a bank, it featured 16-foot-high ceilings without columns, a perfect set-up for Phillips' main auction salesroom, able to seat close to 300 people. Smaller salesrooms located on the third and fourth floors were able to seat 150. Moreover, the new location permitted Phillips to have all of its salesrooms, exhibition spaces, meeting rooms for clients, and executive offices all under the same roof. It was clearly the flagship office of the auction house and Phillips subsequently moved its headquarters from London to New York.

2001 Spring Sale a Disappointment

While Phillips completed the move to its new home it was able to conduct sales in the renovated sections of the 57th Street location. It also continued its practice of extravagant spending in order to acquire market share, very much like a dotcom startup. In February 2001 Phillips purchased an important collection of 19th-century paintings and drawings from Berlin-based dealer Heinz Berggruen. Included were five works by Cezanne and two by van Gogh, the star of the collection being Cezanne's ''La Montagne Ste. Victoire.'' Phillips then used the acquisition as the foundation of the all-important New York spring sale of Impres-

Key Dates:

1796: Harry Phillips founds auction house.
1840: Harry Phillips dies and ownership passes to his son, William Augustus Phillips.
1879: Company name is changed to ''Messrs Phillips & Son.''
1872: Son-in-law joins firm, now called ''Phillips, Son & Neale.''
1939: Longtime London showroom burns down.
1999: LVMH acquires controlling interest.
2000: Phillips merges with de Pury & Luxembourg.
2002: Management-led investors acquire controlling interest.

sionist and modern art, which many saw as a major test for the flashy upstart. Also included in the sale were two highly prized Renoirs owned by financier Henry Kravis. His decision to entrust Phillips rather than Sotheby's, on whose board he sat, became the talk of the art world and continued to generate buzz about the ambitious number three auction house. Clearly the Kravis decision was simply based on the high guaranteed price that Phillips offered, prompting many to criticize Phillips for inflating prices. De Pury maintained that the firm was simply doing what the other houses had practiced for years. In the end, however, the spring sale fell far short of Phillips' expectations, by more than $40 million according to the *Wall Street Journal*, which also speculated that the poor results may have been a ''sign of some reluctance among buyers to trust Phillips price estimates given its financial interests in the property.''

Although Arnault's lavish spending had garnered tremendous attention for Phillips, it also created unusually high expectations that made it difficult for management to portray the spring sale as a positive step for the auction house. Nevertheless, Simon de Pury maintained that Phillips would now be taken seriously in the art world and continued to act on that belief. Shortly after the spring sale he hired a global chief executive officer, a new post for the company, naming Anne Sutherland Fuchs, a woman whose ties to the art world were limited to a trustee position and fundraising for the Whitney Museum of American Art. Her management experience was at The Hearst Corporation's publishing unit, where she headed women's magazines and worked closely with LVMH executives who had involvement with women's and luxury magazines. Like the rest of Phillips' top-heavy stable of executives, she expressed excitement and confidence over the company's boutique approach and focus on select categories of the high-end art world. Arnault, the man who was bankrolling Phillips' entry into this rarified world, apparently began to have second thoughts about the cost of gaining a place at the table with the established auctioneers. When he asked Phillips to trim costs and eliminate its generous price guarantees, sellers simply returned to Christie's or Sotheby's, his money proving to have only leased a temporary share of the art market.

In November 2001 Phillips initiated a restructuring of its business. The U.K. interests were merged with Bonhams & Brooks, another firm with roots that reached back 200 years.

The Bonhams auction house was founded in 1793 and was the smallest of the four London auctioneers. It specialized in collecting esoterica rather than fine art. Brooks was founded in 1989 as a classic and collectors' car auction house, Bonhams and Brooks merged in 2000, less than a year before merging with Phillips, which gained a 49.9 percent stake in the resulting enterprise. Phillips's lower-end art sales were transferred to Bonhams and Brooks, allowing it to focus on its boutique business model. Despite this effort to streamline the business, Arnault was no longer interested in Phillips, and in February 2002 LVHM sold off a controlling interest in the firm to de Pury and other investors.

De Pury quickly moved to replace Fuchs with T. Blouin MacBain, who was a relative newcomer to the art world. Like Fuchs, MacBain had considerable publishing experience; she was the founder of and 14-year CEO of Hebdo Mag Group with nearly 300 publications and over 60 web sites. Perhaps of more importance she knew de Pury from the Hamptons, and according to de Pury, ''She's a very important part of my private life.'' She announced that Phillips would be realigned further, with each department acting as its own profit center. Her approach to woo customers away from Christie's and Sotheby's was to win them over with extra attention, customer service that bordered on pampering. Many in the industry, however, expressed strong doubts that Phillips, at a time when the supply of art was limited, would be able to procure enough works to sell. With the key New York spring sale of Impressionist and modern art fast approaching, Phillips faced a challenge to cobble together enough property to stock its sale. In the end, the auctioneer was unable to convince art sellers and estate attorneys to trust them with important works and it was forced to cancel the sale, an unquestioned humiliation in the art world and a major setback. Phillips's bid to challenge Christie's and Sotheby's, despite the difficulties endured by both, had simply run its course. According to press reports, Phillips now considered relocating its headquarters back to London.

Principal Competitors

Butterfield's; Christie's International plc; Sotheby's Holdings, Inc.

Further Reading

Labi, Aisha, ''The Highest Bidder,'' *Time International,* May 7, 2001, p. 46.

Peers, Alexandra, ''LVMH's Risky Auction Bid,'' *Wall Street Journal,* May 10, 2001, p. B1.

——, ''Phillips Plans to Postpone Big Spring Sale, May Return Base to London,'' *Wall Street Journal,* April 4, 2002, p. B1.

Sorkin, Andrew Ross, and Carol Vogel, ''LVMH Luxury Conglomerate Sells Its Art Auction House,'' *New York Times,* February 20, 2002, p. C1.

Souccar, Miriam Kreinin, ''Phillips Makes Bid to Be a Top House on Auction Block,'' *Crain's New York Business,* May 7, 2001, p. 4.

Vogel, Carol, ''Phillips Buys Cezanne and Van Gogh Collection and Plans an Auction,'' *New York Times,* February 8, 2001, p. E1.

——, ''An Upstart Auctioneer Digs In,'' *New York Times,* February 28, 2002, p. E1.

—Ed Dinger

Pilot Corporation

5508 Lonas Road
Knoxville, Tennessee 37909
U.S.A.
Telephone: (865) 588-7487
Fax: (865) 450-2800
Web site: http://www.pilotcorp.com

Private Company
Incorporated: 1958
Employees: 7,209
Sales: $1.76 billion (2000)
NAIC: 447110 Gasoline Stations with Convenience
    Stores

Pilot Corporation is one of the largest independent retailers of over-the-road diesel fuel, as well as one of the top 25 largest restaurant franchises in the United States. The company operates approximately 235 travel centers spread across 35 states through a joint venture with SuperAmerica LLC, a wholly owned subsidiary of Marathon Ashland Petroleum. CEO James Haslam III and his family own Pilot, which also manages more than 60 convenience stores in Tennessee and Virginia.

One Tiny Gas Station: 1958

The history of Pilot Corporation begins with the story of James A. Haslam II, an athlete who played starting tackle for the University of Tennessee football team. After he graduated in 1952, Haslam joined the U.S. Army and served a tour of duty in the Korean War. Upon his return, he began looking for a job. He began working for Fleet Oil Co., an independent enterprise based in LaFollette, Tennessee.

"Dad always wanted his own business," said James A. Haslam III, son of the founder, in a 1998 interview in *Nation's Restaurant News*. Consequently, in 1958, after saving what money he could from his Fleet Oil job, the elder Haslam went into business for himself, opening the first Pilot gas station "in the heart of the Appalachians," in the small town of Gate City, Virginia.

The first Pilot gas station was a tiny affair, with a mere four pumps for gasoline. In addition to gasoline, Haslam also offered customers the option of purchasing cigarettes and soft drinks at the counter. From these modest beginnings would grow, by the year 2000, an enterprise approaching $2 billion in revenue.

Slowly the company grew, and Haslam added more tiny gas stations here and there throughout the Southeast. In 1965, Pilot Corporation was bringing in some $2 million per year. Casting its acquisitive eye out, Marathon Oil Co.—a fuels giant that began life in 1887 as The Ohio Oil Company—purchased 50 percent of Pilot Corporation. Marathon was focusing, according to its Company Goals, on being "an aggressive, innovative company, constantly seeking improvement, building upon the competitive strengths of our integrated operations, to take advantage of worldwide business opportunities." Marathon thus loaned its tiny new business interest some $4 million, which was earmarked to build new Pilot gas station locations.

Branching Out into the Convenience Store and Restaurant Industries: 1970s–80s

By 1973, Pilot Corporation operated more than 50 stores and was boasting annual sales of $30 million, mostly in gasoline, motor oil, and cigarettes. Pilot's larger partner, Marathon, also continued to grow, acquiring Cleveland-based "Gastown" stations in 1971, Oshkosh-based Consolidated in 1972, and Springfield, Ohio-based Bonded in 1975. It could have turned into a disaster, though. Severe gas shortages hammered the United States in the 1970s. With a huge lack of people with an interest in operating dealer-based gas stations, Marathon was forced to convert many of them into company-operated "Speedway" stores.

Three years later, in 1976, Pilot opened its first convenience store on the Alcoa Highway in Knoxville, Tennessee. The following year, the company bought Lonas Oil Co., also headquartered in Knoxville, converting most of that company's locations into convenience stores.

With 100 convenience stores in 1981, and total annual sales of $175 million, the company opened its first Travel Center in Corbin, Kentucky. The expanded concept included shower facilities for truck drivers on long-haul trips. Some of the first full-length platform scales in the world were installed at some of

Key Dates:

1958: James Haslam II opens the first Pilot in Gate City, Virginia.
1965: Marathon Oil Co. buys half of the $2 million-a-year Pilot and loans $4 million to build new locations.
1973: Pilot has grown to more than 50 stores, with annual sales of $30 million, mostly in gasoline, motor oil, and cigarettes.
1976: Pilot opens its first convenience store on Alcoa Highway in Knoxville, Tennessee.
1977: Pilot buys Lonas Oil Co. in Knoxville, Tennessee, converting most of that company's locations to convenience stores.
1981: With 100 convenience stores and total annual sales of $175 million, Pilot opens its first Travel Center in Corbin, Kentucky.
1985: Pilot adds national restaurant chains to Travel Centers.
1988: Pilot buys out Marathon Oil's one-half interest.
1997: Pilot ranks 99th on *Forbes* magazine's list of the 500 largest privately held companies.
1998: The nation's largest supplier of diesel fuel for over-the-road trucks, Pilot is the 25th largest restaurant franchise in the United States.
2001: Pilot teams with Speedway SuperAmerica LLC to create the joint venture Pilot Travel Centers LLC.

Pilot's Travel Centers by CAT Scale Company. CAT, founded in 1977 by Truckstop entrepreneur Bill Moon, would go on to become the largest truck scale network in the world, supplying scales at most, if not all, Pilot locations, as well as those of some of its competitors, such as Rip Griffin's, Love's Country Stores, and TravelCenters of America.

But in 1981, Pilot's partner, Marathon, was busily fending off a hostile takeover by Mobil Oil. U.S. Steel stepped in to purchase Marathon and then restructured, becoming USX. Marathon Oil, in turn, became the largest and most profitable arm of the new company. USX/Marathon purchased Checker from Exxon in 1983, Ecol in 1984, and Globe in 1985. These brands began appearing in the Speedway stores and in Pilot stores.

In 1984, Pilot started to branch out into the restaurant industry when it opened the first Pilot Kitchen in one of its Travel Centers. It was a deli counter, offering sandwiches, salads, and soups. "It was basically a deli set-up with limited opportunity," said James A. Haslam III in a 1998 interview in *Nation's Restaurant News*. "We realized brands were the way to go." So, Pilot approached Dairy Queen about the possibility of a partnership. DQ liked the idea and, in 1988, the first Pilot Travel Center-based Dairy Queen opened in Hebron, Ohio, and the company's in-store restaurant business was off and running. In 1991, Subway opened its first truck stop location in a Pilot Travel Center.

Also during 1988, some 33 years after Marathon Oil Co. gave Pilot Corporation its much needed infusion of cash, the latter company bought out its larger partner's interest. It would not be the end of the relationship between the two companies, however. Ten years later, in 1998, a merger between Marathon Oil and Ashland Oil divisions created Marathon Ashland Petroleum LLC, which would play a large part in Pilot's life in the 21st century.

Continuing Family Leadership and Company Growth: 1990s and Early 2000s

Somewhere along the way, James Haslam's sons, James A. "Jimmy" Haslam III and William "Bill" Haslam, joined the

family business, taking executive positions. The family followed in the philanthropic footsteps laid down by an earlier generation of Rockefellers and Carnegies. James, the founder, received numerous awards during his career, including two Luminary Awards from the city of Knoxville, for services to the community. He also served as a trustee to the University of Tennessee from 1980–2001; as a key policy advisor to the George W. Bush Administration; as a member of the Knoxville Chapter of the American Marketing Association; and as a member of the board of directors of Tennessee Tomorrow Inc., a public, private, and academic partnership focused on the climate for economic development within Tennessee with emphasis on education and workforce development, among other things. Jimmy would go on to become, in addition to his duties for Pilot, a member of the board of directors of First Tennessee National Corporation and Ruby Tuesday Inc. CEO and President Bill Haslam served on the Knoxville, Tennessee Community Development Corporation from 2001–03. Also during 2001, Bill organized a group of investors (including his brother and father) to purchase the Tennessee Smokies, a local Class AA baseball team, from North Carolina businessman Don Beaver for $7.5 million. "Are we doing this because we think it's the world's greatest financial investment?" asked Bill Haslam in a December 2001 interview in the *Knoxville (Tenn.) News-Sentinel*. "No, that's not why we're doing it. We think it can be a good investment for all of the owners as well as something that is good for the community. And it's fun." It did, however, give the company a chance to be exposed to a broader market by placing advertising in the stadium.

The family also continued to grow the company. By 1997, Pilot Corporation ranked 99th on *Forbes* magazine's list of the

500 largest privately held companies in the United States. In 1998, boasting some 3,000 employees, the company was rated as the nation's largest supplier of diesel fuel for over-the-road trucks, as well as the 25th largest restaurant franchise in the United States. Desiring to add a breakfast restaurant to its roster, Pilot Corporation began looking around and decided to invite T.J. Cinnamons baked goods and coffee shops to join the ranks of the company's in-store partners, which now included Arby's, KFC, Pizza Hut, Steak 'n Shake, Subway, Taco Bell, and Wendy's.

At the end of 2000, the company teamed with Idle-Aire Technologies to test a new system at its Travel Centers designed to provide air conditioning and heating to truck cabs. Telephone, Internet, and cable television access were added to some of the locations as well. Pilot began ramping up to create what essentially amounted to a ''hotel'' for truckers—a place where they could park their trucks, sleep in their cabs, but still enjoy the luxuries of phone and television service, as well as air or heat, without having to leave their engines on and idling.

Early in 2001, Pilot Corporation teamed up with Speedway SuperAmerica LLC (a wholly owned subsidiary of Marathon Ashland Petroleum LLC (MAP), itself a joint venture between Marathon Oil Co. and Ashland Petroleum), to create Pilot Travel Centers LLC. The 50–50 joint venture combined the travel center operations of both companies under the Pilot name and created the largest travel center network in the United States, with approximately 235 locations in 35 states at its inception. CAT Scale Company also was brought into the venture, providing its truck scales to various locations. At the beginning of the 21st century, Pilot Corporation was set to just keep on truckin'.

Principal Competitors

7-Eleven, Inc.; ChevronTexaco; Exxon Mobil Corporation; FFP Marketing; Flying J Inc.; Love's Country Stores; Motiva Enterprises; Petro Stopping Centers; Rip Griffin Truck Service Center; Royal Dutch/Shell Group; Stuckey's, Inc.; TravelCenters of America.

Further Reading

Gates, Nick, and Stan DeLozier, ''Smokies Purchase Nets Pilot a Publicity Vehicle,'' *Knoxville (Tenn.) News-Sentinel,* December 28, 2001.

Gordetsky, Margaret, ''Gingrich on Bandwagon for Truck Stop Heating, Cooling, Entertainment Units,'' *Transport Topics,* December 11, 2000.

Smyth, Whit, ''The NRN Fifty: The Franchisees—Pilot Corp.: Launch into the Restaurant Business Has Sales Taking Off,'' *Nation's Restaurant News,* January 26, 1998.

—Daryl F. Mallett

The PMI Group, Inc.

601 Montgomery Street
San Francisco, California 94111
U.S.A.
Telephone: (415) 788-7878
Toll Free: (800) 288-1970
Fax: (415) 291-6191
Web site: http://www.pmigroup.com

Public Company
Incorporated: 1972 as PMI Investment Corporation
Employees: 1,235
Sales: $936.96 million (2001)
Stock Exchanges: New York
Ticker Symbol: PMI
NAIC: 524126 Direct Property and Casualty Insurance
  Carriers

Based in San Francisco, The PMI Group, Inc., operating through several wholly owned or partially owned subsidiaries, is one of the largest private mortgage insurers in the United States, Australia, New Zealand, and the European Union. PMI is also the largest mortgage guaranty reinsurer in Hong Kong. In recent years the company has looked to diversify beyond the private mortgage insurance market in the United States, expanding internationally as well as licensing its proprietary underwriting system, and providing contract underwriting and title insurance. PMI now portrays itself as an international provider of credit enhancement products and lender services that are designed to promote home ownership and to make mortgages more easily attainable.

Founding of PMI by Preston Martin: 1972

The founder of PMI, Preston Martin, is best known for his public service. The native Californian received a B.A. in finance as well as an M.B.A. from the University of Southern California. He then went on to earn a Ph.D. in monetary economics from the University of Indiana in 1952. During the 1950s he was a Professor of Finance and Director of Executive Programs at USC and went on to found graduate business schools in Italy and Pakistan. Martin also devoted his talents to private enterprise during the 1950s and 1960s, then in 1967 was named the Savings and Loan Commissioner for the State of California and was involved in the development of an important financial services product, the Adjustable Rate Mortgage (ARM). Two years later he gained a national appointment in the Nixon administration, becoming Chairman of the Federal Home Loan Bank Board, and was instrumental in the creation of the Federal Home Loan Mortgage Corporation, Freddie Mac. He held this post until 1972 when he returned to the private sector, securing $25 million in financing from the Allstate Insurance Company to establish a private mortgage insurance company. Drawing on the initials of the product, he named the new company PMI Investment Corporation. Private mortgage insurance protects against loss if a borrower, whose down payment is less than 20 percent of a home's purchase price, is forced to default. Because lenders and mortgage investors are insured, more money is made available to homebuyers, resulting in more people being able to buy a house.

With its first headquarters located in San Francisco's Bank of America Building, PMI initiated operations in April 1973. Also in that year Allstate acquired the company, making it a subsidiary. Martin served as CEO of PMI until 1980, the company's first years devoted to opening regional offices around the country and building a national business. It was the first firm to develop a means to pool insured loans in order to spread risk. Martin left PMI to assume the top position at Seraco Corporation, a venture of Sears Roebuck, the parent corporation of Allstate. He would soon return to public service, becoming vice-chairman of the Federal Reserve Board of Governors during the Reagan Administration.

PMI suffered through a difficult period during the early 1980s, the result of poor economic conditions and difficulties in the oil industry that led to an unusually high number of home loan defaults in such states as Texas, Colorado, and Alaska. The situation became so difficult that PMI was paying out two dollars for every dollar it was collecting in premiums. By 1985, however, the business recovered and the company entered what it called "The New Era," which lasted until 1990. During this period, PMI was reorganized and an Actuary Department developed. PMI also established itself as a company willing to take advantage of high technology, launching a pair of innovative financial

Company Perspectives:

PMI is a leader in mortgage risk management technology providing various products and services for the home mortgage finance industry as well as title insurance.

tools. In 1987 PMI introduced AURA, or Automated Underwriting Risk Analysis, a system that used claim and risk statistical models to predict the chances of a borrower defaulting on a mortgage. In 1988 PMI debuted Economic Real Estate Trends, which was used to analyze local and regional market conditions.

In the early 1990s PMI initiated a strategy to expand beyond the domestic mortgage insurance market. The first step in providing additional mortgage-related services came in 1992 when the company acquired American Pioneer Title Insurance Co., a Florida-based title insurance company. Although APTIC was licensed to conduct business in a number of states, its primary market was Florida, where it offered real estate title insurance on residential property. Its policies protected against loss due to title defects. Also in 1992 PMI agreed to a joint venture with CUNA Mutual Group, creating CMG Mortgage Insurance Company, which provided mortgage insurance for credit union loans. In addition, a Customer Technology department was established to license the use of such technical products as AURA.

Early in 1993 Roger Haughton was named PMI's president and chief executive officer. He had been with PMI since 1985, coming over from Allstate. Under his leadership, PMI continued to make changes in 1993. It stopped writing new business in its mortgage pool segment and entered into an agreement with Forestview, an Allstate subsidiary, to reinsure all its liabilities in connection with its mortgage pool insurance business. Furthermore, in 1993 PMI launched PMI Mortgage Services Co., providing technical products and mortgage underwriting services through 19 field offices. With Haughton at the helm, PMI became deeply involved in the advancement of affordable housing, beginning in 1994 when Haughton was approached by a human resources executive about sponsoring a project with Habitat for Humanity, part of the Jimmy Carter Work Project in South Dakota. Only agreeing to the idea with some reluctance, Houghton later publicly expressed that the project had a profound effect on his life. He told the *Contra Costa Times,* ''That was a real hit between the eyes; there was a commitment born in me that moment.'' PMI would become further involved in affordable housing efforts for Native Americans as well as other housing initiatives.

Spinoff from Allstate: 1995

After more than 20 years operating as an Allstate subsidiary, PMI gained its independence because of events at Sears. In November 1994 Sears announced that it was refocusing on retailing and planned to spin off Allstate to shareholders. In anticipation of the move, Allstate in turn decided to spin off PMI in order to focus on its core property/casualty and life insurance businesses and realize a return on its 20-year investment in the subsidiary. As a result, PMI became the fourth publicly traded mortgage insurer, along with Mortgage Guaranty Insurance Corp., Commonwealth Mortgage Assurance Corp., and Triad

Guaranty Corp. Two separate offerings were completed in April 1995, netting over $1.1 billion. Allstate retained a 30 percent stake, which it would sell off two years later. The initial offering raised $784 million on the sale of 24.5 million common shares at $34 each, which subsequently began trading on the New York Stock Exchange. At the same time, Allstate sold a new issue of 6.7 percent exchangeable notes due 1998, raising an additional $340 million. Haughton remained as president and CEO of PMI, and became a director of the corporation as well. In May 1998 he was elected chairman of the board.

Now an independent, publicly traded company, PMI continued to grow revenues and profits and diversify its business. In 1996 the company topped the $500 million mark in annual revenues while generating record net income of nearly $158 million. PMI also continued to demonstrate an innovative spirit, especially in the leveraging of its technology. In 1995 it created an 800 telephone number to assist both lenders and borrowers, in the process increasing the total volume of mortgage business, a situation clearly to its benefit. The lenders advertised an 800 number assigned by PMI, which prospective borrowers then called to determine how large a loan they would likely receive. Lenders, now possessing a considerable amount of financial information and a credit report, were able to call on the borrower and provide greater assistance, such as connecting the borrower with appropriate real estate agents or builders. PMI Mortgage Connection service was successful enough to warrant the addition of a Spanish language module a few months later. Moreover, this enhancement was an acknowledgment that the demographics of home ownership was changing and that Spanish-speaking Americans were a market with great potential. In 1997 PMI along with Norwest Mortgage Inc. turned to the Internet, taking an important first step in sending encrypted mortgage insurance applications over the Web.

In 1997 private mortgage insurers saw the dollar amount of loans insured drop from the double-digit levels earlier in the decade to just 5 percent. With that amount expected to soon fall to just 3 percent, PMI accelerated its efforts at diversification. PMI acquired CLM Technologies, which developed Reason automated appraisal software. In 1998 it became a principal investor in Bermuda-based startup RAM Reinsurance Company, a reinsurer of investment grade asset-backed and municipal securities. PMI split most of the $80 million capitalization with partners Greenwich Street Capital Partners and Continental Illinois. A year later PMI invested a further $15 million, increasing its stake in RAM to 25 percent.

Entering Hong Kong: 1999

The landscape for private mortgage insurance changed in 1998 when Congress passed legislation that required mortgage insurance to be automatically canceled after borrowers reached 22 percent equity in their homes. A few months later Freddie Mac sought congressional approval to enter the mortgage insurance business. Although the request was rejected, these events concerned investors, driving down the stock prices of firms like PMI. As a result PMI was even more motivated to look overseas in the late 1990s, targeting Asia, Australia, and Europe as the most desirable markets to penetrate. It turned first to Asia and Australia as opportunities became available. In April 1999 PMI

Key Dates:

1972: Preston Marton founds company.
1973: Company is acquired by Allstate.
1980: Martin resigns from the company.
1987: AURA, or Automated Underwriting Risk Analysis, system is introduced to help predict borrower defaults.
1995: Allstate spins off PMI.
1999: Company enters Hong Kong, Australia, and New Zealand markets.
2001: PMI Europe is established.

entered the Hong Kong market, opening an office after signing an agreement with Honk Kong Mortgage Corp. to provide residential mortgage reinsurance. HKMC had been established several years earlier by the Hong Kong government with help from Fannie Mae to introduce residential mortgage insurance to the market. As a result, home ownership rose substantially in the previous three or four years. PMI's role would be to reinsure HKMC's total risk in guaranteeing Hong Kong mortgages. In June 1999 PMI penetrated the Australian and New Zealand markets by establishing a Sydney holding company, PMI Mortgage Insurance Australia, to acquire MGICA Ltd. from AMP General Insurance Holdings Ltd., the country's largest insurance and financial services company, for $77.6 million. MGICA, in business since 1965, was Australia's second largest private mortgage insurer with a 25 percent market share, and generated $3.7 billion of new insurance in 1998. It also controlled as much as 45 percent of the New Zealand market. AMP had decided to divest itself of the insurer in order to concentrate on its core financial services business. For PMI, MGICA was an ideal opportunity to gain access to the second most active mortgage capital market in the world in Australia, which along with Canada and Great Britain were the only non-U.S. countries with a mortgage insurance market. Moreover, PMI looked to leverage its superior technology in the region, which had yet to see mortgage scoring or automated underwriting.

PMI's entry into Asia and Australia quickly proved to be a success, and by the end of 1999 the company was looking aggressively at Europe, in particular targeting the Netherlands, Germany, and Sweden where well-developed mortgage markets already existed and databases on borrowers and credit characteristics were already firmly established. In general, Europe was a large, underserved market for private mortgage insurance. PMI estimated that Europe's outstanding mortgage debt topped $3 trillion, in contrast to the United States' $4 trillion. Because homeownership was lower there and with no mortgage insurance company operating outside of Ireland and the United Kingdom, the continent was especially inviting. PMI entered Europe early in 2000, opening a marketing office in London because of the major financial institutions located there, but after completing some preliminary groundwork, PMI elected to base its European headquarters in Dublin, in large part because the United Kingdom was not part of the European Monetary Union, countries agreeing to a common currency, despite being a part of the European Union. The Dublin unit, PMI Mortgage Insurance Co. Ltd., "PMI Europe," was established in 2001

and capitalized at $75 million. It was licensed by the Irish Department of Enterprise Trade & Employment to offer traditional primary insurance, structured portfolio products, and reinsurance products for loans and securitizations to all of the European Union member states. PMI's products, furthermore, would be tailored to meet the particular needs of lenders and mortgage securitizers in each country.

PMI also strengthened previous expansion efforts in 2001. It acquired Australia's fourth largest mortgage insurance company, Sydney-based CGU Lenders Mortgage Insurance Ltd., paying $40 million to British insurer CGNU PLC. Although CGU controlled just 7 percent of the mortgage insurance market in Australia, it was New Zealand's top insurer. Overall, PMI was now the largest mortgage insurer in both countries. In addition, PMI increased its stake to 45 percent in Fairbanks Capital Holding, which it originally invested in two years earlier. Acquiring, servicing, and resolving nonperforming and underperforming single-family residential mortgages, Salt Lake City-based Fairbanks offered diversification in PMI's domestic market.

Despite a downturn in the economy in 2001 and 2002, PMI remained strong. Its superior technology continued to pay dividends. In 2001, for instance, some 60 percent of PMI's loans were received in an electronic format, resulting in a 30 percent drop in the cost per application over the previous year. PMI continued to emphasize its international efforts, looking to eventually further its business in Asia, but the company was especially optimistic about Europe. PMI Europe had already engaged in a number of mortgage credit default swap agreements, including a major deal in the German market. In all, PMI was well positioned for continued growth in the foreseeable future.

Principal Subsidiaries

American Pioneer Title Insurance Company; CLM Technologies; PMI Mortgage Insurance Australia; PMI Mortgage Insurance Company Limited.

Principal Competitors

Mortgage Guaranty Insurance Corporation; GE Capital Mortgage Insurance Corporation; United Guaranty Residential Insurance Company; Radian Guaranty Inc.; Republic Mortgage Insurance Co.; Triad Guaranty Insurance Corp.

Further Reading

Bergquist, Erick, "More U.S. Insurers Getting Their Feet Wet in Europe," *American Banker,* February 14, 2001, p. 15.
Finkelstein, Brad, "Mortgage Insurer Takes Broader View of Its Mission," *Origination News,* March 2002, p. 12.
Hogue, Robert D., "An Interesting Move for PMI," *Insurance Advocate,* June 6, 1998, p. 32.
"PMI Offers Mortgage Reinsurance in Hong Kong," *Real Estate Finance Today,* April 12, 1999, p. 10.
Smolen, Kelly, "Private Mortgage Firm in Walnut Creek, Calif.-Area Is Building Affordability," *Contra Costa Times,* July 17, 2001.
Taylor, Marshall, "PMI Buys Australian Mortgage Insurer," *Real Estate Finance Today,* June 28, 1999, pp. 10–11.

—Ed Dinger

R.C. Bigelow, Inc.

201 Black Rock Turnpike
Fairfield, Connecticut 06432
U.S.A.
Telephone: (203) 334-1212
Fax: (203) 334-4751
Web site: http://www.rcbigelow.com

Private Company
Incorporated: 1945
Employees: 350
Sales: $80 million (2001 est.)
NAIC: 311920 Coffee and Tea Manufacturing

R.C. Bigelow, Inc. is one of the leading specialty tea manufacturers in the United States and is known particularly for its flagship brand, ''Constant Comment.'' The Fairfield, Connecticut, business is run by the second and third generations of the Bigelow family. David Bigelow is the chairman of the board and his wife Eunice serves as a vice-president. Daughters Cynthia and Lori have also assumed leading roles in the company's operations. In recent years, Bigelow's product lines have expanded beyond tea to include flavored coffees as well as honey spreads.

Company Founder's Beginnings As an Interior Decorator: 1920s

The founder of Bigelow, Ruth Campbell Bigelow, was born in 1896. After attending a design school in Rhode Island she moved to New York City during World War I to continue her education, supporting herself by taking classified ads at the *New York Times* and working in department stores. She got married in 1920 and established her own decorating shop. It was a prosperous time in the city and she found her talents for interior decorating in high demand. Within a few years she was able to move to a fashionable location at Madison and 72nd Street, a corner location where she had two full floors at her disposal. In addition to her work in Manhattan, she often traveled out of town to decorate her clients' second homes in Palm Beach or summer retreats in Maine.

Ruth was at the height of her career when the stock market crash of 1929 and the ensuing Depression had a devastating effect on so much of Manhattan's wealthy set. Her interior decorating skills were a luxury that few could now afford, and as a result she and her family were forced to retrench as well. She relocated her shop to a second floor location on 52nd Street, with her family living in the back. A similar arrangement prevailed at a 57th Street address that next housed her declining business. To make matters worse, in 1931 her husband lost his publishing job at McGraw Hill and would not be employed again until 1940. The couple's resources dwindled during the 1930s, yet in the early 1940s the two were still able to scrape together $8,000 to buy a four-story brownstone located at 241 E. 60th Street. Although the property was perfect for Ruth's decorating business, offering a two-story storefront and large display windows, it would be put to good use in an entirely different line of endeavor.

Ruth decided to quit the decorating business, according to her son David, because she felt she had to start from scratch with each new client, learning their tastes and preferences. She saw the food business as a more desirable occupation: Once an entrepreneur created a product to sell, the customers either liked it or did not. She and her husband established Wilton House Foods in the early 1940s, naming the business after the Connecticut town where the couple had bought a summer house during the flush times of the 1920s. In order to find a product to sell she wrote to manufacturers of sugar, flour, and other commodities, asking for product formulas, which these companies, with the hope of serving as future suppliers, were only too happy to provide. After considering some possibilities, such as rice pudding, Ruth settled on Chinese seasonings. She discovered that the city's Chinese restaurants used a combination of monosodium glutamate (MSG), salt, and milk sugar in virtually all of their cooking. Installing an industrial blender in the first floor of their brownstone, the Bigelows mixed their Chinese seasonings at night, packing the product into tins as small as two-and-half pounds or canisters as large as 50 pounds. During the day the tins would be delivered to the trading companies on Canal Street. According to David Bigelow, Wilton House Foods expanded its outreach to the other boroughs of New York and eventually sold to the major wholesalers in the city. He estimated that the family sold as much as $3,000 each month from this business, just enough to maintain a comfortable living.

The Bigelows continued to sell Chinese seasonings for many years. At the same time, Ruth became interested in the tea business. Although she cared for tea, she was not enamored with the blends of the time, preferring a milder, smoother drink with more flavor. Through a friend named Mrs. Nealy, she learned of a tea recipe from the Colonial period, involving orange peel and spices mixed with tea, which was then allowed to marinate in a crock in a cold cellar before serving. With no specific recipe in hand, just a concept, Ruth began to experiment, eventually settling on a combination of tea, orange, and spices that she considered the best of the batch. According to David Bigelow, his mother and Mrs. Nealy filled a notebook with possible names for the tea before choosing "Constant Comment." The story behind the origin of the name has become a topic of family, and company, lore. She shared some of the tea with a New York socialite, whom she undoubtedly knew through her interior decorating days. The woman served the tea at a party and later reported to Ruth that it was a source of "constant comments."

Marketing "Constant Comment" in 1945

It was around 1945 that Ruth Bigelow began her efforts to market "Constant Comment." It was packaged loose in four-ounce tins with a simple sepia-tone label. To save money she used a neighborhood letter press shop, relying on clip art of two ladies sipping tea at a table and "Constant Comment" printed at the bottom. Her husband, who had limited artistic ability, was enlisted to hand-paint each label—the two ladies in red, the background in green. For distribution of "Constant Comment" she looked to a nearby department store, Bloomingdale's, which featured a gourmet section. According to her son, she went in cold to convince the store's buyer, a Mr. Simon, to take on her product. Simon had a reputation as a difficult man who was not easily persuaded, yet she prevailed and won a valuable asset in selling her tea. She then began her own marketing campaign to take advantage of the Bloomingdale's connection. Using the social section of New York's newspapers as a resource, she hand-painted letters that she sent to select individuals telling them about "Constant Comment" and letting them know the product was available at Bloomingdale's. In the early days, these letters produced enough sales to keep the venture afloat. Nevertheless, at one point her husband commented to their son, "Don't tell your mother this, but I don't think this tea is going to go anywhere."

David Bigelow, after graduating from Yale in 1948, took a more active role in his parents' business. He maintains that his biggest contribution in that period was to convince his parents that the label for "Constant Comment" needed to be upgraded.

He was also instrumental in adding a two-ounce size. By this time "Constant Comment" was sold at several major New York department stores, yet rarely did the company sell more than ten cases a month. It had a single sales representative who covered New England, but in 1948 he resigned the line because the product simply was not selling. Very much like drummers from the 19th century, sales reps of this period pitched a wide variety of products, from corsets to wrought iron. They showed little interest in devoting time to anything that did not sell readily.

Having lost their only salesman, the Bigelows were desperate to find a way to attract new business. Ruth then recalled an experience that happened a few years earlier when she tried to convince a Connecticut grocer to carry "Constant Comment." Busy filling the Saturday morning orders of his regular customers he paid little attention to her sales pitch, but a customer became interested and asked if she could smell the tea, which Ruth at that time had packed in jars. The lady was so impressed that she bought a jar, and later returned to buy the rest of the case that the grocer as a courtesy had allowed Ruth to leave. He still refused to carry "Constant Comment," but the memory of how the customer was affected by the aroma of "Constant Comment" stayed with Ruth Bigelow. A number of the empty jars remained in the basement of the brownstone, and they were now converted into "whiffing jars," one of which replaced a tin of tea in the company's popular "Get Acquainted" case of "Constant Comment." New England gift shops found the whiffing jars perfect for their layouts, and patrons could not resist opening the jars to sample the aroma of "Constant Comment." More and more of these people began to buy the tea and became devoted to it.

Around 1949 sales of "Constant Comment" finally began to take off. By 1950 the company had a half-dozen sales reps spread across the country, selling the tea into gourmet shops, gift shops, and even hardware stores. At this point "Constant Comment" was not a grocery store item. The company maintained thousands of small accounts, relying on Parcel Post or UPS to deliver the orders. Business was proving so successful that in 1950 the Bigelows sold their New York brownstone for $20,000 and bought a factory in Norwalk, Connecticut, part of which they also rented out to another company. Also in 1950 the company became involved with a sales rep named Charles K. Long, who would have a major impact on the fortunes of the Bigelows and their tea business. He was a West Coast salesman who only took on "Constant Comment" because his wife insisted on it. Once he began to sell the product, however, he opened a prodigious number of accounts in California, Arizona, Oregon, and Washington. He would eventually become the company's West Coast sales manager and stay with Bigelow for 30 years.

Although Bigelow was generally regarded to be a one-product company until the mid-1970s, it actually began selling teas other than "Constant Comment" during the 1950s. Getting on the end of Johnson & Johnson runs for flip-top tin boxes used for packaging bandaids, Bigelow began packaging various teas in bags. At first the tea bags were produced offsite, then hand-packed in Norwalk. It was not until 1958, a year after Bigelow moved to a larger plant in Norwalk, that the company bought its first tea bag machine. It was also in the late 1950s that the company began to make the transition from specialty shops to the supermarket. Because grocery stores were receiving requests for "Constant Comment" from their customers, they

Key Dates:

1945: Ruth Campbell Bigelow establishes tea business with ''Constant Comment.''
1950: The company moves to Norwalk, Connecticut.
1963: Son David Bigelow assumes control of the company.
1966: Ruth Bigelow dies.
1984: Company opens a facility in Boise, Idaho.
1987: Company opens a facility in Louisville, Kentucky.
1990: Headquarters moves to Fairfield, Connecticut.

began asking Bigelow for price lists. To accommodate these customers, the company had to recruit food brokers. By the end of the 1960s Bigelow had more accounts from grocery stores than specialty shops. The company was also without its founding spirit. Ruth Bigelow died in 1966, followed by her husband in 1970. David Bigelow had already assumed leadership of the business in 1963.

Expanding Beyond ''Constant Comment'' in the Mid-1970s

Aside from the tea bags Bigelow sold in bandaid boxes in the 1950s, it was not until the mid-1970s that the company truly moved beyond ''Constant Comment,'' and then it was a matter of necessity. Around 1973, according to David Bigelow, a competitor came out with a tea using a label that was virtually identical to the one used for ''Constant Comment.'' Bigelow sued and during the course of the trial it became apparent that the competitor was planning to bring out a complete line of teas using labels in the ''Constant Comment'' vein. Advised by his attorney that the company should bring out its own line of specialty teas, Bigelow initiated a crash program and within a short time produced many of the teas that remain popular today. In addition to ultimately winning protection for its labeling in court, Bigelow now enjoyed the advantages of an expanded product line. Bigelow teas were able to command greater shelf space in supermarkets, and within two years the company doubled its revenues.

With an increase in sales volume, Bigelow began expanding its operations in the 1980s. In 1984 it opened a distribution center in Boise, Idaho, in order to serve its West Coast customers. Tea bag machines were added and the Idaho center soon evolved into Bigelow's largest manufacturing facility, responsible for half of the company's annual production of tea bags. In 1987 Bigelow also opened a small distribution center in Louisville, Kentucky, designed to serve the Southeast and Midwest. In much the way the Boise facility grew, Louisville branched into manufacturing. In addition to making tea bags, it also produced gifts, and became responsible for the bulk of Bige-

low's specialty work. In 1990, after spending some 40 years in Norwalk, Bigelow opened a new headquarters building in Fairfield, Connecticut, featuring test kitchens and an advanced computerized tea blending tower.

During the 1980s and 1990s, Bigelow expanded its product lines in a number of directions. It introduced a line of iced-tea flavors. Looking to capitalize on its reputation with specialty teas, it took on Celestial Seasonings and Lipton in the herbal tea segment. Bigelow also gained an edge over its rivals in the green tea market, an advantage that translated into higher profits when in 1997 studies indicated that green tea helped to prevent some cancers. As a result, green tea sales grew at a pace much higher than the rest of the industry and served as a major driver for Bigelow, which launched a variety of green tea blends. In addition, green tea helped to make tea more than just a seasonable product for consumers who only drink iced tea during warm months. In the late 1990s Bigelow moved beyond tea, introducing a line of honey spreads, and then in 2001 it brought out a line of flavored dessert coffees, including such flavors as French Vanilla and Irish Cream.

To bolster its sales, Bigelow established a mail-order business in the 1990s. It also modernized its management structure, but remained very much a family-run business, operating without an outside board. By 2001 the company's annual revenues were estimated to total in the range of $80 million. Bigelow was a well recognized brand name with established distribution channels, making it a prime target for a much larger food or beverage company. But with a third generation of the Bigelow family fully committed to running the business, there was little chance that the makers of ''Constant Comment'' would change hands in the foreseeable future.

Principal Divisions

Sales; Marketing; Blending; Finance; Operations; Human Resources; Strategic Planning.

Principal Competitors

Celestial Seasonings, Inc.; Thomas J. Lipton Company.

Further Reading

Garfinkel, Perry, ''Honoring Thy Father, the Boss,'' *New York Times,* June 18, 1994, p. A39.

Haar, Dan, ''Industry Fits Them to a Tea,'' *Hartford Courant,* December 11, 1997, p. D1.

Lavoie, Denis, ''Bigelow Vice President Has Tea in Her Blood,'' *Associated Press,* September 20, 1998.

Wittemann, Betsy, ''Infused in the Industry,'' *New York Times,* February 11, 2001, p. CT1.

—Ed Dinger

Ronson PLC

International House
Old Brighton Road
Lowfield Heath
Crawley, West Sussex RH11 0QN
United Kingdom
Telephone: +44 (0)1293 843 600
Fax: +44 (0)1293 843 665
Web site: http://www.ronson.com

Public Company
Incorporated: 1982 as Ronson International Ltd.
Employees: 36
Sales: £8.98 million (2001)
Stock Exchanges: London
Ticker Symbol: RON.L
NAIC: 339999 All Other Miscellaneous Manufacturing

Ronson PLC is the holding company for Ronson International Limited, distributor of Ronson brand lighters and associated products throughout most of the world (excluding the United States, Australia, and Japan). The Ronson name became famous through the innovative and stylish lighters produced since 1913. Metal wares made by the Art Metal Works and other predecessor companies are also collector's items.

Ronson PLC, based in England, is independent from New Jersey-based Ronson Corporation, which produces Ronson-branded lighters and affiliated products for U.S. consumption. The British company was spun off from Ronson Corporation in 1981.

Origins

Louis V. Aronson was born in New York City on Christmas Day 1869 to Jewish immigrant parents. He was drawn to metallurgy at a young age, and in the 1880s developed the Ormolu process of gold plating.

Aronson sold the rights to the Ormolu process and formed the Art Metal Company in 1886. Although the firm would become best known for cigarette lighters, at this time it made a diverse array of metal wares, sometimes on contract for other manufacturers.

Originally based in New York City, the firm relocated to the rapidly growing, industry-friendly city of Newark, New Jersey, in 1897, when it was renamed Art Metal Works (AMW). In the same year, Aronson patented a "Safety Match" that used sulfur instead of phosphorus.

In 1910, AMW trademarked the name "Ronson," an abbreviation of the founder's name. This trademark was first used on toys and other products, rather than lighters.

The company's first pocket lighter, the Wonderliter, was introduced in 1913. It used a wick and a striker made with a newly invented metal alloy. AMW made military products during World War I, and expanded as well. A booming world economy after the war helped sales reach $1 million in 1920.

The company thrived as the Art Deco movement swept the world of design in the 1920s. The style was apparent in AMW's hood ornaments, bookends, clocks, and other products.

Introduction of Banjo Lighter: 1928

Two significant events happened in 1928: the company listed on the stock exchange, and it introduced its $5 Banjo lighter. The Banjo, which could be operated with one motion of the hand, was an instant success; it would fuel the company's growth for years. In 1929, AMW recycled the design in a perfume atomizer called the "Perfu-Mist."

Art Metal Works launched a worldwide expansion in 1929, building a plant in Canada. A U.K. subsidiary, Ronson Products Limited, was established in Battersea in 1930. By this time, the company was focusing on the lucrative cigarette lighter business.

Alexander Harris became the second president of Ronson Art Metal Works in 1940 after the death of Louis Aronson. Harris had begun working for the company 32 years earlier.

During World War II, the company's output was directed towards military products, including, appropriately, flame

---

Company Perspectives:

The Ronson Brand name is world renowned as being synon-ymous with expertly engineered products having unique and innovative designs and offering the consumer a desirable quality product.

---

throwers, as well as fuses for bombs and small components for the aircraft industry. GI humor used the Ronson name as an epithet for the M4 Sherman tank, which caught fire easily when hit. The company's slogan then was "always lights the first time." Ronson's own factory in England was nearly destroyed by German bombing; due to its strategic importance, it was relocated to an old boarding school in London.

The parent company's name was changed to Ronson Art Metal Works, Inc. in 1945. The British subsidiary was relocated to a giant new factory in Leatherhead, south London, in 1952. Employment there was 2,500 during the 1950s.

Diversification: 1950s–70s

Louis V. Aronson II, born in 1923 to the son of the founder, became the firm's third president in 1953 upon the retirement of Alexander Harris. The firm became simply Ronson Corporation in 1954. Sales reached $26 million.

Between the mid-1950s and mid-1960s, Ronson diversified its manufacturing, particularly in the United States, into a wide range for consumers and industry. These included such obvious spinoffs as torches and lighter fluid and extended into special-ized pneumatic and hydraulic valves for the aerospace industry. Ronson also extended the brand into the bathroom with shavers, toothbrushes, and hair dryers, and into the kitchen with carving knives, blenders, can openers, and other appliances.

Varaflame pocket lighters, using the new Multi-Fill fueling system, were introduced in 1957. They were a blazing success; the company was producing 15,000 a day around the world by the end of the decade. The Varaflame Premier was the best-known model; the Adonis Varaflame was a smaller version for women. The plastic, butane-filled "Comet" pocket lighter came out in 1965. Ronson ended the 1960s with 11,000 people working at 17 plants around the world.

Ronson continued to refine the technology for lighting ciga-rettes. Electronic ignition was introduced in 1970. One innova-tion that did not work very well was the Varachem ignition cartridge, which used highly reactive rocket fuel. This system was pulled shortly after its 1976 launch due to dangerous leak-age problems.

Sales reached $128 million in 1974. The British unit was particularly successful in the mid-1970s. However, several fac-tories in the United States were closed as competition from cheap disposable lighters cut into sales. Ronson USA found its diversified businesses in serious trouble as well, and decided to liquidate all the foreign subsidiaries. Ronson rolled out its own Magnum disposable lighter in 1980.

British Unit Spun Off in 1981

Ronson lost $5.5 million in 1980, $3.6 million of it from the U.K. subsidiary Ronson Products. Jeffrey Port bought the busi-ness for $6.1 million that September, reorganizing it as Ronson International a couple of months later. The company entered receivership in July 1982.

Geoffrey Richmond acquired the company in 1983, re-naming it Ronson Exports Limited. The company began im-porting lighters from Asia in 1986. The high value of the British pound depressed sales for a few years.

Halkin Holdings plc acquired Ronson Exports for £10 mil-lion in 1994. It was soon renamed Ronson PLC. The CEO of Halkin was Howard Hodgson, who had in the 1980s trans-formed his family's mortuary into something of a conglomerate.

Hodgson appointed Colgate-Palmolive and Johnson Wax veteran Arthur Till as Ronson's managing director in March 1994. With an eye to capturing the attention of a new generation of consumers, the product line was expanded to 19 lighters, including the Premier Varaflame, and the brand was soon rein-troduced in 50 countries. An updated version of the Comet was rolled out in 1995.

The Newcastle factory suffered a devastating fire in January 1996. Production was restored within a month. Another disaster was the large-scale expansion of the brand into lifestyle products such as watches, pens, luggage, and sunglasses, and the launch of the Rebel, Retro, and Racer lighters. The company lost £11 million in 1997. Hodgson was ousted in the middle of the year.

Victor Kiam, the owner of Remington Products Company and the TV pitchman for the namesake electric razor, acquired a controlling interest in the company and became CEO in July 1998. (He replaced Richard Furse, who had only been confirmed as CEO himself four months earlier.) Kiam presided over a difficult period of cost-cutting, including shutting down produc-tion of the Varaflame Premier in England. He died in May 2001.

Turning Around After 2000

Ronson posted a pretax loss of £1.65 million on turnover down 30 percent to £7.25 million for 2000. The company had lost money on an aborted e-commerce venture, as well as a comprehensive restructuring designed to reorient its products toward the contemporary marketplace. Ronson hired design firms Karim Rashid of New York and London's Factory Design to develop new models. Ronson also dropped a license agree-ment to distribute Pierre Cardin costume jewelry, focusing on the lighter business.

Ronson cut manufacturing costs and trimmed less aggres-sive distributors from its network. It signed a new deal to supply disposable lighters for Tesco, among others. Disposables ac-counted for 60 percent of sales. After a few years of losses, Ronson was able to show a profit of £384,000 on turnover up 24 percent to £8.98 million in 2001.

New products included childproof and windproof lighters and a stylish, refillable one aimed at the growing youth market, along with a new line of cigarette papers. There was also the

Key Dates:

1886: Art Metal Company is formed in New York by Louis V. Aronson.
1897: Art Metal Works, as the company is now known, relocates to New Jersey.
1913: Pocket Lighter is patented.
1928: Company goes public.
1930: U.K. subsidiary is opened.
1956: Varaflame refillable lighters are introduced.
1981: U.K. subsidiary enters liquidation.
1983: Ronson Exports Limited is formed.
1994: Halkin Holdings plc acquires Ronson Exports.
1995: Ronson Exports becomes Ronson plc.
1998: Victor Kiam becomes Ronson plc chairman.
2001: Ronson plc begins to show a profit again as it aims at a younger market.

''Xtreme'' line of lighters; the V2citrus lighter, based on the Premier Varaflame; and the Shark lighter, shaped like the marine predator.

The future for Ronson PLC was anything but clear. However, there could be no doubt that the Ronson name and product line had made a significant impression in the minds of consumers and collectors during the course of its history.

Principal Subsidiaries

Ronson International Limited; Ronson Polska SP z.o.o. (Poland).

Principal Competitors

Alfred Dunhill Ltd.; Bic Corp.; Colibri Corporation; Gillette Corp.; Scripto-Tokai Corporation; Zippo Manufacturing Co.

Further Reading

Batchelor, Charles, ''Ronson Suffers from e-Venture,'' *Financial Times* (London), Companies & Finance, April 10, 2001, p. 24.

Blackwell, David, ''Hodgson Pushed Off Board at Ronson,'' *Financial Times* (London), Companies & Markets, June 3, 1997, p. 21.

——, ''Kiam Steps Up As Ronson Directors Leave,'' *Financial Times* (London), Companies & Finance, July 8, 1998, p. 23.

——, ''Ronson Burned by Lighter Launch,'' *Financial Times* (London), Companies & Finance, October 16, 1997, p. 23.

——, ''Ronson Shares Set to Resume Trading Today,'' *Financial Times* (London), Companies & Finance, September 21, 1998, p. 27.

Booth, Hannah, ''Factory Ignites Ronson's Range of Cigarette Lighters,'' *Design Week,* October 25, 2001, p. 7.

Cummings, Urban K., *The Ronson Book: The World's Greatest Lighter: Wick Lighters 1913–2000,* 2nd ed., n.p., 2001.

''Halkin Gains Further Rights Over Ronson Products,'' *Extel Examiner,* July 15, 1994.

''Hodgson: Resuscitating Another Dying Brand,'' *Financial Times,* March 10, 1994, p. 17.

''The Investment Column: High Debt Levels and Increased Borrowings Make Ronson One to Avoid,'' *Independent* (London), April 18, 2002, p. 19.

''Repayment Hopes for Ronson Intl. Creditors,'' *Financial Times* (London), Sec. I, September 10, 1983, p. 18.

Rigby, Elizabeth, ''Ronson Warning As Simon Russell Alights,'' *Financial Times* (London), Companies & Finance, December 6, 2000, p. 30.

Schneider, Stuart L., *Ronson's Art Metal Works,* Atglen, Pa.: Schiffer Publishing, 2001.

Schneider, Stuart L., and George Fischler, *Cigarette Lighters,* Atglen, Pa.: Schiffer Publishing, 1996.

Schneider, Stuart L., and Ira Pilossof, *Handbook of Lighters,* Atglen, Pa.: Schiffer Publishing, 1999.

Thackray, Rachelle, ''Cigarette Lighters Drag Ronson Sales Down by 31% to £3.5m,'' *Independent* (UK), September 28, 2000, p. 22.

''Turnaround in Results Sparks Hope at Ronson,'' *Evening News* (Edinburgh), August 31, 2001, p. B8.

—Frederick C. Ingram

Royal Dutch/Shell Group

Royal Dutch Petroleum Company
30 Carel Van Bylandtlaan
The Hague
The Netherlands
Telephone: (70) 377 9111
Fax: (70) 377 4848

The "Shell" Transport and Trading Company P.L.C.
Shell Centre
London SE1 7NA
United Kingdom
Telephone: (20) 7934 1234
Fax: (20) 7934 8060
Web site: http://www.shell.com

Public Company
Incorporated: 1890 as Koninklijke Nederlandsche
    Maatschappig Tot Exploitatie van Petroleumbronnen
    in Nederlandschindie and 1897 as The "Shell"
    Transport and Trading Company, Ltd.
Employees: 90,000
Sales: $135.21 billion (2001)
Stock Exchanges: London New York Amsterdam
Ticker Symbols: RDA (Amsterdam); RD (New York); SC
    (New York); SHEL (London)
NAIC: 324110 Petroleum Refineries

The Royal Dutch/Shell Group is the world's third largest oil and gas company. It has a complex corporate organization consisting of hundreds of companies worldwide, ultimately controlled by two publicly traded parent companies. The "Shell" Transport and Trading Company, a U.K.-registered company, has a 40 percent interest in the group, and the remaining 60 percent is owned by the Royal Dutch Petroleum Company, a Netherlands company. Collectively, the group is involved in oil and gas exploration, production, refining, transportation, and marketing. It also has interests in chemicals and diversified activities in coal and metal mining, forestry, solar energy, and biotechnology.

Late 1800s: Two Oil Companies Get Their Start

The Royal Dutch/Shell Group was formed in 1907 when a merging of the interests of Royal Dutch and "Shell" Transport took place, in which each company retained its separate identity. Royal Dutch was established in The Hague in 1890 after receiving a concession to drill for oil in Sumatra, in the Dutch East Indies. It had the support of King William III, hence the name Royal Dutch. The promoters of this venture had found oil in 1885, but needed funds to exploit their discovery. In the early years the firm was directed by J.B. August Kessler under whom, in 1892, it exported its first oil. In 1896 a 30-year-old bookkeeper, Henri Deterding, joined the company and in 1901 he became its chief executive. The predominant use for petroleum in the late 19th century was as paraffin or kerosene, which was used for heating and lighting. However, Sumatra's oil was particularly rich in gasoline, the product used by the internal combustion engine, and it was therefore well placed to take advantage of the growth in demand for oil which the automobile was to bring.

Deterding was one of the great entrepreneurial figures of the 20th century. He combined remarkable strategic vision with acute financial awareness born of his early training as a bookkeeper. His ambition was to build a company to rival the world's largest oil enterprise, John D. Rockefeller's Standard Oil Company of the United States. Deterding preferred to achieve this ambition through alliances and agreements rather than competition. In 1903, as part of this strategy, he formed a marketing company, the Asiatic Petroleum Company, owned jointly by Royal Dutch, Shell, and the Paris branch of the Rothschild family, the last of which had substantial Russian production interests. A crucial intermediary figure in making this alliance was Fred Lane, who had been one of the original directors of "Shell" Transport, but who had become closely identified with the Paris Rothschilds and, by the early 1900s, with Deterding.

The "Shell" Transport and Trading Company's origins lay in the activities of a London merchant, Marcus Samuel, who began his career in the 1830s selling boxes made from shells brought from the East. The business gradually expanded the number of commodities in which it traded. When Marcus Sam-

---

Company Perspectives:

The aim of the Royal Dutch/Shell Group is to meet the energy needs of society in ways that are economically, socially and environmentally viable, now and in the future.

---

uel, Sr., died in 1870, his son Marcus continued to be involved in Far Eastern trade. In 1878 he established with his brother Samuel a partnership known as Marcus Samuel & Co. in London, and Samuel Samuel & Co. in Japan, which became a leading shipping and trading enterprise in the Far East. During the 1880s the Samuels, through intermediary Fred Lane, began selling the Russian oil of the Rothschilds to the Far East, breaking the monopoly previously held by Standard Oil. In 1892 the Suez Canal Company was persuaded to allow oil tankers to pass through the canal, which lowered the cost of Russian oil in the Far East, and allowed the Samuel partnership to rapidly increase its market share. Later in the 1890s fears that Russian supplies might be reduced led the Samuels to search for a secure source of oil nearer their Far Eastern markets, and in 1898 a major oilfield was discovered in Dutch Borneo, a year after the launch of ''Shell'' Transport and Trading.

Early 1900s: Merger of Royal Dutch and ''Shell''

''Shell'' Transport grew rapidly. By 1900 the company possessed oilfields and a refinery in Borneo and a fleet of oil tankers. However, Marcus Samuel was above all a merchant, lacking organizational skills and ignorant of the technicalities of the oil business. After 1900 he lost interest in the details of the business, and in 1902 became lord mayor of London. By the early 1900s ''Shell'' Transport had made a series of costly mistakes, including a disastrous involvement with Texas oil. When Texaco hit a large oil gusher in 1901, Samuel agreed to buy the oil. The flow of oil was not continuous and stopped altogether in the summer of 1902. The formation of the Asiatic Petroleum Company left Deterding in control of Shell's sales in the East. By 1906 Shell's financial situation was so bad that Deterding was able to impose his own terms for a merger of the two concerns, with the Dutch holding 60 percent of what came to be known as the group.

The combined group expanded rapidly under Deterding's leadership. The total assets of Royal Dutch and ''Shell'' Transport grew by more than two and a half times between 1907 and 1914. Major production interests were acquired in Russia in 1910 and Venezuela in 1913. The group also moved into Standard Oil's homeland. In 1912 the Roxana Petroleum Company was formed to operate in Oklahoma, and in 1913 California Oilfields, Ltd. was acquired. By 1915 the group was producing nearly six million barrels of crude oil a year in the United States.

World War I brought mixed fortunes for the group. Its properties in Romania were destroyed, and those in Russia were confiscated after the Russian Revolution in 1917. Shell's exploitation of the Venezuelan oilfields was delayed until late in the war due to difficulties in importing equipment. Shell's cosmopolitan structure was also held in suspicion by some civil servants and ministers within the U.K. government, who feared that it was pro-German and engaged in supplying oil to the enemy through subsidiaries in neutral countries. Various proposals were made by civil servants and several businessmen to merge the group with the Anglo-Persian Oil Company, Burmah Oil, or other U.K. interests in order to make it truly British. However, these wartime proposals were unsuccessful, and regardless of its mixed ownership, the group played an important role in the Allied war effort. In 1919 an agreement was initialed by Deterding and a representative of the U.K. government that provided for an internal rearrangement of the group to allow U.K. interests majority control, but the agreement was never implemented, chiefly because of the delays caused by incoherence and confusion in the official U.K. oil policy of the period. Royal Dutch retained the larger interest in the group.

1920s–40s: Ups and Downs

The 1920s were a decade of growth. In 1919 Shell purchased the large Mexican oilfields controlled by the U.K. oil company Mexican Eagle, led by Lord Cowdray. In 1920 a marketing company was set up in the United Kingdom, Shell-Mex, which represented the Shell and Mexican Eagle interests. Venezuelan oil production expanded very rapidly, much of it controlled by Shell. In 1922 the Shell Union Oil Corporation was formed in the United States to consolidate Shell interests there with those of the Union Oil Company of Delaware, and the American business increased rapidly. By 1929 its U.S. activities had spread to the Atlantic Coast. This decade also saw the first steps in product diversification. In 1929 a new company, N.V. Mekog, was established in the Netherlands to produce nitrogeneous fertilizer from coke-oven gases. This was the group's first venture into chemicals. In the same year the Shell Chemical Company was formed in the United States to produce nitrogeneous fertilizer from natural gas.

The Depression years brought problems. From the late 1920s there was a chronic problem of overcapacity in the oil industry. Deterding's response was to form a worldwide cartel, and in 1928 he organized a meeting in a Scottish castle at Achnacarry with the heads of Standard Oil of New Jersey and the Anglo-Persian Oil Company to achieve this goal. The Achnacarry agreement became an infamous example of cartel exploitation in the oil industry, but the large oil companies were actually unable to control all sources of supply in the world. Achnacarry and subsequent cartel agreements did not last long. The group's oil interests in Mexico were nationalized in 1938—an early warning of later problems in developing countries. Meanwhile Deterding's leadership of the group became suspect. Some managers felt that his leadership style had become very erratic. After his marriage to a German woman in 1936, he resigned as general managing director of Royal Dutch and went to live in Germany.

During World War II and the invasion of the Netherlands, the head offices of the Dutch companies moved to Curaçao in the Dutch West Indies. Once again, Shell played a major role in the Allied war effort. The refineries in the United States produced large quantities of high octane aviation fuel, while the Shell Chemical Company manufactured butadiene for synthetic rubber. All of the group's tankers were placed under U.K. government control, and 87 Shell ships were lost in enemy action.

Key Dates:

1878: The Samuel brothers establish trading companies in London and Japan, which soon begin selling Russian oil to the Far East.

1890: Royal Dutch Petroleum Company is established in The Hague.

1892: Royal Dutch exports its first oil.

1897: The Samuel brothers establish The ''Shell'' Transport and Trading Company and begin searching for oil in the Far East.

1898: ''Shell'' discovers oil in Dutch Borneo.

1907: Royal Dutch and ''Shell'' merge, with Royal Dutch holding 60 percent of the group.

1910: Royal Dutch/Shell obtains production properties in Russia.

1912: Company begins operating in the United States.

1913: Company acquires production properties in Venezuela.

1922: Shell Union Oil is formed in the United States, consolidating Shell's U.S. interests with Union Oil Company of Delaware.

1929: Shell Chemical Company is formed.

1959: Joint Shell and Esso venture discovers one of the world's largest natural gas fields, in the Netherlands.

1971: Shell finds oil in the North Sea.

1974: Shell Coal International is formed.

1995: Shell initiates restructuring.

1998: Shell unveils five-year plan for reducing costs and improving bottom line.

2002: Company acquires Pennzoil-Quaker State.

1950s–80s: Expansion and Diversification

The 1950s and 1960s were golden years of growth for oil companies, as demand for petroleum products expanded. The Shell group and the rest of the ''seven sisters'' of leading international oil companies—British Petroleum, Exxon, Texaco, Chevron, Mobil, and Gulf—retained a strong hold over petroleum production and marketing. The group supplied nearly one-seventh of the world's oil products in these decades. After Deterding's departure, the group was run on a committee basis with no single dominant personality. A stable and respectable image was projected, symbolized by the advertising slogan ''You can be sure of Shell.'' Few Americans, for example, realized that the Shell Oil Company of the United States was not a wholly American oil company.

During the 1950s and 1960s Shell diversified into natural gas and offshore oil production and further expanded its chemicals operations. In 1959 a joint Shell/Esso venture found natural gas in the Netherlands in Groningen. This turned out to be one of the world's largest natural gas fields, and by the early 1970s it provided about half of the natural gas consumed in Europe. Shell was active in the exploration of North Sea oil, and it found oil in the northern North Sea in 1971. In the same year a major offshore gas discovery was made on the Austra-

lian northwest shelf. By the end of the 1960s the Shell group was also manufacturing several hundred chemicals in locations all over the world.

In the late 1960s the group, as well as British Petroleum, attracted widespread criticism because, despite the application of U.N. sanctions, the illegal regime in Rhodesia continued to obtain oil products which were supplied from South Africa. South Africa, of course, made no secret of its support for the illegal regime and did not apply United Nations sanctions.

In the early 1970s it was revealed that the U.K. government had become a party to this discreditable behavior. The Shell group later became the subject of public criticism because of its substantial investment in South Africa.

The structure of the world oil industry was radically altered during the 1973 oil crisis when the Organization of Petroleum Exporting Countries (OPEC) unilaterally raised crude oil prices. The oil companies found themselves forced to allocate scarce oil supplies during the crisis, causing severe problems with several governments. In the United Kingdom, Shell and British Petroleum (BP) had a major clash with the Conservative government led by Edward Heath. Heath demanded that the United Kingdom receive preferential supplies of oil, which the oil companies were attempting to ration between countries. Heath attempted to use the British government's 51 percent shareholding in BP to force that company to supply Britain first, but BP declined. The Shell group, like all the Western oil companies, had much of its crude oil production in developing countries nationalized. The search for oil in non-OPEC areas was stepped up successfully and in the late 1980s it remained responsible for producing 5 percent of the world's oil and 7 percent of its gas.

In response to the problems of the oil industry, the Shell group diversified its business in the 1970s, acquiring coal and metal interests. In 1974 Shell Coal International was established. In 1970 the company acquired the Billiton mining and metals business in the United Kingdom. Chemical manufacture was particularly expanded. This expansion proved unfortunate, since world economic growth after 1973 was much slower than anticipated, with the major recession of the late 1970s and early 1980s causing acute problems. As a result, severe overcapacity developed in the chemical industry. The U.K. company Shell Chemicals experienced problems and was obliged to restructure and reduce capacity. Similar overcapacity occurred in the oil refinery business throughout most of the 1980s. In the 1980s the group rationalized its exposure to chemicals and other noncore businesses. However, the group remained the world's largest producer of petrochemicals and a leading supplier of agrochemicals, in particular insecticides, herbicides, and animal health products and substantial profits were made in the chemicals business.

As the Shell group entered the 1990s, it was an enormous business enterprise and, alongside Unilever, one of the few examples of a successful venture owned and managed by more than one country. The group was the most highly decentralized enterprise in the world oil industry, with its nationally based, integrated operating companies given almost complete autonomy.

1990s: Restructuring

The early 1990s saw higher costs associated with finding and developing oilfields and with refining operations, which had to operate under increasingly stringent environmental controls. At the same time, an abundance of oil on the world market kept prices depressed. While many oil companies scaled back their spending, Shell continued to pump money into both upstream and downstream growth. With Shell aggressively jumping ahead and its competitors drawing back, in 1991 the company overtook Exxon to become the world's largest public oil company.

In 1993, Cornelius Herkstroter became Shell's chairman. He was not in office long before he began to make some radical changes. Despite the fact that Shell was highly profitable—earning a record net profit of $6.3 billion in 1994—it was not performing as well as it should have been. The company's return on average capital employed, which is the key success indicator in the oil industry, had fallen well behind the returns of its competitors. Herkstroter became convinced that Shell's longstanding, extremely decentralized management structure was no longer giving it an advantage. Although the structure had once provided a strategic agility in independent units, it had come to be an unwieldy, inefficient, and expensive bureaucracy.

Herkstroter called in a team of consultants to evaluate the business. The result was a major restructuring that eliminated almost one-third of the jobs at Shell's headquarters. The reorganization also removed some of the power from Shell's dozens of country-specific operating companies—which were accustomed to functioning more as independent companies than as affiliates—and made them accountable to global committees appointed to oversee major areas of operation.

Meanwhile, Shell was coming under heavy fire from environmental groups. In 1995, the company tangled with Germany's Greenpeace group when it attempted to sink its Brent Spar, an offshore oil platform that was no longer used, in the Atlantic Ocean. Enraged environmentalists protested the sinking of the large storage buoy, with its attendant masses of waste that would pollute the waters. As Shell made preparations to tow the Brent Spar from its original location in the North Sea to its planned dumping ground, Greenpeace activists occupied the platform in protest. On land, the group organized a massive boycott of Shell products. Facing a public relations nightmare, Shell ultimately relented, agreeing to dismantle the platform on land—a project that cost exponentially more than sinking it would have. Just a few months after the Brent Spar incident, Shell was again the target of the environmentalists' ire. In November 1995, the Nigerian government executed Ken Saro-Wiwa, an author and activist who had protested the environment-exploiting activities of the oil multinationals in Nigeria—in particular, Shell. Saro-Wiwa's supporters subsequently accused Shell of colluding with the Nigerian government.

The year 1998 was a difficult one for Shell. The company posted its largest ever annual loss—$2.47 billion. On top of

that, consolidation in the industry—the British Petroleum-Amoco merger, and the planned merger of Exxon and Mobil—bumped the company from its post as the largest oil company in the world.

Near the middle of 1998, Cornelius Herkstroter retired from his position as Royal Dutch/Shell's chairman, and was replaced by Mark Moody-Stuart. Under the new leadership, Shell's move toward a more centralized, global structure was immediately accelerated. In December 1998, Moody-Stuart unveiled a five-year plan aimed at streamlining operations, lowering costs, and improving returns. As part of the restructuring, the company announced plans to sell off almost half of its chemicals business, focusing primarily on those chemicals that were most tightly linked to oil refining. It also began consolidating functions wherever possible, more closely integrating its globally far-flung businesses and eliminating some 6,000 jobs in 1999. Along with the divestitures and job cuts came a scaling back in investment; the company reduced overall capital spending by 41 percent in the first three quarters of 1999.

One of the byproducts of the company's more tightly integrated, global structure was its ability to make more consistent and better environmental decisions. In 1997, Shell made a public commitment to contributing to sustainable development. In 1998, it released its first *Shell Report,* an annual publication that documented the actions the company had taken to meet its environmental and social responsibilities.

2000 and Beyond

Shell's efforts to reduce costs proved very effective. While the company had originally expected a $2.5 billion annual savings from its 1998 restructuring, in late 1999 it raised that estimate to $4 billion. The company also continued to cut thousands of jobs and to sell off noncore businesses.

In 2001 and the first part of 2002, although oil and gas prices were volatile, Shell reported solid earnings. In March 2002, the company made a significant acquisition, obtaining Pennzoil-Quaker State Company for $1.8 billion. Pennzoil-Quaker State, the world's largest independent lubricants company, gave Shell a global leadership position in lubricants.

Principal Subsidiaries

Shell Holdings (U.K.) Limited; Shell Oil Company (U.S.A.); Shell Petroleum Inc. (U.S.A.); Shell Petroleum N.V.; Shell U.K. Limited; The Shell Petroleum Company Limited.

Principal Competitors

BP p.l.c.; Exxon Mobil Corporation; TOTAL FINA ELF S.A.

Further Reading

Beaton, K., *Enterprise in Oil: A History of ''Shell'' in the United States,* New York: Brill, 1957.
The First Hundred Years, The Hague: Royal Dutch Petroleum Company, 1990.
Gerretson, F.C., *History of the Royal Dutch,* 4 vols., Leiden: E.J. Brill, 1953–57.

Guyon, Janet, ''Why Is the World's Most Profitable Company Turning Itself Inside Out?'' *Fortune*, August 4, 1997, p. 120.

Henriques, Robert, *Marcus Samuel, First Viscount Bearsted and Founder of the ''Shell' Transport and Trading Company, 1853–1927*, London: Barrie and Rockliff, 1960.

A History of the Royal Dutch/Shell Group of Companies, London: Shell, 1988.

Howarth, Stephen, *A Century in Oil: The ''Shell'' Transport and Trading Company 1897–1997*, London: Weidenfeld & Nicolson Ltd., 1998.

Jones, Geoffrey, ''Frederick Lane'' and ''Marcus Samuel,'' in *Dictionary of Business Biography: A Biographical Dictionary of Business Leaders Active in Britain in the Period, 1860–1980*, 5 vols., edited by David Jeremy, London: Butterworth, 1984–86.

——, *The State and the Emergence of the British Oil Industry*, London: Macmillan, 1981.

Jordan, A. J, and Grant Jordan, *Shell, Greenpeace and the Brent Spar*, New York: Palmgrave, 2001.

Sampson, A., *The Seven Sisters: The Great Oil Companies and the World They Made*, London: Hodder and Stoughton, 1975.

''Shell on the Rocks,'' *Economist*, June 24, 1996, p. 57.

—Geoffrey Jones
—update: Shawna Brynildssen

Sandia National Laboratories

Sandia National Laboratories

1515 Eubank Boulevard SE
Albuquerque, New Mexico 87123
U.S.A.
Telephone: (505) 845-0011
Fax: (505) 845-0098
Web site: http://www.sandia.gov

Nonprofit Corporation
Incorporated: 1949
Employees: 7,450
Sales: $1.4 billion (2001)
NAIC: 541380 Testing Laboratories

Sandia National Laboratories is one of the major national defense engineering and science laboratories in the United States, funded primarily by the Department of Energy and operated as a subsidiary of the Lockheed Martin Company. For more than 50 years Sandia has been responsible for the design of all nonnuclear components of the nation's nuclear weapons. In addition, Sandia has become involved in the detection of nuclear blasts to assist in the verification of arms' treaties, as well as research on the Strategic Defense Initiative, the so-called "Star Wars" program. Although much of the lab's technology has filtered into the private sector over the years, since the early 1990s Sandia has made a concerted effort to team up with industry partners to take full advantage of its talented scientists and state-of-the art facilities. Sandia's main lab is located in New Mexico, with a secondary facility in Livermore, California.

Sandia: A Result of World War II's Manhattan Project

The Manhattan Project was the code name for the United States' World War II crash program to develop an atom bomb. The design, testing, and assembly of the first nuclear weapons were conducted in the remote location of Los Alamos, New Mexico. Although the area was easy to secure, it also presented logistical problems: a lack of housing and utilities and transportation difficulties. To rectify this situation, in July 1945 the

predecessor to Sandia National Laboratories was created, the Z Division of Los Alamos Laboratories, dedicated to the design, testing, and assembly of nonnuclear components used in the atomic bomb. After reviewing a number of possible sites for the new operation, the leaders of the Manhattan Project settled on Kirtland Field, an army staging and training facility located near Albuquerque. East of the airfield was a collection of buildings originally used by the Army Air Corps to train aircraft mechanics and that later served as a convalescent center for wounded airmen; it was named Sandia Base because of the local Sandia Mountains. By the last year of the war it was relegated to the task of dismantling surplus military aircraft. Located near a military airfield, it was deemed the ideal location for the new Z Division. With victory in the war in Europe complete and preparations underway to drop the atomic bombs that would ultimately end the war in the Pacific, the Army constructed new buildings, implemented security measures, and transferred the Manhattan Project's Z Division stockpile of nonnuclear weapons parts to the Sandia Base.

Following the war, the research and control of nuclear weapons was transferred from military to civilian authority, the five-member Atomic Energy Commission (AEC), through the Atomic Energy Act of 1946. In addition, Z Division passed out of military hands, with AEC oversight of the operation provided by a Sandia field office. With the advent of the Cold War and the continued need to develop nuclear weapons, the AEC soon realized the need to upgrade Z Division, which aside from its pool of talented scientists consisted of little more than some prefabricated huts. In 1948 the operation was elevated to laboratory status, becoming a separate branch of Los Alamos called Sandia Laboratory. Under the leadership of its director, Paul Larsen, Sandia moved quickly to upgrade its facilities and recruit new personnel. When it became clear how large an operation Sandia would become, the University of California, which was charged with running Los Alamos, requested that the responsibility for some of Sandia's work be turned over to the Bendix Corporation. Larsen objected, offering a counterproposal: the creation of a nonprofit corporation named Sandia Laboratory, Inc., which would manage the entire operation under the auspices of the AEC. The Air Force recommended that an engineering firm serve as a contract manager, and the heads of the AEC then recruited Bell Laboratories to operate Sandia. Western Electric and its parent corporation, AT&T, shared ownership of Bell Laboratories, and at first AT&T was reluctant to take on the task of running Sandia. It took a personal appeal from President Truman to Leroy Wilson, the president of AT&T, to secure the company's cooperation. Truman wrote that AT&T had "an opportunity to render an exceptional service in the national interest." The language of "exceptional service in the national interest" would become the cornerstone of the lab's ongoing mission.

Becoming an AT&T Subsidiary in 1949

Although the AEC expected AT&T to profit from its management of Sandia, AT&T insisted on a no-profit, no-loss contract, which was signed in October 1949. In turn, Western Electric incorporated Sandia as a wholly owned subsidiary. In this way the AEC would be able to easily transfer the operation to another entity should AT&T decide one day to withdraw from the contract. Thus, on November 1, 1949, Sandia was incorporated under Delaware law with stock valued at $1,000, all of which was owned by AT&T and invested in U.S. savings bonds.

Sandia was charged with the surveillance and maintenance of all nuclear weapon storage sites, a responsibility that would last until 1960, when sealed-pit weapons reduced the need for such a high level of care. Because the Soviet Union detonated its first nuclear explosion in August 1949 and the Korean War would soon begin, Sandia also was forced to quickly ramp up its operation to improve America's nuclear strike capability. Foremost was the need to create smaller components to reduce the size of the metal casing that held the large nuclear devices of the day. The bombs were so heavy that aircraft carrier planes were incapable of delivering them, which greatly limited how the weapon could be deployed. Sandia also became involved in developing suitable nuclear warheads for the military's new guided missile program, which had been jumpstarted by the capture of German scientists. Throughout much of the 1950s Sandia worked on a myriad of nuclear weapons as the United States and the Soviet Union matched achievements. Soon after the United States added fusion, or thermonuclear, weapons, the Soviets followed suit. Sandia became involved in the design of nuclear explosives through its Lawrence Livermore Laboratory, which was established in 1952. Sandia pioneered the "wooden bomb" concept, which led to the creation of nuclear weapons that could be safely stockpiled for a number of years with only a modicum of maintenance yet be ready for immediate use. It also developed the "building-block" concept, which resulted in the sealing of the fissile material of a nuclear weapon, the "physics package," in a capsule that could be used interchangeably with different weapon systems. In addition, Sandia developed the "lay down" concept for delivering nuclear devices. Because an

aircraft was forced to fly low to avoid radar detection and minimize the risk of being shot down, it was unable to escape the blast of the nuclear weapon it dropped. Sandia was instrumental in creating a bomb that could be lobbed in the air as an aircraft escaped and then slowed on its descent to the target by means of a parachute. Making the idea actually work not only required a much stronger chute than was commercially available, it also called for all the parts of the weapon to be significantly strengthened. Instead of exploding in the air, the nuclear device was designed to detonate on impact by means of a spike in the bomb's nose, meaning that all of the components had to be capable of working after surviving what amounted to a 50-mile-an-hour car wreck.

The broad array of problems that Sandia had to solve during the 1950s resulted in its scientists making early use of a number of technologies. In the early 1950s Sandia employed IBM's card-programmed calculators and smaller analog computers, and in some cases designed its own computers for specific uses. By 1954 the lab purchased its first digital computer and soon opened 24-hour-a-day computer centers to handle the large number of calculations its scientists needed in their work. In the mid-1950s Sandia engaged in some early efforts in solar energy. Sandia's nuclear weapons engineering work also involved the use of plastic and microwave circuits. To protect personnel from handling dangerous radioactive material, Sandia entered robotics. In 1958 the lab created Sandy Mobat, a remote-controlled mobile, however lumbering, robot.

The United States and the Soviet Union agreed in 1958 to suspend nuclear testing. With the moratorium holding, Sandia no longer expanded as rapidly as it had during the previous decade. Now it actually faced the possibility of shrinking in size. When the Soviets resumed testing in 1961, however, Sandia saw its responsibilities shifting to other areas of national security. With nuclear weapons deployed to Europe in support of NATO (North Atlantic Treaty Organization), Sandia produced the Permissive Action Link that prevented unauthorized use of the devices. The Limited Test Ban Treaty of 1963, which eliminated atmospheric testing, resulted in Sandia stepping up underground testing as well as efforts to detect nuclear testing around the world. In addition, the lab played a significant role in the design and testing of a number of nuclear weapons, including the warheads for the Minuteman and Poseidon missile systems. During the 1960s, Sandia also took on responsibilities in areas outside of nuclear weaponry. It developed sensors capable of detecting troop movements in the jungles of Vietnam. Its advanced parachute technology would be of particular importance to the NASA space program. Sandia also began to see some of its technology have an impact on private industry. The most important innovation during this period of finding commercial applications was the "clean room," adopted by the medical profession and the pharmaceutical industry. It proved to be pivotal in the development of the modern microelectronics industry. Sandia also invented hot-air solder leveling that greatly benefited the circuit-board industry.

By the early 1970s Sandia was no longer focused on a single mission. It became involved in assessing the safety of America's nuclear reactors. It developed a Safe Secure Trailer (SST) for transporting nuclear weapons and also became involved in the safe disposal of nuclear wastes. Following the terrorist

Key Dates:

1945: Z Division of Los Alamos Laboratory is formed.
1948: Z Division is renamed Sandia Laboratory.
1949: Sandia is incorporated and AT&T takes over as contract manager.
1979: Sandia is designated a national laboratory.
1992: AT&T announces its decision to terminate its management agreement.
1993: Martin Marietta is named the new contract manager.
1997: Sandia wins eight of the international ''R&D 100 Awards.''

attacks at the 1972 Munich Olympics, Sandia became heavily involved in safeguarding all nuclear materials that could be used to create explosive devices. The energy crisis of the early 1970s resulted in Sandia turning its attention to the development of solar, wind, and geothermal power, in addition to improving ways to better obtain fossil fuels. All the while, Sandia continued to work on nuclear weapons, including new warhead subsystems for Minuteman, Poseidon, and Pershing missiles, new cruise missiles, traditional bombs, and even nuclear artillery shells. Moreover, Sandia continued to be responsible for creating sensors to monitor international arms control agreements. To this point in its history, Sandia was little known to the pubic. Then in 1979 it was granted national laboratory status, joining the ranks of the more recognizable facilities at Argonne, Brookhaven, and Oak Ridge.

Becoming Involved in SDI During the Reagan Administration

When Ronald Reagan assumed the presidency in 1981, Sandia adjusted to the new administration's priorities. Funding for energy research was cut, while defense spending increased significantly. During the early 1980s Sandia's expertise in the design of nuclear weapons was applied to conventional weapons. The lab also became heavily involved in conducting research for the Strategic Defense Initiative (SDI). Sandia prospered during this period, but by the close of the 1980s, with the collapse of the Soviet Union and the end of the Cold War, it faced the challenge of adapting to a new era.

In the early 1990s the country stopped developing new nuclear weapons, which placed even greater emphasis on Sandia's role in safeguarding the existing stockpile. The lab also was asked to make its research more readily available for commercial applications. Its national security mission was redefined to include helping the United States stay competitive economically. In 1989 the National Competitiveness Technology Transfer Act was signed into law, which Sandia began implementing two years later. Because its emphasis was on applied engineering rather than basic science, it appeared better suited than the other national laboratories to successfully make the transition to a commercial focus.

Sandia's connection to AT&T was seen as a major asset in making the lab's research commercially relevant, but in 1992 AT&T announced that after more than 40 years of serving as

contract manager it was stepping down, effective September 1993. The U.S. Energy Department, which now oversaw the lab, requested proposals to operate Sandia from 140 organizations, which included four universities, but received bids from less than 30. Martin Marietta was finally selected to run Sandia. Not only did Martin Marietta have experience running the Oak Ridge National Laboratory, it agreed to spend $9.5 million of its own money to fund a nonprofit venture capital corporation that would help commercialize the lab's R&D efforts. (Two years later Martin Marietta merged with Lockheed to become Lockheed Martin.)

Sandia made steady progress during the 1990s in its outreach to private industry, helped in some degree by the Energy Department's decision to allow national laboratories to strike deals with businesses directly, rather than requiring a time-consuming department review. In 1990 Sandia had no Cooperative Research and Development Agreements (CRADAs), but by September 1994 it had 190 in place, worth nearly $600 million. To support its activity in the high-tech arena, Sandia opened an office in San Jose, California, the heart of Silicon Valley. Because so many microelectronic companies were publicly traded and needed to concentrate on short-term profitability, they were unable to engage in lengthy research projects, a situation that offered an opening for Sandia, which had the scientists but not the investor pressure. In addition, the lab also became very active in New Mexico, not only working with area universities to bring new technologies to the attention of venture capitalists, but also lending technical expertise to small businesses, at no cost, through its Small Business Technical Assistance Program. Moreover, Sandia scientists and engineers were granted leave under a new venture program to establish start-up businesses using technologies developed in the lab. Sandia's success in its new commercial mission was reflected in 1997 when it landed eight of the international ''R&D 100 Awards.'' It was especially aggressive in pursuing robotics and ''micromachines,'' which promised a wide range of applications, including delicate surgery, clearing minefields, and cleaning up contaminated sites. To facilitate even greater interaction with private companies, Sandia opened a 200-acre research park in New Mexico, which allowed companies closer access to its researchers.

One of the strengths of Sandia throughout its history was an ability to retain talented scientists and engineers. Careers of 30 and 40 years were not uncommon. In the early 1980s the average age of a weapons designer was nearly 40 years, and by the mid-1990s that average would grow to 45. With the move toward more commercial activity in the 1990s, Sandia found itself competing with private industry for talent. The national laboratories also faced security issues in hiring, following the espionage case of Wen Ho Lee at Los Alamos. Roughly half of all students enrolled in physics and related fields were foreign born, who now faced problems in gaining security clearance. Moreover, the Los Alamos case had an adverse effect on the national laboratories' ability to attract candidates. For instance, not even a single candidate showed up for a recruiting effort at Stanford University in 2000, a visit that would normally result in 200 applicants. Clearly, one of the greatest ongoing challenges facing Sandia was its ability to replenish its ranks with young scientists. Aside from providing compensation on a par with private industry, Sandia and the other national laboratories had to offer candidates something more: the chance to pursue exciting science. Where that science would lead, and into what areas Sandia would expand beyond its military obligations, remained very much an unanswered question.

Principal Operating Units

Albuquerque; Livermore.

Further Reading

Garcia, Kenneth J., ''Weapons Labs Retool for New Era,'' *San Francisco Chronicle,* December 22, 1995, p. A1.

Goodwin, Irwin, ''To Replace AT&T at Sandia, DOE Picks Martin Marietta,'' *Physics Today,* September 1993, p. 53.

Hedden, Carole, ''National Labs Target College Campuses,'' *Aviation Week & Space Technology,* August 6, 2001, p. 64.

Johnson, Leland, *Sandia National Laboratories: A History of Exceptional Service in the National Interest,* Albuquerque: Sandia National Laboratories, 1997.

Mora, Caro J., ''Sandia Turns 50,'' *New Mexico Business Journal,* May-June 1999.

Siemens, Warren, ''The National Labs' Changing Role in New Mexico,'' *New Mexico Business Journal,* June 1997.

Smith, R. Jeffrey, ''Nuclear Labs Asked to Shift Focus,'' *Washington Post,* July 26, 1990, p. A12.

Spohn, Larry, ''Sandia Labs Emerges from the Shadows,'' *New Mexico Business Journal,* April-May 1998, p. 48.

Weber, Jonathan, ''AT&T to Quit As Manager of Weapons Lab,'' *Los Angeles Times,* May 6, 1992, p. D2.

—Ed Dinger

The Sanofi-Synthélabo Group

174, avenue de France
75013 Paris
France
Telephone: (33) 1-53-77-40-00
Fax: (33) 1-53-77-42-96
Web site: http://www.sanofi-synthelabo.com

Public Company
Incorporated: 1973 as the Sanofi Group
Employees: 29,200
Sales: $5.62 billion (2000)
Stock Exchanges: Euronext Paris
Ticker Symbol: SAN
NAIC: 325412 Pharmaceutical Preparation Manufacturing

The history of The Sanofi-Synthélabo Group began in 1973, when the French state-owned Elf Aquitaine oil company consolidated a number of cosmetic, healthcare, and animal nutrition firms into a corporate subsidiary, the Sanofi Group. This undertaking marked an ambitious program of diversification that created a state enterprise capable of competing in the healthcare industry on an international scale. In the past two decades Sanofi has grown from a moderate concern into a major player in the French pharmaceutical industry. After merging with Synthélabo in 1999 the company sold off its cosmetics business and began focusing exclusively on pharmaceuticals. Today the combined company is the fastest growing pharmaceutical firm in Europe.

Managing Diversity: 1973–82

Although Sanofi was created in 1973 in order to form an amalgamation of companies, it was only in 1979 that all of its pharmaceutical activities were regrouped under a single organization. This tactic represented an effort to strengthen research activities and overseas market penetration. Three companies, including Labaz, Parcor, and Galor, all previously affiliated with Sanofi, were now wholly absorbed, and for the first time Sanofi gained a separate stock market quotation through the issuing of public stock on the Paris exchange.

While currency exchange fluctuations caused Parcor to register a profit decline in 1979, that same year Sanofi reported an overall increase in company profits. The following year Sanofi increased its holdings by merging with the Clin-Midy division of CM Industries, a manufacturer of pharmaceuticals, veterinary, chemical, medical-surgical, and food products. This action significantly increased Sanofi's research and development budget and expanded the company's size by 50 percent. Sanofi now ranked among the leading pharmaceutical companies in France.

By mid-1980 Sanofi's profits reached unprecedented heights. A 56 percent increase over the previous year's figures was attributed to benefits gained from the reorganization. Although the sale of pharmaceuticals accounted for a majority of Sanofi's activities, a significant increase was generated from the sale of cosmetics and veterinary products.

Between the years 1978 and 1982 Sanofi's international sales improved by 275 percent. By gaining access to two of the world's most important markets, the United States and Japan, Sanofi's overseas activities generated nearly half of the company's consolidated revenues. A joint subsidiary formed in 1981 with U.S.-based American Home Products was followed by a similar agreement established with the Japanese groups Meiji-Seika-Kaisha and Taisho. Through the operations of these joint ventures, $104 million was generated from the sale of just three drugs. In addition to expanding pharmaceutical operations, Sanofi was successful in tripling its foreign sales in the cosmetics division.

Sanofi's research and development activities, supported by a 34 percent increase in expenditures during 1982, produced a number of potentially profit-making drugs. Among the products undergoing clinical testing were an antiarrhythmic, a third-generation cephalosporin, and a treatment for certain forms of cancer. In addition, research proceeded on a psychotropic drug and on an anticonvulsion drug. Sanofi's pharmaceutical research took place at five laboratories in France as well as at facilities in Brussels and Milan.

One of the most important developments in Sanofi's research activities was the 1983 inauguration of a biotechnology center in Labège, the largest of its kind in France. At the same time the company acquired a minority interest in Entremont, a dairy products firm engaged in researching biotechnological applications. In particular, Sanofi was interested in Entremont's investigation into the production of milk compounds through biotechnology. These two developments marked an important step toward building Sanofi's future position as the biotechnological center of all of Elf Aquitaine's activities.

Expanding Sanofi's Pharmaceutical Business: 1983–89

In addition to advances in the field of biotechnology, Sanofi continued its program of acquisition. In 1983 Choay, a pharmaceutical company specializing in the area of venous thrombosis, was acquired by Sanofi. Sanofi now gained access to a new line of important pharmaceuticals. The animal health division also increased its holdings through the acquisition of Institute Ronchèse, a manufacturer of vaccines and other veterinary medicines.

By 1984 Elf Aquitaine's increasing biotechnological activities compelled the state-owned oil group to reorganize its company structure. Chairman Pecqueur transferred most of Elf Aquitaine's activities in this area, from healthcare to agricultural products, to the control of Sanofi. While Atochem, Elf Aquitaine's chemical subsidiary, maintained control of biotechnological activities in the area of industrial products, Sanofi solidified its role as the center of Elf Aquitaine's innovative technologies.

As a first step in creating Sanofi Elf Bio Industries, Sanofi merged with Rousselot, a gelatine, protein, and glue producer in which Elf Aquitaine formerly held a majority interest. Through the action of this merger, Elf Aquitaine's stake in Sanofi increased to 62 percent. To increase the financial standing of Elf Aquitaine's biotechnological developments, Pecqueur announced plans to double the company budget in this area to $22 million.

By 1985 Sanofi posted an annual sales figure of FFr 15 billion. This marked a significant increase from the FFr 2 billion generated yearly during the 1970s. Yet Sautier, commenting on the weak European market and price controls for pharmaceuticals on the domestic market, initiated a program of internationalization with the hope of recouping investments on foreign markets. Two important targets of this overseas market penetration were the United States and Japan. Thus a sizable amount of cash savings was set aside for any acquisition suitable for this expansion. Additional foreign acquisitions included a Brazilian

subsidiary of Revlon, as well as a 50 percent interest in a South Korean company.

Other significant events that occurred during 1985 included the introduction of the first low molecular weight heparin. This product, developed by the Choay subsidiary, marked a significant step in the prevention of thromboembolic diseases. In addition, Diagnostics Pasteur, a subsidiary in the area of medical equipment, released the Elavia test for detecting the antibody to LAV, a virus associated with AIDS.

Two successful U.S. acquisitions following Sautier's plans for expansion included the Dairyland Food Laboratories, a Wisconsin dairy company, and Dahlgren, a large crop seed producer. Both companies managed a successful biotechnology program. The following year a 35 percent bid for Barberet & Blanc, an Antibes-based specialist in carnations and gerberas, further strengthened Sanofi's operations in plant and genetic technologies. Barberet & Blanc, a small family operation located on the French Riviera, had developed expertise in "in vitro" plant-growing techniques as well as creating new carnation varieties resistant to deadly fungus.

Thus, through a series of acquisitions of small but high-technology concerns, Sanofi gained expertise in the area of biotechnological processes in food additives, dairy products, and large crop seed sectors. Some 25.8 percent of Sanofi's 1985 sales resulted from products developed out of these technologies. In addition to benefits from this product orientation, Pecqueur's plan to internationalize Sanofi's operation resulted in 50 percent of the company's sales being generated from foreign markets.

During the same time that successful biotechnological products emerged from Sanofi's laboratories, the sale of pharmaceuticals continued to account for 46.8 percent of group sales. In the United States, the Food and Drug Administration approved the marketing of Cordarone, a major anti-arrhythmic drug. This drug was marketed through a joint venture between Sanofi and American Home Products.

As Sanofi continued to broaden its activities and generate profits through the sale of healthcare products, cosmetics, additives, seed sectors, and animal pharmaceuticals, the company implemented an employee profit-sharing program. In the late 1980s, a company savings plan and a share purchase option completed this program.

By the end of the decade, the future of Sanofi depended on the company's continuing success in developing innovative products and penetrating foreign markets. The company maintained a strong position as a leading French pharmaceutical concern. As Sanofi's diverse activities suggested, the company would continue to hold this position in the years to come.

The Next Big Step: Mergers and Acquisitions in the 1990s

At the beginning of the 1990s, Sanofi found itself at a crucial juncture in its short history. Recognizing that its core business would ultimately lie in pharmaceuticals, the company began plotting its first steps toward creating an international presence in the rapidly growing drug industry. To achieve this goal, the

Key Dates:

1973: Sanofi Group is formed as a subsidiary of Elf Aquitaine.
1981: Sanofi forms joint subsidiary with American Home Products.
1983: Sanofi opens biotechnology center in Labège, France.
1991: Sanofi enters strategic alliance with Sterling Winthrop.
1999: Sanofi merges with Synthélabo to form the Sanofi-Synthélabo Group.

company would need to set its sights on acquisitions. The company took a big step in 1991, when it entered into a strategic partnership with American drug company Sterling Winthrop, itself a subsidiary of Kodak. Although not a traditional merger—no money was exchanged, and the joint enterprise was run by a team of executives from both companies—the alliance allowed Sanofi to gain an important foothold in the lucrative North American drug market.

At first many industry experts were skeptical that such a ''non-merger'' could work, since it was not clear who would ultimately be leading the venture. Nor could the product of such an alliance be considered a major consolidation. Prior to the agreement, Sanofi and Sterling placed 35th and 37th, respectively, among pharmaceutical companies. What was more significant, however, was the fact that the two companies combined ranked tenth overall in research and development spending, committing more than $500 million annually to developing new drugs. Furthermore, the companies shared similar research philosophies; both utilized a ''mechanistic'' experimental approach, which involved comprehensive screening of chemical compounds. At the same time, each company had experience in unique specialties, Sanofi with thrombosis, Sterling with cancer treatment. The complementary natures of the companies' research interests, along with the similarity of their methods and their shared ambitions, helped push concerns about managerial logistics into the background.

After a year, the agreement was beginning to bear fruit. Operating under the name Sanofi Winthrop, the two companies had established joint ventures in 14 countries by January 1992, with operating units scattered throughout Europe and North and South America. By early 1992 the alliance ranked in the top 20 internationally among pharmaceuticals. In 1994 the venture turned into yet another golden opportunity, when Kodak decided to sell Sterling Winthrop to Sanofi outright for $1.68 billion.

Although Sanofi was now firmly committed to pharmaceuticals, the company had no intention of dumping its other core businesses just yet. Its cosmetic segment, bolstered by the purchase of Yves Saint Laurent in 1993, still boasted excellent sales. Sanofi CEO Jean-Francois Dehecq, however, clearly

viewed these other divisions primarily in terms of financing the growth of the company's pharmaceutical interests. At the same time, if the company wished to continue growing in this market, it would eventually need to sell some of its divisions in order to finance further acquisitions.

The year 1996 was another critical one for the emerging pharmaceutical company. With ten products in late-stage development simultaneously, Sanofi was poised to explode onto the international scene. It was clear, however, that its small size would soon prove a liability if it did not expand its sales and distribution networks, particularly in North America. To this end, Sanofi acquired the Bock Pharmacal Company in July 1996, doubling its U.S. sales and marketing force. This deal was hardly enough, however, to catapult Sanofi into the elite of pharmaceutical corporations. The industry was undergoing intense consolidation in the mid-1990s, with more than $100 billion in mergers and acquisitions occurring between 1994 and 1997. Dwarfed by such numbers, Sanofi was clearly a prime target for a takeover.

Sanofi took a major step toward holding off such an acquisition when it merged with rival French pharmaceutical concern Synthélabo in 1999. The deal allowed Sanofi to sell off its other businesses, and by the following year the company was focusing exclusively on pharmaceuticals. At the same time, Sanofi was gradually moving away from its parent, Elf Aquitaine. Over the course of the 1990s Elf saw its share in its subsidiary fall from 61 percent in 1990 to 52 percent in 1994, and finally to 35.1 percent with the Synthélabo merger. Entering the 21st century, Elf Aquitaine was committed to holding onto its remaining shares in Sanofi until 2004. But with three blockbuster drugs on the market and net profits soaring, Sanofi-Synthélabo was offering some proof that a medium-sized business could survive on its own in the high-powered pharmaceutical industry.

Principal Competitors

Aventis; Eli Lilly and Company; Merck & Co., Inc.

Further Reading

Buchan, David, ''YSL and Elf-Sanofi Form World's Third-Biggest Beauty Group,'' *Financial Times* (London), January 20, 1993, p. 21.
Cookson, Clive, Karen Zagor, and William Dawkins, ''If You Can't Buy 'Em, Join 'Em: Drug Firm Sanofi and Sterling Form a Transatlantic Alliance,'' *Financial Post* (Toronto), January 11, 1991, p. 13.
Firn, David, ''Sanofi Keeps Up with Big Players,'' *Financial Times* (London), February 21, 2001, p. 32.
Owen, David, and David Pilling, ''Partners Plan for Profit Without Tears: Sanofi-Synthélabo Is Sure It Can Elude Predatory Rivals and Make an Impact in a Consolidating Pharmaceuticals Sector,'' *Financial Times* (London), March 17, 2000, p. 37.
Ridding, John, ''Sanofi Shifts Center of Gravity—The Drugs Group Has Taken a Big Strategic Step,'' *Financial Times* (London), June 27, 1994, p. 27.

—update: Steve Meyer

sappi

Sappi Limited

Sappi House
48 Ameshoff Street
Braamfontein
2017 Johannesburg
South Africa
Telephone: (+27) 11 407-8111
Fax: (+27)11 403-1493/8236
Web site: http://www.sappi.com

Public Company
Incorporated: 1936 as South African Pulp and Paper
    Industries
Employees: 18,231
Sales: R 33.29 billion ($4.18 billion) (2001)
Stock Exchanges: Johannesburg Frankfurt New York
    London
Ticker Symbols: SAP; SPP (New York)
NAIC: 322121 Paper (Except Newsprint) Mills; 322110
    Pulp Mills

South Africa's Sappi Limited went on a shopping spree in the 1990s and transformed itself into the world's leading manufacturer of coated fine papers. The company operates 18 pulp and paper mills in southern Africa, North America, and Europe—the company is market leader in each of these regions, holding 20 percent of the European market, 22 percent of the North American market, and 60 percent of the African market. In addition, the company's dissolving pulp production, used for the manufacture of cellulose-derived paper products, has captured the leading position in the global market, with a 15 percent share. Together, the company's operations combined to generate sales of more than R 33 billion ($4.18 billion) in 2001. Sappi—the name derives from its earlier moniker, South African Pulp and Paper Industries—has divided its operations into two primary divisions, London-based Sappi Fine Papers, and Johannesburg's Sappi Forest Products, which includes the company's forestry division, as well as its pulp, particleboard, and cardboard production. Sappi ships its products, which include wood-free coated papers, to more than 100 countries. More than 80 percent of the company's sales and more than three-quarters of the company's

assets are located outside of South Africa. Sappi is targeting the southern Asia region for growth at the beginning of the 21st century, most likely through the establishment of greenfield sites in conjunction with local partners. The company claims that it is unlikely to pursue further megadeals—such as its $1.6 billion purchase of SD Warren in the United States and its nearly $800 million purchase of former Buhrmann subsidiary KNP Leykam in 1997—in the near future. Sappi's transformation has long been led by Chairman and CEO Eugene Van As. The company is listed on the Johannesburg, Frankfurt, and New York stock exchanges.

Afrikaans Pulp and Paper Producer in the 1930s

Sappi started out as South African Pulp and Paper Industries, registered in 1936 in Johannesburg, South Africa. The following year, the company began construction of a pulp and paper mill, located near Springs. Because the mill used straw as its chief raw material, it was given the name Enstra, for "Enterprise Straw." That same flair for fantasy was to enable the company to weather the war years and eye further growth by the end of the 1940s.

South African Pulp and Paper Industries acquired two farms, near the Tugela River in what was known as Zululand. The site was targeted for construction of a second paper mill. In the meantime, the company began its own plantation operations to ensure its raw materials supply. The decision to go ahead with construction of the Tugela Mill was made in 1950. Completed in 1954, the Tugela Mill was devoted to kraft packaging production, while the original Enstra location turned its specialty to the manufacture of fine papers.

By the end of that decade, South African Pulp and Paper Industries sought further growth through acquisition, buying up a controlling share of Union Corrugated Cases in 1959, then taking over Cellulose Products, which made tissue wadding products, the following year. South African Pulp and Paper Industries pursued organic growth as well; among the company's capital investments was the installation of a second machine at the Tugela Mill in 1963. The new machine was dedicated to the production of kraft linerboard products. By then, South African Pulp and Paper Industries had celebrated its one millionth ton of paper produced since the company's inception.

South African Pulp and Paper Industries continued to seek organic growth during the decade, buying up farmland in the Elands River Valley. The company began construction of a new mill, completed in 1966, and called Ngodwana. This mill was dedicated to the production of unbleached kraft pulp. The site also gave the company expanded acreage for its raw materials plantation activities. By the end of that year, South African Pulp and Paper Industries celebrated a new production milestone, reaching the two million ton production mark. The company established a new dedicated timber division in 1968.

That same year, South African Pulp and Paper Industries applied for a patent for a new bleaching process using oxygen instead of chlorine. The process, dubbed Sapoxyl, was put into production in 1970. The steady increases in production made by the company in the late 1960s could be seen with the passage of a new production milestone, that of South African Pulp and Paper Industries' three millionth ton of paper since its founding.

Domestic Expansion in the 1980s

South African Pulp and Paper Industries changed its name to Sappi Limited in 1973. With the growth of its three core operation areas, the company moved to reorganize its operations in 1977, placing its activities into three new operating subsidiaries: Sappi Fine Papers, Sappi Kraft, and Sappi Forests. Each subsidiary operated with its own board of directors. Sappi itself came under control of Gencor, a conglomerate which itself was controlled by finance group Sanlam. This ownership gave Sappi the financial backing to pursue further expansion.

In 1979, Sappi acquired local market rival Stanger Pulp and Paper. The following year, the company branched out into the operation of sawmills, forming a new subsidiary, Sappi Timber Products. That subsidiary acquired a new saw mill in Elandshoek, located near its parent company's Ngodwana mill. This mill was slated to undergo a vast expansion program, representing the company's largest capital investment program to date, to increase its capacity and add newsprint, linerboard, unbleached pulp, and bleached pulp production by 1985. In the meantime, Sappi launched a new kraft linerboard mill in Cape Town. Called Cape Kraft, the new mill's production was based entirely on recycled raw material. Another new product line joined the group in 1982, when Sappi acquired Novobord, adding that company's production of particleboard. The following year, the company acquired another particleboard manufacturer, Timberboard, which was merged into Novobord.

Sappi remained an entirely South African company; nonetheless, exports represented an increasing percentage of the company's production, reaching 50 percent by the end of the 1980s. To encourage this development the company founded

Sappi International, a subsidiary dedicated to international marketing of the company's products, in 1986. A year later, the company expanded its Sappi Novobord operation, adding particleboard manufacturing capacity. Then in 1988, Sappi acquired Usutu Pulp Company, based in Swaziland, giving it a world-leading producer of unbleached kraft pulp. The following year, Sappi made a new acquisition, this time of Saiccor, the world leader in dissolving pulp production. With all of its production going to the export market, the Saiccor acquisition helped Sappi's own exports top half of the company's total production.

These acquisitions helped Sappi gain a strong position in the industry as South Africa at last abandoned apartheid and rejoined the world community. Sappi was quick to expand beyond South Africa and the coming decade was to see the company transform itself from a company with 100 percent of its assets in South Africa to a truly globally operating company, with more than 75 of its assets located away from its home base.

Post-Apartheid Global Market Leader

Among the company's first post-apartheid acquisitions were those of five paper mills in the United Kingdom. Sappi followed up these purchases with the establishment of a new European headquarters, Sappi Europe. That office was soon joined by a new overseas subsidiary, Sappi Trading, which took over Sappi's international trading operations. Founded in 1991, Sappi Trading was formed around another key acquisition, that of Specialty Pulp Services, based in Hong Kong.

Yet, as Sappi moved into the 1990s, it was setting its sights on still higher growth. Led by Eugene Van As, who had joined the company in the late 1970s and took over as CEO and chairman in the 1990s, Sappi began making a small number of large-scale acquisitions. The first of these came in 1992, when Sappi acquired Hannover Papier, the leading manufacturer of coated wood-free paper in Germany. That purchase gave Sappi a position as one of the top three coated wood-free paper makers in the European market. Capitalizing on its new scale, Sappi launched its stock on the London, Frankfurt, and Paris stock exchanges, while maintaining its chief listing on the Johannesburg exchange. A year later, Sappi reorganized its European holdings under a new subsidiary, Sappi Europe SA. At that time, Sappi became an independent operation as Gencor, as well as ultimate parent Sanlam, underwent drastic unbundling operations in an effort to streamline their businesses for the new post-apartheid era.

Sappi turned its sights toward the North American market. In 1994, the company paid $1.6 billion to acquire a 75 percent share of SD Warren, the United States' leading coated wood-free paper producer. That acquisition placed Sappi in the worldwide leadership spot for that paper category. Although Van As was criticized for having paid a premium price for SD Warren, the Sappi CEO was betting on a growing importance for wood-free paper products as the paper and publishing industries increasingly adopted high-technology applications.

Sappi completed its acquisition of SD Warren in 1996. In the meantime, it turned its attention toward renewing its industrial park. In 1995, the company began a R 800 million expansion of its Saiccor subsidiary. The following year, the company completed a modernization of all of its African pulp and paper mills.

Key Dates:

1936: Company registers as South African Pulp and Paper Industries Limited.

1937: Company builds the first paper mill at Springs, called Enstra Mill, for Enterprise Straw, after its chief raw material.

1950: Company begins construction of a second paper mill, Tugela, in Zululand.

1959: Company acquires a controlling stake in Union Corrugated Cases.

1960: Cellulose Products is acquired.

1966: Production begins at a new mill at Ngodwana.

1973: Company changes its name to Sappi Limited.

1982: Company acquires Novobord, entering production of particleboard.

1985: Company completes expansion of the Ngodwana site, adding production facilities for newsprint, linerboard, unbleached pulp, and bleached pulp.

1988: Company acquires Usutu Pulp Company, in Swaziland, gaining the world's largest producer of softwood kraft pulp.

1989: Company acquires Saiccor, world leader in dissolving pulp production.

1990: Company acquires five paper mills in the United Kingdom and establishes Sappi Europe subsidiary.

1992: Company acquires Hannover Papier, of Germany, becoming the European market leader in coated wood-free paper.

1994: Sappi acquires 75 percent of SD Warren (full control in 1996), giving it the leading position in the coated wood-free paper market in the United States.

1997: Company acquires KNP Leykam, European leader in wood-free paper production, making Sappi the world leader in the product segment.

1998: All Sappi operations are rebranded under a single Sappi name.

2000: Company sells Sappi Novobord.

2001: Company sells Sappi Mining Timber and announces its intention to close a number of U.S. paper mills.

Sappi returned to its external growth drive in the second half of the decade. In 1997, Sappi agreed to acquire KNP Leykam, the coated wood-free paper division of Burhmann, paying nearly $800 million. Again criticized for paying a premium price, Sappi with the Leykam acquisition had not only gained the European leader in the wood-free paper category, it had secured for itself the global leadership for that product segment. It also had pushed its debt levels to the limit, resulting in a deep drop in its share price.

Following the Leykam acquisition, Sappi reorganized, splitting its operations into two principal subsidiaries. Sappi Fine Papers took London as its headquarters, grouping all of the company's paper production. Sappi Forest Products, which remained at the parent company's headquarters in Johannesburg, took over the company's pulp, particleboard, and cardboard production, as well as its forestry operations. This move was followed up a year later when the company rebranded its entire organization under the single Sappi name. In that year, Sappi's stock began trading on the New York Stock Exchange as well as the London, Frankfurt, and Johannesburg exchanges.

Sappi came under pressure at the turn of the millennium. On the one hand, the company remained burdened by a heavy debt load generated through its acquisition drive of the 1990s. On the other hand, Sappi was hard hit by a drop in world paper prices, and by the faltering of a number of markets, including Asia and Latin America, and then the weakening economic climate in the United States. As a result, Sappi's share price continued to be pelted, and the company was seen as a potential takeover target.

In 2000, the company began a sell-off of some of its assets, primarily from its Sappi Forest Products subsidiary. That company sold off Sappi Novobord in 2000, exiting the particleboard and mid-density fiberboard market. The following year, the company sold off its Sappi Mining Timber division. The company also announced its intention to close a number of its U.S. paper mills in 2001 and 2002. The company's debt remained relatively high—more than $1.1 billion, equal to some 35 percent of its market value. Yet Sappi's share price was once again on the rise, while takeover rumors lulled.

As Sappi entered 2002, it suggested that its days of large-scale acquisitions were behind it, at least temporarily. Instead, the company intended to continue growth through the acquisition of individual mills. Sappi also was setting its sights on increasing its position in the southern Asia market. However, Sappi suggested that it would pursue growth through a series of greenfield initiatives, linking up with local partners. After transforming itself into a truly global company in just one decade, Sappi looked to continue its successful expansion drive into the Asian market as well.

Principal Subsidiaries

Sappi Manufacturing (Pty) Ltd; Usutu Pulp Company Ltd; Pulp Holdings (Pty) Ltd; Sappi Management Services (Pty) Ltd; Sappi Share Facilitation Co.(Pty) Ltd; SDW Holdings Corporation (U.S.A.); European Paper Holdings SA (France); Sappi Alfeld AG (Switzerland); Sappi Belgium BV; Sappi Ehingen AG (Austria); Sappi Europe SA (France); Sappi Fine Paper plc (U.K.); Sappi Gratkorn GmbH (Germany); Sappi Holding AG (Germany); Sappi International SA (France); Sappi Maastricht BV (Netherlands); Sappi Nijmegen BV (Netherlands); Sappi Papier Holding AG (Netherlands); Sappi Lanaken Presspaper NV (Netherlands); Sappi U.K. Ltd.

Principal Competitors

Arjo Wiggins Appleton Limited; Asia Pulp & Paper Company Ltd.; Domtar Inc.; Georgia-Pacific Corporation; Holmen AB; Hokuetsu Paper Mills, Ltd.; International Paper Company; Stora Enso Oyj; Svenska Cellulosa Aktiebolaget SCA; Unipapel, S.A; UPM-Kymmene Corporation; Votorantim Celulose e Papel S.A.

Further Reading

Fine, Alan, "From Pariahs to Multinationals?," *Business Week,* November 7, 1994.

Innocenti, Nicol, "Sappi Shakes Off Takeover Rumours," *Financial Times,* November 10, 2002.

Kemp, Shirley, "No Mega-Deal for Sappi," *Moneyweb,* January 28, 2002.

Mittner, Martin, " 'Paperless' Van As Takes Sappi to New Heights," *Sake,* March 2, 2002.

Sikhakhane, Jabulani, "Sappi's Paper Trail Leads Offshore," *Business Times (New Zealand),* November 23, 1997.

Walker, Julie, "Sappi Walks Tall Again Despite Heavy Weather," *Business Times (New Zealand),* December 5, 1999.

—M. L. Cohen

Schering-Plough Corporation

2000 Galloping Hill Road
Kenilworth, New Jersey 07033-0530
U.S.A.
Telephone: (908) 298-4000
Fax: (908) 298-2429
Web site: http://www.sch-plough.com

Public Company
Incorporated: 1971
Employees: 28,100
Sales: $9.8 billion (2001)
Stock Exchanges: New York Boston Cincinnati Midwest
    Pacific Philadelphia
Ticker Symbol: SGP
NAIC: 325412 Pharmaceutical Preparation
    Manufacturing; 325620 Toilet Preparation
    Manufacturing; 339113 Surgical Appliance and
    Supplies Manufacturing; 541710 Research and
    Development in the Physical, Engineering, and Life
    Sciences

Schering-Plough Corporation is a major U.S.-based manufacturer of pharmaceuticals. The company's leading prescription drug is the allergy medication Claritin, with 2001 sales of $3.2 billion. Other allergy and respiratory treatments include Clarinex, the firm's next-generation allergy treatment, and Nasonex, a nasal spray for allergies with 2001 sales of $524 million. In the area of anti-infective and anticancer products, Schering-Plough makes Intron A, a treatment for hepatitis C with 2001 sales of $1.4 billion; PEG-Intron, a longer-acting form of Intron A; Temodar, used to treat malignant brain cancer; and Remicade, a treatment for Crohn's disease. Schering-Plough also makes drugs to treat cardiovascular, dermatological, and central nervous system disorders. Overall, pharmaceuticals account for about 85 percent of company sales. Generating about 7 percent of sales are the company's animal health products, which include Nuflor, an antibiotic used to treat bovine respiratory disease. The remaining revenue comes from the sale of consumer products, including Dr. Scholl's foot-care

products, Afrin nasal sprays, and Bain de Soleil and Coppertone sun-care products. On the research side, Schering-Plough is involved in a number of collaborative ventures investigating new drug treatments. Chief among these are partnerships with Merck & Co., Inc. formed in 2000 to develop cholesterol-management and allergy/asthma medications.

History of Schering Corporation

Schering-Plough Corporation was formed in 1971 through the merger of Schering Corporation and Plough, Inc., each with their own long and colorful histories. Schering began in the late 19th century as the U.S. subsidiary of Schering AG, a drug and chemical manufacturer founded in Berlin by Ernst Schering in 1864. In 1894, the company started to export diphtheria medication to the United States, and in 1928 Schering Corporation was incorporated in New York. Until the end of World War II, a sex hormone accounted for up to 75 percent of Schering's sales.

In 1935, on the eve of World War II, the U.S. government took over the assets of Schering Corporation because of its German ownership, thereby changing the course of the company's history. Frank Brown, a New Deal lawyer with no previous experience in the pharmaceutical business, was dealt a hand that would bind his future to Schering. Brown's legal career involved participating in government projects during the 1930s. He joined the Federal Deposit Insurance Corporation (FDIC), a creation of Roosevelt's New Deal policies, and acted as legal counsel to Leo Crowley. Crowley was appointed the Alien Property Custodian, and Brown was given the job of managing Schering. He immediately filled vacated executive positions with associates from the FDIC. In 1943, Brown was formally appointed president of Schering, and under his direction the company soon proved a financial success.

Brown realized that research and development was the key to success in the pharmaceutical industry. To this end, Brown immediately began the development of a research department and, like many other pharmaceutical companies, conducted searches for those scientists and students on the verge of new discoveries or for noteworthy scientific contributions from medical colleges and universities across the country. Established in

1944, the Schering student competition fund has found many worthy recipients over the years.

Because the postwar years marked a reduced demand for sex hormones, the newly expanded research department could not have found a better moment to discover a new antihistamine. Marketed as a proprietary drug (a drug directly advertised to consumers) under the name Trimeton and marketed also as an ethical drug (a drug advertised to healthcare professionals) under the name Chlor-Trimeton, the antihistamine marked a turning point in the history of the Schering Corporation. By 1951, profits had quadrupled with sales reaching over $15 million.

That same year the U.S. attorney general put the company up for sale. A syndicate headed by Merrill Lynch outbid other prospective buyers, purchasing the company in 1952 and then proceeding to take it public that same year through the sale of $1.7 million of stock. The investors, however, asked Brown to remain on as company president. He accepted the offer and directed Schering to even greater profitability through the discovery of Meticorten and Meticortelone, two new corticosteroids that became the envy of the drug industry.

The discovery of synthetic cortisone dated back to 1949 when Merck & Co., an industry competitor, first made public its historic findings. Although the wonder drug's discovery rightfully belonged to Merck, the process for synthesizing the drug conflicted with several other patents for producing sex hormones. Schering was the owner of one of these patents, and through a "cross-licensing" agreement the company gained access to information about cortisone production.

Soon after production of cortisone began, Schering and its competitors raced to discover an improved line of the drug that would eliminate some of the side effects associated with the steroid. They all hoped to modify the cortisone molecule to find a more effective drug and, at the same time, eliminate hypertension, edema (water retention), and osteoporosis (a bone disease), all side effects connected with cortisone therapy. Using microorganisms to convert one chemical into another, Schering scientists discovered a drug in 1954 that fit the desired guidelines. Clinical testing of the drug brought excellent results. When Schering was confronted with the prospect of full-scale production, however, the company realized it had no previous experience in manufacturing by fermentation, the process used to make the new drug. So Schering first tried fermentation in a 150-gallon stainless steel container and later in a 1,000-gallon and finally a 22,000-gallon fermenter. This last container used $100,000 worth of cortisone and a few hundred gallons of microorganisms.

Having established a successful manufacturing technique, Schering released Meticorten in 1955 and Meticortelone soon afterwards. Almost unbelievably, sales for the drugs jumped to over $20 million by the end of the year, $1 million more than total sales in 1954. By the end of 1955 sales for these drugs reached a new high of almost $46 million and by 1957 exceeded $80 million.

Other pharmaceutical companies manufacturing steroids immediately attempted to profit from Schering's success. Lederle, Upjohn, and Merck all developed similar drugs, and soon Schering found itself embroiled in lawsuits over patent and licensing rights. Merck's product arrived on the market only three months after Schering's, but because Schering had spent heavily on advertising it managed to retain a major share of the market. Furthermore, while Schering was forced to arrange licensing agreements with other companies, Brown demanded what other companies regarded as overpriced royalty payments. Although this initiated new litigation, it also allowed Schering profits to remain at an all-time high while agreements were worked out in time-consuming court processes.

In 1957, Schering acquired White Laboratories. During the mid-1960s the company completed a series of important introductions. In 1965, the company debuted Tinactin, an antifungal cream. The following year came the debut of Garamycin, an antibiotic used as a treatment for urinary tract infections and burn victims. This soon became the company's leading product. Schering introduced Afrin, a decongestant, in 1967.

History of Plough and Merger with Schering

Unrelated to Schering's historical development, a consumer product company in Memphis, Tennessee, won recognition for its own success story. Abe Plough, founder of Plough, Inc., began his career in marketing in 1908. He borrowed $125 from his father to create a concoction of linseed oil, carbolic acid, and camphor and sold the potion door-to-door from a horse-drawn buggy as a cure for "any ill of man or beast." Plough's inventory expanded to include a mysteriously named C-2223. This relief for rheumatics became an immediate success; after four years Plough had sold 150,000 packages.

What Plough later claimed to be his shrewdest purchase occurred in 1915 when he paid $900 for the inventory of a bankrupt drug company. He netted a profit of $34,000 peddling the stock in the back woods where there was still a large demand for oxidine chill tonic. In 1920, he bought the St. Joseph Company of Chattanooga, Tennessee, and began manufacturing children's aspirin. By the 1950s, Plough realized that the huge sales figures for the popular aspirin was partially due to children taking overdoses of the product. To prevent this from reoccurring Plough ordered childproof caps added to the aspirin at a time when safety regulations were almost nonexistent. He went on to purchase 27 other companies during the course of his lifetime. In addition to being talented at making important acquisitions, he was also very adept at marketing: 25 percent of all income from sales was routinely spent on advertising. The success of radio advertising, in particular, convinced Plough to buy five AM and FM stations (which were later sold). Plough was best known in his own community for his philanthropic

Key Dates:

1864–Late 1800s: Ernst Schering founds Schering AG as a Berlin-based drug and chemical manufacturer and eventually founds a U.S. subsidiary to which his company begins exporting pharmaceuticals.

1908: Abe Plough begins his career of marketing consumer products by selling a concoction of linseed oil, carbolic acid, and camphor as an "antiseptic healing oil."

1918: Plough incorporates his business as Plough Chemical Co., later known as Plough, Inc.

1920: Plough acquires Chattanooga, Tennessee-based St. Joseph Company, maker of children's aspirin.

1928: Schering Corporation is incorporated in New York.

1935: The U.S. government takes over the assets of Schering Corporation because of its German ownership.

Mid-1940s: Schering establishes a research department and develops a new antihistamine marketed to consumers as Trimeton and as a prescription drug called Chlor-Trimeton.

1950s: Plough adds childproof caps to its children's aspirin products at a time when safety regulations are almost nonexistent.

1952: A syndicate headed by Merrill Lynch purchases Schering from the government and takes the company public.

1955: Schering introduces a new corticosteroid called Meticorten, soon followed by Meticortelone.

1965: Schering introduces Tinactin, an antifungal cream.

1966: Schering introduces Garamycin, an antibiotic used as a treatment for urinary tract infections and burn victims; it will soon become the company's leading product.

1967: Schering introduces the decongestant Afrin.

1971: Schering and Plough merge to form Schering-Plough Corporation, combining Schering's antibiotics, antihistamines, and other pharmaceuticals with Plough's household consumer products such as Coppertone, Di-Gel, and Maybelline cosmetics.

1979: Scholl, Inc., maker of Dr. Scholl's foot-care products, is acquired.

1980: Patent for the company's top product, Garamycin, expires; Wesley-Jensen Inc., maker of vision care products and contact lenses, is acquired.

1982: Drive into biotechnology includes the acquisition of DNAX Research Institute, based in Palo Alto, California.

1986: Schering-Plough's Intron A interferon receives approval from the U.S. Food and Drug Administration (FDA); Key Pharmaceuticals, a maker of allergy, asthma, and cardiovascular drugs, is acquired.

1993: The company introduces Claritin, a nonsedating antihistamine, which quickly achieves blockbuster sales and becomes the firm's number one product.

1995: The firm's contact lens business is sold to Bain Capital.

1997: The animal health division of Mallinckrodt Inc. is acquired for $405 million.

2000: Company enters into a partnership with Merck & Co. to develop cholesterol-management and allergy/asthma medications; the company recalls 59 million asthma inhalers after finding that some of the devices contain little or none of the active ingredient.

2001: The company announces that Clarinex, a next-generation allergy treatment, has been approved by the FDA but that the FDA will likely fine the company as much as $500 million because of protracted manufacturing problems.

---

contributions. Upon his death in 1984 at age 92, flags throughout Memphis were lowered to half-mast.

Years before his death, however, the unlikely friendship between German-born Willibald Hermann Cozen, chief executive officer of Schering Corporation, and Plough was the antecedent to a company merger. At 17, after graduating from Kaiserin Augusta Gymnasium in Koblenz, Cozen began working for Schering AG, the German parent company. When the U.S. subsidiary of Schering AG was seized by the U.S. government in the 1930s and eventually sold to the public, Cozen became the chief executive officer of the new independent company.

Although the 80-year-old Plough had initiated the merger because he was looking for a successor to run his firm, it was Cozen who actually designed the merger and, as a result, became the chief executive officer of Schering-Plough; Plough served as chairman of the new company until 1976. The merger, which was completed in 1971, combined the comprehensive manufacturing of Schering's antibiotics, antihistamines, and other pharmaceuticals, and Plough's household consumer products with names as common as Coppertone, Di-Gel, and Maybelline cosmetics.

1970s: The New Schering-Plough

When the merger of the two companies was finally completed, combined sales reached $500 million in 1971. This marked the fastest sales growth for any merger in the industry. Yet despite an earnings multiple of 46, Cozen, in his typically reserved style, spoke guardedly of continued expansion. The sales for Garamycin reached $90 million by 1972. This income accounted for almost half of both companies' growth for the period. The large profits, however, ironically concealed an "Achilles' heel." Garamycin's patent, scheduled to expire in 1980, signified the beginning of generic competition and the end of Schering-Plough's control over the manufacturing of this drug. The sound of competitors' footsteps could be heard following closely behind; Cozen's cautious remarks on continued expansion were well founded.

In 1974, reduced sales for Garamycin already affected company profit margins. In 1975, the return on equity dropped from 31 to 27 percent and the stock dropped 10 percent from the previous year. Schering-Plough endured the ensuing decline in profits and increased funding for research and development. In 1974, several newly released drugs accounted for $100 million in sales. The following year Schering-Plough introduced Lotrimin AF, an antifungal product, and Vanceril, an antiasthma medicine, debuted in 1976. Similarly, Maybelline introduced a new line of makeup in 1974. The "Fresh and Lovely" cosmetic product line promised to catapult Maybelline into a competitive full-line makeup company.

These moves, however, were not remedies for the ailing profit margin. In 1979, Richard J. Bennet took over as chief executive officer and continued the efforts to solve the Garamycin conundrum. Schering-Plough had historically been a conservative company with no major debts, maintaining an asset-to-liability ratio of 2.2 to 1 and a $350 million cash excess after seven acquisitions. Yet Schering-Plough continued to look like a "one-product" company because of its heavy reliance on Garamycin sales.

In 1979, 40 percent of all profits, or $220 million, was generated solely from Garamycin. Cozen's ineffective attempt to establish company profitability on the sales of a variety of drugs rather than a single product became Bennet's new challenge. Under his management the company released Netromycin, an antibiotic more potent that Garamycin but with fewer side effects. To ensure continued sales of Garamycin when the patent expiration date arrived, the company announced a discount plan to entice former customers into future contracts. Meanwhile, large sums of money continued to pour into the research facilities in the hope of discovering new drugs. Finally, in order to bolster consumer product sales, Schering-Plough purchased Scholl, Inc., the well-established maker of Dr. Scholl's foot-care products, for $30 million. Also acquired that year were the animal health business of Burns-Biotec and Kirby Pharmaceuticals Ltd. The company entered a new sector in 1980 with the acquisition of Wesley-Jensen Inc., maker of vision care products and contact lenses.

Unfortunately, these maneuvers had only a limited effect on the company. Because doctors had already perfected methods for controlling Garamycin's side effects, they actually preferred to wait for generic and therefore cheaper versions of the drug rather than switch to Netromycin. Similarly, despite $75 million a year spent on research and development, no new discoveries were announced. Furthermore, while Scholl, Inc., had yearly revenues of $250 million and earnings of $12 million, its profits had barely kept pace with inflation since 1973.

1980s: Focusing Strongly on Healthcare

Next to all of these disappointments, however, one consumer product did exhibit strong signs of financial success. Maybelline, once known as a manufacturer of "me-too" or imitation products, matured into an aggressive full-line cosmetic company. Bennet claimed in 1980 that Maybelline held 34 percent of the mascara market and 24 percent of the eyeshadow market. Estimated sales for 1980 jumped to $150 million from $75 million in 1976. But after Robert P. Luciano was appointed CEO in 1982, he refocused the company on health care, and Maybelline cosmetics and a household products group were eventually sold.

On May 28, 1980, the day the patent on Garamycin expired, Schering-Plough executives appeared unperturbed. In fact,

stock on that day jumped from $39 to $45 a share. Not only was Netromycin on the market, but 80 percent of the hospitals who were previous customers of Garamycin had signed up for the deferred discount plan. More importantly, however, Schering-Plough had paid $12 million for a 14 percent equity stake in a Swiss genetic engineering company called Biogen. Schering-Plough's interest in the company was significant because it provided them with worldwide rights to the synthesis of human leukocyte interferons using recombinant DNA. The possibilities for using interferon, a chemical produced naturally in the body to fight viruses, were immense. It was hoped that the synthetic drug could be used to treat anything from cancer to the common cold. Moreover, gene-splicing promised to be highly cost-effective; this new method, on the cutting-edge of biotechnology, could produce the same amount of purer proteins in a week than old methods could in a year. Here was the long-awaited breakthrough.

By 1985, in an uncharacteristic move, Schering-Plough had made a more expensive investment in biotechnology than any of its competitors. Expenditures surpassed $100 million. In 1982, Schering-Plough, having reached an agreement to spend $31.5 million over ten years, formed a partnership with West Berlin politicians to establish a research institute on genetic engineering in Berlin. At the same time, plans were announced to build a fermentation and purification plant in Ireland to market the first commercial interferon. Schering-Plough also purchased another biotech firm in Palo Alto, California, called DNAX Research Institute.

Although Schering-Plough was the first to market a commercial Interferon, patent problems with competitors gave Hoffmann-La Roche rights to market alpha interferons in the United States. On June 4, 1986, the U.S. Food and Drug Administration (FDA) approved Schering-Plough's Intron A and Hoffmann-La Roche's Rofeon-A for the U.S. market. Projected market sales for the interferon were $200 million in the United States and $150 million in Europe. By 1994, Intron A had sales of $426 million. With continued expansion in the United States and other international markets, Intron soon grew to be the market leader worldwide. The company continued its study in the field of biotechnology, spending about one-quarter of its research dollars in this area.

In the meantime, Schering-Plough completed additional acquisitions in the late 1980s. In 1986, Key Pharmaceuticals, Inc., a maker of allergy, asthma, and cardiovascular drugs, was acquired. Two years later, Schering-Plough acquired the Cooper Companies' U.S. contact lens solutions business as well as the rights to sell Aquaflex contact lenses in the United States and Japan. Then in 1989 the German animal health business of Byk Gulden was purchased.

The Claritin Decade

In the 1990s, Schering-Plough's largest and fastest-growing therapeutic category was in the area of asthma and allergy. Led by new product introductions, worldwide sales rose 24 percent in 1994 to approximately $1.46 billion. The most successful of these new drugs was Claritin (loratadine), a once-a-day, nonsedating antihistamine. Introduced in April 1993, Claritin was the third nonsedating antihistamine to reach the U.S. market. Despite its late arrival, in its first year on the market, Claritin had sales of nearly $200 million. It then captured the number one position in new prescriptions for plain antihistamines in less than a year and a half on the U.S. market, making it the largest single product for the company. Along with the November 1994 U.S. marketing clearance of Claritin-D, a twice-daily formulation combining the decongestant pseudoephedrine, the company expected to capture a significant share of the antihistamine/decongestant market.

Also in the 1990s, a fear of skin cancer and a depleting ozone layer turned sun care from a cosmetic segment to a healthcare one. With the introduction of Coppertone Kids and Shade UVAGuard, Schering-Plough proved to be a leader in the sun-care market. It heavily promoted Shade UVAGuard, the sunscreen positioned as a drug that protected against year-round UVA and UVB rays, both of which cause skin cancer. Schering was also one of the first companies to market sunless tanning and sport products. The year 1994 marked the 50th anniversary of the Coppertone brand, and, during that year, the company helped launch a national UV (ultraviolet) Index in a joint pilot program with the U.S. Environmental Protection Agency and the National Weather Service to help educate consumers about the importance of proper sun protection. With its broad product lines, Schering-Plough captured major shares in important segments of the entire sun care market, and, in the fast-growing children's market, the company had a 60 percent share with its Coppertone Kids and Water Babies products.

An aging population, the popularity of self-medication, and active lifestyles were other trends that helped boost sales in Schering-Plough's foot-care division and build its position as North America's leading foot-care company. Schering-Plough's brands led in every segment of the market and, according to *Drug Topics* in 1995, Dr. Scholl's had a 72 percent share of the insole/insert category, an 86 percent share of the corn/callus/bunion category, and a 46 percent share of the odor/wetness/grooming category. The company, however, met increased competition from in-store and private-label brands during this time.

Continuing to concentrate more of its attention on pharmaceutical products, Schering-Plough sold off its contact lens business to Bain Capital, Inc. in 1995 for $47.5 million. At the beginning of 1996, Richard J. Kogan succeeded Luciano as CEO. Luciano remained chairman until November 1998, when Kogan took on that position as well. Kogan had served as president and COO since 1986. Also in 1996, Schering-Plough acquired San Diego-based Canji, Inc., a gene therapy firm, for $54.5 million in stock. The following year the company substantially bolstered its animal health unit with the acquisition of the animal health division of Mallinckrodt Inc. for $405 million. Schering-Plough gained Mallinckrodt's lines of antiparasitic drugs and growth-enhancing products for cattle along with that firm's more extensive global distribution network. The newly enlarged animal health unit had annual revenues of about $650 million. In another extension of one of the company's nonpharmaceutical lines, Schering-Plough purchased from Pfizer Inc. the rights to sell Bain de Soleil sun-care products in the United States, Puerto Rico, and certain other markets.

On the pharmaceutical side, Schering-Plough in 1997 introduced Nasonex, a once-daily nasal spray for allergies that by 2000 achieved sales of $415 million. In 1998, the FDA approved a new drug regimen called Rebetron for the treatment of Hepatitis C. Rebetron was developed in partnership with ICN Pharmaceuticals, Inc. and was a combination of Schering-Plough's Intron A and ICN's Ribavirin. The company also purchased the marketing rights to several drugs in 1998, including Remicade, which had been developed by Centocor, Inc. for the treatment of Crohn's disease. During 1999, the FDA granted approval to Schering-Plough's Temodar for treating two serious types of malignant brain cancer.

The New Millennium: Life After Claritin?

With the possible exception of Intron A, which through its various uses was generating $1.4 billion in annual revenues by 2000, none of these new products came close to approaching the blockbuster sales of the Claritin family of products. Worldwide sales of Claritin reached $3 billion in 2000, representing 36 percent of Schering-Plough's pharmaceutical revenues and nearly 31 percent of overall revenues. Part of the reason for the huge sales was the aggressive marketing campaign that had been mounted for the drug, a campaign that took full advantage of the loosening of FDA regulations relating to the advertising of prescription drugs. Claritin, in fact, was the most heavily advertised prescription drug in the United States in the late 1990s. Schering-Plough spent $322 million pitching Claritin to consumers in 1998 and 1999.

With Claritin generating so great a percentage of Schering-Plough's revenues and with the main patent on Claritin set to expire at the end of 2002, the company was faced with a near repeat of the situation it had faced in the late 1970s when the expiration of the patent on Garamycin was approaching. Schering-Plough took a multifaceted approach to the looming prospect of cheap generic competition to its by far top-selling drug. In May 2000, the company entered into a partnership with Merck to develop two new drug combinations. One would combine Claritin with Merck's asthma drug Singulair in the hope of creating a highly effective asthma and allergy medication. Because Singulair's patent was slated to last until 2010, the patent for the combined drug would extend to that year as well. Likewise, the two companies also began investigating a combination of Merck's cholesterol-reducing Zocor with ezetimibe (brand name Zetia), an experimental compound developed by Schering-Plough that interferes with the body's ability to absorb dietary cholesterol. Merck was facing the expiration of Zocor's patent in 2005, but ezetimibe's patent would not expire until 2015.

Schering-Plough also launched an intense lobbying campaign to get the U.S. Congress to extend Claritin's patent. The company argued that because the FDA approval process for Claritin had been so lengthy—lasting nearly six and a half years—the patent on the drug should be extended. These lobbying efforts failed. At the same time, Schering-Plough was attempting to get FDA approval for its next-generation allergy medication, desloratadine, which was to be marketed under the brand name Clarinex. This drug was closely related chemically to Claritin, and among scientists there was some debate about whether there was a marked difference between the two drugs. In any case, Schering-Plough was relying on getting Clarinex approved quickly enough so that it had adequate time to switch patients from Claritin to the new drug before the Claritin generics began flooding the market.

Unfortunately, Schering-Plough was beset by difficulties at its drug manufacturing plants in New Jersey and Puerto Rico, and these troubles delayed the approval of Clarinex. In late 1999 and 2000, the company was forced to recall 59 million asthma inhalers after finding that some of the devices, which were potentially life-saving, contained little or none of the active ingredient. After the facilities failed further inspections, the FDA in February 2001 told the company that Clarinex would not be approved until the manufacturing problems were resolved. Following the uncovering of additional problems at the plants in June 2001, the company's president, Raul E. Cesan, who had been in charge of the manufacturing operations since 1994, was forced to resign. In a further blow, the consumer advocacy group Public Citizen in August 2001 called for a criminal investigation of the company, alleging that 17 deaths were associated with the use of faulty Schering-Plough asthma inhalers. Class-action lawsuits were soon filed related to the defective products and to allegations that the company had failed to alert shareholders to these problems (the company's stock fell substantially during this period).

In April 2001, meantime, Schering-Plough was hit with another lawsuit, this one brought by the Federal Trade Commission (FTC) against the company and two generic drugmakers. In this antitrust suit, the FTC alleged that patent settlements involving Schering-Plough's K-Dur potassium chloride supplement included illegal payments that were made to delay the introduction of generic versions of the drug. The company also faced criticism for its marketing of Rebetron, in which the two-drug combination was sold for about $18,000 for the full year of treatment that was needed. Some patients wanted to take one of the drugs in combination with a drug produced by another company, but Schering-Plough refused to unbundle the drugs, contending that for safety reasons the drugs should only be taken together.

To solve its manufacturing problems, Schering-Plough spent $60 million on plant improvements and the hiring of 500 new employees, many of whom worked in quality control. Finally, in December 2001, the FDA granted approval to Clarinex but at the price of a fine of as much as $500 million for the protracted manufacturing problems at Schering-Plough plants. The company immediately began selling the new drug, but it now had only one year to work at switching patients from Claritin to Clarinex. Further complicating the situation was a petition to the FDA from WellPoint Health Networks Inc. of Thousand Oaks, California, which wanted Claritin and two other popular allergy medications, Allegra and Zyrtec, switched to over-the-counter (OTC) status, a move that would save money for WellPoint and other insurers while costing drugmakers and consumers with prescription drug coverage. After this petition won preliminary FDA approval in 2001, divisions of Johnson & Johnson and American Home Products Corporation filed registrations with the FDA for OTC versions of Claritin. This led Schering-Plough in February 2002 to file separate lawsuits against the two companies to block the OTC versions. At the same time, Schering-Plough was also involved in lawsuits with about 18 companies over generic versions of Claritin. Even if these suits proved unsuccessful, they were likely to delay the introduction of generic and OTC versions of Claritin, thereby buying Schering-Plough some more time.

Schering-Plough clearly faced an uncertain future. The success of Clarinex was by no means assured, and the only other new drug approved in 2001 was PEG-Intron, which was a longer-lasting form of Intron A and which was also used in the treatment of hepatitis C. In late stage development were Zetia, the cholesterol medication being developed with Merck; Asmanex, a next-generation asthma inhaler; and Noxafil (posaconazole), an antifungal designed for patients with HIV or cancer whose immune systems are compromised. None of these were likely to be the blockbuster needed to succeed Claritin, and this left Schering-Plough vulnerable to a takeover, with Merck being a prime candidate given the two companies' status as drug development partners.

Principal Subsidiaries

The Bain de Soleil Company; Canji, Inc.; The Coppertone Corporation; DNAX Research Institute of Molecular & Cellular Biology, Inc.; Dr. Scholl's Foot Comfort Shops, Inc.; Key Pharmaceuticals, Inc.; Schering Corporation; Schering-Plough Products, Inc.; Schering-Plough Veterinary Corporation; Warrick Pharmaceuticals Corporation; White Laboratories, Inc.; Schering-Plough Compania Limitada (Chile); Schering-Plough S.A. (France); Schering-Plough Sante Animale (France); Schering-Plough Veterinaire (France); Schering-Plough S.p.A. (Italy); Schering-Plough S.A de C.V. (Mexico); Schering-Plough Farma Lda. (Portugal); Schering-Plough S.A. (Spain); Schering-Plough Holdings Ltd. (U.K.); Schering-Plough Limited (U.K.); Schering-Plough C.A. (Venezuela).

Principal Operating Units

Schering-Plough International; Schering-Plough HealthCare Products; Schering-Plough Animal Health; Schering-Plough Pharmaceuticals; Schering-Plough Research Institute; Schering Laboratories.

Principal Competitors

Merck & Co., Inc.; Pfizer Inc.; GlaxoSmithKline plc; Bayer AG; Novartis AG; Aventis; Bristol-Myers Squibb Company; Roche Group; Abbott Laboratories; AstraZeneca PLC; American Home Products Corporation.

Further Reading

Babcock, Charles R., "Patent Fight Tests Drug Firm's Clout: Claritin Maker Goes All Out in Congress," *Washington Post*, October 30, 1999, p. A1.
Bailey, Maureen, "Feeling No Pain?: Schering-Plough Suffers Loss of Market Share in Key Drug," *Barron's*, September 22, 1980, p. 11.
Baldo, Anthony, "Unlucky Luciano," *Financial World*, August 6, 1991, pp. 28+.
Bronson, Gail, "Devour Thy Tail," *Forbes*, November 2, 1987, p. 85.
Fischl, Jennifer, "Schering-Plough: Just Say No," *Financial World*, April 15, 1997, pp. 24, 26.
Freudenheim, Milt, "U.S. Decision on New Drug Lifts Schering," *New York Times*, December 25, 2001, p. C1.
Gerena-Morales, Rafael, "Schering-Plough Can Sell Hepatitis C Drug Regimen," *Northern New Jersey Record*, June 5, 1998, p. A3.

Goetzl, David, "How to Follow a Blockbuster?," *Advertising Age,* November 19, 2001, pp. 4, 38.

Hall, Stephen S., "Prescription for Profit," *New York Times Magazine,* March 11, 2001, pp. 60+.

Harris, Gardiner, "Drug Makers Pair Up to Fight Key Patent Losses," *Wall Street Journal,* May 24, 2000, p. B1.

——, "Foul-Ups by Asthma-Drug Maker Draw FDA Fire," *Wall Street Journal,* January 28, 2000, p. B1.

——, "Schering Fines Could Total $500 Million," *Wall Street Journal,* December 24, 2001, p. A3.

Hunter, Kris, "Staff Cutbacks Begin at Schering-Plough," *Memphis Business Journal,* October 17, 1994, pp. 1+.

Jarvis, Lisa, "Manufacturing Problems Cast Pall on Schering-Plough Earnings," *Chemical Market Reporter,* July 9, 2001, p. 8.

Kogan, Richard J., "With Change Comes Opportunity," *Chemical Week,* April 26, 1995, p. 48.

Krause, Carey, "Schering-Plough Becomes Vulnerable to Takeover," *Chemical Market Reporter,* February 18, 2002, p. 10.

Langreth, Robert, "Gene Therapy Is Dealt Setback by the FDA of Gene Drug," *Wall Street Journal,* October 11, 1999, p. B1.

——, "Schering-Plough Corp. to Acquire Mallinckrodt Animal-Health Unit," *Wall Street Journal,* May 20, 1997, p. B6.

Lueck, Sarah, "FDA Considers Unusual Bid to End Allergy Drugs' Prescription Status," *Wall Street Journal,* May 11, 2001, p. B1.

Marcial, Gene G., "Analysts See Schering-Plough on Rough Road As Drug Patent Lapses, Rival Product Gains," *Wall Street Journal,* June 2, 1980.

Nayyar, Seema, "Coppertone Adapts to a Changing World," *Brandweek,* February 22, 1993, p. 28.

Novak, Viveca, "How One Firm Played the Patent Game," *Time,* November 22, 1999, p. 42.

Palmer, Jay, "Say Yes to Drugs? How Schering-Plough Aims to Survive Hillary Clinton," *Barron's,* October 4, 1993, p. 14.

Petersen, Melody, "At Schering, Optimism and Problems," *New York Times,* January 15, 2002, p. C1.

——, "Factory Problems Unresolved, Schering-Plough President Is Out," *New York Times,* June 28, 2001, p. C4.

——, "Group Faults Drug Inhalers in Ten Deaths," *New York Times,* August 10, 2001, p. C1.

Power, Christopher, "Schering May Have a Cure for Anemic Profits," *Business Week,* September 15, 1986, pp. 118+.

"Schering, Plough Agree to Merger Put at $1.5 Billion," *Wall Street Journal,* June 24, 1970.

"Schering-Plough Banking on R&D," *Chemical Marketing Reporter,* July 11, 1994, pp. 7+.

Shaffer, Marjorie, "Schering-Plough: Against the Tide," *Financial World,* June 22, 1993, pp. 16+.

Silverman, Edward R., "Second N.J. Congressman Calls for Probe of Drug's Marketing," *Newark (N.J.) Star-Ledger,* April 27, 1999.

Starr, Cynthia, "Schering's Claritin Promises Quick Onset, No Sedation," *Drug Topics,* June 7, 1993, pp. 22+.

"Step Up to Better Foot Care Sales," *Drug Topics,* March 20, 1995, pp. 68+.

"Touted Schering-Plough Feels the 'Clinton Effect,' " *Chemical Marketing Reporter,* February 22, 1993, pp. 8+.

Twitchell, Evelyn Ellison, "Nothing to Sneeze At: Schering-Plough Looks Like a Blue-Chip Bargain," *Barron's,* September 18, 2000, p. 52.

Verschoor, Curtis C., "Alleged Unethical Behaviors and Schering-Plough," *Strategic Finance,* July 2001, pp. 18, 20.

Waldholz, Michael, "Luciano to Quit Schering Post As Firm's CEO," *Wall Street Journal,* April 26, 1995, p. B7.

Weber, Joseph, "Is Kogan in a Corner?," *Business Week,* July 16, 2001, pp. 68–69.

Wilke, John R., "Schering-Plough to Face Antitrust Charge: FTC to Allege Illegal Deal to Delay Generic Drugs from Reaching Market," *Wall Street Journal,* April 2, 2001, p. A3.

"Will Takeover Fever Strike Schering-Plough?," *Business Week,* October 23, 1989, p. 130.

—updates: **Beth Watson Highman, David E. Salamie**

Scottish Power plc

1 Atlantic Quay
Glasgow G2 8SP
United Kingdom
Telephone: (44) 141-248-8200
Fax: (44) 141-248-8300
Web site: http://www.scottishpower.plc.uk

Public Company
Incorporated: 1989
Employees: 21,981
Sales: $9.0 billion (2001)
Stock Exchanges: London New York
Ticker Symbols: SPW (London); SPI (New York)
NAIC: 212111 Bituminous Coal and Lignite Surface
Mining; 221111 Hydroelectric Power Generation (pt);
221112 Fossil Fuel Electric Power Generation (pt);
221119 Other Electric Power Generation (pt); 221121
Electric Bulk Power Transmission and Control (pt);
221122 Electric Power Distribution (pt); 221210
Natural Gas Distribution; 221320 Sewage Treatment
Facilities; 234920 Power and Communication
Transmission Line Construction; 562119 Other Waste
Collection

Scottish Power plc (ScottishPower) is one of the leading utility companies in the United Kingdom, with more than five million customers in England, Wales, and Scotland. The company operates generating plants, sells electricity and gas, and provides water and wastewater services throughout the United Kingdom. The largest utility company in the country, Scottish-Power is the parent company of Manweb, which sells electricity to customers in Merseyside, Cheshire, and North Wales, and Southern Water, which provides water and wastewater services to customers in Kent, Sussex, Hampshire, and the Isle of Wight, along with designing and installing wastewater treatment plants. In 1999 ScottishPower became the first foreign utility to establish itself in the lucrative American electricity market when it acquired PacifiCorp, which provides electricity to eight states in the western United States.

The Privatization of the Scottish Utilities Industry in the 1980s

ScottishPower was formed in 1989 because of the reorganization of the Scottish electricity industry. The company is the direct successor to all of the nonnuclear operations and activities of the South of Scotland Electricity Board (SSEB). The South of Scotland Electricity Board had been founded in 1955 by the legislation of the Electricity Reorganization Act of 1954, which had merged the two previous boards that provided electricity to customers in the area after nationalization of the industry in 1948.

Prior to the formation of ScottishPower, the Scottish electrical industry consisted of the South of Scotland Electricity Board and the North of Scotland Hydro-Electric Board (NSHEB). Both of these boards, or companies, were operating as vertically integrated monopolies, engaged in such activities as the generation, transmission, distribution, and supply of electrical energy. During this time, all of the expenditures associated with generating and transmitting electricity were shared, and each company's requirements were met according to the determination of the respective boards.

When the British government decided to reorganize the Scottish electrical industry, it summarily rejected the proposal that a single company cover all of the electrical requirements of Scotland. Consequently, when both ScottishPower and Hydro Electric went public in 1991, the British government made the determination that it was best for each of the companies to operate as vertically integrated electrical utility firms, which was in keeping with the tradition established in their earlier history.

One of the most interesting features of the Scottish electrical industry is its large surplus of generating capacity. When the reorganization of the industry took place in Scotland, it was expected that ScottishPower and Hydro Electric would use some of this surplus capacity for export to England and Wales. A large part of the surplus was initially derived from Scotland's nuclear power plants, which existed in a much higher proportion than in any other country in Europe, except for France and Belgium. In fact, at the time of the reorganization, the Scottish nuclear power plants were capable of meeting half of the demand for electricity in the country. Once again, it was determined by the British government that ScottishPower should supervise and operate 74.9 percent of the commercial business of Scottish Nuclear, Ltd., while Hydro Electric took a 25.1 percent interest in the operations of the company.

ScottishPower inherited the entire region previously run by the South of Scotland Electricity Board, an area of 22,950 km that covered the part of Scotland south between the estuaries of the River Tay and River Clyde and encompassed a large area of Northumberland. This land included a significant portion of Scotland's industrial base and was characterized by densely populated urban areas, but also extended to the more rural regions of the Borders and Galloway. The initial customer base was approximately 1.7 million people.

Growth and Expansion in the Early 1990s

Although its main role has always been to supply electricity to the southern part of Scotland, ScottishPower has been in the electrical retail business from its inception. Inheriting 73 retail stores from the South of Scotland Electricity Board, the company sold such items as radios, alarm clocks, and a host of other electrical products, much like the other utility companies across the United Kingdom. When most of the regional electrical companies in England, Wales, and Scotland, including its northern neighbor Hydro Electric, decided to divest all retailing operations, however, management at ScottishPower made the commitment to retain and even expand its network of retail stores, but only on the condition of increasing profitability.

One of the reasons management decided not to abandon retailing operations was that customers who paid their electricity bills in the stores would have been extremely upset. Many people in southern Scotland had grown accustomed to paying their bills while visiting the company's retail stores, and management was well aware of the fact. Consequently, to strengthen its market position, in 1992 ScottishPower acquired a total of 17 units from Rumbelows chain of electrical retail stores owned by Thorn EMI and eight superstores from Atlantis Group, and soon thereafter purchased 50 superstores from the Clydesdale Group, another electrical product retailer with stores in northern England and the Midlands. Having lost £5 million on sales of £32 million in 1990, ScottishPower Retailing Division reported an operating profit of £10 million on sales of £200 million by the end of 1994.

In 1993, ScottishPower was granted a license to enter into the public telecommunications industry, and it immediately installed fibre-optic links within its already existing network of communications between Glasgow and Edinburgh. Carried along its own high-voltage power lines, ScottishPower was soon able to provide extremely high-quality telecommunications services such as the fast transfer of voices, data, and pictures to Scotland's major businesses, including a number of companies in the insurance and banking industries, not to mention engineering firms and universities. Christened "ScottishTelecom," it was one of the fastest growing segments of ScottishPower's business.

Although ScottishPower operated six power generating plants composed of coal, gas, and hydro power, including Longannet at Kincardine on Forth, Cockenzie, Methil, Cruachan, Stonebyres and Bonnington, and Galloway Hydro Scheme, the company was not averse to engaging in more experimental forms of generating energy. In the early 1990s, ScottishPower constructed its first wind farm, located at Penrhyddlan and Llidartywaun in Wales, a unique joint venture between ScottishPower, SeaWest of California, and the Toman Corporation of Japan. The largest such wind farm in Europe, it had a generating capacity of 31 megawatts. Not long afterward, the company established new wind farms in Northern Ireland, Lanarkshire, Cornwall, and Lancashire. By the mid-1990s, ScottishPower had become the largest wind farm operator in the United Kingdom.

Strategic Acquisitions in the Mid-1990s

As opportunities for more customers and increased sales for electricity became limited in Scotland, management at ScottishPower embarked on a strategic acquisitions policy that extended the company's operations into other areas of the United Kingdom. The initial acquisition was Manweb plc, a regional electrical company that provided service to more than 1.3 million commercial, industrial, and residential customers in Merseyside, Cheshire, and rural North Wales. Purchased at a price of £1.1 billion, the transaction was a milestone, since it represented the first merger between two electricity companies in the United Kingdom.

The merger was an efficient move by ScottishPower, since common functions between Manweb and its parent firm were easily integrated, resulting in lower costs to customers and, at the same time, enabling Manweb to focus on developing its electricity distribution and supply network. With a ScottishPower investment of £300 million to improve and enhance Manweb's power system, the new acquisition was able to limit its supply interruptions significantly, reroute electricity supplies to alternative circuits when necessary, and provide better service to sparsely populated countryside in western England and northern Wales. Manweb was also at the forefront of innovations within the electricity industry. The company developed a "live line" technique, by which repairmen are able to carry out maintenance and repairs on overhead distribution lines without needing to interrupt the supply of electricity to customers in the local area. In one of the most original developments in which Manweb was involved, the company conducted experiments with "trenchless technology," which allowed the laying of cable without having to excavate pavements and streets.

Key Dates:

1955: South of Scotland Electricity Board is formed.
1989: Reorganization of electricity industry in Scotland leads to formation of Scottish Power plc (Scottish-Power).
1993: ScottishPower obtains a license to enter the telecommunications business.
1995: ScottishPower acquires Manweb.
1996: ScottishPower acquires Southern Water plc.
1999: ScottishPower acquires PacifiCorp.

In August 1996, ScottishPower acquired Southern Water plc, a water supply and wastewater services company with nearly two million customers in Kent, Sussex, Hampshire, and the Isle of Wight, for £1.67 billion. Supplying approximately 644 million liters of drinking water per day, through an extensive system of pipes that totaled 13,000 kilometers, and treating more than 1,300 liters of sewerage per day, Southern Water at the time of the acquisition was one of the leaders in the water supply and wastewater treatment industry. Over the years, Southern Water had garnered a stellar reputation in the United Kingdom. The company had dramatically improved the quality of drinking water to the geographical region it served and had successfully cleaned up the pollution along an extensive part of the coastline in southern Britain. Southern Water also had cleaned up the rivers within its operating region so that 94 percent of them supported healthy fish stock and allowed for natural breeding.

Under ScottishPower leadership, Southern Water invested £18 million to build a pipeline to transport water from the River Medway in Kent to Bewl Reservoir on the Kent/Sussex boundary. Since very dry summers bordering on drought had plagued that part of Britain during the mid-1990s, ScottishPower and Southern Water were committed to enhancing the region's water resource management. New and improved wastewater treatment plants were also planned by Southern Water, to be built during the late 1990s to comply with the European Union's Urban Wastewater Directive. Perhaps the most important and far-reaching effect of ScottishPower's acquisition of Southern Water was the decrease in prices for all customers in the new subsidiary's region. Consumer prices would be reduced 1 percent in 1997 and 2 percent in 1998 and 1999.

One of the fastest growing segments of ScottishPower's business at the time was its consultancy services. This segment's ever increasing list of customers included, among others, British Petroleum, British Steel, Motorola, and the British Energy Group. The company's consultancy services encompassed a wide variety of activities, such as the design and construction of power plant buildings, the development of control systems and monitoring devices, the hands-on installation and maintenance of boilers, turbines, and other large power plant equipment, the analysis of plant components and water samples, and assistance with environmental management. The design, construction, and project management of new power stations, like Scotland's nuclear generating stations at Hunterston and Torness, were two examples of the company's consultancy activities in the mid-1990s.

In addition, ScottishPower formed a contracting services business during this time, which carried out a full range of electrical contracting services in the areas of security systems, large-scale power plant installations, high- and low-voltage installations, installing electric heating systems, testing and maintaining electrical systems, and facilities management. In the mid-1990s, clients included hospitals, universities, prisons, supermarket chains, and a host of blue-chip corporations such as NEC, Motorola, Coca-Cola, and Vauxhall.

Through its strategic acquisitions, astute management of a growing retail operation, cultivation of new service-oriented consulting businesses, and provision of reliable and inexpensive electricity to its customers, ScottishPower had earned the reputation as one of the best utility companies in the world.

International Expansion: 1997–2002

By the late 1990s ScottishPower was beginning to question the long-term business sense of some of its recent noncore acquisitions. True, the diversity of its holdings provided the company with a foothold in a number of rapidly emerging businesses, and the possibility of high profits made many opportunities too tempting to ignore. Still intent on gaining a dominant position in the lucrative telecommunications industry, the company acquired Demon Internet, the largest service provider in the United Kingdom, in April 1998. The deal, worth £66 million, instantly vaulted Scottish Power into the top tier of European Internet service providers, and added more than two billion minutes of annual traffic to its existing network. During this time the company also began exploring ways to make an entry into the newly privatized British gas industry. In February 1998 it reached an agreement to convert an empty gas field in Yorkshire into a storage facility capable of supplying gas to 250,000 homes. With price controls on transmission and distribution set to expire by 2000, the company was well positioned to reap huge rewards in a fully deregulated market.

These ventures, however, though extremely promising, also threatened to hinder the growth of the company's core electric utilities holdings. By decade's end, expansion of its power transmission and distribution capabilities had become ScottishPower's principal ambition. With this goal in mind, in April 1997 the company undertook a restructuring program, with the aim of selling off 14 of Southern Water's noncore businesses within one year. At the same time ScottishPower began looking for ways to significantly increase its electrical generating capacity in England, which until the late 1990s had been limited to the production from a single 50-megawatt plant. To remedy the situation, the company entered into a joint venture with Seeboard, an electric company operating in southeast England, in October 1997, to build a 500-megawatt generating plant in Sussex. Also in October, the company applied for the right to construct a 1,125-megawatt plant in Leicestershire. This flurry of activity soon paid off, and by November 1998 the company could claim to provide utilities to one-fifth of all homes in the United Kingdom, and was increasing its customer base by 12,000 every week.

ScottishPower's biggest ambition, however, was to gain a foothold in the $230 billion U.S. electricity industry. After failed attempts to purchase two other U.S. utilities—Cinergy, a major supplier of gas and electricity to customers in Kentucky, Indiana, and Ohio, and Florida Progress—ScottishPower became the first foreign company to enter the American market in December 1998, when it reached an agreement to acquire PacifiCorp for $7 billion. Whereas the company was excited by the prospect of blazing a trail into the United States, with the hope of gaining a serious strategic advantage as more and more utilities went up for sale, some analysts regarded the move as a significant risk, primarily because the future course of the deregulated U.S. utilities industry remained uncertain. To be sure, ScottishPower's initial experience running a utility in the United States was far from promising. After spending the majority of 1999 jumping through regulatory hoops, the company immediately implemented cost-cutting measures at PacifiCorp, with the hope of reducing expenses by 22 percent by 2004. Steep rises in U.S. wholesale electricity prices in early 2001, however, exacerbated by the California energy crisis of the following summer, rendered these savings insignificant, while a power plant failure in Utah during this same period cost the company more than $160 million. In order to help maintain its expansion course in its electricity business, ScottishPower began to scale back its telecom interests, and in March 2002 it sold Southern Water. Although the ultimate wisdom of the PacifiCorp acquisition was still uncertain at the beginning of the 21st century, ScottishPower clearly was determined to make its new venture a resounding success.

Principal Subsidiaries

Manweb plc; PacifiCorp (U.S.A.).

Principal Divisions

U.S. Division; U.K. Division; U.K. PowerSystems.

Principal Competitors

Centrica plc; Edison International (U.S.A.); Scottish and Southern Energy plc.

Further Reading

Buxton, James, "Joint Power Plan Set Up by London Underground," *Financial Times* (London), October 11, 1990, p. 8.

Parks, Christopher, "Transatlantic Surge: Scottish Power Is Attempting One of the Most Ambitious Utility Mergers Yet Seen in the U.S.," *Financial Times* (London), December 11, 1998, p. 18.

"ScottishPower," *Financial Times* (London), April 11, 1995, p. 23.

"ScottishPower," *Times London,* March 5, 1994, p. 27.

"ScottishPower Buys," *Times London,* March 5, 1994, p. 26.

"Scottish Telecoms Move," *Times London,* November 23, 1994, p. 26.

Smith, Michael, "Ambitions Lie South," *Financial Times* (London), November 14, 1995, p. III.

——, "On-Shore Gas to Fuel Power Station," *Financial Times* (London), April 14, 1993, p. 10.

"The Song of the Border Reivers," *Financial Times* (London), May 9, 1991, p. 20.

Taylor, Andrew, "Scottish Power Gains Customers," *Financial Times* (London), November 5, 1998, p. 26.

"Telecoms Rival in Pipeline," *Times London,* December 1, 1992, p. 23.

Ward, Andrew, "Scottish Power Cuts Deep at PacifiCorp," *Financial Times* (London), May 5, 2000, p. 30.

"Wired for Success," *Financial Times* (London), June 28, 1995, p. 20.

—Thomas Derdak
—update: Steve Meyer

Shoppers Drug Mart Corporation

243 Consumers Road
Toronto, Ontario M27 4W8
Canada
Telephone: (416) 493-1220
Fax: (416) 490-2700
Web site: http://www.shoppersdrugmart.ca

Public Company
Incorporated: 1962 as Koffler Associated Drug Company
Employees: 31,000
Sales: $2.28 billion (2001)
Stock Exchanges: Toronto
Ticker Symbol: SC
NAIC: 446110 Pharmacies and Drug Stores

Shoppers Drug Mart Corporation is one of the largest retail drugstore chains in Canada, with more than 800 stores, and outlets in every province from the Atlantic to the Pacific. The corporation was the first to build a nationwide chain of drug retailers. Shoppers Drug Mart has outlets in suburban, rural, urban, mall, and strip mall locations, and more than 60 percent of Canadians live within five kilometers of one. Most of the stores operate under the Shoppers Drug Mart name, except in Quebec, where the stores are called Pharmaprix. In addition, the company runs approximately 40 Shoppers Home Health Care stores. About 45 percent of the chain's overall sales come from pharmacy items, with the remainder coming from over-the-counter drugs, health and beauty aids, convenience foods, and other goods. The company markets several of its own exclusive brands, including its Life brand, Rialto Naturals cosmetics and bath and body care products, QUO brand cosmetics, Life Bear baby care products, and Shoppers Drug Mart herbal remedies. The company is structured in a unique franchise arrangement so that individual store owners, called associates, share profits with the chain. The chain grew rapidly through acquisitions and new store openings from the 1960s through the 1990s. The company was owned by Imasco Limited, itself a subsidiary of British American Tobacco PLC, from 1978 through 1999. Shoppers Drug Mart was then bought out by an investment and management group and taken public in 2001.

Early Years As a Family Drugstore

Shoppers Drug Mart began as a small family pharmacy founded by Leon Koffler in a Jewish neighborhood of Toronto. Koffler's family was originally from a small village in Romania, and little is known about them except that Leon and his mother and three older sisters moved to Toronto when Leon was about 15 years old. There he delivered groceries in a horse-drawn wagon. He later went to the Ontario College of Pharmacy and graduated in 1921. He opened his first drugstore two years later, and soon moved to a more propitious corner location. Koffler married in 1921, and he and his family lived above the store. Koffler kept Koffler's Pure Drugs open seven days a week, from eight until midnight or later. In 1930, Koffler opened a second store, on Bathurst Street in the north section of Toronto. The business did well, and the Koffler family became affluent, owning real estate apart from the two stores. But Leon Koffler died suddenly of a heart attack in 1941, when he was only 47 years old.

Running the family business fell to Koffler's eldest child, his son Murray, born in 1924. Murray was 17 when his father died, still in high school, and unprepared to fill his father's shoes. But no one else was able to run the stores either, so Murray started attending pharmacy school while learning the retail business from his father's accountant and lawyer. Koffler graduated in 1946 and continued to run the stores full time. Koffler soon demonstrated a keen eye for retail trends. He was evidently an avid reader of two U.S. trade publications, *Chain Store Age* and *Shopping Center News*. These opened his eyes to the potential of the suburban shopping mall. Koffler's Pure Drugs was still small, and Koffler was turned down from a tenancy at Toronto's first mall. Disappointed, Koffler tried again to get into another development, the York Mills Plaza being built to the north of the city. The York Mills Plaza was backed by Edward Plunket Taylor, a formidable financier comparable to J.P. Morgan in the United States. His conglomerate owned a large brewery, a sugar company, a chemical company, and many other businesses, including Dominion Stores, a chain grocery that had pioneered the self-service notion in Canada. One of Koffler's drugstores was next door to a Dominion market, and Koffler had decided that the self-serve plan would work well for a drugstore. Self-serve is now the norm in

Company Perspectives:

Built on a foundation of professional expertise and personal service, the Shoppers Drug Mart/Pharmaprix organization has been meeting Canadians' health care needs for over 30 years. What was once a small pharmacy in Toronto has grown into an organization of over 800 stores from coast to coast, becoming an indelible part of the lives of Canadians, young and old. Yet despite our growth, we have never forgotten our origins. We have always remained true to our belief that the personal satisfaction of each and every customer is at the root of our success—and it can only be ensured by the commitment of people who realize that success is built one customer at a time.

most retail stores, where the customer walks up and down the aisles picking and choosing. But in the 1940s, Koffler's Pure Drugs was still run with the pharmacist and assistants behind the counter, handing customers what they asked for. Koffler knew that customers were sometimes inhibited or embarrassed about asking for personal items, and he admired the Dominion model. With some trepidation, Koffler met with E.P. Taylor and explained that he wanted to open a new drugstore in York Mills Plaza that would be run like Taylor's Dominion chain. After taking some months to think it over, Taylor agreed. Koffler sold the Bathurst Street drugstore, which had been bringing in approximately $150,000 annually, and in 1953 opened Canada's first self-serve drugstore. Shelving and fixtures for such a store were not available in Canada, and Koffler had to go to a furniture maker in Grand Rapids, Michigan, for some of what he needed. Koffler gave his new store a more modern design, with a black-and-white color scheme.

Expansion Through Franchising: 1950s–70s

Business was slow at first in the new shopping center, which was far enough from town that cows grazed in a field across the street. But Koffler and E.P. Taylor believed in the coming wave of suburbanization, and Koffler negotiated to open more stores in more malls Taylor was developing. Koffler continued to be influenced by retail trends that had not quite made it to Canada yet. Koffler was intrigued by the growing Kentucky Fried Chicken franchise masterminded by Colonel Harland Sanders. Koffler came up with a franchise arrangement whereby his company leased and stocked the store, but it was wholly run by a pharmacist "associate." The associate paid Koffler Drugs 10 percent of gross sales, but accrued any profits beyond that. The associate had an incentive to make the store prosper, while Koffler had time to devote to advertising and promotion and scouting new locations for the chain. Koffler initiated the franchise arrangement in 1955.

In 1959 Koffler became fascinated by another American retail phenomenon, the Detroit-based GEM (for Government Employees' Mart) stores. GEM shoppers paid a small sum for a membership card, which entitled them to shop the stores' deeply discounted goods. Koffler invested in the chain, helping bring the first GEM to Toronto, and arranged to sublease the GEM drug department. Within its first year the GEM drug department brought in roughly $1 million, three or four times what the other Koffler drugstores were doing. Koffler leased drug departments in several other GEM stores in the area.

In 1962, Koffler wanted to run his own drugstore along the lines of GEM, with perpetual discounts and lots of floor space. He leased a spot in a new Toronto mall called Shoppers World. This store debuted with the new name Shoppers Drug Mart. Soon after, Koffler's other stores became Shoppers Drug Marts as well. In 1966 Koffler opened yet another store, this one a 15,000-square-foot "megadrugstore," one of the first of the model now known as a "big box" store. Koffler personally wrote handbills advertising his stores, and took out a free subscription to the local community newspaper for all the nearby residents so they would see his store's advertisement and a store-sponsored medical advice column. That year Koffler also acquired a string of five Sentry drugstores. There were 17 Shoppers Drug Marts in all, under Koffler's umbrella organization Koffler Associated Drug Company.

At this point Koffler wanted to raise capital to expand the chain even further. He continued to be friends with E.P. Taylor, who advised him to take the company public. This he did, first merging with another chain of drugstores, Plaza Drugstores Limited. The Plaza Drugs chain ran 33 stores in Ontario, but it was having financial difficulties and needed a partner. The two chains came together as a single entity, Koffler Stores Limited, which began to sell its stock to the public on June 20, 1968. The new company became a hotly traded stock. Annual sales were about $28 million at that time.

The chain expanded rapidly through acquisition throughout the 1970s. In 1971 it paid $10 million for the 87-store western Canadian chain of Cunningham Drug Stores Limited. These stores were updated and operated under the Shoppers Drug Mart name. The acquisition put the chain into the provinces of British Columbia, Alberta, Saskatchewan, and the Yukon for the first time. Then in 1974 the firm acquired the 26-store chain Lord's Supervalue Pharmacies for $2.4 million. Lord's had locations along the Atlantic seaboard. Shoppers came into Quebec beginning in 1972, under the French name Pharmaprix Ltd. Pharmaprix was run as a joint venture with Quebec's leading grocery chain, but the arrangement had its difficulties. Pharmaprix lost money through at least 1980, when the joint venture fell apart. Shoppers Drug Mart also grew by opening new stores. By the late 1970s, the company had stores all across Canada as well as a handful of stores in the United States.

Under the Imasco Umbrella: 1980s–90s

By 1978, Koffler Stores had about 300 locations, and it was Canada's only nationwide drugstore chain. Murray Koffler was in his 50s, and wondering what would happen to his company after his death. He had five children, and half of Koffler Stores stock was owned by family members. Koffler, his children, and his top managers agreed that the wisest plan would be to sell the company now, to avoid fights between his heirs that might force a sale inopportunely. So that year Koffler Stores Limited became a wholly owned subsidiary of Imasco Limited. The price was approximately $70 million. Murray Koffler stayed on as CEO of the division until 1983, when he was succeeded by

David Bloom. Koffler retired from the company altogether in 1986, and Bloom became CEO and chairman.

Imasco was a Montreal-based conglomerate that had been formed in 1970 by Imperial Tobacco. Imperial Tobacco, which was partially owned by British American Tobacco (BAT), controlled about 50 percent of the Canadian tobacco market, and it had a stable of leading cigarette brands including Players and Du Maurier. With the possibility of a decline in tobacco consumption as health warnings began to appear, the company decided to diversify into several different industries. By the time it bought Koffler Stores, Imasco owned a chain of cigar stores, the Hardees restaurant chain in the United States, and a chain of 63 Top Drug Marts. With the merger, the Top Drug Marts were converted to Shoppers Drug Marts, giving the whole chain close to 400 retail outlets.

David Bloom started his career as a pharmacist at a Shoppers Drug Mart in 1967. He later ran his store as an Associate, but by 1971 he had been recruited for management training. He was only 39 when he became president and CEO in 1983, and he was apparently on a par with Murray Koffler in terms of energy and retail vision. The company had grown rapidly through the 1960s and 1970s, starting as a public company with slightly more than 50 stores and entering the 1980s with about 400. Now with the secure financial backing of Imasco, Bloom planned to double the number of stores. The chain continued to grow by acquisition. In 1986 Shoppers Drug Mart bought up the Super X Drugstores, an Ontario-area chain of 72 stores. Shoppers Drug Mart moved further into the U.S. market in the early 1980s as well, opening about a dozen new locations in Florida. Elsewhere, independent pharmacists became Shoppers Drug Mart associates, giving the chain about a quarter of the Canadian drugstore market by 1980. Sales that year had grown to $700 million, doubling from $350 million two years earlier. Bloom laid out a long-term plan for growing the chain, aiming to triple sales by 1995.

The company continued to advertise heavily, taking advantage of its position as the only Canada-wide drugstore chain. It introduced several in-house brands and positioned itself as a convenience store, with many special promotions, late hours, and the introduction of more food and snack items. In 1993 the

company bought up a chain of ten drugstores called Pinder Stores, and followed this in 1995 with a chain of 24 Bi-Rite Drug Stores based in western Canada. Its largest acquisition was the 135-store Big V Drugstores chain it bought in 1996. Bloom initiated a major reorganization of the company in the mid-1990s to enable it to take better advantage of its nationwide reach. Because each store was run by an individual associate who had lots of independence, the corporate structure was not as tight as that of some other comparable chains. Shoppers Drug Mart overhauled its distribution system in the mid-1990s to give it just three distribution centers, one in the East, one in the West, and another in central Canada. The company also revamped its information technology for handling inventory and accounting, and moved toward a more centralized management, doubling the number of workers in its Toronto office. The chain also moved toward a new store format, with a bigger floor plan. By the late 1990s, the Shoppers chain had more than 800 stores and revenue of C$4 billion.

Public Company Again in the 2000s

Shoppers Drug Mart continued to open new stores in 1999, moving out model stores with redesigned shelving and lighting, a new color scheme, and other features. The company developed new prototype stores for each of its five typical locations—urban, rural, suburban, regional mall, and its so-called "superstore." The chain was still going strong, with plans for more than 20 new stores that year, and renovations and revampings for many older stores. But that year its parent, Imasco, announced that the drugstore chain was for sale. Imasco had been 40 percent owned by BAT, and BAT wanted to buy up the rest of the company, provided it shed its nontobacco businesses. Shoppers received many offers, but finally sold for $1.74 billion to a group of Shoppers managers and outside investors led by the U.S. leveraged buyout firm Kohlberg Kravis Roberts & Co. (KKR). KKR had recently bought out other retail firms, including the grocery chain Safeway, Stop & Shop Companies, and Randall's Food Markets.

David Bloom stayed on as CEO for one year after the buyout, while the chain continued to roll out new stores in new formats. He retired in 2001 and was replaced by Glenn Murphy. Murphy took the company public, hoping to raise money to pay down the company's debt and finance a redoubled expansion effort. The company began selling stock again in November 2001. Shoppers Drug Mart planned to open as many as 30 to 40 stores a year, noting that as the country aged, there was growing demand for drugstores. The number of prescriptions written in Canada was rising, as was the average price of a prescription. About half of Shoppers' sales came from prescription drug sales. The company also seemed well insulated from the business cycles that shook other parts of the economy. One analyst quoted in *Canadian Business* (November 26, 2001) noted, "Regardless of what the economy is like, people are going to continue to get sick and need toilet paper." The chain remained committed to growth, believing that there were still opportunities to consolidate the Canadian pharmacy business.

Principal Competitors

The Jean Coutu Group (PJC) Inc.; Katz Group; London Drugs Ltd.

Further Reading

Branswell, Brenda, ''A Prescription for Prudence and Profits,'' *Maclean's,* August 16, 1999, p. 44.

''Bust It Up, Guys,'' *Canadian Business,* December 12, 1997, p. 33.

Crawford, Purdy, ''The Way to Prosperity,'' *Canadian Business Review,* Autumn 1992, p. 52.

Holloway, Andy, ''Strong Medicine,'' *Canadian Business,* November 26, 2001, p. 20.

''Imasco: Canadian Policy Sparks a Sally into U.S. Drugs and Fast Food,'' *Business Week,* April 20, 1981, pp. 64, 69.

James, Frederick, ''Shoppers Drug Mart Places Focus on Customers, Expansion,'' *Drug Store News,* December 18, 2000, p. 1.

——, ''Shoppers Drug Mart's Bloom to Retire in July,'' *Drug Store News,* March 26, 2001, p. 3.

——, ''Shoppers Goes on the Block As Potential Buyers Emerge,'' *Drug Store News,* August 30, 1999, p. 1.

Kyriakos, Tina, ''Shoppers Pushes Forward Despite Stiff Competition,'' *Drug Store News,* October 20, 1997, p. 82.

Rasky, Frank, *Just a Simple Pharmacist: The Story of Murray Koffler, Builder of the Shoppers Drug Mart Empire,* Toronto: McClelland and Stewart, 1988.

''Shoppers Drug Mart Has Visions of Continuing Success,'' *Drug Store News,* October 20, 1997, p. 13.

''Smooth Transition with Changing of Guard,'' *Drug Store News,* April 23, 2001, p. 122.

Steinmetz, Greg, ''Kohlberg Kravis to Buy Shoppers Drug Mart for $1.74 Billion,'' *Wall Street Journal,* November 19, 1999, p. B5.

''Top Players Add Market Muscle,'' *Drug Store News,* April 29, 2002, p. 129.

—A. Woodward

Société Tunisienne de l'Air-Tunisair

Boulevard du 07 Novembre 1987
Tunis-Carthage 2035
Tunisia
Telephone: (+216 71) 700 100
Fax: (+216 71) 700 008
Web site: http://www.tunisair.com

Public Company (70% Government-Owned)
Incorporated: 1948
Employees: 7,447
Sales: TND 612.99 million ($423.94 million) (2000)
Stock Exchanges: Tunis
Ticker Symbol: TAIR
NAIC: 481111 Scheduled Passenger Air Transportation;
481112 Scheduled Freight Air Transportation; 481212
Nonscheduled Chartered Freight Air Transportation;
481211 Nonscheduled Chartered Passenger Air
Transportation; 721110 Hotels (Except Casino Hotels)
and Motels

Société Tunisienne de l'Air-Tunisair (Tunisair) is Tunisia's state-sponsored international airline. In the Maghreb region of northern Africa, sandwiched between Algeria and Libya, Tunisia has avoided the political extremes of its neighbors while developing an economy based on tourism. (Textiles are the country's second largest industry.) Tunisair, a modern airline that has attained ISO 9002 certification, has been a key player in bringing travelers (particularly from France, Italy, and Germany) to enjoy the country's surf, sunshine, and culture. The Tunisian government owns 70 percent of Tunisair. Tunisair hauled more than 15,000 metric tons of freight in 2000, when its passenger count approached 3.5 million.

Origins

Independence came to many African nations after World War II. Part of this process in Tunisia, a French protectorate between 1881 and 1956, involved setting up a state airline. Société Tunisienne de l'Air (short form: Tunis-Air or Tunis Air; later, Tunisair) was formed in 1948 by the Tunisian government

and Air France (then Compagnie Air-France), whose involvement in the new airline was crucial due to the lack of qualified technical personnel in the area.

The articles of incorporation were approved on October 21, 1948. The government and Air France each took 35 percent holdings, while private French and Tunisian interests divided the remainder. Initial capital was FFr 60 million. The company was headquartered a 1 rue d'Athènes, Tunis. At a company meeting on December 7, 1948, a Mr. Pomey was appointed director general. A board of directors, which included two Tunisians, was named in February 1949.

Flying operations began on April 1, 1949. The new airline took over some of Air France's short-haul routes along the African coast and across the sea to Marseille (cargo only at first), Nice, and Rome. The first North African points in the network were El Aouina, Bône (later called Annaba), Algiers, and Ajaccio and Bastia, Corsica. The network of scheduled routes was steadily expanded, and charters took the airline to still other destinations. Every year, Tunis Air carried thousands of Muslims on the hajj pilgrimage to Jeddah, Saudi Arabia.

First Profit in 1954

In 1954, Tunis Air began a longstanding relationship with the new Club Méditerrannée, or Club Med, which had set up a site on the Tunisian Isle de Djerba. By the mid-1970s, this had become Tunis Air's chief domestic route, illustrating its dependence on international travel. Tunis Air posted its first profit, FFr 3.2 million, in 1954.

Also in 1954, the company bought its first Douglas DC-4 airliner; a second and third were acquired in 1956. Tunis Air had begun operations with four war surplus Douglas DC-3 (C-47 Dakota) transports bought from the U.S. Army, standard equipment for postwar start-up airlines. The purchase price of FFr 56.5 million consumed nearly all of Tunis Air's start-up capital. Two of the planes were dedicated to passengers, the other two to freight.

The company opened its first direct route to Paris in March 1956. Passenger count exceeded 100,000 for the year and Tunis Air showed a profit of FFr 114 million.

Company Perspectives:

Tunisia's affinity for flying took hold at the beginning of avionics at the turn of the 20th century. Since the creation of TUNISAIR in 1948, Tunisia has kept pace with developments and standards in national and international air transport. TUNISAIR's ISO 9002 certification bears witness to this firm commitment.

Moreover, by offering attractive rates and providing quality service to its clientele, TUNISAIR has experienced nonstop growth since the 1960s.

To meet the demands of increasing passenger business, while maintaining the quality services provided, TUNISAIR since 1961 has opted for the continuous renewal of its fleet of aircraft.

Today, known throughout Europe, North Africa and the Middle East, TUNISAIR serves more than 49 destinations with regularly scheduled flights and 80 destinations with charter flight service.

Tunisification Beginning in 1958

A program to staff Tunis Air with Tunisians, "Tunisification," commenced in 1958. Flight crew were trained in France and Morocco; Tunisians were also hired as stewardesses and in other aviation-related occupations.

The company progressed to French-made Caravelle III jets in 1961; the first arrived on September 2. These 76-seat planes, used on routes to Nice and Paris, were phased out in favor of the larger Boeing 727s in the mid-1970s. The company continued to fly DC-3s to Djerba after the third Caravelle was bought in April 1964.

A new airport, El Aouina, opened in Tunis in 1962. In 1965, Tunis Air opened its first foreign offices, in Paris, Geneva, Frankfurt, and Rome.

Tunis Air played an active role in courting tourist business in the 1970s. During this time, a quarter of Tunis Air's passenger traffic was carried on charter flights.

Going the Distance in the 1970s

In August 1972, headquarters were moved to 113 Avenue de la Liberté. Tunis Air then had 1,100 employees. The company acquired a Boeing 727 in 1971. Two more were acquired in 1973. This model allowed Tunis Air to begin flying to London, a ten-hour trip, in April 1973. The number of visitors to Tunisia from England grew by a factor of 30 as a result.

A 1975 article in *Aviation Week & Space Technology* chronicled some of the issues facing Tunis Air in the 1970s. It resisted calls from Libyan Arab Airlines for a single consortium to carry traffic beyond the region. Tunis Air was also increasing its international route network. As armed conflict steered tourists away from Lebanon, traditionally one of the region's top travel destinations, more were coming to Tunis, Algeria, and Morocco. The airline worked closely with the National Office of Tourism on promotions.

By this time, Air Tunis was handling all of its own maintenance work and most of its employees were Tunisian. Its pilots were still being trained by Air France, which still owned 30 percent of the company.

Tunis Air's fleet included ten Boeings by the end of 1977; the last of the Caravelles was retired. Passenger count exceeded one million for the first time.

A new international airport in Towzar-Naftah, in the west central part of Tunisia, was inaugurated in December 1978. Boeing 727 service connected this new tourist destination to Paris, via Monastir (Al Munastir) on Tunisia's eastern shore.

In January 1979, a Boeing 727 flying from Tunis to Djerba was hijacked and taken to Tripoli. The hijackers, demanding release of jailed Tunisian political figures, ultimately surrendered. The company's first two Boeing 737s, mid-sized passenger jets, entered service in the fall of 1979.

A route connecting Tunis with Dakar was opened in March 1982, and a Damas-Athens route was launched three months later. At this time, Tunis Air took delivery of its first Airbus A300, a European-made widebody jet.

Two important new routes debuted in 1985: Monastir-Geneva and Tunis-Athens-Istanbul. Tunis Air posted a loss in 1985 but would remain profitable for the next dozen years. Tunis Air suffered a 13 percent drop in passenger traffic in 1986 due to difficult economic conditions.

1987 Coup

The president of Tunisia, Habib Bourguiba, was deposed in a bloodless coup on November 7, 1987, and was replaced by Zine al-Abidine Ben Ali. Tunis Air Chief Hedi Attia was arrested at the same time and replaced with Mohamed Souissi, and the government set out to reexamine projects, particularly those involving transportation, planned during the Bourguiba administration. Boeing and Airbus were both competing to win a refleeting order of about eight mid-size airliners.

In 1987, Tunisair began to be operated under strictly commercial guidelines, without government subsidies. The company seemed much improved in 1988, with a net operating profit of TND 69 million, up 50 percent from the previous year.

Two Airbus A320s were placed into service in 1990. Another Boeing 737 was added to the fleet in April 1992. Other changes accompanied Tunisair's new commercial focus. The logo was modernized, retaining the trademark gazelle in 1990. The company inaugurated a new headquarters in November 1991.

The route network expanded into Budapest, Lisbon, and Prague in the summer of 1992. The most profitable routes were to Italy and Saudi Arabia, according to *Air Transport World*. The network stretched to Warsaw, Bratislava, Linz, Salzburg, Moscow, and Stockholm in the mid-1990s.

In the early 1990s, the Tunisian government was planning to sell off between 10 and 20 percent of the airline. Air France had decreased its shareholding to 5.5 percent. The government owned the remainder, except for 9.5 percent owned by government agencies.

Key Dates:

1948: Tunisia's state airline is formed with aid of Air France.
1954: First profit is posted; company begins flying to Club Med site on Djerba.
1958: "Tunisification" of the airline begins.
1961: Tunisair begins flying Caravelle jets.
1971: New Boeing 727s allow direct London flights.
1987: Tunisair is restructured following November 7 coup.
1991: New headquarters and new corporate logo are introduced.
1995: Initial public offering takes place on the Tunis Stock Exchange.
1998: First codeshare arrangement is launched with Air France.

Turnover was TND 396 million ($390 million) in 1992, when the airline carried 2.35 million passengers. The company had 3,750 employees. During the year, Tunisair formed a commuter airline subsidiary, Tuninter, that provided feeder traffic with a fleet of three ATR turboprop aircraft. (Tunisair owned 40 percent of it.) Another subsidiary, Aldiana, operated a chain of hotels.

The carrier, noted *Air Transport World*, was regarded as one of the continent's most progressive airlines. However, tourism—the source of 70 percent of Tunisair revenues—had been in decline. Another important source of business was that of carrying laborers to work in oil rich countries, and transporting 7,000 pilgrims a year to Mecca. Cargo (15,000 tons) accounted for $14 million of annual revenue, but was not highly profitable due to government-mandated low rates.

In November 1992, Abdelhamid Fehri, former head of the Tunisia Air Force, became Tunisair's 15th CEO. Around this time, the company completed a new headquarters building at the Tunis Carthage Airport.

Public in 1995

A public offering of 20 percent of the airline's stock was made in June 1995. In the same year, Tunisair introduced its Privilège class of seating as well as the Fidelys frequent flyer program.

Pretax profits rose to TND 26.57 million ($24.2 million) in 1996. The next year, Tunis Air was discussing a possible alliance with several European airlines—Air France, British Airways, Lufthansa, and Swissair.

Ahmed Smaoui succeeded Tahar B. Ali as chairman in late summer 1997. At the time, Tunisair had a market share of 35 percent of tourist charters and 58 percent of scheduled traffic, in spite of competition from 22 scheduled and 80 charter airlines.

Passenger count exceeded three million in 1997. Business class ("L'Espace Privilège") passengers accounted for 13 percent of passengers and 25 percent of total revenues. Revenues were $674.4 million, while net operating profits amounted to $17.6 million, a bit lower yield than usual. A catering division provided $40 million of revenues, and duty-free sales added another $11 million.

Company executives were encouraging early retirement as a way to reduce staff size and increase productivity. The carrier had 7,200 employees at the time, and operated a fleet of two dozen planes (two-thirds Boeing, one-third Airbus). Tunisair was continuing to renew its fleet with the aim of reducing the number of aircraft types (then being Boeing 737s and 727s and Airbus A320s and A319s) to just two.

Tunisair entered its first ever codeshare arrangement (a marketing agreement whereby two airlines shared flight designator codes in computer reservation systems) in 1998 with, not surprisingly, Air France.

In the late 1990s, the government was still talking of selling its stakes in Tunisair, as well as 18 other state-controlled firms. (There were plans to sell off another 49 companies in their entirety, reported *Air Transport World.*) Tunisair lost $20 million in 2000 on revenues of $424 million (TND 613 million), up 4 percent from the previous year. High fuel prices and the cost of financing new planes were cited as reasons for the loss.

Principal Subsidiaries

Aldiana; Tuninter.

Principal Competitors

Air Algerie; Nouvelair Tunisie; Royal Air Maroc.

Further Reading

Ba-Isa, Molouk Y., and Saud Al-Towaim, "Another Saudi 'Hijacker' Turns Up in Tunis," *Middle East Newsfile,* September 18, 2001.
Bowman, Louise, "Digging Deep," *Airfinance Journal,* October 1994, p. 22.
Davies, R.E.G., *A History of the World's Airlines,* London: Oxford University Press, 1964.
Doty, Laurence, "Arabs Seek to Balance Unity, Competition," *Aviation Week & Space Technology,* December 1, 1975, p. 28.
Forward, David C., "Good Things Come in Small Packages," *Airways,* March 2002, pp. 33–37.
"Hijackers Jailed," *Aviation Week & Space Technology,* January 22, 1979, p. 21.
Hill, Leonard, "Nifty Niche Navigator," *Air Transport World,* September 1998, pp. 122–23.
"North African Credit Competition Takes to the Air," *International Trade Finance,* December 17, 1987.
"Tunis Air Plans Growth As Profits Rise," *Flight International,* July 9, 1997.
Vandyk, Anthony, "Tuning Up in Tunis," *Air Transport World,* June 1993, p. 200.
"World Airline Financial Statistics—2000," *Air Transport World,* World Airline Report, July 2001, http://www.atwonline.com.

—Frederick C. Ingram

Sophus Berendsen A/S

Klausdalsbrovej 1
DK-2860 Soborg
Denmark
Telephone: (+45) 39 53 85 00
Fax: (+45) 39 53 85 85
Web site: http://www.berendsen.com

Wholly Owned Subsidiary of The Davis Service Group
*   Plc*
Incorporated: 1897
Employees: 6,791
Sales: DKr 3.87 billion ($483.75 million) (2001)
NAIC: 421830 Industrial Machinery and Equipment
    Wholesalers; 421840 Industrial Supplies Wholesalers;
    421850 Service Establishment Equipment and
    Supplies Wholesalers; 812320 Dry Cleaning and
    Laundry Services (Except Coin-Operated); 812331
    Linen Supply; 812332 Industrial Launderers

Sophus Berendsen A/S is one of Europe's leading business-to-business textile services groups. Based in Denmark, Berendsen is the market leader in that country, as well as in neighboring Sweden and Norway. It also holds strong positions in The Netherlands and Germany and is active in Estonia and Poland. The company provides textile products and services, hygiene products and services, and safety products and services to the hospital, restaurant, hotel, nursing home, public buildings and facilities, and other services providers. The company's services range from providing floor mat services and linen services to supplying work uniforms for various industries. The company also has developed its own range of textile handling and logistical systems and products, including Etage, a textiles and accessories delivery system for hotels, hospitals, and nursing homes; Quickly, a mop and bucket system; Link-Mat, a system for connecting floor mats, enabling modular designs using multiple floor mats; Unilin, a labeling system based on microchips; Unimat, which provides onsite uniform management; and Food-Tex, a range of textiles developed specifically for the food processing, restaurant, and other food-related in-

dustries and sectors. Led by Managing Director Henrik Brandt, Sophus Berendsen has streamlined its operations to focus wholly on textile services at the turn of the century. The company also has become a leader in the consolidation of the European textiles services market, which is expected to take off in earnest in the early years of the new century—in March 2002 the company received a takeover offer from the United Kingdom's Davis Service Group. The merger, approved later that year, created Europe's leading textile services company, and also marked the end of nearly 150 years of independent existence for Sophus Berendsen.

Steel and Glass Shipper in the 19th Century

The Great Exhibition of 1851 in London provided the inspiration for the founding of the Berendsen business. In that year, Sophus Berendsen had traveled to England and was struck by the iron-and-glass construction of the famed Crystal Palace, built especially for the exhibition. The use of iron girders in the Crystal Palace's construction was a novelty at the time. Yet Berendsen recognized the potential of the new building material, particularly for the increasingly crowded urban centers of the Industrial Era.

Berendsen set up his own business in 1854 and began importing iron girders to the Danish market from the United Kingdom and from Belgium. Rapidly expanding Copenhagen, which was seeing its population grow by more than half again before the end of the 1800s, presented a ready market for Berendsen. Iron girders enabled the construction of taller and more fire-safe buildings. Berendsen's early recognition of the potential of iron girders quickly enabled his company to capture the leading share of the import market in Denmark. The company soon expanded, importing glass as well.

Berendsen died in 1884, leaving the business to his wife, who died two years later. The company then was led by their son, Albert Berendsen. The younger Berendsen expanded the business, branching out the company's import operations into other industrial areas, such as materials for the shipbuilding and railroad industries. In 1897, Berendsen formally incorporated the expanded company as Sophus Berendsen A/S. When Albert

Company Perspectives:

Business concept: Berendsen develops and provides value added textile, hygiene and safety solutions. These are aimed at industry, the service sector, hotels, restaurants, hospitals, nursing homes and public institutions. Our aim is to deliver comfort, hygiene and safety to our customers. We wish to add positively to their image, and to give them a better overall financial position through our services. As soon as Berendsen assumes responsibility for handling a customer's textiles, the customer is able to free up time, space, staff and capital. These are resources that can be put to better use in the customer's own business. We call this 'Total Economy'.

Vision: Through innovation and customer relations we will strive to be the leading textile service company in Europe developing future solutions that benefit our customers, employees and shareholders.

Berendsen died that year, leadership of the company was given to Ludvig Elsass.

Just 27 years old when he was appointed the company's managing director, Elsass remained at the company's head into the 1950s and was responsible for leading the company into new directions. One of these, like the company's origins, was inspired by the new urban realities created during the Industrial Revolution. The intense crowding of the world's cities during the time, as well as the generally unsanitary living conditions found in Europe in particular, had brought on a surge in urban rodent populations, especially of disease-carrying rats.

Working in Aalborg, Denmark, pharmacist Georg Neumann discovered a strain of bacteria in 1902 that proved lethal to rats, yet harmless to people. Calling his discovery Ratin, Neumann set up a new business, Bakteriologisk Laboratorium Ratin, in 1904 and began marketing Ratin in Denmark. Sophus Berendsen took an interest in the product, and given its long-standing import relationship with the United Kingdom, acquired the exclusive marketing license for the United Kingdom. The company opened its first U.K. sales office in 1906.

Pest control was to become one of Sophus Berendsen's most lucrative activities. In the meantime, the company continued to diversify its import interests. Beginning in 1912, the company added a range of technical products for such areas as the marine and railroad industries, and installations such as radar and navigation systems.

In 1927, Sophus Berendsen expanded its U.K. sales office as a full-fledged subsidiary company, placing it under the leadership of Karl Gustav Anker Petersen. The new company, called the British Ratin Company, expanded from being a simple sales agent to providing pest control services; it also began a mail-order operation for Ratin, substantially boosting sales. By the following year, however, British Ratin ended sales of the pesticide to concentrate fully on the service sector. Over the following decade, the company expanded rapidly throughout England. By the beginning of the 1940s, British Ratin expanded into insect control services as well, making its first acquisition, of Chelsea Insecticides. The company later brought its insect control division under the subsidiary name Disinfestation Ltd.

By then, Sophus Berendsen had taken over the production of Ratin in Denmark. With the outbreak of World War II, however, the company transferred Ratin production, as well as the division's headquarters, to the United Kingdom. Following the war, Sophus Berendsen, through British Ratin, continued making new acquisitions, as well as entering new services areas. In 1952, for example, British Ratin introduced its first line of termite control treatment products. That segment was to take a jump forward in 1957, when British Ratin acquired woodworm and dry rot control specialist Rentokil.

That company had been founded in 1925 by Harold Maxwell Lefroy, who had developed a means of exterminating the death water beetle, an infestation of which had been threatening Westminster Hall. Lefroy, assisted by Elizabeth Eases, had come up with a formula in 1924, which they called "Ento-Kill." Since a similar name already had been registered as a trade name, Lefroy instead named his insecticide Rentokil, starting up his own business the following year under the same name. Rentokil began offering its own extermination services during World War II, with a focus on termite and dry rot control.

Production of Ratin was phased out during the mid-1950s as the product was replaced by new preparations. The end of Ratin production led British Ratin to change its name, taking on that of Rentokil instead. Sophus Berendsen remained that company's largest shareholder, a position it was to enjoy until the mid-1990s. Yet in 1969, Sophus Berendsen, which itself remained a private company, brought its Rentokil subsidiary to the stock market with a listing on the London Stock Exchange. The Danish company maintained a stake of more than 50 percent in Rentokil; yet its investment position soon evolved to that of a purely financial holding, as Rentokil pursued its own development as an autonomous company.

Shift to Services for a New Century

Berendsen's oversight of Rentokil had by then given it a taste for the services sector. In 1973, the company took its first step into that area, launching a textile services division. At the same time, the company went public, with a listing on the Copenhagen stock exchange. Despite the growth of that division, Berendsen maintained its longstanding commitment to the industrial import market. In 1978, in fact, Berendsen launched a new division, that of Power & Motion Control products. During the 1980s, the distribution of industrial products became Berendsen's primary import focus, and in 1984, the company phased out its steel and glass imports business. That line was replaced the same year with the launch of a new Components division, which was dedicated to the sale and distribution of electronic and related components.

Into the 1990s, Berendsen continued to operate in two primary areas, industrial distribution and textile services. At the start of that decade, Berendsen went on a growth drive, with a particular emphasis on international expansion. In 1991, the company took its textile services operations beyond Denmark when it acquired the Electrolux companies based in Sweden and The Netherlands. The company also took over the textile ser-

Key Dates:

1854: Sophus Berendsen begins importing iron girders for the Danish market from England and Belgium, then adds glass imports.

1886: Albert Berendsen takes over leadership of the company and expands into new import categories, such as materials for the shipbuilding and railroad industries.

1897: The company is incorporated and Ludvig Elsass becomes managing director.

1906: Sophus Berendsen acquires exclusive U.K. rights to Ratin, a rat and mice control product.

1912: Sophus Berendsen adds new import products, including radar and navigation systems components.

1927: Berendsen's U.K. sales office is expanded into a full-fledged subsidiary, British Ratin, which transforms itself into a services company the following year.

1957: British Ratin acquires Rentokil Ltd. and changes its name to Rentokil.

1969: Berendsen forms Rentokil as a public company.

1973: Berendsen lists on the Copenhagen stock exchange and begins textile services operations.

1978: Berendsen creates the Power & Motor Control (PMC) division.

1984: Company phases out its steel and glass imports business.

1991: Company acquires two textile services companies in Sweden and The Netherlands from Electrolux as well as the textile services division of Denmark's ISS.

1993: PMC acquires Lucas Control, based in the United States and Australia.

1996: Rentokil launches a hostile takeover of BET; Berendsen's stake in Rentokil is reduced to 36 percent.

1997: Company acquires Norway's Lillehammer Vask & Rens, Sweden's Norrbottens Läns, and Ster Super Service, based in The Netherlands, all textile services companies.

1998: Company sells off its Component division and splits into two companies, Sophus Berendsen and Ratin A/S.

1999: Company announces its intention to sell off its PMC companies and to become wholly focused on textile services; company acquires Lips Bedrijfsdiensten BV, of The Netherlands.

2000: Company acquires Wäschegut Groáwäscherei GmbH and Catrin Beteiligungsgesellschaft, both in Germany, and Voss Vaskeri A/S of Norway and De Lelie, in The Netherlands.

2001: Berendsen sells off its remaining Rentokil shares and acquires I/S Korova in Denmark, Micronclean in The Netherlands, a clean room specialist, and Denmark's RoBi group, a mat rentals and laundering concern.

2002: Davis Service Group announces takeover offer worth more than $600 million; Berendsen acquires Mors Matteservice Aps, of Denmark and Hovo-de-Maas, a company specializing in workwear based in The Netherlands.

vices division of fellow Danish company ISS. Two years later, the company scored an even bigger coup when its Power & Motion Control subsidiary bought up Lucas Fluid Power, based in the United States and Australia, making Berendsen the world leader in that segment. By then, Berendsen also had begun exploring entry into the textile services sector in the newly opening Eastern European market, establishing its first plant in Poland in 1995.

Berendsen's blossoming interests in textile services, which led it to complete a number of small acquisitions through the second half of the 1990s, led it to begin phasing out its holding in its Rentokil subsidiary, which by then had grown into one of the U.K.'s leading business-to-business services companies with interests extending beyond its pest control origins to embrace such diverse interests as security and guard services; parcel delivery services; plant rentals; office machinery and equipment maintenance; office cleaning services; and healthcare, including washroom services. Led by Clive Thompson since the early 1980s, Rentokil had made more than 300 acquisitions by the mid-1990s, posting annual sales gains of 20 percent.

In 1996, Rentokil's latest and largest acquisition gave Sophus Berendsen an opportunity to begin cashing out its holding in order to finance the growth of its own textile services wing. When Rentokil launched—and won—a £1.9 billion hostile takeover of BET, which held the Initial linen services company among others, Sophus Berendsen reduced its holding in Rentokil to just 36 percent. In support of the takeover,

however, Sophus Berendsen pledged to maintain its interest in Rentokil for at least five more years.

Nonetheless, Berendsen began making preparation for its exit from its stake in Rentokil (renamed Rentokil Initial). In 1998, the company split itself into two companies, Sophus Berendsen A/S, which took over its Textile Services and Industrial Distribution wings, as well as a 10 percent stake in Rentokil Initial; and Ratin A/S, which existed solely as a holding corporation for the company's remaining Rentokil Initial shares. That same year, Sophus Berendsen sold off its poorly performing Components division.

The arrival of CEO Henrik Brandt in 1999 signaled the start of a new era for Sophus Berendsen. The company's Power & Motion Control division had been stumbling in the latter half of the decade, and Sophus Berendsen now announced its intention to sell off that part of the company and refocus itself wholly on its textile services business. The Power & Motion Control business was sold off in 2000.

By 2001, Berendsen was ready to shed its holding in Rentokil Initial, selling off its shares, including selling Ratin A/S to Rentokil itself. The sale of its Rentokil shares—one of the fastest-growing British stocks of the 1990s—helped fund Berendsen's own acquisition drive. Through the end of the decade and into the beginning of the new century, Berendsen added a number of companies, such as Norway's Lillehammer Vask & Rens, Sweden's Norrbottens Läns, and Ster Super

Service, based in The Netherlands, all of which were acquired in 1997. After taking a break for the sale of the Components division and then the Power and Motion Control business, Berendsen returned to its acquisition drive in 1999, adding Lips Bedrijfsdiensten BV, of The Netherlands.

In 2000, Berendsen stepped up its European expansion with the purchase of Wäschegut Großwäscherei GmbH, and of Catrin Beteiligungsgesellschaft, both in Germany. The company acquired Voss Vaskeri A/S of Norway that year, and then purchased De Lelie, in The Netherlands. Through 2001, as the company completed the sale of its Rentokil shares, Berendsen continued its shopping spree, buying up I/S Korova in Denmark, Micronclean in The Netherlands, a clean room specialist, and Denmark's RoBi group, specializing in mat rentals and laundering. The company continued its acquisition drive into 2002, buying up Mors Matteservice Aps, of Denmark, in April, and purchasing Hovo-de-Maas, a company specializing in workwear based in The Netherlands, in June of that year.

Yet, at the beginning of 2001, Berendsen, calling for the consolidation of Europe's textile services market, let it be known that it was willing to entertain acquisition proposals. The company did not have to wait long—in February 2002, fellow Danish services company ISS, which had sold its textile services operations to Berendsen at the beginning of the 1990s and had since used Berendsen as a main subcontractor, announced that it had acquired 10 percent of Berendsen's shares and was interested in acquiring the rest of the company.

Yet, before ISS could complete a formal takeover offer, Berendsen found itself with a new suitor, the United Kingdom's Davis Service Group, with a takeover offer valued at more than $600 million, representing a price some 50 percent more than Berendsen's market value. The purchase of Berendsen by Davis was completed in the summer of 2002, creating Europe's leading textile services company.

Principal Subsidiaries

Berendsen Textil Service A/S; AS Svarmil Ltd. (Estonia); Berendsen GmbH (Germany); Berendsen Textiel Service B.V. (Netherlands); Berendsen Tekstil Service AS (Norway); Berendsen Textile Service Sp. z.o.o. (Poland); Berendsen Textil Service AB (Sweden); Berendsen Safety AB (Sweden).

Principal Competitors

ISS (International Service System A/S); Rentokil Initial plc; Bidvest Group Ltd.; Cintas Corp.; Overall Laundry Services Inc.; Aramark Uniform Services Inc.; Spotless Services Ltd.; Steiner Corp.; Davis Service Group Plc; G and K Services Inc.; Ameripride Services Inc.; Johnson Service Group Plc.

Further Reading

"Berendsen Acquires Hovo-de-Maas," *Nordic Business Report,* June 18, 2002.

Contney, John J., "Sophus Berendsen Finds Growth and Opportunity in a Most Unlikely Location," *Textile Rental Magazine,* November 12, 1999.

"Davis Takes Rival to Cleaners," *Birmingham Post,* March 23, 2002, p. 17.

Dryekilde, Birgitte, "Berendsen May Sell Rentokil Stake to Finance Acquisitions," *Reuters,* March 9, 2001.

Moreira, Peter, "ISS Offers to Buy Sophus Berendsen," *Daily Deal,* January 28, 2002.

——, "Sophus Berendsen Accepts Davis Service Group's Bid," *Daily Deal,* March 22, 2002.

Thomsen, Bech, "Berendsen Bid War Seen As ISS Proposes Takeover," *Reuters,* January 28, 2002.

—M. L. Cohen

SSL International plc

Toft Hall, Toft
Knutsford, Cheshire WA 16 SPD
United Kingdom
Telephone: +44-156-562-4000
Fax: +44-156-562-4001
Web site: http://www.ssl-international.com

Public Company
Incorporated: 1999
Employees: 7,000
Sales: $844.5 million (2002)
Stock Exchanges: London
Ticker Symbol: SSL
NAIC: 325412 Pharmaceutical Preparations Manufacturing; 326299 All Other Rubber Product Manufacturing; 339113 Surgical Appliance and Supplies Manufacturing; 316219 Other Footwear Manufacturing

SSL International plc is one of the United Kingdom's major healthcare companies. It markets and manufactures a variety of well-known brands, including Durex condoms and Dr. Scholl footcare and footwear products. It also makes surgical gloves under the Regent Biogel brand name, and the leading household glove in England, Marigold. Its Hibi line of antiseptics is another major brand. SSL was formed from the merger of several earlier companies. Scholl plc was the non-U.S. arm of the famed Dr. Scholl's footcare line, and this merged with Seton Healthcare Group in 1998 to form Seton Scholl Healthcare. This company then merged with another venerable English company, London International Group, in 1999, to form the current SSL International. London International Group, formerly London Rubber Co., was the oldest and largest manufacturer of condoms in the world. SSL's Durex brand controls about 20 percent of the global market share in condoms, with a much larger market share in the United Kingdom and Europe.

Origins of the Dr. Scholl Brand

The Dr. Scholl brand is one of the world's best-known names in footcare products. Dr. Scholl was William Mathias Scholl, born on a dairy farm in La Porte, Indiana, in 1882. Scholl began attending medical school in Chicago in 1899, and he received his medical degree in 1904. However, his abiding interest was in shoes and feet, and he never practiced general medicine. Scholl had worked in a shoe store to support his studies, and he became convinced that uncomfortable and ill-fitting shoes were responsible for much woe. Even before he completed his medical degree he was granted a patent for a device called the "Foot-Eazer" arch support, and he began his career by peddling his handmade leather shoe inserts to Chicago shoe stores. Scholl's medical training helped him market the Foot-Eazer. He carried a real human skeleton foot with him on his rounds, and used it to demonstrate the stresses unsupported feet were subjected to. In 1907 Scholl incorporated the Scholl Manufacturing Company, and by 1909 the company had its own Chicago factory. Besides the Foot-Eazer, the company made an array of footcare products, including corn plasters, foot powder, special foot soap, and others. Very early on the line was packaged in a distinctive yellow and blue, a color scheme the Dr. Scholl's line still carries.

William Scholl's younger brother Frank joined the firm in 1908, and he became responsible for much of the company's growth in England and the rest of Europe. William Scholl made many trips to Europe, once fitting arch supports for Kaiser Wilhelm II. He also fitted arch supports for the era's famed runner Paavo Nurmi, "the flying Finn." Eventually Scholl dispatched his brother to Europe for good, to develop business there. Frank Scholl's idea was to open a line of retail footcare shops. Over his older brother's objections, Frank opened the first Dr. Scholl Foot Comfort Shop in 1913 in London. His doctor brother was afraid the Foot Comfort Shops would have difficulty competing with the drugstores and shoe stores that already sold Scholl products. But Frank was a magnificent retailer who made the Comfort Shops irresistible. He crammed the large front display windows with products, with posters explaining the products, and then with moving demonstrations of the products. One eye-catcher was a huge sledgehammer endlessly smashing down on the knee of a skeletal leg. Emblazoned "140 pounds, the weight of the average man," the sledgehammer purported to illustrate the ordeal that walking caused the foot and ankle.

In 1933, the Scholl Manufacturing Co. included a line of retail shoe shops selling Dr. Scholl brand shoes. From the 1930s

Company Perspectives:

SSL International plc is a major global healthcare organization committed to developing, manufacturing and marketing premium healthcare brands in its core business areas. SSL's activities will benefit consumers, healthcare professionals and employees worldwide, as well as maximise shareholder value.

through the 1960s the Scholl shops offered a line of comfortable padded shoes designed mainly for people who worked on their feet all day. By the early 1960s, there were about 100 Dr. Scholl's Foot Comfort Shops in the United States, and over 400 overseas. The Scholl shoe line took a huge leap in the 1960s when its wooden exercise sandals became all the rage for young women. The exercise sandal was designed by Frank Scholl's son William, born in London in 1920. William Scholl joined Scholl Manufacturing following World War II, after studying modern languages at Cambridge University. He came across a wooden sandal in Germany in the late 1950s, embellished its design and added a leather strap across the toes. He began marketing it as the ''Original Exercise Sandal,'' claiming that wearing it toned the leg muscles. In the mid-1960s British women discovered the Dr. Scholl's sandals. The bulk of the Scholl shoe line was far from fashionable, designed as they were for people with foot problems and foot fatigue. But the sandals appealed to young people—women in particular—who seemed to like the way they looked with a mini skirt. William Scholl enhanced the distribution of the sandals, making them available in self-service racks in drugstores. The sudden popularity of the exercise sandal brought new recognition to the Dr. Scholl's brand.

Scholl Under New Ownership in the 1970s and 1980s

Founder William M. Scholl died in 1968, and his heirs incorporated Scholl Inc. as a public company to settle his estate. Its first public stock offering was in 1971. Scholl Inc. was split into two parts, each run by one of Scholl's nephews. The U.S. operations were run by Jack Scholl, who was vice-president and general manager, and William Scholl became president of the company, overseeing markets in Europe, Japan, Latin America, Canada, and New Zealand. About 45 percent of Scholl Inc.'s sales came from its non-U.S. operations, and about one-third of its foreign sales came from England. The company as a whole sold over 500 different foot and leg care products as well as its line of shoes. Sales had risen extensively starting in the mid-1960s. Sales were close to $60 million in 1966, and reached over $150 million by 1974.

Sales and earnings remained roughly static over the next few years of the 1970s. In 1978, the company was sold to Schering-Plough Corp., a large New Jersey maker of pharmaceuticals. Schering-Plough paid $130 million for Scholl Inc. William Scholl went to work for the parent company in its overseas markets. He eventually became president of Schering-Plough's international consumer products division, until he retired in 1984. In 1987, Schering-Plough sold the overseas operations of the Dr. Scholl brand. European Home Products of Basingstoke, England, paid $160 million for the Scholl business in Europe, Latin America, and Asia. European Home Products was known

as a manufacturer of household electrical appliances. Following the merger, the company took the name Scholl plc.

London Rubber Co.

London Rubber Co. was another company with a long history that later became part of SSL International. The company was founded by L.A. Jackson in London in 1915 to sell ''barber's sundries.'' Whatever else the sundries were, the stock included rubber condoms, at that time imported from Germany. Condoms made of animal gut had been known in Europe since the 16th century. By the mid-1700s, shops specializing in condoms existed in European cities. It first became possible to manufacture condoms out of rubber beginning in 1843, with the invention of the rubber vulcanization process. In 1915, Jackson's London Rubber Co. was a small affair, selling its imported stock out of a small room behind a tobacconist's shop. In 1929, the company trademarked the brand name that later held a virtual monopoly over the British condom market. The name was Durex, which stood for *Du*rability, *Re*liability, and *Ex*cellence. Though the company continued to import condoms from Germany, London Rubber Co. set up its own factory in England in 1932. The factory made latex condoms, using a process and material that had just been invented. The Durex factory had to increase its production during World War II, when London Rubber Co. was cut off from its suppliers in Germany.

After the war, the company developed more sophisticated manufacturing and testing processes. London Rubber Co. was almost free of competition in Britain and thus enjoyed a huge share of the market there. It incorporated as a public company, trading on the London Stock Exchange, in 1950. The company also exported to Europe in the 1950s under other brand names including London and Hatu. Though there were other manufacturers in Europe, through 1990 the company controlled almost 50 percent of the European condom market. London Rubber ventured into farther flung markets as well. The company began a joint operating agreement with a manufacturer in India in 1961. In 1962 it acquired a U.S. condom maker, Julius Schmid Inc. It sold the Ramses and Sheik brand condoms in the United States, though it had a far smaller market share there than in most of its other markets. In the late 1960s London Rubber began advertising in the United Kingdom for the first time.

But as the birth control pill became more popular, condom sales began to flag. In 1981, the company was run by an American named Alan Woltz. Woltz decided that the company should bolster its sales by diversifying into other product lines. Woltz put London Rubber into a variety of new businesses, including fine china, health and beauty aids, and retail photo finishing. By the mid-1980s, the company was no longer primarily a condom maker, and it changed its name to London International Group (LIG) in 1986. But the diversification strategy did not pay off. The photo processing business in particular was expensive to run, and drained the company of cash. By early 1993, many of LIG's new businesses were in the red, but Woltz managed to cover up this fact, misleading investors. The London Stock Exchange censured LIG in 1993 for hiding its losses, and Alan Woltz resigned.

Woltz's successor was Nicholas Hodges, who had run LIG's European operations and also built up a profitable niche in

Key Dates:

1907: Scholl Manufacturing Company is founded.
1913: First Dr. Scholl's Foot Comfort Shop opens in London.
1915: London Rubber Co. is founded.
1929: Durex brand name is trademarked.
1950: London Rubber Co. goes public.
1971: Scholl Inc. incorporates as public company.
1978: Schering-Plough buys Scholl Inc.
1986: London Rubber changes name to London International Group.
1987: Non-U.S. operations of Scholl are sold to British firm, which takes the name Scholl plc.
1998: Seton Scholl is formed out of Seton Healthcare and Scholl plc.
1999: Seton Scholl buys London International; new company is named SSL International plc.

surgical gloves. Hodges shed the unprofitable divisions, and then began trying to cut costs in the company's core business area, which was again condoms. LIG's profit margin on condom manufacturing was very low, and some insiders thought the company was headed for bankruptcy. LIG shut some of its facilities in England and opened new ones in Malaysia, Thailand, and India, where costs were lower. The company had to take a $220 million charge in 1994 for its discontinued operations, and ended up in the red by some $37 million. This was at a time when it held an 80 percent market share in the British condom market with its Durex brand and a roughly 45 percent market share for its brands in Europe. In addition, the AIDS epidemic had been expected to increase the use of condoms. If the company could not do well under these market conditions, things looked dire.

The company had a strategy for turning itself around. It decided to launch Durex as a global brand, replacing the many brand names its products were sold under outside of England. LIG increased its advertising, for example putting out a new campaign on MTV Europe in 1994, reaching millions of potential customers in 37 countries. It was still the world's largest maker of condoms, and some 15 percent of its sales were to governments and government agencies like the U.S. Agency for International Development. By the late 1990s, LIG had managed to increase its worldwide condom sales by about 3 percent annually. Overall earnings grew 10 to 15 percent annually during 1996 and 1997, and the company hoped to be able to sustain this pace. LIG also hoped to gain a larger share of the U.S. market. The company had a 50 percent market share in Europe by 1998, with a similar market share over much of its Asian markets, but in the U.S. its various brands put together had only about a 20 percent market share. LIG phased out Sheik, Ramses, and its other brand names and unified them as Durex. The company made acquisitions of other condom makers in the 1990s, too, buying up the Malaysian brand Mister in 1995, and the Spanish brand Androtex the next year. In 1996 LIG also bought a U.S. manufacturer of both condoms and medical gloves, Aladan Corporation, for $69.5 million.

Formation of New Company Through Series of Mergers in Late 1990s

Meanwhile, Scholl plc had its ups and downs in the 1990s. It had tried to jump-start its support hosiery business in 1993, hiring a young celebrity to endorse the line and moving distribution into supermarkets. Though the company's sales were up as much as 10 percent for 1994, operating profits were eaten away by the high cost of promotion and distribution. In 1995 Scholl sold off a French cosmetics business it operated and closed down over 20 retail stores. In 1998 Scholl announced it was being acquired for $568 million by Seton Healthcare Group. Seton was another British company which made a variety of consumer healthcare products. It had a line of bandages and skin treatments, as well as the Woodward brand of baby medicines. The merged company took the name Seton Scholl plc, and aimed to focus on its several core brands.

One year later, Seton Scholl embarked on a new merger deal, and acquired LIG for $984.7 million. LIG had not seemed able to find its feet in the 1990s. In 1999, the British Office of Fair Trade announced its second investigation in five years into LIG's trading practices in England, where the company held 70 percent of the condom market. The Office of Fair Trade's Monopolies & Mergers Commission had already put strictures on LIG in 1994, and the condom market was supposed to be open to more competition. In 1999 the commissioned revealed that it was going to look into LIG again. This bad news came just months after LIG announced it would not meet its profit projections, and as a result its share price tumbled 30 percent. The merger placed LIG under new management as part of the new company, now named SSL International plc. The company moved into headquarters in an ancient country estate in Cheshire, Toft Hall.

SSL International found itself with four principal divisions. Its consumer division comprised its condom business, the Dr. Scholl's footcare and footwear lines, and over-the-counter medicines. Besides the Woodward line of baby medicines, the company also had a line of antiseptics, Hibi, that it acquired from AstraZeneca in 2000. Consumer healthcare products made up about 55 percent of the company's sales. Another 33 percent of sales came from its medical products division, which included surgical gloves. Marigold gloves, the leading British household glove brand which came with LIG, accounted for another 8 percent of sales and formed its own division within the new company. A miscellaneous division of other products included various sports and leisure goods. The cost of integrating the merged companies was high. Operating costs also ate into SSL's profits, and in 2002 the company had to issue a warning that it would not meet its profit goals, and it would have to lay off workers. *Investors Chronicle* (May 31, 2002) described the company as having "stumbled from one crisis to the next" ever since the 1999 merger. The company sold 21 of its over-the-counter drug brands in 2002, and announced that it would also sell historic Toft Hall. The company's plans for the future focused on promoting four of its leading brands: Durex condoms, the Dr. Scholl line, Regent surgical gloves, and Hibi antiseptics. SSL shared marketing and technology for its Scholl line with Schering-Plough, which still ran the U.S. operations for the brand. SSL's launch of Flight Socks in 2002 was one of its most successful new products for Dr. Scholl's.

Principal Divisions

Consumer Healthcare; Medical; Marigold Gloves.

Principal Competitors

Ansell Healthcare Inc.; Beiersdorf AG; Safeskin Corp.

Further Reading

"Barriers to Entry," *Economist*, November 30, 1991, p. 71.

Bidlake, Suzanne, "Scholl Pulls Out of Ads with Celebrity Backing," *Marketing*, April 8, 1993, p. 14.

Campanella, Frank W., "Price Increases Step Up Pace of Earnings Recovery at Scholl," *Barron's*, September 2, 1974, p. 23.

Day, Julia, "OFT to Investigate UK Condom Market Again," *Marketing Week*, February 25, 1999, p. 22.

Fox, Harriet Lane, "Durex Stretches Its Brief," *Marketing*, August 10, 1995, p. 14.

"Go Forth and Don't Multiply," *Economist*, June 19, 1999, p. 62.

"Introducing Mr. Rubber," *Institutional Investor*, December 1998, p. 21.

Machan, Dyan, "Condom King," *Forbes*, July 17, 1995, p. 47.

Meek, Vicky, "Making a Business out of Pleasure," *Accountancy*, June 1998, pp. 38–39.

Newland, Francesca, "How Durex's Strength Keeps Entrants at Bay," *Marketing Week*, August 27, 1998, p. 20.

"Obituaries; W. Scholl, 81; Designer of Faddish Dr. Scholl's Sandal," *Los Angeles Times*, March 25, 2002.

"Scholl Starts Well," *Soap, Perfumery & Cosmetics*, May 1995, p. 3.

Seneker, Harold, "Is There Growth in Corn Plasters?" *Forbes*, January 21, 1980, p. 78.

"Seton Healthcare Buying Scholl for $568 Million," *New York Times*, May 7, 1998, p. D8.

"Seton Scholl to Establish Joint Marketing Unit," *Marketing*, September 10, 1998, p. 4.

"SSL International," *Investors Chronicle*, May 31, 2002.

"Those Aching Feet," *Time*, August 24, 1962, pp. 60–62.

Wentz, Laurel, "Condom Marketer Targets the World," *Advertising Age*, September 16, 1996, p. 40.

—A. Woodward

Steria SA

12 rue Paul Dautier
B.P. 58
78142 Vélizy Villacoublay Cedex
France
Telephone: (+33) 1-34-88-60-00
Fax: (+33) 1-34-88-62-62
Web site: http://www.steria.com

Public Company
Incorporated: 1969
Employees: 9,300
Sales: EUR 509 million ($450.9 million) (2001)
Stock Exchanges: Euronext Paris
Ticker Symbol: RIA
NAIC: 541511 Custom Computer Programming Services;
    541512 Computer Systems Design Services; 541330
    Engineering Services

France's Steria SA has leapt onto Europe's computer services scene, claiming the number eight spot in that market after its acquisition of nearly all of Integris, the former IT services wing of faltering French computer legend Bull. With the addition of Integris, Steria's revenues will nearly triple—to a pro forma EUR 1.3 billion—while giving the company, formerly primarily focused on France, a truly international structure. The company expected more than 60 percent of its sales to come from beyond France in 2002. Steria has positioned itself as an end-to-end IT services provider on a European scale, with nearly 10,000 employees and subsidiaries in 12 countries. The company focuses on three core business areas: consulting, systems integration, and outsourcing. Outsourcing provided some 45 percent of the company's pre-acquisition revenues of EUR 509 million in 2001 and is also the company's fastest growing area of operation. Systems Integration remains the company's largest segment, generating 55 percent of Steria's 2001 revenues. Steria's Consulting operations are split about evenly between its outsourcing and systems integration business and represents 20 percent of the company's total revenues. The company focuses on four primary industries: public sector; banking and insurance; telecommunications; and industrial, including energy and transportation. Steria is led by Chairman and CEO François Enaud and is quoted on the Euronext Paris stock exchange.

French IT Pioneer in the 1970s

With backing from BNP (Banque Nationale de Paris), Jean Carterton founded Steria, or the Société d'Etude et de Réalisation en Informatique et Autonomisme, in 1969. BNP initially took 49 percent of the company and was to remain a major shareholder and important client of the company for many years. Yet Carterton, already an industry veteran who had worked in the nascent computer industry since the early 1950s and who had left a position at early IT leader Sema to found Steria, carefully guarded his company's independence. An early feature of the company was that its employees were offered the opportunity to become shareholders; it was one of the first French companies to open its ownership structure in that way.

From the start, Steria's focus was on software development and programming for information and automation systems for the major corporate client market—a new and fast-growing market. Whereas previously hardware and software had been considered a single entity, at the beginning of the 1970s, the development of the microchip and the increasing complexity of software programs led the computer industry to separate the two areas. In France, computer technology had been slow to take hold in the country's industries. By the early 1970s, however, more and more French companies began to embrace the new technologies. While a number of corporations developed in-house IT operations, large numbers turned to specialists like Steria, creating an early outsourcing market.

Steria grew quickly, matching its ambitious sales forecasts to near FFr 10 million by 1971. In that year the company began to expand its operations, opening its first foreign subsidiary, Steriabel, in Brussels. The difficulties of launching a foreign subsidiary, however, soon brought Steria's focus back to the French market, and through most of the next decade the company's growth remained, in large part, domestic. In 1971, the company began building its national network, opening its first branch office in Bordeaux. The following year, Steria added branches in Toulouse and Lyon. Then, in 1973, the company took over the Marseilles office of Honeywell-Bull Service, which had been acquired by BNP.

Yet the company's growth in the 1970s also was due, in large part, to a number of acquisitions, notably that of Frap (Société Française d'Analyse et de Programmation), acquired in 1971, which gave the company a new suite of software, as well as boosting its revenues. The following year, Steria acquired another small company, specialized in computer training, called Orgamatic. A more significant acquisition came in 1973 when the company purchased Société d'Assistance Informatique (SAI), which specialized in real-time automation systems. That group was to play a major role in Steria's first large-scale success, the installation of automated information systems for Agence France Presse, the French news agency, replacing that organization's outdated outmoded manual systems. The fulfillment of that contract quickly led to new contracts from other, foreign news agencies. Steria also was called in by SEP (Société Européenne de Propulsion) to form a partnership, SEP Informatique, which took over SEP's information systems development. That same year, Steria acquired a small French company specialized in creating components based on the new microchip technology, called Intel—the name was quickly changed to Sitintel to avoid confusion with Intel Corporation, based in California.

These events corresponded with a steady rise in company sales through the 1970s, and despite the economic recession brought on by the Arab Oil Embargo. By 1976, Steria's sales had risen to FFr 74 million—a growth rate of some 80 percent per year—and the company featured nearly 550 employees. The company received a number of other large-scale contracts during the decade, such as the technical oversight of the famed Parisian modern art museum and library, Centre Pompidou, then under construction, as well as work on the massive La Défense complex and the development of a simulator for an automated control system for the Parisian rail authority, RATP.

Significantly, Steria also had become an early participant in the rapidly developing telecommunications sector, in part through its Sitintel subsidiary. The race was on in Europe to develop text and video delivery systems. In the late 1970s, Steria became one of the driving forces behind the development of France's Teletel system, through the Teletel 3V, which in turn led to the launch of the Minitel system in 1981—a precursor to the online and Internet systems that developed elsewhere in the world in the late 1980s and early 1990s.

Sleeping Beauty in the 1980s

With BNP as a major shareholder, Steria had developed extensive experience with banking systems, and numbered such important clients as the Banque de l'Indochine, Banque de Bruxelles, and the United Overseas Bank in Geneva, Switzerland. This latter contract led the company to its first international expansion since the early 1970s, with the purchase of a small company based in Geneva in 1975. The company then found a partner in Switzerland, Galenica, a pharmaceuticals distribution company that had set up its own IT services subsidiary with offices in Geneva, Berne, and Zurich. The two companies combined their Swiss operations, creating Galenica Informatique, and attempted to expand into the German-speaking region of Switzerland. Yet that effort proved a distinct failure, to the point where the joint venture collapsed. Steria gained control of Galenica Informatique and renamed it Steria Informatic.

Steria had grown strongly in the 1970s and by 1985 had seen its sales top FFr 550 million. Yet the company was to earn itself a reputation as the "Sleeping Beauty" of the French IT services industry as its growth slowed. Nonetheless, the company completed a number of large-scale contracts, including the development of the information system for the Central Bank of Saudi Arabia, at the time the largest foreign contract ever awarded to a French IT services company. The company also completed another important contract in the late 1980s, that of the creation of the driverless train system for the Paris RER A line.

Toward the end of the 1980s, Steria—which had sold off its Steriabel subsidiary in 1986—returned to the international market. In 1987, the company made its first attempt to enter the lucrative German market, with a focus on the banking sector, creating a new subsidiary, Steria GmbH. Yet access to the German banking industry proved difficult for foreign corporations, and in 1990 Steria reinforced its position with the acquisition of Software Partner, based in Darmstadt. Nevertheless, the company found it difficult to crack the German market, and its subsidiary there grew only slowly through the 1990s.

Steria found more success in Spain, which the company entered with the creation of subsidiary Steria Iberica in 1987. The following year, the company acquired majority control of Audinsa, based in Barcelona. The purchase of Solinsa, also based in Barcelona, in 1990, led Steria to regoup all of its Spanish operations into a single subsidiary, Steria Solinsa. Through the 1990s, the Spanish market grew to become the company's most important foreign market, together with Switzerland. Meanwhile, the company returned to Belgium, buying up Générale de Banque subsidiary Gecosys, originally a specialist in artificial intelligence applications. That purchase formed the basis of a new subsidiary, Steria SA/NV.

In France, Steria had grown through acquisitions as well, buying three companies from Systmark: ECL, an IT services company specializing in industrial applications; Sysinter, a temporary agency focused on the IT services market; and C-Mips, an early specialist in systems integration and outsourcing. If two of the three were to have little substantial impact on the company—ECL was folded into subsidiary Steria Ingénierie, and Sysinter remained a peripheral operation—C-Mips enabled Steria to turn in a new direction. The computer industry was changing rapidly

Key Dates:

1969: Steria is created by Jean Carteron, with backing from BNP.
1971: The first French branch office opens in Bordeaux; the Belgian subsidiary Steriabel is created.
1973: Three companies—Frap, Orgamatics, and SAI—are acquired; a contract for the automation of Agence France Presse is obtained.
1978: Steria Informatic is formed in Switzerland.
1981: The Minitel system, based on software architecture developed by Steria, is launched.
1986: Steriabel is sold.
1988: ECL, Sysinter, and C-Mips are acquired from Systmark; C-Mips forms the basis of Steria Exploitation, marking the company's entry into systems integration and management market.
1996: Steria adopts a new strategy, making systems integration a key target area.
1998: François Enaud is appointed chairman and CEO to replace Jean Carteron.
1999: Steria goes public on the Paris stock exchange; subsidiaries are formed in the United Kingdom and Singapore.
2000: Steria acquires TECSI, EQIP, Métanoïques, and the outsourcing operations of Experian; company founds e-business consulting subsidiary Net and B.
2002: Steria completes the acquisition of Integris Europe, tripling its revenues and placing it in the top ten of European IT services companies.

at the end of the 1980s, abandoning the former mainframe-based systems for multiplatform client/server-based information systems. The purchase of C-Mips enabled Steria to become an early player in the fast-growing systems integration and services market. That company was renamed Steria Exploitation.

Reaching the Top Ten in the New Century

At the beginning of the 1990s, Steria formed two significant joint venture partnerships, the first with Bull, called Bull-Steria Génie Logiciel, offering consulting and applications development services, and the second with IBM, called Ishtme, which proved to be primarily a commercialization vehicle for IBM products.

Steria recorded a number of further triumphs in the early 1990s, such as the development of the information system for the Jakarta airport in 1993 and the creation of the French inter-bank management system in 1994. Despite these important projects, the company was hit hard by the recession of the early 1990s and in 1993 the company recorded its first-ever net losses.

Recovering from its difficulties, Steria quickly recognized that the economic recession had helped transform its market—French and European companies now began to embrace the outsourcing of their information systems needs in an effort to control costs and to concentrate on core competencies. Steria Exploitation placed Steria in a good position to take a major

share of the fast-growing market, and in 1996 the company adopted a new strategy to make systems management one of the company's key operational areas.

The "Sleeping Beauty" of the French IT services industry was preparing to wake up, and in 1997 Carteron found the company's Prince Charming in the form of 38-year-old François Enaud, who had joined Steria as a programmer in the early 1980s. Yet Enaud nearly found himself out of a job, when Steria was confronted by a hostile takeover attempt from Compagnie des Signaux. The company was able to fend off the takeover attempt, however, and Enaud took the company's reins in 1998.

Under Enaud, Steria resumed its expansion, opening new subsidiaries in the United Kingdom and in Singapore, as well as a new branch office in Düsseldorf in 1999. That year, also, Steria went public with a listing on the Euronext Paris stock exchange's secondary market. The public offering enabled Steria to begin making acquisitions, and in 2000 the company acquired several businesses, including TECSI, EQIP, Métanoïques, and the outsourcing operations of Experian, all based in France. The company also founded an e-business consulting subsidiary, Net and B.

Steria had succeeded in gaining one of the top spots in the French IT services market. Yet the increasing international positioning of its major clients placed the company in a difficult position—by 2000, international revenues accounted for just 16 percent of the company's total sales of EUR 389 million. Steria began looking for a means to expand onto the European scene on a larger scale.

The company soon located its target—Integris, the IT services division of troubled French computer group Bull. The eventual agreement worked out by the sides (Bull had attempted to cancel the companies' original acquisition agreement) gave Steria control of nearly all of Integris Europe, with the exception of its French operations, unwanted by Steria, and most of its Italian and Greek operations, which were kept by Bull. The acquisition of Integris, based in the United Kingdom, propelled Steria into the top ten of European IT services companies, tripling its sales, to a pro forma EUR 1.13 billion for 2002. Steria had successfully negotiated its transformation into a truly international company, with more than 60 percent of its sales coming from beyond France.

Principal Subsidiaries

BSGL; Diamis (50%); Temis; Intest; Net and B; Sysinter; Clearsy; Mix RH; Steria GmbH (Germany); Steria SA/NV (Belgium); Steria Solinsa SA (Spain); Steria Informatic SA/AG (Switzerland); Steria UK Ltd; Steria Ltd (U.K.); Steria SA (Saudi Arabia); Steria Asia Pte Ltd (Singapore); Steria Sud America (Argentina).

Principal Competitors

Cap Gemini Ernst & Young; Atos Origin PF; Getronics NV; Logica; CMG; WIM Data; Tieto Enator; GFI Informatique SA; Unilog SA; Sopra SA; Transiciel SA; Sylis SA.

Further Reading

Bremer, Catherine, "Bull Sells Integris to Steria for 190 mln Euros," *Reuters,* August 31, 2001.

Carterton, Jean, *Steria: 30 ans de création continue,* Paris: Le Cherche Midi Editeur, 1999.

Guillaume, Philippe, "L'introduction de Steria: Un véritable project d'entreprise," *Les Echos,* November 9, 1999, p. 48.

Laugier, Edouard, "Steria, du Minitel à Bull," *Nouvel Economiste,* May 3, 2002.

"Le prince charmant d'une SSII endormie," *Challenges,* September 15, 2001.

"Steria Emerges As Europe's Eight Computer Services Company," *European Report,* January 16, 2002.

"Steria to Pursue Active M&A Strategy," *Computergram International,* February 4, 1999.

—M. L. Cohen

Tanger Factory Outlet Centers, Inc.

3200 Northline Avenue, Suite 360
Greensboro, North Carolina 27408
U.S.A.
Telephone: (336) 292-3010
Fax: (336) 852-2096
Web site: http://www.tangeroutlet.com

Public Company
Incorporated: 1981 as Stanley K. Tanger & Co.
Employees: 275
Sales: $111.1 million (2001)
Stock Exchanges: New York
Ticker Symbol: SKT
NAIC: 525930 Real Estate Investment Trusts

For more than 20 years, Tanger Factory Outlet Centers, Inc. has been developing shopping centers catering to bargain-hunting consumers. The company acquires, develops, owns and operates multi-unit shopping centers, leasing the individual stores to tenant companies who wish to offer factory overruns or imperfect merchandise directly to consumers at a substantial discount over retail prices. Tanger has 29 outlet centers in 20 states, most of them located either in a resort area or on a thoroughfare between two major cities. With occupancy rates close to 95 percent, the centers generally contain about 70 stores run by manufacturers of upscale clothing and household items. Prominent tenants include Liz Claiborne, Polo Ralph Lauren, and Banana Republic. The company went public as a Real Estate Investment Trust (REIT) in 1993, becoming the first outlet-only REIT to do so. Tanger expanded rapidly in the early 1990s, developed a more conservative growth pattern later in the decade, and has been shoring up its bottom line with a campaign to replace lower-volume tenants with high-profile brand names. Company founder Stanley K. Tanger acts as chairman and chief executive officer, while his son Steven B. Tanger is president and chief operating officer. The Tanger family owns about 30 percent of the company.

Introducing the Outlet Center Concept: 1981–93

Before he pioneered the development of outlet centers, Stanley K. Tanger spent many years at the head of a shirt manufacturing company. Creighton, Inc., located in Reidsville, North Carolina, was founded by Stanley's father Moe Tanger in 1920. The company made private-label shirts for department stores as well as uniform shirts for sale to the military. Stanley became head of management at Creighton in 1948. Under his leadership, the factory opened five small outlet stores to sell shirts directly to customers. The stores were successful, suggesting that a factory outlet enterprise on a larger scale could be viable. But Tanger was occupied with running the factory and lacked the time to pursue large-scale development of outlet centers. In 1979, however, tired of dealing with department stores and banks, he sold the shirt manufacturer to its employees. The outlet center idea resurfaced as he found himself retired with plenty of time on his hands.

Having spent three decades in the shirt manufacturing business, Tanger had firsthand experience of how much excess merchandise was generated by returns and factory overruns. The potential for factory outlet centers was apparent. Accordingly, in 1981 he formed Stanley K. Tanger & Co. with the purpose of developing shopping centers. Four banks turned him down before he obtained a loan to launch the business. The first outlet center opened in North Carolina in 1981: a 50,000-square-foot project at the Burlington Manufacturer's Outlet Center. Five years later Stanley Tanger's son Steven B. Tanger joined the growing company.

The outlet business did well from the start, laying the ground for expansion. Stores in the early centers were only about 2,500 feet in size, but by the late 1980s Tanger was building complexes with stores of 10,000 to 15,000 square feet each. The tenant mix tended toward upscale manufacturers of men's and women's clothing, with early tenants including Anne Klein, Liz Claiborne, OshKosh B'Gosh, and Van Heusen. Tanger sought to avoid upsetting regular-price clothing retailers by keeping its centers at least 25 miles away from traditional malls. As a result, outlet centers sprang up along interstates between major metro areas. The Casa Grande, Arizona center, for example,

Company Perspectives:

"Our goal is to increase shareholder value by creating superior shopping environments where consumers can purchase quality merchandise directly from brand name manufacturers at a true value.

Our success begins and ends with our core principles: Understand customer needs and satisfy them; Hire good people and empower them; Focus on solutions—not problems; Do what we say we are going to do; Have fun; Above all—play to win."—Stanley K. Tanger, chairman

which opened in November 1991, was about halfway between Phoenix and Tucson. Other centers were constructed near popular vacation destinations, such as the Pigeon Forge, Tennessee center in the Smoky Mountains.

Each site was carefully chosen to maximize the center's chances for success. Eventually, specific guidelines were developed to evaluate a potential location: a viable project had to be near a resort area with an annual minimum of five million visitors, or on an interstate frequented by at least 50,000 cars a day. Each center also had to be less than an hour's drive away from a minimum population of five million. The small communities that were chosen to host a Tanger outlet center often reaped significant economic benefits from the development. The city of Stroud, Oklahoma, for example, with a population of slightly more than 3,000, saw its sales tax revenue nearly triple after a Tanger mall opened there in 1992. The *Tulsa World* reported that the city was able to buy four new police cars and a new computer system for the city with the added revenue, and that a host of new businesses revived the city's downtown.

IPO and Expansion: 1993–95

By 1993, there were 17 Tanger outlet centers in 15 states. The company had added 50 percent to its base square footage in 1992 alone, reaching a total of about 1.5 million square feet of real estate. Stanley Tanger explained the centers' appeal to Brenda Lloyd of the *Daily News Record* in 1993: "The consumer loves this type of buying. And buying at bargain prices is contagious. And at the same time we're entertaining people. They're beating the system and they love it." Value-minded shoppers were now able to visit Tanger outlets in Boaz, Alabama; Casa Grande, Arizona; Commerce, Georgia; Williamsburg, Iowa; North Branch, Minnesota; North Conway, New Hampshire; Stroud, Oklahoma; Pigeon Forge, Tennessee; Martinsburg, West Virginia; and three centers in Kittery, Maine. In addition, new centers had just opened at Gonzales, Louisiana, between New Orleans and Baton Rouge, and at San Marcos, Texas, on a major thoroughfare from San Antonio to Austin.

But Tanger found itself facing a formidable amount of debt after such rapid expansion. Hitherto owned 100 percent by the Tanger family, in June 1993 the company turned to outside investors for financing with an initial public offering (IPO) on the New York Stock Exchange. The IPO raised about $104 million, enough to pay off $75 million in bank financing and support further expansion. Tanger changed its name to Tanger

Factory Outlet Centers, Inc. and became the first outlet-only Real Estate Investment Trust (REIT) to listed on the New York Stock Exchange. The Tanger family was left with a 44 percent stake in the company. Later in 1993 outlet centers opened in Lawrence, Kansas, and McMinnville, Oregon, and five existing centers were expanded. Net revenue for the year was $30.4 million, with net income at $1.9 million. Sales volume at the outlet stores was close to half a billion dollars.

Expansion continued into 1994, when Tanger added six new centers to its portfolio. The Riverhead, New York center was built on Long Island to attract vacationers as well as New York City residents. The center eventually became one of Tanger's largest. The first tenant to open its doors at Riverhead was Liz Claiborne, a company that also had been a pioneering tenant at many of Tanger's earlier centers. Claiborne was one of a core group of retailers, including Brooks Brothers, Reebok, London Fog, and Bugle Boy, that followed along with Tanger's expansion, opening a new store at almost every new location. Aside from the Riverhead site, two other resort-area centers opened in 1994: the Lancaster, Pennsylvania center drew shoppers from the Amish Country tourist area, and the center in Branson, Missouri, was close to the Music City vacation area. Also in 1994, the Terrel, Texas center, located on the interstate 30 miles from Dallas, became the second Tanger center in that state, and the Locust Grove center was the second to be built in Georgia. Another new center was built at Seymour, Indiana, on the way from Indianapolis to Louisville. Net revenues for 1994 grew to $46 million. Funds from operations—an earnings measure used by REITs—rose 59 percent to $23.4 million.

At the start of 1995 Steven Tanger took over as president of Tanger, while his father Stanley continued in the positions of chairman and CEO. By this time, several competing outlet centers were attracting bargain hunters, and Tanger felt the need to demonstrate that its centers offered unmatched value. In the second half of 1995, the company introduced its "Relax, It's Guaranteed" program, offering a cash refund equal to the difference in price if a customer found the same name brand product for less anywhere else. The guarantee was remarkable because Tanger was only the site developer and had no control over the prices set by its tenants. Nevertheless, the company invited customers to come to company offices at the outlet centers for refunds. The strategy proved successful, as Tanger was able to reinforce its reputation for bargains and never refunded more than $1,000 a year. Funds from operations in 1995 grew close to 30 percent over the previous year, reaching $29.6 million as the previous year's expansions were integrated into the company portfolio.

Prudent Strategies for Reliable Growth: 1996–2002

During a time when other outlet center developers were building rapidly, Tanger moderated its growth after the rapid expansions of 1993 and 1994. The company increased its square footage by only 181,000 square feet in 1996, compared with a 1.2 million-square-foot expansion in 1994. Revenues increased modestly that year, with funds from operations standing at $32.3 million and net revenue at $74.7 million. The company's conservative approach was vindicated when outlet mall stocks entered a difficult period. In the summer of 1997, Tanger was

Key Dates:	
1948:	Stanley K. Tanger takes over his father's shirt manufacturing business.
1979:	Tanger sells the shirt factory to his employees.
1981:	Tanger opens his first project at a Burlington Manufacturer's Outlet Center.
1986:	Stanley's son Steven Tanger joins the company.
1993:	With a total of 17 outlet centers, Tanger Factory Outlet Centers makes its initial public offering on the New York Stock Exchange.
1995:	Tanger introduces its 30-day lowest price guarantee and concludes a period of rapid growth.
1997:	Tanger begins a re-merchandising policy to bring in higher-volume tenants.
2002:	Tanger has 29 outlet centers in 20 states.

one of only two outlet companies, out of six that were booming in 1994, that was trading above its IPO price.

After taking a break from building, the company was once again ready for prudent expansion. A stock offering in the fall of 1997 raised $29 million, financing the acquisition of outlet centers in Sevierville, Tennessee; Blowing Rock, North Carolina; and Nags Head, North Carolina. A new center in Commerce, Georgia, became the third in that state, opening its doors across the interstate from an already existing center that was one of Tanger's most popular sites. In addition, a phase two expansion was completed at the Riverhead location on Long Island, which had the company's second highest sales per square foot after the Pigeon Forge, Tennessee center. The Riverhead expansion marked a turn toward high-volume, trendier tenants, including such stores as DKNY, Calvin Klein, and Saks Fifth Avenue. The Tanger family was able to monitor the Riverhead location from its vacation home in the Hamptons resort area.

Expansions in 1997 totaled more than 705,000 square feet, and funds from operations that year rose 11 percent to $35.8 million. The second generation of tenants at the Riverhead location was typical of Tanger's newly adopted re-merchandising strategy. The company now embarked on a long-term effort to replace low-volume tenants with higher-volume stores calculated to appeal to consumers based on the market demographics outlet center visitors. By 1999, Tanger had retenanted more than 9 percent of its portfolio, with brand names such as The Gap, Banana Republic, Polo Ralph Lauren, Tommy Hilfiger, and Old Navy replacing older tenants. Same-space sales grew over the same period. The strategy kept the company's revenues growing at a steady rate even as REIT stock prices fell in 1998. That year the company added 569,000 square feet to its portfolio with the purchase of Dalton Factory Stores in Dalton, Georgia, and Sanibel Factory Stores in Fort Myers, Florida. Funds from operations for the year grew 11 percent to $39.7 million.

In April 1999 the REIT stock sector was boosted when investor Warren Buffett bought a 5 percent stake in Tanger. The company's stock went up 14 percent to $23.625 as a result, slightly higher than its IPO price of $22.50, but still well down from peak periods when it had been trading at more than $30. A natural disaster hit one of the company's sites later that spring, when a tornado destroyed the outlet mall in Stroud, Oklahoma. Tanger at first expressed its intention to rebuild the mall, but soon decided to sell the site, saying that too few tenants were interested in reopening their stores. The company sold the property for $723,500 in December 2000, taking a loss of more than $1 million.

Ever vigilant in maintaining a steady path of profitability, Tanger took some steps to cut costs as the turn of the millennium approached. The company took over its own property management duties in 1999. In June 2000 Tanger sold two poorly performing properties in Lawrence, Kansas, and McMinnville, Oregon. Square-foot sales at the two centers were low, and Tanger planned to use the $7.1 million generated by the sale for expansion of more successful sites, as well as for debt reduction. The company completed 216,000 square feet in expansions in 2000. That summer it also set up a joint venture, Tanger-Warren Development, with C. Randy Warren, Jr. Warren had been the senior vice-president of Leasing for Tanger since 1997; now he would leave the company to devote his time exclusively to identifying, acquiring, and developing new outlet sites.

Later in the year a proposed site in Dania Beach, Florida, fell through. Tanger had bought a property just off Interstate 95 in November 1999 and leased a building there to Bass Pro Outdoor World. At the time of the initial purchase, Tanger also agreed to buy an adjacent parcel and build a mall there. The company dropped the deal in November, however, alleging that certain conditions for purchase had not been met. Bass Pro contested Tanger's explanation and sued the company for breach of contract.

Other development projects were more successful. In the fall of 2001 Tanger began construction of a resort-area site at Myrtle Beach, South Carolina, in a 50–50 joint venture with Rosen-Warren Myrtle Beach LLC. The terrorist attacks of September 2001 had little negative effect on Tanger's bottom line. In fact, traffic at the company's Long Island site went up as New Yorkers were vacationing closer to home and preferred the outlet center's design to an enclosed mall. Traffic at all stores was up 4.5 percent in 2001. Funds from operations were up slightly to $38.2 million, net revenue continued a gradual climb to $111.1 million, and net income improved over 2000 to reach $7.2 million. Tanger reported continued growth for the first quarter of 2002. After two decades in business, the company had shown an ability to maintain profits through the ups and downs of the outlet mall industry. Nevertheless, Tanger faced the challenge of continually renewing the leases on its properties. Skillful management would be necessary to maintain the company's high occupancy rates and continue to attract consumers to the outlet malls.

Principal Competitors

Prime Retail; Chelsea Property Group.

Further Reading

Abelson, Jenn, "Tanger's Treasure," *LI Business News,* November 23, 2001, p. 1A.

Hartnett, Dwayne, ''Former Shirt Manufacturer Finds Second Career in Setting Up Outlet Stores,'' *Knight-Ridder/Tribune Business News,* October 17, 1994.

Kaplan, Don, ''Listening to Consumers: Tanger's Refunds,'' *Daily News Record,* February 16, 1996, p. 3.

Kirkpatrick, David D., ''REIT Interest: FelCor Aims to Be Hotel Landlord of Choice,'' *Wall Street Journal,* July 30, 1997, p. B10.

Lloyd, Brenda, ''Outlet King Goes Public,'' *Daily News Record,* June 11, 1993, p. 12.

Martinez, Barbara, ''Tanger Jumps 14% on News of Stake Taken by Buffett,'' *Wall Street Journal,* April 13, 1999, p. B5.

Sheridan, Terry, ''Tangled Lines: Scuttled $12 Million Deal for Land Near High-Profile Bass Pro Outdoor World Leads to Fight with Mall Company,'' *Daily Business Review* (Miami, Fla.), January 3, 2001, p. A1.

—Sarah Ruth Lorenz

TDK Corporation

1-13-1, Nihonbashi
Chuo-ku
Tokyo 103-8272
Japan
Telephone: (03) 5201-7102
Fax: (03) 5201-7114
Web site: http://www.tdk.co.jp

Public Company
Incorporated: 1935 as Tokyo Denkikagaku Kogyo K.K. (TDK Electronics Company, Ltd.)
Employees: 32,249
Sales. ¥575.03 billion ($4.32 billion) (2002)
Stock Exchanges: Tokyo Osaka New York Amsterdam London Paris Swiss
NAIC: 334112 Computer Storage Device Manufacturing; 334413 Semiconductor and Related Device Manufacturing; 334414 Electronic Capacitor Manufacturing; 334415 Electronic Resistor Manufacturing; 334416 Electronic Coil, Transformer, and Other Inductor Manufacturing; 334419 Other Electronic Component Manufacturing; 334613 Magnetic and Optical Recording Media Manufacturing

TDK Corporation is best-known as one of the world's leading makers of recording media and systems, including high-quality audio and videotape, CD-R and CD-RW discs and drives, minidiscs, and rewritable DVD discs. Recording media and systems, however, account for only about one-quarter of the company's revenues. In fiscal 2002, electronic materials generated about 28 percent of sales; these included multilayer chip capacitors and ferrite cores and magnets. Another 18 percent of sales came from electronic devices, such as inductive devices, high-frequency components, and power supplies. Generating more than one-quarter of 2002 revenues were recording devices, with the main product in this sector being magnetic recording heads used in computer hard disk drives. Semiconductors, including those used in local area network devices, set-top boxes, and modems, accounted for just over 3 percent of 2002 sales. TDK's research and development efforts have been responsible for many discoveries in the application of magnetic materials over the years, and the company continues to drive the cutting edge of this technology in the 21st century.

Originated As a Marketer of Ferrite Technology

The success of TDK parallels the commercial development of a remarkably versatile material known as ferrite, a magnetic material with ceramic properties. Ferrite is composed of ferric oxide and any of a number of other metallic oxides, but usually zinc. Ferrite can be produced in several variations, each with somewhat different properties, and it can be categorized in two groups: hard and soft. Hard ferrite can be easily and permanently magnetized. Soft ferrite, on the other hand, does not stay magnetized for any great length of time but has other properties that make it suitable for many electronics applications. In the 1990s TDK supplied about half of the world's ferrite.

Ferrite was invented in 1933 by two Japanese scientists, Dr. Yogoro Kato and Dr. Takeshi Takei, at the Tokyo Institute of Technology. Two years later a man named Kenzo Saito founded TDK Corporation (originally known as Tokyo Denkikagaku Kogyo K.K., or TDK Electronics Company, Ltd.) to market the scientists' discovery. Saito had been searching for a manufacturing business that he could establish in his hometown, which was wholly dependent on agriculture. When Kato and Saito met by chance, each was impressed by the other, and soon Kato granted Saito the use of the ferrite technology he and Takei had developed.

TDK's first application was a soft ferrite product, marketed as an "oxide core" and employed in transformers and coils. The demand for ferrite was very limited at this time, however, and TDK's first years were hard. But as the number of electrical appliances in the world increased, demand for TDK's ferrite cores increased dramatically. Early in its history, TDK made research and development a priority by exploring the properties of ferrite and finding new ways to employ it. Soon, the use of ferrite cores became widespread in consumer electronic products such as radios and televisions, markets that grew considerably during the 1940s and 1950s. Saito left TDK in 1946 and later became a member of the Diet.

Diversifying Manufacturing and Expanding Overseas: 1950s–60s

Eventually TDK branched into the manufacture of materials other than ferrite. In 1951 the company began to produce ceramic capacitors. These components are used to store electrical energy, inhibit the flow of direct current, or facilitate the flow of alternating current, and are widely used in the production of electronic devices. Establishing itself as a key components manufacturer, TDK would benefit as the Japanese electronics industry grew.

In 1952 TDK introduced its first magnetic recording tape. TDK's line of recording tape eventually became the industry standard: at one point it accounted for half of the company's sales. In Japan TDK led the development of recording tape, becoming the first domestic manufacturer of audiocassettes in 1966. Two years later the company defied skeptics when it produced the world's first high-fidelity cassettes, marketed by TDK as Super Dynamic (SD) tape. Meanwhile, a TDK researcher named Yasuo Imaoka was looking for a material that could be used to replace chromium dioxide in video and audiotapes. Chromium dioxide, while offering excellent sound quality, is rare and expensive. Imaoka and his team came up with a process that combined ferric oxide with metal cobalt. The resulting material was named Avilyn, and it had a greater coercivity—a measure of magnetic substances—than chromium dioxide. Avilyn videotapes hit the market in 1973. The formula was soon improved by using cobalt hydroxide instead of metal cobalt, and the resulting Super Avilyn audiotapes revolutionized the industry when TDK unveiled its SA line, the first nonchrome high-bias tape, in 1975. In 1985 the Japanese Council of Industrial Patents named Avilyn as one of the country's top 53 inventions of the century.

As TDK developed technological innovations, its marketing strength also improved. The company entered foreign markets as early as 1959, opening a representative office in New York City. TDK opened a second American office in Los Angeles four years later, and TDK Electronics Corporation, the first overseas subsidiary, was established in New York in 1965. TDK's international operations grew extensively during the late

1960s and the 1970s. In 1968, TDK set up a subsidiary in Taiwan to manufacture ferrite cores, ceramic capacitors, and coil components. Over the course of the next ten years, TDK established subsidiaries in West Germany, Hong Kong, Great Britain, Brazil, Korea, Mexico, the United States, Singapore, and Australia. To ease trade imbalances and to insulate the company from currency fluctuations, TDK set up manufacturing facilities in many of these countries. TDK or its subsidiaries began producing magnetic heads in the United States in 1972 and audiotape a year later, ferrite cores in Korea in 1973, ferrite magnets in Mexico in 1974, ferrite cores in Brazil in 1979, and videotape in the United States in 1980. By the mid-1980s nearly half of TDK's business was generated outside of Japan. In the meantime, TDK went public in 1961 with a listing on the Tokyo Stock Exchange.

VCRs Spur Tremendous Growth

In the mid-1970s TDK's already impressive growth rate took off for a number of reasons. Technological developments in consumer electronics created new demand for the company's expertise in ferrite and other materials. More sensitive audio equipment created strong demand for TDK's SA tapes, and the introduction of videocassette recorders (VCRs) to the consumer market created new demand for both the software (videotapes) and hardware (magnetic tape heads and other components) that TDK was capable of producing. The company's sales went through the roof as the videocassette market expanded 60 percent each year in the late 1970s.

Videocassettes and audiocassettes made up half of TDK's sales in the early 1980s. In 1983, however, an oversupply of videotapes sent prices into a downward spiral. While TDK's audiotapes sales continued to improve, revenue from videotape declined even though total volume increased. Just as the videotape crunch was at its worst, Yutaka Otoshi, the former chief of the tapes division, took over as TDK president and CEO. Otoshi increased TDK's research and development budget from 3.4 percent to 5 percent of sales to ensure the company's technological edge. New products such as the compact 8mm camcorders and players and recordable optical videodiscs were expected to give a boost to the market. Nonetheless, Otoshi focused on expanding TDK's nontape business. As he told *Business Week* in 1983, "we have never thought it was a good idea to concentrate too much on one product." Also in 1983, the company changed its name to TDK Corporation.

R&D Successes in the 1980s

In 1984 TDK launched its Components Engineering Laboratory (CEL) in Los Angeles. At this lab TDK's researchers worked with marketing personnel to develop custom prototypes of transformers, microwave products, and other components for use by American customers. In addition to customization, the new lab reduced the time required to go from product development to full-scale production. TDK's research efforts also resulted in the development of a number of new products in the 1980s. The company made breakthroughs in the development of thin-film heads for increased recording sensitivity, in multilayer hybrid circuits that allow equalization in headphone cassette players to be performed in one-third the usual space, and in sensor technology.

Key Dates:

1935: Kenzo Saito founds Tokyo Denkikagaku Kogyo K.K. (TDK Electronics Company, Ltd.) to market ferrite cores.

1951: Company diversifies, launching production of ceramic capacitors.

1952: TDK begins production of magnetic recording tape.

1959: Overseas expansion begins with the opening of an office in New York City.

1961: Company goes public with a listing on the Tokyo Stock Exchange.

1965: TDK Electronics Corporation, the first overseas subsidiary, is established in New York.

1966: Production of audiocassettes begins.

1968: Company debuts the world's first high-fidelity cassettes, marketed as Super Dynamic tape.

1973: Avilyn videotapes are introduced.

1975: TDK launches Super Avilyn audiotapes, the first nonchrome high-bias tape.

1982: Floppy disks are produced for the first time.

1983: Company's name is changed to TDK Corporation.

1993: Production of CD-R discs commences.

2000: TDK acquires Headway Technologies, Inc., producer of recording heads.

2001: Slumping technology market leads the company to announce that it will cut 8,800 jobs, or 20 percent of its workforce, by March 2004.

2002: Company posts its first net loss since it began reporting consolidated earnings results in 1975.

Another area in which TDK excelled in the 1980s was the field of anechoic chambers—rooms lined with a material that absorbs radiowaves. Anechoic chambers are used to measure the electromagnetic emission of electronic products and also a product's vulnerability to interference from such emissions. TDK's success with anechoic chambers grew out of its experience with microwave absorption. The company first began research in that field in 1964 and by 1968 had marketed its first ferrite-based microwave absorbers. The popularity of microwave ovens, which use a ferrite and rubber compound to keep the cooking process inside the oven, bolstered TDK's bottom line. In 1975 the company applied its expertise in microwave absorption to anechoic chambers, and in the 1980s, as demand for these facilities grew on the back of a booming electronics industry, TDK became a major force in the field.

In 1987 the company embarked on a joint venture with the Allen-Bradley Company, of the United States, to produce motor magnets for the automobile industry. Allen-Bradley/TDK Magnetics began production at a plant in Oklahoma in April of that year. TDK benefited from its partner's longstanding relationship with American automakers, and Allen-Bradley benefited from TDK's magnetics expertise.

The late 1980s also saw the miniaturization of and increased demand for higher-density circuits and components. Manufacturers of these products required extremely precise equipment for their production facilities. TDK's Avimount and Avisert automated assembly equipment was in greater demand as a result. Sales in 1988 were up 25 percent over the previous year and were expected to continue to rise.

TDK's focus on broadening its nontape products was successful; by 1988 the nontape sector accounted for 64 percent of the company's total sales. But TDK did not neglect its recording-media development. TDK's floppy disks, first produced in 1982, garnered a respectable market share partly based on the company's excellent reputation in audio and video recording media. In 1987 the company introduced digital audio tape (DAT)—tapes able to play and record music digitally, like compact discs—in Japan and prepared to enter foreign markets as soon as copyright problems were settled. In 1988, it introduced a top-of-the-line videotape called Super Strong, a new product that allowed TDK to raise prices and still maintain market share.

TDK continued to grow on its own and make acquisitions when appropriate. In 1988 the company acquired Display Components Inc. (Discom), of Westford, Massachusetts. The purchase allowed Discom access to TDK's advanced production techniques while TDK received Discom's state-of-the-art magnetic field technology.

Overseas Production and Increasing R&D: Early to Mid-1990s

In 1989 TDK purchased a large American manufacturer of mixed-signal integrated circuits, Silicon Systems Inc. (SSI), for $200 million, further diversifying its range of products. SSI proved to be a problematic acquisition for TDK, however. SSI struggled during its first few years under TDK, even after a $100-million-plus infusion from the parent to help SSI beef up its U.S. production. By the mid-1990s, even this had not provided SSI with the capacity it needed to compete with the giants of the semiconductor industry. Rather than sinking more money into the troubled firm, TDK decided to sell SSI in 1996 and found a willing buyer among these same giants, namely Texas Instruments Incorporated. Terms were $575 million in cash plus a long-term note that could bring TDK another $50 million in contingent payments. This sale did not mark TDK's complete withdrawal from semiconductor-related areas, however. Not included in the deal were SSI's Communications Products Division and TDK Systems Division, leaving TDK with such products as PC cards and integrated circuits for telecommunications. These were not insignificant, as evidenced particularly by TDK's success in the area of fax/modem PC cards, a product that experienced explosive sales growth in the mid-1990s as the Internet and online services became everyday business and personal tools.

In the early to mid-1990s, TDK had to contend with a glut in the videotape market and the consequences of an extremely strong yen, both of which depressed company sales, and consequently earnings. TDK moved aggressively to cut costs, consolidating Japanese production of blank audio and videotapes in one factory in 1993. To mitigate the effects of the strong yen, TDK shifted much of its production overseas. Ferrite products began to be manufactured in Dalian, China, in 1993. By 1995, more than half of TDK's audio and videotapes were produced outside Japan—in Luxembourg, the United States, and Thailand. In May 1996, TDK announced a plan to shift all its floppy disk manufacturing overseas, some to a California subsidiary, some to several Southeast Asian companies. In the fall of 1996, a new plant in Hungary began manufacturing transformers, ferrite cores, and other components.

Under the guidance of President Hiroshi Sato, TDK further bolstered R&D by spending 6 percent of overall sales on new product development. One product area targeted was that of ceramic filters for mobile telecommunications, another high-growth sector. Overall, R&D was directed to make TDK even less dependent on the mature areas of magnetic products and tapes. An example of the company's search for nontape revenue was the joint venture with Duracell International Inc. announced in early 1996, whereby the two companies would jointly develop and manufacture ion electrode sets, a key component in the increasingly popular lithium-ion rechargeable battery.

The production shifts and emphasis on new products began to pay off in 1996, with TDK posting healthy increases of 11.6 percent in net sales and 41.1 percent in operating profit over 1995, which represented the best consolidated results in five years. The company cited electronic components for computers, home electronics, and telecommunications products as the main contributors to these gains. Continued strong sales in overseas markets and the yen's weakness against the dollar sent sales and profits soaring still higher in fiscal 1997. Revenues increased another 15 percent, and operating profits surged by nearly 43 percent.

Turn of the Millennium: Acquisitions, GMR Heads, and a Technology Slump

Continuing its policy of making strategic acquisitions, TDK acquired Grey Cell Systems Limited in September 1997. Based in the United Kingdom, Grey Cell specialized in PC card and software-based data communications products. Grey Cell was later renamed TDK Systems Europe Ltd. Having produced CD-Rs (rewritable compact discs) for the first time in 1993, TDK maintained its position on the cutting edge of recording media by launching production of DVD-R discs in April 1998, well in advance of any sizable market for the product. In June 1998 Sato retired from his position as president of TDK and was succeeded by Hajime Sawabe.

By the late 1990s one of TDK's key product areas was that of magnetoresistive recording heads, which are a key component of computer disk drives. TDK was one of the leading makers of an advanced version of these heads that were known as giant magnetoresistive (GMR) heads, and much of the company's profits were derived from the sale of GMR heads. In March 2000 TDK bolstered its position in this sector with the purchase of Headway Technologies, Inc. for about $122 million. Based in Milpitas, California, and founded in 1994, Headway produced a variety of recording heads but was particularly strong in the area of GMR heads. The company reported net income of $1 million on sales of $160 million for 1999.

Despite TDK's commitment to remaining on the cutting edge of technological development and its selected use of acquisitions and strategic alliances as growth generators, profits came under increasing pressure around the turn of the millennium as the Japanese economy continued to struggle. One response to this profit squeeze was a restructuring of the product lines. Products were now arranged into five sectors: electronic materials, electronic devices, recording devices, semiconductors, and recording media. Another strategy was diversification, and TDK in 2000 moved beyond its traditional position as provider of recording media by branching out into the manufacture of related hardware devices to be sold to consumers. Early in 2000 the company began selling TDK brand CD-R/RW drives for personal computers. In November of that year the company introduced its first audio CD recorder, and in January 2001 TDK began selling computer speakers. Meanwhile, in December 2000, TDK paid $26 million for U.S. semiconductor maker Sierra Research and Technology Inc. Established in 1993, Sierra specialized in the design of CMOS (complementary metal-oxide semiconductor) products for networking and data communications applications.

By late 2001 TDK was forced to launch a major restructuring effort as the technology market entered a severe slump precipitated by a slowdown in the U.S. economy and by a global downturn in information technology investment. Inventories for a broad range of electronic components soared as the predictions for worldwide demand for mobile phones and personal computers proved to be far too optimistic. The huge inventories placed downward pressure on prices, cutting into revenues. In October 2001 TDK responded by announcing that it would cut 8,800 jobs, or 20 percent of its workforce by March 2004, with 2,300 of the job cuts earmarked for the company's domestic operations. Two manufacturing plants in Japan and one in Germany were closed, and several subsidiaries were consolidated to improve efficiencies. The number of jobs to be eliminated was increased by 400 in February 2002. Restructuring charges for the fiscal year ending in March 2002 totaled ¥25.87 billion ($194.5 million). This led to TDK's first net loss since it began reporting consolidated earnings results in 1975. For fiscal 2002, the company lost ¥25.77 billion ($193.8 million) on net sales of ¥575.03 billion ($4.32 billion). The sales figure represented a 16.7 percent decline from the previous year, despite a further weakening in the yen. More job cuts and plant closures were likely as TDK hoped to return to profitability by fiscal 2003.

Principal Subsidiaries

TDK Akita Manufacturing Co., Ltd.; TKD-MCC Co., Ltd.; TDK Shonai Manufacturing Co., Ltd.; Iida TDK Co., Ltd; Tsuruoka TDK Co., Ltd.; Yashima TDK Co., Ltd.; Ujo TDK Co., Ltd.; TDK Service Co., Ltd.; TDK Design Core Co., Ltd.; Iwaki Kogyo Co., Ltd.; Yuri TDK Co., Ltd.; TDK Core Co., Ltd.; TDK Distributor Co., Ltd.; Honjo TDK Co., Ltd.; Kofu TDK Co., Ltd.; Toso TDK Co., Ltd.; TDK (Australia) Pty. Ltd.; TDK do Brasil Ind. e Com. Ltda. (Brazil); TDK Dalian Corporation (China); TDK (Tianjin) Co., Ltd. (China); TDK (Shanghai) International Trading Co., Ltd. (China); Qingdao TDK Electronics Co., Ltd. (China); TDK (Guangzhou) Co., Ltd. (China); TDK Xiamen Co., Ltd. (China); TDK Recording Media France SARL; TDK Electronics Europe GmbH (Germany); TDK Hong Kong Co., Ltd.; TDK Recording Media (Hong Kong) Co., Ltd.; SAE Magnetics (H.K.) Ltd. (Hong Kong); TDK Italia S.p.A. (Italy); Korea TDK Co., Ltd. (99.4%); TDK Recording Media Europe S.A. (Luxembourg); TDK (Malaysia) Sdn. Bhd.; TDK Softec (M) Sdn. Bhd. (Malaysia); TDK de Mexico S.A. de C.V.; TDK Philippines Corporation; TDK

Polska Sp. z.o.o. (Poland); TDK Singapore (Pte) Ltd.; TDK Scandinavia A.B. (Sweden); TDK Taiwan Corporation (80.95%); TDK (Thailand) Co., Ltd.; TDK UK Limited; TDK Systems Europe Ltd. (U.K.); TDK U.S.A. Corporation; TDK Electronics Corporation (U.S.A.); TDK Online Services Corporation (U.S.A.); TDK Corporation of America (U.S.A.); TDK Components U.S.A., Inc.; Headway Technologies, Inc. (U.S.A.); Husko Inc. (U.S.A.); Saki Magnetics, Inc. (U.S.A.); TDK Ferrites Corporation (U.S.A.); TDK Texas Corporation (U.S.A.); TDK Semiconductor Corporation (U.S.A.); TDK RF Solutions Inc. (U.S.A.).

Principal Divisions

Electronic Components Business Group; Data Storage Components Business Group; Recording Media & Systems Business Group; Semiconductors Division.

Principal Competitors

Imation Corp.; Murata Manufacturing Co., Ltd.; Kyocera Corporation; Pioneer Corporation; Fuji Photo Film Co., Ltd.; Sony Corporation; Hitachi, Ltd.; Vishay Intertechnology, Inc.; AVX Corporation; EPCOS AG; Read-Rite Corporation.

Further Reading

McCartney, Scott, ''Texas Instruments to Buy TDK Unit, Broadening Its Role in Chip-Making,'' *Wall Street Journal,* June 5, 1996, p. B4.

Palenchar, Joseph, ''TDK Drives for Diversification,'' *Twice,* October 9, 2000, p. 10.

Sprackland, Teri, ''How Silicon Systems Turns Yen into Dollars,'' *Electronic Business,* January 21, 1991, pp. 38–39.

''TDK Agrees to Buy Si Systems,'' *Electronic News,* April 17, 1989, p. 25.

''TDK Launches New Round of Product Development,'' *Tokyo Business Today,* July 1995, p. 18.

Zaczkiewicz, Arthur, ''TDK Cautiously Adds Capacity,'' *Electronic Buyers' News,* May 15, 2000, p. 52.

—update: David E. Salamie

TD **Bank Financial Group**

The Toronto-Dominion Bank

Post Office Box 1
King Street West and Bay Street
Toronto, Ontario M5K 1A2
Canada
Telephone: (416) 982-8222
Fax: (416) 982-5671
Web site: http://www.td.com

Public Company
Incorporated: 1955
Employees: 51,000
Total Assets: $300.7 billion (2002)
Stock Exchanges: Toronto London New York Tokyo
Ticker Symbol: TD
NAIC: 551111 Offices of Bank Holding Companies;
    522110 Commercial Banking; 523110 Investment
    Banking and Securities Dealing; 523120 Securities
    Brokerage; 523920 Portfolio Management; 523930
    Investment Advice

The Toronto-Dominion Bank (commonly called TD Bank) ranks as Canada's second largest bank in terms of assets, trailing only RBC Financial Group. The bank's operations are divided into four main businesses. TD Canada Trust consists of the retail banking operations that serve about ten million individual, small business, and commercial customers in Canada. A full range of financial services are offered through about 1,000 branches and more than 2,700 automated teller machines. TD Securities is the wholesale banking arm, serving corporate, government, and institutional clients and focusing on five main areas: investment banking, debt capital markets, institutional equities, private equity, and foreign exchange. TD Waterhouse offers discount and online brokerage services to individuals interested in self-directed investing; it serves customers in the United States, Canada, the United Kingdom, Australia, Japan, Luxembourg, Hong Kong, and India. TD Wealth Management offers asset management and financial planning services as well as a full-service brokerage; it serves individuals as well as pension funds, corporations, institutions, endowments, and foundations. TD Bank and its subsidiaries are collectively referred to as TD Bank Financial Group.

Toronto-Dominion Bank's hyphenated name suggests its origins: the amalgamation of the Bank of Toronto and of the Dominion Bank. The Bank of Toronto missed celebrating its centennial by six weeks when the new bank's charter was signed on February 1, 1955.

Development of the Predecessor Banks

Founded by flour producers who wanted their own banking facilities, the Bank of Toronto was originally chartered on March 18, 1855. The Millers' Association of Canada West, as Ontario was then known, coordinated its preliminary affairs, and on July 8, 1856, the bank opened its doors to the public.

From its initial service to wheat farmers, millers, and merchants, the Bank of Toronto quickly expanded to the lumber industry and to other agricultural interests, mirroring the expansion of business activities on Canada's frontier as pioneers pushed west. In addition to this expansion, railroad booms both in England and in the United States increased the demand for flour and timber. Unfortunately, both booms collapsed at the same time, sharply curtailing the Canadian economy and with it, the westward growth of railroads and towns. Entire communities that had borrowed heavily to finance the building of rail service to their areas went bankrupt.

Although geographically in the middle of this national crisis, the Bank of Toronto was not as imperiled as many other businesses that had invested in the promise of the railroads because it had been established too late to provide much of the financing to the industry. Nor was it directly affected by the radical swings in real estate prices, dependent on the coming of the railroad, because its first officers did not believe in investing in an asset that fluctuated in value. While the business of the bank did contract, wheat was still grown, milled, and shipped.

The Canadian economy rebounded when markets in the United States reopened after the American Civil War in 1865. Fledgling businesses in leather, tanning, and liquor distillation sprang up, but the harvest still formed the backbone of business

---

Company Perspectives:

They say that organizations are more than the sum of their parts, and that's certainly true for TD.

We are a personal and commercial bank, a wholesale bank, a self-directed brokerage and an asset manager advisor and distributor. But we're also much more. We are a team of over 51,000 people with a shared goal: to be the best Canadian-based financial institution in North America.

---

for native Ontario banks. A good year brought prosperity and a bad one meant hardship.

The Bank of Toronto was not without competition. The Bank of Montreal, older and larger, attempted to have the new bank's status limited to that of a community bank with no authority to establish branches. This debate was settled by Lord Durham's Report of 1850, which established branch banking as the national structure for the industry and guaranteed that successful banks could compete within their provinces and beyond, giving all institutions the opportunity to establish national identities.

The volume of business in Ontario in general and in Toronto specifically encouraged a group of professional men to seek a charter and to found the Dominion Bank, which was chartered in 1869 and opened for business on February 1, 1871. The Toronto-Dominion Bank was foreshadowed from the start: stock subscriptions for the Dominion Bank were deposited in the Bank of Toronto. Although originally incorporated to facilitate and promote agricultural and commercial growth, the Dominion Bank stressed the commercial end of banking, investing heavily in railway and construction ventures as well as in the needle trade in Ontario and Montreal.

Over the next several decades, through a series of booms and busts, Canada's economy grew and new industries were established: dairying, textiles, pulpwood, mining, and petroleum. Both the Bank of Toronto and the Dominion Bank responded to the opening of the prairies with a pioneering spirit. Many a new office shared the counter of a town's single general store, while a one-man staff slept with deposits beneath his mattress and a revolver under his pillow.

The outbreak of World War I brought great demand for Canada's natural resources. Within a year the country had erased its trade deficit and become a creditor nation. A few brief years of prosperity followed Germany's surrender in 1918, but the depression and panic preceding World War II appeared at the Dominion Bank on October 23, 1923. Sometime that Friday morning a foreign customer presented a check that was uncashable because of insufficient funds in the account. The teller attempted to overcome the customer's lack of fluency by raising his voice. "No money in the bank," he said. Those five words began a run that lasted until Tuesday afternoon, when rational voices finally overruled rumors.

Hastily established branches were another symptom of the shaky ground on which growth was built. For example, when three banks, one of them the Bank of Toronto, decided simultaneously to open an office at Cold Lake, Manitoba, the Bank of

Toronto's officer rushed to be the first—with the help of Western Canada Airways. Although undocumented, he claimed it was the first bank in the world to open with the help of aviation.

The impact of the 1929 stock market crash in New York was compounded in Canada by the beginning of a seven-year drought. Foreign trade decreased, inventories accumulated, and factories closed. Both banks compensated by closing unprofitable branches, writing off bad debts, and reducing assets. Public criticism abounded. Partly as a response to the outcry but also as an attempt to coordinate the industry, the Bank of Canada was founded in 1934 to issue currency, set interest rates, and formulate national monetary policy. During World War II, the Foreign Exchange Control Board had issued regulations for all foreign transactions. Both banks worked under these restrictions and cooperated with the Bank of Canada to raise $12.5 billion from Canadian citizens to finance the war effort. In another major contribution, 707 employees of the Dominion Bank and more than 500 of the Bank of Toronto, approximately half of each staff, served with the Canadian forces while their jobs were held for them.

Creation of TD Bank in the Mid-1950s

By 1954, both the Bank of Toronto and the Dominion Bank occupied a special position among the nine major banks in Canada. Each had achieved national prominence through its own efforts rather than through merger or acquisition. Each bank, however, realized that to retain its position, it needed to improve its capital base. Only a merger would support the size of industrial loans, which had grown from thousands to millions of dollars. The Minister of Finance approved the merger on November 1, 1954, and it was enacted on the following February 1, the first amalgamation of chartered banks since 1908 and only the third in the nation's history.

On opening day, The Toronto-Dominion Bank operated 450 branches, including offices in New York and London. It controlled assets of $1.1 billion and a loan portfolio of $479 million. During its first 15 years the new bank devoted a great deal of effort to establishing a unified image. In 1967, it moved into the 56-story Toronto-Dominion Bank Tower of Toronto-Dominion Centre. During the 1970s, the bank began to expand internationally—within three years it opened branches in such diverse locations as Bangkok, Frankfurt, and Beirut. During the mid-1970s, Toronto-Dominion issued the $65 million offering for the Toronto Eaton Centre, a 15-acre urban redevelopment project in downtown Toronto.

Toronto-Dominion prospered during the late 1970s and 1980s under the leadership of Richard Murray Thomson, who became chairman in 1976. By the late 1980s the bank was consistently outperforming its rivals both in return on assets and in stock performance, and was one of only two non-regional banks in North America to enjoy an AAA credit rating. Thomson was independent enough during the 1980s to refuse the government's request to provide free services to retail depositors, and to have led the opposition against the bailout of two regional banks in Alberta. On the other hand, he willingly stopped the flow of money to Canadian firms for the purchase of foreign oil companies because it was causing a run on the already weak dollar in 1981. During the 1980s, in fact, Thom-

Key Dates:

1855: The Bank of Toronto is chartered.

1869: The Dominion Bank is chartered.

1955: Bank of Toronto and Dominion Bank merge to form The Toronto-Dominion Bank, with 450 branches and assets of $1.1 billion.

1984: Bank enters the discount brokerage business by establishing Green Line Investor Services.

1987: Canadian regulators begin allowing chartered banks to own securities firms, leading TD Bank to establish an investment bank called TD Securities Inc.

1996: U.S. discount broker Waterhouse Investor Services, Inc. is acquired.

1998: TD Bank's proposed merger with Canadian Imperial Bank of Commerce is blocked by the Canadian government.

2000: The bank acquires CT Financial Services Inc. (Canada Trust) for C$8 billion.

son and Toronto-Dominion were credited with two major successes: reducing problems related to third world debt and helping to finance the largest merger in Canadian history.

Indeed, developing countries offered a financial frontier for large banks during the 1960s and 1970s. By 1987, though, Brazil's debt alone totaled $90.4 billion. Of that amount, Brazil owed $7.1 billion to Canadian creditors, including $836 million to Toronto-Dominion. In February 1987, Brazil suspended payment on the entire debt. After months of negotiation, a settlement was reached in which several Canadian banks, including Toronto-Dominion, agreed to assist Brazil with a $2 billion interest payment to the United States by loaning the country an additional $6 billion. This action protected the U.S. banks from classifying Brazil's loans of $37 billion as uncollectible and preempted a banking crisis in that country. Internally, Toronto-Dominion reclassified most of its Brazilian loans as non-accruing in the second quarter of 1987. Thomson reduced the risk from all third world debt further by selling off $411 million in loans for 66 cents on the dollar.

The other major liability resolved under Thomson's guidance involved a merger between Dome Petroleum and Conoco, Inc. Problems began in 1981 when Dome purchased Conoco for US$1.7 billion. As oil prices fell, Dome attempted to restructure its debt, but succeeded only in prolonging the inevitable. By early 1987, Dome was entertaining buyout discussions with several different companies. Amoco Canada Petroleum emerged as the early leader among the bidders and signed an agreement with Dome in April. It took eight months and an additional $400 million for Dome's creditors to approve the largest buyout in Canadian history. The final $5.5 billion offer provided 95.4 cents on the dollar to each secured creditor.

A key development in the Canadian banking sector in the late 1980s was the enactment of deregulatory legislation in 1987 that enabled chartered banks to own securities firms. Many of the top Canadian banks moved quickly to acquire investment banks, but TD Bank took a different approach. It

established its own investment bank, TD Securities Inc., and built it up from scratch.

Expanding and Diversifying in the 1990s

Toronto-Dominion continued to prosper in the late 1980s and to expand into new businesses and regions. Some analysts criticized the bank's performance during that period, implying that it was failing to take advantage of real estate industry gains. Fortunately, though, Toronto-Dominion stayed the conservative course. The real estate market crashed, bringing many banks along with it. Toronto-Dominion suffered during the downturn, which lingered throughout the early 1990s. But it continued to post profits, increase its asset base, and enter new service businesses. After bottoming out in 1992 at about $6.14 billion, the bank's sales jumped to about $7 billion in 1994 as net income recovered to about $640 million. Meanwhile, Toronto-Dominion's asset base swelled past $100 billion early in 1995 from just $67 billion in 1990.

Toronto-Dominion's gains following the banking industry downturn of the early 1990s reflected its healthy future prospects. Besides building its traditional banking operations, the organization was aggressively chasing new markets in an effort to keep pace with changing technology and to compete against new competitors in the financial services arena. To that end, Toronto-Dominion was among the first Canadian banks to offer mutual funds. By 1995 the bank was offering nearly 50 different funds. Toronto-Dominion was also boosting its investments in electronic and home banking services, trust administration, retail brokerage, and credit card services. Importantly, Toronto-Dominion was permitted by the federal government to enter the property and casualty insurance business beginning in 1995. In the first month following the announcement the bank received 40,000 inquiries and 1,000 new customers.

Also in 1995 A. Charles Baillie was named president of Toronto-Dominion, having moved up through the ranks of TD Bank's investment banking operations. He succeeded Thomson as CEO in February 1997 and then as chairman one year later. Baillie (whose grandfather had been an executive with Dominion Bank) led Toronto-Dominion through a dizzying series of acquisitions from the mid-1990s through the early 2000s that transformed the bank into a well-diversified financial services powerhouse whose assets had tripled from 1994 (C$99.76 billion) to 2002 (C$300.7 billion).

During the mid-1990s it was the bank's discount brokerage operations that were the object of the bulk of the expansion activities. TD Bank had first entered the sector in 1984 by establishing Green Line Investor Services, which quickly became the dominant discount broker in Canada and by 1996 held about 70 percent of the Canadian market. Running out of room to expand Green Line in its home market, Toronto-Dominion completed a series of acquisitions to create an international discount brokerage operation. In October 1996 TD Bank acquired New York-based Waterhouse Investor Services, Inc., the number four discount broker in the United States, for C$714 million (US$525 million). As part of the conditions of the cash-and-stock deal for the publicly traded Waterhouse, Toronto-Dominion's stock began trading on the New York Stock Exchange. During 1997 Toronto-Dominion added two Australian discount brokers to the fold, Pont Securities Ltd. and Rivkin Croll Smith, thereby gaining 50 percent of that market. Then in October 1997 the bank spent C$214 million to acquire Kennedy, Cabot & Co., a closely held discount broker based in Beverly Hills, California. In March 1998 another California discount broker, Jack White & Co., which was headquartered in San Diego, was acquired for US$100 million. TD Bank also established a discount brokerage in London, England, in 1997 and was using an operation that had been established in Hong Kong as a beachhead for further expansion in Asia.

Toronto-Dominion entered 1998 as the smallest of Canada's "Big Five" banks, with assets of C$163.85 billion. Despite a wave of megamergers in the North American banking and financial services sector, including the proposed merger of Royal Bank of Canada (RBC) and Bank of Montreal, two of the top five Canadian banks, it appeared that TD Bank was content to go it alone. But in April 1998 the bank agreed to merge with the number two Canadian bank, Canadian Imperial Bank of Commerce (CIBC), to create what would have been the ninth-largest bank in North America. In December of that year, however, Finance Minister Paul Martin rejected both the proposed merger between TD Bank and CIBC and that of RBC and Bank of Montreal. Ignoring the banks' insistence that they needed to merge in order to compete in the increasingly globalized financial services market, Martin concluded that from the standpoint of Canadians the mergers would create two banks with too much power and would severely reduce competition.

During 1999 Toronto-Dominion combined its global discount brokerage operations, including Waterhouse and Green Line, under a new holding company called TD Waterhouse Group, Inc. and then sold an 11.2 percent stake in the new company to the public via an IPO on the New York Stock Exchange. The offering raised just over US$1 billion. In December 1999 Bank of Tokyo-Mitsubishi Ltd. and TD Waterhouse entered into an alliance to launch an online brokerage business for the Japanese market. By this time TD Waterhouse was the number two discount broker in the world and had also expanded into India.

Acquiring Canada Trust in 2000

Despite the scuttling of the proposed merger with CIBC, Toronto-Dominion appeared to be holding its own in the highly competitive global financial services marketplace. The bank reported net income of C$3.03 billion for the year ending in October 1999, the largest such figure on record by a Canadian bank. The profit figure was aided greatly by the funds raised through the TD Waterhouse IPO. TD Bank was also able to complete a major acquisition in early 2000—in fact, the largest financial services takeover in Canadian history—although it was not at the level of the earlier megamergers. In February 2000 Toronto-Dominion paid nearly C$8 billion in cash for CT Financial Services Inc., a Toronto-based financial services holding company operating under the name Canada Trust. CT Financial was a subsidiary of Imasco Limited, which was majority owned by British American Tobacco PLC (BAT), and TD Bank's purchase of Canada Trust was part of BAT's deal to acquire the shares in Imasco it did not already own. For Toronto-Dominion, the purchase of Canada Trust enabled it to jump to the number three position among Canadian banks in

terms of total assets and made the newly named TD Canada Trust unit the leading retail banking operation in Canada. The deal added more than 400 branches to TD Bank's network of nearly 900 branches, although plans were in place to close as many as 275 branches postmerger as well as cut about 4,900 jobs nationwide. The merger was expected to reduce annual expenses by about C$450 million. The addition of Canada Trust also bolstered the TD Wealth Management unit with the addition of CT's mutual funds operations. One condition for securing regulatory approval was that CT's MasterCard credit portfolio had to be sold off (they were sold to Citibank Canada) because TD Bank was already an issuer of Visa credit cards.

As it worked to integrate Canada Trust into its operations in the early 2000s, Toronto-Dominion was also attempting to gain a larger presence in the U.S. retail banking market. One approach was stepping up the activities of a U.S. retail bank called TD Waterhouse Bank that had been inherited when Waterhouse was acquired (it had been known as Waterhouse National Bank). This online bank worked in conjunction with TD Waterhouse to sell banking services, such as credit cards, checking accounts, and wealth-management products, to the customers of the discount brokerage. By mid-2001 TD Waterhouse Bank had US$5.6 billion in federally insured deposits. In September 2001 Toronto-Dominion announced plans to begin offering banking services within U.S. units of discount retail giant Wal-Mart Stores, Inc., but U.S. regulators rejected the planned alliance because of concerns that Wal-Mart would be in control of the operation, a situation that would violate U.S. laws that bar commercial businesses from operating banking establishments.

During 2001 and 2002, TD Waterhouse was once again at the center of much of the bank's activities. In October 2001 TD Bank regained full control of TD Waterhouse by acquiring the 12 percent publicly traded stake for US$386 million. Later in 2001, TD Waterhouse acquired the British online brokerage DLJdirect Ltd. from Credit Suisse First Boston Corp. and also the Australian operations of archrival Charles Schwab Corporation. In July 2002 the U.K. operations of TD Waterhouse were further bolstered through the purchase of 50 percent of NatWest Stockbrokers, which had been wholly owned by the Royal Bank of Scotland Group plc. Meantime, in early 2002 Toronto-Dominion announced that it would begin to use the TD Waterhouse brand for all of its investment management businesses. As a result, the discount brokerage itself would be renamed TD Waterhouse Discount Brokerage, the bank's full-service brokerage, TD Evergreen, would be renamed TD Waterhouse Full Service Brokerage, and TD Financial Planning, part of TD Wealth Management, would become TD Waterhouse Financial Planning.

Toronto-Dominion Bank continued to be one of the most profitable Canadian banks in the early 21st century, and the bank reported net income of C$1.3 billion for fiscal 2001. Under Baillie's leadership, the bank had a well-diversified and growing array of financial services operations, highlighted by the newly bolstered TD Canada Trust retail banking unit and the rapidly expanding TD Waterhouse unit. By the turbulent economic times of 2002, however, the bank's future was becoming clouded by its exposure to losses from loans connected to Argentina, which was in a state of financial crisis, and to the battered telecommunications sector, in which the bank had made heavy investments. By the end of the third quarter of fiscal

2002 TD Bank had been forced to take one-time loan-loss provisions of C$2.1 billion.

Principal Subsidiaries

Meloche Monnex Inc.; Newcrest Holdings Inc.; TD Asset Management Inc.; TD Capital Group Limited; TD Capital Trust; TD Mortgage Corporation; TD Mortgage Investment Corporation; TD Nordique Inc.; TD Realty Limited; TD Securities Inc.; TD North American Limited Partnership (U.S.A.); TD Waterhouse Holdings, Inc. (U.S.A.); TD Waterhouse Group, Inc. (U.S.A.); Toronto Dominion Holdings (U.S.A.), Inc.; TD Haddington Services B.V. (Netherlands); Haddington Investments Ltd. (Cayman Islands; 70%); TD Ireland; Toronto Dominion Australia Limited; Toronto Dominion Jersey Holdings Limited; Toronto Dominion International Inc. (Barbados); Toronto Dominion Investments B.V. (Netherlands); Toronto Dominion (South East Asia) Limited (Singapore).

Principal Operating Units

TD Canada Trust; TD Waterhouse; TD Wealth Management; TD Securities.

Principal Competitors

RBC Financial Group; Canadian Imperial Bank of Commerce; The Bank of Nova Scotia; Bank of Montreal.

Further Reading

Blackwell, Richard, "TD Bank Licensed to Sell Home and Auto Insurance," *Financial Post,* February 8, 1995, Section 1, p. 3.

——, "TD, National Profits Higher," *Financial Post,* February 24, 1995, Section 1, p. 5.

Cone, Edward F., "Do It My Way," *Forbes,* August 8, 1988, pp. 50+.

Craig, Susanne, "Angry Bankers Face an Uncertain Future," *Globe and Mail,* December 15, 1998, p. A1.

——, "TD to Spin Off 10 Percent of Global Brokerage," *Globe and Mail,* April 1, 1999, p. B1.

Dalglish, Brenda, "Opening the Bank," *Maclean's,* November 16, 1992, p. 54.

DeCloet, Derek, "What's Big, Green, and User-Friendly?," *Canadian Business,* August 27, 1999, p. 40.

Haliechuk, Rick, "TD Bank, National Bank Post Solid Profit Gains," *Toronto Star,* February 24, 1995, Section B, p. 4.

Harris, Jonathan, "Single and Proud," *Canadian Business,* April 10, 1998, pp. 47+.

Howlett, Karen, "TD Faces New Challenges with Canada Trust Merger," *Globe and Mail,* May 23, 2000, p. B1.

——, "TD Takes Provision on Telecom Exposure," *Globe and Mail,* July 19, 2002, p. B1.

McFarland, Janet, "Baillie to Become TD President," *Financial Post,* September 23, 1994, Section 1, p. 7.

——, "TD Buys Canada Trust, Expects Martin's Approval," *Globe and Mail,* August 4, 1999, p. A1.

McQueen, Rod, "Thomson Insists on Hand-Picking His Heir," *Financial Post,* September 24, 1994, Section 1, p. 4.

Newman, Peter C., "The Biggest Threat to Canada's Future," *Maclean's,* March 8, 1999, p. 44.

Noble, Kimberley, "Bitterness on Bay Street: Ottawa Hands the Banks a Resounding Defeat," *Maclean's,* December 28, 1998, pp. 70–73.

——, "How the Banks Blew It," *Maclean's,* December 7, 1998, pp. 26–30.

Partridge, John, "TD Nails Deal with U.S. Broker," *Globe and Mail,* April 11, 1996, p. B1.

——, "TD Raises Loss Provisions: Cites Trouble in Argentina, Telecom Sector," *Globe and Mail,* February 6, 2002, p. B1.

Schull, Joseph, *100 Years of Banking in Canada: A History of the Toronto-Dominion Bank,* Toronto: Copp Clark, 1958, 222 p.

Willoughby, Jack, "Prime Cuts," *Barron's,* June 21, 1999, p. 38.

Wilson-Smith, Anthony, "The Challengers," *Maclean's,* April 27, 1998, pp. 40–44.

—updates: Dave Mote, David E. Salamie

Transport Corporation of America, Inc.

1715 Yankee Doodle Road
Eagan, Minnesota 55121
U.S.A.
Telephone: (651) 686-2500
Fax: (651) 686-2551
Web site: http://www.transportamerica.com

Public Company
Incorporated: 1984
Employees: 1,815
Sales: $290.6 million (2000)
Stock Exchanges: NASDAQ
Ticker Symbol: TCAM
NAIC: 484121 General Freight Trucking, Long-Distance, Truckload; 484110 General Freight Trucking, Local; 484122 General Freight Trucking, Long-Distance, Less Than Truckload; 541614 Process, Physical Distribution, and Logistics Consulting Services

Transport America, legally named Transport Corporation of America, Inc., is a trucking firm headquartered in Eagan, Minnesota, with a fleet of some 2,200 cabs, or ''tractors,'' pulling nearly 6,000 trailers throughout the United States and Canada. Transport America's trucking routes are primarily in the Midwest, East, and Southeast. Transport America offers customers a wide range of transportation services for cargo requiring various shipment distances. The company has a strong commitment to customer service, providing detailed and customized ''logistics'' services to help clients manage their inventory traffic. Transport America has the capability of offering ''time-definite'' pick-up and delivery to support a growing industry trend of ''just-in-time'' delivery, designed to reduce warehouse and inventory management. Transport America has regional and local operations that offer line haul (from point A to point B), loading and unloading capabilities and multiple stops, temperature-controlled trailers, trailers to support decking, satellite monitored transport, electronic data interchange, load optimization, and information technology services. The company can even coordinate transportation details with third-party transpor-

tation providers. Transport America primarily moves freight in retailing, manufacturing, consumer goods, and recreational products. The company's primary customers include Sears, General Mills, Dupont, S.C. Johnson and Sons, Target, 3M, Federal Express, and Ford Motor Company.

1980s: Founding and Early Growth

Founder James Aronson founded Transport Corporation of America in 1984. Aronson had been a driver and held management positions with Overland Express, Inc. The company espoused a strong commitment to high-quality customer service. Aronson was a hands-on manager, focusing on marketing and operations. He was known for his excellent rapport with customers and commitment to timely deliveries. In Transport America's first full year of operation in 1985, it recorded $15 million in revenues.

Early on, Transport America was seen as a technological leader in the industry. By the late 1980s the company was testing the use of technology to maximize efficiency and reliability in the trucking industry. For Aronson, use of technology offered one more avenue for enhancing customer service. In 1988, the company implemented an automated interactive voice-response system that interfaced with the computer to allow drivers to communicate locations by phone. Soon after, Transport America was using satellite tracking to trace freight movement and share information with drivers via two-way information exchange. The company gradually expanded the size of its fleet and service centers and established small service centers in various locations. By 1993 Transport America's expanding fleet pushed the company to purchase a new, larger headquarters building in Eagan.

1994–98: Going Public and Financial Growth

In 1994 Transport America went public as the Transport Corporation of America, Inc. The company's initial public offering raised $14.5 million. The infusion of revenue helped the company keep abreast of the competition in an industry that relied heavily on capital resources to routinely replace $150,000 trucks every 46–60 months.

The first quarter of 1995 showed Transport America with noticeably improved earnings. The most impressive statistic was the ratio of operating expenses to operating revenue from 96.9 percent in the previous year's first quarter to 93.4 percent the current first quarter. While many competitors had experienced lower demand in the transportation business, Transport America credited their gains to increased freight activity from current customers. By June 1995, the company's operating revenue grew some 12.5 percent, gains due again to growing business from existing customers. The company's operating efficiency (the ratio of expenses to revenue) had improved from 5.1 percent to 7.4 percent in one year.

In the first quarter of 1996 the company recorded double-digit growth in revenue. This good news was dampened by other factors that hurt profit margins: Winter storms and very low temperatures caused reduced utilization of equipment. Rising fuel costs also contributed to increased costs of truck operations. Second quarter growth was even more promising—an 18 percent rise in operating revenue. Growth continued in the remaining two quarters that year. Transport America continued to resist declining business trends in the transportation industry through 1996. Another promising statistic was that the ratio of operating expenses to revenue for the year was down from previous years—91.2 percent, compared with 92.3 percent in 1994. The company reported revenues of $164.7 million and a net income of $6.3 million.

By 1997 the fleet had grown to 1,350 tractors and 3,500 trailers, operating out of ten service centers. In January the Transport America board of directors approved a stock repurchase program allowing repurchase of up to 350,000 shares of common stock. In addition, the board initiated a shareholder rights plan to ensure fair and equal treatment for all shareholders in case of a bid by another party or shareholder to take over the company. At the time there was no indication that anyone was considering taking control of the company.

Transport America also created Transport International Express (TIE), as a new wholly owned subsidiary. TIE was designed to transport goods between major cities by land that had previously most often been shipped by air even though they did not require next-day delivery. TIE would coordinate expedited and time-specific service for moving products that did not have to constitute an entire truckload. Companies could spend a fraction of the cost to have cargo hauled by truck and would enlist the customized logistics services of Transport America to coordinate with the airlines and other freight companies to meet their needs.

The company continued to grow along with the economy. CEO Aronson led concerted efforts to improve driver retention and use of company assets. Aronson became chairman of the board, and Robert Meyers stepped up as president and chief operating officer. Meyers had been executive vice-president since 1994 and chief financial officer since 1993. With a background in technology and accounting, Meyers was credited with implementing the company's state-of-the-art information system.

1997: Local and National Recognition

In August 1997 CEO James Aronson was recognized by *Twin Cities Business Monthly* magazine as one of a small number of Minnesota entrepreneurs of the year. He was recognized in the area of service. The magazine commended Aronson's leadership of the company and his commitment to cutting-edge technology in the transportation industry with global positioning systems installed in his entire fleet, at a price tag of more than $4,000 per vehicle. The computerized tracking system, or global positioning system, enabled customers to determine the locations of their shipments at any given time, within 25 yards anywhere in the country. Transport's trucking technology made it possible to transfer information about driving routes and freight details from company headquarters directly to drivers on the road. In addition, the truck's computer system could diagnose mechanical problems and inform the driver and headquarters.

The magazine also noted the transportation software Transport America had created and tailored specifically for its business to help coordinate schedules and assure timeliness of services. Aronson's successful practice of being very knowledgeable about the business of his customers was also applauded. The company's intimate knowledge of its customers' businesses assisted it in managing supply chains, specifically to better implement "just-in-time delivery" to simplify inventory coordination and reduce warehousing costs. At the time, Transport America recorded an on-time arrival rate of more than 98 percent, an important indicator of company success given the growing popularity of "just-in-time" deliveries.

Aronson was credited with "putting a new face on an old industry" through new transportation technologies. The magazine quoted Aronson as saying, "The thing we've got to realize is trucks are only there to support business and industry. We don't just drive around. When you go to the grocery store or anywhere else and buy something, there's no doubt that a truck brought it there."

Aronson moved Transport America beyond the typical realm of trucking business by implementing the "Trucker Buddy Program" to educate young people about the business. Transport America drivers from several areas of the country partnered with elementary school classes and visited frequently to update young schoolchildren about their profession. The program also included field trips to service centers so kids could

Key Dates:

1984: Transport Corporation of America begins operations.
1990: Satellite tracing is implemented.
1994: The initial public offering raises $14.5 million.
1997: Transport International Express is established; the company is ranked 179 on *Forbes* magazine's list of the top 200 small U.S. businesses; CEO James Aronson is recognized as a local "Entrepreneur of the Year"; Aronson becomes chairman of the board and Robert Meyers becomes president.
1998: Company purchases North Star Transport Inc.
1999: Company acquires Robert Hansen Trucking; founder James Aronson dies of cancer at age 61.
2000: Company agrees to be acquired by USFreightways, but the deal is canceled.
2001: Michael Paxton is named president and CEO; Robert Meyers heads offshoot Techgistics.

learn about the trucks firsthand. The company also had a comprehensive training and certification program for drivers that helped increase the number of company-owned tractors at a time when the industry had a driver shortage.

Transport America gained additional recognition, this time nationally, in November 1997 when it made *Forbes* magazine's list of the 200 Best Small Companies in the United States. The magazine ranked Transport America number 170, based on a 16.2 percent five-year average return on equity.

By 1998 Transport America's fleet had grown to 2,000 tractors and 5,000 trailers. In February of that year Transport America acquired a local, privately held company called North Star Transport Inc. The purchase was for a cash and stock combination valued at approximately $34 million. The acquisition was a good fit because North Star was an operation similar to that of Transport America, focusing on using experienced and highly qualified drivers. North Star had a fleet of 625 owner-operated vehicles, employed about 100, and posted annual revenues of $75 million. Company leaders said North Star would help them better serve the needs of a greater variety of clients and become more competitive in the industry.

The company's major customer, Sears, named Transport America a Sears Partners in Progress Award winner for 1998. In addition, strong business and the purchase of North Star helped Transport America achieve high growth and record profits in 1998. Late that year the company announced plans to develop a new 123,000-square-foot corporate headquarters at a nearby Eagan location. Because of plans for further growth and because the acquisition of North Star added some 30 percent to the operation, Transport America wanted to consolidate its business sites to one location.

1999–2001: A Weaker Market

In January 1999 Transport America sold Transport International Express because the subsidiary had not met company performance expectations. Transport America sold the assets

and operations of TIE to Express America Inc. and maintained some ownership interest, but was not a controlling shareholder.

Later that year Transport America expanded its fleet further with the purchase of privately held Robert Hansen Trucking Inc., a $24 million operation based in Delavan, Wisconsin. The deal to acquire, through cash, stock, and assumption of debt, was completed in May. Robert Hansen Trucking had 200 company trucks, primarily serving the eastern market. Transport America reportedly acquired the firm for approximately $2.2 million in cash, 350,000 shares of Transport America stock, and a $16 million debt assumption.

Unlike recent years, Transport America experienced some financial difficulties in 1999, with earnings falling below expectations in the last quarter. Sadly, late that year Transport America founder James Aronson died of cancer at the age of 61. Robert Meyers was elected chief executive officer.

Around the same time, Transport America formed a wholly owned subsidiary, Transport America Logistics, or TA Logistics. TA Logistics was designed to provide transportation procurement and logistics services, basically assuming management of all the details of a customer's shipping traffic needs. Operations of the company began in 2000. The subsidiary was selected to partner in the development and operation of a Logistics Management Center for Polaris Industries.

Early in 2000 Transport America began discussions about a merger agreement with a wholly owned subsidiary of USFreightways Corporation. It would be a stock-for-stock transaction with a value of $149 million. CEO Meyers described the marriage of the two companies as a positive one, noting Transport America's leadership in services and dedicated truckload transportation, and Freightways' leadership in the areas of logistics, supply-chain coordination, and less-than-truckload regional operations. In February, however, by mutual agreement of both companies' boards, the deal between Freightways and Transport was dissolved. The purchase would have resulted in Freightways' trucking arm becoming one of the top ten publicly traded truckload carriers.

When the deal collapsed, Transport America's stock price fell. Soon after, the company announced plans to repurchase stock under the existing share repurchase plan. The company faced additional challenges in 2000 with driver retention and rising fuel costs. Profits also were impacted because a key customer temporarily decreased operations. Despite these problems, tractor productivity increased from the previous quarter and year, and the number of empty miles that were nonrevenue-producing was reduced.

In 2001 Transport America experienced declining revenues due to continuing weak economic conditions and a reduced number of shipments by primary customers in manufacturing, automotive, industrial, and retail. The company also was affected by less cargo movement in general in its primary geographic service areas. Reports for 2001 reflected a softer demand for freight movement, more empty miles, and fewer fuel surcharge dollars.

Transport America's third quarter operating ratio in 2001 was 96.3 percent, compared with 93.1 percent for the same quarter the previous year. Third quarter net earnings were

$478,000 (0.7 percent of operating revenues), compared with $1.6 million (2.2 percent of operating revenues) for the same quarter in 2000. A sluggish economy reduced demand for Transport America's services by its primary customers.

2001: New Leadership and Technology Offshoot

Late in 2001 Transport America announced changes in its management team, naming Michael Paxton as president and chief executive officer. Paxton had served on the Transport America Board for more than six years. He was also president and CEO of Sunbeam Health and Safety Company. Robert Meyers was appointed president and CEO of a Transport America offshoot, Techgistics, a separate technology arm through which the company intended to pursue advancements in transportation technology. The company planned to enhance and market its internally designed and customized trucking software package through Techgistics.

Transport America's 2,200 tractors and nearly 6,000 trailers operated out of the Minnesota headquarters as well as service centers and terminals in Indiana, Wisconsin, Ohio, Iowa, Missouri, Texas, South Carolina, Georgia, and Pennsylvania. Its customer list in the early 21st century included many who relied on pickup and delivery of goods carried out in a narrow time frame. Its clients included Hon Company, P.P.G. Industries, Polaris Industries, Toys-R-Us, Wal-Mart, Sears, General Mills, Dupont, S.C. Johnson, Target, 3M, Federal Express, and Ford Motor Company.

A big part of the company's success continued to derive from its reputation for providing 100 percent on-time pickup and delivery within narrowly defined time frames, using minimal transit time, and conscientiously handling freight traffic details for customers. Transport America's biggest challenge in the early 21st century appeared to be maintaining its competitive edge against companies with greater financial resources, more equipment, and more hauling capability, not only other trucking firms, but also rail and air freight rivals.

Principal Subsidiaries

TA Logistics; Techgistics.

Principal Competitors

Covenant Transport; U.S. Xpress; Werner.

Further Reading

Elmstrom, Dave, ''Entrepreneurs of the Year: James Aronson Transport Corporation of America, Inc.,'' *Twin Cities Business Monthly,* August 1997, p. 44.

Gaw, Jonathan, ''Transportation Technology; Satellite Communications Help Dispatchers, Semitrailer Truck Drivers Keep on Trucking,'' *Minneapolis Star Tribune,* August 11, 1996, p. 1D.

''Hansen Trucking Sold to Minnesota Firm,'' *Milwaukee Journal Sentinel,* April 14, 1999, p. 2.

Roberts, Richado, ''Cratered Deals—New Buyer Should Drive Up for Transport: Down the Road, Trucking Co. Will Likely Hook Up with Another Partner,'' *Mergers & Acquisitions Report,* February 28, 2000.

''Transport America's James Aronson Dies,'' *Journal of Commerce,* December 17, 1999, p. 6.

''Transport Sells Units to Express America,'' *Journal of Commerce,* January 15, 1999, p. 12A.

''Trucking Companies Merge in $149 Million Stock Deal,'' *New York Times,* January 19, 2000, p. C4.

''Trucking Company's Stock Falls with Buyout Deal Off,'' *New York Times,* February 10, 2000, p. C4.

''Transport Corp. Plans to Repurchase Stock,'' *Journal of Commerce,* April 10, 2000, p. 5.

''Transport Corporation Bucks Earnings Trend,'' *Journal of Commerce,* February 14, 1996, p. 2B.

''Transportation Briefs: At Transport Corp.,'' *Journal of Commerce,* April 26, 1995, p. 2B.

Weintraub, Adam, ''Transport Corp. of America Projects Fast Growth: Trucking Firm Building New Eagan Headquarters,'' *Minneapolis-St. Paul CityBusiness,* December 18, 1998, p. 6.

Wolf, Liz, ''Eagan Trucking Company Plans New Local HQ,'' *Minnesota Real Estate Journal,* December 14, 1998, p. 10.

—Mary Heer-Forsberg

Trinity Mirror plc

One Canada Square
Canary Wharf
London E14 5AP
United Kingdom
Telephone: 44 20 7293 3000
Fax: 44 20 7293 3476
Web site: http://www.trinity.plc.uk

Public Company
Incorporated: 1999
Employees: 14,000
Sales: £1.13 billion (2001)
Stock Exchanges: London
Ticker Symbol: TNI
NAIC: 511110 Newspaper Publishers

Trinity Mirror plc is the largest newspaper publisher in the United Kingdom, with more than 250 regional and national newspaper titles. The result of a 1999 merger of the regional newspaper publisher Trinity plc and the primarily national newspaper publisher Mirror Group plc, Trinity Mirror reaped the benefits of the newspaper consolidation of the 1980s and 1990s. With three of the top ten regional evening newspapers and three of the top six regional Sunday papers, Trinity Mirror led the nation in 2002 in regional newspaper readership. In addition, for much of the 20th century, the company's *Daily Mirror* had been one of the world's most popular newspapers, a pioneer of what has been characterized variously as New Journalism, the popular press, or, less charitably, the scandal sheet. As Europe's fourth largest selling newspaper, the *Mirror* continued to anchor Trinity Mirror's national holdings, along with *Sunday People* and the *Daily Record.* As of 2002, Trinity Mirror also owned more than 50 trade magazines, ran an equal number of web sites, and published several popular sporting newspapers.

Although the company officially incorporated in 1999, the history of some of its titles can be traced back hundreds of years. In addition to holding some of the oldest, continuously published English-language newspapers, the two merging companies had made significant contributions to the development of newspaper publishing. To fully appreciate the rich history of Trinity Mirror, one must look to the history of its two progenitors, Mirror Group plc and Trinity plc.

Trinity's 19th-Century Beginnings

When Trinity merged with Mirror Group in 1999, it already boasted a long history. It published the *News Letter* in Belfast, which first hit the streets in 1737, making it the oldest surviving English-language newspaper in the world. Trinity also published the *Belfast Telegraph:* Launched in 1870, it became Northern Ireland's best-selling newspaper. In addition, Trinity published the *South Wales Echo,* first issued in 1884, and the *Coventry Evening Telegraph,* first printed in 1891. Although Trinity had acquired these and other long-running papers rather late in its history, the company's direct precursor, the Liverpool Post & Echo, had a history equally distinguished.

In the mid-1800s the owner of the weekly newspaper the *Liverpool Journal,* Michael James Whitty, approached a Select Committee of MPs with a proposal. At the time, a Stamp Act was in place that taxed newspapers, an arrangement that Whitty claimed restricted enterprise. If the act were repealed, he promised, he would publish a daily paper to be sold for just one penny. On June 11, 1855, Whitty launched the *Daily Post.* True to his word, the eight-page paper had a cover price of one penny.

The paper was a success, and 14 years later Edward Russell was appointed the editor of the *Daily Post.* He ran the paper for nearly a half-century and oversaw several important events.

In 1879 the *Daily Post*'s sister paper, the *Liverpool Echo,* was launched. Alexander Jeans, the former manager of the *Daily Post,* founded the paper, and it was produced in the same facility as the *Daily Post.* The *Liverpool Echo* had ten editions a day and sold for a mere halfpenny. It managed to continue at that price for almost 40 years; in 1917 the price rose to a whole penny.

Both the *Daily Post* and the *Liverpool Echo* were known for their Liberal editorial slant, despite their location in a predominantly Tory city. Russell, editor of the *Daily Post,* supported Gladstone, campaigned for Irish Home Rule, and generally advocated Liberal positions on issues through the paper.

In 1905, Liverpool's Licensing Magistrates brought a case of criminal libel against Russell and the paper. Decided in favor of Russell, the case was considered an important success for freedom of the press.

In another step on its road to becoming a newspaper empire, the *Daily Post* merged with its competitor the *Liverpool Mercury* in 1904. A public company was established, with Alexander Jeans as its managing director. Jeans ran the company until his son Alan succeeded him. Alan Jeans increased the company's publishing concerns, over the years purchasing additional newspaper titles in the area. He died in 1961, and management of the company passed to another Jeans, this time Alan's son Alick.

Alick Jeans continued his father's policies of expansion. By the time of his death in 1972, Liverpool Daily Post & Echo Ltd. had become a diversified international company. Along with the *Daily Post* and the *Liverpool Echo,* the company published numerous regional weeklies in Britain and North America. In addition, the company manufactured cardboard and paper products for the printing and packaging industries.

Liverpool Daily Post & Echo was affected in the 1980s by the city's rapidly shrinking population and rampant unemployment. The company relaunched both papers as tabloids and managed to hold its readership to a steady level.

Trinity Expansion in the 1980s and 1990s

In 1985, the company restructured itself to better support its various businesses. A new parent company was established, Trinity International Holdings plc. Liverpool Daily Post & Echo Ltd. was reorganized as a subsidiary, primarily responsible for publishing the *Post* and the *Echo.* Other subsidiaries ran the British weeklies, the North American newspapers, and the paper manufacturing and answered directly to Trinity International. Three years later, the company shortened its name to Trinity plc.

Regional newspapers suffered in the late 1980s and early 1990s from falling subscriptions and rising newsprint costs. Their ad revenues were generally falling, and they had trouble attracting a younger audience. As a result, most of the largest publishers were dumping their regional titles. Trinity, however, saw an opportunity to rise from its position as the 14th largest regional press in Britain.

In 1988, Trinity purchased the North Wales weeklies series. Then, in 1990, the company's American division bought Pitts-

burgh Pennysaver for $13.5 million. The acquisition was expected to raise the revenues of Trinity's U.S. newspaper group to $40 million annually. With additional small purchases, Trinity was soon in the ranks of the five largest regional newspaper publishers in Britain.

Trinity took the lead in 1995 when it bought five British newspapers from the Thomson Corporation of Canada. The $522.4 million purchase included the *Belfast Telegraph* in Northern Ireland and the *Western Mail* in Cardiff, Wales. The acquisitions brought Trinity's British portfolio to 50 titles, making it the largest publisher of regional newspapers in the nation.

Two years later, in an effort to focus on its British holdings, Trinity sold 33 Canadian titles to Black Press Ltd. for $58 million. In 1998, the company sold its U.S. subsidiary, Trinity Holdings Inc., to a management-led group for $57 million.

By the late 1990s, Trinity's investment in regional publishing seemed to be paying off. Regional papers were enjoying sales rises and increased ad revenues, while national papers were experiencing a drop in circulation. Analysts ascribed the success of the regionals to efficiencies created by the consolidation of the industry and to the general strength of the economy. Some, however, also saw an increased desire on the part of advertisers to tailor their appeals to local audiences, resulting in double-digit increases in national advertising in regional papers. In 1998, Trinity's sales increased 5.4 percent, to $564 million. Profits leaped 43 percent, to $101 million.

That same year, Trinity began to pursue the acquisition of a major national newspaper publisher. The company began talks with the Mirror Group, a financially unstable but prominent publisher. Although the two companies eventually would merge, the negotiations were long and contentious.

Early History of Mirror Group

The history of Mirror Group rightly begins with the history of Alfred Harmsworth (Lord Northcliffe), the founder of the company's flagship paper, the *Daily Mirror.* In the words of the *Times* of London, Harmsworth was "unquestionably the greatest journalist of his time." The creation of the *Daily Mirror* was a critical episode in the revolution in British journalism wrought by Alfred Harmsworth and his brother Harold (later Lord Rothermere). Until the end of the 19th century, British newspapers and magazines had been written by and for the aristocracy and professional middle class, a relatively small percentage of the country's total population. Compared to most of the industrialized nations, Britain had developed a vigorous and often vitriolic press, but not until the last half of the 19th century did anyone propose seriously to publish a newspaper for the lower-middle and lower classes. Alfred and Harold Harmsworth, born to the family of an impoverished schoolteacher, eventually amassed fortunes, wielded enormous political power, and became members of the House of Lords.

Alfred Harmsworth exhibited his gifts for writing and self-promotion at an early age. As a grammar school student outside London he founded and edited the school newspaper. The young man pursued a career in journalism and began to contribute short pieces to the popular periodicals then coming into their own, such as *Young Folk Tales* and *Tit-Bits.* In 1887 he founded

Key Dates:

1737: The *News Letter,* published by Trinity and the oldest surviving English-language newspaper in the world, makes its first appearance in Belfast.

1855: The *Daily Post,* with a cover price of one penny, is launched by Liverpool Daily Post & Echo Ltd.

1870: Trinity introduces the *Belfast Telegraph,* which becomes Northern Ireland's best-selling newspaper.

1894: Alfred Harmsworth buys the *London Evening News* for £25,000.

1896: Alfred and Harold Harmsworth found the *Daily Mail.*

1911: The *Daily Mirror* becomes the first daily paper with a circulation greater than one million.

1951: Cecil Harmsworth King becomes chairman of the *Mirror.*

1961: The *Mirror* and its newly acquired magazine empire are merged to form the International Publishing Corporation (IPC).

1968: Cecil King is forced to resign.

1970: The merger of IPC and Albert E. Reed & Co. Ltd., one of the largest paper products companies in Europe, creates Reed International.

1984: Robert Maxwell purchases the Mirror papers for about £90 million, and the Mirror Group Newspapers Ltd. (MGN) becomes a pillar of his business empire.

1985: Trinity International Holdings plc is established as a new parent company for Liverpool Daily Post & Echo Ltd.

1988: Trinity International Holdings shortens its name to Trinity plc.

1991: Robert Maxwell is found dead, presumably from drowning.

1994: A consortium led by the Mirror Group purchases the *Independent* for an estimated $110 million.

1995: Trinity buys five British newspapers, including the *Belfast Telegraph* in Northern Ireland and the *Western Mail* in Cardiff, Wales, from Canada's Thomson Corporation.

1997: Mirror Group acquires Midland Independent Newspaper plc.

1998: Mirror Group sells its stake in the *Independent.*

1999: Trinity announces its purchase of Mirror Group and the combined company is named Trinity Mirror plc.

2002: Trinity Mirror announces plans to earmark an additional £25 million for editorial revamping and marketing for the *Daily Mirror.*

his own popular periodical called *Answers to Correspondents.* The magazine's title suggested its format, a collection of letters to the editor and his answers.

The title also suggested the nature of New Journalism as a whole. England's advanced economy had created a large middle class whose members, such as Alfred Harmsworth himself, were literate and curious about the world at large but uninterested in the higher arcana of politics, theology, and *belles lettres.* These readers, Harmsworth felt, hungered for publications that reflected and commented on their own middle-class lives, free of cultural pretensions, informative but simply written, and spiced with stories of love and violent crime.

In 1894 Harmsworth bought the moribund *London Evening News* for £25,000 and completed the triumph of popular daily journalism, aided by a talented young editor named Kennedy Jones and by his brother Harold, who would remain the financial and administrative director of the Harmsworth syndicate. Two years later the Harmsworth brothers founded the *Daily Mail,* a morning paper that experienced astonishing success from its initial publication date, when it already boasted the world's largest daily circulation. The secret of Harmsworth's success was summed up in his phrase, "explain, clarify, simplify," or perhaps more frankly in the formula articulated by Kennedy Jones: "Crime, love, money and food." In truth, the *Mail* (and later the *Mirror*) did not seem to follow any particular editorial philosophy. It did combine elements of ultranationalist politics, sex and violence, sports, cartoons, and advice columns, all written in brisk humorous prose and framed by bold black headlines.

These were papers for the plain-speaking common man, a market long associated with the United States but mostly unrec-ognized in England until Harmsworth provided the "daily mirror" in which they could recognize themselves. Nor were women excluded from this democratic awakening; the *Daily Mirror* owed its origin to Alfred Harmsworth's rare sensitivity to women as a newly emerging force in the political and cultural life of England. In 1903 Harmsworth established a paper written entirely by and for women. This "enlightened" experiment lasted about a year, the women of England for unknown reasons failing to rally around the *Mirror* as anticipated. The *Mirror*'s weekly losses of £3,000 soon convinced Harmsworth that "women can't write and don't want to read." He dismissed the female staff, replacing them with the usual gang of cigar-smoking men and relaunched the paper in 1904 with a lead story entitled, "How I Dropped £100,000 on the *Mirror.*"

The success of the new *Mirror* was not predicated on the gender of its editors, however. Harmsworth took advantage of recently evolved technology to make the *Daily Mirror* the first halfpenny paper in England illustrated with photographs, which until that time had appeared in newspapers rarely and at substantial cost. The *Mirror*'s photographs were sharp and clear and inexpensive, and the paper soon was known for its front-page photos of the royal family, war scenes, and famous criminals. The liberal use of photographs, combined with the usual Harmsworth mix of letters, gossip, contests, and short news articles, proved to be a powerful lure for the English working class. Circulation shot upward to 350,000 in 1905 and six years later topped the one million mark, making the *Mirror* the world's first daily to reach that figure.

The *Mirror* was edited in these years by Alexander Kenealy, an Irishman whose instinct for sensational news had been honed by years of work with publishing magnate William Randolph

Hearst in the United States. Under Kenealy, the *Mirror* took a further turn toward the journalism of titillation and sensationalism, eventually going too far to suit Alfred Harmsworth himself. The publisher, who was made a baronet in 1905, wanted to exercise power in the political as well as commercial sphere and he found the *Mirror* something of an embarrassment. In 1908 Harmsworth bought the *Times* of London and rapidly lost interest in the *Mirror,* which he sold to his brother Harold in 1914. The elder Harmsworth went on to a career of frustrated political campaigns and a growing megalomania; he was remembered by Prime Minister Lloyd George, as "far and away the most redoubtable figure of all the Press barons of my time. He created the popular daily, and the more the other journals scoffed . . . the more popular it became." More typical of upper-class feelings, however, were the words of Lord Salisbury, who charged that Harmsworth had "invented a paper for those who could read but could not think, and another for those who could see but could not read."

The **Mirror** *in the World Wars*

Harold Harmsworth (Lord Rothermere) was a businessman of talent, and for some years the *Mirror* prospered under his ownership, helped especially by the public's hunger for photographs of the fighting in World War I. By 1917 the *Mirror* was the most popular daily in Great Britain, but Rothermere's obsessive criticism of governmental waste eroded the paper's circulation base in the 1920s. Like his brother, Rothermere could not resist trying to play the power broker in his nation's political life. The *Mirror* remained essentially conservative, as it had always been, but Rothermere used the paper as a vehicle for voicing his private feelings about the leaders of the Tory Party, for years attacking the government for alleged inefficiency and corruption. The culmination of this campaign was Rothermere's founding of the United Empire Party in the late 1920s, a short-lived far right-wing party whose jingoistic statements presaged Rothermere's later support for fascism.

Rothermere's fulminations were politically ineffectual and eventually proved to be bad for business as well. With the *Mirror's* circulation sinking quickly Rothermere sold his shares in 1931, his reputation permanently damaged by the rebukes of fellow conservatives such as Stanley Baldwin. "What the proprietorship of these pages is aiming at," said Baldwin in a famous 1930 speech, "is power, and power without responsibility—the prerogative of the harlot through the ages."

The politically turbulent 1930s witnessed the birth of a new, radical *Daily Mirror.* While Lord Rothermere formally adopted the fascist philosophy of Hitler and Mussolini, his former paper became one of England's leading advocates of democratic rights and armed resistance to Hitler's growing power in the east. Of the four men chiefly responsible for the new *Mirror,* three of them—editors H.G. Bartholomew and Hugh Cudlipp, and columnist William Connor (pen name "Cassandra")— were by birth and temperament sympathetic to the working classes; the fourth, Cecil Harmsworth King, was the nephew of founder Alfred Harmsworth. Together these four men created the *Daily Mirror* of which historian A.J.P. Taylor would later remark, "The English people had at last found their voice."

It was an irreverent, loud voice, in which could be heard elements of both high principle and low culture, semi-pornographic cartoons side by side with early and accurate warnings about the menace of Hitler. In 1934, years before most of England's high-brow papers gave up the rhetoric of "appeasement," the *Daily Mirror* characterized the German dictator with startling prescience as "the hysterical Austrian, with his megalomania, based on an acute inferiority complex, his neurasthenia, his oratorical brilliance." The *Mirror's* enthusiasm for confrontation would vary in the years following, but from 1937 onward it was England's leading proponent of the rearmament needed to deal with "the gangsters" of Europe.

In this sentiment it found an ally in none other than Winston Churchill, one aristocrat whom the *Mirror* supported during the 1930s and the first years of war. As the symbol of embattled Britain, Churchill could rely on the applause of the *Mirror,* which if nothing else had always identified itself with the interests of England. The *Mirror,* though, was an essentially iconoclastic journal with leftist leanings and soon it was criticizing the coalition government for various failings, in 1942 nearly suffering censorship for publishing what Churchill believed were demoralizing statements. By war's end the *Mirror* had fully resumed its prewar support for the Labour Party, helping defeat Churchill in the 1945 election. As always, the *Mirror* reflected and amplified the beliefs of its two million-plus readers, who in 1945 were overwhelmingly pacifist and neo-Socialist in their feelings.

Postwar Influence

In 1951 Cecil Harmsworth King deposed H.G. Bartholomew as chairman of the *Mirror.* The paper was probably then at the peak of its influence, the leading daily in all of Great Britain (possibly in the world) and the voice of the New Left that would dominate the country's politics for the next 30 years. Cecil King took the paper several steps further, however; it was under King's leadership that the *Mirror* expanded from newspaper to "Group." For years the *Mirror* had published a successful weekend edition called the *Sunday Pictorial,* and to this core King added a vast collection of magazines by taking over the Amalgamated Press in 1958 and Odhams Press a few years later. The holdings from the latter deal included a leading Labour newspaper, the *Daily Herald.* Along with the *Daily Record* and *Sunday Mail,* both of Glasgow, Scotland, the *Mirror* and its newly acquired magazine empire were all merged in the early 1960s into the International Publishing Corporation (IPC), described by Hugh Cudlipp in his 1962 book *At Your Peril* as "the greatest publishing operation the world has ever seen."

IPC owned the leading publications in virtually every category of British journalism, its power so great that in 1961 a parliamentary committee was formed to determine whether the *Mirror* takeover of Odham should not be prohibited by the government for reasons of free trade and the general good. The merger went through anyway, and IPC became one of the world's first "media conglomerates," as they would later be called, and Cecil King, like his uncle Alfred Harmsworth, established himself as a "media baron."

King's long and remarkable career ended abruptly in 1968 with his resignation under pressure from the board of directors.

IPC's profits apparently were suffering from the entrenched power of its printing unions, power fought for and won with the help of newspapers like IPC's own *Daily Mirror.* The English printers union was a strong one, and it adamantly opposed new technologies that would cut costs at the expense of union jobs. Cecil King despaired of the situation, and two years after his departure IPC was merged with Albert E. Reed & Co. Ltd., one of the largest paper products companies in Europe. IPC had long been the largest shareholder in Reed (the Harmsworth brothers became involved in the Canadian paper business as early as 1906) and in 1970 the two firms banded together in the interests of vertical integration under the name of Reed International.

The Maxwell Years: 1984–91

Reed had no more luck with the printing unions than had IPC, and one by one the pieces of its publishing empire were sold off during the 1970s, starting with the magazines. Last to go were the Mirror newspapers, which then as now consisted of the *Daily Mirror, Daily Record, Sunday Mirror, The People* (a glossy Sunday spread), the *Sunday Mail,* the *Sporting Life,* and the *Sporting Life Weekender.* Reed could find no buyer for the Mirror newspapers, however, and a plan to float the group on the public exchange was ruined when Price Waterhouse discovered gross union laxities and described them in its prospectus statement. At the last minute an unlikely white knight appeared in the form of Robert Maxwell, Czech-born business dealer extraordinaire, who purchased the Mirror papers for about £90 million in 1984.

Mirror Group Newspapers Ltd. (MGN) became a pillar of Robert Maxwell's incredibly tangled business empire, a mysterious world in which the distinction between private and public companies was regularly ignored by Maxwell and his sons Ian and Kevin. A former MP for the Labour Party and a professed friend of the working man, Maxwell, according to many critics, had little regard for anything beyond his own insatiable desire for fame, and he had long coveted a public platform such as MGN offered. He took over MGN editorial policy while denying that he would even be interested in doing so, and by threat of company closure persuaded the unions to cut their employee levels and relinquish a host of archaic union rules.

For the same reason, Maxwell did not hesitate to break the law when his financial network began unraveling in the late 1980s. His 1988 purchase of Macmillan, Inc., the American publisher, and Official Airline Guides, Inc., for which he borrowed a combined $3.35 billion, pushed his empire further into precarious territory. The anemic economy in 1989 sent the price of stock at Maxwell Communications Corporation (MCC) spiraling downward. MCC was the holding company for Maxwell's American interests and the collateral for many of the huge loans made to Maxwell's private holding companies at the top of the pyramid. To bolster MCC's falling share price, Maxwell engaged in a blur of desperate transactions, including the use of Mirror Group pension funds and other cash accounts to buy MCC shares and provide collateral for further new loans. Shortly after the first signs of imminent personal bankruptcy appeared in November 1991, Maxwell's body was found floating off the stern of his yacht, at which point his conglomerate fell to pieces in a welter of bankruptcy filings and criminal investigations.

Of all of Maxwell's holdings, MGN was probably the soundest at the time of his death, but the company sustained serious losses due to Maxwell's illegal business dealings. In its 1992 annual report MGN noted a one-time extraordinary loss of £421 million to cover the cost of repairs, but the company also showed a healthy operating profit of £91 million on revenues of £460 million.

Mirror Group Expansion in the 1990s

After years of litigation, Mirror Group recovered a portion of its lost pension funds, and the shaken company seemed on its feet again. Hopes for economic security were based on further expansion. In 1994, the Mirror Group led a consortium of media interests in the takeover of the *Independent.* The *Independent* was founded in 1986 as a nonpartisan London daily. The paper at first prospered, as it was perceived to offer respectable and unbiased reporting, in contrast to the *London Times,* which was regarded by many as having declined in quality since being taken over by media magnate Rupert Murdoch. But financial losses in the early 1990s, coupled with gradual ebbing of circulation to its wealthier rival paper, eventually led the *Independent* to solicit a buyer. The consortium led by Mirror Group paid an estimated $110 million for the paper, and MGN was to have a 25 to 30 percent share. Its share was later upped to 46 percent.

Mirror Group's other significant expansion at this time was the launch of its cable television channel, Live TV. MGN put £2.9 million into the cable channel, which featured an irreverent take on the news. One of its most popular innovations was the News Bunny, nothing more than a broadcaster delivering the news while dressed as a rabbit. After a rocky start, Live TV gained a significant share of the British cable market.

By 1995, Mirror Group seemed to have put its financial troubles behind it. Profits that year were up 12 percent, and circulation of its flagship *Daily Mirror* inched up almost 2 percent. Meanwhile, its rival the *Sun* lost almost 3 percent of its circulation. The Group's other titles also showed increasing circulation. Management claimed that it had bolstered its papers by editorial improvement and strong marketing, not by cutting cover prices.

Further expansion came in 1997, when Mirror Group paid £297 million ($502.1 million) for Midland Independent Newspaper plc, publisher of the *Birmingham Post* and the *Birmingham Evening Mail.* This purchase was expected to boost MGN's presence in the Birmingham area, where its Live TV station was already popular.

Mirror Group was constrained from further television expansion by antimonopoly laws, and competition among the top newspaper conglomerates made every tenth of a percentage point fluctuation in circulation a battle. In 1998, the company reshuffled top management, bringing Live TV's managing director, Kelvin MacKenzie, in as managing director for the whole group. MacKenzie had formerly managed the *Sun,* the main competitor to the *Daily Mirror.* This shake-up came as the director of the Group's Scottish papers resigned and circulation of the Group's Sunday papers appeared to be falling.

When the Group announced its 1997 fiscal results in March 1998, profits were up 12 percent, and sales had climbed slightly less than 4 percent, to £559 million. Nevertheless, circulations at its papers were now declining, and the Group was forced to drop its cover prices in response to its competitors lowering theirs. The flagship paper *Daily Mirror,* long number two to the *Sun,* was in danger of losing its place to the *Daily Mail.* In addition, the *Independent,* which Mirror Group had acquired four years earlier, was suffering greatly in response to price cuts and promotions by its two main rivals, Rupert Murdoch's *Times* and the *Daily Telegraph.* Losses at the *Independent* had approached £10 million for the past several years, and Mirror Group announced in March 1998 that it would sell its stake in the ailing paper. This bad news overshadowed the rosy fiscal picture.

Merger of Trinity and Mirror Group

Intense competition between the leading national newspapers continued, and in 1998 the *Daily Mirror* lost more market share, falling into third behind the *Daily Mail.* The company's stock fell to a low of 136 pence a share in October 1998, and two companies made serious bids to take over the Mirror Group. Trinity made an all-stock offer of 160 pence a share, and Candover Investment Trust offered 200 pence a share. Mirror Group turned them both down, and an internal struggle between Mirror Group's chief executive, David Montgomery, and the nonexecutive chairman, Victor Blank, came to a head.

Montgomery, who was credited with saving the company after Maxwell's plundering, had seen his popularity decline through the mid-1990s. Journalists, many of whom had lost their jobs to Montgomery's cost-cutting, criticized him heavily. When takeover offers appeared, Montgomery was accused of thwarting their success in an effort to protect his position in the company. In January 1999, Blank threatened to call for a no-confidence vote at a board meeting. When Montgomery failed to get the company's institutional investors to back him, he resigned.

Trinity upped its offer to 210 pence a share in March, which valued Mirror Group at $1.53 billion. Mirror Group refused again, and continued in talks with Candover Investment. In July 1999, however, Trinity announced its purchase of Mirror Group for £1.24 billion, or approximately $2 billion. The combined company, named Trinity Mirror plc, would be the largest newspaper publisher in Britain. Philip Graf, chief executive of Trinity, was appointed to the same position for Trinity Mirror. Regulators required Trinity to sell its newspapers in Northern Ireland, including the *Belfast Telegraph,* to complete the deal.

Soon after the merger, scandal disturbed the new company. Trinity Mirror admitted that it had overstated the circulation figures for its Birmingham newspapers. For six years, the company had inflated the figures for the *Birmingham Evening Mail* and the *Sunday Mercury* by about 17 percent and the figures for the *Birmingham Post* by about 10 percent. The company agreed to compensate advertisers, who paid for ads based on circulation figures.

In 2000, Trinity Mirror purchased Southnews, a newspaper publisher based in London, for £284.6 million. The company also completed its required sale of the *Belfast Telegraph;* Independent News & Media purchased the title for £300 million. The same year, Trinity Mirror expanded its ic brand of web

sites, with several new regional web sites, including icscotland.com, and several content-based web sites, including icshowbiz.com.

Trinity Mirror sold its Internet service provider, ic24, in 2001. It also announced plans in July of that year to reduce its workforce by 800 jobs over the next three years in an effort to reduce costs. In addition, the company suffered a downturn in advertising sales in 2001, along with the rest of the industry. Following the September 11 terrorist attacks on the World Trade Center, advertising went into a severe decline, with a 10 percent drop for the *Daily Mirror* and the *Sunday People* in October and a greater than 21 percent drop in November. In response, the company's shares fell by 14 pence.

Although advertising revenues continued to fall in the first quarter of 2002, Trinity Mirror announced plans to spend an additional £25 million in editorial revamping and marketing for the *Daily Mirror.* An effort to reposition the paper as a more serious tabloid had met with a positive response from readers. To cut costs, Trinity Mirror contracted its national advertising sales for the *Mirror, Sunday Mirror, Sunday People,* the *Daily Record,* and the *Sunday Mail* to Apollo Sales, a new sales subsidiary of the Telegraph Group. Although Apollo Sales also would handle advertising sales for the *Daily Telegraph* and the *Sunday Telegraph,* analysts foresaw little chance for Apollo to abuse its position with cross-selling.

In addition to continued declines in advertising revenue, newsprint prices were rising. The crunch for Trinity Mirror led the company to raise its expected job cuts to 1,100 by 2003.

Principal Subsidiaries

MGN Limited; Century Newspapers Ltd.; Derry Journal Ltd.; The Sunday Business Post; Scottish Daily Record & Sunday Mail Limited (Scotland); Scottish & Universal Newspapers Ltd. (Scotland); Insider Group Ltd.; Newcastle Chronicle & Journal Ltd.; Gazette Media Company Ltd.; Liverpool Daily Post & Echo Ltd.; The Chester Chronicle & Associated Newspapers Ltd.; Examiner News & Information Services Ltd.; Wheatley Dyson & Son Ltd.; Birmingham Post & Mail Ltd.; Coventry Newspapers Ltd.; Trinity Publications Ltd.; Midland Weekly Media Ltd.; Trinity Mirror Southern; Inside Communications Ltd.; Western Mail & Echo Ltd.

Principal Divisions

Regional; National; Sport; Magazines and Exhibitions; Digital Media.

Principal Competitors

Daily Mail and General Trust plc; Guardian Media Group; Johnston Press plc; Newsquest plc.

Further Reading

Berti, Pat, ''Pennysaver Sold to Gateway Parent,'' *Pittsburgh Business Times,* February 12, 1990, p. 2.

Bower, Tom, *Maxwell the Outsider,* New York: Viking, 1992.

Cook, Richard, ''The Devolution Effect,'' *Campaign,* June 12, 1998, p. 30.

Cowell, Alan, "Mirror Group Chief Resigns in Showdown," *New York Times,* January 27, 1999, p. C7.

——, "Mirror Rejects Trinity's Sweetened Bid," *New York Times,* March 2, 1999, p. C4.

Crawford, Anne-Marie, "Trinity Hits Back at IPA," *Marketing,* December 9, 1999, p. 3.

Dignam, Conor, "Mirror Group Profits Mask Its TV Troubles," *Marketing,* September 21, 1995, p. 12.

Edelman, Maurice, *The Mirror: A Political History,* London: Hamish Mailton, 1966.

Escott, T.H.S., *Masters of English Journalism,* London: T. Fisher Unwin, 1911.

Gapper, John, "Reshuffle at Mirror Group As Kane Resigns," *Financial Times,* January 15, 1998, p. 26.

Johnson, Branwell, "The Cost of Trinity Teaming Up with Telegraph Sales," *Marketing Week,* March 7, 2002, p. 16.

MacMillan, Gordon, "Wanderer Returns to Claim His Newspaper Crown," *Campaign,* July 19, 1996, p. 11.

Maremont, Mark, and Mark Landler, "An Empire Up for Grabs," *Business Week,* December 23, 1991.

McIntosh, Bill, "Mirror Group Sale of Independent on Track for This Week," *Dow Jones News Service,* March 9, 1998.

O'Connor, Robert, "British Papers' Purchase Ruled Not a Monopoly," *Editor & Publisher,* April 30, 1994, pp. 30–31.

"Pressing Ahead in the North," *Marketing,* February 21, 1991, p. 29.

Snoddy, Raymond, "Maxwell—the Legacy: Media Interests Flourish Under New Ownership," *Financial Times,* January 20, 1996, p. 5.

Sorkin, Andrew Ross, "Merger in Britain Creates Largest Publisher," *New York Times,* July 31, 1999, p. C2.

"Thomson in Deal to Sell 5 Newspapers in Britain," *New York Times,* July 11, 1997, p. D5.

"Trinity Mirror Acquiring Southnews plc," *Marketing,* November 2, 2000, p. 11.

"Trinity Mirror Claims Nationals' Ad Sales Plummet," *Media Business,* December 17, 2001, p. 15.

"Trinity Mirror Digital Unveils 'ic'-Branded Showbiz Site," *Marketing Week,* December 14, 2000, p. 15.

"U.K. Newspaper Publisher Plans £25 Million Boost for Flagship Titles," *Evening Standard,* February 28, 2002.

"U.K.'s Mirror Group Offers $502.1 Million for Midland Newspapers," *Dow Jones Online News,* July 4, 1997.

—Jonathan Martin
—updates: A. Woodward, Susan Windisch Brown

Triple Five Group Ltd.

Canadian Executive Offices
Suite 3000
8882-170 Street
Edmonton, Alberta T5T 4M2
Canada
Telephone: (780) 444-8100
Fax: (780) 444-5232
Web site: http://www.triplefive.com

U.S.A. Executive Offices
9510 West Sahara
Las Vegas, Nevada 89117
U.S.A.
Telephone: (702) 242-6937
Fax: (702) 242-6941

Private Company
Founded: 1965 as Germez Developments
Employees: 1,400
NAIC: 233110 Land Subdivision and Land Development;
    551112 Offices of Other Holding Companies

Triple Five Group Ltd. of Edmonton, Alberta, Canada, is most widely recognized as the owner of the world's largest mega-mall, recreation, and amusement complex—the West Edmonton Mall. The 5.2 million-square-foot mall is a mixed-use, tourism, retail, and entertainment center that attracts more than 60 million visitors annually. Triple Five also has ownership in the Mall of America in Bloomington, Minnesota, the largest mall in the United States. Triple Five owns and operates several other shopping and entertainment complexes, hotels, and commercial, industrial, and residential properties throughout the United States and Canada. The private company is owned by the Ghermezian family, a large, close-knit orthodox Jewish family, who emigrated from Iran. The company web site lists Triple Five Group divisions in technology, venture capital, mining, real estate, and banking, in addition to the two mega-malls. The many arms of the business appear to overlap considerably. The technology division, for instance, offers "venture capital" for technology businesses such as multimedia, telecommunications, biotechnology, Internet, fiber optics, networking, e-commerce, and more. Triple Five also owns Peoples Trust, a federally regulated and chartered bank with several branches throughout Canada, and First Nuclear Corporation, which pursues growth in resource development and exploration.

From Rugs to Real Estate: 1920s–60s

The roots of Triple Five corporation began with family patriarch Jacob Ghermezian, who was just 17 years old in 1919 when he started the business in Iran. In the 1920s he erected what could later be seen as the small-scale model of his grandiose-scale mega-malls. It was a multi-use, retail-apartment-office-recreational complex in Tehran. Family history has it that in 1943 that complex hosted an historic meeting of Franklin Roosevelt, Winston Churchill, and Joseph Stalin, which resulted in a united action against the Nazis.

Ghermezian left Iran with his family in the late 1940s and settled in New York. His oldest sons later moved to Montreal for education at McGill University and to begin establishing a business there. The family business of importing Persian rugs was flourishing. By 1964 they owned 16 retail stores throughout the United States and Canada.

Between the 1950s and 1970s, these carpet importers transformed their business focus to real estate development. In 1965 Jacob Ghermezian established a real estate business, Germez Developments, which was later named Triple Five, to purchase land and resell it to builders in the Ottawa area. Two years later Jacob and the oldest of his four sons moved to Edmonton and began purchasing land there, beginning with a hotel and other properties. Thanks to the region's oil boom in the 1970s, the Ghermezians' real estate investments prospered. Eventually the entire family moved to Edmonton—Jacob's four sons Raphael, Eskander, Nader, and Bahman and their families. In addition to two hotels and the Northtown Mall in Edmonton, they opened several boutiques in major cities throughout Canada and the United States and developed more shopping centers, office buildings, and residential communities.

Company Perspectives:

Together we are committed to providing an exceptional entertainment and shopping experience in a safe and friendly environment.

According to author Peter C. Newman in his 1998 book *Titans,* ''Their flagship Triple Five Corp. was formed with the backing of 551 silent partners, Iranians who needed a secret conduit to reinvest their wealth in order to avoid Iran's notoriously capricious habit of retroactive taxation.'' The actual founding date is unclear, as is the meaning of the name Triple Five. A 20th anniversary publication of the West Edmonton Mall offers this guess as an explanation: Triple Five is the ''business of three countries, plus the sum of four brothers and a father.'' The true meaning, however, remains a mystery.

The Making of the First Mega-Mall: 1979–85

The Ghermezians' early real estate investments paid off. In 1979 Canada's provincial government purchased undeveloped land from Triple Five, giving the family a reported $18 million profit, which they used to finance their dream of building Canada's largest shopping center, the West Edmonton Mall. They had been lobbying the local government for concessions and trying to maneuver several obstacles to build the planned 225-store mall. They were successful in getting tax concessions, rezoning, and land purchase deals to secure enough acreage to build the mall.

Phase I of the West Edmonton Mall opened in July 1981. The 1.1 million-square-foot facility offered 220 stores and services and was modeled after a typical Persian bazaar serving as a hub at the center of town. The mall reportedly cost Triple Five about $200 million to build. The new mall was a success, grossing $113 million in revenues the first year. Phase II followed in September 1983. It increased the Mall's size by 1.13 million square feet and included an ice skating rink, amusement park, and another 240 shops and services. A full-scale replica of Bourbon Street in New Orleans was another popular feature of Phase II. Phase II cost the Ghermezians another $250 million.

But that was not enough to fulfill the grand dreams of Triple Five's owners. After months of debate with local officials over Phase III, the Ghermezians were eventually successful at negotiating the plans with a $20 million concession package. Phase III featured a water park, submarine ride, dolphin tank, golf course, and hotel. The brothers bolstered their lobbying efforts by promising to donate all profits from the amusement park to local charities. They also pledged to build a $600 million shopping and office complex in downtown Edmonton, with an Eaton's department store as the primary anchor. They were, however, demanding massive tax concessions from the local government, which were narrowly approved. The government later granted Triple Five $30 million worth of tax and parking concessions to build the Eaton Center Mall. Phase III of the West Edmonton Mall opened in September 1985. The mall had grown to 5.2 million square feet, occupying a total of 120 acres.

1985: Opening of People's Trust Company

In the midst of all the mall development, Triple Five announced plans in 1985 to open a trust company called People's Trust Company. The first branch was located in the West Edmonton Mall, and the bank eventually spread across Canada. At the time of the trust opening, Triple Five Managing Director Nader Ghermezian hinted that Triple Five might some day become a publicly traded corporation.

In 1986 Triple Five completed the Fantasyland luxury hotel, which was attached to the West Edmonton Mall's phase III arm. The Fantasyland Hotel, with 350 rooms, offered guests executive-style guest rooms or ''fantasy'' suites featuring decorative themes of different countries, time periods, and interests, such as Roman, Arabian, Polynesian, and Eskimo rooms.

By the mid-1980s the West Edmonton Mall boasted visitor statistics exceeding the number of tourists visiting nearby Banff National Park. The mall's estimated economic impact annually in the province was $1.2 billion. Despite the West Edmonton Mall's notoriety as the site of the planet's largest mall, parking lot, indoor wave pool, indoor lake, and world-record status amusement park and roller coaster, the $700 million mall was straining company finances. The company issued a $400 million bond offer, Canada's largest to date, which was unsuccessful in attracting investors. The bond offer was withdrawn as the province was in recession. Triple Five eventually negotiated with the banks for a $450 million loan refinance package.

The process of making the Edmonton mega-mall a reality created and reinforced the mystique of the very private Ghermezian family. The brothers gained a public reputation as big dreamers, shrewd salesmen, extremely aggressive businessmen, and relentless and obviously successful lobbyists for government concessions. It was no surprise, then, that they took that formula on the road.

1986–92: Selling the Mega-Mall Model

Not ones to rest on their laurels, the Ghermezians were busy hatching dreams of mega-retail centers in other communities. In 1986 they were chosen to develop the Mall of America in Bloomington, a suburb of Minneapolis, Minnesota. It would be the largest indoor mall in the United States with more than 200 specialty stores, an amusement park, and convention center (which was later dropped from the proposal). The mall would be built on the vacant site of the former Metropolitan Stadium, where Minnesota's professional baseball and football teams once played. Bloomingdale's and Nordstrom (which had no Minnesota presence at that time) agreed to be anchor stores.

But the road to building the mall was not a smooth one, and the Ghermezians had to work hard to make all the pieces fit. Triple Five leaders lobbied state and local officials doggedly for direct subsidies and tax breaks. The city of Bloomington granted Triple Five $60 million in municipal aid and concessions to build there. Minnesota legislators, however, rejected providing any operating subsidies to the developers and reduced the size of the initial development proposal. They did, however, authorize use of funds for improvements on and around the mall site.

Despite the state and local aid, Triple Five had difficulty securing all of the necessary financing for the Mall of America.

Key Dates:

1917: Jacob Ghermezian establishes his own business in Iran.

1920: Ghermezian erects his first multi-use facility in Tehran.

1940s: Jacob Ghermezian moves to the United States with his family.

1959: Ghermezian relocates to Edmonton, Alberta, Canada.

1965: Ghermezian establishes a real estate development focus with Germez Developments (later named Triple Five).

1981: Triple Five Group opens Phase I of West Edmonton Mall, followed by Phase II in 1983 and Phase III in 1985.

1989: Triple Five breaks ground for the Mall of America.

1992: The Mall of America opens in Bloomington, Minnesota; Ghermezian family is awarded the Great Canadian Order of Canada Award.

2001: West Edmonton Mall records its best year ever.

Finally in November 1987 Triple Five Group announced that it had partnered with American retail developer Melvin Simon and Associates of Indianapolis and with Teachers Insurance and Annuity Association (TIAA) to finance the project. Triple Five and Simon each held 22.5 ownership, and TIAA held the majority 55 percent share. Simon was given management control of the mall. The price tag of the 4.2 million-square-foot Mall of America was estimated at $600 million. They broke ground in Bloomington in 1989. Completion was expected in 1992.

While the Mall of America was being developed, the Ghermezians also floated proposals to build mega-mall entertainment complexes in upstate New York and Toronto, apparently pitting the New York and Canadian officials at odds for the project. For these proposals the Ghermezians were asking for tax concessions, reduced price of government-owned properties, and commitments from local public officials to create utility services and new roads to the shopping centers. Despite Triple Five's aggressive, persistent lobbying and sales pitches, its proposals for building additional mega-malls in England, Moscow, Germany, and even Beijing encountered roadblocks, as did the plans for New York, Ontario, and California. Rumors began circulating about the developer having tax problems related to the expensive West Edmonton Mall.

In 1992 Mall of America opened with fanfare and crowds of shoppers. Also that year the Ghermezians, particularly father Jacob, were honored for their contributions in development and other community-building projects throughout western Canada. The Governor General of Canada presented them with the Great Canadian Order of Canada Award.

1994–96: Financial Questions and Silver Spring Proposal

Talk of the West Edmonton Mall's financial problems tainted the company's positive public relations. The mall was reportedly $9 million in arrears for property tax payments, as high debt payments decreased Triple Five's cash flow. In 1994, the company apparently defaulted on $450 million worth of loans on the West Edmonton Mall. In addition, the store vacancy rate was growing as several mall tenants left. Evidently the company had difficulty finding another lender when their bank, Royal Trust, failed. Alternative refinancing was eventually secured. During this time Triple Five sold several real estate holdings in Edmonton to offset the lack of mall profits, selling a handful of retail, hotel, and housing complexes in Edmonton.

Triple Five continued pursuing leads for erecting mega-malls, giving its pitch a theme of urban renewal in Silver Spring, Maryland. Billed in part to revitalize an economically precarious downtown area, Triple Five proposed building a two million-square-foot retail and entertainment complex—the American Dream Mall. With an estimated cost of $600 million, this mall would include a skating rink, indoor amusement park, indoor wave pool, more than 20 movie theaters, and a 500-room hotel.

Again the Ghermezian brothers pushed hard with their sales and lobbying efforts to make the American Dream Mall a reality. Critics of the Silver Spring project publicly raised questions about the company's financial stability, particularly the recent loan default. Company officials admitted that they were in "technical default" on the loan, but said the problem was due to the bankruptcy of their primary lender, and added that they were able to refinance with another bank at a lower interest rate. Triple Five's PR image in Silver Spring improved somewhat, when in November 1995 an independent consultant's report gave the company's finances a positive report, indicating that their main asset, the West Edmonton Mall, was financially healthy.

Planning on the American Dream Mall moved ahead and evolved to include a multimedia educational facility, sports club, and wellness center. The local 46-member advisory board approved the project in early 1996, requesting the addition of a performing arts center and mini-golf course. Although the local community was still divided on the project, Triple Five explored using either taxable or tax-exempt bonds backed by project revenues to cover approximately half the costs. The project was later postponed and then canceled in late 1996 due to lack of private sector investors to help finance the project.

1998: West Edmonton Mall Beginning a Turnaround

Despite the failure of the once promising Silver Spring project, financial troubles of the West Edmonton Mall had begun to turn around, improving the overall health and stability of the company. The mall got a makeover of sorts, with Triple Five investing $18.3 million in renovations and maintenance and giving it a smaller retail focus. The Ghermezians reduced retail presence at the mall from 80 to 60 percent and created more round-the-clock uses for the mall, primarily through entertainment venues. Entertainment additions included a bowling alley and the Palace Casino with slot machines, poker games, and blackjack tables. Although available retail space was less, the overall store vacancy rate declined to just 3 percent.

In 1998 Triple Five completed Phase IV of the mall, bringing total square feet to 5.3 million. Phase IV offered an IMAX theater, more restaurants and specialty stores, and mega-versions of traditionally smaller stores.

In the late 1990s Triple Five pursued smaller development projects in other cities such as Las Vegas and Phoenix. These were large retail-focused projects, not mega-malls. Triple Five's development firm in Nevada opened a large retail center in Las Vegas with an 18-screen movie theater, restaurants, a hotel, a public library, and a fine arts museum. Another Triple Five Nevada development, called Peccole Town Center, featured high-priced boutiques, professional offices, restaurants, art galleries, and an outdoor amphitheater. Triple Five officials continued to spread novel mall concepts throughout the United States. In Mesa, Arizona, they proposed a $200 million trendy urban village where people could live, work, shop, and find plenty of entertainment opportunities.

1998–2001: On Both Sides of Legal Disputes

In 1998 The Ghermezians were served a lawsuit by the Alberta Treasury Branch (owned by the province) alleging that the family bribed a former bank official to obtain a loan when the West Edmonton Mall was financially struggling. The suit contended the former bank superintendent received money from the Ghermezians after he approved a controversial $300 million refinancing package in 1994. The Ghermezians and the former superintendent countersued and denied any wrongdoing.

Meanwhile in Minnesota, Triple Five found itself on the initiating end of a lawsuit, this time with Mall of America business partner Simon Property Group. Their suit accused Simon Property and related businesses of secretly negotiating a deal to obtain majority ownership of the Mall of America to keep Triple Five from future potential profits. Apparently, TIAA sold 27.5 percent of its share in the property to Simon without the Ghermezians' knowledge, giving Simon majority ownership of the Mall of America. By mid-2002, neither the Alberta or Minnesota lawsuit had been resolved.

2001 and Beyond: The Future of the Malls and Triple Five Looking Bright

Despite the court battle with Simon Properties, the companies continued to pursue developing phase II of the Mall of America, which was still in the early planning stages. Despite skepticism by many Minnesotans, the mega-mall, which was made a reality by Triple Five, had been an unquestionable success. In less than ten years it became the nation's most popular tourist attraction with more annual visitors (an estimated 42.5 million) than Disney World, Graceland, and the Grand Canyon attracted together. An economic impact report on the Mall indicated that it attracted more than 2.5 million international visitors annually and resulted in $1.4 billion of positive economic impact for the state. Twin Cities business spinoffs from the mall increased sales tax revenues and helped create an estimated 10,000 new jobs in the area.

The West Edmonton Mall also was thriving. The mall recorded its best year ever in 2001, setting new records for sales, revenue, and visitor traffic, with the lowest vacancy rate in its history. The mall's performance was aided by the fact that Alberta boasted North America's lowest unemployment rate.

Although most of North America was experiencing a recession, northern Alberta's oil resources were driving its healthy economy. Triple Five also had plans to continue the growth of the West Edmonton Mall property, hoping to add stadiums, a professional office tower, an adult living residence, and another hotel.

At the beginning of the 21st century Triple Five's corporate offices were located in the West Edmonton Mall. The company had satellite offices in California, Washington, Colorado, Minnesota, Arizona, Nevada, New York, and Florida, working on a variety of development projects. Hotels were common development projects, but to own a string of cookie-cutter hotel properties would be contrary to the innovative Ghermezian spirit. Triple Five's hotels, often constructed along with shopping and entertainment facilities, were designed to complement specific market opportunities and needs, such as an all-suite hotel, convention facility, or apartment hotel.

Triple Five's Peoples Trust Bank, a federally regulated and government CDIC insured chartered trust company, had offices in Vancouver, Calgary, Victoria, Edmonton, and Toronto. Peoples Trust provided investment and lending services, estate and trust asset management, and mortgage servicing, plus other banking services, and had in excess of $1 billion of assets directly held or under management.

Although founder Jacob Ghermezian died in January 2000 at the age of 97, his sons continued doing business in the "outside the box" spirit with which their father founded the company. The West Edmonton Mall's 20th Anniversary celebration booklet described Jacob as "a visionary, the quintessential cross between dreamer and businessman. And the existence of the Mall is a testament to his uncanny ability to marry the fantastic and the whimsical with community spirit and an eye on the bottom line." No doubt the Ghermezian brothers would (as the anniversary booklet promised) "continue to entertain ideas about businesses that will take them beyond the common and into the extraordinary."

Principal Subsidiaries

Triam Development Corporation; Triple Five Nevada Development Corporation; Triple Five National Development Corporation; Triple Five Florida Development Corporation; First Nuclear Corporation; Peoples Trust of Canada; West Edmonton Mall Property Inc.

Principal Divisions

West Edmonton Mall and Mall of America; Technology; Resource Development and Mining; Venture Capital; Real Estate Division; Finance and Banking.

Principal Competitors

General Growth Properties; The Rouse Company; Simon Property Group, Inc.

Further Reading

"American Dream Mall: Breaking the Mold for Urban Renewal," *Stores*, May 1996, pp. 60–61.

Carlisle, Tamsin, "Canadian Mall Hit with Creditor Suit Over Receivership," *Wall Street Journal,* August 27, 1998.

——, "Property Report: Gamble by the World's Biggest Mall Pays Off," *Wall Street Journal,* March 7, 1997, p. B1.

Denton, Herbert, "Invasion of the Mammoth Shopping Malls; Creators of Edmonton Center Seek to Build Replicas in Minnesota, Upstate New York," *Washington Post,* August 10, 1986, p. K7.

Finkel, David, "Mall Is Beautiful," *Washington Post,* December 10, 1995, p. W16.

"Ghermezians and Triple Five Reveal Plans to Open Trust Firm," *Toronto Star,* September 11, 1985, p. E3.

Henton, Darcy, "Mall Bankruptcy Probers Smell a Rat," *Montreal Gazette,* June 18, 2001, p. A9.

Hutchinson, Brian, "Trouble in Big Mall Country," *Canadian Business,* September 1994, p. 68.

Laucius, Joanne, "West Edmonton Mall a Family Legacy," *Ottawa Citizen,* January 4, 2000, p. A5.

"Mall Mogul Dies at 97," *Toronto Star,* January 4, 2000.

"The Mall of Dreams," *Economist,* May 4, 1996, p. 23.

Moore, Janet, "Ghermezian Brothers Are Still at It, Chasing Their Big Retail Dreams," *Minneapolis Star and Tribune,* August 4, 1997 p. 6A.

Moore, Janet, and Phelps, David, "Mega Brawl; A Lawsuit Over the Sale of a Stake in Bloomington's Mall of America," *Minneapolis Star and Tribune,* April 9, 2000, p. 1D.

Newman, Peter C., *Titans,* New York: Viking Press, 1998.

"Obituaries: Jacob Ghermezian; Built World's Largest Mall," *Los Angeles Times,* January 10, 2000.

Padgett, Mike, "Canadian Builder Plans Unique Mesa Destination," *Business Journal* (Phoenix), October 30, 1998, p. 4.

Pinney, Gregor W., and Randy Furst, "Two Bills Offer No Direct Aid to Mall," *Minneapolis Star and Tribune,* February 14, 1986, p. 1A.

Pressler, Margaret Webb, "Thinking Big: Brothers Propose a Mega-Mall in Silver Spring," *Washington Post,* September 4, 1995, p. 1.

Pressler, Margaret Webb, and Louis Aguilar, "Mall Builder's Finances Called Sound; Consultant's Report Boosts Supporters of Huge Silver Spring Complex," *Washington Post,* November 29, 1995, p. F01.

Queenan, Joe, "Will Wonders Never Cease?," *Forbes,* September 4, 1989, p. 72.

Resnick, Amy B., "Builder of Maryland Mall Complex Looks into Partial Bond Financing," *Bond Buyer,* October 22, 1996, p. 3.

——, "Plans for Maryland Mall Scrapped Due to Lack of Private Funds," *Bond Buyer,* November 13, 1996, p. 3.

—Mary Heer-Forsberg

Tsingtao Brewery Group

Tsingtao Beer Tower, 56 Dengzhou Road
Qingdao, Shandong 266071
China
Telephone: +86 (532) 571-1119
Fax: +86 (532) 571-4719
Web site: http://www.tsingtaobeer.com

Public Company
Incorporated: 1997
Employees: 5,200
Sales: $416.6 million (2000)
Stock Exchanges: OTC
Ticker Symbol: TSGTY
NAIC: 312120 Malt Beverages

Tsingtao Brewery Group is the parent of publicly traded Tsingtao Brewery Company Limited, which is renowned for its Tsingtao beer, the top-selling beer in China as well as that country's leading export beer. Tsingtao was part of the "China Nine," the first group of Chinese companies to sell stock on the public market in 1993. Tsingtao has been aggressively growing in recent years, acquiring companies and increasing its production output.

Early 1900s: British and German Roots

In 1903, the Qingdao Brewery Factory was founded by a group of businessmen from Great Britain and Germany. The process, equipment, and raw material were all German imports, but the local water in Qingdao, China, was the ingredient that made the beer distinctive. The spring water used in the recipe was from the mountain area of Laoshan. The beer was awarded a gold medal at the Munich International Exhibition in 1906.

Germany had been a presence in China since 1861, focusing on the Qingdao region specifically. In 1897, after the murder of two German missionaries, Germany began an official occupation of the Shangdong Province and Kiaochou peninsula, obtaining a 99-year lease in 1898. The area was then considered a colony and administered by the German navy.

1910s–80s: War and Foreign Control

The history of Tsingtao Brewery essentially paralleled the history of modern-day China. When China was occupied, so was the brewery. As China embraced Communism, so the brewery became a state-owned business. When China opened its doors, Tsingtao was one of the first products to be exported.

Japan, an Allied power in World War I, seized the city from Germany on November 7, 1914. Germany's presence in China was greatly depleted, and Germany lost all of its colonies at the end of the war. Then, in 1922, the city Qingdao as well as the Tsingtao brewery were absorbed into China. During World War II, the Japanese again took control, but then a few years after the war, China became a Communist country. The brewery then became a state-owned business.

Tsingtao was first exported in 1954, but it was in 1979, as China was opening its doors to the world, that Tsingtao became well known outside the country. The government in Beijing named Tsingtao the official export beer of China.

Early 1990s: New Tsingtao Leading the Way in Public Markets

Tsingtao Brewery Company Limited was formed in 1993 when the four breweries that produced the beer merged to form one company. The merger into one larger state-owned company preceded the historic listing of Tsingtao Brewery and eight other companies on the Hong Kong Stock Exchange. Prior to 1993, no Chinese companies had been publicly sold.

"Tsingtao Beer is China's most popular brand of beer and is regarded by foreign beer drinkers as one of China's best products," said Zhang Yadong, chairman of the newly formed company in the *South China Morning Post*, June 15, 1993. "It is a frequent award-winner in overseas beer competitions such as in the United States and Belgium."

The Hong Kong exchange rules stipulated that at least 25 percent of each company be offered when the "China Nine," as they were identified, went public. Tsingtao issued 317.6 million H shares at $2.80 per share and raised HK$900 million. In July

1993, Tsingtao became the first of the nine Chinese state-owned companies to list on the Hong Kong Stock Exchange. After the stock sale, the Qingdao State-Owned Asset Bureau owned 44 percent of Tsingtao, the Bank of China and other People's Republic parties owned 10 percent, and another 35 percent was owned publicly, including 5 percent purchased by the U.S. company Anheuser-Busch in the initial public offering.

Investors were attracted to the Tsingtao stock because, of the nine companies, Tsingtao had the most recognizable name outside of China and because Tsingtao was considered to have high growth potential. Per capita beer consumption was low in China compared with other companies, but with a population of 1.2 billion people, the Chinese market was identified as one of the largest beer markets in the world, with the potential to become even larger. While some analysts had predicted a tremendous oversubscription for the stock offer, the reality was a modest oversubscription. The stock opened at 27 percent higher than the public offering price.

Controversy soon surrounded the newly listed stock as Tsingtao refused to announce interim results for the first half of 1993. The Hong Kong exchange responded by acknowledging that Tsingtao was not obligated to release the results for the first interim but would be required to publish full disclosure of results for the end of the year. The company cited ''administrative reasons'' for the failure to announce results. Both investors and analysts were disappointed by the company's decision. Tsingtao assured those concerned that future results would be published promptly and that it would meet the profit forecast for the full year.

Tsingtao met those forecasts when it announced a jump in profits for 1993. Profits were up 316.2 percent to HK$168.7 million. ''The board of directors is pleased with the results and the company's achievements throughout the year,'' said Zhang Yadong, chairman of Tsingtao in the April 28, 1994 issue of the *South China Morning Post*.

Despite the fact that Tsingtao fulfilled its profit expectations, its refusal to release interim results in the months after it became public prompted a change in the listing rules on the Hong Kong Stock Exchange. As of June 1, 1994, newly listed companies were required to issue interim results for the first period after becoming listed on the exchange.

In July 1994, Zhang Yadong, the chairman of Tsingtao, resigned as chairman and general manager but retained his position as the Communist Party committee secretary at Tsingtao. ''He worked diligently and seriously and made im-

portant contributions in the reorganization of the company into a joint stock company, in introducing the company to the international community, in raising capital from local and foreign sources and in the overall planning design of the company,'' announced company secretaries Yan Wen-ming and Cheung Yuk-tong in the July 26, 1994 issue of the *South China Morning Post*. Tsingtao announced that Liu Deyuan would become chairman while Shao Ruiqi was named general manager. Liu had been a director of the company, and Shao had worked in the management area of Tsingtao.

Despite rising costs for raw materials, results for the first half of 1994 showed a profit due to an increase in sales to overseas markets. The company announced that the cost for raw materials had increased by 15 to 20 percent. The company won a court award in 1994 when it sued a competitor over brand-name copyright infringement. The competitor, Ming Zhu Brewery, was ordered to pay 1.09 million yuan in damages to Tsingtao. Also, the company announced that sales in the European market had increased 31 percent. In October 1994, Tsingtao expanded production by purchasing the Yangzhou Brewery in Jiangsu province for 80 million yuan (HK$72 million).

1995 to 2000: Growing Pains for Tsingtao

Anheuser-Busch Companies, owner of 5 percent of Tsingtao, purchased 80 percent of another Chinese brewer, Zhongde Brewery in Wuhuan, in 1995 and announced that it was interested in increasing its investment in Tsingtao as well. The announcement resulted in a 13.1 percent increase in the share price of Tsingtao. Tsingtao was enthusiastic about the proposed increase in investment by Anheuser-Busch.

However, soon the company was being questioned about its practice of lending money to third-party businesses. According to an April 9, 1995 article in the *South China Morning Post*, the company had been lending funds raised from its stock shares to ''just about anyone who needs it.'' Analysts had alleged that Tsingtao was now short of expansion funds because of overextending its lending business. The company responded by announcing that only surplus working capital was being used as short-term loans. Tsingtao requested that sale of its stock be suspended for a day amid the controversy and attempted to assure investors that the loans were not a risk to the company's future. The loans, stated Tsingtao, were secured and guaranteed by the Shandong branch of the Bank of China. Despite the assurances from the company, the existence of the loans left Tsingtao with a shortfall of 1.3 billion yuan for announced expansion plans and an uncertainty of how that money would be raised.

The controversy, combined with a 42 percent drop in profits, caused stock prices to fall and questions to rise about Tsingtao and its business practices. The company abruptly changed its plans to expand existing production facilities and instead presented a strategy for building new plants. Tsingtao's goal, to increase production by 400 percent by the year 2000, was planned to keep up with the projected growth in the domestic beer market and increase the brewery's share of the Chinese market from a little over 2 percent to 10 percent. In spite of only having 2.2 percent of the fragmented market, Tsingtao was the largest of the 800 Chinese breweries.

Key Dates:

1903: German and English businessmen found Tsingtao Brewery.
1914: Japan seizes Tsingtao Brewery.
1922: Tsingtao again becomes a Chinese company.
1949: Communists take control of China.
1954: Tsingtao exports beer.
1979: Beijing names Tsingtao official export beer of China.
1993: Tsingtao Brewery Company Limited is formed; Tsingtao offers IPO on Hong Kong Stock Exchange.
1994: Zhang Yadong retires as chairman, replaced by Liu Deyuan.
1996: Li Guirong becomes chairman after company reorganization.
1997: Tsingtao is restructured as a holding company.
1999: Tsingtao produces over one million tons of beer.
2000: China joins the World Trade Organization.

A December 7, 1995 article in the *New York Times* highlighted several problems facing Tsingtao. In addition to the questionable loans granted by Tsingtao to other businesses, the article stated that the negotiations between Anheuser-Busch and Tsingtao had stalled because Anheuser-Busch, a U.S. company, was disappointed in Tsingtao's performance and unsure about Tsingtao's ability to expand its market share. Foreign markets made up only 10 percent of Tsingtao's sales, and the company refused to advertise to boost sales. A distributor quoted in the article stated, ''They're amazingly arrogant. They say, 'We're Tsingtao, we don't need to advertise.' It's so ridiculous. Even Coca-Cola has to advertise.''

Another decline was reported for 1995, with profits falling 9.59 percent. Production and sales continued to rise, but the company noted that the cost of raw materials had again increased. Foreign competition from labels such as Foster's, Carlsberg, and San Miguel kept Tsingtao from gaining more than a few tenths of a percentage in market share. Talks between Anheuser-Busch and Tsingtao were officially ended in 1996, and Anheuser-Busch aligned with one of Tsingtao's rivals while planning to begin selling Budweiser beer in China. Budweiser's name is Bai Wie Pijiu in China.

As the possibility of obtaining expansion money from foreign investors faded, Tsingtao looked to the government and the People's Bank of China for a loan of 100 million yuan. Other changes at the company included the retirement of Chairman Liu Deyuan and the assignment of Vice-Chairman Shao Ruiqi to a government post, along with former Chairman Zhang Yadong. Li Guirong was appointed as the chairman of the company in 1996.

By 1997, China was forecasted to become the world's biggest beer market, overtaking the U.S. market by the year 2000. However, the forecast did not soften the blow for Tsingtao as it announced a net profit loss in 1996 of 73.7 percent. The company announced that the 1996 figures were

attributable to the switch in strategy and leadership that happened during July of that year. Despite the profit loss announced in April, Tsingtao moved forward with its expansion plans to purchase more breweries in the last half of 1997.

Purchases of Nanjizhou Brewery Group, Rongcheng Brewery, Anqui Brewery, Maanshan Brewery, and Huangshi Brewery were completed in the first half of 1997. They helped expand Tsingtao's production capacity by 200,000 tons. In 1997, Tsingtao seized 8 percent of the domestic market to secure its leading brewer status. In July 1997, Tsingtao restructured its organization by establishing a holding company backed by the Shandong provincial government.

In early 1999, Tsingtao again went to battle over its trademark and filed a lawsuit against China Beer (Hong Kong). China Beer had been Tsingtao's distributor in Hong Kong, but after January 1999, Tsingtao switched to Tsingtao Beverage (Hong Kong) Co., Ltd. for its Hong Kong distribution. China Beer's aggressive advertising campaign hindered Tsingtao's distributor change. In August, Tsingtao won the lawsuit and reclaimed use of its trademark.

A 1998 increase in profits was announced in April 1999. Profits increased 34.8 percent and annual beer production rose as well. In September 1999, Tsingtao acquired the assets of Shanghai Brewery Co., Ltd. to further expand production. The acquisition was part of an 80 percent production increase for 1999 that resulted in over one million tons of beer production, a company record.

2000 and Beyond: WTO Further Opening World for Tsingtao

In 2000, China joined the World Trade Organization and agreed to eliminate tariffs and trade barriers that had provided protection for the government-owned companies in the Communist country. While some Chinese companies feared the foreign competition, Tsingtao had been competing in the world market for decades. The company was ready for the transition and had made many changes since its 1993 IPO. The company implemented increased advertising and promotions as well as strict reporting to stockholders and analysts in response to the lessons learned since 1993. ''Some industries are afraid of foreign competition. Competing with foreign brands, we learned how markets worked,'' said Peng Zuo Yi, Chief Executive of Tsingtao in a January 18, 2000 article in *USA Today*.

Tsingtao continued its aggressive brewery acquisitions and purchased Carlsberg Hong Kong, Asia Shuang He Sheng Five Star Beer Co., Ltd., Three Ring Asia Pacific Beer Co., Ltd., and New Laoshan Brewery. The company's 2000 results included a net profit increase of 52 percent. In 2001, Tsingtao chairman Li Guirong announced that the company would be continuing to increase production but that the major acquisitions had been completed. The new goals of the company, he announced, would be to further increase production quantities and to raise Tsingtao's share of the domestic market from 10.7 percent to 15 percent by 2004. Profits for 2001 increased 31 percent, and Tsingtao increased its share of the Chinese market to 11 percent.

As Tsingtao Brewery entered the first years of the 21st century, it was poised to build on the successes and lessons of a century of company history. The company worked to increase and seize market share, realizing its opportunity in the high growth potential of its own country as well as abroad.

Principal Subsidiaries

Tsingtao Brewery Company Limited.

Principal Competitors

Anheuser-Busch Company, Inc.; Yanjing; CBR Brewing.

Further Reading

Alexander, Garth, "China Issue Sparks Anger," *Sunday Times*, October 31, 1993.

Beveridge, Dirk, "War in Hong Kong Over Tsingtao Beer Has Both Sides Frothing," *Pittsburgh Post-Gazette*, January 14, 1999, p. F6.

"Big Thirst for Hong Kong's First Chinese Share Offer," *Independent (London)*, July 6, 1993, p. 27.

Carey, Christopher, "Busch Buys into Chinese Brewery," *St. Louis Post-Dispatch*, June 29, 1993, p. 6B.

Chan, Christine, "Tsingtao Brewery Outlines Detailed Strategy for Hong Kong Listing," *South China Morning Post*, June 16, 1993, p. B2.

——, "Tsingtao Bubbles with 316pc Leap in Results," *South China Morning Post*, April 28, 1994, p. B1.

——, "Tsingtao Profit Falls 49pc, High Costs and Rivalry Knock Back Brewer's Interim Gains," *South China Morning Post*, August 29, 1995, p. B1.

——, "Tsingtao Public Offer Subscribed 111 Times," *South China Morning Post*, July 8, 1993, p. B3.

Chan, Christine, and Carrie Lee, "Tsingtao Set to Lead China Nine with $900m Issue," *South China Morning Post*, June 26, 1993, p. B1.

Chapel, Chris, "Beer Offer Spilling Over," *South China Morning Post*, July 1, 1993, p. B20.

——, "Tsingtao to Smash Listing Records," *South China Morning Post*, July 1, 1993, p. B1.

"China Brewery to List in Colony," *Nikkei Weekly*, July 5, 1993, p. 24.

Clifford, Mark L., "It's Enough to Make You Drink," *Business Week*, September 29, 1997, p. 124.

"Corporate Revamp at Tsingtao," *South China Morning Post*, June 15, 1993, p. B2.

Cramb, Gordon, "China's Drinkers Head for Top of World Beer League," *Financial Times (London)*, February 11, 1997, p. 4.

Davies, Simon, and Nikki Tait, "Anheuser-Busch Takes Five Percent Stake in Chinese Brewer," *Financial Times (London)*, June 29, 1993, p.26.

Doebele, Justin, "Bear in the China Shop," *Forbes Magazine*, May 5, 1997, p. 18.

Evans, Mark, "Brewers Thirst for Vast Profits," *South China Morning Post*, July 2, 1993, p. B5.

——, "Law Laid Down on Interim Results," *South China Morning Post*, May 26, 1994, p. B3.

Faison, Seth, "A Long March to Capitalism," *New York Times*, December 27, 1995, p. D1.

Fluendy, Simon, "Beer Giants in a Froth Over China," *South China Morning Post*, September 15, 1994, p. B6.

Fung, Noel, "Tsingtao Decision Draws Fire," *South China Morning Post*, October 26, 1993, p. B1.

——, "Tsingtao Response 'Surprisingly' Quiet," *South China Morning Post*, July 3, 1993, p. B1.

Harding, James, "Changes Afoot at Tsingtao," *Financial Times (London)*, September 9, 1997, p. 29.

——, "Cuts Strengthen Tsingtao Results," *Financial Times (London)*, August 22, 1997, p. 21.

Heath, Ray, "Super Dry on Data," *South China Morning Post*, October 26, 1993, p. B18.

Hewett, Gareth, "Speaking Out Will Help Bring More Tsingtaos," *South China Morning Post*, July 16, 1993, p. B14.

——, "Tsingtao Listing Brings Cheer to the Exchange," *South China Morning Post*, July 16, 1993, p. B1.

Holberton, Simon, "Blue Chip Offers from Beijing: The First Chinese Companies to Be Partially Sold in Hong Kong," *Financial Times (London)*, June 18, 1993, p. 14.

——, "Business and the Law: Solutions to Chinese Puzzle—The Challenges Posed By Listing Mainland Companies on Hong Kong's Stock Exchange," *Financial Times (London)*, July 13, 1993, p. 12.

——, "Rush to Buy Chinese Brewer's HK Offering," *Financial Times (London)*, July 8, 1993, p. 34.

Holberton, Simon, and Louise Lucas, "Chinese Stocks Lose Their Shine—Caution Is the Watchword," *Financial Times (London)*, May 6, 1994, p. 30.

Ibison, David, "Anheuser Deal Could Still Leave Tsingtao Short of Cash," *South China Morning Post*, April 30, 1995, p. 1.

——, "Hangover Feeling at Tsingtao," *South China Morning Post*, April 16, 1995, p. 3.

——, "Tsingtao Mystery Loans to Come Under Scrutiny," *South China Morning Post*, April 9, 1995, p. 1.

"Investors Souring on Actions of China's Tsingtao Beer Managers," *Los Angeles Times*, May 19, 1995, p. D7.

Janofsky, Michael, "Anheuser-Busch Buys Stake in Leading Chinese Brewer," *New York Times*, June 29, 1993, p. D6.

Johnson, Ian, "China's Tantalizing Stocks," *Baltimore Sun*, January 24, 1994, p. 11C.

Ko, Kenneth, "Tsingtao Defends Decision on Interim Results," *South China Morning Post*, October 29, 1993, p. B3.

Lai, Renee, "Beijing Is Encouraging Larger Beer Producers to Fend Off Competition from International Rivals; Brewers Turn Their Backs on Foreigners," *South China Morning Post*, September 12, 1996, p. 8.

——, "Financial Set Lose Taste for Tsingtao," *South China Morning Post*, April 27, 1995, p. 28.

——, "Foreigners' Taste for Tsingtao Helps Beat Rising Cost of Raw Materials," *South China Morning Post*, August 18, 1994, p. B1.

——, "Tsingtao Acquiring Breweries to Plug Shortfall," *South China Morning Post*, May 2, 1995, p. 3.

——, "Tsingtao Asks Partner to Fund New Brewery," *South China Morning Post*, August 20, 1996, p. B2.

——, "Tsingtao in Move for Loans of $93m," *South China Morning Post*, July 11, 1996, p. B4.

——, "Tsingtao Pauses Before Next Round of Buying," *South China Morning Post*, August 28, 1996, p. B3.

——, "Tsingtao Poised to Swallow Two Breweries in Shandong," *South China Morning Post*, November 5, 1997, p. 3.

——, "Tsingtao Sees Earnings Dip As Costs Squeeze Profit Margins," *South China Morning Post*, April 17, 1996, p. 1.

——, "Tsingtao Takes on the Challenges," *South China Morning Post*, May 2, 1995, p. 22.

——, "Yuan Unification Drains Tsingtao," *South China Morning Post*, August 24, 1994, p. B1.

Lee, Carrie, "Tsingtao Chairman Decides His Cup Has Overflowed," *South China Morning Post*, July 26, 1994, p. B1.

Lee, Teresa, "Tsingtao Will Stick to Its Buying Line," *Hong Kong Standard*, August 25, 1999.

Linn, Gene, " 'China Nine' Likely to Spur Hong Kong Stock Exchange," *Journal of Commerce*, August 31, 1993, p. 11A.

Lucas, Louise, "Companies and Finance: Asia-Pacific: Higher Costs Drag Tsingtao to Surprise 9.6 Percent Fall," *Financial Times(London)*, April 17, 1996, p. 37.

——, "Provisions Hit Chinese Brewery," *Financial Times (London)*, April 21, 1998, p. 36.

——, "Tsingtao Brewery Ahead," *Financial Times (London)*, August 23, 1996, p. 20.

——, "Tsingtao Tumbles 74 Percent in Full Year," *Financial Times (London)*, April 25, 1997, p. 30.

Manor, Robert, "Anheuser-Busch, Tsingtao Brewery Co., to Part Company," *St. Louis Post-Dispatch*, April 22, 1996.

McGregor, Richard, "Brewing War Leaves a Bitter Taste," *Financial Times (London)*, June 23, 2001, p. 18.

Poole, Teresa, "Hong Kong Exchange to Take First Sip of Tsingtao; Teresa Poole Reports on a Milestone in Chinese Reform," *Independent (London)*, June 29, 1993, p. 23.

Qi, Zhi, "Beer Market in China (2000)," China Economic Forum, Department of Botany, University of Wisconsin-Madison, October 23, 2000.

Reynolds, Nicholas, "Leap in Tsingtao Profit Expected," *South China Morning Post*, January 12, 1997, p. 7.

Ridding, John, "Tsingtao in Restructuring to Cut Costs," *Financial Times (London)*, July 11, 1997, p. 22.

Roberts, Dexter, and Alysha Webb, "China: Buying Binge," *Business Week*, January 29, 2001, p. 48.

Sawyer, John, "Busch May Build Brewery in China," *St. Louis Post-Dispatch*, December 8, 1993, p. 1C.

"Stock Offer of Chinese Brewery Is Oversubscribed," *New York Times*, July 8, 1993, p. D4.

Tong, Ivan, "Banking on a Familiar Face," *South China Morning Post*, June 19, 1993, p. B3.

——, "This Bud's for China," *South China Morning Post*, June 29, 1993, p. B16.

——, "Tsingtao Attracts Top U.S. Brewer," *South China Morning Post*, June 29, 1993, p. B1.

Tsang, Denise, "Cheung Set to Sell Brewery Stake; Yiu Wing Moves to Cultivate Stable Income Generator," *South China Morning Post*, July 29, 1996, p. B3.

"Tsingtao Buys Jiangsu Brewer," *South China Morning Post*, October 29, 1994, p. B5.

"Tsingtao's Champagne Debut with HK Suitors," *South China Morning Post*, July 1, 1993, p. B5.

Vines, Stephen, "Subscription for Tsingtao's HK Listing Lower Than Expected," *Business Times (Singapore)*, July 3, 1993, p. 1.

Walker, Tony, "Tsingtao Loses Much of Its Froth—Chinese Brewer Fails to Live up to Listing Promises," *Financial Times (London)*, August 29, 1995, p. 17.

Wiseman, Paul, "Chinese Beer Barrels up to the World's Bar; Tsingtao Learns to Compete in International Market," *USA Today*, January 18, 2000, p. 1B.

Wong, Kerry, "Key Sectors Braced for Bumpy Ride When China Joins WTO," *South China Morning Post*, February 5, 1995, p. 2.

Yau, Winston, "Tsingtao Takes Stakes in Four Breweries," *South China Morning Post*, November 15, 2001, p. B4.

——, "Tsingtao Targets Expansion Via Buyouts As Rivals Lift Presence," *South China Morning Post*, June 26, 2001, p. B3.

——, "Tsingtao to Grow by Consolidation," *South China Morning Post*, September 4, 2001, p. B2.

—Melissa Rigney Baxter

24/7 Real Media, Inc.

1250 Broadway
New York, New York 10001
U.S.A.
Telephone: (212) 231-7100
Fax: (212) 760-1774
Web site: http://www.247realmedia.com

Public Company
Incorporated: 1998 as 24/7 Media Inc.
Employees: 308
Sales: $52.4 million (2001)
Stock Exchanges: NASDAQ
Ticker Symbol: TFSM
NAIC: 541810 Advertising Agencies; 541840 Media
Representatives

Formed in early 1998 as 24/7 Media Inc., the company, renamed 24/7 Real Media, Inc., specializes in providing services to support Internet-enabled online advertising and marketing. A successful initial public offering (IPO) in August 1998 has enabled it to pursue a fairly aggressive acquisitions strategy. As spending on Internet advertising has grown, 24/7 Media's revenue has increased dramatically. It has expanded internationally and into related areas such as e-mail marketing and online promotions. When Internet ad spending slowed in the second half of 2000, 24/7 Media began to sell off some of its noncore businesses. It has refocused on its North American core businesses, which include ad serving technology, online media representation, integrated marketing solutions, e-mail list management and brokerage, online promotions, and search engine optimization. In October 2001 24/7 Media merged with Real Media, Inc. to form 24/7 Real Media. Although the company has yet to achieve profitability or a positive cash flow, it hopes to break even by the fourth quarter of 2002.

Pursuing Aggressive Growth Strategy in 1998

The formation of 24/7 Media Inc., a new media company that would provide interactive advertising solutions for Internet advertisers and publishers, was announced at the end of 1997 and completed in April 1998. 24/7 Media was created as the result of a merger between Petry Interactive, Inc., the former Katz Millennium Marketing, and Interactive Imaginations, Inc. Petry and Katz were formerly interactive divisions of major media advertising agencies, and Interactive Imaginations was the owner of the Commonwealth Network and an online marketing innovator. David J. Moore, CEO of Petry Interactive, was named CEO of 24/7 Media, while Jay Friesel, president and CEO of Katz Millennium Marketing, became executive vice-president of sales and administration. Interactive Imaginations' CEO Michael Paolucci joined 24/7 Media as a member of the board of directors.

24/7 Media began with an initial investment of $10 million from a variety of institutional investors. From its inception, 24/7 Media represented a large number of web sites that included an aggregation of smaller sites as well as prominent sites such as AT&T Worldnet, Columbia House, Comedy Central, Fox News, Reuters MoneyNet, AOL NetFind, Frommer's Travel Guide, Rolling Stone, Modern Bride, and Better Homes and Gardens Online.

In April 1998 24/7 Media added advanced e-commerce technology and an advanced advertising management system to its capabilities with the acquisition of Intelligent Interactions Corp. for $7.7 million. Intelligent Interactions' flagship product was 24/7 Connect, an advanced advertising management system that enabled advertisers and web sites to target and deliver ads to specific audience segments on the basis of demographic and lifestyle information. Its e-commerce product, dbCommerce, utilized database marketing techniques to deliver personalized promotions to distinct audience segments and individual customers. Following the acquisition, Intelligent Interactions' management team joined 24/7 Media. The company continued to operate independently from its headquarters in Alexandria, Virginia, while expanding its operations in New York City.

Pursuing an aggressive growth strategy, 24/7 Media acquired the CLIQNOW! Sales Group, the Internet advertising representative division of K2 Design, Inc., for $4 million in cash and stock. CLIQNOW! represented more than 75 web sites

Company Perspectives:

24/7 Real Media provides marketing and technology solutions to online marketers and publishers. Our products and services are designed to meet the needs of marketers and publishers in all new media.

and served some 75 million ad impressions per month through eight branded networks.

In August 1998 24/7 Media went public, offering 3.25 million shares at $14 per share. In January 1999 the company filed for an additional public offering of four million shares, of which two million were offered by existing stockholders. For 1998, 24/7 Media reported revenue of $19.9 million and a net loss of $24.7 million, compared to revenue of $3.1 million and a net loss of $5.3 million in 1997. By December 1998 the company was delivering an aggregate of approximately one billion ad impressions per month.

International Expansion, Entry into E-Mail Marketing, and Enhanced Domestic Services in the Late 1990s

Before the end of 1998 24/7 Media entered into a strategic partnership with Hong Kong-based China.com Corp. to introduce 24/7 Media to Asia. The 24/7 Media Network-Asia was launched in October 1998 and was operated by China.com.

24/7 Media further expanded its operations internationally in 1999 and 2000 through a series of acquisitions and strategic partnerships. In January 1999 the company launched 24/7 Media Europe through a strategic partnership with London-based InterAd Holdings Ltd., Europe's first international Internet advertising sales firm. Under the terms of the deal, which was valued at $4 million, 24/7 Media obtained a 60 percent interest in InterAd Holdings and its regionally incorporated offices throughout Europe. In exchange, 24/7 Media purchased the interest of a selling stockholder and provided the company's European operations with a significant investment. The 24/7 Media Europe Network initially consisted of 64 high-demand web sites represented by eight sales offices in seven European countries. In August 1999 24/7 Media Europe launched 24/7 Suomi, an ad sales network devoted to Finnish advertisers and web sites.

In mid-1999 24/7 Media acquired ClickThrough Interactive, a Toronto, Canada-based Internet advertising sales network. It was Canada's largest network and represented more than 65 premium Canadian web sites, including the Toronto Stock Exchange, Canada Newswire, and others.

With the launch of 24/7 Latino in October 1999, 24/7 Media became the first online ad sales company to open a network across the entire Latin American continent. 24/7 Latino began with offices in Mexico City, Sao Paulo, Buenos Aires, and Lima, with regional headquarters located in Miami.

24/7 Media's entry into e-mail marketing began with the acquisition in March 1999 of Sift, Inc. for $22 million in stock. Sift was a full-service provider of e-mail direct marketing ser-

vices, including an e-mail distribution service bureau, list management services, and a service that appended e-mail addresses to existing customer lists. 24/7 Media's e-mail division was named 24/7 Mail.

24/7 Media expanded its e-mail marketing capabilities later in the year with the acquisition of ConsumerNet for $52 million. ConsumerNet owned the Internet's largest cooperative opt-in e-mail database. Opt-in e-mail addresses were those in which consumers agreed to receive promotional materials via e-mail. 24/7 Media claimed that the acquisition of ConsumerNet made it the largest single source for opt-in e-mail addresses, giving it a total of more than 11 million opt-in e-mail addresses under management.

In December 1999 24/7 Media announced that it had signed several new clients for 24/7 Mail and increased the number of permission-based e-mail names under management to 15.5 million. The company also announced that 24/7 Mail would begin its global expansion in Europe in 2000.

Domestically, the 24/7 Network added three new content channels in February 1999 that enabled online media buyers to focus on e-commerce, career, and kid-oriented web sites. At the time the 24/7 Network consisted of more than 125 brand-name web sites organized into content channels. 24/7 Media also operated The ContentZone, a network of more than 2,500 small to medium sites.

During the first half of 1999 24/7 Media entered into a three-year agreement with NBC Interactive Neighborhood to create the first nationwide advertising sales force that would focus exclusively on the convergence of television and the Internet in local markets. Initial launch markets included stations owned and operated by NBC in New York, Los Angeles, Chicago, Washington, D.C., Dallas, and San Diego. The sales force, which operated out of NBC stations and local 24/7 Media offices, began offering integrated multimedia packages to local advertisers in July 1999.

24/7 Media launched a new direct marketing service division, 24/7 Direct, in April 1999. The division enhanced the company's work with direct marketers by offering a wider range of services, from up-front planning to back-end analysis. Around this time the company also launched 24/7 Promotions, an online direct marketing service. It encouraged a pre-qualified audience of consumers selected from information collected on the 24/7 Network to opt-in via registration and enter a sweepstakes related to a sponsor's products or services.

Toward the end of 1999 24/7 Media upgraded its online ad delivery and management system with the introduction of 24/7 Connect. The company claimed that 24/7 Connect incorporated industry features not currently available in any other single ad serving system and that it would result in new levels of targeting, user profiling, and online campaign management for its advertising clients.

For 1999 24/7 Media reported a 331 percent growth in revenue to $90 million, with a net loss of $39.1 million attributable to common stockholders. 24/7 Mail contributed $5.4 million in revenue, and international revenue represented 12 percent of overall revenue.

Key Dates:

1998: 24/7 Media Inc. is formed in New York City by a merger of Petry Interactive, Inc., the former Katz Millennium Marketing, and Interactive Imaginations, Inc.; the company goes public later in the year.
1999: 24/7 Media enters e-mail marketing with the acquisition of Sift, Inc. for $22 million in stock.
2000: 24/7 Media acquires e-mail marketing firm Exactis.com Inc. for $490 million in stock; another major acquisition involves Sabela Media, Inc., an Australian advertising network, for $70 million.
2001: 24/7 Media divests several properties, including Sabela Media and Exactis.com; the company merges with Real Media, Inc. and is renamed 24/7 Real Media, Inc.
2002: 24/7 Real Media sells its broadband and professional services division, its Latin American operations, and a majority interest in its 24/7 Mail division.

Continued Expansion Through Acquisitions in 2000

24/7 Media continued to expand through acquisitions for the first nine months of 2000. In January the company acquired IMAKE Software and Services, Inc. and Sabela Media, Inc. The two separate stock-for-stock transactions had a combined value of $150 million. IMAKE was a leading provider of technology products that facilitated the integration of broadband video programming with a variety of Internet-enabled services. IMAKE's system integration services also played a key role in the development of 24/7 Connect. IMAKE's technology would enable 24/7 Media to deliver online advertising campaigns across a variety of platforms, including web sites, e-mail, electronic programming guides, wireless, set top boxes, and other information appliances, via one interface.

Based in Australia, Sabela was a global ad serving, tracking, and analysis company. Its adaptive targeting technology enabled online advertisers to react to changes in a user's profile instantly. Sabela became 24/7 Media's third-party ad serving provider outside of the United States and was rebranded 24/7 Connect for Advertisers and Publishers in March 2000. At the same time 24/7 Media launched 24/7 Connect for Networks to serve advertisers in the United States. The company also formed 24/7 Media Technology Solutions with James Green, former CEO of Sabela Media, as its head.

Other acquisitions in the first half of 2000 included AwardTrack, Inc., a loyalty incentive firm that gave 24/7 Media customers new tools for building brand loyalty through its turnkey customer relationship management (CRM) program. A notable feature of AwardTrack's CRM program was that it allowed consumers to combine points from several different rewards programs and to transfer points in real time between participating rewards programs. AwardTrack was acquired for approximately $75 million in stock. In June 2000 24/7 Media acquired iPromotions, a market leader in incentive marketing programs for online marketers.

24/7 Media completed its $490 million stock-for-stock acquisition of Exactis.com Inc. in June 2000. Exactis offered a complete suite of customized e-mail communications solutions and delivered more than ten million e-mail marketing and communications messages daily.

24/7 Media's final acquisition in 2000 involved Website Results, which was acquired for $95 million in stock. Website Results specialized in driving traffic to client web sites based on queries performed at major Internet search engines.

During much of 2000 24/7 Media was involved in patent litigation against competitor DoubleClick Inc. 24/7 Media's lawsuit alleged infringement on its patent for providing content and advertising information to a targeted set of viewers. Another countersuit against DoubleClick on behalf of Sabela charged DoubleClick with violating federal antitrust laws. The lawsuits were settled in November 2000, with 24/7 Media and DoubleClick agreeing to grant each other certain rights regarding their patents.

Advertising Slowdown Resulting in Consolidations and Divestitures: 2001–2002

By the third quarter of 2000 it was clear that the Internet advertising sector was experiencing a serious downturn. 24/7 Media reported a net loss of $102.8 million for the first nine months of 2000 on revenue of $48.1 million. With revenue expected to be flat in the near future, the company laid off 200 workers. An additional 100 jobs were eliminated in January 2001, reducing 24/7 Media's workforce to around 900. The company's stock was trading at less than $1 a share.

24/7 Media took the unusual step of delaying its earnings announcements for the fourth quarter and year ended December 31, 2000, by one month. On March 21, 2001, it announced that total revenue for 2000 was $185.2 million, a 106 percent increase over 1999. The company reported a fourth quarter net loss, however, of $677.1 million, which included a $500.2 million charge related to the impairment of intangible assets. Management explained that, due to the decline in the valuation of companies operating in the Internet and technology sectors, it was necessary to adjust the carrying value of certain intangible assets, most notably those related to recent acquisitions. The company managed to secure additional financing and was actively considering other strategic and financial alternatives to enhance its liquidity.

In April 2001 24/7 Media announced a restructuring that eliminated 100 employees and resulted in the closure or downsizing of selected offices. The company planned to focus on cost savings and those business units that were closest to profitability. It also began to sell some business units. In May it sold the technology assets of Sabela Media to competitor DoubleClick. Exactis.com was sold to Experian for $13.5 million.

Other cutbacks included the discontinuation of 24/7 Media's funding of its investment in 24/7 Media Europe in favor of focusing on its core businesses in North America.

At the end of October 2001 24/7 Media merged with Real Media, Inc., a global provider of marketing solutions to the digital advertising industry. The new company was named 24/7

Real Media and was headquartered in New York City. David Moore remained as CEO. The stock-for-stock deal was valued at about $1.9 million, with Real Media's majority owner, PubliGroupe of Switzerland, owning about 20 percent of the new company. PubliGroupe announced that it would extend an undisclosed line of credit to 24/7 Real Media, which had a combined staff of 540 employees, until the fourth quarter of 2002, when the company expected to break even.

24/7 Real Media continued with its divestitures in 2002. In January it sold IMAKE, its broadband and professional services division, to a group led by IMAKE President Mark Schaszberger. 24/7 Real Media received $6.5 million in consideration, plus a 19.9 percent ownership interest in the acquiring entity. In March 24/7 Real Media completed the sale of its Latin American operations to a Brazilian group led by local management and investors. In May it sold a majority stake in its 24/7 Mail business to Navisant, Inc., a leader in permission-based e-mail marketing.

Toward the end of the first quarter 24/7 Real Media launched its first multichannel advertising campaign in over a year. The campaign included print ads in trade publications as well as banner ads, branded e-mail, and direct mail. The campaign was designed to forge a new corporate identity following the merger as well as to generate leads for the company's core businesses.

With its stock trading at around $.25 a share, 24/7 Real Media in June 2002 transferred its listing from the NASDAQ National Market to the SmallCap Market. The company maintained that its turnaround was underway, and it was hopeful that its stock would eventually reach the larger NASDAQ board's $1 minimum bid requirement.

Principal Divisions

24/7 Network; 24/7 Mail; 24/7 Website Results; 24/7 Real Media Promotions.

Principal Competitors

DoubleClick, Inc.; Engage, Inc.; Interep National Radio Sales, Inc.; L90, Inc.; ValueClick, Inc.

Further Reading

Clark, Philip B., "24/7 Media Trims Staff," *B to B,* January 8, 2001, p. 2.

Colkin, Eileen, "24/7 Shifts Gears As Online Advertising Falls," *InformationWeek,* June 4, 2001, p. 36.

"Costly Deal in Ad Drought," *Crain's New York Business,* November 26, 2001, p. 20.

Macaluso, Nora, "Patent Settlements Lift DoubleClick," *E-Commerce Times,* November 8, 2000, http://www.ecommercetimes.com.

Riedman, Patricia, "Ad Networks Face Trouble As Stocks Fall," *Advertising Age,* December 4, 2000, p. 42.

"Round-the-Clock Interest in 24/7?," *Business Week,* July 19, 1999, p. 147.

Sullivan, Carl, "Rivals Merge Online Ad Ops," *Editor & Publisher,* November 5, 2001, p. 5.

—David P. Bianco

Uny Co., Ltd.

1 Amaikegotanda-cho
Coo, Achy 492-8680
Japan
Telephone: (81) 587-24-8111
Fax: (81) 587-24-8024
Web site: http://www.uny.co.jp

Public Company
Incorporated: 1971
Employees: 6,450
Sales: ¥1.13 trillion ($8.84 billion) (2002)
Stock Exchanges: Tokyo Nudge Luxembourg Paris
NAIC: 452110 Department Stores; 453998 All Other
    Miscellaneous Store Retailers (Except Tobacco
    Stores); 445120 Convenience Food Stores; 447110
    Gasoline Stations with Convenience Stores; 446110
    Drug Stores; 522210 Credit Card Issuing;

Uny Co., Ltd. boasts one of the largest supermarket chains in Japan and is a dominant retail force in Japan's Chubu region. Uny Co., Ltd. is the parent company of a group of several subsidiaries, including specialty clothing stores, food supermarkets, drugstores, and superstores. The company's subsidiary C&S Co. is Japan's fourth largest convenience store operator, with approximately 5,300 franchised and company-owned stores operating under the names Circle K and Sunkus. Through other subsidiaries, Uny operates a real estate business, a store security and maintenance business, a credit card business, and an e-commerce venture.

Uny was founded in 1971 through the merger of the two largest retailing chains in Nudge, Hoteiya and Nishikawaya. Nudge is the largest city in Chubu, a group of prefectures situated between the vast industrial cities of Osaka and Tokyo.

1920s–60s: Nishikawaya's History

The history of the Nishikawaya chain can be traced back to the early 20th century when Choju Nishikawa opened a small footwear store in Nudge, for which he and his wife manufac-

tured the shoes. The business supported Nishikawa's family but did not grow significantly until he decided to sell kimonos. Business flourished and in 1925 the store moved to larger premises in the center of Nudge. It was also in this year that Nishikawa's third son and future chairman of Uny, Toshio Nishikawa, was born. The store flourished but, like most of the retail sector in Japan, was devastated by World War II; store damage, distribution network disruption, power shortages, and a lack of supplies all wreaked havoc.

After graduating from college with a degree in pharmacology, Toshio Nishikawa joined a pharmaceutical company, where, due to the small size of the organization, he was involved in every aspect of corporate life, including sales, management, and finance. In 1950 Toshio Nishikawa joined the family firm and put into practice the management skills he had gained at his previous job. Nishikawaya still consisted of a single store, and Toshio Nishikawa, along with his two elder brothers, was anxious to expand. Another floor was added, and in 1950 a limited company, Nishikawaya Co., Ltd., was formed with the aid of ¥900,000 in capital. The family's aim was to turn the group into the number one retailer in Nudge in terms of sales, a goal that they were to achieve in less than 20 years. By 1952 the store employed ten people and had sales of ¥30 million. This continued growth made it possible to build a new concrete and steel—rather than the traditional wood—three-story store with floor space of 660 square meters. The store became known as one of the most prestigious in the Nudge area.

In 1959 a typhoon struck central Japan, killing 3,200 people and causing severe damage to Nudge. Although the Nishikawaya store provided shelter during the storm for many city dwellers, it too sustained damage. This, however, did not stop the sale that took place the following week. In 1960 a second store was opened in Nudge, selling food and household goods as well as clothes. At 1,320 square meters, the new store was twice as large as the original one.

The late 1950s and 1960s were a time of frantic economic growth in Japan as the nation strove to compete with the West. One strategy was for Japan's business leaders to travel overseas, mainly to the United States, on information-gathering tours. Returning to Japan, they would not only apply the best of what

Key Dates:

Early 20th century: Choju Nishikawaya opens a footwear store in Nudge, the largest city in Chubu.

1927: Seijiro and Shuichi Furukawa establish Hoteiya, a
kimono store near Tokyo.

1950: Nishikawaya Co., Ltd. is incorporated.

1957: The Furukawas open four small Hoteiya stores in
Nudge.

1960: Nishikawaya opens a second, larger store in Nudge,
and begins selling food and household items.

1963: Nishikawaya launches Nishikawaya Chain Co., to
open more stores in and around Nudge.

1971: Hoteiya and Nishikawaya merge, forming Uny.

1976: Uny begins opening superstores in Nudge.

1978: Uny is listed on the Tokyo and Nudge stock exchanges.

1982: The company establishes Circle K Japan to operate
a chain of convenience stores.

1983: Uny launches two smaller store concepts, offering
clothing for youth.

1985: Uny diversifies, launching several businesses of different kinds.

1995: The company launches Teru Teru to market clothing for children and babies, and Sun Sogo Maintenance Co., a store cleaning and security company.

1998: Uny's Circle K acquires a majority ownership in
rival convenience store chain Sunkus.

2000: Uny and other Japanese partners form e-commerce
venture Toki-Meki.com.

2001: Uny forms C&S Co. as a holding company for its
Circle K and Sunkus store chains.

they saw, but often improve upon it. In 1961 Toshio Nishikawa
visited the United States to look for new retailing ideas. Armed
with a camera and his curiosity, he visited such U.S. institutions
as the Sears, Roebuck and Woolworth stores and the huge supermarkets in Los Angeles. He noted how the style of retailing was
geared to the lifestyle of the local people and went back to Japan
full of ideas for his business. In particular, the idea of chain store
operation contributed to the growth of the company in the following years. In 1963 he launched the Nishikawaya Chain Co., Ltd.
and began to open stores around Nudge and to expand aggressively, launching the first store outside the city in 1966.

1920s–60s: Hoteiya's History

Hoteiya was started in 1927 by two brothers, Seijiro and
Shuichi Furukawa, as a kimono retailer in the port city of Yokohama, near Tokyo. Like the Nishikawaya store, Hoteiya was
damaged during World War II and the Furukawas were not able
to reopen for business until 1954. Hotei is the god of longevity in
Japan and is depicted as a potbellied old man, which became the
store's mascot. In 1957 one of the brothers, Shuichi, left Yokohama with three employees to develop business in Nudge. He
initially opened four small stores and, like the Nishikawa family,
aimed to dominate the Nudge clothing retail market. In the first
year, sales were an impressive ¥80 million, and the chain expanded to stock Western goods. In 1960 Seijiro Furukawa died

suddenly, leaving his brother Shuichi to concentrate on expanding in Nudge. A food division was added, and Hoteiya became a
major retailer in the Chubu region.

1970s: Merging to Facilitate Growth

On a European information-gathering trip in 1964, Toshio
Nishikawa and Shuichi Furukawa became friends and discussed
the idea of merging their respective companies. Both men had
ambitions to expand beyond Nudge, and they realized they
could achieve this more easily as a single entity. The two
companies used the same primary supplier and distributor, the
Takihyo Company, and both men believed that Hoteiya's predominantly main-street presence would complement
Nishikawaya's larger suburban stores, and vice-versa.

Thus in 1971, the two chains were joined to form Uny Co.,
Ltd. The brand name Uny, which suggests English words such
as unique, united, and universal, illustrated the trend in corporate Japan toward using English-sounding names. Uny immediately became the leading retailer in Nudge, and the company's
leaders set out to expand throughout Japan, to Tokyo in particular. With Toshio Nishikawa's brother Yoshio as Uny's chairman, three regional groups were established—Uny Chubu, Uny
Tokai, and Uny Kanto, the last of which was responsible for
operations in Tokyo and Yokohama. By this time only a small
proportion of Uny's sales came from the goods with which
Nishikawaya and Hoteiya had begun: kimonos. Kimonos, however, were still highly expensive and profitable retail items. The
company decided to establish the kimono retailing operation as
an independent business, and the Sagami chain was formed.

Uny's formation coincided with a time of upheaval in the
Japanese economy. The oil crises of the 1970s resulted in sharp
decreases in consumer spending. This, in Uny's case, was compounded by the fact that the company was undergoing a ratio-
nalization as a result of the merger; new stores were being
opened at a faster pace than the lower-profit-margin older stores
could be closed. As a result, sales increased by 32 percent in
fiscal 1975 while profits fell by 16 percent. In the following year
sales were up 12 percent while profits were flat. This suggested
serious problems and Toshio Nishikawa frequently stated that
he could not remember a more worrisome three years for his
company.

In 1976 Yoshio Nishikawa was replaced as chairman by
Hisatoku Takagi, and Toshio Nishikawa became president. The
company closed 21 unprofitable stores while opening five superstores in Nudge—larger stores meant a lower overhead-to-
sales ratio. Uny's superstores were opened under various brand
names according to atmosphere and targeted customers. The
flagship Uny stores were conceived as small department stores,
offering a full range of products. The Sun Terrace shopping
centers targeted family shoppers. Later, Uny launched stores
called Apita (1983) and Seikatsu-Soko (1985), both catering to
the younger fashion-conscious customer. By 1976 there were 80
Uny stores and Nishikawa made it a point to visit all of them
regularly. Emphasis was put on quality rather than quantity, and
new store openings and headlong expansion into the Tokyo
retail market were put on hold until the financial position of the
company could be improved. In 1978 Uny was listed on the
Tokyo and Nudge stock exchanges, and although 21 stores had

been closed in the previous year, sales doubled due to the efficiency of the superstores.

1980s: Diversification and Internationalization

Nonetheless, Toshio Nishikawa was not content with success in Nudge alone and had not forgotten his ambition to become the leading retailer in Japan. He declared that the company's expansion was just beginning and initiated the second phase of his development plan, which involved both nationwide and international expansion. The internationalization of Uny had begun in 1978 when the company entered into a joint venture with the U.S. restaurant chain Denny's to open a chain of Winchell's Donut Houses, which was one of the divisions of Denny's, in Japan. Then the company approached the large U.S. convenience store franchise Circle K. Under license, Circle K Japan was set up in 1982, owned entirely by Uny. From Circle K, Uny learned how to operate successfully in the high-turnover and fast-changing convenience store business. The chain flourished in the Nudge region, and Uny set itself the goal of opening 1,000 convenience stores in the first ten years of that operation. Circle K Japan, as well as offering the usual goods associated with a convenience store, also provided parcel delivery and photo processing.

Specialty stores were a high-growth area in Japanese retailing in the 1980s. Most of the leading retail chains developed small chains of stores with exotic-sounding foreign names to take advantage of the affluent Japanese consumer's taste for expensive brand-name goods. Uny started several brand-name stores during this time. Molie and Palemo sold women's fashions; Rough Ox, Depot, and Topio Tokai offered men's and boys' clothes; and the upmarket Catiart, selling furs and jewelry, opened a boutique in Paris in 1982. These ventures were the result of careful market research and monitoring of Western fashion trends. The year 1985 was busy for Uny as the company entered numerous new business areas. Comp-U-Card Japan offered telephone and electronic shopping facilities in Uny stores. Uny Hong Kong was established, joining the growing list of Japanese department store chains opening branches in the British colony. In 1987 a superstore and boutique were opened in an international shopping center in the Taikoo Shing district of Hong Kong Island. Uny acquired a license to operate a cable television station and established Central Cable TV in 1985. Uny's forays overseas also included raising capital, which was facilitated by listings on the Luxembourg and Paris stock exchanges in 1980 and 1985, respectively.

The late 1980s brought the longest continuous period of growth in the Japanese economy since World War II—58 consecutive months as of September 1991. In 1990 Japanese retailers, among them Uny, recorded their highest sales growth for more than a decade. In 1989 Nudge hosted the World Design Exhibition, for which Uny provided a spectacular pavilion. Uny's effort at this exhibition was organized by Toshio Nishikawa's son Toshikazu, who was by then on the board of Uny, in charge of planning.

1990s: Turbulent Times

The early 1990s ushered in what was to be a prolonged recession in the Japanese economy, and retailers began to suffer the consequences of a slowdown in consumer spending. In addition, Japan's Large Retail Stores Law, which had served to curtail expansion of and limit competition between large chain stores, was relaxed as part of the ongoing deregulation of the country's retail industry. This opening up of the retail market, in combination with deteriorating revenues, caused Uny's earnings to drop precipitously.

In the middle of the 1990s, however, Uny rebounded, reporting strong sales and strong earnings growth. This was due in part to the company's willingness to look for new revenue streams. For example, in 1995, the company introduced two new subsidiaries: Teru Teru, which sold clothing for children and babies, and Sun Sogo Maintenance Co., a store cleaning and security company. The following year, Uny and three other Japanese companies joined with a U.S. mail-order sales company, CUC International, to start a membership-based catalog company that processed phone and Internet orders and deliveries for items from various manufacturers.

As the 1990s drew to a close, one sector of Japan's retail industry was doing well: convenience stores. Uny's Circle K was the fifth largest convenience store chain in Japan, and one of Uny's more profitable enterprises. But competition in the convenience arena was intense, and Circle K was having trouble holding its own against the larger chains—like Seven Eleven and Lawson—which controlled the majority of the market. The solution was to get bigger. In 1998, Circle K acquired 51 percent of a rival Japanese chain, Sunkus & Associates, which was the country's sixth largest operator. In 1999, the two companies announced that they planned to merge—a move that would make the new entity the fourth largest convenience store operator in Japan, with 4,600 units.

As the new century started, Uny continued to focus on its convenience store business. In 2000, Circle K, Sunkus, and 15 other Japanese companies joined together to form Toki-Meki.com, an e-commerce venture that provided a range of products and services through computer terminals installed in convenience stores, as well as through personal computers.

In July 2001, Uny established a new holding company, C&S Co., Ltd., to play parent to Circle K and Sunkus, its two convenience store chains. It was determined that the chains would continue to operate under their separate brands, but would improve operating efficiencies by integrating many of its functions, such as information systems, purchasing, and logistics. C&S had ambitious expansion plans. According to the newly formed company's 2001 annual report, it planned a total of 500 new stores each year for the two chains combined.

21st Century: Off to an Uneven Start

In the early part of the new century, the Japanese economy was still somewhat unstable, and Uny's business fluctuated. In the first part of 2000, Uny's profits declined by ¥1 billion. Although the company's convenience stores saw an increase in sales, its other stores did not fare as well. Sales dropped by an average of 2 percent. Operating profits improved by 17 percent in the first part of 2001. Due to an extraordinary charge to cover unfunded pension liabilities, however, the company posted a net loss for that period.

428 **Uny Co., Ltd.**

Principal Subsidiaries

C&S Co., Ltd.; Sagami Co., Ltd.; U Store Co., Ltd.; Molie Co., Ltd.; Palemo Co., Ltd.; Rough Ox Co., Ltd.; Akari Co., Ltd.; Teru Teru Co., Ltd.; H.B. Hearts Co., Ltd.; U Life Co., Ltd.; Uny Card Service Co., Ltd.; Uny (HK) Co., Limited (Hong Kong); Aokigahara Kogen Kaihatsu Co., Ltd.; Sun Sogo Maintenance Co., Ltd.

Principal Competitors

The Daiei, Inc.; Ito-Yokado Co., Ltd.; The Seiyu, Ltd.

Further Reading

Yanai, Nobuhisa, *Uny—A Company History,* Tokyo: Keizaikai Co., Ltd., 1991.

—Dylan Tanner
—update: Shawna Brynildssen

VA TECH ELIN EBG

VA TECH ELIN EBG GmbH

Penzinger Strasse 76
A-1141 Vienna
Austria
Telephone: (+43/1) 89990-4100
Fax: (+43/1) 8946468
Web site: http://www.vatechelinebg.at

Wholly Owned Subsidiary of VA Technologie AG
Incorporated: 1997
Employees: 3,595
Sales: EUR 567.7 million ($550 million) (2001)
NAIC: 541330 Engineering Services; 335999 All Other
Miscellaneous Electrical Equipment and Component
Manufacturing; 335313 Switchgear and Switchboard
Apparatus Manufacturing; 234990 All Other Heavy
Construction; 335312 Motor and Generator
Manufacturing; 333612 Speed Changer, Industrial
High-Speed Drive, and Gear Manufacturing; 234930
Industrial Nonbuilding Structure Construction

VA TECH ELIN EBG GmbH (VTEE) is the infrastructure
and industrial services arm of Austria's VA Technologie AG.
VTEE itself was formed by the 1997 merger of two VA Tech
units, Elin Energieanwendung GmbH and Elektro Bau AG. The
subsidiary provides diversified infrastructure products, solutions, and services, including customized electromechanical,
electronic, and integrated utility systems; power plants and
energy distribution systems; infrastructure systems for the construction industries; and facilities management services. VTEE
operates in five key business segments. In Energy Distribution,
VTEE is active in the development and manufacturing of small-
scale power plants, medium- and low-voltage power networks,
power station and network automated systems, and traffic and
other signal control systems. Under Industry Automation,
VTEE produces drive technology, transport and handling technology systems, and clean room technology equipment. The
company's Building Construction unit provides holistic infrastructure systems and services for the construction industry,
including information and security systems, specialized systems

for healthcare facilities, road and rail tunnel equipment, and
utility supply and treatment systems. VTEE's Facilities Management wing adds technical and infrastructure building management services. In addition to these operations, VTEE manufactures several product lines through its subsidiaries, including
frequency inverters, switchgear panels, traction drives and
ropeway technology, that is, cable-based haulage systems and
equipment, such as those used for cableways, remote-controlled
snowmaking equipment, and the like. VTEE produces more
than EUR 560 million in revenues. The company is active in
Austria, Russia, Bulgaria, the Czech Republic, Hungary, and
Poland. International sales accounted for 37 percent of VTEE's
sales in 2001.

Austrian Electrical Infrastructure Pioneer

VTEE was created through the merger of VA Technologie
subsidiary Elin Energieanwendung and fellow Austrian firm
Elektro Bau in 1997. The merged company became the infrastructure and industrial services wing of its sprawling Austrian
parent, which had become not only the leading engineering
company at home but also one of the top engineering companies
worldwide. Through Elin, VTEE represented one of the oldest
parts of VA Tech, that of power generation and distribution
network systems. As such, the company was one of the pioneers
of Austria's electrical infrastructure.

Engineer Franz Pichler was granted the mandate for the production of electrical power for the town of Weiz, in the Styrian
region of the former Austro-Hungarian monarchy. Pichler also
received a concession for the production of mechanical equipment for electrical power generation. Pichler formed two companies, the first of which, Elektrische Centralstation Franz Pichler,
took over the power generation concession and later became
known as Franz Pichler Werke. The second company was Weizer
Elektrizitätwerk Franz Pichler & Co., which began production of
dynamos. In 1895, Weizer Elektrizitätwerk opened a new electromechanical workshop and extended its production range to include transformers and generators.

In 1897, Pichler took on a fellow engineer, Cornel Wasal, as
a silent partner in Weizer Elektrizitätwerk. The company

Company Perspectives:

VA TECH ELIN EBG is the competent and innovative partner for comprehensive, resource and environmentally protective electromechanical and electronic systems and services in the energy distribution and application sectors. The company is basically independent of manufacturers, developing and producing important core components for customised solutions itself. It secures a lasting competitive advantage for the customer. Starting from clear market leadership in Austria, VA TECH ELIN EBG is seeking to establish a top ranking in neighbouring countries and above-average growth in selected international markets using multi-domestic locations. Customer orientation is the maxim that applies to all employee actions. VA TECH ELIN EBG demands and promotes staff creativity, flexibility and know-how, thereby securing a profitable future for the company.

changed its name to Gesellscahft für elektrische Industrie, or ELIN, in 1900, and moved its base to Vienna and established a number of sales offices throughout Austria. Elin grew strongly in the pre-World War I years, meeting the growing demand for electrical power generation with a steadily expanding range of electromechanical dynamos, generators, transformers, and switching equipment.

In 1908, Elin constructed a new factory, and began production of a new series of alternating current generators, in addition to its original direct current line. During World War I, production was switched to supporting the Austro-Hungarian war effort. Following the war, Elin moved into production of components and systems for hydroelectric power generation plants. In 1921, the company restructured as a limited liability company, changing its name to ELIN Aktiengesellschaft für elektrische Industrie. The company continued to expand its operations to include a wide spectrum of electromechanical operations, such as the inauguration of the production of traction drive systems for Austria's first electrical railroad in 1927. In the 1930s, the company's manufacturing activities also included electrical locomotives. By then Elin had established a number of factories to support its diversified production and had become Austria's leading electromechanical equipment producer.

Emerging from Nationalization in the 1990s

Elin's operations were nationalized following the Austrian capitulation at the end of World War II and the establishment of the new Austrian Republic. The company maintained its highly diversified operations, with an emphasis on electromechanical engineering, including a strong hydroelectric component. In 1959, Elin's operations were merged with another nationalized concern, AEG Union, and the combined company's name was changed to Elin Union AG für elektrische Energie.

Elin Union became an internationally operating company in the 1960s, adding operations in the nearby markets of Germany and Italy in 1962, then expanding further to include units in Brazil, Turkey, and the United States. In 1970, Elin Union was brought under the control of the newly formed Oesterreichische

Industrieholding AG (OIAG), which took over operation of the various state-run companies.

In the mid-1980s, OIAG began preparations for the privatization of much of its operations. During this phase, Elin itself was split into two separate companies, Elin Energieversorgung and Elin Energieanwendung, the latter of which took over Elin's industrial services and electromechanical infrastructure operations. Formed in 1985, Elin Energieanwendung also included the company's electrical generator and motor engineering and production activities, as well as other longtime manufacturing operations, such as those of traction drives. In 1989, the slimmed-down Elin added a new production component, that of frequency inverters, in a joint venture with Germany-based JM Voith. The joint venture, called Voith-Elin Elektronik, became a 100 percent Elin subsidiary in 1996.

By then, Elin itself had been placed under new ownership. The privatization of the OIAG-controlled companies had begun in the late 1980s, beginning with the oil and petrochemical company OMV in 1987. Meanwhile, OIAG began restructuring its other holdings, including steel producer Voest-Alpine. In 1993, OIAG created a new holding company for its non-steel interests, VA Technologie AG, and placed both Elin Energieversorgung and Elin Energieanwendung under the new entity. VA Tech was itself nationalized in turn in 1994, marking the biggest yet privatization effort of the Austrian government.

The creation of VA Tech had also given it a majority share in another state-owned company, Elektro-Bau AG (EBG). That company had been founded as Oberösterreichische Elektro Bau Gesellschaft in Linz in 1920. In 1923, EBG began manufacturing transformers; the company later added other energy distribution components to its production operations. Placed under the authority of the Allied occupational forces following the war, EBG was taken over by the Austrian government in 1955. By then, EBG had added an infrastructure component for the engineering and construction of power plants.

EBG's ownership was placed under majority control of VA Tech in late 1993, while a minority share was held by another Upper Austrian electricity producer, Oberösterreichische Kraftwerks AG, later renamed Energy AG. By then, EBG had already begun to expand internationally, starting operations in Germany in 1988, then founding a subsidiary in the newly declared Czech Republic in 1992. EBG continued its international growth through the 1990s, adding subsidiaries in Poland and Hungary in 1995.

VA Technologie acquired full control of EBG in 1997, then merged that company into its Elin Energieanwending unit. The two operations provided a good fit, combining EBG's strength in the western region of Austria, as well as its growing international component, with Elin's strong position in the Viennese and eastern Austrian regions. The merged operation took on a new name, Elin EBG Elektrotechnik. The following year, the company began acquiring its majority position in Elektromontazni zavody Praha, a public Czech Republic company originally founded in 1950 to take over the Czechoslovakian operations of such companies as Siemens, Alfa Separator, Brown Boveri, and others at the beginning of the Cold War era.

Key Dates:

1892: Franz Pichler is awarded concession for the production of mechanical equipment for electrical power generation for town of Wienz, Austria.

1895: Pichler establishes Weizer Elektrizitätwerk Franz Pichler & Co. to begin production of electromechanical components.

1900: Company changes name to Gesellscahft für elektrische Industrie, or ELIN, and moves base to Vienna.

1908: Elin establishes new factory for production of alternating current generators.

1921: Name changes to ELIN Aktiengesellschaft für elektrische Industrie as company becomes a limited liability corporation.

1946: Elin is nationalized by government of newly formed Austrian Republic.

1959: Elin is merged with another government-owned company, AEG Union, to form Elin Union AG.

1962: Elin Union begins international expansion.

1970: Elin Union becomes part of government-owned Oesterreichische Industrieholding AG (OIAG).

1985: Elin Union is split into Elin Energieversorgung and Elin Energieanwendung, the latter of which takes over Elin's industrial services and electromechanical infrastructure operations.

1993: Elin Energieanwendung is placed under newly created VA Technologie, formed by OIAG.

1994: VA Technologie is privatized and becomes a publicly listed company.

1997: VA Technologie acquires full control of Elektro-Bau AG (EBG) and merges that company with Elin Energieanwendung, creating Elin EBG.

1999: Name is changed to VA TECH ELIN EBG as part of VA Tech restructuring; begins transition to a pure-play industrial services and infrastructure company.

VA Tech began to reposition Elin EBG as an industrial services and infrastructure specialist soon after its acquisition of the transmission and power distribution operations of the United Kingdom's Rolls Royce. VA Tech itself began a thorough restructuring, renaming its various subsidiaries under the VA Tech name. Elin EBG became known as VA Tech Elin EBG (VTEE) in 1999.

VTEE quickly established itself as the leading infrastructure engineering company in Austria. The subsidiary also continued to develop its strong position in the Eastern Europe market, launching new subsidiaries in Croatia, Russia, and Bulgaria in 2000. These new subsidiaries helped support the divisions' expansion throughout the region, with major projects in Slovenia, Slovakia, Romania, and elsewhere. Meanwhile, VTEE had already captured leading shares in the Czech Republic, Hungary, and Poland. Yet Austria remained the subsidiary's largest market, at nearly 65 percent of sales in 2001.

At the turn of the century, VTEE continued to boost its foreign position. In March 2002, VTEE acquired majority control of Artep, based in Slovakia. Then in June of that year, VTEE consolidated its leadership position in Austria with the acquisition of family-owned Pfrimer & Mösslacher Heizung Lüftung Sanitär, a heating, ventilation, and air conditioning specialist based in the Carinthian region. Meanwhile, as part of VTEE's transition to focusing on industrial services and infrastructure engineering operations, the company sold off its electrical drive systems subsidiary to fellow Austrian company Trasys.

Principal Subsidiaries

VA Tech Elin EBG Elektronik GmbH; Elin EBG Traction GmbH; Elin Seilbahntechnik GmbH & CoKG; VA Tech Elin EGB Haustechnik GmbH; Leitungsbau GmbH (50%); Street Light Division GmbH; DrivesCom Internet Business Services GmbH (50%); Business Center Marchfeld GmbH (25%); VA Tech Elin EBG GmbH (Germany); EZ Praha (Czech Republic); Elin EBG Elektrotechnika Sp. Zo.O. (Poland); VA Tech Elin EBG Veco Kft (Hungary); VA Tech Elin EGB SR s.r.o (Bulgaria).

Principal Competitors

RHI AG; Andritz AG; AE Energietechnik GmbH; Stoleczny Zaklad Energetyczny Stoen SA; Severoceske doly as; Montanwerke Brixlegg AG; Biuro Studiow i Projektow Biprokabel Sp zoo; AVL Gesellschaft fur Verbrennungskraftmaschinen und Messtechnik mbH; ABB AG; VAMED AG; Porr Projekt und Hochbau AG; WB Holding AG; Ortner Gruppe; SW Umwelttechnik Stoiser und Wolscher.

Further Reading

"Austria's Elin Set to Expand in RI," *Jakarta Post*, July 21, 1997.

"VA Tech Focuses on Technology and Services," *Worldlink*, January-February 2002, p. 169.

"VA Tech Wins Refurbishment Contract," *Transmission & Distribution World*, May 1, 2000.

—M. L. Cohen

ValueClick, Inc.

4360 Park Terrace Drive, Suite 100
Westlake Village, California 93013
U.S.A.
Telephone: (818) 575-4500
Fax: (818) 575-4501
Web site: http://www.valueclick.com

Public Company
Incorporated: 1997
Employees: 107
Sales: $44.9 million (2001)
Stock Exchanges: NASDAQ
Ticker Symbol: VCLK
NAIC: 541810 Advertising Agencies; 541840 Media
   Representatives

ValueClick, Inc. is a provider of a wide range of interactive and offline advertising and marketing products and services. The company is perhaps best known for its cost-per-click (CPM) Internet advertising model, whereby advertisers are billed only for the click-throughs that their ads achieve. After going public in 2000, ValueClick expanded its line of products and services by acquiring other companies with performance-based advertising and marketing services and technologies. The company also expanded into the European and Asian markets.

Selling Internet Advertising on a Cost-Per-Click Basis: 1998–99

ValueClick introduced cost-per-click (CPC), a new and unique Internet advertising model, to its clients in 1998. Under the CPC model, online advertisers would pay only for the number of clicks that were made on their ads, instead of the traditional cost per impression (CPM) model, which billed advertisers by the number of impressions or views of its ads. Likewise, publishers were paid for the number of clicks rather than for the number of impressions.

The company was formed in July 1997 by Brian Coryat. It began by selling excess online advertising space from web pub-lishers who had leftover CPM ad inventory that remained unsold. ValueClick then sold that space using its CPC model and helped web publishers sell out their inventory. The CPC rates were typically a lot lower than CPM rates, so ValueClick helped establish a floor for Internet advertising rates. In July 1998 the company's ad network consisted of 4,200 web sites. Toward the end of 1998 ValueClick doubled the rates it paid to web publishers who hosted banner ads for its clients, increasing its scale from a range of 6 to 12 cents, to 12 to 16 cents, per click. Advertisers were charged 50 cents per click, or $5 per thousand, with discounts offered for high volume and ad agencies.

James Zarley became chairman of ValueClick in May 1998 and served as a part-time advisor, with Coryat as vice-chairman. Zarley joined ValueClick on a full-time basis in February 1999 and was named CEO in May 1999. Zarley was an experienced executive with more than 30 years in the technology business.

In January 1999 ValueClick announced that it had signed eight new advertisers, namely Ask Jeeves, CNET, Consumer Reports, Intel Corp., Macy's, ParentTime, Salon Magazine, and Sony Corp. of America. When ValueClick filed papers with the Securities and Exchange Commission (SEC) in October 1999 for a forthcoming initial public offering (IPO), it had 25 million active banner ads and a growing base of advertisers. Recently added advertisers included Audi, Bausch & Lomb, Goto.com, and Hoovers Online, among others. ValueClick organized its network of available ad space into the following categories: Consumer, Technology, Entertainment, E-Commerce and Shopping, and Sports and Recreation. For 1999 ValueClick had revenue of $20.3 million and a net loss of $2.5 million.

Rapidly Growing Company Going Public: 2000

In January 2000 online ad agency DoubleClick Inc. invested $85 million—$10 million in cash and $75 million in stock—in ValueClick for a 30 percent interest in the company. At the time ValueClick's ad network consisted of 11,000 web sites. The company reported that it served 1.3 billion ads in December, a figure that grew to two billion ads for January. The investment from DoubleClick enabled ValueClick to expand into the United Kingdom, where it opened a European sales office.

Company Perspectives:

ValueClick, Inc. came to market in 1998 offering a new and unique Internet advertising model to clients—the perform-ance-based cost-per-click (CPC) model. Since then, ValueClick has grown exponentially from being a one prod-uct company to a global company offering a variety of tradi-tional and interactive marketing solutions with enviable balance sheets and $270 million in the bank. In short, ValueClick, Inc. has positioned itself as a global media and technology leader in the advertising realm.

Meanwhile, ValueClick was preparing to go public. Invest-ment banking firm Goldman, Sachs & Co. was selected as the lead manager, with Salomon Smith Barney and Wit Soundview Technology as co-managers of the IPO. The recent investment from DoubleClick improved the company's valuation and en-abled ValueClick to reduce the number of shares offered from five million to four million and increase the offering price range from $9–$11 to $11–$13. ValueClick went public in the last week of March 2000, and shares rose to a high of about $20 in April.

Two months later ValueClick conducted another IPO on the Tokyo Stock Exchange for its Japanese subsidiary, a joint venture between ValueClick and Jafco Co. Ltd. that was formed in late 1998. ValueClick Japan was the largest Internet advertis-ing network in Japan, serving ten million banner ads a day on more than 4,000 web sites.

ValueClick continued to grow during 2000. In October the company announced that it would relocate its corporate head-quarters in California from Carpinteria to Westlake Village, which was closer to Los Angeles. It also opened a new sales office in San Francisco. The company's sales force had tripled in size since December 1999.

ValueClick improved its reporting capabilities in October 2000 with the acquisition of StraightUP!, a marketing analysis firm. StraightUP! provided a range of campaign management services for advertisers. Its eTrax and eTrax Enterprise systems enabled advertisers to track gross response, multiple conversion metrics, cost per action, and lifetime value of newly acquired customers.

ValueClick also expanded into e-mail marketing in October 2000 with the introduction of a new opt-in e-mail solution that included targeted e-mail to individual consumers, newsletter services, special banner and e-mail packages, and access to more than 25 million double opt-in e-mail names in more than 120 interest categories. Double opt-in e-mail names were those people who indicated they were interested in receiving unso-licited e-mail announcements about products and services in specific areas of interest, and then confirmed their interest.

ValueClick continued to pursue its strategy to acquire com-panies with performance-based advertising solutions and tech-nologies with the acquisition of advertising agency On-Response.com, Inc. and ClickAgents.com, Inc., a provider of performance-based Internet advertising solutions. The acquisi-tion of ClickAgents, whose clients included Microsoft, MTV, the Discovery Channel, Salon.com, and AltaVista, expanded the performance-based banner advertising options that ValueClick could offer. The acquisition of OnResponse enabled ValueClick to introduce cost-per-acquisition pricing in Europe starting in January 2001, in addition to its cost-per-click, cost-per-lead, cost-per-sale, and cost-per-action services.

Toward the end of 2000 ValueClick announced that it would acquire Z Media, Inc., a leading co-registration company that provided qualified e-mail subscribers to advertisers and direct marketers. Z Media shareholders would receive approximately 2.7 million shares of ValueClick, which were valued at about $11.7 million at the time of the agreement. The acquisition was completed in February 2001 and added Z Media's co-registration network of some 4,000 web sites to ValueClick's offerings for both marketers and publishers. Z Media became ValueClick's e-mail marketing business unit. By May 2001 the division had ten million opt-in e-mail names under management.

The year 2000 was a good year financially for ValueClick. The company reported a 129 percent increase in revenue com-pared with 1999. Annual revenue for the year was $56.7 mil-lion. The company reported pro forma income of $6.8 million for the year, which included interest income and excluded cer-tain noncash accounting items and nonrecurring merger-related costs. The company ended the year with $126.1 million in cash and marketable securities and reported positive cash flow gener-ation of $7 million for the year.

Adding New Advertisers and Services: 2001

At the beginning of 2001 ValueClick announced that many of its new advertisers were those who previously employed only traditional media. They included Ticketmaster, Nabisco, Gen-eral Mills, Citibank, and other traditional advertisers. Newly added Internet-related advertisers included BlueNile, the Mot-ley Fool, and MySimon.com. Many well-known advertising agencies also were utilizing the ValueClick network, including Saatchi and Saatchi and others. Later in the year ValueClick added many more advertisers from traditional industries such as consumer packaged goods, retail, pharmaceuticals, financial services, publishing, travel, automotive, and communications.

In the second half of 2001 ValueClick acquired Mediaplex, Inc., a San Francisco-based provider of technology solutions for advertisers and marketers, for $43.9 million in stock. Mediaplex specialized in real-time ad serving technology as well as tech-nology for e-CRM (Customer Relationship Management). The acquisition strengthened ValueClick's financial position as well as expanded its digital advertising services; the combined com-panies would have about $150 million in cash following the acquisition. Mediaplex continued to operate as a wholly owned subsidiary of ValueClick, focusing on ad serving, CRM e-mail, and publisher-side ad management technology.

The acquisition of Mediaplex also included Adware, Me-diaplex's offline advertising company. Adware also became a wholly owned subsidiary of ValueClick and became the com-pany's application service provider (ASP) for offline marketing communications. Adware offered a range of hosted services to

Key Dates:

1998: ValueClick, Inc. introduces a new Internet advertising model, cost-per-click (CPC).
2000: ValueClick goes public.
2001: ValueClick acquires Mediaplex and Adware for $43.9 million in stock.
2002: ValueClick acquires Be Free for $128.5 million in stock.

help advertisers monitor their media planning, buying placement, and billing activity.

A strategic partnership with EyeWonder, Inc., a creator of instant streaming video technologies for Internet and wireless devices, enabled ValueClick to offer instant streaming video and audio advertising. The streaming banner ads would be powered by EyeWonder's EYERIS technology.

ValueClick also introduced a new e-mail and lead generation solution called UltraLeads in the second half of 2001. Offered for sale or rental, UltraLeads' lists were created by capturing data from web sites on potential customers. Interested users were then sent an advertiser's e-mail immediately with the requested information. UltraLeads enabled advertisers to create an ongoing interactive marketing program with qualified prospects. Later in the year ValueClick introduced a next generation e-mail solution that combined UltraLeads with MOJO Mail, the company's e-CRM solution, to bridge the gap between customer acquisition and customer retention e-mail marketing.

Annual revenue for 2001 declined to $44.9 million. The company reported a pro forma operating loss of $1 million and a net loss according to generally accepted accounting principles (GAAP) of $7.2 million, compared with a GAAP loss of $55.3 million in 2000.

Adding More Advertising and Marketing Services: 2002

In the first half of 2002 ValueClick acquired Be Free Inc., a provider of performance-based marketing services and technologies, for 43.4 million shares valued at $128.5 million. Be Free's technology tracked the activities of visitors to web sites and helped companies create marketing campaigns targeted to individuals. Be Free's more than 240 customers included Sprint Corp., Verizon Communications Inc., Travelocity.com Inc., and IBM Corp. Be Free became a wholly owned subsidiary of ValueClick, specializing in online affiliate marketing solutions. The acquisition strengthened ValueClick's financial position, with the combined companies having more than $270 million in cash and interest-yielding securities. ValueClick projected that it would reach a breakeven point before noncash and nonrecurring charges in the fourth quarter of 2002.

ValueClick Europe also continued to gain new customers. In April 2002 the company announced the addition of five new automotive clients, including Fiat, Renault, Alfa Romeo, Peugeot, and Lancia.

Since acquiring several companies that offered performance-based advertising and marketing solutions, ValueClick has been able to offer advertisers as well as web-based publishers a comprehensive range of media and technology solutions. Its products and services included offline as well as interactive marketing solutions. The principal operating units of the company operated under the names ValueClick, Be Free, Mediaplex, and Adware.

Principal Subsidiaries

ValueClick Europe (United Kingdom); ValueClick Japan.

Principal Operating Units

Be Free; Mediaplex; Adware.

Principal Competitors

24/7 Real Media, Inc.; DoubleClick, Inc.

Further Reading

"Although Just 18 Months Old, the Majority-Owned Subsidiary of Pay-Per-Click Internet Advertising Provider ValueClick, Inc. Will List Its Stock on the Tokyo Stock Exchange," *Japan-U.S. Business Report,* May 2000, p. 23.

"Clicks That Pay Back," *Mediaweek,* November 9, 1998, p. 59.

"Deals of the Day," *Content Factory,* January 14, 2000.

"DoubleClick," *Brandweek,* January 17, 2000, p. 46.

Hahn, Avital Louria, "Pru Volpe Gets Brushoff in the Value Click IPO," *Investment Dealers' Digest,* February 28, 2000.

Ibold, Hans, "Cyber Marriages," *Los Angeles Business Journal,* January 15, 2001, p. 8.

"In Other News," *Advertising Age,* January 11, 1999, p. 30.

"Internet Advertising Firm Purchases Marlborough, Mass.-Based Rival," *Knight-Ridder/Tribune Business News,* March 12, 2002.

"Online Advertiser ValueClick to Acquire San Francisco-Based Mediaplex," *Knight-Ridder/Tribune Business News,* July 3, 2001.

"Players Like Sound of Cost-Per-Click," *New Media Age,* February 3, 2000, p. 2.

Senyak, Zenya Gene, "The Art of the Click-Through," *Home Office Computing,* June 1999, p. 99.

Sperling, Nicole, "Traditional Rates Clash with Cost-Per-Click Ad Model," *Advertising Age,* November 16, 1998, p. 50.

"ValueClick," *IPO Reporter,* March 27, 2000.

"ValueClick Chairman and CEO James Zarley Named One of Digital Coast Reporter's Top 100 Internet Executives," *Canadian Corporate News,* January 30, 2001.

"ValueClick Completes Acquisition of Z Media," *Canadian Corporate News,* February 6, 2001.

"ValueClick Continues to Provide Ad Solutions As Network Grows," *Electronic Advertising & Marketplace Report,* October 19, 1999.

"ValueClick to Extend Result-Driven Pricing," *New Media Age,* November 30, 2000, p. 2.

"Ventura County Star, Calif., Roger Harris Column," *Knight-Ridder/Tribune Business News,* August 20, 2001.

Weisul, Kimberly, "ValueClick Could Live Up to Its Name," *Inter@ctive Week,* March 27, 2000, p. 92.

Whiddon, Robert L., "ValueClick Awaits Its Turn for an IPO," *IPO Reporter,* March 13, 2000.

—David P. Bianco

Vebego International BV

Postbus 23092
Cortenbach 1
NL-6367 Voerendaal
The Netherlands
Telephone: +31 45 562 83 33
Fax: +31 45 562 83 34
Web site: http://www.vebego.com

Private Company
Incorporated: 1943 as Hago
Employees: 14,736
Sales: EUR 505.86 million ($500 million) (2001)
NAIC: 551112 Offices of Other Holding Companies;
561320 Temporary Help Services; 561720 Janitorial
Services; 561210 Facilities Support Services

Vebego International BV is a private, family-owned holding company specializing in the services industry. Based in Voerendaal, in the Netherlands, Vebego is active in four primary areas: Cleaning and Facilities Services; Facilities Management; Personnel Services; Products and Systems. The company also operates a Greenfields division responsible for the development of innovative business areas. Cleaning and facilities services, the company's founding business, remains its largest component, generating more than 67 percent of Vebego's revenues of EUR 506 million in 2001. In the Netherlands, the company's Cleaning and Facilities Services operations are carried out by subsidiaries Hago, Fortron, Westerveld Schoonhouders, Stoffels Cleaning, and Bleijenberg. Vebego has also established a strong international cleaning services component, notably through subsidiaries Care, in Belgium, Ambach Hospach in Switzerland, Hago in Germany, Carrard in France, and Indigo in the United Kingdom. Personnel Services is Vebego's second largest component, generating nearly 24 percent of sales, principally through the company's Tence! (Netherlands) and Tence! Interim (Belgium) subsidiaries. Vebego's Facilities Management operations are grouped under subsidiary Prisma Facility Management, operating in the Netherlands and Germany. Facility Management produced 4.3 per-

cent of the company's sales. Products and Systems supplies technical cleaning products through subsidiary Alpheios, in the Netherlands, Belgium, and France. This subsidiary generated nearly 5 percent of company sales in 2001. In terms of geographic breakdown, the Netherlands remains by far the company's core business area, at more than 55 percent of sales. France, Belgium, and Switzerland combine to add more than 30 percent of sales, while the United Kingdom (7.3 percent) and Germany (3.5 percent) are also important growth regions for the company. Vebego also has operations in Italy and Portugal. The company is owned and run by brothers Ton and Ronald Goedmakers, sons of founder Ton Goedmakers.

Cleaning Start in Wartime

Vebego had its start during World War II when Ton Goedmakers founded a cleaning company called Hago in Voerenlaan, in the Netherlands. Goedmakers at first concentrated on window-cleaning services. The company quickly signed on a number of high-profile customers, including Dutch State Mines (later DSM), and Dutch electronics giant Philips. Hago's work for Philips enabled the company to expand to include a wider range of cleaning services. Hago's relationship with Philips soon extended to contracts for cleaning Philips facilities throughout much of the Netherlands, enabling the company to establish itself on a national level.

Another early and important customer was the Diaconnessenhuis hospital in Eindhoven. This contract brought Hago into the healthcare cleaning services segment for the first time. Healthcare was to become one of Hago's most prominent markets, and the company later gained a position as the leading provider of cleaning services to the healthcare industry in the Netherlands. By then, Hago had more or less completed its national coverage, with five regional companies.

In the 1950s, Hago's growing operations brought it into contact with Swiss cleaning products and systems developer Wetrok AG. Hago became the exclusive importer of Wetrok products for the Netherlands. Initially, Hago reserved the Wetrok line for its own cleaning operations. In 1958, however, the company set up a new subsidiary, Alpheios, which began sales and distribution of Wetrok products and systems for other Netherlands-based contract cleaning companies. Alpheios developed a full range of technical cleaning products and systems, while Wetrok and its products continued to play an important role in the company. Meanwhile, Alpheios expanded internationally, opening subsidiaries in Belgium and France.

Alpheios represented a move into industrial cleaning products. In the 1960s, Hago became interested in extending its cleaning expertise into the consumer market as well. The company began importing bulk quantities of cleaning products and in 1968 formed a new subsidiary, Toron. At the beginning, that subsidiary merely repackaged its bulk imports into consumer-sized containers. In the 1970s, however, Toron began acquiring licenses for the manufacture of cleaning supplies for third-party brand names. In 1979, Toron branched out, forming the Dicom manufacturing partnership to produce bath soap and shampoos.

By then, Ton Goedmakers had been joined by son Ton Goedmakers, Jr. Together, the father-son team restructured the company's now diversified operations under a holding company, Vebego, a name adapted from the longer name Verenigde Bedrijven Goedmakers (Goedmakers United Businesses). Vebego then began to plot its national and international development.

Diversified Holding Company in the 1980s

At the end of the 1970s, Vebego made a number of expansion moves. In addition to creating the Dicom consumer cleaning products joint venture, Vebego gathered its window-cleaning operations under a new specialist subsidiary, Fortron. The company began to expand its Hago cleaning services businesses as well, opening a subsidiary in Germany. International growth remained a company target, and in 1979 the company, building on its relationship with Wetrok, extended its Cleaning and Facilities Services business into Switzerland.

In that year, the company made its first significant acquisition, that of Amberg Hospach AG. Founded in 1972, Amberg Hospach had chiefly developed business in the Zurich region. Under Vebego, the subsidiary extended its operations with a series of branch openings throughout much of German-speaking Switzerland, before entering the French-speaking region in the early 1990s.

Vebego continued building its Cleaning and Facilities Services division in the 1980s, notably with the acquisition of Westerveld Schoonhouders in 1990, based in Hilversum. That company, founded in 1945, was active in the western region of

the Netherlands. The following year, the company acquired a stake in Stoffels Cleaning, based in Terneuzen. Founded in 1954, Stoffels added a new regional component to Vebego's Cleaning and Facilities Services operations with a focus on the Dutch southwest. By the end of the decade, Vebego had taken full control of Stoffels Cleaning. By then, the company had acquired another regional component, with a stake in Bleijenberg, based in Vlissingen.

The 1980s was also a time of strong international growth for Vebego. A series of partnerships brought it into a number of new foreign markets, beginning with Belgium and Spain, and then extending to France, through subsidiary Carrard Propreté; Italy, through Impresa Pulizia, based in Cuneo; and the United Kingdom, through Indigo Services UK, based in Romford, England. In 1989, the company strengthened its position in the Belgian market with the acquisition of Care NV. Established in 1974, Care was, like many of the Vebego companies—and like Vebego itself—a family-owned company. Vebego's respect for the family-oriented nature of many of its subsidiaries led the company to adopt, in 1987, a decentralized management structure, which allowed its subsidiaries to operate as more or less autonomous businesses, under the central guidance of the Vebego holding company.

Vebego had by then extended its operations into a new area, that of Personnel Services. In 1985 the company acquired a stake in temp agency Uitzendburo Walcheren, before taking full control of that business. Vebego quickly made a series of acquisitions, including that of Bis, based in Roosendaal; Interval, based in Weert; and Spring Time, based in Amsterdam. The company also launched its own business, in a partnership located in Zeeland, called Zuidgeest. By the end of the decade, however, Vebego united all of its temp agency businesses under a single banner, Tènce!

Family Commitment in the 21st Century

In the late 1980s, Vebego began preparing a move into a new service category, Facilities Management. By 1990, the company had finished development of this new arm, and launched subsidiary Prisma Facility Management, as a partnership. Soon after, Vebego decided to sell off its Consumer Products operations, a process begun in 1995. Vebego nonetheless maintained its Alpheios industrial cleaning products and systems subsidiary, which also served as a research and development facility for products and systems used by other Vebego subsidiaries.

The exit from consumer products allowed the company to focus on developing its remaining businesses. In 1996, the company acquired a 50 percent stake in two Belgian personnel services companies, Interwork and Locamet, which together formed a network of 11 offices in that country, and had been owned by venture capital firm Brant Beheer. Vebego renamed its new Belgian operations as Tènce! Interim; later that year, Vebego acquired full control of Tènce! Interim. At the same time, Vebego acquired full ownership of Prisma Facility Management. In 1998, the company began expanding that business into Belgium, then launched a second Prisma subsidiary in Germany.

Vebego grew steadily throughout the 1990s, starting the decade with sales of approximately EUR 275 million, and

Key Dates:

1943: Ton Goedmakers establishes Hago as a window-cleaning service.

1958: Alpheios, a cleaning products and systems distribution subsidiary, is formed.

1968: Toron consumer products subsidiary is formed.

1976: Firm changes structure to that of holding company under the name Vebego.

1979: Vebego enters Switzerland with acquisition of cleaning services company Amberg Hospach.

1985: Vebego begins acquiring personnel services companies and launches new subsidiary Tènce! Uitzendburo; acquires Westerveld Schoonhouders.

1986: Company acquires Stoffels Cleaning.

1987: Company adopts decentralized management structure.

1990: Vebego launches Prisma Facility Management subsidiary.

1995: Company sells off Consumer Products division.

1996: Company acquires two Belgian personnel services companies and forms Tence! Interim subsidiary for Belgium.

1998: Prisma extends operations into Belgium and opens subsidiary in Germany.

2000: Vebego launches Vitz Consultants Vitaliseringsdiensten subsidiary as part of new Greenfields division.

2001: Belfien, another Greenfields project, is established to offer cleaning and other services to households and residential properties.

beginning the new century with revenues of more than EUR 500 million. Despite suggestions that the company might ultimately go public, Vebego steadfastly remained committed to its family-owned status. Meanwhile, the company launched a new division, called Greenfields, dedicated to exploring new and innovative business areas. One of the first of these was launched in the year 2000, with the founding of Vitz Consultants Vitaliseringsdiensten, a consulting service specialized in helping customers define and improve their in-house cleaning services operations. Then, in 2001, Vebego created another new subsidiary, Belfien, a company dedicated to providing a range of ''comfort and convenience'' services, including housecleaning, gardening, security and other services, to homeowners and residential properties. At nearly 60 years, Vebego had captured a leading share of the Netherlands' cleaning and facilities ser-

vices markets, a strong share in the personnel services market, and a growing presence on the European market.

Principal Subsidiaries

Alpheios International B.V.; Alpheios B.V.; Alpheios Belgium N.V.; Alpheios France S.A.S.; Amhoco AG Zug (Switzerland); Belfien B.V.(50%); Care N.V. Deurne (Belgium); Carrard S.A.S. Reims (France); CIP SRL Cuneo (Italy); Groupe Service Ouest S.A.S. (France); Hago Nederland B.V.; Hago Huiszorg B.V.; Hago Gebäude-Service GmbH & Co KG (Germany); Indigo Services Group B.V.; Indigo Airport Services Ltd. (U.K.); Indigo B.V.; L'activité S.A.S. (France); PCL Ltd. Yately (UK) 51; Peters Cleaning B.V.; Prisma Facility Management B.V.; Prisma Facility Management N.V. (Belgium); Prisma Facility Management GmbH & Co KG (Germany); Prisma Facility Management S.A. (France); SBV Holding B.V. 50%); Schoonmaakbedrijf Fortron B.V.; Stoffels Cleaning B.V.; Tènce! Interim N.V. (Belgium); Tènce! Personeel & Projecten B.V.; Tènce! Uitzendbureau B.V.; Toron B.V.; Uitleenbedrijf De Pooter Axel B.V. (50%); Uitzendbureau Zuidgeest B.V. (50%); Vebego International B.V.; Vebego Management Consultancy B.V.; Vebego Products B.V.; Vebego Products N.V. (Netherlands Antilles); Vebego Services — Amberg Hospach AG (Switzerland); Vebego Services B.V.; Vebego Services S.A.S. (France); Vebego Services GmbH (Germany); Vebego Services Serviços de Limpeza S.A. (Portugal); Vitz Consultants Vitaliseringsdiensten B.V.; Westerveld B.V.

Principal Divisions

Cleaning and Facilities Services; Facilities Management; Personnel Services; Products and Systems.

Principal Competitors

ISS-International Service System A/S; Facilicom Bedrijfsdiensten BV; CSU Total Care BV; Asito BV; Tennant NV; Euroclean SA; Iris SA; Etablissements Francis Laurenty SA; ELVIA Reiseversicherungs-Gesellschaft.

Further Reading

''Nederland voor meeste bedrijven niet groot genoeg,'' *Het Financieele Dagblad*, December 3, 2001.

Omnink, Gert, ''De inhaalrace van de schoonmakers,'' *Rotterdams Dagblad*, 1997.

''Schoonmaken op de serieuze kaart zeten,'' *De Ondernemer*, December 2000.

—M. L. Cohen

Velocity Express Corporation

7803 Glenroy Road
Four Paramount Plaza, Suite 200
Minneapolis, Minnesota 55439
U.S.A.
Telephone: (612) 492-2400
Toll Free: (800) 433-1066
Fax: (612) 492-2499
Web site: http://www.velocityexpress.com

Public Company
Incorporated: 1993 as U.S. Delivery Systems, Inc.
Employees: 10,300
Sales: $471.7 million (2001)
Stock Exchanges: NASDAQ
Ticker Symbol: VEXP
NAIC: 484110 General Freight Trucking, Local; 492110
    Couriers; 492210 Local Messengers and Local
    Delivery; 541614 Process, Physical Distribution, and
    Logistics Consulting Services

Velocity Express Corporation is one of the largest providers of same-day delivery and distribution/logistics services in the United States. In contrast to the next-day delivery business, which is dominated by major national players, such as FedEx Corporation and United Parcel Service, Inc. (UPS), the same-day sector of the delivery business is highly fragmented, with close to 6,000 firms in operation in the United States, most of them conducting business only locally. Velocity Express has been a leading consolidator within this sector. By mid-2001 the company had in place a network of 200 locations in 86 of the top 100 U.S. metropolitan areas. The company fleet included about 7,000 vehicles, and there were more than 1,500 Velocity Express agents in North America. The firm was making in excess of 150,000 deliveries every day, with a record of 98 percent on-time performance—a particular point of pride given Velocity's emphasis on service reliability. In addition to its same-day ground delivery services, Velocity Express also offers supply chain management services, fleet replacement, warehousing and storage, and limited long-haul services. The wide range of businesses served by the company includes finan-cial institutions, healthcare and medical organizations, retailers, petrochemical firms, and technology companies.

From Idea to IPO to National Network

The origins of the same-day delivery operations that are the core of Velocity Express can be traced back to those of U.S. Delivery Systems, Inc., which was founded by Clayton K. Trier, a one-time accountant who eventually developed a reputation as an acquirer and consolidator. Prior to founding U.S. Delivery, Trier had served as co-CEO in the late 1980s of a Houston firm called Allwaste, Inc., which grew rapidly through a string of acquisitions of small companies within the highly fragmented industrial waste cleaning business† In 1993 Trier was approached by his friend Michael Baker, head of a venture capital firm called Notre Capital Ventures, about taking a similar approach to the same-day, local delivery market. According to a 1995 *Forbes* article, Trier's immediate reaction was, ''You mean those spiky-haired guys on bicycles?''

Of course, the market was much bigger than just the bicycle messenger business. In the mid-1990s, U.S. businesses were spending $15 billion for the services of same-day local delivery companies. This segment of the market was highly fragmented, consisting of about 10,000 companies, most of which were privately held and operated in only one market. None of the firms held more than 2 percent of the national market share. The idea was to create a national same-day delivery service, following the example set by FedEx in the overnight delivery sector.

As he researched his friend's idea further, Trier found a number of trends that indicated that the time might be right for a national same-day delivery company. First, companies were increasingly turning to outsourcing for noncore activities, one of which was local delivery operations. Second, to maintain lower levels of inventories, companies were using sophisticated inventory control systems along with just-in-time delivery of components and materials; this increased the demand for same-day delivery services. Third, the same general trend toward a quicker pace of business that had earlier increased the demand for second-day and next-day delivery services (and that continued to be driven by the increasing speed of communication in the high-tech world) was now tending to increase the demand for same-day deliveries. Finally, major companies with locations scattered around the country were clamoring for the efficiencies and cost-savings that could be realized by being able to deal with just one same-day delivery firm rather than the dozens that they had been relying on. There was also an operational advantage to building a national network in that the delivery company itself could realize savings in overhead and certain operating expenses.

Having convinced himself through his research of the merit of the idea, Trier, with the backing of Notre Capital Ventures, formed U.S. Delivery Systems, Inc. in November 1993, basing the firm in Houston. Trier was named chairman, president, and CEO. The firm had no operations at the time, but in a clever maneuver, Trier planned to complete an initial public offering simultaneous with the acquisition of six local delivery companies and one telemarketing services firm, thereby raising the needed funding. On May 20, 1994, the company completed its IPO, selling three million shares of common stock on the New York Stock Exchange at $10 per share. This represented 40 percent of the company's equity. The remaining shares were retained by the initial investors, who saw the value of their investment skyrocket. At the time of the IPO, for example, the 10 percent stake that Baker's Notre Capital Ventures had gained for $2.3 million was worth $7.5 million. Out of the $29.2 million netted from the IPO, about $19.4 million in cash went toward purchasing the seven founding companies. In addition to the cash, the acquisitions also involved 3.4 million shares of U.S. Delivery common stock.

The seven founding companies had combined for about $108 million in revenues in 1993. The six local delivery companies had operations in a number of major markets and therefore formed a solid base upon which to grow. Eastway Transportation Services, Inc. operated in eastern Texas and Louisiana. First National Courier Systems Inc. had locations in Woodside, New York, and in Boston. Grace Courier Service, Inc. had operations in New York City, White Plains, and Long Island City, New York; Paramus and Edison, New Jersey; Newington, Virginia, a suburb of Washington, D.C.; and Tampa and Fort Lauderdale, Florida. U.S. Courier Corporation of San Francisco had been serving the San Francisco Bay area for 15 years. U.S. Service Corporation of America had locations in Los Angeles, San Diego, Chicago, and Milwaukee. ViaNet, Inc. was serving markets in Texas, Louisiana, and Tennessee. The telemarketing firm, CallCenter Services, Inc., was based in Salisbury, Maryland, and provided inbound telemarketing services that were used to process home delivery orders for catalog retailers.

From the start, U.S. Delivery offered several different types of same-day delivery services. Scheduled and routed delivery services were offered for time-sensitive local deliveries that were recurrent. Financial institutions were the prototypical users of this type of service, with an example being a bank needing to have canceled checks or ATM receipts picked up from various locations and then transported to a central processing center. A second type of service was "dedicated vehicle,"

or what the company later called "distribution services." In this case, a customer, usually a wholesale distributor, needed a bulk supply of some product divided up into smaller batches for delivery to several locations. For example, a pharmaceutical wholesaler might need a shipment of a particular drug delivered to several local drugstores. On-demand delivery comprised the third category and was usually offered 24 hours a day, seven days a week. In this case, a customer could request immediate pickup and delivery of the item(s) in question, choosing from one-hour, two-hour, and four-hour service. As part of its on-demand services, U.S. Delivery also offered air-courier/freight services. Other services offered by the firm included delivery management, warehousing, and just-in-time delivery services.

Working quickly toward its goal of creating a nationwide network, U.S. Delivery completed the acquisition of an additional 18 businesses by the end of 1994. Among the additional markets added via these purchases were Atlanta, Baltimore, Charlotte, Jacksonville, Orlando, Philadelphia, Phoenix, and Salt Lake City. For the year, the company reported net income of $5.3 million on revenues of $127.9 million. At this point, Trier was involved more in the acquisitions side of the business, while the day-to-day operations were being headed up by Gary W. Grant, who had been named senior vice-president and COO in March 1994. Grant had been one of the founders of ViaNet.

During 1995 U.S. Delivery completed more than two dozen additional acquisitions. By the end of the year, the firm had more than 150 locations that served 70 major markets using more than 6,500 delivery vehicles. The workforce had swelled to 6,400. Also in 1995, U.S. Delivery entered the contract logistics business through the purchase of American Distribution System, Inc. Based in Keego Harbour, Michigan, American Distribution provided logistics management services, which entailed the coordination, distribution, and warehousing of products for commercial and industrial clients.

Subsidiary of Corporate Express: 1996–99

Rather than continuing to expand on its own, U.S. Delivery agreed in January 1996 to be bought by Corporate Express, Inc. in a stock swap valued at about $410 million. Since its founding in 1986, Corporate Express had grown into a national powerhouse in the supplying of large companies with office products and services the same way that U.S. Delivery had built its national delivery network: through the acquisition of small, local, privately held firms. Corporate Express completed the acquisition of U.S. Delivery in March 1, 1996. Both companies viewed the merger as a way of enhancing their national networks, and there were obvious synergies in terms of both firms serving a similar clientele. The executives at U.S. Delivery also anticipated that the merger would enable the company to grow at a faster pace through both acquisition and internal expansion and would give the firm access to highly evolved information systems that had been developed at Corporate Express.

Following the merger, Trier briefly joined the Corporate Express board of directors, and Grant also joined the firm as president of the delivery operations, which became a subsidiary of Corporate Express that was eventually renamed Corporate Express Delivery Systems, Inc. (CEDS). The headquarters for CEDS remained in Houston. For the fiscal year ending on

Key Dates:

1993: U.S. Delivery Systems, Inc. is founded to establish a nationwide network of same-day delivery services.

1994: Simultaneous with an IPO that raises $29.2 million, U.S. Delivery acquires seven companies, including six local delivery firms; an additional 18 local delivery companies are acquired by U.S. Delivery following the IPO.

1996: Firm is acquired by Corporate Express, Inc., becoming a subsidiary known as Corporate Express Delivery Systems, Inc. (CEDS).

1997: United TransNet, Inc., the second largest same-day delivery company in the nation, is acquired.

1998: Under new Chairman and CEO Peter Lytle, Minneapolis-based U-Ship, Inc. enters the same-day shipping business.

1999: U-Ship changes its name to United Shipping & Technology, Inc.; Corporate Express sells CEDS to United Shipping for about $60 million.

2000: United Shipping changes the name of its same-day delivery operations to Velocity Express.

2002: United Shipping changes its name to Velocity Express Corporation.

March 2, 1996, the delivery subsidiary accounted for $342.5 million of Corporate Express's total revenues of $1.59 billion.

The pace of acquisition was initially faster for CEDS, with 20 more delivery companies acquired during the fiscal year ending on March 1, 1997. The most significant of these was the purchase of Roswell, Georgia-based United TransNet, Inc., the second largest same-day delivery company in the nation. The transaction, completed in November 1996, involved $138 million in Corporate Express stock. Founded only in 1994, United TransNet had combined a number of local same-day delivery companies into a growing national concern whose 1995 revenues were about $254 million. The firm's operations were centered mainly in the eastern United States. With the addition of United TransNet and the other acquired companies, revenues for CEDS more than doubled during fiscal 1996, reaching $759.8 million.

In 1997 but particularly in 1998 Corporate Express began running into problems digesting all of the acquisitions it had made, the acquisition pace slowed considerably, and the company stock price took a beating. The integration of United TransNet into CEDS proved especially nettlesome, and the same-day delivery subsidiary began losing money. In January 1999 Corporate Express announced it intended to either reduce its ownership interest in CEDS or sell it outright. The delivery business was declared to be a discontinued operation.

Reemerging As an Independent Firm Called Velocity Express

Takeover rumors began swirling around Corporate Express because of its troubles as the firm posted a net loss for fiscal 1998 and the stock continued to languish. Finally, in July 1999, the Dutch firm Buhrmann N.V. reached an agreement to purchase Corporate Express for $2.3 billion. The deal was contingent upon Corporate Express finding a buyer for CEDS. In September 1999 Corporate Express sold CEDS to Minneapolis-based United Shipping & Technology, Inc. for about $60 million.

United Shipping, which was known as U-Ship, Inc. from its founding in 1991 to May 1999, had been mainly involved in making and operating self-service, automated shipping systems that were used by consumers and small business shippers to ship packages and express letters through major carriers such as UPS. Although touted for their convenience (customers could access them 24 hours a day), the shipping centers never really caught on with consumers or businesspeople, and U-Ship posted a string of losses, including a loss of $2.5 million on revenues of just $917,000 for the fiscal year ending in June 1997. By December 1997 the company was close to running out of money and faced a possible delisting from the NASDAQ SmallCap Market. Peter Lytle, a business strategist and turnaround specialist, was brought in as chairman and CEO in early 1998 to save the firm from bankruptcy and revamp the company strategy.

Lytle quickly brought U-Ship back from the brink by raising $2.6 million in new equity through private placements. Then in July 1998 Lytle made the critical decision to expand the company's operations by moving into same-day delivery services the same way that U.S. Delivery had: by buying up existing local delivery firms and consolidating them into a larger and larger entity. Initially this was viewed as an extension of the company's shipping kiosk business, and Lytle believed that the firm's advanced shipping technology would give it a competitive advantage. U-Ship created a new subsidiary called Advanced Courier Services, Inc. as its platform for same-day delivery acquisitions in September 1998, and in late 1998 the first acquisition was completed, that of JEL Trucking, Inc., which operated in the Minneapolis—St. Paul metropolitan area. A second company, Twin Cities Transportation, Inc., was acquired in January 1999. U-Ship then changed its name to United Shipping & Technology in May 1999.

After learning that Corporate Express Delivery Systems was for sale, Lytle boldly suggested to his board of directors that United Shipping make a bid, despite his company having revenues of less than $2 million compared to the more than $600 million of CEDS. Nevertheless, if the acquisition could be pulled off, United Shipping would instantly achieve its goal of operating a nationwide same-day delivery service. Lytle was able to pull off the deal—beating out 21 other bidders in the process—completing the acquisition of CEDS in September 1999 for about $60 million, plus the assumption of $60 million in debt. CEDS's name was then changed to UST Delivery Systems, Inc., which was set up as a subsidiary of United Shipping.

Riding high on its acquisition coup and beginning to see the dividends of a new strategy aimed at going after e-commerce clients, United Shipping saw its stock trade well in excess of $10 a share by early 2000. Just two years earlier, the stock was going for 12 cents per share and the company verged on bankruptcy. The firm significantly improved its balance sheet in May 2000 by selling 2.8 million preferred shares, which were convertible to about 13 percent of the outstanding common stock, for $9 each to TH Lee.Putnam Internet Partners, a venture capital firm specializing in e-commerce. The $25.2 million thus raised was used to pay down debt that had been incurred to acquire CEDS and also provided United Shipping with additional working capital. One month later, the company unveiled its new brand for the same-day delivery service, Velocity Express; UST Delivery Systems was renamed Velocity Express, Inc. For the year ending July 1, 2000, United Shipping reported a net loss of $28.2 million on revenues of $471.2 million.

In October 2000 Jeffry J. Parell was named president and CEO of Velocity Express. Parell had been president of the North American Rental Group of AutoNation, Inc., where he was responsible for rental operations. Just four months later, Parell took over as CEO of United Shipping, with Lytle remaining chairman. Meantime, in November 2000, United Shipping sold one of its two air courier units, Tricor America, Inc., in a paring back of a noncore operation. By the early months of 2001 United Shipping was struggling again—it continued to lose money, bad winter weather and a stumbling economy were not helping matters, and the share price had made a precipitous drop to below $1 a share. The company was forced to scale back on its ambitious growth plans—talk of becoming a $1 billion company at least temporarily disappeared—and it launched an $11 million cost-cutting program that involved the streamlining of its existing operations through the consolidation or elimination of loss-making delivery locations. Nearly 250 jobs were eliminated from the workforce as a result of this restructuring. To improve the working capital situation, United Shipping raised $15 million through another private placement of preferred shares. The revenues of $471.7 million were nearly flat for the fiscal year ending June 30, 2001, while the net loss widened to $35.3 million thanks to a $7.1 million restructuring charge.

United Shipping was able to further strengthen its balance sheet in July 2001 by reaching an agreement with Corporate Express in a follow-up to the acquisition of CEDS. Through the agreement, United Shipping was able to eliminate $43 million in liabilities from its balance sheet. The company's improved financial position enabled it to stave off another threatened delisting from the NASDAQ exchange. In August 2001 Lytle retired from the company board and was replaced as chairman by Vince Wasik, a cofounder and principal of MCG Global, a private equity firm that had helped United Shipping with its restructuring efforts and its negotiations with Corporate Express and had also taken a stake in the company. United Shipping in October 2001 completed its exit from the air courier business by selling its remaining air unit, Air Courier Dispatch, Inc., to an investment group. One month later, United Shipping added two high-profile names to its board of directors: William S. Cohen, former U.S. Secretary of Defense, and Jack Kemp, former Secretary of Housing and Urban Development.

In January 2002 United Shipping was merged into its Velocity Express subsidiary and was renamed Velocity Express Corporation. In April of that year, Velocity Express executed a five-for-one reverse stock split, thereby increasing the share price to a level that it was hoped would make the stock more appealing to institutional investors. Through the first nine months of the 2002 fiscal year, the company saw its income fall significantly, from $365 million to $261.7 million, as a result of the elimination of unprofitable delivery locations, the divestment of the air

courier business, and the faltering U.S. economy. On the positive side, the net loss of $11.4 million was a major improvement over the $26.7 million of the previous nine-month period, and the firm was able to report operating income of $231,000, compared to an operating loss of $21.8 million a year earlier. Although its long-term prospects still seemed somewhat shaky, Velocity Express was certainly on more solid ground as a result of its restructuring efforts and its focus on strengthening the balance sheet.

Principal Subsidiaries

Velocity Express, Inc.; U-Ship International Ltd.; U-Ship America, Inc.; Intelligent Kiosk Company; Advanced Courier Services, Inc.; United Acquisitions, Inc.; United Vehicle Leasing, Inc.

Principal Competitors

Dynamex Inc.; Dispatch Management Services Corp.; CD&L, Inc.; FedEx Corporation; United Parcel Service, Inc.; United States Postal Service; Airborne, Inc.; DHL Worldwide Express, Inc.

Further Reading

Barshay, Jill J., "Seeking More Growth, Edina-Based U-Ship Inc. Names Director CEO," *Minneapolis Star Tribune*, June 7, 1997, p. 2D.

Boisseau, Charles, "Delivering the Goods with Gusto," *Houston Chronicle*, June 27, 1995.

Goldberg, Laura, "Delivering the Goods: Corporate Express Caters to E-commerce," *Houston Chronicle*, May 4, 2000.

Hassell, Greg, "Houston Firm Wants to Take Local Delivery Nationwide," *Houston Chronicle*, August 15, 1994.

Jean, Sheryl, "Plymouth, Minn.-Based Shipping Firm Believes Same-Day Delivery Will Grow," *St. Paul Pioneer Press*, September 6, 2000.

Ketelsen, James, "Learning the Hard Way," *Forbes*, December 18, 1995, pp. 130+.

Niemela, Jennifer, "Get Educated," *Minneapolis-St. Paul CityBusiness*, April 7, 2000, p. S14.

Pybus, Kenneth R., "Allwaste Ex-President Goes Public with Nationwide Delivery Network: U.S. Delivery Systems Seeking $48 Million to Buy Seven Businesses," *Houston Business Journal*, April 11, 1994, pp. 1+.

——, "Forging a Delivery Network from Fragments," *Houston Business Journal*, November 4, 1994, pp. 12+.

——, "U.S. Delivery Breaks New Ground in Purchasing Michigan Company," *Houston Business Journal*, February 24, 1995, p. 2.

St. Anthony, Neal, "Cold Winter, Cool Economy Hurt United Shipping," *Minneapolis Star Tribune*, May 18, 2001, p. 1D.

——, "Stock Deal Gives Shipping Company Cash and Credibility," *Minneapolis Star Tribune*, May 19, 2000, p. 1D.

Stone, Adam, "Gaining Velocity," *Minneapolis-St. Paul CityBusiness*, September 14, 2001, p. 13.

Yip, Pamela, "U.S. Delivery Systems Offered Buyout: Colorado Firm Proposes $410 Million Deal," *Houston Chronicle*, January 8, 1996.

Youngblood, Dick, "U-Ship, Long at Sea, Tries to Set Profitable Course Under New Management," *Minneapolis Star Tribune*, June 24, 1998, p. 2D.

—David E. Salamie

Vought Aircraft Industries, Inc.

9314 W. Jefferson Boulevard
Dallas, Texas 75211
U.S.A.
Telephone: (972) 946-2011
Fax: (972) 946-3465
Web site: http://www.voughtaircraft.com

Private Company
Incorporated: 1917 as Lewis and Vought Company
Employees: 4,800
Sales: $1 billion (2001 est.)
NAIC: 336411 Aircraft Manufacturing; 541710 Research
and Development in the Physical, Engineering, and
Life Sciences

Vought Aircraft Industries, Inc. is the world's largest independent aerostructures manufacturer. The firm traces its origins back to the pioneering designer Chance Vought. From its heritage as a manufacturer of innovative naval aircraft, Vought has evolved into a major aerospace subcontractor, supplying large, complex aerostructures for many commercial and military aircraft. The Carlyle Group, a Washington, D.C.-based defense industry investment firm, owns about 90 percent of the company.

Launch During World War I

Chance Vought, born in 1890 as Chauncey Milton Vought, became known as one of the most creative American aircraft designers during World War I. He designed his first complete plane (the PLV) in 1914, only a couple of years after becoming a pilot himself. Vought landed jobs at Simplex Aircraft and, later, the Wright Company, where he was chief engineer of the legendary firm for a short time.

With backing from sportsman Birdseye B. Lewis, Vought founded Lewis and Vought Company in Long Island, New York, on June 18, 1917, to make aircraft needed during World War I. The VE-7 "Bluebird" trainer was the company's first product. While serving on General Pershing's staff, Lewis died

in a plane crash in France in 1918. The Lewis and Vought firm would survive the drop-off in demand that accompanied the end of the war.

Pioneering Naval Aviation Between the Wars

In the 1920s, Vought pioneered the field of naval aviation. In 1922, a VE-7SF fighter made the first carrier take-off from the *USS Langley*. In May 1922, Lewis and Vought was reorganized as the Chance Vought Corporation, with Chance Vought's father being brought in as company president. In 1926, the O2U-1 Corsair entered production. It had been designed by Rex B. Beisel, who by then had already joined the staff at Curtiss.

During World War I, Vought met Pratt & Whitney founder Frederick Rentschler and began using his firm's Wasp engine in his designs. When Boeing Airplane and Transport acquired Pratt & Whitney Aircraft, Chance Vought Aircraft was brought into the new United Aircraft and Transport Corporation, incorporated on February 1, 1929, along with propeller manufacturer Hamilton Aero.

Chance Vought died from septicemia (blood poisoning) on July 25, 1930, at the age of 40 (aviation pioneer Glenn H. Curtis had passed away just two days earlier). His replacement as chief engineer was Rex Beisel, who rejoined the company in September 1931.

United Aircraft and Transport was dissolved on September 26, 1934. Within a few months, Chance Vought, Pratt & Whitney, Sikorsky, and Hamilton Standard were all made part of the new United Aircraft Manufacturing Company.

Winning Wings in World War II

Vought continued to make a small number of naval aircraft until the outbreak of World War II. The SB2U Vindicator, a light bomber, first flew in 1936 but was obsolescent by the start of the war in spite of its low-winged monoplane configuration. Two other designs were more successful. The OS2U Kingfisher began production in 1940 and excelled in its role as an observation aircraft. The F4U Corsair would become one of the most respected fighters of the era and Vought's best-known aircraft.

In 1938, Rex Beisel had launched a design effort for a new fighter specification calling for use of a powerful 4,000 horsepower engine; when the F4U Corsair began flight tests it was the first American fighter to top 400 mph. The famous gull-winged fighter was the plane that decisively bested the Japanese Zero as the two fought for domination of the Pacific skies. The Corsair was flown by Col. Gregory "Pappy" Boyington, USMC, leader of the legendary Black Sheep Squadron. In a ten-year production run that ended in December 1952, 12,571 Corsairs were made.

The legendary Igor Sikorsky had been part of the design team for the F4U Corsair. Sikorsky Aircraft had joined the United Aircraft and Transport Corporation on July 30, 1929. This was combined into United Aircraft's Vought-Sikorsky Division on April 1, 1939.

Towards the end of the war, Vought was developing the XF5U "Flying Pancake," a twin-engine flying wing designed to excel at low speed flight and carrier operations. In 1948, the program was canceled by the Navy, which was by then emphasizing jet fighters. Vought developed one of the first naval jets, the F6U Pirate. Its successor, the revolutionary but troublesome F7U Cutlass, borrowed heavily from German jet technology.

Postwar Relocation

Chance Vought relocated to Dallas in 1948, taking over the "B" Plant formerly occupied by North American Aviation. The move was initiated by the Navy, which did not want both of its main aircraft suppliers (the other being Grumman) located on the East Coast. Involving 1,500 employees and 50 million pounds of equipment, it was the largest industrial move to date, yet the production lines were barely disturbed.

Chance Vought became an independent company again on July 1, 1954. The company was spun off (first as a subsidiary in January 1954) owing to concerns that it might gain unfair advantage from Pratt & Whitney's dealings with other manufacturers.

The F7U Cutlass was succeeded by the F8U Crusader, later designated F-8, which first flew in March 1955 and remained in production until 1965. This fighter, used by the navies of the United States and France, was unique in employing a variable-incidence wing to facilitate carrier landings. The U.S. Navy's first single-engine supersonic fighter, the F-8 remained in the fleet for 31 years.

Part of a Conglomerate in the 1960s and 1970s

Chance Vought was renamed Chance Vought Corporation in December 1960, but was soon a takeover target of Ling-Temco

Electronics, which had been formed through the acquisition of the former Texas Engineering and Manufacturing Company by Ling-Altec Electronics. Antitrust suits failed to stop the merger with Vought, and the Ling-Temco-Vought Corporation was formed on August 31, 1961, in a leveraged buyout. Fred Detweiler, who had become head of Vought after Rex Beisel stepped down in the early 1950s, resigned in protest. Texas industrialist James J. Ling, the man behind his namesake company, himself was forced to step down as CEO by his creditors and was succeeded by Robert McCulloch.

The Chance Vought Corporation name survived until a reorganization of Ling-Temco-Vought on October 20, 1963. Chance Vought operations formed the bulk of the LTV Aerosystems Corporation, formed in 1965 as a subsidiary of Ling-Temco-Vought.

In spite of the success of the new A-7 attack jet, the parent company accrued massive debts in the late 1960s, and Ling was forced to relinquish his chairmanship of Ling-Temco-Vought. Vought head and former test pilot W. Paul Thayer became Ling-Temco-Vought's new CEO in 1970. He sold off holdings such as Braniff Airways Inc. and Okonite Co. to reduce debt.

When Ling-Temco-Vought was renamed LTV Corporation in the early 1970s, it had three operating divisions: LTV Aerosystems, LTV Electrosystems, and LTV Ling-Altec. By this time, LTV Aerosystems was comprised of Vought Aeronautics Company, a few other units, and Vought Helicopters, Inc., a unit set up in 1969 to market Aérospatiale helicopters in North America. This subsidiary was sold to Aérospatiale in 1974 and renamed Vought Helicopter Corp.

In 1972, the Vought units were reorganized as the Vought Systems Division of LTV Aerospace, which itself was renamed Vought Corporation on January 1, 1976. The parent company LTV Corporation had become a $4 billion diversified conglomerate, with significant holdings in steel and food processing. With revenues exceeding $500 million and pretax profits of $41 million, Vought Corp. accounted for 12 percent of LTV's sales in 1975.

At this time, Vought's only prime contracts were the A-7 Corsair II attack jets being produced for the Navy and the Army's Lance missiles. *Business Week* reported that the A-7 program had brought Vought $3.3 billion in business between 1964 and 1977.

A New Focus in the 1980s

By 1980, reported *Aviation Week & Space Technology,* Vought's corporate strategy had shifted to becoming a major prime contractor in missiles, projected to be a growth market for the coming decade. Vought had already produced more than 3,000 Lance missiles, used by the United States and several European armies. Subcontracting work had already become a significant part of Vought's business. Vought was conducting unique research in the areas of hypervelocity (low-explosive projectiles achieving speeds of up to 5,000 feet per second) and lethality.

LTV Corporation made an attempt to acquire 70 percent of rival Grumman Corp. in 1981, but the sale was blocked on antitrust grounds. Two years later, CEO Paul Thayer left LTV

Key Dates:

1917: Lewis and Vought Company is founded.
1929: Vought joins Pratt & Whitney-led United Aircraft and Transport Corporation.
1935: Chance Vought becomes part of new United Aircraft Manufacturing Company.
1939: Vought-Sikorsky Division is formed as division of United Aircraft.
1948: Chance Vought moves to Dallas plant.
1954: Chance Vought becomes an independent corporation again.
1968: Grand Prairie plant is built.
1976: LTV Aerospace becomes Vought Corporation.
1983: Vought Corporation is renamed LTV Aerospace and Defense Company.
1992: Carlyle Group and Northrop acquire LTV Aircraft Division, which is renamed Vought Aircraft Company.
1994: Northrop Grumman acquires remainder of Vought from Carlyle.
2000: Carlyle Group buys Northrop Grumman's aerostructures business and revives the Vought name.

for a stint as deputy secretary of defense. A restructuring in April 1983 renamed Vought Corporation as LTV Aerospace and Defense Company, and it was organized into two divisions: Missiles and Advanced Programs, and Aero Products. These were renamed the Missiles and Electronics Group and the Aircraft Products Group at the end of September 1986.

Poor results in LTV's steel and energy businesses forced the company to enter a long and litigious bankruptcy in July 1986. LTV Aerospace and Defense Co., however, was consistently profitable, posting operating earnings of $164 million on sales of $2.3 billion in 1985.

In the late 1980s, LTV was placing its hopes on the YA-7F, an upgrade of the A-7 Corsair II attack jet. This was the company's last program as a prime contractor; the Air Force preferred the General Dynamics F-16. LTV Aircraft had sales of about $700 million in 1989.

New Owners in the 1990s

LTV's bankruptcy resulted in the Aerospace and Defense division being offered for sale in May 1991. Martin Marietta and Lockheed together bid $355 million for the unit. A competing bid launched by Thomson SA, the French aerospace giant, raised political questions regarding foreign ownership in the defense industry.

In the end, LTV Aircraft went to Northrop and the Carlyle Group, which had also backed Thomson's bid, for $230 million. The whole unit was renamed Vought Aircraft Company. Loral paid $244 million for the LTV Missiles and Space Division, renaming it Loral Vought Systems. Both transactions closed on August 31, 1992.

Vought Aircraft attained sales of $1 billion in 1992, while reducing staffing levels 30 percent in three years to 7,300 employees. The company had diversified its subcontracting business to a nearly 50–50 split of commercial and defense work. It was involved in a handful of major programs: the Boeing 747, 757, and 767 on the civil side and the Northrop B-2 stealth bomber and McDonnell Douglas C-17 military transport. In June 1993, Gulfstream selected Vought to produce the wings for its new Gulfstream V business jet.

Vought President Gordon Williams credited the company's improvement on a commitment to total quality management (TQM). He rated Vought as one of the top two composite material structures fabricators in the United States, next to Boeing. Vought had also invested in advanced, flexible manufacturing equipment for large aluminum and titanium parts.

Vought was fielding cooperative bids for two major military aircraft contracts. It was on the McDonnell Douglas-led team to develop a successor to the Grumman A-6 naval strike aircraft designated A/F-X. The Pampa 2000 was a venture with FMA of Argentina to field an entrant for the USAF/US Navy Joint Primary Aircraft Training System (JPATS) program.

The commercial aviation business suffered from a world recession and effects of the Persian Gulf War in the early 1990s, and Boeing's cutback prompted Vought to cut 1,500 jobs in 1993.

Northrop Grumman Corp. exercised an option to buy the Carlyle Group's 51 percent share of Vought Aircraft Co. in July 1994. Northrop had earlier acquired Grumman Corp. for $2.2 billion. Northrop Grumman paid $130 million for Vought, which eventually became part of its Integrated Systems and Aerostructures sector.

Carlyle Buying Again in 2000

Northrop Grumman sold its aerostructures unit to the Carlyle Group in a deal worth $1.2 billion in July 2000. Carlyle renamed the business Vought Aircraft Industries. Sales at the unit had fallen from $1.6 billion to $1.4 billion in 1999, and Northrop Grumman preferred to focus on growth opportunities in defense electronics and information technology.

Vought Aircraft Industries cut 20 percent of its 6,000 strong workforce in late 2001 following a downturn in the civil aviation market and a downturn in Boeing business. At the same time, the company began closing a plant in Perry, Georgia, and moving its operations to its factory in Stuart, Florida. Grumman had opened the latter site in 1950 as a flight-testing facility.

Vought CEO Gordon Williams left the company to become chairman of the Carlyle Group in January 2002. He was succeeded at Vought by Tom Risley.

Principal Operating Units

Dallas; Hawthorne; Midgeville; Perry; Stuart.

Principal Competitors

CPI Aerostructures, Inc.; Goodrich Corporation; LMI Aerospace, Inc.

Further Reading

"Aerospatiale's US Subsidiary Aims at North American Market," *Aviation Week & Space Technology,* June 2, 1975, p. 127.

Brown, Stanley H., *Ling: The Rise, Fall and Return of a Texas Titan,* New York: Atheneum, 1972.

Bulban, Erwin J., "Vought Sees Missiles As Area of Growth," *Aviation Week & Space Technology,* July 28, 1980, p. 67.

"Commander Sees Need for Interim A-10 Replacement," *Aviation Week & Space Technology,* September 23, 1985, p. 16.

"FTC to Block LTV Takeover of Grumman," *Aviation Week & Space Technology,* November 2, 1981, p. 22.

Guyton, Boone T., *Whistling Death: The Test Pilot's Story of the F4U Corsair,* Atglen, Pa.: Schiffer Military/Aviation History, 1994.

"LTV Corp. Files for Chapter 11," *Aviation Week & Space Technology,* July 21, 1986, p. 28.

"LTV's Campaign to Save Vought," *Business Week,* March 7, 1977, p. 24.

"LTV: Weak Growth in Mature Industries," *Business Week,* April 5, 1976, p. 50.

Marshall, Rick, "Automation Leads at Vought," *Defense & Foreign Affairs,* September 1984, p. 32.

Martinez, Amy, "Carlyle Closes Northrop Deal; Stuart Plant Now Vought Air," *Palm Beach Post,* July 25, 2000, p. 7B.

Millot, Bernard, *Les avions Vought,* Paris: Editions Lariviére, 1983.

Moran, Gerard P., *Aeroplanes Vought, 1917–1977,* Temple City, Calif.: Historical Aviation Album, 1978.

Pattillo, Donald M., *Pushing the Envelope: The American Aircraft Industry,* Ann Arbor: University of Michigan Press, 1998.

Peltz, James F., "Northrop to Buy Rest of Vought," *Los Angeles Times,* July 13, 1994, p. D2.

Phillips, Edward H., "Vought Pursuing Seat on Sonic Cruiser Team," *Aviation Week & Space Technology,* April 15, 2002, pp. 69–70.

Ropelewski, Robert, "Role Shift Keeps Vought Taut, Viable," *Interavia Aerospace World,* August 1993, pp. 17–21.

Ruesink, David C., and Michael C. Kleibrink, "Mexican-Americans from the Rio Grande to Ling-Temco-Vought," *Labor Law Journal,* August 1969, pp. 473–79.

Stevenson, Richard W., "Making a Difference; An Aerospace Executive with Good Reason to Smile," *New York Times,* March 1, 1992, Sec. 3, p. 10.

Tillman, Barrett, *Corsair: The F4U in World War II and Korea,* Annapolis, Md.: Naval Institute Press, 2002.

——, *Vought F4U Corsair,* rev. Ed., North Branch, Minn.: Specialty Press, 2001.

Veronico, Nick, and John M. and Donna Campbell, *F4U Corsair,* Osceola, Wis.: Motorbooks International, 1994.

"Vought Sees Reagan Policy Increasing Exports of A-7s," *Aviation Week & Space Technology,* September 28, 1981, p. 66.

"Vought Submits Proposal to Navy for New A-7X," *Aviation Week & Space Technology,* May 25, 1981, p. 21.

"Why Grumman Insists and LTV Deal Won't Fly," *Business Week,* October 12, 1981, p. 46.

—Frederick C. Ingram

W.P. Carey & Co. LLC

50 Rockefeller Plaza
New York, New York 10020
U.S.A.
Telephone: (212) 492-1100
Toll Free: (800) 972-2739
Fax: (212) 492-8922
Web site: http://www.wpcarey.com

Public Company
Incorporated: 1998 as Carey Diversified LLC
Employees: 95
Sales: $139.4 million (2001)
Stock Exchanges: New York
Ticker Symbol: WPC
NAIC: 531190 Lessors of Other Real Estate Property

W.P. Carey & Co. LLC, an investment firm headquartered in New York City's Rockefeller Plaza, is the preeminent provider of corporate real estate financing solutions. The company specializes in acquiring properties which are then leased back to the tenant company. As a result, the real estate is removed from the tenant company's balance sheet, unlocking capital that can be utilized for corporate initiatives such as funding future growth, paying down debt, facility expansion, or build-to-suits. Major corporations engaged in such leasing arrangements with W.P. Carey include Federal Express, Wal-Mart, and PETsMART, Inc. In addition, W.P. Carey works closely with private equity firms seeking to optimize the capital structure of their portfolio companies through the sale-leaseback of owned real estate. Transactions are typically with a single-tenanted property with a lease structure based on a triple net lease arrangement, in which the tenant, in addition to rent, pays for maintenance, taxes, and insurance on the property. In addition to acquiring properties, W.P. Carey also serves as the manager of four real estate investment trusts (REITs), including the Corporate Property Associates series of funds—CPA:12, CPA:14, and CPA:15—and Carey Institutional Properties Incorporated (CIP). In all, W.P. Carey owns and/or manages more than 450 properties located across the United States and Europe, totaling more than 55 million square feet of space.

Founding of W.P. Carey: 1973

Wm. Polk Carey founded W.P. Carey in 1973. Born in 1930 in Baltimore, Maryland, he grew up during the Depression. Having firsthand experience of difficult times would lead him to adopt a conscientious and careful approach to real estate investments. He attended Princeton University from 1948 to 1950 and ultimately earned a B.S. in Economics from the University of Pennsylvania's Wharton School. Following a two-year stint in the United States Air Force, he went to work for A.J. Orbach Co. in Plainfield, New Jersey, rising to the level of vice-president and general manager. In 1959, at the age of 28, he decided to strike out on his own and form his first company—International Leasing Corporation, a name he chose primarily because it was available. At first, he leased equipment and vehicles to corporate customers and arranged the private placement of debt. He later took on the leasing of aircraft and complete factories. His first major deal, completed in 1960, was historic, the first direct investment that the government of Australia ever permitted. The client was L.J. Hooker, an Australian whose seven million acres of land made him the world's largest private landowner. Carey arranged financing so that Hooker could expand his business empire, which included hotels and livestock.

Carey's first business taught him valuable lessons that he would apply to future endeavors. He learned that equipment leasing was both a highly competitive and risky business—you could not count on the lessee to properly maintain the equipment and were uncertain of its residual value when the lease expired. Carey realized that by using a net lease approach, the lessee would be responsible for maintenance and operating costs. Carey recognized that net leasing real estate would be even more advantageous, since the residual value of the property was easier to gauge. Furthermore, Carey learned that he could borrow against the credit of the lessee. If the lessee had a solid credit rating and could meet the lease payments, Carey could go to a bank and arrange to finance a major share of the capital needed to buy the equipment being leased. In a similar way he would be able to receive a mortgage on the real estate.

446

It was when Carey merged International Leasing with Hubbard, Westervelt & Mottelay in 1964 that he became involved in the net leasing of corporate real estate. In 1967, he joined Loeb, Rhoades & Co., which ultimately became a part of Lehman Brothers, to head the Real Estate and Equipment Financing department. In 1971, he went to work as the director of corporate finance for duPont Glore Forgan Inc. In 1973, he resigned and at the age of 43 faced a crossroads in his life. According to a speech he delivered to the Newcomen Society, "I was being wooed by Lazard Freres, among others. I was quite content to be part of a large organization—the opportunities real and challenging, the compensation appropriate and the atmosphere congenial. But I despised the office politics that big, competitive operations often breed, and I hadn't forgotten the pleasures of being the boss. I made up my mind when I saw some really cheap office space at 67 Wall Street. The rent was less than we now pay for flowers."

Beginning Business in 1973

Although his new company, named W.P. Carey & Co., began business with an impressive address, it was unable to arrange for directors and officers liability insurance. As a result, the board of directors numbered just three: Carey; his brother Frank, a practicing attorney; and brother-in-law Raymond C. Clark, who headed Baltimore's Canton Co., operator of the world's largest privately owned marine terminal. Carey hired an acquisitions officer, Jim Umlauf, who had worked in the corporate finance department at duPont Glore Forgan. Umlauf was charged with the unenviable task of drumming up the company's initial business. According to Carey, Umlauf called "all one thousand of the *Fortune* 1000 companies. Nine-hundred ninety-seven turned us down, but three agreed to give us some business. Even so, we came close to selling the firm to First Boston Corporation, despite unfavorable terms, because it took so long for our first deal to close and cash to start flowing." To provide some security to the business, Carey combined transaction-related income with asset management income. In an interview with *Global Real Estate Now,* he explained, "In the asset management aspect, our asset management fees would cover the main overhead of the company so that if the transaction didn't work out, we would still be able to survive."

During the first years of its existence, W.P. Carey focused on lease-back ventures which served more as tax shelters than revenue producers. Although many high-flying firms were engaged in the same activity, Carey quickly grew wary of these tax-advantaged transactions. Because so many companies were pushing the boundaries on tax shelters, he felt that it was only a

matter of time before the government cracked down. That day of reckoning would come in 1986, by which time W.P. Carey had long since abandoned tax shelter deals. The company turned to real estate limited partnerships (RELPs) in 1979, launching CPA:1, the first in a series of Corporate Property Associates investment funds. Only later, when the Tax Reform Act of 1986 made it more attractive, would W.P. Carey turn to real estate investment trust (REIT) funds. CPA:1, with $20 million in capital, was designed to provide a consistent return for its investors, the only tax shelter component being a function of depreciation. All of the CPA funds focused on long-term leases, offered stable returns and served as an effective hedge against the cyclical nature of the stock market.

Carey took steps to make sure that the company was making sound investment decisions, creating an independent investment committee to be involved in the approval of all acquisitions. "Basically, I set it up," Carey conceded, "because I'm a deal man, and I wanted to protect myself against myself." A key player on the committee, George E. Stoddard, was hired shortly before the first CPA fund was launched. Stoddard had 30 years of experience with the Equitable Life Assurance Society of the United States, where he was in charge of a multibillion-dollar portfolio of investments. Carey convinced him to join the company, despite a number of attractive offers Stoddard received from other Wall Street firms. According to Carey, "George works closely with our acquisition staff, but his compensation, unlike theirs, does not depend on the number or size of our acquisitions. His goal is not to poke holes in their deals, but to make certain there ARE no holes, and to be sure the terms give us a return that is commensurate with the real risks." The importance of paying attention to detail became evident in problems associated with the firm's first RELP. A major tenant in the Denver area, which was overbuilt, had financial trouble and was forced to vacate three buildings. Finding new tenants proved difficult and the RELP's return was adversely affected.

With the investment committee in place, W.P. Carey developed a consistent acquisitions procedure for its new funds. The first step involved the careful selection of target properties and the sorting through of hundreds of potential deals brought to the firm's attention in the course of a year. In addition, W.P. Carey's acquisition staff searched for companies that were attractive candidates of lease-back deals. Credit worthiness was clearly important, but the firm was more than willing to take a chance on a company with potential that had not yet been recognized in the marketplace. Also relevant, but to a lesser degree, was the location of the property—only important in the event that the property had to be re-let or sold. Once the acquisition staff put together a deal, it still had to pass muster with Stoddard, then receive unanimous approval from the investment committee, which was comprised of other highly experienced executives. Only then would an acquisition be forwarded to the firm's board of directors for consideration. To further protect the interest of its investors, W.P. Carey was also diligent about spreading out the risk in its portfolio, diversifying investments by industry, geography, and property type.

Debut of First REIT: 1990

W.P. Carey's thoroughness resulted in steady returns on investments, good relations with lessees, and a sterling reputa-

Key Dates:

1959:   William Polk Carey forms his first company, International Leasing Corporation.
1973:   Carey forms W.P. Carey & Co., Inc.
1979:   First Corporate Property Associates investment fund is launched.
1990:   First real estate investment trust fund is offered.
1994:   Assets under management tops $1 billion.
1998:   Early CPA funds are used to create Carey Diversified LLC.
2000:   W.P. Carey & Co merges with Carey Diversified to create W.P. Carey & Co. LLC.

tion in the business world. As a result, while other companies suffered through the economic slump of the early 1990s, W.P. Carey maintained high occupancy rates and consistent profits. Unfortunately, it still suffered somewhat as a result of ''guilt by association.'' In 1990 the firm launched its first REIT fund, CPA:10, and had difficulty raising capital for it despite W.P. Carey's track record of above-average returns.

W.P. Carey launched CPA:11 in 1991, later called Carey Institutional Properties (CIP), because of its attractiveness to institutional investors. By 1994, the firm topped the $1 billion mark in assets under its management. That amount would surpass $2 billion in 1997. At this time, the earlier CPA funds had reached a point at which they could be closed down. According to Carey, the firm faced a dilemma: ''If we simply dissolved the funds and sold the assets, our investors—whose support and goodwill we had labored so tirelessly to earn and keep—would be saddled with huge, immediate taxes on $350 million in capital gains, just because we had been so successful. Many real estate operators were doing just that,'' he said. ''It wasn't easy, but we found a way for our investors to have their cake and eat it, too. In January 1998, with the overwhelming consent of the investors, we consolidated the first nine funds in the series, CPAs 1 through 9, into Carey Diversified, a Limited Liability Company headed by Frank Carey, which we immediately listed on the New York Stock Exchange.'' Because investors could swap their partnership interest for shares in the new company they not only avoided capital gains taxes, they were now in a position to achieve instant liquidity and decide for themselves when they wanted to realize capital gains.

The next step in the evolution of the firm came in June 2000 when its management company, W.P. Carey & Co., Inc., was merged with Carey Diversified LLC to form W.P. Carey & Co. LLC. The result was a fully integrated investment company—the nation's largest net lease firm and the world's largest publicly traded LLC, which was subsequently listed on the New York Stock Exchange and the Pacific Exchange. Not only did shareholders in the company enjoy the consistent returns of

Carey Diversified's net lease operations, they also benefited from the asset management business, which included the newer CPA series of REITs.

Altogether, the company had approximately $3.5 billion under ownership or management. In addition, it owned part of W.P. Carey International LLC, which was created to buy foreign properties for the public company's family of funds. Inroads were made in Europe, with acquisitions in France, The Netherlands, Finland, and the United Kingdom, as W.P. Carey also began to cast an eye towards the potentially lucrative markets of India and China.

The U.S. market, however, would continue to be a major focus for W.P. Carey going forward. With the economy struggling during the early years of a new century, an increasing number of companies were looking to sell their buildings and lease them back. With its reputation and expertise in net-leasing, W.P. Carey was well positioned to take full advantage of that rising trend. The founder of the firm, now more than 70 years of age, was optimistic and confident in the abilities of several young executives he had groomed to take over control of the business. Edward V. LaPuma was tabbed to oversee global operations and Gordon F. DuGan, the firm's president, was poised to run the domestic company. Carey stated his intention to remain as chairman ''for the foreseeable future but in a less hands-on fashion. I want to spend more time helping with the international side because I have a solid feel for it, having been in the business as a young man, and I enjoy it.'' There was every reason to believe that Carey would continue to make a valuable contribution and that the firm bearing his name would thrive for many years to come.

Principal Subsidiaries

Carey Asset Management Corp.; Carey Financial Corporation; W.P. Carey Development, Inc.

Principal Competitors

CarrAmerica; Crescent Real Estate Equities; Lexington Corporate Properties Trust.

Further Reading

Brown, Steve, ''To Tap into Cash, Many Firms Are Selling Their Buildings, Leasing Them Back,'' *Dallas Morning News,* January 25, 2002.

Carey, Wm. Polk, ''W.P. Carey & Co. LLC.,'' New York: The Newcomen Society of the United States of America, 2001.

Grant, Peter, ''Investor Backlash Hits Sober Syndicator,'' *Crain's New York Business,* November 19, 1990, p. 9.

''W.P. Carey & Co. LLC: Looking Global in 2002,'' *Global Real Estate Now,* Spring 2002, pp. 7–13.

—Ed Dinger

William Hill Organization Limited

Greenside House
50 Station Road
Wood Green
London N22 7TP
United Kingdom
Telephone: (+44) 870-600-0479
Fax: (+44) 113-291-2007
Web site: http://www.williamhill.co.uk

Public Company
Incorporated: 1939 as William Hill (Park Lane) Ltd.
Employees: 9,877
Sales: £2.45 billion ($3.92 billion) (2001)
Stock Exchanges: London
Ticker Symbol: WHO
NAIC: 713290 Other Gambling Industries 713210
    Casinos (Except Casino Hotels)

William Hill Organization Limited is the United Kingdom's second largest betting shop owner, with more than 1,500 shops, placing it behind Ladbrokes, part of the Hilton Group. That operation registers an average of 750,000 bets per day, covering 16 sports and some 38,000 sporting events per year. Yet William Hill also has become known for its quirky "amusement" bets, which have included taking odds on the outcome of the *Dallas* TV episode "Who Shot J.R.?," and whether the winter season will see a white Christmas. Since the late 1990s, William Hill has expanded successfully beyond its storefront betting parlors to capture the leading shares in the telephone betting market—the company has more than 400,000 registered telephone bettors, of which more than 150,000 are active bettors. The company also has extended its telephone betting services across Europe, and especially into Germany and Italy. William Hill also has taken a leading position in the online betting market, setting up its online sportsbook and casino operations in 1998. Set up in the Dutch Antilles in order to skirt stiff British betting taxes, the company's online business, available in ten languages and 12 currencies, attracted more than 12 million customers from 150 countries in 2001. After aborting a public offering in 1999, William Hill finally listed its stock on the London Stock Exchange in June 2002.

Origins in the 1920s

Born in Birmingham, England, in 1903, William Hill was already taking illicit, or off-track, bets at area pubs by 1920. While cash-based betting had been illegal since the 1850s, bookmakers were allowed to take bets based on credit. In 1925, Hill made his first attempt to enter credit-based bookmaking, with a focus on horse racing. But that operation quickly folded when Hill lost his start-up capital.

The legalization of organized greyhound racing in 1926 gave Hill his next opportunity. Hill moved to London in 1929, placing bets on the greyhound races held there. Hill's success enabled him to become a part owner of the Northholt Park racetrack. By 1934, Hill was able to open his first off-track betting parlor for credit-based bets. Hill's new business flourished, and, after moving to a new location on Park Lane, Hill incorporated his company as William Hill (Park Lane) Ltd.

From his new offices, Hill expanded his betting operations, offering ante-post odds and then adding fixed odds for soccer—known as football in the United Kingdom—matches. The football operation proved particularly successful, and in 1944 Hill moved that business to its own quarters, establishing a second business, William Hill (Football) Ltd. By then, Hill also had extended his operation outside of London, opening up a subsidiary office in Scotland.

By the early 1950s, Hill was able to claim more than 400,000 customers. He also had proven himself to be a skilled breeder, after winning the Derby with his horse, Nimbus. Meanwhile, the company's continued success led it to go public in that decade. In addition to taking credit-based bets, the company also accepted postal bets—as long as they were postmarked before the day of a race. Meanwhile, the restrictions on cash bets had created a vibrant black market industry, often operated in collusion with corrupted officials.

The British government legalized cash-based betting in 1961, and bookmakers were allowed to open off-track betting

Company Perspectives:

William Hill intends to pursue a strategy aimed at delivering sustainable earnings growth and value for shareholders. The key elements of this strategy are to: Continue to enhance traditional earnings and maximise organic growth opportunities; profitably exploit new platforms; capitalise on opportunities arising from regulatory, fiscal and technological change; and selectively pursue value-enhancing acquisitions.

parlors. Nonetheless, the new shops were placed under a number of restrictions—such as being forced to black out their windows, limitations on opening hours, and the barring of food and beverages—which combined to give the off-track betting parlor an unsavory reputation. William Hill himself decided not to enter the newly legalized category and refused to open off-track betting parlors.

Hill gave in on his stance as the off-track betting parlors rose in popularity into the mid-1960s. In 1966, Hill entered that business by buying up a number of shops. This was a costlier move than setting up his own shops at the outset would have been, particularly since bookmaking had suffered two significant blows. In 1964, the British government imposed a hefty 25 percent gambling tax on fixed odds betting, William Hill's mainstay. Then, in 1966, a new betting duty was instituted. Initially set at a 2.5 percent rate, the duty was steadily increased, hitting 6 percent by the 1970s, and 10 percent by the 1990s.

Changing Hands in the 1970s and 1980s

Throughout the late 1960s and 1970s, William Hill continued to open new betting shops, while adding others through a string of acquisitions. The company was able to impose itself as one of the leaders of the vast market—which had seen the opening of nearly 15,000 off-track betting parlors across the United Kingdom by the mid-1970s. William Hill's network continued to expand, growing to 800 shops by the mid-1980s.

Beyond sports and race bets, William Hill also was branching out into so-called "amusement" bets, such as accepting a bet, at 1,000-to-1 odds, that a man would walk on the moon before 1970—a bet the company lost in 1969. Another amusement bet gained the company worldwide publicity in 1980, when the company fixed odds on the culprit behind the "Who Shot J.R.?" mystery in the television program *Dallas*. By then, the company changed hands, when it was bought by British retail giant Sears Ltd. after William Hill's death in 1971.

Under its new owners, William Hill branched out in racing sponsorships, backing such races as the William Hill Futurity at the Doncaster racing grounds—a race won by the company's own stable of thoroughbreds in 1976. By then, William Hill had become the United Kingdom's largest horse racing sponsor. In 1981, the company, on the back of its "Who Shot JR?" notoriety, attempted to break into the U.S. market as well, sponsoring the William Hill Trophy at the Belmont Park racetrack in New York.

Television coverage of races was allowed into betting parlors in 1986 for the first time, although restrictions remained on the size and number of televisions allowed in the shop. The introduction of television enabled William Hill to introduce, in 1987, its Hillsport system of text and audio to its network of shops. By then, the betting sector had begun its first round of consolidation, and in 1988, William Hill was sold to Grand Metropolitan (later renamed Diageo) for £330 million. That company already controlled its own bookmakers network, Mecca Bookmakers.

The combination of William Hill with Mecca, into an enlarged William Hill Organization, created the United Kingdom's second largest bookmaker, behind Hilton Group-controlled Ladbrokes, with 1,800 shops. Meanwhile, William Hill had continued building up other areas of its business, notably its historic credit betting operation, which, after the addition of Mecca, became the world's largest. The company was also rapidly building a telephone betting operation. William Hill had garnered a number of other prestigious titles, including the award in 1975 of an exclusive license to make book for the Wimbledon Championships. In 1989, the company was named the official bookmaker for the PGA Golf Tournament. These were followed in the 1990s by exclusives on such events and venues as Wembley Stadium and the Rugby Union World Cup.

William Hill's stint with Grand Metropolitan lasted only a year. In 1989 fast-growing Pubmaster owner Brent Walker Ltd., led by former professional boxer George Walker, acquired William Hill for £650 million (the figure was later slightly reduced after a lawsuit alleging that Grand Metropolitan misrepresented William Hill's profitability). Under Chairman John Brown, who had begun with William Hill as a "tea boy" in the 1950s, the company continued to innovate. In 1990, William Hill added credit card services for the Grand National; the following year, it introduced a debit card-based telephone betting service.

New Technology Leaders for the 21st Century

The company extended its telephone services beyond the United Kingdom for the first time in 1992, when it began offering betting services in Germany and Italy—complete with German- and Italian-speaking operators. The company later extended the service elsewhere in Europe. In 1993, changes in legislation gave off-track operators more flexibility in their opening times, in particular, allowing parlors to remain open until 10 p.m. William Hill promptly added evening hours across its entire network.

In 1994, William Hill launched Accolade, a loyalty system that rewarded its customers according to their betting levels. In that year, also, U.K. betting shops were granted the right to accept fixed odds bets on football matches, a move made in preparation for a broader series of legislative changes to come the following year. In the meantime, the off-track betting industry faced a crisis with the launch of the first British National Lottery, which threatened to cut into the off-track gambling business.

The year 1975 saw a number of significant changes that not only liberalized the legal gambling industry, but did much to enhance the image of the off-track parlor. Significantly, parlors were no longer required to black out their windows; instead, parlors were allowed to use shop windows to advertise their services. On the inside, shops were now allowed to serve food and beverages, and the size restrictions on televisions were

<table>
<tr><td colspan="2">Key Dates:</td></tr>
<tr><td>1920:</td><td>William Hill, then 17 years old, begins acting as a bookmaker in the Birmingham, England region.</td></tr>
<tr><td>1934:</td><td>Hill opens his first credit-based betting business.</td></tr>
<tr><td>1939:</td><td>Hill incorporates his company as William Hill (Park Lane) Ltd.</td></tr>
<tr><td>1966:</td><td>William Hill acquires its first off-track betting parlors, which had been legalized in 1961.</td></tr>
<tr><td>1971:</td><td>After its founder's death, William Hill is bought by Sears Ltd.</td></tr>
<tr><td>1976:</td><td>William Hill branches out into horse-racing sponsorships.</td></tr>
<tr><td>1987:</td><td>Company introduces Hillsport text and audio service after betting parlors are allowed to install televisions the year before.</td></tr>
<tr><td>1988:</td><td>William Hill is acquired for £330 million by Grand Metropolitan, which combines the company with its Mecca Bookmakers operations to create the second largest betting parlor group in the United Kingdom.</td></tr>
<tr><td>1989:</td><td>Brent Walker Ltd. acquires William Hill for £845 million.</td></tr>
<tr><td>1995:</td><td>The first of a series of liberalized legislation on betting parlors is introduced.</td></tr>
<tr><td>1997:</td><td>Japanese banking group Nomura acquires William Hill for £700 million.</td></tr>
<tr><td>1998:</td><td>William Hill launches its online sports betting and casino web sites.</td></tr>
<tr><td>1999:</td><td>Nomura attempts to take William Hill public, but instead sells the company to CVC and Cinven for £825 million.</td></tr>
<tr><td>2002:</td><td>William Hill goes public in June, with an initial market value of more than £1 billion.</td></tr>
</table>

lifted. In addition, parlors were granted the right to sell the National Lottery's instant lottery cards.

William Hill introduced spread betting in 1995. Meanwhile, the betting industry continued to be liberalized. In 1996, shops were granted the right to install slot machines and similar "amusement" machines. The shops also were given the right to sell racing forms and magazines. Then, in 1997, shops were allowed to place advertisements in telephone directories and newspapers for the first time.

The year 1997 marked a new turning point for William Hill. Brent Walker's rapid expansion had brought the company under a crushing debt load—which had already led to George Walker's ouster at the beginning of the 1990s. By 1997, Brent Walker was forced to liquidate its holdings, and, after a sharp bidding war, the company was sold to Japan's Nomura for £700 million, beating out such rivals as investment firms Cinven and CVC Capital Partners. Despite the change, John Brown remained the company's chairman and CEO.

In 1998, William Hill, eager to skirt the hefty gambling taxes and duties imposed on bets from British residents, turned to the Internet, setting up an online betting and casino service. The company quickly established an offshore company, based in the

Dutch Antilles, to take over its online operations, enabling the company and its customers to reduce duty fees to just 5 percent. The company continued to lobby for a reduction, if not the abolishment of such taxes, notably with the establishment of an offshore telephone betting service, run through a call center in Ireland, where gambling duties were limited to just 3 percent.

By then, William Hill had suffered a serious setback. In 1999, Nomura announced its intention to float William Hill on the London stock exchange, a move that was greeted with enthusiasm by the industry. Yet at the last moment the company's financial advisors decided to cut the initial quote price, slashing the estimated value of the offering to £400 million. Instead, Nomura turned around and accepted an offer from Cinven and CVC Capital Partners, which offered £845 million for William Hill.

In 2000, William Hill launched a new, international online site, which enabled British gamblers to place duty- and tax-free bets for the first time. This move forced the British government's hand, and, just as it had been forced to accept cash-based betting in the 1960s, the British government now abolished the betting duty. This was replaced by a more equitable Gross Profits Tax in 2001. As a result, William Hill shut down its Ireland-based call center, combining that operation with its existing British facilities. That year, also, the company sold off its spread betting operation to IG Index, and refocused its business on its fixed odds operations.

William Hill at last made good on its public offering in June 2002. Led by new CEO David Harding, who took over after Brown's retirement in 2000, the highly successful floatation, oversubscribed by some ten times, gave William Hill a market valuation of more than £1 billion. By then, the William Hill Organization consisted of nearly 1,600 betting shops, a strong telephone betting service—the company claimed to be the U.K. market leader, with a 40 percent market share—and one of the industry's only profitable online betting operations. Continued legislative changes, including further reductions on slot machine and advertising restrictions, gave William Hill good reason to bet on its own future.

Principal Subsidiaries

William Hill Holdings Limited; William Hill Investments Limited; William Hill Organization Limited; William Hill Finance plc; Camec Limited; Laystall Limited; William Hill Casino NV (Netherlands Antilles); Betwilliamhill.com Limited (Antigua and Barbuda); Brooke Bookmakers Limited; Evenmedia Limited; Eventip Limited; Gearnet Limited; Ixora Company Limited (Antigua and Barbuda); James Lane Group Limited; Matsbest Limited; Vynplex Limited; William Hill Bookmakers (Ireland) Limited; William Hill (Caledonian) Limited; William Hill Call Centre Limited; William Hill Credit Limited; William Hill (IOM) Limited (Isle of Man); Windsors (Sporting Investments) Limited.

Principal Competitors

Camelot Group Plc; Ladbrokes Plc; Coral Eurobet plc; Sportingbet.com (U.K.) Plc; Stanley Leisure PLC; Horserace Totalisator Board; Victor Chandler International Ltd.

Further Reading

Cave, Andrew, ''Stock Market Favourite Who's Looking for Results,'' *Daily Telegraph,* June 22, 2002.

Cope, Nigel, ''Bookie Takes a Punt on the Stock Market,'' *Independent,* May 27, 2002, p. 19.

Dunne, Helen, ''The Green-Eyed Monster That Tripped Up Small Investors' Nap,'' *Daily Telegraph,* February 27, 1999, p. 1.

Osborne, Alistair, ''Buoyant William Hill Considers Going Public,'' *Daily Telegraph,* May 3, 2002.

——, ''Frontrunner in Cyberspace Race,'' *Daily Telegraph,* January 29, 2000, p. 33.

——, ''William Hill Eyes Bookies for Takeover As Float Price Is Fixed,'' *Daily Telegraph,* May 30, 2002.

—M. L. Cohen

WOODWARD

Woodward Governor Company

5001 North Second Street
P.O. Box 7001
Rockford, Illinois 61125-7001
U.S.A.
Telephone: (815) 877-7441
Fax: (815) 639-6033
Web site: http://www.woodward.com

Public Company
Incorporated: 1902
Employees: 3,654
Sales: $678.8 million (2001)
Stock Exchanges: NASDAQ
Ticker Symbol: WGOV
NAIC: 333611 Turbine and Turbine Generator Set Unit Manufacturing; 335314 Relay and Industrial Control Manufacturing; 336412 Aircraft Engine and Engine Parts Manufacturing

Woodward Governor Company is the world's oldest and one of the largest manufacturers of energy control systems and components for industrial and aircraft engines, turbines, and other power equipment. Examples of the company's products include ignition systems, fuel injection systems, integrated fuel systems, and power management controls. The main markets served by the company are power generation, transportation, process industries (such as the processing of oil and gas, petrochemicals, paper, and sugar), and aerospace. The bulk of Woodward Governor's sales are to original equipment manufacturers (OEMs), with General Electric Company accounting for nearly one-third of overall revenues. Other customers include Caterpillar Inc., Honeywell Inc., MAN AG, Pratt & Whitney, and Rolls-Royce plc. The company operates eight plants in the United States, two each in the United Kingdom and Germany, and one each in the Netherlands and Japan. Woodward Governor is also distinguished by a unique and proven management philosophy called the Corporate Partnership.

First Product: Waterwheel Governor

The company that would become Woodward Governor was founded in 1870 by Amos W. Woodward. Woodward was descended from the Woodward family that helped to settle Watertown, Massachusetts, in the 1630s. Born in 1829 in Winthrop, Maine, Woodward attended Kents Hill Academy for only one term. In that short time, however, he mastered higher mathematics and physics and was considered by many to be a genius. Woodward eventually went to work in a factory in Worcester, Massachusetts, before migrating to the Midwest, specifically Rockford, Illinois, in 1856. An inveterate tinkerer and inventor, Woodward managed to earn a modest salary by selling his innovations. He also held various mechanic jobs. It was through one of those positions, in fact, that he became intrigued with a major dilemma of the day: how to control the speed at which waterwheels turned.

Woodward solved the problem by designing a mechanism—the mechanical noncompensating waterwheel governor—in 1869. He received a patent for the device in 1870 and started a company to manufacture the governors. Despite the usefulness of Woodward's invention, the new company struggled. Besides lacking capital, Woodward also lacked the desire to build a profitable business. Like many other inventors, he was more interested in developing new ideas. Fortunately, his son Elmer Woodward had a greater knack for business. Elmer had started working in his father's shop as a boy and had, like his father, shown himself to be gifted in math and physics. On one occasion, for example, Elmer devised a contraption that automatically controlled the cutting speed and feeder of a machine that he was operating. Elmer was caught reading a book while the machine worked away.

Elmer Woodward's desire for learning stemmed from what he considered a poor formal education. To make up for the deficiency, he spent years studying technical books after dinner until midnight. As he got older, he became increasingly involved in the company's business affairs. It was then that the enterprise began to prosper. In 1891 the business had three employees and was selling about $8,000 worth of governors annually. During the 1890s, though, the company grew and

453

Company Perspectives:

Woodward is a world-class company with customer-focused engineering capabilities. We design and manufacture efficient, low-emission, cost-effective products. Woodward takes an aggressive approach to gaining market share and expanding our customer base. We will achieve these objectives using strategic acquisitions and alliances, as well as organic growth.

Woodward is rapidly becoming the preferred supplier for leading global equipment manufacturers—a system solution supplier.

---

even expanded into a larger manufacturing facility. At the same time that he was helping to run the business, Elmer Woodward, like his father, continued to invent. Importantly, in 1898, when he was 36 years old, Elmer received a patent for a governor that was an improvement over the one his father had designed. The breakthrough device gave the company an important advantage in the burgeoning market for governors needed to control new hydroelectric generators.

In 1902 Amos and Elmer Woodward incorporated as Woodward Governor Company. By that time they were employing 25 men at their Rockford manufacturing facility. As the hydroelectric power market surged during the 1910s and 1920s, so did Woodward Governor's sales. The company also expanded overseas into Europe, Japan, New Zealand, and elsewhere throughout the world. Indeed, by the 1920s the company was making more than 35 percent of its sales to foreign buyers. In 1910 Woodward Governor moved its operations to a new five-story plant. Elmer Woodward continued to tweak and improve the company's governors in an effort to meet new needs in the marketplace, helping the company's revenues to climb. Amos Woodward died in 1919, a few years short of his 90th birthday, and his son continued to lead Woodward throughout the 1920s. Early in 1929, when he was 67 years old, Elmer Woodward hired son-in-law Irl Martin to take over day-to-day operations, while he continued to design new products and make pivotal contributions to the company well into his 70s.

By 1929, Woodward Governor was employing 50 workers and had established itself as a leader in the design and manufacture of prime mover controls (prime movers are machines that convert either heat or hydraulic energy into mechanical or electrical energy); that year, the firm posted net income of $65,000 on sales of $318,000. Unfortunately, the company's fortunes were about to change for reasons outside of its control. The stock market crash of 1929 quashed demand for Woodward's waterwheel and hydropower governors. Martin was faced with a crisis, his handling of which would demonstrate his legendary management abilities and philosophies. Rather than lay off staff, Martin called all of the workers together and offered them a choice: either fill existing orders and hope for more, or keep everyone on the payroll at 20 hours per week and at a cut in pay until business improved. The workers elected to scale back hours and pay. Until the crisis was over, Elmer Woodward paid much of their wages out of his own pocket—a practice that was, and still is, almost unheard of in any kind of

corporation. It was later discovered that Woodward had borrowed against his own life insurance to meet the payroll.

Expanding the Product Line in the 1930s

The company's shipments began to pick up in 1932 and 1933, although the company was still lagging. Woodward and Martin realized that the company would be forced to find new sources of revenue to supplant lost demand. To that end, Woodward began developing a governor to control diesel engines that were being used at the time as auxiliary systems in hydroelectric plants. Under his supervision, the company perfected a governor for diesel engines in 1933 that would become the core of the company's product line for several years. The pivotal breakthrough provided an important boost to the company's sagging bottom line. In fact, Woodward Governor's elated workers were soon making up for lost time with 60-hour weeks. Unfortunately, the federal government, concerned with underemployment, forced the company to cut them back to 40 hours. Martin feared that the company would be unable to meet demand, but their workers, realizing the urgency of the situation, continued to work 60 hours per week at only 40 hours of pay.

Woodward Governor introduced another major product breakthrough in 1934: a governor that could control the pitch of an airplane propeller. An aviation company had approached the company about creating such a control, and several of the company's younger members had gone to work to design the contraption. Unable to solve the problem, they eventually called on 73-year-old Elmer Woodward to finish the job. Within several months his team delivered a perfected governor that would give Woodward Governor a much needed entry into the aviation industry.

Although sales surged during the mid-1930s as a result of the new innovations—and reached $1.4 million by 1939, exceeding the $1 million mark for the first time—the company's equipment and facilities had depreciated by the end of the decade. Rather than borrow the cash to renew the plant, Martin again called the employees together. They all agreed that everyone in the company should forego a pay raise in order to pay cash for new equipment. Thus, Woodward Governor emerged from the Depression with a broader product line, new equipment, little debt, and a family-like bond between labor and management that would distinguish the company in American industry. This bond also led the company to undertake a recapitalization in 1940 that greatly increased the number of shares of common stock, enabling employees to become stockholders in the company; coupled with the recapitalization was an initial public offering of the company stock, which also took place in 1940.

Much of Woodward Governor's success in the 1930s, and even over the next several decades, was attributable to Martin's unique management techniques. In the 1930s, for example, Martin realized that some of his skilled machinists and mechanics were not producing as much as he believed they could. He believed the problem was psychological and was attributable to the workers' poor self-image. To solve the problem, he instituted a dress code that included a tie and smock, and began requiring that all employees remain neatly shaven. The workers also agreed to begin keeping their work areas extremely clean and neat. Worker productivity improved greatly and, according to Martin,

Key Dates:

1870: Amos W. Woodward receives a patent for the mechanical noncompensating waterwheel governor and soon begins selling the devices, marking the beginning of Rockford, Illinois-based A.W. Woodward Company.

1902: Company is incorporated as Woodward Governor Company, with Amos's son Elmer Woodward now largely in charge of the firm.

1929: Elmer Woodward's son-in-law Irl Martin takes over day-to-day operations.

1930s: Company expands into controls for diesel engines and for airplane propellers.

1940: Woodward Governor goes public.

1946: Martin institutes the Corporate Partnership management scheme.

1955: Company builds first company factory outside Rockford, in Fort Collins, Colorado.

1976: Calvin C. Covert succeeds Martin as chairman and CEO.

1994: Company posts its first loss since 1940.

1995: John Halbrook takes over as chairman and CEO following Covert's death.

1997: Company stock is moved from OTC trading to the NASDAQ market.

1998: Fuel Systems Textron, Inc. is acquired for $174.8 million and is renamed Woodward FST, Inc.

2000: Company receives a five-year, $500 million contract from GE Power Systems.

the workers began to realize the true value of their contribution to the company and society. Among other of Martin's management innovations was aptitude testing, which was used to help determine where a worker would perform most effectively and happily. He also introduced a cutting edge health insurance program that focused on personal preventive medicine.

On December 31, 1940, 78-year-old Elmer Woodward, or "Pops" as he had come to be called, worked a full day, returned home, and then died of a heart attack. His exemplary service to the company spanned 64 years. Among other attributes, the soft-spoken Elmer was known for treating everyone as his equal, regardless of position or stature, as well as for earning the respect of all those who knew him. Irl Martin assumed complete leadership of the company after Elmer's death, just as Woodward Governor was entering the greatest growth phase in its history. Indeed, World War II placed huge demands on the company's production facilities as orders for its advanced propeller controls boomed; the advantage that the controls offered was that they reduced vibration in airplanes and ships by synchronizing and phasing the propellers of two or more engines.

Woodward Governor continued to innovate during the war, introducing, for example, the first aircraft turbine control in 1943, and sales skyrocketed. Amazingly, the company's ranks swelled from just 50 in 1935 to more than 1,600 during the war's peak. The explosive growth virtually changed the face of the company, which had moved its operations into a large new

factory at the very start of the war. Again, Martin consulted his workers about the new facility and they all agreed to forgo some compensation to build it. The facility was completely state-of-the-art, and was designed with worker productivity and satisfaction in mind. The plant became much less crowded after the war, when the workforce shrank to a more manageable 500. Although demand faded during that period, sales growth resumed in the wake of the postwar economic boom of the 1950s and 1960s.

Instituting the Corporate Partnership in 1946

In 1946 Martin instituted what would become one of his most noted management schemes: the Corporate Partnership. This plan led to a number of innovative management solutions. For example, Martin was concerned about the problem of determining equitable pay rates for everyone in the company, including himself. After much thought, he decided to present a solution to the employees. Under the new system, every employee, or "member," would receive no more and no less than ten times that of the least valuable category of worker. In addition, a bonus system was put in place. At the end of each year, workers and management would rank everyone in their department according to a given set of criteria. The rankings were combined and every employee then received a ranking within the entire company. That rank was used to determine an employee's percentage of the aggregate annual bonus.

During the mid-1950s Woodward Governor expanded its product line to include main fuel controls for aircraft gas turbines and electronic analog controls. Among the recognized innovations during the 1950s and 1960s were: the electrical cabinet actuator in 1957; the first truly electric governor in 1960; fuel valves for aerodrive turbines in 1962; control for turboprop engines in 1964; and a unique new electronic control system in 1965. As demand for the company's products increased, Martin expanded the company. In 1955 Woodward Governor built a new factory in Fort Collins, Colorado. Subsequently, Martin oversaw the installation of production facilities throughout the world in the Netherlands, England, Japan, and Australia. By the late 1960s, Woodward was generating annual revenues of about $70 million.

Although the 65-year-old Martin officially retired from the presidency in 1960, he remained as chairman of the board and led Woodward Governor into the 1970s. The company continued to introduce new products during the early 1970s and to strengthen its Corporate Partnership program. In fact, Martin became a sought-after speaker in the Midwest by groups wanting to hear about his unique management philosophy. Unfortunately, Martin's health began deteriorating in 1975. He resigned in March 1976 and died on April 22 after 55 years of service to Woodward Governor.

Thriving Under Covert's Leadership: 1976–89

Martin was succeeded by Calvin C. Covert. Covert had joined the company in 1942, going to work in the lowly "snagging" room, where he shaved rough spots off of castings. "One day Mr. Martin came out and said, 'Sonny boy, you made,'" Covert recalled in the January 1988 *Rockford Magazine*. Covert continued, "I said, 'made what.' And he said, 'I gave you one of the dirtiest jobs. Now what the hell do you want to do?' '' That began Covert's rise up the corporate ladder. By the time he took the helm in 1976, he had been working in top management for most of his career. Under his direction, Woodward Governor continued to create new products and to refine its management techniques. Major new products in the 1970s included an eight-bit microprocessor synchronizer and a digital synchronizer for aircraft. Covert also stepped up Woodward Governor's international expansion in 1977 with a new plant in Brazil.

The company thrived under Covert's leadership. It experienced a downturn in its important turbine division in the early 1980s, but by the mid-1980s its sales were approaching the $200 million mark. During the mid-1990s the company whipped its internal operations into shape and stepped up its growth pace. Indeed, $100 invested in Woodward Governor in 1976 would have grown to nearly $1,500 by 1988. That growth was largely the result of an economic upswing and increased demand from defense and aerospace industries during the mid- and late 1980s. Woodward Governor's sales leapt 13 percent in 1987 to $275 million as net earnings rose 37 percent to $24 million. By the end of the decade, moreover, the company was generating more than $300 million in revenues annually.

Although Woodward Governor was helped by strong markets during much of the 1980s, its success was also attributed to its proven management style, which was getting increased attention within American industry as a result of the company's ability to compete with Japan and other countries. As it turned out, Woodward Governor had long been practicing management techniques (such as employee empowerment and performance-based incentives) that were emerging as major trends in the 1980s. For example, the company's president received only $247,000 in total salary and bonuses in 1986, in keeping with the company rule of not making more than ten times the amount of the lowest job category. Likewise, new Woodward Governor employees were brought into the company by way of a solemn ceremony; other employees attended, and even joined in prayer, as the new employees were inducted into the Woodward "family." Finally, while Woodward Governor's workers received only about 80 to 90 percent of the salary of their U.S. industrial counterparts, their bonuses consistently placed them well above the national average in compensation.

Early 1990s Setback

Woodward Governor entered the 1990s with record sales and profits; revenues hit $362 million in 1991. Unfortunately, waning defense and aerospace markets were beginning to take their toll on the company's bottom line. Woodward Governor had been trying to reduce its dependence on the aircraft market since the mid-1980s, when over 60 percent of sales were attributable to that sector. But by the early 1990s the company was still getting more than 50 percent of its revenues from the aircraft market and was scurrying to beef up its activity in other sectors. Similarly, the company had seen the percentage of its sales attributable to defense markets fall from 20 percent in 1990 to less than 15 percent by 1993. To make up for the shortfall, Woodward Governor began concentrating on its industrial controls division, its only major segment other than aircraft controls.

Sagging key markets hurt Woodward Governor in 1993 and 1994. Sales slipped to $333 million in 1994, and the company

posted its first loss since 1940. By that time, John Halbrook had been brought on board as president and chief executive. Under his leadership, the company instituted aggressive cost-cutting measures in 1994 that resulted in a $24 million restructuring charge, which pinched its net earnings. The charge also forced the company to cut its aircraft division workforce by 20 percent, resulting in one of the biggest layoffs ever conducted by the organization. The restructuring also included the closing of a plant in Stevens Point, Wisconsin. Covert passed away in December 1994 at the age of 70, and Halbrook assumed his position as chairman, announcing his commitment to continue cutting costs and improving the company's market stance.

Despite setbacks going into the mid-1990s, Woodward Governor continued to research and introduce new products. It brought out innovative new digital controls in 1992 and 1993, for example, and had several advanced devices for both aircraft and industrial markets under development. Acquisitions were also completed, including the purchase of HSC Controls of Buffalo, New York, which made electromechanical devices for integrated control systems, especially for aircraft engines; and a small maker of fuel injection nozzles based in Kelbra, Germany, which became part of Woodward Governor Germany GmbH. In 1995, the year of Woodward Governor's 125th anniversary, the company bounced back, posting net income of $11.9 million on revenues of $379.7 million.

Growing Steadily, Late 1990s Through Early 2000s

Woodward Governor enjoyed steady growth from the late 1990s into the early 21st century, growth that was fueled by continual expansion of the product line, strategic acquisitions, and alliance formation. In July 1996 the company acquired Deltec Fuel Systems Holding B.V., a Netherlands firm specializing in fuel control systems for natural gas engines. The purchase was part of a company push to grab a share of the burgeoning market for natural gas engines. In October 1996 Woodward Governor and Mountain View, California-based Catalytica, Inc. created a joint venture called GENXON Power Systems, LLC to market an aftermarket emission control system for industrial gas turbines.

Early in 1997 Woodward Governor executed a four-for-one split of its stock. The increased liquidity set the stage for the company to take what many observers considered to be a long-overdue move: listing the stock on the NASDAQ. The move brought a heightened awareness to both the stock and the company because the company's shares had previously traded only via over-the-counter "pink sheets," a trading area usually used only for small start-up companies. The move to the NASDAQ, along with the company's increasing emphasis on acquisitions and alliances, highlighted a shift from the more conservative management style of the past to a much more aggressive approach.

The bold new approach was more than evident in the June 1998 acquisition of Fuel Systems Textron, Inc. from Textron Inc. for $174.8 million—by far the largest acquisition in company history. Based in Zeeland, Michigan, Fuel Systems Textron produced fuel injection nozzles, spray manifolds, and fuel metering and distribution valves for gas turbine engines used in both aircraft and industrial applications. The acquired company, which had revenues of $82 million in 1997, was subsequently renamed Woodward FST, Inc. The acquisition resulted in a substantial increase in revenues for the 1999 fiscal year, with revenues surging from $490.5 million to $596.9 million. Meantime, the company also acquired Baker Electrical Products, Inc. of Memphis, Michigan, in May 1998, gaining a supplier of electromagnetic coils for antilock braking systems; and formed an alliance with Lockheed Martin Control Systems to create a company called AESYS that was charged with creating fuel delivery systems for aircraft engine OEMs.

In June 2000 Woodward Generator received the largest single contract in its history, a five-year deal with GE Power Systems valued at more than $500 million. GE Power Systems was a unit of General Electric Company, which had long been Woodward Generator's largest customer. Under the contract, the company would supply GE Power Systems with fuel and combustion control systems and components for GE's array of industrial gas turbines for the power generation, oil and gas processing, and marine markets. At the time, power generation was considered a particularly key market as growing demand for power was leading to utilities building new generating plants. Woodward Generator also completed one acquisition during 2000: Hoeflich Controls, Inc., a maker of ignition systems for industrial gas engines, purchased in November.

In June 2001 the company acquired the Bryce diesel fuel injection business of Delphi Automotive Systems, which included a plant in Cheltenham, England. For the fiscal year ending in September 2001, Woodward Generator posted record profits of $53.1 million on record sales of $678.8 million. Hoping to get in on the ground floor of a potentially burgeoning new sector, the company announced in December 2001 that it was entering the market for fuel cell control systems.

Acquisitions continued in 2002. In March the company bolstered its power generation sector by acquiring Leonhard-Reglerbau, which produced monitoring devices for power generation equipment at its plant in Stuttgart, Germany. The company had 1991 sales of $13 million. Also acquired in March 2002 was Nolff's Carburetion, Inc., a private company in Romulus, Michigan, that produced fuel management systems for small industrial engines that use cleaner-burning fuels such as propane and natural gas. That same month, Woodward Generator entered into a joint venture with MotoTron, a subsidiary of Brunswick Corporation that had developed electronic controls technology for pleasure boat engines. Woodward Generator in April 2002 struck a seven-year, $350 million deal with GE Aircraft Engines to supply fuel delivery systems for engines used in regional and single-aisle aircraft. One month later, the company joined forces with one of its chief competitors, Hamilton Sundstrand Corporation, to establish a joint venture in China to repair jet engine parts, including fuel controls.

Many of Woodward Governor's initiatives in the early 2000s were aimed at bolstering the firm's industrial control operations, thereby continuing the drive to lessen dependence on the aircraft market. By 2002 industrial controls were generating about 60 percent of overall revenues. This trend became particularly important with the slump in the airline and aircraft industries that followed in the wake of the events of September 11, 2001. Despite the dismal economic conditions that prevailed into the following year, which were also slowing demand in the power generation sector, Woodward Generator managed through the first nine months of its 2002 fiscal year to post slightly higher profits and revenues. The company seemed well positioned to survive the turbulent economic times and to thrive in the long run.

Principal Subsidiaries

Baker Electrical Products, Inc.; Woodward FST, Inc.; Woodward Foreign Sales Corporation (U.S. Virgin Islands); Woodward HSC, Inc.; Woodward International, Inc.; Woodward Tianjin Controls Company Limited (China); Woodward Governor de Mexico S.A. de C.V.; Woodward Governor Asia/Pacific PTE. LTD. (Singapore); Woodward Governor France S.A.R.L.; Woodward Governor Germany GmbH; Woodward Governor GmbH (Switzerland); Woodward Governor India PTE. LTD.; Woodward Governor Nederland B.V. (Netherlands); Woodward Governor Poland, Limited; Woodward Governor (Japan) Ltd.; Woodward Governor (Quebec) Inc. (Canada); Woodward Governor (Reguladores) Limitada (Brazil); Woodward Governor (U.K.) Limited.

Principal Competitors

Hamilton Sundstrand Corporation; Parker Hannifin Corporation; Wabtec Corporation.

Further Reading

Anason, Dean, "This Isn't the Place to Rest," *Atlanta Business Chronicle,* May 26, 1995, p. 1B.

Braun, Georgette, "Smaller Is More for Woodward," *Rockford (Ill.) Register Star,* March 19, 2002, p. 1B.

——, "Two Local Firms to Team Up in China," *Rockford (Ill.) Register Star,* May 23, 2002, p. 1B.

——, "Woodward Buy Boosts Power Unit," *Rockford (Ill.) Register Star,* March 7, 2002, p. 2C.

——, "Woodward Inks $350 Million Engine Deal with GE," *Rockford (Ill.) Register Star,* April 3, 2002, p. 1B.

Bremner, Brian, "Caught in Crunch: Growth Crimps Woodward Governor," *Crain's Chicago Business,* January 25, 1988, p. 20.

A Gentleman Named Woodward, Rockford, Ill.: Woodward Governor Company, 1974.

Hodge, Bob, *The Woodward Way: A History of the Woodward Governor Company, Rockford, Illinois, USA, 1870–1995,* Rockford, Ill.: Woodward Governor Company, 1997, 224 p.

Knapp, Kevin, "Surging Power Demand Gives Turbine Parts Maker a Boost," *Crain's Chicago Business,* September 18, 2000, p. 47.

Knowles, Francine, "Woodward Governor Split Powers Stock," *Chicago Sun-Times,* November 22, 1996, p. 49.

McGough, Robert, "How to Win the Class Struggle," *Forbes,* November 3, 1986, p. 153.

Murphy, H. Lee, "Move to Big Leagues Ignites Woodward Governor's Stock," *Crain's Chicago Business,* January 27, 1997, p. 12.

——, "Shrinking Markets Put Squeeze on Woodward," *Crain's Chicago Business,* January 24, 1994, p. 19.

Osbourne, Randy, "An Officer and a Gentleman," *Rockford (Ill.) Magazine,* January 1988.

Palmer, Ann Therese, "Cost Controls Key for Woodward Governor," *Crain's Chicago Business,* February 6, 1995, p. 24.

Pride, Jackie, "Woodward Eliminates 200 Jobs," *Wausau (Wisc.) Daily Herald,* April 2, 1993.

Spivak, Cary, "Woodward Shifts Facilities to Handle Product Demand," *Crain's Chicago Business,* January 27, 1986, p. 18.

Weingarten, Paul, "Woodward's Way," *Chicago Tribune Magazine,* July 29, 1984.

—Dave Mote
—update: David E. Salamie

YAMATO TRANSPORT CO., LTD.

Yamato Transport Co. Ltd.

16-10, Ginza 2-chome
Chuo-ku
Tokyo 104-8125
Japan
Telephone: (3) 3541 3411
Fax: (3) 3542 3887
Web site: http://www.kuronekoyamato.co.jp

Public Company
Incorporated: 1929
Employees: 101,784
Sales: ¥906.95 billion ($7.31 billion) (2001)
Stock Exchanges: Tokyo
NAIC: 492210 Local Messengers and Local Delivery;
     561431 Private Mail Centers; 492110 Couriers

Yamato Transport Co. Ltd. is the founder of the private parcel delivery service industry in Japan, and the largest player in the market today. The company delivers approximately 900 million parcels each year. Links with United Parcel Service allow Yamato to deliver in more than 200 countries. A strong menu of domestic services includes home moving, delivery of refrigerated goods, magazine and catalog delivery, roundtrip delivery service, and B2B (business-to-business) and B2C (business-to-consumer) logistics services. The company also operates a virtual mall, handling the shipping and logistics needs of its retail ''tenants.''

Early 20th Century: Tokyo's First Courier Service

Yamato was founded in 1919 in the Chuo ward of Tokyo, although it was not incorporated as a company until ten years later. The company's founder was a young entrepreneur, Koshin Kogura, who began with ¥100,000 in capital and four new trucks. The establishment of the company came at a time when Tokyo and the rest of Japan, to a lesser extent, were rapidly building the transport and industrial infrastructure necessary to sustain Japan's growing economic power. Kogura's business, delivering business documents and parcels throughout the Tokyo area, boomed. It was, in effect, the city's first courier service.

By 1923 the range of delivery was extended to the adjacent city of Yokohama, and in the same year Yamato was contracted by Tokyo's most prestigious department store, Mitsukoshi, to deliver purchases to customers. Mitsukoshi generally catered to upper-class clientele and the items to be delivered were usually expensive Western imported goods. Yamato obtained its second prestigious client in 1925 when it was appointed by the Imperial household as its official courier and delivery service. The ministry of communications also used Yamato for the speedy delivery of important documents.

By 1929, with Kogura as its first president, the Yamato Transport Co. Ltd. was officially incorporated. A regular Tokyo to Yokohama delivery service was initiated, running several times a day. Customers could rely on Yamato, as opposed to the postal service, for swift delivery of mail within the Tokyo-Yokohama area. In the 1930s Yamato concentrated on expanding its network in the city of Tokyo and surrounding suburbs, and by 1940 claimed that it could deliver anywhere within the Kanto region within one day. Yamato bought a controlling interest in Kawase Cars Co. Ltd., a Tokyo-based operator of taxis and rental cars, to add to its network in the city. This was followed by the purchase of Sanwa Transport Co. Ltd., a competitor in the courier business, in 1944.

Mid-20th Century: Overseas Deliveries

Like many essential infrastructure-related businesses in wartime Japan, Yamato was forced by the military government to aid in the war effort. This in effect meant that the company's resources were directed mainly at supplying goods for military use. The company played a role in the military's communication network within the city of Tokyo.

The U.S. Air Force's bombing campaign during the summer of 1945 left Tokyo in ruins and much of its transport infrastructure in disarray. Yamato was asked by the city authorities and the U.S. occupation forces to assist in the transport of vital goods within the city. Yamato's fleet of trucks was used extensively in the rebuilding of certain areas of Tokyo. Yamato thrived in the immediate postwar period and in 1949 obtained a listing on the Tokyo Stock Exchange for the first time. New branch offices were opened in Tokyo near the main stations of Akihabara and Idabashi in 1950.

In the same year Yamato signed an agreement with the Tokyo municipal authorities that allowed the company to act as clearing agents at customs. By acting as such, Yamato was in a position to deliver parcels efficiently overseas. The company did this in 1951 by setting up a liaison office in Haneda Airport, Tokyo, and forming an agreement with CAT Airlines Co. Ltd. to transport parcels. An overseas freight service from Haneda followed in 1952, allowing Yamato to ship large-scale items for customers. An agreement with the port authorities in nearby Yokohama allowed Yamato to clear goods through customs in this important port. In 1954 Yamato bought a controlling stake in one of its competitors in Tokyo, Teito Transport Co. Ltd. Three years later Yamato made another acquisition, the Tokyo-based Chiyoda Konpo Kogyo Co. Ltd., a packaging and moving company.

Yamato's plans for developing an international delivery service received a boost in 1954 when the International Association of Transport Airlines (IATA) certified the company as fit to handle packages and goods transported by its member aircargo companies. Yamato was now in a position to set up representative offices at all of Japan's major airports. Japan's largest airline, Japan Airlines Co. Ltd., named Yamato as the internal distributor of its cargo goods in 1958, and in 1960 Yamato began handling freight to New York in conjunction with Japan Airlines and others. The now familiar logo, visible on thousands of trucks all over Japan, was introduced in 1957. It depicts a mother cat carrying a kitten between its teeth, symbolizing the careful and efficient handling of goods. Yamato's history of assisting governmental agencies continued in 1965, when the company was involved in helping the post office to ensure that its year-end rush of letters and packages was delivered on time. This was to be repeated in the ensuing years.

Strengthening the Domestic Network in the 1960s

During this period, Yamato was increasingly expanding its main business—the delivery of parcels within Japan. One of the goals of the company, with founder Kogura still at the helm, was to develop the capacity to deliver goods nationwide. This was achieved by the establishment of subsidiaries throughout Japan and by strategic alliances and acquisitions of regional delivery companies.

In 1967 Yamato took advantage of its growing network by diversifying into the travel business and offering package tours. Due to the increasing complexity of its network, Yamato began computerizing all of its operations in 1969. The company was, however, slow to realize the need for this and lagged behind other business sectors, such as retailing, in the introduction of computers. Yamato soon realized that information technology would play a major role in the company's operations and established a subsidiary, Yamato Computer Systems Development Co. Ltd., in 1973. This company was primarily set up to

offer systems support to Yamato but would later also work for other organizations. In 1974 the company succeeded in establishing an online system for the control of a package to its destination. This system greatly reduced instances of delayed or lost goods and improved overall efficiency.

Since 1958, when it arranged the safe transport of a Van Gogh exhibition to Tokyo from Europe, Yamato prided itself on being able to handle almost any goods for transport. In 1970, when Japan hosted the World Expo, Yamato was responsible for the shipment of works of art and expensive machinery from all over the world to the exhibition site. In 1972 Yamato was asked to aid in the transport of the Chinese National Theater's set during the group's tour of Japan. In the same year, founding President Koshin Kogura received the Third Order of Merit from the emperor for his achievements in the Japanese business world.

Birth of Takkyubin in the 1970s

At this time Japan was becoming one of the major exporting nations in the world. Many Japanese companies were setting up subsidiaries overseas, notably in the United States. Mainly to serve this market, Yamato opened a representative office in New York in 1971, which dealt with the delivery of business packages between the United States and Japan. On the domestic front, Yamato established freight train operations between Osaka and the southern island of Kyushu, in conjunction with the regional railway company Shimabara Railroad Co. Ltd.

In 1975 Yamato underwent a reorganization and six divisions were formed, representing the major regional areas of Japan: Hokkaido, Kanto, Tohoku, Chubu, Kansai, and Kyushu. The vast majority of Japan's population is concentrated within these regions and Yamato planned to develop the capability to reach all of these regions with its delivery services. The year 1976 marked the establishment of the now well-known Takkyubin parcel delivery service aimed at both the business and consumer markets. Initially, the service offered to deliver a parcel anywhere in the Kanto area within one working day. This was soon extended to cover most of Japan, with the delivery time varying according to distance and accessibility. The Takkyubin, which means literally "home express post," is now the cornerstone of Yamato's business. During the late 1970s the company focused on the expansion of the Takkyubin service, which extended to Niigata on the west coast of Japan, in 1978. The year 1979 marked the delivery of the ten millionth Takkyubin parcel. In the same year Yamato's founder and president, Koshin Kogura, died.

Building an International Network in the 1980s

At the start of the 1980s, with a comprehensive Japanese domestic network in place, Yamato embarked on a program to establish an international delivery service network. A subsidiary, Yamato Transport USA Inc., was established and based in New York. In the same year representative offices were set up in Singapore and Frankfurt. Yamato used these offices to market its services and coordinate operations with Japan Airlines, and in 1983 the Takkyubin service was extended to include overseas destinations. Yamato's 1981 upgrade to the First Section of the Tokyo Stock Exchange from the Second Section was followed by domestic and overseas fundraising activities on the world's

Key Dates:

1919: Koshin Kogura forms Yamato in the Chuo ward of Tokyo.
1923: Yamato expands its range of delivery to the adjacent city of Yokohama; the company is contracted to deliver purchases for Tokyo's most prestigious department store.
1929: Yamato Transport Co. Ltd. is incorporated.
1949: Yamato obtains a listing on the Tokyo Stock Exchange.
1952: The company establishes an overseas freight service from Haneda Airport.
1957: Yamato begins using its cat logo.
1960: Yamato begins handling freight to New York, in conjunction with Japan Airlines and other airlines.
1969: The company computerizes all of its operations.
1971: Yamato opens a representative office in New York.
1976: Yamato's Takkyubin service is introduced.
Early 1980s: Yamato partners with UPS to provide worldwide delivery services.
1986: Yamato introduces its collection service.
1996: The company establishes a logistics unit to help companies with their distribution.
1998: Yamato creates an online mall for retailers who need shipping services.
1999: Yamato forms an alliance with a Taiwanese company to provide courier service to Taiwanese consumers.
2000: The company spins off its logistics unit, forming a new subsidiary.
2001: Yamato begins courier service in Taiwan.

money markets. The company raised SFr 50 million and $40 million in two separate bond issues in 1982. An agreement with United Parcel Service (UPS), a leading U.S. courier company with its own fleet of planes, marked the beginning of the realization of Yamato's worldwide delivery service network. Yamato's Takkyubin could now deliver to 175 countries around the globe. In the same year Yamato established overseas subsidiaries in the United Kingdom, Germany, The Netherlands, and France. In 1986, the company introduced its Collect Service—a program in which the company collected payments for products delivered on behalf of the companies that had sold and shipped the products. In 1987 Yamato added Cool Takkyubin to its list of services. This offered the delivery of refrigerated goods within Japan. The service was supported by a fleet of refrigerated trucks.

In 1990 Yamato solidified its link with UPS by the formation of a joint venture company, UPS Yamato Co. Ltd. Virtually all of Yamato's air-forwarding operations were transferred to this company, which managed every step of the shipment process, from receipt to delivery.

End of the 20th Century: Preparing for a New Economy

The 1990s were to bring changes to Yamato, as to many Japanese businesses. Virtually every sector of the country's economy was hurt by the prolonged recession that started at the beginning of the decade and lasted throughout. The ensuing deregulation of many industries created still more turmoil, in the form of increased competition from foreign interests.

One change that the 1990s brought, however, proved highly advantageous to Yamato: the advent of e-commerce. The company had already inadvertently positioned itself for the coming Internet economy when it initiated its collection service in the mid-1980s. When online shopping became an option, this collection service stood in good stead with the large number of Japanese consumers who felt uneasy about providing credit card information over the Internet. With Yamato, they could still order over the Internet without worrying about being defrauded.

By the middle of the decade, Yamato believed that a surge in online retailing was imminent—and it began preparing. Reasoning that every purchase made on the Internet would require delivery, Yamato took steps to secure its share of that market. In 1996, the company established a special unit to handle distribution services—including storage, inventory management, packing, delivery, and customer services—for web-based retailers. In 1998, it went a step further, establishing a virtual mall— called ''Kuroneko Tankentai''—that played host to thousands of merchants. Yamato provided these retailers with a free storefront and online parcel tracking, but charged them for delivery and payment collections services.

While preparing for the online retailing boom, Yamato also was broadening its range of services in other directions as well. One new service followed on the heels of another throughout most of the 1990s. In 1992, the company added a variation of its highly successful Takkyubin delivery service: Takkyubin Time Service, which guaranteed delivery by 10 a.m. the following day. In 1994 and 1995, Yamato introduced two new complete moving packages—one designed to appeal to the budget-conscious and one to target families and individuals moving internationally. The year 1996 saw the addition of Yamato's Pickup and Storage Service, in which the company transported and stored customers' personal belongings in its own storage facilities. In 1997, the company added Kuroneko Mail to its menu of service offerings. Aimed at the business-to-consumer market, Kuroneko Mail delivered magazines, catalogs, and product samples to Japanese consumers' mailboxes. The main new service offering of 1998 was Round Trip service, which allowed customers to send packages to a destination, and then back again, in a single transaction. This service was originally designed to appeal to golfers, skiers, and other sports enthusiasts who were likely to transport gear to and from a destination.

Business in the New Millennium

As the 1990s gave way to the new century, Yamato began looking at ways to expand into other parts of Asia. In late October 1999, the company partnered with the Uni-President Group, a convenience store chain in Taiwan, to establish a national courier service in that country in early 2001. A second Taiwan alliance followed in June 2000—with the Shihlin Electric & Engineering Group. Together Yamato and Shihlin planned to build a business-to-business and business-to-consumer e-commerce enterprise. If these alliances proved successful, they could serve as entrée into southeast Asia and mainland China.

Also in 2000, the company separated out the logistics business it had started in 1996, launching it as a new subsidiary. The subsidiary, Yamato Logistics Produce, was dedicated to developing distribution services in the business-to-business sector.

In 2001, Yamato closed its travel business, which it had operated since 1963, and closed its four travel sales offices. That same year, the company furthered its commitment to the new economy by launching Kuroneko@Payment Credit Card Service, a third-party credit card account settlement system to be used for online and mail-order accounts.

As Yamato looked to the future, both outside analysts and company executives believed that much of the company's future success hinged on how well it could respond to the growth of e-commerce. Yamato's B2B and B2C logistics business was expected to play an especially important role in this arena.

Principal Subsidiaries

Yamato System Development Co., Ltd.; Chiyoda Packaging Industry Ltd.; Konan Industry Co., Ltd.; Kyushu Yamato Transport Co., Ltd.; Kyoto Yamato Transport Co., Ltd.; Shikoku Yamato Transport Co., Ltd.; Kobe Yamato Transport Co., Ltd.; Okinawa Yamato Transport Co., Ltd.; Yamato Shoji Co., Ltd.; Yamato Home Service Co., Ltd.; Chubu Yamato Home Service Co., Ltd.; Kansai Yamato Home Service Co., Ltd.; Chugoku Yamato Home Service Co., Ltd.; Kyushu Yamato Home Service Co., Ltd.; Tohoku Yamato Home Service Co., Ltd.; Hokushinetsu Yamato Home Service Co., Ltd.; Shikoku Yamato Home Service Co., Ltd.; Book Service Co., Ltd.; Yamato Collect Service Co., Ltd.; Yamato Lease Co., Ltd.; Yamato Parcel Service Co., Ltd.; Miyagi Green Liner Co., Ltd.; Iwate Green Liner Co., Ltd.; Saitama Green Liner Co., Ltd.; Niigata Green Liner Co., Ltd.; Aichi Green Liner Co., Ltd.; Chugoku Green Liner Co., Ltd.; Fukuoka Green Liner Co., Ltd.; Yamato Logistics Produce Co., Ltd.; Swan Co., Ltd.; Swan Net Co., Ltd.; Minami Kyushu Green Co., Ltd.; Shikoku Yamato Distribution Service Co., Ltd.; Yamato Career Service Co., Ltd.; Yamato UPS International Air Cargo Co., Ltd.; UPS Yamato Co., Ltd. (50%); UPS Yamato Express Co., Ltd.; Yamato Transport U.S.A., Inc. (50%); Yamato Customs Brokers U.S.A., Inc. (50%); Yamato International Forwarding, Inc. (50%); UPS Yamato Partnership USA; Yamato Systems U.S.A., Inc.; Yamato Transport (Canada) Inc.; Yamato Transport (U.K.) Ltd.; Yamato Transport Europe B.V.; Yamato Transport (Deutschland) GmbH.; Yamato Transport (Hong Kong) Ltd.; Yamato Travel Hong Kong Ltd.; Yamato Transport (S) Pte. Ltd.; Yamato Transport (M) Sdn. Bhd.; Yamato Transport Taiwan Ltd.; Yamato Unyu (Thailand) Co., Ltd.

Principal Competitors

DHL Worldwide Express, Inc.; Japan Postal Service; Nippon Express Co., Ltd.

Further Reading

"Delivery King Sheds Bureaucratic Ways: The Father of 'Black Cat' Door-to-Door Deliveries Bypassed Japan's Customs," *Orlando Sentinel*, April 20, 1997, p. H4.

Kunii, Irene, "A Trucker Finds a Niche in Cyberspace," *Business Week*, September 4, 2000, p. 27.

——, "A Trucker for the Information Highway," *Business Week*, December 13, 1999, p. 42.

—Dylan Tanner
—update: Shawna Brynildssen

INDEX TO COMPANIES

Index to Companies

Listings in this index are arranged in alphabetical order under the company name. Company names beginning with a letter or proper name such as Eli Lilly & Co. will be found under the first letter of the company name. Definite articles (The, Le, La) are ignored for alphabetical purposes as are forms of incorporation that precede the company name (AB, NV). Company names printed in bold type have full, historical essays on the page numbers appearing in bold. Updates to entries that appeared in earlier volumes are signified by the notation (**upd.**). Company names in light type are references within an essay to that company, not full historical essays. This index is cumulative with volume numbers printed in bold type.

A & A Die Casting Company, **25** 312
A and A Limousine Renting, Inc., **26** 62
A & C Black Ltd., **7** 165
A&E Plastics, **12** 377
A&E Television Networks, **IV** 627; **19** 204; **32** 3–7; **46** 232
A. & J. McKenna, **13** 295
A&K Petroleum Company. *See* Kerr-McGee Corporation.
A & M Instrument Co., **9** 323
A&M Records, **23** 389
A&N Foods Co., **II** 553
A&P. *See* Great Atlantic & Pacific Tea Company, Inc.
A&P Water and Sewer Supplies, Inc., **6** 487
A. and T. McKenna Brass and Copper Works, **13** 295
A & W Brands, Inc., **II** 595; **25** 3–5
A-1 Supply. *See* International Game Technology.
A-R Technologies, **48** 275
A.A. Housman & Co., **II** 424; **13** 340
A.A. Mathews. *See* CRSS Inc.
A. Ahlström Oy, **IV** 276–77
A.B. Chance Industries Co., Inc., **II** 20; **31** 259
A.B.Dick Company, **II** 25; **28** 6–8
A.B. Hemmings, Ltd., **13** 51
A.B. Leasing Corp., **13** 111–12
A-B Nippondenso, **III** 593
A.B. Watley Group Inc., **45** 3–5
A-BEC Mobility, **11** 487
A.C. Delco, **26** 347, 349
A.C. Moore Arts & Crafts, Inc., **30** 3–5
A.C. Nielsen Company, **IV** 605; **13** 3–5. *See also* ACNielsen Corporation.
A.C. Wickman, **13** 296
A.D. International (Australia) Pty. Ltd., **10** 272
A. Dager & Co., **I** 404
A. Dunkelsbuhler & Co., **IV** 20–21, 65; **7** 122
A/E/C/ Systems International, **27** 362
A.E. Fitkin & Company, **6** 592–93

A.E. Gutman, **16** 486
A.E. LePage, **II** 457
A.E. Lottes, **29** 86
A.G. Becker, **II** 259–60; **11** 318; **20** 260
A.G. Edwards, Inc., **8** 3–5; **19** 502; **32** 17–21 (upd.)
A.G. Industries, Inc., **7** 24
A.G. Morris, **12** 427
A.G. Spalding & Bros., Inc., **I** 428–29; **24** 402–03
A.G. Stanley Ltd., **V** 17, 19; **24** 75
A. Gettelman, Co., **I** 269
A. Goertz and Co., **IV** 91
A.H. Belo Corporation, **IV** 605; **10** 3–5; **28** 367, 369; **30** 13–17 (upd.)
A.H. Robins Co., **10** 70; **12** 188; **16** 438
A. Hirsh & Son, **30** 408
A.I. Credit Corp., **III** 196
A.J. Caley and Son. Ltd., **II** 569
A.J. Oster Co., **III** 681
A. Johnson & Co. *See* Axel Johnson Group.
A.L. Laboratories Inc., **12** 3
A.L. Pharma Inc., **12** 3–5. *See also* Alpharma Inc.
A.L. Van Houtte Inc. *See* Van Houtte Inc.
A. Lambert International Inc., **16** 80
A. Leon Capel and Sons, Inc. *See* Capel Incorporated.
A.M. Castle & Co., **25** 6–8
A.M. Collins Manufacturing Co., **IV** 286
A. Michel et Cie., **49** 84
A.O. Smith Corporation, **7** 139; **22** 181, **11** 3–6; **24** 499; **40** 3–8 (upd.)
A-1 Steak Sauce Co., **I** 259
A-1 Supply, **10** 375
A.P. Green Refractories, **22** 285
A.R. Pechiney, **IV** 173
A. Roger Perretti, **II** 484
A.S. Abell Co., **IV** 678
A.S. Aloe, **III** 443
A.S. Cameron Steam Pump Works, **III** 525
A/S Titan, **III** 418
A.S. Watson & Company, **18** 254
A.S. Yakovlev Design Bureau, **15** 3–6

A. Schilling & Company. *See* McCormick & Company, Incorporated.
A. Schulman, Inc., **8** 6–8; **49** 3–7 (upd.)
A. Sulka & Co., **29** 457
A.T. Cross Company, **17** 3–5; **49** 8–12 (upd.)
A.T. Massey Coal Company, **34** 164
A-T-O Inc. *See* Figgie International, Inc.
A.V. Roe & Co., **I** 50, 81; **III** 508; **24** 85
A.W. Bain Holdings, **III** 523
A.W. Shaw Co., **IV** 635
A.W. Sijthoff, **14** 555
A-Z International Companies, **III** 569; **20** 361
AA Development Corp., **I** 91
AA Distributors, **22** 14
AA Energy Corp., **I** 91
AAA Development Corp., **17** 238
Aaardman Animations, **43** 143
Aachener und Münchener Feuer-Versicherungs-Gesellschaft, **III** 376
Aachener und Münchener Gruppe, **III** 349–50
Aachener Union, **II** 385
AAE Ahaus Alstatter Eisenbahn Holding AG, **25** 171
AAF-McQuay Incorporated, **26** 3–5
AAI Corporation, **37** 399
Aalborg, **6** 367
Aansworth Shirt Makers, **8** 406
AAON, Inc., **22** 3–6
AAR Corp., **III** 687; **IV** 60; **28** 3–5
Aargauische Portlandcement-Fabrik Holderbank-Wildegg, **III** 701
Aaron Brothers, Inc., **17** 320, 322
Aaron Rents, Inc., **14** 3–5; **33** 368; **35** 3–6 (upd.)
AARP, **27** 3–5
Aasche Transportation, **27** 404
Aastrom Biosciences, Inc., **13** 161
AAV Cos., **13** 48; **41** 22
Aavant Health Management Group, Inc., **11** 394
Aavid Thermal Technologies, Inc., **29** 3–6

AB Capital & Investment Corporation, **23** 381

AB Ingredients Limited, **41** 32

AB-PT. *See* American Broadcasting-Paramount Theatres, Inc.

ABA. *See* Aktiebolaget Aerotransport.

Abacus Direct Corporation, **46** 156

Abacus Fund, Inc., **II** 445; **22** 405

ABACUS International Holdings Ltd., **26** 429

Abana Pharmaceuticals, **24** 257

Abar Staffing, **25** 434

ABB Asea Brown Boveri Ltd., **II** 1–4, 13; **III** 427, 466, 631–32; **IV** 66, 109, 204, 300; **15** 483; **22** 7–12 **(upd.)**, 64, 288; **28** 39; **34** 132

ABB Hafo AB. *See* Mitel Corp.

ABB RDM Service, **41** 326

Abba Seafood AB, **18** 396

Abbatoir St.-Valerien Inc., **II** 652

Abbey Business Consultants, **14** 36

Abbey Home Entertainment, **23** 391

Abbey Life Group PLC, **II** 309

Abbey Medical, Inc., **11** 486; **13** 366–67

Abbey National plc, **10** 6–8; **39** 3–6 **(upd.)**

Abbey Rents, **II** 572

Abbey Road Building Society, **10** 6–7

Abbott Laboratories, **I** 619–21, 686, 690, 705; **II** 539; **10** 70, 78, 126; **11** 7–9 **(upd.)**, 91, 494; **12** 4; **14** 98, 389; **22** 75; **25** 55; **36** 38–39; **40** 9–13 **(upd.)**; **46** 394–95

Abbott, Proctor & Paine, **II** 445; **22** 405

ABC Appliance, Inc., **10** 9–11

ABC Carpet & Home Co. Inc., **26** 6–8

ABC, Inc., **I** 463–64; **II** 89, 129–33, 151, 156, 170, 173; **III** 188, 214, 251–52; **6** 157–59, 164; **11** 197–98; **17** 150; **XVIII** 65; **19** 201; **21** 25; **24** 516–17; **32** 3. *See also* Capital Cities/ABC Inc.

ABC Markets, **17** 558

ABC Rail Products Corporation, **18** 3–5

ABC Records, **II** 144

ABC Supply Co., Inc., **22** 13–16

ABC Treadco, **19** 455

ABD Securities Corp., **II** 239, 283

ABECOR. *See* Associated Banks of Europe Corp.

Abell-Howe Construction Inc., **42** 434

Abercom Holdings, **IV** 92

Abercrombie & Fitch Co., **V** 116; **15** 7–9; **17** 369; **25** 90; **35** 7–10 **(upd.)**

Aberthaw Cement, **III** 671

Abex Aerospace, **III** 512

Abex Corp., **I** 456; **10** 553; **18** 3

Abex Friction Products, **III** 512

ABF. *See* Associated British Foods PLC.

ABF Freight System, Inc., **16** 39–41

ABI. *See* American Furniture Company, Inc.

Abigail Adams National Bancorp, Inc., **23** 3–5

Abilis, **49** 222

Abington Shoe Company. *See* The Timberland Company.

Abiomed, Inc., **47** 3–6

Abitec Corporation, **41** 32–33

Abitibi-Consolidated, Inc., **25** 9–13 **(upd.)**; **26** 445

Abitibi-Price Inc., **IV** 245–47, 721; **9** 391

Abko Realty Inc., **IV** 449

ABM Industries Incorporated, **25** 14–16 **(upd.)**

ABN. *See* Algemene Bank Nederland N.V.

ABN AMRO Rothschild, **39** 295

Above The Belt, Inc., **16** 37

ABR Foods, **II** 466

Abraham & Straus, **V** 168; **8** 443; **9** 209; **31** 192

Abraham Schaaffhausenscher Bankverein, **IV** 104

Abrams Industries Inc., **23** 6–8

Abri Bank Bern, **II** 378

Absolut Company, **31** 458, 460

Abu Dhabi National Oil Company, **IV** 363–64, 476; **45** 6–9 **(upd.)**

Abu Qir Fertilizer and Chemical Industries Co., **IV** 413

AC Design Inc., **22** 196

AC Humko Corporation, **41** 32–33

AC Roma SpA, **44** 388

ACA Corporation, **25** 368

Academic Press, **IV** 622–23

Academy Sports & Outdoors, **27** 6–8

Acadia Entities, **24** 456

Acadia Investors, **23** 99

Acadia Partners, **21** 92

Acadian Ambulance & Air Med Services, Inc., **39** 7–10

Access Dynamics Inc., **17** 255

Access Graphics Technology Inc., **13** 128

Access Technology, **6** 225

Accessory Network Group, Inc., **8** 219

Accident and Casualty Insurance Co., **III** 230–31

Acclaim Entertainment Inc., **13** 115; **24** 3–8, 538

ACCO World Corporation, **7** 3–5; **12** 264

Accolade Inc., **35** 227

Accor SA, **10** 12–14; **13** 364; **27** 9–12 **(upd.)**; **48** 199; **49** 126

Accord Energy, **18** 367; **49** 120

Accountants on Call, **6** 10

Accounting and Tabulating Corporation of Great Britain, **6** 240

Acctex Information Systems, **17** 468

Accuralite Company, **10** 492

Accurate Forming Co., **III** 643

AccuRead Limited, **42** 165, 167

Accuride Corp., **IV** 179

Accuscan, Inc., **14** 380

AccuStaff Inc. *See* MPS Group, Inc.

ACE Cash Express, Inc., **33** 3–6

Ace Comb Company, **12** 216

Ace Electric Co., **I** 156

Ace Hardware Corporation, **12** 6–8; **35** 11–14 **(upd.)**

ACE Limited, **45** 109

Ace Medical Company, **30** 164

Ace Novelty Company, **26** 374

Ace Refrigeration Ltd., **I** 315; **25** 81

Acer Inc., **6** 244; **10** 257; **16** 3–6; **47** 385

Acer Sertek, **24** 31

Aceralia, **42** 414

Aceros Fortuna S.A. de C.V., **13** 141

Aceto Corp., **38** 3–5

ACF Industries, **30** 282

Acheson Graphite Corp, **I** 399; **9** 517

ACI. *See* Advance Circuits Inc.

ACI Holdings Inc., **I** 91; **28** 24

ACI Ltd., **29** 478

Aciéries de Ploërmel, **16** 514

Aciéries et Minières de la Sambre, **IV** 52

Aciéries Réunies de Burbach-Eich-Dudelange S.A. *See* ARBED S.A.

Acker Drill Company, **26** 70

Ackerley Communications, Inc., **9** 3–5

Acklin Stamping Company, **8** 515

ACLC. *See* Allegheny County Light Company.

ACLI Government Securities Inc., **II** 422

ACM. *See* Advanced Custom Molders, Inc.

Acme Boot, **I** 440–41

Acme Brick Company, **19** 231–32

Acme Can Co., **I** 601; **13** 188

Acme Carton Co., **IV** 333

Acme-Cleveland Corp., **I** 531; **13** 6–8

Acme Corrugated Cases, **IV** 258

Acme Cotton Products, **13** 366

Acme-Delta Company, **11** 411

Acme Fast Freight Inc., **27** 473

Acme Market. *See* American Stores Company.

Acme Newspictures, **25** 507

Acme Quality Paint Co., **III** 744

Acme Quilting Co., Inc., **19** 304

Acme Road Machinery, **21** 502

Acme Screw Products, **14** 181

ACMI, **21** 118–19

ACNielsen Corporation, **38** 6–9 **(upd.)**

Acordis, **41** 10

Acorn Computer, **III** 145

Acorn Financial Corp., **15** 328

Acoustics Development Corporation, **6** 313

Acova S.A., **26** 4

Acquired Systems Enhancement Corporation, **24** 31

ACR. *See* American Capital and Research Corp.

AcroMed Corporation, **30** 164

Acsys, Inc., **44** 3–5

ACT Group, **45** 280

Act III Theatres, **25** 453

Actava Group, **14** 332

Action, **6** 393

Action Furniture by Lane, **17** 183

Action Gaming Inc., **44** 337

Action Labs Inc., **37** 285

Action Performance Companies, Inc., **27** 13–15; **32** 344; **37** 319

Action Temporary Services, **29** 273

Active Apparel Group. *See* Everlast Worldwide Inc.

Activenture Corporation, **16** 253; **43** 209

Activision, Inc., **24** 3; **32** 8–11

Acton Bolt Ltd., **IV** 658

Acumos, **11** 57

Acuson Corporation, **10** 15–17; **36** 3–6 **(upd.)**

ACX Technologies, **13** 11; **36** 15

Acxiom Corporation, **35** 15–18

Ad Astra Aero, **I** 121

AD-AM Gas Company, **11** 28

Adage Systems International, Inc., **19** 438

Adam, Meldrum & Anderson Company (AM&A), **16** 61–62

Adam Opel AG, **7** 6–8; **11** 549; **18** 125; **21** 3–7 **(upd.)**

Adams Childrenswear, **V** 177

Adams Express Co., **II** 380–81, 395–96; **10** 59–60; **12** 533

Adams Golf, Inc., **37** 3–5; **45** 76

Adams Industries, **19** 414

Adams/Cates Company, **21** 257

Adanac General Insurance Company, **13** 63

Adaptec, Inc., **11** 56; **31** 3–6

Adaptive Data Systems, **25** 531

Adar Associates, Inc. *See* Scientific-Atlanta, Inc.

ADC of Greater Kansas City, Inc., **22** 443

ADC Telecommunications, Inc., 10 18–21; **30 6–9 (upd.)**; **44** 69
Adco Products, **I** 374
Addison Communications Plc, **45** 272
Addison Corporation, **31** 399
Addison Structural Services, Inc., **26** 433
Addison Wesley, **IV** 659
Addressograph-Multigraph, **11** 494
Adecco S.A., 26 240; **35** 441–42; **36 7–11 (upd.)**
Adelphi Pharmaceutical Manufacturing Co., **I** 496
Adelphia Communications Corp., 17 6–8
Ademco. *See* Alarm Device Manufacturing Company.
Adero Inc., **45** 202
ADESA Corporation, **34** 286
Adesso-Madden, Inc., **37** 372
Adger Assuranceselskab, **III** 310
Adhere Paper Co., **IV** 252; **17** 29
ADI Group Limited. *See* AHL Services, Inc.
Adia S.A., 6 9–11; **9** 327. *See also* Adecco S.A.
Adiainvest S.A., **6** 9, 11
adidas AG, 8 392–93; **13** 513; **14 6–9**; **17** 244; **22** 202; **23** 472, 474; **25** 205, 207; **36** 344, 346
adidas-Salomon AG, 33 7–11 (upd.)
Adirondack Industries, **24** 403
Adjusters Auto Rental Inc. **16** 380
Adler, **23** 219
Adler and Shaykin, **III** 56; **11** 556–57
Adler Line. *See* Transatlantische Dampfschiffahrts Gesellschaft.
Adley Express, **14** 567
ADM. *See* Archer-Daniels-Midland Co.
Administracion Corporativa y Mercantil, S.A. de C.V., **37** 178
Admiral Co., **II** 86; **III** 573
Admiral Cruise Lines, **6** 368; **27** 91
Adnan Dabbagh, **6** 115
ADNOC. *See* Abu Dhabi National Oil Company.
Adobe Systems Incorporated, 10 22–24; **15** 149; **20** 46, 237; **33 12–16 (upd.)**; **43** 151
Adolf Würth GmbH & Co. KG, 49 13–15
Adolph Coors Company, I 236–38, 255, 273; **13 9–11 (upd.)**; **18** 72; **26** 303, 306; **34** 37; **36 12–16 (upd.)**; **44** 198
Adolphe Lafont, **17** 210
Adonis Radio Corp., **9** 320
Adorence, **16** 482
ADP. *See* Automatic Data Processing, Inc.
Adria Produtos Alimenticios, Ltd., **12** 411
Adria Steamship Company, **6** 425
Adrian Hope and Company, **14** 46
Adriatico Banco d'Assicurazione, **III** 206, 345–46
Adrienne Vittadini, **15** 291
ADS. *See* Aerospace Display Systems.
Adsega, **II** 677
Adstaff Associates, Ltd., **26** 240
ADT Ltd., **26** 410; **28** 486
ADT Security Services, Inc., 44 6–9 (upd.)
ADT Security Systems, Inc., 12 9–11
Adtel, Inc., **10** 358
Adtran Inc., 22 17–20
Adtranz **34** 128, 132–33, 136; **42** 45. *See also* ABB ASEA Brown Boveri Ltd.
Advacel, **18** 20; **43** 17

Advance Chemical Company, **25** 15
Advance Circuits Inc., **49** 234
Advance Foundry, **14** 42
Advance Publications Inc., **IV 581–84**; **13** 178, 180, 429; **19 3–7 (upd.)**; **31** 376, 378
Advance-Rumely Thresher Co., **13** 16
Advance Transformer Co., **13** 397
Advance/Newhouse Communications, **42** 114
Advanced Casino Systems Corporation, **21** 277
Advanced Communications Engineering. *See* Scientific-Atlanta, Inc.
Advanced Communications Inc. *See* Metrocall, Inc.
Advanced Custom Molders, Inc., **17** 533
Advanced Data Management Group S.A., **23** 212
Advanced Entertainment Group, **10** 286
Advanced Fiberoptic Technologies, **30** 267
Advanced Gravis, **28** 244
Advanced Logic Research, Inc., **27** 169
Advanced Marine Enterprises, Inc., **18** 370
Advanced Marketing Services, Inc., 24 354; **34 3–6**
Advanced Medical Technologies, **III** 512
Advanced Metal Technologies Inc., **17** 234
Advanced Metallurgy, Inc., **29** 460
Advanced Micro Devices, Inc., 6 215–17; **9** 115; **10** 367; **11** 308; **16** 316; **18** 18–19, 382; **19** 312; **20** 175; **30 10–12 (upd.)**; **32** 498; **43** 15–16; **47** 384
Advanced MobilComm, **10** 432
Advanced Plasma Systems, Inc., **48** 299
Advanced Structures, Inc., **18** 163
Advanced System Applications, **11** 395
Advanced Technology Laboratories, Inc., 9 6–8
Advanced Telecommunications Corporation, **8** 311
Advanced Tissue Sciences Inc., **41** 377
Advanced Web Technologies, **22** 357
AdvanceMed LLC, **45** 146
Advanstar Communications, **27** 361
Advanta Corporation, 8 9–11; **11** 123; **38 10–14 (upd.)**
Advanta Partners, LP, **42** 322
Advantage Company, **8** 311; **27** 306
The Advantage Group, Inc., **25** 185–86
Advantage Health Plans, Inc., **11** 379
Advantage Health Systems, Inc., **25** 383
Advantage Insurers, Inc., **25** 185, 187
Advantage Publishers Group, **34** 5
Advantest, **39** 350, 353
Advantica Restaurant Group, Inc., 27 16–19 (upd.); **29** 150
Advent Corporation, **22** 97
Advertising Unlimited, Inc., **10** 461
Advo, Inc., 6 12–14
Advocat Inc., 46 3–5
AEA. *See* United Kingdom Atomic Energy Authority.
AEA Investors Inc., **II** 628; **13** 97; **22** 169, 171; **28** 380; **30** 328
AEG A.G., I 151, 193, **409–11**; **II** 12, 119, 279; **III** 466, 479; **IV** 167; **6** 489; **IX** 11; **14** 169; **15** 142; **22** 28; **23** 495; **34** 131–32
Aegis Group plc, 6 15–16
Aegis Insurance Co., **III** 273
AEGON N.V., III 177–79, 201, 273; **33** 418–20. *See also* Transamerica–An AEGON Company

AEI Music Network Inc., 35 19–21
AEL Ventures Ltd., **9** 512
Aeneas Venture Corp., **26** 502
AEON Group, **V** 96–99; **11** 498–99; **31** 430–31; **37** 227
AEP. *See* American Electric Power Company.
AEP Industries, Inc., 36 17–19
AEP-Span, **8** 546
Aer Lingus Group plc, 6 59; **12** 367–68; **34 7–10**; **35** 382–84; **36** 230–31
Aera Energy LLC, **41** 359
Aérazur, **36** 529
Aerial Communications Inc., **31** 452
Aeritalia, **I** 51, 74–75, 467; **24** 86
Aero-Coupling Corp., **III** 641
Aero Engines, **9** 418
Aero International (Regional) SAS, **24** 88
Aero International Inc., **14** 43
Aero Mayflower Transit Company. *See* Mayflower Group Inc.
Aero O/Y, **6** 87–88
Aero-Portuguesa, **6** 125
Aeroflot—Russian International Airlines, 29 7–10 (upd.)
Aeroflot Soviet Airlines, I 105, 110, 118; **6 57–59**; **14** 73; **27** 475
Aerojet, **8** 206, 208
Aerojet-General Corp., **9** 266
Aerolíneas Argentinas S.A., I 107; **6** 97; **33 17–19**; **36** 281
Aeroméxico, **20** 168
Aeronautics Leasing, Inc., **39** 33
Aeronca Inc., 46 6–8; **48** 274
Aéroports de Paris, 33 20–22
Aeroquip Corporation, III 640–42; **V** 255; **16 7–9**; **19** 508
Aerospace Avionics, **III** 509
Aerospace Display Systems, **36** 158
Aerospace International Services, **41** 38
Aerospace Products International, Inc., **49** 141
The Aérospatiale Group, I 41–42, 46, 50, 74, 94; **7 9–12**; **12** 190–91; **14** 72; **21 8–11 (upd.)**; **24** 84–86, 88–89; **26** 179
Aerostar, **33** 359–61
The AES Corporation, 10 25–27; **13 12–15 (upd.)**; **24** 359
Aetna, Inc., 20 59; **21 12–16 (upd.)**, 95; **22** 139, 142–43; **30** 364
Aetna Life and Casualty Company, II 170–71, 319; **III** 78, **180–82**, 209, 223, 226, 236, 254, 296, 298, 305, 313, 329, 389; **IV** 123, 703; **10** 75–76; **12** 367; **15** 26; **17** 324; **23** 135; **40** 199
Aetna National Bank, **13** 466
Aetna Oil Co., **IV** 373
AF Insurance Agency, **44** 33
AFC Enterprises, Inc., 32 12–16 (upd.); **36** 517, 520
AFCO Industries, Inc., **III** 241; **IV** 341
Afcol, **I** 289; **24** 449–50
AFE Ltd., **IV** 241
Affiliated Enterprises Inc., **I** 114
Affiliated Hospital Products Inc., **37** 400
Affiliated Music Publishing, **22** 193
Affiliated Paper Companies, Inc., **31** 359, 361
Affiliated Physicians Network, Inc., **45** 194
Affiliated Products Inc., **I** 622
Affiliated Publications, Inc., 6 323; **7 13–16**; **19** 285
Affordable Inns, **13** 364
AFG Industries Inc., **I** 483; **9** 248; **48** 42

AFIA, **22** 143; **45** 104, 108
Afianzadora Insurgentes Serfin, **19** 190
AFL. *See* American Football League.
**AFLAC Incorporated, 10 28–30 (upd.);
38 15–19 (upd.)**
AFP. *See* Australian Forest Products.
AFRA Enterprises Inc., **26** 102
African and European Investment, **IV** 96
African Coasters, **IV** 91
African Explosive and Chemical Industries,
IV 22
AFT. *See* Advanced Fiberoptic
Technologies.
AFW Fabric Corp., **16** 124
AG&E. *See* American Electric Power
Company.
**Ag-Chem Equipment Company, Inc., 17
9–11**
AG Communication Systems Corporation,
15 194; **43** 446
AGA, **I** 358
Agan Chemical Manufacturers Ltd., **25**
266–67
Agar Manufacturing Company, **8** 2
Agatha Christie Ltd., **31** 63 67
AGCO Corp., 13 16–18
Agefi, **34** 13
AGEL&P. *See* Albuquerque Gas, Electric
Light and Power Company.
Agence France-Presse, IV 670; **34 11–14**
Agency, **6** 393
Agency Rent-A-Car, **16** 379
AGF, **III** 185; **27** 515
AGFA, **I** 310–11
Agfa-Ansco Corporation, **I** 337–38; **22**
225–27
Agfa-Gevaert, **III** 487; **18** 50, 184–86; **26**
540–41
Aggregate Industries plc, 36 20–22
Aggreko Plc, 45 10–13
Agiba Petroleum, **IV** 414
Agilent Technologies Inc., 38 20–23
Agip SpA, **IV** 419–21, 454, 466, 472–74,
498; **12** 153
Agiv AG, **39** 40–41
AGLP, **IV** 618
AGO, **III** 177, 179, 273, 310
Agor Manufacturing Co., **IV** 286
Agouron Pharmaceuticals, Inc., **38** 365
AGRAN, **IV** 505
AGRANA, **27** 436, 439
AgriBank FCB, **8** 489
Agribrands International, Inc., **40** 89
Agrico Chemical Company, **IV** 82, 84,
576; **7** 188; **31** 470
Agricole de Roquefort et Maria Grimal, **23**
219
Agricultural Insurance Co., **III** 191
Agricultural Minerals and Chemicals Inc.,
IV 84; **13** 504
Agrifan, **II** 355
Agrifull, **22** 380
Agrigenetics, Inc., **I** 361. *See also*
Mycogen Corporation.
Agrippina Versicherungs AG, **III** 403, 412
Agrobios S.A., **23** 172
Agroferm Hungarian Japanese
Fermentation Industry, **III** 43
Agromán S.A., **40** 218
AGTL. *See* Alberta Gas Trunk Line
Company, Ltd.
Agua de la Falda S.A., **38** 231
Agua Pura Water Company, **24** 467

Aguila (Mexican Eagle) Oil Co. Ltd., **IV**
657
Agusta S.p.A., **46** 66
**Agway, Inc., 7 17–18; 21 17–19 (upd.);
36** 440
AHL Services, Inc., 26 149; **27 20–23; 45**
379
Ahmanson. *See* H.F. Ahmanson &
Company.
AHMSA. *See* Altos Hornos de México,
S.A. de C.V.
Ahold. *See* Koninklijke Ahold NV.
AHP. *See* American Home Products
Corporation.
AHS. *See* American Hospital Supply
Corporation.
AHSC Holdings Corp., **III** 9–10
Ahtna AGA Security, Inc., **14** 541
AI Automotive, **24** 204
AIC. *See* Allied Import Company.
AICA, **16** 421; **43** 308
Aichi Bank, **II** 373
Aichi Kogyo Co., **III** 415
Aichi Steel Works, **III** 637
AICPA. *See* The American Institute of
Certified Public Accountants.
Aid Auto, **18** 144
Aida Corporation, **11** 504
AIG. *See* American International Group,
Inc.
AIGlobal, **III** 197
Aiken Stores, Inc., **14** 92
Aikenhead's Home Improvement
Warehouse, **18** 240; **26** 306
Aikoku Sekiyu, **IV** 554
AIL Technologies, **46** 160
AIM Create Co., Ltd., **V** 127
AIMCO. *See* Apartment Investment and
Management Company.
Ainsworth National, **14** 528
AIP. *See* Amorim Investimentos e
Participaço.
**Air & Water Technologies Corporation,
6 441–42.** *See also* Aqua Alliance Inc.
Air BP, **7** 141
Air Brasil, **6** 134; **29** 496
Air Canada, 6 60–62; 23 9–12 (upd.); 29
302; **36** 230
Air China, 46 9–11
Air Compak, **12** 182
Air de Cologne, **27** 474
**Air Express International Corporation,
13 19–20; 40** 138; **46** 71
Air France, **I** 93–94, 104, 110, 120; **II**
163; **6** 69, 373; **8** 313; **12** 190; **24** 86;
27 26; **33** 21, 50, 377. *See also* Groupe
Air France *and* Societe Air France.
**Air-India Limited, 6 63–64; 27 24–26
(upd.); 41** 336–37
Air Inter. *See* Groupe Air France.
Air La Carte Inc., **13** 48
Air Lanka Catering Services Ltd., **6**
123–24; **27** 464
Air Liberté, **6** 208
Air Liquide. *See* L'Air Liquide SA.
Air London International, **36** 190
Air Micronesia, **I** 97; **21** 142
Air Midwest, Inc., **11** 299
Air New Zealand Limited, 14 10–12; 24
399–400; **27** 475; **38 24–27 (upd.)**
Air Nippon Co., Ltd., **6** 70
Air Pacific, **24** 396, 400

Air Products and Chemicals, Inc., I
297–99, 315, 358, 674; **10 31–33**
(upd.); 11 403; **14** 125
Air Russia, **24** 400
Air Sea Broker AG, **47** 286–87
Air Southwest Co. *See* Southwest Airlines
Co.
Air Spec, Inc., **III** 643
Airborne Accessories, **II** 81
Airborne Freight Corporation, 6 345–47
345; **13** 19; **14** 517; **18** 177; **34 15–18**
(upd.); 46 72
Airbus Industrie, **6** 74; **7** 9–11, 504; **9** 418;
10 164; **13** 356; **21** 8; **24 84–89; 34**
128, 135; **48** 219. *See also* G.I.E. Airbus
Industrie.
AirCal, **I** 91
Airco, **25** 81–82; **26** 94
Aircraft Marine Products, **II** 7; **14** 26
Aircraft Modular Products, **30** 73
Aircraft Services International, **I** 449
Aircraft Transport & Travel Ltd., **I** 92
Aircraft Turbine Center, Inc., **28** 3
Airex Corporation, **16** 337
Airguard Industries, Inc., **17** 104, 106
Airlease International, **II** 422
Airline Interiors Inc., **41** 368–69
Airlines of Britain Holdings, **34** 398; **38**
105–06
Airlink, **24** 396
Airmark Plastics Corp., **18** 497–98
Airmec-AEI Ltd., **II** 81
Airpax Electronics, Inc., **13** 398
Airport Ground Service Co., **I** 104, 106
Airshop Ltd., **25** 246
Airstream. *See* Thor Industries, Inc.
Airtel, **IV** 640
AirTouch Communications, 11 10–12.
See also Vodafone Group PLC.
Airtours Plc, II 164; **27 27–29,** 90, 92
AirTran Holdings, Inc., 22 21–23; 28
266; **33** 302; **34** 32
AirWair Ltd., **23** 399, 401–02
AirWays Corporation. *See* AirTran
Holdings, Inc.
Airways Housing Trust Ltd., **I** 95
Airwick Industries, **II** 567
Aisin Seiki Co., Ltd., III 415–16; **14** 64;
48 3–5 (upd.)
AIT Worldwide, **47** 286–87
Aitken, Inc., **26** 433
AITS. *See* American International Travel
Service.
Aiuruoca, **25** 85
Aiwa Co., Ltd., 28 360; **30 18–20**
Ajax, **6** 349
Ajax Iron Works, **II** 16
Ajinomoto Co., Inc., II 463–64, 475; **III**
705; **28 9–11 (upd.)**
Ajman Cement, **III** 760
AJS Auto Parts Inc., **15** 246
AK Steel Holding Corporation, 19 8–9;
41 3–6 (upd.)
Akane Securities Co. Ltd., **II** 443
Akashic Memories, **11** 234
Akemi, **17** 310; **24** 160
Aker RGI, **32** 99
AKH Co. Inc., **20** 63
**Akin, Gump, Strauss, Hauer & Feld,
L.L.P., 18** 366; **33 23–25; 47** 140
AKO Bank, **II** 378
Akorn, Inc., 32 22–24
Akro-Mills Inc., **19** 277–78
Akron Brass Manufacturing Co., **9** 419

Akron Corp., **IV** 290
Akroyd & Smithers, **14** 419
Akseli Gallen-Kallela, **IV** 314
Aktiebolaget Aerotransport, **I** 119
Aktiebolaget Electrolux, 22 24–28 **(upd.)**
Aktiebolaget SKF, III 622–25; **IV** 203; **38** 28–33 **(upd.)**
Aktiengesellschaft für Berg- und Hüttenbetriebe, **IV** 201
Aktiengesellschaft für Maschinenpapier-Zellstoff-Fabrikation, **IV** 323
Aktiv Placering A.B., **II** 352
Akzo Nobel N.V., I 674; **II** 572; **III** 44; **13** 21–23, 545; **14** 27; **15** 436; **16** 69, 462; **21** 466; **41** 7–10 **(upd.)**
Al Copeland Enterprises, Inc., **7** 26–28; **32** 13–15
Alaadin Middle East-Ersan, **IV** 564
Alabama Bancorp., **17** 152
Alabama Gas Corporation, **21** 207–08
Alabama Power Company, **38** 445, 447–48
Alabama Shipyards Inc., **21** 39–40
Alabaster Co., **III** 762
Aladdin Industries, **16** 487
Aladdin Mills Inc., **19** 276
Aladdin's Castle, **III** 430, 431
Alagasco, **21** 207–08
Alagroup, **45** 337
Alais et Camargue, **IV** 173
Alamac Knit Fabrics, Inc., **16** 533–34; **21** 192
Alamito Company, **6** 590
Alamo Engine Company, **8** 514
Alamo Group Inc., 32 25–28
Alamo Rent A Car, Inc., 6 348–50; **24** 9–12 **(upd.)**; **25** 93; **26** 409
Alania, **24** 88
ALANTEC Corporation, **25** 162
Alarm Device Manufacturing Company, **9** 413–15
Alaron Inc., **16** 357
Alascom, **6** 325–28; **26** 358
Alaska Air Group, Inc., 6 65–67; **11** 50; **29** 11–14 **(upd.)**; **48** 219
Alaska Co., **III** 439
Alaska Commercial Company, **12** 363
Alaska Hydro-Train, **6** 382; **9** 510
Alaska Junk Co., **19** 380
Alaska Natural Gas Transportation System, **V** 673, 683
Alaska Pulp Co., **IV** 284, 297, 321
Alaska Steel Co., **19** 381
Alatas Mammoet, **26** 279
Alba Foods, **III** 619–20; **27** 197; **43** 218
Alba-Waldensian, Inc., 30 21–23
Albany and Susquehanna Railroad, **II** 329
Albany Assurance Co., Ltd., **III** 293
Albany Cheese, **23** 219
Albany Felt Company. *See* Albany International Corp.
Albany International Corp., 8 12–14
Albemarle Paper Co., **I** 334–35; **10** 289
Albers Brothers Milling Co., **II** 487
Albert E. Reed & Co. Ltd. *See* Reed International PLC.
The Albert Fisher Group plc, 41 11–13
Albert Heijn NV, **II** 641–42; **38** 200, 202
Albert Nipon, Inc., **8** 323
Albert Willcox & Co., **14** 278
Alberta Distillers, **I** 377
Alberta Energy Company Ltd., 16 10–12; **43** 3–6 **(upd.)**
Alberta Gas Trunk Line Company, Ltd., **V** 673–74

Alberta Sulphate Ltd., **IV** 165
Alberto-Culver Company, II 641–42; **8** 15–17; **36** 23–27 **(upd.)**
Albertson's Inc., II 601–03, 604–05, 637; **7** 19–22 **(upd.)**; **8** 474; **15** 178, 480; **16** 249; **18** 8; **22** 38; **27** 247, 290, 292; **30** 24–28 **(upd.)**; **33** 306; **40** 366
Albi Enterprises, **III** 24
Albion Industries, Inc., **16** 357
Albion Reid Proprietary, **III** 673
Albright & Friel, **I** 313; **10** 154
Albright & Wilson Ltd., **I** 527; **IV** 165; **12** 351; **16** 461; **38** 378, 380
Albuquerque Gas & Electric Company. *See* Public Service Company of New Mexico.
Albuquerque Gas, Electric Light and Power Company, **6** 561–62
Albury Brickworks, **III** 673
Alcan Aluminium Limited, II 415; **IV** 9–13, 14, 59, 154–55; **9** 512; **14** 35; **31** 7–12 **(upd.)**; **45** 337
Alcantara and Sores, **III** 582
Alcatel Alsthom Compagnie Générale d'Electricité, II 13, 69, 117; **6** 304; **7** 9; **9** 9–11, 32; **11** 59, 198; **15** 125; **17** 353; **18** 155; **19** 164, 166; **21** 233
Alcatel S.A., 36 28–31 **(upd.)**; **42** 375–76
Alchem Capital Corp., **8** 141, 143
Alchem Plastics, **19** 414
Alco Capital Group, Inc., **27** 288
Alco Health Services Corporation, III 9–10. *See also* AmeriSource Health Corporation.
Alco Hydro-Aeroplane, **I** 64
Alco Office Products Inc., **24** 362
Alco Standard Corporation, I 412–13; **III** 9; **9** 261; **16** 473–74
ALCO Trade Show Services, **26** 102
Alcoa. *See* Aluminum Company of America.
Alcon Laboratories, **II** 547; **7** 382; **10** 46, 48; **30** 30–31
Alcudia, **IV** 528
Alden Merrell Corporation, **23** 169
Aldermac Mines Ltd., **IV** 164
Aldi Group, 11 240; **13** 24–26; **17** 125
Aldila Inc., 46 12–14
Aldine Press, **10** 34
Aldiscon, **37** 232
Aldrich Chemical Co., **I** 690
Aldus Corporation, 10 34–36
Aldwarke Main & Car House Collieries, **I** 573
Alenia, **7** 9, 11
Alert Centre Inc., **32** 373
Alert Management Systems Inc., **12** 380
Alessio Tubi, **IV** 228
Alestra, **19** 12
Alex & Ivy, **10** 166–68
Alex Lee Inc., 18 6–9; **44** 10–14 **(upd.)**
Alexander & Alexander Services Inc., III 280; **10** 37–39; **13** 476; **22** 318
Alexander & Baldwin, Inc., I 417; **10** 40–42; **24** 32; **29** 307; **40** 14–19 **(upd.)**
Alexander and Lord, **13** 482
Alexander Grant & Co., **I** 481, 656
Alexander Hamilton Life Insurance Co., **II** 420; **29** 256
Alexander Howden Group, **III** 280; **10** 38–39; **22** 318
Alexander Martin Co., **I** 374
Alexander-Schroder Lumber Company, **18** 514

Alexander Smith, Inc., **19** 275
Alexander's, Inc., 10 282; **12** 221; **26** 111; **45** 14–16
Alexis Lichine, **III** 43
Alfa-Laval AB, III 417–21; **IV** 203; **8** 376
Alfa Romeo, I 163, 167; **11** 102, 104, 139, 205; **13** 27–29, 218–19; **36** 32–35 **(upd.)**, 196–97
Alfa, S.A. de C.V., II 262; **11** 386; **19** 10–12; **37** 176
Alfa Trading Company, **23** 358
Alfalfa's Markets, **19** 500–02
Alfinal, **III** 420
Alfred A. Knopf, Inc., **13** 428, 429; **31** 376–79
Alfred Bullows & Sons, Ltd., **21** 64
Alfred Dunhill Limited, **19** 369; **27** 487–89
Alfred Hickman Ltd., **III** 751
Alfred Marks Bureau, Ltd., **6** 9–10
Alfred Nobel & Co., **III** 693
Alfred Teves, **I** 193
Alfried Krupp von Bohlen und Halbach Foundation, **IV** 89
ALG. *See* Arkla, Inc.
Alga, **24** 83
Algemeen Burgerlijk Pensioenfonds, **26** 421
Algemeene Bankvereeniging en Volksbank van Leuven, **II** 304
Algemeene Friesche, **III** 177–79
N.V. Algemeene Maatschappij tot Exploitatie van Verzekeringsmaatschappijen, **III** 199
Algemeene Maatschappij van Levensverzekering en Lijfrente, **III** 178
Algemeene Maatschappij voor Nijverheidskrediet, **II** 304–05
Algemeene Nederlandsche Maatschappij ter begunstiging van de Volksvlijt, **II** 294
Algemene Bank Nederland N.V., II 183–84, 185, 239, 527; **III** 200
Algo Group Inc., 24 13–15
Algoma Steel Corp., **IV** 74; **8** 544–45; **24** 143
Algonquin Energy, Inc., **6** 487
Algonquin Gas Transmission Company, **6** 486; **14** 124–26
ALI. *See* Aeronautics Leasing, Inc.
Alidata, **6** 69
Aligro Inc., **II** 664
Alimenta (USA), Inc., **17** 207
Alimentana S.A., **II** 547
Alimondo, **17** 505
Alitalia–Linee Aeree Italiana, S.p.A., I 110, 466–67; **6** 96, 68–69; **24** 311; **29** 15–17 **(upd.)**
Alken, **II** 474
Oy Alkoholiliike Ab, **IV** 469
Alkor-Oerlikon Plastic GmbH, **7** 141
All American Airways. *See* USAir Group, Inc.
All American Communications Inc., 20 3–7; **25** 138
All American Gourmet Co., **12** 178, 199
All American Sports Co., **22** 458–59
All British Escarpment Company LTD, **25** 430
All-Clad Metalcrafters Inc., **34** 493, 496–97
All Nippon Airways Co., Ltd., I 106, 493; **6** 70–71 118, 427; **16** 168; **24** 326; **33** 50–51; **38** 34–37 **(upd.)**

All Seasons Vehicles, Inc. *See* ASV, Inc.
All Woods, Inc., **18** 514
Allami Biztosito, **III** 209; **15** 30
Allcom, **16** 392
Alldays plc, 49 16–19
Allders plc, 37 6–8
Alleanza & Unione Mediterranea, **III** 208
Alleanza-Securitas-Esperia, **III** 208
Alleghany Corporation, **II** 398; **IV**
   180–81; **10 43–45**; **19** 319; **22** 494
Allegheny Airlines. *See* USAir Group, Inc.
   and US Airways Group, Inc.
Allegheny Beverage Corp., **7** 472–73
Allegheny County Light Company, **6**
   483–84
Allegheny Energy, Inc., 38 38–41 (upd.)
Allegheny International, Inc., **III** 732; **8**
   545; **9** 484; **22** 3, 436
Allegheny Ludlum Corporation, **I** 307; **II**
   402; **8 18–20**; **9** 484; **21** 489
Allegheny Power System, Inc., V 543–45
Allegheny Steel and Iron Company, **9** 484
Allegiance Life Insurance Company, **22**
   268
Allegis, Inc. *See* United Airlines.
Allegmeine Transpotmittel
   Aktiengesellschaft, **6** 394; **25** 169
Allegretti & Co., **22** 26
Allen & Co., **I** 512, 701; **II** 136; **12** 496;
   13 366; **25** 270
Allen & Ginter, **12** 108
Allen & Hanbury's, **I** 640
Allen-Bradley Co., **I** 80; **II** 110; **III** 593;
   11 429–30; **17** 478; **22** 373; **23** 211
Allen-Liversidge Ltd., **I** 315; **25** 80
Allen Organ Company, 33 26–29
Allen-Stuart Equipment Company, **49** 160
Allen Tank Ltd., **21** 499
Allen's Convenience Stores, Inc., **17** 170
Allergan, Inc., 10 46–49; **23** 196; **30**
   29–33 (upd.)
Allforms Packaging Corp., **13** 442
Allgemeine Deutsche Creditanstalt, **II** 211,
   238, 383; **12** 536
Allgemeine Eisenbahn-Versicherungs-
   Gesellschaft, **III** 399
Allgemeine Elektricitäts-Gesellschaft. *See*
   AEG A.G.
Allgemeine Handelsgesellschaft der
   Verbraucher AG. *See* AVA AG.
Allgemeine Rentenstalt Lebens- und
   Rentenversicherung, **II** 258
Allgemeine Schweizerische Uhrenindustrie,
   26 480
Allgemeine Versicherungs-Gesellschaft
   Helvetia, **III** 375
Alliance Agro-Alimentaires S.A., **II** 577
Alliance Amusement Company, **10** 319
Alliance Assurance Co., **III** 369–73
Alliance Atlantis Communications Inc.,
   35 69; **39 11–14**
Alliance Brothers, **V** 356
Alliance Capital Management Corp., **22**
   189
Alliance Entertainment Corp., 17 12–14;
   35 430
Alliance Gaming Corp., **15** 539; **24** 36
Alliance Insurance Co., **III** 224
Alliance Manufacturing Co., **13** 397
Alliance Marine, **III** 373
Alliance Mortgage Co., **I** 610
Alliance Packaging, **13** 443
Alliance Paper Group, **IV** 316

Alliance Tire and Rubber Co., **II** 47; **25**
   267
AllianceWare, Inc., **16** 321
Alliant Energy Corp., **39** 261
Alliant Techsystems Inc., 8 21–23; 30
   34–37 (upd.)
Allianz AG Holding, **I** 411, 426; **II** 239,
   257, 279–80; **III 183–86**, 200, 250, 252,
   299–301, 347–48, 373, 377, 393; **IV**
   222; **14** 169–70; **15 10–14 (upd.)**
Allibert, **III** 614
Allied Bakeries Ltd., **II** 465–66; **13** 52–53
Allied Breweries Ltd., **I** 215; **III** 105; **IV**
   712
Allied Chemical, **I** 310, 332, 351–52; **8**
   526; **9** 521–22; **13** 76; **22** 5. *See also*
   General Chemical Corp.
Allied Chemical & Dye Corp., **I** 414; **7**
   262; **9** 154; **22** 29
Allied Color Industries, **8** 347
Allied Communications Group, **18** 77; **22**
   297
Allied Construction Products, **17** 384
Allied Container Corp., **IV** 345
Allied Corporation, **I** 68, 141, 143, 414,
   534; **III** 118, 511; **6** 599; **7** 356; **9** 134;
   11 435; **24** 164; **25** 224; **31** 135. *See*
   also AlliedSignal Inc.
Allied Crude Vegetable Oil Refining Co.,
   II 398; **10** 62
Allied Distributing Co., **12** 106
Allied Domecq PLC, **24** 220; **29 18–20**,
   85
Allied Dunbar, **I** 427
Allied Engineering Co., **8** 177
Allied Fibers, **19** 275
Allied Food Markets, **II** 662
Allied Gas Company, **6** 529
Allied Grape Growers, **I** 261
Allied Health and Scientific Products
   Company, **8** 215
Allied Healthcare Products, Inc., 24
   16–19
Allied Holdings, Inc., **24** 411
Allied Import Company, **V** 96
Allied Irish Banks, plc, 16 13–15; **43**
   7–10 (upd.)
Allied Leisure, **40** 296–98
Allied-Lyons plc, **I 215–16**, 258, 264,
   438; **IV** 721; **9** 100, 391; **10** 170; **13**
   258; **21** 228, 323; **29** 18, 84
Allied Maintenance Corp., **I** 514
Allied Mills, Inc., **10** 249; **13** 186; **43** 121
Allied Oil Co., **IV** 373
Allied Overseas Trading Ltd., **I** 216
Allied Plywood Corporation, **12** 397
Allied Polymer Group, **I** 429
Allied Products Corporation, 21 20–22
Allied Radio, **19** 310
Allied Safety, Inc., **V** 215
Allied Shoe Corp., **22** 213
Allied-Signal Corp., **I** 85, 141, 143,
   414–16; **III** 511–12; **V** 605; **6** 599–600;
   9 519; **11** 435, 444; **13** 227; **16** 436; **17**
   20; **21** 200, 396–97; **40** 35; **43** 320
Allied Signal Engines, 9 12–15
Allied Steel and Conveyors, **18** 493
Allied Steel and Wire Ltd., **III** 495
Allied Stores Corporation, **II** 350, 611–12;
   V 25–28; **9** 211; **10** 282; **13** 43; **15** 94,
   274; **16** 60; **22** 110; **23** 59–60; **25** 249;
   31 192; **37**
Allied Structural Steel Company, **10** 44
Allied Supermarkets, Inc., **7** 570; **28** 511

Allied Suppliers, **II** 609
Allied Telephone Company. *See* Alltel
   Corporation.
Allied Tin Box Makers Ltd., **I** 604
Allied Towers Merchants Ltd., **II** 649
Allied Van Lines Inc., **6** 412, 414; **14** 37.
   See also Allied Worldwide, Inc.
Allied Vintners, **I** 215
Allied Worldwide, Inc., 49 20–23
AlliedSignal Inc., 22 29–32 (upd.); **29**
   408; **31** 154; **37** 158
Allis Chalmers Corporation, **I** 163; **II** 98,
   121; **III** 543–44; **9** 17; **11** 104; **12** 545;
   13 16–17, 563; **14** 446; **21** 502–03; **22**
   380
Allis-Gleaner Corp. *See* AGCO Corp.
Allison Engine Company, **21** 436
Allison Engineering Company. *See* Rolls-
   Royce Allison.
Allison Gas Turbine Division, **9 16–19**,
   417; **10** 537; **11** 473
Allmanna Svenska Elektriska Aktiebolaget.
   See ABB ASEA Brown Boveri Ltd.
Allmänna Telefonaktiebolaget L.M.
   Ericsson, **V** 334
Allnatt London & Guildhall Properties, **IV**
   724
Allnet, **10** 19
Allo Pro, **III** 633
Allor Leasing Corp., **9** 323
Allou Health & Beauty Care, Inc., 28
   12–14
Alloy & Stainless, Inc., **IV** 228
Alloys Unlimited, **II** 82
Allserve Inc., **25** 367
Allsport plc., **31** 216, 218
The Allstate Corporation, **I** 23; **III**
   231–32, 259, 294; **V** 180, 182; **6** 12; **10**
   50–52; **13** 539; **18** 475; **21** 96–97; **22**
   495; **23** 286–87; **25** 155; **27 30–33**
   (upd.); **29** 397; **49** 332
ALLTEL Corporation, **6** 299–301; **16**
   318; **20** 440; **46 15–19 (upd.)**
Alltrans Group, **27** 472
Alltrista Corporation, 30 38–41
Allwaste, Inc., 18 10–13
Almac Electronics Corporation, **10** 113
Almac's Inc., **17** 558–59
Almacenes de Baja y Media, **39** 201, 204
Almaden Vineyards, **I** 377–78; **13** 134; **34**
   89
Almanij NV, 44 15–18. *See also*
   Algemeene Maatschappij voor
   Nijverheidskrediet.
Almay, Inc., **III** 54
Almeida Banking House. *See* Banco
   Bradesco S.A.
Almours Security Co., **IV** 311; **19** 266
Almys, **24** 461
Aloe Vera of America, **17** 187
Aloha Airlines, Incorporated, **I** 97; **9**
   271–72; **21** 142; **22** 251; **24 20–22**
ALP. *See* Associated London Properties.
Alp Sport Sandals, **22** 173
Alpen-Elektrowerke Aktiengesellschaft, **IV**
   230
Alpex Computer Corp., **III** 157
Alpex, S.A. de C.V., **19** 12
Alpha Beta Co., **II** 605, 625, 653; **17** 559
Alpha Engineering Group, Inc., **16** 259–60
Alpha Healthcare Ltd., **25** 455
Alpha Processor Inc., **41** 349
Alpha Technical Systems, **19** 279
Alphaform, **40** 214–15

Alphanumeric Publication Systems, Inc., **26** 518

Alpharma Inc., 35 22–26 (upd.)

Alphonse Allard Inc., **II** 652

Alpina Versicherungs-Aktiengesellschaft, **III** 412

Alpine, **IV** 234

Alpine Electronics, Inc., II 5; **13 30–31**

Alpine Lace Brands, Inc., 18 14–16

Alpine Securities Corporation, **22** 5

Alpre, **19** 192

Alps Electric Co., Ltd., II 5–6; 13 30; **44 19–21 (upd.)**

Alric Packing, **II** 466

Alsen-Breitenbury, **III** 702

ALSO Holding AG, **29** 419, 422

Alsons Corp., **III** 571; **20** 362

Alsthom, **II** 12

Alsthom-Atlantique, **9** 9

Alta Dena, **25** 83, 85

Alta Electric Company, **25** 15

Alta Gold Co., **IV** 76

ALTA Health Strategies, Inc., **11** 113

Alta Holidays Ltd., **I** 95

Altamil Corp., **IV** 137

Altana AG, **23** 498

AltaVista Company, 43 11–13

Alte Leipziger, **III** 242

Altec Electronics, **I** 489–90

ALTEC International, **21** 107–09

Altenburg & Gooding, **22** 428

Altera Corporation, 18 17–20; 43 14–18 (upd.); 47 384

Alternate Postal Delivery, **6** 14

Alternative Living Services. *See* Alterra Healthcare Corporation.

Alternative Youth Services, Inc., **29** 399–400

Alterra Healthcare Corporation, 42 3–5

Altex, **19** 192–93

Althoff KG, **V** 101

Althouse Chemical Company, **9** 153

Althus Corp, **I** 361

Altman Weil Pensa, **29** 237

Alton & Eastern Railroad Company, **6** 504

Alton Box Board Co., **IV** 295; **19** 225

Altos Computer Systems, **6** 279; **10** 362

Altos Hornos de México, S.A. de C.V., 13 144; **19** 220; **39** 188; **42 6–8**

Altron Incorporated, 20 8–10

Altura Energy Ltd., **41** 359

Aluar. *See* Aluminios Argentinos.

Aluma Systems Corp., **9** 512; **22** 14

Alumax Inc., **I** 508; **III** 758; **IV 18–19; 8** 505–06; **22** 286

Alumina Partners of Jamaica, **IV** 123

Aluminate Sales Corp, **I** 373

Aluminio de Galicia, **IV** 174

Aluminios Argentinos, **26** 433

Aluminium Co. of London, **IV** 69

L'Aluminium Francais, **IV** 173

Aluminium Ltd., **IV** 9–11, 14, 153

Aluminium-Oxid Stade GmbH, **IV** 231

Aluminium Plant and Vessel Co., **III** 419

Aluminum Can Co., **I** 607

Aluminum Company of America, I 373, 599; **II** 315, 402, 422; **III** 490–91, 613; **IV** 9–12, **14–16**, 56, 59, 121–22, 131, 173, 703; **6** 39; **12** 346; **19** 240, 292; **20 11–14 (upd.); 22** 455; **42** 438

Aluminum Company of Canada Ltd., **II** 345; **IV** 10–12, 154

Aluminum Cooking Utensil Co., **IV** 14

Aluminum Forge Co., **IV** 137

Aluminum Norf GmbH, **IV** 231

Aluminum of Korea, **III** 516

Aluminum Rolling Mills, **17** 280

Aluminum Sales Corporation, **12** 346

Aluminum Seating Corp., **I** 201

Alun Cathcart, **6** 357

Alup-Kompressoren Pressorun, **III** 570; **20** 361

Alupak, A.G., **12** 377

Alusaf, **IV** 92

Alusuisse Lonza Group Ltd., **IV** 12; **31** 11

Alva Jams Pty., **I** 437

Alvic Group, **20** 363

Alvis Plc, 47 7–9

Alyeska Pipeline Service Co., **IV** 522, 571; **14** 542; **24** 521; **40** 356

Alyeska Seafoods Co., **II** 578

ALZA Corporation, 10 53–55; 36 36–39 (upd.); 40 11; **41** 200–01

Alzwerke GmbH, **IV** 230

AM Acquisition, **8** 559–60

AM Cosmetics, Inc., **31** 89

Am-Par Records, **II** 129

Am-Safe, Inc., **16** 357

AM-TEX Corp., Inc., **12** 443

Amagasaki Co., **I** 492; **24** 325

Amagasaki Spinners Ltd., **V** 387

Amagasaki Steel Co., Ltd., **IV** 130

Amalgamaize Co., **14** 18

Amalgamated Chemicals, Ltd., **IV** 401

Amalgamated Dental International, **10** 271–72

Amalgamated Distilled Products, **II** 609

Amalgamated Press, **IV** 666; **7** 244, 342; **17** 397

Amalgamated Roadstone Corp., **III** 752; **28** 449

Amalgamated Sugar Co., **14** 18; **19** 467–68

Amalgamated Weatherware, **IV** 696

Amana Refrigeration Company, **II** 86; **11** 413; **18** 226; **38** 374; **42** 159

Amaray International Corporation, **12** 264

Amarillo Gas Company. *See* Atmos Energy Corporation.

Amarillo Railcar Services, **6** 580

Amarin Plastics, **IV** 290

Amax Gold, **36** 316

AMAX Inc., **I** 508; **III** 687; **IV 17–19**, 46, 139, 171, 239, 387; **6** 148; **12** 244; **22** 106, 286

Amazon.com, Inc., 25 17–19

Amazôna Mineracao SA, **IV** 56

Ambac Industries, **I** 85

AmBase Corp., **III** 264

Amber's Stores, Inc., **17** 360

Amberg Hospach AG, **49** 436

Amblin Entertainment, 21 23–27; 33 431

AMBRA, Inc., **48** 209

Ambrose Shardlow, **III** 494

AMC Entertainment Inc., 12 12–14; 14 87; **21** 362; **23** 126; **35 27–29 (upd.)**

AMCA International Corporation, **7** 513; **8** 545; **10** 329; **23** 299

AMCC. *See* Applied Micro Circuits Corporation.

Amcell. *See* American Cellular Network.

Amchem Products Inc., **I** 666

AMCO, Inc., **13** 159

Amcor Limited, IV 248–50; 19 13–16 (upd.)

AMCORE Financial Inc., 44 22–26

Amcraft Building Products Co., Inc., **22** 15

AMD. *See* Advanced Micro Devices, Inc.

Amdahl Corporation, III 109–11, 140; **6** 272; **12** 238; **13** 202; **14 13–16 (upd.); 16** 194, 225–26; **22** 293; **25** 87; **40 20–25 (upd.); 42** 147. *See also* Fujitsu Limited.

Amdocs Ltd., 47 10–12

AME Finanziaria, **IV** 587; **19** 19

AMEC plc, **I** 568; **36** 322; **49** 65

Amedco, **6** 295

Amer Group plc, 24 530; **41 14–16**

Amer Sport, **22** 202

Amerada Hess Corporation, IV 365–67, 400, 454, 522, 571, 658; **11** 353; **21 28–31 (upd.); 24** 521

Amerco, 6 351–52

AmerGen Energy LLC, **49** 65, 67

Ameri-Kart Corp., **19** 277, 279

America Japan Sheet Glass Co., **III** 714

America Latina Companhia de Seguros, **III** 289

America Online, Inc., 10 56–58, 237; **13** 147; **15** 54, 265, 321; **18** 24; **19** 41; **22** 52, 519, 522; **26 16–20 (upd.); 27** 20, 106, 301, 430, 517–18; **29** 143, 227; **32** 163; **33** 254; **34** 361; **35** 304, 306; **38** 269–71; **49** 311–12. *See also* CompuServe Interactive Services, Inc.

America Publishing Company, **18** 213

America Today, **13** 545

America Unplugged, **18** 77

America West Airlines, 6 72–74, 121

America West Express, **32** 334

America West Holdings Corporation, 34 22–26 (upd.)

America's Favorite Chicken Company, Inc., 7 26–28. *See also* AFC Enterprises, Inc.

American & Efird, Inc., **12** 501; **23** 260

American Acquisitions, Inc., **49** 279

American Agricultural Chemical Co., **IV** 401

American Air Conditioning, **25** 15

American Air Filter, **26** 3–4

American Airlines, I 30–31, 48, 71, **89–91**, 97, 106, 115, 118, 124–26, 130, 132, 512, 530; **III** 102; **6** 60, 81, **75–77 (upd.)**, 121, 129–31; **9** 271–72; **10** 163; **11** 279; **12** 190, 192, 379, 381, 487, **13** 173; **14** 73; **16** 146; **18** 73; **21** 141, 143; **24** 21, 399–400; **25** 90–91, 403, 421–22; **26** 427–28, 441; **31** 103, 306; **33** 270, 302; **34** 118; **38** 105. *See also* AMR Corporation.

American Alliance Co., **III** 191

American Allsafe Co., **8** 386

American Amusements, Inc., **III** 430

American Appliance Co., **II** 85; **11** 411

American Arithmometer Company. *See* Burroughs Corporation.

American Asiatic Underwriters, **III** 195

American Association of Retired Persons, **9** 348. *See also* AARP.

American Austin Quality Foods Inc., **44** 40

American Automar Inc., **12** 29

American Automated, **11** 111

American Automobile Insurance Co., **III** 251

American Aviation and General Insurance Co., **III** 230

American Aviation Manufacturing Corp., **15** 246

American Avitron Inc, **I** 481

American Bakeries Company, **12** 275–76

American Bancorp, **11** 295

American Bancshares, Inc., **11** 457
American Bank, **9** 474–75
American Bank Note, **IV** 599
American Bank of Vicksburg, **14** 41
American Bankcorp, Inc., **8** 188
American Banker/Bond Buyer, **8** 526
American Banknote Corporation, 30 42–45
American Bar Association, 35 30–33
American Barge and Towing Company, **11** 194
American Beauty Cover Company, **12** 472
American Beef Packers, Inc., **16** 473
American Beet Sugar Company, **11** 13–14
American Bell Telephone Company, **V** 259; **14** 336
American Beryllium Co., Inc., **9** 323
American Beverage Corp., **II** 528
American Biltrite Inc., 16 16–18; 18 116, 118; **43 19–22 (upd.)**
American Biodyne Inc., **9** 348
American Biomedical Corporation, **11** 333
American Biscuit Co., **II** 542
American Bottling, **49** 78
American Box Board Company, **12** 376
American Box Co., **IV** 137
American Brake Shoe and Foundry Company, **I** 456. *See also* ABC Rail Products Corporation.
American Brands, Inc., II 468, 477; **IV** 251; **V 395–97**, 398–99, 405; **7** 3–4; **9** 408; **12** 87, 344; **14** 95, 271–72; **16** 108, 110, 242; **19** 168–69; **38** 169; **49** 150–51, 153. *See also* Fortune Brands, Inc.
American Bridge Co., **II** 330; **IV** 572; **7** 549
American Broadcasting Co., **25** 418. *See also* ABC, Inc. *and* Capital Cities/ABC Inc.
American Builders & Contractors Supply Co. *See* ABC Supply Co., Inc.
American Builders, Inc., **8** 436
American Building Maintenance Industries, Inc., 6 17–19. *See also* ABM Industries Incorporated.
American Bus Lines Inc., **24** 118
American Business Information, Inc., 18 21–25
American Business Interiors. *See* American Furniture Company, Inc.
American Business Products, Inc., 20 15–17
American Cable Systems, Inc. *See* Comcast Corporation.
American Cablesystems, **7** 99
American Cafe, **I** 547
American Can Co., **IV** 36, 290; **8** 476; **10** 130; **11** 29, 197; **12** 408; **13** 255; **15** 127–28; **17** 106; **22** 210; **23** 98; **49** 293. *See also* Primerica Corp.
The American Cancer Society, 24 23–25
American Capital and Research Corp., **28** 201
American Car & Foundry Inc., **21** 503
American Carbide Corporation, **7** 584
American Cash Register Co., **III** 150; **6** 264
American Casualty Co., **III** 230–31, 404
American Casualty Co. of Dallas, **III** 203
American Cellular Network, **7** 91; **24** 122
American Cellulose and Chemical Manufacturing Co., **I** 317

American Cement Co. *See* Giant Cement Holding, Inc.
American Central Insurance Co., **III** 241
American Cereal Co., **II** 558; **12** 409
American Chicle Co., **I** 711; **21** 54; **38** 363–64
American Chocolate & Citrus Co., **IV** 409
American Chrome, **III** 699
American Classic Voyages Company, 22 340, 27 34–37
American Clay Forming Company, **8** 178
American Clip Company, **7** 3
American Coin Merchandising, Inc., 28 15–17
American Colloid Co., 13 32–35
American Colonial Insurance Company, **44** 356
American Commercial Bank, **II** 336
American Commercial Lines Inc., **22** 164, 166–67
American Commonwealths Power Corporation, **6** 579
American Community Grocers, **II** 670
American Computer Systems. *See* American Software Inc.
American Construction Lending Services, Inc., **39** 380, 382
American Continental Insurance Co., **III** 191–92
American Cotton Cooperative Association, **17** 207; **33** 85
American Cotton Oil Co., **II** 497
American Council on Education, **12** 141
American Courier Express, Inc., **24** 126
American Crayon Company, **12** 115
American Credit Corporation, **II** 236; **20** 59
American Crystal Sugar Company, 7 377; **11 13–15; 32 29–33 (upd.)**
American Cyanamid, I 300–02, 619; **III** 22; **IV** 345, 552; **8 24–26 (upd.)**; **10** 269; **11** 494; **13** 231–32; **14** 254, 256; **16** 68; **22** 147; **27** 115–16
American Dairy Queen Corporation, **10** 373
American Data Technology, Inc., **11** 111
American Digital Communications, Inc., **33** 329
American Distilling Co., **I** 226; **10** 180–81
American District Telegraph Co., **III** 644; **12** 9
American Diversified Foods, Inc., **14** 351
American Drew, Inc., **12** 301
American Drug Company, **13** 367
American Eagle Airlines, Inc., **28** 22
American Eagle Fire Insurance Co., **III** 240–41
American Eagle Outfitters, Inc., 14 427; **24 26–28; 25** 121
American Education Press, **10** 479
American Electric Company, **II** 27; **12** 193; **22** 10
American Electric Power Company, II 3; **IV** 181; **V 546–49; 6** 449, 524; **11** 516; **45 17–21 (upd.)**
American Empire Insurance Co., **III** 191
American Emulsions Co., **8** 455
American Encaustic Tiling Co., **22** 170
American Energy Management Inc., **39** 261
American Envelope Co., **III** 40; **16** 303; **28** 251; **43** 257
American Equipment Co., **I** 571
American Export Steamship Lines, **I** 89

American Express Company, I 26–27, 480, 614; **II** 108, 176, 309, 380–82, **395–99**, 450–52, 544; **III** 251–52, 319, 340, 389; **IV** 637, 721; **6** 206–07, 409; **8** 118; **9** 335, 343, 391, 468–69, 538; **10** 44–45, **59–64 (upd.); 11** 41, 416–17, 532; **12** 533; **14** 106; **15** 50; **18** 60, 112, 516, 543; **21** 97, 127; **23** 229; **26** 516; **33** 394–96; **38 42–48 (upd.)**
American Factors, Ltd. *See* Amfac/JMB Hawaii L.L.C.
American Family Corporation, III 187–89. *See also* AFLAC Inc.
American Family Life Insurance Company, **33** 407
American Family Publishers, **23** 393–94
American Feldmühle Corp., **II** 51; **21** 330
American Filtrona Corp., **IV** 260–61
American Finance Systems, **II** 349
American Financial Corporation, II 596; **III 190–92**, 221; **8** 537; **9** 452; **18** 549
American Financial Group Inc., 48 6–10 (upd.)
American Fine Wire, Inc., **33** 248
American First National Supermarkets, **16** 313
American Fitness Centers, **25** 40
American Fitness Products, Inc., **47** 128
American Flange, **30** 397
American Flavor & Fragrance Company, **9** 154
American Flyer Trains, **16** 336–37
American Food Management, **6** 45
American Foods Group, 43 23–27
American Football League, **29** 346
American Fore Group, **III** 241–42
American Foreign Insurance Association, **III** 223, 226. *See also* AFIA.
American Forest Products Co., **IV** 282; **9** 260
American Freightways Corporation, **42** 141
American Fructose Corp., **14** 18–19
American Fur Company, **25** 220
American Furniture Company, Inc., 12 300; **21 32–34**
American Gage Co., **I** 472
American Gaming and Electronics, Inc., **43** 461
American Gas & Electric. *See* American Electric Power Company.
American Gasoline Co., **IV** 540
American General Capital Corp., **I** 614
American General Corporation, III 193–94; 10 65–67 (upd.); 11 16; **46 20–23 (upd.); 47** 15
American General Finance Corp., 11 16–17
American General Life Insurance Company, **6** 294
American Golf Corporation, 45 22–24
American Graphics, **23** 100
American Greetings Corporation, 7 23–25; 12 207–08; **15** 507; **16** 256; **21** 426–28; **22 33–36 (upd.)**
American Grinder and Manufacturing Company, **9** 26
American Hardware & Supply Company. *See* TruServ Corporation.
American Harvester, **II** 262
American Hawaii Cruises, **27** 34
American Health & Life Insurance Company, **27** 47
American Healthcorp Inc., **48** 25
American Heritage Savings, **II** 420

American Hoechst Corporation. *See* Hoechst Celanese Corporation.
American Hoist & Derrick Co., **8** 544
American Home Assurance Co., **III** 196–97
American Home Assurance Co. of New York, **III** 203
American Home Mortgage Holdings, Inc., 46 24–26
American Home Patients Centers Inc., **46** 4
American Home Products, I 527, **622–24**, 631, 676–77, 696, 700; **III** 18, 36, 444; **8** 282–83; **10 68–70 (upd.)**, 528; **11** 35; **15** 64–65; **16** 191, 438; **21** 466; **24** 288; **25** 477; **36** 87; **38** 365; **49** 349–50
American Home Publishing Co., Inc., **14** 460
American Home Shield, **6** 46; **23** 428, 430
American Home Video, **9** 186
American Homestar Corporation, 18 26–29; **41 17–20 (upd.)**
American Homeware Inc., **15** 501
American Honda Motor Co., **I** 174; **10** 352
American Hospital Association, **10** 159
American Hospital Supply Co., **I** 627, 629; **III** 80; **10** 141–43; **11** 459, 486; **19** 103; **21** 118; **30** 496
American Hydron, **13** 366; **25** 55
American I.G. Chemical Corporation. *See* GAF Corporation.
American Impacts Corporation, **8** 464
American Improved Cements. *See* Giant Cement Holding, Inc.
American Independent Oil Co., **IV** 522, 537. *See also* Aminoil, Inc.
American Industrial Manufacturing Co., **I** 481
American Information Services, Inc., **11** 111
American Institute of Certified Public Accountants (AICPA), 44 27–30
American Institutional Products, Inc., **18** 246
American Instrument Co., **I** 628; **13** 233
American Insurance Agency, **III** 191, 352
American Insurance Co., **III** 251
American International Airways, Inc., **17** 318; **22** 311
American International Group, Inc., II 422; **III 195–98**, 200; **6** 349; **10** 39; **11** 532–33; **15 15–19 (upd.)**; **18** 159; **45** 109; **46** 20; **47 13–19 (upd.)**; **48** 219
American International Travel Service, **6** 367; **27** 90
American Iron and Steel Manufacturing Co., **IV** 35; **7** 48
American Isuzu Motors, Inc. *See* Isuzu Motors, Ltd.
American Italian Pasta Company, 27 38–40
American Janitor Service, **25** 15
American Jet Industries, **7** 205
American Ka-Ro, **8** 476
American Knitting Mills of Miami, Inc., **22** 213
American La-France, **10** 296
American Laboratories, **III** 73
American Land Cruiser Company. *See* Cruise America Inc.
American Lawyer Media Holdings, Inc., 32 34–37
American Learning Corporation, **7** 168
American Life Insurance Co., **III** 195–96

American Light and Traction. *See* MCN Corporation.
American Lightwave Systems, Inc., **10** 19
American Limestone Co., **IV** 33
American Limousine Corp., **26** 62
American Linseed Co, **II** 497
American Locker Group Incorporated, 34 19–21
American Lung Association, 48 11–14
American Machine and Foundry Co., **II** 7; **III** 443; **7** 211–13; **11** 397; **25** 197
American Machine and Metals, **9** 23
American Machinist Press, **IV** 634
American Magnesium Products Co., **I** 404
American Maize-Products Co., 14 17–20; **23** 464
American Management Systems, Inc., 11 18–20
American Manufacturers Mutual Insurance Co., **III** 269, 271; **15** 257
American-Marietta Corp., **I** 68, 405
American Materials & Technologies Corporation, **27** 117
American Media, Inc., 27 41–44
American Medical Association, 39 15–18
American Medical International, Inc., III 73–75, 79; **14** 232
American Medical Optics, **25** 55
American Medical Response, Inc., 39 19–22
American Medical Services, **II** 679–80; **14** 209
American Medicorp, Inc., **III** 81; **6** 191; **14** 432; **24** 230
American Melamine, **27** 317
American Merchandising Associates Inc., **14** 411
American Merchants Union Express Co., **II** 396
American Metal Climax, Inc. *See* AMAX.
American Metal Co. Ltd. *See* AMAX.
American Metal Products Company. *See* Lear Seating Corporation.
American Metal Products Corp., **I** 481
American Metals and Alloys, Inc., **19** 432
American Metals Corp., **III** 569; **20** 361
American Micro Devices, Inc., **16** 549
American Microsystems, **I** 193
American Milk Products Corp., **II** 487
The American Mineral Spirits Company, **8** 99–100
American Motorists Insurance Co., **III** 269, 271; **15** 257
American Motors Corp., I 135–37, 145, 152, 190; **II** 60, 313; **III** 543; **6** 27, 50; **8** 373; **10** 262, 264; **18** 493; **26** 403
American Movie Classics Co., **II** 161
American Multi-Cinema. *See* AMC Entertainment Inc.
American National Bank, **13** 221–22
American National Bank and Trust Co., **II** 286
American National Can Co., **III** 536; **IV** 173, 175; **26** 230; **45** 336
American National Corp., **II** 286
American National Fire Insurance Co., **III** 191
American National General Agencies Inc., **III** 221; **14** 109; **37** 85
American National Insurance Company, 8 27–29; **27 45–48 (upd.)**; **39** 158
American Natural Resources Co., **I** 678; **IV** 395; **13** 416
American Natural Snacks Inc., **29** 480

American Newspaper Publishers Association, **6** 13
American of Philadelphia, **III** 234
American Oil Co., **IV** 369–70; **7** 101; **14** 22
American Olean Tile Company, **III** 424; **22** 48, 170
American Optical Co., **I** 711–12; **III** 607; **7** 436; **38** 363–64
American Overseas Airlines, **12** 380
American Overseas Holdings, **III** 350
American Pad & Paper Company, 20 18–21
American Paging, **9** 494–96
American-Palestine Trading Corp., **II** 205–06
American Paper Box Company, **12** 376
American Patriot Insurance, **22** 15
American Payment Systems, Inc., **21** 514
American Petrofina, Inc., **IV** 498; **7** 179–80; **19** 11
American Pfauter, **24** 186
American Phone Centers, Inc., **21** 135
American Photographic Group, **III** 475; **7** 161
American Physicians Service Group, Inc., **6** 45; **23** 430
American Platinum Works, **IV** 78
American Port Services (Amports), **45** 29
American Postage Meter Co., **III** 156
American Potash and Chemical Corporation, **IV** 95, 446; **22** 302
American Power & Light Co., **6** 545, 596–97; **12** 542; **49** 143
American Power Conversion Corporation, 24 29–31
American Premier Underwriters, Inc., 10 71–74; **48** 9
American Prepaid Professional Services, Inc. *See* CompDent Corporation.
American President Companies Ltd., III 512; **6 353–55**
American Printing House for the Blind, 26 13–15
American Prospecting Equipment Co., **49** 174
American Protective Mutual Insurance Co. Against Burglary, **III** 230
American Public Automotive Group, **37** 115
American Publishing Co., **IV** 597; **24** 222
American Pure Oil Co., **IV** 497
American Radiator & Standard Sanitary Corp., **III** 663–64
American Railway Express Co., **II** 382, 397; **10** 61
American Railway Publishing Co., **IV** 634
American Re Corporation, III 182; **10 75–77**; **35 34–37 (upd.)**; **46** 303
American Record Corp., **II** 132
American Recreation Company Holdings, Inc., **16** 53; **44** 53–54
American Red Cross, 40 26–29
American Ref-Fuel, **V** 751
American Refrigeration Products S.A, **7** 429
American Republic Assurance Co., **III** 332
American Research and Development Corp., **II** 85; **III** 132; **6** 233; **19** 103
American Residential Mortgage Corporation, 8 30–31
American Residential Services, **33** 141
American Resorts Group, **III** 103

American Retirement Corporation, 42 9–12; **43** 46

American Rice, Inc., 17 161–62; **33** 30–33

American River Transportation Co., **I** 421; **11** 23

American Robot Corp., **III** 461

American Rolling Mill Co., **IV** 28; **8** 176–77

American Royalty Trust Co., **IV** 84; **7** 188

American Rug Craftsmen, **19** 275

American RX Pharmacy, **III** 73

American Safety Equipment Corp., **IV** 136

American Safety Razor Company, III 27–29; **20** 22–24

American Saint-Gobain, **16** 121

American Sales Book Co., Ltd., **IV** 644

American Salt Co., **12** 199

American Satellite Co., **6** 279; **15** 195

American Savings & Loan, **10** 117

American Savings Bank, **9** 276; **17** 528, 531

American Sealants Company. *See* Loctite Corporation.

American Seating Co., **I** 447; **21** 33

American Seaway Foods, Inc, **9** 451

American Service Corporation, **19** 223

American Sheet Steel Co., **IV** 572; **7** 549

American Shipbuilding, **18** 318

American Skiing Company, 28 18–21; **31** 67, 229

American Sky Broadcasting, **27** 305; **35** 156

American Smelting and Refining Co., **IV** 31–33. *See also* ASARCO.

The American Society of Composers, Authors and Publishers (ASCAP), 29 21–24

American Software Inc., 22 214; **25** 20–22

American-South African Investment Co. Ltd., **IV** 79

American Southern Insurance Co., **17** 196

American Standard Companies Inc., 30 46–50 **(upd.)**

American Standard Inc., **III** 437, 663–65; **19** 455; **22** 4, 6; **28** 486; **40** 452

American States Insurance Co., **III** 276

American States Water Company, 46 27–30

American Steamship Company, **6** 394–95; **25** 168, 170

American Steel & Wire Co., **I** 355; **IV** 572; **7** 549; **13** 97–98; **40** 70, 72

American Steel Foundries, **7** 29–30

American Stock Exchange, **10** 416–17

American Stores Company, II 604–06; **12** 63, 333; **13** 395; **17** 559; **18** 89; **22** 37–40 **(upd.)**; **25** 297; **27** 290–92; **30** 24, 26–27

American Sugar Refining Company. *See* Domino Sugar Corporation.

American Sumatra Tobacco Corp., **15** 138

American Superconductor Corporation, **41** 141

American Surety Co., **26** 486

American Systems Technologies, Inc., **18** 5

American Teaching Aids Inc., **19** 405

American Star Technical Services Company. *See* American Building Maintenance Industries, Inc. *and* ABM Industries Incorporated.

American Telephone and Telegraph Company. *See* AT&T.

American Television and Communications Corp., **I** 534–35; **II** 161; **IV** 596, 675; **7** 528–30; **18** 65

American Textile Co., **III** 571; **20** 362

American Thermos Bottle Company. *See* Thermos Company.

American Tile Supply Company, **19** 233

American Tin Plate Co., **IV** 572; **7** 549

American Tissue Company, **29** 136

American Title Insurance, **III** 242

American Tobacco Co., **I** 12–14, 28, 37, 425; **V** 395–97, 399, 408–09, 417–18, 600; **14** 77, 79; **15** 137–38; **16** 242; **18** 416; **27** 128–29; **33** 82; **43** 126. *See also* American Brands Inc., B.A.T. Industries PLC., *and* Fortune Brands, Inc.

American Tool & Machinery, **III** 420

American Tool Company, **13** 563

American Totalisator Corporation, **10** 319–20

American Tourister, Inc., 10 350; **13** 451, 453; **16** 19–21. *See also* Samsonite Corporation.

American Tower Corporation, 33 34–38

American Tractor Corporation, **10** 379

American Trading and Production Corporation, **7** 101

American Trans Air, **34** 31

American Transport Lines, **6** 384

American Trust and Savings Bank, **II** 261

American Trust Co., **II** 336, 382; **12** 535

American Twist Drill Co., **23** 82

American Ultramar Ltd., **IV** 567

American Vanguard Corporation, 47 20–22

American VIP Limousine, Inc., **26** 62

American Viscose Corp. *See* Avisco.

American Water Works Company, Inc., V 543–44; **6** 443–45; **26** 451; **38** 49–52 **(upd.)**

American Window Glass, **16** 120

American Wood Reduction Company, **14** 174

American Woodmark Corporation, 31 13–16

American Woolen, **I** 529

American Yard Products, **22** 26, 28

American Yearbook Company, **7** 255; **25** 252

American-Strevell Inc., **II** 625

Americana Entertainment Group, Inc., **19** 435

Americana Foods, Inc., **17** 474–75

Americana Healthcare Corp., **15** 522

Americana Hotel, **12** 316

AmeriFirst Bank, **11** 258

Amerifirst Federal Savings, **10** 340

AmeriGas Partners, L.P., **12** 498

AmeriGas Propane, Inc., **12** 500

Amerihost Properties, Inc., 30 51–53

AmeriKing Corp., **36** 309

Amerimark Inc., **II** 682

Amerin Corporation. *See* Radian Group Inc.

AmeriServe Food Distribution. *See* Holberg Industries, Inc.

AmeriSource Health Corporation, 37 9–11 **(upd.)**

Ameristar Casinos, Inc., 33 39–42

Amerisystems, **8** 328

Ameritech Corporation, V 265–68; **6** 248; **7** 118; **10** 431; **11** 382; **12** 137; **14**

252–53, 257, 259–61, 364; **15** 197; **18** 30–34 **(upd.)**; **25** 499; **41** 288–90; **43** 447; **44** 49

Ameritech Illinois. *See* Illinois Bell Telephone Company.

Ameritrade Holding Corporation, 34 27–30

Ameritrust Corporation, **9** 476

Ameriwood Industries International Corp., 17 15–17

Amerock Corp., **13** 41

Amerotron, **I** 529

Amersil Co., **IV** 78

Ames Department Stores, Inc., V 197–98; **9** 20–22; **10** 497; **15** 88; **19** 449; **30** 54–57 **(upd.)**

Ametek Inc., **9** 23–25; **12** 88; **38** 169

N.V. Amev, III 199–202

Amey Plc, 47 23–25; **49** 320

AMF Bowling, Inc., 19 312; **23** 450; **40** 30–33

Amfac Inc., I 417–18, 566; **IV** 703; **10** 42; **23** 320

Amfac/JMB Hawaii L.L.C., 24 32–35 **(upd.)**

Amfas, **III** 310

AMFM Inc., **35** 221, 245, 248; **37** 104; bf]XLI 384

Amgen, Inc., I 266; **8** 216–17; **10** 78–81; **13** 240; **14** 255; **21** 320; **30** 58–61 **(upd.)**; **38** 204

Amherst Coal Co., **IV** 410; **7** 309

AMI. *See* Advanced Metallurgy, Inc.

Amiga Corporation, **7** 96

Aminoil, Inc., **IV** 523. *See also* American Independent Oil Co.

AMISA, **IV** 136

Amisys Managed Care Information Systems, **16** 94

Amitron S.A., **10** 113

Amity Leather Products Company. *See* AR Accessories Group, Inc.

AMK Corporation, **II** 595; **7** 85; **21** 111

Amkor, **23** 17

AMLI Realty Company, **33** 418, 420

Amling Co., **25** 89

Ammirati Puris Lintas, **14** 316; **22** 294

Ammo-Phos, **I** 300; **8** 24

L'Ammoniac Sarro-Lorrain S.a.r.l., **IV** 197

Amoco Corporation, I 516, 202; **II** 376; **III** 611; **IV** 368–71, 412, 424–25, 453, 525; **7** 107, 443; **10** 83–84; **11** 441; **12** 18; **14** 21–25 **(upd.)**; 494; **18** 365; **19** 297; **26** 369. *See also* BP p.l.c.

Amorim Investimentos e Participaço, **48** 117, 119

Amorim Revestimentos, **48** 118

Amoseas, **IV** 453–54

Amoskeag Company, 6 356; **8** 32–33; **9** 213–14, 217; **22** 54; **31** 199

Amot Controls Corporation, **15** 404

AMP, Inc., II 7–8; **11** 319; **13** 344; **14** 26–28 **(upd.)**; **17** 274; **22** 542; **28** 486; **36** 158

Ampad Holding Corporation. *See* American Pad & Paper Company.

AMPAL. *See* American-Palestine Trading Corp.

AMPCO Auto Parks, Inc. *See* American Building Maintenance Industries, Inc. *and* ABM Industries Incorporated.

Ampeg Company, **48** 353

AMPEP, **III** 625

Ampex Corporation, III 549; **6** 272; **17** 18–20

Amphenol Corporation, 40 34–37

Ampol Petroleum Ltd., **III** 729; **27** 473

Ampro, **25** 504–05

AMR. *See* American Medical Response, Inc.

AMR Combs Inc., **36** 190

AMR Corporation, I 90–91; **6** 76; **8** 315; **22** 252; **26** 427–28; **28** 22–26 **(upd.)**; **29** 409; **33** 19; **34** 119

AMR Information Services, **9** 95

Amram's Distributing Limited, **12** 425

AMRE, **III** 211

AMREP Corporation, I 563; **21** 35–37; **24** 78

Amro. *See* Amsterdam-Rotterdam Bank N.V.

Amrop International Australasia, **34** 249

AMS. *See* Advanced Marketing Services, Inc.

AMS Trading Co., **III** 112

Amsco International, **29** 450

Amserve Ltd., **48** 23

AmSouth Bancorporation, 12 15–17; **48** 15–18 **(upd.)**

Amstar Corp., **14** 18

Amstar Sugar Corporation, **II** 582; **7** 466–67; **26** 122

Amsted Industries Incorporated, 7 29–31

Amstel Brewery, **I** 257; **34** 201

Amsterdam-Rotterdam Bank N.V., II 184, **185–86**, 279, 295, 319; **III** 200; **14** 169; **17** 324

Amstrad plc, III 112–14; **48** 19–23 **(upd.)**

AmSurg Corporation, 48 24–27

AMT. *See* American Materials & Technologies Corporation.

Amtech. *See* American Building Maintenance Industries, Inc. *and* ABM Industries Incorporated.

Amtech Systems Corporation, **11** 65; **27** 405

Amtel, Inc., **8** 545; **10** 136

Amtliches Bayerisches Reisebüro, **II** 163

Amtorg, **13** 365

Amtrak, **II** 2; **10** 73; **19** 141; **26** 440. *See also* National Railroad Passenger Corporation.

Amtran, Inc., 34 31–33

AmTrans. *See* American Transport Lines.

Amvac Chemical Corporation, **47** 20

Amvent Inc., **25** 120

Amway Corporation, III 11–14; **13** 36–39 **(upd.)**; **17** 186; **18** 67, 164; **20** 435; **23** 509; **29** 493; **30** 62–66 **(upd.)**; **31** 327

Amylum, **II** 582

ANA. *See* All Nippon Airways Co., Ltd.

Anacomp, Inc., **11** 19

Anaconda Aluminum, **11** 38

Anaconda Co., **III** 644; **IV** 33, 376; **7** 261–63

Anaconda-Jurden Associates, **8** 415

Anadarko Petroleum Corporation, 10 82–84

Anadex, Inc., **18** 435–36

Anaheim Imaging, **19** 336

Analog Devices, Inc., 10 85–87; **18** 20; **19** 67; **38** 54; **43** 17, 311; **47** 384

Analogic Corporation, 23 13–16

Analysts International Corporation, 36 40–42

Analytic Sciences Corporation, 10 88–90; **13** 417

Analytical Surveys, Inc., 33 43–45

Anam Group, 21 239; **23** 17–19

Anamax Mining Co., **IV** 33

AnAmo Co., **IV** 458

Anarad, Inc., **18** 515

Anaren Microwave, Inc., 33 46–48

ANB Bank, **I** 55

Anchor Bancorp, Inc., 10 91–93

Anchor Brake Shoe, **18** 5

Anchor Brewing Company, 47 26–28

Anchor Corporation, **12** 525

Anchor Gaming, 24 36–39; **41** 216

Anchor Hocking Glassware, I 609–10; **13** 40–42; **14** 483; **26** 353; **49** 253

Anchor Motor Freight, Inc., **12** 309–10

Anchor National Financial Services, Inc., **11** 482

Anchor National Life Insurance Company, **11** 482

Anchor Oil and Gas Co., **IV** 521

Anchor Records, **II** 130

Ancienne Mutuelle, **III** 210

Anders Wilhelmsen & Co., **22** 471

Andersen Consulting, **38** 430

Andersen Corporation, 9 344; **10** 94–95; **11** 305; **22** 346; **39** 324

Andersen Worldwide, 29 25–28 **(upd.)**

Anderson & Kerr Drilling Co., **IV** 445

Anderson and Campbell, **II** 479

Anderson Box Co., **IV** 342; **8** 267

Anderson Clayton & Co., **II** 560; **12** 411

Anderson, Greenwood & Co., **11** 225–26

Anderson Testing Company, Inc., **6** 441

The Andersons, Inc., 31 17–21

Anderton, **III** 624

Andes Candies, **II** 520–21

Andian National Corp. Ltd., **IV** 415–16

André Courrèges, **III** 47; **8** 342–43

Andreas Christ, **26** 243

Andreas Stihl, 16 22–24

Andrew Corporation, 10 96–98; **32** 38–41 **(upd.)**

Andrew Jergens Co., **III** 38; **25** 56

Andrew Weir & Co., **III** 273

Andrews, Clark & Company, **IV** 426; **7** 169

Andrews Group, Inc., **10** 402

Andrews McMeel Universal, 40 38–41

Andrews Office Supply and Equipment Co., **25** 500

Andritz AG, **27** 269

Anfor, **IV** 249–50

Angele Ghigi, **II** 475

Angelica Corporation, 15 20–22; **43** 28–31 **(upd.)**

Angelo's Supermarkets, Inc., **II** 674

ANGI Ltd., **11** 28

Angle Steel, **25** 261

Anglian Water Plc, **38** 51

Anglo-American Chewing Gum Ltd., **II** 569

Anglo-American Clays Corp., **III** 691; **IV** 346

Anglo American Corporation of South Africa Limited, I 289, 423; **IV** 20–23, 56–57, 64–68, 79–80, 90, 92, 94–96, 118–20, 191, 239–40; **7** 121–23, 125; **16** 25–30 **(upd.)**, 292; **21** 211, 354; **22** 233; **28** 88, 93; **49** 232–34

Anglo-American Oil Company Limited, **IV** 427; **7** 170

Anglo American Paper Co., **IV** 286

Anglo-American Telegraph Company Ltd., **IV** 668; **25** 98

Anglo-Belge, **II** 474

Anglo-Canadian, **III** 704

Anglo-Canadian Mining & Refining, **IV** 110

Anglo-Canadian Telephone Company of Montreal. *See* British Columbia Telephone Company.

Anglo-Celtic Watch Company, **25** 430

Anglo Company, Ltd., **9** 363

Anglo-Dutch Unilever group, **9** 317

Anglo-Egyptian D.C.O., **II** 236

Anglo-Egyptian Oilfields, **IV** 412, 414

Anglo-Elementar-Versicherungs-AG, **III** 185

Anglo Energy, Ltd., **9** 364

Anglo-Huronian Ltd., **IV** 164

Anglo-Iranian Oil Co., **IV** 379, 419, 435, 450, 466, 559; **7** 57, 141; **21** 81

Anglo-Lautaro Nitrate Corporation, **9** 363

Anglo Mexican Petroleum Co. Ltd., **IV** 657

Anglo-Palestine Co., **II** 204

Anglo-Persian Oil Co., **IV** 363, 378–79, 381, 429, 450, 466, 515, 524, 531, 557–59; **7** 56–57, 140; **21** 80–81; **45** 47

Anglo-Swiss Condensed Milk Co., **II** 545

Anglo-Thai Corp., **III** 523

Anglo-Transvaal Consolidated, **IV** 534

Anglovaal Industries Ltd., **20** 263

Angus Hill Holdings, **IV** 249

Anheuser-Busch Companies, Inc., 34 34–37 **(upd.)**; **36** 12–15, 163

Anheuser-Busch Company, Inc., I 32, **217–19**, 236–37, 254–55, 258, 265, 269–70, 290–91, 598; **IV** 624; **6** 20–21, 48; **9** 100; **10** 99–101 **(upd.)**, 130; **11** 421; **12** 337–38; **13** 5, 10, 258, 366; **15** 429; **17** 256; **18** 65, 70, 72–73, 499, 501; **19** 221, 223; **21** 229, 319–20; **22** 421; **23** 403; **25** 281–82, 368; **26** 432; **29** 84–85; **29** 218; **31** 381, 383

ANIC Gela, **IV** 421

Anikem, **I** 374

Anitec Image Technology Corp., **IV** 287; **15** 229

Annabelle's, **II** 480–81; **26** 57

Anne Klein & Co., **15** 145–46; **24** 299; **40** 277–78

Anneplas, **25** 464

AnnTaylor Stores Corporation, V 26–27; **13** 43–45; **15** 9; **25** 120–22; **37** 12–15 **(upd.)**

Annuaries Marcotte Ltd., **10** 461

Anocout Engineering Co., **23** 82

Anonima Infortunia, **III** 208

ANR Pipeline Co., 17 21–23; **31** 119

Ansa Software, **9** 81

Ansaldo, **II** 191

Ansbacher-Siegle Corp., **13** 460

Anschütz & Co. GmbH, **III** 446

The Anschutz Corporation, 12 18–20; **36** 43–47 **(upd.)**; **37** 312

Anschütz-Kaempfe, **III** 446

Ansell, **I** 215

Ansell Rubber Company, **10** 445

Anselmo L. Morvillo S.A., **19** 336

Ansett Airlines, **6** 73; **14** 11; **27** 475

Ansett Australia, **24** 398, 400; **26** 113

Ansett Transport Industries Limited, **V** 523–25; **27** 473

Ansonia Brass and Battery Co., **IV** 176–77

Ansonia Manufacturing Co., **IV** 176

ANSYS Technologies Inc., **48** 410
Ant Nachrichtentechnik GmbH., **I** 411
Anta Corporation, **6** 188; **25** 308
Antalis, **34** 38, 40
Antar group, **IV** 544, 546
Antares Alliance Group, **14** 15
Antares Electronics, Inc., **10** 257
Ante Corp., **22** 222
Antenna Company, **32** 40
ANTEX. *See* American National Life Insurance Company of Texas.
Anthem Electronics, Inc., **13** 46–47; **17** 276
Anthem P&C Holdings, **15** 257
Anthes Imperial Ltd., **I** 274; **26** 304
Anthes Industries Inc., **9** 512
Anthony Industries Inc. *See* K2 Inc.
Anthony Stumpf Publishing Company, **10** 460
Anthropologie, **14** 524–25
Antillaase Bank-Unie N.V., **II** 184
Antinori. *See* Marchesi Antinori SRL.
The Antioch Company, **40** 42–45
Antique Street Lamps, **19** 212
ANTK Tupolev. *See* Aviacionny Nauchno-Tehnicheskii Komplex im. A.N. Tupoleva.
Antoine Saladin, **III** 675
Antwerp Co., **IV** 497
ANZ. *See* Australia and New Zealand Banking Group Ltd.
ANZ Securities, **24** 400
Anzon Limited, **III** 681; **44** 118–19
AO Sidanco, **45** 50
AOE Plastic GmbH, **7** 141
Aoki Corporation, **9** 547, 549; **29** 508
AOL. *See* America Online, Inc.
AOL Time Warner Inc., **45** 201; **47** 271
Aon Corporation, **III** 203–05; **22** 495; **45** 25–28 (upd.)
AP. *See* The Associated Press.
AP Bank, Ltd., **13** 439
AP Support Services, **25** 13
AP&L. *See* American Power & Light Co.
AP-Dow Jones/Telerate Company, **10** 277
APAC, Inc., **IV** 374
Apache Corporation, **10** 102–04; **11** 28; **18** 366; **32** 42–46 (upd.)
Apache Energy Ltd., **25** 471
APACHE Medical Systems, Inc., **16** 94
Apartment Furniture Rental, **26** 102
Apartment Investment and Management Company, **49** 24–26
APCOA/Standard Parking. *See* Holberg Industries, Inc.
Apex, **17** 363
Apex Financial Corp., **8** 10
Apex Oil, **37** 310–11
Apex One Inc., **31** 137
Apex Smelting Co., **IV** 18
APH. *See* American Printing House for the Blind.
Apita, **V** 210
APL. *See* American President Companies Ltd.
APL Corporation, **9** 346
APL Ltd., **41** 399
Aplex Industries, Inc., **26** 363
Apline Guild, **12** 173
Aplix, **19** 477
APM Ltd., **IV** 248–49
APN. *See* Affiliated Physicians Network, Inc.

Apogee Enterprises, Inc., **8** 34–36; **22** 347
Apollo Advisors L.P., **16** 37; **26** 500, 502; **43** 438
Apollo Apparel Partners, L.P., **12** 431
Apollo Computer, **III** 143; **6** 238; **9** 471; **11** 284
Apollo Group, Inc., **24** 40–42
Apollo Heating & Air Conditioning Inc., **15** 411
Apollo Investment Fund Ltd., **31** 211; **39** 174
Apollo Ski Partners LP of New York, **11** 543, 545
Apollo Technologies, **I** 332
Apotekarnes Droghandel A.B., **I** 664–65
Apotekernes Laboratorium A.S., **12** 3–5
Appalachian Computer Services, **11** 112
Appalachian Travel Services, Inc., **25** 185, 187
Applause Inc., **17** 461; **24** 43–46
Apple Computer, Inc., **II** 6, 62, 103, 107, 124; **III** 114, **115–16**, 121, 125, 149, 172; **6** 218–20 (upd.), 222, 225, 231, 244, 248, 254–58, 260, 289; **8** 138; **9** 166, 170–71, 368, 464; **10** 22–23, 34, 57, 233, 235, 404, 458–59, 518–19; **11** 45, 50, 57, 62, 490; **12** 139, 183, 335, 449, 455, 470; **13** 90, 388, 482; **16** 195, 367–68, 372, 417–18; **18** 93, 511, 521; **20** 31; **21** 391; **23** 209; **24** 370; **25** 299–300, 348, 530–31; **28** 244–45; **33** 12–14; **34** 512; **36** 48–51 (upd.), 168; **38** 69
Apple Container Corp., **III** 536; **26** 230
Apple Orthodontix, Inc., **35** 325
Apple South, Inc., **21** 362; **35** 39. *See also* Avado Brands, Inc.
Applebee's International Inc., **14** 29–31; **19** 258; **20** 159; **21** 362; **31** 40; **35** 38–41 (upd.)
Appleton & Cox, **III** 242
Appleton Papers, **I** 426
Appleton Wire Works Corp., **8** 13
Appliance Buyers Credit Corp., **III** 653
Appliance Recycling Centers of America, Inc., **42** 13–16
Applica Incorporated, **43** 32–36 (upd.)
Les Applications du Roulement, **III** 623
Applied Beverage Systems Ltd., **21** 339
Applied Biomedical Corp., **47** 4
Applied Bioscience International, Inc., **10** 105–07
Applied Color Systems, **III** 424
Applied Communications, Inc., **6** 280; **11** 151; **25** 496; **29** 477–79
Applied Data Research, Inc., **6** 225; **18** 31–32
Applied Digital Data Systems Inc., **II** 83; **9** 514
Applied Engineering Services, Inc. *See* The AES Corporation.
Applied Films Corporation, **12** 121; **35** 148; **48** 28–31
Applied Industrial Materials Corporation, **22** 544, 547
Applied Komatsu Technology, Inc., **10** 109
Applied Laser Systems, **31** 124
Applied Learning International, **IV** 680
Applied Materials, Inc., **10** 108–09; **18** 382–84; **46** 31–34 (upd.)
Applied Micro Circuits Corporation, **38** 53–55
Applied Network Technology, Inc., **25** 162

Applied Power Inc., **9** 26–28; **32** 47–51 (upd.)
Applied Programming Technologies, Inc., **12** 61
Applied Solar Energy, **8** 26
Applied Technology Corp., **11** 87
Applied Thermal Technologies, Inc., **29** 5
Approvisionnement Atlantique, **II** 652
Appryl, **I** 303
Apria Healthcare Inc., **43** 266
Aprilia SpA, **17** 24–26
APS. *See* Arizona Public Service Company.
APS Healthcare, **17** 166, 168
Apura GmbH, **IV** 325
APUTCO, **6** 383
Aqua Alliance Inc., **32** 52–54 (upd.)
Aqua-Chem, Inc., **I** 234; **10** 227
Aqua Glass, **III** 570; **20** 362
Aqua Pure Water Co., **III** 21
Aquafin N.V., **12** 443; **38** 427
Aquarium Supply Co., **12** 230
Aquarius Group, **6** 207
Aquila, **IV** 486
Aquila Energy Corp., **6** 593
Aquitaine. *See* Société Nationale des Petroles d'Aquitaine.
AR Accessories Group, Inc., **23** 20–22
AR-TIK Systems, Inc., **10** 372
ARA Services, **II** 607–08; **21** 507; **25** 181
Arab Contractors, **III** 753
Arab Japanese Insurance Co., **III** 296
Arab Petroleum Pipeline Co., **IV** 412
Arabian American Oil Co., **I** 570; **IV** 386, 429, 464–65, 512, 536–39, 552, 553, 559; **7** 172, 352; **14** 492–93; **41** 392. *See also* Saudi Arabian Oil Co.
Arabian Gulf Oil Co., **IV** 454
Arabian Investment Banking Corp., **15** 94; **26** 53; **47** 361
Arabian Oil Co., **IV** 451
Aral, **IV** 487
ARAMARK Corporation, **13** 48–50; **16** 228; **21** 114–15; **35** 415; **41** 21–24
Aramco. *See* Arabian American Oil Co. *and* Saudi Arabian Oil Company.
Aramis Inc., **30** 191
Arandell Corporation, **37** 16–18
Arapuã. *See* Lojas Arapuã S.A.
Aratex Inc., **13** 49
Aratsu Sekiyu, **IV** 554
ARBED S.A., **IV** 24–27, 53; **22** 41–45 (upd.); **26** 83; **42** 414
Arbeitsgemeinschaft der öffentlich-rechtlichen Rundfunkanstalten der Bundesrepublik. *See* ARD.
The Arbitron Company, **III** 128; **10** 255, 359; **13** 5; **38** 56–61
Arbor Acres, **13** 103
Arbor Drugs Inc., **12** 21–23. *See also* CVS Corporation.
Arbor International, **18** 542
Arbor Living Centers Inc., **6** 478
Arbuthnot & Co., **III** 522
Arby's Inc., **II** 614; **8** 536–37; **14** 32–34, 351
ARC. *See* American Rug Craftsmen.
ARC International Corporation, **27** 57
ARC Ltd., **III** 501
ARC Materials Corp., **III** 688
ARC Propulsion, **13** 462
ARCA. *See* Appliance Recycling Centers of America, Inc.
Arcadia Company, **14** 138

Arcadia Group plc, **28** 27–30 (upd.), 95–96
Arcadia Partners, **17** 321
Arcadian Corporation, **18** 433; **27** 317–18
Arcadian Marine Service, Inc., **6** 530
Arcadis NV, **26** 21–24
Arcata Corporation, **12** 413
Arcata National Corp., **9** 305
Arcelik, **I** 478
Arch Mineral Corporation, **IV** 374; **7** 32–34
Arch Petroleum Inc., **39** 331
Arch Wireless, Inc., **39** 23–26; **41** 265, 267
Archbold Container Co., **35** 390
Archbold Ladder Co., **12** 433
Archer-Daniels-Midland Co., **I** 419–21; **IV** 373; **7** 432–33, 241 **8** 53; **11** 21–23 (upd.); **17** 207; **22** 85, 426; **23** 384; **25** 241; **31** 234; **32** 55–59 (upd.)
Archer Drug, **III** 10
Archer Management Services Inc., **24** 360
Archers Gilles & Co., **II** 187
Archibald Candy Corporation, **36** 309
Archipelago RediBook, **48** 226, 228
Archstone-Smith Trust, **49** 27–30
Archway Cookies, Inc., **29** 29–31
ARCO. *See* Atlantic Richfield Company.
ARCO Chemical Company, **IV** 376–77, 456–57; **10** 110–11
ARCO Comfort Products Co., **26** 4
Arco Electronics, **9** 323
Arco Pharmaceuticals, Inc., **31** 346
Arco Societa Per L'Industria Elettrotecnica, **II** 82
Arcon Corporation, **26** 287
Arctco, Inc., **12** 400–01; **16** 31–34; **35** 349, 351
Arctic, **III** 479
Arctic Alaska Fisheries Corporation, **14** 515
Arctic Cat Inc., **40** 46–50 (upd.)
Arctic Enterprises, **34** 44
Arctic Slope Regional Corporation, **38** 62–65
ARD, **41** 25–29
Ardal og Sunndal Verk AS, **10** 439
Arden Group, Inc., **29** 32–35
Ardent Computer Corp., **III** 553
Ardent Risk Services, Inc. *See* General Re Corporation.
Areal Technologies, **III** 715
Argbeit-Gemeinschaft Lurgi und Ruhrchemie, **IV** 534; **47** 342
Argenbright Security Inc. *See* Securicor Plc.
Argentaria Caja Postal y Banco Hipotecario S.A. *See* Banco Bilbao Vizcaya Argentaria S.A.
Argentine National Bank, **14** 46
Argo Communications Corporation, **6** 300
Argon Medical, **12** 327
Argonaut, **I** 523–24; **10** 520–22
Argos, **I** 426; **22** 72
Argos Retail Group, **47** 165, 169
Argos Soditic, **43** 147, 149
Argosy Gaming Company, **21** 38–41
Argosy Group LP, **27** 197
Argus Chemical Co., **I** 405
Argus Corp., **IV** 22, 272, 611
Argus Energy, **7** 538
Argus Motor Company, **16** 7
Argyle Television Inc., **19** 204

Argyll Group PLC, **I** 241; **II** 609–10, 656; **12** 152–53; **24** 418
Aria Communications, Inc. *See* Ascend Communications, Inc.
Ariba Inc., **38** 432
Ariel Capital Management, **28** 421
Ariens Company, **48** 32–34
Aries Technology, **25** 305
Aris Industries, Inc., **15** 275; **16** 35–38
Aristech Chemical Corp., **12** 342
Arizona Airways, **22** 219
Arizona Copper Co., **IV** 177
Arizona Edison Co., **6** 545
Arizona Growth Capital, Inc., **18** 513
AriZona Iced Tea. *See* Ferolito, Vultaggio & Sons.
Arizona One, **24** 455
Arizona Public Service Company, **6** 545–47; **19** 376, 412; **26** 359; **28** 425–26
Arizona Refrigeration Supplies, **14** 297–98
Arjo Wiggins Appleton p.l.c., **13** 458; **27** 513; **34** 38–40
Ark Restaurants Corp., **20** 25–27
Ark Securities Co., **II** 233
Arkady Co., Ltd., **I** 421; **11** 23
Arkansas Best Corporation, **16** 39–41; **19** 455; **42** 410
Arkansas Breeders, **II** 585
Arkansas Chemicals Inc., **I** 341
Arkansas Louisiana Gas Company. *See* Arkla, Inc.
Arkansas Power & Light, **V** 618
Arkay Computer, **6** 224
ARKE, **II** 164
Arkia, **23** 184, 186–87
Arkla, Inc., **V** 550–51; **11** 441
Arla Foods amba, **48** 35–38
Arlesey Lime and Portland Cement Co., **III** 669
Arlington Corporation, **6** 295
Arlington Motor Holdings, **II** 587
Arlington Securities plc, **24** 84, 87–89
Arlon, Inc., **28** 42, 45
Armani. *See* Giorgio Armani S.p.A.
Armaturindistri, **III** 569
Armco Inc., **III** 259, 721; **IV** 28–30, 125, 171; **10** 448; **11** 5, 255; **12** 353; **19** 8; **26** 407; **30** 282–83; **41** 3, 5
Armin Corp., **III** 645
Armin Poly Film Corp., **III** 645
Armitage Shanks, **III** 671
Armor All Products Corp., **12** 333; **15** 507; **16** 42–44; **22** 148; **26** 349; **47** 235
Armor Elevator, **11** 5
Armor Holdings, Inc., **27** 49–51
Armour. *See* Tommy Armour Golf Co.
Armour & Company, **8** 144; **12** 198; **13** 21, 506; **23** 173
Armour-Dial, **I** 14; **8** 144; **23** 173–74
Armour Food Co., **I** 449–50, 452; **II** 494, 518; **12** 81, 370; **13** 270; **42** 92
Armour Pharmaceutical Co., **III** 56
Armstrong Advertising Co., **I** 36
Armstrong Air Conditioning Inc. *See* Lennox International Inc.
Armstrong Autoparts, **III** 495
Armstrong Communications, **IV** 640
Armstrong Cork Co., **III** 118
Armstrong Nurseries, **I** 272
Armstrong Rees Ederer Inc., **IV** 290
Armstrong-Siddeley Co., **III** 508
Armstrong Tire Co., **15** 355

Armstrong, Whitworth & Co. Ltd., **I** 50; **III** 508; **IV** 257; **24** 85
Armstrong World Industries, Inc., **III** 422–24; **9** 466; **12** 474–75; **22** 46–50 (upd.), 170–71; **26** 507
Armtek, **7** 297
Army and Air Force Exchange Service, **39** 27–29
Army Cooperative Fire Insurance Company, **10** 541
Army Ordnance, **19** 430
Army Signal Corps Laboratories, **10** 96
Arndale, **IV** 696
Arno Press, **IV** 648; **19** 285
Arnold & Porter, **35** 42–44
Arnold Communications, **25** 381
Arnold Electric Company, **17** 213
Arnold Foods Co., **II** 498
Arnold Industries Inc., **35** 297
Arnold, Schwinn & Company. *See* Schwinn Cycle and Fitness L.P.
Arnold Thomas Co., **9** 411
Arnoldo Mondadori Editore S.p.A., **IV** 585–88, 675; **19** 17–21 (upd.)
Arnotts Ltd., **II** 481; **26** 57–59
Aro Corp., **III** 527; **14** 477, 508; **15** 225
Aromat Corporation, **III** 710; **7** 303
Aromatic Industries, **18** 69
Arpet Petroleum, **III** 740; **IV** 550
Arpic, **III** 426
Arrosto Coffee Company, **25** 263
Arrow Electronics, Inc., **10** 112–14; **13** 47; **19** 310–11, 313; **29** 414; **30** 175
Arrow Food Distributor, **II** 675
Arrow Furniture Co., **21** 32
Arrow Oil Co., **IV** 401
Arrow Oil Tools, **III** 570; **20** 360
Arrow Pacific Plastics, **48** 334
Arrow Pump Co., **I** 185
Arrow Shirt Co., **24** 384
Arrow Specialty Company, **III** 570; **20** 360
Arrowhead Mills Inc., **27** 197–98; **43** 218–19
Arrowsmith & Silver, **I** 428
Arsam Investment Co., **26** 261
A.B. Arsenalen, **II** 352
Arsynco, Inc., **38** 4
The Art Institute of Chicago, **29** 36–38
Art Van Furniture, Inc., **28** 31–33
Artal Luxembourg SA, **33** 446, 449
Artal NV, **40** 51
Artec, **III** 420; **12** 297
Artech Digital Entertainments, Inc., **15** 133
Artek Systems Corporation, **13** 194
Artémis Group, **27** 513
Artesian Manufacturing and Bottling Company, **9** 177
Artesian Resources Corporation, **45** 277
Artesyn Solutions Inc., **48** 369
Artesyn Technologies Inc., **46** 35–38 (upd.)
Artex Enterprises, **7** 256; **25** 167, 253
Arthur Andersen & Company, Société Coopérative, **III** 143; **6** 244; **10** 115–17, 174; **16** 92; **25** 358; **29** 392; **46** 186. *See also* Andersen Worldwide.
Arthur D. Little, Inc., **35** 45–48
Arthur H. Fulton, Inc., **42** 363
Arthur Murray International, Inc., **32** 60–62
Arthur Ovens Motor Freight Co., **6** 371
Arthur Rank Organisation, **25** 328
Arthur Tappan & Co., **IV** 604

Arthur Young & Company, **IV** 119; **10** 386; **19** 311; **33** 235. *See also* Ernst & Young.

Artisan Entertainment Inc., 32 63–66 (upd.)

Artisan Life Insurance Cooperative, **24** 104

Artisoft, Inc., **18** 143

Artistic Direct, Inc., **37** 108

Artists & Writers Press, Inc., **13** 560

Artists Management Group, **38** 164

ArtMold Products Corporation, **26** 342

Artra Group Inc., **40** 119–20

Arts and Entertainment Network. *See* A&E Television Networks.

Arundel Corp., **46** 196

Arvey Corp., **IV** 287

Arvida Corp., **IV** 703

Arvin Industries, Inc., 8 37–40

ASA Holdings, **47** 30

ASAB, **III** 480

Asahi Breweries, Ltd., I 220–21, 282, 520; **13** 454; **20 28–30 (upd.)**; **21** 230, 319–20; **26** 456; **36** 404–05

Asahi Chemical Industry Co., **I** 221; **III** 760; **IV** 326

Asahi Corporation, **16** 84; **40** 93

Asahi Glass Company, Ltd., I 363; III 666–68; 11 234–35; 48 39–42 (upd.)

Asahi Kasei Industry Co. Ltd., **IV** 476

Asahi Komag Co., Ltd., **11** 234

Asahi Kyoei Co., **I** 221

Asahi Manufacturing, **III** 592

Asahi Medix Co., Ltd., **36** 420

Asahi Milk Products, **II** 538

Asahi National Broadcasting Company, Ltd., 9 29–31

Asahi Oil, **IV** 542

Asahi Real Estate Facilities Co., Ltd., **6** 427

Asahi Seiko, **III** 595

Asahi Shimbun, **9** 29–30

Asahi Trust & Banking, **II** 323

Asano Group, **III** 718

Asanté Technologies, Inc., 20 31–33

ASARCO Incorporated, I 142; **IV** 31–34; **40** 220–22, 411

ASB Agency, Inc., **10** 92

ASB Air, **47** 286–87

Asbury Associates Inc., **22** 354–55

Asbury Group, **26** 501

ASCAP. *See* The American Society of Composers, Authors and Publishers.

Ascend Communications, Inc., 24 47–51; **34** 258

Aschaffenburger Zellstoffwerke AG, **IV** 323–24

ASCO Healthcare, Inc., **18** 195–97

Asco Products, Inc., **22** 413

Ascom AG, 9 32–34; **15** 125

Ascometal, **IV** 227

Ascotts, **19** 122

ASD, **IV** 228

ASDA Group plc, II 611–12, 513, 629; **11** 240; **28 34–36 (upd.)**

ASEA AB. *See* ABB ASEA Brown Boveri Ltd.

Asean Bintulu Fertilizer, **IV** 518

Asepak Corp., **16** 339

A.B. Asesores Bursatiles, **III** 197–98; **15** 18

ASF. *See* American Steel Foundries.

Asgrow Florida Company, **13** 503

Asgrow Seed Co., **29** 435; **41** 306

Ash Company, **10** 271

Ash Resources Ltd., **31** 398–99

Ashanti Goldfields Company Limited, 43 37–40

Ashbourne PLC, **25** 455

Ashitaka Rinsan Kogyo, **IV** 269

Ashland Inc., 19 22–25; **27** 316, 318

Ashland Iron and Mining Co., **IV** 28

Ashland Oil, Inc., I 420; **IV** 71, 198, 366, **372–74**, 472, 658; **7** 32–33; **8** 99; **9** 108; **11** 22; **18** 279

Ashley Furniture Industries, Inc., 35 49–51

Ashtead Group plc, 34 41–43

Ashton Joint Venture, **IV** 60, 67

Ashton Mining, **IV** 60

Ashton-Tate Corporation, **9** 81–82; **10** 504–05

Ashworth, Inc., 26 25–28

Asia Life Insurance Co., **III** 195–96

Asia Oil Co., Ltd., **IV** 404, 476

Asia Pulp & Paper, **38** 227

Asia Shuang He Sheng Five Star Beer Co., Ltd., **49** 418

Asia Television, **IV** 718; **38** 320

Asia Terminals Ltd., **IV** 718; **38** 319

AsiaInfo Holdings, Inc., 43 41–44

Asian Football Confederation, **27** 150

Asiatic Petroleum Co., **IV** 434, 530

ASICS Corp., **24** 404

Asil çelik, **I** 479

ASK Group, Inc., 9 35–37; **25** 34

Ask Mr. Foster Agency, **22** 127; **26** 308

Asland SA, **III** 705, 740

ASMI. *See* Acer Semiconductor Manufacturing Inc.

Aso Cement, **III** 705

Aspect Telecommunications Corporation, 16 392–93; **22 51–53**

Aspen Imaging International, Inc., **17** 384

Aspen Mountain Gas Co., **6** 568

Aspen Skiing Company, II 170; **15 23–26**, 234; **43 438**

Aspen Systems, **14** 555

Asplundh Tree Expert Co., 20 34–36

Assam Co. Ltd., **III** 522–23

Assam Oil Co., **IV** 441, 483–84

Asset Management Company, **25** 86

Asset Marketing Inc. *See* Commercial Financial Services, Inc.

L'Assicuratrice Italiana, **III** 346–47

Assicurazioni Generali SpA, II 192; **III 206–09**, 211, 296, 298; **14** 85; **15 27–31 (upd.)**

Assisted Living Concepts, Inc., 43 45–47

Associate Venture Investors, **16** 418

Associated Anglo-Atlantic Corp., **III** 670

Associated Aviation Underwriters, **III** 220

Associated Banks of Europe Corp., **II** 184, 239

Associated Biscuit Co., **II** 631

Associated Book Publishers, **8** 527

Associated Bowater Industries, **IV** 258

Associated Brewing Co., **I** 254

Associated British Foods plc, II 465–66, 565, 609; **11** 526; **13 51–53 (upd.)**; **24** 475; **41 30–33 (upd.)**

Associated British Maltsters, **II** 500

Associated British Picture Corporation, **I** 531; **II** 157; **22** 193

Associated British Ports Holdings Plc, 45 29–32

Associated Bulk Carriers Ltd., **38** 345

Associated City Investment Trust, **IV** 696

Associated Communications Companies, **7** 78; **23** 479

Associated Container Transportation, **23** 161

Associated Cooperative Investment Trust Ltd., **IV** 696

Associated Dairies Ltd., **II** 611

Associated Dry Goods Corp., **V** 134; **12** 54–55; **24** 298

Associated Electrical Industries, Ltd., **II** 25; **III** 502

Associated Employers General Agency, **III** 248

Associated Estates Realty Corporation, 25 23–25

Associated Fire Marine Insurance Co., **26** 486

Associated Food Holdings Ltd., **II** 628

Associated Fresh Foods, **II** 611–12; **48** 37

Associated Fuel Pump Systems Corp., **III** 593

Associated Gas & Electric Company, **V** 621, 629–30; **6** 534; **14** 124

Associated Gas Services, Inc., **11** 28

Associated Grocers, Incorporated, 9 38–40; **19** 301; **31 22–26 (upd.)**

Associated Grocers of Arizona, **II** 625

Associated Grocers of Colorado, **II** 670

The Associated Group, **10** 45

Associated Hospital Service of New York, **III** 245–46

Associated Iliffe Press, **IV** 666; **17** 397

Associated Indemnity Co., **III** 251

Associated Inns and Restaurants Company of America, **14** 106; **25** 309; **26** 459

Associated Insurance Cos., **III** 194

Associated International Insurance Co. *See* Gryphon Holdings, Inc.

Associated Lead Manufacturers Ltd., **III** 679, 680–81

Associated London Properties, **IV** 705; **49** 247

Associated Madison Insurance, **I** 614

Associated Merchandisers, Inc., **27** 246

Associated Merchandising Corp., **16** 215

Associated Milk Producers, Inc., 11 24–26; **48 43–46 (upd.)**

Associated National Insurance of Australia, **III** 309

Associated Natural Gas Corporation, 11 27–28

Associated Newspapers Holdings P.L.C., **IV** 686; **19** 118, 120; **37** 121

Associated Octel Company Limited, **10** 290

Associated Oil Co., **IV** 460

Associated Pipeline Contractors, **III** 559

Associated Piping & Engineering Corp., **III** 535

Associated Portland Cement Manufacturers (1900) Ltd., **III** 669–71

The Associated Press, IV 629, 669–70; **7** 158; **10** 277; **13 54–56**; **25** 506; **31 27–30 (upd.)**; **34** 11

Associated Publishing Company, **19** 201

Associated Pulp & Paper Mills, **IV** 328

Associated Sales Agency, **16** 389

Associated Spring Co., **III** 581; **13** 73

Associated Stationers, **14** 521, 523

Associated Television, **7** 78

Associated Timber Exporters of British Columbia Ltd., **IV** 307

Associated TV, **IV** 666; **17** 397

Associates First Capital Corporation, **22** 207

Associates Investment Co., **I** 452

Association des Centres Distributeurs E. Leclerc, 37 19–21

Assubel, **III** 273

Assurances du Groupe de Paris, **III** 211

Assurances Générales de France, **III** 351; **27** 513; **42** 151

AST Holding Corp., **III** 663, 665

AST Research, Inc., 9 41–43; **10** 459, 518–19; **12** 470; **18** 260

Asta Pharma AG, **IV** 71

Asta Werke AG, **IV** 71

Astech, **18** 370

Asteroid, **IV** 97

Astley & Pearce, **10** 277

Aston Brooke Software, **14** 392

Aston Villa plc, 41 34–36

Astor Holdings Inc., **22** 32

Astor Trust Co., **II** 229

Astoria Financial Corporation, 44 31–34; **46** 316

Astra AB, I 625–26, 635, 651; **11** 290; **20** 37–40 **(upd.)**; **34** 282, 284

Astra Resources, **12** 543

Astrolac, **IV** 498

Astronics Corporation, 35 52–54

Astrotech Space Operations, L.P., **11** 429; **37** 365

Astrum International Corp., **12** 88; **13** 453; **16** 20–21; **43** 355

Asur. *See* Grupo Aeropuerto del Sureste, S.A. de C.V.

ASV, Inc., 34 44–47

ASW. *See* American Steel & Wire Corp.

Asylum Life Assurance Co., **III** 371

Asylum Records, **23** 33; **26** 150

Asymetrix, **6** 259

AT&E Corp., **17** 430

AT&T Bell Laboratories, Inc., 13 57–59; **22** 17

AT&T Corp., I 462; **II** 13, 54, 61, 66, 80, 88, 120, 125, 252, 403, 430–31, 448; **III** 99, 110–11, 130, 145, 149, 160, 162, 167, 246, 282; **IV** 95, 287; **V** 259–64, 265–68, 269, 272–75, 302–04, 308–12, 318–19, 326–30, 334–36, 339, 341–342, 344–346; **6** 267, 299, 306–07, 326–27, 338–40; **7** 88, 118–19, 146, 288–89, 333; **8** 310–11; **9** 32, 43, 106–07, 138, 320, 321, 344, 478–80, 495, 514; **10** 19, 58, 87, 97, 175, 202–03, 277–78, 286, 431, 433, 455–57; **11** 10, 59, 91, 183, 185, 196, 198, 302, 395, 500–01; **12** 9, 135–36, 162, 544; **13** 212–13, 326, 402, 448; **14** 15, 95, 251–53, 257–61, 318, 336–37, 345, 347, 354, 363–64; **15** 125–26, 228, 455; **16** 223, 318, 368, 467; **18** 30, 32, 74, 76, 111–12, 155, 164–65, 368, 516–18, 569–70; **19** 12, 41; **20** 34, 313; **21** 70, 200–01, 514; **22** 51; **23** 135; **25** 100, 256, 301, 495–99; **26** 187, 225, 431, 520; **27** 363; **28** 242; **29** 59, 39–45 **(upd.)**; **30** 99, 339; **33** 34–35, 37, 91, 93–94; **34** 257–59; **38** 269–70, 416; **42** 224; **43** 50, 222, 443; **44** 47; **46** 373; **47** 319–20; **49** 70, 346–47

AT&T Istel Ltd., 14 35–36

At Home Corporation, 43 48–51

Ataka & Co., **I** 433; **II** 361

Atari Corporation, II 176; **III** 587; **IV** 676; **6** 244; **7** 395–96; **9** 44–47; **10** 284,

482, 485; **13** 472; **23** 23–26 **(upd.)**; **28** 319; **32** 8

ATAS International, **26** 527, 530

ATC, **III** 760; **13** 280

Atchison Casting Corporation, 24 144; **39 30–32**

Atchison, Topeka and Santa Fe Railroad, **V** 507–08; **12** 19–20; **27** 86

ATCO Ltd., **13** 132

ATD Group, **10** 113

ATE Investment, **6** 449

Atelier de Construction Electrique de Delle, **9** 9

ATEQ Corp., **III** 533

Atex, Inc., **III** 476; **7** 162; **10** 34; **36** 172, 174

ATH AG, **IV** 221

Atha Tool Co., **III** 627

Athalon Products, Ltd., **10** 181; **12** 313

Athena Assurances, **27** 513, 515

Athenia Steel Co., **13** 369

Athens National Bank, **III** 190

Athens Piraeus Electricity Co., **IV** 658

Athern, **16** 337

Athlete's Foot, **29** 186

Athletic Attic, **19** 230

Athletic Shoe Company, **17** 243

Athletic Textile Company, Inc., **13** 532

Athletic X-Press, **14** 293

Athleticum Sportmarket, **48** 279

Athol Machine Co., **13** 301

ATI, **IV** 651; **7** 390

Atlalait, **19** 50

Atlanta Gas Light Company, 6 446–48; **23 27–30 (upd.)**

Atlanta-LaSalle Corporation, **43** 54

Atlanta National Bank, **16** 521

Atlanta National League Baseball Club, Inc., 43 52–55

Atlanta Paper Co., **IV** 311; **19** 267

Atlantic & Pacific Tea Company (A&P). *See* Great Atlantic & Pacific Tea Company, Inc.

Atlantic Acceptance Corporation, **7** 95

Atlantic Aircraft Corp., **I** 34; **17** 197

Atlantic American Corporation, 23 413; **44 35–37**

Atlantic Auto Finance Corp. *See* United Auto Group, Inc.

Atlantic Cellular, **43** 341

Atlantic Cement Co., **III** 671

Atlantic Coast Carton Company, **19** 77

Atlantic Coast Line Railroad Company. *See* CSX Corporation.

Atlantic Computers, **14** 35

Atlantic Container Lines Ltd., **23** 161

Atlantic Energy, Inc., 6 449–50

The Atlantic Group, 23 31–33

Atlantic Gulf and Caribbean Airways, **I** 115

Atlantic Import, **I** 285

Atlantic Mills, **27** 188

Atlantic Mutual, **41** 65

Atlantic Precision Instrument Company, **13** 234

Atlantic Precision Works, **9** 72

Atlantic Records, **II** 176; **18** 458; **26** 150

Atlantic Refining Co., **III** 497; **III** 498; **IV** 375–76, 456, 504, 566, 570; **24** 520–21

Atlantic Research Corp., **13** 462

Atlantic Richfield Company, I 452; **II** 90, 425; **III** 740; **IV** 375–77, 379, 435, 454, 456–57, 467, 494, 522, 536, 571; **7** 57, 108, 537–38, 558–59; **8** 184, 416; **10**

110; **13** 13, 341; **19** 175; **24** 521, 524; **26** 4, 372; **31 31–34 (upd.)**; **40** 358; **45** 49, 55, 252

Atlantic Sea Products, **13** 103

The Atlantic Seaboard Dispatch. *See* GATX.

Atlantic Securities Ltd., **II** 223; **III** 98

Atlantic Southeast Airlines, Inc., 26 439; **47 29–31**

Atlantic Southern Properties, Inc., **6** 449–50

Atlantic Surety Co., **III** 396

Atlantic Transport Company, **19** 198

Atlantic-Union Oil, **IV** 570; **24** 520

Atlantic Wholesalers, **II** 631

Atlantis Energy Inc., **44** 182

Atlantis Group, Inc., **17** 16; **19** 50, 390

Atlantis Ltd., **II** 566

Atlantis Resort and Casino. *See* Sun International Hotels Limited.

Atlas Air, Inc., 39 33–35

Atlas America, Inc., **42** 311

Atlas Assurance Co., **III** 370

Atlas Cement Company, **31** 252

Atlas Chemical Industries, **I** 353

Atlas Copco AB, III 425–27, 480; **IV** 203; **28 37–41 (upd.)**

Atlas Corp., **I** 58, 512; **10** 316

Atlas Eléctrica S.A., **22** 27

Atlas Hotels, Inc., **V** 164

Atlas Petroleum Ltd., **IV** 449

Atlas Plastics, **19** 414

Atlas Powder Company, **I** 343–44; **22** 260

Atlas Securities, **47** 160

Atlas Shipping, **I** 285

Atlas Steel Works, **I** 572

Atlas Steels, **IV** 191

Atlas Supply Co., **IV** 369

Atlas Tag & Label, **9** 72

Atlas Van Lines, Inc., 14 37–39

Atlas Ventures, **25** 96

Atlas-Werke AG, **IV** 88

Atlas Works, **I** 531

Atlatec SA de CV, **39** 192

Atle Byrnestad, **6** 368; **27** 92

Atmel Corporation, 17 32–34; **19** 313

Atmos Energy Corporation, 43 56–58

Atmos Lebensmitteltechnik, **III** 420

Atmospherix Ltd. *See* Blyth Industries, Inc.

ATO Chimie, **I** 303; **IV** 560

Atochem S.A., I 303–04, 676; **IV** 525, 547; **7** 484–85

AtoHaas Americas, **26** 425

Atom-Energi, **II** 2; **22** 9

Atomic Austria GmbH, **41** 14–16

ATR, **7** 9, 11

ATS. *See* Magasins Armand Thiéry et Sigrand.

ATT Microelectrica España, **V** 339

Attachmate Corp., **11** 520

ATTC Manufacturing Inc., **48** 5

Atvidabergs Industrier, **25** 463

Atwater McMillian. *See* St. Paul Companies, Inc.

Atwood Resources Inc., **17** 372

ATX Technologies, Inc., **32** 374

ATx Telecom Systems Inc., **31** 124

Au Bon Marché, **26** 160

Au Bon Pain Co., Inc., 18 35–38; **44** 327

Au Printemps S.A., V 9–11; **17** 124; **41** 114. *See also* Pinault-Printemps-Redoute S.A.

Aubrey G. Lanston Co., **II** 301

Auchan, 10 205; **23** 230; **27** 94; **37**
    22–24; 39 183–85
AUDI AG, **I** 202; **IV** 570; **34** 55
Audio Accessories, Inc., **37** 301
Audio Development Company, **10** 18
Audio International Inc., **36** 159
Audio King Corporation, 24 52–54
Audio/Video Affiliates, Inc., **10** 468–69
Audiofina, **44** 377
Audiotronic Holdings, **III** 112
Audiovox Corporation, 34 48–50
Audits & Surveys Worldwide Inc., **28** 501,
    504
Aufina Bank, **II** 378
Aug. Stenman A.B., **III** 493
Aughton Group, **II** 466
Augsburger Aktienbank, **III** 377
Auguri Mondadori S.p.A., **IV** 586
August Max Woman, **V** 207–08
August Schell's Brewing Co., **22** 421
August Thyssen-Hütte AG, **IV** 221–22
Auguste Metz et Cie, **IV** 24
Ault Incorporated, 34 51–54
Aunor Gold Mines, Ltd., **IV** 164
Aunt Fanny's Bakery, **7** 429
Auntie Anne's, Inc., 35 55–57
Aura Books plc, **34** 5
Aurec Information and Directory Systems.
    See Amdocs Ltd.
Aurora Dairy Corporation, **37** 195, 198
Aurora Foods Inc., 26 384; **32** 67–69
Aurora Products, **II** 543
Aurora Systems, Inc., **21** 135
Aurrera S.A., **35** 459
Aurum Corp., **38** 431
Ausilio Generale di Sicurezza, **III** 206
Ausimont N.V., **8** 271
Ausplay, **13** 319
AUSSAT Ltd., **6** 341
Aussedat-Rey, **IV** 288; **23** 366, 368
The Austin Company, 8 41–44
Austin Industries, **25** 402
Austin-Morris, **III** 494
Austin Motor Company, **I** 183; **III** 554; **7**
    458
Austin Nichols, **I** 248, 261, 280–81
Austin Quality Foods, **36** 313
Austin Rover, **14** 321
Austral Waste Products, **IV** 248
Australasian Paper and Pulp Co. Ltd., **IV**
    248
Australasian Sugar Co., **III** 686
Australasian United Steam Navigation Co.,
    III 522
Australia and New Zealand Banking
    Group Ltd., II 187–90
Australia Gilt Co. Group, **II** 422
Australia National Bank, Limited, **10** 170
Australian Airlines, **6** 91, 112; **24**
    399–400; **27** 475
Australian and Kandos Cement (Holdings)
    Ltd., **III** 687, 728; **28** 83
Australian and Overseas
    Telecommunications Corporation, **6**
    341–42
Australian Associated Press, **IV** 669
Australian Automotive Air, Pty. Ltd., **III**
    593
Australian Blue Asbestos, **III** 687
Australian Consolidated Investments,
    Limited, **10** 170
Australian Consolidated Press, **27** 42
Australian Forest Products, **I** 438–39

Australian Guarantee Corporation Ltd., **II**
    389–90; **48** 427
Australian Gypsum Industries, **III** 673
Australian Iron & Steel Company, **IV** 45;
    22 105
Australian Metal Co., **IV** 139
Australian Mutual Provident Society, **IV**
    61, 697
Australian Paper Co., **IV** 248
Australian Petroleum Pty. Ltd., **25** 471
Australian Tankerships Pty. Ltd., **25** 471
Australian Telecommunications
    Corporation, **6** 342
Australian United Corp., **II** 389
Australian Window Glass, **III** 726
Austrian Airlines AG (Österreichische
    Luftverkehrs AG), 27 26; **33** 49–52; **34**
    398; **48** 258, 259
Austrian Industries, **IV** 485, 486
Austrian National Bank, **IV** 230
Austrian Star Gastronomie GmbH, **48** 63
Austro-Americana, **6** 425
Austro-Daimler, **I** 138, 206; **11** 31
Authentic Fitness Corp., 16 511; **20**
    41–43; 46 450
Auto Avio Costruzione, **13** 219
Auto Coil Springs, **III** 581
Auto-Flo Corp., **III** 569; **20** 360
Auto Ordnance Corporation, **19** 430–31
Auto Parts Wholesale, **26** 348
Auto Shack. *See* AutoZone, Inc.
Auto Strop Safety Razor Co., **III** 27–28
Auto-Trol Technology, **14** 15
Auto Union, **I** 150
Auto Value Associates, Inc., 25 26–28
Autobytel Inc., 47 32–34
Autodesk, Inc., 10 118–20
Autogrill SpA, 24 195; **49** 31–33
Autolite, **I** 29, 142; **III** 555
Autoliv AB, **41** 369
Autologic Information International,
    Inc., 20 44–46; **26** 518–20
Automat, **II** 614
Automated Building Components, **III** 735
Automated Communications, Inc., **8** 311
Automated Design Systems, **25** 348
Automated Loss Prevention Systems, **11**
    445
Automated Security (Holdings) PLC, **11**
    444
Automated Wagering Systems, **III** 128
Automatic Coil Corp., **33** 359, 361
Automatic Data Processing, Inc., III
    117–19; 9 48–51 (upd.), 125, 173; **21**
    69; **46** 333; **47** 35–39 (upd.)
Automatic Fire Alarm Co., **III** 644
Automatic Manufacturing Corporation, **10**
    319
Automatic Payrolls, Inc., **III** 117
Automatic Retailers of America, Inc., **II**
    607; **13** 48
Automatic Sprinkler Corp. of America. *See*
    Figgie International, Inc.
Automatic Telephone & Electric, **II** 81
Automatic Toll Systems, **19** 111
Automatic Vaudeville Arcades Co., **II** 154
Automatic Voting Machine Corporation.
    See American Locker Group
    Incorporated.
Automobile Insurance Co., **III** 181–82
Automobiles Citroen, I 162, 188; **III** 676;
    IV 722; **V** 237; **7** 35–38; **11** 103; **16**
    121, 420

Automobili Lamborghini Holding S.p.A.,
    34 55–58 (upd.)
Automobili Lamborghini S.p.A., 13
    60–62, 219
Automotive Components Group
    Worldwide, **10** 325
Automotive Diagnostics, **10** 492
Automotive Group. *See* Lear Seating
    Corporation.
Automotive Industries Holding Inc., **16** 323
AutoNation USA, **41** 239. *See also*
    Republic Industries, Inc.
Autonet, **6** 435
Autonom Computer, **47** 36
Autophon AG, **9** 32
Autosite.com, **47** 34
Autotote Corporation, 20 47–49
AutoTrol Technology, **III** 111
Autoweb.com, **47** 34
AUTOWORKS Holdings, Inc., **24** 205
AutoZone, Inc., 9 52–54; **26** 348; **31**
    35–38 (upd.); **36** 364
AVA AG (Allgemeine
    Handelsgesellschaft der Verbraucher
    AG), 33 53–56
Avado Brands, Inc., 31 39–42; **46** 234
Avalon Publishing Group. *See* Publishers
    Group, Inc.
Avana Group, **II** 565
Avantel, **27** 304
Avaya Inc., **41** 287, 289–90
Avco. *See* Aviation Corp. of the Americas.
Avco Corp., **34** 433
Avco Financial Services Inc., 13 63–65
Avco National Bank, **II** 420
Avdel, **34** 433
Avecor Cardiovascular Inc., **8** 347; **22** 360
Aveda Corporation, 24 55–57
Avedis Zildjian Co., 38 66–68
Avendt Group, Inc., **IV** 137
Avenir, **III** 393
Avenor Inc., **25** 13
Aventis, **34** 280, 283–84; **38** 378, 380
Avery Dennison Corporation, IV
    251–54; 15 229, 401; **17** 27–31 (upd.),
    445; **49** 34–40 (upd.)
Avesta Steel Works Co., **I** 553–54
AvestaPolarit, **49** 104
Avex Electronics Inc., **40** 68
Avfuel, **11** 538
Avgain Marine A/S, **7** 40; **41** 42
Avia Group International, Inc., **V** 376–77;
    26 397–99
Aviacion y Comercio, **6** 95–96
Aviacionny Nauchno-Tehnicheskii
    Komplex im. A.N. Tupoleva, **24** 58–60
AVIACO. *See* Aviacion y Comercio.
Avianca Aerovías Nacionales de
    Colombia SA, 36 52–55
Aviation Corp. of the Americas, **I** 48, 78,
    89, 115, 530; **III** 66; **6** 75; **9** 497–99; **10**
    163; **11** 261, 427; **12** 379, 383; **13** 64
Aviation Inventory Management Co., **28** 5
Aviation Power Supply, **II** 16
Aviation Sales Company, 41 37–39
Aviation Services West, Inc. *See* Scenic
    Airlines, Inc.
Avid Technology Inc., 38 69–73
Avimo, **47** 7–8
Avion Coach Corporation, **I** 76; **III** 484;
    11 363; **22** 206
Avions Marcel Dassault-Breguet
    Aviation, I 44–46; **7** 11; **7** 205; **8** 314.
    See also Groupe Dassault Aviation SA.

Avis, Inc., I 30, 446, 463; II 468; III 502; IV 370; **6** 348–49, **356–58,** 392–93; **8** 33; **9** 284; **10** 419; **11** 198; **16** 379–80; **22** 524

Avis Rent A Car, Inc., 22 54–57 (upd.); **24** 9; **25** 93, 143, 420–22

Avisco, I 317, 365, 442–43; **V** 359; **17** 117

Avisun Corp., IV 371

Avnet Electronics Supply Co., **19** 311, 313

Avnet Inc., 9 55–57; 10 112–13; **13** 47

Avon Products, Inc., III 13, 15–16, 62; **8** 329; **9** 331; **11** 282, 366; **12** 314, 435; **13** 38; **14** 501–02; **17** 186; **19 26–29** **(upd.),** 253; **21** 49, 51; **25** 292; 456; **27** 429; **30** 64, 308–09; **46 43–46 (upd.)**

Avon Publications, Inc., IV 627; **19** 201, 204

Avon Rubber plc, **23** 146

Avoncraft Construction Co., I 512

Avondale Industries, Inc., I 512–14; **7** 39–41; **41 40–43 (upd.)**

Avondale Mills, Inc., **8** 558–60; **9** 466

Avondown Properties Ltd., IV 711

Avro. *See* A.V. Roe & Company.

AVS, III 200

Avstar, **38** 72

Avtech Corp., **36** 159

Avtex Fibers Inc., I 443; **11** 134

AVX Corporation, **21** 329, 331

AW North Carolina Inc., **48** 5

AWA. *See* America West Holdings Corporation.

AWA Defence Industries (AWADI). *See* British Aerospace Defence Industries.

Award Foods, II 528

AwardTrack, Inc., **49** 423

Awesome Transportation, Inc., **22** 549

AXA Colonia Konzern AG, III 209, **210–12; 15** 30; **21** 147; **27 52–55; 49** **41–45 (upd.)**

Axe-Houghton Associates Inc., **41** 208

Axel Johnson Group, I 553–55

Axel Springer Verlag AG, IV **589–91; 20** **50–53 (upd.); 23** 86; **35** 452

Axelrod Foods, II 528

Axon Systems Inc., **7** 336

Ayco Corp., II 398; **10** 62

Aydin Corp., 19 30–32

Ayerst, I 623

Ayr-Way Stores, **27** 452

AYS. *See* Alternative Youth Services, Inc.

Ayshire Collieries, IV 18

Azcon Corporation, 23 34–36

Azerty, **25** 13

Azienda Generale Italiana Petroli. *See* Agip SpA.

Azienda Nazionale Idrogenazione Combustibili, IV 419–22

AZL Resources, **7** 538

Aznar International, **14** 225

Azon Limited, **22** 282

AZP Group Inc., **6** 546

Aztar Corporation, 13 66–68

Azteca, **18** 211, 213

Azuma Leather Co. Ltd., **V** 380

Azuma Shiki Manufacturing, IV 326

Azusa Valley Savings Bank, II 382

B&D. *See* Barker & Dobson.

B&G Foods, Inc., 40 51–54

B & K Steel Fabrications, Inc., **26** 432

B&M Baked Beans, **40** 53

B & O. *See* Baltimore and Ohio Railroad.

B&Q plc, **V** 106, 108; **24** 266, 269–70

B&S. *See* Binney & Smith Inc.

B&W Diesel, III 513

B.A.T. Industries PLC, 14 77; **16** 242; **22** **70–73 (upd.); 25** 154–56; **29** 196. *See also* Brown & Williamson Tobacco Corporation

B. B. & R. Knight Brothers, **8** 200; **25** 164

B.B. Foods, **13** 244

B-Bar-B Corp., **16** 340

B.C. Rail Telecommunications, **6** 311

B.C. Sugar, II 664

B.C. Ziegler and Co. *See* The Ziegler Companies, Inc.

B. Dalton Bookseller Inc., 10 136; **13** 545; **16** 160; **18** 136; **25 29–31; 30** 68

B-E Holdings, **17** 60

B/E Aerospace, Inc., 30 72–74

B.F. Ehlers, I 417; **24** 32

B.F. Goodrich Co. *See* The BFGoodrich Company.

B.F. Walker, Inc., **11** 354

B.I.C. America, **17** 15, 17

B.J.'s Wholesale, **12** 335

The B. Manischewitz Company, LLC, 31 **43–46**

B. Perini & Sons, Inc., **8** 418

B.R. Simmons, III 527

B.S. Bull & Company. *See* Supervalu Inc.

B. Stroh Brewing Co., I 290

B.T.I. Chemicals Ltd., I 313; **10** 154

B Ticino, **21** 350

B.V. Tabak Export & Import Compagnie, **12** 109

BA. *See* British Airways.

BAA plc, 10 121–23; **29** 509, 511; **33** **57–61 (upd.); 37** 8

Bålforsens Kraft AB, **28** 444

Baan Company, 25 32–34; 26 496, 498

Babbage's, Inc., 10 124–25

Babcock & Wilcox Co., III 465–66, 516, 559–60; **V** 621; **23** 199; **37** 242–45

BABE. *See* British Aerospace plc.

Baby Dairy Products, **48** 438

Baby Furniture and Toy Supermarket, **V** 203

Baby Phat. *See* Phat Fashions LLC.

Baby Superstore, Inc., 15 32–34

Babybird Co., Ltd., **V** 150

BabyCenter.com, **37** 130

Babyliss, S.A., **17** 110

BAC. *See* Barclays American Corp. *and* British Aircraft Corporation.

Bacardi Limited, 18 39–42

Baccarat, 23 241; **24 61–63; 27** 421, 423

Bache & Company, III 340; **8** 349

Bachman Foods, **15** 139

Bachman Holdings, Inc., **14** 165; **34** 144–45

Bachman's Inc., 22 58–60; 24 513

Bachoco. *See* Industrias Bacholo, S.A. de C.V.

Bachrach Advertising, **6** 40

Back Bay Restaurant Group, Inc., 20 **54–56**

Back Yard Burgers, 45 33–36

Backer & Spielvogel, I 33; **12** 168; **14** 48–49; **22** 296

Backer Spielvogel Bates Worldwide **42** 329. *See also* Bates Worldwide, Inc.

Backroom Systems Group, II 317

Bacon & Matheson Drop Forge Co., I 185

Bacova Guild, Ltd., **17** 76

Bad Boy Entertainment, **31** 269

Baddour, Inc. *See* Fred's, Inc.

Badger Co., II 86

Badger Illuminating Company, **6** 601

Badger Meter, Inc., 22 61–65

Badger Paint and Hardware Stores, II 419

Badger Paper Mills, Inc., 15 35–37

Badin-Defforey, **27** 93

Badische Analin & Soda Fabrik A.G., I 305

BAe. *See* British Aerospace plc.

BAE Systems, **41** 412

BAFS. *See* Bangkok Aviation Fuel Services Ltd.

Bahia de San Francisco Television, IV 621

Bahlsen GmbH & Co. KG, 44 38–41

Bailey, Banks & Biddle, **16** 559

Bailey Controls, III 560

Bailey's Pub and Grille. *See* Total Entertainment Restaurant Corporation.

Bain & Co., III 429; **9** 343; **21** 143

Bain Capital, Inc., **14** 244–45; **16** 466; **20** 18; **24** 456, 482; **25** 254; **26** 184; **38** 107–09

Baird, **7** 235, 237

Bairnco Corporation, 28 42–45

Bajaj Auto Limited, 39 36–38

BAKAB. *See* Bålforsens Kraft AB.

Bakelite Corp., I 399; **9** 517; **13** 231

Baker and Botts, L.L.P., 28 46–49

Baker & Co., IV 78

Baker & Crane, II 318; **17** 323

Baker & Hostetler LLP, 40 55–58

Baker & McKenzie, 10 126–28; 42 **17–20 (upd.)**

Baker & Taylor Corporation, I 548; **16** **45–47; 43 59–62 (upd.)**

Baker Casing Shoe Co., III 429

Baker Cummins Pharmaceuticals Inc., **11** 208

Baker Extract Co., **27** 299

Baker Hughes Incorporated, III **428–29;** **11** 513; **22 66–69 (upd.); 25** 74

Baker Industries, Inc., III 440; **8** 476; **13** 124

Baker International Corp., III 428–29

Baker Oil Tools. *See* Baker Hughes Incorporated.

Baker-Raulang Co., **13** 385

Bakers Best Snack Food Corporation, **24** 241

Bakers Square. *See* VICORP Restaurants, Inc.

Bakersfield Savings and Loan, **10** 339

Bakery Products Inc., IV 410

Balair Ltd., I 122

Balance Bar Company, 32 70–72

Balchem Corporation, 42 21–23

Balco, Inc., **7** 479–80; **27** 415

Balcor Co., II 398; IV 703

Balcor, Inc., **10** 62

Bald Eagle Corporation, **45** 126

Baldor Electric Company, 21 42–44

Baldwin-Ehret-Hill Inc., **28** 42

Baldwin Filters, Inc., **17** 104

Baldwin Hardware Manufacturing Co., III 570; **20** 361

Baldwin-Montrose Chemical Co., Inc., **31** 110

Baldwin Piano & Organ Company, 16 201; **18 43–46**

Baldwin Rubber Industries, **13** 79

Baldwin Technology Company, Inc., 25 **35–39**

Baldwin-United Corp., III 254, 293

Baldwins Ltd., **III** 494
Bålforsens Kraft AB, **IV** 339–40; **28** 444
Balfour Beatty Construction Ltd., III 433–34; **36 56–60 (upd.)**
Balfour Company, L.G., **19** 451–52
Balikpapan Forest Industries, **I** 504
Ball & Young Adhesives, **9** 92
Ball-Bartoe Aircraft Corp., **I** 598; **10** 130
Ball Corporation, I 597–98; **10 129–31 (upd.); 13** 254, 256; **15** 129; **16** 123; **30** 38
The Ball Ground Reps, Inc., **26** 257
Ball Industries, Inc., **26** 539
Ball Stalker Inc., **14** 4
Ballantine & Sons Ltd., **I** 263
Ballantine Beer, **6** 27
Ballantine Books, **13** 429; **31** 376–77, 379
Ballantyne of Omaha, Inc., 27 56–58
Ballard & Ballard Co., **II** 555
Ballard Medical Products, 21 45–48
Ballast Nedam Group, **24** 87–88
Balli Group plc, **26** 527, 530
Bally Entertainment Corp., **19** 205, 207
Bally Gaming International, **15** 539
Bally Manufacturing Corporation, III 430–32; **6** 210; **10** 375, 482; **12** 107; **15** 538–39; **17** 316–17, 443; **41** 214–15
Bally Total Fitness Holding Corp., 25 40–42
Bâloise-Holding, 40 59–62
Baltek Corporation, 34 59–61
AB Baltic, **III** 418–19
Baltic Cable, **15** 521
Baltica, **27** 54
Baltimar Overseas Limited, **25** 469
Baltimore & Ohio Railroad, **I** 584; **II** 329. *See also* CSX Corporation.
Baltimore Aircoil Company, **7** 30–31
Baltimore Gas and Electric Company, V 552–54; **11** 388; **25 43–46 (upd.)**
Baltimore Paper Box Company, **8** 102
Baltimore Technologies Plc, 42 24–26
Baltino Foods, **13** 383
Balzaretti-Modigliani, **III** 676; **16** 121
Balzers Process Systems GmbH, **48** 30
Bamberger's of New Jersey, **V** 169; **8** 443
Banamex, **22** 285; **23** 170; **34** 81. *See also* Banco Nacional de Mexico.
Banana Boat Holding Corp., **15** 359
Banana Brothers, **31** 229
Banana Importers of Ireland, **38** 197
Banana Republic Inc., V 61–62; **18** 193–94; **25 47–49; 31** 51–52
Banc Internacional d'Andorra-Banca Mora, **48** 51
Banc One Corporation, 9 475; **10** 132–34; **11** 181. *See also* Bank One Corporation.
Banca Brasiliana Italo-Belga, **II** 270
Banca Coloniale di Credito, **II** 271
Banca Commerciale Italiana SpA, I 368, 465, 467; **II 191–93**, 242, 271, 278, 295, 319; **III** 207–08, 347; **17** 324
BancA Corp., **11** 305
Banca d'America e d'Italia, **II** 280
Banca Dalmata di Sconto, **II** 271
Banca de Gottardo, **II** 361
Banca di Genova, **II** 270
Banca Internazionale Lombarda, **II** 192
Banca Italiana di Sconto, **II** 191
Banca Italo-Cinese, **II** 270
Banca Italo-Viennese, **II** 270
Banca Jacquet e Hijos, **II** 196
Banca Luis Roy Sobrino, **II** 196

Banca Nazionale de Lavoro, **II** 239
Banca Nazionale dell'Agricoltura, **II** 272
Banca Nazionale di Credito, **II** 271
Banca Serfin. *See* Grupo Financiero Serfin, S.A.
Banca Unione di Credito, **II** 270
Bancard Systems, **24** 395
BancBoston Capital, **48** 412
BancFinancial Services Corporation, **25** 187
BancItaly Corp., **II** 226–27, 288, 536; **13** 528
BancMortgage Financial Corp., **25** 185, 187
Banco Aleman-Panameno, **II** 521
Banco Aliança S.A., **19** 34
Banco Azteca, **19** 189
Banco Bilbao Vizcaya Argentaria S.A., 48 47–51 (upd.)
Banco Bilbao Vizcaya, S.A., II 194–96
Banco Bradesco S.A., 13 69–71; 19 33
Banco Capitalizador de Monterrey, **19** 189
Banco Central, II 197–98. *See also* Banco Santander Central Hispano S.A.
Banco Central de Crédito. *See* Banco Itaú.
Banco Chemical (Portugal) S.A. *See* Chemical Banking Corp.
Banco Comercial, **19** 188
Banco Comercial de Puerto Rico, **41** 311
Banco Credito y Ahorro Ponceno, **41** 312
Banco da América, **19** 34
Banco de Credito Local, **48** 51
Banco de Londres, Mexico y Sudamerica. *See* Grupo Financiero Serfin, S.A.
Banco de Madrid, **40** 147
Banco de Mexico, **19** 189
Banco de Ponce, **41** 313
Banco del Norte, **19** 189
Banco di Roma, **I** 465, 467; **II** 191, 257, 271
Banco di Santo Spirito, **I** 467
Banco do Brasil S.A., II 199–200
Banco Español de Credito, **II** 195, 198; **IV** 160
Banco Espírito Santo e Comercial de Lisboa S.A., 15 38–40
Banco Federal de Crédito. *See* Banco Itaú.
Banco Frances y Brasiliero, **19** 34
Banco Industrial de Bilbao, **II** 195
Banco Industrial de Monterrey, **19** 189
Banco Italo-Belga, **II** 270, 271
Banco Italo-Egiziano, **II** 271
Banco Itaú S.A., 19 33–35
Banco Nacional de Cuba, **II** 345
Banco Nacional de Mexico, **9** 333; **19** 188, 193
Banco Pinto de Mahalhães, **19** 34
Banco Popular, **III** 348; **6** 97. *See also* Popular, Inc.
Banco Português do Brasil S.A., **19** 34
Banco Santander Central Hispano S.A., 36 61–64 (upd.); 42 349
Banco Serfin, **34** 82
Banco Sul Americano S.A., **19** 34
Banco Trento & Bolanzo, **II** 240
Banco União Comercial, **19** 34
Banco Vascongado, **II** 196
BancOhio National Bank in Columbus, **9** 475
Bancomer S.A., **19** 12; **48** 47
Bancorp Leasing, Inc., **14** 529
BancorpSouth, Inc., **14** 40–41
Bancroft Racket Co., **III** 24
BancSystems Association Inc., **9** 475, 476

Bandag, Inc., 19 36–38, 454–56
Bandai America Inc., **23** 388; **25** 488
Bandai Co., Ltd., 38 415
Banesto. *See* Banco Español de Credito.
Banexi, **II** 233
Banfi Products Corp., 36 65–67
Bang & Olufsen Holding A/S, 37 25–28
Bangkok Airport Hotel, **6** 123–24
Bangkok Aviation Fuel Services Ltd., **6** 123–24
Bangladesh Krishi Bank, **31** 220
Bangor and Aroostook Railroad Company, **8** 33
Bangor Mills, **13** 169
Bangor Punta Alegre Sugar Corp., **30** 425
Bangor Punta Corp., **I** 452, 482; **II** 403
Banister Continental Corp. *See* BFC Construction Corporation.
Bank Austria AG, 23 37–39
Bank Brussels Lambert, **II 201–03**, 295, 407
Bank Bumiputra, **IV** 519
Bank Central Asia, **18** 181
Bank CIC-Union Européenne A.G., **II** 272
Bank du Louvre, **27** 423
Bank Européene de Credità Moyen Terme, **II** 319; **17** 324
Bank for International Settlements, **II** 368
Bank für Elektrische Unternehmungen. *See* Elektrowatt AG.
Bank für Gemeinwirtschaft, **II** 239
Bank Hapoalim B.M., II 204–06; 25 266, 268
Bank Hofmann, **21** 146–47
Bank Leu, **I** 252; **21** 146–47
Bank Leumi Le-Israel, **25** 268
Bank of Adelaide, **II** 189
Bank of America Corporation, I 536–37; **II** 252–55, 280, 288–89, 347, 382; **III** 218; **6** 385; **9** 50, 123–24, 333, 536; **12** 106, 466; **14** 170; **18** 516; **22** 542; **25** 432; **26** 486; **46 47–54 (upd.); 47** 37
Bank of Antwerp, **IV** 497
Bank of Asheville, **II** 336
Bank of Australasia, **II** 187–89
The Bank of Bishop and Co., Ltd., **11** 114
Bank of Boston Corporation, II 207–09; 7 114; **12** 31; **13** 467; **14** 90
Bank of Brandywine Valley, **25** 542
Bank of Britain, **14** 46–47
Bank of British Columbia, **II** 244, 298
Bank of British Honduras, **II** 344
Bank of British North America, **II** 220
Bank of California, **II** 322, 490. *See also* Union Bank of California.
Bank of Canada, **II** 210, 376
Bank of Central and South America, **II** 344
Bank of Chicago, **III** 270
Bank of China, **II** 298
Bank of Chosen, **II** 338
Bank of Commerce, **II** 331
Bank of Delaware, **25** 542
Bank of England, **II** 217, 235–36, 306–07, 318–19, 333–34, 357, 421–22, 427–28; **III** 234, 280; **IV** 119, 366, 382, 705, 711; **10** 8, 336; **14** 45–46; **17** 324–25; **47** 227
Bank of Finland, **III** 648
Bank of France, **II** 232, 264–65, 354; **III** 391
Bank of Hamilton, **II** 244
Bank of Hindustan, **IV** 699
Bank of Ireland, **16** 13–14; **19** 198
Bank of Israel, **II** 206

Bank of Italy, **I** 536; **II** 192, 226, 271–72, 288; **III** 209, 347; **8** 45

The Bank of Jacksonville, **9** 58

Bank of Japan, **I** 519; **II** 291, 325

Bank of Kobe, **II** 371

Bank of Lee County, **14** 40

Bank of Liverpool, **II** 236

Bank of London and South America, **II** 308

Bank of Manhattan Co., **II** 247–48

Bank of Mexico Ltd., **19** 188

The Bank of Milwaukee, **14** 529

Bank of Mississippi, Inc., 14 40–41

Bank of Montreal, II 210–12, 231, 375; **26** 304; **46 55–58 (upd.)**

Bank of Nettleton, **14** 40

Bank of New Brunswick, **II** 221

Bank of New England Corporation, II 213–15; **9** 229

Bank of New Orleans, **11** 106

Bank of New Queensland, **II** 188

Bank of New South Wales, **II** 188–89. *See also* Westpac Banking Corporation.

Bank of New York Company, Inc., II 192, **216–19**, 247; **34** 82; **46 59–63 (upd.)**

Bank of North Mississippi, **14** 41

Bank of Nova Scotia, II 220–23, 345; **IV** 644

Bank of Oklahoma, **22** 4

Bank of Ontario, **II** 210

Bank of Osaka, **II** 360

Bank of Ottawa, **II** 221

Bank of Pasadena, **II** 382

Bank of Queensland, **II** 188

The Bank of Scotland. *See* The Governor and Company of the Bank of Scotland.

Bank of Sherman, **14** 40

Bank of Spain, **II** 194, 197

Bank of the Ohio Valley, **13** 221

Bank of the People, **II** 210

Bank of the United States, **II** 207, 216, 247

Bank of the West, **II** 233

Bank of Tokyo, Ltd., II 224–25, 276, 301, 341, 358; **IV** 151; **12** 138; **16** 496, 498; **24** 358

Bank of Tokyo-Mitsubishi Ltd., 15 41–43 (upd.), 431; **26** 454, 457; **38** 387

Bank of Toronto, **II** 375–76

Bank of Tupelo, **14** 40

Bank of Upper Canada, **II** 210

Bank of Wales, **10** 336, 338

Bank of Western Australia, **II** 187

Bank of Winterthur, **II** 378

Bank One Corporation, 36 68–75 (upd.)

Bank Powszechny Depozytowy, **IV** 119

Bank-R Systems Inc., **18** 517

Bank voor Handel en Nijverheid, **II** 304

BankAmerica Corporation, II 226–28, 436; **8 45–48 (upd.)**, 295, 469, 471; **13** 69; **17** 546; **18** 518; **25** 187; **26** 65; **47** 401. *See also* Bank of America

BankBoston. *See* FleetBoston Financial Corporation.

BankCard America, Inc., **24** 394

Bankers and Shippers Insurance Co., **III** 389

Bankers Co., **II** 230

Bankers Corporation, **14** 473

Bankers Investment, **II** 349

Bankers Life and Casualty Co., **10** 247; **16** 207; **33** 110

Bankers Life Co., **III** 328–30

Bankers National Bank, **II** 261

Bankers National Life Insurance Co., **II** 182; **10** 246

Bankers Trust Co., **38** 411

Bankers Trust New York Corporation, I 601; **II** 211, **229–31**, 330, 339; **III** 84–86; **10** 425; **11** 416; **12** 165, 209; **13** 188, 466; **17** 559; **19** 34; **22** 102; **25** 268; 317

Bankhaus IG Herstatt, **II** 242

BankVermont Corp., **II** 208

BankWatch, **37** 143, 145

Banner Aerospace, Inc., 14 42–44; **37 29–32 (upd.)**

Banner International, **13** 20

Banner Life Insurance Company, **III** 273; **24** 284

BanPonce Corporation, **41** 312

Banque Belge et Internationale en Egypte, **II** 295

Banque Belge pour l'Etranger, **II** 294

Banque Belgo-Zairoise, **II** 294

Banque Bruxelles Lambert. *See* Bank Brussels Lambert.

Banque Commerciale du Maroc, **II** 272

Banque Commerciale-Basle, **II** 270

Banque d'Anvers/Bank van Antwerpen, **II** 294–95

Banque de Bruxelles, **II** 201–02, 239

Banque de Credit et de Depot des Pays Bas, **II** 259

Banque de France, **14** 45–46

Banque de l'Indochine et de Suez, **II** 259

Banque de l'Union Européenne, **II** 94

Banque de l'Union Parisienne, **II** 270; **IV** 497, 557

Banque de la Construction et les Travaux Public, **II** 319; **17** 324

Banque de la Société Générale de Belgique, **II** 294–95

Banque de Louvain, **II** 202

Banque de Paris et des Pays-Bas, **II** 136, 259; **10** 346; **19** 188–89; **33** 179

Banque de Reports et de Depots, **II** 201

Banque du Congo Belge, **II** 294

Banque Européenne pour l'Amerique Latine, **II** 294

Banque Française et Espagnol en Paris, **II** 196

Banque Francaise pour le Commerce et l'Industrie, **II** 232, 270

Banque Génerale des Pays Roumains, **II** 270

Banque Générale du Luxembourg, **II** 294

Banque Indosuez, **II** 429

Banque Internationale de Bruxelles, **II** 201–02

Banque Internationale de Luxembourg, **II** 239; **42** 111

Banque Italo-Belge, **II** 294

Banque Italo-Francaise de Credit, **II** 271

Banque Lambert, **II** 201–02

Banque Nationale de Paris S.A., II 232–34, 239; **III** 201, 392–94; **9** 148; **13** 203; **15** 309; **19** 51; **33** 119; **49** 382. *See also* BNP Paribas Group.

Banque Nationale Pour le Commerce et l'Industrie, **II** 232–33

Banque Nordique du Commerce, **II** 366

Banque Orea, **II** 378

Banque Paribas, **II** 192, 260; **IV** 295; **19** 225. *See* BNP Paribas Group.

Banque Rothschild, **IV** 107

Banque Sino-Belge, **II** 294

Banque Stern, **II** 369

La Banque Suisse et Française. *See* Crédit Commercial de France.

Banque Transatlantique, **II** 271

Banque Worms, **III** 393; **27** 514

Banquet Foods Corp., **II** 90, 494; **12** 81; **42** 91

Banta Corporation, 12 24–26; 19 333; **32 73–77 (upd.)**

Bantam Ball Bearing Company, **13** 522

Bantam Books, Inc., **III** 190–91

Bantam Doubleday Dell Publishing Group, **IV** 594; **13** 429; **15** 51; **27** 222; **31** 375–76, 378

Banyan Systems Inc., 25 50–52

Banyu Pharmaceutical Co., **I** 651; **11** 290; **34** 283

Baoshan Iron and Steel, **19** 220

BAP of New York, Inc., **15** 246

BAPCO, **III** 745

Bar Technologies, Inc., **26** 408

Barat. *See* Barclays PLC.

Barber Dental Supply Inc., **19** 291

Barber-Greene, **21** 502

Barberet & Blanc, **I** 677; **49** 350

Barcel, **19** 192

Barclay Furniture Co., **12** 300

Barclay Group, **I** 335; **10** 290

Barclay White Inc., **38** 436

Barclays Business Credit, **13** 468

Barclays PLC, I 604–05; **II** 202, 204, **235–37**, 239, 244, 308, 319, 333, 383, 422, 429; **III** 516; **IV** 23, 722; **7** 332–33; **8** 118; **11** 29–30; **17** 324–25; **20 57–60 (upd.)**; **25** 101; **28** 167; **47** 227

BarclaysAmerican Mortgage Corporation, 11 29–30

Barco Manufacturing Co., **16** 8; **26** 541

Barco NV, 44 42–45

Barcolo Manufacturing, **15** 103; **26** 100

Barden Cablevision, **IV** 640; **26** 273

Bardon Group. *See* Aggregate Industries plc.

Bareco Products, **15** 352

Barefoot Inc., **23** 428, 431

Bari Shoes, Inc., **22** 213

Barilla G. e R. Fratelli S.p.A., 17 35–37

Baring Brothers & Co., Ltd., **39** 5

Barings PLC, III 699; **14 45–47**

Barker & Dobson, **II** 629; **47** 367

Barker and Company, Ltd., **13** 286

Barlow Rand Ltd., I 288–89, **422–24**; **IV** 22, 96

Barlow Specialty Advertising, Inc., **26** 341

Barmag AG, 39 39–42

Barmer Bankverein, **II** 238, 241

Barnato Brothers, **IV** 21, 65; **7** 122

Barneda Carton SA, **41** 326

Barnes & Noble, Inc., 10 135–37; 12 172; **13** 494, 545; **14** 61–62; **15** 62; **16** 160; **17** 524; **23** 370; **25** 17, 29–30; **30 67–71 (upd.)**; **41** 61; **43** 78, 408

Barnes Group, **III** 581

Barnes-Hind, **III** 56, 727

Barnett Banks, Inc., 9 58–60

Barnett Brass & Copper Inc., **9** 543

Barnett Inc., 28 50–52

Barnetts, Hoares, Hanbury and Lloyds, **II** 306

Barney's, Inc., 28 53–55; **36** 290, 292

Barnstead/Thermolyne Corporation, **14** 479–80

Baroid, **19** 467–68

Baron Philippe de Rothschild S.A., 39 43–46
Barr & Stroud Ltd., **III** 727
Barr Laboratories, Inc., 26 29–31
Barracuda Technologies, **47** 7, 9
Barranquilla Investments, **II** 138; **24** 193
Barratt Developments plc, I 556–57
Barret Fitch North, **II** 445; **22** 405
Barrett Burston, **I** 437
Barrett Business Services, Inc., 16 48–50
The Barrett Co., **I** 414–15; **18** 116; **22** 29
Barricini Foods Inc., **27** 197
Barrick Gold Corporation, 34 62–65; 38 232
Barris Industries, Inc., **23** 225
Barry & Co., **III** 522
Barry Callebaut AG, 29 46–48
Barry Wright Corporation, **9** 27; **32** 49
Barry's Jewelers. *See* Samuels Jewelers Incorporated.
Barsab Investment Trust. *See* South African Breweries Ltd.
Barsotti's, Inc., **6** 146
Bart Starr, **12** 284
Barth Smelting Corp., **I** 513
Bartlett & Co., **33** 261
Barton & Ludwig, Inc., **21** 96
Barton Beers, Ltd., **29** 219
Barton Brands, **I** 227; **II** 609; **10** 181
Barton, Duer & Koch, **IV** 282; **9** 261
Barton Incorporated, **13** 134; **24** 140; **34** 89
Bartow Food Company, **25** 332
Barwig Medizinische Systeme. *See* OEC Medical Systems, Inc.
Basel AG, **39** 304
BASF Aktiengesellschaft, I 275, 305–08, 309, 319, 346–47, 632, 638; **II** 554; **IV** 70–71; **13** 75; **14** 308; **16** 462; **18** **47–51 (upd.)**, 186, 234; **21** 544; **24** 75; **26** 305, 368; **27** 22; **28** 194; **41** 45
Bashas' Inc., 33 62–64
Basic American Retirement Communities, **III** 103
Basic Resources, Inc., **V** 725
Basics, **14** 295
BASIS Information Technologies, Inc., **11** 112–13, 132
Baskin-Robbins Ice Cream Co., **I** 215; **7** 128, 372; **17** 474–75; **25** 366; **29** 18
Basle A.G., **I** 632–33, 671–72; **8** 108–09
Basle Air Transport, **I** 121
Basler Bankverein, **II** 368
Bass & Co., **I** 142
Bass Brewers Ltd., **15** 441; **29** 85
Bass Brothers Enterprises Inc., **28** 107; **36** 472
Bass Charington, **29** 84
Bass PLC, I 222–24; III 94–95; 9 99, 425–26; **15 44–47 (upd.)**; **16** 263; **23** 482; **24** 194; **33** 127; **35** 396; **38 74–78** **(upd.)**; **43** 226
Bass Pro Shops, Inc., 42 27–30
Bassett Boat Company, **30** 303
Bassett Foods, **II** 478
Bassett Furniture Industries, Inc., 18 **52–55; 19** 275
Bassett-Walker Inc., **V** 390–91; **17** 512
Bassins Food Chain, **II** 649
BAT. *See* British-American Tobacco Co., Ltd.
BAT Industries plc, I 425–27, 605; **II** 628; **III** 66, 185, 522; **9** 312; **23** 427; **30** 273
Bataafsche Petroleum Maatschappij, **V** 658

Batavia Wine Company, **13** 134
Batchelors Ltd., **I** 315; **25** 81
Bateaux Parisiens, **29** 442
Bateman Eichler Hill Richards, **III** 270
Bates, **16** 545
Bates & Robins, **II** 318; **17** 323
Bates Chemical Company, **9** 154
Bates Manufacturing Company, **10** 314
Bates Worldwide, Inc., 14 48–51; 26 500; **33 65–69 (upd.)**
Batesville Casket Company, **10** 349–50
Bath & Body Works, **11** 41; **24** 237
Bath Industries Inc., **18** 117–18
Bath Iron Works Corporation, 12 **27–29; 36 76–79 (upd.)**
Bathurst Bank, **II** 187
Baton Rouge Gas Light Company. *See* Gulf States Utilities Company.
Battelle Laboratories, **25** 260
Battelle Memorial Institute, Inc., 6 288; **10 138–40**
Batten Barton Durstine & Osborn, **I** 25, 28–31, 33; **16** 70; **41** 88
Battle Creek Food Company, **14** 557–58
Battle Creek Toasted Corn Flake Co., **II** 523; **13** 291
Battle Mountain Gold Company, IV 490; **23 40–42**
Battlefield Equipment Rentals, **21** 499, 501
BATUS Inc., **9** 312; **18** 136; **30** 273
Bauborg, **I** 560–61
Baudhuin-Anderson Company, **8** 553
Bauer Audio Visual, Inc., **24** 96
Bauer Nike Hockey Inc., **36** 347
Bauer Publishing Group, 7 42–43; 20 53
Baume & Mercier, **27** 487, 489
Bausch & Lomb Inc., III 446; **7 44–47;** **10** 46–47; **13** 365–66; **25** 22, **53–57** **(upd.)**, 183; **30** 30; **42** 66
Bavaria SA, **36** 52
Bavarian Brewing Limited, **25** 280
Bavarian Railway, **II** 241
Bavarian Specialty Foods, **13** 383
Baxter Estates, **II** 649
Baxter Healthcare, **36** 497–98
Baxter International Inc., I 627–29; 9 346; **10 141–43 (upd.)**, 198–99; **11** 459–60; **12** 325; **18** 469; **22** 361; **25** 82; **26** 433; **36** 92
Baxter Travenol, **21** 119; **24** 75
The Bay, **16** 216
Bay Area Review Course, Inc., **IV** 623
Bay Cities Transportation Company, **6** 382
Bay City, **21** 502
Bay City Cash Way Company, **V** 222; **25** 534
Bay Colony Life Insurance Co., **III** 254
Bay Harbour Management L.C., **28** 55
Bay Networks, Inc., **20** 33, 69; **26** 276; **36** 352
Bay Petroleum, **I** 526
Bay Ridge Savings Bank, **10** 91
Bay Shipbuilding Corporation, **18** 320
Bay State Gas Company, 38 79–82
Bay State Glass Co., **III** 683
Bay State Iron Manufacturing Co., **13** 16
Bay State Tap and Die Company, **13** 7
Bay West Paper Corporation. *See* Mosinee Paper Corporation.
Bayard SA, 49 46–49
BayBanks, Inc., 12 30–32
Bayer A.G., I 305–06, 309–11, 319, 346–47, 350; **II** 279; **12** 364; **13 75–77** **(upd.)**; **14** 169; **16** 439; **18** 47, 49, 51,

234; **21** 544; **22** 225; **41 44–48 (upd.);** **45** 255
Bayer S.p.A., **8** 179
Bayerische Aluminium AG, **IV** 230
Bayerische Hypotheken- und Wechsel- **Bank AG, II 238–40,** 241–42; **IV** 323
Bayerische Kraftwerke AG, **IV** 229–30
Bayerische Landesbank, **II** 257–58, 280; **14** 170; **47** 83
Bayerische Motoren Werke A.G., I 73, 75, **138–40,** 198; **II** 5; **III** 543, 556, 591; **11 31–33 (upd.)**; **13** 30; **17** 25; **21** 441; **27** 20, 203; **38 83–87 (upd.)**
Bayerische Rückversicherung AG, **III** 377
Bayerische Rumpler Werke, **I** 73
Bayerische Stickstoff-Werke AG, **IV** 229–30
Bayerische Vereinsbank A.G., II 239–40, **241–43; III** 401
Bayerische Versicherungsbank, **II** 238; **III** 377
Bayerische Wagnisbeteiligung GmbH, **27** 192
Bayerische Wasserkraftwerke Aktiengesellschaft, **IV** 231
Bayerische Zellstoff, **IV** 325
Bayernwerk AG, IV 231–32, 323; **V** **555–58,** 698–700; **23 43–47 (upd.)**; **39** 57
Bayliner Marine Corporation, **22** 116
Bayou Boeuf Fabricators, **III** 559
Bayou Steel Corporation, IV 234; **31** **47–49**
Bayside National Bank, **II** 230
Baystate Corporation, **12** 30
Baytree Investors Inc., **15** 87
Bayview, **III** 673
Bayview Water Company, **45** 277
Bazaar & Novelty. *See* Stuart Entertainment Inc.
Bazar de l'Hotel de Ville, **19** 308
BBA. *See* Bush Boake Allen Inc.
BBAG Osterreichische Brau- **Beteiligungs-AG, 38 88–90**
BBC. *See* British Broadcasting Corp.
BBC Brown, Boveri Ltd. *See* ABB ASEA Brown Boveri Ltd.
BBDO. *See* Batten Barton Durstine & Osborn.
BBDO Worldwide Network, **22** 394
BBME. *See* British Bank of the Middle East.
BBN Corp., 19 39–42
BBO & Co., **14** 433
BBVA. *See* Banco Bilbao Vizcaya Argentaria S.A.
BC Development, **16** 481
BC TEL. *See* British Columbia Telephone Company.
BCal. *See* British Caledonian Airways.
BCC, **24** 266, 270
BCE, Inc., V 269–71; 6 307; **7** 333; **12** 413; **18** 32; **36** 351; **44 46–50 (upd.)**
BCI. *See* Banca Commerciale Italiana SpA.
Bcom3 Group, Inc., **40** 142
BCOP. *See* Boise Cascade Office Products.
BCP Corporation, **16** 228–29
BCPA. *See* British Commonwealth Pacific Airways.
BDB. *See* British Digital Broadcasting plc.
BDB Corp., **10** 136
BDDP. *See* Wells Rich Greene BDDP.
Be Free Inc., **49** 434
BEA Systems, Inc., 36 80–83

Beach Hill Investments Pty Ltd., **48** 427
Beach Patrol Inc., **29** 181
BeachviLime Ltd., **IV** 74; **24** 143, 144
Beacon Communications Group, **23** 135
Beacon Manufacturing Company, **I** 377; **19** 304–05
Beacon Oil, **IV** 566
Beacon Participations, **III** 98
Beacon Publishing Co., **IV** 629
Beall-Ladymon, Inc., **24** 458
Bealls, **24** 456
Beamach Group Ltd., **17** 182–83
Beaman Corporation, **16** 96; **25** 390
Bean Fiberglass Inc., **15** 247
Bear Automotive Service Equipment Company, **10** 494
Bear Creek Corporation, 12 444–45; **38 91–94; 39** 361
Bear Instruments Inc., **48** 410
Bear Stearns Companies, Inc., II 400–01, 450; **10 144–45 (upd.)**, 382; **20** 313; **24** 272
Beard & Stone Electric Co., **I** 451
Bearings, Inc., I 158–59; **13 78–80**
Beasley Industries, Inc., **19** 125–26
Beatrice Company, I 353; **440–41; II 467–69**, 475; **III** 118, 437; **6** 357; **9** 318; **12** 82, 87, 93; **13** 162–63, 452; **14** 149–50; **15** 213–14, 358; **16** 160, 396; **19** 290; **24** 273; **26** 476, 494; **28** 475; **42** 92. *See also* TLC Beatrice International Holdings, Inc.
Beatrice Foods, **21** 322–24, 507, 545; **25** 277–78; **38** 169; **43** 355
Beauharnois Power Company, **6** 502
Beaulieu of America, **19** 276
Beaulieu Winery, **I** 260
Beaumont-Bennett Group, **6** 27
Beauté Prestige International S.A. *See* Shiseido Company Limited.
BeautiControl Cosmetics, Inc., 21 49–52
Beauty Biz Inc., **18** 230
Beaver Lumber Company Limited, **I** 274; **26** 303, 305–06
Beazer Homes USA, Inc., 17 38–41
Beazer Plc., **7** 209
bebe stores, inc., 31 50–52
BEC Group Inc., **22** 35
Bechtel Group, Inc., I 558–59, 563; **III** 248; **IV** 171, 576; **6** 148–49, 556; **13** 13; **24 64–67 (upd.)**; **25** 402; **26** 220
Beck & Gregg Hardware Co., **9** 253
Beck's North America, Inc. *See* Brauerei Beck & Co.
Becker Drill, Inc., **19** 247
Becker Group of Germany, **26** 231
Becker Paribas Futures, **II** 445; **22** 406
Becker Warburg Paribas, **II** 259
Beckett Papers, 23 48–50
Beckley-Cardy Co., **IV** 623–24
Beckman Coulter, Inc., 22 74–77
Beckman Instruments, Inc., I 694; **14 52–54; 16** 94
BECOL. *See* Belize Electric Company Limited.
Becton, Dickinson & Company, I 630–31; 11 34–36 (upd.); 36 84–89 (upd.); 42 182–83
Bed Bath & Beyond Inc., 13 81–83; 14 61; **18** 239; **24** 292; **33** 384; **41 49–52 (upd.)**
Bedcovers, Inc., **19** 304
Beddor Companies, **12** 25
Bedford Chemical, **8** 177

Bedford-Stuyvesant Restoration Corp., **II** 673
Bee Chemicals, **I** 372
Bee Discount, **26** 476
Bee Gee Shoe Corporation, **10** 281
Bee Gee Shrimp, **I** 473
Beech Aircraft Corporation, II 87; **8 49–52**, 313; **11** 411, 413; **27** 98; **38** 375; **46** 354
Beech Holdings Corp., **9** 94
Beech-Nut Nutrition Corporation, I 695; **II** 489; **21 53–56; 46** 290
Beecham Group PLC, **I** 626, 640, 668; **II** 331, 543; **III** 18, 65–66; **9** 264; **14** 53; **16** 438
Beechwood Insurance Agency, Inc., **14** 472
Beeck-Feinkost GmbH, **26** 59
ZAO BeeOnLine-Portal, **48** 419
Beerman Stores, Inc., **10** 281
Beers Construction Company, **38** 437
Beghin Say S.A., **II** 540
Behr-Manning Company, **8** 396
Behringwerke AG, **14** 255
Beiersdorf AG, 29 49–53; 41 374–77
Beijerinvest Group, **I** 210
Beijing Contact Lens Ltd., **25** 56
Beijing Dentsu, **16** 168
Beijing Liyuan Co., **22** 487
Beijing Machinery and Equipment Corp., **II** 442
Beijing Yanshan Petrochemical Company, **22** 263
Beijing ZF North Drive Systems Technical Co. Ltd., **48** 450
Beirao, Pinto, Silva and Co. *See* Banco Espírito Santo e Comercial de Lisboa S.A.
Bejam Group PLC, **II** 678; **33** 206–07
Beker Industries, **IV** 84
Bekins Company, 15 48–50; 26 197
Bel. *See* Fromageries Bel.
Bel Air Markets, **14** 397
Belairbus, **I** 42; **12** 191
Belcher New England, Inc., **IV** 394
Belcher Oil Co., **IV** 394
Belco Oil & Gas Corp., 23 219; **40 63–65**
Belden Inc., II 16; **19 43–45**
Beldis, **23** 219
Beldoch Industries Corp., **17** 137–38
Belfast Banking Co., **II** 318; **17** 323
Belgacom, 6 302–04
Belgian De Vaderlandsche, **III** 309
Belgian Rapid Access to Information Network Services, **6** 304
Belgian Société Internationale Forestière et Minière, **IV** 65
Belglas, **16** 420; **43** 307
Belgo Group plc, **31** 41
Belgochim, **IV** 499
Belize Electric Company Limited, **47** 137
Belize Sugar Industries, **II** 582
Belk Stores Services, Inc., V 12–13; **19 46–48 (upd.)**
Bell (Quarry and Concrete), **III** 674
Bell Aerospace, **I** 530; **24** 442; **34** 432–33
Bell Aircraft Company, **I** 529; **11** 267; **13** 267; **34** 431
Bell and Howell Company, I 463; **IV** 642; **9** 33, **61–64; 11** 197; **14** 569; **15** 71; **29 54–58 (upd.)**, 159
Bell Atlantic Corporation, V 272–74; **9** 171; **10** 232, 456; **11** 59, 87, 274; **12** 137; **13** 399; **18** 33; **25 58–62 (upd.)**,

91, 497; **27** 22, 365. *See also* Verizon Communications.
Bell Canada Enterprises Inc. *See* BCE, Inc.
Bell Canada International, Inc., V 269, 308–09; **6 305–08; 12** 413; **21** 308; **25** 102
Bell Communications Research, **13** 58; **25** 496
Bell Fibre Products, **12** 377
Bell Helicopter Textron Inc., 46 64–67
Bell Helmets Inc., **22** 458
Bell Industries, Inc., 13 47; **18** 498; **19** 311; **47 40–43**
Bell Laboratories, **II** 33, 60–61, 101, 112; **V** 259–64; **8** 157; **9** 171; **10** 108; **11** 327, 500–01; **12** 61; **14** 52, 281–82; **23** 181; **29** 41, 44; **34** 257–58. *See also* AT&T Bell Labroatories, Inc.
Bell Mountain Partnership, Ltd., **15** 26
Bell-Northern Research, Ltd., **V** 269–71; **15** 131
Bell Pharmacal Labs, **12** 387
Bell Resources, **I** 437–38; **III** 729; **10** 170; **27** 473
Bell Sports Corporation, 16 51–53; 44 51–54 (upd.)
Bell System, **II** 72, 230; **6** 338–40; **7** 99, 333; **11** 500; **16** 392–93
Bell Telephone Company, **I** 409; **6** 332, 334
Bell Telephone Company of Pennsylvania, **I** 585
Bell Telephone Manufacturing, **II** 13
Bell's Asbestos and Engineering, **I** 428
Bellcore. *See* Bell Communications Research.
Belle Alkali Co., **IV** 409; **7** 308
Belledune Fertilizer Ltd., **IV** 165
Bellefonte Insurance Co., **IV** 29
Bellemead Development Corp., **III** 220; **14** 108; **37** 84
Bellofram Corp., **14** 43
BellSouth Corporation, V 276–78; **9** 171, 321; **10** 431, 501; **15** 197; **18** 23, 74, 76; **19** 254–55; **22** 19; **27** 20; **29 59–62 (upd.)**; **43** 447; **45** 390
Bellway Plc, 45 37–39
Belmin Systems, **14** 36
Belmont Electronics, **II** 85–86; **11** 412
Belmont Plaza, **12** 316
Belmont Savings and Loan, **10** 339
Belmont Springs Water Company, Inc., **I** 234; **10** 227
Belo Corporation. *See* A.H. Belo Corporation
Beloit Corporation, 8 243; **14 55–57; 34** 358; **38** 224, 226–28
Beloit Tool Company. *See* Regal-Beloit Corporation.
Beloit Woodlands, **10** 380
Belridge Oil Co., **IV** 541
Belzer Group, **IV** 198–99
Bemis Company, Inc., 8 53–55; 26 43
Bemrose group, **IV** 650
Ben & Jerry's Homemade, Inc., 10 146–48; 35 58–62
Ben Franklin Retail Stores, Inc. *See* FoxMeyer Health Corporation.
Ben Franklin Savings & Trust, **10** 117
Ben Hill Griffin, **III** 53
Ben Johnson & Co. Ltd., **IV** 661
Ben Line, **6** 398
Ben Myerson Candy Co., Inc., **26** 468

Ben Venue Laboratories Inc., **16** 439; **39** 73

Benchmark Capital, 49 50–52

Benchmark Electronics, Inc., 40 66–69

Benckiser Group, **37** 269

Benckiser N.V. *See* Reckitt Benckiser plc.

Bendicks, **I** 592

Bendix Corporation, I 68, **141–43**, 154, 166, 192, 416; **II** 33; **III** 166, 555; **7** 356; **8** 545; **9** 16–17; **10** 260, 279; **11** 138; **13** 356–57; **15** 284; **17** 564; **21** 416; **22** 31

Beneficial Corporation, II 236; **8 56–58**, 117; **10** 490

Beneficial Finance Company, **27** 428–29

Beneficial National Bank USA, **II** 286

Beneficial Standard Life, **10** 247

Benefit Consultants, Inc., **16** 145

Benelli Arms S.p.A., **39** 151

Benesse Corporation, **13** 91, 93; **39** 49

Benetton Group S.p.A., 8 171; **10 149–52**; **15** 369; **18** 193; **25** 56; **49** 31

Bengal Iron and Steel Co., **IV** 205–06

Benihana, Inc., 18 56–59

Benjamin Allen & Co., **IV** 660

Benjamin Moore and Co., 13 84–87; **38 95–99 (upd.)**

Benlox Holdings PLC, **16** 465

Benn Bros. plc, **IV** 687

Bennett Biscuit Co., **II** 543

Bennett Industries, Inc., **17** 371–73

Bennett's Smokehouse and Saloon, **19** 122; **29** 201

Bennigan's, **II** 556–57; **7** 336; **12** 373; **13** 408; **19** 286; **25** 181

Bensdorp, **29** 47

Benson & Hedges, Ltd., **V** 398–99; **15** 137; **19** 171; **49** 151, 153

Benson Wholesale Co., **II** 624

Bentalls, **37** 6, 8

Bentex Holding S.A., **48** 209

Bentley Laboratories, **22** 360

Bentley Mills, Inc., **8** 272

Bentley Motor Ltd., **I** 194; **21** 435

Bentley Systems, **6** 247

Benton & Bowles, **I** 33; **6** 20, 22

Benton International, Inc., **29** 376

Benton Oil and Gas Company, 47 44–46

Benwood Iron Works, **17** 355

Benxi Iron and Steel Corp., **IV** 167

Benzina, **IV** 487

Benzinol, **IV** 487

N.V. Benzit. *See* N.V. Gemeenschappelijk Benzit van Aandeelen Philips Gloeilampenfabriken.

Bercy Management. *See* Elior SA.

Berec Group, **III** 502; **7** 208

Beresford International plc, **24** 335; **27** 159

Beretta. *See* Fabbrica D' Armi Pietro Beretta S.p.A.

Berg Manufacturing Sales Co., **I** 156

Berg- und Metallbank, **IV** 139–40

Bergdorf Goodman, **I** 246; **V** 30–31; **25** 177

Bergedorfer Eisenwerk, **III** 417–20

Bergen Bank, **II** 352

Bergen Brunswig Corporation, I 413; **V 14–16**, 152; **13 88–90 (upd.)**; **18** 97

Berger Associates, Inc., **26** 233

Berger, Jenson and Nicholson, **I** 347; **18** 236

Berger Manufacturing Company, **26** 405

Bergische-Markische Bank, **II** 278

Berglen, **III** 570; **20** 362

Bergmann & Co., **II** 27

Bergstrom Paper Company, **8** 413

Bergswerksgesellschaft Hibernia, **I** 349; **IV** 194

Bergvik & Ala, **IV** 336, 338–39

Beringer Wine Estates Holdings, Inc., 22 78–81; **36** 472

Berisford International plc, **19** 492, 494

Berjaya Group, **22** 464–65

Berkeley Computers, **III** 109; **14** 13

Berkeley Farms, Inc., 46 68–70

Berkey Photo Inc., **I** 447; **III** 475; **36** 171

Berkley Dean & Co., **15** 525

Berkline Corp., **17** 183; **20** 363; **39** 267

Berkshire Hathaway Inc., III 213–15; **18 60–63 (upd.)**; **29** 191; **30** 411; **36** 191; **38** 98; **40** 196, 199, 398; **39** 232, 235; **42 31–36 (upd.)**

Berkshire International, **V** 390–91; **17** 512

Berkshire Partners, **10** 393

Berkshire Realty Holdings, L.P., 49 53–55

Berleca Ltd., **9** 395; **42** 269

Berlex Laboratories, **I** 682; **10** 214

Berli Jucker, **18** 180–82

Berlin Exchange, **I** 409

Berlin Göring-Werke, **IV** 233

BerlinDat Gesellschaft für Informationsverarbeitung und Systemtechnik GmbH, **39** 57

Berliner Bank, **II** 256

Berliner Bankverein, **II** 278

Berliner Handels- und Frankfurter Bank, **II** 242

Berliner Union, **I** 409

Berlinische Bodengesellschaft, **I** 560

Berlitz International, Inc., IV 643; **7** 286, 312; **13 91–93**; **39 47–50 (upd.)**

Berman Brothers Fur Co., **21** 525

Berman Buckskin, **21** 525

Bernard C. Harris Publishing Company, Inc., 39 51–53

Bernard Chaus, Inc., 27 59–61

Bernardin Ltd., **30** 39

Berndorf Austria, **44** 206

Berndorf Switzerland, **44** 206

Bernheim-Meyer: A l'Innovation. *See* GIB Group.

Berni Inns, **I** 247

Bernie Schulman's, **12** 132

Bernina Holding AG, 47 47–50

Bernstein Macauley, Inc., **II** 450

Berrios Enterprises, **14** 236

Berry Bearing Company, **9** 254

Berry Industries, **III** 628

Berry Petroleum Company, 47 51–53

Berry Plastics Corporation, 21 57–59

Bert L. Smokler & Company, **11** 257

Bertea Corp., **III** 603

Bertelsmann A.G., IV 592–94, 614–15; **10** 196; **15 51–54 (upd.)**; **17** 399; **19** 285; **22** 194; **26** 19, 43; **30** 67, 70; **31** 375, 378; **43 63–67 (upd.)**, 422; **44** 377

Bertolini's Authentic Trattorias, **30** 329

Bertram & Graf Gmbh, **28** 45

Bertron Griscom & Company, **V** 641

Bertucci's Inc., 16 54–56, 447

Berwick Industries, Inc., **35** 130–31

Berwind Corp., **14** 18

Beryl Corp., **26** 149

Beryllium Resources, **14** 80

Berzelius Metallhütten Gesellschaft, **IV** 141

Berzelius Umwelt-Service, **III** 625; **IV** 141

Besi, **26** 498

Besnier SA, 19 49–51; **23** 217, 219; **24** 444–45; **25** 83, 85

Bess Mfg., **8** 510

Bessemer Capital Partners L.P., **15** 505

Bessemer Gas Engine Co., **II** 15; **20** 163

Bessemer Limestone & Cement Co., **IV** 409; **31** 454

Bessemer Steamship, **IV** 572; **7** 549

Besser Vibrapac, **III** 673

Best Apparel, **V** 156

Best Buy Co., Inc., 9 65–66; **10** 305; **17** 489; **18** 532–33; **19** 362; **23 51–53 (upd.)**; **24** 52, 502; **29** 120, 123; **30** 464, 466; **38** 315

best energy GmbH, **39** 54, 57

Best Fabric Outlets, **16** 198

Best Holding Corporation. *See* Arkansas Best Corporation.

Best Manufacturing, **15** 490

Best Power, **24** 29

Best Products Inc., **19** 396–97

Best Read Guides Franchise Corp., **36** 341

Best Western, **14** 106; **25** 308

Bestfoods, II 496–97; **22 82–86 (upd.)**

Bestline Products, **17** 227

Bestop Inc., **16** 184

Bestwall Gypsum Co., **IV** 281; **9** 259

Bestway Distribution Services, Inc., **24** 126

Bestway Transportation, **14** 505

Beswick, **II** 17

BET Holdings, Inc., 18 64–66; **22** 224; **25** 213; **34** 43

Beta West Properties, **25** 496–97

Bethesda Research Laboratories, Inc., **I** 321; **17** 287, 289

Bethlehem Steel Corporation, IV 35–37, 228, 572–73; **6** 540; **7 48–51 (upd.)**, 447, 549–50; **11** 65; **12** 354; **13** 97, 157; **18** 378; **22** 285; **23** 305; **25** 45; **26** 405; **27 62–66 (upd.)**

Beton Union, **III** 738

Better Brands Ltd., **32** 518–19

Better Communications, **IV** 597

Betz Laboratories, Inc., I 312–13; **10 153–55 (upd.)**; **15** 536

Bevan and Wedd Durlacher Morduant & Co., **II** 237

Beveridge-Marvellum Company, **8** 483

Beverly Enterprises, Inc., III 76–77, 80; **14** 242; **16 57–59 (upd.)**; **25** 309

Beverly Hills Savings, **II** 420

Beverly Pest Control, **25** 15

Bevis Custom Furniture, Inc., **12** 263

Bevrachtingskantoor, **26** 280

Bewag AG, 38 449; **39 54–57**

Bezeq, **25** 266

BFC Construction Corporation, 25 63–65

The BFGoodrich Company, I 28, 428, 440; **II** 414; **III** 118, 443; **V 231–33**; **8** 80–81, 290; **9** 12, 96, 133; **10** 438; **11** 158; **19 52–55 (upd.)**; **20** 260, 262; **21** 260; **22** 114; **23** 170; **25** 70; **30** 158; **31** 135. *See also* Goodrich Corporation.

BFI. *See* Browning-Ferris Industries, Inc.

BFP Holdings Corp. *See* Big Flower Press Holdings, Inc.

BG Freight Line Holding B.V., **30** 318

BG plc, **29** 104

BG&E. *See* Baltimore Gas and Electric Company.

BGC Finance, **II** 420

BGJ Enterprises, Inc. *See* Brown Printing Company.
BH Acquisition Corporation, **22** 439
Bharat Coking Coal Ltd., **IV** 48–49
Bharat Petroleum Ltd., **IV** 441
Bharti Telecom, **16** 84
BHC Communications, Inc., 9 119; **26** 32–34; **31** 109
BHP. *See* Broken Hill Proprietary Company Ltd.
BHP Steel of Australia, **18** 380
BHPC Marketing, Inc., **45** 41
Bhs plc, 16 466; **17 42–44,** 334–35
BHV. *See* Bazar de l'Hotel de Ville.
Bi-Lo Inc., **II** 641; **V** 35; **16** 313
Biacore International AB, **25** 377
Bianchi, **13** 27
Bibb Co., **31** 199
BIC Corporation, III 29; **8 59–61; 20** 23; **23 54–57 (upd.)**
BICC PLC, III 433–34; 11 520. *See also* Balfour Beatty plc.
BICE Med Grille, **16** 447
Bicoastal Corporation, II 9–11
Bidermann Industries, **22** 122; **41** 129
Biederman & Company, **14** 160
Biedermann Motech, **37** 112
Bieffe, **16** 52
Bienfaisance, **III** 391
Bierbrauerei Wilhelm Remmer, **9** 86
Biesemeyer Manufacturing Corporation, **26** 363
Biffa Waste Services Ltd. *See* Severn Trent PLC.
Big B, Inc., 17 45–47
Big Bear Stores Co., 13 94–96
Big Boy, **III** 102–03
Big D Construction Corporation, 42 432
Big Dog Holdings, Inc., 45 40–42
Big 5 Sporting Goods, **12** 477
Big Flower Press Holdings, Inc., 21 60–62; 32 465–66
Big Foot Cattle Co., **14** 537
Big Horn Mining Co., **8** 423
Big Idea Productions, Inc., 49 56–59
Big M, **8** 409–10
Big O Tires, Inc., 20 61–63
Big Rivers Electric Corporation, 11 37–39
Big Sky Western Bank, **35** 197, 199
Big Three Industries, **I** 358
Big V Supermarkets, Inc., 25 66–68
Big Y Foods, Inc., **23** 169
Bigelow-Sanford, Inc., **31** 199
BII. *See* Banana Importers of Ireland.
Bike Athletics, **23** 449
BIL. *See* Brierley Investments.
Bilbao Insurance Group, **III** 200
Bilfinger & Berger Bau A.G., I 560–61
Bill & Melinda Gates Foundation, 41 53–55, 119
Bill Acceptance Corporation Ltd., **48** 427
Bill Blass Ltd., 32 78–80
Bill France Racing, **19** 222
Billabong International Ltd., 44 55–58
Billboard Publications, Inc., **7** 15
Billerud, **IV** 336
Billing Concepts Corp., 26 35–38
Billiton International, **IV** 56, 532; **22** 237
Bill's Casino, **9** 426
Bilsom, **40** 96–97
Bilt-Rite Chase-Pitkin, Inc., **41** 416
Biltwell Company, **8** 249
Bimar Foods Inc., **19** 192

Bimbo Bakeries USA, **29** 341
Bimbo, S.A., **36** 162, 164
Binder Hamlyn, **IV** 685
Binderline Development, Inc., **22** 175
Bindley Western Industries, Inc., 9 67–69
Bing Crosby Productions, **IV** 595
Bingham Dana LLP, 43 68–71
Binghamton Container Company, **8** 102
Bingo King. *See* Stuart Entertainment Inc.
Binks Sames Corporation, 21 63–66
Binney & Smith Inc., II 525; **IV** 621; **13** 293; **25 69–72**
Binnie & Partners, **22** 89
Binny & Co. Ltd., **III** 522
Binter Canarias, **6** 97
Bio-Clinic, **11** 486–87
Bio-Dental Technologies Corporation, **46** 466
Bio-Dynamics, Inc., **10** 105, 107; **37** 111
Bio Foods Inc. *See* Balance Bar Company.
Bio Synthetics, Inc., **21** 386
Bio-Toxicological Research Laboratories, **IV** 409
Biodevelopment Laboratories, Inc., **35** 47
Biofermin Pharmaceutical, **I** 704
Biogen Inc., I 638, 685; **8** 210; **14 58–60; 36 90–93 (upd.)**
Bioindustrias, **19** 475
Biokyowa, **III** 43; **48** 250
Biological Research, **III** 443
Biological Technology Corp., **IV** 252; **17** 29
Biomedical Reference Laboratories of North Carolina, **11** 424
Biomega Corp., **18** 422
Biomet, Inc., 10 156–58
Bionaire, Inc., **19** 360
BioSensor A.B., **I** 665
Biotechnica International, **I** 286
Bioteknik-Gruppen, **I** 665
Bioter-Biona, S.A., **II** 493
Bioter S.A., **III** 420
Biotherm, **III** 47
Biovail Corporation, 47 54–56
Biralo Pty Ltd., **48** 427
Bird & Sons, **22** 14
Bird Corporation, 19 56–58
Birdair, Inc., **35** 99–100
Birds Eye, **32** 474
Birdsall, Inc., **6** 529, 531
Bireley's, **22** 515
Birfield S.A., **III** 494
Birkbeck, **10** 6
Birkenstock Footprint Sandals, Inc., 12 33–35; 42 37–40 (upd.)
Birmingham & Midland Bank. *See* Midland Bank plc.
Birmingham Joint Stock Bank, **II** 307
Birmingham Screw Co., **III** 493
Birmingham Slag Company, **7** 572–73, 575
Birmingham Steel Corporation, 13 97–98; 18 379–80; **19** 380; **40 70–73 (upd.)**
Birra Moretti, **25** 281–82
Birtman Electric Co., **III** 653; **12** 548
Biscayne Bank. *See* Banco Espírito Santo e Comercial de Lisboa S.A.
Biscayne Federal Savings and Loan Association, **11** 481
Biscuiterie Nantaise, **II** 502; **10** 323
Biscuits Belin, **II** 543
Biscuits Delacre, **II** 480; **26** 56

Biscuits Gondolo, **II** 543
Bishop & Babcock Manufacturing Co., **II** 41
Bishop & Co. Savings Bank, **11** 114
Bishop National Bank of Hawaii, **11** 114
Bishopsgate Insurance, **III** 200
BISSELL, Inc., 9 70–72; 30 75–78 (upd.)
Bit Software, Inc., **12** 62
Bits & Pieces, **26** 439
Bitumax Proprietary, **III** 672
Bitumen & Oil Refineries (Australia) Ltd., **III** 672–73
BIW. *See* Bath Iron Works.
BIZ Enterprises, **23** 390
BizBuyer.com, **39** 25
Bizmark, **13** 176
BizMart, **6** 244–45; **8** 404–05
BJ Services Company, 15 534, 536; **25 73–75**
BJ's Pizza & Grill, **44** 85
BJ's Restaurant & Brewhouse, **44** 85
BJ's Wholesale Club, **12** 221; **13** 547–49; **33** 198
BJK&E. *See* Bozell Worldwide Inc.
Björknäs Nya Sågverks, **IV** 338
BK Tag, **28** 157
BKW, **IV** 229
BL Ltd., **I** 175; **10** 354
BL Systems. *See* AT&T Istel Ltd.
BL Universal PLC, **47** 168
The Black & Decker Corporation, I 667; **III 435–37,** 628, 665; **8** 332, 349; **15** 417–18; **16** 384; **17** 215; **20 64–68 (upd.); 22** 334; **43** 101, 289
Black & Veatch LLP, 22 87–90
Black Arrow Leasing, **II** 138; **34** 193
Black Box Corporation, 20 69–71
Black Clawson Company, **24** 478
Black Entertainment Television. *See* BET Holdings, Inc.
Black Flag Co., **I** 622
Black Hawk Broadcasting Group, **III** 188; **10** 29; **38** 17
Black Hills Corporation, 20 72–74
Black Pearl Software, Inc., **39** 396
Black Spread Eagle, **II** 235
Blackburn Group, **III** 508; **24** 85
Blackhawk Holdings, Inc. *See* PW Eagle Inc.
Blackhorse Agencies, **II** 309; **47** 227
Blackmer Pump Co., **III** 468
Blacks Leisure Group plc, 39 58–60
Blackstone Capital Partners L.P., **V** 223; **6** 378; **17** 366
The Blackstone Group, **II** 434, 444; **IV** 718; **11** 177, 179; **13** 170; **17** 238, 443; **22** 404, 416; **26** 408; **37** 309, 311
Blackstone Hotel Acquisition Co., **24** 195
Blaine Construction Company, **8** 546
Blair and Co., **II** 227
Blair Corporation, 25 76–78; 31 53–55
Blair Paving, **III** 674
Blair Radio, **6** 33
Blakiston Co., **IV** 636
Blane Products, **I** 403
Blanes, S.A. de C.V., **34** 197
Blatz Breweries, **I** 254
Blaupunkt-Werke, **I** 192–93
BLC Insurance Co., **III** 330
BLD Europe, **16** 168
Bleichröder, **II** 191
Blendax, **III** 53; **8** 434; **26** 384
Blessings Corp., 14 550; **19 59–61**

Blimpie International, Inc., 15 55–57; **17**
501; **32** 444; bf]XLIX **60–64 (upd.)**
Bliss Manufacturing Co., **17** 234–35
Blitz-Weinhart Brewing, **18** 71–72
Bloch & Guggenheimer, Inc., **40** 51–52
Blochman Lawrence Goldfree, **I** 697
Block Drug Company, Inc., 6 26; **8**
62–64; 27 67–70 (upd.)
Block Financial Corporation, **17** 265; **29**
227
Block Management, **29** 226
Block Medical, Inc., **10** 351
Blockbuster Entertainment Corporation,
II 161; **IV** 597; **9 73–75,** 361; **11**
556–58; **12** 43, 515; **13** 494; **18** 64, 66;
19 417; **22** 161–62; **23** 88, 503; **25**
208–10, 222; **26** 409; **28** 296; **29** 504
Blockbuster Inc., 31 56–60 (upd.),
339–40
Blockson Chemical, **I** 380; **13** 379
Bloedel, Stewart & Welch, **IV** 306–07
Blohm & Voss, **I** 74
Blonder Tongue Laboratories, Inc., 48
52–55
Bloomberg L.P., 18 24; **21 67–71**
Bloomingdale's Inc., I 90; **III** 63; **IV** 651,
703; **9** 209, 393; **10** 487; **12 36–38,** 307,
403–04; **16** 328; **23** 210; **25** 257; **31** 190
Blount International, Inc., I 563; **12**
39–41; 24 78; **26** 117, 119, 363; **48**
56–60 (upd.)
BLP Group Companies. *See* Boron, LePore
& Associates, Inc.
BLT Ventures, **25** 270
Blue Arrow PLC, **II** 334–35; **9** 327; **30**
300
Blue Bell Creameries L.P., 30 79–81
Blue Bell, Inc., **V** 390–91; **12** 205; **17** 512
Blue Bird Corporation, 35 63–66
Blue Bunny Ice Cream. *See* Wells' Dairy,
Inc.
Blue Byte, **41** 409
Blue Chip Stamps, **III** 213–14; **30** 412
Blue Circle Industries PLC, III 669–71,
702
Blue Cross and Blue Shield Association,
10 159–61; **14** 84
Blue Cross and Blue Shield Mutual of
Northern Ohio, **12** 176
Blue Cross and Blue Shield of Colorado,
11 175
Blue Cross and Blue Shield of Greater
New York, **III** 245, 246
Blue Cross and Blue Shield of Ohio, **15**
114
Blue Cross Blue Shield of Michigan, **12** 22
Blue Cross of California, **25** 525
Blue Cross of Northeastern New York, **III**
245–46
Blue Diamond Growers, 28 56–58
Blue Dot Services, **37** 280, 283
Blue Funnel Line, **I** 521; **6** 415–17
Blue Line Distributing, **7** 278–79
Blue Metal Industries, **III** 687; **28** 82
Blue Mountain Arts, Inc., IV 621; **29**
63–66
Blue Mountain Springs Ltd., **48** 97
Blue Ribbon Beef Pack, Inc., **II** 515–16
Blue Ribbon Sports. *See* Nike, Inc.
Blue Ridge Grocery Co., **II** 625
Blue Ridge Lumber Ltd., **16** 11
Blue Shield of California, **25** 527
Blue Square Israel Ltd., 41 56–58
Blue Tee Corporation, **23** 34, 36

Blue Water Food Service, **13** 244
Bluebird Inc., **10** 443
Bluffton Grocery Co., **II** 668
Blumberg Communications Inc., **24** 96
Blunt Ellis & Loewi, **III** 270
Blyth and Co., **I** 537; **13** 448, 529
Blyth Eastman Dillon & Company, **II** 445;
22 405–06
Blyth Industries, Inc., 18 67–69
Blyth Merrill Lynch, **II** 448
Blythe Colours BV, **IV** 119
BMC Industries, Inc., 6 275; **17 48–51**
BMC Software Inc., **14** 391
BMG/Music, **IV** 594; **15** 51; **37** 192–93
BMI. *See* Broadcast Music Inc.
BMI Ltd., **III** 673
BMI Systems Inc., **12** 174
BMO Corp., **III** 209
BMO Nesbitt Burns, **46** 55
BMW. *See* Bayerische Motoren Werke.
BNA. *See* Banca Nazionale
    dell'Agricoltura *or* Bureau of National
    Affairs, Inc.
BNCI. *See* Banque Nationale Pour le
    Commerce et l'Industrie.
BNE. *See* Bank of New England Corp.
BNG, Inc., **19** 487
BNP Paribas Group, 36 94–97 (upd.); 42
349
BNS Acquisitions, **26** 247
Boa Shoe Company, **42** 325
BOAC. *See* British Overseas Airways
    Corp.
Boardwalk Regency, **6** 201
Boart and Hard Metals, **IV** 22
Boart Longyear Company, 26 39–42, 69
Boase Massimi Pollitt, **6** 48
Boatmen's Bancshares Inc., 15 58–60
BoatsDirect.com, **37** 398
Bob Evans Farms, Inc., 9 76–79; 10 259;
35 83–84
Bobbie Brooks Inc., **17** 384
Bobbs-Merrill, **11** 198
Bobingen A.G., **I** 347
Bobro Products. *See* BWP Distributors.
BOC Group plc, I 314–16, 358; **11** 402;
12 500; **25 79–82 (upd.)**
Boca Resorts, Inc., 37 33–36
BOCAP Corp., **37** 372
Bochumer Verein für Gusstahlfabrikation,
IV 88
Bock Bearing Co., **8** 530
Bodcaw Co., **IV** 287; **15** 228
Boddington, **21** 247
Bodegas, **8** 556
Bodeker Drug Company, **16** 399
Bodum Design Group AG, 47 57–59
The Body Shop International PLC, 11
40–42
Boehringer Ingelheim GmbH. *See* C.H.
    Boehringer Sohn.
Boehringer Mannheim Companies, **37**
111–12
The Boeing Company, I 41–43, **47–49,**
50, 55–56, 58, 61, 67–68, 70–72, 74,
77, 82, 84–85, 90, 92–93, 96–97, 100,
102, 104–05, 108, 111–13, 116,
121–22, 126, 128, 130, 195, 489–90,
511, 530; **II** 7, 32–33, 62, 442; **III** 512,
539; **IV** 171, 576; **6** 68, 96, 130, 327; **7**
11, 456, 504; **8** 81, 313, 315; **9** 12, 18,
128, 194, 206, 232, 396, 416–17,
458–60, 498; **10 162–65 (upd.),** 262,
316, 369, 536; **11** 164, 267, 277–79,

363, 427; **12** 180, 190–91, 380; **13**
356–58; **21** 140, 143, 436; **24** 21, 84,
85–86, 88–89, 442; **25** 34, 224, 430–31;
26 117; **28** 195, 225; **32 81–87 (upd.);**
36 122, 190; **38** 372; **48** 218–20
Boeke & Huidekooper, **III** 417
Boerenbond, **II** 304
Boettcher & Co., **III** 271
Bofors Nobel Inc., **9** 380–81; **13** 22
Bogen Company, **15** 213
Bohemia, Inc., 13 99–101; 31 467
Bohm-Allen Jewelry, **12** 112
Böhme-Fettchemie, Chenmitz, **III** 32
Bohn Aluminum & Brass, **10** 439
Boise Cascade Corporation, I 142; **III**
499, 648, 664; **IV 255–56,** 333; **6** 577;
7 356; **8 65–67 (upd.),** 477; **15** 229; **16**
510; **19** 269, 445–46; **22** 154; **31** 13; **32**
88–92 (upd.); 36 509; **37** 140
Bokaro Steel Ltd., **IV** 206
Bolands Ltd., **II** 649
Bolar Pharmaceutical Co., **16** 529
Boley G.m.b.H., **21** 123
Boliden Mining, **II** 366
Bolinder-Munktell, **I** 209; **II** 366
Bolitho Bank, **II** 235
Bölkow GmbH, **I** 74
Bolles & Houghton, **10** 355
The Bolsa Chica Company, **8** 300
Bolt, Beranek & Newman Inc., **26** 520
Bolt Security, **32** 373
BOMAG, **8** 544, 546
Bombadier Defence Services UK, **41** 412
Bombardier Aerospace Group, **36** 190–91
Bombardier, Inc., **12** 400–01; **16** 78; **25**
423; **27** 281, 284; **34** 118–19; **35**
350–51; **42 41–46 (upd.)**
The Bombay Company, Inc., III 581; **10**
166–68; 27 429
Bon Appetit Holding AG, II 656; **48**
61–63
Bon Dente International Inc., **39** 320
The Bon Marché, Inc., V 25; **9** 209; **19**
88, 306, 309; **23 58–60; 26** 158, 160
Bon Secours Health System, Inc., 24
68–71
The Bon-Ton Stores, Inc., 16 60–62
Bonanza, **7** 336; **10** 331; **15** 361–63
Bonanza Steakhouse, **17** 320
Bonaventura, **IV** 611
Bonaventure Liquor Store Co., **I** 284
Bond Brewing International, **23** 405
Bond Corporation Holdings Limited, I
253, 255; **10 169–71**
Bondex International, **8** 456
Bonduel Pickling Co. Inc., **25** 517
Bongrain SA, 19 50; **23** 217, 219; **25**
83–85
Boni & Liveright, **13** 428
Bonifiche Siele, **II** 272
Bonimart, **II** 649
Bonneville International Corporation, 29
67–70; 30 15
Bontrager Bicycles, **16** 495
Bonwit Teller, **13** 43; **17** 43
Book-Mart Press, Inc., **41** 111
Book-of-the-Month Club, Inc., IV 661,
675; **7** 529; **13 105–07**
Booker plc, 13 102–04; 31 61–64 (upd.)
Booker Tate, **13** 102
Booklink Technologies, **26** 19
Bookmasters, **10** 136
Books-A-Million, Inc., 14 61–62; 16 161;
41 59–62 (upd.)

Bookstop, **10** 136
Boole & Babbage, Inc., 25 86–88
Booth Bay, Ltd., **16** 37
Booth Creek Ski Holdings, Inc., 31
65–67
Booth Fisheries, **II** 571
Booth, Inc., **II** 420
Booth-Kelly Lumber Co., **IV** 281; **9** 259
Booth Leasing, **I** 449
Bootprint Entertainment, **31** 240
The Boots Company PLC, I 640, 668,
708; **II** 650; **V** 17–19; **8** 548; **19** 122;
24 72–76 **(upd.)**
Boots Pharmaceuticals, **18** 51
Booz Allen & Hamilton Inc., 10 172–75
Boral Limited, III 672–74; **43** 72–76
(upd.)
Borax Holdings, **IV** 191
Bordas, **IV** 615
Borden Cabinet Corporation, **12** 296
Borden, Inc., II 470–73, 486, 498, 538,
545; **IV** 569; **7** 127, 129, 380; **11** 173;
15 490; **16** 43; **17** 56; **22** 84, **91–96**
(upd.); **24** 273, 288, 520; **27** 38, 40,
316, 318
Border Fine Arts, **11** 95
Border Television, **41** 352
Borders Group, Inc., 9 361; **10** 137; **15**
61–62; **17** 522; **18** 286; **25** 17; **30** 69;
43 77–79 **(upd.)**, 408; **47** 211
Borders, Perrin and Norrander, **23** 480
Borealis A/S, **30** 205; **45** 8
Borg Instruments, **23** 494
Borg-Warner Australia, **47** 280
Borg-Warner Automotive, Inc., 14
63–66; **23** 171; **32** 93–97 **(upd.)**
Borg-Warner Corporation, I 193, 339,
393; **III** 428, **438–41**; **14** 63, 357; **22**
228; **25** 74, 253
Borg-Warner Security Corporation, **13**
123–25; **14** 63, 65, 541; **41** 79
Borland International, Inc., 6 255–56; **9**
80–82; **10** 237, 509, 519, 558; **15** 492;
25 300–01, 349; **38** 417
Borman's, Inc., **II** 638; **16** 249
Borneo Airways. *See* Malaysian Airlines
System BHD.
Borneo Co., **III** 523
Boron, LePore & Associates, Inc., 45
43–45
Borregaard Osterreich AG, **18** 395
Borror Corporation. *See* Dominion Homes,
Inc.
Borsheim's, **III** 215; **18** 60
Borun Bros., **12** 477
Bosanquet, Salt and Co., **II** 306
Bosch. *See* Robert Bosch GmbH.
Boschert, **III** 434
Boscov's Department Store, Inc., 31
68–70
Bose Corporation, 13 108–10; **36** 98–101
(upd.)
Bosendorfer, L., Klavierfabrik, A.G., **12**
297
Bosert Industrial Supply, Inc., **V** 215
Boso Condensed Milk, **II** 538
Bost Sports Clubs. *See* Town Sports
International, Inc.
Bostich, **III** 628
Boston Acoustics, Inc., 22 97–99
Boston and Maine Corporation, **16** 350
Boston Beer Company, 18 70–73; 22
422; **31** 383
Boston Brewing Company, **18** 502

Boston Casualty Co., **III** 203
Boston Celtics Limited Partnership, 14
67–69
Boston Chicken, Inc., 12 42–44; 23 266;
29 170, 172. *See also* Boston Market
Corporation.
Boston Co., **II** 451–52
Boston Consulting Group, **I** 532; **9** 343; **18**
70; **22** 193
Boston Corp., **25** 66
Boston Distributors, **9** 453
Boston Edison Company, 12 45–47
Boston Educational Research, **27** 373
Boston Fruit Co., **II** 595
Boston Garden Arena Corporation, **14** 67
Boston Gas Company, **6** 486–88
Boston Globe, **7** 13–16
Boston Herald, **7** 15
Boston Industries Corp., **III** 735
Boston Marine Insurance Co., **III** 242
Boston Market Corporation, 48 64–67
(upd.)
Boston National Bank, **13** 465
Boston News Bureau, **IV** 601
Boston Overseas Financial Corp., **II** 208
Boston Popcorn Co., **27** 197–98; **43** 218
Boston Professional Hockey Association
Inc., 39 61–63
Boston Properties, Inc., 22 100–02
Boston Scientific Corporation, 37 37–40
Boston Technology, **43** 117
Boston Ventures Limited Partnership, **17**
444; **27** 41, 393
Boston Whaler, Inc., **V** 376–77; **10**
215–16; **26** 398
Bostrom Seating, Inc., **23** 306
BOTAS, **IV** 563
Botsford Ketchum, Inc., **6** 40
Botswana General Insurance Company, **22**
495
Botto, Rossner, Horne & Messinger, **6** 40
Bottu, **II** 475
BOTWEB, Inc., **39** 95
Bougainville Copper Pty., **IV** 60–61
Boulanger, **37** 22
Boulder Creek Steaks & Saloon, **16** 447
Boulder Natural Gas Company, **19** 411
Boulet Dru DuPuy Petit Group. *See* Wells
Rich Greene BDDP.
Boulevard Bancorp, **12** 165
Boulton & Paul Ltd., **31** 398–400
Boundary Gas, **6** 457
Boundary Healthcare, **12** 327
Bouquet, **V** 114
Bourdon, **19** 49
Bourjois, **12** 57
Boussois Souchon Neuvesel, **II** 474; **III**
677; **16** 121–22
Bouygues S.A., I 562–64; **13** 206; **23**
475–76; **24** 77–80 **(upd.)**; **31** 126, 128;
48 204
Bouzan Mines Ltd., **IV** 164
Bovaird Seyfang Manufacturing Co., **III**
471
Bovis Construction, **38** 344–45
Bovis Ltd., **I** 588
Bow Bangles, **17** 101, 103
Bow Flex of America, Inc. *See* Direct
Focus, Inc.
Bow Valley Energy Inc., **47** 397
Bowater PLC, III 501–02; **IV** 257–59; **7**
208; **8** 483–84; **25** 13; **30** 229
Bower Roller Bearing Company. *See*
Federal-Mogul Corporation.

Bowers and Merena Galleries Inc., **48** 99
Bowery and East River National Bank, **II**
226
Bowery Savings Bank, **II** 182; **9** 173
Bowes Co., **II** 631
Bowman Gum, Inc., **13** 520
Bowman Instruments, **II** 113; **11** 506
Bowne & Co., Inc., 18 331–32; **23 61–64**
Bowthorpe plc, 33 70–72
Box Innards Inc., **13** 442
Box Office Attraction Co., **II** 169
BoxCrow Cement Company, **8** 259
The Boy Scouts of America, 34 66–69
Boyd Bros. Transportation Inc., 39
64–66
Boyd Gaming Corporation, 43 80–82
The Boyds Collection, Ltd., 29 71–73
Boyer Brothers, Inc., **14** 17–18
Boyer's International, Inc., **20** 83
Boykin Enterprises, **IV** 136
Boyles Bros. Drilling Company. *See*
Christensen Boyles Corporation.
Boys Market, **17** 558–59
Boz, **IV** 697–98
Bozel Électrométallurgie, **IV** 174
Bozell, Jacobs, Kenyon, and Eckhardt Inc.
See True North Communications Inc.
Bozell Worldwide Inc., 25 89–91
Bozkurt, **27** 188
Bozzuto's, Inc., 13 111–12
BP. *See* British Petroleum Company PLC.
BP Amoco plc, **31** 31, 34; **40** 358
BP Canada. *See* Talisman Energy Inc.
BP p.l.c., 45 46–56 (upd.), 409, 412
BPB, **III** 736
BPD, **13** 356
BPI Communications, Inc., **7** 15; **19** 285;
27 500
BR. *See* British Rail.
Braas, **III** 734, 736
Braathens ASA, 47 60–62
Brabant, **III** 199, 201
Brabazon, **III** 555
Brach and Brock Confections, Inc., 15
63–65; **29** 47
Brad Foote Gear Works, **18** 453
Bradbury Agnew and Co., **IV** 686
Braden Manufacturing, **23** 299–301
Bradford District Bank, **II** 333
Bradford Exchange Ltd. Inc., **21** 269
Bradford Insulation Group, **III** 687
Bradford Pennine, **III** 373
Bradlees Discount Department Store
Company, II 666–67; **12 48–50; 24**
461
Bradley Lumber Company, **8** 430
Bradley Producing Corp., **IV** 459
Bradstreet Co., **IV** 604–05; **19** 133
Braegen Corp., **13** 127
Bragussa, **IV** 71
BRAINS. *See* Belgian Rapid Access to
Information Network Services.
Brake Bros plc, 45 57–59
Bramalea Ltd., 9 83–85; 10 530–31
Brambles Industries Limited, III 494–95;
24 400; **42 47–50**
Bramco, **III** 600
Bramwell Gates, **II** 586
Bran & Lübbe, **III** 420
Brand Companies, Inc., **9** 110; **11** 436
Branded Restaurant Group, Inc., **12** 372
Brandeis & Sons, **19** 511
Brandenburgische Motorenwerke, **I** 138
Brandt Zwieback-Biskuits GmbH, **44** 40

Brandywine Asset Management, Inc., **33** 261

Brandywine Holdings Ltd., **45** 109

Brandywine Insurance Agency, Inc., **25** 540

Brandywine Iron Works and Nail Factory, **14** 323

Brandywine Valley Railroad Co., **14** 324

Braniff Airlines, **I** 97, 489, 548; **II** 445; **6** 50, 119–20; **16** 274; **17** 504; **21** 142; **22** 406; **36** 231

Branigar Organization, Inc., **IV** 345

Brannock Device Company, 48 68–70

Brascade Resources, **IV** 308

Brascan Ltd., **II** 456; **IV** 165, 330; **25** 281

Braspetro, **IV** 454, 501–02

Brass Craft Manufacturing Co., **III** 570; **20** 361

Brass Eagle Inc., 34 70–72

Brasseries Kronenbourg, **II** 474–75

Braswell Motor Freight, **14** 567

Braud & Faucheux. *See* Manitou BF S.A.

Brauerei Beck & Co., 9 86–87; 33 73–76 (upd.)

Braun, **III** 29; **17** 214–15; **26** 335

Braunkohlenwerk Golpa-Jessnitz AG, **IV** 230

Brauns Fashions Corporation. *See* Christopher & Banks Corporation.

Brazilian Central Bank, **IV** 56

Brazos Gas Compressing, **7** 345

Brazos Sportswear, Inc., 23 65–67

Breakstone Bros., Inc., **II** 533

Breakthrough Software, **10** 507

Breckenridge-Remy, **18** 216

Breco Holding Company, **17** 558, 561

Bredel Exploitatie B.V., **8** 546

Bredell Paint Co., **III** 745

Bredero's Bouwbedrijf of Utrecht, **IV** 707–08, 724

BREED Technologies, Inc., **22** 31

Breedband NV, **IV** 133

Brega Petroleum Marketing Co., **IV** 453, 455

Breguet Aviation, **I** 44; **24** 86

Breitenburger Cementfabrik, **III** 701

Bremer Financial Corp., 45 60–63

Bremner Biscuit Co., **II** 562; **13** 426

Brenco Inc., **16** 514

Brenda Mines Ltd., **7** 399

Brennan College Services, **12** 173

Brenntag AG, 8 68–69, 496; 23 68–70 (upd.), 23 453–54

Brent Walker Ltd., **49** 450–51

Brentwood Associates Buyout Fund II LP, **44** 54

Bresler's Industries, Inc., **35** 121

Breslube Enterprises, **8** 464

Bresser Optik, **41** 264

Brewster Lines, **6** 410

Breyers Ice Cream Co. *See* Good Humor-Breyers.

BRI Bar Review Institute, Inc., **IV** 623; **12** 224

BRI International, **21** 425

Brian Mills, **V** 118

Briarpatch, Inc., **12** 109

Brickwood Breweries, **I** 294

Bricorama, **23** 231

Bricotruc, **37** 259

Bridas S.A., **24** 522

Bridel, **19** 49–50; **25** 85

Bridge Communications Inc., **34** 442–43

Bridge Oil Ltd., **I** 438

Bridge Technology, Inc., **10** 395

Bridgeman Creameries, **II** 536

Bridgeport Brass, **I** 377

Bridgeport Machines, Inc., 17 52–54

Bridgestone Corporation, V 234–35; 15 355; **20** 262; **21 72–75 (upd.)**

Bridgestone Liquefied Gas, **IV** 364

Bridgestone/Firestone, **19** 454, 456

Bridgeway Plan for Health, **6** 186

Bridgford Company, **13** 382

Bridgford Foods Corporation, 27 71–73

Brier Hill, **IV** 114

Brierly Investment Limited, **19** 156; **24** 399

Briggs & Stratton Corporation, III 597; **8 70–73; 27 74–78 (upd.)**

Briggs and Lundy Lumber Cos., **14** 18

Brigham's Inc., **15** 71

Bright Horizons Family Solutions, Inc., 31 71–73

Bright of America Inc., **12** 426

Bright Star Technologies, **13** 92; **15** 455; **41** 362

Brighter Vision Learning Adventures, **29** 470, 472

Brighton & Hove Bus and Coach Company, **28** 155–56

Brighton Federal Savings and Loan Assoc., **II** 420

Brightpoint, Inc., 18 74–77

Brightwork Development Inc., **25** 348

Briker, **23** 231

Brillion Iron Works Inc., **23** 306

Brimsdown Lead Co., **III** 680

Brin's Oxygen Company Limited. *See* BOC Group plc.

Brinco Ltd., **II** 211

Brink's, Inc., **IV** 180–82; **19** 319

Brinker International, Inc., 10 176–78; **18** 438; **38 100–03 (upd.)**

Brinson Partners Inc., **41** 198

BRIntec, **III** 434

Brinton Carpets, **III** 423

BRIO AB, 24 81–83

Brio Technology, **25** 97

Briones Alonso y Martin, **42** 19

Brisbane Gas Co., **III** 673

Brisco Engineering, **41** 412

Bristol Aeroplane, **I** 50, 197; **10** 261; **24** 85

Bristol-BTR, **I** 429

Bristol-Erickson, **13** 297

Bristol Gaming Corporation, **21** 298

Bristol Hotel Company, 23 71–73; 38 77

Bristol-Myers Squibb Company, I 26, 30, 37, 301, 696, 700, 703; **III 17–19,** 36, 67; **IV** 272; **6** 27; **7** 255; **8** 210, 282–83; **9 88–91 (upd.); 10** 70; **11** 289; **12** 126–27; **16** 438; **21** 546; **25** 91, 253, 365; **32** 213; **34** 280, 282, 284; **37** **41–45 (upd.)**

Bristol PLC, **IV** 83

Bristol-Siddeley, Ltd., **I** 50; **24** 85

Britannia Airways, **8** 525–26

Britannia Security Group PLC, **12** 10

Britannia Soft Drinks Limited, **38** 77

Britannica Software, **7** 168

Britannica.com, **39** 140, 144

Britches of Georgetowne, **10** 215–16

BRITE. *See* Granada Group PLC.

Brite Voice Systems, Inc., 20 75–78

BriteSmile, Inc., **35** 325

British & Commonwealth Shipping Company, **10** 277

British Aerospace plc, **48** 81, 274

British Aerospace plc, I 42, 46, **50–53,** 55, 74, 83, 132, 532; **III** 458, 507; **V** 339; **7** 9, 11, 458–59; **8** 315; **9** 499; **11** 413; **12** 191; **14** 36; **18** 125; **21** 8, 443; **24 84–90 (upd.); 27** 474

British Airways plc, I 34, 83, **92–95,** 109; **IV** 658; **6** 60, 78–79, 118, 132; **14** **70–74 (upd.); 18** 80; **22** 52; **24** 86, 311, 396, 399–400; **26** 115; **27** 20–21, 466; **28** 25, 508; **31** 103; **33** 270; **34** 398; **37** 232; **38** 104–05; **39** 137–38; **43 83–88 (upd.)**

British Aluminium, Ltd., **II** 422; **IV** 15

British American Cosmetics, **I** 427

British American Financial Services, **42** 450

British American Insurance Co., **III** 350

British American Nickel, **IV** 110

British-American Tobacco Co., Ltd., **V** 396, 401–02, 417; **9** 312; **29** 194–95; **34** 39; **49** 367, 369

British and Dominion Film Corp., **II** 157

British and Foreign Marine, **III** 350

British and Foreign Steam Navigation Company, **23** 160

British and French Bank, **II** 232–33

British and North American Royal Mail Steam Packet Company. *See* Cunard Line Ltd.

British Bank of North America, **II** 210

British Bank of the Middle East, **II** 298

British-Borneo Oil & Gas PLC, 34 73–75

British Borneo Timber Co., **III** 699

British Broadcasting Corporation Ltd., III 163; **IV** 651; **7 52–55; 21 76–79 (upd.); 24** 192; **39** 198; **42** 114, 116

British Caledonian Airways, **I** 94–95; **6** 79

British Can Co., **I** 604

British Car Auctions, **14** 321

British Celanese Ltd., **I** 317

British Cellulose and Chemical Manufacturing Co., **I** 317

British Chrome, **III** 699

British Coal Corporation, IV 38–40

British Columbia Forest Products Ltd., **IV** 279; **19** 155

British Columbia Packers, **II** 631–32

British Columbia Resources Investment Corp., **IV** 308

British Columbia Telephone Company, IV 308; **6 309–11**

British Commonwealth Insurance, **III** 273

British Commonwealth Pacific Airways, **6** 110; **24** 398

British Continental Airlines, **I** 92

British Credit Trust, **10** 443

British Data Management, Ltd., **33** 212, 214

British Digital Broadcasting plc, **24** 192, 194

British Dyestuffs Corp., **I** 351

British Dynamite Co., **I** 351

British Electric Traction Company. *See* Rentokil Initial Plc.

British Energy Plc, 19 391; **49 65–68.** *See also* British Nuclear Fuels PLC.

British Engine, **III** 350

British European Airways, **I** 93, 466

British Executive and General Aviation, **I** 50; **24** 85

British Fuels, **III** 735

British Gas plc, II 260; **V 559–63; 6** 478–79; **11** 97; **18** 365–67; **38** 408; **49** 120–21. *See also* Centrica plc.

British Gauge and Instrument Company, **13** 234

British General, **III** 234

British General Post Office, **25** 99–100

British Goodrich Tyre Co., **I** 428

British Home Stores PLC. *See* Storehouse PLC.

British Hovercraft Corp., **I** 120

British Independent Television Enterprises Ltd. *See* Granada Group PLC.

British India and Queensland Agency Co. Ltd., **III** 522

British India Steam Navigation Co., **III** 521–22

British Industrial Solvents Ltd., **IV** 70

British Industry, **III** 335

British Insulated and Helsby Cables Ltd., **III** 433–34

British Interactive Broadcasting Ltd., **20** 79

British Isles Transport Co. Ltd., **II** 564

British Land Company PLC, **10** 6; **47** 168

British Leyland Motor Corporation, **I** 175, 186; **III** 516, 523; **13** 286–87; **14** 35–36; **47** 8

British Linen Bank, **10** 336

British Marine Air Navigation, **I** 92

British Metal Corp., **IV** 140, 164

British Midland plc, 34 398; **38 104–06**

British Motor Corporation, **III** 555; **7** 459; **13** 286

British Motor Holdings, **7** 459

British National Films Ltd., **II** 157

British National Oil Corp., **IV** 40

British Newfoundland Corporation, **6** 502

British Nuclear Fuels PLC, I 573; **6 451–54; 13** 458

British Nylon Spinners (BNS), **17** 118

British Overseas Airways Corp., **I** 51, 93, 120–21; **III** 522; **6** 78–79, 100, 110, 112, 117; **14** 71; **24** 86, 397

British Oxygen Co. *See* BOC Group.

The British Petroleum Company plc, I 241, 303; **II** 449, 563; **IV** 61, 280, 363–64, **378–80**, 381–82, 412–13, 450–54, 456, 466, 472, 486, 497–99, 505, 515, 524–25, 531–32, 557; **6** 304; **7 56–59 (upd.)**, 140–41, 332–33, 516, 559; **9** 490, 519; **11** 538; **13** 449; **14** 317; **16** 394, 461–62; **19** 155, 391; **21 80–84 (upd.)**, 352; **25** 101; **26** 366, 369; **30** 86, 88; **47** 393. *See also* BP p.l.c.

British Plasterboard, **III** 734

British Portland Cement Manufacturers, **III** 669–70

British Printing and Communications Corp., **IV** 623–24, 642; **7** 312; **12** 224

British Prudential Assurance Co., **III** 335

British Rail, **III** 509; **V** 421–24; **10** 122; **27** 474

British Railways, **6** 413

British Railways Board, V 421–24

British Road Services, **6** 413

British Royal Insurance Co., Ltd., **III** 242

British Satellite Broadcasting, **10** 170

British Shoe Corporation, **V** 178

British Sky Broadcasting Group Plc, 20 79–81; 24 192, 194

British South Africa Co., **IV** 23, 94

British South American Airways, **I** 93

British South American Corporation, **6** 95

British Steel Brickworks, **III** 501; **7** 207

British Steel plc, III 494–95; **IV** 40, **41–43**, 128; **17** 481; **19 62–65 (upd.)**, 391; **24** 302; **49** 98, 101, 104

British Sugar plc, **II** 514, 581–82; **13** 53; **41** 30, 32–33

British Tabulating Machine Company, **6** 240

British Telecommunications plc, I 83, 330; **II** 82; **V 279–82; 6** 323; **7** 332–33; **8** 153; **9** 32; **11** 59, 185, 547; **15 66–70 (upd.)**, 131; **16** 468; **18** 155, 345; **20** 81; **21** 233; **24** 370; **25** 101–02, 301; **27** 304; **29** 44. *See also* BT Group plc.

British Thermoplastics and Rubber. *See* BTR plc.

British Timken Ltd., **8** 530

British Trimmings Ltd., **29** 133

British Twin Disc Ltd., **21** 504

British Tyre and Rubber Co., **I** 428

British United Airways, **I** 94

British Vita plc, 9 92–93; 19 413–15; **33 77–79 (upd.)**

British World Airlines Ltd., 18 78–80

British Zaire Diamond Distributors Ltd., **IV** 67

Britoil, **IV** 380; **21** 82

Britt Airways, **I** 118

Britt Lumber Co., Inc., **8** 348

Brittains Bricks, **III** 673

Brittania Sportswear, **16** 509

Britvic Soft Drinks Limited, **38** 74, 77

BritWill Healthcare Corp., **25** 504

BRK Brands, Inc., **28** 134

BRK Electronics, **9** 414

Bro-Well, **17** 56

Broad, Inc., **11** 482

Broad River Power Company, **6** 575

Broadband Networks Inc., **36** 352

Broadbandtalentneet.com, **44** 164

Broadcast Music Inc., 23 74–77; 29 22–23

Broadcast Technology Systems, Inc., **13** 398

Broadcaster Press, **36** 341

Broadcom Corporation, 34 76–79; 36 123

Broadcom Eireann Research, **7** 510

Broadcort Capital Corp., **13** 342

The Broadmoor Hotel, 30 82–85

BroadPark, **II** 415

BroadVision Inc., **18** 543; **38** 432

Broadway & Seymour Inc., **17** 264; **18** 112

Broadway-Hale Stores, Inc., **12** 356

Broadway Stores, Inc., **31** 193

Brobeck, Phleger & Harrison, LLP, 31 74–76

Brock Candy Company. *See* Brach and Brock Confections, Inc.

Brock Hotel Corp., **13** 472–73; **31** 94

Brock Residence Inn, **9** 426

Brockway Glass Co., **I** 524; **15** 128

Brockway Standard Holdings Corporation. *See* BWAY Corporation.

Broder Bros. Co., 38 107–09

Broderbund Software, Inc., 10 285; **13 113–16; 25** 118; **29 74–78 (upd.)**

Les broderies Lesage, **49** 83

Broederlijke Liefdebeurs, **III** 177

Broken Hill Proprietary Company Ltd., I 437–39; **II** 30; **III** 494; **IV 44–47**, 58, 61, 171, 484; **10** 170; **21** 227; **22 103–08 (upd.); 26** 248

The Bronfman Group, **6** 161, 163; **23** 124–25

Bronson Laboratories, Inc., **34** 460

Bronson Pharmaceuticals, **24** 257

Brooke Bond, **32** 475

Brooke Group Ltd., 15 71–73. *See also* Vector Group Ltd.

Brooke Partners L.P., **11** 275

Brookfield Athletic Shoe Company, **17** 244

Brookfield International Inc., **35** 388

Brooklyn Flint Glass Co., **III** 683

Brooklyn Trust Co., **II** 312

Brooklyn Union Gas, 6 455–57; 27 264–66

Brooks Brothers Inc., V 26–27; **13** 43; **22 109–12; 24** 313, 316

Brooks Fashion, **29** 164

Brooks Fiber Communications, **41** 289–90

Brooks Fiber Properties, Inc., **27** 301, 307

Brooks, Harvey & Company, Inc., **II** 431; **16** 376

Brooks-Scanlon Lumber Co., **IV** 306

Brooks Shoe Manufacturing Co., **16** 546

Brooks, Shoobridge and Co., **III** 669

Brooks Sports Inc., 32 98–101

Brookshire Grocery Company, 16 63–66

Brookstone, Inc., II 560; **12** 411; **18 81–83**

Brookville Telephone Company, **6** 300

Brookwood Health Services, **III** 73

Brother Industries, Ltd., 13 478; **14 75–76**

Brother International, **23** 212

Brothers Foods, **18** 7

Brothers Gourmet Coffees, Inc., 20 82–85

Brotherton Chemicals, **29** 113

Broughton Foods Co., 17 55–57

Brown & Bigelow, **27** 193

Brown & Brown, Inc., 41 63–66

Brown & Dureau Ltd., **IV** 248–49; **19** 14

Brown & Haley, 23 78–80

Brown & Root, Inc., III 498–99, 559; **13 117–19; 25** 190–91; **37** 244; **38** 481

Brown & Sharpe Manufacturing Co., 23 81–84

Brown and Williamson Tobacco Corporation, I 426; **14 77–79; 15** 72; **22** 72–73; **33 80–83 (upd.)**

Brown Bibby & Gregory, **I** 605

Brown Boveri. *See* BBC Brown Boveri.

Brown Brothers Harriman & Co., 45 64–67

Brown Co., **I** 452; **IV** 289

Brown Corp., **IV** 286

Brown Drug, **III** 9

Brown-Forman Corporation, I 225–27; **III** 286; **10 179–82 (upd.); 12** 313; **18** 69; **38 110–14 (upd.)**

Brown Foundation, **III** 498

Brown Group, Inc., V 351–53; 9 192; **10** 282; **16** 198; **20 86–89 (upd.)**

Brown Institute, **45** 87

Brown Instrument Co., **II** 41

Brown Jordan Co., **12** 301

Brown Oil Tools, **III** 428

Brown Paper Mill Co., **I** 380; **13** 379

Brown Printing Company, 26 43–45

Brown-Service Insurance Company, **9** 507

Brown Shipbuilding Company. *See* Brown & Root, Inc.

Brown, Shipley & Co., Limited, **II** 425; **13** 341; **45** 65

Brown Shoe Co., **V** 351–52; **14** 294

Browne & Nolan Ltd., **IV** 294; **19** 225

Browning-Ferris Industries, Inc., V 749–53; **8** 562; **10** 33; **17** 552; **18** 10; **20 90–93 (upd.)**; **23** 491; **33** 382; **46** 456

Browning Manufacturing, **II** 19

Browning Telephone Corp., **14** 258

Broyhill Furniture Industries, Inc., III 528, 530; **10 183–85**; **12** 308; **39** 170, 173–74

BRS Ltd., **6** 412–13

Bruce Foods Corporation, 39 67–69

Bruce Power LP, **49** 65, 67

Bruce's Furniture Stores, **14** 235

Bruckmann, Rosser, Sherill & Co., **27** 247; **40** 51

Bruegger's Bagel Bakery, **29** 171

Brufina, **II** 201–02

Brugman, **27** 502

Brummer Seal Company, **14** 64

Brunner Mond and Co., **I** 351

Bruno's Inc., 7 60–62; **13** 404, 406; **23** 261; **26 46–48 (upd.)**

Brunswick Corporation, III 442–44, 599; **9** 67, 119; **10** 262; **17** 453; **21** 291; **22 113–17 (upd.)**, 118; **30** 303; **40** 30; **45** 175

Brunswick Pulp & Paper Co., **IV** 282, 311, 329; **9** 260; **19** 266

The Brush Electric Light Company, **11** 387; **25** 44

Brush Electrical Machines, **III** 507–09

Brush Moore Newspaper, Inc., **8** 527

Brush Wellman Inc., 14 80–82

Bryan Bros. Packing, **II** 572

Bryant Heater Co., **III** 471

Bryce & Co., **I** 547

Bryce Brothers, **12** 313

Bryce Grace & Co., **I** 547

Brylane Inc., **29** 106–07

Brymbo Steel Works, **III** 494

Bryn Mawr Stereo & Video, **30** 465

Brynwood Partners, **13** 19

BSA. *See* The Boy Scouts of America.

BSB, **IV** 653; **7** 392

BSC. *See* Birmingham Steel Corporation.

BSC (Industry) Ltd., **IV** 42

BSkyB, **IV** 653; **7** 392; **29** 369, 371; **34** 85

BSN Groupe S.A., II 474–75, 544; **22** 458; **23** 448. *See also* Groupe Danone

BSN Medical, **41** 374, 377

BSR, **II** 82

BT Group plc, 49 69–74 (upd.)

BTG, Inc., 45 68–70

BTI Services, **9** 59

BTM. *See* British Tabulating Machine Company.

BTR Dunlop Holdings, Inc., **21** 432

BTR plc, I 428–30; **III** 185, 727; **8** 397; **24** 88

BTR Siebe plc, 27 79–81

Buca, Inc., 38 115–17

Buchanan, **I** 239–40

Buchanan Electric Steel Company, **8** 114

Buck Consultants Inc., **32** 459

Buck Knives Inc., 48 71–74

Buckaroo International. *See* Bugle Boy Industries, Inc.

Buckeye Business Products Inc., **17** 384

Buckeye Technologies, Inc., 42 51–54

Buckeye Tractor Ditcher, **21** 502

Buckeye Union Casualty Co., **III** 242

Buckhorn, Inc., **19** 277–78

Buckingham Corp., **I** 440, 468

The Buckle, Inc., 18 84–86

Buckler Broadcast Group, **IV** 597

Buckley/DeCerchio New York, **25** 180

Bucyrus Blades, Inc., **14** 81

Bucyrus-Erie Company, **7** 513

Bucyrus International, Inc., 17 58–61

Bud Bailey Construction, **43** 400

Budapest Bank, **16** 14

The Budd Company, III 568; **IV** 222; **8 74–76**; **20** 359

Buderus AG, III 692, 694–95; **37 46–49**

Budget Group, Inc., 25 92–94

Budget Rent a Car Corporation, I 537; **6** 348–49, 393; **9 94–95**; **13** 529; **22** 524; **24** 12, 409; **25** 143; **39** 370; **41** 402

Budgetel Inn. *See* Marcus Corporation.

Budweiser, **18** 70

Budweiser Japan Co., **21** 320

Buena Vista Distribution, **II** 172; **6** 174; **30** 487

Buena Vista Music Group, **44** 164

Bufete Industrial, S.A. de C.V., 34 80–82

Buffalo Forge Company, **7** 70–71

Buffalo Insurance Co., **III** 208

Buffalo Mining Co., **IV** 181

Buffalo News, **18** 60

Buffalo Paperboard, **19** 78

Buffalo-Springfield, **21** 502

Buffets, Inc., 10 186–87; **22** 465; **32 102–04 (upd.)**

Buffett Partnership, Ltd., **III** 213

Bugaboo Creek Steak House Inc., **19** 342

Bugatti Industries, **14** 321

Bugle Boy Industries, Inc., 18 87–88

Buhrmann NV, 41 67–69; **47 90–91**; **49** 440

Buick Motor Co., **I** 171; **III** 438; **8** 74; **10** 325

Builders Emporium, **13** 169; **25** 535

Builders Square, **V** 112; **9** 400; **12** 345, 385; **14** 61; **16** 210; **31** 20; **35** 11, 13; **47** 209

Building One Services Corporation. *See* Encompass Services Corporation.

Building Products of Canada Limited, **25** 232

Buitoni SpA, **II** 548; **17** 36

Bulgari S.p.A., 20 94–97

Bulgarian Oil Co., **IV** 454

Bulgheroni SpA, **27** 105

Bulkships, **27** 473

Bull. *See* Compagnie des Machines Bull S.A.

Bull-GE, **III** 123

Bull HN Information Systems, **III** 122–23

Bull Motors, **11** 5

Bull Run Corp., **24** 404

Bull S.A., **III** 122–23; **43 89–91 (upd.)**

Bull Tractor Company, **7** 534; **16** 178; **26** 492

Bull-Zenith, **25** 531

Bulldog Computer Products, **10** 519

Bullock's, **III** 63; **31** 191

Bulolo Gold Dredging, **IV** 95

Bulova Corporation, I 488; **II** 101; **III** 454–55; **12** 316–17, 453; **13 120–22**; **14** 501; **21** 121–22; **36** 325; **41 70–73 (upd.)**

Bumble Bee Seafoods, Inc., **II** 491, 508, 557; **24** 114

Bumkor-Ramo Corp., **I** 539

Bunawerke Hüls GmbH., **I** 350

Bundy Corporation, 17 62–65, 480

Bunker Ramo Info Systems, **III** 118

Bunte Candy, **12** 427

Bunzl plc, **IV** 260–62; **12** 264; **31 77–80 (upd.)**

Buquet, **19** 49

Burbank Aircraft Supply, Inc., **14** 42–43; **37** 29, 31

Burberry Ltd., 41 74–76 (upd.); **47** 167, 169

Burberrys Ltd., V 68; **10** 122; **17 66–68**; **19** 181

Burda Holding GmbH. & Co., 20 53; **23 85–89**

Burdines, **9** 209; **31** 192

Bureau de Recherches de Pétrole, **IV** 544–46, 559–60; **7** 481–83; **21** 203–04

The Bureau of National Affairs, Inc., 23 90–93

Burelle S.A., 23 94–96

Burger and Aschenbrenner, **16** 486

Burger Boy Food-A-Rama, **8** 564

Burger Chef, **II** 532

Burger King Corporation, I 21, 278; **II** 556–57, **613–15**, 647; **7** 316; **8** 564; **9** 178; **10** 122; **12** 43, 553; **13** 408–09; **14** 25, 32, 212, 214, 452; **16** 95–97, 396; **17 69–72 (upd.)**, 501; **18** 437; **21** 25, 362; **23** 505; **24** 140–41; **25** 228; **26** 284; **33** 240–41; **36** 517, 519

Burgess, Anderson & Tate Inc., **25** 500

Bürhle, **17** 36

Burhmann-Tetterode, **22** 154

Burke Scaffolding Co., **9** 512

BURLE Industries Inc., **11** 444

Burlesdon Brick Co., **III** 734

Burlington Coat Factory Warehouse Corporation, 10 188–89

Burlington Homes of New England, **14** 138

Burlington Industries, Inc., V 118, **354–55**; **8** 234; **9** 231; **12** 501; **17 73–76 (upd.)**, 304–05; **19** 275

Burlington Mills Corporation, **12** 117–18

Burlington Motor Holdings, **30** 114

Burlington Northern, Inc., IV 182; **V 425–28**; **10** 190–91; **11** 315; **12** 145, 278

Burlington Northern Santa Fe Corporation, 27 82–89 (upd.); **28** 495

Burlington Resources Inc., 10 190–92; **11** 135; **12** 144; **47** 238

Burmah Castrol PLC, IV 378, **381–84**, 440–41, 483–84, 531; **7** 56; **15** 246; **21** 80; **30 86–91 (upd.)**; **45** 55

Burmeister & Wain, **III** 417–18

Burn & Co., **IV** 205

Burn Standard Co. Ltd., **IV** 484

Burnards, **II** 677

Burndy, **19** 166

Burnham and Co., **II** 407–08; **6** 599; **8** 388

Burns & Ricker, Inc., **40** 51, 53

Burns & Wilcox Ltd., **6** 290

Burns-Alton Corp., **21** 154–55

Burns Companies, **III** 569; **20** 360

Burns Fry Ltd., **II** 349

Burns International Security Services, III 440; **13 123–25**; **42** 338. *See also* Securitas AB.

Burns International Services Corporation, 41 77–80 (upd.)

Burns Philp & Company Limited, **21** 496–98

Burnup & Sims, Inc., **19** 254; **26** 324

Burpee & Co. *See* W. Atlee Burpee & Co.

Burr & Co., **II** 424; **13** 340

Burr-Brown Corporation, 19 66–68

Burrill & Housman, **II** 424; **13** 340

Burris Industries, **14** 303
Burroughs Corp., **I** 142, 478; **III** 132, 148–49, 152, 165–66; **6** 233, 266, 281–83; **18** 386, 542. *See also* Unisys Corporation.
Burroughs Mfg. Co., **16** 321
Burroughs Wellcome & Co., **I** 713; **8** 216
Burrows, Marsh & McLennan, **III** 282
Burrups Ltd., **18** 331, 333; **47** 243
Burry, **II** 560; **12** 410
Bursley & Co., **II** 668
Burt Claster Enterprises, **III** 505
Burthy China Clays, **III** 690
Burton-Furber Co., **IV** 180
Burton Group plc, V 20–22. *See also* Arcadia Group plc.
Burton J. Vincent, Chesley & Co., **III** 271
Burton, Parsons and Co. Inc., **II** 547
Burton Retail, **V** 21
Burton Rubber Processing, **8** 347
Burton Snowboards Inc., 22 118–20, 460
Burtons Gold Medal Biscuits Limited, **II** 466; **13** 53
Burwell Brick, **14** 248
Bury Group, **II** 581
Busch Entertainment Corporation, **34** 36
Bush Boake Allen Inc., IV 346; **30 92–94; 38** 247
Bush Brothers & Company, 45 71–73
Bush Hog, **21** 20–22
Bush Industries, Inc., 20 98–100
Bush Terminal Company, **15** 138
Business Communications Group, Inc. *See* Caribiner International, Inc.
Business Depot, Limited, **10** 498
Business Expansion Capital Corp., **12** 42
Business Express Airlines, Inc., **28** 22
Business Information Technology, Inc., **18** 112
Business Men's Assurance Company of America, III 209; **13** 476; **14 83–85; 15** 30
Business Objects S.A., 25 95–97
Business Post Group plc, 46 71–73
Business Resources Corp., **23** 489, 491
Business Science Computing, **14** 36
Business Software Association, **10** 35
Business Software Technology, **10** 394
Business Wire, **25** 240
Businessland Inc., **III** 153; **6** 267; **10** 235; **13** 175–76, 277, 482
Busse Broadcasting Corporation, **7** 200; **24** 199
Büssing Automobilwerke AG, **IV** 201
Buster Brown, **V** 351–52
BUT S.A., **24** 266, 270
Butano, **IV** 528
Butler Bros., **21** 96
Butler Cox PLC, **6** 229
Butler Group, Inc., **30** 310–11
Butler Manufacturing Co., 12 51–53; 43 130
Butler Shoes, **16** 560
Butterfield & Butterfield, **32** 162
Butterfield & Swire. *See* Swire Pacific Ltd.
Butterfield, Wasson & Co., **II** 380, 395; **10** 59; **12** 533
Butterick Co., Inc., 23 97–99
Butterley Company, **III** 501; **7** 207
Butterworth & Co. (Publishers) Ltd., **IV** 641; **7** 311; **17** 398
Buttrey Food & Drug Stores Co., 18 89–91

Butz Thermo-Electric Regulator Co., **II** 40; **12** 246
Buxton, **III** 28; **23** 21
buy.com, Inc., 46 74–77
Buzzard Electrical & Plumbing Supply, **9** 399; **16** 186
BVA Investment Corp., **11** 446–47
BVD, **25** 166
BWAY Corporation, 24 91–93
BWP Distributors, **29** 86, 88
Byerly's, Inc. *See* Lund Food Holdings, Inc.
Byers Machines, **21** 502
Byrnes Long Island Motor Cargo, Inc., **6** 370
Byron Jackson, **III** 428, 439. *See also* BJ Services Company.
Byron Weston Company, **26** 105
Bytrex, Inc., **III** 643

C&A, 40 74–77 (upd.)
C&A Brenninkmeyer KG, V 23–24
C&E Software, **10** 507
C.&E. Cooper Co., **II** 14
C & G Systems, **19** 442
C.&G. Cooper Company, **II** 14; **20** 162
C & H Distributors, Inc., **27** 177
C & O. *See* Chesapeake and Ohio Railway.
C&R Clothiers, **17** 313
C&S Bank, **10** 425–26
C&S Co., Ltd., **49** 425, 427
C&S/Sovran Corporation, **10** 425–27; **18** 518; **26** 453; **46** 52
C&W. *See* Cable and Wireless plc.
C-COR.net Corp., 38 118–21
C-Cube Microsystems, Inc., 37 50–54; 43 221–22
C.A. Delaney Capital Management Ltd., **32** 437
C.A. Pillsbury and Co., **II** 555
C.A. Reed Co., **IV** 353; **19** 498
C.A.S. Sports Agency Inc., **22** 460, 462
C.A. Swanson & Sons. *See* Vlasic Foods International Inc.
C. Bechstein, **III** 657
C. Brewer, **I** 417; **24** 32
C.D. Haupt, **IV** 296; **19** 226
C.D. Kenny Co., **II** 571
C.D. Magirus AG, **III** 541
C.E. Chappell & Sons, Inc., **16** 61–62
C.E.T. *See* Club Européen du Tourisme.
C.F. Burns and Son, Inc., **21** 154
C.F. Hathaway Company, **12** 522
C.F. Martin & Co., Inc., 42 55–58; 48 231
C.F. Mueller Co., **I** 497–98; **12** 332; **47** 234
C.F. Orvis Company. *See* The Orvis Company, Inc.
C. Francis, Son and Co., **III** 669
C.G. Conn, **7** 286
C.H. Boehringer Sohn, 39 70–73
C.H. Dexter & Co., **I** 320
C.H. Heist Corporation, 24 111–13
C.H. Knorr Company, **II** 497; **22** 83
C.H. Masland & Sons. *See* Masland Corporation.
C.H. Musselman Co., **7** 429
C.H. Robinson, Inc., 8 379–80; **11** 43–44; **23** 357
C.H. Robinson Worldwide, Inc., 40 78–81 (upd.)
C-I-L, Inc., **III** 745; **13** 470

C. Itoh & Co., I 431–33, 492, 510; **II** 273, 292, 361, 442, 679; **IV** 269, 326, 516, 543; **7** 529; **10** 500; **17** 124; **24** 324–25; **26** 456. *See also* ITOCHU Corporation.
C.J. Devine, **II** 425
C.J. Lawrence, Morgan Grenfell Inc., **II** 429
C.J. Smith and Sons, **11** 3
C.L. Bencard, **III** 66
C. Lee Cook Co., **III** 467
C.M. Aikman & Co., **13** 168
C.M. Armstrong, Inc., **14** 17
C.M. Barnes Company, **10** 135
C.M. Page, **14** 112
C-MAC Industries Inc., **48** 369
C.O. Lovette Company, **6** 370
C.O.M.B. Company, **18** 131–33
C/P Utility Services Company, **14** 138
C.P.U., Inc., **18** 111–12
C.R. Anthony Company, **24** 458
C.R. Bard Inc., IV 287; **9 96–98; 22** 360–61
C.R. Eggs, Inc., **25** 332
C. Reichenbach'sche Maschinenfabrik, **III** 561
C. Rowbotham & Sons, **III** 740
C.S. Rolls & Co., **I** 194
C.T. Bowring, **III** 280, 283; **22** 318
C-Tec Corp. *See* Commonwealth Telephone Enterprises, Inc.
C.V. Buchan & Co., **I** 567
C.V. Gebroeders Pel, **7** 429
C.V. Mosby Co., **IV** 677–78
C.W. Acquisitions, **27** 288
C.W. Costello & Associates Inc., **31** 131
C.W. Holt & Co., **III** 450
C.W. Zumbiel Company, **11** 422
C. Wuppesahl & Co. Assekuranzmakler, **25** 538
CAA. *See* Creative Artists Agency LLC.
Cabana (Holdings) Ltd., **44** 318
Cabela's Inc., 26 49–51
Cable & Wireless HKT, 30 95–98 (upd.). *See also* Hong Kong Telecomminications Ltd.
Cable and Wireless plc, IV 695; **V 283–86; 7** 332–33; **11** 547; **15** 69, 521; **17** 419; **18** 253; **25 98–102 (upd.); 26** 332; **27** 307; **49** 70, 73
Cable Communications Operations, Inc., **6** 313
Cable London, **25** 497
Cable Management Advertising Control System, **25** 497
Cable News Network, **II** 166–68; **6** 171–73; **9** 30; **12** 546
Cablec Corp., **III** 433–34
Cableform, **I** 592
Cabletron Systems, Inc., 10 193–94; 10 511; **20** 8; **24** 183; **26** 276
Cablevision Electronic Instruments, Inc., 32 105–07
Cablevision Systems Corporation, 7 63–65; 18 211; **30 99–103 (upd.)** 106; **47** 421. *See also* Cablevision Electronic Instruments, Inc.
Cabot, Cabot & Forbes, **22** 100
Cabot Corporation, 8 77–79; 29 79–82 (upd.)
Cabot Medical Corporation, **21** 117, 119
Cabot-Morgan Real Estate Co., **16** 159
Cabot Noble Inc., **18** 503, 507
Cabrera Vulcan Shoe Corp., **22** 213

Cache Incorporated, 30 104–06
CACI International Inc., 21 85–87
Cacique, 24 237
Cadadia, II 641–42
Cadbury Schweppes PLC, I 25–26, 220, 288; **II 476–78**, 510, 512, 592; **III** 554; **6** 51–52; **9** 178; **15** 221; **22** 513; **25** 3, 5; **39** 383, 385; **49 75–79 (upd.)**
CADCAM Technology Inc., 22 196
Caddell Construction Company, 12 41
Cademartori, 23 219
Cadence Design Systems, Inc., 6 247; **10** 118; **11 45–48**, 285, 490–91; **24** 235; **35** 346; **38** 188; **48 75–79 (upd.)**
Cadence Industries Corporation, 10 401–02
Cadet Uniform Services Ltd., 21 116
Cadillac Automobile Co., I 171; 10 325
Cadillac Fairview Corp., IV 703
Cadillac Plastic, 8 347
Cadisys Corporation, 10 119
Cadmus Communications Corporation, 16 531; **23 100–03**
Cadoricin, III 47
CAE USA Inc., 8 519; **48 80–82**
Caere Corporation, 20 101–03
Caesar-Wollheim-Gruppe, IV 197
Caesars World, Inc., 6 199–202; **17** 318
Caf'Casino, 12 152
Café Express, 47 443
Café Grand Mère, II 520
Caffarel, 27 105
CAFO, III 241
Cagiva Group, 17 24; **30** 172; **39** 37
Cagle's, Inc., 20 104–07
Cahners Business Information, 43 92–95
Cahners Publishing, IV 667; 12 561; 17 398; 22 442
CAI Corp., 12 79
Cailler, II 546
Cain Chemical, IV 481
Cains Marcelle Potato Chips Inc., 15 139
Caisse Commericale de Bruxelles, II 270
Caisse de dépôt et placement du Quebec, II 664
Caisse des Dépôts, 6 206
Caisse des Dépôts—Développement (C3D), 48 107
Caisse National de Crédit Agricole, II 264–66
Caisse Nationale de Crédit Agricole, 15 38–39
Caithness Glass Limited, 38 402
Caja General de Depositos, II 194
Cajun Bayou Distributors and Management, Inc., 19 301
Cajun Electric Power Cooperative, Inc., 21 470
CAK Universal Credit Corp., 32 80
CAL. See China Airlines.
Cal Circuit Abco Inc., 13 387
CAL Corporation, 21 199, 201
Cal-Dive International Inc., 25 104–05
Cal-Van Tools. See Chemi-Trol Chemical Co.
Cal/Ink, 13 228
Cala, 17 558
Calais Railroad Company, 16 348
Calavo Growers, Inc., 47 63–66
Calcined Coke Corp., IV 402
Calcitherm Group, 24 144
Calco, I 300–01
CalComp Inc., 13 126–29
Calcot Ltd., 33 84–87

Calculating-Tabulating-Recording Company. See International Business Machines Corporation.
Calcutta & Burmah Steam Navigation Co., III 521
Caldbeck Macgregor & Co., III 523
Calder Race Course, Inc., 29 118
Caldera Systems Inc., 38 416, 420
Caldor Inc., 12 54–56, 508; **30** 57
Caledonian Airways. See British Caledonian Airways.
Caledonian Bank, 10 337
Caledonian Paper plc, IV 302
Calédonickel, IV 107
Calgary Power Company. See TransAlta Utilities Corporation.
Calgene, Inc., 29 330; 41 155
Calgon Corporation, 6 27; 16 387; 34 281
Calgon Vestal Laboratories, 37 44
Calgon Water Management, 15 154; 40 176
Cali Realty. See Mack-Cali Realty Corporation.
California Arabian Standard Oil Co., IV 536, 552
California Automated Design, Inc., 11 284
California Bank, II 289
California Charter Inc., 24 118
California Cheese, 24 444
California Computer Products, Inc. See CalComp Inc.
California Cooler Inc., I 227, 244; 10 181
California Dental Supply Co., 19 289
California Design Studio, 31 52
California Federal Bank, 22 275
California First, II 358
California Fruit Growers Exchange. See Sunkist Growers, Inc.
California Ink Company, 13 227
California Institute of Technology, 9 367
California Insurance Co., III 234
California Oilfields, Ltd., IV 531, 540
California Pacific, 22 172
California Perfume Co., III 15
California Petroleum Co., IV 551–52
California Pizza Kitchen Inc., 15 74–76
California Plant Protection, 9 408
California Portland Cement Co., III 718; 19 69
California Pro Sports Inc., 24 404
California Slim, 27 197
California Steel Industries, IV 125
California Telephone and Light, II 490
California Test Bureau, IV 636
California Texas Oil Co., III 672
California Tile, III 673
California-Western States Life Insurance Co., III 193–94
California Woodfiber Corp., IV 266
Caligen, 9 92
Caligor. See Henry Schein Medical.
Call-Chronicle Newspapers, Inc., IV 678
Callaghan & Company, 8 526
Callard and Bowser, II 594
Callaway Golf Company, 15 77–79; **16** 109; **19** 430, 432; **23** 267, 474; **37** 4; **45 74–77 (upd.)**; **46** 13
Callaway Wines, I 264
Callebaut, II 520–21
Callender's Cable and Construction Co. Ltd., III 433–34
Callon Petroleum Company, 47 67–69
Calloway's Nursery Inc., 12 200
Calma, II 30; 12 196

Calmar Co., 12 127
CalMat Co., III 718; **19 69–72**
Calmic Ltd., I 715
Calor Group, IV 383
Caloric Corp., II 86
Calpine Corporation, 36 102–04
Calsil Ltd., III 674
Caltex Petroleum Corporation, II 53; **III** 672; **IV** 397, 434, 440–41, 479, 484, 492, 519, 527, 536, 545–46, 552, 560, 562, 718; **7** 483; **19 73–75**; **21** 204; **25** 471; **38** 320; **41** 392–93
Calumatic Group, 25 82
Calumet & Arizona Mining Co., IV 177
Calumet Electric Company, 6 532
Calvert & Co., I 293
Calvert Insurance Co. See Gryphon Holdings, Inc.
Calvin Bullock Ltd., I 472
Calvin Klein, Inc., 9 203; **22 121–24**; **25** 258; **27** 329; **32** 476
Calyx & Corolla Inc., 37 162–63
Camargo Foods, 12 531
Camas. See Aggregate Industries plc.
CamBar. See Cameron & Barkley Company.
Camber Corporation, 25 405
Cambex, 46 164
Cambrex Corporation, 12 147–48; **16** 67–69; **44 59–62 (upd.)**
Cambria Steel Company, IV 35; 7 48
Cambrian Wagon Works Ltd., 31 369
Cambridge Applied Nutrition Toxicology and Biosciences Ltd., 10 105
Cambridge Biotech Corp., 13 241
Cambridge Electric Co., 14 124, 126
Cambridge Gas Co., 14 124
The Cambridge Instrument Company, 35 272
Cambridge Interactive Systems Ltd., 10 241
Cambridge SoundWorks, 36 101; **Inc., 48 83–86**
Cambridge Steam Corp., 14 124
Cambridge Technology Partners, Inc., 36 105–08
Cambridge Tool & Mfg. Co. Inc., 48 268
Camco Inc., IV 658
Camden Wire Co., Inc., 7 408; 31 354–55
CAMECO, IV 436
Camelot Barthropp Ltd., 26 62
Camelot Group plc, 34 140
Camelot Music, Inc., 26 52–54
Cameron & Barkley Company, 13 79; **28 59–61**
Cameron Ashley Inc., 19 57
Cameron-Brown Company, 10 298
Cameron Iron Works, II 17
Cameron Oil Co., IV 365
CAMI Automotive, III 581
Camintonn, 9 41–42
Camp Manufacturing Co., IV 345; 8 102
Campbell Box & Tag Co., IV 333
Campbell Cereal Company. See Malt-O-Meal Company.
Campbell, Cowperthwait & Co., 17 498
Campbell-Ewald Co., I 16–17
Campbell Hausfeld. See Scott Fetzer Company.
Campbell Industries, Inc., 11 534
Campbell-Mithun-Esty, Inc., 13 516; **16 70–72**
Campbell Soup Company, I 21, 26, 31, 599, 601; **II 479–81**, 508, 684; **7 66–69**

(upd.), 340; **10** 382; **11** 172; **18** 58; **25** 516; **26 55–59 (upd.)**; **33** 32; **43** 121; **44** 295

Campbell Taggart, Inc., **I** 219; **19** 135–36, 191; **34** 36

Campeau Corporation, **IV** 721; **V 25–28**; **9** 209, 211, 391; **12** 36–37; **13** 43; **15** 94; **17** 560; **22** 110; **23** 60; **31** 192; **37** 13

Campo Electronics, Appliances & Computers, Inc., **16 73–75**

Campo Lindo, **25** 85

Campofrio Alimentacion, S.A., **18** 247

CAMPSA. *See* Compañia Arrendataria del Monopolio de Petróleos Sociedad Anónima.

Campus Services, Inc., **12** 173

Canada & Dominion Sugar Co., **II** 581

Canada Cable & Wire Company, **9** 11

Canada Cement, **III** 704–05

Canada Cup, **IV** 290

Canada Development Corp., **IV** 252; **17** 29

Canada Dry, **I** 281

Canada, Limited, **24** 143

Canada Packers Inc., **II 482–85**; **41** 249

Canada Safeway Ltd., **II** 650, 654

Canada Surety Co., **26** 486

Canada Trust. *See* CT Financial Services Inc.

Canada Tungsten Mining Corp., Ltd., **IV** 18

Canada Wire & Cable Company, Ltd., **IV** 164–65; **7** 397–99

Canadair, Inc., **I** 58; **7** 205; **13** 358; **16 76–78**

Canadian Ad-Check Services Inc., **26** 270

Canadian Airlines International Ltd., **6** 61–62, 101; **12** 192; **23** 10; **24** 400

Canadian Bank of Commerce, **II** 244–45

Canadian British Aluminum, **IV** 11

The Canadian Broadcasting Corporation (CBC), **37 55–58**

Canadian Cellucotton Products Ltd., **III** 40; **16** 302; **43** 256

Canadian Copper, **IV** 110

Canadian Copper Refiners, Ltd., **IV** 164

Canadian Dominion Steel and Coal Corp., **III** 508

Canadian Eastern Finance, **IV** 693

Canadian Fina Oil, **IV** 498

Canadian Football League, **12** 457

Canadian Forest Products, **IV** 270. *See also* Canfor Corporation.

Canadian Freightways, Ltd., **48** 113

Canadian Fuel Marketers, **IV** 566

Canadian General Electric Co., **8** 544–45

Canadian Government Merchant Marine, **6** 360–61

Canadian Gridoil Ltd., **IV** 373

Canadian Imperial Bank of Commerce, **II 244–46**; **IV** 693; **7** 26–28; **10** 8; **32** 12, 14

Canadian Industrial Alcohol Company Limited, **14** 141

Canadian International Paper Co., **IV** 286–87; **15** 228

Canadian Keyes Fibre Company, Limited of Nova Scotia, **9** 305

Canadian National Railway System, **I** 284; **6 359–62**; **12** 278–79; **22** 444; **23** 10

Canadian Niagara Power Company, **47** 137

Canadian Odeon Theatres, **6** 161; **23** 123

Canadian Overseas Telecommunications Corporation, **25** 100

Canadian Pacific Enterprises, **III** 611

Canadian Pacific Limited, **V 429–31**; **8** 544–46

Canadian Pacific Railway Limited, **I** 573; **II** 210, 220, 344; **III** 260; **IV** 272, 308, 437; **6** 359–60; **25** 230; **45 78–83 (upd.)**

Canadian Packing Co. Ltd., **II** 482

Canadian Petrofina, **IV** 498

Canadian Radio-Television and Telecommunications Commission, **6** 309

Canadian Steel Foundries, Ltd., **39** 31

Canadian Telephones and Supplies, **6** 310

Canadian Tire Corporation, Limited, **25** 144

Canadian Transport Co., **IV** 308

Canadian Utilities Limited, **13 130–32**

Canadian Vickers, **16** 76

Canal Bank, **11** 105

Canal Electric Co., **14** 125–26

Canal Plus, **III** 48; **7** 392; **10 195–97**, 345, 347; **23** 476; **29** 369, 371; **31** 330; **33** 181; **34 83–86 (upd.)**

CanalSatellite, **29** 369, 371

CanAmera Foods, **7** 82

Canandaigua Brands, Inc., **34 87–91 (upd.)**

Canandaigua Wine Company, Inc., **13 133–35**

Cananwill, **III** 344

Canary Wharf Group Plc, **30 107–09**

Candela Corporation, **48 87–89**

Candie's, Inc., **31 81–84**

Candle Corporation of America. *See* Blyth Industries, Inc.

Candlewood Hotel Company, Inc., **41 81–83**

Candy SpA, **22** 350

Canfor Corporation, **IV** 321; **17** 540; **42 59–61**

Cannell Communications, **25** 418

Cannon Assurance Ltd., **III** 276

Cannon Mills, Co., **9** 214–16

Cannondale Corporation, **16** 494; **21 88–90**; **26** 183, 412

Canon Inc., **I** 494; **II** 103, 292; **III** 120–21, 143, 172, 575, 583–84; **6** 238, 289; **9** 251; **10** 23; **13** 482; **15** 150; **18 92–95 (upd.)**, 186, 341–42, 383, 386–87; **24** 324; **26** 213; **33** 13; **43** 152, 283–84

Canpet Exploration Ltd., **IV** 566

Canpotex Ltd., **18** 432

Canrad-Hanovia, **27** 57

Cans Inc., **I** 607

Canstar Sports Inc., **15** 396–97; **16 79–81**

Canteen Corp., **I** 127; **II** 679–80; **12** 489; **13** 321

Cantel Corp., **11** 184; **18** 32; **20** 76; **30** 388

Canterbury Park Holding Corporation, **42 62–65**

Canterra Energy Ltd., **47** 180

Canton Chemical, **I** 323; **8** 147

Canton Railway Corp., **IV** 718; **38** 320

Cantor Fitzgerald Securities Corporation, **10** 276–78

CanWest Global Communications Corporation, **35 67–70**; **39** 13

Canyon Cafes, **31** 41

Cap Gemini Ernst & Young, **37 59–61**

Cap Rock Energy Corporation, **6** 580; **46 78–81**

Capacity of Texas, Inc., **33** 105–06

CAPCO. *See* Central Area Power Coordination Group *or* Custom Academic Publishing Company.

Capco Energy, Inc., **33** 296

Capcom Co., **7** 396

Cape and Vineyard Electric Co., **14** 124–25

Cape Cod-Cricket Lane, Inc., **8** 289

Cape Cod Potato Chip Company, Inc., **41** 233

Cape Horn Methanol, **III** 512

Cape May Light and Power Company, **6** 449

Cape PLC, **22** 49

Cape Wine and Distillers, **I** 289

Capel Incorporated, **45 84–86**

Capex, **6** 224

AB Capital & Investment Corporation, **6** 108; **23** 381

Capital Advisors, Inc., **22** 4

Capital Airlines, **I** 128; **III** 102; **6** 128

Capital and Counties Bank, **II** 307; **IV** 91

Capital Bank N.A., **16** 162

Capital Cities/ABC Inc., **II 129–31**; **III** 214; **IV** 608–09, 613, 652; **11** 331; **15** 464; **18** 60, 62–63, 329; **30** 490; **42** 31, 33–34. *See also* ABC, Inc.

Capital Concrete Pipe Company, **14** 250

Capital Controls Co., Inc. *See* Severn Trent PLC.

Capital Distributing Co., **21** 37

Capital Financial Services, **III** 242

Capital-Gazette Communications, Inc., **12** 302

Capital Grille, **19** 342

Capital Group, **26** 187

Capital Holding Corporation, **III 216–19**

Capital Life Insurance Company, **11** 482–83

Capital Management Services. *See* CB Commercial Real Estate Services Group, Inc.

Capital One, **18** 535

Capital Radio plc, **35 71–73**; **39** 199

Capital Trust Corp., **17** 498

Capitol-EMI, **I** 531–32; **11** 557

Capitol Film + TV International, **IV** 591

Capitol Films, **25** 270

Capitol Pack, Inc., **13** 350

Capitol Printing Ink Company, **13** 227–28

Capitol Publishing, **13** 560

Capitol Radio Engineering Institute, **IV** 636

Capitol Records, **22** 192–93

Capper Pass, **IV** 191

Capseals, Ltd., **8** 476

CapStar Hotel Company, **21 91–93**

Capsugel, **I** 712

Car-lac Electronic Industrial Sales Inc., **9** 420

Car-X, **10** 415

Caracas Petroleum Sociedad Anónima, **IV** 565–66

Caradco, Inc., **45** 216

Caradon plc, **18** 561; **20 108–12 (upd.)**. *See also* Novar plc.

Carando Foods, **7** 174–75

Carat Group, **6** 15–16

Caratti Sports, Ltd., **26** 184

Caraustar Industries, Inc., 19 76–78; **44** 63–67 (upd.)
Caravali, **13** 493–94
Caravelle Foods, **21** 500
The Carbide/Graphite Group, Inc., 40 82–84
Carbide Router Co., **III** 436
Carbis China Clay & Brick Co., **III** 690
Carbocol, **IV** 417
Carboline Co., **8** 455
CarboMedics, **11** 458–60
Carbon Research Laboratories, **9** 517
Carbone Lorraine S.A., 33 88–90
La Carbonique, **23** 217, 219
Carborundum Company, III 610; **15** 80–82
Cardàpio, **29** 444
Cardboard Containers, **IV** 249
Cardem Insurance Co., **III** 767; **22** 546
Cardiac Pacemakers, Inc., **I** 646; **11** 90; **11** 458; **22** 361
Cardinal Distributors Ltd., **II** 663
Cardinal Freight Carriers, Inc., **42** 365
Cardinal Health, Inc., 18 96–98
Cardiotronics Systems, Inc., **21** 47
Cardo, **49** 156
Cardon-Phonocraft Company, **18** 492
Care Advantage, Inc., **25** 383
Care Group, **22** 276
Career Education Corporation, 45 87–89
Career Horizons Inc., **49** 265
CareerCom Corp., **25** 253
CareerStaff Unlimited Inc., **25** 455
Caremark International Inc., 10 143, 198–200; **33** 185
Carenes, SA, **12** 377
CarePlus, **6** 42
CareUnit, Inc., **15** 123
CareWise, Inc., **36** 365, 367–68
Carey Canada Inc., **III** 766; **22** 546
Carey Diversified LLC. See W.P. Carey & Co. LLC.
Carey International, Inc., 26 60–63
Carey-McFall Corp., **V** 379; **19** 421
Carey Straw Mill, **12** 376
S.A. CARFUEL, **12** 152
Cargill, Incorporated, II 494, 517, 616–18; **11** 92; **13** 136–38 (upd.), 186, 351; **18** 378, 380; **21** 290, 500; **22** 85, 426; **25** 332; **31** 17, 20; **40** 85–90 (upd.); **41** 306
Cargill Trust Co., **13** 467
Cargo Express, **16** 198
Cargo Furniture, **31** 436
Cargolux Airlines International S.A., 47 287; **49** 80–82
CARGOSUR, **6** 96
Carhartt, Inc., 30 110–12
Cariani Sausage Co., **II** 518
Caribair, **I** 102
Caribbean Chemicals S.A., **I** 512
Caribe Co., **II** 493
Caribe Shoe Corp., **III** 529
Caribiner International, Inc., 24 94–97
Cariboo Pulp & Paper Co., **IV** 269
Caribou Coffee Company, Inc., 28 62–65
Carintusa Inc., **8** 271
CARIPLO, **III** 347
Carisam International Corp., **29** 511
Carita S.A., **III** 63; **22** 487
Caritas Foundation, **22** 411, 413
Carl Byoir & Associates, **I** 14

Carl Ed. Meyer GmbH, **48** 119
Carl I. Brown and Company, **48** 178
Carl Karcher Enterprises, Inc., **19** 435; **46** 94
Carl Marks & Co., **11** 260–61
Carl-Zeiss-Stiftung, III 445–47, 583; **33** 218; **34** 92–97 (upd.)
Carl's Jr. See CKE Restaurants, Inc.
Carl's Superstores, **9** 452
Carlan, **III** 614
Carless Lubricants, **IV** 451
Carleton Financial Computations Inc., **II** 317
Carlin Gold Mining Company, **7** 386–87
Carling O'Keefe Ltd., **I** 218, 229, 254, 269, 438–39; **7** 183; **12** 337; **26** 305
Carlingford, **II** 298
Carlisle Companies Incorporated, 8 80–82
Carlisle Memory Products, **14** 535
Carlo Erba S.p.A., **I** 635
Carlon, **13** 304–06
Carlova, Inc., **21** 54
Carlsberg A/S, I 247; **9** 99–101; **29** 83–85 (upd.)
Carlson Companies, Inc., 6 363–66; **22** 125–29 (upd.); **26** 147, 439–40; **27** 9, 11; **29** 200; **38** 387
Carlton and United Breweries Ltd., I 228–29, 437–39; **7** 182–83
Carlton Cards, **39** 87
Carlton Communications plc, 15 83–85; **23** 111, 113; **24** 194
Carlton Investments L.P., **22** 514
The Carlyle Group, **11** 364; **14** 43; **16** 47; **21** 97; **30** 472; **43** 60; **49** 444
CarMax, **26** 410; **29** 120, 123
Carmeda AB, **10** 439
Carmichael Lynch Inc., 28 66–68
Carmike Cinemas, Inc., 14 86–88; **21** 362; **37** 62–65 (upd.)
Carmine's Prime Meats, Inc., **35** 84
Carnation Company, I 269; **II** 486–89, 518, 548; **7** 339, 383, 429; **10** 382; **12** 337; **28** 311
Carnaud Basse-Indre, **IV** 228
Carnaud MetalBox, **13** 190; **20** 111; **32** 125–26; **49** 295
Carnegie Brothers & Co., Ltd., **9** 407
Carnegie Corporation of New York, 35 74–77; **45** 403–05
Carnegie Foundation for the Advancement of Teaching, **12** 141
Carnegie Group, **41** 371–72
Carnegie Steel Co., **II** 330; **IV** 572; **7** 549; **35** 74
Carnival Corporation, 27 90–92 (upd.); **36** 194
Carnival Cruise Lines, Inc., 6 367–68; **21** 106; **22** 444–46, 470; **27** 27
Caro Produce and Institutional Foods, **31** 359–61
Carol-Braugh-Robinson Co., **II** 624
Carol Moberg, Inc., **6** 40
Carol's Shoe Corp., **22** 213
Carolco Pictures Inc., **III** 48; **10** 196
Carolina Biological Supply, **11** 424
Carolina Coach Co., **13** 397–98
Carolina Coin Caterers Corporation, **10** 222
Carolina Energies, Inc., **6** 576
Carolina First Corporation, 31 85–87
Carolina First National, **II** 336
Carolina Freight Corporation, 6 369–72

Carolina Paper Board Corporation. See Caraustar Industries, Inc.
Carolina Power & Light Company, V 564–66; **23** 104–07 (upd.)
Carolina Telephone and Telegraph Company, 10 201–03
Carolinas Capital Funds Group, **29** 132
Carolinas-Virginia Nuclear Power Association, **27** 130
Carpenter Investment and Development Corporation, **31** 279
Carpenter Paper Co., **IV** 282; **9** 261
Carpenter Technology Corporation, 13 139–41
CarpetMAX, **25** 320
Carpets International Plc., **8** 270–71
CARQUEST Corporation, 26 348; **29** 86–89
Carr Fowler, **III** 673
Carr-Gottstein Foods Co., 17 77–80
Carr-Lowrey Glass Co., **13** 40
Carr-Union Line, **6** 397
Carr's of Carlisle, **I** 604; **II** 594
Carrabba's Italian Grill, **12** 373–75
Carre Orban International, **34** 248
Carrefour SA, II 628; **8** 404–05; **10** 204–06; **12** 153; **19** 98, 309; **21** 225; **23** 230–32, 246–47, 364; **24** 475; **27** 207, 93–96 (upd.); **34** 198; **37** 21, 23
Carreras, Limited, **V** 411–12; **19** 367–69
Carriage Services, Inc., 37 66–68
Carrier Access Corporation, 44 68–73
Carrier Corporation, I 85; **III** 329; **7** 70–73; **13** 507; **22** 6; **26** 4; **29** 216
Carrington Laboratories, **33** 282
Carrington Viyella, **44** 105
Carroll County Electric Company, **6** 511
Carroll Reed Ski Shops, Inc., **10** 215
Carroll's Foods, Inc., 7 477; **22** 368; **43** 382; **46** 82–85
Carrows, **27** 16, 19
Carry Machine Supply, Inc., **18** 513
The Carsey-Werner Company, L.L.C., 37 69–72
Carsmart.com, **47** 34
Carso Global Telecom S.A. de C.V., **34** 362
Carson, Inc., 31 88–90; **46** 278
Carson Pirie Scott & Company, II 669; **9** 142; **15** 86–88; **19** 324, 511–12; **41** 343–44
Carson Water Company, **19** 411
CART. See Championship Auto Racing Teams, Inc.
Carte Blanche, **9** 335
CarTemps USA. See Republic Industries, Inc.
Carter & Co., **IV** 644
Carter Automotive Co., **I** 159
Carter, Berlind, Potoma & Weill, **II** 450
Carter Hawley Hale Stores, I 246; **V** 29–32; **8** 160; **12** 356; **15** 88; **16** 466; **17** 43, 523; **18** 488; **25** 177
Carter Holt Harvey Ltd., **IV** 280; **15** 229; **19** 155
Carter Lumber Company, 45 90–92
Carter Oil Company, **IV** 171; **11** 353
Carter-Wallace, Inc., 6 27; **8** 83–86; **38** 122–26 (upd.)
Carteret Savings Bank, **III** 263–64; **10** 340
Carterphone, **22** 17
Cartier, **27** 329, 487–89
Cartier Monde, IV 93; **V** 411, 413; **29** 90–92

Cartier Refined Sugars Ltd., **II** 662–63
Cartiera F.A. Marsoni, **IV** 587
Cartiere Ascoli Piceno, **IV** 586
Cartiers Superfoods, **II** 678
Cartillon Importers, Ltd., **6** 48
Carton Titan S.A. de C.V., **37** 176–77
Cartotech, Inc., **33** 44
Carvel Corporation, **35** 78–81
Carver Pump Co., **19** 36
Carworth Inc., **I** 630; **11** 34
Cary-Davis Tug and Barge Company. *See* Puget Sound Tug and Barge Company.
CASA. *See* Construcciones Aeronautics S.A.
Casa Bancária Almeida e Companhia. *See* Banco Bradesco S.A.
Casa Bonita, **II** 587
Casa Cuervo, S.A. de C.V., **31** 91–93
Casa Ley, S.A. de C.V., **24** 416
Casa Saba. *See* Grupo Casa Saba, S.A. de C.V.
Casablanca Records, **23** 390
Casalee, Inc., **48** 406
Casarotto Security, **24** 510
Cascade Communications Corp., **16** 468; **20** 8; **24** 50
Cascade Fertilizers Ltd., **25** 232
Cascade Fiber, **13** 99
Cascade Lumber Co., **IV** 255; **8** 65
Cascade Natural Gas Corporation, **6** 568; **9** 102–04
Cascade Steel Rolling Mills, Inc., **19** 380–81
CasChem, Inc. *See* Cambrex Corporation.
Casco Northern Bank, **14** 89–91
Casden Properties, **49** 26
Case Corporation. *See* CNH Global N.V.
Case Manufacturing Corp., **I** 512
Case, Pomeroy & Co., Inc., **IV** 76
Case Technologies, Inc., **11** 504
Casein Co. of America, **II** 471
Casey's General Stores, Inc., **19** 79–81
Cash America International, Inc., **20** 113–15; **33** 4
Cash Wise Foods and Liquor, **30** 133
Casino, **10** 205; **23** 231; **26** 160; **27** 93–94
Casino. *See* Etablissements Economiques de Casino Guichard, Perrachon et Cie, S.C.A.
Casino America, Inc. *See* Isle of Capri Casinos, Inc., **41** 218
Casino Frozen Foods, Inc., **16** 453
Casino Guichard S.A., **37** 23
Casino S.A., **22** 515
Casino USA, **16** 452
Casinos International Inc., **21** 300
CASIO Computer Co., Ltd., **III** 448–49, 455; **IV** 599; **10** 57; **16** 82–84 (upd.); **21** 123; **26** 18; **40** 91–95 (upd.)
Caspian Pipeline Consortium, **47** 75
Cassa Generale Ungherese di Risparmio, **III** 207
Cassady Broiler Co., **II** 585
Cassandra Group, **42** 272
Cassatt, **II** 424
Cassco Ice & Cold Storage, Inc., **21** 534–35
CAST Inc., **18** 20; **43** 17
Cast-Matic Corporation, **16** 475
Castex, **13** 501
Castings, Inc., **29** 98
Castle & Cooke, Inc., **I** 417; **II** 490–92; **9** 175–76; **10** 40; **20** 116–19 (upd.); **24**

32, 115. *See also* Dole Food Company, Inc.
Castle Brewery, **I** 287
Castle Cement, **31** 400
Castle Communications plc, **17** 13
Castle Harlan Investment Partners III, **36** 468; **47**
Castle Rock Pictures, **23** 392
Castle Rubber Co., **17** 371
Castle Tretheway Mines Ltd., **IV** 164
Castlemaine Tooheys, **10** 169–70
Castorama S.A., **37** 258–60. *See also* Groupe Castorama-Dubois Investissements.
Castro Convertibles. *See* Krause's Furniture, Inc.
Castrol Ltd., **IV** 382–83
Castrorama, **10** 205; **27** 95
Casual Corner Group, Inc., **V** 207–08; **25** 121; **43** 96–98
CAT Scale Company, **49** 329–30
Catalina Lighting, Inc., **43** 99–102 (upd.)
Catalina Marketing Corporation, **18** 99–102
Catalogue Marketing, Inc., **17** 232
Catalyst Telecom, **29** 414–15
Catalytica Energy Systems, Inc., **44** 74–77
Catamaran Cruisers, **29** 442
Catamount Petroleum Corp., **17** 121
Cataract, Inc., **34** 373
CATCO. *See* Crowley All Terrain Corporation.
Catellus Development Corporation, **24** 98–101; **27** 88
Caterair International Corporation, **16** 396
Caterpillar Inc., **I** 147, 181, 186, 422; **III** 450–53, 458, 463, 545–46; **9** 310; **10** 274, 377, 381, 429; **11** 473; **12** 90; **13** 513; **15** 89–93 (upd.), 225; **16** 180, 309–10; **18** 125; **19** 293; **21** 173, 499–501, 503; **22** 542; **34** 44, 46–47
Cathay Insurance Co., **III** 221; **14** 109
Cathay Pacific Airways Limited, **I** 522; **II** 298; **6** 71, 78–80; **16** 480–81; **18** 114–15; **34** 98–102 (upd.)
Catherines Stores Corporation, **15** 94–97; **38** 129
Cathodic Protection Services Co., **14** 325
Catholic Digest, **49** 48
Catholic Order of Foresters, **24** 102–05
CatiCentre Ltd. Co, **48** 224
Cato Corporation, **14** 92–94
Cato Oil and Grease Company, **IV** 446; **22** 302
Catteau S.A., **24** 475
Cattleman's, Inc., **20** 120–22
Cattybrook Brick Company, **14** 249
CATV, **10** 319
Caudill Rowlett Scott. *See* CRSS Inc.
Caudle Engraving, **12** 471
CAV, **III** 554–55
Cavallo Pipeline Company, **11** 441
Cavedon Chemical Co., **I** 341
Cavendish International Holdings, **IV** 695
Cavendish Land, **III** 273
Cavenham Ltd., **7** 202–03; **28** 163
Caves Altovisto, **22** 344
Caves de Roquefort, **19** 51; **24** 445
Cawoods Holdings, **III** 735
Caxton Holdings, **IV** 641
CB Commercial Real Estate Services Group, Inc., **21** 94–98
CB&I, **7** 76–77

CB&Q. *See* Chicago, Burlington and Quincy Railroad Company.
CB&T. *See* Synovus Financial Corp.
CBC Film Sales Co., **II** 135
CBE Technologies Inc., **39** 346
CBI Industries, Inc., **7** 74–77; **22** 228; **48** 323
CBM Realty Corp., **III** 643
CBN Cable Network, **13** 279–81
CBN Satellite Services, **13** 279
CBOT. *See* Chicago Board of Trade.
CBR-HCI Construction Materials Corp., **31** 253
CBRL Group, Inc., **35** 82–85 (upd.)
CBS Corporation, **28** 69–73 (upd.); **30** 269, 272
CBS Inc., **I** 29, 488; **II** 61, 89, 102–03, 129–31, **132–34**, 136, 152, 166–67; **III** 55, 188; **IV** 605, 623, 652, 675, 703; **6** **157–60** (upd.); **11** 327; **12** 75, 561; **16** 201–02; **17** 150, 182; **19** 210, 426, 428; **21** 24; **24** 516–17; **25** 330, 418; **26** 102; **36** 326; **43** 170–71
CBS.MarketWatch.com, **49** 290
CBS Musical Instruments, **16** 201–02; **43** 170–71
CBS Radio Group, **37** 192; **48** 217
CBS Records, **II** 103, 134, 177; **6** 159; **22** 194; **23** 33; **28** 419; **40** 406
CBSI. *See* Complete Business Solutions, Inc.
CBT Corp., **II** 213–14
CBW Inc., **42** 129
CBWL-Hayden Stone, **II** 450
CC Beverage Corporation, **48** 97
CC Soft Drinks Ltd., **I** 248
cc:Mail, Inc., **25** 300
CCA. *See* Container Corporation of America *and* Corrections Corporation of America.
CCAir Inc., **11** 300
CCB Financial Corp., **33** 293
CCC Franchising Corporation. *See* Primedex Health Systems, Inc.
CCG. *See* The Clark Construction Group, Inc.
CCH Computax, **7** 93–94
CCH Inc., **7** 93; **14** 95–97; **33** 461
CCI Asia-Pacific Ltd., **27** 362
CCI Electronique, **10** 113
CCL Industries, Ltd., **15** 129
CCM Inc. *See* The Hockey Company.
CCM Sport Maska, Inc., **15** 396
CCN Group Ltd., **45** 154
CCP Insurance, Inc., **10** 248
CCR, Inc. *See* Rica Foods, Inc.
CCS Automation Systems Inc., **I** 124
CCT. *See* Crowley Caribbean Transport.
CD Titles, Inc., **22** 409
CDC. *See* Canada Development Corporation *or* Control Data Corporation.
CdF-Chimie, **I** 303; **IV** 174, 198, 525
CDG Books Canada Inc., **27** 224
CDI. *See* Centre de Dechets Industriels Group.
CDI Corporation, **6** 139–41
CDMS. *See* Credit and Data Marketing Services.
CDR. *See* Consortium de Realisation.
CDR International, **13** 228
CDS Holding Corp., **22** 475
CDW Computer Centers, Inc., **16** 85–87
CDX Audio Development, Inc., **18** 208

CE-Minerals, **IV** 109
CEAG AG, **23** 498
Ceat Ltd., **III** 434; **20** 263
CEC Entertainment, Inc., 31 94–98 (upd.)
Ceco Doors, **8** 544–46
Ceco Industries, Inc. *See* Robertson-Ceco Corporation.
CeCorr Inc., **47** 149
CECOS International, Inc., **V** 750
Cedar Engineering, **III** 126
Cedar Fair, L.P., 22 130–32
Cedarapids, Inc., **11** 413; **38** 374, 376; **40** 432
Cedec S.A., **14** 43
Cederroth International AB, **8** 17; **36** 25–26
CEDIS, **12** 153
Cedric Chivers, **35** 243–44
Cegedur, **IV** 174
Cegetel SA, **38** 300
CEIR, **10** 255
Celadon Group Inc., 30 113–16
Celanese Corp., **I** 317–19, 347; **19** 192. *See also* Hoechst Celanese Corporation.
Celebrity Entertainment, Inc., **27** 43
Celebrity, Inc., 22 133–35, 472
Celeron Corporation, **20** 258, 262–63
Celestial Farms, **13** 383
Celestial Seasonings, Inc., II 534; **16** 88–91; **49** 336. *See also* The Hain Celestial Group, Inc.
Celestron International, **41** 262–63
Celfor Tool Company. *See* Clark Equipment Company.
Celite Corporation, **III** 706; **7** 291; **10** 43, 45
Cell-Tel Monitoring, Inc., **46** 386
Cella Italian Wines, **10** 181
CellAccess Technology, Inc., **25** 162
CellLife International, **49** 280
Cellnet Data Systems, **11** 547; **22** 65
Cellonit-Gesellschaft Dreyfus & Cie., **I** 317
Cellstar Corporation, **18** 74
Cellu-Products Co., **14** 430
Cellular America, **6** 300
Cellular One, **9** 321
Cellular 2000. *See* Rural Cellular Corporation.
CellularOne. *See* Rural Cellular Corporation.
CellularVision, **13** 399
Cellulosa d'Italia, **IV** 272
Cellulose & Chemical Manufacturing Co., **I** 317
Cellulose & Specialties, **8** 434
Cellulose du Pin, **III** 677, 704; **16** 121–22; **19** 226–27
Celotex Corporation, **III** 766–67; **22** 545
Celsius Energy Company, **6** 569
Celtex **I** 388–89. *See also* Pricel.
Cement Products, **46** 196
Cementia, **III** 705
Cementos Portland Moctezuma, **21** 261
Cementownia Chelm, **31** 398, 400
Cemex SA de CV, 20 123–26
Cemij, **IV** 132
Cemp Investments Ltd., **16** 79–80
Cemsto, **13** 545
CenCall Communications, **10** 433
Cenco, Inc., **6** 188; **10** 262–63; **25** 308; **35** 135
Cencor, **25** 432
Cendant Corporation, **48** 234–35

Cendant Corporation, 41 363; **44 78–84 (upd.)**
Cenex Cooperative, **21** 342
Cenex Inc., **II** 536; **19** 160
Cengas, **6** 313
Centaur Communications, **43** 204, 206
Centel Corporation, 6 312–15, 593; **9** 106, 480; **10** 203; **14** 258; **16** 318; **17** 7
Centennial Communications Corporation, 39 74–76
Centennial Technologies Inc., **48** 369
Center Co., Ltd., **48** 182
Center Rental & Sales Inc., **28** 387
Centerior Energy Corporation, V 567–68
Centerra Corporation, **24** 79
Centertel, **18** 33
Centex Corporation, 8 87–89, 461; **11** 302; **23** 327; **29 93–96 (upd.)**
Centocor Inc., 14 98–100; **36** 306
CentraBank, **II** 337; **10** 426
Central Alloy Steel Corporation. *See* Republic Engineered Steels, Inc.
Central and South West Corporation, V 569–70; **21** 197–98; **45** 21
Central Area Power Coordination Group, **V** 677
Central Arizona Light & Power Company, **6** 545
Central Asia Gas Pipeline Ltd., **24** 522
Central Bancorp of Cincinnati, **II** 342
Central Bank for Railway Securities, **II** 281
Central Bank of Italy, **II** 403
Central Bank of London, **II** 318; **17** 323
Central Bank of Oman, **IV** 516
Central Bank of Scotland, **10** 337
Central Coalfields Ltd., **IV** 48–49
Central Computer Systems Inc., **11** 65
Central Covenants, **II** 222
Central Detallista, S.A. de C.V., **12** 154; **16** 453
Central Electric & Gas Company. *See* Centel Corporation.
Central Electric and Telephone Company, Inc. *See* Centel Corporation.
Central Elevator Co., **19** 111
Central Fiber Products Company, **12** 376
Central Finance Corporation of Canada, **II** 418; **21** 282
Central Florida Press, **23** 101
Central Foam Corp., **I** 481, 563; **16** 322
Central Garden & Pet Company, 23 108–10
Central Hankyu Ltd., **V** 71
Central Hardware, **III** 530
Central Hudson Gas And Electricity Corporation, 6 458–60
Central Illinois Public Service Company. *See* CIPSCO Inc.
Central Independent Television, 7 78–80; **15** 84; **23 111–14 (upd.)**
Central India Spinning, Weaving and Manufacturing Co., **IV** 217
Central Indiana Power Company, **6** 556
Central Investment Corp., **12** 184
Central Japan Heavy Industries, **III** 578–79; **7** 348
Central Japan Railway Company, 43 103–06
Central Maine Power, 6 461–64; **14** 126
Central Maloney Transformer, **I** 434
Central Mining and Investment Corp., **IV** 23, 79, 95–96, 524, 565

Central National Bank, **9** 475
Central National Bank & Trust Co., **13** 467
Central National Life Insurance Co., **III** 463; **21** 174
Central Nebraska Packing, **10** 250
Central Newspapers, Inc., 10 207–09
Central Pacific Railroad, **II** 381; **13** 372
Central Park Bank of Buffalo, **11** 108
Central Parking Corporation, 18 103–05
Central Penn National Corp., **11** 295
Central Planning & Design Institute, **IV** 48
Central Point Software, **10** 509
Central Public Service Corporation, **6** 447; **23** 28
Central Public Utility Corp., **13** 397
Central Research Laboratories, **22** 194
Central Savings and Loan, **10** 339
Central Solvents & Chemicals Company, **8** 100
Central Songs, **22** 193
Central Soya Company, Inc., 7 81–83; **31** 20; **36** 185, 187
Central Sprinkler Corporation, 29 97–99
Central States Indemnity, **18** 62
Central Supply Company. *See* Granite Rock Company.
Central Telephone & Utilities Corporation. *See* Centel Corporation.
Central Terminal Company, **6** 504
Central Textile, **16** 36
Central Transformer, **I** 434
Central Trust Co., **II** 313; **11** 110
Central Union Telephone Company, **14** 251, 257
Central Union Trust Co. of New York, **II** 313
Central West Public Service Company. *See* Centel Corporation.
Centralab Inc., **13** 398
Centrale Verzorgingsdienst Cotrans N.V., **12** 443
Centran Corp., **9** 475
Centre de Dechets Industriels Group, **IV** 296; **19** 226
Centre Investissements et Loisirs, **48** 107
Centre Lait, **II** 577
Centre Partners Management LLC, **18** 355; **24** 482
Centrica plc, 29 100–05 (upd.)
Centron DPL Company, Inc., **25** 171
Centronics Corp., **16** 192
Centros Commerciales Pryca, **23** 246, 248
Centrum Communications Inc., **11** 520
CenTrust Federal Savings, **10** 340
Centura Software, **10** 244
Centurion Brick, **14** 250
Century Bakery. *See* Dawn Food Products, Inc.
Century Bank, **II** 312
Century Brewing Company. *See* Rainier Brewing Company.
Century Cellular Network, Inc., **18** 74
Century Communications Corp., 10 210–12
Century Data Systems, Inc., **13** 127
Century Electric Company, **13** 273
Century Finance, **25** 432
Century Hutchinson, Ltd., **13** 429
Century Manufacturing Company, **26** 363
Century Papers, Inc., **16** 387
Century Savings Assoc. of Kansas, **II** 420
Century Supply Corporation, **39** 346

Century Telephone Enterprises, Inc., 9 105–07
Century Theatres, Inc., 31 99–101
Century Tool Co., **III** 569; **20** 360
Century 21 Real Estate, **I** 127; **II** 679; **III** 293; **11** 292; **12** 489; **21** 97; **25** 444
CEPA. *See* Consolidated Electric Power Asia.
CEPAM, **21** 438
CEPCO. *See* Chugoku Electric Power Company Inc.
Cephalon, Inc., 45 93–96
CEPSA. *See* Compañia Española de Petroleos S.A.
Cera Trading Co., **III** 756
Ceramesh, **11** 361
Ceramic Art Company, **12** 312
Ceramic Supply Company, **8** 177
Cerberus Limited, **6** 490
Cereal and Fruit Products, **32** 519
Cereal Industries, **II** 466
Cereal Packaging, Ltd., **13** 294
Cereal Partners Worldwide, **10** 324; **13** 294; **36** 234, 237
Cerebos, **II** 565
Cereol, **36** 185
Cerestar, **36** 185, 187
Ceresucre, **36** 185
Cerex, **IV** 290
Ceridian Corporation, **10** 257; **38** 58
Cermalloy, **IV** 100
Cerner Corporation, 16 92–94
Cerro Corp., **IV** 11, 136
Cerro de Pasco Corp., **IV** 33; **40** 411
Cerro Metal Products Company, **16** 357
CertainTeed Corporation, III 621, 677–78, 762; **16** 8, 121–22; **19** 58; **35** **86–89**
Certanium Alloys and Research Co., **9** 419
Certified Grocers of Florida, Inc., **15** 139
Certified Laboratories, **8** 385
Certified TV and Appliance Company, **9** 120
Certus International Corp., **10** 509
Cerus, **23** 492
Cerveceria Cuahtémoc Moctezuma, **25** 281
Cerveceria Cuauhtemoc, **19** 10
Cerveceria Moctezuma, **23** 170
Cerveceria Polar, I 230–31
Cessna Aircraft Company, III 512; **8** 49–51, 90–93, 313–14; **26** 117; **27** **97–101 (upd.); 34** 431, 433; **36** 190; **44** 309
CET. *See* Compagnie Européenne de Télésecurité.
Cetelem S.A., 21 99–102
Cetus Corp., **I** 637; **III** 53; **7** 427; **10** 78, 214; **41** 201
CF AirFreight, **6** 390; **25** 149
CF Braun, **13** 119
CF Holding Corporation, **12** 71
CF Industries, **IV** 576
CF&I Steel Corporation, **8** 135
CFC Investment Company, **16** 104
CFM. *See* Compagnie Française du Méthane.
CFP. *See* Compagnie Française des Pétroles.
CFS Continental, Inc., **II** 675; **26** 504
CG&E. *See* Cincinnati Gas & Electric Company.
CGCT, **I** 563
CGE. *See* Alcatel Alsthom.
CGM. *See* Compagnie Générale Maritime.

CGR-MeV, **III** 635
Chace Precision Metals, Inc., **29** 460–61
Chaco Energy Corporation, **V** 724–25
Chadbourne & Parke, 36 109–12
Chadwick's of Boston, Ltd., V 197–98; **27** 348; **29 106–08**
Chalet Suisse International, Inc., **13** 362
Chalk's International Airlines, **12** 420
Challenge Corp. Ltd. *See* Fletcher Challenge Ltd.
Challenger Airlines, **22** 219
Challenger Minerals Inc., **9** 267
The Chalone Wine Group, Ltd., 36 **113–16**
Chamberlain Group, Ltd., **23** 82
Chambers Corporation, **8** 298; **17** 548–49
Chambosse Brokerage Co., **29** 33
Champ Industries, Inc., **22** 15
Champalimaud, **36** 63
Champcork–Rolhas de Champanhe SA, **48** 118
Champion Engineering Co., **III** 582
Champion Enterprises, Inc., 17 81–84; **22** 207
Champion Forge Co., **41** 366
Champion, Inc., **8** 459; **12** 457
Champion Industries, Inc., 28 74–76
Champion International Corporation, **III** 215; **IV** 263–65, 334; **12** 130; **15** 229; **18** 62; **20 127–30 (upd.); 22** 352; **26** 444; **47** 189, 191
Champion Modular Restaurant Company, Inc. *See* Checkers Drive-Up Restaurants Inc.
Champion Products Inc., **27** 194
Champion Spark Plug Co., **II** 17; **III** 593
Champion Valley Farms, **II** 480; **26** 56
Championship Auto Racing Teams, Inc., **37 73–75**
Champlin Petroleum Company, **10** 83
Champps Americana, **27** 480–82
Champs Sports, **14** 293, 295. *See also* Venator Group Inc.
Chance Bros., **III** 724–27
Chance Vought Aircraft Co., **I** 67–68, 84–85, 489–91
Chancellor Media Corporation, 24 **106–10; 35** 247
Chancery Law Publishing Ltd., **17** 272
Chanco Medical Industries, **III** 73
Chandeleur Homes, Inc., **17** 83
The Chandris Group, **11** 377
Chanel SA, 12 57–59; 23 241; **49 83–86** **(upd.)**
Changchun Terumo Medical Products Co. Ltd., **48** 395
Channel Master Corporation, **II** 91; **15** 134
Channel One Communications Corp., **22** 442
Channel Tunnel Group, **13** 206
Chansam Investments, **23** 388
Chantex Inc., **18** 519
Chantiers de l'Atlantique, **9** 9
Chaparral Steel Co., 8 522–24; **13** **142–44; 18** 379; **19** 380
Chapman Printing Company. *See* Champion Industries, Inc.
Chapman Valve Manufacturing Company, **8** 135
Chappel Music, **23** 389
Charan Industries Inc., **18** 519
Charan Toy Co., Inc., **18** 519
Chargeurs International, 6 373–75, 379; **20** 79; **21 103–06 (upd.); 29** 369, 371

Charise Charles Ltd., **9** 68
Charisma Communications, **6** 323
Charles A. Eaton Co., **III** 24
Charles B. Perkins Co., **II** 667; **24** 461
Charles Barker, plc, **25** 91
Charles D. Burnes Co., Inc. *See* The Holson Burnes Group, Inc.
Charles E. Smith Residential Realty Inc., **49** 29
Charles Hobson, **6** 27
Charles Huston & Sons, **14** 323
Charles Luckman Assoc., **I** 513
Charles M. Schulz Creative Associates, **39** 95
Charles of the Ritz Group Ltd., **I** 695–97; **III** 56; **23** 237
Charles Pfizer Co., **I** 96
Charles Phillips & Co. Ltd., **II** 677
Charles R. McCormick Lumber Company, **12** 407
Charles River Laboratories **International, Inc., 25** 55; **42 66–69**
The Charles Schwab Corporation, II 228; **8 94–96; 18** 552; **22** 52; **26 64–67** **(upd.); 34** 407; **38** 430
Charles Scribner's Sons, **7** 166
The Charles Stark Draper Laboratory, **Inc., 35 90–92**
Charlesbank Capital Partners LLC, **44** 54
Charleston Consolidated Railway, Gas and Electric Company, **6** 574
Charlestown Foundry, **III** 690
Charley Brothers, **II** 669
Charley's Eating & Drinking Saloon, **20** 54
Charlie Browns, **24** 269–70
Charlotte Russe Holding, Inc., 35 93–96
Charmin Paper Co., **III** 52; **IV** 329; **8** 433; **26** 383
Charming Shoppes, Inc., 8 97–98; 38 **127–29; 39** 287, 289
Charrington & Co., **I** 223
Charrington United Breweries, **38** 76
Chart House Enterprises, Inc., II 556, 613–14; **17** 70, 71, **85–88**
Chart Industries, Inc., 21 107–09
Charter Bank, **II** 348
Charter Club, **9** 315
Charter Communications, Inc., 33 91–94
Charter Consolidated, **IV** 23, 119–20; **16** 293; **49** 234
Charter Corp., **III** 254; **14** 460
Charter Golf, Inc. *See* Ashworth, Inc.
Charter Medical Corporation, **31** 356
Charter National Life Insurance Company, **11** 261
Charter Oil Co., **II** 620; **12** 240
Charter Security Life Insurance Cos., **III** 293
Chartered Bank, **II** 357
Chartered Co. of British New Guinea, **III** 698
Chartered Mercantile Bank of India, London and China, **II** 298
Charterhouse Japhet, **24** 269
Charterhouse Petroleum, **IV** 499
ChartHouse International Learning **Corporation, 49 87–89**
Chartwell Associates, **III** 16; **9** 331
Chartwell Investments, **44** 54
Chartwell Land plc, **V 106; 24** 266, 269
Chas. A. Stevens & Co., **IV** 660
Chas. H. Tompkins Co., **16** 285–86
Chase & Sanborn, **II** 544
Chase Corp., **II** 402

Chase Drier & Chemical Co., **8** 177
Chase, Harris, Forbes, **II** 402
The Chase Manhattan Corporation, **I**
    123, 334, 451; **II** 202, 227, **247–49**,
    256–57, 262, 286, 317, 385, 397, 402;
    III 104, 248; **IV** 33; **6** 52; **9** 124; **10** 61;
    13 145–48 (upd.), 476; **14** 48, 103; **15**
    38–39; **16** 460; **17** 498; **23** 482; **36** 358;
    46 316. See J.P. Morgan Chase & Co.
Chase National Bank, **25** 114
Chastain-Roberts Company, **II** 669; **18** 504
Chaston Medical & Surgical Products, **13**
    366
Chateau Cheese Co. Ltd., **II** 471
Chateau Communities, Inc., **37 76–79**
Chateau Grower Winery Co., **II** 575
Chateau St. Jean, **22** 80
Chateau Souverain, **22** 80
Chateau Ste. Michelle Winery, **42** 245, 247
Chateaux St. Jacques, **24** 307
Chatfield & Woods Co., **IV** 311; **19** 267
Chatfield Paper Co., **IV** 282; **9** 261
Chatham and Phenix National Bank of
    New York, **II** 312
Chatham Bank, **II** 312
Chatham Technologies Inc., **38** 189
Chatillon. See John Chatillon & Sons Inc.
Chattanooga Gas Company, Inc., **6** 577
Chattanooga Gas Light Company, **6** 448;
    23 30
Chattanooga Medicine Company. See
    Chattem, Inc.
Chattem, Inc., **17 89–92**
Chatto, Virago, Bodley Head & Jonathan
    Cape, Ltd., **13** 429; **31** 376
Chautauqua Airlines, Inc., **38 130–32**
Chaux et Ciments de Lafarge et du Teil,
    III 703–04
Chaux et Ciments du Maroc, **III** 703
Check Express, **33** 4–5
Check Point Software Technologies Ltd.,
    20 238
Checker Auto Parts. See CSK Auto
    Corporation.
Checker Holding, **10** 370
Checker Motors Corp., **10** 369
Checkers Drive-Up Restaurants Inc., **14**
    452; **16 95–98**; **46** 98
CheckFree Corporation, **22** 522
Checkpoint Systems, Inc., **39 77–80**
The Cheesecake Factory Inc., **17 93–96**
Chef-Boy-Ar-Dee Quality Foods Inc., **I**
    622
Chef Boyardee, **10** 70
Chef Francisco, **13** 383
Chef Pierre, **II** 572
Chef's Orchard Airline Caterers Inc., **I** 513
Cheil Sugar Co., **I** 515
Cheil Wool Textile Co., **I** 515
Chelan Power Company, **6** 596
Chelsea GCA Realty, Inc., **27** 401
Chelsea Milling Company, **29 109–11**
Chem-Nuclear Systems, Inc., **9** 109–10
Chemap, **III** 420
Chemcentral Corporation, **8 99–101**
Chemcut, **I** 682
Chemdal Corp., **13** 34
Chemed Corporation, **13 149–50**; **15**
    409–11; **16** 386–87; **49** 307–08
Chemetron Process Equipment, Inc., **8** 545
Chemex Pharmaceuticals, Inc., **8** 63; **27** 69
Chemfab Corporation, **35 97–101**
ChemFirst, Inc., **27** 316
Chemgas Holding BV, **41** 340

Chemgrout, **26** 42
Chemi-Trol Chemical Co., **16 99–101**
Chemical Banking Corporation, **II** 234,
    250–52, 254; **9** 124, 361; **12** 15, 31; **13**
    49, 147, 411; **14 101–04 (upd.)**; **15** 39;
    21 138; **26** 453; **38** 253
Chemical Coatings Co., **I** 321
Chemical Process Co., **IV** 409; **7** 308
Chemical Products Company, **13** 295
Chemical Specialties Inc., **I** 512
Chemical Waste Management, Inc., **V**
    753; **9 108–10**; **11** 435–36
Chemie Linz, **16** 439
Chemins de fer de Paris à Lyon et à la
    Méditerranée, **6** 424
Chemins de fer du Midi, **6** 425
Chemins de Fer Fédéraux, **V** 519
Chemisch-Pharmazeutische AG, **IV** 70
Chemische Fabrik auf Actien, **I** 681
Chemische Fabrik Friesheim Elektron AG,
    IV 229
Chemische Fabrik vormals Sandoz, **I** 671
Chemische Fabrik Wesseling AG, **IV**
    70–71
Chemische Werke Hüls GmbH. See Hüls
    A.G.
Chemise Lacoste, **9** 157
ChemLawn, **13** 199; **23** 428, 431; **34** 153
Chemmar Associates, Inc., **8** 271
Chemonics Industries–Fire-Trol, **17**
    161–62
Chemonics International–Consulting, **17**
    161–62
Chempump, **8** 135
Chemurgic Corporation, **6** 148
Chemway Corp., **III** 423
Cheney Bigelow Wire Works, **13** 370
CHEP Pty Ltd., **42** 50
Cheplin Laboratories, **III** 17
Cherokee Inc., **18 106–09**
Cherokee Insurance Co., **I** 153; **10** 265
Cherry-Burrell Process Equipment, **8**
    544–45
Cherry Company Ltd., **I** 266; **21** 319
Cherry Hill Cheese, **7** 429
Cherry-Levis Co., **26** 172
Chesapeake and Ohio Railroad, **II** 329; **V**
    438–40; **10** 43; **13** 372. See also CSX
    Corporation.
Chesapeake Corporation, **8 102–04**; **10**
    540; **25** 44; **30 117–20 (upd.)**
Chesapeake Microwave Technologies, Inc.,
    32 41
Chesapeake Paperboard Company, **44** 66
Chesebrough-Pond's USA, Inc., **II** 590; **7**
    544; **8 105–07**; **9** 319; **17** 224–25; **22**
    123; **32** 475
Cheshire Wholefoods, **II** 528
Chester Engineers, **10** 412
Chester G. Luby, **I** 183
Chester Oil Co., **IV** 368
Cheung Kong (Holdings) Limited, **I** 470;
    IV 693–95; **18** 252; **20 131–34 (upd.)**;
    23 278, 280; **49** 199. See also Hutchison
    Whampoa Ltd.
Chevignon, **44** 296
Chevrolet, **V** 494; **9** 17; **19** 221, 223; **21**
    153; **26** 500
Chevron Corporation, **II** 143; **IV** 367,
    385–87, 452, 464, 466, 479, 484, 490,
    523, 531, 536, 539, 563, 721; **9** 391; **10**
    119; **12** 20; **17** 121–22; **18** 365, 367; **19**
    73, 75, **82–85 (upd.)**; **25** 444; **29** 385;
    40 354, 357–58; **41** 391, 394–95; **49**

121. See also ChevronTexaco
    Corporation.
Chevron U.K. Ltd., **15** 352
ChevronTexaco Corporation, **47 70–76**
    (upd.), 343
Chevy Chase Savings Bank, **13** 439
Chevy's, Inc., **33** 140
Chevy's Mexican Restaurants, **27** 226
ChexSystems, **22** 181
Cheyenne Software, Inc., **12 60–62**; **25**
    348–49
CHF. See Chase, Harris, Forbes.
Chi-Chi's Inc., **13 151–53**; **14** 195; **25**
    181
Chiat/Day Inc. Advertising, **9** 438; **11**
    49–52. See also TBWA/Chiat/Day.
Chiba Riverment and Cement, **III** 760
**Chibu Electric Power Company,
    Incorporated**, **V 571–73**
Chic by H.I.S, Inc., **20 135–37**
Chicago & Calumet Terminal Railroad, **IV**
    368
Chicago and Alton Railroad, **I** 456
**Chicago and North Western Holdings
    Corporation**, **I** 440; **6 376–78**
Chicago and Southern Airlines Inc., **I** 100;
    6 81
Chicago Bears Football Club, Inc., **IV**
    703 **33 95–97**
Chicago Board of Trade, **41 84–87**
Chicago Bridge & Iron Company, **7 74–77**
Chicago Burlington and Quincy Railroad,
    III 282; **V 425–28**
Chicago Chemical Co., **I** 373; **12** 346
Chicago Corp., **I** 526
Chicago Cubs, **IV 682–83**
Chicago Cutlery, **16** 234
Chicago Directory Co., **IV 660–61**
Chicago Edison, **IV** 169
Chicago Faucet Company, **49** 161, 163
Chicago Flexible Shaft Company, **9** 484
Chicago Heater Company, Inc., **8** 135
Chicago Magnet Wire Corp., **13** 397
Chicago Medical Equipment Co., **31** 255
Chicago Motor Club, **10** 126
Chicago Musical Instrument Company, **16**
    238
Chicago Pacific Corp., **I** 530; **III** 573; **12**
    251; **22** 349; **23** 244; **34** 432
Chicago Pizza & Brewery, Inc., **44**
    85–88
Chicago Pneumatic Tool Co., **III** 427, 452;
    7 480; **21** 502; **26** 41; **28** 40
Chicago Radio Laboratory, **II** 123
Chicago Rawhide Manufacturing Company,
    8 462–63
Chicago Rock Island and Peoria Railway
    Co., **I** 558
Chicago Rollerskate, **15** 395
Chicago Screw Co., **12** 344
Chicago Shipbuilding Company, **18** 318
Chicago Steel Works, **IV** 113
Chicago Sun-Times Distribution Systems, **6**
    14
Chicago Times, **11** 251
Chicago Title and Trust Co., **III** 276; **10**
    43–45
Chicago Tribune. See Tribune Company.
Chick-fil-A Inc., **23 115–18**
Chicken of the Sea International, **24**
    114–16 (upd.)
Chico's FAS, Inc., **45 97–99**
Chicopee Manufacturing Corp., **III** 35
Chief Auto Parts, **II** 661; **32** 416

Chieftain Development Company, Ltd., **16** 11

Chiers-Chatillon-Neuves Maisons, **IV** 227

Chilcott Laboratories Inc., **I** 710–11

Child World Inc., **13** 166; **18** 524

Childers Products Co., **21** 108

Children's Book-of-the-Month Club, **13** 105

Children's Comprehensive Services, Inc., 42 70–72

The Children's Place Retail Stores, Inc., 37 80–82

Children's Record Guild, **13** 105

Children's Television Workshop, **12** 495; **13** 560; **35** 75

Children's World Learning Centers, **II** 608; **V** 17, 19; **13** 48; **24** 75

Childtime Learning Centers, Inc., 34 103–06

Chiles Offshore Corporation, 9 111–13

Chili's Grill & Bar, **10** 331; **12** 373–74; **19** 258; **20** 159

Chillicothe Co., **IV** 310; **19** 266

Chilton Corp., **III** 440; **25** 239; **27** 361

Chilton Publications. *See* Cahners Business Information.

Chiminter, **III** 48

Chimio, **I** 669–70; **8** 451–52

Chimney Rock Winery, **48** 392

China Airlines, 6 71; **34** 107–10; **39** 33–34

China Borneo Co., **III** 698

China Canada Investment and Development Co., **II** 457

China Coast, **10** 322, 324; **16** 156, 158

China.com Corp., **49** 422

China Communications System Company, Inc. (Chinacom), **18** 34

China Development Corporation, **16** 4

China Eastern Airlines Co. Ltd., 31 102–04; **46** 10

China Electric, **II** 67

China Foreign Transportation Corporation, **6** 386

China Industries Co., **II** 325

China International Capital Corp., **16** 377

China International Trade and Investment Corporation, **II** 442; **IV** 695; **6** 80; **18** 113, 253; **19** 156; **25** 101; **34** 100. *See also* CITIC Pacific Ltd.

China Light & Power, **6** 499; **23** 278–80

China Mutual Steam Navigation Company Ltd., **6** 416

China National Automotive Industry Import and Export Corp., **III** 581

China National Aviation Corp., **I** 96; **18** 115; **21** 140

China National Cereals, Oils & Foodstuffs Import and Export Corporation, **24** 359

China National Chemicals Import and Export Corp., **IV** 395; **31** 120

China National Heavy Duty Truck Corporation, **21** 274

China National Machinery Import and Export Corporation, **8** 279

China National Petroleum Corporation, 18 483; **46** 86–89

China Navigation Co., **I** 521; **16** 479–80

China Orient Leasing Co., **II** 442

China Resources (Shenyang) Snowflake Brewery Co., **21** 320

China Southern Airlines Company Ltd., 31 102; **33** 98–100; **46** 10

China Unicom, **47** 320–21

China Zhouyang Fishery Co. Ltd., **II** 578

Chinese Electronics Import and Export Corp., **I** 535

Chinese Metallurgical Import and Export Corp., **IV** 61

Chinese Petroleum Corporation, IV 388–90, 493, 519; **31 105–108 (upd.)**

Chinese Steel Corp., **IV** 184

The Chinet Company, **30** 397

Chino Mines Co., **IV** 179

Chinon Industries, **III** 477; **7** 163

Chipcom, **16** 392

Chippewa Shoe, **19** 232

CHIPS and Technologies, Inc., 6 217; **9** 114–17

Chiquita Brands International, Inc., II 595–96; **III** 28; **7** 84–86; **21** 110–13 **(upd.)**; **38** 197

ChiRex, **38** 380

Chiro Tool Manufacturing Corp., **III** 629

Chiron Corporation, 7 427; **10** 213–14; **36** 117–20 **(upd.)**; **45** 94

Chisholm-Mingo Group, Inc., 41 88–90

Chisso Chemical, **II** 301

Chiswick Products, **II** 566

Chita Oil Co., **IV** 476

Chitaka Foods International, **24** 365

Chivers, **II** 477

Chiyoda Bank, **I** 503; **II** 321

Chiyoda Chemical, **I** 433

Chiyoda Fire and Marine, **III** 404

Chiyoda Kogaku Seiko Kabushiki Kaisha, **III** 574–75; **43** 282

Chiyoda Konpo Kogyo Co. Ltd., **V** 536

Chiyoda Mutual, **II** 374

Chloé Chimie, **I** 303

Chloride S.A., **I** 423

Choay, **I** 676–77

Chock Full o'Nuts Corp., 17 97–100; **20** 83

Chocoladefabriken Lindt & Sprüngli AG, 27 102–05; **30** 220

Chocolat Ibled S.A., **II** 569

Chocolat-Menier S.A., **II** 569

Chocolat Poulait, **II** 478

Chogoku Kogyo, **II** 325

Choice Hotels International Inc., 6 187, 189; **14** 105–07; **25** 309–10; **26** 460

ChoiceCare Corporation, **24** 231

ChoicePoint Services, Inc., **31** 358

Chorlton Metal Co., **I** 531

Chorus Line Corporation, 25 247; **30** 121–23

Chosen Sekiyu, **IV** 554

Chotin Transportation Co., **6** 487

Chouinard Equipment. *See* Lost Arrow Inc.

Chow Tai Fook Jewellery Co., **IV** 717

Chris-Craft Industries, Inc., II 176, 403; **III** 599–600; **9** 118–19; **26** 32; **31** 109–112 **(upd.)**; **46** 313

Christal Radio, **6** 33

Christensen Boyles Corporation, 19 247; **26** 68–71

Christensen Company, **8** 397

Christiaensen, **26** 160

Christian Bourgois, **IV** 614–15

Christian Broadcasting Network, **13** 279

Christian Dalloz SA, 40 96–98

Christian Dior S.A., I 272; **19** 86–88; **23** 237, 242; **49** 90–93 **(upd.)**

Christian Salvesen Plc, 45 10, 100–03

Christian Supply Centers, Inc., **45** 352

Christiana Bank og Kredietklasse, **40** 336

Christie, Mitchell & Mitchell, **7** 344

Christie's International plc, 15 98–101; **39** 81–85 **(upd.)**; **49** 325

Christofle Orfevrerie, **44** 206

Christofle SA, 40 99–102

Christopher & Banks Corporation, 42 73–75

Christopher Charters, Inc. *See* Kitty Hawk, Inc.

Chromalloy American Corp., **13** 461

Chromalloy Gas Turbine Corp., **13** 462

Chromatic Color, **13** 227–28

Chromcraft Revington, Inc., 15 102–05; **26** 100

Chrompack, Inc., **48** 410

The Chronicle Publishing Company, Inc., 23 119–22

Chronimed Inc., 26 72–75

Chronoservice, **27** 475

Chrysalis Group plc, 22 194; **40** 103–06

Chrysler Corporation, I 10, 17, 28, 38, 59, 79, 136, **144–45**, 152, 162–63, 172, 178, 182, 188, 190, 207, 420, 504, 516, 525, 540; **II** 5, 313, 403, 448; **III** 439, 517, 544, 568, 591, 607, 637–38; **IV** 22, 449, 676, 703; **7** 205, 233, 461; **8** 74–75, 315, 505–07; **9** 118, 349–51, 472; **10** 174, 198, 264–65, 290, 317, 353, 430; **11 53–55 (upd.)**, 103–04, 429; **13** 28–29, 61, 448, 501, 555; **14** 321, 367, 457; **16** 184, 322, 484; **17** 184; **18** 173–74, 308, 493; **20** 359–60; **22** 52, 55, 175, 330; **23** 352–54; **25** 89–91, 93, 142–44, 329; **26** 403, 501; **31** 130; **36** 34, 242; **38** 480–81; **43** 163–64; **47** 436. *See also* DaimlerChrysler AG

Chrysler Financial Company, LLC, **45** 262

CH2M Hill Ltd., 22 136–38

Chu Ito & Co., **IV** 476

Chubb Corporation, II 84; **III** 190, 220–22, 368; **11** 481; **14** 108–10 **(upd.)**; **29** 256; **37** 83–87 **(upd.)**; **45** 109

Chubb Security plc, **44** 258

Chubu Electric Power Company, Inc., 46 90–93 **(upd.)**

Chuck E. Cheese, **13** 472–74; **31** 94

Chugai Boyeki Co. Ltd., **44** 441

Chugai Pharmaceutical Company, **8** 215–16; **10** 79

Chugai Shogyo Shimposha, **IV** 654–55

Chugoku Electric Power Company Inc., V 574–76

Chunghwa Picture Tubes, **23** 469

Chunghwa Trust & Banking Co. *See* Yasuda Trust and Banking Company, Limited.

Chupa Chups S.A., 38 133–35

Church & Company, **45** 342, 344

Church & Dwight Co., Inc., 29 112–15

Church and Tower Group, **19** 254

Church, Goodman, and Donnelley, **IV** 660

Church's Fried Chicken, Inc., **I** 260; **7** 26–28; **15** 345; **23** 468; **32** 13–14

Churchill Downs Incorporated, 29 116–19

Churchill Insurance Co. Ltd., **III** 404

Churny Co. Inc., **II** 534

Cianbro Corporation, 14 111–13

Cianchette Brothers, Inc. *See* Cianbro Corporation.

Ciba-Geigy Ltd., I 625, **632–34**, 671, 690, 701; **III** 55; **IV** 288; **8** 63, **108–11 (upd.)**, 376–77; **9** 153, 441; **10** 53–54, 213; **15** 229; **18** 51; **21** 386; **23** 195–96;

25 55; **27** 69; **28** 193, 195; **30** 327; **36** 36, 119. *See also* Novartis AG.
CIBC. *See* Canadian Imperial Bank of Commerce.
CIBC Wood Gundy Securities Corp., **24** 482
Ciber, Inc., 18 110–12
Ciby 2000, **24** 79
CICI, **11** 184
CIDLA, **IV** 504–06
Cie Continental d'Importation, **10** 249
Cie des Lampes, **9** 9
Cie Générale d'Electro-Ceramique, **9** 9
Cie. Generale des Eaux S.A., **24** 327
Cifra, S.A. de C.V., 8 556; **12 63–65; 26** 524; **34** 197–98; **35** 320. *See also* Wal-Mart de Mexico, S.A. de C.V.
Cigarrera La Moderna, **21** 260; **22** 73
Cigarros la Tabacelera Mexicana (Cigatam), **21** 259
CIGNA Corporation, III 197, **223–27**, 389; **10** 30; **11** 243; **22 139–44 (upd.),** 269; **38** 18; **45 104–10 (upd.)**
CIGWELD, **19** 442
Cii-HB, **III** 123, 678; **16** 122
Cilag-Chemie, **III** 35–36; **8** 282
Cilbarco, **II** 25
Cilva Holdings PLC, **6** 358
Cima, **14** 224–25
Cimaron Communications Corp., **38** 54
Cimarron Utilities Company, **6** 580
CIMCO Ltd., **21** 499–501
Cimenteries CBR S.A., **23** 325, 327
Ciments d'Obourg, **III** 701
Ciments de Chalkis Portland Artificiels, **III** 701
Ciments de Champagnole, **III** 702
Ciments de l'Adour, **III** 702
Ciments Français, 40 107–10
Ciments Lafarge France, **III** 704
Ciments Lafarge Quebec, **III** 704
Cimos, **7** 37
Cinar Corporation, 40 111–14
Cincinnati Bell, Inc., 6 316–18; 29 250, 252
Cincinnati Chemical Works, **I** 633
Cincinnati Electronics Corp., **II** 25
Cincinnati Financial Corporation, 16 102–04; 44 89–92 (upd.)
Cincinnati Gas & Electric Company, 6 465–68, 481–82
Cincinnati Milacron Inc., 12 66–69
Cincom Systems Inc., 15 106–08
Cine-Groupe, **35** 279
Cineamerica, **IV** 676
Cinecentrum, **IV** 591
Cinema International Corp., **II** 149
Cinemark, **21** 362; **23** 125
Cinemax, **IV** 675; **7** 222–24, 528–29; **23** 276
Cineplex Odeon Corporation, II 145, **6 161–63; 14** 87; **23 123–26 (upd.); 33** 432
Cinnabon Inc., 13 435–37; 23 127–29; 32 12, 15
Cinquième Saison, **38** 200, 202
Cinram International, Inc., 43 107–10
Cintas Corporation, 16 228; **21 114–16,** 507; **30** 455
Cintel, **II** 158
Cintra. *See* Concesiones de Infraestructuras de Transportes, S.A. *or* Corporacion Internacional de Aviacion, S.A. de C.V.
Cinven, **49** 451

Cipal-Parc Astérix, **27** 10
Ciprial S.A., **27** 260
CIPSCO Inc., 6 469–72, 505–06
Circa Pharmaceuticals, **16** 529
Circle A Ginger Ale Company, **9** 177
Circle International, Inc., **17** 216
The Circle K Company, II 619–20; V 210; **7** 113–14, 372, 374; **20 138–40 (upd.); 25** 125; **26** 447; **49** 17, 427
Circle Plastics, **9** 323
Circon Corporation, 21 117–20
Circuit City Stores, Inc., 9 65–66, **120–22; 10** 235, 305–06, 334–35, 468–69; **12** 335; **14** 61; **15** 215; **16** 73, 75; **17** 489; **18** 533; **19** 362; **23** 51–53, 363; **24** 52, 502; **26** 410; **29 120–24 (upd.); 30** 464–65
Circus Circus Enterprises, Inc., 6 201, **203–05; 19** 377, 379
Circus Knie, **29** 126
Circus World, **16** 389–90
Cirque du Soleil Inc., 29 125–28
Cirrus Design Corporation, 44 93–95
Cirrus Logic, Inc., 9 334; **11 56–57; 25** 117; **48 90–93 (upd.)**
Cisco Systems, Inc., 11 58–60, 520; **13** 482; **16** 468; **19** 310; **20** 8, 33, 69, 237; **25** 499; **26** 276–77; **34 111–15 (upd.),** 441, 444; **36** 300; **38** 430; **43** 251
Cise, **24** 79
Cisneros Group, **47** 312
CIT Alcatel, **9** 9–10
CIT Financial Corp., **II** 90, 313; **8** 117; **12** 207
CIT Group/Business Credit, Inc., **13** 446
CIT Group/Commercial Services, **13** 536
Citadel Communications Corporation, 35 102–05
Citadel General, **III** 404
Citadel, Inc., **27** 46
CitFed Bancorp, Inc., 16 105–07
CITGO Petroleum Corporation, II 660–61; **IV 391–93,** 508; **7** 491; **31 113–117 (upd.); 32** 414, 416–17; **45** 252, 254
Citibanc Group, Inc., **11** 456
Citibank, **II** 227, 230, 248, 250–51, 253–55, 331, 350, 358, 415; **III** 243, 340; **6** 51; **9** 124; **10** 150; **11** 418; **13** 146; **14** 101; **23** 3–4, 482; **25** 180, 542. *See also* Citigroup Inc
Citibank of Mexico, **34** 82
CITIC Pacific Ltd., 16 481; **18 113–15; 20** 134. *See also* China International Trade and Investment Corporation.
Citicasters Inc., **23** 293–94
Citicorp, II 214, **253–55,** 268, 275, 319, 331, 361, 398, 411, 445; **III** 10, 220, 397; **7** 212–13; **8** 196; **9 123–26 (upd.),** 441; **10** 463, 469; **11** 140; **12** 30, 310, 334; **13** 535; **14** 103, 108, 235; **15** 94, 146, 281; **17** 324, 559; **21** 69, 145; **22** 169, 406; **25** 198, 542
Cities Service Company, **IV** 376, 391–92, 481, 575; **12** 542; **22** 172
Citifor, **19** 156
Citigroup Inc., 30 124–28 (upd.); 42 332; **46** 316
Citinet. *See* Hongkong Telecommunications Ltd.
Citivision PLC, **9** 75
Citizen Watch Co., Ltd., III 454–56, 549; **13** 121–22; **21 121–24 (upd.); 23** 212; **41** 71–82

Citizen's Electric Light & Power Company, **V** 641
Citizen's Federal Savings Bank, **10** 93
Citizen's Fidelity Corp., **II** 342
Citizen's Industrial Bank, **14** 529
Citizens and Southern Bank, **II** 337; **10** 426
Citizens Bank, **11** 105
Citizens Bank of Hamilton, **9** 475
Citizens Bank of Savannah, **10** 426
Citizens Building & Loan Association, **14** 191
Citizens Federal Savings and Loan Association, **9** 476
Citizens Financial Group, Inc., 12 422; **42 76–80**
Citizens Gas Co., **6** 529
Citizens Gas Fuel Company. *See* MCN Corporation.
Citizens Gas Light Co., **6** 455
Citizens Gas Supply Corporation, **6** 527
Citizens Mutual Savings Bank, **17** 529–30
Citizens National Bank, **II** 251; **13** 466; **25** 114; **41** 312
Citizens National Gas Company, **6** 527
Citizens Saving and Trust Company, **17** 356
Citizens Savings & Loan Association, **9** 173
Citizens Savings and Loan Society. *See* Citizens Mutual Savings Bank.
Citizens State Bank, **41** 178, 180
Citizens Telephone Company, **14** 257–58
Citizens Trust Co., **II** 312
Citizens Utilities Company, 7 87–89; 37 124–27
Citizens' Savings and Loan, **10** 339
Citrix Systems, Inc., 44 96–99
Citroën. *See* Automobiles Citroen *and* PSA Peugeot Citroen S.A.
City and St. James, **III** 501
City and Suburban Telegraph Association and Telephonic Exchange, **6** 316–17
City and Village Automobile Insurance Co., **III** 363
City Auto Stamping Co., **I** 201
City Bank Farmers' Trust Co., **II** 254; **9** 124
City Bank of New York, **II** 250, 253
City Brewery, **I** 253
City Capital Associates, **31** 211
City Centre Properties Ltd., **IV** 705–06; **49** 248
City Finance Company, **10** 340; **11** 261
City Ice Delivery, Ltd., **II** 660
City Investing Co., **III** 263; **IV** 721; **9** 391; **13** 363
City Light and Traction Company, **6** 593
City Light and Water Company, **6** 579
City Market Inc., **12** 112
City Mutual Life Assurance Society, **III** 672–73
City National Bank of Baton Rouge, **11** 107
City National Leasing, **II** 457
City of London Real Property Co. Ltd., **IV** 706; **49** 248
City of Seattle Water Department, **12** 443
The City Post Publishing Corp., **12** 359
City Products Corp., **II** 419
City Public Service, 6 473–75
City Savings, **10** 340
City Stores Company, **16** 207
Cityhome Corp., **III** 263

Civic Drugs, **12** 21
Civic Parking LLC, **18** 105
Civil & Civic Pty. Ltd., **IV** 707–08; **17** 286
Civil Aviation Administration of China, **31** 102; **33** 98
Civil Service Employees Insurance Co., **III** 214
CJ Banks. *See* Christopher & Banks Corporation.
CKE Restaurants, Inc., 19 89–93, 433, 435; **25** 389; **27** 19; **29** 203; **37** 349–51; **46 94–99 (upd.)**
CKS Group Inc. *See* marchFIRST, Inc.
CKS Inc., **23** 479
Clabir Corp., **12** 199
Claeys, **22** 379–80
Claire's Stores, Inc., 17 101–03; 18 411
Clairol, **III** 17–18; **17** 110
Clairton Steel Co., **IV** 572; **7** 550
Clal Electronic Industries Ltd., **24** 429
Clal Group, **18** 154
CLAM Petroleum, **7** 282
Clancy Paul Inc., **13** 276
Clapp-Eastham Company. *See* GenRad, Inc.
Clara Candy, **15** 65
Clarcor Inc., 17 104–07
Claremont Technology Group Inc., **31** 131
Clares Equipment Co., **I** 252
Clariden Bank, **21** 146–47
Claridge Group, **25** 266, 268
Clarify Corp., **38** 431
Clarion Hotels and Resorts, **25** 309
Clark & Co., **IV** 301
Clark & McKenney Hardware Co. *See* Clarcor Inc.
Clark & Rockefeller, **IV** 426
Clark Bros. Co., **III** 471
The Clark Construction Group, Inc., 8 112–13
Clark, Dietz & Associates-Engineers. *See* CRSS Inc.
Clark Equipment Company, I 153; **7** 513–14; **8** 114–16; **10** 265; **13** 500; **15** 226
Clark Estates Inc., **8** 13
Clark Filter, Inc., **17** 104
Clark Materials Handling Company, **7** 514
Clark Motor Co., **I** 158; **10** 292
Clark Retail Enterprises Inc., **37** 311
Clark-Schwebel, Inc., **28** 195
Clarkins, Inc., **16** 35–36
Clarkson International Tools, **I** 531
CLASSA. *See* Compañia de Líneas Aéreas Subvencionadas S.A.
Classic FM plc, **39** 198–200
Classic Vacation Group, Inc., 46 100–03
Claudel Roustand Galac, **19** 50
Claussen Pickle Co., **12** 371
Clayco Construction Company, **41** 225–26
Clayton Brown Holding Company, **15** 232
Clayton Dubilier & Rice Inc., **III** 25; **25** 501; **29** 408; **40** 370; **49** 22
Clayton Homes Incorporated, 13 154–55; 37 77
Clayton-Marcus Co., **12** 300
Clayton/National Courier Systems, Inc., **24** 126
CLE. *See* Compagnie Laitière Européenne.
Clean Window Remodelings Co., **III** 757
Cleanaway Ltd., **III** 495
Cleancoal Terminal, **7** 582, 584

Clear Channel Communications, Inc., 23 130–32, 294; **25** 418; **27** 278; **33** 322, 324; **35** 219–21, 233; **36** 422, 424; **37** 104–05
Clear Shield Inc., **17** 157, 159
Clearing Inc., **III** 514
Clearly Canadian Beverage Corporation, 48 94–97
Clearwater Tissue Mills, Inc., **8** 430
Cleary, Gottlieb, Steen & Hamilton, 35 106–09
Cleco Corporation, 37 88–91
Clef, **IV** 125
Clemente Capital Inc., **25** 542
Clements Energy, Inc., **7** 376
Cleo Inc., **12** 207–09; **35** 131
Le Clerc, **21** 225–26
Cletrac Corp., **IV** 366
Cleve-Co Jig Boring Co., **23** 82
Cleveland and Western Coal Company, **7** 369
Cleveland-Cliffs Inc., 13 156–58; 17 355
Cleveland Cotton Products Co., **37** 393
Cleveland Electric Illuminating Company. *See* Centerior Energy Theodor.
Cleveland Fabric Centers, Inc. *See* Fabri-Centers of America Inc.
Cleveland Grinding Machine Co., **23** 82
Cleveland Indians Baseball Company, Inc., 37 92–94
Cleveland Iron Mining Company. *See* Cleveland-Cliffs Inc.
Cleveland Oil Co., **I** 341
Cleveland Paper Co., **IV** 311; **19** 267
Cleveland Pneumatic Co., **I** 457; **III** 512
Cleveland Precision Instruments, Inc., **23** 82
Cleveland Twist Drill Company. *See* Acme-Cleveland Corp.
Clevepak Corporation, **8** 229; **13** 442
Clevite Corporation, **14** 207
CLF Research, **16** 202; **43** 170
Click Messenger Service, Inc., **24** 126
ClickAgents.com, Inc., **49** 433
Clifford & Wills, **12** 280–81
Clifford Chance LLP, 38 136–39
Cliffs Corporation, **13** 157; **27** 224
Climax Molybdenum Co., **IV** 17–19
Clinchfield Coal Corp., **IV** 180–81; **19** 320
Clinical Assays, **I** 628
Clinical Partners, Inc., **26** 74
Clinical Pathology Facility, Inc., **26** 391
Clinical Science Research Ltd., **10** 106
Clinique Laboratories, Inc., **30** 191
Clinton Cards plc, 39 86–88
Clinton Pharmaceutical Co., **III** 17; **37** 41
Clipper Group, **12** 439
Clipper, Inc., **IV** 597
Clipper Manufacturing Company, **7** 3
Clipper Seafoods, **II** 587
La Cloche d'Or, **25** 85
Clopay Corp., **34** 195
The Clorox Company, III 20–22, 52; **8** 433; **22 145–48 (upd.),** 436; **26** 383
Close Brothers Group plc, 39 89–92
The Clothestime, Inc., 20 141–44
Clouterie et Tréfilerie des Flandres, **IV** 25–26
Clover Club, **44** 348
Clover Leaf Creamery, **II** 528
Clover Milk Products Co., **II** 575
Clovis Water Co., **6** 580
CLRP. *See* City of London Real Property Company Ltd.

CLSI Inc., **15** 372; **43** 182
Club Aurrera, **8** 556
Club Corporation of America, **26** 27
Club de Hockey Canadien Inc., **26** 305
Club Européen du Tourisme, **6** 207
Club Méditerranée S.A., I 286; **6 206–08; 21 125–28 (upd.); 27** 10
ClubCorp, Inc., 33 101–04
Clubhôtel, **6** 207
Cluett Corporation, **22** 133
Cluett, Peabody & Co., Inc., **II** 414; **8** 567–68
Clyde Iron Works, **8** 545
Clydebank Engineering & Shipbuilding Co., **I** 573
Clydesdale Group, **19** 390
Clyne Maxon Agency, **I** 29
CM&M Equilease, **7** 344
CM&P. *See* Cresap, McCormick and Paget.
CM Industries, **I** 676
CMAC Investment Corporation. *See* Radian Group Inc.
CMB Acier, **IV** 228
CMB Packaging SA, **8** 477; **49** 295
CMC. *See* Commercial Metals Company.
CME. *See* Campbell-Mithun-Esty, Inc.
CMGI, Inc., **43** 11, 13, 420, 422
CMI International, Inc., **27** 202, 204
CML Group, Inc., 10 215–18; 22 382, 536; **38** 238
CMP Media Inc., 26 76–80; 28 504
CMP Properties Inc., **15** 122
CMS Energy Corporation, IV 23; **V 577–79; 8** 466; **14 114–16 (upd.)**
CMS Healthcare, **29** 412
CMT Enterprises, Inc., **22** 249
CN. *See* Canadian National Railway System.
CNA Financial Corporation, I 488; **III 228–32,** 339; **12** 317; **36** 325, 327; **38 140–46 (upd.)**
CNA Health Plans, **III** 84
CNB Bancshares Inc., **31** 207
CNBC, Inc., **28** 298
CNC Holding Corp., **13** 166
CNCA. *See* Caisse National de Crédit Agricole.
CNEP. *See* Comptoir National d'Escompte de Paris.
CNET Networks, Inc., 47 77–80
CNF Transportation. *See* Consolidated Freightways, Inc.
CNG. *See* Consolidated Natural Gas Company.
CNH Global N.V., 38 147–56 (upd.)
CNI. *See* Community Networks Inc.
CNN. *See* Cable News Network.
CNP. *See* Compagnie Nationale à Portefeuille.
CNPC. *See* China National Petroleum Corporation.
CNS, Inc., 20 145–47
Co-Axial Systems Engineering Co., **IV** 677
Co-Counsel, Inc., **29** 364
Co. Luxemburgeoise de Banque S.A., **II** 282
Co. of London Insurers, **III** 369
Co-Op Blue Square Consumer Cooperative Society, **41** 56–58
Co-Steel International Ltd., **8** 523–24; **13** 142–43; **24** 144
Coach and Car Equipment Corp., **41** 369
Coach, Inc., 45 111–15 (upd.)
Coach Leatherware, 10 219–21; 12 559

Coach Specialties Co. *See* Fleetwood Enterprises, Inc.

Coach USA, Inc., 24 117–19; **30** 431, 433

Coachmen Industries Inc., **21** 153; **39** 393

Coal India Ltd., IV 48–50; **44** 100–03 (upd.)

Coalport, **12** 528

Coast American Corporation, **13** 216

Coast Consolidators, Inc., **14** 505

Coast to Coast Hardware. *See* TruServ Corporation.

Coast-to-Coast Stores, **II** 419; **12** 8

Coastal Coca-Cola Bottling Co., **10** 223

Coastal Container Line Inc., **30** 318

Coastal Corporation, IV 366, 394–95; **7** 553–54; **31** 118–121 (upd.)

Coastal Lumber, S.A., **18** 514

Coastal States Corporation, **11** 481

Coastal States Life Insurance Company, **11** 482

Coastal Valley Canning Co., **I** 260

CoastAmerica Corp., **13** 176

Coates/Lorilleux, **14** 308

Coating Products, Inc., **III** 643

Coats plc, 44 104–07 (upd.)

Coats Viyella Plc, V 356–58. *See also* Coats plc.

CoBank. *See* National Bank for Cooperatives.

Cobb & Branham, **14** 257

Cobb, Inc., **II** 585; **14** 515

COBE Laboratories, Inc., 13 159–61; **22** 360; **49** 156

Cobham plc, 30 129–32

Coborn's, Inc., 30 133–35

Cobra Electronics Corporation, 14 117–19

Cobra Golf Inc., 16 108–10; **23** 474

Cobra Ventilation Products, **22** 229

Coburn Optical Industries, **III** 56

Coburn Vision Care, **III** 727

Coca-Cola Bottling Co. Consolidated, II 170, 468; **10** 222–24; **15** 299

Coca-Cola Bottling Company of Northern New England, Inc., **21** 319

The Coca-Cola Company, I 17, 232–35, 244, 248, 278–79, 286, 289, 440, 457; **II** 103, 136–37, 477–78; **III** 215; **IV** 297; **6** 20–21, 30; **7** 155, 383, 466; **8** 399; **9** 86, 177; **10** 130, 222–23, **225–28** (upd.); **11** 421, 450–51; **12** 74; **13** 284; **14** 18, 453; **15** 428; **16** 480–81; **17** 207; **18** 60, 62–63, 68, 467–68; **19** 391; **21** 337–39, 401; **23** 418–20; **24** 516; **25** 183; **27** 21, 150; **28** 271, 473; **29** 85; **31** 243; **32** 59, 111–16 (upd.); **40** 350–52; **42** 31, 34–35; **47** 289, 291; **49** 77–78

Coca-Cola Enterprises, Inc., 10 223; **13** 162–64; **23** 455–57; **32** 115

Cochrane Corporation, **8** 135

Cochrane Foil Co., **15** 128

Cockburn & Campbell Ltd., **38** 501

Cockburn-Adelaide Cement, **31** 398, 400

Cockerill Sambre Group, IV 26–27, 51–53; **22** 44; **26** 81–84 (upd.); **42** 416

Coco's, **I** 547; **27** 16, 19

Code Hennessey & Simmons Limited, **39** 358

Codec, **19** 328

Codelco. *See* Corporacion Nacional del Cobre de Chile.

Codex Corp., **II** 61

Codville Distributors Ltd., **II** 649

Coelba. *See* Companhia de Electricidade da Bahia.

Coeur d'Alene Mines Corporation, 20 148–51

Coffee People, Inc., **40** 152–54

Cofica, **21** 99

COFINA, **III** 347

COFIRED, **IV** 108

Cofitel SA, **25** 466

Coflexip S.A., 25 103–05

Cofroma, **23** 219

Cogéma, **IV** 108

COGEMA Canada, **IV** 436

Cogeneracion Prat SA, **41** 325, 327

Cogeneration Development Corp., **42** 387–88

Cogent Data Technologies, Inc., **31** 5

Cogentrix Energy, Inc., 10 229–31

Cogetex, **14** 225

Cogifer, S.A., **18** 4; **31** 156, 158

Cognex Corp., **22** 373

CogniSeis Development, Inc., **18** 513, 515

Cognitive Solutions, Inc., **18** 140

Cognos Inc., 11 78; **25** 97; **44** 108–11

Cohasset Savings Bank, **13** 468

Coherent, Inc., 31 122–25

Coherix Corporation, **48** 446

Cohn-Hall-Marx Co. *See* United Merchants & Manufacturers, Inc.

Cohoes Bancorp Inc., **41** 212

Cohu, Inc., 32 117–19

Coils Plus, Inc., **22** 4

Coinamatic Laundry Equipment, **II** 650

Coinmach Laundry Corporation, 20 152–54

Coinstar, Inc., 44 112–14

Coktel Vision, **15** 455

Colas S.A., 31 126–29

Colbert Television Sales, **9** 306

Colchester Car Auctions, **II** 587

Cold Spring Granite Company, 16 111–14

Coldwater Creek Inc., 21 129–31

Coldwell Banker, **IV** 715, 727; **V** 180, 182; **11** 292; **12** 97; **18** 475, 478; **27** 32. *See also* CB Commercial Real Estate Services Group, Inc.

Cole & Weber Inc., **I** 27

Cole Haan Holdings Incorporated, **36** 346

Cole National Corporation, 13 165–67, 391

Cole Sewell Corporation, **39** 322, 324

Cole's Craft Showcase, **13** 166

Coleco Industries, Inc., **III** 506; **18** 520; **21** 375; **43** 229, 232

Coleman & Co., **II** 230

The Coleman Company, Inc., III 485; **9** 127–29; **22** 207; **26** 119; **28** 135, 247; **30** 136–39 (upd.)

Coleman Outdoor Products Inc., **21** 293

Colemans Ltd., **11** 241

Coles Book Stores Ltd., **7** 486, 488–89

Coles Express Inc., 15 109–11

Coles Myer Ltd., V 33–35; **18** 286; **20** 155–58 (upd.)

Colex Data, **14** 556

Colgate-Palmolive Company, I 260; **II** 672; **III** 23–26; **IV** 285; **9** 291; **11** 219, 317; **14** 120–23 (upd.), 279; **17** 106; **25** 365; **27** 212–13, 390; **35** 110–15 (upd.)

Colgens, **22** 193

Collabra Software Inc., **15** 322

Collectors Universe, Inc., 48 98–100

College Construction Loan Insurance Assoc., **II** 455; **25** 427

College Entrance Examination Board, **12** 141

College Survival, Inc., **10** 357

Collegiate Arlington Sports Inc., **II** 652

Collett Dickinson Pearce International Group, **I** 33; **16** 168

Collins & Aikman Corporation, I 483; **13** 168–70; **25** 535; **41** 91–95 (upd.)

Collins Industries, Inc., 33 105–07

Collins Radio Co., **III** 136; **11** 429

Collins Stewart, **41** 371–72

Colo-Macco. *See* CRSS Inc.

Cologne Re. *See* General Re Corporation *or* Kölnische Rückversicherungs-Gesellschaft AG.

Cologne Reinsurance Co., **III** 273, 299

Colombia Graphophone Company, **22** 192

Colombo, **25** 84

Colonia Insurance Company (UK) Ltd., **III** 273, 394; **49** 43

Colonia Versicherung Aktiengesellschaft. *See* AXA Colonia Konzern AG.

Colonial & General, **III** 359–60

Colonial Air Transport, **I** 89, 115; **12** 379

Colonial Airlines, **I** 102

Colonial Bancorp, **II** 208

Colonial Bank, **II** 236

Colonial Candle of Cape Cod, **18** 69

Colonial Container, **8** 359

Colonial Food Stores, **7** 373

Colonial Healthcare Supply Co., **13** 90

Colonial Insurance Co., **IV** 575–76

Colonial Life Assurance Co., **III** 359

Colonial Life Insurance Co. of America, **III** 220–21; **14** 108–09

Colonial Life Insurance Company, **11** 481

Colonial National Bank, **8** 9; **38** 10–12

Colonial National Leasing, Inc., **8** 9

Colonial Packaging Corporation, **12** 150

Colonial Penn Group Insurance Co., **11** 262; **27** 4

Colonial Penn Life Insurance Co., **V** 624; **49** 144–45

Colonial Rubber Works, **8** 347

Colonial Stores, **II** 397

Colonial Sugar Refining Co. Ltd. *See* CSR Limited.

Colony Capital, Inc., **27** 201

Colony Communications, **7** 99

Colony Gift Corporation, Ltd., **18** 67, 69

Color-Box, Inc., **8** 103

Color Corporation of America, **8** 553

Color Me Mine, **25** 263

Color Tile, **31** 435

Colorado Belle Casino, **6** 204

Colorado Cooler Co., **I** 292

Colorado Electric Company. *See* Public Service Company of Colorado.

Colorado Fuel & Iron (CF&I), **14** 369

Colorado Gaming & Entertainment Co., **21** 335

Colorado Gathering & Processing Corporation, **11** 27

Colorado Interstate Gas Co., **IV** 394

Colorado MEDtech, Inc., 48 101–05

Colorado National Bank, **12** 165

Colorado Technical University, Inc., **41** 419

Colorcraft, **I** 447

Colorfoto Inc., **I** 447

Coloroll, **44** 148

Colortree. *See* National Envelope Corporation.
ColorTyme, Inc., **45** 367
Colossal Pictures, **10** 286
Colson Co., **III** 96; **IV** 135–36
Colt, **19** 430–31
Colt Industries Inc., **I** 434–36, 482, 524; **III** 435
Colt Pistol Factory, **9** 416
COLT Telecom Group plc, 41 96–99
Colt's Manufacturing Company, Inc., 12 70–72
Coltec Industries Inc., **30** 158; **32** 96; **46** 213
Columbia Brewery, **25** 281
Columbia Broadcasting System. *See* CBS Corporation.
Columbia Chemical Co. *See* PPG Industries, Inc.
Columbia Electric Street Railway, Light and Power Company, **6** 575
Columbia Forest Products, **IV** 358
Columbia Gas & Electric Company, **6** 466. *See also* Columbia Gas System, Inc.
Columbia Gas Light Company, **6** 574
Columbia Gas of New York, Inc., **6** 536
The Columbia Gas System, Inc., **V** 580–82; **16** 115–18 (upd.)
Columbia Gas Transmission Corporation, **6** 467
Columbia General Life Insurance Company of Indiana, **11** 378
Columbia Hat Company, **19** 94
Columbia House, **IV** 676
Columbia Insurance Co., **III** 214
Columbia News Service, **II** 132
Columbia Paper Co., **IV** 311; **19** 266
Columbia Pictures Entertainment, Inc., **II** 103, 134, **135–37**, 170, 234, 619; **IV** 675; **10** 227; **12** 73, 455; **21** 360; **22** 193; **25** 139; **28** 71. *See also* Columbia TriStar Motion Pictures Companies.
Columbia Railroad, Gas and Electric Company, **6** 575
Columbia Records, **II** 132; **16** 201; **26** 150
Columbia Records Distribution Corp., **43** 170
Columbia River Packers, **II** 491
Columbia Savings & Loan, **II** 144
Columbia Sportswear Company, 19 94–96; **41** 100–03 (upd.)
Columbia Steamship Company, **17** 356
Columbia Steel Co., **IV** 28, 573; **7** 550
Columbia Transportation Co., **17** 357
Columbia TriStar Motion Pictures Companies, 12 73–76 (upd.); **28** 71
Columbia TriStar Television Distribution, **17** 149
Columbia/HCA Healthcare Corporation, **13** 90; **15** 112–14; **22** 409–10; **27** 356
Columbian Carbon Company, **25** 70–71
Columbian Chemicals Co., **IV** 179; **28** 352, 356
Columbian Peanut Co., **I** 421; **11** 23
Columbus & Southern Ohio Electric Company (CSO), **6** 467, 481–82
Columbus Bank & Trust. *See* Synovus Financial Corp.
Columbus McKinnon Corporation, 37 95–98
Columbus-Milpar, **I** 544
Columbus Realty Trust, **26** 378
Columbus Savings and Loan Society, **I** 536; **13** 528

Colwell Systems, **19** 291; **22** 181
Com Dev, Inc., **32** 435
Com Ed. *See* Commonwealth Edison.
Com-Link 21, Inc., **8** 310
Comair Holdings Inc., **13 171–73**; **31** 420; **34** 116–20 (upd.)
Comalco Fabricators (Hong Kong) Ltd., **III** 758
Comalco Ltd., **IV** 59–61, 122, 191
Comark, **24** 316; **25** 417–18
Comat Services Pte. Ltd., **10** 514
Comau, **I** 163
Combibloc Inc., **16** 339
Combined American Insurance Co. of Dallas, **III** 203
Combined Casualty Co. of Philadelphia, **III** 203
Combined Communications Corp., **II** 619; **IV** 612; **7** 191
Combined Insurance Company of America, **III** 203–04; **45** 25–26
Combined International Corp., **III** 203–04
Combined Mutual Casualty Co. of Chicago, **III** 203
Combined Properties, Inc., **16** 160
Combined Registry Co., **III** 203
Combustion Engineering Group, **22** 11; **25** 534
Combustiveis Industriais e Domésticos. *See* CIDLA.
Comcast Corporation, 7 90–92; **9** 428; **10** 432–33; **17** 148; **22** 162; **24 120–24** (upd.); **27** 342, 344; **49** 175
ComCore Semiconductor, Inc., **26** 330
Comdata, **19** 160
Comdial Corporation, 21 132–35
Comdisco, Inc., 9 130–32; **11** 47, 86, 484, 490
Comdor Flugdienst GmbH., **I** 111
Comer Motor Express, **6** 370
Comerci. *See* Controladora Comercial Mexicana, S.A. de C.V.
Comercial Mexicana, S.A. *See* Controladora Comercial Mexicana, S.A. de C.V.
Comerco, **III** 21; **22** 147
Comerica Incorporated, 40 115–17
Comet, **II** 139; **V** 106–09; **24** 194, 266, 269–70
Comet American Marketing, **33** 31
Comet Rice, Inc., **33** 31
Cometra Oil, **IV** 576
ComFed Bancorp, **11** 29
COMFORCE Corporation, 40 118–20
Comfort Inns, **21** 362
Comforto GmbH, **8** 252; **39** 206
Cominco Ltd., 37 99–102 55
Comision Federal de Electricidad de Mexico (CFE), **21** 196–97
Comitato Interministrale per la Ricostruzione, **I** 465
Comm-Quip, **6** 313
CommAir. *See* American Building Maintenance Industries, Inc.
Commander Foods, **8** 409
Commander-Larabee Co., **I** 419; **25** 242
Commemorative Brands Inc., **19** 453
Commentry, **III** 676; **16** 120
Commerce and Industry Insurance Co., **III** 196, 203
Commerce Clearing House, Inc., 7 93–94. *See also* CCH Inc.
Commerce Group, **III** 393
Commerce.TV, **42** 323

Commerce Union, **10** 426
Commercial & General Life Assurance Co., **III** 371
Commercial Air Conditioning of Northern California, **25** 15
Commercial Air Lines, Inc., **23** 380
Commercial Alliance Corp. of New York, **II** 289
Commercial Aseguradora Suizo Americana, S.A., **III** 243
Commercial Assurance, **III** 359
Commercial Bank of Australia Ltd., **II** 189, 319, 388–89; **17** 324; **48** 425
Commercial Bank of London, **II** 334
Commercial Bank of Tasmania, **II** 188
Commercial Banking Co. of Sydney, **II** 187–89
Commercial Bureau (Australia) Pty., **I** 438
Commercial Chemical Company, **16** 99
Commercial Credit Company, III 127–28; **8 117–19**; **10** 255–56; **15** 464
Commercial Exchange Bank, **II** 254; **9** 124
Commercial Federal Corporation, 12 77–79
Commercial Filters Corp., **I** 512
Commercial Financial Services, Inc., 26 85–89
Commercial Insurance Co. of Newark, **III** 242
Commercial Life, **III** 243
Commercial Life Assurance Co. of Canada, **III** 309
Commercial Metals Company, 15 115–17; **42 81–84** (upd.)
Commercial Motor Freight, Inc., **14** 42
Commercial National Bank, **II** 261; **10** 425
Commercial National Bank & Trust Co., **II** 230
Commercial National Bank of Charlotte, **II** 336
Commercial Realty Services Group, **21** 257
Commercial Ship Repair Co., **I** 185
Commercial Union plc, **II** 272, 308; **III** 185, **233–35**, 350, 373; **IV** 711
Commerzbank A.G., **II** 239, 242, **256–58**, 280, 282, 385; **IV** 222; **9** 283; **14** 170; **47 81–84** (upd.)
Commerzfilm, **IV** 591
CommLink Corp., **17** 264
Commodity Credit Corp., **11** 24
Commodore Corporation, **8** 229
Commodore International, Ltd., **II** 6; **III** 112; **6** 243–44; **7 95–97**, 532; **9** 46; **10** 56, 284; **23** 25; **26** 16
Commonwealth & Southern Corporation, **V** 676
Commonwealth Aluminium Corp., Ltd. *See* Comalco Ltd.
Commonwealth Bank, **II** 188, 389
Commonwealth Board Mills, **IV** 248
Commonwealth Edison, **II** 28, 425; **III** 653; **IV** 169; **V 583–85**; **6** 505, 529, 531; **12** 548; **13** 341; **15** 422; **48** 163
Commonwealth Energy System, 14 124–26
Commonwealth Hospitality Ltd., **III** 95
Commonwealth Industrial Gases, **25** 82
Commonwealth Industries, **III** 569; **11** 536; **20** 360
Commonwealth Insurance Co., **III** 264
Commonwealth Land Title Insurance Co., **III** 343
Commonwealth Life and Accident Insurance Company, **27** 46–47

Commonwealth Life Insurance Co., **III** 216–19

Commonwealth Limousine Services, Ltd., **26** 62

Commonwealth Mortgage Assurance Co., **III** 344

Commonwealth National Financial Corp., **II** 316; **44** 280

Commonwealth Oil Refining Company, **II** 402; **7** 517; **45** 410

Commonwealth Power Railway and Light Company, **14** 134

Commonwealth Southern Corporation, **14** 134

Commonwealth Telephone Enterprises, Inc., 25 106–08

Commtron, Inc., **V** 14, 16; **11** 195; **13** 90

Communication Services Ltd. See Hongkong Telecommunications Ltd.

Communications and Systems Specialists, **18** 370

Communications Consultants, Inc., **16** 393

Communications Corp. of America, **25** 418

Communications Data Services, Inc., **IV** 627; **19** 204

Communications Industries Inc., **25** 496

Communications Network Consultants, **29** 400

Communications Properties, Inc., **IV** 677

Communications Solutions Inc., **11** 520

Communications Technology Corp. (CTC), **13** 7–8

Communicorp, **III** 188; **10** 29; **38** 17

Community Direct, Inc., **7** 16

Community HealthCare Services, **6** 182

Community Hospital of San Gabriel, **6** 149

Community Medical Care, Inc., **III** 245

Community National Bank, **9** 474

Community Networks Inc., **45** 69

Community Newspapers, Inc., **45** 352

Community Power & Light Company, **6** 579–80

Community Psychiatric Centers, 15 118–20

Community Public Service Company, **6** 514

Community Savings and Loan, **II** 317

Comnet Corporation, **9** 347

Comp-U-Card of America, Inc. See CUC International Inc.

Compac Corp., **11** 535

Compactom, **I** 588

Compagnia di Assicurazioni, **III** 345

Compagnia di Genova, **III** 347

Compagnia di Participazioni Assicurative ed Industriali S.p.A., **24** 341

Compagnie Auxiliaire de Navigation, **IV** 558

Compagnie Bancaire, **II** 259; **21** 99–100

Compagnie Belge pour l'industrie, **II** 202

Compagnie Continentale, **I** 409–10

Compagnie d'Assurances Générales, **III** 391

Compagnie d'assurances Mutuelles contre l'incendie dans les départements de la Seine Inférieure et de l'Eure, **III** 210

Compagnie d'Investissements de Paris, **II** 233

Compagnie de Compteurs, **III** 617; **17** 418

Compagnie de Five-Lille, **IV** 469

Compagnie de Mokta, **IV** 107–08

Compagnie de Navigation Mixte, **III** 185

Compagnie de Reassurance Nord-Atlantique, **III** 276

Compagnie de Recherche et d'Exploitation du Pétrole du Sahara, **IV** 545; **21** 203

Compagnie de Saint-Gobain S.A., II 117, 474–75; **III** 675–78, 704; **8** 395, 397; **15** 80; **16 119–23 (upd.)**; **19** 58, 226; **21** 222; **26** 446; **33** 338, 340; **35** 86, 88

Compagnie de Transport Aerien, **I** 122

Compagnie des Alpes, 48 106–08

Compagnie des Cristalleries de Baccarat. See Baccarat.

Compagnie des Machines Bull S.A., II 40, 42, 70, 125; **III 122–23**, 154; **IV** 600; **12** 139; **13** 574; **25** 33. See also Bull S.A. and Groupe Bull.

Compagnie des Messageries Maritimes, **6** 379

Compagnie des Produits Chimiques et Électrométallurgiques d'Alais, Froges et Camargue, **IV** 173–74

Compagnie du Midi, **III** 209, 211

Compagnie du Nord, **IV** 108

Compagnie Européenne de Publication, **IV** 614–15

Compagnie Européenne de Télésecurité, **32** 374

Compagnie Financier Richemont AG, **19** 367, 369–70

Compagnie Financiere Alcatel, **9** 10

Compagnie Financière Belge des Pétroles. See PetroFina S.A.

Compagnie Financière de Paribas, II 192, **259–60**; **III** 185; **21** 99; **27** 138; **33** 339. See also BNP Paribas Group.

Compagnie Financière de Richemont AG, **29** 90

Compagnie Financière de Suez. See Suez Lyonnaise des Eaux.

Compagnie Financière du Groupe Victoire, **27** 54; **49** 44

Compagnie Financière Richemont AG, **27** 487; **29** 91–92

Compagnie Française Chaufour Investissement, **27** 100

Compagnie Française de Distribution en Afrique, **IV** 559

Compagnie Française de Manutention, **27** 295

Compagnie Française de Raffinage, **IV** 558–60

Compagnie Française des Lubricants, **I** 341

Compagnie Française des Minerais d'Uranium, **IV** 108

Compagnie Française des Mines de Diamants du Cap, **IV** 64; **7** 121

Compagnie Française des Pétroles. See TOTAL S.A.

Compagnie Française des Produits d'Orangina, **I** 281

Compagnie Française du Méthane, **V** 626

Compagnie Française Thomson-Houston, **I** 357; **II** 116. See also Thales S.A.

Compagnie Fromagère de la Vallée de l'Ance, **25** 84

Compagnie Générale d'Électricité, I 193; **II 12–13**, 25; **IV** 174, 615; **9** 9–10

Compagnie Generale de Cartons Ondules, **IV** 296; **19** 226

Compagnie Generale de Radiologie, **II** 117

Compagnie Generale de Telegraphie Sans Fils, **II** 116

Compagnie Générale des Eaux, **V** 632–33; **6** 441. See also Vivendi SA.

Compagnie Générale des Établissements Michelin, V 236–39; **19** 508; **42 85–89 (upd.)**

Compagnie Générale Maritime et Financière, 6 379–81

Compagnie Industriali Riunite S.p.A., **IV** 587–88

Compagnie Industrielle de Matérials de Manutention, **27** 296

Compagnie Industrielle des Fillers. See L'Entreprise Jean Lefebvre.

Compagnie Internationale de l'Informatique, **III** 123

Compagnie Internationale Express, **25** 120

Compagnie Internationale Pirelli S.A., **V** 249

Compagnie Laitière Européenne, **25** 83, 85

Compagnie Luxembourgeoise de Télédiffusion, **15** 54

Compagnie Nationale à Portefeuille, **29** 48

Compagnie Nationale de Navigation, **27** 515

Compagnie Navale Des Pétroles, **IV** 558

Compagnie Parisienne de Garantie, **III** 211

Compagnie Pneumatique Commerciale, **III** 426

Compagnie Tunisienne de Ressorts a Lames, **III** 581

Compagnie Union des Assurances de Paris (UAP), **49** 44

Compal, **47** 152–53

Companhia Brasileira de Aluminio, **IV** 55

Companhia Brasileira de Mineracão e Siderugica, **IV** 54

Companhia de Celulose do Caima, **14** 250

Companhia de Diamantes de Angola, **IV** 21

Companhia de Electricidade da Bahia, **49** 211

Companhia de Minerales y Metales, **IV** 139

Companhia de Pesquisas Mineras de Angola, **IV** 65; **7** 122

Companhia de Seguros Argos Fluminense, **III** 221

Companhia de Seguros Tranquilidade Vida, S.A. See Banco Espírito Santo e Comercial de Lisboa S.A.

Companhia Siderúrgica de Tubarao, **IV** 125

Companhia Siderúrgica Mannesmann S.A., **III** 565–66

Companhia Siderúrgica Nacional, **II** 199; **43** 112

Companhia Uniao Fabril, **IV** 505

Companhia Vale do Rio Doce, IV 54–57; **43 111–14 (upd.)**

Compañia Arrendataria del Monopolio de Petróleos Sociedad Anónima, **IV** 396–97, 527–29

Compañia de Investigacion y Exploitaciones Petrolifera, **IV** 397

Compañia de Líneas Aéreas Subvencionadas S.A., **6** 95

Compañia Española de Petroleos S.A., IV 396–98, 527

Compania Fresnillo, **22** 286

Compania General de Aceptaciones. See Financiera Aceptaciones.

Compania Hulera Euzkadi, **21** 260; **23** 170

Compañia Mexicana de Transportación Aérea, **20** 167

Compania Minera de Penoles. See Industrias Penoles, S.A. de C.V.

Compañia Minera La India, **IV** 164
Compania Minera Las Torres, **22** 286
Compañia Nacional Minera Petrólia del
Táchira, **IV** 507
Compania Siderurgica Huachipato, **24** 209
Compañía Telefónica Nacional de España
S.A., **V** 337
Compaq Computer Corporation, II 45;
III 114, **124–25; 6** 217, **221–23 (upd.),**
230–31, 235, 243–44; **9** 42–43, 166,
170–71, 472; **10** 87, 232–33, 366, 459,
518–19; **12** 61, 183, 335, 470; **13** 388,
483; **16** 4, 196, 367–68; **17** 274; **21** 123,
391; **22** 288; **25** 184, 239, 498, 531; **26**
90–93 (upd.); 27 365; **28** 191; **29** 439;
30 12; **36** 384; **43** 13; **47** 153
Compart, **24** 341
Compass Airlines, **27** 475
Compass Design Automation, **16** 520
Compass Group PLC, 6 193; **24** 194; **27**
482; **34 121–24**
CompDent Corporation, 22 149–51
Compeda, Ltd., **10** 240
Competence ApS, **26** 240
Competition Tire East/West, **V** 494; **19** 292
Competrol Ltd., **22** 189
Compex, **II** 233
CompHealth Inc., 25 109–12
Complete Business Solutions, Inc., 31
130–33
Completion Bond Co., **26** 487
Components Agents Ltd., **10** 113
Composite Craft Inc., **I** 387
Composite Research & Management Co.,
17 528, 530
Comprehensive Care Corporation, 15
121–23
Comprehensive Resources Corp., **IV** 83
Compressed Industrial Gases, **I** 297
Compression Labs Inc., **10** 456; **16** 392,
394; **27** 365
Compressor Controls Corporation, **15** 404
Comptoir d'Escompte de Mulhouse, **II** 232
Comptoir des Textiles Artificielles, **I** 122,
388–89
Comptoir Général de la Photographie. *See*
Gaumont SA.
Comptoir Métallurgique Luxembourgeois,
IV 25
Comptoir National d'Escompte de Paris, **II**
232–33, 270
Comptoirs Modernes S.A., 19 97–99
Compton Communications, **I** 33
Compton Foods, **II** 675
Compton's MultiMedia Publishing Group,
Inc., **7** 165
Compton's New Media, Inc., **7** 168
Compu-Notes, Inc., **22** 413
CompuAdd Computer Corporation, 11
61–63
CompuChem Corporation, **11** 425
CompuCom Systems, Inc., 10 232–34,
474; **13** 176
Compugraphic, **III** 168; **6** 284
Compumech Technologies, **19** 312
Compumotor, **III** 603
CompuPharm, Inc., **14** 210
CompUSA, Inc., 10 235–36; 35 116–18
(upd.)
CompuServe Incorporated, 9 268–70; **10**
237–39; 12 562; **13** 147; **15** 265; **16**
467, 508; **26** 16; **29** 224, 226–27; **34**
361. *See also* America Online, Inc.

CompuServe Interactive Services, Inc.,
27 106, **106–08 (upd.),** 301, 307. *See
also* America Online, Inc.
Computax, **6** 227–28
Computer Associates International, Inc.,
6 224–26; 10 394; **12** 62; **14** 392; **27**
492; **49 94–97 (upd.)**
Computer City, **12** 470; **36** 387
The Computer Company, **11** 112
Computer Consoles Inc., **III** 164
Computer Data Systems, Inc., 14 127–29
The Computer Department, Ltd., **10** 89
Computer Depot, **6** 243
Computer Discount Corporation. *See*
Comdisco, Inc.
Computer Dynamics, Inc., **6** 10
Computer Engineering Associates, **25** 303
Computer Factory, Inc., **13** 176
Computer Learning Centers, Inc., 26
94–96
Computer Network, **20** 237
Computer Peripheral Manufacturers
Association, **13** 127
Computer Plaza K.K., **IV** 542–43
Computer Power, **6** 301
Computer Renaissance, Inc., **18** 207–8
Computer Research Corp., **III** 151; **6** 265
Computer Resources Management, Inc., **26**
36
Computer Sciences Corporation, 6 25,
227–29; 13 462; **15** 474; **18** 370
Computer Shoppe, **V** 191–92
Computer Systems and Applications, **12**
442
Computer Systems Division (CDS), **13** 201
Computer Terminal Corporation, **11** 67–68
ComputerCity, **10** 235
ComputerCraft, **27** 163
Computerized Lodging Systems, Inc., **11**
275
Computerized Waste Systems, **46** 248
ComputerLand Corp., 6 243; **9** 116; **10**
233, 563; **12** 335; **13 174–76,** 277; **33**
341–42
Computervision Corporation, 6 246–47;
7 498; **10 240–42; 11** 275; **13** 201; **24**
234
Computing Scale Company of America.
See International Business Machines
Corporation.
Computing-Tabulating-Recording Co., **III**
147
Compuware Corporation, 10 243–45; 30
140–43 (upd.); 38 482
CompX International, Inc., **19** 466, 468
Comsat Corporation, II 425; **12** 19; **13**
341; **23 133–36; 28** 241; **29** 42
Comshare Inc., 23 137–39
Comstock Canada, **9** 301
Comstock Resources, Inc., 47 85–87
Comtel Electronics, Inc., **22** 409
Comunicaciones Avanzados, S.A. de C.V.,
39 195
Comverse Technology, Inc., 15 124–26;
43 115–18 (upd.)
Comviq GSM AB, **26** 331–33
Con Ed. *See* Consolidated Edison, Inc.
Con-Ferro Paint and Varnish Company, **8**
553
ConAgra, Inc., II 493–95, 517, 585; **7**
432, 525; **8** 53, 499–500; **12 80–82**
(upd.); 13 138, 294, 350, 352; **14** 515;
17 56, 240–41; **18** 247, 290; **21** 290; **23**

320; **25** 243, 278; **26** 172, 174; **36** 416;
42 90–94 (upd.)
Conahay & Lyon, **6** 27
Conair Corp., 16 539; **17 108–10; 24**
131; **25** 56
Concept, Inc., **23** 154
Concepts Direct, Inc., 39 93–96
Concepts in Community Living, Inc., **43** 46
Concert Communications Company, **15** 69;
27 304–05; **49** 72
Concesiones de Infraestructuras de
Transportes, S.A., **40** 217
Concession Air, **16** 446
Concha y Toro. *See* Viña Concha y Toro
S.A.
Concord Camera Corporation, 41
104–07
Concord Fabrics, Inc., 16 124–26
Concord International, **II** 298
Concord Watch Company, S.A., **28** 291
Concorde Hotels, **27** 421
Concordia, **IV** 497
Concrete Industries (Monier) Ltd., **III** 735
Concurrent Logic, **17** 34
The Condé Nast Publications Inc., IV
583–84; **13 177–81; 19** 5; **23** 98
Condor Systems Inc., **15** 530
Cone Communications, **25** 258
Cone Mills Corporation, 8 120–22
Conelectron, **13** 398
Conestoga National Bank, **II** 316
Conexant Systems, Inc., 36 121–25; 43
328
Confectionaire, **25** 283
Confederacion Norte-Centromericana y del
Caribe de Futbol, **27** 150
Confederacion Sudamericana de Futbol, **27**
150
Confederation Africaine de Football, **27**
150
Confederation Freezers, **21** 501
Confederation of Engineering Industry, **IV**
484
Confidata Corporation, **11** 111
Confindustria, **I** 162
Confiserie-Group Hofbauer, **27** 105
Congas Engineering Canada Ltd., **6** 478
Congoleum Corp., 12 28; **16** 18; **18**
116–19; 36 77–78; **43** 19, 21
Congress Financial Corp., **13** 305–06; **19**
108; **27** 276
Congressional Information Services, **IV**
610
Conic, **9** 324
Conifer Group, **II** 214
Conill Corp., **II** 261
Coniston Partners, **I** 130; **II** 680; **III** 29; **6**
130; **10** 302
CONNA Corp., **7** 113; **25** 125
Connect Group Corporation, **28** 242
Connecticut Bank and Trust Co., **II**
213–14
Connecticut General Corporation. *See*
CIGNA Corporation.
Connecticut Health Enterprises Network,
22 425
Connecticut Light and Power Co., 13
182–84; 21 514; **48** 305
Connecticut Mutual Life Insurance
Company, III 225, **236–38,** 254, 285
Connecticut National Bank, **13** 467
Connecticut River Banking Company, **13**
467

Connecticut Telephone Company. *See* Southern New England Telecommunications Corporation.
Connecticut Trust and Safe Deposit Co., **II** 213
Connecticut Yankee Atomic Power Company, **21** 513
Connecting Point of America, **6** 244
The Connection Group, Inc., **26** 257
Connectix Corporation, **28** 245
The Connell Company, 29 129–31
Conner Corp., **15** 327
Conner Peripherals, Inc., 6 230–32; 10 403, 459, 463–64, 519; **11** 56, 234; **18** 260
Connie Lee. *See* College Construction Loan Insurance Assoc.
Connoisseur Communications, **37** 104
Connolly Data Systems, **11** 66
Connolly Tool and Machine Company, **21** 215
Connors Brothers, **II** 631–32
Connors Steel Co., **15** 116
Conoco Inc., I 286, 329, 346, 402–04; **II** 376; **IV** 365, 382, 389, **399–402**, 413, 429, 454, 476; **6** 539; **7** 346, 559; **8** 152, 154, 556; **11** 97, 400; **16 127–32 (upd.);** **18** 366; **21** 29; **26** 125, 127
Conorada Petroleum Corp., **IV** 365, 400
Conover Furniture Company, **10** 183
ConQuest Telecommunication Services Inc., **16** 319
Conquistador Films, **25** 270
Conrad International Hotels, **III** 91–93
Conrail Inc., **22** 167, 376. *See also* Consolidated Rail Corporation.
Conran Associates, **17** 43
Conrock Co., **19** 70
Conseco Inc., 10 246–48; 15 257; 33 **108–12 (upd.)**
Consgold. *See* Consolidated Gold Fields of South Africa Ltd. *and* Consolidated Gold Fields PLC.
Conshu Holdings, **24** 450
Conso International Corporation, 29 **132–34**
Consodata S.A., **47** 345, 347
Consolidated Aircraft Corporation, **9** 16, 497
Consolidated Aluminum Corp., **IV** 178
Consolidated Asset Management Company, Inc., **25** 204
Consolidated-Bathurst Inc., **IV** 246–47, 334; **25** 11; **26** 445
Consolidated Brands Inc., **14** 18
Consolidated Cable Utilities, **6** 313
Consolidated Cement Corp., **III** 704
Consolidated Cigar Holdings, Inc., **I** 452–53; **15** 137–38; **27** 139–40; **28** 247
Consolidated Coal Co., **IV** 82, 170–71
Consolidated Coin Caterers Corporation, **10** 222
Consolidated Controls, **I** 155
Consolidated Converting Co., **19** 109
Consolidated Copper Corp., **13** 503
Consolidated Delivery & Logistics, Inc., **24 125–28**
Consolidated Denison Mines Ltd., **8** 418
Consolidated Diamond Mines of South-West Africa Ltd., **IV** 21, 65–67; **7** 122–25; **16** 26
Consolidated Distillers Ltd., **I** 263

Consolidated Edison Company of New **York, Inc., I** 28; **V 586–89; 6** 456; **35** 479
Consolidated Edison, Inc., 45 116–20 **(upd.)**
Consolidated Electric & Gas, **6** 447; **23** 28
Consolidated Electric Power Asia, **38** 448
Consolidated Electric Supply Inc., **15** 385
Consolidated Electronics Industries Corp. (Conelco), **13** 397–98
Consolidated Foods Corp., **II** 571–73, 584; **III** 480; **12** 159, 494; **22** 27; **29** 132
Consolidated Freightways Corporation, **V 432–34; 6** 280, 388; **12** 278, 309; **13** 19; **14** 567; **21 136–39 (upd.); 25** 148–50; **48 109–13 (upd.)**
Consolidated Gas Company. *See* Baltimore Gas and Electric Company.
Consolidated Gold Fields of South Africa Ltd., **IV** 94, 96, 118, 565, 566
Consolidated Gold Fields PLC, **II** 422; **III** 501, 503; **IV** 23, 67, 94, 97, 171; **7** 125, 209, 387
Consolidated Grocers Corp., **II** 571
Consolidated Insurances of Australia, **III** 347
Consolidated Marketing, Inc., **IV** 282; **9** 261
Consolidated Mines Selection Co., **IV** 20, 23
Consolidated Mining and Smelting Co., **IV** 75
Consolidated National Life Insurance Co., **10** 246
Consolidated Natural Gas Company, V **590–91; 19 100–02 (upd.)**
Consolidated Oatmeal Co., **II** 558
Consolidated Papers, Inc., 8 123–25; 36 **126–30 (upd.)**
Consolidated Plantations Berhad, **36** 434–35
Consolidated Power & Light Company, **6** 580
Consolidated Power & Telephone Company, **11** 342
Consolidated Press Holdings, **8** 551; **37** 408–09
Consolidated Products, Inc., 14 130–32, 352
Consolidated Rail Corporation, II 449; **V 435–37**, 485; **10** 44; **12** 278; **13** 449; **14** 324; **29** 360; **35** 291. *See also* Conrail Inc.
Consolidated Rand-Transvaal Mining Group, **IV** 90; **22** 233
Consolidated Rock Products Co., **19** 69
Consolidated Specialty Restaurants, Inc., **14** 131–32
Consolidated Steel, **I** 558; **IV** 570; **24** 520
Consolidated Stores Corp., **13** 543; **29** 311; **35** 254
Consolidated Temperature Controlling Co., **II** 40; **12** 246
Consolidated Theaters, Inc., **14** 87
Consolidated Tire Company, **20** 258
Consolidated Trust Inc., **22** 540
Consolidated Tyre Services Ltd., **IV** 241
Consolidated Vultee, **II** 7, 32
Consolidated Zinc Corp., **IV** 58–59, 122, 189, 191
Consolidation Coal Co., **IV** 401; **8** 154, 346–47
Consolidation Services, **44** 10, 13

Consorcio G Grupo Dina, S.A. de C.V., **36 131–33**
Consortium, **34** 373
Consortium de Realisation, **25** 329
Consortium De Realization SAS, **23** 392
Consoweld Corporation, **8** 124
Constar International Inc., **8** 562; **13** 190; **32** 125
Constellation, **III** 335
Constellation Energy Corporation, **24** 29
Constellation Enterprises Inc., **25** 46
Constellation Insurance Co., **III** 191–92
Constinsouza, **25** 174
Construcciones Aeronauticas S.A., **I** 41–42; **7** 9; **12** 190; **24** 88
Construcciones y Contratas, **II** 198
Construction DJL Inc., **23** 332–33
Construtora Moderna SARL, **IV** 505
Consul Restaurant Corp., **13** 152
Consumer Access Limited, **24** 95
Consumer Products Company, **30** 39
Consumer Value Stores, **V** 136–37; **9** 67; **18** 199; **24** 290
Consumer's Gas Co., **I** 264
ConsumerNet, **49** 422
Consumers Cooperative Association, **7** 174. *See also* Farmland Industries, Inc.
Consumers Distributing Co. Ltd., **II** 649, 652–53
Consumers Electric Light and Power, **6** 582
The Consumers Gas Company Ltd., 6 **476–79; 43** 154. *See also* Enbridge Inc.
Consumers Mutual Gas Light Company. *See* Baltimore Gas and Electric Company.
Consumers Power Co., V 577–79, 593–94; **14** 114–15, **133–36**
Consumers Public Power District, **29** 352
Consumers Union, 26 97–99
Consumers Water Company, 14 137–39; **39** 329
Contact Software International Inc., **10** 509
Contadina, **II** 488–89
Container Corporation of America, **IV** 295, 465; **V** 147; **7** 353; **8** 476; **19** 225; **26** 446
The Container Store, 36 134–36
Container Transport International, **III** 344
Containers Packaging, **IV** 249
Contaminant Recovery Systems, Inc., **18** 162
CONTAQ Microsystems Inc., **48** 127
Conte S.A., **12** 262
Contech, **10** 493
Contel Corporation, **II** 117; **V** 294–98; **6** 323; **13** 212; **14** 259; **15** 192; **43** 447
Contempo Associates, **14** 105; **25** 307
Contempo Casuals, Inc. *See* The Wet Seal, Inc.
Contemporary Books, **22** 522
Content Technologies Inc., **42** 24–25
Contex Graphics Systems Inc., **24** 428
Contherm Corp., **III** 420
Conti-Carriers & Terminals Inc., **22** 167
ContiCommodity Services, Inc., **10** 250–51
ContiGroup Companies, Inc., 43 119–22 **(upd.)**
Continental AG, **9** 248; **15** 355
Continental Airlines, Inc., I 96–98, 103, 118, 123–24, 129–30; **6** 52, 61, 105, 120–21, 129–30; **12** 381; **20** 84, 262; **21** **140–43 (upd.); 22** 80, 220; **25** 420, 423; **26** 439–40; **34** 398

Continental Aktiengesellschaft, V **240–43**, 250–51, 256; **8** 212–14; **19** 508

Continental American Life Insurance Company, **7** 102

Continental Assurance Co., **III** 228–30

Continental Baking Co., **I** 463–64; **II** 562–63; **7** 320–21; **11** 198; **12** 276; **13** 427; **19** 192; **27** 309–10; **38** 252

Continental Bancor, **II** 248

Continental Bank and Trust Co., **II** 251; **14** 102

Continental Bank Corporation, **I** 526; **II** **261–63**, 285, 289, 348; **IV** 702; **47** 231

Continental Bio-Clinical Laboratories, **26** 391

Continental Blacks Inc., **I** 403

Continental Cablevision, Inc., **7 98–100**; **17** 148; **19** 201

Continental Can Co., Inc., **I** 597; **II** 34, 414; **III** 471; **10** 130; **13** 255; **15 49** 293–94**127–30**; **24** 428; **26** 117, 449; **32** 125;

Continental-Caoutchouc und Gutta-Percha Compagnie, **V** 240

Continental Carbon Co., **I** 403–05; **II** 53; **IV** 401; **36** 146–48

Continental Care Group, **10** 252–53

Continental Casualty Co., **III** 196, 228–32; **16** 204

Continental Cities Corp., **III** 344

Continental Corporation, **III** 230, **239–44**, 273; **10** 561; **12** 318; **15** 30; **38** 142

Continental Cos., **III** 248

Continental Divide Insurance Co., **III** 214

Continental Electronics Corporation, **18** 513–14

Continental Emsco, **I** 490–91; **24** 305

Continental Equipment Company, **13** 225

Continental Express, **11** 299

Continental Fiber Drum, **8** 476

Continental Gas & Electric Corporation, **6** 511

Continental General Tire Corp., **23** **140–42**

Continental Grain Company, **10 249–51**; **13 185–87 (upd.)**; **30** 353, 355; **40** 87. *See also* ContiGroup Companies, Inc.

Continental Group Co., **I 599–600**, 601–02, 604–05; 609, 612–13, 615; **IV** 334; **8** 175, 424; **17** 106

Continental Gummi-Werke Aktiengesellschaft, **V** 241; **9** 248

Continental Hair Products, Inc. *See* Conair Corp.

Continental Health Affiliates, **17** 307

Continental Homes, **26** 291

Continental Illinois Corp. *See* Continental Bank Corporation.

Continental Illinois Venture Co., **IV** 702

Continental Insurance Co., **III** 239–42, 372–73, 386

Continental Insurance Cos. of New York, **III** 230

Continental Investment Corporation, **9** 507; **12** 463; **22** 541; **33** 407

Continental Life Insurance Co., **III** 225

Continental Medical Systems, Inc., **10** **252–54**; **11** 282; **14** 233; **25** 111; **33** 185

Continental Milling Company, **10** 250

Continental Modules, Inc., **45** 328

Continental Motors Corp., **I** 199, 524–25; **10** 521–22

Continental Mutual Savings Bank, **17** 529

Continental National American Group, **III** 230, 404

Continental National Bank, **II** 261; **11** 119

Continental-National Group, **III** 230

Continental Oil Co., **IV** 39, 365, 382, 399–401, 476, 517, 575–76

Continental Packaging Inc., **13** 255

Continental Plastic Containers, Inc., **25** 512

Continental Radio, **IV** 607

Continental Reinsurance, **11** 533

Continental Research Corporation, **22** 541

Continental Restaurant Systems, **12** 510

Continental Risk Services, **III** 243

Continental Savouries, **II** 500

Continental Scale Works, **14** 229–30

Continental Securities Corporation, **II** 444; **22** 404

Continental Telephone Company, **V** 296–97; **9** 494–95; **11** 500; **15** 195

Continental Wood Preservers, Inc., **12** 397

Continentale Allgemeine, **III** 347

ContinueCare Corporation, **25** 41

Contran Corporation, **19** 467

Contrans Acquisitions, Inc., **14** 38

Contred Ltd., **20** 263

Control Data Corporation, **17** 49; **19** 110, 513–15; **25** 496; **30** 338; **38** 58; **46** 35

Control Data Systems, Inc., **III** 118, **126–28**, 129, 131, 149, 152, 165; **6** 228, 252, 266; **8** 117–18, 467; **10 255–57**, 359, 458–59; **11** 469; **16** 137

Controladora Comercial Mexicana, S.A. de C.V., **36 137–39**

Controladora PROSA, **18** 516, 518

Controlled Materials and Equipment Transportation, **29** 354

Controlonics Corporation, **13** 195

Controls Company of America, **9** 67

Controlware GmbH, **22** 53

Convair, **I** 82, 121, 123, 126, 131; **II** 33; **9** 18, 498; **13** 357

Convenient Food Mart Inc., **7** 114; **25** 125

Convergent Technologies, **III** 166; **6** 283; **11** 519

Converse Inc., **III** 528–29; **V** 376; **9** **133–36**, 234; **12** 308; **31 134–138** **(upd.)**, 211; **39** 170, 172–74

Conway Computer Group, **18** 370

Conwest Exploration Company Ltd., **16** 10, 12; **43** 3

Conycon. *See* Construcciones y Contratas.

Conzinc Riotinto of Australia. *See* CRA Limited.

Cook Bates Inc., **40** 347–48

Cook Data Services, Inc., **9** 73

Cook Industrial Coatings, **I** 307

Cook Standard Tool Co., **13** 369

Cook United, **V** 172

Cooke Engineering Company, **13** 194

The Cooker Restaurant Corporation, **20** **159–61**

Cooking and Crafts Club, **13** 106

Cookson Group plc, **III 679–82**; **16** 290; **44 115–20 (upd.)**; **49** 234–35

CoolBrands International Inc., **35** **119–22**

Coolerator, **I** 463

Coolidge Mutual Savings Bank, **17** 529

Coop Schweiz Genossenschaftsverband, **48** 114–16

Cooper Cameron Corporation, **20** **162–66 (upd.)**

Cooper Canada Ltd., **16** 80

The Cooper Companies, Inc., **39 97–100**

Cooper Industries, Inc., **II 14–17**; **14** 564; **19** 43, 45, 140; **30** 266; **44 121–25** **(upd.)**; **49** 159

Cooper Laboratories, **I** 667, 682

Cooper LaserSonics Inc., **IV** 100

Cooper McDougall & Robertson Ltd., **I** 715

Cooper Tire & Rubber Company, **8** **126–28**; **23 143–46 (upd.)**

Cooper-Weymouth, **10** 412

Cooper's, Inc., **12** 283

Cooperative Grange League Federation Exchange, **7** 17

Coopers & Lybrand, **9 137–38**; **12** 391; **25** 383. *See also* PricewaterhouseCoopers.

CooperVision, **7** 46; **25** 55

Coordinated Caribbean Transport. *See* Crowley Caribbean Transport.

Coors Company. *See* Adolph Coors Company.

Coorsh and Bittner, **7** 430

Coos Bay Lumber Co., **IV** 281; **9** 259

Coosa River Newsprint Co., **III** 40; **16** 303; **43** 257

Coote & Jurgenson, **14** 64

Cooymans, **I** 281

Copart Inc., **23 147–49**, 285, 287

Copeland Corp., **II** 20

Copeman Ridley, **13** 103

Copico, **44** 273

Copland Brewing Co., **I** 268; **25** 280

Copley Pharmaceuticals Inc., **13** 264

The Copley Press, Inc., **23 150–52**

Copley Real Estate Advisors, **III** 313

Copolymer Corporation, **9** 242

Copper Queen Consolidated Mining Co., **IV** 176–77

Copper Range Company, **IV** 76; **7** 281–82

Copperweld Steel Co., **IV** 108–09, 237

The Copps Corporation, **32 120–22**

Copycat Ltd., **8** 383

Cor Therapeutics, **47** 251

Cora Verlag, **IV** 590

Coral Drilling, **I** 570

Coral Energy, **41** 359

Coral Leisure Group, **I** 248

Coral Petroleum, **IV** 395

Corange, Ltd., **37** 111–13

Corbett Canyon. *See* The Wine Group, Inc.

Corbett Enterprises Inc., **13** 270

Corbis Corporation, **31 139–42**

Corby Distilleries Limited, **14 140–42**

Corchos de Mérida S.A., **48** 349

Corco. *See* Commonwealth Oil Refining Company.

Corco, Inc. *See* Liqui-Box Corporation.

Corcoran & Riggs. *See* Riggs National Corporation.

Cordant plc. *See* Saatchi & Saatchi plc.

Cordis Corporation, **19 103–05**; **36** 306; **46 104–07 (upd.)**

Cordon & Gotch, **IV** 619

Le Cordon Bleu, **II** 609; **45** 88; **45** 88

Cordovan Corp., **IV** 608

Core Laboratories Inc., **I** 486; **11** 265

Corel Corporation, **15 131–33**; **33** **113–16 (upd.)**

CoreStates Financial Corp, **17 111–15**

CoreTek, Inc., **36** 353

Corfuerte S.A. de C.V., **23** 171

Corimon, **12** 218

Corinthian Broadcasting Corporation, **IV** 605; **10** 4

Corinthian Colleges, Inc., **39** 101–04
Corio Inc., **38** 188, 432
Cormetech, **III** 685
Corn Exchange Bank, **II** 316
Corn Exchange Bank Trust Co., **II** 251; **14** 102
Corn Exchange National Bank, **II** 261
Corn Products Company. *See* Bestfoods.
Corn Sweetners Inc., **I** 421; **11** 23
Cornelia Insurance Agency. *See* Advantage Insurers, Inc.
Cornell Corrections, **28** 255
Cornerstone Direct Marketing, **8** 385–86
Cornerstone Propane Partners, L.P., **37** 280, 283
Cornerstone Title Company, **8** 461
Cornhill Insurance Co., **I** 429; **III** 185, 385
Cornhusker Casualty Co., **III** 213
Corning Asahi Video Products Co., **III** 667
Corning Clinical Laboratories, **26** 390–92
Corning Consumer Products Company, **27** 288
Corning Inc., **I** 609; **III** 434, 667, **683–85**, 720–21; **8** 468; **11** 334; **13** 398; **22** 454; **25** 254; **30** 151–52; **44 126–30** (upd.)
Coro International A.V.V., **39** 346
Coronado Corp., **II** 112
Coronet Industries, Inc., **II** 90; **14** 436
Corporacion Durango, S.A. de C.V., **37** 178
Corporacion Estatal Petrolera Ecuatoriana, **IV** 510–11
Corporación Internacional de Aviación, S.A. de C.V. (Cintra), **20 167–69**
Corporación Moctezuma, **21** 261
Corporacion Nacional del Cobre de Chile, **38** 231; **40 121–23**
Corporacion Siderurgica Integral, **22** 44
Corporación Venezolana de Petroleo, **IV** 507
Corporate Childcare Development, Inc. *See* Bright Horizons Family Solutions, Inc.
Corporate Express, Inc., **22 152–55**, 531; **41** 67–69; **47 88–92 (upd.)**; **49** 440
Corporate Microsystems, Inc., **10** 395
Corporate Partners, **12** 391
Corporate Software Inc., **9 139–41**
CorporateFamily Solutions. *See* Bright Horizons Family Solutions, Inc.
Corporation for Public Broadcasting, **14 143–45**; **47** 259
Corporation of Lloyd's, **III** 278–79
Corporation Trust Co. *See* CCH Inc.
Corpoven, **IV** 508
Corrado Passera, **IV** 588
Corral Midwest, Inc., **10** 333
Correctional Services Corporation, **30 144–46**
Corrections Corporation of America, **23 153–55**; **28** 255
Corrigan-McKinney Steel Company, **13** 157
Corrigan's, **16** 559
Corroon & Black. *See* Willis Corroon Group Plc.
Corrpro Companies, Inc., **20 170–73**
Corrugated Paper, **IV** 249
CORT Business Services Corporation, **26 100–02**
El Corte Inglés Group, **26 128–31 (upd.)**
Cortec Corporation, **14** 430

Corticeira Amorim, Sociedade Gestora de Participaço es Sociais, S.A., **48 117–20**, 349
Corus Group plc, **49 98–105 (upd.)**
Corvallis Lumber Co., **IV** 358
Cory Bros & Co. Ltd., **31** 367, 369
Cory Components, **36** 158
Cory Corp., **II** 511
Cory Food Services, Inc., **II** 608
Cory Orchard and Turf. *See* Chemi-Trol Chemical Co.
Cosco Pacific, **20** 313
Cosden Petroleum Corp., **IV** 498; **26** 367
Cosgrove & Co., **III** 283
Cosmair Inc., **III** 47–48; **8 129–32**, 342–44; **12** 404; **31** 418; **46** 278
Cosmar Corp., **37** 269–71
The Cosmetic Center, Inc., **22 156–58**
Cosmetic Technology International, Inc., **22** 409
Cosmo Oil Co., Ltd., **IV 403–04**
Cosmopolitan Cosmetics GmbH, **48** 420, 422
Cosmopolitan Productions, **IV** 626; **19** 203
Cosmotel, **46** 401
Cosorzio Interprovinciale Vini, **10** 181
Cost Plus, Inc., **12** 393; **27 109–11**; **34** 337, 340
Costa Apple Products, **II** 480; **26** 57
Costa Cruise Lines, **27** 29, 90, 92
Costa e Ribeiro Ltd., **IV** 504
Costa Rica International, Inc., **41** 329
Costain Civil Engineering Ltd., **III** 495; **13** 206
Costain Homes, **31** 386
Costco Wholesale Corporation, **V** 36; **10** 206; **11** 240; **14** 393–95; **15** 470; **25** 235; **27** 95; **43 123–25 (upd.)**
Costruzioni Meccaniche Nazionalia, **13** 218
Côte d'Or, **II** 521
Cott Beverage Corporation, **9** 291
Cottees General Foods, **II** 477
Cotter & Company, **V** 37–38; **12** 8. *See also* TruServ Corporation.
Cotter Corporation, **29** 488
Cotton Incorporated, **46 108–11**
Cotton Producers Association. *See* Gold Kist Inc.
Coty, Inc., **36 140–42**; **37** 270
Coudert Brothers, **30 147–50**
Coulter Corporation. *See* Beckman Coulter, Inc.
Counsel Corp., **46** 3
Counselor Co., **14** 230
Country Fresh, Inc., **26** 449
Country Kitchen Foods, **III** 21
Country Kitchen International, **22** 127
Country Music Television, **11** 153
Country Poultry, Inc., **II** 494
Country Seat Stores, Inc., **15** 87
Country Store of Concord, Inc., **10** 216
Countrywide Credit Industries, Inc., **16 133–36**
County Bank, **II** 333
County Catering Co., **13** 103
County Data Corporation, **18** 24
County Fire Insurance Co., **III** 191
County Market, **II** 670
County NatWest, **II** 334–35
County Perfumery, **III** 65
County Seat Stores Inc., **II** 669; **9 142–43**
County Trust Co., **II** 230
Cour des Comptes, **II** 233

Courage Brewing Group., **I** 229, 438–39; **III** 503
Courcoux-Bouvet, **II** 260
Courier Corporation, **41 108–12**
Courir S.A., **39** 183–85
Courrèges Parfums, **III** 48; **8** 343
The Courseware Developers, **11** 19
Court Courier Systems, Inc., **24** 126
Court House Square, **10** 44
Courtaulds plc, **I** 321; **IV** 261, 670; **V** 356–57, **359–61**; **12** 103; **17 116–19 (upd.)**; **33** 134; **41** 9
Courtney Wines International, **II** 477
Courtot Investments, **II** 222
Courts Plc, **45 121–24**
Courtyard by Marriott, **9** 427
Cousins Mortgage and Equity Investments, **12** 393
Coutts & Co., **II** 333–34
Couvrette & Provost Ltd., **II** 651
Covance Inc., **30 151–53**
Covantage, **11** 379
Covenant Life Insurance, **III** 314
Coventry Climax Engines, Ltd., **13** 286
Coventry Co., **III** 213
Coventry Corporation, **17** 166, 168
Coventry Machinists Company, **7** 458
Coventry Ordnance Works, **I** 573
Coventry Union Banking Co., **II** 318; **17** 323
Covidea, **II** 252
Coville Inc., **16** 353
Covington & Burling, **40 124–27**
Cow & Gate Ltd., **II** 586–87
Cowham Engineering, **III** 704
Cowles Media Company, **IV** 613, 648; **7** 191; **19** 285; **23 156–58**; 344
Cox & Co., **II** 236, 307–08
Cox Cable Communications, Inc., **42** 114
Cox Enterprises, Inc., **IV** 246, 595–97; **6** 32; **7** 327; **9** 74; **17** 148; **22 159–63 (upd.)**; **24** 120; **30** 217; **38** 307–08
Cox Medical Enterprises, Inc., **21** 47
Cox Newsprint, Inc., **25** 11
Cox Pharmaceuticals, **35** 25
Cox Woodlands Company, **25** 11
Coz Chemical Co., **21** 20, 22
CP. *See* Canadian Pacific Limited.
CP/AAON. *See* AAON, Inc.
CP Air, **6** 60–61
CP National, **6** 300; **19** 412
CP Ships, **45** 80
CPC International Inc., **II** 463, **496–98**; **27** 40. *See also* Bestfoods.
CP8, **43** 89
CPI Corp., **38 157–60**
CPL. *See* Carolina Power & Light Company.
CR2A Holding, **48** 402
CRA Limited, **IV 58–61**, 67, 192; **7** 124. *See also* Rio Tinto plc.
Crabtree Electricals, **III** 503; **7** 210
Cracker Barrel Old Country Store, Inc., **10 258–59**. *See also* CBRL Group, Inc.
Craft House Corp., **8** 456
Craftique, Inc., **33** 350–51
Craftmade International, Inc., **44 131–33**
Craig Bit Company, **13** 297
Crain Communications, Inc., **12 83–86**; **35 123–27 (upd.)**
Cramer, Berkowitz & Co., **34 125–27**
Cramer Electronics, **10** 112
Cranberry Canners, Inc. *See* Ocean Spray Cranberries, Inc.

Crane & Co., Inc., 26 103–06; 30 42
Crane Carton Co., **44** 66
Crane Co., 8 133–36, 179; **24** 332; **30 154–58 (upd.)**
Crane Packing Company, **19** 311
Crane Supply Company, **8** 135
Cranston Mills, **13** 168
Cranswick plc, 40 128–30
Crate and Barrel, 9 144–46; 27 429; **36** 135. See also Euromarket Designs Inc.
Cravath, Swaine & Moore, 27 325; **43 126–28**
Craven Tasker Ltd., **I** 573–74
Crawford and Watson, **IV** 278
Crawford Gosho Co., Ltd., **IV** 442
Crawford Group, Inc., **17** 372
Crawford Supply Company, **6** 392
Cray Research, Inc., III 126, 128, **129–31; 10** 256; **16 137–40 (upd.); 21** 391; **22** 428; **29** 440
Crayfish Company, Ltd., **36** 153
Crazy Eddie Inc., **23** 373
Crazy Shirts, Inc., **45** 42
CRD Total France, **IV** 560
Cream City Railway Company, **6** 601
Cream of Wheat Corp., **II** 543; **22** 427
Cream Wine Company, **48** 392
Creamola Food Products, **II** 569
Creasy Co., **II** 682
Creative Artists Agency LLC, 10 228; **22** 297; **23** 512, 514; **32** 115; **38 161–64**
Creative Artists Associates, **43** 235
Creative BioMolecules, Inc., **29** 454
Creative Business Concepts, Inc., **39** 346
Creative Concepts in Advertising, **27** 194
Creative Displays, Inc., **27** 279
Creative Engineering Inc., **13** 472
Creative Food 'N Fun Co., **14** 29
Creative Forming, Inc., **8** 562
Creative Homes, Inc., **IV** 341
Creative Integration and Design Inc., **20** 146
Creative Memories, **40** 44
Creative Technologies Corp., **15** 401
Creative Technology, Inc., **48** 83
Credit & Risk Management Associates, Inc., **18** 170
Credit Acceptance Corporation, 18 120–22
Crédit Agricole, II 264–66, 355; **19** 51
Credit and Data Marketing Services, **V** 118
Credit Clearing House, **IV** 605
Crédit Commercial de France, **25** 173
Crédit Communal de Belgique, **42** 111
Credit du Nord, **II** 260
Crédit Foncier, **II** 264
Crédit Général de Belgique, **II** 304
Credit Immobilier, **7** 538
Crédit Liégiois, **II** 270
Crédit Local de France, **42** 111
Crédit Lyonnais, II 242, 257, 354; **6** 396; **7** 12; **9 147–49; 19** 34, 51, 166; **21** 226; **25** 170, 329; **33 117–21 (upd.)**
Credit Mobilier, **II** 294
Crédit National S.A., 9 150–52
Credit Service Exchange, **6** 24
Credit Suisse First Boston. See Financière Crédit Suisse-First Boston.
Crédit Suisse Group, II 267–69, 369–70, 378–79, 402–04; **21 144–47 (upd.).** See also Schweizerische Kreditanstalt.
Credit Union Federation, **48** 290
Creditanstalt-Bankverein, **II** 242, 295
CrediThrift Financial, **11** 16

Credithrift Financial of Indiana, **III** 194
Credito de la Union Minera, **II** 194
Credito Italiano, I 368, 465, 567; **II** 191, **270–72; III** 347
Credito Minero y Mercantil, S.A., **22** 285
Credito Provincial Hipotecario, **19** 189
Creditrust Corp., **42** 259
Cree Research, Inc., **13** 399
Crellin Holding, Inc., **8** 477
Crellin Plastics, **8** 13
Crenlo Corp., **16** 180
Creo Inc., 48 121–24
Creole Petroleum Corporation, **IV** 428; **7** 171
Cresap, McCormick and Paget, **32** 458
Crescendo Productions, **6** 27
Crescent Box & Printing Co., **13** 442
Crescent Capital, **44** 95
Crescent Chemical, **I** 374
Crescent Niagara Corp., **II** 16
Crescent Real Estate Equities Company, **25** 454
Crescent Software Inc., **15** 373
Crescent Vert Company, Ltd., **II** 51; **21** 330
Crescent Washing Machine Company, **8** 298
Crescott, Inc., **15** 501
Cressbrook Dairy Co., **II** 546
Cressey Dockham & Co., **II** 682
Crest Fruit Co., **17** 458
Crest Ridge Homes, Inc., **17** 83
Crest Service Company, **9** 364
Crestbrook Forest Industries Ltd., **IV** 285
Crestmont Financial Corporation, **14** 472
Creusot-Loire, **II** 93–94; **19** 166
Crevettes du Cameroun, **13** 244
CRH plc, **37** 203, 206
Crimson Associates L.P., **26** 48
Crist Partners, **34** 249
Criterion Casualty Company, **10** 312
Criterion Life Insurance Company, **10** 311
Critikon, Inc., **III** 36
Crocker National Bank, **II** 226, 317, 319, 383; **13** 535; **17** 324–25
Crocker National Corporation, **12** 536
Crockett Container Corporation, **8** 268
Croda International Plc, IV 383; **45 125–28**
Croitex S.A., **26** 374
Crompton & Knowles Corp., I 633; **9 153–55**
Crompton Corporation, 36 143–50 (upd.)
Crop Production Services, Inc., **IV** 576
Crosby Enterprises, **17** 19
Croscill Home Fashions, **8** 510
Croscill, Inc., 42 95–97
Crosfield, Lampard & Co., **III** 696
Cross & Trecker Corporation, **10** 330
Cross Company. See A.T. Cross Company.
Cross-Continent Auto Retailers, **26** 501
Cross Country Group, **25** 358
Cross Creek Apparel, Inc., **30** 400
Cross Pointe Paper Corporation, **26** 363
Cross/Tessitore & Associates, **16** 259
Crossair AG. See Swiss International Air Lines Ltd.
Crosse and Blackwell, **II** 547
Crossett Lumber Co., **IV** 281; **9** 259
Crossland Capital Corp., **III** 293
Crossley Motors, Ltd., **13** 285
Crothall, **6** 44
Crothers Properties, Ltd., **21** 500

Crouse-Hinds Co., **II** 16; **19** 45
Crow Catchpole, **III** 752; **28** 448
Crowell-Collier Publishing Company, **IV** 310; **7** 286
Crowell Publishing Company, **19** 266
Crowley Foods, Inc., **II** 528
Crowley Maritime Corporation, 6 382–84; 9 510–11; 28 77–80 (upd.)
Crowley, Milner & Company, 19 106–08
Crown Advertising Agency. See King Kullen Grocery Co., Inc.
Crown Aluminum, **I** 544
Crown America Corp., **13** 393
Crown Books Corporation, 14 61; **16** 159–61; **21 148–50; 41** 61
Crown Can Co., **I** 601
Crown Center Redevelopment Corp., **IV** 621
Crown Central Petroleum Corporation, 7 101–03
Crown, Cork & Seal Company, Inc., I 601–03; 13 188–90 (upd.); 15 129; **17** 106; **24** 264; **30** 475; **32 123–27 (upd.)**
Crown Courier Systems, Inc., **24** 126
Crown Crafts, Inc., 16 141–43
Crown Drugs, **II** 673
Crown Equipment Corporation, 15 134–36
Crown Forest Industries, **IV** 279; **19** 155
Crown House Engineering, **44** 148
Crown Life Insurance Company, **III** 261; **6** 181–82
Crown Media Holdings, Inc., 45 129–32
Crown Oil and Refining Company, **7** 101
Crown Packaging, **19** 155
Crown Pet Foods Ltd., **39** 356
Crown Point Ventures, **49** 316
Crown Publishing Group, **IV** 584; **13** 429; **31** 376, 379
Crown Radio, **17** 123–24; **41** 114
Crown Technical Systems, Inc., **37** 215
Crown Vantage Inc., 29 135–37
Crown Zellerbach Corporation, **IV** 290, 345; **8** 261; **22** 210; **24** 247
Crownx Inc., **6** 181–82
Crowson and Son Ltd., **23** 219
CRSS Inc., 6 142–44; 23 491
CRTC. See Canadian Radio-Television and Telecommunications Commission.
Crucible Steel, **I** 434–35
Crude Oil Pipe Line Co., **IV** 400
Cruden Investments Pty Ltd., **IV** 651; **7** 390
Cruise America Inc., 21 151–53
Cruise Associates, **22** 471
Crum & Forster Holdings, Inc., **II** 448; **III** 172; **6** 290; **13** 448; **26** 546
Crump E & S, **6** 290
Crump Inc., **I** 584
Crush International, **II** 478; **III** 53
Crushed Stone Sales Ltd., **IV** 241
Cruzan Rum Distillery, Ltd., **27** 478
Cruzcampo, **18** 501
Cruzeiro do Sul Airlines, **6** 133
Cryenco Sciences Inc., **21** 109
CryoLife, Inc., 46 112–14
Cryomedics Inc., **I** 667
Crystal Brands, Inc., 9 156–58; 12 431
Crystal Market, **41** 174
Crystal Oil Co., **IV** 180, 548
CS Crable Sportswear Inc., **23** 66
CS First Boston Inc., II 269, **402–04; III** 289; **12** 209; **21** 146. See also Credit Suisse Group.

CS Holding. *See* Credit Suisse Group.
CS Life, **21** 146–47
CSA. *See* China Southern Airlines Company Ltd.
CSA Press, **IV** 661
CSC. *See* Computer Sciences Corporation.
CSC Holdings, Inc., **32** 105
CSC Industries, Inc., **IV** 63
CSE Corp., **III** 214
CSFB. *See* Financière Crédit Suisse-First Boston *and* Credit Suisse Group.
CSFBdirect Inc., **46** 55
CSI Computer Systems, **47** 36
CSK, **10** 482
CSK Auto Corporation, 38 165–67
CSO. *See* Columbus & Southern Ohio Electric Company.
CSR Limited, III 686–88, 728, 735–36; **IV** 46; **22** 106; **28 81–84 (upd.)**
CSR Rinker Materials Corp., **46** 197
CSS Industries, Inc., 35 128–31
CST Office Products, **15** 36; **42** 416
CSX Corporation, V 438–40, 485; **6** 340; **9** 59; **13** 462; **22 164–68 (upd.)**; **29** 360–61
CSY Agri-Processing, **7** 81–82
CT Financial Services Inc., **V** 401–02; **49** 397
CT&T. *See* Carolina Telephone and Telegraph Company.
CTA. *See* Comptoir des Textiles Artificielles.
CTB International Corporation, 43 129–31 (upd.)
CTG, Inc., 11 64–66
CTI. *See* Cosmetic Technology International, Inc.
CTNE, **I** 462
CTR. *See* International Business Machines Corporation.
CTS Corporation, 19 104; **39 105–08**
CTV Network, **35** 69
C2B Technologies, **45** 201
CTX Mortgage Company, **8** 88
Cub Foods, **II** 669–70; **14** 411; **17** 302; **18** 505; **22** 327
Cuban-American Manganese Corp., **IV** 81; **7** 186
Cuban American Nickel Co., **IV** 82; **7** 186
Cuban American Oil Company, **8** 348
Cuban Telephone Co., **I** 462–63
Cubic Corporation, 19 109–11
Cubitts Nigeria, **III** 753
CUC International Inc., 16 144–46. *See also* Cendant Corporation.
Cuckler Steel Span Co., **I** 481
Cudahy Corp., **12** 199
Cuisinart Corporation, 17 110; **24 129–32**
Culbro Corporation, 14 19; **15 137–39**
Culinary Foods, Inc., **14** 516
Cullen/Frost Bankers, Inc., 25 113–16
Culligan International Company, I 373; **II** 468; **12 87–88**, 346; **16** 20
Culligan Water Technologies, Inc., 38 168–70 (upd.)
Cullinet Software Corporation, **6** 225; **14** 390; **15** 108
Cullman Bros. *See* Culbro Corporation.
Cullum Companies, **II** 670
Culp, Inc., 29 138–40
Culter Industries, Inc., **22** 353
Cumberland Farms, Inc., 17 120–22; **26** 450

Cumberland Federal Bancorporation, **13** 223; **31** 206
Cumberland Newspapers, **IV** 650; **7** 389
Cumberland Packing Corporation, 26 107–09
Cumberland Paper Board Mills Ltd., **IV** 248
Cumberland Pipeline Co., **IV** 372
Cumberland Property Investment Trust Ltd., **IV** 711
Cummins Cogeneration Co. *See* Cogeneration Development Corp.
Cummins Engine Co., Inc., I 146–48, 186; **III** 545; **IV** 252; **10** 273–74; **12 89–92 (upd.)**; **16** 297; **17** 29; **19** 293; **21** 503; **26** 256; **40 131–35 (upd.)**; **42** 387
Cumo Sports, **16** 109
Cumulus Media Inc., 37 103–05
CUNA Mutual Insurance Group, **11** 495
Cunard Line Ltd., I 573; **23 159–62**; **27** 90, 92; **36** 323; **38** 341, 344
Cuno Kourten, **13** 353
Cupples Products Co., **IV** 15
Current, Inc., 37 106–09
Currys Group PLC, **V** 49; **19** 123; **49** 112
Cursenir, **I** 280
Curtice-Burns Foods, Inc., 7 17–18, **104–06**; **21** 18, **154–57 (upd.)**
Curtin & Pease/Peneco, **27** 361
Curtis Circulation Co., **IV** 619
Curtis Homes, **22** 127
Curtis Industries, **13** 165
Curtis 1000 Inc. *See* American Business Products, Inc.
Curtis Squire Inc., **18** 455
Curtiss Candy Co., **II** 544
Curtiss-Wright Corporation, I 524; **III** 464; **7** 263; **8** 49; **9** 14, 244, 341, 417; **10 260–63**; **11** 427; **21** 174; **23** 340; **35 132–37 (upd.)**
Curver Group, **III** 614
Curver-Rubbermaid, **III** 615
Cushman Motor Works, **III** 598
Custom Academic Publishing Company, **12** 174
Custom Chrome, Inc., 16 147–49
Custom Electronics, Inc., **9** 120
Custom Expressions, Inc., **7** 24; **22** 35
Custom Hoists, Inc., **17** 458
Custom, Ltd., **46** 197
Custom Metal Products, Inc., **III** 643
Custom Organics, **8** 464
Custom Primers, **17** 288
Custom Products Inc., **III** 643
Custom Publishing Group, **27** 361
Custom Technologies Corp., **19** 152
Custom Thermoform, **24** 512
Custom Tool and Manufacturing Company, **41** 366
Custom Transportation Services, Inc., **26** 62
Custom Woodwork & Plastics Inc., **36** 159
Customized Transportation Inc., **22** 164, 167
AB Custos, **25** 464
Cutler-Hammer Inc., **I** 155; **III** 644–45
Cutter & Buck Inc., 27 112–14
Cutter Laboratories, **I** 310
Cutter Precision Metals, Inc., **25** 7
CVC Capital Partners, **49** 451
CVE Corporation, Inc., **24** 395
CVG Aviation, **34** 118
CVI Incorporated, **21** 108

CVL Inc., **II** 457
CVN Companies, **9** 218
CVS Corporation, 32 166, 170; **34** 285; **45 133–38 (upd.)**
CWM. *See* Chemical Waste Management, Inc.
CWP. *See* Custom Woodwork & Plastics Inc.
CWT Farms International Inc., **13** 103
CXT Inc., **33** 257
Cyber Communications Inc., **16** 168
CyberCash Inc., **18** 541, 543
Cybermedia, 25 117–19, 349
Cybernet Electronics Corp., **II** 51; **21** 330
Cybernex, **10** 463
CyberSource Corp., **26** 441
CYBERTEK Corporation, **11** 395
CyberTel, **IV** 596–97
CyberTrust Solutions Inc., **42** 24–25
Cybex International, Inc., 49 106–09
Cycle & Carriage Ltd., **20** 313
Cycle Video Inc., **7** 590
Cyclo Chemical Corp., **I** 627
Cyclo Getriebebau Lorenz Braren GmbH, **III** 634
Cyclone Co. of Australia, **III** 673
Cyclops Corporation, **10** 45; **13** 157
Cydsa. *See* Grupo Cydsa, S.A. de C.V.
Cygna Energy Services, **13** 367
Cygne Designs, Inc., 25 120–23; **37** 14
Cymbal Co., Ltd., **V** 150
Cynosure Inc., **11** 88
Cyphernetics Corp., **III** 118
Cypress Amax Minerals Co., **13** 158; **22** 285–86
Cypress Insurance Co., **III** 214
Cypress Semiconductor Corporation, 6 216; **18** 17, 383; **20 174–76**; **43** 14; **48 125–29 (upd.)**
Cyprus Amax Coal Company, **35** 367
Cyprus Amax Minerals Company, 21 158–61
Cyprus Minerals Company, 7 107–09
Cyrix Corp., **10** 367; **26** 329
Cyrk Inc., 19 112–14; **21** 516; **33** 416
Cytec Industries Inc., 27 115–17
Czarnikow-Rionda Company, Inc., 32 128–30

D&D Enterprises, Inc., **24** 96
D&F Industries, Inc., **17** 227; **41** 204
D&K Wholesale Drug, Inc., 14 146–48
D&N Systems, Inc., **10** 505
D&O Inc., **17** 363
D & P Studios, **II** 157
D&W Computer Stores, **13** 176
D & W Food Stores, Inc., **8** 482; **27** 314
D.B. Kaplan's, **26** 263
D.B. Marron & Company, **II** 445; **22** 406
D.C. Heath & Co., **II** 86; **11** 413; **36** 273; **38** 374
D.C. National Bancorp, **10** 426
D. Connelly Boiler Company, **6** 145
D. de Ricci-G. Selnet et Associes, **28** 141
d.e.m.o., **28** 345
D.E. Makepeace Co., **IV** 78
D.E. Shaw & Co., **25** 17; **38** 269
D.E. Winebrenner Co., **7** 429
D.G. Calhoun, **12** 112
D.G. Yuengling & Son, Inc., 38 171–73
D. Hald & Co., **III** 417
D.I. Manufacturing Inc., **37** 351
D.K. Gold, **17** 138
D.L. Rogers Group, **37** 363

D.L. Saslow Co., **19** 290
D.M. Nacional, **23** 170
D.M. Osborne Co., **III** 650
D.R. Horton Inc., **25** 217; **26** 291
D.W. Mikesell Co. *See* Mike-Sell's Inc.
Da Gama Textiles Company, **24** 450
Dabney, Morgan & Co., **II** 329
D'Addario & Company, Inc. *See* J.
  D'Addario & Company, Inc.
Dade Reagents Inc., **19** 103
Dade Wholesale Products, **6** 199
DADG. *See* Deutsch-Australische
  Dampfschiffs-Gesellschaft.
Dae Won Kang Up Co., **III** 581
Daejin Shipping Company, **6** 98; **27** 271
Daesung Heavy Industries, **I** 516
Daewoo Group, **I** 516; **II** 53; **III** 457–59,
  749; **12** 211; **18** 123–27 **(upd.)**; **30** 185
DAF, **I** 186; **III** 543; **7** 566–67
Daffy's Inc., **26** 110–12
NV Dagblad De Telegraaf. *See* N.V.
  Holdingmaatschappij De Telegraaf.
Dage-Bell, **II** 86
Dagincourt. *See* Compagnie de Saint-
  Gobain S.A.
D'Agostino Supermarkets Inc., **19**
  115–17
Dagsbladunie, **IV** 611
DAH. *See* DeCrane Aircraft Holdings Inc.
Dahl Manufacturing, Inc., **17** 106
Dahlberg, Inc., **18** 207–08
Dahlgren, **I** 677
Dahlonega Equipment and Supply
  Company, **12** 377
Dai-Ichi. *See also listings under* Daiichi.
Dai-Ichi Bank, **I** 507, 511; **IV** 148
Dai-Ichi Kangyo Bank Ltd., **II** 273–75,
  325–26, 360–61, 374; **III** 188
Dai-Ichi Mokko Co., **III** 758
Dai-Ichi Mutual Life Insurance Co., **II**
  118; **III** 277, 401; **25** 289; **26** 511; **38**
  18
Dai Nippon. *See also listings under*
  Dainippon.
Dai Nippon Brewery Co., **I** 220, 282; **21**
  319
Dai Nippon Ink and Chemicals, **I** 303
Dai Nippon Mujin, **II** 371
Dai Nippon Printing Co., Ltd., **IV**
  598–600, 631, 679–80
Dai Nippon X-ray Inc., **II** 75
Dai Nippon Yuben Kai, **IV** 631–32
Daido Boeki, **24** 325
Daido Spring Co., **III** 580
Daido Steel Co., Ltd., **IV** 62–63
Daido Trading, **I** 432, 492; **24** 324
The Daiei, Inc., **V** 11, 39–40; **17** 123–25
  (upd.); **18** 186, 285; **19** 308; **36** 418–19;
  41 113–16 **(upd.)**
Daig Corporation, **43** 349–50
Daignault Rolland, **24** 404
Daihatsu Motor Company, Ltd., **7**
  110–12; **21** 162–64 **(upd.)**; **38** 415
Daiichi. *See also listings under* Dai-Ichi.
Daiichi Atomic Power Industry Group, **II**
  22
Daiichi Bussan Kaisha Ltd., **I** 505, 507
Daiichi Fire, **III** 405
Daijugo Bank, **I** 507
Daiken Company. *See* Marubeni
  Corporation.
Daikin Industries, Ltd., **III** 460–61
Daikyo Oil Co., Ltd., **IV** 403–04, 476
Dailey & Associates, **I** 16

Daily Chronicle Investment Group, **IV** 685
Daily Mail and General Trust plc, **19**
  118–20; **39** 198–99
Daily Mirror, **IV** 665–66; **17** 397
Daily Press Inc., **IV** 684; **22** 522
The Daimaru, Inc., **V** 41–42, 130; **42**
  98–100 (upd.)
Daimler Airway, **I** 92
Daimler-Benz Aerospace AG, **16** 150–52;
  24 84
Daimler-Benz AG, **I** 27, 138, **149–51**,
  186–87, 192, 194, 198, 411, 549; **II**
  257, 279–80, 283; **III** 495, 523, 562,
  563, 695, 750; **7** 219; **10** 261, 274; **11**
  31; **12** 192, 342; **13** 30, 286, 414; **14**
  169; **15 140–44 (upd.)**; **20** 312–13; **22**
  11; **26** 481, 498
DaimlerChrysler AG, **34 128–37 (upd.)**,
  306
Dain Bosworth Inc., **15** 231–33, 486
Dain Rauscher Corporation, **35 138–41**
  (upd.)
Daina Seikosha, **III** 620
Daini-Denden Incorporated, **12** 136–37
Daini-Denden Kikaku Company, Ltd., **II**
  51. *See also* DDI Corporation.
Dainippon. *See also listings under* Dai-
  Nippon.
Dainippon Celluloid Company, **I** 509; **III**
  486; **18** 183
Dainippon Ink & Chemicals, Inc., **IV** 397;
  10 466–67; **13** 308, 461; **17** 363; **28** 194
Dainippon Shurui, **III** 42
Dainippon Spinning Company, **V** 387
Daio Paper Corporation, **IV** 266–67, 269
Dairy Crest Group plc, **32** 131–33
Dairy Farm Ice and Cold Storage Co., **IV**
  700; **47** 176
Dairy Farm Management Services Ltd., **I**
  471; **20** 312
Dairy Farmers of America Inc., **48** 45
Dairy Fresh, Inc., **26** 449
Dairy Maid Products Cooperative, **II** 536
Dairy Mart Convenience Stores, Inc., **7**
  113–15; **17** 501; **25** 124–27 **(upd.)**
Dairy Queen. *See* International Dairy
  Queen, Inc.
Dairy Queen National Development
  Company, **10** 372
Dairy Supply Co., **II** 586; **III** 418, 420
Dairyland Food Laboratories, **I** 677
Dairymen, Inc., **11** 24
Daishowa Paper Manufacturing Co.,
  Ltd. II 361; **IV** 268–70, 326, 667; **17**
  398
Daisy Manufacturing Company, Inc., **34** 72
Daisy Systems Corp., **11** 46, 284–85, 489
Daisy/Cadnetix Inc., **6** 248; **24** 235
Daisytek International Corporation, **18**
  128–30
Daiwa Bank, Ltd., **II 276–77**, 347, 438;
  26 457; **39 109–11 (upd.)**
Daiwa Securities Company, Limited, **II**
  276, 300, **405–06**, 434; **9** 377
Daka, Inc. *See* Unique Casual Restaurants,
  Inc.
Dakin Inc., **24** 44; **33** 415
Dakota Power Company, **6** 580; **20** 73
Dakotah Mills, **8** 558–59; **16** 353
Daksoft, Inc., **20** 74
Daktronics, Inc., **32 134–37**
Dal-Tile International Inc., **22** 46, 49,
  169–71
Dalberg Co., **II** 61

Dale Carnegie Training, Inc., **28 85–87**
Dale Electronics, **21** 519
Daleville & Middletown Telephone
  Company, **14** 258
Dalfort Corp., **15** 281
Dalgety PLC, **II 499–500**; **III** 21; **12** 411;
  22 147; **27** 258, 260. *See also* PIC
  International Group PLC
Dalian, **14** 556
Dalian Cement Factory, **III** 718
Dalian International Nordic Tire Co., **20**
  263
D'Allaird's, **24** 315–16
Dallas Airmotive, **II** 16
Dallas Ceramic Co. *See* Dal-Tile
  International Inc.
Dallas Cowboys Football Club, Ltd., **33**
  122–25
Dallas-Fort Worth Suburban Newspapers,
  Inc., **10** 3
Dallas Lumber and Supply Co., **IV** 358
Dallas Power & Light Company, **V** 724
Dallas Semiconductor Corporation, **13**
  191–93; **31 143–46 (upd.)**
Dallas Southland Ice Co., **II** 660
Daltex General Agency, Inc., **25** 115
Damar, **IV** 610
Damark International, Inc., **18 131–34**
Damart, **25** 523
Dameron-Pierson Co., **25** 500
Dames & Moore, Inc., **25 128–31**. *See
  also* URS Corporation.
Dammann Asphalt, **III** 673
Damodar Valley Corp., **IV** 49
Damon, **21** 153
Damon Clinical Laboratories Inc., **26** 392
Damon Corporation, **11** 334
Dan River Inc., **35 142–46**
Dan's Supreme, **24** 528
Dana Alexander Inc., **27** 197; **43** 218
Dana Corporation, **I 152–53**; **10 264–66**
  (upd.); **23** 170–71; **47** 376
Dana Design Ltd., **16** 297
Danaher Corporation, **7 116–17**
Danair A/S, **I** 120
Danapak Holding Ltd., **11** 422
Danapak Riverwood Multipack A/S, **48**
  344
Danat-Bank, **I** 138
Danbury Mint, **34** 370
Danbury Phamacal Inc., **31** 254
Dancer Fitzgerald Sample, **I** 33; **23** 505
Daniel Industries, Inc., **16 153–55**
Daniel International Corp., **I** 570–71; **8**
  192
Daniel James Insurance Group, **41** 64
Daniel P. Creed Co., Inc., **8** 386
Daniel's Jewelers, **16** 559
Danieli & C. Officine Meccaniche, **13** 98
Daniels Linseed Co., **I** 419
Daniels Packaging, **12** 25
Daniels Pharmaceuticals, Inc., **24** 257
Danisco A/S, **44 134–37**
Danish Aalborg, **27** 91
Danish Almindelige Brand-Assurance-
  Compagni, **III** 299
Danley Machine Corp., **I** 514
Danner Shoe Manufacturing Co., **18** 300
Dannon Co., Inc., **II** 468, 474–75; **14**
  149–51
Danone Group, **25** 85; **35** 394, 397
Danray, **12** 135
Dansk Bioprotein, **IV** 406–07

Dansk International Designs Ltd., **10** 179, 181; **12** 313
Dansk Metal and Armaturindistri, **III** 569; **20** 361
Dansk Rejsebureau, **I** 120
Danskin, Inc., 12 93–95; 15 358
Danville Resources, Inc., **13** 502
Danzas Group, V 441–43; 40 136–39 (upd.)
DAP, Inc., **III** 66; **12** 7; **18** 549
DAP Products Inc., **36** 396
Dara Michelle, **17** 101–03
D'Arcy Masius Benton & Bowles, Inc., I 233–34; **6 20–22; 10** 226–27; **26** 187; **28** 137; **32 138–43 (upd.)**
Darden Restaurants, Inc., 16 156–58; 36 238; **44 138–42 (upd.)**
Darigold, Inc., 9 159–61
Darling and Hodgson, **IV** 91
Darling, Brown & Sharpe. *See* Brown & Sharpe Manufacturing Co.
Darmstadter, **II** 282
Darracq, **7** 6
Darrell J. Sekin Transport Co., **17** 218
Dart & Kraft Financial Corp., **II** 534; **III** 610–11; **7** 276; **12** 310; **14** 547
Dart Group Corporation, II 645, 656, 667, 674; **12** 49; **15** 270; **16 159–62; 21** 148; **23** 370; **24** 418; **27** 158; **32** 168
Dart Industries, **II** 533–34; **III** 610; **9** 179–80. *See also* Premark International Inc.
Dart Transit Co., **13** 550
Dart Truck Co., **I** 185
Dartex, **18** 434
Darty S.A., 27 118–20
Darvel Realty Trust, **14** 126
Darya-Varia Laboratoria, **18** 182
DASA. *See* Daimler-Benz Aerospace AG *or* Deutsche Aerospace Airbus.
Dashwood Industries, **19** 446
Dassault Aviation SA, **21** 11
Dassault-Breguet. *See* Avions Marcel Dassault-Breguet Aviation.
Dassault Systèmes S.A., 25 132–34; 26 179. *See also* Groupe Dassault Aviation SA.
Dassler, **14** 6
Dastek Inc., **10** 464; **11** 234–35
DAT GmbH, **10** 514
Dat Jidosha Seizo Co., **I** 183
Data Acquisition Systems, Inc., **16** 300
Data Architects, **14** 318
Data Base Management Inc., **11** 19
Data-Beam Corp., **25** 301
Data Broadcasting Corporation, 31 147–50
Data Business Forms, **IV** 640
Data Card Corp., **IV** 680
Data Corp., **IV** 311; **19** 267
Data Documents, **III** 157
Data Force Inc., **11** 65
Data General Corporation, II 208; **III** 124, 133; **6** 221, 234; **8 137–40; 9** 297; **10** 499; **12** 162; **13** 201; **16** 418; **20** 8
Data One Corporation, **11** 111
Data Preparation, Inc., **11** 112
Data Printer, Inc., **18** 435
Data Resources, Inc., **IV** 637
Data Specialties Inc. *See* Zebra Technologies Corporation.
Data Structures Inc., **11** 65
Data Systems Technology, **11** 57; **38** 375
Data Technology Corp., **18** 510

Data 3 Systems, **9** 36
Datac plc, **18** 140
Datachecker Systems, **II** 64–65; **III** 164; **11** 150
Datacraft Corp., **II** 38
DataFocus, Inc., **18** 112
Datamatic Corp., **II** 41, 86; **12** 247
Datapoint Corporation, 11 67–70
Datapro Research Corp., **IV** 637
Dataquest Inc., **10** 558; **21** 235, 237; **22** 51; **25** 347
Datas Incorporated, **I** 99; **6** 81
Datascope Corporation, 39 112–14
Dataset Communications Inc., **23** 100
Datastream International Ltd., **IV** 605; **10** 89; **13** 417
DataTimes Corporation, **29** 58
Datavision Inc., **11** 444
Datec, **22** 17
Datek Online Holdings Corp., 32 144–46; 48 225–27
Datext, **IV** 596–97
Datran, **11** 468
Datsun. *See* Nissan Motor Company, Ltd.
Datteln, **IV** 141
Datura Corp., **14** 391
Dauphin Deposit Corporation, 14 152–54
Dauphin Distribution Services. *See* Exel Logistics Ltd.
Daut + Rietz and Connectors Pontarlier, **19** 166
Dave & Buster's, Inc., 33 126–29
Davenport & Walter, **III** 765
Davenport Mammoet Heavy Transport Inc., **26** 280
The Davey Tree Expert Company, 11 71–73
The David and Lucile Packard Foundation, 41 117–19
David B. Smith & Company, **13** 243
David Berg & Co., **14** 537
David Brown & Son. *See* Brown & Sharpe Manufacturing Co.
David Brown, Ltd., **10** 380
David Clark, **30** 357
David Crystal, Inc., **II** 502; **9** 156; **10** 323
David Hafler Company, **43** 323
The David J. Joseph Company, 14 155–56; 19 380
David Sandeman Group, **I** 592
David Sassoon & Co., **II** 296
David Williams and Partners, **6** 40
David Wilson Homes Ltd., **45** 442–43
David's Bridal, Inc., 33 130–32; 46 288
David's Supermarkets, **17** 180
Davidson & Associates, **16** 146
Davidson & Leigh, **21** 94
Davidson Automatic Merchandising Co. Inc., **II** 607
Davidson Brothers Co., **19** 510
Davies, William Ltd., **II** 482
Davis & Geck, **I** 301; **27** 115
Davis & Henderson Ltd., **IV** 640
Davis Coal & Coke Co., **IV** 180
Davis Estates, **I** 592
Davis Manufacturing Company, **10** 380
Davis Polk & Wardwell, 36 151–54
Davis Service Group PLC, 45 139–41; 49 374, 377
Davis-Standard Company, **9** 154; **36** 144
Davis Vision, Inc., **27** 209
Davis Wholesale Company, **9** 20
Davison Chemical Corp., **IV** 190

Davlyn Industries, Inc., **22** 487
Davox Corporation, **18** 31
Davy Bamag GmbH, **IV** 142
Davy McKee AG, **IV** 142
DAW Technologies, Inc., 25 135–37
Dawe's Laboratories, Inc., **12** 3
Dawn Food Products, Inc., 17 126–28
Dawnay Day, **III** 501
Dawson Holdings PLC, 43 132–34
Dawson Mills, **II** 536
Day & Zimmermann Inc., 6 579; **9 162–64; 31 151–155 (upd.)**
Day Brite Lighting, **II** 19
Day-Glo Color Corp., **8** 456
Day International, **8** 347
Day-Lee Meats, **II** 550
Day-N-Nite, **II** 620
Day Runner, Inc., 14 157–58; 41 120–23 (upd.)
Daybridge Learning Centers, **13** 49, 299
Dayco Products, **7** 297
Daylin Corporation, **46** 271
Days Inns of America, Inc., **III** 344; **11** 178; **13** 362, 364; **21** 362
Daystar International Inc., **11** 44
Daystrom, **III** 617; **17** 418
Daytex, Inc., **II** 669; **18** 505
Dayton Engineering Laboratories, **I** 171; **9** 416; **10** 325
Dayton Flexible Products Co., **I** 627
Dayton Hudson Corporation, V 43–44; 8 35; **9** 360; **10** 136, 391–93, 409–10, 515–16; **13** 330; **14** 376; **16** 176, 559; **18** 108, **135–37 (upd.); 22** 59
Dayton Power & Light Company, **6** 467, 480–82
Dayton Walther Corp., **III** 650, 652
Daytron Mortgage Systems, **11** 485
Dazey Corp., **16** 384; **43** 289
DB. *See* Deutsche Bundesbahn.
DB Reise & Touristik AG, **37** 250
DBA Holdings, Inc., **18** 24
DBMS Inc., **14** 390
DC Comics Inc., 25 138–41
DCA Advertising, **16** 168
DCA Food Industries, **II** 554; **27** 258–60, 299
DCL BioMedical, Inc., **11** 333
DCMS Holdings Inc., **7** 114; **25** 125
DDB Needham Worldwide, 14 159–61; 22 394
DDD Energy, Inc., **47** 348, 350
DDI Corporation, 7 118–20; 13 482; **21** 330–31
NV De Beer and Partners, **45** 386
De Beers Consolidated Mines Limited / De Beers Centenary AG, I 107; **IV** 20–21, 23, 60, **64–68**, 79, 94; **7 121–26 (upd.); 16** 25–26, 29; **21** 345–46; **28 88–94 (upd.)**
De Bono Industries, **24** 443
De Dietrich & Cie., 31 156–59
De Grenswisselkantoren NV, **III** 201
De Groote Bossche, **III** 200
de Havilland Aircraft Co., **I** 82, 92–93, 104, 195; **III** 507–08; **7** 11. *See also* Bombardier Inc.
de Havilland Holdings, Ltd., **24** 85–86
De La Rue plc, 10 267–69; 34 138–43 (upd.); 46 251
De Laurentiis Entertainment Group, **III** 84; **25** 317
De Laval Turbine Company, **III** 418–20; **7** 236–37

De Leuw, Cather & Company, **8** 416
De Nederlandse Bank, **IV** 132
De Paepe, **45** 386
De-sta-Co., **III** 468
De Ster 1905 NV, **III** 200
De Streekkrant-De Weekkrantgroep NV, **48** 347
De Tomaso Industries, **11** 104
De Trey Gesellchaft, **10** 271
De Vito/Verdi, **26** 111
De Walt, **III** 436
de Wendel, **IV** 226–27
DEA Group, **23** 83
Dealer Equipment and Services, **10** 492
Dean & Barry Co., **8** 455
Dean & DeLuca, Inc., 36 155–57
Dean-Dempsy Corp., **IV** 334
Dean Foods Company, 7 127–29; 17 56; **21** 157, **165–68 (upd.); 26** 447; **29** 434; **46** 70
Dean Witter, Discover & Co., II 445; **IV** 186; **V** 180, 182; **7** 213; **12 96–98; 18** 475; **21** 97; **22** 405–07. *See also* Morgan Stanley Dean Witter & Company.
Dearborn Publishing Group, **42** 211
Death Row Records, 27 121–23
Deb Shops, Inc., 16 163–65
DeBartolo Realty Corp., **27** 401
Debenhams Plc, V 20–22; **28** 29–30, **95–97; 39** 88
Debevoise & Plimpton, 39 115–17
Debis, **26** 498
DeBoles Nutritional Foods Inc., **27** 197–98; **43** 218–19
Debron Investments Plc., **8** 271
DEC. *See* Digital Equipment Corp.
Decafin SpA, **26** 278, 280
Decathlon S.A., **39** 183–84
Decca Record Company Ltd., **II** 81, 83, 144; **23** 389
Dechert, 43 135–38
Decision Base Resources, **6** 14
Decision Systems Israel Ltd. (DSI), **21** 239
DecisionQuest, Inc., **25** 130
Decker, Howell & Co., **26** 451
Deckers Outdoor Corporation, 22 172–74
Deco Industries, Inc., **18** 5
Deco Purchasing Company, **39** 211
Decoflex Ltd., **IV** 645
Decolletage S.A. St.-Maurice, **14** 27
Decora Industries, Inc., 31 160–62
DeCrane Aircraft Holdings Inc., 36 158–60
Dee and Cee Toy Co., **25** 312
Dee Corporation plc, **I** 549; **II** 628–29, 642; **24** 269
Deeks McBride, **III** 704
Deep Ocean Services, L.L.C., **44** 203
Deep Oil Technology, **I** 570
Deep Rock Oil Company. *See* Kerr-McGee Corporation.
Deep Rock Water Co., **III** 21
DeepFlex Production Partners, L.P., **21** 171
Deepsea Ventures, Inc., **IV** 152; **24** 358
DeepTech International Inc., 21 169–71
Deepwater Light and Power Company, **6** 449
Deer Park Spring Water Co., **III** 21
Deere & Company, I 181, 527; **III** **462–64**, 651; **10** 377–78, 380, 429; **11** 472; **13** 16–17, 267; **16** 179; **17** 533; **21**

172–76 (upd.); 22 542; **26** 492; **42** **101–06 (upd.)**
Deering Harvesting Machinery Company. *See* Navistar.
Deering Milliken & Co. *See* Milliken & Co.
Def Jam Records, Inc., **23** 389, 391; **31** 269; **33** 373–75
Defense Plant Corp., **IV** 10, 408
Defense Technology Corporation of America, **27** 50
Defiance, Inc., 22 175–78
Deflecta-Shield Corporation, **40** 299–300
Deft Software, Inc., **10** 505
DEG. *See* Deutsche Edison Gesellschaft.
Degussa Group, I 303; **IV 69–72**, 118
Degussa-Hüls AG, 32 147–53 (upd.); 34 209
Deinhard, **I** 281
DEKA Research & Development Corporation. *See* Segway LLC.
DeKalb AgResearch Inc., **9** 411; **41** 304–06
Dekalb Energy Company, **18** 366
DeKalb Farmers Market, **23** 263–64
DeKalb Genetics Corporation, 17 129–31; 29 330
DeKalb Office Supply, **25** 500
Del Laboratories, Inc., 28 98–100
Del Mar Avionics, **26** 491
Del Monte Corporation, II 595; **7 130–32; 12** 439; **14** 287; **25** 234
Del Monte Foods Company, 23 163–66 (upd.); 36 472; **38** 198
Del-Rey Petroleum, **I** 526
Del Webb Corporation, 14 162–64; 17 186–87; **19** 377–78; **26** 291
Delafield, Harvey, Tabrell, Inc., **17** 498
Delafield Industries, **12** 418
Delagrange, **I** 635
Delaware and Hudson Railway Company, Inc., **16** 350; **45** 78
Delaware Charter Guarantee & Trust Co., **III** 330
Delaware Guarantee and Trust Co. *See* Wilmington Trust Company.
Delaware Lackawanna & Western, **I** 584
Delaware Management Holdings, **III** 386
Delaware North Companies Incorporated, 7 133–36
Delbard, **I** 272
Delchamps, Inc., **II** 638; **27** 247
Delco Electronics Corporation, **II** 32–35; **III** 151; **6** 265; **25** 223–24; **45** 142–43
Delek Investment & Properties Ltd., **45** 170
Delhaize ''Le Lion'' S.A., II 626; **15** 176; **27** 94; **44 143–46**
Delhi Gas Pipeline Corporation, **7** 551
Delhi International Oil Corp., **III** 687; **28** 83
Deli Universal, **13** 545
dELiA*s Inc., 29 141–44
Delicious Foods, **13** 383
Delimaatschappij, **13** 545
Dell Computer Corporation, 9 165–66; 10 309, 459; **11** 62; **16** 5, 196; **24** 31; **25** 254; **27** 168; **31 163–166 (upd.); 47** 323
Dell Distributing, **25** 483
Dell Publishing Co., **13** 560
Dellwood Elevator Co., **I** 419
Delmar Chemicals Ltd., **II** 484
Delmar Paper Box Co., **IV** 333
Delmarva Properties, Inc., **8** 103; **30** 118

Delmonico Foods Inc., **II** 511
Delmonico International, **II** 101
Deloitte & Touche, 9 167–69, 423; **24** 29
Deloitte Touche Tohmatsu International, 29 145–48 (upd.)
DeLong Engineering Co., **III** 558
DeLorean Motor Co., **10** 117; **14** 321
Delphax, **IV** 252; **17** 29
Delphi Automotive Systems Corporation, 22 52; **36** 243; **25** 223; **37** 429; **45 142–44**
Delprat, **IV** 58
Delta and Pine Land Company, **21** 386; **33 133–37**
Delta Acceptance Corporation Limited, **13** 63
Delta Air Lines, Inc., I 29, 91, 97, **99–100**, 102, 106, 120, 132; **6** 61, **81–83 (upd.)**, 117, 131–32, 383; **12** 149, 381; **13** 171–72; **14** 73; **21** 141, 143; **22** 22; **25** 420, 422–23; **26** 439; **27** 20, 409; **33** 50–51, 377; **34** 116–17, 119; **39 118–21 (upd.); 47** 29
Delta Biologicals S.r.l., **11** 208
Delta Biotechnology Ltd., **25** 82
Delta Campground Management Corp., **33** 399
Delta Communications, **IV** 610
Delta Education, **29** 470, 472
Delta Faucet Co., **III** 568–69; **39** 263
Delta International Machinery Corp., **26** 361–63
Delta Lloyd, **III** 235
Delta Manufacturing, **II** 85
Delta Motors, **III** 580
Delta Play, Ltd., **44** 261
Delta Pride Catfish Inc., **18** 247
Delta Queen Steamboat Company, **27** 34–35
Delta Resources Inc., **26** 519
Delta Savings Assoc. of Texas, **IV** 343
Delta Steamship Lines, **9** 425–26
Delta V Technologies, Inc., **33** 348
Delta Woodside Industries, Inc., 8 141–43; 17 329; **30 159–61 (upd.); 42** 118
Deltak Corp., **23** 300
Deltic Timber Corporation, 32 339, 341; **46 115–17**
Deluxe Corporation, 7 137–39; 19 291; **22 179–82 (upd.); 37** 107–08
Deluxe Data, **18** 518
DeLuxe Laboratories, **IV** 652
Deluxe Upholstering Ltd., **14** 303
Delvag Luftürsicherungs A.G., **I** 111
Demag AG, **II** 22; **III** 566; **IV** 206
Demerara Company, **13** 102
Deminex, **IV** 413, 424
Deming Company, **8** 135
Demka, **IV** 132–33
Demko, **30** 469
DeMoulas / Market Basket Inc., 23 167–69
Dempsey & Siders Agency, **III** 190
Den Fujita, **9** 74
Den Norske Bank, **22** 275
Den norske Creditbank, **II** 366
Den Norske Stats Oljeselskap AS, IV 405–07, 486
Den-Tal-Ez, **I** 702
Denain-Nord-Est-Longwy, **IV** 227
DenAmerica Corporation, 29 149–51
Denault Ltd., **II** 651
Denby Group plc, 44 147–50

Denison International plc, 46 118–20
Denison Mines, Ltd., **12** 198
Denker & Goodwin, **17** 498
Denki Seikosho, **IV** 62
Denmark Tiscali A/S, **48** 398
Denney-Reyburn, **8** 360
Dennison Manufacturing Company. *See*
    Avery Dennison Corporation.
Denny's Restaurants Inc., **II** 680; **III** 103;
    V 88–89; **12** 511; **13** 526; **27** 16–18
Denshi Media Services, **IV** 680
DENSO Corporation, 46 121–26 (upd.)
Dent & Co., **II** 296
Dental Capital Corp., **19** 290
Dental Research, **25** 56
DentiCare, Inc., **22** 149
Dentons Green Brewery, **21** 246
Dentsply International Inc., 10 270–72
Dentsu Inc., I 9–11, 36, 38; **6** 29; **9** 30;
    13 204; **16 166–69 (upd.); 25** 91; **40**
    140–44 (upd.)
Denver & Rio Grande Railroad, **12** 18–19
Denver Chemical Company, **8** 84; **38** 124
Denver Gas & Electric Company. *See*
    Public Service Company of Colorado.
DEP Corporation, 20 177–80; 34 209
Department 56, Inc., 14 165–67; 22 59;
    34 144–47 (upd.)
Department Stores International, **I** 426; **22**
    72
Deposit Guaranty Corporation, 17
    132–35
Deposito and Administratie Bank, **II** 185
Depositors National Bank of Durham, **II**
    336
DePree Company, **17** 90–91
DePuy, Inc., 10 156–57; 30 162–65; 36
    306; **37 110–13 (upd.)**
Der Anker, **III** 177
Derby Commercial Bank, **II** 318; **17** 323
Derby Outdoor, **27** 280
Derbyshire Stone and William Briggs, **III**
    752
Deritend Computers, **14** 36
Dermablend, Inc., **31** 89
Deruluft, **6** 57
Derwent Publications, **8** 526
Des Moines Electric Light Company, **6** 504
DESA Industries, **8** 545
Desc, S.A. de C.V., 23 170–72
Deseret Management Corporation, **29** 67
Deseret National Bank, **11** 118
Deseret Pharmaceutical Company, **21** 45
Desert Partners, **III** 763
Design-Center Southwest, **19** 411
Design Craft Ltd., **IV** 640
Design Trend, Inc., **37** 394
Designcraft Inc. *See* Sloan's Supermarkets
    Inc.
Designer Holdings Ltd., 20 181–84; 22
    123
Desmarais Frères, **IV** 557, 559
DeSoto, Inc., **8** 553; **13** 471
Desoutter Brothers plc, **III** 427; **28** 40
Destec Energy, Inc., 12 99–101; 49 121
Det Danske/Norske Luftartselskab, **I** 119
Det Danske Rengorings Selskab A/S, **49**
    221
Detroit Aircraft Corp., **I** 64; **11** 266
Detroit Automobile Co., **I** 164
Detroit Ball Bearing Co., **13** 78
Detroit Chemical Coatings, **8** 553
Detroit City Gas Company. *See* MCN
    Corporation.

Detroit Copper Co., **IV** 176–77
Detroit Diesel Corporation, V 494–95; 9
    18; **10 273–75; 11** 471; **12** 90–91; **18**
    308; **19** 292–94; **21** 503
The Detroit Edison Company, I 164; **V**
    592–95; 7 377–78; **11** 136; **14** 135; **18**
    320. *See also* DTE Energy Co.
Detroit Fire & Marine Insurance Co., **III**
    191
Detroit Gear and Machine Co., **III** 439
Detroit-Graphite Company, **8** 553
The Detroit Pistons Basketball
    Company, 41 124–27
Detroit Radiator Co., **III** 663
Detroit Red Wings, **7** 278–79; **24** 293; **37**
    207; **46** 127
Detroit Steel Products Co., Inc., **IV** 136;
    13 157; **16** 357
Detroit Stoker Company, **37** 399–401
Detroit Tigers Baseball Club, Inc., 24
    293; **37** 207; **46 127–30**
Detroit Toledo & Ironton Railroad, **I** 165
Detroit Vapor Stove Co., **III** 439
Detrola, **II** 60
Dettmers Industries Inc., **36** 159–60
Deutsch-Australische Dampfschiffs-
    Gesellschaft, **6** 398
Deutsch Erdol A.G., **IV** 552
Deutsch, Inc., 42 107–10
Deutsch-Luxembergische Bergwerks und
    Hütten AG, **I** 542; **IV** 105
Deutsch-Österreichische
    Mannesmannröhren-Werke
    Aktiengesellschaft, **III** 564–65
Deutsch Shea & Evans Inc., **I** 15
Deutsch-Skandinavische Bank, **II** 352
Deutsche Aerospace Airbus, **I** 41–42; **7** 9,
    11; **12** 190–91; **21** 8
Deutsche Allgemeine Versicherungs-
    Aktiengesellschaft, **III** 412
Deutsche Anlagen Leasing GmbH, **II** 386
Deutsche-Asiatische Bank, **II** 238, 256
Deutsche BA, **14** 73; **24** 400; **26** 115
Deutsche Babcock AG, II 386; **III**
    465–66
Deutsche Bahn AG, 37 250, 253; **46**
    131–35 (upd.)
Deutsche Bank AG, I 151, 409, 549; **II**
    98, 191, 239, 241–42, 256–58, **278–80,**
    281–82, 295, 319, 385, 427, 429; **III**
    154–55, 692, 695; **IV** 91, 141, 229, 232,
    378, 557; **V** 241–42; **14 168–71 (upd.);**
    15 13; **16** 364–65; **17** 324; **21** 147, **34**
    29; **40 145–51 (upd.); 47** 81–84; **49** 44
Deutsche Börse, **37** 131–32
Deutsche BP Aktiengesellschaft, 7
    140–43
Deutsche Bundepost Telekom, V 287–90;
    18 155
Deutsche Bundesbahn, V 444–47; 6
    424–26
Deutsche Edelstahlwerke AG, **IV** 222
Deutsche Edison Gesellschaft, **I** 409–10
Deutsche Erdol Aktiengesellschaft, **7** 140
Deutsche Gold-und Silber-Scheideanstalt
    vormals Roessler, **IV** 69, 118, 139
Deutsche Grammophon Gesellschaft, **23**
    389
Deutsche Herold, **49** 44
Deutsche Hydrierwerke, **III** 32
Deutsche Industriewerke AG, **IV** 230
Deutsche Kreditbank, **14** 170
Deutsche Länderbank, **II** 379

Deutsche Lufthansa Aktiengesellschaft, I
    94, **110–11,** 120; **6** 59–60, 69, 95–96,
    386; **12** 191; **25** 159; **26 113–16 (upd.);**
    27 465; **33** 49; **36** 426; **48** 258
Deutsche Marathon Petroleum, **IV** 487
Deutsche Mineralöl-
    Explorationsgesellschaft mbH, **IV** 197
Deutsche-Nalco-Chemie GmbH., **I** 373
Deutsche Nippon Seiko, **III** 589
Deutsche Petroleum-Verkaufsgesellschaft
    mbH, **7** 140
Deutsche Post AG, 29 152–58; 40 138
Deutsche Reichsbahn. *See* Deutsche
    Bundesbahn.
Deutsche Schiff-und Maschinenbau
    Aktiengesellschaft ''Deschimag,'' **IV** 87
Deutsche Shell, **7** 140
Deutsche Spezialglas AG, **III** 446
Deutsche Strassen und Lokalbahn A.G., **I**
    410
Deutsche Telekom AG, 18 155; **25** 102;
    38 296; **48 130–35 (upd.)**
Deutsche Texaco, **V** 709
Deutsche Union, **III** 693–94
Deutsche Union-Bank, **II** 278
Deutsche Wagnisfinanzierung, **II** 258; **47**
    83
Deutsche Werke AG, **IV** 230
Deutscher Aero Lloyd, **I** 110
Deutscher Automobil Schutz Allgemeine
    Rechtsschutz-Versicherung AG, **III** 400
Deutscher Kommunal-Verlag Dr. Naujoks
    & Behrendt, **14** 556
Deutscher Ring, **40** 61
Deutsches Reisebüro DeR, **II** 163
Deutz AG, III 541; **39 122–26**
Deutz-Allis, **III** 544. *See also* AGCO Corp.
Deutz Farm Equipment, **13** 17
Devanlay SA, **48** 279
Devcon Corporation, **III** 519; **22** 282
Deveaux S.A., 41 128–30
Developer's Mortgage Corp., **16** 347
Development Finance Corp., **II** 189
Devenish, **21** 247
DeVilbiss Company, **8** 230
DeVilbiss Health Care, Inc., **11** 488
Deville, **27** 421
Devoe & Raynolds Co., **12** 217
Devoke Company, **18** 362
Devon Energy Corporation, **22** 304
DeVry Incorporated, 9 63; **29** 56, **159–61**
Dewars Brothers, **I** 239–40
Dewey & Almy Chemical Co., **I** 548
Dewey Ballantine LLP, 48 136–39
Dexer Corporation, **41** 10
Dexia Group, 42 111–13
The Dexter Corporation, I 320–22; **12**
    102–04 (upd.); 17 287
Dexter Lock Company, **45** 269
Dexter Shoe, **18** 60, 63
DFS Dorland Worldwide, **I** 35
DFS Group Ltd., **33** 276
DFW Printing Company, **10** 3
DG Bank, **33** 358
DG&E. *See* Denver Gas & Electric
    Company.
DH Compounding, **8** 347
DH Technology, Inc., 18 138–40
Dharma Juice, **31** 350
DHI Corp., **II** 680
DHJ Industries, Inc., **12** 118
DHL Worldwide Express, 6 385–87; 18
    177, 316; **24 133–36 (upd.); 26** 441; **27**
    471, 475; **29** 152

Di Giorgio Corp., **II** 602; **12** 105–07; **24** 528–29
Di-Rite Company, **11** 534
Dia Prosim, S.A., **IV** 409
Diageo plc, **24** 137–41 (upd.); **25** 411; **29** 19; **31** 92; **34** 89; **36** 404; **42** 223
Diagnostic Health Corporation, **14** 233
Diagnostic Imaging Services, Inc., **25** 384
Diagnostics Pasteur, **I** 677
Dial-A-Mattress Operating Corporation, **32** 427; **46** 136–39
The Dial Corporation, **8** 144–46; **23** 173–75 (upd.); **29** 114; **32** 230; **34** 209
Dial Home Shopping Ltd., **28** 30
Dial-Net Inc., **27** 306
Dialight Corp., **13** 397–98
Dialog Information Services, Inc., **IV** 630
Dialogic Corporation, **18** 141–43
Diamandis Communications Inc., **IV** 619, 678
Diamang, **IV** 65, 67
Diamedix, **11** 207
Diamond Animal Health, Inc., **39** 216
Diamond Communications, **10** 288
Diamond Corporation Ltd., **IV** 21, 66–67; **7** 123
Diamond Crystal Brands, Inc., **32** 274, 277
Diamond Electronics, **24** 510
Diamond Fields Resources Inc., **27** 457
Diamond Head Resources, Inc. See AAON, Inc.
Diamond International Corp., **IV** 290, 295; **13** 254–55; **19** 225; **26** 446
Diamond M Offshore Inc., **12** 318
Diamond Match Company, **14** 163
Diamond Offshore Drilling, Inc., **36** 325; **43** 202
Diamond Oil Co., **IV** 548
Diamond Park Fine Jewelers, **16** 559
Diamond Rug & Carpet Mills, **19** 276
Diamond Savings & Loan, **II** 420
Diamond Shamrock Corporation, **IV** 408–11, 481; **7** 34, 308–099, 345; **13** 118; **19** 177; **45** 411. See also Ultramar Diamond Shamrock Corporation.
Diamond-Star Motors Corporation, **9** 349–51
Diamond Trading Company, **IV** 66–67; **7** 123
Diamond Walnut Growers, **7** 496–97
Dianatel, **18** 143
Diapositive, **44** 296
Diasonics Ultrasound, Inc., **27** 355
Dibrell Brothers, Incorporated, **12** 108–10; **13** 492
dick clark productions, inc., **16** 170–73
Dick Simon Trucking, Inc. See Simon Transporation Services Inc.
Dickerman, **8** 366
Dickson Forest Products, Inc., **15** 305
Dickstein Partners, L.P., **13** 261
Dictaphone Corp., **III** 157
Didier Lamarthe, **17** 210
Didier Werke AG, **IV** 232
Diebold, Incorporated, **7** 144–46; **22** 183–87 (upd.)
Diedrich Coffee, Inc., **40** 152–54
Diehl Manufacturing Co., **II** 9
Diemakers Inc., **IV** 443
Diesel Nacional, S.A. See Consorcio G Grupo Dina, S.A. de C.V.
Diesel SpA, **40** 155–57
Diesel United Co., **III** 533
AB Diesels Motorer, **III** 425–26

Diet Center, **10** 383
Dieter Hein Co., **14** 537
Dieterich Standard Corp., **III** 468
Dietrich & Cie. See De Dietrich & Cie.
Dietrich Corp., **II** 512; **15** 221
Dietrich's Bakeries, **II** 631
DiFeo Automotive Group, **26** 500–01
DiFranza Williamson, **6** 40
DIG Acquisition Corp., **12** 107
Digex, Inc., **45** 201; **46** 140–43
Digi International Inc., **9** 170–72; **20** 237
Digicom, **22** 17
Digidesign Inc., **38** 70, 72
DiGiorgio Corporation, **25** 421
Digital Audio Disk Corp., **II** 103
Digital City, Inc., **22** 522
Digital Data Systems Company, **11** 408
Digital Devices, Inc., **III** 643
Digital Directory Assistance, **18** 24
Digital Entertainment Network, **42** 272
Digital Equipment Corporation, **II** 8, 62, 108; **III** 118, 128, **132–35**, 142, 149, 166; **6** 225, **233–36 (upd.)**, 237–38, 242, 246–47, 279, 287; **8** 137–39, 519; **9** 35, 43, 57, 166, 170–71, 514; **10** 22–23, 34, 86, 242, 361, 463, 477; **11** 46, 86–88, 274, 491, 518–19; **12** 147, 162, 470; **13** 127, 202, 482; **14** 318; **15** 108; **16** 394, 418; **18** 143, 345; **19** 310; **21** 123; **25** 499; **26** 90, 93; **34** 441–43; **36** 81, 287; **43** 13; **45** 201
Digital Marketing, Inc., **22** 357
Digital Research in Electronic Acoustics and Music S.A., **17** 34
Digitech, **19** 414
Dii Group Inc., **38** 188–89
Diligent Engine Co., **III** 342
Dill & Collins, **IV** 311; **19** 266
Dill Enterprises, Inc., **14** 18
Dillard Department Stores, Inc., **V** 45–47; **10** 488; **11** 349; **12** 64; **13** 544–45; **16** 174–77 (upd.), 559; **19** 48, 324; **27** 61
Dillard Paper Company, **11** 74–76
Dillingham Construction Corporation, **44** 151–54 (upd.)
Dillingham Corp., **I** 565–66
Dillingham Holdings Inc., **9** 511
Dillon Companies Inc., **II** 645; **12** 111–13; **15** 267; **22** 194
Dillon Paper, **IV** 288
Dillon, Read, and Co., Inc., **I** 144, 559; **III** 151, 389; **6** 265; **11** 53; **20** 259; **24** 66
Dime Bancorp, **44** 32–33; **46** 316
Dime Banking and Loan Association of Rochester, **10** 91
Dime Savings Bank of New York, F.S.B., **9** 173–74
Dimeling, Schreiber & Park, **11** 63; **44** 309
Dimensions in Sport, Ltd., **37** 5
Dimeric Development Corporation, **14** 392
DIMON Inc., **12** 110; **27** 124–27
Dina. See Consorcio G Grupo Dina, S.A. de C.V.
Dinamica, S.A., **19** 12
Dine S.A., **23** 170–72
Dineen Mechanical Contractors, Inc., **48** 238
Diners Club, **II** 397; **6** 62; **9** 335; **10** 61
Dinner Bell Foods, Inc., **11** 93
de Dion, **III** 523
Dionex Corporation, **46** 144–46
Dior. See Christian Dior S.A.

Dirección General de Correos y Telecomunicaciónes, **V** 337
Dirección Nacional de los Yacimientos Petrolíferos Fiscales, **IV** 577–78
Direct Container Lines, **14** 505
Direct Focus, Inc., **47** 93–95
Direct Friends, **25** 91
Direct Line, **12** 422
Direct Mail Services Pty. Ltd., **10** 461
Direct Marketing Technology Inc., **19** 184
Direct Spanish Telegraph Co., **I** 428
Direct Transit, Inc., **42** 364
Direction Générale des Télécommunications, **V** 471
DirectLine Insurance, **22** 52
Directorate General of Telecommunications, **7** 147–49
DIRECTV, Inc., **21** 70; **35** 156, 158–59; **38** 174–77
Dirr's Gold Seal Meats, **6** 199
Disc Go Round, **18** 207, 209
Disc Manufacturing, Inc., **15** 378
Disclosure, Inc., **18** 24
Disco SA, **V** 11; **19** 308–09
Disconto-Gesellschaft, **II** 238, 279
Discount Auto Parts, Inc., **18** 144–46; **26** 348
Discount Bank, **II** 205
Discount Corporation, **12** 565
Discount Drug Mart, Inc., **14** 172–73
Discount Investment Corporation Ltd., **24** 429
Discount Labels, Inc., **20** 15
Discount Tire Co., **19** 294; **20** 263
Discover, **9** 335; **12** 97
Discovery Communications, Inc., **42** 114–17
Discovery Toys, Inc., **19** 28
Discovery Zone, **31** 97
DiscoVision Associates, **III** 605
Discreet Logic Inc., **20** 185–87
Disctronics, Ltd., **15** 380
Disney Channel, **6** 174–75; **13** 280
Disney Co. See The Walt Disney Company.
Disney Studios, **II** 408; **6** 174, 176; **43** 229–30, 233
Disneyland, **6** 175
Disneyland Paris. See Euro Disneyland SCA.
Dispatch Communications, **10** 432
Display Components Inc., **II** 110; **17** 479
Displayco Midwest Inc., **8** 103
Disposable Hospital Products, **I** 627
Distillers and Cattle Feeders Trust, **I** 376
Distillers Co. plc, **I** 239–41, 252, 263, 284–85; **II** 429, 609–10; **IV** 70; **43** 214
Distillers Securities, **I** 376
Distinctive Printing and Packaging Co., **8** 103
Distinctive Software Inc., **10** 285
Distribuidora Bega, S.A. de C.V., **31** 92
Distribution Centers Incorporated. See Exel Logistics Ltd.
Distribution Services, Inc., **10** 287
Distribution Solutions International, Inc., **24** 126
District Bank, **II** 333
District Cablevision, **II** 160
District News Co., **II** 607
Distrigas, **IV** 425
DITAS, **IV** 563
Ditzler Color Co., **III** 732
DIVAL, **III** 347

Divani & Divani. *See* Industrie Natuzzi S.p.A.
Divco-Wayne Corp., **17** 82
DIVE!, **26** 264
Diversey Corp., **I** 275, 333; **13** 150, 199; **26** 305–06; **32** 476
Diversified Agency Services, **I** 32
Diversified Foods Inc., **25** 179
Diversified Retailing Co., **III** 214
Diversified Services, **9** 95
Diversifoods Inc., **II** 556; **13** 408
Diversity Consultants Inc., **32** 459
DiviCom, **43** 221–22
Dixie Airline, **25** 420
Dixie Bearings, Inc., **13** 78
Dixie Carriers, Inc., **18** 277
Dixie Container Corporation, **12** 377
Dixie Crystals Brands, Inc., **32** 277
The Dixie Group, Inc., **20** 188–90
Dixie Hi-Fi, **9** 120–21
Dixie Home Stores, **II** 683
Dixie-Narco Inc., **III** 573; **22** 349
Dixie Paper, **I** 612–14
Dixie Power & Light Company, **6** 514
Dixie Yarns, Inc., **9** 466; **19** 305
Dixieland Food Stores, **II** 624
Dixie Industries, Inc., 26 117–19; **48** 59
Dixon Ticonderoga Company, 12 114–16
Dixons Group plc, II 139; **V** 48–50; **9** 65; **10** 45, 306; **19** 121–24 (upd.); **23** 52; **24** 194, 269–70; **49** 110–13 (upd.)
DIY Home Warehouse, **16** 210
DJ Moldings Corp., **18** 276
DJ Pharma, Inc., **47** 56
Djedi Holding SA, **23** 242
DKB. *See* Dai-Ichi Kangyo Bank Ltd.
DLC. *See* Duquesne Light Company.
DLJ. *See* Donaldson, Lufkin & Jenrette.
DLJ Merchant Banking Partners II, **21** 188; **36** 158–59
DM Associates Limited Partnership, **25** 127
DMA, **18** 510
DMB&B. *See* D'Arcy Masius Benton & Bowles.
DMGT. *See* Daily Mail and General Trust.
DMI Furniture, Inc., 44 132; **46** 147–50
DMP Mineralöl Petrochemie GmbH, **IV** 487
DNATA, **39** 137, 139
DNAX Research Institute, **I** 685; **14** 424
DNEL-Usinor, **IV** 227
DNN Galvanizing Limited Partnership, **24** 144
DNP DENMARK A/S, **IV** 600
Do It All, **24** 75
Do it Best Corporation, 30 166–70
Dobbs House, **21** 54
Dobbs Houses Inc., **I** 696–97; **15** 87
Dobrolet, **6** 57
Dobson Park Industries, **38** 227
Docks de France, **37** 23; **39** 183–84
Doctors' Hospital, **6** 191
Documentation Resources, **11** 65
Documentum, Inc., 46 151–53
DOD Electronics Corp., **15** 215
Dodd, Mead & Co., **14** 498
Dodge & Day. *See* Day & Zimmermann, Inc.
Dodge Corp., **I** 144; **8** 74; **11** 53
The Dodge Group, **11** 78
Dodge Manufacturing Company, **9** 440
Dodge Motor Company, **20** 259
Doduco Corporation, **29** 460–61

Dodwell & Co., **III** 523
Doe Run Company, **12** 244
Doeflex PLC, **33** 79
Dofasco Inc., IV 73–74; **24** 142–44 (upd.)
Doherty Clifford Steers & Sherfield Inc., **I** 31
Doherty, Mann & Olshan. *See* Wells Rich Greene BDDP.
Dolan Design, Inc., **44** 133
Dolby Laboratories Inc., 20 191–93
Dole Corporation, **44** 152
Dole Food Company, Inc., I 565; **II** 491–92; **9** 175–76; **20** 116; **31** 167–170 (upd.)
Dolland & Aitchison Group, **V** 399
Dollar Bills, Inc. *See* Dollar Tree Stores, Inc.
Dollar General, **26** 533
Dollar Rent A Car, **6** 349; **24** 10
Dollar Steamship Lines, **6** 353
Dollar Thrifty Automotive Group, Inc., 25 92, 142–45
Dollar Tree Stores, Inc., 16 161; **23** 176–78
Dollfus Mieg & Cie. *See* Groupe DMC.
Dollond & Aitchison Group, **49** 151–52
Dolphin Book Club, **13** 106
Dolphin Services, Inc., **44** 203
Dom Perignon, **25** 258
Domain Technology, **6** 231
Domaine Carneros, **43** 401
Domaine Chandon, **I** 272
Domaines Barons de Rothschild, **36** 113, 115
Dombrico, Inc., **8** 545
Domco Industries, **19** 407
Dome Laboratories, **I** 654
Dome Petroleum, Ltd., **II** 222, 245, 262, 376; **IV** 371, 401, 494; **12** 364
Domestic Electric Co., **III** 435
Domestic Operating Co., **III** 36
Dominick International Corp., **12** 131
Dominick's Finer Foods, **9** 451; **13** 25, 516; **17** 558, 560–61
Dominion Bank, **II** 375–76
Dominion Bridge Company, Limited, **8** 544
Dominion Cellular, **6** 322
Dominion Dairies, **7** 429
Dominion Engineering Works Ltd., **8** 544
Dominion Far East Line, **I** 469; **20** 311
Dominion Foils Ltd., **17** 280
Dominion Foundries and Steel, Ltd., **IV** 73–74
Dominion Hoist & Shovel Co., **8** 544
Dominion Homes, Inc., 19 125–27
Dominion Industries Ltd., **15** 229
Dominion Life Assurance Co., **III** 276
Dominion Mushroom Co., **II** 649–50
Dominion Ornamental, **III** 641
Dominion Paper Box Co. Ltd., **IV** 645
Dominion Resources, Inc., V 591, **596–99**
Dominion Securities, **II** 345; **21** 447
Dominion Steel Castings Company, Ltd. *See* Dofasco Inc.
Dominion Stores Ltd., **II** 650, 652
Dominion Tar & Chemical Co. Ltd., **IV** 271–72
Dominion Terminal Associates, **IV** 171; **7** 582, 584
Dominion Textile Inc., V 355; **8** 559–60; **12** 117–19

Domino Sugar Corporation, 26 120–22; **42** 370
Domino Supermarkets, **24** 528
Domino's Pizza, Inc., 7 150–53; **9** 74; **12** 123; **15** 344, 346; **16** 447; **21** 177–81 (upd.); **22** 353; **24** 295; **25** 179–80, 227–28; **26** 177; **33** 388; **37** 208
Domtar Inc., IV 271–73, 308
Don Baxter Intravenous Products Co., **I** 627
Don Massey Cadillac, Inc., 37 114–16
Don's Foods, Inc., **26** 164
Donac Company, **V** 681
Donald L. Bren Co., **IV** 287
Donaldson Company, Inc., 16 178–81; **49** 114–18 (upd.)
Donaldson, Lufkin & Jenrette, Inc., II 422, 451; **III** 247–48; **9** 115, 142, 360–61; **18** 68; **22** 188–91; **26** 348; **35** 247; **41** 197
Donaldson's Department Stores, **15** 274
Doncaster Newspapers Ltd., **IV** 686
Dong-A Motor, **III** 749
Dong-Myung Industrial Co. Ltd., **II** 540
Dongbang Life Insurance Co., **I** 515
Dongguan Shilong Kyocera Optics Co., Ltd., **21** 331
Dongil Frozen Foods Co., **II** 553
Dongsu Industrial Company, **III** 516; **7** 232
Donn, Inc., **18** 162
Donna Karan Company, 15 145–47; **24** 299; **25** 294, 523
Donnelley, Gassette & Loyd, **IV** 660
Donnellon McCarthy Inc., **12** 184
Donnelly Coated Corporation, **48** 28
Donnelly Corporation, 12 120–22; **35** 147–50 (upd.)
Donnkenny, Inc., 17 136–38
Donohue Inc., **12** 412
Donohue Meehan Publishing Co., **27** 362
Donruss Leaf Inc., **19** 386
Donzi Marine Corp., **III** 600
Dooner Laboratories, **I** 667
Door-to-Door, **6** 14
Dorado Beach Development Inc., **I** 103
Dordrecht, **III** 177–78
Dorenbecher Properties, **19** 381
Doric Corp., **19** 290
Dorling Kindersley Holdings plc, 20 194–96
Dorman Long & Co. Ltd., **IV** 658
Dorman's, Inc., **27** 291
Dorney Park, **22** 130
Dornier, **I** 46, 74, 151; **15** 142; **34** 131
Dorothy Hamill International, **13** 279, 281
Dorothy Perkins, **V** 21
Dorr-Oliver Inc., **35** 134–35
Dorset Capital, **49** 189
Dorsey & Whitney LLP, 47 96–99
Dortmunder Union, **II** 240; **IV** 103, 105
Doskocil Companies, Inc., 12 123–25. *See also* Foodbrands America, Inc.
Dot Wireless Inc., **46** 422
Doty Agency, Inc., **41** 178, 180
Double A Products Co., **23** 82–83
DoubleClick Inc., 46 154–57; **49** 423, 432
Doubleday Book Shops, Inc., **10** 136; **25** 31; **30** 68
Doubleday-Dell, **IV** 594, 636
Doubletree Corporation, 21 182–85; **41** 81–82
Doughty Handson, **49** 163

Douglas & Lomason Company, 16 182–85
Douglas Aircraft Co., **I** 48, 70, 76, 96, 104, 195; **II** 32, 425; **III** 601; **9** 12, 18, 206; **10** 163; **13** 48, 341; **16** 77; **21** 141; **24** 375
Douglas-Dahlin Co., **I** 158–59
Douglas Dynamics L.L.C., **41** 3
Douglas Oil Co., **IV** 401
Doulton Glass Industries Ltd., **IV** 659
Douwe Egberts, **II** 572
Dove International, **7** 299–300
Dover Corporation, III 467–69; 28 101–05 (upd.)
Dover Downs Entertainment, Inc., 43 139–41
Dover Publications Inc., 34 148–50; 41 111
Dovrat Shrem, **15** 470
Dow Chemical Co., I 323–25, 334, 341–42, 360, 370–71, 708; **II** 440, 457; **III** 617, 760; **IV** 83, 417; **8 147–50 (upd.)**, 153, 261–62, 548; **9** 328–29, 500–1; **10** 289; **11** 271; **12** 99–100, 254, 364; **14** 114, 217; **16** 99; **17** 418; **18** 279; **21** 387; **28** 411; **38** 187
Dow Corning, **II** 54; **III** 683, 685; **44** 129
Dow Jones & Company, Inc., IV 601–03, 654, 656, 670, 678; **7** 99; **10** 276–78, 407; **13** 55; **15** 335–36; **19 128–31 (upd.)**, 204; **21** 68–70; **23** 157; **47 100–04 (upd.)**
Dow Jones Telerate, Inc., **10** 276–78
DOW Stereo/Video Inc., **30** 466
Dowdings Ltd., **IV** 349
DowElanco, **21** 385, 387
Dowell Australia Ltd., **III** 674
Dowell Schlumberger. *See* Schlumberger Limited.
Dowidat GmbH, **IV** 197
Dowlais Iron Co., **III** 493
Down River International, Inc., **15** 188
Downe Communications, Inc., **14** 460
Downingtown Paper Company, **8** 476
Downyflake Foods, **7** 429
Dowty Aerospace, **17** 480
Doyle Dane Bernbach, **I** 9, 20, 28, 30–31, 33, 37, 206; **11** 549; **14** 159; **22** 396
DP&L. *See* Dayton Power & Light Company.
DPCE, **II** 139; **24** 194
DPF, Inc., **12** 275; **38** 250–51
DPL Inc., 6 480–82
DQE, **6 483–85; 38** 40
Dr. Gerhard Mann Pharma, **25** 56
DR Holdings, Inc., **10** 242
Dr. Ing he F. Porsche GmbH, **13** 413–14
Dr. Karl Thomae GmbH, **39** 72–73
Dr. Martens, **23** 399, 401
Dr. Miles' Medical Co., **I** 653
Dr Pepper/Seven Up, Inc., I 245; **II** 477; **9** 177–78; **32 154–57 (upd.); 49** 78
Dr. Richter & Co., **IV** 70
Dr. Solomon's Software Ltd., **25** 349
Dr. Tigges-Fahrten, **II** 163–64; **44** 432
Drackett Professional Products, III 17; **12 126–28**
DraftDirect Worldwide, **22** 297
Draftline Engineering Co., **22** 175
Dragados y Construcciones S.A., **II** 198
Dragon, **III** 391
Dragon International, **18** 87
Dragonair, **16** 481; **18** 114. *See also* Hong Kong Dragon Airlines.

The Drake, **12** 316
Drake Bakeries, **II** 562
Drake Beam Morin, Inc., IV 623; **44 155–57**
Drake Steel Supply Co., **19** 343
Drallos Potato Company, **25** 332
Draper & Kramer, **IV** 724
Draper Corporation, **14** 219; **15** 384
Drathen Co., **I** 220
Dravo Corp., **6** 143
Draw-Tite, Inc., **II** 535
Drayton Corp., **II** 319; **17** 324
DreamWorks SKG, 17 72; **21** 23, 26; **26** 150, 188; **43 142–46**
The Drees Company, Inc., 41 131–33
Dreher Breweries, **24** 450
Dresdner Bank A.G., I 411; **II** 191, 238–39, 241–42, 256–57, 279–80, **281–83**, 385; **III** 201, 289, 401; **IV** 141; **14** 169–70; **15** 13; **47** 81–84
Dresdner Feuer-Versicherungs-Gesellschaft, **III** 376
Dresdner RCM Global Investors, **33** 128
The Dress Barn, Inc., 24 145–46
Dresser Industries, Inc., I 486; **III** 429, **470–73**; 499, 527, 545–46; **12** 539; **14** 325; **15** 225–26, 468; **16** 310; **18** 219; **24** 208; **25** 188, 191
Dresser Power, **6** 555
Drew Graphics, Inc., **13** 227–28
Drew Industries Inc., 28 106–08
Drewry Photocolor, **I** 447
Drexel Burnham Lambert Incorporated, **II** 167, 329–30, **407–09**, 482; **III** 10, 253, 254–55, 531, 721; **IV** 334; **6** 210–11; **7** 305; **8** 327, 349, 388–90, 568; **9** 346; **12** 229; **13** 169, 299, 449; **14** 43; **15** 71, 281, 464; **16** 535, 561; **20** 415; **22** 55, 189; **24** 273; **25** 313; **33** 253. *See also* New Street Capital Inc.
Drexel Heritage Furnishings Inc., III 571; **11** 534; **12 129–31; 20** 362; **39** 266
Dreyer's Grand Ice Cream, Inc., 10 147–48; **17 139–41; 30** 81; **35** 59–61
Dreyfus Interstate Development Corp., **11** 257
DRI. *See* Dominion Resources, Inc.
Dribeck Importers Inc., **9** 87
Drip In Irrigation, **26** 494
Drogueros S.A., **39** 188
Drott Manufacturing Company, **10** 379
Drouot Group, **III** 211
DRS Investment Group, **27** 370
Drug City, **II** 649
Drug Emporium, Inc., 12 132–34, 477
Drug House, **III** 9
Drug, Inc., **III** 17; **37** 42
Drummond Lighterage. *See* Puget Sound Tug and Barge Company.
Drummonds' Bank, **12** 422
Druout, **I** 563; **24** 78
Dry Milks Inc., **I** 248
DryClean U.S.A., **14** 25
Dryden and Co., **III** 340
Drypers Corporation, 18 147–49
Drysdale Government Securities, **10** 117
DSC Communications Corporation, 9 170; **12 135–37**
DSL Group Ltd., **27** 49
DSM Melamine America, **27** 316–18
DSM N.V., I 326–27; III 614; **15** 229
DST Systems Inc., **6** 400–02; **26** 233
DTAG. *See* Dollar Thrifty Automotive Group, Inc.

DTE Energy Company, 20 197–201 (upd.)
Du Bouzet, **II** 233
Du Mont Company, **8** 517
Du Pareil au Même, 43 147–49
Du Pont. *See* E.I. du Pont de Nemours & Co.
Du Pont Fabricators, **III** 559
Du Pont Glore Forgan, Inc., **III** 137
Du Pont Photomask, **IV** 600
Duane Reade Holding Corp., 21 186–88
Dublin and London Steam Packet Company, **V** 490
DuBois Chemicals Division, **13** 149–50; **22** 188; **26** 306
Ducatel-Duval, **II** 369
Ducati Motor Holding S.p.A., 17 24; **30 171–73; 36** 472
Duck Head Apparel Company, Inc., 8 141–43; **30** 159; **42 118–21**
Ducks Unlimited, **28** 306
Duckwall-ALCO Stores, Inc., 24 147–49
Duco Ltd., **25** 104–05
Ducommun Incorporated, 30 174–76
Ducon Group, **II** 81
Ducros, **36** 185, 187–88
Dudley Stationery Ltd., **25** 501
Duff & Phelps Credit Rating, **37** 143, 145
Duff Bros., **III** 9–10
Duffy Meats, **27** 259
Duffy-Mott, **II** 477
Duke Energy Corporation, 27 128–31 (upd.); 40 354, 358
Duke Energy Field Services, Inc., **24** 379; **40** 354, 358
Duke Power Company, V 600–02
Dumes SA, **13** 206
Dumez, **V** 655–57
Dumont Broadcasting Corporation, **7** 335
The Dun & Bradstreet Corporation, I 540; **IV 604–05**, 643, 661; **8** 526; **9** 505; **10** 4, 358; **13** 3–4; **19 132–34 (upd.); 38** 6
Dun & Bradstreet Software Services Inc., 11 77–79; 43 183
Dunbar-Stark Drillings, Inc., **19** 247
Duncan Foods Corp., **I** 234; **10** 227
Duncan, Sherman & Co., **II** 329
Duncanson & Holt, Inc., **13** 539
Dundee Acquisition Corp., **19** 421
Dundee Bancorp, **36** 314
Dundee Cement Co., **III** 702; **8** 258–59
Dunfey Brothers Capital Group, **12** 368
Dunfey Hotels Corporation, **12** 367
Dunhams Stores Corporation, **V** 111
Dunhill Holdings, **IV** 93; **V** 411
Dunkin' Donuts, **II** 619; **21** 323; **29** 18–19
Dunlop Coflexip Umbilicals Ltd. *See* Duco Ltd.
Dunlop Holdings, **I** 429; **III** 697; **V** 250, 252–53
Dunlop Ltd., **25** 104
Dunn Bennett, **38** 401
Dunn Bros., **28** 63
Dunn Manufacturing Company, **25** 74
Dunn Paper Co., **IV** 290
Dunning Industries, **12** 109
Dunoyer. *See* Compagnie de Saint-Gobain S.A.
Dunwoodie Manufacturing Co., **17** 136
Duo-Bed Corp., **14** 435
Dupey Enterprises, Inc., **17** 320
Dupil-Color, Inc., **III** 745
Duplainville Transport, **19** 333–34

Duplex Products, Inc., 17 142–44, 445
Dupol, **III** 614
Dupont. *See* E.I. du Pont de Nemours &
    Company.
Dupont Chamber Works, **6** 449
Duquesne Light Company, **6** 483–84
Duquesne Systems, **10** 394
Dura Convertible Systems, **13** 170
Dura Corp., **I** 476
Dura-Vent, **III** 468
Duracell International Inc., 9 179–81; **12**
    559; **13** 433; **17** 31; **24** 274; **39** 336, 339
Durametallic, 17 147; **21** 189–91
Durand & Huguenin, **I** 672
Durango-Mapimi Mining Co., **22** 284
Duray, Inc., **12** 215
Durban Breweries and Distillers, **I** 287
D'Urban, Inc., **41** 169
Durham Chemicals Distributors Ltd., **III**
    699
Durham Raw Materials Ltd., **III** 699
Duriron Company Inc., 17 145–47; **21**
    189, 191
Durkee Famous Foods, **II** 567; **7** 314; **8**
    222; **17** 106; **27** 297
Dürr AG, 44 158–61
Durr-Fillauer Medical Inc., **13** 90; **18** 97
Dutch Boy, **II** 649; **III** 745; **10** 434–35
Dutch Crude Oil Company. *See*
    Nederlandse Aardolie Maatschappij.
Dutch East Indies Post, Telegraph and
    Telephone Service, **II** 67
Dutch Nuts Chocoladefabriek B.V., **II** 569
Dutch Pantry, **II** 497
Dutch State Mines. *See* DSM N.V.
Dutchland Farms, **25** 124
Dutton Brewery, **I** 294
Duttons Ltd., **24** 267
Duty Free International, Inc., 11 80–82.
    See also World Duty Free Americas,
    Inc.
Duval Corp., **IV** 489–90; **7** 280; **25** 461
DWG Corporation. *See* Triarc Companies,
    Inc.
Dyckerhoff AG, 35 151–54
Dyersburg Corporation, 21 192–95
Dyke and Dryden, Ltd., **31** 417
Dylex Limited, 29 162–65
Dymed Corporation. *See* Palomar Medical
    Technologies, Inc.
Dynaco Corporation, **III** 643; **22** 409
Dynalectric Co., **45** 146
DynaMark, Inc., **18** 168, 170, 516, 518
Dynamatic Corp., **I** 154
Dynamem Corporation, **22** 409
Dynamic Capital Corp., **16** 80
Dynamic Controls, **11** 202
Dynamic Microprocessor Associated Inc.,
    10 508
Dynamics Corporation of America, **39** 106
Dynamit Nobel AG, **III** 692–95; **16** 364;
    18 559
Dynamix, **15** 455
Dynapar, **7** 116–17
Dynaplast, **40** 214–15
Dynascan AK, **14** 118
Dynasty Footwear, Ltd., **18** 88
Dynatech Corporation, 13 194–96
Dynatron/Bondo Corporation, **8** 456
DynCorp, 45 145–47
Dynegy Inc., 47 70; **49** 119–22 **(upd.)**
Dynell Electronics, **I** 85
Dyno Industrier AS, **13** 555
Dyonics Inc., **I** 667

DYR, **I** 38; **16** 167
Dystrybucja, **41** 340

E. & B. Carpet Mills, **III** 423
E&B Company, **9** 72
E&B Marine, Inc., **17** 542–43
E & H Utility Sales Inc., **6** 487
E. & J. Gallo Winery, I 27, 242–44, 260;
    7 154–56 **(upd.)**; **15** 391; **28** 109–11
    (upd.), 223
E&M Laboratories, **18** 514
E & S Retail Ltd. *See* Powerhouse.
E! Entertainment Television Inc., 17
    148–50; **24** 120, 123; **47** 78
E-Stamp Corporation, **34** 474
E-Systems, Inc., I 490; **9** 182–85
E*Trade Group, Inc., **20** 206–08; **38** 439;
    45 4
E-II Holdings Inc., **II** 468; **9** 449; **12** 87;
    43 355. *See also* Astrum International
    Corp.
E-Z Haul, **24** 409
E-Z Serve Corporation, 15 270; **17**
    169–71
E.A. Miller, Inc., **II** 494
E.A. Pierce & Co., **II** 424; **13** 340
E.A. Stearns & Co., **III** 627
E.B. Badger Co., **11** 413
E.B. Eddy Forest Products, **II** 631
E.C. Snodgrass Company, **14** 112
E.C. Steed, **13** 103
E. de Trey & Sons, **10** 270–71
E.F. Hutton Group, **I** 402; **II** 399, 450–51;
    8 139; **9** 469; **10** 63
E.F. Hutton LBO, **24** 148
E. Gluck Trading Co., **III** 645
E.H. Bindley & Company, **9** 67
E.I. du Pont de Nemours & Company, I
    21, 28, 305, 317–19, 323, **328–30**, 334,
    337–38, 343–44, 346–48, 351–53, 365,
    377, 379, 383, 402–03, 545, 548, 675;
    III 21; **IV** 69, 78, 263, 371, 399,
    401–02, 409, 481, 599; **V** 360; **7** 546; **8**
    151–54 (upd.), 485; **9** 154, 216, 352,
    466; **10** 289; **11** 432; **12** 68, 365,
    416–17; **13** 21, 124; **16** 127, 130, 201,
    439, 461–62; **19** 11, 223; **21** 544; **22**
    147, 260, 405; **24** 111, 388; **25** 152,
    540; **26 123–27 (upd.)**; **34** 80, 283–84;
    37 111; **40** 370; **45** 246
E.J. Brach & Sons, **II** 521. *See also* Brach
    and Brock Confections, Inc.
E.J. Longyear Company. *See* Boart
    Longyear Company.
E. Katz Special Advertising Agency. *See*
    Katz Communications, Inc.
E.L. Phillips and Company, **V** 652–53
E.M. Warburg Pincus & Co., **7** 305; **13**
    176; **16** 319; **25** 313; **29** 262
E. Missel GmbH, **20** 363
E.N.V. Engineering, **I** 154
E.piphany, Inc., 49 123–25
E.R.R. Enterprises, **44** 227
E.R. Squibb, **I** 695; **21** 54–55
E. Rabinowe & Co., Inc., **13** 367
E.S. Friedman & Co., **II** 241
E.S. International Holding S.A. *See* Banco
    Espírito Santo e Comercial de Lisboa
    S.A.
E.W. Bliss, **I** 452
E.W. Oakes & Co. Ltd., **IV** 118
The E.W. Scripps Company, IV 606–09;
    7 157–59 **(upd.)**; **24** 122; **25** 507; **28**
    122–26 (upd.)

E.W.T. Mayer Ltd., **III** 681
EADS. *See* European Aeronautic Defence
    and Space Company.
Eagle Airways Ltd., **23** 161
Eagle Credit Corp., **10** 248
Eagle Distributing Co., **37** 351
Eagle Family Foods, Inc., **22** 95
Eagle Floor Care, Inc., **13** 501; **33** 392
Eagle Gaming, L.P., **16** 263; **43** 226
Eagle Hardware & Garden, Inc., 9 399;
    16 186–89; **17** 539–40
Eagle Industries Inc., **8** 230; **22** 282; **25**
    536
Eagle-Lion Films, **II** 147; **25** 328
Eagle Managed Care Corp., **19** 354, 357
Eagle Oil Transport Co. Ltd., **IV** 657
Eagle-Picher Industries, Inc., 8 155–58;
    23 179–83 (upd.)
Eagle Plastics, **19** 414
Eagle Printing Co. Ltd., **IV** 295; **19** 225
Eagle Sentry Inc., **32** 373
Eagle Snacks Inc., **I** 219; **34** 36–37
Eagle Square Manufacturing Co., **III** 627
Eagle Star Insurance Co., **I** 426–27; **III**
    185, 200
Eagle Supermarket, **II** 571
Eagle Thrifty Drug, **14** 397
Eagle Travel Ltd., **IV** 241
Earl Scheib, Inc., 32 158–61
Early American Insurance Co., **22** 230
Early Learning Centre, **39** 240, 242
Earth Resources Company, **IV** 459; **17** 320
Earth Wise, Inc., **16** 90
Earth's Best, Inc., **21** 56; **36** 256
The Earthgrains Company, 36 161–65
EarthLink, Inc., 33 92; **36 166–68**; **38**
    269
EAS. *See* Executive Aircraft Services.
Easco Hand Tools, Inc., **7** 117
Eason Oil Company, **6** 578; **11** 198
East African External Communications
    Limited, **25** 100
East Chicago Iron and Forge Co., **IV** 113
East Hartford Trust Co., **13** 467
East India Co., **I** 468; **III** 521, 696; **IV** 48;
    20 309
East Japan Heavy Industries, **III** 578–79; **7**
    348
East Japan Railway Company, V 448–50
East Midlands Electricity, **V** 605
The East New York Savings Bank, **11**
    108–09
East of Scotland, **III** 359
East Texas Pulp and Paper Co., **IV** 342,
    674; **7** 528
East-West Airlines, **27** 475
East-West Federal Bank, **16** 484
East West Motor Express, Inc., **39** 377
Easter Enterprises, **8** 380; **23** 358
Easterday Supply Company, **25** 15
Eastern Air Group Co., **31** 102
Eastern Airlines, I 41, 66, 78, 90, 98–99,
    101–03, 116, 118, 123–25; **III** 102; **6**
    73, 81–82, 104–05; **8** 416; **9** 17–18, 80;
    11 268, 427; **12** 191, 487; **21** 142, 143;
    23 483; **26** 339, 439; **39** 120
Eastern Associated Coal Corp., **6** 487
Eastern Australia Airlines, **24** 396
Eastern Aviation Group, **23** 408
Eastern Bank, **II** 357
Eastern Carolina Bottling Company, **10**
    223
Eastern Coal Corp., **IV** 181
Eastern Coalfields Ltd., **IV** 48–49

The Eastern Company, 48 140–43
Eastern Corp., **IV** 703
Eastern Electricity, **13** 485
Eastern Enterprises, IV 171; **6 486–88**
Eastern Gas and Fuel Associates, **I** 354; **IV** 171
Eastern Indiana Gas Corporation, **6** 466
Eastern Kansas Utilities, **6** 511
Eastern Machine Screw Products Co., **13** 7
Eastern Market Beef Processing Corp., **20** 120
Eastern Operating Co., **III** 23
Eastern Pine Sales Corporation, **13** 249
Eastern Software Distributors, Inc., **16** 125
Eastern States Farmers Exchange, **7** 17
Eastern Telegraph Company, **V** 283–84; **25** 99–100
Eastern Texas Electric. *See* Gulf States Utilities Company.
Eastern Tool Co., **IV** 249
Eastern Torpedo Company, **25** 74
Eastern Wisconsin Power, **6** 604
Eastern Wisconsin Railway and Light Company, **6** 601
Eastex Pulp and Paper Co., **IV** 341–42
Eastman Chemical Company, 14 174–75; 25 22; **38 178–81 (upd.)**
Eastman Christensen Company, **22** 68
Eastman Kodak Company, I 19, 30, 90, 323, 337–38, 690; **II** 103; **III** 171–72, **474–77**, 486–88, 547–48, 550, 584, 607–09; **IV** 260–61; **6** 288–89; **7 160–64 (upd.)**, 436–38; **8** 376–77; **9** 62, 231; **10** 24; **12** 342; **14** 174–75, 534; **16** 168, 449; **18** 184–86, 342, 510; **25** 153; **29** 370; **36 169–76 (upd.)**; **38** 178–79; **41** 104, 106; **43** 284; **45** 284
Eastman Radio, **6** 33
Eastmaque Gold Mines, Ltd., **7** 356
Eastover Mining, **27** 130
Eastpak, Inc., **30** 138
Eastwynn Theatres, Inc., **37** 63
easyJet Airline Company Limited, 39 127–29
Eatco, Inc., **15** 246
Eateries, Inc., 33 138–40
Eaton Axle Co., **I** 154
Eaton, Cole & Burnham Company, **8** 134
Eaton Corporation, I 154–55, 186; **III** 645; **10 279–80 (upd.)**; **12** 547; **27** 100
Eaton Vance Corporation, 18 150–53
EAudio, Inc., **48** 92
Eavey Co., **II** 668
Ebamsa, **II** 474
EBASCO. *See* Electric Bond and Share Company.
Ebasco Services, **III** 499; **V** 612; **IV** 255–56
eBay Inc., 32 162–65; 49 51
EBC Amro Ltd., **II** 186
Eberhard Faber, **12** 115
Eberhard Foods, **8** 482
Eberhard Manufacturing Company, **48** 141
EBIC. *See* European Banks' International Co.
Ebiex S.A., **25** 312
EBS. *See* Electric Bond & Share Company *or* Electronic Bookshelf.
EBSCO Industries, Inc., 17 151–53; 40 158–61 (upd.)
EC Comics, **25** 139
EC Erdolchemie GmbH, **7** 141
ECAD Inc., **48** 75
ECC. *See* Educational Credit Corporation.

ECC Group plc, III 689–91. *See also* English China Clays plc.
ECC International Corp., 42 122–24
Ecce, **41** 129
ECCO. *See* Adecco S.A.
Echigoya Saburobei Shoten, **IV** 292
Echlin Inc., I 156–57; 11 83–85 (upd.); 15 310
Echo Bay Mines Ltd., IV 75–77; 23 40; **38 182–85 (upd.)**
Les Echos, **IV** 659
EchoStar Communications Corporation, 35 155–59
EchoStar Satellite Corp., **39** 400
ECI Telecom Ltd., 18 154–56
Eckerd Corporation, 9 186–87; 18 272; **24** 263; **43** 247. *See also* J.C. Penney Company, Inc.
Eckert-Mauchly Corp., **III** 166
Ecko-Ensign Design, **I** 531
Ecko Products, **I** 527
ECL, **16** 238
Eclipse Candles, Ltd., **18** 67, 69
Eclipse Machine Co., **I** 141
Eclipse Telecommunications, Inc., **29** 252
Eco Hotels, **14** 107
Eco SA, **48** 224
Ecolab Inc., I 331–33; 13 197–200 (upd.); 26 306; **34 151–56 (upd.)**, 205, 208
Ecology and Environment, Inc., 39 130–33
Econo Lodges of America, **25** 309
Econo-Travel Corporation, **13** 362
Economist Group, **15** 265
Economy Book Store, **10** 135
Economy Fire & Casualty, **22** 495
Economy Grocery Stores Company. *See* The Stop & Shop Companies, Inc.
Ecopetrol. *See* Empresa Colombiana de Petróleos.
EcoSystems Software, Inc., **10** 245; **30** 142
EcoWater Systems, Inc., **16** 357
ECS S.A, 12 138–40
Ecton, Inc., **36** 5
Ecusta Corporation, **8** 414
ed bazinet international, inc., **34** 144–45
Edah, **13** 544–45
Eddie Bauer, Inc., II 503; V 160; **9 188–90; 9** 316; **10** 324, 489, 491; **11** 498; **15** 339; **25** 48; **27** 427, 429–30; **29** 278; **36 177–81 (upd.)**
Eddy Bakeries, Inc., **12** 198
Eddy Paper Co., **II** 631
Edeka Zentrale A.G., II 621–23; 33 56; **47 105–07 (upd.)**
edel music AG, 44 162–65
Edelbrock Corporation, 37 117–19
Edelhoff AG & Co., **39** 415
Edelstahlwerke Buderus AG, **III** 695
Edenhall Group, **III** 673
Edenton Cotton Mills, **12** 503
EDF. *See* Electricité de France.
Edgars, **I** 289
Edgcomb Metals, **IV** 575–76; **31** 470–71
Edge Research, **25** 301
Edgell Communications Inc., **IV** 624
Edgewater Hotel and Casino, **6** 204–05
EDI, **26** 441
Edina Realty Inc., **13** 348
Edison Brothers Stores, Inc., 9 191–93; 17 369, 409; **33** 126–28
Edison Electric Appliance Co., **II** 28; **12** 194

Edison Electric Co., **I** 368; **II** 330; **III** 433; **6** 572
Edison Electric Illuminating Co., **II** 402; **6** 595, 601; **14** 124
Edison Electric Illuminating Company of Boston, **12** 45
Edison Electric Light & Power, **6** 510
Edison Electric Light Co., **II** 27; **6** 565, 595; **11** 387; **12** 193
Edison General Electric Co., **II** 27, 120, 278; **12** 193; **14** 168; **26** 451
Edison Machine Works, **II** 27
Edison Phonograph, **III** 443
Edison Schools Inc., 37 120–23
Editions Albert Premier, **IV** 614
Editions Bernard Grasset, **IV** 618
Editions Dalloz, **IV** 615
Editions Jean-Baptiste Baillière, **25** 285
Editions Nathan, **IV** 615
Editions Ramsay, **25** 174
Editorial Centro de Estudios Ramón Areces, S.A., **V** 52; **26** 130
Editorial Televisa, **18** 211, 213; **23** 417
Editoriale L'Espresso, **IV** 586–87
Editoriale Le Gazzette, **IV** 587
EdK. *See* Edeka Zentrale A.G.
Edmark Corporation, 14 176–78; 41 134–37 (upd.)
Edmonton City Bakery, **II** 631
EDO Corporation, 46 158–61
Edogawa Oil Co., **IV** 403
EdoWater Systems, Inc., **IV** 137
EDP Group. *See* Electricidade de Portugal, S.A.
Edper Equities, **II** 456
EDS. *See* Electronic Data Systems Corporation.
Education Association Mutual Assurance Company. *See* Horace Mann Educators Corporation.
The Education Finance Group, **33** 418, 420
Education Funds, Inc., **II** 419
Education Management Corporation, 35 160–63
Education Systems Corporation, **7** 256; **25** 253
Educational & Recreational Services, Inc., **II** 607
Educational Broadcasting Corporation, 48 144–47
Educational Computer International, Inc. *See* ECC International Corp.
Educational Credit Corporation, **8** 10; **38** 12
Educational Loan Administration Group, Inc., **33** 420
Educational Publishing Corporation, **22** 519, 522
Educational Supply Company, **7** 255; **25** 252
Educational Testing Service, 12 141–43; 42 209–10, 290
Educorp, Inc., **39** 103
EduQuest, **6** 245
EduServ Technologies, Inc., **33** 420
Edusoft Ltd., **40** 113
EduTrek International, Inc., **45** 88
Edw. C. Levy Co., 42 125–27
Edward Ford Plate Glass Co., **III** 640–41, 731
Edward J. DeBartolo Corporation, V 116; **8 159–62**
Edward Jones, 30 177–79
Edward Lloyd Ltd., **IV** 258

Edward P. Allis Company, **13** 16
Edward Smith & Company, **8** 553
Edwards & Jones, **11** 360
Edwards Dunlop & Co. Ltd., **IV** 249
Edwards Food Warehouse, **II** 642
Edwards George and Co., **III** 283
Edwards Industries, **IV** 256
Edwards Theatres Circuit, Inc., 31 171–73
Edwardstone Partners, **14** 377
EEC Environmental, Inc., **16** 259
EEGSA. *See* Empresa Eléctrica de Guatemala S.A.
Eerste Nederlandsche, **III** 177–79
Eff Laboratories, **I** 622
Effectenbank, **II** 268; **21** 145
EFM Media Management, **23** 294
Efnadruck GmbH, **IV** 325
Efrat Future Technology Ltd. *See* Comverse Technology, Inc.
EFTEC, **32** 257
EG&G Incorporated, 8 163–65; **18** 219; **22** 410; **29 166–69 (upd.)**
EGAM, **IV** 422
Egerton Hubbard & Co., **IV** 274
Egg plc, **48** 328
Egghead Inc., 9 194–95; **10** 284
Egghead.com, Inc., 31 174–177 (upd.)
EGPC. *See* Egyptian General Petroleum Corporation.
EGUZKIA-NHK, **III** 581
EgyptAir, I 107; **6 84–86**; **27 132–35 (upd.)**
Egyptian General Petroleum Corporation, IV 412–14; **32** 45
EHAPE Einheitspreis Handels Gesellschaft mbH. *See* Kaufhalle AG.
eHow.com, **49** 290
Ehrlich-Rominger, **48** 204
Eidgenössische Bank, **II** 378
Eidgenössische Versicherungs- Aktien-Gesellschaft, **III** 403
Eiffage, 27 136–38
Eiffel Construction Metallique, **27** 138
800-JR Cigar, Inc., 27 139–41
84 Lumber Company, 9 196–97; **39 134–36 (upd.)**
Eildon Electronics Ltd., **15** 385
EIMCO, **I** 512
Einstein/Noah Bagel Corporation, 29 170–73; **44** 313
eircom plc, 31 178–181 (upd.)
EIS Automotive Corp., **III** 603
EIS, Inc., **45** 176, 179
Eisai Company, **13** 77
Eisen-und Stahlwerk Haspe AG, **IV** 126
Eisen-und Stahlwerk Hoesch, **IV** 103
Eisenhower Mining Co., **IV** 33
EJ Financial Enterprises Inc., **48** 308–09
EKA AB, **I** 330; **8** 153
Eka Nobel AB, **9** 380
Ekco Group, Inc., 12 377; **16 190–93**
EKT, Inc., **44** 4
El Al Israel Airlines Ltd., I 30; **23 184–87**
El Camino Resources International, Inc., 11 86–88
El Chico Restaurants, Inc., 19 135–38; **36** 162–63
El Corte Inglés, S.A., V 51–53; **26 128–31 (upd.)**
El Dorado Investment Company, **6** 546–47
El-Mel-Parts Ltd., **21** 499
El Paso & Southwestern Railroad, **IV** 177

El Paso Electric Company, 21 196–98
El Paso Healthcare System, Ltd., **15** 112; **35** 215
El Paso Natural Gas Company, 10 190; **11** 28; **12 144–46**; **19** 411; **27** 86
El Pollo Loco, **II** 680; **27** 16–18
El Taco, **7** 505
ELAN, **IV** 486
Elan Corp. plc, **10** 54
Elan Ski Company, **22** 483
Elanco Animal Health, **47** 112
Elano Corporation, 14 179–81
Elantis, **48** 290
Elastic Reality Inc., **38** 70
Elcat Company, **17** 91
Elco Corporation, **21** 329, 331
Elco Industries Inc., **22** 282
Elco Motor Yacht, **I** 57
Elda Trading Co., **II** 48; **25** 267
Elder-Beerman Stores Corporation, 10 281–83; **19** 362
Elder Dempster Line, **6** 416–17
Elder Smith Goldsbrough Mort Ltd., **21** 227
Elder's Insurance Co., **III** 370
Elders IXL Ltd., I 216, 228–29, 264, **437–39**, 592–93; **7** 182–83; **21** 227; **26** 305; **28** 201
Elders Keep, **13** 440
Eldorado Gold Corporation, **22** 237
ele Corporation, **23** 251
Electra Corp., **III** 569; **20** 361–62
Electra/Midland Corp., **13** 398
Electralab Electronics Corp., **III** 643
Electric Boat Co., **I** 57–59, 527; **II** 7; **10** 315
Electric Bond & Share Company, **V** 564–65; **6** 596
Electric Clearinghouse, Inc., **18** 365, 367
Electric Energy, Inc., **6** 470, 505
Electric Fuels Corp., **V** 621; **23** 200
Electric Heat Regulator Co., **II** 40; **12** 246
Electric Iron and Steel, **IV** 162
Electric Light and Power Company, **6** 483
Electric Light Company of Atlantic City. *See* Atlantic Energy, Inc.
Electric Lightwave, Inc., 37 124–27
Electric Storage Battery Co., **39** 338
Electric Thermostat Co., **II** 40; **12** 246
Electric Transit, Inc., **37** 399–400
Electrical Lamp Service Co. *See* EMI Group plc.
Electricidade de Portugal, S.A., 47 108–11; **49** 211
Electricité de France, I 303; **V 603–05**, 626–28; **41 138–41 (upd.)**
Electro-Alkaline Company. *See* The Clorox Company.
Electro-Chemische Fabrik Natrium GmbH, **IV** 69–70
Electro Dynamics Corp., **I** 57, 484; **11** 263
Electro-Flo, Inc., **9** 27
Electro-Mechanical Research, **III** 617; **17** 417
Electro Metallurgical Co., **I** 400; **9** 517; **11** 402
Electro-Motive Engineering Company, **10** 273
Electro-Nite International N.V., **IV** 100
Electro-Optical Systems, **III** 172; **6** 289
Electro Refractories and Abrasives Company, **8** 178
Electro String Instrument Corporation, **16** 201; **43** 169

Electrobel, **II** 202
ElectroData Corp., **III** 165; **6** 281
Electrolux Group, II 69, 572; **III** 420, **478–81**; **IV** 338; **6** 69; **11** 439; **12** 158–59, 250; **13** 562, 564; **17** 353; **21** 383. *See also* Aktiebolaget Electrolux.
Electromagnetic Sciences Inc., 21 199–201
Electromedics, **11** 460
Electronic Arts Inc., 10 284–86; **13** 115; **29** 76; **35** 227
Electronic Banking Systems, **9** 173
Electronic Book Technologies, Inc., **26** 216 **29** 427
Electronic Data Systems Corporation, I 172; **II** 65; **III 136–38**, 326; **6** 226; **9** 36; **10** 325, 327; **11** 62, 123, 131; **13** 482; **14** 15, 318; **22** 266; **27** 380; **28 112–16 (upd.)**; **241**; **XXIX** 375; **36** 242; **49** 116, 311, 313. *See also* Perot Systems Corporation.
Electronic Engineering Co., **16** 393
Electronic Hair Styling, Inc., **41** 228
Electronic Rentals Group PLC, **II** 139; **24** 194
Electronic Tool Company, **16** 100
Electronics Corp. of Israel Ltd. *See* ECI Telecom Ltd.
Electronics for Imaging, Inc., 15 148–50; **43 150–53 (upd.)**
Electrorail, **II** 93; **18** 472
Electrowatt Ltd., **21** 146–47
Electrowerke AG, **IV** 230
Elekom, **31** 176
Elektra. *See* Grupo Elektra, S.A. de C.V.
Elektra Records, **III** 480; **23** 33
Elektriska Aktiebolaget. *See* ABB Asea Brown Boveri Ltd.
Elektrizitäts-Gesellschaft Laufenburg, **6** 490
Elektrizitätswerk Wesertal GmbH, **30** 206
Elektrizitätswerk Westfalen AG, **V** 744
ElektroHelios, **III** 479; **22** 26
Elektromekaniska AB, **III** 478
Elektromekano, **II** 1
Elektrowatt AG, 6 489–91
Eleme Petrochemicals Co., **IV** 473
Elementis plc, 40 162–68 (upd.)
Eletson Corp., **13** 374
Elettra Broadcasting Corporation, **14** 509
Elettrofinanziaria Spa, **9** 152
Eleventh National Bank, **II** 373
Elf Aquitaine SA, 21 202–06 (upd.); **23** 236, 238; **24** 494; **25** 104; **26** 369, 425; **49** 349–51. *See also* Société Nationale Elf Aquitaine.
Elfa International, **36** 134–35
Elgin Blenders, Inc., **7** 128
Elgin Exploration, Inc., **19** 247; **26** 70
Eli Lilly and Company, I 637, **645–47**, 666, 679, 687, 701; **III** 18–19, 60–61; **8** 168, 209; **9** 89–90; **10** 535; **11** 9, **89–91 (upd.)**, 458, 460; **12** 187, 278, 333; **14** 99–100, 259; **17** 437; **18** 420, 422; **19** 105; **21** 387; **26** 31; **32** 212; **44** 175; **45** 382; **47 112–16 (upd.)**, 221, 236
Eli Witt Company, **15** 137, 139; **43** 205
Elias Brothers Restaurants, **III** 103
Elior SA, 49 126–28
Elit Circuits Inc., **I** 330; **8** 153
Elite Microelectronics, **9** 116
Elite Sewing Machine Mfg. Co. Ltd., **III** 415; **48** 5

Elizabeth Arden, Inc., I 646, III 48; **8 166–68,** 344; **9** 201–02, 428, 449; **11** 90; **12** 314; **30** 188; **32** 476; **40 169–72 (upd.);** **47** 113
Eljer Industries, Inc., II 420; **24 150–52**
Elk River Resources, Inc., **IV** 550
Elka, **III** 54
Elke Corporation, **10** 514
Elkjop ASA, **49** 113
Elko-Lamoille Power Company, **11** 343
Ellanef Manufacturing Corp., **48** 274
Ellenville Electric Company, **6** 459
Ellerbe Becket, 41 142–45
Ellesse International S.p.A., **V** 376; **26** 397–98
Ellett Brothers, Inc., 17 154–56
Ellington Recycling Center, **12** 377
Elliot Group Limited, **45** 139–40
Elliott Automation, **II** 25; **6** 241; **13** 225
Elliott Bay Design Group, **22** 276
Elliott Paint and Varnish, **8** 553
Ellipse Programmes, **48** 164–65
Ellis & Everard, **41** 341
Ellis Adding-Typewriter Co., **III** 151; **6** 265
Ellis Banks, **II** 336
Ellis, Chafflin & Co. *See* Mead Corporation.
Ellis-Don Ltd., **38** 481
Ellis Paperboard Products Inc., **13** 442
Ellis Park Race Course, **29** 118
Ellisco Co., **35** 130
Ellos A.B., **II** 640
ELMA Electronic, **III** 632
Elmendorf Board, **IV** 343
Elmer's Products, Inc. *See* Borden, Inc.
Elmer's Restaurants, Inc., 42 128–30
Elmo Semiconductor Corp., **48** 246
Elphinstone, **21** 501
Elrick & Lavidge, **6** 24
Elrick Industries, Inc., **19** 278
Elscint Ltd., 20 202–05
Elsevier NV, IV 610–11, 643, 659; **7** 244; **14** 555–56; **17** 396, 399. *See also* Reed Elsevier.
Elsi, **II** 86
Elsinore Corporation, 36 158; **48 148–51**
ELTO Outboard Motor Co., **III** 597
Eltra Corporation, **I** 416, 524; **22** 31; **31** 135
Elwerath, **IV** 485
ELYO, **42** 387–88
Elyria Telephone Company, **6** 299
Email Ltd., **III** 672–73
EMAP plc, 35 71–72, **164–66,** 242–44
Emballage, **III** 704
Embankment Trust Ltd., **IV** 659
Embassy Book Co., Ltd., **IV** 635
Embassy Hotel Group, **I** 216; **9** 426
Embassy Suites, **9** 425; **24** 253
Embedded Support Tools Corporation, **37** 419, 421
Embers America Restaurants, 30 180–82
Embotelladora Central, S.A., **47** 291
Embraer. *See* Empresa Brasileira de Aeronáutica S.A.
Embry-Riddle, **I** 89
EMC Corporation, 12 147–49; 20 8; **46 162–66 (upd.)**
EMC Technology Services, Inc., **30** 469
Emco, **III** 569; **20** 361
EMD Technologies, **27** 21; **40** 67
Emerald Coast Water Co., **III** 21
Emerald Technology, Inc., **10** 97

Emerson, 46 167–71 (upd.)
Emerson-Brantingham Company, **10** 378
Emerson Drug, **I** 711
Emerson Electric Co., II 18–21, 92; III 625; **8** 298; **12** 248; **13** 225; **14** 357; **15** 405–06; **21** 43; **22** 64; **25** 530; **36** 400
Emerson Foote, Inc., **25** 90
Emerson Radio Corp., 30 183–86
Emery Air Freight Corporation, 6 345–46, 386, **388–91; 18** 177. *See also* Emery Worldwide Airlines, Inc.
Emery Group, **I** 377; **III** 33
Emery Worldwide Airlines, Inc., 21 139; **25 146–50 (upd.)**
Emeryville Chemical Co., **IV** 408
Emge Packing Co., Inc., 11 92–93
Emhart Corp., **III** 437; **8** 332; **20** 67
EMI Group plc, I 531; **6** 240; **22 192–95 (upd.); 24** 485; **26** 188, 314. *See also* Thorne EMI plc.
The Emirates Group, 24 400; **39 137–39**
Emmis Communications Corporation, 47 117–21
Empain, **18** 472; **19** 165
Empain-Schneider, **II** 93
Empaques de Carton Titan, **19** 10–11
Empex Hose, **19** 37
Empi, Inc., 27 132–35
Empire Blue Cross and Blue Shield, III 245–46; 6 195
Empire Brewery, **I** 253
Empire Co., **II** 653
Empire Cos., **IV** 391
Empire District Electric, **IV** 391
Empire Family Restaurants Inc., **15** 362
Empire Gas & Fuel, **IV** 391
Empire Hanna Coal Co., Ltd., **8** 346
Empire Inc., **II** 682
Empire Life and Accident Insurance Co., **III** 217
Empire National Bank, **II** 218
Empire of America, **11** 110
Empire Pencil, **III** 505; **43** 230
Empire Savings, Building & Loan Association, **8** 424
Empire State Group, **IV** 612
Empire State Petroleum, **IV** 374
Empire State Pickling Company, **21** 155
Empire Steel Castings, Inc., **39** 31–32
Empire Stores, **19** 309
Empire Trust Co., **II** 218
Employee Solutions, Inc., 18 157–60
employeesavings.com, **39** 25
Employers' Liability Assurance, **III** 235
Employer's Overload, **25** 432
Employers Reinsurance Corp., **II** 31; **12** 197
Empresa Brasileira de Aeronáutica S.A. (Embraer), 36 182–84
Empresa Colombiana de Petróleos, IV 415–18
Empresa de Obras y Montajes Ovalle Moore, S.A., **34** 81
Empresa Eléctrica de Guatemala S.A., **49** 211
Empresa Nacional de Electridad, **I** 459
Empresa Nacional del Petroleo, **IV** 528
Empresa Nacional Electrica de Cordoba, **V** 607
Empresa Nacional Hidro-Electrica del Ribagorzana, **I** 459; **V** 607
Empresa Nacional Hulleras del Norte, **I** 460
Empresas Emel S.A., **41** 316

Empresas Frisco, **21** 259
Empresas ICA, **34** 82
Empresas ICA Sociedad Controladora, S.A. de C.V., 41 146–49
Empresas La Moderna, **21** 413; **29** 435
Empresas Tolteca, **20** 123
Emprise Corporation, **7** 134–35
EMS-Chemie Holding AG, **III** 760; **32** 257
EMS Technologies, Inc., **21** 199, 201; **22** 173
Enagas, **IV** 528
Enbridge Inc., 43 154–58
ENCAD, Incorporated, 25 151–53
ENCASO, **IV** 528
ENCI, **IV** 132
Encompass Services Corporation, 33 141–44
Encon Safety Products, Inc., **45** 424
Encor Inc., **47** 396
Encore Computer Corporation, 13 201–02
Encore Distributors Inc., **17** 12–13
Encryption Technology Corporation, **23** 102
Encyclopedia Britannica, Inc., 7 165–68; 12 435, 554–55; **16** 252; **39 140–44 (upd.); 43** 208
Endata, Inc., **11** 112
Endemol Entertainment Holding NV, 46 172–74
ENDESA S.A., V 606–08; 46 175–79 (upd.); 49 210–11
Endevco Inc., **11** 28
Endiama, **IV** 67
Endicott Trust Company, **11** 110
Endo Vascular Technologies, Inc., **11** 460
Endovations, Inc., **21** 47
ENECO. *See* Empresa Nacional Electrica de Cordoba.
ENEL. *See* Ente Nazionale per l'Energia Elettrica.
Enerchange LLC, **18** 366
Enercon, Inc., **6** 25
Energas Company, **43** 56–57
Energen Corporation, 6 583; **21 207–09**
Energie-Verwaltungs-Gesellschaft, **V** 746
Energieversorgung Ostbayern AG, **23** 47
Energis plc, 44 363; **47 122–25**
Energizer Holdings, Inc., 9 180; **32 171–74; 39** 336, 339
Energy & Minerals, Inc., **42** 354
Energy Absorption Systems, Inc., **15** 378
Energy Biosystems Corp., **15** 352
Energy Coatings Co., **14** 325
Energy Corp. of Louisiana, **V** 619
Energy Film Library, **31** 216, 218
Energy Foundation, **34** 386
The Energy Group, **26** 359
Energy Increments Inc., **19** 411
Energy National, Inc., **27** 485
Energy Resources, **27** 216
Energy Steel Corporation, **19** 472
Energy Systems Group, Inc., **13** 489
Energy Transportation Systems, Inc., **27** 88
Energy Ventures, Inc., **49** 181
Energyline Systems, **26** 5
EnergyOne, **19** 487
Enerplus Resources, **21** 500
Enesco Corporation, 11 94–96; 15 475, 477–78
Engelhard Corporation, II 54; **IV** 23, **78–80; 16** 28; **21 210–14 (upd.)**
Engen, **IV** 93; **22** 236
Engineered Polymers Co., **I** 202

Engineering Co. of Nigeria, **IV** 473
Engineering Company, **9** 16
Engineering for the Petroleum and Process Industries, **IV** 414
Engineering Plastics, Ltd., **8** 377
Engineering Research Associates, **III** 126, 129
Engineers & Fabricators, Inc., **18** 513
England Corsair Furniture, **14** 302
Englander Co., **I** 400
Engle Homes, Inc., 46 180–82
Engles Management Corp., **26** 448
English China Clays Ltd., III 689–91; **15** 151–54 (upd.); **36** 20; **40** 173–77 (upd.)
English Condensed Milk Co., **II** 545
English Electric Co., **I** 50; **II** 25, 81; **6** 241; **24** 85
English Mercantile & General Insurance Co., **III** 376
English Property Corp., **IV** 712
English, Scottish and Australian Bank Ltd., **II** 187–89
Engraph, Inc., 12 150–51
Enhanced Services Billing, Inc. *See* Billing Concepts Corp.
ENHER. *See* Empresa Nacional Hidro-Electrica del Ribagorzana.
ENI. *See* Ente Nazionale Idrocarburi.
ENI S.p.A., **34** 75
ENIEPSA, **IV** 528
Enimont, **IV** 422, 525
Ennia, **III** 177, 179, 310
Ennis Business Forms, Inc., 21 215–17
Eno Proprietaries, **III** 65
Enocell Oy, **IV** 277
The Enoch F. Bills Co., **25** 365
Enogex, Inc., **6** 539–40
Enova Corporation. *See* Sempra Energy.
ENPAC Corporation, **18** 162
Enpetrol, **IV** 528
Enquirer/Star Group, Inc., 10 287–88; 12 358. *See also* American Media, Inc.
Enrich International, Inc., 33 145–48; 37 340, 342
Enron Corporation, III 197; **V** 609–10; **6** 457, 593; **18** 365; **19** 139–41, 162, 487; **27** 266; **34** 82; **46 183–86 (upd.); 49** 121–22
Enseco, **III** 684
Enserch Corp., V 611–13
Ensidesa, **I** 460
Ensign Oil Company, **9** 490
Enskilda S.A., **II** 352–53
Enso-Gutzeit Oy, IV 274–77; **17** 539. *See also* Stora Enso Oyj
ENSTAR Corporation, **IV** 567; **11** 441
Enstar Group Inc., **13** 299
Ensys Environmental Products, Inc., **10** 107
ENTASA, **IV** 528
Ente Gestione Aziende Minerarie, **I** 466
Ente Nazionale di Energia Elettrica, **I** 466
Ente Nazionale Idrocarburi, I 369; **IV** 412, **419–22**, 424, 453, 466, 470, 486, 546; **V** 614–17
Ente Nazionale per l'Energia Elettrica, V 614–17
Entenmann's Bakery, **I** 246, 712; **10** 551; **35** 415; **38** 364
Entercom, **48** 272
Entergy Corporation, V 618–20; **6** 496–97; **45 148–51 (upd.)**
Enterprise Development Company, **15** 413

Enterprise Electronics Corporation, **18** 513–15
Enterprise Federal Savings & Loan, **21** 524
Enterprise Integration Technologies, **18** 541
Enterprise Leasing, 6 392–93
Enterprise Metals Pty. Ltd., **IV** 61
Enterprise Oil plc, 11 97–99
Enterprise Rent-A-Car, Inc., **16** 380; **33** 192
Enterra Corp., **25** 546
Entertainment Publications, **16** 146
Entertainment UK, **24** 266, 269
Entertainment Zone, Inc., **15** 212
Entex Information Services, **24** 29
Entity Software, **11** 469
Entrada Industries Incorporated, **6** 568–69; **26** 387
Entravision Communications Corporation, 41 150–52
Entré Computer Centers, **6** 243–44; **13** 175
Entremont, **I** 676
Entreprise de Recherches et d'Activités Pétrolières, **IV** 453, 467, 544, 560; **7** 481, 483–84
Entreprise Nationale Sonatrach, IV 423–25; **V** 626, 692; **10** 83–84; **12** 145
Entrex, Inc., **III** 154
Entrust Financial Corp., **16** 347
Envergure, **27** 421
Envirex, **11** 361
Envirodrill Services, Inc., **19** 247
Envirodyne Industries, Inc., 17 157–60
EnviroLease, Inc., **25** 171
ENVIRON International Corporation, **10** 106
Environmental Defense Fund, **9** 305
Environmental Industries, Inc., 31 182–85
Environmental Mediation, Inc., **47** 20
Environmental Planning & Research. *See* CRSS Inc.
Environmental Research and Technology, Inc., **23** 135
Environmental Systems Corporation, **9** 109
Environmental Testing and Certification Corporation, **10** 106–07
Environmentals Incorporated. *See* Angelica Corporation.
Envirosciences Pty. Ltd., **16** 260
Envision Corporation, **24** 96
Enwright Environmental Consulting Laboratories, **9** 110
Enzafruit Worldwide, **38** 202
Enzo Biochem, Inc., 41 153–55
Enzyme Bio-Systems, Ltd., **21** 386
Enzyme Technologies Corp., **I** 342; **14** 217
Eon Productions, **II** 147; **25** 328
Eon Systems, **III** 143; **6** 238; **38** 409
l'Epargne, **12** 152
EPE Technologies, **18** 473
EPI. *See* Essentially Pure Ingredients.
EPI Group Limited, **26** 137
Epic Express, **48** 113
Les Epiceries Presto Limitée, **II** 651
Epiphone, **16** 238–39
Epoch Software, Plc, **49** 290
Epoch Systems Inc., **9** 140; **12** 149
ePOWER International, **33** 3, 6
Eppler, Guerin & Turner, Inc., **III** 330
Eppley, **III** 99
Epsilon Trading Corporation, **6** 81
Epson, **18** 386–87, 435
Equator Bank, **II** 298

EQUICOR-Equitable HCA Corp., **III** 80, 226; **45** 104, 109
Equicor Group Ltd., **29** 343
Equifax, Inc., 6 23–25; 25 182, 358; **28 117–21 (upd.)**
Equilink Licensing Group, **22** 458
Equilon Enterprises LLC, **41** 359, 395
Equistar Chemicals, LP, **45** 252, 254
EquiStar Hotel Investors L.P. *See* CapStar Hotel Co.
Equitable Bancorporation, **12** 329
Equitable Equipment Company, **7** 540
Equitable Life Assurance Society of the United States, II 330; **III** 80, 229, 237, **247–49**, 274, 289, 291, 305–06, 316, 329, 359; **IV** 171, 576, 711; **6** 23; **13** 539; **19** 324, 511; **22** 188–90; **23** 370, 482; **27** 46
Equitable Resources, Inc., 6 492–94
Equitable Trust Co., **II** 247, 397; **10** 61
Equitas, **22** 315
Equitec Financial Group, **11** 483
Equitex Inc., **16** 431
Equity & Law, **III** 211
Equity Corp. Tasman, **III** 735
Equity Corporation, **6** 599; **37** 67–68
Equity Group Investment, Inc., **22** 339
Equity Marketing, Inc., 26 136–38
Equity Residential, 49 55, **129–32**
Equity Title Services Company, **13** 348
Equivalent Company, **12** 421
Equus Capital Corp., **23** 65
Equus Computer Systems, Inc., 49 133–35
Equus II Inc., **18** 11
Eramet, **IV** 108
ERAP. *See* Entreprise de Recherches et d'Activités Pétrolières.
Erasco Group, **II** 556; **26** 58
EraSoft Technologies, **27** 492
Ercea, **41** 128–29
ERCO Systems Group, **16** 461–63
Ercon Corp., **49** 181
ERDA Inc., **36** 160
Erdal, **II** 572
Erdölsproduktions-Gesellschaft AG, **IV** 485
Erftwerk AG, **IV** 229
ERGO Versicherungsgruppe AG, 44 166–69, 443
Ericson Yachts, **10** 215
Ericssan, AB, **11** 501
Ericsson, **9** 32–33; **11** 196; **17** 33, 353; **18** 74; **47** 321. *See also* Telefonaktiebolaget LM Ericsson.
Eridania Béghin-Say S.A., 14 17, 19; **36 185–88**
Erie and Pennyslvania, **I** 584
Erie County Bank, **9** 474
Erie Indemnity Company, 35 167–69
Erie Railroad, **I** 584; **II** 329; **IV** 180
Erie Scientific Company, **14** 479–80
Eritsusha, **IV** 326
erizon, **36** 264
ERKA. *See* Reichs Kredit-Gesellschaft mbH.
ERLY Industries Inc., 17 161–62; 33 30–31
Ernest Oppenheimer and Sons, **IV** 21, 79
Ernst & Young, I 412; **9 198–200**, 309, 311; **10** 115; **25** 358; **29 174–77 (upd.)**, 236, 392
Ernst Göhner Foundation, **47** 286–87
Ernst, Homans, Ware & Keelips, **37** 224
Erol's, **9** 74; **11** 556

ERPI, **7** 167

Ersco Corporation, **17** 310; **24** 160

Erste Allgemeine, **III** 207–08

The Ertl Company, **37** 318

Erving Distributor Products Co., **IV** 282; **9** 260

Erving Healthcare, **13** 150

Erwin Wasey & Co., **I** 17, 22

Erzbergbau Salzgitter AG, **IV** 201

ES&A. *See* English, Scottish and Australian Bank Ltd.

Esanda, **II** 189

Esaote Biomedica, **29** 298

ESB Inc., **IV** 112; **18** 488

Esbjerg Thermoplast, **9** 92

Escada AG, **14** 467

Escalade, Incorporated, 19 142–44

Escambia Chemicals, **I** 298

Escan, **22** 354

Escanaba Paper Co., **IV** 311; **19** 266

Escaut et Meuse, **IV** 227

Escher Wyss, **III** 539, 632

Eschweiler Bergwerks-Verein AG, **IV** 25–26, 193

ESCO Electronics Corporation, **17** 246, 248; **24** 425

Esco Trading, **10** 482

Escoffier Ltd., **I** 259

Escotel Mobile Communications, **18** 180

Esdon de Castro, **8** 137

ESE Sports Co. Ltd., **V** 376; **26** 397

ESGM. *See* Elder Smith Goldsbrough Mort.

ESGO B.V., **49** 222

ESI Energy, Inc., **V** 623–24

Eskay Screw Corporation, **11** 536

Eskilstuna Separator, **III** 419

Eskimo Pie Corporation, 21 218–20; 35 119, 121

Esmark, Inc., **I** 441; **II** 448, 468–69; **6** 357; **12** 93; **13** 448; **15** 357; **19** 290; **22** 55, 513

Esperance-Longdoz, **IV** 51–52

Espírito Santo. *See* Banco Espírito Santo e Comercial de Lisboa S.A.

ESPN Inc., **II** 131; **IV** 627; **19** 201, 204; **24** 516; **46** 232

Esporta plc, 35 170–72

Esprit de Corp., 8 169–72; 29 178–82 (upd.)

La Espuela Oil Company, Ltd., **IV** 81–82; **7** 186

Esquire Education Group, **12** 173

Esquire Inc., **I** 453; **IV** 672; **13** 178; **19** 405

ESS Technology, Inc., 22 196–98

Essanelle Salon Co., **18** 455

Essantee Theatres, Inc., **14** 86

Essef Corporation, 18 161–63

Esselte Leitz GmbH & Co. KG, 48 152–55

Esselte Pendaflex Corporation, 11 100–01

Essence Communications, Inc., 24 153–55

Essener Reisebüro, **II** 164

Essentially Pure Ingredients, **49** 275–76

Essex International Ltd., **19** 452

Essex Outfitters Inc., **9** 394; **42** 268–69

Essilor International, 18 392; 21 221–23; 40 96–98

Esso Petroleum, **I** 52; **II** 628; **III** 673; **IV** 46, 276, 397, 421, 423, 432–33, 439, 441, 454, 470, 484, 486, 517–19, 531,

555, 563; **7** 140, 171; **11** 97; **13** 558; **22** 106; **24** 86; **25** 229, 231–32. *See also* Imperial Oil Limited *and* Standard Oil Company of New Jersey.

Essroc Corporation, **40** 108

Estat Telecom Group plc, **31** 180

Estech, Inc., **19** 290

Estee Corp., **27** 197; **43** 218

The Estée Lauder Companies Inc., 30 187–91 (upd.)

Estée Lauder Inc., I 696; **III** 56; **8** 131; **9** 201–04; **11** 41; **24** 55

Estel N.V., **IV** 105, 133

Esterline Technologies Corp., 15 155–57

Eston Chemical, **6** 148

Estronicks, Inc., **19** 290

ETA Systems, Inc., **10** 256–57

Etablissement Mesnel, **I** 202

Etablissement Poulenc-Frères, **I** 388

Etablissements Badin-Defforey, **19** 98

Etablissements Braud. *See* Manitou BF S.A.

Etablissements Economiques du Casino Guichard, Perrachon et ie, S.C.A., 12 152–54; 16 452

Etablissements Pierre Lemonnier S.A., **II** 532

Etablissements Robert Ouvrie S.A., **22** 436

Etam Developpement SA, 35 308; 44 170–72

Eteq Microsystems, **9** 116

Ethan Allen Interiors, Inc., III 530–31; **10** 184; **12** 307; **12** 155–57; **39 145–48 (upd.)**, **39** 173–74

Ethical Personal Care Products, Ltd., **17** 108

Ethicon, Inc., III 35; **8** 281; **10** 213; **23 188–90**

Ethyl Corp., I 334–36, 342; **IV** 289; **10 289–91 (upd.)**; **14** 217

Etienne Aigner, **14** 224

Etimex Kunststoffwerke GmbH, **7** 141

Etkin Skanska, **38** 437

L'Etoile, **II** 139

Etos, **II** 641

EToys, Inc., 37 128–30

ETPM Entrêpose, **IV** 468

ETS. *See* Educational Testing Service.

Euclid, **I** 147; **12** 90

Euclid Chemical Co., **8** 455–56

Euclid Crane & Hoist Co., **13** 385

Euralux, **III** 209

Eurasbank, **II** 279–80; **14** 169

The Eureka Company, III 478, 480; **12 158–60**; **15** 416; **22** 26. *See also* White Consolidated Industries Inc.

Eureka Insurance Co., **III** 343

Eureka Specialty Printing, **IV** 253; **17** 30

Eureka Technology, **18** 20; **43** 17

Eureka Tent & Awning Co., **III** 59

Eureka X-Ray Tube, Inc., **10** 272

Eurex, **41** 84, 87

Euris, **22** 365

Euro Disneyland SCA, 6 174, 176; **20 209–12**

Euro-Pacific Finance, **II** 389

Euro RSCG Worldwide S.A., 10 345, 347; **13 203–05**; **16** 168; **33** 181

Eurobel, **II** 139; **III** 200; **24** 193

Eurobrokers Investment Corp., **II** 457

Eurocan Pulp & Paper Co. Ltd., **III** 648; **IV** 276, 300

Eurocard France, **II** 265

Eurocom S.A. *See* Euro RSCG Worldwide S.A.

Eurocopter SA, **7** 9, 11; **21** 8

EuroCross, **48** 381

Eurodis, **46** 71

EuroDollar Rent A Car. *See* Republic Industries, Inc.

Eurofighter Jagdflugzeug GmbH, **24** 84

Eurofilter Airfilters Ltd., **17** 106

Eurogroup, **V** 65

Euroimpex, **18** 163

Euromarché SA, **10** 205; **19** 308–09; **23** 231; **27** 94–95

Euromarket Designs Inc., 9 144; **31 186–89 (upd.)**; **34** 324, 327

Euromissile Dynamics Group, **7** 9; **24** 84

Euromoney Publications, **19** 118, 120

Euronext Paris S.A., 37 131–33

Euronova S.R.L., **15** 340

Europa Discount Sud-Ouest, **23** 248

Europa Metalli, **IV** 174

Europaischen Tanklager- und Transport AG, **7** 141

Europate, S.A., 36 162–63

Europcar Chauffeur Drive U.K. International, **26** 62

Europcar International Corporation, Limited, **25** 142, 144; **27** 9, 11

Europcar Interrent, **10** 419

Europe Computer Systems. *See* ECS S.A.

Europe Craft Imports, Inc., **16** 37

Europe Publications, **44** 416

European Aeronautic Defence and Space Company, **34** 128, 135

European-American Bank & Trust Company, **14** 169

European-American Banking Corp., **II** 279, 295

European and African Investments Ltd., **IV** 21

European Banking Co., **II** 186

European Banks' International Co., **II** 184–86, 295

European Coal and Steel, **II** 402

European Gas Turbines, **13** 356

European Health Spa, **46** 431

European Investment Bank, **6** 97

European Periodicals, Publicity and Advertising Corp., **IV** 641; **7** 311

European Petroleum Co., **IV** 562

European Retail Alliance (ERA), **12** 152–53

European Silicon Structures, **17** 34

European Software Company, **25** 87

Europeia, **III** 403

Europemballage, **I** 600

Europene du Zirconium (Cezus), **21** 491

Europensiones, **III** 348

Europoligrafico SpA, **41** 326

Eurosar S.A., **25** 455

Eurotec, **IV** 128

Eurotech BV, **25** 101

Eurotechnique, **III** 678; **16** 122

Eurotunnel Group, 37 134–38 (upd.)

Eurotunnel PLC, 13 206–08

Eurovida, **III** 348

Euthenics Systems Corp., **14** 334

EVA Airways Corporation, **13** 211

Evaluation Associates, Inc., **III** 306

Evan Picone, **III** 55

Evans, **V** 21

Evans & Sutherland Computer Corporation, 19 145–49

Evans-Aristocrat Industries, **III** 570; **20** 361

Evans Drumhead Company, **48** 232

Evans, Inc., 30 192–94

Evans Products Co., **13** 249–50, 550

Evans Rents, **26** 101

Evansville Veneer and Lumber Co., **12** 296

Eve of Roma, **III** 28

Evelyn Haddon, **IV** 91

Evelyn Wood, Inc., **7** 165, 168

Evence Coppée, **III** 704–05

Evenflo Companies, Inc., **19** 144

Evening News Association, **IV** 612; **7** 191

Ever Ready Label Corp., **IV** 253; **17** 30

Ever Ready Ltd., **7** 209; **9** 179–80; **30** 231

Everan Capital Corp., **15** 257

Everest & Jennings, **11** 200

Everett Pulp & Paper Company, **17** 440

Everex Systems, Inc., 12 162; **16 194–96**

Everfresh Beverages Inc., **26** 326

Evergenius, **13** 210

Evergreen Healthcare, Inc., **14** 210

Evergreen Marine Corporation Taiwan Ltd., 13 209–11

Evergreen Media Corporation, **24** 106

Evergreen Resources, Inc., **11** 28

Everlast Worldwide Inc., 47 126–29

Everlaurel, **13** 210

Everready Battery Co., **13** 433; **39** 338

Eversharp, **III** 28

Everyday Learning Corporation, **22** 519, 522

Everything for the Office, **22** 154

Everything Yogurt, **25** 180

Everything's A Dollar Inc. (EAD), **13** 541–43

EVI, Inc., **39** 416

Evian, **6** 47, 49

Evinrude-ELTO, **III** 597

Evinrude Motor Co., **III** 597–99

Evinrude Outboard Motor Company, **27** 75

Ewell Industries, **III** 739

Ewo Breweries, **I** 469; **20** 311

Ex-Cell-O Corp., **IV** 297

Ex-Lax Inc., **15** 138–39

Exabyte Corporation, 12 161–63; **26** 256; **40 178–81 (upd.)**

Exacta, **III** 122

Exactis.com Inc., **49** 423

ExamOne World Wide, **48** 256

Exar Corp., 14 182–84

Exatec A/S, **10** 113

Exbud, **38** 437

Excaliber, **6** 205

EXCEL Communications Inc., 18 164–67

Excel Corporation, **11** 92–93; **13** 138, 351

Excel Mining Systems, Inc., **13** 98

Excelsior Life Insurance Co., **III** 182; **21** 14

Excelsior Printing Company, **26** 105

Excerpta Medica International, **IV** 610

Exchange & Discount Bank, **II** 318; **17** 323

Exchange Bank of Yarmouth, **II** 210

Exchange Oil & Gas Corp., **IV** 282; **9** 260

Excite, Inc., **22** 519; **27** 517. *See also* At Home Corporation.

Exco International, **10** 277

Execu-Fit Health Programs, **11** 379

Executive Aircraft Services, **27** 21

Executive Airlines, Inc., **28** 22

Executive Fund Life Insurance Company, **27** 47

Executive Gallery, Inc., **12** 264

Executive Income Life Insurance Co., **10** 246

Executive Jet, Inc., 36 189–91; 42 35

Executive Life Insurance Co., **III** 253–55; **11** 483

Executive Risk Inc., **37** 86

Executive Systems, Inc., **11** 18

Executone Information Systems, Inc., 13 212–14; 15 195

ExecuTrain. *See* International Data Group, Inc.

Executrans, Inc., **21** 96

Exel Logistics Ltd., **6** 412, 414

Exel Ltd., **13** 150

Exelon Corporation, 48 156–63 **(upd.)**; **49** 65

Exeter & Hampton Electric Company, **37** 406

Exeter Oil Co., **IV** 550

Exide Electronics Group, Inc., 9 10; **20 213–15; 24** 29

Exmark Manufacturing Company, Inc., **26** 494

Exors. of James Mills, **III** 493

Exp@nets, **37** 280, 283

Expand SA, 48 164–66

Expedia Inc., **46** 101, 103; **47** 421

Expeditors International of Washington Inc., 17 163–65

Expercom, **6** 303

Experian Information Solutions Inc., 28 120; **45 152–55**

Experian Ltd., **47** 165, 168–69

Experience, **III** 359

Exploitasi Tambang Minyak Sumatra Utara, **IV** 492

Explorer Motor Home Corp., **16** 296

Explosive Fabricators Corp., **III** 643

Export & Domestic Can Co., **15** 127

Export-Import Bank, **IV** 33, 184

Express Airlines, Inc., **28** 266

Express Baggage Reclaim Services Limited, **27** 21

Express Foods Inc., **I** 247–48

Express Newspapers plc, **IV** 687; **28** 503

Express Rent-a-Tire, Ltd., **20** 113

Express Scripts Inc., 17 166–68; **44 173–76 (upd.)**

Expression Homes, **22** 205, 207

Extel Corp., **II** 142; **III** 269–70

Extel Financial Ltd., **IV** 687

Extended Stay America, Inc., 41 156–58

Extendicare Health Services, Inc., III 81; **6 181–83**

Extracorporeal Medical Specialties, **III** 36

Extron International Inc., **16** 538; **43** 33

Exx Inc., **40** 334

Exxon Corporation, I 16–17, 360, 364; **II** 16, 62, 431, 451; **IV** 171, 363, 365, 403, 406, **426–30**, 431–33, 437–38, 454, 466, 506, 508, 512, 515, 522, 537–39, 554; **V** 605; **7 169–73 (upd.)**, 230, 538, 559; **9** 440–41; **11** 353; **14** 24–25, 291, 494; **12** 348; **16** 489, 548; **20** 262; **23** 317; **25** 229–30; **26** 102, 369; **27** 217; **32 175–82 (upd.)**; **45** 54

Exxon Mobil Corporation, **40** 358

Eye Masters Ltd., **23** 329

Eyeful Home Co., **III** 758

Eyelab, **II** 560; **12** 411

EZ Paintr Corporation, **9** 374

EZCORP Inc., 43 159–61

EZPor Corporation, **12** 377

F. & F. Koenigkramer Company, **10** 272

F&G International Insurance, **III** 397

F. & J. Heinz, **II** 507

F & J Meat Packers, Inc., **22** 548–49

F & M Distributors, **12** 132

F. & M. Schaefer Brewing Corporation, **I** 253, 291, **III** 137; **18** 500

F & M Scientific Corp., **III** 142; **6** 237

F & R Builders, Inc., **11** 257

F.A. Computer Technologies, Inc., **12** 60

F.A. Ensign Company, **6** 38

F.A.I. Insurances, **III** 729

F.A.O. Schwarz, **I** 548

F. Atkins & Co., **I** 604

F.B. McFarren, Ltd., **21** 499–500

F.C. Internazionale Milano SpA, **44** 387

F.E. Compton Company, **7** 167

F. Egger Co., **22** 49

F.F. Dalley Co., **II** 497

F.F. Publishing and Broadsystem Ltd., **IV** 652; **7** 392

F.H. Tomkins Buckle Company Ltd., **11** 525

F. Hoffmann-La Roche & Co. A.G., I 637, 640, **642–44**, 657, 685, 693, 710; **7** 427; **9** 264; **10** 80, 549; **11** 424–25; **14** 406; **32** 211–12

F.J. Walker Ltd., **I** 438

F.K.I. Babcock, **III** 466

F. Kanematsu & Co., Ltd. *See* Kanematsu Corporation.

F.L. Industries Inc., **I** 481, 483

F.L. Moseley Co., **III** 142; **6** 237

F.N. Burt Co., **IV** 644

F. Perkins, **III** 651–52

F.S. Smithers, **II** 445; **22** 405

F.W. Dodge Corp., **IV** 636–37

F.W. Means & Company, **11** 337

F.W. Sickles Company, **10** 319

F.W. Williams Holdings, **III** 728

F.W. Woolworth & Co. Ltd. *See* Kingfisher plc.

F.W. Woolworth Co. *See* Woolworth Corporation.

F.X. Matt Brewing Co., **18** 72

Fab-Asia, Inc., **22** 354–55

Fab Industries, Inc., 27 142–44

Fab 9, **26** 431

Fabbrica D' Armi Pietro Beretta S.p.A., 39 149–51

Fabco Automotive Corp., **23** 306; **27** 203

Fabergé, Inc., **II** 590; **III** 48; **8** 168, 344; **11** 90; **32** 475; **47** 114

Fabri-Centers of America Inc., 15 329; **16 197–99; 18** 223; **43** 291

Fabrica de Cemento El Melan, **III** 671

Fabtek Inc., **48** 59

Facchin Foods Co., **I** 457

Facit, **III** 480; **22** 26

Facom S.A., 32 183–85; 37 143, 145

Facts on File, Inc., **14** 96–97; **22** 443

FAE Fluid Air Energy SA, **49** 162–63

Fafnir Bearing Company, **13** 523

FAG Kugelfischer Georg Schafer AG, **11** 84; **47** 280

Fagersta, **II** 366; **IV** 203

Fahr AG, **III** 543

Fahrzeugwerke Eisenach, **I** 138

FAI, **III** 545–46

Failsafe, **14** 35

Fair Grounds Corporation, 44 177–80

Fair, Isaac and Company, 18 168–71, 516, 518

Fairbanks Morse Co., **I** 158, 434–35; **10** 292; **12** 71

Fairchild Aircraft, Inc., 9 205–08, 460; **11** 278

Fairchild Camera and Instrument Corp., **II** 50, 63; **III** 110, 141, 455, 618; **6** 261–62; **7** 531; **10** 108; **11** 503; **13** 323–24; **14** 14; **17** 418; **21** 122, 330; **26** 327

Fairchild Communications Service, **8** 328

The Fairchild Corporation, **37** 30

Fairchild Dornier GmbH, 48 167–71 (upd.)

Fairchild Industries, **I** 71, 198; **11** 438; **14** 43; **15** 195; **34** 117

Fairchild Semiconductor Corporation, **II** 44–45, 63–65; **III** 115; **6** 215, 247; **10** 365–66; **16** 332; **24** 235; **41** 201

Fairclough Construction Group plc, I 567–68

Fairey Industries Ltd., **IV** 659

Fairfax, **IV** 650

Fairfield Communities, Inc., 36 192–95

The Fairfield Group, **33** 259–60

Fairfield Manufacturing Co., **14** 43

Fairfield Publishing, **13** 165

Fairmont Foods Co., **7** 430; **15** 139

Fairmont Hotels and Resorts Inc., **45** 80

Fairmont Insurance Co., **26** 487

Fairmount Glass Company, **8** 267

Fairport Machine Shop, Inc., **17** 357

Fairway Marketing Group, Inc., **24** 394

Fairway Outdoor Advertising, Inc., **36** 340, 342

Faiveley S.A., 39 152–54

Falcon Drilling Co. *See* Transocean Sedco Forex Inc.

Falcon Oil Co., **IV** 396

Falcon Products, Inc., 33 149–51

Falcon Seaboard Inc., **II** 86; **IV** 410; **7** 309

Falconbridge Limited, IV 111, 165–66; **49 136–39**

Falconet Corp., **I** 45

Falley's, Inc., **17** 558, 560–61

Fallon McElligott Inc., 22 199–201

Falls Financial Inc., **13** 223; **31** 206

Falls National Bank of Niagara Falls, **11** 108

Falls Rubber Company, **8** 126

FAME Plastics, Inc., **18** 162

Family Bookstores, **24** 548

Family Channel. *See* International Family Entertainment Inc.

Family Dollar Stores, Inc., 13 215–17

Family Golf Centers, Inc., 29 183–85

Family Health Program, **6** 184

Family Life Insurance Co., **II** 425; **13** 341

Family Mart Group, **V** 188; **36** 418, 420

Family Restaurants, Inc., **14** 194

Family Steak Houses of Florida, Inc., **15** 420

Famosa Bakery, **II** 543

Famous Amos Chocolate Chip Cookie Corporation, **27** 332

Famous Atlantic Fish Company, **20** 5

Famous-Barr, **46** 288

Famous Dave's of America, Inc., 40 182–84 4

Famous Players-Lasky Corp., **I** 451; **II** 154; **6** 161–62; **23** 123

Famous Restaurants Inc., **33** 139–40

FAN, **13** 370

Fancom Holding B.V., **43** 130

Fannie Mae, 45 156–59 (upd.)

Fannie May Candy Shops Inc., **36** 309

Fansteel Inc., 19 150–52

Fantastic Sam's, **26** 476

Fanthing Electrical Corp., **44** 132

Fantle's Drug Stores, **16** 160

Fantus Co., **IV** 605

Fanuc Ltd., III 482–83; **17 172–74 (upd.)**

Fanzz, **29** 282

FAO Schwarz, 46 187–90

Faprena, **25** 85

Far East Airlines, **6** 70

Far East Machinery Co., **III** 581

Far Eastern Air Transport, Inc., **23** 380

Far West Restaurants, **I** 547

Faraday National Corporation, **10** 269

Farah Incorporated, 24 156–58

Farben. *See* I.G. Farbenindustrie AG.

Farbenfabriken Bayer A.G., **I** 309

Farberware, Inc., **27** 287–88

Farbro Corp., **45** 15

Farbwerke Hoechst A.G., **I** 346–47; **IV** 486; **13** 262

Farine Lactée Henri Nestlé, **II** 545

Farinon Corp., **II** 38

Farley Candy Co., **15** 190

Farley Industries, **25** 166

Farley Northwest Industries Inc., I 440–41

Farm Credit Bank of St. Louis, **8** 489

Farm Credit Bank of St. Paul, **8** 489–90

Farm Electric Services Ltd., **6** 586

Farm Family Holdings, Inc., 39 155–58

Farm Fresh Foods, **25** 332

Farm Journal Corporation, 42 131–34

Farm Power Laboratory, **6** 565

Farmer Jack, **16** 247; **44** 145

Farmers and Mechanics Bank of Georgetown, **13** 439

Farmers and Merchants Bank, **II** 349

Farmers Bank of Delaware, **II** 315–16

Farmers Insurance Group of Companies, **23** 286; **25 154–56**; **29** 397

Farmers' Loan and Trust Co., **II** 254; **9** 124

Farmers National Bank & Trust Co., **9** 474

Farmers Petroleum, Inc., **48** 175

Farmers Regional Cooperative, **II** 536

Farmland Foods, Inc., IV 474; **7** 17, **7 174–75**

Farmland Industries, Inc., 39 282; **48 172–75**

Farnam Cheshire Lime Co., **III** 763

Farrar, Straus and Giroux Inc., 15 158–60; **35** 451

FASC. *See* First Analysis Securities Corporation.

Fasco Consumer Products, **19** 360

Fasco Industries, **III** 509; **13** 369

Faserwerke Hüls GmbH., **I** 350

Fashion Bar, Inc., **24** 457

Fashion Bug, **8** 97

Fashion Co., **II** 503; **10** 324

Fasquelle, **IV** 618

Fasson. *See* Avery Dennison Corporation.

Fast Air, **31** 305

Fast Fare, **7** 102

Fastenal Company, **14 185–87**; **42 135–38 (upd.)**

Fata European Group, **IV** 187; **19** 348

Fateco Förlag, **14** 556

FATS, Inc., **27** 156, 158

Fatum, **III** 308

Faugere et Jutheau, **III** 283

Faulkner, Dawkins & Sullivan, **II** 450

Fauquet, **25** 85

Favorite Plastics, **19** 414

FAvS. *See* First Aviation Services Inc.

Fawcett Books, **13** 429

Fay's Inc., 17 175–77

Fayette Tubular Products, **7** 116–17

Fayva, **13** 359–61

Fazoli's Systems, Inc., 13 321; **27 145–47**

FB&T Corporation, **14** 154

FBC. *See* First Boston Corp.

FBO. *See* Film Booking Office of America.

FC Holdings, Inc., **26** 363

FCBC, **IV** 174

FCC. *See* Federal Communications Commission.

FCC National Bank, **II** 286

FCI. *See* Framatome SA.

FDIC. *See* Federal Deposit Insurance Corp.

Fearn International, **II** 525; **13** 293

Feather Fine, **27** 361

Featherlite Inc., 28 127–29

Feature Enterprises Inc., **19** 452

Fechheimer Bros. Co., **III** 215; **18** 60, 62

Fedders Corporation, **18 172–75**; **43 162–67 (upd.)**

Federal Barge Lines, **6** 487

Federal Bearing and Bushing, **I** 158–59

Federal Bicycle Corporation of America, **11** 3

Federal Cartridge, **26** 363

Federal Coca-Cola Bottling Co., **10** 222

Federal Communications Commission, **6** 164–65; **9** 321

Federal Deposit Insurance Corp., **II** 261–62, 285, 337; **12** 30, 79

Federal Electric, **I** 463; **III** 653

Federal Express Corporation, **II** 620; **V 451–53**; **6** 345–46, 385–86, 389; **12** 180, 192; **13** 19; **14** 517; **17** 504–05; **18** 315–17, 368, 370; **24** 22, 133; **25** 148; **26** 441; **27** 20, 22, 471, 475; **34** 15, 17; **39** 33, 35; **41** 245–47. *See also* FedEx Corporation.

Federal Home Life Insurance Co., **III** 263; **IV** 623

Federal Home Loan Bank, **II** 182

Federal Home Loan Mortgage Corp., **18** 168; **25** 427

Federal Insurance Co., **III** 220–21; **14** 108–109; **37** 83–85

Federal Lead Co., **IV** 32

Federal Light and Traction Company, **6** 561–62

Federal Mining and Smelting Co., **IV** 32

Federal-Mogul Corporation, **I** 158–60; **III** 596; **10 292–94 (upd.)**; **26 139–43 (upd.)**; **47** 279

Federal National Mortgage Association, **II 410–11**; **18** 168; **25** 427. *See also* Fannie Mae.

Federal Pacific Electric, **II** 121; **9** 440

Federal Packaging and Partition Co., **8** 476

Federal Packaging Corp., **19** 78

Federal Paper Board Company, Inc., I 524; **8 173–75**; **15** 229; **47** 189

Federal Paper Mills, **IV** 248

Federal Power, **18** 473

Federal Prison Industries, Inc., 34 157–60

Federal Reserve Bank of New York, **21** 68

Federal Savings and Loan Insurance Corp., **16** 346

Federal Signal Corp., 10 295–97

Federal Steel Co., **II** 330; **IV** 572; **7** 549
Federal Trade Commission, **6** 260; **9** 370
Federal Yeast Corp., **IV** 410
Federale Mynbou, **IV** 90–93
Federated Department Stores Inc., IV 703; **V** 25–28; **9** 209–12; **10** 282; **11** 349; **12** 37, 523; **13** 43, 260; **15** 88; **16** 61, 206; **17** 560; **18** 523; **22** 406; **23** 60; **27** 346–48; **30** 379; **31** 190–194 **(upd.)**; **35** 368; **36** 201, 204; **37** 13
Federated Development Company, **8** 349
Federated Metals Corp., **IV** 32
Federated Publications, **IV** 612; **7** 191
Federated Timbers, **I** 422
Fédération Internationale de Football Association, 27 148–51
Federation Nationale d'Achats des Cadres. *See* FNAC.
FedEx Corporation, 18 128, **176–79 (upd.)**, 535; **33** 20, 22; **34** 474; **42** 139–44 **(upd.)**; **46** 71
Fedmart, **V** 162
FEE Technology, **29** 461–62
Feed-Rite Controls, Inc., **16** 270
Feffer & Simons, **16** 46
Feikes & Sohn KG, **IV** 325
Feinblech-Contiglühe, **IV** 103
Felco. *See* Farmers Regional Cooperative.
Feld Entertainment, Inc., 32 186–89 **(upd.)**
Feldmühle Nobel AG, II 50–51; **III** 692–95; **IV** 142, 325, 337; **21** 330; **36** 449
Felixstowe Ltd., **18** 254
Fellowes Manufacturing Company, 28 130–32
Felten & Guilleaume, **IV** 25
Femsa, **19** 473. *See also* Formento Económico Mexicano, S.A. de C.V.
Femtech, **8** 513
Fendall Company, **40** 96, 98
Fendel Schiffahrts-Aktiengesellschaft, **6** 426
Fender Musical Instruments Company, 16 200–02; **43** 168–72 **(upd.)**
Fendi S.p.A., **45** 344
Fenestra Inc., **IV** 136
Fenicia Group, **22** 320
Fenn, Wright & Manson, **25** 121–22
Fenner & Beane, **II** 424
Fenton Hill American Limited, **29** 510
Fenwal Laboratories, **I** 627; **10** 141
Fenway Partners, **47** 361
Fenwick & West LLP, 34 161–63, 512
Ferembal S.A., **25** 512
Ferfin, **24** 341
Fergus Brush Electric Company, **18** 402
Ferguson Machine Co., **8** 135
Ferguson Manufacturing Company, **25** 164
Ferguson Radio Corp., **I** 531–32
Ferienreise GmbH., **II** 164
Fermec Manufacturing Limited, **40** 432
Fermentaciones Mexicanas S.A. de C.V., **III** 43; **48** 250
Fernando Roqué, **6** 404; **26** 243
Ferngas, **IV** 486
Ferolito, Vultaggio & Sons, 27 152–55
Ferranti Business Communications, **20** 75
Ferranti Ltd., **II** 81; **6** 240
Ferrari S.p.A., I 162; **11** 103; **13** 218–20; **36** 196–200 **(upd.)**
Ferrellgas Partners, L.P., 35 173–75
Ferrier Hodgson, **10** 170

Ferro Corporation, III 536; **8 176–79**; **9** 10; **26** 230
Ferro Engineering Co., **17** 357
Ferrocarril del Noreste, S.A. de C.V. *See* Grupo Transportación Ferroviaria Mexicana, S.A. de C.V.
Ferrovial. *See* Grupo Ferrovail
Ferroxcube Corp. of America, **13** 397
Ferrum Inc., **24** 144
Ferruzzi Agricola Finanziario, **I** 369; **7** 81–83
Ferruzzi Finanziaria S.p.A., **24** 341; **36** 186
Fesca, **III** 417–18
Fetzer Vineyards, **10** 182
FFI Fragrances. *See* Elizabeth Arden, Inc.
FHP International Corporation, 6 184–86; **17** 166, 168; **44** 174
Fianzas Monterrey, **19** 189
Fiat S.p.A., I 154, 157, **161–63**, 459–60, 466, 479; **II** 280; **III** 206, 543, 591; **IV** 420; **9** 10; **11** 102–04 **(upd.)**, 139; **13** 17, 27–29, 218–20; **16** 322; **17** 24; **22** 379–81; **36** 32–34, 196–97, 199, 240, 243
Fibamex, **17** 106
Fibar, **44** 261
Fiber Chemical Corporation, **7** 308
Fiberglas Canada, **III** 722
Fiberite, Inc., **27** 117; **28** 195
FiberMark, Inc., 37 139–42
Fibermux Corporation, **10** 19; **30** 7
Fibic Corp., **18** 118
Fibre Containers, **IV** 249
Fibreboard Corporation, IV 304; **12** 318; **14** 110; **16 203–05**
FibreChem, Inc., **8** 347
Fibro Tambor, S.A. de C.V., **8** 476
Fichtel & Sachs AG, **III** 566; **14** 328; **38** 299
Fidata Corp., **II** 317
Fidelco Capital Group, **10** 420
Fidelio Software GmbH, **18** 335, 337
Fidelity and Casualty Co. of New York, **III** 242
Fidelity and Guaranty Life Insurance Co., **III** 396–97
Fidelity Exploration & Production Company, **42** 249, 253
Fidelity Federal Savings and Loan, **II** 420
Fidelity Fire Insurance Co., **III** 240
Fidelity Insurance of Canada, **III** 396–97
Fidelity Investments Inc., II 412–13; **III** 588; **8** 194; **9** 239; **14 188–90 (upd.)**; **18** 552; **19** 113; **21** 147; **22** 52. *See also* FMR Corp.
Fidelity Leasing Corporation, **42** 312–13
Fidelity Life Association, **III** 269
Fidelity Mutual Insurance Co., **III** 231
Fidelity National Life Insurance Co., **III** 191
Fidelity National Title, **19** 92
Fidelity Oil Group, **7** 324
Fidelity-Phenix Fire Insurance Co., **III** 240–42
Fidelity Title and Trust Co., **II** 315
Fidelity Trust Co., **II** 230; **33** 293
Fidelity Union Life Insurance Co., **III** 185
Fidenas Investment Ltd., **30** 185
Fides Holding, **21** 146
Field Corporation, **18** 355
Field Enterprises Educational Corporation, **16** 252; **26** 15; **43** 208
Field Enterprises, Inc., **IV** 672; **12** 554; **19** 404

Field Group plc, **30** 120
Field Limited Partnership, **22** 441
Field Oy, **10** 113
Fieldale Farms Corporation, 23 191–93; **25** 185–86
Fieldco Guide Dog Foundation, **42** 207
Fieldcrest Cannon, Inc., 8 32–33; **9** 213–17; **16** 535; **19** 276, 305; **31** 195–200 **(upd.)**; **41** 299–301
Fieldstone Cabinetry, **III** 571; **20** 362
Fielmann AG, 31 201–03
Fiesta Restaurants Inc., **33** 139–40
FIFA. *See* Fédération Internationale de Football Association.
Fifa International, **39** 58
Fifteen Oil, **I** 526
Fifth Generation Systems Inc., **10** 509
Fifth Third Bancorp, II 291; **9** 475; **11** 466; **13** 221–23; **31** 204–208 **(upd.)**
50-Off Stores, **23** 177. *See also* LOT$OFF Corporation.
Figgie International Inc., 7 176–78; **24** 403–04
Figi's Inc., **9** 218, 220
FII Limited, **38** 197
Fil-Mag Group, **29** 461
Fila Holding S.p.A., 20 216–18; **39** 60
Filene's, **V** 132, 134
Filene's Basement. *See* Value City Department Stores, Inc.
Filergie S.A., **15** 355
Filipacchi Medias S.A. *See* Hachette Filipacchi Medias S.A.
Filiz Lastex, S.A., **15** 386
Filles S.A. de C.V., **7** 115; **25** 126
Film Booking Office of America, **II** 88
Films for the Humanities, Inc., **22** 441
Filofax Inc., **41** 120, 123
Filter Queen-Canada, **17** 234
Filterfresh Corporation, **39** 409
Filtertek, Inc., **24** 425
Filtrol Corp., **IV** 123
Filtrona International Ltd., **31** 77
Filtros Baldwin de Mexico, **17** 106
Filtros Continental, **17** 106
Fimalac S.A., 37 143–45
Fimaser, **21** 101
Fimestic, **21** 101
Fin. Comit SpA, **II** 192
FINA, Inc., 7 179–81; **26** 368
Finalrealm Limited, **42** 404
Finance Oil Corp., **49** 304
Financial Computer Services, Inc., **11** 111
Financial Corp. of Indonesia, **II** 257
Financial Data Services, Inc., **11** 111
Financial Investment Corp. of Asia, **III** 197
Financial Network Marketing Company, **11** 482
Financial News Ltd., **IV** 658
Financial News Network, Inc., **25** 507; **31** 147
Financial Security Assurance Inc., **III** 765; **25** 497
Financial Services Corp., **III** 306–07
Financial Services Corporation of Michigan, **11** 163
Financial Systems, Inc., **11** 111
Financial Technologies International, **17** 497
The Financial Times Group, **46** 337
Financiera Aceptaciones, **19** 189
Financière Crédit Suisse-First Boston, **II** 268, 402–04

Financiere de Suez, **II** 295
Financière Saint Dominique, **9** 151–52
FinansSkandic A.B., **II** 352–53
Finast. *See* First National Supermarkets, Inc.
Fincantieri, **I** 466–67
Find-A-Home Service, Inc., **21** 96
Findomestic, **21** 101
Findus, **II** 547; **25** 85
Fine Art Developments Ltd., **15** 340
Fine Fare, **II** 465, 609, 628–29
Fine Fragrances, **22** 213
Finelettrica, **I** 465–66
Finesco, LLC, **37** 200–01
Finevest Services Inc., **15** 526
Fingerhut Companies, Inc., **I** 613; **V** 148; **9** 218–20; **15** 401; **18** 133; **31** 190; **34** 232; **36** 201–05 (upd.); **37** 130
Fininvest Group, **IV** 587–88
The Finish Line, Inc., 29 186–88
FinishMaster, Inc., 17 310–11; **24** 159–61
Finland Wood Co., **IV** 275
Finlay Enterprises, Inc., 16 206–08
Finlay Forest Industries, **IV** 297
Finmare, **I** 465, 467
Finmeccanica S.p.A., **II** 86; **13** 28; **23** 83; **36** 34
Finnair Oy, **I** 120; **6** 87–89; **25** 157–60 (upd.); **33** 50; **34** 398
Finnforest Oy, **IV** 316
Finnigan Corporation, **11** 513
Finnish Cable Works, **II** 69; **17** 352
Finnish Fiberboard Ltd., **IV** 302
Oy Finnish Peroxides Ab, **IV** 300
Finnish Rubber Works, **II** 69; **17** 352
Oy Finnlines Ltd., **IV** 276
Finsa, **II** 196
FinSer Capital Corporation, **17** 262
Finservizi SpA, **II** 192
Finsider, **I** 465–66; **IV** 125
Firan Motor Coach, Inc., **17** 83
Fire Association of Philadelphia, **III** 342–43
Firearms Training Systems, Inc., 27 156–58
Fireman's Fund Insurance Company, **I** 418; **II** 398, 457; **III** 214, 250–52, 263; **10** 62
Firemen's Insurance Co. of Newark, **III** 241–42
Firestone Tire and Rubber Co., **III** 440, 697; **V** 234–35; **8** 80; **9** 247; **15** 355; **17** 182; **18** 320; **20** 259–62; **21** 73–74
Firma Hamburger Kaffee-Import- Geschäft Emil Tengelmann. *See* Tengelmann Group.
Firma Huter Vorfertigung GmbH, **49** 163
The First, **10** 340
First Acadiana National Bank, **11** 107
First Albany Companies Inc., 37 146–48
First Alert, Inc., 28 133–35
First American. *See* Bremer Financial Corp.
First American Bank Corporation, **8** 188; **41** 178
First American Media, Inc., **24** 199
First American National Bank, **19** 378
First American National Bank-Eastern, **11** 111
First Analysis Securities Corporation, **22** 5
First and Merchants, **10** 426
First Atlanta Corporation, **16** 523
First Atlantic Capital, Ltd., **28** 340, 342

First Aviation Services Inc., 49 140–42
First Bancard, Inc., **11** 106
First BanCorporation, **13** 467
First Bank and Trust of Mechanicsburg, **II** 342
First Bank of Savannah, **16** 522
First Bank of the United States, **II** 213, 253
First Bank System Inc., 11 130; **12** 164–66; **13** 347–48; **24** 393. *See also* U.S. Bancorp
First Boston Corp., **II** 208, 257, 267–69, 402–04, 406–07, 426, 434, 441; **9** 378, 386; **12** 439; **13** 152, 342; **21** 145–46. *See also* CSFB.
First Brands Corporation, 8 180–82; **16** 44
First Capital Financial, **8** 229
First Carolina Investors Inc., **17** 357
First Chicago Corporation, II 284–87. *See also* Bank One Corporation.
First Chicago Venture Capital, **24** 516
First Choice Holidays PLC, 40 185–87, 284–85
First Cincinnati, Inc., **41** 133
First City Bank of Rosemead, **II** 348
First Colony Farms, **II** 584
First Colony Life Insurance, **I** 334–35; **10** 290
First Commerce Bancshares, Inc., 15 161–63
First Commerce Corporation, 11 105–07
First Commercial Savings and Loan, **10** 340
First Consumers National Bank, **10** 491; **27** 429
First Dallas, Ltd., **II** 415
First Data Corporation, 10 63; **18** 516–18, 537; **24** 393 **30** 195–98 (upd.); **46** 250
First Data Management Company of Oklahoma City, **11** 112
First Delaware Life Insurance Co., **III** 254
First Deposit Corp., **III** 218–19
First Empire State Corporation, 11 108–10
First Engine and Boiler Insurance Co. Ltd., **III** 406
First Executive Corporation, III 253–55
First Express, **48** 177
First Federal Savings & Loan Assoc., **IV** 343; **9** 173
First Federal Savings and Loan Association of Crisp County, **10** 92
First Federal Savings and Loan Association of Hamburg, **10** 91
First Federal Savings and Loan Association of Fort Myers, **9** 476
First Federal Savings and Loan Association of Kalamazoo, **9** 482
First Federal Savings Bank of Brunswick, **10** 92
First Fidelity Bank, N.A., New Jersey, 9 221–23
First Fidelity Bank of Rockville, **13** 440
First Financial Insurance, **41** 178
First Financial Management Corporation, 11 111–13; **18** 542; **25** 183; **30** 195
First Florida Banks, **9** 59
First Hawaiian, Inc., 11 114–16
First Health, **III** 373
FIRST HEALTH Strategies, **11** 113
First Healthcare, **14** 242

First Heights, fsa, **8** 437
First Hospital Corp., **15** 122
First Industrial Corp., **II** 41
First Insurance Agency, Inc., **17** 527
First Insurance Co. of Hawaii, **III** 191, 242
First International Trust, **IV** 91
First Interstate Bancorp, II 228, **288–90**; **8** 295; **9** 334; **17** 546
First Investment Advisors, **11** 106
First Investors Management Corp., **11** 106
First Jersey National Bank, **II** 334
First Leisure Corporation plc. *See* Esporta plc.
First Liberty Financial Corporation, **11** 457
First Line Insurance Services, Inc., **8** 436
First Madison Bank, **14** 192
First Maryland Bancorp, **16** 14
First Mid America, **II** 445; **22** 406
First Mississippi Corporation, 8 183–86. *See also* ChemFirst, Inc.
First Mississippi National, **14** 41
First National Bank, **10** 298; **13** 467
First National Bank (Revere), **II** 208
First National Bank and Trust Company, **22** 4
First National Bank and Trust Company of Kalamazoo, **8** 187–88
First National Bank and Trust of Oklahoma City, **II** 289
First National Bank in Albuquerque, **11** 119
First National Bank of Akron, **9** 475
First National Bank of Allentown, **11** 296
First National Bank of Atlanta, **16** 522
First National Bank of Azusa, **II** 382
First National Bank of Boston, **II** 207–08, 402; **12** 310; **13** 446
First National Bank of Carrollton, **9** 475
First National Bank of Chicago, **II** 242, 257, 284–87; **III** 96–97; **IV** 135–36
First National Bank of Commerce, **11** 106
First National Bank of Harrington, Delaware. *See* J.C. Penny National Bank.
First National Bank of Hartford, **13** 466
First National Bank of Hawaii, **11** 114
First National Bank of Highland, **11** 109
First National Bank of Houma, **21** 522
The First National Bank of Lafayette, **11** 107
The First National Bank of Lake Charles, **11** 107
First National Bank of Lake City, **II** 336; **10** 425
First National Bank of Mexico, New York, **II** 231
First National Bank of Minneapolis, **22** 426–27
First National Bank of New York, **II** 254, 330
First National Bank of Raleigh, **II** 336
First National Bank of Salt Lake, **11** 118
First National Bank of Seattle, **8** 469–70
First National Bank of York, **II** 317
First National Bankshares, Inc., **21** 524
First National Boston Corp., **II** 208
First National Casualty Co., **III** 203
First National City Bank, **9** 124; **16** 13
First National City Bank of New York, **II** 254; **9** 124
First National City Corp., **III** 220–21
First National Holding Corporation, **16** 522
First National Insurance Co., **III** 352
First National Life Insurance Co., **III** 218

First National Supermarkets, Inc., **II** 641–42; **9** 452

First Nations Gaming, Ltd., **44** 334

First Nationwide Bank, 8 30; **14 191–93**

First Nationwide Financial Corp., **I** 167; **11** 139

First Nationwide Holdings Inc., **28** 246

First New England Bankshares Corp., **13** 467

First Nitrogen, Inc., **8** 184

First Nuclear Corporation, **49** 411

First of America Bank Corporation, 8 187–89

First of America Bank-Monroe, **9** 476

First of Boston, **II** 402–03

First Omni Bank NA, **16** 14; **18** 518; **43** 8

First Pacific Company Limited, 18 180–82

First Penn-Pacific Life Insurance Co., **III** 276

First Physician Care, Inc., **36** 367

First Pick Stores, **12** 458

First Railroad and Banking Company, **11** 111

First Republic Bank of Texas, **II** 336

First Republic Corp., **III** 383; **14** 483

First RepublicBank Corporation, **II** 337; **10** 425–26

First Savings and Loan, **10** 339

First Seattle Dexter Horton National Bank, **8** 470

First Security Bank of Missoula, **35** 197–99

First Security Corporation, 11 117–19; 38 491

First Signature Bank and Trust Co., **III** 268

First Sport Ltd., **39** 60

1st State Bank & Trust, **9** 474

First State Bank Southwest Indiana, **41** 178–79

First SunAmerican Life Insurance Company, **11** 482

First Team Sports, Inc., 15 396–97; **22 202–04**

First Tennessee National Corporation, 11 120–21; 48 176–79 (upd.)

First Texas Pharmaceuticals, **I** 678

First Trust and Savings Bank, **II** 284

First Trust Bank, **16** 14

First Union Corporation, 10 298–300; 24 482; **37** 148. See also Wachovia Corporation.

First Union Trust and Savings Bank, **II** 284–85; **11** 126; **22** 52

First United Financial Services Inc., **II** 286

First USA, Inc., 11 122–24

First USA Paymentech, **24** 393

First Virginia Banks, Inc., 11 125–26

First Westchester National Bank of New Rochelle, **II** 236

First Western Bank and Trust Co., **II** 289

First Women's Bank of New York, **23** 3

First Worth Corporation, **19** 232

The First Years Inc., 46 191–94

FirstAir Inc., **48** 113

Firstamerica Bancorporation, **II** 288–89

Firstar Corporation, 11 127–29; 33 152–55 (upd.)

FirstBancorp., **13** 467

FirstGroup plc, **38** 321

FirstMiss, Inc., **8** 185

FirstPage USA Inc., **41** 265

Firth Carpet, **19** 275

Fischbach & Moore, **III** 535

Fischbach Corp., **III** 198; **8** 536–37

FISCOT, **10** 337

Fiserv Inc., 11 130–32; 33 156–60 (upd.)

Fisher & Company, **9** 16

Fisher Body Company, **I** 171; **10** 325

Fisher Broadcasting Co., **15** 164

Fisher-Camuto Corp., **14** 441

Fisher Companies, Inc., 15 164–66

Fisher Controls International, Inc., 13 224–26; 15 405, 407; **29** 330; **46** 171

Fisher Foods, Inc., **II** 602; **9** 451, 452; **13** 237; **41** 11, 13

Fisher Marine, **III** 444; **22** 116

Fisher Nut, **14** 275

Fisher-Price Inc., II 559–60; **12 167–69,** 410–11; **13** 317; **25** 314, 380; **32 190–94 (upd.); 34** 365

Fisher Scientific International Inc., III 511–12; **24 162–66; 25** 260

Fishers Agricultural Holdings, **II** 466

Fishers Nutrition, **II** 466

Fishers Seed and Grain, **II** 466

Fishery Department of Tamura Kisen Co., **II** 552

Fisk Telephone Systems, **6** 313

Fiskars Corporation, 33 161–64

Fiskeby Board AB, **48** 344

Fisons plc, 9 224–27; 23 194–97 (upd.)

Fitch IBCA Inc., **37** 143, 145

Fitch Lovell PLC, **13** 103

Fitchburg Daily News Co., **IV** 581

Fitchburg Gas and Electric Light, **37** 406

Fitchell and Sachs, **III** 495

Fitel, **III** 491

Fitzsimmons Stores Inc., **16** 452

Fitzwilton Public Limited Company, **12** 529; **34** 496

Five Bros. Inc., **19** 456

Five Star Entertainment Inc., **28** 241

546274 Alberta Ltd., **48** 97

FKM Advertising, **27** 280

FL Industries Holdings, Inc., **11** 516

Flachglass A.G., **II** 474

Flagship Resources, **22** 495

Flagstar Companies, Inc., 10 301–03; 29 150. See also Advantica Restaurant Group, Inc.

Flair Corporation, **18** 467

Flair Fold, **25** 11

Flanagan McAdam Resources Inc., **IV** 76

Flapdoodles, **15** 291

Flashes Publishers, Inc., **36** 341

Flatbush Gas Co., **6** 455–56

Flatiron Mandolin Company, **16** 239

Flatow, Moore, Bryan, and Fairburn, **21** 33

Flavors Holdings Inc., **38** 294

Fleck Controls, Inc., **26** 361, 363

Fleer Corporation, 10 402; **13** 519; **15 167–69; 19** 386; **34** 447; **37** 295

Fleet Aerospace Corporation. See Magellan Aerospace Corporation.

Fleet Call, Inc., **10** 431–32

Fleet Financial Group, Inc., IV 687; **9 228–30; 12** 31; **13** 468; **18** 535; **38** 13, 393

Fleet Holdings, **28** 503

FleetBoston Financial Corporation, 36 206–14 (upd.)

Fleetway, **7** 244

Fleetwood Enterprises, Inc., III 484–85; 13 155; **17** 83; **21** 153; **22 205–08 (upd.); 33** 399

Fleischmann Co., **II** 544; **7** 367

Fleischmann Malting Co., **I** 420–21; **11** 22

Fleming Chinese Restaurants Inc., **37** 297

Fleming Companies, Inc., II 624–25, 671; **7** 450; **12** 107, 125; **13** 335–37; **17 178–81 (upd.); 18** 506–07; **23** 407; **24** 529; **26** 449; **28** 152, 154; **31** 25; **34** 198

Fleming Foodservice, **26** 504

Fleming Machine Co., **III** 435

Fleming-Wilson Co., **II** 624

Fletcher Challenge Ltd., III 687; **IV** 250, **278–80; 19 153–57 (upd.); 25** 12

Fleury Michon S.A., 39 159–61

Fleuve Noir, **IV** 614

Flex Elektrowerkzeuge GmbH, **26** 363

Flex Interim, **16** 421; **43** 308

Flex-O-Lite, **14** 325

Flexsteel Industries Inc., 15 170–72; 41 159–62 (upd.)

Flextronics International Ltd., 12 451; **38 186–89**

Flexsys, **16** 462

FLGI Holding Company, **10** 321

Flick Industrial Group, **II** 280, 283; **III** 692–95

Flight One Logistics, Inc., **22** 311

Flight Refuelling Limited. See Cobham plc.

Flight Transportation Co., **II** 408

FlightSafety International, Inc., 9 231–33; 29 189–92 (upd.)

Flint and Walling Water Systems, **III** 570; **20** 362

Flint Eaton & Co., **I** 627

Flint Ink Corporation, 13 227–29; 41 163–66 (upd.)

Flip Chip Technologies, LLC, **33** 248

Florafax International, Inc., **37** 162

Floral City Furniture Company, **14** 302–03

Flori Roberts, Inc., **11** 208

Florida Crystals Inc., 35 176–78

Florida Cypress Gardens, Inc., **IV** 623

Florida Distillers Company, **27** 479

Florida East Coast Railway Company, **8** 486–87; **12** 278

Florida Flavors, **44** 137

Florida Frozen Foods, **13** 244

Florida Gaming Corporation, 47 130–33

Florida Gas Co., **15** 129

Florida Gas Transmission Company, **6** 578

Florida National Banks of Florida, Inc., **II** 252

Florida Panthers Hockey Club, Ltd., **37** 33, 35

Florida Power & Light Company. See FPL Group, Inc.

Florida Presbyterian College, **9** 187

Florida Progress Corp., V 621–22; 23 198–200 (upd.)

Florida Rock Industries, Inc., 23 326; **46 195–97**

Florida Steel Corp., **14** 156

Florida Telephone Company, **6** 323

Florida's Natural Growers, 45 160–62

FloridaGulf Airlines, **11** 300

Florimex Verwaltungsgesellschaft mbH, **12** 109

Florists' Transworld Delivery, Inc., 28 136–38

Florsheim Shoe Group Inc., III 528–29; **9** 135, 234–36; **12** 308; **16** 546; **31 209–212 (upd.); 39** 170, 172, 174

Flour City International, Inc., 44 181–83

Flow Laboratories, **14** 98

Flow Measurement, **26** 293
Flower Gate Inc., **I** 266; **21** 320
Flower Time, Inc., **12** 179, 200
**Flowers Industries, Inc., 12 170–71; 35
179–82 (upd.).** *See also* Keebler Foods
Company.
Flowserve Corporation, 33 165–68
Floyd West & Co., **6** 290
Fluent, Inc., **29** 4–6
Fluf N'Stuf, Inc., **12** 425
Fluke Corporation, 15 173–75
Flunch, **37** 22
Fluor Corporation, I 569–71, 586; **III**
248; **IV** 171, 533, 535, 576; **6** 148–49;
8 190–93 (upd.); 12 244; **26** 220, 433;
34 164–69 (upd.); 47 340
Fluor Daniel Inc., **41** 148
The Fluorocarbon Company. *See* Furon
Company.
Flushing Federal Savings & Loan
Association, **16** 346
Flushing National Bank, **II** 230
Flying J Inc., 19 158–60
Flying Tiger Line, **V** 452; **6** 388; **25** 146;
39 33
Flymo, **III** 478, 480; **22** 26
FMC Corp., I 442–44, 679; **II** 513; **11
133–35 (upd.); 14** 457; **22** 415; **30** 471;
47 238
FMR Corp., II 412; **8 194–96; 14** 188; **22**
413; **30** 331; **32 195–200 (upd.)**
FMXI, Inc. *See* Foamex International Inc.
FN Life Insurance Co., **III** 192
FN Manufacturing Co., **12** 71
FNAC, 21 224–26; 26 160
FNC Comercio, **III** 221
FNCB. *See* First National City Bank of
New York.
FNK. *See* Finance Oil Corp.
FNMA. *See* Federal National Mortgage
Association.
FNN. *See* Financial News Network.
**Foamex International Inc., 17 182–85;
26** 500
Focal Surgery, Inc., **27** 355
Focke-Wulf, **III** 641; **16** 7
FOCUS, **44** 402
Fodens Ltd., **I** 186
Fodor's Travel Guides, **13** 429
Fogdog Inc., **36** 347
Fokker. *See* N.V. Koninklijke Nederlandse
Vliegtuigenfabriek Fokker.
Fokker Aircraft Corporation of America, **9**
16
Fokker-VFW, **I** 41–42; **12** 191
Foley & Lardner, 28 139–42
Folgers, **III** 52
Folksamerica Holding Company, Inc., **48**
431
Folland Aircraft, **I** 50; **III** 508; **24** 85
Follett Corporation, 12 172–74; 16 47;
39 162–65 (upd.); 43 61
Follis DeVito Verdi. *See* De Vito/Verdi.
Fomento de Valores, S.A. de C.V., **23** 170
Fomento Economico Mexicano, S.A. de
C.V. *See* Femsa.
Fonda Group, **36** 462
Fondiaria Group, **III** 351
Fonditalia Management, **III** 347
Font & Vaamonde, **6** 27
Font Vella, **II** 474
FONTAC, **II** 73
Fontana Asphalt, **III** 674
Food City, **II** 649–50

Food Fair, **19** 480
Food 4 Less Supermarkets, Inc., **II** 624; **17**
558–61
Food Giant, **II** 670
Food Ingredients Technologies, **25** 367
Food Investments Ltd., **II** 465
Food Lion, Inc., II 626–27; 7 450; **15
176–78 (upd.),** 270; **18** 8; **21** 508; **33**
306; **44** 145
Food Machinery Corp. *See* FMC Corp.
Food Marketing Corp., **II** 668; **18** 504
Food Town Inc., **II** 626–27
Food World, **26** 46; **31** 372
**Foodarama Supermarkets, Inc., 28
143–45**
FoodBrands America, Inc., 21 290; **22**
510; **23 201–04.** *See also* Doskocil
Companies, Inc.
FoodLand Distributors, **II** 625, 645, 682
Foodmaker, Inc., II 562; **13** 152, 426; **14
194–96**
Foodstuffs, **9** 144
Foodtown, **II** 626; **V** 35; **15** 177; **24** 528
FoodUSA.com, **43** 24
Foodways National, Inc., **12** 531; **13** 383
Foot Locker, **V** 226; **14** 293–95. *See also*
Venator Group Inc.
Footaction. *See* Footstar, Incorporated.
**Foote Cone & Belding Communications
Inc., I 12–15,** 28, 34; **11** 51; **13** 517; **22**
395; **25** 90–91. *See also* True North
Communications Inc.
Foote Mineral Company, **7** 386–87
Footquarters, **14** 293, 295
Footstar, Incorporated, 24 167–69
Forages et Exploitations Pétrolières. *See*
Forex.
Forbes Inc., 30 199–201
The Ford Foundation, 34 170–72
Ford Motor Company, I 10, 14, 20–21,
136, 142, 145, 152, 154–55, 162–63,
164–68, 172, 183, 186, 201, 203–04,
280, 297, 337, 354, 423, 478, 484, 540,
693; **II** 7–8, 33, 60, 86, 143, 415; **III**
58, 259, 283, 439, 452, 495, 515, 555,
568, 591, 603, 637–38, 651, 725; **IV** 22,
187, 597, 722; **6** 27, 51; **7** 377, 461,
520–21; **8** 70, 74–75, 117, 372–73, 375,
505–06; **9** 94, 118, 126, 190, 283–84,
325, 341–43; **10** 32, 241, 260, 264–65,
279–80, 290, 353, 407, 430, 460, 465;
11 53–54, 103–04, **136–40 (upd.),** 263,
326, 339, 350, 528–29; **12** 68, 91, 294,
311; **13** 28, 219, 285, 287, 345, 555; **14**
191–92; **15** 91, 171, 513, 515; **16**
321–22; **17** 183, 303–04; **18** 112, 308,
319; **19** 11, 125, 221, 223, 482, 484; **20**
359; **21** 153, 200, 503; **22** 175, 380–81;
23 143, 339–41, 434; **24** 12; **25** 90, 93,
142–43, 224, 226, 358; **26** 176, 452,
501; **27** 20, 202; **29** 265; **34** 133–34,
136, 303, 305; **36** 34, 180, 198, **215–21
(upd.),** 242–43; **38** 86, 458–59; **40** 134;
41 280–81
**Ford Motor Company, S.A. de C.V., 20
219–21**
Ford New Holland, Inc. *See* New Holland
N.V.
Ford Transport Co., **I** 112; **6** 103
Fording Inc., **45** 80
Fordyce Lumber Co., **IV** 281; **9** 259
FORE Systems, Inc., 25 161–63; 33 289
Forefront Communications, **22** 194

Foreman State Banks, **II** 285
Foremost Dairies, **47** 234–35
Foremost Dairy of California, **I** 496–97
Foremost-McKesson Inc., **I** 496–97, **III**
10; **11** 211; **12** 332
Foremost Warehouse Corp., **14** 372
Forenza, **V** 116
Forest City Auto Parts, **23** 491
Forest City Enterprises, Inc., 16 209–11
Forest City Ratner Companies, **17** 318
Forest E. Olson, Inc., **21** 96
Forest Laboratories, Inc., 11 141–43; 47
55
Forest Oil Corporation, 19 161–63
Forest Products, **III** 645
Forestry Corporation of New Zealand, **19**
156
Företagsfinans, **25** 464
Forethought Group, Inc., **10** 350
**Forever Living Products International
Inc., 17 186–88**
Forex Chemical Corp., **I** 341; **14** 216; **17**
418
Forex-Neptune, **III** 617
Forge Books. *See* Tom Doherty Associates
Inc.
Forges d'Eich–Le Gallais, Metz et Cie, **IV**
24; **22** 42
Forges de la Providence, **IV** 52
Forjas Metalicas, S.A. de C.V. (Formet),
44 193
Formento Económico Mexicano, S.A. de
C.V., **25** 279, 281
Formica Corporation, 10 269; **13 230–32**
Forming Technology Co., **III** 569; **20** 361
Formonix, **20** 101
Formosa Plastics Corporation, 11 159;
14 197–99; 16 194, 196
Formosa Plastics Group, **31** 108
Formosa Springs, **I** 269; **12** 337
Formularios y Procedimientos Moore, **IV**
645
Formule 1, **13** 364; **27** 10
Forney Fiber Company, **8** 475
Forsakrings A.B. Volvia, **I** 20
Forstmann Little & Co., I 446, 483; **II**
478, 544; **III** 56; **7** 206; **10** 321; **12** 344,
562; **14** 166; **16** 322; **19** 372–73, 432;
22 32, 60; **30** 426; **34** 145, 448; **36** 523;
38 190–92
Fort Associates, **I** 418
Fort Bend Utilities Company, **12** 269
Fort Dummer Mills, **III** 213
Fort Garry Brewery, **26** 304
Fort Howard Corporation, 8 197–99; 15
305; **22** 209. *See also* Fort James
Corporation.
**Fort James Corporation, 22 209–12
(upd.); 29** 136
Fort Mill Manufacturing Co., **V** 378
Fort William Power Co., **IV** 246; **25** 10
Forte Plc, **15** 46; **16** 446; **24** 195; **29** 443
Forte's Holdings Ltd., **III** 104–05
Fortis, Inc., 15 179–82; 47 134–37 (upd.)
Fortum Corporation, 30 202–07 (upd.)
Fortun Foods, **26** 59
Fortuna Coffee Co., **I** 451
Fortune Brands, Inc., 19 168; **29 193–97
(upd.); 45** 269; **49** 153
Fortune Enterprises, **12** 60
**Fortunoff Fine Jewelry and Silverware
Inc., 24 144–46**
Forum Cafeterias, **19** 299–300
Forum Hotels, **I** 248

Foseco plc, **IV** 383
Fosgate Electronics, **43** 322
Foss Maritime Co., **9** 509, 511
Fossil, Inc., 17 189–91
Foster & Kleiser, **7** 335; **14** 331
Foster & Marshall, **II** 398; **10** 62
Foster and Braithwaite, **III** 697
Foster Forbes, **16** 123
Foster Grant, **I** 670; **II** 595–96; **12** 214
Foster Management Co., **11** 366–67
Foster Medical Corp., **III** 16; **11** 282
Foster Poultry Farms, 32 201–04
Foster-Probyn Ltd., **38** 501
Foster Sand & Gravel, **14** 112
Foster Wheeler Corporation, I 82; **6**
    145–47; 23 205–08 (upd.); 25 82
Foster's Brewing Group Ltd., 7 182–84;
    21 227–30 (upd.); 26 303, 305–06; **36**
    15
Fotomat Corp., **III** 549
Fougerolle, **27** 136, 138
Foundation Computer Systems, Inc., **13**
    201
Foundation Fieldbus, **22** 373
Foundation Health Corporation, 11 174;
    12 175–77
Founders Equity Inc., **14** 235
Founders of American Investment Corp.,
    15 247
Fountain Powerboats Industries, Inc., 28
    146–48
Four Media Co., **33** 403
Four-Phase Systems, Inc., **II** 61; **11** 327
Four Queens Hotel and Casino. *See* The
    Elsinore Corporation.
Four Seasons Hotels Inc., II 531; **9**
    237–38; 29 198–200 (upd.)
Four Seasons Nursing Centers, Inc., **6** 188;
    25 308
Four Winds, **21** 153
Four Winns, **III** 600
Fournier Furniture, Inc., **12** 301
4P, **30** 396–98
Fourth Financial Corporation, 11
    144–46; 15 60
Foussard Associates, **I** 333
Fowler Road Construction Proprietary, **III**
    672
Fowler, Roenau & Geary, LLC, **37** 224
Fowler-Waring Cables Co., **III** 162
Fox and Hound English Pub and Grille.
    See Total Entertainment Restaurant
    Corporation.
Fox & Jacobs, **8** 87
Fox Broadcasting Company, **II** 156; **IV**
    608, 652; **7** 391–92; **9** 428; **21** 25, 360;
    24 517; **25** 174, 417–18; **46** 311
Fox Children's Network, **21** 26
Fox Entertainment Group, Inc., 43
    173–76
Fox Family Worldwide, Inc., 24 170–72
Fox Film Corp., **II** 146–47, 154–55, 169;
    25 327–28
Fox, Fowler & Co., **II** 307
Fox Glacier Mints Ltd., **II** 569
Fox Grocery Co., **II** 682
Fox, Inc., **12** 359; **25** 490
Fox Network, **29** 426
Fox Paper Company, **8** 102
Fox Photo, **III** 475; **7** 161
Fox-Vliet Drug Company, **16** 212
Foxboro Company, 13 233–35; 27 81
FoxMeyer Health Corporation, V
    152–53; **8** 55; **16 212–14**

Foxmoor, **29** 163
Foxx Hy-Reach, **28** 387
FP&L. *See* Florida Power & Light Co.
FPK LLC, **26** 343
FPL Group, Inc., V 623–25; 45 150; **49**
    143–46 (upd.)
FR Corp., **18** 340; **43** 282
Fragrance Express Inc., **37** 271
Fram Corp., **I** 142, 567
Framatome SA, 9 10; **19 164–67**
Framingham Electric Company, **12** 45
Franc-Or Resources, **38** 231–32
France Cables et Radio, **6** 303
France 5, **6** 374; **21** 105
France-Loisirs, **IV** 615–16, 619
France Quick, **12** 152; **26** 160–61; **27** 10
France Telecom Group, V 291–93, 471;
    9 32; **14** 489; **18** 33; **21 231–34 (upd.);**
    25 96, 102; **34** 13; **47** 214
Franchise Associates, Inc., **17** 238
Franchise Business Systems, Inc., **18** 207
Franchise Finance Corp. of America, **19**
    159; **37** 351
Francis H. Leggett & Co., **24** 527
Franciscan Vineyards, Inc., **34** 89
Franco-Américaine de Constructions
    Atomiques, **19** 165
Franco-American Food Co., **I** 428; **II** 479
Frank & Hirsch, **III** 608
Frank & Schulte GmbH, **8** 496
Frank Dry Goods Company, **9** 121
Frank H. Nott Inc., **14** 156
Frank J. Rooney, Inc., **8** 87
Frank J. Zamboni & Co., Inc., 34
    173–76
Frank Russell Company, 45 316; **46**
    198–200
Frank Schaffer Publications, **19** 405; **29**
    470, 472
Frank W. Horner, Ltd., **38** 123
Frank's Nursery & Crafts, Inc., 12
    178–79, 198–200
Frankel & Co., 39 166–69
Fränkel & Selz, **II** 239
Frankenberry, Laughlin & Constable, **9** 393
Frankford-Quaker Grocery Co., **II** 625
Frankfort Oil Co., **I** 285
Frankfurter Allgemeine Versicherungs-
    AG, **III** 184
Franklin Assurances, **III** 211
Franklin Baker's Coconut, **II** 531
Franklin Brass Manufacturing Company,
    20 363
Franklin Container Corp., **IV** 312; **19** 267
Franklin Corp., **14** 130; **41** 388
Franklin Covey Company, 37 149–52
    (upd.)
Franklin Electric Company, Inc., 43
    177–80
Franklin Electronic Publishers, Inc., 23
    209–13
Franklin Life Insurance Co., **III** 242–43; **V**
    397; **29** 195
Franklin Mint, **IV** 676; **9** 428; **37** 337–38
Franklin National Bank, **9** 536
Franklin Plastics, **19** 414
Franklin Quest Co., 11 147–49; 41 121.
    See also Franklin Covey Company.
Franklin Rayon Yarn Dyeing Corp., **I** 529
Franklin Research & Development, **11** 41
Franklin Resources, Inc., 9 239–40
Franklin Sports, Inc., **17** 243
Franklin Steamship Corp., **8** 346
Franks Chemical Products Inc., **I** 405

Frans Maas Beheer BV, **14** 568
Franz and Frieder Burda, **IV** 661
Franz Foods, Inc., **II** 584
Franz Ströher AG, **III** 68–69
Franzia. *See* The Wine Group, Inc.
Fraser & Chalmers, **13** 16
Fraser Cos. Ltd., **IV** 165
Fratelli Manzoli, **IV** 585
Fratelli Treves, **IV** 585
Fraternal Assurance Society of America,
    III 274
Fray Data International, **14** 319
Frazer & Jones, **48** 141
Fre Kote Inc., **I** 321
Frears, **II** 543
Fred Campbell Auto Supply, **26** 347
Fred Harvey Hotels, **I** 417
Fred Meyer, Inc., II 669; **V 54–56; 18**
    505; **20 222–25 (upd.); 35** 370
Fred S. James and Co., **III** 280; **I** 537; **22**
    318
Fred Sammons Co., **9** 72
Fred Sammons Company of Chicago, **30**
    77
Fred Sands Realtors, **IV** 727
Fred Schmid Appliance & T.V. Co., Inc.,
    10 305; **18** 532
The Fred W. Albrecht Grocery Co., 13
    236–38
Fred's, Inc., 23 214–16
Freddie Mac. *See* Federal Home Loan
    Mortgage Corporation.
Fredelle, **14** 295
Frederick & Nelson, **17** 462
Frederick Atkins Inc., 16 215–17
Frederick Bayer & Company, **22** 225
Frederick Gas Company, **19** 487
Frederick Manufacturing Corporation, **26**
    119; **48** 59
Frederick Miller Brewing Co., **I** 269
Frederick's of Hollywood Inc., 16
    218–20; 25 521
Free-lance Uitzendburo, **26** 240
Freeborn Farms, **13** 244
Freedom Communications, Inc., 36
    222–25
Freedom Group Inc., **42** 10–11
Freedom Technology, **11** 486
Freedom-Valvoline Oil Co., **IV** 373; **19** 23
Freeman, Spogli & Co., **17** 366; **18** 90; **32**
    12, 15; **35** 276; **36** 358–59; **47** 142–43
Freemans, **V** 177
FreeMark Communications, **38** 269
Freeport-McMoRan Inc., IV 81–84; 7
    185–89 (upd.); 16 29; **23** 40
Freeport Power, **38** 448
Freezer House, **II** 398; **10** 62
Freezer Queen Foods, Inc., **21** 509
Freezer Shirt Corporation, **8** 406
Freiberger Papierfabrik, **IV** 323
Freight Car Services, Inc., **23** 306
Freight Outlet, **17** 297
Freightliner, **I** 150; **6** 413
FreightMaster, **III** 498
Frejlack Ice Cream Co., **II** 646; **7** 317
Fremlin Breweries, **I** 294
Fremont Butter and Egg Co., **II** 467
Fremont Canning Company, **7** 196
Fremont Group, **21** 97
Fremont Investors, **30** 268
Fremont Partners, **24** 265
Fremont Savings Bank, **9** 474–75
French and Richards & Co., **I** 692
French Bank of California, **II** 233

French Connection Group plc, 41 **167–69**

French Fragrances, Inc., 22 213–15; 40 170. *See also* Elizabeth Arden, Inc.

French Kier, **I** 568

French Petrofina, **IV** 497

French Quarter Coffee Co., **27** 480–81

Frequency Sources Inc., **9** 324

Fresenius AG, **22** 360; **49** 155–56

Fresh America Corporation, 20 226–28

Fresh Choice, Inc., 20 229–32

Fresh Fields, **19** 501

Fresh Foods, Inc., 25 391; 29 201–03

Fresh Start Bakeries, **26** 58

Freshbake Foods Group PLC, **II** 481; **7** 68; **25** 518; **26** 57

Fretter, Inc., 9 65; **10** 9–10, **304–06**, 502; **19** 124; **23** 52

Freudenberg & Co., 41 170–73

Frialco, **IV** 165

Frictiontech Inc., **11** 84

Friday's Front Row Sports Grill, **22** 128

Friden, Inc., **II** 10; **30** 418

Fridy-Gauker & Fridy, **I** 313; **10** 154

Fried, Frank, Harris, Shriver & **Jacobson, 35 183–86**

Fried. Krupp AG Hoesch- Krupp. *See* Thyssen Krupp AG.

Fried. Krupp GmbH, II 257; **IV** 60, **85–89**, 104, 128, 203, 206, 222, 234

Friedman's Inc., 29 204–06

Friedrich Flick Industrial Corp., **I** 548; **III** 692

Friedrich Roessler Söhne, **IV** 69

Friedrichshütte, **III** 694

Friendly Hotels PLC, **14** 107

Friendly Ice Cream Corp., II 511–12; **15** 221; **30 208–10**

Friesch-Groningsche Hypotheekbank, **III** 179

Frigidaire Home Products, III 572; **13** 564; **19** 361; **22** 28, **216–18**, 349

Frigo, **II** 587

Friguia, **IV** 165

Frisby P.M.C. Incorporated, **16** 475

Frisch's Restaurants, Inc., 35 187–89

Frisdranken Industries Winters B.V., **22** 515

Frisia Group, **IV** 197–98

Frito-Lay Company, I 219, 278–79; **III** 136; **22** 95; **32 205–10**; **38** 347; **44** 348

Fritz Companies, Inc., 12 180–82

Fritz Gegauf AG. *See* Bernina Holding AG.

Fritz Thyssen Stiftung, **IV** 222

Fritz W. Glitsch and Sons, Inc. *See* Glitsch International, Inc.

Fritzsche Dodge and Ollcott, **I** 307

Froebel-Kan, **IV** 679

Frolic, **16** 545

Fromagerie d'Illoud. *See* Bongrain SA.

La Fromagerie du Velay, **25** 85

Fromagerie Paul Renard, **25** 85

Fromageries Bel, II 518; **6** 47; **19** 51; **23** **217–19; 25 83–84**

Fromageries des Chaumes, **25** 84

Fromarsac, **25** 84

Frome Broken Hill Co., **IV** 59

Fromm & Sichel, **I** 285

Frontec, **13** 132

Frontenac Co., **24** 45

Frontier Airlines, Inc., I 97–98, 103, 118, 124, 129–30; **6** 129; **11** 298; **21** 141–42; **22 219–21; 25** 421; **26** 439–40; **39** 33

Frontier Communications, **32** 216, 218

Frontier Corp., 16 221–23; 18 164

Frontier Electronics, **19** 311

Frontier Expeditors, Inc., **12** 363

Frontier Oil Co., **IV** 373

Frontier Pacific Insurance Company, **21** 263

FrontLine Capital Group, **47** 330–31

Frontline Ltd., 45 163–65

Frosch Touristik, **27** 29

Frost National Bank. *See* Cullen/Frost Bankers, Inc.

Frozen Food Express Industries, Inc., 20 **233–35; 27** 404

Fru-Con Corp., **I** 561

Fruehauf Corp., I 169–70, 480; **II** 425; **III** 652; **7** 259–60, 513–14; **13** 341; **27** 202–03, 251; **40** 432

Fruit of the Loom, Inc., 8 200–02; 16 535; **25 164–67 (upd.)**

The Frustum Group Inc., **45** 280

Fry's Diecastings, **III** 681

Fry's Food Stores, **12** 112

Fry's Metal Foundries, **III** 681

Frye Copy Systems, **6** 599

Frymaster Corporation, 27 159–62

FSA Corporation, **25** 349

FSI International, Inc., 17 192–94. *See* *also* FlightSafety International, Inc.

FSP. *See* Frank Schaffer Publications.

FTD, **26** 344. *See also* Florists Transworld Delivery, Inc.

F3 Software Corp., **15** 474

FTP Software, Inc., 20 236–38

Fubu, 29 207–09

Fuddruckers, **27** 480–82

Fuel Pipeline Transportation Ltd., **6** 123–24; **27** 464

Fuel Resources Development Co., **6** 558–59

Fuel Resources Inc., **6** 457

FuelMaker Corporation, **6** 569

Fuji Bank, Ltd., I 494; **II 291–93**, 360–61, 391, 422, 459, 554; **III** 405, 408–09; **17** 556–57; **24** 324; **26** 455

Fuji Electric Co., Ltd., II 22–23, 98, 103; **III** 139; **13** 356; **18** 511; **22** 373; **42** 145; **48 180–82 (upd.)**

Fuji Gen-Gakki, **16** 202; **43** 171

Fuji Heavy Industries, **I** 207; **III** 581; **9** 294; **12** 400; **13** 499–501; **23** 290; **36** 240, 243

Fuji Iron & Steel Co., Ltd., **I** 493; **II** 300; **IV** 130, 157, 212; **17** 349–50; **24** 325

Fuji Kaolin Co., **III** 691

Fuji Paper, **IV** 320

Fuji Photo Film Co., Ltd., III 172, 476, **486–89**, 549–50; **6** 289; **7** 162; **18** 94, **183–87 (upd.)**, 341–42; **36** 172, 174; **43** 284

Fuji Photo Film USA, Inc., **45** 284

Fuji Seito, **I** 511

Fuji Television, **7** 249; **9** 29

Fuji Xerox. *See* Xerox Corporation.

Fuji Yoshiten Co., **IV** 292

Fujian Hualong Carburetor, **13** 555

Fujikoshi Kozai, **III** 595

Fujimoto Bill Broker & Securities Co., **II** 405

Fujisawa Pharmaceutical Co., I 635–36; **III** 47; **8** 343

Fujita Airways, **6** 70

Fujitsu-ICL Systems Inc., 11 150–51

Fujitsu Limited, I 455, 541; **II** 22–23, 56, 68, 73, 274; **III** 109–11, 130, **139–41**, 164, 482; **V** 339; **6** 217, 240–42; **10** 238; **11** 308, 542; **13** 482; **14** 13–15, 512; **16** 139, **224–27 (upd.)**; **17** 172; **21** 390; **27** 107; **40** 20; **145–50 (upd.)**; **43** 285

Fujitsu Takamisawa, **28** 131

Fujiyi Confectionery Co., **II** 569

Fukuin Electric Works, Ltd., **III** 604

Fukuin Shokai Denki Seisakusho, **III** 604

Fukuju Fire, **III** 384

Fukuoka Paper Co., Ltd., **IV** 285

Fukutake Publishing Co., Ltd., **13** 91, 93

Ful-O-Pep, **10** 250

Fulbright & Jaworski L.L.P., 22 4; **47** **138–41**

Fulcrum Communications, **10** 19

The Fulfillment Corporation of America, **21** 37

Fulham Brothers, **13** 244

Fullbright & Jaworski, **28** 48

Fuller Brush Co., **II** 572; **15** 475–76, 78

Fuller Co., **6** 395–96; **25** 169–70

Fuller Manufacturing Company **I** 154. *See* *also* H.B. Fuller Company.

Fuller Smith & Turner P.L.C., 38 **193–95**

Fulton Bank, **14** 40

Fulton Co., **III** 569; **20** 361

Fulton Insurance Co., **III** 463; **21** 173

Fulton Manufacturing Co., **11** 535

Fulton Municipal Gas Company, **6** 455

Fulton Performance Products, Inc., **11** 535

Funai-Amstrad, **III** 113

Funco, Inc., 20 239–41

Fund American Companies. *See* White Mountains Insurance Group, Ltd.

Fundimensions, **16** 337

Funk & Wagnalls, **IV** 605; **22** 441

Funk Software Inc., **6** 255; **25** 299

Funnel Cake Factory, **24** 241

Fuqua Enterprises, Inc., 17 195–98

Fuqua Industries Inc., I 445–47, 452; **8** 545; **12** 251; **14** 86; **37** 62

Furalco, **IV** 15

Furnishings International Inc., **20** 359, 363; **39** 267

Furniture Brands International, Inc., 31 246, 248; **39 170–75 (upd.)**

The Furniture Center, Inc., **14** 236

Furon Company, 28 149–51

Furr's Supermarkets, Inc., II 601; **28** **152–54**

Furst Group, **17** 106

Furukawa Electric Co., Ltd., II 22; **III** 139, **490–92**; **IV** 15, 26, 153; **15** 514; **22** 44

Fusi Denki, **II** 98

Fuso Marine Insurance Co., **III** 367

Fuso Metal Industries, **IV** 212

Futabu Co., Ltd., **V** 96

Futronix Corporation, **17** 276

Future Diagnostics, Inc., **25** 384

Future Graphics, **18** 387

Future Now, Inc., 6 245; **12 183–85**

Futurestep, Inc., **34** 247, 249

Fuyo Group, **II** 274, 291–93, 391–92, 554

FWD Corporation, **7** 513

Fyffes Plc, 38 196–99, 201

G&G Shops, Inc., **8** 425–26

G & H Products, **III** 419

G&K Services, Inc., 16 228–30; 21 115

G&L Albu, **IV** 90
G&L Inc., **16** 202; **43** 170
G&R Pasta Co., Inc., **II** 512
G. and T. Earle, **III** 669, 670
G.A. Serlachius Oy, **IV** 314–15
G.B. Lewis Company, **8** 359
G. Bruss GmbH and Co. KG, **26** 141
G.C.E. International Inc., **III** 96–97
G.C. Murphy Company, **9** 21
G.C. Smith, **I** 423
G.D. Searle & Co., I 365–66, **686–89; III**
  47, 53; **8** 343, 398, 434; **9** 356–57; **10**
  54; **12 186–89 (upd.); 16** 527; **26** 108,
  383; **29** 331; **29** 331; **34 177–82 (upd.)**
G. Felsenthal & Sons, **17** 106
G.H. Bass & Co., **15** 406; **24** 383
G.H. Besselaar Associates, **30** 151
G.H. Rinck NV, **V** 49; **19** 122–23; **49** 111
G.H. Wetterau & Sons Grocery Co., **II** 681
G. Heileman Brewing Co., I 253–55,
  270; **10** 169–70; **12** 338; **18** 501; **23**
  403, 405
G.I.E. Airbus Industrie, I
G.I. Joe's, Inc., 30 221–23 41–43, 49–52,
  55–56, 70, 72, 74–76, 107, 111, 116,
  121; **9** 458, 460; **11** 279, 363; **12**
  190–92 (upd.)
G-III Apparel Group, Ltd., 22 222–24
G.J. Coles & Coy. Ltd., **20** 155
G.L. Kelty & Co., **13** 168
G.L. Rexroth GmbH, **III** 566; **38** 298, 300
G.M. Pfaff AG, **30** 419–20
G.P. Group, **12** 358
G.P. Putnam's Sons, **II** 144
G.R. Foods, Inc. *See* Ground Round, Inc.
G.R. Herberger's Department Stores, **19**
  324–25; **41** 343–44
G.R. Kinney Corporation, **V** 226, 352; **14**
  293; **20** 88
G. Riedel Kälte- und Klimatechnik, **III** 420
G.S. Blodgett Corporation, 15 183–85;
  22 350
G.S. Capital Partners II L.P. *See* Goldman,
  Sachs & Company.
G. Washington Coffee Refining Co., **I** 622
Gabelli Asset Management Inc., 13 561;
  30 211–14. *See also* Lynch Corporation.
Gable House Properties, **II** 141
Gables Residential Trust, 49 147–49
Gabriel Industries, **II** 532
GAC. *See* The Goodyear Tire & Rubber
  Company.
GAC Corp., **II** 182; **III** 592
GAC Holdings L.P., **7** 204; **28** 164
Gadzooks, Inc., 18 188–90; 33 203
GAF, I 337–40, 524–25, 549; **II** 378; **III**
  440; **8** 180; **9** 518; **18** 215; **22** 14,
  225–29 (upd.); 25 464
Gage Marketing Group, 26 147–49; 27
  21
Gagliardi Brothers, **13** 383
Gaiam, Inc., 41 174–77
Gail Borden, Jr., and Company. *See*
  Borden, Inc.
Gain Technology, Inc., **10** 505
Gaines Dog Food Co., **II** 531
Gaines Furniture Manufacturing, Inc., **43**
  315
Gainsborough Craftsmen Ltd., **II** 569
Gainsco, Inc., 22 230–32
Gair Paper Co., **I** 599
Galas Harland, S.A., **17** 266, 268
Galavision, Inc., **24** 515–17
Galaxy Carpet Mills Inc., **19** 276

Galaxy Energies Inc., **11** 28
Galbreath Escott, **16** 474
The Gale Group, Inc., **34** 437
Gale Research Inc., **8** 526; **23** 440
Galen Health Care, **15** 112; **35** 215–16
Galen Laboratories, **13** 160
Galerías Preciados, **26** 130
Galeries Lafayette S.A., V 57–59; **23**
  220–23 (upd.)
Galesburg Coulter Disc Co., **III** 439–40
Galey & Lord, Inc., 20 242–45
Gallaher Group Plc, 49 150–54 (upd.)
Gallaher Limited, IV 260; **V** 398–400; **19**
  168–71 (upd.); 29 195
Gallatin Bank, **II** 312
Gallatin Steel Company, **18** 380; **24** 144
Galletas, **II** 543
Gallimard, **IV** 618
Gallo Winery. *See* E. & J. Gallo Winery.
Gallop Johnson & Neuman, L.C., **26** 348
The Gallup Organization, 37 153–56; 41
  196–97
Galoob Toys. *See* Lewis Galoob Toys Inc.
Galor, **I** 676
GALP, **IV** 505; **48** 117, 119
Galvanizing Co., **IV** 159
Galveston *Daily News*, **10** 3
Galvin Manufacturing Corp., **II** 60; **11** 326
GALVSTAR, L.P., **26** 530
Galyan's Trading Company, Inc., 47
  142–44s
Gamble-Skogmo Inc., **13** 169; **25** 535
The Gambrinus Company, 29 219; **40**
  188–90
Gambro AB, **13** 159–61, 327–28; **49**
  155–57
Gamebusters, **41** 409
Gamesa, **II** 544; **19** 192
GameTime, Inc., **19** 387; **27** 370–71
GAMI. *See* Great American Management
  and Investment, Inc.
Gamlestaden, **9** 381–82
Gamlestadens Fabriker, **III** 622
Gamma Capital Corp., **24** 3
Gammalink, **18** 143
Gander Mountain, Inc., 20 246–48
Gang-Nail Systems, **III** 735
Gannett Co., Inc., III 159; **IV 612–13,**
  629–30; **7 190–92 (upd.); 9** 3; **18** 63;
  23 157–58, 293; **24** 224; **25** 371; **30**
  215–17 (upd.); 32 354–55; **41** 197–98
Gannett Supply, **17** 282
Gantos, Inc., 17 199–201
The Gap, Inc., V 60–62; **9** 142, 360; **11**
  499; **18 191–94 (upd.); 24** 27; **25**
  47–48; **31** 51–52
GAR Holdings, **19** 78
Garamond Press, **23** 100
Garan, Inc., 16 231–33
Garantie Mutuelle des Fonctionnaires, **21**
  225
Garden Botanika, **11** 41
Garden City Newspapers Inc., **38** 308
Garden Escape, **26** 441
Garden Fresh Restaurant Corporation,
  31 213–15
Garden of Eatin' Inc., **27** 198; **43** 218–19
Garden Ridge Corporation, 27 163–65
Garden State BancShares, Inc., **14** 472
Garden State Life Insurance Company, **10**
  312; **27** 47–48
Garden State Paper, **38** 307–08
Gardenburger, Inc., 33 169–71
Gardener's Eden, **17** 548–49

Gardenia, **II** 587
Gardner & Harvey Container Corporation,
  8 267
Gardner Advertising. *See* Wells Rich Green
  BDDP.
Gardner Cryogenics, **13** 140
Gardner Denver, Inc., II 16; **49 158–60**
Gardner Merchant Ltd., **III** 104; **11** 325;
  29 442–44
Gardner Rubber Co. *See* Tillotson Corp.
Garelick Farms, Inc., **26** 449
Garfield Weston, **13** 51
Garfinckel, Brooks Brothers, Miller &
  Rhodes, Inc., **15** 94; **22** 110
Garfinckels, **37** 12
Garland Publishing, **44** 416
Garland-Compton, **42** 328
Garlock, **I** 435
Garnier, **III** 47
A.B. Garnisonen, **II** 352
Garrard Engineering, **II** 82
Garrett, **9** 18; **11** 472
Garrett & Company, **27** 326
Garrett AiResearch, **9** 18
Garrett-Buchanan, **I** 412
Garrett Poultry Co., **II** 584; **14** 514
Garrick Investment Holdings Ltd., **16** 293
Garrido y Compania, **26** 448
Gart Sports Company, 24 173–75
Gartner Group, Inc., 21 235–37; 25 22
Gartrell White, **II** 465
Garuda Indonesia, I 107; **6 90–91**
Gary Fisher Mountain Bike Company, **16**
  494
Gary Industries, **7** 4
Gary-Wheaton Corp., **II** 286
Gary-Williams Energy Corporation, **19** 177
Gas Authority of India Ltd., **IV** 484
Gas Corp. of Queensland, **III** 673
Gas Energy Inc., **6** 457
Gas Group, **III** 673
Gas Light and Coke Company. *See* British
  Gas plc.
Gas Light Company. *See* Baltimore Gas
  and Electric Company.
Gas Machinery Co., **I** 412
Gas Natural, **49** 211
Gas Service Company, **6** 593; **12** 542
Gas Supply Co., **III** 672
Gas Tech, Inc., **11** 513
Gas Utilities Company, **6** 471
Gaston Paper Stock Co., Inc., **8** 476
Gasunie. *See* N.V. Nederlandse Gasunie.
GATC. *See* General American Tank Car
  Company.
Gate City Company, **6** 446
The Gates Corporation, 9 241–43
Gates Distribution Company, **12** 60
Gates Radio Co., **II** 37
Gates Rubber, **26** 349
Gates/FA Distributing Inc., **29** 413–14
Gateway Books, **14** 61
Gateway Corporation Ltd., II 612,
  628–30, 638, 642; **10** 442; **16** 249; **25**
  119. *See also* Somerfield plc.
Gateway Foodmarkets Ltd., **II** 628; **13** 26
Gateway, Inc., 27 166–69 (upd.)
Gateway International Motorsports
  Corporation, Inc., **43** 139–40
Gateway State Bank, **39** 381–82
Gateway Technologies, Inc., **46** 387
Gateway 2000, Inc., 10 307–09; 11 240;
  22 99; **24** 31; **25** 531
Gatliff Coal Co., **6** 583

Gattini, **40** 215

Gatwick Handling, **28** 157

GATX, 6 394–96; 25 168–71 (upd.); 47 298

Gaultier. *See* Groupe Jean-Paul Gaultier.

Gaumont SA, II 157–58; **25 172–75; 29** 369–71

Gauntlet Developments, **IV** 724

Gavilan Computer Corp., **III** 124; **6** 221

Gaya Motor, P.T. **23** 290

Gaylord Container Corporation, 8 203–05; **24** 92

Gaylord Entertainment Company, 11 152–54; **36 226–29 (upd.); 38** 456

Gaymer Group, **25** 82

Gaz de France, IV 425; **V 626–28; 38** 407; **40 191–95 (upd.)**

Gazelle Graphics Systems, **28** 244

Gazprom, **18** 50; **30** 205. *See also* OAO Gazprom.

GB Foods Inc., **19** 92

GB-Inno-BM, **II** 658; **V** 63

GB Papers, **IV** 290

GB s.a. *See* GIB Group.

GB Stores, Inc., **14** 427

GBL, **IV** 499

GC Companies, Inc., 25 176–78

GCFC. *See* General Cinema Finance Co.

GD Express Worldwide, **27** 472, 475; **30** 463

GDE Systems, Inc., **17** 492

GDF. *See* Gaz de France.

GDS, **29** 412

GE. *See* General Electric Company.

GE Aircraft Engines, 9 244–46

GE Capital Aviation Services, 36 230–33

GE Capital Corporation, **29** 428, 430

GE Capital Services, **27** 276; **49** 240

GE SeaCo SRL, **29** 428, 431

GEA AG, 27 170–74

GEAC Computer Corporation Ltd., 43 181–85

Geant Casino, **12** 152

Gear Products, Inc., **48** 59

Gearhart Industries Inc., **III** 499; **15** 467

Gearmatic, **I** 185

Geberit AG, 49 161–64

Gebrüder Kiessel GmbH, **IV** 197

Gebrüder Sulzer Aktiengesellschaft. *See* Sulzer Brothers Limited.

Gebrüder Volkart, **III** 402

Gebrueder Ahle GmbH, **III** 581

GEC. *See* General Electric Company.

GECAS. *See* GE Capital Aviation Services.

Gecina SA, 42 151–53

GECO, **III** 618; **17** 419

Geco Mines Ltd., **IV** 165; **7** 398

Geer Drug, **III** 9–10

Geerlings & Wade, Inc., 45 166–68

Geest Plc, 38 198, **200–02**

Geffen Records Inc., 21 26; **23** 33; **26** 150–52; **43** 143

GEGC, **III** 434

GEHE AG, 27 175–78

Gehl Company, 19 172–74

GEICO Corporation, III 214, 248, 252, 273, 448; **10 310–12; 18** 60, 61, 63; **40** 196–99 (upd.); **42** 31–34

Gelatin Products Co., **I** 678

Gelco Express, **18** 177

Gelco Truck Services, **19** 293

Gellatly, Hankey and Sewell, **III** 521

Gelsenberg AG, **IV** 454; **7** 141

Gelsenkirchener Bergwerks AG, **I** 542; **IV** 194

Gelson's, **29** 32

Gem State Utilities, **6** 325, 328

GEMA Gesellschaft für Maschinen- und Apparatebau mbH, **IV** 198

GemChem, Inc., **47** 20

Gemco, **17** 366

Gemcolite Company, **8** 178

N.V. Gemeenschappelijk Benzit van Aandeelen Philips Gloeilampenfabrieken, **II** 79; **13** 396

Gemeinhardt Co., **16** 201; **43** 170

Gemey, **III** 47

Gemina, **I** 369

Gemini Computer Systems, **III** 109; **14** 13; **37** 59–60

Gemini Group Limited Partnership, **23** 10

Gemini Industries, **17** 215

GemPlus, **18** 543

Gemstar-TV Guide International, **43** 431

Genbel Investments Ltd., **IV** 92

GenCare Health Systems, **17** 166–67

Gencor Ltd., I 423; **IV 90–93, 95; 22** 233–37 (upd.); **49** 353

GenCorp Inc., 8 206–08; 9 247–49; 13 381

Gendex Corp., **10** 270, 272

Gene Reid Drilling, **IV** 480

Gene Upton Co., **13** 166

Genencor International Inc., **44** 134, 136

Genender International Incorporated, **31** 52

Genentech Inc., I 628, **637–38; III** 43; **8** **209–11 (upd.)**, 216–17; **10** 78, 80, 142, 199; **17** 289; **29** 386; **30** 164; **32 211–15** **(upd.); 37** 112; **38** 204, 206; **41** 153, 155

General Accident plc, III 256–57, 350

General America Corp., **III** 352–53

General American Oil Co., **IV** 523

General American Tank Car Company. *See* GATX Corporation.

General Aniline and Film Corporation. *See* GAF Corporation.

General Aquatics, Inc., **16** 297

General Artificial Silk Co., **IV** 310; **19** 265

General Atlantic Partners, **25** 34; **26** 94

General Automotive Parts Corp., **I** 62; **9** 254

General Aviation Corp., **I** 54; **9** 16

General Battery Corp., **I** 440–41

General Bearing Corporation, 45 169–71

General Binding Corporation, 10 313–14

General Box Corp., **IV** 342

General Brewing Corp, **I** 269

General Bussan Kaisha, Ltd., **IV** 431–32, 555

General Cable Corporation, IV 32; **7** 288; **8** 367; **18** 549; **40 200–03**

General Casualty Co., **III** 258, 343, 352, 404

The General Chemical Group Inc., I 414; **22** 29, 115, 193, 349, 541; **29** 114; **37 157–60**

General Chocolate, **II** 521

General Cigar Company, **43** 204–05. *See also* Culbro Corporation.

General Cigar Holdings, Inc., **27** 139–40

General Cinema Corporation, I 245–46; **II** 478; **IV** 624; **12** 12–13, 226, 356; **14** 87; **19** 362; **26** 468; **27** 481

General Cinema Finance Co., **II** 157–58

General Cinema Theaters. *See* GC Companies, Inc.

General Co. for Life Insurance and Superannuation, **III** 309

General Corporation, **9** 173

General Credit Ltd., **II** 389

General Crude Oil Co., **II** 403; **IV** 287; **15** 228

General DataComm Industries, Inc., 14 200–02

General Diaper Corporation, **14** 550

General Dynamics Corporation, I 55, **57–60**, 62, 71, 74, 77, 482, 525, 527, 597; **6** 79, 229; **7** 520; **8** 51, 92, 315, 338; **9** 206, 323, 417–18, 498; **10** 315–18 (upd.), 522, 527; **11** 67, 165, 269, 278, 364; **13** 374; **16** 77–78; **18** 62, 554; **27** 100; **30** 471; **36** 76, 78–79; **40** 204–10 (upd.)

General Electric Capital Aviation Services, **48** 218–19

General Electric Capital Corp., **15** 257, 282; **19** 190

General Electric Company, I 41, 52, 82–85, 195, 321, 454, 478, 532, 534, 537; **II** 2, 16, 19, 22, 24, **27–31**, 38–39, 41, 56, 58–59, 66, 82, 86, 88–90, 98–99, 116–17, 119–21, 143, 151–52, 330, 349, 431, 604; **III** 16, 110, 122–23, 132, 149, 152, 154, 170–71, 340, 437, 440, 443, 475, 483, 502, 526, 572–73, 614, 655; **IV** 66, 203, 287, 596, 675; **V** 564; **6** 13, 27, 32, 164–66, 240, 261, 266, 288, 452, 517; **7** 123, 125, 161, 456, 520, 532; **8** 157, 262, 332, 377; **9** 14–18, 27, 128, 162, 244, 246, 352–53, 417–18, 439, 514; **10** 16, 241, 536–37; **11** 46, 313, 318, 422, 472, 490; **12** 68, 190, **193–97 (upd.)**, 237, 247, 250, 252, 484, 544–45, 550; **13** 30, 124, 326, 396, 398, 501, 529, 554, 563–64; **15** 196, 228, 285, 380, 403, 467; **17** 149, 173, 272; **18** 228, 369; **19** 110, 164–66, 210, 335; **20** 8, 152; **22** 37, 218, 406; **23** 104–05, 181; **26** 371; **28** 4–5, 8, 298; **30** 490; **31** 123; **34 183–90 (upd.)**; **41** 366; **43** 447, 466; **45** 17, 19, 117; **47** 351

General Electric Company, PLC, I 411, 423; **II** 3, 12, **24–26**, 31, 58, 72, 80–83; **III** 509; **9** 9–10; **13** 356; **20** 290; **24** 87; **42** 373, 377. *See also* Marconi plc.

General Electric Credit Corporation, **19** 293; **20** 42

General Electric Railcar Wheel and Parts Services Corporation, **18** 4

General Electric Venture Capital Corporation, **9** 140; **10** 108

General Electronics Co., **III** 160

General Elevator Corporation, **25** 15

General Europea S.A., **V** 607

General Export Iron and Metals Company, **15** 116

General Felt Industries Inc., **I** 202; **14** 300; **17** 182–83

General Film Distributors Ltd., **II** 157

General Finance Corp., **II** 419; **III** 194, 232; **11** 16

General Finance Service Corp., **11** 447

General Fire and Casualty, **I** 449

General Fire Extinguisher Co. *See* Grinnell Corp.

General Foods Corp., **I** 26, 36, 608, 712; **II** 414, 463, 477, 497, 502, 525, 530–34, 557, 569; **III** 66; **V** 407; **7** 272–74; **10**

323, 551; **12** 167, 372; **13** 293; **18** 416, 419; **25** 517; **26** 251; **36** 236; **44** 341

General Foods, Ltd., **7** 577

General Furniture Leasing. *See* CORT Business Services Corporation.

General Gas Co., **IV** 432

General Glass Corporation, **13** 40

General Growth Properties, **III** 248

General Health Services, **III** 79

General Host Corporation, **7** 372; **12** 178–79, **198–200**, 275; **15** 362; **17** 230–31

General Housewares Corporation, **16** **234–36**; **18** 69

General Instrument Corporation, **II** 5, 112, 160; **10 319–21**; **17** 33; **34** 298

General Insurance Co. of America, **III** 352–53

General Jones Processed Food, **I** 438

General Learning Corp., **IV** 675; **7** 528

General Leisure, **16** 33

General Life Insurance Co. of America, **III** 353

General Medical Corp., **18** 469

General Merchandise Company, **V** 91

General Merchandise Services, Inc., **15** 480

General Milk Co., **II** 487; **7** 429

General Milk Products of Canada Ltd., **II** 586

General Mills, Inc., **II** 493, **501–03**, 525, 556, 576, 684; **III** 505; **7** 547; **8** 53–54; **9** 156, 189–90, 291; **10** 177, **322–24** (upd.); **11** 15, 497–98; **12** 80, 167–68, 275; **13** 244, 293–94, 408, 516; **15** 189; **16** 71, 156–58, 337; **18** 225, 523; **22** 337–38, 239, 241, 243, 253; **30** 286; **31** 429–31; **33** 359; **36** 179–80, **234–39** (upd.); **44** 138–40

General Mining and Finance Corporation. *See* Gencor Ltd.

General Mortgage and Credit Corp., **II** 256

General Motors Acceptance Corporation, **21** 146; **22** 55

General Motors Corporation, **I** 10, 14, 16–17, 54, 58, 78–80, 85, 101–02, 125, 136, 141, 144–45, 147, 154–55, 162–63, 165–67, **171–73**, 181, 183, 186–87, 203, 205–06, 280, 328–29, 334–35, 360, 448, 464, 481–82, 529, 540; **II** 2, 5, 15, 32–35, 268, 431, 608; **III** 55, 136–38, 292, 442, 458, 482–83, 536, 555, 563, 581, 590–91, 637–38, 640–42, 760; **6** 140, 256, 336, 356, 358; **7** 6–8, 427, 461–64, 513, 565, 567, 599; **8** 151–52, 505–07; **9** 16–18, 36, 283, 293–95, 341, 343, 344, 439, 487–89; **10** 198, 232, 262, 264, 273–74, 279–80, 288–89, **325–27** (upd.), 419–20, 429, 460, 537; **11** 5, 29, 53, 103–04, 137–39, 339, 350, 427–29, 437–39, 471–72, 528, 530; **12** 90, 160, 309, 311, 487; **13** 109, 124, 179, 344–45, 357; **16** 321–22, 436, 484; **17** 173, 184, 304; **18** 125–26, 168, 308; **19** 293–94, 482, 484; **21** 3, 6, 444; **22** 13, 169, 175, 216; **23** 267–69, 288–91, 340, 459–61; **25** 142–43, 149, 223–24, 300; **29** 375, 407–08; **34** 133–35, 303; **36** 32, **240–44 (upd.)**, 298; **38** 86, 458, 461; **43** 319; **45** 142, 170

General Nucleonics Corp., **III** 643

General Nutrition Companies, Inc., **11** **155–57**; **24** 480; **29 210–14 (upd.)**; **31** 347; **37** 340, 342; **45** 210

General Office Products Co., **25** 500

General Packing Service, Inc., **19** 78

General Parts Inc., **29** 86

General Petroleum and Mineral Organization of Saudi Arabia, **IV** 537–39

General Petroleum Corp., **IV** 412, 431, 464; **7** 352

General Physics Corporation, **13** 367

General Portland Cement Co., **III** 704–05; **17** 497

General Portland Inc., **28** 229

General Precision Equipment Corp., **II** 10; **30** 418

General Printing and Paper, **II** 624–25

General Printing Ink Corp. *See* Sequa Corp.

General Property Trust, **IV** 708

General Public Utilities Corporation, **V** **629–31**; **6** 484, 534, 579–80; **11** 388; **20** 73

General Radio Company. *See* GenRad, Inc.

General Railway Signal Company. *See* General Signal Corporation.

General Re Corporation, **III** 258–59, 276; **24 176–78 (upd.)**; **42** 31, 35

General Rent A Car, **6** 349; **25** 142–43

General Research Corp., **14** 98

General Seafoods Corp., **II** 531

General Sekiyu K.K., **IV** 431–33, 555; **16** 490

General Signal Corporation, **III** 645; **9** **250–52**; **11** 232

General Spring Products, **16** 321

General Steel Industries Inc., **14** 324

General Supermarkets, **II** 673

General Telephone and Electronics Corp., **II** 47; **V** 295, 345–46; **13** 398; **19** 40; **25** 267

General Telephone Corporation, **V** 294–95; **9** 478, 494

General Time Corporation, **16** 483

General Tire, Inc., **8** 206–08, **212–14**; **9** 247–48; **20** 260, 262; **22** 219

General Transistor Corporation, **10** 319

General Utilities Company, **6** 555

General Waterworks Corporation, **40** 449

Generale Bank, **II 294–95**

Générale Biscuit S.A., **II** 475

Générale de Banque, **36** 458

Générale de Mécanique Aéronautique, **I** 46

Générale de Restauration, **49** 126

Générale des Eaux Group, **V 632–34**; **21** 226. *See* Vivendi Universal S.A.

Generale du Jouet, **16** 428

Générale Occidentale, **II** 475; **IV** 614–15

Générale Restauration S.A., **34** 123

Generali. *See* Assicurazioni Generali.

Génération Y2K, **35** 204, 207

GenerComit Gestione SpA, **II** 192

Genesco Inc., **14** 501; **17 202–06**; **27** 59

Genesee & Wyoming Inc., **27 179–81**

Genesee Brewing Co., **18** 72

Genesee Iron Works. *See* Wickes Inc.

Genesis, **II** 176–77

Genesis Health Ventures, Inc., **18** **195–97**; **25** 310

Genetic Anomalies, Inc., **39** 395

Genetic Systems Corp., **I** 654; **III** 18; **37** 43

Genetics Institute, Inc., **8 215–18**; **10** 70, 78–80

Geneva Metal Wheel Company, **20** 261

Geneva Pharmaceuticals, Inc., **8** 549; **22** 37, 40

Geneva Rubber Co., **17** 373

Geneva Steel, **7 193–95**

Genex Corp., **I** 355–56; **26** 246

GENIX, **V** 152

Genix Group. *See* MCN Corporation.

Genmar Holdings, Inc., **45 172–75**

Genossenschaftsbank Edeka, **II** 621–22

Genosys Biotechnologies, Inc., **36** 431

Genovese Drug Stores, Inc., **18 198–200**; **21** 187; **32** 170; **43** 249

Genpack Corporation, **21** 58

GenRad, Inc., **24 179–83**

GenSet, **19** 442

Genstar, **22** 14; **23** 327

Genstar Gypsum Products Co., **IV** 273

Genstar Stone Products Co., **III** 735; **15** 154; **40** 176

GenTek Inc., **37** 157; **41** 236

Gentex Corporation, **26 153–57**; **35** 148–49

Gentex Optics, **17** 50; **18** 392

GenTrac, **24** 257

Gentry Associates, Inc., **14** 378

Gentry International, **I** 497; **47** 234

Genty-Cathiard, **39** 183–84

Genuardi's Family Markets, Inc., **35** **190–92**

Genuin Golf & Dress of America, Inc., **32** 447

Genuine Parts Company, **9 253–55**; **45** **176–79 (upd.)**

Genung's, **II** 673

Genus, **18** 382–83

Genzyme Corporation, **13 239–42**; **38** **203–07 (upd.)**; **47** 4

Genzyme Transgenics Corp., **37** 44

Geo Space Corporation, **18** 513

GEO Specialty Chemicals, Inc., **27** 117

Geo. W. Wheelwright Co., **IV** 311; **19** 266

geobra Brandstätter GmbH & Co. KG, **48 183–86**

Geodynamics Oil & Gas Inc., **IV** 83

Geographics, Inc., **25** 183

Geomarine Systems, **11** 202

The Geon Company, **11 158–61**

Geon Industries, Inc. *See* Johnston Industries, Inc.

Geophysical Service, Inc., **II** 112; **III** 499–500; **IV** 365

GeoQuest Systems Inc., **17** 419

Georesources, Inc., **19** 247

Georg Fischer Foundries Group, **38** 214

George A. Hormel and Company, **II** **504–06**; **7** 547; **12** 123–24; **18** 244. *See also* Hormel Foods Corporation.

George A. Touche & Co., **9** 167

George Batten Co., **I** 28

George Booker & Co., **13** 102

George Buckton & Sons Limited, **40** 129

George Fischer, Ltd., **III** 638

George H. Dentler & Sons, **7** 429

The George Hyman Construction Company, **8** 112–13; **25** 403

George J. Ball, Inc., **27** 507

George K. Baum & Company, **25** 433

George K. Smith & Co., **I** 692

George Kent, **II** 3; **22** 10

George Newnes Company, **IV** 641; **7** 244

George Peabody & Co., **II** 329, 427

George R. Newell Company. *See* Supervalu Inc.

George R. Rich Manufacturing Company. *See* Clark Equipment Company.

George Smith Financial Corporation, **21** 257

George W. Neare & Co., **III** 224

George Weston Limited, II 631–32; 36 245–48 (upd.); 41 30, 33

George Wimpey PLC, 12 201–03; 28 450

Georges Renault SA, **III** 427; **28** 40

Georgetown Group, Inc., **26** 187

Georgetown Steel Corp., **IV** 228

Georgia Carpet Outlets, **25** 320

Georgia Cotton Producers Association. *See* Gold Kist Inc.

Georgia Credit Exchange, **6** 24

Georgia Federal Bank, **I** 447; **11** 112–13; **30** 196

Georgia Gulf Corporation, IV 282; **9 256–58**, 260

Georgia Hardwood Lumber Co., **IV** 281; **9** 259

Georgia International Life Insurance Co., **III** 218

Georgia Kraft Co., **IV** 312, 342–43; **8** 267–68; **19** 268

Georgia Natural Gas Corporation, **6** 447–48

Georgia-Pacific Corporation, IV 281–83, 288, 304, 345, 358; **9** 256–58, **259–62 (upd.); 12** 19, 377; **15** 229; **22** 415, 489; **31** 314; **44** 66; **47 145–51 (upd.)**

Georgia Power & Light Co., **V** 621; **6** 447, 537; **23** 28; **27** 20

Georgia Power Company, **38** 446–48; **49** 145

Georgia Railway and Electric Company, **6** 446–47; **23** 28

Georgie Pie, **V** 35

GeoScience Corporation, **18** 515; **44** 422

Geosource Inc., **III** 182; **21** 14; **22** 189

Geotec Boyles Brothers, S.A., **19** 247

Geotek Communications Inc., 21 238–40

GeoTel Communications Corp., **34** 114

Geothermal Resources International, **11** 271

GeoVideo Networks, **34** 259

Geoworks Corporation, **25** 509

Geraghty & Miller Inc., **26** 23

Gerald Stevens, Inc., 37 161–63

Gérard, **25** 84

Gerber Products Company, II 481; **III** 19; **7 196–98**, 547; **9** 90; **11** 173; **21** 53–55, **241–44 (upd); 25** 366; **34** 103; **36** 256

Gerber Scientific, Inc., 12 204–06

Gerbes Super Markets, Inc., **12** 112

Gerbo Telecommunicacoes e Servicos Ltda., **32** 40

Geren Associates. *See* CRSS Inc.

Geriatrics Inc., **13** 49

Gericom AG, 47 152–54

Gerling of Cologne, **III** 695

Germaine Monteil Cosmetiques Corp., **I** 426; **III** 56

German American Bancorp, 41 178–80

German-American Car Company. *See* GATX.

German-American Securities, **II** 283

German Cargo Service GmbH., **I** 111

German Mills American Oatmeal Factory, **II** 558; **12** 409

The German Society. *See* The Legal Aid Society.

Germania Refining Co., **IV** 488–89

Germplasm Resource Management, **III** 740

Gerresheimer Glas AG, II 386; **IV** 232; **43 186–89**

Gerrity Oil & Gas Corporation, **11** 28; **24** 379–80

Gervais Danone, **II** 474

GESA. *See* General Europea S.A.

Gesbancaya, **II** 196

Gesellschaft für Chemische Industrie im Basel, **I** 632

Gesellschaft für den Bau von Untergrundbahnen, **I** 410

Gesellschaft für Linde's Eisenmachinen, **I** 581

Gesellschaft für Markt- und Kühlhallen, **I** 581

Gesparal, **III** 47; **8** 342

Gestettner, **II** 159

Gestione Pubblicitaria Editoriale, **IV** 586

GET Manufacturing Inc., **36** 300

Getronics NV, 39 176–78

Getty Images, Inc., 31 216–18

Getty Oil Co., **II** 448; **IV** 367, 423, 429, 461, 479, 488, 490, 551, 553; **6** 457; **8** 526; **11** 27; **13** 448; **17** 501; **18** 488; **27** 216; **41** 391, 394–95; bf]XLVII 436

Getz Corp., **IV** 137

Geyser Peak Winery, **I** 291

Geysers Geothermal Co., **IV** 84, 523; **7** 188

GFI Informatique SA, 49 165–68

GfK Aktiengesellschaft, 49 169–72

GFS. *See* Gordon Food Service Inc.

GFS Realty Inc., **II** 633

GGT Group, **44** 198

GHH, **II** 257

GHI, **28** 155, 157

Ghirardelli Chocolate Company, 24 480; **27** 105; **30 218–20**

GI Communications, **10** 321

GI Export Corp. *See* Johnston Industries, Inc.

GIAG, **16** 122

Gianni Versace SpA, 22 238–40

Giant Bicycle Inc., **19** 384

Giant Cement Holding, Inc., 23 224–26

Giant Eagle, Inc., **12** 390–91; **13** 237

Giant Food Inc., II 633–35, 656; **13** 282, 284; **15** 532; **16** 313; **22 241–44 (upd.); 24** 462

Giant Industries, Inc., 19 175–77

Giant Resources, **III** 729

Giant Stores, Inc., **7** 113; **25** 124

Giant TC, Inc. *See* Campo Electronics, Appliances & Computers, Inc.

Giant Tire & Rubber Company, **8** 126

Giant Video Corporation, **29** 503

Giant Wholesale, **II** 625

GIB Group, V 63–66; 22 478; **23** 231; **26 158–62 (upd.)**

Gibbons, Green, van Amerongen Ltd., **II** 605; **9** 94; **12** 28; **19** 360

Gibbs Automatic Molding Co., **III** 569; **20** 360

Gibbs Construction, **25** 404

GIBCO Corp., **I** 321; **17** 287, 289

Gibraltar Casualty Co., **III** 340

Gibraltar Financial Corp., **III** 270–71

Gibraltar Steel Corporation, 37 164–67

Gibson, Dunn & Crutcher LLP, 36 249–52; 37 292

Gibson Greetings, Inc., 7 24; **12 207–10; 16** 256; **21** 426–28; **22** 34–35

Gibson Guitar Corp., 16 237–40

Gibson McDonald Furniture Co., **14** 236

GIC. *See* The Goodyear Tire & Rubber Company.

Giddings & Lewis, Inc., 8 545–46; **10 328–30; 23** 299; **28** 455

Giftmaster Inc., **26** 439–40

Gil-Wel Manufacturing Company, **17** 440

Gilbane, Inc., 34 191–93

Gilbert & John Greenall Limited, **21** 246

Gilbert-Ash Ltd., **I** 588

Gilbert Lane Personnel, Inc., **9** 326

Gilde-Verlag, **IV** 590

Gilde-Versicherung AG, **III** 400

Gildon Metal Enterprises, **7** 96

Gilkey Bros. *See* Puget Sound Tug and Barge Company.

Gill and Duffus, **II** 500

Gill Industries, **II** 161

Gill Interprovincial Lines, **27** 473

Gillett Holdings, Inc., 7 199–201; 11 543, 545; **43** 437–38

The Gillette Company, III 27–30, 114, 215; **IV** 722; **8** 59–60; **9** 381, 413; **17** 104–05; **18** 60, 62, 215, 228; **20 249–53 (upd.); 23** 54–57; **26** 334; **28** 247; **39** 336

Gilliam Furniture Inc., **12** 475

Gilliam Manufacturing Co., **8** 530

Gilman & Co., **III** 523

Gilman Fanfold Corp., Ltd., **IV** 644

Gilman Paper Co., **37** 178

Gilmore Brother's, **I** 707

Gilmore Steel Corporation. *See* Oregon Steel Mills, Inc.

Gilroy Foods, **27** 299

Giltspur, **II** 587

Gimbel Brothers, Inc. *See* Saks Holdings, Inc.

Gimbel's Department Store, **I** 426–27; **8** 59; **22** 72

Gindick Productions, **6** 28

Ginn & Co., **IV** 672; **19** 405

Ginnie Mae. *See* Government National Mortgage Association.

Gino's, **III** 103

Gino's East, **21** 362

Ginsber Beer Group, **15** 47; **38** 77

Giorgio Armani S.p.A., 45 180–83

Giorgio Beverly Hills, Inc., **26** 384

Giorgio, Inc., **III** 16; **19** 28

Girard Bank, **II** 315–16; **44** 280

Girbaud, **17** 513; **31** 261

Girl Scouts of the USA, 35 193–96

Girling, **III** 556

Giro Sport Designs International Inc., **16** 53; **44** 53–54

Girod, **19** 50

Girsa S.A., **23** 170

Girvin, Inc., **16** 297

Gist-Brocades Co., **III** 53; **26** 384

The Gitano Group, Inc., 8 219–21; 20 136 **25** 167; **37** 81

Givaudan SA, 43 190–93

GJM International Ltd., **25** 121–22

GK Technologies Incorporated, **10** 547

GKH Partners, **29** 295

GKN plc, III 493–96, 554, 556; **38 208–13 (upd.); 42** 47; **47** 7, 9, 279–80

Glaceries de Saint-Roch, **III** 677; **16** 121

Glaces de Boussois, **II** 474–75

Glacier Bancorp, Inc., 35 197–200

Glacier Park Co., **10** 191

Glacier Water Services, Inc., 47 155–58

Gladieux Corp., **III** 103

Glamar Group plc, **14** 224
Glamor Shops, Inc., **14** 93
Glanbia Group, **38** 196, 198
Glasrock Home Health Care, **I** 316; **25** 81
Glass Containers Corp., **I** 609–10
Glass Fibres Ltd., **III** 726
Glasstite, Inc., **33** 360–61
GlasTec, **II** 420
Glastron. *See* Genmar Holdings, Inc.
Glatfelter Wood Pulp Company, **8** 413
Glaverbel, **III** 667
Glaxo Holdings plc, I 639–41, 643, 668,
    675, 693; **III** 66; **6** 346; **9 263–65**
    (upd.); **10** 551; **11** 173; **20** 39; **26** 31;
    34 284; **38** 365
GlaxoSmithKline plc, 46 201–08 (upd.)
Gleason Corporation, 24 184–87
Glen & Co, **I** 453
Glen Alden Corp., **15** 247
Glen Cove Mutual Insurance Co., **III** 269
Glen-Gery Corporation, **14** 249
Glen Iris Bricks, **III** 673
Glen Line, **6** 416
Glencairn Ltd., **25** 418
Glendale Federal Savings, **IV** 29
The Glenlyte Group, **29** 469
Glenlyte Thomas Group LLC, **29** 466
Glenn Advertising Agency, **25** 90
Glenn Pleass Holdings Pty. Ltd., **21** 339
Glens Falls Insurance Co., **III** 242
GLF-Eastern States Association, **7** 17
The Glidden Company, I 353; 8 222–24;
    21 545
Glimcher Co., **26** 262
Glitsch International, Inc., **6** 146; **23** 206,
    208
Global Access, **31** 469
Global Apparel Sourcing Ltd., **22** 223
Global Communications of New York,
    Inc., **45** 261
Global Crossing Ltd., 32 216–19
Global Energy Group, **II** 345
Global Engineering Company, **9** 266
Global Health Care Partners, **42** 68
Global Industries, Ltd., 37 168–72
Global Information Solutions, **34** 257
Global Interactive Communications
    Corporation, **28** 242
Global Marine Inc., 9 266–67; 11 87
Global Natural Resources, **II** 401; **10** 145
Global Outdoors, Inc., 49 173–76
Global Telesystems Ltd. *See* Global
    Crossing Ltd.
Global Transport Organization, **6** 383
Global Vacations Group. *See* Classic
    Vacation Group, Inc.
Global Van Lines. *See* Allied Worldwide,
    Inc.
GlobalCom Telecommunications, Inc., **24**
    122
GlobaLex, **28** 141
GlobalSantaFe Corporation, 48 187–92
    (upd.)
Globe & Rutgers Insurance Co., **III**
    195–96
Globe Business Furniture, **39** 207
Globe Co. **I** 201
Globe Electric Co., **III** 536
Globe Feather & Down, **19** 304
Globe Files Co., **I** 201
Globe Grain and Milling Co., **II** 555
Globe Industries, **I** 540
Globe Insurance Co., **III** 350

Globe Life Insurance Co., **III** 187; **10** 28;
    38 15
Globe National Bank, **II** 261
Globe Newspaper Co., **7** 15
Globe Pequot Press, **36** 339, 341
Globe Petroleum Ltd., **IV** 401
Globe Steel Abrasive Co., **17** 371
Globe Telegraph and Trust Company, **25**
    99
Globe-Union, **III** 536; **26** 229
Globe-Wernicke Co., **I** 201
Globelle Corp., **43** 368
Globetrotter Communications, **7** 199
Globo, **18** 211
Glock Ges.m.b.H., 42 154–56
Gloria Jean's Gourmet Coffees, **20** 83
La Gloria Oil and Gas Company, **7** 102
Gloria Separator GmbH Berlin, **III** 418
Glosser Brothers, **13** 394
Gloster Aircraft, **I** 50; **III** 508; **24** 85
Gloucester Cold Storage and Warehouse
    Company, **13** 243
Glovatorium, **III** 152; **6** 266; **30** 339
Glowlite Corporation, **48** 359
Glycomed Inc., **13** 241; **47** 222
Glyn, Mills and Co., **II** 308; **12** 422
GM. *See* General Motors Corp.
GM Hughes Electronics Corporation, II
    32–36; 10 325. *See also* Hughes
    Electronics Corporation.
GMARA, **II** 608
GMFanuc Robotics, **III** 482–83
GMR Properties, **21** 257
GNB International Battery Group, **10** 445
GND Holdings Corp., **7** 204; **28** 164
GNMA. *See* Government National
    Mortgage Association.
Gnôme & Rhône, **46** 369
The Go-Ahead Group Plc, 28 155–57
Go Fly Ltd., **39** 128
Go-Gro Industries, Ltd., **43** 99
Go Sport. *See* Groupe Go Sport S.A.
Go-Video, Inc. *See* Sensory Science
    Corporation.
Goal Systems International Inc., **10** 394
Godfather's Pizza Incorporated, II
    556–57; **11** 50; **12** 123; **14** 351; **17** 86;
    25 179–81
Godfrey Co., **II** 625
Godfrey L. Cabot, Inc., **8** 77
Godiva Chocolatier, **II** 480; **26** 56
Godo Shusei, **III** 42
Godsell, **10** 277
Godtfred Kristiansen, **13** 310–11
Goebel & Wetterau Grocery Co., **II** 681
Goelitz Confectionary. *See* Herman
    Goelitz, Inc.
Goering Werke, **II** 282
Göhner AG, **6** 491
Gokey Company, **10** 216; **28** 339
Gold Bond Stamp Company, **6** 363–64; **22**
    125
Gold Crust Bakeries, **II** 465
Gold Dust Corp., **II** 497
Gold Exploration and Mining Co. Limited
    Partnership, **13** 503
Gold Fields of South Africa Ltd., I 423;
    IV 91, **94–97**
Gold Kist Inc., 7 432; **17 207–09; 26**
    166–68
Gold Lance Inc., **19** 451–52
Gold Lion, **20** 263
Gold Prospectors' Association of America,
    49 173

Gold Seal, **II** 567
Gold Star Foods Co., **IV** 410
Gold's Gym Enterprises, **25** 450
Goldblatt Bros., **IV** 135
Goldblatt's Department Stores, **15** 240–42
Golden Bear International, **33** 103; **42** 433;
    45 300
Golden Belt Manufacturing Co., 16
    241–43
Golden Books Family Entertainment,
    Inc., 28 158–61
Golden Circle Financial Services, **15** 328
Golden Corral Corporation, 10 331–33
Golden Eagle Exploration, **IV** 566–67
Golden Enterprises, Inc., 26 163–65
Golden Gate Airlines, **25** 421
Golden Grain Macaroni Co., **II** 560; **12**
    411; **30** 219; **34** 366
Golden Hope Rubber Estate, **III** 697, 699
Golden Moores Finance Company, **48** 286
Golden Nugget, Inc. *See* Mirage Resorts,
    Incorporated.
Golden Ocean Group, **45** 164
Golden Partners, **10** 333
Golden Peanut Company, **17** 207
Golden Poultry Company, **26** 168
Golden Press, Inc., **13** 559–61
Golden Sea Produce, **10** 439
Golden Skillet, **10** 373
Golden State Bank, **II** 348
Golden State Foods Corporation, 32
    220–22
Golden State Newsprint Co. Inc., **IV** 296;
    19 226; **23** 225
Golden State Sanwa Bank, **II** 348
Golden State Vintners, Inc., 33 172–74
Golden Tulip International, **I** 109
Golden West Financial Corporation, 47
    159–61
Golden West Homes, **15** 328
Golden West Publishing Corp., **38** 307–08
Golden Wonder, **II** 500; **III** 503
Golden Youth, **17** 227
Goldenberg Group, Inc., **12** 396
Goldenlay Eggs, **II** 500
Goldfield Corp., **12** 198
Goldfine's Inc., **16** 36
Goldkuhl & Broström, **III** 419
Goldline Laboratories Inc., **11** 208
Goldman, Sachs & Co., II 11, 268, 326,
    361, **414–16**, 432, 434, 448; **III** 80, 531;
    IV 611; **9** 378, 441; **10** 423; **12** 405; **13**
    95, 448, 554; **15** 397; **16** 195; **20**
    254–57 (upd.), 258; **21** 146; **22** 427–28;
    26 456; **27** 317; **29** 508; **36** 190–91; **38**
    289, 291
Goldner Hawn Johnson & Morrison Inc.,
    48 412
Goldome Savings Bank, **11** 110; **17** 488
Goldsbrough Mort & Co., **I** 437
Goldsmith's, **9** 209
Goldstar Co., Ltd., II 5, 53–54; **III** 517;
    7 233; **12 211–13; 13** 213; **30** 184; **43**
    428
Goldwell, **III** 38
Goldwin Golf, **45** 76
Goldwyn Films. *See* Metro-Goldwyn-
    Mayer Inc.
Goleta National Bank, **33** 5
Golf Day, **22** 517
The Golub Corporation, 26 169–71
Gomoljak, **14** 250
Gonnella Baking Company, 40 211–13
Good Foods, Inc., **II** 497

The Good Guys!, Inc., 10 334–35; 30 224–27 (upd.)
The Good Humor-Breyers Ice Cream Company, II 533; 14 203–05; 15 222; 17 140–41; 32 474, 476
Good Natural Café, 27 481
Good Times, Inc., 8 303
Good Vibrations, Inc., 28 345
Good Weather International Inc., III 221; 14 109
Goodbody & Company, II 425; 13 341; 22 428
Goodbody James Capel, 16 14
Goodby, Berlin & Silverstein, 10 484
Goodebodies, 11 41
Gooderham and Worts, I 216, 263–64
Goodlass, Wall & Co., III 680–81
Goodman Bros. Mfg. Co., 14 436
Goodman Fielder, 44 137
Goodman Fielder, Wattie's, Ltd., II 565; 7 577
Goodman Holding Company, 42 157–60
GoodMark Foods, Inc., 26 172–74
Goodrich Corporation, 46 209–13 (upd.)
Goodrich Oil Co., IV 365
Goodrich, Tew and Company, V 231
Goodrich Tire Company, V 240–41; 6 27
Goodson Newspaper Group, 29 262
GoodTimes Entertainment Ltd., 31 238; 48 193–95
Goodwill Industries International, Inc., 15 511; 16 244–46
Goodwin & Co., 12 108
Goodwin, Dannenbaum, Littman & Wingfield, 16 72
Goody Products, Inc., 12 214–16
Goody's Family Clothing, Inc., 20 265–67
The Goodyear Tire & Rubber Company, I 21; II 304; III 452; V 244–48; 8 81, 291–92, 339; 9 324; 10 445; 15 91; 16 474; 19 221, 223, 455; 20 259–64 (upd.); 21 72–74
Gordon A. Freisen, International, III 73
Gordon B. Miller & Co., 7 256; 25 254
Gordon Capital Corp., II 245
Gordon Food Service Inc., 8 225–27; 39 179–82 (upd.)
Gordon Investment Corp., II 245
Gordon Jewelry Corporation, 16 559, 561; 40 472
Gordon Manufacturing Co., 11 256
Gordon Publications, IV 610
Gordon S. Black Corporation, 41 197–98
Gordon-Van Cheese Company, 8 225
Gordy Company, 26 314
Gore Newspapers Company, IV 683; 22 521
Gorges Foodservice, Inc., 14 516
Gorham Silver, 12 313
Gorilla Sports Club, 25 42
Gorman Eckert & Co., 27 299
The Gorman-Rupp Company, 18 201–03
Gormully & Jeffrey, IV 660
Gorton's, II 502; 10 323; 13 243–44
The Gosho Co. See Kanematsu Corporation.
Goss Holdings, Inc., 43 194–97
Gotaas-Larsen Shipping Corp., 6 368; 27 91
Götabanken, II 303, 353
Göteborgs Handelsbank, II 351
Göteborgs Handelskompani, III 425

Gothenburg Light & Power Company, 6 580
Gothenburg Tramways Co., II 1
Gott Corp., III 614; 21 293
Gottleib Group, 38 437
Gottschalks, Inc., 18 204–06; 26 130
Goulard and Olena, I 412
Gould Electronics, Inc., III 745; 11 45; 13 127, 201; 14 206–08; 21 43
Goulding Industries Ltd., IV 295; 19 225
Goulds Pumps Inc., 24 188–91
Gourmet Award Foods, 29 480–81
Gourmet Foods, II 528
Government Bond Department, 9 369
Government Employees Insurance Company. See GEICO Corporation.
Government National Mortgage Assoc., II 410
Government Technology Services Inc., 45 69
Governor and Company of Adventurers of England. See Hudson's Bay Company.
The Governor and Company of the Bank of Scotland, II 422; III 360; V 166; 10 336–38
Goya Foods Inc., 22 245–47; 24 516
GP Group Acquisition Limited Partnership, 10 288; 27 41–42
GPAA. See Gold Prospectors' Association of America.
GPE. See General Precision Equipment Corporation.
GPI. See General Parts Inc.
GPM Gas Corporation, 40 357–58
GPS Pool Supply, 29 34
GPT, 15 125
GPU. See General Public Utilities Corporation.
GPU, Inc., 27 182–85 (upd.)
Graber Industries, Inc., V 379; 19 421
Grace. See W.R. Grace & Co.
Grace Drilling Company, 9 365
Grace-Sierra Horticultural Products Co., 22 475
Graco Inc., 19 178–80
Gradco Systems, Inc., 6 290
Gradiaz, Annis & Co., 15 138
Gradmann & Holler, III 283
Graef & Schmidt, III 54
Graf, 23 219
Graf Bertel Dominique/New York, 6 48
Graficas e Instrumentos S.A., 13 234
Graficas Monte Alban S.A., 47 326
Graftek Press, Inc., 26 44
Graham Brothers, 27 267, 269
Graham Container Corp., 8 477
Graham Page, III 568; 20 359
Grahams Builders Merchants, I 429
Gralla, IV 687
Grameen Bank, 31 219–22
Gramercy Pictures, 23 391
Gramophone Company, 22 192
Grampian Electricity Supply Company, 13 457
Gran Central Corporation, 8 487
Gran Dorado, 48 315
Granada Group PLC, II 70, 138–40; 17 353; 24 192–95 (upd.), 269; 25 270; 32 404
Granada Royale Hometels, 9 426
Granaria Holdings B.V., 23 183
GranCare, Inc., 14 209–11; 25 310
Grand Bazaar Innovations Bon Marché, 13 284; 26 159–60

Grand Casinos, Inc., 20 268–70; 21 526; 25 386
Grand Department Store, 19 510
Grand Hotel Krasnapolsky N.V., 23 227–29
Grand Magasin de Nouveautés Fournier d'Annecy, 27 93
Grand Metropolitan plc, I 247–49, 259, 261; II 555–57, 565, 608, 613–15; 9 99; 13 391, 407, 409; 14 212–15 (upd.); 15 72; 17 69, 71; 20 452; 21 401; 26 58; 33 276; 34 121; 35 438; 42 223; 43 215. See also Diageo plc.
Grand Ole Opry. See Gaylord Entertainment Company.
Grand Prix Association of Long Beach, Inc., 43 139–40
Grand Rapids Carpet Sweeper Company, 9 70
Grand Rapids Gas Light Company. See MCN Corporation.
Grand Rapids Wholesale Grocery Company, 8 481
Grand Trunk Corp., 6 359–61
Grand Union Company, II 637, 662; 7 202–04; 8 410; 13 394; 16 249; 28 162–65 (upd.)
Grand Valley Gas Company, 11 28
Grand-Perret, 39 152–53
Grandes Superficies S.A., 23 247
Grandmet USA, I 248
Les Grands Magasins Au Bon Marché, 26 159–60
Grands Magasins L. Tietz, V 103
GrandVision S.A., 43 198–200
Grandy's, 15 345
Granger Associates, 12 136
Gränges, III 480; 22 27
Granite Broadcasting Corporation, 42 161–64
Granite City Steel Company, 12 353
Granite Furniture Co., 14 235
Granite Rock Company, 26 175–78
Granite State Bankshares, Inc., 37 173–75
Grant Oil Tool Co., III 569; 20 361
Grant Street National Bank, II 317; 44 280
Grantham, Mayo, Van Otterloo & Co. LLC, 24 407
Grantree Corp., 14 4; 33 398
Graphic Controls Corp., IV 678
Graphic Industries Inc., 25 182–84; 36 508
Graphic Research, Inc., 13 344–45
Graphic Services, III 166; 6 282
Graphics Systems Software, III 169; 6 285; 8 519
Graphite Oil Product Co., I 360
Graphix Zone, 31 238
Grass Valley Group, 8 518, 520
Grasselli Chemical Company, 22 225
Grasselli Dyestuffs Corp., I 337
Grasset, IV 617–18
Grasso Production Management Inc., 37 289
Grattan Plc, V 160; 29 356
The Graver Company, 16 357
Gray Communications Systems, Inc., 24 196–200
Gray Dawes & Co., III 522–23
Gray Drug Stores, III 745
Gray Dunn and Co., II 569
Gray Line, 24 118

Gray, Siefert & Co., Inc., **10** 44; **33** 259–60

Grayarc, **III** 157

Grayrock Capital, **I** 275

Grays Harbor Mutual Savings Bank, **17** 530

Greaseater, Ltd., **8** 463–64

Great Alaska Tobacco Co., **17** 80

Great American Bagel and Coffee Co., **27** 482

Great American Broadcasting Inc., **18** 65–66; **22** 131; **23** 257–58

Great American Cookie Company. *See* Mrs. Fields' Original Cookies, Inc.

Great American Entertainment Company, **13** 279; **48** 194

Great American First Savings Bank of San Diego, **II** 420

Great American Insurance Company, **48** 9

Great American Life Insurance Co., **III** 190–92

Great American Lines Inc., **12** 29

Great American Management and Investment, Inc., 8 228–31; **49** 130

Great American Reserve Insurance Co., **IV** 343; **10** 247

Great American Restaurants, **13** 321

The Great Atlantic & Pacific Tea Company, Inc., II 636–38, 629, 655–56, 666; **13** 25, 127, 237; **15** 259; **16** 63–64, **247–50 (upd.); 17** 106; **18** 6; **19** 479–80; **24** 417; **26** 463; **33** 434

Great Bagel and Coffee Co., **27** 480–81

Great Beam Co., **III** 690

Great Eastern Railway, **6** 424

Great 5¢ Store, **V** 224

Great Halviggan, **III** 690

Great Harvest Bread Company, 44 184–86

Great Lakes Bancorp, 8 232–33

Great Lakes Bankgroup, **II** 457

Great Lakes Carbon Corporation, **12** 99

Great Lakes Chemical Corp., I 341–42; 8 262; **14 216–18 (upd.)**

Great Lakes Corp., **IV** 136

Great Lakes Energy Corp., **39** 261

Great Lakes Pipe Line Co., **IV** 400, 575; **31** 470

Great Lakes Steel Corp., **IV** 236; **8** 346; **12** 352; **26** 528

Great Lakes Window, Inc., **12** 397

Great Land Seafoods, Inc., **II** 553

Great Northern, **III** 282

Great Northern Import Co., **I** 292

Great Northern Nekoosa Corp., **IV** 282–83, 300; **9** 260–61; **47** 148

Great Northern Railway Company, **6** 596

Great Plains Software Inc., **38** 432

Great Plains Transportation, **18** 226

Great Shoshone & Twin Falls Water Power Company, **12** 265

The Great Universal Stores plc, V 67–69; 15 83; **17** 66, 68; **19 181–84 (upd.); 41** 74, 76; **45** 152. *See also* GUS plc.

Great-West Lifeco Inc., III 260–61; 21 447. *See also* Power Corporation of Canada.

The Great Western Auction House & Clothing Store, **19** 261

Great Western Bank, **47** 160

Great Western Billiard Manufactory, **III** 442

Great Western Financial Corporation, 10 339–41

Great Western Foam Co., **17** 182

Great Western Railway, **III** 272

Great World Foods, Inc., **17** 93

Greatamerica Corp., **I** 489; **10** 419; **24** 303

Greater All American Markets, **II** 601; **7** 19

Greater New York Film Rental Co., **II** 169

Greater Washington Investments, Inc., **15** 248

Greb Industries Ltd., **16** 79, 545

Grebner GmbH, **26** 21

Grede Foundries, Inc., 38 214–17

Greeley Beef Plant, **13** 350

Greeley Gas Company, **43** 56–57

Green Acquisition Co., **18** 107

Green Bay Food Company, **7** 127

The Green Bay Packers, Inc., 32 223–26

Green Capital Investors L.P., **23** 413–14

Green Cross K.K., **I** 665

Green Giant, **II** 556; **13** 408; **14** 212, 214; **24** 140–41

Green Island Cement (Holdings) Ltd. Group, **IV** 694–95

Green Line Investor Services, **18** 553

Green Mountain Coffee, Inc., 31 227–30

Green Power & Light Company. *See* UtiliCorp United Inc.

Green River Electric Corporation, **11** 37

Green Thumb, **II** 562

Green Tree Financial Corporation, 11 162–63. *See also* Conseco, Inc.

The Greenalls Group PLC, 21 245–47

The Greenbrier Companies, 19 185–87

Greene King plc, 31 223–26

Greenfield Healthy Foods, **26** 58

Greenfield Industries Inc., **13** 8

Greenham Construction Materials, **38** 451–52

Greenleaf Corp., **IV** 203

Greenman Brothers Inc. *See* Noodle Kidoodle.

GreenPoint Financial Corp., 28 166–68

Greensboro Life Insurance Company, **11** 213

Greenville Insulating Board Corp., **III** 763

Greenville Tube Corporation, **21** 108

Greenwell Montagu Gilt-Edged, **II** 319; **17** 325

Greenwich Associates, **19** 117

Greenwich Capital Markets, **II** 311

Greenwood Mills, Inc., 14 219–21

Greenwood Publishing Group, **IV** 610

Greenwood Trust Company, **18** 478

Gregg Publishing Co., **IV** 636

Greif Bros. Corporation, 15 186–88

Greiner Engineering Inc., **45** 421

Grenfell and Colegrave Ltd., **II** 245

Gresham Insurance Company Limited, **24** 285

Gresham Life Assurance, **III** 200, 272–73

GretagMacbeth Holdings AG, **18** 291

Gretel's Pretzels, **35** 56

Grey Advertising, Inc., I 175, 623; **6** 26–28; **10** 69; **14** 150; **22** 396; **25** 166, 381

Grey United Stores, **II** 666

Grey Wolf, Inc., 43 201–03

Greyhound Corp., I 448–50; **II** 445; **6** 27; **8** 144–45; **10** 72; **12** 199; **16** 349; **22** 406, 427; **23** 173–74; **27** 480; **42** 394

Greyhound Lines, Inc., 32 227–31 (upd.); 48 319

Greyhound Temporary Services, **25** 432

Greylock Mills, **III** 213

GRiD Systems Corp., **II** 107

Griesheim Elektron, **IV** 140

Grieveson, Grant and Co., **II** 422–23

Griffin and Sons, **II** 543

Griffin Bacal, **25** 381

Griffin Land & Nurseries, Inc., 43 204–06

Griffin Pipe Products Co., **7** 30–31

Griffin Wheel Company, **7** 29–30

Griffon Corporation, 34 194–96

Griffon Cutlery Corp., **13** 166

Grigg, Elliot & Co., **14** 555

Grimes Aerospace, **22** 32

Grindlays Bank, **II** 189

Gringoir/Broussard, **II** 556

Grinnell Corp., III 643–45; **11** 198; **13** 245–47

Grip Printing & Publishing Co., **IV** 644

Grisewood & Dempsey, **IV** 616

Grist Mill Company, 15 189–91; **22** 338

Gristede Brothers, **23** 407; **24** 528–29

Gristede's Sloan's, Inc., 31 231–33

GRM Industries Inc., **15** 247–48

Grocer Publishing Co., **IV** 638

Grocery Store Products Co., **III** 21

Grocery Warehouse, **II** 602

Groen Manufacturing, **III** 468

Grogan-Cochran Land Company, **7** 345

Grolier Inc., IV 619; **16** 251–54; **43** 207–11 (upd.)

Grolier Interactive, **41** 409

Groot-Noordhollandsche, **III** 177–79

Groovy Beverages, **II** 477

Gross Brothers Laundry. *See* G&K Services, Inc.

Gross Townsend Frank Hoffman, **6** 28

Grosset & Dunlap, Inc., **II** 144; **III** 190–91

Grosskraftwerk Franken AG, **23** 47

Grossman's Inc., 13 248–50

Grossmith Agricultural Industries, **II** 500

Grosvenor Marketing Co., **II** 465

Groton Victory Yard, **I** 661

Ground Round, Inc., 21 248–51

Ground Services Inc., **13** 49

Group Arnault, **32** 146

Group 4 Falck A/S, 42 165–68, 338

Group Health Cooperative, 41 181–84

Group Hospitalization and Medical Services, **10** 161

Group Lotus, **13** 357

Group Maeva SA, **48** 316

Group Maintenance America Corp. *See* Encompass Services Corporation.

Group Schneider S.A., **20** 214

Groupe AB, **19** 204

Groupe AG, **III** 201–02

Groupe Air France, 6 92–94. *See also* Air France *and* Societe Air France.

Groupe Ancienne Mutuelle, **III** 210–11

Groupe André, 17 210–12

Groupe Axime, **37** 232

Groupe Barrière SA, **48** 199

Groupe Barthelmey, **III** 373

Groupe Bisset, **24** 510

Groupe Bollore, **37** 21

Groupe Bruxelles Lambert, **26** 368

Groupe Bull, **10** 563–64; **12** 246; **21** 391; **34** 517. *See also* Compagnie des Machines Bull.

Groupe Casino. *See* Etablissements Economiques de Casino Guichard, Perrachon et Cie, S.C.A.

Groupe Castorama-Dubois Investissements, 23 230–32

Groupe Danone, 14 150; 32 232–36 (upd.)

Le Groupe Darty, **24** 266, 270

Groupe Dassault Aviation SA, 26 179–82 (upd.); 42 373, 376

Groupe de la Cité, IV 614–16, 617

Groupe de la Financière d'Angers, **IV** 108

Groupe DMC (Dollfus Mieg & Cie), 27 186–88

Groupe Fournier SA, 44 187–89

Groupe Go Sport S.A., 39 183–85

Groupe Guillin SA, 40 214–16

Groupe Jean-Claude Darmon, 44 190–92

Groupe Jean Didier, **12** 413

Groupe Jean-Paul Gaultier, **34** 214

Groupe Lagardère S.A., **15** 293; **21** 265, 267

Groupe Lapeyre S.A., 33 175–77

Groupe Legris Industries, 23 233–35

Groupe Les Echos, 25 283–85

Groupe Partouche SA, 48 196–99

Groupe Pechiney, **33** 89

Groupe Pinault-Printemps-Redoute, **19** 306, 309; **21** 224, 226

Groupe Poron, **35** 206

Groupe Promodès S.A., 19 326–28

Groupe Rallye, **39** 183–85

Groupe Rothschild, **22** 365

Groupe Rougier SA, 21 438–40

Groupe Roussin, **34** 13

Groupe Salvat, **IV** 619

Groupe SEB, 35 201–03

Groupe Sidel S.A., 21 252–55

Groupe Victoire, **III** 394

Groupe Vidéotron Ltée., 20 271–73

Groupe Yves Saint Laurent, 23 236–39

Groupe Zannier S.A., 35 204–07

Groupement des Exploitants Pétroliers, **IV** 545

Groupement des Mousquetaires. *See* ITM Entreprises SA.

Groupement Français pour l'Investissement Immobilier, **42** 153

Groupement Laitier du Perche, **19** 50

Groupement pour le Financement de la Construction. *See* Gecina SA.

GroupMAC. *See* Encompass Services Corporation.

Groux Beverage Corporation, **11** 451

Grove Manufacturing Co., **I** 476–77; **9** 393

Grow Biz International, Inc., 18 207–10

Grow Group Inc., 12 217–19, 387–88

Growing Healthy Inc., **27** 197; **43** 218

Growmark, **I** 421; **11** 23

Growth International, Inc., **17** 371

Grubb & Ellis Company, 21 256–58

Gruene Apotheke, **I** 681

Gruma, S.A. de C.V., 19 192; **31 234–36**

Grumman Corp., I 58–59, **61–63,** 67–68, 78, 84, 490, 511; **7** 205; **8** 51; **9** 17, 206–07, 417, 460; **10** 316–17, 536; **11 164–67 (upd.),** 363–65, 428; **15** 285; **28** 169

Grün & Bilfinger A.G., **I** 560–61

Grundig AG, I 411; **II** 80, 117; **12** 162; **13** 402–03; **15** 514; **27 189–92; 48** 383

Grunenthal, **I** 240

Gruner + Jahr AG & Co., **IV** 590, 593; **7** 245; **15** 51; **20** 53; **22** 442; **23** 85

Gruntal & Co., L.L.C., III 263; **20 274–76**

Gruntal Financial Corp., **III** 264

Grupo Acerero del Norte,

Grupo Acerero del Norte, S.A. de C.V., **22** 286; **42** 6

Grupo Aeropuerto del Sureste, S.A. de C.V., 48 200–02

Grupo Bimbo, S.A. de C.V., **31** 236

Grupo Bufete. *See* Bufete Industrial, S.A. de C.V.

Grupo Cabal S.A., **23** 166

Grupo Campi, S.A. de C.V., **39** 230

Grupo Carso, S.A. de C.V., 14 489; **21 259–61**

Grupo Casa Saba, S.A. de C.V., 39 186–89

Grupo Corvi S.A. de C.V., **7** 115; **25** 126

Grupo Cruzcampo S.A., **34** 202

Grupo Cuervo, S.A. de C.V., **31** 91–92

Grupo Cydsa, S.A. de C.V., 39 190–93

Grupo de Ingenieria Ecologica, **16** 260

Grupo Dina. *See* Consorcio G Grupo Dina, S.A. de C.V.

Grupo DST, **41** 405–06

Grupo Elektra, S.A. de C.V., 39 194–97

Grupo Ferrovial, S.A., 40 217–19

Grupo Financiero Banamex-Accival, **27** 304

Grupo Financiero Inbursa, **21** 259

Grupo Financiero Inverlat, S.A., **39** 188

Grupo Financiero Serfin, S.A., 19 188–90, 474; **36** 63

Grupo Gigante, S.A. de C.V., 34 197–99

Grupo Hecali, S.A., **39** 196

Grupo Herdez, S.A. de C.V., 35 208–10

Grupo Hermes, **24** 359

Grupo IMSA, S.A. de C.V., 44 193–96

Grupo Industrial Alfa, S.A. de C.V., **44** 332. *See also* Alfa, S.A. de C.V.

Grupo Industrial Atenquique, S.A. de C.V., **37** 176

Grupo Industrial Bimbo, 19 191–93; 29 338

Grupo Industrial Durango, S.A. de C.V., 37 176–78

Grupo Industrial Maseca S.A. de C.V. (Gimsa). *See* Gruma, S.A. de C.V.

Grupo Irsa, **23** 171

Grupo Mexico, S.A. de C.V., 40 220–23, 413

Grupo Modelo, S.A. de C.V., 29 218–20

Grupo Nacional Provincial, **22** 285

Grupo Pipsamex S.A., **37** 178

Grupo Protexa, **16** 210

Grupo Pulsar. *See* Pulsar Internacional S.A.

Grupo Quan, **19** 192–93

Grupo Salinas, **39** 196

Grupo Sanborns S.A. de C.V., **35** 118

Grupo TACA, 38 218–20

Grupo Televisa, S.A., 9 429; **18 211–14; 19** 10; **24** 515–17; **39** 188, 398

Grupo Transportación Ferroviaria Mexicana, S.A. de C.V., 47 162–64

Grupo Tribasa, **34** 82

Grupo Tudor, **IV** 471

Grupo Xtra, **39** 186, 188

Grupo Zeta, **IV** 652–53; **7** 392

Gruppo Buffetti S.p.A., **47** 345–46

Gruppo Coin S.p.A., 41 185–87

Gruppo GFT, **22** 123

Gruppo IRI, **V** 325–27

Gryphon Development, **24** 237

Gryphon Holdings, Inc., 21 262–64

GSD&M Advertising, 44 197–200

GSG&T, **6** 495

GSG Holdings Ltd., **39** 87

GSI. *See* Geophysical Service, Inc.

GSI Acquisition Co. L.P., **17** 488

GSR, Inc., **17** 338

GSU. *See* Gulf States Utilities Company.

GT Bicycles, 26 183–85, 412

GT Interactive Software, 19 405; **31 237–41.** *See also* Infogrames Entertainment S.A.

GTE Corporation, II 38, 47, 80; **III** 475; **V 294–98; 9** 49, 171, 478–80; **10** 19, 97, 431; **11** 500; **14** 259, 433; **15 192–97 (upd.); 18** 74, 111, 543; **22** 19; **25** 20–21, 91; **26** 520; **27** 302, 305; **46** 373. *See also* British Columbia Telephone Company *and* Verizon Communications.

GTE Northwest Inc., **37** 124–26

GTECH Holdings, Inc., **27** 381

GTI Corporation, **29** 461–62

GTM-Entrepose, **23** 332

GTM Group, **43** 450, 452

GTO. *See* Global Transport Organization.

GTS Duratek, Inc., **13** 367–68

GTSI. *See* Government Technology Services Inc.

Guangzhou M. C. Packaging, **10** 130

Guangzhou Pearl River Piano Group Ltd., 49 177–79

Guaranty Bank & Trust Company, **13** 440

Guaranty Federal Bank, F.S.B., **31** 441

Guaranty Federal Savings & Loan Assoc., **IV** 343

Guaranty Properties Ltd., **11** 258

Guaranty Savings and Loan, **10** 339

Guaranty Trust Co., **II** 329–32, 428; **IV** 20; **16** 25; **22** 110; **36** 152

Guardforce Limited, **45** 378

Guardian, **III** 721

Guardian Bank, **13** 468

Guardian Federal Savings and Loan Association, **10** 91

Guardian Mortgage Company, **8** 460

Guardian National Bank, **I** 165; **11** 137

Guardian Refrigerator Company. *See* Frigidaire Home Products.

Guardian Royal Exchange Plc, III 350; **11 168–70; 33** 319

Gubor Schokoladen, **15** 221

Gucci Group N.V., **45** 343–44

Guccio Gucci, S.p.A., 12 281; **15 198–200; 27** 329

GUD Holdings, Ltd., **17** 106

Guelph Dolime, **IV** 74

Guerbet Group, 46 214–16

Guerdon Homes, Inc., **41** 19

Guerlain, 23 240–42; 33 272

Guernsey Banking Co., **II** 333

Guess, Inc., 15 201–03; 17 466; **23** 309; **24** 157; **27** 329

Guest, Keen and Nettlefolds plc. *See* GKN plc.

Guest Supply, Inc., 18 215–17

Gueyraud et Fils Cadet, **III** 703

Guidant Corp., **30** 316; **37** 39; **43** 351

Guideoutdoors.com Inc., **36** 446

Guilbert S.A., 42 169–71

Guild Press, Inc., **13** 559

Guild Wineries, **13** 134; **34** 89

Guilford Industries, **8** 270–72

Guilford Mills Inc., 8 234–36; 40 224–27 (upd.)

Guilford of Maine, Inc., **29** 246
Guilford Transportation Industries, Inc., **16** 348, 350
Guillemot Corporation, 41 188–91, 407, 409
Guillin. *See* Groupe Guillin SA
Guinness Mahon, **36** 231
Guinness Overseas Ltd., **25** 281
Guinness Peat Aviation, **10** 277; **36** 426
Guinness plc, **I** 239, 241, **250–52**, 268, 272, 282; **II** 428–29, 610; **9** 100, 449; **10** 399; **13** 454; **18** 62, 501; **29** 84; **33** 276; **36** 405–06. *See also* Diageo plc.
Guinness/UDV, 43 212–16 (upd.)
Guitar Center, Inc., 29 221–23
Gujarat State Fertilizer Co., **III** 513
Gulco Industries, Inc., **11** 194
Güldner Aschaffenburg, **I** 582
Gulf + Western Inc., I 418, **451–53**, 540; **II** 147, 154–56, 177; **III** 642, 745; **IV** 289, 672; **7** 64; **10** 482; **13** 121, 169, 470; **22** 210; **24** 33; **25** 328, 535; **33** 3; **41** 71
Gulf + Western Industries, **22** 122. *See also* Paramount Communications.
Gulf Air, **6** 63; **27** 25; **39** 137–38
Gulf Canada Ltd., **I** 216, 262, 264; **IV** 495, 721; **6** 478; **9** 391; **13** 557–58
Gulf Caribbean Marine Lines, **6** 383
Gulf Coast Sportswear Inc., **23** 65
Gulf Energy Development, **22** 107
Gulf Engineering Co. Ltd., **IV** 131
Gulf Exploration Co., **IV** 454
Gulf Island Fabrication, Inc., 44 201–03
Gulf Marine & Maintenance Offshore Service Company, **22** 276
Gulf Mobile and Northern Railroad, **I** 456
Gulf Mobile and Ohio Railroad, **I** 456; **11** 187
Gulf of Suez Petroleum Co., **IV** 412–14
Gulf Oil Chemical Co., **13** 502
Gulf Oil Corp., **I** 37, 584; **II** 315, 402, 408, 448; **III** 225, 231, 259, 497; **IV** 198, 287, 385–87, 392, 421, 450–51, 466, 470, 472–73, 476, 484, 508, 510, 512, 531, 538, 565, 570, 576; **17** 121–22; **21** 494; **24** 521; **25** 444; **33** 253
Gulf Plains Corp., **III** 471
Gulf Power Company, **38** 446, 448
Gulf Public Service Company, Inc, **6** 580; **37** 89
Gulf Resources & Chemical Corp., **15** 464
Gulf States Paper, **IV** 345
Gulf States Steel, **I** 491
Gulf States Utilities Company, 6 495–97; **12** 99
Gulf United Corp., **III** 194
GulfMark Offshore, Inc., 49 180–82
Gulfstream Aerospace Corporation, 7 205–06; **13** 358; **24** 465; **28 169–72 (upd.)**; **36** 190–91
Gulfstream Banks, **II** 336
Gulfwind Marine USA, **30** 303
Gulistan Holdings Inc., **28** 219
Gulton Industries Inc., **7** 297; **19** 31
Gummi Werke, **I** 208; **44** 218
Gump's, **7** 286
Gunder & Associates, **12** 553
Gunderson, Inc. *See* The Greenbrier Companies.
Gunfred Group, **I** 387
Gunite Corporation, **23** 306
The Gunlocke Company, 12 299; **13** 269; **23 243–45**

Gunnite, **27** 203
Gunns Ltd., **II** 482
Gunpowder Trust, **I** 379; **13** 379
Gunter Wulff Automaten, **III** 430
Gunther, S.A., **8** 477
Gupta, **15** 492
Gurneys, Birkbeck, Barclay & Buxton, **II** 235
Gurwitch Bristow Products, LLC, **49** 285
GUS plc, 47 165–70 (upd.)
Gusswerk Paul Saalmann & Sohne, **I** 582
Gustav Schickendanz KG, **V** 165
Gustavus A. Pfeiffer & Co., **I** 710
Gustin-Bacon Group, **16** 8
Gutehoffnungshütte Aktienverein AG, **III** 561, 563; **IV** 104, 201
Guthrie Balfour, **II** 499–500
Guthy-Renker Corporation, 32 237–40
Gutta Percha Co., **I** 428
Gutteridge, Haskins & Davey, **22** 138
Gutzeit. *See* W. Gutzeit & Co.
Guy Carpenter & Co., **III** 282
Guy Degrenne SA, 44 204–07
Guy Motors, **13** 286
Guy Pease Associates, **34** 248
Guy Salmon Service, Ltd., **6** 349
Guyenne et Gascogne, 23 246–48
Guyomarc'h, **39** 356
GW Utilities Ltd., **I** 264; **6** 478
Gwathmey Siegel & Associates Architects LLC, **II** 424; **13** 340; **26 186–88**
GWC. *See* General Waterworks Corporation.
GWK GmbH, **45** 378
GWR Group plc, 39 198–200
Gymboree Corporation, 15 204–06
Gynecare Inc., **23** 190
Gynetics, Inc., **26** 31
Gypsum, Lime, & Alabastine Canada Ltd., **IV** 271

H&D. *See* Hinde & Dauch Paper Company.
H&H Craft & Floral, **17** 322
H & H Plastics Co., **25** 312
H & R Block, Incorporated, 9 268–70; **25** 434; **27** 106, 307; **29 224–28 (upd.)**; **48** 234, 236
H.A. Job, **II** 587
H.B. Claflin Company, **V** 139
H.B. Fenn and Company Ltd., **25** 485
H.B. Fuller Company, 8 237–40; 32 254–58 (upd.)
H.B. Nickerson & Sons Ltd., **14** 339
H.B. Reese Candy Co., **II** 511
H.B. Tuttle and Company, **17** 355
H.B. Viney Company, Inc., **11** 211
H. Berlind Inc., **16** 388
H.C. Christians Co., **II** 536
H.C. Frick Coke Co., **IV** 573; **7** 550
H.C. Petersen & Co., **III** 417
H.C. Prange Co., **19** 511–12
H Curry & Sons. *See* Currys Group PLC.
H.D. Lee Company, Inc. *See* Lee Apparel Company, Inc.
H.D. Pochin & Co., **III** 690
H.D. Vest, Inc., 46 217–19
H. Douglas Barclay, **8** 296
H.E. Butt Grocery Company, 13 251–53; 32 259–62 (upd.); **33** 307
H.E. Moss and Company Tankers Ltd., **23** 161

H.F. Ahmanson & Company, **II 181–82**; **10 342–44 (upd.)**; **28** 167; **47** 160
H. Fairweather and Co., **I** 592
H.G. Anderson Equipment Corporation, **6** 441
H.H. Brown Shoe Company, **18** 60, **18** 62
H.H. Cutler Company, **17** 513
H.H. Robertson, Inc., **19** 366
H.H. West Co., **25** 501
H. Hackfeld & Co., **I** 417
H. Hamilton Pty, Ltd., **III** 420
H.I.G. Capital L.L.C., **30** 235
H.I. Rowntree and Co., **II** 568
H.J. Green, **II** 556
H.J. Heinz Company, **I** 30–31, 605, 612; **II** 414, 480, 450, **507–09**, 547; **III** 21; **7** 382, 448, 576, 578; **8** 499; **10** 151; **11 171–73 (upd.)**; **12** 411, 529, 531–32; **13** 383; **21** 55, 500–01; **22** 147; **25** 517; **27** 197–98; **33** 446–49; **36 253–57 (upd.)**; **43** 217–18
H.J. Justin & Sons. *See* Justin Industries, Inc.
H.K. Ferguson Company, **7** 355
H.K. Porter Company, Inc., **19** 152
H.L. Green Company, Inc., **9** 448
H.L. Judd Co., **III** 628
H.L. Yoh Company. *See* Day & Zimmerman, Inc.
H. Lewis and Sons, **14** 294
H. Lundbeck A/S, 44 208–11
H.M. Byllesby & Company, Inc., **6** 539
H.M. Goush Co., **IV** 677–78
H.M. Spalding Electric Light Plant, **6** 592
H. Miller & Sons, Inc., **11** 258
H N Norton Co., **11** 208
H.O. Houghton & Company, **10** 355
H.O. Systems, Inc., **47** 430
H-P. *See* Hewlett-Packard Co.
H.P. Foods, **II** 475
H.P. Hood, **7** 17–18
H.P. Smith Paper Co., **IV** 290
H.R. MacMillan Export Co., **IV** 306–08
H. Reeve Angel & Co., **IV** 300
H. Salt Fish and Chips, **13** 320
H.T. Cherry Company, **12** 376
H.V. McKay Proprietary, **III** 651
H.W. Heidmann, **I** 542
H.W. Johns Manufacturing Co., **III** 663, 706–08; **7** 291
H.W. Madison Co., **11** 211
H.W.S. Solutions, **21** 37
H.W. Wilson Company, **17** 152; **23** 440
H. Williams and Co., Ltd., **II** 678
Ha-Lo Industries, Inc., 27 193–95
Häagen-Dazs, **II** 556–57, 631; **10** 147; **14** 212, 214; **19** 116; **24** 140, 141
Haake-Beck Brauerei AG, **9** 86
Haas, Baruch & Co. *See* Smart & Final, Inc.
Haas Corp., **I** 481
Haas Publishing Companies, Inc., **22** 442
Haas Wheat & Partners, **15** 357
Habersham Bancorp, 25 185–87
Habirshaw Cable and Wire Corp., **IV** 177
Habitat for Humanity International, 36 258–61
Habitat/Mothercare PLC. *See* Storehouse PLC.
Hach Co., 14 309; **18 218–21**
Hachette Filipacchi Medias S.A., 21 265–67; **33** 310
Hachette S.A., **IV** 614–15, **617–19**, 675; **10** 288; **11** 293; **12** 359; **16** 253–54; **17**

399; **21** 266; **22** 441–42; **23** 476; **43** 210. *See also* Matra-Hachette S.A.

Hachmeister, Inc., **II** 508; **11** 172

Hacker-Pschorr Brau, **II** 242; **35** 331

Hackman Oyj Adp, 44 204, **212–15**

Hadco Corporation, 24 201–03

Hadleigh-Crowther, **I** 715

Haemocell, **11** 476

Haemonetics Corporation, 20 277–79

Hafez Insurance Co., **III** 242

Hagemeyer N.V., 18 180–82; **39 201–04**; **45** 426

Haggar Corporation, 19 194–96; 24 158

Haggen Inc., 38 221–23

Haggie, **IV** 91

Hägglunds Vehicle AB, **47** 7, 9

Hahn Automotive Warehouse, Inc., 24 204–06

Hahn Department Stores. *See* Allied Stores Corp.

Hahn, Inc., **17** 9

Haile Mines, Inc., **12** 253

The Hain Celestial Group, Inc., 43 217–20 (upd.)

Hain Food Group, Inc., I 514; **27 196–98; 36** 256

Hainaut-Sambre, **IV** 52

A.B. Hakon Swenson, **II** 639

Hakuhodo, Inc., 6 29–31, 48–49; **16** 167; **42 172–75 (upd.)**

Hakunetsusha & Company, **12** 483

HAL Inc., 6 104; **9 271–73**. *See also* Hawaiian Airlines, Inc.

Halcon International, **IV** 456

Hale and Dorr, **31** 75

Haleko Hanseatisches Lebensmittel Kontor GmbH, **29** 500

Halewood, **21** 246

Half Price Books, Records, Magazines Inc., 37 179–82

Halfords Ltd., **IV** 17, 19, 382–83; **24** 75

Halifax Banking Co., **II** 220

Halifax Timber, **I** 335

Halkin Holdings plc, **49** 338–39

Hall & Levine Agency, **I** 14

Hall and Co., **III** 737

Hall and Ham River, **III** 739

Hall Bros. Co., **IV** 620–21; **7** 23

Hall Containers, **III** 739

Hall Laboratories, Inc., **45** 209

Hall-Mark Electronics, **23** 490

Hallamore Manufacturing Co., **I** 481

La Halle aux Chaussures, **17** 210

Haller, Raymond & Brown, Inc., **II** 10

Halliburton Company, I 112; **III** 473, **497–500**, 617; **11** 505; **13** 118–19; **17** 417; **25 188–92 (upd.)**

Hallivet China Clay Co., **III** 690

Hallmark Cards, Inc., IV 620–21; 7 23–25; **12** 207, 209; **16 255–57 (upd.)**, 427; **18** 67, 69, 213; **21** 426–28; **22** 33, 36; **24** 44, 516–17; **25** 69, 71, 368; **28** 160; **29** 64; **39** 87; **40 228–32 (upd.)**; **45** 131

Hallmark Chemical Corp., **8** 386

Hallmark Investment Corp., **21** 92

Hallmark Residential Group, Inc., **45** 221

Halo Lighting, **30** 266

Haloid Company. *See* Xerox Corporation.

Halsam Company, **25** 380

Halsey, Stuart & Co., **II** 431; **III** 276

Halstead Industries, **26** 4

Halter Marine, **22** 276

Hamada Printing Press, **IV** 326

Hamashbir Lata'asiya, **II** 47; **25** 267

Hambrecht & Quist Group, **10** 463, 504; **26** 66; **27** 447; **31** 349

Hambro American Bank & Trust Co., **11** 109

Hambro Countrywide Security, **32** 374

Hambro Life Assurance Ltd., **I** 426; **III** 339

Hambros Bank, **II** 422; **16** 14; **27** 474; **43** 7

Hamburg-Amerikanische-Packetfahrt-Actien-Gesellschaft, **6** 397–98

Hamburg Banco, **II** 351

Hamburg-Amerika, **I** 542

Hamburger Flugzeubau GmbH., **I** 74

Hamelin Group, Inc., **19** 415

Hamer Hammer Service, Inc., **11** 523

Hamersley Holdings, **IV** 59–61

Hamil Textiles Ltd. *See* Algo Group Inc.

Hamilton Aero Manufacturing, **I** 47, 84; **10** 162

Hamilton Beach/Proctor-Silex Inc., 7 369–70; **16** 384; **17 213–15; 24** 435; **43** 289

Hamilton Blast Furnace Co., **IV** 208

Hamilton Brown Shoe Co., **III** 528

Hamilton Group Limited, **15** 478

Hamilton Industries, Inc., **25** 261

Hamilton Malleable Iron Co., **IV** 73; **24** 142

Hamilton National Bank, **13** 465

Hamilton Oil Corp., **IV** 47; **22** 107

Hamilton Standard, **9** 417

Hamilton Steel and Iron Co., **IV** 208

Hamilton/Hall-Mark, **19** 313

Hamish Hamilton, **IV** 659; **8** 526

Hammacher Schlemmer & Company, 21 268–70; 26 439–40

Hammamatsu Commerce Bank, **II** 291

Hammarplast, **13** 493

Hammarsforsens Kraft, **IV** 339

Hammerich & Lesser, **IV** 589

Hammermill Paper Co., **IV** 287; **15** 229; **23** 48–49; **47** 189

Hammers Plastic Recycling, **6** 441

Hammerson plc, 40 233–35

Hammerson Property Investment and Development Corporation PLC, IV 696–98; 26 420

Hammery Furniture Company, **14** 302–03

Hammes Co., **38** 482

Hamming-Whitman Publishing Co., **13** 559

Hammond Corp., **IV** 136

Hammond Lumber Co., **IV** 281; **9** 259

Hammond's, **II** 556

Hammonton Electric Light Company, **6** 449

Hamomag AG, **III** 546

Hampton Industries, Inc., 20 280–82

Hampton Inns, **9** 425–26

Hampton Roads Food, Inc., **25** 389

Hamworthy Engineering Ltd., **31** 367, 369

Han Kook Fertilizer, **I** 516

Hanbury, Taylor, Lloyd and Bowman, **II** 306

Hancock Fabrics, Inc., 16 197–99; **18 222–24**

Hancock Holding Company, 15 207–09

Hancock Jaffe Laboratories, **11** 460

Hancock Park Associates. *See* Leslie's Poolmart, Inc.

Hancock Textile Co., Inc., **27** 291

Hand in Hand, **III** 234

Handelsbank of Basel, **III** 375

Handelsfinanz Bank of Geneva, **II** 319; **17** 324

Handelsmaatschappij Montan N.V., **IV** 127

Handelsunion AG, **IV** 222

Handleman Company, 15 210–12

Handley Page Transport Ltd., **I** 50, 92–93; **24** 85

Handspring Inc., 49 183–86

Handy & Harman, 23 249–52

Handy Andy Home Improvement Centers, Inc., **16** 210; **26** 160–61

Handy Dan, **V** 75

Hanes Corp., **II** 572–73; **8** 202, 288; **15** 436; **25** 166

Hanes Holding Company, **11** 256; **48** 267

Hang Chong, **18** 114

Hang Seng Bank, **II** 298; **IV** 717

Hanger Orthopedic Group, Inc., 41 192–95

Haniel & Cie. GmbH, **27** 175

Hanil Development Company, **6** 98

Hanjin Group, **6** 98; **27 271–72**

Hankook Tyre Manufacturing Company, **V** 255–56; **19** 508

Hankuk Glass Industry Co., **III** 715

Hankyu Corporation, V 454–56; 23 253–56 (upd.)

Hankyu Department Stores, Inc., V 70–71

Hanley Brick, **14** 250

Hanmi Citizen Precision Industry, **III** 455

Hanna Andersson Corp., 49 187–90

Hanna-Barbera Cartoons Inc., 7 306; **18** 65; **23 257–59**, 387; **25** 313; **33** 432

Hanna Iron Ore Co., **IV** 236; **26** 528

Hanna Mining Co., **8** 346–47

Hanna Ore Mining Company, **12** 352

Hannaford Bros. Co., 12 220–22

Hannen Brauerei GmbH, **9** 100

Hannifin Corp., **III** 602

Hannover Papier, **49** 353

Hannoversche Bank, **II** 278

Hanover Bank, **II** 312–13

Hanover Direct, Inc., 36 262–65

Hanover Foods Corporation, 35 211–14

Hanover House, Inc., **24** 154

Hanovia Co., **IV** 78

Hanrstoffe-und Düngemittelwerk Saar-Lothringen GmbH, **IV** 197

Hans Grohe, **III** 570; **20** 362

Hansa Linie, **26 279–80**

Hanseco Reinsurance Co., **III** 343

Hansen Natural Corporation, 31 242–45

Hanson Industries, **44** 257

Hanson PLC, I 438, 475, 477; **III 501–03**, 506; **IV** 23, 94, 97, 169, 171, 173, 290; **7 207–10 (upd.)**; **13** 478–79; **17** 39–40, 325; **23** 296–97; **27** 287–88; **30 228–32 (upd.)**, 441; **37** 6–7, 205; **39** 345; **45** 332

Hansvedt Industries Inc., **25** 195

Hapag-Lloyd Ag, 6 397–99; 42 283

Happy Air Exchangers Ltd., **21** 499

Happy Eater Ltd., **III** 106

Happy Kids Inc., 30 233–35

Haralambos Beverage Corporation, **11** 451

Harald Quant Group, **III** 377

Harbert Corporation, 13 98; **14 222–23**

Harbison-Walker Refractories Company, III 472; **24 207–09**

Harbor Group, **41 262–63**

Harbor Tug and Barge Co., **6** 382

Harborlite Corporation, **10** 45

Harbour Group, **24** 16

Harco, Inc., **37** 31
Harcourt Brace and Co., IV 622; **12 223–26**
Harcourt Brace Jovanovich, Inc., II 133–34; **III** 118; **IV** 622–24, 642, 672; **7** 312; **12** 224; **13** 106; **14** 177; **19** 404; **25** 177
Harcourt General, Inc., 12 226; **20 283–87 (upd.)**; **25** 178; **49** 286
Harcros Chemical Group, **III** 699
Harcros Investment Trust Ltd., **III** 698–99
Hard Rock Cafe International, Inc., 12 227–29; **25** 387; **27** 201; **32 241–45 (upd.)**; **37** 191; **41** 308
Hardee's Food Systems Inc., **II** 679; **7** 430; **8** 564; **9** 178; **15** 345; **16** 95; **19** 93; **23** 505; **27** 16–18; **46** 98
Hardin Stockton, **21** 96
Harding Lawson Associates Group, Inc., 16 258–60
Hardinge, 25 193–95
Hardison & Stewart Oil, **IV** 569; **24** 519
Hardman Inc., **III** 699
Hardware Wholesalers Inc., **12** 8. *See also* Do it Best Corporation.
Hardwick Stove Company, **III** 573; **22** 349
Hardy Oil & Gas, **34** 75
Hardy Spicer, **III** 595
HARIBO GmbH & Co. KG, 44 216–19
Harima Shipbuilding & Engineering Co., Ltd., **I** 511, 534; **III** 513, 533; **12** 484
Harima Zosenjo, Ltd., **IV** 129
Harken Energy Corporation, **17** 169–70
Harland and Wolff Holdings plc, 19 197–200
Harlem Globetrotters, **7** 199, 335
Harlequin Enterprises Ltd., **IV** 587, 590, 617, 619, 672; **19** 405; **29** 470–71, 473
Harley-Davidson, Inc., III 658; **7 211–14**; **13** 513; **16** 147–49; **21** 153; **23** 299–301; **25** 22, **196–200 (upd.)**; **40** 31
Harleysville Group Inc., 37 183–86
Harlow Metal Co. Ltd., **IV** 119
Harman International Industries Inc., 15 213–15; **36** 101
Harmon Industries, Inc., 25 201–04
Harmon Publishing Company, **12** 231
Harmonic Inc., 43 221–23
Harmsworth Brothers, **17** 396
Harmsworth Publishing, **19** 118, 120
Harnischfeger Industries, Inc., I 186; **8 241–44**; **14** 56; **26** 355; **38 224–28 (upd.)**
Harold A. Wilson & Co., **I** 405
Harold's Stores, Inc., 22 248–50
Harp Lager Ltd., **15** 442; **35** 395, 397
Harper Group Inc., 12 180; **13** 20; **17 216–19**
Harper House, Inc. *See* Day Runner, Inc.
Harper Robinson and Company, **17** 163
HarperCollins Publishers, IV 652; **7** 389, 391; **14** 555–56; **15 216–18**; **23** 156, 210; **24** 546; **46** 196, 311
Harpers, Inc., **12** 298; **48** 245
Harpo Entertainment Group, 28 173–75; **30** 270
Harrah's Entertainment, Inc., 9 425–27; **16 261–63**; **27** 200; **43 224–28 (upd.)**
Harrell International, **III** 21; **22** 146
Harriman Co., **IV** 310; **19** 266
Harriman, Ripley and Co., **II** 407
Harris Abattoir Co., **II** 482
Harris Adacom Corporation B.V., **21** 239
Harris Bankcorp, **II** 211; **46** 55

Harris Corporation, II 37–39; **11** 46, 286, 490; **20 288–92 (upd.)**; **27** 364
Harris Daishowa (Australia) Pty., Ltd., **IV** 268
Harris-Emery Co., **19** 510
Harris Financial, Inc., **11** 482
Harris Interactive Inc., 41 196–99
Harris Laboratories, **II** 483; **14** 549
Harris Manufacturing Company, **25** 464
Harris Microwave Semiconductors, **14** 417
Harris Oil Company, **17** 170
Harris Pharmaceuticals Ltd., **11** 208
Harris Publications, **13** 179
Harris Publishing. *See* Bernard C. Harris Publishing Company, Inc.
Harris Queensway, **24** 269
Harris Teeter Inc., 23 260–62
Harris Transducer Corporation, **10** 319
Harrisburg National Bank and Trust Co., **II** 315–16
Harrison & Sons (Hanley) Ltd., **III** 681
Harrisons & Crosfield plc, III 696–700. *See also* Elementis plc.
Harrods Holdings, , 21 353; **45** 188; **47 171–74**
Harrow Stores Ltd., **II** 677
Harry and David. *See* Bear Creek Corporation.
Harry F. Allsman Co., **III** 558
Harry Ferguson Co., **III** 651
Harry N. Abrams, Inc., **IV** 677; **17** 486
Harry Winston Inc., 45 184–87
Harry's Farmers Market Inc., 23 263–66
Harry's Premium Snacks, **27** 197; **43** 218
Harsah Ceramics, **25** 267
Harsco Corporation, 8 245–47; **11** 135; **30** 471
Harshaw Chemical Company, **9** 154; **17** 363
Harshaw/Filtrol Partnership, **IV** 80
Hart Glass Manufacturing, **III** 423
Hart Press, **12** 25
Hart Schaffner & Marx. *See* Hartmarx Corporation.
Hart Son and Co., **I** 592
Harte & Co., **IV** 409; **7** 308
Harte-Hanks Communications, Inc., 17 220–22
Harter Bank & Trust, **9** 474–75
Hartford Container Company, **8** 359
Hartford Electric Light Co., **13** 183
Hartford Financial Services Group, **41** 64
Hartford Fire Insurance, **11** 198
Hartford Insurance Group, **I** 463–64; **22** 428
Hartford Machine Screw Co., **12** 344
Hartford National Bank and Trust Co., **13** 396
Hartford National Corporation, **13** 464, 466–67
Hartford Trust Co., **II** 213
Hartley's, **II** 477
Hartmann & Braun, **III** 566; **38** 299
Hartmann Fibre, **12** 377
Hartmann Luggage, **12** 313
Hartmarx Corporation, 8 248–50; **25** 258; **32 246–50 (upd.)**
The Hartstone Group plc, 14 224–26
The Hartz Mountain Corporation, 12 230–32; **46 220–23 (upd.)**
Harvard Private Capital Group Inc., **26** 500, 502
Harvard Sports, Inc., **19** 144
Harvard Table Tennis, Inc., **19** 143–44

Harvard Ventures, **25** 358
Harvest Day, **27** 291
Harvest International, **III** 201
Harvest Partners, Inc., **40** 300
Harvestore, **11** 5
Harvey Aluminum Inc., **I** 68; **22** 188
Harvey Benjamin Fuller, **8** 237–38
Harvey Group, **19** 312
Harvey Hotel Corporation, **23** 71, 73
Harvey Lumber and Supply Co., **III** 559
Harveys Casino Resorts, 27 199–201
Harwood Homes, **31** 386
Harza Engineering Company, 14 227–28
Has.net, **48** 402
Hasbro, Inc., III 504–06; **IV** 676; **7** 305, 529; **12** 168–69, 495; **13** 561; **16 264–68 (upd.)**; **17** 243; **18** 520–21; **21** 375; **25** 313, 380–81, 487–89; **28** 159; **34** 369; **43 229–34 (upd.)**
Haslemere Estates, **26** 420
Hasler Holding AG, **9** 32
Hassenfeld Brothers Inc., **III** 504
Hasten Bancorp, **11** 371
Hastings Entertainment, Inc., 29 229–31
Hastings Filters, Inc., **17** 104
Hastings Manufacturing Company, **17** 106
Hatch Grinding, **29** 86, 88
Hatersley & Davidson, **16** 80
Hatfield Jewelers, **30** 408
Hathaway Manfacturing Co., **III** 213
Hathaway Shirt Co., **I** 25–26
Hatteras Yachts Inc., **45** 175
Hattori Seiko Co., Ltd. *See* Seiko Corporation.
Hauser, Inc., 46 224–27
Hausted, Inc., **29** 451
Havas, SA, IV 616; **10** 195–96, **345–48**; **13** 203–04; **33 178–82 (upd.)**; **34** 83. *See also* Vivendi Universal Publishing
Haven Automation International, **III** 420
Haverty Furniture Companies, Inc., 31 246–49
Havertys, **39** 174
Haviland Candy Co., **15** 325
Hawaii National Bank, **11** 114
Hawaiian Airlines Inc., 9 271–73; **22 251–53 (upd.)**; **24** 20–22; **26** 339. *See also* HAL Inc.
Hawaiian Dredging & Construction Co., **I** 565–66
Hawaiian Electric Industries, Inc., 9 274–77
Hawaiian Fertilizer Co., **II** 490
Hawaiian Pineapple Co., **II** 491
Hawaiian Tug & Barge, **9** 276
Hawaiian Tuna Packers, **II** 491
Hawker Siddeley Group Public Limited Company, I 41–42, 50, 71, 470; **III 507–10**; **8** 51; **12** 190; **20** 311; **24** 85–86
Hawkeye Cablevision, **II** 161
Hawkins Chemical, Inc., 16 269–72
Hawley & Hazel Chemical Co., **III** 25
Hawley Group Limited, **12** 10
Hawley Products, **16** 20
Haworth Inc., 8 251–52; **27** 434; **39 205–08 (upd.)**
Hawthorn Company, **8** 287
Hawthorn-Mellody, **I** 446; **11** 25
Hawthorne Appliance and Electronics, **10** 9–11
Haxton Foods Inc., **21** 155
Hay Group, **I** 33; **42** 329–30
Hayakawa Electrical Industries, **II** 95–96

Hayakawa Metal Industrial Laboratory, **II** 95; **12** 447
Hayaku Zenjiro, **III** 408
Hayama Oil, **IV** 542
Hayashi Kane Shoten, **II** 578
Hayashikane Shoten K.K., **II** 578
Hayden Clinton National Bank, **11** 180
Hayden Publications, **27** 499
Hayden Stone, **II** 450; **9** 468
Hayes Conyngham & Robinson, **24** 75
Hayes Corporation, 24 210–14
Hayes Industries Inc., **16** 7
Hayes Lemmerz International, Inc., 27 202–04
Hayes Microcomputer Products, **9** 515
Hayes Wheel Company, **7** 258
Hayne, Miller & Swearingen, Inc., **22** 202
Hays Petroleum Services, **IV** 451
Hays Plc, 27 205–07
Hazard, **I** 328
HAZCO International, Inc., **9** 110
Hazel-Atlas Glass Co., **I** 599; **15** 128
Hazel Bishop, **III** 55
Hazelden Foundation, 28 176–79
Hazell Sun Ltd., **IV** 642; **7** 312
Hazeltine, Inc., **II** 20
Hazlenut Growers of Oregon, **7** 496–97
Hazleton Laboratories Corp., **30** 151
Hazlewood Foods plc, 32 251–53
Hazzard and Associates, **34** 248
HBO. *See* Home Box Office Inc.
HCA - The Healthcare Company, 35 215–18 (upd.)
HCI Holdings, **I** 264
HCL America, **10** 505
HCL Sybase, **10** 505
HCR Manor Care, **25** 306, 310
HCS Technology, **26** 496–97
HDM Worldwide Direct, **13** 204; **16** 168
HDR Inc., I 563; 48 203–05
HDS. *See* Heartland Express, Inc.
Head Sportswear International, **15** 368; **16** 296–97; **43** 374
Headrick Outdoor, **27** 280
Heads and Threads, **10** 43
Headway Corporate Resources, Inc., 40 236–38
Headway Technologies, Inc., **49** 392–93
Heal's, **13** 307
Heald Machine Co., **12** 67
Healey & Baker, **IV** 705
Healing Arts Publishing, Inc., **41** 177
Healix Health Services Inc., **48** 310
Health & Tennis Corp., **III** 431; **25** 40
Health and Diet Group, **29** 212
Health Care & Retirement Corporation, III 79; **22** 254–56; **25** 306, 310
Health Care International, **13** 328
Health Development Corp., **46** 432
Health Maintenance Organization of Pennsylvania. *See* U.S. Healthcare, Inc.
Health Maintenance Organizations, **I** 545
Health Management Center West, **17** 559
Health-Mor Inc. *See* HMI Industries.
Health O Meter Products Inc., 14 229–31; 15 307
Health Plan of America, **11** 379
Health Plan of Virginia, **III** 389
Health Products Inc., **I** 387
Health Risk Management, Inc., 24 215–17
Health Services, Inc., **10** 160
Health Systems International, Inc., 11 174–76; 25 527

Health Way, Inc., **II** 538
HealthAmerica Corp., **III** 84
Healthcare, L.L.C., **29** 412
HealthCare USA, **III** 84, 86
HealthCo International, Inc., **19** 290
Healthdyne, Inc., **17** 306–09; **25** 82
Healthmagic, Inc., **29** 412
HealthRider Corporation, **38** 238
HealthRite, Inc., **45** 209
Healthshares L.L.C, **18** 370
Healthsource Inc., **22** 143; **45** 104, 109
HealthSouth Corporation, 33 183–86 (upd.)
HealthSouth Rehabilitation Corporation, 14 232–34; 25 111
Healthtex, Inc., 17 223–25, 513
HealthTrust, **III** 80; **15** 112; **35** 215, 217
Healthy Choice, **12** 531
The Hearst Corporation, IV 582, 596, 608, **625–27; 12** 358–59; **19 201–204 (upd.); 21** 404; **22** 161; **32** 3; **46 228–32 (upd.)**
Hearthstone Insurance Co. of Massachusetts, **III** 203
Heartland Building Products, **II** 582
Heartland Components, **III** 519; **22** 282
Heartland Express, Inc., 13 550–51; 18 225–27
Heartland Homes, Inc., **41** 19
Heartland Industrial Partners L.P., **41** 94
Heartland Securities Corp., **32** 145
Heartstream Inc., **18** 423
Heat Transfer Pty. Ltd., **III** 420
Heatcraft Inc., **8** 320–22
Heath Co., **II** 124; **13** 573; **34** 516
Heath Steele Mines Ltd., **IV** 18
Heatilator Inc., **13** 269
Heavy Duty Parts, Inc., **19** 37
Hebrew National Kosher Foods, **III** 24
Hechinger Company, 12 233–36; 28 51
Hecker-H-O Co., **II** 497
Heckett Technology Services Inc., **8** 246–47
Heckler & Koch GmbH, **24** 88
Hecla Mining Company, 17 363; **20** 149, **293–96**
Heco Envelope Co., **IV** 282; **9** 261
Hede Nielsen A/S, **47** 219
Heekin Can Inc., 10 130; **13 254–56**
HEFCO, **17** 106
Hefei Rongshida Group Corporation, **22** 350
HEI Investment Corp., **9** 276
HEICO Corporation, 15 380; **30 236–38**
Heidelberger Druckmaschinen AG, III 701; **33** 346; **40 239–41**
Heidelberger Zement AG, 23 325–26; **31 250–53**
Heidelburger Drueck, **III** 301
Heidemij. *See* Arcadis NV.
Heidi Bakery, **II** 633
Heidrick & Struggles International, Inc., 14 464; **28 180–82**
Heights of Texas, fsb, **8** 437
Heil Company, **28** 103
Heil-Quaker Corp., **III** 654
Heileman Brewing Co. *See* G. Heileman Brewing Co.
Heilig-Meyers Company, 14 235–37; 23 412, 414; **40 242–46 (upd.)**
Heim-Plan Unternehmensgruppe, **25** 455
Heimstatt Bauspar AG, **III** 401
Heineken N.V., I 219, **256–58**, 266, 288; **II** 642; **13 257–59 (upd.); 14** 35; **17**

256; **18** 72; **21** 319; **25** 21–22; **26** 305; **34 200–04 (upd.)**
Heinkel Co., **I** 74
Heinrich Bauer North America, **7** 42–43
Heinrich Bauer Verlag, **23** 85–86
Heinrich Koppers GmbH, **IV** 89
Heinrich Lanz, **III** 463; **21** 173
Heinz Co. *See* H.J. Heinz Company.
Heinz Deichert KG, **11** 95
Heinz Italia S.p.A., **15** 221
Heisers Inc., **I** 185
Heisey Glasswork Company, **19** 210
Heiwa Sogo Bank, **II** 326, 361
Heizer Corp., III 109–11; **14** 13–15
HEL&P. *See* Houston Electric Light & Power Company.
Helados La Menorquina S.A., **22** 515
Helemano Co., **II** 491
Helen of Troy Corporation, 18 228–30
Helen's Arts & Crafts, **17** 321
Helena Rubenstein, Inc., **III** 24, 48; **8** 343–44; **9** 201–02; **14** 121; **30** 188; **35** 111; **46** 277
Helene Curtis Industries, Inc., I 403; **8 253–54; 18** 217; **22** 487; **28 183–85 (upd.); 32** 476
Heliotrope Studios, Inc., **39** 396
Helix Biocore, **11** 458
Hellefors Jernverk, **III** 623
Heller, Ehrman, White & McAuliffe, 41 200–02
Heller Financial, Inc., **7** 213; **16** 37; **25** 198
Hellman, Haas & Co. *See* Smart & Final, Inc.
Hellschreiber, **IV** 669
Helly Hansen ASA, 18 396; **25 205–07**
Helme Products, Inc., **15** 139
Helmerich & Payne, Inc., 18 231–33
Helmsley Enterprises, Inc., 9 278–80; 39 209–12 (upd.)
Helmut Delhey, **6** 428
Helmut Hardkopf Bunker GmbH, **7** 141
Help-U-Sell, Inc., **III** 304
Helvetia General, **III** 376
Helvetia Milk Condensing Co., **II** 486; **7** 428
Helvetia Schweizerische Feuerversicherungs-Gesellschaft St. Gallen, **III** 375
Hely Group, **IV** 294; **19** 225
Helzberg Diamonds, 18 60, 63; **40 247–49**
Hemelinger Aktienbrauerei, **9** 86
Hemex, **11** 458
Hemlo Gold Mines Inc., 9 281–82; 23 40, 42
Hemma, **IV** 616
A.B. Hemmings, Ltd., **II** 465
Henderson Brothers Holdings, Inc., **37** 225
Henderson-Union Electric Cooperative, **11** 37
Henderson's Industries, **III** 581
Henijean & Cie, **III** 283
Henkel KGaA, III 21, **31–34**, 45; **IV** 70; **9** 382; **13** 197, 199; **22** 145, 257; **30** 291; **34** 153, **205–10 (upd.)**
Henkel Manco Inc., 22 257–59
Henley Drilling Company, **9** 364
The Henley Group, Inc., I 416; **III** 511–12; **6** 599–600; **9** 298; **11** 435; **12** 325; **17** 20; **37** 158
Henlys Group plc, **35** 63, 65
Hennes & Mauritz AB, 29 232–34
Hennessy Company, **19** 272

Henney Motor Company, **12** 159
Henredon Furniture Industries, **III** 571; **11** 534; **20** 362; **39** 266
Henri Bendel Inc., **17** 203–04
Henry Broderick, Inc., **21** 96
Henry Denny & Sons, **27** 259
Henry Grant & Co., **I** 604
Henry Holt & Co., **IV** 622–23; **13** 105; **27** 223; **35** 451
Henry I. Siegel Co., **20** 136
Henry J. Kaiser Company, Ltd., **28** 200
Henry J. Tully Corporation, **13** 531
The Henry Jones Co-op Ltd., **7** 577
Henry Jones Foods, **I** 437–38, 592; **7** 182; **11** 212
Henry L. Doherty & Company, **IV** 391; **12** 542
Henry Lee Company, **16** 451, 453
Henry, Leonard & Thomas Inc., **9** 533
Henry Meadows, Ltd., **13** 286
Henry Modell & Company Inc., 32 263–65
Henry Pratt Company, **7** 30–31
Henry S. King & Co., **II** 307
Henry S. Miller Companies, **21** 257
Henry Schein, Inc., 29 298; **31 254–56**
Henry Tate & Sons, **II** 580
Henry Telfer, **II** 513
Henry Waugh Ltd., **I** 469; **20** 311
Henry Willis & Co. *See* Willis Corroon Group Plc.
Henthy Realty Co., **III** 190
HEPCO. *See* Hokkaido Electric Power Company Inc.
Hepworth plc, **44** 438
Her Majesty's Stationery Office, 7 215–18
Heraeus Holding GmbH, IV 98–100, 118
Herald and Weekly Times, **IV** 650, 652; **7** 389, 391
Herald Publishing Company, **12** 150
Heralds of Liberty, **9** 506
Herbalife International, Inc., 17 226–29; 18 164; **41 203–06 (upd.)**
Herbert Clough Inc., **24** 176
Herbert W. Davis & Co., **III** 344
Herby's Foods, **36** 163
Herco Technology, **IV** 680
Hercofina, **IV** 499
Hercules Filter, **III** 419
Hercules Inc., I 343–45, 347; **III** 241; **19** 11; **22 260–63 (upd.); 28** 195; **30** 36
Hercules Nut Corp., **II** 593
Hercules Offshore Drilling, **28** 347–48
Hereford Paper and Allied Products Ltd., **14** 430
Herff Jones, **II** 488; **25** 254
Heritage Bankcorp, **9** 482
Heritage Communications, **II** 160–61
Heritage Federal Savings and Loan Association of Huntington, **10** 92
Heritage House of America Inc., **III** 81
Heritage Life Assurance, **III** 248
Heritage Media Group, **25** 418
Heritage National Health Plan, **III** 464
Heritage Springfield $$Heritage Springfield, **14** 245
Herley Industries, Inc., 33 187–89
Herman Goelitz, Inc., 28 186–88
Herman Miller, Inc., 8 251–52, **255–57; 39** 205–07
Herman's World of Sports, **I** 548; **II** 628–29; **15** 470; **16** 457; **43** 385
Hermann Pfauter Group, **24** 186

Hermannshütte, **IV** 103, 105
Hermès International S.A., 34 211–14 (upd.); 49 83
Hermes Kreditversicherungsbank, **III** 300
Hermès S.A., 14 238–40
Herrburger Brooks P.L.C., **12** 297
Herrick, Waddell & Reed. *See* Waddell & Reed, Inc.
Herring-Hall-Marvin Safe Co. of Hamilton, Ohio, **7** 145
Hersey Products, Inc., **III** 645
Hershey Bank, **II** 342
Hershey Foods Corporation, I 26–27; **II** 478, 508, **510–12,** 569; **7** 300; **11** 15; **12** 480–81; **15** 63–64, **219–22 (upd.),** 323; **27** 38–40; **30** 208–09
Hertel AG, **13** 297
Hertford Industrial Estates, **IV** 724
Hertie Waren- und Kaufhaus GmbH, V 72–74; 19 234, 237
Herts & Beds Petroleum Co., **IV** 566
Herts Pharmaceuticals, **17** 450; **41** 375–76
The Hertz Corporation, I 130; **II** 90; **6** 52, 129, 348–50, 356–57, 392–93; **V** 494; **9 283–85; 10** 419; **11** 494; **16** 379; **21** 151; **22** 54, 56, 524; **24** 9, 409; **25** 143; **33 190–93 (upd.); 36** 215
Hertz-Penske Leasing. *See* Penske Corporation.
Hervillier, **27** 188
Heska Corporation, 39 213–16
Hespeler Hockey Inc., **22** 204
Hess Department Stores Inc., **16** 61–62; **19** 323–24; **41** 343
Hess Oil & Chemical Corp., **IV** 366
Hessische Berg- und Hüttenwerke AG, **III** 695
Hessische Landesbank, **II** 385–86
Hessische Ludwigs-Eisenbahn-Gesellschaft, **6** 424
Hesston Corporation, **13** 17; **22** 380
Hetteen Hoist & Derrick. *See* Polaris Industries Inc.
Heublein Inc., I 226, 246, 249, **259–61,** 281; **7** 266–67; **10** 180; **14** 214; **21** 314–15; **24** 140; **25** 177; **31** 92; **34** 89
Heuer. *See* TAG Heuer International SA.
Heuga Holdings B.V., **8** 271
Hewitt & Tuttle, **IV** 426; **17** 355–56
Hewitt Motor Company, **I** 177; **22** 329
Hewlett-Packard Company, II 62; **III** 116, **142–43; 6** 219–20, 225, **237–39 (upd.),** 244, 248, 278–79, 304; **8** 139, 467; **9** 7, 35–36, 57, 115, 471; **10** 15, 34, 86, 232, 257, 363, 404, 459, 464, 499, 501; **11** 46, 234, 274, 284, 382, 491, 518; **12** 61, 147, 162, 183, 470; **13** 128, 326, 501; **14** 354; **15** 125; **16** 5, 139–40, 299, 301, 367, 394, 550; **18** 386–87, 434, 436, 571; **19** 515; **20** 8; **25** 96, 118, 151–53, 499, 531; **26** 177, 520; **27** 221; **28 189–92 (upd.); 33** 15; **36** 3, 81–82, 299–300; **38** 20, 187, 417–19; **41** 117, 288; **43** 294
Hexalon, **26** 420
Hexatec Polymers, **III** 742
Hexcel Corporation, 11 475; **27** 50; **28 193–95**
Heyden Newport Chemical Corp., **I** 526
Heyer-Schulte, **26** 286
Heytesbury Party Ltd., **34** 422
HFC. *See* Household Finance Corporation.
HFS Inc., **21** 97; **22** 54, 56
HG Hawker Engineering Co. Ltd., **III** 508

HGCC. *See* Hysol Grafil Composite Components Co.
HH Finch Ltd., **38** 501
HI. *See* Houston Industries Incorporated.
Hi-Bred Corn Company, **9** 410
Hi-Lo Automotive, Inc., **26** 348–49
Hi-Mirror Co., **III** 715
Hi Tech Consignments, **18** 208
Hi-Tek Polymers, Inc., **8** 554
Hibbett Sporting Goods, Inc., 26 189–91
Hibbing Transportation, **I** 448
Hibernia & Shamrock-Bergwerksgesellschaft zu Berlin, **I** 542–43
Hibernia Bank, **18** 181
Hibernia Corporation, 37 187–90
Hibernian Banking Assoc., **II** 261
Hickman Coward & Wattles, **24** 444
Hickory Farms, Inc., 12 178, 199; **17 230–32**
Hickorycraft, **III** 571; **20** 362
Hicks & Greist, **6** 40
Hicks & Haas, **II** 478
Hicks, Muse, Tate & Furst, Inc., **24** 106; **30** 220; **36** 423
Hicksgas Gifford, Inc., **6** 529
Hidden Creek Industries, Inc., **16** 397; **24** 498
HiFi Buys, **30** 465
Higginson et Hanckar, **IV** 107
Higgs & Young Inc., **I** 412
High Point Chemical Corp., **III** 38
High Retail System Co., Ltd., **V** 195; **47** 391
Highgate Hotels, Inc., **21** 93
Highland Container Co., **IV** 345
Highland Superstores, **9** 65–66; **10** 9–10, 304–05, 468; **23** 51–52
Highland Telephone Company, **6** 334
Highlander Publications, **38** 307–08
Highlands Insurance Co., **III** 498
Highmark Inc., I 109; **27 208–11**
Highveld Steel and Vanadium Corp., **IV** 22
Higo Bank, **II** 291
Hilbun Poultry, **10** 250
Hilco Technologies, **III** 143; **6** 238
Hildebrandt International, 29 235–38
Hilex Poly Co., Inc., **8** 477
Hill & Knowlton Inc. *See* WPP Group PLC.
Hill Publishing Co., **IV** 634
Hill-Rom Company, **10** 349–50
Hill Stores, **II** 683
Hill's Pet Nutrition, Inc., 14 123; **26** 207; **27 212–14,** 390. *See also* Colgate-Palmolive Company.
Hillard Oil and Gas Company, Inc., **11** 523
Hillards, PLC, **II** 678
Hillenbrand Industries, Inc., 6 295; **10 349–51; 16** 20
Hiller Aircraft Company, **9** 205; **48** 167
Hiller Group, **14** 286
Hillerich & Bradsby Co., **24** 403
The Hillhaven Corporation, III 76, 87–88; **6** 188; **14 241–43; 16** 57, 515, 517; **25** 307, 456
Hillin Oil, **IV** 658
Hillman, **I** 183
Hills & Dales Railway Co. *See* Dayton Power & Light Company.
Hills Brothers Inc., **II** 548; **7** 383; **28** 311
Hills Pet Products, **III** 25
Hills Stores Company, 11 228; **13 260–61; 21** 459; **30** 57

Hillsborough Holdings Corporation. *See* Walter Industries, Inc.

Hillsdale Machine & Tool Company, **8** 514

Hillsdown Holdings, PLC, II 513–14; 24 218–21 (upd.); 28 490; **41** 252

Hillshire Farm, **II** 572

Hillside Industries Inc., **18** 118

Hilo Electric Light Company, **9** 276

Hilton, Anderson and Co., **III** 669

Hilton Athletic Apparel, **16** 296–97

Hilton Gravel, **III** 670

Hilton Group plc, 49 191–95 (upd.), 449–50

Hilton Hotels Corporation, II 208; **III 91–93,** 98–99, 102; **IV** 703; **6** 201, 210; **9** 95, 426; **19 205–08 (upd.); 21** 91, 93, 182, 333, 363; **23** 482; **27** 10. *See also* Hilton Group plc.

Hilton International Co., **6** 385; **12** 489

Himley Brick, **14** 248

Himolene, Inc., **8** 181

Hinde & Dauch Ltd., **IV** 272

Hinde & Dauch Paper Company, **19** 496

Hindell's Dairy Farmers Ltd., **II** 611–12

Hinds, Hayden & Eldredge, **10** 135

Hindustan Petroleum Corp. Ltd., **IV** 441

Hindustan Shipyard, **IV** 484

Hindustan Steel Ltd., **IV** 205–07

Hines Horticulture, Inc., 49 196–98

Hino Motors, Ltd., 7 219–21; 21 163, **271–74 (upd.); 23** 288

Hinode Life Insurance Co., Ltd., **II** 360; **III** 365

Hinomaru Truck Co., **6** 428

HIP Health Plan, **22** 425

Hip Hing Construction Company Limited, **IV** 717; **38** 319

Hipercor, S.A., **V** 52; **26** 129

Hiram Walker Resources Ltd., I 216, **262–64; IV** 721; **6** 478; **9** 391; **18** 41

Hiram Walker-Consumers' Home Ltd. *See* Consumers' Gas Company Ltd.

Hiram Walker-Gooderham & Worts Ltd., **29** 18

Hire-Purchase Company of Ireland, **16** 13; **43** 7

Hiroshima Yakult Co., **25** 449

The Hirsh Company, **17** 279

Hirth-Krause Company. *See* Wolverine World Wide Inc.

Hirz, **25** 85

Hispanic Broadcasting Corporation, 35 219–22; 41 383, 385

Hispanica de Petroleos, **IV** 424, 527, 546

Hispano Aviacion, **I** 74

HISPANOBRAS, **IV** 55

Hispanoil. *See* Hispanica de Petroleos.

Hispeed Tools, **I** 573

Hisshin-DCA foods, **II** 554

History Book Club, **13** 105–06

HIT Entertainment PLC, 40 250–52

Hit or Miss, **V** 197–98

Hitachi, Ltd., I 454–55, 494, 534; **II** 5, 30, 59, 64–65, 68, 70, 73, 75, 114, 273–74, 292–91; **III** 130, 140, 143, 464, 482; **IV** 101; **6** 238, 262; **7** 425; **9** 297; **11** 45, 308, 507; **12 237–39 (upd.),** 484; **14** 201; **16** 139; **17** 353, 556; **18** 383; **19** 11; **21** 174–75, 390; **23** 53; **24** 324; **40 253–57 (upd.)**

Hitachi Metals, Ltd., IV 101–02

Hitachi Zosen Corporation, III 513–14; 8 449

Hitchiner Manufacturing Co., Inc., 23 267–70

Hitco, **III** 721–22

Hjalmar Blomqvist A.B., **II** 639

HL&P. *See* Houston Lighting and Power Company.

HLH Products, **7** 229

HMI Industries, Inc., 17 233–35

HMO-PA. *See* U.S. Healthcare, Inc.

HMSHost, **49** 31

HMT Technology Corp., **IV** 102

HMV, **I** 531

Hoan Products Ltd. *See* Lifetime Hoan Corporation.

Hoare Govett Ltd., **II** 349

HOB Entertainment, Inc., 37 191–94

Hobart Corporation, **II** 534; **III** 610–11, 654; **7** 276; **12** 549; **22** 282, 353

Hobart Manufacturing Company, **8** 298

Hobbes Manufacturing, **I** 169–70

Hobby Lobby Stores, Inc., **17** 360

Hobson, Bates & Partners, Ltd., **14** 48

Hochschild, Kohn Department Stores, **II** 673

Hochtief AG, 14 298; **17** 376; **24** 88; **33 194–97**

The Hockey Company, 34 215–18

Hocking Glass Company, **13** 40

Hoden Oil, **IV** 478

Hodenpyl-Walbridge & Company, **14** 134

Hodgart Consulting. *See* Hildebrandt International.

Hodgkin, Barnett, Pease, Spence & Co., **II** 307

Hoechst AG, I 305–06, 309, 317, **346–48,** 605, 632, 669–70; **IV** 451; **8** 262, 451–53; **13** 75, 262–64; **18** 47, 49, 51, **234–37 (upd.),** 401; **21** 544; **22** 32; **25** 376; **34** 284; **35** 455–57; **38** 380

Hoechst Celanese Corporation, 8 562; **11** 436; **12** 118; **13** 118, **262–65; 22** 278; **24** 151; **26** 108

Hoeganaes Corporation, **8** 274–75

Hoenig Group Inc., 41 207–09

Hoerner Waldorf Corp., **IV** 264; **20** 129

Hoesch AG, IV 103–06, 128, 133, 195, 228, 232, 323

Hofbräubierzentrale GmbH Saarbrücken, **41** 222

Hoffman Enclosures Inc., **26** 361, 363

Hoffmann-La Roche & Co. *See* F. Hoffmann- La Roche & Co.

Hoffritz, **27** 288

Hofmann Herbold & Partner, **34** 249

Hogan & Hartson L.L.P., 44 220–23; 47 445–46

Högbo Stål & Jernwerks, **IV** 202

Högforsin Tehdas Osakeyhtiö, **IV** 300

Hojalata y Laminas S.A., **19** 10

Hojgaard & Schultz, **38** 436

Hokkaido Butter Co., **II** 575

Hokkaido Colonial Bank, **II** 310

Hokkaido Dairy Cooperative, **II** 574

Hokkaido Dairy Farm Assoc., **II** 538

Hokkaido Electric Power Company Inc., V 635–37

Hokkaido Forwarding, **6** 428

Hokkaido Rakuno Kosha Co., **II** 574

Hokkaido Takushoku Bank, **II** 300

Hokoku Cement, **III** 713

Hokoku Fire, **III** 384

Hokuetsu Paper Manufacturing, **IV** 327

Hokuriku Electric Power Company, V 638–40

Hokusin Kai, **IV** 475

Hokuyo Sangyo Co., Ltd., **IV** 285

Holberg Industries, Inc., 36 266–69

Holbrook Grocery Co., **II** 682

Holco BV, **41** 12

Holcroft & Company, **7** 521

Hold Everything, **17** 548–50

Holden Group, **II** 457

Holderbank Financière Glaris Ltd., III 701–02; 8 258–59, 456; **39** 217. *See also* Holnam Inc

N.V. Holdingmaatschappij De Telegraaf, 23 271–73

Holec Control Systems, **26** 496

Holes-Webway Company, **40** 44

Holga, Inc., **13** 269

Holgate Toys, **25** 379–80

Holiday Corp., **16** 263; **22** 418; **38** 76; **43** 226

Holiday Inns, Inc., I 224; **III 94–95,** 99–100; **6** 383; **9** 425–26; **10** 12; **11** 178, 242; **13** 362; **14** 106; **15** 44, 46; **16** 262; **18** 216; **21** 361–62; **23** 71; **24** 253; **25** 386; **27** 21. *See also* The Promus Cos., Inc.

Holiday Magic, Inc., **17** 227

Holiday Mart, **17** 124; **41** 114–15

Holiday Rambler Corporation, **7** 213; **25** 198

Holiday RV Superstores, Incorporated, 26 192–95

Holland & Barrett, **13** 103; **31** 346, 348

Holland & Holland, **49** 84

Holland America Line, **6** 367–68; **26** 279; **27** 90–91

Holland Burgerville USA, 44 224–26

Holland Casino, **23** 229

Holland Electro B.V., **17** 234

Holland Hannen and Cubitts, **III** 753

Holland House, **I** 377–78

Holland Motor Express, **14** 505

Holland Studio Craft, **38** 402

Holland van 1859, **III** 200

Hollandsche Bank-Unie, **II** 184–85

Hollandse Signaalapparaten, **13** 402

Holley Carburetor, **I** 434

Hollinger International Inc., 24 222–25; 32 358

Hollingsead International, Inc., **36** 158–60

Hollingsworth & Whitney Co., **IV** 329

Hollostone, **III** 673

Holly Corporation, 12 240–42

Holly Farms Corp., **II** 585; **7** 422–24; **14** 515; **23** 376–77

Holly Sugar Company. *See* Imperial Holly Corporation.

Hollywood Casino Corporation, 21 275–77

Hollywood Entertainment Corporation, 25 208–10; 29 504; **31** 339

Hollywood Park, Inc., 20 297–300

Hollywood Park Race Track, **29** 118

Hollywood Pictures, **II** 174; **30** 487

Hollywood Records, **6** 176

Holme Roberts & Owen LLP, 28 196–99

Holmen Hygiene, **IV** 315

Holmen S.A., **IV** 325

Holmens Bruk, **IV** 317–18

Holmes Electric Protective Co., **III** 644

Holmes International. *See* Miller Industries, Inc.

Holmsund & Kramfors, **IV** 338

Holnam Inc., III 702; **8** 258–60; **39 217–20 (upd.)**

Holophane Corporation, 19 209–12
Holson Burnes Group, Inc., 14 244–45
Holsten Brauerei AG, **35** 256, 258
Holt Manufacturing Co., **III** 450–51
Holt, Rinehart and Winston, Inc., **IV** 623–24; **12** 224
Holt's Cigar Holdings, Inc., 42 176–78
Holthouse Furniture Corp., **14** 236
Holtzbrinck. *See* Verlagsgruppe Georg von Holtzbrinck.
Holvick Corp., **11** 65
Holvis AG, **15** 229
Holyman Sally Ltd., **29** 431
Holyoke Food Mart Inc., **19** 480
Holzer and Co., **III** 569; **20** 361
Holzverkohlungs-Industrie AG, **IV** 70
Homart Development, **V** 182
Home & Automobile Insurance Co., **III** 214
Home and Community Care, Inc., **43** 46
Home Box Office Inc., II 134, 136, 166–67, 176–77; **IV** 675; **7** 222–24, 528–29; **10** 196; **12** 75; **18** 65; **23** 274–77 **(upd.)**, 500; **25** 498; **28** 71
Home Builders Supply, Inc. *See* Scotty's, Inc.
Home Centers of America, Inc., **18** 286
Home Charm Group PLC, **II** 141
Home Choice Holdings, Inc., **33** 366–67
The Home Depot, Inc., V 75–76; **9** 400; **10** 235; **11** 384–86; **12** 7, 235, 345, 385; **13** 250, 548; **16** 187–88, 457; **17** 366; **18 238–40 (upd.)**; **19** 248, 250; **21** 356, 358; **22** 477; **23** 232; **26** 306; **27** 416, 481; **31** 20; **35** 11–13; **39** 134; **43** 385; **44** 332–33
Home Entertainment of Texas, Inc., **30** 466
Home Furnace Co., **I** 481
Home Insurance Company, I 440; **III** 262–64
Home Interiors, **15** 475, 477
Home Nutritional Services, **17** 308
Home Office Reference Laboratory, Inc., **22** 266
Home Oil Company Ltd., **I** 264; **6** 477–78
Home Products Corp., **18** 492
Home Properties Co., Inc., **21** 95
Home Properties of New York, Inc., 42 179–81
Home Quarters Warehouse, Inc., **12** 233, 235
Home Savings of America, **II** 181–82; **10** 342–43; **16** 346; **28** 167; **47** 160
The Home School, Inc., **41** 111
Home Shopping Network, Inc., V 77–78; **9** 428; **18** 76; **24** 517; **25 211–15 (upd.)**; **26** 441; **33** 322
Home Telephone and Telegraph Company, **10** 201
Home Telephone Company. *See* Rochester Telephone Corporation.
Home Vision Entertainment Inc., **31** 339–40
HomeBase, Inc., II 658; **13** 547–48; **33 198–201 (upd.)**
HomeClub Inc., **13** 547–48; **16** 187; **17** 366. *See also* HomeBase, Inc.
Homécourt, **IV** 226
HomeFed Bank, **10** 340
Homegrocer.com Inc., **38** 223
Homelite, **21** 175
Homemade Ice Cream Company, **10** 371
Homemakers Furniture. *See* John M. Smyth Co.

HomeMax, Inc., **41** 20
Homer McKee Advertising, **I** 22
Homes By Oakwood, Inc., **15** 328
Homeserve.net Ltd., **46** 72
Homestake Mining Company, IV 18, 76; **12** 243–45; **20** 72; **27** 456; **38** 229–32 **(upd.)**
Hometown Auto Retailers, Inc., 44 227–29
HomeTown Buffet, Inc., **19** 435; **22** 465. *See also* Buffets, Inc
Homette Corporation, **30** 423
Homewood Stores Co., **IV** 573; **7** 550
Homewood Suites, **9** 425–26
Hominal Developments Inc., **9** 512
Hon Industries Inc., 13 266–69; **23** 243–45
Honam Oil Refinery, **II** 53
Honcho Real Estate, **IV** 225; **24** 489
Honda Giken Kogyo Kabushiki Kaisha. *See* Honda Motor Company Limited.
Honda Motor Company Limited, I 9–10, 32, **174–76**, 184, 193; **II** 5; **III** 495, 517, 536, 603, 657–58, 667; **IV** 443; **7** 212–13, 459; **8** 71–72; **9** 294, 340–42; **10 352–54 (upd.)**; **11** 33, 49–50, 352; **12** 122, 401; **13** 30; **16** 167; **17** 25; **21** 153; **23** 289–90, 338, 340; **25** 197–99; **27** 76; **29 239–42 (upd.)**; **34** 305–06; **36** 243
Hondo Oil & Gas Co., **IV** 375–76
Honeywell Inc., I 63; **II** 30, **40–43**, 54, 68; **III** 122–23, 149, 152, 165, 535, 548–49, 732; **6** 266, 281, 283, 314; **8** 21; **9** 171, 324; **11** 198, 265; **12 246–49 (upd.)**; **13** 234, 499; **17** 33; **18** 341; **22** 373, 436; **23** 471; **29** 464; **30** 34; **33** 334, 337; **43** 284
Hong Kong Aircraft Engineering Co., **I** 522; **6** 79; **16** 480
Hong Kong Airways, **6** 78–79; **16** 480
Hong Kong and Kowloon Wharf and Godown Co., **I** 470; **IV** 699
Hong Kong Dragon Airlines, **18** 114
Hong Kong Industrial Co., Ltd., **25** 312
Hong Kong Island Line Co., **IV** 718
Hong Kong Mass Transit Railway Corp., **19** 111
Hong Kong Resort Co., **IV** 718; **38** 320
Hong Kong Telecommunications Ltd., IV 700; **V** 285–86; **6** 319–21; **18** 114; **25** 101–02. *See also* Cable & Wireless HKT.
Hong Kong Telephone Company, **47** 177
Hong Leong Corp., **III** 718
Hong Leong Group Malaysia, **26** 3, 5
Hongkong & Kowloon Wharf & Godown Company, **20** 312
Hongkong and Shanghai Banking Corporation Limited, II 257, **296–99**, 320, 358; **III** 289; **17** 325; **18** 253; **25** 12. *See also* HSBC Holdings plc.
Hongkong Electric Company Ltd., 6 498–500; **20** 134
Hongkong Electric Holdings Ltd., 23 278–81 **(upd.)**; **47** 177
Hongkong Land Holdings Ltd., I 470–71; **IV** 699–701; **6** 498–99; **20** 312–13; **23** 280; **47 175–78 (upd.)**
Honig-Copper & Harrington, **I** 14
Honjo Copper Smeltery, **III** 490
Honolua Plantation Land Company, Inc., **29** 308
Honolulu Oil, **II** 491

Honolulu Sugar Refining Co., **II** 490
Honshu Paper Co., Ltd., IV 268, **284–85**, 292, 297, 321, 326
Hood Rubber Company, **15** 488–89
Hood Sailmakers, Inc., **10** 215
Hoogovens. *See* Koninklijke Nederlandsche Hoogovens en Staalfabricken NV.
Hooiberg, **I** 256
Hook's Drug Stores, **9** 67
Hooker Chemical, **IV** 481
Hooker Corp., **19** 324
Hooker Furniture Corp. *See* Bassett Furniture Industries, Inc.
Hooker Petroleum, **IV** 264
Hooper Holmes, Inc., 22 264–67
Hoosier Park L.P., **29** 118
Hooters of America, Inc., 18 241–43
Hoover Ball and Bearing Co., **III** 589
The Hoover Company, II 7; **III** 478; **12** 158, **250–52**; **15** 416, 418; **21** 383; **30** 75, 78; **40 258–62 (upd.)**
Hoover Group Inc., **18** 11
Hoover Industrial, **III** 536; **26** 230
Hoover-NSK Bearings, **III** 589
Hoover Treated Wood Products, Inc., **12** 396
Hopkinton LNG Corp., **14** 126
Hopper Soliday and Co. Inc., **14** 154
Hops Restaurant Bar and Brewery, 31 41; **46 233–36**
Hopwood & Company, **22** 427
Horace Mann Educators Corporation, 22 268–70
Horizon Air Industries, Inc. *See* Alaska Air Group, Inc.
Horizon Bancorp, **II** 252; **14** 103
Horizon Corporation, **8** 348
Horizon Group Inc., **27** 221
Horizon Healthcare Corporation, **25** 456
Horizon Holidays, **14** 36
Horizon Industries, **19** 275
Horizon Lamps, **48** 299
Horizon Organic Holding Corporation, 37 195–99
Horizon Travel Group, **8** 527
Horizon/CMS Healthcare Corp., **25** 111, 457; **33** 185
Horizons Laitiers, **25** 85
Hormel Foods Corporation, 18 244–47 (upd.)
Horn & Hardart, **II** 614
Horn Silver Mines Co., **IV** 83; **7** 187
Horn Venture Partners, **22** 464
Hornblower & Co., **II** 450
Hornbrook, Inc., **14** 112
Horne's, **I** 449; **16** 62
Hornsberg Land Co., **I** 553
Horsham Corp. *See* TrizecHahn.
Horst Breuer GmbH, **20** 363
Horst Salons Inc., **24** 56
Horten, **II** 622; **47** 107
Horton Homes, Inc., 25 216–18
Hospal SA, **49** 156
Hospital Corporation of America, II 331; **III 78–80**; **15** 112; **23** 153; **27** 237. *See also* HCA - The Healthcare Company.
Hospital Cost Consultants, **11** 113
Hospital Products, Inc., **10** 534
Hospital Service Association of Pittsburgh, **III** 325
Hospital Specialty Co., **37** 392
Hospitality Franchise Systems, Inc., 11 177–79; **14** 106; **17** 236. *See also* Cendant Corporation.

Hospitality Worldwide Services, Inc., 26 **196–98**
Hosposable Products, Inc. *See* Wyant Corporation.
Host Communications Inc., **24** 404
Host Marriott Corporation, **21** 366
Host Marriott Services Corp., **III** 103; **16** 446; **17** 95. *See also* HMSHost
Hot 'n Now, **16** 96–97
Hot Dog Construction Co., **12** 372
Hot Sam Co., **12** 179, 199. *See also* Mrs. Fields' Original Cookies, Inc.
Hot Shoppes Inc., **III** 102
Hot Topic, Inc., 33 202–04
Hotchkiss-Brandt, **II** 116; **42** 378
Hoteiya, **V** 209–10
Hotel Corporation of America, **16** 337
Hotel Corporation of India, **27** 26
Hotel Properties Ltd., **30** 107
Hotel Reservations Network, Inc., **47** 420
Hotel Scandinavia K/S, **I** 120
HotRail Inc., **36** 124
HotWired, **45** 200
Houbigant, **37** 270
Houdry Chemicals, **I** 298
Houghton Mifflin Company, 10 355–57; **26** 215; **36** 270–74 (upd.); **46** 441
Houlihan's Restaurant Group, **25** 546
Housatonic Power Co., **13** 182
House and Land Syndicate, **IV** 710
House of Blues, **32** 241, 244
House of Fabrics, Inc., 16 197–98; **18** 223; **21 278–80**
House of Fraser PLC, 21 353; **37** 6, 8; **45** **188–91**; **47** 173. *See also* Harrods Holdings.
House of Miniatures, **12** 264
House of Windsor, Inc., **9** 533
Household International, Inc., I 31; **II** **417–20,** 605; **7** 569–70; **8** 117; **10** 419; **16** 487–88; **21 281–86 (upd.);** **22** 38, 542; **24** 152
Household Products Inc., **I** 622; **10** 68
Household Rental Systems, **17** 234
Housing Development Finance Corporation, **20** 313
Housmex Inc., **23** 171
Houston, Effler & Partners Inc., **9** 135
Houston Electric Light & Power Company, **44** 368
Houston General Insurance, **III** 248
Houston Industries Incorporated, V **641–44**; **7** 376. *See also* Reliant Energy Inc.
Houston International Teleport, Inc., **11** 184
Houston Natural Gas Corp., **IV** 395; **V** 610
Houston Oil & Minerals Corp., **11** 440–41
Houston Oil Co., **IV** 342, 674
Houston Pipe Line Company, **45** 21
Hoveringham Group, **III** 753; **28** 450
Hoving Corp., **14** 501
Hovis-McDougall Co., **II** 565
Hovnanian Enterprises, Inc., 29 243–45
Howaldtswerke-Deutsche Werft AG, **IV** 201
Howard B. Stark Candy Co., **15** 325
Howard Flint Ink Company, **13** 227
Howard H. Sweet & Son, Inc., **14** 502
Howard Hughes Medical Institute, II 33, 35; **39 221–24**
Howard Hughes Properties, Ltd., **17** 317
Howard Humphreys, **13** 119

Howard Johnson International, Inc., III 94, 102–03; **6** 27; **7** 266; **11** 177–78; **15** 36; **16** 156; **17 236–39**; **25** 309
Howard Printing Co., **III** 188; **10** 29
Howard Research and Development Corporation, **15** 412, 414
Howard, Smith & Levin, **40** 126
Howard Smith Paper Mills Ltd., **IV** 271–72
Howden. *See* Alexander Howden Group.
Howdy Company, **9** 177
Howe & Fant, Inc., **23** 82
Howe and Brainbridge Inc., **I** 321
Howe Sound Co., **12** 253
Howe Sound Inc., **IV** 174
Howe Sound Pulp and Paper Ltd., **IV** 321
Howmedica, **29** 455
Howmet Corporation, 12 IV 174; **253–55; 22** 506
Hoya Corp., **III** 715
Hoyt Archery Company, **10** 216
HPI Health Care Services, **49** 307–08
HQ Global Workplaces, Inc., **47** 331
HQ Office International, **8** 405; **23** 364
HRB Business Services, **29** 227
Hrubitz Oil Company, **12** 244
HSBC Holdings plc, 12 256–58; 17 323, 325–26; **26 199–204 (upd.)**
HSN Inc., **25** 411
HSS Hire Service Group PLC, **45** 139–41
HTH, **12** 464
HTM Goedkoop, **26** 278–79
H2O Plus, **11** 41
Hua Bei Oxygen, **25** 82
Huaneng Raw Material Corp., **III** 718
Hub Group, Inc., 26 533; **38 233–35**
Hub Services, Inc., **18** 366
Hubbard Air Transport, **10** 162
Hubbard, Baker & Rice, **10** 126
Hubbard Broadcasting Inc., 24 226–28
Hubbard Construction Co., **23** 332
Hubbard, Westervelt & Motteley, **II** 425; **13** 341
Hubbell Incorporated, 9 286–87; **31** **257–259 (upd.)**
Hubinger Co., **II** 508; **11** 172; **36** 254
Huck Manufacturing Company, **22** 506
Huddart Parker, **III** 672
Hudepohl-Schoenling Brewing Co., **18** 72
Hudnut, **I** 710
Hudson Automobile Company, **18** 492
The Hudson Bay Mining and Smelting **Company, Limited, 12** 259–61; **13** 502–03; **16** 29
Hudson Engineering Corp., **III** 559
Hudson Foods Inc., 13 270–72
Hudson Housewares Corp., **16** 389
Hudson Motor Car Co., **I** 135, 158; **III** 568; **10** 292; **20** 359
Hudson Packaging & Paper Co., **IV** 257
Hudson Pharmaceutical Corp., **31** 347
Hudson River Bancorp, Inc., 41 210–13
Hudson River Railroad, **II** 396
Hudson River Rubber Company, **V** 231
Hudson Scott & Sons, **I** 604
Hudson Software, **13** 481
Hudson Underground Telephone Company, **6** 299
Hudson's. *See* Dayton Hudson Corporation.
Hudson's Bay Company, I 284; **IV** 400–01, 437; **V 79–81**; **6** 359; **8** 525; **12** 361; **25 219–22 (upd.)**, 230
Hue International, **8** 324
Hueppe Duscha, **III** 571; **20** 362

Huff Daland Dusters, **I** 99; **6** 81
Huffco, **IV** 492
Huffman Manufacturing Company, **7** 225–26
Huffy Bicycles Co., **19** 383
Huffy Corporation, 7 225–27; 26 184, 412; **30 239–42 (upd.)**
Hugerot, **19** 50
Hugh O'Neill Auto Co., **12** 309
Hughes Air West, **25** 421
Hughes Aircraft Corporation, **I** 172, 484, 539; **III** 428, 539; **7** 426–27; **9** 409; **10** 327; **11** 263, 540; **13** 356, 398; **15** 528, 530; **21** 201; **23** 134; **24** 442; **25** 86, 223; **30** 175. *See also* GM Hughes Electronics Corporation.
Hughes Communications, Inc., **13** 398; **18** 211
Hughes Corp., **18** 535
Hughes Electric Heating Co., **II** 28; **12** 194
Hughes Electronics Corporation, 25 **223–25; 36** 240, 243; **38** 175, 375; **46** 327
Hughes Helicopter, **26** 431; **46** 65
Hughes Hubbard & Reed LLP, 44 **230–32**
Hughes Markets, Inc., 22 271–73
Hughes Network Systems Inc., **21** 239
Hughes Properties, Inc., **17** 317
Hughes Space and Communications Company, **33** 47–48
Hughes Supply, Inc., 14 246–47; 39 360
Hughes Television Network, **11** 184
Hughes Tool Co., **I** 126; **II** 32; **12** 488; **15** 467; **25** 74; **35** 425. *See also* Baker Hughes Incorporated.
Hugo Boss AG, 48 206–09
Hugo Neu Corporation, **19** 381–82
Hugo Stinnes GmbH, **I** 542; **8** 69, 494–95
Huguenot Fenal, **IV** 108
Huhtamaki, **30** 396, 398
Hulman & Company, 44 233–36; 46 245
Hüls A.G., **I** 349–50; **25** 82. *See also* Degussa-Hüls AG.
Hulton, **17** 397
Hulton Getty, **31** 216–17
Humana Inc., III 79, **81–83**; **6** 28, 191–92, 279; **15** 113; **24 229–32 (upd.);** **35** 215–16
Humanetics Corporation, **29** 213
Humanities Software, **39** 341
Humason Manufacturing Co., **III** 628
Humber, **I** 197
Humberside Sea & Land Services, **31** 367
Humble Oil & Refining Company, **III** 497; **IV** 373, 428; **7** 171; **13** 118; **14** 291. *See also* Exxon.
Humboldt-Deutz-Motoren AG, **III** 541–42, 543; **IV** 126
Hummel, **II** 163–64
Hummel Lanolin Corporation, **45** 126
Hummel-Reise, **44** 432
Hummer, Winblad Venture Partners, **36** 157
Hummingbird, **18** 313
Humongous Entertainment, Inc., **31** 238–40
Humphrey Instruments, **I** 693
Humphrey's Estate and Finance, **IV** 700
Humphreys & Glasgow Ltd., **V** 612
Hunco Ltd., **IV** 640; **26** 273
Hungária Biztositó, **III** 185
Hungarian-Soviet Civil Air Transport Joint Stock Company. *See* Maláev Plc.

Hungarotex, **V** 166
Hungry Howie's Pizza and Subs, Inc., 25 **226–28**
Hunt Consolidated, Inc., 27 215–18 **(upd.)**
Hunt Lumber Co., **IV** 358
Hunt Manufacturing Company, 12 **262–64**
Hunt Oil Company, **IV** 367, 453–54; **7** **228–30**, 378. *See also* Hunt Consolidated, Inc.
Hunt-Wesson, Inc., 17 240–42; 25 278
Hunter-Douglas, **8** 235
Hunter Engineering Co., **IV** 18
Hunter Fan Company, 13 273–75
Hunter-Hayes Elevator Co., **III** 467
Hunters' Foods, **II** 500
Hunting Aircraft, **I** 50; **24** 85
Huntingdon Life Sciences Group plc, 42 **182–85**
Huntington Bancshares Inc., 11 180–82
Huntley and Palmer Foods, **II** 544
Huntley Boorne & Stevens, **I** 604
Hunton & Williams, 35 223–26
Huntsman Chemical Corporation, 8 **261–63; 9** 305
Hupp Motor Car Company, **III** 601; **8** 74; **10** 261
Hurd & Houghton, **10** 355
Hurlburt Paper Co., **IV** 311; **19** 267
Huron Steel Company, Inc., **16** 357
Huse Food Group, **14** 352
Husky Energy Inc., 47 179–82; 49 203
Husky Oil Ltd., **IV** 454, 695; **V** 673–75; **18** 253–54; **19** 159
Husqvarna Forest & Garden Company, **III** 480; **13** 564; **22** 26–27
Hussmann Corporation, **I** 457–58; **7** 429–30; **10** 554; **13** 268; **22** 353–54
Hutcheson & Grundy, **29** 286
Hutchinson-Mapa, **IV** 560
Hutchinson Technology Incorporated, 18 **248–51**
Hutchinson Wholesale Grocery Co., **II** 624
Hutchison Microtel, **11** 548
Hutchison Whampoa Limited, I 470; **IV** 694–95; **18** 114, **252–55; 20** 131, 312–13; **25** 101; **47** 181; **49 199–204** **(upd.)**
Huth Manufacturing Corporation, **10** 414
Hüttenwerk Oberhausen AG, **IV** 222
Hüttenwerk Salzgitter AG, **IV** 201
Huttig Building Products, **31** 398, 400
Huttig Sash & Door Company, **8** 135
Hutton, E.F. *See* E.F. Hutton.
Huyck Corp., **I** 429
Hvide Marine Incorporated, 22 274–76
HWI. *See* Hardware Wholesalers, Inc.
Hy-Form Products, Inc., **22** 175
Hy-Vee, Inc., 36 275–78; 42 432
Hyatt-Clark Industries Inc., **45** 170
Hyatt Corporation, II 442; **III** 92, **96–97;** **9** 426; **16 273–75 (upd.); 22** 101; **23** 482; **48** 148
Hyatt Legal Services, **20** 435; **29** 226
Hyatt Medical Enterprises, **III** 73
Hyatt Roller Bearing Co., **I** 171–72; **9** 17; **10** 326
Hybridtech, **III** 18
Hyde Athletic Industries, Inc., 17 **243–45.** *See* Saucony Inc.
Hyde Company, A.L., **7** 116–17
Hyder plc, 34 219–21
Hydra Computer Systems, Inc., **13** 201

Hydrac GmbH, **38** 300
Hydraulic Brake Co., **I** 141
Hydril Company, 46 237–39
Hydro-Aire Incorporated, **8** 135
Hydro Carbide Corp., **19** 152
Hydro-Carbon Light Company, **9** 127
Hydro Electric, **19** 389–90; **49** 363–64
Hydro-Electric Power Commission of Ontario, **6** 541; **9** 461
Hydro Med Sciences, **13** 367
Hydro-Quebéc, 6 501–03; 32 266–69 **(upd.)**
Hydrocarbon Services of Nigeria Co., **IV** 473
Hydroponic Chemical Co., **III** 28
Hydrox Corp., **II** 533
Hyer Boot, **19** 232
Hygeia Sciences, Inc., **8** 85, 512
Hygienic Ice Co., **IV** 722
Hygrade Containers Ltd., **IV** 286
Hygrade Foods, **III** 502; **7** 208; **14** 536
Hyland Laboratories, **I** 627
Hylsa. *See* Hojalata y Laminas S.A.
Hylsamex, S.A. de C.V., 39 225–27
Hyosung Group, **III** 749
Hyper Shoppes, Inc., **II** 670; **18** 507
Hypercom Corporation, 27 219–21
Hyperion Press, **6** 176
Hyperion Software Corporation, 22 **277–79**
Hypermart USA, **8** 555–56
Hyplains Beef, **7** 175
Hypo-Bank. *See* Bayerische Hypotheken-und Wechsel-Bank AG.
Hypobaruk, **III** 348
Hyponex Corp., **22** 475
Hypro Engineering Inc., **I** 481
Hysol Corp., **I** 321; **12** 103
Hyster Company, 17 246–48; 33 364
Hyster-Yale Materials Handling, Inc., **I** 424; **7** 369–71
Hystron Fibers Inc., **I** 347
Hyundai Group, I 207, 516; **II** 53–54, 122; **III** 457–59, **515–17; 7 231–34** **(upd.); 9** 350; **10** 404; **12** 211, 546; **13** 280, 293–94; **18** 124; **23** 353; **25** 469; **29** 264, 266
Hyundai Motors, **47** 279

I Can't Believe It's Yogurt, Inc., **17** 474; **35** 121
I Pellettieri d'Italia S.p.A., **45** 342
I. Appel, **30** 23
I.B. Kleinert Rubber Company, **37** 399
I.C.H. Corp., **I** 528
I.C. Isaacs & Company, 31 260–62
I.C. Johnson and Co., **III** 669
I.D. Systems, Inc., **11** 444
I-DIKA Milan SRL, **12** 182
I. Feldman Co., **31** 359
I.G. Farbenindustrie AG, **I** 305–06, 309–11, 337, 346–53, 619, 632–33, 698–99; **II** 257; **III** 677, 694; **IV** 111, 485; **8** 108–09; **11** 7; **13** 75–76, 262; **16** 121; **18** 47; **21** 544; **22** 225–26; **26** 452. *See also* BASF A.G. *and* Bayer A.G. *and* Hoechst A.G.
I.J. Stokes Corp., **I** 383
I.M. Pei & Associates, **I** 580; **III** 267; **41** 143
I.M. Singer and Co., **II** 9
I. Magnin Inc., **8** 444; **15** 86; **24** 422; **30** 383; **31** 191, 193
I.N. Kote, **IV** 116; **19** 219

I.N. Tek, **IV** 116; **19** 219
I.R. Maxwell & Co. Ltd., **IV** 641; **7** 311
I-T-E Circuit Breaker, **II** 121
I-X Corp., **22** 416
Iacon, Inc., **49** 299, 301
IAL. *See* International Aeradio Limited.
IAM/Environmental, **18** 11
Iams Company, 26 205–07; 27 213
IAWS Group plc, 46 405; **49 205–08**
IBANCO, **26** 515
IBC Holdings Corporation, **12** 276
IBCA. *See* International Banking and Credit Analysis.
Iberdrola, S.A., V 608; **47** 110; **49** **209–12**
Iberia Líneas Aéreas De España S.A., I 110; **6 95–97; 33** 18; **36 279–83 (upd.)**
IBERIABANK Corporation, 37 200–02
Ibero-Amerika Bank, **II** 521
Iberswiss Catering, **6** 96
Ibex Engineering Co., **III** 420
IBH Holding AG, **7** 513
IBJ. *See* The Industrial Bank of Japan Ltd.
IBM. *See* International Business Machines Corporation.
IBP, Inc., II 515–17; **7** 525; **21 287–90** **(upd.); 23** 201
IBS Conversions Inc., **27** 492
Ibstock Brick Ltd., 37 203–06 (upd.)
Ibstock plc, III 735; **14 248–50**
IC Designs, Inc., **48** 127
IC Industries Inc., I 456–58; **III** 512; **7** 430; **10** 414, 553; **18** 3; **22** 197; **43** 217. *See also* Whitman Corporation.
ICA AB, II 639–40
ICA Fluor Daniel, S. de R.L. de C.V., **41** 148
ICA Mortgage Corporation, **8** 30
ICA Technologies, Ltd., **III** 533
Icahn Capital Corp., **35** 143
Icarus Consulting AG, **29** 376
ICE, **I** 333
ICEE-USA, **24** 240
Iceland Group plc, 33 205–07
Icelandic Air, **49** 80
ICF Kaiser International, Inc., 28 **200–04**
ICH Corporation, **19** 468
Ichikoh Industries Ltd., **26** 154
ICI. *See* Imperial Chemical Industries plc.
ICI Canada, **22** 436
ICL plc, II 65, 81; **III** 141, 164; **6** **240–42; 11** 150; **16** 226
ICM Mortgage Corporation, **8** 436
ICOA Life Insurance, **III** 253
Icon Health & Fitness, Inc., 38 236–39
Icon International, **24** 445
iConcepts, Inc., **39** 95
Icot Corp., **18** 543
ICS. *See* International Care Services.
ICS, **26** 119
ICX, **IV** 136
ID, Inc., **9** 193
id Software, **31** 237–38; **32** 9
Idaho Frozen Foods, **II** 572–73
Idaho Power Company, 12 265–67
IDB Communications Group, Inc., 11 **183–85; 20** 48; **27** 301, 307
IDC, **25** 101
Ide Megumi, **III** 549
Ideal Basic Industries, III 701–02; **8** 258–59; **12** 18
Ideal Corp., **III** 602; **23** 335
Ideal Loisirs Group, **23** 388

IDEC Pharmaceuticals Corporation, **32** 214
Idemitso Petrochemicals, **8** 153
Idemitsu Kosan Co., Ltd., 49 213–16 (upd.)
Idemitsu Kosan K.K., II 361; **IV 434–36,** 476, 519
Identification Business, Inc., **18** 140
Identix Inc., 44 237–40
IDEXX Laboratories, Inc., 23 282–84
IDG Books Worldwide, Inc., 27 222–24. See also International Data Group, Inc.
IDG Communications, Inc, **7** 238
IDG World Expo Corporation, **7** 239
IDI, **22** 365
IDI Temps, **34** 372
IDO. See Nippon Idou Tsushin.
IDS Ltd., **22** 76
IDT Corporation, 34 222–24
IEC Electronics Corp., 42 186–88
IEL. See Industrial Equity Ltd.
IFC Disposables, Inc., **30** 496–98
IFF. See International Flavors & Fragrances Inc.
IFI, **I** 161–62; **III** 347
Ifil, **27** 515
IFM, **25** 85
IFS Industries, **6** 294
IG. See Integrated Genetics.
IG Farben. See I.G. Farbenindustrie AG.
IG Holdings, **27** 430
IGA, **II** 624, 649, 668, 681–82; **7** 451; **15** 479; **18** 6, 9; **25** 234
Iggesund Bruk, **IV** 317–18
Igloo Products Corp., 21 291–93; 22 116
IGT-International, **10** 375–76
IGT-North America, **10** 375
IHI. See Ishikawajima Harima Heavy Industries.
IHI Granitech Corp., **III** 533
IHOP Corporation, 17 249–51; 19 435, 455
Iida & Co., **I** 493; **24** 325
IinteCom, **III** 169
IIS, **26** 441
IISCO-Ujjain Pipe and Foundry Co. Ltd., **IV** 206
IJ Holdings Corp., **45** 173
IK Coach, Ltd., **23** 290
IKEA Group, V 82–84
IKEA International A/S, 26 161, **208–11 (upd.)**
Il Fornaio (America) Corporation, 27 225–28
Il Giornale, **13** 493
Ilaco, **26** 22
ILFC. See International Lease Finance Corporation.
Ilitch Holdings Inc., 37 207–210; 46 130
Illco Toy Co. USA, **12** 496
Illinois Bell Telephone Company, IV 660; **14 251–53; 18** 30
Illinois Central Corporation, I 456, 584; **8** 410; **10** 553; **11 186–89**
Illinois Glass Co., **I** 609
Illinois Lock Company, **48** 142
Illinois Merchants Trust Co., **II** 261
Illinois National Bank & Trust Co., **III** 213–14
Illinois Power Company, 6 470, **504–07; 49** 119, 121
Illinois Steel Co., **IV** 572; **7** 549; **8** 114
Illinois Terminal Company, **6** 504
Illinois Tool Works Inc., III 518–20; 22 280–83 (upd.); 44 193

Illinois Traction Company, **6** 504
Illinois Trust and Savings Bank, **II** 261
Illinova Energy Partners, **27** 247
Illuminet Holdings Inc., 47 430
Ilmor Engineering of Great Britain, **V** 494
Ilse-Bergbau AG, **IV** 229–30
Ilselder Hütte, **IV** 201
Ilwaco Telephone and Telegraph Company. See Pacific Telecom, Inc.
Ilyushin, **24** 60
IMA Bancard, Inc., **24** 395
IMA Holdings Corp., **III** 73–74
Imabari, **25** 469
Image Business Systems Corp., **11** 66
Image Industries, Inc., **25** 320–21
Image Technologies Corporation, **12** 264
Imageline Inc., **25** 348
ImageTag Inc., **49** 290
Imagine Entertainment, **43** 144
Imagine Manufacturing Solutions Inc., **48** 410
ImagiNet, **41** 97
Imaging Technologies, **25** 183
Imaje, S.A., **28** 104
IMAKE Software and Services, Inc., **49** 423–24
IMall Inc., **26** 441
Imasa Group, **IV** 34
Imasco Limited, I 514; **II** 605; **V 401–02; 49** 367–68
Imation Corporation, 20 301–04; 33 348. See also Minnesota Mining & Manufacturing Company.
Imatran Voima Oy, **IV** 469. See also Fortum Corporation
Imax Corporation, 21 362; **28 205–08; 46** 422
IMC. See Intertec Marine Corporation.
IMC Drilling Mud, **III** 499
IMC Fertilizer Group, Inc., 8 264–66
Imcera Group, Inc., **8** 264, 266
IMCO Recycling, Incorporated, 32 270–73
IMED Corp., **I** 712; **III** 511–12; **10** 551; **38** 364
Imerys S.A., 40 176, **263–66 (upd.)**
Imetal S.A., IV 107–09
IMG. See International Management Group.
IMI plc, III 593; **9 288–89; 29** 364
Imigest Fondo Imicapital, **III** 347
Imlo, **26** 22
Immersion Corporation, **28** 245
Immobilier Batibail, **42** 152
Immunex Corporation, 8 26; **14 254–56**
Immuno Serums, Inc., **V** 174–75
Immuno Therapeutics, Inc., **25** 382
Imo Industries Inc., 7 235–37; 27 229–32 (upd.)
IMO Ltd., **III** 539
Impala Platinum Holdings, **IV** 91–93
Impark Limited, **42** 433
IMPATH Inc., 45 192–94
Imperial Airways. See British Overseas Airways Corporation.
Imperial and International Communications Limited, **25** 100
Imperial Bank of Canada, **II** 244–45
Imperial Bank of Persia, **II** 298
Imperial British East Africa Co., **III** 522
Imperial Business Forms, **9** 72
Imperial Chemical Industries plc, I 303, **351–53,** 374, 605, 633; **II** 448, 565; **III** 522, 667, 677, 680, 745; **IV** 38, 110,

698; **7** 209; **8** 179, 222, 224; **9** 154, 288; **10** 436; **11** 97, 361; **12** 347; **13** 448, 470; **16** 121; **17** 118; **18** 50; **21** 544; **44** 116–17; **49** 268, 270
Imperial Feather Company, **19** 304
Imperial Fire Co., **III** 373
Imperial Goonbarrow, **III** 690
Imperial Group Ltd., **II** 513; **III** 503; **7** 209; **17** 238
Imperial Holly Corporation, 12 268–70. See also Imperial Sugar Company.
Imperial Japanese Government Steel Works, **17** 349–50
Imperial Life Co., **III** 288, 373
Imperial Marine Insurance Co., **III** 384, 405–06
Imperial Metal Industries Ltd. See IMI plc.
Imperial Oil Limited, IV 428, **437–39,** 494; **25 229–33 (upd.); 32** 179–80
Imperial Outdoor, **27** 280
Imperial Packing Co. See Beech-Nut Nutrition Corp.
Imperial Paper, **13** 169
Imperial Pneumatic Tool Co., **III** 525
Imperial Premium Finance, **III** 264
Imperial Savings Association, **8** 30–31
Imperial Smelting Corp., **IV** 58
Imperial Sports, **19** 230
Imperial Sugar Company, 32 274–78 (upd.)
Imperial Tobacco Company, **I** 425–26, 605; **IV** 260; **V** 401; **49** 153. See also B.A.T. Industries PLC.
IMPO Import Parfumerien, **48** 116
Imported Auto Parts, Inc., **15** 246
Impressions Software, **15** 455
Imprimis, **8** 467
Impulse, **9** 122
Impulse Designs, **31** 435–36
IMRA America Inc., **48** 5
Imreg, **10** 473–74
IMRS. See Hyperion Software Corporation.
IMS International, Inc., **10** 105
In Focus Systems, Inc., 22 287–90
In Home Health, Inc., **25** 306, 309–10
In-N-Out Burger, 19 213–15
In-Sink-Erator, **II** 19
INA Corporation, **II** 403; **III** 79, 208, 223–25, 226; **11** 481; **22** 269. See also CIGNA Corporation.
INA-Naftaplin, **IV** 454
INA Wälzlager Schaeffler, **III** 595; **47** 278
Inabata & Co., **I** 398
InaCom Corporation, 13 176, **276–78; 19** 471
Incasso Bank, **II** 185
Incentive Group, **27** 269
Inchcape PLC, II 233; **III 521–24; 16 276–80 (upd.)**
Incheon Iron & Steel Co., **III** 516
Inchon Heavy Industrial Corp., **IV** 183
INCO-Banco Indústria e Comércio de Santa Catarina, **13** 70
Inco Limited, IV 75, 78, **110–12; 39** 338; **45 195–99 (upd.)**
Incola, S.A., **II** 471; **22** 93
Incon Research Inc., **41** 198
InControl Inc., **11** 460
Incredible Universe, **12** 470; **17** 489; **36** 387
Ind Coope, **I** 215
Indemnité, **III** 391
Indemnity Insurance Company. See CIGNA Corporation.

Indentimat Corp., **14** 542
Independent Breweries Company, **9** 178
Independent Delivery Services, Inc., **37** 409
Independent Election Corp. of America, **47** 37
Independent Exhibitions Ltd., **27** 362
Independent Grocers Alliance. *See* IGA.
Independent Lock Co., **13** 166
Independent Metal Products Co., **I** 169
Independent Oil & Gas Co., **IV** 521
Independent Petrochemical, **14** 461
Independent Power Generators, **V** 605
Independent Stave Company, **28** 223
Independent Torpedo Company, **25** 73
Independent Warehouses, Inc., **IV** 180
India Exotics, Inc., **22** 133
India General Steam Navigation and Railway Co., **III** 522
India Life Assurance Co., **III** 359
India Rubber, Gutta Percha & Telegraph Works Co., **I** 428
Indian Airlines Corporation. *See* Air-India.
Indian Airlines Ltd., 46 240–42
Indian Archery and Toy Corp., **19** 142–43
Indian Iron & Steel Co. Ltd., **IV** 49, 205–07
Indian Oil Corporation Ltd., IV 440–41, 483; **48 210–13 (upd.)**
Indian Point Farm Supply, Inc., **IV** 458–59
Indiana Bearings, Inc., **13** 78
Indiana Bell Telephone Company, Incorporated, 14 257–61; 18 30
Indiana Board and Filler Company, **12** 376
Indiana Electric Corporation, **6** 555
Indiana Energy, Inc., 27 233–36
Indiana Gaming Company, **21** 40
Indiana Gas & Water Company, **6** 556
Indiana Group, **I** 378
Indiana Oil Purchasing Co., **IV** 370
Indiana Parts and Warehouse, **29** 86, 88
Indiana Power Company, **6** 555
Indiana Refining Co., **IV** 552
Indiana Tube Co., **23** 250
Indianapolis Air Pump Company, **8** 37
Indianapolis Brush Electric Light & Power Company, **6** 508
Indianapolis Cablevision, **6** 508–09
Indianapolis Light and Power Company, **6** 508
Indianapolis Motor Speedway Corporation, 9 16; **46 243–46**
Indianapolis Power & Light Company, **6** 508–09
Indianapolis Pump and Tube Company, **8** 37
Indianhead Truck Lines, **6** 371
IndianOil Companies. *See* Indian Oil Corporation Ltd.
Indigo NV, 26 212–14, 540–41
Indo-Asahi Glass Co., Ltd., **III** 667
Indo-China Steam Navigation Co., **I** 469; **20** 311
Indo Mobil Ltd., **48** 212
Indola Cosmetics B.V., **8** 16
Indonesia Petroleum Co., **IV** 516
Indresco, Inc., **22** 285
Induba, S.A. de C.V., **39** 230
Induban, **II** 196
Indura SA Industria Y Commercio, **25** 82
Industri Kapital, **27** 269
Industria Gelati Sammontana, **II** 575
Industria Metalgrafica, **I** 231
Industria Raffinazione Oli Minerali, **IV** 419

Industrial & Trade Shows of Canada, **IV** 639
Industrial Acceptance Bank, **I** 337
Industrial Air Products, **19** 380–81
Industrial Air Tool, **28** 387
Industrial Bancorp, **9** 229
Industrial Bank of Japan, Ltd., II 300–01, 310–11, 338, 369, 433, 459; **17** 121
Industrial Bank of Scotland, **10** 337
Industrial Bio-Test Laboratories, **I** 374, 702
Industrial Cartonera, **IV** 295; **19** 226
Industrial Chemical and Equipment, **16** 271
Industrial Circuits, **IV** 680
Industrial Computer Corp., **11** 78
Industrial Development Corp., **IV** 22, 92, 534
Industrial Development Corp. of Zambia Ltd., **IV** 239–41
Industrial Devices Inc., **48** 359
Industrial Engineering, **III** 598
Industrial Engineering Associates, Inc., **II** 112
Industrial Equity Ltd., **I** 438; **17** 357
Industrial Fuel Supply Co., **I** 569
Industrial Gas Equipment Co., **I** 297
Industrial Gases Lagos, **25** 82
Industrial Instrument Company. *See* Foxboro Company.
Industrial Light & Magic, **12** 322
Industrial Mutual Insurance, **III** 264
Industrial National Bank, **9** 229
Industrial Powder Coatings, Inc., **16** 475
Industrial Publishing Company, **9** 413; **27** 361
Industrial Reorganization Corp., **III** 502, 556
Industrial Resources, **6** 144
Industrial Services of America, Inc., 46 247–49
Industrial Shows of America, **27** 362
Industrial Tectonics Corp., **18** 276
Industrial Trade & Consumer Shows Inc., **IV** 639; **26** 272
Industrial Trust Co. of Wilmington, **25** 540
Industrial Trust Company, **9** 228
Industrial Vehicles Corp. B.V., **III** 543–44
Industrias Bachoco, S.A. de C.V., 39 228–31
Industrias del Atlantico SA, **47** 291
Industrias Nacobre, **21** 259
Industrias Negromex, **23** 170
Industrias Penoles, S.A. de C.V., 22 284–86
Industrias Resistol S.A., **23** 170–71
Industrias y Confecciones, S.A. **V** 51; **26** 129
Industrie-Aktiengesellschaft, **IV** 201
Industrie Natuzzi S.p.A., 18 256–58
Industrie Regionale du Bâtiment, **IV** 108
Industriegas GmbH., **I** 581
Les Industries Ling, **13** 443
Industriförvaltnings AB Kinnevik, **26** 331–33; **36** 335
Industrionics Control, Inc., **III** 643
AB Industrivärden, **II** 366; **32** 397
Induyco. *See* Industrias y Confecciones, S.A.
Indy Lighting, **30** 266
Indy Racing League, **37** 74
Inelco Peripheriques, **10** 459
Inespo, **16** 322
Inexco Oil Co., **7** 282

Infinity Broadcasting Corporation, 11 190–92; 22 97; **23** 510; **28** 72; **35** 232; **48 214–17 (upd.)**
Infinity Enterprises, Inc., **44** 4
Infinity Partners, **36** 160
INFLEX, S.A., **8** 247
Inflight Sales Group Limited, **11** 82; **29** 511
InfoAsia, **28** 241
Infobase Services, **6** 14
Infocom, **32** 8
Infogrames Entertainment S.A., 35 227–30; 41 407
Infonet Services Corporation, **6** 303; **27** 304
Infoplan, **14** 36
Informatics General Corporation, **III** 248; **11** 468; **25** 86
Informatics Legal Systems, **III** 169; **6** 285
Information Access Company, 12 560–62; 17 252–55; 34 438. *See also* The Thomson Corporation.
Information and Communication Group, **14** 555
Information Associates Inc., **11** 78
Information Builders, Inc., 14 16; **22 291–93**
Information Consulting Group, **9** 345
Information, Dissemination and Retrieval Inc., **IV** 670
Information Holdings Inc., 47 183–86
Information International. *See* Autologic Information International, Inc.
Information Management Reporting Services. *See* Hyperion Software Corporation.
Information Management Science Associates, Inc., **13** 174
Information Please LLC, **26** 216
Information Resources, Inc., 10 358–60; 13 4; **25** 366
Information Unlimited Software, **6** 224
Informix Corporation, 10 361–64, 505; **30 243–46 (upd.)**
Infoseek Corporation, **27** 517; **30** 490
InfoSoft International, Inc. *See* Inso Corporation.
Infostrada S.p.A., **38** 300
Infosys Technologies Ltd., 38 240–43
Infotech Enterprises, Ltd., **33** 45
Infotechnology Inc., **25** 507–08
Infrasud, **I** 466
Infun, S.A., **23** 269
ING, B.V., **14** 45, 47
Ing. C. Olivetti & C., S.p.A., III 122, **144–46,** 549, 678; **10** 499; **16** 122; **25** 33. *See also* Olivetti S.p.A
Ingalls Quinn and Johnson, **9** 135
Ingalls Shipbuilding, Inc., I 485; **11** 264–65; **12** 28, **271–73; 36** 78–79; **41** 42
Ingear, **10** 216
Ingenico—Compagnie Industrielle et Financière d'Ingénierie, 46 250–52
Ingenious Designs Inc., **47** 420
Ingersoll-Rand Company, III 473, **525–27; 10** 262; **13** 27, 523; **15** 187, **223–26 (upd.); 22** 542; **33** 168; **34** 46
Ingka Holding B.V. *See* IKEA International A/S.
Ingleby Enterprises Inc. *See* Caribiner International, Inc.
Inglenook Vineyards, **13** 134; **34** 89
Ingles Markets, Inc., 20 305–08

Inglis Ltd., **III** 654; **12** 549
Ingram Book Group, **30** 70
Ingram Corp. Ltd., **III** 559; **IV** 249
Ingram Industries, Inc., 10 518–19; **11** 193–95; **13** 90, 482; **49 217–20 (upd.)**
Ingram Micro Corporation, **24** 29
AB Ingredients, **II** 466
Ingredients Technology Corp., **9** 154
Ingres Corporation, **9** 36–37; **25** 87
Ingwerson and Co., **II** 356
INH. *See* Instituto Nacional de Hidrocarboros.
Inha Works Ltd., **33** 164
Inhalation Therapy Services, **III** 73
INI. *See* Instituto Nacional de Industria.
Initial Towel Supply. *See* Rentokil Initial Plc.
Inktomi Corporation, 41 98; **45 200–04**
Inland Container Corporation, IV 311, 341–42, 675; **7** 528; **8 267–69**; **19** 267
Inland Motors Corporation, **18** 291
Inland Paperboard and Packaging, Inc., **31** 438
Inland Pollution Control, **9** 110
Inland Specialty Chemical Corp., **I** 342; **14** 217
Inland Steel Industries, Inc., II 403; **IV** 113–16, 158, 703; **7** 447; **13** 157; **15** 249–50; **17** 351; **19** 9, **216–20 (upd.)**, 311, 381; **23** 35; **30** 254; **40** 269, 381; **41** 4
Inland Valley, **23** 321
Inmac, Inc., **16** 373
Inmos Ltd., **I** 532; **11** 307; **29** 323
InnCOGEN Limited, **35** 480
InnerCity Foods Joint Venture Company, **16** 97
Inno-BM, **26** 158, 161
Inno-France. *See* Societe des Grandes Entreprises de Distribution, Inno-France.
Innova International Corporation, **26** 333
Innovacom, **25** 96
Innovation, **26** 158
Innovative Marketing Systems. *See* Bloomberg L.P.
Innovative Pork Concepts, **7** 82
Innovative Products & Peripherals Corporation, **14** 379
Innovative Software Inc., **10** 362
Innovative Sports Systems, Inc., **15** 396
Innovative Valve Technologies Inc., **33** 167
Innovex Ltd., **21** 425
Inns and Co., **III** 734
Innwerk AG, **IV** 229
Inoue Electric Manufacturing Co., **II** 75–76
Inpaco, **16** 340
Inpacsa, **19** 226
Inprise/Borland Corporation, **33** 115
Input/Output, Inc., **11** 538
INS. *See* International News Service.
Insalaco Markets Inc., **13** 394
INSCO, **III** 242
Inserra Supermarkets, 25 234–36
Insight Enterprises, Inc., 18 259–61
Insight Marques SARL IMS SA, **48** 224
Insilco Corporation, I 473; **12** 472; **16** **281–83**; **23** 212; **36** 469–70
Insley Manufacturing Co., **8** 545
Inso Corporation, 26 215–19; **36** 273
Inspiration Resources Corporation, **12** 260; **13** 502–03
Inspirations PLC, **22** 129

Insta-Care Holdings Inc., **16** 59
Insta-Care Pharmacy Services, **9** 186
Instant Auto Insurance, **33** 3, 5
Instant Interiors Corporation, **26** 102
Instant Milk Co., **II** 488
Instapak Corporation, **14** 429
Instinet Corporation, 34 225–27; **48** 227–28
Institut de Sérothérapie Hémopoiétique, **I** 669
Institut für Gemeinwohl, **IV** 139
Institut Merieux, **I** 389
Institut Ronchese, **I** 676
Institute de Development Industriel, **19** 87
Institute for Professional Development, **24** 40
Institute for Scientific Information, **8** 525, 528
Institution Food House. *See* Alex Lee Inc.
Institutional Financing Services, **23** 491
Instituto Nacional de Hidrocarboros, **IV** 528
Instituto Nacional de Industria, I **459–61**; **V** 606–07; **6** 95–96
Instituto per la Ricostruzione Industriale, **V** 614
Instone Airline, **I** 92
Instromet International, **22** 65
Instrument Systems Corp. *See* Griffon Corporation.
Instrumentarium Corp., **13** 328; **25** 82
Instrumentation Laboratory Inc., **III** 511–12; **22** 75
Instrumentation Scientifique de Laboratoire, S.A., **15** 404
Insulite Co. of Finland, **IV** 275
Insurance Auto Auctions, Inc., 23 148, **285–87**
Insurance Co. against Fire Damage, **III** 308
Insurance Co. of Scotland, **III** 358
Insurance Co. of the State of Pennsylvania, **III** 196
Insurance Company of North America. *See* CIGNA Corporation.
Insurance Corp. of Ireland (Life), **III** 335
Insurance Partners L.P., **15** 257
InSync Communications, **42** 425
Intabex Holdings Worldwide, S.A., **27** 126
Intalco Aluminum Corp., **12** 254
Intamin, **17** 443
Intarsia Corp., **38** 187
Intat Precision Inc., **48** 5
INTEC, **6** 428
InteCom Inc., **6** 285
Integon Corp., **IV** 374
Integra-A Hotel and Restaurant Company, **13** 473
Integral Corporation, **14** 381; **23** 446; **33** 331
Integrated Business Information Services, **13** 5
Integrated Computer Systems. *See* Learning Tree International Inc.
Integrated Data Services Co., **IV** 473
Integrated Defense Technologies, **44** 423
Integrated Genetics, **I** 638; **8** 210; **13** 239; **38** 204, 206
Integrated Health Services, Inc., **11** 282
Integrated Medical Systems Inc., **12** 333; **47** 236
Integrated Resources, Inc., **11** 483; **16** 54; **19** 393

Integrated Silicon Solutions, Inc., **18** 20; **43** 17; **47** 384
Integrated Software Systems Corporation, **6** 224; **11** 469
Integrated Systems Operations. *See* Xerox Corporation.
Integrated Systems Solutions Corp., **9** 284; **11** 395; **17** 264
Integrated Technology, Inc., **6** 279
Integrated Telecom Technologies, **14** 417
Integris Europe, **49** 382, 384
Integrity Inc., 44 241–43
Integrity Life Insurance, **III** 249
Intel Corporation, II 44–46, 62, 64; **III** 115, 125, 455; **6** 215–17, 222, 231, 233, 235, 257; **9** 42–43, 57, 114–15, 165–66; **10 365–67 (upd.)**, 477; **11** 62, 308, 328, 490, 503, 518, 520; **12** 61, 449; **13** 47; **16** 139–40, 146, 394; **17** 32–33; **18** 18, 260; **19** 310, 312; **20** 69, 175; **21** 36, 122; **22** 542; **24** 233, 236, 371; **25** 418, 498; **26** 91, 432; **27** 365–66; **30** 10; **34** 441; **36** 123, **284–88 (upd.)**; **38** 71, 416; **41** 408; **43** 14–16; **47** 153
Intelcom Support Services, Inc., **14** 334
Intelicom Solutions Corp., **6** 229
IntelliCorp, Inc., 9 310; **31** 298; **45** **205–07**
Intelligent Electronics, Inc., 6 243–45; **12** 184; **13** 176, 277
Intelligent Interactions Corp., **49** 421
Intelligent Software Ltd., **26** 275
Intelligraphics Inc., **33** 44
Intellimetrics Instrument Corporation, **16** 93
Intellisys, **48** 257
Inter American Aviation, Inc. *See* SkyWest, Inc.
Inter-American Development Bank, **IV** 55
Inter-American Satellite Television Network, **7** 391
Inter-City Gas Ltd., **III** 654; **19** 159
Inter-City Western Bakeries Ltd., **II** 631
Inter-City Wholesale Electric Inc., **15** 385
Inter-Comm Telephone, Inc., **8** 310
Inter-Continental Hotels and Resorts, **38** 77
Inter IKEA Systems B.V., **V** 82
Inter-Island Airways, Ltd., **22** 251; **24** 20
Inter-Island Steam Navigation Co. *See* Hawaiian Airlines.
Inter Island Telephone, **6** 326, 328
Inter-Mountain Telephone Co., **V** 344
Inter-Ocean Corporation, **16** 103; **44** 90
Inter Parfums Inc., 35 235–38
Inter-Regional Financial Group, Inc., 15 **231–33**. *See also* Dain Rauscher Corporation.
Inter State Telephone, **6** 338
Inter Techniek, **16** 421
Interactive Computer Design, Inc., **23** 489, 491
Interactive Systems, **7** 500
InterAd Holdings Ltd., **49** 422
Interamericana de Talleras SA de CV, **10** 415
Interbake Foods, **II** 631
InterBold, **7** 146; **11** 151
Interbrás, **IV** 503
Interbrew S.A., 16 397; **17 256–58**; **25** 279, 282; **26** 306; **34** 202; **38** 74, 78
Interchemical Corp., **13** 460
Intercity Food Services, Inc., **II** 663
Interco Incorporated, III 528–31; **9** 133, 135, 192, 234–35; **10** 184; **12** 156,

306–08; **22** 49; **29** 294; **31** 136–37, 210; **39** 146. *See also* Furniture Brands International, Inc.
Intercolonial, **6** 360
Intercomi, **II** 233
Intercontessa AG, **35** 401; **36** 294
Intercontinental Apparel, **8** 249
Intercontinental Breweries, **I** 289
Intercontinental Electronics Corp. *See* IEC Electronics Corp.
Intercontinental Hotels, **I** 248–49
Intercontinental Mortgage Company, **8** 436
Intercontinental Rubber Co., **II** 112
Intercontinentale, **III** 404
Intercord, **22** 194
Intercostal Steel Corp., **13** 97
Interdesign, **16** 421
Interdiscount/Radio TV Steiner AG, **48** 116
Interealty Corp., **43** 184
Interedi-Cosmopolitan, **III** 47
Interep National Radio Sales Inc., 35 231–34
Interessen Gemeinschaft Farbenwerke. *See* I.G. Farbenindustrie AG.
Interface Group, **13** 483
Interface, Inc., 8 270–72; 18 112; 29 246–49 (upd.)
Interferon Sciences, Inc., **13** 366–67
Interfinancial, **III** 200
InterFirst Bankcorp, Inc., **9** 482
Interfood Ltd., **II** 520–21, 540
Interglas S.A., **22** 515
Intergram, Inc., **27** 21
Intergraph Corporation, 6 246–49; 10 257; 24 233–36 (upd.)
Interhandel, **I** 337–38; **II** 378; **22** 226
INTERIM Services, Inc., **9** 268, 270; **25** 434; **29** 224, 227
Interinvest S.A., **33** 19
Interlabor, **16** 420–21
Interlabor Interim, **43** 308
The Interlake Corporation, 8 273–75; 38 210
Interlake Steamship Company, **15** 302
Intermaco S.R.L., **43** 368
Intermagnetics General Corp., **9** 10
Intermarché, **35** 398, 401. *See also* ITM Entreprises SA.
Intermark, Inc., **12** 394; **34** 338–39
Intermec Corporation, **29** 414
Intermed, **I** 429
Intermedia, **25** 499
Intermedics, **III** 633; **11** 458–59; **12** 325–26; **40** 66–67
Intermedics Intraocular Inc., **I** 665
Intermet Corporation, 32 279–82
Intermoda, **V** 166
Intermountain Broadcasting and Television Corp., **IV** 674
Intermountain Health Care, Inc., 27 237–40
ITM International, **IV** 239
International Aeradio Limited, **47** 352
International Aero Engines, **9** 418
International Agricultural Corporation, **8** 264–65
International Air Service Co., **24** 21
International Assurance Co., **III** 195
International Bank, **II** 261
International Bank of Japan, **17** 122
International Bank of Moscow, **IV** 242
International Banking and Credit Analysis (IBCA), **37** 144
International Banking Corp., **II** 253; **9** 123

International Banking Technologies, Inc., **11** 113
International Basic Economy Corporation, **13** 103
International Beauty Supply, Ltd. *See* L.L. Knickerbocker Co., Inc.
International Beverage Corporation. *See* Clearly Canadian Beverage Corporation.
International Brewing Holdings Pty., **21** 229
International Brotherhood of Teamsters, 37 211–14
International Business Directories, Inc., **26** 484
International Business Machines Corporation, I 26, 455, 523, 534, 541; **II** 6, 8, 10, 42, 44–45, 56, 62, 68, 70, 73, 86, 99, 107, 113, 134, 159, 211, 274, 326, 379, 397, 432, 440; **III** 9, 109–11, 113–18, 121–28, 130, 132–34, 136, 139–43, 145, **147–49**, 151–52, 154–55, 157, 165–72, 200, 246, 313, 319, 326, 458, 475, 549, 618, 685; **IV** 443, 711; **6** 51, 218–25, 233–35, 237, 240–42, 244–48, **250–53 (upd.),** 254–60, 262, 265, 269–71, 275–77, 279, 281–89, 320, 324, 346, 390, 428; **7** 145–46, 161; **8** 138–39, 466–67; **9** 36, 41–42, 48, 50, 114–15, 131, 139, 165–66, 170–71, 184, 194, 284, 296–97, 310, 327, 463–64; **10** 19, 22–24, 58, 119, 125, 161, 194, 232, 237, 243–44, 255–56, 309, 361–62, 366–67, 394, 456, 463, 474, 500–01, 505, 510, 512–13, 518–19, 542; **11** 19, 45, 50, 59, 61–62, 64–65, 68, 86–88, 150, 273–74, 285, 364, 395, 469, 485, 491, 494, 506, 519; **12** 61, 138–39, 147–49, 161–62, 183, 204, 238, 278, 335, 442, 450, 469–70, 484; **13** 47, 127, 174, 214, 326, 345, 387–88, 403, 482; **14** 13–15, 106, 268–69, 318, 354, 391, 401, 432–33, 446, 533; **15** 106, 440, 454–55, 491–92; **16** 4, 94, 140, 224–26, 301, 367–68, 372; **17** 353, 418, 532–34; **18** 94, 110, 112, 162, 250, 292, 305–07, 344, 434–36; **19** 41, 110, 310, 312, 437; **20** 237, 313; **21** 86, 391; **23** 135, 138, 209, 470; **24** 234; **25** 20–21, 34, 86–87, 96, 133–34, 149, 298–301, 356, 358, 530–32; **26** 90, 187, 275–76, 427, 429, 441, 540, 542; **28** 112, 189; **29** 375, 414; **30** 247–51 (upd.), 140, 300, 337–38; **34** 442–46; **36** 81–82, 171, 480–81; **38** 54–55, 250, 417; **43** 126–27; **46** 165; **47** 153; **49** 94
International Care Services, **6** 182
International Cellucotton Products Co., **III** 40; **16** 302–03; **43** 256–57
International Cementers Inc., **25** 74
International Commercial Bank, **II** 257
International Communication Materials, Inc., **18** 387
International Computers. *See* ICL plc.
International Controls Corporation, 10 368–70
International Corona Corporation, **12** 244
International Creative Management, Inc., 38 161; **43 235–37**
International Credit Card Business Assoc., **II** 436
International Dairy Queen, Inc., 7 266; **10 371–74; 39 232–36 (upd.)**

International Data Group, Inc., 7 238–40; 12 561; **25 237–40 (upd.); 27** 222
International Development Bank, **IV** 417
International Digital Communications, Inc., **6** 327
International Distillers & Vintners Ltd., **31** 92
International Egyptian Oil Co., **IV** 412
International Engineering Company, Inc., **7** 355
International Epicure, **12** 280
International Equities Corp., **III** 98
International Factoring Corp., **II** 436
International Factors, Limited, **II** 208
International Family Entertainment Inc., 13 279–81
International Finance Corp., **19** 192
International Flavors & Fragrances Inc., 9 290–92; 38 244–48 (upd.)
International Foods, **II** 468
International Fuel Cells Inc., **39** 394
International Game Technology, 10 375–76; 24 37 **25** 313; **41 214–16 (upd.)**
International Graphics Corp., **IV** 645
International Group, **13** 277
International Harvester Co., **III** 473, 650, 651; **10** 264, 280, 378, 380, 528; **13** 16; **17** 158; **22** 380. *See also* Navistar International Corporation.
International Healthcare, **III** 197
International Home Foods, Inc., **42** 94
International House of Pancakes. *See* IHOP Corporation.
International Hydron, **10** 47; **13** 367
International Imaging Limited, **29** 58
International Income Property, **IV** 708
International Industries, **17** 249
International Learning Systems Corp. Ltd., **IV** 641–42; **7** 311
International Lease Finance Corporation, III 198; **6** 67; **36** 231; **48 218–20**
International Light Metals Corp., **IV** 163
International MacGregor, **27** 269
International Management Group, 18 262–65
International Marine Oil Co., **IV** 363
International Marine Services, **22** 276
International Match, **12** 463
International Mercantile Marine Co., **II** 330
International Milling. *See* International Multifoods Corporation.
International Mineral & Chemical, Inc., **8** 265–66
International Minerals and Chemical Corporation, **19** 253
International Multifoods Corporation, II 493; **7 241–43; 12** 80, 125; **14** 515; **21** 289; **23** 203; **25 241–44 (upd.); 28** 238
International Music Co., **16** 202; **43** 171
International News Service, **IV** 626–27; **19** 203; **25** 507
International Nickel Co. of Canada, Ltd. *See* Inco Limited.
International Nutrition Laboratories, **14** 558
International Olympic Committee, 44 244–47
International Organization of Consumers Unions, **26** 98
International Pacific Corp., **II** 389
International Paper Company, I 27; **II** 208, 403; **III** 693, 764; **IV** 16, 245,

286–88, 289, 326; **8** 267; **11** 76, 311; **15** 227–30 (upd.); **16** 349; **17** 446; **23** 48–49, 366, 368; **25** 9; **26** 444; **30** 92, 94; **32** 91, 346; **47 187–92 (upd.)**
International Parts Corporation, **10** 414
International Periodical Distributors, **34** 5
International Permalite, **22** 229
International Petroleum Co., Ltd., **IV** 415–16, 438, 478; **25** 230
International Petroleum Corp., **IV** 454, 484
International Playtex, Inc., **12** 93
International Products Corporation. *See* The Terlato Wine Group.
International Proteins Corporation, **21** 248
International Publishing Corp., **IV** 641, 666–67; **7** 343; **17** 397; **23** 350; **49** 407
International Raw Materials, Ltd., **31** 20
International Rectifier Corporation, 31 263–66
International Roofing Company, **22** 13–14
International Sealants Corporation, **8** 333
International Shipholding Corporation, Inc., 27 241–44
International Shoe Co., **III** 528–30
International Silver Company, **I** 30; **12** 472; **14** 482–83
International Specialty Products, Inc., **22** 225, 228–29
International Speedway Corporation, 19 221–23; **32** 439
International Standard Electric, **II** 66–68
International Stores, **I** 427
International Supply Consortium, **13** 79
International Talent Group, **25** 281
International Talent Management, Inc. *See* Motown Records Company L.P.
International Telcell Group, **7** 336
International Telecommunications Satellite Organization, **46** 328
International Telephone & Telegraph Corporation, I 434, 446, **462–64**, 544; **II** 13, 66, 68, 86, 130, 331; **III** 98–99, 162–64, 166, 644–45, 684; **V** 334–35, 337–38; **6** 356; **8** 157; **9** 10–11, 324; **10** 19, 44, 301; **11 196–99 (upd.)**, 337, 516; **12** 18; **13** 246; **14** 332, 488; **19** 131, 205, 208; **22** 55; **25** 100, 432; **46** 412
International Television Corporation Entertainment Group, **23** 391
International Thomson Organisation Ltd. *See* The Thomson Corporation.
International Thomson Organization Ltd., **23** 92
International Time Recording Company. *See* International Business Machines Corporation.
International Total Services, Inc., 37 215–18
International Trust and Investment Corp., **II** 577
International Trust Co., **II** 207
International Utilities Corp., **IV** 75–76; **6** 444
International Western Electric Co., **I** 462; **II** 66; **III** 162; **11** 196
International Wind Systems, **6** 581
International Wine & Spirits Ltd., **9** 533
International Wire Works Corp., **8** 13
International Wireless Inc., **21** 261
Internationale Industriële Beleggung Maatschappij Amsterdam BV, **IV** 128
Internationale Nederlanden Group, **24** 88
Internet Shopping Network, **26** 441

InterNorth, Inc., **II** 16; **V** 610
Interocean Management Corp., **9** 509–11
Interpac Belgium, **6** 303
Interprovincial Pipe Line Ltd., **I** 264; **IV** 439; **25** 231. *See also* Enbridge Inc.
The Interpublic Group of Companies, Inc., I 16–18, 31, 36; **6** 53; **14** 315; **16** 70, 72, 167; **20** 5; **22 294–97 (upd.)**; **23** 478; **28** 66–67; **32** 142; **42** 107
Interra Financial. *See* Dain Rauscher Corporation.
InterRedec, Inc., **17** 196
Interscience, **17** 271
Interscope Communications, Inc., **23** 389, 391; **27** 121
Interscope Music Group, 31 267–69
Intersec, Inc., **27** 21
Intersil Inc., **II** 30; **12** 196; **16** 358
Interstate & Ocean Transport, **6** 577
Interstate Bag, **I** 335
Interstate Bakeries Corporation, 7 320; **12 274–76**; **27** 310; **38 249–52 (upd.)**
Interstate Brick Company, **6** 568–69
Interstate Electric Manufacturing Company. *See* McGraw Electric Company.
Interstate Finance Corp., **11** 16
Interstate Financial Corporation, **9** 475
Interstate Iron and Steel Company. *See* Republic Engineered Steels, Inc.
Interstate Logos, Inc., **27** 278
Interstate Paint Distributors, Inc., **13** 367
Interstate Power Company, **6** 555, 605; **18** 404
Interstate Properties Inc., **45** 15–16
Interstate Public Service Company, **6** 555
Interstate Stores Inc., **V** 203; **15** 469; **18** 522
Interstate Supply Company. *See* McGraw Electric Company.
Interstate United Corporation, **II** 679; **III** 502; **13** 435
Intertec Design, Inc., **34** 371–72
Intertec Publishing Corp., **22** 441
Intertechnique SA, **36** 530
Interturbine Holland, **19** 150
Intertype Corp., **II** 37
Interunfall, **III** 346
Intervideo TV Productions-A.B., **II** 640
Intervision Express, **24** 510
Interweb, **IV** 661
InterWest Partners, **16** 418
Intimate Brands, Inc., 24 237–39'; **29** 357
InTouch Systems, Inc., **43** 118
Intrac Handelsgesellschaft mbH, **7** 142
Intradal, **II** 572
Intraph South Africa Ltd., **6** 247
IntraWest Bank, **II** 289
The Intrawest Corporation, 15 234–36; **31** 67; **43** 438
Intrepid Corporation, **16** 493
IntroGene B.V., **13** 241
Intuit Inc., 13 147; **14 262–64**; **23** 457; **33 208–11 (upd.)**
Invacare Corporation, 11 200–02, 486; **47 193–98 (upd.)**
Invenex Laboratories, **17** 287
Invento Products Corporation, **21** 269
Invep S.p.A., **10** 150
Inveresk Paper Co., **III** 693; **IV** 685
Invergordon Distillers, **III** 509
Inverness Medical Innovations, Inc., **45** 208
Inverness Medical Technology, Inc., **45** 210

Inversale, **9** 92
INVESCO MIM Management Limited, **21** 397
Invesgen S.A., **26** 129
InvestCorp International, **15** 200; **24** 195, 420; **25** 205, 207
Investcorp S.A. *See* Arabian Investment Banking Corp.
Investimentos Itaú S.A., **19** 33
Investors Bank and Trust Company, **18** 152
Investors Diversified Services, Inc., **II** 398; **6** 199; **8** 348–49; **10** 43–45, 59, 62; **21** 305; **25** 248; **38** 42
Investors Group, **III** 261. *See also* Power Corporation of Canada.
Investors Management Corp., **10** 331
Investors Overseas Services, **10** 368–69
Investrónica S.A., **26** 129
Invista Capital Management, **III** 330
The Invus Group, Ltd., **33** 449
Iolab Corp., **III** 36
Iomega Corporation, 18 509–10; **21 294–97**
IONA Technologies plc, 43 238–41
Ionpure Technologies Corporation, **6** 486–88
Iowa Beef Packers, **21** 287
Iowa Beef Processors, **II** 516–17; **IV** 481–82; **13** 351
Iowa Manufacturing, **II** 86
Iowa Mold Tooling Co., Inc., **16** 475
Iowa Public Service Company, **6** 524–25
IP Gas Supply Company, **6** 506
IP Services, Inc., **IV** 597
IP Timberlands Ltd., **IV** 288
IP&L. *See* Illinois Power & Light Corporation.
Ipalco Enterprises, Inc., 6 508–09
IPC. *See* International Publishing Corp.
IPC Communications, Inc., **15** 196
IPC Magazines Limited, IV 650; **7 244–47**
IPD. *See* International Periodical Distributors.
IPEC Holdings Ltd., **27** 474–75
Iphotonics Inc., **48** 369
Ipko-Amcor, **14** 225
IPL Energy Inc. *See* Enbridge Inc.
IPS Praha a.s., **38** 437
IPS Publishing, **39** 341–42
IPSOA Editore, **14** 555
Ipsos SA, 24 355; **48 221–24**
IQUE, Inc., **21** 194
Iran Air, **6** 101
Iran Pan American Oil Co., **IV** 466
Iranian Oil Exploration and Producing Co., **IV** 466–67
Iraq Petroleum Co., **IV** 363, 386, 429, 450, 464, 558–60
Irby-Gilliland Company, **9** 127
Irdeto, **31** 330
IRI. *See* Instituto per la Ricostruzione Industriale.
Irideon, Inc., **35** 435
Iris Associates, Inc., **25** 299, 301
IRIS Holding Co., **III** 347
Irish Agricultural Wholesale Society Ltd. *See* IAWS Group plc.
Irish Air. *See* Aer Lingus Group plc.
Irish Life Assurance Company, **16** 14; **43** 7
Irish Paper Sacks Ltd., **IV** 295; **19** 225
Irish Sugar Co., **II** 508
Iron and Steel Corp., **IV** 22, 41, 92, 533–34

Iron and Steel Press Company, **27** 360
Iron Cliffs Mining Company, **13** 156
Iron Mountain Forge, **13** 319
Iron Mountain, Inc., 33 212–14
Iron Ore Company of Canada, **8** 347
Iroquois Gas Corporation, **6** 526
Irvin Feld & Kenneth Feld Productions, Inc., 15 237–39. *See also* Feld Entertainment, Inc.
Irving Bank Corp., **II** 192
Irving Tanning Company, **17** 195
Irving Trust Coompany, **II** 257; **22** 55
Irvington Smelting, **IV** 78
Irwin Lehrhoff Associates, **11** 366
Irwin Toy Limited, 14 265–67
Isabela Shoe Corporation, **13** 360
Isagro S.p.A., **26** 425
Iscor. *See* Iron and Steel Corporation.
Isetan Company Limited, V 85–87; 36 289–93 (upd.)
Iseya Tanji Drapery, **V** 85
Ishikawajima-Harima Heavy Industries Co., Ltd., I 508, 511, 534; **II** 274; **III** 532–33; **9** 293; **12** 484; **41** 41
Ishizaki Honten, **III** 715
Isis Distributed Systems, Inc., **10** 501
Island Air, **24** 22
The Island ECN, Inc., 48 225–29
Island Equipment Co., **19** 381
Island Holiday, **I** 417
Island Pictures Corp., **23** 389
Island Records, **23** 389
Islands Restaurants, **17** 85–87
Isle of Capri Casinos, Inc., 33 41; 41 217–19
Isolite Insulating Products Co., **III** 714
Isosceles PLC, **II** 628–29; **24** 270; **47** 367–68
Isotec Communications Incorporated, **13** 213
Isover, **III** 676; **16** 121
Ispat Inland Inc., 40 267–72 (upd.), 381
Ispat International N.V., 30 252–54
ISS A/S, 49 221–23, 376
ISS International Service System, Inc., **8** 271
ISS Securitas, **42** 165, 167
ISSI. *See* Integrated Silicon Solutions Inc.
Istanbul Fertilizer Industry, **IV** 563
Istante Vesa s.r.l., **22** 239
Istituto Farmacologico Serono S.p.A. *See* Serono S.A.
Istituto per la Ricostruzione Industriale S.p.A., I 207, 459, 465–67; **II** 191–92, 270–71; **IV** 419; **11 203–06; 13** 28, 218
Isuzu Motors, Ltd., II 274; **III** 581, 593; **7** 8, 219; **9 293–95; 10** 354; **23 288–91 (upd.); 36** 240, 243
Isuzu Motors of Japan, **21** 6
IT Group, **28** 203
IT International, **V** 255
IT-Software Companies, **48** 402
Itabira Iron Ore Co. Ltd., **IV** 54; **43** 111
ITABRASCO, **IV** 55
Italcarta, **IV** 339
Italcementi, **IV** 420
Italcimenti Group, **40** 107–08
Italianni's, **22** 128
Italiatour, **6** 69
Italmobiliare, **III** 347
Italstate. *See* Societa per la Infrastrutture e l'Assetto del Territoria.
Italtel, **V** 326–27
Italware, **27** 94

Itaú. *See* Banco Itaú S.A.
Itaú Winterthur Seguradura S.A., **III** 404
Itaúsa. *See* Investimentos Itaú S.A.
Itek Corp., **I** 486; **11** 265
Itel Corporation, II 64; **III** 512; **6** 262, 354; **9** 49, **296–99; 15** 107; **22** 339; **26** 328, 519; **47** 37
Items International Airwalk Inc., 17 259–61
Ithaca Gas & Electric. *See* New York State Electric and Gas.
ITI Education Corporation, **29** 472
ITM Entreprises SA, 36 294–97
Ito Carnation Co., **II** 518
Ito Food Processing Co., **II** 518
Ito Gofuku Co. Ltd., **V** 129
Ito Meat Processing Co., **II** 518
Ito Processed Food Co., **II** 518
Ito-Yokado Co., Ltd., II 661; **V 88–89; 32** 414, 416–17; **42 189–92 (upd.)**
Itochu and Renown, Inc., **12** 281
ITOCHU Corporation, 19 9; **32 283–87 (upd.); 34** 231; **42** 342
Itochu Housing, **38** 415
Itochu of Japan, **14** 550
Itoh. *See* C. Itoh & Co.
Itoham Foods Inc., II 518–19
Itokin, **III** 48
Itoman & Co., **26** 456
ITT, **21** 200; **24** 188, 405; **30** 101; **47** 103. *See also* International Telephone and Telegraph Corporation.
ITT Aerospace, **33** 48
ITT Educational Services, Inc., 33 215–17
ITT Sheraton Corporation, III 98–101; 23 484
ITT World Directories, **27** 498, 500
iTurf Inc., **29** 142–43
ITW. *See* Illinois Tool Works Inc.
ITW Devcon, **12** 7
IU International, **23** 40
IURA Edition, **14** 556
IV Therapy Associates, **16** 440
IVAC Corp., **I** 646; **11** 90
IVACO Industries Inc., **11** 207
Ivanhoe, Inc., **II** 662, 664
IVAX Corporation, 11 207–09; 41 420–21
IVC Industries, Inc., 45 208–11
Iveco, **I** 148; **12** 91
Ives Trains, **16** 336
iVillage Inc., 46 232, **253–56**
Ivy Mortgage Corp., **39** 380, 382
Iwai & Co., **I** 492, 509–10; **IV** 151; **24** 325, 358
Iwata Air Compressor, **III** 427
Iwerks Entertainment, Inc., 33 127; **34 228–30**
IXC Communications, Inc., 29 250–52; 37 127
IXI Ltd., **38** 418–19
IYG Holding Company of Japan, **7** 492; **32** 414, 417
The IZOD Gant Corporation, **24** 385
Izod Lacoste, **II** 502–03; **9** 156–57; **10** 324
Izukyu Corporation, **47** 408
Izumi Fudosan, **IV** 726
Izumiya, **V** 477; **36** 418

J&E Davy, **16** 14
J&G Meakin, **12** 529
J&J Colman, **II** 566

J&J Corrugated Box Corp., **IV** 282; **9** 261
J & J Snack Foods Corporation, 24 240–42
J&L Industrial Supply, **13** 297
J&L Steel. *See* Jones & Laughlin Steel Corp.
J & M Laboratories, **48** 299
J&R Electronics Inc., 26 224–26
J. & W. Seligman and Co., **17** 498
J.A. Baldwin Manufacturing Company, **17** 106
J.A. Jones, Inc., 16 284–86; 17 377
J. Aron & Co., **II** 415
J.B. Hudson & Son, **18** 136
J.B. Hunt Transport Services Inc., 12 277–79; 15 440; **26** 533
J.B. Lippincott & Company, **IV** 652; **14** 554–56; **33** 460
J.B. McLean Publishing Co., Ltd., **IV** 638
J.B. Williams Company, **III** 66; **8** 63
J.B. Wolters Publishing Company, **14** 554
J. Baker, Inc., 13 361; **31 270–73**
J. Beres & Son, **24** 444–45
J Bibby & Sons, **I** 424
J Bibby Agriculture Limited, **13** 53
J. Bulova Company. *See* Bulova Corporation.
J. Byrons, **9** 186
J.C. Baxter Co., **15** 501
J.C. Hillary's, **20** 54
J.C. Penney Company, Inc., I 516; **V 90–92; 6** 336; **8** 288, 555; **9** 156, 210, 213, 219, 346–94; **10** 409, 490; **11** 349; **12** 111, 431, 522; **14** 62; **16** 37, 327–28; **17** 124, 175, 177, 366, 460; **18** 108, 136, 168, 200, **269–73 (upd.),** 373, 478; **19** 300; **21** 24, 527; **25** 91, 254, 368; **26** 161; **27** 346, 429; **31** 260–61; **32** 166, 168–70; **39** 270; **41** 114–15; **43 245–50 (upd.)**
J. Crew Group Inc., 12 280–82; 25 48; **34 231–34 (upd.); 36** 472
J.D. Bassett Manufacturing Co. *See* Bassett Furniture Industries, Inc.
J.D. Edwards & Company, 14 268–70; 38 431
J.D. Power and Associates, 9 166; **32 297–301**
J. D'Addario & Company, Inc., 48 230–33
J.E. Baxter Co., **I** 429
J.E. Nolan, **11** 486
J.E. Sirrine. *See* CRSS Inc.
J.E. Smith Box & Printing Co., **13** 441
J. Edward Connelly Associates, Inc., **22** 438
J. Evershed & Son, **13** 103
J.F. Corporation, **V** 87
J.F. Lauman and Co., **II** 681
J. Fielding & Co., **IV** 249
J.G. McMullen Dredging Co., **III** 558
J. Gadsden Paper Products, **IV** 249
J. George Leyner Engineering Works Co., **III** 525–26
J.H. Heafner Co., **20** 263
J.H. Stone & Sons, **IV** 332
J.H. Whitney & Company, **9** 250; **32** 100
J. Homestock. *See* R.H. Macy & Co.
J. Horner's, **48** 415
J.I. Case Company, I 148, 527; **III** 651; **10 377–81; 13** 17; **22** 380. *See also* CNH Global N.V.
The J. Jill Group, Inc., 35 239–41
J.K. Armsby Co., **7** 130–31

J.K. Starley and Company Ltd, **7** 458
J.L. Clark, Inc. *See* Clarcor Inc.
J.L. Hudson Company. *See* Dayton Hudson
   Corporation.
J.L. Kraft & Bros. Co., **II** 532
J.L. Shiely Co., **III** 691
J.L. Wright Company, **25** 379
J. Levin & Co., Inc., **13** 367
J. Lyons & Co., **I** 215
J.M. Brunswick & Brothers, **III** 442
J.M. Douglas & Company Limited, **14** 141
J.M. Horton Ice Cream Co., **II** 471
J.M. Huber Corporation, **40** 68
J.M. Jones Co., **II** 668; **18** 504
J.M. Kohler Sons Company, **7** 269
The **J.M. Smucker Company, 11** 210–12
J.M. Tull Metals Co., Inc., **IV** 116; **15** 250;
   19 219
J.M. Voith AG, 33 222–25
J. Mandelbaum & Sons, **19** 510
J-Mar Associates, **31** 435–36
J-Mass, **IV** 289
J. Muirhead Ltd., **I** 315; **25** 81
J.P. Heilwell Industries, **II** 420
J.P. Morgan & Co. Incorporated, II 281,
   329–32, 407, 419, 427–28, 430–31,
   441; **III** 237, 245, 380; **IV** 20, 180, 400;
   9 386; **11** 421; **12** 165; **13** 13; **16** 25,
   375; **19** 190; **26** 66, 500; **30** 261–65
   (upd.); **33** 464; **35** 74; **36** 151–53
J.P. Morgan Chase & Co., 38 253–59
   (upd.)
J.P. Stevens Inc., **8** 234; **12** 404; **16**
   533–35; **17** 75; **19** 420; **27** 468–69; **28**
   218
J.P. Wood, **II** 587
J.R. Brown & Sharpe. *See* Brown &
   Sharpe Manufacturing Co.
J.R. Geigy S.A., **I** 632–33, 635, 671; **8**
   108–10; **39** 72
J.R. Parkington Co., **I** 280
J.R. Simplot Company, 16 287–89; **21**
   508; **26** 309
J.R. Wyllie & Sons, **I** 437
J. Ray McDermott & Co., **III** 558–59
J.S. Fry & Sons, **II** 476
J.S. Morgan & Co., **II** 329, 427
J Sainsbury plc, II 657–59, 677–78; **10**
   442; **11** 239, 241; **13** 282–84 **(upd.)**; **17**
   42; **21** 335; **22** 241; **32** 253; **38** 260–65
   (upd.)
J. Sanders & Sons, **IV** 711
J. Sears & Company, **V** 177
J. Spiegel and Company. *See* Spiegel, Inc.
J.T. Wing and Co., **I** 158
J.U. Dickson Sawmill Inc. *See* Dickson
   Forest Products, Inc.
J.W. Bateson, **8** 87
J.W. Buderus and Sons, **III** 694
J.W. Charles Financial Services Inc., **25**
   542
J.W. Childs Associates, L.P., **46** 220
J.W. Childs Equity Partners LP, **40** 274
J.W. Foster and Sons, Inc. *See* Reebok
   International Ltd.
J.W. Higman & Co., **III** 690
J.W. Spear, **25** 314
J.W. Wassall Ltd. *See* Wassall PLC.
J. Walter Thompson Co., **I** 9, 17, 25, 37,
   251, 354, 623; **10** 69; **11** 51; **12** 168; **16**
   167; **48** 442
J. Weingarten Inc., **7** 203; **28** 163
J. Wiss & Sons Co., **II** 16
J.Z. Sales Corp., **16** 36

J. Zinmeister Co., **II** 682
Jabil Circuit, Inc., 36 298–301
Jacintoport Corporation, **7** 281
Jack Daniel Distillery, **10** 180
Jack Daniel's. *See* Brown-Forman
   Corporation.
Jack Eckerd Corp., **16** 160; **19** 467
Jack Frain Enterprises, **16** 471
Jack Henry and Associates, Inc., 17
   262–65
Jack Houston Exploration Company, **7** 345
Jack in the Box, Inc. *See* Foodmaster, Inc.
Jack Schwartz Shoes, Inc., 18 266–68
Jackpot Enterprises Inc., 21 298–300; **24**
   36
Jackson & Curtis, **II** 444; **22** 405
Jackson & Perkins. *See* Bear Creek
   Corporation.
Jackson Box Co., **IV** 311; **19** 267
Jackson Cushion Spring Co., **13** 397
Jackson Furniture of Danville, LLC., **48**
   246
Jackson Hewitt, Inc., 48 234–36
Jackson Ice Cream Co., **12** 112
Jackson Marine Corp., **III** 499
Jackson Mercantile Co. *See* Jitney-Jungle
   Stores of America, Inc.
Jackson National Life Insurance
   Company, III 335–36; **8 276–77; 48**
   327
Jackson Purchase Electric Cooperative
   Corporation, **11** 37
Jacksonville Shipyards, **I** 170
Jaco Electronics, Inc., 19 311; **30 255–57**
Jacob Holm & Sons A/S, **22** 263
Jacob Leinenkugel Brewing Company,
   12 338; **28 209–11**
Jacobs Brake Manufacturing Company, **7**
   116–17
Jacobs Engineering Group Inc., 6
   148–50; 26 220–23 (upd.)
Jacobs Suchard (AG), II 520–22, 540,
   569; **15** 64; **29** 46–47. *See also* Kraft
   Jacobs Suchard AG.
Jacobson Stores Inc., 21 301–03
Jacoby & Meyers, **20** 435
Jacor Communications, Inc., 6 33; **23**
   292–95; 24 108; **27** 339; **35** 220
Jacques Borel International, **II** 641; **10** 12;
   49 126
Jacques Fath Perfumes, **III** 47
Jacuzzi Inc., 7 207, 209; **23 296–98**
Jade Accessories, **14** 224
Jade KK, **25** 349
Jadepoint, **18** 79–80
JAF Pampryl, **I** 281
Jafco Co. Ltd., **49** 433
Jafra Cosmetics, **15** 475, 477
Jagenberg AG, **9** 445–46; **14** 57
Jaguar Cars, Ltd., III 439, 495; **11** 140;
   13 28, 219, **285–87,** 414; **36** 198, 217.
   See also Ford Motor Company.
JAI Parabolic Spring Ltd., **III** 582
JAIX Leasing Company, **23** 306
Ab Jakobstads Cellulosa-Pietarsaaren
   Selluloosa Oy, **IV** 302
JAL. *See* Japan Air Lines.
Jalate Inc., 25 245–47
Jaluzot & Cie. *See* Pinault-Printemps-
   Redoute S.A.
Jamaica Gas Light Co., **6** 455
Jamaica Plain Trust Co., **II** 207
Jamaica Water Supply Company. *See* JWP
   Inc.

Jamba Juice Company, 47 199–202
JAMCO, **III** 589
James A. Ryder Transportation (Jartran), **V**
   505
James Bay Development Corporation, **6**
   502
James Beam Distilling Co., **I** 226; **10** 180
James Beattie plc, 43 242–44
James Burn/American, Inc., **17** 458
James C. Heintz Company, **19** 278
James Ericson, **III** 324
James Felt Realty, Inc., **21** 257
James Fison and Sons. *See* Fisons plc.
James Fleming, **II** 500
James G. Fast Company. *See* Angelica
   Corporation.
James Gulliver Associates, **II** 609
James Hardie Industries Limited, **IV** 249;
   26 494
James Hartley & Son, **III** 724
James Heekin and Company, **13** 254
James Lyne Hancock Ltd., **I** 428
James Magee & Sons Ltd., **IV** 294; **19** 224
James McNaughton Ltd., **IV** 325
James O. Welch Co., **II** 543
James Publishing Group, **17** 272
James R. Osgood & Company, **10** 356
James River Corporation of Virginia, IV
   289–91; 8 483; **22** 209; **29** 136. *See also*
   Fort James Corporation.
James Stedman Ltd., **II** 569
James Talcott, Inc., **11** 260–61
James Thompson, **IV** 22
James Wellbeloved, **39** 354, 356
James Wholesale Company, **18** 7
James Wrigley & Sons, **IV** 257
Jamestown Publishers, **22** 522
Jamesway Corporation, **IV** 136; **13** 261; **23**
   177
Jamie Scott, Inc., **27** 348
Jamieson & Co., **22** 428
Jamna Auto Industries Pvt. Ltd., **III** 581
Jämsänkoski Oy, **IV** 347
Jan Bell Marketing Inc., **24** 335. *See also*
   Mayor's Jewelers, Inc.
Janata Bank, **31** 219
Jane Jones Enterprises, **16** 422; **43** 309
Jane's Information Group, **8** 525
Janesville Electric, **6** 604
Janet Frazer, **V** 118
Janin, S.A., **36** 163
Janna Systems Inc., **38** 433
Janson Publications, **22** 522
Janssen-Kyowa, **III** 43
N.V. Janssen M&L, **17** 147
Janssen Pharmaceutica, **III** 36; **8** 282
JANT Pty. Ltd., **IV** 285
Jantzen Inc., **V** 391; **17** 513
Janus Capital Corporation, **6** 401–02; **26**
   233
Japan Acoustics, **II** 118
Japan Advertising Ltd., **16** 166
Japan Air Filter Co., Ltd., **III** 634
Japan Airlines Company, Ltd., I 104–06;
   6 70–71, 118, 123, 386, 427; **24**
   399–400; **27** 464; **32 288–92 (upd.)**; **49**
   459
Japan Brewery. *See* Kirin Brewery
   Company, Limited.
Japan Broadcasting Corporation, I 586;
   II 66, 101, 118; **7 248–50; 9** 31
Japan-California Bank, **II** 274
Japan Commerce Bank, **II** 291

Japan Copper Manufacturing Co., **II** 104; **IV** 211
Japan Cotton Co., **IV** 150; **24** 357
Japan Creative Tours Co., **I** 106
Japan Credit Bureau, **II** 348
Japan Dairy Products, **II** 538
Japan Day & Night Bank, **II** 292
Japan Development Bank, **II** 300, 403
Japan Dyestuff Manufacturing Co., **I** 397
Japan Elanco Company, Ltd., **17** 437
Japan Electricity Generation and Transmission Company (JEGTCO), **V** 574
Japan Energy Corporation, **13** 202; **14** 206, 208
Japan Food Corporation, **14** 288
Japan International Bank, **II** 292
Japan International Liquor, **I** 220
Japan Iron & Steel Co., Ltd., **IV** 157; **17** 349–50
Japan Leasing Corporation, 8 278–80; 11 87
Japan Medico, **25** 431
Japan National Oil Corp., **IV** 516
Japan National Railway, **V** 448–50; **6** 70
Japan Oil Development Co., **IV** 364
Japan Petroleum Development Corp., **IV** 461
Japan Petroleum Exploration Co., **IV** 516
Japan Pulp and Paper Company Limited, IV 292–93, 680
Japan Reconstruction Finance Bank, **II** 300
Japan Special Steel Co., Ltd., **IV** 63
Japan Steel Manufacturing Co., **IV** 211
Japan Steel Works, **I** 508
Japan Telecom, **7** 118; **13** 482
Japan Telegraphic Communication Company (Nihon Denpo-Tsushin Sha), **16** 166
Japan Tobacco Inc., V 403–04; 30 387; **46 257–60 (upd.)**
Japan Trust Bank, **II** 292
Japan Try Co., **III** 758
Japan Vilene Company Ltd., **41** 170–72
Japanese and Asian Development Bank, **IV** 518
Japanese Electronic Computer Co., **III** 140
Japanese Enterprise Co., **IV** 728
Japanese National Railway, **I** 579; **III** 491; **43** 103
Japanese Victor Co., **II** 118
Japex Oman Co., **IV** 516
Japonica Partners, **9** 485
Jara Enterprises, Inc., **31** 276
Jarcho Brothers Inc., **I** 513
Jardinay Manufacturing Corp., **24** 335
Jardine Matheson Holdings Limited, I 468–71, 521–22, 577, 592; **II** 296; **IV** 189, 699–700; **16** 479–80; **18** 114; **20 309–14 (upd.); 47** 175–78
Jartran Inc., **V** 505; **24** 410
Järvenpään Kotelo Oy, **IV** 315
Jarvis plc, 39 237–39
Jas, Hennessy & Co., **I** 272
Jas. I. Miller Co., **13** 491
JASCO Products, **III** 581
Jason Incorporated, 23 299–301
Jasper Corporation, **III** 767; **22** 546. See also Kimball International, Inc.
JAT, **27** 475
Jato, **II** 652
Jauch & Hübener, **14** 279
Java-China-Japan Line, **6** 403–04; **26** 242
Java Software, **30** 453

Javelin Software Corporation, **10** 359
Javex Co., **IV** 272
Jax, **9** 452
Jay Cooke and Co., **III** 237; **9** 370
Jay Jacobs, Inc., 15 243–45
Jay-Ro Services, **III** 419
Jay's Washateria, Inc., **7** 372
Jayco Inc., 13 288–90
Jaywoth Industries, **III** 673
Jazzercise, Inc., 45 212–14
JB Oxford Holdings, Inc., 32 293–96
JBA Holdings PLC, **43** 184
JBL, **22** 97
JCB, **14** 321
JCJL. See Java-China-Japan Line.
JD Wetherspoon plc, 30 258–60
JDS Uniphase Corporation, 34 235–37
The Jean Coutu Group (PJC) Inc., 46 261–65
Jean-Jacques, **19** 50
Jean Lassale, **III** 619–20; **17** 430
Jean Lincet, **19** 50
Jean Nate, **I** 695
Jean Pagées et Fils, **III** 420
Jean-Philippe Fragrances, Inc. See Inter Parfums, Inc.
Jean Prouvost, **IV** 618
Jeanmarie Creations, Inc., **18** 67, 69
Jeanne Piaubert, **III** 47
Jefferies Group, Inc., 25 248–51
Jefferson Bancorp, Inc., **37** 201
Jefferson Chemical Co., **IV** 552
Jefferson Fire Insurance Co., **III** 239
Jefferson National Life Group, **10** 247
Jefferson-Pilot Corporation, 11 213–15; 29 253–56 (upd.)
Jefferson Properties, Inc. See JPI.
Jefferson Smurfit Group plc, IV 294–96; 16 122; **19 224–27 (upd.); 49 224–29 (upd.).** See also Smurfit-Stone Container Corporation.
Jefferson Standard Life Insurance, **11** 213–14
Jefferson Ward, **12** 48–49
Jefferson Warrior Railroad Company, **III** 767; **22** 546
Jeffery Sons & Co. Ltd., **IV** 711
Jeffrey Galion, **III** 472
JEGTCO. See Japan Electricity Generation and Transmission Company (JEGTCO).
Jeld-Wen, Inc., 33 409; 45 215–17
Jell-O Co., **II** 531
Jem Development, **17** 233
Jenaer Glaswerk Schott & Genossen, **III** 445, 447
Jenn-Air Corporation, **III** 573; **22** 349
Jennie-O Foods, **II** 506
Jennifer Convertibles, Inc., 31 274–76
Jenny Craig, Inc., 10 382–84; 12 531; **29 257–60 (upd.)**
Jeno's, **13** 516; **26** 436
Jenoptik AG, 33 218–21
Jensen Salsbery, **I** 715
Jenson, Woodward & Lozier, Inc., **21** 96
JEORA Co., **IV** 564
Jeppesen Sanderson, Inc., **IV** 677; **17** 486
Jepson Corporation, **8** 230
Jeri-Jo Knitwear, Inc., **27** 346, 348
Jerome Increase Case Machinery Company. See J.I. Case Company.
Jerrico Inc., **27** 145
Jerrold Corporation, **10** 319–20
Jerry Bassin Inc., **17** 12–14
Jerry's Famous Deli Inc., 24 243–45

Jerry's Restaurants, **13** 320
Jersey Central Power & Light Company, **27** 182
Jersey Paper, **IV** 261
Jersey Standard. See Standard Oil Co. of New Jersey.
Jervis B. Webb Company, 24 246–49
Jesse Jones Sausage Co. See GoodMark Foods, Inc.
Jesse L. Lasky Feature Play Co., **II** 154
Jessup & Moore Paper Co., **IV** 351; **19** 495
Jet America Airlines, **I** 100; **6** 67, 82
Jet Capital Corp., **I** 123
Jet Petroleum, Ltd., **IV** 401
Jet Research Center, **III** 498
Jet Set Corporation, **18** 513
JetBlue Airways Corporation, 44 248–50
Jetro Cash & Carry Enterprises Inc., 38 266–68
Jetway Systems, **III** 512
Jeumont-Industrie, **II** 93
Jeumont-Schneider Industries, **II** 93–94; **9** 10; **18** 473
Jevic Transportation, Inc., **45** 448
Jewel Companies, Inc., **II** 605; **6** 531; **12** 63; **18** 89; **22** 38; **26** 476; **27** 291
Jewel Food Stores, **7** 127–28; **13** 25
Jewell Ridge Coal Corp., **IV** 181
JFD-Encino, **24** 243
JG Industries, Inc., 15 240–42
Jheri Redding Products, Inc., **17** 108
JHT, Inc., **39** 377
Jiamusi Combine Harvester Factory, **21** 175
Jiangsu General Ball & Roller Co., Ltd., **45** 170
JIB Group plc, **20** 313
Jiffee Chemical Corporation, **III** 21; **22** 146
Jiffy Auto Rental, **16** 380
Jiffy Convenience Stores, **II** 627
Jiffy Lube International, Inc., **IV** 490; **21** 541; **24** 339; **25** 443–45
Jiffy Mixes, **29** 109–10
Jiffy Packaging, **14** 430
Jiji, **16** 166
Jil Sander A.G., **45** 342, 344
Jillian's Entertainment Holdings, Inc., 40 273–75
Jim Beam Brands Co., 14 271–73; 29 196
Jim Cole Enterprises, Inc., **19** 247
The Jim Henson Company, 23 302–04; 45 130
The Jim Pattison Group, 37 219–22
Jim Walter Corporation. See Walter Industries, Inc.
Jim Walter Papers, **IV** 282; **9** 261
Jimmy Carter Work Project. See Habitat for Humanity International.
Jintan Taionkei Co. See Terumo Corporation.
Jitney-Jungle Stores of America, Inc., 27 245–48
Jitsugyo no Nihon-sha, **IV** 631
Jitsuyo Jidosha Seizo Co., **I** 183
JJB Sports plc, 32 302–04
JLA Credit, **8** 279
JLL. See Jones Lang LaSalle Incorporated.
JMB Internacionale S.A., **25** 121
JMB Realty Corporation, IV 702–03. See also Amfac/JMB Hawaii L.L.C.

Jno. H. Swisher & Son. *See* Swisher International Group Inc.
JNR. *See* Japan National Railway.
Jo-Ann Fabrics and Crafts, **16** 197
Jo-Gal Shoe Company, Inc., **13** 360
Joanna Cotton Mills, **14** 220
Joannes Brothers, **II** 668
Jobete Music. *See* Motown Records Company L.P.
JobWorks Agency, Inc., **16** 50
Jockey International, Inc., 12 283–85; 34 238–42 (upd.)
Joe Alexander Press, **12** 472; **36** 469
Joe B. Hughes, **III** 498
Joe's American Bar & Grill, **20** 54
Joe's Crab Shack, **15** 279
Joh. A. Benckiser GmbH, **36** 140
Joh. Parviaisen Tehtaat Oy, **IV** 276
Johann Jakob Rieter & Co., **III** 402
Johannesburg Consolidated Investment Co. Ltd., **IV** 21–22, 118; **16** 293
John A. Frye Shoe Company, **V** 376; **8** 16; **26** 397–98; **36** 24
John A. Pratt and Associates, **22** 181
John Alden Life Insurance, **10** 340
John B. Sanfilippo & Son, Inc., 14 274–76
John Bean Spray Pump Co., **I** 442
John Blair & Company, **6** 13
John Brown plc, I 572–74
John Bull, **II** 550
John Carr Group, **31** 398–400
John Chatillon & Sons Inc., **29** 460
John Crane International, **17** 480
John Crosland Company, **8** 88
The John D. and Catherine T. MacArthur Foundation, 34 243–46
John de Kuyper and Son, **I** 377
John Deere. *See* Deere & Company.
John F. Jelke Company, **9** 318
John F. Murray Co., **I** 623; **10** 69
John Fairfax Holdings Limited, 7 251–54
John Gardner Catering, **III** 104
John Govett & Co., **II** 349
John Gund Brewing Co., **I** 253
John H. Harland Company, 17 266–69
John H.R. Molson & Bros. *See* The Molson Companies Limited.
John Hancock Financial Services, Inc., 42 193–98 (upd.)
John Hancock Mutual Life Insurance Company, III 265–68, 291, 313, 332, 400; **IV** 283; **13** 530; **25** 528
John Hill and Son, **II** 569
John Holroyd & Co. of Great Britain, **7** 236
John L. Wortham & Son Agency, **III** 193
John Labatt Ltd., **I** 267; **II** 582; **8** 399; **16** 397; **17** 256–57. *See also* Labatt Brewing Company Limited.
John Laing plc, I 575–76, 588
John Lewis Partnership plc, V 93–95; 13 307; **42 199–203 (upd.)**
John Lucas Co., **III** 745
John Lysaght, **III** 493–95
John M. Hart Company, **9** 304
John M. Smyth Co., **15** 282
John Macfarlane and Sons, **II** 593
John Mackintosh and Sons, **II** 568–69
John McConnell & Co., **13** 102
John McLean and Sons Ltd., **III** 753
John Menzies plc, 39 240–43
John Morrell and Co., **II** 595–96; **21** 111

John Nicholls & Co., **III** 690
The John Nuveen Company, III 356; **21 304–06; 22** 492, 494–95
John Oster Manufacturing Company. *See* Sunbeam-Oster.
John Paul Mitchell Systems, 24 250–52
John Pew & Company, **13** 243
John Q. Hammons Hotels, Inc., 24 253–55
John R. Figg, Inc., **II** 681
John Rogers Co., **9** 253
John Sands, **22** 35
John Schroeder Lumber Company, **25** 379
John Sexton & Co., **26** 503
John Strange Paper Company, **8** 358
John Swire & Sons Ltd. *See* Swire Pacific Ltd.
John W. Danforth Company, 48 237–39
John Walker & Sons, **I** 239–40
John Wanamaker, **22** 110
John Wiley & Sons, Inc., 17 270–72
John Williams, **III** 691
John Wyeth & Bro., **I** 713
John Yokley Company, **11** 194
John Zink Company, **22** 3–4; **25** 403
Johnny Rockets Group, Inc., 31 277–81
Johns Manville Corporation, **III** 708; **7** 293; **11** 420; **19** 211–12
John Perry, **III** 673
Johnsen, Jorgensen and Wettre, **14** 249
Johnson. *See* Axel Johnson Group.
Johnson & Higgins, 14 277–80
Johnson and Howe Furniture Corporation, **33** 151
Johnson & Johnson, III 18, 35–37; **IV** 285, 722; **7** 45–46; **8 281–83 (upd.),** 399, 511–12; **9** 89–90; **10** 47, 69, 78, 80, 534–35; **15** 357–58, 360; **16** 168, 440; **17** 104–05, 340, 342–43, 533; **19** 103, 105; **25** 55–56; **34** 280, 283–84; **36 302–07 (upd.); 37** 110–11, 113; **41** 154–55; **46** 104
Johnson and Patan, **III** 671
Johnson and Sons Smelting Works Ltd., **IV** 119
Johnson Brothers, **12** 528
Johnson, Carruthers & Rand Shoe Co., **III** 528
Johnson Controls, Inc., III 534–37; 13 398; **16** 184, 322; **26 227–32 (upd.)**
Johnson Diversified, Inc., **III** 59
Johnson Engineering Corporation, **37** 365
Johnson Matthey PLC, II 390; **IV** 23, **117–20; 16** 28, **290–94 (upd.),** 439; **49 230–35 (upd.)**
Johnson Motor Co., **III** 597–99
Johnson Products Co., Inc., **11** 208; **31** 89
Johnson Publishing Company, Inc., 27 361; **28 212–14**
Johnson Systems, **6** 224
Johnson Wax. *See* S.C. Johnson & Son, Inc.
Johnson Worldwide Associates, Inc., 24 530; **28 215–17,** 412
Johnson Coca-Cola Bottling Company of Chattanooga, **13** 163–64
Johnston Evans & Co., **IV** 704
Johnston Foil Co., **IV** 18
Johnston Harvester Co., **III** 650
Johnston Industries, Inc., 15 246–48
Johnston Press plc, 35 242–44
Johnstown America Industries, Inc., 23 305–07
Johnstown Sanitary Dairy, **13** 393

Jointless Rim Ltd., **I** 428
Jokisch, **II** 556
Jonathan Backhouse & Co., **II** 235
Jonathan Logan Inc., **13** 536
Jonell Shoe Manufacturing Corporation, **13** 360
Jones & Babson, Inc., **14** 85
Jones & Johnson, **14** 277
Jones & Laughlin Steel Corp., **I** 463, 489–91; **IV** 228; **11** 197
Jones Apparel Group, Inc., 11 216–18; 27 60; **30 310–11; 39 244–47 (upd.),** 301, 303
Jones Brothers Tea Co., **7** 202
Jones, Day, Reavis & Pogue, 33 226–29
Jones Environmental, **11** 361
Jones Financial Companies, L.P. *See* Edward Jones.
Jones Intercable, Inc., 14 260; **17** 7; **21 307–09; 24** 123; **25** 212
Jones Janitor Service, **25** 15
Jones Lang LaSalle Incorporated, 49 236–38
Jones Medical Industries, Inc., 24 256–58; 34 460
Jones Motor Co., **10** 44
Jones-Rodolfo Corp. *See* Cutter & Buck, Inc.
Jonker Fris, **II** 571
Jonkoping & Vulcan, **12** 462
Jordache Enterprises, Inc., 15 201–02; **23 308–10**
The Jordan Co., **11** 261; **16** 149
Jordan Industries, Inc., 36 308–10
Jordan Marsh, **III** 608; **V** 26; **9** 209
Jordan Valley Electric Cooperative, **12** 265
Jos. A. Bank Clothiers, Inc., II 560; **12** 411; **31 282–85**
The Joseph & Feiss Company, **48** 209
Joseph Bellamy and Sons Ltd., **II** 569
Joseph Campbell Company. *See* Campbell Soup Company.
Joseph Crosfield, **III** 31
Joseph E. Seagram & Sons Inc., **I** 266, 285; **21** 319
Joseph Garneau Co., **I** 226; **10** 180
Joseph Leavitt Corporation, **9** 20
Joseph Littlejohn & Levy, **27** 204
Joseph Lucas & Son, **III** 554–56
Joseph Lumber Company, **25** 379
Joseph Magnin, **I** 417–18; **17** 124; **41** 114
Joseph Malecki Corp., **24** 444–45
Joseph Nathan & Co., **I** 629–40
Joseph Rank Limited, **II** 564
Joseph Schlitz Brewing Company, **25** 281
Joseph T. Ryerson & Son, Inc., IV 114; **15** 249–51; **19** 217, 381. *See also* Ryerson Tull, Inc.
Josephson International, **27** 392; **43** 235
Joshin Denki, **13** 481
Joshu Railway Company, **6** 431
Joshua's Christian Bookstores, **31** 435–36
Josiah Wedgwood and Sons Limited. *See* Waterford Wedgwood plc.
Jostens, Inc., 7 255–57; **25 252–55 (upd.); 36** 470
Journal Register Company, 29 261–63
Journey's End Corporation, **14** 107
Jovan, **III** 66
Jove Publications, Inc., **II** 144; **IV** 623; **12** 224
Jovi, **II** 652
Joy Manufacturing, **III** 526

Joy Planning Co., **III** 533
Joy Technologies Inc., **II** 17; **26** 70; **38** 227
Joyce International, Inc., **16** 68
JP Foodservice Inc., **24** 445
JP Household Supply Co. Ltd., **IV** 293
JP Information Center Co., Ltd., **IV** 293
JP Planning Co. Ltd., **IV** 293
JPC Co., **IV** 155
JPF Holdings, Inc. *See* U.S. Foodservice.
JPI, 49 239–41
JPS Automotive L.P., **17** 182–84
JPS Textile Group, Inc., 28 218–20
JPT Publishing, **8** 528
JR Central, **43** 103
JR Tokai, **43** 103
JSC MMC Norilsk Nickel, 48 300–02
JT Aquisitions, **II** 661
JTL Corporation, **13** 162–63
JTN Acquisition Corp., **19** 233
JTS Corporation, **23** 23, 26
Jude Hanbury, **I** 294
Judel Glassware Co., Inc., **14** 502
Judson Dunaway Corp., **12** 127
Judson Steel Corp., **13** 97
Jugend & Volk, **14** 556
Jugo Bank, **II** 325
Juice Bowl Products, **II** 480–81; **26** 57
Juice Works, **26** 57
Jujamycn, **24** 439
Jujo Paper Co., Ltd., **IV** 268, 284–85, 292–93, **297–98,** 321, 326, 328, 356
JuJu Media, Inc., **41** 385
Julius Berger-Bauboag A.G., **I** 560–61
Julius Garfinckel & Co., Inc., **22** 110
Jumping-Jacks Shoes, Inc., **17** 390
Jung-Pumpen, **III** 570; **20** 361
Junghans Uhren, **10** 152
Juniper Networks, Inc., 43 251–55
Junkers Luftverkehr, **I** 110, 197; **6** 87–88
Juno Lighting, Inc., 30 266–68
Juno Online Services, Inc., 38 269–72; 39 25–26
Juovo Pignone, **13** 356
Jupiter National, **15** 247–48; **19** 166
Jupiter Tyndall, **47** 84
Jurgens, **II** 588–89
Jurgensen's, **17** 558
Jurgovan & Blair, **III** 197
Juristförlaget, **14** 556
Jusco Car Life Company, **23** 290
JUSCO Co., Ltd., **V** 96–99; **11** 498; **36** 419; **43** 386
Jusco Group, **31** 430
Just Born, Inc., 32 305–07
Just For Feet, Inc., 19 228–30
Just Squeezed, **31** 350
Just Toys, Inc., **29** 476
Justin Industries, Inc., 19 231–33
Juventus F.C. S.p.A., **44** 387–88
JVC. *See* Victor Company of Japan, Ltd.
JW Aluminum Company, **22** 544
JW Bernard & Zn., **39** 203
JWD Group, Inc., **48** 238
JWP Inc., 9 300–02; 13 176
JWT Group Inc., I 9, 19–21, 23; **6** 53. *See also* WPP Group plc.
Jylhävaara, **IV** 348
JZC. *See* John Zink Company.

K&B Inc., 12 286–88; 17 244
K&F Manufacturing. *See* Fender Musical Instruments.

K & G Men's Center, Inc., 21 310–12; 48 286
K&K Insurance Group, **26** 487
K&K Toys, Inc., **23** 176
K&L, **6** 48
K&M Associates L.P., **16** 18; **43** 19
K & R Warehouse Corporation, **9** 20
K-C Aviation, **III** 41; **16** 304; **43** 258
K-Graphics Inc., **16** 306; **43** 261
K-Group, **27** 261
K-H Corporation, **7** 260
K-Swiss, Inc., 33 243–45
K-tel International, Inc., 21 325–28
K-III Holdings. *See* Primedia Inc.
K.C.C. Holding Co., **III** 192
K.F. Kline Co., **7** 145; **22** 184
K.H. Wheel Company, **27** 202
K. Hattori & Co., Ltd., **III** 454–55, 619–20. *See also* Seiko Corporation.
k.k. Staatsbahnen, **6** 419
K Line. *See* Kawasaki Kisen Kaisha, Ltd.
K.O. Lester Co., **31** 359, 361
K.W. Muth Company, **17** 305
KA Teletech, **27** 365
Ka Wah AMEV Insurance, **III** 200–01
Kabelvision AB, **26** 331–33
Kable News Company. *See* AMREP Corporation.
Kable Printing Co., **13** 559
Kaduna Refining and Petrochemicals Co., **IV** 473
Kaepa, **16** 546
Kaestner & Hecht Co., **II** 120
Kafte Inc., **28** 63
Kaga Forwarding Co., **6** 428
Kagami Crystal Works, **III** 714
Kagle Home Health Care, **11** 282
Kagoshima Central Research Laboratory, **21** 330
Kahan and Lessin, **II** 624–25
Kahn's Meats, **II** 572
Kai Tak Land Investment Co., **IV** 717
Kaiser + Kraft GmbH, **27** 175
Kaiser Aluminum & Chemical Corporation, **IV** 11–12, 15, 59–60, **121–23,** 191; **6** 148; **12** 377; **8** 348, 350; **22** 455. *See also* ICF Kaiser International, Inc.
Kaiser Cement, **III** 501, 760; **IV** 272
Kaiser Company, **6** 184
Kaiser Engineering, **IV** 218
Kaiser Industries, **III** 760
Kaiser Packaging, **12** 377
Kaiser Permanente Corp., **6** 279; **12** 175; **24** 231; **25** 434, 527; **41** 183
Kaiser Steel, **IV** 59
Kaiser's Kaffee Geschäft AG, **27** 461
Kaizosha, **IV** 632
Kajaani Oy, **II** 302; **IV** 350
Kajima Corp., I 577–78
Kal Kan Foods, Inc., 22 298–300
Kalamazoo Paper Co., **IV** 281; **9** 259
Kalbfleish, **I** 300
Kaldveer & Associates, **14** 228
Kaliningradnefteprodukt, **48** 378
Kalitta Group, **22** 311
Kalua Koi Corporation, **7** 281
Kalumburu Joint Venture, **IV** 67
Kamaishi, **IV** 157; **17** 349
Kaman Corporation, 12 289–92; 16 202; **42 204–08 (upd.); 43** 171
Kamewa Group, **27** 494, 496
Kaminski/Engles Capital Corp. *See* Suiza Foods Corporation.

Kamioka Mining & Smelting Co., Ltd., **IV** 145, 148
Kammer Valves, A.G., **17** 147
Kampgrounds of America, Inc., 33 230–33
Kamps AG, 44 251–54
Kanagawa Bank, **II** 291
Kanda Shokai, **16** 202; **43** 171
Kanders Florida Holdings, Inc., **27** 50
Kane Financial Corp., **III** 231
Kane Foods, **III** 43
Kane Freight Lines, **6** 370
Kane-Miller Corp., **12** 106
Kanebo Spinning Inc., **IV** 442
Kanegafuchi Shoji, **IV** 225
Kanematsu Corporation, **IV** 442–44; **24 259–62 (upd.)**
Kangaroo. *See* Seino Transportation Company, Ltd.
Kangol Ltd., **IV** 136
Kangyo Bank, **II** 300, 310, 361
Kanhym, **IV** 91–92
Kanoldt, **24** 75
Kansai Electric Power Co., Inc., **IV** 492; **V 645–48**
Kansai Seiyu Ltd., **V** 188
Kansai Sogo Bank, **II** 361
Kansallis-Osake-Pankki, **II** 242, **302–03,** 366; **IV** 349
Kansas City Ingredient Technologies, Inc., **49** 261
Kansas City Power & Light Company, 6 510–12, 592; **12** 541–42
Kansas City Securities Corporation, **22** 541
Kansas City Southern Industries, Inc., 6 400–02; 26 233–36 (upd.); 29 333; **47** 162
Kansas City White Goods Company. *See* Angelica Corporation.
Kansas Fire & Casualty Co., **III** 214
Kansas Power Company, **6** 312
Kansas Public Service Company, **12** 541
Kansas Utilities Company, **6** 580
The Kantar Group, **48** 442
Kanto Steel Co., Ltd., **IV** 63
Kao Corporation, **III** 38–39, 48; **16** 168; **20 315–17 (upd.)**
Kaohsiung Refinery, **IV** 388
Kaolin Australia Pty Ltd., **III** 691
Kapalua Land Company, Ltd., **29** 307–08
Kaplan Educational Centers, **12** 143
Kaplan, Inc., 42 209–12, 290
Kaplan Musical String Company, **48** 231
Kapok Computers, **47** 153
Kapy, **II** 139; **24** 194
Karafuto Industry, **IV** 320
Karan Co. *See* Donna Karan Company.
Karastan Bigelow, **19** 276
Karg'sche Familienstiftung, **V** 73
Karl Kani Infinity, Inc., 49 242–45
Karlsberg Brauerei GmbH & Co KG, 41 220–23
Karmelkorn Shoppes, Inc., **10** 371, 373; **39** 232, 235
Karstadt Aktiengesellschaft, **V** 100–02; **19 234–37 (upd.)**
Kasado Dockyard, **III** 760
Kasai Securities, **II** 434
Kasco Corporation, **28** 42, 45
Kaset Rojananil, **6** 123
Kash n' Karry Food Stores, Inc., 20 318–20; 44 145

Kasmarov, **9** 18
Kaspare Cohn Commercial & Savings Bank. *See* Union Bank of California.
Kasper A.S.L., Ltd., 40 276–79
Kast Metals, **III** 452; **15** 92
Kasuga Radio Company. *See* Kenwood Corporation.
Kat-Em International Inc., **16** 125
Katalco, **I** 374
Kataoka Electric Co., **II** 5
Kate Spade LLC, **49** 285
Katelise Group, **III** 739–40
Katharine Gibbs Schools Inc., **22** 442
Kathleen Investment (Australia) Ltd., **III** 729
Kathy's Ranch Markets, **19** 500–01
Katies, **V** 35
Kativo Chemical Industries Ltd., **8** 239; **32** 256
Katy Industries Inc., I 472–74; 14 483–84; **16** 282
Katz Communications, Inc., 6 32–34
Katz Drug, **II** 604
Katz Media Group, Inc., 35 232, **245–48**
Kauffman-Lattimer, **III** 9–10
Kaufhalle AG, **V** 104; **23** 311; **41** 186–87
Kaufhof Holding AG, II 257; **V 103–05**
Kaufhof Warenhaus AG, 23 311–14 (upd.)
Kaufman and Broad Home Corporation, 8 284–86; 11 481–83. *See also* KB Home.
Kaufmann Department Stores, Inc., **V** 132–33; **6** 243; **19** 262
Kaufring AG, 35 249–52
Kaukaan Tehdas Osakeyhtiö, **IV** 301
Oy Kaukas Ab, **IV** 300–02; **19** 462
Kaukauna Cheese Inc., **23** 217, 219
Kauppaosakeyhtiö Kymmene Aktiebolag, **IV** 299
Kauppiaitten Oy, **8** 293
Kautex-Bayern GmbH, **IV** 128
Kautex-Ostfriedland GmbH, **IV** 128
Kautex Werke Reinold Hagen AG, **IV** 128
Kawachi Bank, **II** 361; **26** 455
Kawamata, **11** 350
Kawasaki Denki Seizo, **II** 22
Kawasaki Heavy Industries, Ltd., I 75; **II** 273–74; **III** 482, 513, 516, **538–40**, 756; **IV** 124; **7** 232; **8** 72; **23** 290
Kawasaki Kisen Kaisha, Ltd., V 457–60
Kawasaki Steel Corporation, I 432; **II** 274; **III** 539, 760; **IV** 30, **124–25**, 154, 212–13; **13** 324; **19** 8
Kawashimaya Shoten Inc. Ltd., **II** 433
Kawecki Berylco Industries, **8** 78
Kawneer GmbH., **IV** 18
Kawsmouth Electric Light Company. *See* Kansas City Power & Light Company.
Kay-Bee Toy Stores, V 137; **15 252–53; 16** 389–90. *See also* KB Toys.
Kay County Gas Co., **IV** 399
Kay Home Products, **17** 372
Kay's Drive-In Food Service, **II** 619
Kaydon Corporation, 18 274–76
Kaye, Scholer, Fierman, Hays & Handler, **47** 436
Kayex, **9** 251
Kaynar Manufacturing Company, **8** 366
Kayser Aluminum & Chemicals, **8** 229
Kayser Roth Corp., **8** 288; **22** 122
Kaysersberg, S.A., **IV** 290
KB Home, 45 218–22 (upd.)
AO KB Impuls, **48** 419

KB Toys, 35 253–55 (upd.)
KBLCOM Incorporated, **V** 644
KC. *See* Kenneth Cole Productions, Inc.
KC Holdings, Inc., **11** 229–30
KCI Konecranes International, **27** 269
KCPL. *See* Kansas City Power & Light Company.
KCS Industries, **12** 25–26
KCSI. *See* Kansas City Southern Industries, Inc.
KCSR. *See* Kansas City Southern Railway.
KD Acquisition Corporation, **34** 103–04
KD Manitou, Inc. *See* Manitou BF S.A.
KDT Industries, Inc., **9** 20
Keane Inc., **38** 431
The Keds Corp., **37** 377, 379
Keebler Foods Company, II 594; **35** 181; **36 311–13**
Keefe Manufacturing Courtesy Coffee Company, **6** 392
Keegan Management Co., **27** 274
Keen, Robinson and Co., **II** 566
Keene Packaging Co., **28** 43
KEG Productions Ltd., **IV** 640; **26** 272
Keihan JUSCO, **V** 96
Keil Chemical Company, **8** 178
Keio Teito Electric Railway Company, V 461–62
Keisei Electric Railway, **II** 301
Keith-Albee-Orpheum, **II** 88
Keith Prowse Music Publishing, **22** 193
Keithley Instruments Inc., 16 299–301; 48 445
Kelco, **34** 281
Kelda Group plc, 45 223–26
Keller Builders, **43** 400
Keller-Dorian Graveurs, S.A., **17** 458
Kelley & Partners, Ltd., **14** 130
Kelley Drye & Warren LLP, 40 280–83
Kellock, **10** 336
Kellogg Company, I 22–23; **II** 463, 502–03, **523–26**, 530, 560; **10** 323–24; **12** 411; **13** 3, **291–94 (upd.); 15** 189; **18** 65, 225–26; **22** 336, 338; **25** 90; **27** 39; **29** 30, 110; **36 236–38**
Kellogg Foundation, **41** 118
Kellwood Company, V 181–82; **8 287–89**
Kelly & Associates, **III** 306
Kelly & Cohen, **10** 468
Kelly, Douglas and Co., **II** 631
Kelly Nason, Inc., **13** 203
Kelly Services, Inc., 6 35–37, 140; **9** 326; **16** 48; **25** 356, 432; **26 237–40 (upd.); 40** 236, 238; **49** 264–65
The Kelly-Springfield Tire Company, 8 290–92; 20 260, 263
Kelsey-Hayes Group of Companies, I 170; **III** 650, 652; **7 258–60; 27 249–52 (upd.)**
Kelso & Co., **III** 663, 665; **12** 436; **19** 455; **21** 490; **30** 48–49; **33** 92
Kelty Pack, Inc., **10** 215
Kelvinator Inc., **17** 487
KemaNobel, **9** 380–81; **13** 22
Kemet Corp., 14 281–83
Kemi Oy, **IV** 316
Kemira, Inc., **III** 760; **6** 152
Kemp's Biscuits Limited, **II** 594
Kemper Corporation, III 269–71, 339; **15 254–58 (upd.); 22** 495; **33** 111; **42** 451
Kemper Financial Services, **26** 234
Kemper Motorenfabrik, **I** 197
Kemper Snowboards, **22** 460

Kemperco Inc., **III** 269–70
Kempinski Group, **II** 258
Kemps Biscuits, **II** 594
Ken-L-Ration, **II** 559
Kendall International, Inc., I 529; **III** 24–25; **IV** 288; **11 219–21; 14** 121; **15** 229; **28** 486
Kendall-Jackson Winery, Ltd., 28 111, **221–23**
Kenetech Corporation, 11 222–24
Kennametal, Inc., IV 203; **13 295–97**
Kennecott Corporation, III 248; **IV** 33–34, 79, 170–71, 179, 192, 288, 576; **7 261–64; 10** 262, 448; **12** 244; **27 253–57 (upd.); 35** 135; **38** 231; **45** 332
Kennedy Automatic Products Co., **16** 8
Kenner, **II** 502; **10** 323; **12** 168
Kenner Parker Toys, Inc., **II** 503; **9** 156; **10** 324; **14** 266; **16** 337; **25** 488–89
Kenneth Cole Productions, Inc., 22 223; **25 256–58**
Kenneth O. Lester, Inc., **21** 508
Kenny Rogers' Roasters, **22** 464; **29** 342, 344
Kenroy International, Inc., **13** 274
Kent Drugs Ltd., **II** 640, 650
Kent Electronics Corporation, 17 273–76
Kent Fire, **III** 350
Kent-Moore Corp., **I** 200; **10** 492–93
Kentland-Elkhorn Coal Corp., **IV** 181
Kentrox Industries, **30** 7
Kentucky Bonded Funeral Co., **III** 217
Kentucky Electric Steel, Inc., 31 286–88
Kentucky Fried Chicken, **I** 260–61; **II** 533; **III** 78, 104, 106; **6** 200; **7 26–28**, 433; **8** 563; **12** 42; **13** 336; **16** 97; **18** 8, 538; **19** 92; **21** 361; **22** 464; **23** 384, 504. *See also* KFC Corporation.
Kentucky Institution for the Education of the Blind. *See* American Printing House for the Blind.
Kentucky Utilities Company, 6 513–15; 11 37, 236–38
Kenway, **I** 155
Kenwood Corporation, I 532; **19** 360; **23** 53; **31 289–91**
Kenwood Silver Company, Inc., **31** 352
Kenworth Motor Truck Corp., **I** 185–86; **26** 354
Kenyon & Eckhardt Advertising Agency, **25** 89–91
Kenyon Corp., **18** 276
Kenyon Sons and Craven Ltd., **II** 593–94
Kenzo, **25** 122
Keo Cutters, Inc., **III** 569; **20** 360
KEPCO. *See* Kyushu Electric Power Company Inc.
Kerlick, Switzer & Johnson, **6** 48
Kerlyn Oil Co., **IV** 445–46
Kern County Land Co., **I** 527; **10** 379, 527
Kernite SA, **8** 386
Kernkraftwerke Lippe-Ems, **V** 747
Kernridge Oil Co., **IV** 541
Kerr-Addison Mines Ltd., **IV** 165
Kerr Concrete Pipe Company, **14** 250
Kerr Corporation, **14** 481
Kerr Drug Stores, **32** 170
Kerr Group Inc., III 423; **10** 130; **22** 48; **24 263–65; 30** 39
Kerr-McGee Corporation, IV 445–47; 13 118; **22 301–04 (upd.)**
Kerry Group plc, 27 258–60
Kerry Properties Limited, 22 305–08; 24 388

Keski-Suomen Tukkukauppa Oy, **8** 293
Kesko Ltd (Kesko Oy), 8 293–94; **27 261–63 (upd.)**
Ketchikan International Sales Co., **IV** 304
Ketchikan Paper Company, **31** 316
Ketchikan Pulp Co., **IV** 304
Ketchum Communications Inc., 6 38–40
Ketner and Milner Stores, **II** 683
Kettle Foods Inc., 26 58; **48 240–42**
Kettle Restaurants, Inc., **29** 149
Keumkang Co., **III** 515; **7** 231
Kewanee Public Service Company, **6** 505
Kewaunee Scientific Corporation, 25 259–62
Key Computer Laboratories, Inc., **14** 15
Key Industries, Inc., **26** 342
Key Markets, **II** 628
Key Pharmaceuticals, Inc., **11** 207; **41** 419
Key Tronic Corporation, 14 284–86
KeyCorp, 8 295–97; **11** 110; **14** 90
Keyes Fibre Company, 9 303–05
Keypage. *See* Rural Cellular Corporation.
KeySpan Energy Co., 27 264–66
Keystone Aircraft, **I** 61; **11** 164
Keystone Consolidated Industries, Inc., **19** 467
Keystone Custodian Fund, **IV** 458
Keystone Foods Corporation, **10** 443
Keystone Franklin, Inc., **III** 570; **9** 543; **20** 362
Keystone Frozen Foods, **17** 536
Keystone Gas Co., **IV** 548
Keystone Health Plan West, Inc., **27** 211
Keystone Insurance and Investment Co., **12** 564
Keystone International, Inc., 11 225–27; **28** 486
Keystone Life Insurance Co., **III** 389; **33** 419
Keystone Paint and Varnish, **8** 553
Keystone Pipe and Supply Co., **IV** 136
Keystone Portland Cement Co., **23** 225
Keystone Savings and Loan, **II** 420
Keystone Tube Inc., **25** 8
Keytronics, **18** 541
KFC Corporation, 7 265–68; **10** 450; **21 313–17 (upd.);** **23** 115, 117, 153; **32** 12–14
KFF Management, **37** 350
Khalda Petroleum Co., **IV** 413
KHBB, **16** 72
KHD AG. *See* Klöckner-Humboldt-Deutz AG.
KHD Konzern, III 541–44
KHL. *See* Koninklijke Hollandsche Lloyd.
Kia Motors Corporation, I 167; **12 293–95; 29 264–67 (upd.)**
Kiabi, **37** 22–23
Kickers Worldwide, **35** 204, 207
Kidd, Kamm & Co., **21** 482
Kidde Inc., I 475–76; **III** 503; **7** 209; **23** 297; **39 344–46**
Kidde plc, 44 255–59 (upd.)
Kidder, Peabody & Co., **II** 31, 207, 430; **IV** 84; **7** 310; **12** 197; **13** 465–67, 534; **16** 322; **22** 406
Kidder Press Co., **IV** 644
Kiddie Products, Inc. *See* The First Years Inc.
Kids ''R'' Us, **V** 203–05; **9** 394; **37** 81
Kids Foot Locker, **14** 293, 295
Kidston Mines, **I** 438
Kiekhaefer Corporation, **III** 443; **22** 115
Kien, **13** 545

Kienzle Apparate GmbH, **III** 566; **38** 299
Kierulff Electronics, **10** 113
Kieser Verlag, **14** 555
Kiewit Diversified Group Inc., **11** 301
Kiewit-Murdock Investment Corp., **15** 129
Kijkshop/Best-Sellers, **13** 545
Kikkoman Corporation, I 9; **14 287–89; 47 203–06 (upd.)**
Kilburn & Co., **III** 522
Kilgo Motor Express, **6** 370
Kilgore Ceramics, **III** 671
Kilgore Federal Savings and Loan Assoc., **IV** 343
Killington, Ltd., **28** 21
Kilpatrick's Department Store, **19** 511
Kilsby Tubesupply, **I** 570
Kimball International, Inc., 12 296–98; **48 243–47 (upd.)**
Kimbell Inc., **II** 684
Kimberley Central Mining Co., **IV** 64; **7** 121
Kimberly-Clark Corporation, I 14, 413; **III** 36, 40–41; **IV** 249, 254, 297–98, 329, 648, 665; **8** 282; **15** 357; **16 302–05 (upd.);** **17** 30, 397; **18** 147–49; **19** 14, 284, 478; **22** 209; **43 256–60 (upd.)**
Kimco Realty Corporation, 11 228–30
Kimowelt Medien, **39** 13
Kincaid Furniture Company, **14** 302–03
Kindai Golf Company, **32** 447
Kinden Corporation, **7** 303
Kinder Morgan, Inc., 45 227–30
KinderCare Learning Centers, Inc., 13 298–300; 34 105; **35** 408
Kinear Moodie, **III** 753
Kineret Acquisition Corp. *See* The Hain Celestial Group, Inc.
Kinetic Concepts, Inc., 20 321–23
King & Spalding, 23 315–18
The King Arthur Flour Company, 31 292–95
King Bearing, Inc., **13** 79
King Cullen, **II** 644
King Features Syndicate, **IV** 626; **19** 201, 203–04; **46** 232
King Folding Box Co., **13** 441
King Fook Gold and Jewellery Co., **IV** 717
King Hickory, **17** 183
King Kullen Grocery Co., Inc., 15 259–61; 19 481; **24** 528
King Ranch, Inc., 14 290–92
King-Seeley, **II** 419; **16** 487
King Soopers Inc., **12** 112–13
King World Productions, Inc., 9 306–08; **28** 174; **30 269–72 (upd.)**
King's Lynn Glass, **12** 528
Kingbird Media Group LLC, **26** 80
Kingfisher plc, V 106–09; **10** 498; **19** 123; **24 266–71 (upd.);** **27** 118, 120; **28** 34, 36; **49** 112–13
Kings, **24** 528
Kings County Lighting Company, **6** 456
Kings County Research Laboratories, **11** 424
Kings Mills, Inc., **13** 532
Kings Super Markets, **24** 313, 316
Kingsford Corporation, **III** 21; **22** 146
Kingsin Line, **6** 397
Kingsport Pulp Corp., **IV** 310; **19** 266
Kingston Technology Corporation, 20 324–26; 38 441
Kinki Nippon Railway Company Ltd., V 463–65

Kinko's Inc., 12 174; **16** 306–08; **18** 363–64; **43 261–64 (upd.)**
Kinnevik. *See* Industriförvaltnings AB Kinnevik.
Kinney Corporation, **23** 32; **24** 373
Kinney National Service Inc., **II** 176; **IV** 672; **19** 404; **25** 140
Kinney Services, **6** 293
Kinney Shoe Corp., V 226; **11** 349; **14 293–95**
Kinney Tobacco Co., **12** 108
Kinoshita Sansho Steel Co., **I** 508
Kinpo Electronic, **23** 212
Kinross Gold Corporation, 36 314–16
Kinson Resources Inc., **27** 38
Kintec Corp., **10** 97
Kirby. *See* Scott Fetzer Company.
Kirby Corporation, 18 277–79; 22 275
Kirby Forest Industries, **IV** 305
Kirch Gruppe, **10** 196; **35** 452
Kirchner, Moore, and Co., **II** 408
KirchPayTV, **46** 402
Kirin Brewery Company, Limited, I 220, 258, 265–66, 282; **10** 78, 80; **13** 258, 454; **20** 28; **21 318–21 (upd.);** **36** 404–05
Kirk Stieff Company, **10** 181; **12** 313
Kirkland Messina, Inc., **19** 392, 394
Kirkstall Forge Engineering, **III** 494
Kirsch Co., **II** 16
Kirschner Manufacturing Co., **16** 296
Kishimoto & Co., **I** 432, 492; **24** 325
Kishimoto Shoten Co., Ltd., **IV** 168
Kistler, Lesh & Co., **III** 528
Kit Manufacturing Co., 18 280–82
Kita Consolidated, Ltd., **16** 142
Kita Karafunto Oil Co., **IV** 475
Kita Nippon Paper Co., **IV** 321
Kitagawa & Co. Ltd., **IV** 442
Kitchell Corporation, 14 296–98
KitchenAid, III 611, 653–54; **8 298–99**
Kitchenbell, **III** 43
Kitchens of Sara Lee, **II** 571–73
Kittery Electric Light Co., **14** 124
Kittinger, **10** 324
Kitty Hawk, Inc., 22 309–11
Kiwi International Airlines Inc., 20 327–29
Kiwi Packaging, **IV** 250
Kiwi Polish Co., **15** 507
KJJ. *See* Klaus J. Jacobs Holdings.
Kjøbenhavns Bandelsbank, **II** 366
KJPCL. *See* Royal Interocean Lines.
KKK Shipping, **II** 274
KKR. *See* Kohlberg Kravis Roberts & Co.
KLA Instruments Corporation, 11 231–33; 20 8
KLA-Tencor Corporation, 45 231–34 (upd.)
Klaus J. Jacobs Holdings, **29** 46–47
KLC/New City Televentures, **25** 269
Klein Bicycles, **16** 495
Klein Sleep Products Inc., **32** 426
Kleiner, Perkins, Caufield & Byers, **I** 637; **6** 278; **10** 15, 504; **14** 263; **16** 418; **27** 447
Kleinwort Benson Group PLC, II 379, 421–23; **IV** 191; **22** 55
Kline Manufacturing, **II** 16
KLLM Transport Services, **27** 404
KLM Royal Dutch Airlines, **26** 33924 311, 396–97; **27** 474; **29** 15, 17; **33** 49, 51; **34** 397; **47** 60–61. *See also* Koninklijke Luftvaart Maatschappij N.V.

Klöckner-Humboldt-Deutz AG, **I** 542; **III** 541–44; **IV** 126–27; **13** 16–17

Klöckner-Werke AG, IV 43, 60, **126–28**, 201; **19** 64; **39** 125

Klondike, **14** 205

Klopman International, **12** 118

Kloth-Senking, **IV** 201

Klüber Lubrication München KG, **41** 170

Kluwer Publishers, **IV** 611; **14** 555

Klynveld Main Goerdeler, **10** 387

Klynveld Peat Marwick Goerdeler. *See* KPMG Worldwide.

KM&G. *See* Ketchum Communications Inc.

Kmart Canada Co., **25** 222

Kmart Corporation, I 516; **V** 35, **110–12**; **6** 13; **7** 61, 444; **9** 361, 400, 482; **10** 137, 410, 490, 497, 515–16; **12** 48, 54–55, 430, 477–78, 507–08; **13** 42, 260–61, 274, 317–18, 444, 446; **14** 192, 394; **15** 61–62, 210–11, 330–31, 470; **16** 35–37, 61, 187, 210, 447, 457; **17** 297, 460–61, 523–24; **18** 137, **283–87** (**upd.**), 477; **19** 511; **20** 155–56; **21** 73; **22** 258, 328; **23** 210, 329; **24** 322–23; **25** 121; **26** 348, 524; **27** 313, 429, 451, 481; **32** 169; **43** 77–78, 293, 385; **47** **207–12 (upd.**); **48** 331

Kmart Mexico, **36** 139

KMC Enterprises, Inc., **27** 274

KMP Holdings, **I** 531

KN. *See* Kühne & Nagel Group.

KN Energy. *See* Kinder Morgan, Inc.

Kna-Shoe Manufacturing Company, **14** 302

Knape & Vogt Manufacturing Company, 17 277–79

Knapp & Tubbs, **III** 423

Knapp Communications Corporation, **II** 656; **13** 180; **24** 418

Knapp-Monarch, **12** 251

Knauf, **III** 721, 736

KNI Retail A/S, **12** 363

Knickerbocker Toy Co., **III** 505

Knickerbocker Trust Company, **13** 465

Knife River Coal Mining Company, **7** 322–25

Knife River Corporation, **42** 249, 253

Knight Paper Co., III 766; **22** 545

Knight-Ridder, Inc., III 190; **IV** 597, 613, **628–30**, 670; **6** 323; **7** 191, 327; **10** 407; **15 262–66 (upd.**); **18** 323; **30** 216; **38** 307

Knightsbridge Partners, **26** 476

KNILM, **24** 397

Knoff-Bremse, **I** 138

Knogo Corp., **11** 444; **39** 78

Knoll Group Inc., I 202; **14 299–301**

Knoll Pharmaceutical, **I** 682

Knomark, **III** 55

Knorr-Bremse, **11** 31

Knorr Co. *See* C.H. Knorr Co.

Knorr Foods Co., Ltd., **28** 10

Knott, **III** 98

Knott's Berry Farm, 18 288–90; 22 130

Knowledge Systems Concepts, **11** 469

KnowledgeWare Inc., 9 309–11; 27 491; **31 296–298 (upd.**); **45** 206

Knox County Insurance, **41** 178

Knox Reeves Advertising Agency, **25** 90

Knoxville Glove Co., **34** 159

Knoxville Paper Box Co., Inc., **13** 442

KNP BT. *See* Buhrmann NV.

KNP Leykam, **49** 352, 354

KNSM. *See* Koninklijke Nederlandsche Stoomboot Maatschappij.

Knudsen & Sons, Inc., **11** 211

Knudsen Foods, **27** 330

Knutange, **IV** 226

Knutson Construction, **25** 331

KOA. *See* Kampgrounds of America, Inc.

Koala Corporation, 44 260–62

Kobacker Co., **18** 414–15

Kobayashi Tomijiro Shoten, **III** 44

Kobe Shipbuilding & Engine Works, **II** 57

Kobe Steel, Ltd., I 511; **II** 274; **IV** 16, **129–31**, 212–13; **8** 242; **11** 234–35; **13** 297; **19 238–41 (upd.**); **38** 225–26

Kobelco America Inc., **19** 241

Kobelco Middle East, **IV** 131

Kobold. *See* Vorwerk & Co.

Kobrand Corporation, **24** 308; **43** 402

Koç Holdings A.S., I 167, **478–80**; **11** 139; **27** 188

Koch Enterprises, Inc., 29 215–17

Koch Industries, Inc., IV 448–49; 20 330–32 (upd.); **21** 108; **22** 3

Koch-Light Laboratories, **13** 239; **38** 203–04

Kockos Brothers, Inc., **II** 624

Kodak. *See* Eastman Kodak Company.

Kodansha Ltd., IV 631–33; 38 273–76 (upd.)

Ködel & Böhn GmbH, **III** 543

Koehring Company, **8** 545; **23** 299

Koehring Cranes & Excavators, **7** 513

Koei Real Estate Ltd., **V** 195; **47** 390

Koenig Plastics Co., **19** 414

Kogaku Co., Ltd., **48** 295

Kohl's Corporation, 9 312–13; 22 72; **30 273–75 (upd.**)

Kohl's Food Stores, Inc., **I** 426–27; **16** 247, 249

Kohlberg Kravis Roberts & Co., I 566, 609–11; **II** 370, 452, 468, 544, 645, 654, 656, 667; **III** 263, 765–67; **IV** 642–43; **V** 55–56, 408, 410, 415; **6** 357; **7** 130, 132, 200; **9** 53, 180, 230, 469, 522; **10** 75–77, 302; **12** 559; **13** 163, 166, 363, 453; **14** 42; **15** 270; **17** 471; **18** 3; **19** 493; **22** 55, 91, 441, 513, 544; **23** 163; **24** 92, **272–74**, 416, 418; **25** 11, 278; **26** 46, 48, 352; **27** 11; **28** 389, 475; **30** 386; **32** 408; **33** 255; **35** 35; **38** 190; **40** 34, 36, 366; **43** 355; **44** 153; **45** 243; **49** 369

Kohler Bros., **IV** 91

Kohler Company, 7 269–71; 10 119; **24** 150; **32 308–12 (upd.**)

Kohler Mix Specialties, Inc., **25** 333

Kohner Brothers, **II** 531

Koholyt AG, **III** 693

Koike Shoten, **II** 458

Kojiro Matsukata, **V** 457–58

Kokkola Chemicals Oy, **17** 362–63

Kokomo Gas and Fuel Company, **6** 533

Kokuei Paper Co., Ltd., **IV** 327

Kokura Sekiyu Co. Ltd., **IV** 554

Kokura Steel Manufacturing Co., Ltd., **IV** 212

Kokusai Kisen, **V** 457–58

Kokusaku Kiko Co., Ltd., **IV** 327

Kokusaku Pulp Co., **IV** 327

Kolb-Lena, **25** 85

Kolbenschmidt, **IV** 141

Kolker Chemical Works, Inc., **IV** 409; **7** 308

The Koll Company, 8 300–02; 21 97; **25** 449

Kollmorgen Corporation, 18 291–94

Kölnische Rückversicherungs- Gesellschaft AG, **24** 178

Komag, Inc., 11 234–35

Komatsu Ltd., III 453, 473, **545–46**; **15** 92; **16 309–11 (upd.**)

Kommanditgesellschaft S. Elkan & Co., **IV** 140

Kommunale Energie-Beteiligungsgesellschaft, **V** 746

Kompro Computer Leasing, **II** 457

Konan Camera Institute, **III** 487

Kone Corporation, 27 267–70

Kongl. Elektriska Telegraf-Verket, **V** 331

Kongo Bearing Co., **III** 595

Konica Corporation, III 547–50; 30 276–81 (upd.); **43** 284

König Brauerei GmbH & Co. KG, 35 256–58 (upd.)

Koninklijke Ahold N.V., II 641–42; 12 152–53; **16 312–14 (upd.**)

Koninklijke Bols Wessanen, N.V., **29** 480–81

Koninklijke Distilleerderijen der Erven Lucas Böls, **I** 226

Koninklijke Hoogovens NV, **26** 527, 530. *See also* Koninklijke Nederlandsche Hoogovens en Staalfabrieken NV.

Koninklijke Java-China Paketvaart Lijnen. *See* Royal Interocean Lines.

NV Koninklijke KNP BT. *See* Buhrmann NV.

Koninklijke KPN N.V. *See* Royal KPN N.V.

Koninklijke Luchtvaart Maatschappij N.V., I 55, **107–09**, 119, 121; **6** 95, 105, 109–10; **14** 73; **28 224–27 (upd.**)

Koninklijke Nederlandsche Hoogovens en Staalfabrieken NV, IV 105, 123, **132–34**; **49** 98, 101

Koninklijke Nederlandsche Maatschappig Tot Exploitatie van Petroleumbronnen in Nederlandsch-indie, **IV** 530

Koninklijke Nederlandsche Petroleum Maatschappij, **IV** 491

Koninklijke Nederlandsche Stoomboot Maatschappij, **26** 241

N.V. Koninklijke Nederlandse Vliegtuigenfabriek Fokker, I 46, **54–56**, 75, 82, 107, 115, 121–22; **28 327–30 (upd.**)

Koninklijke Nedlloyd Groep N.V., 6 403–05

Koninklijke Nedlloyd N.V., 26 241–44 (upd.)

Koninklijke Numico N.V. *See* Royal Numico N.V.

Koninklijke Paketvaart Maatschappij, **26** 242

Koninklijke PTT Nederland NV, V 299–301; 27 471–72, 475. *See also* Royal KPN NV.

Koninklijke Van Ommeren, **22** 275

Koninklijke Wessanen N.V., II 527–29

Koninklijke West-Indische Maildienst, **26** 242

Koniphoto Corp., **III** 548

Konishi Honten, **III** 547

Konishi Pharmaceutical, **I** 704

Konishiroku Honten Co., Ltd., **III** 487, 547–49

Konoike Bank, **II** 347

Konrad Hornschuch AG, **31** 161–62
Koo Koo Roo, Inc., 25 263–65
Koop Nautic Holland, **41** 412
Koopman & Co., **III** 419
Koor Industries Ltd., II 47–49; **22** 501; **25** 266–68 (upd.)
Koors Perry & Associates, Inc., **24** 95
Koortrade, **II** 48
Kop-Coat, Inc., **8** 456
Kopin Corp., **13** 399
Köpings Mekaniska Verkstad, **26** 10
Koppel Steel, **26** 407
Koppens Machinenfabriek, **III** 420
Kopper United, **I** 354
Koppers Inc., I 199, 354–56; **III** 645, 735; **6** 486; **17** 38–39
Koppers Industries, Inc., 26 245–48 (upd.)
Koracorp Industries Inc., **16** 327
Korbel, **I** 226
Korea Automotive Fuel Systems Ltd., **13** 555
Korea Automotive Motor Corp., **16** 436; **43** 319
Korea Development Leasing Corp., **II** 442
Korea Steel Co., **III** 459
Korea Telecommunications Co, **I** 516
Korean Air Lines Co. Ltd., II 442; **6** 98–99; **24** 443; **27** 271–73 (upd.); **46** 40
Korean Development Bank, **III** 459
Korean Tungsten Mining Co., **IV** 183
Kori Kollo Corp., **23** 41
Korn/Ferry International, 34 247–49
Koro Corp., **19** 414
Korrekt Gebäudereinigung, **16** 420; **43** 307
KorrVu, **14** 430
Kortbetalning Servo A.B., **II** 353
Kortgruppen Eurocard-Köpkort A.B., **II** 353
Korvettes, E.J., **14** 426
Koryeo Industrial Development Co., **III** 516; **7** 232
Koryo Fire and Marine Insurance Co., **III** 747
Koss Corporation, 38 277–79
Kosset Carpets, Ltd., **9** 467
Kotobukiya Co., Ltd., V 113–14
Kowa Metal Manufacturing Co., **III** 758
Koyo Seiko, **III** 595–96, 623–24
KPM. *See* Koninklijke Paketvaart Maatschappij.
KPMG International, 29 176; **33** 234–38 (upd.)
KPMG Worldwide, 7 266; **10** 115, 385–87
KPN. *See* Koninklijke PTT Nederland N.V.
KPR Holdings Inc., **23** 203
Kraft Foods Inc., II 129, 530–34, 556; **V** 407; **III** 610; **7** 272–77 (upd.), 339, 433, 547; **8** 399, 499; **9** 180, 290, 318; **11** 15; **12** 372, 532; **13** 408, 515, 517; **14** 204; **16** 88, 90; **17** 56; **18** 67, 246, 416, 419; **19** 51; **22** 82, 85; **23** 219, 384; **25** 366, 517; **26** 249, 251; **28** 479; **44** 342; **45** 235–44 (upd.); **48** 331
Kraft Foodservice, **26** 504; **31** 359–60
Kraft Jacobs Suchard AG, 26 249–52 (upd.)
Kraft-Versicherungs-AG, **III** 183
Kraftco Corporation, **II** 533; **14** 204
KraftMaid Cabinetry, Inc., **20** 363; **39** 267
Kraftwerk Union, **I** 411; **III** 466

Kragen Auto Supply Co., **27** 291. *See also* CSK Auto Corporation.
Kramer, **III** 48
Krämer & Grebe, **III** 420
Kramer Guitar, **29** 222
Kramer Machine and Engineering Company, **26** 117
Krames Communications Co., **22** 441, 443
Kransco, **25** 314
Krasnapolsky Restaurant and Wintergarden Company Ltd., **23** 228
Kraus-Anderson, Incorporated, 36 317–20
Krause Publications, Inc., 35 259–61
Krause's Furniture, Inc., 27 274–77
Krauss-Maffei AG, **I** 75; **II** 242; **III** 566, 695; **14** 328; **38** 299
Kravco, **III** 248
Kredietbank N.V., II 295, 304–05
Kreditanstalt für Wiederaufbau, IV 231–32; **29** 268–72
Kreft, **III** 480; **22** 26
Kreher Steel Co., **25** 8
Krelitz Industries, Inc., **14** 147
Krema Hollywood Chewing Gum Co. S.A., **II** 532
Kremers-Urban, **I** 667
Kresge Foundation, **V** 110
Kreuger & Toll, **IV** 338; **12** 462–63
Kreymborg, **13** 544–45
Kriegschemikalien AG, **IV** 229
Kriegsmetall AG, **IV** 229
Kriegswollbedarfs AG, **IV** 229
Krislex Knits, Inc., **8** 235
Krispy Kitchens, Inc., **II** 584
Krispy Kreme Doughnut Corporation, 21 322–24
Kroeze, **25** 82
The Kroger Company, II 605, 632, 643–45, 682; **III** 218; **6** 364; **7** 61; **12** 111–13; **13** 25, 237, 395; **15** 259, 267–70 (upd.), 449; **16** 63–64; **18** 6; **21** 323, 508; **22** 37, 126; **24** 416; **25** 234; **28** 512; **30** 24, 27; **40** 366
Krohn-Fechheimer Shoe Company, **V** 207
Krone AG, **33** 220
Krones A.G., **I** 266; **21** 319
Kronos, Inc., 18 295–97; **19** 468
Krovtex, **8** 80
Kroy Tanning Company, **17** 195
Krueger Insurance Company, **21** 257
Kruger Inc., 17 280–82
Krumbhaar Chemical Inc., **14** 308
Krupp, **17** 214; **22** 364; **49** 53–55. *See also* Fried. Krupp GmbH *and* Thyssen Krupp AG.
Krupp Widia GmbH, **12** 66
Kruse International, **32** 162
The Krystal Company, 33 239–42
KSSU Group, **I** 107–08, 120–21
KT Contract Services, **24** 118
KTR. *See* Keio Teito Electric Railway Company.
K2 Inc., 16 295–98; **22** 481, 483; **23** 474; **43** 389
KU Energy Corporation, 6 513, 515; **11** 236–38
Kubota Corporation, I 494; **III** 551–53; **10** 404; **12** 91, 161; **21** 385–86; **24** 324; **39** 37; **40** 134
Kubota, Gonshiro. *See* Gonshiro Oode.
Kudelski Group SA, 44 263–66
Kuhara Mining Co., **IV** 475
Kuhlman Corporation, 20 333–35

Kuhlmann, **III** 677; **IV** 174; **16** 121
Kühn + Bayer, **24** 165
Kuhn Loeb, **II** 402–03
Kühne & Nagel International AG, V 466–69
Kuitu Oy, **IV** 348
KUK, **III** 577, 712
Kukje Group, **III** 458
Kulicke and Soffa Industries, Inc., 33 246–48
Kulka Smith Inc., **13** 398
Kulmobelwerk G.H. Walb and Co., **I** 581
Kum-Kleen Products, **IV** 252; **17** 29
Kumagai Gumi Co., I 579–80
Kumsung Companies, **III** 747–48
Kunkel Industries, **19** 143
Kunst und Technik Verlag, **IV** 590
Kuo International Ltd., **I** 566; **44** 153
Kuok Group, **28** 84
Kuoni Travel Holding Ltd., 40 284–86
The Kuppenheimer Company, **8** 248–50; **32** 247
Kureha Chemical Industry, **I** 675
Kureha Spinning, **24** 325
Kureha Textiles, **I** 432, 492
Kurosawa Construction Co., Ltd., **IV** 155
Kurose, **III** 420
Kurt Möller Verlag, **7** 42
Kurushima Dockyard, **II** 339
The Kushner-Locke Company, 25 269–71
Kuusankoski Aktiebolag, **IV** 299
Kuwait Airways, **27** 135
Kuwait Investment Office, **II** 198; **IV** 380, 452; **27** 206
Kuwait Petroleum Corporation, IV 364, 450–52, 567; **18** 234; **38** 424
Kvaerner ASA, 20 313; **31** 367, 370; **36** 321–23
KW, Inc. *See* Coca-Cola Bottling Company of Northern New England, Inc.
Kwaishinsha Motor Car Works, **I** 183
Kwik Save Group plc, 11 239–41; **13** 26; **47** 368
Kwik Shop, Inc., **12** 112
Kwikasair Ltd., **27** 473
KWIM. *See* Koninklijke West-Indische Maildienst.
KWV, **I** 289
Kygnus Sekiyu K.K., **IV** 555
Kymi Paper Mills Ltd., **IV** 302
Kymmene Corporation, IV 276–77, 299–303, 337. *See also* UPM-Kymmene Corporation.
Kyocera Corporation, II 50–52; **III** 693; **7** 118; **21** 329–32 (upd.)
Kyodo, **16** 166
Kyodo Dieworks Thailand Co., **III** 758
Kyodo Gyogyo Kaisha, Limited, **II** 552
Kyodo Kako, **IV** 680
Kyodo Kokusan K.K., **21** 271
Kyodo Oil Co. Ltd., **IV** 476
Kyodo Securities Co., Ltd., **II** 433
Kyodo Unyu Kaisha, **I** 502–03, 506; **IV** 713; **V** 481
Kyoei Mutual Fire and Marine Insurance Co., **III** 273
Kyoritsu Pharmaceutical Industry Co., **I** 667
Kyosai Trust Co. *See* Yasuda Trust and Banking Company, Limited.
Kyoto Bank, **II** 291
Kyoto Ceramic Co., Ltd. *See* Kyocera Corporation.

Kyoto Ouchi Bank, **II** 292
Kyowa Hakko Kogyo Co., Ltd., III
  42–43; 45 94; **48 248–50 (upd.)**
Kyusha Refining Co., **IV** 403
Kyushu Electric Power Company Inc.,
  IV 492; **V 649–51; 17** 349
Kyushu Oil Refinery Co. Ltd., **IV** 434
Kywan Petroleum Ltd., **13** 556
KYZ International, **9** 427
KZO, **13** 21

L & G, **27** 291
L. & H. Sales Co., **16** 389
L&W Supply Corp., **III** 764
L-3 Communications Holdings, Inc., 48
  251–53
L.A. Darling Co., **IV** 135–36; **16** 357
L.A. Gear, Inc., 8 303–06; 11 349; **31**
  413; **32 313–17 (upd.)**
L.A. Mex. See Checkers Drive-Up
  Restaurants Inc.
L.A. T Sportswear, Inc., 26 257–59
L.B. DeLong, **III** 558
L.B. Foster Company, 33 255–58
L. Bamberger & Co., **V** 169; **8** 443
L. Bosendorfer Klavierfabrik, A.G., **12** 297
L.C. Bassford, **III** 653
L.D. Canocéan, **25** 104
The L.D. Caulk Company, **10** 271
L. Fish, **14** 236
L.G. Balfour Company, **12** 472; **19**
  451–52; **36** 469
L. Greif & Bro. Inc., **17** 203–05
L. Grossman and Sons. See Grossman's
  Inc.
L.H. Parke Co., **II** 571
L.J. Knowles & Bros., **9** 153
L.J. Melody & Co., **21** 97
L.K. Liggett Company, **24** 74
L. Kellenberger & Co. AG, **25** 194
L.L. Bean, Inc., 9 190, 316; **10 388–90;**
  12 280; **19** 333; **21** 131; **22** 173; **25** 48,
  206; **29** 278; **36** 180, 420; **38 280–83**
  (upd.)
The L.L. Knickerbocker Co., Inc., 25
  272–75
L. Luria & Son, Inc., 19 242–44
L.M. Electronics, **I** 489
L.M. Ericsson, **I** 462; **II** 1, 70, 81–82, 365;
  III 479–80; **11** 46, 439; **14** 488. See
  also Telefonaktiebolaget LM Ericsson.
L-N Glass Co., **III** 715
L-N Safety Glass, **III** 715
L-O-F Glass Co. See Libbey-Owens-Ford
  Glass Co.
L. Prang & Co., **12** 207
L.S. DuBois Son and Co., **III** 10
L.S. Starrett Co., 13 301–03
L. Straus and Sons, **V** 168
L.W. Hammerson & Co., **IV** 696
L.W. Pierce Co., Inc. See Pierce Leahy
  Corporation.
L.W. Singer, **13** 429
La Banque Suisse et Française. See Crédit
  Commercial de France.
La Barge Mirrors, **III** 571; **20** 362
La Cerus, **IV** 615
La Choy Food Products Inc., II 467–68;
  17 241; **25 276–78**
La Cinq, **IV** 619
La Cloche d'Or, **25** 85
La Concorde, **III** 208
La Crosse Telephone Corporation, **9** 106
La Cruz del Campo S.A., **9** 100

La Favorita Bakery, **II** 543
La Fromagerie du Velay, **25** 85
La Grange Foundry, Inc., **39** 31
La Halle aux Chaussures, **17** 210
La India Co., **II** 532
La Madeleine French Bakery & Café, 33
  249–51
La Oroya, **22** 286
La Petite Academy, **13** 299
La Pizza Loca Inc., **44** 86
La Poste, V 270–72;], **47 213–16 (upd.)**
The La Quinta Companies, 42 213–16
  (upd.)
La Quinta Inns, Inc., 11 242–44; 21 362
La Redoute S.A., **19** 306, 309
La Rinascente, **12** 153
La-Ru Truck Rental Company, Inc., **16** 386
La Ruche Meridionale, **12** 153
La 7, **47** 345, 347
La Societe Anonyme Francaise Holophane,
  19 211
La Vie Claire, **13** 103
La-Z-Boy Chair Company, 14 302–04;
  31 248
Laakirchen, **IV** 339–40; **28** 445
LAB. See Lloyd Aereo de Bolivia.
The Lab, Inc., **37** 263
LaB Investing Co. L.L.C, **37** 224
LaBakelite S.A., **I** 387
LaBarge Inc., 41 224–26
Labatt Brewing Company Limited, I
  267–68; 18 72; **25 279–82 (upd.); 26**
  303, 306
Labaz, **I** 676; **IV** 546
Labelcraft, Inc., **8** 360
LaBelle Iron Works, **7** 586
LabOne, Inc., 48 254–57
Labor für Impulstechnik, **III** 154
Labor Ready, Inc., 29 273–75
Laboratoire L. Lafon, **45** 94
Laboratoire Michel Robilliard, **IV** 546
Laboratoire Roger Bellon, **I** 389
Laboratoires d'Anglas, **III** 47
Laboratoires de Biologie Végétale Yves
  Rocher, 35 262–65
Laboratoires Goupil, **III** 48
Laboratoires Roche Posay, **III** 48
Laboratoires Ruby d'Anglas, **III** 48
Laboratorios Grossman, **III** 55
Laboratorios Liade S.A., **24** 75
Laboratory Corporation of America
  Holdings, 42 217–20 (upd.)
Laboratory for Electronics, **III** 168; **6** 284
LaBour Pump, **I** 473
LaBow, Haynes Co., **III** 270
LaBranche & Co. Inc., 37 223–25
Labsphere, Inc., **48** 446
Labtronics, Inc., **49** 307–08
Lachine Rapids Hydraulic and Land
  Company, **6** 501
Laci Le Beau Tea, **49** 275–76
Lackawanna Steel & Ordnance Co., **IV** 35,
  114; **7** 48
Laclede Steel Company, 15 271–73
Lacombe Electric. See Public Service
  Company of Colorado.
Lacquer Products Co., **I** 321
LaCrosse Footwear, Inc., 18 298–301
Lacto Ibérica, **23** 219
Lactos, **25** 85
Lacy Diversified Industries, Ltd., **24**
  159–61
Ladbroke Group PLC, II 139, 141–42;
  19 208; **21 333–36 (upd.); 24** 194; **42**

64; **49** 449–50. See also Hilton Group
  plc.
Ladd and Tilton, **14** 527–28
LADD Furniture, Inc., 12 299–301; 23
  244
Ladd Petroleum Corp., **II** 30
LADECO, **6** 97; **31** 304; **36** 281
Ladenburg, Thalmann & Co. Inc., **17** 346
Ladenso, **IV** 277
Ladish Co., Inc., 30 282–84
Lady Foot Locker, **V** 226; **14** 293, 295
Lady Lee, **27** 291
Laerdal Medical, **18** 423
Lafarge Coppée S.A., III 702, **703–05,**
  736; **8** 258; **10** 422–23; **23** 333
Lafarge Corporation, **24** 332; **28 228–31**
Lafayette Manufacturing Co., **12** 296
Lafayette Radio Electronics Corporation, **9**
  121–22
Laflin & Rand Powder Co., **I** 328; **III** 525
Lafuma S.A., 39 248–50
LAG&E. See Los Angeles Gas and Electric
  Company.
LaGard Inc., **20** 363
Lagardère Groupe SCA, **16** 254; **24** 84, 88;
  34 83
Lagoven, **IV** 508
Laidlaw Inc., **39** 19, 21
Laidlaw Transportation, Inc., **6** 410; **32**
  227, 231
Laing, **IV** 696
Laing's Properties Ltd., **I** 575
L'Air Liquide SA, I 303, **357–59; 11** 402;
  47 217–20 (upd.)
Laitaatsillan Konepaja, **IV** 275
Laiterie Centrale Krompholtz, **25** 84
Laiterie de la Vallée du Dropt, **25** 84
Laiterie Ekabe, **19** 50
SA Laiterie Walhorn Molkerel, **19** 50
Laiteries Prairies de l'Orne, **19** 50
Lake Arrowhead Development Co., **IV** 255
Lake Central Airlines, **I** 131; **6** 131
Lake Erie Screw Corp., **11** 534, 536
Lake Odessa Machine Products, **18** 494
Lake Superior Consolidated Mines
  Company, **IV** 572; **7** 549; **17** 355–56
Lake Superior Paper Industries, **26** 363
Lakehead Pipe Line Partners, L.P., **43** 155
Lakeland Fire and Casualty Co., **III** 213
Lakeland Industries, Inc., 45 245–48
Läkemedels-Industri Föreningen, **I** 664
Laker Airways, **I** 94; **6** 79; **24** 399
Lakeside Laboratories, **III** 24
The Lakeside Publishing and Printing Co.,
  IV 660
Lakestone Systems, Inc., **11** 469
Lam Research Corporation, IV 213; **11**
  245–47; 18 383; **31 299–302 (upd.)**
Lamar Advertising Company, 27 278–80
The Lamaur Corporation, 41 227–29
Lamb Technicon Corp., **I** 486
Lamb Weston, Inc., I 417; **23 319–21; 24**
  33–34
Lambda Electronics Inc., **32** 411
Lambert Brothers, Inc., **7** 573
Lambert Brussels Financial Corporation, **II**
  407; **11** 532
Lambert Frères, **33** 339
Lambert Kay Company, **8** 84
Lambert Pharmacal Co., **I** 710–11; **III** 28
Lambert Rivière, **41** 340
Lamborghini. See Automobili Lamborghini
  S.p.A.
Lamkin Brothers, Inc., **8** 386

Lamons Metal Gasket Co., **III** 570; **11** 535; **20** 361

Lamontagne Ltd., **II** 651

Lamonts Apparel, Inc., 15 274–76

Lampadaires Feralux, Inc., **19** 472

Lamson & Sessions Co., 13 304–06

Lamson Bros., **II** 451

Lamson Corporation, **7** 145; **49** 159

Lamson Industries Ltd., **IV** 645

Lamson Store Service Co., **IV** 644

Lan Chile S.A., 31 303–06; 33

Lanca, **14** 224

Lancashire, **III** 350

Lancaster Caramel Co., **II** 510

Lancaster Colony Corporation, 8 307–09

Lancaster Cork Works, **III** 422

Lancaster Financial Ltd., **14** 472

Lancaster National Bank, **9** 475

Lancaster Press, **23** 102

Lance, Inc., 14 305–07; 41 230–33 (upd.)

Lancel, **27** 487, 489

Lancer Corporation, 21 337–39

Lanchester Motor Company, Ltd., **13** 286

Lancia, **I** 162; **11** 102

Lancôme, **III** 46–48; **8** 342

Land O'Lakes, Inc., II 535–37; 7 339; **13** 351; **21 340–43 (upd.)**

Land-O-Sun Dairies, L.L.C., **26** 449

Land Securities PLC, IV 704–06; 49 246–50 (upd.)

Land-Wheelwright Laboratories, **III** 607; **7** 436

Lander Alarm Co., **III** 740

Lander Company, **21** 54

Länderbank, **II** 282

Landesbank für Westfalen Girozentrale, Münster, **II** 385

Landis International, Inc., **10** 105–06

Landmark Banks, **10** 426

Landmark Communications, Inc., 12 302–05; 22 442

Landmark Financial Services Inc., **11** 447

Landmark Target Media, **IV** 597

Landmark Union Trust, **18** 517

Landoll, Inc., **22** 522

Landor Associates, **I** 94

Landry's Seafood Restaurants, Inc., 15 277–79

Lands' End, Inc., 9 314–16; 12 280; **16** 37; **19** 333; **26** 439; **27** 374, 429; **29 276–79 (upd.)**

Landstar, **26** 533

Lane Bryant, **V** 115–16

The Lane Co., Inc., III 528, 530; 12 306–08; 39 170, 173–74

Lane Drug Company, **12** 132

Lane, Piper, and Jaffray, Inc. *See* Piper Jaffray Companies.

Lane Processing Inc., **II** 585

Lane Publishing Co., **IV** 676; **7** 529

Lane Rossi, **IV** 421

Laneco, Inc., **II** 682

Lang Exploratory Drilling, **26** 42

Langdon Rieder Corp., **21** 97

Lange International S.A., **15** 462; **43** 375–76

Lange, Maxwell & Springer, **IV** 641; **7** 311

Langford Labs, **8** 25

Lanier Business Products, Inc., **II** 39; **8** 407; **20** 290

Lanman Companies, Inc., **23** 101

Lannet Data Communications Ltd., **18** 345–46; **26** 275–77

Lano Corp., **I** 446

Lansi-Suomen Osake-Pankki, **II** 303

Lanson Pere et Fils, **II** 475

Lantic Industries, Inc., **II** 664

Lanvin, **I** 696; **III** 48; **8** 343

LAPE. *See* Líneas Aéreas Postales Españolas.

Lapeyre S.A. *See* Groupe Lapeyre S.A.

LaPine Technology, **II** 51; **21** 331

Laporte Industries Ltd., **I** 303; **IV** 300

Lapp, **8** 229

Lara, **19** 192

Larami Corp., **14** 486

Lareco, **26** 22

Largardère Groupe, **43** 210

Largo Entertainment, **25** 329

Laroche Navarron, **I** 703

Larousse Group, **IV** 614–15

Larrowe Milling Co., **II** 501; **10** 322

Larry Flynt Publishing Inc., 31 307–10

Larry H. Miller Group, 29 280–83

Larry's Food Products, **36** 163

Larsen & Toubro, **IV** 484

Larsen Company, **7** 128

Larson Boats. *See* Genmar Holdings, Inc.

Larson Lumber Co., **IV** 306

Larwin Group, **III** 231

Las Vegas Gas Company, **19** 411

LaSalle Investment Management, Inc., **49** 238

LaSalle Machine Tool, Inc., **13** 7–8

LaSalle National Bank, **II** 184

LaSalle Partners, **49** 28

LaSalle Steel Corporation, **28** 314

LaSalles & Koch Co., **8** 443

Lasco Shipping Co., **19** 380

Laser Tech Color, **21** 60

Lasercharge Pty Ltd., **18** 130

LaserSoft, **24** 349

Oy Läskelä Ab, **IV** 300

Lasky's, **II** 141; **24** 269

Lasmo, **IV** 455, 499

Lason, Inc., 31 311–13

Latham & Watkins, 33 252–54; 37 292

Latin Communications Group Inc., **41** 151

Latitude Communications, **22** 52

Latrobe Brewing Co., **25** 281

Latrobe Steel Company, **8** 529–31

Lattice Semiconductor Corp., 16 315–17; 43 17

Lauda Air Luftfahrt AG, 48 258–60

Lauder Chemical, **17** 363

Laura Ashley Holdings plc, 13 307–09; 37 226–29 (upd.)

Laura Scudders, **7** 429; **44** 348

Laurel Glen, **34** 3, 5

Laurent-Perrier SA, 42 221–23

Laurentian Group, **48** 290

Laurentien Hotel Co., **III** 99

Lauson Engine Company, **8** 515

LaVista Equipment Supply Co., **14** 545

Lavold, **16** 421; **43** 308

Law Life Assurance Society, **III** 372

Lawn Boy Inc., **7** 535–36; **8** 72; **26** 494

Lawrence Manufacturing Co., **III** 526

Lawrence Warehouse Co., **II** 397–98; **10** 62

Lawrenceburg Gas Company, **6** 466

The Lawson Co., **7** 113; **25** 125

Lawson Inc., **41** 113, 115

Lawson Milk, **II** 572

Lawson Software, 38 284–88

Lawter International Inc., 14 308–10; 18 220

Lawyers Cooperative, **8** 527–28

Lawyers Trust Co., **II** 230

Layer Five, **43** 252

Layne & Bowler Pump, **11** 5

Layne Christensen Company, 19 245–47; 26 71

Layton Homes Corporation, **30** 423

Lazard Freres & Co., **II** 268, 402, 422; **IV** 23, 79, 658–59; **6** 356; **7** 287, 446; **10** 399; **12** 165, 391, 547, 562; **21** 145

Lazard LLC, 38 289–92

Lazare Kaplan International Inc., 21 344–47

Lazio. *See* Societá Sportiva Lazio SpA.

LBO Holdings, **15** 459

LBS Communications, **6** 28

LCI International, Inc., 16 318–20

LCP Hotels. *See* CapStar Hotel Co.

LDDS-Metro Communications, Inc., 8 310–12

LDDS WorldCom, Inc., **16** 467–68

LDI. *See* Lacy Diversified Industries, Ltd.

LDMA-AU, Inc., **49** 173

LDS Health Services Corporation, **27** 237

LDX NET, Inc., **IV** 576

Le Bon Marché. *See* Bon Marché.

Le Brun and Sons, **III** 291

Le Buffet System-Gastronomie, **V** 74

Le Chameau, **39** 250

Le Clerc, **21** 225–26

Le Courviour S.A., **10** 351

Le Monde S.A., 33 308–10

Le Rocher, Compagnie de Reassurance, **III** 340

Le Touquet's, SA, **48** 197

Lea & Perrins, **II** 475

Lea County Gas Co., **6** 580

Lea Lumber & Plywood Co., **12** 300

Lea Manufacturing, **23** 299

Leach McMicking, **13** 274

Lead Industries Group Ltd., **III** 681; **IV** 108

Leadership Housing Inc., **IV** 136

Leaf River Forest Products Inc., **IV** 282, 300; **9** 261

Leahy & Co. *See* Pierce Leahy Corporation.

Leamington Priors & Warwickshire Banking Co., **II** 318; **17** 323

Lean Cuisine, **12** 531

Lear Corporation, **17** 303, 305

Lear Inc., **II** 61; **8** 49, 51

Lear Romec Corp., **8** 135

Lear Seating Corporation, 16 321–23

Lear Siegler Holdings Corporation, **25** 431

Lear Siegler Inc., I 481–83; III 581; 8 313; **13** 169, 358, 398; **19 371–72; 30** 426; **44** 308

Learjet Inc., 8 313–16; 9 242; **27 281–85 (upd.)**

The Learning Company Inc., 24 275–78, 480; 29 74, 77; **41** 409

Learning Tree International Inc., 24 279–82

LeaRonal, Inc., 23 322–24

Leasco Data Processing Equipment Corp., **III** 342–44; **IV** 641–42; **7** 311

Lease International SA, **6** 358

Leaseway Personnel Corp., **18** 159

Leaseway Transportation Corp., V 494; 12 309–11; 19 293

Leatherback Industries, **22** 229

LeBoeuf, Lamb, Greene & MacRae, L.L.P., 29 284–86

Lebr Associates Inc., **25** 246
Lech Brewery, **24** 450
Lechmere Inc., 10 391–93
Lechters, Inc., 11 248–50; 39 251–54 (upd.)
Leclerc. *See* Association des Centres Distributeurs E. Leclerc.
LeCroy Corporation, 41 234–37
Lectorum Publications, **29** 426
Ledcor Industries Limited, 46 266–69
Lederle Laboratories, **I** 300–02, 657, 684; **8** 24–25; **14** 254, 256, 423; **27** 115
Lederle Standard Products, **26** 29
Lee Ackerman Investment Company, **18** 513
Lee Apparel Company, Inc., 8 317–19; 17 512, 514
Lee Brands, **II** 500
Lee Company, **V** 390–92
Lee Cooper Group Ltd., **49** 259
Lee Enterprises, Incorporated, 11 251–53; 47 120
Lee Hecht Harrison, **6** 10
Lee International, **24** 373
Lee National Corporation, **26** 234
Lee Optical, **13** 390
Lee Rubber and Tire Corp., **16** 8
Lee Telephone Company, **6** 313
Lee Way Holding Co., **14** 42
Lee Way Motor Freight, **I** 278
Leeann Chin, Inc., 30 285–88
Leeds & County Bank, **II** 318; **17** 323
Leeds & Northrup Co., **III** 644–45; **28** 484
Lees Carpets, **17** 76
Leewards Creative Crafts Inc., **17** 322
Lefeldt, **III** 417, 418
Lefrak Organization Inc., 8 357; 26 260–62
Legacy Homes Ltd., **26** 290
Legal & General Group plc, III 272–73; IV 705, 712; **24 283–85 (upd.); 30** 494; **33** 319
The Legal Aid Society, 48 261–64
Legal Technologies, Inc., **15** 378
Legault and Masse, **II** 664
Legent Corporation, 10 394–96; 14 392
Legetojsfabrikken LEGO Billund A/S. *See* Lego A/S.
Legg Mason, Inc., 11 493; 33 259–62
Leggett & Platt, Inc., 9 93; 11 254–56; 48 265–68 (upd.)
Leggett Stores Inc., **19** 48
Lego A/S, 12 495; 13 310–13; 40 287–91 (upd.)
Legrand SA, 21 348–50
Lehigh Acquisition Corp., **34** 286
Lehigh Portland Cement Company, 23 325–27; 31 252
Lehigh Railroad, **III** 258
Lehman Brothers, **I** 78, 125, 484; **II** 192, 259, 398, 448, 450–51; **6** 199; **10** 62–63; **11** 263–64; **13** 448; **14** 145; **22** 445; **25** 301; **38** 411; **48** 59
Lehman Merchant Bank Partners, **19** 324
Lehmer Company. *See* Centel Corporation.
Lehn & Fink, **I** 699
Lehnkering AG, **IV** 140
Lehrman Bros., **III** 419
Lehser Communications, Inc., **15** 265
Leica Camera AG, 35 266–69
Leica Microsystems Holdings GmbH, 35 270–73
Leigh-Mardon Security Group, **30** 44
Leighton Holdings Ltd., **19** 402

Leinenkugel Brewing Company. *See* Jacob Leinenkugel Brewing Company.
Leiner Health Products Inc., 34 250–52
The Leisure Company, **34** 22
Leisure Lodges, **III** 76
Leisure System Inc., **12** 359
Leitz, **III** 583–84
LeMaster Litho Supply, **13** 228
Lemmerz Holding GmbH, **27** 202, 204
Lempereur, **13** 297
Lena Goldfields Ltd., **IV** 94
Lenc-Smith, **III** 430
Lend Lease Corporation Limited, IV 707–09; 17 283–86 (upd.); 47 410
Lender's Bagel, **32** 69
Lending Textiles, **29** 132
Lenel Systems International Inc., **24** 510
Lennar Corporation, 11 257–59
Lennon's, **II** 628
Lennox Industries, Inc., **22** 6
Lennox International Inc., 8 320–22; 28 232–36 (upd.)
Lenoir Furniture Corporation, **10** 183
Lenox, Inc., I 227; **10** 179, 181; **12** 312–13; **18** 69; **38** 113
Lens, Inc., **30** 267–68
LensCrafters Inc., **V** 207–08; **13** 391; **17** 294; **23** 328–30; **43** 199
Lentheric, **I** 426
L'Entreprise Jean Lefebvre, 23 331–33
Leo Burnett Company, Inc., I 22–24, 25, 31, 37; **11** 51, 212; **12** 439; **20 336–39 (upd.)**
The Leo Group, **32** 140; **40** 140
Léon Gaumont et Cie. *See* Gaumont SA.
Leonard Bernstein Music Publishing Company, **23** 391
Leonard Development Group, **10** 508
Leonard Express, Inc., **6** 371
Leonard Green & Partners LP, **12** 477–78; **24** 173
Leonard Machinery Corp., **16** 124
Leonard Parker Company, **26** 196
Leonard Silver, **14** 482
Leonardi Manufacturing, **48** 70
Leonardo Editore, **IV** 587
Leonberger Bausparkasse, **II** 258
Lepco Co., **III** 596
Leprino Foods Company, 28 237–39
Lern, Inc., **II** 420
Lerner Plastics, **9** 323
Lerner Stores, **V** 116
Leroy-Merlin, **23** 230; **37** 24
Les broderies Lesage, **49** 83
Les Chantiers de l'Atlantique, **II** 13
Les Echos. *See* Groupe Les Echos.
Les Grands Magasins Au Bon Marché: Etablissements Vaxelaire-Claes, **26** 159–60
Les Industries Ling, **13** 443
Les Papeteries du Limousin, **19** 227
L'Escaut, **III** 335
Lesco Inc., 19 248–50
The Leslie Fay Companies, Inc., 8 323–25
The Leslie Fay Company, Inc., 39 255–58 (upd.); 40 276–77
Leslie Paper, **IV** 288
Leslie's Poolmart, Inc., 18 302–04
Lesser-Goldman, **II** 18
Lester B. Knight & Associates, **II** 19
Lester Ink and Coatings Company, **13** 228
Lestrem Group, **IV** 296; **19** 226
Let op Uw Einde, **III** 199

Létang et Rémy, **44** 205
Lettuce Entertain You Enterprises, **38** 103
Leucadia National Corporation, 6 396; **11** ; **25** 170 **260–62**
Leuna-Werke AG, **7** 142
Level Five Research, Inc., **22** 292
N.V. Levensverzekering Maatschappji Utrecht, **III** 199–200
Lever Brothers Company, I 17, 21, 26, 30, 333; **II** 497, 588–89; **III** 31; **7** 542–43, 545; **9** 291, **317–19**; **13** 199; **14** 314. *See also* Unilever.
Levi Strauss & Co., I 15; **II** 634, 669; **V** 60–61, **362–65**; **9** 142; **12** 430; **16 324–28 (upd.)**, 509, 511; **17** 512; **18** 191–92; **19** 196; **23** 422; **24** 158; **25** 47
Leviathan Gas Pipeline Company, **21** 171
Levine, Huntley, Vick & Beaver, **6** 28
Levitt & Sons, **IV** 728
Levitt Corp., **21** 471
Levitt Homes, **I** 464; **11** 198
Levitt Industries, **17** 331
Levitt Investment Company, **26** 102
Levitz Furniture Inc., 15 280–82; 23 412, 414
Levtex Hotel Ventures, **21** 363
Levy Bakery Goods, **I** 30
Levy Restaurants L.P., 26 263–65
Lew Liberbaum & Co., **27** 197
The Lewin Group, Inc., **21** 425
Lewis and Marks, **IV** 21–22, 96; **16** 27
Lewis Batting Company, **11** 219
Lewis Construction, **IV** 22
Lewis Galoob Toys Inc., 16 329–31
Lewis Grocer Co., **II** 669; **18** 504
Lewis Homes, **45** 221
Lewis-Howe Co., **III** 56
Lewis Refrigeration Company, **21** 500
Lewis's, **V** 178
Lewis's Bank, **II** 308
Lex Electronics, **10** 113
Lex Service plc, **19** 312
Lexecon, Inc., **26** 187
Lexington Broadcast Services, **6** 27
Lexington Furniture Industries, **III** 571; **20** 362
Lexington Ice Company, **6** 514
Lexington Insurance Co., **III** 197
Lexington Utilities Company, **6** 514; **11** 237
LEXIS-NEXIS Group, 17 399; **18** 542; **21** 70; **31** 388, 393; **33 263–67**
Lexitron, **II** 87
Lexmark International, Inc., 9 116; **10** 519; **18 305–07; 30** 250
Leybold GmbH, **IV** 71; **48** 30
Leyland and Birmingham Rubber Co., **I** 429
Leyland Motor Corporation, **7** 459
LFC Financial, **10** 339
LFC Holdings Corp. *See* Levitz Furniture Inc.
LFE Corp., **7** 297
LG Chemical Ltd., **26** 425
LG Electronics Inc., **13** 572, 575; **43** 428
LG Group, **18** 124; **34** 514, 517–18
LG&E Energy Corp., 6 516–18; 18 366–67
Lhomme S.A., **8** 477
Liaison Agency, **31** 216–17
Lianozovo Dairy, **48** 438
Liaoyang Automotive Spring Factory, **III** 581
Libbey Inc., 49 251–54

Libbey-Owens-Ford Company, **I** 609; **III** 640–42, 707, 714–15, 725–26, 731; **IV** 421; **7** 292; **16** 7–9; **22** 434; **23** 83; **26** 353; **31** 355

Libby, **II** 547; **7** 382

Libby McNeil & Libby Inc., **II** 489

Libeltex, **9** 92

Liber, **14** 556

Liberty Bank of Buffalo, **9** 229

Liberty Brokerage Investment Company, **10** 278

Liberty Can and Sign Company, **17** 105–06

The Liberty Corporation, 22 312–14

Liberty Gauge Company, **17** 213

Liberty Hardware Manufacturing Corporation, **20** 363

Liberty House, **I** 417–18

Liberty Life, **IV** 91, 97

Liberty Livewire Corporation, 42 224–27

Liberty Media Corporation, **18** 66; **19** 282; **25** 214; **34** 224; **42** 114, 224; **47** 414, 416, 418. *See also* Liberty Livewire Corporation.

Liberty Mexicana, **III** 415

Liberty Mutual Insurance Group, **I** 28; **11** 379; **48** 271

Liberty Mutual Savings Bank, **17** 530

Liberty National Bank, **II** 229

Liberty National Insurance Holding Company. *See* Torchmark Corporation.

Liberty National Life Insurance Co., **III** 217; **9** 506–07

Liberty Natural Gas Co., **11** 441

Liberty Software, Inc., **17** 264

Liberty Surf UK, **48** 399

Liberty Tax Service, **48** 236

Liberty's, **13** 307

Libra Bank Ltd., **II** 271

Librairie de Jacques-Francois Brétif, **IV** 617

Librairie Fayard, **IV** 618

Librairie Générale Francaise, **IV** 618

Librairie Larousse, **IV** 614–16

Librairie Louis Hachette, **IV** 617–18

Librairie Nathan, **IV** 614, 616

Librairie Victor Lecou, **IV** 617

Librizol India Pvt. Ltd., **48** 212

Libyan Arab Airline, **6** 85

Libyan Arab Foreign Bank, **IV** 454

Libyan National Oil Corporation, IV 453–55

Libyan-Turkish Engineering and Consultancy Corp., **IV** 563

Lidköpings Mekaniska Verkstad AB, **III** 623

Lieberman Enterprises, **24** 349

Liebert Corp., **II** 20

Life and Casualty Insurance Co. of Tennessee, **III** 193

Life Assoc. of Scotland, **III** 310

Life Fitness Inc., **III** 431

Life Insurance Co. of Georgia, **III** 310

Life Insurance Co. of Scotland, **III** 358

Life Insurance Co. of Virginia, **III** 204

Life Insurance Securities, Ltd., **III** 288

Life Investors International Ltd., **III** 179; **12** 199

Life of Eire, **III** 273

Life Partners Group, Inc., **33** 111

Life Retail Stores. *See* Angelica Corporation.

Life Savers Corp., **II** 129, 544; **7** 367; **21** 54

Life Science Research, Inc., **10** 105–07

Life Technologies, Inc., I 321; **12** 103; **17** 287–89

Life Uniform Shops. *See* Angelica Corporation.

Lifecycle, Inc., **III** 431; **25** 40

Lifeline Systems, Inc., **32** 374

LifeLink, **11** 378

Lifemark Corp., **III** 74; **14** 232; **33** 183

Lifestyle Fitness Clubs, **46** 432

LIFETIME, **IV** 627; **19** 204

Lifetime Corp., **29** 363–64

Lifetime Foam Products, Inc., **12** 439

Lifetime Hoan Corporation, 27 286–89

Lift Parts Manufacturing, **I** 157

Ligand Pharmaceuticals Incorporated, 10 48; **47 221–23**

Liggett & Meyers, **V** 396, 405, 417–18; **18** 416; **29** 195

Liggett-Ducat, **49** 153

Liggett Group Inc., **I** 248; **7** 105; **14** 213; **15** 71; **16** 242; **37** 295. *See also* Vector Group Inc.

Light & Power Company, **12** 265

Light Corrugated Box Co., **IV** 332

Light Savers U.S.A., Inc. *See* Hospitality Worldwide Services, Inc.

Light-Servicos de Eletricidade S.A., **II** 456

Lightel Inc., **6** 311

Lighthouse, Ltd., **24** 95

Lighting Corp. of America, **I** 476

LIGHTNET, **IV** 576

Lightwell Co., **III** 634

Lignum Oil Co., **IV** 658

Lil' Champ Food Stores, Inc., **36** 359

LILCO. *See* Long Island Lighting Company.

Lilia Limited, **17** 449

Lille Bonnières et Colombes, **37** 143–44

Lillian Vernon Corporation, 12 314–15; 35 274–77 (upd.)

Lillie Rubin, **30** 104–06

Lilliput Group plc, **11** 95; **15** 478

Lilly & Co. *See* Eli Lilly & Co.

Lilly Industries, **22** 437

Lillybrook Coal Co., **IV** 180

Lillywhites Ltd., **III** 105

Lily Tulip Co., **I** 609, 611; **8** 198

Limburger Fabrik und Hüttenverein, **IV** 103

Limhamns Golvindustri AB. *See* Tarkett Sommer AG.

The Limited, Inc., V 115–16; **9** 142; **12** 280, 356; **15** 7, 9; **16** 219; **18** 193, 215, 217, 410; **20 340–43 (upd.)**; **24** 237; **25** 120–21, 123; **28** 344; **47** 142–43

Limmer and Trinidad Ltd., **III** 752

LIN Broadcasting Corp., II 331; **6** 323; **9** 320–22; **11** 330

Lin Data Corp., **11** 234

Linamar Corporation, 18 308–10

Lincare Holdings Inc., 43 265–67

Lincoln American Life Insurance Co., **10** 246

Lincoln Automotive, **26** 363

Lincoln Benefit Life Company, **10** 51

Lincoln Electric Co., II 19; **13 314–16**

Lincoln Electric Motor Works, **9** 439

Lincoln Federal Savings, **16** 106

Lincoln First Bank, **II** 248

Lincoln Income Life Insurance Co., **10** 246

Lincoln Liberty Life Insurance Co., **III** 254

Lincoln Marketing, Inc., **18** 518

Lincoln Motor Co., **I** 165

Lincoln National Corporation, III 274–77; **6** 195; **10** 44; **22** 144; **25** 286–90 (upd.)

Lincoln Property Company, 8 326–28

Lincoln Savings, **10** 340

Lincoln Savings & Loan, **9** 199

Lincoln Snacks Company, 24 286–88

Lincoln Telephone & Telegraph Company, 14 311–13

LinCom Corp., **8** 327

Lindal Cedar Homes, Inc., 29 287–89

Linde A.G., **I** 297–98, 315, 581–83; **9** 16, 516; **10** 31–32; **11** 402–03; **25** 81; **48** 323

Lindemann's, **I** 220

Lindex, **II** 640

Lindsay Manufacturing Co., 20 344–46

Lindsay Parkinson & Co., **I** 567

Lindt & Sprüngli. *See* Chocoladefabriken Lindt & Sprüngli AG.

Lindustries, **III** 502; **7** 208

Linear Corp., **III** 643

Linear Technology, Inc., 16 332–34

Líneas Aéreas Postales Españolas, **6** 95

Linens 'n Things, Inc., 13 81–82; **24** 289–92; **33** 384; **41** 50

Linfood Cash & Carry, **13** 103

Linfood Holdings Ltd., **II** 628–29

Ling Products, **12** 25

Ling-Temco-Vought. *See* LTV Corporation.

Lingerie Time, **20** 143

Linguaphone Group, **43** 204, 206

Linjeflyg, **I** 120

Link-Belt Corp., **I** 443; **IV** 660

Link House Publications PLC, **IV** 687

Link Motor Supply Company, **26** 347

Linmark Westman International Limited, **25** 221–22

Linroz Manufacturing Company L.P., **25** 245

Lintas: Worldwide, I 18; **6** 30; **14** 314–16

Lintott Engineering, Ltd., **10** 108

Linz, **16** 559

Lion Corporation, III 44–45

Lion Manufacturing, **III** 430; **25** 40

Lion Match Company, **24** 450

Lion Oil, **I** 365

Lion's Head Brewery. *See* The Stroh Brewery Company.

Lionel L.L.C., 12 494; **16 335–38**; **18** 524

Lionex Corporation, **13** 46

Lions Gate Entertainment Corporation, 35 278–81

Liontech, **16** 337–38

Lippincott & Margulies, **III** 283

Lippincott-Raven Publishers, **14** 556

Lipschutz Bros., Inc., **29** 511

Lipton. *See* Thomas J. Lipton Company.

Liqui-Box Corporation, 16 339–41

Liquid Ag Systems Inc., **26** 494

Liquid Carbonic, **7** 74, 77

Liquid Holdings, Inc., **45** 168

Liquor Barn, **II** 656

Liquorland, **V** 35

Liquorsave, **II** 609–10

LIRCA, **III** 48

Liris, **23** 212

Lisbon Coal and Oil Fuel Co., **IV** 504

Liscaya, **II** 196

Listening Library Inc., **31** 379

Lister, **21** 503
Litco Bancorp., **II** 192
LiTel Communications, Inc., **16** 318
Lithia Motors, Inc., 41 238–40
Litho-Krome Corp., **IV** 621
LitleNet, **26** 441
Litronix, **III** 455; **21** 122
Littelfuse, Inc., 26 266–69
Little, Brown & Company, **IV** 675; **7** 528;
    10 355; **36** 270
**Little Caesar Enterprises, Inc., 24
    293–96 (upd.); 27** 481. *See also* Ilitch
    Holdings Inc.
**Little Caesar International, Inc., 7
    278–79; 7** 278–79; **15** 344, 346; **16** 447;
    25 179, 227–28
Little Chef Ltd., **III** 105–06
Little General, **II** 620; **12** 179, 200
Little Giant Pump Company, **8** 515
Little League Baseball, Incorporated, **23**
    450
Little Leather Library, **13** 105
Little, Royal, **I** 529–30; **8** 545; **13** 63
Little Switzerland, **19** 451
Little Tikes Co., III 614; **12** 169; **13
    317–19**
Littlewoods Financial Services, **30** 494
**Littlewoods Organisation PLC, V
    117–19; 24** 316
Littlewoods plc, 42 228–32 (upd.)
Litton Industries Inc., I 85, 452, 476,
    484–86, 523–24; **II** 33; **III** 293, 473,
    732; **IV** 253; **6** 599; **10** 520–21, 537; **11
    263–65 (upd.),** 435; **12** 248, 271–72,
    538–40; **15** 287; **17** 30; **19** 31, 110, 290;
    21 86; **22** 436; **45** 306; **48** 383. *See also*
    Avondale Industries.
Litwin Engineers & Constructors, **8** 546
Livanos, **III** 516
LIVE Entertainment Inc., 18 64, 66; **20
    347–49; 24** 349
Liverpool and London and Globe Insurance
    Co., **III** 234, 350
Liverpool and London Fire and Life
    Insurance Co., **III** 349
Liverpool Daily Post & Echo Ltd., **49** 405
Liverpool Fire and Life Insurance Co., **III**
    350
Liverpool Mexico S.A., **16** 216
Livia, **I** 154; **10** 279
Living Arts, Inc., **41** 174
Living Centers of America, **13** 49
Living Videotext, **10** 508
Livingston Communications, **6** 313
Livingston, Fargo and Co., **II** 380, 395; **10**
    59
LivingWell Inc., **12** 326
Liz Claiborne, Inc., 8 329–31; 16 37, 61;
    25 258, **291–94 (upd.)**
LKB-Produkter AB, **I** 665
Lloyd A. Fry Roofing, **III** 721
Lloyd Adriatico S.p.A., **III** 377
Lloyd Aereo de Bolivia, **6** 97
Lloyd Creative Staffing, **27** 21
Lloyd George Management, **18** 152
Lloyd Instruments, Ltd., **29** 460–61
Lloyd Italico, **III** 351
Lloyd Thompson Group plc, **20** 313
Lloyd-Truax Ltd., **21** 499
Lloyd's Electronics, **14** 118
Lloyd's of London, III 234, **278–81; 9**
    297; **10** 38; **11** 533; **22 315–19 (upd.)**
Lloyds Bank PLC, II 306–09 319, 334,
    358; **17** 324–25; **48** 373

Lloyds Chemists plc, **27** 177
Lloyds Life Assurance, **III** 351
Lloyds TSB Group plc, 39 6; **47 224–29
    (upd.)**
LM Ericsson. *See* Telefonaktiebolaget LM
    Ericsson.
LMC Metals, **19** 380
LME. *See* Telefonaktiebolaget LM
    Ericsson.
LNG Co., **IV** 473–74
LNM Group, **30** 252
Lo-Cost, **II** 609
Lo-Vaca Gathering Co., **IV** 394; **7** 553
Loadometer Co., **III** 435
Lobitos Oilfields Ltd., **IV** 381–82
Loblaw Companies Limited, II 631–32;
    19 116; **43 268–72.** *See also* George
    Weston Limited.
Local Data, Inc., **10** 97
Locations, Inc., **IV** 727
Locke, Lancaster and W.W.&R. Johnson &
    Sons, **III** 680
Lockhart Catering, **III** 104
Lockhart Corporation, **12** 564
Lockheed Corporation, I 13, 41, 48, 50,
    52, 54, 61, 63, **64–66,** 67–68, 71–72,
    74, 76–77, 82, 84, 90, 92–94, 100, 102,
    107, 110, 113, 121, 126, 195, 493–94,
    529; **II** 19, 32–33; **III** 84, 539, 601; **IV**
    15; **6** 71; **9** 12, 17–18, 272, 417,
    458–60, 501; **10** 163, 262–63, 317, 536;
    11 164, 166, **266–69 (upd.),** 278–79,
    363–65; **12** 190; **13** 126, 128; **17** 306;
    21 140; **22** 506; **24** 84–85, 87, 311, 326,
    375, 397; **25** 303, 316, 347; **34** 371
**Lockheed Martin Corporation, 15
    283–86 (upd.); 21** 86; **24** 88; **29** 409;
    32 437; **33** 47–48; **38** 372, 376; **45** 306;
    48 251; **49** 345, 347
Lockwood Banc Group, Inc., **11** 306
Lockwood Greene Engineers, Inc., **17** 377
Lockwood National Bank, **25** 114
Lockwood Technology, Inc., **19** 179
Lockwoods Foods Ltd., **II** 513
**Loctite Corporation, 8 332–34; 30
    289–91 (upd.); 34** 209
Lodding Engineering, **7** 521
Lodestar Group, **10** 19
Lodge-Cottrell, **III** 472
Lodge Plus, Ltd., **25** 430
**LodgeNet Entertainment Corporation,
    26** 441; **28 240–42**
The Lodging Group, **12** 297; **48** 245
Loeb Rhoades, Hornblower & Co., **II**
    450–51; **9** 469
Loehmann's Inc., 24 297–99
Loening Aeronautical, **I** 61; **11** 164
Loew's Consolidated Enterprises, **II** 154
Loew's, Inc., **31** 99
The Loewen Group, Inc., 16 342–44; 37
    67–68; **40 292–95 (upd.)**
Loewenstein Furniture Group, Inc., **21**
    531–33
Loewi Financial Cos., **III** 270
Loews Cineplex Entertainment Corp., **37**
    64
Loews Corporation, I 245, **487–88; II**
    134, 148–49, 169; **III** 228, 231; **12
    316–18 (upd.),** 418; **13** 120–21; **19** 362;
    22 73; **25** 177, 326–28; **36 324–28
    (upd.); 38** 142; **41** 70, 72
LOF Plastics, Inc. *See* Libbey-Owens-Ford.
Loffland Brothers Company, **9** 364
Loft Inc., **I** 276; **10** 451

Logan's Roadhouse, Inc., 19 287–88; **22**
    464; **29 290–92; 35** 84
Logged Off Land Co., **IV** 355–56
Logic Modeling, **11** 491
Logica plc, 14 317–19; 37 230–33 (upd.)
Logicon Inc., 20 350–52; 45 68, 310
Logility, **25** 20, 22
Logistics, **III** 431
Logistics Data Systems, **13** 4
Logistics Industries Corporation, **39** 77
Logistics Management Systems, Inc., **8** 33
Logitech International SA, 9 116; **28
    243–45**
Logo Athletic, Inc., **35** 363
Logo 7, Inc., **13** 533
Logon, Inc., **14** 377
LoJack Corporation, 48 269–73
Lojas Arapuã S.A., 22 320–22
Loma Linda Foods, **14** 557–58
Lomak Petroleum, Inc., **24** 380
Lomas & Nettleton Financial Corporation,
    III 249; **11** 122
Lombard North Central, **II** 442
Lombard Orient Leasing Ltd., **II** 442
London and County Bank, **II** 334
London and Hanseatic Bank, **II** 256
London & Hull, **III** 211
London and Lancashire Insurance Co., **III**
    350
London & Leeds Development Corp., **II**
    141
London & Midland Bank. *See* Midland
    Bank plc.
London & Overseas Freighters plc. *See*
    Frontline Ltd.
London & Rhodesia Mining & Land
    Company. *See* Lonrho Plc.
London and Scottish Marine Oil, **11** 98
London & Western Trust, **39** 90
London and Westminster Bank, **II** 333–34
London Asiastic, **III** 699
London Assurance Corp., **III** 278, 369–71,
    373
London Brick Co., **III** 502; **7** 208; **14** 249
London Brokers Ltd., **6** 290
London Buses Limited, **6** 406
London Cargo Group, **25** 82
London Central, **28** 155–56
London Chartered Bank of Australia, **II**
    188
London Clermont Club, **III** 431
London County and Westminster Bank, **II**
    334
London County Freehold & Leasehold
    Properties, **IV** 711
London Drugs Ltd., 46 270–73
London East India Company, **12** 421
London, Edinburgh and Dublin Insurance
    Co., **III** 350
London Electricity, **12** 443; **41** 141
London Film Productions Ltd., **II** 157; **14**
    399
London Fog Industries, Inc., 16 61; **29
    293–96**
London General Omnibus Company, **6** 406
London Guarantee and Accident Co., **III**
    372
London Insurance Group, **III** 373; **36** 372
London International Group. *See* SSL
    International plc.
London Joint-Stock Bank, **II** 318, 388; **17**
    324
London Life Assoc., **IV** 711
London Life Insurance Co., **II** 456–57

London Precision Machine & Tool, Ltd., **39** 32

London, Provincial and South Western Bank, **II** 235

London Records, **23** 390

London Regional Transport, 6 406–08

London Rubber Co., **49** 380

London South Partnership, **25** 497

London Stock Exchange Limited, 34 253–56; 37 131–33

London Transport, **19** 111

London Weekend Television, **IV** 650–51; **7** 389

Londontown Manufacturing Company. *See* London Fog Industries, Inc.

Lone Star and Crescent Oil Co., **IV** 548

Lone Star Brewing Co., **I** 255

Lone Star Gas Corp., **V** 609, 611

Lone Star Industries, **III** 718, 729, 753; **IV** 304; **23** 326; **28** 450; **35** 154

Lone Star Steakhouse, **21** 250

Lone Star Steel, **I** 440–41

Lone Star Technologies, Inc., **22** 3

Long-Airdox Co., **IV** 136

Long Distance Discount Services, Inc., **8** 310; **27** 305

Long Distance/USA, **9** 479

Long Island Airways, **I** 115; **12** 379

Long Island Bancorp, Inc., 16 345–47; **44** 33

Long Island Cable Communication Development Company, **7** 63

Long Island Daily Press Publishing Co., **IV** 582–83

Long Island Lighting Company, V 652–54; 6 456; **27** 264

Long Island Power Authority, **27** 265

Long Island Rail Road, **35** 290

Long Island Trust Co., **II** 192, 218

Long John Silver's Restaurants Inc., 13 320–22

Long Lac Mineral Exploration, **9** 282

Long Life Fish Food Products, **12** 230

Long Manufacturing Co., **III** 439; **14** 63

Long-Term Credit Bank of Japan, Ltd., II 301, **310–11**, 338, 369

Long Valley Power Cooperative, **12** 265

The Longaberger Company, 12 319–21; 44 267–70 (upd.)

Longchamps, Inc., **38** 385; **41** 388

LongHorn Steaks Inc., **19** 341

Longines-Wittenauer Watch Co., **II** 121

Longman Group Ltd., **IV** 611, 658

Longmat Foods, **II** 494

Longs Drug Stores Corporation, V 120; 25 295–97 (upd.)

Longview Fibre Company, 8 335–37; 37 234–37 (upd.)

Longwy, **IV** 227

Lonrho Plc, IV 651–52; **10** 170; **21 351–55; 43** 38

Lonsdale Investment Trust, **II** 421

Lonvest Corp., **II** 456–57

Loomis Armored Car Service Limited, **45** 378

Loomis Fargo Group, **42** 338

Loomis, Sayles & Co., **III** 313

Loose Leaf Metals Co., Inc., **10** 314

Lor-Al, Inc., **17** 10

Loral Corporation, II 38; **7** 9; **8 338–40; 9 323–25; 13** 356; **15** 283, 285; **20** 262; **47** 319

Lord & Taylor, **13** 44; **14** 376; **15** 86; **18** 137, 372; **21** 302

Lord & Thomas, **I** 12–14; **IV** 660

Lord Baltimore Press, Inc., **IV** 286

L'Oréal, II 547; **III 46–49**, 62; **7** 382–83; **8** 129–31; **341–44 (upd.); 11** 41; **23** 238, 242; **31** 418; **46 274–79 (upd.)**

Lorenz, **I** 463

Lorillard Industries, **I** 488; **V** 396, 407, 417; **12** 317; **18** 416; **22** 73; **29** 195; **36** 324, 327

Lorimar Telepictures, **II** 149, 177; **25** 90–91, 329

Loronix Inc., **24** 509

Lorraine-Escaut, **IV** 227

Lorvic Corp., **I** 679

Los Angeles Can Co., **I** 599

Los Angeles Drug Co., **12** 106

Los Angeles Gas and Electric Company, **V** 682; **25** 413

Los Angeles Steamship Co., **II** 490

Los Lagos Corp., **12** 175

Los Nietos Co., **IV** 570; **24** 520

Loss Prevention Inc., **24** 509

Lost Arrow Inc., 22 323–25

LOT Polish Airlines (Polskie Linie Lotnicze S.A.), 33 268–71

Lothringer Bergwerks- und Hüttenverein Aumetz-Friede AG, **IV** 126

LOT$OFF Corporation, 24 300–01

Lotus Cars Ltd., 14 320–22

Lotus Development Corporation, IV 597; **6** 224–25, 227, **254–56**, 258–60, 270–71, 273; **9** 81, 140; **10** 24, 505; **12** 335; **16** 392, 394; **20** 238; **21** 86; **22** 161; **25 298–302 (upd.); 30** 251; **38** 417

Lotus Publishing Corporation, **7** 239; **25** 239

Lotus Radio, **I** 531

Louart Corporation, **29** 33–34

Loucks, Hoffman & Company, **8** 412

Loudcloud, Inc. *See* Opsware Inc.

Loughead Aircraft Manufacturing Co., **I** 64

Louis Allis, **15** 288

Louis B. Mayer Productions, **II** 148; **25** 326–27

Louis C. Edwards, **II** 609

Louis Dreyfus Energy Corp., **28** 471

Louis Harris & Associates, Inc., **22** 188

Louis Kemp Seafood Company, **14** 515

Louis Marx Toys, **II** 559; **12** 410

Louis Rich, Inc., **II** 532; **12** 372

Louis Vuitton, I 272; **III** 48; **8** 343; **10 397–99.** *See also* LVMH Moët Hennessy Louis Vuitton SA.

Louisiana & Southern Life Insurance Co., **14** 460

Louisiana Bank & Trust, **11** 106

Louisiana Corporation, **19** 301

Louisiana Energy Services, **27** 130

The Louisiana Land and Exploration Company, IV 76, 365, 367; **7 280–83**

Louisiana-Pacific Corporation, IV 282, **304–05; 9** 260; **16** 203; **22** 491; **31 314–317 (upd.); 32** 91

Louisville Cement Co., **IV** 409

Louisville Gas and Electric Company, **49** 120. *See also* LG&E Energy Corporation.

Louisville Home Telephone Company, **14** 258

Loup River Public Power District, **29** 352

Louthan Manufacturing Company, **8** 178

LoVaca Gathering Company. *See* The Coastal Corporation.

Lovelace Truck Service, Inc., **14** 42

Loveman's, Inc., **19** 323

Lovering China Clays, **III** 690

Lowe Bros. Co., **III** 745

Lowe Group, **22** 294

Lowe's Companies, Inc., V 122–23; 11 384; **12** 234, 345; **18** 239; **21** 324, **356–58 (upd.); 27** 416; **44** 333

Lowell Bearing Co., **IV** 136

Lowell Shoe, Inc., **13** 360

Löwenbräu, **I** 220, 257; **II** 240

Lower Manhattan Development Corporation, **47** 360

Lowes Food Stores. *See* Alex Lee Inc.

Lowney/Moirs, **II** 512

Lowrance Electronics, Inc., 18 311–14

Lowrey's Meat Specialties, Inc., **21** 156

Loyalty Group, **III** 241–43

LPL Investment Group, **40** 35–36

LRL International, **II** 477

LSI. *See* Lear Siegler Inc.

LSI Logic Corporation, 13 323–25; 18 382

LTA Ltd., **IV** 22

LTU Group Holding GmbH, 37 238–41

LTV Aerospace. *See* Vought Aircraft Industries, Inc.

The LTV Corporation, I 62–63, **489–91; 7** 107–08; **8** 157, 315; **10** 419; **11** 166, 364; **12** 124; **17** 357; **18** 110, 378; **19** 466; **24 302–06 (upd.); 26** 406; **45** 306

Luberef, **IV** 538

The Lubrizol Corporation, 30 292–95 (upd.)

Lubrizol Enterprises, Inc., I 360–62; **21** 385–87

Luby's Cafeteria's, Inc., 17 290–93; 19 301

Luby's, Inc., 42 233–38 (upd.)

Lucas Bols, **II** 642

Lucas Digital Ltd., **12** 322

Lucas Girling, **I** 157

Lucas Industries Plc, III 509, **554–57; 27** 251

Lucas Ingredients, **27** 258

Lucas-Milhaupt, Inc., **23** 250

LucasArts Entertainment Company, **32** 9

Lucasfilm Ltd., 9 368, 472; **12 322–24; 22** 459; **34** 350; **38** 70

LucasVarity plc, **27** 249, 251

Lucchini, **IV** 228

Lucent Technologies Inc., 18 154, 180; **20** 8; **22** 19; **26** 275, 277; **29** 44, 414; **34 257–60; 36** 122, 124; **41** 289–90; **44** 426; **48** 92

Lucille Farms, Inc., 45 249–51

Lucky Brand Dungarees, **18** 85

Lucky-Goldstar, II 53–54; **III** 457; **13** 574. *See also* Goldstar Co., Ltd.

Lucky Lager Brewing Co., **I** 268; **25** 280

Lucky Stores Inc., **II** 605, 653; **6** 355; **8** 474; **12** 48; **17** 369, 559; **22** 39; **27** 290–93

Lucky Strike, **II** 143

Ludi Wap S.A., **41** 409

Ludlow Corp., **III** 645

Ludovico, **25** 85

Lufkin Rule Co., **II** 16

Luftag, **I** 110

Lufthansa. *See* Deutsche Lufthansa Aktiengesellschaft.

The Luggage Company, **14** 224

Lukens Inc., 14 323–25; 27 65

Lukey Mufflers, **IV** 249

LUKOIL. *See* OAO LUKOIL.

Lum's, **6** 199–200
Lumac B.V., **I** 387
Lumbermen's Investment Corp., **IV** 341
Lumbermens Mutual Casualty Co., **III** 269–71; **15** 257
Lumex, Inc., **17** 197
La Lumière Economique, **II** 79
Luminar Plc, 40 296–98
Lummus Crest, **IV** 469; **26** 496
Lumonics Inc., **III** 635
Lunar Corporation, 29 297–99
Luncheon Voucher, **27** 10
Lund Boat Co. *See* Genmar Holdings, Inc.
Lund Food Holdings, Inc., 22 326–28
Lund International Holdings, Inc., 40 299–301
Lundstrom Jewelers, **24** 319
Lunenburg Sea Products Limited, **14** 339
Lunevale Products Ltd., **I** 341
L'Unite Hermetique S.A., **8** 515
Lunn Poly, **8** 525–26
Luotto-Pankki Oy, **II** 303
Lurgei, **6** 599
LURGI. *See* Metallurgische Gesellschaft Aktiengesellschaft.
Luria Bros. and Co., **I** 512–13; **6** 151
Lutèce, **20** 26
Luther's Bar-B-Q, **II** 556
Lutheran Brotherhood, 31 318–21
Lux, **III** 478
Lux Mercantile Co., **II** 624
Luxair, **49** 80
Luxor, **II** 69; **6** 205; **17** 353
Luxottica SpA, **17** 294–96; **23** 328; **43** 96; **49** 301. *See also* Casual Corner Group, Inc.
LuxSonor Semiconductor Inc., **48** 92
Luxury Linens, **13** 81–82
LVMH Moët Hennessy Louis Vuitton SA, I 272; **19** 86; **24** 137, 140; **33** 272–77 **(upd.)**; **45** 344; **46** 277; **49** 90, 326. *See also* Christian Dior S.A.
LVO Cable Inc., **IV** 596
LXE Inc., **21** 199–201
Lycos, **27** 517; **37** 384; **47** 420. *See also* Terra Lycos, Inc.
Lydex, **I** 527
Lykes Corp., **I** 490–91; **24** 303
Lyn Knight Currency Auctions, Inc, **48** 100
Lynch Corporation, 43 273–76; 301–02
Lynde Company, **16** 269–71
Lynx Express Delivery, **6** 412, 414
Lyon & Healy, **IV** 660
Lyon's Technological Products Ltd., **III** 745
Lyondell Chemical Company, 45 252–55 (upd.)
Lyondell Petrochemical Company, IV 377, 456–57; **10** 110
Lyonnaise Communications, **10** 196; **25** 497
Lyonnaise des Eaux-Dumez, I 576; **V** 655–57; **23** 332. *See also* Suez Lyonnaise des Eaux.
Lyons. *See* J. Lyons & Co. Ltd.
LyphoMed Inc., **IV** 333; **17** 287
Oy Lypsyniemen Konepaja, **IV** 275–76
Lysaght, **24** 143
Lysaght's Canada, Ltd., **IV** 73
Lystads, **I** 333
Lytag Ltd., **31** 398–99

M & C Saatchi, **42** 330

M&F Worldwide Corp., 38 293–95
M and G Fund Management, **III** 699
M&G Group plc, **48** 328
M&J Diesel Locomotive Filter Co., **17** 106
M&M Limited, **7** 299
M and M Manufacturing Company, **23** 143
M&M/Mars, **14** 48; **15** 63–64; **21** 219
M & S Computing. *See* Intergraph Corporation.
M&T Capital Corporation, **11** 109
M/A Com Inc., **6** 336; **14** 26–27
M.A. Hanna Company, 8 345–47; **12** 352
M.A.N., **III** 561–63; **IV** 86
M.B. McGerry, **21** 94
M-Cell Ltd., **31** 329
M.D.C., **11** 258
M.E.P.C. Ltd., **IV** 711
M.F. Patterson Dental Supply Co. *See* Patterson Dental Co.
M.G. Waldbaum Company, **25** 332–33
M. Guggenheim's Sons, **IV** 31
M.H. McLean Wholesaler Grocery Company, **8** 380
M.H. Meyerson & Co., Inc., 46 280–83
M. Hensoldt & Söhne Wetzlar Optische Werke AG, **III** 446
M-I Drilling Fluids Co., **III** 473; **15** 468
M.I. Schottenstein Homes Inc., **19** 125–26
M.J. Brock Corporation, **8** 460
M.J. Designs, Inc., **17** 360
M.L.C. Partners Limited Partnership, **22** 459
M. Loeb Ltd., **II** 652
M. Lowenstein Corp., **V** 379
M.M. Warburg. *See* SBC Warburg.
M.P. Burke PLC, **13** 485–86
M.P. Pumps, Inc., **8** 515
M. Polaner Inc., **10** 70; **40** 51–52
M-R Group plc, **31** 312–13
M.S. Carriers, Inc., **42** 363, 365
M. Samuel & Co., **II** 208
M. Sobol, Inc., **28** 12
M Stores Inc., **II** 664
M.T.G.I. Textile Manufacturers Group, **25** 121
M.W. Carr, **14** 245
M.W. Kellogg Co., **III** 470; **IV** 408, 534; **34** 81
M-Web Holdings Ltd., **31** 329–30
Ma. Ma-Macaroni Co., **II** 554
Maakauppiaitten Oy, **8** 293–94
Maakuntain Keskus-Pankki, **II** 303
MaasGlas, **III** 667
Maatschappij tot Exploitatie van de Onderneming Krasnapolsky. *See* Grand Hotel Krasnapolsky N.V.
Maatschappij tot Exploitatie van Steenfabrieken Udenhout, voorheen Weyers, **14** 249
MABAG Maschinen- und Apparatebau GmbH, **IV** 198
Mabley & Carew, **10** 282
Mac Frugal's Bargains - Closeouts Inc., 17 297–99
Mac-Gray Corporation, 44 271–73
Mac Publications LLC, **25** 240
Mac Tools, **III** 628
MacAndrews & Forbes Holdings Inc., II 679; **III** 56; **9** 129; **11** 334; **28** 246–49; **30** 138; **38** 293–94
MacArthur Foundation. *See* The John D. and Catherine T. MacArthur Foundation.
Macau Telephone, **18** 114
Maccabees Life Insurance Co., **III** 350

MacCall Management, **19** 158
MacDermid Incorporated, 32 318–21
MacDonald Companies, **15** 87
MacDonald Dettwiler and Associates, **32** 436
MacDonald, Halsted, and Laybourne, **10** 127
Macdonald Hamilton & Co., **III** 522–23
Macey Furniture Co., **7** 493
Macfarlane Lang & Co., **II** 592–93
Macfield Inc., **12** 502
MacFrugal's Bargains Close-Outs Inc., **29** 312
MacGregor Sporting Goods Inc., **III** 443; **22** 115, 458; **23** 449
Mach Performance, Inc., **28** 147
Machine Vision International Inc., **10** 232
Macintosh. *See* Apple Computer, Inc.
Mack-Cali Realty Corporation, 42 239–41
Mack Trucks, Inc., I 147, **177–79;** **9** 416; **12** 90; **22** 329–32 **(upd.)**
Mack-Wayne Plastics, **42** 439
Mackay Envelope Corporation, 45 256–59
MacKay-Shields Financial Corp., **III** 316
MacKenzie & Co., **II** 361
Mackenzie Hill, **IV** 724
Mackenzie Mann & Co. Limited, **6** 360
Mackey Airways, **I** 102
Mackie Designs Inc., 30 406; 33 278–81
Mackinnon Mackenzie & Co., **III** 521–22
Maclaren Power and Paper Co., **IV** 165
Maclean Hunter Limited, III 65; **IV** 638–40; **22** 442; **23** 98
Maclean Hunter Publishing Limited, 26 270–74 (upd.); 30 388
Maclin Co., **12** 127
Macluan Capital Corporation, **49** 196
The MacManus Group, **32** 140; **40** 140
MacMark Corp., **22** 459
MacMarr Stores, **II** 654
Macmillan & Co. Ltd., **35** 452
MacMillan Bloedel Limited, IV 165, 272, **306–09,** 721; **9** 391; **19** 444, 446; **25** 12; **26** 445
Macmillan, Inc., IV 637, 641–43; **7** 284–86, 311–12, 343; **9** 63; **12** 226; **13** 91, 93; **17** 399; **18** 329; **22** 441–42; **23** 350, 503; **25** 484; **27** 222–23
Macnaughton Blair, **III** 671
The MacNeal-Schwendler Corporation, 25 303–05
Macneill & Co., **III** 522
Macon Gas Company, **6** 447; **23** 28
Macon Kraft Co., **IV** 311; **11** 421; **19** 267
Maconochie Bros., **II** 569
Macrodata, **18** 87
Macwhyte Company, **27** 415
Macy's. *See* R.H. Macy & Co., Inc.
Macy's California, **21** 129
Mad Dog Athletics, **19** 385
Maddingley Brown Coal Pty Ltd., **IV** 249
Maddux Air Lines, **I** 125; **12** 487
Madeira Wine Company, S.A., 49 255–57
Madge Networks N.V., 18 346; **26** 275–77
Madison & Sullivan, Inc., **10** 215
Madison Dearborn Capital Partners, L.P., **46** 289; **49** 197
Madison Financial Corp., **16** 145
Madison Foods, **14** 557
Madison Furniture Industries, **14** 436

Madison Gas and Electric Company, 6 605–06; **39 259–62**
Madison Resources, Inc., 13 502
Madison Square Garden, I 452
MAEFORT Hungarian Air Transport Joint Stock Company, 24 310
Maersk Lines, 22 167
Maes Group Breweries, II 475
Maeva Group, 6 206
Mafco Holdings, Inc., 28 248; 38 293–95
Magasins Armand Thiéry et Sigrand, V 11; 19 308
Magazine and Book Services, 13 48
Magazins Réal Stores, II 651
Magcobar, III 472
MagCorp, 28 198
Magdeburg Insurance Group, III 377
Magdeburger Versicherungsgruppe, III 377
Magee Company, 31 435–36
Magellan Aerospace Corporation, 46 8; **48 274–76**
Magellan Corporation, 22 403
Magic Chef Co., III 573; 8 298; 22 349
Magic City Food Products Company. *See* Golden Enterprises, Inc.
Magic Marker, 29 372
Magic Pan, II 559–60; 12 410
Magic Pantry Foods, 10 382
Magicsilk, Inc., 22 133
MagicSoft Inc., 10 557
Magirus, IV 126
Maglificio di Ponzano Veneto dei Fratelli Benetton. *See* Benetton.
Magma Copper Company, 7 287–90, 385–87; **22 107**
Magma Power Company, 11 270–72
Magna Computer Corporation, 12 149; 13 97
Magna Distribuidora Ltda., 43 368
Magnaflux, III 519; 22 282
Magnavox Co., 13 398; 19 393
Magne Corp., IV 160
Magnesium Metal Co., IV 118
Magnet Cove Barium Corp., III 472
MagneTek, Inc., 15 287–89; **41 241–44(upd.)**
Magnetic Controls Company, 10 18
Magnetic Peripherals Inc., 19 513–14
Magnivision, 22 35
Magnolia Petroleum Co., III 497; IV 82, 464
Magnus Co., I 331; 13 197
La Magona d'Italia, IV 228
Magor Railcar Co., I 170
Magro, 48 63
MAGroup Inc., 11 123
Magyar Viscosa, 37 428
Mahalo Air, 22 252; 24 22
Maharam Fabric, 8 455
Mahir, I 37
Mahir & Numan A.S., 48 154
Mahou, II 474
Mai Nap Rt, IV 652; 7 392
MAI PLC, 28 504
MAI Systems Corporation, 10 242; **11 273–76**; 26 497, 499
Maidenform Worldwide Inc., 20 352–55
Mail Boxes Etc., 18 315–17; 25 500; **41 245–48 (upd.)**. *See also* U.S. Office Products Company.
Mail.com Inc., 38 271
Mail-Well, Inc., 25 184; **28 250–52**
Mailson Ferreira da Nobrega, II 200
Mailtek, Inc., 18 518

MAIN. *See* Mid-American Interpool Network.
Main Event Management Corp., III 194
Main Plaza Corporation, 25 115
Main Street Advertising USA, IV 597
Maine Central Railroad Company, 16 348–50
Mainline Industrial Distributors, Inc., 13 79
Mainline Travel, I 114
Maison Blanche Department Stores Group, 35 129
Maison Bouygues, I 563
Maison de Schreiber and Aronson, 25 283
Maison de Valérie, 19 309
Maison Louis Jadot, 24 307–09
Maizuru Heavy Industries, III 514
Majestic Contractors Ltd., 8 419–20
Majestic Industries, Inc., 43 459
Majestic Wine Warehouses Ltd., II 656
The Major Automotive Companies, Inc., 45 260–62
Major League Baseball, 12 457
Major Video Concepts, 6 410
Major Video, Inc., 9 74
MaK Maschinenbau GmbH, IV 88
Mak van Waay, 11 453
Makepeace Preserving Co., 25 365
Makhteshim Chemical Works Ltd., II 47; 25 266–67
Makita Corporation, III 436; 20 66; **22 333–35**
Makiyama, I 363
Makovsky & Company, 12 394
Makro Inc., 18 286
Malama Pacific Corporation, 9 276
Malapai Resources, 6 546
Malayan Breweries, I 256
Malayan Motor and General Underwriters, III 201
Malaysia LNG, IV 518–19
Malaysian Airlines System Berhad, 6 71, 100–02, 117, 415; **29 300–03 (upd.)**
Malaysian International Shipping Co., IV 518
Malaysian Sheet Glass, III 715
Malbak Ltd., IV 92–93
Malcolm Pirnie, Inc., 42 242–44
Malcolm's Diary & Time-Table, III 256
Malcus Industri, III 624
Malden Mills Industries, Inc., 16 351–53
Malév Plc, 24 310–12; 27 474; 29 17
Malheur Cooperative Electric Association, 12 265
Malibu, 25 141
Mall.com, 38 271
Mallard Bay Drilling, Inc., 28 347–48
Malleable Iron Works, II 34
Mallinckrodt Group Inc., III 16; IV 146; 8 85; 19 28, 251–53
Malmö Aviation, 47 61
Malmö Flygindustri, I 198
Malmö Woodworking Factory. *See* Tarkett Sommer AG.
Malmsten & Bergvalls, I 664
Malone & Hyde, Inc., II 625, 670–71; 9 52–53; 14 147; 18 506
Malrite Communications Group, IV 596
Malt-A-Milk Co., II 487
Malt-O-Meal Company, 15 189; **22 336–38**
Mameco International, 8 455
Mammoet Transport B.V., 26 241, 278–80
Man Aktiengesellschaft, III 301, 561–63

MAN Gutehoffnungshütte AG, 15 226
Management and Training Corporation, 28 253–56
Management By Information Inc., 48 307
Management Decision Systems, Inc., 10 358
Management Engineering and Development Co., IV 310; 19 266
Management Recruiters International, 6 140
Management Science America, Inc., 11 77; 25 20
Manbré and Garton, II 582
Manchester and Liverpool District Banking Co., II 307, 333
Manchester Board and Paper Co., 19 77
Manchester Commercial Buildings Co., IV 711
Manchester United Football Club plc, 30 296–98; 44 388
Manco, Inc., 13 166. *See also* Henkel Manco Inc.
Mancuso & Co., 22 116
Mandabach & Simms, 6 40
Mandalay Pictures, 35 278–80
Mandalay Resort Group, 32 322–26 (upd.)
Mandarin, Inc., 33 128
Mandarin Oriental Hotel Group International Ltd., I 471; IV 700; 20 312
Mandarin Oriental International Limited, 47 177
Mandel Bros., IV 660
Manetta Mills, Inc., 19 304
Manhattan Card Co., 18 114
Manhattan, Co., II 217, 247
Manhattan Construction Company. *See* Rooney Brothers Co.
Manhattan Electrical Supply Co., 9 517
Manhattan Fund, I 614
Manhattan International Limousine Network Ltd., 26 62
Manhattan Trust Co., II 229
Manheim Auctions, Inc. *See* Cox Enterprises, Inc.
Manifatture Cotoniere Meridionali, I 466
Manischewitz Company. *See* B. Manischewitz Company.
Manistique Papers Inc., 17 282
Manistique Pulp and Paper Co., IV 311; 19 266
Manitoba Bridge and Engineering Works Ltd., 8 544
Manitoba Paper Co., IV 245–46; 25 10
Manitoba Rolling Mill Ltd., 8 544
Manitou BF S.A., 27 294–96
Manitowoc Company, Inc., 18 318–21
Mann Egerton & Co., III 523
Mann Theatres Chain, I 245; 25 177
Mann's Wine Company, Ltd., 14 288
Mann's Wine Pub Co., Ltd., 47 206
Mannatech Inc., 33 282–85
Manne Tossbergs Eftr., II 639
Mannesmann AG, I 411; III 564–67; IV 222, 469; 14 326–29 (upd.); 34 319; 38 296–301 (upd.). *See also* Vodafone Group PLC.
Mannheimer Bank, IV 558
Manning, Selvage & Lee, 6 22
Mannstaedt, IV 128
Manor AG, 48 279
Manor Care, Inc., 6 187–90; 14 105–07; 15 522; 25 306–10 (upd.)
Manor Healthcare Corporation, 26 459

Manorfield Investments, **II** 158
Manos Enterprises, **14** 87
Manpower, Inc., **6** 10, 140; **9 326–27**; **16** 48; **25** 432; **30 299–302 (upd.)**; **40** 236, 238; **44** 157; **49** 264–65
Mantrec S.A., **27** 296
Mantua Metal Products. *See* Tyco Toys, Inc.
Manufactured Home Communities, Inc., **22 339–41**; **46** 378
Manufacturers & Merchants Indemnity Co., **III** 191
Manufacturers and Traders Trust Company, **11** 108–09
Manufacturers Casualty Insurance Co., **26** 486
Manufacturers Fire Insurance Co., **26** 486
Manufacturers Hanover Corporation, **II** 230, 254, **312–14**, 403; **III** 194; **9** 124; **11** 16, 54, 415; **13** 536; **14** 103; **16** 207; **17** 559; **22** 406; **26** 453; **38** 253
Manufacturers National Bank of Brooklyn, **II** 312
Manufacturers National Bank of Detroit, **I** 165; **11** 137; **40** 116
Manufacturers Railway, **I** 219; **34** 36
Manufacturing Management Inc., **19** 381
Manus Nu-Pulse, **III** 420
Manville Corporation, **III 706–09**, 721; **7 291–95 (upd.)**; **10** 43, 45; **11** 420–22. *See also* Riverwood International Corporation.
Manweb plc, **19** 389–90; **49** 363–64
MAP. *See* Marathon Ashland Petroleum LLC.
MAPCO Inc., **IV 458–59**; **26** 234; **31** 469, 471
Mapelli Brothers Food Distribution Co., **13** 350
Maple Grove Farms of Vermont, Inc., **40** 51–52
Maple Leaf Foods Inc., **41 249–53**
Maple Leaf Mills, **II** 513–14; **41** 252
MAPP. *See* Mid-Continent Area Power Planner.
Mapra Industria e Comercio Ltda., **32** 40
MAR Associates, **48** 54
Mar-O-Bar Company, **7** 299
A.B. Marabou, **II** 511
Marantha! Music, **14** 499
Marantz Co., **14** 118
Marathon Ashland Petroleum LLC, **49** 329–30
Marathon Insurance Co., **26** 486
Marathon Oil Co., **IV** 365, 454, 487, 572, 574; **7** 549, 551; **13** 458; **49** 328, 330
Marathon Paper Products, **I** 612, 614
Marauder Company, **26** 433
Maraven, **IV** 508
Marblehead Communications, Inc., **23** 101
Marbodal, **12** 464
Marboro Books, Inc., **10** 136
Marbro Lamp Co., **III** 571; **20** 362
Marc's Big Boy. *See* The Marcus Corporation.
Marcade Group. *See* Aris Industries, Inc.
Marceau Investments, **II** 356
March-Davis Bicycle Company, **19** 383
March of Dimes, **31 322–25**
March Plasma Systems, Inc., **48** 299
Marchand, **13** 27
Marchesi Antinori SRL, **42 245–48**
marchFIRST, Inc., **34 261–64**
Marchland Holdings Ltd., **II** 649

Marchon Eyewear, **22** 123
Marciano Investments, Inc., **24** 157
Marcillat, **19** 49
Marcon Coating, Inc., **22** 347
Marconi plc, **33 286–90 (upd.)**
Marconi Wireless Telegraph Co. of America, **II** 25, 88
Marconiphone, **I** 531
The Marcus Corporation, **21 359–63**
Marcus Samuel & Co., **IV** 530
Marcy Fitness Products, Inc., **19** 142, 144
Mardon Packaging International, **I** 426–27
Mardorf, Peach and Co., **II** 466
Maremont Corporation, **8** 39–40
Margarete Steiff GmbH, **23 334–37**
Margarine Unie N.V. *See* Unilever PLC (Unilever N.V.).
Marge Carson, Inc., **III** 571; **20** 362
Margo's La Mode, **10** 281–82; **45** 15
Marico Acquisition Corporation, **8** 448, 450
Marie Brizard & Roger International S.A., **22 342–44**
Marie Callender's Restaurant & Bakery, Inc., **13** 66; **28 257–59**
Marie-Claire Album, **III** 47
Marigold Foods Inc., **II** 528
Marina Mortgage Company, **46** 25
Marinduque Mining & Industrial Corp., **IV** 146
Marine Bank and Trust Co., **11** 105
Marine Bank of Erie, **II** 342
Marine Computer Systems, **6** 242
Marine Diamond Corp., **IV** 66; **7** 123
Marine-Firminy, **IV** 227
Marine Group, **III** 444; **22** 116
Marine Harvest International, **13** 103
Marine Midland Corp., **I** 548; **II** 298; **9** 475–76; **11** 108; **17** 325
Marine Office of America, **III** 220, 241–42
Marine United Inc., **42** 361
Marinela, **19** 192–93
Marineland Amusements Corp., **IV** 623
MarineMax, Inc., **30 303–05**; **37** 396
Marion Brick, **14** 249
Marion Foods, Inc., **17** 434
Marion Freight Lines, **6** 370
Marion Laboratories Inc., **I 648–49**; **8** 149; **9 328–29**; **16** 438
Marion Manufacturing, **9** 72
Marion Merrell Dow, Inc., **9 328–29 (upd.)**
Marionet Corp., **IV** 680–81
Marisa Christina, Inc., **15 290–92**; **25** 245
Maritime Electric Company, Limited, **15** 182; **47 136–37**
Maritz Inc., **38 302–05**
Mark Controls Corporation, **30** 157
Mark Cross, Inc., **17** 4–5
Mark Goldston, **8** 305
Mark Hopkins, **12** 316
Mark IV Industries, Inc., **7 296–98**; **21** 418; **28 260–64 (upd.)**
Mark Travel Corporation, **30** 448
Mark Trouser, Inc., **17** 338
Markborough Properties, **II** 222; **V** 81; **8** 525; **25** 221
Market Growth Resources, **23** 480
Market Horizons, **6** 27
Market National Bank, **13** 465
Marketime, **V** 55
Marketing Data Systems, Inc., **18** 24
Marketing Equities International, **26** 136

Marketing Information Services, **6** 24
MarketSpan Corp. *See* KeySpan Energy Co.
Markham & Co., **I** 573–74
Marks and Spencer p.l.c., **I** 588; **II** 513, 678; **V 124–26**; **10** 442; **17** 42, 124; **22** 109, 111; **24** 268, 270; **313–17 (upd.)**, 474; **28** 96; **35** 308, 310; **41** 114; **42** 231
Marks-Baer Inc., **11** 64
Marks Brothers Jewelers, Inc., **24 318–20**
Marland Refining Co., **IV** 399–400
Marlene Industries Corp., **16** 36–37
MarLennan Corp., **III** 283
Marley Co., **19** 360
Marley Holdings, L.P., **19** 246
Marley Tile, **III** 735
Marlin-Rockwell Corp., **I** 539; **14** 510
Marlow Foods, **II** 565
Marman Products Company, **16** 8
The Marmon Group, **III** 97; **IV 135–38**; **16 354–57 (upd.)**
Marmon-Perry Light Company, **6** 508
Marolf Dakota Farms, Inc., **18** 14–15
Marotte, **21** 438
Marquam Commercial Brokerage Company, **21** 257
Marquardt Aircraft, **I** 380; **13** 379
Marquette Electronics, Inc., **13 326–28**
Marquette Paper Corporation, **III** 766; **22** 545
Marquis Who's Who, **17** 398
Marriage Mailers, **6** 12
Marriner Group, **13** 175
Marriot Inc., **29** 442
Marriot Management Services, **29** 444
Marriott Corporation, **II** 173, 608; **III** 92, 94, 99–100, **102–03**, 248; **7** 474–75; **9** 95, 426; **15** 87; **17** 238; **18** 216; **19** 433–34; **21** 91, 364; **22** 131; **23** 436–38; **27** 334; **38** 386; **41** 82
Marriott International, Inc., **21** 182, **364–67 (upd.)**; **29** 403, 406; **41 156–58**
Mars, Incorporated, **II** 510–11; **III** 114; **7 299–301**; **22** 298, 528; **40 302–05 (upd.)**
Marschke Manufacturing Co., **III** 435
Marsene Corp., **III** 440
Marsh & McLennan Companies, Inc., **III** 280, **282–84**; **10** 39; **14** 279; **22** 318; **45** 28, **263–67 (upd.)**
Marsh Supermarkets, Inc., **17 300–02**
Marshalk Company, **I** 16; **22** 294
Marshall Die Casting, **13** 225
Marshall Field & Co., **I** 13, 426; **III** 329; **IV** 660; **V** 43–44; **8** 33; **9** 213; **12** 283; **15** 86; **18** 136–37, 488; **22** 72
Marshall Industries, **19** 311
Marshalls Incorporated, **13 329–31**; **14** 62
Marsin Medical Supply Co., **III** 9
Marstellar, **13** 204
The Mart, **9** 120
Marten Transport, **27** 404
Martha, **IV** 486
Martha Lane Adams, **27** 428
Martha Stewart Living Omnimedia, L.L.C., **24 321–23**; **47** 211
Martin & Pagenstecher GMBH, **24** 208
Martin Bros. Tobacco Co., **14** 19
Martin-Brower Corp., **II** 500; **III** 21; **17** 475
Martin Collet, **19** 50
Martin Dennis Co., **IV** 409

Martin Dunitz, **44** 416
Martin Electric Co., **III** 98
Martin Guitar Company. *See* C.F. Martin & Co., Inc.
Martin Industries, Inc., 44 274–77
Martin Marietta Corporation, I 47, **67–69**, 71, 102, 112, 142–43, 184, 416; **II** 32, 67; **III** 671; **IV** 60, 163; **7** 356, 520; **8** 315; **9** 310; **10** 162, 199, 484; **11** 166, 277–78, 364; **12** 127, 290; **13** 327, 356; **15** 283; **17** 564; **18** 369; **19** 70; **22** 400; **28** 288. *See also* Lockheed Martin Corporation.
Martin Mathys, **8** 456
Martin Rooks & Co., **I** 95
Martin-Senour Co., **III** 744
Martin Sorrell, **6** 54
Martin Theaters, **14** 86
Martin-Yale Industries, Inc., **19** 142–44
Martin Zippel Co., **16** 389
Martin's, **12** 221
Martindale-Hubbell, **17** 398
Martineau and Bland, **I** 293
Martini & Rossi, **18** 41
Martins Bank, **II** 236, 308
Martinus Nijhoff, **14** 555; **25** 85
Marubeni Corporation, 24 324–27 **(upd.)**
Marubeni K.K., I 432, **492–95**, 510; **II** 292, 391; **III** 760; **IV** 266, 525; **12** 147; **17** 556
Maruei & Co., **IV** 151; **24** 358
Maruetsu, **17** 124; **41** 114
Marufuku Co., Ltd., **III** 586; **7** 394
Marui Co. Ltd., V 127
Marukuni Kogyo Co., Ltd., **IV** 327
Marutaka Kinitsu Store Ltd., **V** 194; **47** 389
Maruzen Co., Limited, II 348; **IV** 403–04, 476, 554; **18 322–24**
Marvel Entertainment Group, Inc., 10 400–02; **18** 426, 520–21; **21** 404; **25** 141; **34** 449
Marvel Metal Products, **III** 570; **20** 361
Marvel-Schebler Carburetor Corp., **III** 438; **14** 63–64
Marvin & Leonard Advertising, **13** 511–12
Marvin H. Sugarman Productions Inc., **20** 48
Marvin Lumber & Cedar Company, 10 95; **22 345–47**
Marwick, Mitchell & Company, **10** 385
Marwitz & Hauser, **III** 446
Marx, **12** 494
Mary Ann Co. Ltd., **V** 89
Mary Ann Restivo, Inc., **8** 323
Mary Ellen's, Inc., **11** 211
Mary Kathleen Uranium, **IV** 59–60
Mary Kay Corporation, III 16; **9 330–32**; **12** 435; **15** 475, 477; **18** 67, 164; **21** 49, 51; **30 306–09 (upd.)**
Maryland Casualty Co., **III** 193, 412
Maryland Cup Company, **8** 197
Maryland Distillers, **I** 285
Maryland Medical Laboratory Inc., **26** 391
Maryland National Corp., **11** 287
Maryland National Mortgage Corporation, **11** 121; **48** 177
Maryland Shipbuilding and Drydock Co., **I** 170
Maryland Steel Co., **IV** 35; **7** 48
Marzotto S.p.A., 20 356–58; **48** 206–07
Masayoshi Son, **13** 481–82
Mascan Corp., **IV** 697

Maschinenbauanstalt Humboldt AG, **III** 541
Maschinenfabrik Augsburg-Nürnberg. *See* M.A.N.
Maschinenfabrik Deutschland, **IV** 103
Maschinenfabrik für den Bergbau von Sievers & Co., **III** 541
Maschinenfabrik Gebr. Meer, **III** 565
Maschinenfabrik Sürth, **I** 581
Masco Corporation, III 568–71; **11** 385, 534–35; **12** 129, 131, 344; **13** 338; **18** 68; **20 359–63 (upd.)**; **39 263–68 (upd.)**
Masco Optical, **13** 165
Mascon Toy Co., **III** 569; **20** 360
MASCOR, **14** 13
Mase Westpac Limited, **11** 418
Maserati. *See* Officine Alfieri Maserati S.p.A.
Mashantucket Pequot Gaming Enterprise Inc., 35 282–85
Masinfabriks A.B. Scania, **I** 197
MASkargo Ltd., **6** 101
Masland Corporation, 17 303–05; **19** 408
Mason & Hamlin, **III** 656
Mason Best Co., **IV** 343
Masonite Corp., **III** 764; **47** 189
Masonite Holdings, **III** 687
Mass Rapid Transit Corp., **19** 111
Massachusetts Bank, **II** 207
Massachusetts Capital Resources Corp., **III** 314
Massachusetts Mutual Life Insurance Company, III 110, **285–87**, 305; **14** 14; **25** 528
Massachusetts Technology Development Corporation, **18** 570
Massachusetts's General Electric Company, **32** 267
Massey Burch Investment Grou Master Boot Polish Co., **II** 566
Master Builders, **I** 673
Master Electric Company, **15** 134
Master Glass & Color, **24** 159–60
Master Lock Company, 45 268–71
Master Pneumatic Tool Co., **III** 436
Master Processing, **19** 37
Master Products, **14** 162
Master Shield Inc., **7** 116
Master Tank and Welding Company, **7** 541
Master Tek International, Inc., **47** 372
MasterBrand Industries Inc., **12** 344–45
MasterCard International, Inc., 9 333–35; **18** 337, 543; **25** 41; **26** 515; **41** 201
Mastercraft Homes, Inc., **11** 257
Mastercraft Industries Corp., **III** 654
Mastex Industries, **29** 132
Maszovlet. *See* Malév Plc.
Matador Records, **22** 194
Matairco, **9** 27
Matalan PLC, 49 258–60
Matane Pulp & Paper Company, **17** 281
Matchbox Toys Ltd., **12** 168
MatchLogic, Inc., **41** 198
Matco Tools, **7** 116
Material Management and Services Inc., **28** 61
Materials Services Corp., **I** 58
Mathematica, Inc., **22** 291
Mather & Crother Advertising Agency, **I** 25
Mather Co., **I** 159
Mather Metals, **III** 582
Matheson & Co., **IV** 189

Mathews Conveyor Co., **14** 43
Mathieson Chemical Corp., **I** 379–80, 695; **13** 379
Matra, **II** 38, 70; **IV** 617–19; **13** 356; **17** 354; **24** 88
Matra Aerospace Inc., **22** 402
Matra-Hachette S.A., 15 293–97 (upd.); **21** 267
Matria Healthcare, Inc., 17 306–09
Matrix Science Corp., **II** 8; **14** 27
Matson Navigation Company, Inc., **II** 490–91; **10** 40; **41** 399
Matsumoto Medical Instruments, Inc., **11** 476; **29** 455
Matsushita Electric Industrial Co., Ltd., II 5, **55–56**, 58, 61, 91–92, 102, 117–19, 361, 455; **III** 476, 710; **6** 36; **7** 163, 302; **10** 286, 389, 403, 432; **11** 487; **12** 448; **13** 398; **18** 18; **20** 81; **26** 511; **33** 432; **36** 399–400, 420
Matsushita Electric Works, Ltd., III 710–11; **7 302–03 (upd.)**; **12** 454; **16** 167; **27** 342
Matsushita Kotobuki Electronics Industries, Ltd., **10** 458–59
Matsuura Trading Co., Ltd., **IV** 327
Matsuzakaya Company, V 129–31
Mattatuck Bank & Trust Co., **13** 467
Mattel, Inc., II 136; **III** 506; **7 304–07**; **12** 74, 168–69, 495; **13** 560–61; **15** 238; **16** 264, 428; **17** 243; **18** 520–21; **25 311–15 (upd.)**, 381, 488; **27** 20, 373, 375; **28** 159; **29** 74, 78; **32** 187; **34** 369–70; **43** 229, 232–33
Matthes & Weber, **III** 32
Matthew Bender & Company, Inc., **IV** 677; **7** 94; **14** 97; **17** 486
Matthews International Corporation, 29 304–06
Matthews Paint Co., **22** 437
Maud Foster Mill, **II** 566
Maui Electric Company, **9** 276
Maui Land & Pineapple Company, Inc., 29 307–09
Maui Tacos International, Inc., **49** 60
Mauna Kea Properties, **6** 129
Maurice H. Needham Co., **I** 31
Maus Frères SA, 19 307; **48 277–79**
Maus-Nordmann, **V** 10; **19** 308
Max & Erma's Restaurants Inc., 19 258–60
Max Factor & Co., **III** 54, 56; **6** 51; **12** 314
Max-Grundig-Stiftung, **27** 190–91
Max Klein, Inc., **II** 572
Max Media Properties LLC, **25** 419
Max Television Co., **25** 418
Maxcell Telecom Plus, **6** 323
Maxco Inc., 17 310–11; **24** 159, 160
Maxell Corp., **I** 500; **14** 534
Maxi-Papier-Markt, **10** 498; **24** 270
Maxi Vac, Inc., **9** 72
Maxicare Health Plans, Inc., III 84–86; **25 316–19 (upd.)**; **44** 174
Maxie's of America, **25** 389
The Maxim Group, 25 88, **320–22**
Maxim Integrated Products, Inc., 16 358–60
MAXIMUS, Inc., 43 277–80
Maxis Software, **13** 115
Maxoptix Corporation, **10** 404
Maxpro Sports Inc., **22** 458
Maxpro Systems, **24** 509–10

Maxtor Corporation, **6** 230; **10 403–05**, 459, 463–64

Maxus Energy Corporation, **IV** 410; **7 308–10**; **10** 191; **31** 456

Maxwell Communication Corporation plc, **IV** 605, 611, **641–43**; **7** 286, **311–13** (upd.), 343; **10** 288; **13** 91–93; **23** 350; **39** 49; **47** 326; **49** 408

Maxwell Morton Corp, **I** 144, 414

Maxwell Shoe Company, Inc., **30 310–12**

Maxwell Travel Inc., **33** 396

MAXXAM Inc., **IV** 121, 123; **8 348–50**

Maxxim Medical Inc., **12 325–27**

May and Baker, **I** 388

May & Speh Inc., **35** 17

The May Department Stores Company, **I** 540; **II** 414; **V 132–35**; **8** 288; **11** 349; **12** 55, 507–08; **13** 42, 361; **15** 275; **16** 62, 160, 206–07; **18** 414–15; **19 261–64** (upd.); **23** 345; **27** 61, 291, 346, 348; **33** 471, 473; **46 284–88** (upd.)

Maybelline, **I** 684

Mayer & Schweitzer, **26** 66

Mayer, Brown, Rowe & Maw, **47 230–32**

Mayfair Foods, **I** 438; **16** 314

Mayfield Dairy Farms, Inc., **7** 128

Mayflower Group Inc., **6 409–11**; **15** 50

Mayne Nickless Ltd., **IV** 248

Mayo Foundation, **9 336–39**; **13** 326; **34 265–69** (upd.)

Mayor's Jewelers, Inc., **41 254–57**

Maytag Corporation, **III 572–73**; **12** 252, 300; **21** 141; **22** 218, **348–51** (upd.); **23** 244; **42** 159; **43** 166

Mayville Metal Products Co., **I** 513

Mazda Motor Corporation, **I** 520; **II** 4, 361; **III** 603; **9 340–42**; **11** 86; **13** 414; **16** 322; **23 338–41** (upd.); **36** 215

Mazel Stores, Inc., **29 310–12**

MB Group, **20** 108. *See also* Novar plc.

MBB. *See* Messerschmitt-Bölkow-Blohm.

MBC. *See* Middle East Broadcasting Centre, Ltd.

MBC Holding Company, **40 306–09**

MBE. *See* Mail Boxes Etc.

MBNA Corporation, **11** 123; **12 328–30**; **33 291–94** (upd.)

MBPXL Corp., **II** 494

MC Distribution Services, Inc., **35** 298

MCA Inc., **II 143–45**; **6** 162–63; **10** 286; **11** 557; **17** 317; **21** 23, 25–26; **22** 131, 194; **23** 125; **25** 411; **26** 151, 314; **33** 431

McAfee Associates. *See* Network Associates, Inc.

The McAlpin Company, **19** 272

McAndrew & Forbes Holdings Inc., **23** 407; **26** 119

McArthur Glen Realty, **10** 122; **33** 59

MCC. *See* Maxwell Communications Corporation *and* Morris Communications Corporation.

McCaffrey & McCall, **I** 33; **11** 496

McCain Feeds Ltd., **II** 484

McCain Foods, **41** 252

McCall Pattern Company, **22** 512; **23** 99

McCall Printing Co., **14** 460

McCall's Corp., **23** 393

McCann-Erickson Worldwide, **I** 10, 14, 16–17, 234; **6** 30; **10** 227; **14** 315; **16** 167; **18** 68; **22** 294; **32** 114

McCann-Erickson Hakuhodo, Ltd., **42** 174

McCarthy Building Companies, Inc., **48 280–82**

McCarthy Milling, **II** 631; **27** 245–47

McCaughan Dyson and Co., **II** 189

McCaw Cellular Communications, Inc., **II** 331; **6** 274, **322–24**; **7** 15; **9** 320–21; **10** 433; **15** 125, 196; **27** 341, 343–44; **29** 44, 61; **36** 514–15; **43** 447; **49** 71–72

McClanahan Oil Co., **I** 341; **14** 216

McClatchy Newspapers, Inc., **23** 156, 158, **342–44**

McCleary, Wallin and Crouse, **19** 274

McClintic-Marshall, **IV** 36; **7** 49

The McCloskey Corporation, **8** 553

The McClure Syndicate, **25** 138

McColl-Frontenac Petroleum Inc., **IV** 439; **25** 232

McComb Manufacturing Co., **8** 287

McCormack & Dodge, **IV** 605; **11** 77

McCormick & Company, Incorporated, **7 314–16**; **17** 104, 106; **21** 497; **27 297–300** (upd.); **36** 185, 188

McCormick & Schmick's, **31** 41

McCormick Harvesting Machine Co., **I** 180; **II** 330

McCown De Leeuw & Co., **16** 510

McCracken Brooks, **23** 479; **25** 91

McCrory Stores, **II** 424; **9** 447–48; **13** 340

McCulloch Corp., **III** 436; **8** 348–49

McCullough Environmental Services, **12** 443

McDermott International, Inc., **III 558–60**; **37 242–46** (upd.)

McDonald Glass Grocery Co. Inc., **II** 669

McDonald's Company (Japan) Ltd., **V** 205

McDonald's Corporation, **I** 23, 31, 129; **II** 500, 613–15 **646–48**; **III** 63, 94, 103; **6** 13; **7** 128, 266–67, 316, **317–19** (upd.), 435, 505–06; **8** 261–62, 564; **9** 74, 178, 290, 292, 305; **10** 122; **11** 82, 308; **12** 43, 180, 553; **13** 494; **14** 25, 32, 106, 195, 452–53; **16** 95–97, 289; **17** 69–71; **19** 85, 192, 214; **21** 25, 315, 362; **23** 505; **25** 179, 309, 387; **26 281–85** (upd.); **31** 278; **32** 442–44; **33** 240; **36** 517, 519–20; **39** 166, 168; **48** 67

McDonnell Douglas Corporation, **I** 41–43, 45, 48, 50–52, 54–56, 58–59, 61–62, 67–68, **70–72**, 76–77, 82, 84–85, 90, 105, 108, 111, 121–22, 321, 364, 490, 511; **II** 442; **III** 512, 654; **6** 68; **7** 456, 504; **8** 49–51, 315; **9** 18, 183, 206, 231, 271–72, 418, 458, 460; **10** 163–64, 317, 536; **11** 164–65, 267, **277–80** (upd.), 285, 363–65; **12** 190–91, 549; **13** 356; **15** 283; **16** 78, 94; **18** 368; **24** 84–85, 87; **28** 225; **32** 81, 83, 85

McDonough Co., **II** 16; **III** 502

McDougal, Littell & Company, **10** 357

McDowell Energy Center, **6** 543

McDowell Furniture Company, **10** 183

McDuff, **10** 305

McElligott Wright Morrison and White, **12** 511

McFadden Holdings L.P., **27** 41

McFadden Industries, **III** 21

McFadden Publishing, **6** 13

McGaughy, Marsha 584, **634–37**, 643, 656, 674; **10** 62; **12** 359; **13** 417; **18 325–30** (upd.); **26** 79; **27** 360

McGaw Inc., **11** 208

McGill Manufacturing, **III** 625

McGraw-Edison Co., **II** 17, 87

McGraw Electric Company. *See* Centel Corporation.

The McGraw-Hill Companies, Inc., **II** 398; **IV** 584, **634–37**, 643, 656, 674; **10** 62; **12** 359; **13** 417; **18 325–30** (upd.); **26** 79; **27** 360

McGregor Corporation, **6** 415; **26** 102

McGrew Color Graphics, **7** 430

MCI. *See* Manitou Costruzioni Industriali SRL. *or* Melamine Chemicals, Inc.

MCI Communications Corporation, **II** 408; **III** 13, 149, 684; **V 302–04**; **6** 51–52, 300, 322; **7** 118–19; **8** 310; **9** 171, 478–80; **10** 19, 80, 89, 97, 433, 500; **11** 59, 183, 185, 302, 409, 500; **12** 135–37; **13** 38; **14** 252–53, 260, 364; **15** 222; **16** 318; **18** 32, 112, 164–66, 569–70; **19** 255; **25** 358; **26** 102, 441; **27** 430; **29** 42; **46** 374; **49** 72–73

MCI WorldCom, Inc., **27 301–08** (upd.)

McIlhenny Company, **20 364–67**

McIlwraith McEachern Limited, **27** 474

McJunkin Corp., **13** 79; **28** 61

McKechnie plc, **34 270–72**

McKee Foods Corporation, **7 320–21**; **27 309–11** (upd.)

McKenna Metals Company, **13** 295–96

McKesson Corporation, **I** 413, **496–98**, 713; **II** 652; **III** 10; **6** 279; **8** 464; **9** 532; **11** 91; **12 331–33** (upd.); **16** 43; **18** 97; **37** 10; **41** 340; **47 233–37** (upd.)

McKesson General Medical, **29** 299

McKinsey & Company, Inc., **I** 108, 144, 437, 497; **III** 47, 85, 670; **9 343–45**; **10** 175; **13** 138; **18** 68; **25** 34, 317; **26** 161

McLain Grocery, **II** 625

McLane America, Inc., **29** 481

McLane Company, Inc., **V** 217; **8** 556; **13 332–34**; **36** 269

McLaren Consolidated Cone Corp., **II** 543; **7** 366

McLaughlin Motor Company of Canada, **I** 171; **10** 325

McLean Clinic, **11** 379

McLeodUSA Incorporated, **32 327–30**; **38** 192

McLouth Steel Products, **13** 158

MCM Electronics, **9** 420

McMahan's Furniture Co., **14** 236

McMan Oil and Gas Co., **IV** 369

McManus, John & Adams, Inc., **6** 21

McMoCo, **IV** 82–83; **7** 187

McMoRan, **IV** 81–83; **V** 739; **7** 185, 187

McMullen & Yee Publishing, **22** 442

McMurtry Manufacturing, **8** 553

MCN Corporation, **6 519–22**; **13** 416; **17** 21–23; **45** 254

McNeil Corporation, **26** 363

McNeil Laboratories, **III** 35–36; **8** 282–83

McNellan Resources Inc., **IV** 76

MCO Holdings Inc., **8** 348–49

MCorp, **10** 134; **11** 122

McPaper AG, **29** 152

McQuay International. *See* AAF-McQuay Incorporated.

McRae's, Inc., **19** 324–25; **41** 343–44

MCS, Inc., **10** 412

MCSi, Inc., **41 258–60**

MCT Dairies, Inc., **18** 14–16

McTeigue & Co., **14** 502

McVitie & Price, **II** 592–93

McWhorter Inc., **8** 553; **27** 280

MD Distribution Inc., **15** 139
MD Foods (Mejeriselskabet Danmark Foods), **48** 35
MD Pharmaceuticals, **III** 10
MDC. *See* Mead Data Central, Inc.
MDI Co., Ltd., **IV** 327
MDS/Bankmark, **10** 247
MDU Resources Group, Inc., 7 322–25; 42 249–53 (upd.)
The Mead Corporation, IV 310–13, 327, 329, 342–43; **8** 267; **9** 261; **10** 406; **11** 421–22; **17** 399; **19 265–69 (upd.); 20** 18; **33** 263, 265
Mead Cycle Co., **IV** 660
Mead Data Central, Inc., IV 312; **7** 581; **10 406–08; 19** 268. *See also* LEXIS-NEXIS Group.
Mead John & Co., **19** 103
Mead Johnson, **III** 17
Mead Packaging, **12** 151
Meade County Rural Electric Cooperative Corporation, **11** 37
Meade Instruments Corporation, 41 261–64
Meadow Gold Dairies, Inc., **II** 473
Meadowcraft, Inc., 29 313–15
Means Services, Inc., **II** 607
Mears & Phillips, **II** 237
Measurex Corporation, **8** 243; **14** 56; **38** 227
Mebetoys, **25** 312
MEC - Hawaii, UK & USA, **IV** 714
MECA Software, Inc., **18** 363
Mecair, S.p.A., **17** 147
Mecca Bookmakers, **49** 450
Mecca Leisure PLC, **I** 248; **12** 229; **32** 243
Mechanics Exchange Savings Bank, **9** 173
Mechanics Machine Co., **III** 438; **14** 63
Mecklermedia Corporation, 24 328–30; **26** 441; **27** 360, 362
Meconic, **49** 230, 235
Medal Distributing Co., **9** 542
Medallion Pictures Corp., **9** 320
Medar, Inc., **17** 310–11
Medco Containment Services Inc., 9 346–48; 11 291; **12** 333; **44** 175
Medcom Inc., **I** 628
Medeco Security Locks, Inc., **10** 350
Medfield Corp., **III** 87
Medford, Inc., **19** 467–68
Medi Mart Drug Store Company. *See* The Stop & Shop Companies, Inc.
Media Arts Group, Inc., 42 254–57
Media Exchange International, **25** 509
Media General, Inc., III 214; **7 326–28;** **18** 61; **23** 225; **38 306–09 (upd.)**
Media Groep West B.V., **23** 271
Media News Corporation, **25** 507
Media Play. *See* Musicland Stores Corporation.
MediaBay, **41** 61
Mediacom Inc., **25** 373
Mediamark Research, **28** 501, 504
Mediamatics, Inc., **26** 329
MediaOne Group Inc. *See* U S West, Inc.
Mediaplex, Inc., **49** 433
Medic Computer Systems LLC, **16** 94; **45** 279–80
Medical Care America, Inc., **15** 112, 114; **35** 215–17
Medical Development Corp. *See* Cordis Corp.
Medical Development Services, Inc., **25** 307

Medical Economics Data, **23** 211
Medical Expense Fund, **III** 245
Medical Indemnity of America, **10** 160
Medical Innovations Corporation, **21** 46
Medical Marketing Group Inc., **9** 348
Medical Service Assoc. of Pennsylvania, **III** 325–26
Medical Tribune Group, **IV** 591; **20** 53
Medicare-Glaser, **17** 167
Medicine Bow Coal Company, **7** 33–34
Medicine Shoppe International. *See* Cardinal Health, Inc.
Medicor, Inc., **36** 496
Medicus Intercon International, **6** 22
Medifinancial Solutions, Inc., **18** 370
MedImmune, Inc., 35 286–89
Medinol Ltd., **37** 39
Mediobanca Banca di Credito Finanziario SpA, **II** 191, 271; **III** 208–09; **11** 205
The Mediplex Group, Inc., **III** 16; **11** 282
Medis Health and Pharmaceuticals Services Inc., **II** 653
Medite Corporation, **19** 467–68
Meditrust, 11 281–83
Medlabs Inc., **III** 73
MedPartners, **36** 367
Medtech, Ltd., **13** 60–62
Medtronic, Inc., 8 351–54; 11 459; **18** 421; **19** 103; **22** 359–61; **26** 132; **30 313–17 (upd.); 37** 39; **43** 349
Medusa Corporation, 8 135; **24 331–33; 30** 156
Mees & Hope, **II** 184
The MEGA Life and Health Insurance Co., **33** 418–20
MEGA Natural Gas Company, **11** 28
MegaBingo, Inc., **41** 273, 275
Megafoods Stores Inc., 13 335–37; 17 560
MegaKnowledge Inc., **45** 206
Megasong Publishing, **44** 164
Megasource, Inc., **16** 94
Meggitt PLC, 34 273–76; 48 432, 434
MEI Diversified Inc., **18** 455
Mei Foo Investments Ltd., **IV** 718; **38** 319
Meier & Frank Co., 23 345–47
Meijer Incorporated, 7 329–31; 15 449; **17** 302; **27 312–15 (upd.)**
Meiji Commerce Bank, **II** 291
Meiji Fire Insurance Co., **III** 384–85
Meiji Milk Products Company, Limited, II 538–39
Meiji Mutual Life Insurance Company, II 323; **III 288–89**
Meiji Seika Kaisha, Ltd., I 676; **II 540–41**
Meikosha Co., **II** 72
Meinecke Muffler Company, **III** 495; **10** 415
Meineke Discount Muffler Shops, **38** 208
Meis of Illiana, **10** 282
Meisei Electric, **III** 742
Meisel. *See* Samuel Meisel & Co.
Meisenzahl Auto Parts, Inc., **24** 205
Meissner, Ackermann & Co., **IV** 463; **7** 351
Meister, Lucious and Company, **13** 262
Meiwa Manufacturing Co., **III** 758
N.V. Mekog, **IV** 531
Mel Farr Automotive Group, 20 368–70
Mel Klein and Partners, **III** 74
Melaleuca Inc., 31 326–28
Melamine Chemicals, Inc., 27 316–18
Melbourne Engineering Co., **23** 83

Melbur China Clay Co., **III** 690
Melco, **II** 58; **44** 285
Meldisco. *See* Footstar, Incorporated.
Melkunie-Holland, **II** 575
Mellbank Security Co., **II** 316
Mello Smello. *See* The Miner Group International.
Mellon Bank Corporation, I 67–68, 584; **II 315–17,** 342, 402; **III** 275; **9** 470; **13** 410–11; **18** 112
Mellon Financial Corporation, 42 76; **44 278–82 (upd.)**
Mellon Indemnity Corp., **III** 258–59; **24** 177
Mellon-Stuart Co., I 584–85; 14 334
Melmarkets, **24** 462
Mélotte, **III** 418
Meloy Laboratories, Inc., **11** 333
Melroe Company, **8** 115–16; **34** 46
Melville Corporation, V 136–38; 9 192; **13** 82, 329–30; **14** 426; **15** 252–53;, **16** 390; **19** 449; **21** 526; **23** 176; **24** 167, 290; **35** 253. *See also* CVS Corporation.
Melvin Simon and Associates, Inc., 8 355–57; 26 262. *See also* Simon Property Group, Inc.
Melwire Group, **III** 673
MEM, **37** 270–71
Memco, **12** 48
Memorex Corp., **III** 110, 166; **6** 282–83
Memphis International Motorsports Corporation Inc., **43** 139–40
The Men's Wearhouse, Inc., 17 312–15; 21 311; **48 283–87 (upd.)**
Menasco Manufacturing Co., **I** 435; **III** 415
Menasha Corporation, 8 358–61
Menck, **8** 544
Mendelssohn & Co., **II** 241
Meneven, **IV** 508
Menka Gesellschaft, **IV** 150; **24** 357
The Mennen Company, **I** 19; **6** 26; **14** 122; **18** 69; **35** 113
Mental Health Programs Inc., **15** 122
The Mentholatum Company Inc., IV 722; **32 331–33**
Mentor Corporation, 26 286–88
Mentor Graphics Corporation, III 143; **8** 519; **11** 46–47, 284–86, 490; **13** 128
MEPC plc, IV 710–12
Mepco/Electra Inc., **13** 398
MeraBank, **6** 546
MERBCO, Inc., **33** 456
Mercantile Agency, **IV** 604
Mercantile and General Reinsurance Co., **III** 335, 377
Mercantile Bancorporation Inc., **33** 155
Mercantile Bank, **II** 298
Mercantile Bankshares Corp., 11 287–88
Mercantile Credit Co., **16** 13
Mercantile Estate and Property Corp. Ltd., **IV** 710
Mercantile Fire Insurance, **III** 234
Mercantile Mutual, **III** 310
Mercantile Property Corp. Ltd., **IV** 710
Mercantile Security Life, **III** 136
Mercantile Stores Company, Inc., V 139; 19 270–73 (upd.)
Mercantile Trust Co., **II** 229, 247
Mercator & Noordstar N.V., **40** 61
Mercedes Benz. *See* Daimler-Benz A.G.
Mercedes Benz of North America, **22** 52
Merchant Bank Services, **18** 516, 518
Merchant Co., **III** 104

Merchant Distributors, Inc., **20** 306
Merchants & Farmers Bank of Ecru, **14** 40
Merchants Bank, **II** 213
Merchants Bank & Trust Co., **21** 524
Merchants Bank of Canada, **II** 210
Merchants Bank of Halifax, **II** 344
Merchants Dispatch, **II** 395–96; **10** 60
Merchants Distributors Inc. *See* Alex Lee Inc.
Merchants Fire Assurance Corp., **III** 396–97
Merchants Home Delivery Service, **6** 414
Merchants Indemnity Corp., **III** 396–97
Merchants Life Insurance Co., **III** 275
Merchants National Bank, **9** 228; **14** 528; **17** 135
Merchants National Bank of Boston, **II** 213
Merchants Union Express Co., **II** 396; **10** 60
Merchants' Assoc., **II** 261
Merchants' Loan and Trust, **II** 261; **III** 518
Merchants' Savings, Loan and Trust Co., **II** 261
Mercier, **I** 272
Merck & Co., Inc., I 640, 646, **650–52**, 683–84, 708; **II** 414; **III** 42, 60, 66, 299; **8** 154, 548; **10** 213; **11** 9, 90, **289–91 (upd.)**; **12** 325, 333; **14** 58, 422; **15** 154; **16** 440; **20** 39, 59; **26** 126; **34** **280–85 (upd.)**; **36** 91, 93, 305; **38** 380; **44** 175; **47** 236
Mercury Air Group, Inc., 20 371–73
Mercury Asset Management (MAM), **14** 420; **40** 313
Mercury Communications, Ltd., V 280–82; **7 332–34**; **10** 456; **11** 547–48; **25** 101–02; **27** 365; **49** 70–71, 73
Mercury General Corporation, 25 323–25
Mercury, Inc., **8** 311
Mercury Mail, Inc., **22** 519, 522
Mercury Records, **13** 397; **23** 389, 391
Mercury Telecommunications Limited, **15** 67, 69
Meredith and Drew, **II** 593
Meredith Corporation, IV 661–62; **11** **292–94**; **17** 394; **18** 239; **23** 393; **29** **316–19 (upd.)**
Merfin International, **42** 53
Merial, **34** 284
Merico, Inc., **36** 161–64
Meridian Bancorp, Inc., 11 295–97; **17** 111, 114
Meridian Emerging Markets Ltd., **25** 509
Meridian Gold, Incorporated, 47 238–40
Meridian Healthcare, **18** 197
Meridian Insurance Co., **III** 332
Meridian Investment and Development Corp., **22** 189
Meridian Oil Inc., **10** 190–91
Meridian Publishing, Inc., **28** 254
Merillat Industries Inc., III 570; **13** **338–39**; **20** 362; **39** 266, 268
Merisel, Inc., 10 518–19; **12 334–36**; **13** 174, 176, 482
Merit Distribution Services, **13** 333
Merit Medical Systems, Inc., 29 320–22; **36** 497
Merit Tank Testing, Inc., **IV** 411
Merita/Cotton's Bakeries, **38** 251
Meritage Corporation, 26 289–92
MeritaNordbanken, **40** 336
Meritor Automotive Inc., **43** 328
Merivienti Oy, **IV** 276

Merix Corporation, 36 329–31
Merkur Direktwerbegesellschaft, **29** 152
Merla Manufacturing, **I** 524
Merlin Gérin, **II** 93–94; **18** 473; **19** 165
Merpati Nusantara Airlines, **6** 90–91
Merrell, **22** 173
Merrell Dow, **16** 438
Merrell Drug, **I** 325
Merrell-Soule Co., **II** 471
Merriam and Morgan Paraffine Co., **IV** 548
Merriam-Webster, Inc., **7** 165, 167; **23** 209–10; **39** 140, 143
Merrill Corporation, 18 331–34; **47** **241–44 (upd.)**
Merrill Gas Company, **9** 554
Merrill Lynch & Co., Inc., I 26, 339, 681, 683, 697; **II** 149, 257, 260, 268, 403, 407–08, 412, **424–26**, 441, 445, 449, 451, 456, 654–55, 680; **III** 119, 253, 340, 440; **6** 244; **7** 130; **8** 94; **9** 125, 187, 239, 301, 386; **11** 29, 122, 348, 557; **13** 44, 125, **340–43 (upd.)**, 448–49, 512; **14** 65; **15** 463; **16** 195; **17** 137; **21** 68–70, 145; **22** 404–06, 542; **23** 370; **25** 89–90, 329; **29** 295; **32** 14, 168; **40 310–15 (upd.)**; **49** 130
Merrill Lynch Capital Partners, **47** 363
Merrill, Pickard, Anderson & Eyre **IV**, **11** 490
Merrill Publishing, **IV** 643; **7** 312; **9** 63; **29** 57
Merrimack Services Corp., **37** 303
Merry-Go-Round Enterprises, Inc., 8 **362–64**; **24** 27
Merry Group, **III** 673
Merry Maids, **6** 46; **23** 428, 430
Merryhill Schools, Inc., **37** 279
The Mersey Docks and Harbour Company, 30 318–20
Mersey Paper Co., **IV** 258
Mersey White Lead Co., **III** 680
Merv Griffin Enterprises, **II** 137; **12** 75; **22** 431
Mervyn's, V 43–44; **10 409–10**; **13** 526; **18** 136–37; **27** 452
Mervyn's California, 39 269–71 (upd.)
Mesa Air Group, Inc., 32 334–37 (upd.)
Mesa Airlines, Inc., 11 298–300
Mesa LP, **IV** 410, 523; **11** 441; **40** 357
Mesa Petroleum, **IV** 392, 571; **24** 521, 522; **27** 217
Mesaba Holdings, Inc., I 448; **22** 21; **28** **265–67**
Messageries du Livre, **IV** 614
Messerschmitt-Bölkow-Blohm GmbH., I 41–42, 46, 51–52, 55, **73–75**, 111; **II** 242; **III** 539; **11** 267; **24** 86
Messner, Vetere, Berger, Carey, Schmetterer, **13** 204
Mesta Machine Co., **22** 415
Mestek, Inc., 10 411–13
Met Food Corp. *See* White Rose Food Corp.
Met-Mex Penoles. *See* Industrias Penoles, S.A. de C.V.
META Group, Inc., **37** 147
Metabio-Joullie, **III** 47
Metaframe Corp., **25** 312
Metal Box plc, I 604–06; **20** 108. *See also* Novar plc.
Metal-Cal. *See* Avery Dennison Corporation.

Metal Casting Technology, Inc., **23** 267, 269
Metal Closures, **I** 615
Metal Industries, **I** 531–32
Metal Manufactures, **III** 433–34
Metal Office Furniture Company, **7** 493
Metales y Contactos, **29** 461–62
Metaleurop S.A., IV 108–09; **21 368–71**
MetalExchange, **26** 530
Metall Mining Corp., **IV** 141; **27** 456
Metallgesellschaft AG, IV 17, **139–42**, 229; **16 361–66 (upd.)**
MetalOptics Inc., **19** 212
MetalPro, Inc., **IV** 168
Metals and Controls Corp., **II** 113
Metals Exploration, **IV** 82
Metalurgica Mexicana Penoles, S.A. *See* Industrias Penoles, S.A. de C.V.
Metaphase Technology, Inc., **10** 257
Metatec International, Inc., 47 245–48
Metcalf & Eddy Companies, Inc., **6** 143, 441; **32** 52
Meteor Film Productions, **23** 391
Meteor Industries Inc., 33 295–97
Methane Development Corporation, **6** 457
Methanex Corporation, 12 365; **19** 155–56; **40 316–19**
Methode Electronics, Inc., 13 344–46
Metinox Steel Ltd., **IV** 203
MetLife General Insurance Agency, **III** 293; **45** 294
MetLife HealthCare, **36** 366
MetMor Financial, Inc., **III** 293
Meto AG, **39** 79
MetPath, Inc., **III** 684; **26** 390
Metra Steel, **19** 381
Metrastock Ltd., **34** 5
Metric Constructors, Inc., **16** 286
Metric Systems Corporation, **18** 513; **44** 420
Metris Companies, **25** 41
Metro AG, **23** 311
Metro Distributors Inc., **14** 545
Metro Drug Corporation, **II** 649–50; **18** 181
Metro Glass, **II** 533
Metro-Goldwyn-Mayer Inc., 25 173, 253, **326–30 (upd.)**; **33**
Metro Holding AG, **38** 266
Metro Information Services, Inc., 36 **332–34**
Metro International SA, **36** 335
Metro-Mark Integrated Systems Inc., **11** 469
Metro-North Commuter Railroad Company, **35** 292
Metro Pacific, **18** 180, 182
Metro-Richelieu Inc., **II** 653
Metro Southwest Construction. *See* CRSS Inc.
Metro Support Services, Inc., **48** 171
Metro Vermögensverwaltung GmbH & Co. of Dusseldorf, **V** 104
Metro-Verwegensverwaltung, **II** 257
Metrocall, Inc., 18 77; **39** 25; **41 265–68**
Metrol Security Services, Inc., **32** 373
Metroland Printing, Publishing and Distributing Ltd., **29** 471
Metromail Corp., **IV** 661; **18** 170; **38** 370
Metromedia Companies, II 171; **6** 33, 168–69; **7** 91, **335–37**; **14 298–300**
Metropolitan Accident Co., **III** 228
Metropolitan Bank, **II** 221, 318; **III** 239; **IV** 644; **17** 323

Metropolitan Baseball Club Inc., 39 272–75

Metropolitan Broadcasting Corporation, **7** 335

Metropolitan Clothing Co., **19** 362

Metropolitan Distributors, **9** 283

Metropolitan District Railway Company, **6** 406

Metropolitan Edison Company, **27** 182

Metropolitan Estate and Property Corp. Ltd., **IV** 710–11

Metropolitan Financial Corporation, 12 165; **13** 347–49

Metropolitan Furniture Leasing, **14** 4

Metropolitan Gas Light Co., **6** 455

Metropolitan Housing Corp. Ltd., **IV** 710

Metropolitan Life Insurance Company, II 679; **III** 265–66, 272, **290–94**, 313, 329, 337, 339–40, 706; **IV** 283; **6** 256; **8** 326–27; **11** 482; **22** 266; **25** 300; **42** 194; **45** 411

Metropolitan National Bank, **II** 284

Metropolitan Opera Association, Inc., 40 320–23

Metropolitan Petroleum Corp., **IV** 180–81; **19** 319

Metropolitan Railway, **6** 407

Metropolitan Railways Surplus Lands Co., **IV** 711

Metropolitan Reference Laboratories Inc., **26** 391

Metropolitan Tobacco Co., **15** 138

Metropolitan Transportation Authority, 35 290–92

Metropolitan Vickers, **III** 670

METSA, Inc., **15** 363

Metsä-Serla Oy, IV 314–16, 318, 350

Metso Corporation, 30 321–25 (upd.)

Mettler-Toledo International Inc., 30 326–28

Mettler United States Inc., **9** 441

Metwest, **26** 391

Metz Baking Company, **36** 164

Metzdorf Advertising Agency, **30** 80

Metzeler Kautschuk, **15** 354

Mexican Eagle Oil Co., **IV** 365, 531

Mexican Metal Co. See Industrias Penoles, S.A. de C.V.

Mexican Original Products, Inc., **II** 585; **14** 515

Mexican Restaurants, Inc., 41 269–71

Mexofina, S.A. de C.V., **IV** 401

Meyer and Charlton, **IV** 90

Meyer Brothers Drug Company, **16** 212

Meyer Corporation, **27** 288

Meyerland Company, **19** 366

Meyers and Co., **III** 9

Meyers & Muldoon, **6** 40

Meyers Motor Supply, **26** 347

Meyers Parking, **18** 104

Meyr Melnhof Karton AG, **41** 325–27

Meyrin, **I** 122

MFI, **II** 612

MFS Communications Company, Inc., 11 301–03; **14** 253; **27** 301, 307

MG&E. See Madison Gas & Electric.

MG Holdings. See Mayflower Group Inc.

MG Ltd., **IV** 141

MGD Graphics Systems. See Goss Holdings, Inc.

MGIC Investment Corp., **45** 320

MGM. See McKesson General Medical.

MGM Grand Inc., III 431; **6** 210; **17** 316–19; **18** 336–37

MGM Mirage. See Mirage Resorts, Incorporated.

MGM/UA Communications Company, I 286, 487; **II** 103, 135, **146–50**, 155, 161, 167, 169, 174–75, 408; **IV** 676; **6** 172–73; **12** 73, 316, 323, 455; **15** 84; **17** 316. See also Metro-Goldwyn-Mayer Inc.

MGN. See Mirror Group Newspapers Ltd.

MH Alshaya Group, **28** 96

mh Bausparkasse AG, **III** 377

MH Media Monitoring Limited, **26** 270

MHI Group, Inc., **13** 356; **16** 344

MHS Holding Corp., **26** 101

MHT. See Manufacturers Hanover Trust Co.

MI. See Masco Corporation.

Miami Computer Supply Corporation. See MCSi, Inc.

Miami Power Corporation, **6** 466

Miami Subs Corp., **29** 342, 344

Micamold Electronics Manufacturing Corporation, **10** 319

Mich-Wis. See Michigan Wisconsin Pipe Line.

Michael Anthony Jewelers, Inc., 24 334–36

Michael Baker Corp., 14 333–35

MICHAEL Business Systems Plc, **10** 257

Michael Foods, Inc., 25 331–34; **39** 319–321

Michael Joseph, **IV** 659

Michael Page International plc, 45 272–74

Michael Reese Health Plan Inc., **III** 82

Michael's Fair-Mart Food Stores, Inc., **19** 479

Michaels Stores, Inc., 17 320–22, 360; **25** 368

MichCon. See MCN Corporation.

Michelin, **III** 697; **7** 36–37; **8** 74; **11** 158, 473; **20** 261–62; **21** 72, 74; **28** 372. See also Compagnie Générale des Établissements Michelin.

Michelin et Compagnie, **V** 236

Michiana Merchandising, **III** 10

Michie Co., **IV** 312; **19** 268; **33** 264–65

Michigan Automotive Compressor, Inc., **III** 593, 638–39

Michigan Automotive Research Corporation, **23** 183

Michigan Bell Telephone Co., 14 336–38; **18** 30

Michigan Carpet Sweeper Company, **9** 70

Michigan Consolidated Gas Company. See MCN Corporation.

Michigan Fruit Canners, **II** 571

Michigan General, **II** 408

Michigan International Speedway, **V** 494

Michigan Livestock Exchange, **36** 442

Michigan Motor Freight Lines, **14** 567

Michigan National Corporation, 11 304–06; **18** 517

Michigan Oil Company, **18** 494

Michigan Packaging Company, **15** 188

Michigan Plating and Stamping Co., **I** 451

Michigan Radiator & Iron Co., **III** 663

Michigan Shoe Makers. See Wolverine World Wide Inc.

Michigan Spring Company, **17** 106

Michigan State Life Insurance Co., **III** 274

Michigan Steel Corporation, **12** 352

Michigan Tag Company, **9** 72

Michigan Wisconsin Pipe Line, **39** 260

Mick's Inc., **30** 329

Mickey Shorr Mobile Electronics, **10** 9–11

Micro-Circuit, Inc., **III** 645

Micro Contract Manufacturing Inc., **44** 441

Micro D, Inc., **11** 194

Micro Decisionware, Inc., **10** 506

Micro Focus Inc., **27** 491

Micro Magic, Inc., **43** 254

Micro Peripherals, Inc., **18** 138

Micro-Power Corp., **III** 643

Micro Power Systems Inc., **14** 183

Micro Switch, **14** 284

Micro/Vest, **13** 175

Micro Warehouse, Inc., 16 371–73

MicroAge, Inc., 16 367–70; **29** 414

Microamerica, **12** 334

Microban Products Company, **27** 288

MicroBilt Corporation, **11** 112

Microcom, Inc., **26** 93

MicroComputer Accessories, **III** 614

Microcomputer Asset Management Services, **9** 168

Microcomputer Systems, **22** 389

Microdot Inc., I 440; **8** 365–68, 545

Microfal, **I** 341

Microform International Marketing Corp., **IV** 642; **7** 312

Microfral, **14** 216

MicroFridge, **44** 273

Micromass Ltd., **43** 455

Micromedex, **19** 268

Micron Technology, Inc., III 113; **11** 307–09; **29** 323–26 (upd.)

Micropolis Corp., **10** 403, 458, 463

MicroPro International Corp., **10** 556. See also The Learning Company Inc.

Microprocessor Systems, **13** 235

Microprose Inc., **24** 538

Micros Systems, Inc., 18 335–38

Microseal Corp., **I** 341

Microsensor Systems Inc., **43** 366

Microsoft Corporation, III 116; **6** 219–20, 224, 227, 231, 235, 254–56, **257–60**, 269–71; **9** 81, 140, 171, 195, 472; **10** 22, 34, 57, 87, 119, 237–38, 362–63, 408, 477, 484, 504, 557–58; **11** 59, 77–78, 306, 519–20; **12** 180, 335; **13** 115, 128, 147, 482, 509; **14** 262–64, 318; **15** 132–33, 321, 371, 483, 492, 511; **16** 4, 94, 367, 392, 394, 444; **18** 24, 64, 66, 306–7, 345, 349, 367, 541, 543; **19** 310; **20** 237; **21** 86; **24** 120, 233, 236, 371; **25** 21, 32, 34, 96, 117, 119, 184, 298–301, 498–99, 509; **26** 17, 294–95, 441, 520; **27** 319–23 (upd.), 448, 517; **28** 245, 301; **29** 65, 439; **30** 391, 450; **33** 115–16, 210; **34** 443, 445, 513; **36** 384; **37** 383; **38** 71, 416; **41** 53–54; **42** 424; **43** 240; **44** 97; **45** 200–02; **47** 419–21

Microsoft Network, **38** 270–71

Microtek, **22** 413

Microtel Limited, **6** 309–10

Microware Surgical Instruments Corp., **IV** 137

Microwave Communications, Inc., **V** 302; **27** 302

Mid-America Capital Resources, Inc., **6** 508

Mid-America Dairymen, Inc., II 536; **7** 338–40; **11** 24; **21** 342; **22** 95; **26** 448

Mid-America Industries, **III** 495

Mid-America Interpool Network, **6** 506, 602

Mid-America Packaging, Inc., **8** 203
Mid-America Tag & Label, **8** 360
Mid Bus Inc., **33** 107
Mid-Central Fish and Frozen Foods Inc., **II** 675
Mid-Continent Area Power Planner, **V** 672
Mid-Continent Computer Services, **11** 111
Mid-Continent Life Insurance Co., **23** 200
Mid-Continent Telephone Corporation. *See* Alltel Corporation.
Mid-Georgia Gas Company, **6** 448
Mid-Illinois Gas Co., **6** 529
Mid-Pacific Airlines, **9** 271; **24** 21–22
Mid-Packaging Group Inc., **19** 78
Mid-South Towing, **6** 583
Mid-States Development, Inc., **18** 405
Mid-Texas Communications Systems, **6** 313
Mid-Valley Dairy, **14** 397
Mid-West Drive-In Theatres Inc., **I** 245
Mid-West Paper Ltd., **IV** 286
MidAmerican Communications Corporation, **8** 311
Midas International Corporation, **I** 457–58; **10** 414–15, 554; **24** 337
MIDCO, **III** 340
MidCon, **IV** 481; **25** 363
Middle East Broadcasting Centre, Ltd., **25** 506, 508
Middle East Tube Co. Ltd., **25** 266
Middle South Utilities. *See* Entergy Corporation.
Middle West Corporation, **6** 469–70
Middle West Utilities Company, **V** 583–84; **6** 555–56, 604–05; **14** 227; **21** 468–69
Middle Wisconsin Power, **6** 604
Middleburg Steel and Alloys Group, **I** 423
The Middleby Corporation, **22** 352–55
Middlesex Bank, **II** 334
Middlesex Water Company, **45** 275–78
Middleton Aerospace, **48** 275
Middleton Packaging, **12** 377
Middleton's Starch Works, **II** 566
Middletown Manufacturing Co., Inc., **16** 321
Middletown National Bank, **13** 467
Midhurst Corp., **IV** 658
Midial, **II** 478
Midland Bank plc, **II** 208, 236, 279, 295, 298, **318–20**, 334, 383; **9** 505; **12** 257; **14** 169; **17 323–26 (upd.)**; **19** 198; **26** 202; **33** 395
Midland Brick, **14** 250
Midland Cooperative, **II** 536
Midland Counties Dairies, **II** 587
Midland Electric Coal Co., **IV** 170
Midland Enterprises Inc., **6** 486–88
Midland Gravel Co., **III** 670
Midland Independent Newspaper plc, **23** 351
Midland Industrial Finishes Co., **I** 321
Midland Insurance, **I** 473
Midland International, **8** 56–57
Midland Investment Co., **II** 7
Midland Linseed Products Co., **I** 419
Midland National Bank, **11** 130
Midland Railway Co., **II** 306
Midland-Ross Corporation, **14** 369
Midland Southwest Corp., **8** 347
Midland Steel Products Co., **13** 305–06
Midland United, **6** 556; **25** 89
Midland Utilities Company, **6** 532
Midlands Electricity, **13** 485

Midlands Energy Co., **IV** 83; **7** 188
Midlantic Corp., **13** 411
Midlantic Hotels Ltd., **41** 83
Midrange Performance Group, **12** 149
Midrex Corp., **IV** 130
Midvale Steel and Ordnance Co., **IV** 35, 114; **7** 48
Midway Airlines Corporation, **6** 105, 120–21; **33 301–03**
Midway Games, Inc., **25 335–38**
Midway Manufacturing Company, **III** 430; **15** 539
Midwest Agri-Commodities Company, **11** 15; **32** 29
Midwest Air Charter, **6** 345
Midwest Biscuit Company, **14** 306
Midwest Com of Indiana, Inc., **11** 112
Midwest Dairy Products, **II** 661
Midwest Express Holdings, Inc., **35 293–95**; **43** 258
Midwest Federal Savings & Loan Association, **11** 162–63
Midwest Financial Group, Inc., **8** 188
Midwest Foundry Co., **IV** 137
Midwest Grain Products, Inc., **49 261–63**
Midwest Manufacturing Co., **12** 296
Midwest Realty Exchange, Inc., **21** 257
Midwest Refining Co., **IV** 368
Midwest Resources Inc., **6 523–25**
Midwest Staffing Systems, **27** 21
Midwest Steel Corporation, **13** 157
Midwest Synthetics, **8** 553
Midwinter, **12** 529
Miele & Cie., **III** 418
MIG Realty Advisors, Inc., **25** 23, 25
Miguel Galas S.A., **17** 268
MIH Limited, **31 329–32**
Mikasa, Inc., **28 268–70**
Mike-Sell's Inc., **15 298–300**
Mikemitch Realty Corp., **16** 36
Mikko, **II** 70
Mikko Kaloinen Oy, **IV** 349
Mikohn Gaming Corporation, **39 276–79**
Mikon, Ltd., **13** 345
Milac, **27** 259
Milan A.C., S.p.A., **44** 387
Milani Foods, **II** 556; **36** 24
Milbank Insurance Co., **III** 350
Milbank, Tweed, Hadley & McCloy, **27 324–27**
Milbank, Tweed, Hope & Webb, **II** 471
Milcor Steel Co., **IV** 114
Miles Druce & Co., **III** 494
Miles Inc., **22** 148
Miles Kimball Co., **9** 393
Miles Laboratories, **I** 310, **653–55**, 674, 678; **6** 50; **13** 76; **14** 558
Miles Redfern, **I** 429
Milgo Electronic Corp., **II** 83; **11** 408
Milgram Food Stores Inc., **II** 682
Milgray Electronics Inc., **19** 311; **47** 41
Milk Producers, Inc., **11** 24
Milk Specialties Co., **12** 199
Mill-Power Supply Company, **27** 129–30
Millbrook Press Inc., **IV** 616
Millennium Chemicals Inc., **30** 231; **45** 252, 254
Millennium Pharmaceuticals, Inc., **47 249–52**
Miller Brewing Company, **I** 218–19, 236–37, 254–55, 257–58, **269–70**, 283, 290–91, 548; **10** 100; **11** 421; **12 337–39 (upd.)**, 372; **13** 10, 258; **15** 429; **17** 256; **18** 70, 72, 418, 499, 501; **21**

230; **22** 199, 422; **26** 303, 306; **27** 374; **28** 209–10; **34** 36–37; **36** 12–15; **44** 342
Miller Chemical & Fertilizer Corp., **I** 412
Miller Companies, **17** 182
Miller Container Corporation, **8** 102
Miller Freeman, Inc., **IV** 687; **27** 362; **28** 501, 504
Miller Group Ltd., **22** 282
Miller Industries, Inc., **26 293–95**
Miller, Mason and Dickenson, **III** 204–05
Miller, Tabak, Hirsch & Co., **13** 394; **28** 164
Millet, **39** 250
Millet's Leisure, **V** 177–78
Millicom, **11** 547; **18** 254
Milliken & Co., **V 366–68**; **8** 270–71; **17 327–30 (upd.)**; **29** 246
Milliken, Tomlinson Co., **II** 682
Millipore Corporation, **9** 396; **23** 284; **25 339–43**; **43** 454
Mills Clothing, Inc. *See* The Buckle, Inc.
Millstone Point Company, **V** 668–69
Millville Electric Light Company, **6** 449
Millway Foods, **25** 85
Milne & Craighead, **48** 113
Milne Fruit Products, Inc., **25** 366
Milner, **III** 98
Milnot Company, **46 289–91**
Milsco Manufacturing Co., **23** 299, 300
Milton Bradley Company, **III 504–06**; **16** 267; **17** 105; **21 372–75**; **25** 380; **43** 229, 232
Milton Light & Power Company, **12** 45
Milton Roy Co., **8** 135
Milupa S.A., **37** 341
Milwaukee Brewers Baseball Club, **37 247–49**
Milwaukee Cheese Co. Inc., **25** 517
Milwaukee Electric Manufacturing Co., **III** 534
Milwaukee Electric Railway and Light Company, **6** 601–02, 604–05
Milwaukee Electric Tool, **28** 40
Milwaukee Insurance Co., **III** 242
Milwaukee Mutual Fire Insurance Co., **III** 321
Minatome, **IV** 560
Mindpearl, **48** 381
Mindport, **31** 329
Mindset Corp., **42** 424–25
Mindspring Enterprises, Inc., **36** 168
Mine Safety Appliances Company, **31 333–35**
Minemet Recherche, **IV** 108
The Miner Group International, **22 356–58**
Mineral Point Public Service Company, **6** 604
Minerales y Metales, S.A. *See* Industrias Penoles, S.A. de C.V.
Minerals & Chemicals Philipp, **IV** 79–80
Minerals & Metals Trading Corporation of India Ltd., **IV 143–44**
Minerals and Resources Corporation Limited, **IV** 23; **13** 502. *See also* Minorco.
Minerals Technologies Inc., **11 310–12**
Minerec Corporation, **9** 363
Minerva, **III** 359
Minerve, **6** 208
Mines et Usines du Nord et de l'Est, **IV** 226
Minet Group, **III** 357; **22** 494–95

Mini Stop, **V** 97
Mining and Technical Services, **IV** 67
Mining Corp. of Canada Ltd., **IV** 164
Mining Development Corp., **IV** 239–40
Mining Trust Ltd., **IV** 32
MiniScribe, Inc., **6** 230; **10** 404
Minister of Finance Inc., **IV** 519
Minitel, **21** 233
Minivator Ltd., **11** 486
Minneapolis General Electric of Minnesota, **V** 670
Minneapolis Heat Regulator Co., **II** 40–41; **12** 246
Minneapolis-Honeywell Regulator Co., **II** 40–41, 86; **8** 21; **12** 247; **22** 427
Minneapolis Millers Association, **10** 322
Minneapolis Steel and Machinery Company, **21** 502
Minnesota Brewing Company. *See* MBC Holding Company.
Minnesota Cooperative Creamery Association, Inc., **II** 535; **21** 340
Minnesota Linseed Oil Co., **8** 552
Minnesota Mining & Manufacturing Company, **I** 28, 387, **499–501**; **II** 39; **III** 476, 487, 549; **IV** 251, 253–54; **6** 231; **7** 162; **8** 35, **369–71 (upd.)**; **11** 494; **13** 326; **17** 29–30; **22** 427; **25** 96, 372; **26 296–99 (upd.)**
Minnesota Paints, **8** 552–53
Minnesota Power & Light Company, **11 313–16**
Minnesota Power, Inc., **34 286–91 (upd.)**
Minnesota Sugar Company, **11** 13
Minnesota Valley Canning Co., **I** 22
Minnetonka Corp., **II** 590; **III** 25; **22** 122–23
Minntech Corporation, **22 359–61**
Minn-Dak Farmers Cooperative, **32** 29
Minolta Camera Co., Ltd., **III 574–76**, 583–84
Minolta Co., Ltd., **18** 93, 186, **339–42 (upd.)**; **43 281–85 (upd.)**
Minorco, **III** 503; **IV** 67–68, 84, 97; **16** 28, 293
Minstar Inc., **11** 397; **15** 49; **45** 174
Minton China, **38** 401
The Minute Maid Company, **I** 234; **10** 227; **28 271–74**, 473; **32** 116
Minute Tapioca, **II** 531
Minuteman International Inc., **46 292–95**
Minyard Food Stores, Inc., **33 304–07**
Mippon Paper, **21** 546
MIPS Computer Systems, **II** 45; **11** 491
Miracle Food Mart, **16** 247, 249–50
Miracle-Gro Products, Inc., **22** 474
Miraflores Designs Inc., **18** 216
Mirage Resorts, Incorporated, **6 209–12**; **15** 238; **28 275–79 (upd.)**; **29** 127; **43** 82
Miramar Hotel & Investment Co., **IV** 717; **38** 318
Mirant, **39** 54, 57
Mircali Asset Management, **III** 340
Mircor Inc., **12** 413
Mirrlees Blackstone, **III** 509
Mirror Group Newspapers plc, **IV** 641; **7** 244, 312, **341–43**; **23 348–51 (upd.)**; **49** 408
Mirror Printing and Binding House, **IV** 677
Misceramic Tile, Inc., **14** 42
Misr Airwork. *See* AirEgypt.
Misr Bank of Cairo, **27** 132

Misrair. *See* AirEgypt.
Miss Erika, Inc., **27** 346, 348
Miss Selfridge, **V** 177–78
Misset Publishers, **IV** 611
Mission Energy Company, **V** 715
Mission First Financial, **V** 715
Mission Group, **V** 715, 717
Mission Insurance Co., **III** 192
Mission Jewelers, **30** 408
Mississippi Chemical Corporation, **8** 183; **IV** 367; **27** 316; **39 280–83**
Mississippi Drug, **III** 10
Mississippi Gas Company, **6** 577
Mississippi Power & Light, **V** 619
Mississippi Power Company, **38** 446–47
Mississippi River Corporation, **10** 44
Mississippi River Recycling, **31** 47, 49
Missoula Bancshares, Inc., **35** 198–99
Missouri Book Co., **10** 136
Missouri Fur Company, **25** 220
Missouri Gaming Company, **21** 39
Missouri Gas & Electric Service Company, **6** 593
Missouri-Kansas-Texas Railroad, **I** 472; **IV** 458
Missouri Pacific Railroad, **10** 43–44
Missouri Public Service Company. *See* UtiliCorp United Inc.
Missouri Utilities Company, **6** 580
Mist Assist, Inc. *See* Ballard Medical Products.
Mistik Beverages, **18** 71
Mistral Plastics Pty Ltd., **IV** 295; **19** 225
Misys PLC, **45 279–81**; **46 296–99**
Mitchel & King Skates Ltd., **17** 244
Mitchell Construction, **III** 753
Mitchell Energy and Development Corporation, **7 344–46**
Mitchell Home Savings and Loan, **13** 347
Mitchell Hutchins, Inc., **II** 445; **22** 405–06
Mitchell International, **8** 526
Mitchells & Butler, **I** 223
Mitchum Co., **III** 55
Mitchum, Jones & Templeton, **II** 445; **22** 405
MiTek Industries Inc., **IV** 259
MiTek Wood Products, **IV** 305
Mitel Corporation, **15** 131–32; **18 343–46**
MitNer Group, **7** 377
MITRE Corporation, **26 300–02**
Mitre Sport U.K., **17** 204–05
MITROPA AG, **37 250–53**
Mitsubishi Aircraft Co., **III** 578; **7** 348; **9** 349; **11** 164
Mitsubishi Bank, Ltd., **II** 57, 273–74, 276, **321–22**, 323, 392, 459; **III** 289, 577–78; **7** 348; **15** 41; **16** 496, 498. *See also* Bank of Tokyo-Mitsubishi Ltd.
Mitsubishi Chemical Industries Ltd., **I** 319, **363–64**, 398; **II** 57; **III** 666, 760; **11** 207
Mitsubishi Corporation, **I** 261, 431–32, 492, **502–04**, 505–06, 510, 515, 519–20; **II** 57, 59, 101, 118, 224, 292, 321–25, 374; **III** 577–78; **IV** 285, 518, 713; **6** 499; **7** 82, 233, 590; **9** 294; **12 340–43 (upd.)**; **17** 349, 556; **24** 325, 359; **27** 511
Mitsubishi Electric Corporation, **II** 53, **57–59**, 68, 73, 94, 122; **III** 577, 586; **7** 347, 394; **18** 18; **23** 52–53; **43** 15; **44 283–87 (upd.)**

Mitsubishi Estate Company, Limited, **IV 713–14**
Mitsubishi Foods, **24** 114
Mitsubishi Group, **V** 481–82; **7** 377; **21** 390
Mitsubishi Heavy Industries, Ltd., **II** 57, 75, 323, 440; **III** 452–53, 487, 532, 538, **577–79**, 685, 713; **IV** 184, 713; **7 347–50 (upd.)**; **8** 51; **9** 349–50; **10** 33; **13** 507; **15** 92; **24** 359; **40 324–28 (upd.)**
Mitsubishi International Corp., **16** 462
Mitsubishi Kasei Corp., **III** 47–48, 477; **8** 343; **14** 535
Mitsubishi Kasei Industry Co. Ltd., **IV** 476
Mitsubishi Kasei Vinyl Company, **49** 5
Mitsubishi Marine, **III** 385
Mitsubishi Materials Corporation, **III 712–13**; **IV** 554; **38** 463
Mitsubishi Motors Corporation, **III** 516–17, 578–79; **6** 28; **7** 219, 348–49; **8** 72, 374; **9** 349–51; **23 352–55 (upd.)**; **34** 128, 136; **40** 326
Mitsubishi Oil Co., Ltd., **IV 460–62**, 479, 492
Mitsubishi Paper Co., **III** 547
Mitsubishi Rayon Co. Ltd., **I** 330; **V 369–71**; **8** 153
Mitsubishi Sha Holdings, **IV** 554
Mitsubishi Shipbuilding Co. Ltd., **II** 57; **III** 513, 577–78; **7** 348; **9** 349
Mitsubishi Shokai, **III** 577; **IV** 713; **7** 347
Mitsubishi Trading Co., **IV** 460
Mitsubishi Trust & Banking Corporation, **II 323–24**; **III** 289
Mitsui & Co., Ltd., **I** 282; **IV** 18, 224, 432, 654–55; **V** 142; **6** 346; **7** 303; **13** 356; **24** 325, 488–89; **27** 337; **28 280–85 (upd.)**
Mitsui Bank, Ltd., **II** 273–74, 291, **325–27**, 328, 372; **III** 295–97; **IV** 147, 320; **V** 142; **17** 556
Mitsui Bussan K.K., **I** 363, 431–32, 469, 492, 502–04, **505–08**, 510, 515, 519, 533; **II** 57, 66, 101, 224, 292, 323, 325–28, 392; **III** 295–96, 717–18; **IV** 147, 431; **9** 352–53. *See also* Mitsui & Co., Ltd.
Mitsui Gomei Kaisha, **IV** 715
Mitsui Group, **9** 352; **16** 84; **20** 310; **21** 72
Mitsui House Code, **V** 142
Mitsui Light Metal Processing Co., **III** 758
Mitsui Marine and Fire Insurance Company, Limited, **III** 209, **295–96**, 297
Mitsui Mining & Smelting Co., Ltd., **IV 145–46**, 147–48
Mitsui Mining Company, Limited, **IV** 145, **147–49**
Mitsui Mutual Life Insurance Company, **III 297–98**; **39 284–86 (upd.)**
Mitsui-no-Mori Co., Ltd., **IV** 716
Mitsui O.S.K. Lines, Ltd., **I** 520; **IV** 383; **V 473–76**; **6** 398; **26 278–80**
Mitsui Petrochemical Industries, Ltd., **I** 390, 516; **9 352–54**
Mitsui Real Estate Development Co., Ltd., **IV 715–16**
Mitsui Shipbuilding and Engineering Co., **III** 295, 513
Mitsui Toatsu, **9** 353–54
Mitsui Trading, **III** 636
Mitsui Trust & Banking Company, Ltd., **II** 328; **III** 297

Mitsukoshi Ltd., **I** 508; **V** 142–44; **14** 502; **41** 114; **47** 391
Mitsuya Foods Co., **I** 221
Mitteldeutsche Creditbank, **II** 256
Mitteldeutsche Energieversorgung AG, **V** 747
Mitteldeutsche Privatbank, **II** 256
Mitteldeutsche Stickstoff-Werke Ag, **IV** 229–30
Mitteldeutsches Kraftwerk, **IV** 229
Mity Enterprises, Inc., **38** 310–12
Mixconcrete (Holdings), **III** 729
Miyoshi Electrical Manufacturing Co., **II** 6
Mizuno Corporation, **25** 344–46
Mizushima Ethylene Co. Ltd., **IV** 476
MJB Coffee Co., **I** 28
MK-Ferguson Company, **7** 356
MLC Ltd., **IV** 709
MLH&P. *See* Montreal Light, Heat & Power Company.
MLT Vacations Inc., **30** 446
MMAR Group Inc., **19** 131
MMC Networks Inc., **38** 53, 55
MML Investors Services, **III** 286
MMS America Corp., **26** 317
MNC Financial. *See* MBNA Corporation.
MNC Financial Corp., **11** 447
MND Drilling, **7** 345
MNet, **11** 122
Mo och Domsjö AB, **IV** 315, **317–19**, 340
Moa Bay Mining Co., **IV** 82; **7** 186
Mobay, **I** 310–11; **13** 76
Mobil Corporation, **I** 30, 34, 403, 478; **II** 379; **IV** 93, 295, 363, 386, 401, 403, 406, 423, 428, 454, **463–65**, 466, 472–74, 486, 492, 504–05, 515, 517, 522, 531, 538–39, 545, 554–55, 564, 570–71; **V** 147–48; **6** 530; **7** 171, **351–54 (upd.)**; **8** 552–53; **9** 546; **10** 440; **12** 348; **16** 489; **17** 363, 415; **19** 140, 225, 297; **21 376–80 (upd.)**; **24** 496, 521; **25** 232, 445; **26** 369; **32** 175, 179, 181; **45** 50
Mobil Oil Australia, **24** 399
Mobile America Housing Corporation. *See* American Homestar Corporation.
Mobile and Ohio Railroad, **I** 456
Mobile Corporation, **25** 232
Mobile Mini, Inc., **21** 476
Mobile Telecommunications Technologies Corp., **V** 277–78; **6** 323; **16** 74; **18** 347–49
Mobile Telesystems, **48** 419
Mobilefone, Inc., **25** 108
MobileMedia Corp., **39** 23, 24
MobileStar Network Corp., **26** 429
Mobira, **II** 69; **17** 353
Mobley Chemical, **I** 342
Mobu Company, **6** 431
Mobujidosha Bus Company, **6** 431
MOÇACOR, **IV** 505
Mocatta and Goldsmid Ltd., **II** 357
Mochida Pharmaceutical Co. Ltd., **II** 553
Moctezuma Copper Co., **IV** 176–77
Modar, **17** 279
Mode 1 Communications, Inc., **48** 305
Modell's Shoppers World, **16** 35–36
Modell's Sporting Goods. *See* Henry Modell & Company Inc.
Modeluxe Linge Services SA, **45** 139–40
Modem Media, **23** 479
Modern Equipment Co., **I** 412
Modern Furniture Rentals Inc., **14** 4; **27** 163

Modern Handling Methods Ltd., **21** 499
Modern Maid Food Products, **II** 500
Modern Merchandising Inc., **19** 396
Modern Patterns and Plastics, **III** 641
Modern Times Group AB, **36** 335–38
Modernistic Industries Inc., **7** 589
Modine Manufacturing Company, **8** 372–75
Modis Professional Services. *See* MPS Group, Inc.
MoDo. *See* Mo och Domsjö AB.
MoDo Paper AB, **28** 446
Moen Incorporated, **12** 344–45
Moët-Hennessy, **I** 271–72; **10** 397–98; **23** 238, 240, 242. *See also* LVMH Moët Hennessy Louis Vuitton SA.
Mogen David. *See* The Wine Group, Inc.
Mogul Corp., **I** 321; **17** 287
The Mogul Metal Company. *See* Federal-Mogul Corporation.
Mohasco Corporation, **15** 102; **26** 100–01
Mohawk & Hudson Railroad, **9** 369
Mohawk Airlines, **I** 131; **6** 131
Mohawk Carpet Corp., **26** 101
Mohawk Industries, Inc., **19** 274–76; **31** 199
Mohawk Rubber Co. Ltd., **V** 256; **7** 116; **19** 508
Mohegan Tribal Gaming Authority, **37** 254–57
Mohr-Value Stores, **8** 555
Moilliet and Sons, **II** 306
Mojave Foods Corporation, **27** 299
Mojo MDA Group Ltd., **11** 50–51; **43** 412
Mokta. *See* Compagnie de Mokta.
MOL. *See* Mitsui O.S.K. Lines, Ltd.
Molecular Biosystems, **III** 61
Molex Incorporated, **II** 8; **11** 317–19; **14** 27
Moline National Bank, **III** 463; **21** 173
Molinera de México S.A. de C.V., **31** 236
Molinos de Puerto Rico, **II** 493
Molinos Nacionales C.A., **7** 242–43; **25** 241
Molins Co., **IV** 326
Molkerie-Zentrak Sud GmbH, **II** 575
Moll Plasticrafters, L.P., **17** 534
Molloy Manufacturing Co., **III** 569; **20** 360
Mölnlycke AB, **IV** 338–39; **28** 443–45; **36** 26
The Molson Companies Limited, **I** 273–75, 333; **II** 210; **7** 183–84; **12** 338; **13** 150, 199; **21** 320; **23** 404; **25** 279; **26** 303–07 (upd.); **36** 15
Molycorp, **IV** 571; **24** 521
Mon-Dak Chemical Inc., **16** 270
Mon-Valley Transportation Company, **11** 194
Mona Meyer McGrath & Gavin, **47** 97
MONACA. *See* Molinos Nacionales C.A.
Monaco Coach Corporation, **31** 336–38
Monadnock Paper Mills, Inc., **21** 381–84
Monarch Air Lines, **22** 219
Monarch Development Corporation, **38** 451–52
Monarch Food Ltd., **II** 571
Monarch Foods, **26** 503
Monarch Marking Systems, **III** 157
MonArk Boat, **III** 444; **22** 116
Mond Nickel Co., **IV** 110–11
Mondadori. *See* Arnoldo Monadori Editore S.p.A.
Mondex International, **18** 543

Mondi Foods BV, **41** 12
Mondi Paper Co., **IV** 22
Moneris Solutions Corp., **46** 55
Monet Jewelry, **II** 502–03; **9** 156–57; **10** 323–24
Money Access Service Corp., **11** 467
Monfort, Inc., **13** 350–52
Monheim Group, **II** 521
Monier Roof Tile, **III** 687, 735
Monis Wineries, **I** 288
Monitor Dynamics Inc., **24** 510
Monitor Group Inc., **33** 257
Monk-Austin Inc., **12** 110
Monmouth Pharmaceuticals Ltd., **16** 439
Monochem, **II** 472; **22** 93
Monogram Aerospace Fasteners, Inc., **11** 536
Monogram Models, **25** 312
Monogramme Confections, **6** 392
Monolithic Memories Inc., **6** 216; **16** 316–17, 549
Monon Corp., **13** 550
Monon Railroad, **I** 472
Monongahela Power, **38** 40
Monoprix, **V** 57–59
Monro Muffler Brake, Inc., **24** 337–40
Monroe Auto Equipment, **I** 527
Monroe Calculating Machine Co., **I** 476, 484
Monroe Cheese Co., **II** 471
Monroe Savings Bank, **11** 109
Monrovia Aviation Corp., **I** 544
Monsanto Company, **I** 310, 363, **365–67**, 402, 631, 666, 686, 688; **III** 741; **IV** 290, 367, 379, 401; **8** 398; **9** 318, **355–57 (upd.)**; 466; **12** 186; **13** 76, 225; **16** 460–62; **17** 131; **18** 112; **22** 107; **23** 170–71; **26** 108; **29 327–31 (upd.)**; **33** 135; **34** 179; **41** 306
Monsavon, **III** 46–47
Monsoon plc, **39** 287–89
Mont Blanc, **17** 5; **27** 487, 489
Montabert S.A., **15** 226
Montan TNT Pty Ltd., **27** 473
Montan Transport GmbH, **IV** 140
Montana-Dakota Utilities Co., **7** 322–23; **37** 281–82; **42** 249–50, 252
Montana Enterprises Inc., **I** 114
The Montana Power Company, **6** 566; **7** 322; **11** 320–22; **37** 280, 283; **44** 288–92 (upd.)
Montana Refining Company, **12** 240–41
Montana Resources, Inc., **IV** 34
Montaup Electric Co., **14** 125
MontBell America, Inc., **29** 279
Montecatini, **I** 368; **IV** 421, 470, 486
Montedison S.p.A., **I** 368–69; **IV** 413, 421–22, 454, 499; **14** 17; **22** 262; **24** 341–44 (upd.); **26** 367; **36** 185–86, 188
Montefibre, **I** 369
Montefina, **IV** 499; **26** 367
Montell N.V., **24** 343
Monterey Homes Corporation. *See* Meritage Corporation.
Monterey Mfg. Co., **12** 439
Monterey's Acquisition Corp., **41** 270
Monterey's Tex-Mex Cafes, **13** 473
Monterrey, Compania de Seguros sobre la Vida. *See* Seguros Monterrey.
Monterrey Group, **19** 10–11, 189
Montfort of Colorado, Inc., **II** 494
Montgomery Elevator Company, **27** 269
Montgomery Ward & Co., Incorporated, **III** 762; **IV** 465; **V** 145–48; **7** 353; **8**

509; **9** 210; **10** 10, 116, 172, 305, 391, 393, 490–91; **12** 48, 309, 315, 335, 430; **13** 165; **15** 330, 470; **17** 460; **18** 477; **20** 263, **374–79 (upd.)**, 433; **22** 535; **25** 144; **27** 428–30; **43** 292
Montiel Corporation, **17** 321
Montinex, **24** 270
Montreal Bank, **II** 210
Montreal Engineering Company, **6** 585
Montreal Light, Heat & Power Consolidated, **6** 501–02
Montreal Mining Co., **17** 357
Montres Rolex S.A., **8** 477; **13 353–55**; **19** 452; **34 292–95 (upd.)**
Montrose Capital, **36** 358
Montrose Chemical Company, **9** 118, 119
Montrose Chrome, **IV** 92
Monument Property Trust Ltd., **IV** 710
Monumental Corp., **III** 179
MONYCo., **III** 306
Moody's Investment Service, **IV** 605; **16** 506; **19** 133; **22** 189
Moog Inc., **13 356–58**
Moon-Hopkins Billing Machine, **III** 165
Mooney Chemicals, Inc. *See* OM Group, Inc.
Moonlight Mushrooms, Inc. *See* Sylvan, Inc.
Moonstone Mountaineering, Inc., **29** 181
Moore and McCormack Co. Inc., **19** 40
Moore Corporation Limited, **IV 644–46**, 679; **15** 473; **16** 450; **36** 508
Moore Gardner & Associates, **22** 88
The Moore Group Ltd., **20** 363
Moore-Handley, Inc., **IV** 345–46; **39 290–92**
Moore McCormack Resources Inc., **14** 455
Moore Medical Corp., **17 331–33**
Moorhouse, **II** 477
Moran Group Inc., **II** 682
Moran Health Care Group Ltd., **25** 455
MoRan Oil & Gas Co., **IV** 82–83
Moran Towing Corporation, Inc., **15 301–03**
Morana, Inc., **9** 290
Moreland and Watson, **IV** 208
Moretti-Harrah Marble Co., **III** 691
Morgan & Banks Limited, **30** 460
Morgan & Cie International S.A., **II** 431
Morgan Construction Company, **8** 448
Morgan Edwards, **II** 609
Morgan Engineering Co., **8** 545
Morgan Grampian Group, **IV** 687
Morgan Grenfell Group PLC, **II** 280, 329, **427–29**; **IV** 21, 712
The Morgan Group, Inc., **46 300–02**
Morgan Guaranty International Banking Corp., **II** 331; **9** 124
Morgan Guaranty Trust Co. of New York, **I** 26; **II** 208, 254, 262, 329–32, 339, 428, 431, 448; **III** 80; **10** 150
Morgan Guaranty Trust Company, **11** 421; **13** 49, 448; **14** 297; **25** 541; **30** 261
Morgan, Harjes & Co., **II** 329
Morgan, J.P. & Co. Inc. *See* J.P. Morgan & Co. Incorporated.
Morgan, Lewis & Bockius LLP, **29 332–34**
Morgan, Lewis, Githens & Ahn, Inc., **6** 410
Morgan Mitsubishi Development, **IV** 714
Morgan Schiff & Co., **29** 205

Morgan Stanley Dean Witter & Company, **33 311–14 (upd.)**; **38** 289, 291, 411
Morgan Stanley Group, Inc., **I** 34; **II** 211, 330, 403, 406–08, 422, 428, **430–32**, 441; **IV** 295, 447, 714; **9** 386; **11** 258; **12** 529; **16 374–78 (upd.)**; **18** 448–49; **20** 60, 363; **22** 404, 407; **25** 542; **30** 353–55; **34** 496; **36** 153
Morgan Yacht Corp., **II** 468
Morgan's Brewery, **I** 287
Mori Bank, **II** 291
Moria Informatique, **6** 229
Morino Associates, **10** 394
Morita & Co., **II** 103
Mormac Marine Group, **15** 302
Morning Star Technologies Inc., **24** 49
Morning Sun, Inc., **23** 66
Morris Air, **24** 455
Morris Communications Corporation, **36 339–42**
Morris Motors, **III** 256; **7** 459
Morris Travel Services L.L.C., **26 308–11**
Morrison Industries Ltd., **IV** 278; **19** 153
Morrison Knudsen Corporation, **IV** 55; **7 355–58**; **11** 401, 553; **28 286–90 (upd.)**; **33** 442. *See also* The Washington Companies.
Morrison Machine Products Inc., **25** 193
Morrison Restaurants Inc., **11 323–25**; **18** 464
Morse Chain Co., **III** 439; **14** 63
Morse Equalizing Spring Company, **14** 63
Morse Industrial, **14** 64
Morse Shoe Inc., **13 359–61**
Morss and White, **III** 643
Morstan Development Co., Inc., **II** 432
Mortgage & Trust Co., **II** 251
Mortgage Associates, **9** 229
Mortgage Insurance Co. of Canada, **II** 222
Mortgage Resources, Inc., **10** 91
Morton Foods, Inc., **II** 502; **10** 323; **27** 258
Morton International Inc., **9 358–59 (upd.)**, 500–01; **16** 436; **22** 505–06; **43** 319
Morton Thiokol Inc., **I** 325, **370–72**; **19** 508; **28** 253–54. *See also* Thiokol Corporation.
Morton's Restaurant Group, Inc., **28** 401; **30 329–31**
Mos Magnetics, **18** 140
MOS Technology, **7** 95
Mosby-Year Book, Inc., **IV** 678; **17** 486
Moseley, Hallgarten, Estabrook, and Weeden, **III** 389
Mosher Steel Company, **7** 540
Mosinee Paper Corporation, **15 304–06**
Moskatel's, Inc., **17** 321
Mosler Safe Co., **III** 664–65; **7** 144, 146; **22** 184
Moss-Rouse Company, **15** 412
Mossgas, **IV** 93
Mossimo, Inc., **27 328–30**
Mostek Corp., **I** 85; **II** 64; **11** 307–08; **13** 191; **20** 175; **29** 323
Mostjet Ltd. *See* British World Airlines Ltd.
Móstoles Industrial S.A., **26** 129
Mostra Importaciones S.A., **34** 38, 40
Motel 6 Corporation, **10** 13; **13 362–64**. *See also* Accor SA
Mother Karen's, **10** 216

Mother's Oats, **II** 558–59; **12** 409
Mothercare Stores, Inc., **16** 466
Mothercare UK Ltd., **17** 42–43, **334–36**
Mothers Work, Inc., **18 350–52**
Motif Inc., **22** 288
Motion Designs, **11** 486
Motion Factory, Inc., **38** 72
Motion Picture Association of America, **37** 353–54
Motion Picture Corporation of America, **25** 326, 329
Motiva Enterprises LLC, **41** 359, 395
MotivePower. *See* Wabtec Corporation.
The Motley Fool, Inc., **40 329–31**
Moto Photo, Inc., **45 282–84**
Moto-Truc Co., **13** 385
Motor Cargo Industries, Inc., **35 296–99**
Motor Club of America Insurance Company, **44** 354
Motor Coaches Industries International Inc., **36** 132
Motor Haulage Co., **IV** 181
Motor Parts Industries, Inc., **9** 363
Motor Transit Corp., **I** 448; **10** 72
Motor Wheel Corporation, **20** 261; **27** 202–04
Motorcar Parts & Accessories, Inc., **47 253–55**
Motoren-und-Turbinen-Union, **I** 151; **III** 563; **9** 418; **15** 142; **34** 128, 131, 133
Motoren-Werke Mannheim AG, **III** 544
Motorenfabrik Deutz AG, **III** 541
Motorenfabrik Oberursel, **III** 541
Motornetic Corp., **III** 590
Motorola, Inc., **I** 534; **II** 5, 34, 44–45, 56, **60–62**, 64; **III** 455; **6** 238; **7** 119, 494, 533; **8** 139; **9** 515; **10** 87, 365, 367, 431–33; **11** 45, 308, **326–29 (upd.)**, 381–82; **12** 136–37, 162; **13** 30, 356, 501; **17** 33, 193; **18** 18, 74, 76, 260, 382; **19** 391; **20** 8, 439; **21** 123; **22** 17, 19, 288, 542; **26** 431–32; **27** 20, 341–42, 344; **33** 47–48; **34 296–302 (upd.)**; **38** 188; **43** 15; **44** 97, 357, 359; **45** 346, 348; **47** 318, 320, 385; **48** 270, 272
Motown Records Company L.P., **II** 145; **22** 194; **23** 389, 391; **26 312–14**
Moulinex S.A., **22 362–65**
Mound Metalcraft. *See* Tonka Corporation.
Mount. *See also* Mt.
Mount Hood Credit Life Insurance Agency, **14** 529
Mount Isa Mines, **IV** 61
Mount Vernon Group, **8** 14
Mountain Fuel Supply Company. *See* Questar Corporation.
Mountain Fuel Supply Company, **6** 568–69
Mountain Pass Canning Co., **7** 429
Mountain Safety Research, **18** 445–46
Mountain State Telephone Company, **6** 300
Mountain States Mortgage Centers, Inc., **29 335–37**
Mountain States Power Company. *See* PacifiCorp.
Mountain States Telephone & Telegraph Co., **V** 341; **25** 495
Mountain States Wholesale, **II** 602; **30** 25
Mountain Valley Indemnity Co., **44** 356
Mountain West Bank, **35** 197
Mountleigh PLC, **16** 465
Mounts Wire Industries, **III** 673
Mountsorrel Granite Co., **III** 734

Mouvement des Caisses Desjardins, **48** 288–91

Movado Group, Inc., **28** 291–94

Movado-Zenith-Mondia Holding, **II** 124

Movie Gallery, Inc., **31** 339–41

Movie Star Inc., **17** 337–39

Movies To Go, Inc., **9** 74; **31** 57

Movil@ccess, S.A. de C.V., **39** 25, 194

Moving Co. Ltd., **V** 127

The Moving Picture Company, **15** 83

The Mowry Co., **23** 102

MP3.com, **43** 109

MPB Corporation, **8** 529, 531

MPI. *See* Michael Page International plc.

MPM, **III** 735

MPS Group, Inc., **49** 264–67

Mr. Bricolage S.A., **37** 258–60

Mr. Coffee, Inc., **14** 229–31; **15** 307–09; **17** 215; **27** 275; **39** 406

Mr. D's Food Centers, **12** 112

Mr. Donut, **21** 323

Mr. Gasket Inc., **11** 84; **15** 310–12

Mr. Gatti's, **15** 345

Mr. Goodbuys, **13** 545

Mr. How, **V** 191–92

Mr. M Food Stores, **7** 373

Mr. Maintenance, **25** 15

Mr. Payroll Corp., **20** 113

MRC Bearings, **III** 624

MRN Radio Network, **19** 223

Mrs. Baird's Bakeries, **29** 338–41

Mrs. Fields' Original Cookies, Inc., **27** 331–35

Mrs. Paul's Kitchens, **II** 480; **26** 57–58

Mrs. Smith's Frozen Foods, **II** 525; **13** 293–94; **35** 181

MS-Relais GmbH, **III** 710; **7** 302–03

MSAS Cargo International, **6** 415, 417

MSE Corporation, **33** 44

MSI Data Corp., **10** 523; **15** 482

M6. *See* Métropole Télévision.

MSL Industries, **10** 44

MSNBC, **28** 301

MSR. *See* Mountain Safety Research.

MSU. *See* Middle South Utilities.

Mt. *See also* Mount.

Mt. Beacon Insurance Co., **26** 486

Mt. Carmel Public Utility Company, **6** 506

Mt. Goldsworthy Mining Associates, **IV** 47

Mt. Lyell Investments, **III** 672–73

Mt. Olive Pickle Company, Inc., **44** 293–95

Mt. Summit Rural Telephone Company, **14** 258

Mt. Vernon Iron Works, **II** 14

MTC. *See* Management and Training Corporation.

MTC Pharmaceuticals, **II** 483

MTel. *See* Mobile Telecommunications Technologies Corp.

MTG. *See* Modern Times Group AB.

MTM Entertainment Inc., **13** 279, 281

MTS Inc., **37** 261–64

MTV, **31** 239

MTV Asia, **23** 390

MTVi Group, **37** 194

Muehlens KG, **48** 422

Mueller Co., **III** 645; **28** 485

Mueller Furniture Company, **8** 252; **39** 206

Mueller Industries, Inc., **7** 359–61

Mujirushi Ryohin, **V** 188

Mukluk Freight Lines, **6** 383

Mule Battery Manufacturing Co., **III** 643

Mule-Hide Products Co., **22** 15

Mülheimer Bergwerksvereins, **I** 542

Mullen Advertising, **13** 513

Mullens & Co., **14** 419

Multex Systems, **21** 70

Multi Restaurants, **II** 664

Multibank, Inc., **11** 281

Multicom Publishing Inc., **11** 294

Multilink, Inc., **27** 364–65

MultiMed, **11** 379

Multimedia Games, Inc., **41** 272–76

Multimedia, Inc., **IV** 591; **11** 330–32; **30** 217

Multimedia Security Services, Inc., **32** 374

Multiple Access Systems Corp., **III** 109

Multiple Properties, **I** 588

MultiScope Inc., **10** 508

Multitech International. *See* Acer Inc.

Multiview Cable, **24** 121

Münchener Rückversicherungs-Gesellschaft. *See* Munich Re.

Munford, Inc., **17** 499

Mungana Mines, **I** 438

Munich Re (Münchener Rückversicherungs-Gesellschaft Aktiengesellschaft in München), **II** 239; **III** 183–84, 202, 299–301, 400–01, 747; **35** 34, 37; **46** 303–07 **(upd.)**

Municipal Assistance Corp., **II** 448

Munising Paper Co., **III** 40; **13** 156; **16** 303; **43** 257

Munising Woodenware Company, **13** 156

Munksjö, **19** 227

Munksund, **IV** 338

Munsingwear, Inc., **22** 427; **25** 90; **27** 443, 445; **41** 291. *See also* PremiumWear, Inc.

Munson Transportation Inc., **18** 227

Munster and Leinster Bank Ltd., **16** 13

Mura Corporation, **23** 209

Murata, **37** 347

Murdock Madaus Schwabe, **26** 315–19, 470

Murfin Inc., **8** 360

Murmic, Inc., **9** 120

Murphey Favre, Inc., **17** 528, 530

Murphy Family Farms Inc., **7** 477; **21** 503; **22** 366–68; **46** 84

Murphy Oil Corporation, **7** 362–64; **32** 338–41 **(upd.)**

Murphy-Phoenix Company, **14** 122

Murray Bay Paper Co., **IV** 246; **25** 10

Murray Corp. of America, **III** 443

Murray Goulburn Snow, **II** 575

Murray Inc., **19** 383

Murrayfield, **IV** 696

Murtaugh Light & Power Company, **12** 265

Musashino Railway Company, **V** 510

Muscatine Journal, **11** 251

Muscocho Explorations Ltd., **IV** 76

Muse Air Corporation, **6** 120; **24** 454

Muse, Cordero, Chen, **41** 89

Music and Video Club, **24** 266, 270

Music-Appreciation Records, **13** 105

Music Corporation of America. *See* MCA Inc.

Music Go Round, **18** 207–09

Music Man, Inc., **16** 202; **43** 170

Music Plus, **9** 75

Musical America Publishing, Inc., **22** 441

Musician's Friend, **29** 221, 223

Musicland Stores Corporation, **9** 360–62; **11** 558; **19** 417; **37** 263; **38** 313–17 **(upd.)**

Musitek, **16** 202; **43** 170

Muskegon Gas Company. *See* MCN Corporation.

Musotte & Girard, **I** 553

Mutoh Industries, Ltd., **6** 247; **24** 234

Mutual Benefit Life Insurance Company, **III** 243, 302–04

Mutual Broadcasting System, **23** 509

Mutual Gaslight Company. *See* MCN Corporation.

Mutual Life Insurance Co. of the State of Wisconsin, **III** 321

Mutual Life Insurance Company of New York, **II** 331; **III** 247, 290, 305–07, 316, 321, 380

Mutual Marine Office Inc., **41** 284

Mutual Medical Aid and Accident Insurance Co., **III** 331

Mutual of Omaha, **III** 365; **25** 89–90; **27** 47

Mutual Oil Co., **IV** 399

Mutual Papers Co., **14** 522

Mutual Safety Insurance Co., **III** 305

Mutual Savings & Loan Association, **III** 215; **18** 60

Mutualité Générale, **III** 210

Mutuelle d'Orléans, **III** 210

Mutuelle de l'Ouest, **III** 211

Mutuelle Vie, **III** 210

Mutuelles Unies, **III** 211

Muzak, Inc., **7** 90–91; **18** 353–56; **35** 19–20

Muzzy-Lyon Company. *See* Federal-Mogul Corporation.

MVC. *See* Music and Video Club.

MVR Products Pte Limited, **47** 255

Mwinilunga Canneries Ltd., **IV** 241

MXL Industries, **13** 367

MY Holdings, **IV** 92

Myanmar Oil and Gas Enterprise, **IV** 519

MYCAL Group, **V** 154

Myco-Sci, Inc. *See* Sylvan, Inc.

Mycogen Corporation, **21** 385–87

Mycrom, **14** 36

Myer Emporium Ltd., **20** 156

Myers Industries, Inc., **19** 277–79

Mygind International, **8** 477

Mylan Laboratories Inc., **I** 656–57; **20** 380–82 **(upd.)**

Myllykoski Träsliperi AB, **IV** 347–48

Myokenya, **III** 757

Myrna Knitwear, Inc., **16** 231

Myson Group PLC, **III** 671

Mysore State Iron Works, **IV** 205

N.A. Otto & Cie., **III** 541

N.A. Woodworth, **III** 519; **22** 282

N. Boynton & Co., **16** 534

N.C. Cameron & Sons, Ltd., **11** 95

N.C. Monroe Construction Company, **14** 112

N.E.M., **23** 228

N.H. Geotech. *See* New Holland N.V.

N.K. Fairbank Co., **II** 497

N.L. Industries, **19** 212

N M Electronics, **II** 44

N M Rothschild & Sons Limited, **IV** 64, 712; **24** 267; **39** 293–95

N.M.U. Transport Ltd., **II** 569

N.R.F. Gallimard, **IV** 618

N. Shure Company, **15** 477

N.V. *see under first word of company name*
N.W. Ayer & Son, **I** 36; **II** 542
N.W. Ayer and Partners, **32** 140
N.Y.P. Holdings Inc., **12** 360
Na Pali, S.A. *See* Quiksilver, Inc.
Naamloze Vennootschap tot Exploitatie van het Café Krasnapolsky. *See* Grand Hotel Krasnapolsky N.V.
Nabisco, **24** 358
Nabisco Brands, Inc., II 475, 512, **542–44**; **7** 128, 365–67; **12** 167; **25** 366. *See also* RJR Nabisco.
Nabisco Foods Group, 7 365–68 (upd.); **9** 318; **14** 48. *See also* Kraft Foods Inc.
Nabisco Holdings Corporation, **25** 181; **42** 408; **44** 342
Nabisco Ltd., **24** 288
Nabors Industries, Inc., 9 363–65
Nacamar Internet Services, **48** 398
NACCO Industries, Inc., 7 369–71; **17** 213–15, 246, 248
Nacional de Drogas, S.A. de C.V., **39** 188
Nacional Financiera, **IV** 513
NACO Finance Corp., **33** 398
Nadler Sportswear. *See* Donnkenny, Inc.
Naegele Outdoor Advertising Inc., **36** 340
Naf Naf SA, 44 296–98
NAFI Corp. *See* Chris-Craft Industries, Inc.
Nagano Seiyu Ltd., **V** 188
Nagasaki Shipyard, **I** 502
Nagasakiya Co., Ltd., V 149–51
Nagasco, Inc., **18** 366
Nagase & Company, Ltd., 8 376–78
Nagase-Alfa, **III** 420
Nagel Meat Markets and Packing House, **II** 643
Nagoya Bank, **II** 373
Nagoya Electric Light Co., **IV** 62
NAI. *See* Natural Alternatives International, Inc. *and* Network Associates, Inc.
Naigai Tsushin Hakuhodo, **6** 29
Naikoku Tsu-un Kabushiki Kaisha, **V** 477
Naiman Co., **25** 449
Nairn Linoleum Co., **18** 116
Nakai Shoten Ltd., **IV** 292
Nakano Vinegar Co. Ltd., **26** 58
Nalco Chemical Corporation, I 373–75; **12 346–48 (upd.)**
Nalfloc, **I** 374
Nalge Co., **14** 479–80
NAM. *See* Nederlandse Aardolie Maatschappij.
Namco, **III** 431
Namibia Breweries Ltd., **33** 75
Namkwang Engineering & Construction Co. Ltd., **III** 749
NAMM. *See* North American Medical Management Company, Inc.
Nampack, **I** 423
Nan Ya Plastics Corp., **14** 197–98
NANA Regional Corporation, **7** 558
Nanfang South China Motor Corp., **34** 132
Nankai Kogyo, **IV** 225; **24** 489
Nansei Sekiyu, **IV** 432
Nantucket Allserve, Inc., 22 369–71
Nantucket Corporation, **6** 226
Nantucket Mills, **12** 285; **34** 240
Nanyo Bussan, **I** 493; **24** 326
NAPA. *See* National Automotive Parts Association.
NAPC. *See* North American Philips Corp.
Napier, **I** 194
NAPP Systems, Inc., **11** 253

Narmco Industries, **I** 544
NAS. *See* National Audubon Society.
NASA. *See* National Aeronautics and Space Administration.
NASCAR. *See* National Association for Stock Car Auto Racing.
NASDAQ, **37** 132
Nash DeCamp Company, **23** 356–57
Nash Finch Company, 8 379–81; **11** 43; **23 356–58 (upd.)**; **40** 80
Nash-Kelvinator Corp., **I** 135; **12** 158
Nash Motors Co., **I** 135; **8** 75
Nashaming Valley Information Processing, **III** 204
Nashua Corporation, 8 382–84
The Nashville Network, **11** 153
Nashville Speedway USA, Inc., **43** 139–41
Nassau Gas Light Co., **6** 455
Nassco Holdings Inc., **36** 79
NASTECH, **III** 590
Nasu Aluminium Manufacturing Co., **IV** 153
Nasu Nikon Co., Ltd., **48** 295
Nat Robbins, **37** 269–70
Natal Brewery Syndicate, **I** 287
Natco Corp., **I** 445
NaTec Ltd. *See* CRSS Inc.
Nathan's Famous, Inc., 29 342–44
National, **10** 419
National Acme Company. *See* Acme-Cleveland Corp.
National Advanced Systems, **II** 64–65
National Advertising Company, **27** 280
National Aeronautics and Space Administration, **II** 139; **6** 227–29, 327; **11** 201, 408; **12** 489; **37** 364–65
National Air Transport Co., **I** 128; **6** 128; **9** 416; **11** 427
National Airlines, **I** 97, 116; **6** 388; **21** 141; **25** 146
National Allied Publications. *See* DC Comics Inc.
National Aluminate Corp., **I** 373; **12** 346
National Aluminum Company, **11** 38
National American Corporation, **33** 399
National American Life Insurance Co. of California, **II** 181
National American Title Insurance Co., **II** 181
National Amusements Inc., 28 295–97
National Aniline & Chemical Coompany, **I** 414; **22** 29
National Association for Stock Car Auto Racing, 32 342–44
National Association of Securities Dealers, Inc., 10 416–18
National Audubon Society, 26 320–23
National Australia Bank, **III** 673
National Auto Credit, Inc., 16 379–81
National Automobile and Casualty Insurance Co., **III** 270
National Automotive Fibers, Inc. *See* Chris-Craft Industries, Inc.
National Automotive Parts Association, **26** 348
National Aviation, **I** 117
National Baby Shop, **V** 203
National Bancard Corporation, **11** 111–13
National Bancorp of Arizona, **12** 565
National Bank, **II** 312
National Bank for Cooperatives, **8** 489–90
National Bank für Deutschland, **II** 270
National Bank of Belgium, **II** 294

National Bank of Commerce, **II** 331; **9** 536; **11** 105–06; **13** 467
National Bank of Commerce Trust & Savings Association, **15** 161
National Bank of Detroit, **I** 165. *See also* NBD Bancorp, Inc.
National Bank of Egypt, **II** 355
National Bank of Greece, 41 277–79
The National Bank of Jacksonville, **9** 58
National Bank of New Zealand, **II** 308; **19** 155
National Bank of North America, **II** 334
National Bank of South Africa Ltd., **II** 236
National Bank of the City of New York, **II** 312
National Bank of Turkey, **IV** 557
National Bank of Washington, **13** 440
National BankAmericard Inc. *See* Visa International.
National Bankers Express Co., **II** 396; **10** 60
National Basketball Association, **12** 457
National Bell Telephone Company, **V** 259
National-Ben Franklin Insurance Co., **III** 242
National Benefit and Casualty Co., **III** 228
National Benefit Co., **III** 228
National Beverage Corp., 26 324–26
National Binding Company, **8** 382
National BioSystems, **47** 37
National Biscuit Co., **IV** 152; **22** 336. *See also* Nabisco.
National Bridge Company of Canada, Ltd., **8** 544
National Broach & Machine Co., **I** 481–82
National Broadcasting Company, Inc., II 30, 88–90, 129–33, **151–53**, 170, 173, 487, 543; **III** 188, 329; **IV** 596, 608, 652; **6** 157–59, **164–66 (upd.)**; **10** 173; **17** 149–50; **19** 201, 210; **21** 24; **23** 120; **28** 69, **298–301 (upd.)**; **30** 99; **32** 3; **33** 324; **34** 186; **42** 161, 163. *See also* General Electric Company.
National Building Society, **10** 6–7
National Cable & Manufacturing Co., **13** 369
National Cable Television Association, **18** 64
National Can Corp., I 601–02, **607–08**; **IV** 154; **13** 255
National Car Rental System, Inc., I 489; **II** 419–20, 445; **6** 348–49; **10** 373, **419–20**; **21** 284; **22** 406, 524; **24** 9; **25** 93, 143. *See also* Republic Industries, Inc.
National Carbon Co., Inc., **I** 400; **9** 516; **11** 402
National Carriers, **6** 413–14
National Cash Register Company. *See* NCR Corporation.
National Cement Co., **35** 419
National Cheerleaders Association, **15** 516–18
National Chemsearch Corp. *See* NCH Corporation.
National Child Care Centers, Inc., **II** 607
National City Bank, **9** 475
National City Bank of New York, **I** 337, 462; **II** 253–54; **III** 380; **IV** 81
National City Co., **II** 254; **9** 124
National City Corp., 9 475; **15 313–16**
National Cleaning Contractors, **II** 176
National Coal Board, **IV** 38–40
National Coal Development Corp., **IV** 48

National Comics Publications. *See* DC Comics Inc.

National Commercial Bank, **11** 108; **12** 422; **13** 476

National Components Industries, Inc., **13** 398

National Container Corp., **I** 609

National Convenience Stores Incorporated, 7 372–75; 20 140

National Cranberry Association. *See* Ocean Spray Cranberries, Inc.

National Credit Office, **IV** 604

National CSS, **IV** 605

National Dairy Products Corp., **II** 533; **7** 275; **14** 204

National Data Corporation, **24** 393

National Demographics & Lifestyles Inc., **10** 461

National Development Bank, **IV** 56

National Discount Brokers Group, Inc., 28 302–04

National Disinfectant Company. *See* NCH Corporation.

National Distillers and Chemical Corporation, I 226, **376–78; IV** 11; **8** 439–41; **9** 231; **10** 181; **30** 441

National Drive-In Grocery Corporation, **7** 372

National Drug Ltd., **II** 652

National Economic Research Associates, **III** 283

National Education Association, **9** 367

National Educational Corporation, **26** 95

National Educational Music Co. Ltd., 47 256–58

National Electric Company, **11** 388

National Electric Instruments Co., **IV** 78

National Electric Products Corp., **IV** 177

National Employers Life Assurance Co. Ltd., **13** 539

National Enquirer, **10** 287–88

National Envelope Corporation, 32 345–47

National Executive Service. *See* Carey International, Inc.

National Express Laboratories, Inc., **10** 107

National Family Opinion. *See* NFO Worldwide, Inc.

National Fence Manufacturing Co., Inc., **45** 327

National Fidelity Life Insurance Co., **10** 246

National Fidelity Life Insurance Co. of Kansas, **III** 194; **IV** 343

National Finance Corp., **IV** 22–23

National Fire & Marine Insurance Co., **III** 213–14; **42** 32

National Fire Insurance Co., **III** 229–30

National Football League, 12 457; **29 345–47; 37** 294

National Freight Corporation, **6** 412–13

National Fuel Gas Company, 6 526–28

National Gateway Telecom, **6** 326–27

National General Corp., **III** 190–91; **48** 7

National Geographic Society, 9 366–68; 30 332–35 (upd.); 42 115, 117

National Golf Properties, Inc. *See* American Golf Corporation

National Grape Co-operative Association, Inc., 20 383–85

National Greyhound Racing Club, **II** 142

National Grid Group plc, **11** 399–400; **12** 349; **13** 484; **45** 298–99; **47** 122

National Grocers of Ontario, **II** 631

National Guardian Corp., **18** 33

National Gypsum Company, 8 43; **10 421–24; 13** 169; **22** 48, 170; **25** 535

National Health Enterprises, **III** 87

National Health Laboratories Incorporated, 11 333–35. *See also* Laboratory Corporation of America Holdings.

National Hockey League, 35 300–03

National Home Centers, Inc., 44 299–301

National Hotel Co., **III** 91

National Housing Systems, Inc., **18** 27

National Hydrocarbon Corp., **IV** 543

National ICEE Corporation, **24** 242

National Import and Export Corp. Ltd., **IV** 240

National Indemnity Co., **III** 213–14; **42** 32–33

National India Rubber Company, **9** 228

National Industries, **I** 446

National Inking Appliance Company, **14** 52

National Instruments Corporation, 22 372–74

National Integrity Life Insurance, **III** 249

National Intergroup, Inc., IV 237, 574; **V 152–53; 12** 354; **16** 212; **26** 529. *See also* FoxMeyer Health Corporation.

National Iranian Oil Company, III 748; **IV** 370, 374, **466–68**, 484, 512, 535; **47** 342

National Key Company. *See* Cole National Corporation.

National Kinney Corp., **IV** 720; **9** 391

National Law Publishing Company, Inc., **32** 35

National Lead Co., **III** 681; **IV** 32; **21** 489

National Leisure Group, **47** 421

National Liability and Fire Insurance Co., **III** 214

National Liberty Corp., **III** 218–19

National Life and Accident Insurance Co., **III** 194

National Life Insurance Co., **III** 290

National Life Insurance Co. of Canada, **III** 243

National Living Centers, **13** 49

National Loss Control Service Corp., **III** 269

National Lumber Co. *See* National Home Centers, Inc.

National Magazine Company Limited, **19** 201

National Manufacturing Co., **III** 150; **6** 264; **13** 6

National Marine Service, **6** 530

National Market System, **9** 369

National Media Corporation, 27 336–40

National Medical Care, **22** 360

National Medical Enterprises, Inc., III 79, **87–88; 6** 188; **10** 252; **14** 233; **25** 307–08; **33** 185

National Minerals Development Corp., **IV** 143–44

National Mobility Corp., **30** 436

National Mortgage Agency of New Zealand Ltd., **IV** 278; **19** 153

National Mortgage Assoc. of Washington, **II** 410

The National Motor Bearing Company. *See* Federal-Mogul Corporation.

The National Motor Club of America, Inc., **33** 418

National Mutual Life Assurance of Australasia, **III** 249

National Office Furniture, **12** 297

National Oil Corp. *See* Libyan National Oil Corporation.

National Oil Distribution Co., **IV** 524

National Old Line Insurance Co., **III** 179

National Packaging, **IV** 333

National Paper Co., **8** 476

National Parks Transportation Company, **25** 420–22

National Patent Development Corporation, 7 45; **13 365–68; 25** 54

National Periodical Publications. *See* DC Comics Inc.

National Permanent Mutual Benefit Building Society, **10** 6

National Petrochemical Co., **IV** 467

National Petroleum Publishing Co., **IV** 636

National Petroleum Refiners of South Africa, **47** 340

National Pharmacies, **9** 346

National Picture & Frame Company, 24 345–47

National Pig Development Co., **46** 84

National Postal Meter Company, **14** 52

National Potash Co., **IV** 82; **7** 186

National Power PLC, 11 399–400; 12 349–51; 13 458, 484

National Presto Industries, Inc., 16 382–85; 43 286–90 (upd.)

National Processing, Inc., **24** 394

National Propane Corporation, **8** 535–37

National Provident Institution for Mutual Life Assurance, **IV** 711

National Provincial Bank, **II** 319–20, 333–34; **IV** 722; **17** 324

National Public Radio, 19 280–82; 47 259–62 (upd.)

National Publishing Company, **41** 110

National Quotation Bureau, Inc., **14** 96–97

National R.V. Holdings, Inc., 32 348–51

National Railroad Passenger Corporation, 22 375–78

National Railways of Mexico, **IV** 512

National Record Mart, Inc., 29 348–50

National Register Publishing Co., **17** 399; **23** 442

National Regulator Co., **II** 41

National Reinsurance Corporation. *See* General Re Corporation.

National Rent-A-Car, **6** 392–93

National Research Corporation, **8** 397

National Restaurants Management, Inc., **38** 385–87

National Revenue Corporation, **22** 181

National Rifle Association of America, 37 265–68

National Rubber Machinery Corporation, **8** 298

National Sanitary Supply Co., 13 149–50; **16 386–87**

National Satellite Paging, **18** 348

National School Studios, **7** 255; **25** 252

National Science Foundation, **9** 266

National Sea Products Ltd., 14 339–41

National Seal, **I** 158

National Semiconductor Corporation, II 63–65; III 455, 618, 678; **6** 215, **261–63; 9** 297; **11** 45–46, 308, 463; **16** 122, 332; **17** 418; **18** 18; **19** 312; **21** 123; **26 327–30 (upd.); 43** 15

National Service Industries, Inc., 11 336–38

National Shoe Products Corp., **16** 17
National Slicing Machine Company, **19** 359
National-Southwire Aluminum Company, **11** 38; **12** 353
National Stamping & Electric Works, **12** 159
National Standard Co., IV 137; **13 369–71**
National Star Brick & Tile Co., **III** 501; **7** 207
National Starch and Chemical Company, II 496; **IV** 253; **17** 30; **32** 256–57; **49 268–70**
National Steel and Shipbuilding Company, **7** 356
National Steel Car Corp., **IV** 73; **24** 143–44
National Steel Corporation, I 491; **IV** 74, 163, 236–37, 572; **V** 152–53; **7** 549; **8** 346, 479–80; **11** 315; **12** 352–54; **14** 191; **16** 212; **23** 445; **24** 144; **26** 527–29; **28** 325. See also FoxMeyer Health Corporation.
National Student Marketing Corporation, **10** 385–86
National Supply Co., **IV** 29
National Surety Co. of New York, **III** 395
National System Company, **9** 41; **11** 469
National Tanker Fleet, **IV** 502
National Tea, **II** 631–32
National Technical Laboratories, **14** 52
National TechTeam, Inc., 41 280–83
National Telecommunications of Austin, **8** 311
National Telephone and Telegraph Corporation. See British Columbia Telephone Company.
National Telephone Co., **III** 162; **7** 332, 508
National Theatres, Inc., **III** 190
National Trading Manufacturing, Inc., **22** 213
National Transcontinental, **6** 360
National Travelers' Insurance Co., **III** 290
National Trust Life Insurance Co., **III** 218
National Tube Co., **II** 330; **IV** 572; **7** 549
National Union Electric Corporation, **12** 159
National Union Fire Insurance Co. of Pittsburgh, Pa., **III** 195–97
National Union Life and Limb Insurance Co., **III** 290
National Utilities & Industries Corporation, **9** 363
National Westminster Bank PLC, II 237, **333–35; IV** 642; **13** 206
National Wine & Spirits, Inc., 49 271–74
Nationalbank, **I** 409
Nationale Bank Vereeniging, **II** 185
Nationale-Nederlanden N.V., III 179, 200–01, **308–11; IV** 697
Nationar, **9** 174
NationsBank Corporation, 6 357; **10 425–27; 11** 126; **13** 147; **18** 516, 518; **23** 455; **25** 91, 186; **26** 348, 453. See also Bank of America Corporation
NationsRent, **28** 388
Nationwide Cellular Service, Inc., **27** 305
Nationwide Credit, **11** 112
Nationwide Group, **25** 155
Nationwide Income Tax Service, **9** 326
Nationwide Logistics Corp., **14** 504
Nationwide Mutual Insurance Co., **26** 488

NATIOVIE, **II** 234
Native Plants, **III** 43
NATM Buying Corporation, **10** 9, 468
Natomas Co., **IV** 410; **6** 353–54; **7** 309; **11** 271
Natref. See National Petroleum Refiners of South Africa.
Natrol, Inc., 49 275–78
Natronag, **IV** 325
Natronzellstoff-und Papierfabriken AG, **IV** 324
NatSteel Electronics Ltd., **48** 369
NatTeknik, **26** 333
Natudryl Manufacturing Company, **10** 271
Natural Alternatives International, Inc., 49 279–82
Natural Gas Clearinghouse, **11** 355. See also NGC Corporation.
Natural Gas Corp., **19** 155
Natural Gas Pipeline Company, **6** 530, 543; **7** 344–45
Natural Gas Service of Arizona, **19** 411
Natural Wonders Inc., 14 342–44
NaturaLife International, **26** 470
The Nature Company, **10** 215–16; **14** 343; **26** 439; **27** 429; **28** 306
The Nature Conservancy, 26 323; **28 305–07,** 422
Nature's Sunshine Products, Inc., 15 317–19; 26 470; **27** 353; **33** 145
Nature's Way Products Inc., **26** 315
Natuzzi Group. See Industrie Natuzzi S.p.A.
NatWest Bancorp, **38** 393
NatWest Bank, **22** 52. See also National Westminster Bank PLC.
Naugles, **7** 506
Nautica Enterprises, Inc., 16 61; **18 357–60; 25** 258; **27** 60; **44 302–06 (upd.)**
Nautilus International, Inc., **III** 315–16; **13** 532; **25** 40; **30** 161
Nautor Ab, **IV** 302
Navaho Freight Line, **16** 41
Navajo Refining Company, **12** 240
Navajo Shippers, Inc., **42** 364
Navale, **III** 209
Navan Resources, **38** 231
Navarre Corporation, 22 536; **24 348–51**
Naviera Vizcaina, **IV** 528
Navigant International, Inc., 47 263–66
Navigation Mixte, **III** 348
Navire Cargo Gear, **27** 269
Navisant, Inc., **49** 424
Navistar International Corporation, I 152, 155, **180–82,** 186, 525, 527; **II** 330; **10** 280, **428–30 (upd.); 17** 327; **33** 254. See also International Harvester Co.
Navy Exchange Service Command, 31 342–45
Navy Federal Credit Union, 33 315–17
Naxon Utilities Corp., **19** 359
Naylor, Hutchinson, Vickers & Company. See Vickers PLC.
NBC **24** 516–17. See also National Broadcasting Company, Inc.
NBC Bankshares, Inc., **21** 524
NBC/Computer Services Corporation, **15** 163
NBD Bancorp, Inc., 9 476; **11 339–41,** 466. See also Bank One Corporation.
NBTY, Inc., 31 346–48
NCA Corporation, **9** 36, 57, 171

NCB. See National City Bank of New York.
NCB Brickworks, **III** 501; **7** 207
NCC L.P., **15** 139
NCH Corporation, 8 385–87
Nchanga Consolidated Copper Mines, **IV** 239–40
nChip, **38** 187–88
NCNB Corporation, II 336–37; 12 519; **26** 453
NCO Group, Inc., 42 258–60
NCR Corporation, I 540–41; **III** 147–52, **150–53,** 157, 165–66; **IV** 298; **V** 263; **6** 250, **264–68 (upd.),** 281–82; **9** 416; **11** 62, 151, 542; **12** 162, 148, 246, 484; **16** 65; **29** 44; **30 336–41 (upd.); 36** 81
NCS. See Norstan, Inc.
NCTI (Noise Cancellation Technologies Inc.), **19** 483–84
nCube Corp., **14** 15; **22** 293
ND Marston, **III** 593
NDB. See National Discount Brokers Group, Inc.
NDL. See Norddeutscher Lloyd.
NEA. See Newspaper Enterprise Association.
NEAC Inc., **I** 201–02
Nearly Me, **25** 313
Neatherlin Homes Inc., **22** 547
Nebraska Bell Company, **14** 311
Nebraska Cellular Telephone Company, **14** 312
Nebraska Consolidated Mills Company, **II** 493; **III** 52; **8** 433; **26** 383
Nebraska Furniture Mart, **III** 214–15; **18** 60–61, 63
Nebraska Light & Power Company, **6** 580
Nebraska Power Company, **25** 89
Nebraska Public Power District, 29 351–54
NEBS. See New England Business Services, Inc.
NEC Corporation, I 455, 520; **II** 40, 42, 45, 56–57, **66–68,** 73, 82, 91, 104, 361; **III** 122–23, 130, 140, 715; **6** 101, 231, 244, 287; **9** 42, 115; **10** 257, 366, 463, 500; **11** 46, 308, 490; **13** 482; **16** 139; **18** 382–83; **19** 391; **21 388–91 (upd.); 25** 82, 531; **36** 286, 299–300; **47** 320
Neches Butane Products Co., **IV** 552
Neckermann Versand AG, **V** 100–02
Nedbank, **IV** 23
Nederland Line. See Stoomvaart Maatschappij Nederland.
Nederlander Organization, **24** 439
Nederlands Talen Institut, **13** 544
Nederlandsche Electriciteits Maatschappij. See N.E.M.
Nederlandsche Handel Maatschappij, **26** 242
Nederlandsche Heide Maatschappij, **III** 199
Nederlandsche Heidenmaatschappij. See Arcadis NV.
Nederlandsche Kunstzijdebariek, **13** 21
Nederlandsche Nieuw Guinea Petroleum Maatschappij, **IV** 491
Nederlandsche Stoomvart Maatschappij Oceaan, **6** 416
Nederlandse Cement Industrie, **III** 701
Nederlandse Credietbank N.V., **II** 248
Nederlandse Dagbladunie NV, **IV** 610
N.V. Nederlandse Gasunie, I 326; **V** 627, **658–61; 38** 407

Nederlandse Handel Maatschappij, **II** 183, 527; **IV** 132–33
Nederlandse Vliegtuigenfabriek, **I** 54
Nedlloyd Group. *See* Koninklijke Nedlloyd N.V.
Nedsual, **IV** 23; **16** 28
Neeco, Inc., **9** 301
Needham Harper Worldwide, **I** 23, 28, 30–33; **13** 203; **14** 159
Needlecraft, **II** 560; **12** 410
Needleworks, Inc., **23** 66
Neenah Paper Co., **III** 40; **16** 303; **43** 257
Neenah Printing, **8** 360
NEES. *See* New England Electric System.
Neff Corp., 32 352–53
Negromex, **23** 171–72
Neighborhood Restaurants of America, **18** 241
Neilson/Cadbury, **II** 631
Neiman Bearings Co., **13** 78
The Neiman Marcus Group, Inc., I 246; **II** 478; **V** 10, 31; **12 355–57; 15** 50, 86, 291; **17** 43; **21** 302; **25** 177–78; **27** 429; **49 283–87 (upd.)**
Neisler Laboratories, **I** 400
Neisner Brothers, Inc., **9** 20
Nekoosa Edwards Paper Co., **IV** 282; **9** 261
NEL Equity Services Co., **III** 314
Nelio Chemicals, Inc., **IV** 345
Nelson Bros., **14** 236
Nelson Entertainment Group, **47** 272
Nelson Publications, **22** 442
Nemuro Bank, **II** 291
Nenuco, **II** 567
Neo Products Co., **37** 401
Neodata, **11** 293
Neos, **21** 438
Neoterics Inc., **11** 65
Neozyme I Corp., **13** 240
Nepera, Inc., **I** 682; **16** 69
Neptun Maritime Oyj, **29** 431
Neptune Orient Lines Limited, 47 267–70
NER Auction Group, **23** 148
NERCO, Inc., V 689, **7 376–79**
Nesbitt Thomson, **II** 211
Nesco Inc., **28** 6, 8
Nescott, Inc., **16** 36
Nesher Israel Cement Enterprises Ltd., **II** 47; **25** 266
Nespak SpA, **40** 214–15
Neste Oy, IV 435, **469–71**, 519. *See also* Fortum Corporation
Nestlé S.A., I 15, 17, 251–52, 369, 605; **II** 379, 456, 478, 486–89, 521, **545–49**, 568–70; **III** 47–48; **6** 16; **7 380–84 (upd.)**; **8** 131, 342–44, 498–500; **10** 47, 324; **11** 15, 205; **12** 480–81; **13** 294; **14** 214; **15** 63; **16** 168; **19** 50–51; **21** 55–56, 219; **22** 78, 80; **23** 219; **24** 388; **25** 21, 85, 366; **28 308–13 (upd.)**; **32** 115, 234; **36** 234, 237; **44** 351; **46** 274
NetCom Systems AB, 26 331–33
NetCreations, **47** 345, 347
Netherland Bank for Russian Trade, **II** 183
Netherlands Fire Insurance Co. of Tiel, **III** 308, 310
Netherlands India Steam Navigation Co., **III** 521
Netherlands Insurance Co., **III** 179, 308–10
Netherlands Trading Co. *See* Nederlandse Handel Maatschappij.

NetHold B.V., **31** 330
NetLabs, **25** 117
NetMarket Company, **16** 146
NetPlane Systems, **36** 124
Netron, **II** 390
Netscape Communications Corporation, 15 320–22; 35 304–07 (upd.); 44 97
NetStar Communications Inc., **24** 49; **35** 69
NetStar Inc.,
Nettai Sangyo, **I** 507
Nettingsdorfer, **19** 227
Nettle Creek Corporation, **19** 304
Nettlefolds Ltd., **III** 493
Netto, **11** 240
Net2Phone Inc., **34** 224
NetWest Securities, **25** 450
Network Associates, Inc., 25 119, **347–49**
Network Communications Associates, Inc., **11** 409
Network Solutions, Inc., **47** 430
Network Ten, **35** 68–69
NetZero Inc., **38** 271
Neue Frankfurter Allgemeine Versicherungs-AG, **III** 184
Neue Holding AG, **III** 377
Neuenberger Versicherungs-Gruppe, **III** 404
Neuralgyline Co., **I** 698
Neuro Navigational Corporation, **21** 47
Neutrogena Corporation, 17 340–44; 36 305
Nevada Bell Telephone Company, V 318–20; **14 345–47**
Nevada Community Bank, **11** 119
Nevada National Bank, **II** 381; **12** 534
Nevada Natural Gas Pipe Line Co., **19** 411
Nevada Power Company, 11 342–44; 12 265
Nevada Savings and Loan Association, **19** 412
Nevada Southern Gas Company, **19** 411
Neversink Dyeing Company, **9** 153
Nevex Software Technologies, **42** 24, 26
New Access Communications, **43** 252
New America Publishing Inc., **10** 288
New Asahi Co., **I** 221
New Balance Athletic Shoe, Inc., 17 245; **25 350–52; 35** 388
New Bedford Gas & Edison Light Co., **14** 124–25
New Broken Hill Consolidated, **IV** 58–61
New Brunswick Scientific Co., Inc., 45 285–87
New Century Network, **13** 180; **19** 204, 285
New City Releasing, Inc., **25** 269
New Consolidated Canadian Exploration Co., **IV** 96
New Consolidated Gold Fields, **IV** 21, 95–96
New CORT Holdings Corporation. *See* CORT Business Services Corporation.
New Daido Steel Co., Ltd., **IV** 62–63
New Dana Perfumes Company, 37 269–71
New Departure, **9** 17
New Departure Hyatt, **III** 590
New England Audio Company, Inc. *See* Tweeter Home Entertainment Group, Inc.
New England Business Services, Inc., 18 361–64
New England Confectionery Co., 15 323–25

New England CRInc, **8** 562
New England Electric System, V 662–64
New England Gas & Electric Association, **14** 124–25
New England Glass Co., **III** 640
New England Life Insurance Co., **III** 261
New England Merchants National Bank, **II** 213–14; **III** 313
New England Mutual Life Insurance Co., III 312–14
New England National Bank of Boston, **II** 213
New England Network, Inc., **12** 31
New England Nuclear Corporation, **I** 329; **8** 152
New England Power Association, **V** 662
New England Trust Co., **II** 213
New Fire Office, **III** 371
New Found Industries, Inc., **9** 465
New Galveston Company, Inc., **25** 116
New Guinea Goldfields, **IV** 95
New Halwyn China Clays, **III** 690
New Hampshire Gas & Electric Co., **14** 124
New Hampshire Insurance Co., **III** 196–97
New Hampshire Oak, **III** 512
New Hampton, Inc., **27** 429
New Haven District Telephone Company. *See* Southern New England Telecommunications Corporation.
New Haven Electric Co., **21** 512
New Hokkai Hotel Co., Ltd., **IV** 327
New Holland N.V., 22 379–81. *See also* CNH Global N.V.
New Horizon Manufactured Homes, Ltd., **17** 83
New Hotel Showboat, Inc. *See* Showboat, Inc.
New Ireland, **III** 393
New Jersey Bell, **9** 321
New Jersey Educational Music Company. *See* National Educational Music Co. Ltd.
New Jersey Hot Water Heating Company, **6** 449
New Jersey Shale, **14** 250
New Jersey Tobacco Co., **15** 138
New Jersey Zinc, **I** 451
New Laoshan Brewery, **49** 418
New Line Cinema, Inc., 47 271–74
New London City National Bank, **13** 467
New London Ship & Engine, **I** 57
New Look Group plc, 35 308–10
New Materials Ltd., **48** 344
New Mather Metals, **III** 582
New Mitsui Bussan, **I** 507; **III** 296
New Nippon Electric Co., **II** 67
New Orleans Canal and Banking Company, **11** 105
New Orleans Refining Co., **IV** 540
The New Piper Aircraft, Inc., 44 307–10
New Plan Realty Trust, 11 345–47
New Process Company, **25** 76–77
New Process Cork Company Inc., **I** 601; **13** 188
New South Wales Health System, **16** 94
New Street Capital Inc., 8 388–90 (upd.). *See also* Drexel Burnham Lambert Incorporated.
New Sulzer Diesel, **III** 633
New Times, Inc., 45 288–90
New Toyo Group, **19** 227
New Trading Company. *See* SBC Warburg.
New United Motor Manufacturing Inc., **I** 205; **38** 461

New UPI Inc., **25** 507

New Valley Corporation, 17 345–47

New Vanden Borre, **24** 266–70

New World Coffee-Manhattan Bagel, Inc., **32** 15

New World Communications Group, **22** 442; **28** 248

New World Development Company Limited, IV 717–19; **8** 500; **38 318–22 (upd.)**

New World Entertainment, **17** 149

New World Hotel (Holdings) Ltd., **IV** 717; **13** 66

New World Restaurant Group, Inc., 44 311–14

New York Air, **I** 90, 103, 118, 129; **6** 129

New York Airways, **I** 123–24

New York and Richmond Gas Company, **6** 456

New York and Suburban Savings and Loan Association, **10** 91

New York Biscuit Co., **II** 542

New York Capital Bank, **41** 312

New York Central Railroad Company, **II** 329, 369; **IV** 181; **9** 228; **10** 43–44, 71–73; **17** 496

New York Chemical Manufacturing Co., **II** 250

New York City Transit Authority, **8** 75

New York Condensed Milk Co., **II** 470

New York Daily News, 32 357–60

New York Electric Corporation. *See* New York State Electric and Gas.

New York Envelope Co., **32** 346

New York Evening Enquirer, **10** 287

New York Fabrics and Crafts, **16** 197

New York Gas Light Company. *See* Consolidated Edison Company of New York.

New York Glucose Co., **II** 496

New York Guaranty and Indemnity Co., **II** 331

New York Harlem Railroad Co., **II** 250

New York Improved Patents Corp., **I** 601; **13** 188

New York, Lake Erie & Western Railroad, **II** 395; **10** 59

New York Life Insurance Company, II 217–18, 330; **III** 291, 305, **315–17**, 332; **10** 382; **45 291–95 (upd.)**

New York Magazine Co., **IV** 651; **7** 390; **12** 359

New York Manufacturing Co., **II** 312

New York Marine and Gotham Insurance, **41** 284

New York Marine Underwriters, **III** 220

New York Quinine and Chemical Works, **I** 496

New York Quotation Company, **9** 370

New York Restaurant Group, Inc., 32 361–63

New York, Rio and Buenos Aires Airlines, **I** 115

New York Sports Clubs. *See* Town Sports International, Inc.

New York State Board of Tourism, **6** 51

New York State Electric and Gas Corporation, 6 534–36

New York Stock Exchange, Inc., 9 369–72; 10 416–17; **34** 254; **39 296–300 (upd.)**

New York Telephone Co., **9** 321

The New York Times Company, III 40; **IV 647–49**; **6** 13; **15** 54; **16** 302; **19 283–85 (upd.)**; **23** 158; **32** 508; **43** 256

New York Trust Co., **I** 378; **II** 251

New York, West Shore and Buffalo Railroad, **II** 329

New York Zoological Society. *See* Wildlife Conservation Society.

New York's Bankers Trust Co., **12** 107

New York-Newport Air Service Co., **I** 61

New Zealand Aluminum Smelters, **IV** 59

New Zealand Co., **II** 187

New Zealand Countrywide Banking Corporation, **10** 336

New Zealand Forest Products, **IV** 249–50

New Zealand Press Assoc., **IV** 669

New Zealand Sugar Co., **III** 686

New Zealand Wire Ltd., **IV** 279; **19** 154

Newark Electronics Co., **9** 420

Newco Waste Systems, **V** 750

Newcor, Inc., 40 332–35

Newcrest Mining Ltd., **IV** 47; **22** 107

Newell and Harrison Company. *See* Supervalu Inc.

Newell Co., 9 373–76; 12 216; **13** 40–41; **22** 35; **25** 22

Newell Rubbermaid Inc., **49** 253

Newey and Eyre, **I** 429

Newfoundland Brewery, **26** 304

Newfoundland Energy, Ltd., **17** 121

Newfoundland Light & Power Co. *See* Fortis, Inc.

Newfoundland Processing Ltd. *See* Newfoundland Energy, Ltd.

Newgateway PLC, **II** 629

Newhall Land and Farming Company, 14 348–50

Newhouse Broadcasting, **6** 33

Newman's Own, Inc., 37 272–75

Newmark & Lewis Inc., **23** 373

Newmont Mining Corporation, III 248; **IV** 17, 20, 33, 171, 576; **7** 287–89, **385–88**; **12** 244; **16** 25; **23** 40; **38** 231–32; **40** 411–12

Newnes, **17** 397

Newport News Shipbuilding and Dry Dock Co., I 58, 527; **13 372–75**; **27** 36

Newport News Shipbuilding Inc., 38 323–27 (upd.); **41** 42; **45** 306

News & Observer Publishing Company, **23** 343

News America Publishing Inc., 12 358–60; **27** 42; **37** 408

News and Westminster Ltd., **IV** 685

News Communications & Media Plc, **35** 242

News Corporation Limited, II 169; **IV 650–53**; **7 389–93 (upd.)**; **8** 551; **9** 429; **12** 358–60; **17** 398; **18** 211, 213, 254; **22** 194, 441; **23** 121; **24** 224; **25** 490; **26** 32; **27** 305, 473; **32** 239; **35** 157–58; **37** 408; **43** 174, 433; **46 308–13 (upd.)**

News International Corp., **20** 79

News of the World Organization (NOTW), **46** 309

Newsco NV, **48** 347

Newsfoto Publishing Company, **12** 472; **36** 469

Newspaper Co-op Couponing, **8** 551

Newspaper Enterprise Association, **7** 157–58

Newspaper Proprietors' Assoc., **IV** 669

Newspaper Supply Co., **IV** 607

Newsquest plc, 32 354–56

Newsweek, Inc., **IV** 688

Newth-Morris Box Co. *See* Rock-Tenn Company.

Newtherm Oil Burners, Ltd., **13** 286

Newton Yarn Mills, **19** 305

Newtown Gas Co., **6** 455

Nexar Technologies, Inc., **22** 409

NEXCOM. *See* Navy Exchange Service Command.

NeXT Incorporated, **III** 116, 121; **6** 219; **18** 93; **34** 348; **36** 49

Next plc, 6 25; **29 355–57**

Nextel Communications, Inc., 10 431–33; **21** 239; **26** 389; **27 341–45 (upd.)**

NEXTLINK Communications, Inc., **38** 192

Neyveli Lignite Corp. Ltd., **IV** 49

NFC plc, 6 412–14; **14** 547

NFL Properties, Inc., **22** 223

NFO Worldwide, Inc., 24 352–55

NGC Corporation, 18 365–67. *See also* Dynegy Inc.

NGI International Precious Metals, Ltd., **24** 335

NHK. *See* Japan Broadcasting Corporation.

NHK Spring Co., Ltd., III 580–82

NI Industries, **20** 362

Niagara Corporation, 28 314–16

Niagara Fire Insurance Co., **III** 241–42

Niagara First Savings and Loan Association, **10** 91

Niagara Insurance Co. (Bermuda) Ltd., **III** 242

Niagara Mohawk Holdings Inc., 45 296–99 (upd.)

Niagara Mohawk Power Corporation, V 665–67; **6** 535; **25** 130

Niagara of Wisconsin, **26** 362–63

Niagara Silver Co., **IV** 644

Niagara Sprayer and Chemical Co., **I** 442

NIBRASCO, **IV** 55

Nicaro Nickel Co., **IV** 82, 111; **7** 186

Nice Day, Inc., **II** 539

Nice Systems, **11** 520

NiceCom Ltd., **11** 520

Nichi-Doku Shashinki Shoten, **III** 574; **43** 281

Nichia Steel, **IV** 159

Nichibo, **V** 387

Nichii Co., Ltd., V 154–55; **15** 470; **36** 418

Nichimen Corporation, II 442; **IV 150–52**, 154; **10** 439; **24 356–59 (upd.)**

Nichimo Sekiyu Co. Ltd., **IV** 555; **16** 490

Nicholas Kiwi Ltd., **II** 572; **15** 436

Nicholas Turkey Breeding Farms, **13** 103

Nicholas Ungar, **V** 156

Nichols & Company, **8** 561

Nichols Copper Co., **IV** 164, 177

Nichols-Homeshield, **22** 14

Nichols plc, 44 315–18

Nichols Research Corporation, 18 368–70

Nicholson File Co., **II** 16

Nicholson Graham & Jones, **28** 141

Le Nickel. *See* Société Le Nickel.

Nickelodeon, **25** 381

Nicklaus Companies, 45 300–03

Nicolai Pavdinsky Co., **IV** 118

Nicolet Instrument Company, **11** 513

NICOR Inc., 6 529–31

Niederbayerische Cellulosewerke, **IV** 324

Niederrheinische Hütte AG, **IV** 222

Niehler Maschinenfabrick, **III** 602

Nielsen, **10** 358

Nielsen & Petersen, **III** 417
Nielsen Marketing Research. *See* A.C. Nielsen Company.
Niemann Chemie, **8** 464
Niese & Coast Products Co., **II** 681
Niesmann & Bischoff, **22** 207
Nieuw Rotterdam, **27** 54
Nieuwe Eerste Nederlandsche, **III** 177–79
Nieuwe HAV-Bank of Schiedam, **III** 200
Nigeria Airways, **I** 107
Nigerian National Petroleum Corporation, IV 472–74
Nigerian Shipping Operations, **27** 473
Nihol Repol Corp., **III** 757
Nihon Denko, **II** 118
Nihon Keizai Shimbun, Inc., IV 654–56
Nihon Kensetsu Sangyo Ltd., **I** 520
Nihon Kohden Corporation, **13** 328
Nihon Lumber Land Co., **III** 758
Nihon Sangyo Co., **I** 183; **II** 118
Nihon Sugar, **I** 511
Nihon Synopsis, **11** 491
Nihon Teppan, **IV** 159
Nihon Timken K.K., **8** 530
Nihon Waters K.K., **43** 456
Nihon Yusen Kaisha, **I** 503, 506; **III** 577, 712
Nihron Yupro Corp., **III** 756
NII. *See* National Intergroup, Inc.
Niitsu Oil, **IV** 542
NIKE, Inc., V 372–74, 376; **8** 303–04, **391–94 (upd.); 9** 134–35, 437; **10** 525; **11** 50, 349; **13** 513; **14** 8; **15** 397; **16** 79, 81; **17** 244–45, 260–61; **18** 264, 266–67, 392; **22** 173; **25** 352; **27** 20; **29** 187–88; **31** 413–14; **36 343–48 (upd.)**
Nikka Oil Co., **IV** 150; **24** 357
Nikka Whisky Distilling Co., **I** 220
Nikkei. *See also* Nihon Keizai Shimbun, Inc.
Nikkei Aluminium Co., **IV** 153–55
Nikkei Shimbun Toei, **9** 29
Nikkelverk, **49** 136
Nikken Global Inc., 32 364–67
Nikken Stainless Fittings Co., Ltd., **IV** 160
Nikko Copper Electrolyzing Refinery, **III** 490
Nikko International Hotels, **I** 106
Nikko Kido Company, **6** 431
Nikko Petrochemical Co. Ltd., **IV** 476
The Nikko Securities Company Limited, II 300, 323, 383, **433–35; 9 377–79 (upd.); 12** 536
Nikko Trading Co., **I** 106
Nikolaiev, **19** 49, 51
Nikon Corporation, III 120–21, 575, **583–85; 9** 251; **12** 340; **18** 93, 186, 340, 342; **43** 282; **48 292–95 (upd.)**
Nile Faucet Corp., **III** 569; **20** 360
Nillmij, **III** 177–79
Nilpeter, **26** 540, 542
Nimas Corp., **III** 570; **20** 362
Nimbus CD International, Inc., 20 386–90
9 Telecom, **24** 79
Nine West Group Inc., 11 348–49; 14 441; **23** 330; **39** 247, **301–03 (upd.)**
Nineteen Hundred Washer Co., **III** 653; **12** 548
99¢ Only Stores, 25 353–55
Ningbo General Bearing Co., Ltd., **45** 170
Nintendo Co., Ltd., III 586–88; 7 394–96 (upd.); 10 124–25, 284–86, 483–84; **13**

403; **15** 539; **16** 168, 331; **18** 520; **23** 26; **28 317–21 (upd.); 31** 237; **38** 415
Nintendo of America, **24** 4
NIOC. *See* National Iranian Oil Company.
Nippon ARC Co., **III** 715
Nippon Breweries Ltd. *See* Sapporo Breweries Ltd.
Nippon Broilers Co., **II** 550
Nippon Cable Company, **15** 235
Nippon Cargo Airlines, **6** 71
Nippon Chemical Industries, **I** 363
Nippon Credit Bank, II 310, **338–39; 38** 439
Nippon Del Monte Corporation, **47** 206
Nippon Educational Television (NET). *See* Asahi National Broadcasting Company, Ltd.
Nippon Electric Company, Limited. *See* NEC Corporation.
Nippon Express Co., Ltd., II 273; **V 477–80**
Nippon-Fisher, **13** 225
Nippon Fruehauf Co., **IV** 154
Nippon Fukokin Kinyu Koku, **II** 300
Nippon Funtai Kogyo Co., **III** 714
Nippon Gakki Co., Ltd., **III** 656–58; **16** 554, 557
Nippon Ginko, **III** 408
Nippon Gyomo Sengu Co. Ltd., **IV** 555
Nippon Hatsujo Kabushikikaisha. *See* NHK Spring Co., Ltd.
Nippon Helicopter & Aeroplane Transport Co., Ltd., **6** 70
Nippon Hoso Kyokai. *See* Japan Broadcasting Corporation.
Nippon Idou Tsushin, **7** 119–20
Nippon International Container Services, **8** 278
Nippon Interrent, **10** 419–20
Nippon K.K. *See* Nikon Corporation.
Nippon Kairiku Insurance Co., **III** 384
Nippon Kakoh Seishi, **IV** 293
Nippon Kogaku K.K. *See* Nikon Corporation.
Nippon Kogyo Co. Ltd. *See* Nippon Mining Co. Ltd.
Nippon Kokan K.K., **IV** 161–63, 184, 212; **8** 449; **12** 354
Nippon Life Insurance Company, II 374, 451; **III** 273, 288, **318–20; IV** 727; **9** 469
Nippon Light Metal Company, Ltd., IV 153–55
Nippon Machinery Trading, **I** 507
Nippon Meat Packers, Inc., II 550–51
Nippon Menka Kaisha. *See* Nichimen Corporation.
Nippon Merck-Banyu, **I** 651; **11** 290
Nippon Mining Co., Ltd., III 759; **IV 475–77; 14** 207
Nippon Mitsubishi Oil Corporation, **49** 216
Nippon Motorola Manufacturing Co., **II** 62
Nippon New Zealand Trading Co. Ltd., **IV** 327
Nippon Oil Company, Limited, IV 434, 475–76, **478–79,** 554; **19** 74
Nippon Onkyo, **II** 118
Nippon Paint Co., Ltd, **11** 252
Nippon Pelnox Corp., **III** 715
Nippon Phonogram, **23** 390
Nippon Polaroid Kabushiki Kaisha, **III** 608; **7** 437; **18** 570
Nippon Pulp Industries, **IV** 321
Nippon Rayon, **V** 387

Nippon Sangyo Co., Ltd., **IV** 475
Nippon Sanso Corp., **I** 359; **16** 486, 488
Nippon Seiko K.K., III 589–90, 595; **47** 278
Nippon Sekiyu Co. *See* Nippon Oil Company, Limited.
Nippon Sheet Glass Company, Limited, III 714–16
Nippon Shinpan Company, Ltd., II 436–37, 442; **8** 118
Nippon Silica Kogyo Co., **III** 715
Nippon Soda, **II** 301
Nippon Soken, **III** 592
Nippon Steel Chemical Co., **10** 439
Nippon Steel Corporation, I 466, 493–94, 509; **II** 300, 391; **IV** 116, 130, **156–58,** 184, 212, 228, 298; **6** 274; **14** 369; **17 348–51 (upd.),** 556; **19** 219; **24** 324–25, 370
Nippon Suisan Kaisha, Limited, II 552–53
Nippon Tar, **I** 363
Nippon Telegraph and Telephone Corporation, II 51, 62; **III** 139–40; **V 305–07; 7** 118–20; **10** 119; **13** 482; **16** 224; **21** 330; **25** 301; **27** 327, 365
Nippon Television, **7** 249; **9** 29
Nippon Tire Co., Ltd. *See* Bridgestone Corporation.
Nippon Trust Bank Ltd., **II** 405; **15** 42
Nippon Typewriter, **II** 459
Nippon Victor (Europe) GmbH, **II** 119
Nippon Wiper Blade Co., Ltd., **III** 592
Nippon Yusen Kabushiki Kaisha, IV 713; **V 481–83; 6** 398
Nippon Yusoki Company, Ltd., **13** 501
Nippondenso Co., Ltd., III 591–94, 637–38. *See also* DENSO Corporation.
NIPSCO Industries, Inc., 6 532–33
Nishi Taiyo Gyogyo Tosei K.K., **II** 578
Nishikawaya Co., Ltd., **V** 209
Nishimbo Industries Inc., **IV** 442
Nishizono Ironworks, **III** 595
NiSource, Inc., **38** 81
Nissan Construction, **V** 154
Nissan Motor Acceptance Corporation, **22** 207
Nissan Motor Co., Ltd., I 9–10, **183–84,** 207, 494; **II** 118, 292–93, 391; **III** 485, 517, 536, 579, 591, 742, 750; **IV** 63; **7** 111, 120, 219; **9** 243, 340–42; **10** 353; **11** 50–51, 350, **350–52 (upd.); 16** 167; **17** 556; **23** 338–40, 289; **24** 324; **27** 203; **34** 133, **303–07 (upd.)**
Nissan Trading Company, Ltd., **13** 533
Nisshin Chemical Industries, **I** 397
Nisshin Chemicals Co., **II** 554
Nisshin Flour Milling Company, Ltd., II 554
Nisshin Pharaceutical Co., **II** 554
Nisshin Steel Co., Ltd., I 432; **IV** 130, **159–60; 7** 588
Nissho Iwai K.K., I 432, **509–11; IV** 160, 383; **V** 373; **6** 386; **8** 75, 392; **15** 373; **25** 449; **27** 107; **36** 345
Nissho Kosan Co., **III** 715
Nissui. *See* Nippon Suisan Kaisha.
Nitratos de Portugal, **IV** 505
Nitroglycerin AB, **13** 22
Nitroglycerin Ltd., **9** 380
Nittetsu Curtainwall Corp., **III** 758
Nittetsu Sash Sales Corp., **III** 758
Nitto Warehousing Co., **I** 507
Nittoku Metal Industries, Ltd., **III** 635

Nittsu. *See* Nippon Express Co., Ltd.
Niugini Mining Ltd., **23** 42
Nixdorf Computer AG, I 193; **II** 279; **III** 109, **154–55; 12** 162; **14** 13, 169; **26** 497
Nixdorf-Krein Industries Inc. *See* Laclede Steel Company.
Nizhny Novgorod Dairy, **48** 438
NKK Corporation, IV 74, **161–63,** 212–13; **V** 152; **24** 144; **28 322–26 (upd.)**
NL Industries, Inc., III 681; **10 434–36; 19** 466–68
NLG. *See* National Leisure Group.
NLM City-Hopper, **I** 109
NLM Dutch Airlines, **I** 108
NLT Corp., **II** 122; **III** 194; **10** 66; **12** 546
NM Acquisition Corp., **27** 346
NMC Laboratories Inc., **12** 4
NMH Stahlwerke GmbH, **IV** 128
NMT. *See* Nordic Mobile Telephone.
NNG. *See* Northern Natural Gas Company.
No-Leak-O Piston Ring Company, **10** 492
No-Sag Spring Co., **16** 321
Noah's New York Bagels, **13** 494. *See also* Einstein/Noah Bagel Corporation.
Nobel-Bozel, **I** 669
Nobel Drilling Corporation, **26** 243
Nobel-Hoechst Chimie, **I** 669
Nobel Industries AB, I 351; **9 380–82; 16** 69. *See also* Akzo Nobel N.V.
Nobel Learning Communities, Inc., 37 276–79
Noble Affiliates, Inc., 11 353–55; 18 366
Noble Broadcast Group, Inc., **23** 293
Noble Roman's Inc., 14 351–53
Nobles Industries, **13** 501
Noblesville Telephone Company, **14** 258
Noblitt-Sparks Industries, Inc., **8** 37–38
Nobody Beats the Wiz. *See* Cablevision Electronic Instruments, Inc.
Nocona Belt Company, **31** 435–36
Nocona Boot Co. *See* Justin Industries, Inc.
Noel Group, Inc., **24** 286–88
Noell, **IV** 201
NOK Corporation, **41** 170–72
Nokia Corporation, II 69–71; **IV** 296; **6** 242; **15** 125; **17** 33, **352–54 (upd.); 18** 74, 76; **19** 226; **20** 439; **38 328–31 (upd.); 47** 318–19
NOL Group. *See* Neptune Orient Lines Limited.
Noland Company, 35 311–14
Nolo.com, Inc., 49 288–91
Nolte Mastenfabriek B.V., **19** 472
Noma Industries, **11** 526
Nomai Inc., **18** 510
Nomura Bank of Japan, **34** 221
Nomura Holdings, Inc., **49** 451
Nomura Securities Company, Limited, II 276, 326, 434, **438–41; 9** 377, **383–86 (upd.); 39** 109
Nomura Toys Ltd., **16** 267; **43** 232
Non-Fiction Book Club, **13** 105
Non-Stop Fashions, Inc., **8** 323
Nonpareil Refining Co., **IV** 488
Noodle Kidoodle, 16 388–91
Noordwinning Group, **IV** 134
NOP Research Group, **28** 501, 504
Nopco Chemical Co., **IV** 409; **7** 308
Nopri, **V** 63–65
Nor-Am Agricultural Products, **I** 682
Nor-Cal Engineering Co. GmbH, **18** 162
Nora Industrier A/S, **18** 395

NORAND, **9** 411
Noranda Inc., IV 164–66; 7 397–99 (upd.); 9 282; **26** 363; **49** 136
Norandex, **16** 204
Norbro Corporation. *See* Stuart Entertainment Inc.
Norcast Manufacturing Ltd., **IV** 165
Norcen Energy Resources, Ltd., **8** 347
Norcliff Thayer, **III** 66
Norco Plastics, **8** 553
Norcon, Inc., **7** 558–59
Norcore Plastics, Inc., **33** 361
Nord-Aviation, **I** 45, 74, 82, 195; **7** 10
Nordarmatur, **I** 198
Nordbanken, **9** 382
Norddeutsche Affinerie, **IV** 141
Norddeutsche Bank A.G., **II** 279
Norddeutscher-Lloyd, **I** 542; **6** 397–98
Nordea AB, 40 336–39
Nordfinanzbank, **II** 366
Nordic Baltic Holding. *See* Nordea AB.
Nordic Bank Ltd., **II** 366
Nordic Joint Stock Bank, **II** 302
Nordic Mobile Telephone, **II** 70
Nordica, **10** 151; **15** 396–97
NordicTrack, 10 215–17; **22 382–84; 38** 238. *See also* Icon Health & Fitness, Inc.
Nordland Papier GmbH, **IV** 300, 302
Nordson Corporation, 11 356–58; 48 296–99 **(upd.)**
Nordstahl AG, **IV** 201
Nordstjernan, **I** 553–54
Nordstrom, Inc., V 156–58; 11 349; **13** 494; **14** 376; **17** 313; **18 371–74 (upd.); 21** 302; **22** 173
Nordwestdeutsche Kraftwerke AG, **III** 466; **V** 698–700
Norelco, **17** 110
Norelco Consumer Products Co., 12 439; **26 334–36**
Norelec, **27** 138
Norex Laboratories, **I** 699
Norex Leasing, Inc., **16** 397
Norfolk Carolina Telephone Company, **10** 202
Norfolk Southern Corporation, V 484–86; 6 436, 487; **12** 278; **22** 167; **29 358–61 (upd.)**
Norfolk Steel, **13** 97
Norge Co., **III** 439–40; **18** 173–74; **43** 163–64
Noric Corporation, **39** 332
Norinchukin Bank, II 340–41
NORIS Bank GmbH, **V** 166
Norlin, **16** 238–39
Norm Thompson Outfitters, Inc., 47 275–77
Norma Cie., **III** 622
Norman BV, **9** 93; **33** 78
Norman J. Hurll Group, **III** 673
Normandy Mining Ltd., **23** 42
Normark Corporation. *See* Rapala-Normark Group, Ltd.
Normond/CMS, **7** 117
Norrell Corporation, I 696; **6** 46; **23** 431; **25 356–59**
Norris Cylinder Company, **11** 535
Norris Grain Co., **14** 537
Norris Oil Company, **47** 52
Norsk Hydro ASA, 10 437–40; 35 315–19 (upd.); 36 322
Norsk Rengjorings Selskap a.s., **49** 221
Norstan, Inc., 16 392–94
Norstar Bancorp, **9** 229

Nortek, Inc., I 482; **14** 482; **22** 4; **26** 101; **34 308–12; 37** 331
Nortel Networks Corporation, 36 349–54 (upd.)
Nortex International, **7** 96; **19** 338
North & South Wales Bank, **II** 318; **17** 323
North Advertising, Inc., **6** 27
North African Petroleum Ltd., **IV** 455
North American Aviation, **I** 48, 71, 78, 81, 101; **7** 520; **9** 16; **10** 163; **11** 278, 427
North American Bancorp, **II** 192
North American Carbon, **19** 499
North American Cellular Network, **9** 322
North American Coal Corporation, **7** 369–71
North American Company, **6** 443, 552–53, 601–02
North American Dräger, **13** 328
North American Energy Conservation, Inc., **35** 480
North American Insurance Co., **II** 181
North American InTeleCom, Inc., **IV** 411
North American Life and Casualty Co., **III** 185, 306
North American Light & Power Company, **V** 609; **6** 504–05; **12** 541
North American Managers, Inc., **III** 196
North American Medical Management Company, Inc., **36** 366
North American Mogul Products Co. *See* Mogul Corp.
North American Philips Corporation, **II** 79–80; **19** 393; **21** 520
North American Printed Circuit Corp., **III** 643
North American Printing Ink Company, **13** 228
North American Reinsurance Corp., **III** 377
North American Rockwell Corp., **10** 173
North American Systems, **14** 230
North American Training Corporation. *See* Rollerblade, Inc.
North American Van Lines, **I** 278; **14** 37. *See also* Allied Worldwide, Inc.
North American Watch Company. *See* Movado Group, Inc.
North Atlantic Energy Corporation, **21** 411
North Atlantic Packing, **13** 243
North British Insurance Co., **III** 234–35
North British Rubber Company, **20** 258
North Broken Hill Peko, **IV** 61
North Carolina Motor Speedway, Inc., **19** 294
North Carolina National Bank Corporation, **II** 336; **10** 425–27; **18** 518; **46** 52
North Carolina Natural Gas Corporation, **6** 578
North Carolina Shipbuilding Co., **13** 373
North Central Airlines, **I** 132
North Central Finance, **II** 333
North Central Financial Corp., **9** 475
North Central Utilities, Inc., **18** 405
North Cornwall China Clay Co., **III** 690
North East Insurance Company, **44** 356
North Eastern Bricks, **14** 249
North Eastern Coalfields Ltd., **IV** 48
The North Face, Inc., 8 169; **18 375–77; 25** 206; **41** 103
North Fork Bancorporation, Inc., 44 33; **46 314–17**
North Goonbarrow, **III** 690
North Holland Publishing Co., **IV** 610

North New York Savings Bank, **10** 91

North of Scotland Bank, **II** 318; **17** 324

North of Scotland Hydro-Electric Board, **19** 389

North Pacific Paper Corp., **IV** 298

North Pacific Railroad, **II** 330

North Sea Ferries, **26** 241, 243

North Sea Oil and Gas, **10** 337

North Sea Sun Oil Co. Ltd., **IV** 550

North Shore Gas Company, **6** 543–44

North Shore Land Co., **17** 357

North Shore Medical Centre Pty, Ltd., **IV** 708

North Star Egg Case Company, **12** 376

North Star Marketing Cooperative, **7** 338

North Star Mill, **12** 376

North Star Steel Company, 13 138; **18 378–81**; **19** 380; **40** 87

North Star Transport Inc., **49** 402

North Star Universal, Inc., **25** 331, 333

North Supply, **27** 364

The North West Company, Inc., 12 361–63; **25** 219–20

North-West Telecommunications, **6** 327

North West Water Group plc, 11 359–62

Northamptonshire Union Bank, **II** 333

Northbrook Corporation, **24** 32

Northbrook Holdings, Inc., **22** 495

Northcliffe Newspapers, **IV** 685; **19** 118

Northeast Airlines Inc., **I** 99–100; **6** 81

Northeast Federal Corp., **13** 468

Northeast Petroleum Industries, Inc., **11** 194; **14** 461

Northeast Savings Bank, **12** 31; **13** 467–68

Northeast Utilities, V 668–69; 13 182–84; **21** 408, 411; **48 303–06 (upd.)**

Northeastern Bancorp of Scranton, **II** 342

Northeastern New York Medical Service, Inc., **III** 246

Northern Aluminum Co. Ltd., **IV** 9–10

Northern and Employers Assurance, **III** 235

Northern Arizona Light & Power Co., **6** 545

Northern Border Pipeline Co., **V** 609–10

Northern California Savings, **10** 340

Northern Crown Bank, **II** 344

Northern Dairies, **10** 441

Northern Development Co., **IV** 282

Northern Drug Company, **14** 147

Northern Electric Company. *See* Northern Telecom Limited.

Northern Energy Resources Company. *See* NERCO, Inc.

Northern Engineering Industries Plc, **21** 436

Northern Fibre Products Co., **I** 202

Northern Foods PLC, I 248; **II** 587; **10 441–43**

Northern Illinois Gas Co., **6** 529–31

Northern Indiana Power Company, **6** 556

Northern Indiana Public Service Company, **6** 532–33

Northern Infrastructure Maintenance Company, **39** 238

Northern Joint Stock Bank, **II** 303

Northern Leisure, **40** 296–98

Northern Light Electric Company, **18** 402–03

Northern National Bank, **14** 90

Northern Natural Gas Co., **V** 609–10; **49** 122

Northern Pacific Corp., **15** 274

Northern Pacific Railroad, **II** 278, 329; **III** 228, 282; **14** 168; **26** 451

Northern Paper, **I** 614

Northern Pipeline Construction Co., **19** 410, 412

Northern Rock plc, 33 318–21

Northern Star Co., **25** 332

Northern States Life Insurance Co., **III** 275

Northern States Power Company, V 670–72; 18 404; **20 391–95 (upd.)**

Northern Stores, Inc., **12** 362

Northern Sugar Company, **11** 13

Northern Telecom Limited, II 70; **III** 143, 164; **V** 271; **V 308–10**; **6** 242, 307, 310; **9** 479; **10** 19, 432; **11** 69; **12** 162; **14** 259; **16** 392, 468; **17** 353; **18** 111; **20** 439; **22** 51; **25** 34; **27** 342; **47** 318–20. *See also* Nortel Networks Corporation.

Northern Trust Company, III 518; **9 387–89**; **22** 280

Northfield Metal Products, **11** 256

Northgate Computer Corp., **16** 196

Northland. *See* Scott Fetzer Company.

Northland Cranberries, Inc., 38 332–34

Northland Publishing, **19** 231

NorthPrint International, **22** 356

Northrop Corporation, I 47, 49, 55, 59, **76–77**, 80, 84, 197, 525; **III** 84; **9** 416, 418; **10** 162; **11** 164, 166, 266, 269, **363–65 (upd.)**; **25** 316

Northrop Grumman Corporation, 41 43; **45 304–12 (upd.)**; **49** 444

Northrup King Co., **I** 672

NorthStar Computers, **10** 313

Northwest Airlines Inc., I 42, 64, 91, 97, 100, 104, **112–14**, 125, 127; **6** 66, 74, 82 **103–05 (upd.)**, 123; **9** 273; **11** 266, 315; **12** 191, 487; **21** 141, 143; **22** 252; **26 337–40 (upd.)**, 441; **27** 20; **28** 226, 265–66; **30** 447; **31** 419–20; **33** 50–51, 302. *See also* Mesaba Holdings, Inc.

Northwest Benefit Assoc., **III** 228

Northwest Engineering, **21** 502

Northwest Engineering Co. *See* Terex Corporation.

Northwest Express. *See* Bear Creek Corporation.

Northwest Industries, **I** 342; **II** 468 **8** 367; **25** 165–66. *See also* Chicago and North Western Holdings Corporation.

Northwest Instruments, **8** 519

Northwest Linen Co., **16** 228

Northwest Natural Gas Company, 45 313–15

Northwest Outdoor, **27** 280

Northwest Paper Company, **8** 430

Northwest Steel Rolling Mills Inc., **13** 97

Northwest Telecommunications Inc., **6** 598

Northwestern Bell Telephone Co., **V** 341; **25** 495

Northwestern Benevolent Society, **III** 228

NorthWestern Corporation, 37 280–83

Northwestern Engraving, **12** 25

Northwestern Expanded Metal Co., **III** 763

Northwestern Financial Corporation, **11** 29

Northwestern Industries, **III** 263

Northwestern Manufacturing Company, **8** 133

Northwestern Mutual Life Insurance Company, III 321–24, 352; **IV** 333; **45 316–21 (upd.)**; **46** 198

Northwestern National Bank, **16** 71

Northwestern National Insurance Co., **IV** 29

Northwestern National Life Insurance Co., **14** 233

Northwestern Public Service Company, **6** 524

Northwestern States Portland Cement Co., **III** 702

Northwestern Telephone Systems, **6** 325, 328

Norton Company, III 678; **8 395–97**; **16** 122; **22** 68; **26** 70

Norton Healthcare Ltd., **11** 208

Norton McNaughton, Inc., 25 245; **27 346–49**

Norton Opax PLC, **IV** 259; **34** 140

Norton Professional Books. *See* W.W. Norton & Company, Inc.

Norton Simon Industries, **I** 446; **IV** 672; **6** 356; **19** 404; **22** 513

Norwales Development Ltd., **11** 239

Norwalk Truck Lines, **14** 567

NORWEB plc, **13** 458; **24** 270

Norwegian Assurance, **III** 258

Norwegian Caribbean Line, **27** 90

Norwegian Globe, **III** 258

Norwegian Petroleum Consultants, **III** 499

Norweld Holding A.A., **13** 316

Norwest Bank, **19** 412

Norwest Corp., **16** 135

Norwest Mortgage Inc., **11** 29

Norwest Publishing, **IV** 661

Norwich-Eaton Pharmaceuticals, **III** 53; **8** 434; **26** 383

Norwich Pharmaceuticals, **I** 370–71; **9** 358

Norwich Union Fire Insurance Society, Ltd., **III** 242, 273, 404; **IV** 705

Norwich Winterthur Group, **III** 404

Norwood Company, **13** 168

Norwood Promotional Products, Inc., 26 341–43

Nostell Brick & Tile, **14** 249

Notre Capital Ventures II, L.P., **24** 117

Nottingham Manufacturing Co., **V** 357

Nouvelle Compagnie Havraise Pénninsulaire, **27** 514

Nouvelles Galeries Réunies, **10** 205; **19** 308; **27** 95

Nouvelles Messageries de la Presse Parisienne, **IV** 618

Nova Corporation, **18** 365–67; **24** 395; **49** 120–21

Nova Corporation of Alberta, V 673–75; **12** 364–66

Nova Information Systems, **24** 393

Nova Mechanical Contractors, **48** 238

Nova Pharmaceuticals, **14** 46

Nova Scotia Steel Company, **19** 186

NovaCare, Inc., 11 366–68; **14** 233; **33** 185; **41** 194

Novacor Chemicals Ltd., 12 364–66

Novaction Argentina SA, **48** 224

Novagas Clearinghouse Ltd., **18** 367; **49** 120

Novalta Resources Inc., **11** 441

Novamax Technologies Inc., **34** 209

Novanet Semiconductor, **36** 124

Novar plc, 49 292–96 (upd.)

Novartis AG, 18 51; **34** 284; **39 304–10 (upd.)**

Novell, Inc., 6 255–56, 260, **269–71**; **9** 170–71; **10** 232, 363, 473–74, 558, 565; **11** 59, 519–20; **12** 335; **13** 482; **15** 131, 133, 373, 492; **16** 392, 394; **20** 237; **21** 133–34; **23 359–62 (upd.)**; **25** 50–51,

117, 300, 499; **33** 113, 115; **34** 442–43; **36** 80; **38** 418–19
Novello and Co., **II** 139; **24** 193
Novellus Systems, Inc., 18 382–85
Novgorodnefteprodukt, **48** 378
Novo Industri A/S, I 658–60, 697
Novobord, **49** 353
Novotel. *See* Accor SA.
NOVUM. *See* Industrie Natuzzi S.p.A.
NOVUS Financial Corporation, **33** 314
Nowell Wholesale Grocery Co., **II** 681
Nowsco Well Services Ltd., **25** 73
Nox Ltd., **I** 588
Noxell Corporation, **III** 53; **8** 434; **26** 384
NPC International, Inc., 40 340–42
NPD Group, **13** 4
NPD Trading (USA), Inc., **13** 367
NPR. *See* National Public Radio, Inc.
NPS Waste Technologies, **13** 366
NRG Energy, Inc., **11** 401
NS. *See* Norfolk Southern Corporation.
NS Group, **31** 287
NS Petites Inc., **8** 323
NSG Information System Co., **III** 715
NSK. *See* Nippon Seiko K.K.
NSK Ltd., **42** 384
NSK-Warner, **14** 64
NSMO. *See* Nederlandsche Stoomvart Maatschappij Oceaan.
NSN Network Services, **23** 292, 294
NSP. *See* Northern States Power Company.
NSU Werke, **10** 261
NTC Publishing Group, **22** 519, 522
NTCL. *See* Northern Telecom Limited.
NTN Corporation, III 595–96, 623; **28** 241; **47 278–81 (upd.)**
NTRON, **11** 486
NTT. *See* Nippon Telegraph and Telephone Corp.
NTTPC. *See* Nippon Telegraph and Telephone Public Corporation.
NU. *See* Northeast Utilities.
Nu-Era Gear, **14** 64
Nu-kote Holding, Inc., 18
Nu Skin Enterprises, Inc., 27 350–53; 31 327 **386–89**
Nuclear Electric, **6** 453; **11** 399–401; **12** 349; **13** 484
Nuclear Power International, **19** 166
Nucoa Butter Co., **II** 497
Nucor Corporation, 7 400–02; 13 143, 423; **14** 156; **18** 378–80; **19** 380; **21 392–95 (upd.)**; **26** 407
Nucorp Energy, **II** 262, 620
NUG Optimus Lebensmittel-Einzelhandelgesellschaft mbH, **V** 74
Nugget Polish Co. Ltd., **II** 566
NUMAR Corporation, **25** 192
Numerax, Inc., **IV** 637
NUMMI. *See* New United Motor Manufacturing, Inc.
Nuovo Pignone, **IV** 420–22
NUR Touristic GmbH, **V** 100–02
Nurad, **III** 468
Nurotoco Inc. *See* Roto-Rooter Service Company.
Nursefinders, **6** 10
Nutmeg Industries, Inc., **17** 513
Nutraceutical International Corporation, 37 284–86
NutraSweet Company, II 463, 582; **8 398–400; 26** 108; **29** 331
Nutrena, **II** 617; **13** 137
Nutri-Foods International, **18** 467–68

Nutri/System Inc., **29** 258
Nutrilite Co., **III** 11–12
NutriSystem, **10** 383; **12** 531
Nutrition for Life International Inc., 22 385–88
Nuveen. *See* John Nuveen Company.
NV Dagblad De Telegraaf. *See* N.V. Holdingmaatschappij De Telegraaf.
NVR L.P., 8 401–03
NWA, Inc. *See* Northwest Airlines Corporation.
NWK. *See* Nordwestdeutsche Kraftwerke AG.
NWL Control Systems, **III** 512
NWS BANK plc, **10** 336–37
Nya AB Atlas, **III** 425–26
Nydqvist & Holm, **III** 426
Nyhamms Cellulosa, **IV** 338
NYK. *See* Nihon Yusen Kaisha, Nippon Yusen Kabushiki Kaisha *and* Nippon Yusen Kaisha.
Nyland Mattor, **25** 464
NYLCare Health Plans, **45** 293–94
Nylex Corp., **I** 429
NYLife Care Health Plans, Inc., **17** 166
Nylon de Mexico, S.A., **19** 10, 12
NYMAGIC, Inc., 41 284–86
Nyman & Schultz Affarsresbyraer A.B., **I** 120
Nymofil, Ltd., **16** 297
NYNEX Corporation, V 311–13; 6 340; **11** 19, 87; **13** 176; **25** 61–62, 102; **26** 520; **43** 445
NYRG. *See* New York Restaurant Group, Inc.
Nyrop, **I** 113
Nysco Laboratories, **III** 55
NYSEG. *See* New York State Electric and Gas Corporation.
NZI Corp., **III** 257

O&K Rolltreppen, **27** 269
O&Y. *See* Olympia & York Developments Ltd.
O.B. McClintock Co., **7** 144–45
O.G. Wilson, **16** 560
O. Kraft & Sons, **12** 363
O.N.E. Color Communications L.L.C., **29** 306
O-Pee-Chee, **34** 447–48
O.S. Designs Inc., **15** 396
O.Y.L. Industries Berhad, **26** 3, 5
Oahu Railway & Land Co., **I** 565–66
Oak Creek Homes Inc., **41** 18
Oak Farms Dairies, **II** 660
Oak Hill Investment Partners, **11** 490
Oak Hill Sportswear Corp., **17** 137–38
Oak Industries Inc., III 512; **21 396–98**
Oak Technology, Inc., 22 389–93
OakBrook Investments, LLC, **48** 18
Oakley, Inc., 18 390–93; 49 297–302 (upd.)
OakStone Financial Corporation, **11** 448
Oaktree Capital Management, **30** 185
OakTree Health Plan Inc., **16** 404
Oakville, **7** 518
Oakwood Homes Corporation, 13 155; **15 326–28**
OAO Gazprom, 42 261–65
OAO LUKOIL, 40 343–46
OAO NK YUKOS, 47 282–85; 49 304
OAO Siberian Oil Company (Sibneft), 49 303–06
OAO Tatneft, 45 322–26

OASIS, **IV** 454
Oasis Group P.L.C., **10** 506
OASYS, Inc., **18** 112
Obayashi Corp., **44** 154
ÖBB. *See* Österreichische Bundesbahnen GmbH.
Obbola Linerboard, **IV** 339
Oberheim Corporation, **16** 239
Oberland, **16** 122
Oberrheinische Bank, **II** 278
Oberschlesische Stickstoff-Werge AG, **IV** 229
Oberusel AG, **III** 541
Obi, **23** 231
Object Design, Inc., **15** 372
O'Boy Inc. *See* Happy Kids Inc.
O'Brien Kreitzberg, Inc., **25** 130
Obunsha, **9** 29
Occidental Bank, **16** 497
Occidental Chemical Corporation, **19** 414; **45** 254
Occidental Insurance Co., **III** 251
Occidental Life Insurance Company, **I** 536–37; **13** 529; **26** 486–87; **41** 401
Occidental Overseas Ltd., **11** 97
Occidental Petroleum Corporation, I 527; **II** 432, 516; **IV** 264, 312, 392, 410, 417, 453–54, 467, **480–82**, 486, 515–16; **7** 376; **8** 526; **12** 100; **19** 268; **25 360–63 (upd.)**; **29** 113; **31** 115, 456; **37** 309, 311; **45** 252, 254
Occidental Petroleum Great Britain Inc., **21** 206
Océ N.V., 24 360–63
Ocean, **III** 234
Ocean Combustion Services, **9** 109
Ocean Drilling and Exploration Company. *See* ODECO.
Ocean Group plc, 6 415–17
Ocean Reef Management, **19** 242, 244
Ocean Salvage and Towage Co., **I** 592
Ocean Scientific, Inc., **15** 380
Ocean Specialty Tankers Corporation, **22** 275
Ocean Spray Cranberries, Inc., 7 403–05; 10 525; **19** 278; **25 364–67 (upd.); 38** 334
Ocean Steam Ship Company. *See* Malaysian Airlines System BHD.
Ocean Systems Inc., **I** 400
Ocean Transport & Trading Ltd., **6** 417
Oceania Football Confederation, **27** 150
Oceanic Contractors, **III** 559
Oceanic Properties, **II** 491–92
Oceanic Steam Navigation Company, **19** 197; **23** 160
Oceans of Fun, **22** 130
Ocelet Industries Ltd., **25** 232
O'Charley's Inc., 19 286–88
OCL. *See* Overseas Containers Ltd.
Ocoma Foods, **II** 584
Octane Software, **49** 124
Octek, **13** 235
Octel Communications Corp., III 143; **14** 217, **354–56; 16** 394
Octel Messaging, 41 287–90 (upd.)
Octopus Publishing, **IV** 667; **17** 398
Oculinum, Inc., **10** 48
Odakyu Electric Railway Company Limited, V 487–89
Odam's and Plaistow Wharves, **II** 580–81
Odd Job Trading Corp., **29** 311–12
Odd Lot Trading Company, **V** 172–73
Odda Smelteverk A/S, **25** 82

Odeco Drilling, Inc., **7** 362–64; **11** 522; **12** 318; **32** 338, 340

Odegard Outdoor Advertising, L.L.C., **27** 280

Odeon Theatres Ltd., **II** 157–59

Odetics Inc., 14 357–59

Odhams Press Ltd., **IV** 259, 666–67; **7** 244, 342; **17** 397–98

ODM, **26** 490

ODME. *See* Toolex International N.V.

O'Donnell-Usen Fisheries, **II** 494

Odwalla, Inc., 31 349–51

Odyssey Holdings, Inc., **18** 376

Odyssey Partners Group, **II** 679; **V** 135; **12** 55; **13** 94; **17** 137; **28** 218

Odyssey Press, **13** 560

Odyssey Publications Inc., **48** 99

OEC Medical Systems, Inc., 27 354–56

Oelwerken Julius Schindler GmbH, **7** 141

OEN Connectors, **19** 166

Oertel Brewing Co., **I** 226; **10** 180

Oësterreichischer Phönix in Wien, **III** 376

Oetker Group, **I** 219

Off the Rax, **II** 667; **24** 461

Off Wall Street Consulting Group, **42** 313

Office Depot Incorporated, 8 404–05; 10 235, 497; **12** 335; **13** 268; **15** 331; **18** 24, 388; **22** 154, 412–13; **23 363–65 (upd.); 27** 95; **34** 198; **43** 293

Office Mart Holdings Corporation, **10** 498

Office National du Crédit Agricole, **II** 264

Office Systems Inc., **15** 407

The Office Works, Inc., **13** 277; **25** 500

OfficeMax Inc., 8 404; **15 329–31; 18** 286, 388; **20** 103; **22** 154; **23** 364–65; **43 291–95 (upd.)**

Official Airline Guides, Inc., **IV** 605, 643; **7** 312, 343; **17** 399

Officine Alfieri Maserati S.p.A., 11 104; **13** 28, **376–78**

Offset Gerhard Kaiser GmbH, **IV** 325

The Offshore Company, **III** 558; **6** 577; **37** 243

Offshore Food Services Inc., **I** 514

Offshore Logistics, Inc., 37 287–89

Offshore Transportation Corporation, **11** 523

Ogden Corporation, I 512–14, 701; **6 151–53,** 600; **7** 39; **25** 16; **27** 21, 196; **41** 40–41; **43** 217

Ogden Food Products, **7** 430

Ogden Gas Co., **6** 568

Ogden Ground Services, **39** 240, 242

Ogilvie Flour Mills Co., **I** 268; **IV** 245; **25** 9, 281

Ogilvy & Mather, **22** 200

Ogilvy Group Inc., I 20, 25–27, 31, 37, 244; **6** 53; **9** 180. *See also* WPP Group.

Oglebay Norton Company, 17 355–58

Oglethorpe Power Corporation, 6 537–38

O'Gorman and Cozens-Hardy, **III** 725

Ogura Oil, **IV** 479

Oh la la!, **14** 107

Ohbayashi Corporation, I 586–87

The Ohio Art Company, 14 360–62

Ohio Ball Bearing. *See* Bearings Inc.

Ohio Barge Lines, Inc., **11** 194

Ohio Bell Telephone Company, 14 363–65; 18 30

Ohio Boxboard Company, **12** 376

Ohio Brass Co., **II** 2

Ohio Casualty Corp., III 190; **11 369–70**

Ohio Crankshaft Co. *See* Park-Ohio Industries Inc.

Ohio Edison Company, V 676–78

Ohio Electric Railway Co., **III** 388

Ohio Mattress Co., **12 438–39**

Ohio Oil Co., **IV** 365, 400, 574; **6** 568; **7** 551

Ohio Pizza Enterprises, Inc., **7** 152

Ohio Power Shovel, **21** 502

Ohio Pure Foods Group, **II** 528

Ohio River Company, **6** 487

Ohio-Sealy Mattress Mfg. Co., **12 438–39**

Ohio Valley Electric Corporation, **6** 517

Ohio Ware Basket Company, **12** 319

Ohlmeyer Communications, **I** 275; **26** 305

Ohlsson's Cape Breweries, **I** 287–88; **24** 449

OHM Corp., **17** 553

Ohmeda. *See* BOC Group plc.

Ohmite Manufacturing Co., **13** 397

Ohrbach's Department Store, **I** 30

Ohta Keibin Railway Company, **6** 430

ÖIAG, **IV** 234

Oil Acquisition Corp., **I** 611

Oil and Natural Gas Commission, IV 440–41, **483–84**

Oil and Solvent Process Company, **9** 109

Oil City Oil and Grease Co., **IV** 489

Oil Co. of Australia, **III** 673

Oil Distribution Public Corp., **IV** 434

Oil-Dri Corporation of America, 20 396–99

Oil Drilling, Incorporated, **7** 344

Oil Dynamics Inc., **43** 178

Oil Equipment Manufacturing Company, **16** 8

Oil India Ltd., **IV** 440, 483–84

Oil Shale Corp., **IV** 522; **7** 537

Oilfield Industrial Lines Inc., **I** 477

Oilfield Service Corp. of America, **I** 342

Oita Co., **III** 718

Oji Paper Co., Ltd., I 506, 508; **II** 326; **IV** 268, 284–85, 292–93, 297–98, **320–22,** 326–27

OJSC Wimm-Bill-Dann Foods, 48 436–39

OK Bazaars, **I** 289; **24** 450

OK Turbines, Inc., **22** 311

Okadaya Co. Ltd., **V** 96

O'Keefe Marketing, **23** 102

Oki Electric Industry Company, Limited, II 68, **72–74; 15** 125; **21** 390

Okidata, **9** 57; **18** 435

Okinoyama Coal Mine, **III** 759

Oklahoma Airmotive, **8** 349

Oklahoma Entertainment, Inc., **9** 74

Oklahoma Gas and Electric Company, 6 539–40; 7 409–11

Oklahoma Oil Co., **I** 31

Oklahoma Publishing Company, **11** 152–53; **30** 84

Okonite, **I** 489

Okura & Co., Ltd., I 282; **IV 167–68**

Oland & Sons Limited, **25** 281

Olathe Manufacturing, **26** 494

OLC. *See* Orient Leasing Co., Ltd.

Olcott & McKesson, **I** 496

Old America Stores, Inc., 17 359–61

Old Colony Envelope Co., **32** 345–46

Old Colony Trust Co., **II** 207; **12** 30

Old Country Buffet Restaurant Co. (OCB). *See* Buffets, Inc.

Old Dominion Power Company, **6** 513, 515

Old El Paso, **I** 457; **14** 212; **24** 140–41

Old Harbor Candles, **18** 68

Old Kent Financial Corp., 11 371–72

Old Line Life Insurance Co., **III** 275

Old Mutual, **IV** 23, 535

Old National Bancorp, 14 529; **15 332–34**

Old Navy Clothing Company, **18** 193

Old Quaker Paint Company, **13** 471

Old Republic International Corp., 11 373–75

Old Spaghetti Factory International Inc., 24 364–66

Old Stone Trust Company, **13** 468

Oldach Window Corp., **19** 446

Oldham Estate, **IV** 712

Oldover Corp., **23** 225

Olds Motor Vehicle Co., **I** 171; **10** 325

Olds Oil Corp., **I** 341

Ole's Innovative Sports. *See* Rollerblade, Inc.

Olean Tile Co., **22** 170

Oleochim, **IV** 498–99

OLEX. *See* Deutsche BP Aktiengesellschaft.

Olex Cables Ltd., **10** 445

Olin Corporation, I 318, 330, **379–81,** 434, 695; **III** 667; **IV** 482; **8** 23, 153; **11** 420; **13 379–81 (upd.); 16** 68, 297; **32** 319

Olinkraft, Inc., **II** 432; **III** 708–09; **11** 420; **16** 376

Olins Rent-a-Car, **6** 348

Olinvest, **IV** 454

Olive Garden Italian Restaurants, **10** 322, 324; **16** 156–58; **19** 258; **35** 83

Oliver Rubber Company, **19** 454, 456

Olivetti S.p.A., 34 316–20 (upd.); 38 300

Olivine Industries, Inc., **II** 508; **11** 172; **36** 255

Olmstead Products Co., **23** 82

OLN. *See* Outdoor Life Network.

Olofsson, **I** 573

Olohana Corp., **I** 129; **6** 129

Olsen Dredging Co., **III** 558

Olson & Wright, **I** 120; **34** 398

Olsonite Corp., **I** 201

Olsten Corporation, 6 41–43; 9 327; **29 362–65 (upd.); 49** 265. *See also* Adecco S.A.

Olveh, **III** 177–79

Olympia & York Developments Ltd., IV 245, 247, 712, **720–21; 6** 478; **8** 327; **9 390–92 (upd.); 25** 11–12; **30** 108

Olympia Arenas, Inc., **7** 278–79; **24** 294

Olympia Brewing, **I** 260; **11** 50

Olympia Entertainment, **37** 207

Olympia Floor & Tile Co., **IV** 720

Olympiaki, **III** 401

Olympic Airways, **II** 442

Olympic Courier Systems, Inc., **24** 126

Olympic Fastening Systems, **III** 722

Olympic Insurance Co., **26** 486

Olympic Packaging, **13** 443

Olympus Communications L.P., **17** 7

Olympus Optical Company, Ltd., **15** 483

Olympus Sport, **V** 177–78

Olympus Symbol, Inc., **15** 483

OM Group, Inc., 17 362–64

Omaha Cold Store Co., **II** 571

Omaha Public Power District, **29** 353

Oman Oil Refinery Co., **IV** 516

Omega Gas Company, **8** 349

Omega Gold Mines, **IV** 164

Omega Protein Corporation, **25** 546
O'Melveny & Myers, 37 290–93
Omex Corporation, **6** 272
OMI Corporation, **IV** 34; **9** 111–12; **22** 275
Omlon, **II** 75
Ommium Française de Pétroles, **IV** 559
Omnes, **17** 419
Omni Construction Company, Inc., **8** 112–13
Omni Hearing Aid Systems, **I** 667
Omni Hotels Corp., 12 367–69
Omni-Pac, **12** 377
Omni Products International, **II** 420
Omnibus Corporation, **9** 283
Omnicad Corporation, **48** 75
Omnicare, Inc., 13 150; **49 307–10**
Omnicom Group Inc., I 28–32, 33, 36; **14** 160; **22 394–99 (upd.); 23** 478; **43** 410. *See also* TBWA Worldwide.
Omnipoint Communications Inc., **18** 77
OmniSource Corporation, 14 366–67
Omnitel Pronto Italia SpA, **38** 300
Omron Corporation, 28 331–35 (upd.)
Omron Tateisi Electronics Company, II 75–77; III 549
ÖMV Aktiengesellschaft, IV 234, 454, **485–87**
On Assignment, Inc., 20 400–02
On Command Video Corp., **23** 135
On Cue, **9** 360
On-Line Software International Inc., **6** 225
On-Line Systems. *See* Sierra On-Line Inc.
Onan Corporation, **8** 72
Onbancorp Inc., **11** 110
Once Upon A Child, Inc., **18** 207–8
Oncogen, **III** 18
Ondal Industrietechnik GmbH, **III** 69; **48** 423
Ondulato Imolese, **IV** 296; **19** 226
1-800-FLOWERS, Inc., 26 344–46; 28 137
1-800-Mattress. *See* Dial-A-Mattress Operating Corporation.
One For All, **39** 405
One Hundred Thirtieth National Bank, **II** 291
One Hundredth Bank, **II** 321
One Price Clothing Stores, Inc., 20 403–05
O'Neal, Jones & Feldman Inc., **11** 142
OneBeacon Insurance Group LLC, **48** 431
Oneida Bank & Trust Company, **9** 229
Oneida County Creameries Co., **7** 202
Oneida Gas Company, **9** 554
Oneida Ltd., 7 406–08; 31 352–355 (upd.)
ONEOK Inc., 7 409–12
Onex Corporation, 16 395–97; 22 513; **24** 498; **25** 282
OneZero Media, Inc., **31** 240
Onitsuka Tiger Co., **V** 372; **8** 391; **36** 343–44
Online Distributed Processing Corporation, **6** 201
Online Financial Communication Systems, **11** 112
Only One Dollar, Inc. *See* Dollar Tree Stores, Inc.
Onoda Cement Co., Ltd., I 508; **III 717–19**
Onomichi, **25** 469
OnResponse.com, Inc., **49** 433
Onsale Inc., **31** 177

Onstead Foods, **21** 501
OnTarget Inc., **38** 432
Ontario Hydro Services Company, 6 541–42; 9 461; **32 368–71 (upd.)**
Ontario Power Generation, **49** 65, 67
Ontel Corporation, **6** 201
OnTrak Systems Inc., **31** 301
Oode Casting Iron Works, **III** 551
O'okiep Copper Company, Ltd., **7** 385–86
Opel. *See* Adam Opel AG.
Open Board of Brokers, **9** 369
Open Cellular Systems, Inc., **41** 225–26
Open Market, Inc., **22** 522
OpenTV, Inc., **31** 330–31
Operadora de Bolsa Serfin. *See* Grupo Financiero Serfin, S.A.
Operon Technologies Inc., **39** 335
Opinion Research Corporation, 35 47; **46 318–22**
Opp and Micolas Mills, **15** 247–48
Oppenheimer. *See* Ernest Oppenheimer and Sons.
Oppenheimer & Co., **17** 137; **21** 235; **22** 405; **25** 450
Opryland USA, **11** 152–53; **25** 403; **36** 229
Opsware Inc., 49 311–14
Optel Corp., **17** 331
OPTi Computer, **9** 116
Opti-Ray, Inc., **12** 215
Optical Radiation Corporation, **27** 57
Optilink Corporation, **12** 137
Optima Pharmacy Services, **17** 177
Optimum Financial Services Ltd., **II** 457
Option Care Inc., 48 307–10
Optische Werke G. Rodenstock, 44 319–23
Opto-Electronics Corp., **15** 483
Optronics, Inc., **6** 247; **24** 234
Optus Communications, **25** 102
Optus Vision, **17** 150
Opus Group, 34 321–23
OPW, **III** 467–68
Oracle Corporation, 24 367–71 (upd.); **25** 34, 96–97, 499
Oracle Systems Corporation, 6 272–74; **10** 361, 363, 505; **11** 78; **13** 483; **14** 16; **15** 492; **18** 541, 543; **19** 310; **21** 86; **22** 154, 293
Orange and Rockland Utilities, Inc., **45** 116, 120
Orange Julius of America, **10** 371, 373; **39** 232, 235
Orange Line Bus Company, **6** 604
Orange PLC, **24** 89; **38** 300
Orb Books. *See* Tom Doherty Associates Inc.
Orbis Entertainment Co., **20** 6
Orbis Graphic Arts. *See* Anaheim Imaging.
Orbital Engine Corporation Ltd., **17** 24
Orbital Sciences Corporation, 22 400–03
Orchard Supply Hardware Stores Corporation, 17 365–67; 25 535
Orcofi, **III** 48
OrderTrust LLP, **26** 440
Ore and Chemical Corp., **IV** 140
Ore-Ida Foods Incorporated, II 508; **11** 172; **12** 531; **13 382–83; 36** 254, 256
Orebehoved Fanerfabrik, **25** 464
Oregon Ale and Beer Company, **18** 72
Oregon Chai, Inc., 49 315–17
Oregon Craft & Floral Supply, **17** 322
Oregon Cutting Systems, **26** 119

Oregon Metallurgical Corporation, 20 406–08
Oregon Pacific and Eastern Railway, **13** 100
Oregon Steel Mills, Inc., 14 368–70; 19 380
O'Reilly Automotive, Inc., 26 347–49
Orenda Aerospace, **48** 274
Orford Copper Co., **IV** 110
Organización Soriana, S.A. de C.V., 35 320–22
Organon, **I** 665
Orico Life Insurance Co., **48** 328
Oriel Foods, **II** 609
Orient, **21** 122
Orient Express Hotels Inc., **29** 429–30
Orient Glass, **III** 715
Orient Leasing. *See* Orix Corporation.
Orient Overseas, **18** 254
Oriental Brewery Co., Ltd., **21** 320
Oriental Cotton Trading. *See* Tomen Corporation.
Oriental Land Co., Ltd., **IV** 715
Oriental Precision Company, **13** 213
Oriental Trading Corp., **22** 213
Oriental Yeast Co., **17** 288
Origin Energy Limited, **43** 75. *See also* Boral Limited.
Origin Systems Inc., **10** 285
Origin Technology, **14** 183
Original Arizona Jean Company. *See* J.C. Penney Company, Inc.
Original Cookie Co., **13** 166. *See also* Mrs. Fields' Original Cookies, Inc.
Original Musical Instrument Company (O.M.I.), **16** 239
Original Wassertragers Hummel, **II** 163
Origins Natural Resources Inc., **30** 190
Orinoco Oilfields, Ltd., **IV** 565
Orion, **III** 310
Orion Bank Ltd., **II** 271, 345, 385
Orion Healthcare Ltd., **11** 168
Orion Personal Insurances Ltd., **11** 168
Orion Pictures Corporation, II 147; **6 167–70; 7** 336; **14** 330, 332; **25** 326, 328–29; **31** 100
Orit Corp., **8** 219–20
ORIX Corporation, II 442–43, 259, 348; **44 324–26 (upd.)**
Orkem, **IV** 547, 560; **21** 205
Orkin Pest Control, **11** 431–32, 434
Orkla A/S, 18 394–98; 25 205–07; **36** 266
Orlimar Golf Equipment Co., **45** 76
Orm Bergold Chemie, **8** 464
Ormco Corporation, **14** 481
ÖROP, **IV** 485–86
Orowheat Baking Company, **10** 250
La Oroya, **22** 286
ORSCO, Inc., **26** 363
Ortho Diagnostic Systems, Inc., **10** 213; **22** 75
Ortho Pharmaceutical Corporation, **III** 35; **8** 281; **10** 79–80; **30** 59–60
Orthodontic Centers of America, Inc., 35 323–26
Orthopedic Services, Inc., **11** 366
Orval Kent Food Company, Inc., **7** 430
Orville Redenbacher/Swiss Miss Foods Co., **17** 241
The Orvis Company, Inc., 28 336–39
Oryx Energy Company, IV 550; **7 413–15**
Osaka Aluminium Co., **IV** 153

Osaka Beer Brewing Co., **I** 220, 282; **20** 28

Osaka Electric Tramway, **V** 463

Osaka Gas Co., Ltd., V 679–81

Osaka General Bussan, **IV** 431

Osaka Iron Works, **III** 513

Osaka Marine and Fire Insurance Co., **III** 367

Osaka Nomura Bank, **II** 276, 438–39

Osaka North Harbor Co. Ltd., **I** 518

Osaka Shinyo Kumiai, **15** 495

Osaka Shosen Kaisha, **I** 503; **V** 473–74, 481–82

Osaka Spinning Company, **V** 387

Osaka Sumitomo Marine and Fire Insurance Co., Ltd., **III** 367

Osaka Textile Co., **I** 506

Osakeyhtiö Gustaf Cederberg & Co., **IV** 301

Osakeyhtiö T. & J. Salvesen, **IV** 301

Osborn Group Inc., **48** 256

Osborne Books, **IV** 637

Oscar Mayer Foods Corp., II 532; **7** 274, 276; **12** 123, **370–72**

Osco Drug, **II** 604–05

OSF Japan Ltd., **24** 365

Oshawa Group Limited, II 649–50

OshKosh B'Gosh, Inc., 9 393–95; 42 266–70 (upd.)

Oshkosh Electric Power, **9** 553

Oshkosh Gas Light Company, **9** 553

Oshkosh Truck Corporation, 7 416–18; 14 458

Oshman's Sporting Goods, Inc., 16 560; **17 368–70; 27** 7

OSi Specialties, Inc., **16** 543; **36** 148–49

Osiris Holding Company, **16** 344

OSK. See Osaka Shosen Kaisha.

Osmonics, Inc., 18 399–401

Oster. See Sunbeam-Oster.

Österreichische Brau-Beteiligungs AG. See BBAG Österreichische Brau-Beteiligungs AG.

Österreichische Bundesbahnen GmbH, 6 418–20

Österreichische Creditanstalt-Wiener Bankverein, **IV** 230

Österreichische Elektrowerke, **IV** 230

Österreichische Industrieholding AG, **IV** 486–87

Österreichische Industriekredit AG, **IV** 230

Österreichische Länderbank, **II** 239; **23** 37

Österreichische Luftverkehrs AG. See Austrian Airlines AG.

Österreichische Mineralölverwaltung AG, **IV** 485

Österreichische Post- und Telegraphenverwaltung, V 314–17

Österreichische Stickstoffswerke, **IV** 486

Ostravar A.S., **38** 77

Ostschweizer Zementwerke, **III** 701

O'Sullivan Industries Holdings, Inc., 34 313–15

Osuuskunta Metsäliito, **IV** 316

Oswald Tillotson Ltd., **III** 501; **7** 207

Otagiri Mercantile Co., **11** 95

Otake Paper Manufacturing Co., **IV** 327

OTC, **10** 492

Other Options, **29** 400

Otis Company, **6** 579

Otis Elevator Company, Inc., I 85, **III** 467, 663; **13 384–86; 27** 267, 268; **29** 422; **39 311–15 (upd.)**

Otis Engineering Corp., **III** 498

Otis Spunkmeyer, Inc., 28 340–42

Otosan, **I** 167, 479–80

OTP, Incorporated, **48** 446

OTR Express, Inc., 25 368–70

Otsego Falls Paper Company, **8** 358

Ott and Brewer Company, **12** 312

Ottawa Fruit Supply Ltd., **II** 662

Ottaway Newspapers, Inc., 15 335–37

Otter Tail Power Company, 18 402–05; 37 282

Otter-Westelaken, **16** 420; **43** 308

Otto Bremer Foundation. See Bremer Financial Corp.

Otto-Epoka mbH, **15** 340

Otto Sumisho Inc., **V** 161

Otto Versand GmbH & Co., V 159–61; 10 489–90; **15 338–40 (upd.); 27** 427, 429; **31** 188; **34 324–28 (upd.); 36** 177, 180

Ottumwa Daily Courier, **11** 251

Ourso Investment Corporation, **16** 344

Outback Steakhouse, Inc., 12 373–75; 34 329–32 (upd.)

Outboard Marine Corporation, III 329, 597–600; **8** 71; **16** 383; **20 409–12 (upd.); 26** 494; **42** 45; **43** 287; **45** 174

Outdoor Channel, Inc. See Global Outdoors, Inc.

The Outdoor Group Limited, **39** 58, 60

Outdoor Systems, Inc., 25 371–73; 27 278–80; **48** 217

Outdoor World. See Bass Pro Shops, Inc.

The Outdoorsman, Inc., **10** 216

Outlet, **6** 33

Outlet Retail Stores, Inc., **27** 286

Outlook Group Corporation, 37 294–96

Outlook Window Partnership, **19** 446

Outokumpu Metals Group. See OM Group, Inc.

Outokumpu Oyj, IV 276; **38 335–37**

Ovako Oy, **III** 624

Ovation, **19** 285

OVC, Inc., **6** 313

Overhill Farms, **10** 382

Overland Energy Company, **14** 567

Overland Mail Co., **II** 380–81, 395; **10** 60; **12** 533

Overland Western Ltd., **27** 473

Overnite Transportation Co., 14 371–73; 28 492

Overseas Air Travel Ltd., **I** 95

Overseas Containers Ltd., **6** 398, 415–16

Overseas Petroleum and Investment Corp., **IV** 389

Overseas Shipholding Group, Inc., 11 376–77

Overseas Telecommunications Commission, **6** 341–42

Overseas Telecommunications, Inc., **27** 304

Ovox Fitness Clubs, **46** 432

Owatonna Tool Co., **I** 200; **10** 493

Owen Owen, **37** 8

Owen Steel Co. Inc., **15** 117

Owens & Minor, Inc., 10 143; **16 398–401**

Owens Corning Corporation, I 609; **III** 683, 720–23; **8** 177; **13** 169; **20 413–17 (upd.); 25** 535; **30** 283; **35** 98–99

Owens-Corning Fiberglas, **44** 127

Owens-Illinois Inc., I 609–11, 615; **II** 386; **III** 640, 720–21; **IV** 282, 343; **9** 261; **16** 123; **22** 254; **24** 92; **26 350–53 (upd.); 42** 438; **43** 188; **49** 253

Owens Yacht Company, **III** 443; **22** 115

Owensboro Municipal Utilities, **11** 37

Owosso Corporation, 29 366–68

Oxdon Investments, **II** 664

Oxfam America, **13** 13

Oxford-AnsCo Development Co., **12** 18

Oxford Biscuit Fabrik, **II** 543

Oxford Bus Company, **28** 155–56

Oxford Chemical Corp., **II** 572

Oxford Financial Group, **22** 456

Oxford Health Plans, Inc., 16 402–04

Oxford Industries, Inc., 8 406–08; 24 158

Oxford Instruments, **III** 491

Oxford Learning Centres, **34** 105

Oxford Paper Co., **I** 334–35; **10** 289

Oxford Realty Financial Group, Inc., **49** 26

Oxford University Press, **23** 211

Oxirane Chemical Co., **IV** 456

OXO International, **16** 234

Oxy Petrochemicals Inc., **IV** 481

Oxy Process Chemicals, **III** 33

Oxycal Laboratories Inc., **46** 466

OxyChem, **11** 160

Oxygen Media, **28** 175

Ozalid Corporation, **I** 337–38; **IV** 563; **22** 226

Ozark Airlines, **I** 127; **12** 489

Ozark Automotive Distributors, **26** 347–48

Ozark Pipe Line Corp., **IV** 540

Ozark Utility Company, **6** 593

OZM. See OneZero Media, Inc.

P&C Foods Inc., 8 409–11; 13 95, 394

P&C Groep N.V., **46** 344

P & F Industries, Inc., 45 327–29

P&F Technologies Ltd., **26** 363

P&G. See Procter & Gamble Company.

P&L Coal Holdings Corporation, **45** 333

P & M Manufacturing Company, **8** 386

P & O. See Peninsular & Oriental Steam Navigation Company.

P&O Nedlloyd, **26** 241, 243

P.A. Bergner & Company, **9** 142; **15** 87–88

P.A. Geier Company. See Royal Appliance Manufacturing Company.

P.A.J.W. Corporation, **9** 111–12

P.A. Rentrop-Hubbert & Wagner Fahrzeugausstattungen GmbH, **III** 582

P.C. Hanford Oil Co., **IV** 368

P.C. Richard & Son Corp., 23 372–74

P. D'Aoust Ltd., **II** 651

P.D. Associated Collieries Ltd., **31** 369

P.D. Kadi International, **I** 580

P.D. Magnetics, **I** 330; **8** 153

P.E.C. Israel Economic Corporation, **24** 429

P.F. Chang's China Bistro, Inc., 37 297–99

P.G. Realty, **III** 340

P.H. Glatfelter Company, 8 412–14; 30 349–52 (upd.)

P.Ink Press, **24** 430

P.L. Porter Co., **III** 580

P.R. Mallory, **9** 179

P.S.L. Food Market, Inc., **22** 549

P. Sharples, **III** 418

P.T. Bridgeport Perkasa Machine Tools, **17** 54

P.T. Dai Nippon Printing Indonesia, **IV** 599

P.T. Darya-Varia Laboratoria, **18** 180

P.T. Gaya Motor, **23** 290

P.T. Muaratewe Spring, **III** 581

P.T. Semen Nusantara, **III** 718
P.W. Huntington & Company, **11** 180
P.W.J. Surridge & Sons, Ltd., **43** 132
Pabst, **I** 217, 255; **10** 99; **18** 502
Pac-Am Food Concepts, **10** 178; **38** 102
Pac-Fab, Inc., **18** 161
PAC Insurance Services, **12** 175; **27** 258
PACCAR Inc., **I** 155, **185–86**; **10** 280; **26** **354–56 (upd.)**; **40** 135
Pace-Arrow, Inc., **III** 484; **22** 206
Pace Companies, **6** 149; **26** 221
PACE Entertainment Corp., **36** 423–24
Pace Express Pty. Ltd., **13** 20
Pace Foods Ltd., **26** 58
Pace Management Service Corp., **21** 91
PACE Membership Warehouse, Inc., **V** 112; **10** 107; **12** 50; **18** 286; **40** 387; **47** 209
Pace Pharmaceuticals, **16** 439
Pacer Technology, 40 347–49
Pacer Tool and Mold, **17** 310
Pachena Industries Ltd., **6** 310
Pacific Advantage, **43** 253
Pacific Aero Products Co., **I** 47; **10** 162
Pacific Air Freight, Incorporated, **6** 345
Pacific Air Transport, **I** 47, 128; **6** 128; **9** 416
Pacific Alaska Fuel Services, **6** 383
Pacific and European Telegraph Company, **25** 99
Pacific Bell, **V** 318–20; **11** 59; **12** 137; **21** 285; **22** 19; **37** 126
Pacific Brick Proprietary, **III** 673
Pacific-Burt Co., Ltd., **IV** 644
Pacific Car & Foundry Company. See PACCAR Inc.
Pacific Cascade Land Co., **IV** 255
Pacific Coast Co., **IV** 165
Pacific Coast Condensed Milk Co., **II** 486
Pacific Coast Oil Co., **IV** 385
Pacific Communication Sciences, **11** 57
Pacific Dry Dock and Repair Co., **6** 382
Pacific Dunlop Limited, 10 444–46
Pacific Electric Heating Co., **II** 28; **12** 194
Pacific Electric Light Company, **6** 565
Pacific Enterprises, **V** 682–84; **12** 477. See also Sempra Energy.
Pacific Express Co., **II** 381
Pacific Finance Corp., **I** 537; **9** 536; **13** 529; **26** 486
Pacific Fur Company, **25** 220
Pacific Gamble Robinson, **9** 39
Pacific Gas and Electric Company, **I** 96; **V 685–87**; **11** 270; **12** 100, 106; **19** 411; **25** 415. See also PG&E Corporation.
Pacific Glass Corp., **48** 42
Pacific Guardian Life Insurance Co., **III** 289
Pacific Health Beverage Co., **I** 292
Pacific Home Furnishings, **14** 436
Pacific Indemnity Corp., **III** 220; **14** 108, 110; **16** 204
Pacific Lighting Corp., **IV** 492; **V** 682–84; **12** 477; **16** 496. See also Sempra Energy.
Pacific Linens, **13** 81–82
Pacific Link Communication, **18** 180
Pacific Lumber Company, **III** 254; **8** 348–50
Pacific Magazines and Printing, **7** 392
Pacific Mail Steamship Company, **6** 353
Pacific Manifolding Book/Box Co., **IV** 644
Pacific Media K.K., **18** 101

Pacific Metal Bearing Co., **I** 159
Pacific Monolothics Inc., **11** 520
Pacific National Bank, **II** 349
Pacific National Insurance Co. See TIG Holdings, Inc.
Pacific Natural Gas Corp., **9** 102
Pacific Northern, **6** 66
Pacific Northwest Bell Telephone Co., **V** 341; **25** 495
Pacific Northwest Laboratories, **10** 139
Pacific Northwest Pipeline Corporation, **9** 102–104, 540; **12** 144
Pacific Northwest Power Company, **6** 597
Pacific Pearl, **I** 417
Pacific Petroleums Ltd., **IV** 494; **9** 102
Pacific Plastics, Inc., **48** 334
Pacific Platers Ltd., **IV** 100
Pacific Power & Light Company. See PacifiCorp.
Pacific Pride Bakeries, **19** 192
Pacific Recycling Co. Inc., **IV** 296; **19** 226; **23** 225
Pacific Refining Co., **IV** 394–95
Pacific Resources Inc., **IV** 47; **22** 107
Pacific Sentinel Gold Corp., **27** 456
Pacific-Sierra Research, **I** 155
Pacific Silver Corp., **IV** 76
Pacific/Southern Wine & Spirits, **48** 392
Pacific Southwest Airlines Inc., **I** 132; **6** 132
Pacific Steel Ltd., **IV** 279; **19** 154
Pacific Stock Exchange, **48** 226
Pacific Sunwear of California, Inc., 28 343–45; **47** 425
Pacific Telecom, Inc., **V** 689; **6 325–28**; **25** 101
Pacific Telesis Group, **V** 318–20; **6** 324; **9** 321; **11** 10–11; **14** 345, 347; **15** 125; **25** 499; **26** 520; **29** 387; **47** 318
Pacific Teletronics, Inc., **7** 15
Pacific Towboat. See Puget Sound Tug and Barge Company.
Pacific Trading Co., Ltd., **IV** 442
Pacific Trail Inc., **17** 462; **29** 293, 295–96
Pacific Western Extruded Plastics Company, **17** 441. See also PW Eagle Inc.
Pacific Western Oil Co., **IV** 537
Pacific Wine Co., **18** 71
PacifiCare Health Systems, Inc., **III** 85; **11 378–80**; **25** 318
PacifiCorp, Inc., **V 688–90**; **6** 325–26, 328; **7** 376–78; **26 357–60 (upd.)**; **27** 327, 483, 485; **32** 372; **49** 363, 366
Package Products Company, Inc., **12** 150
Packaged Ice, Inc., **21** 338; **26** 449
Packaging Corporation of America, **I** 526; **12 376–78**, 397; **16** 191
Packard Bell Electronics, Inc., **I** 524; **II** 86; **10** 521, 564; **11** 413; **13 387–89**, 483; **21** 391; **23** 471
Packard Motor Co., **I** 81; **8** 74; **9** 17
Packer's Consolidated Press, **IV** 651
Packerland Packing Company, **7** 199, 201
Pacolet Manufacturing Company, **17** 327
PacTel. See Pacific Telesis Group.
Paddington Corp., **I** 248
PAFS. See Pacific Alaska Fuel Services.
Page, Bacon & Co., **II** 380; **12** 533
Page Boy Inc., **9** 320
PageAhead Software, **15** 492
Pageland Coca-Cola Bottling Works, **10** 222
PageMart Wireless, Inc., **18** 164, 166

Paging Network Inc., 11 381–83; **39** 24–25; **41** 266–67
Pagoda Trading Company, Inc., **V** 351, 353; **20** 86
Paid Prescriptions, **9** 346
Paige Publications, **18** 66
PaineWebber Group Inc., **I** 245; **II** **444–46**, 449; **III** 409; **13** 449; **22** 352, **404–07 (upd.)**, 542; **25** 433
Painter Carpet Mills, **13** 169
Painton Co., **II** 81
PairGain Technologies, **36** 299
Paisley Products, **32** 255
La Paix, **III** 273
Pak-a-Sak, **II** 661
Pak-All Products, Inc., **IV** 345
Pak Arab Fertilizers Ltd., **IV** 364
Pak Mail Centers, **18** 316
Pak-Paino, **IV** 315
Pak Sak Industries, **17** 310; **24** 160
Pak-Well, **IV** 282; **9** 261
Pakhoed Holding, N.V., **9** 532; **26** 420; **41** 339–40
Pakistan International Airlines Corporation, 46 323–26
Pakkasakku Oy, **IV** 471
Paknet, **11** 548
Pakway Container Corporation, **8** 268
PAL. See Philippine Airlines, Inc.
Pal Plywood Co., Ltd., **IV** 327
Palace Station Hotel & Casino. See Station Casinos Inc.
Palais Royal, Inc., **24** 456
Palatine Insurance Co., **III** 234
Palco Industries, **19** 440
Pale Ski & Sports GmbH, **22** 461
Palestine Coca-Cola Bottling Co., **13** 163
PALIC. See Pan-American Life Insurance Company.
Pall Corporation, 9 396–98
Palm Beach Holdings, **9** 157
Palm Harbor Homes, Inc., 39 316–18
Palm, Inc., 34 441, 445; **36 355–57**; **38** 433; **49** 184
Palm Shipping Inc., **25** 468–70
Palmafina, **IV** 498–99
Palmax, **47** 153
Palmer Communications, **25** 418
Palmer G. Lewis Co., **8** 135
Palmer Tyre Ltd., **I** 428–29
Palmolive Co. See Colgate-Palmolive Company.
Palo Alto Brewing, **22** 421
Palo Alto Products International, Inc., **29** 6
Palo Alto Research Center, **10** 510
Palomar Medical Technologies, Inc., 22 408–10; **31** 124
PAM Group, **27** 462
Pamida Holdings Corporation, 15 341–43
Pamour Porcupine Mines, Ltd., **IV** 164
Pampa OTT, **27** 473
The Pampered Chef, Ltd., 18 406–08
Pamplemousse, **14** 225
Pamplin Corp. See R.B. Pamplin Corp.
Pan-Alberta Gas Ltd., **16** 11
Pan American Banks, **II** 336
Pan-American Life Insurance Company, 48 311–13
Pan American Petroleum & Transport Co., **IV** 368–70
Pan American World Airways, Inc., **I** 20, 31, 44, 64, 67, 89–90, 92, 99, 103–04, 112–13, **115–16**, 121, 124,

126, 129, 132, 248, 452, 530, 547–48; **III** 536; **6** 51, 65–66, 71, 74–76, 81–82, 103–05, 110–11, 123, 129–30; **9** 231, 417; **10** 561; **11** 266; **12** 191, **379–81 (upd.)**, 419; **13** 19; **14** 73; **24** 397; **29** 189; **36** 52–53; **39** 120

Pan European Publishing Co., **IV** 611

Pan Geo Atlas Corporation, **18** 513

Pan Ocean, **IV** 473

Pan Pacific Fisheries, **24** 114

Panagra, I 547–48; **36** 53

Panalpina World Transport (Holding) Ltd., 47 286–88; **49** 81–82

Panama Refining and Petrochemical Co., **IV** 566

Panamerican Beverages, Inc., 47 289–91

PanAmSat Corporation, 18 211, 213; **46** 327–29

Panarctic Oils, **IV** 494

Panasonic, **9** 180; **10** 125; **12** 470; **43** 427

Panatech Research & Development Corp., **III** 160

Panavia Aircraft GmbH, **24** 84, 86–87

Panavia Consortium, **I** 74–75

Panavision Inc., 24 372–74; 28 249; **38** 295

PanCanadian Petroleum Ltd., **27** 217; **45** 80

Pancho's Mexican Buffet, Inc., 46 330–32

Panda Management Company, Inc., 35 327–29

Pandair, **13** 20

Pandel, Inc., **8** 271

Pandick Press Inc., **23** 63

PanEnergy Corporation, **27** 128, 131

Panera Bread Company, 44 186, **327–29**

Panerai, **27** 489

Panhandle Eastern Corporation, I 377, 569; **IV** 425; **V** 691–92; **10** 82–84; **11** 28; **14** 135; **17** 21

Panhandle Oil Corp., **IV** 498

Panhandle Power & Light Company, **6** 580

Panhard, **I** 194

Panhard-Levassor, **I** 149

Panificadora Bimbo, **19** 191

AB Pankakoski, **IV** 274

Panmure Gordon, **II** 337

Pannill Knitting Company, **13** 531

Panocean Storage & Transport, **6** 415, 417

Panola Pipeline Co., **7** 228

Panosh Place, **12** 168

Pansophic Systems Inc., **6** 225

Pantepec Oil Co., **IV** 559, 570; **24** 520

Pantera Energy Corporation, **11** 27

Pantheon Books, **13** 429; **31** 376

Panther, **III** 750

Panther Express International Company, **6** 346

The Pantry, Inc., 36 358–60

Pantry Pride Inc., **I** 668; **II** 670, 674; **III** 56; **23** 407–08

Pants Corral, **II** 634

Papa John's International, Inc., 15 344–46; 16 447; **24** 295

Pape and Co., Ltd., **10** 441

Papelera General, S.A. de C.V., **39** 188

Papelera Navarra, **IV** 295; **19** 226

Papeleria Calparsoro S.A., **IV** 325

Papeles Venezolanos C.A., **17** 281

Paper Direct, **37** 107–08

The Paper Factory of Wisconsin, Inc., **12** 209

Paper Magic Group, **35** 130–31

Paper Makers Chemical Corp., **I** 344

Paper Recycling International, **V** 754

Paper Software, Inc., **15** 322

Paper Stock Dealers, Inc., **8** 476

PaperMate, **III** 28; **23** 54

Paperituote Oy, **IV** 347–48

Paperwork Data-Comm Services Inc., **11** 64

Papeterie de Pont Sainte Maxence, **IV** 318

Papeteries Aussedat, **III** 122

Papeteries Boucher S.A., **IV** 300

Les Papeteries de la Chapelle-Darblay, **IV** 258–59, 302, 337

Papeteries de Lancey, 23 366–68

Les Papeteries du Limousin, **19** 227

Papeteries Navarre, **III** 677; **16** 121

Papetti's Hygrade Egg Products, Inc., 25 332–33; **39 319–21**

Papierfabrik Salach, **IV** 324

Papierwaren Fleischer, **IV** 325

Papierwerke Waldhof-Aschaffenburg AG, **IV** 323–24

Papyrus Design Group, **IV** 336; **15** 455

Para-Med Health Services, **6** 181–82

Parachute Press, **29** 426

Parade Gasoline Co., **7** 228

Paradigm Entertainment, **35** 227

Paradise Creations, **29** 373

Paradise Island Resort and Casino. *See* Sun International Hotels Limited.

Paradise Music & Entertainment, Inc., 42 271–74

Paradyne, **22** 19

Paragon Communications, **44** 372

Paragon Corporate Holdings, Inc., **IV** 552; **28** 6, 8

Paragon Vineyard Company, **36** 114

Paragren Technologies Inc., **38** 432

Parallax Software Inc., **38** 70

Paramax, **6** 281–83

Parametric Technology Corp., 16 405–07

Parametrics Corp., **25** 134

Paramount Communications Inc., **16** 338; **19** 403–04; **28** 296

Paramount Fire Insurance Co., **26** 486

Paramount Oil Company, **18** 467

Paramount Paper Products, **8** 383

Paramount Pictures Corporation, I 451–52; **II** 129, 135, 146–47, **154–56**, 171, 173, 175, 177; **IV** 671–72, 675; **7** 528; **9** 119, 428–29; **10** 175; **12** 73, 323; **19** 404; **21** 23–25; **23** 503; **24** 327; **25** 88, 311, 327–29, 418; **31** 99; **35** 279

Parashop SA, **48** 279

Parasitix Corporation. *See* Mycogen Corporation.

Parasole Restaurant Holdings, Inc., **38** 117

Paravision International, **III** 48; **8** 343

Parcelforce, **V** 498

PARCO Co., Ltd., **V** 184–85; **42** 341

Parcor, **I** 676

ParentWatch, **34** 105

Parfums Chanel, **12** 57

Parfums Christian Dior, **I** 272

Parfums Rochas S.A., **I** 670; **III** 68; **8** 452; **48** 422

Parfums Stern, **III** 16

Pargas, **I** 378

Paribas. *See* Banque de Paris et des Pays-Bas, BNP Paribas Group *and* Compagnie Financiere de Paribas.

Paridoc and Giant, **12** 153

Paris Bourse, **34** 13

Paris Corporation, 22 411–13

Paris Group, **17** 137

Paris Playground Equipment, **13** 319

Parisian, Inc., 14 374–76; 19 324–25; **41** 343–44

Park Acquisitions, Inc., **38** 308

Park-Brannock Shoe Company, **48** 69

Park Consolidated Motels, Inc., **6** 187; **14** 105; **25** 306

Park Corp., 22 414–16

Park Drop Forge Co. *See* Park-Ohio Industries Inc.

Park Hall Leisure, **II** 140; **24** 194

Park Inn International, **11** 178

Park-Ohio Industries Inc., 17 371–73

Park Ridge Corporation, **9** 284

Park View Hospital, Inc., **III** 78

Parkdale State Bank, **25** 114

Parkdale Wines, **I** 268; **25** 281

Parke-Bernet, **11** 453

Parke, Davis & Co. *See* Warner-Lambert Co.

Parker, **III** 33

Parker Appliance Co., **III** 601–02

Parker Brothers, **II** 502; **III** 505; **10** 323; **16** 337; **21** 375; **25** 489; **43** 229, 232

Parker Drilling Company, 28 346–48

Parker Drilling Company of Canada, **9** 363

Parker-Hannifin Corporation, III 601–03; **21** 108; **24 375–78 (upd.)**

Parker Pattern Works Co., **46** 293

Parker Pen Corp., **III** 218; **9** 326

Parker's Pharmacy, Inc., **15** 524

Parkinson Cowan, **I** 531

Parkmount Hospitality Corp., **II** 142

Parks-Belk Co., **19** 324

Parks Box & Printing Co., **13** 442

Parkway Distributors, **17** 331

Parr's Bank, **II** 334; **III** 724

Parson and Hyman Co., Inc., **8** 112

Parsons Brinckerhoff, Inc., 34 333–36

The Parsons Corporation, III 749; **8 415–17**

Parsons International Trading Business, **27** 195

Parsons Place Apparel Company, **8** 289

Partech, **28** 346, 348

Partek Corporation, **11** 312

Partex, **IV** 515

Parthénon, **27** 10

Parthenon Insurance Co., **III** 79

Participating Annuity Life Insurance Co., **III** 182; **21** 14

La Participation, **III** 210

Partlow Corporation, **7** 116

Partnership Pacific Ltd., **II** 389

Partouche SA. *See* Groupe Partouche SA.

Parts Industries Corp., **III** 494–95

Parts Plus, **26** 348

PartyLite Gifts, Inc., **18** 67, 69

Pascagoula Lumber Company, **28** 306

Pascale & Associates, **12** 476

Paschen Contractors Inc., **I** 585

Pasha Pillows, **12** 393

Pasminco, **IV** 61

Pasqua Inc., **28** 64

Pass & Seymour, **21** 348–49

Passive Power Products, Inc., **32** 41

Patagonia, **16** 352; **18** 376; **21** 193; **25** 206. *See also* Lost Arrow Inc.

Patak Spices Ltd., **18** 247

Pataling Rubber Estates Syndicate, **III** 697, 699

Patch Rubber Co., **19** 277–78

Patchoque-Plymouth Co., **IV** 371

PATCO. *See* Philippine Airlines, Inc.

Patent Arms Manufacturing Company, **12** 70

Patent Nut & Bolt Co., **III** 493

Patent Slip and Dock Co., **I** 592

La Paternelle, **III** 210

Paterno Wines International, **48** 392

Paternoster Stores plc, **V** 108; **24** 269

Paterson Candy Ltd., **22** 89

Paterson, Simons & Co., **I** 592

Path-Tek Laboratories, Inc., **6** 41

Pathé Cinéma, **6** 374

Pathe Communications Co., **IV** 676; **7** 529; **25** 329

Pathé Fréres, **IV** 626; **19** 203

Pathé SA, 29 369–71. *See also* Chargeurs International.

Pathmark Stores, Inc., II 672–74; **9** 173; **15** 260; **18** 6; **19** 479, 481; **23** 369–71; **33** 436

PathoGenesis Corporation, **36** 119

Patience & Nicholson, **III** 674

Patient Care, Inc., **13** 150

Patil Systems, **11** 56

Patina Oil & Gas Corporation, 24 379–81

Patino N.V., **17** 380

Patrick Industries, Inc., 30 342–45

Patrick Raulet, S.A., **36** 164

Patricof & Company, **24** 45

Patriot American Hospitality, Inc., **21** 184

Patriot Co., **IV** 582

Patriot Life Insurance Co., **III** 193

PATS Inc., **36** 159

Patterson Dental Co., 19 289–91

Patterson Industries, Inc., **14** 42

Pattison & Bowns, Inc., **IV** 180

Patton Electric Company, Inc., **19** 360

Patton Paint Company. *See* PPG Industries, Inc.

Paul A. Brands, **11** 19

Paul Andra KG, **33** 393

Paul Boechat & Cie, **21** 515

Paul C. Dodge Company, **6** 579

Paul Davril, Inc., **25** 258

Paul H. Rose Corporation, **13** 445

Paul Harris Stores, Inc., 15 245; **18** 409–12

Paul, Hastings, Janofsky & Walker LLP, 27 357–59

Paul Koss Supply Co., **16** 387

Paul Marshall Products Inc., **16** 36

Paul Masson, **I** 285

Paul Ramsay Group, **41** 323

The Paul Revere Corporation, 12 382–83

Paul Revere Insurance, **34** 433

Paul Wahl & Co., **IV** 277

Paul, Weiss, Rifkind, Wharton & Garrison, 47 292–94

Paul Williams Copier Corp., **IV** 252; **17** 28

Paul Wurth, **IV** 25

Paulaner Brauerei GmbH & Co. KG, 35 330–33

Pauls Plc, **III** 699

Pavallier, **18** 35

Pavex Construction Company. *See* Granite Rock Company.

Pawnee Industries, Inc., **19** 415

Paxall, Inc., **8** 545

Paxson Communications Corporation, 33 322–26

Pay 'N Pak Stores, Inc., 9 399–401; **16** 186–88

Pay 'n Save Corp., **12** 477; **15** 274; **17** 366

Pay Less, **II** 601, 604

Paychex, Inc., 15 347–49; **46** 333–36 (upd.)

PayConnect Solutions, **47** 39

Payless Cashways, Inc., 11 384–86; **13** 274; **44** 330–33 (upd.)

Payless DIY, **V** 17, 19

PayLess Drug Stores, **12** 477–78; **18** 286; **22** 39

Payless ShoeSource, Inc., V 132, 135; **13** 361; **18** 413–15; **26** 441

PBF Corp. *See* Paris Corporation.

PBL. *See* Publishing and Broadcasting Ltd.

PBS. *See* Public Broadcasting Stations.

PC Connection, Inc., 37 300–04

PC Globe, Inc., **13** 114

PC Realty, Canada Ltd., **III** 340

PCA-Budafok Paperboard Ltd., **12** 377

pcBoat.com, **37** 398

PCI Acquisition, **11** 385

PCI/Mac-Pak Group, **IV** 261

PCI NewCo Inc., **36** 159

PCI Services, Inc. *See* Cardinal Health, Inc.

PCL Industries Ltd., **IV** 296; **19** 226

PCO, **III** 685

PCS. *See* Potash Corp. of Saskatchewan Inc.

PCS Health Systems Inc., **12** 333; **47** 115, 235–36

PCX. *See* Pacific Stock Exchange.

PDA Engineering, **25** 305

PDA Inc., **19** 290

PDI, Inc., **49** 25

PDO. *See* Petroleum Development Oman.

PDQ Transportation Inc., **18** 226

PDS Gaming Corporation, 44 334–37

PDV America, Inc., **31** 113

PDVSA. *See* Petróleos de Venezuela S.A.

Peabody Coal Company, I 559; **III** 248; **IV** 47, 169–71, 576; **7** 387–88; **10** 447–49

Peabody Energy Corporation, 45 330–33 (upd.)

Peabody Holding Company, Inc., IV 19, 169–72; **6** 487; **7** 209

Peabody, Riggs & Co., **II** 427

Peaches Entertainment Corporation, **24** 502

Peachtree Doors, **10** 95

Peachtree Federal Savings and Loan Association of Atlanta, **10** 92

Peachtree Software Inc., **18** 364

Peak Audio Inc., **48** 92

Peak Oilfield Service Company, **9** 364

The Peak Technologies Group, Inc., 14 377–80

Peakstone, **III** 740

Peapod, Inc., 22 522; **30** 346–48

Pearce-Uible Co., **14** 460

Pearl Health Services, **I** 249

Pearl Package Co., Ltd., **IV** 327

Pearle Vision, Inc., I 688; **12** 188; **13** 390–92; **14** 214; **23** 329; **24** 140; **34** 179

Pearson plc, IV 611, 652, 657–59; **14** 414; **25** 283, 285; **32** 355; **38** 402; **46** 337–41 (upd.)

Peasant Restaurants Inc., **30** 330

Pease Industries, **39** 322, 324

Peat Marwick. *See* KPMG Peat Marwick.

Peaudouce, **IV** 339

Peavey Electronics Corporation, II 494; **12** 81; **16** 408–10

Peavey Paper Mills, Inc., **26** 362

Pebble Beach Corp., **II** 170

PEC Plastics, **9** 92

Pechelbronn Oil Company, **III** 616; **17** 416–17

Pechenganickel MMC, **48** 300

Pechiney S.A., I 190, 341; **IV** 12, 59, 108, 173–75, 560; **V** 605; **12** 253–54; **14** 216; **26** 403; **31** 11; **45** 334–37 (upd.)

Péchiney-Saint-Gobain, **I** 389; **III** 677; **16** 121

PECO Energy Company, 11 387–90. *See also* Exelon Corporation.

Pediatric Services of America, Inc., 31 356–58

Pedigree Petfoods, **22** 298

Peebles Inc., 16 411–13; **43** 296–99 (upd.)

Peek & Cloppenburg KG, 46 342–45

Peekskill Chemical Works. *See* Binney & Smith Inc.

Peel-Conner Telephone Works, **II** 24

Peerless, **III** 467; **8** 74; **11** 534

Peerless Gear & Machine Company, **8** 515

Peerless Industries, Inc., **III** 569; **20** 360; **39** 264

Peerless Paper Co., **IV** 310; **19** 266

Peerless Pump Co., **I** 442

Peerless Spinning Corporation, **13** 532

Peerless Systems, Inc., **17** 263

Peet's Coffee & Tea, Inc., 13 493; **18** 37; **38** 338–40

Pegulan, **I** 426–27; **25** 464

PEI. *See* Process Engineering Inc.

Peine, **IV** 201

Pekema Oy, **IV** 470–71

Peko-Wallsend Ltd., **13** 97

Pel-Tex Oil Co., **IV** 84; **7** 188

Pelican and British Empire Life Office, **III** 372

Pelican Homestead and Savings, **11** 107

Pelican Insurance Co., **III** 349

Pelican Life Assurance, **III** 371–72

Pelikan Holding AG, **18** 388

Pella Corporation, 10 95; **12** 384–86; **22** 346; **39** 322–25 (upd.)

Pelto Oil Corporation, **14** 455; **44** 362

PEM International Ltd., **28** 350

Pemex. *See* Petróleos Mexicanos.

Pen Computing Group, **49** 10

Peñarroya, **IV** 107–08

Penauille Polyservices SA, 49 318–21

Penda Corp., **19** 415

Pendexcare Ltd., **6** 181

Pendle Travel Services Ltd. *See* Airtours Plc.

Pendleton Woolen Mills, Inc., 42 275–78

Pengrowth Gas Corp., **25** 232

The Penguin Group, **46** 337

Penguin Publishing Co. Ltd., **IV** 585, 659

Penhaligon's, **24** 237

Peninsula Stores, Ltd. *See* Lucky Stores, Inc.

The Peninsular and Oriental Steam Navigation Company, II 296; **III** 521–22, 712; **V** 490–93; **22** 444; **26** 241, 243; **37** 137; **38** 341–46 (upd.)

Peninsular and Oriental Steam Navigation Company (Bovis Division), I 588–89

Peninsular Portland Cement, **III** 704

Peninsular Power, **6** 602
Peninsular Railroad Company, **17** 440
Penn Advertising, **27** 280
Penn-American Refining Co., **IV** 489
Penn Central Corp., **I** 435; **II** 255; **IV** 576; **10** 71, 73, 547; **17** 443
Penn Champ Co., **9** 72
Penn Controls, **III** 535–36; **26** 229
Penn Corp., **13** 561
Penn Cress Ice Cream, **13** 393
Penn Engineering & Manufacturing Corp., **28** 349–51
Penn Fuel Co., **IV** 548
Penn Health, **III** 85
Penn National Gaming, Inc., **33** 327–29
Penn Square Bank, **II** 248, 262
Penn-Texas Corporation, **I** 434; **12** 71
Penn Traffic Company, **8** 409–10; **13** 95, 393–95
Penn-Western Gas and Electric, **6** 524
Pennaco Hosiery, Inc., **12** 93
Pennington Drug, **III** 10
Pennon Group Plc, **45** 338–41
Pennroad Corp., **IV** 458
Pennsalt Chemical Corp., **I** 383
Pennsylvania Blue Shield, **III** 325–27
Pennsylvania Coal & Coke Corp., **I** 434
Pennsylvania Coal Co., **IV** 180
Pennsylvania Electric Company, **6** 535; **27** 182
Pennsylvania Farm Bureau Cooperative Association, **7** 17–18
Pennsylvania Gas and Water Company, **38** 51
Pennsylvania General Fire Insurance Assoc., **III** 257
Pennsylvania General Insurance Company, **48** 431
Pennsylvania Glass Sand Co., **I** 464; **11** 198
Pennsylvania House, Inc., **10** 324; **12** 301
Pennsylvania International Raceway, **V** 494
Pennsylvania Life Insurance Company, **27** 47
Pennsylvania Power & Light Company, **V** 676, 693–94; **11** 388
Pennsylvania Pump and Compressor Co., **II** 16
Pennsylvania Railroad, **I** 456, 472; **II** 329, 490; **6** 436; **10** 71–73; **26** 295
Pennsylvania Refining Co., **IV** 488–89
Pennsylvania Salt Manufacturing Co., **I** 383
Pennsylvania Steel Co., **IV** 35; **7** 48
Pennsylvania Steel Foundry and Machine Co., **39** 32
Pennsylvania Water & Power Company, **25** 44
Pennwalt Corporation, **I** 382–84; **IV** 547; **12** 18; **21** 205
Penny Curtiss Baking Co., Inc., **13** 395
Pennzoil Company, **IV** 488–90, 551, 553; **10** 190; **14** 491, 493; **20** 418–22 (upd.); **23** 40–41; **25** 443, 445; **39** 330; **41** 391, 394; **47** 436
Pennzoil-Quaker State Company, **49** 343
Penray, **I** 373
Penrod Drilling Corporation, **7** 228, 558
Pension Benefit Guaranty Corp., **III** 255; **12** 489
Penske Corporation, **V** 494–95; **19** 223, 292–94 (upd.); **20** 263
Penske Motorsports, **32** 440
Penske Truck Rental, **24** 445

Pentair, Inc., **III** 715; **7** 419–21; **11** 315; **26** 361–64 (upd.)
Pental Insurance Company, Ltd., **11** 523
Pentane Partners, **7** 518
Pentastar Transportation Group, Inc. *See* Dollar Thrifty Automotive Group, Inc.
Pentaverken A.B., **I** 209
Pentech International, Inc., **14** 217; **29** 372–74
Pentes Play, Inc., **27** 370, 372
Pentland Group plc, **20** 423–25; **35** 204, 206–07
Pentland Industries PLC, **V** 375; **26** 396–97
Penton Media, Inc., **9** 414; **27** 360–62; **33** 335–36
People Express Airlines Inc., **I** 90, 98, 103, **117–18**, 123–24, 129–30; **6** 129; **21** 142; **22** 220
People That Love (PTL) Television, **13** 279
People's Bank of Halifax, **II** 210
People's Bank of New Brunswick, **II** 210
People's Drug Store, **II** 604–05; **22** 37–38
People's Ice and Refrigeration Company, **9** 274
People's Insurance Co., **III** 368
People's Natural Gas, **IV** 548; **6** 593
People's Radio Network, **25** 508
People's Trust Co. of Brooklyn, **II** 254; **9** 124
People's Trust Company, **49** 412
Peoples, **24** 315–16
Peoples Bancorp, **14** 529
Peoples Bank, **13** 467; **17** 302
Peoples Bank & Trust Co., **31** 207
Peoples Bank of Youngstown, **9** 474
Peoples Energy Corporation, **6** 543–44
Peoples Finance Co., **II** 418
Peoples Gas Light & Coke Co., **IV** 169; **6** 529, 543–44
Peoples Gas Light Co., **6** 455; **25** 44
Peoples Jewelers of Canada, **16** 561; **40** 472
Peoples Life Insurance Co., **III** 218
Peoples National Bank, **41** 178–79
Peoples Natural Gas Company of South Carolina, **6** 576
Peoples Restaurants, Inc., **17** 320–21
Peoples Savings of Monroe, **9** 482
Peoples Security Insurance Co., **III** 219
Peoples Trust of Canada, **49** 411
PeopleServe, Inc., **29** 401
PeopleSoft Inc., **11** 78; **14** 381–83; **33** 330–33 (upd.); **38** 432
The Pep Boys—Manny, Moe & Jack, **11** 391–93; **16** 160; **26** 348; **36** 361–64 (upd.)
PEPCO. *See* Portland Electric Power Company *and* Potomac Electric Power Company.
Pepe Clothing Co., **18** 85
Pepper Hamilton LLP, **43** 300–03
Pepperell Manufacturing Company, **16** 533–34
Pepperidge Farm, **I** 29; **II** 480–81; **7** 67–68; **26** 56–57, 59
The Pepsi Bottling Group, Inc., **40** 350–53
PepsiCo, Inc., **I** 234, 244–46, 257, 269, **276–79**, 281, 291; **II** 103, 448, 477, 608; **III** 106, 116, 588; **7** 265, 267, 396, 404, 434–35, 466, 505–06; **8** 399; **9** 177, 343; **10** 130, 199, 227, 324,

450–54 (upd.); **11** 421, 450; **12** 337, 453; **13** 162, 284, 448, 494; **15** 72, 75, 380; **16** 96; **18** 65; **19** 114, 221; **21** 143, 313, 315–16, 362, 401, 405, 485–86; **22** 95, 353; **23** 418, 420; **25** 91, 177–78, 366, 411; **28** 271, 473, 476; **31** 243; **32** 59, 114, 205; **36** 234, 237; **38** 347–54 (upd.); **40** 340–42, 350–52; **49** 77
Pepsodent Company, **I** 14; **9** 318
Perception Technology, **10** 500
Percy Bilton Investment Trust Ltd., **IV** 710
Percy Street Investments Ltd., **IV** 711
Perdue Farms Inc., **7** 422–24, 432; **23** 375–78 (upd.); **32** 203
Perfect Circle Corp., **I** 152
Perfect Fit Industries, **17** 182–84
Perfect-Ventil GmbH, **9** 413
Performance Contracting, Inc., **III** 722; **20** 415
Performance Food Group Company, **31** 359–62
Performance Technologies, Inc., **10** 395
Perfumania, Inc., **22** 157
Pergamon Holdings, **15** 83
Pergamon Press, **IV** 611, 641–43, 687; **7** 311–12
Perini Corporation, **8** 418–21; **38** 481
Perisem, **I** 281
The Perkin-Elmer Corporation, **III** 455, 727; **7** 425–27; **9** 514; **13** 326; **21** 123
Perkins, **I** 147; **12** 90
Perkins Bacon & Co., **10** 267
Perkins Cake & Steak, **9** 425
Perkins Engines Ltd., **III** 545, 652; **10** 274; **11** 472; **19** 294; **27** 203
Perkins Family Restaurants, L.P., **22** 417–19
Perkins Oil Well Cementing Co., **III** 497
Perkins Products Co., **II** 531
Perl Pillow, **19** 304
Perland Environmental Technologies Inc., **8** 420
Permal Group, **27** 276, 513
Permaneer Corp., **IV** 281; **9** 259. *See also* Spartech Corporation.
Permanent General Companies, Inc., **11** 194
Permanent Pigments Inc., **25** 71
Permanente Cement Company, **I** 565; **44** 152
Permanente Metals Corp., **IV** 15, 121–22
Permian Corporation, **V** 152–53
PERMIGAN, **IV** 492
Permodalan, **III** 699
Pernod Ricard S.A., **I** 248, 280–81; **21** 399–401 (upd.)
Pernvo Inc., **I** 387
Perot Systems Corporation, **13** 482; **29** 375–78
Perret-Olivier, **III** 676; **16** 120
Perrier, **19** 50
Perrier Corporation of America, **16** 341
Perrigo Company, **12** 218, 387–89
Perrin, **IV** 614
Perrot Brake Co., **I** 141
Perrow Motor Freight Lines, **6** 370
Perry Brothers, Inc., **24** 149
Perry Capital Corp., **28** 138
Perry Drug Stores Inc., **12** 21; **26** 476
Perry Ellis International, Inc., **16** 37; **41** 291–94
Perry Manufacturing Co., **16** 37
Perry Sports, **13** 545; **13** 545
Perry Tritech, **25** 103–05

Perry's Shoes Inc., **16** 36
Perscombinatie, **IV** 611
Pershing & Co., **22** 189
Personal Care Corp., **17** 235
Personal Performance Consultants, **9** 348
Personal Products Company, **III** 35; **8** 281, 511
Personnel Pool of America, **29** 224, 26–27
Perstorp A.B., I 385–87
PERTAMINA, IV 383, 461, **491–93**, 517, 567
Pertec Computer Corp., **17** 49; **18** 434
Pertech Computers Ltd., **18** 75
Perusahaan Minyak Republik Indonesia, **IV** 491
Peruvian Corp., **I** 547
Pet Food & Supply, **14** 385
Pet Foods Plus Inc., **39** 355
Pet Incorporated, I 457; **II** 486–87; **7** **428–31**; **10** 554; **12** 124; **13** 409; **14** 214; **24** 140; **27** 196; **43** 217; **46** 290
Petco Animal Supplies, Inc., 29 379–81
Pete's Brewing Company, 18 72, 502; **22** **420–22**
Peter Bawden Drilling, **IV** 570; **24** 521
Peter, Cailler, Kohler, Chocolats Suisses S.A., **II** 546; **7** 381
Peter Cundill & Associates Ltd., **15** 504
Peter Gast Shipping GmbH, **7** 40; **41** 42
Peter J. Schmitt Co., **13** 394; **24** 444–45
Peter J. Schweitzer, Inc., **III** 40; **16** 303; **43** 257
Peter Jones, **V** 94
Peter Kiewit Sons' Inc., I 599–600; **III** 198; **8** **422–24**; **15** 18; **25** 512, 514
Peter Norton Computing Group, **10** 508–09
Peter Paul/Cadbury, **II** 477, 512; **15** 221
Peterbilt Motors Co., **I** 185–86; **26** 355
Peters-Revington Corporation, **26** 100. *See also* Chromcraft Revington, Inc.
Peters Shoe Co., **III** 528
Petersen Publishing Company, 21 **402–04**
Peterson, Howell & Heather, **V** 496
Peterson Soybean Seed Co., **9** 411
Petit Bateau, **35** 263
La Petite Academy, **13** 299
Petite Sophisticate, **V** 207–08
Petoseed Co. Inc., **29** 435
Petrie Stores Corporation, 8 425–27
Petrini's, **II** 653
Petro-Canada Limited, IV 367, **494–96**, 499; **13** 557
Petro/Chem Environmental Services, Inc., **IV** 411
Petro-Coke Co. Ltd., **IV** 476
Petro-Lewis Corp., **IV** 84; **7** 188
Petroamazonas, **IV** 511
Petrobas, **21** 31
Petrobel, **IV** 412
Petrobrás. *See* Petróleo Brasileiro S.A.
Petrocarbona GmbH, **IV** 197–98
Petrocel, S.A., **19** 12
Petrochemical Industries Co., **IV** 451
Petrochemicals Company, **17** 90–91
Petrochemie Danubia GmbH, **IV** 486–87
Petrochim, **IV** 498
PetroChina Company Ltd., **46** 86
Petrocomercial, **IV** 511
Petrocorp. *See* Petroleum Company of New Zealand.
Petroecuador. *See* Petróleos del Ecuador.
Petrofertil, **IV** 501

PetroFina S.A., IV 455, 495, **497–500**, 576; **7** 179; **26 365–69 (upd.)**
Petrogal. *See* Petróleos de Portugal.
Petroindustria, **IV** 511
Petrol, **IV** 487
Petrol Ofisi Anonim Sirketi, **IV** 564
Petrolane Properties, **17** 558
Petróleo Brasileiro S.A., IV 424, **501–03**
Petróleo Mecânica Alfa, **IV** 505
Petróleos de Portugal S.A., IV 504–06
Petróleos de Venezuela S.A., II 661; **IV** 391–93, **507–09**, 571; **24** 522; **31** 113
Petróleos del Ecuador, IV 510–11
Petróleos Mexicanos, IV 512–14, 528; **19** 10, **295–98 (upd.)**; **41** 147
Petroleum and Chemical Corp., **III** 672
Petroleum Authority of Thailand, **IV** 519
Petroleum Company of New Zealand, **IV** 279; **19** 155
Petroleum Development (Qatar) Ltd., **IV** 524
Petroleum Development (Trucial States) Ltd., **IV** 363
Petroleum Development Corp. of the Republic of Korea, **IV** 455
Petroleum Development Oman LLC, IV **515–16**
Petroleum Helicopters, Inc., 35 334–36; **37** 288; **39** 8
Petroleum Projects Co., **IV** 414
Petroleum Research and Engineering Co. Ltd., **IV** 473
Petrolgroup, Inc., **6** 441
Petroliam Nasional Bhd. *See* Petronas.
Petrolite Corporation, 15 350–52
Petrolube, **IV** 538
Petromex. *See* Petróleos de Mexico S.A.
Petromin Lubricating Oil Co., **17** 415
Petronas, IV 517–20; 21 501
Petronor, **IV** 514, 528
Petropeninsula, **IV** 511
Petroproduccion, **IV** 511
Petroquímica de Venezuela SA, **IV** 508
Petroquimica Española, **I** 402
Petroquisa, **IV** 501
PETROSUL, **IV** 504, 506
Petrotransporte, **IV** 511
PETsMART, Inc., 14 384–86; 27 95; **29** 379–80; **41 295–98 (upd.)**; **45** 42
Petstuff, Inc., **14** 386; **41** 297
Pettibone Corporation, **19** 365
Petzazz, **14** 386
Peugeot S.A., I 163, 187–88; **II** 13; **III** 508; **11** 104; **26** 11. *See also* PSA Peugeot Citroen S.A.
The Pew Charitable Trusts, 35 337–40
Pez Candy, Inc., 38 355–57
Pfaff-Pegasus of U.S.A. Inc., **15** 385
Pfaltz & Bauer, Inc., **38** 3
The Pfaltzgraff Co. *See* Susquehanna Pfaltzgraff Company.
Pfaudler Vacuum Co., **I** 287
Pfauter-Maag Cutting Tools, **24** 186
PFCI. *See* Pulte Financial Companies, Inc.
PFD Supply, Inc., **47** 304
PFI Acquisition Corp., **17** 184
Pfizer, Hoechst Celanese Corp., **8** 399
Pfizer Inc., I 301, 367, **661–63**, 668; **9** 356, **402–05 (upd.)**; **10** 53–54; **11** 207, 310–11, 459; **12** 4; **17** 131; **19** 105; **38** **358–67 (upd.)**; **44** 175
Pflueger Corporation, **22** 483

PG&E Corporation, 26 370–73 (upd.); **27** 131. *See also* Portland General Electric.
PGA. *See* The Professional Golfers' Association.
PGH Bricks and Pipes, **III** 735
Phaostron Instruments and Electronic Co., **18** 497–98
Phar-Mor Inc., 12 209, **390–92**, 477; **18** 507; **21** 459; **22** 157
Pharma Plus Drugmarts, **II** 649–50
PharmaCare Management Services, Inc., **45** 136
Pharmacia & Upjohn Inc., 25 22, **374–78 (upd.)**; **34** 177, 179
Pharmacia A.B., I 211, **664–65**
Pharmaco Dynamics Research, Inc., **10** 106–07
Pharmacom Systems Ltd., **II** 652
Pharmacy Corporation of America, **16** 57
PharmaKinetics Laboratories, Inc., **10** 106
Pharmanex, Inc., **27** 352
Pharmaprix Ltd., **II** 663; **49** 368
Pharmazell GmbH, **IV** 324
Pharmedix, **11** 207
Pharos, **9** 381
Phat Fashions LLC, 49 322–24
Phelan & Collender, **III** 442
Phelan Faust Paint, **8** 553
Phelps Dodge Corporation, IV 33, **176–79**, 216; **7** 261–63, 288; **19** 375; **28** **352–57 (upd.)**; **40** 411
Phenix Bank, **II** 312
Phenix Cheese Corp., **II** 533
Phenix Insurance Co., **III** 240
Phenix Mills Ltd., **II** 662
PHF Life Insurance Co., **III** 263; **IV** 623
PHH Corporation, V 496–97; **6** 357; **22** 55
PHI. *See* Pizza Hut, Inc.
Phibro Corporation, **II** 447–48; **IV** 80; **13** 447–48; **21** 67
Philadelphia and Reading Corp., **I** 440; **II** 329; **6** 377; **25** 165
Philadelphia Carpet Company, **9** 465
Philadelphia Coke Company, **6** 487
Philadelphia Company, **6** 484, 493
Philadelphia Drug Exchange, **I** 692
Philadelphia Eagles, 37 305–08
Philadelphia Electric Company, V **695–97**; **6** 450
Philadelphia Life, **I** 527
Philadelphia Smelting and Refining Co., **IV** 31
Philadelphia Sports Clubs. *See* Town Sports International, Inc.
Philadelphia Suburban Corporation, 39 **326–29**
Philco Corp., **I** 167, 531; **II** 86; **III** 604; **13** 402
Phildar, **37** 22
Phildrew Ventures, **44** 147
Philip Environmental Inc., 16 414–16
Philip Morris Companies Inc., I 23, 269; **II** 530–34; **V** 397, 404, **405–07**, 409, 417; **6** 52; **7** 272, 274, 276, 548; **8** 53; **9** 180; **12** 337, 372; **13** 138, 517; **15** 64, 72–73, 137; **18** 72, **416–19 (upd.)**; **19** 112, 369; **20** 23; **22** 73, 338; **23** 427; **26** 249, 251; **29** 46–47; **32** 472, 476; **44** **338–43 (upd.)**. *See also* Kraft Foods Inc.
Philip Smith Theatrical Enterprises. *See* GC Companies, Inc.

Philipp Abm. Cohen, **IV** 139
Philipp Brothers Chemicals, Inc., **II** 447;
   IV 79–0; **25** 82
Philipp Holzmann AG, **II** 279, 386; **14**
   169; **16** 284, 286; **17 374–77**
Philippine Aerospace Development
   Corporation, **27** 475
Philippine Airlines, Inc., **I** 107; **6 106–08**,
   122–23; **23 379–82 (upd.)**; **27** 464
Philippine American Life Insurance Co.,
   III 195
Philippine Sinter Corp., **IV** 125
Philips, **V** 339; **6** 101; **10** 269; **22** 194
Philips Electronics N.V., **8** 153; **9** 75; **10**
   16; **12** 475, 549; **13** 396, **400–03 (upd.)**;
   14 446; **23** 389; **26** 334; **27** 190–92; **32**
   373; **34** 258; **37** 121; **47** 383–86
**Philips Electronics North America
   Corp.**, **13 396–99**; **26** 334
N.V. Philips Gloeilampenfabriken, **I** 107,
   330; **II** 25, 56, 58, **78–80**, 99, 102, 117,
   119; **III** 479, 654–55; **IV** 680; **12** 454.
   See also Philips Electronics N.V.
Philips Medical Systems, **29** 299
Phillip Hawkins, **III** 169; **6** 285
Phillip Securities, **16** 14; **43** 8
Phillippe of California, **8** 16; **36** 24
Phillips & Drew, **II** 379
Phillips & Jacobs, Inc., **14** 486
Phillips Cables, **III** 433
Phillips Carbon Black, **IV** 421
Phillips Colleges Inc., **22** 442; **39** 102
Phillips, de Pury & Luxembourg, **49
   325–27**
Phillips Manufacturing Company, **8** 464
Phillips Petroleum Company, **I** 377; **II**
   15, 408; **III** 752; **IV** 71, 290, 366, 405,
   412, 414, 445, 453, 498, **521–23**, 567,
   570–71, 575; **10** 84, 440; **11** 522; **13**
   356, 485; **17** 422; **19** 176; **24** 521; **31**
   457; **38** 407; **40 354–59 (upd.)**; **47** 70
Phillips Sheet and Tin Plate Co., **IV** 236
Phillips-Van Heusen Corporation, **24
   382–85**
PHLCorp., **11** 261
PHM Corp., **8** 461
Phoenicia Glass, **25** 266–67
Phoenix Assurance Co., **III** 242, 257, 369,
   370–74
Phoenix Financial Services, **11** 115
Phoenix Fire Office, **III** 234
Phoenix Insurance Co., **III** 389; **IV** 711
Phoenix Microsystems Inc., **13** 8
Phoenix Mutual Life Insurance, **16** 207
Phoenix Oil and Transport Co., **IV** 90
Phoenix-Rheinrohr AG, **IV** 222
Phoenix State Bank and Trust Co., **II** 213
Phoenix Technologies Ltd., **13** 482
Phone America of Carolina, **8** 311
Phonogram, **23** 389
PhotoChannel Networks, Inc., **45** 283
Photocircuits Corp., **18** 291–93
PhotoDisc Inc., **31** 216, 218
PHP Healthcare Corporation, **22 423–25**
Phuket Air Catering Company Ltd., **6**
   123–24; **27** 464
PhyCor, Inc., **36 365–69**
Physical Measurements Information, **31**
   357
Physician Corporation of America, **24** 231
Physician Sales & Service, Inc., **14
   387–89**
Physician's Weight Loss Center, **10** 383
Physicians Formula Cosmetics, **8** 512

Physicians Placement, **13** 49
Physio-Control International Corp., **18
   420–23**; **30** 316
Physiotherapy Associates Inc., **29** 453
Piaget, **27** 487, 489
Piaggio & C. S.p.A., **17** 24; **20 426–29**;
   36 472; **39** 36–37
Piam Pty. Ltd., **48** 364
PIC International Group PLC, **24
   386–88 (upd.)**
Pic 'N' Save, **17** 298–99
PIC Realty Corp., **III** 339
Picard Surgeles, **27** 93
Picault, **19** 50
Piccadilly Cafeterias, Inc., **19 299–302**
Pick, **III** 98
Pick-N-Pay, **II** 642; **9** 452
Pick Pay, **48** 63
Pickands Mather, **13** 158
Picker International Corporation, **II** 25; **8**
   352; **30** 314
Pickfords Ltd., **6** 412–14
Pickfords Removals, **49** 22
Pickland Mather & Co., **IV** 409
PickOmatic Systems, **8** 135
Pickwick Dress Co., **III** 54
Pickwick International, **I** 613; **9** 360; **38**
   315
Piclands Mather, **7** 308
Pico Ski Area Management Company, **28**
   21
Picture Classified Network, **IV** 597
PictureTel Corp., **10 455–57**; **27 363–66
   (upd.)**
Piece Goods Shops, **16** 198
Piedmont Airlines, Inc., **6** 132; **12** 490; **28**
   507
Piedmont Coca-Cola Bottling Partnership,
   10 223
Piedmont Concrete, **III** 739
Piedmont Natural Gas Company, Inc.,
   27 367–69
Piedmont Pulp and Paper Co. *See*
   Westvaco Corporation.
Pier 1 Imports, Inc., **12** 179, 200,
   393–95; **34 337–41 (upd.)**
Pierburg GmbH, **9** 445–46
Pierce, **IV** 478
Pierce Brothers, **6** 295
Pierce Leahy Corporation, **24 389–92**.
   See also Iron Mountain Inc.
Pierce National Life, **22** 314
Pierce Steam Heating Co., **III** 663
Piercing Pagoda, Inc., **29 382–84**; **40** 472
Pierre & Vacances SA, **48 314–16**
Pierre Foods, **13** 270–72; **29** 203
Pierson, Heldring, and Pierson, **II** 185
Pietrafesa Corporation, **29** 208
Pietro's Pizza Parlors, **II** 480–81; **26**
   56–57; **44** 85
Piezo Electric Product, Inc., **16** 239
Pig Improvement Co., **II** 500
Piggly Wiggly Southern, Inc., **II** 571,
   624; **13** 251–52, **404–06**; **18** 6, 8; **21**
   455; **22** 127; **26** 47; **27** 245; **31** 406,
   408; **32** 260
Pignone, **IV** 420
Pike Adding Machine, **III** 165
Pike Corporation of America, **I** 570; **8** 191
Pikrose and Co. Ltd., **IV** 136
Pilgrim Curtain Co., **III** 213
Pilgrim's Pride Corporation, **7 432–33**;
   23 383–85 (upd.); **39** 229

Pilkington plc, **I** 429; **II** 475; **III** 56,
   641–42, 676–77, 714–15, **724–27**; **16** 7,
   9, 120–21; **22** 434; **34 342–47 (upd.)**
Pillar Holdings, **IV** 191
Pilliod Furniture, Inc., **12** 300
Pillowtex Corporation, **19 303–05**; **31**
   200; **41 299–302 (upd.)**
Pillsbury Company, **II** 133, 414, 493–94,
   511, **555–57**, 575, 613–15; **7** 106, 128,
   277, 469, 547; **8** 53–54; **10** 147, 176; **11**
   23; **12** 80, 510; **13 407–09 (upd.)**, 516;
   14 212, 214; **15** 64; **16** 71; **17** 70–71,
   434; **22** 59, 426; **24** 140–41; **25** 179,
   241; **27** 196, 287; **29** 433; **32** 32, 67; **38**
   100
Pillsbury Madison & Sutro LLP, **29
   385–88**
Pilot, **I** 531
Pilot Corporation, **49 328–30**
Pilot Freight Carriers, **27** 474
Pilot Insurance Agency, **III** 204
Pinal-Dome Oil, **IV** 569; **24** 520
Pinault-Printemps-Redoute S.A., **15** 386;
   19 306–09 (upd.); **22** 362; **27** 513; **41**
   185–86; **42** 171
Pincus & Co., **7** 305
Pine Tree Casting. *See* Sturm, Ruger &
   Company, Inc.
Pinecliff Publishing Company, **10** 357
Pinelands, Inc., **9** 119; **26** 33
Pinelands Water Company, **45** 275, 277
Pineville Kraft Corp., **IV** 276
Pinewood Studios, **II** 157
Pininfarina, **I** 188
Pinkerton's Inc., **9 406–09**; **13** 124–25;
   14 541; **16** 48; **41** 77, 79. *See also*
   Securitas AB.
Pinnacle Art and Frame, **31** 436
Pinnacle Books, **25** 483
Pinnacle Fitness, **25** 42
Pinnacle West Capital Corporation, **6
   545–47**; **26** 359
Pinsetter Corp., **III** 443
Pinto Island Metals Company, **15** 116
Pioneer Airlines, **I** 96; **21** 141
Pioneer Asphalt Co., **I** 404; **36** 146–47
Pioneer Asphalts Pty. Ltd., **III** 728
Pioneer Bank, **41** 312
Pioneer Concrete Services Ltd., **III** 728–29
Pioneer Cotton Mill, **12** 503
Pioneer Electronic Corporation, **II** 103;
   III 604–06; **28 358–61 (upd.)**
Pioneer Federal Savings Bank, **10** 340; **11**
   115
Pioneer Financial Corp., **11** 447
Pioneer Food Stores Co-op, **24** 528
Pioneer Hi-Bred International, Inc., **9
   410–12**; **17** 131; **21** 387; **41 303–06
   (upd.)**
Pioneer International Limited, **III** 687,
   728–30; **28** 83
Pioneer Life Insurance Co., **III** 274
Pioneer Natural Gas Company, **10** 82
Pioneer Outdoor, **27** 280
Pioneer Plastics Corporation, **31** 399–400
Pioneer Readymixed Concrete and Mortar
   Proprietary Ltd., **III** 728
Pioneer Saws Ltd., **III** 598
Pioneer-Standard Electronics Inc., **13** 47;
   19 310–14
Pipasa, **41** 329
Pipe Line Service Company. *See* Plexco.
Pipeline and Products Marketing Co., **IV**
   473

Piper Aircraft Corp., **I** 482; **II** 403; **8** 49–50

Piper Jaffray Companies Inc., 22 426–30, 465. *See also* U.S. Bancorp.

Pirelli S.p.A., IV 174, 420; **V** 249–51; **10** 319; **15** 353–56 **(upd.)**; **16** 318; **21** 73; **28** 262

Piscataquis Canal and Railroad Company, **16** 348

Pisces Inc., **13** 321

Pispalan Werhoomo Oy, **I** 387

The Piston Ring Company, **I** 199; **10** 492

Pitcairn Aviation, **I** 101

Pitney Bowes, Inc., III 156–58, 159; **19** 315–18 **(upd.)**; **47** 295–99 **(upd.)**

Pittman Company, **28** 350

Pittsburgh & Lake Angeline Iron Company, **13** 156

Pittsburgh & Lake Erie Railroad, **I** 472

Pittsburgh Aluminum Alloys Inc., **12** 353

Pittsburgh Brewing Co., **10** 169–70; **18** 70, 72

Pittsburgh Chemical Co., **IV** 573; **7** 551

Pittsburgh Consolidation Coal Co., **8** 346

Pittsburgh Corning Corp., **III** 683

Pittsburgh Life, **III** 274

Pittsburgh National Bank, **II** 317, 342; **22** 55

Pittsburgh National Corp., **II** 342

Pittsburgh Paint & Glass. *See* PPG Industries, Inc.

Pittsburgh Plate Glass Co. *See* PPG Industries, Inc.

Pittsburgh Railway Company, **9** 413

Pittsburgh Reduction Co., **II** 315; **IV** 9, 14

Pittsburgh Steel Company, **7** 587

Pittsburgh Trust and Savings, **II** 342

The Pittston Company, IV 180–82, 566; **10** 44; **19** 319–22 **(upd.)**

Pittway Corporation, 9 413–15; **27** 361–62; **28** 133–34; **33** 334–37 **(upd.)**

Pixar Animation Studios, 34 348–51

Pixel Semiconductor, **11** 57

Pizitz, Inc., **19** 324

Pizza Dispatch. *See* Dominos's Pizza, Inc.

Pizza Hut Inc., I 221, 278, 294; **II** 614; **7** 152–53, 267, 434–35, 506; **10** 450; **11** 50; **12** 123; **13** 336, 516; **14** 107; **15** 344–46; **16** 446; **17** 71, 537; **21** 24–25, 315, 405–07 **(upd.)**; **22** 353; **24** 295; **25** 179–80, 227; **28** 238; **33** 388; **40** 340

Pizza Inn, Inc., 46 346–49; **16** 447; **25** 179

PizzaCo, Inc., **7** 152

Pizzeria Uno, **25** 178

PJS Publications, **22** 442

PKbanken, **II** 353

Place Two, **V** 156

Placer Cego Petroleum Ltd., **IV** 367

Placer Development Ltd., **IV** 19

Placer Dome Inc., IV 571; **20** 430–33; **24** 522; **36** 314

Placid Oil Co., **7** 228

Plaid Holdings Corp., **9** 157

Plain Jane Dress Company, **8** 169

Plainwell Paper Co., Inc., **8** 103

Planet Hollywood International, Inc., 18 424–26; **25** 387–88; **32** 241, 243–44; **41** 307–10 **(upd.)**

Planet Insurance Co., **III** 343

Planet Waves, **48** 232

Plank Road Brewery, **I** 269; **12** 337

Plankinton Packing Co., **III** 534

Plant Genetics Inc., **I** 266; **21** 320

Planters Company, **24** 287

Planters Lifesavers, **14** 274–75

Planters Nut & Chocolate Co., **I** 219; **II** 544

Plas-Techs, Inc., **15** 35

Plastic Coating Corporation, **IV** 330; **8** 483

Plastic Containers, Inc., **15** 129; **25** 512

Plastic Engineered Products Company. *See* Ballard Medical Products.

Plastic Parts, Inc., **19** 277

Plasticos Metalgrafica, **I** 231

Plastics, Inc., **13** 41

Plasto Bambola. *See* BRIO AB.

Plastrier. *See* Compagnie de Saint-Gobain S.A.

Plate Glass Group, **24** 450

Plateau Holdings, Inc., **12** 260; **13** 502

Platinum Entertainment, Inc., 35 341–44

PLATINUM Technology, Inc., 14 390–92

Plato Learning, Inc., 44 344–47

Platt & Co., **I** 506

Platt Bros., **III** 636

Platt's Price Service, Inc., **IV** 636–37

Play by Play Toys & Novelties, Inc., 26 374–76

Play It Again Sam (PIAS), **44** 164

Play It Again Sports, **18** 207–08

Playboy Enterprises, Inc., 18 427–30; **48** 148

PlayCore, Inc., 27 370–72

Players International, Inc., 16 263, 275; **19** 402; **22** 431–33; **33** 41; **43** 226–27

Playland, **16** 389

Playmates Toys, 23 386–88

Playmobil. *See* geobra Brandstätter GmbH & Co. KG.

Playskool, Inc., III 504, 506; **12** 169; **13** 317; **16** 267; **25** 379–81; **43** 229, 232

Playtex Products, Inc., II 448, 468; **8** 511; **13** 448; **15** 357–60; **24** 480

Playworld, **16** 389–90

Plaza Coloso S.A. de C.V., **10** 189

Plaza Medical Group, **6** 184

Plaza Securities, **I** 170

PLC. *See* Prescription Learning Corporation.

Pleasant Company, 25 314; **27** 373–75

Pleasurama PLC, **I** 248; **12** 228; **32** 243

Plessey Company, PLC, I 25, 39, 81–82; **IV** 100; **6** 241; **33** 287–88

Plews Manufacturing Co., **III** 602

Plexco, **7** 30–31

Plexus Corporation, 35 345–47

Plezall Wipers, Inc., **15** 502

Plitt Theatres, Inc., **6** 162; **23** 126

Plon et Juillard, **IV** 614

Plough Inc., **I** 684; **49** 356

Plum Associates, **12** 270

Plum Creek Timber Company, Inc., 43 304–06

Pluma, Inc., 27 376–78

Plumb Tool, **II** 16

Plus Development Corporation, **10** 458–59

Plus Mark, Inc., **7** 24

Plus System Inc., **9** 537

Plus-Ultra, **II** 196

Plus Vita, **36** 162

Pluto Technologies International Inc., **38** 72

Ply Gem Industries Inc., 12 396–98; **23** 225

Plymouth County Electric Co., **14** 124

Plymouth Mills Inc., **23** 66

PMC Contract Research AB, **21** 425

PMC Specialties Group, **III** 745

PMI Corporation, **6** 140. *See also* Physical Measurements Information

The PMI Group, Inc., 49 331–33

PMI Mortgage Insurance Company, **10** 50

PMS Consolidated, **8** 347

PMT Services, Inc., 24 393–95

PN Pertambangan Minyak Dan Gas Bumi Negara, **IV** 492

PNC Bank Corp., 13 410–12 **(upd.)**; **14** 103; **18** 63

PNC Financial Corporation, **II** 317, 342–43; **9** 476; **17** 114

The PNC Financial Services Group Inc., 46 350–53 **(upd.)**

Pneumo Abex Corp., **I** 456–58; **III** 512; **10** 553–54; **38** 293–94

Pneumo Dynamics Corporation, **8** 409

PNL. *See* Pacific Northwest Laboratories.

PNM. *See* Public Service Company of New Mexico.

PNP. *See* Pacific Northwest Power Company.

POAS, **IV** 563

POB Polyolefine Burghausen GmbH, **IV** 487

Pocahontas Foods USA, **31** 359, 361

Pocket Books, Inc., **10** 480; **13** 559–60

Poclain Company, **10** 380

Poe & Associates, Inc., **41** 63–64

Pogo Producing Company, I 441; **39** 330–32

Pohang Iron and Steel Company Ltd., IV 183–85; **17** 351

Pohjan Sellu Oy, **IV** 316

Pohjoismainen Osakepankki, **II** 302

Pohjola Voima Oy, **IV** 348

Pohjolan Osakepankki, **II** 303

Point Chehalis Packers, **13** 244

Polak & Schwarz Essencefabricken, **9** 290

Poland Spring Natural Spring Water Co., **31** 229

Polar Manufacturing Company, **16** 32

Polar Star Milling Company, **7** 241

Polaris Industries Inc., 12 399–402; **35** 348–53 **(upd.)**; **40** 47, 50

Polaroid Corporation, I 30–31; **II** 412; **III** 475–77, 549, 584, 607–09; **IV** 330; **7** 161–62, 436–39 **(upd.)**; **12** 180; **28** 362–66 **(upd.)**; **36** 171–73; **41** 104, 106

Polbeth Packaging Limited, **12** 377

Polenghi, **25** 84

Policy Management Systems Corporation, 11 394–95

Poliet S.A., 33 175–77, 338–40; **40** 108

Polioles, S.A. de C.V., **19** 10, 12

Politos, S.A. de C.V., **23** 171

Polk Audio, Inc., 34 352–54

Pollenex Corp., **19** 360

Polo Food Corporation, **10** 250

Polo/Ralph Lauren Corporation, 9 157; **12** 403–05; **16** 61; **25** 48

Polser, **19** 49, 51

Polskie Linie Lotnicze S.A. *See* LOT Polish Airlines.

Poly-Glas Systems, Inc., **21** 65

Poly-Hi Corporation, **8** 359

Poly P, Inc., **IV** 458

Poly Version, Inc., **III** 645

Polyblend Corporation, **7** 4

Polycell Holdings, **IV** 666; **17** 397

Polydesign België, **16** 421

Polydesign Nederland, **16** 421

Polydor B.V., **23** 389

Polydor KK, **23** 390
Polydress Plastic GmbH, **7** 141
Polygon Networks Inc., **41** 73
PolyGram N.V., **13** 402; **22** 194; **23** 389–92; **25** 411; **26** 152, 314, 394; **31** 269
Polyken Technologies, **11** 220
Polymer Technologies Corporation, **26** 287
Polysar Energy & Chemical Corporation of Toronto, **V** 674
Polysius AG, **IV** 89
Pomeroy Computer Resources, Inc., **33** 341–44
Pomeroy's, **16** 61
Pommersche Papierfabrik Hohenkrug, **III** 692
Pommery et Greno, **II** 475
Ponderosa Steakhouse, **7** 336; **12** 373; **14** 331; **15** 361–64
Ponderosa System Inc., **12** 199
Pont-à-Mousson S.A., **III** 675, 677–78, 704; **16** 119, 121–22; **21** 253
Pont Royal SA, **48** 316
Pontiac, **III** 458; **10** 353
Pontificia, **III** 207
Ponto Frio Bonzao, **22** 321
Pony Express, **II** 380–81, 395
Poore Brothers, Inc., **44** 348–50
Poorman-Douglas Corporation, **13** 468
Pop.com, **43** 144
Pope and Talbot, Inc., **12** 406–08
Pope Cable and Wire B.V., **19** 45
Pope Tin Plate Co., **IV** 236; **26** 527
Popeye's/Church's, **23** 115, 117
Popeyes Famous Fried Chicken and Biscuits, Inc., **7** 26–28; **32** 13
Pophitt Cereals, Inc., **22** 337
Poppe Tyson Inc., **23** 479; **25** 91
Poppin' Fresh Pies, Inc., **12** 510
Popsicle, **II** 573; **14** 205
Popular Aviation Company, **12** 560
Popular Club Plan, **12** 280; **34** 232
Popular, Inc., **41** 311–13
Popular Merchandise, Inc., **12** 280
Pori, **IV** 350
Poron Diffusion, **9** 394
Poron, S.A., **42** 268–69
Porsche AG, **13** 28, 219, 413–15; **31** 363–366 (upd.); **36** 198
Port Arthur Finance Corp., **37** 309
The Port Authority of New York and New Jersey, **47** 359; **48** 317–20
Port Blakely Mill Company, **17** 438
Port Dickson Power Sdn. Bhd., **36** 435–36
Port Harcourt Refining Co., **IV** 473
Port of London Authority, **48** 317
Port Stockton Food Distributors, Inc., **16** 451, 453
Portage Industries Corp., **19** 415
Portal Software, Inc., **47** 300–03
Portals Water Treatment, **11** 510
Porter-Cable Corporation, **26** 361–63
Porter Chadburn plc, **28** 252
Porter Shoe Manufacturing Company, **13** 360
Portex, **25** 431
Portia Management Services Ltd., **30** 318
Portland General Corporation, **6** 548–51
Portland General Electric, **45** 313
Portland Heavy Industries, **10** 369
Portland Plastics, **25** 430–31
Portland-Zementwerke Heidelberg A.G., **23** 326
Portnet, **6** 435

Portsmouth & Sunderland, **35** 242, 244
Portugalia, **46** 398
Portways, **9** 92
Poseidon Exploration Ltd., **IV** 84; **7** 188
Posey, Quest, Genova, **6** 48
Positive Response Television, Inc., **27** 337–38
Post Office Counters, **V** 496
Post Office Group, **V** 498–501
Post Properties, Inc., **26** 377–79
PostBank, **II** 189
La Poste, **V** 470–72
Posti- Ja Telelaitos, **6** 329–31
PostScript, **17** 177
Postum Cereal Company, **II** 497, 523, 530–31; **7** 272–73; **13** 291
Potash Corporation of Saskatchewan Inc., **18** 51, 431–33; **27** 318
Potlatch Corporation, **IV** 282; **8** 428–30; **9** 260; **19** 445; **34** 355–59 (upd.)
Potomac Edison Company, **38** 39–40
Potomac Electric Power Company, **6** 552–54; **25** 46
Potomac Insurance Co., **III** 257
Potomac Leasing, **III** 137
Potter & Brumfield Inc., **11** 396–98
Pottery Barn, **13** 42; **17** 548–50
Potts, **IV** 58
Poulan/Weed Eater. *See* White Consolidated Industries Inc.
Poulsen Wireless, **II** 490
PowCon, Inc., **17** 534
Powell Duffryn plc, **III** 502; **IV** 38; **31** 367–70
Powell Energy Products, **8** 321
Powell Group, **33** 32
Powell River Co. Ltd., **IV** 306–07
Powell's Books, Inc., **37** 181; **40** 360–63
Power Applications & Manufacturing Company, Inc., **6** 441
Power Corporation of Canada, **36** 370–74 (upd.)
Power Financial Corp., **III** 260–61
Power Jets Ltd., **I** 81
Power Parts Co., **7** 358
Power Products, **8** 515
Power Specialty Company, **6** 145
Power Team, **10** 492
PowerBar Inc., **44** 351–53
Powercor. *See* PacifiCorp.
PowerFone Holdings, **10** 433
PowerGen PLC, **11** 399–401; **12** 349; **13** 458, 484
Powerhouse Technologies, Inc., **13** 485; **27** 379–81
Powers Accounting Machine Company, **6** 240
Powers Regulator, **III** 535
Powers-Samas, **6** 240
PowerSoft Corp., **11** 77; **15** 374
Powertel Inc., **48** 130
Pozzi-Renati Millwork Products, Inc., **8** 135
PP&L. *See* Pennsylvania Power & Light Company.
PP&L Global, Inc., **44** 291
PPG Industries, Inc., **I** 330, 341–42; **III** 21, 641, 667, 676, 722, 725, **731–33**; **8** 153, 222, 224; **16** 120–21; **20** 415; **21** 221, 223; **22** 147, **434–37 (upd.)**; **37** 73; **39** 292
PPI. *See* Precision Pattern Inc.
PPL Corporation, **41** 314–17 **(upd.)**
PR Holdings, **23** 382

PR Newswire, **35** 354–56
Prac, **I** 281
Practical and Educational Books, **13** 105
Practical Business Solutions, Inc., **18** 112
Prada Holding B.V., **45** 342–45
Pragma Bio-Tech, Inc., **11** 424
Prairie Farmer Publishing Co., **II** 129
Prairie Farms Dairy, Inc., **47** 304–07
Prairie Holding Co., **IV** 571; **24** 522
Prairie Oil and Gas Co., **IV** 368
Prairielands Energy Marketing, Inc., **7** 322, 325
Prakla Seismos, **17** 419
Pratt & Whitney, **I** 47, 78, 82–85, 128, 434; **II** 48; **III** 482; **6** 128; **7** 456; **9** 14, 16–18, 244–46, **416–18**; **10** 162; **11** 299, 427; **12** 71; **13** 386; **14** 564; **24** 312; **25** 267; **39** 313
Pratt Holding, Ltd., **IV** 312; **19** 268
Pratt Hotel Corporation, **21** 275; **22** 438
Pratt Properties Inc., **8** 349
Pratta Electronic Materials, Inc., **26** 425
Praxair, Inc., **11** 402–04; **16** 462; **43** 265; **48** 321–24 **(upd.)**
Praxis Biologics, **8** 26; **27** 115
Praxis Corporation, **30** 499
Pre-Fab Cushioning, **9** 93
Pre-Paid Legal Services, Inc., **20** 434–37
PreAnalytiX, **39** 335
Precious Metals Development, **IV** 79
Precise Fabrication Corporation, **33** 257
Precise Imports Corp., **21** 516
Precision Castparts Corp., **15** 365–67
Precision Games, **16** 471
Precision Husky Corporation, **26** 494
Precision Interconnect Corporation, **14** 27
Precision LensCrafters, **13** 391
Precision Moulds, Ltd., **25** 312
Precision Optical Co., **III** 120, 575
Precision Optical Industry Company, Ltd. *See* Canon Inc.
Precision Pattern Inc., **36** 159
Precision Power, Inc., **21** 514
Precision Response Corporation, **47** 420
Precision Software Corp., **14** 319
Precision Studios, **12** 529
Precision Tube Formers, Inc., **17** 234
Precor, **III** 610–11
Predica, **II** 266
Predicasts Inc., **12** 562; **17** 254
Preferred Medical Products. *See* Ballard Medical Products.
Preferred Products, Inc., **II** 669; **18** 504
PREINCO Holdings, Inc., **11** 532
PREL&P. *See* Portland Railway Electric Light & Power Company.
Prelude Corp., **III** 643
Premark International, Inc., **II** 534; **III** 610–12; **14** 548; **28** 479–80
Premcor Inc., **37** 309–11
Premex A.G., **II** 369
Premier (Transvaal) Diamond Mining Co., **IV** 65–66
Premier & Potter Printing Press Co., Inc., **II** 37
Premier Brands Foods, **II** 514
Premier Consolidated Oilfields PLC, **IV** 383
Premier Cruise Lines, **6** 368; **27** 92
Premier Diamond Mining Company, **7** 122
Premier Health Alliance Inc., **10** 143
Premier Industrial Corporation, **9** 419–21; **19** 311
Premier Insurance Co., **26** 487

Premier Medical Services, **31** 357
Premier Milling Co., **II** 465
Premier One Products, Inc., **37** 285
Premier Parks, Inc., 27 382–84
Premier Radio Networks, Inc., **23** 292, 294
Premier Rehabilitation Centers, **29** 400
Premier Sport Group Inc., **23** 66
Premiere Products, **I** 403
Premisteres S.A., **II** 663
Premium Standard Farms, Inc., 30 353–55
PremiumWear, Inc., 30 356–59
Prémontré, **III** 676; **16** 120
Prentice Hall Computer Publishing, **10** 24
Prentice Hall Inc., **I** 453; **IV** 672; **19** 405; **23** 503
Prescott Ball & Turben, **III** 271; **12** 60
Prescott Investors, **14** 303
Prescription Learning Corporation, **7** 256; **25** 253
Présence, **III** 211
La Preservatrice, **III** 242
Preserver Group, Inc., 44 354–56
Preserves and Honey, Inc., **II** 497
President Baking Co., **36** 313
President Casinos, Inc., 22 438–40
President Riverboat Casino-Mississippi Inc., **21** 300
Presidential Airlines, **I** 117
Presidents Island Steel & Wire Company. *See* Laclede Steel Company.
Presidio Oil Co., **III** 197; **IV** 123
Press Associates, **IV** 669; **19** 334
Press Trust of India, **IV** 669
Presse Pocket, **IV** 614
Pressed Steel Car Co., **6** 395; **25** 169
Presses de la Cité, **IV** 614–15
Presstar Printing, **25** 183
Presstek, Inc., 33 345–48
Pressware International, **12** 377
Prest-O-Lite Co., Inc., **I** 399; **9** 16, 516; **11** 402
Prestage Farms, **46** 83
Prestige et Collections, **III** 48
Prestige Fragrance & Cosmetics, Inc., **22** 158
The Prestige Group plc., **19** 171
Prestige International, **33** 284
Prestige Leather Creations, **31** 435–36
Prestige Properties, **23** 388
Presto Products, Inc., **II** 609–10; **IV** 187; **19** 348
Preston Corporation, 6 421–23; 14 566, 568
Prestone Products Corp., **22** 32; **26** 349
Prestwick Mortgage Group, **25** 187
Pretty Good Privacy, Inc., **25** 349
Pretty Neat Corp., **12** 216
Pretty Paper Inc., **14** 499
Pretty Polly, **I** 429
Pretzel Time. *See* Mrs. Fields' Original Cookies, Inc.
Pretzelmaker. *See* Mrs. Fields' Original Cookies, Inc.
Pretzels Incorporated, **24** 241
Preussag AG, I 542–43; **II** 386; **IV** 109, 201, 231; **17 378–82; 21** 370; **28** 454; **42 279–83 (upd.); 44** 432
Preussenelektra Aktiengesellschaft, I 542; **V 698–700; 39** 57
Preval, **19** 49–50
Previews, Inc., **21** 96
PreVision Marketing, Inc., **37** 409
Priam Corporation, **10** 458

Priba, **26** 158, 160
Pribina, **25** 85
Price Chopper Supermarkets. *See* The Golub Corporation.
Price Club, **V** 162–64
Price Co., **34** 198
Price Communications Corporation, 42 284–86
Price Company Ltd, II 664; **IV** 246–47; **V** 162–64; **14** 393–94; **25** 11
Price Enterprises, Inc., **14** 395
Price, McCormick & Co., **26** 451
Price Rite, **25** 67
Price Waterhouse LLP, III 84, 420, 527; **9** 422–24; **14** 245; **26** 439. *See also* PricewaterhouseCoopers
PriceCostco, Inc., 14 393–95
Pricel, **6** 373; **21** 103
Pricesearch Ltd Co, **48** 224
PricewaterhouseCoopers, 29 389–94 (upd.)
Prichard and Constance, **III** 65
Pride & Clarke, **III** 523
Pride Petroleum Services. *See* DeKalb Genetics Corporation.
Priggen Steel Building Co., **8** 545
Primadonna Resorts Inc., **17** 318
Primark Corp., 10 89–90; **13 416–18**
Prime Care International, Inc., **36** 367
Prime Computer, Inc. *See* Computervision Corporation.
Prime Motor Inns Inc., **III** 103; **IV** 718; **11** 177; **17** 238
The Prime-Mover Co., **13** 267
Prime Service, Inc., **28** 40
Prime Telecommunications Corporation, **8** 311
PrimeAmerica, **III** 340
Primedex Health Systems, Inc., 25 382–85
Primedia Inc., 7 286; **12** 306; **21** 403–04; **22 441–43; 23** 156, 158, 344, 417; **24** 274
Primergy Corp., **39** 261
Primerica Corporation, I 597, 599–602, 604, 607–09, **612–14**, 615; **II** 422; **III** 283 **8** 118; **9** 218–19, 360–61; **11** 29; **15** 464; **27** 47; **36** 202. *See also* American Can Co.
Primerica Financial Services, **30** 124
PriMerit Bank, **19** 412
Primes Régal Inc., **II** 651
PrimeSource, **26** 542
Primestar, **38** 176
PRIMESTAR Partners L.P., **28** 241
Primex Fibre Ltd., **IV** 328
Primo Foods Ltd., **I** 457; **7** 430
Prince Co., **II** 473
Prince Gardner Company, **17** 465; **23** 21
Prince Golf International, Ltd., **23** 450
Prince Holding Corporation, **26** 231
Prince Motor Co. Ltd., **I** 184
Prince of Wales Hotels, PLC, **14** 106; **25** 308
Prince Sports Group, Inc., 15 368–70
Prince Street Technologies, Ltd., **8** 271
Prince William Bank, **II** 337; **10** 425
Princess Cruise Lines, IV 256; **22 444–46**
Princess Dorothy Coal Co., **IV** 29
Princess Hotel Group, **21** 353
Princess Hotels International Inc., **45** 82
Princess Metropole, **21** 354
Princeton Gas Service Company, **6** 529

Princeton Laboratories Products Company, **8** 84; **38** 124
The Princeton Review, Inc., 12 142; **42** 210, **287–90**
Princeton Telecommunications Corporation, **26** 38
Princeville Airlines, **24** 22
Principal Mutual Life Insurance Company, III 328–30
Principles, **V** 21–22
Princor Financial Services Corp., **III** 329
Pringle Barge Line Co., **17** 357
Print Technologies, Inc., **22** 357
Printex Corporation, **9** 363
Printrak, A Motorola Company, 44 357–59
Printronix, Inc., 14 377–78; **18 434–36**
Priority Records, **22** 194
Pripps Ringnes, **18** 394, 396–97
Prism Systems Inc., **6** 310
Prismo Universal, **III** 735
Prisunic SA, **V** 9–11; **19 307–09**
Prisunic-Uniprix, **26** 160
Pritchard Corporation. *See* Black & Veatch, Inc.
Pritzker & Pritzker, **III** 96–97
Privatbanken, **II** 352
Pro-Fac Cooperative, Inc., **7** 104–06; **21** 154–55, 157
Pro-Lawn, **19** 250
Pro-Line Corporation, **36** 26
Pro-optik AG, **31** 203
Probe Exploration Inc., **25** 232
Process Engineering Inc., **21** 108
Process Systems International, **21** 108
Processing Technologies International. *See* Food Ingredients Technologies.
Procino-Rossi Corp., **II** 511
Procor Limited, **16** 357
Procordia Foods, **II** 478; **18** 396
Procter & Gamble Company, I 34, 129, 290, 331, 366; **II** 478, 493, 544, 590, 684, 616; **III** 20–25, 36–38, 40–41, 44, **50–53; IV** 282, 290, 329–30; **6** 26–27, 50–52, 129, 363; **7** 277, 300, 419; **8** 63, 106–07, 253, 282, 344, 399, **431–35 (upd.)**, 477, 511–12; **9** 260, 291, 317–19, 552; **10** 54, 288; **11** 41, 421; **12** 80, 126–27, 439; **13** 39, 197, 199, 215; **14** 121–22, 262, 275; **15** 357; **16** 302–04, 440; **18** 68, 147–49, 217, 229; **22** 146–47, 210; **26 380–85 (upd.); 32** 208, 474–77; **35** 111, 113; **37** 270; **38** 365; **42** 51; **43** 257–58
Proctor & Collier, **I** 19
Proctor & Schwartz, **17** 213
Proctor-Silex. *See* Hamilton Beach/Proctor-Silex Inc.
Prodega Ltd. *See* Bon Appetit Holding AG.
Prodigy Communications Corporation, 10 237–38; **12** 562; **13** 92; **27** 517; **34 360–62**
Product Components, Inc., **19** 415
Production Association Kirishinefteorgsintez, **48** 378
Productos Ortiz, **II** 594
Produits Chimiques Ugine Kuhlmann, **I** 303; **IV** 547
Produits Jaeger, **27** 258
Profarmaco Nobel S.r.l., **16** 69
Professional Care Service, **6** 42
Professional Computer Resources, Inc., **10** 513

Professional Education Systems, Inc., **17** 272

The Professional Golfers' Association of America, **41** 318–21

Professional Health Care Management Inc., **14** 209

Professional Research, **III** 73

Proffitt's, Inc., **19** 323–25, 510, 512. *See also* Saks Holdings, Inc.

Profile Extrusion Company, **22** 337

Profimatics, Inc., **11** 66

PROFITCo., **II** 231

Progenx, Inc., **47** 221

Progil, **I** 389

Progress Development Organisation, **10** 169

Progress Software Corporation, **15** 371–74

Progressive Bagel Concepts, Inc. *See* Einstein/Noah Bagel Corporation.

Progressive Corporation, **11** 405–07; **29** 395–98 (upd.)

Progressive Distributions Systems, **44** 334

Progressive Distributors, **12** 220

Progressive Grocery Stores, **7** 202

Progressive Networks, **37** 193

Progresso, **I** 514; **14** 212

Project Carriers. *See* Hansa Linie.

Projexions Video Supply, Inc., **24** 96

Projiis, **II** 356

ProLab Nutrition, Inc., **49** 275, 277

Prolabo, **I** 388

Proland, **12** 139

Proler International Corp., **13** 98; **19** 380–81

Promarkt Holding GmbH, **24** 266, 270

Promigas, **IV** 418

Promodès Group, **24** 475; **26** 158, 161; **37** 21

Promotional Graphics, **15** 474

Promstroybank, **II** 242

Promus Companies, Inc., **III** 95; **9** 425–27; **15** 46; **16** 263; **22** 537; **38** 76–77; **43** 225–26

Pronto Pacific, **II** 488

Prontophot Holding Limited, **6** 490

Prontor-Werk Alfred Gauthier GmbH, **III** 446

Propaganda Films, Inc., **23** 389, 391

Property Automation Software Corporation, **49** 290

Prophet Foods, **I** 449

Propwix, **IV** 605

ProSiebenSat.1 Media AG, **46** 403

Prosim, S.A., **IV** 409

Proskauer Rose LLP, **47** 308–10

ProSource Distribution Services, Inc., **16** 397; **17** 475

Prospect Farms, Inc., **II** 584; **14** 514

The Prospect Group, Inc., **11** 188

Prospect Provisions, Inc. *See* King Kullen Grocery Co., Inc.

Prospectors Airways, **IV** 165

Protan & Fagertun, **25** 464

Protection One, Inc., **32** 372–75

Protective Closures, **7** 296–97

La Protectrice, **III** 346–47

Protek, **III** 633

Proto Industrial Tools, **III** 628

Protogene Laboratories Inc., **17** 288

Proveedora de Seguridad del Golfo, S.A. de C.V., **45** 425–26

Proventus A.B., **II** 303

Proventus Handels AB, **35** 362

Provi-Soir, **II** 652

Provi-Viande, **II** 652

Provibec, **II** 652

The Providence Journal Company, **28** 367–69; **30** 15

La Providence, **III** 210–11

Providence National Bank, **9** 228

Providence Steam and Gas Pipe Co. *See* Grinnell Corp.

Providencia, **III** 208

Provident Bank, **III** 190

Provident Institution for Savings, **13** 467

Provident Life and Accident Insurance Company of America, **III** 331–33, 404

Provident National Bank, **II** 342

Provident Services, Inc., **6** 295

Provident Travelers Mortgage Securities Corp., **III** 389

Provigo Inc., **II** 651–53; **12** 413

Provimi, **36** 185

Les Provinces Réunies, **III** 235

Provincetown-Boston Airlines, **I** 118

Provincial Bank of Ireland Ltd., **16** 13

Provincial Engineering Ltd, **8** 544

Provincial Gas Company, **6** 526

Provincial Insurance Co., **III** 373

Provincial Newspapers Ltd., **IV** 685–86; **28** 502

Provincial Traders Holding Ltd., **I** 437

Provinzial-Hülfskasse, **II** 385

Provost & Provost, **II** 651

PROWA, **22** 89

Proximity Technology, **23** 210

Prudential Assurance Company, **24** 314

Prudential Bache Securities, **9** 441

Prudential-Bache Trade Corporation, **II** 51; **21** 331

Prudential Corporation plc, **II** 319; **III** 334–36; **IV** 711; **8** 276–77. *See also* Prudential plc.

Prudential Insurance Company of America, **I** 19, 334, 402; **II** 103, 456; **III** 79, 92, 249, 259, 265–67, 273, 291–93, 313, 329, **337–41**; **IV** 410, 458; **10** 199; **11** 243; **12** 28, 453, 500; **13** 561; **14** 95, 561; **16** 135, 497; **17** 325; **22** 266; **23** 226; **25** 399; **30** 360–64 (upd.); **36** 77–78; **42** 193, 196; **45** 294

Prudential Oil & Gas, Inc., **6** 495–96

Prudential plc, **48** 325–29 (upd.)

Prudential Refining Co., **IV** 400

Prudential Steel, **IV** 74; **24** 143–44

PSA. *See* Pacific Southwest Airlines.

PSA Peugeot Citroen S.A., **7** 35; **28** 370–74 (upd.)

PSB Company, **36** 517

PSCCo. *See* Public Service Company of Colorado.

PSE, Inc., **12** 100

PSF. *See* Premium Standard Farms, Inc.

PSI. *See* Process Systems International.

PSI Resources, **6** 555–57

Psion PLC, **45** 346–49

Psychiatric Institutes of America, **III** 87–88

Psychological Corp., **IV** 623; **12** 223

PT Components, **14** 43

PT PERMINA, **IV** 492, 517

PTI Communications, Inc. *See* Pacific Telecom, Inc.

PTT Nederland N.V., **27** 472; **30** 393–94

PTT Telecom BV, **V** 299–301; **6** 303

PTV. *See* Österreichische Post- und Telegraphenverwaltung.

Pubco Corporation, **17** 383–85

Publi-Graphics, **16** 168

Public Broadcasting Stations, **29** 426

Public Home Trust Co., **III** 104

Public National Bank, **II** 230

Public Savings Insurance Co., **III** 219

Public Service Co., **14** 124

Public Service Company of Colorado, **6** 558–60

Public Service Company of Indiana. *See* PSI Energy.

Public Service Company of New Hampshire, **21** 408–12

Public Service Company of New Mexico, **6** 561–64; **27** 486

Public Service Corporation of New Jersey, **44** 360

Public Service Electric and Gas Company, **IV** 366; **V** 701–03; **11** 388

Public Service Enterprise Group Inc., **V** 701–03; **44** 360–63 (upd.)

Public Service Market. *See* The Golub Corporation.

Public Storage, Inc., **21** 476

Public/Hacienda Resorts, Inc. *See* Santa Fe Gaming Corporation.

Publicaciones Citem, S.A. de C.V., **39** 188

Publicis S.A., **13** 204; **19** 329–32; **21** 265–66; **23** 478, 480; **25** 91; **33** 180; **39** 166, 168; **42** 328, 331

Publicker Industries Inc., **I** 226; **10** 180

PubliGroupe, **49** 424

Publishers Clearing House, **23** 393–95; **27** 20

Publishers Group, Inc., **35** 357–59

Publishers Paper Co., **IV** 295, 677–78; **19** 225

Publishers Press Assoc., **IV** 607; **25** 506

Publishing and Broadcasting Ltd., **19** 400–01

Publix Super Markets Inc., **II** 155, 627; **7** 440–42; **9** 186; **20** 84, 306; **23** 261; **31** 371–374 (upd.)

Puck Holdings, **35** 474, 476

Puck Lazaroff Inc. *See* The Wolfgang Puck Food Company, Inc.

Pueblo Xtra International, Inc., **47** 311–13

Puente Oil, **IV** 385

Puerto Rican Aqueduct and Sewer Authority, **6** 441

Puerto Rican-American Insurance Co., **III** 242

Puerto Rico Electric Power Authority, **47** 314–16

Puget Mill Company, **12** 406–07

Puget Sound Alaska Van Lines. *See* Alaska Hydro-Train.

Puget Sound National Bank, **8** 469–70

Puget Sound Power And Light Company, **6** 565–67

Puget Sound Pulp and Timber Co., **IV** 281; **9** 259

Puget Sound Tug and Barge Company, **6** 382

Pulaski Furniture Corporation, **33** 349–52

Pulitzer Publishing Company, **15** 375–77

Pullman Co., **II** 403; **III** 94, 744

Pullman Savings and Loan Association, **17** 529

Pullman Standard, **7** 540

Pulsar Internacional S.A., **21** 413–15

Pulse Engineering, Inc., **29** 461

Pulte Corporation, **8** 436–38; **22** 205, 207
Pulte Homes, Inc., **42** 291–94 (upd.)
Puma AG Rudolf Dassler Sport, **35** 360–63; **36** 344, 346
AB Pump-Separator, **III** 418–19
Pumpkin Masters, Inc., **48** 330–32
Punchcraft, Inc., **III** 569; **20** 360
Purdue Fredrick Company, **13** 367
Pure-Gar, Inc., **49** 276
Pure Milk Products Cooperative, **11** 24
Pure Oil Co., **III** 497; **IV** 570; **24** 521
Pure Packed Foods, **II** 525; **13** 293
Purex Corporation, **I** 450; **III** 21; **22** 146
Purex Pool Systems, **I** 13, 342; **18** 163
Purfina, **IV** 497
Purina Mills, Inc., **32** 376–79
Puris Inc., **14** 316
Puritan-Bennett Corporation, **13** 419–21
Puritan Chemical Co., **I** 321
Puritan Fashions Corp., **22** 122
Purity Stores, **I** 146
Purity Supreme, Inc., **II** 674; **24** 462
Purle Bros., **III** 735
Purnell & Sons Ltd., **IV** 642; **7** 312
Purodenso Co., **III** 593
Purolator Courier, Inc., **6** 345–46, 390; **16** 397; **18** 177; **25** 148
Purolator Products Company, **III** 593; **21** 416–18; **28** 263
Puros de Villa Gonzales, **23** 465
Purup-Eskofot, **44** 44
Push Records, Inc., **42** 271
Puss 'n Boots, **II** 559
Putnam Investments Inc., **25** 387; **30** 355. *See also* Marsh & McLennan Companies, Inc.
Putnam Management Co., **III** 283
Putnam Reinsurance Co., **III** 198
Putt-Putt Golf Courses of America, Inc., **23** 396–98
PW Eagle, Inc., **48** 333–36
PWA Group, **IV** 323–25; **28** 446
PWS Holding Corporation, **13** 406; **26** 47
PWT Projects Ltd., **22** 89
PWT Worldwide, **11** 510
PYA/Monarch, **II** 675; **26** 504
Pyramid Breweries Inc., **33** 353–55
Pyramid Communications, Inc., **IV** 623
Pyramid Electric Company, **10** 319
Pyramid Electronics Supply, Inc., **17** 275
Pyramid Technology Corporation, **10** 504; **27** 448
Pytchley Autocar Co. Ltd., **IV** 722
Pyxis. *See* Cardinal Health, Inc.
Pyxis Resources Co., **IV** 182

Q Lube, Inc., **18** 145; **24** 339
Qantas Airways Limited, **I** 92–93; **6** 79, 91, 100, 105, **109–13**, 117; **14** 70, 73; **24 396–401** (upd.); **27** 466; **31** 104; **38** 24
Qatar General Petroleum Corporation, **IV** 524–26
Qiagen N.V., **39** 333–35
Qintex Australia Ltd., **II** 150; **25** 329
QMS Ltd., **43** 284
QO Chemicals, Inc., **14** 217
QSP, Inc., **IV** 664
Qtera Corporation, **36** 352
Quad/Graphics, Inc., **19** 333–36
Quail Oil Tools, **28** 347–48
Quaker Alloy, Inc., **39** 31–32
Quaker Fabric Corp., **19** 337–39

Quaker Oats Company, **I** 30; **II** 558–60, 575, 684; **12** 167, 169, **409–12** (upd.); **13** 186; **22** 131, 337–38; **25** 90, 314; **27** 197; **30** 219; **31** 282; **34 363–67** (upd.); **38** 349; **43** 121, 218
Quaker State Corporation, **7** 443–45; **21 419–22** (upd.); **25** 90; **26** 349
QUALCOMM Incorporated, **20** 438–41; **26** 532; **38** 271; **39** 64; **41** 289; **43** 312–13; **46** 410, 422; **47 317–21** (upd.)
Qualicare, Inc., **6** 192
QualiTROL Corporation, **7** 116–17
Quality Bakers of America, **12** 170
Quality Care Inc., **I** 249
Quality Chekd Dairies, Inc., **48** 337–39
Quality Courts Motels, Inc., **14** 105. *See also* Choice Hotels International, Inc.
Quality Dining, Inc., **18** 437–40
Quality Food Centers, Inc., **17** 386–88; **22** 271, 273
Quality Importers, **I** 226; **10** 180
Quality Inns International, **13** 363; **14** 105. *See also* Choice Hotels International, Inc.
Quality Markets, Inc., **13** 393
Quality Oil Co., **II** 624–25
Quality Paperback Book Club (QPB), **13** 105–07
Quality Products, Inc., **18** 162
Qualtec, Inc., **V** 623; **49** 145
Quanex Corporation, **13** 422–24
Quanta Computer Inc., **47** 322–24
Quantex Microsystems Inc., **24** 31
Quantum Chemical Corporation, **8 439–41**; **11** 441; **30** 231, 441
Quantum Computer Services, Inc. *See* America Online, Inc.
Quantum Corporation, **6** 230–31; **10** 56, 403, **458–59**, 463; **25** 530; **36** 299–300
Quantum Health Resources, **29** 364
Quantum Marketing International, Inc., **27** 336
Quantum Offshore Contractors, **25** 104
Quantum Overseas N.V., **7** 360
Quantum Restaurant Group, Inc., **30** 330
Quarex Industries, Inc. *See* Western Beef, Inc.
Quark, Inc., **36** 375–79
Quarrie Corporation, **12** 554
Quasi-Arc Co., **I** 315; **25** 80
Quebec Bank, **II** 344
Quebec Credit Union League, **48** 290
Québec Hydro-Electric Commission. *See* Hydro-Quebec.
Quebecor Inc., **12** 412–14; **19** 333; **26** 44; **29** 471; **47 325–28** (upd.)
Queen Casuals, **III** 530
Queen City Broadcasting, **42** 162
Queen Insurance Co., **III** 350
Queens Isetan Co., Ltd., **V** 87
Queensborough Holdings PLC, **38** 103
Queensland Alumina, **IV** 59
Queensland and Northern Territories Air Service. *See* Qantas Airways Limited.
Queensland Mines Ltd., **III** 729
Queensland Oil Refineries, **III** 672
Queiroz Pereira, **IV** 504
Quelle Group, **V** 165–67
Quennessen, **IV** 118
Quesarias Ibéricas, **23** 219
Quesnel River Pulp Co., **IV** 269
Quest Aerospace Education, Inc., **18** 521
Quest Diagnostics Inc., **26** 390–92
Quest Education Corporation, **42** 212

Quest Pharmacies Inc., **25** 504–05
Questar Corporation, **6** 568–70; **10** 432; **26 386–89** (upd.)
Questor Partners, **I** 332; **26** 185
The Quick & Reilly Group, Inc., **18** 552; **20 442–44**; **26** 65
QUICK Corp., **IV** 656
Quick-Shop, **II** 619
Quicken.com. *See* Intuit Inc.
Quickie Designs, **11** 202, 487–88
Quik Stop Markets, Inc., **12** 112
Quiksilver, Inc., **18** 441–43; **27** 329
QuikTrip Corporation, **36** 380–83
QuikWok Inc., **II** 556; **13** 408
Quill Corporation, **28** 375–77
Quillery, **27** 138
Quilter Goodison, **II** 260
Quimica Industrial Huels Do Brasil Ltda., **I** 350
Quimicos Industriales Penoles. *See* Industrias Penoles, S.A. de C.V.
Quincy Compressor Co., **I** 434–35
Quincy Family Steak House, **II** 679; **10** 331; **19** 287; **27** 17, 19
Quintana Roo, Inc., **17** 243, 245; **25** 42
Quintex Australia Limited, **25** 329
Quintiles Transnational Corporation, **21** 423–25
Quinton Hazell Automotive, **III** 495; **IV** 382–83
Quintron, Inc., **11** 475
Quintus Computer Systems, **6** 248
Quixote Corporation, **15** 378–80
Quixtar Inc., **30** 62
Quixx Corporation, **6** 580
The Quizno's Corporation, **32** 444; **42** 295–98
Quoddy Products Inc., **17** 389, 390
Quotron Systems, Inc., **III** 119; **IV** 670; **9** 49, 125; **30** 127; **47** 37
QVC Network Inc., **9** 428–29; **10** 175; **12** 315; **18** 132; **20** 75; **24** 120, 123
Qwest Communications International, Inc., **25** 499; **26** 36; **32** 218; **36** 43–44; **37** 126, **312–17**; **49** 312
QwikSilver II, Inc., **37** 119

R&B Falcon Corp. *See* Transocean Sedco Forex Inc.
R & B Manufacturing Co., **III** 569; **20** 361
R&O Software-Technik GmbH, **27** 492
R&S Technology Inc., **48** 410
R. and W. Hawaii Wholesale, Inc., **22** 15
R-Anell Custom Homes Inc., **41** 19
R-B. *See* Arby's, Inc.
R-Byte, **12** 162
R-C Holding Inc. *See* Air & Water Technologies Corporation.
R.A. Waller & Co., **III** 282
R.B. Pamplin Corp., **45** 350–52
R. Buckland & Son Ltd., **IV** 119
R.C. Bigelow, Inc., **16** 90; **49** 334–36
R.C. Willey Home Furnishings, **18** 60
R. Cubed Composites Inc., **I** 387
R.E. Funsten Co., **7** 429
R.G. Barry Corp., **17** 389–91; **44** 364–67 (upd.)
R.G. Dun-Bradstreet Corp., **IV** 604–05
R. Griggs Group Limited, **23** 399–402; **31** 413–14
R.H. Macy & Co., Inc., **I** 30; **V** 168–70; **8** 442–45 (upd.); **10** 282; **11** 349; **13** 42; **15** 281; **16** 206–07, 328, 388, 561;

23 60; 27 60, 481; 30 379–83 (upd.); 31
190, 192–93; 45 15
R.H. Squire, III 283
R.H. Stengel & Company, 13 479
R. Hoe & Co., I 602; 13 189
R. Hornibrook (NSW), I 592
R.J. Brown Co., IV 373
R.J. Reynolds, I 259, 261, 363; II 542,
544; III 16; IV 523; V 396, 404–05,
407–10, 413, 415, 417–18; 7 130, 132,
267, 365, 367; 9 533; 13 490; 14 78; 15
72–73; 16 242; 18 416; 19 369; 21 315;
27 125; 29 195; 32 344. See also RJR
Nabisco.
R.J. Reynolds Tobacco Holdings, Inc., 30
384–87 (upd.)
R.J. Tower Corporation. See Tower
Automotive, Inc.
R.K. Brown, 14 112
R.L. Crain Limited, 15 473
R.L. Manning Company, 9 363–64
R.L. Polk & Co., 10 460–62
R.N. Coate, I 216
R-O Realty, Inc., 43 314
R.O. Hull Co., I 361
R.P.M., Inc., 25 228
R.P. Scherer Corporation, I 678–80; 33
145
R.R. Bowker Co., 17 398; 23 440
R.R. Donnelley & Sons Company, IV
660–62, 673; 9 430–32 (upd.); 11 293;
12 414, 557, 559; 18 331; 19 333; 38
368–71 (upd.)
R.S.R. Corporation, 31 48
R.S. Stokvis Company, 13 499
R. Scott Associates, 11 57
R. Stock AG, IV 198
R-T Investors LC, 42 323–24
R.T. French USA, II 567
R.T. Securities, II 457
R.W. Beck, 29 353
R.W. Harmon & Sons, Inc., 6 410
R.W. Sears Watch Company, V 180
RABA PLC, 10 274
Rabbit Software Corp., 10 474
Rabobank Group, 26 419; 33 356–58
Racal-Datacom Inc., 11 408–10
Racal Electronics PLC, II 83–84; 11 408,
547; 42 373, 376
Race Z, Inc. See Action Peformance
Companies, Inc.
Rachel's Dairy Ltd., 37 197–98
Racine Hardware Co., III 58
Racine Hidraulica, 21 430
Racine Threshing Machine Works, 10 377
Racing Champions. See Action
Performance Companies, Inc.
Racing Champions Corporation, 37
318–20
Racing Collectables Club of America, Inc.
See Action Performance Companies, Inc.
Rack Rite Distributors, V 174
Racket Store. See Duckwall-ALCO Stores,
Inc.
Rada Corp., IV 250
Radian Group Inc., 42 299–301
Radiant Lamp Corp., 13 398
Radiation Dynamics, III 634–35
Radiation, Inc., II 37–38
Radiation-Medical Products Corp., I 202
Radiator Specialty Co., III 570; 20 362
Radio & Allied Industries, II 25
Radio & Television Equipment Company
(Radio-Tel), 16 200–01; 43 168–69

Radio Austria A.G., V 314–16
Radio Cap Company. See Norwood
Promotional Products, Inc.
Radio City Productions, 30 102
Radio Corporation of America. See RCA
Corporation.
Radio Flyer Inc., 34 368–70
Radio-Keith-Orpheum, II 32, 88, 135,
146–48, 175; III 428; 9 247; 12 73; 31
99
Radio Receptor Company, Inc., 10 319
Radio Shack, II 106–08; 12 470; 13 174
Radio Vertrieb Fürth. See Grundig AG.
Radiocel, 39 194
Radiometer A/S, 17 287
Radiometrics, Inc., 18 369
RadioShack Canada Inc., 30 391
RadioShack Corporation, 36 384–88
(upd.)
Radiotelevision Española, 7 511
Radisson Hotels Worldwide, 22 126–27
Radium Pharmacy, I 704
Radius Inc., 16 417–19
Radix Group, Inc., 13 20
RadNet Managed Imaging Services, Inc.,
25 382–84
Radnor Venture Partners, LP, 10 474
Raet, 39 177
Raf, Haarla Oy, IV 349
Raffinerie Tirlemontoise S.A., 27 436
Raffineriegesellschaft Vohburg/Ingolstadt
mbH, 7 141
RAG AG, 35 364–67
Rag Shops, Inc., 30 365–67
Ragan Outdoor, 27 280
Ragazzi's, 10 331
Ragnar Benson Inc., 8 43–43
RAI, I 466
Rail Link, Inc., 27 181
Railroad Enterprises, Inc., 27 347
RailTex, Inc., 20 445–47
Railtrack, 39 238
Railway Express Agency, I 456; II 382; 6
388–89; 25 146–48
Railway Maintenance Equipment Co., 14
43
Railway Officials and Employees Accident
Assoc., III 228
Railway Passengers Assurance Co., III
178, 410
Rainbow Crafts, II 502; 10 323
Rainbow Home Shopping Ltd., V 160
Rainbow Media, 47 421
Rainbow Production Corp., I 412
Rainbow Programming Holdings, 7 63–64
Rainbow Resources, IV 576
RainbowBridge Communications, Inc., 25
162
Raincoast Book Distribution, 34 5
Rainer Pulp & Paper Company, 17 439
Rainfair, Inc., 18 298, 300
Rainforest Café, Inc., 25 386–88; 32 241,
244
Rainier Brewing Company, 23 403–05
Rainier Pulp and Paper Company. See
Rayonier Inc.
Rainy River Forest Products, Inc., 26 445
Rajastan Breweries, Ltd., 18 502
Raky-Danubia, IV 485
Ralcorp Holdings, Inc., 13 293, 425, 427;
15 189, 235; 21 53, 56; 22 337; 36 238;
43 438. See also Ralston Purina
Company.
Raley's Inc., 14 396–98

Ralli International, III 502; IV 259
Rally's Hamburgers, Inc., 25 389–91; 46
97
Rally's Inc., 14 452; 15 345; 16 96–97; 23
225
Rallye S.A., 12 154. See also Casino.
Ralph & Kacoo's. See Piccadilly
Cafeterias, Inc.
Ralph Lauren. See Polo/Ralph Lauren
Corportion.
The Ralph M. Parsons Company. See The
Parsons Corporation.
Ralph Wilson Plastics, III 610–11
Ralph's Industries, 31 191
Ralphs Grocery Company, 35 368–70
Ralston Purina Company, I 608, II 544,
560, 561–63, 617; III 588; 6 50–52; 7
209, 396, 547, 556; 8 180; 9 180; 12
276, 411, 510; 13 137, 270, 293,
425–27 (upd.); 14 194–95, 558; 18 312;
21 56; 23 191. See also Ralcorp
Holdings, Inc.
Ram dis Ticaret, I 479
Ram Golf Corp., III 24; 32 447
Ram's Insurance, III 370
Ramada International Hotels & Resorts, II
142; III 99; IV 718; 9 426; 11 177; 13
66; 21 366; 25 309; 28 258; 38 320
Ramazotti, I 281
Rambol, 25 84
Ramo-Woolridge Corp., I 539; 14 510
Ramón Areces Foundation, V 52
Rampage Clothing Co., 35 94
Ramsay Youth Services, Inc., 41 322–24
Ranbar Packing, Inc. See Western Beef,
Inc.
Ranchers Packing Corp. See Western Beef,
Inc.
Rand American Investments Limited, IV
79; 21 211
Rand Capital Corp., 35 52–53
Rand Drill Co., III 525
Rand Group, Inc., 6 247; 24 234
Rand McNally & Company, 28 378–81
Rand Mines Ltd., I 422; IV 22, 79, 94
Rand Selection Corp. Ltd., IV 79
Randall's Food Markets, Inc., 40 364–67
Random House, Inc., II 90; IV 583–84,
637, 648; 13 113, 115, 178, 428–30; 14
260; 18 329; 19 6, 285; 31 375–380
(upd.); 42 287
Randon Meldkamer, 43 307
Randstad Holding n.v., 16 420–22; 43
307–10 (upd.)
Randsworth Trust P.L.C., IV 703
Range Resources Corporation, 45
353–55
Rank Organisation PLC, II 139, 147,
157–59; III 171; IV 698; 6 288; 12 229;
14 399–402 (upd.); 24 194; 26 543,
546; 32 241, 243–44; 34 140; 40 296,
298
Ranks Hovis McDougall Limited, II 157,
564–65; 28 382–85 (upd.)
Ransburg Corporation, 22 282
Ransom and Randolph Company, 10 271
Ransomes America Corp., III 600
RAO Unified Energy System of Russia,
45 356–60
Rapala-Normark Group, Ltd., 30 368–71
Rapicom, III 159
Rapid American, I 440
Rapides Bank & Trust Company, 11 107
Rapidforms, Inc., 35 130–31

Rapifax of Canada, **III** 160
Rare Hospitality International Inc., 19 340–42
RAS. *See* Riunione Adriatica di Sicurtà SpA.
Rascal House, **24** 243
Rassini Rheem, **III** 581
Ratin A/S, **49** 376
Rational GmbH, **22** 354
Rational Systems Inc., **6** 255; **25** 299
Ratti Vallensasca, **25** 312
Raufast et Fils, **35** 205
Rauland Corp., **II** 124; **13** 573
Rauma-Repola Oy, **II** 302; **IV** 316, 340, 349–50. *See also* Metso Corporation
Rauscher Pierce Refsnes, Inc., **15** 233
Raven Industries, Inc., 33 359–61
Raven Press, **14** 555
Ravenhead, **16** 120
Ravenna Metal Products Corp., **12** 344
Ravenseft Properties Ltd., **IV** 696, 704–05; **49** 246, 248
RAVIcad, **18** 20; **43** 17
Rawlings Sporting Goods Co., Inc., 7 177; **23** 449; **24 402–04**
Rawlplug Co. Ltd., **IV** 382–83
Rawls Brothers Co., **13** 369
Rawson, Holdsworth & Co., **I** 464
Ray Industries, **22** 116
Ray Simon, **24** 94
Ray Strauss Unlimited, **22** 123
Ray's Printing of Topeka, **II** 624
Raychem Corporation, III 492; **8 446–47**
Raycom Sports, **6** 33
Raymar Book Corporation, **11** 194
Raymond International Inc., **28** 201
Raymond, Jones & Co., **IV** 647
Raymond, Trice & Company, **14** 40
Raynet Corporation, **8** 447
Rayonese Textile, Inc., **29** 140
Rayonier Inc., 24 405–07
Rayovac Corporation, 13 431–34; 17 105; **23** 497; **24** 480; **39 336–40 (upd.)**
Raytheon Aircraft Holdings Inc., 46 354–57
Raytheon Company, I 463, 485, 544; **II** 41, 73, **85–87; III** 643; **8** 51, 157; **11** 197, **411–14 (upd.); 12** 46, 247; **14** 223; **17** 419, 553, 564; **21** 200; **23** 181; **24** 88; **25** 223; **36** 190–91; **38 372–77 (upd.); 42** 373, 376; **48** 252
Razorback Acquisitions, **19** 455
Razorfish, Inc., 37 321–24
RB&W Corp., **17** 372
RBC Dominion Securities, **25** 12
RCA Corporation, I 142, 454, 463; **II** 29–31, 34, 38, 56, 61, 85–86, **88–90,** 96, 102, 117–18, 120, 124, 129, 132–33, 151–52, 313, 609, 645; **III** 118, 122, 132, 149, 152, 165, 171, 569, 653–54; **IV** 252, 583, 594; **6** 164–66, 240, 266, 281, 288, 334; **7** 520; **8** 157; **9** 283; **10** 173; **11** 197, 318, 411; **12** 204, 208, 237, 454, 544, 548; **13** 106, 398, 429, 506, 573; **14** 357, 436; **16** 549; **17** 29; **20** 361; **21** 151; **22** 541; **23** 181; **26** 358, 511; **28** 349; **31** 376; **34** 186, 516; **38** 373
RCA Global Communications, Inc., **27** 304
RCG International, Inc., **III** 344
RCM Technologies, Inc., 34 371–74
RCN Corp., **25** 107
RDO Equipment Company, 33 362–65
REA. *See* Railway Express Agency.

Rea & Derick, **II** 605
Rea Construction Company, **17** 377
Rea Magnet Wire Co., **IV** 15
React-Rite, Inc., **8** 271
Read, R.L., **II** 417
Read-Rite Corp., 10 403–04, **463–64; 18** 250
The Reader's Digest Association, Inc., IV 663–64; **17 392–95 (upd.)**
Reader's Garden Inc., **22** 441
Reading & Bates Corp. *See* Transocean Sedco Forex Inc.
Reading Railroad, **9** 407
Ready Mixed Concrete, **III** 687, 737–40; **28** 82
Real Decisions, **21** 236
Real Estate Maintenance, **25** 15
Real Fresh, **25** 85
Real Goods Trading Company, **41** 177
Real-Share, Inc., **18** 542
RealCom Communications Corporation, **15** 196
Reale Mutuale, **III** 273
Reality Group Limited, **47** 165, 169
The Really Useful Group, 23 390; **26 393–95; 34** 422
Realty Development Co. *See* King Kullen Grocery Co., Inc.
Realty Investment Group, **25** 127
Realty Parking Properties II L.P., **18** 104
Réassurances, **III** 392
Reavis & McGrath, **47** 139
Recaro North America Inc., **26** 231
Reckitt & Colman plc, II 566–67; 15 46, 360; **18** 556; **22** 148; **27** 69
Reckitt Benckiser plc, 42 302–06 (upd.)
Reckson Associates Realty Corp., 47 329–31
Reconstruction Bank of Holland, **IV** 707
Reconstruction Finance Bank, **II** 292
Reconstruction Finance Corp., **I** 67, 203; **II** 261; **IV** 10, 333
Record Bar / Licorice Pizza, **9** 361
Record Merchandisers. *See* Entertainment UK.
Record World Inc., **9** 361
Recoton Corp., 15 381–83
Recoupe Recycling Technologies, **8** 104
Recovery Centers of America, **III** 88
Recovery Engineering, Inc., 25 392–94
Recreational Equipment, Inc., 18 444–47; 22 173
Recticel S.A., **III** 581; **17** 182–84
Rectigraph Co., **III** 171
Recycled Paper Greetings, Inc., 21 426–28
RED, **44** 164
Red & White, **II** 682
The Red Adair Company, **37** 171
Red Ant Entertainment, **17** 14
Red Apple Group, Inc., 23 406–08; 24 528–29; **31** 231
Red Arrow, **II** 138
Red Ball, Inc., **18** 300
Red Brick Systems Inc., **30** 246
Red Bull, **31** 244
Red Carpet Food Systems, **39** 409
Red Food Stores, Inc., **19** 327–28
Red Hat, Inc., 45 361–64
Red House Books Ltd., **29** 426
Red Kap, **V** 390–91
Red L Foods, **13** 244
Red Line HealthCare Corporation, **47** 236
Red Lion Entertainment, **29** 503

Red Lobster Inns of America, **16** 156–58
Red Lobster Restaurants, **II** 502–03; **6** 28; **10** 322–24; **19** 258
Red Oak Consulting, **42** 244
Red Owl Stores, Inc., **II** 670; **18** 506
Red Roof Inns, Inc., 13 363; **18 448–49; 21** 362
Red Rooster, **V** 35
Red Sea Insurance Co., **III** 251
Red Star Express, **14** 505
Red Star Milling Co., **II** 501; **6** 397; **10** 322
Red Storm, **41** 409
The Red Wing Co., Inc., **28** 382
Red Wing Shoe Company, Inc., 9 433–35; 30 372–75 (upd.)
Redactron, **III** 166; **6** 282
Redbook Florists Service, **28** 138
Redbook Publishing Co., **14** 460
Reddy Elevator Co., **III** 467
Reddy Ice, **II** 661
Redentza, **IV** 504
Redgate Communications, **26** 19
Redhill Tile Co., **III** 734
Redhook Ale Brewery, Inc., 31 381–84
Redi, **IV** 610
Rediffusion, **II** 139; **24** 194
Reditab S.p.A., **12** 109
Redken Laboratories, **8** 131; **24** 251
Redland Plasterboard, **28** 83
Redland plc, III 495, 688, **734–36; 14** 249, 739; **15** 154; **37** 205
Redlaw Industries Inc., **15** 247
Redman Industries, Inc., **17** 81, 83
Redmond & Co., **I** 376
La Redoute, S.A., **V** 11; **19** 306, 309
Redpath Industries, **II** 581–82
Redrow Group plc, 31 385–87
Redwood Design Automation, **11** 47; **16** 520
Redwood Fire & Casualty Insurance Co., **III** 214
Redwood Systems, **48** 112
Reebok International Ltd., V 375–77; 8 171, 303–04, 393; **9** 134–35, **436–38 (upd.); 11** 50–51, 349; **13** 513; **14** 8; **17** 244–45, 260; **18** 266; **19** 112; **22** 173; **25** 258, 352, 450; **26 396–400 (upd.); 36** 346
Reed & Ellis, **17** 439
Reed & Gamage, **13** 243
Reed Corrugated Containers, **IV** 249
Reed Elsevier plc, 19 268; **23** 271, 273; **31 388–394 (upd.); 32** 354; **33** 263, 265–66, 458; **34** 438; **43** 92–93
Reed International PLC, I 423; **IV** 270, 642, **665–67,** 711; **7** 244–45, 343; **10** 407; **12** 359; **17 396–99 (upd.); 23** 350; **49** 408
Reed Tool Coompany, **III** 429; **22** 68
Reeder Light, Ice & Fuel Company, **6** 592
Redpack, **IV** 339–40, 667; **28** 445
Reeds Jewelers, Inc., 22 447–49
Reese Finer Foods, Inc., **7** 429
Reese Products, **III** 569; **11** 535; **20** 361
Reeves Banking and Trust Company, **11** 181
Reeves Brothers, **17** 182
Reeves Pulley Company, **9** 440
Refco, Inc., **10** 251; **22** 189
Reference Software International, **10** 558
Refined Sugars, **II** 582
Reflectone Inc. *See* CAE USA Inc.

Reflex Winkelmann & Pannhoff GmbH, **18** 163

Reform Rt, **IV** 652; **7** 392

Refractarios Mexicanos, S.A. de C.V., **22** 285

Refrigeração Paraná S.A., **22** 27

Refrigerantes do Oeste, SA, **47** 291

Regal-Beloit Corporation, 18 450–53

Regal Drugs, **V** 171

Regal Inns, **13** 364

Regal Manufacturing Co., **15** 385

Regency, **12** 316

Regency Electronics, **II** 101

Regency Health Services Inc., **25** 457

Regency International, **10** 196

Regenerative Environmental Equipment Company, Inc., **6** 441

Regeneron Pharmaceuticals Inc., **10** 80

Regent Canal Co., **III** 272

Regent Carolina Corporation, **37** 226

Regent Communications Inc., **23** 294

Regent Insurance Co., **III** 343

Regent International Hotels Limited, **9** 238; **29** 200

Régie Autonome des Pétroles, **IV** 544–46; **21** 202–04

Régie des Mines de la Sarre, **IV** 196

Régie des Télégraphes et Téléphones. *See* Belgacom.

Régie Nationale des Usines Renault, I 136, 145, 148, 178–79, 183, **189–91,** 207, 210; **II** 13; **III** 392, 523; **7** 566–67; **11** 104; **12** 91; **15** 514; **19** 50; **22** 331. *See also* Renault SA.

Regina Verwaltungsgesellschaft, **II** 257

Regional Bell Operating Companies, **15** 125; **18** 111–12, 373

Regis Corporation, 18 454–56; 22 157; **26** 475, 477

Register & Tribune Co. *See* Cowles Media Company.

Registered Vitamin Company, **V** 171

Regnecentralen AS, **III** 164

Rego Supermarkets and American Seaway Foods, Inc., **9** 451; **13** 237

Rehab Hospital Services Corp., **III** 88; **10** 252

RehabClinics Inc., **11** 367

REI. *See* Recreational Equipment, Inc.

Reich, Landman and Berry, **18** 263

Reichart Furniture Corp., **14** 236

Reichhold Chemicals, Inc., I 386, 524; **8** 554; **10 465–67**

Reichs-Kredit-Gesellschaft mbH, **IV** 230

Reichs-Kredit- und Krontrollstelle GmbH, **IV** 230

Reichswerke AG für Berg- und Hüttenbetriebe Hermann Göring, **IV** 200

Reichswerke AG für Erzbergbau und Eisenhütten, **IV** 200

Reichswerke Hermann Göring, **IV** 233

Reid Bros. & Carr Proprietary, **III** 672–73

Reid Dominion Packaging Ltd., **IV** 645

Reid Ice Cream Corp., **II** 471

Reid, Murdoch and Co., **II** 571

Reid Press Ltd., **IV** 645

Reidman Corporation, **41** 65

Reidsville Fashions, Inc., **13** 532

Reigel Products Corp., **IV** 289

Reimersholms, **31** 458–60

Reims Aviation, **8** 92; **27** 100

Rein Elektronik, **10** 459

Reinsurance Agency, **III** 204–05

Reisebüro Bangemann, **II** 164

Reisholz AG, **III** 693

Reisland GmbH, **15** 340

Reiue Nationale des Usines Renault, **7** 220

Rekkof Restart NV, **28** 327

Relational Courseware, Inc., **21** 235–36

Relational Database Systems Inc., **10** 361–62

Relational Technology Inc., **10** 361

Relationship Marketing Group, Inc., **37** 409

Release Technologies, **8** 484

Reliable Stores Inc., **14** 236

Reliable Tool, **II** 488

Reliance Electric Company, IV 429; **9 439–42**

Reliance Group Holdings, Inc., II 173; **III 342–44; IV** 642

Reliance Life Insurance Co., **III** 275–76

Reliance National Indemnity Company, **18** 159

Reliance Steel & Aluminum Co., 19 343–45

Reliant Energy Inc., 44 368–73 (upd.)

ReLife Inc., **14** 233; **33** 185

Relocation Central. *See* CORT Business Services Corporation.

Rembrandt Group, **I** 289; **IV** 91, 93, 97; **V** 411–13; **19** 367–69; **24** 449

RemedyTemp, Inc., 20 448–50

Remgro, **IV** 97

Remington Arms Company, Inc., I 329; **8** 152; **12 415–17; 26** 125; **40 368–71 (upd.)**

Remington Products Company, L.L.C., 42 307–10

Remington Rand, **III** 122, 126, 148, 151, 165–66, 642; **6** 251, 265, 281–82; **10** 255; **12** 416; **19** 430; **30** 337

Remmele Engineering, Inc., **17** 534

Rémy Cointreau S.A., 20 451–53

Remy Martin, **48** 348–49

REN Corp. USA, Inc., **13** 161

REN Corporation, **49** 156

Renaissance Communications Corp., **22** 522

Renaissance Connects, **16** 394

Renaissance Cosmetics Inc. *See* New Dana Perfumes Co.

Renaissance Energy Ltd., **47** 181

Renaissance Hotel Group N.V., **38** 321

Renaissance Learning Systems, Inc., 39 341–43

Renal Systems, Inc. *See* Minntech Corporation.

Renault. *See* Régie Nationale des Usines Renault.

Renault S.A., 26 11, **401–04 (upd.); 34** 303, 306

Rendeck International, **11** 66

Rendic International, **13** 228

René Garraud, **III** 68

Renfro Corp., **25** 167

Rengo Co., Ltd., IV 326

Renishaw plc, 46 358–60

RENK AG, 37 325–28

Rennies Consolidated Holdings, **I** 470; **20** 312

Reno Air Inc., 23 409–11; 24 400; **28** 25

Reno de Medici S.p.A., 41 325–27

Réno-Dépôt Inc., **26** 306

Reno Technologies, **12** 124

Rent-A-Center, Inc., 22 194; **24** 485; **33** 366, 368; **45 365–67**

Rent-Way, Inc., 33 366–68

Rental Service Corporation, 28 386–88

Renters Choice Inc. *See* Rent-A-Center, Inc.

Rentokil Initial Plc, 34 43; **47 332–35; 49** 375–77

Rentrak Corporation, 35 371–74

Rentz, **23** 219

Renwick Technologies, Inc., **48** 286

Reo Products. *See* Lifetime Hoan Corporation.

Repco Ltd., **15** 246

REPESA, **IV** 528

Replacement Enterprises Inc., **16** 380

Repligen Inc., **13** 241

Repola Ltd., **19** 465; **30** 325

Repola Oy, **IV** 316, 347, 350

Repsol S.A., IV 396–97, 506, 514, **527–29; 16 423–26 (upd.); 49** 211

Repsol-YPF S.A., 40 372–76 (upd.)

Repubblica, **IV** 587

Republic Aircraft Co., **I** 89

Republic Airlines, **I** 113, 132; **6** 104; **25** 421; **28** 265

Republic Aviation Corporation, **I** 55; **9** 205–07; **48** 167

Republic Broadcasting Corp., **23** 292

Republic Corp., **I** 447

Republic Engineered Steels, Inc., 7 446–47; **26 405–08 (upd.)**

Republic Freight Systems, **14** 567

Republic Indemnity Co. of America, **III** 191

Republic Industries, Inc., 24 12; **26 409–11,** 501

Republic Insurance, **III** 404

Republic National Bank, **19** 466

Republic New York Corporation, 11 415–19

Republic Pictures, **9** 75

Republic Powdered Metals, Inc., **8** 454

Republic Realty Mortgage Corp., **II** 289

Republic Rubber, **III** 641

Republic Steel Corp., **I** 491; **IV** 114; **7** 446; **12** 353; **13** 169, 157; **14** 155; **24** 304. *See also* Republic Engineered Steels, Inc.

Republic Supply Co. of California, **I** 570

Res-Care, Inc., 29 399–402

Research Analysis Corporation, **7** 15

Research Cottrell, Inc., **6** 441

Research Polymers International, **I** 321; **12** 103

Research Publications, **8** 526

Resem SpA, **I** 387

Reserve Mining Co., **17** 356

Reservoir Productions, **17** 150

Residence Inns, **III** 103; **9** 426

Residential Funding Corporation, **10** 92–93

Resin Exchange, **19** 414

Resinous Products, **I** 392

ResNet Communications Inc., **28** 241

Resolution Systems, Inc., **13** 201

Resolution Trust Corp., **10** 117, 134; **11** 371; **12** 368

Resorts International, Inc., I 452; **12 418–20; 19** 402; **26** 462

Resource America, Inc., 42 311–14

Resource Associates of Alaska, Inc., **7** 376

The Resource Club, **32** 80

Resource Electronics, **8** 385

Resource Group International, **25** 207

ReSource NE, Inc., **17** 553

reSOURCE PARTNER, INC., **22** 95

Response Oncology, Inc., 27 385–87

Rest Assured, **I** 429

The Restaurant Company, **22** 417
Restaurant Enterprises Group Inc., **14** 195
Restaurant Franchise Industries, **6** 200
Restaurant Property Master, **19** 468
Restaurants Les Pres Limitée, **II** 652
Restaurants Universal Espana S.A., **26** 374
**Restaurants Unlimited, Inc., 13 435–37;
23** 127–29
Restoration Hardware, Inc., 30 376–78
Resurgens Communications Group, **7** 336;
8 311; **27** 306
Retail Association Pskovnefteprodukt, **48**
378
Retail Credit Company. *See* Equifax.
Retail Systems Consulting, Inc., **24** 395
Retail Ventures Inc., **14** 427; **24** 26
Retailers Commercial Agency, Inc., **6** 24
Retequattro, **19** 19
Retirement Care Associates Inc., **25** 457
Retirement Inns of America, Inc., **III** 16;
11 282
Reuben H. Donnelley Corp., **IV** 605, 661;
19 133
Reunion Properties, **I** 470; **20** 311–12
Reuters Holdings PLC, IV 259, 652, 654,
656, **668–70; 10** 277, 407; **21** 68–70; **22**
450–53 (upd.); 34 11, 227
Revco D.S., Inc., II 449; **III** 10; **V**
171–73; 9 67, 187; **12** 4; **13** 449; **16**
560; **19** 357; **32** 169–70; **45** 136
Revell-Monogram Inc., 16 427–29; 25
71; **27** 14
Revere Copper and Brass Co., **IV** 32. *See
also* The Paul Revere Corporation.
Revere Foil Containers, Inc., **12** 377
Revere Furniture and Equipment Company,
14 105; **25** 307
Revere Ware Corporation, 22 454–56
Revlon Inc., I 29, 449, 620, 633, 668, 677,
693, 696; **II** 498, 679; **III** 29, 46,
54–57, 727; **6** 27; **8** 131, 341; **9**
202–03, 291; **11** 8, 333–34; **12** 314; **16**
439; **17** 110, **400–04 (upd.); 18** 229; **22**
157; **25** 55; **26** 384; **28** 246–47; **30**
188–89
Revson Bros., **III** 54
Rewe Group, **37** 241
Rewe-Liebbrand, **28** 152
Rex Pulp Products Company, **9** 304
REX Stores Corp., 10 468–69; 19 362
Rexall Drug & Chemical Co., **II** 533–34;
III 610; **13** 525; **14** 547
Rexall Sundown, Inc., **37** 340, 342
Rexam PLC, 32 380–85 (upd.); 45 337
Rexel, Inc., 15 384–87
Rexene Products Co., **III** 760; **IV** 457
Rexham Inc., **IV** 259; **8** 483–84
Rexnord Corporation, I 524; **14** 43; **21**
429–32; 37 30
Reycan, **49** 104
Reydel Industries, **23** 95–96
Reyes Holdings, Inc., **24** 388
Reymer & Bros., Inc., **II** 508; **11** 172
Reymersholm, **II** 366
Reynolds and Reynolds Company, **17** 142,
144
Reynolds Electric Co., **22** 353
Reynolds Metals Company, II 421–22;
IV 11–12, 15, 59, **186–88; IV** 122; **12**
278; **19 346–48 (upd.); 21** 218; **22** 455;
25 22
RF Communications, **II** 38
RF Micro Devices, Inc., 43 311–13
RF Monolithics Inc., **13** 193

RHC Holding Corp., **10** 13; **13** 364; **27** 11
RHD Holdings, **23** 413
Rhee Syngman, **I** 516; **12** 293
Rheem Manufacturing, **25** 368
Rhein-Elbe Gelsenkirchener Bergwerks
A.G., **IV** 25
Rheinelbe Union, **I** 542
Rheinisch Kalksteinwerke Wulfrath, **III**
738
Rheinisch Oelfinwerke, **I** 306
Rheinisch-Westfalische Bank A.G., **II** 279
Rheinisch-Westfälischer Sprengstoff AG,
III 694
Rheinisch-Westfälisches Elektrizatätswerke
AG, **I** 542–43; **III** 154; **IV** 231; **V** 744;
25 102
Rheinische Aktiengesellschaft für
Braunkohlenbergbau, **V** 708
Rheinische Creditbank, **II** 278
Rheinische Metallwaaren- und
Maschinenfabrik AG, **9** 443–44
Rheinische Wasserglasfabrik, **III** 31
Rheinische Zuckerwarenfabrik GmbH, **27**
460
Rheinmetall Berlin AG, 9 443–46
Rheinsche Girozentrale und Provinzialbank,
Düsseldorf, **II** 385
Rheinstahl AG, **IV** 222
Rheinstahl Union Brueckenbau, **8** 242
Rheintalische Zementfabrik, **III** 701
Rhenus-Weichelt AG, **6** 424, 426
RHI Entertainment Inc., **16** 257
Rhino Entertainment Company, 18
457–60; 21 326
RHM. *See* Ranks Hovis McDougall.
Rhodes & Co., **8** 345
Rhodes Inc., 23 412–14
Rhodesian Anglo American Ltd., **IV** 21,
23; **16** 26
Rhodesian Development Corp., **I** 422
Rhodesian Selection Trust, Ltd., **IV** 17–18,
21
Rhodesian Sugar Refineries, **II** 581
Rhodia SA, 38 378–80
Rhodiaceta, **I** 388–89
Rhokana Corp., **IV** 191
Rhône Moulage Industrie, **39** 152, 154
Rhône-Poulenc S.A., I 303–04, 371,
388–90, 670, 672, 692; **III** 677; **IV** 174,
487, 547; **8** 153, 452; **9** 358; **10 470–72**
(upd.); 16 121, 438; **21** 466; **23** 194,
197; **34** 284; **38** 379
Rhymey Breweries, **I** 294
Rhymney Iron Company, **31** 369
Rhythm Watch Co., Ltd., **III** 454; **21** 121
La Riassicuratrice, **III** 346
Rica Foods, Inc., 41 328–30
Ricard, **I** 280
Riccar, **17** 124; **41** 114
Riccardo's Restaurant, **18** 538
Rice Broadcasting Co., Inc., **II** 166
Rice-Stix Dry Goods, **II** 414
Riceland Foods, Inc., **27** 390
**Rich Products Corporation, 7 448–49;
38 381–84 (upd.)**
Rich's Inc., **9** 209; **10** 515; **31** 191
Richard A. Shaw, Inc., **7** 128
Richard D. Irwin Inc., **IV** 602–03, 678; **47**
102
Richard Hellman Co., **II** 497
Richard Manufacturing Co., **I** 667
Richard P. Simmons, **8** 19
Richard Shops, **III** 502
Richard Thomas & Baldwins, **IV** 42

Richards & O'Neil LLP, **43** 70
Richards Bay Minerals, **IV** 91
Richardson Company, **36** 147
Richardson Electronics, Ltd., 17 405–07
Richardson-Vicks Company, **III** 53; **8** 434;
26 383
Richardson's, **21** 246
Richfield Oil Corp., **IV** 375–76, 456
Richfood Holdings, Inc., 7 450–51
Richland Co-op Creamery Company, **7** 592
Richland Gas Company, **8** 349
Richmon Hill & Queens County Gas Light
Companies, **6** 455
Richmond American Homes of Florida,
Inc., **11** 258
Richmond Carousel Corporation, **9** 120
Richmond Cedar Works Manufacturing
Co., **12** 109; **19** 360
Richmond Corp., **I** 600; **15** 129
Richmond Paperboard Corp., **19** 78
Richmond Pulp and Paper Company, **17**
281
Richton International Corporation, 39
344–46
Richway, **10** 515
Richwood Building Products, Inc., **12** 397
Richwood Sewell Coal Co., **17** 357
Ricils, **III** 47
Rickards, Roloson & Company, **22** 427
Rickel Home Centers, **II** 673
Ricky Shaw's Oriental Express, **25** 181
Ricoh Company, Ltd., III 121, 157,
159–61, 172, 454; **6** 289; **8** 278; **18** 386,
527; **19** 317; **21** 122; **24** 429; **36 389–93**
(upd.)
Ricolino, **19** 192
Riddell Inc., **33** 467
Riddell Sports Inc., 22 457–59; 23 449
Ridder Publications, **IV** 612–13, 629; **7**
191
Ride, Inc., 22 460–63
Ridge Tool Co., **II** 19
Ridgewell's Inc., **15** 87
Ridgewood Properties Inc., **12** 394
Ridgway Co., **23** 98
Ridgway Color, **13** 227–28
Rieck-McJunkin Dairy Co., **II** 533
Riedel-de Haën AG, **22** 32; **36** 431
Riegel Bag & Paper Co., **IV** 344
Rieke Corp., **III** 569; **11** 535; **20** 361
The Riese Organization, 38 385–88
Rieter Holding AG, 42 315–17
Rieter Machine Works, **III** 638
Rig Tenders Company, **6** 383
Riggin & Robbins, **13** 244
Riggs National Corporation, 13 438–40
Right Associates, **27** 21; **44** 156
Right Management Consultants, Inc., 42
318–21
Right Source, Inc., **24** 96
RightPoint, Inc., **49** 124
RightSide Up, Inc., **27** 21
Rijnhaave Information Systems, **25** 21
Rike's, **10** 282
Riken Corp., **IV** 160; **10** 493
Riken Kagaku Co. Ltd., **48** 250
Riken Kankoshi Co. Ltd., **III** 159
Riken Optical Co., **III** 159
Riklis Family Corp., 9 447–50; 12 87; **13**
453; **38** 169; **43** 355
Riku-un Moto Kaisha, **V** 477
La Rinascente, **12** 153
Ring King Visibles, Inc., **13** 269
Ring Ltd., **43** 99

Ringier America, **19** 333
Ringköpkedjan, **II** 640
Ringling Bros., Barnum & Bailey Circus, **25** 312–13
Ringnes Bryggeri, **18** 396
Rini-Rego Supermarkets Inc., **13** 238
Rini Supermarkets, **9** 451; **13** 237
Rinker Materials Corp., **III** 688
Rio Grande Industries, Inc., **12** 18–19
Rio Grande Oil Co., **IV** 375, 456
Rio Grande Servaas, S.A. de C.V., **23** 145
Rio Grande Valley Gas Co., **IV** 394
Rio Sportswear Inc., **42** 269
Rio Sul Airlines, **6** 133
Rio Tinto plc, 19 349–53 (upd.); **27** 253; **42** 395
Rio Tinto-Zinc Corp., **II** 628; **IV** 56, 58–61, 189–91, 380; **21** 352
Rioblanco, **II** 477
Riordan Freeman & Spogli, **13** 406
Riordan Holdings Ltd., **I** 457; **10** 554
Riser Foods, Inc., 9 451–54; **13** 237–38
Rising Sun Petroleum Co., **IV** 431, 460, 542
Risk Management Partners Ltd., **35** 36
Risk Planners, **II** 669
Rit Dye Co., **II** 497
Ritchie Bros. Auctioneers Inc., 41 331–34
Rite Aid Corporation, V 174–76; **9** 187, 346; **12** 221, 333; **16** 389; **18** 199, 286; **19 354–57 (upd.);** **23** 407; **29** 213; **31** 232; **32** 166, 169–70
Rite-Way Department Store, **II** 649
Riteway Distributor, **26** 183
Rittenhouse and Embree, **III** 269
Rittenhouse Financial Services, **22** 495
Ritter Co. *See* Sybron Corp.
Ritz Camera Centers, 18 186; **34 375–77**
Ritz-Carlton Hotel Company L.L.C., 9 455–57; **21** 366; **29 403–06 (upd.)**
Ritz Firma, **13** 512
Riunione Adriatica di Sicurtà SpA, III 185, 206, **345–48**
The Rival Company, 17 215; **19 358–60**
Rivarossi, **16** 337
Rivaud Group, **29** 370
River Boat Casino, **9** 425–26
River City Broadcasting, **25** 418
River North Studios. *See* Platinum Entertainment, Inc.
River Oaks Furniture, Inc., 43 314–16
River-Raisin Paper Co., **IV** 345
River Ranch Fresh Foods—Salinas, Inc., **41** 11
River Steam Navigation Co., **III** 522
River Thames Insurance Co., Ltd., **26** 487
Riverdeep Group plc, **41** 137
Riverside Chemical Company, **13** 502
Riverside Furniture, **19** 455
Riverside Insurance Co. of America, **26** 487
Riverside Iron Works, Ltd., **8** 544
Riverside National Bank of Buffalo, **11** 108
Riverside Press, **10** 355–56
Riverside Publishing Company, **36** 272
Riverwood International Corporation, 7 294; **11 420–23;** **48 340–44 (upd.)**
Riviana Foods, **III** 24, 25; **27 388–91**
Riyadh Armed Forces Hospital, **16** 94
Rizzoli Publishing, **IV** 586, 588; **19** 19; **23** 88
RJMJ, Inc., **16** 37

RJR Nabisco Holdings Corp., I 249, 259, 261; **II** 370, 426, 477–78, 542–44; **V 408–10, 415;** **7** 130, 132, 277, 596; **9** 469; **12** 82, 559; **13** 342; **14** 214, 274; **17** 471; **22** 73, 95, 441; **23** 163; **24** 273; **30** 384; **32** 234; **33** 228; **36** 151, 153; **46** 259; **49** 77–78. *See also* R.J Reynolds Tobacco Holdings Inc., Nabisco Brands, Inc. *and* R.J. Reynolds Industries, Inc.
RKO. *See* Radio-Keith-Orpheum.
RKO-General, Inc., **8** 207
RKO Radio Sales, **6** 33
RLA Polymers, **9** 92
RM Marketing, **6** 14
RMC Group p.l.c., III 734, 737–40; **34 378–83 (upd.)**
RMF Inc., **I** 412
RMH Teleservices, Inc., 42 322–24
RMP International, Limited, **8** 417
Roadhouse Grill, Inc., 22 464–66
Roadline, **6** 413–14
Roadmaster Industries, Inc., 16 430–33; **22** 116
Roadmaster Transport Company, **18** 27; **41** 18
RoadOne. *See* Miller Industries, Inc.
Roadway Express, Inc., 25 395–98 (upd.)
Roadway Services, Inc., V 502–03; **12** 278, 309; **14** 567; **15** 111
Roaman's, **V** 115
Roan Selection Trust Ltd., **IV** 18, 239–40
Roanoke Capital Ltd., **27** 113–14
Roanoke Electric Steel Corporation, 45 368–70
Roanoke Fashions Group, **13** 532
Robb Engineering Works, **8** 544
Robbins & Myers Inc., 13 273; **15 388–90**
Robbins Co., **III** 546
Robeco Group, **IV** 193; **26** 419–20
Roberds Inc., 19 361–63
Roberk Co., **III** 603
Robert Allen Companies, **III** 571; **20** 362
Robert Benson, Lonsdale & Co. Ltd., **II** 232, 421–22; **IV** 191
Robert Bosch GmbH, I 392–93, 411; **III** 554, 555, 591, 593; **13** 398; **16 434–37 (upd.);** **22** 31; **43 317–21 (upd.)**
Robert E. McKee Corporation, **6** 150
Robert Fleming Holdings Ltd., **I** 471; **IV** 79; **11** 495
Robert Gair Co., **15** 128
Robert Garrett & Sons, Inc., **9** 363
Robert Grace Contracting Co., **I** 584
Robert Half International Inc., 18 461–63
Robert Hall Clothes, Inc., **13** 535
Robert Hansen Trucking Inc., **49** 402
Robert Johnson, **8** 281–82
Robert McLane Company. *See* McLane Company, Inc.
Robert McNish & Company Limited, **14** 141
Robert Mondavi Corporation, 15 391–94; **39** 45
Robert R. Mullen & Co., **I** 20
Robert Skeels & Company, **33** 467
Robert Stigwood Organization Ltd., **23** 390
Robert W. Baird & Co., **III** 324; **7** 495
Robert Warschauer and Co., **II** 270
Robert Watson & Co. Ltd., **I** 568
Robert Wood Johnson Foundation, 35 375–78
Robertet SA, 39 347–49

Roberts Express, **V** 503
Roberts, Johnson & Rand Shoe Co., **III** 528–29
Roberts Pharmaceutical Corporation, 16 438–40
Robertson Building Products, **8** 546
Robertson-Ceco Corporation, 8 546; **19 364–66**
Robertson, Stephens & Co., **22** 465
Robin Hood Flour Mills, Ltd., **7** 241–43; **25** 241
Robin International Inc., **24** 14
Robinair, **10** 492, 494
Robinson & Clark Hardware. *See* Clarcor Inc.
Robinson Clubs, **II** 163–64
Robinson-Danforth Commission Co., **II** 561
Robinson-Humphrey, **II** 398; **10** 62
Robinson Industries, **24** 425
Robinson Radio Rentals, **I** 531
Robinson Smith & Robert Haas, Inc., **13** 428
Robinson's Japan Co. Ltd., **V** 89; **42** 191
Robinsons Soft Drinks Limited, **38** 77
Robot Manufacturing Co., **16** 8
Robotic Vision Systems, Inc., **16** 68
ROC Communities, Inc., **I** 272; **22** 341
Roccade, **39** 177
Roch, S.A., **23** 83
Roche Biomedical Laboratories, Inc., 8 209–10; **11 424–26**. *See also* Laboratory Corporation of America Holdings.
Roche Bioscience, 14 403–06 (upd.)
Roche Holding AG, **30** 164; **32** 211, 213–14; **37** 113
Roche Products Ltd., **I** 643
Rocher Soleil, **48** 315
Rochester American Insurance Co., **III** 191
Rochester Gas And Electric Corporation, 6 571–73
Rochester German Insurance Co., **III** 191
Rochester Instrument Systems, Inc., **16** 357
Rochester Telephone Corporation, 6 332–34; **12** 136; **16** 221
Röchling Industrie Verwaltung GmbH, **9** 443
Rock Bottom Restaurants, Inc., 25 399–401
Rock Island Oil & Refining Co., **IV** 448–49
Rock Island Plow Company, **10** 378
Rock of Ages Corporation, 37 329–32
Rock Systems Inc., **18** 337
Rock-Tenn Company, IV 312; **13 441–43;** **19** 268
Rockcor Inc., **I** 381; **13** 380
Rockcote Paint Company, **8** 552–53
The Rockefeller Foundation, 34 384–87
Rockefeller Group, **IV** 714
Rocket Chemical Company. *See* WD-40 Company.
Rockford Corporation, 43 322–25
Rockford Drilling Co., **III** 439
Rockhaven Asset Management, LLC, **48** 18
Rocking Horse Child Care Centers of America Inc. *See* Nobel Learning Communities, Inc.
Rockland Corp., **8** 271
Rockland React-Rite, Inc., **8** 270
Rockmoor Grocery, **II** 683
Rockower of Canada Ltd., **II** 649

Rockport Company, **V** 376–77; **26** 397
Rockresorts, Inc., **22** 166
RockShox, Inc., 26 412–14
Rockwell Automation, 43 326–31 (upd.)
Rockwell International Corporation, I
   71, **78–80**, 154–55, 186; **II** 3, 94, 379;
   6 263; **7** 420; **8** 165; **9** 10; **10** 279–80;
   11 268, 278, **427–30 (upd.)**, 473; **12**
   135, 248, 506; **13** 228; **18** 369, 571; **22**
   51, 53, 63–64; **32** 81, 84–85; **33** 27; **35**
   91; **36** 121–22; **39** 30; **44** 357
Rocky Mountain Bankcard, **24** 393
Rocky Mountain Financial Corporation, **13**
   348
Rocky Mountain Pipe Line Co., **IV** 400
Rocky River Power Co. See Connecticut
   Light and Power Co.
Rocky Shoes & Boots, Inc., 26 415–18
Rod's Food Products, **36** 163
Rodale, Inc., 47 336–39 (upd.)
Rodale Press, Inc., 22 443; **23 415–17**
Rodamco N.V., IV 698; **26 419–21**
Rodel, Inc., **26** 425
Röder & Co., **34** 38, 40
Rodeway Inns of America, **II** 142; **III** 94;
   11 242; **25** 309
Rodgers Instrument Corporation, **38** 391
Rodney Square Management Corp., **25** 542
Rodven Records, **23** 391
Roederstein GmbH, **21** 520
Roegelein Co., **13** 271
Roehr Products Co., **III** 443
Roermond, **IV** 276
Roessler & Hasslacher Chemical Co., **IV**
   69
Roger Cleveland Golf Company, **15** 462;
   43 375–76
Roger Williams Foods, **II** 682
Rogers & Oling, Inc., **17** 533
Rogers Bros., **I** 672
Rogers CanGuard, Inc., **32** 374
Rogers Communications Inc., 30 388–92
   (upd.). See also Maclean Hunter
   Publishing Limited.
Rohde & Schwarz GmbH & Co. KG, 39
   350–53
Rohe Scientific Corp., **13** 398
Röhm and Haas Company, I 391–93; 14
   182–83; **26 422–26 (upd.)**
ROHN Industries, Inc., 22 467–69
Rohölgewinnungs AG, **IV** 485
Rohr Gruppe, **20** 100
Rohr Incorporated, I 62; **9 458–60; 11**
   165
Roja, **III** 47
The Rokke Group, **16** 546; **32** 100
Rokuosha, **III** 547
Rol Oil, **IV** 451
Rola Group, **II** 81
Roland Berger & Partner GmbH, 37
   333–36
Roland Corporation, 38 389–91
Roland Murten A.G., 7 452–53
Roland NV, **41** 340
Rolex. See Montres Rolex S.A.
Roll International Corporation, 37
   337–39
Rollalong, **III** 502; **7** 208
Rollerblade, Inc., 15 395–98; 22 202–03;
   34 388–92 (upd.)
Rolling Stones Records, **23** 33
Rollins Burdick Hunter Company, **III** 204;
   45 27
Rollins Communications, **II** 161

Rollins, Inc., 11 431–34
Rollins Specialty Group, **III** 204
Rollo's, **16** 95
Rolls-Royce Allison, 29 407–09 (upd.)
Rolls-Royce Motors Ltd., I 25–26,
   81–82, 166, **194–96; III** 652; **9** 16–18,
   417–18; **11** 138, 403; **21** 435
Rolls-Royce plc, I 41, 55, 65, **81–83**, 481;
   III 507, 556; **7 454–57 (upd.); 9** 244;
   11 268; **12** 190; **13** 414; **21 433–37**
   (upd.); 24 85; **27** 495–96; **46** 358–59;
   47 7, 9
Rolm Corp., **II** 99; **III** 149; **18** 344; **22** 51;
   34 512
Rolodex Electronics, **23** 209, 212
Rolscreen. See Pella Corporation.
Rombas, **IV** 226
Rome Cable and Wire Co., **IV** 15
Rome Network, Inc., **24** 95
Romper Room Enterprises, Inc., **16** 267
Rompetrol, **IV** 454
Ron Nagle, **I** 247
Ronco, Inc., 15 399–401; 21 327
Rondel's, Inc., **8** 135
Ronel, **13** 274
Roni-Linda Productions, Inc., **27** 347
Ronnebyredds Trävaru, **25** 463
Ronningen-Petter, **III** 468
Ronson PLC, 49 337–39
Ronzoni Foods Corp., **15** 221
Roombar S.A., **28** 241
Rooms To Go Inc., 28 389–92
Rooney Brothers Co., 25 402–04
Roots Canada Ltd., 27 194; **42 325–27**
Roots-Connersville Blower Corp., **III** 472
Roper Industries Inc., III 655; **12** 550; **15**
   402–04; 25 89
Ropert Group, **18** 67
Ropes & Gray, 40 377–80
RoProperty Services BV. See Rodamco
   N.V.
Rorer Group, I 666–68; 12 4; **16** 438; **24**
   257
Rosaen Co., **23** 82
Rosarita Food Company, **25** 278
Rose & Co., **26** 65
Rose Exterminator Company, **25** 15
Rose Foundation, **9** 348
Rose's Stores, Inc., 13 261, **444–46; 23**
   215
Rosebud Dolls Ltd., **25** 312
Rosefield Packing Co., **II** 497
Rosehaugh, **24** 269
RoseJohnson Incorporated, **14** 303
Rosemount Inc., II 20; **13** 226; **15**
   405–08; 46 171
Rosen Enterprises, Ltd., **10** 482
Rosenblads Patenter, **III** 419
Rosenbluth International Inc., 14 407–09
Rosenfeld Hat Company. See Columbia
   Hat Company.
Rosenmund-Guèdu, **31** 158
Rosenthal A.G., **I** 347; **18** 236; **34** 493,
   496
Rosevear, **III** 690
Rosewood Financial, Inc., **24** 383
Roshco, Inc., **27** 288
Roslyn Bancorp, **46** 316
Ross Carrier Company, **8** 115
Ross Clouston, **13** 244
Ross Gear & Tool Co., **I** 539; **14** 510
Ross Hall Corp., **I** 417
Ross Stores, Inc., 17 408–10; 43 332–35
   (upd.)

Rossendale Combining Company, **9** 92
Rossignol Ski Company, Inc. See Skis
   Rossignol S.A.
Rössing Uranium Ltd., **IV** 191
Rossville Union Distillery, **I** 285
Rostocker Brauerei VEB, **9** 87
Roswell Public Service Company, **6** 579
Rota Bolt Ltd., **III** 581
Rotadisk, **16** 7
Rotan Mosle Financial Corporation, **II** 445;
   22 406
Rotary International, 31 395–97
Rotary Lift, **III** 467–68
Rotax, **III** 555–56. See also Orbital Engine
   Corporation Ltd.
Rote. See Avery Dennison Corporation.
Rotelcom Data Inc., **6** 334; **16** 222
Rotex, **IV** 253
Roth Co., **16** 493
Roth Freres SA, **26** 231
Rothmans International BV, **33** 82
Rothmans International p.l.c., I 438; **IV**
   93; **V 411–13; 27** 488
Rothmans UK Holdings Limited, 19
   367–70 (upd.)
Rothschild Financial Corporation, **13** 347
Rothschild Group, **6** 206
Rothschild Investment Trust, **I** 248; **III** 699
Roto-Rooter Corp., 13 149–50; **15**
   409–11; 16 387
Rotodiesel, **III** 556
Rotor Tool Co., **II** 16
Rotork plc, 46 361–64
Rotterdam Bank, **II** 183–85
Rotterdam Beleggings (Investment)
   Consortium. See Robeco.
Rotterdam Lloyd, **6** 403–04; **26** 241–42
The Rottlund Company, Inc., 28 393–95
Rouge et Or, **IV** 614
Rouge Steel Company, 8 448–50
Roughdales Brickworks, **14** 249
Rougier. See Groupe Rougier, SA.
Roularta Media Group NV, 48 345–47
Round Hill Foods, **21** 535
Round Table, **16** 447
Roundup Wholesale Grocery Company, **V**
   55
Roundy's Inc., 14 410–12
The Rouse Company, II 445; **15 412–15;**
   22 406
Roussel Uclaf, I 669–70; 8 451–53
   (upd.); 18 236; **19** 51; **25** 285; **38** 379
Rousselot, **I** 677
Routh Robbins Companies, **21** 96
Roux Séguéla Cayzac & Goudard. See
   Euro RSCG Worldwide S.A.
Rover Group Ltd., I 186; **7 458–60; 11**
   31, 33; **14** 36; **21 441–44 (upd.); 24**
   87–88; **38** 83, 85–86
Rowan Companies, Inc., 43 336–39
Rowe & Pitman, **14** 419
Rowe Bros. & Co., **III** 680
Rowe Price-Fleming International, Inc., **11**
   495
Rowell Welding Works, **26** 433
Rowenta. See Groupe SEB.
Rowland Communications Worldwide, **42**
   328, 331
Rowntree and Co., **27** 104
Rowntree Mackintosh PLC, II 476, 511,
   521, 548, **568–70; 7** 383; **28** 311
Roxana Petroleum Co., **IV** 531, 540
Roxell, N.V., **43** 129
Roxoil Drilling, **7** 344

Roy and Charles Moore Crane Company, **18** 319
Roy F. Weston, Inc., 33 369–72
Roy Farrell Import-Export Company, **6** 78
Roy Rogers, **III** 102
Royal Ahold. *See* Koninklijke Ahold N.V.
Royal Aluminium Ltd., **IV** 9
Royal Appliance Manufacturing Company, 15 416–18; 17 233
Royal Baking Powder Co., **II** 544; **14** 17
Royal Bank of Australia, **II** 188
The Royal Bank of Canada, II 344–46; 21 445–48 (upd.)
Royal Bank of Ireland Ltd., **16** 13
Royal Bank of Queensland, **II** 188
The Royal Bank of Scotland Group plc, II 298, 358; **10 336–37; 12 421–23; 38** 13, **392–99 (upd.); 42** 76
Royal Bankgroup of Acadiana, Inc., **37** 201
Royal Brewing Co., **I** 269; **12** 337
Royal Business Machines, **I** 207, 485; **III** 549
Royal Canada, **III** 349
Royal Canin S.A., 39 354–57
Royal Caribbean Cruises Ltd., 6 368; **22** 444–46; **470–73; 27** 29, 91
Royal Copenhagen A/S, **9** 99
Royal Crown Company, Inc., II 468; **6** 21, 50; **8 536–37; 14 32–33; 23 418–20**
Royal Data, Inc. *See* King Kullen Grocery Co., Inc.
Royal Doulton plc, IV 659; **14 413–15; 34** 497; **38 400–04 (upd.)**
Royal Dutch Harbour Co., **IV** 707
Royal Dutch Paper Co., **IV** 307
Royal Dutch Petroleum Company, IV 530–32, 657; **24** 496. *See also* Shell Transport and Trading Company p.l.c.
Royal Dutch/Shell Group, **I** 368, 504; **III** 616; **IV** 132–33, 378, 406, 413, 429, 434, 453–54, 460, 491–92, 512, 515, 517–18, 530–32, 540–45, 557–58, 569; **7** 56–57, 172–73, 481–82; **17** 417; **19** 73, 75; **21** 203; **22** 237; **24** 520; **32** 175, 180; **41** 356–57, 359; **45** 47; **49 340–44 (upd.)**
Royal Electric Company, **6** 501
Royal Exchange Assurance Corp., **III** 233–34, 278, 349, 369–71, 373
Royal Farms, **24** 528
Royal Food Distributors, **II** 625
Royal Food Products, **24** 528–29; **36** 163
Royal General Insurance Co., **III** 242
Royal Hawaiian Macadamia Nut Co., **II** 491
Royal Industries, Inc., **19** 371
Royal Insurance Holdings plc, III 349–51
Royal International, **II** 457; **III** 349
Royal Interocean Lines, **6** 404; **26** 243
Royal Jackson, **14** 236
Royal Jordanian, **6** 101
Royal KPN N.V., 30 393–95, 461, 463
Royal London Mutual Insurance, **IV** 697
Royal Mail Group, **V** 498; **6** 416; **19** 198
Royal Nedlloyd. *See* Koninglijke Nedlloyd N.V.
Royal Nepal Airline Corporation, 41 335–38
Royal Netherlands Steamship Company. *See* KNSM.
Royal Numico N.V., 33 145, 147; **37 340–42**
Royal Orchid Holidays, **6** 122–23

Royal Ordnance plc, **13** 356; **24** 87–88
Royal Packaging Industries Van Leer N.V., 9 305; **30 396–98**
Royal Pakhoed N.V., **9** 532
Royal PTT Post, **30** 463
Royal Re, **III** 349
Royal Sash Manufacturing Co., **III** 757
Royal Securities Company, **6** 585
Royal Securities Corp. of Canada, **II** 425
Royal Sporting House Pte. Ltd., **21** 483
Royal Trust Co., **II** 456–57; **V** 25
Royal Union Life Insurance Co., **III** 275
Royal USA, **III** 349
Royal Vopak NV, 41 339–41
Royal Wessanen, **II** 527
Royale Belge, **III** 177, 200, 394
Royale Inns of America, **25** 307
Royalite, **I** 285
Royce Electronics, **III** 569; **18** 68; **20** 361
Royce Ltd., **I** 194
Royster-Clark, Inc., **13** 504
Rozes, **I** 272
RPC Industries, **III** 635
RPI. *See* Research Polymers International.
RPM Inc., 8 III 598; **454–57; 36 394–98 (upd.)**
RSA Security Inc., 46 365–68; 47 430
RSC. *See* Rental Service Corporation.
RSI Corp., **8** 141–42; **30** 160
RSO Records, **23** 390
RSV, **26** 496
RTE Corp., **II** 17
RTL Group SA, 41 29; **44 374–78**
RTL-Véeronique, **IV** 611
RTZ Corporation PLC, IV 189–92; 7 261, 263; **27** 256
RTZ-CRA Group. *See* Rio Tinto plc.
Rubber Latex Limited, **9** 92
Rubbermaid Incorporated, III 613–15; 12 168–69; **13** 317–18; **19** 407; **20** 262, **454–57 (upd.); 21** 293; **28** 479; **31** 160–61; **34** 369
Ruberoid Corporation, **I** 339; **22** 227
Rubicon Group plc, **32** 50
Rubio's Restaurants, Inc., 35 379–81
Rubloff Inc., **II** 442
Rubo Lederwaren, **14** 225
Rubry Owen, **I** 154
Ruby, **III** 47
Ruby Tuesday, Inc., 18 464–66
Rubyco, Inc., **15** 386
La Ruche Meridionale, **12** 153
Ruddick Corporation, **23** 260
Rudisill Printing Co., **IV** 661
Rudolf Wolff & Co., **IV** 165
Rudolph Fluor & Brother, **I** 569
Ruel Smith Transportation Services, Inc., **39** 66
Ruff Hewn, **25** 48
Rug Corporation of America, **12** 393
The Rugby Group plc, 31 398–400; 34 380
Ruger Corporation, **19** 431
Ruhr-Zink, **IV** 141
Ruhrgas AG, V 704–06; 7 141; **18** 50; **38 405–09 (upd.); 42** 263
Ruhrkohle AG, IV 193–95. *See also* RAG AG.
Ruinart Père et Fils, **I** 272
Rumbelows, **I** 532
Runcorn White Lead Co., **III** 680
Runnymede Construction Co., **8** 544
Runo-Everth Treibstoff und Ol AG, **7** 141
Rural Bank, **IV** 279; **19** 155

Rural Cellular Corporation, 43 340–42
Rural/Metro Corporation, 28 396–98; 39 22
Rurhkohle AG, **V** 747
Rush Communications, 33 373–75. *See also* Phat Fashions LLC.
Rush Laboratories, Inc., **6** 41
Russ Berrie and Company, Inc., 12 424–26
Russell & Co., **II** 296
Russell Corporation, 8 458–59; 12 458; **30 399–401 (upd.)**
Russell Electric, **11** 412
Russell Electronics, **II** 85
Russell Kelly Office Services, Inc. *See* Kelly Services Inc.
Russell, Majors & Waddell, **II** 381
Russell Reynolds Associates Inc., 38 410–12
Russell Stover Candies Inc., 12 427–29
Russwerke Dortmund GmbH, **IV** 70
Rust Craft Greeting Cards Incorporated, **12** 561
Rust International Inc., V 754; **6** 599–600; **11 435–36**
Rust-Oleum Corporation, **36** 396
Rustenburg Platinum Co., **IV** 96, 118, 120
Rütgerswerke AG, **IV** 193; **8** 81
Ruth's Chris Steak House, 28 399–401; 37 297
Rutherford Hill Winery, **48** 392
Ruti Machinery Works, **III** 638
Rutland Plastics, **I** 321; **12** 103
RWE Group, V 707–10; 33 194, 196
RxAmerica, **22** 40; **25** 297
Ryan Aeronautical, **I** 525; **10** 522; **11** 428
Ryan Aircraft Company, **9** 458
Ryan Homes, Inc., **8** 401–02
Ryan Insurance Company, **III** 204; **45** 26
Ryan Milk Company of Kentucky, **7** 128
Ryan's Family Steak Houses, Inc., 15 419–21; 19 287; **22** 464
Ryanair Holdings plc, 35 382–85
Rycade Corp., **IV** 365, 658
Rydelle-Lion, **III** 45
Ryder System, Inc., V 504–06; 13 192; **19** 293; **24 408–11 (upd.); 25** 93, 144; **28** 3; **41** 37
Ryerson Tull, Inc., 19 216; **40** 269, **381–84 (upd.)**
Rykoff-Sexton, Inc., **21** 497; **26** 503, 505
The Ryland Group, Inc., 8 460–61; 19 126; **37 343–45 (upd.)**
Ryobi Ltd., **I** 202
Ryohin Keikaku Co., Ltd., **36** 420
Rypper Corp., **16** 43
Rysher Entertainment, **22** 162; **25** 329
Ryukyu Cement, **III** 760
The Ryvita Company Limited, **II** 466; **13** 52; **41** 31

S&A Restaurant Corp., **7** 336; **10** 176; **14** 331; **15** 363; **38** 100–01
S&C Electric Company, 15 422–24
S&H. *See* Sperry and Hutchinson Co.
S&H Diving Corporation, **6** 578
S&K Famous Brands, Inc., 23 421–23
S&V Screen Inks, **13** 227–28
S. & W. Berisford, **II** 514, 528
S&W Fine Foods, **12** 105
S + T Gesellschaft fur Reprotechnik mbH, **29** 306
S.A. CARFUEL, **12** 152

S.A. Cockerill Sambre. *See* Cockerill Sambre Group.
S.A. de C.V., **29** 461
S.A. des Ateliers d'Aviation Louis Breguet. *See* Groupe Dassault Aviation SA.
s.a. GB-Inno-BM. *See* GIB Group.
S.A. Greetings Corporation, **22** 35
S.A. Innovation—Bon Marché N.V., **26** 160
S.A. Schonbrunn & Co., **14** 18
S.B. Irving Trust Bank Corp., **II** 218
S.B. Penick & Co., **I** 708; **8** 548
S.C. Johnson & Son, Inc., **I** 14; **III** 45, **58–59**; **8** 130; **10** 173; **12** 126–28; **17** 215; **21** 386; **28** 215, **409–12 (upd.)**
S-C-S Box Company, **8** 173
S.D. Cohn & Company, **10** 455; **27** 364
S.D. Warren Co., **IV** 329–30
S-E Bank Group, **II** 351–53
S.E. Massengill, **III** 66
S.E. Rykoff & Co., **26** 503
S.F. Braun, **IV** 451
S.G. Warburg and Co., **II** 232, 259–60, 422, 629; **14** 419; **16** 377. *See also* SBC Warburg.
S. Grumbacher & Son. *See* The Bon-Ton Stores, Inc.
S.H. Benson Ltd., **I** 25–26
S.H. Kress & Co., **17** 203–04
S.I.P., Co., **8** 416
S-K-I Limited, **15 457–59**
S.K. Wellman, **14** 81
S. Kuhn & Sons, **13** 221
S.M.A. Corp., **I** 622
S.P. Richards Co., **45** 177–79
S Pearson & Son Ltd., **IV** 657–59; **38** 290
S.R. Dresser Manufacturing Co., **III** 470–71
S.S. Kresge Company. *See* Kmart Corporation.
S.S.V. Inc., **36** 420
S.S. White Dental Manufacturing Co., **I** 383
S. Smith & Sons. *See* Smiths Industries PLC.
S.T. Cooper & Sons, **12** 283
S.T. Dupont Company, **III** 28; **23** 55
S.W.M. Chard, **27** 259
SA Alliance Air, **28** 404
SA Express, **28** 404
Sa SFC NA, **18** 163
Sa SFC NV, **18** 162
SAA. *See* South African Airways.
SAA (Pty) Ltd., **28 402–04**
SAAB. *See* Svenska Aeroplan Aktiebolaget.
Saab Automobile AB, **32 386–89 (upd.)**; **36** 242–43
Saab-Scania A.B., **I** 197–98, 210; **III** 556; **V** 339; **10** 86; **11 437–39 (upd.)**; **16** 322; **34** 117
Saarberg-Konzern, **IV 196–99**
Saarstahl AG, **IV** 228
Saatchi & Saatchi plc, **I** 21, 28, **33–35**, 36; **6** 53, 229; **14** 49–50; **16** 72; **21** 236; **22** 296; **33** 65, 67; **328–31 (upd.)**
SAB. *See* South African Breweries Ltd.
Sabah Timber Co., **III** 699
Saban Entertainment, **24** 171
Sabaté Diosos SA, **48 348–50**
Sabela Media, Inc., **49** 423
Sabena S.A./N.V., **6** 96; **18** 80; **33** 49, 51, **376–79**; **34** 398
Saber Energy, Inc., **7** 553–54

Saber Software Corp., **25** 348
Sabi International Ltd., **22** 464
Sabian Ltd., **38** 68
SABIM Sable, **12** 152
Sabine Corporation, **7** 229
Sabine Investment Co. of Texas, Inc., **IV** 341
SABO Maschinenfabrik AG, **21** 175
Sabratek Corporation, **29 410–12**
SABRE Group Holdings, Inc., **25** 144; **26 427–30**; **28** 22
Sabre Interactive, **46** 434
Sacer, **31** 127–28
Sachs-Dolmer G.m.b.H., **22** 334
Sachsgruppe, **IV** 201
Sacilor, **IV** 174, 226–27
Sackett Plasterboard Co., **III** 762
Sacks Industries, **8** 561
OY Saco AB, **23** 268
SACOR, **IV** 250, 504–06
Sacramento Savings & Loan Association, **10** 43, 45
SADE Ingenieria y Construccions S.A., **38** 435, 437
SAE Magnetics Ltd., **18** 250
Saeger Carbide Corp., **IV** 203
Saes, **III** 347
SAFECO Corporation, **III 352–54**; **10** 44
Safeguard Scientifics, Inc., **10** 232–34, **473–75**; **27** 338
Safelite Glass Corp., **19 371–73**
Safer, Inc., **21** 385–86
Safeskin Corporation, **18 467–70**
Safety 1st, Inc., **24 412–15**; **46** 192
Safety Fund Bank, **II** 207
Safety-Kleen Corp., **8 462–65**
Safety Rehab, **11** 486
Safety Savings and Loan, **10** 339
Safeway Inc., **II** 424, 601, 604–05, 609–10, 628, 632, 637, **654–56**; **6** 364; **7** 61, 569; **9** 39; **10** 442; **11** 239, 241; **12** 113, 209, 559; **13** 90, 336, 340; **16** 64, 160, 249, 452; **22** 37, 126; **24** 273, **416–19 (upd.)**; **25** 296; **27** 292; **28** 510; **30** 24, 27; **33** 305; **40** 366
Saffa SpA, **41** 325–26
Safilo, **40** 155–56
Safmarine, **IV** 22
SAFR. *See* Société Anonyme des Fermiers Reúnis.
Safrap, **IV** 472
Saga Communications, Inc., **II** 608; **III** 103; **IV** 406; **27** 226, **392–94**
Saga Petroleum ASA, **35** 318
Sagami Optical Co., Ltd., **48** 295
The Sage Group, **43 343–46**
Sagebrush Sales, Inc., **12** 397
Sagebrush Steakhouse, **29** 201
SAGEM S.A., **37 346–48**
Saginaw Dock & Terminal Co., **17** 357
Sagitta Arzneimittel, **18** 51
Sagittarius Productions Inc., **I** 286
Sahara Casino Partners L.P., **19** 379
Sahara Resorts. *See* Santa Fe Gaming Corporation.
SAI. *See* Stamos Associates Inc.
Sai Baba, **12** 228
Saia Motor Freight Line, Inc., **6** 421–23; **45** 448
Saibu Gas, **IV** 518–19
SAIC Velcorex, **12** 153; **27** 188
Saiccor, **IV** 92; **49** 353
Sainrapt et Brice, **9** 9
Sainsbury's. *See* J Sainsbury PLC.

St. Alban Boissons S.A., **22** 515
St. Alban's Sand and Gravel, **III** 739
St. Andrews Insurance, **III** 397
St. Charles Manufacturing Co., **III** 654
St. Clair Industries Inc., **I** 482
St. Clair Press, **IV** 570
St. Croix Paper Co., **IV** 281; **9** 259
St. George Reinsurance, **III** 397
Saint-Gobain. *See* Compagnie de Saint Gobain S.A.
St. Helens Crown Glass Co., **III** 724
St. Ives Laboratories Inc., **36** 26
St Ives plc, **34 393–95**
St. James Associates, **32** 362–63
The St. Joe Company, **31 422–25**
St. Joe Gold, **23** 40
St. Joe Minerals Corp., **I** 569, 571; **8** 192
St. Joe Paper Company, **8 485–88**
St. John Knits, Inc., **14 466–68**
St. John's Wood Railway Company, **6** 406
St. Joseph Company, **I** 286, 684; **49** 357
St. Jude Medical, Inc., **6** 345; **11 458–61**; **43 347–52 (upd.)**
St. Laurent Paperboard Inc., **30** 119
St. Lawrence Cement Inc., **III** 702; **8** 258–59
St. Lawrence Corp. Ltd., **IV** 272
St. Lawrence Steamboat Co., **I** 273; **26** 303
St. Louis and Illinois Belt Railway, **6** 504
Saint Louis Bread Company, **18** 35, 37; **44** 327
St. Louis Concessions Inc., **21** 39
St. Louis Music, Inc., **48 351–54**
St. Louis Refrigerator Car Co., **I** 219; **34** 36
St. Louis Troy and Eastern Railroad Company, **6** 504
St. Martin's Press, **25** 484–85; **35** 452
St. Michel-Grellier S.A., **44** 40
St. Paul Bank for Cooperatives, **8 489–90**
St. Paul Book and Stationery, Inc., **47** 90
The St. Paul Companies, **III 355–57**; **15** 257; **21** 305; **22** 154, **492–95 (upd.)**
St. Paul Fire and Marine Insurance Co., **III** 355–56
St. Paul Venture Capital Inc., **34** 405–06
Saint-Quirin, **III** 676; **16** 120
St. Regis Corp., **I** 153; **IV** 264, 282; **9** 260; **10** 265; **20** 129
St. Regis Paper Co., **IV** 289, 339; **12** 377; **22** 209
Sainte Anne Paper Co., **IV** 245–46; **25** 10
Saipem, **IV** 420–22, 453
SAirGroup, **29** 376; **33** 268, 271; **37** 241; **46** 398; **47** 287
SAirLogistics, **49** 80–81
Saison Group, **V** 184–85, 187–89; **36** 417–18, 420; **42** 340–41
Saito Ltd., **IV** 268
Saiwa, **II** 543
Sako Ltd., **39** 151
Saks Fifth Avenue, **I** 426; **15** 291; **18** 372; **21** 302; **22** 72; **25** 205; **27** 329
Saks Holdings, Inc., **24 420–23**
Saks Inc., **41 342–45 (upd.)**
Sakura Bank, **39** 286
Sakurai Co., **IV** 327
Salada Foods, **II** 525; **13** 293
Salant Corporation, **12 430–32**; **27** 445
Sale Knitting Company, **12** 501. *See also* Tultex Corporation.
Salem Broadcasting, **25** 508
Salem Carpet Mills, Inc., **9** 467

Salem Sportswear, **25** 167
Salen Energy A.B., **IV** 563
Salick Health Care, Inc., **21** 544, 546
Salim Group, **18** 180–81
Salinas Equipment Distributors, Inc., **33** 364
Sallie Mae. *See* SLM Holding Corp. *and* Student Loan Marketing Association.
Sally Beauty Company, Inc., **8** 15–17; **36** 23–26
Salmon Carriers, **6** 383
Salmon River Power & Light Company, **12** 265
Salomon Brothers Inc., **28** 164
Salomon Inc., **I** 630–31; **II** 268, 400, 403, 406, 426, 432, 434, 441, **447–49**; **III** 221, 215, 721; **IV** 80, 137; **7** 114; **9** 378–79, 386; **11** 35, 371; **13** 331, **447–50 (upd.)** Inc.; **18** 60, 62; **19** 293; **21** 67, 146; **22** 102; **23** 472–74; **25** 12, 125; **42** 34
Salomon Smith Barney, **30** 124
Salomon Worldwide, **20** 458–60; **33** 7.
See also adidas-Salomon AG.
Salora, **II** 69; **17** 353
Salsåkers Ångsågs, **IV** 338
Salt River Project, **19 374–76**
Salton, Inc., **30 402–04**
Saltos del Sil, **II** 197
Salvagnini Company, **22** 6
The Salvation Army USA, **15** 510–11; **32 390–93**
Salzgitter AG, **IV** 128, 198, **200–01**; **17** 381
SAM. *See* Sociedad Aeronáutica de Medellín, S.A.
Sam & Libby Inc., **30** 311
Sam Ash Music Corporation, **30 405–07**
Sam Goody, **I** 613; **9** 360–61
Sam's Club, **V** 216–17; **8** 555–57; **12** 221, 335; **13** 548; **14** 393; **15** 470; **16** 64; **25** 235; **40 385–87**; **41** 254–56
Samancor Ltd., **IV** 92–93
Samaritan Senior Services Inc., **25** 503
Samas-Groep N.V., **47** 91
Sambo's, **12** 510
Sambre-et-Moselle, **IV** 52
Samcor Glass, **III** 685
Samedan Oil Corporation, **11** 353
Sames, S.A., **21** 65–66
Samim, **IV** 422
Samkong Fat Ltd. Co., **III** 747
Samna Corp., **6** 256; **25** 300
Sampson's, **12** 220–21
Samson Technologies Corp., **30** 406
Samsonite Corporation, **6** 50; **13** 311, **451–53**; **16** 20–21; **38** 169; **43 353–57 (upd.)**
Samsung-Calex, **17** 483
Samsung Electronics Co., Ltd., **14 416–18**; **18** 139, 260; **41 346–49 (upd.)**
Samsung Group, **I 515–17**; **II** 53–54; **III** 143, 457–58, 517, 749; **IV** 519; **7** 233; **12** 211–12; **13** 387; **18** 124; **29** 207–08
Samuel Austin & Son Company, **8** 41
Samuel Meisel & Company, Inc., **11** 80–81; **29** 509, 511
Samuel Montagu & Co., **II** 319; **17** 324–25
Samuel Moore & Co., **I** 155
Samuel Samuel & Co., **IV** 530, 542
Samuel, Son & Co. Ltd., **24** 144
Samuels Jewelers Incorporated, **30 408–10**

Samwha Paper Co., **III** 748
San Antonio Public Service Company, **6** 473
San Diego Gas & Electric Company, **V 711–14**; **6** 590; **11** 272; **25** 416
San Francisco Mines of Mexico Ltd., **22** 285
San Gabriel Light & Power Company, **16** 496
San Giorgio Macaroni Inc., **II** 511
SAN-MIC Trading Co., **IV** 327
San Miguel Corporation, **I** 221; **15 428–30**; **23** 379
Sanborn Co., **III** 142; **6** 237
Sanborn Hermanos, S.A., **20 461–63**; **21** 259
Sanborn Manufacturing Company, **30** 138
Sandcastle 5 Productions, **25** 269–70
Sanders Associates, Inc., **9** 324; **13** 127–28
Sanderson & Porter, **I** 376
Sanderson Computers, **10** 500
Sanderson Farms, Inc., **15 425–27**
Sandia National Laboratories, **49 345–48**
Sandoz Ltd., **I** 632–33, **671–73**, 675; **7** 315, 452; **8** 108–09, 215; **10** 48, 199; **11** 173; **12** 388; **15** 139; **18** 51; **22** 475; **27** 299. *See also* Novartis AG.
Sandoz Nutrition Corp., **24** 286
SandPoint Corp., **12** 562; **17** 254
Sandusky Plastics, Inc., **17** 157
Sandusky Portland Cement Company, **24** 331
Sandvik AB, **III** 426–27; **IV 202–04**; **32 394–98 (upd.)**
Sandwell, Inc., **6** 491
Sandwich Chef, Inc. *See* Wall Street Deli, Inc.
Sandy's Pool Supply, Inc. *See* Leslie's Poolmart, Inc.
SANFLO Co., Ltd., **IV** 327
Sanford-Brown College, Inc., **41** 419–20
Sangu Express Company, **V** 463
Sanichem Manufacturing Company, **16** 386
Sanitary Farm Dairies, Inc., **7** 372
Sanitas Food Co., **II** 523
Sanitation Systems, Inc. *See* HMI Industries.
Sanjushi Bank, **II** 347
Sanka Coffee Corp., **II** 531
Sankin Kai Group, **II** 274
Sanko Kabushiki Kaisha. *See* Marubeni Corporation.
Sankyo Company Ltd., **I** 330, **674–75**; **III** 760; **8** 153
Sanlam, **IV** 91, 93, 535; **49** 353
Sano Railway Company, **6** 430
Sanofi Group, **I** 304, **676–77**; **III** 18; **IV** 546; **7** 484–85; **21** 205; **23** 236, 238, 242; **35** 262–63, 265
The Sanofi-Synthélabo Group, **49 349–51 (upd.)**
Sanrio Company, Ltd., **38 413–15**
Sanseisha Co., **IV** 326
Santa Ana Savings and Loan, **10** 339
Santa Ana Wholesale Company, **16** 451
Santa Barbara Restaurant Group, Inc., **37 349–52**
The Santa Cruz Operation, Inc., **6** 244; **38 416–21**
Santa Cruz Portland Cement, **II** 490
Santa Fe Gaming Corporation, **19 377–79**
Santa Fe Gold Corporation, **38** 232

Santa Fe Industries, **II** 448; **12** 19; **13** 448; **28** 498
Santa Fe International Corporation, **IV** 451–52; **38 422–24**
Santa Fe Pacific Corporation, **V 507–09**; **24** 98. *See also* Burlington Northern Santa Fe Corporation.
Santa Fe Railway, **12** 278; **18** 4
Santa Fe Southern Pacific Corp., **III** 512; **IV** 721; **6** 150, 599; **9** 391; **22** 491
Santa Rosa Savings and Loan, **10** 339
Santal, **26** 160
Santiam Lumber Co., **IV** 358
Santone Industries Inc., **16** 327
Sanus Corp. Health Systems, **III** 317
Sanwa Bank, Ltd., **II** 276, 326, **347–48**, 442, 511; **III** 188, 759; **IV** 150–51; **7** 119; **15** 43, **431–33 (upd.)**; **24** 356, 358
Sanyo Chemical Manufacturing Co., **III** 758
Sanyo Electric Co., Ltd., **I** 516; **II** 55–56, **91–92**; **III** 569, 654; **6** 101; **14** 535; **20** 361; **36 399–403 (upd.)**
Sanyo Ethylene Co. Ltd., **IV** 476
Sanyo-Kokusaku Pulp Co., Ltd., **IV** 326, **327–28**
Sanyo Petrochemical Co. Ltd., **IV** 476
Sanyo Railway Co., **I** 506; **II** 325
Sanyo Semiconductor, **17** 33
SAP AG, **11** 78; **16 441–44**; **25** 34; **26** 496, 498; **43 358–63 (upd.)**
SAP America Inc., **38** 431–32
SAPAC. *See* Société Parisienne d'Achats en Commun.
Sapirstein Greeting Card Company. *See* American Greetings Corporation.
Sappi Limited, **IV** 91–93; **49 352–55**
Sapporo Breweries Limited, **I** 282–83; **13 454–56 (upd.)**; **20** 28–29; **21** 319–20; **36 404–07 (upd.)**
Sara Lee Corporation, **I** 15, 30; **II 571–73**, 675; **7** 113 **8** 262; **10** 219–20; **11** 15, 486; **12** 494, 502, 531; **15** 359, **434–37 (upd.)**, 507; **19** 192; **25** 91, 125, 166, 523; **26** 325, 503; **29** 132; **38** 381; **45** 111–12, 114; **49** 10
Saracen's Head Brewery, **21** 245
Saratoga Partners, **24** 436
Sarawak Trading, **14** 448
Sargent & Lundy, **6** 556
Sarget S.A., **IV** 71
SARL, **12** 152
Sarma, **III** 623–24; **26** 159–61
Sarmag, **26** 161
Saros Corp., **15** 474
Sarotti A.G., **II** 546
Sarpe, **IV** 591
Sarrià S.A., **41** 325–26
Sartek Industries Inc., **44** 441
The SAS Group, **34 396–99 (upd.)**
SAS Institute Inc., **10 476–78**; **38** 432
Saseba Heavy Industries, **II** 274
Saskatchewan Oil and Gas Corporation, **13** 556–57
Sasol Limited, **IV 533–35**; **47 340–44 (upd.)**
Sason Corporation, **V** 187
SAT. *See* Stockholms Allmänna Telefonaktiebolag.
Satcom Group of Companies, **32** 40
Satellite Business Systems, **III** 182; **21** 14; **23** 135; **27** 304
Satellite Information Services, **II** 141
Satellite Software International, **10** 556

Satellite Television PLC, **IV** 652; **7** 391; **23** 135

Satellite Transmission and Reception Specialist Company, **11** 184

Säteri Oy, **IV** 349

Sato Yasusaburo, **I** 266

Saturday Evening Post Co., **II** 208; **9** 320

Saturn Corporation, **III** 593, 760; **7** 461–64; **21** 449–53 (upd.); **22** 154; **36** 242

Saturn Industries, Inc., **23** 489

SATV. *See* Satellite Television PLC.

Saucona Iron Co., **IV** 35; **7** 48

Saucony Inc., **35** 386–89

Sauder Woodworking Co., **12** 433–34; **35** 390–93 (upd.)

Saudi Arabian Airlines, **6** 84, 114–16; **27** 132, 395–98 (upd.)

Saudi Arabian Oil Company, **IV** 536–39; **17** 411–15 (upd.). *See also* Arabian American Oil Co.

Saudi Arabian Parsons Limited, **8** 416

Saudi British Bank, **II** 298

Saudi Consolidated Electric Co., **IV** 538; **17** 414

Saudi Refining Inc., **IV** 539; **17** 414

Saudia. *See* Saudi Arabian Airlines.

Sauer Motor Company, **I** 177; **22** 329

Saul Lerner & Co., **II** 450

Saunders Karp & Co., **26** 190

Saunders, Karp, and Megrue, LP, **28** 258

Saunders-Roe Ltd., **IV** 658

Sauza, **31** 92

Sav-on Drug, **II** 605; **12** 477

Sav-X, **9** 186

Sava Group, **20** 263

Savacentre Ltd., **II** 658; **13** 284

Savage, **19** 430

Savage Shoes, Ltd., **III** 529

Savannah Electric & Power Company, **38** 448

Savannah Foods & Industries, Inc., **7** 465–67; **32** 274, 277; **35** 178

Savannah Gas Company, **6** 448; **23** 29

Save & Prosper Group, **10** 277

Save-A-Lot, **II** 682; **11** 228

Save Mart, **14** 397; **27** 292

Save.com, **37** 409

Savia S.A. de C.V., **29** 435

Saviem, **III** 543

Savin, **III** 159; **26** 497

Savings of America, **II** 182

Savio, **IV** 422

Oy Savo-Karjalan Tukkuliike, **8** 293

Savon Sellu Mills, **IV** 315

Savory Milln, **II** 369

Savoy Group, **I** 248; **IV** 705; **24** 195; **49** 247

Savoy Industries, **12** 495

Savoy Pictures Entertainment Inc., **25** 214

Sawdust Pencil Company, **29** 372

Sawgrass Asset Management, LLC, **48** 18

Sawhill Tubular Products, **41** 3

Sawtek Inc., **43** 364–66 (upd.)

Sawyer Electrical Manufacturing Company, **11** 4

Sawyer Industries, Inc., **13** 532

Sawyer Research Products, Inc., **14** 81

Saxby, S.A., **13** 385

Saxon and Norman Cement Co., **III** 670

Saxon Oil, **11** 97

Saxon Petroleum, Inc., **19** 162

Sayama Sekiyu, **IV** 554

SB Acquisitions, Inc., **46** 74

SBAR, Inc., **30** 4

Sbarro, Inc., **16** 445–47; **19** 435; **27** 146

SBC Communications Inc., **25** 498–99; **29** 62; **32** 399–403 (upd.); **34** 362; **43** 447; **47** 10

SBC Warburg, **II** 369; **14** 419–21; **15** 197

Sberbank, **II** 242

SBK Entertainment World, Inc., **22** 194; **24** 485; **26** 187

SBS Technologies, Inc., **25** 405–07

SCA. *See* Svenska Cellulosa Aktiebolaget.

SCA Services, Inc., **V** 754; **9** 109

Scaldia Paper BV, **15** 229

Scali, McCabe & Sloves, **I** 27; **22** 200

Scan Screen, **IV** 600

Scana Corporation, **6** 574–76; **19** 499

Scanair, **34** 397–98

Scancem, **38** 437

Scandic Hotels AB, **49** 193

Scandinavian Airlines System, **I** 107, 119–20, 121; **6** 96, 122; **25** 159; **26** 113; **27** 26, 463, 474; **31** 305; **33** 50; **38** 105. *See also* The SAS Group.

Scandinavian Bank, **II** 352

Scandinavian Trading Co., **I** 210

ScanDust, **III** 625

Scania-Vabis. *See* Saab-Scania AB.

ScanSource, Inc., **29** 413–15

Scantron Corporation, **17** 266–68

Scarborough Public Utilities Commission, **9** 461–62

Scaturro Supermarkets, **24** 528

SCB Computer Technology, Inc., **29** 416–18

SCEcorp, **V** 713–14, **715–17**; **6** 590

Scenic Airlines, Inc., **25** 420, 423

Scenographic Designs, **21** 277

Schäfer, **31** 158

Schaffhausenschor Bankverein, **II** 281

Schaper Mfg. Co., **12** 168

Scharff-Koken Manufacturing Co., **IV** 286

Scharnow-Reisen, **II** 163–64; **44** 432

Schaum Publishing Co., **IV** 636

Schauman Wood Oy, **IV** 277, 302

Schawk, Inc., **24** 424–26

Schein Pharmaceutical Inc., **13** 77

Schenker-Rhenus Ag, **6** 424–26

Schenley Industries Inc., **I** 226, 285; **9** 449; **10** 181; **24** 140

Scherer. *See* R.P. Scherer.

Schering A.G., **I** 681–82, 684, 701; **10** 214; **14** 60; **16** 543; **36** 92, 148

Schering-Plough Corporation, **I** 682, 683–85; **II** 590; **III** 45, 61; **11** 142, 207; **14** 58, 60, **422–25** (upd.); **36** 91–92; **45** 382; **49** 356–62 (upd.)

Schiavi Homes, Inc., **14** 138

Schibsted ASA, **31** 401–05

Schicht Co., **II** 588

Schick Products, **41** 366

Schick Shaving, **I** 711; **III** 55; **38** 363, 365

Schieffelin & Co., **I** 272

Schindler Holding AG, **II** 122; **12** 546; **27** 267; **29** 419–22

Schlage Lock Co., **III** 526

Schleppschiffahrtsgesellschaft Unterweser, **IV** 140

Schlesischer Bankverein, **II** 278

Schlitz Brewing Co., **I** 218, 255, 268, 270, 291, 600; **10** 100; **12** 338; **18** 500; **23** 403

Schlotzsky's, Inc., **36** 408–10

Schlumberger Limited, **III** 429, 499, 616–18; **13** 323; **17** 416–19 (upd.); **22** 64, 68; **25** 191; **43** 91, 338; **45** 418; **49** 305

Schmalbach-Lubeca-Werke A.G., **15** 128

Schmid, **19** 166

Schmidt, **I** 255

Schmitt Music Company, **40** 388–90

Schneider Co., **III** 113

Schneider et Cie, **IV** 25; **22** 42

Schneider National, Inc., **36** 411–13; **47** 318–19

Schneider S.A., **II** 93–94; **18** 471–74 (upd.); **19** 165–66; **37** 39

Schneiderman's Furniture Inc., **28** 405–08

Schnitzer Steel Industries, Inc., **19** 380–82

Schnoll Foods, **24** 528

Schober Direktmarketing, **18** 170

Schocken Books, **13** 429

Schoeller & Hoesch Group, **30** 349, 352

Schoenfeld Industries, **16** 511

Scholastic Corporation, **10** 479–81; **29** 143, 423–27 (upd.)

Scholl Inc., **I** 685; **14** 424; **49** 359, 380

Schöller, **27** 436, 439

Scholz Homes Inc., **IV** 115

Schott Glass Technologies Inc., **34** 94

Schott Glaswerke, **III** 445–47

Schott-Zwiesel-Glaswerke AG, **34** 94

Schottenstein Stores Corp., **14** 426–28; **19** 108; **24** 26; **38** 475. *See also* American Eagle Outfitters, Inc.

Schrader Bellows, **III** 603

Schreiber Foods, **26** 432

Schreiber Frères. *See* Groupe Les Echos.

Schrock Cabinet Company, **13** 564

Schroder Darling & Co., **II** 389

Schroders plc, **42** 332–35

Schroders Ventures, **18** 345

Schroeter, White and Johnson, **III** 204

Schroff Inc., **26** 361, 363

Schubach, **30** 408

Schubert & Salzer GmbH, **42** 316

Schuck's Auto Supply. *See* CSK Auto Corporation.

Schuff Steel Company, **26** 431–34

Schuitema, **II** 642; **16** 312–13

Schuler Chocolates, **15** 65

Schuller International, Inc., **11** 421

Schultz Sav-O Stores, Inc., **21** 454–56; **31** 406–08

Schumacher Co., **II** 624

Schuykill Energy Resources, **12** 41

Schwabe-Verlag, **7** 42

Schwabel Corporation, **19** 453

Schwan's Sales Enterprises, Inc., **7** 468–70; **26** 435–38 (upd.)

Schwartz Iron & Metal Co., **13** 142

Schwarze Pumpe, **38** 408

Schweitzer-Maudit International Inc., **16** 304; **43** 258

Schweiz Allgemeine, **III** 377

Schweiz Transport-Vericherungs-Gesellschaft, **III** 410

Schweizer Rück Holding AG, **III** 377

Schweizerische Bankgesellschaft AG, **II** 379; **V** 104

Schweizerische Kreditanstalt, **III** 375, 410; **6** 489

Schweizerische Nordostbahn, **6** 424

Schweizerische Post-, Telefon- und Telegrafen-Betriebe, **V** 321–24

Schweizerische Ruckversicherungs-Gesellschaft. *See* Swiss Reinsurance Company.

Schweizerische Unfallversicherungs-Actiengesellschaft in Winterthur, **III** 402

Schweizerische Unionbank, **II** 368

Schweizerischer Bankverein, **II** 368

Schweppe, Paul & Gosse, **II** 476

Schweppes Ltd. *See* Cadbury Schweppes PLC.

Schwinn Cycle and Fitness L.P., 16 494; **19 383–85; 26** 412; **47** 95

The Schwinn GT Co., **26** 185

Schwitzer, **II** 420

SCI. *See* Service Corporation International *or* Société Centrale d'Investissement.

SCI Systems, Inc., 9 463–64; 12 451

Scicon International, **14** 317; **49** 165

SciCor Inc., **30** 152

Science Applications International Corporation, 15 438–40

Scientific-Atlanta, Inc., 6 335–37; 45 371–75 (upd.)

Scientific Communications, Inc., **10** 97

Scientific Data Systems, **II** 44; **III** 172; **6** 289; **10** 365

Scientific Games Holding Corp., **III** 431; **20** 48

Scientific Materials Company, **24** 162

SciMed Life Systems, **III** 18–19; **37** 43

Scioto Bank, **9** 475

Scitex Corporation Ltd., 15 148, 229; **24 427–32; 26** 212; **43** 150; **48** 123

SCM Corp., **I** 29; **III** 502; **IV** 330; **7** 208; **8** 223–24; **17** 213

SCO. *See* Santa Cruz Operation, Inc.

SCOA Industries, Inc., **13** 260

Scopus Technology Inc., **38** 431

SCOR S.A., III 394; **20 464–66**

The Score Board, Inc., 19 386–88

Score! Learning, Inc., **42** 211

Scot Bowyers, **II** 587

Scot Lad Foods, **14** 411

Scotch House Ltd., **19** 181

Scotia Securities, **II** 223

Scotiabank. *See* The Bank of Nova Scotia.

Scotsman Industries, Inc., II 420; **16** 397; **20 467–69**

Scott-Ballantyne Company. *See* Ballantyne of Omaha, Inc.

Scott Communications, Inc., **10** 97

Scott Fetzer Company, III 214; **12 435–37,** 554–55; **17** 233; **18** 60, 62–63; **42** 33

Scott, Foresman, **IV** 675

Scott Graphics, **IV** 289; **8** 483

Scott Health Care, **28** 445

Scott Holdings, **19** 384

Scott Lithgow, **III** 516; **7** 232

Scott-McDuff, **II** 107

Scott Paper Company, III 749; **IV** 258, 289–90, 311, 325, 327, **329–31; 8** 483; **16** 302, 304; **17** 182; **18** 181; **19** 266; **22** 210; **29** 333; **31 409–412 (upd.); 43** 258

Scott Transport, **27** 473

Scotti Brothers, **20** 3

Scottish & Newcastle plc, 15 441–44; 35 394–97 (upd.)

Scottish Amicable plc, **48** 328

Scottish Aviation, **I** 50; **24** 85–86

Scottish Brick, **14** 250

Scottish Electric, **6** 453

Scottish General Fire Assurance Corp., **III** 256

Scottish Hydro-Electric PLC, 13 457–59

Scottish Inns of America, Inc., **13** 362

Scottish Land Development, **III** 501; **7** 207

Scottish Malt Distillers, **I** 240

Scottish Media Group plc, 32 404–06; 41 350–52

Scottish Mutual plc, **39** 5–6

Scottish Nuclear, Ltd., **19** 389

Scottish Power plc, 49 363–66 (upd.)

Scottish Radio Holding plc, 41 350–52

Scottish Sealand Oil Services Ltd., **25** 171

Scottish Union Co., **III** 358

Scottish Universal Investments, **45** 189

ScottishPower plc, 19 389–91; 27 483, 486

ScottishTelecom plc, **19** 389

The Scotts Company, 22 474–76

Scotts Stores, **I** 289

Scotty's, Inc., 12 234; **22 477–80; 26** 160–61

Scovill Fasteners Inc., IV 11; **22** 364; **24 433–36**

SCP Pool Corporation, 39 358–60

Scranton Corrugated Box Company, Inc., **8** 102

Scranton Plastics Laminating Corporation, **8** 359

Screen Gems, **II** 135–36; **12** 74; **22** 193

Screg Group, **I** 563; **24** 79; **31** 128

Scribbans-Kemp Ltd., **II** 594

Scriha & Deyhle, **10** 196

Scripps-Howard, Inc., **IV** 607–09, 628; **7** 64, 157–59. *See also* The E.W. Scripps Company.

Scrivner Inc., **17** 180

SCS Interactive, **44** 261

Scudder Kemper Investments. *See* Zurich Financial Services.

Scudder, Stevens & Clark, **II** 448; **13** 448

Scurlock Oil Co., **IV** 374

SD-Scicon plc, **24** 87

SD Warren, **49** 352–53

SDA Systems Inc., **48** 75

SDC Coatings, **III** 715

SDGE. *See* San Diego Gas & Electric Company.

SDK Health Care Information Systems, **16** 94

SDK Parks, **IV** 724

Sea-Alaska Products, **II** 494

Sea Containers Ltd., 29 428–31

Sea Diamonds Ltd., **IV** 66; **7** 123

Sea Far of Norway, **II** 484

Sea Insurance Co. Ltd., **III** 220

Sea-Land Service Inc., **I** 476; **9** 510–11; **22** 164, 166

Sea Life Centre Aquariums, **10** 439

Sea Ray, **III** 444

Sea Star Line, **41** 399

Sea World, Inc., **IV** 623–24; **12** 224

Seabee Corp., **18** 276

Seaboard Air Line Railroad. *See* CSX Corporation.

Seaboard Corporation, 36 414–16

Seaboard Finance Company, **13** 63

Seaboard Fire and Marine Insurance Co., **III** 242

Seaboard Life Insurance Co., **III** 193

Seaboard Lumber Sales, **IV** 307

Seaboard Oil Co., **IV** 552

Seaboard Surety Company, **III** 357; **22** 494

Seabourn Cruise Lines, **6** 368; **27** 90, 92

Seabrook Farms Co., **24** 527–28

Seabulk Offshore International. *See* Hvide Marine Incorporated.

Seabury & Smith, **III** 283

Seacat-Zapata Off-Shore Company, **18** 513

Seacoast Products, **III** 502

Seafield Capital Corporation, **27** 385, 387. *See also* LabOne, Inc.

Seafield Estate and Consolidated Plantations Berhad, **14** 448

Seafirst. *See* Seattle First National Bank, Inc.

SeaFirst Corp., **II** 228; **17** 462

Seagate Technology, Inc., 6 230–31; **8 466–68; 9** 57; **10** 257, 403–04, 459; **11** 56, 234; **13** 483; **18** 250; **25** 530; **34 400–04 (upd.); 45** 429

The Seagram Company Ltd., I 26, 240, 244, **284–86,** 329, 403; **II** 456, 468; **IV** 401; **7** 155; **18** 72; **21** 26, 401; **22** 194; **23** 125; **25** 266, 268, 366, **408–12 (upd.); 26** 125, 127, 152; **28** 475; **29** 196; **31** 269; **33** 375, 424, 432; **46** 438; **47** 418–20

Seagull Energy Corporation, 11 440–42

Seahawk Services Ltd., **37** 289

Seal Products, Inc., **12** 264

Seal Sands Chemicals, **16** 69

Sealand Petroleum Co., **IV** 400

Sealectro, **III** 434

Sealed Air Corporation, 14 429–31

Sealed Power Corporation, I 199–200; 10 492–94. *See also* SPX Corporation.

Sealright Co., Inc., 17 420–23

SealRite Windows, **19** 446

Sealtest, **14** 205

Sealy Inc., 12 438–40; 28 416; **34** 407

Seaman Furniture Company, Inc., 28 389; **32 407–09**

Seamless Rubber Co., **III** 613

Seaquist Manufacturing Corporation, **9** 413–14; **33** 335–36

Searle & Co. *See* G.D. Searle & Co.

Sears Canada Inc., **25** 221

Sears Logistics Services, **18** 225–26

Sears plc, V 177–79

Sears, Roebuck and Co., I 26, 146, 516, 556; **II** 18, 60, 134, 331, 411, 414; **III** 259, 265, 340, 536, 598, 653–55; **V 180–83; 6** 12–13; **7** 166, 479; **8** 224, 287–89; **9** 44, 65–66 156, 210, 213, 219, 235–36, 430–31, 538; **10** 10, 50–52, 199, 236–37, 288, 304–05, 490–91; **11** 62, 349, 393, 498; **12** 54, 96–98, 309, 311, 315, 430–31, 439, 522, 548, 557; **13** 165, 260, 268, 277, 411, 545, 550, 562–63; **14** 62; **15** 402, 470; **16** 73, 75, 160, 327–28, 560; **17** 366, 460, 487; **18** 65, 168, 283, 445, **475–79 (upd.); 19** 143, 221, 309, 490; **20** 259, 263; **21** 73, 94, 96–97; **23** 23, 52, 210; **25** 221, 357, 535; **27** 30, 32, 163, 347–48, 416, 428–30; **33** 311–12; **36** 418

Sears Roebuck de México, S.A. de C.V., 20 470–72; 21 259; **34** 340

Seashore Transportation Co., **13** 398

Season-all Industries, **III** 735

SEAT. *See* Sociedad Española de Automoviles de Turismo.

Seat Pagine Gialle S.p.A., 47 345–47

Seatrain International, **27** 474

Seattle Brewing and Malting Company. *See* Rainier Brewing Company.

Seattle Coffee Company, **32** 12, 15

Seattle Electric Company, **6** 565
Seattle FilmWorks, Inc., 20 473–75
Seattle First National Bank Inc., 8 469–71
Seattle Times Company, 15 445–47
Seaview Oil Co., **IV** 393
Seaway Express, **9** 510
Seaway Food Town, Inc., 9 452; **15 448–50**
SeaWest, **19** 390
SEB-Fastigheter A.B., **II** 352
SEB S.A. *See* Groupe SEB.
Sebastian International, **48** 422
Sebastiani Vineyards, Inc., 28 413–15; 39 421
SECA, **IV** 401
SECDO, **III** 618
SECO Industries, **III** 614
Seco Products Corporation, **22** 354
Secon GmbH, **13** 160
Second Bank of the United States, **II** 213; **9** 369
Second Harvest, 29 432–34
Second National Bank, **II** 254
Second National Bank of Bucyrus, **9** 474
Second National Bank of Ravenna, **9** 474
Secoroc, **III** 427
Le Secours, **III** 211
SecPac. *See* Security Pacific Corporation.
Secure Horizons, **11** 378–79
Secure Networks, Inc., **25** 349
Securicor Plc, 11 547; **45 376–79**
Securitas AB, 41 77, 80; **42** 165–66, **336–39**
Securitas Esperia, **III** 208
Securities Industry Automation Corporation, **9** 370
Securities International, Inc., **II** 440–41
Securities Management & Research, Inc., **27** 46
Security Bancorp, **25** 186–87
Security Capital Corporation, 17 424–27; 21 476; **48** 330–31; **49** 28–29
Security Connecticut Life Insurance Co., **III** 276
Security Data Group, **32** 373
Security Dynamics Technologies, Inc., **46** 367
Security Engineering, **III** 472
Security Express, **10** 269
Security First National Bank of Los Angeles, **II** 349
Security Life and Annuity Company, **11** 213
Security Management Company, **8** 535–36
Security National Bank, **II** 251, 336
Security National Corp., **10** 246
Security Pacific Corporation, II 349–50, 422; **III** 366; **8** 45, 48; **11** 447; **17** 137
Security Trust Company, **9** 229, 388
Security Union Title Insurance Co., **10** 43–44
SED International Holdings, Inc., 43 367–69
Sedat Eldem, **13** 475
SEDCO, **17** 418
Sedgwick Group PLC, **I** 427; **III** 280, 366; **10** 38; **22** 318
Sedgwick Sales, Inc., **29** 384
SEDTCO Pty., **13** 61
See's Candies, Inc., III 213; **18** 60–61; **30 411–13**
Seeburg Corporation, **II** 22; **III** 430; **15** 538

Seed Restaurant Group Inc., **13** 321; **27** 145
Seed Solutions, Inc., **11** 491
Seeger-Orbis, **III** 624
Seeger Refrigerator Co., **III** 653; **12** 548
Seeman Brothers. *See* White Rose, Inc.
SEEQ Technology, Inc., **9** 114; **13** 47; **17** 32, 34
SEG, **I** 463
Sega Enterprises, Ltd., **28** 320
Sega of America, Inc., 7 396; **10** 124–25, 284–86, **482–85; 18** 520
Sega of Japan, **24** 4
Segespar, **II** 265
Sego Milk Products Company, **7** 428
Seguros Comercial America, **21** 413
Seguros El Corte Inglés, **V** 52
Seguros Monterrey Aetna, **19** 189; **45** 294
Seguros Serfin S.A., **25** 290
Segway LLC, 48 355–57
Seibels, Bruce & Co., **11** 394–95
Seiberling Rubber Company, **V** 244; **20** 259
Seibu Allstate Life Insurance Company, Ltd., **27** 31
Seibu Department Stores, Ltd., II 273; **V 184–86; 42 340–43 (upd.)**
Seibu Group, **36** 417–18; **47** 408–09
Seibu Railway Co. Ltd., V 187, **510–11,** 526
Seibu Saison, **6** 207
Seifu Co. Ltd., **48** 250
Seigle's Home and Building Centers, Inc., 41 353–55
Seijo Green Plaza Co., **I** 283
Seikatsu-Soko, **V** 210
Seiko Corporation, I 488; **III** 445, **619–21;** 11 46; **12** 317; **13** 122; **16** 168, 549; **17 428–31 (upd.); 21** 122–23; **22** 413; **41** 72
Seiko Instruments USA Inc., **23** 210
Seimi Chemical Co. Ltd., **48** 41
Seine, **III** 391
Seino Transportation Company, Ltd., 6 427–29
Seismograph Service Limited, **II** 86; **11** 413; **17** 419
Seita, 23 424–27
Seitel, Inc., 47 348–50
Seiwa Fudosan Co., **I** 283
The Seiyu, Ltd., V 187–89; **36 417–21 (upd.)**
Seizo-sha, **12** 483
Sekisui Chemical Co., Ltd., III 741–43
SEL, **I** 193, 463
Selat Marine Services, **22** 276
Selby Shoe Company, **48** 69
Selden, **I** 164, 300
Select Comfort Corporation, 34 405–08
Select Energy, Inc., **48** 305
Select-Line Industries, **9** 543
Select Theatres Corp. *See* Shubert Organization Inc.
Selection Trust, **IV** 67, 380, 565
Selective Auto and Fire Insurance Co. of America, **III** 353
Selective Insurance Co., **III** 191
Selectronics Inc., **23** 210
Selectrons Ltd., **41** 367
Selena Coffee Inc., **39** 409
Selenia, **I** 467; **II** 86; **38** 374
Self Auto, **23** 232
The Self-Locking Carton Company, **14** 163
Self-Service Drive Thru, Inc., **25** 389

Self Service Restaurants, **II** 613
Selfridges Plc, V 94, 177–78; **34 409–11**
Seligman & Latz, **18** 455
Selkirk Communications Ltd., **26** 273
Selleck Nicholls, **III** 691
Sells-Floto, **32** 186
The Selmer Company, Inc., 19 392–94, 426, 428
Seltel International Inc., **6** 33; **35** 246
Semarca, **11** 523
Sematech, **18** 384, 481
Sembler Company, **11** 346
SEMCO Energy, Inc., 44 379–82
Semet-Solvay, **22** 29
Seminis, Inc., 21 413; **29 435–37**
Seminole Electric Cooperative, **6** 583
Seminole Fertilizer, **7** 537–38
Seminole National Bank, **41** 312
Semitic, Inc., **33** 248
Semitool, Inc., 18 480–82
Sempra Energy, 25 413–16 (upd.)
Semrau and Sons, **II** 601
Semtech Corporation, 32 410–13
SEN AG, **IV** 128
Sencel Aero Engineering Corporation, **16** 483
Seneca Foods Corporation, 17 432–34
Senelle-Maubeuge, **IV** 227
Senior Corp., **11** 261
Senshusha, **I** 506
Sensi, Inc., **22** 173
Sensormatic Electronics Corp., 11 443–45; 49 77–79
Sensory Science Corporation, 37 353–56
Sentinel Foam & Envelope Corporation, **14** 430
Sentinel Group, **6** 295
Sentinel Savings and Loan, **10** 339
Sentinel-Star Company, **IV** 683; **22** 521
Sentinel Technologies, **III** 38
Sentrust, **IV** 92
Sentry, **II** 624
Sentry Insurance Company, **10** 210
Senyo Kosakuki Kenkyujo, **III** 595
Seohan Development Co., **III** 516; **7** 232
Sepa, **II** 594
Sepal, Ltd., **39** 152, 154
AB Separator, **III** 417–19
SEPECAT, **24** 86
SEPIC, **I** 330
Sepracor Inc., 45 380–83
Sept, **IV** 325
Sequa Corp., 13 460–63
Séquanaise, **III** 391–92
Sequel Corporation, **41** 193
Sequent Computer Systems Inc., **10** 363
Sequoia Athletic Company, **25** 450
Sequoia Insurance, **III** 270
Sequoia Pharmacy Group, **13** 150
Sera-Tec Biologicals, Inc., **V** 175–76; **19** 355
Seraco Group, **V** 182
Seragen Inc., **47** 223
Serck Group, **I** 429
Serco Group plc, 47 351–53
SEREB, **I** 45; **7** 10
Sereg Valves, S.A., **17** 147
Serewatt AG, **6** 491
Sergeant Drill Co., **III** 525
Sero-Genics, Inc., **V** 174–75
Serono S.A., 47 354–57
Serta, Inc., 28 416–18
Serval Marketing, **18** 393

Servam Corp., **7** 471–73
Servel Inc., **III** 479; **22** 25
Service America Corp., 7 471–73; 27 480–81
Service Bureau Corp., **III** 127
Service Co., Ltd., **48** 182
Service Control Corp. *See* Angelica Corporation.
Service Corporation International, 6 **293–95**; **16** 343–44; **37** 66–68
Service Corporation of America, **17** 552
Service Games Company, **10** 482
Service Master L.P., **34** 153
Service Merchandise Company, Inc., V **190–92**; **6** 287; **9** 400; **19 395–99** **(upd.)**
Service Partner, **I** 120
Service Pipe Line Co., **IV** 370
Service Q. General Service Co., **I** 109
Service Systems, **III** 103
ServiceMaster Inc., 23 428–31 (upd.)
Servicemaster Limited Partnership, 6 **44–46**; **13** 199
Services Maritimes des Messageries Impériales. *See* Compagnie des Messageries Maritimes.
ServiceWare, Inc., **25** 118
Servicios Financieros Quadrum S.A., **14** 156
Servisair Plc, **49** 320
Servisco, **II** 608
ServiStar Coast to Coast Corporation. *See* TruServ Corporation.
ServoChem A.B., **I** 387
Servomation Corporation, **7** 472–73
Servomation Wilbur. *See* Service America Corp.
Servoplan, S.A., **8** 272
SES Staffing Solutions, **27** 21
Sesame Street Book Club, **13** 560
Sesamee Mexicana, **48** 142
Sespe Oil, **IV** 569; **24** 519
Sessler Inc., **19** 381
SET, **I** 466
Setagaya Industry Co., Ltd., **48** 295
SETCAR, **14** 458
Seton Scholl. *See* SSL International plc.
Settsu Marine and Fire Insurance Co., **III** 367
Seven Arts Limited, **25** 328
Seven Arts Productions, Ltd., **II** 147, 176
7-Eleven, Inc., 32 414–18 (upd.); **36** 358
Seven-Eleven Japan Co., **41** 115. *See also* Ito-Yokado Co., Ltd.
Seven Generation, Inc., **41** 177
Seven Network Limited, **25** 329
Seven-Up Bottling Co. of Los Angeles, **II** 121
Seven-Up Co., **I** 245, 257; **II** 468, 477; **18** 418
Sevenson Environmental Services, Inc., **42 344–46**
Severn Trent PLC, 12 441–43; 38 **425–29 (upd.)**
Severonickel Combine, **48** 300
Seversky Aircraft Corporation, **9** 205
Sevin-Rosen Partners, **III** 124; **6** 221
Sewell Coal Co., **IV** 181
Sewell Plastics, Inc., **10** 222
Sextant In-Flight Systems, LLC, **30** 74
Seybold Machine Co., **II** 37; **6** 602
Seymour Electric Light Co., **13** 182
Seymour International Press Distributor Ltd., **IV** 619

Seymour Press, **IV** 619
Seymour Trust Co., **13** 467
SFIC Holdings (Cayman) Inc., **38** 422
SFIM Industries, **37** 348
SFNGR. *See* Nouvelles Galeries Réunies.
SFS Bancorp Inc., **41** 212
SFX Broadcasting Inc., **24** 107
SFX Entertainment, Inc., 36 422–25; 37 383–84
SGC. *See* Supermarkets General Corporation.
SGE. *See* Vinci.
SGI, 29 438–41 (upd.)
SGL Carbon Group, **40** 83; **46** 14
SGLG, Inc., **13** 367
SGS Corp., **II** 117; **11** 46
Shaffer Clarke, **II** 594
Shakespeare Company, 16 296; **22** **481–84**
Shakey's Pizza, **16** 447
Shaklee Corporation, 12 444–46; 17 186; **38** 93; **39 361–64 (upd.)**
Shalco Systems, **13** 7
Shampaine Industries, Inc., **37** 399
Shamrock Advisors, Inc., **8** 305
Shamrock Broadcasting Inc., **24** 107
Shamrock Capital L.P., **7** 81–82
Shamrock Holdings, **III** 609; **7** 438; **9** 75; **11** 556; **25** 268
Shamrock Oil & Gas Co., **I** 403–04; **IV** 409; **7** 308
Shan-Chih Business Association, **23** 469
Shandwick International, **47** 97
Shanghai Crown Maling Packaging Co. Ltd., **13** 190
Shanghai General Bearing Co., Ltd., **45** 170
Shanghai Hotels Co., **IV** 717
Shanghai International Finance Company Limited, **15** 433
Shanghai Kyocera Electronics Co., Ltd., **21** 331
Shanghai Petrochemical Co., Ltd., 18 **483–85**; **21** 83; **45** 50
Shanghai Tobacco, **49** 150, 153
Shangri-La Asia Ltd., **22** 305
Shanks Group plc, 45 384–87
Shannon Aerospace Ltd., 36 426–28
Shannon Group, Inc., **18** 318, 320
Shansby Group, **27** 197; **43** 218
Share Drug plc, **24** 269
Shared Financial Systems, Inc., **10** 501
Shared Medical Systems Corporation, 14 **432–34**
Shared Technologies Inc., **12** 71
Shared Use Network Systems, Inc., **8** 311
ShareWave Inc., **48** 92
Shari Lewis Enterprises, Inc., **28** 160
Sharon Steel Corp., **I** 497; **7** 360–61; **8** 536; **13** 158, 249; **47** 234
Sharon Tank Car Corporation, **6** 394; **25** 169
Sharp & Dohme, Incorporated, **I** 650; **11** 289, 494
Sharp Corporation, I 476; **II 95–96**; **III** 14, 428, 455, 480; **6** 217, 231; **11** 45; **12** **447–49 (upd.)**; **13** 481; **16** 83; **21** 123; **22** 197; **40 391–95 (upd.)**
The Sharper Image Corporation, 10 **486–88**; **23** 210; **26** 439; **27** 429
Sharples Co., **I** 383
Sharples Separator Co., **III** 418–20
Shasta Beverages. *See* National Beverage Corp.

Shaw Communications Inc., **26** 274; **35** 69
Shaw Industries, Inc., 9 465–67; 19 274, 276; **25** 320; **40 396–99 (upd.)**
Shaw's Supermarkets, Inc., **II** 658–59; **23** 169
Shawell Precast Products, **14** 248
Shawinigan Water and Power Company, **6** 501–02
Shawmut National Corporation, II 207; **12** 31; **13 464–68**
Shea's Winnipeg Brewery Ltd., **I** 268; **25** 280
Sheaffer Group, **23** 54, 57
Shearman & Sterling, 32 419–22; **35** 467
Shearson Hammill & Company, **22** 405–06
Shearson Lehman Brothers Holdings **Inc., I** 202; **II** 398–99, 450, 478; **III** 319; **8** 118; **9 468–70 (upd.)**; **10** 62–63; **11** 418; **12** 459; **15** 124, 463–64
Shearson Lehman Hutton Group, **49** 181
Shearson Lehman Hutton Holdings Inc., **II** 339, 445, **450–52**; **III** 119; **9** 125; **10** 59, 63; **17** 38–39
Shedd's Food Products Company, **9** 318
Sheepbridge Engineering, **III** 495
Sheffield Banking Co., **II** 333
Sheffield Exploration Company, **28** 470
Sheffield Forgemasters Group Ltd., **39** 32
Sheffield Motor Co., **I** 158; **10** 292
Sheffield Twist Drill & Steel Co., **III** 624
Shekou Container Terminal, **16** 481; **38** 345
Shelby Insurance Company, **10** 44–45
Shelby Steel Tube Co., **IV** 572; **7** 550
Shelby Williams Industries, Inc., 14 **435–37**
Shelco, **22** 146
Sheldahl Inc., 23 432–35
Shelf Life Inc. *See* King Kullen Grocery Co., Inc.
Shell. *See* Shell Transport and Trading Company p.l.c. *and* Shell Oil Company.
Shell Australia Ltd., **III** 728
Shell BV, **IV** 518
Shell Canada Limited, **32** 45
Shell Chemical Corporation, **IV** 410, 481, 531–32, 540; **8** 415; **24** 151
Shell Coal International, **IV** 532
Shell Forestry, **21** 546
Shell France, **12** 153
Shell Nederland BV, **V** 658–59
Shell Oil Company, I 20, 26, 569; **III** 559; **IV** 392, 400, 531, **540–41**; **6** 382, 457; **8** 261–62; **11** 522; **14** 25, **438–40** **(upd.)**; **17** 417; **19** 175–76; **21** 546; **22** 274; **24** 520; **25** 96, 232, 469; **26** 496; **41 356–60 (upd.)**, 395; **45** 54
Shell Transport and Trading Company **p.l.c., I** 605; **II** 436, 459; **III** 522, 735; **IV** 363, 378–79, 381–82, 403, 412, 423, 425, 429, 440, 454, 466, 470, 472, 474, 484–86, 491, 505, 508, **530–32**, 564; **31** 127–28. *See also* Royal Dutch Petroleum Company *and* Royal Dutch/ Shell.
Shell Western E & P, **7** 323
Shell Winning, **IV** 413–14
Sheller-Globe Corporation, I 201–02; **17** 182
Shells Seafood Restaurants, Inc., 43 **370–72**
Shelly Brothers, Inc., **15** 65
Shenley Laboratories, **I** 699
Shepard Warner Elevator Co., **III** 467

Shepard's Citations, Inc., **IV** 636–37
Shepherd Hardware Products Ltd., **16** 357
Shepherd Neame Limited, 30 414–16
Shepherd Plating and Finishing Company, **13** 233
Shepler Equipment Co., **9** 512
Sheraton Corp. of America, **I** 463–64, 487; **III** 98–99; **11** 198; **13** 362–63; **21** 91
Sherborne Group Inc./NH Holding Inc., **17** 20
Sherbrooke Paper Products Ltd., **17** 281
Sheridan Bakery, **II** 633
Sheridan Catheter & Instrument Corp., **III** 443
Sherix Chemical, **I** 682
Sherr-Gold, **23** 40
Sherritt Gordon Mines, **7** 386–87; **12** 260
The Sherwin-Williams Company, III 744–46; 8 222, 224; **11** 384; **12** 7; **13 469–71 (upd.); 19** 180; **24** 323; **30** 474
Sherwood Equity Group Ltd. *See* National Discount Brokers Group, Inc.
Sherwood Medical Group, **I** 624; **III** 443–44; **10** 70
SHI Resort Development Co., **III** 635
ShianFu Optical Fiber, **III** 491
Shibaura Seisakusho Works, **I** 533; **12** 483
Shieh Chi Industrial Co., **19** 508
Shields & Co., **9** 118
Shihlin Electric & Engineering Group, **49** 460
Shikoku Drinks Co., **IV** 297
Shikoku Electric Power Company, Inc., V 718–20
Shikoku Machinery Co., **III** 634
Shiley, Inc., **38** 361
Shillito's, **31** 192
Shimizu Construction Company Ltd., **44** 153
Shimotsuke Electric Railway Company, **6** 431
Shimura Kako, **IV** 63
Shin-Nihon Glass Co., **I** 221
Shin Nippon Machine Manufacturing, **III** 634
Shinano Bank, **II** 291
Shinko Electric Co., Ltd., **IV** 129
Shinko Rayon Ltd., **I** 363; **V** 369–70
Shinriken Kogyo, **IV** 63
Shintech, **11** 159–60
Shinwa Pharmaceutical Co. Ltd., **48** 250
Shinwa Tsushinki Co., **III** 593
Shiomi Casting, **III** 551
Shionogi & Co., Ltd., I 646, 651; **III 60–61; 11** 90, 290; **17** 435–37 (upd.)
Ship 'n Shore, **II** 503; **9** 156–57; **10** 324
Shipley Co. Inc., **26** 425
Shipowners and Merchants Tugboat Company, **6** 382
Shipper Group, **16** 344
Shipstad & Johnson's Ice Follies, **25** 313
Shiro Co., Ltd., **V** 96
Shirokiya Co., Ltd., **V** 199
Shiseido Company, Limited, II 273–74, 436; **III** 46, 48, 62–64; **8** 341, 343; **22 485–88 (upd.)**
SHL Systemhouse Inc., **27** 305
Shochiku Company Ltd., **28** 461
Shockley Electronics, **20** 174
Shoe Carnival Inc., 14 441–43
Shoe Corp., **I** 289
Shoe Supply, Inc., **22** 213
Shoe-Town Inc., **23** 310
Shoe Works Inc., **18** 415

Shohin Kaihatsu Kenkyusho, **III** 595
Shoman Milk Co., **II** 538
Shonac Corp., **14** 427
Shonco, Inc., **18** 438
Shoney's, Inc., 7 474–76; **14** 453; **19** 286; **23** 436–39 (upd.); **29** 290–91
Shop & Go, **II** 620
Shop 'n Bag, **II** 624
Shop 'n Save, **II** 669, 682; **12** 220–21
Shop Rite Foods Inc., **II** 672–74; **7** 105; **19** 479. *See also* Big V Supermarkets, Inc.
ShopKo Stores Inc., II 669–70; **18** 505–07; **21** 457–59
Shoppers Drug Mart Corporation, 49 367–70
Shoppers Food Warehouse Corporation, **16** 159, 161
Shoppers World Stores, Inc. *See* LOT$OFF Corporation.
ShopRite, **24** 528. *See also* Foodarama Supermarkets, Inc.
Shopwell/Food Emporium, **II** 638; **16** 247, 249
Shore Manufacturing, **13** 165
Shorewood Packaging Corporation, 28 419–21; **47** 189
Short Aircraft Co., **I** 50, 55, 92
Short Brothers, **24** 85
Shoseido Co., **17** 110
Shoshi-Gaisha, **IV** 320
Shotton Paper Co. Ltd., **IV** 350
Showa Aircraft Industry Co., **I** 507–08
Showa Aluminum Corporation, **8** 374
Showa Bank, **II** 291–92
Showa Bearing Manufacturing Co., **III** 595
Showa Cotton Co., Ltd., **IV** 442
Showa Denko, **I** 493–94; **II** 292; **IV** 61; **24** 324–25
Showa Marutsutsu Co. Ltd., **8** 477
Showa Paper Co., **IV** 268
Showa Photo Industry, **III** 548
Showa Products Company, **8** 476
Showa Shell Sekiyu K.K., II 459; **IV** 542–43
ShowBiz Pizza Time, Inc., 12 123; **13** 472–74; **15** 73; **16** 447. *See also* CEC Entertainment, Inc.
Showboat, Inc., 19 400–02; **43** 227
Showcase of Fine Fabrics, **16** 197
Showco, Inc., **35** 436
Showerings, **I** 215
Showscan Entertainment Inc., **34** 230
Showscan Film Corporation, **28** 206
Showtime, **II** 173; **7** 222–23; **9** 74; **23** 274–75, 391, 503; **25** 329–30
Shredded Wheat Co., **II** 543; **7** 366
Shreve and Company, **12** 312
Shreveport Refrigeration, **16** 74
Shrewsbury and Welshpool Old Bank, **II** 307
Shu Uemura, **III** 43
Shubert Organization Inc., 24 437–39
Shubrooks International Ltd., **11** 65
Shueisha, **IV** 598
Shuford Mills, Inc., **14** 430
Shugart Associates, **6** 230; **8** 466; **22** 189
Shull Lumber & Shingle Co., **IV** 306
Shulman Transport Enterprises Inc., **27** 473
Shun Fung Ironworks, **IV** 717
Shunan Shigyo Co., Ltd., **IV** 160
Shurgard Storage Centers of Seattle, **21** 476

Shuttleworth Brothers Company. *See* Mohawk Industries, Inc.
Shuwa Corp., **22** 101; **36** 292
SHV Holdings N.V., **IV** 383; **14** 156
SI Holdings Inc., **10** 481; **29** 425
SIAS, **19** 192
SIAS-MPA, **I** 281
SIATA S.p.A., **26** 363
SIB Financial Services, **39** 382
Sibco Universal, S.A., **14** 429
Sibel, **48** 350
Siberian Moloko, **48** 438
Sibneft. *See* OAO Siberian Oil Company.
Siboney Shoe Corp., **22** 213
SIBV/MS Holdings, **IV** 295; **19** 226
Sicard Inc., **I** 185
SICC. *See* Univision Communications Inc.
Sichuan Station Wagon Factory, **38** 462
Sick's Brewery, **26** 304
Siclet, **25** 84
Sicma Aero Seat, **36** 529
Siddeley Autocar Co., **III** 508
Sidel. *See* Groupe Sidel S.A.
Sidélor, **IV** 226
Siderbrás, **IV** 125
Siderca S.A.I.C., **41** 405–06
Sidermex, **III** 581
Sidérurgie Maritime, **IV** 26
Sidley Austin Brown & Wood, 40 400–03
SIDMAR NV, **IV** 128
Siebe plc, **13** 235. *See also* BTR Siebe plc.
Siebel Group, **13** 544–45
Siebel Marketing Group, **27** 195
Siebel Systems, Inc., 38 430–34
Siebert Financial Corp., 32 423–25
Siegas, **III** 480; **22** 26
Siegler Heater Corp., **I** 481
Siemens AG, I 74, 192, 409–11, 462, 478, 542; **II** 22, 25, 38, 80–82, 97–100, 122, 257, 279; **III** 139, 154–55, 466, 482, 516, 724; **6** 215–16; **7** 232; **9** 11, 32, 44; **10** 16, 363; **11** 59, 196, 235, 397–98, 460; **12** 546; **13** 402; **14** 169, 444–47 (upd.); **15** 125; **16** 392; **18** 32; **19** 166, 313; **20** 290; **22** 19, 373–74; **23** 389, 452, 494–95; **24** 88; **30** 11; **33** 225, 288
Siemens Solar Industries L.P., **44** 182
The Sierra Club, 28 422–24
Sierra Designs, Inc., **10** 215–16
Sierra Health Services, Inc., 15 451–53
Sierra Leone External Telegraph Limited, **25** 100
Sierra Leone Selection Trust, **IV** 66
Sierra On-Line, Inc., 13 92, 114; **14** 263; **15** 454–56; **16** 146; **29** 75; **41** 361–64 (upd.)
Sierra Pacific Industries, 22 489–91
Sierrita Resources, Inc., **6** 590
SIFCO Industries, Inc., 41
Sight & Sound Entertainment, **35** 21
Sigma-Aldrich Corporation, I 690–91; **36** 429–32 (upd.)
Sigma Alimentos, S.A. de C.V., **19** 11–12
Sigma Coatings, **IV** 499
Sigma Network Systems, **11** 464
Sigmor Corp., **IV** 410; **31** 455
Signal Companies, Inc. *See* AlliedSignal Inc.
Signal Galaxies, **13** 127
Signal Oil & Gas Inc., **I** 71, 178; **IV** 382; **7** 537; **11** 278; **19** 175; **22** 331
Signalite, Inc., **10** 319

Signature Brands USA Inc., **28** 135; **30** 139

Signature Corporation, **22** 412–13

Signature Flight Support Services Corporation, **47** 450

Signature Group, **V** 145

Signature Health Care Corp., **25** 504

Signet Banking Corporation, 11 446–48

Signet Communications Corp., **16** 195

Signetics Co., **III** 684; **11** 56; **18** 383; **44** 127

Signode Industries, **III** 519; **22** 282

Sika Finanz AG, **28** 195

SIKEL NV, **IV** 128

Sikes Corporation, **III** 612

Sikorsky Aircraft Corporation, I 47, 84, 115, 530; **III** 458, 602; **9** 416; **10** 162; **18** 125; **24 440–43**; **41** 368; **46** 65

SIL&P. *See* Southern Illinois Light & Power Company.

SILA. *See* Swedish Intercontinental Airlines.

Silband Sports Corp., **33** 102

Silenka B.V., **III** 733; **22** 436

Silex. *See* Hamilton Beach/Proctor-Silex Inc.

Silgan Holdings Inc., **26** 59

Silicon Beach Software, **10** 35

Silicon Compiler Systems, **11** 285

Silicon Engineering, **18** 20; **43** 17

Silicon Graphics Inc., 9 471–73; **10** 119, 257; **12** 323; **15** 149, 320; **16** 137, 140; **20** 8; **25** 96; **28** 320; **38** 69; **43** 151. *See also* SGI.

Silicon Light Machines Corporation, **48** 128

Silicon Magnetic Systems, **48** 128

Silicon Microstructures, Inc., **14** 183

Silicon Systems Inc., **II** 110

Silo Electronics, **16** 73, 75

Silo Holdings, **9** 65; **23** 52

Silo Inc., **V** 50; **10** 306, 468; **19** 123; **49** 112

Silver & Co., **I** 428

Silver Burdett Co., **IV** 672, 675; **7** 528; **19** 405

Silver City Airways. *See* British World Airlines Ltd.

Silver City Casino, **6** 204

Silver Dollar Mining Company, **20** 149

Silver Dolphin, **34** 3, 5

Silver Furniture Co., Inc., **15** 102, 104

Silver King Communications, **25** 213

Silver King Mines, **IV** 76

Silver Screen Partners, **II** 174

Silver's India Rubber Works & Telegraph Cable Co., **I** 428

Silverado Banking, **9** 199

Silverado Partners Acquisition Corp., **22** 80

Silverline, Inc., **16** 33

Silvermans Menswear, Inc., **24** 26

SilverPlatter Information Inc., 23 440–43

Silvershoe Partners, **17** 245

Silverstar Ltd. S.p.A., **10** 113

Silverstein Properties, Inc., 47 358–60; **48** 320

Silvertown Rubber Co., **I** 428

Silvey Corp., **III** 350

Simca, **I** 154, 162; **11** 103

Simco S.A., 37 357–59

Sime Darby Berhad, 14 448–50; 36 433–36 (upd.)

Simeira Comercio e Industria Ltda., **22** 320

SIMEL S.A., **14** 27

Simer Pump Company, **19** 360

SIMEST, **24** 311

Simi Winery, Inc., **34** 89

Simicon Co., **26** 153

Simkins Industries, Inc., **8** 174–75

Simmons Company, 34 407; **47 361–64**

Simms, **III** 556

Simon & Schuster Inc., II 155; **IV** 671–72; **13** 559; **19 403–05 (upd.)**; **23** 503; **28** 158

Simon Adhesive Products, **IV** 253; **17** 30

Simon de Wit, **II** 641

Simon DeBartolo Group Inc., **26** 146; **27** 401

Simon Engineering, **11** 510

Simon Marketing, Inc., **19** 112, 114

Simon Property Group, Inc., 27 399–402; **49** 414

Simon Transportation Services Inc., 27 403–06

Simonius'sche Cellulosefabriken AG, **IV** 324

Simonize, **I** 371

Simons Inc., **26** 412

AB Simpele, **IV** 347

Simple Shoes, Inc., **22** 173

Simplex Industries, Inc., **16** 296

Simplex Technologies Inc., 21 460–63

Simplex Wire and Cable Co., **III** 643–45

Simplicity Pattern Company, **I** 447; **8** 349; **23** 98; **29** 134

Simpson Investment Company, 17 438–41

Simpson Marketing, **12** 553

Simpson Thacher & Bartlett, 27 327; **39 365–68**

Simpson Timber Company. *See* PW Eagle Inc.

Simpsons, **V** 80; **25** 221

Sims Telephone Company, **14** 258

Simsmetal USA Corporation, **19** 380

SimuFlite, **II** 10

Simula, Inc., 41 368–70

Sinai Kosher Foods, **14** 537

Sincat, **IV** 453

Sinclair Broadcast Group, Inc., 25 417–19; **47** 120

Sinclair Coal Co., **IV** 170; **10** 447–48

Sinclair Crude Oil Purchasing Co., **IV** 369

Sinclair Oil Corp., **I** 355, 569; **IV** 376, 394, 456–57, 512, 575

Sinclair Paint Company, **12** 219

Sinclair Petrochemicals Inc., **IV** 456

Sinclair Pipe Line Co., **IV** 368–69

Sinclair Research Ltd., **III** 113

Sindo Ricoh Co., **III** 160

Sinfor Holding, **48** 402

Sing Tao Holdings Ltd., **29** 470–71

Singapore Airlines Ltd., 6 100, **117–18**, 123; **12** 192; **20** 313; **24** 399; **26** 115; **27** 26, **407–09 (upd.)**, 464, 466; **29** 301; **38** 26

Singapore Alpine Electronics Asia Pte. Ltd., **13** 31

Singapore Candle Company, **12** 393

Singapore Cement, **III** 718

Singapore Petroleum Co., **IV** 452

Singapore Shinei Sangyo Pte Ltd., **48** 369

Singapore Straits Steamship Company, **6** 117

Singapore Telecom, **18** 348

Singapour, **II** 556

Singareni Collieries Ltd., **IV** 48–49

Singer & Friedlander Group plc, I 592; **41 371–73**

Singer Company, **I** 540; **II** 9–11; **6** 27, 241; **9** 232; **11** 150; **13** 521–22; **19** 211; **22** 4; **26** 3; **29** 190. *See also* Bicoastal Corp.

The Singer Company N.V., 30 417–20 (upd.)

Singer Controls, **I** 155

Singer Hardware & Supply Co., **9** 542

Singer Sewing Machine Co., **12** 46

Singer Supermarkets, **25** 235

Single Service Containers Inc., **IV** 286

Singleton Seafood, **II** 494

Singular Software, **9** 80

Sinister Games, **41** 409

Sinkers Inc., **21** 68

Sinochem. *See* China National Chemicals Import and Export Corp.

Sinopec. *See* China National Petroleum Corporation.

Sintel, S.A., **19** 256

Sioux City Gas and Electric Company, **6** 523–24

SIP. *See* Società Italiana per L'Esercizio delle Telecommunicazioni p.A.

Siporex, S.A., **31** 253

Sir Speedy, Inc., 16 448–50; 33 231

SIRCOMA, **10** 375

SIREM, **23** 95

The Sirena Apparel Group Inc., **25** 245

Sirloin Stockade, **10** 331

Sirrine. *See* CRSS Inc.

Sirrine Environmental Consultants, **9** 110

Sirte Oil Co., **IV** 454

Sisters Chicken & Biscuits, **8** 564

Sisters of Bon Secours USA. *See* Bon Secours Health System, Inc.

SIT-Siemens. *See* Italtel.

Sitca Corporation, **16** 297

Sithe Energies, Inc., **24** 327

Sitintel, **49** 383

Sitmar Cruises, **22** 445

Sitzmann & Heinlein GmbH, **IV** 198–99

Six Companies, Inc., **IV** 121; **7** 355

Six Flags Theme Parks, Inc., III 431; **IV** 676; **17 442–44**

600 Fanuc Robotics, **III** 482–83

Six Industries, Inc., **26** 433

61 Going to the Game!, **14** 293

Sixt AG, 39 369–72

Sizeler Property Investors Inc., **49** 27

Sizes Unlimited, **V** 115

Sizzler International Inc., **15** 361–62. *See also* Worldwide Restaurant Concepts, Inc.

SJB Equities, Inc., **30** 53

The SK Equity Fund, L.P., **23** 177

Skånes Enskilda Bank, **II** 351

Skånska Ättiksfabriken, **I** 385

Skadden, Arps, Slate, Meagher & Flom, 10 126–27; **18 486–88**; **27** 325, 327

Skaggs-Albertson's Properties, **II** 604

Skaggs Companies, **22** 37

Skaggs Drug Centers, Inc., **II** 602–04; **7** 20; **27** 291; **30** 25–27

Skagit Nuclear Power Plant, **6** 566

Skandia, **25** 85

Skandinaviska Enskilda Banken, II 351–53, 365–66; **IV** 203

Skanska AB, IV 204; **25** 463; **32** 396; **38** 435–38

Skanza Mammoet Transport Sdn Bhd, **26** 280

Skechers U.S.A. Inc., **31** 413–15
Skelly Oil Co., **IV** 575
Sketchley plc, **19** 124
SKF. *See* Aktiebolaget SKF.
SKF Industries Inc. *See* AB Volvo.
Ski-Doo. *See* Bombardier Inc.
Skidmore, Owings & Merrill, **13** 475–76
Skil-Craft Playthings, Inc., **13** 560
Skillern, **16** 560
Skillware, **9** 326
Skinner Macaroni Co., **II** 511
Skis Rossignol S.A., **15** 460–62; **43** 373–76 **(upd.)**
Skoda Auto a.s., **39** 373–75
SKODA Group, **37** 399–400
Skönvik, **IV** 338
SKS Group, **20** 363
SKW Nature's Products, Inc., **25** 332
SKW-Trostberg AG, **IV** 232
Sky Channel, **IV** 652
Sky Chefs, Inc., **16** 397
Sky Climber Inc., **11** 436
Sky Courier, **6** 345
Sky Merchant, Inc., **V** 78
Sky Television, **IV** 652–53; **7** 391–92
Skyband, Inc., **IV** 652; **7** 391; **12** 359
SkyBox International Inc., **15** 72–73
Skylight, **25** 508
Skyline Corporation, **30** 421–23
Skyline Homes, **17** 82
SkyMall, Inc., **26** 439–41; **28** 241
Skypak, **27** 474
Skyservice Airlines Inc., **42** 327
SkyTel Corp., **18** 349; **23** 212
Skywalker Sound, **12** 322
Skyway Airlines, **6** 78; **11** 299; **32** 335; **35** 293–94
SkyWest, Inc., **25** 420–24
SL Green Realty Corporation, **44** 383–85
SL Holdings. *See* Finlay Enterprises, Inc.
Slade Gorton & Company, **13** 243
Slater Co. Foods, **II** 607
Slater Electric, **21** 349
Slater Systems, Inc., **13** 48
Slautterback Corporation, **48** 299
Slavneft, **49** 306
Sleepy's Inc., **32** 426–28
SLI, Inc., **48** 358–61
Slick Airways, **6** 388; **25** 146
Slim-Fast Nutritional Foods International, Inc., **12** 531; **18** 489–91; **27** 196
Slim Jim, Inc. *See* GoodMark Foods, Inc.
Slingerland Drum Company, **16** 239
Slip-X Safety Treads, **9** 72
SLJFB Vedrenne, **22** 344
SLM Holding Corp., **25** 425–28 **(upd.)**
SLM International Inc. *See* The Hockey Company.
SLN-Peñarroya, **IV** 108
Sloan's Supermarkets Inc. *See* Gristede's Sloan's, Inc.
Sloman Neptun Schiffahrts, **26** 279
Slope Indicator Company, **26** 42
Sloss Industries Corporation, **22** 544
Slots-A-Fun, **6** 204
Slough Estates plc, **IV** 722–25
AB Small Business Investment Co., Inc., **13** 111–12
Small Tube Products, Inc., **23** 517
SMALLCO, **III** 340
Smalley Transportation Company, **6** 421–23

SMAN. *See* Societe Mecanique Automobile du Nord.
Smart & Final, Inc., **12** 153–54; **16** 451–53
Smart Communications, **18** 180, 182
Smart Products, **44** 261
Smart Shirts Ltd., **8** 288–89
Smart Talk Network, Inc., **16** 319
SmartCash, **18** 543
SmartForce PLC, **43** 377–80
SmarTTarget Marketing, **36** 342
Smead Manufacturing Co., **17** 445–48
Smed International, **39** 207
Smedley's, **II** 513
Smethwick Drop Forgings, **III** 494
SMH. *See* The Swatch Group SA.
SMI Industries, **25** 15
Smiles Holdings Ltd., **38** 501
Smirnoff, **14** 212; **18** 41
Smit International, **26** 241
Smith and Bell Insurance, **41** 178, 180
Smith & Butterfield Co., Inc., **28** 74
Smith & Hawken, **10** 215, 217
Smith & Nephew plc, **17** 449–52; **41** 374–78 **(upd.)**
Smith & Wesson Corporation, **30** 424–27
Smith & Weston, **19** 430
Smith & Wollensky Operating Corp., **32** 362
Smith Barney Inc., **I** 614; **III** 569; **6** 410; **10** 63; **13** 328; **15** 463–65; **19** 385; **20** 360; **22** 406
Smith Bros., **I** 711
Smith Corona Corp., **III** 502; **7** 209; **13** 477–80; **14** 76; **23** 210
Smith-Higgins, **III** 9–10
Smith International, Inc., **III** 429; **15** 466–68
Smith Mackenzie & Co., **III** 522
Smith McDonell Stone and Co., **14** 97
Smith Meter Co., **11** 4
Smith New Court PLC, **13** 342; **40** 313
Smith Packaging Ltd., **14** 429
Smith Parts Co., **11** 3
Smith Transfer Corp., **II** 607–08; **13** 49
Smith Wall Associates, **32** 145
Smith's Food & Drug Centers, Inc., **8** 472–74; **17** 558, 561; **24** 36; **26** 432
Smith's Stampings, **III** 494
Smithfield Foods, Inc., **7** 477–78, 524–25; **22** 509, 511; **43** 25, 381–84 **(upd.)**; **46** 83
SmithKline Beckman Corporation, **I** 389, 636, 640, 644, 646, 657, **692–94**, 696; **II** 331; **III** 65–66; **14** 46, 53; **26** 391; **30** 29–31. *See also* GlaxoSmithKline plc.
SmithKline Beecham plc, **III** 65–67; **8** 210; **9** 347; **10** 47, 471; **11** 9, 90, 337; **13** 77; **14** 58; **16** 438; **17** 287; **24** 88; **25** 82; **32** 212–13, **429–34 (upd.)**; **36** 91; **38** 362. *See also* GlaxoSmithKline plc.
Smiths Bank, **II** 333
Smiths Food Group, Ltd., **II** 502; **10** 323
Smiths Industries PLC, **III** 555; **25** 429–31
Smithsonian Institution, **27** 410–13
Smithway Motor Xpress Corporation, **39** 376–79
Smitty's Super Valu Inc., **II** 663–64; **12** 391; **17** 560–61
Smittybilt, Incorporated, **40** 299–300
Smoothie Island, **49** 60
SMP Clothing, Inc., **22** 462

SMS, **IV** 226; **7** 401
Smucker. *See* The J.M. Smucker Company.
Smurfit Companies. *See* Jefferson Smurfit Group plc.
Smurfit-Stone Container Corporation, **26** 442–46 **(upd.)**
SN Repal. *See* Société Nationale de Recherche de Pétrole en Algérie.
Snack Ventures Europe, **10** 324; **36** 234, 237
Snake River Sugar Company, **19** 468
Snam Montaggi, **IV** 420
Snam Progetti, **IV** 420, 422
Snap-On, Incorporated, **27** 414–16 **(upd.)**; **32** 397
Snap-on Tools Corporation, **III** 628; **7** 479–80; **25** 34
Snapper, **I** 447
Snapple Beverage Corporation, **11** 449–51; **12** 411; **24** 480; **27** 153; **31** 243; **34** 366; **39** 383, 386
Snapps Drive-Thru, **25** 389
Snappy Car Rental, Inc., **6** 393; **25** 142–43. *See also* Republic Industries, Inc.
SNE Enterprises, Inc., **12** 397
SNEA. *See* Société Nationale Elf Aquitaine.
Snecma Group, **17** 482; **46** 369–72
Snell & Wilmer L.L.P., **28** 425–28
Snell Acoustics, **22** 99
SNET. *See* Southern New England Telecommunications Corporation.
SNMC Management Corporation, **11** 121; **48** 177
Snoqualmie Falls Plant, **6** 565
Snow Brand Milk Products Company, Ltd., **II** 574–75; **48** 362–65 **(upd.)**
Snow King Frozen Foods, **II** 480; **26** 57
Snow White Dairies Inc. *See* Dairy Mart Convenience Stores, Inc.
Snowy Mountains Hydroelectric Authority, **IV** 707; **13** 118
SNPA, **IV** 453
Snyder Communications, **35** 462, 465
Snyder Oil Company, **24** 379–81; **45** 354
Snyder's of Hanover, **35** 213
SnyderGeneral Corp., **8** 321. *See also* AAF-McQuay Incorporated.
Soap Opera Magazine, **10** 287
Sobrom, **I** 341
Sobu Railway Company, **6** 431
Socal. *See* Standard Oil Company (California).
Socamel-Rescaset, **40** 214, 216
Socar, Incorporated, **IV** 505; **45** 370
Sochiku, **9** 30
Sociade Intercontinental de Compressores Hermeticos SICOM, S.A., **8** 515
La Sociale di A. Mondadori & C., **IV** 585
La Sociale, **IV** 585
Sociedad Aeronáutica de Medellín, S.A., **36** 53
Sociedad Alfa-Laval, **III** 419
Sociedad Bilbaina General de Credito, **II** 194
Sociedad Española de Automobiles del Turismo S.A. (SEAT), **I** 207, 459–60; **6** 47–48; **11** 550
Sociedad Financiera Mexicana, **19** 189
Sociedade Anónima Concessionária de Refinacao em Portugal. *See* SACOR.
Sociedade de Lubrificantes e Combustiveis, **IV** 505

Sociedade Nacional de Petróleos, **IV** 504
Sociedade Portuguesa de Petroquimica, **IV** 505
Società Anonima Fabbrica Italiana di Automobili, **I** 161
Società Anonima Lombarda Fabbrica Automobili, **13** 27
Società Azionaria Imprese Perforazioni, **IV** 419–20
Società Concessioni e Costruzioni Autostrade, **I** 466
Società Edison, **II** 86
Societa Esercizio Fabbriche Automobili e Corse Ferrari, **13** 219
Società Finanziaria Idrocarburi, **IV** 421
Società Finanziaria Telefonica per Azioni, **I** 465–66; **V** 325–27
Società Generale di Credito Mobiliare, **II** 191
Società Idrolettrica Piemonte, **I** 465–66
Societa Industria Meccanica Stampaggio S.p.A., **24** 500
Società Italiana Gestione Sistemi Multi Accesso, **6** 69
Società Italiana per L'Esercizio delle Telecommunicazioni p.A., **I** 466–67; **V** 325–27
Società Italiana per la Infrastrutture e l'Assetto del Territoria, **I** 466
Società Italiana Pirelli, **V** 249
Società Italiana Vetro, **IV** 421
Società Meridionale Finanziaria, **49** 31
Società Nazionale Metanodotti, **IV** 419–21
Società Ravennate Metano, **IV** 420
Società Reale Mutua, **III** 207
Società Sportiva Lazio SpA, **44 386–88**
Société Africaine de Déroulage des Ets Rougier, **21** 439
Société Air France, **27 417–20 (upd.)**. *See also* Groupe Air France.
Société Alsacienne de Magasins SA, **19** 308
Societe Anonima Italiana Ing. Nicola Romeo & Company, **13** 27
Societe Anonomie Alfa Romeo, **13** 28
Societe Anonyme Automobiles Citroen, **7** 35–36. *See also* PSA Peugeot Citroen S.A.
Société Anonyme Belge des Magasins Prisunic-Uniprix, **26** 159
Société Anonyme de la Manufactures des Glaces et Produits Chimiques de Saint-Gobain, Chauny et Cirey. *See* Compagnie de Saint-Gobain S.A.
Société Anonyme des Ciments Luxembourgeois, **IV** 25
Société Anonyme des Fermiers Reúnis, **23** 219
Société Anonyme des Hauts Fourneaux et Aciéries de Differdange-St. Ingbert-Rumelange, **IV** 26
Société Anonyme des Hauts Fourneaux et Forges de Dudelange, **22** 42
Société Anonyme des Mines du Luxembourg et des Forges de Sarrebruck, **IV** 24; **22** 42
La Societe Anonyme Francaise Holophane, **19** 211
Societe Anonyme Francaise Timken, **8** 530
Société Anonyme Telecommunications, **III** 164
Société, Auxiliaire d'Entrepreses SA, **13** 206
Société Belge de Banque, **II** 294–95

Société BIC, S.A., **III** 29; **8** 60–61; **23** 55–57
Société Calédonia, **IV** 107
Société Centrale d'Investissement, **29** 48
Société Centrale Union des Assurances de Paris, **III** 391, 393
Société Chimiques des Usines du Rhône, **I** 388
Société Civil des Mousquetaires. *See* ITM Entreprises SA.
Société Civile Valoptec, **21** 222
Societe Commerciale Citroen, **7** 36
Société Congolaise des Grands Magasins Au Bon Marché, **26** 159
Société d'Emboutissage de Bourgogne. *See* Groupe SEB.
Société d'Investissement de Travaux Publics, **31** 128
Société d'Ougrée-Marihaye, **IV** 51
Société de Collecte des Prodicteirs de Preval, **19** 50
Societe de Construction des Batignolles, **II** 93
Société de Crédit Agricole, **II** 264
Société de Développements et d'Innovations des Marchés Agricoles et Alimentaires, **II** 576
Société de Diffusion de Marques, **II** 576
Société de Diffusion Internationale Agro-Alimentaire, **II** 577
Société de Fiducie du Québec, **48** 289
Société de garantie des Crédits à court terme, **II** 233
Société de l'Oléoduc de la Sarre a.r.l., **IV** 197
Société de Prospection Électrique, **III** 616; **17** 416
La Société de Traitement des Minerais de Nickel, Cobalt et Autres, **IV** 107
Société des Caves de Roquefort, **24** 444
Société des Caves et des Producteurs Reunis de Roquefort, **19** 49
Société des Ciments Français, **33** 339
Société des Eaux d'Evian, **II** 474
Société des Etablissements Gaumont. *See* Gaumont SA.
Société des Forges d'Eich–Metz et Cie, **IV** 24
Société des Forges et Aciéries du Nord-Est, **IV** 226
Société des Forges et Fonderies de Montataire, **IV** 226
Société des Grandes Entreprises de Distribution, Inno-France, **V** 58
Société des Hauts Fourneaux et Forges de Denain-Anzin, **IV** 226
Société des Immeubles de France, **37** 357, 359
Société des Mines du Luxembourg et de Sarrebruck, **IV** 25
Société des Moteurs Gnôme, **46** 369
Société des Pétroles d'Afrique Equatoriale, **IV** 545; **7** 482
Société des Usines Chimiques des Laboratoires Français, **I** 669
Société des Vins de France, **I** 281
Société du Louvre, 27 421–23
Société Economique de Rennes, **19** 98
Société Électrométallurgique Française, **IV** 173
Société European de Semi-Remorques, **7** 513
Societé Européenne de Brasseries, **II** 474–75

Société Européenne de Production de L'avion E.C.A.T. *See* SEPECAT.
Société Financiére Européenne, **II** 202–03, 233
Societe Financiere pour l caise pour l'Exploitation du Pétrole, **IV** 557
Société Française de Casinos, **48** 198
Société Gélis-Poudenx-Sans, **IV** 108
Société General de Banque, **17** 324
Société Générale, **II** 233, 266, 295, **354–56**; **9** 148; **13** 203, 206; **19** 51; **33** 118–19; **42 347–51 (upd.)**; **47** 411–12
Société Générale de Banque, **II** 279, 295, 319; **14** 169
Société Générale de Belgique S.A., **II** 270, 294–95; **IV** 26; **10** 13; **22** 44; **26** 368; **27** 11; **36** 456
Société Générale des Entreprises. *See* Vinci.
Société Générale du Telephones, **21** 231
Société Générale pour favoriser l'Industrie nationale, **II** 294
Societe-Hydro-Air S.a.r.L., **9** 27
Société Industrielle Belge des Pétroles, **IV** 498–99
Société Internationale Pirelli S.A., **V** 250
Société Irano-Italienne des Pétroles, **IV** 466
Société Laitière Vendômoise, **23** 219
Société Le Nickel, **IV** 107–08, 110
Societe Mecanique Automobile de l'Est/du Nord, **7** 37
Société Métallurgique, **IV** 25–26, 227
Société Minière de Bakwanga, **IV** 67
Société Minière des Terres Rouges, **IV** 25–26
Société Nationale de Programmes de Télévision Française 1. *See* Télévision Française 1.
Société Nationale de Recherche de Pétrole en Algérie, **IV** 545, 559; **7** 482
Société Nationale de Transport et de Commercialisation des Hydrocarbures, **IV** 423
Société Nationale des Chemins de Fer Français, V 512–15
Société Nationale des Pétroles d'Aquitaine, **21** 203–05
Société Nationale Elf Aquitaine, I 303–04, 670, 676–77; **II** 260; **IV** 174, 397–98, 424, 451, 453–54, 472–74, 499, 506, 515–16, 518, 525, 535, **544–47**, 559–60; **V** 628; **7 481–85 (upd.)**; **8** 452; **11** 97; **12** 153
Société Nationale pour la Recherche, la Production, le Transport, la Transformation et la Commercialisation des Hydrocarbures, **IV** 423–24
Société Nord Africaine des Ciments Lafarge, **III** 703
Société Nouvelle d'Achat de Bijouterie, **16** 207
Société Nouvelle des Etablissements Gaumont. *See* Gaumont SA.
Société Parisienne d'Achats en Commun, **19** 307
Societe Parisienne pour l'Industrie Electrique, **II** 93
Société Parisienne Raveau-Cartier, **31** 128
Société pour l'Eportation de Grandes Marques, **I** 281
Société pour l'Étude et la Realisation d'Engins Balistiques. *See* SEREB.
Société pour L'Exploitation de la Cinquième Chaîne, **6** 374

Société pour le Financement de l'Industrie Laitière, **19** 51
Société Samos, **23** 219
Société Savoyarde des Fromagers du Reblochon, **25** 84
Société Succursaliste S.A. d'Approvisonnements Guyenne et Gascogne. *See* Guyenne et Gascogne.
Société Suisse de Microelectronique & d'Horlogerie. *See* The Swatch Group SA.
Société Tefal. *See* Groupe SEB.
Société Tunisienne de l'Air-Tunisair, 49 371–73
Societe Vendeenne des Embalages, **9** 305
Society Corporation, 9 474–77
Society of Lloyd's, **III** 278–79
SOCO Chemical Inc., **8** 69
Socombel, **IV** 497
Socony. *See* Standard Oil Co. (New York).
Socony Mobil Oil Co., Inc., **IV** 465; **7** 353
Socony-Vacuum Oil Company. *See* Mobil Corporation.
Sodak Gaming, Inc., **9** 427; **41** 216
Sodastream Holdings, **II** 477
Sodexho Alliance SA, 23 154; **29 442–44; 47** 201
Sodiaal S.A., II 577; **19** 50; **36 437–39 (upd.)**
SODIMA. *See* Sodiaal S.A.
Sodiso, **23** 247
Sodyeco, **I** 673
Soekor, **IV** 93
Soffo, **22** 365
Soficom, **27** 136
SOFIL. *See* Société pour le Financement de l'Industrie Laitière.
Sofimex. *See* Sociedad Financiera Mexicana.
Sofiran, **IV** 467
Sofitam, S.A., **21** 493, 495
Sofitels. *See* Accor SA.
Sofrem, **IV** 174
Soft Lenses Inc., **25** 55
Soft Sheen Products, Inc., 31 416–18; 46 278
Soft*Switch, **25** 301
Softbank Corp., 12 562; **13 481–83; 16** 168; **27** 516, 518; **36** 523; **38 439–44 (upd.)**
Softimage Inc., **38** 71–72
SoftKat. *See* Baker & Taylor, Inc.
SoftKey Software Products Inc., **24** 276
Softsel Computer Products, **12** 334–35
SoftSolutions Technology Corporation, **10** 558
Software AG, **11** 18
Software Arts, **6** 254; **25** 299
Software Development Pty., Ltd., **15** 107
Software Dimensions, Inc. *See* ASK Group, Inc.
Software, Etc., **13** 545
The Software Group Inc., **23** 489, 491
Software International, **6** 224
Software Plus, Inc., **10** 514
Software Publishing Corp., **14** 262
Softwood Holdings Ltd., **III** 688
Sogara S.A., **23** 246–48
Sogebra S.A., **I** 257
Sogedis, **23** 219
Sogen International Corp., **II** 355
Sogexport, **II** 355
Soginnove, **II** 355–56
Sogo Co., **42** 342

Sohio Chemical Company, **13** 502
Sohken Kako Co., Ltd., **IV** 327
Soil Teq, Inc., **17** 10
Soilserv, Inc. *See* Mycogen Corporation.
Soinlahti Sawmill and Brick Works, **IV** 300
Sola Holdings, **III** 727
Solair Inc., **14** 43; **37** 30–31
La Solana Corp., **IV** 726
Solar, **IV** 614
Solar Electric Corp., **13** 398
Solaray, Inc., **37** 284–85
Solect Technology Group, **47** 12
Solectron Corporation, 12 161–62, **450–52; 38** 186, 189; **46** 38; **48 366–70 (upd.)**
Solel Boneh Construction, **II** 47; **25** 266–67
Soletanche Co., **I** 586
Solid Beheer B.V., **10** 514
Solid State Dielectrics, **I** 329; **8** 152
Solite Corp., **23** 224–25
Söll, **40** 96, 98
Sollac, **IV** 226–27; **24** 144; **25** 96
Solley's Delicatessen and Bakery, **24** 243
Solmer, **IV** 227
Solo Serve Corporation, 23 177; **28 429–31**
Soloman Brothers, **17** 561
Solomon Smith Barney Inc., **22** 404
Solomon Valley Milling Company, **6** 592
Solon Automated Services, **II** 607
Solsound Industries, **16** 393
Soltam, **25** 266
Solutia Inc., **29** 330
Solvay & Cie S.A., I 303, **394–96,** 414–15; **III** 677; **IV** 300; **16** 121; **21** 254, **464–67 (upd.)**
Solvay Animal Health Inc., **12** 5
Solvent Resource Recovery, Inc., **9** 109
Solvents Recovery Service of New Jersey, Inc., **8** 464
SOMABRI, **12** 152
SOMACA, **12** 152
Somali Bank, **31** 220
Someal, **27** 513, 515
Somerfield plc, 47 365–69 (upd.)
Somerville Electric Light Company, **12** 45
Somerville Packaging Group, **28** 420
Sommer-Allibert S.A., 19 406–09; 22 49; **25** 462, 464
Sommers Drug Stores, **9** 186
SONAP, **IV** 504–06
Sonat, Inc., 6 577–78; 22 68
Sonatrach. *See* Entreprise Nationale Sonatrach.
Sonecor Systems, **6** 340
Sonergy, Inc., **49** 280
Sonesson, **I** 211
Sonesta International Hotels Corporation, 44 389–91
Sonet Media AB, **23** 390
Sonic Corp., 37 14 451–53; **16** 387; **360–63 (upd.)**
Sonic Duo, **48** 419
Sonic Restaurants, **31** 279
Sonneborn Chemical and Refinery Co., **I** 405
Sonnen Basserman, **II** 475
SonnenBraune, **22** 460
Sonoco Products Company, 8 475–77; 12 150–51; **16** 340
The Sonoma Group, **25** 246
Sonoma Mortgage Corp., **II** 382

Sonometrics Inc., **I** 667
Sony Corporation, I 30, 534; **II** 56, 58, 91–92, **101–03,** 117–19, 124, 134, 137, 440; **III** 141, 143, 340, 658; **6** 30; **7** 118; **9** 385; **10** 86, 119, 403; **11** 46, 490–91, 557; **12** 75, 161, 448, **453–56 (upd.); 13** 399, 403, 482, 573; **14** 534; **16** 94; **17** 533; **18** 18; **19** 67; **20** 439; **21** 129; **22** 194; **24** 4; **25** 22; **26** 188, 433, 489, 511; **28** 241; **30** 18; **31** 239; **40 404–10 (upd.); 43** 15; **47** 318–20, 410
Sonzogno, **IV** 585
Soo Line Corporation, **V** 429–30; **24** 533; **45** 80
Soo Line Mills, **II** 631
Sooner Trailer Manufacturing Co., **29** 367
Soparind, **25** 83–85
Sope Creek, **30** 457
SOPEAL, **III** 738
Sophia Jocoba GmbH, **IV** 193
Sophus Berendsen A/S, 49 374–77
SOPI, **IV** 401
SOPORCEL, **34** 38–39
Sopwith Aviation Co., **III** 507–08
Soravie, **II** 265
Sorbents Products Co. Inc., **31** 20
Sorbus, **6** 242
Sorcim, **6** 224
Soreal, **8** 344
Sorenson Research Company, **36** 496
Sorg Paper Company. *See* Mosinee Paper Corporation.
Soriana. *See* Organización Soriana, S.A. de C.V.
Soros Fund Management LLC, 27 198; **28 432–34; 43** 218
Sorrento, Inc., 19 51; **24 444–46; 26** 505
SOS Co., **II** 531
SOS Staffing Services, 25 432–35
Sosa, Bromley, Aguilar & Associates, **6** 22
Soterra, Inc., **15** 188
Sotheby's Holdings, Inc., 11 452–54; 15 98–100; **29 445–48 (upd.); 32** 164; **39** 81–84; **49** 325
Sound Advice, Inc., 41 379–82
Sound of Music Inc. *See* Best Buy Co., Inc.
Sound Trek, **16** 74
Sound Video Unlimited, **16** 46; **43** 60
Sound Warehouse, **9** 75
Souplantation Incorporated. *See* Garden Fresh Restaurant Corporation.
Source One Mortgage Services Corp., **12** 79
Source Perrier, **7** 383; **24** 444
Souriau, **19** 166
South African Airways Ltd., **6** 84, 433, 435; **27** 132
The South African Breweries Limited, I 287–89, 422; **24 447–51 (upd.); 26** 462
South African Coal, Oil and Gas Corp., **IV** 533
South African Railways, **6** 434–35
South African Torbanite Mining and Refining Co., **IV** 534
South African Transport Services, **6** 433, 435
South American Cable Co., **I** 428
South Asia Tyres, **20** 263
South Bend Toy Manufacturing Company, **25** 380
South Carolina Electric & Gas Company, **6** 574–76
South Carolina Industries, **IV** 333

South Carolina National Corporation, **16** 523, 526

South Carolina Power Company, **38** 446–47

South Central Bell Telephone Co. **V** 276–78

South Central Railroad Co., **14** 325

South China Morning Post (Holdings) Ltd., **II** 298; **IV** 652; **7** 392

South Coast Gas Compression Company, Inc., **11** 523

South Coast Terminals, Inc., **16** 475

South Dakota Public Service Company, **6** 524

South Fulton Light & Power Company, **6** 514

South Improvement Co., **IV** 427

South Jersey Industries, Inc., 42 352–55

South Manchuria Railroad Co. Ltd., **IV** 434

South of Scotland Electricity Board, **19** 389–90

South Penn Oil Co., **IV** 488–89

South Puerto Rico Sugar Co., **I** 452

South Puerto Rico Telephone Co., **I** 462

South Sea Textile, **III** 705

South Texas Stevedore Co., **IV** 81

South Wales Electric Company, **34** 219

South West Water Plc. *See* Pennon Group Plc.

South Western Electricity plc, **38** 448; **41** 316

South-Western Publishing Co., **8** 526–28

Southam Inc., 7 486–89; 15 265; **24** 223; **36** 374

Southco, **II** 602–03; **7** 20–21; **30** 26

Southcorp Holdings Ltd., **17** 373; **22** 350

Southdown, Inc., 14 454–56

Southeast Bank of Florida, **11** 112

Southeast Banking Corp., **II** 252; **14** 103

Southeast Public Service Company, **8** 536

Southeastern Personnel. *See* Norrell Corporation.

Southeastern Power and Light Company, **6** 447; **23** 28

Southeastern Telephone Company, **6** 312

Southern and Phillips Gas Ltd., **13** 485

Southern Australia Airlines, **24** 396

Southern Bank, **10** 426

Southern Bearings Co., **13** 78

Southern Bell, **10** 202

Southern Biscuit Co., **II** 631

Southern Blvd. Supermarkets, Inc., **22** 549

Southern Box Corp., **13** 441

Southern California Edison Co., **II** 402; **V** 711, 713–15, 717; **11** 272; **12** 106; **35** 479

Southern California Financial Corporation, **27** 46

Southern California Fruit Growers Exchange. *See* Sunkist Growers, Inc.

Southern California Gas Co., **I** 569; **25** 413–14, 416

Southern Casualty Insurance Co., **III** 214

Southern Clay Products, **III** 691

Southern Clays Inc., **IV** 82

Southern Co., **24** 525

Southern Colorado Power Company, **6** 312

Southern Comfort Corp., **I** 227

The Southern Company, 38 445–49 (upd.)

Southern Connecticut Newspapers Inc., **IV** 677

Southern Cotton Co., **IV** 224; **24** 488

Southern Cotton Oil Co., **I** 421; **11** 23

Southern Cross Paints, **38** 98

Southern Discount Company of Atlanta, **9** 229

Southern Electric PLC, 13 484–86

Southern Electric Supply Co., **15** 386

Southern Electronics Corp. *See* SED International Holdings, Inc.

Southern Equipment & Supply Co., **19** 344

Southern Extract Co., **IV** 310; **19** 266

Southern Forest Products, Inc., **6** 577

Southern Gage, **III** 519; **22** 282

Southern Graphic Arts, **13** 405

Southern Guaranty Cos., **III** 404

Southern Idaho Water Power Company, **12** 265

Southern Illinois Light & Power Company, **6** 504

Southern Indiana Gas and Electric Company, 13 487–89

Southern Japan Trust Bank, **V** 114

Southern Kraft Corp., **IV** 286

Southern Lumber Company, **8** 430

Southern Manufacturing Company, **8** 458

Southern Minnesota Beet Sugar Cooperative, **32** 29

Southern National Bankshares of Atlanta, **II** 337; **10** 425

Southern Natural Gas Co., **III** 558; **6** 447–48, 577

Southern Nevada Power Company, **11** 343

Southern Nevada Telephone Company, **6** 313; **11** 343

Southern New England Telecommunications Corporation, 6 338–40

Southern Nitrogen Co., **IV** 123

Southern Oregon Broadcasting Co., **7** 15

Southern Pacific Communications Corporation, **9** 478–79

Southern Pacific Rail Corp., **12** 18–20. *See also* Union Pacific Corporation.

Southern Pacific Railroad, **I** 13; **II** 329, 381, 448; **IV** 625; **19** 202

Southern Pacific Transportation Company, V 516–18; 12 278; **26** 235; **37** 312

Southern Peru Copper Corp.,

Southern Peru Copper Corporation, IV 3; **40** 220, 222, **411–13**

Southern Phenix Textiles Inc., **15** 247–48

Southern Pine Lumber Co., **IV** 341

Southern Power Company. *See* Duke Energy Corporation.

Southern Railway Company, **V** 484–85; **29** 359

Southern Science Applications, Inc., **22** 88

Southern States Cooperative Incorporated, 36 440–42

Southern States Trust Co., **II** 336

Southern Sun Hotel Corporation. *See* South African Breweries Ltd. and *Sun International Hotels Limited.*

Southern Surety Co., **III** 332

Southern Telephone Company, **14** 257

Southern Television Corp., **II** 158; **IV** 650; **7** 389

Southern Union Company, 12 542; **27 424–26**

Southern Utah Fuel Co., **IV** 394

Southern Video Partnership, **9** 74

Southern Water plc, **19** 389–91; **49** 363, 365–66

Southgate Medical Laboratory System, **26** 391

The Southland Corporation, II 449, 620, **660–61; IV** 392, 508; **V** 89; **7** 114, 374, **490–92 (upd.); 9** 178; **13** 333, 449, 525; **23** 406–07; **25** 125; **26** 447; **31** 115, 231; **42** 191. *See also* 7-Eleven, Inc.

Southland Mobilcom Inc., **15** 196

Southland Paper, **13** 118

Southland Royal Company, **27** 86

Southland Royalty Co., **10** 190

Southlife Holding Co., **III** 218

Southmark Corp., **11** 483; **33** 398

Southport, Inc., **44** 203

Southtrust Corporation, 11 455–57

Southview Pulp Co., **IV** 329

Southwest Airlines Co., I 106; **6** 72–74, **119–21; 21** 143; **22** 22; **24** 452–55 **(upd.); 25** 404; **26** 308, 439–40; **33** 301–02; **35** 383; **44** 197, 248

Southwest Airmotive Co., **II** 16

Southwest Convenience Stores, LLC, **26** 368

Southwest Converting, **19** 414

Southwest Enterprise Associates, **13** 191

Southwest Forest Industries, **IV** 287, 289, 334

Southwest Gas Corporation, 19 410–12

Southwest Hide Co., **16** 546

Southwest Potash Corp., **IV** 18; **6** 148–49

Southwest Water Company, 47 370–73

Southwestern Bell Corporation, V 328–30; 6 324; **10** 431, 500; **14** 489; **17** 110; **18** 22. *See also* SBC Communications Inc.

Southwestern Bell Publications, **26** 520

Southwestern Electric Power Co., 21 468–70

Southwestern Gas Pipeline, **7** 344

Southwestern Illinois Coal Company, **7** 33

Southwestern Life Insurance, **I** 527; **III** 136

Southwestern Pipe, **III** 498

Southwestern Public Service Company, 6 579–81

Southwestern Refining Company, Inc., **IV** 446; **22** 303

Southwestern Textile Company, **12** 393

Southwire Company, Inc., 8 478–80; 12 353; **23 444–47 (upd.)**

Souvall Brothers, **8** 473

Sovereign Corp., **III** 221; **14** 109; **37** 84

Sovran Financial, **10** 425–26

SovTransavto, **6** 410

Soyland Power Cooperative, **6** 506

SP Reifenwerke, **V** 253

SP Tyres, **V** 253

Space Control GmbH, **28** 243–44

Space Craft Inc., **9** 463

Space Data Corporation, **22** 401

Space Systems Corporation. *See* Orbital Sciences Corporation.

Space Systems/Loral, **9** 325

Spacehab, Inc., 37 364–66

Spacemakers Inc., **IV** 287

Spaghetti Warehouse, Inc., 25 436–38

Spagnesi, **18** 258

Spago. *See* The Wolfgang Puck Food Company, Inc.

Spalding & Evenflo, **24** 530

Spalding, Inc., **17** 243; **23** 449

Spangler Candy Company, 44 392–95

Spanish Broadcasting System, Inc., 41 383–86

Spanish International Communications Corp. *See* Univision Communications Inc.

Spanish River Pulp and Paper Mills, **IV** 246; **25** 10

SPAO, **39** 184

Spar Aerospace Limited, 32 435–37

SPAR Handels AG, 35 398–401; 36 296

Sparbanken Bank, **18** 543

SPARC International, **7** 499

Spare Change, **10** 282

Sparklets Ltd., **I** 315; **25** 80

Sparks Computerized Car Care Centers, **25** 445

Sparks Family Hospital, **6** 191

Sparks-Withington Company. *See* Sparton Corporation.

Sparrow Records, **22** 194

Sparta, Inc., **18** 369

Sparta Surgical Corporation, **33** 456

Spartan Communications, **38** 308–09

Spartan Industries, Inc., **45** 15

Spartan Insurance Co., **26** 486

Spartan Motors Inc., 14 457–59

Spartan Stores Inc., I 127; **II** 679–80; **8** 481–82; **10** 302; **12** 489; **14** 412

Spartech Corporation, 9 92; **19 413–15; 33** 78–79

Sparton Corporation, 18 492–95

SPCM, Inc., **14** 477

Spec's Music, Inc., 19 416–18

Spécia, **I** 388

Special Agent Investigators, Inc., **14** 541

Special Foods, **14** 557

Special Light Alloy Co., **IV** 153

Special Zone Limited, **26** 491

Specialized Bicycle Components Inc., **19** 384

Specialty Brands Inc., **25** 518

Specialty Coatings Inc., 8 483–84

Specialty Equipment Companies, Inc., 25 439–42

Specialty Foods Corporation, **29** 29, 31

Specialty Papers Co., **IV** 290

Specialty Products Co., **8** 386

Specialty Retailers, Inc., **24** 456

Spectra-Physics AB, **9** 380–81

Spectra Star, Inc., **18** 521

Spectradyne, **28** 241

Spectral Dynamics Corporation. *See* Scientific- Atlanta, Inc.

Spectron MicroSystems, **18** 143

Spectrum Club, **25** 448–50

Spectrum Communications Holdings International Limited, **24** 95

Spectrum Concepts, **10** 394–95

Spectrum Data Systems, Inc., **24** 96

Spectrum Dyed Yarns of New York, **8** 559

Spectrum Health Care Services, **13** 48

Spectrum Medical Technologies, Inc., **22** 409

Spectrum Technology Group, Inc., **7** 378; **18** 112

Spectrumedia, **21** 361

Speed-O-Lac Chemical, **8** 553

SpeeDee Marts, **II** 661

SpeeDee Oil Change and Tune-Up, 25 443–47

Speedway Motorsports, Inc., 32 438–41

Speedway SuperAmerica LLC, **49** 330

Speedy Auto Glass, **30** 501

Speedy Muffler King, **10** 415; **24** 337, 339

Speidel Newspaper Group, **IV** 612; **7** 191

Speizman Industries, Inc., 44 396–98

Spelling Entertainment, 14 460–62; 35 402–04 (upd.)

Spencer & Spencer Systems, Inc., **18** 112

Spencer Beef, **II** 536

Spencer Gifts, Inc., **II** 144; **15** 464

Spencer Stuart and Associates, Inc., 14 463–65

Spenco Medical Corp., **III** 41; **16** 303; **43** 257

Sperry & Hutchinson Co., **12** 299; **23** 243–44

Sperry Aerospace Group, **II** 40, 86; **6** 283; **12** 246, 248

Sperry Corporation, **I** 101, 167; **III** 165, 642; **6** 281–82; **8** 92; **11** 139; **12** 39; **13** 511; **18** 386, 542; **22** 379; **36** 481. *See also* Unisys Corporation.

Sperry Milling Co., **II** 501; **10** 322

Sperry New Holland. *See* New Holland N.V.

Sperry Rand Corp., **II** 63, 73; **III** 126, 129, 149, 166, 329, 642; **6** 241, 261, 281–82; **16** 137

Sperry Top-Sider, Inc., **37** 377, 379

Sphere Inc., **8** 526; **13** 92

Sphere SA, **27** 9

Spherion Corporation, **45** 272, 274

Spicer Manufacturing Co., **I** 152; **III** 568; **20** 359; **23** 170–71

Spider Software, Inc., **46** 38

Spie Batignolles SA, **I** 563; **II** 93–94; **13** 206; **18** 471–73; **24** 79

Spiegel, Inc., III 598; **V** 160; **8** 56–58; **10** 168, 489–91; **11** 498; **9** 190, 219; **13** 179; **15** 339; **27 427–31 (upd.); 34** 232, 324, 326; **36** 177, 180

SPIEGEL-Verlag Rudolf Augstein GmbH & Co. KG, 44 399–402

Spillers, **II** 500

Spin Physics, **III** 475–76; **7** 163

SpinCircuit Inc., **38** 188

Spinnaker Industries, Inc., **43** 276

Spinnaker Software Corp., **24** 276

SPIRE Corporation, **14** 477

Spire, Inc., **25** 183

Spirella Company of Great Britain Ltd., **V** 356; **44** 105

Spirit Airlines, Inc., 31 419–21

Spirit Cruises, **29** 442–43

Spliethoff, **26** 280

Spoerle Electronic, **10** 113

Spokane Falls Electric Light and Power Company. *See* Edison Electric Illuminating Company.

Spokane Falls Water Power Company, **6** 595

Spokane Gas and Fuel, **IV** 391

Spokane Natural Gas Company, **6** 597

Spokane Street Railway Company, **6** 595

Spokane Traction Company, **6** 596

Spom Japan, **IV** 600

Spon Press, **44** 416

Spoor Behrins Campbell and Young, **II** 289

Spoornet, **6** 435

Sporis, **27** 151

Sporloisirs S.A., **9** 157

Sport Chalet, Inc., 16 454–56

Sport Developpement SCA, **33** 10

Sport Supply Group, Inc., 22 458–59; **23 448–50; 30** 185

Sporting Dog Specialties, Inc., **14** 386

Sporting News Publishing Co., **IV** 677–78

Sportland, **26** 160

Sportmagazine NV, **48** 347

Sportmart, Inc., 15 469–71. *See also* Gart Sports Company.

Sports & Co. *See* Hibbett Sporting Goods, Inc.

Sports & Recreation, Inc., 15 470; **17 453–55**

The Sports Authority, Inc., 15 470; **16 457–59; 17** 453; **18** 286; **24** 173; **43 385–88 (upd.)**

The Sports Club Company, 25 448–51

Sports Experts Inc., **II** 652

Sports Holdings Corp., **34** 217

Sports Inc., **14** 8; **33** 10

Sports Plus, **44** 192

Sports-Tech Inc., **21** 300

Sports Traders, Inc., **18** 208

Sportservice Corporation, **7** 133–35

The Sportsman's Guide, Inc., 36 443–46

Sportstown, Inc., **15** 470

Sportsystems Corporation, **7** 133, 135

Sprague Co., **I** 410

Sprague Devices, Inc., **11** 84

Sprague Electric Company, **6** 261

Sprague Electric Railway and Motor Co., **II** 27; **12** 193

Sprague Technologies, **21** 520

Sprague, Warner & Co., **II** 571

Spray-Rite, **I** 366

Sprayon Products, **III** 745

Spraysafe, **29** 98

Sprecher & Schub, **9** 10

Spreckels Sugar Company, Inc., **32** 274, 277

Spring Co., **21** 96, 246

Spring Forge Mill, **8** 412

Spring Grove Services, **45** 139–40

Spring Industries, Inc., V 378–79

Spring Valley Brewery. *See* Kirin Brewery Company, Limited.

Springbok Editions, **IV** 621

Springer Verlag GmbH & Co., **IV** 611, 641

Springfield Bank, **9** 474

Springfield Gas Light Company, **38** 81

Springhouse Corp., **IV** 610

Springhouse Financial Corp., **III** 204

Springmaid International, Inc., **19** 421

Springs Industries, Inc., 19 419–22 (upd.); 29 132; **31** 199

Sprint Canada Inc., **44** 49

Sprint Communications Company, L.P., 9 478–80; 10 19, 57, 97, 201–03; **11** 183, 185, 500–01; **18** 32, 164–65, 569–70; **22** 19, 162; **24** 120, 122; **25** 102; **26** 17; **27** 365; **36** 167. *See also* Sprint Corporation and *US Sprint Communications.*

Sprint Corporation, 46 373–76 (upd.)

Sprint PCS, **33** 34, 36–37; **38** 433

Sprout Group, **37** 121

Spruce Falls Power and Paper Co., **III** 40; **IV** 648; **16** 302, 304; **19** 284; **43** 256

SPS Technologies, Inc., 30 428–30

Spun Yarns, Inc., **12** 503

Spur Oil Co., **7** 362

SPX Corporation, 10 492–95; 47 374–79 (upd.)

SPZ, Inc., **26** 257

SQ Software, Inc., **10** 505

SQL Solutions, Inc., **10** 505

Square D Company, **18** 473

Square Industries, **18** 103, 105

Squibb Beech-Nut. *See* Beech-Nut Nutrition Corp.

Squibb Corporation, **I** 380–81, 631, 651, 659, 675, **695–97**; **III** 17, 19, 67; **8** 166; **9** 6–7; **13** 379–80; **16** 438–39[see_aslo]Bristol-Myers Squibb Company.

Squire Fashions Inc. *See* Norton McNaughton of Squire, Inc.

SR. *See* Southern Railway.

SR Beteiligungen Aktiengesellschaft, **III** 377

SRI International, **10** 139

SRI Strategic Resources Inc., **6** 310

SS Cars, Ltd. *See* Jaguar Cars, Ltd.

SS Lazio. *See* Societá Sportiva Lazio SpA.

SSA. *See* Stevedoring Services of America Inc.

Ssangyong Cement Industrial Co., Ltd., **III 747–50**; **IV** 536–37, 539

Ssangyong Motor Company, **34** 132

SSC&B-Lintas, **I** 16–17; **14** 315

SSDS, Inc., **18** 537; **43** 433

SSI Medical Services, Inc., **10** 350

SSL International plc, **49 378–81**

SSMC Inc., **II** 10

SSP Company, Inc., **17** 434

St. *See under* Saint

Staal Bankiers, **13** 544

Stackpole Fibers, **37** 427

Stadia Colorado Corporation, **18** 140

Stadt Corporation, **26** 109

Städtische Electkricitäts-Werke A.G., **I** 410

Staefa Control System Limited, **6** 490

Staff International, **40** 157

StaffAmerica, Inc., **16** 50

Stafford-Lowdon, **31** 435

Stafford Old Bank, **II** 307

Stag Cañon Fuel Co., **IV** 177

Stage Stores, Inc., **24 456–59**

Stagecoach Holdings plc, **30 431–33**

Stags' Leap Winery, **22** 80

Stahl-Urban Company, **8** 287–88

Stahlwerke Peine-Salzgitter AG, **IV** 201

Stahlwerke Röchling AG, **III** 694–95

Stahlwerke Südwestfalen AG, **IV** 89

Stakis plc, **49** 193

Stal-Astra GmbH, **III** 420

Staley Continental, **II** 582

Stamford Drug Group, **9** 68

Stamford FHI Acquisition Corp., **27** 117

Stamos Associates Inc., **29** 377

Stamps.com Inc., **34** 474

Stanadyne Automotive Corporation, **37 367–70**

Stanadyne, Inc., **7** 336; **12** 344

Standard & Poor's Corp., **IV** 29, 482, 636–37; **12** 310; **25** 542

Standard Accident Co., **III** 332

Standard Aero, **III** 509

Standard Aircraft Equipment, **II** 16

Standard Alaska, **7** 559

Standard Bank, **17** 324

Standard Bank of Canada, **II** 244

Standard Box Co., **IV** 357

Standard Brands, **I** 248; **II** 542, 544; **7** 365, 367; **18** 538

Standard Car Truck, **18** 5

Standard Chartered plc, **II** 298, 309, 319, **357–59**, 386; **10** 170; **47** 227; **48 371–74 (upd.)**

Standard Chemical Products, **III** 33

Standard Commercial Corporation, **12** 110; **13 490–92**; **27** 126

Standard Drug Co., **V** 171

Standard Electric Time Company, **13** 233

Standard Electrica, **II** 13

Standard Elektrik Lorenz A.G., **II** 13, 70; **17** 353

Standard Equities Corp., **III** 98

Standard Federal Bank, **9 481–83**

Standard Fire Insurance Co., **III** 181–82

Standard Fruit and Steamship Co. of New Orleans, **II** 491; **31** 168

Standard Gauge Manufacturing Company, **13** 233

Standard General Insurance, **III** 208

Standard Gypsum Corp., **19** 77

Standard Industrial Group Ltd., **IV** 658

Standard Insert Co., **28** 350

Standard Insulation Co., **I** 321

Standard Insurance Co. of New York, **III** 385

Standard Investing Corp., **III** 98

Standard Kollsman Industries Inc., **13** 461

Standard Life & Accident Insurance Company, **27** 47–48

Standard Life Assurance Company, **III 358–61**; **IV** 696–98

Standard Life Insurance Company, **11** 481

Standard Magnesium & Chemical Co., **IV** 123

Standard Metals Corp., **IV** 76

Standard Microsystems Corporation, **11 462–64**

Standard Milling Co., **II** 497

Standard Motor Co., **III** 651

Standard Motor Products, Inc., **40 414–17**

Standard of America Life Insurance Co., **III** 324

Standard of Georgia Insurance Agency, Inc., **10** 92

Standard Oil Co., **III** 470, 513; **IV** 46, 372, 399, 426–29, 434, 463, 478, 488–89, 530–31, 540, 542, 551, 574, 577–78, 657; **V** 590, 601; **6** 455; **7** 169–72, 263, 351, 414, 551; **8** 415; **10** 110, 289; **14** 21, 491–92; **25** 230; **27** 129. *See also* Exxon Corporation.

Standard Oil Co. (California), **II** 448; **IV** 18–19, 385–87, 403, 429, 464, 536–37, 545, 552, 560, 578; **6** 353; **7** 172, 352, 483; **13** 448

Standard Oil Co. (Illinois), **IV** 368

Standard Oil Co. (Indiana), **II** 262; **IV** 366, 368–71, 466–67; **7** 443; **10** 86; **14** 222

Standard Oil Co. (Minnesota), **IV** 368

Standard Oil Co. (New York), **IV** 428–29, 431, 460, 463–65, 485, 504, 537, 549, 558; **7** 171, 351–52

Standard Oil Co. of Iowa, **IV** 385

Standard Oil Co. of Kentucky, **IV** 387

Standard Oil Co. of New Jersey, **I** 334, 337, 370; **II** 16, 496; **IV** 378–79, 385–86, 400, 415–16, 419, 426–29, 431–33, 438, 460, 463–64, 488, 522, 531, 537–38, 544, 558, 565, 571; **V** 658–59; **7** 170–72, 253, 351; **13** 124; **17** 412–13; **24** 521

Standard Oil Co. of Ohio, **IV** 373, 379, 427, 452, 463, 522, 571; **7** 57, 171, 263; **12** 309; **21** 82; **24** 521

Standard Oil Development Co., **IV** 554

Standard Oil Trust, **IV** 31, 368, 375, 385–86, 427, 463

Standard Plastics, **25** 312

Standard Printing Company, **19** 333

Standard Process & Engraving, Inc., **26** 105

Standard Products Company, **19** 454

Standard Rate & Data Service, **IV** 639; **7** 286

Standard Register Co., **15 472–74**

Standard Sanitary, **III** 663–64

Standard Screw Co., **12** 344

Standard Shares, **9** 413–14

Standard Steel Propeller, **I** 47, 84; **9** 416; **10** 162

Standard Telephone and Radio, **II** 13

Standard Telephones and Cables, Ltd., **III** 162–63; **6** 242

Standard Tin Plate Co., **15** 127

Standard-Vacuum Oil Co., **IV** 431–32, 440, 460, 464, 491–92, 554–55; **7** 352

Standex International Corporation, **16** 470–71; **17 456–59**; **44 403–06 (upd.)**

Stanhome Inc., **9** 330; **11 94–96**; **15 475–78**

Stanhome Worldwide Direct Selling, **35** 262, 264

STANIC, **IV** 419, 421

Stanko Fanuc Service, **III** 483

Stanley Electric Manufacturing Co., **II** 28; **12** 194

Stanley Furniture Company, Inc., **34 412–14**

Stanley Home Products, Incorporated. *See* Stanhome Inc.

Stanley Mining Services, Ltd., **19** 247

The Stanley Works, **III** 626–29; **7** 480; **9** 543; **13** 41; **20 476–80 (upd.)**

StanMont, Inc., **24** 425

Stanolind Oil & Gas Co., **III** 498; **IV** 365, 369–70

Stant Corporation, **15** 503, 505

Staples, Inc., **8** 404–05; **10 496–98**; **18** 24, 388; **20** 99; **22** 154; **23** 363, 365; **24** 270

Star, **10** 287–88

Star Air Service. *See* Alaska Air Group, Inc.

Star Alliance, **26** 113; **33** 51; **38** 36

Star Banc Corporation, **11** 465–67; **13** 222; **31** 206. *See also* Firstar Corporation.

Star Building Systems, Inc., **19** 366

Star Engraving, **12** 471

Star Enterprise, **IV** 536, 539, 553

Star Enterprises, Inc., **6** 457

Star Finishing Co., **9** 465

Star Laboratories Inc., **24** 251

Star Markets Company, Inc., **23** 169

Star Medical Technologies, Inc., **22** 409; **31** 124

Star Paper Ltd., **IV** 300

Star Paper Tube, Inc., **19** 76–78

Star Sportwear Manufacturing Corp., **29** 294

Star Video, Inc., **6** 313

Starber International, **12** 181

Starbucks Corporation, **13** 493–94; **18** 37; **22** 370; **25** 178, 501; **28** 63; **34 415–19 (upd.)**; **36** 156–57; **37** 181; **38** 340; **40** 152–53; **44** 313

Starcraft Corporation, **III** 444; **13** 113; **22** 116; **30 434–36**

Stardent Computer Inc., **III** 553; **26** 256

Starfish Software, **23** 212

Stark Record and Tape Service. *See* Camelot Music, Inc.

StarKist Foods, **II** 508; **11** 172; **36 254–55**

Starlawerken, **I** 527
Starlen Labs, Ltd., **31** 346
Starlight Networks, Inc., **27** 366
Starline Optical Corp., **22** 123
StarMed Staffing Corporation, **6** 10
Starpointe Savings Bank, **9** 173
Starrett Corporation, 21 471–74
Star's Discount Department Stores, **16** 36
Startech Semiconductor Inc., **14** 183
Startel Corp., **15** 125
Starter Corp., 12 457–458
Starwood Capital, **29** 508
Starwood Hotels and Resorts Worldwide Inc., **33** 217
State Bank of Albany, **9** 228
State Farm Insurance Companies, **27** 30; **29** 397; **39** 155
State Farm Mutual Automobile Insurance Company, III 362–64; **10** 50; **22** 266; **23** 286; **25** 155; **41** 313
State Finance and Thrift Company, **14** 529
State Leed, **13** 367
State Metal Works, **III** 647
State-o-Maine, **18** 357–59
State-Record Co., **IV** 630
State Savings Bank and Trust Co., **11** 180; **42** 429
State Street Boston Corporation, 8 491–93
State Trading Corp. of India Ltd., **IV** 143
Staten Island Advance Corp., **IV** 581–82; **19** 4
Staten Island Bancorp, Inc., 39 380–82
Stater Brothers, **17** 558
Statex Petroleum, Inc., **19** 70
Static, Inc., **14** 430
Station Casinos Inc., 25 452–54
Stationers Distributing Company, **14** 523
Stationers, Inc., **28** 74
Statler Hotel Co., **III** 92, 98; **19** 206
Statoil. *See* Den Norske Stats Oljeselskap AS.
StatScript Management Services, **26** 73
Statter, Inc., **6** 27
Staubli International, **II** 122; **12** 546
Stauffer Chemical Company, **8** 105–07; **21** 545
Stauffer Communications, Inc., **36** 339–41
Stauffer-Meiji, **II** 540
Stax Records, **23** 32
STC PLC, III 141, 162–64; **25** 497; **36** 351
Stead & Miller, **13** 169
Steag AG, **IV** 193
Steak & Ale, **II** 556–57; **7** 336; **12** 373; **13** 408–09
The Steak n Shake Company, 14 130–31; **41 387–90**
Steam and Gas Pipe Co., **III** 644
Steam Boiler Works, **18** 318
Steamboat Ski and Resort Corporation, **28** 21
Stearman, **I** 47, 84; **9** 416; **10** 162
Stearns & Foster, **12** 439
Stearns Catalytic World Corp., **II** 87; **11** 413
Stearns Coal & Lumber, **6** 514
Stearns, Inc., 43 389–91
Stearns Manufacturing Co., **16** 297
Steaua-Romana, **IV** 557
Steego Auto Paints, **24** 160
Steel and Tube Co. of America, **IV** 114
Steel Authority of India Ltd., IV 205–07

Steel Ceilings and Aluminum Works, **IV** 22
Steel Co. of Canada Ltd., **IV** 208
Steel Dynamics, Inc., **18** 380; **26** 530
Steel Mills Ltd., **III** 673
Steel Products Engineering Co., **I** 169
Steel Stamping Co., **III** 569; **20** 360
Steelcase Inc., 7 493–95; 8 251–52, 255, 405; **25** 500; **27 432–35 (upd.); 39** 205–07
Steelmade Inc., **I** 513
Steely, **IV** 109
Steenfabriek De Ruiterwaard, **14** 249
Steenkolen Handelsvereniging, **IV** 132; **39** 176
Steering Aluminum, **I** 159
Stefany, **12** 152
Stegbar Pty Ltd., **31** 398–400
Steger Furniture Manufacturing Co., **18** 493
Steiff. *See* Margarete Steiff GmbH.
Steil, Inc., **8** 271
Stein Mart Inc., 19 423–25
Stein Printing Company, **25** 183
Stein Robaire Helm, **22** 173
Steinbach Inc., **IV** 226; **14** 427
Steinbach Stores, Inc., **19** 108
Steinberg Incorporated, II 652–53, 662–65; **V** 163
Steinberger, **16** 239
Steinheil Optronik GmbH, **24** 87
Steinman & Grey, **6** 27
Steinmüller Verwaltungsgesellschaft, **V** 747
Steinway & Sons, **16** 201; **43** 170
Steinway Musical Properties, Inc., 19 392, 394, **426–29**
Stelco Inc., IV 208–10; **24** 144
Stella Bella Corporation, **19** 436
Stella D'Oro Company, **7** 367
Stellar Systems, Inc., **III** 553; **14** 542
Stellenbosch Farmers Winery, **I** 288
Stelux Manufacturing Company, **13** 121; **41** 71
Stena AB, **25** 105; **29** 429–30
Stena Line AB, **38** 345
Stena-Sealink, **37** 137
Stens Corporation, **48** 34
Stensmölla Kemiska Tekniska Industri, **I** 385
Stentor Canadian Network Management, **6** 310
Stenval Sud, **19** 50
Stepan Company, 30 437–39
Stephen F. Whitman & Son, Inc., **7** 429
Stephens Inc., **III** 76; **16** 59; **18** 223
Stephenson Clarke and Company, **31** 368–69
Sterchi Bros. Co., **14** 236
Steria SA, 49 382–85
Stericycle Inc., 33 380–82
STERIS Corporation, 29 449–52
Sterling Chemicals, Inc., 16 460–63; 27 117
Sterling Drug Inc., I 309–10, **698–700**; **III** 477; **7** 163; **13** 76–77; **36** 173; **41** 45
Sterling Electronics Corp., 18 496–98; 19 311
Sterling Engineered Products, **III** 640, 642; **16** 9
Sterling Forest Corp., **III** 264
Sterling House Corp., **42** 4
Sterling Industries, **13** 166
Sterling Information Services, Ltd., **IV** 675; **7** 528

Sterling Manhattan, **7** 63
Sterling Oil, **I** 526
Sterling Oil & Development, **II** 490
Sterling Organics Ltd., **12** 351
Sterling Plastics, **III** 642
Sterling Plastics Inc., **16** 9
Sterling Products Inc., **I** 622; **10** 68
Sterling Remedy Co., **I** 698
Sterling Software, Inc., 11 468–70; 31 296
Sterling Stores Co. Inc., **24** 148
Sterling Winthrop, **7** 164; **36** 174; **49** 351
Stern & Stern Textiles, **11** 261
Stern-Auer Shoe Company, **V** 207
Stern Bros. Investment Bank, **V** 362–65; **19** 359
Stern Bros., LLC, **37** 224
Stern Publishing, **38** 478
Stern's, **9** 209
Sternco Industries, **12** 230–31
STET. *See* Società Finanziaria Telefonica per Azioni.
Steuben Glass, **III** 683
Stevcoknit Fabrics Company, **8** 141–43
Stevedoring Services of America Inc., 28 435–37
Steven Madden, Ltd., 37 371–73
Stevens Linen Associates, Inc., **8** 272
Stevens Park Osteopathic Hospital, **6** 192
Stevens Sound Proofing Co., **III** 706; **7** 291
Stevens, Thompson & Runyan, Inc. *See* CRSS Inc.
Steve's Ice Cream, **16** 54–55
Steward Esplen and Greenhough, **II** 569
Stewards Foundation, **6** 191
Stewart & Stevenson Services Inc., 11 471–73
Stewart Bolling Co., **IV** 130
Stewart Cash Stores, **II** 465
Stewart Enterprises, Inc., 16 344; **20 481–83; 37** 67
Stewart P. Orr Associates, **6** 224
Stewart Systems, Inc., **22** 352–53
Stewart's Beverages, 39 383–86
Steyr Walzlager, **III** 625
Stichting Continuïteit AMEV, **III** 202
Stieber Rollkupplung GmbH, **14** 63
Stihl Inc. *See* Andreas Stihl.
Stilecraft, **24** 16
Stillwater Mining Company, 47 380–82
Stimson & Valentine, **8** 552
Stimsonite Corporation, **49** 38
Stinnes AG, 6 424, 426; **8** 68–69, **494–97; 23** 68–70, **451–54 (upd.); 33** 195
Stirling Readymix Concrete, **III** 737–38
STM Systems Corp., **11** 485
Stock, **IV** 617–18
Stock Clearing Corporation, **9** 370
Stock Yards Packing Co., Inc., 37 374–76
Stockholder Systems Inc., **11** 485
Stockholm Southern Transportation Co., **I** 553
Stockholms Allmänna Telefonaktiebolag, **V** 334
Stockholms Enskilda Bank, **II** 1, 351, 365–66; **III** 419, 425–26
Stockholms Intecknings Garanti, **II** 366
Stockpack Ltd., **44** 318
Stockton and Hartlepool Railway, **III** 272
Stockton Wheel Co., **III** 450
Stoelting Brothers Company, **10** 371

Stokely Van Camp, **II** 560, 575; **12** 411; **22** 338

Stokvis/De Nederlandsche Kroon Rijwiefabrieken, **13** 499

Stoll-Moss Theatres Ltd., 34 420–22

Stolt-Nielsen S.A., 42 356–59

Stone & Webster, Inc., 13 495–98

Stone and Kimball, **IV** 660

Stone-Consolidated Corporation, **25** 9, 12

Stone Container Corporation, IV 332–34; 8 203–04; **15** 129; **17** 106; **25** 12. *See also* Smurfit-Stone Container Corporation.

Stone Exploration Corp., **IV** 83; **7** 187

Stone Manufacturing Company, 14 469–71; 43 392–96 (upd.)

Stonega Coke & Coal Co. *See* Westmoreland Coal Company.

Stoner Associates. *See* Severn Trent PLC.

Stonewall Insurance Co., **III** 192

Stonington Partners, **19** 318

StonyBrook Services Inc., **24** 49

Stoody Co., **19** 440

Stoof, **26** 278–79

Stoomvaart Maatschappij Nederland, **6** 403–04; **26** 241

The Stop & Shop Companies, Inc., II 666–67; 9 451, 453; **12** 48–49; **16** 160, 314; **23** 169; **24 460–62 (upd.)**

Stop N Go, **7** 373; **25** 126

Stoppenbauch Inc., **23** 202

Stora Enso Oyj, 36 128, **447–55 (upd.)**

Stora Kopparbergs Bergslags AB, III 693, 695; **IV 335–37**, 340; **12** 464; **28** 445–46

Storage Dimensions Inc., **10** 404

Storage Technology Corporation, III 110; **6 275–77**; **12** 148, 161; **16** 194; **28** 198

Storage USA, Inc., 21 475–77

Storebrand Insurance Co., **III** 122

Storehouse PLC, II 658; **13** 284; **16 464–66**; **17** 42–43, 335; **24** 75

Storer Communications, **II** 161; **IV** 596; **7** 91–92, 200–1; **24** 122

Storer Leasing Inc., **I** 99; **6** 81

Storm Technology, **28** 245

Storz Instruments Co., **I** 678; **25** 56; **27** 115

Stouffer Corp., I 485; **II** 489, 547; **6** 40; **7** 382; **8 498–501**

Stouffer Foods Corporation, **28** 238

Stout Air Services, **I** 128; **6** 128

Stout Airlines, **I** 47, 84; **9** 416; **10** 162

Stout Metal Airplane Co., **I** 165

Stowe Machine Co., Inc., **30** 283

Stowe Woodward, **I** 428–29

STP, **19** 223; **26** 349

STRAAM Engineers. *See* CRSS Inc.

Straits Steamship Co. *See* Malaysian Airlines System.

Stran, **8** 546

Strata Energy, Inc., **IV** 29

StrataCom, Inc., 11 59; **16 467–69**; **34** 113

Strategic Implications International, Inc., **45** 44

Strategix Solutions, **43** 309

Stratford Corporation, **15** 103; **26** 100

Strathmore Consolidated Investments, **IV** 90

Stratos Boat Co., Ltd., **III** 600

Stratton Oakmont Inc., **37** 372–73; **46** 282

Stratton Ski Corporation, **15** 235

Stratus Computer, Inc., 6 279; **10 499–501**

Straus-Frank Company, **29** 86, 88

Strauss Turnbull and Co., **II** 355

Strawberries, **30** 465

Strawbridge & Clothier's, **6** 243

Stream International, **48** 369

Stream Machine Co., **48** 92

Streamline Holdings, **39** 237–38

De Streekkrant-De Weekkrantgroep NV, **48** 347

Street & Smith Publications, Inc., **IV** 583; **13** 178

The Stride Rite Corporation, 8 502–04; 9 437; **33** 244; **37 377–80 (upd.)**

Stroehmann Bakeries, **II** 631

Stroh and Co., **IV** 486

The Stroh Brewery Company, I 32, 255, **290–92**; **13** 10–11, 455; **18** 72, **499–502 (upd.)**; **22** 422; **23** 403, 405; **36** 14–15

Strömberg, **IV** 300; **27** 267, 268

Stromberg Carburetor Co., **I** 141

Stromberg-Carlson, **II** 82

Stromeyer GmbH, **7** 141

Strong Brewery, **I** 294

Strong Electric Corporation, **19** 211

Strong International, **27** 57

Stroock & Stroock & Lavan LLP, 40 418–21

Strother Drug, **III** 9–10

Strouds, Inc., 33 383–86

Structural Dynamics Research Corporation, **10** 257

Structural Fibers, Inc. *See* Essef Corporation.

Structural Iberica S.A., **18** 163

Struebel Group, **18** 170

Strydel, Inc., **14** 361

Stryker Corporation, 10 351; **11 474–76; 29 453–55 (upd.)**

Stuart & Sons Ltd., **34** 493, 496

Stuart Co., **I** 584

Stuart Entertainment Inc., 16 470–72

Stuart Hall Co., **17** 445

Stuart Medical, Inc., **10** 143; **16** 400

Stuart Perlman, **6** 200

Stuckey's, Inc., **7** 429

Studebaker Co., **I** 141–42, 451; **8** 74; **9** 27

Studebaker-Packard, **9** 118; **10** 261

Studebaker Wagon Co., **IV** 660

Student Loan Marketing Association, II 453–55. *See also* SLM Holding Corp.

Studiengesellschaft, **I** 409

StudioCanal, **48** 164–65

Studley Products Inc., **12** 396

Stuffit Co., **IV** 597

Stuller Settings, Inc., 35 405–07

Sturbridge Yankee Workshop, Inc., **10** 216

Sturgeon Bay Shipbuilding and DryDock Company, **18** 320

Sturm, Ruger & Company, Inc., 19 430–32

Stuttgart Gas Works, **I** 391

Stuttgarter Verein Versicherungs-AG, **III** 184

Stuyvesant Insurance Group, **II** 182

Style Magazine BV, **48** 347

Styleclick.com, Inc., **47** 420

Stylus Writing Instruments, **27** 416

Stymer Oy, **IV** 470–71

SU214, **28** 27, 30

Suave Shoe Corporation. *See* French Fragrances, Inc.

Sub-Zero Freezer Co., Inc., 31 426–28

Subaru, **6** 28; **23** 290

Suber Suisse S.A., **48** 350

SubLogic, **15** 455

Submarine Boat Co., **I** 57

Submarine Signal Co., **II** 85–86; **11** 412

Suburban Cablevision, **IV** 640

Suburban Coastal Corporation, **10** 92

Suburban Cos., **IV** 575–76

Suburban Light and Power Company, **12** 45

Suburban Propane Partners, L.P., I 378; **30 440–42[ro**

Suburban Savings and Loan Association, **10** 92

Subway, 15 56–57; **32 442–44**

Successories, Inc., 30 443–45[ro

Suchard Co., **II** 520

Sud-Aviation, **I** 44–45; **7** 10; **8** 313

Sudbury Inc., 16 473–75; 17 373

Sudbury River Consulting Group, **31** 131

Suddeutsche Bank A.G., **II** 279

Süddeutsche Donau- Dampfschiffahrts-Gesellschaft, **6** 425

Süddeutsche Kalkstickstoffwerke AG, **IV** 229, 232

Sudler & Hennessey, **I** 37

Südpetrol, **IV** 421

Südzucker AG, 27 436–39

Suez Bank, **IV** 108

Suez Canal Co., **IV** 530

Suez Lyonnaise des Eaux, 36 456–59 (upd.); **38** 321; **40** 447, 449; **42** 386, 388; **45** 277; **47** 219

Suez Oil Co., **IV** 413–14

Suffolk County Federal Savings and Loan Association, **16** 346

Sugar Land State Bank, **25** 114

Sugar Mount Capital, LLC, **33** 355

Sugarland Industries. *See* Imperial Holly Corporation.

SugarLoaf Creations, Inc. *See* American Coin Merchandising, Inc.

Sugarloaf Mountain Corporation, **28** 21

Suita Brewery, **I** 220

Suito Sangyo Co., Ltd. *See* Seino Transportation Company, Ltd.

SUITS. *See* Scottish Universal Investments.

Suiza Foods Corporation, 25 512, 514; **26 447–50; 37** 197; **38** 381

Sukhoi Design Bureau Aviation Scientific-Industrial Complex, 24 463–65

Sullair Co., **I** 435

Sullivan & Cromwell, 26 451–53; 27 327; **47** 437

Sullivan-Schein Dental Products Inc., **31** 256

Sullivan, Stauffer, Colwell & Bayles, **14** 314

Sullivan Systems, **III** 420

Sulpetro Limited, **25** 232

Sulphide Corp., **IV** 58

Sulzbach, **I** 409

Sulzer Brothers Limited, III 402, 516, **630–33**, 638

Sumergrade Corporation, **19** 304; **41** 300

Suminoe Textile Co., **8** 235

Sumisei Secpac Investment Advisors, **III** 366

Sumisho Electronics Co. Ltd., **18** 170

Sumitomo Bank, Limited, I 587; **II** 104, 224, 273–74, 347, **360–62**, 363, 392, 415; **IV** 269, 726; **9** 341–42; **18** 170; **23** 340; **26 454–57 (upd.)**

Sumitomo Chemical Company Ltd., I 363, **397–98**; **II** 361; **III** 715; **IV** 432

Sumitomo Corporation, I 431–32, 492, 502, 504–05, 510–11, 515, **518–20**; **III** 43, 365; **V** 161; **7** 357; **11 477–80 (upd.)**, 490; **15** 340; **17** 556; **18** 170; **24** 325; **28** 288; **36** 420; **45** 115

Sumitomo Electric Industries, I 105; **II 104–05**; **III** 490, 684; **IV** 179; **V** 252

Sumitomo Heavy Industries, Ltd., III 533, **634–35**; **10** 381; **42 360–62 (upd.)**

Sumitomo Life Insurance Co., II 104, 360, 422; **III** 288, **365–66**

Sumitomo Marine and Fire Insurance Company, Limited, III 367–68

Sumitomo Metal Industries, Ltd., I 390; **II** 104, 361; **IV** 130, **211–13**, 216; **10** 463–64; **11** 246; **24** 302

Sumitomo Metal Mining Co., Ltd., IV 214–16; **9** 340; **23** 338

Sumitomo Realty & Development Co., Ltd., IV 726–27

Sumitomo Rubber Industries, Ltd., V 252–53; **20** 263

Sumitomo Trading, **45** 8

Sumitomo Trust & Banking Company, Ltd., II 104, **363–64**; **IV** 726

Sumitomo Wire Company, **16** 555

Summa Corporation, **9** 266; **17** 317

Summer Paper Tube, **19** 78

SummerGate Inc., **48** 148

Summers Group Inc., **15** 386

The Summit Bancorporation, 14 472–74

Summit Constructors. *See* CRSS Inc.

Summit Engineering Corp., **I** 153

Summit Family Restaurants Inc., 19 89, 92, **433–36**

Summit Gear Company, **16** 392–93

Summit Management Co., Inc., **17** 498

Summit Screen Inks, **13** 228

Summit Systems Inc., **45** 280

Summit Technology Inc., **30** 485

Sun Aire, **25** 421–22

Sun Alliance Group PLC, III 296, **369–74**, 400; **37** 86

Sun Apparel Inc., **39** 247

Sun Chemical Corp. *See* Sequa Corp.

Sun Communities Inc., 46 377–79

Sun Company, Inc., I 286, 631; **IV** 449, **548–50**; **7** 114, 414; **11** 484; **12** 459; **17** 537; **25** 126

Sun Country Airlines, I 114; **30 446–49**

Sun-Diamond Growers of California, 7 496–97

Sun Distributors L.P., 12 459–461

Sun Electric, **15** 288

Sun Electronics, **9** 116

Sun Equities Corporation, **15** 449

Sun-Fast Color, **13** 227

Sun Federal, **7** 498

Sun Federal Savings and Loan Association of Tallahassee, **10** 92

Sun Financial Group, Inc., **25** 171

Sun Fire Coal Company, **7** 281

Sun Fire Office, **III** 349, 369–71

Sun Foods, **12** 220–21

Sun Gro Horticulture Inc., **49** 196, 198

Sun Healthcare Group Inc., 25 455–58

Sun International Hotels Limited, 12 420; **26 462–65**; **37** 254–55

Sun Kyowa, **III** 43

Sun Life Assurance Co. of Canada, **IV** 165

Sun Life Group of America, **11** 482

Sun-Maid Growers of California, **7** 496–97

Sun Mark, Inc., **21** 483

Sun Media, **27** 280; **29** 471–72; **47** 327

Sun Men's Shop Co., Ltd., **V** 150

Sun Microsystems, Inc., II 45, 62; **III** 125; **6** 222, 235, 238, 244; **7 498–501**; **9** 36, 471; **10** 118, 242, 257, 504; **11** 45–46, 490–91, 507; **12** 162; **14** 15–16, 268; **15** 321; **16** 140, 195, 418–19; **18** 537; **20** 175, 237; **21** 86; **22** 154; **23** 471; **25** 348, 499; **26** 19; **27** 448; **30 450–54 (upd.)**; **36** 80–81; **38** 416, 418; **43** 238–40; **44** 97; **45** 200; **49** 124

Sun Newspapers, **III** 213–14

Sun Oil Co., **III** 497; **IV** 371, 424, 548–50; **7** 413–14; **11** 35; **18** 233; **19** 162; **36** 86–87. *See also* Sunoco, Inc.

Sun Optical Co., Ltd., **V** 150

Sun Pac Foods, **45** 161

Sun-Pat Products, **II** 569

Sun Pharmaceuticals, **24** 480

Sun Shades 501 Ltd., **21** 483

Sun Ship, **IV** 549

Sun Sportswear, Inc., 17 460–63; **23** 65–66

Sun State Marine Services, Inc. *See* Hvide Marine Incorporated.

Sun Techno Services Co., Ltd., **V** 150

Sun Technology Enterprises, **7** 500

Sun Television & Appliances Inc., 10 502–03; **19** 362

Sun Valley Equipment Corp., **33** 363

SunAir, **11** 300

SunAmerica Inc., 11 481–83

Sunbeam-Oster Co., Inc., 9 484–86; **14** 230; **16** 488; **17** 215; **19** 305; **22** 3; **28** 135, 246; **30** 136; **42** 309

Sunbelt Beverage Corporation, **32** 520

Sunbelt Coca-Cola, **10** 223

Sunbelt Nursery Group, Inc., **12** 179, 200, 394

Sunbelt Rentals Inc., **34** 42

Sunbird, **III** 600; **V** 150

Sunburst Hospitality Corporation, 26 458–61

Sunburst Technology Corporation, **36** 273

Sunburst Yarns, Inc., **13** 532

Sunciti Manufacturers Ltd., **III** 454; **21** 122

Sunclipse Inc., **IV** 250

Sunco N.V., **22** 515

Suncoast Motion Picture Company, **9** 360

SunCor Development Company, **6** 546–47

Suncor Energy, **33** 167

Sundance Publishing, **IV** 609; **12** 559

Sunday Pictorial, **IV** 665–66; **17** 397

Sundheim & Doetsch, **IV** 189

Sunds Defibrator AG, **IV** 338–40, 350; **28** 444

Sundstrand Corporation, 7 502–04; **21 478–81 (upd.)**

Sundt Corp., 24 466–69

SunGard Data Systems Inc., 11 484–85

Sunglass Hut International, Inc., 18 393; **21 482–84**

Sunglee Electronics Co. Ltd., **III** 748–49

Sunila Oy, **IV** 348–49

Sunkiss Thermoreactors, **21** 65

Sunkist Growers, Inc., 7 496; **25** 366; **26 466–69**; **47** 63

Sunkist Soft Drinks Inc., **I** 13

Sunkus & Associates, **49** 427

Sunkus Co. Ltd., **V** 150

Sunlight Services Group Limited, **45** 139

Sunlit Industries, **44** 132

Sunnybrook Farms, **25** 124

Sunoco, Inc., 28 438–42 (upd.)

SunQuest HealthCare Corp. *See* Unison HealthCare Corporation.

Sunquest Information Systems Inc., **45** 279, 281

Sunray DX Oil Co., **IV** 550, 575; **7** 414

The Sunrider Corporation, 26 316, **470–74**; **27** 353

SunRise Imaging, **44** 358

Sunrise Medical Inc., 11 202, **486–88**

Sunrise Test Systems, **11** 491

Sunsations Sunglass Company, **21** 483

Sunshine Biscuit Co., **35** 181; **36** 313

Sunshine Bullion Co., **25** 542

Sunshine Jr. Stores, Inc., **17** 170

Sunshine Mining Company, **20** 149

SunSoft Inc., **7** 500; **43** 238

Sunstate, **24** 396

Sunsweet Growers, **7** 496

Suntory Ltd., **13** 454; **21** 320; **36** 404

SunTrust Banks Inc., 23 455–58; **33** 293

Sunward Technologies, Inc., **10** 464

Supasnaps, **V** 50

Supelco, Inc., **36** 431

Super Bazars, **26** 159

Super D Drugs, **9** 52

Super Dart. *See* Dart Group Corporation.

Super 8 Motels, Inc., **11** 178

Super Food Services, Inc., 15 479–81; **18** 8

Super Oil Seals & Gaskets Ltd., **16** 8

Super 1 Stores. *See* Brookshire Grocery Company.

Super-Power Company, **6** 505

Super Quick, Inc., **7** 372

Super Rite Foods, Inc., **V** 176; **19** 356

Super Sagless Spring Corp., **15** 103

Super Sol Ltd., **41** 56–57

Super Store Industries, **14** 397

Super Valu Stores, Inc., II 632, **668–71**; **6** 364; **7** 450; **8** 380; **14** 411; **17** 180; **22** 126; **23** 357–58. *See also* Supervalu Inc.

SuperAmerica Group, Inc., **IV** 374

Superbrix, **14** 248

Supercomputer Systems, Inc., **III** 130; **16** 138

Supercuts Inc., 26 475–78

Superdrug plc, **V** 175; **24** 266, 269–70

Superenvases Envalic, **I** 231

Superior Bearings Company. *See* Federal-Mogul Corporation.

Superior Foam and Polymers, Inc., **44** 261

Superior Healthcare Group, Inc., **11** 221

Superior Industries International, Inc., 8 505–07

Superior Oil Co., **III** 558; **IV** 400, 465, 524; **7** 353; **49** 137

Superior Recycled Fiber Industries, **26** 363

Superior Transfer, **12** 309

Superior Uniform Group, Inc., 30 455–57

SuperMac Technology Inc., **16** 419

Supermarchés GB, **26** 159

Supermarchés Montréal, **II** 662–63

Supermarkets General Holdings Corporation, II 672–74; **16** 160; **23** 369–70

Supermart Books, **10** 136

Supersaver Wholesale Clubs, **8** 555

Supersnaps, **19** 124

SuperStation WTBS, **6** 171

Supertest Petroleum Corporation, **9** 490

Supervalu Inc., **18** 503–08 (upd.); **21** 457–57; **22** 327. *See also* Super Valu Stores, Inc.

Supervalue Corp., **13** 393

Supervised Investors Services, **III** 270

SupeRx, **II** 644

Supplyon AG, **48** 450

Suprema Specialties, Inc., 27 440–42

Supreme International Corporation, 27 443–46; 30 358; **41** 291

Supreme Life Insurance Company of America, **28** 212

Supreme Sugar Co., **I** 421; **11** 23

Supron Energy Corp., **15** 129

Surety Life Insurance Company, **10** 51

SureWay Air Traffic Corporation, **24** 126

Surgical Health Corporation, **14** 233

Surgical Mechanical Research Inc., **I** 678

Surgical Plastics, **25** 430–31

Surgikos, Inc., **III** 35

Surgitool, **I** 628

OAO Surgutneftegaz, 48 375–78

Suroflex GmbH, **23** 300

Surpass Software Systems, Inc., **9** 81

Surplus Software, **31** 176

Surridge Dawson Ltd. *See* Dawson Holdings PLC.

Survey Research Group, **10** 360

SurVivaLink, **18** 423

Susan Bristol, **16** 61

Susan Kay Cosmetics. *See* The Cosmetic Center, Inc.

SuSE Linux AG, **45** 363

Susie's Casuals, **14** 294

Susquehanna Pfaltzgraff Company, 8 508–10

Sussex Group, **15** 449

Sussex Trust Company, **25** 541

Sutherland Lumber Co., **19** 233

Sutter Corp., **15** 113

Sutter Health, **12** 175–76

Sutter Home Winery Inc., 16 476–78

Sutton & Towne, Inc., **21** 96

Sutton Laboratories, **22** 228

Suunto Oy, **41** 14, 16

Suwa Seikosha, **III** 620

Suzaki Hajime, **V** 113–14

Suzannah Farms, **7** 524

Suze, **I** 280

Suzhou Elevator Company, **29** 420

Suzuki & Co., **I** 509–10; **IV** 129; **9** 341–42; **23** 340

Suzuki Motor Corporation, III 581, 657; **7** 110; **8** 72; **9** 487–89; **23** 290, **459–62** (upd.); **36** 240, 243; **39** 38

Suzuki Shoten Co., **V** 380, 457–58

Suzy Shier, **18** 562

Svea Choklad A.G., **II** 640

Svensk Fastighetskredit A.B., **II** 352

Svensk Golvindustri, **25** 463

Svenska A.B. Humber & Co., **I** 197

Svenska Aeroplan Aktiebolaget. *See* Saab-Scania AB.

Svenska Cellulosa Aktiebolaget SCA, II 365–66; **IV** 295–96, 325, 336, **338–40,** 667; **17** 398; **19** 225–26; **28 443–46** (upd.)

Svenska Centrifug AB, **III** 418

Svenska Elektron, **III** 478

A.B. Svenska Flaktfabriken, **II** 2; **22** 8

Svenska Flygmotor A.B., **I** 209; **26** 10

Svenska Handelsbanken, II 353, 365–67; **IV** 338–39; **28** 443–44

Svenska Järnvagsverkstäderna A.B., **I** 197

Svenska Kullagerfabriken A.B., **I** 209; **III** 622; **7** 565; **26** 9. *See also* AB Volvo.

Svenska Oljeslageri AB, **IV** 318

Svenska Stålpressnings AB, **26** 11

Svenska Varv, **6** 367

Svenska Varv, **27** 91

Svenskt Stål AB, **IV** 336

Sverdrup Corporation, 14 475–78

Sverker Martin-Löf, **IV** 339

SVF. *See* Société des Vins de France.

SVIDO, **17** 250

Sviluppo Iniziative Stradali Italiene, **IV** 420

SVPW, **I** 215

Swallow Airplane Company, **8** 49; **27** 98

Swallow Sidecar and Coach Building Company, **13** 285

Swan, **10** 170

Swan Electric Light Co., **I** 410

Swan's Down Cake Flour, **II** 531

Swank Inc., 17 464–66

Swann Corp., **I** 366

Swarovski International Holding AG, 40 422–25

The Swatch Group SA, 7 532–33; **25** 481; **26 479–81**

Swearingen Aircraft Company, **9** 207; **48** 169

SwedeChrome, **III** 625

Swedish Ericsson Group, **17** 353

Swedish Furniture Research Institute, **V** 82

Swedish Intercontinental Airlines, **I** 119; **34** 396

Swedish Match AB, 39 387–90 (upd.)

Swedish Match S.A., IV 336–37; **9** 381; **12 462–64; 23** 55; **25** 464

Swedish Ordnance-FFV/Bofors AB, **9** 381–82

Swedish Telecom, V 331–33

Sweedor, **12** 464

Sweeney Specialty Restaurants, **14** 131

Sweeney's, **16** 559

Sweet & Maxwell, **8** 527

Sweet Life Foods Inc., **18** 507

Sweet Traditions LLC, **21** 323

Sweetheart Cup Company, Inc., 36 460–64

Swenson Granite Company, Inc., **37** 331

Swett & Crawford Group, **III** 357; **22** 494

Swift & Co., **II** 447, 550; **13** 351, 448; **17** 124; **41** 114

Swift Adhesives, **10** 467

Swift-Armour S.A., **II** 480

Swift-Armour S.A. Argentina, **25** 517; **26** 57

Swift-Eckrich, **II** 467

Swift Independent Packing Co., **II** 494; **13** 350, 352; **42** 92

Swift Textiles, Inc., **12** 118; **15** 247

Swift Transportation Co., Inc., 26 533; **33** 468; **42 363–66**

Swinerton Inc., 43 397–400

Swing-N-Slide, Inc. *See* PlayCore, Inc.

Swingline, Inc., **7** 3–5

Swire Group, **34** 100

Swire Pacific Ltd., I 469–70, **521–22; 6** 78; **16 479–81 (upd.); 18** 114; **20** 310, 312

Swisher International Group Inc., 14 17–19; **23 463–65; 27** 139

Swiss Air Transport Company Ltd., I 107, 119; **121–22; 24** 312; **27** 409; **33** 49, 51, 271

Swiss-American Corporation, **II** 267; **21** 145

Swiss Banca de Gottardo, **26** 456

Swiss Banca della Svizzera Italiano, **II** 192

Swiss Bank Corporation, II 267, **368–70,** 378–79; **14** 419–20; **21** 145–46

Swiss Cement-Industrie-Gesellschaft, **III** 701

Swiss Colony Wines, **I** 377

Swiss Drilling Co., **IV** 372; **19** 22

Swiss Federal Railways (Schweizerische Bundesbahnen), V 519–22

Swiss General Chocolate Co., **II** 545–46; **7** 380–81

Swiss International Air Lines Ltd., 48 379–81

Swiss Locomotive and Machine Works, **III** 631–32

Swiss Oil Co., **IV** 372–73

Swiss Reinsurance Company (Schweizerische Rückversicherungs-Gesellschaft), III 299, 301, 335, **375–78; 15** 13; **21** 146; **45** 110; **46 380–84 (upd.)**

Swiss Saurer AG, **39** 39, 41

Swiss Time Australia Pty Ltd, **25** 461

Swiss Volksbank, **21** 146–47

Swissair Associated Co., **I** 122; **6** 60, 96, 117; **34** 397–98; **36** 426

Swissair Group, **47** 286–87; **49** 80–81

SwissCargo, **49** 81

Switchboard Inc., **25** 52

SXI Limited, **17** 458

Sybase, Inc., 6 255, 279; **10** 361, **504–06; 11** 77–78; **15** 492; **25** 96, 299; **27 447–50 (upd.)**

SyberVision, **10** 216

Sybra, Inc., **19** 466–68

Sybron International Corp., 14 479–81; 19 289–90

Sycamore Networks, Inc., 45 388–91

SYCOM, Inc., **18** 363

Sydney Electricity, **12** 443

Sydney Paper Mills Ltd., **IV** 248

Sydney Ross Co., **I** 698–99

Syfrets Trust Co., **IV** 23

Sykes Enterprises, Inc., 45 392–95

Sylacauga Calcium Products, **III** 691

Syllogic B.V., **29** 376

Sylvan, Inc., 22 496–99

Sylvan Lake Telephone Company, **6** 334

Sylvan Learning Systems, Inc., 35 408–11

Sylvan Learning Systems Inc., **13** 299; **34** 439

Sylvania Companies, **I** 463; **II** 63; **III** 165, 475; **V** 295; **7** 161; **8** 157; **11** 197; **13** 402; **23** 181

Sylvia Paperboard Co., **IV** 310; **19** 266

Symantec Corporation, 10 507–09; 25 348–49

Symbian Ltd., **45** 346, 348

Symbios Logic Inc., **19** 312; **31** 5

Symbiosis Corp., **10** 70

Symbol Technologies, Inc., 10 363, 523–24; **15 482–84**

Symington-Wayne, **III** 472

Symphony International, **14** 224

Syms Corporation, 29 456–58

Symtron Systems Inc., **37** 399–400

Symtronix Corporation, **18** 515

Syn-Optics, Inc., **29** 454

Synbiotics Corporation, **23** 284

Syncordia Corp., **15** 69

Syncrocom, Inc., **10** 513
Syncrude Canada Limited, **25** 232
Synercom Technology Inc., **14** 319
Synercon Corporation, **25** 538
Synergen Inc., **13** 241
Synergy Dataworks, Inc., **11** 285
Synergy Software Inc., **31** 131
Synetic, Inc., **16** 59
Synfloor SA, **25** 464
Synopsis, Inc., 11 489–92; **18** 20; **43** 17
SynOptics Communications, Inc., 10 194, **510–12**; **11** 475; **16** 392; **22** 52
Synovus Financial Corp., 12 465–67; **18** 516–17
Syntax Ophthalmic Inc., **III** 727
Syntex Corporation, I 512, **701–03**; **III** 18, 53; **8** 216–17, 434, 548; **10** 53; **12** 322; **26** 384
Syntex Pharmaceuticals Ltd., **21** 425
Synthecolor S.A., **8** 347
Synthélabo, **III** 47–48
Synthetic Blood Corp., **15** 380
Synthetic Pillows, Inc., **19** 304
Syntron, Inc., **18** 513–15
SyQuest Technology, Inc., 18 509–12
Syracuse China, **8** 510
Syratech Corp., 14 482–84; **27** 288
Syrian Airways, **6** 85; **27** 133
Syroco, **14** 483–84
SYSCO Corporation, II 675–76; **9** 453; **16** 387; **18** 67; **24 470–72 (upd.)**, 528; **26** 504; **47** 457
Syscon Corporation, **38** 227
Sysorex Information Systems, **11** 62
SysScan, **V** 339
Systech Environmental Corporation, **28** 228–29
System Designers plc. *See* SD-Scicon plc.
System Development Co., **III** 166; **6** 282
System Fuels, Inc., **11** 194
System Integrators, Inc., **6** 279
System Parking West, **25** 16
System Software Associates, Inc., 10 513–14
Systematic Business Services, Inc., **48** 256–57
Systematics Inc., **6** 301; **11** 131
Systembolaget, **31** 459–60
Systems & Computer Technology Corp., 19 437–39
Systems and Services Company. *See* SYSCO Corporation.
Systems Center, Inc., **6** 279; **11** 469
Systems Construction Ltd., **II** 649
Systems Development Corp., **25** 117
Systems Engineering and Manufacturing Company, **11** 225
Systems Engineering Labs (SEL), **11** 45; **13** 201
Systems Exploration Inc., **10** 547
Systems Magnetic Co., **IV** 101
Systems Marketing Inc., **12** 78
Systronics, **13** 235
Sytner Group plc, 45 396–98
Syufy Enterprises. *See* Century Theatres, Inc.
Szabo, **II** 608

T. and J. Brocklebank Ltd., **23** 160
T&N PLC, **26** 141
T-Fal. *See* Groupe SEB.
T-Netix, Inc., 46 385–88
T.G.I. Friday's, **10** 331; **19** 258; **20** 159; **21** 250; **22** 127; **44** 349

T.J. Falgout, **11** 523
T.J. Maxx, **V** 197–98; **13** 329–30; **14** 62
T. Kobayashi & Co., Ltd., **III** 44
T.L. Smith & Company, **21** 502
T/Maker, **9** 81
T. Mellon & Sons, **II** 315
T. Rowe Price Associates, Inc., 10 89; **11** 493–96; **34 423–27 (upd.)**
T.S. Farley, Limited, **10** 319
T-Shirt Brokerage Services, Inc., **26** 257
T-Tech Industries, **26** 363
T. Wear Company S.r.l., **25** 121
TA Associates Inc., **10** 382; **32** 146
TA Logistics, **49** 402
TA Media AG, **15** 31
TA Triumph-Adler AG, 48 382–85
TAB Products Co., 17 467–69
Tabacalera, S.A., V 414–16; **15** 139; **17** 470–73 (upd.)
TABCORP Holdings Limited, 44 407–10
Table Supply Stores, **II** 683
Tabulating Machine Company. *See* International Business Machines Corporation.
TACA. *See* Grupo TACA.
Taco Bell Corp., I 278; **7** 267, **505–07**; **9** 178; **10** 450; **13** 336, 494; **14** 453; **15** 486; **16** 96–97; **17** 537; **21** 315, **485–88 (upd.)**; **25** 178; **37** 349, 351
Taco Cabana, Inc., 23 466–68
Taco John's International Inc., 15 485–87
Taco Kid, **7** 506
Tadiran Telecommunications Ltd., **II** 47; **25** 266–67
Taehan Cement, **III** 748
Taft Broadcasting Co. *See* Great American Broadcasting Inc.
TAG Heuer International SA, 7 554; **25 459–61**
TAG Pharmaceuticals, **22** 501
Taguchi Automobile. *See* Seino Transportation Company, Ltd.
Tahoe Joe's, Inc., **32** 102 **32** 249
TAI, Ltd., **34** 397
Taiba Corporation, **8** 250
Taiheiyo Bank, **15** 495
Taikoo Dockyard Co., **I** 521; **16** 480
Taikoo Sugar Refinery, **I** 521; **16** 480
Taio Paper Mfg. Co., Ltd. *See* Daio Paper Co., Ltd.
Taisho America, **III** 295
Taisho Marine and Fire Insurance Co., Ltd., **III** 209, 295–96
Taisho Pharmaceutical, **I** 676; **II** 361
Taittinger S.A., 27 421; **43 401–05**
Taiwan Aerospace Corp., **11** 279; **24** 88
Taiwan Auto Glass, **III** 715
Taiwan Power Company, **22** 89
Taiwan Semiconductor Manufacturing Company Ltd., 18 20; **22** 197; **43** 17; **47 383–87**
Taiway, **III** 596
Taiyo Bussan, **IV** 225; **24** 489
Taiyo Fishery Company, Limited, II 578–79
Taiyo Kobe Bank, Ltd., II 326, **371–72**
Taiyo Kogyo Corporation, **35** 98, 100
Taiyo Metal Manufacturing Co., **III** 757
Takada & Co., **IV** 151; **24** 358
Takanashi Milk Products Ltd., **37** 197
Takara, **25** 488
Takaro Shuzo, **III** 42

Takashimaya Company, Limited, V 193–96; **41** 114; **47 388–92 (upd.)**
Take-Two Interactive Software, Inc., 46 389–91
Takeda Chemical Industries, Ltd., I 704–06; **III** 760; **46 392–95 (upd.)**
Takeda Riken, **11** 504
Takeuchi Mining Co., **III** 545
Takihyo, **15** 145
Takkyubin, **V** 537
Tako Oy, **IV** 314
The Talbots, Inc., II 503; **10** 324; **11** 497–99; **12** 280; **31 429–432 (upd.)**
Talcott National Corporation, **11** 260–61
Talegen Holdings Inc., **26** 546
Talent Net Inc., **44** 164
Taliq Corp., **III** 715
Talisman Energy Inc., 9 490–93; **47** 393–98 (upd.)
TALK Corporation, **34** 48
Talk Radio Network, Inc., **23** 294
Talley Industries, Inc., 10 386; **16 482–85**
Tally Corp., **18** 434
Talmadge Farms, Inc., **20** 105
TAM Ceramics Inc., **III** 681; **44** 118–19
Tamar Bank, **II** 187
Tamarkin Co., **12** 390
Tambrands Inc., III 40; **8 511–13**; **12** 439; **15** 359–60, 501; **16** 303; **26** 384; **37** 394
Tamco, **12** 390; **19** 380
TAMET, **IV** 25
Tamglass Automotive OY, **22** 436
Tampa Electric Company, **6** 582–83
Tampax Inc. *See* Tambrands Inc.
Oy Tampella Ab, **II** 47; **III** 648; **IV** 276; **25** 266
Tampere Paper Board and Roofing Felt Mill, **IV** 314
Tampereen Osake-Pankki, **II** 303
Tampimex Oil, **11** 194
TAMSA. *See* Tubos de Acero de Mexico, S.A.
Tamura Kisan Co., **II** 552
Tanaka, **6** 71
Tanaka Kikinzoku Kogyo KK, **IV** 119
Tanaka Matthey KK, **IV** 119
Tandem Computers, Inc., 6 278–80; **10** 499; **11** 18; **14** 318; **26** 93; **29** 477–79
Tandon, **25** 531
Tandy Corporation, II 70, **106–08**; **6** 257–58; **9** 43, 115, 165; **10** 56–57, 166–67, 236; **12 468–70 (upd.)**; **13** 174; **14** 117; **16** 84; **17** 353–54; **24** 502; **25** 531; **26** 18; **34** 198; **49** 183. *See also* RadioShack Corporation.
Tandycrafts, Inc., 31 433–37
Tangent Industries, **15** 83
Tangent Systems, **6** 247–48
Tanger Factory Outlet Centers, Inc., 49 386–89
Tangiers International. *See* Algo Group Inc.
Tangram Rehabilitation Network, Inc., **29** 401
Tanjong Pagar Dock Co., **I** 592
Tanks Oil and Gas, **11** 97
Tanne-Arden, Inc., **27** 291
Tanner-Brice Company, **13** 404
Tantalum Mining Corporation, **29** 81
TAP—Air Portugal Transportes Aéreos Portugueses S.A., 46 396–99 (upd.)
Tapiola Insurance, **IV** 316

Tapis-St. Maclou, **37** 22

Tappan. *See* White Consolidated Industries Inc.

Tara Exploration and Development Ltd., **IV** 165

Tara Foods, **II** 645

Target Rock Corporation, **35** 134–36

Target Stores, V 35, 43–44; **10** 284, **515–17; 12** 508; **13** 261, 274, 446; **14** 398; **15** 275; **16** 390; **17** 460–61; **18** 108, 137, 283, 286; **20** 155; **22** 328; **27** 315, **451–54 (upd.);** **39** 269, 271

Tarkett Sommer AG, 12 464; **25 462–64**

Tarmac plc, III 734, **751–54; 14** 250; **28** **447–51 (upd.);** **36** 21

TarMacadam (Purnell Hooley's Patent) Syndicate Ltd., **III** 751

Tarragon Oil and Gas Ltd., **24** 522

Tarragon Realty Investors, Inc., 45 **399–402**

Tarslag, **III** 752

TASC. *See* Analytical Sciences Corp.

Tashima Shoten, **III** 574

Tasman Pulp and Paper Co. Ltd. *See* Fletcher Challenge Ltd.

Tasman U.E.B., **IV** 249

Tasmanian Fibre Containers, **IV** 249

Tastee Freeze, **39** 234

Tasty Baking Company, 14 485–87; **35** **412–16 (upd.)**

TAT European Airlines, **14** 70, 73; **24** 400

Tata Airlines. *See* Air-India Limited.

Tata Enterprises, **III** 43

Tata Industries, **20** 313; **21** 74

Tata Iron & Steel Co. Ltd., IV 48, 205–07, **217–19; 44 411–15 (upd.)**

Tate & Lyle PLC, II 514, **580–83; 7** 466–67; **13** 102; **26** 120; **42 367–72** **(upd.)**

Tatebayashi Flour Milling Co., **II** 554

Tateisi Electric Manufacturing, **II** 75

Tateisi Medical Electronics Manufacturing Co., **II** 75

Tatham Corporation, **21** 169, 171

Tatham/RSCG, **13** 204

Tati SA, 25 465–67

Tatneft. *See* OAO Tatneft.

Tattered Cover Book Store, 43 406–09

Tatung Co., III 482; **13** 387; **23 469–71**

Taurus Exploration, **21** 208

Taurus Programming Services, **10** 196

TaurusHolding GmbH & Co. KG, 46 **400–03**

Tax Management, Inc., **23** 92

Taylor & Francis Group plc, 44 416–19

Taylor Aircraft Corporation, **44** 307

Taylor Corporation, 36 465–67; 37 108

Taylor Diving and Salvage Co., **III** 499

Taylor-Evans Seed Co., **IV** 409

Taylor Guitars, 48 386–89

Taylor Made Golf Co., 23 270, **472–74;** **33** 7

Taylor Material Handling, **13** 499

Taylor Medical, **14** 388

Taylor Nelson Sofres plc, 34 428–30; 37 144

Taylor Petroleum, Inc., **17** 170

Taylor Publishing Company, 12 471–73; **25** 254; **36 468–71 (upd.)**

Taylor Rental Corp., **III** 628

Taylor Wines Co., **I** 234; **10** 227

Taylor Woodrow plc, I 590–91; **III** 739; **13** 206; **38 450–53 (upd.)**

Taylors and Lloyds, **II** 306

Tayto Ltd., **22** 515

Tazuke & Co., **IV** 151; **24** 358

TBC Corp., **20** 63

TBS. *See* Turner Broadcasting System, Inc.

TBWA Advertising, Inc., 6 47–49; 22 394

TBWA Worldwide, 42 175; **43** 412

TBWA\Chiat\Day, 43 410–14 (upd.)

TC Advertising. *See* Treasure Chest Advertising, Inc.

TC Debica, **20** 264

TCA. *See* Air Canada.

TCBC. *See* Todays Computers Business Centers.

TCBY Enterprises Inc., 17 474–76

TCF. *See* Tokyo City Finance.

TCF Financial Corporation, 47 399–402

TCF Holdings, Inc., **II** 170–71

TCH Corporation, **12** 477

TCI. *See* Tele-Communications, Inc.

TCI Communications, **29** 39

TCI Inc., **33** 92–93

TCI International Inc., **43** 48

TCM Investments, Inc., **49** 159

TCPL. *See* TransCanada PipeLines Ltd.

TCS Management Group, Inc., **22** 53

TCW Capital, **19** 414–15

TD Bank. *See* The Toronto-Dominion Bank.

TDK Corporation, I 500; **II** 109–11; **IV** 680; **17 477–79 (upd.);** **49 390–94** **(upd.)**

TDL Group Ltd., 46 404–06

TDL Infomedia Ltd., **47** 347

TDS. *See* Telephone and Data Systems, Inc.

Teaberry Electronics Corp., **III** 569; **20** 361

Teachers Insurance and Annuity **Association, III 379–82; 22** 268; **35** 75; **47** 331; **49** 413

Teachers Insurance and Annuity **Association-College Retirement** **Equities Fund, 45 403–07 (upd.)**

Teachers Service Organization, Inc., **8** 9–10

Team America, **9** 435

Team Penske, **V** 494

Team Rental Group. *See* Budget Group, Inc.

Teams, Inc., **37** 247

Teamsters Central States Pension Fund, **19** 378

Teamsters Union, **13** 19

TearDrop Golf Company, 32 445–48

Tebel Maschinefabrieken, **III** 420

Tebel Pneumatiek, **III** 420

Tech Data Corporation, 10 518–19

Tech Pacific International, **18** 180; **39** 201, 203

Tech-Sym Corporation, 18 513–15; 44 **420–23 (upd.)**

Tech Textiles, USA, **15** 247–48

Techalloy Co., **IV** 228

Techgistics, **49** 403

Technair Packaging Laboratories, **18** 216

Technical Ceramics Laboratories, Inc., **13** 141

Technical Coatings Co., **13** 85; **38** 96–97

Technical Materials, Inc., **14** 81

Technical Olympic USA, **46** 180

Technical Publishing, **IV** 605

Technicare, **11** 200

Technicolor Inc., **28** 246

Technicon Instruments Corporation, **III** 56; **11** 333–34; **22** 75

Technifax, **8** 483

Techniques d'Avant-Garde. *See* TAG Heuer International SA.

Technisch Bureau Visser, **16** 421

Technitrol, Inc., 29 459–62

Techno-Success Company, **V** 719

AB Technology, **II** 466

Technology Management Group, Inc., **18** 112

Technology Resources International Ltd., **18** 76

Technology Venture Investors, **11** 490; **14** 263

Technophone Ltd., **17** 354

TechTeam Europe, Ltd., **41** 281

Teck Corporation, 9 282; **27 455–58**

Tecnamotor S.p.A., **8** 72, 515

Tecneco, **IV** 422

Tecnifax Corp., **IV** 330

Tecnipublicaciones, **14** 555

Tecnost S.p.A., **34** 319

TECO Energy, Inc., 6 582–84

Tecom Industries, Inc., **18** 513–14

Tecstar, Inc., **30** 436

Tectrix Fitness Equipment, Inc., **49** 108

Tecumseh Products Company, 8 72, **514–16**

Ted Bates, Inc., **I** 33, 623; **10** 69; **16** 71–72

Teddy's Shoe Store. *See* Morse Shoe Inc.

Tedelex, **IV** 91–92

Teekay Shipping Corporation, 25 **468–71**

Tees and Hartlepool, **31** 367, 369

Tefal. *See* Groupe SEB.

TEFSA, **17** 182

TEIC. *See* B.V. Tabak Export & Import Compagnie.

Teijin Limited, I 511; **V 380–82**

Teikoku Bank, **I** 507; **II** 273, 325–26

Teikoku Hormone, **I** 704

Teikoku Jinken. *See* Teijin Limited.

Teikoku Sekiyu Co. Ltd., **IV** 475

Teikoku Shiki, **IV** 326

Teito Electric Railway, **V** 461

Teito Transport Co. Ltd., **V** 536

Tejas Gas Co., **41** 359

Tejas Snacks LP, **44** 349

Tejon Ranch Company, 35 417–20

Teklogix International, **45** 346, 348

Tekmunc A/S, **17** 288

Teknekron Infoswitch Corporation, **22** 51

Teknika Electronics Corporation, **43** 459

Tekrad, Inc. *See* Tektronix, Inc.

Tekton Corp., **IV** 346

Tektronix, Inc., II 101; **8 517–21; 10** 24; **11** 284–86; **12** 454; **36** 331; **38** 71; **39** 350, 353; **41** 235

Tel-A-Data Limited, **11** 111

TelAutograph Corporation, **29** 33–34

Telcon. *See* Telegraph Construction and Maintenance Company.

Tele-Communications, Inc., II 160–62, 167; **10** 484, 506; **11** 479; **13** 280; **15** 264–65; **17** 148; **18** 64–66, 211, 213, 535; **19** 282; **21** 307, 309; **23** 121, 502; **24** 6, 120; **25** 213–14; **26** 33; **28** 241; **38** 114–15; **43** 433

Tele Consulte, **14** 555

Télé Luxembourg, **44** 376

Telebook, **25** 19

Telec Centre S.A., **19** 472

TeleCheck Services, **18** 542
TeleCheck Services, Inc., **11** 113
TeleChef, **33** 387, 389
Teleclub, **IV** 590
Teleco Oilfield Services Inc., **6** 578; **22** 68
TeleColumbus, **11** 184
Telecom Australia, 6 341–42
Telecom Canada. *See* Stentor Canadian Network Management.
Telecom Eireann, 7 508–10. *See also* eircom plc.
Telecom Italia S.p.A., 15 355; **24** 79; **34** 316, 319; **43 415–19**; **47** 345–46
Telecom New Zealand, **18** 33
Telecom One, Inc., **29** 252
Telecom*USA, **27** 304
Telecommunications of Jamaica Ltd., **25** 101
Telecomputing Corp., **I** 544
Telecredit, Inc., **6** 25
Telectronic Pacing Systems, **10** 445
Teledyne Inc., I 486, **523–25**; **II** 33, 44; **10** 262–63, 365, **520–22 (upd.)**; **11** 265; **13** 387; **17** 109; **18** 369; **29** 400; **35** 136
Teleflora Inc., **28** 1 8–90; **19** 12; **21** 259
Teleflora LLC, **37** 337
Telefonaktiebolaget LM Ericsson, V 334–36; **46** 407–11 **(upd.)**
Telefónica de España, S.A., V 337–40; **43** 422
Telefónica S.A., 46 172, **412–17 (upd.)**
Telefonos de Mexico S.A. de C.V., 14 488–90
Téléfrance, **25** 174
Telefunken Fernseh & Rundfunk GmbH., **I** 411; **II** 117
telegate AG, **18** 155; **47** 345, 347
Teleglobe Inc., **14** 512
Telegraph Condenser Co., **II** 81
Telegraph Construction and Maintenance Company, **25** 98–100
Telegraph Manufacturing Co., **III** 433
Telegraph Works, **III** 433
Telegraphic Service Company, **16** 166
Telekomunikacja S.A., **18** 33
Telelistas Editors Ltda., **26** 520
TeleMarketing Corporation of Louisiana, **8** 311
Telemarketing Investments, Ltd., **8** 311
Telematics International Inc., **18** 154, 156
Télémécanique, **II** 94; **18** 473; **19** 166
Telemundo Group, Inc., **III** 344; **24** 516
Telenet Communications, **18** 32
Telenet Information Services, **47** 37
Telenor, **31** 221
Telenorma, **I** 193
Telenova, **III** 169; **6** 285
Teleos Communications Inc., **26** 277
Telephone and Data Systems, Inc., 9 494–96, 527–529; **31** 449
Telephone Company of Ireland, **7** 508
Telephone Exchange Company of Indianapolis, **14** 257
Telephone Management Corporation, **8** 310
Telephone Utilities, Inc. *See* Pacific Telecom, Inc.
Telephone Utilities of Washington, **6** 325, 328
Telepictures, **II** 177
TelePizza S.A., 33 387–89
Teleport Communications Group, **14** 253; **24** 122
Teleprompter Corp., **II** 122; **7** 222; **10** 210; **18** 355

Telerate Systems Inc., **IV** 603, 670; **10** 276–78; **21** 68; **47** 102–03
Teleregister Corp., **I** 512
Telerent Europe. *See* Granada Group PLC.
TeleRep, **IV** 596
Telesat Cable TV, Inc., **23** 293
Telesis Oil and Gas, **6** 478
Telesistema, **18** 212
Telesistema Mexico. *See* Grupo Televisa.
TeleSite, U.S.A., Inc., **44** 442
Telesphere Network, Inc., **8** 310
Telesystems SLW Inc., **10** 524
Telettra S.p.A., **V** 326; **9** 10; **11** 205
Tele2 AB, **26** 331–33
Teletype Corp., **14** 569
Televimex, S.A., **18** 212
Television de Mexico, S.A., **18** 212
Television Española, S.A., 7 511–12; **18** 211
Télévision Française 1, 23 475–77
Television Sales and Marketing Services Ltd., **7** 79–80
Teleway Japan, **7** 118–19; **13** 482
Telex Corporation, **II** 87; **13** 127
Telfin, **V** 339
Telia Mobitel, **11** 19; **26** 332
Telihoras Corporation, **10** 319
Telinfo, **6** 303
Telinq Inc., **10** 19
Telios Pharmaceuticals, Inc., **11** 460; **17** 288
Tellabs, Inc., 11 500–01; **40 426–29 (upd.)**; **45** 390
Telmex. *See* Teléfonos de México S.A. de C.V.
Telpar, Inc., **14** 377
Telport, **14** 260
Telrad Telecommunications Ltd., **II** 48; **25** 266–67
Telxon Corporation, 10 523–25
Tembec, Inc., **IV** 296; **19** 226
Temco Electronics and Missile Co., **I** 489
Temenggong of Jahore, **I** 592
Temerlin McClain, **23** 479; **25** 91
TEMIC TELEFUNKEN, **34** 128, 133, 135
Temp Force, **16** 421–22; **43** 308
Temp World, Inc., **6** 10
Temple, Barker & Sloan/Strategic Planning Associates, **III** 283
Temple Frosted Foods, **25** 278
Temple Inks Company, **13** 227
Temple-Inland Inc., IV 312, **341–43**, 675; **8** 267–69; **19** 268; **31 438–442 (upd.)**
Temple Press Ltd., **IV** 294–95; **19** 225
Templeton, **II** 609
TEMPO Enterprises, **II** 162
Tempo-Team, **16** 420; **43** 307
Tempus Expeditions, **13** 358
Tempus Group plc, **48** 442
TemTech Ltd., **13** 326
10 Sen Kinitsu Markets, **V** 194
Ten Speed Press, **27** 223
Tenacqco Bridge Partnership, **17** 170
Tenby Industries Limited, **21** 350
Tencor Instruments, Inc. *See* KLA-Tencor Corporation.
TenFold Corporation, 35 421–23
Tengelmann Group, II 636–38; **16** 249–50; **27 459–62**; **35** 401
Tengelmann Warenhandelsgesellschaft OHG, **47** 107
Tengen Inc., **III** 587; **7** 395
Tennant Company, 13 499–501; **33 390–93 (upd.)**

Tenneco Inc., I 182, **526–28**; **IV** 76, 152, 283, 371, 499; **6** 531; **10** 379–80, 430, **526–28 (upd.)**; **11** 440; **12** 91, 376; **13** 372–73; **16** 191, 461; **19** 78, 483; **21** 170; **22** 275, 380; **24** 358; **38** 325, 380; **40** 134; **45** 354
Tennessee Book Company, **11** 193
Tennessee Coal, Iron and Railroad Co., **IV** 573; **7** 550
Tennessee Eastman Corporation, **III** 475; **7** 161. *See also* Eastman Chemical Company.
Tennessee Electric Power Co., **III** 332
Tennessee Gas Pipeline Co., **14** 126
Tennessee Gas Transmission Co., **I** 526; **13** 496; **14** 125
Tennessee Insurance Company, **11** 193–94
Tennessee Paper Mills Inc. *See* Rock-Tenn Company.
Tennessee Restaurant Company, **9** 426; **30** 208–9
Tennessee River Pulp & Paper Co., **12** 376–77
Tennessee Trifting, **13** 169
Tennessee Valley Authority, **II** 2–3, 121; **IV** 181; **22** 10; **38** 447
Tennessee Woolen Mills, Inc., **19** 304
Tenngasco, **I** 527
Teollisuusosuuskunta Metsä-Saimaa, **IV** 315
TEP. *See* Tucson Electric Power Company.
Tequila Sauza, **31** 91
Tequilera de Los Altos, **31** 92
TeraBeam Networks Inc., **41** 261, 263–64
Teradata Corporation, **6** 267; **30** 339–40
Teradyne, Inc., 11 502–04
Terex Corporation, 7 513–15; **8** 116; **40 430–34 (upd.)**
Teril Stationers Inc., **16** 36
The Terlato Wine Group, 48 390–92
Terminal Transfer and Storage, Inc., **6** 371
Terminix International, **6** 45–46; **11** 433; **23** 428, 430; **25** 16
Terra Industries, Inc., 13 277, **502–04**
Terra Lycos, Inc., 43 420–25; **46** 416
Terrace Park Dairies, **II** 536
Terracor, **11** 260–61
Terragrafics, **14** 245
Terrain King, **32** 26
Terre Haute Electric, **6** 555
Terre Lune, **25** 91
Territorial Hotel Co., **II** 490
Territory Ahead, Inc., **29** 279
Territory Enterprises Ltd., **IV** 59
Terry Coach Industries, Inc., **III** 484; **22** 206
Terry's of York, **II** 594
Terumo Corporation, 48 393–95
Tesa, S.A., **23** 82
TESC. *See* The European Software Company.
Tesco PLC, II 513, **677–78**; **10** 442; **11** 239, 241; **24 473–76 (upd.)**
Tesoro Bolivia Petroleum Company, **25** 546
Tesoro Petroleum Corporation, 7 516–19; **45 408–13 (upd.)**
Tesseract Inc., **11** 78; **33** 331
Tessman Seed, Inc., **16** 270–71
Testor Corporation, **8** 455
TETI, **I** 466
Tetley Inc., **I** 215; **14** 18
Tetra Plastics Inc., **V** 374; **8** 393
Tetra Tech, Inc., 29 463–65

Teutonia National Bank, **IV** 310; **19** 265

Teva Pharmaceutical Industries Ltd., 22 500–03; 47 55

Tex-Mex Partners L.C., **41** 270

Tex-Star Oil & Gas Corp., **IV** 574; **7** 551

Texaco Canada Inc., **25** 232

Texaco Inc., I 21, 360; **II** 31, 313, 448; **III** 760; **IV** 386, 403, 418, 425, 429, 439, 461, 464, 466, 472–73, 479–80, 484, 488, 490, 510–11, 530–31, 536–39, 545, **551–53**, 560, 565–66, 570, 575; **7** 172, 280, 483; **9** 232; **10** 190; **12** 20; **13** 448; **14 491–94 (upd.); 17** 412; **18** 488; **41** 359, **391–96 (upd.) 19** 73, 75, 176; **24** 521; **27** 481; **28** 47; **47** 72, 436. *See also* ChevronTexaco Corporation.

Texada Mines, Ltd., **IV** 123

Texas Air Corporation, I 97, 100, 103, 118, **123–24**, 127, 130; **6** 82, 129; **12** 489; **21** 142–43; **35** 427

Texas Almanac, **10** 3

Texas Bus Lines, **24** 118

Texas Butadiene and Chemical Corp., **IV** 456

Texas Co., **III** 497; **IV** 386, 400, 464, 536, 551–52; **7** 352

Texas Commerce Bankshares, **II** 252

Texas Eastern Corp., **6** 487; **11** 97, 354; **14** 126

Texas Eastern Transmission Company, **11** 28

Texas Eastman, **III** 475; **7** 161

Texas Electric Service Company, **V** 724

Texas Gas Resources Corporation, **IV** 395; **22** 166

Texas Gypsum, **IV** 341

Texas Homecare, **21** 335

Texas Industries, Inc., 8 522–24; 13 142–43

Texas Instruments Incorporated, I 315, 482, 523, 620; **II** 64, **112–15**; **III** 120, 124–25, 142, 499; **IV** 130, 365, 681; **6** 216, 221–22, 237, 241, 257, 259; **7** 531; **8** 157; **9** 43, 116, 310; **10** 22, 87, 307; **11** 61, 308, 490, 494, **505–08 (upd.); 12** 135, 238; **14** 42–43; **16** 4, 333; **17** 192; **18** 18, 436; **21** 123; **23** 181, 210; **25** 81, 96, 531; **38** 375; **43** 15; **46 418–23 (upd.)**

Texas International Airlines, **I** 117, 123; **II** 408; **IV** 413; **21** 142

Texas Life Insurance Co., **III** 293

Texas Metal Fabricating Company, **7** 540

Texas-New Mexico Utilities Company, **6** 580

Texas Oil & Gas Corp., **IV** 499, 572, 574; **7** 549, 551

Texas Overseas Petroleum Co., **IV** 552

Texas Pacific Coal and Oil Co., **I** 285–86

Texas Pacific Group Inc., 22 80; **23** 163, 166; **30** 171; **34** 231; **36 472–74**

Texas Pacific Oil Co., **IV** 550

Texas Pipe Line Co., **IV** 552

Texas Power & Light Company, **V** 724

Texas Public Utilities, **II** 660

Texas Super Duper Markets, Inc., **7** 372

Texas Trust Savings Bank, **8** 88

Texas United Insurance Co., **III** 214

Texas Utilities Company, V 724–25; 12 99; **25 472–74 (upd.); 35** 479

Texasgulf Inc., **IV** 546–47; **13** 557; **18** 433

Texboard, **IV** 296; **19** 226

Texize, **I** 325, 371

Texkan Oil Co., **IV** 566

Texstar Petroleum Company, **7** 516

Texstyrene Corp., **IV** 331

Textile Diffusion, **25** 466

Textile Paper Tube Company, Ltd., **8** 475

Textile Rubber and Chemical Company, **15** 490

Textron Inc., I 186, **529–30**; **II** 420; **III** 66, 628; **8** 93, 157, 315, 545; **9** 497, 499; **11** 261; **12** 251, 382–83, 400–01; **13** 63–64; **17** 53; **21** 175; **22** 32; **27** 100; **34 431–34 (upd.); 35** 350–51; **46** 65

Textron Lycoming Turbine Engine, 9 497–99

Texwood Industries, Inc., **20** 363

TF-I, **I** 563

TFC. *See* Times Fiber Communications, Inc.

TFM. *See* Grupo Transportación Ferroviaria Mexicana, S.A. de C.V.

TFN Group Communications, Inc., **8** 311

TF1 **24** 79. *See also* Télévision Française 1

TFP, Inc., **44** 358–59

TGEL&PCo. *See* Tucson Gas, Electric Light & Power Company.

Th. Pilter, **III** 417

TH:s Group, **10** 113

Thai Airways International Ltd., I 119; **II** 442; **6 122–24**

Thai Airways International Public Company Limited, 27 463–66 (upd.)

Thai Aluminium Co. Ltd., **IV** 155

Thai Union International Inc., **24** 116

Thalassa International, **10** 14; **27** 11

Thales S.A., 42 373–76; 47 9; **49** 165, 167

Thalhimer Brothers, **V** 31

Thames Board Ltd., **IV** 318

Thames Television Ltd., **I** 532

Thames Trains, **28** 157

Thames Water plc, 11 509–11; 22 89

Thameslink, **28** 157

Tharsis Co., **IV** 189–90

Thatcher Glass, **I** 610

THAW. *See* Recreational Equipment, Inc.

Thayer Laboratories, **III** 55

Theatrical Syndicate, **24** 437

Theo H. Davies & Co., **I** 470; **20** 311

Theo Hamm Brewing Co., **I** 260

Théraplix, **I** 388

Therm-o-Disc, **II** 19

Therm-X Company, **8** 178

Thermacote Welco Company, **6** 146

Thermadyne Holding Corporation, 19 440–43

Thermal Dynamics, **19** 441

Thermal Energies, Inc., **21** 514

Thermal Power Company, **11** 270

Thermal Snowboards, Inc., **22** 462

Thermal Transfer Ltd., **13** 485

ThermaStor Technologies, Ltd., **44** 366

Thermo BioAnalysis Corp., 25 475–78

Thermo Electron Corporation, 7 520–22; 11 512–13; **13** 421; **24** 477; **25** 475–76

Thermo Fibertek, Inc., 24 477–79

Thermo Instrument Systems Inc., 11 512–14; 25 475–77

Thermo King Corporation, 13 505–07

Thermodynamics Corp., **III** 645

Thermoforming USA, **16** 339

Thermogas Co., **IV** 458–59; **35** 175

Thermolase Corporation, **22** 410

Thermoplast und Apparatebau GmbH, **IV** 198

Thermos Company, **16 486–88**

TheStreet.com, **34** 125

Thies Companies, **13** 270

Thiess, **III** 687

Thiess Dampier Mitsui, **IV** 47

Things Remembered, **13** 165–66

Think Entertainment, **II** 161

Think Technologies, **10** 508

Thiokol Corporation, I 370; **8** 472; **9** 358–59, **500–02 (upd.); 12** 68; **22 504–07 (upd.)**

Third National Bank. *See* Fifth Third Bancorp.

Third National Bank of Dayton, **9** 475

Third National Bank of New York, **II** 253

Third Wave Publishing Corp. *See* Acer Inc.

ThirdAge.com, **49** 290

Thirteen/WNET. *See* Educational Broadcasting Corporation.

Thistle Group, **9** 365

Thom McAn, **V** 136–37; **11** 349

Thomas & Betts Corp., II 8; **11 515–17; 14** 27

Thomas and Hochwalt, **I** 365

Thomas & Howard Co., **II** 682; **18** 8

Thomas and Judith Pyle, **13** 433

Thomas Barlow & Sons Ltd., **I** 288, 422; **IV** 22

Thomas Bros. Maps, **28** 380

Thomas Cook Group Ltd., **17** 325

Thomas Cook Travel Inc., 6 84; **9 503–05; 27** 133; **33 394–96 (upd.); 42** 282

Thomas De La Rue and Company, Ltd., **44** 357–58

Thomas Firth & Sons, **I** 573

Thomas H. Lee Co., 11 156, 450; **14** 230–31; **15** 309; **19** 371, 373; **24** 480–83; **25** 67; **28** 134; **30** 219; **32** 362

Thomas Industries Inc., 29 466–69

Thomas J. Lipton Company, II 609, 657; **11** 450; **14 495–97; 16** 90; **32** 474

Thomas Jefferson Life Insurance Co., **III** 397

Thomas Kinkade Galleries. *See* Media Arts Group, Inc.

Thomas Linnell & Co. Ltd., **II** 628

Thomas Nationwide Transport. *See* TNT.

Thomas Nationwide Transport Limited. *See* TNT Post Group N.V.

Thomas Nelson Inc., 8 526; **14 498–99; 24** 548; **38 454–57 (upd.)**

Thomas Publishing Company, 26 482–85

Thomas Tilling plc, **I** 429

Thomas Y. Crowell, **IV** 605

Thomaston Mills, Inc., 27 467–70

Thomasville Furniture Industries, Inc., III 423; **12 474–76; 22** 48; **28** 406; **31** 248; **39** 170, 174

Thompson and Formby, **16** 44

Thompson Aircraft Tire Corp., **14** 42

Thompson-Hayward Chemical Co., **13** 397

Thompson Medical Company. *See* Slim-Fast Nutritional Foods International Inc.

Thompson Nutritional Products, **37** 286

Thompson PBE Inc., **24** 160–61

Thompson Products Co., **I** 539

Thompson-Ramo-Woolridge, **I** 539

Thompson-Werke, **III** 32

Thomson BankWatch Inc., **19** 34

Thomson-Bennett, **III** 554

Thomson-Brandt, **I** 411; **II** 13, 116–17; **9** 9

The Thomson Corporation, **IV** 651, 686; **7** 390; **8 525–28**; **10** 407; **12** 361, 562; **17** 255; **22** 441; **34 435–40 (upd.)**; **44** 155

Thomson-CSF, **II** 116–17; **III** 556. *See also* Thales S.A.

Thomson-Houston Electric Co., **II** 27, 116, 330; **12** 193

Thomson International, **37** 143

Thomson-Jenson Energy Limited, **13** 558

Thomson-Lucas, **III** 556

THOMSON multimedia S.A., **18** 126; **36** 384; **42 377–80 (upd.)**

Thomson-Ramo-Woolridge. *See* TRW Inc.

Thomson S.A., **I** 411; **II** 31, **116–17**; **7** 9; **13** 402. *See also* THOMSON multimedia S.A.

Thomson T-Line, **II** 142

Thomson Travel Group, **27** 27

Thonet Industries Inc., **14** 435–36

Thor Industries, Inc., **39 391–94**

Thorn Apple Valley, Inc., **7 523–25**; **12** 125; **22 508–11 (upd.)**; **23** 203

Thorn EMI plc, **I** 52, 411, **531–32**; **II** 117, 119; **III** 480; **19** 390; **22** 27, 192–94; **24** 87, 484–85; **26** 151; **40** 105

Thorn plc, **24 484–87**

Thorncraft Inc., **25** 379

Thorndike, Doran, Paine and Lewis, Inc., **14** 530

Thornton, **III** 547

Thornton & Co., **II** 283

Thornton Stores, **14** 235

Thorntons plc, **46 424–26**

Thoroughgood, **II** 658

Thorsen Realtors, **21** 96

Thos. & Wm. Molson & Company. *See* The Molson Companies Limited.

Thousand Trails, Inc., **13** 494; **33 397–99**

Thousands Springs Power Company, **12** 265

THQ, Inc., **39 395–97**

Threads for Life, **49** 244

Threadz, **25** 300

Three-Diamond Company. *See* Mitsubishi Shokai.

The 3DO Company, **10** 286; **43 426–30**

3 Guys, **II** 678, **V** 35

3-in-One Oil Co., **I** 622

3 Maj, **25** 469

Three Ring Asia Pacific Beer Co., Ltd., **49** 418

Three Rivers Pulp and Paper Company, **17** 281

Three Score, **23** 100

3 Suisses International, **12** 281

3Com Corporation, **III** 143; **6** 238, 269; **10** 237; **11 518–21**; **20** 8, 33; **26** 276; **34 441–45 (upd.)**; **36** 122, 300, 357; **49** 184. *See also* Palm, Inc.

3D Planet SpA, **41** 409

3M. *See* Minnesota Mining & Manufacturing Co.

3S Systems Support Services Ltd., **6** 310

360networks inc., **46** 268

Threlfall Breweries, **I** 294

Threshold Entertainment, **25** 270

Thrif D Discount Center, **V** 174

Thrift Drug, **V** 92

Thrift Mart, **16** 65

ThriftiCheck Service Corporation, **7** 145

Thriftimart Inc., **12** 153; **16** 452

Thriftway Food Drug, **21** 530

Thriftway Foods, **II** 624

Thrifty Corporation, **25** 413, 415–16

Thrifty PayLess, Inc., **V** 682, 684; ; **12** **477–79**; **18** 286; **19** 357; **25** 297

Thrifty Rent-A-Car, **6** 349; **24** 10; **44** 355. *See also* Dollar Thrifty Automotive Group, Inc.

Throwing Corporation of America, **12** 501

Thrustmaster S.A., **41** 190

Thummel Schutze & Partner, **28** 141

Thunder Bay Press, **34** 3–5

Thuringia Insurance Co., **III** 299

Thurmond Chemicals, Inc., **27** 291

Thurston Motor Lines Inc., **12** 310

Thy-Marcinelle, **IV** 52

Thyssen AG, **II** 279; **III** 566; **IV** 195, **221–23**, 228; **8** 75–76; **14** 169, 328

Thyssen Krupp AG, **28** 104, **452–60 (upd.)**; **42** 417

Thyssen-Krupp Stahl AG, **26** 83

Thyssengas, **38** 406–07

TI. *See* Texas Instruments.

TI Corporation, **10** 44

TI Group plc, **17 480–83**

TIAA-CREF. *See* Teachers Insurance and Annuity Association-College Retirement Equities Fund.

Tianjin Agricultural Industry and Commerce Corp., **II** 577

Tianjin Automobile Industry Group, **21** 164

Tianjin Bohai Brewing Company, **21** 230

Tibbals Floring Co., **III** 611

Tibbett & Britten Group plc, **32 449–52**

Tiber Construction Company, **16** 286

Tichenor Media System Inc., **35** 220

Ticino Societa d'Assicurazioni Sulla Vita, **III** 197

Ticketmaster Corp., **13 508–10**; **25** 214; **36** 423–24

Ticketmaster Group, Inc., **37 381–84 (upd.)**; **47** 419, 421

Ticketron, **13** 508–09; **24** 438; **37** 381–82

Tichnor & Fields, **10** 356

Tickometer Co., **III** 157

Ticor Title Insurance Co., **10** 45

Tidel Systems, **II** 661; **32** 416

Tidewater Inc., **11 522–24**; **37 385–88 (upd.)**

Tidewater Oil Co., **IV** 434, 460, 489, 522

Tidewater Utilities, Inc., **45** 275, 277

Tidi Wholesale, **13** 150

Tidy House Products Co., **II** 556

TIE. *See* Transport International Express.

Tiel Utrecht Fire Insurance Co., **III** 309–10

Tien Wah Press (Pte.) Ltd., **IV** 600

Le Tierce S.A., **II** 141

Tierco Group, Inc., **27** 382

Tierney & Partners, **23** 480

Tiffany & Co., **III** 16; **12** 312; **14** **500–03**; **15** 95; **19** 27; **26** 145; **27** 329; **41** 256

TIG Holdings, Inc., **26 486–88**

Tiger Accessories, **18** 88

Tiger International, Inc., **17** 505; **18** 178; **42** 141

Tiger Management Associates, **13** 158, 256

Tiger Oats, **I** 424

Tigon Corporation, **V** 265–68; **41** 288

Tilcon, **I** 429

Tilden Interrent, **10** 419

Tile & Coal Company, **14** 248

Tilgate Pallets, **I** 592

Tillie Lewis Foods Inc., **I** 513–14

Tillinghast, Nelson & Warren Inc., **32** 459

Tillotson Corp., **14** 64; **15 488–90**

Tim-Bar Corp., **IV** 312; **19** 267

Tim Horton's Restaurants, **23** 507; **47** 443. *See also* TDL Group Ltd.

Timber Lodge Steakhouse, Inc., **37** 351–52

Timber Realization Co., **IV** 305

The Timberland Company, **11** 349; **13** **511–14**; **17** 245; **19** 112; **22** 173; **25** 206

Timberline Software Corporation, **15** **491–93**

TIMCO. *See* Triad International Maintenance Corp.

Time Distribution Services, **13** 179

Time Electronics, **19** 311

Time Industries, **IV** 294; **19** 225; **26** 445

Time-Life Books, Inc. **44** 447, 449. *See also* Time Warner Inc.

Time Life Music, **44** 242

Time-O-Stat Controls Corp., **II** 41; **12** 247

Time Saver Stores, Inc., **12** 112; **17** 170

Time-Sharing Information, **10** 357

Time Warner Inc., **II** 155, 161, 168, 175–177, 252, 452; **III** 245; **IV** 341–42, 636, **673–76**; **6** 293; **7** 63, 222–24, 396, **526–30 (upd.)**; **8** 267–68, 527; **9** 119, 469, 472; **10** 168, 286, 484, 488, 491; **12** 531; **13** 105–06, 399; **14** 260; **15** 51, 54; **16** 146, 223; **17** 148, 442–44; **18** 66, 535; **19** 6, 336; **22** 52, 194, 522; **23** 31, 33, 257, 274, 276, 393; **24** 321–22; **25** 141, 498–99; **26** 33, 151, 441; **27** 121, 429–30; **43** 55

Timely Brands, **I** 259

Timeplex, **III** 166; **6** 283; **9** 32

Times Fiber Communications, Inc., **40** 35–36

Times Media Ltd., **IV** 22

The Times Mirror Company, **I** 90; **IV** 583, 630, **677–78**; **14** 97; **17 484–86 (upd.)**; **21** 404; **22** 162, 443; **26** 446; **35** 419

Times Newspapers, **8** 527

Times-Picayune Publishing Co., **IV** 583

TIMET. *See* Titanium Metals Corporation.

Timex Corporation, **25 479–82 (upd.)**

Timex Enterprises Inc., **III** 455; **7** **531–33**; **10** 152; **12** 317; **21** 123; **25** 22

The Timken Company, **III** 596; **7** 447; **8** **529–31**; **15** 225; **42 381–85 (upd.)**

Timothy Whites, **24** 74

Timpte Industries, **II** 488

Tioxide Group plc, **III** 680; **44** 117, 119

Tip Corp., **I** 278

Tip Top Drugstores plc, **24** 269

Tip Top Tailors, **29** 162

TIPC Network. *See* Gateway 2000.

Tiphook PLC, **13** 530

Tipton Centers Inc., **V** 50; **19** 123; **49** 112

Tiroler Hauptbank, **II** 270

Tiscali SpA, **48 396–99**

TISCO. *See* Tata Iron & Steel Company Ltd.

Tishman Realty and Construction, **III** 248

Tishman Speyer Properties, L.P., **47** **403–06**

Tissue Papers Ltd., **IV** 260

Tissue Technologies, Inc., **22** 409

The Titan Corporation, **36 475–78**; **45** 68, 70

Titan Manufacturing Company, **19** 359

Titanium Metals Corporation, **10** 434; **21** **489–92**

Titanium Technology Corporation, **13** 140

Titanium Enterprises, **IV** 345

TITISA, **9** 109
Title Guarantee & Trust Co., **II** 230
Titmus Optical Inc., **III** 446
Titmuss Sainer Dechert. *See* Dechert.
Tivoli Audio, **48** 85
Tivoli Systems, Inc., **14** 392
TJ International, Inc., 19 444–47
The TJX Companies, Inc., V 197–98; **13**
548; **14** 426; **19 448–50 (upd.)**; **29** 106
TKD Electronics Corp., **II** 109
TKM Foods, **II** 513
TKR Cable Co., **15** 264
TLC Associates, **11** 261
TLC Beatrice International Holdings,
Inc., 22 512–15
TLC Gift Company, **26** 375
TLC Group, **II** 468
TLO, **25** 82
TMB Industries, **24** 144
TMC Industries Ltd., **22** 352
TML Information Services Inc., **9** 95
TMP Worldwide Inc., 30 458–60
TMS, Inc., **7** 358
TMS Marketing, **26** 440
TMS Systems, Inc., **10** 18
TMT. *See* Trailer Marine Transport.
TMW Capital Inc., **48** 286
TN Technologies Inc., **23** 479
TNT Crust, Inc., **23** 203
TNT Freightways Corporation, IV 651;
14 504–06
TNT Limited, V 523–25; **6** 346
TNT Post Group N.V., 27 471–76 (upd.);
30 393, 461–63 (upd.)
Toa Airlines, **I** 106; **6** 427
Toa Fire & Marine Reinsurance Co., **III**
385
Toa Kyoseki Co. Ltd., **IV** 476
Toa Medical Electronics Ltd., **22** 75
Toa Nenryo Kogyo, **IV** 432
Toa Oil Co. Ltd., **IV** 476, 543
Toa Tanker Co. Ltd., **IV** 555
Toasted Corn Flake Co., **II** 523; **13** 291
Toastmaster, **17** 215; **22** 353
Tobacco Group PLC, **30** 231
Tobacco Products Corporation, **18** 416
Tobata Imaon Co., **I** 183
Tobias, **16** 239
Tobler Co., **II** 520–21
Tobu Railway Co Ltd, 6 430–32
TOC Retail Inc., **17** 170
Tocom, Inc., **10** 320
Today's Man, Inc., 20 484–87; **21** 311
Todays Computers Business Centers, **6**
243–44
Todays Temporary, **6** 140
The Todd-AO Corporation, 33 400–04.
See also Liberty Livewire Corporation.
Todd Shipyards Corporation, IV 121; **7**
138; **14 507–09**
Todhunter International, Inc., 27 477–79
Todito.com, S.A. de C.V., **39** 194, 196
Todorovich Agency, **III** 204
Toei Co. Ltd., **9** 29–30; **28** 462
Tofas, **I** 479–80
Toggenburger Bank, **II** 378
Togo's Eatery, **29** 19
Toho Co., Ltd., I 363; **IV** 403; **24** 327; **28**
461–63
Tohoku Alps, **II** 5
Tohoku Pulp Co., **IV** 297
Tohokushinsha Film Corporation, **18** 429
Tohuku Electric Power Company, Inc.,
V 724, 732

Tojo Railway Company, **6** 430
Tokai Aircraft Co., Ltd., **III** 415
The Tokai Bank, Limited, II 373–74; **15**
494–96 (upd.)
Tokai Kogyo Co. Ltd., **I** 615; **48** 42
Tokai Paper Industries, **IV** 679
Tokheim Corporation, 21 493–95
Tokio Marine and Fire Insurance Co.,
Ltd., II 323; **III** 248, 289, 295, **383–86**
Tokos Medical Corporation, **17** 306,
308–09
Tokushima Ham Co., **II** 550
Tokushima Meat Processing Factory, **II**
550
Tokushu Seiko, Ltd., **IV** 63
Tokuyama Soda, **I** 509
Tokuyama Teppan Kabushikigaisha, **IV**
159
Tokyo Broadcasting System, **7** 249; **9** 29;
16 167
Tokyo Car Manufacturing Co., **I** 105
Tokyo City Finance, **36** 419–20
Tokyo Confectionery Co., **II** 538
Tokyo Corporation, **V** 199
Tokyo Dairy Industry, **II** 538
Tokyo Denki Kogaku Kogyo, **II** 109
Tokyo Dento Company, **6** 430
Tokyo Disneyland, **IV** 715; **6** 123, 176
Tokyo Electric Company, Ltd., **I** 533; **12**
483
Tokyo Electric Express Railway Co., **IV**
728
Tokyo Electric Light Co., **IV** 153
Tokyo Electric Power Company, IV 167,
518; **V 729–33**
Tokyo Electronic Corp., **11** 232
Tokyo Express Highway Co., Ltd., **IV**
713–14
Tokyo Express Railway Company, **V** 510,
526
Tokyo Fire Insurance Co. Ltd., **III** 405–06,
408
Tokyo Food Products, **I** 507
Tokyo Fuhansen Co., **I** 502, 506
Tokyo Gas and Electric Industrial
Company, **9** 293
Tokyo Gas Co., Ltd., IV 518; **V 734–36**
Tokyo Ishikawajima Shipbuilding and
Engineering Company, **III** 532; **9** 293
Tokyo Maritime Insurance Co., **III** 288
Tokyo Motors. *See* Isuzu Motors, Ltd.
Tokyo Sanyo Electric, **II** 91–92
Tokyo Shibaura Electric Company, Ltd., **I**
507, 533; **12** 483
Tokyo Steel Works Co., Ltd., **IV** 63
Tokyo Stock Exchange, **34** 254
Tokyo Tanker Co., Ltd., **IV** 479
Tokyo Telecommunications Engineering
Corp. *See* Tokyo Tsushin Kogyo K.K.
Tokyo Trust & Banking Co., **II** 328
Tokyo Tsushin Kogyo K.K., **II** 101, 103
Tokyo Yokohama Electric Railways Co.,
Ltd., **V** 199
Tokyu Corporation, IV 728; **V** 199,
526–28; **47 407–10 (upd.)**
Tokyu Department Store Co., Ltd., V
199–202; **32 453–57 (upd.)**
Toledo Edison Company. *See* Centerior
Energy Corporation.
Toledo Milk Processing, Inc., **15** 449
Toledo Scale Corp., **9** 441; **30** 327
Toledo Seed & Oil Co., **I** 419
Toll Brothers Inc., 15 497–99

Tollgrade Communications, Inc., 44
424–27
Tom Bowling Lamp Works, **III** 554
Tom Brown, Inc., 37 389–91
Tom Doherty Associates Inc., 25 483–86
Tom Huston Peanut Co., **II** 502; **10** 323
Tom Piper Ltd., **I** 437
Tom Snyder Productions, **29** 470, 472
Tom Thumb, **40** 365–66
Tom Thumb-Page, **16** 64
Tom's of Maine, Inc., 45 414–16
Tomakomai Paper Co., Ltd., **IV** 321
Toman Corporation, **19** 390
Tombstone Pizza Corporation, 13
515–17
Tomei Fire and Marine Insurance Co., **III**
384–85
Tomen Corporation, IV 224–25; **19** 256;
24 488–91 (upd.)
Tomen Transportgerate, **III** 638
Tomkins-Johnson Company, **16** 8
Tomkins plc, 11 525–27; **28** 382, 384; **30**
424, 426; **44 428–31 (upd.)**
Tomlee Tool Company, **7** 535; **26** 493
Tommy Armour Golf Co., **32** 446–47
Tommy Hilfiger Corporation, 16 61; **20**
488–90; **25** 258
Tomoe Trading Co., **III** 595
Tonami Transportation Company, **6** 346
Tone Brothers, Inc., 21 496–98
Tone Coca-Cola Bottling Company, Ltd.,
14 288; **47** 206
Tonen Corporation, IV 554–56; **16**
489–92 (upd.)
Tong Yang Group, **III** 304
Toni Co., **III** 28; **9** 413
Tonka Corporation, 12 169; **14** 266; **16**
267; **25** 380, **487–89**; **43** 229, 232
Tonkin, Inc., **19** 114
Tony Lama Company Inc., **19** 233
Tony Roma's, A Place for Ribs Inc., 40
340–41
Tony Stone Images, **31** 216–17
Toohey, **10** 170
Toolex International N.V., 26 489–91
Tootal Group, **V** 356–57
Tootsie Roll Industries Inc., 12 480–82;
15 323
Top End Wheelchair Sports, **11** 202
Top Green International, **17** 475
Top Man, **V** 21
Top Shop, **V** 21
Top Tool Company, Inc., **25** 75
Top Value Stamp Co., **II** 644–45; **6** 364;
22 126
Topco Associates, **17** 78
Topkapi, **17** 101–03
Toppan Printing Co., Ltd., IV 598–99,
679–81
Topps Company, Inc., 13 518–20; **19**
386; **34 446–49 (upd.)**
Topps Markets, **16** 314
Tops Appliance City, Inc., 17 487–89
TopTip, **48** 116
Topy Industries, Limited, **8** 506–07
Tor Books. *See* Tom Doherty Associates
Inc.
Toray Industries, Inc., V 380, 383; **17**
287
Torbensen Gear & Axle Co., **I** 154
Torchmark Corporation, III 194; **9**
506–08; **10** 66; **11** 17; **22** 540–43; **33**
405–08 (upd.)
Torfeaco Industries Limited, **19** 304

Torise Ham Co., **II** 550
Tornator Osakeyhtiö, **IV** 275–76
Toro Assicurazioni, **III** 347
The Toro Company, **III** 600; **7 534–36**; **26 492–95 (upd.)**
Toromont Industries, Ltd., 21 499–501
Toronto and Scarborough Electric Railway, **9** 461
The Toronto-Dominion Bank, **II** 319, **375–77**, 456; **16** 13–14; **17** 324; **18** 551–53; **21** 447; **43** 7; **49 395–99 (upd.)**
Toronto Electric Light Company, **9** 461
Toronto Sun Publishing Company. *See* Sun Media.
Torpshammars, **IV** 338
Torrey Canyon Oil, **IV** 569; **24** 519
The Torrington Company, **III** 526, 589–90; **13 521–24**
Torrington National Bank & Trust Co., **13** 467
Torstar Corporation, **IV** 672; **7** 488–89; **19** 405; **29 470–73**
Tosa Electric Railway Co., **II** 458
Toscany Co., **13** 42
Tosco Corporation, **7 537–39**; **12** 240; **20** 138; **24** 522; **36** 359; **40** 358
Toshiba Corporation, **I** 221, 507–08, **533–35**; **II** 5, 56, 59, 62, 68, 73, 99, 102, 118, 122, 326, 440; **III** 298, 461, 533, 604; **6** 101, 231, 244, 287; **7** 529; **9** 7, 181; **10** 518–19; **11** 46, 328; **12** 454, **483–86 (upd.)**, 546; **13** 324, 399, 482; **14** 117, 446; **16** 5, 167; **17** 533; **18** 18, 260; **21** 390; **22** 193, 373; **23** 471; **40 435–40 (upd.)**; **43** 15;
Toshiba Corporation, **47** 153–54
Toshin Kaihatsu Ltd., **V** 195; **47** 390
Toshin Paper Co., Ltd., **IV** 285
Tostem. *See* Toyo Sash Co., Ltd.
Total Audio Visual Services, **24** 95
Total Beverage Corporation, **16** 159, 161
Total Compagnie Française des Pétroles S.A., **I** 303; **II** 259; **III** 673; **IV** 363–64, 423–25, 466, 486, 498, 504, 515, 525, 544–47, **557–61**; **V** 628; **7** 481–84; **13** 557; **21** 203
Total Entertainment Restaurant Corporation, 46 427–29
Total Exploration S.A., **11** 537
Total Fina Elf S.A., **47** 342, 365, 368
Total Global Sourcing, Inc., **10** 498
Total Home Entertainment (THE), **39** 240, 242
Total Petroleum Corporation, **21** 500
TOTAL S.A., 24 492–97 (upd.), 522; **25** 104; **26** 369
Total System Services, Inc., **12** 465–66; **18** 168, 170, **516–18**
Totem Resources Corporation, 9 509–11
Totino's Finer Foods, **II** 556; **13** 516; **26** 436
Toto Bank, **II** 326
TOTO LTD., III 755–56; **28 464–66 (upd.)**
Totsu Co., **I** 493; **24** 325
Touch America Inc., **37** 127; **44** 288
Touch-It Corp., **22** 413
Touche Remnant Holdings Ltd., **II** 356
Touche Ross. *See* Deloitte Touche Tohmatsu International.
Touchstone Films, **II** 172–74; **6** 174–76; **30** 487
Le Touquet's, SA, **48** 197

Tour d'Argent, **II** 518
Tourang Limited, **7** 253
Touristik Union International GmbH. and Company K.G., **II** 163–65; **46** 460
Touron y Cia, **III** 419
Touropa, **II** 163–64; **44** 432
Toval Japon, **IV** 680
Towa Nenryo Kogyo Co. Ltd., **IV** 554–55
Towa Optical Manufacturing Company, **41** 261–63
Tower Air, Inc., 28 467–69
Tower Automotive, Inc., 24 498–500
Tower Records, **9** 361; **10** 335; **11** 558; **30** 224. *See also* MTS Inc.
Towers, **II** 649
Towers Perrin, 32 458–60
Towle Manufacturing Co., **14** 482–83; **18** 69
Town & City, **IV** 696
Town & Country Corporation, **7** 372; **16** 546; **19 451–53**; **25** 254
Town Investments, **IV** 711
Town Sports International, Inc., 46 430–33
Townsend Hook, **IV** 296, 650, 652; **19** 226
Toxicol Laboratories, Ltd., **21** 424
Toy Biz, Inc., **10** 402; **18 519–21**
Toy Liquidators, **13** 541–43
Toy Park, **16** 390
Toyad Corp., **7** 296
Toymax International, Inc., 29 474–76
Toyo Bearing Manufacturing, **III** 595
Toyo Cotton Co., **IV** 224–25
Toyo Ink Manufacturing, **26** 213
Toyo Kogyo, **I** 167; **II** 361; **11** 139
Toyo Marine and Fire, **III** 385
Toyo Menka Kaisha Ltd. *See* Tomen Corporation.
Toyo Microsystems Corporation, **11** 464
Toyo Oil Co., **IV** 403
Toyo Pulp Co., **IV** 322
Toyo Rayon, **V** 381, 383
Toyo Sash Co., Ltd., III 757–58
Toyo Seikan Kaisha Ltd., I 615–16
Toyo Soda, **II** 301
Toyo Tire & Rubber Co., **V** 255–56; **9** 248
Toyo Toki Co., Ltd., **III** 755
Toyo Tozo Co., **I** 265; **21** 319
Toyo Trust and Banking Co., **II** 347, 371; **17** 349
Toyoda Automatic Loom Works, Ltd., I 203; **III** 591, 593, 632, **636–39**
Toyokawa Works, **I** 579
Toyoko Co., Ltd., **V** 199
Toyoko Kogyo, **V** 199
Toyomenka (America) Inc., **IV** 224
Toyomenka (Australia) Pty., Ltd., **IV** 224
Toyota Gossei, **I** 321
Toyota Industrial Equipment, **27** 294, 296
Toyota Motor Corporation, **I** 9–10, 174, 184, **203–05**, 507–08, 587; **II** 373; **III** 415, 495, 521, 523, 536, 579, 581, 591–93, 624, 636–38, 667, 715, 742; **IV** 702; **6** 514; **7** 111, 118, 212, 219–21; **8** 315; **9** 294, 340–42; **10** 353, 407; **11** 351, 377, 487, **528–31 (upd.)**; **14** 321; **15** 495; **21** 162, 273; **23** 289–90, 338–40; **25** 198; **34** 303, 305–06; **38 458–62 (upd.)**
Toyota Tsusho America, Inc., **13** 371
Toys 'R' Us, Inc., **III** 588; **V 203–06**; **7** 396; **10** 235, 284, 484; **12** 178; **13** 166; **14** 61; **15** 469; **16** 389–90, 457; **18**

522–25 (upd.); **24** 412; **25** 314; **31** 477–78; **37** 129; **43** 385
Tozer Kemsley & Milbourn, **II** 208
TP Transportation, **39** 377
TPA. *See* Aloha Airlines Incorporated.
TPCR Corporation, **V** 163; **14** 394
TPG. *See* TNT Post Group N.V.
Trac Inc., **44** 355
Trace International Holdings, Inc., **17** 182–83; **26** 502
Tracey Bros., **IV** 416
Tracey-Locke, **II** 660
Tracinda Corporation, **25** 329–30
Tracker Marine. *See* Bass Pro Shops, Inc.
Tracker Services, Inc., **9** 110
Traco International N.V., **8** 250; **32** 249
Tracor Inc., **10** 547; **17 490–92**; **26** 267
Tractebel S.A., 20 491–93. *See also* Suez Lyonnaise des Eaux.
Tractor Supply Corp., **I** 446
Tradax, **II** 617; **13** 137
Trade Assoc. of Bilbao, **II** 194
Trade Development Bank, **11** 415–17
Trade Source International, **44** 132
Trade Waste Incineration, Inc., **9** 109
Trade Winds Campers, **III** 599
TradeARBED, **IV** 25
Trader Joe's Co., **13 525–27**; **41** 422
Trader Publications, Inc., **IV** 597
Trader Publishing Company, **12** 302
Traders & General Insurance, **III** 248
Traders Bank of Canada, **II** 344
Traders Group Ltd., **11** 258
Tradesmens National Bank of Philadelphia, **II** 342
The Trading Service, **10** 278
Traex Corporation, **8** 359
Trafalgar House Investments Ltd., **I** 248–49, 572–74; **IV** 259, 711; **20** 313; **23** 161; **24** 88; **36** 322
Trafalgar House PLC, **47** 178
Trafiroad NV, **39** 239
Trailer Bridge, Inc., 41 397–99
Trailer Marine Transport, **6** 383
Trailways Lines, Inc., **I** 450; **9** 425; **32** 230
Trak Auto Corporation, **16** 159–62
TRAK Communications Inc., **44** 420
TRAK Microwave Corporation, **18** 497, 513
Trammell Crow Company, **IV** 343; **8** 326–28, **532–34**; **49** 147–48
Tran Telecommunications Corp., **III** 110; **14** 14
Trane Company, **III** 663, 665; **10** 525; **21** 107; **22** 6; **26** 4; **30** 46, 48–49
Trans Air System, **6** 367; **27** 90
Trans-Arabian Pipe Line Co., **IV** 537, 552
Trans-Australia Airlines, **6** 110–12
Trans-Canada Air Lines. *See* Air Canada.
Trans Colorado, **11** 299
Trans-Continental Leaf Tobacco Company, (TCLTC), **13** 491
Trans Freight Lines, **27** 473–74
Trans International Airlines, **I** 537; **13** 529; **41** 402
Trans Louisiana Gas Company, **43** 56–57
Trans-Mex, Inc. S.A. de C.V., **42** 365
Trans-Natal Coal Corp., **IV** 93
Trans Ocean Products, **II** 578; **8** 510
Trans-Pacific Airlines, **22** 251. *See also* Aloha Airlines Incorporated.
Trans Rent-A-Car, **6** 348
Trans-Resources Inc., **13** 299
Trans Union Corp., **IV** 137; **6** 25; **28** 119

Trans Western Publishing, **25** 496
Trans World Airlines, Inc., **I** 58, 70, 90, 97, 99–100, 102, 113, 121, 123–24, **125–27**, 132, 466; **II** 32–33, 142, 425, 679; **III** 92, 428; **6** 50, 68, 71, 74, 76–77, 81–82, 114, 130; **9** 17, 232; **10** 301–03, 316; **11** 277, 427; **12** 381, **487–90 (upd.)**; **13** 341; **14** 73; **15** 419; **21** 141–42; **22** 22, 219; **26** 439; **29** 190; **35 424–29 (upd.)**
Trans-World Corp., **19** 456; **47** 231
Trans World Entertainment Corporation, **24 501–03**
Trans World International, **18** 262–63
Trans World Life Insurance Company, **27** 46–47
Trans World Music, **9** 361
Trans World Seafood, Inc., **13** 244
Transaction Systems Architects, Inc., **29 477–79**
Transaction Technology, **12** 334
TransAlta Utilities Corporation, **6 585–87**
Transamerica—An AEGON Company, **41 400–03 (upd.)**
Transamerica Corporation, **I 536–38**; **II** 147–48, 227, 288–89, 422; **III** 332, 344; **7** 236–37; **8** 46; **11** 273, 533; **13 528–30 (upd.)**; **21** 285; **25** 328; **27** 230; **46** 48. See also TIG Holdings, Inc.
Transamerica Pawn Holdings. See EZCORP Inc.
TransAmerican Waste Industries Inc., **41** 414
Transat. See Compagnie Générale Transatlantique (Transat).
Transatlantic Holdings, Inc., **III** 198; **11 532–33**; **15** 18
Transatlantische Dampfschiffahrts Gesellschaft, **6** 397
Transatlantische Gruppe, **III** 404
TransBrasil S/A Linhas Aéreas, **6** 134; **29** 495; **31 443–45**; **46** 398
TransCanada PipeLines Limited, **I** 264; **V** 270–71, **737–38**; **17** 22–23
Transco Energy Company, **IV** 367; **V** 739–40; **6** 143; **18** 366
Transcontinental Air Transport, **I** 125; **9** 17; **11** 427; **12** 487
Transcontinental and Western Air Lines, **9** 416; **12** 487
Transcontinental Gas Pipe Line Corporation, **V** 739; **6** 447
Transcontinental Pipeline Company, **6** 456–57
Transcontinental Services Group N.V., **16** 207
TransCor America, Inc., **23** 154
Transelco, Inc., **8** 178
TransEuropa, **II** 164
Transfer Drivers, Inc., **46** 301
Transflash, **6** 404; **26** 243
Transfracht, **6** 426
Transiciel SA, **48 400–02**
Transinternational Life, **II** 422
Transit Homes of America, Inc., **46** 301
Transit Mix Concrete and Materials Company, **7** 541
Transitions Optical Inc., **21** 221, 223
Transitron, **16** 332
Transking Inc. See King Kullen Grocery Co., Inc.
Transkrit Corp., **IV** 640; **26** 273
Translite, **III** 495

Transmanche-Link, **13** 206–08; **37** 135
Transmedia Network Inc., **20 494–97**
Transmedica International, Inc., **41** 225
Transmisiones y Equipos Mecanicos, S.A. de C.V., **23** 171
Transmitter Equipment Manufacturing Co., **13** 385
TransMontaigne Inc., **28 470–72**
Transmontane Rod and Gun Club, **43** 435–36
Transnet Ltd., **6 433–35**
TransOcean Oil, **III** 559
Transocean Sedco Forex Inc., **45 417–19**
Transpac, **IV** 325
Transport Corporation of America, Inc., **49 400–03**
Transport Management Co., **III** 192
Transport- und Unfall-Versicherungs-Aktiengesellschaft Zürich, **III** 411
Transportacion Maritima Mexicana S.A. de C.V., **12** 279; **26** 236; **47** 162
Transportation Insurance Co., **III** 229
Transportation.com, **45** 451
Transportes Aéreas Centro-Americanos. See Grupo TACA.
Transportes Aereos Portugueses, S.A., **6 125–27**. See also TAP—Air Portugal Transportes Aéreos Portugueses S.A.
Transportes Aeromar, **39** 188
Transrack S.A., **26** 363
Transtar, **6** 120–21; **24** 454
Transue & Williams Steel Forging Corp., **13** 302
Transvaal Silver and Base Metals, **IV** 90
Transway International Corp., **10** 369
Transworld Communications, **35** 165
Transworld Corp., **14** 209
Transworld Drilling Company Limited. See Kerr-McGee Corporation.
The Tranzonic Companies, **8** 512; **15 500–02**; **37 392–95**
Trapper's, **19** 286
Trasgo, S.A. de C.V., **14** 516
Trausch Baking Co., **I** 255
Trävaru Svartvik, **IV** 338
Travel Air Manufacturing Company, **8** 49; **27** 97
Travel Automation Services Ltd., **I** 95
Travel Inc., **26** 309
Travel Information Group, **17** 398
Travel Ports of America, Inc., **17 493–95**
Travelers Bank & Trust Company, **13** 467
Travelers Book Club, **13** 105
Travelers Corporation, **I** 37, 545; **III** 313, 329, **387–90**, 707–08; **6** 12; **15** 463 124. See also Citigroup Inc.
Travelers/Aetna Property Casualty Corp., **21** 15
Traveller's Express, **I** 449
Travelocity.com, Inc., **46 434–37**
TraveLodge, **III** 94, 104–06
Travenol Laboratories, **I** 627–28; **10** 141–43
Travers Morgan Ltd., **42** 183
Travis Boats & Motors, Inc., **37 396–98**
Travis Perkins plc, **34 450–52**
Travocéan, **25** 104
Trayco, **III** 570; **20** 362
Traylor Engineering & Manufacturing Company, **6** 395; **25** 169
TRC. See Tennessee Restaurant Company.
TRC Companies, Inc., **32 461–64**
TRE Corp., **23** 225
Treadco, Inc., **16** 39; **19** 38, **454–56**

Treasure Chest Advertising Company, Inc., **21** 60; **32 465–67**
Treasure House Stores, Inc., **17** 322
Treatment Centers of America, **11** 379
Trebuhs Realty Co., **24** 438
Trechmann, Weekes and Co., **III** 669
Tredegar Industries, Inc., **10** 291
Tree of Life, Inc., **II** 528; **29 480–82**
Tree Sweet Products Corp., **12** 105; **26** 325
Tree Tavern, Inc., **27** 197
TrefilARBED, **IV** 26
Tréfimétaux, **IV** 174
Trefoil Capital Investors, L.P., **8** 305
Trek, **IV** 90, 92–93
Trek Bicycle Corporation, **16 493–95**; **19** 384–85
Trelleborg A.B., **III** 625; **IV** 166
Tremec. See Transmisiones y Equipos Mecanicos, S.A. de C.V.
Tremletts Ltd., **IV** 294; **19** 225
Tremont Corporation, **21** 490
Trencherwood Plc, **45** 443
Trend International Ltd., **13** 502
Trend-Lines, Inc., **22 516–18**
Trends Magazine NV, **48** 347
Trendwest Resorts, Inc., **12** 439; **33 409–11**. See also Jeld-Wen, Inc.
Trent Tube, **I** 435
Trenton Foods, **II** 488
TrentonWorks Limited. See The Greenbrier Companies.
Tresco, **8** 514
Trethowal China Clay Co., **III** 690
Tri-City Federal Savings and Loan Association, **10** 92
Tri-City Utilities Company, **6** 514
Tri-County National Bank, **9** 474
Tri-Marine International Inc., **24** 116
Tri-Miller Packing Company, **7** 524
Tri-Sonics, Inc., **16** 202; **43** 170
Tri-State Improvement Company, **6** 465–66
Tri-State Publishing & Communications, Inc., **22** 442
Tri-State Recycling Corporation, **15** 117
Tri-State Refining Co., **IV** 372
Tri-Union Seafoods LLC, **24** 116
Tri Valley Growers, **32 468–71**
Triad, **14** 224
Triad Artists Inc., **23** 514
Triad International Maintenance Corp., **13** 417
Triad Nitrogen, Inc., **27** 316, 318
Triad Systems Corp., **38** 96
Triangle Auto Springs Co., **IV** 136
The Triangle Group, **16** 357
Triangle Industries Inc., **I** 602, 607–08, 614; **II** 480–81; **14** 43
Triangle Manufacturing, **26** 57
Triangle Portfolio Associates, **II** 317
Triangle Publications, Inc., **IV** 652; **7** 391; **12** 359–60
Triangle Refineries, **IV** 446; **22** 302
Triangle Sheet Metal Works, Inc., **45** 327
Triarc Companies, Inc., **8 535–37**; **13** 322; **14** 32–33; **34 453–57 (upd.)**; **39** 383, 385
Triathlon Leasing, **II** 457
Tribe Computer Works. See Zoom Telephonics.
Tribune Company, **III** 329; **IV 682–84**; **10** 56; **11** 331; **22 519–23 (upd.)**; **26** 17; **32** 358–59; **38** 306; **42** 133
Trical Resources, **IV** 84

Tricity Cookers, **I** 531–32
Trick & Murray, **22** 153
Trico Products Corporation, **I** 186; **15 503–05**
Tricon Global Restaurants, Inc., **21** 313, 317, 405, 407, 485; **40** 342
Tridel Enterprises Inc., **9 512–13**
Trident NGL Holdings Inc., **18** 365, 367
Trident Seafoods, **II** 494
Trifari, Krussman & Fishel, Inc., **9** 157
Trigen Energy Corporation, **6** 512; **42 386–89**
Trigon Industries, **13** 195; **14** 431
Trilan Developments Ltd., **9** 512
Trilogy Fabrics, Inc., **16** 125
Trilon Financial Corporation, **II 456–57**; **IV** 721; **9** 391
Trimac Ltd., **25** 64
TriMas Corp., **III** 571; **11 534–36**; **20** 359, 362; **39** 266
Trimble Navigation Limited, **40 441–43**
Trimel Corp., **47** 54
Trinidad and Tobago External Telecommunications Company, **25** 100
Trinidad Oil Co., **IV** 95, 552
Trinidad-Tesoro Petroleum Company Limited, **7** 516, 518
Trinity Beverage Corporation, **11** 451
Trinity Broadcasting, **13** 279
Trinity Capital Opportunity Corp., **17** 13
Trinity Distributors, **15** 139
Trinity Industries, Incorporated, **7 540–41**
Trinity Mirror plc, **49 404–10 (upd.)**
Trinkaus und Burkhardt, **II** 319; **17** 324
TRINOVA Corporation, **III 640–42**, 731; **13** 8; **16** 7, 9
Trintex, **6** 158
Triology Corp., **III** 110
Triple Five Group Ltd., **49 411–15**
Triple P N.V., **26 496–99**
Triplex, **6** 279
Triplex (Northern) Ltd., **III** 725
Trippe Manufacturing Co., **10** 474; **24** 29
Triquet Paper Co., **IV** 282; **9** 261
TriStar Pictures, **I** 234; **II** 134, 136–37; **6** 158; **10** 227; **12** 75, 455; **23** 275; **28** 462; **32** 114. *See also* Columbia TriStar Motion Pictures Companies.
Triton Bioscience, **III** 53; **26** 384
Triton Cellular Partners, L.P., **43** 341
Triton Energy Corporation, **11 537–39**
Triton Group Ltd., **I** 447; **31** 287; **34** 339
Triton Oil, **IV** 519
Triton Systems Corp., **22** 186
Triumph-Adler, **I** 485; **III** 145; **11** 265. *See also* TA Triumph-Adler AG.
Triumph American, Inc., **12** 199
Triumph Films, **25** 174
Triumph, Finlay, and Philips Petroleum, **11** 28
Triumph Group, Inc., **21** 153; **31 446–48**
Trivest, Inc., **II** 457; **21** 531–32
Trizec Corporation Ltd., **9** 84–85; **10 529–32**
TrizecHahn, **37** 311
TRM Copy Centers Corporation, **18 526–28**
Trojan, **III** 674
Troll, **13** 561
Trolley Barn Brewery Inc., **25** 401
Trona Corp., **IV** 95
Tropical Marine Centre, **40** 128–29
Tropical Oil Co., **IV** 415–16

Tropical Shipping, Inc., **6** 529, 531
Tropical Sportswear Int'l Corporation, **42** 120
Tropicana Products, Inc., **II** 468, 525; **13** 293; **25** 366; **28** 271, **473–77**; **38** 349; **45** 160–62
Trotter, Inc., **49** 108
Trotter-Yoder & Associates, **22** 88
Troxel Cycling, **16** 53
Troy & Nichols, Inc., **13** 147
Troy Metal Products. *See* KitchenAid.
Troyfel Ltd., **III** 699
TRT Communications, Inc., **6** 327; **11** 185
Tru-Run Inc., **16** 207
Tru-Stitch, **16** 545
Tru-Trac Therapy Products, **11** 486
Truck Components Inc., **23** 306
Trudeau Marketing Group, Inc., **22** 386
True Form Boot Co., **V** 177
True North Communications Inc., **23 478–80**; **25** 91
True Temper Hardware Co., **30** 241–42
True Value Hardware Stores, **V** 37–38; **30** 168. *See also* TruServ Corporation.
Trugg-Hansa Holding AB, **III** 264
TruGreen, **23** 428, 430
Truitt Bros., **10** 382
Truman Dunham Co., **III** 744
Truman Hanburg, **I** 247
Trumball Asphalt, **III** 721
Trümmer-Verwertungs-Gesellschaft, **IV** 140
Trump Organization, **16** 262; **23 481–84**; **43** 225
Trunkline Gas Company, **6** 544; **14** 135
Trunkline LNG Co., **IV** 425
Trus Joist Corporation. *See* TJ International, Inc.
TruServ Corporation, **24 504–07**
Trussdeck Corporation. *See* TJ International, Inc.
Trust Company of the West, **19** 414; **42** 347
Trustcorp, Inc., **9** 475–76
Trusted Information Systems, Inc., **25** 349
Trustees, Executors and Agency Co. Ltd., **II** 189
Trusthouse Forte PLC, **I** 215; **III 104–06**; **16** 446
TRW Inc., **I 539–41**; **II** 33; **6** 25; **8** 416; **9** 18, 359; **10** 293; **11** 68, **540–42 (upd.)**; **12** 238; **14 510–13 (upd.)**; **16** 484; **17** 372; **18** 275; **19** 184; **23** 134; **24** 480; **26** 141; **28** 119; **32** 437; **33** 47; **34** 76; **43** 311, 313; **45** 152
TRW Vehicle Safety Systems Inc., **41** 369
Tryart Pty. Limited, **7** 253
TSA. *See* Transaction Systems Architects, Inc.
Tsai Management & Research Corp., **III** 230–31
TSB Group plc, **12 491–93**; **16** 14
TSI Inc., **38** 206
TSI Soccer Corporation, **29** 142–43
Tsingtao Brewery Group, **49 416–20**
TSMC. *See* Taiwan Semiconductor Manufacturing Company Ltd.
TSO. *See* Teacher's Service Organization, Inc.
TSO Financial Corp., **II** 420; **8** 10
Tsogo Sun Gaming & Entertainment, **17** 318
TSP. *See* Tom Snyder Productions.
TSR Inc., **24** 538

Tsuang Hine Co., **III** 582
Tsubakimoto-Morse, **14** 64
Tsukumo Shokai, **I** 502; **III** 712
Tsumeb Corp., **IV** 17–18
Tsurumi Steelmaking and Shipbuilding Co., **IV** 162
Tsurusaki Pulp Co., Ltd., **IV** 285
Tsutsunaka Plastic Industry Co., **III** 714; **8** 359
TSYS. *See* Total System Services, Inc.
TTK. *See* Tokyo Tsushin Kogyo K.K.
TTX Company, **6 436–37**
Tube Fab Ltd., **17** 234
Tube Forming, Inc., **23** 517
Tube Investments, **II** 422; **IV** 15
Tube Reducing Corp., **16** 321
Tube Service Co., **19** 344
Tubed Chemicals Corporation, **27** 299
Tuborg, **9** 99
Tubos de Acero de Mexico, S.A. (TAMSA), **41 404–06**
Tuboscope, **42** 420
Tucker, Lynch & Coldwell. *See* CB Commercial Real Estate Services Group, Inc.
TUCO, Inc., **8** 78
Tucson Electric Power Company, **V** 713; **6 588–91**; **42** 388
Tucson Gas & Electric, **19** 411–12
Tuesday Morning Corporation, **18 529–31**
Tuff Stuff Publications, **23** 101
TUI. *See* Touristik Union International GmbH. and Company K.G.
TUI Group GmbH, **42** 283; **44 432–35**
Tuileries et Briqueteries d'Hennuyeres et de Wanlin, **14** 249
TUJA, **27** 21
Tultex Corporation, **13 531–33**
Tumbleweed, Inc., **33 412–14**
Tunhems Industri A.B., **I** 387
Tunisair. *See* Société Tunisienne de l'Air-Tunisair.
Tupolev Aviation and Scientific Technical Complex, **24 58–60**
Tupperware Corporation, **I** 29; **II** 534; **III** 610–12;, **15** 475, 477; **17** 186; **18** 67; **28 478–81**
Turbinbolaget, **III** 419
Turbine Engine Asset Management LLC, **28** 5
TurboLinux Inc., **45** 363
Turcot Paperboard Mills Ltd., **17** 281
Turkish Engineering, Consultancy and Contracting Corp., **IV** 563
Turkish Petroleum Co. *See* Türkiye Petrolleri Anonim Ortakliği.
Türkiye Garanti Bankasi, **I** 479
Türkiye Petrolleri Anonim Ortakliği, **IV** 464, 557–58, **562–64**; **7** 352
Turnbull, **III** 468
Turner Broadcasting System, Inc., **II** 134, 149, 161 **166–68**; **IV** 676; **6 171–73 (upd.)**; **7** 64, 99, 306, 529; **23** 33, 257; **25** 313, 329, 498; **28** 71; **30** 100; **47** 272
The Turner Corporation, **8 538–40**; **23 485–88 (upd.)**; **25** 402; **33** 197
Turner Entertainment Co., **18** 459
Turner Glass Company, **13** 40
Turner Network Television, **21** 24
Turner's Turkeys, **II** 587
Turnstone Systems, **44** 426
TURPAS, **IV** 563

Turtle Wax, Inc., 15 506–09; 16 43; 26 349

Tuscarora Inc., 17 155; 29 483–85

Tussauds Group Ltd., IV 659

Tutt Bryant Industries PLY Ltd., 26 231

Tuttle, Oglebay and Company. *See* Oglebay Norton Company.

TV & Stereo Town, 10 468

TV Asahi, 7 249

TV Azteca, S.A. de C.V., 39 194–95, **398–401**

TV Food Network, 22 522

TV Guide, Inc., 43 431–34 (upd.)

TVA. *See* Tennessee Valley Authority.

TVE. *See* Television Española, S.A.

TVE Holdings, 22 307

TVH Acquisition Corp., III 262, 264

TVI, Inc., 15 510–12

TVN Entertainment Corporation, 32 239

TVS Entertainment PLC, 13 281

TVW Enterprises, 7 78

TVX, II 449; 13 449

TW Kutter, III 420

TW Services, Inc., II 679–80; 10 301–03

TWA. *See* Trans World Airlines *and* Transcontinental & Western Airways.

Tweco Co., 19 441

Tweeds, 12 280

Tweeter Home Entertainment Group, Inc., 30 464–66; 41 379, 381

Twen-Tours International, II 164

Twentieth Century Fox Film Corporation, II 133, 135, 146, 155–56, **169–71**, 175; IV 652; 7 391–92; 12 73, 322, 359; 15 23, 25, 234; 25 327, **490–94 (upd.); 43** 173; **46** 311

Twentsche Bank, II 183

"21" International Holdings, 17 182

21 Invest International Holdings Ltd., 14 322

21st Century Food Products. *See* Hain Food Group, Inc.

21st Century Mortgage, 18 28

Twenty-Second National Bank, II 291

Twenty-third Publications, 49 48

24/7 Real Media, Inc., 49 421–24

TWI. *See* Trans World International.

Twin City Wholesale Drug Company, 14 147

Twin Disc, Inc., 21 502–04

Twin Hill Acquisition Company, Inc., 48 286

Twining Crosfield Group, II 465; 13 52

Twinings' Foods International, II 465–66; III 696

Twinings Tea, 41 31

Twinlab Corporation, 34 458–61

Twinpak, IV 250

Two Guys, 12 49

2-in-1 Shinola Bixby Corp., II 497

21st Century Mortgage, 41 18, 20

TWW Plc, 26 62

TXEN, Inc., 18 370

TXL Oil Corp., IV 552

TXP Operation Co., IV 367

TxPort Inc., 13 8

Ty-D-Bol, III 55

Ty Inc., 33 415–17

Tyco International Ltd., 21 462; **28 482–87 (upd.); 30** 157; **44** 6

Tyco Laboratories, Inc., III 643–46; 13 245–47

Tyco Submarine Systems Ltd., 32 217

Tyco Toys, Inc., 12 494–97; 13 312, 319; **18** 520–21; **25** 314

Tyler Corporation, 23 489–91

Tymnet, 18 542

Tyndall Fund-Unit Assurance Co., III 273

Typhoo Tea, II 477

Typpi Oy, IV 469

Tyrolean Airways, 9 233; 33 50

Tyrväan Oy, IV 348

Tyskie Brewery, 24 450

Tyson Foods, Inc., II 584–85; 7 422–23, 432; **14 514–16 (upd.); 21** 535; **23** 376, 384; **26** 168; **39** 229

U.C.L.A.F. *See* Roussel-Uclaf.

U-Haul International Inc. *See* Amerco.

U.K. Corrugated, IV 296; 19 226

U.S. Aggregates, Inc., 42 390–92

U.S. Appliances, 26 336

U.S. Bancorp, 12 165; **14 527–29; 36 489–95 (upd.)**

U.S. Bank of Washington, 14 527

U.S. Banknote Company, 30 43

U.S. Bearings Company. *See* Federal-Mogul Corporation.

U.S. Billing, Inc. *See* Billing Concepts Corp.

U.S. Biomedicals Corporation, 27 69

U.S. Bioscience, Inc., 35 286, 288

U.S. Borax, Inc., 42 393–96

U.S. Brass., 24 151

U.S. Can Corporation, 30 474–76

U.S. Cellular Corporation, 31 449–452 (upd.)

U.S. Computer of North America Inc., 43 368

U.S. Delivery Systems, Inc., 22 153, **531–33; 47** 90. *See also* Velocity Express Corporation.

U.S. Electrical Motors, II 19

U.S. Elevator Corporation, 19 109–11

U.S. Envelope, 19 498

U.S. Food Products Co., I 376

U.S. Foodservice, 26 503–06; 37 374, 376

U.S.G. Co., III 762

U.S. Generating Company, 26 373

U.S. Geological Survey, 9 367

U.S. Graphite. *See* Wickes Inc.

U.S. Guarantee Co., III 220; 14 108

U.S. Healthcare, Inc., 6 194–96; 21 16

U.S. Home Corporation, 8 541–43

U.S. Industries, Inc., 7 208; 18 467; 23 296; 24 150; 27 288

U.S. Intec, 22 229

U.S. International Reinsurance, III 264

U.S. Investigations Services Inc., 35 44

U.S. Land Co., IV 255

U.S. Lawns, 31 182, 184

U.S. Life Insurance, III 194

U.S. Lines, I 476; III 459; 11 194

U.S. Lock Corporation, 9 543; 28 50–52

U.S. Long Distance Corp. *See* Billing Concepts Corp.

U.S. Marine Corp., III 444

U.S. News and World Report Inc., 30 477–80

U.S. Office Products Company, 25 500–02; 41 69, 247; **47** 91

U.S. Overall Company, 14 549

U.S. Plywood Corp. *See* United States Plywood Corp.

U.S. Realty and Improvement Co., III 98

U.S. RingBinder Corp., 10 313–14

U.S. Robotics Inc., 9 514–15; 20 8, 69; **22** 17; **24** 212; **34** 444; **36** 122, 357; **48** 369; **49** 184

U.S. Rubber Company, I 478; 10 388

U.S. Satellite Broadcasting Company, Inc., 20 505–07

U.S. Satellite Systems, III 169; 6 285

U.S. Shoe Corporation, 43 98; 44 365

U.S. Smelting Refining and Mining, 7 360

U.S. Software Inc., 29 479

U.S. Steel Corp. *See* United States Steel Corp.

U.S. Telephone Communications, 9 478

U.S. Tile Co., III 674

U.S. Timberlands Company, L.P., 42 397–400

U.S. Time Corporation, 13 120

U.S. Trust Co. of New York, II 274

U.S. Trust Corp., 17 496–98

U.S. Vanadium Co., 9 517

U.S. Venture Partners, 15 204–05

U.S. Vitamin & Pharmaceutical Corp., III 55

U S West, Inc., V 341–43; 11 12, 59, 547; **25** 101, **495–99 (upd.); 32** 218; **36** 43; **37** 124–27

U.S. Windpower, 11 222–23

U.S. Xpress Enterprises, Inc., 18 159

U-Tote'M, II 620; 7 372

UA. *See* Metro- Goldwyn-Mayer Inc., MGM/UA Communications Company, *and* United Artists Corp.

UAA. *See* EgyptAir.

UAL Corporation, 34 462–65 (upd.)

UAL, Inc. *See* United Airlines.

UAP. *See* Union des Assurances de Paris.

UAP Inc., 45 179

UARCO Inc., 15 473–74

UAT. *See* UTA.

Ub Iwerks, 6 174

Ube Industries, Ltd., III 759–61; 38 463–67 (upd.)

Uberseebank A.G., III 197

Ubi Soft Entertainment S.A., 41 188–89, **407–09**

Ubique Ltd., 25 301

UBL Educational Loan Center, 42 211

UBS. *See* Union Bank of Switzerland.

Ucabail, II 265

UCAR International, Inc., 40 83

UCC-Communications Systems, Inc., II 38

Uccel, 6 224

Uchiyama, V 727

UCI, IV 92; 25 173

UCPMI, IV 226

Uddeholm and Bohler, IV 234

Udet Flugzeugwerke, I 73

Udo Fischer Co., 8 477

UE Automotive Manufacturing, III 580

Ueda Kotsu Company, 47 408

UETA Inc., 29 510–11

Ufa Sports, 44 190

Ugg Holdings, Inc., 22 173

UGI. *See* United Gas Improvement.

UGI Corporation, 12 498–500

Ugine-Kuhlmann, IV 108, 174

Ugine S.A., IV 174; **20 498–500**

Ugine Steels, IV 227

Ugly Duckling Corporation, 22 524–27

Uhlmans Inc., 24 458

UI International, 6 444

UIB. *See* United Independent Broadcasters, Inc.

UICI, 33 418–21

Uinta Co., **6** 568
Uintah National Corp., **11** 260
UIS Co., **13** 554–55; **15** 324
Uitgeversmaatschappij Elsevier, **IV** 610
Uitzendbureau Amstelveen. *See* Randstad Holding n.v.
UJB Financial Corp., **14** 473
UK Paper, **IV** 279; **19** 155
UKF. *See* Unie van Kunstmestfabrieken.
Ukrop's Super Market's, Inc., 39 402–04
UL. *See* Underwriters Laboratories, Inc.
Ullrich Copper, Inc., **6** 146
Ullstein AV Produktions-und Vertriebsgesellschaft, **IV** 590
Ullstein Langen Müller, **IV** 591
Ullstein Tele Video, **IV** 590
ULN. *See* Union Laitière Normande.
ULPAC, **II** 576
Ulstein Holding ASA, **27** 494
Ulster Bank, **II** 334
Ultimate Electronics, Inc., 18 532–34; 21 33; **24** 52, 269
Ultra Bancorp, **II** 334
Ultra High Pressure Units Ltd., **IV** 66; **7** 123
Ultra Mart, **16** 250
Ultra Pac, Inc., 24 512–14
Ultra Radio & Television, **I** 531
UltraCam. *See* Ultrak Inc.
UltraCare Products, **18** 148
Ultrak Inc., 24 508–11
Ultralar, **13** 544
Ultramar Diamond Shamrock Corporation, 31 453–457 (upd.)
Ultramar PLC, IV 565–68
Ultrametl Mfg. Co., **17** 234
Ultronic Systems Corp., **IV** 669
UM Technopolymer, **III** 760
Umacs of Canada Inc., **9** 513
Umberto's of New Hyde Park Pizzeria, **16** 447
Umbro Holdings Ltd., **43** 392. *See also* Stone Manufacturing Company.
UMC. *See* United Microelectronics Corp.
UMG. *See* Universal Music Group.
UMI Company, **29** 58
NV Umicore SA, 47 411–13
Umm-al-Jawabi Oil Co., **IV** 454
Umpqua River Navigation Company, **13** 100
Unadulterated Food Products, Inc., **11** 449
UNAT, **III** 197–98
Unbrako Socket Screw Company Ltd., **30** 429
Uncas-Merchants National Bank, **13** 467
Uncle Ben's Inc., 22 528–30
Under Sea Industries, **III** 59
Underground Group, **6** 407
Underwood, **III** 145; **24** 269
Underwriters Adjusting Co., **III** 242
Underwriters Laboratories, Inc., 30 467–70
Underwriters Reinsurance Co., **10** 45
Unefon, S.A., **39** 194, 196
UNELCO. *See* Union Electrica de Canarias S.A.
Unelec, Inc., **13** 398
Unfall, **III** 207
Ungermann-Bass, Inc., **6** 279
Uni-Cardan AG, **III** 494
Uni-Cast. *See* Sturm, Ruger & Company, Inc.
Uni-Charm, **III** 749
Uni Europe, **III** 211

Uni-Marts, Inc., 17 499–502
Uni-President Group, **49** 460
Uni-Sankyo, **I** 675
Unibail SA, 40 444–46
Unibank, **40** 336
Unic, **V** 63
Unicapital, Inc., **15** 281
Unicare Health Facilities, **6** 182; **25** 525
Unicco Security Services, **27** 22
Unicel. *See* Rural Cellular Corporation.
Unicer, **9** 100
Unichem, **25** 73
Unichema International, **13** 228
Unicoa, **I** 524
Unicom Corporation, 29 486–90 (upd.). *See also* Exelon Corporation.
Unicomi, **II** 265
Unicon Producing Co., **10** 191
Unicoolait, **19** 51
UNICOR. *See* Federal Prison Industries, Inc.
Unicord, **24** 115
Unicorn Shipping Lines, **IV** 91
UniCorp, **8** 228
Unicorp Financial, **III** 248
Unicredit, **II** 265
Uniden, **14** 117
Unidrive, **47** 280
UniDynamics Corporation, **8** 135
Unie van Kunstmestfabrieken, **I** 326
Uniface Holding B.V., **10** 245; **30** 142
Unifi, Inc., 12 501–03
Unified Energy System of Russia. *See* RAO Unified Energy System of Russia.
Unified Management Corp., **III** 306
Unified Western Grocers, **31** 25
UniFirst Corporation, 16 228; 21 115, 505–07
Uniforce Services Inc., **40** 119
Unigate PLC, II 586–87; 28 488–91 (upd.); 29 150
Unigep Group, **III** 495
Unigesco Inc., **II** 653
Uniglory, **13** 211
Unigroup, **15** 50
UniHealth America, **11** 378–79
Unijoh Sdn, Bhd, **47** 255
Unik S.A., **23** 170–171
Unilab Corp., **26** 391
Unilac Inc., **II** 547
Unilever PLC/Unilever N.V., I 369, 590, 605; **II** 547, **588–91; III** 31–32, 46, 52, 495; **IV** 532; **7** 382, **542–45 (upd.),** 577; **8** 105–07, 166, 168, 341, 344; **9** 449; **11** 205, 421; **13** 243–44; **14** 204–05; **18** 395, 397; **19** 193; **21** 219; **22** 123; **23** 242; **26** 306; **28** 183, 185; **30** 396–97; **32** 472–78 (upd.); **36** 237; **49** 269
Unilife Assurance Group, **III** 273
UniLife Insurance Co., **22** 149
Unilog SA, 42 401–03
UniMac Companies, **11** 413
Unimat, **II** 265
Unimation, **II** 122
Unimetal, **IV** 227; **30** 252
Uninsa, **I** 460
Union, **III** 391–93
Union & NHK Auto Parts, **III** 580
Union Acceptances Ltd., **IV** 23
Unión Aérea Española, **6** 95
Union Aéromaritime de Transport. *See* UTA.
Union Assurance, **III** 234

Union Bag–Camp Paper Corp., **IV** 344–45
Union Bancorp of California, **II** 358
Union Bank. *See* State Street Boston Corporation.
Union Bank of Australia, **II** 187–89
Union Bank of Birmingham, **II** 318; **17** 323
Union Bank of California, 16 496–98
Union Bank of Canada, **II** 344
Union Bank of England, **II** 188
Union Bank of Finland, **II** 302, 352
Union Bank of Halifax, **II** 344
Union Bank of London, **II** 235
Union Bank of New London, **II** 213
Union Bank of New York, **9** 229
Union Bank of Prince Edward Island, **II** 220
Union Bank of Scotland, **10** 337
Union Bank of Switzerland, II 257, 267, 334, 369, 370, **378–79; 21** 146
Union Battery Co., **III** 536
Union Bay Sportswear, **17** 460
Union Camp Corporation, IV 344–46; 8 102; **39** 291; **47** 189
Union-Capitalisation, **III** 392
Union Carbide Corporation, I 334, 339, 347, 374, 390, **399–401,** 582, 666; **II** 103, 313, 562; **III** 742, 760; **IV** 92, 374, 379, 521; **7** 376; **8** 180, 182, 376; **9** 16, **516–20 (upd.); 10** 289, 472; **11** 402–03; **12** 46, 347; **13** 118; **14** 281–82; **16** 461; **17** 159; **18** 235; **22** 228, 235; **43** 265–66; **48** 321
Union Cervecera, **9** 100
Union Colliery Company, **V** 741
Union Commerce Corporation, **11** 181
Union Commerciale, **19** 98
Union Corporation. *See* Gencor Ltd.
Union d'Etudes et d'Investissements, **II** 265
Union des Assurances de Paris, II 234; **III** 201, **391–94**
Union des Coopératives Bressor, **25** 85
Union des Cooperatives Laitières. *See* Unicoolait.
Union des Transports Aériens. *See* UTA.
Union Electric Company, V 741–43; **6** 505–06; **26** 451
Union Electrica de Canarias S.A., **V** 607
Union Equity Co-Operative Exchange, **7** 175
Union et Prévoyance, **III** 403
Union Fertilizer, **I** 412
Union Fidelity Corporation, **III** 204; **45** 26
Union Financiera, **19** 189
Union Gas & Electric Co., **6** 529
Union Générale de Savonnerie, **III** 33
l'Union Générale des Pétroles, **IV** 545–46, 560; **7** 482–83
Union Glass Co., **III** 683
Union Hardware, **III** 443; **22** 115
Union Hop Growers, **I** 287
Union Laitière Normande, **19** 50. *See also* Compagnie Laitière Européenne.
Union Levantina de Seguros, **III** 179
Union Light, Heat & Power Company, **6** 466
Union Marine, **III** 372
Union Minière. *See* NV Umicore SA.
Union Mutual Life Insurance Company. *See* UNUM Corp.
Union National Bank, **II** 284; **10** 298
Union National Bank of Wilmington, **25** 540

Union of European Football Association, **27** 150

Union of Food Co-ops, **II** 622

Union of London, **II** 333

Union Oil Associates, **IV** 569

Union Oil Co., **9** 266

Union Oil Co. of California, **I** 13; **IV** 385, 400, 403, 434, 522, 531, 540, 569, 575; **11** 271. *See also* Unocal Corporation.

Union Pacific Corporation, **I** 473; **II** 381; **III** 229; **V 529–32**; **12** 18–20, 278; **14** 371–72; **28 492–500 (upd.)**; **36** 43–44

Union Pacific Tea Co., **7** 202

Union Paper Bag Machine Co., **IV** 344

Union Petroleum Corp., **IV** 394

L'Union pour le Developement Régional, **II** 265

Union Power Company, **12** 541

Union Rückversicherungs-Gesellschaft, **III** 377

Union Savings, **II** 316

Union Savings and Loan Association of Phoenix, **19** 412

Union Savings Bank, **9** 173

Union Savings Bank and Trust Company, **13** 221

Union Steam Ship Co., **IV** 279; **19** 154

Union Steamship Co. of New Zealand Ltd., **27** 473

Union Steel Co., **IV** 22, 572; **7** 550

Union Sugar, **II** 573

Union Suisse des Coopératives de Consommation. *See* Coop Schweiz.

Union Sulphur Co., **IV** 81; **7** 185

Union Supply Co., **IV** 573; **7** 550

Union Tank Car Co., **IV** 137

Union Telecard Alliance, LLC, **34** 223

Union Telephone Company, **14** 258

Union Texas Petroleum Holdings, Inc., **I** 415; **7** 379; **9 521–23**; **22** 31

Union-Transport, **6** 404; **26** 243

Union Trust Co., **II** 284, 313, 315–16, 382; **9** 228; **13** 222

The Union Underwear Company, **I** 440–41; **8** 200–01; **25** 164–66

Union Wine, **I** 289

Unionamerica, Inc., **16** 497

Unionamerica Insurance Group, **III** 243

UnionBay Sportswear Co., **27** 112

Unione Manifatture, S.p.A., **19** 338

Uniphase Corporation. *See* JDS Uniphase Corporation.

Uniplex Business Software, **41** 281

Unique Casual Restaurants, Inc., **27 480–82**

Uniroy of Hempstead, Inc. *See* Aris Industries, Inc.

Uniroyal Chemical Corporation, **36** 145

Uniroyal Corp., **I** 30–31; **II** 472; **V** 242; **8** 503; **11** 159; **20** 262

Uniroyal Goodrich, **42** 88

Uniroyal Holdings Ltd., **21** 73

Unishops, Inc. *See* Aris Industries, Inc.

Unison HealthCare Corporation, **25 503–05**

Unisource Worldwide, Inc., **I** 413, **47** 149

Unistar Radio Networks, **23** 510

Unisys Corporation, **II** 42; **III 165–67**; **6 281–83 (upd.)**; **8** 92; **9** 32, 59; **12** 149, 162; **17** 11, 262; **18** 345, 386, 434, 542; **21** 86; **36 479–84 (upd.)**

The Unit Companies, Inc., **6** 394, 396; **25** 170

Unit Group plc, **8** 477

Unitech plc, **27** 81

United Acquisitions, **7** 114; **25** 125

United Advertising Periodicals, **12** 231

United Agri Products, **II** 494

United AgriSeeds, Inc., **21** 387

United Air Express. *See* United Parcel Service of America Inc.

United Air Fleet, **23** 408

United Aircraft and Transportation Co., **I** 48, 76, 78, 85–86, 96, 441, 489; **9** 416, 418; **10** 162, 260; **12** 289; **21** 140

United Airlines, **I** 23, 47, 71, 84, 90, 97, 113, 116, 118, 124, **128–30**; **II** 142, 419, 680; **III** 225; **6** 71, 75–77, 104, 121, 123, **128–30 (upd.)**, 131, 388–89; **9** 271–72, 283, 416, 549; **10** 162, 199, 301, 561; **11** 299; **12** 192, 381; **14** 73; **21** 141; **22** 199, 220; **24** 21, 22; **25** 146, 148, 421–23; **26** 113, 338–39, 440; **27** 20; **29** 507; **38** 105. *See also* UAL Corporation.

United Alaska Drilling, Inc., **7** 558

United Alkalai Co., **I** 351

United Alloy Steel Company, **26** 405

United-American Car, **13** 305

United American Insurance Company of Dallas, **9** 508; **33** 407

United American Lines, **6** 398

United Arab Airlines. *See* EgyptAir.

United Artists Corp., **I** 537; **II** 135, 146–48, 149, 157–58, 160, 167, 169; **III** 721; **IV** 676; **6** 167; **9** 74; **12** 13, 73; **13** 529; **14** 87, 399; **21** 362; **23** 389; **26** 487; **36** 47; **41** 402. *See also* MGM/UA Communications Company *and* Metro-Goldwyn-Mayer Inc.

United Artists Theatre Circuit, Inc., **37** 63–64

United Auto Group, Inc., **45** 261

United Auto Group, Inc., **26 500–02**

United Bank of Arizona, **II** 358

United Biscuits (Holdings) plc, **II** 466, 540, **592–94**; **III** 503; **26** 59; **36** 313; **42 404–09 (upd.)**

United Brands Company, **II 595–97**; **III** 28; **7** 84–85; **12** 215; **21** 110, 112; **25** 4

United Breweries Ltd. **I** 221, 223, 288; **24** 449. *See also* Carlsberg A/S.

United Broadcasting Corporation Public Company Ltd., **31** 330

United Cable Television Corporation, **II** 160; **9** 74; **18** 65; **43** 431

United California Bank, **II** 289

United Car, **I** 540; **14** 511

United Carbon Co., **IV** 373

United Central Oil Corporation, **7** 101

United Cigar Manufacturers Company, **II** 414. *See also* Culbro Corporation.

United Cities Gas Company, **43** 56, 58

United City Property Trust, **IV** 705

United Co., **I** 70

United Communications Systems, Inc. **V** 346

United Computer Services, Inc., **11** 111

United Consolidated Industries, **24** 204

United Corp., **10** 44

United County Banks, **II** 235

United Dairies, **II** 586–87

United Dairy Farmers, **III** 190

United Defense, L.P., **30 471–73**

United Distiller & Vintners, **43** 215. *See also* Diageo plc.

United Distillers Glenmore, Inc., **34** 89

United Dominion Corp., **III** 200

United Dominion Industries Limited, **IV** 288; **8 544–46**; **16 499–502 (upd.)**; **47** 378

United Drapery Stores, **III** 502; **7** 208

United Drug Co., **II** 533

United Electric Light and Water Co., **13** 182

United Engineering Steels, **III** 495

United Engineers & Constructors, **II** 86; **11** 413

United Express, **11** 299

United Factors Corp., **13** 534–35

United Features Syndicate, Inc., **IV** 607–08

United Federal Savings and Loan of Waycross, **10** 92

United Financial Corporation, **12** 353

United Financial Group, Inc., **8** 349

United 5 and 10 Cent Stores, **13** 444

United Foods, Inc., **21 508–11**

United Fruit Co., **I** 529, 566; **II** 120, 595; **IV** 308; **7** 84–85; **21** 110–11; **44** 152

United Funds, Inc., **22** 540–41

United Gas and Electric Company of New Albany, **6** 555

United Gas and Improvement Co., **13** 182

United Gas Corp., **IV** 488–90

United Gas Improvement Co., **IV** 549; **V** 696; **6** 446, 523; **11** 388

United Gas Industries, **III** 502; **7** 208

United Gas Pipe Line Co., **IV** 489–90

United Geophysical Corp., **I** 142

United Graphics, **12** 25

United Grocers, **II** 625

United Guaranty Corp., **III** 197

United Health Maintenance, Inc., **6** 181–82

United HealthCare Corporation, **9 524–26**; **24** 229, 231. *See also* Humana Inc.

The United Illuminating Company, **21 512–14**

United Image Entertainment, **18** 64, 66

United Independent Broadcasters, Inc., **II** 132

United Industrial Corporation, **37 399–402**

United Industrial Syndicate, **8** 545

United Information Systems, Inc., **V** 346

United Insurance Co., **I** 523

Oy United International, **IV** 349

United International Holdings Inc., **28** 198

United International Pictures, **II** 155

United Investors Life Insurance Company, **22** 540; **33** 407

United Iron & Metal Co., **14** 156

United Jewish Communities, **33 422–25**

United Kent Fire, **III** 350

United Kingdom Atomic Energy Authority, **6** 451–52

United Knitting, Inc., **21** 192, 194

United Liberty Life Insurance Co., **III** 190–92

United Life & Accident Insurance Co., **III** 220–21; **14** 109

United Life Insurance Company, **12** 541

United Light & Railway Co., **V** 609

United Light and Power, **6** 511

United Machinery Co., **15** 127

United Match Factories, **12** 462

United Media, **22** 442

United Medical Service, Inc., **III** 245–46

United Merchandising Corp., **12** 477

United Merchants & Manufacturers, Inc., **13 534–37**; **31** 160

United Meridian Corporation, **8** 350

United Metals Selling Co., **IV** 31
United Microelectronics Corporation, **22** 197; **47** 384, 386
United Micronesian, **I** 97; **21** 142
United Molasses, **II** 582
United Mortgage Servicing, **16** 133
United Natural Foods, Inc., 32 479–82
United Natural Gas Company, **6** 526
United Netherlands Navigation Company. *See* Vereenigde Nederlandsche Scheepvaartmaatschappij.
United News & Media plc, 28 501–05 (upd.); 35 354
United Newspapers plc, IV 685–87
United of Omaha, **III** 365
United Office Products, **11** 64
United Oil Co., **IV** 399
United Optical, **10** 151
United Pacific Financial Services, **III** 344
United Pacific Insurance Co., **III** 343
United Pacific Life Insurance Co., **III** 343–44
United Pacific Reliance Life Insurance Co. of New York, **III** 343
United Packages, **IV** 249
United Pan-Europe Communications NV, 47 414–17
United Paper Mills Ltd., II 302; **IV** 316, **347–50**
United Paramount Network, **25** 418–19; **26** 32; **31** 109
United Paramount Theatres, **II** 129
United Parcel Service of America Inc., V 533–35; 6 345–46, 385–86, 390; **11** 11; **12** 309, 334; **13** 19, 416; **14** 517; **17 503–06 (upd.); 18** 82, 177, 315–17; **24** 22, 133; **25** 148, 150, 356; **27** 471, 475; **34** 15, 17, 473; **39** 33; **41** 245; **42** 140; **49** 460
United Pipeline Co., **IV** 394
United Power and Light Corporation, **6** 473; **12** 541
United Presidential Life Insurance Company, **12** 524, 526
United Press International, Inc., IV 607, 627, 669–70; **7** 158–59; **16** 166; **19** 203; **22** 453; **25 506–09**
United Railways & Electric Company, **25** 44
United Refining Co., **23** 406, 408
United Rentals, Inc., 28 386, 388; **34 466–69; 48** 272
United Resources, Inc., **21** 514
United Retail Group Inc., 33 426–28
United Retail Merchants Stores Inc., **9** 39
United Roasters, **III** 24; **14** 121
United Satellite Television, **10** 320
United Savings of Texas, **8** 349
United Scientific Holdings, **47** 8
United Servomation, **7** 471–72
United Shipping & Technology, Inc., **49** 440
United Shirt Shops, Inc. *See* Aris Industries, Inc.
United Skates of America, **8** 303
United Software Consultants Inc., **11** 65
United States Aluminum Co., **17** 213
United States Aviation Underwriters, Inc., **24** 176
United States Baking Co., **II** 542
United States Can Co., **15** 127, 129
United States Cellular Corporation, 9 494–96, **527–29.** *See also* U.S. Cellular Corporation.

United States Department of Defense, **6** 327
United States Distributing Corp., **IV** 180–82
United States Electric and Gas Company, **6** 447
United States Electric Light and Power Company, **25** 44
The United States Electric Lighting Company, **11** 387
United States Export-Import Bank, **IV** 55
United States Express Co., **II** 381, 395–96; **10** 59–60; **12** 534
United States Fidelity and Guaranty Co., **III** 395
United States Filter Corporation, I 429; **IV** 374; **20 501–04; 38** 168, 170
United States Foil Co., **IV** 186; **19** 346
United States Football League, **29** 347
United States Glucose Co., **II** 496
United States Graphite Company, **V** 221–22
United States Gypsum Co., **III** 762–64
United States Health Care Systems, Inc. *See* U.S. Healthcare, Inc.
United States Independent Telephone Company, **6** 332
United States Leasing Corp., **II** 442
United States Mail Steamship Co., **23** 160
United States Medical Finance Corp., **18** 516, 518
United States Mortgage & Trust Company, **II** 251; **14** 102
United States National Bancshares, **25** 114
United States National Bank of Galveston. *See* Cullen/Frost Bankers, Inc.
United States National Bank of Oregon, **14** 527
The United States National Bank of Portland, **14** 527–28
United States National Bank of San Diego, **II** 355
United States Pipe and Foundry Co., **III** 766; **22** 544–45
United States Plywood Corp., **IV** 264, 282, 341; **9** 260; **13** 100; **20** 128
United States Postal Service, 10 60; **14 517–20; 34 470–75 (upd.); 42** 140
United States Realty-Sheraton Corp., **III** 98
United States Satellite Broadcasting Company Inc., **24** 226; **38** 176
United States Security Trust Co., **13** 466
United States Shoe Corporation, V 207–08; 17 296, 390; **23** 328; **39** 301
United States Steel Corp., **I** 298, 491; **II** 129, 330; **III** 282, 326, 379; **IV** 35, 56, 110, 158, 572–74; **6** 514; **7** 48, 70–73, 401–02, 549–51; **10** 32; **11** 194; **12** 353–54; **17** 350, 356; **18** 378; **26** 405, 451. *See also* USX Corporation.
United States Sugar Refining Co., **II** 496
United States Surgical Corporation, 10 533–35; 13 365; **21** 119–20; **28** 486; **34 476–80 (upd.)**
United States Tobacco Company, **9** 533
United States Trucking Corp., **IV** 180–81
United States Trust Co. of New York. *See* U.S. Trust Corp.
United States Underseas Cable Corp., **IV** 178
United States Zinc Co., **IV** 32
United Stationers Inc., 14 521–23; 25 13; **36** 508
United Steel, **III** 494

United Steel Mills Ltd., **25** 266
United Supers, **II** 624
United Technologies Automotive Inc., 15 513–15
United Technologies Corporation, I 68, **84–86,** 143, 411, 530, 559; **II** 64, 82; **III** 74; **9** 18, 418; **10 536–38 (upd.); 11** 308; **12** 289; **13** 191, 384–86; **22** 6; **34** 371–72, 432, **481–85 (upd.); 39** 311, 313
United Telecommunications, Inc., V 344–47; 8 310; **9** 478–80; **10** 202; **12** 541
United Telephone Company, **7** 508; **14** 257
United Telephone Company of the Carolinas, **10** 202
United Telephone of Indiana, **14** 259
United Telephone System, Inc., **V** 346
United Telespectrum, **6** 314
United Television, Inc., **9** 119; **26** 32
United Television Programs, **II** 143
United Thermal Corp., **42** 388
United Transportation Co., **6** 382
United Truck Lines, **14** 505
United Utilities, Inc., **V** 344; **10** 202
United Van Lines, **14** 37; **15** 50
United Verde Copper Co., **IV** 178
United Video Satellite Group, 18 535–37. *See also* TV Guide, Inc.
United Vintners, **I** 243, 260–61
United Water Resources, Inc., 40 447–50; 45 277
United Way of America, 36 485–88
United Westburne Inc., **19** 313
United Westphalia Electricity Co., **IV** 127
Unitek Corp., **III** 18
Unitika Ltd., V 387–89
Unitil Corporation, 37 403–06
Unitog Co., 16 228; **19 457–60; 21** 115
Unitransa, **27** 474
Unitrin Inc., 16 503–05
Unitron Medical Communications, **29** 412
Unity Cellular Systems, Inc. *See* Rural Cellular Corporation.
Unity Financial Corp., **19** 411
Unity Joint-Stock Bank, **II** 334
UNIVAC, **III** 133, 152, 313; **6** 233, 240, 266
Univar Corporation, 8 99; **9 530–32; 12** 333; **41** 340
Univas, **13** 203 **23** 171
Univasa, **39** 229
Univel Inc., **38** 418
Universal Adding Machine, **III** 165
Universal American, **I** 452
Universal Atlas Cement Co., **IV** 573–74; **7** 550–51
Universal Belo Productions, **10** 5
Universal Cheerleaders Association. *See* Varsity Spirit Corp.
Universal Cigar Corp., **14** 19
Universal Consumer Products Group, **30** 123
Universal Containers, **IV** 249
Universal Controls, Inc., **10** 319
Universal Cooler Corp., **8** 515
Universal Corporation, V 417–18; 48 403–06 (upd.)
Universal Data Systems, **II** 61; **22** 17
Universal Electronics Inc., 39 405–08
Universal Foods Corporation, 7 546–48; 21 498

Universal Footcare Products Inc., **31** 255
Universal Forest Products Inc., 10 539–40
Universal Frozen Foods, **23** 321
Universal Furniture, **III** 571; **20** 362
Universal Genève, **13** 121
Universal Guaranty Life Insurance Company, **11** 482
Universal Health Services, Inc., 6 191–93
Universal Highways, **III** 735
Universal Industries, Inc., **10** 380; **13** 533
Universal Instruments Corp., **III** 468
Universal International, Inc., 25 353, 355, **510–11**
Universal Juice Co., **21** 55
Universal Leaf Tobacco Company. *See* Universal Corporation.
Universal Manufacturing, **I** 440–41; **25** 167
Universal Marking Systems, **25** 331
Universal Match, **12** 464
Universal Matchbox Group, **12** 495
Universal Matthey Products Ltd., **IV** 119
Universal Music Group, **22** 194; **26** 152; **37** 193
Universal Paper Bag Co., **IV** 345
Universal Pictures, **II** 102, 135, 144, 154–55, 157; **10** 196; **14** 399; **25** 271. *See also* Universal Studios, Inc.
Universal Press Syndicate, **10** 4; **40** 38
Universal Records, **27** 123
Universal Resources Corporation, **6** 569; **26** 388
Universal Shoes, Inc., **22** 213
Universal Stamping Machine Co., **III** 156
Universal Studios Florida, **14** 399
Universal Studios, Inc., II 143–44; **12** 73; **21** 23–26; **25** 411; **33** 429–33; **47** 419–21
Universal Telephone, **9** 106
Universal Television, **II** 144
Universal Textured Yarns, **12** 501
Universal Transfers Co. Ltd., **IV** 119
University Computing Corp., **II** 38; **11** 468; **17** 320; **25** 87
University Microfilms, **III** 172; **6** 289
University of Phoenix, **24** 40
Univisa, **24** 516
Univision Communications Inc., IV 621; **18** 213; **24 515–18; 41** 150–52
Unix System Laboratories Inc., **6** 225; **25** 20–21; **38** 418
UNM. *See* United News & Media plc.
Uno-e Bank, **48** 51
Uno Restaurant Corporation, 16 447; **18** 465, **538–40**
Uno-Ven, **IV** 571; **24** 522
Unocal Corporation, IV 508, **569–71; 24 519–23 (upd.)**
UNR Industries, Inc. *See* ROHN Industries, Inc.
Unterberg Harris, **25** 433
UNUM Corp., III 236; **13 538–40**
Uny Co., Ltd., II 619; **V 209–10**, 154; **13** 545; **36** 419; **49 425–28 (upd.)**
UPC. *See* United Pan-Europe Communications NV.
UPI. *See* United Press International.
Upjohn Company, I 675, 684, 686, 700, **707–09; III** 18, 53; **6** 42; **8 547–49 (upd.); 10** 79; **12** 186; **13** 503; **14** 423; **16** 440; **29** 363. *See also* Pharmacia & Upjohn Inc.

UPM-Kymmene Corporation, 19 461–65; 25 12; **30** 325
UPN. *See* United Paramount Network.
Upper Deck Company, LLC, **34** 448; **37** 295
UPS. *See* United Parcel Service of America Inc.
UPSHOT, **27** 195
Upton Machine Company, **12** 548
Uraga Dock Co., **II** 361; **III** 634
Uraga Heavy Industries, **III** 634
Urbaine, **III** 391–92
Urban Investment and Development Co., **IV** 703
Urban Outfitters, Inc., 14 524–26
Urban Systems Development Corp., **II** 121
Urenco, **6** 452
URS Corporation, 45 420–23
Urwick Orr, **II** 609
US Airways Express, **32** 334; **38** 130
US Airways Group, Inc., 28 506–09 (upd.); 33 303
US Industrial Chemicals, Inc., **I** 377; **8** 440
US Industries Inc., **30** 231
US 1 Industries, **27** 404
US Order, Inc., **10** 560, 562
US Sprint Communications Company, **V** 295–96, 346–47; **6** 314; **8** 310; **9** 32; **10** 543; **11** 302; **12** 136, 541; **14** 252–53; **15** 196; **16** 318, 392; **25** 101; **29** 44; **43** 447. *See also* Sprint Communications Company, L.P.
US Telecom, **9** 478–79
US West Communications Services, Inc., **19** 255; **21** 285; **29** 39, 45, 478; **37** 312, 315–16. *See also* Regional Bell Operating Companies.
USA Cafes, **14** 331
USA Floral Products Inc., **27** 126
USA Interactive, Inc., 47 418–22 (upd.)
USA Networks Inc., **25** 330, 411; **33** 432; **37** 381, 383–84; **43** 422
USA Security Systems, Inc., **27** 21
USA Truck, Inc., 42 410–13
USAA, 10 541–43
USAir Group, Inc., I 55, **131–32; III** 215; **6** 121, **131–32 (upd.); 11** 300; **14** 70, 73; **18** 62; **21** 143; **24** 400; **26** 429; **42** 34. *See also* US Airways Group, Inc.
USANA, Inc., 27 353; **29 491–93**
USCC. *See* United States Cellular Corporation.
USCP-WESCO Inc., **II** 682
Usego AG., **48** 63
USF&G Corporation, III 395–98; 11 494–95; **19** 190
USFL. *See* United States Football League.
USFreightways Corporation, **27** 475; **49** 402
USG Corporation, III 762–64; 26 507–10 (upd.)
USH. *See* United Scientific Holdings.
Usines de l'Espérance, **IV** 226
Usines Métallurgiques de Hainaut, **IV** 52
Usinor SA, 42 414–17 (upd.)
Usinor Sacilor, IV 226–28; **22** 44; **24** 144; **26** 81, 84
USLD Communications Corp. *See* Billing Concepts Corp.
USLIFE, **III** 194
USM, **10** 44
Usource LLC, **37** 406
USPS. *See* United States Postal Service.

USSC. *See* United States Surgical Corporation.
USSI. *See* U.S. Software Inc.
UST Inc., 9 533–35; 42 79
UST Wilderness Management Corporation, **33** 399
Usutu Pulp Company, **49** 353
USV Pharmaceutical Corporation, **11** 333
USWeb/CKS. *See* marchFIRST, Inc.
USX Corporation, I 466; **IV** 130, 228, **572–74; 7** 193–94, **549–52 (upd.)**
UT Starcom, **44** 426
UTA, **I** 119, 121; **6** 373–74, 93; **34** 397
Utag, **11** 510
Utah Construction & Mining Co., **I** 570; **IV** 146; **14** 296
Utah Federal Savings Bank, **17** 530
Utah Gas and Coke Company, **6** 568
Utah Group Health Plan, **6** 184
Utah International, **II** 30; **12** 196
Utah Medical Products, Inc., 36 496–99
Utah Mines Ltd., **IV** 47; **22** 107
Utah Oil Refining Co., **IV** 370
Utah Power and Light Company, 9 536; **12** 266; **27 483–86**. *See also* PacifiCorp.
UTI Energy Corp., **12** 500
Utilicom, **6** 572
Utilicorp United Inc., 6 592–94
UtiliTech Solutions, **37** 88
Utilities Power & Light Corporation, **I** 512; **6** 508
Utility Constructors Incorporated, **6** 527
Utility Engineering Corporation, **6** 580
Utility Fuels, **7** 377
Utility Service Affiliates, Inc., **45** 277
Utility Services, Inc., **42** 249, 253
Utility Supply Co. *See* United Stationers Inc.
AB Utra Wood Co., **IV** 274
Utrecht Allerlei Risico's, **III** 200
UUNET, 38 468–72
UV Industries, Inc., **7** 360; **9** 440

V & V Cos., **I** 412
V&S Variety Stores, **V** 37
V.A.W. of America Inc., **IV** 231
V.L. Churchill Group, **10** 493
VA Linux Systems, **45** 363
VA TECH ELIN EBG GmbH, 49 429–31
Vabis, **I** 197
Vacheron Constantin, **27** 487, 489
Vaco, **38** 200, 202
Vaculator Division. *See* Lancer Corporation.
Vacuum Metallurgical Company, **11** 234
Vacuum Oil Co., **IV** 463–64, 504, 549; **7** 351–52
Vadic Corp., **II** 83
Vadoise Vie, **III** 273
Vagnfabriks A.B., **I** 197
Vail Associates, Inc., 11 543–46; 31 65, 67
Vail Resorts, Inc., 43 435–39 (upd.)
Vaillant GmbH, 44 436–39
Val Corp., **24** 149
Val-Pak Direct Marketing Systems, Inc., **22** 162
Val Royal LaSalle, **II** 652
Valassis Communications, Inc., 8 550–51; 37 407–10 (upd.)
Valcambi S.A., **II** 268; **21** 145
Valcom, **13** 176
ValCom Inc. *See* InaCom Corporation.

Valdi Foods Inc., **II** 663–64
Valdosta Drug Co., **III** 9–10
Vale do Rio Doce Navegacao SA—
  Docenave, **43** 112
Vale Harmon Enterprises, Ltd., **25** 204
Vale Power Company, **12** 265
Valentine & Company, **8** 552–53
Valeo, III 593; **23 492–94**
Valero Energy Corporation, IV 394; **7
  553–55**; **19** 140; **31** 119
Valhi, Inc., 10 435–36; **19 466–68**
Valid Logic Systems Inc., **11** 46, 284; **48**
  77
Valio-Finnish Co-operative Dairies' Assoc.,
  II 575
Valke Oy, **IV** 348
Vallen Corporation, 45 424–26
Valley Bank of Helena, **35** 197, 199
Valley Bank of Maryland, **46** 25
Valley Bank of Nevada, **19** 378
Valley Crest Tree Company, **31** 182–83
Valley Deli Inc., **24** 243
Valley East Medical Center, **6** 185
Valley Falls Co., **III** 213
Valley Fashions Corp., **16** 535
Valley Federal of California, **11** 163
Valley Fig Growers, **7** 496–97
Valley Forge Life Insurance Co., **III** 230
Valley Media Inc., 35 430–33
Valley National Bank, **II** 420
Valley-Todeco, Inc., **13** 305–06
Valley Transport Co., **II** 569
Valleyfair, **22** 130
Vallourec, **IV** 227
Valmac Industries, **II** 585
Valmet Corporation, I 198; **III 647–49**;
  IV 276, 350, 471
Valmet Oy. *See* Metso Corporation.
Valmont Industries, Inc., 13 276; **19** 50,
  469–72
Valores Industriales S.A., 19 10, 12, 189,
  473–75; **29** 219
The Valspar Corporation, 8 552–54; **32
  483–86 (upd.)**
Valtec Industries, **III** 684
Valtek International, Inc., **17** 147
Valtur, **6** 207; **48** 316
Value America, **29** 312
Value City Department Stores,
Value City Department Stores, Inc., 29
  311; **38 473–75**
Value Foods Ltd., **11** 239
Value Giant Stores, **12** 478
Value House, **II** 673
Value Investors, **III** 330
Value Line, Inc., 16 506–08
Value Merchants Inc., 13 541–43
Value Rent-A-Car, **9** 350; **23** 354
ValueClick, Inc., 49 432–34
Valueland, **8** 482
**ValueVision International, Inc., 22
  534–36**; **27** 337
ValuJet, Inc. *See* AirTran Holdings, Inc.
Valvoline, Inc., **I** 291; **IV** 374
Valvtron, **11** 226
Van Ameringen-Haebler, Inc., **9** 290
Van Brunt Manufacturing Co., **III** 462; **21**
  173
Van Camp Seafood Company, Inc., II
  562–63; **7 556–57**; **13** 426. *See also*
  Chicken of the Sea International.
Van Cleef & Arpels Inc., **26** 145
Van de Kamp's, Inc., **II** 556–57; **7** 430; **32**
  67

Van den Bergh Foods, **II** 588; **9** 319
Van der Horst Corp. of America, **III** 471
Van der Moolen Holding NV, **37** 224
Van Dorn Company, **13** 190
Van Dorn Electric Tool Co., **III** 435
Van Gend and Loos, **6** 404; **26** 241, 243
Van Houton, **II** 521
Van Houtte Inc., 39 409–11
Van Kirk Chocolate, **7** 429
Van Kok-Ede, **II** 642
Van Leer Containers Inc., **30** 397
Van Leer Holding, Inc., **9** 303, 305
Van Leer N.V. *See* Royal Packaging
  Industries Van Leer N.V.
Van Mar, Inc., **18** 88
Van Munching & Company, Inc., **I** 256; **13**
  257, 259; **34** 202
Van Nostrand Reinhold, **8** 526
Van Ommeren, **41** 339–40
Van Ryn Gold Mines Estate, **IV** 90
Van Schaardenburg, **II** 528
Van Sickle, **IV** 485
Van Waters & Rogers, **8** 99; **41** 340
Van Wezel, **26** 278–79
Van Wijcks Waalsteenfabrieken, **14** 249
Vanadium Alloys Steel Company
  (VASCO), **13** 295–96
Vanant Packaging Corporation, **8** 359
Vance International Airways, **8** 349
Vancouver Pacific Paper Co., **IV** 286
Vanderbilt Mortgage and Finance, **13** 154
Vanderlip-Swenson-Tilghman Syndicate,
  IV 81; **7** 185
Vanessa and Biffi, **11** 226
**The Vanguard Group, Inc., 34 486–89
  (upd.)**
**The Vanguard Group of Investment
  Companies, 9** 239; **14 530–32**
Vanguard International Semiconductor
  Corp., **47** 385
Vanity Fair Mills, Inc., **V** 390–91
Vanity Fair Paper Mills, **IV** 281; **9** 259
Vans, Inc., 16 509–11; **17** 259–61; **47
  423–26 (upd.)**
Vansickle Industries, **III** 603
Vanstar, **13** 176
Vantage Analysis Systems, Inc., **11** 490
Vantive Corporation, **33** 333; **38** 431–32
Vantona Group Ltd., **V** 356; **44** 105
Vantress Pedigree, Inc., **II** 585
Vapor Corp., **III** 444
Varco International, Inc., 42 418–20
Varco-Pruden, Inc., **8** 544–46
Vare Corporation, **8** 366
Vari-Lite International, Inc., 35 434–36
Variable Annuity Life Insurance Co., **III**
  193–94
Varian Associates Inc., 12 504–06
Varian, Inc., 48 407–11 (upd.)
Varibus Corporation, **6** 495
Variform, Inc., **12** 397
**VARIG S.A. (Viação Aérea Rio-
  Grandense), 6 133–35**; **26** 113; **29
  494–97 (upd.)**; **31** 443–45; **33** 19
Varity Corporation, III 650–52; **7** 258,
  260; **19** 294; **27** 203, 251
Varlen Corporation, 16 512–14
Varney Air Lines, **I** 47, 128; **6** 128; **9** 416
Varney Speed Lines. *See* Continental
  Airlines, Inc.
Varo, **7** 235, 237
Varsity Spirit Corp., 15 516–18; **22** 459
Varta AG, **III** 536; **9** 180–81; **23 495–99**;
  26 230

Vasco Metals Corp., **I** 523; **10** 520, 522
Vascoloy-Ramet, **13** 295
VASP (Viaçao Aérea de Sao Paulo), **6**
  134; **29** 495; **31** 444–45
Vasset, S.A., **17** 362–63
Vast Solutions, **39** 24
Vastar Resources, Inc., 24 524–26; **38**
  445, 448
Vaughan Harmon Systems Ltd., **25** 204
Vaughan Printers Inc., **23** 100
Vaungarde, Inc., **22** 175
Vauxhall, **19** 391
VAW Leichtmetall GmbH, **IV** 231
VBB Viag-Bayernwerk-Beteiligungs-
  Gesellschaft mbH, **IV** 232
VDM Nickel-Technologie AG, **IV** 89
VEB Londa, **III** 69
Veba A.G., I 349–50, **542–43**; **III** 695;
  IV 194–95, 199, 455, 508; **8** 69,
  494–495; **15 519–21 (upd.)**; **23** 69, 451,
  453–54; **24** 79; **25** 102; **26** 423; **32** 147
Vebego International BV, 49 435–37
VECO International, Inc., 7 558–59
Vector Automotive Corporation, **13** 61
Vector Casa de Bolsa, **21** 413
Vector Gas Ltd., **13** 458
Vector Group Ltd., 35 437–40 (upd.)
Vector Video, Inc., **9** 74
Vedelectric, **13** 544
Vedior NV, 35 441–43; **44** 5
Veeco Instruments Inc., 32 487–90
Veeder-Root Company, **7** 116–17
VeggieTales. *See* Big Idea Productions,
  Inc.
Veit Companies, 43 440–42
Vel-Tex Chemical, **16** 270
Velcarta S.p.A., **17** 281
Velcro Industries N.V., 19 476–78
Velda Farms, Inc., **26** 448
Vellumoid Co., **I** 159
VeloBind, Inc., **10** 314
Velocity Express Corporation, 49 438–41
Velsicol, **I** 342, 440
Velva-Sheen Manufacturing Co., **23** 66
Vemar, **7** 558
Venator Group Inc., 35 444–49 (upd.)
Vencemos, **20** 124
Vencor, Inc., IV 402; **14** 243; **16 515–17**;
  25 456
Vendex International N.V., 10 136–37;
  13 544–46; **26** 160; **46** 187, 189
Vendôme Luxury Group plc, 27 487–89;
  29 90, 92
Vendors Supply of America, Inc., **7**
  241–42; **25** 241
**Venetian Casino Resort, LLC, 47
  427–29**
Venevision, **24** 516, 517
Vennootschap Nederland, **III** 177–78
Ventshade Company, **40** 299–300
Ventura, **29** 356–57
Venture Out RV, **26** 193
Venture Stores Inc., V 134; **12 507–09**
Ventures Limited, **49** 137
Venturi, Inc., **9** 72
Vepco. *See* Virginia Electric and Power
  Company.
Vera Cruz Electric Light, Power and
  Traction Co. Ltd., **IV** 658
Vera Imported Parts, **11** 84
Verafumos Ltd., **12** 109
Veragon Corporation. *See* Drypers
  Corporation.
Veratex Group, **13** 149–50

Veravision, **24** 510
Verbatim Corporation, **III** 477; **7** 163; **14** 533–35; **36** 173
Verbundnetz Gas AG, **38** 408
Verd-A-Fay, **13** 398
Vereenigde Nederlandsche Scheepvaartmaatschappij, **6** 404; **26** 242
Vereeniging Refractories, **IV** 22
Vereeniging Tiles, **III** 734
Verein für Chemische Industrie, **IV** 70
Vereinigte Aluminium Werke AG, **IV** 229–30, 232
Vereinigte Deutsche Metallwerke AG, **IV** 140
Vereinigte Elektrizitäts und Bergwerke A.G., **I** 542
Vereinigte Elektrizitätswerke Westfalen AG, **IV** 195; **V** 744–47
Vereinigte Energiewerke AG, **V** 709
Vereinigte Flugtechnische Werke GmbH., **I** 42, 55, 74–75
Vereinigte Glanzstoff-Fabriken, **13** 21
Vereinigte Industrie-Unternehmungen Aktiengesellschaft, **IV** 229–30
Vereinigte Leichtmetall-Werke GmbH, **IV** 231
Vereinigte Papierwarenfabriken GmbH, **IV** 323
Vereinigte Papierwerke Schickedanz AG, **26** 384
Vereinigte Stahlwerke AG, **III** 565; **IV** 87, 104–05, 132, 221; **14** 327
Vereinigte Versicherungsgruppe, **III** 377
Vereinigten Westdeutsche Waggonfabriken AG, **III** 542–43
Vereinsbank Wismar, **II** 256
Vereinte Versicherungen, **III** 377
Verenigde Bedrijven Bredero, **26** 280
N.V. Verenigde Fabrieken Wessanen and Laan, **II** 527
Verenigde Nederlandse Uitgeverijen. *See* VNU N.V.
Verenigde Spaarbank Groep. *See* VSB Groep.
Verienigte Schweizerbahnen, **6** 424
Verifact Inc. (IVI), **46** 251
VeriFone, Inc., **15** 321; **18** 541–44; **27** 219–21; **28** 191
Verilyte Gold, Inc., **19** 452
VeriSign, Inc., **47** 430–34
Veritas Capital Fund L.P., **44** 420, 423
Veritas Capital Partners, **26** 408
Veritas Software Corporation, **45** 427–31
Veritec Technologies, Inc., **48** 299
Veritus Inc., **27** 208–09
Verizon Communications, **43** 443–49 **(upd.)**
Verizon Wireless, Inc., **42** 284
Verlagsgruppe Georg von Holtzbrinck GmbH, **15** 158, 160; **25** 485; **35** 450–53
Vermeer Manufacturing Company, **17** 507–10
The Vermont Teddy Bear Co., Inc., **36** 500–02
Verneuil Holding Co, **21** 387
Vernitron Corporation, **18** 293
Vernon and Nelson Telephone Company. *See* British Columbia Telephone Company.
Vernon Graphics, **III** 499
Vernon Paving, **III** 674
Vernon Savings & Loan, **9** 199
Vernons, **IV** 651

Vernors, Inc., **25** 4
Vero, **III** 434
La Verrerie Souchon-Neuvesel, **II** 474
Verreries Champenoises, **II** 475
Versace. *See* Gianni Versace SpA.
Versatec Inc., **13** 128
Versatile Farm and Equipment Co., **22** 380
Versax, S.A. de C.V., **19** 12
Versicherungs-Verein, **III** 402, 410–11
Verson Allsteel Press Co., **21** 20, 22
Vert Baudet, **19** 309
Vertical Technology Industries, **14** 571
Verticom, **25** 531
Verve Records, **23** 389
Vessel Management Services, Inc., **28** 80
Vestar Capital Partners, **42** 309
Vestek Systems, Inc., **13** 417
Vestro, **19** 309
Vesuvius Crucible Co., **III** 681
Vesuvius USA Corporation, **8** 179
Veszpremtej, **25** 85
Veterinary Cos. of America, **III** 25
VEW AG, **IV** 234; **39** 412–15
Vexlar, **18** 313
VF Corporation, **V** 390–92; **12** 205; **13** 512; **17** 223, 225, **511–14 (upd.)**; **25** 22; **31** 261
VFW-Fokker B.V., **I** 41, 55, 74–75
VHA Long Term Care, **23** 431
VH1 Inc., **23** 503
VI-Jon Laboratories, Inc., **12** 388
VIA/Rhin et Moselle, **III** 185
Via-Générale de Transport et d'Industrie SA, **28** 155
Viacao Aerea Rio Grandense of South America. *See* VARIG, SA.
Viacom Enterprises, **6** 33; **7** 336
Viacom Inc., **23** 274–76, **500–03 (upd.)**; **24** 106, 327; **26** 32; **28** 295; **30** 101; **31** 59, 109; **35** 402; **48** 214. *See also* National Amusements Inc.
Viacom International Inc., **7** 222–24, 530, **560–62**; **9** 429; **10** 175; **19** 403
Viag AG, **IV** 229–32, 323; **25** 332; **32** 153; **43** 188–89
Viajes El Corte Inglés, S.A., **26** 129
VIASA, **I** 107; **6** 97; **36** 281
Viasoft Inc., **27** 490–93
Viatech Continental Can Company, Inc., **25** 512–15 **(upd.)**
Vichy, **III** 46
Vickers-Armstrong Ltd., **I** 50, 57, 82; **24** 85
Vickers Inc., **III** 640, 642; **13** 8; **23** 83
Vickers plc, **I** 194–95; **II** 3; **III** 555, 652, 725; **16** 9; **21** 435; **27** 494–97; **47** 9
VICOM, **48** 415
Vicon Industries, Inc., **44** 440–42
Vicoreen Instrument Co., **I** 202
VICORP Restaurants, Inc., **12** 510–12; **48** 412–15 **(upd.)**
Vicra Sterile Products, **I** 628
Vicsodrive Japan, **III** 495
Victor Company, **10** 483
Victor Company of Japan, Ltd., **I** 411; **II** 55–56, 91, 102, **118–19**; **III** 605; **IV** 599; **12** 454; **26** 511–13 **(upd.)**
Victor Comptometer, **I** 676; **III** 154
Victor Equipment Co., **19** 440
Victor Manufacturing and Gasket Co., **I** 152
Victor Musical Industries Inc., **II** 119; **10** 285
Victor Talking Machine Co., **II** 88, 118

Victor Value, **II** 678
Victoria, **III** 308
Victoria & Co., **39** 247
Victoria & Legal & General, **III** 359
Victoria Coach Station, **6** 406
Victoria Creations Inc., **13** 536
Victoria Group, **44** 443–46 **(upd.)**
VICTORIA Holding AG, **III** 399–401. *See also* Victoria Group.
Victoria Paper Co., **IV** 286
Victoria Sugar Co., **III** 686
Victoria Wine Co., **I** 216
Victoria's Secret, **V** 115–16; **11** 498; **12** 557, 559; **16** 219; **18** 215; **24** 237; **25** 120–22, 521
Victorinox AG, **21** 515–17
Victory Fire Insurance Co., **III** 343
Victory Insurance, **III** 273
Victory Oil Co., **IV** 550
Victory Refrigeration Company, **22** 355
Victory Savings and Loan, **10** 339
Victory Supermarket. *See* Big V Supermarkets, Inc.
Vidal Sassoon, **17** 110
Video Concepts, **9** 186
Video Independent Theatres, Inc., **14** 86
Video Library, Inc., **9** 74
Video News International, **19** 285
Video Superstores Master Limited Partnership, **9** 74
Videoconcepts, **II** 107
VideoFusion, Inc., **16** 419
Videotex Network Japan, **IV** 680
Videotron, **25** 102
VideV, **24** 509
La Vie Claire, **13** 103
Vielle Montaign, **22** 285
Vienna Sausage Manufacturing Co., **14** 536–37
Viessmann Werke GmbH & Co., **37** 411–14
View-Master/Ideal Group, **12** 496
Viewdata Corp., **IV** 630; **15** 264
Viewer's Edge, **27** 429
Viewlogic, **11** 490
ViewStar Corp., **20** 103
Viewtel, **14** 36
ViewTrade Holding Corp., **46** 282
Vigilance-Vie, **III** 393
Vigilant Insurance Co., **III** 220; **14** 108; **37** 83
Vigoro, **22** 340
Vigortone, **II** 582
Viiala Oy, **IV** 302
Viking, **II** 10; **IV** 659
Viking Brush, **III** 614
Viking Building Products, **22** 15
Viking Computer Services, Inc., **14** 147
Viking Consolidated Shipping Corp, **25** 470
Viking Direct Limited, **10** 545
Viking Foods, Inc., **8** 482; **14** 411
Viking Industries, **39** 322, 324
Viking Office Products, Inc., **10** 544–46
Viking Penguin, **IV** 611
Viking Press, **12** 25
Viking Pump Company, **21** 499–500
Viking Star Shipping, Inc. *See* Teekay Shipping Corporation.
Viktor Achter, **9** 92
Village Inn. *See* VICORP Restaurants, Inc.
Village Super Market, Inc., **7** 563–64
Village Voice Media, Inc., **38** 476–79
Villager, Inc., **11** 216; **39** 244

Villazon & Co., **27** 139
Villeroy & Boch AG, 37 415–18
VILPAC, S.A., **26** 356
AO VimpelCom, 48 416–19
Vimto. *See* Nichols plc.
Vin & Spirit AB, 31 458–61
Viña Concha y Toro S.A., 45 432–34
Vinci, 27 54; **43 450–52; 49** 44
Vine Products Ltd., **I** 215
Viner Bros., **16** 546
Vingaarden A/S, **9** 100
Vingresor A.B., **I** 120
Vining Industries, **12** 128
Viniprix SA, **10** 205; **19** 309; **27** 95
Vinland Web-Print, **8** 360
Vinson & Elkins L.L.P., 28 48; **30**
    481–83; 47 139–40, 447
Vintage Petroleum, Inc., 42 421–23
Vintners International, **34** 89
Vinyl Maid, Inc., **IV** 401
Vipont Pharmaceutical, **III** 25; **14** 122
VIPS, **11** 113
Viratec Thin Films, Inc., **22** 347
Virco Manufacturing Corporation, 17
    515–17
Virgin Atlantic Airlines. *See* Virgin Group
    PLC.
Virgin Express, **35** 384
Virgin Group PLC, 12 513–15; 14 73; **18**
    80; **22** 194; **24** 486; **29** 302; **32 491–96**
    (upd.)
The Virgin Islands Telephone Co., **19** 256
Virgin Retail Group Ltd., **9** 75, 361; **37**
    262
Virginia Eastern Shore Sustainable
    Development Corporation, **28** 307
Virginia Electric and Power Company, **V**
    596–98
Virginia Fibre Corporation, **15** 188
Virginia Folding Box Company, **IV** 352;
    19 497
Virginia Laminating, **10** 313
Virginia Mason Medical Center, **41** 183
Virginia National Bankshares, **10** 426
Virginia Railway and Power Company
    (VR&P), **V** 596
Virginia Trading Corp., **II** 422
Viridor Waste Limited, **45** 338
Viromedics, **25** 382
Visa. *See* Valores Industriales S.A.
Visa International, II 200; **9** 333–35,
    536–38; 18 543; **20** 59; **26 514–17**
    (upd.); 41 200–01
Visco Products Co., **I** 373; **12** 346
Viscodrive GmbH, **III** 495
Viscount Industries Limited, **6** 310
Vishay Intertechnology, Inc., 11 516; **21**
    518–21
VisiCorp, **6** 254; **25** 298
Vision Centers, **I** 688; **12** 188
Vision Technology Group Ltd., **19** 124; **49**
    113
Visionware Ltd., **38** 419
Visionworks, **9** 186
Viskase Corporation, **17** 157, 159
Visking Co., **I** 400
Visnews Ltd., **IV** 668, 670
VisQueen, **I** 334
Vista Bakery Inc., **14** 306
Vista Chemical Company, I 402–03; V
    709
Vista Concepts, Inc., **11** 19
Vista Resources, Inc., **17** 195
Vista 2000, Inc., **36** 444

Vistana, Inc., 22 537–39; 26 464
Visual Action Holdings plc, **24** 96, 374
Visual Information Technologies, **11** 57
Visual Technology, **6** 201
VISX, Incorporated, 30 484–86
Vita-Achter, **9** 92
Vita Lebensversicherungs-Gesellschaft, **III**
    412
Vita Liquid Polymers, **9** 92
Vitafoam Incorporated, **9** 93; **33** 78
Vital Health Corporation, **13** 150
Vital Processing Services LLC, **18** 516,
    518
Vitalink Communications Corp., **11** 520;
    34 444
Vitalink Pharmacy Services, Inc., 15
    522–24; 25 309–10
Vitalscheme, **38** 426
Vitamin World, **31** 346–48
Vitesse Semiconductor Corporation, 32
    497–500
Vitex Foods, **10** 382
Vitoria-Minas Railroad, **43** 111
Vitro Corp., 8 178; **10** 547–48; **17** 492
Vitro Corporativo S.A. de C.V., 34
    490–92
Vitro S.A., **19** 189
VIVA, **23** 390
Viva Home Co., **III** 757
Vivendi Universal S.A., 29 369, 371; **32**
    52, 54; **33** 178, 181; **34** 83, 85; **38** 168,
    170; **40** 408; **41** 361; **43** 450, 452; **44**
    190; **46 438–41 (upd.); 47** 420–21; **48**
    164–65
Vivendia, **40** 449
Vivesvata Iron and Steel Ltd., **IV** 207
Viviane Woodard Cosmetic Corp., **II** 531
Vivra, Inc., 15 119; **18 545–47**
VK Mason Construction Ltd., **II** 222
VKI Technologies Inc., **39** 409
Vladivostok Dairy, **48** 438
Vlasic Foods International Inc., II
    480–81; **7** 67–68; **25 516–19; 26** 56, 59
VLN Corp., **I** 201
VLSI Technology, Inc., 11 246; **16**
    518–20; 31 300
VMG Products. *See* Drypers Corporation.
VMX Inc., **14** 355; **41** 289
VND, **III** 593
Vnesheconbank, **II** 242
VNG. *See* Verbundnetz Gas AG.
VNS. *See* Vereenigde Nederlandsche
    Scheepvaartmaatschappij.
VNU N.V., 27 361, **498–501; 38** 8
VNU/Claritas, **6** 14
Vobis Microcomputer, **20** 103; **23** 311
VocalTec, Inc., **18** 143
Vodac, **11** 548
Vodacom World Online Ltd, **48** 399
Vodafone Group Plc, II 84; **11 547–48;**
    34 85; **36 503–06 (upd.); 38** 296, 300
Vodapage, **11** 548
Vodata, **11** 548
Vodavi Technology Corporation, **13** 213
Voest-Alpine Stahl AG, IV 233–35; 31
    47–48
Vogel Peterson Furniture Company, **7** 4–5
Vogoro Corp., **13** 503
Voice Data Systems, **15** 125
Voice Powered Technology International,
    Inc., **23** 212
Voice Response, Inc., **11** 253
VoiceStream Wireless Corporation, **48** 130

Voith Sulzer Papiermaschinen GmbH. *See*
    J.M. Voith AG.
Vokes, **I** 429
Volition, Inc., **39** 395
Volkert Stampings, **III** 628
Volkswagen Aktiengesellschaft, I 30, 32,
    186, 192, **206–08**, 460; **II** 279; **IV** 231;
    7 8; **10** 14; **11** 104, **549–51 (upd.); 13**
    413; **14** 169; **16** 322; **19** 484; **26** 12; **27**
    11, 496; **31** 363–65; **32 501–05 (upd.);**
    34 55, 130; **39** 373–74
Volt Information Sciences Inc., 26
    518–21
Volta Aluminium Co., Ltd., **IV** 122
Volume Distributors. *See* Payless
    ShoeSource, Inc.
Volume Service Company. *See* Restaurants
    Unlimited, Inc.
Volume Shoe Corporation. *See* Payless
    ShoeSource,Inc.
Voluntary Hospitals of America, **6** 45
Volunteer Leather Company, **17** 202, 205
Volunteer State Life Insurance Co., **III**
    221; **37** 84
AB Volvo, I 186, 192, 198, **209–11; II** 5,
    366; **III** 543, 591, 623, 648; **IV** 336; **7**
    565–68 (upd.); 9 283–84, 350, 381; **10**
    274; **12** 68, 342; **13** 30, 356; **14** 321; **15**
    226; **16** 322; **18** 394; **23** 354; **26 9–12**
    (upd.), 401, 403; **33** 191, 364; **39** 126.
    See also Ford Motor Company.
Volvo-Penta, **21** 503
von Roll, **6** 599
Von Ruden Manufacturing Co., **17** 532
von Weise Gear Co., **III** 509
Von's Grocery Co., **II** 419; **8** 474; **17** 559
The Vons Companies, Incorporated, II
    655; **7 569–71; 12** 209; **24** 418; **28**
    510–13 (upd.); 35 328
VOP Acquisition Corporation, **10** 544
Vornado Realty Trust, 20 508–10; 39
    211; **45** 14–16; **47** 360
Voroba Hearing Systems, **25** 56
Vortex Management, Inc., **41** 207
Vorwerk & Co., 27 502–04
Vosper Thornycroft Holding plc, 41
    410–12
Votainer International, **13** 20
Vought Aircraft Industries, Inc., 11 364;
    45 309; **49 442–45**
Voxson, **I** 531; **22** 193
Voyage Conseil, **II** 265
Voyager Communications Inc., **24** 5
Voyager Energy, **IV** 84
Voyager Ltd., **12** 514
Voyager Petroleum Ltd., **IV** 83; **7** 188
Voyageur Travel Insurance Ltd., **21** 447
VR&P. *See* Virginia Railway and Power
    Company.
Vratislavice A.S., **38** 77
VRG International. *See* Roberts
    Pharmaceutical Corporation.
Vroom & Dreesmann, **13** 544–46
Vrumona B.V., **I** 257
VS Services, **13** 49
VSA. *See* Vendors Supply of America, Inc.
VSB Groep, **III** 199, 201
VSD Communications, Inc., **22** 443
VSEL, **24** 88
VSM. *See* Village Super Market, Inc.
VST. *See* Vision Technology Group Ltd.
Vtel Corporation, **10** 456; **27** 365
VTR Incorporated, **16** 46; **43** 60
Vu-Tech Communications, Inc., **48** 54

Vulcan Materials Company, 7 572–75;
  12 39; **25** 266; **41** 147, 149
Vulcan Ventures Inc., **32** 145; **43** 144
Vulcraft, **7** 400–02
VVM, **III** 200
VW&R. *See* Van Waters & Rogers.
VWR Textiles & Supplies, Inc., **11** 256
VWR United Company, **9** 531
Vycor Corporation, **25** 349
Vyvx, **31** 469

W&A Manufacturing Co., LLC, **26** 530
W&F Fish Products, **13** 103
W. & G. Turnbull & Co., **IV** 278; **19** 153
W & J Sloane Home Furnishings Group,
  35 129
W. & M. Duncan, **II** 569
W.A. Bechtel Co., **I** 558
W.A. Harriman & Co., **III** 471
W.A. Krueger Co., **19** 333–35
W. Atlee Burpee & Co., II 532; **11** 198;
  27 505–08
W.B. Constructions, **III** 672
W.B. Doner & Company, **10** 420; **12** 208;
  28 138
W.B. Saunders Co., **IV** 623–24
W.C. Bradley Company, **18** 516
W.C.G. Sports Industries Ltd. *See* Canstar
  Sports Inc.
W.C. Heraeus GmbH, **IV** 100
W.C. Norris, **III** 467
W.C. Platt Co., **IV** 636
W.C. Ritchie & Co., **IV** 333
W.C. Smith & Company Limited, **14** 339
W. Duke & Sons, **V** 395, 600
W. Duke Sons & Company, **27** 128
W.E. Andrews Co., Inc., **25** 182
W.E. Dillon Company, Ltd., **21** 499
W.F. Linton Company, **9** 373
W. Gunson & Co., **IV** 278; **19** 153
W. Gutzeit & Co., **IV** 274–77
W.H. Brady Co., 17 518–21
W.H. Gunlocke Chair Co. *See* Gunlocke
  Company.
W.H. McElwain Co., **III** 528
W.H. Morton & Co., **II** 398; **10** 62
W.H. Smith & Son (Alacra) Ltd., **15** 473
W H Smith Group PLC, V 211–13
W.J. Noble and Sons, **IV** 294; **19** 225
W.L. Gore & Associates, Inc., 14
  538–40; 26 417
W.M. Bassett Furniture Co. *See* Bassett
  Furniture Industries, Inc.
W.M. Ritter Lumber Co., **IV** 281; **9** 259
W.O. Daley & Company, **10** 387
W.P. Carey & Co. LLC, 49 446–48
W.R. Bean & Son, **19** 335
W.R. Berkley Corp., III 248; **15** 525–27
W.R. Breen Company, **11** 486
W.R. Case & Sons Cutlery Company, **18**
  567
W.R. Grace & Company, I 547–50; **III**
  525, 695; **IV** 454; **11** 216; **12** 337; **13**
  149, 502, 544; **14** 29; **16** 45–47; **17** 308,
  365–66; **21** 213, 507, 526; **22** 188, 501;
  25 535; **35** 38, 40; **43** 59–60; **49** 307
W. Rosenlew, **IV** 350
W.S. Barstow & Company, **6** 575
W.T. Grant Co., **16** 487
W.T. Rawleigh, **17** 105
W.T. Young Foods, **III** 52; **8** 433; **26** 383
W. Ullberg & Co., **I** 553
W.V. Bowater & Sons, Ltd., **IV** 257–58
W.W. Cargill and Brother, **II** 616; **13** 136

W.W. Grainger, Inc., V 214–15; **13** 297;
  26 537–39 (upd.)
W.W. Kimball Company, **12** 296; **18** 44
W.W. Norton & Company, Inc., 28
  518–20
Waban Inc., **V** 198; **13** 547–49; **19** 449.
  See also HomeBase, Inc.
Wabash National Corp., 13 550–52
Wabash Valley Power Association, **6** 556
Wabtec Corporation, 40 451–54
Wabush Iron Co., **IV** 73; **24** 143
Wachbrit Insurance Agency, **21** 96
Wachovia Bank of Georgia, N.A., 16
  521–23
Wachovia Bank of South Carolina, N.A.,
  16 524–26
Wachovia Corporation, II 336; **10** 425;
  12 16, **516–20**; **16** 521, 524, 526; **23**
  455; **46** 442–49 (upd.)
Wachtell, Lipton, Rosen & Katz, 47
  435–38
The Wackenhut Corporation, 13 124–25;
  14 541–43; **28** 255; **41** 80
Wacker-Chemie GmbH, 35 454–58
Wacker Oil Inc., **11** 441
Waco Aircraft Company, **27** 98
Wacoal Corp., 25 520–24
Waddell & Reed, Inc., 22 540–43; **33**
  405, 407
Wade Smith, **28** 27, 30
Wadsworth Inc., **8** 526
WaferTech, **18** 20; **43** 17; **47** 385
Waffle House Inc., 14 544–45
Wagenseller & Durst, **25** 249
Waggener Edstrom, 42 424–26
The Wagner & Brown Investment Group, **9**
  248
Wagner Castings Company, **16** 474–75
Wagner Litho Machinery Co., **13** 369–70
Wagner Spray Tech, **18** 555
Wagonlit Travel, **22** 128
Wagons-Lits, **27** 11; **29** 443; **37** 250–52
Wah Chang Corp., **I** 523–24; **10** 520–21
AB Wahlbecks, **25** 464
Wahlstrom & Co., **23** 480
Waialua Agricultural Co., **II** 491
Waitaki International Biosciences Co., **17**
  288
Waite Amulet Mines Ltd., **IV** 164
Waitrose Ltd. *See* John Lewis Partnership
  plc.
Wakefern Food Corporation, II 672; **7**
  563–64; **18** 6; **25** 66, 234–35; **28** 143;
  33 434–37
Wako Shoji Co. Ltd. *See* Wacoal Corp.
Wakodo Co., **I** 674
Wal-Mart de Mexico, S.A. de C.V., 35
  322, 459–61 (upd.)
Wal-Mart Stores, Inc., II 108; **V** 216–17;
  6 287; **7** 61, 331; **8** 33, 295, 555–57
  (upd.); **9** 187, 361; **10** 236, 284,
  515–16, 524; **11** 292; **12** 48, 53–55,
  63–64, 97, 208–09, 221, 277, 333, 477,
  507–08; **13** 42, 215–17, 260–61, 274,
  332–33, 444, 446; **14** 235; **15** 139, 275;
  16 61–62, 65, 390; **17** 297, 321,
  460–61; **18** 108, 137, 186, 283, 286; **19**
  511; **20** 263; **21** 457–58; **22** 224, 257,
  328; **23** 214; **24** 148, 149, 334; **25**
  221–22, 254, 314; **26** 522–26 (upd.),
  549; **27** 286, 313, 315, 416, 451; **29**
  230, 314, 318; **32** 169, 338, 341; **33**
  307; **34** 198; **37** 64; **41** 61, 115; **45** 408,
  412

Walbridge Aldinger Co., 38 480–82
Walbro Corporation, 13 553–55
Walchenseewerk AG, **23** 44
Waldbaum, Inc., II 638; **15** 260; **16** 247,
  249; **19** 479–81; **24** 528
Walden Book Company Inc., V 112; **10**
  136–37; **16** 160; **17** 522–24; **25** 30; **47**
  209
Waldes Truarc Inc., **III** 624
Oy Waldhof AB, **IV** 324
Wales & Company, **14** 257
Walgreen Co., V 218–20; **9** 346; **18** 199;
  20 511–13 (upd.); **21** 186; **24** 263; **32**
  166, 170; **45** 133, 137
Walk Haydel & Associates, Inc., **25** 130
Walk Softly, Inc., **25** 118
Walker & Lee, **10** 340
Walker Cain, **I** 215
Walker Dickson Group Limited, **26** 363
Walker Interactive Systems, **11** 78; **25** 86
Walker Manufacturing Company, I 527;
  19 482–84
Walker McDonald Manufacturing Co., **III**
  569; **20** 361
Walkers Parker and Co., **III** 679–80
Walki GmbH, **IV** 349
AB Walkiakoski, **IV** 347
Walkins Manufacturing Corp., **III** 571; **20**
  362
Walkup's Merchant Express Inc., **27** 473
Wall Drug Store, Inc., 40 455–57
Wall Paper Manufacturers, **IV** 666; **17** 397
Wall Street Deli, Inc., 33 438–41
Wall Street Leasing, **III** 137
Wallace and Tiernan, **I** 383; **11** 361
The Wallace Berrie Company. *See*
  Applause Inc.
Wallace Computer Services, Inc., 36
  507–10
Wallace International Silversmiths, **I** 473;
  14 482–83
Wallace Murray Corp., **II** 420
Wallbergs Fabriks A.B., **8** 14
Wallens Dairy Co., **II** 586
Wallin & Nordstrom, **V** 156
Wallingford Bank and Trust Co., **II** 213
Wallis, **V** 177
Wallis Arnold Enterprises, Inc., **21** 483
Wallis Tin Stamping Co., **I** 605
Wallis Tractor Company, **21** 502
Walrus, Inc., **18** 446
Walsin-Lihwa, **13** 141
Walston & Co., **II** 450; **III** 137
Walt Disney Company, II 102, 122, 129,
  156, **172–74**; **III** 142, 504, 586; **IV** 585,
  675, 703; **6** 15, **174–77** (upd.); **36** 7
  305; **8** 160; **10** 420; **12** 168, 208, 229,
  323, 495–96; **13** 551; **14** 260; **15** 197;
  16 143, 336; **17** 243, 317, 442–43; **21**
  23–26, 360–61; **23** 257–58, 303, 335,
  476, 514; **25** 172, 268, 312–13; **27** 92,
  287; **30** 487–91 (upd.); **34** 348; **43** 142,
  447
Walt Disney World, **6** 82, 175–76; **18** 290
Walter Baker's Chocolate, **II** 531
Walter Bau, **27** 136, 138
Walter E. Heller, **17** 324
Walter Herzog GmbH, **16** 514
Walter Industries, Inc., III 765–67; **22**
  544–47 (upd.)
Walter Kidde & Co., **I** 475, 524; **27** 287
Walter Pierce Oil Co., **IV** 657
Walter Wilson, **49** 18
Walter Wright Mammoet, **26** 280

Walton Manufacturing, **11** 486
Walton Monroe Mills, Inc., 8 558–60
Wander Ltd., **I** 672
Wanderer Werke, **III** 154
Wang Global, **39** 176–78
Wang Laboratories, Inc., II 208; **III** 168–70; **6 284–87 (upd.)**; **8** 139; **9** 171; **10** 34; **11** 68, 274; **12** 183; **18** 138; **19** 40; **20** 237
Wanishi, **IV** 157; **17** 349
WAP, **26** 420
Waples-Platter Co., **II** 625
War Damage Corp., **III** 353, 356; **22** 493
War Emergency Tankers Inc., **IV** 552
Warbasse-Cogeneration Technologies Partnership, **35** 479
Warburg, Pincus Capital Corp., **6** 13; **9** 524; **14** 42; **24** 373
Warburg USB, **38** 291
Warburtons Bakery Cafe, Inc., **18** 37
Ward Manufacturing Inc., **IV** 101
Ward's Communications, **22** 441
Wardley Ltd., **II** 298
Wards. See Circuit City Stores, Inc.
Waring and LaRosa, **12** 167
The Warnaco Group Inc., 9 156; **12 521–23**; **22** 123; **25** 122, 523; **46 450–54 (upd.).** See also Authentic Fitness Corp.
Warner & Swasey Co., **III** 168; **6** 284; **8** 545
Warner Brothers, **25** 327–28; **26** 102
Warner Communications Inc., II 88, 129, 135, 146–47, 154–55, 169–70, **175–77**, 208, 452; **III** 443, 505; **IV** 623, 673, 675–76; **7** 526, 528–30 **8** 527; **9** 44–45, 119, 469; **10** 196; **11** 557; **12** 73, 495–96; **17** 65, 149, 442–43; **21** 23–25, 360; **22** 519, 522; **23** 23–24, 390, 501; **24** 373; **25** 418–19, 498; **26** 151. See also Time Warner Inc.
Warner Cosmetics, **III** 48; **8** 129
Warner Gear Co., **III** 438–39; **14** 63–64
Warner-Lambert Co., I 643, 674, 679, 696, **710–12**; **7** 596; **8** 62–63; **10 549–52 (upd.)**; **12** 480, 482; **13** 366; **16** 439; **20** 23; **25** 55, 366; **34** 284; **38** 366
Warner Records, **II** 177
Warner Sugar Refining Co., **II** 496
Warren Apparel Group Ltd., **39** 257
Warren Bank, **13** 464
Warren, Gorham & Lamont, **8** 526
Warren Oilfield Services, **9** 363
Warren Petroleum, **18** 365, 367; **49** 121
Warri Refining and Petrochemicals Co., **IV** 473
Warrick Industries, **31** 338
Warringah Brick, **III** 673
Warrington Products Ltd. See Canstar Sports Inc.
Warrior River Coal Company, **7** 281
Wartsila Marine Industries Inc., **III** 649
Warwick Chemicals, **13** 461
Warwick Electronics, **III** 654
Warwick International Ltd., **13** 462
Wasa, **I** 672–73
Wasag-Chemie AG, **III** 694
Wasatch Gas Co., **6** 568
Wascana Energy Inc., 13 556–58
Washburn Crosby Co., **II** 501, 555; **10** 322
Washburn Graphics Inc., **23** 100
The Washington Companies, 33 442–45
Washington Duke Sons & Co., **12** 108
Washington Federal, Inc., 17 525–27

Washington Football, Inc., 35 462–65
Washington Gas Light Company, 19 485–88
Washington Inventory Service, **30** 239
Washington Mills Company, **13** 532
Washington Mutual, Inc., 17 528–31
Washington National Corporation, 11 482; **12 524–26**
Washington Natural Gas Company, 9 539–41
The Washington Post Company, III 214; **IV 688–90**; **6** 323; **11** 331; **18** 60, 61, 63; **20 515–18 (upd.)**; **23** 157–58; **42** 31, 33–34, 209–10
Washington Railway and Electric Company, **6** 552–53
Washington Scientific Industries, Inc., 17 532–34
Washington Specialty Metals Corp., **14** 323, 325
Washington Sports Clubs. See Town Sports International, Inc.
Washington Steel Corp., **14** 323, 325
Washington Water Power Company, 6 566, **595–98**
Washtenaw Gas Company. See MCN Corporation.
Wassall Plc, 18 548–50
Wasserstein Perella Partners, **II** 629; **III** 512, 530–31; **V** 223; **17** 366
Waste Connections, Inc., 46 455–57
Waste Control Specialists LLC, **19** 466, 468
Waste Holdings, Inc., 41 413–15
Waste Management, Inc., V 749–51, **752–54**; **6** 46, 600; **9** 73, 108–09; **11** 435–36; **18** 10; **20** 90; **23** 430
Water Engineering, **11** 360
Water Pik Technologies, Inc., I 524–25; **34 498–501**
Water Products Group, **6** 487–88
Water Street Corporate Recovery Fund, **10** 423
The Waterbury Companies, **16** 482
Waterford Wedgwood Holdings PLC, IV 296; **12 527–29**
Waterford Wedgwood plc, 34 493–97 (upd.); **38** 403
Waterhouse Investor Services, Inc., 18 551–53; **49** 397
Waterloo Gasoline Engine Co., **III** 462; **21** 173
Waterlow and Sons, **10** 269
Waterman Marine Corporation, **27** 242
The Waterman Pen Company. See BIC Corporation.
WaterPro Supplies Corporation, **6** 486, 488
Waters Corporation, 43 453–57
Waterstone's, **42** 444
Waterstreet Inc., **17** 293
Watertown Insurance Co., **III** 370
Watkins-Johnson Company, 15 528–30
Watkins Manufacturing Co., **I** 159
Watkins-Strathmore Co., **13** 560
Watmough and Son Ltd., **II** 594
Watney Mann and Truman Brewers, **I** 228, 247; **9** 99
Watson & Philip. See Alldays plc.
Watson-Haas Lumber Company, **33** 257
Watson Pharmaceuticals Inc., 16 527–29
Watson-Triangle, **16** 388, 390
Watson-Wilson Transportation System, **V** 540; **14** 567
Watson Wyatt Worldwide, 42 427–30

Watt & Shand, **16** 61
Watt AG, **6** 491
Watt Electronic Products, Limited, **10** 319
The Watt Stopper, **21** 348, 350
Wattie Pict Ltd., **I** 437
Wattie's Ltd., 7 576–78; **11** 173
Watts Industries, Inc., 19 489–91
Watts/Silverstein, Inc., **24** 96
Waukesha Engine Servicenter, **6** 441
Waukesha Foundry Company, **11** 187
Waukesha Motor Co., **III** 472
Wausau Paper Mills, **15** 305
Wausau Sulphate Fibre Co. See Mosinee Paper Corporation.
Wavelength Corporate Communications Pty Limited, **24** 95
Waverly, Inc., 10 135; **16 530–32**; **19** 358
Waverly Oil Works, **I** 405
Waverly Pharmaceutical Limited, **11** 208
Wawa Inc., 17 535–37
Waxman Industries, Inc., III 570; **9 542–44**; **20** 362; **28** 50–51
Wayco Foods, **14** 411
Waycross-Douglas Coca-Cola Bottling, **10** 222
Wayne Home Equipment. See Scott Fetzer Company.
Wayne Oakland Bank, **8** 188
WB. See Warner Communications Inc.
WBI Holdings, Inc., **42** 249, 253
WCI Holdings Corporation, **V** 223; **13** 170; **41** 94
WCK, Inc., **14** 236
WCRS Group plc, **6** 15
WCT Live Communication Limited, **24** 95
WD-40 Company, 18 554–57
Wear-Ever, **17** 213
WearGuard, **13** 48
Wearne Brothers, **6** 117
The Weather Department, Ltd., **10** 89
Weather Guard, **IV** 305
Weatherford International, Inc., 39 416–18
Weathers-Lowin, Leeam, **11** 408
Weaver, **III** 468
Webb & Knapp, **10** 43
Webb Corbett and Beswick, **38** 402
Webber Gage Co., **13** 302
WeBco International LLC, **26** 530
Webco Securities, Inc., **37** 225
Weber, **16** 488
Weber Aircraft Inc., **41** 369
Weber Metal, **30** 283–84
Weber-Stephen Products Co., 40 458–60
Webers, **I** 409
Weblock, **I** 109
WebLogic Inc., **36** 81
Webster Publishing Co., **IV** 636
Webtron Corp., **10** 313
Webvan Group Inc., **38** 223
Wedgwood. See Waterford Wedgewood Holdings PLC.
Week's Dairy, **II** 528
Wegert Verwaltungs-GmbH and Co. Beteiligungs-KG, **24** 270
Wegmans Food Markets, Inc., 9 545–46; **24** 445; **41 416–18 (upd.)**
Weidemann Brewing Co., **I** 254
Weider Health and Fitness, Inc., **38** 238
Weider Nutrition International, Inc., 29 498–501; **33** 146–47; **34** 459
Weider Sporting Goods, **16** 80
Weifang Power Machine Fittings Ltd., **17** 106

Weight Watchers Gourmet Food Co., **43** 218

Weight Watchers International Inc., II 508; **10** 383; **11** 172; **12** 530–32; **13** 383; **27** 197; **33** 446–49 (upd.); **36** 255–56

Weiner's Stores, Inc., 33 450–53

Weirton Steel Corporation, I 297; **IV** 236–38; **7** 447, 598; **8** 346, 450; **10** 31–32; **12** 352, 354; **26** 407, **527–30** (upd.)

Weis Markets, Inc., 15 531–33

The Weitz Company, Inc., 42 431–34

Welbecson, **III** 501

Welbilt Corp., 19 492–94; **27** 159

Welborn Transport Co., **39** 64, 65

Welch's, **25** 366

Welcome Wagon International Inc., **III** 28; **16** 146

Weldless Steel Company, **8** 530

Welex Jet Services, **III** 498–99

Wella AG, 48 420–23 (upd.)

Wella Group, III 68–70

Wellby Super Drug Stores, **12** 220

Wellcome Foundation Ltd., I 638, **713–15**; **8** 210, 452; **9** 265; **10** 551; **32** 212

Wellcome Trust, **41** 119

Weller Electric Corp., **II** 16

Wellington, **II** 457

Wellington Management Company, **14** 530–31; **23** 226

Wellington Sears Co., **15** 247–48

Wellman, Inc., 8 561–62; **21** 193

Wellmark, Inc., **10** 89

Wellness Co., Ltd., **IV** 716

WellPoint Health Networks Inc., 25 **525–29**

Wells Aircraft, **12** 112

Wells Fargo & Company, II 380–84, 319, 395; **III** 440; **10** 59–60; **12** 165, **533–37** (upd.); **17** 325; **18** 60, 543; **19** 411; **22** 542; **25** 434; **27** 292; **32** 373; **38** 44, **483–92** (upd.); **41** 200–01; **46** 217. See also American Express Company.

Wells Fargo HSBC Trade Bank, **26** 203

Wells-Gardner Electronics Corporation, **43** 458–61

Wells Lamont, **IV** 136

Wells Rich Greene BDDP, 6 48, **50–52**

Wells' Dairy, Inc., 36 511–13

Wellspring Associates L.L.C., **16** 338

Wellspring Resources LLC, **42** 429

Welsbach Mantle, **6** 446

Welsh Associated Collieries Ltd., **31** 369

Welsh Water. See Hyder plc.

Weltkunst Verlag GmbH, **IV** 590

Wendy's International, Inc., II 614–15, 647; **7** 433; **8** 563–65; **9** 178; **12** 553; **13** 494; **14** 453; **16** 95, 97; **17** 71, 124; **19** 215; **23** 384, **504–07** (upd.); **26** 284; **33** 240; **36** 517, 519; **41** 114; **46** 404–05; **47** 439–44 (upd.)

Wenger S.A., **III** 419; **21** 515

Wenlock Brewery Co., I 223

Wenner Media, Inc., 32 506–09

Wenstroms & Granstoms Electriska Kraftbolag, **II** 1

Werkhof GmbH, **13** 491

Werknet, **16** 420; **43** 308

Werner Baldessarini Design GmbH, **48** 209

Werner Enterprises, Inc., 26 531–33

Werner International, **III** 344; **14** 225

Wernicke Co., I 201

Wertheim Schroder & Company, **17** 443

Weru Aktiengesellschaft, 18 558–61; **49** 295

Wesco Financial Corp., **III** 213, 215; **18** 62; **42** 32–34

Wesco Food Co., **II** 644

Wescot Decisison Systems, **6** 25

Weserflug, I 74

Wesper Co., **26** 4

Wesray and Management, **17** 213

Wesray Capital Corporation, **6** 357; **13** 41; **17** 443; **47** 363

Wesray Corporation, **22** 55

Wesray Holdings Corp., **13** 255

Wesray Transportation, Inc., **14** 38

Wessanen. See Koninklijke Wessanen N.V.

Wessanen and Laan, **II** 527

Wessanen Cacao, **II** 528

Wessanen USA, **II** 528; **29** 480

Wessanen's Koninklijke Fabrieken N.V., **II** 527

Wesson/Peter Pan Foods Co., **17** 241

West Australia Land Holdings, Limited, **10** 169

West Bend Co., III 610–11; **14** 546–48; **16** 384; **43** 289

West Coast Entertainment Corporation, **29** 502–04

West Coast Grocery Co., **II** 670; **18** 506

West Coast Machinery, **13** 385

West Coast of America Telegraph, I 428

West Coast Power Company, **12** 265

West Coast Restaurant Enterprises, **25** 390

West Coast Savings and Loan, **10** 339

West Coast Telecom, **III** 38

West Corporation, 42 435–37

West End Family Pharmacy, Inc., **15** 523

West Fraser Timber Co. Ltd., IV 276; **17** 538–40

West Georgia Coca-Cola Bottlers, Inc., **13** 163

West Group, 34 438, **502–06** (upd.)

West Ham Gutta Percha Co., I 428

West Harrison Gas & Electric Company, **6** 466

West India Oil Co., **IV** 416, 428

West Japan Heavy Industries, **III** 578–79; **7** 348

West Jersey Electric Company, **6** 449

West Lynn Creamery, Inc., **26** 450

West Marine, Inc., 17 541–43; **37** 398

West Missouri Power Company. See UtiliCorp United Inc.

West Newton Savings Bank, **13** 468

West Newton Telephone Company, **14** 258

West of England, **III** 690

West of England Sack Holdings, **III** 501; **7** 207

West One Bancorp, 11 552–55; **36** 491

West Penn Electric. See Allegheny Power System, Inc.

West Penn Power Company, **38** 38–40

West Pharmaceutical Services, Inc., 42 438–41

West Point-Pepperell, Inc., 8 566–69; **9** 466; **15** 247; **25** 20; **28** 218. See also WestPoint Stevens Inc. and JPS Textile Group, Inc.

West Publishing Co., IV 312; **7** 579–81; **10** 407; **19** 268; **33** 264–65. See also The West Group.

West Rand Consolidated Mines, **IV** 90

West Rand Investment Trust, **IV** 21; **16** 27

West Richfield Telephone Company, **6** 299

West Side Bank, **II** 312

West Side Printing Co., **13** 559

West Surrey Central Dairy Co. Ltd., **II** 586

West TeleServices Corporation. See West Corporation.

West Texas Utilities Company, **6** 580

West Union Corporation, **22** 517

West Virginia Bearings, Inc., **13** 78

West Virginia Pulp and Paper Co. See Westvaco Corporation.

West Witwatersrand Areas Ltd., **IV** 94–96

West Yorkshire Bank, **II** 307

West's Holderness Corn Mill, **II** 564

Westaff Inc., 33 454–57

WestAir Holding Inc., **11** 300; **25** 423; **32** 336

Westamerica Bancorporation, 17 544–47

Westbrae Natural, Inc., **27** 197–98; **43** 218

Westburne Group of Companies, **9** 364

Westchester County Savings & Loan, **9** 173

Westchester Specialty Group, Inc., **26** 546

Westclox Seth Thomas, **16** 483

Westcott Communications Inc., **22** 442

Westdeutsche Landesbank Girozentrale, **II** 257–58, **385–87**; **33** 395; **46** 458–61 (upd.); **47** 83

Westec Corporation. See Tech-Sym Corporation.

Western Aerospace Ltd., **14** 564

Western Air Express, I 125; **III** 225; **9** 17

Western Air Lines, I 98, 100, 106; **6** 82; **21** 142; **25** 421–23

Western Alaska Fisheries, **II** 578

Western American Bank, **II** 383

Western Assurance Co., **III** 350

Western Atlas Inc., III 473; **12** 538–40; **17** 419

Western Australian Specialty Alloys Proprietary Ltd., **14** 564

Western Auto, **19** 223

Western Auto Supply Co., **8** 56; **11** 392

Western Automatic Machine Screw Co., **12** 344

Western Bancorporation, I 536; **II** 288–89; **13** 529

Western Bank, **17** 530

Western Beef, Inc., 22 548–50

Western Bingo, **16** 471

Western California Canners Inc., I 513

Western Canada Airways, **II** 376

Western Coalfields Ltd., **IV** 48–49

Western Company of North America, 15 **534–36**; **25** 73, 75

Western Condensing Co., **II** 488

Western Copper Mills Ltd., **IV** 164

Western Corrugated Box Co., **IV** 358

Western Crude, **11** 27

Western Dairy Products, I 248

Western Data Products, Inc., **19** 110

Western Digital Corp., 10 403, 463; **11** 56, 463; **25** 530–32

Western Edison, **6** 601

Western Electric Co., **II** 57, 66, 88, 101, 112; **III** 162–63, 440; **IV** 181, 660; **V** 259–64; **VII** 288; **11** 500–01; **12** 136; **13** 57; **49** 346

Western Empire Construction. See CRSS Inc.

Western Equities, Inc. See Tech-Sym Corporation.

Western Family Foods, **47** 457

Western Federal Savings & Loan, **9** 199

Western Fire Equipment Co., **9** 420

Western Gas Resources, Inc., 45 435–37
Western Geophysical, **I** 485; **11** 265; **12** 538–39
Western Glucose Co., **14** 17
Western Grocers, Inc., **II** 631, 670
Western Hotels Inc. *See* Westin Hotels and Resorts Worldwide.
Western Illinois Power Cooperative, **6** 506
Western Inland Lock Navigation Company, **9** 228
Western International Communications, **35** 68
Western International Hotels, **I** 129; **6** 129
Western International Media, **22** 294
Western International University, **24** 40
Western Kentucky Gas Company, **43** 56–57
Western Kraft Corp., **IV** 358; **8** 476
Western Life Insurance Co., **III** 356; **22** 494
Western Light & Telephone Company. *See* Western Power & Gas Company.
Western Light and Power. *See* Public Service Company of Colorado.
Western Massachusetts Co., **13** 183
Western Medical Services, **33** 456
Western Merchandise, Inc., **8** 556
Western Merchandisers, Inc., **29** 229–30
Western Mining Corp., **IV** 61, 95
Western-Mobile, **III** 735
Western Mortgage Corporation, **16** 497
Western National Life Company, **10** 246; **14** 473
Western Natural Gas Company, **7** 362
Western New York State Lines, Inc., **6** 370
Western Newell Manufacturing Company. *See* Newell Co.
Western Nuclear, Inc., **IV** 179
Western Offset Publishing, **6** 13
Western Offshore Drilling and Exploration Co., **I** 570
Western Pacific, **22** 220
Western Pacific Industries, **10** 357
Western Paper Box Co., **IV** 333
Western Pioneer, Inc., **18** 279
Western Piping and Engineering Co., **III** 535
Western Platinum, **21** 353
Western Playing Card Co., **13** 559
Western Powder Co., **I** 379; **13** 379
Western Power & Gas Company. *See* Centel Corporation.
Western Printing and Lithographing Company, **19** 404
Western Public Service Corporation, **6** 568
Western Publishing Group, Inc., IV 671; **13** 114, **559–61**; **15** 455; **25** 254, 313; **28** 159; **29** 76
Western Reserve Bank of Lake County, **9** 474
Western Reserve Telephone Company. *See* Alltel Corporation.
Western Reserves, **12** 442
Western Resources, Inc., 12 541–43; **27** 425; **32** 372–75
Western Rosin Company, **8** 99
Western Sizzlin', **10** 331; **19** 288
Western Slope Gas, **6** 559
Western Steel Group, **26** 407
Western Steer Family Restaurant, **10** 331; **18** 8
Western Sugar Co., **II** 582; **42** 371
Western Telegraph Company, **25** 99
Western Telephone Company, **14** 257

Western Union Corporation, **I** 512; **III** 644; **6** 227–28, 338, 386; **9** 536; **10** 263; **12** 9; **14** 363; **15** 72; **17** 345–46; **21** 25; **24** 515
Western Union Insurance Co., **III** 310
Western Vending, **13** 48; **41** 22
Western Veneer and Plywood Co., **IV** 358
Western Wireless Corporation, 36 514–16
Westfair Foods Ltd., **II** 649
Westfalenbank of Bochum, **II** 239
Westfalia AG, **III** 418–19
Westfalia Dinnendahl Gröppel AG, **III** 543
Westfälische Transport AG, **6** 426
Westfälische Verbands- Elektrizitätswerk, **V** 744
Westgate House Investments Ltd., **IV** 711
Westimex, **II** 594
Westin Hotel Co., I 129–30; **6** 129; **9** 283, **547–49**; **21** 91
Westin Hotels and Resorts Worldwide, 29 505–08 (upd.)
Westinghouse Air Brake Company. *See* Wabtec Corporation.
Westinghouse Brake & Signal, **III** 509
Westinghouse Cubic Ltd., **19** 111
Westinghouse Electric Corporation, I 4, 7, 19, 22, 28, 33, 82, 84–85, 524; **II** 57–58, 59, 80, 86, 88, 94, 98–99, **120–22**, 151; **III** 440, 467, 641; **IV** 59, 401; **6** 39, 164, 261, 452, 483, 556; **9** 12, 17, 128, 162, 245, 417, 439–40, 553; **10** 280, 536; **11** 318; **12** 194, **544–47 (upd.)**; **13** 230, 398, 402, 506–07; **14** 300–01; **16** 8; **17** 488; **18** 320, 335–37, 355; **19** 164–66, 210; **21** 43; **26** 102; **27** 269; **28** 69; **33** 253; **36** 327; **41** 366; **45** 306; **48** 217. *See also* CBS Radio Group.
WestJet Airlines Ltd., 38 493–95
Westland Aircraft Ltd., **I** 50, 573; **IV** 658; **24** 85
WestLB. *See* Westdeutsche Landesbank Girozentrale.
Westmark Mortgage Corp., **13** 417
Westmark Realty Advisors, **21** 97
Westmark Systems, Inc., **26** 268
Westmill Foods, **II** 466
Westminster Bank Ltd., **II** 257, 319, 320, 333–34; **17** 324
Westminster Press Ltd., **IV** 658
Westminster Trust Ltd., **IV** 706
Westmoreland Coal Company, 7 582–85
Westmount Enterprises, **I** 286
Weston and Mead, **IV** 310
Weston Bakeries, **II** 631
Weston Foods Inc. *See* George Weston Limited.
Weston Pharmaceuticals, **V** 49; **19** 122–23; **49** 111–12
Weston Presidio, **49** 189
Weston Resources, **II** 631–32
Westpac Banking Corporation, II 388–90; **17** 285; **48 424–27 (upd.)**
Westphalian Provinzialbank-Hülfskasse, **II** 385
WestPoint Stevens Inc., 16 533–36; **21** 194; **28** 219. *See also* JPS Textile Group, Inc.
Westport Woman, **24** 145
Westvaco Corporation, I 442; **IV** **351–54**; **19 495–99 (upd.)**
The Westwood Group, **20** 54
Westwood One, Inc., 17 150; **23 508–11**

Westwood Pharmaceuticals, **III** 19
Westwools Holdings, **I** 438
Westworld Resources Inc., **23** 41
Westwynn Theatres, **14** 87
The Wet Seal, Inc., 18 562–64; **49** 285
Wetterau Incorporated, II 645, **681–82**; **7** 450; **18** 507; **32** 222
Wexpro Company, **6** 568–69
Weyco Group, Incorporated, 32 510–13
Weyerhaeuser Company, I 26; **IV** 266, 289, 298, 304, 308, **355–56**, 358; **8** 428, 434; **9 550–52 (upd.)**; **19** 445–46, 499; **22** 489; **26** 384; **28 514–17 (upd.)**; **31** 468; **32** 91; **42** 397; **49** 196–97
Weyman-Burton Co., **9** 533
WFSC. *See* World Fuel Services Corporation.
WGM Safety Corp., **40** 96–97
WH Smith PLC, 42 442–47 (upd.)
Whalstrom & Co., **I** 14
Wharf Holdings Limited, **12** 367–68; **18** 114
Whatman plc, 46 462–65
Wheat, First Securities, **19** 304–05
Wheaton Industries, 8 570–73
Wheatsheaf Investment, **27** 94
Wheel Horse, **7** 535
Wheel Restaurants Inc., **14** 131
Wheelabrator Technologies, Inc., I 298; **II** 403; **III** 511–12; **V** 754; **6 599–600**; **10** 32; **11** 435
Wheeled Coach Industries, Inc., **33** 105–06
Wheeler Condenser & Engineering Company, **6** 145
Wheeler, Fisher & Co., **IV** 344
Wheeling-Pittsburgh Corp., 7 586–88
Wheelock Marden, **I** 470; **20** 312
Whemco, **22** 415
Whemo Denko, **I** 359
Wherehouse Entertainment Incorporated, 9 361; **11 556–58**; **29** 350; **35** 431–32
WHI Inc., **14** 545
Whippet Motor Lines Corporation, **6** 370
Whippoorwill Associates Inc., **28** 55
Whirl-A-Way Motors, **11** 4
Whirlpool Corporation, I 30; **II** 80; **III** 572, 573, **653–55**; **8** 298–99; **11** 318; **12** 252, 309, **548–50 (upd.)**; **13** 402–03, 563; **15** 403; **18** 225–26; **22** 218, 349; **23** 53; **25** 261
Whirlwind, Inc., **6** 233; **7** 535
Whiskey Trust, **I** 376
Whistler Corporation, **13** 195
Whitaker-Glessner Company, **7** 586
Whitaker Health Services, **III** 389
Whitall Tatum, **III** 423
Whitbread PLC, I 288, **293–94**; **18** 73; **20 519–22 (upd.)**; **29** 19; **35** 395; **42** 247
Whitby Pharmaceuticals, Inc., **10** 289
White & Case LLP, 35 466–69
White Automotive, **10** 9, 11
White Brand, **V** 97
White Brothers, **39** 83, 84
White Bus Line, **I** 448
White Castle System, Inc., 12 551–53; **33** 239; **36 517–20 (upd.)**
White Consolidated Industries Inc., II 122; **III** 480, 654, 573; **8** 298; **12** 252, 546; **13 562–64**; **22** 26–28, 216–17, 349
White Discount Department Stores, **16** 36
White Eagle Oil & Refining Co., **IV** 464; **7** 352

White Fuel Corp., **IV** 552
White Industrial Power, **II** 25
White Miller Construction Company, **14** 162
White Motor Co., **II** 16
White Mountain Freezers, **19** 360
White Mountains Insurance Group, Ltd., **48 428–31**
White-New Idea, **13** 18
White Oil Corporation, **7** 101
White Rock Corp., **I** 377; **27** 198; **43** 218
White-Rodgers, **II** 19
White Rose, Inc., 12 106; **24 527–29**
White Star Line, **23** 161
White Stores, **II** 419–20
White Swan Foodservice, **II** 625
White Tractor, **13** 17
White Wave, 43 462–64
White Weld, **II** 268; **21** 145
White-Westinghouse. *See* White Consolidated Industries Inc.
Whiteaway Laidlaw, **V** 68
Whitehall Canadian Oils Ltd., **IV** 658
Whitehall Company Jewellers, **24** 319
Whitehall Electric Investments Ltd., **IV** 658
Whitehall Labs, **8** 63
Whitehall Petroleum Corp. Ltd., **IV** 657–58
Whitehall Securities Corp., **IV** 658
Whitehall Trust Ltd., **IV** 658
Whitewater Group, **10** 508
Whitewear Manufacturing Company. *See* Angelica Corporation.
Whitman Corporation, 7 430; **10** 414–15, **553–55 (upd.); 11** 188; **22** 353–54; **27** 196; **43** 217
Whitman Education Group, Inc., 41 419–21
Whitman Publishing Co., **13** 559–60
Whitman's Chocolates, **I** 457; **7** 431; **12** 429
Whitmire Distribution. *See* Cardinal Health, Inc.
Whitney Communications Corp., **IV** 608
Whitney Group, **40** 236–38
Whitney Holding Corporation, 21 522–24
Whitney National Bank, **12** 16
Whitney Partners, L.L.C., **40** 237
Whittaker Corporation, I 544–46; **III** 389, 444; **34** 275; **48 432–35 (upd.)**
Whittar Steel Strip Co., **IV** 74; **24** 143
Whitteways, **I** 215
Whittle Communications L.P., **IV** 675; **7** 528; **13** 403; **22** 442
Whittman-Hart Inc. *See* marchFIRST, Inc.
Whitworth Brothers Company, **27** 360
Whole Foods Market, Inc., 19 501–02; **20 523–27; 41** 422–23; **47** 200
Wholesale Cellular USA. *See* Brightpoint, Inc.
The Wholesale Club, Inc., **8** 556
Wholesale Depot, **13** 547
Wholesale Food Supply, Inc., **13** 333
Wholesome Foods, L.L.C., **32** 274, 277
Wholly Harvest, **19** 502
Whyte & Mackay Distillers Ltd., **V** 399; **19** 171; **49** 152
Wicanders Group, **48** 119
Wicat Systems, **7** 255–56; **25** 254
Wichita Industries, **11** 27
Wickes Companies, Inc., I 453, 483; **II** 262; **III** 580, 721; **V 221–23; 10** 423;

13 169–70; **15** 281; **17** 365–66; **19** 503–04; **20** 415; **41** 93
Wickes Inc., 25 533–36 (upd.)
Wickman-Wimet, **IV** 203
Widows and Orphans Friendly Society, **III** 337
Wielkopolski Bank Kredytowy, **16** 14
Wien Air Alaska, **II** 420
Wienerwald Holding, **17** 249
Wiesner, Inc., **22** 442
Wifstavarfs, **IV** 325
Wiggins Teape Ltd., **I** 426; **IV** 290
Wild by Nature. *See* King Cullen Grocery Co., Inc.
Wild Leitz G.m.b.H., **23** 83
Wild Oats Markets, Inc., 19 500–02; 29 213; **41 422–25 (upd.)**
Wildlife Conservation Society, 31 462–64
Wildwater Kingdom, **22** 130
Wiles Group Ltd., **III** 501; **7** 207
Wiley Manufacturing Co., **8** 545
Oy Wilh. Schauman AB, **IV** 300–02; **19** 463
Wilhelm Fette GmbH, **IV** 198–99
Wilhelm Weber GmbH, **22** 95
Wilhelm Wilhelmsen Ltd., **7** 40; **41** 42
Wilkins Department Store, **19** 510
Wilkinson, Gaddis & Co., **24** 527
Wilkinson Sword Co., **III** 23, 28–29; **12** 464; **38** 365
Willamette Falls Electric Company. *See* Portland General Corporation.
Willamette Industries, Inc., IV 357–59; **13** 99, 101; **16** 340; **28** 517; **31 465–468 (upd.)**
Willcox & Gibbs Sewing Machine Co., **15** 384
Willetts Manufacturing Company, **12** 312
William A. Rogers Ltd., **IV** 644
William B. Tanner Co., **7** 327
William Barnet and Son, Inc., **III** 246
William Barry Co., **II** 566
William Benton Foundation, **7** 165, 167
William Bonnel Co., **I** 334; **10** 289
The William Brooks Shoe Company. *See* Rocky Shoes & Boots, Inc.
William Burdon, **III** 626
William Byrd Press Inc., **23** 100
William Carter Company, **17** 224
William Colgate and Co., **III** 23
William Collins & Sons, **II** 138; **IV** 651–52; **7** 390–91; **24** 193
William Cory & Son Ltd., **6** 417
William Crawford and Sons, **II** 593
William Douglas McAdams Inc., **I** 662; **9** 403
William Duff & Sons, **I** 509
William E. Pollack Government Securities, **II** 390
William E. Wright Company, **9** 375
William Esty Company, **16** 72
William Gaymer and Son Ltd., **I** 216
William George Company, **32** 519
William Grant Company, **22** 343
William H. Rorer Inc., **I** 666
William Hancock & Co., **I** 223
William Hewlett, **41** 117
William Hill Organization Limited, 49 449–52
William Hodges & Company, **33** 150
William Hollins & Company Ltd., **44** 105
William J. Hough Co., **8** 99–100
William Lyon Homes, **III** 664

William M. Mercer Cos. Inc., **III** 283; **32** 459
William Mackinnon & Co., **III** 522
William McDonald & Sons, **II** 593
William Morris Agency, Inc., III 554; **23 512–14; 43** 235–36
William Morrow & Company, **19** 201
William Neilson, **II** 631
William Odhams Ltd., **7** 244
William P. Young Contruction, **43** 400
William Penn Cos., **III** 243, 273
William Penn Life Insurance Company of New York, **24** 285
William Press, **I** 568
William R. Warner & Co., **I** 710
William S. Kimball & Co., **12** 108
William Southam and Sons, **7** 487
William T. Blackwell & Company, **V** 395
William Underwood Co., **I** 246, 457; **7** 430
William Varcoe & Sons, **III** 690
William Zinsser & Co., **8** 456
Williams & Connolly LLP, 47 445–48
Williams & Glyn's Bank Ltd., **12** 422
Williams & Wilkins. *See* Waverly, Inc.
Williams Brother Offshore Ltd., **I** 429
Williams Communications Group, Inc., 6 340; **25** 499; **34 507–10**
The Williams Companies, Inc., III 248; **IV** 84, 171, **575–76; 27** 307; **31 469–472 (upd.)**
Williams Deacon's Bank, **12** 422
Williams, Donnelley and Co., **IV** 660
Williams Electronics, **III** 431; **12** 419
Williams Electronics Games, Inc., **15** 539
Williams Gold Refining Co., **14** 81
The Williams Manufacturing Company, **19** 142–43
Williams/Nintendo Inc., **15** 537
Williams Oil-O-Matic Heating Corporation, **12** 158; **21** 42
Williams plc, **44** 255
Williams Printing Company. *See* Graphic Industries Inc.
Williams-Sonoma, Inc., 13 42; **15** 50; **17 548–50; 27** 225, 429; **44 447–50 (upd.)**
Williamsburg Gas Light Co., **6** 455
Williamson-Dickie Manufacturing Company, 14 549–50; 45 438–41 (upd.)
Willie G's, **15** 279
Willis Corroon Group plc, III 280, 747; **22** 318; **25 537–39**
Willis Stein & Partners, **21** 404
Williston Basin Interstate Pipeline Company, **7** 322, 324. *See also* WBI Holdings, Inc.
Willor Manufacturing Corp., **9** 323
Willys-Overland, **I** 183; **8** 74
Wilmington Coca-Cola Bottling Works, Inc., **10** 223
Wilmington Trust Corporation, 25 540–43
Wilsdorf & Davis, **13** 353–54
Wilshire Real Estate Investment Trust Inc., **30** 223
Wilshire Restaurant Group Inc., **13** 66; **28** 258
Wilson & Co., **I** 490
Wilson Bowden Plc, 45 442–44
Wilson Brothers, **8** 536
Wilson Foods Corp., **I** 489, 513; **II** 584–85; **12** 124; **14** 515; **22** 510
Wilson, H.W., Company. *See* H.W. Wilson Company.

Wilson Jones Company, **7** 4–5

Wilson Learning Group, **17** 272

Wilson-Maeulen Company, **13** 234

Wilson Pharmaceuticals & Chemical, **I** 489

Wilson Sonsini Goodrich & Rosati, 34 511–13

Wilson Sporting Goods Company, **I** 278, 489; **13** 317; **16** 52; **23** 449; **24** 403, **530–32**; **25** 167; **41** 14–16

Wilson's Motor Transit, **6** 370

Wilson's Supermarkets, **12** 220–21

Wilsons The Leather Experts Inc., 21 525–27

WilTel Network Services, **27** 301, 307

Wilts and Dorset Banking Co., **II** 307

Wiltshire United Dairies, **II** 586

Wimpey International Ltd., **13** 206

Wimpey's plc, **I** 315, 556

Win-Chance Foods, **II** 508; **36** 255

Win Schuler Foods, **II** 480; **25** 517; **26** 57

Wincanton Group, **II** 586–87

Winchell's Donut Shops, **II** 680

Winchester Arms, **I** 379–81, 434; **13** 379

Wind River Systems, Inc., 37 419–22

Windmere Corporation, 16 537–39. *See also* Applica Incorporated.

Windmere-Durable Holdings, Inc., **30** 404

WindowVisions, Inc., **29** 288

Windsor Forestry Tools, Inc., **48** 59

Windsor Manufacturing Company, **13** 6

Windsor Trust Co., **13** 467

Windstar Sail Cruises, **6** 368; **27** 90–91

Windsurfing International, **23** 55

Windward Capital Partners, **28** 152, 154

The Wine Group, Inc., 39 419–21

Wine World, Inc., **22** 78, 80

Winfire, Inc., **37** 194

Wingate Partners, **14** 521, 523

Wings & Wheels, **13** 19

Wings Luggage, Inc., **10** 181

WingspanBank.com, **38** 270

Winkelman Stores, Inc., **8** 425–26

Winkler-Grimm Wagon Co., **I** 141

Winlet Fashions, **22** 223

Winmar Co., **III** 353

Winn-Dixie Stores, Inc., **II** 626–27, 670, **683–84**; **7** 61; **11** 228; **15** 178; **16** 314; **18** 8; **21 528–30 (upd.)**; **34** 269

Winnebago Industries Inc., **7** 589–91; **22** 207; **27 509–12 (upd.)**

Winners Apparel Ltd., **V** 197

Winning International, **21** 403

Winschermann group, **IV** 198

WinsLoew Furniture, Inc., 21 531–33

Winston & Newell Company. *See* Supervalu Inc.

Winston & Strawn, 35 470–73

Winston Furniture Company, Inc., **21** 531–33

Winston Group, **10** 333

Winston, Harper, Fisher Co., **II** 668

WinterBrook Corp., **26** 326

Winterflood Securities Limited, **39** 89, 91

Wintershall AG, **I** 306; **IV** 485; **18** 49; **38** 408

Winterthur Insurance, **21** 144, 146–47

Winterthur Schweizerische Versicherungs-Gesellschaft, III 343, **402–04**

Winthrop Laboratories, **I** 698–99

Winthrop Lawrence Corporation, **25** 541

Winton Engines, **10** 273

Winton Motor Car Company, **V** 231

Wipro Limited, 43 465–68

Wire and Cable Specialties Corporation, **17** 276

Wire and Plastic Products PLC. *See* WPP Group PLC.

Wireless Hong Kong. *See* Hong Kong Telecommunications Ltd.

Wireless LLC, **18** 77

Wireless Management Company, **11** 12

Wireless Speciality Co., **II** 120

Wirtz Productions Ltd., **15** 238

Wisaforest Oy AB, **IV** 302

Wisconsin Bell, Inc., 14 551–53; **18** 30

Wisconsin Central Transportation Corporation, **12** 278; **24 533–36**

Wisconsin Dairies, 7 592–93

Wisconsin Energy Corporation, 6 601–03, 605

Wisconsin Gas Company, **17** 22–23

Wisconsin Knife Works, **III** 436

Wisconsin Power and Light, **22** 13; **39** 260

Wisconsin Public Service Corporation, **6** 604–06; **9 553–54**

Wisconsin Steel, **10** 430; **17** 158–59

Wisconsin Tissue Mills Inc., **8** 103

Wisconsin Toy Company. *See* Value Merchants Inc.

Wisconsin Wire and Steel, **17** 310; **24** 160

Wise Foods, Inc., **22** 95

Wiser's De Luxe Whiskey, **14** 141

Wishnick-Tumpeer Chemical Co., **I** 403–05

Wispark Corporation, **6** 601, 603

Wisser Service Holdings AG, **18** 105

Wisvest Corporation, **6** 601, 603

Witco Corporation, **I** 403, **404–06**; **16 540–43 (upd.)**

Wite-Out Products, Inc., **23** 56–57

Witech Corporation, **6** 601, 603

Withington Company. *See* Sparton Corporation.

Wittington Investments Ltd., **13** 51

The Wiz. *See* Cablevision Electronic Instruments, Inc.

Wizards of the Coast Inc., **24 537–40**; **43** 229, 233

WizardWorks Group, Inc., **31** 238–39

WLIW-TV. *See* Educational Broadcasting Corporation.

WLR Foods, Inc., 14 516; **21 534–36**

WM Investment Company, **34** 512

Wm. Morrison Supermarkets PLC, 38 496–98

Wm. Underwood Company, **40** 53

Wm. Wrigley Jr. Company, 7 594–97

WMC, Limited, 43 469–72

WMS Industries, Inc., III 431; **15 537–39**; **41** 215–16

WMX Technologies Inc., 11 435–36; **17** 551–54; **26** 409

Woermann and German East African Lines, **I** 542

Wöhlk, **III** 446

Wolf Furniture Enterprises, **14** 236

Wolfe & Associates, **25** 434

Wolfe Industries, Inc., **22** 255

Wolff Printing Co., **13** 559

The Wolfgang Puck Food Company, Inc., 26 534–36

Wolohan Lumber Co., 19 503–05; **25** 535

Wolters Kluwer NV, **IV** 611; **14 554–56**; **31** 389, 394; **33 458–61 (upd.)**

Wolvercote Paper Mill, **IV** 300

Wolverine Die Cast Group, **IV** 165

Wolverine Insurance Co., **26** 487

Wolverine Tube Inc., 23 515–17

Wolverine World Wide Inc., 16 544–47; **17** 390; **32** 99; **44** 365

Womack Development Company, **11** 257

Women's Specialty Retailing Group. *See* Casual Corner Group, Inc.

Women's World, **15** 96

Wometco Coca-Cola Bottling Co., **10** 222

Wometco Coffee Time, **I** 514

Wometco Enterprises, **I** 246, 514

Wonderware Corp., **22** 374

Wong International Holdings, **16** 195

Wood Fiberboard Co., **IV** 358

Wood Gundy, **II** 345; **21** 447

Wood Hall Trust plc, I 438, **592–93**

Wood-Metal Industries, Inc. *See* Wood-Mode, Inc.

Wood-Mode, Inc., 23 518–20

Wood River Oil and Refining Company, **11** 193

Wood Shovel and Tool Company, **9** 71

Wood, Struthers & Winthrop, Inc., **22** 189

Wood Wyant Inc., **30** 496–98

Woodall Industries, **III** 641; **14** 303

Woodard-Walker Lumber Co., **IV** 358

Woodbury Co., **19** 380

Woodcock, Hess & Co., **9** 370

Woodfab, **IV** 295; **19** 225

Woodhaven Gas Light Co., **6** 455

Woodhill Chemical Sales Company, **8** 333

Woodland Publishing, Inc., **37** 286

Woodlands, **7** 345–46

Woods and Co., **II** 235

Woods Equipment Company, **32** 28

Woodside Travel Trust, **26** 310

Woodville Appliances, Inc., **9** 121

Woodward-Clyde Group Inc., **45** 421

Woodward Corp., **IV** 311; **19** 267

Woodward Governor Company, **13** **565–68**; **49 453–57 (upd.)**

Woodworkers Warehouse, **22** 517

Woolco Department Stores, **II** 634; **7** 444; **V** 107, 225–26; **14** 294; **22** 242

The Woolwich plc, 30 492–95

Woolworth Corporation, **II** 414; **6** 344; **V** 106–09, **224–27**; **8** 509; **14** 293–95; **17** 42, 335; **20 528–32 (upd.)**; **25** 22. *See also* Venator Group Inc.

Woolworth Holdings, **II** 139; **V** 108; **19** 123; **24** 194

Woolworth's Ltd., **II** 656. *See also* Kingfisher plc.

Wooster Preserving Company, **11** 211

Wooster Rubber Co., **III** 613

Worcester City and County Bank, **II** 307

Worcester Gas Light Co., **14** 124

Worcester Wire Works, **13** 369

Word, Inc., **14** 499; **38** 456

Word Processors Personnel Service, **6** 10

WordPerfect Corporation, **6** 256; **10** 519, **556–59**; **12** 335; **25** 300; **41** 281. *See also* Corel Corporation.

WordStar International, **15** 149; **43** 151. *See also* The Learning Company Inc.

Work Wear Corp., **II** 607; **16** 229

Working Assets Funding Service, 43 473–76

Working Title Films, **23** 389

Workscape Inc., **42** 430

World Air Network, Ltd., **6** 71

World Airways, **10** 560–62; **28** 404

World Bank Group, 33 462–65

World Book Group. *See* Scott Fetzer Company.
World Book, Inc., IV 622; **12 554–56**
World Championship Wrestling (WCW), **32** 516
World Color Press Inc., 12 557–59; 19 333; **21** 61
World Commerce Corporation, **25** 461
World Communications, Inc., **11** 184
World Duty Free Americas, Inc., 29 509–12 (upd.)
World Duty Free plc, **33** 59
World Film Studio, **24** 437
World Financial Network National Bank, **V** 116
World Flight Crew Services, **10** 560
World Foot Locker, **14** 293
World Fuel Services Corporation, 47 449–51
World Gift Company, **9** 330
World International Holdings Limited, **12** 368
World Journal Tribune Inc., **IV** 608
World Machinery Company, **45** 170–71
World Online, **48** 398–39
World Publishing Co., **8** 423
World Savings and Loan, **19** 412; **47** 159–60
World Service Life Insurance Company, **27** 47
World Trade Corporation. *See* International Business Machines Corporation.
World Trans, Inc., **33** 105
World-Wide Shipping Group, **II** 298; **III** 517
World Wrestling Federation Entertainment, Inc., 32 514–17
World Yacht Enterprises, **22** 438
World's Finest Chocolate Inc., 39 422–24
WorldCom, Inc., **14** 330, 332; **18** 33, 164, 166; **29** 227; **38** 269–70, 468; **46** 376. *See also* MCI WorldCom, Inc.
WorldCorp, Inc., 10 560–62
WorldGames, **10** 560
WorldMark, The Club, **33** 409
Worlds of Fun, **22** 130
Worlds of Wonder, Inc., **25** 381; **26** 548
Worldview Systems Corporation, **26** 428; **46** 434
WorldWay Corporation, **16** 41
Worldwide Fiber Inc., **46** 267
Worldwide Insurance Co., **48** 9
Worldwide Logistics, **17** 505
Worldwide Restaurant Concepts, Inc., 47 452–55
Worldwide Semiconductor Manufacturing Co., **47** 386
Worldwide Underwriters Insurance Co., **III** 218–19
Wormald International Ltd., **13** 245, 247
Worms et Cie, 27 275–76, **513–15**
Wormser, **III** 760
Worth Corp., **27** 274
Wortham, Gus Sessions, **III** 193; **10** 65
Worthen Banking Corporation, **15** 60
Worthington & Co., **I** 223
Worthington Corp., **I** 142
Worthington Foods, Inc., I 653; **14 557–59**; **33** 170
Worthington Industries, Inc., 7 598–600; 8 450; **21 537–40 (upd.)**
Worthington Telephone Company, **6** 312
Woven Belting Co., **8** 13

WPL Holdings, 6 604–06
WPM. *See* Wall Paper Manufacturers.
WPP Group plc, I 21; **6 53–54; 22** 201, 296; **23** 480; **48 440–42 (upd.).** *See also* Ogilvy Group Inc.
Wrather Corporation, **18** 354
Wrenn Furniture Company, **10** 184
WRG. *See* Wells Rich Greene BDDP.
Wright & Company Realtors, **21** 257
Wright Aeronautical, **9** 16
Wright Airplane Co., **III** 151; **6** 265
Wright and Son, **II** 593
Wright Company, **9** 416
Wright Engine Company, **11** 427
Wright Group, **22** 519, 522
Wright Manufacturing Company, **8** 407
Wright Plastic Products, **17** 310; **24** 160
Wright, Robertson & Co. *See* Fletcher Challenge Ltd.
Wright Stephenson & Co., **IV** 278
Wrightson Limited, **19** 155
Write Right Manufacturing Co., **IV** 345
WS Atkins Plc, 45 445–47
WSGC Holdings, Inc., **24** 530
WSI Corporation, **10** 88–89
WSM Inc., **11** 152
WSMC. *See* Worldwide Semiconductor Manufacturing Co.
WSMP, Inc., **29** 202
WTC Airlines, Inc., **IV** 182
WTD Industries, Inc., 20 533–36
Wührer, **II** 474
Wunderlich Ltd., **III** 687
Wunderman, Ricotta & Kline, **I** 37
Wurlitzer Co., **17** 468; **18** 45
Württembergische Landes- Elektrizitäts AG, **IV** 230
WVPP. *See* Westvaco Corporation.
WWG Industries, Inc., **22** 352–53
WWTV, **18** 493
Wyandotte Chemicals Corporation, **18** 49
Wyandotte Corp., **I** 306
Wyant Corporation, 30 496–98
Wycombe Bus Company, **28** 155–56
Wyeth-Ayerst Laboratories, **25** 477; **27** 69
Wyeth Laboratories, **I** 623; **10** 69
Wyle Electronics, 14 560–62; 19 311
Wyly Corporation, **11** 468
Wyman-Gordon Company, 14 563–65; 30 282–83; **41** 367
Wymore Oil Co., **IV** 394
Wynkoop Brewing Company, **43** 407
Wynn's International, Inc., 22 458; **33 466–70**
Wynncor Ltd., **IV** 693
Wyoming Mineral Corp., **IV** 401
Wyse Technology, Inc., 10 362; **15 540–42**

X-Acto, **12** 263
X-Chem Oil Field Chemicals, **8** 385
X-Rite, Inc., 48 443–46
XA Systems Corporation, **10** 244
Xaos Tools, Inc., **10** 119
Xcelite, **II** 16
Xcor International, **III** 431; **15** 538
Xeikon NV, 26 540–42
Xenell Corporation, **48** 358
Xenia National Bank, **9** 474
Xenotech, **27** 58
Xerox Corporation, I 31–32, 338, 490, 693; **II** 10, 117, 157, 159, 412, 448; **III** 110, 116, 120–21, 157, 159, **171–73**, 475; **IV** 252, 703; **6** 244, **288–90 (upd.)**,

390; **7** 45, 161; **8** 164; **10** 22, 139, 430, 510–11; **11** 68, 494, 518; **13** 127, 448; **14** 399; **17** 28–29, 328–29; **18** 93, 111–12; **22** 411–12; **25** 54–55, 148, 152; **26** 213, 540, 542, **543–47 (upd.)**; **28** 115; **36** 171; **40** 394; **41** 197; **46** 151
Xiamen Airlines, **33** 99
Xilinx, Inc., 16 317, **548–50**; **18** 17, 19; **19** 405; **43** 15–16
XMR, Inc., **42** 361
XP, **27** 474
Xpert Recruitment, Ltd., **26** 240
Xpress Automotive Group, Inc., **24** 339
XR Ventures LLC, **48** 446
XRAL Storage and Terminaling Co., **IV** 411
Xros, Inc., **36** 353
XTRA Corp., **18** 67
XTX Corp., **13** 127
Xynetics, **9** 251
Xytek Corp., **13** 127

Y & S Candies Inc., **II** 511
Yacimientos Petrolíferos Fiscales Sociedad Anónima, **IV** 578
Yageo Corporation, 16 551–53
Yahoo! Inc., 25 18; **27 516–19; 38** 439; **45** 201
Yakovlev, **24** 60
Yale & Towne Manufacturing Co., **I** 154–55; **10** 279
Yamabun Oil Co., **IV** 403
Yamagata Enterprises, **26** 310
Yamaguchi Bank, **II** 347
Yamaha Corporation, III 366, 599, **656–59**; **11** 50; **12** 401; **16** 410, **554–58 (upd.)**; **17** 25; **18** 250; **19** 428; **22** 196; **33** 28; **40 461–66 (upd.)**; **49** 178
Yamaha Musical Instruments, **16** 202; **43** 170
Yamaichi Capital Management, **42** 349
Yamaichi Securities Company, Limited, II 300, 323, 434, **458–59**; **9** 377
Yamano Music, **16** 202; **43** 171
Yamanouchi Consumer Inc., **39** 361
Yamanouchi Pharmaceutical Co., Ltd., **12** 444–45; **38** 93
Yamatame Securities, **II** 326
Yamato Transport Co. Ltd., V 536–38; 49 458–61 (upd.)
Yamazaki Baking Co., **II** 543; **IV** 152; **24** 358
Yanbian Industrial Technology Training Institute, **12** 294
Yangzhou Motor Coach Manufacturing Co., **34** 132
The Yankee Candle Company, Inc., 37 423–26; 38 192
Yankee Energy Gas System, Inc., **13** 184
Yankee Gas Services Company, **48** 305
YankeeNets LLC, 35 474–77
Yankton Gas Company, **6** 524
Yarmouth Group, Inc., **17** 285
Yaryan, **I** 343
Yashica Co., Ltd., **II** 50–51; **21** 330
Yasuda Fire and Marine Insurance Company, Limited, II 292, 391; **III 405–07**, 408; **45** 110
Yasuda Mutual Life Insurance Company, II 292, 391, 446; **III** 288, 405, **408–09; 22** 406–07; **39 425–28 (upd.)**

The Yasuda Trust and Banking Company, Limited, II 273, 291, 391–92; 17 555–57 (upd.)
Yates-Barco Ltd., 16 8
Yates Circuit Foil, IV 26
Yawata Iron & Steel Co., Ltd., I 493, 509; II 300; IV 130, 157, 212; 17 350; 24 325
Year Book Medical Publishers, IV 677–78
Yearbooks, Inc., 12 472
Yeargin Construction Co., II 87; 11 413
Yellow Cab Co., I 125; V 539; 10 370; 12 487; 24 118
Yellow Corporation, 14 566–68; 45 448–51 (upd.)
Yellow Freight System, Inc. of Deleware, V 503, 539–41; 12 278
Yeomans & Foote, I 13
Yeomans & Partners Ltd., I 588
YES! Entertainment Corporation, 10 306; 26 548–50
Yesco Audio Environments, 18 353, 355
Yeti Cycles Inc., 19 385
Yeung Chi Shing Estates, IV 717
YGK Inc., 6 465, 467
Yhtyneet Paperitehtaat Oy. See United Paper Mills Ltd.
Yili Food Co., II 544
YKK, 19 477
YMCA of the USA, 31 473–76
Ymos A.G., IV 53; 26 83
YOCREAM International, Inc., 47 456–58
Yogen Fruz World-Wide, Inc. See CoolBrands International Inc.
Yokado Clothing Store, V 88
Yokogawa Electric Corp., III 142–43, 536; 26 230
Yokogawa Electric Works, Limited, 6 237; 13 234
Yokohama Bottle Plant, 21 319
Yokohama Cooperative Wharf Co., IV 728
Yokohama Electric Cable Manufacturing Co., III 490
The Yokohama Rubber Co., Ltd., V 254–56; 19 506–09 (upd.)
Yokohama Specie Bank, I 431; II 224
Yokohama Tokyu Deppartment Store Co., Ltd., 32 457
Yoosung Enterprise Co., Ltd., 23 269
Yoplait S.A. See Sodiaal S.A.
York & London, III 359
The York Bank and Trust Company, 16 14; 43 8
York-Benimaru, V 88
York Corp., III 440
York Developments, IV 720
York International Corp., 13 569–71; 22 6
York Research Corporation, 35 478–80
York Manufacturing Co $$York Manufacturing Co., 13 385
York Safe & Lock Company, 7 144–45; 22 184
York Steak House, 16 157
York Wastewater Consultants, Inc., 6 441
Yorkshire and Pacific Securities Ltd., IV 723
Yorkshire Energies, 45 21
Yorkshire Insurance Co., III 241–42, 257
Yorkshire Paper Mills Ltd., IV 300
Yorkshire Post Newspapers, IV 686; 28 503
Yorkshire Television Ltd., IV 659

Yorkshire-Tyne Tees Television, 24 194
Yorkshire Water Services Ltd. See Kelda Group plc.
Yorkville Group, IV 640
Yosemite Park & Curry Co., II 144
Yoshikazu Taguchi, 6 428
Yoshitomi Pharmaceutical, I 704
Young & Co.'s Brewery, P.L.C., 38 499–502
Young & Rubicam Inc., I 9–11, 25, 36–38; II 129; 6 14, 47; 9 314; 13 204; 16 166–68; 22 551–54 (upd.); 41 89–90, 198; 48 442
Young & Selden, 7 145
Young & Son, II 334
Young Broadcasting Inc., 40 467–69; 42 163
Young Innovations, Inc., 44 451–53
Young Readers of America, 13 105
Young's Engineering Company Limited, IV 717; 38 319
Young's Market Company, LLC, 32 518–20
Youngblood Truck Lines, 16 40
Youngs Drug Products Corporation, 8 85; 38 124
Youngstown, IV 114
Youngstown Pressed Steel Co., III 763
Youngstown Sheet & Tube, I 490–91; 13 157
Younkers, Inc., 19 324–25, 510–12; 41 343–44
Yount-Lee Oil Co., IV 369
Youth Centre Inc., 16 36
Youth Services International, Inc., 21 541–43; 30 146
Youthtrack, Inc., 29 399–400
Yoxall Instrument Company, 13 234
Yoyoteiki Cargo Co., Ltd., 6 428
YPF Sociedad Anónima, IV 577–78. See also Repsol-YPF S.A.
Yside Investment Group, 16 196
YTT. See Yorkshire-Tyne Tees Television.
Yuasa Battery Co., III 556
Yuba Heat Transfer Corp., I 514
The Yucaipa Cos., 17 558–62; 22 39; 32 222; 35 369
Yugraneft, 49 306
Yukon Pacific Corporation, 22 164, 166
YUKOS, 49 305–06. See also OAO NK YUKOS.
Yurakucho Seibu Co., Ltd., V 185
Yurakucho Seibu Co., Ltd., V 185
Yutani Heavy Industries, Ltd., IV 130
Yves Rocher. See Laboratoires de Biologie Végétale Yves Rocher.
Yves Saint Laurent, I 697; 12 37
Yves Soulié, II 266
YWCA of the U.S.A., 45 452–54

Z Media, Inc., 49 433
Z-Spanish Media Corp., 35 220; 41 151
Z.C. Mines, IV 61
Zaadunie B.V., I 672
Zagara's Inc., 35 190–91
Zahnfabrik Weinand Sohne & Co. G.m.b.H., 10 271
Zahnradfabrik Friedrichshafen, III 415
Zale Corporation, 16 206, 559–61; 17 369; 19 452; 23 60; 40 470–74 (upd.)
Zambezi Saw Mills (1968) Ltd., IV 241
Zambia Breweries, 25 281
Zambia Industrial and Mining Corporation Ltd., IV 239–41

Zamboni. See Frank J. Zamboni & Co., Inc.
Zander & Ingeström, III 419
Zanders Feinpapiere AG, IV 288; 15 229
Zanussi, III 480; 22 27
Zany Brainy, Inc., 31 477–79; 36 502
Zap, Inc., 25 546
Zapata Corporation, 17 157, 160; 25 544–46
Zapata Drilling Co., IV 489
Zapata Gulf Marine Corporation, 11 524
Zapata Offshore Co., IV 489
Zapata Petroleum Corp., IV 489
Zaring Premier Homes, 41 133
Zausner, 25 83
Zayre Corp., V 197–98; 9 20–21; 13 547–48; 19 448; 29 106; 30 55–56; 33 198
ZCMI. See Zion's Cooperative Mercantile Institution.
ZDF, 41 28–29
ZDNet, 36 523
Zealand Mines S.A., 23 41
Zebco, 22 115
Zebra Technologies Corporation, 14 378, 569–71
Zecco, Inc., III 443; 6 441
Zee Medical, Inc., 47 235
Zehrmart, II 631
Zeiss Ikon AG, III 446
Zell Bros., 16 559
Zell/Chilmark Fund LP, 12 439; 19 384
Zellers, V 80; 25 221
Zellstoff AG, III 400
Zellstoffabrik Waldhof AG, IV 323–24
Zellweger Telecommunications AG, 9 32
Zeneca Group PLC, 21 544–46
Zengine, Inc., 41 258–59
Zenit Bank, 45 322
Zenith Data Systems, Inc., II 124–25; III 123; 6 231; 10 563–65; 36 299
Zenith Electronics Corporation, II 102, 123–25; 10 563; 11 62, 318; 12 183, 454; 13 109, 398, 572–75 (upd.); 18 421; 34 514–19 (upd.)
Zenith Media, 42 330–31
Zentec Corp., I 482
Zentralsparkasse und Kommerzialbank Wien, 23 37
Zentronics, 19 313
Zeppelin Luftschifftechnik GmbH, 48 450
Zergo Holdings, 42 24–25
Zero Corporation, 17 563–65
Zero Plus Dialing, Inc. See Billing Concepts Corp.
Zetor s.p., 21 175
Zeus Components, Inc., 10 113
Zewawell AG, IV 324
ZF Friedrichshafen AG, 48 447–51
Zhongbei Building Material Products Company, 26 510
Zhongde Brewery, 49 417
Ziebart International Corporation, 30 499–501
The Ziegler Companies, Inc., 24 541–45
Ziff Communications Company, 7 239–40; 12 359, 560–63; 13 483; 16 371; 17 152, 253; 25 238, 240; 41 12
Ziff Davis Media Inc., 36 521–26 (upd.); 47 77, 79. See also CNET Networks, Inc.
Ziff-Davis Publishing Co., 38 441
Zijlker, IV 491
Zila, Inc., 46 466–69

Zilber Ltd., **13** 541
Zildjian. *See* Avedis Zildjian Co.
Zilkha & Company, **12** 72
Zilog, Inc., 15 543–45; **16** 548–49; **22** 390
Zimbabwe Sugar Refineries, **II** 581
Zimmer AG, **IV** 142
Zimmer Holdings, Inc., 45 455–57
Zimmer Inc., **10** 156–57; **11** 475
Zimmer Manufacturing Co., **III** 18; **37** 110, 113
Zinc Corp., **IV** 58–59, 61
Zinc Products Company, **30** 39
Zion Foods, **23** 408
Zion's Cooperative Mercantile Institution, 33 471–74
Zions Bancorporation, 12 564–66; **24** 395
Zippo Manufacturing Company, 18 565–68
Zipps Drive-Thru, Inc., **25** 389
Zippy Mart, **7** 102
Zircotube, **IV** 174
Zivnostenska, **II** 282
Zodiac S.A., 36 527–30
Zody's Department Stores, **9** 120–22
Zoecon, **I** 673
Zoll Medical, **18** 423
Zoloto Mining Ltd., **38** 231
Zoltek Companies, Inc., 37 427–30
Zondervan Publishing House, 14 499; **24 546–49**
Zoom Telephonics, Inc., 18 569–71
Zortech Inc., **10** 508
Zotos International, Inc., **III** 63; **17** 110; **22** 487; **41** 228
ZPT Radom, **23** 427
ZS Sun Limited Partnership, **10** 502
Zuari Cement, **40** 107, 109
Zuellig Group N.A., Inc., **46** 226
Zuid Nederlandsche Handelsbank, **II** 185
Zuka Juice, **47** 201
Zürcher Bankverein, **II** 368
Zurich Financial Services, 40 59, 61; **42 448–53 (upd.)**
Zurich Insurance Group, **15** 257; **25** 154, 156
Zürich Versicherungs-Gesellschaft, III 194, 402–03, **410–12**. *See also* Zurich Financial Services
Zurn Industries, Inc., **24** 150
Zwarovski, **16** 561
Zweckform Büro-Produkte G.m.b.H., **49** 38
Zycad Corp., **11** 489–91
Zycon Corporation, **24** 201
Zygo Corporation, 42 454–57
Zymaise, **II** 582
ZyMOS Corp., **III** 458
Zytec Corporation, 19 513–15. *See also* Artesyn Technologies Inc.

INDEX TO INDUSTRIES

Index to Industries

ACCOUNTING

American Institute of Certified Public
  Accountants (AICPA), 44
Andersen Worldwide, 29 (upd.)
Automatic Data Processing, Inc., 47 (upd.)
Deloitte & Touche, 9
Deloitte Touche Tohmatsu International, 29
  (upd.)
Ernst & Young, 9; 29 (upd.)
KPMG International, 33 (upd.)
L.S. Starrett Co., 13
McLane Company, Inc., 13
NCO Group, Inc., 42
Paychex, Inc., 46 (upd.)
Price Waterhouse, 9
PricewaterhouseCoopers, 29 (upd.)
Robert Wood Johnson Foundation, 35
Univision Communications Inc., 24

ADVERTISING & OTHER BUSINESS SERVICES

A.C. Nielsen Company, 13
ABM Industries Incorporated, 25 (upd.)
Ackerley Communications, Inc., 9
ACNielsen Corporation, 38 (upd.)
Acsys, Inc., 44
Adecco S.A., 36 (upd.)
Adia S.A., 6
Advo, Inc., 6
Aegis Group plc, 6
AHL Services, Inc., 27
Amdocs Ltd., 47
American Building Maintenance Industries,
  Inc., 6
The American Society of Composers,
  Authors and Publishers (ASCAP), 29
Amey Plc, 47
Analysts International Corporation, 36
The Arbitron Company, 38
Armor Holdings, Inc., 27
Ashtead Group plc, 34
The Associated Press, 13
Barrett Business Services, Inc., 16
Bates Worldwide, Inc., 14; 33 (upd.)
Bearings, Inc., 13
Berlitz International, Inc., 13
Big Flower Press Holdings, Inc., 21
Boron, LePore & Associates, Inc., 45
Bozell Worldwide Inc., 25
Bright Horizons Family Solutions, Inc., 31
Broadcast Music Inc., 23
Burns International Services Corporation,
  13; 41 (upd.)
Cambridge Technology Partners, Inc., 36
Campbell-Mithun-Esty, Inc., 16
Career Education Corporation, 45
Carmichael Lynch Inc., 28
Central Parking Corporation, 18
ChartHouse International Learning
  Corporation, 49
Chiat/Day Inc. Advertising, 11
Chicago Board of Trade, 41
Chisholm-Mingo Group, Inc., 41
Christie's International plc, 15; 39 (upd.)

Cintas Corporation, 21
COMFORCE Corporation, 40
Computer Learning Centers, Inc., 26
Corporate Express, Inc., 47 (upd.)
CORT Business Services Corporation, 26
Cox Enterprises, Inc., 22 (upd.)
Creative Artists Agency LLC, 38
Cyrk Inc., 19
Dale Carnegie Training, Inc., 28
D'Arcy Masius Benton & Bowles, Inc., 6;
  32 (upd.)
Dawson Holdings PLC, 43
DDB Needham Worldwide, 14
Deluxe Corporation, 22 (upd.)
Dentsu Inc., I; 16 (upd.); 40 (upd.)
Deutsch, Inc., 42
Deutsche Post AG, 29
DoubleClick Inc., 46
Drake Beam Morin, Inc., 44
Earl Scheib, Inc., 32
EBSCO Industries, Inc., 17
Ecology and Environment, Inc., 39
Edison Schools Inc., 37
Education Management Corporation, 35
Employee Solutions, Inc., 18
Ennis Business Forms, Inc., 21
Equifax Inc., 6; 28 (upd.)
Equity Marketing, Inc., 26
ERLY Industries Inc., 17
Euro RSCG Worldwide S.A., 13
Fallon McElligott Inc., 22
Fiserv, Inc., 33 (upd.)
FlightSafety International, Inc., 29 (upd.)
Florists' Transworld Delivery, Inc., 28
Foote, Cone & Belding Communications,
  Inc., I
Frankel & Co., 39
Franklin Covey Company, 37 (upd.)
Gage Marketing Group, 26
The Gallup Organization, 37
GfK Aktiengesellschaft, 49
Grey Advertising, Inc., 6
Group 4 Falck A/S, 42
Groupe Jean-Claude Darmon, 44
GSD&M Advertising, 44
Gwathmey Siegel & Associates Architects
  LLC, 26
Ha-Lo Industries, Inc., 27
Hakuhodo, Inc., 6; 42 (upd.)
Handleman Company, 15
Havas SA, 33 (upd.)
Hays Plc, 27
Headway Corporate Resources, Inc., 40
Heidrick & Struggles International, Inc., 28
Hildebrandt International, 29
Interep National Radio Sales Inc., 35
International Brotherhood of Teamsters, 37
International Management Group, 18
International Total Services, Inc., 37
The Interpublic Group of Companies, Inc.,
  I; 22 (upd.)
Ipsos SA, 48
Iron Mountain, Inc., 33
ITT Educational Services, Inc., 33
J.D. Power and Associates, 32

Jackson Hewitt, Inc., 48
Japan Leasing Corporation, 8
Jostens, Inc., 25 (upd.)
JWT Group Inc., I
Katz Communications, Inc., 6
Katz Media Group, Inc., 35
Kelly Services Inc., 6; 26 (upd.)
Ketchum Communications Inc., 6
Kinko's Inc., 16; 43 (upd.)
Korn/Ferry International, 34
Labor Ready, Inc., 29
Lamar Advertising Company, 27
Learning Tree International Inc., 24
Leo Burnett Company Inc., I; 20 (upd.)
Lintas: Worldwide, 14
Mail Boxes Etc., 18; 41 (upd.)
Manpower, Inc., 30 (upd.)
marchFIRST, Inc., 34
Maritz Inc., 38
MAXIMUS, Inc., 43
MPS Group, Inc., 49
National Media Corporation, 27
New England Business Services, Inc., 18
New Valley Corporation, 17
NFO Worldwide, Inc., 24
Nobel Learning Communities, Inc., 37
Norrell Corporation, 25
Norwood Promotional Products, Inc., 26
The Ogilvy Group, Inc., I
Olsten Corporation, 6; 29 (upd.)
Omnicom Group, I; 22 (upd.)
On Assignment, Inc., 20
1-800-FLOWERS, Inc., 26
Opinion Research Corporation, 46
Outdoor Systems, Inc., 25
Paris Corporation, 22
Paychex, Inc., 15
Penauille Polyservices SA, 49
Phillips, de Pury & Luxembourg, 49
Pierce Leahy Corporation, 24
Pinkerton's Inc., 9
PMT Services, Inc., 24
Publicis S.A., 19
Publishers Clearing House, 23
Randstad Holding n.v., 16; 43 (upd.)
RemedyTemp, Inc., 20
Rental Service Corporation, 28
Rentokil Initial Plc, 47
Right Management Consultants, Inc., 42
Ritchie Bros. Auctioneers Inc., 41
Robert Half International Inc., 18
Roland Berger & Partner GmbH, 37
Ronco, Inc., 15
Russell Reynolds Associates Inc., 38
Saatchi & Saatchi, I; 42 (upd.)
Securitas AB, 42
ServiceMaster Limited Partnership, 6
Shared Medical Systems Corporation, 14
Sir Speedy, Inc., 16
Skidmore, Owings & Merrill, 13
SmartForce PLC, 43
SOS Staffing Services, 25
Sotheby's Holdings, Inc., 11; 29 (upd.)
Spencer Stuart and Associates, Inc., 14
Superior Uniform Group, Inc., 30

Sykes Enterprises, Inc., 45
Sylvan Learning Systems, Inc., 35
TA Triumph-Adler AG, 48
Taylor Nelson Sofres plc, 34
TBWA Advertising, Inc., 6
TBWA\Chiat\Day, 43 (upd.)
Thomas Cook Travel Inc., 33 (upd.)
Ticketmaster Group, Inc., 13; 37 (upd.)
TMP Worldwide Inc., 30
TNT Post Group N.V., 30
Towers Perrin, 32
Transmedia Network Inc., 20
Treasure Chest Advertising Company, Inc.,
  32
TRM Copy Centers Corporation, 18
True North Communications Inc., 23
24/7 Real Media, Inc., 49
Tyler Corporation, 23
U.S. Office Products Company, 25
UniFirst Corporation, 21
United News & Media plc, 28 (upd.)
Unitog Co., 19
Valassis Communications, Inc., 37 (upd.)
ValueClick, Inc., 49
Vebego International BV, 49
Vedior NV, 35
The Wackenhut Corporation, 14
Waggener Edstrom, 42
Wells Rich Greene BDDP, 6
Westaff Inc., 33
Whitman Education Group, Inc., 41
William Morris Agency, Inc., 23
WPP Group plc, 6; 48 (upd.)
Young & Rubicam, Inc., I; 22 (upd.)

AEROSPACE

A.S. Yakovlev Design Bureau, 15
Aeronca Inc., 46
The Aerospatiale Group, 7; 21 (upd.)
Alliant Techsystems Inc., 30 (upd.)
Aviacionny Nauchno-Tehnicheskii
  Komplex im. A.N. Tupoleva, 24
Avions Marcel Dassault-Breguet Aviation,
  I
B/E Aerospace, Inc., 30
Banner Aerospace, Inc., 14
Beech Aircraft Corporation, 8
Bell Helicopter Textron Inc., 46
The Boeing Company, I; 10 (upd.); 32
  (upd.)
Bombardier Inc., 42 (upd.)
British Aerospace plc, I; 24 (upd.)
CAE USA Inc., 48
Canadair, Inc., 16
Cessna Aircraft Company, 8
Cirrus Design Corporation, 44
Cobham plc, 30
Daimler-Benz Aerospace AG, 16
DeCrane Aircraft Holdings Inc., 36
Ducommun Incorporated, 30
Empresa Brasileira de Aeronáutica S.A.
  (Embraer), 36
Fairchild Aircraft, Inc., 9
Fairchild Dornier GmbH, 48 (upd.)
First Aviation Services Inc., 49
G.I.E. Airbus Industrie, I; 12 (upd.)
General Dynamics Corporation, I; 10
  (upd.); 40 (upd.)
GKN plc, 38 (upd.)
Goodrich Corporation, 46 (upd.)
Groupe Dassault Aviation SA, 26 (upd.)
Grumman Corporation, I; 11 (upd.)
Grupo Aeropuerto del Sureste, S.A. de
  C.V., 48
Gulfstream Aerospace Corporation, 7; 28
  (upd.)
HEICO Corporation, 30
International Lease Finance Corporation,
  48
N.V. Koninklijke Nederlandse
  Vliegtuigenfabriek Fokker, I; 28 (upd.)
Learjet Inc., 8; 27 (upd.)
Lockheed Corporation, I; 11 (upd.)
Lockheed Martin Corporation, 15 (upd.)
Magellan Aerospace Corporation, 48
Martin Marietta Corporation, I
McDonnell Douglas Corporation, I; 11 (upd.)
Meggitt PLC, 34
Messerschmitt-Bölkow-Blohm GmbH., I
Moog Inc., 13
The New Piper Aircraft, Inc., 44
Northrop Corporation, I; 11 (upd.)
Northrop Grumman Corporation, 45 (upd.)
Orbital Sciences Corporation, 22
Pratt & Whitney, 9
Raytheon Aircraft Holdings Inc., 46
Rockwell International Corporation, I; 11
  (upd.)
Rolls-Royce Allison, 29 (upd.)
Rolls-Royce plc, I; 7 (upd.); 21 (upd.)
Sequa Corp., 13
Shannon Aerospace Ltd., 36
Sikorsky Aircraft Corporation, 24
Smiths Industries PLC, 25
Snecma Group, 46
Société Air France, 27 (upd.)
Spacehab, Inc., 37
Spar Aerospace Limited, 32
Sukhoi Design Bureau Aviation Scientific-
  Industrial Complex, 24
Sundstrand Corporation, 7; 21 (upd.)
Textron Lycoming Turbine Engine, 9
Thales S.A., 42
Thiokol Corporation, 9; 22 (upd.)
United Technologies Corporation, I; 10
  (upd.)
Vought Aircraft Industries, Inc., 49
Whittaker Corporation, 48 (upd.)
Woodward Governor Company, 49 (upd.)
Zodiac S.A., 36

AIRLINES

Aer Lingus Group plc, 34
Aeroflot—Russian International Airlines, 6;
  29 (upd.)
Aerolíneas Argentinas S.A., 33
Air Canada, 6; 23 (upd.)
Air China, 46
Air New Zealand Limited, 14; 38 (upd.)
Air-India Limited, 6; 27 (upd.)
AirTran Holdings, Inc., 22
Alaska Air Group, Inc., 6; 29 (upd.)
Alitalia-Linee Aeree Italiana, S.p.A., 6; 29
  (upd.)
All Nippon Airways Company Limited, 6;
  38 (upd.)
Aloha Airlines, Incorporated, 24
America West Holdings Corporation, 6; 34
  (upd.)
American Airlines, I; 6 (upd.)
AMR Corporation, 28 (upd.)
Amtran, Inc., 34
Asiana Airlines, Inc., 46
Atlantic Southeast Airlines, Inc., 47
Atlas Air, Inc., 39
Austrian Airlines AG (Österreichische
  Luftverkehrs AG), 33
Aviacionny Nauchno-Tehnicheskii
  Komplex im. A.N. Tupoleva, 24
Avianca Aerovías Nacionales de Colombia
  SA, 36
Banner Aerospace, Inc., 37 (upd.)
Braathens ASA, 47
British Airways PLC, I; 14 (upd.); 43
  (upd.)
British Midland plc, 38
British World Airlines Ltd., 18
Cargolux Airlines International S.A., 49
Cathay Pacific Airways Limited, 6; 34
  (upd.)
Chautauqua Airlines, Inc., 38
China Airlines, 34
China Eastern Airlines Co. Ltd., 31
China Southern Airlines Company Ltd., 33
Comair Holdings Inc., 13; 34 (upd.)
Continental Airlines, Inc., I; 21 (upd.)
Corporación Internacional de Aviación,
  S.A. de C.V. (Cintra), 20
Delta Air Lines, Inc., I; 6 (upd.); 39 (upd.)
Deutsche Lufthansa Aktiengesellschaft, I;
  26 (upd.)
Eastern Airlines, I
easyJet Airline Company Limited, 39
EgyptAir, 6; 27 (upd.)
El Al Israel Airlines Ltd., 23
The Emirates Group, 39
Finnair Oy, 6; 25 (upd.)
Frontier Airlines, Inc., 22
Garuda Indonesia, 6
Groupe Air France, 6
Grupo TACA, 38
HAL Inc., 9
Hawaiian Airlines, Inc., 22 (upd.)
Iberia Líneas Aéreas de España S.A., 6; 36
  (upd.)
Indian Airlines Ltd., 46
Japan Air Lines Company Ltd., I; 32 (upd.)
JetBlue Airways Corporation, 44
Kitty Hawk, Inc., 22
Kiwi International Airlines Inc., 20
Koninklijke Luchtvaart Maatschappij, N.V.
  (KLM Royal Dutch Airlines), I; 28 (upd.)
Korean Air Lines Co., Ltd., 6; 27 (upd.)
Lan Chile S.A., 31
Lauda Air Luftfahrt AG, 48
LOT Polish Airlines (Polskie Linie
  Lotnicze S.A.), 33
LTU Group Holding GmbH, 37
Malév Plc, 24
Malaysian Airlines System Berhad, 6; 29
  (upd.)
Mesa Air Group, Inc., 32 (upd.)
Mesa Airlines, Inc., 11
Mesaba Holdings, Inc., 28
Midway Airlines Corporation, 33
Midwest Express Holdings, Inc., 35
Northwest Airlines Corporation, I; 6 (upd.);
  26 (upd.)
Offshore Logistics, Inc., 37
Pakistan International Airlines Corporation,
  46
Pan American World Airways, Inc., I; 12
  (upd.)
Panalpina World Transport (Holding) Ltd.,
  47
People Express Airlines, Inc., I
Petroleum Helicopters, Inc., 35
Philippine Airlines, Inc., 6; 23 (upd.)
Preussag AG, 42 (upd.)
Qantas Airways Limited, 6; 24 (upd.)
Reno Air Inc., 23
Royal Nepal Airline Corporation, 41
Ryanair Holdings plc, 35
SAA (Pty) Ltd., 28
Sabena S.A./N.V., 33
The SAS Group, 34 (upd.)
Saudi Arabian Airlines, 6; 27 (upd.)
Scandinavian Airlines System, I
Singapore Airlines Ltd., 6; 27 (upd.)
SkyWest, Inc., 25
Société Tunisienne de l'Air-Tunisair, 49

Southwest Airlines Co., 6; 24 (upd.)
Spirit Airlines, Inc., 31
Sun Country Airlines, 30
Swiss Air Transport Company, Ltd., I
Swiss International Air Lines Ltd., 48
TAP—Air Portugal Transportes Aéreos
    Portugueses S.A., 46
Texas Air Corporation, I
Thai Airways International Public
    Company Limited, 6; 27 (upd.)
Tower Air, Inc., 28
Trans World Airlines, Inc., I; 12 (upd.); 35
    (upd.)
TransBrasil S/A Linhas Aéreas, 31
Transportes Aereos Portugueses, S.A., 6
TV Guide, Inc., 43 (upd.)
UAL Corporation, 34 (upd.)
United Airlines, I; 6 (upd.)
US Airways Group, Inc., 28 (upd.)
USAir Group, Inc., I; 6 (upd.)
VARIG S.A. (Viação Aérea Rio-
    Grandense), 6; 29 (upd.)
WestJet Airlines Ltd., 38

AUTOMOTIVE

AB Volvo, I; 7 (upd.); 26 (upd.)
Adam Opel AG, 7; 21 (upd.)
Aisin Seiki Co., Ltd., 48 (upd.)
Alfa Romeo, 13; 36 (upd.)
Alvis Plc, 47
American Motors Corporation, I
Applied Power Inc., 32 (upd.)
Arvin Industries, Inc., 8
Automobiles Citroen, 7
Automobili Lamborghini Holding S.p.A.,
    13; 34 (upd.)
Bajaj Auto Limited, 39
Bayerische Motoren Werke AG, I; 11
    (upd.); 38 (upd.)
Bendix Corporation, I
Blue Bird Corporation, 35
Bombardier Inc., 42 (upd.)
Borg-Warner Automotive, Inc., 14; 32
    (upd.)
The Budd Company, 8
CARQUEST Corporation, 29
Chrysler Corporation, I; 11 (upd.)
CNH Global N.V., 38 (upd.)
Consorcio G Grupo Dina, S.A. de C.V., 36
CSK Auto Corporation, 38
Cummins Engine Company, Inc., I; 12
    (upd.); 40 (upd.)
Custom Chrome, Inc., 16
Daihatsu Motor Company, Ltd., 7; 21
    (upd.)
Daimler-Benz A.G., I; 15 (upd.)
DaimlerChrysler AG, 34 (upd.)
Dana Corporation, I; 10 (upd.)
Deere & Company, 42 (upd.)
Delphi Automotive Systems Corporation,
    45
Don Massey Cadillac, Inc., 37
Donaldson Company, Inc., 49 (upd.)
Douglas & Lomason Company, 16
Ducati Motor Holding S.p.A., 30
Eaton Corporation, I; 10 (upd.)
Echlin Inc., I; 11 (upd.)
Edelbrock Corporation, 37
Federal-Mogul Corporation, I; 10 (upd.);
    26 (upd.)
Ferrari S.p.A., 13; 36 (upd.)
Fiat S.p.A, I; 11 (upd.)
FinishMaster, Inc., 24
Ford Motor Company, I; 11 (upd.); 36
    (upd.)
Ford Motor Company, S.A. de C.V., 20
Fruehauf Corporation, I

General Motors Corporation, I; 10 (upd.);
    36 (upd.)
Gentex Corporation, 26
Genuine Parts Company, 9; 45 (upd.)
GKN plc, 38 (upd.)
Harley-Davidson Inc., 7; 25 (upd.)
Hayes Lemmerz International, Inc., 27
The Hertz Corporation, 33 (upd.)
Hino Motors, Ltd., 7; 21 (upd.)
Hometown Auto Retailers, Inc., 44
Honda Motor Company Limited (Honda
    Giken Kogyo Kabushiki Kaisha), I; 10
    (upd.); 29 (upd.)
Insurance Auto Auctions, Inc., 23
Isuzu Motors, Ltd., 9; 23 (upd.)
Kelsey-Hayes Group of Companies, 7; 27
    (upd.)
Kia Motors Corporation, 12; 29 (upd.)
Lear Seating Corporation, 16
Lithia Motors, Inc., 41
Lotus Cars Ltd., 14
Lund International Holdings, Inc., 40
Mack Trucks, Inc., I; 22 (upd.)
The Major Automotive Companies, Inc., 45
Masland Corporation, 17
Mazda Motor Corporation, 9; 23 (upd.)
Mel Farr Automotive Group, 20
Metso Corporation, 30 (upd.)
Midas International Corporation, 10
Mitsubishi Motors Corporation, 9; 23
    (upd.)
Monaco Coach Corporation, 31
Monro Muffler Brake, Inc., 24
National R.V. Holdings, Inc., 32
Navistar International Corporation, I; 10
    (upd.)
Nissan Motor Co., Ltd., I; 11 (upd.); 34
    (upd.)
O'Reilly Automotive, Inc., 26
Officine Alfieri Maserati S.p.A., 13
Oshkosh Truck Corporation, 7
Paccar Inc., I
PACCAR Inc., 26 (upd.)
Pennzoil Company, 20 (upd.)
Penske Corporation, 19 (upd.)
The Pep Boys—Manny, Moe & Jack, 11;
    36 (upd.)
Peugeot S.A., I
Piaggio & C. S.p.A., 20
Porsche AG, 13; 31 (upd.)
PSA Peugeot Citroen S.A., 28 (upd.)
Regie Nationale des Usines Renault, I
Renault S.A., 26 (upd.)
Republic Industries, Inc., 26
Robert Bosch GmbH., I; 16 (upd.); 43
    (upd.)
RockShox, Inc., 26
Rockwell Automation, 43 (upd.)
Rolls-Royce plc, I; 21 (upd.)
Rover Group Ltd., 7; 21 (upd.)
Saab Automobile AB, 32 (upd.)
Saab-Scania A.B., I; 11 (upd.)
Safelite Glass Corp., 19
Saturn Corporation, 7; 21 (upd.)
Sealed Power Corporation, I
Sheller-Globe Corporation, I
Sixt AG, 39
Skoda Auto a.s., 39
Spartan Motors Inc., 14
SpeeDee Oil Change and Tune-Up, 25
SPX Corporation, 10; 47 (upd.)
Standard Motor Products, Inc., 40
Superior Industries International, Inc., 8
Suzuki Motor Corporation, 9; 23 (upd.)
Sytner Group plc, 45
Tower Automotive, Inc., 24
Toyota Motor Corporation, I; 11 (upd.); 38
    (upd.)

TRW Inc., 14 (upd.)
Ugly Duckling Corporation, 22
United Auto Group, Inc., 26
United Technologies Automotive Inc., 15
Valeo, 23
Volkswagen Aktiengesellschaft, I; 11
    (upd.); 32 (upd.)
Walker Manufacturing Company, 19
Winnebago Industries Inc., 7; 27 (upd.)
Woodward Governor Company, 49 (upd.)
ZF Friedrichshafen AG, 48
Ziebart International Corporation, 30

BEVERAGES

A & W Brands, Inc., 25
Adolph Coors Company, I; 13 (upd.); 36
    (upd.)
Allied Domecq PLC, 29
Allied-Lyons PLC, I
Anchor Brewing Company, 47
Anheuser-Busch Companies, Inc., I; 10
    (upd.); 34 (upd.)
Asahi Breweries, Ltd., I; 20 (upd.)
Bacardi Limited, 18
Banfi Products Corp., 36
Baron Philippe de Rothschild S.A., 39
Bass PLC, I; 15 (upd.); 38 (upd.)
BBAG Osterreichische Brau-Beteiligungs-
    AG, 38
Beringer Wine Estates Holdings, Inc., 22
Boston Beer Company, 18
Brauerei Beck & Co., 9; 33 (upd.)
Brown-Forman Corporation, I; 10 (upd.);
    38 (upd.)
Cadbury Schweppes PLC, 49 (upd.)
Canandaigua Brands, Inc., 34 (upd.)
Canandaigua Wine Company, Inc., 13
Carlsberg A/S, 9; 29 (upd.)
Carlton and United Breweries Ltd., I
Casa Cuervo, S.A. de C.V., 31
Cerveceria Polar, I
The Chalone Wine Group, Ltd., 36
Clearly Canadian Beverage Corporation, 48
Coca Cola Bottling Co. Consolidated, 10
The Coca-Cola Company, I; 10 (upd.); 32
    (upd.)
Corby Distilleries Limited, 14
D.G. Yuengling & Son, Inc., 38
Dean Foods Company, 21 (upd.)
Distillers Company PLC, I
Dr Pepper/Seven Up, Inc., 9; 32 (upd.)
E. & J. Gallo Winery, I; 7 (upd.); 28 (upd.)
Ferolito, Vultaggio & Sons, 27
Florida's Natural Growers, 45
Foster's Brewing Group Ltd., 7; 21 (upd.)
Fuller Smith & Turner P.L.C., 38
G. Heileman Brewing Company Inc., I
The Gambrinus Company, 40
Geerlings & Wade, Inc., 45
General Cinema Corporation, I
Golden State Vintners, Inc., 33
Grand Metropolitan PLC, I
Green Mountain Coffee, Inc., 31
The Greenalls Group PLC, 21
Greene King plc, 31
Grupo Modelo, S.A. de C.V., 29
Guinness/UDV, I; 43 (upd.)
The Hain Celestial Group, Inc., 43 (upd.)
Hansen Natural Corporation, 31
Heineken N.V, I; 13 (upd.); 34 (upd.)
Heublein, Inc., I
Hiram Walker Resources, Ltd., I
Interbrew S.A., 17
Jacob Leinenkugel Brewing Company, 28
JD Wetherspoon plc, 30
Karlsberg Brauerei GmbH & Co KG, 41
Kendall-Jackson Winery, Ltd., 28

Kikkoman Corporation, 14
Kirin Brewery Company, Limited, I; 21 (upd.)
König Brauerei GmbH & Co. KG, 35 (upd.)
Labatt Brewing Company Limited, I; 25 (upd.)
Laurent-Perrier SA, 42
Madeira Wine Company, S.A., 49
Maison Louis Jadot, 24
Marchesi Antinori SRL, 42
Marie Brizard & Roger International S.A., 22
MBC Holding Company, 40
Miller Brewing Company, I; 12 (upd.)
The Minute Maid Company, 28
Moët-Hennessy, I
The Molson Companies Limited, I, 26 (upd.)
National Beverage Corp., 26
National Grape Cooperative Association, Inc., 20
National Wine & Spirits, Inc., 49
Nichols plc, 44
Ocean Spray Cranberries, Inc., 25 (upd.)
Odwalla, Inc., 31
Oregon Chai, Inc., 49
Panamerican Beverages, Inc., 47
Paulaner Brauerei GmbH & Co. KG, 35
Peet's Coffee & Tea, Inc., 38
The Pepsi Bottling Group, Inc., 40
Pepsico, Inc., I; 10 (upd.); 38 (upd.)
Pernod Ricard S.A., I; 21 (upd.)
Pete's Brewing Company, 22
Philip Morris Companies Inc., 18 (upd.)
Pyramid Breweries Inc., 33
R.C. Bigelow, Inc., 49
Rainier Brewing Company, 23
Redhook Ale Brewery, Inc., 31
Rémy Cointreau S.A., 20
Robert Mondavi Corporation, 15
Royal Crown Company, Inc., 23
Sapporo Breweries Limited, I; 13 (upd.); 36 (upd.)
Scottish & Newcastle plc, 15; 35 (upd.)
The Seagram Company Ltd., I; 25 (upd.)
Sebastiani Vineyards, Inc., 28
Shepherd Neame Limited, 30
Snapple Beverage Corporation, 11
The South African Breweries Limited, I; 24 (upd.)
Starbucks Corporation, 13; 34 (upd.)
Stewart's Beverages, 39
The Stroh Brewery Company, I; 18 (upd.)
Sutter Home Winery Inc., 16
Taittinger S.A., 43
The Terlato Wine Group, 48
Todhunter International, Inc., 27
Triarc Companies, Inc., 34 (upd.)
Tsingtao Brewery Group, 49
Van Houtte Inc., 39
Vin & Spirit AB, 31
Viña Concha y Toro S.A., 45
Whitbread and Company PLC, I
The Wine Group, Inc., 39
Young & Co.'s Brewery, P.L.C., 38

BIOTECHNOLOGY

Amgen, Inc., 10; 30 (upd.)
Biogen Inc., 14; 36 (upd.)
Cambrex Corporation, 44 (upd.)
Centocor Inc., 14
Charles River Laboratories International, Inc., 42
Chiron Corporation, 10; 36 (upd.)
Covance Inc., 30
CryoLife, Inc., 46

Delta and Pine Land Company, 33
Dionex Corporation, 46
Enzo Biochem, Inc., 41
Genentech, Inc., 32 (upd.)
Genzyme Corporation, 38 (upd.)
Howard Hughes Medical Institute, 39
Huntingdon Life Sciences Group plc, 42
IDEXX Laboratories, Inc., 23
Immunex Corporation, 14
IMPATH Inc., 45
Life Technologies, Inc., 17
Medtronic, Inc., 30 (upd.)
Millipore Corporation, 25
Minntech Corporation, 22
Mycogen Corporation, 21
New Brunswick Scientific Co., Inc., 45
Qiagen N.V., 39
Quintiles Transnational Corporation, 21
Seminis, Inc., 29
Sigma-Aldrich Corporation, 36 (upd.)
STERIS Corporation, 29
Waters Corporation, 43
Whatman plc, 46

CHEMICALS

A. Schulman, Inc., 8
Aceto Corp., 38
Air Products and Chemicals, Inc., I; 10 (upd.)
Akzo Nobel N.V., 13
AlliedSignal Inc., 22 (upd.)
American Cyanamid, I; 8 (upd.)
American Vanguard Corporation, 47
ARCO Chemical Company, 10
Atochem S.A., I
Baker Hughes Incorporated, 22 (upd.)
Balchem Corporation, 42
BASF Aktiengesellschaft, I; 18 (upd.)
Bayer A.G., I; 13 (upd.); 41 (upd.)
Betz Laboratories, Inc., I; 10 (upd.)
The BFGoodrich Company, 19 (upd.)
BOC Group plc, I; 25 (upd.)
Brenntag AG, 8; 23 (upd.)
Burmah Castrol PLC, 30 (upd.)
Cabot Corporation, 8; 29 (upd.)
Cambrex Corporation, 16
Catalytica Energy Systems, Inc., 44
Celanese Corporation, I
Chemcentral Corporation, 8
Chemi-Trol Chemical Co., 16
Church & Dwight Co., Inc., 29
Ciba-Geigy Ltd., I; 8 (upd.)
The Clorox Company, 22 (upd.)
Croda International Plc, 45
Crompton & Knowles, 9
Crompton Corporation, 36 (upd.)
Cytec Industries Inc., 27
Degussa-Hüls AG, 32 (upd.)
DeKalb Genetics Corporation, 17
The Dexter Corporation, I; 12 (upd.)
Dionex Corporation, 46
The Dow Chemical Company, I; 8 (upd.)
DSM, N.V, I
E.I. du Pont de Nemours & Company, I; 8 (upd.); 26 (upd.)
Eastman Chemical Company, 14; 38 (upd.)
Ecolab Inc., I; 13 (upd.); 34 (upd.)
Elementis plc, 40 (upd.)
English China Clays Ltd., 15 (upd.); 40 (upd.)
ERLY Industries Inc., 17
Ethyl Corporation, I; 10 (upd.)
Ferro Corporation, 8
First Mississippi Corporation, 8
Formosa Plastics Corporation, 14
Fort James Corporation, 22 (upd.)
G.A.F., I

The General Chemical Group Inc., 37
Georgia Gulf Corporation, 9
Givaudan SA, 43
Great Lakes Chemical Corporation, I; 14 (upd.)
Guerbet Group, 46
H.B. Fuller Company, 32 (upd.)
Hauser, Inc., 46
Hawkins Chemical, Inc., 16
Henkel KGaA, 34 (upd.)
Hercules Inc., I; 22 (upd.)
Hoechst A.G., I; 18 (upd.)
Hoechst Celanese Corporation, 13
Huls A.G., I
Huntsman Chemical Corporation, 8
IMC Fertilizer Group, Inc., 8
Imperial Chemical Industries PLC, I
International Flavors & Fragrances Inc., 9; 38 (upd.)
Koppers Industries, Inc., I; 26 (upd.)
L'Air Liquide SA, I; 47 (upd.)
Lawter International Inc., 14
LeaRonal, Inc., 23
Loctite Corporation, 30 (upd.)
Lubrizol Corporation, I; 30 (upd.)
Lyondell Chemical Company, 45 (upd.)
M.A. Hanna Company, 8
MacDermid Incorporated, 32
Mallinckrodt Group Inc., 19
MBC Holding Company, 40
Melamine Chemicals, Inc., 27
Methanex Corporation, 40
Mississippi Chemical Corporation, 39
Mitsubishi Chemical Industries, Ltd., I
Mitsui Petrochemical Industries, Ltd., 9
Monsanto Company, I; 9 (upd.); 29 (upd.)
Montedison SpA, I
Morton International Inc., 9 (upd.)
Morton Thiokol, Inc., I
Nagase & Company, Ltd., 8
Nalco Chemical Corporation, I; 12 (upd.)
National Distillers and Chemical Corporation, I
National Sanitary Supply Co., 16
National Starch and Chemical Company, 49
NCH Corporation, 8
NL Industries, Inc., 10
Nobel Industries AB, 9
Norsk Hydro ASA, 35 (upd.)
Novacor Chemicals Ltd., 12
NutraSweet Company, 8
Olin Corporation, I; 13 (upd.)
OM Group, Inc., 17
Pennwalt Corporation, I
Perstorp A.B., I
Petrolite Corporation, 15
Pioneer Hi-Bred International, Inc., 41 (upd.)
Praxair, Inc., 11
Quantum Chemical Corporation, 8
Reichhold Chemicals, Inc., 10
Rhodia SA, 38
Rhône-Poulenc S.A., I; 10 (upd.)
Robertet SA, 39
Rohm and Haas Company, I; 26 (upd.)
Roussel Uclaf, I; 8 (upd.)
RPM, Inc., 36 (upd.)
The Scotts Company, 22
SCP Pool Corporation, 39
Sequa Corp., 13
Shanghai Petrochemical Co., Ltd., 18
Sigma-Aldrich Corporation, 36 (upd.)
Solvay & Cie S.A., I; 21 (upd.)
Stepan Company, 30
Sterling Chemicals, Inc., 16
Sumitomo Chemical Company Ltd., I
Takeda Chemical Industries, Ltd., 46 (upd.)

Terra Industries, Inc., 13
Teva Pharmaceutical Industries Ltd., 22
TOTAL S.A., 24 (upd.)
Ube Industries, Ltd., 38 (upd.)
Union Carbide Corporation, I; 9 (upd.)
Univar Corporation, 9
The Valspar Corporation, 32 (upd.)
Vista Chemical Company, I
Witco Corporation, I; 16 (upd.)
Zeneca Group PLC, 21

CONGLOMERATES

Accor SA, 10; 27 (upd.)
AEG A.G., I
Alcatel Alsthom Compagnie Générale
 d'Electricité, 9
Alco Standard Corporation, I
Alexander & Baldwin, Inc., 40 (upd.)
Alfa, S.A. de C.V., 19
Allied Domecq PLC, 29
Allied-Signal Inc., I
AMFAC Inc., I
The Anschutz Corporation, 36 (upd.)
Aramark Corporation, 13
ARAMARK Corporation, 41
Archer-Daniels-Midland Company, I; 11
 (upd.)
Arkansas Best Corporation, 16
Associated British Ports Holdings Plc, 45
BAA plc, 33 (upd.)
Barlow Rand Ltd., I
Bat Industries PLC, I
Berkshire Hathaway Inc., 42 (upd.)
Bond Corporation Holdings Limited, 10
BTR PLC, I
Bunzl plc, 31 (upd.)
Burlington Northern Santa Fe Corporation,
 27 (upd.)
Business Post Group plc, 46
C. Itoh & Company Ltd., I
Cargill, Incorporated, 13 (upd.); 40 (upd.)
CBI Industries, Inc., 7
Chemed Corporation, 13
Chesebrough-Pond's USA, Inc., 8
CITIC Pacific Ltd., 18
Colt Industries Inc., I
The Connell Company, 29
CSR Limited, 28 (upd.)
Daewoo Group, 18 (upd.)
De Dietrich & Cie., 31
Deere & Company, 21 (upd.)
Delaware North Companies Incorporated, 7
Desc, S.A. de C.V., 23
The Dial Corp., 8
EBSCO Industries, Inc., 40 (upd.)
El Corte Inglés Group, 26 (upd.)
Elders IXL Ltd., I
Engelhard Corporation, 21 (upd.)
Farley Northwest Industries, Inc., I
Fimalac S.A., 37
First Pacific Company Limited, 18
Fisher Companies, Inc., 15
Fletcher Challenge Ltd., 19 (upd.)
FMC Corporation, I; 11 (upd.)
Fortune Brands, Inc., 29 (upd.)
Fuqua Industries, Inc., I
General Electric Company, 34 (upd.)
GIB Group, 26 (upd.)
Gillett Holdings, Inc., 7
Grand Metropolitan PLC, 14 (upd.)
Great American Management and
 Investment, Inc., 8
Greyhound Corporation, I
Grupo Carso, S.A. de C.V., 21
Grupo Industrial Bimbo, 19
Gulf & Western Inc., I
Hagemeyer N.V., 39

Hankyu Corporation, 23 (upd.)
Hanson PLC, III; 7 (upd.)
Hitachi, Ltd., I; 12 (upd.); 40 (upd.)
Hutchison Whampoa Limited, 18; 49
 (upd.)
IC Industries, Inc., I
Ilitch Holdings Inc., 37
Inchcape plc, 16 (upd.)
Ingram Industries, Inc., 11; 49 (upd.)
Instituto Nacional de Industria, I
International Controls Corporation, 10
International Telephone & Telegraph
 Corporation, I; 11 (upd.)
Istituto per la Ricostruzione Industriale, I
ITOCHU Corporation, 32 (upd.)
Jardine Matheson Holdings Limited, I; 20
 (upd.)
Jason Incorporated, 23
Jefferson Smurfit Group plc, 19 (upd.)
The Jim Pattison Group, 37
Jordan Industries, Inc., 36
Justin Industries, Inc., 19
Kanematsu Corporation, 24 (upd.)
Kao Corporation, 20 (upd.)
Katy Industries, Inc., I
Kesko Ltd. (Kesko Oy), 8; 27 (upd.)
Kidde plc, 44 (upd.)
Kidde, Inc., I
KOC Holding A.S., I
Koninklijke Nedlloyd N.V., 26 (upd.)
Koor Industries Ltd., 25 (upd.)
K2 Inc., 16
The L.L. Knickerbocker Co., Inc., 25
Lancaster Colony Corporation, 8
Larry H. Miller Group, 29
Lear Siegler, Inc., I
Lefrak Organization Inc., 26
Leucadia National Corporation, 11
Litton Industries, Inc., I; 11 (upd.)
Loews Corporation, I; 12 (upd.); 36 (upd.)
Loral Corporation, 8
LTV Corporation, I
LVMH Moët Hennessy Louis Vuitton SA,
 33 (upd.)
Marubeni Corporation, 24 (upd.)
Marubeni K.K., I
MAXXAM Inc., 8
McKesson Corporation, I
Menasha Corporation, 8
Metallgesellschaft AG, 16 (upd.)
Metromedia Co., 7
Minnesota Mining & Manufacturing
 Company (3M), I; 8 (upd.); 26 (upd.)
Mitsubishi Corporation, I; 12 (upd.)
Mitsubishi Heavy Industries, Ltd., 40
 (upd.)
Mitsui & Co., Ltd., 28 (upd.)
Mitsui Bussan K.K., I
The Molson Companies Limited, I; 26
 (upd.)
Montedison S.p.A., 24 (upd.)
NACCO Industries, Inc., 7
National Service Industries, Inc., 11
New World Development Company
 Limited, 38 (upd.)
Nichimen Corporation, 24 (upd.)
Nissho Iwai K.K., I
Norsk Hydro A.S., 10
Novar plc, 49 (upd.)
Ogden Corporation, I
Onex Corporation, 16
Orkla A/S, 18
Park-Ohio Industries Inc., 17
Pentair, Inc., 7
Philip Morris Companies Inc., 44 (upd.)
Poliet S.A., 33
Powell Duffryn plc, 31
Power Corporation of Canada, 36 (upd.)

Preussag AG, 17
Pubco Corporation, 17
Pulsar Internacional S.A., 21
R.B. Pamplin Corp., 45
The Rank Organisation Plc, 14 (upd.)
Red Apple Group, Inc., 23
Roll International Corporation, 37
Rubbermaid Incorporated, 20 (upd.)
Samsung Group, I
San Miguel Corporation, 15
Sara Lee Corporation, 15 (upd.)
Schindler Holding AG, 29
Sea Containers Ltd., 29
Seaboard Corporation, 36
ServiceMaster Inc., 23 (upd.)
Sime Darby Berhad, 14; 36 (upd.)
Société du Louvre, 27
Standex International Corporation, 17; 44
 (upd.)
Stinnes AG, 23 (upd.)
Sudbury Inc., 16
Sumitomo Corporation, I; 11 (upd.)
Swire Pacific Ltd., I; 16 (upd.)
Talley Industries, Inc., 16
Tandycrafts, Inc., 31
TaurusHolding GmbH & Co. KG, 46
Teledyne, Inc., I; 10 (upd.)
Tenneco, Inc., I; 10 (upd.)
Textron Inc., I; 34 (upd.)
Thomas H. Lee Co., 24
Thorn Emi PLC, I
Thorn plc, 24
TI Group plc, 17
Time Warner Inc., IV; 7 (upd.)
Tokyu Corporation, 47 (upd.)
Tomen Corporation, 24 (upd.)
Tomkins plc, 11; 44 (upd.)
Toshiba Corporation, I; 12 (upd.); 40
 (upd.)
Tractebel S.A., 20
Transamerica–An AEGON Company, I; 13
 (upd.); 41 (upd.)
The Tranzonic Cos., 15
Triarc Companies, Inc., 8
Triple Five Group Ltd., 49
TRW Inc., I; 11 (upd.)
Unilever, II; 7 (upd.); 32 (upd.)
United Technologies Corporation, 34 (upd.)
Universal Studios, Inc., 33
Valhi, Inc., 19
Valores Industriales S.A., 19
Veba A.G., I; 15 (upd.)
Vendôme Luxury Group plc, 27
Viacom Inc., 23 (upd.)
Virgin Group, 12; 32 (upd.)
W.R. Grace & Company, I
The Washington Companies, 33
Wheaton Industries, 8
Whitbread PLC, 20 (upd.)
Whitman Corporation, 10 (upd.)
Whittaker Corporation, I
WorldCorp, Inc., 10
Worms et Cie, 27
Yamaha Corporation, 40 (upd.)

CONSTRUCTION

A. Johnson & Company H.B., I
ABC Supply Co., Inc., 22
Abrams Industries Inc., 23
AMREP Corporation, 21
ASV, Inc., 34
The Austin Company, 8
Balfour Beatty plc, 36 (upd.)
Baratt Developments PLC, I
Beazer Homes USA, Inc., 17
Bechtel Group, Inc., I; 24 (upd.)
Bellway Plc, 45

BFC Construction Corporation, 25
Bilfinger & Berger Bau A.G., I
Bird Corporation, 19
Black & Veatch LLP, 22
Boral Limited, 43 (upd.)
Bouygues S.A., I; 24 (upd.)
Brown & Root, Inc., 13
Bufete Industrial, S.A. de C.V., 34
CalMat Co., 19
Centex Corporation, 8; 29 (upd.)
Cianbro Corporation, 14
The Clark Construction Group, Inc., 8
Colas S.A., 31
Day & Zimmermann, Inc., 31 (upd.)
Dillingham Construction Corporation, I; 44
    (upd.)
Dominion Homes, Inc., 19
The Drees Company, Inc., 41
Edw. C. Levy Co., 42
Eiffage, 27
Ellerbe Becket, 41
Empresas ICA Sociedad Controladora, S.A.
    de C.V., 41
Encompass Services Corporation, 33
Engle Homes, Inc., 46
Environmental Industries, Inc., 31
Eurotunnel PLC, 13
Fairclough Construction Group PLC, I
Fleetwood Enterprises, Inc., 22 (upd.)
Fluor Corporation, I; 8 (upd.); 34 (upd.)
George Wimpey PLC, 12
Gilbane, Inc., 34
Granite Rock Company, 26
Grupo Ferrovial, S.A., 40
Habitat for Humanity International, 36
Hillsdown Holdings plc, 24 (upd.)
Hochtief AG, 33
Horton Homes, Inc., 25
Hospitality Worldwide Services, Inc., 26
Hovnanian Enterprises, Inc., 29
J.A. Jones, Inc., 16
Jarvis plc, 39
John Brown PLC, I
John Laing PLC, I
John W. Danforth Company, 48
Kajima Corporation, I
Kaufman and Broad Home Corporation, 8
KB Home, 45 (upd.)
Kitchell Corporation, 14
The Koll Company, 8
Komatsu Ltd., 16 (upd.)
Kraus-Anderson, Incorporated, 36
Kumagai Gumi Company, Ltd., I
L'Entreprise Jean Lefebvre, 23
Ledcor Industries Limited, 46
Lennar Corporation, 11
Lincoln Property Company, 8
Lindal Cedar Homes, Inc., 29
Linde A.G., I
McCarthy Building Companies, Inc., 48
Mellon-Stuart Company, I
Michael Baker Corp., 14
Morrison Knudsen Corporation, 7; 28
    (upd.)
New Holland N.V., 22
NVR L.P., 8
Ohbayashi Corporation, I
Opus Group, 34
The Peninsular & Oriental Steam
    Navigation Company (Bovis Division), I
Perini Corporation, 8
Peter Kiewit Sons' Inc., 8
Philipp Holzmann AG, 17
Post Properties, Inc., 26
Pulte Homes, Inc., 8; 42 (upd.)
Redrow Group plc, 31
RMC Group p.l.c., 34 (upd.)
Rooney Brothers Co., 25

The Rottlund Company, Inc., 28
The Ryland Group, Inc., 8; 37 (upd.)
Sandvik AB, 32 (upd.)
Schuff Steel Company, 26
Shorewood Packaging Corporation, 28
Simon Property Group, Inc., 27
Skanska AB, 38
Sundt Corp., 24
Swinerton Inc., 43
Taylor Woodrow plc, I; 38 (upd.)
Thyssen Krupp AG, 28 (upd.)
Toll Brothers Inc., 15
Trammell Crow Company, 8
Tridel Enterprises Inc., 9
The Turner Corporation, 8; 23 (upd.)
U.S. Aggregates, Inc., 42
U.S. Home Corporation, 8
VA TECH ELIN EBG GmbH, 49
Veit Companies, 43
Walbridge Aldinger Co., 38
Walter Industries, Inc., 22 (upd.)
The Weitz Company, Inc., 42
Wilson Bowden Plc, 45
Wood Hall Trust PLC, I

CONTAINERS

Ball Corporation, I; 10 (upd.)
BWAY Corporation, 24
Clarcor Inc., 17
Continental Can Co., Inc., 15
Continental Group Company, I
Crown Cork & Seal Company, Inc., I; 13
    (upd.); 32 (upd.)
Gaylord Container Corporation, 8
Golden Belt Manufacturing Co., 16
Greif Bros. Corporation, 15
Grupo Industrial Durango, S.A. de C.V.,
    37
Inland Container Corporation, 8
Kerr Group Inc., 24
Keyes Fibre Company, 9
Libbey Inc., 49
Liqui-Box Corporation, 16
The Longaberger Company, 12
Longview Fibre Company, 8
The Mead Corporation, 19 (upd.)
Metal Box PLC, I
National Can Corporation, I
Owens-Illinois, Inc., I; 26 (upd.)
Primerica Corporation, I
Reynolds Metals Company, 19 (upd.)
Royal Packaging Industries Van Leer N.V.,
    30
Sealright Co., Inc., 17
Smurfit-Stone Container Corporation, 26
    (upd.)
Sonoco Products Company, 8
Thermos Company, 16
Toyo Seikan Kaisha, Ltd., I
U.S. Can Corporation, 30
Ultra Pac, Inc., 24
Viatech Continental Can Company, Inc., 25
    (upd.)
Vitro Corporativo S.A. de C.V., 34

DRUGS/PHARMACEUTICALS

A.L. Pharma Inc., 12
Abbott Laboratories, I; 11 (upd.); 40 (upd.)
Akorn, Inc., 32
Alpharma Inc., 35 (upd.)
ALZA Corporation, 10; 36 (upd.)
American Home Products, I; 10 (upd.)
Amgen, Inc., 10
Astra AB, I; 20 (upd.)
Barr Laboratories, Inc., 26
Bayer A.G., I; 13 (upd.)
Biovail Corporation, 47

Block Drug Company, Inc., 8
Bristol-Myers Squibb Company, III; 9
    (upd.); 37 (upd.)
C.H. Boehringer Sohn, 39
Carter-Wallace, Inc., 8; 38 (upd.)
Cephalon, Inc., 45
Chiron Corporation, 10
Ciba-Geigy Ltd., I; 8 (upd.)
D&K Wholesale Drug, Inc., 14
Eli Lilly and Company, I; 11 (upd.); 47
    (upd.)
Express Scripts Inc., 44 (upd.)
F. Hoffmann-Laroche & Company A.G., I
Fisons plc, 9; 23 (upd.)
FoxMeyer Health Corporation, 16
Fujisawa Pharmaceutical Company Ltd., I
G.D. Searle & Co., I; 12 (upd.); 34 (upd.)
GEHE AG, 27
Genentech, Inc., I; 8 (upd.)
Genetics Institute, Inc., 8
Genzyme Corporation, 13
Glaxo Holdings PLC, I; 9 (upd.)
GlaxoSmithKline plc, 46 (upd.)
Groupe Fournier SA, 44
H. Lundbeck A/S, 44
Hauser, Inc., 46
Heska Corporation, 39
Huntingdon Life Sciences Group plc, 42
Johnson & Johnson, III; 8 (upd.)
Jones Medical Industries, Inc., 24
Kyowa Hakko Kogyo Co., Ltd., 48 (upd.)
Leiner Health Products Inc., 34
Ligand Pharmaceuticals Incorporated, 47
Marion Merrell Dow, Inc., I; 9 (upd.)
McKesson Corporation, 12; 47 (upd.)
MedImmune, Inc., 35
Merck & Co., Inc., I; 11 (upd.)
Miles Laboratories, I
Millennium Pharmaceuticals, Inc., 47
Monsanto Company, 29 (upd.)
Moore Medical Corp., 17
Murdock Madaus Schwabe, 26
Mylan Laboratories Inc., I; 20 (upd.)
National Patent Development Corporation,
    13
Natrol, Inc., 49
Natural Alternatives International, Inc., 49
Novartis AG, 39 (upd.)
Novo Industri A/S, I
Omnicare, Inc., 49
Pfizer Inc., I; 9 (upd.); 38 (upd.)
Pharmacia & Upjohn Inc., I; 25 (upd.)
Quintiles Transnational Corporation, 21
R.P. Scherer, I
Roberts Pharmaceutical Corporation, 16
Roche Bioscience, 14 (upd.)
Rorer Group, I
Roussel Uclaf, I; 8 (upd.)
Sandoz Ltd., I
Sankyo Company, Ltd., I
Sanofi Group, I
The Sanofi-Synthélabo Group, 49 (upd.)
Schering A.G., I
Schering-Plough Corporation, I; 14 (upd.);
    49 (upd.)
Sepracor Inc., 45
Serono S.A., 47
Shionogi & Co., Ltd., 17 (upd.)
Sigma-Aldrich Corporation, I; 36 (upd.)
SmithKline Beckman Corporation, I
SmithKline Beecham plc, 32 (upd.)
Squibb Corporation, I
Sterling Drug, Inc., I
The Sunrider Corporation, 26
Syntex Corporation, I
Takeda Chemical Industries, Ltd., I
Teva Pharmaceutical Industries Ltd., 22
The Upjohn Company, I; 8 (upd.)

Vitalink Pharmacy Services, Inc., 15
Warner-Lambert Co., I; 10 (upd.)
Watson Pharmaceuticals Inc., 16
The Wellcome Foundation Ltd., I
Zila, Inc., 46

ELECTRICAL & ELECTRONICS

ABB ASEA Brown Boveri Ltd., II; 22
   (upd.)
Acer Inc., 16
Acuson Corporation, 10; 36 (upd.)
ADC Telecommunications, Inc., 30 (upd.)
Adtran Inc., 22
Advanced Micro Devices, Inc., 30 (upd.)
Advanced Technology Laboratories, Inc., 9
Agilent Technologies Inc., 38
Aiwa Co., Ltd., 30
Akzo Nobel N.V., 41 (upd.)
Alliant Techsystems Inc., 30 (upd.)
AlliedSignal Inc., 22 (upd.)
Alpine Electronics, Inc., 13
Alps Electric Co., Ltd., II
Altera Corporation, 18; 43 (upd.)
Altron Incorporated, 20
Amdahl Corporation, 40 (upd.)
American Power Conversion Corporation,
   24
AMP Incorporated, II; 14 (upd.)
Amphenol Corporation, 40
Amstrad plc, 48 (upd.)
Analog Devices, Inc., 10
Analogic Corporation, 23
Anam Group, 23
Anaren Microwave, Inc., 33
Andrew Corporation, 10; 32 (upd.)
Apple Computer, Inc., 36 (upd.)
Applied Power Inc., 32 (upd.)
Arrow Electronics, Inc., 10
Ascend Communications, Inc., 24
Astronics Corporation, 35
Atari Corporation, 9; 23 (upd.)
Atmel Corporation, 17
Audiovox Corporation, 34
Ault Incorporated, 34
Autodesk, Inc., 10
Avnet Inc., 9
Bang & Olufsen Holding A/S, 37
Barco NV, 44
Benchmark Electronics, Inc., 40
Bicoastal Corporation, II
Blonder Tongue Laboratories, Inc., 48
Bose Corporation, 13; 36 (upd.)
Boston Acoustics, Inc., 22
Bowthorpe plc, 33
Broadcom Corporation, 34
Bull S.A., 43 (upd.)
Burr-Brown Corporation, 19
C-COR.net Corp., 38
Cabletron Systems, Inc., 10
Cadence Design Systems, Inc., 48 (upd.)
Cambridge SoundWorks, Inc., 48
Canon Inc., 18 (upd.)
Carbone Lorraine S.A., 33
Carl-Zeiss-Stiftung, 34 (upd.)
CASIO Computer Co., Ltd., 16 (upd.); 40
   (upd.)
Checkpoint Systems, Inc., 39
Cirrus Logic, Inc., 48 (upd.)
Cisco Systems, Inc., 34 (upd.)
Citizen Watch Co., Ltd., 21 (upd.)
Cobham plc, 30
Cobra Electronics Corporation, 14
Coherent, Inc., 31
Cohu, Inc., 32
Compagnie Générale d'Électricité, II
Conexant Systems, Inc., 36
Cooper Industries, Inc., II

Cray Research, Inc., 16 (upd.)
CTS Corporation, 39
Cubic Corporation, 19
Cypress Semiconductor Corporation, 20; 48
   (upd.)
Daktronics, Inc., 32
Dallas Semiconductor Corporation, 13; 31
   (upd.)
De La Rue plc, 34 (upd.)
Dell Computer Corporation, 31 (upd.)
DH Technology, Inc., 18
Digi International Inc., 9
Discreet Logic Inc., 20
Dixons Group plc, 19 (upd.)
Dolby Laboratories Inc., 20
Dynatech Corporation, 13
E-Systems, Inc., 9
Electronics for Imaging, Inc., 15; 43 (upd.)
Emerson, 46 (upd.)
Emerson Electric Co., II
Emerson Radio Corp., 30
ENCAD, Incorporated, 25
Equus Computer Systems, Inc., 49
ESS Technology, Inc., 22
Everex Systems, Inc., 16
Exabyte Corporation, 40 (upd.)
Exar Corp., 14
Exide Electronics Group, Inc., 20
Flextronics International Ltd., 38
Fluke Corporation, 15
Foxboro Company, 13
Fuji Electric Co., Ltd., II; 48 (upd.)
Fujitsu Limited, 16 (upd.); 42 (upd.)
General Dynamics Corporation, 40 (upd.)
General Electric Company, II; 12 (upd.)
General Electric Company, PLC, II
General Instrument Corporation, 10
General Signal Corporation, 9
GenRad, Inc., 24
GM Hughes Electronics Corporation, II
Goldstar Co., Ltd., 12
Gould Electronics, Inc., 14
Grundig AG, 27
Guillemot Corporation, 41
Hadco Corporation, 24
Hamilton Beach/Proctor-Silex Inc., 17
Harman International Industries Inc., 15
Harris Corporation, II; 20 (upd.)
Hayes Corporation, 24
Herley Industries, Inc., 33
Hewlett-Packard Company, 28 (upd.)
Holophane Corporation, 19
Honeywell Inc., II; 12 (upd.)
Hubbell Incorporated, 9; 31 (upd.)
Hughes Supply, Inc., 14
Hutchinson Technology Incorporated, 18
Hypercom Corporation, 27
IEC Electronics Corp., 42
Imax Corporation, 28
In Focus Systems, Inc., 22
Indigo NV, 26
Intel Corporation, II; 10 (upd.)
International Business Machines
   Corporation, 30 (upd.)
International Rectifier Corporation, 31
Itel Corporation, 9
Jabil Circuit, Inc., 36
Jaco Electronics, Inc., 30
JDS Uniphase Corporation, 34
Juno Lighting, Inc., 30
Keithley Instruments Inc., 16
Kemet Corp., 14
Kent Electronics Corporation, 17
Kenwood Corporation, 31
Kimball International, Inc., 48 (upd.)
Kingston Technology Corporation, 20
KitchenAid, 8
KLA-Tencor Corporation, 45 (upd.)

KnowledgeWare Inc., 9
Kollmorgen Corporation, 18
Konica Corporation, 30 (upd.)
Koor Industries Ltd., II
Koss Corporation, 38
Kudelski Group SA, 44
Kulicke and Soffa Industries, Inc., 33
Kyocera Corporation, II
LaBarge Inc., 41
Lattice Semiconductor Corp., 16
LeCroy Corporation, 41
Legrand SA, 21
Linear Technology, Inc., 16
Littelfuse, Inc., 26
Loral Corporation, 9
Lowrance Electronics, Inc., 18
LSI Logic Corporation, 13
Lucent Technologies Inc., 34
Lucky-Goldstar, II
Lunar Corporation, 29
Mackie Designs Inc., 33
MagneTek, Inc., 15; 41 (upd.)
Marconi plc, 33 (upd.)
Marquette Electronics, Inc., 13
Matsushita Electric Industrial Co., Ltd., II
Maxim Integrated Products, Inc., 16
Merix Corporation, 36
Methode Electronics, Inc., 13
Mitel Corporation, 18
MITRE Corporation, 26
Mitsubishi Electric Corporation, II; 44
   (upd.)
Motorola, Inc., II; 11 (upd.); 34 (upd.)
National Instruments Corporation, 22
National Presto Industries, Inc., 16; 43
   (upd.)
National Semiconductor Corporation, II; 26
   (upd.)
NEC Corporation, II; 21 (upd.)
Nintendo Co., Ltd., 28 (upd.)
Nokia Corporation, II; 17 (upd.); 38 (upd.)
Nortel Networks Corporation, 36 (upd.)
Northrop Grumman Corporation, 45 (upd.)
Oak Technology, Inc., 22
Oki Electric Industry Company, Limited, II
Omron Corporation, II; 28 (upd.)
Otter Tail Power Company, 18
Palm, Inc., 36
Palomar Medical Technologies, Inc., 22
The Peak Technologies Group, Inc., 14
Peavey Electronics Corporation, 16
Philips Electronics N.V., II; 13 (upd.)
Philips Electronics North America Corp.,
   13
Pioneer Electronic Corporation, 28 (upd.)
Pioneer-Standard Electronics Inc., 19
Pitney Bowes Inc., 47 (upd.)
Pittway Corporation, 9
The Plessey Company, PLC, II
Plexus Corporation, 35
Polk Audio, Inc., 34
Potter & Brumfield Inc., 11
Premier Industrial Corporation, 9
Protection One, Inc., 32
Quanta Computer Inc., 47
Racal Electronics PLC, II
RadioShack Corporation, 36 (upd.)
Radius Inc., 16
Raychem Corporation, 8
Rayovac Corporation, 13
Raytheon Company, II; 11 (upd.); 38
   (upd.)
RCA Corporation, II
Read-Rite Corp., 10
Reliance Electric Company, 9
Rexel, Inc., 15
Richardson Electronics, Ltd., 17
Ricoh Company, Ltd., 36 (upd.)

The Rival Company, 19
Rockford Corporation, 43
S&C Electric Company, 15
SAGEM S.A., 37
St. Louis Music, Inc., 48
Sam Ash Music Corporation, 30
Samsung Electronics Co., Ltd., 14; 41 (upd.)
SANYO Electric Co., Ltd., II; 36 (upd.)
ScanSource, Inc., 29
Schneider S.A., II; 18 (upd.)
SCI Systems, Inc., 9
Scientific-Atlanta, Inc., 45 (upd.)
Scitex Corporation Ltd., 24
Seagate Technology, Inc., 34 (upd.)
Semtech Corporation, 32
Sensormatic Electronics Corp., 11
Sensory Science Corporation, 37
SGI, 29 (upd.)
Sharp Corporation, II; 12 (upd.); 40 (upd.)
Sheldahl Inc., 23
Siemens A.G., II; 14 (upd.)
Silicon Graphics Incorporated, 9
Smiths Industries PLC, 25
Solectron Corporation, 12; 48 (upd.)
Sony Corporation, II; 12 (upd.); 40 (upd.)
SPX Corporation, 47 (upd.)
Sterling Electronics Corp., 18
Sumitomo Electric Industries, Ltd., II
Sun Microsystems, Inc., 30 (upd.)
Sunbeam-Oster Co., Inc., 9
SyQuest Technology, Inc., 18
Tandy Corporation, II; 12 (upd.)
Tatung Co., 23
TDK Corporation, II; 17 (upd.); 49 (upd.)
Tech-Sym Corporation, 18
Technitrol, Inc., 29
Tektronix, Inc., 8
Telxon Corporation, 10
Teradyne, Inc., 11
Texas Instruments Inc., II; 11 (upd.); 46 (upd.)
Thales S.A., 42
THOMSON multimedia S.A., II; 42 (upd.)
The Titan Corporation, 36
Tops Appliance City, Inc., 17
Toromont Industries, Ltd., 21
Trimble Navigation Limited, 40
Tweeter Home Entertainment Group, Inc., 30
Ultrak Inc., 24
Universal Electronics Inc., 39
Varian Associates Inc., 12
Veeco Instruments Inc., 32
Vicon Industries, Inc., 44
Victor Company of Japan, Limited, II; 26 (upd.)
Vishay Intertechnology, Inc., 21
Vitesse Semiconductor Corporation, 32
Vitro Corp., 10
VLSI Technology, Inc., 16
Wells-Gardner Electronics Corporation, 43
Westinghouse Electric Corporation, II; 12 (upd.)
Wyle Electronics, 14
Yageo Corporation, 16
York Research Corporation, 35
Zenith Data Systems, Inc., 10
Zenith Electronics Corporation, II; 13 (upd.); 34 (upd.)
Zoom Telephonics, Inc., 18
Zytec Corporation, 19

ENGINEERING & MANAGEMENT SERVICES

AAON, Inc., 22
Aavid Thermal Technologies, Inc., 29
Alliant Techsystems Inc., 30 (upd.)
Amey Plc, 47
Analytic Sciences Corporation, 10
Arcadis NV, 26
Arthur D. Little, Inc., 35
The Austin Company, 8
Balfour Beatty plc, 36 (upd.)
Brown & Root, Inc., 13
Bufete Industrial, S.A. de C.V., 34
C.H. Heist Corporation, 24
CDI Corporation, 6
CH2M Hill Ltd., 22
The Charles Stark Draper Laboratory, Inc., 35
Coflexip S.A., 25
Corrections Corporation of America, 23
CRSS Inc., 6
Dames & Moore, Inc., 25
DAW Technologies, Inc., 25
Day & Zimmermann Inc., 9; 31 (upd.)
Donaldson Co. Inc., 16
EG&G Incorporated, 8; 29 (upd.)
Eiffage, 27
Essef Corporation, 18
Fluor Corporation, 34 (upd.)
Foster Wheeler Corporation, 6; 23 (upd.)
Framatome SA, 19
Gilbane, Inc., 34
Halliburton Company, 25 (upd.)
Harding Lawson Associates Group, Inc., 16
Harza Engineering Company, 14
HDR Inc., 48
ICF Kaiser International, Inc., 28
Jacobs Engineering Group Inc., 6; 26 (upd.)
JWP Inc., 9
Kvaerner ASA, 36
Layne Christensen Company, 19
The MacNeal-Schwendler Corporation, 25
Malcolm Pirnie, Inc., 42
McDermott International, Inc., 37 (upd.)
McKinsey & Company, Inc., 9
Ogden Corporation, 6
Opus Group, 34
Parsons Brinckerhoff, Inc., 34
The Parsons Corporation, 8
RCM Technologies, Inc., 34
Renishaw plc, 46
Rosemount Inc., 15
Roy F. Weston, Inc., 33
Royal Vopak NV, 41
Rust International Inc., 11
Sandia National Laboratories, 49
Sandvik AB, 32 (upd.)
Science Applications International Corporation, 15
Serco Group plc, 47
Stone & Webster, Inc., 13
Susquehanna Pfaltzgraff Company, 8
Sverdrup Corporation, 14
Tech-Sym Corporation, 44 (upd.)
Tetra Tech, Inc., 29
Thyssen Krupp AG, 28 (upd.)
Towers Perrin, 32
Tracor Inc., 17
TRC Companies, Inc., 32
Underwriters Laboratories, Inc., 30
United Dominion Industries Limited, 8; 16 (upd.)
URS Corporation, 45
VA TECH ELIN EBG GmbH, 49
VECO International, Inc., 7
Vinci, 43
WS Atkins Plc, 45

ENTERTAINMENT & LEISURE

A&E Television Networks, 32
Acclaim Entertainment Inc., 24
Activision, Inc., 32
AEI Music Network Inc., 35
Airtours Plc, 27
All American Communications Inc., 20
Alliance Entertainment Corp., 17
Amblin Entertainment, 21
AMC Entertainment Inc., 12; 35 (upd.)
American Golf Corporation, 45
American Skiing Company, 28
Ameristar Casinos, Inc., 33
AMF Bowling, Inc., 40
Anchor Gaming, 24
Applause Inc., 24
Aprilia SpA, 17
Argosy Gaming Company, 21
The Art Institute of Chicago, 29
Artisan Entertainment Inc., 32 (upd.)
Asahi National Broadcasting Company, Ltd., 9
Aspen Skiing Company, 15
Aston Villa plc, 41
Atlanta National League Baseball Club, Inc., 43
The Atlantic Group, 23
Autotote Corporation, 20
Aztar Corporation, 13
Baker & Taylor Corporation, 43 (upd.)
Baker & Taylor, Inc., 16
Bally Total Fitness Holding Corp., 25
Bertelsmann A.G., 15 (upd.); 43 (upd.)
Bertucci's Inc., 16
Big Idea Productions, Inc., 49
Blockbuster Inc., 9; 31 (upd.)
Boca Resorts, Inc., 37
Bonneville International Corporation, 29
Booth Creek Ski Holdings, Inc., 31
Boston Celtics Limited Partnership, 14
Boston Professional Hockey Association Inc., 39
The Boy Scouts of America, 34
British Broadcasting Corporation Ltd., 7; 21 (upd.)
British Sky Broadcasting Group Plc, 20
Cablevision Systems Corporation, 7
Callaway Golf Company, 45 (upd.)
Canterbury Park Holding Corporation, 42
Capital Cities/ABC Inc., II
Carlson Companies, Inc., 22 (upd.)
Carmike Cinemas, Inc., 14; 37 (upd.)
Carnival Corporation, 27 (upd.)
Carnival Cruise Lines, Inc., 6
The Carsey-Werner Company, L.L.C., 37
CBS Inc., II; 6 (upd.)
Cedar Fair, L.P., 22
Central Independent Television, 7; 23 (upd.)
Century Theatres, Inc., 31
Championship Auto Racing Teams, Inc., 37
Chicago Bears Football Club, Inc., 33
Chris-Craft Industries, Inc., 31 (upd.)
Chrysalis Group plc, 40
Churchill Downs Incorporated, 29
Cinar Corporation, 40
Cineplex Odeon Corporation, 6; 23 (upd.)
Cinram International, Inc., 43
Cirque du Soleil Inc., 29
Classic Vacation Group, Inc., 46
Cleveland Indians Baseball Company, Inc., 37
ClubCorp, Inc., 33
Columbia Pictures Entertainment, Inc., II
Columbia TriStar Motion Pictures Companies, 12 (upd.)
Comcast Corporation, 7
Compagnie des Alpes, 48
Continental Cablevision, Inc., 7

Corporation for Public Broadcasting, 14
Cox Enterprises, Inc., 22 (upd.)
Crown Media Holdings, Inc., 45
Cruise America Inc., 21
Cunard Line Ltd., 23
Dallas Cowboys Football Club, Ltd., 33
Dave & Buster's, Inc., 33
Death Row Records, 27
The Detroit Pistons Basketball Company, 41
Detroit Tigers Baseball Club, Inc., 46
dick clark productions, inc., 16
DIRECTV, Inc., 38
Dover Downs Entertainment, Inc., 43
DreamWorks SKG, 43
E! Entertainment Television Inc., 17
edel music AG, 44
Educational Broadcasting Corporation, 48
Edwards Theatres Circuit, Inc., 31
Elsinore Corporation, 48
Endemol Entertainment Holding NV, 46
Equity Marketing, Inc., 26
Esporta plc, 35
Euro Disneyland SCA, 20
Fair Grounds Corporation, 44
Family Golf Centers, Inc., 29
FAO Schwarz, 46
Fédération Internationale de Football Association, 27
Feld Entertainment, Inc., 32 (upd.)
First Choice Holidays PLC, 40
First Team Sports, Inc., 22
Fisher-Price Inc., 32 (upd.)
Florida Gaming Corporation, 47
Fox Entertainment Group, Inc., 43
Fox Family Worldwide, Inc., 24
Gaumont SA, 25
Gaylord Entertainment Company, 11; 36 (upd.)
GC Companies, Inc., 25
Geffen Records Inc., 26
Gibson Guitar Corp., 16
Girl Scouts of the USA, 35
Global Outdoors, Inc., 49
GoodTimes Entertainment Ltd., 48
Granada Group PLC, II; 24 (upd.)
Grand Casinos, Inc., 20
The Green Bay Packers, Inc., 32
Groupe Partouche SA, 48
Hallmark Cards, Inc., 40 (upd.)
Hanna-Barbera Cartoons Inc., 23
Hard Rock Cafe International, Inc., 32 (upd.)
Harpo Entertainment Group, 28
Harrah's Entertainment, Inc., 16; 43 (upd.)
Harveys Casino Resorts, 27
Hasbro, Inc., 43 (upd.)
Hastings Entertainment, Inc., 29
The Hearst Corporation, 46 (upd.)
Hilton Group plc, 49 (upd.)
HIT Entertainment PLC, 40
HOB Entertainment, Inc., 37
Hollywood Casino Corporation, 21
Hollywood Entertainment Corporation, 25
Hollywood Park, Inc., 20
Home Box Office Inc., 7; 23 (upd.)
Imax Corporation, 28
Indianapolis Motor Speedway Corporation, 46
Infinity Broadcasting Corporation, 48 (upd.)
Infogrames Entertainment S.A., 35
Integrity Inc., 44
International Creative Management, Inc., 43
International Family Entertainment Inc., 13
International Game Technology, 41 (upd.)
International Olympic Committee, 44

International Speedway Corporation, 19
Interscope Music Group, 31
The Intrawest Corporation, 15
Irvin Feld & Kenneth Feld Productions, Inc., 15
Isle of Capri Casinos, Inc., 41
iVillage Inc., 46
Iwerks Entertainment, Inc., 34
Jackpot Enterprises Inc., 21
Japan Broadcasting Corporation, 7
Jazzercise, Inc., 45
Jillian's Entertainment Holdings, Inc., 40
The Jim Henson Company, 23
Kampgrounds of America, Inc. (KOA), 33
King World Productions, Inc., 9; 30 (upd.)
Knott's Berry Farm, 18
Kuoni Travel Holding Ltd., 40
The Kushner-Locke Company, 25
Ladbroke Group PLC, II; 21 (upd.)
Lego A/S, 13; 40 (upd.)
Liberty Livewire Corporation, 42
Lionel L.L.C., 16
Lions Gate Entertainment Corporation, 35
LIVE Entertainment Inc., 20
LodgeNet Entertainment Corporation, 28
Lucasfilm Ltd., 12
Luminar Plc, 40
Manchester United Football Club plc, 30
Mandalay Resort Group, 32 (upd.)
The Marcus Corporation, 21
Mashantucket Pequot Gaming Enterprise Inc., 35
MCA Inc., II
Media General, Inc., 7
Metro-Goldwyn-Mayer Inc., 25 (upd.)
Metromedia Companies, 14
Métropole Télévision, 33
Metropolitan Baseball Club Inc., 39
Metropolitan Opera Association, Inc., 40
MGM Grand Inc., 17
MGM/UA Communications Company, II
Midway Games, Inc., 25
Mikohn Gaming Corporation, 39
Milwaukee Brewers Baseball Club, 37
Mizuno Corporation, 25
Mohegan Tribal Gaming Authority, 37
Motown Records Company L.P., 26
Movie Gallery, Inc., 31
Multimedia Games, Inc., 41
Muzak, Inc., 18
National Amusements Inc., 28
National Association for Stock Car Auto Racing, 32
National Broadcasting Company, Inc., II; 6 (upd.)
National Football League, 29
National Hockey League, 35
National Public Radio, Inc., 19; 47 (upd.)
National Rifle Association of America, 37
Navarre Corporation, 24
Navigant International, Inc., 47
New Line Cinema, Inc., 47
News Corporation Limited, 46 (upd.)
Nicklaus Companies, 45
Nintendo Co., Ltd., 28 (upd.)
O'Charley's Inc., 19
Orion Pictures Corporation, 6
Paradise Music & Entertainment, Inc., 42
Paramount Pictures Corporation, II
Pathé SA, 29
PDS Gaming Corporation, 44
Penn National Gaming, Inc., 33
Philadelphia Eagles, 37
Pierre & Vacances SA, 48
Pixar Animation Studios, 34
Platinum Entertainment, Inc., 35
Play by Play Toys & Novelties, Inc., 26
Players International, Inc., 22

PolyGram N.V., 23
Powerhouse Technologies, Inc., 27
Premier Parks, Inc., 27
President Casinos, Inc., 22
Preussag AG, 42 (upd.)
Princess Cruise Lines, 22
The Professional Golfers' Association of America, 41
Promus Companies, Inc., 9
Putt-Putt Golf Courses of America, Inc., 23
Rainforest Cafe, Inc., 25
Rank Organisation PLC, II
Rawlings Sporting Goods Co., Inc., 24
The Really Useful Group, 26
Rentrak Corporation, 35
Rhino Entertainment Company, 18
Ride, Inc., 22
Rollerblade, Inc., 34 (upd.)
Roularta Media Group NV, 48
Royal Caribbean Cruises Ltd., 22
RTL Group SA, 44
Rush Communications, 33
S-K-I Limited, 15
Salomon Worldwide, 20
Santa Fe Gaming Corporation, 19
Schwinn Cycle and Fitness L.P., 19
Scottish Radio Holding plc, 41
Seattle FilmWorks, Inc., 20
Sega of America, Inc., 10
SFX Entertainment, Inc., 36
Showboat, Inc., 19
Shubert Organization Inc., 24
Six Flags Theme Parks, Inc., 17
Smithsonian Institution, 27
Società Sportiva Lazio SpA, 44
Sony Corporation, 40 (upd.)
Speedway Motorsports, Inc., 32
Spelling Entertainment Group, Inc., 14
The Sports Club Company, 25
Station Casinos Inc., 25
Stoll-Moss Theatres Ltd., 34
Stuart Entertainment Inc., 16
TABCORP Holdings Limited, 44
Take-Two Interactive Software, Inc., 46
Tele-Communications, Inc., II
Television Española, S.A., 7
Thomas Cook Travel Inc., 9
The Thomson Corporation, 8
Thousand Trails, Inc., 33
THQ, Inc., 39
Ticketmaster Corp., 13
The Todd-AO Corporation, 33
Toho Co., Ltd., 28
The Topps Company, Inc., 34 (upd.)
Touristik Union International GmbH. and Company K.G., II
Town Sports International, Inc., 46
Toy Biz, Inc., 18
Trans World Entertainment Corporation, 24
Travelocity.com, Inc., 46
TUI Group GmbH, 44
Turner Broadcasting System, Inc., II; 6 (upd.)
Twentieth Century Fox Film Corporation, II; 25 (upd.)
Ubi Soft Entertainment S.A., 41
United Pan-Europe Communications NV, 47
Universal Studios, Inc., 33
Univision Communications Inc., 24
USA Interactive, Inc., 47 (upd.)
Vail Resorts, Inc., 11; 43 (upd.)
Venetian Casino Resort, LLC, 47
Viacom Inc., 7; 23 (upd.)
Vivendi Universal S.A., 46 (upd.)
Walt Disney Company, II; 6 (upd.); 30 (upd.)
Warner Communications Inc., II

Washington Football, Inc., 35
West Coast Entertainment Corporation, 29
Wherehouse Entertainment Incorporated, 11
Wildlife Conservation Society, 31
William Hill Organization Limited, 49
Wilson Sporting Goods Company, 24
Wizards of the Coast Inc., 24
World Wrestling Federation Entertainment, Inc., 32
YankeeNets LLC, 35
YES! Entertainment Corporation, 26
YMCA of the USA, 31
Young Broadcasting Inc., 40

FINANCIAL SERVICES: BANKS

Abbey National plc, 10; 39 (upd.)
Abigail Adams National Bancorp, Inc., 23
Algemene Bank Nederland N.V., II
Allied Irish Banks, plc, 16; 43 (upd.)
Almanij NV, 44
AMCORE Financial Inc., 44
American Residential Mortgage Corporation, 8
AmSouth Bancorporation,12; 48 (upd.)
Amsterdam-Rotterdam Bank N.V., II
Anchor Bancorp, Inc., 10
Astoria Financial Corporation, 44
Australia and New Zealand Banking Group Ltd., II
Banc One Corporation, 10
Banca Commerciale Italiana SpA, II
Banco Bilbao Vizcaya Argentaria S.A., 48 (upd.)
Banco Bilbao Vizcaya, S.A., II
Banco Bradesco S.A., 13
Banco Central, II
Banco do Brasil S.A., II
Banco Espírito Santo e Comercial de Lisboa S.A., 15
Banco Itaú S.A., 19
Banco Santander Central Hispano S.A., 36 (upd.)
Bank Austria AG, 23
Bank Brussels Lambert, II
Bank Hapoalim B.M., II
Bank of America Corporation, 46 (upd.)
Bank of Boston Corporation, II
Bank of Mississippi, Inc., 14
Bank of Montreal, II; 46 (upd.)
Bank of New England Corporation, II
The Bank of New York Company, Inc., II; 46 (upd.)
The Bank of Nova Scotia, II
Bank of Tokyo-Mitsubishi Ltd., II; 15 (upd.)
Bank One Corporation, 36 (upd.)
BankAmerica Corporation, II; 8 (upd.)
Bankers Trust New York Corporation, II
Banque Nationale de Paris S.A., II
Barclays PLC, II; 20 (upd.)
BarclaysAmerican Mortgage Corporation, 11
Barings PLC, 14
Barnett Banks, Inc., 9
BayBanks, Inc., 12
Bayerische Hypotheken- und Wechsel- Bank AG, II
Bayerische Vereinsbank A.G., II
Beneficial Corporation, 8
BNP Paribas Group, 36 (upd.)
Boatmen's Bancshares Inc., 15
Bremer Financial Corp., 45
Brown Brothers Harriman & Co., 45
Canadian Imperial Bank of Commerce, II
Carolina First Corporation, 31
Casco Northern Bank, 14

The Chase Manhattan Corporation, II; 13 (upd.)
Chemical Banking Corporation, II; 14 (upd.)
Citicorp, II; 9 (upd.)
Citigroup Inc., 30 (upd.)
Citizens Financial Group, Inc., 42
Close Brothers Group plc, 39
Commercial Credit Company, 8
Commercial Federal Corporation, 12
Commerzbank A.G., II; 47 (upd.)
Compagnie Financiere de Paribas, II
Continental Bank Corporation, II
CoreStates Financial Corp, 17
Countrywide Credit Industries, Inc., 16
Crédit Agricole, II
Crédit Lyonnais, 9; 33 (upd.)
Crédit National S.A., 9
Credit Suisse Group, II; 21 (upd.)
Credito Italiano, II
Cullen/Frost Bankers, Inc., 25
The Dai-Ichi Kangyo Bank Ltd., II
The Daiwa Bank, Ltd., II; 39 (upd.)
Dauphin Deposit Corporation, 14
Deposit Guaranty Corporation, 17
Deutsche Bank AG, II; 14 (upd.); 40 (upd.)
Dexia Group, 42
Dime Savings Bank of New York, F.S.B., 9
Donaldson, Lufkin & Jenrette, Inc., 22
Dresdner Bank A.G., II
Fifth Third Bancorp, 13; 31 (upd.)
First Bank System Inc., 12
First Chicago Corporation, II
First Commerce Bancshares, Inc., 15
First Commerce Corporation, 11
First Empire State Corporation, 11
First Fidelity Bank, N.A., New Jersey, 9
First Hawaiian, Inc., 11
First Interstate Bancorp, II
First Nationwide Bank, 14
First of America Bank Corporation, 8
First Security Corporation, 11
First Tennessee National Corporation, 11; 48 (upd.)
First Union Corporation, 10
First Virginia Banks, Inc., 11
Firstar Corporation, 11; 33 (upd.)
Fleet Financial Group, Inc., 9
FleetBoston Financial Corporation, 36 (upd.)
Fourth Financial Corporation, 11
The Fuji Bank, Ltd., II
Generale Bank, II
German American Bancorp, 41
Glacier Bancorp, Inc., 35
Golden West Financial Corporation, 47
The Governor and Company of the Bank of Scotland, 10
Grameen Bank, 31
Granite State Bankshares, Inc., 37
Great Lakes Bancorp, 8
Great Western Financial Corporation, 10
GreenPoint Financial Corp., 28
Grupo Financiero Serfin, S.A., 19
H.F. Ahmanson & Company, II; 10 (upd.)
Habersham Bancorp, 25
Hancock Holding Company, 15
Hibernia Corporation, 37
The Hongkong and Shanghai Banking Corporation Limited, II
HSBC Holdings plc, 12; 26 (upd.)
Hudson River Bancorp, Inc., 41
Huntington Bancshares Inc., 11
IBERIABANK Corporation, 37
The Industrial Bank of Japan, Ltd., II
J Sainsbury plc, 38 (upd.)

J.P. Morgan & Co. Incorporated, II; 30 (upd.)
J.P. Morgan Chase & Co., 38 (upd.)
Japan Leasing Corporation, 8
Kansallis-Osake-Pankki, II
KeyCorp, 8
Kredietbank N.V., II
Kreditanstalt für Wiederaufbau, 29
Lloyds Bank PLC, II
Lloyds TSB Group plc, 47 (upd.)
Long Island Bancorp, Inc., 16
Long-Term Credit Bank of Japan, Ltd., II
Manufacturers Hanover Corporation, II
MBNA Corporation, 12
Mellon Bank Corporation, II
Mellon Financial Corporation, 44 (upd.)
Mercantile Bankshares Corp., 11
Meridian Bancorp, Inc., 11
Metropolitan Financial Corporation, 13
Michigan National Corporation, 11
Midland Bank PLC, II; 17 (upd.)
The Mitsubishi Bank, Ltd., II
The Mitsubishi Trust & Banking Corporation, II
The Mitsui Bank, Ltd., II
The Mitsui Trust & Banking Company, Ltd., II
Mouvement des Caisses Desjardins, 48
N M Rothschild & Sons Limited, 39
National Bank of Greece, 41
National City Corp., 15
National Westminster Bank PLC, II
NationsBank Corporation, 10
NBD Bancorp, Inc., 11
NCNB Corporation, II
Nippon Credit Bank, II
Nordea AB, 40
Norinchukin Bank, II
North Fork Bancorporation, Inc., 46
Northern Rock plc, 33
Northern Trust Company, 9
NVR L.P., 8
Old Kent Financial Corp., 11
Old National Bancorp, 15
PNC Bank Corp., II; 13 (upd.)
The PNC Financial Services Group Inc., 46 (upd.)
Popular, Inc., 41
Pulte Corporation, 8
Rabobank Group, 33
Republic New York Corporation, 11
Riggs National Corporation, 13
The Royal Bank of Canada, II; 21 (upd.)
The Royal Bank of Scotland Group plc, 12; 38 (upd.)
The Ryland Group, Inc., 8
St. Paul Bank for Cooperatives, 8
The Sanwa Bank, Ltd., II; 15 (upd.)
SBC Warburg, 14
Seattle First National Bank Inc., 8
Security Capital Corporation, 17
Security Pacific Corporation, II
Shawmut National Corporation, 13
Signet Banking Corporation, 11
Singer & Friedlander Group plc, 41
Skandinaviska Enskilda Banken, II
Société Générale, II; 42 (upd.)
Society Corporation, 9
Southtrust Corporation, 11
Standard Chartered plc, II; 48 (upd.)
Standard Federal Bank, 9
Star Banc Corporation, 11
State Street Boston Corporation, 8
Staten Island Bancorp, Inc., 39
The Sumitomo Bank, Limited, II; 26 (upd.)
The Sumitomo Trust & Banking Company, Ltd., II
The Summit Bancorporation, 14

SunTrust Banks Inc., 23
Svenska Handelsbanken, II
Swiss Bank Corporation, II
Synovus Financial Corp., 12
The Taiyo Kobe Bank, Ltd., II
TCF Financial Corporation, 47
The Tokai Bank, Limited, II; 15 (upd.)
The Toronto-Dominion Bank, II; 49 (upd.)
TSB Group plc, 12
U.S. Bancorp, 14; 36 (upd.)
U.S. Trust Corp., 17
Union Bank of California, 16
Union Bank of Switzerland, II
Wachovia Bank of Georgia, N.A., 16
Wachovia Bank of South Carolina, N.A.,
  16
Wachovia Corporation, 12
Washington Mutual, Inc., 17
Wells Fargo & Company, II; 12 (upd.); 38
  (upd.)
West One Bancorp, 11
Westamerica Bancorporation, 17
Westdeutsche Landesbank Girozentrale, II;
  46 (upd.)
Westpac Banking Corporation, II; 48 (upd.)
Whitney Holding Corporation, 21
Wilmington Trust Corporation, 25
The Woolwich plc, 30
World Bank Group, 33
The Yasuda Trust and Banking Company,
  Ltd., II; 17 (upd.)
Zions Bancorporation, 12

FINANCIAL SERVICES: NON-BANKS

A.B. Watley Group Inc., 45
A.G. Edwards, Inc., 8; 32 (upd.)
ACE Cash Express, Inc., 33
ADVANTA Corp., 8
Advanta Corporation, 38 (upd.)
American Express Company, II; 10 (upd.);
  38 (upd.)
American General Finance Corp., 11
American Home Mortgage Holdings, Inc.,
  46
Ameritrade Holding Corporation, 34
Arthur Andersen & Company, Société
  Coopérative, 10
Avco Financial Services Inc., 13
Bear Stearns Companies, Inc., II; 10 (upd.)
Benchmark Capital, 49
Bill & Melinda Gates Foundation, 41
Bozzuto's, Inc., 13
Carnegie Corporation of New York, 35
Cash America International, Inc., 20
Cendant Corporation, 44 (upd.)
Cetelem S.A., 21
The Charles Schwab Corporation, 8; 26
  (upd.)
Citfed Bancorp, Inc., 16
Coinstar, Inc., 44
Comerica Incorporated, 40
Commercial Financial Services, Inc., 26
Coopers & Lybrand, 9
Cramer, Berkowitz & Co., 34
Credit Acceptance Corporation, 18
CS First Boston Inc., II
Dain Rauscher Corporation, 35 (upd.)
Daiwa Securities Company, Limited, II
Datek Online Holdings Corp., 32
The David and Lucile Packard Foundation,
  41
Dean Witter, Discover & Co., 12
Dow Jones Telerate, Inc., 10
Drexel Burnham Lambert Incorporated, II
E*Trade Group, Inc., 20
Eaton Vance Corporation, 18

Edward Jones, 30
Euronext Paris S.A., 37
Experian Information Solutions Inc., 45
Fair, Isaac and Company, 18
Fannie Mae, 45 (upd.)
Federal National Mortgage Association, II
Fidelity Investments Inc., II; 14 (upd.)
First Albany Companies Inc., 37
First Data Corporation, 30 (upd.)
First USA, Inc., 11
FMR Corp., 8; 32 (upd.)
Forstmann Little & Co., 38
Fortis, Inc., 15
Frank Russell Company, 46
Franklin Resources, Inc., 9
Gabelli Asset Management Inc., 30
Goldman, Sachs & Co., II; 20 (upd.)
Grede Foundries, Inc., 38
Green Tree Financial Corporation, 11
Gruntal & Co., L.L.C., 20
H & R Block, Incorporated, 9; 29 (upd.)
H.D. Vest, Inc., 46
Hoenig Group Inc., 41
Household International, Inc., II; 21 (upd.)
Ingenico—Compagnie Industrielle et
  Financière d'Ingénierie, 46
Instinet Corporation, 34
Inter-Regional Financial Group, Inc., 15
The Island ECN, Inc., 48
Istituto per la Ricostruzione Industriale
  S.p.A., 11
JB Oxford Holdings, Inc., 32
Jefferies Group, Inc., 25
John Hancock Financial Services, Inc., 42
  (upd.)
The John Nuveen Company, 21
Jones Lang LaSalle Incorporated, 49
Kansas City Southern Industries, Inc., 26
  (upd.)
Kleinwort Benson Group PLC, II
Kohlberg Kravis Roberts & Co., 24
KPMG Worldwide, 10
La Poste, 47 (upd.)
LaBranche & Co. Inc., 37
Lazard LLC, 38
Legg Mason, Inc., 33
London Stock Exchange Limited, 34
M.H. Meyerson & Co., Inc., 46
MacAndrews & Forbes Holdings Inc., 28
MasterCard International, Inc., 9
MBNA Corporation, 33 (upd.)
Merrill Lynch & Co., Inc., II; 13 (upd.); 40
  (upd.)
Morgan Grenfell Group PLC, II
Morgan Stanley Dean Witter & Company,
  II; 16 (upd.); 33 (upd.)
Mountain States Mortgage Centers, Inc., 29
National Association of Securities Dealers,
  Inc., 10
National Auto Credit, Inc., 16
National Discount Brokers Group, Inc., 28
Navy Federal Credit Union, 33
New Street Capital Inc., 8
New York Stock Exchange, Inc., 9; 39
  (upd.)
The Nikko Securities Company Limited, II;
  9 (upd.)
Nippon Shinpan Company, Ltd., II
Nomura Securities Company, Limited, II; 9
  (upd.)
Orix Corporation, II
ORIX Corporation, 44 (upd.)
PaineWebber Group Inc., II; 22 (upd.)
The Pew Charitable Trusts, 35
Piper Jaffray Companies Inc., 22
Pitney Bowes Inc., 47 (upd.)
The Prudential Insurance Company of
  America, 30 (upd.)

The Quick & Reilly Group, Inc., 20
Resource America, Inc., 42
Safeguard Scientifics, Inc., 10
Salomon Inc., II; 13 (upd.)
SBC Warburg, 14
Schroders plc, 42
Shearson Lehman Brothers Holdings Inc.,
  II; 9 (upd.)
Siebert Financial Corp., 32
SLM Holding Corp., 25 (upd.)
Smith Barney Inc., 15
Soros Fund Management LLC, 28
State Street Boston Corporation, 8
Student Loan Marketing Association, II
T. Rowe Price Associates, Inc., 11; 34
  (upd.)
Teachers Insurance and Annuity
  Association-College Retirement Equities
  Fund, 45 (upd.)
Texas Pacific Group Inc., 36
Total System Services, Inc., 18
Trilon Financial Corporation, II
United Jewish Communities, 33
The Vanguard Group of Investment
  Companies, 14
The Vanguard Group, Inc., 34 (upd.)
VeriFone, Inc., 18
Visa International, 9; 26 (upd.)
Wachovia Corporation, 46 (upd.)
Waddell & Reed, Inc., 22
Washington Federal, Inc., 17
Waterhouse Investor Services, Inc., 18
Watson Wyatt Worldwide, 42
Working Assets Funding Service, 43
Yamaichi Securities Company, Limited, II
The Ziegler Companies, Inc., 24
Zurich Financial Services, 42 (upd.)

FOOD PRODUCTS

Agway, Inc., 7
Ajinomoto Co., Inc., II; 28 (upd.)
The Albert Fisher Group plc, 41
Alberto-Culver Company, 8
Aldi Group, 13
Alpine Lace Brands, Inc., 18
American Crystal Sugar Company, 11; 32
  (upd.)
American Foods Group, 43
American Italian Pasta Company, 27
American Maize-Products Co., 14
American Rice, Inc., 33
Amfac/JMB Hawaii L.L.C., 24 (upd.)
Archer-Daniels-Midland Company, 32
  (upd.)
Archway Cookies, Inc., 29
Arla Foods amba, 48
Associated British Foods plc, II; 13 (upd.);
  41 (upd.)
Associated Milk Producers, Inc., 11; 48
  (upd.)
Aurora Foods Inc., 32
B&G Foods, Inc., 40
The B. Manischewitz Company, LLC, 31
Bahlsen GmbH & Co. KG, 44
Balance Bar Company, 32
Baltek Corporation, 34
Barilla G. e R. Fratelli S.p.A., 17
Bear Creek Corporation, 38
Beatrice Company, II
Beech-Nut Nutrition Corporation, 21
Ben & Jerry's Homemade, Inc., 10; 35
Berkeley Farms, Inc., 46
Besnier SA, 19
Bestfoods, 22 (upd.)
Blue Bell Creameries L.P., 30
Blue Diamond Growers, 28
Bongrain SA, 25

Booker PLC, 13; 31 (upd.)
Borden, Inc., II; 22 (upd.)
Brach and Brock Confections, Inc., 15
Brake Bros plc, 45
Bridgford Foods Corporation, 27
Brothers Gourmet Coffees, Inc., 20
Broughton Foods Co., 17
Brown & Haley, 23
Bruce Foods Corporation, 39
BSN Groupe S.A., II
Burger King Corporation, 17 (upd.)
Bush Boake Allen Inc., 30
Bush Brothers & Company, 45
C.H. Robinson Worldwide, Inc., 40 (upd.)
Cadbury Schweppes PLC, II; 49 (upd.)
Cagle's, Inc., 20
Calavo Growers, Inc., 47
Calcot Ltd., 33
Campbell Soup Company, II; 7 (upd.); 26 (upd.)
Canada Packers Inc., II
Cargill Inc., 13 (upd.)
Carnation Company, II
Carroll's Foods, Inc., 46
Carvel Corporation, 35
Castle & Cooke, Inc., II; 20 (upd.)
Cattleman's, Inc., 20
Celestial Seasonings, Inc., 16
Central Soya Company, Inc., 7
Chelsea Milling Company, 29
Chicken of the Sea International, 24 (upd.)
Chiquita Brands International, Inc., 7; 21 (upd.)
Chock Full o'Nuts Corp., 17
Chocoladefabriken Lindt & Sprüngli AG, 27
Chupa Chups S.A., 38
The Clorox Company, 22 (upd.)
Coca-Cola Enterprises, Inc., 13
ConAgra Foods, Inc., 42 (upd.)
Conagra, Inc., II; 12 (upd.)
The Connell Company, 29
ContiGroup Companies, Inc., 43 (upd.)
Continental Grain Company, 10; 13 (upd.)
CoolBrands International Inc., 35
CPC International Inc., II
Cranswick plc, 40
Cumberland Packing Corporation, 26
Curtice-Burns Foods, Inc., 7; 21 (upd.)
Czarnikow-Rionda Company, Inc., 32
Dairy Crest Group plc, 32
Dalgery, PLC, II
Danisco A/S, 44
Dannon Co., Inc., 14
Darigold, Inc., 9
Dawn Food Products, Inc., 17
Dean Foods Company, 7; 21 (upd.)
DeKalb Genetics Corporation, 17
Del Monte Foods Company, 7; 23 (upd.)
Di Giorgio Corp., 12
Diageo plc, 24 (upd.)
Dole Food Company, Inc., 9; 31 (upd.)
Domino Sugar Corporation, 26
Doskocil Companies, Inc., 12
Dreyer's Grand Ice Cream, Inc., 17
The Earthgrains Company, 36
Emge Packing Co., Inc., 11
Eridania Béghin-Say S.A., 36
ERLY Industries Inc., 17
Eskimo Pie Corporation, 21
Farmland Foods, Inc., 7
Farmland Industries, Inc., 48
Fieldale Farms Corporation, 23
Fleer Corporation, 15
Fleury Michon S.A., 39
Florida Crystals Inc., 35
Flowers Industries, Inc., 12; 35 (upd.)
FoodBrands America, Inc., 23

Foster Poultry Farms, 32
Fresh America Corporation, 20
Fresh Foods, Inc., 29
Frito-Lay Company, 32
Fromageries Bel, 23
Fyffes Plc, 38
Gardenburger, Inc., 33
Geest Plc, 38
General Mills, Inc., II; 10 (upd.); 36 (upd.)
George A. Hormel and Company, II
George Weston Limited, 36 (upd.)
Gerber Products Company, 7; 21 (upd.)
Ghirardelli Chocolate Company, 30
Givaudan SA, 43
Gold Kist Inc., 17; 26 (upd.)
Golden Enterprises, Inc., 26
Gonnella Baking Company, 40
Good Humor-Breyers Ice Cream Company, 14
GoodMark Foods, Inc., 26
Gorton's, 13
Goya Foods Inc., 22
Great Harvest Bread Company, 44
Grist Mill Company, 15
Groupe Danone, 32 (upd.)
Gruma, S.A. de C.V., 31
Grupo Herdez, S.A. de C.V., 35
H.J. Heinz Company, II; 11 (upd.); 36 (upd.)
The Hain Celestial Group, Inc., 27; 43 (upd.)
Hanover Foods Corporation, 35
HARIBO GmbH & Co. KG, 44
The Hartz Mountain Corporation, 12
Hazlewood Foods plc, 32
Herman Goelitz, Inc., 28
Hershey Foods Corporation, II; 15 (upd.)
Hill's Pet Nutrition, Inc., 27
Hillsdown Holdings plc, II; 24 (upd.)
Horizon Organic Holding Corporation, 37
Hormel Foods Corporation, 18 (upd.)
Hudson Foods Inc., 13
Hulman & Company, 44
Hunt-Wesson, Inc., 17
Iams Company, 26
IAWS Group plc, 49
IBP, Inc., II; 21 (upd.)
Iceland Group plc, 33
Imperial Holly Corporation, 12
Imperial Sugar Company, 32 (upd.)
Industrias Bachoco, S.A. de C.V., 39
International Multifoods Corporation, 7; 25 (upd.)
Interstate Bakeries Corporation, 12; 38 (upd.)
Itoham Foods Inc., II
J & J Snack Foods Corporation, 24
The J.M. Smucker Company, 11
J.R. Simplot Company, 16
Jacobs Suchard A.G., II
Jim Beam Brands Co., 14
John B. Sanfilippo & Son, Inc., 14
Just Born, Inc., 32
Kal Kan Foods, Inc., 22
Kamps AG, 44
Keebler Foods Company, 36
Kellogg Company, II; 13 (upd.)
Kerry Group plc, 27
Kettle Foods Inc., 48
Kikkoman Corporation, 14; 47 (upd.)
The King Arthur Flour Company, 31
King Ranch, Inc., 14
Koninklijke Wessanen N.V., II
Kraft Foods Inc., 45 (upd.)
Kraft General Foods Inc., II; 7 (upd.)
Kraft Jacobs Suchard AG, 26 (upd.)
Krispy Kreme Doughnut Corporation, 21
La Choy Food Products Inc., 25

Lamb Weston, Inc., 23
Lance, Inc., 14; 41 (upd.)
Land O'Lakes, Inc., II; 21 (upd.)
Leprino Foods Company, 28
Lincoln Snacks Company, 24
Lucille Farms, Inc., 45
Malt-O-Meal Company, 22
Maple Leaf Foods Inc., 41
Mars, Incorporated, 7; 40 (upd.)
Maui Land & Pineapple Company, Inc., 29
McCormick & Company, Incorporated, 7; 27 (upd.)
McIlhenny Company, 20
McKee Foods Corporation, 7; 27 (upd.)
Meiji Milk Products Company, Limited, II
Meiji Seika Kaisha, Ltd., II
Michael Foods, Inc., 25
Mid-America Dairymen, Inc., 7
Midwest Grain Products, Inc., 49
Mike-Sell's Inc., 15
Milnot Company, 46
Monfort, Inc., 13
Mrs. Baird's Bakeries, 29
Mt. Olive Pickle Company, Inc., 44
Murphy Family Farms Inc., 22
Nabisco Foods Group, II; 7 (upd.)
Nantucket Allserve, Inc., 22
Nathan's Famous, Inc., 29
National Presto Industries, Inc., 43 (upd.)
National Sea Products Ltd., 14
Nestlé S.A., II; 7 (upd.); 28 (upd.)
New England Confectionery Co., 15
Newhall Land and Farming Company, 14
Newman's Own, Inc., 37
Nippon Meat Packers, Inc., II
Nippon Suisan Kaisha, Limited, II
Nisshin Flour Milling Company, Ltd., II
Northern Foods PLC, 10
Northland Cranberries, Inc., 38
Nutraceutical International Corporation, 37
NutraSweet Company, 8
Ocean Spray Cranberries, Inc., 7; 25 (upd.)
OJSC Wimm-Bill-Dann Foods, 48
Ore-Ida Foods Incorporated, 13
Oscar Mayer Foods Corp., 12
Otis Spunkmeyer, Inc., 28
Papetti's Hygrade Egg Products, Inc., 39
PepsiCo, Inc., 38 (upd.)
Perdue Farms Inc., 7; 23 (upd.)
Pet Incorporated, 7
Pez Candy, Inc., 38
Philip Morris Companies Inc., 18 (upd.)
PIC International Group PLC, 24 (upd.)
Pilgrim's Pride Corporation, 7; 23 (upd.)
Pillsbury Company, II; 13 (upd.)
Pioneer Hi-Bred International, Inc., 9
Pizza Inn, Inc., 46
Poore Brothers, Inc., 44
PowerBar Inc., 44
Prairie Farms Dairy, Inc., 47
Premium Standard Farms, Inc., 30
The Procter & Gamble Company, III; 8 (upd.); 26 (upd.)
Purina Mills, Inc., 32
Quaker Oats Company, II; 12 (upd.); 34 (upd.)
Quality Chekd Dairies, Inc., 48
Ralston Purina Company, II; 13 (upd.)
Ranks Hovis McDougall Limited, II; 28 (upd.)
Reckitt & Colman PLC, II
Reckitt Benckiser plc, 42 (upd.)
Rica Foods, Inc., 41
Rich Products Corporation, 7; 38 (upd.)
Riviana Foods Inc., 27
Roland Murten A.G., 7
Rowntree Mackintosh, II
Royal Numico N.V., 37

Russell Stover Candies Inc., 12
Sanderson Farms, Inc., 15
Sara Lee Corporation, II; 15 (upd.)
Savannah Foods & Industries, Inc., 7
Schlotzsky's, Inc., 36
Schwan's Sales Enterprises, Inc., 7
See's Candies, Inc., 30
Seminis, Inc., 29
Smithfield Foods, Inc., 7; 43 (upd.)
Snow Brand Milk Products Company, Ltd.,
    II; 48 (upd.)
Sodiaal S.A., 36 (upd.)
SODIMA, II
Sorrento, Inc., 24
Spangler Candy Company, 44
Stock Yards Packing Co., Inc., 37
Stolt-Nielsen S.A., 42
Stouffer Corp., 8
Südzucker AG, 27
Suiza Foods Corporation, 26
Sun-Diamond Growers of California, 7
Sunkist Growers, Inc., 26
Supervalu Inc., 18 (upd.)
Suprema Specialties, Inc., 27
Sylvan, Inc., 22
Taiyo Fishery Company, Limited, II
Tasty Baking Company, 14; 35 (upd.)
Tate & Lyle PLC, II; 42 (upd.)
TCBY Enterprises Inc., 17
TDL Group Ltd., 46
Thomas J. Lipton Company, 14
Thorn Apple Valley, Inc., 7; 22 (upd.)
Thorntons plc, 46
TLC Beatrice International Holdings, Inc.,
    22
Tombstone Pizza Corporation, 13
Tone Brothers, Inc., 21
Tootsie Roll Industries Inc., 12
Tri Valley Growers, 32
Tropicana Products, Inc., 28
Tyson Foods, Incorporated, II; 14 (upd.)
U.S. Foodservice, 26
Uncle Ben's Inc., 22
Unigate PLC, II; 28 (upd.)
United Biscuits (Holdings) plc, II; 42
    (upd.)
United Brands Company, II
United Foods, Inc., 21
Universal Foods Corporation, 7
Van Camp Seafood Company, Inc., 7
Vienna Sausage Manufacturing Co., 14
Vlasic Foods International Inc., 25
Wattie's Ltd., 7
Wells' Dairy, Inc., 36
White Wave, 43
OJSC Wimm-Bill-Dann Foods, 48
Wisconsin Dairies, 7
WLR Foods, Inc., 21
Wm. Wrigley Jr. Company, 7
World's Finest Chocolate Inc., 39
Worthington Foods, Inc., 14
YOCREAM International, Inc., 47

FOOD SERVICES & RETAILERS

Advantica Restaurant Group, Inc., 27
    (upd.)
AFC Enterprises, Inc., 32 (upd.)
Albertson's Inc., II; 7 (upd.); 30 (upd.)
Aldi Group, 13
Alex Lee Inc., 18; 44 (upd.)
America's Favorite Chicken Company,
    Inc., 7
American Stores Company, II
Applebee's International, Inc., 14; 35
    (upd.)
ARA Services, II
Arby's Inc., 14

Arden Group, Inc., 29
Argyll Group PLC, II
Ark Restaurants Corp., 20
Asahi Breweries, Ltd., 20 (upd.)
Asda Group PLC, II
ASDA Group plc, 28 (upd.)
Associated Grocers, Incorporated, 9; 31
    (upd.)
Association des Centres Distributeurs E.
    Leclerc, 37
Au Bon Pain Co., Inc., 18
Auchan, 37
Auntie Anne's, Inc., 35
Autogrill SpA, 49
Avado Brands, Inc., 31
Back Bay Restaurant Group, Inc., 20
Back Yard Burgers, Inc., 45
Bashas' Inc., 33
Bear Creek Corporation, 38
Benihana, Inc., 18
Big Bear Stores Co., 13
Big V Supermarkets, Inc., 25
Blimpie International, Inc., 15; 49 (upd.)
Bob Evans Farms, Inc., 9
Bon Appetit Holding AG, 48
Boston Chicken, Inc., 12
Boston Market Corporation, 48 (upd.)
Brinker International, Inc., 10; 38 (upd.)
Brookshire Grocery Company, 16
Bruno's, Inc., 7; 26 (upd.)
Buca, Inc., 38
Buffets, Inc., 10; 32 (upd.)
Burger King Corporation, II
C.H. Robinson, Inc., 11
California Pizza Kitchen Inc., 15
Cargill, Inc., II
Caribou Coffee Company, Inc., 28
Carlson Companies, Inc., 22 (upd.)
Carr-Gottstein Foods Co., 17
Casey's General Stores, Inc., 19
CBRL Group, Inc., 35 (upd.)
CEC Entertainment, Inc., 31 (upd.)
Chart House Enterprises, Inc., 17
Checkers Drive-Up Restaurants Inc., 16
The Cheesecake Factory Inc., 17
Chi-Chi's Inc., 13
Chicago Pizza & Brewery, Inc., 44
Chick-fil-A Inc., 23
Cinnabon Inc., 23
The Circle K Corporation, II
CKE Restaurants, Inc., 19; 46 (upd.)
Coborn's, Inc., 30
Compass Group PLC, 34
Comptoirs Modernes S.A., 19
Consolidated Products Inc., 14
Controladora Comercial Mexicana, S.A. de
    C.V., 36
The Cooker Restaurant Corporation, 20
The Copps Corporation, 32
Cracker Barrel Old Country Store, Inc., 10
D'Agostino Supermarkets Inc., 19
Dairy Mart Convenience Stores, Inc., 7; 25
    (upd.)
Darden Restaurants, Inc., 16; 44 (upd.)
Dean & DeLuca, Inc., 36
Delhaize "Le Lion" S.A., 44
DeMoulas / Market Basket Inc., 23
DenAmerica Corporation, 29
Diedrich Coffee, Inc., 40
Domino's Pizza, Inc., 7; 21 (upd.)
Eateries, Inc., 33
Edeka Zentrale A.G., II; 47 (upd.)
Einstein/Noah Bagel Corporation, 29
El Chico Restaurants, Inc., 19
Elior SA, 49
Elmer's Restaurants, Inc., 42
Embers America Restaurants, 30

Etablissements Economiques du Casino
    Guichard, Perrachon et Cie, S.C.A., 12
Famous Dave's of America, Inc., 40
Fazoli's Systems, Inc., 27
Flagstar Companies, Inc., 10
Fleming Companies, Inc., II
Food Lion, Inc., II; 15 (upd.)
Foodarama Supermarkets, Inc., 28
Foodmaker, Inc., 14
The Fred W. Albrecht Grocery Co., 13
Fresh Choice, Inc., 20
Fresh Foods, Inc., 29
Friendly Ice Cream Corp., 30
Frisch's Restaurants, Inc., 35
Fuller Smith & Turner P.L.C., 38
Furr's Supermarkets, Inc., 28
Garden Fresh Restaurant Corporation, 31
The Gateway Corporation Ltd., II
Genuardi's Family Markets, Inc., 35
George Weston Limited, II; 36 (upd.)
Ghirardelli Chocolate Company, 30
Giant Food Inc., II; 22 (upd.)
Godfather's Pizza Incorporated, 25
Golden Corral Corporation, 10
Golden State Foods Corporation, 32
The Golub Corporation, 26
Gordon Food Service Inc., 8; 39 (upd.)
The Grand Union Company, 7; 28 (upd.)
The Great Atlantic & Pacific Tea
    Company, Inc., II; 16 (upd.)
Gristede's Sloan's, Inc., 31
Ground Round, Inc., 21
Groupe Promodès S.A., 19
Guyenne et Gascogne, 23
H.E. Butt Grocery Co., 13; 32 (upd.)
Haggen Inc., 38
Hannaford Bros. Co., 12
Hard Rock Cafe International, Inc., 12
Harris Teeter Inc., 23
Harry's Farmers Market Inc., 23
Hickory Farms, Inc., 17
Holberg Industries, Inc., 36
Holland Burgerville USA, 44
Hooters of America, Inc., 18
Hops Restaurant Bar and Brewery, 46
Hughes Markets, Inc., 22
Hungry Howie's Pizza and Subs, Inc., 25
Hy-Vee, Inc., 36
ICA AB, II
Iceland Group plc, 33
IHOP Corporation, 17
Il Fornaio (America) Corporation, 27
In-N-Out Burger, 19
Ingles Markets, Inc., 20
Inserra Supermarkets, 25
International Dairy Queen, Inc., 10; 39
    (upd.)
ITM Entreprises SA, 36
Ito-Yokado Co., Ltd., 42 (upd.)
J Sainsbury plc, II; 13 (upd.); 38 (upd.)
Jamba Juice Company, 47
JD Wetherspoon plc, 30
Jerry's Famous Deli Inc., 24
Jitney-Jungle Stores of America, Inc., 27
John Lewis Partnership plc, 42 (upd.)
Johnny Rockets Group, Inc., 31
KFC Corporation, 7; 21 (upd.)
King Kullen Grocery Co., Inc., 15
Koninklijke Ahold N.V. (Royal Ahold), II;
    16 (upd.)
Koo Koo Roo, Inc., 25
The Kroger Company, II; 15 (upd.)
The Krystal Company, 33
Kwik Save Group plc, 11
La Madeleine French Bakery & Café, 33
Landry's Seafood Restaurants, Inc., 15
Leeann Chin, Inc., 30
Levy Restaurants L.P., 26

Little Caesar Enterprises, Inc., 7; 24 (upd.)
Loblaw Companies Limited, 43
Logan's Roadhouse, Inc., 29
Long John Silver's Restaurants Inc., 13
Luby's Cafeteria's, Inc., 17
Luby's, Inc., 42 (upd.)
Lucky Stores, Inc., 27
Lund Food Holdings, Inc., 22
Marie Callender's Restaurant & Bakery, Inc., 28
Marsh Supermarkets, Inc., 17
Max & Erma's Restaurants Inc., 19
McDonald's Corporation, II; 7 (upd.); 26 (upd.)
Megafoods Stores Inc., 13
Meijer Incorporated, 7
Metromedia Companies, 14
Mexican Restaurants, Inc., 41
The Middleby Corporation, 22
Minyard Food Stores, Inc., 33
MITROPA AG, 37
Morrison Restaurants Inc., 11
Morton's Restaurant Group, Inc., 30
Mrs. Fields' Original Cookies, Inc., 27
Nash Finch Company, 8; 23 (upd.)
Nathan's Famous, Inc., 29
National Convenience Stores Incorporated, 7
New World Restaurant Group, Inc., 44
New York Restaurant Group, Inc., 32
Noble Roman's Inc., 14
NPC International, Inc., 40
O'Charley's Inc., 19
Old Spaghetti Factory International Inc., 24
The Oshawa Group Limited, II
Outback Steakhouse, Inc., 12; 34 (upd.)
P&C Foods Inc., 8
P.F. Chang's China Bistro, Inc., 37
Pancho's Mexican Buffet, Inc., 46
Panda Management Company, Inc., 35
Panera Bread Company, 44
Papa John's International, Inc., 15
Pathmark Stores, Inc., 23
Peapod, Inc., 30
Penn Traffic Company, 13
Performance Food Group Company, 31
Perkins Family Restaurants, L.P., 22
Piccadilly Cafeterias, Inc., 19
Piggly Wiggly Southern, Inc., 13
Pizza Hut Inc., 7; 21 (upd.)
Planet Hollywood International, Inc., 18; 41 (upd.)
Players International, Inc., 22
Ponderosa Steakhouse, 15
Provigo Inc., II
Publix Super Markets Inc., 7; 31 (upd.)
Pueblo Xtra International, Inc., 47
Quality Dining, Inc., 18
Quality Food Centers, Inc., 17
The Quizno's Corporation, 42
Rally's Hamburgers, Inc., 25
Ralphs Grocery Company, 35
Randall's Food Markets, Inc., 40
Rare Hospitality International Inc., 19
Restaurants Unlimited, Inc., 13
Richfood Holdings, Inc., 7
The Riese Organization, 38
Riser Foods, Inc., 9
Roadhouse Grill, Inc., 22
Rock Bottom Restaurants, Inc., 25
Rubio's Restaurants, Inc., 35
Ruby Tuesday, Inc., 18
Ruth's Chris Steak House, 28
Ryan's Family Steak Houses, Inc., 15
Safeway Inc., II; 24 (upd.)
Santa Barbara Restaurant Group, Inc., 37
Sbarro, Inc., 16
Schlotzsky's, Inc., 36

Schultz Sav-O Stores, Inc., 21
Schwan's Sales Enterprises, Inc., 26 (upd.)
Seaway Food Town, Inc., 15
Second Harvest, 29
See's Candies, Inc., 30
Seneca Foods Corporation, 17
Service America Corp., 7
Shells Seafood Restaurants, Inc., 43
Shoney's, Inc., 7; 23 (upd.)
ShowBiz Pizza Time, Inc., 13
Smart & Final, Inc., 16
Smith's Food & Drug Centers, Inc., 8
Sodexho Alliance SA, 29
Somerfield plc, 47 (upd.)
Sonic Corporation, 14; 37 (upd.)
The Southland Corporation, II; 7 (upd.)
Spaghetti Warehouse, Inc., 25
SPAR Handels AG, 35
Spartan Stores Inc., 8
The Steak n Shake Company, 41
Steinberg Incorporated, II
The Stop & Shop Companies, Inc., II
Subway, 32
Super Food Services, Inc., 15
Super Valu Stores, Inc., II
Supermarkets General Holdings Corporation, II
Supervalu Inc., 18 (upd.)
SYSCO Corporation, II; 24 (upd.)
Taco Bell Corp., 7; 21 (upd.)
Taco Cabana, Inc., 23
Taco John's International Inc., 15
TelePizza S.A., 33
Tesco PLC, II
Total Entertainment Restaurant Corporation, 46
Trader Joe's Co., 13
Travel Ports of America, Inc., 17
Tree of Life, Inc., 29
Triarc Companies, Inc., 34 (upd.)
Tumbleweed, Inc., 33
TW Services, Inc., II
Ukrop's Super Market's, Inc., 39
Unique Casual Restaurants, Inc., 27
United Natural Foods, Inc., 32
Uno Restaurant Corporation, 18
Vail Resorts, Inc., 43 (upd.)
VICORP Restaurants, Inc., 12; 48 (upd.)
Village Super Market, Inc., 7
The Vons Companies, Incorporated, 7; 28 (upd.)
Waffle House Inc., 14
Wakefern Food Corporation, 33
Waldbaum, Inc., 19
Wall Street Deli, Inc., 33
Wawa Inc., 17
Wegmans Food Markets, Inc., 9; 41 (upd.)
Weis Markets, Inc., 15
Wendy's International, Inc., 8; 23 (upd.); 47 (upd.)
Wetterau Incorporated, II
White Castle System, Inc., 12; 36 (upd.)
White Rose, Inc., 24
Wild Oats Markets, Inc., 19; 41 (upd.)
Winn-Dixie Stores, Inc., II; 21 (upd.)
Wm. Morrison Supermarkets PLC, 38
The Wolfgang Puck Food Company, Inc., 26
Worldwide Restaurant Concepts, Inc., 47
Young & Co.'s Brewery, P.L.C., 38
Yucaipa Cos., 17

HEALTH & PERSONAL CARE PRODUCTS

Akorn, Inc., 32
Alberto-Culver Company, 8
Alco Health Services Corporation, III

Allergan, Inc., 10; 30 (upd.)
American Safety Razor Company, 20
American Stores Company, 22 (upd.)
Amway Corporation, III; 13 (upd.)
Aveda Corporation, 24
Avon Products, Inc., III; 19 (upd.); 46 (upd.)
Bally Total Fitness Holding Corp., 25
Bausch & Lomb Inc., 7; 25 (upd.)
Baxter International Inc., I; 10 (upd.)
BeautiControl Cosmetics, Inc., 21
Becton, Dickinson & Company, I; 11 (upd.)
Beiersdorf AG, 29
Big B, Inc., 17
Bindley Western Industries, Inc., 9
Block Drug Company, Inc., 8; 27 (upd.)
The Boots Company PLC, 24 (upd.)
Bristol-Myers Squibb Company, III; 9 (upd.)
C.R. Bard Inc., 9
Candela Corporation, 48
Cardinal Health, Inc., 18
Carson, Inc., 31
Carter-Wallace, Inc., 8
Chattem, Inc., 17
Chesebrough-Pond's USA, Inc., 8
Chronimed Inc., 26
The Clorox Company, III
CNS, Inc., 20
Colgate-Palmolive Company, III; 14 (upd.); 35 (upd.)
Conair Corp., 17
Cordis Corp., 19
Cosmair, Inc., 8
Coty, Inc., 36
Cybex International, Inc., 49
Datascope Corporation, 39
Del Laboratories, Inc., 28
Dentsply International Inc., 10
DEP Corporation, 20
DePuy, Inc., 30
The Dial Corp., 23 (upd.)
Direct Focus, Inc., 47
Drackett Professional Products, 12
Elizabeth Arden, Inc., 8; 40 (upd.)
Empi, Inc., 26
Enrich International, Inc., 33
The Estée Lauder Companies Inc., 9; 30 (upd.)
Ethicon, Inc., 23
Forest Laboratories, Inc., 11
Forever Living Products International Inc., 17
French Fragrances, Inc., 22
Gambro AB, 49
General Nutrition Companies, Inc., 11; 29 (upd.)
Genzyme Corporation, 13
The Gillette Company, III; 20 (upd.)
Groupe Yves Saint Laurent, 23
Guerlain, 23
Guest Supply, Inc., 18
Hanger Orthopedic Group, Inc., 41
Helen of Troy Corporation, 18
Helene Curtis Industries, Inc., 8; 28 (upd.)
Henkel KGaA, III
Henry Schein, Inc., 31
Herbalife International, Inc., 17; 41 (upd.)
Inter Parfums Inc., 35
Invacare Corporation, 11
IVAX Corporation, 11
IVC Industries, Inc., 45
The Jean Coutu Group (PJC) Inc., 46
John Paul Mitchell Systems, 24
Johnson & Johnson, III; 8 (upd.); 36 (upd.)
Kao Corporation, III
Kendall International, Inc., 11

Kimberly-Clark Corporation, III; 16 (upd.); 43 (upd.)
Kyowa Hakko Kogyo Co., Ltd., III
L'Oréal SA, III; 8 (upd.); 46 (upd.)
Laboratoires de Biologie Végétale Yves Rocher, 35
The Lamaur Corporation, 41
Lever Brothers Company, 9
Lion Corporation, III
Luxottica SpA, 17
Mannatech Inc., 33
Mary Kay Corporation, 9; 30 (upd.)
Maxxim Medical Inc., 12
Medco Containment Services Inc., 9
Medtronic, Inc., 8
Melaleuca Inc., 31
The Mentholatum Company Inc., 32
Mentor Corporation, 26
Merck & Co., Inc., 34 (upd.)
Merit Medical Systems, Inc., 29
Nature's Sunshine Products, Inc., 15
NBTY, Inc., 31
Neutrogena Corporation, 17
New Dana Perfumes Company, 37
Nikken Global Inc., 32
Nutrition for Life International Inc., 22
OEC Medical Systems, Inc., 27
Patterson Dental Co., 19
Perrigo Company, 12
Physician Sales & Service, Inc., 14
Playtex Products, Inc., 15
The Procter & Gamble Company, III; 8 (upd.); 26 (upd.)
Revlon Inc., III; 17 (upd.)
Roche Biomedical Laboratories, Inc., 11
S.C. Johnson & Son, Inc., III
Safety 1st, Inc., 24
Schering-Plough Corporation, 14 (upd.)
Shaklee Corporation, 39 (upd.)
Shionogi & Co., Ltd., III
Shiseido Company, Limited, III; 22 (upd.)
Slim-Fast Nutritional Foods International, Inc., 18
Smith & Nephew plc, 17
SmithKline Beecham PLC, III
Soft Sheen Products, Inc., 31
Sunrise Medical Inc., 11
Tambrands Inc., 8
Terumo Corporation, 48
Tom's of Maine, Inc., 45
The Tranzonic Companies, 37
Turtle Wax, Inc., 15
United States Surgical Corporation, 10; 34 (upd.)
USANA, Inc., 29
Utah Medical Products, Inc., 36
VISX, Incorporated, 30
Water Pik Technologies, Inc., 34
Weider Nutrition International, Inc., 29
Wella AG, 48 (upd.)
Wella Group, III
West Pharmaceutical Services, Inc., 42
Zila, Inc., 46
Zimmer Holdings, Inc., 45

HEALTH CARE SERVICES

Acadian Ambulance & Air Med Services, Inc., 39
Advocat Inc., 46
Alterra Healthcare Corporation, 42
The American Cancer Society, 24
American Lung Association, 48
American Medical Association, 39
American Medical International, Inc., III
American Medical Response, Inc., 39
American Red Cross, 40
AmeriSource Health Corporation, 37 (upd.)

AmSurg Corporation, 48
Applied Bioscience International, Inc., 10
Assisted Living Concepts, Inc., 43
Beverly Enterprises, Inc., III; 16 (upd.)
Bon Secours Health System, Inc., 24
Caremark International Inc., 10
Children's Comprehensive Services, Inc., 42
Chronimed Inc., 26
COBE Laboratories, Inc., 13
Columbia/HCA Healthcare Corporation, 15
Community Psychiatric Centers, 15
CompDent Corporation, 22
CompHealth Inc., 25
Comprehensive Care Corporation, 15
Continental Medical Systems, Inc., 10
Express Scripts Incorporated, 17
Extendicare Health Services, Inc., 6
FHP International Corporation, 6
Genesis Health Ventures, Inc., 18
GranCare, Inc., 14
Group Health Cooperative, 41
Hazelden Foundation, 28
HCA - The Healthcare Company, 35 (upd.)
Health Care & Retirement Corporation, 22
Health Risk Management, Inc., 24
Health Systems International, Inc., 11
HealthSouth Corporation, 14; 33 (upd.)
Highmark Inc., 27
The Hillhaven Corporation, 14
Hooper Holmes, Inc., 22
Hospital Corporation of America, III
Howard Hughes Medical Institute, 39
Humana Inc., III; 24 (upd.)
Intermountain Health Care, Inc., 27
Jenny Craig, Inc., 10; 29 (upd.)
Kinetic Concepts, Inc. (KCI), 20
LabOne, Inc., 48
Laboratory Corporation of America Holdings, 42 (upd.)
Lincare Holdings Inc., 43
Manor Care, Inc., 6; 25 (upd.)
March of Dimes, 31
Matria Healthcare, Inc., 17
Maxicare Health Plans, Inc., III; 25 (upd.)
Mayo Foundation, 9; 34 (upd.)
Merit Medical Systems, Inc., 29
National Health Laboratories Incorporated, 11
National Medical Enterprises, Inc., III
NovaCare, Inc., 11
Option Care Inc., 48
Orthodontic Centers of America, Inc., 35
Oxford Health Plans, Inc., 16
PacifiCare Health Systems, Inc., 11
Palomar Medical Technologies, Inc., 22
Pediatric Services of America, Inc., 31
PHP Healthcare Corporation, 22
PhyCor, Inc., 36
Primedex Health Systems, Inc., 25
Quest Diagnostics Inc., 26
Ramsay Youth Services, Inc., 41
Res-Care, Inc., 29
Response Oncology, Inc., 27
Rural/Metro Corporation, 28
Sabratek Corporation, 29
St. Jude Medical, Inc., 11; 43 (upd.)
Sierra Health Services, Inc., 15
Smith & Nephew plc, 41 (upd.)
The Sports Club Company, 25
SSL International plc, 49
Stericycle Inc., 33
Sun Healthcare Group Inc., 25
Twinlab Corporation, 34
U.S. Healthcare, Inc., 6
Unison HealthCare Corporation, 25
United HealthCare Corporation, 9
United Way of America, 36

Universal Health Services, Inc., 6
Vencor, Inc., 16
VISX, Incorporated, 30
Vivra, Inc., 18
WellPoint Health Networks Inc., 25
YWCA of the U.S.A., 45

HOTELS

Amerihost Properties, Inc., 30
Aztar Corporation, 13
Bass PLC, 38 (upd.)
Boca Resorts, Inc., 37
Boyd Gaming Corporation, 43
Bristol Hotel Company, 23
The Broadmoor Hotel, 30
Caesars World, Inc., 6
Candlewood Hotel Company, Inc., 41
Carlson Companies, Inc., 22 (upd.)
Castle & Cooke, Inc., 20 (upd.)
Cedar Fair, L.P., 22
Cendant Corporation, 44 (upd.)
Choice Hotels International Inc., 14
Circus Circus Enterprises, Inc., 6
Club Mediterranée S.A., 6; 21 (upd.)
Doubletree Corporation, 21
Extended Stay America, Inc., 41
Fibreboard Corporation, 16
Four Seasons Hotels Inc., 9; 29 (upd.)
Fuller Smith & Turner P.L.C., 38
Gables Residential Trust, 49
Gaylord Entertainment Company, 36 (upd.)
Granada Group PLC, 24 (upd.)
Grand Casinos, Inc., 20
Grand Hotel Krasnapolsky N.V., 23
Helmsley Enterprises, Inc., 9
Hilton Group plc, 49 (upd.)
Hilton Hotels Corporation, III; 19 (upd.)
Holiday Inns, Inc., III
Hospitality Franchise Systems, Inc., 11
Howard Johnson International, Inc., 17
Hyatt Corporation, III; 16 (upd.)
ITT Sheraton Corporation, III
JD Wetherspoon plc, 30
John Q. Hammons Hotels, Inc., 24
The La Quinta Companies, 11; 42 (upd.)
Ladbroke Group PLC, 21 (upd.)
Mandalay Resort Group, 32 (upd.)
Manor Care, Inc., 25 (upd.)
The Marcus Corporation, 21
Marriott International, Inc., III; 21 (upd.)
Mirage Resorts, Incorporated, 6; 28 (upd.)
Motel 6 Corporation, 13
Omni Hotels Corp., 12
Park Corp., 22
Players International, Inc., 22
Preussag AG, 42 (upd.)
Promus Companies, Inc., 9
Red Roof Inns, Inc., 18
Resorts International, Inc., 12
Ritz-Carlton Hotel Company L.L.C., 9; 29 (upd.)
Santa Fe Gaming Corporation, 19
The SAS Group, 34 (upd.)
Showboat, Inc., 19
Sonesta International Hotels Corporation, 44
Sun International Hotels Limited, 26
Sunburst Hospitality Corporation, 26
Trusthouse Forte PLC, III
Vail Resorts, Inc., 43 (upd.)
The Walt Disney Company, 30 (upd.)
Westin Hotels and Resorts Worldwide, 9; 29 (upd.)
Young & Co.'s Brewery, P.L.C., 38

INFORMATION TECHNOLOGY

A.B. Watley Group Inc., 45

Acxiom Corporation, 35
Adaptec, Inc., 31
Adobe Systems Incorporated, 10; 33 (upd.)
Advanced Micro Devices, Inc., 6
Agence France-Presse, 34
Agilent Technologies Inc., 38
Aldus Corporation, 10
AltaVista Company, 43
Amdahl Corporation, III; 14 (upd.); 40 (upd.)
Amdocs Ltd., 47
America Online, Inc., 10 ; 26 (upd.)
American Business Information, Inc., 18
American Management Systems, Inc., 11
American Software Inc., 25
Amstrad PLC, III
Analytic Sciences Corporation, 10
Analytical Surveys, Inc., 33
Apollo Group, Inc., 24
Apple Computer, Inc., III; 6 (upd.)
The Arbitron Company, 38
Asanté Technologies, Inc., 20
AsiaInfo Holdings, Inc., 43
ASK Group, Inc., 9
AST Research Inc., 9
At Home Corporation, 43
AT&T Bell Laboratories, Inc., 13
AT&T Corporation, 29 (upd.)
AT&T Istel Ltd., 14
Autologic Information International, Inc., 20
Automatic Data Processing, Inc., III; 9 (upd.)
Autotote Corporation, 20
Avid Technology Inc., 38
Aydin Corp., 19
Baan Company, 25
Baltimore Technologies Plc, 42
Banyan Systems Inc., 25
Battelle Memorial Institute, Inc., 10
BBN Corp., 19
BEA Systems, Inc., 36
Bell and Howell Company, 9; 29 (upd.)
Bell Industries, Inc., 47
Billing Concepts Corp., 26
Bloomberg L.P., 21
Boole & Babbage, Inc., 25
Booz Allen & Hamilton Inc., 10
Borland International, Inc., 9
Bowne & Co., Inc., 23
Brite Voice Systems, Inc., 20
Broderbund Software, 29 (upd.)
Broderbund Software, Inc., 13
BTG, Inc., 45
Bull S.A., 43 (upd.)
Business Objects S.A., 25
C-Cube Microsystems, Inc., 37
CACI International Inc., 21
Cadence Design Systems, Inc., 11
Caere Corporation, 20
Cahners Business Information, 43
CalComp Inc., 13
Cambridge Technology Partners, Inc., 36
Canon Inc., III
Cap Gemini Ernst & Young, 37
Caribiner International, Inc., 24
Catalina Marketing Corporation, 18
CDW Computer Centers, Inc., 16
Cerner Corporation, 16
Cheyenne Software, Inc., 12
CHIPS and Technologies, Inc., 9
Ciber, Inc., 18
Cincom Systems Inc., 15
Cirrus Logic, Incorporated, 11
Cisco Systems, Inc., 11
Citizen Watch Co., Ltd., 21 (upd.)
Citrix Systems, Inc., 44
CNET Networks, Inc., 47

Cognos Inc., 44
Commodore International Ltd., 7
Compagnie des Machines Bull S.A., III
Compaq Computer Corporation, III; 6 (upd.); 26 (upd.)
Complete Business Solutions, Inc., 31
CompuAdd Computer Corporation, 11
CompuCom Systems, Inc., 10
CompUSA, Inc., 35 (upd.)
CompuServe Incorporated, 10
CompuServe Interactive Services, Inc., 27 (upd.)
Computer Associates International, Inc., 6; 49 (upd.)
Computer Data Systems, Inc., 14
Computer Sciences Corporation, 6
Computervision Corporation, 10
Compuware Corporation, 10; 30 (upd.)
Comshare Inc., 23
Conner Peripherals, Inc., 6
Control Data Corporation, III
Control Data Systems, Inc., 10
Corbis Corporation, 31
Corel Corporation, 15; 33 (upd.)
Corporate Software Inc., 9
Cray Research, Inc., III
CTG, Inc., 11
Cybermedia, Inc., 25
Dassault Systèmes S.A., 25
Data Broadcasting Corporation, 31
Data General Corporation, 8
Datapoint Corporation, 11
Dell Computer Corp., 9
Dialogic Corporation, 18
Digex, Inc., 46
Digital Equipment Corporation, III; 6 (upd.)
Documentum, Inc., 46
The Dun & Bradstreet Corporation, IV; 19 (upd.)
Dun & Bradstreet Software Services Inc., 11
DynCorp, 45
E.piphany, Inc., 49
EarthLink, Inc., 36
ECS S.A, 12
Edmark Corporation, 14; 41 (upd.)
Egghead Inc., 9
El Camino Resources International, Inc., 11
Electronic Arts Inc., 10
Electronic Data Systems Corporation, III; 28 (upd.)
Electronics for Imaging, Inc., 43 (upd.)
EMC Corporation, 12; 46 (upd.)
Encore Computer Corporation, 13
Evans & Sutherland Computer Corporation, 19
Exabyte Corporation, 12
Experian Information Solutions Inc., 45
First Financial Management Corporation, 11
Fiserv Inc., 11
FlightSafety International, Inc., 9
FORE Systems, Inc., 25
Franklin Electronic Publishers, Inc., 23
FTP Software, Inc., 20
Fujitsu Limited, III; 42 (upd.)
Fujitsu-ICL Systems Inc., 11
Future Now, Inc., 12
Gartner Group, Inc., 21
Gateway 2000, Inc., 10
Gateway, Inc., 27 (upd.)
GEAC Computer Corporation Ltd., 43
Gericom AG, 47
Getronics NV, 39
GFI Informatique SA, 49
GT Interactive Software, 31
Guthy-Renker Corporation, 32

Handspring Inc., 49
Hewlett-Packard Company, III; 6 (upd.)
Hyperion Software Corporation, 22
ICL plc, 6
Identix Inc., 44
Imation Corporation, 20
Information Access Company, 17
Information Builders, Inc., 22
Information Resources, Inc., 10
Informix Corporation, 10; 30 (upd.)
Infosys Technologies Ltd., 38
Ing. C. Olivetti & C., S.p.a., III
Inktomi Corporation, 45
Inso Corporation, 26
Intel Corporation, 36 (upd.)
IntelliCorp, Inc., 45
Intelligent Electronics, Inc., 6
Intergraph Corporation, 6; 24 (upd.)
International Business Machines Corporation, III; 6 (upd.); 30 (upd.)
Intuit Inc., 14; 33 (upd.)
Iomega Corporation, 21
IONA Technologies plc, 43
J.D. Edwards & Company, 14
Jack Henry and Associates, Inc., 17
Juniper Networks, Inc., 43
Juno Online Services, Inc., 38
KLA Instruments Corporation, 11
KnowledgeWare Inc., 31 (upd.)
Komag, Inc., 11
Kronos, Inc., 18
Lam Research Corporation, 11
Lason, Inc., 31
Lawson Software, 38
The Learning Company Inc., 24
Learning Tree International Inc., 24
Legent Corporation, 10
LEXIS-NEXIS Group, 33
Logica plc, 14; 37 (upd.)
Logicon Inc., 20
Logitech International SA, 28
LoJack Corporation, 48
Lotus Development Corporation, 6; 25 (upd.)
The MacNeal-Schwendler Corporation, 25
Madge Networks N.V., 26
MAI Systems Corporation, 11
Maxtor Corporation, 10
Mead Data Central, Inc., 10
Mecklermedia Corporation, 24
Mentor Graphics Corporation, 11
Merisel, Inc., 12
Metatec International, Inc., 47
Metro Information Services, Inc., 36
Micro Warehouse, Inc., 16
Micron Technology, Inc., 11; 29 (upd.)
Micros Systems, Inc., 18
Microsoft Corporation, 6; 27 (upd.)
Misys plc, 45; 46
MITRE Corporation, 26
The Motley Fool, Inc., 40
National Semiconductor Corporation, 6
National TechTeam, Inc., 41
Navarre Corporation, 24
NCR Corporation, III; 6 (upd.); 30 (upd.)
Netscape Communications Corporation, 15; 35 (upd.)
Network Associates, Inc., 25
Nextel Communications, Inc., 10
NFO Worldwide, Inc., 24
Nichols Research Corporation, 18
Nimbus CD International, Inc., 20
Nixdorf Computer AG, III
Novell, Inc., 6; 23 (upd.)
Océ N.V., 24
Odetics Inc., 14
Opsware Inc., 49
Oracle Corporation, 24 (upd.)

Oracle Systems Corporation, 6
Packard Bell Electronics, Inc., 13
Parametric Technology Corp., 16
PC Connection, Inc., 37
PeopleSoft Inc., 14; 33 (upd.)
Perot Systems Corporation, 29
Pitney Bowes Inc., III
PLATINUM Technology, Inc., 14
Policy Management Systems Corporation, 11
Portal Software, Inc., 47
Primark Corp., 13
The Princeton Review, Inc., 42
Printrak, A Motorola Company, 44
Printronix, Inc., 18
Prodigy Communications Corporation, 34
Progress Software Corporation, 15
Psion PLC, 45
Quantum Corporation, 10
Quark, Inc., 36
Racal-Datacom Inc., 11
Razorfish, Inc., 37
RCM Technologies, Inc., 34
Red Hat, Inc., 45
Renaissance Learning Systems, Inc., 39
Reuters Holdings PLC, 22 (upd.)
Ricoh Company, Ltd., III
RSA Security Inc., 46
SABRE Group Holdings, Inc., 26
The Sage Group, 43
The Santa Cruz Operation, Inc., 38
SAP AG, 16; 43 (upd.)
SAS Institute Inc., 10
SBS Technologies, Inc., 25
SCB Computer Technology, Inc., 29
Schawk, Inc., 24
Seagate Technology, Inc., 8
Siebel Systems, Inc., 38
Sierra On-Line, Inc., 15; 41 (upd.)
SilverPlatter Information Inc., 23
SmartForce PLC, 43
Softbank Corp., 13; 38 (upd.)
Standard Microsystems Corporation, 11
STC PLC, III
Steria SA, 49
Sterling Software, Inc., 11
Storage Technology Corporation, 6
Stratus Computer, Inc., 10
Sun Microsystems, Inc., 7; 30 (upd.)
SunGard Data Systems Inc., 11
Sybase, Inc., 10; 27 (upd.)
Sykes Enterprises, Inc., 45
Symantec Corporation, 10
Symbol Technologies, Inc., 15
Synopsis, Inc., 11
System Software Associates, Inc., 10
Systems & Computer Technology Corp., 19
Tandem Computers, Inc., 6
TenFold Corporation, 35
Terra Lycos, Inc., 43
The Thomson Corporation, 34 (upd.)
3Com Corporation, 11; 34 (upd.)
The 3DO Company, 43
Timberline Software Corporation, 15
Transaction Systems Architects, Inc., 29
Transiciel SA, 48
Triple P N.V., 26
Ubi Soft Entertainment S.A., 41
Unilog SA, 42
Unisys Corporation, III; 6 (upd.); 36 (upd.)
UUNET, 38
Verbatim Corporation, 14
VeriFone, Inc., 18
VeriSign, Inc., 47
Veritas Software Corporation, 45
Viasoft Inc., 27
Volt Information Sciences Inc., 26

Wang Laboratories, Inc., III; 6 (upd.)
West Group, 34 (upd.)
Western Digital Corp., 25
Wind River Systems, Inc., 37
Wipro Limited, 43
Wolters Kluwer NV, 33 (upd.)
WordPerfect Corporation, 10
Wyse Technology, Inc., 15
Xerox Corporation, III; 6 (upd.); 26 (upd.)
Xilinx, Inc., 16
Yahoo! Inc., 27
Zapata Corporation, 25
Ziff Davis Media Inc., 36 (upd.)
Zilog, Inc., 15

INSURANCE

AEGON N.V., III
Aetna, Inc., III; 21 (upd.)
AFLAC Incorporated, 10 (upd.); 38 (upd.)
Alexander & Alexander Services Inc., 10
Alleghany Corporation, 10
Allianz Aktiengesellschaft Holding, III; 15 (upd.)
The Allstate Corporation, 10; 27 (upd.)
American Family Corporation, III
American Financial Corporation, III
American Financial Group Inc., 48 (upd.)
American General Corporation, III; 10 (upd.); 46 (upd.)
American International Group, Inc., III; 15 (upd.); 47 (upd.)
American National Insurance Company, 8; 27 (upd.)
American Premier Underwriters, Inc., 10
American Re Corporation, 10; 35 (upd.)
N.V. AMEV, III
Aon Corporation, III; 45 (upd.)
Assicurazioni Generali SpA, III; 15 (upd.)
Atlantic American Corporation, 44
Axa, III
AXA Colonia Konzern AG, 27; 49 (upd.)
B.A.T. Industries PLC, 22 (upd.)
Bâloise-Holding, 40
Berkshire Hathaway Inc., III; 18 (upd.)
Blue Cross and Blue Shield Association, 10
Brown & Brown, Inc., 41
Business Men's Assurance Company of America, 14
Capital Holding Corporation, III
Catholic Order of Foresters, 24
The Chubb Corporation, III; 14 (upd.); 37 (upd.)
CIGNA Corporation, III; 22 (upd.); 45 (upd.)
Cincinnati Financial Corporation, 16; 44 (upd.)
CNA Financial Corporation, III; 38 (upd.)
Commercial Union PLC, III
Connecticut Mutual Life Insurance Company, III
Conseco Inc., 10; 33 (upd.)
The Continental Corporation, III
Empire Blue Cross and Blue Shield, III
Enbridge Inc., 43
Engle Homes, Inc., 46
The Equitable Life Assurance Society of the United States Fireman's Fund Insurance Company, III
ERGO Versicherungsgruppe AG, 44
Erie Indemnity Company, 35
Farm Family Holdings, Inc., 39
Farmers Insurance Group of Companies, 25
First Executive Corporation, III
Foundation Health Corporation, 12
Gainsco, Inc., 22
GEICO Corporation, 10; 40 (upd.)

General Accident PLC, III
General Re Corporation, III; 24 (upd.)
Great-West Lifeco Inc., III
Gryphon Holdings, Inc., 21
Guardian Royal Exchange Plc, 11
Harleysville Group Inc., 37
The Home Insurance Company, III
Horace Mann Educators Corporation, 22
Household International, Inc., 21 (upd.)
Jackson National Life Insurance Company, 8
Jefferson-Pilot Corporation, 11; 29 (upd.)
John Hancock Financial Services, Inc., III; 42 (upd.)
Johnson & Higgins, 14
Kemper Corporation, III; 15 (upd.)
Legal & General Group plc, III; 24 (upd.)
The Liberty Corporation, 22
Lincoln National Corporation, III; 25 (upd.)
Lloyd's of London, III; 22 (upd.)
The Loewen Group Inc., 40 (upd.)
Lutheran Brotherhood, 31
Marsh & McLennan Companies, Inc., III; 45 (upd.)
Massachusetts Mutual Life Insurance Company, III
The Meiji Mutual Life Insurance Company, III
Mercury General Corporation, 25
Metropolitan Life Insurance Company, III
Mitsui Marine and Fire Insurance Company, Limited, III
Mitsui Mutual Life Insurance Company, III; 39 (upd.)
Munich Re (Münchener Rückversicherungs-Gesellschaft Aktiengesellschaft in München), III; 46 (upd.)
The Mutual Benefit Life Insurance Company, III
The Mutual Life Insurance Company of New York, III
Nationale-Nederlanden N.V., III
New England Mutual Life Insurance Company, III
New York Life Insurance Company, III; 45 (upd.)
Nippon Life Insurance Company, III
Northwestern Mutual Life Insurance Company, III; 45 (upd.)
NYMAGIC, Inc., 41
Ohio Casualty Corp., 11
Old Republic International Corp., 11
Pan-American Life Insurance Company, 48
The Paul Revere Corporation, 12
Pennsylvania Blue Shield, III
The PMI Group, Inc., 49
Preserver Group, Inc., 44
Principal Mutual Life Insurance Company, III
The Progressive Corporation, 11; 29 (upd.)
Provident Life and Accident Insurance Company of America, III
Prudential Corporation PLC, III
The Prudential Insurance Company of America, III; 30 (upd.)
Prudential plc, 48 (upd.)
Radian Group Inc., 42
Reliance Group Holdings, Inc., III
Riunione Adriatica di Sicurtà SpA, III
Royal Insurance Holdings PLC, III
SAFECO Corporaton, III
The St. Paul Companies, Inc., III; 22 (upd.)
SCOR S.A., 20
The Standard Life Assurance Company, III
State Farm Mutual Automobile Insurance Company, III

Sumitomo Life Insurance Company, III
The Sumitomo Marine and Fire Insurance Company, Limited, III
Sun Alliance Group PLC, III
SunAmerica Inc., 11
Swiss Reinsurance Company (Schweizerische Rückversicherungs-Gesellschaft), III; 46 (upd.)
Teachers Insurance and Annuity Association-College Retirement Equities Fund, III; 45 (upd.)
Texas Industries, Inc., 8
TIG Holdings, Inc., 26
The Tokio Marine and Fire Insurance Co., Ltd., III
Torchmark Corporation, 9; 33 (upd.)
Transatlantic Holdings, Inc., 11
The Travelers Corporation, III
UICI, 33
Union des Assurances de Pans, III
Unitrin Inc., 16
UNUM Corp., 13
USAA, 10
USF&G Corporation, III
Victoria Group, 44 (upd.)
VICTORIA Holding AG, III
W.R. Berkley Corp., 15
Washington National Corporation, 12
White Mountains Insurance Group, Ltd., 48
Willis Corroon Group plc, 25
''Winterthur'' Schweizerische Versicherungs-Gesellschaft, III
The Yasuda Fire and Marine Insurance Company, Limited, III
The Yasuda Mutual Life Insurance Company, III; 39 (upd.)
''Zürich'' Versicherungs-Gesellschaft, III

LEGAL SERVICES

Akin, Gump, Strauss, Hauer & Feld, L.L.P., 33
American Bar Association, 35
American Lawyer Media Holdings, Inc., 32
Arnold & Porter, 35
Baker & Hostetler LLP, 40
Baker & McKenzie, 10; 42 (upd.)
Baker and Botts, L.L.P., 28
Bingham Dana LLP, 43
Brobeck, Phleger & Harrison, LLP, 31
Cadwalader, Wickersham & Taft, 32
Chadbourne & Parke, 36
Cleary, Gottlieb, Steen & Hamilton, 35
Clifford Chance LLP, 38
Coudert Brothers, 30
Covington & Burling, 40
Cravath, Swaine & Moore, 43
Davis Polk & Wardwell, 36
Debevoise & Plimpton, 39
Dechert, 43
Dewey Ballantine LLP, 48
Dorsey & Whitney LLP, 47
Fenwick & West LLP, 34
Foley & Lardner, 28
Fried, Frank, Harris, Shriver & Jacobson, 35
Fulbright & Jaworski L.L.P., 47
Gibson, Dunn & Crutcher LLP, 36
Heller, Ehrman, White & McAuliffe, 41
Hildebrandt International, 29
Hogan & Hartson L.L.P., 44
Holme Roberts & Owen LLP, 28
Hughes Hubbard & Reed LLP, 44
Hunton & Williams, 35
Jones, Day, Reavis & Pogue, 33
Kelley Drye & Warren LLP, 40
King & Spalding, 23
Latham & Watkins, 33
LeBoeuf, Lamb, Greene & MacRae, L.L.P., 29
The Legal Aid Society, 48
Mayer, Brown, Rowe & Maw, 47
Milbank, Tweed, Hadley & McCloy, 27
Morgan, Lewis & Bockius LLP, 29
O'Melveny & Myers, 37
Paul, Hastings, Janofsky & Walker LLP, 27
Paul, Weiss, Rifkind, Wharton & Garrison, 47
Pepper Hamilton LLP, 43
Pillsbury Madison & Sutro LLP, 29
Pre-Paid Legal Services, Inc., 20
Proskauer Rose LLP, 47
Ropes & Gray, 40
Shearman & Sterling, 32
Sidley Austin Brown & Wood, 40
Simpson Thacher & Bartlett, 39
Skadden, Arps, Slate, Meagher & Flom, 18
Snell & Wilmer L.L.P., 28
Stroock & Stroock & Lavan LLP, 40
Sullivan & Cromwell, 26
Vinson & Elkins L.L.P., 30
Wachtell, Lipton, Rosen & Katz, 47
White & Case LLP, 35
Williams & Connolly LLP, 47
Wilson Sonsini Goodrich & Rosati, 34
Winston & Strawn, 35

MANUFACTURING

A. Schulman, Inc., 49 (upd.)
A.B.Dick Company, 28
A.O. Smith Corporation, 11; 40 (upd.)
A.T. Cross Company, 17; 49 (upd.)
AAF-McQuay Incorporated, 26
AAON, Inc., 22
AAR Corp., 28
ABC Rail Products Corporation, 18
Abiomed, Inc., 47
ACCO World Corporation, 7
Acme-Cleveland Corp., 13
Acuson Corporation, 36 (upd.)
Adams Golf, Inc., 37
Adolf Würth GmbH & Co. KG, 49
AEP Industries, Inc., 36
Ag-Chem Equipment Company, Inc., 17
AGCO Corp., 13
Aisin Seiki Co., Ltd., III
AK Steel Holding Corporation, 41 (upd.)
Aktiebolaget Electrolux, 22 (upd.)
Aktiebolaget SKF, III; 38 (upd.)
Alamo Group Inc., 32
Alberto-Culver Company, 36 (upd.)
Aldila Inc., 46
Alfa-Laval AB, III
Allen Organ Company, 33
Alliant Techsystems Inc., 8; 30 (upd.)
Allied Healthcare Products, Inc., 24
Allied Products Corporation, 21
Allied Signal Engines, 9
AlliedSignal Inc., 22 (upd.)
Allison Gas Turbine Division, 9
Alltrista Corporation, 30
Alps Electric Co., Ltd., 44 (upd.)
Alvis Plc, 47
Amer Group plc, 41
American Biltrite Inc., 43 (upd.)
American Business Products, Inc., 20
American Homestar Corporation, 18; 41 (upd.)
American Locker Group Incorporated, 34
American Standard Companies Inc., 30 (upd.)
American Tourister, Inc., 16
American Woodmark Corporation, 31
Ameriwood Industries International Corp., 17
AMETEK, Inc., 9
AMF Bowling, Inc., 40
Ampex Corporation, 17
Amway Corporation, 30 (upd.)
Analogic Corporation, 23
Anchor Hocking Glassware, 13
Andersen Corporation, 10
The Andersons, Inc., 31
Andreas Stihl, 16
Anthem Electronics, Inc., 13
Applica Incorporated, 43 (upd.)
Applied Films Corporation, 48
Applied Materials, Inc., 10; 46 (upd.)
Applied Micro Circuits Corporation, 38
Applied Power Inc., 9; 32 (upd.)
ARBED S.A., 22 (upd.)
Arctco, Inc., 16
Arctic Cat Inc., 40 (upd.)
Ariens Company, 48
Armor All Products Corp., 16
Armstrong World Industries, Inc., III; 22 (upd.)
Artesyn Technologies Inc., 46 (upd.)
Asahi Glass Company, Ltd., 48 (upd.)
Ashley Furniture Industries, Inc., 35
Astronics Corporation, 35
ASV, Inc., 34
Atlas Copco AB, III; 28 (upd.)
Avedis Zildjian Co., 38
Avery Dennison Corporation, 17 (upd.); 49 (upd.)
Avondale Industries, 7; 41 (upd.)
Badger Meter, Inc., 22
Baker Hughes Incorporated, III
Baldor Electric Company, 21
Baldwin Piano & Organ Company, 18
Baldwin Technology Company, Inc., 25
Balfour Beatty plc, 36 (upd.)
Ballantyne of Omaha, Inc., 27
Ballard Medical Products, 21
Bally Manufacturing Corporation, III
Baltek Corporation, 34
Barmag AG, 39
Barnes Group Inc., 13
Barry Callebaut AG, 29
Bassett Furniture Industries, Inc., 18
Bath Iron Works, 12; 36 (upd.)
Beckman Coulter, Inc., 22
Beckman Instruments, Inc., 14
Becton, Dickinson & Company, 36 (upd.)
Beiersdorf AG, 29
Belden Inc., 19
Bell Sports Corporation, 16; 44 (upd.)
Beloit Corporation, 14
Benjamin Moore & Co., 13; 38 (upd.)
Bernina Holding AG, 47
Berry Plastics Corporation, 21
BIC Corporation, 8; 23 (upd.)
BICC PLC, III
Billabong International Ltd., 44
Binks Sames Corporation, 21
Binney & Smith Inc., 25
Biomet, Inc., 10
BISSELL Inc., 9; 30 (upd.)
The Black & Decker Corporation, III; 20 (upd.)
Blount International, Inc., 48 (upd.)
Blount, Inc., 12
Blyth Industries, Inc., 18
BMC Industries, Inc., 17
Bodum Design Group AG, 47
Boral Limited, 43 (upd.)
Borden, Inc., 22 (upd.)
Borg-Warner Automotive, Inc., 14
Borg-Warner Corporation, III
Boston Scientific Corporation, 37

The Boyds Collection, Ltd., 29
Brannock Device Company, 48
Brass Eagle Inc., 34
Bridgeport Machines, Inc., 17
Briggs & Stratton Corporation, 8; 27 (upd.)
BRIO AB, 24
British Vita plc, 33 (upd.)
Brother Industries, Ltd., 14
Brown & Sharpe Manufacturing Co., 23
Brown-Forman Corporation, 38 (upd.)
Broyhill Furniture Industries, Inc., 10
Brunswick Corporation, III; 22 (upd.)
BTR Siebe plc, 27
Buck Knives Inc., 48
Buckeye Technologies, Inc., 42
Bucyrus International, Inc., 17
Bugle Boy Industries, Inc., 18
Bulgari S.p.A., 20
Bulova Corporation, 13; 41 (upd.)
Bundy Corporation, 17
Burelle S.A., 23
Burton Snowboards Inc., 22
Bush Boake Allen Inc., 30
Bush Industries, Inc., 20
Butler Manufacturing Co., 12
C.F. Martin & Co., Inc., 42
Callaway Golf Company, 15; 45 (upd.)
Cannondale Corporation, 21
Caradon plc, 20 (upd.)
The Carbide/Graphite Group, Inc., 40
Carbone Lorraine S.A., 33
Carl-Zeiss-Stiftung, III; 34 (upd.)
Carrier Corporation, 7
CASIO Computer Co., Ltd., III; 40 (upd.)
Catalina Lighting, Inc., 43 (upd.)
Caterpillar Inc., III; 15 (upd.)
Central Sprinkler Corporation, 29
Cessna Aircraft Company, 27 (upd.)
Champion Enterprises, Inc., 17
Chanel, 12
Chanel SA, 49 (upd.)
Chart Industries, Inc., 21
Chris-Craft Industries, Inc., 31 (upd.)
Christian Dalloz SA, 40
Christofle SA, 40
Chromcraft Revington, Inc., 15
Ciments Français, 40
Cincinnati Milacron Inc., 12
Cinram International, Inc., 43
Circon Corporation, 21
Cirrus Design Corporation, 44
Citizen Watch Co., Ltd., III
Clarcor Inc., 17
Clark Equipment Company, 8
Clayton Homes Incorporated, 13
The Clorox Company, 22 (upd.)
CNH Global N.V., 38 (upd.)
Coach, 45 (upd.)
Cobra Golf Inc., 16
Cockerill Sambre Group, 26 (upd.)
Cohu, Inc., 32
Colas S.A., 31
The Coleman Company, Inc., 30 (upd.)
Collins & Aikman Corporation, 41 (upd.)
Collins Industries, Inc., 33
Colorado MEDtech, Inc., 48
Colt's Manufacturing Company, Inc., 12
Columbia Sportswear Company, 19
Columbus McKinnon Corporation, 37
Concord Camera Corporation, 41
Congoleum Corp., 18
Conso International Corporation, 29
Consorcio G Grupo Dina, S.A. de C.V., 36
Converse Inc., 9
The Cooper Companies, Inc., 39
Cooper Industries, Inc., 44 (upd.)
Cordis Corporation, 46 (upd.)
Corning Inc., 44 (upd.)

Corrpro Companies, Inc., 20
Corticeira Amorim, Sociedade Gestora de
    Participaço es Sociais, S.A., 48
Crane Co., 8; 30 (upd.)
Creo Inc., 48
Crown Equipment Corporation, 15
CTB International Corporation, 43 (upd.)
Cuisinart Corporation, 24
Culligan Water Technologies, Inc., 12; 38
    (upd.)
Cummins Engine Company, Inc., 40 (upd.)
Curtiss-Wright Corporation, 10; 35 (upd.)
Cutter & Buck Inc., 27
Cybex International, Inc., 49
Daewoo Group, III
Daikin Industries, Ltd., III
Danaher Corporation, 7
Daniel Industries, Inc., 16
Danisco A/S, 44
Day Runner, Inc., 41 (upd.)
Decora Industries, Inc., 31
DeCrane Aircraft Holdings Inc., 36
Deere & Company, III; 42 (upd.)
Defiance, Inc., 22
Denby Group plc, 44
Denison International plc, 46
DENSO Corporation, 46 (upd.)
Department 56, Inc., 14
DePuy Inc., 37 (upd.)
Detroit Diesel Corporation, 10
Deutsche Babcock A.G., III
Deutz AG, 39
Dial-A-Mattress Operating Corporation, 46
Diebold, Incorporated, 7; 22 (upd.)
Diesel SpA, 40
Dixon Industries, Inc., 26
Dixon Ticonderoga Company, 12
DMI Furniture, Inc., 46
Donaldson Company, Inc., 49 (upd.)
Donnelly Corporation, 12; 35 (upd.)
Douglas & Lomason Company, 16
Dover Corporation, III; 28 (upd.)
Dresser Industries, Inc., III
Drew Industries, Inc., 28
Drexel Heritage Furnishings Inc., 12
Drypers Corporation, 18
Ducommun Incorporated, 30
Duracell International Inc., 9
Durametallic, 21
Duriron Company Inc., 17
Dürr AG, 44
Eagle-Picher Industries, Inc., 8; 23 (upd.)
The Eastern Company, 48
Eastman Kodak Company, III; 7 (upd.); 36
    (upd.)
ECC International Corp., 42
Ecolab Inc., 34 (upd.)
Eddie Bauer Inc., 9
EDO Corporation, 46
EG&G Incorporated, 29 (upd.)
Ekco Group, Inc., 16
Elano Corporation, 14
Electrolux Group, III
Eljer Industries, Inc., 24
Elscint Ltd., 20
Encompass Services Corporation, 33
Energizer Holdings, Inc., 32
Enesco Corporation, 11
English China Clays Ltd., 40 (upd.)
Escalade, Incorporated, 19
Esselte Leitz GmbH & Co. KG, 48
Essilor International, 21
Esterline Technologies Corp., 15
Ethan Allen Interiors, Inc., 12; 39 (upd.)
The Eureka Company, 12
Everlast Worldwide Inc., 47
Fabbrica D' Armi Pietro Beretta S.p.A., 39
Facom S.A., 32

Faiveley S.A., 39
Falcon Products, Inc., 33
Fanuc Ltd., III; 17 (upd.)
Farah Incorporated, 24
Fastenal Company, 42 (upd.)
Featherlite Inc., 28
Fedders Corporation, 18; 43 (upd.)
Federal Prison Industries, Inc., 34
Federal Signal Corp., 10
Fellowes Manufacturing Company, 28
Fender Musical Instruments Company, 16;
    43 (upd.)
Figgie International Inc., 7
Firearms Training Systems, Inc., 27
First Alert, Inc., 28
First Brands Corporation, 8
The First Years Inc., 46
Fisher Controls International, Inc., 13
Fisher Scientific International Inc., 24
Fisher-Price Inc., 12; 32 (upd.)
Fiskars Corporation, 33
Fisons plc, 9
Fleetwood Enterprises, Inc., III; 22 (upd.)
Flexsteel Industries Inc., 15; 41 (upd.)
Flextronics International Ltd., 38
Flint Ink Corporation, 41 (upd.)
Florsheim Shoe Company, 9
Flour City International, Inc., 44
Flowserve Corporation, 33
Fort James Corporation, 22 (upd.)
Fountain Powerboats Industries, Inc., 28
Foxboro Company, 13
Framatome SA, 19
Frank J. Zamboni & Co., Inc., 34
Franklin Electric Company, Inc., 43
Freudenberg & Co., 41
Frigidaire Home Products, 22
Frymaster Corporation, 27
FSI International, Inc., 17
Fuji Photo Film Co., Ltd., III; 18 (upd.)
Fuqua Enterprises, Inc., 17
Furniture Brands International, Inc., 39
    (upd.)
Furon Company, 28
The Furukawa Electric Co., Ltd., III
G.S. Blodgett Corporation, 15
Gardner Denver, Inc., 49
The Gates Corporation, 9
GE Aircraft Engines, 9
GEA AG, 27
Geberit AG, 49
Gehl Company, 19
GenCorp Inc., 8; 9 (upd.)
General Bearing Corporation, 45
General Cable Corporation, 40
General Dynamics Corporation, 40 (upd.)
General Housewares Corporation, 16
Genmar Holdings, Inc., 45
geobra Brandstätter GmbH & Co. KG, 48
Gerber Scientific, Inc., 12
Gerresheimer Glas AG, 43
Giddings & Lewis, Inc., 10
The Gillette Company, 20 (upd.)
GKN plc, III; 38 (upd.)
Gleason Corporation, 24
The Glidden Company, 8
Glock Ges.m.b.H., 42
Goodman Holding Company, 42
Goodrich Corporation, 46 (upd.)
Goody Products, Inc., 12
The Gorman-Rupp Company, 18
Goss Holdings, Inc., 43
Goulds Pumps Inc., 24
Graco Inc., 19
Griffon Corporation, 34
Grinnell Corp., 13
Groupe André, 17
Groupe Guillin SA, 40

Groupe Legis Industries, 23
Groupe SEB, 35
Grow Group Inc., 12
Grupo Cydsa, S.A. de C.V., 39
Grupo IMSA, S.A. de C.V., 44
Guangzhou Pearl River Piano Group Ltd., 49
Gulf Island Fabrication, Inc., 44
The Gunlocke Company, 23
Guy Degrenne SA, 44
H.B. Fuller Company, 8; 32 (upd.)
Hach Co., 18
Hackman Oyj Adp, 44
Haemonetics Corporation, 20
Halliburton Company, III
Hallmark Cards, Inc., 40 (upd.)
Hanson PLC, 30 (upd.)
Hardinge Inc., 25
Harland and Wolff Holdings plc, 19
Harmon Industries, Inc., 25
Harnischfeger Industries, Inc., 8; 38 (upd.)
Harsco Corporation, 8
Hartmarx Corporation, 32 (upd.)
The Hartz Mountain Corporation, 46 (upd.)
Hasbro, Inc., III; 16 (upd.)
Hawker Siddeley Group Public Limited
    Company, III
Haworth Inc., 8; 39 (upd.)
Health O Meter Products Inc., 14
Heekin Can Inc., 13
HEICO Corporation, 30
Heidelberger Druckmaschinen AG, 40
Henkel Manco Inc., 22
The Henley Group, Inc., III
Herman Miller, Inc., 8
Hermès International S.A., 34 (upd.)
Hillenbrand Industries, Inc., 10
Hillsdown Holdings plc, 24 (upd.)
Hitachi Zosen Corporation, III
Hitchiner Manufacturing Co., Inc., 23
HMI Industries, Inc., 17
Holnam Inc., 8
Holson Burnes Group, Inc., 14
HON INDUSTRIES Inc., 13
The Hoover Company, 12; 40 (upd.)
Huffy Corporation, 7; 30 (upd.)
Hunt Manufacturing Company, 12
Hunter Fan Company, 13
Hydril Company, 46
Hyster Company, 17
Hyundai Group, III; 7 (upd.)
Icon Health & Fitness, Inc., 38
Igloo Products Corp., 21
Illinois Tool Works Inc., III; 22 (upd.)
IMI plc, 9
Imo Industries Inc., 7; 27 (upd.)
Inchcape PLC, III; 16 (upd.)
Industrie Natuzzi S.p.A., 18
Ingalls Shipbuilding, Inc., 12
Ingersoll-Rand Company, III; 15 (upd.)
Insilco Corporation, 16
Interco Incorporated, III
Interface, Inc., 8
The Interlake Corporation, 8
International Controls Corporation, 10
International Flavors & Fragrances Inc., 38
    (upd.)
International Game Technology, 10
Invacare Corporation, 47 (upd.)
Irwin Toy Limited, 14
Ishikawajima-Harima Heavy Industries Co.,
    Ltd., III
J. D'Addario & Company, Inc., 48
J.I. Case Company, 10
J.M. Voith AG, 33
Jabil Circuit, Inc., 36
Jacuzzi Inc., 23
Japan Tobacco Inc., 46 (upd.)

Jayco Inc., 13
Jeld-Wen, Inc., 45
Jenoptik AG, 33
Jervis B. Webb Company, 24
Johnson Controls, Inc., III; 26 (upd.)
Johnson Matthey PLC, 49 (upd.)
Johnson Worldwide Associates, Inc., 28
Johnstown America Industries, Inc., 23
Jones Apparel Group, Inc., 11
Jostens, Inc., 7; 25 (upd.)
Kaman Corporation, 12; 42 (upd.)
Kasper A.S.L., Ltd., 40
Kawasaki Heavy Industries, Ltd., III
Kaydon Corporation, 18
KB Toys, 35 (upd.)
Kerr Group Inc., 24
Kewaunee Scientific Corporation, 25
Key Tronic Corporation, 14
Keystone International, Inc., 11
KHD Konzern, III
Kimball International, Inc., 12; 48 (upd.)
Kit Manufacturing Co., 18
Knape & Vogt Manufacturing Company,
    17
Knoll Group Inc., 14
Koala Corporation, 44
Kobe Steel, Ltd., IV; 19 (upd.)
Koch Enterprises, Inc., 29
Kohler Company, 7; 32 (upd.)
Komatsu Ltd., III; 16 (upd.)
Kone Corporation, 27
Konica Corporation, III
Kubota Corporation, III; 26 (upd.)
Kuhlman Corporation, 20
Kyocera Corporation, 21 (upd.)
L-3 Communications Holdings, Inc., 48
L.B. Foster Company, 33
LADD Furniture, Inc., 12
Ladish Co., Inc., 30
Lafarge Corporation, 28
Lafuma S.A., 39
Lakeland Industries, Inc., 45
Lam Research Corporation, 31 (upd.)
Lamson & Sessions Co., 13
Lancer Corporation, 21
The Lane Co., Inc., 12
Leggett & Platt, Inc., 11; 48 (upd.)
Leica Camera AG, 35
Leica Microsystems Holdings GmbH, 35
Lennox International Inc., 8; 28 (upd.)
Lenox, Inc., 12
Lexmark International, Inc., 18
Linamar Corporation, 18
Lincoln Electric Co., 13
Lindal Cedar Homes, Inc., 29
Lindsay Manufacturing Co., 20
Little Tikes Co., 13
Loctite Corporation, 8
Logitech International SA, 28
The Longaberger Company, 12; 44 (upd.)
Louis Vuitton, 10
Lucas Industries PLC, III
Lynch Corporation, 43
M&F Worldwide Corp., 38
MacAndrews & Forbes Holdings Inc., 28
Mackay Envelope Corporation, 45
Mail-Well, Inc., 28
Makita Corporation, 22
MAN Aktiengesellschaft, III
Manitou BF S.A., 27
Manitowoc Company, Inc., 18
Mannesmann AG, III; 14 (upd.)
Margarete Steiff GmbH, 23
Marisa Christina, Inc., 15
Mark IV Industries, Inc., 7; 28 (upd.)
The Marmon Group, 16 (upd.)
Martin Industries, Inc., 44
Marvin Lumber & Cedar Company, 22

Mary Kay, Inc., 30 (upd.)
Masco Corporation, III; 20 (upd.); 39
    (upd.)
Master Lock Company, 45
Mattel, Inc., 7; 25 (upd.)
Matthews International Corporation, 29
Maxco Inc., 17
Maxwell Shoe Company, Inc., 30
Maytag Corporation, III; 22 (upd.)
McDermott International, Inc., III
McKechnie plc, 34
Meade Instruments Corporation, 41
Meadowcraft, Inc., 29
Meggitt PLC, 34
Merck & Co., Inc., 34 (upd.)
Merillat Industries Inc., 13
Mestek Inc., 10
Metso Corporation, 30 (upd.)
Mettler-Toledo International Inc., 30
Michael Anthony Jewelers, Inc., 24
Microdot Inc., 8
Midwest Grain Products, Inc., 49
Mikasa, Inc., 28
Mikohn Gaming Corporation, 39
Miller Industries, Inc., 26
Milton Bradley Company, 21
Mine Safety Appliances Company, 31
Minolta Co., Ltd., III; 18 (upd.); 43 (upd.)
Minuteman International Inc., 46
Mitsubishi Heavy Industries, Ltd., III; 7
    (upd.)
Mity Enterprises, Inc., 38
Modine Manufacturing Company, 8
Moen Incorporated, 12
Mohawk Industries, Inc., 19
Molex Incorporated, 11
Montres Rolex S.A., 13; 34 (upd.)
Motorcar Parts & Accessories, Inc., 47
Moulinex S.A., 22
Movado Group, Inc., 28
Mr. Coffee, Inc., 15
Mr. Gasket Inc., 15
Mueller Industries, Inc., 7
Nashua Corporation, 8
National Envelope Corporation, 32
National Gypsum Company, 10
National Picture & Frame Company, 24
National Standard Co., 13
National Starch and Chemical Company,
    49
Natrol, Inc., 49
Natural Alternatives International, Inc., 49
NCR Corporation, 30 (upd.)
New Balance Athletic Shoe, Inc., 25
New Holland N.V., 22
Newcor, Inc., 40
Newell Co., 9
Newport News Shipbuilding Inc., 13; 38
    (upd.)
NHK Spring Co., Ltd., III
NIKE, Inc., 36 (upd.)
Nikon Corporation, III; 48 (upd.)
Nintendo Co., Ltd., III; 7 (upd.)
Nippon Seiko K.K., III
Nippondenso Co., Ltd., III
NKK Corporation, 28 (upd.)
NordicTrack, 22
Nordson Corporation, 11; 48 (upd.)
Nortek, Inc., 34
Norton Company, 8
Norton McNaughton, Inc., 27
Novellus Systems, Inc., 18
NTN Corporation, III; 47 (upd.)
Nu-kote Holding, Inc., 18
O'Sullivan Industries Holdings, Inc., 34
Oak Industries Inc., 21
Oakley, Inc., 49 (upd.)
Oakwood Homes Corporation, 15

The Ohio Art Company, 14
Oil-Dri Corporation of America, 20
Oneida Ltd., 7; 31 (upd.)
Optische Werke G. Rodenstock, 44
Osmonics, Inc., 18
Otis Elevator Company, Inc., 13; 39 (upd.)
Outboard Marine Corporation, III; 20 (upd.)
Owens Corning Corporation, 20 (upd.)
Owosso Corporation, 29
P & F Industries, Inc., 45
Pacer Technology, 40
Pacific Dunlop Limited, 10
Pall Corporation, 9
Palm Harbor Homes, Inc., 39
Panavision Inc., 24
Park Corp., 22
Parker-Hannifin Corporation, III; 24 (upd.)
Patrick Industries, Inc., 30
Pechiney SA, 45 (upd.)
Pella Corporation, 12; 39 (upd.)
Penn Engineering & Manufacturing Corp., 28
Pentair, Inc., 26 (upd.)
Pentech International, Inc., 29
The Perkin-Elmer Corporation, 7
Phillips-Van Heusen Corporation, 24
Physio-Control International Corp., 18
Pilkington plc, 34 (upd.)
Pioneer Electronic Corporation, III
Pitney Bowes, Inc., 19
Pittway Corporation, 33 (upd.)
PlayCore, Inc., 27
Playmates Toys, 23
Playskool, Inc., 25
Pleasant Company, 27
Ply Gem Industries Inc., 12
Polaris Industries Inc., 12; 35 (upd.)
Polaroid Corporation, III; 7 (upd.); 28 (upd.)
PPG Industries, Inc., 22 (upd.)
Prada Holding B.V., 45
Praxair, Inc., 48 (upd.)
Precision Castparts Corp., 15
Premark International, Inc., III
Presstek, Inc., 33
Prince Sports Group, Inc., 15
Printronix, Inc., 18
Pulaski Furniture Corporation, 33
Pumpkin Masters, Inc., 48
Puritan-Bennett Corporation, 13
Purolator Products Company, 21
PW Eagle, Inc., 48
Quixote Corporation, 15
R. Griggs Group Limited, 23
Racing Champions Corporation, 37
Radio Flyer Inc., 34
Rapala-Normark Group, Ltd., 30
Raven Industries, Inc., 33
Raychem Corporation, 8
Rayovac Corporation, 39 (upd.)
Recovery Engineering, Inc., 25
Red Wing Shoe Company, Inc., 9
Regal-Beloit Corporation, 18
Reichhold Chemicals, Inc., 10
Remington Arms Company, Inc., 12; 40 (upd.)
Remington Products Company, L.L.C., 42
RENK AG, 37
Revell-Monogram Inc., 16
Revere Ware Corporation, 22
Rexam PLC, 32 (upd.)
Rexnord Corporation, 21
RF Micro Devices, Inc., 43
Rheinmetall Berlin AG, 9
Riddell Sports Inc., 22
Rieter Holding AG, 42
River Oaks Furniture, Inc., 43

RMC Group p.l.c., 34 (upd.)
Roadmaster Industries, Inc., 16
Robbins & Myers Inc., 15
Robertson-Ceco Corporation, 19
RockShox, Inc., 26
Rockwell Automation, 43 (upd.)
Rohde & Schwarz GmbH & Co. KG, 39
ROHN Industries, Inc., 22
Rohr Incorporated, 9
Roland Corporation, 38
Rollerblade, Inc., 15; 34 (upd.)
Ronson PLC, 49
Roper Industries Inc., 15
Rotork plc, 46
Royal Appliance Manufacturing Company, 15
Royal Canin S.A., 39
Royal Doulton plc, 14; 38 (upd.)
RPM, Inc., 8; 36 (upd.)
Rubbermaid Incorporated, III
Russ Berrie and Company, Inc., 12
S.C. Johnson & Son, Inc., 28 (upd.)
Sabaté Diosos SA, 48
Safeskin Corporation, 18
Salant Corporation, 12
Salton, Inc., 30
Samsonite Corporation, 13; 43 (upd.)
Sandvik AB, 32 (upd.)
Sanrio Company, Ltd., 38
Sauder Woodworking Company, 12; 35 (upd.)
Sawtek Inc., 43 (upd.)
Schindler Holding AG, 29
Schlumberger Limited, III
Scotsman Industries, Inc., 20
Scott Fetzer Company, 12
The Scotts Company, 22
Scovill Fasteners Inc., 24
Sealed Air Corporation, 14
Sealy Inc., 12
Segway LLC, 48
Seiko Corporation, III; 17 (upd.)
Select Comfort Corporation, 34
The Selmer Company, Inc., 19
Semitool, Inc., 18
Sequa Corp., 13
Serta, Inc., 28
Shakespeare Company, 22
Shelby Williams Industries, Inc., 14
Shorewood Packaging Corporation, 28
SIFCO Industries, Inc., 41
Simmons Company, 47
Simula, Inc., 41
The Singer Company N.V., 30 (upd.)
Skis Rossignol S.A., 15; 43 (upd.)
Skyline Corporation, 30
SLI, Inc., 48
Smead Manufacturing Co., 17
Smith & Wesson Corporation, 30
Smith Corona Corp., 13
Smith International, Inc., 15
Smiths Industries PLC, 25
Snap-on Tools Corporation, 7
Snap-On, Incorporated, 27 (upd.)
Sparton Corporation, 18
Specialty Equipment Companies, Inc., 25
Speizman Industries, Inc., 44
SPS Technologies, Inc., 30
SPX Corporation, 47 (upd.)
Stanadyne Automotive Corporation, 37
Standex International Corporation, 17
Stanley Furniture Company, Inc., 34
The Stanley Works, III; 20 (upd.)
Stearns, Inc., 43
Steelcase, Inc., 7; 27 (upd.)
Steinway Musical Properties, Inc., 19
Stewart & Stevenson Services Inc., 11
Stryker Corporation, 11; 29 (upd.)

Sturm, Ruger & Company, Inc., 19
Sub-Zero Freezer Co., Inc., 31
Sudbury Inc., 16
Sulzer Brothers Limited (Gebruder Sulzer Aktiengesellschaft), III
Sumitomo Heavy Industries, Ltd., III; 42 (upd.)
Susquehanna Pfaltzgraff Company, 8
Swank Inc., 17
Swarovski International Holding AG, 40
The Swatch Group SA, 26
Swedish Match AB, 12; 39 (upd.)
Sweetheart Cup Company, Inc., 36
Sybron International Corp., 14
Syratech Corp., 14
TAB Products Co., 17
TAG Heuer International SA, 25
Taiwan Semiconductor Manufacturing Company Ltd., 47
Tarkett Sommer AG, 25
Taylor Guitars, 48
Taylor Made Golf Co., 23
TDK Corporation, 49 (upd.)
TearDrop Golf Company, 32
Tecumseh Products Company, 8
Tektronix, Inc., 8
Tennant Company, 13; 33 (upd.)
Terex Corporation, 7; 40 (upd.)
Thales S.A., 42
Thermadyne Holding Corporation, 19
Thermo BioAnalysis Corp., 25
Thermo Electron Corporation, 7
Thermo Fibertek, Inc., 24
Thermo Instrument Systems Inc., 11
Thermo King Corporation, 13
Thiokol Corporation, 22 (upd.)
Thomas & Betts Corp., 11
Thomas Industries Inc., 29
Thomasville Furniture Industries, Inc., 12
Thor Industries, Inc., 39
Thyssen Krupp AG, 28 (upd.)
Timex Corporation, 7; 25 (upd.)
The Timken Company, 8; 42 (upd.)
TJ International, Inc., 19
Todd Shipyards Corporation, 14
Tokheim Corporation, 21
Tonka Corporation, 25
Toolex International N.V., 26
Topps Company, Inc., 13
The Toro Company, 7; 26 (upd.)
The Torrington Company, 13
TOTO LTD., 28 (upd.)
Town & Country Corporation, 19
Toymax International, Inc., 29
Toyoda Automatic Loom Works, Ltd., III
Trek Bicycle Corporation, 16
Trico Products Corporation, 15
TriMas Corp., 11
Trinity Industries, Incorporated, 7
TRINOVA Corporation, III
Triumph Group, Inc., 31
Tubos de Acero de Mexico, S.A. (TAMSA), 41
Tultex Corporation, 13
Tupperware Corporation, 28
Twin Disc, Inc., 21
Ty Inc., 33
Tyco International Ltd., III; 28 (upd.)
Tyco Toys, Inc., 12
U.S. Robotics Inc., 9
Ube Industries, Ltd., 38 (upd.)
United Defense, L.P., 30
United Dominion Industries Limited, 8; 16 (upd.)
United Industrial Corporation, 37
United States Filter Corporation, 20
Unitog Co., 19
Utah Medical Products, Inc., 36

VA TECH ELIN EBG GmbH, 49
Vaillant GmbH, 44
Valmet Corporation (Valmet Oy), III
Valmont Industries, Inc., 19
The Valspar Corporation, 8
Vari-Lite International, Inc., 35
Varian, Inc., 48 (upd.)
Varity Corporation, III
Varlen Corporation, 16
Varta AG, 23
Velcro Industries N.V., 19
Vermeer Manufacturing Company, 17
Vickers plc, 27
Victorinox AG, 21
Viessmann Werke GmbH & Co., 37
Villeroy & Boch AG, 37
Virco Manufacturing Corporation, 17
Vitro Corporativo S.A. de C.V., 34
Vorwerk & Co., 27
Vosper Thornycroft Holding plc, 41
W.H. Brady Co., 17
W.L. Gore & Associates, Inc., 14
W.W. Grainger, Inc., 26 (upd.)
Wabash National Corp., 13
Wabtec Corporation, 40
Walbro Corporation, 13
Washington Scientific Industries, Inc., 17
Wassall Plc, 18
Waterford Wedgwood plc, 12; 34 (upd.)
Waters Corporation, 43
Watts Industries, Inc., 19
WD-40 Company, 18
Weber-Stephen Products Co., 40
Welbilt Corp., 19
Wellman, Inc., 8
Weru Aktiengesellschaft, 18
West Bend Co., 14
Western Digital Corp., 25
Whirlpool Corporation, III; 12 (upd.)
White Consolidated Industries Inc., 13
Williamson-Dickie Manufacturing
  Company, 45 (upd.)
Wilson Sporting Goods Company, 24
Windmere Corporation, 16
WinsLoew Furniture, Inc., 21
WMS Industries, Inc., 15
Wolverine Tube Inc., 23
Wood-Mode, Inc., 23
Woodward Governor Company, 13; 49
  (upd.)
Wyant Corporation, 30
Wyman-Gordon Company, 14
Wynn's International, Inc., 33
X-Rite, Inc., 48
Yamaha Corporation, III; 16 (upd.)
York International Corp., 13
Young Innovations, Inc., 44
Zero Corporation, 17
Zippo Manufacturing Company, 18
Zodiac S.A., 36
Zygo Corporation, 42

MATERIALS

AK Steel Holding Corporation, 19
American Biltrite Inc., 16
American Colloid Co., 13
American Standard Inc., III
Ameriwood Industries International Corp.,
  17
Apogee Enterprises, Inc., 8
Asahi Glass Company, Limited, III
Bairnco Corporation, 28
Bayou Steel Corporation, 31
Blessings Corp., 19
Blue Circle Industries PLC, III
Boral Limited, III
British Vita PLC, 9

Cameron & Barkley Company, 28
Carborundum Company, 15
Carl-Zeiss-Stiftung, 34 (upd.)
Carlisle Companies Incorporated, 8
Cemex SA de CV, 20
CertainTeed Corporation, 35
Chargeurs International, 21 (upd.)
Chemfab Corporation, 35
Compagnie de Saint-Gobain S.A., III; 16
  (upd.)
Cookson Group plc, III; 44 (upd.)
Corning Incorporated, III
CSR Limited, III
Dal-Tile International Inc., 22
The David J. Joseph Company, 14
The Dexter Corporation, 12 (upd.)
Dyckerhoff AG, 35
ECC Group plc, III
Edw. C. Levy Co., 42
84 Lumber Company, 9; 39 (upd.)
English China Clays Ltd., 15 (upd.); 40
  (upd.)
Envirodyne Industries, Inc., 17
Feldmuhle Nobel A.G., III
Fibreboard Corporation, 16
Florida Rock Industries, Inc., 46
Foamex International Inc., 17
Formica Corporation, 13
GAF Corporation, 22 (upd.)
The Geon Company, 11
Giant Cement Holding, Inc., 23
Gibraltar Steel Corporation, 37
Granite Rock Company, 26
Groupe Sidel S.A., 21
Harbison-Walker Refractories Company, 24
Harrisons & Crosfield plc, III
Heidelberger Zement AG, 31
Hexcel Corporation, 28
''Holderbank'' Financière Glaris Ltd., III
Holnam Inc., 39 (upd.)
Howmet Corp., 12
Ibstock Brick Ltd., 14; 37 (upd.)
Imerys S.A., 40 (upd.)
Joseph T. Ryerson & Son, Inc., 15
Lafarge Coppée S.A., III
Lafarge Corporation, 28
Lehigh Portland Cement Company, 23
Manville Corporation, III; 7 (upd.)
Matsushita Electric Works, Ltd., III; 7
  (upd.)
Medusa Corporation, 24
Mitsubishi Materials Corporation, III
Nippon Sheet Glass Company, Limited, III
OmniSource Corporation, 14
Onoda Cement Co., Ltd., III
Owens-Corning Fiberglass Corporation, III
Pilkington plc, III; 34 (upd.)
Pioneer International Limited, III
PPG Industries, Inc., III
Redland plc, III
RMC Group p.l.c., III
Rock of Ages Corporation, 37
The Rugby Group plc, 31
Schuff Steel Company, 26
Sekisui Chemical Co., Ltd., III
Shaw Industries, 9
The Sherwin-Williams Company, III; 13
  (upd.)
Simplex Technologies Inc., 21
Sommer-Allibert S.A., 19
Southdown, Inc., 14
Spartech Corporation, 19
Ssangyong Cement Industrial Co., Ltd., III
Sun Distributors L.P., 12
Tarmac PLC, III
Tarmac plc, 28 (upd.)
TOTO LTD., III; 28 (upd.)
Toyo Sash Co., Ltd., III

Tuscarora Inc., 29
U.S. Aggregates, Inc., 42
Ube Industries, Ltd., III
USG Corporation, III; 26 (upd.)
Vulcan Materials Company, 7
Wacker-Chemie GmbH, 35
Walter Industries, Inc., III
Waxman Industries, Inc., 9
Zoltek Companies, Inc., 37

MINING & METALS

A.M. Castle & Co., 25
Aggregate Industries plc, 36
Aktiebolaget SKF, 38 (upd.)
Alcan Aluminium Limited, IV; 31 (upd.)
Alleghany Corporation, 10
Allegheny Ludlum Corporation, 8
Altos Hornos de México, S.A. de C.V., 42
Aluminum Company of America, IV; 20
  (upd.)
AMAX Inc., IV
Amsted Industries Incorporated, 7
Anglo American Corporation of South
  Africa Limited, IV; 16 (upd.)
ARBED S.A., IV; 22 (upd.)
Arch Mineral Corporation, 7
Armco Inc., IV
ASARCO Incorporated, IV
Ashanti Goldfields Company Limited, 43
Atchison Casting Corporation, 39
Barrick Gold Corporation, 34
Battle Mountain Gold Company, 23
Bethlehem Steel Corporation, IV; 7 (upd.);
  27 (upd.)
Birmingham Steel Corporation, 13; 40
  (upd.)
Boart Longyear Company, 26
Boral Limited, 43 (upd.)
British Coal Corporation, IV
British Steel plc, IV; 19 (upd.)
Broken Hill Proprietary Company Ltd., IV,
  22 (upd.)
Brush Wellman Inc., 14
Buderus AG, 37
Carpenter Technology Corporation, 13
Chaparral Steel Co., 13
Christensen Boyles Corporation, 26
Cleveland-Cliffs Inc., 13
Coal India Ltd., IV; 44 (upd.)
Cockerill Sambre Group, IV; 26 (upd.)
Coeur d'Alene Mines Corporation, 20
Cold Spring Granite Company, 16
Cominco Ltd., 37
Commercial Metals Company, 15; 42
  (upd.)
Companhia Vale do Rio Doce, 43
Companhia Vale do Rio Duce, IV
Corporacion Nacional del Cobre de Chile,
  40
Corus Group plc, 49 (upd.)
CRA Limited, IV
Cyprus Amax Minerals Company, 21
Cyprus Minerals Company, 7
Daido Steel Co., Ltd., IV
De Beers Consolidated Mines Limited/De
  Beers Centenary AG, IV; 7 (upd.); 28
  (upd.)
Degussa Group, IV
Dofasco Inc., IV; 24 (upd.)
Echo Bay Mines Ltd., IV; 38 (upd.)
Engelhard Corporation, IV
Falconbridge Limited, 49
Fansteel Inc., 19
Fluor Corporation, 34 (upd.)
Freeport-McMoRan Inc., IV; 7 (upd.)
Fried. Krupp GmbH, IV
Gencor Ltd., IV, 22 (upd.)

Geneva Steel, 7
Gold Fields of South Africa Ltd., IV
Grupo Mexico, S.A. de C.V., 40
Handy & Harman, 23
Hanson PLC, 30 (upd.)
Hecla Mining Company, 20
Hemlo Gold Mines Inc., 9
Heraeus Holding GmbH, IV
Hitachi Metals, Ltd., IV
Hoesch AG, IV
Homestake Mining Company, 12; 38 (upd.)
The Hudson Bay Mining and Smelting
    Company, Limited, 12
Hylsamex, S.A. de C.V., 39
IMCO Recycling, Incorporated, 32
Imerys S.A., 40 (upd.)
Imetal S.A., IV
Inco Limited, IV; 45 (upd.)
Industrias Penoles, S.A. de C.V., 22
Inland Steel Industries, Inc., IV; 19 (upd.)
Intermet Corporation, 32
Ispat Inland Inc., 40 (upd.)
Ispat International N.V., 30
Johnson Matthey PLC, IV; 16 (upd.)
JSC MMC Norilsk Nickel, 48
Kaiser Aluminum & Chemical Corporation,
    IV
Kawasaki Steel Corporation, IV
Kennecott Corporation, 7; 27 (upd.)
Kentucky Electric Steel, Inc., 31
Kerr-McGee Corporation, 22 (upd.)
Kinross Gold Corporation, 36
Klockner-Werke AG, IV
Kobe Steel, Ltd., IV; 19 (upd.)
Koninklijke Nederlandsche Hoogovens en
    Staalfabrieken NV, IV
Laclede Steel Company, 15
Layne Christensen Company, 19
Lonrho Plc, 21
The LTV Corporation, 24 (upd.)
Lukens Inc., 14
Magma Copper Company, 7
The Marmon Group, IV; 16 (upd.)
MAXXAM Inc., 8
Meridian Gold, Incorporated, 47
Metaleurop S.A., 21
Metallgesellschaft AG, IV
Minerals and Metals Trading Corporation
    of India Ltd., IV
Minerals Technologies Inc., 11
Mitsui Mining & Smelting Co., Ltd., IV
Mitsui Mining Company, Limited, IV
National Steel Corporation, 12
NERCO, Inc., 7
Newmont Mining Corporation, 7
Niagara Corporation, 28
Nichimen Corporation, IV
Nippon Light Metal Company, Ltd., IV
Nippon Steel Corporation, IV; 17 (upd.)
Nisshin Steel Co., Ltd., IV
NKK Corporation, IV; 28 (upd.)
Noranda Inc., IV; 7 (upd.)
North Star Steel Company, 18
Nucor Corporation, 7; 21 (upd.)
Oglebay Norton Company, 17
Okura & Co., Ltd., IV
Oregon Metallurgical Corporation, 20
Oregon Steel Mills, Inc., 14
Outokumpu Oyj, 38
Park Corp., 22
Peabody Coal Company, 10
Peabody Energy Corporation, 45 (upd.)
Peabody Holding Company, Inc., IV
Pechiney, IV
Pechiney SA, 45 (upd.)
Peter Kiewit Sons' Inc., 8
Phelps Dodge Corporation, IV; 28 (upd.)
The Pittston Company, IV; 19 (upd.)

Placer Dome Inc., 20
Pohang Iron and Steel Company Ltd., IV
Potash Corporation of Saskatchewan Inc.,
    18
Quanex Corporation, 13
RAG AG, 35
Reliance Steel & Aluminum Co., 19
Republic Engineered Steels, Inc., 7; 26
    (upd.)
Reynolds Metals Company, IV
Rio Tinto plc, 19 (upd.)
RMC Group p.l.c., 34 (upd.)
Roanoke Electric Steel Corporation, 45
Rouge Steel Company, 8
The RTZ Corporation PLC, IV
Ruhrkohle AG, IV
Ryerson Tull, Inc., 40 (upd.)
Saarberg-Konzern, IV
Salzgitter AG, IV
Sandvik AB, IV
Schnitzer Steel Industries, Inc., 19
Southern Peru Copper Corporation, 40
Southwire Company, Inc., 8; 23 (upd.)
Steel Authority of India Ltd., IV
Stelco Inc., IV
Stillwater Mining Company, 47
Sumitomo Metal Industries, Ltd., IV
Sumitomo Metal Mining Co., Ltd., IV
Tata Iron & Steel Co. Ltd., IV; 44 (upd.)
Teck Corporation, 27
Texas Industries, Inc., 8
Thyssen AG, IV
The Timken Company, 8; 42 (upd.)
Titanium Metals Corporation, 21
Tomen Corporation, IV
U.S. Borax, Inc., 42
Ugine S.A., 20
NV Umicore SA, 47
Usinor SA, IV; 42 (upd.)
Usinor Sacilor, IV
VIAG Aktiengesellschaft, IV
Voest-Alpine Stahl AG, IV
Walter Industries, Inc., 22 (upd.)
Weirton Steel Corporation, IV; 26 (upd.)
Westmoreland Coal Company, 7
Wheeling-Pittsburgh Corp., 7
WMC, Limited, 43
Worthington Industries, Inc., 7; 21 (upd.)
Zambia Industrial and Mining Corporation
    Ltd., IV

PAPER & FORESTRY

Abitibi-Consolidated, Inc., 25 (upd.)
Abitibi-Price Inc., IV
Amcor Limited, IV; 19 (upd.)
American Pad & Paper Company, 20
Arjo Wiggins Appleton p.l.c., 34
Asplundh Tree Expert Co., 20
Avery Dennison Corporation, IV
Badger Paper Mills, Inc., 15
Beckett Papers, 23
Bemis Company, Inc., 8
Bohemia, Inc., 13
Boise Cascade Corporation, IV; 8 (upd.);
    32 (upd.)
Bowater PLC, IV
Bunzl plc, IV
Canfor Corporation, 42
Caraustar Industries, Inc., 19; 44 (upd.)
Carter Lumber Company, 45
Champion International Corporation, IV;
    20 (upd.)
Chesapeake Corporation, 8; 30 (upd.)
Consolidated Papers, Inc., 8; 36 (upd.)
Crane & Co., Inc., 26
Crown Vantage Inc., 29
CSS Industries, Inc., 35

Daio Paper Corporation, IV
Daishowa Paper Manufacturing Co., Ltd.,
    IV
Deltic Timber Corporation, 46
Dillard Paper Company, 11
Domtar Inc., IV
Enso-Gutzeit Oy, IV
Esselte Pendaflex Corporation, 11
Federal Paper Board Company, Inc., 8
FiberMark, Inc., 37
Fletcher Challenge Ltd., IV
Fort Howard Corporation, 8
Fort James Corporation, 22 (upd.)
Georgia-Pacific Corporation, IV; 9 (upd.);
    47 (upd.)
Groupe Rougier SA, 21
Guilbert S.A., 42
Honshu Paper Co., Ltd., IV
International Paper Company, IV; 15
    (upd.); 47 (upd.)
James River Corporation of Virginia, IV
Japan Pulp and Paper Company Limited,
    IV
Jefferson Smurfit Group plc, IV; 49 (upd.)
Jujo Paper Co., Ltd., IV
Kimberly-Clark Corporation, 16 (upd.); 43
    (upd.)
Kruger Inc., 17
Kymmene Corporation, IV
Longview Fibre Company, 8; 37 (upd.)
Louisiana-Pacific Corporation, IV; 31
    (upd.)
MacMillan Bloedel Limited, IV
The Mead Corporation, IV; 19 (upd.)
Metsa-Serla Oy, IV
Mo och Domsjö AB, IV
Monadnock Paper Mills, Inc., 21
Mosinee Paper Corporation, 15
Nashua Corporation, 8
National Envelope Corporation, 32
NCH Corporation, 8
Oji Paper Co., Ltd., IV
P.H. Glatfelter Company, 8; 30 (upd.)
Packaging Corporation of America, 12
Papeteries de Lancey, 23
Plum Creek Timber Company, Inc., 43
Pope and Talbot, Inc., 12
Potlatch Corporation, 8; 34 (upd.)
PWA Group, IV
Rayonier Inc., 24
Rengo Co., Ltd., IV
Reno de Medici S.p.A., 41
Rexam PLC, 32 (upd.)
Riverwood International Corporation, 11;
    48 (upd.)
Rock-Tenn Company, 13
St. Joe Paper Company, 8
Sanyo-Kokusaku Pulp Co., Ltd., IV
Sappi Limited, 49
Scott Paper Company, IV; 31 (upd.)
Sealed Air Corporation, 14
Sierra Pacific Industries, 22
Simpson Investment Company, 17
Specialty Coatings Inc., 8
Stone Container Corporation, IV
Stora Enso Oyj, 36 (upd.)
Stora Kopparbergs Bergslags AB, IV
Svenska Cellulosa Aktiebolaget SCA, IV;
    28 (upd.)
Temple-Inland Inc., IV; 31 (upd.)
TJ International, Inc., 19
U.S. Timberlands Company, L.P., 42
Union Camp Corporation, IV
United Paper Mills Ltd. (Yhtyneet
    Paperitehtaat Oy), IV
Universal Forest Products Inc., 10
UPM-Kymmene Corporation, 19
West Fraser Timber Co. Ltd., 17

Westvaco Corporation, IV; 19 (upd.)
Weyerhaeuser Company, IV; 9 (upd.); 28
    (upd.)
Wickes Inc., 25 (upd.)
Willamette Industries, Inc., IV; 31 (upd.)
WTD Industries, Inc., 20

PERSONAL SERVICES

AARP, 27
ADT Security Services, Inc., 12; 44 (upd.)
American Retirement Corporation, 42
Arthur Murray International, Inc., 32
Berlitz International, Inc., 39 (upd.)
Carriage Services, Inc., 37
Childtime Learning Centers, Inc., 34
Corinthian Colleges, Inc., 39
Correctional Services Corporation, 30
CUC International Inc., 16
Davis Service Group PLC, 45
DeVry Incorporated, 29
Educational Testing Service, 12
The Ford Foundation, 34
Franklin Quest Co., 11
Goodwill Industries International, Inc., 16
Jazzercise, Inc., 45
The John D. and Catherine T. MacArthur
    Foundation, 34
Kaplan, Inc., 42
KinderCare Learning Centers, Inc., 13
The Loewen Group Inc., 16; 40 (upd.)
Management and Training Corporation, 28
Manpower, Inc., 9
Michael Page International plc, 45
Regis Corporation, 18
The Rockefeller Foundation, 34
Rollins, Inc., 11
Rosenbluth International Inc., 14
Rotary International, 31
The Salvation Army USA, 32
Service Corporation International, 6
SOS Staffing Services, 25
Stewart Enterprises, Inc., 20
Supercuts Inc., 26
Weight Watchers International Inc., 12; 33
    (upd.)
Youth Services International, Inc., 21
YWCA of the U.S.A., 45

PETROLEUM

Abu Dhabi National Oil Company, IV; 45
    (upd.)
Agway, Inc., 21 (upd.)
Alberta Energy Company Ltd., 16; 43
    (upd.)
Amerada Hess Corporation, IV; 21 (upd.)
Amoco Corporation, IV; 14 (upd.)
Anadarko Petroleum Corporation, 10
ANR Pipeline Co., 17
Anschutz Corp., 12
Apache Corporation, 10; 32 (upd.)
Arctic Slope Regional Corporation, 38
Ashland Inc., 19
Ashland Oil, Inc., IV
Atlantic Richfield Company, IV; 31 (upd.)
Baker Hughes Incorporated, 22 (upd.)
Belco Oil & Gas Corp., 40
Benton Oil and Gas Company, 47
Berry Petroleum Company, 47
BJ Services Company, 25
BP p.l.c., 45 (upd.)
The British Petroleum Company plc, IV; 7
    (upd.); 21 (upd.)
British-Borneo Oil & Gas PLC, 34
Broken Hill Proprietary Company Ltd., 22
    (upd.)
Burlington Resources Inc., 10
Burmah Castrol PLC, IV; 30 (upd.)

Callon Petroleum Company, 47
Caltex Petroleum Corporation, 19
Chevron Corporation, IV; 19 (upd.)
ChevronTexaco Corporation, 47 (upd.)
Chiles Offshore Corporation, 9
China National Petroleum Corporation, 46
Chinese Petroleum Corporation, IV; 31
    (upd.)
CITGO Petroleum Corporation, IV; 31
    (upd.)
The Coastal Corporation, IV; 31 (upd.)
Compañia Española de Petróleos S.A., IV
Comstock Resources, Inc., 47
Conoco Inc., IV; 16 (upd.)
Cooper Cameron Corporation, 20 (upd.)
Cosmo Oil Co., Ltd., IV
Crown Central Petroleum Corporation, 7
DeepTech International Inc., 21
Den Norse Stats Oljeselskap AS, IV
Deutsche BP Aktiengesellschaft, 7
Diamond Shamrock, Inc., IV
Dynegy Inc., 49 (upd.)
Egyptian General Petroluem Corporation,
    IV
Elf Aquitaine SA, 21 (upd.)
Empresa Colombiana de Petróleos, IV
Enbridge Inc., 43
Energen Corporation, 21
Enron Corporation, 19
Ente Nazionale Idrocarburi, IV
Enterprise Oil plc, 11
Entreprise Nationale Sonatrach, IV
Exxon Corporation, IV; 7 (upd.); 32 (upd.)
Ferrellgas Partners, L.P., 35
FINA, Inc., 7
Flying J Inc., 19
Forest Oil Corporation, 19
OAO Gazprom, 42
General Sekiyu K.K., IV
Giant Industries, Inc., 19
Global Industries, Ltd., 37
Global Marine Inc., 9
GlobalSantaFe Corporation, 48 (upd.)
Grey Wolf, Inc., 43
Halliburton Company, 25 (upd.)
Helmerich & Payne, Inc., 18
Holly Corporation, 12
Hunt Consolidated, Inc., 27 (upd.)
Hunt Oil Company, 7
Husky Energy Inc., 47
Idemitsu Kosan Co., Ltd., 49 (upd.)
Idemitsu Kosan K.K., IV
Imperial Oil Limited, IV; 25 (upd.)
Indian Oil Corporation Ltd., IV; 48 (upd.)
Kanematsu Corporation, IV
Kerr-McGee Corporation, IV; 22 (upd.)
Kinder Morgan, Inc., 45
King Ranch, Inc., 14
Koch Industries, Inc., IV; 20 (upd.)
Koppers Industries, Inc., 26 (upd.)
Kuwait Petroleum Corporation, IV
Libyan National Oil Corporation, IV
The Louisiana Land and Exploration
    Company, 7
OAO LUKOIL, 40
Lyondell Petrochemical Company, IV
MAPCO Inc., IV
Maxus Energy Corporation, 7
McDermott International, Inc., 37 (upd.)
Meteor Industries Inc., 33
Mitchell Energy and Development
    Corporation, 7
Mitsubishi Oil Co., Ltd., IV
Mobil Corporation, IV; 7 (upd.); 21 (upd.)
Murphy Oil Corporation, 7; 32 (upd.)
Nabors Industries, Inc., 9
National Iranian Oil Company, IV
Neste Oy, IV

NGC Corporation, 18
Nigerian National Petroleum Corporation,
    IV
Nippon Oil Company, Limited, IV
OAO NK YUKOS, 47
Noble Affiliates, Inc., 11
OAO Gazprom, 42
OAO LUKOIL, 40
OAO NK YUKOS, 47
OAO Siberian Oil Company (Sibneft), 49
OAO Surgutneftegaz, 48
OAO Tatneft, 45
Occidental Petroleum Corporation, IV; 25
    (upd.)
Oil and Natural Gas Commission, IV
ÖMV Aktiengesellschaft, IV
Oryx Energy Company, 7
Parker Drilling Company, 28
Patina Oil & Gas Corporation, 24
Pennzoil Company, IV; 20 (upd.)
PERTAMINA, IV
Petro-Canada Limited, IV
PetroFina S.A., IV; 26 (upd.)
Petróleo Brasileiro S.A., IV
Petróleos de Portugal S.A., IV
Petróleos de Venezuela S.A., IV
Petróleos del Ecuador, IV
Petróleos Mexicanos, IV; 19 (upd.)
Petroleum Development Oman LLC, IV
Petronas, IV
Phillips Petroleum Company, IV; 40 (upd.)
Pogo Producing Company, 39
Premcor Inc., 37
Qatar General Petroleum Corporation, IV
Quaker State Corporation, 7; 21 (upd.)
Range Resources Corporation, 45
Repsol S.A., IV; 16 (upd.)
Repsol-YPF S.A., 40 (upd.)
Resource America, Inc., 42
Rowan Companies, Inc., 43
Royal Dutch Petroleum Company/ The
    ''Shell'' Transport and Trading Company
    p.l.c., IV
Royal Dutch/Shell Group, 49 (upd.)
Santa Fe International Corporation, 38
Sasol Limited, IV; 47 (upd.)
Saudi Arabian Oil Company, IV; 17 (upd.)
Schlumberger Limited, 17 (upd.)
Seagull Energy Corporation, 11
Seitel, Inc., 47
Shanghai Petrochemical Co., Ltd., 18
Shell Oil Company, IV; 14 (upd.); 41
    (upd.)
Showa Shell Sekiyu K.K., IV
OAO Siberian Oil Company (Sibneft), 49
Société Nationale Elf Aquitaine, IV; 7
    (upd.)
Suburban Propane Partners, L.P., 30
Sun Company, Inc., IV
Sunoco, Inc., 28 (upd.)
OAO Surgutneftegaz, 48
Talisman Energy Inc., 9; 47 (upd.)
OAO Tatneft, 45
Tesoro Petroleum Corporation, 7; 45 (upd.)
Texaco Inc., IV; 14 (upd.); 41 (upd.)
Tidewater Inc., 37 (upd.)
Tom Brown, Inc., 37
Tonen Corporation, IV; 16 (upd.)
Tosco Corporation, 7
TOTAL S.A., IV; 24 (upd.)
TransMontaigne Inc., 28
Transocean Sedco Forex Inc., 45
Travel Ports of America, Inc., 17
Triton Energy Corporation, 11
Türkiye Petrolleri Anonim Ortakliği, IV
Ultramar Diamond Shamrock Corporation,
    IV; 31 (upd.)
Union Texas Petroleum Holdings, Inc., 9

Unocal Corporation, IV; 24 (upd.)
USX Corporation, IV; 7 (upd.)
Valero Energy Corporation, 7
Varco International, Inc., 42
Vastar Resources, Inc., 24
Vintage Petroleum, Inc., 42
Wascana Energy Inc., 13
Weatherford International, Inc., 39
Western Atlas Inc., 12
Western Company of North America, 15
Western Gas Resources, Inc., 45
The Williams Companies, Inc., IV; 31 (upd.)
World Fuel Services Corporation, 47
YPF Sociedad Anonima, IV

PUBLISHING & PRINTING

A.B.Dick Company, 28
A.H. Belo Corporation, 10; 30 (upd.)
Advance Publications Inc., IV; 19 (upd.)
Advanced Marketing Services, Inc., 34
Affiliated Publications, Inc., 7
Agence France-Presse, 34
American Banknote Corporation, 30
American Greetings Corporation, 7, 22 (upd.)
American Media, Inc., 27
American Printing House for the Blind, 26
Andrews McMeel Universal, 40
The Antioch Company, 40
Arandell Corporation, 37
Arnoldo Mondadori Editore S.p.A., IV; 19 (upd.)
The Associated Press, 31 (upd.)
The Atlantic Group, 23
Axel Springer Verlag AG, IV; 20 (upd.)
Banta Corporation, 12; 32 (upd.)
Bauer Publishing Group, 7
Bayard SA, 49
Berlitz International, Inc., 13
Bernard C. Harris Publishing Company, Inc., 39
Bertelsmann A.G., IV; 15 (upd.); 43 (upd.)
Big Flower Press Holdings, Inc., 21
Blue Mountain Arts, Inc., 29
Book-of-the-Month Club, Inc., 13
Bowne & Co., Inc., 23
Broderbund Software, 29 (upd.)
Brown Printing Company, 26
Burda Holding GmbH. & Co., 23
The Bureau of National Affairs, Inc., 23
Butterick Co., Inc., 23
Cadmus Communications Corporation, 23
Cahners Business Information, 43
CCH Inc., 14
Central Newspapers, Inc., 10
Champion Industries, Inc., 28
The Chronicle Publishing Company, Inc., 23
Chrysalis Group plc, 40
CMP Media Inc., 26
Commerce Clearing House, Inc., 7
Concepts Direct, Inc., 39
The Condé Nast Publications Inc., 13
Consumers Union, 26
The Copley Press, Inc., 23
Courier Corporation, 41
Cowles Media Company, 23
Cox Enterprises, Inc., IV; 22 (upd.)
Crain Communications, Inc., 12; 35 (upd.)
Current, Inc., 37
Dai Nippon Printing Co., Ltd., IV
Daily Mail and General Trust plc, 19
Dawson Holdings PLC, 43
Day Runner, Inc., 14
DC Comics Inc., 25
De La Rue plc, 10; 34 (upd.)

Deluxe Corporation, 7; 22 (upd.)
Dorling Kindersley Holdings plc, 20
Dover Publications Inc., 34
Dow Jones & Company, Inc., IV; 19 (upd.); 47 (upd.)
The Dun & Bradstreet Corporation, IV; 19 (upd.)
Duplex Products Inc., 17
The E.W. Scripps Company, IV; 7 (upd.); 28 (upd.)
Edmark Corporation, 14
Electronics for Imaging, Inc., 43 (upd.)
Elsevier N.V., IV
EMAP plc, 35
EMI Group plc, 22 (upd.)
Encyclopaedia Britannica, Inc., 7; 39 (upd.)
Engraph, Inc., 12
Enquirer/Star Group, Inc., 10
Entravision Communications Corporation, 41
Essence Communications, Inc., 24
Farm Journal Corporation, 42
Farrar, Straus and Giroux Inc., 15
Flint Ink Corporation, 13
Follett Corporation, 12; 39 (upd.)
Forbes Inc., 30
Franklin Electronic Publishers, Inc., 23
Freedom Communications, Inc., 36
Gannett Co., Inc., IV; 7 (upd.); 30 (upd.)
Gibson Greetings, Inc., 12
Golden Books Family Entertainment, Inc., 28
Goss Holdings, Inc., 43
Graphic Industries Inc., 25
Gray Communications Systems, Inc., 24
Grolier Incorporated, 16; 43 (upd.)
Groupe de la Cite, IV
Groupe Les Echos, 25
Hachette, IV
Hachette Filipacchi Medias S.A., 21
Hallmark Cards, Inc., IV; 16 (upd.); 40 (upd.)
Harcourt Brace and Co., 12
Harcourt Brace Jovanovich, Inc., IV
Harcourt General, Inc., 20 (upd.)
HarperCollins Publishers, 15
Harris Interactive, 41
Harte-Hanks Communications, Inc., 17
Havas SA, 10; 33 (upd.)
Hazelden Foundation, 28
The Hearst Corporation, IV; 19 (upd.); 46 (upd.)
Her Majesty's Stationery Office, 7
N.V. Holdingmaatschappij De Telegraaf, 23
Hollinger International Inc., 24
Houghton Mifflin Company, 10; 36 (upd.)
IDG Books Worldwide, Inc., 27
Information Holdings Inc., 47
International Data Group, Inc., 7; 25 (upd.)
IPC Magazines Limited, 7
John Fairfax Holdings Limited, 7
John H. Harland Company, 17
John Wiley & Sons, Inc., 17
Johnson Publishing Company, Inc., 28
Johnston Press plc, 35
Jostens, Inc., 25 (upd.)
Journal Register Company, 29
Kaplan, Inc., 42
Kinko's, Inc., 43 (upd.)
Knight-Ridder, Inc., IV; 15 (upd.)
Kodansha Ltd., IV; 38 (upd.)
Krause Publications, Inc., 35
Landmark Communications, Inc., 12
Larry Flynt Publishing Inc., 31
Le Monde S.A., 33
Lee Enterprises, Incorporated, 11
LEXIS-NEXIS Group, 33

Maclean Hunter Publishing Limited, IV; 26 (upd.)
Macmillan, Inc., 7
Martha Stewart Living Omnimedia, L.L.C., 24
Marvel Entertainment Group, Inc., 10
Matra-Hachette S.A., 15 (upd.)
Maxwell Communication Corporation plc, IV; 7 (upd.)
McClatchy Newspapers, Inc., 23
The McGraw-Hill Companies, Inc., IV; 18 (upd.)
Mecklermedia Corporation, 24
Media General, Inc., 38 (upd.)
Meredith Corporation, 11; 29 (upd.)
Merrill Corporation, 18; 47 (upd.)
The Miner Group International, 22
Mirror Group Newspapers plc, 7; 23 (upd.)
Moore Corporation Limited, IV
Morris Communications Corporation, 36
Multimedia, Inc., 11
National Audubon Society, 26
National Geographic Society, 9; 30 (upd.)
New Times, Inc., 45
New York Daily News, 32
The New York Times Company, IV; 19 (upd.)
News America Publishing Inc., 12
News Corporation Limited, IV; 7 (upd.)
Newsquest plc, 32
Nihon Keizai Shimbun, Inc., IV
Nolo.com, Inc., 49
Ottaway Newspapers, Inc., 15
Outlook Group Corporation, 37
Pearson plc, IV; 46 (upd.)
Penton Media, Inc., 27
Petersen Publishing Company, 21
Plato Learning, Inc., 44
Playboy Enterprises, Inc., 18
Pleasant Company, 27
PR Newswire, 35
Primedia Inc., 22
The Providence Journal Company, 28
Publishers Group, Inc., 35
Pulitzer Publishing Company, 15
Quad/Graphics, Inc., 19
Quebecor Inc., 12; 47 (upd.)
R.L. Polk & Co., 10
R.R. Donnelley & Sons Company, IV; 9 (upd.); 38 (upd.)
Rand McNally & Company, 28
Random House Inc., 13; 31 (upd.)
The Reader's Digest Association, Inc., IV; 17 (upd.)
Recycled Paper Greetings, Inc., 21
Reed Elsevier plc, 31 (upd.)
Reed International PLC, IV; 17 (upd.)
Reuters Holdings PLC, IV; 22 (upd.)
Rodale Press, Inc., 23
Rodale, Inc., 47 (upd.)
Rogers Communications Inc., 30 (upd.)
St Ives plc, 34
Schawk, Inc., 24
Schibsted ASA, 31
Scholastic Corporation, 10; 29 (upd.)
Scott Fetzer Company, 12
Scottish Media Group plc, 32
Seat Pagine Gialle S.p.A., 47
Seattle Times Company, 15
The Sierra Club, 28
Simon & Schuster Inc., IV; 19 (upd.)
Sir Speedy, Inc., 16
SkyMall, Inc., 26
Softbank Corp., 13
Southam Inc., 7
SPIEGEL-Verlag Rudolf Augstein GmbH & Co. KG, 44
Standard Register Co., 15

Taylor & Francis Group plc, 44
Taylor Corporation, 36
Taylor Publishing Company, 12; 36 (upd.)
Thomas Nelson, Inc., 14; 38 (upd.)
Thomas Publishing Company, 26
The Thomson Corporation, 8; 34 (upd.)
The Times Mirror Company, IV; 17 (upd.)
Tom Doherty Associates Inc., 25
Toppan Printing Co., Ltd., IV
The Topps Company, Inc., 34 (upd.)
Torstar Corporation, 29
Tribune Company, IV, 22 (upd.)
Trinity Mirror plc, 49 (upd.)
U.S. News and World Report Inc., 30
United News & Media plc, 28 (upd.)
United Newspapers plc, IV
United Press International, Inc., 25
Valassis Communications, Inc., 8
Value Line, Inc., 16
Verlagsgruppe Georg von Holtzbrinck GmbH, 35
Village Voice Media, Inc., 38
VNU N.V., 27
Volt Information Sciences Inc., 26
W.W. Norton & Company, Inc., 28
Wallace Computer Services, Inc., 36
The Washington Post Company, IV; 20 (upd.)
Waverly, Inc., 16
Wenner Media, Inc., 32
West Group, 7; 34 (upd.)
Western Publishing Group, Inc., 13
WH Smith PLC, 42 (upd.)
Wolters Kluwer NV, 14; 33 (upd.)
World Book, Inc., 12
World Color Press Inc., 12
Xeikon NV, 26
Zebra Technologies Corporation, 14
Ziff Communications Company, 12
Ziff Davis Media Inc., 36 (upd.)
Zondervan Publishing House, 24

REAL ESTATE

Alexander's, Inc., 45
Amfac/JMB Hawaii L.L.C., 24 (upd.)
Apartment Investment and Management Company, 49
Archstone-Smith Trust, 49
Associated Estates Realty Corporation, 25
Berkshire Realty Holdings, L.P., 49
Boston Properties, Inc., 22
Bramalea Ltd., 9
Canary Wharf Group Plc, 30
CapStar Hotel Company, 21
Castle & Cooke, Inc., 20 (upd.)
Catellus Development Corporation, 24
CB Commercial Real Estate Services Group, Inc., 21
Chateau Communities, Inc., 37
Cheung Kong (Holdings) Limited, IV; 20 (upd.)
Del Webb Corporation, 14
The Edward J. DeBartolo Corporation, 8
Equity Residential, 49
Fairfield Communities, Inc., 36
Forest City Enterprises, Inc., 16
Gecina SA, 42
Griffin Land & Nurseries, Inc., 43
Grubb & Ellis Company, 21
The Haminerson Property Investment and Development Corporation plc, IV
Hammerson plc, 40
Harbert Corporation, 14
Helmsley Enterprises, Inc., 39 (upd.)
Home Properties of New York, Inc., 42
Hongkong Land Holdings Limited, IV; 47 (upd.)

Hyatt Corporation, 16 (upd.)
JMB Realty Corporation, IV
Jones Lang LaSalle Incorporated, 49
JPI, 49
Kaufman and Broad Home Corporation, 8
Kerry Properties Limited, 22
Kimco Realty Corporation, 11
The Koll Company, 8
Land Securities PLC, IV; 49 (upd.)
Lefrak Organization Inc., 26
Lend Lease Corporation Limited, IV; 17 (upd.)
Lincoln Property Company, 8
The Loewen Group Inc., 40 (upd.)
Mack-Cali Realty Corporation, 42
Manufactured Home Communities, Inc., 22
Maui Land & Pineapple Company, Inc., 29
Maxco Inc., 17
Meditrust, 11
Melvin Simon and Associates, Inc., 8
MEPC plc, IV
Meritage Corporation, 26
Mitsubishi Estate Company, Limited, IV
Mitsui Real Estate Development Co., Ltd., IV
The Nature Conservancy, 28
New Plan Realty Trust, 11
New World Development Company Ltd., IV
Newhall Land and Farming Company, 14
Olympia & York Developments Ltd., IV; 9 (upd.)
Park Corp., 22
Perini Corporation, 8
Post Properties, Inc., 26
Reckson Associates Realty Corp., 47
Rodamco N.V., 26
The Rouse Company, 15
Shubert Organization Inc., 24
The Sierra Club, 28
Silverstein Properties, Inc., 47
Simco S.A., 37
SL Green Realty Corporation, 44
Slough Estates PLC, IV
Starrett Corporation, 21
Storage USA, Inc., 21
Sumitomo Realty & Development Co., Ltd., IV
Sun Communities Inc., 46
Tanger Factory Outlet Centers, Inc., 49
Tarragon Realty Investors, Inc., 45
Taylor Woodrow plc, 38 (upd.)
Tejon Ranch Company, 35
Tishman Speyer Properties, L.P., 47
Tokyu Land Corporation, IV
Trammell Crow Company, 8
Trendwest Resorts, Inc., 33
Tridel Enterprises Inc., 9
Trizec Corporation Ltd., 10
Trump Organization, 23
Unibail SA, 40
Vistana, Inc., 22
Vornado Realty Trust, 20
W.P. Carey & Co. LLC, 49

RETAIL & WHOLESALE

A.C. Moore Arts & Crafts, Inc., 30
A.T. Cross Company, 49 (upd.)
Aaron Rents, Inc., 14; 35 (upd.)
ABC Appliance, Inc., 10
ABC Carpet & Home Co. Inc., 26
Abercrombie & Fitch Co., 15
Academy Sports & Outdoors, 27
Ace Hardware Corporation, 12; 35 (upd.)
Action Performance Companies, Inc., 27
Alba-Waldensian, Inc., 30
Alberto-Culver Company, 36 (upd.)

Alldays plc, 49
Allders plc, 37
Allou Health & Beauty Care, Inc., 28
Amazon.com, Inc., 25
American Coin Merchandising, Inc., 28
American Eagle Outfitters, Inc., 24
American Furniture Company, Inc., 21
American Stores Company, 22 (upd.)
AmeriSource Health Corporation, 37 (upd.)
Ames Department Stores, Inc., 9; 30 (upd.)
Amway Corporation, 13; 30 (upd.)
The Andersons, Inc., 31
AnnTaylor Stores Corporation, 13; 37 (upd.)
Appliance Recycling Centers of America, Inc., 42
Arbor Drugs Inc., 12
Arcadia Group plc, 28 (upd.)
Army and Air Force Exchange Service, 39
Art Van Furniture, Inc., 28
ASDA Group plc, 28 (upd.)
Ashworth, Inc., 26
Au Printemps S.A., V
Audio King Corporation, 24
Authentic Fitness Corp., 20
Auto Value Associates, Inc., 25
Autobytel Inc., 47
AutoZone, Inc., 9; 31 (upd.)
AVA AG (Allgemeine Handelsgesellschaft der Verbraucher AG), 33
Aveda Corporation, 24
Aviation Sales Company, 41
B. Dalton Bookseller Inc., 25
Babbage's, Inc., 10
Baby Superstore, Inc., 15
Baccarat, 24
Bachman's Inc., 22
Banana Republic Inc., 25
Barnes & Noble, Inc., 10; 30 (upd.)
Barnett Inc., 28
Barney's, Inc., 28
Bass Pro Shops, Inc., 42
Bear Creek Corporation, 38
Bearings, Inc., 13
bebe stores, inc., 31
Bed Bath & Beyond Inc., 13; 41 (upd.)
Belk Stores Services, Inc., V; 19 (upd.)
Bergen Brunswig Corporation, V; 13 (upd.)
Bernard Chaus, Inc., 27
Best Buy Co., Inc., 9; 23 (upd.)
Bhs plc, 17
Big Dog Holdings, Inc., 45
Big O Tires, Inc., 20
Birkenstock Footprint Sandals, Inc., 42 (upd.)
Black Box Corporation, 20
Blacks Leisure Group plc, 39
Blair Corporation, 25; 31 (upd.)
Bloomingdale's Inc., 12
Blue Square Israel Ltd., 41
Blyth Industries, Inc., 18
The Body Shop International PLC, 11
The Bombay Company, Inc., 10
The Bon Marché, Inc., 23
The Bon-Ton Stores, Inc., 16
Books-A-Million, Inc., 14; 41 (upd.)
The Boots Company PLC, V; 24 (upd.)
Borders Group, Inc., 15; 43 (upd.)
Boscov's Department Store, Inc., 31
Bozzuto's, Inc., 13
Bradlees Discount Department Store Company, 12
Brambles Industries Limited, 42
Broder Bros. Co., 38
Brooks Brothers Inc., 22
Brookstone, Inc., 18
The Buckle, Inc., 18
Buhrmann NV, 41

Burlington Coat Factory Warehouse Corporation, 10
The Burton Group plc, V
Buttrey Food & Drug Stores Co., 18
buy.com, Inc., 46
C&A, V; 40 (upd.)
Cabela's Inc., 26
Cablevision Electronic Instruments, Inc., 32
Cache Incorporated, 30
Caldor Inc., 12
Camelot Music, Inc., 26
Campeau Corporation, V
Campo Electronics, Appliances & Computers, Inc., 16
Carrefour SA, 10; 27 (upd.)
Carson Pirie Scott & Company, 15
Carter Hawley Hale Stores, Inc., V
Carter Lumber Company, 45
Cartier Monde, 29
Casual Corner Group, Inc., 43
Catherines Stores Corporation, 15
Cato Corporation, 14
CDW Computer Centers, Inc., 16
Celebrity, Inc., 22
Central Garden & Pet Company, 23
Chadwick's of Boston, Ltd., 29
Charlotte Russe Holding, Inc., 35
Charming Shoppes, Inc., 38
ChevronTexaco Corporation, 47 (upd.)
The Children's Place Retail Stores, Inc., 37
Christian Dior S.A., 49 (upd.)
Christopher & Banks Corporation, 42
Cifra, S.A. de C.V., 12
The Circle K Company, 20 (upd.)
Circuit City Stores, Inc., 9; 29 (upd.)
Clinton Cards plc, 39
The Clothestime, Inc., 20
CML Group, Inc., 10
Coach, Inc., 45 (upd.)
Coborn's, Inc., 30
Coinmach Laundry Corporation, 20
Coldwater Creek Inc., 21
Cole National Corporation, 13
Coles Myer Ltd., V; 20 (upd.)
Collectors Universe, Inc., 48
Comdisco, Inc., 9
CompUSA, Inc., 10
Computerland Corp., 13
Concepts Direct, Inc., 39
The Container Store, 36
Controladora Comercial Mexicana, S.A. de C.V., 36
Coop Schweiz Genossenschaftsverband, 48
Corby Distilleries Limited, 14
Corporate Express, Inc., 22; 47 (upd.)
The Cosmetic Center, Inc., 22
Cost Plus, Inc., 27
Costco Wholesale Corporation, V; 43 (upd.)
Cotter & Company, V
County Seat Stores Inc., 9
Courts Plc, 45
CPI Corp., 38
Crate and Barrel, 9
Croscill, Inc., 42
Crowley, Milner & Company, 19
Crown Books Corporation, 21
Cumberland Farms, Inc., 17
CVS Corporation, 45 (upd.)
Daffy's Inc., 26
The Daiei, Inc., V; 17 (upd.); 41 (upd.)
The Daimaru, Inc., V; 42 (upd.)
Dairy Mart Convenience Stores, Inc., 25 (upd.)
Daisytek International Corporation, 18
Damark International, Inc., 18
Dart Group Corporation, 16
Darty S.A., 27

David's Bridal, Inc., 33
Dayton Hudson Corporation, V; 18 (upd.)
Deb Shops, Inc., 16
Debenhams Plc, 28
dELiA*s Inc., 29
Department 56, Inc., 34 (upd.)
Designer Holdings Ltd., 20
Deveaux S.A., 41
Diesel SpA, 40
Dillard Department Stores, Inc., V; 16 (upd.)
Dillon Companies Inc., 12
Discount Auto Parts, Inc., 18
Discount Drug Mart, Inc., 14
Dixons Group plc, V; 19 (upd.); 49 (upd.)
Do it Best Corporation, 30
Dollar Tree Stores, Inc., 23
The Dress Barn, Inc., 24
Drug Emporium, Inc., 12
Du Pareil au Même, 43
Duane Reade Holding Corp., 21
Duckwall-ALCO Stores, Inc., 24
Duty Free International, Inc., 11
Dylex Limited, 29
E-Z Serve Corporation, 17
Eagle Hardware & Garden, Inc., 16
eBay Inc., 32
Eckerd Corporation, 9; 32 (upd.)
Eddie Bauer, Inc., 36 (upd.)
Egghead.com, Inc., 31 (upd.)
El Corte Inglés Group, V
Elder-Beerman Stores Corporation, 10
Ellett Brothers, Inc., 17
EMI Group plc, 22 (upd.)
Ethan Allen Interiors, Inc., 39 (upd.)
EToys, Inc., 37
Euromarket Designs Inc., 31 (upd.)
Evans, Inc., 30
EZCORP Inc., 43
Family Dollar Stores, Inc., 13
Fastenal Company, 14; 42 (upd.)
Fay's Inc., 17
Federated Department Stores, Inc., 9; 31 (upd.)
Fielmann AG, 31
Fila Holding S.p.A., 20
Fingerhut Companies, Inc., 9; 36 (upd.)
The Finish Line, Inc., 29
Finlay Enterprises, Inc., 16
Fleming Companies, Inc., 17 (upd.)
Florsheim Shoe Group Inc., 9; 31 (upd.)
FNAC, 21
Follett Corporation, 12
Footstar, Incorporated, 24
Fortunoff Fine Jewelry and Silverware Inc., 26
Frank's Nursery & Crafts, Inc., 12
Fred Meyer, Inc., V; 20 (upd.)
Fred's, Inc., 23
Frederick Atkins Inc., 16
Fretter, Inc., 10
Friedman's Inc., 29
Funco, Inc., 20
G.I. Joe's, Inc., 30
Gadzooks, Inc., 18
Gaiam, Inc., 41
Galeries Lafayette S.A., V; 23 (upd.)
Galyan's Trading Company, Inc., 47
Gander Mountain, Inc., 20
Gantos, Inc., 17
The Gap, Inc., V; 18 (upd.)
Garden Ridge Corporation, 27
Gart Sports Company, 24
GEHE AG, 27
General Binding Corporation, 10
General Host Corporation, 12
Genesco Inc., 17
Genovese Drug Stores, Inc., 18

Genuine Parts Company, 45 (upd.)
Gerald Stevens, Inc., 37
Giant Food Inc., 22 (upd.)
GIB Group, V; 26 (upd.)
Glacier Water Services, Inc., 47
The Good Guys, Inc., 10; 30 (upd.)
Goodwill Industries International, Inc., 16
Goody's Family Clothing, Inc., 20
Gottschalks, Inc., 18
GrandVision S.A., 43
The Great Universal Stores plc, V; 19 (upd.)
Griffin Land & Nurseries, Inc., 43
Grossman's Inc., 13
Groupe Castorama-Dubois Investissements, 23
Groupe DMC (Dollfus Mieg & Cie), 27
Groupe Go Sport S.A., 39
Groupe Lapeyre S.A., 33
Groupe Zannier S.A., 35
Grow Biz International, Inc., 18
Grupo Casa Saba, S.A. de C.V., 39
Grupo Elektra, S.A. de C.V., 39
Grupo Gigante, S.A. de C.V., 34
Gruppo Coin S.p.A., 41
GT Bicycles, 26
Guccio Gucci, S.p.A., 15
Guilbert S.A., 42
Guitar Center, Inc., 29
GUS plc, 47 (upd.)
Hahn Automotive Warehouse, Inc., 24
Half Price Books, Records, Magazines Inc., 37
Hallmark Cards, Inc., 40 (upd.)
Hammacher Schlemmer & Company, 21
Hancock Fabrics, Inc., 18
Hankyu Department Stores, Inc., V
Hanna Andersson Corp., 49
Hanover Direct, Inc., 36
Harold's Stores, Inc., 22
Harrods Holdings, 47
Harry Winston Inc., 45
Hasbro, Inc., 43 (upd.)
Haverty Furniture Companies, Inc., 31
Hechinger Company, 12
Heilig-Meyers Company, 14; 40 (upd.)
Helzberg Diamonds, 40
Hennes & Mauritz AB, 29
Henry Modell & Company Inc., 32
Hertie Waren- und Kaufhaus GmbH, V
Hibbett Sporting Goods, Inc., 26
Hills Stores Company, 13
Hines Horticulture, Inc., 49
The Hockey Company, 34
Holiday RV Superstores, Incorporated, 26
Holt's Cigar Holdings, Inc., 42
The Home Depot, Inc., V; 18 (upd.)
Home Shopping Network, Inc., V; 25 (upd.)
HomeBase, Inc., 33 (upd.)
Hot Topic, Inc., 33
House of Fabrics, Inc., 21
House of Fraser PLC, 45
Hudson's Bay Company, V; 25 (upd.)
IKEA International A/S, V; 26 (upd.)
InaCom Corporation, 13
Insight Enterprises, Inc., 18
Intimate Brands, Inc., 24
Isetan Company Limited, V; 36 (upd.)
Ito-Yokado Co., Ltd., V; 42 (upd.)
J&R Electronics Inc., 26
J. Baker, Inc., 31
The J. Jill Group, Inc., 35
J.C. Penney Company, Inc., V; 18 (upd.); 43 (upd.)
Jack Schwartz Shoes, Inc., 18
Jacobson Stores Inc., 21
Jalate Inc., 25

James Beattie plc, 43
Jay Jacobs, Inc., 15
Jennifer Convertibles, Inc., 31
Jetro Cash & Carry Enterprises Inc., 38
JG Industries, Inc., 15
JJB Sports plc, 32
John Lewis Partnership plc, V; 42 (upd.)
JUSCO Co., Ltd., V
Just For Feet, Inc., 19
K & B Inc., 12
K & G Men's Center, Inc., 21
K-tel International, Inc., 21
Karstadt Aktiengesellschaft, V; 19 (upd.)
Kash n' Karry Food Stores, Inc., 20
Kasper A.S.L., Ltd., 40
Kaufhof Warenhaus AG, V; 23 (upd.)
Kaufring AG, 35
Kay-Bee Toy Stores, 15
Kingfisher plc, V; 24 (upd.)
Kinney Shoe Corp., 14
Kmart Corporation, V; 18 (upd.); 47 (upd.)
Knoll Group Inc., 14
Kohl's Corporation, 9; 30 (upd.)
Kotobukiya Co., Ltd., V
Krause's Furniture, Inc., 27
L. Luria & Son, Inc., 19
L.A. T Sportswear, Inc., 26
L.L. Bean, Inc., 38 (upd.)
La-Z-Boy Chair Company, 14
Lamonts Apparel, Inc., 15
Lands' End, Inc., 9; 29 (upd.)
Laura Ashley Holdings plc, 37 (upd.)
Lazare Kaplan International Inc., 21
Lechmere Inc., 10
Lechters, Inc., 11; 39 (upd.)
LensCrafters Inc., 23
Lesco Inc., 19
Leslie's Poolmart, Inc., 18
Levitz Furniture Inc., 15
Lewis Galoob Toys Inc., 16
Lifetime Hoan Corporation, 27
Lillian Vernon Corporation, 12; 35
The Limited, Inc., V; 20 (upd.)
Linens 'n Things, Inc., 24
The Littlewoods Organisation PLC, V
Littlewoods plc, 42 (upd.)
Liz Claiborne, Inc., 25 (upd.)
Loehmann's Inc., 24
Lojas Arapuã S.A., 22
London Drugs Ltd., 46
Longs Drug Stores Corporation, V; 25
   (upd.)
Lost Arrow Inc., 22
LOT$OFF Corporation, 24
Lowe's Companies, Inc., V; 21 (upd.)
Mac Frugal's Bargains - Closeouts Inc., 17
Mac-Gray Corporation, 44
MarineMax, Inc., 30
Marks and Spencer p.l.c., V; 24 (upd.)
Marks Brothers Jewelers, Inc., 24
Marshalls Incorporated, 13
Marui Co., Ltd., V
Maruzen Co., Limited, 18
Mary Kay, Inc., 30 (upd.)
Matalan PLC, 49
Matsuzakaya Company Limited, V
Maus Frères SA, 48
The Maxim Group, 25
The May Department Stores Company, V;
   19 (upd.); 46 (upd.)
Mayor's Jewelers, Inc., 41
Mazel Stores, Inc., 29
McKesson Corporation, 47 (upd.)
McLane Company, Inc., 13
MCSi, Inc., 41
Media Arts Group, Inc., 42
Meier & Frank Co., 23
Meijer Incorporated, 27 (upd.)

Melville Corporation, V
The Men's Wearhouse, Inc., 17; 48 (upd.)
Menard, Inc., 34
Mercantile Stores Company, Inc., V; 19
   (upd.)
Merry-Go-Round Enterprises, Inc., 8
Mervyn's California, 10; 39 (upd.)
Michaels Stores, Inc., 17
Micro Warehouse, Inc., 16
MicroAge, Inc., 16
Mitsukoshi Ltd., V
Monsoon plc, 39
Montgomery Ward & Co., Incorporated, V;
   20 (upd.)
Moore-Handley, Inc., 39
Morse Shoe Inc., 13
Mothers Work, Inc., 18
Moto Photo, Inc., 45
Mr. Bricolage S.A., 37
MTS Inc., 37
Musicland Stores Corporation, 9; 38 (upd.)
Nagasakiya Co., Ltd., V
National Educational Music Co. Ltd., 47
National Home Centers, Inc., 44
National Intergroup, Inc., V
National Record Mart, Inc., 29
National Wine & Spirits, Inc., 49
Natural Wonders Inc., 14
Navy Exchange Service Command, 31
Neff Corp., 32
Neiman Marcus Co., 12
The Neiman Marcus Group, Inc., 49 (upd.)
New Look Group plc, 35
Next plc, 29
Nichii Co., Ltd., V
NIKE, Inc., 36 (upd.)
Nine West Group Inc., 11
99¢ Only Stores, 25
Noland Company, 35
Noodle Kidoodle, 16
Nordstrom, Inc., V; 18 (upd.)
Norelco Consumer Products Co., 26
Norm Thompson Outfitters, Inc., 47
The North West Company, Inc., 12
Norton McNaughton, Inc., 27
Nu Skin Enterprises, Inc., 27
Oakley, Inc., 49 (upd.)
Office Depot Incorporated, 8; 23 (upd.)
OfficeMax, Inc., 15; 43 (upd.)
Old America Stores, Inc., 17
One Price Clothing Stores, Inc., 20
Orchard Supply Hardware Stores
   Corporation, 17
Organización Soriana, S.A. de C.V., 35
The Orvis Company, Inc., 28
OshKosh B'Gosh, Inc., 42 (upd.)
Oshman's Sporting Goods, Inc., 17
Otto Versand (GmbH & Co.), V; 15 (upd.);
   34 (upd.)
Owens & Minor, Inc., 16
P.C. Richard & Son Corp., 23
Pamida Holdings Corporation, 15
The Pampered Chef, Ltd., 18
The Pantry, Inc., 36
Parisian, Inc., 14
Paul Harris Stores, Inc., 18
Pay 'N Pak Stores, Inc., 9
Payless Cashways, Inc., 11; 44 (upd.)
Payless ShoeSource, Inc., 18
Pearle Vision, Inc., 13
Peebles Inc., 16; 43 (upd.)
Peet's Coffee & Tea, Inc., 38
Petco Animal Supplies, Inc., 29
Petrie Stores Corporation, 8
PETsMART, Inc., 14; 41 (upd.)
Phar-Mor Inc., 12
Pier 1 Imports, Inc., 12; 34 (upd.)
Piercing Pagoda, Inc., 29

Pilot Corporation, 49
Pinault-Printemps Redoute S.A., 19 (upd.)
Pomeroy Computer Resources, Inc., 33
Powell's Books, Inc., 40
The Price Company, V
PriceCostco, Inc., 14
Proffitt's, Inc., 19
Purina Mills, Inc., 32
Quelle Group, V
QuikTrip Corporation, 36
Quill Corporation, 28
R.H. Macy & Co., Inc., V; 8 (upd.); 30
   (upd.)
RadioShack Corporation, 36 (upd.)
Rag Shops, Inc., 30
Raley's Inc., 14
Rapala-Normark Group, Ltd., 30
RDO Equipment Company, 33
Reckitt Benckiser plc, 42 (upd.)
Recoton Corp., 15
Recreational Equipment, Inc., 18
Reeds Jewelers, Inc., 22
Rent-A-Center, Inc., 45
Rent-Way, Inc., 33
Restoration Hardware, Inc., 30
Revco D.S., Inc., V
REX Stores Corp., 10
Rhodes Inc., 23
Richton International Corporation, 39
Riklis Family Corp., 9
Rite Aid Corporation, V; 19 (upd.)
Ritz Camera Centers, 34
Roberds Inc., 19
Rocky Shoes & Boots, Inc., 26
Rogers Communications Inc., 30 (upd.)
Rooms To Go Inc., 28
Roots Canada Ltd., 42
Rose's Stores, Inc., 13
Ross Stores, Inc., 17; 43 (upd.)
Roundy's Inc., 14
S&K Famous Brands, Inc., 23
Saks Holdings, Inc., 24
Saks Inc., 41 (upd.)
Sam Ash Music Corporation, 30
Sam's Club, 40
Samuels Jewelers Incorporated, 30
Sanborn Hermanos, S.A., 20
Schmitt Music Company, 40
Schneiderman's Furniture Inc., 28
Schottenstein Stores Corp., 14
Schultz Sav-O Stores, Inc., 31
The Score Board, Inc., 19
Scotty's, Inc., 22
SCP Pool Corporation, 39
Seaman Furniture Company, Inc., 32
Sears plc, V
Sears Roebuck de México, S.A. de C.V.,
   20
Sears, Roebuck and Co., V; 18 (upd.)
SED International Holdings, Inc., 43
Seibu Department Stores, Ltd., V; 42
   (upd.)
Seigle's Home and Building Centers, Inc.,
   41
The Seiyu, Ltd., V; 36 (upd.)
Selfridges Plc, 34
Service Merchandise Company, Inc., V; 19
   (upd.)
7-Eleven, Inc., 32 (upd.)
Shaklee Corporation, 12
The Sharper Image Corporation, 10
Shoe Carnival Inc., 14
ShopKo Stores Inc., 21
Shoppers Drug Mart Corporation, 49
SkyMall, Inc., 26
Sleepy's Inc., 32
Solo Serve Corporation, 28
Sophus Berendsen A/S, 49

Sound Advice, Inc., 41
Southern States Cooperative Incorporated, 36
Spec's Music, Inc., 19
Spiegel, Inc., 10; 27 (upd.)
Sport Chalet, Inc., 16
Sport Supply Group, Inc., 23
Sportmart, Inc., 15
Sports & Recreation, Inc., 17
The Sports Authority, Inc., 16; 43 (upd.)
The Sportsman's Guide, Inc., 36
Stage Stores, Inc., 24
Stanhome Inc., 15
Staples, Inc., 10
Starbucks Corporation, 34 (upd.)
Starcraft Corporation, 30
Stein Mart Inc., 19
Stinnes AG, 8
The Stop & Shop Companies, Inc., 24 (upd.)
Storehouse PLC, 16
Stride Rite Corporation, 8
Strouds, Inc., 33
Stuller Settings, Inc., 35
Successories, Inc., 30
Sun Television & Appliances Inc., 10
Sunglass Hut International, Inc., 21
Supreme International Corporation, 27
Swarovski International Holding AG, 40
Syms Corporation, 29
Takashimaya Company, Limited, V; 47 (upd.)
The Talbots, Inc., 11; 31 (upd.)
Target Stores, 10; 27 (upd.)
Tati SA, 25
Tattered Cover Book Store, 43
Tech Data Corporation, 10
Tengelmann Group, 27
Tesco PLC, 24 (upd.)
Thrifty PayLess, Inc., 12
Tiffany & Co., 14
The TJX Companies, Inc., V; 19 (upd.)
Today's Man, Inc., 20
Tokyu Department Store Co., Ltd., V; 32 (upd.)
Tops Appliance City, Inc., 17
Toys "R" Us, Inc., V; 18 (upd.)
Travis Boats & Motors, Inc., 37
Travis Perkins plc, 34
Trend-Lines, Inc., 22
TruServ Corporation, 24
Tuesday Morning Corporation, 18
Tupperware Corporation, 28
TVI, Inc., 15
Tweeter Home Entertainment Group, Inc., 30
Ultimate Electronics, Inc., 18
Ultramar Diamond Shamrock Corporation, 31 (upd.)
Uni-Marts, Inc., 17
United Rentals, Inc., 34
The United States Shoe Corporation, V
United Stationers Inc., 14
Universal International, Inc., 25
Uny Co., Ltd., V; 49 (upd.)
Urban Outfitters, Inc., 14
Vallen Corporation, 45
Valley Media Inc., 35
Value City Department Stores, Inc., 38
Value Merchants Inc., 13
ValueVision International, Inc., 22
Vans, Inc., 47 (upd.)
Venator Group Inc., 35 (upd.)
Vendex International N.V., 13
Venture Stores Inc., 12
The Vermont Teddy Bear Co., Inc., 36
Viking Office Products, Inc., 10
Vorwerk & Co., 27

W. Atlee Burpee & Co., 27
W H Smith Group PLC, V
W.W. Grainger, Inc., V
Waban Inc., 13
Wacoal Corp., 25
Wal-Mart de Mexico, S.A. de C.V., 35 (upd.)
Wal-Mart Stores, Inc., V; 8 (upd.); 26 (upd.)
Walden Book Company Inc., 17
Walgreen Co., V; 20 (upd.)
Wall Drug Store, Inc., 40
Weiner's Stores, Inc., 33
West Marine, Inc., 17
Western Beef, Inc., 22
The Wet Seal, Inc., 18
Weyco Group, Incorporated, 32
WH Smith PLC, 42 (upd.)
Whole Foods Market, Inc., 20
Wickes Inc., V; 25 (upd.)
Williams-Sonoma, Inc., 17; 44 (upd.)
Wilsons The Leather Experts Inc., 21
Wolohan Lumber Co., 19
Woolworth Corporation, V; 20 (upd.)
World Duty Free Americas, Inc., 29 (upd.)
The Yankee Candle Company, Inc., 37
Young's Market Company, LLC, 32
Younkers, Inc., 19
Zale Corporation, 16; 40 (upd.)
Zany Brainy, Inc., 31
Ziebart International Corporation, 30
Zion's Cooperative Mercantile Institution, 33

RUBBER & TIRE

Aeroquip Corporation, 16
Bandag, Inc., 19
The BFGoodrich Company, V
Bridgestone Corporation, V; 21 (upd.)
Carlisle Companies Incorporated, 8
Compagnie Générale des Établissements Michelin, V; 42 (upd.)
Continental Aktiengesellschaft, V
Continental General Tire Corp., 23
Cooper Tire & Rubber Company, 8; 23 (upd.)
Elementis plc, 40 (upd.)
General Tire, Inc., 8
The Goodyear Tire & Rubber Company, V; 20 (upd.)
The Kelly-Springfield Tire Company, 8
Myers Industries, Inc., 19
Pirelli S.p.A., V; 15 (upd.)
Safeskin Corporation, 18
Sumitomo Rubber Industries, Ltd., V
Tillotson Corp., 15
Treadco, Inc., 19
Ube Industries, Ltd., 38 (upd.)
The Yokohama Rubber Co., Ltd., V; 19 (upd.)

TELECOMMUNICATIONS

A.H. Belo Corporation, 30 (upd.)
Acme-Cleveland Corp., 13
ADC Telecommunications, Inc., 10
Adelphia Communications Corp., 17
Adtran Inc., 22
AEI Music Network Inc., 35
AirTouch Communications, 11
Alcatel S.A., 36 (upd.)
Alliance Atlantis Communications Inc., 39
ALLTEL Corporation, 6; 46 (upd.)
American Telephone and Telegraph Company, V
American Tower Corporation, 33
Ameritech Corporation, V; 18 (upd.)
Amstrad plc, 48 (upd.)

AO VimpelCom, 48
Arch Wireless, Inc., 39
ARD, 41
Ascom AG, 9
Aspect Telecommunications Corporation, 22
AT&T Bell Laboratories, Inc., 13
AT&T Corporation, 29 (upd.)
BCE, Inc., V; 44 (upd.)
Belgacom, 6
Bell Atlantic Corporation, V; 25 (upd.)
Bell Canada, 6
BellSouth Corporation, V; 29 (upd.)
BET Holdings, Inc., 18
BHC Communications, Inc., 26
Bonneville International Corporation, 29
Bouygues S.A., 24 (upd.)
Brightpoint, Inc., 18
Brite Voice Systems, Inc., 20
British Columbia Telephone Company, 6
British Telecommunications plc, V; 15 (upd.)
BT Group plc, 49 (upd.)
C-COR.net Corp., 38
Cable & Wireless HKT, 30 (upd.)
Cable and Wireless plc, V; 25 (upd.)
Cablevision Systems Corporation, 30 (upd.)
The Canadian Broadcasting Corporation (CBC), 37
Canal Plus, 10; 34 (upd.)
CanWest Global Communications Corporation, 35
Capital Radio plc, 35
Carlton Communications plc, 15
Carolina Telephone and Telegraph Company, 10
Carrier Access Corporation, 44
CBS Corporation, 28 (upd.)
Centel Corporation, 6
Centennial Communications Corporation, 39
Century Communications Corp., 10
Century Telephone Enterprises, Inc., 9
Chancellor Media Corporation, 24
Charter Communications, Inc., 33
Chris-Craft Industries, Inc., 9
Chrysalis Group plc, 40
Cincinnati Bell, Inc., 6
Citadel Communications Corporation, 35
Clear Channel Communications, Inc., 23
COLT Telecom Group plc, 41
Comcast Corporation, 24 (upd.)
Comdial Corporation, 21
Commonwealth Telephone Enterprises, Inc., 25
Comsat Corporation, 23
Comverse Technology, Inc., 15; 43 (upd.)
Corning Inc., 44 (upd.)
Craftmade International, Inc., 44
Cumulus Media Inc., 37
DDI Corporation, 7
Deutsche Bundespost TELEKOM, V
Deutsche Telekom AG, 48 (upd.)
Dialogic Corporation, 18
Directorate General of Telecommunications, 7
DIRECTV, Inc., 38
Discovery Communications, Inc., 42
DSC Communications Corporation, 12
EchoStar Communications Corporation, 35
ECI Telecom Ltd., 18
eircom plc, 31 (upd.)
Electric Lightwave, Inc., 37
Electromagnetic Sciences Inc., 21
Emmis Communications Corporation, 47
Energis plc, 47
Entravision Communications Corporation, 41

EXCEL Communications Inc., 18
Executone Information Systems, Inc., 13
Expand SA, 48
Fox Family Worldwide, Inc., 24
France Télécom Group, V; 21 (upd.)
Frontier Corp., 16
Gannett Co., Inc., 30 (upd.)
Gaylord Entertainment Company, 36 (upd.)
General DataComm Industries, Inc., 14
Geotek Communications Inc., 21
Getty Images, Inc., 31
Global Crossing Ltd., 32
Granite Broadcasting Corporation, 42
Gray Communications Systems, Inc., 24
Groupe Vidéotron Ltée., 20
Grupo Televisa, S.A., 18
GTE Corporation, V; 15 (upd.)
Guthy-Renker Corporation, 32
GWR Group plc, 39
Harmonic Inc., 43
Havas, SA, 10
Hispanic Broadcasting Corporation, 35
Hong Kong Telecommunications Ltd., 6
Hubbard Broadcasting Inc., 24
Hughes Electronics Corporation, 25
IDB Communications Group, Inc., 11
IDT Corporation, 34
Illinois Bell Telephone Company, 14
Indiana Bell Telephone Company,
    Incorporated, 14
Infinity Broadcasting Corporation, 11
IXC Communications, Inc., 29
Jacor Communications, Inc., 23
Jones Intercable, Inc., 21
Koninklijke PTT Nederland NV, V
LCI International, Inc., 16
LDDS-Metro Communications, Inc., 8
LIN Broadcasting Corp., 9
Lincoln Telephone & Telegraph Company,
    14
LodgeNet Entertainment Corporation, 28
Mannesmann AG, 38 (upd.)
MasTec, Inc., 19
McCaw Cellular Communications, Inc., 6
MCI WorldCom, Inc., V; 27 (upd.)
McLeodUSA Incorporated, 32
Mercury Communications, Ltd., 7
Metrocall, Inc., 41
Metromedia Companies, 14
Métropole Télévision, 33
MFS Communications Company, Inc., 11
Michigan Bell Telephone Co., 14
MIH Limited, 31
MITRE Corporation, 26
Mobile Telecommunications Technologies
    Corp., 18
Modern Times Group AB, 36
The Montana Power Company, 44 (upd.)
Multimedia, Inc., 11
National Broadcasting Company, Inc., 28
    (upd.)
NCR Corporation, 30 (upd.)
NetCom Systems AB, 26
Nevada Bell Telephone Company, 14
New Valley Corporation, 17
Nextel Communications, Inc., 27 (upd.)
Nippon Telegraph and Telephone
    Corporation, V
Norstan, Inc., 16
Nortel Networks Corporation, 36 (upd.)
Northern Telecom Limited, V
NYNEX Corporation, V
Octel Communications Corp., 14
Octel Messaging, 41 (upd.)
Ohio Bell Telephone Company, 14
Olivetti S.p.A., 34 (upd.)
Österreichische Post- und
    Telegraphenverwaltung, V

Pacific Telecom, Inc., 6
Pacific Telesis Group, V
Paging Network Inc., 11
PanAmSat Corporation, 46
Paxson Communications Corporation, 33
PictureTel Corp., 10; 27 (upd.)
Posti- ja Telelaitos, 6
Price Communications Corporation, 42
QUALCOMM Incorporated, 20; 47 (upd.)
QVC Network Inc., 9
Qwest Communications International, Inc.,
    37
RMH Teleservices, Inc., 42
Rochester Telephone Corporation, 6
Rogers Communications Inc., 30 (upd.)
Royal KPN N.V., 30
Rural Cellular Corporation, 43
Saga Communications, Inc., 27
Sawtek Inc., 43 (upd.)
SBC Communications Inc., 32 (upd.)
Schweizerische Post-, Telefon- und
    Telegrafen-Betriebe, V
Scientific-Atlanta, Inc., 6; 45 (upd.)
Seat Pagine Gialle S.p.A., 47
Securicor Plc, 45
Sinclair Broadcast Group, Inc., 25
Società Finanziaria Telefonica per Azioni,
    V
Southern New England
    Telecommunications Corporation, 6
Southwestern Bell Corporation, V
Spanish Broadcasting System, Inc., 41
Spelling Entertainment, 35 (upd.)
Sprint Communications Company, L.P., 9
Sprint Corporation, 46 (upd.)
StrataCom, Inc., 16
Swedish Telecom, V
Sycamore Networks, Inc., 45
SynOptics Communications, Inc., 10
T-Netix, Inc., 46
Telecom Australia, 6
Telecom Eireann, 7
Telecom Italia S.p.A., 43
Telefonaktiebolaget LM Ericsson, V; 46
    (upd.)
Telefónica de España, S.A., V
Telefónica S.A., 46 (upd.)
Telefonos de Mexico S.A. de C.V., 14
Telephone and Data Systems, Inc., 9
Télévision Française 1, 23
Tellabs, Inc., 11; 40 (upd.)
Tiscali SpA, 48
The Titan Corporation, 36
Tollgrade Communications, Inc., 44
TV Azteca, S.A. de C.V., 39
U.S. Satellite Broadcasting Company, Inc.,
    20
U S West, Inc., V; 25 (upd.)
U.S. Cellular Corporation, 9; 31 (upd.)
United Pan-Europe Communications NV,
    47
United Telecommunications, Inc., V
United Video Satellite Group, 18
USA Interactive, Inc., 47 (upd.)
Verizon Communications, 43 (upd.)
Vivendi Universal S.A., 46 (upd.)
Vodafone Group PLC, 11; 36 (upd.)
The Walt Disney Company, 30 (upd.)
Watkins-Johnson Company, 15
West Corporation, 42
Western Wireless Corporation, 36
Westwood One, Inc., 23
Williams Communications Group, Inc., 34
The Williams Companies, Inc., 31 (upd.)
Wipro Limited, 43
Wisconsin Bell, Inc., 14
Working Assets Funding Service, 43
Young Broadcasting Inc., 40

TEXTILES & APPAREL

Abercrombie & Fitch Co., 35 (upd.)
Adidas AG, 14
adidas-Salomon AG, 33 (upd.)
Alba-Waldensian, Inc., 30
Albany International Corp., 8
Algo Group Inc., 24
American Safety Razor Company, 20
Amoskeag Company, 8
Angelica Corporation, 15; 43 (upd.)
AR Accessories Group, Inc., 23
Aris Industries, Inc., 16
Authentic Fitness Corp., 20
Banana Republic Inc., 25
Benetton Group S.p.A., 10
Bill Blass Ltd., 32
Birkenstock Footprint Sandals, Inc., 12
Blair Corporation, 25
Brazos Sportswear, Inc., 23
Brooks Brothers Inc., 22
Brooks Sports Inc., 32
Brown Group, Inc., V; 20 (upd.)
Bugle Boy Industries, Inc., 18
Burberry Ltd., 17; 41 (upd.)
Burlington Industries, Inc., V; 17 (upd.)
Calcot Ltd., 33
Calvin Klein, Inc., 22
Candie's, Inc., 31
Canstar Sports Inc., 16
Capel Incorporated, 45
Carhartt, Inc., 30
Cato Corporation, 14
Chargeurs International, 21 (upd.)
Charming Shoppes, Inc., 8
Cherokee Inc., 18
Chic by H.I.S, Inc., 20
Chico's FAS, Inc., 45
Chorus Line Corporation, 30
Christian Dior S.A., 19; 49 (upd.)
Christopher & Banks Corporation, 42
Claire's Stores, Inc., 17
Coach Leatherware, 10
Coats plc, 44 (upd.)
Coats Viyella Plc, V
Collins & Aikman Corporation, 13
Columbia Sportswear Company, 19; 41
    (upd.)
Concord Fabrics, Inc., 16
Cone Mills Corporation, 8
Converse Inc., 31 (upd.)
Cotton Incorporated, 46
Courtaulds plc, V; 17 (upd.)
Croscill, Inc., 42
Crown Crafts, Inc., 16
Crystal Brands, Inc., 9
Culp, Inc., 29
Cygne Designs, Inc., 25
Dan River Inc., 35
Danskin, Inc., 12
Deckers Outdoor Corporation, 22
Delta Woodside Industries, Inc., 8; 30
    (upd.)
Designer Holdings Ltd., 20
The Dixie Group, Inc., 20
Dominion Textile Inc., 12
Donna Karan Company, 15
Donnkenny, Inc., 17
Duck Head Apparel Company, Inc., 42
Dyersburg Corporation, 21
Edison Brothers Stores, Inc., 9
Esprit de Corp., 8; 29 (upd.)
Etam Developpement SA, 44
Evans, Inc., 30
Fab Industries, Inc., 27
Fabri-Centers of America Inc., 16
Fieldcrest Cannon, Inc., 9; 31 (upd.)
Fila Holding S.p.A., 20

Florsheim Shoe Group Inc., 31 (upd.)
Fossil, Inc., 17
Frederick's of Hollywood Inc., 16
French Connection Group plc, 41
Fruit of the Loom, Inc., 8; 25 (upd.)
Fubu, 29
G&K Services, Inc., 16
G-III Apparel Group, Ltd., 22
Galey & Lord, Inc., 20
Garan, Inc., 16
Gianni Versace SpA, 22
Giorgio Armani S.p.A., 45
The Gitano Group, Inc. 8
Greenwood Mills, Inc., 14
Groupe DMC (Dollfus Mieg & Cie), 27
Groupe Yves Saint Laurent, 23
Guccio Gucci, S.p.A., 15
Guess, Inc., 15
Guilford Mills Inc., 8; 40 (upd.)
Gymboree Corporation, 15
Haggar Corporation, 19
Hampton Industries, Inc., 20
Happy Kids Inc., 30
Hartmarx Corporation, 8
The Hartstone Group plc, 14
Healthtex, Inc., 17
Helly Hansen ASA, 25
Hermès S.A., 14
The Hockey Company, 34
Hugo Boss AG, 48
Hyde Athletic Industries, Inc., 17
I.C. Isaacs & Company, 31
Interface, Inc., 8; 29 (upd.)
Irwin Toy Limited, 14
Items International Airwalk Inc., 17
J. Crew Group, Inc., 12; 34 (upd.)
Jockey International, Inc., 12; 34 (upd.)
Johnston Industries, Inc., 15
Jones Apparel Group, Inc., 39 (upd.)
Jordache Enterprises, Inc., 23
Jos. A. Bank Clothiers, Inc., 31
JPS Textile Group, Inc., 28
K-Swiss, Inc., 33
Karl Kani Infinity, Inc., 49
Kellwood Company, 8
Kenneth Cole Productions, Inc., 25
Kinney Shoe Corp., 14
L.A. Gear, Inc., 8; 32 (upd.)
L.L. Bean, Inc., 10; 38 (upd.)
LaCrosse Footwear, Inc., 18
Laura Ashley Holdings plc, 13
Lee Apparel Company, Inc., 8
The Leslie Fay Company, Inc., 8; 39 (upd.)
Levi Strauss & Co., V; 16 (upd.)
Liz Claiborne, Inc., 8
London Fog Industries, Inc., 29
Lost Arrow Inc., 22
Maidenform Worldwide Inc., 20
Malden Mills Industries, Inc., 16
Marzotto S.p.A., 20
Milliken & Co., V; 17 (upd.)
Mitsubishi Rayon Co., Ltd., V
Mossimo, Inc., 27
Mothercare UK Ltd., 17
Movie Star Inc., 17
Naf Naf SA, 44
Nautica Enterprises, Inc., 18; 44 (upd.)
New Balance Athletic Shoe, Inc., 25
Nike, Inc., V; 8 (upd.)
Nine West Group, Inc., 39 (upd.)
The North Face, Inc., 18
Oakley, Inc., 18
OshKosh B'Gosh, Inc., 9; 42 (upd.)
Oxford Industries, Inc., 8
Pacific Sunwear of California, Inc., 28
Peek & Cloppenburg KG, 46
Pendleton Woolen Mills, Inc., 42
Pentland Group plc, 20

Perry Ellis International, Inc., 41
Phat Fashions LLC, 49
Pillowtex Corporation, 19; 41 (upd.)
Pluma, Inc., 27
Polo/Ralph Lauren Corporation, 12
Prada Holding B.V., 45
PremiumWear, Inc., 30
Puma AG Rudolf Dassler Sport, 35
Quaker Fabric Corp., 19
Quiksilver, Inc., 18
R.G. Barry Corporation, 17; 44 (upd.)
Recreational Equipment, Inc., 18
Red Wing Shoe Company, Inc., 30 (upd.)
Reebok International Ltd., V; 9 (upd.); 26 (upd.)
Rieter Holding AG, 42
Rollerblade, Inc., 15
Russell Corporation, 8; 30 (upd.)
St. John Knits, Inc., 14
Saucony Inc., 35
Shaw Industries, Inc., 40 (upd.)
Shelby Williams Industries, Inc., 14
Skechers U.S.A. Inc., 31
Sophus Berendsen A/S, 49
Springs Industries, Inc., V; 19 (upd.)
Starter Corp., 12
Steven Madden, Ltd., 37
Stone Manufacturing Company, 14; 43 (upd.)
The Stride Rite Corporation, 8; 37 (upd.)
Sun Sportswear, Inc., 17
Superior Uniform Group, Inc., 30
Teijin Limited, V
Thomaston Mills, Inc., 27
The Timberland Company, 13
Tommy Hilfiger Corporation, 20
Toray Industries, Inc., V
Tultex Corporation, 13
Unifi, Inc., 12
United Merchants & Manufacturers, Inc., 13
United Retail Group Inc., 33
Unitika Ltd., V
Vans, Inc., 16; 47 (upd.)
Varsity Spirit Corp., 15
VF Corporation, V; 17 (upd.)
Walton Monroe Mills, Inc., 8
The Warnaco Group Inc., 12; 46 (upd.)
Wellman, Inc., 8
West Point-Pepperell, Inc., 8
WestPoint Stevens Inc., 16
Weyco Group, Incorporated, 32
Williamson-Dickie Manufacturing Company, 14
Wolverine World Wide Inc., 16

TOBACCO

American Brands, Inc., V
B.A.T. Industries PLC, 22 (upd.)
Brooke Group Ltd., 15
Brown & Williamson Tobacco Corporation, 14; 33 (upd.)
Culbro Corporation, 15
Dibrell Brothers, Incorporated, 12
DIMON Inc., 27
800-JR Cigar, Inc., 27
Gallaher Group Plc, 49 (upd.)
Gallaher Limited, V; 19 (upd.)
Holt's Cigar Holdings, Inc., 42
Imasco Limited, V
Japan Tobacco Incorporated, V
Philip Morris Companies Inc., V; 18 (upd.)
R.J. Reynolds Tobacco Holdings, Inc., 30 (upd.)
RJR Nabisco Holdings Corp., V
Rothmans UK Holdings Limited, V; 19 (upd.)

Seita, 23
Standard Commercial Corporation, 13
Swisher International Group Inc., 23
Tabacalera, S.A., V; 17 (upd.)
Universal Corporation, V; 48 (upd.)
UST Inc., 9
Vector Group Ltd., 35 (upd.)

TRANSPORT SERVICES

Aéroports de Paris, 33
Air Express International Corporation, 13
Airborne Freight Corporation, 6; 34 (upd.)
Alamo Rent A Car, Inc., 6; 24 (upd.)
Alexander & Baldwin, Inc., 10
Allied Worldwide, Inc., 49
Amerco, 6
American Classic Voyages Company, 27
American President Companies Ltd., 6
Anschutz Corp., 12
Aqua Alliance Inc., 32 (upd.)
Atlas Van Lines, Inc., 14
Avis Rent A Car, Inc., 6; 22 (upd.)
BAA plc, 10
Bekins Company, 15
Boyd Bros. Transportation Inc., 39
Brambles Industries Limited, 42
British Railways Board, V
Broken Hill Proprietary Company Ltd., 22 (upd.)
Budget Group, Inc., 25
Budget Rent a Car Corporation, 9
Burlington Northern Santa Fe Corporation, V; 27 (upd.)
C.H. Robinson Worldwide, Inc., 40 (upd.)
Canadian National Railway System, 6
Canadian Pacific Railway Limited, V; 45 (upd.)
Carey International, Inc., 26
Carlson Companies, Inc., 6
Carolina Freight Corporation, 6
Celadon Group Inc., 30
Central Japan Railway Company, 43
Chargeurs, 6
Chicago and North Western Holdings Corporation, 6
Christian Salvesen Plc, 45
Coach USA, Inc., 24
Coles Express Inc., 15
Compagnie Générale Maritime et Financière, 6
Consolidated Delivery & Logistics, Inc., 24
Consolidated Freightways Corporation, V; 21 (upd.); 48 (upd.)
Consolidated Rail Corporation, V
Crowley Maritime Corporation, 6; 28 (upd.)
CSX Corporation, V; 22 (upd.)
Danzas Group, V; 40 (upd.)
Deutsche Bahn AG, 46 (upd.)
Deutsche Bundesbahn, V
DHL Worldwide Express, 6; 24 (upd.)
Dollar Thrifty Automotive Group, Inc., 25
East Japan Railway Company, V
Emery Air Freight Corporation, 6
Emery Worldwide Airlines, Inc., 25 (upd.)
Enterprise Rent-A-Car Company, 6
Eurotunnel Group, 37 (upd.)
Evergreen Marine Corporation Taiwan Ltd., 13
Executive Jet, Inc., 36
Expeditors International of Washington Inc., 17
Federal Express Corporation, V
FedEx Corporation, 18 (upd.); 42 (upd.)
Fritz Companies, Inc., 12
Frontline Ltd., 45
Frozen Food Express Industries, Inc., 20

GATX Corporation, 6; 25 (upd.)
GE Capital Aviation Services, 36
Genesee & Wyoming Inc., 27
The Go-Ahead Group Plc, 28
The Greenbrier Companies, 19
Greyhound Lines, Inc., 32 (upd.)
Grupo Transportación Ferroviaria
    Mexicana, S.A. de C.V., 47
GulfMark Offshore, Inc., 49
Hankyu Corporation, V; 23 (upd.)
Hapag-Lloyd AG, 6
Harland and Wolff Holdings plc, 19
Harper Group Inc., 17
Heartland Express, Inc., 18
The Hertz Corporation, 9
Holberg Industries, Inc., 36
Hospitality Worldwide Services, Inc., 26
Hub Group, Inc., 38
Hvide Marine Incorporated, 22
Illinois Central Corporation, 11
International Shipholding Corporation, Inc.,
    27
J.B. Hunt Transport Services Inc., 12
John Menzies plc, 39
Kansas City Southern Industries, Inc., 6; 26
    (upd.)
Kawasaki Kisen Kaisha, Ltd., V
Keio Teito Electric Railway Company, V
Kinki Nippon Railway Company Ltd., V
Kirby Corporation, 18
Koninklijke Nedlloyd Groep N.V., 6
Kuhne & Nagel International A.G., V
La Poste, V; 47 (upd.)
Leaseway Transportation Corp., 12
London Regional Transport, 6
Maine Central Railroad Company, 16
Mammoet Transport B.V., 26
Mayflower Group Inc., 6
Mercury Air Group, Inc., 20
The Mersey Docks and Harbour Company,
    30
Metropolitan Transportation Authority, 35
Miller Industries, Inc., 26
Mitsui O.S.K. Lines, Ltd., V
Moran Towing Corporation, Inc., 15
The Morgan Group, Inc., 46
Morris Travel Services L.L.C., 26
Motor Cargo Industries, Inc., 35
National Car Rental System, Inc., 10
National Railroad Passenger Corporation,
    22
Neptune Orient Lines Limited, 47
NFC plc, 6
Nippon Express Co., Ltd., V
Nippon Yusen Kabushiki Kaisha, V
Norfolk Southern Corporation, V; 29 (upd.)
Ocean Group plc, 6
Odakyu Electric Railway Company
    Limited, V
Oglebay Norton Company, 17
Österreichische Bundesbahnen GmbH, 6
OTR Express, Inc., 25
Overnite Transportation Co., 14
Overseas Shipholding Group, Inc., 11
The Peninsular and Oriental Steam
    Navigation Company, V; 38 (upd.)
Penske Corporation, V
PHH Corporation, V
The Port Authority of New York and New
    Jersey, 48
Post Office Group, V
Preston Corporation, 6
RailTex, Inc., 20
Roadway Express, Inc., 25 (upd.)
Roadway Services, Inc., V
Royal Vopak NV, 41
Ryder System, Inc., V; 24 (upd.)
Santa Fe Pacific Corporation, V

Schenker-Rhenus AG, 6
Schneider National, Inc., 36
Securicor Plc, 45
Seibu Railway Co. Ltd., V
Seino Transportation Company, Ltd., 6
Simon Transportation Services Inc., 27
Smithway Motor Xpress Corporation, 39
Société Nationale des Chemins de Fer
    Français, V
Southern Pacific Transportation Company,
    V
Stagecoach Holdings plc, 30
Stevedoring Services of America Inc., 28
Stinnes AG, 8
Stolt-Nielsen S.A., 42
Sunoco, Inc., 28 (upd.)
Swift Transportation Co., Inc., 42
The Swiss Federal Railways
    (Schweizerische Bundesbahnen), V
Teekay Shipping Corporation, 25
Tibbett & Britten Group plc, 32
Tidewater Inc., 11; 37 (upd.)
TNT Freightways Corporation, 14
TNT Post Group N.V., V; 27 (upd.); 30
    (upd.)
Tobu Railway Co Ltd, 6
Tokyu Corporation, V
Totem Resources Corporation, 9
Trailer Bridge, Inc., 41
Transnet Ltd., 6
Transport Corporation of America, Inc., 49
TTX Company, 6
U.S. Delivery Systems, Inc., 22
Union Pacific Corporation, V; 28 (upd.)
United Parcel Service of America Inc., V;
    17 (upd.)
United States Postal Service, 14; 34 (upd.)
USA Truck, Inc., 42
Velocity Express Corporation, 49
Werner Enterprises, Inc., 26
Wisconsin Central Transportation
    Corporation, 24
Yamato Transport Co. Ltd., V; 49 (upd.)
Yellow Corporation, 14; 45 (upd.)
Yellow Freight System, Inc. of Delaware,
    V

UTILITIES

The AES Corporation, 10; 13 (upd.)
Aggreko Plc, 45
Air & Water Technologies Corporation, 6
Alberta Energy Company Ltd., 16; 43
    (upd.)
Allegheny Energy, Inc., 38 (upd.)
Allegheny Power System, Inc., V
American Electric Power Company, Inc.,
    V; 45 (upd.)
American States Water Company, 46
American Water Works Company, Inc., 6;
    38 (upd.)
Arkla, Inc., V
Associated Natural Gas Corporation, 11
Atlanta Gas Light Company, 6; 23 (upd.)
Atlantic Energy, Inc., 6
Atmos Energy Corporation, 43
Baltimore Gas and Electric Company, V;
    25 (upd.)
Bay State Gas Company, 38
Bayernwerk AG, V; 23 (upd.)
Bewag AG, 39
Big Rivers Electric Corporation, 11
Black Hills Corporation, 20
Boston Edison Company, 12
Bouygues S.A., 24 (upd.)
British Energy Plc, 49
British Gas plc, V
British Nuclear Fuels plc, 6

Brooklyn Union Gas, 6
Calpine Corporation, 36
Canadian Utilities Limited, 13
Cap Rock Energy Corporation, 46
Carolina Power & Light Company, V; 23
    (upd.)
Cascade Natural Gas Corporation, 9
Centerior Energy Corporation, V
Central and South West Corporation, V
Central Hudson Gas and Electricity
    Corporation, 6
Central Maine Power, 6
Centrica plc, 29 (upd.)
Chubu Electric Power Company, Inc., V;
    46 (upd.)
Chugoku Electric Power Company Inc., V
Cincinnati Gas & Electric Company, 6
CIPSCO Inc., 6
Citizens Utilities Company, 7
City Public Service, 6
Cleco Corporation, 37
CMS Energy Corporation, V, 14
The Coastal Corporation, 31 (upd.)
Cogentrix Energy, Inc., 10
The Coleman Company, Inc., 9
The Columbia Gas System, Inc., V; 16
    (upd.)
Commonwealth Edison Company, V
Commonwealth Energy System, 14
Connecticut Light and Power Co., 13
Consolidated Edison, Inc., V; 45 (upd.)
Consolidated Natural Gas Company, V; 19
    (upd.)
Consumers Power Co., 14
Consumers Water Company, 14
Consumers' Gas Company Ltd., 6
Destec Energy, Inc., 12
The Detroit Edison Company, V
Dominion Resources, Inc., V
DPL Inc., 6
DQE, Inc., 6
DTE Energy Company, 20 (upd.)
Duke Energy Corporation, V; 27 (upd.)
Eastern Enterprises, 6
El Paso Electric Company, 21
El Paso Natural Gas Company, 12
Electricidade de Portugal, S.A., 47
Électricité de France, V; 41 (upd.)
Elektrowatt AG, 6
Enbridge Inc., 43
ENDESA Group, V
ENDESA S.A., 46 (upd.)
Enron Corporation, V; 46 (upd.)
Enserch Corporation, V
Ente Nazionale per L'Energia Elettrica, V
Entergy Corporation, V; 45 (upd.)
Equitable Resources, Inc., 6
Exelon Corporation, 48 (upd.)
Florida Progress Corporation, V; 23 (upd.)
Fortis, Inc., 15; 47 (upd.)
Fortum Corporation, 30 (upd.)
FPL Group, Inc., V; 49 (upd.)
Gaz de France, V; 40 (upd.)
General Public Utilities Corporation, V
Générale des Eaux Group, V
GPU, Inc., 27 (upd.)
Gulf States Utilities Company, 6
Hawaiian Electric Industries, Inc., 9
Hokkaido Electric Power Company Inc., V
Hokuriku Electric Power Company, V
Hongkong Electric Holdings Ltd., 6; 23
    (upd.)
Houston Industries Incorporated, V
Hyder plc, 34
Hydro-Québec, 6; 32 (upd.)
Iberdrola, S.A., 49
Idaho Power Company, 12
Illinois Bell Telephone Company, 14

Illinois Power Company, 6
Indiana Energy, Inc., 27
IPALCO Enterprises, Inc., 6
The Kansai Electric Power Co., Inc., V
Kansas City Power & Light Company, 6
Kelda Group plc, 45
Kenetech Corporation, 11
Kentucky Utilities Company, 6
KeySpan Energy Co., 27
KU Energy Corporation, 11
Kyushu Electric Power Company Inc., V
LG&E Energy Corporation, 6
Long Island Lighting Company, V
Lyonnaise des Eaux-Dumez, V
Madison Gas and Electric Company, 39
Magma Power Company, 11
MCN Corporation, 6
MDU Resources Group, Inc., 7; 42 (upd.)
Middlesex Water Company, 45
Midwest Resources Inc., 6
Minnesota Power, Inc., 11; 34 (upd.)
The Montana Power Company, 11; 44
  (upd.)
National Fuel Gas Company, 6
National Power PLC, 12
Nebraska Public Power District, 29
N.V. Nederlandse Gasunie, V
Nevada Power Company, 11
New England Electric System, V
New York State Electric and Gas, 6
Niagara Mohawk Holdings Inc., V; 45
  (upd.)
NICOR Inc., 6
NIPSCO Industries, Inc., 6
North West Water Group plc, 11
Northeast Utilities, V; 48 (upd.)
Northern States Power Company, V; 20
  (upd.)
Northwest Natural Gas Company, 45
NorthWestern Corporation, 37
Nova Corporation of Alberta, V
Oglethorpe Power Corporation, 6
Ohio Edison Company, V
Oklahoma Gas and Electric Company, 6
ONEOK Inc., 7
Ontario Hydro Services Company, 6; 32
  (upd.)
Osaka Gas Co., Ltd., V
Otter Tail Power Company, 18
Pacific Enterprises, V
Pacific Gas and Electric Company, V
PacifiCorp, V; 26 (upd.)
Panhandle Eastern Corporation, V
PECO Energy Company, 11
Pennon Group Plc, 45
Pennsylvania Power & Light Company, V
Peoples Energy Corporation, 6
PG&E Corporation, 26 (upd.)
Philadelphia Electric Company, V
Philadelphia Suburban Corporation, 39
Piedmont Natural Gas Company, Inc., 27
Pinnacle West Capital Corporation, 6
Portland General Corporation, 6
Potomac Electric Power Company, 6
PowerGen PLC, 11
PPL Corporation, 41 (upd.)
PreussenElektra Aktiengesellschaft, V
PSI Resources, 6
Public Service Company of Colorado, 6
Public Service Company of New
  Hampshire, 21
Public Service Company of New Mexico, 6
Public Service Enterprise Group Inc., V;
  44 (upd.)
Puerto Rico Electric Power Authority, 47
Puget Sound Power and Light Company, 6
Questar Corporation, 6; 26 (upd.)
RAO Unified Energy System of Russia, 45

Reliant Energy Inc., 44 (upd.)
Rochester Gas and Electric Corporation, 6
Ruhrgas AG, V; 38 (upd.)
RWE Group, V
Salt River Project, 19
San Diego Gas & Electric Company, V
SCANA Corporation, 6
Scarborough Public Utilities Commission,
  9
SCEcorp, V
Scottish Hydro-Electric PLC, 13
Scottish Power plc, 49 (upd.)
ScottishPower plc, 19
SEMCO Energy, Inc., 44
Sempra Energy, 25 (upd.)
Severn Trent PLC, 12; 38 (upd.)
Shikoku Electric Power Company, Inc., V
Sonat, Inc., 6
South Jersey Industries, Inc., 42
The Southern Company, V; 38 (upd.)
Southern Electric PLC, 13
Southern Indiana Gas and Electric
  Company, 13
Southern Union Company, 27
Southwest Gas Corporation, 19
Southwest Water Company, 47
Southwestern Electric Power Co., 21
Southwestern Public Service Company, 6
Suez Lyonnaise des Eaux, 36 (upd.)
TECO Energy, Inc., 6
Texas Utilities Company, V; 25 (upd.)
Thames Water plc, 11
Tohoku Electric Power Company, Inc., V
The Tokyo Electric Power Company,
  Incorporated, V
Tokyo Gas Co., Ltd., V
TransAlta Utilities Corporation, 6
TransCanada PipeLines Limited, V
Transco Energy Company, V
Trigen Energy Corporation, 42
Tucson Electric Power Company, 6
UGI Corporation, 12
Unicom Corporation, 29 (upd.)
Union Electric Company, V
The United Illuminating Company, 21
United Water Resources, Inc., 40
Unitil Corporation, 37
Utah Power and Light Company, 27
UtiliCorp United Inc., 6
Vereinigte Elektrizitätswerke Westfalen
  AG, V
VEW AG, 39
Washington Gas Light Company, 19
Washington Natural Gas Company, 9
Washington Water Power Company, 6
Western Resources, Inc., 12
Wheelabrator Technologies, Inc., 6
Wisconsin Energy Corporation, 6
Wisconsin Public Service Corporation, 9
WPL Holdings, Inc., 6

WASTE SERVICES

Allwaste, Inc., 18
Appliance Recycling Centers of America,
  Inc., 42
Azcon Corporation, 23
Brambles Industries Limited, 42
Browning-Ferris Industries, Inc., V; 20
  (upd.)
Chemical Waste Management, Inc., 9
Copart Inc., 23
Ecology and Environment, Inc., 39
Industrial Services of America, Inc., 46
ISS A/S, 49
Kelda Group plc, 45
Pennon Group Plc, 45
Philip Environmental Inc., 16

Roto-Rooter Corp., 15
Safety-Kleen Corp., 8
Sevenson Environmental Services, Inc., 42
Severn Trent PLC, 38 (upd.)
Shanks Group plc, 45
Stericycle Inc., 33
TRC Companies, Inc., 32
Veit Companies, 43
Waste Connections, Inc., 46
Waste Holdings, Inc., 41
Waste Management, Inc., V
WMX Technologies Inc., 17

GEOGRAPHIC INDEX

Geographic Index

Algeria

Entreprise Nationale Sonatrach, IV

Argentina

Aerolíneas Argentinas S.A., 33
YPF Sociedad Anonima, IV

Australia

Amcor Limited, IV; 19 (upd.)
Australia and New Zealand Banking Group Ltd., II
Billabong International Ltd., 44
Bond Corporation Holdings Limited, 10
Boral Limited, III; 43 (upd.)
Brambles Industries Limited, 42
Broken Hill Proprietary Company Ltd., IV; 22 (upd.)
Carlton and United Breweries Ltd., I
Coles Myer Ltd., V; 20 (upd.)
CRA Limited, IV
CSR Limited, III; 28 (upd.)
Elders IXL Ltd., I
Foster's Brewing Group Ltd., 7; 21 (upd.)
John Fairfax Holdings Limited, 7
Lend Lease Corporation Limited, IV; 17 (upd.)
News Corporation Limited, IV; 7 (upd.); 46 (upd.)
Pacific Dunlop Limited, 10
Pioneer International Limited, III
Qantas Airways Limited, 6; 24 (upd.)
TABCORP Holdings Limited, 44
Telecom Australia, 6
Westpac Banking Corporation, II; 48 (upd.)
WMC, Limited, 43

Austria

Austrian Airlines AG (Österreichische Luftverkehrs AG), 33
Bank Austria AG, 23
BBAG Osterreichische Brau-Beteiligungs-AG, 38
Gericom AG, 47
Glock Ges.m.b.H., 42
Lauda Air Luftfahrt AG, 48
ÖMV Aktiengesellschaft, IV
Österreichische Bundesbahnen GmbH, 6
Österreichische Post- und Telegraphenverwaltung, V
VA TECH ELIN EBG GmbH, 49
Voest-Alpine Stahl AG, IV

Bahamas

Sun International Hotels Limited, 26
Teekay Shipping Corporation, 25

Bangladesh

Grameen Bank, 31

Belgium

Almanij NV, 44
Bank Brussels Lambert, II
Barco NV, 44
Belgacom, 6
C&A, 40 (upd.)
Cockerill Sambre Group, IV; 26 (upd.)
Delhaize "Le Lion" S.A., 44
Generale Bank, II
GIB Group, V; 26 (upd.)
Interbrew S.A., 17
Kredietbank N.V., II
PetroFina S.A., IV; 26 (upd.)
Roularta Media Group NV, 48
Sabena S.A./N.V., 33
Solvay & Cie S.A., I; 21 (upd.)
Tractebel S.A., 20
NV Umicore SA, 47
Xeikon NV, 26

Bermuda

Bacardi Limited, 18
Frontline Ltd., 45
Jardine Matheson Holdings Limited, I; 20 (upd.)
Sea Containers Ltd., 29
Tyco International Ltd., III; 28 (upd.)
White Mountains Insurance Group, Ltd., 48

Brazil

Banco Bradesco S.A., 13
Banco Itaú S.A., 19
Companhia Vale do Rio Doce, IV; 43 (upd.)
Empresa Brasileira de Aeronáutica S.A. (Embraer), 36
Lojas Arapua S.A., 22
Petróleo Brasileiro S.A., IV
TransBrasil S/A Linhas Aéreas, 31
VARIG S.A. (Viaçâo Aérea Rio-Grandense), 6; 29 (upd.)

Canada

Abitibi-Consolidated, Inc., V; 25 (upd.)
Abitibi-Price Inc., IV
Air Canada, 6; 23 (upd.)
Alberta Energy Company Ltd., 16; 43 (upd.)
Alcan Aluminium Limited, IV; 31 (upd.)
Algo Group Inc., 24
Alliance Atlantis Communications Inc., 39
Bank of Montreal, II; 46 (upd.)
Bank of Nova Scotia, The, II
Barrick Gold Corporation, 34
BCE Inc., V; 44 (upd.)
Bell Canada, 6
BFC Construction Corporation, 25
Biovail Corporation, 47
Bombardier Inc., 42 (upd.)
Bramalea Ltd., 9
British Columbia Telephone Company, 6
Campeau Corporation, V
Canada Packers Inc., II
Canadair, Inc., 16
Canadian Broadcasting Corporation (CBC), The, 37
Canadian Imperial Bank of Commerce, II
Canadian National Railway System, 6
Canadian Pacific Railway Limited, V; 45 (upd.)
Canadian Utilities Limited, 13
Canfor Corporation, 42
Canstar Sports Inc., 16
CanWest Global Communications Corporation, 35
Cinar Corporation, 40
Cineplex Odeon Corporation, 6; 23 (upd.)
Cinram International, Inc., 43
Cirque du Soleil Inc., 29
Clearly Canadian Beverage Corporation, 48
Cognos Inc., 44
Cominco Ltd., 37
Consumers' Gas Company Ltd., 6
CoolBrands International Inc., 35
Corby Distilleries Limited, 14
Corel Corporation, 15; 33 (upd.)
Creo Inc., 48
Discreet Logic Inc., 20
Dofasco Inc., IV; 24 (upd.)
Dominion Textile Inc., 12
Domtar Inc., IV
Dylex Limited, 29
Echo Bay Mines Ltd., IV; 38 (upd.)
Enbridge Inc., 43
Extendicare Health Services, Inc., 6
Falconbridge Limited, 49
Fortis, Inc., 15; 47 (upd.)
Four Seasons Hotels Inc., 9; 29 (upd.)
GEAC Computer Corporation Ltd., 43
George Weston Limited, II; 36 (upd.)
Great-West Lifeco Inc., III
Groupe Vidéotron Ltée., 20
Hemlo Gold Mines Inc., 9
Hiram Walker Resources, Ltd., I
Hockey Company, The, 34
Hudson Bay Mining and Smelting Company, Limited, The, 12
Hudson's Bay Company, V; 25 (upd.)
Husky Energy Inc., 47
Hydro-Québec, 6; 32 (upd.)
Imasco Limited, V
Imax Corporation, 28
Imperial Oil Limited, IV; 25 (upd.)
Inco Limited, IV; 45 (upd.)
Intrawest Corporation, The, 15
Irwin Toy Limited, 14
Jean Coutu Group (PJC) Inc., The, 46
Jim Pattison Group, The, 37
Kinross Gold Corporation, 36
Kruger Inc., 17
Labatt Brewing Company Limited, I; 25 (upd.)
Ledcor Industries Limited, 46
Linamar Corporation, 18
Lions Gate Entertainment Corporation, 35
Loblaw Companies Limited, 43
Loewen Group, Inc., The, 16; 40 (upd.)
London Drugs Ltd., 46

Canada (continued)

Maclean Hunter Publishing Limited, IV; 26
  (upd.)
MacMillan Bloedel Limited, IV
Magellan Aerospace Corporation, 48
Maple Leaf Foods Inc., 41
Methanex Corporation, 40
Mitel Corporation, 18
Molson Companies Limited, The, I; 26
  (upd.)
Moore Corporation Limited, IV
Mouvement des Caisses Desjardins, 48
National Sea Products Ltd., 14
Noranda Inc., IV; 7 (upd.)
Nortel Networks Corporation, 36 (upd.)
North West Company, Inc., The, 12
Northern Telecom Limited, V
Nova Corporation of Alberta, V
Novacor Chemicals Ltd., 12
Olympia & York Developments Ltd., IV; 9
  (upd.)
Onex Corporation, 16
Ontario Hydro Services Company, 6; 32
  (upd.)
Oshawa Group Limited, The, II
Petro-Canada Limited, IV
Philip Environmental Inc., 16
Placer Dome Inc., 20
Potash Corporation of Saskatchewan Inc.,
  18
Power Corporation of Canada, 36 (upd.)
Provigo Inc., II
Quebecor Inc., 12; 47 (upd.)
Ritchie Bros. Auctioneers Inc., 41
Rogers Communications Inc., 30 (upd.)
Roots Canada Ltd., 42
Royal Bank of Canada, The, II; 21 (upd.)
Scarborough Public Utilities Commission,
  9
Seagram Company Ltd., The, I; 25 (upd.)
Shoppers Drug Mart Corporation, 49
Southam Inc., 7
Spar Aerospace Limited, 32
Steinberg Incorporated, II
Stelco Inc., IV
Talisman Energy Inc., 9; 47 (upd.)
TDL Group Ltd., 46
Teck Corporation, 27
Thomson Corporation, The, 8; 34 (upd.)
Toromont Industries, Ltd., 21
Toronto-Dominion Bank, The, II; 49 (upd.)
Torstar Corporation, 29
TransAlta Utilities Corporation, 6
TransCanada PipeLines Limited, V
Tridel Enterprises Inc., 9
Trilon Financial Corporation, II
Triple Five Group Ltd., 49
Trizec Corporation Ltd., 10
Van Houtte Inc., 39
Varity Corporation, III
Wascana Energy Inc., 13
West Fraser Timber Co. Ltd., 17
WestJet Airlines Ltd., 38

Chile

Corporacion Nacional del Cobre de Chile,
  40
Lan Chile S.A., 31
Viña Concha y Toro S.A., 45

China

Air China, 46
Asia Info Holdings, Inc., 43
China Eastern Airlines Co. Ltd., 31
China National Petroleum Corporation, 46
China Southern Airlines Company Ltd., 33
Chinese Petroleum Corporation, IV; 31
  (upd.)
Directorate General of
  Telecommunications, 7
Guangzhou Pearl River Piano Group Ltd.,
  49
Hongkong and Shanghai Banking
  Corporation Limited, The, II
Shanghai Petrochemical Co., Ltd., 18
Tsingtao Brewery Group, 49

Colombia

Avianca Aerovías Nacionales de Colombia
  SA, 36
Empresa Colombiana de Petróleos, IV

Czech Republic

Skoda Auto a.s., 39

Denmark

Arla Foods amba, 48
Bang & Olufsen Holding A/S, 37
Carlsberg A/S, 9; 29 (upd.)
Danisco A/S, 44
Group 4 Falck A/S, 42
H. Lundbeck A/S, 44
IKEA International A/S, V; 26 (upd.)
ISS A/S, 49
Lego A/S, 13; 40 (upd.)
Novo Industri A/S, I
Sophus Berendsen A/S, 49

Ecuador

Petróleos del Ecuador, IV

Egypt

EgyptAir, 6; 27 (upd.)
Egyptian General Petroluem Corporation,
  IV

El Salvador

Grupo TACA, 38

Finland

Amer Group plc, 41
Enso-Gutzeit Oy, IV
Finnair Oy, 6; 25 (upd.)
Fiskars Corporation, 33
Fortum Corporation, 30 (upd.)
Hackman Oyj Adp, 44
Kansallis-Osake-Pankki, II
Kesko Ltd. (Kesko Oy), 8; 27 (upd.)
Kone Corporation, 27
Kymmene Corporation, IV
Metsa-Serla Oy, IV
Metso Corporation, 30 (upd.)
Neste Oy, IV
Nokia Corporation, II; 17 (upd.); 38 (upd.)
Outokumpu Oyj, 38
Posti- ja Telelaitos, 6
Stora Enso Oyj, 36 (upd.)
United Paper Mills Ltd. (Yhtyneet
  Paperitehtaat Oy), IV
UPM-Kymmene Corporation, 19
Valmet Corporation (Valmet Oy), III

France

Accor SA, 10; 27 (upd.)
Aéroports de Paris, 33
Aerospatiale Group, The, 7; 21 (upd.)
Agence France-Presse, 34
Alcatel Alsthom Compagnie Générale
  d'Electricité, 9
Alcatel S.A., 36 (upd.)
Association des Centres Distributeurs E.
  Leclerc, 37
Atochem S.A., I
Au Printemps S.A., V
Auchan, 37
Automobiles Citroen, 7
Avions Marcel Dassault-Breguet Aviation,
  I
Axa, III
Baccarat, 24
Banque Nationale de Paris S.A., II
Baron Philippe de Rothschild S.A., 39
Bayard SA, 49
Besnier SA, 19
BNP Paribas Group, 36 (upd.)
Bongrain SA, 25
Bouygues S.A., I; 24 (upd.)
BSN Groupe S.A., II
Bull S.A., 43 (upd.)
Burelle S.A., 23
Business Objects S.A., 25
Canal Plus, 10; 34 (upd.)
Cap Gemini Ernst & Young, 37
Carbone Lorraine S.A., 33
Carrefour SA, 10; 27 (upd.)
Cetelem S.A., 21
Chanel, 12
Chanel SA, 49 (upd.)
Chargeurs International, 6; 21 (upd.)
Christian Dalloz SA, 40
Christian Dior S.A., 19; 49 (upd.)
Christofle SA, 40
Ciments Français, 40
Club Mediterranée S.A., 6; 21 (upd.)
Coflexip S.A., 25
Colas S.A., 31
Compagnie de Saint-Gobain S.A., III; 16
  (upd.)
Compagnie des Alpes, 48
Compagnie des Machines Bull S.A., III
Compagnie Financiere de Paribas, II
Compagnie Générale d'Électricité, II
Compagnie Générale des Établissements
  Michelin, V; 42 (upd.)
Compagnie Générale Maritime et
  Financière, 6
Comptoirs Modernes S.A., 19
Crédit Agricole, II
Crédit Lyonnais, 9; 33 (upd.)
Crédit National S.A., 9
Darty S.A., 27
Dassault Systèmes S.A., 25
De Dietrich & Cie., 31
Deveaux S.A., 41
Dexia Group, 42
Du Pareil au Même, 43
ECS S.A., 12
Eiffage, 27
Electricité de France, V; 41 (upd.)
Elf Aquitaine SA, 21 (upd.)
Elior SA, 49
Eridania Béghin-Say S.A., 36
Essilor International, 21
Etablissements Economiques du Casino
  Guichard, Perrachon et Cie, S.C.A., 12
Etam Developpement SA, 44
Euro Disneyland SCA, 20
Euro RSCG Worldwide S.A., 13
Euronext Paris S.A., 37
Expand SA, 48
Facom S.A., 32
Faiveley S.A., 39
Fimalac S.A., 37
Fleury Michon S.A., 39
FNAC, 21
Framatome SA, 19
France Télécom Group, V; 21 (upd.)
Fromageries Bel, 23

G.I.E. Airbus Industrie, I; 12 (upd.)
Galeries Lafayette S.A., V; 23 (upd.)
Gaumont SA, 25
Gaz de France, V; 40 (upd.)
Gecina SA, 42
Générale des Eaux Group, V
GFI Informatique SA, 49
GrandVision S.A., 43
Groupe Air France, 6
Groupe André, 17
Groupe Castorama-Dubois Investissements, 23
Groupe Danone, 32 (upd.)
Groupe Dassault Aviation SA, 26 (upd.)
Groupe de la Cite, IV
Groupe DMC (Dollfus Mieg & Cie), 27
Groupe Fournier SA, 44
Groupe Go Sport S.A., 39
Groupe Guillin SA, 40
Groupe Jean-Claude Darmon, 44
Groupe Lapeyre S.A., 33
Groupe Legris Industries, 23
Groupe Les Echos, 25
Groupe Partouche SA, 48
Groupe Promodès S.A., 19
Groupe Rougier SA, 21
Groupe SEB, 35
Groupe Sidel S.A., 21
Groupe Yves Saint Laurent, 23
Groupe Zannier S.A., 35
Guerbet Group, 46
Guerlain, 23
Guilbert S.A., 42
Guillemot Corporation, 41
Guy Degrenne SA, 44
Guyenne et Gascogne, 23
Hachette, IV
Hachette Filipacchi Medias S.A., 21
Havas, SA, 10; 33 (upd.)
Hermès International S.A., 14; 34 (upd.)
Imerys S.A., 40 (upd.)
Imetal S.A., IV
Infogrames Entertainment S.A., 35
Ingenico—Compagnie Industrielle et Financière d'Ingénierie, 46
ITM Entreprises SA, 36
L'Air Liquide SA, I; 47 (upd.)
L'Entreprise Jean Lefebvre, 23
L'Oreal, III; 8 (upd.)
L'Oréal SA, 46 (upd.)
La Poste, V; 47 (upd.)
Laboratoires de Biologie Végétale Yves Rocher, 35
Lafarge Coppée S.A., III
Lafuma S.A., 39
Laurent-Perrier SA, 42
Lazard LLC, 38
Le Monde S.A., 33
Legrand SA, 21
Louis Vuitton, 10
LVMH Möet Hennessy Louis Vuitton SA, 33 (upd.)
Lyonnaise des Eaux-Dumez, V
Maison Louis Jadot, 24
Manitou BF S.A., 27
Marie Brizard & Roger International S.A., 22
Matra-Hachette S.A., 15 (upd.)
Metaleurop S.A., 21
Métropole Télévision, 33
Moët-Hennessy, I
Moulinex S.A., 22
Mr. Bricolage S.A., 37
Naf Naf SA, 44
Papeteries de Lancey, 23
Pathé SA, 29
Pechiney SA, IV; 45 (upd.)
Penauille Polyservices SA, 49

Pernod Ricard S.A., I; 21 (upd.)
Peugeot S.A., I
Pierre & Vacances SA, 48
Pinault-Printemps Redoute S.A., 19 (upd.)
Poliet S.A., 33
PSA Peugeot Citroen S.A., 28 (upd.)
Publicis S.A., 19
Regie Nationale des Usines Renault, I
Rémy Cointreau S.A., 20
Renault S.A., 26 (upd.)
Rhodia SA, 38
Rhône-Poulenc S.A., I; 10 (upd.)
Robertet SA, 39
Roussel Uclaf, I; 8 (upd.)
Royal Canin S.A., 39
Sabaté Diosos SA, 48
SAGEM S.A., 37
Salomon Worldwide, 20
Sanofi Group, I
Sanofi-Synthélabo Group, The, 49 (upd.)
Schneider S.A., II; 18 (upd.)
SCOR S.A., 20
Seita, 23
Simco S.A., 37
Skis Rossignol S.A., 15; 43 (upd.)
Snecma Group, 46
Société Air France, 27 (upd.)
Société du Louvre, 27
Société Générale, II; 42 (upd.)
Société Nationale des Chemins de Fer Français, V
Société Nationale Elf Aquitaine, IV; 7 (upd.)
Sodexho Alliance SA, 29
Sodiaal S.A., 36 (upd.)
SODIMA, II
Sommer-Allibert S.A., 19
Steria SA, 49
Suez Lyonnaise des Eaux, 36 (upd.)
Taittinger S.A., 43
Tati SA, 25
Télévision Française 1, 23
Thales S.A., 42
THOMSON multimedia S.A., II; 42 (upd.)
TOTAL S.A., IV; 24 (upd.)
Transiciel SA, 48
Ubi Soft Entertainment S.A., 41
Ugine S.A., 20
Unibail SA, 40
Unilog SA, 42
Union des Assurances de Pans, III
Usinor S.A., 42 (upd.)
Usinor Sacilor, IV
Valeo, 23
Vinci, 43
Vivendi Universal S.A., 46 (upd.)
Worms et Cie, 27
Zodiac S.A., 36

Germany

Adam Opel AG, 7; 21 (upd.)
Adidas AG, 14
adidas-Salomon AG, 33 (upd.)
Adolf Würth GmbH & Co. KG, 49
AEG A.G., I
Aldi Group, 13
Allianz Aktiengesellschaft Holding, III; 15 (upd.)
Andreas Stihl, 16
ARD, 41
AVA AG (Allgemeine Handelsgesellschaft der Verbraucher AG), 33
AXA Colonia Konzern AG, 27; 49 (upd.)
Axel Springer Verlag AG, IV; 20 (upd.)
Bahlsen GmbH & Co. KG, 44
Barmag AG, 39
BASF Aktiengesellschaft, I; 18 (upd.)

Bauer Publishing Group, 7
Bayer A.G., I; 13 (upd.); 41 (upd.)
Bayerische Hypotheken- und Wechsel-Bank AG, II
Bayerische Motoren Werke AG, I; 11 (upd.); 38 (upd.)
Bayerische Vereinsbank A.G., II
Bayernwerk AG, V; 23 (upd.)
Beiersdorf AG, 29
Bertelsmann A.G., IV; 15 (upd.); 43 (upd.)
Bewag AG, 39
Bilfinger & Berger Bau A.G., I
Brauerei Beck & Co., 9; 33 (upd.)
Brenntag AG, 8; 23 (upd.)
Buderus AG, 37
Burda Holding GmbH. & Co., 23
C&A Brenninkmeyer KG, V
C.H. Boehringer Sohn, 39
Carl-Zeiss-Stiftung, III; 34 (upd.)
Commerzbank A.G., II; 47 (upd.)
Continental Aktiengesellschaft, V
Daimler-Benz A.G., I; 15 (upd.)
Daimler-Benz Aerospace AG, 16
DaimlerChrysler AG, 34 (upd.)
Degussa Group, IV
Degussa-Huls AG, 32 (upd.)
Deutsche Babcock A.G., III
Deutsche Bahn AG, 46 (upd.)
Deutsche Bank A.G., II; 14 (upd.); 40 (upd.)
Deutsche BP Aktiengesellschaft, 7
Deutsche Bundesbahn, V
Deutsche Bundespost TELEKOM, V
Deutsche Lufthansa Aktiengesellschaft, I; 26 (upd.)
Deutsche Post AG, 29
Deutsche Telekom AG, 48 (upd.)
Deutz AG, 39
Dresdner Bank A.G., II
Dürr AG, 44
Dyckerhoff AG, 35
Edeka Zentrale A.G., II; 47 (upd.)
edel music AG, 44
ERGO Versicherungsgruppe AG, 44
Esselte Leitz GmbH & Co. KG, 48
Fairchild Dornier GmbH, 48 (upd.)
Feldmuhle Nobel A.G., III
Fielmann AG, 31
Freudenberg & Co., 41
Fried. Krupp GmbH, IV
GEA AG, 27
GEHE AG, 27
geobra Brandstätter GmbH & Co. KG, 48
Gerresheimer Glas AG, 43
GfK Aktiengesellschaft, 49
Grundig AG, 27
Hapag-Lloyd AG, 6
HARIBO GmbH & Co. KG, 44
Heidelberger Druckmaschinen AG, 40
Heidelberger Zement AG, 31
Henkel KGaA, III; 34 (upd.)
Heraeus Holding GmbH, IV
Hertie Waren- und Kaufhaus GmbH, V
Hochtief AG, 33
Hoechst A.G., I; 18 (upd.)
Hoesch AG, IV
Hugo Boss AG, 48
Huls A.G., I
J.M. Voith AG, 33
Jenoptik AG, 33
Kamps AG, 44
Karlsberg Brauerei GmbH & Co KG, 41
Karstadt Aktiengesellschaft, V; 19 (upd.)
Kaufhof Holding AG, V
Kaufhof Warenhaus AG, 23 (upd.)
Kaufring AG, 35
KHD Konzern, III
Klockner-Werke AG, IV

Germany (*continued*)

König Brauerei GmbH & Co. KG, 35 (upd.)
Kreditanstalt für Wiederaufbau, 29
Leica Camera AG, 35
Leica Microsystems Holdings GmbH, 35
Linde A.G., I
LTU Group Holding GmbH, 37
MAN Aktiengesellschaft, III
Mannesmann AG, III; 14 (upd.); 38 (upd.)
Margarete Steiff GmbH, 23
Messerschmitt-Bölkow-Blohm GmbH., I
Metallgesellschaft AG, IV; 16 (upd.)
MITROPA AG, 37
Munich Re (Münchener Rückversicherungs-Gesellschaft Aktiengesellschaft in München), III; 46 (upd.)
Nixdorf Computer AG, III
Optische Werke G. Rodenstock, 44
Otto Versand GmbH & Co., V; 15 (upd.); 34 (upd.)
Paulaner Brauerei GmbH & Co. KG, 35
Peek & Cloppenburg KG, 46
Philipp Holzmann AG, 17
Porsche AG, 13; 31 (upd.)
Preussag AG, 17; 42 (upd.)
PreussenElektra Aktiengesellschaft, V
Puma AG Rudolf Dassler Sport, 35
PWA Group, IV
Qiagen N.V., 39
Quelle Group, V
RAG AG, 35
RENK AG, 37
Rheinmetall Berlin AG, 9
Robert Bosch GmbH, I; 16 (upd.); 43 (upd.)
Rohde & Schwarz GmbH & Co. KG, 39
Roland Berger & Partner GmbH, 37
Ruhrgas AG, V; 38 (upd.)
Ruhrkohle AG, IV
RWE Group, V
Saarberg-Konzern, IV
Salzgitter AG, IV
SAP AG, 16; 43 (upd.)
Schenker-Rhenus AG, 6
Schering AG, I
Siemens A.G., II; 14 (upd.)
Sixt AG, 39
SPAR Handels AG, 35
SPIEGEL-Verlag Rudolf Augstein GmbH & Co. KG, 44
Stinnes AG, 8; 23 (upd.)
Südzucker AG, 27
TA Triumph-Adler AG, 48
Tarkett Sommer AG, 25
TaurusHolding GmbH & Co. KG, 46
Tengelmann Group, 27
Thyssen Krupp AG, IV; 28 (upd.)
Touristik Union International GmbH. and Company K.G., II
TUI Group GmbH, 44
Vaillant GmbH, 44
Varta AG, 23
Veba A.G., I; 15 (upd.)
Vereinigte Elektrizitätswerke Westfalen AG, V
Verlagsgruppe Georg von Holtzbrinck GmbH, 35
VEW AG, 39
Victoria Group, 44 (upd.)
VICTORIA Holding AG, III
Viessmann Werke GmbH & Co., 37
Villeroy & Boch AG, 37
Volkswagen Aktiengesellschaft, I; 11 (upd.); 32 (upd.)

Vorwerk & Co., 27
Wacker-Chemie GmbH, 35
Wella AG, 48 (upd.)
Wella Group, III
Weru Aktiengesellschaft, 18
Westdeutsche Landesbank Girozentrale, II; 46 (upd.)
ZF Friedrichshafen AG, 48

Ghana

Ashanti Goldfields Company Limited, 43

Greece

National Bank of Greece, 41

Hong Kong

Cable & Wireless HKT, 30 (upd.)
Cathay Pacific Airways Limited, 6; 34 (upd.)
Cheung Kong (Holdings) Limited, IV; 20 (upd.)
CITIC Pacific Ltd., 18
First Pacific Company Limited, 18
Hong Kong Telecommunications Ltd., 6
Hongkong Electric Holdings Ltd., 6; 23 (upd.)
Hongkong Land Holdings Limited, IV; 47 (upd.)
Hutchison Whampoa Limited, 18; 49 (upd.)
Kerry Properties Limited, 22
New World Development Company Limited, IV; 38 (upd.)
Playmates Toys, 23
Singer Company N.V., The, 30 (upd.)
Swire Pacific Ltd., I; 16 (upd.)
Tommy Hilfiger Corporation, 20

Hungary

Malév Plc, 24

India

Air-India Limited, 6; 27 (upd.)
Bajaj Auto Limited, 39
Coal India Limited, IV; 44 (upd.)
Indian Airlines Ltd., 46
Indian Oil Corporation Ltd., IV; 48 (upd.)
Infosys Technologies Ltd., 38
Minerals and Metals Trading Corporation of India Ltd., IV
Oil and Natural Gas Commission, IV
Steel Authority of India Ltd., IV
Tata Iron & Steel Co. Ltd., IV; 44 (upd.)
Wipro Limited, 43

Indonesia

Garuda Indonesia, 6
PERTAMINA, IV

Iran

National Iranian Oil Company, IV

Ireland

Aer Lingus Group plc, 34
Allied Irish Banks, plc, 16; 43 (upd.)
Baltimore Technologies Plc, 42
eircom plc, 31 (upd.)
Fyffes Plc, 38
Harland and Wolff Holdings plc, 19
IAWS Group plc, 49
IONA Technologies plc, 43
Jefferson Smurfit Group plc, IV; 19 (upd.); 49 (upd.)
Kerry Group plc, 27

Ryanair Holdings plc, 35
Shannon Aerospace Ltd., 36
Telecom Eireann, 7
Waterford Wedgwood plc, 34 (upd.)

Israel

Amdocs Ltd., 47
Bank Hapoalim B.M., II
Blue Square Israel Ltd., 41
ECI Telecom Ltd., 18
El Al Israel Airlines Ltd., 23
Elscint Ltd., 20
Koor Industries Ltd., II; 25 (upd.)
Scitex Corporation Ltd., 24
Teva Pharmaceutical Industries Ltd., 22

Italy

Alfa Romeo, 13; 36 (upd.)
Alitalia-Linee Aeree Italiana, S.p.A., 6; 29 (upd.)
Aprilia SpA, 17
Arnoldo Mondadori Editore S.p.A., IV; 19 (upd.)
Assicurazioni Generali SpA, III; 15 (upd.)
Autogrill SpA, 49
Automobili Lamborghini Holding S.p.A., 34 (upd.)
Automobili Lamborghini S.p.A., 13
Banca Commerciale Italiana SpA, II
Barilla G. e R. Fratelli S.p.A., 17
Benetton Group S.p.A., 10
Bulgari S.p.A., 20
Credito Italiano, II
Diesel SpA, 40
Ducati Motor Holding S.p.A., 30
Ente Nazionale Idrocarburi, IV
Ente Nazionale per L'Energia Elettrica, V
Fabbrica D' Armi Pietro Beretta S.p.A., 39
Ferrari S.p.A., 13; 36 (upd.)
Fiat S.p.A., I; 11 (upd.)
Fila Holding S.p.A., 20
Gianni Versace SpA, 22
Giorgio Armani S.p.A., 45
Gruppo Coin S.p.A., 41
Guccio Gucci, S.p.A., 15
Industrie Natuzzi S.p.A., 18
Ing. C. Olivetti & C., S.p.a., III
Istituto per la Ricostruzione Industriale S.p.A., I; 11
Luxottica SpA, 17
Marchesi Antinori SRL, 42
Marzotto S.p.A., 20
Montedison SpA, I; 24 (upd.)
Officine Alfieri Maserati S.p.A., 13
Olivetti S.p.A., 34 (upd.)
Piaggio & C. S.p.A., 20
Pirelli S.p.A., V; 15 (upd.)
Reno de Medici S.p.A., 41
Riunione Adriatica di Sicurtè SpA, III
Seat Pagine Gialle S.p.A., 47
Società Finanziaria Telefonica per Azioni, V
Società Sportiva Lazio SpA, 44
Telecom Italia S.p.A., 43
Tiscali SpA, 48

Japan

Aisin Seiki Co., Ltd., III; 48 (upd.)
Aiwa Co., Ltd., 30
Ajinomoto Co., Inc., II; 28 (upd.)
All Nippon Airways Co., Ltd., 6; 38 (upd.)
Alpine Electronics, Inc., 13
Alps Electric Co., Ltd., II; 44 (upd.)
Asahi Breweries, Ltd., I; 20 (upd.)
Asahi Glass Company, Ltd., III; 48 (upd.)

Asahi National Broadcasting Company, Ltd., 9
Bank of Tokyo-Mitsubishi Ltd., II; 15 (upd.)
Bridgestone Corporation, V; 21 (upd.)
Brother Industries, Ltd., 14
C. Itoh & Company Ltd., I
Canon Inc., III; 18 (upd.)
CASIO Computer Co., Ltd., III; 16 (upd.); 40 (upd.)
Central Japan Railway Company, 43
Chubu Electric Power Company, Inc., V; 46 (upd.)
Chugoku Electric Power Company Inc., V
Citizen Watch Co., Ltd., III; 21 (upd.)
Cosmo Oil Co., Ltd., IV
Dai Nippon Printing Co., Ltd., IV
Dai-Ichi Kangyo Bank Ltd., The, II
Daido Steel Co., Ltd., IV
Daiei, Inc., The, V; 17 (upd.); 41 (upd.)
Daihatsu Motor Company, Ltd., 7; 21 (upd.)
Daikin Industries, Ltd., III
Daimaru, Inc., The, V; 42 (upd.)
Daio Paper Corporation, IV
Daishowa Paper Manufacturing Co., Ltd., IV
Daiwa Bank, Ltd., The, II; 39 (upd.)
Daiwa Securities Company, Limited, II
DDI Corporation, 7
DENSO Corporation, 46 (upd.)
Dentsu Inc., I; 16 (upd.); 40 (upd.)
East Japan Railway Company, V
Fanuc Ltd., III; 17 (upd.)
Fuji Bank, Ltd., The, II
Fuji Electric Co., Ltd., II; 48 (upd.)
Fuji Photo Film Co., Ltd., III; 18 (upd.)
Fujisawa Pharmaceutical Company Ltd., I
Fujitsu Limited, III; 16 (upd.); 42 (upd.)
Furukawa Electric Co., Ltd., The, III
General Sekiyu K.K., IV
Hakuhodo, Inc., 6; 42 (upd.)
Hankyu Corporation, V; 23 (upd.)
Hino Motors, Ltd., 7; 21 (upd.)
Hitachi Ltd., I; 12 (upd.)
Hitachi Metals, Ltd., IV
Hitachi Zosen Corporation, III
Hitachi, Ltd., 40 (upd.)
Hokkaido Electric Power Company Inc., V
Hokuriku Electric Power Company, V
Honda Motor Company Limited, I; 10 (upd.); 29 (upd.)
Honshu Paper Co., Ltd., IV
Idemitsu Kosan Co., Ltd., 49 (upd.)
Idemitsu Kosan K.K., IV
Industrial Bank of Japan, Ltd., The, II
Isetan Company Limited, V; 36 (upd.)
Ishikawajima-Harima Heavy Industries Co., Ltd., III
Isuzu Motors, Ltd., 9; 23 (upd.)
Ito-Yokado Co., Ltd., V; 42 (upd.)
ITOCHU Corporation, 32 (upd.)
Itoham Foods Inc., II
Japan Airlines Company, Ltd., I; 32 (upd.)
Japan Broadcasting Corporation, 7
Japan Leasing Corporation, 8
Japan Pulp and Paper Company Limited, IV
Japan Tobacco Inc., V; 46 (upd.)
Jujo Paper Co., Ltd., IV
JUSCO Co., Ltd., V
Kajima Corporation, I
Kanematsu Corporation, IV; 24 (upd.)
Kansai Electric Power Co., Inc., The, V
Kao Corporation, III; 20 (upd.)
Kawasaki Heavy Industries, Ltd., III
Kawasaki Kisen Kaisha, Ltd., V
Kawasaki Steel Corporation, IV

Keio Teito Electric Railway Company, V
Kenwood Corporation, 31
Kikkoman Corporation, 14; 47 (upd.)
Kinki Nippon Railway Company Ltd., V
Kirin Brewery Company, Limited, I; 21 (upd.)
Kobe Steel, Ltd., IV; 19 (upd.)
Kodansha Ltd., IV; 38 (upd.)
Komatsu Ltd., III; 16 (upd.)
Konica Corporation, III; 30 (upd.)
Kotobukiya Co., Ltd., V
Kubota Corporation, III; 26 (upd.)
Kumagai Gumi Company, Ltd., I
Kyocera Corporation, II; 21 (upd.)
Kyowa Hakko Kogyo Co., Ltd., III; 48 (upd.)
Kyushu Electric Power Company Inc., V
Lion Corporation, III
Long-Term Credit Bank of Japan, Ltd., II
Makita Corporation, 22
Marubeni Corporation, I; 24 (upd.)
Marui Co., Ltd., V
Maruzen Co., Limited, 18
Matsushita Electric Industrial Co., Ltd., II
Matsushita Electric Works, Ltd., III; 7 (upd.)
Matsuzakaya Company Limited, V
Mazda Motor Corporation, 9; 23 (upd.)
Meiji Milk Products Company, Limited, II
Meiji Mutual Life Insurance Company, The, III
Meiji Seika Kaisha, Ltd., II
Minolta Co., Ltd., III; 18 (upd.); 43 (upd.)
Mitsubishi Bank, Ltd., The, II
Mitsubishi Chemical Industries, Ltd., I
Mitsubishi Corporation, I; 12 (upd.)
Mitsubishi Electric Corporation, II; 44 (upd.)
Mitsubishi Estate Company, Limited, IV
Mitsubishi Heavy Industries, Ltd., III; 7 (upd.); 40 (upd.)
Mitsubishi Materials Corporation, III
Mitsubishi Motors Corporation, 9; 23 (upd.)
Mitsubishi Oil Co., Ltd., IV
Mitsubishi Rayon Co., Ltd., V
Mitsubishi Trust & Banking Corporation, The, II
Mitsui & Co., Ltd., 28 (upd.)
Mitsui Bank, Ltd., The, II
Mitsui Bussan K.K., I
Mitsui Marine and Fire Insurance Company, Limited, III
Mitsui Mining & Smelting Co., Ltd., IV
Mitsui Mining Company, Limited, IV
Mitsui Mutual Life Insurance Company, III; 39 (upd.)
Mitsui O.S.K. Lines, Ltd., V
Mitsui Petrochemical Industries, Ltd., 9
Mitsui Real Estate Development Co., Ltd., IV
Mitsui Trust & Banking Company, Ltd., The, II
Mitsukoshi Ltd., V
Mizuno Corporation, 25
Nagasakiya Co., Ltd., V
Nagase & Company, Ltd., 8
NEC Corporation, II; 21 (upd.)
NHK Spring Co., Ltd., III
Nichii Co., Ltd., V
Nichimen Corporation, IV; 24 (upd.)
Nihon Keizai Shimbun, Inc., IV
Nikko Securities Company Limited, The, II; 9 (upd.)
Nikon Corporation, III; 48 (upd.)
Nintendo Co., Ltd., III; 7 (upd.); 28 (upd.)
Nippon Credit Bank, II
Nippon Express Co., Ltd., V

Nippon Life Insurance Company, III
Nippon Light Metal Company, Ltd., IV
Nippon Meat Packers, Inc., II
Nippon Oil Company, Limited, IV
Nippon Seiko K.K., III
Nippon Sheet Glass Company, Limited, III
Nippon Shinpan Company, Ltd., II
Nippon Steel Corporation, IV; 17 (upd.)
Nippon Suisan Kaisha, Limited, II
Nippon Telegraph and Telephone Corporation, V
Nippon Yusen Kabushiki Kaisha, V
Nippondenso Co., Ltd., III
Nissan Motor Company Ltd., I; 11 (upd.); 34 (upd.)
Nisshin Flour Milling Company, Ltd., II
Nisshin Steel Co., Ltd., IV
Nissho Iwai K.K., I
NKK Corporation, IV; 28 (upd.)
Nomura Securities Company, Limited, II; 9 (upd.)
Norinchukin Bank, II
NTN Corporation, III; 47 (upd.)
Odakyu Electric Railway Company Limited, V
Ohbayashi Corporation, I
Oji Paper Co., Ltd., IV
Oki Electric Industry Company, Limited, II
Okura & Co., Ltd., IV
Omron Corporation, II; 28 (upd.)
Onoda Cement Co., Ltd., III
Orix Corporation, II
ORIX Corporation, 44 (upd.)
Osaka Gas Co., Ltd., V
Pioneer Electronic Corporation, III; 28 (upd.)
Rengo Co., Ltd., IV
Ricoh Company, Ltd., III; 36 (upd.)
Roland Corporation, 38
Sankyo Company, Ltd., I
Sanrio Company, Ltd., 38
Sanwa Bank, Ltd., The, II; 15 (upd.)
SANYO Electric Company, Ltd., II; 36 (upd.)
Sanyo-Kokusaku Pulp Co., Ltd., IV
Sapporo Breweries, Ltd., I; 13 (upd.); 36 (upd.)
Seibu Department Stores, Ltd., V; 42 (upd.)
Seibu Railway Co. Ltd., V
Seiko Corporation, III; 17 (upd.)
Seino Transportation Company, Ltd., 6
Seiyu, Ltd., The, V; 36 (upd.)
Sekisui Chemical Co., Ltd., III
Sharp Corporation, II; 12 (upd.); 40 (upd.)
Shikoku Electric Power Company, Inc., V
Shionogi & Co., Ltd., III; 17 (upd.)
Shiseido Company, Limited, III; 22 (upd.)
Showa Shell Sekiyu K.K., IV
Snow Brand Milk Products Company, Ltd., II; 48 (upd.)
Softbank Corp., 13; 38 (upd.)
Sony Corporation, II; 12 (upd.); 40 (upd.)
Sumitomo Bank, Limited, The, II; 26 (upd.)
Sumitomo Chemical Company Ltd., I
Sumitomo Corporation, I; 11 (upd.)
Sumitomo Electric Industries, Ltd., II
Sumitomo Heavy Industries, Ltd., III; 42 (upd.)
Sumitomo Life Insurance Company, III
Sumitomo Marine and Fire Insurance Company, Limited, The, III
Sumitomo Metal Industries, Ltd., IV
Sumitomo Metal Mining Co., Ltd., IV
Sumitomo Realty & Development Co., Ltd., IV
Sumitomo Rubber Industries, Ltd., V

Japan (*continued*)

Sumitomo Trust & Banking Company, Ltd., The, II
Suzuki Motor Corporation, 9; 23 (upd.)
Taiyo Fishery Company, Limited, II
Taiyo Kobe Bank, Ltd., The, II
Takashimaya Company, Limited, V; 47 (upd.)
Takeda Chemical Industries, Ltd., I; 46 (upd.)
TDK Corporation, II; 17 (upd.); 49 (upd.)
Teijin Limited, V
Terumo Corporation, 48
Tobu Railway Co Ltd, 6
Toho Co., Ltd., 28
Tohoku Electric Power Company, Inc., V
Tokai Bank, Limited, The, II; 15 (upd.)
Tokio Marine and Fire Insurance Co., Ltd., The, III
Tokyo Electric Power Company, Incorporated, The, V
Tokyo Gas Co., Ltd., V
Tokyu Corporation, V; 47 (upd.)
Tokyu Department Store Co., Ltd., V; 32 (upd.)
Tokyu Land Corporation, IV
Tomen Corporation, IV; 24 (upd.)
Tonen Corporation, IV; 16 (upd.)
Toppan Printing Co., Ltd., IV
Toray Industries, Inc., V
Toshiba Corporation, I; 12 (upd.); 40 (upd.)
TOTO LTD., III; 28 (upd.)
Toyo Sash Co., Ltd., III
Toyo Seikan Kaisha, Ltd., I
Toyoda Automatic Loom Works, Ltd., III
Toyota Motor Corporation, I; 11 (upd.); 38 (upd.)
Ube Industries, Ltd., III; 38 (upd.)
Unitika Ltd., V
Uny Co., Ltd., V; 49 (upd.)
Victor Company of Japan, Limited, II; 26 (upd.)
Wacoal Corp., 25
Yamaha Corporation, III; 16 (upd.); 40 (upd.)
Yamaichi Securities Company, Limited, II
Yamato Transport Co. Ltd., V; 49 (upd.)
Yasuda Fire and Marine Insurance Company, Limited, The, III
Yasuda Mutual Life Insurance Company, The, III; 39 (upd.)
Yasuda Trust and Banking Company, Ltd., The, II; 17 (upd.)
Yokohama Rubber Co., Ltd., The, V; 19 (upd.)

Korea

Anam Group, 23
Asiana Airlines, Inc., 46
Daewoo Group, III; 18 (upd.)
Electronics Co., Ltd., 14
Goldstar Co., Ltd., 12
Hyundai Group, III; 7 (upd.)
Kia Motors Corporation, 12; 29 (upd.)
Korean Air Lines Co., Ltd., 6; 27 (upd.)
Lucky-Goldstar, II
Pohang Iron and Steel Company Ltd., IV
Samsung Electronics Co., Ltd., 41 (upd.)
Samsung Group, I
Ssangyong Cement Industrial Co., Ltd., III

Kuwait

Kuwait Petroleum Corporation, IV

Luxembourg

ARBED S.A., IV; 22 (upd.)
Cargolux Airlines International S.A., 49
RTL Group SA, 44

Lybia

Libyan National Oil Corporation, IV

Madeira

Madeira Wine Company, S.A., 49

Malaysia

Malaysian Airlines System Berhad, 6; 29 (upd.)
Petronas, IV
Sime Darby Berhad, 14; 36 (upd.)

Mexico

Alfa, S.A. de C.V., 19
Altos Hornos de México, S.A. de C.V., 42
Bufete Industrial, S.A. de C.V., 34
Casa Cuervo, S.A. de C.V., 31
Cemex SA de CV, 20
Cifra, S.A. de C.V., 12
Consorcio G Grupo Dina, S.A. de C.V., 36
Controladora Comercial Mexicana, S.A. de C.V., 36
Corporación Internacional de Aviación, S.A. de C.V. (Cintra), 20
Desc, S.A. de C.V., 23
Empresas ICA Sociedad Controladora, S.A. de C.V., 41
Gruma, S.A. de C.V., 31
Grupo Aeropuerto del Sureste, S.A. de C.V., 48
Grupo Carso, S.A. de C.V., 21
Grupo Casa Saba, S.A. de C.V., 39
Grupo Cydsa, S.A. de C.V., 39
Grupo Elektra, S.A. de C.V., 39
Grupo Financiero Serfin, S.A., 19
Grupo Gigante, S.A. de C.V., 34
Grupo Herdez, S.A. de C.V., 35
Grupo IMSA, S.A. de C.V., 44
Grupo Industrial Bimbo, 19
Grupo Industrial Durango, S.A. de C.V., 37
Grupo Mexico, S.A. de C.V., 40
Grupo Modelo, S.A. de C.V., 29
Grupo Televisa, S.A., 18
Grupo Transportación Ferroviaria Mexicana, S.A. de C.V., 47
Hylsamex, S.A. de C.V., 39
Industrias Bachoco, S.A. de C.V., 39
Industrias Penoles, S.A. de C.V., 22
Organización Soriana, S.A. de C.V., 35
Petróleos Mexicanos, IV; 19 (upd.)
Pulsar Internacional S.A., 21
Sanborn Hermanos, S.A., 20
Sears Roebuck de México, S.A. de C.V., 20
Telefonos de Mexico S.A. de C.V., 14
Tubos de Acero de Mexico, S.A. (TAMSA), 41
TV Azteca, S.A. de C.V., 39
Valores Industriales S.A., 19
Vitro Corporativo S.A. de C.V., 34
Wal-Mart de Mexico, S.A. de C.V., 35 (upd.)

Nepal

Royal Nepal Airline Corporation, 41

New Zealand

Air New Zealand Limited, 14; 38 (upd.)
Fletcher Challenge Ltd., IV; 19 (upd.)
Wattie's Ltd., 7

Nigeria

Nigerian National Petroleum Corporation, IV

Norway

Braathens ASA, 47
Den Norse Stats Oljeselskap AS, IV
Helly Hansen ASA, 25
Kvaerner ASA, 36
Norsk Hydro ASA, 10; 35 (upd.)
Orkla A/S, 18
Schibsted ASA, 31

Oman

Petroleum Development Oman LLC, IV

Pakistan

Pakistan International Airlines Corporation, 46

Panama

Panamerican Beverages, Inc., 47

Peru

Southern Peru Copper Corporation, 40

Philippines

Philippine Airlines, Inc., 6; 23 (upd.)
San Miguel Corporation, 15

Poland

LOT Polish Airlines (Polskie Linie Lotnicze S.A.), 33

Portugal

Banco Espírito Santo e Comercial de Lisboa S.A., 15
Corticeira Amorim, Sociedade Gestora de Participaço es Sociais, S.A., 48
Electricidade de Portugal, S.A., 47
Petróleos de Portugal S.A., IV
TAP—Air Portugal Transportes Aéreos Portugueses S.A., 46
Transportes Aereos Portugueses, S.A., 6

Puerto Rico

Puerto Rico Electric Power Authority, 47

Qatar

Qatar General Petroleum Corporation, IV

Russia

A.S. Yakovlev Design Bureau, 15
Aeroflot—Russian International Airlines, 6; 29 (upd.)
AO VimpelCom, 48
Aviacionny Nauchno-Tehnicheskii Komplex im. A.N. Tupoleva, 24
JSC MMC Norilsk Nickel, 48
OAO Gazprom, 42
OAO LUKOIL, 40
OAO NK YUKOS, 47
OAO Siberian Oil Company (Sibneft), 49
OAO Surgutneftegaz, 48
OAO Tatneft, 45
OJSC Wimm-Bill-Dann Foods, 48
RAO Unified Energy System of Russia, 45
OAO Siberian Oil Company (Sibneft), 49
Sukhoi Design Bureau Aviation Scientific-Industrial Complex, 24

OAO Surgutneftegaz, 48
AO VimpelCom, 48
OJSC Wimm-Bill-Dann Foods, 48

Saudi Arabia

Saudi Arabian Airlines, 6; 27 (upd.)
Saudi Arabian Oil Company, IV; 17 (upd.)

Scotland

Distillers Company PLC, I
General Accident PLC, III
Governor and Company of the Bank of
    Scotland, The, 10
Royal Bank of Scotland Group plc, The,
    12
Scottish & Newcastle plc, 15
Scottish Hydro-Electric PLC, 13
Scottish Media Group plc, 32
ScottishPower plc, 19
Stagecoach Holdings plc, 30
Standard Life Assurance Company, The,
    III

Singapore

Flextronics International Ltd., 38
Neptune Orient Lines Limited, 47
Singapore Airlines Ltd., 6; 27 (upd.)

South Africa

Anglo American Corporation of South
    Africa Limited, IV; 16 (upd.)
Barlow Rand Ltd., I
De Beers Consolidated Mines Limited/De
    Beers Centenary AG, IV; 7 (upd.); 28
    (upd.)
Gencor Ltd., IV; 22 (upd.)
Gold Fields of South Africa Ltd., IV
SAA (Pty) Ltd., 28
Sappi Limited, 49
Sasol Limited, IV; 47 (upd.)
South African Breweries Limited, The, I;
    24 (upd.)
Transnet Ltd., 6

Spain

Banco Bilbao Vizcaya Argentaria S.A., 48
    (upd.)
Banco Bilbao Vizcaya, S.A., II
Banco Central, II
Banco do Brasil S.A., II
Banco Santander Central Hispano S.A., 36
    (upd.)
Chupa Chups S.A., 38
Compañia Española de Petróleos S.A., IV
El Corte Inglés Group, V; 26 (upd.)
ENDESA Group, V
ENDESA S.A., 46 (upd.)
Grupo Ferrovial, S.A., 40
Iberdrola, S.A., 49
Iberia Líneas Aéreas de España S.A., 6; 36
    (upd.)
Instituto Nacional de Industria, I
Repsol S.A., IV; 16 (upd.)
Repsol-YPF S.A., 40 (upd.)
Tabacalera, S.A., V; 17 (upd.)
Telefónica de España, S.A., V
Telefónica S.A., 46 (upd.)
TelePizza S.A., 33
Television Española, S.A., 7
Terra Lycos, Inc., 43

Sweden

A. Johnson & Company H.B., I
AB Volvo, I; 7 (upd.); 26 (upd.)
Aktiebolaget Electrolux, 22 (upd.)

Aktiebolaget SKF, III; 38 (upd.)
Alfa-Laval AB, III
Astra AB, I; 20 (upd.)
Atlas Copco AB, III; 28 (upd.)
BRIO AB, 24
Electrolux Group, III
Gambro AB, 49
Hennes & Mauritz AB, 29
ICA AB, II
Mo och Domsjö AB, IV
Modern Times Group AB, 36
NetCom Systems AB, 26
Nobel Industries AB, 9
Nordea AB, 40
Perstorp A.B., I
Saab Automobile AB, 32 (upd.)
Saab-Scania A.B., I; 11 (upd.)
Sandvik AB, IV; 32 (upd.)
SAS Group, The, 34 (upd.)
Scandinavian Airlines System, I
Securitas AB, 42
Skandinaviska Enskilda Banken, II
Skanska AB, 38
Stora Kopparbergs Bergslags AB, IV
Svenska Cellulosa Aktiebolaget SCA, IV;
    28 (upd.)
Svenska Handelsbanken, II
Swedish Match AB, 39 (upd.)
Swedish Telecom, V
Telefonaktiebolaget LM Ericsson, V; 46
    (upd.)
Vin & Spirit AB, 31

Switzerland

ABB ASEA Brown Boveri Ltd., II; 22
    (upd.)
Adecco S.A., 36 (upd.)
Adia S.A., 6
Arthur Andersen & Company, Société
    Coopérative, 10
Ascom AG, 9
Bâloise-Holding, 40
Barry Callebaut AG, 29
Bernina Holding AG, 47
Bodum Design Group AG, 47
Bon Appetit Holding AG, 48
Chocoladefabriken Lindt & Sprüngli AG,
    27
Ciba-Geigy Ltd., I; 8 (upd.)
Coop Schweiz Genossenschaftsverband, 48
Credit Suisse Group, II; 21 (upd.)
Danzas Group, V; 40 (upd.)
De Beers Consolidated Mines Limited/De
    Beers Centenary AG, IV; 7 (upd.); 28
    (upd.)
Elektrowatt AG, 6
F. Hoffmann-Laroche & Company A.G., I
Fédération Internationale de Football
    Association, 27
Geberit AG, 49
Givaudan SA, 43
Holderbank Financière Glaris Ltd., III
International Olympic Committee, 44
Jacobs Suchard A.G., II
Kraft Jacobs Suchard AG, 26 (upd.)
Kudelski Group SA, 44
Kuhne & Nagel International A.G., V
Kuoni Travel Holding Ltd., 40
Logitech International SA, 28
Maus Frères SA, 48
Mettler-Toledo International Inc., 30
Montres Rolex S.A., 13; 34 (upd.)
Nestlé S.A., II; 7 (upd.); 28 (upd.)
Novartis AG, 39 (upd.)
Panalpina World Transport (Holding) Ltd.,
    47
Rieter Holding AG, 42

Roland Murten A.G., 7
Sandoz Ltd., I
Schindler Holding AG, 29
Schweizerische Post-, Telefon- und
    Telegrafen-Betriebe, V
Serono S.A., 47
Sulzer Brothers Limited (Gebruder Sulzer
    Aktiengesellschaft), III
Swarovski International Holding AG, 40
Swatch Group SA, The, 26
Swedish Match S.A., 12
Swiss Air Transport Company, Ltd., I
Swiss Bank Corporation, II
Swiss Federal Railways (Schweizerische
    Bundesbahnen), The, V
Swiss International Air Lines Ltd., 48
Swiss Reinsurance Company
    (Schweizerische Rückversicherungs-
    Gesellschaft), III; 46 (upd.)
TAG Heuer International SA, 25
Union Bank of Switzerland, II
Victorinox AG, 21
Winterthur Schweizerische Versicherungs-
    Gesellschaft, III
Zurich Financial Services, 42 (upd.)
Zürich Versicherungs-Gesellschaft, III

Taiwan

Acer Inc., 16
China Airlines, 34
Evergreen Marine Corporation Taiwan
    Ltd., 13
Formosa Plastics Corporation, 14
Quanta Computer Inc., 47
Taiwan Semiconductor Manufacturing
    Company Ltd., 47
Tatung Co., 23
Yageo Corporation, 16

Thailand

Thai Airways International Public
    Company Limited, 6; 27 (upd.)

The Netherlands

AEGON N.V., III
Akzo Nobel N.V., 13; 41 (upd.)
Algemene Bank Nederland N.V., II
Amsterdam-Rotterdam Bank N.V., II
Arcadis NV, 26
Baan Company, 25
Buhrmann NV, 41
CNH Global N.V., 38 (upd.)
DSM, N.V., I
Elsevier N.V., IV
Endemol Entertainment Holding NV, 46
Getronics NV, 39
Grand Hotel Krasnapolsky N.V., 23
Hagemeyer N.V., 39
Heineken N.V., I; 13 (upd.); 34 (upd.)
Indigo NV, 26
Ispat International N.V., 30
Koninklijke Ahold N.V. (Royal Ahold), II;
    16 (upd.)
Koninklijke Luchtvaart Maatschappij, N.V.
    (KLM Royal Dutch Airlines), I; 28 (upd.)
Koninklijke Nederlandsche Hoogovens en
    Staalfabrieken NV, IV
Koninklijke Nedlloyd N.V., 6; 26 (upd.)
Koninklijke PTT Nederland NV, V
Koninklijke Wessanen N.V., II
KPMG International, 10; 33 (upd.)
Mammoet Transport B.V., 26
MIH Limited, 31
N.V. AMEV, III
N.V. Holdingmaatschappij De Telegraaf,
    23

The Netherlands (*continued*)

N.V. Koninklijke Nederlandse
    Vliegtuigenfabriek Fokker, I; 28 (upd.)
N.V. Nederlandse Gasunie, V
Nationale-Nederlanden N.V., III
New Holland N.V., 22
Océ N.V., 24
Philips Electronics N.V., II; 13 (upd.)
PolyGram N.V., 23
Prada Holding B.V., 45
Qiagen N.V., 39
Rabobank Group, 33
Randstad Holding n.v., 16; 43 (upd.)
Rodamco N.V., 26
Royal Dutch Petroleum Company/ The
    Shell Transport and Trading Company
    p.l.c., IV
Royal Dutch/Shell Group, 49 (upd.)
Royal KPN N.V., 30
Royal Numico N.V., 37
Royal Packaging Industries Van Leer N.V.,
    30
Royal Vopak NV, 41
TNT Post Group N.V., V; 27 (upd.); 30
    (upd.)
Toolex International N.V., 26
Triple P N.V., 26
Unilever N.V., II; 7 (upd.); 32 (upd.)
United Pan-Europe Communications NV,
    47
Vebego International BV, 49
Vedior NV, 35
Velcro Industries N.V., 19
Vendex International N.V., 13
VNU N.V., 27
Wolters Kluwer NV, 14; 33 (upd.)

Tunisia

Société Tunisienne de l'Air-Tunisair, 49

Turkey

KOC Holding A.S., I
Türkiye Petrolleri Anonim Ortakliği, IV

United Arab Emirates

Abu Dhabi National Oil Company, IV; 45
    (upd.)
Emirates Group, The, 39

United Kingdom

Abbey National plc, 10; 39 (upd.)
Aegis Group plc, 6
Aggregate Industries plc, 36
Aggreko Plc, 45
Airtours Plc, 27
Albert Fisher Group plc, The, 41
Alldays plc, 49
Allders plc, 37
Allied Domecq PLC, 29
Allied-Lyons PLC, I
Alvis Plc, 47
Amey Plc, 47
Amstrad plc, III; 48 (upd.)
Arcadia Group plc, 28 (upd.)
Argyll Group PLC, II
Arjo Wiggins Appleton p.l.c., 34
ASDA Group plc, II; 28 (upd.)
Ashtead Group plc, 34
Associated British Foods plc, II; 13 (upd.);
    41 (upd.)
Associated British Ports Holdings Plc, 45
Aston Villa plc, 41
AT&T Istel Ltd., 14
B.A.T. Industries PLC, I; 22 (upd.)
BAA plc, 10; 33 (upd.)
Balfour Beatty plc, 36 (upd.)

Barclays PLC, II; 20 (upd.)
Barings PLC, 14
Barratt Developments PLC, I
Bass PLC, I; 15 (upd.); 38 (upd.)
Bat Industries PLC, I; 20 (upd.)
Bellway Plc, 45
Bhs plc, 17
BICC PLC, III
Blacks Leisure Group plc, 39
Blue Circle Industries PLC, III
BOC Group plc, I; 25 (upd.)
Body Shop International PLC, The, 11
Booker plc, 13; 31 (upd.)
Boots Company PLC, The, V; 24 (upd.)
Bowater PLC, IV
Bowthorpe plc, 33
BP p.l.c., 45 (upd.)
Brake Bros plc, 45
British Aerospace plc, I; 24 (upd.)
British Airways PLC, I; 14 (upd.); 43
    (upd.)
British Broadcasting Corporation Ltd., 7;
    21 (upd.)
British Coal Corporation, IV
British Energy Plc, 49
British Gas plc, V
British Midland plc, 38
British Nuclear Fuels plc, 6
British Petroleum Company plc, The, IV; 7
    (upd.); 21 (upd.)
British Railways Board, V
British Sky Broadcasting Group Plc, 20
British Steel plc, IV; 19 (upd.)
British Telecommunications plc, V; 15
    (upd.)
British Vita plc, 9; 33 (upd.)
British World Airlines Ltd., 18
British-Borneo Oil & Gas PLC, 34
BT Group plc, 49 (upd.)
BTR PLC, I
BTR Siebe plc, 27
Bunzl plc, IV; 31 (upd.)
Burberry Ltd., 17; 41 (upd.)
Burmah Castrol PLC, IV; 30 (upd.)
Burton Group plc, The, V
Business Post Group plc, 46
Cable and Wireless plc, V; 25 (upd.)
Cadbury Schweppes PLC, II; 49 (upd.)
Canary Wharf Group plc, 30
Capital Radio plc, 35
Caradon plc, 20 (upd.)
Carlton Communications plc, 15
Cartier Monde, 29
Central Independent Television, 7; 23
    (upd.)
Centrica plc, 29 (upd.)
Christian Salvesen Plc, 45
Christie's International plc, 15; 39 (upd.)
Chrysalis Group plc, 40
Clifford Chance LLP, 38
Clinton Cards plc, 39
Close Brothers Group plc, 39
Coats plc, 44 (upd.)
Coats Viyella Plc, V
Cobham plc, 30
COLT Telecom Group plc, 41
Commercial Union PLC, III
Compass Group PLC, 34
Cookson Group PLC, III; 44 (upd.)
Corus Group plc, 49 (upd.)
Courtaulds plc, V; 17 (upd.)
Courts Plc, 45
Cranswick plc, 40
Croda International Plc, 45
Daily Mail and General Trust plc, 19
Dairy Crest Group plc, 32
Dalgety, PLC, II
Davis Service Group PLC, 45

Dawson Holdings PLC, 43
De La Rue plc, 10; 34 (upd.)
Debenhams Plc, 28
Denby Group plc, 44
Denison International plc, 46
Diageo plc, 24 (upd.)
Dixons Group plc, V; 19 (upd.); 49 (upd.)
Dorling Kindersley Holdings plc, 20
easyJet Airline Company Limited, 39
ECC Group plc, III
Elementis plc, 40 (upd.)
EMAP plc, 35
EMI Group plc, 22 (upd.)
Energis plc, 47
English China Clays Ltd., 15 (upd.); 40
    (upd.)
Enterprise Oil plc, 11
Esporta plc, 35
Eurotunnel Group, 37 (upd.)
Eurotunnel PLC, 13
Fairclough Construction Group PLC, I
First Choice Holidays PLC, 40
Fisons plc, 9; 23 (upd.)
French Connection Group plc, 41
Fuller Smith & Turner P.L.C., 38
Gallaher Group Plc, 49 (upd.)
Gallaher Limited, V; 19 (upd.)
Gateway Corporation Ltd., The, II
Geest Plc, 38
General Electric Company PLC, II
George Wimpey PLC, 12
GKN plc, III; 38 (upd.)
Glaxo Holdings PLC, I; 9 (upd.)
GlaxoSmithKline plc, 46 (upd.)
Go-Ahead Group Plc, The, 28
Granada Group PLC, II; 24 (upd.)
Grand Metropolitan PLC, I; 14 (upd.)
Great Universal Stores plc, The, V; 19
    (upd.)
Greenalls Group PLC, The, 21
Greene King plc, 31
Guardian Royal Exchange Plc, 11
Guinness/UDV, I; 43 (upd.)
GUS plc, 47 (upd.)
GWR Group plc, 39
Hammerson plc, 40
Hammerson Property Investment and
    Development Corporation plc, The, IV
Hanson PLC, III; 7 (upd.); 30 (upd.)
Harrisons & Crosfield plc, III
Harrods Holdings, 47
Hartstone Group plc, The, 14
Hawker Siddeley Group Public Limited
    Company, III
Hays Plc, 27
Hazlewood Foods plc, 32
Her Majesty's Stationery Office, 7
Hillsdown Holdings plc, II; 24 (upd.)
Hilton Group plc, 49 (upd.)
HIT Entertainment PLC, 40
House of Fraser PLC, 45
HSBC Holdings plc, 12; 26 (upd.)
Huntingdon Life Sciences Group plc, 42
Ibstock Brick Ltd., 14; 37 (upd.)
ICL plc, 6
IMI plc, 9
Imperial Chemical Industries PLC, I
Inchcape PLC, III; 16 (upd.)
IPC Magazines Limited, 7
J Sainsbury plc, II; 13 (upd.); 38 (upd.)
James Beattie plc, 43
Jarvis plc, 39
JD Wetherspoon plc, 30
JJB Sports plc, 32
John Brown PLC, I
John Laing PLC, I
John Lewis Partnership plc, V; 42 (upd.)
John Menzies plc, 39

Johnson Matthey PLC, IV; 16 (upd.); 49 (upd.)
Johnston Press plc, 35
Kelda Group plc, 45
Kennecott Corporation, 7; 27 (upd.)
Kidde plc, 44 (upd.)
Kingfisher plc, V; 24 (upd.)
Kleinwort Benson Group PLC, II
Kvaerner ASA, 36
Ladbroke Group PLC, II; 21 (upd.)
Land Securities PLC, IV; 49 (upd.)
Laura Ashley Holdings plc, 13; 37 (upd.)
Legal & General Group plc, III; 24 (upd.)
Littlewoods plc, V; 42 (upd.)
Lloyd's of London, III; 22 (upd.)
Lloyds Bank PLC, II
Lloyds TSB Group plc, 47 (upd.)
Logica plc, 14; 37 (upd.)
London Regional Transport, 6
London Stock Exchange Limited, 34
Lonrho Plc, 21
Lotus Cars Ltd., 14
Lucas Industries PLC, III
Luminar Plc, 40
Madge Networks N.V., 26
Manchester United Football Club plc, 30
Marconi plc, 33 (upd.)
Marks and Spencer p.l.c., V; 24 (upd.)
Matalan PLC, 49
Maxwell Communication Corporation plc, IV; 7 (upd.)
McKechnie plc, 34
Meggitt PLC, 34
MEPC plc, IV
Mercury Communications, Ltd., 7
Mersey Docks and Harbour Company, The, 30
Metal Box PLC, I
Michael Page International plc, 45
Midland Bank PLC, II; 17 (upd.)
Mirror Group Newspapers plc, 7; 23 (upd.)
Misys plc, 45; 46
Monsoon plc, 39
Morgan Grenfell Group PLC, II
Mothercare UK Ltd., 17
N M Rothschild & Sons Limited, 39
National Power PLC, 12
National Westminster Bank PLC, II
New Look Group plc, 35
Newsquest plc, 32
Next plc, 29
NFC plc, 6
Nichols plc, 44
North West Water Group plc, 11
Northern Foods PLC, 10
Northern Rock plc, 33
Novar plc, 49 (upd.)
Ocean Group plc, 6
Pearson plc, IV; 46 (upd.)
Peninsular & Oriental Steam Navigation Company (Bovis Division), The, I
Peninsular and Oriental Steam Navigation Company, The, V; 38 (upd.)
Pennon Group Plc, 45
Pentland Group plc, 20
PIC International Group PLC, 24 (upd.)
Pilkington plc, III; 34 (upd.)
Plessey Company, PLC, The, II
Post Office Group, V
Powell Duffryn plc, 31
PowerGen PLC, 11
Prudential plc, 48 (upd.)
Psion PLC, 45
R. Griggs Group Limited, 23
Racal Electronics PLC, II
Rank Organisation Plc, The, II; 14 (upd.)
Ranks Hovis McDougall Limited, II; 28 (upd.)

Really Useful Group, The, 26
Reckitt Benckiser plc, II; 42 (upd.)
Redland plc, III
Redrow Group plc, 31
Reed Elsevier plc, IV; 17 (upd.); 31 (upd.)
Renishaw plc, 46
Rentokil Initial Plc, 47
Reuters Holdings PLC, IV; 22 (upd.)
Rexam PLC, 32 (upd.)
Rio Tinto plc, 19 (upd.)
RMC Group p.l.c., III ; 34 (upd.)
Rolls-Royce Motors Ltd., I
Rolls-Royce plc, I; 7 (upd.); 21 (upd.)
Ronson PLC, 49
Rothmans International p.l.c., V
Rothmans UK Holdings Limited, 19 (upd.)
Rotork plc, 46
Rover Group Ltd., 7; 21 (upd.)
Rowntree Mackintosh, II
Royal Bank of Scotland Group plc, The, 38 (upd.)
Royal Doulton plc, 14; 38 (upd.)
Royal Dutch Petroleum Company/ The Shell Transport and Trading Company p.l.c., IV
Royal Insurance Holdings PLC, III
RTZ Corporation PLC, The, IV
Rugby Group plc, The, 31
Saatchi & Saatchi PLC, I
Sage Group, The, 43
SBC Warburg, 14
Schroders plc, 42
Scottish & Newcastle plc, 35 (upd.)
Scottish Power plc, 49 (upd.)
Scottish Radio Holding plc, 41
Sea Containers Ltd., 29
Sears plc, V
Securicor Plc, 45
Selfridges Plc, 34
Serco Group plc, 47
Severn Trent PLC, 12; 38 (upd.)
Shanks Group plc, 45
Shepherd Neame Limited, 30
Singer & Friedlander Group plc, 41
Slough Estates PLC, IV
Smith & Nephew plc, 17;41 (upd.)
SmithKline Beecham plc, III; 32 (upd.)
Smiths Industries PLC, 25
Somerfield plc, 47 (upd.)
Southern Electric PLC, 13
SSL International plc, 49
St Ives plc, 34
Standard Chartered plc, II; 48 (upd.)
STC PLC, III
Stoll-Moss Theatres Ltd., 34
Stolt-Nielsen S.A., 42
Storehouse PLC, 16
Sun Alliance Group PLC, III
Sytner Group plc, 45
Tarmac plc, III; 28 (upd.)
Tate & Lyle PLC, II; 42 (upd.)
Taylor & Francis Group plc, 44
Taylor Nelson Sofres plc, 34
Taylor Woodrow plc, I; 38 (upd.)
Tesco PLC, II; 24 (upd.)
Thames Water plc, 11
Thorn Emi PLC, I
Thorn plc, 24
Thorntons plc, 46
TI Group plc, 17
Tibbett & Britten Group plc, 32
Tomkins plc, 11; 44 (upd.)
Travis Perkins plc, 34
Trinity Mirror plc, 49 (upd.)
Trusthouse Forte PLC, III
TSB Group plc, 12
Ultramar PLC, IV
Unigate plc, II; 28 (upd.)

Unilever PLC, II; 7 (upd.); 32 (upd.)
United Biscuits (Holdings) plc, II; 42 (upd.)
United News & Media plc, 28 (upd.)
United Newspapers plc, IV
Vendôme Luxury Group plc, 27
Vickers plc, 27
Virgin Group, 12; 32 (upd.)
Vodafone Group PLC, 11; 36 (upd.)
Vosper Thornycroft Holding plc, 41
W H Smith Group PLC, V
Wassall Plc, 18
Waterford Wedgwood Holdings PLC, 12
Watson Wyatt Worldwide, 42
Wellcome Foundation Ltd., The, I
WH Smith PLC, 42 (upd.)
Whatman plc, 46
Whitbread PLC, I; 20 (upd.)
William Hill Organization Limited, 49
Willis Corroon Group plc, 25
Wilson Bowden Plc, 45
Wm. Morrison Supermarkets PLC, 38
Wood Hall Trust PLC, I
Woolwich plc, The, 30
WPP Group plc, 6; 48 (upd.)
WS Atkins Plc, 45
Young & Co.'s Brewery, P.L.C., 38
Zeneca Group PLC, 21

United States

A & E Television Networks, 32
A & W Brands, Inc., 25
A. Schulman, Inc., 8; 49 (upd.)
A.B. Watley Group Inc., 45
A.B.Dick Company, 28
A.C. Moore Arts & Crafts, Inc., 30
A.C. Nielsen Company, 13
A.G. Edwards, Inc., 8; 32
A.H. Belo Corporation, 10; 30 (upd.)
A.L. Pharma Inc., 12
A.M. Castle & Co., 25
A.O. Smith Corporation, 11; 40 (upd.)
A.T. Cross Company, 17; 49 (upd.)
AAF-McQuay Incorporated, 26
AAON, Inc., 22
AAR Corp., 28
Aaron Rents, Inc., 14; 35 (upd.)
AARP, 27
Aavid Thermal Technologies, Inc., 29
Abbott Laboratories, I; 11 (upd.); 40 (upd.)
ABC Appliance, Inc., 10
ABC Carpet & Home Co. Inc., 26
ABC Rail Products Corporation, 18
ABC Supply Co., Inc., 22
Abercrombie & Fitch Co., 15; 35 (upd.)
Abigail Adams National Bancorp, Inc., 23
Abiomed, Inc., 47
ABM Industries Incorporated, 25 (upd.)
Abrams Industries Inc., 23
Academy Sports & Outdoors, 27
Acadian Ambulance & Air Med Services, Inc., 39
Acclaim Entertainment Inc., 24
ACCO World Corporation, 7
ACE Cash Express, Inc., 33
Ace Hardware Corporation, 12; 35 (upd.)
Aceto Corp., 38
Ackerley Communications, Inc., 9
Acme-Cleveland Corp., 13
ACNielsen Corporation, 38 (upd.)
Acsys, Inc., 44
Action Performance Companies, Inc., 27
Activision, Inc., 32
Acuson Corporation, 10; 36 (upd.)
Acxiom Corporation, 35
Adams Golf, Inc., 37
Adaptec, Inc., 31

United States (*continued*)

ADC Telecommunications, Inc., 10; 30 (upd.)
Adelphia Communications Corp., 17
Adobe Systems Inc., 10; 33 (upd.)
Adolph Coors Company, I; 13 (upd.); 36 (upd.)
ADT Security Services, Inc., 12; 44 (upd.)
Adtran Inc., 22
Advance Publications Inc., IV; 19 (upd.)
Advanced Marketing Services, Inc., 34
Advanced Micro Devices, Inc., 6; 30 (upd.)
Advanced Technology Laboratories, Inc., 9
Advanta Corporation, 8; 38 (upd.)
Advantica Restaurant Group, Inc., 27 (upd.)
Advo, Inc., 6
Advocat Inc., 46
AEI Music Network Inc., 35
AEP Industries, Inc., 36
Aeronca Inc., 46
Aeroquip Corporation, 16
AES Corporation, The, 10; 13 (upd.)
Aetna, Inc., III; 21 (upd.)
AFC Enterprises, Inc., 32
Affiliated Publications, Inc., 7
AFLAC Incorporated, 10 (upd.); 38 (upd.)
Ag-Chem Equipment Company, Inc., 17
AGCO Corp., 13
Agilent Technologies Inc., 38
Agway, Inc., 7; 21 (upd.)
AHL Services, Inc., 27
Air & Water Technologies Corporation, 6
Air Express International Corporation, 13
Air Products and Chemicals, Inc., I; 10 (upd.)
Airborne Freight Corporation, 6; 34 (upd.)
AirTouch Communications, 11
AirTran Holdings, Inc., 22
AK Steel Holding Corporation, 19; 41 (upd.)
Akin, Gump, Strauss, Hauer & Feld, L.L.P., 33
Akorn, Inc., 32
Alamo Group Inc., 32
Alamo Rent A Car, Inc., 6; 24 (upd.)
Alaska Air Group, Inc., 6; 29 (upd.)
Alba-Waldensian, Inc., 30
Albany International Corp., 8
Alberto-Culver Company, 8; 36 (upd.)
Albertson's Inc., II; 7 (upd.); 30 (upd.)
Alco Health Services Corporation, III
Alco Standard Corporation, I
Aldila Inc., 46
Aldus Corporation, 10
Alex Lee Inc., 18; 44 (upd.)
Alexander & Alexander Services Inc., 10
Alexander & Baldwin, Inc., 10; 40 (upd.)
Alexander's, Inc., 45
All American Communications Inc., 20
Alleghany Corporation, 10
Allegheny Energy, Inc., 38 (upd.)
Allegheny Ludlum Corporation, 8
Allegheny Power System, Inc., V
Allen Organ Company, 33
Allergan, Inc., 10; 30 (upd.)
Alliance Entertainment Corp., 17
Alliant Techsystems Inc., 8; 30 (upd.)
Allied Healthcare Products, Inc., 24
Allied Products Corporation, 21
Allied Signal Engines, 9
Allied Worldwide, Inc., 49
AlliedSignal Inc., I; 22 (upd.)
Allison Gas Turbine Division, 9
Allou Health & Beauty Care, Inc., 28
Allstate Corporation, The, 10; 27 (upd.)
ALLTEL Corporation, 6; 46 (upd.)

Alltrista Corporation, 30
Allwaste, Inc., 18
Aloha Airlines, Incorporated, 24
Alpharma Inc., 35 (upd.)
Alpine Lace Brands, Inc., 18
AltaVista Company, 43
Altera Corporation, 18; 43 (upd.)
Alterra Healthcare Corporation, 42
Altron Incorporated, 20
Aluminum Company of America, IV; 20 (upd.)
ALZA Corporation, 10; 36 (upd.)
AMAX Inc., IV
Amazon.com, Inc., 25
Amblin Entertainment, 21
AMC Entertainment Inc., 12; 35 (upd.)
AMCORE Financial Inc., 44
Amdahl Corporation, III; 14 (upd.); 40 (upd.)
Amdocs Ltd., 47
Amerada Hess Corporation, IV; 21 (upd.)
Amerco, 6
America Online, Inc., 10 ; 26 (upd.)
America West Airlines, 6
America West Holdings Corporation, 34 (upd.)
America's Favorite Chicken Company, Inc., 7
American Airlines, I; 6 (upd.)
American Banknote Corporation, 30
American Bar Association, 35
American Biltrite Inc., 16; 43 (upd.)
American Brands, Inc., V
American Building Maintenance Industries, Inc., 6
American Business Information, Inc., 18
American Business Products, Inc., 20
American Cancer Society, The, 24
American Classic Voyages Company, 27
American Coin Merchandising, Inc., 28
American Colloid Co., 13
American Crystal Sugar Company, 9; 32 (upd.)
American Cyanamid, I; 8 (upd.)
American Eagle Outfitters, Inc., 24
American Electric Power Company, Inc., V; 45 (upd.)
American Express Company, II; 10 (upd.); 38 (upd.)
American Family Corporation, III
American Financial Corporation, III
American Financial Group Inc., 48 (upd.)
American Foods Group, 43
American Furniture Company, Inc., 21
American General Corporation, III; 10 (upd.); 46 (upd.)
American General Finance Corp., 11
American Golf Corporation, 45
American Greetings Corporation, 7; 22 (upd.)
American Home Mortgage Holdings, Inc., 46
American Home Products, I; 10 (upd.)
American Homestar Corporation, 18; 41 (upd.)
American Institute of Certified Public Accountants (AICPA), 44
American International Group, Inc., III; 15 (upd.); 47 (upd.)
American Italian Pasta Company, 27
American Lawyer Media Holdings, Inc., 32
American Locker Group Incorporated, 34
American Lung Association, 48
American Maize-Products Co., 14
American Management Systems, Inc., 11
American Media, Inc., 27
American Medical Association, 39
American Medical International, Inc., III

American Medical Response, Inc., 39
American Motors Corporation, I
American National Insurance Company, 8; 27 (upd.)
American Pad & Paper Company, 20
American Power Conversion Corporation, 24
American Premier Underwriters, Inc., 10
American President Companies Ltd., 6
American Printing House for the Blind, 26
American Re Corporation, 10; 35 (upd.)
American Red Cross, 40
American Residential Mortgage Corporation, 8
American Retirement Corporation, 42
American Rice, Inc., 33
American Safety Razor Company, 20
American Skiing Company, 28
American Society of Composers, Authors and Publishers (ASCAP), The, 29
American Software Inc., 25
American Standard Companies Inc., III; 30 (upd.)
American States Water Company, 46
American Stores Company, II; 22 (upd.)
American Telephone and Telegraph Company, V
American Tourister, Inc., 16
American Tower Corporation, 33
American Vanguard Corporation, 47
American Water Works Company, Inc., 6; 38 (upd.)
American Woodmark Corporation, 31
Amerihost Properties, Inc., 30
AmeriSource Health Corporation, 37 (upd.)
Ameristar Casinos, Inc., 33
Ameritech Corporation, V; 18 (upd.)
Ameritrade Holding Corporation, 34
Ameriwood Industries International Corp., 17
Ames Department Stores, Inc., 9; 30 (upd.)
AMETEK, Inc., 9
AMF Bowling, Inc., 40
Amfac/JMB Hawaii L.L.C., I; 24 (upd.)
Amgen, Inc., 10; 30 (upd.)
Amoco Corporation, IV; 14 (upd.)
Amoskeag Company, 8
AMP Incorporated, II; 14 (upd.)
Ampex Corporation, 17
Amphenol Corporation, 40
AMR Corporation, 28 (upd.)
AMREP Corporation, 21
AmSouth Bancorporation, 12; 48 (upd.)
Amsted Industries Incorporated, 7
AmSurg Corporation, 48
Amtran, Inc., 34
Amway Corporation, III; 13 (upd.); 30 (upd.)
Anadarko Petroleum Corporation, 10
Analog Devices, Inc., 10
Analogic Corporation, 23
Analysts International Corporation, 36
Analytic Sciences Corporation, 10
Analytical Surveys, Inc., 33
Anaren Microwave, Inc., 33
Anchor Bancorp, Inc., 10
Anchor Brewing Company, 47
Anchor Gaming, 24
Anchor Hocking Glassware, 13
Andersen Corporation, 10
Andersen Worldwide, 29 (upd.)
Andersons, Inc., The, 31
Andrew Corporation, 10; 32 (upd.)
Andrews McMeel Universal, 40
Angelica Corporation, 15; 43 (upd.)
Anheuser-Busch Companies, Inc., I; 10 (upd.); 34 (upd.)

AnnTaylor Stores Corporation, 13; 37 (upd.)
ANR Pipeline Co., 17
Anschutz Corporation, The, 12; 36 (upd.)
Anthem Electronics, Inc., 13
Antioch Company, The, 40
Aon Corporation, III; 45 (upd.)
Apache Corporation, 10; 32 (upd.)
Apartment Investment and Management Company, 49
Apogee Enterprises, Inc., 8
Apollo Group, Inc., 24
Applause Inc., 24
Apple Computer, Inc., III; 6 (upd.); 36 (upd.)
Applebee's International Inc., 14; 35 (upd.)
Appliance Recycling Centers of America, Inc., 42
Applica Incorporated, 43 (upd.)
Applied Bioscience International, Inc., 10
Applied Films Corporation, 48
Applied Materials, Inc., 10; 46 (upd.)
Applied Micro Circuits Corporation, 38
Applied Power, Inc., 9; 32 (upd.)
Aqua Alliance Inc., 32 (upd.)
AR Accessories Group, Inc., 23
ARA Services, II
ARAMARK Corporation, 13; 41 (upd.)
Arandell Corporation, 37
Arbitron Company, The, 38
Arbor Drugs Inc., 12
Arby's Inc., 14
Arch Mineral Corporation, 7
Arch Wireless, Inc., 39
Archer-Daniels-Midland Company, I; 11 (upd.); 32 (upd.)
Archstone-Smith Trust, 49
Archway Cookies, Inc., 29
ARCO Chemical Company, 10
Arctco, Inc., 16
Arctic Cat Inc., 40 (upd.)
Arctic Slope Regional Corporation, 38
Arden Group, Inc., 29
Argosy Gaming Company, 21
Ariens Company, 48
Aris Industries, Inc., 16
Ark Restaurants Corp., 20
Arkansas Best Corporation, 16
Arkla, Inc., V
Armco Inc., IV
Armor All Products Corp., 16
Armor Holdings, Inc., 27
Armstrong World Industries, Inc., III; 22 (upd.)
Army and Air Force Exchange Service, 39
Arnold & Porter, 35
Arrow Electronics, Inc., 10
Art Institute of Chicago, The, 29
Art Van Furniture, Inc., 28
Artesyn Technologies Inc., 46 (upd.)
Arthur D. Little, Inc., 35
Arthur Murray International, Inc., 32
Artisan Entertainment Inc., 32 (upd.)
Arvin Industries, Inc., 8
Asanté Technologies, Inc., 20
ASARCO Incorporated, IV
Ascend Communications, Inc., 24
Ashland Inc., 19
Ashland Oil, Inc., IV
Ashley Furniture Industries, Inc., 35
Ashworth, Inc., 26
ASK Group, Inc., 9
Aspect Telecommunications Corporation, 22
Aspen Skiing Company, 15
Asplundh Tree Expert Co., 20
Assisted Living Concepts, Inc., 43
Associated Estates Realty Corporation, 25

Associated Grocers, Incorporated, 9; 31 (upd.)
Associated Milk Producers, Inc., 11; 48 (upd.)
Associated Natural Gas Corporation, 11
Associated Press, The, 13; 31 (upd.)
AST Research Inc., 9
Astoria Financial Corporation, 44
Astronics Corporation, 35
ASV, Inc., 34
At Home Corporation, 43
AT&T Bell Laboratories, Inc., 13
AT&T Corporation, 29 (upd.)
Atari Corporation, 9; 23 (upd.)
Atchison Casting Corporation, 39
Atlanta Gas Light Company, 6; 23 (upd.)
Atlanta National League Baseball Club, Inc., 43
Atlantic American Corporation, 44
Atlantic Energy, Inc., 6
Atlantic Group, The, 23
Atlantic Richfield Company, IV; 31 (upd.)
Atlantic Southeast Airlines, Inc., 47
Atlas Air, Inc., 39
Atlas Van Lines, Inc., 14
Atmel Corporation, 17
Atmos Energy Corporation, 43
Au Bon Pain Co., Inc., 18
Audio King Corporation, 24
Audiovox Corporation, 34
Ault Incorporated, 34
Auntie Anne's, Inc., 35
Aurora Foods Inc., 32
Austin Company, The, 8
Authentic Fitness Corp., 20
Auto Value Associates, Inc., 25
Autobytel Inc., 47
Autodesk, Inc., 10
Autologic Information International, Inc., 20
Automatic Data Processing, Inc., III; 9 (upd.); 47 (upd.)
Autotote Corporation, 20
AutoZone, Inc., 9; 31 (upd.)
Avado Brands, Inc., 31
Avco Financial Services Inc., 13
Aveda Corporation, 24
Avedis Zildjian Co., 38
Avery Dennison Corporation, IV; 17 (upd.); 49 (upd.)
Aviation Sales Company, 41
Avid Technology Inc., 38
Avis Rent A Car, Inc., 6; 22 (upd.)
Avnet Inc., 9
Avon Products, Inc., III; 19 (upd.); 46 (upd.)
Avondale Industries, 7; 41 (upd.)
Aydin Corp., 19
Azcon Corporation, 23
Aztar Corporation, 13
B&G Foods, Inc., 40
B. Dalton Bookseller Inc., 25
B. Manischewitz Company, LLC, The, 31
B/E Aerospace, Inc., 30
Babbage's, Inc., 10
Baby Superstore, Inc., 15
Bachman's Inc., 22
Back Bay Restaurant Group, Inc., 20
Back Yard Burgers, Inc., 45
Badger Meter, Inc., 22
Badger Paper Mills, Inc., 15
Bairnco Corporation, 28
Baker & Hostetler LLP, 40
Baker & McKenzie, 10; 42 (upd.)
Baker & Taylor Corporation, 16; 43 (upd.)
Baker and Botts, L.L.P., 28
Baker Hughes Incorporated, III; 22 (upd.)
Balance Bar Company, 32

Balchem Corporation, 42
Baldor Electric Company, 21
Baldwin Piano & Organ Company, 18
Baldwin Technology Company, Inc., 25
Ball Corporation, I; 10 (upd.)
Ballantyne of Omaha, Inc., 27
Ballard Medical Products, 21
Bally Manufacturing Corporation, III
Bally Total Fitness Holding Corp., 25
Baltek Corporation, 34
Baltimore Gas and Electric Company, V; 25 (upd.)
Banana Republic Inc., 25
Banc One Corporation, 10
Bandag, Inc., 19
Banfi Products Corp., 36
Bank of America Corporation, 46 (upd.)
Bank of Boston Corporation, II
Bank of Mississippi, Inc., 14
Bank of New England Corporation, II
Bank of New York Company, Inc., The, II; 46 (upd.)
Bank One Corporation, 36 (upd.)
BankAmerica Corporation, II; 8 (upd.)
Bankers Trust New York Corporation, II
Banner Aerospace, Inc., 14; 37 (upd.)
Banta Corporation, 12; 32 (upd.)
Banyan Systems Inc., 25
BarclaysAmerican Mortgage Corporation, 11
Barnes & Noble, Inc., 10; 30 (upd.)
Barnes Group Inc., 13
Barnett Banks, Inc., 9
Barnett Inc., 28
Barney's, Inc., 28
Barr Laboratories, Inc., 26
Barrett Business Services, Inc., 16
Bashas' Inc., 33
Bass Pro Shops, Inc., 42
Bassett Furniture Industries, Inc., 18
Bates Worldwide, Inc., 14; 33 (upd.)
Bath Iron Works, 12; 36 (upd.)
Battelle Memorial Institute, Inc., 10
Battle Mountain Gold Company, 23
Bausch & Lomb Inc., 7; 25 (upd.)
Baxter International Inc., I; 10 (upd.)
Bay State Gas Company, 38
BayBanks, Inc., 12
Bayou Steel Corporation, 31
BBN Corp., 19
BEA Systems, Inc., 36
Bear Creek Corporation, 38
Bear Stearns Companies, Inc., II; 10 (upd.)
Bearings, Inc., 13
Beatrice Company, II
BeautiControl Cosmetics, Inc., 21
Beazer Homes USA, Inc., 17
bebe stores, inc., 31
Bechtel Group, Inc., I; 24 (upd.)
Beckett Papers, 23
Beckman Coulter, Inc., 22
Beckman Instruments, Inc., 14
Becton, Dickinson & Company, I; 11 (upd.); 36 (upd.)
Bed Bath & Beyond Inc., 13; 41 (upd.)
Beech Aircraft Corporation, 8
Beech-Nut Nutrition Corporation, 21
Bekins Company, 15
Belco Oil & Gas Corp., 40
Belden, Inc., 19
Belk Stores Services, Inc., V; 19 (upd.)
Bell and Howell Company, 9; 29 (upd.)
Bell Atlantic Corporation, V; 25 (upd.)
Bell Helicopter Textron Inc., 46
Bell Industries, Inc., 47
Bell Sports Corporation, 16; 44 (upd.)
BellSouth Corporation, V; 29 (upd.)
Beloit Corporation, 14

United States (*continued*)

Bemis Company, Inc., 8
Ben & Jerry's Homemade, Inc., 10; 35 (upd.)
Benchmark Capital, 49
Benchmark Electronics, Inc., 40
Bendix Corporation, I
Beneficial Corporation, 8
Benihana, Inc., 18
Benjamin Moore & Co., 13; 38 (upd.)
Benton Oil and Gas Company, 47
Bergen Brunswig Corporation, V; 13 (upd.)
Beringer Wine Estates Holdings, Inc., 22
Berkeley Farms, Inc., 46
Berkshire Hathaway Inc., III; 18 (upd.); 42 (upd.)
Berkshire Realty Holdings, L.P., 49
Berlitz International, Inc., 13; 39 (upd.)
Bernard C. Harris Publishing Company, Inc., 39
Bernard Chaus, Inc., 27
Berry Petroleum Company, 47
Berry Plastics Corporation, 21
Bertucci's Inc., 16
Best Buy Co., Inc., 9; 23 (upd.)
Bestfoods, 22 (upd.)
BET Holdings, Inc., 18
Bethlehem Steel Corporation, IV; 7 (upd.); 27 (upd.)
Betz Laboratories, Inc., I; 10 (upd.)
Beverly Enterprises, Inc., III; 16 (upd.)
BFGoodrich Company, The, V; 19 (upd.)
BHC Communications, Inc., 26
BIC Corporation, 8; 23 (upd.)
Bicoastal Corporation, II
Big V Supermarkets, Inc., 25
Big B, Inc., 17
Big Bear Stores Co., 13
Big Dog Holdings, Inc., 45
Big Flower Press Holdings, Inc., 21
Big Idea Productions, Inc., 49
Big O Tires, Inc., 20
Big Rivers Electric Corporation, 11
Bill & Melinda Gates Foundation, 41
Bill Blass Ltd., 32
Billing Concepts Corp., 26
Bindley Western Industries, Inc., 9
Bingham Dana LLP, 43
Binks Sames Corporation, 21
Binney & Smith Inc., 25
Biogen Inc., 14; 36 (upd.)
Biomet, Inc., 10
Bird Corporation, 19
Birkenstock Footprint Sandals, Inc., 12; 42 (upd.)
Birmingham Steel Corporation, 13; 40 (upd.)
BISSELL Inc., 9; 30 (upd.)
BJ Services Company, 25
Black & Decker Corporation, The, III; 20 (upd.)
Black & Veatch LLP, 22
Black Box Corporation, 20
Black Hills Corporation, 20
Blair Corporation, 25; 31
Blessings Corp., 19
Blimpie International, Inc., 15; 49 (upd.)
Block Drug Company, Inc., 8; 27 (upd.)
Blockbuster Inc., 9; 31 (upd.)
Blonder Tongue Laboratories, Inc., 48
Bloomberg L.P., 21
Bloomingdale's Inc., 12
Blount International, Inc., 48 (upd.)
Blount, Inc., 12
Blue Bell Creameries L.P., 30
Blue Bird Corporation, 35

Blue Cross and Blue Shield Association, 10
Blue Diamond Growers, 28
Blue Mountain Arts, Inc., 29
Blyth Industries, Inc., 18
BMC Industries, Inc., 17
Boart Longyear Company, 26
Boatmen's Bancshares Inc., 15
Bob Evans Farms, Inc., 9
Boca Resorts, Inc., 37
Boeing Company, The, I; 10 (upd.); 32 (upd.)
Bohemia, Inc., 13
Boise Cascade Corporation, IV; 8 (upd.); 32 (upd.)
Bombay Company, Inc., The, 10
Bon Marché, Inc., The, 23
Bon Secours Health System, Inc., 24
Bon-Ton Stores, Inc., The, 16
Bonneville International Corporation, 29
Book-of-the-Month Club, Inc., 13
Books-A-Million, Inc., 14; 41 (upd.)
Boole & Babbage, Inc., 25
Booth Creek Ski Holdings, Inc., 31
Booz Allen & Hamilton Inc., 10
Borden, Inc., II; 22 (upd.)
Borders Group, Inc., 15; 43 (upd.)
Borg-Warner Automotive, Inc., 14; 32 (upd.)
Borg-Warner Corporation, III
Borland International, Inc., 9
Boron, LePore & Associates, Inc., 45
Boscov's Department Store, Inc., 31
Bose Corporation, 13; 36 (upd.)
Boston Acoustics, Inc., 22
Boston Beer Company, 18
Boston Celtics Limited Partnership, 14
Boston Chicken, Inc., 12
Boston Edison Company, 12
Boston Market Corporation, 48 (upd.)
Boston Professional Hockey Association Inc., 39
Boston Properties, Inc., 22
Boston Scientific Corporation, 37
Bowne & Co., Inc., 23
Boy Scouts of America, The, 34
Boyd Bros. Transportation Inc., 39
Boyd Gaming Corporation, 43
Boyds Collection, Ltd., The, 29
Bozell Worldwide Inc., 25
Bozzuto's, Inc., 13
Brach and Brock Confections, Inc., 15
Bradlees Discount Department Store Company, 12
Brannock Device Company, 48
Brass Eagle Inc., 34
Brazos Sportswear, Inc., 23
Bremer Financial Corp., 45
Bridgeport Machines, Inc., 17
Bridgford Foods Corporation, 27
Briggs & Stratton Corporation, 8; 27 (upd.)
Bright Horizons Family Solutions, Inc., 31
Brightpoint, Inc., 18
Brinker International, Inc., 10; 38 (upd.)
Bristol Hotel Company, 23
Bristol-Myers Squibb Company, III; 9 (upd.); 37 (upd.)
Brite Voice Systems, Inc., 20
Broadcast Music Inc., 23
Broadcom Corporation, 34
Broadmoor Hotel, The, 30
Brobeck, Phleger & Harrison, LLP, 31
Broder Bros. Co., 38
Broderbund Software, Inc., 13; 29 (upd.)
Brooke Group Ltd., 15
Brooklyn Union Gas, 6
Brooks Brothers Inc., 22
Brooks Sports Inc., 32

Brookshire Grocery Company, 16
Brookstone, Inc., 18
Brothers Gourmet Coffees, Inc., 20
Broughton Foods Co., 17
Brown & Brown, Inc., 41
Brown & Haley, 23
Brown & Root, Inc., 13
Brown & Sharpe Manufacturing Co., 23
Brown & Williamson Tobacco Corporation, 14; 33 (upd.)
Brown Brothers Harriman & Co., 45
Brown Group, Inc., V; 20 (upd.)
Brown Printing Company, 26
Brown-Forman Corporation, I; 10 (upd.); 38 (upd.)
Browning-Ferris Industries, Inc., V; 20 (upd.)
Broyhill Furniture Industries, Inc., 10
Bruce Foods Corporation, 39
Bruno's, Inc., 7; 26 (upd.)
Brunswick Corporation, III; 22 (upd.)
Brush Wellman Inc., 14
BTG, Inc., 45
Buca, Inc., 38
Buck Knives Inc., 48
Buckeye Technologies, Inc., 42
Buckle, Inc., The, 18
Bucyrus International, Inc., 17
Budd Company, The, 8
Budget Group, Inc., 25
Budget Rent a Car Corporation, 9
Buffets, Inc., 10; 32 (upd.)
Bugle Boy Industries, Inc., 18
Bulova Corporation, 13; 41 (upd.)
Bundy Corporation, 17
Bureau of National Affairs, Inc.,The 23
Burger King Corporation, II; 17 (upd.)
Burlington Coat Factory Warehouse Corporation, 10
Burlington Industries, Inc., V; 17 (upd.)
Burlington Northern Santa Fe Corporation, V; 27 (upd.)
Burlington Resources Inc., 10
Burns International Services Corporation, 13; 41 (upd.)
Burr-Brown Corporation, 19
Burton Snowboards Inc., 22
Bush Boake Allen Inc., 30
Bush Brothers & Company, 45
Bush Industries, Inc., 20
Business Men's Assurance Company of America, 14
Butler Manufacturing Co., 12
Butterick Co., Inc., 23
Buttrey Food & Drug Stores Co., 18
buy.com, Inc., 46
BWAY Corporation, 24
C-COR.net Corp., 38
C-Cube Microsystems, Inc., 37
C.F. Martin & Co., Inc., 42
C.H. Heist Corporation, 24
C.H. Robinson Worldwide, Inc., 11; 40 (upd.)
C.R. Bard Inc., 9
Cabela's Inc., 26
Cabletron Systems, Inc., 10
Cablevision Electronic Instruments, Inc., 32
Cablevision Systems Corporation, 7; 30 (upd.)
Cabot Corporation, 8; 29 (upd.)
Cache Incorporated, 30
CACI International Inc., 21
Cadence Design Systems, Inc., 11; 48 (upd.)
Cadmus Communications Corporation, 23
Cadwalader, Wickersham & Taft, 32
CAE USA Inc., 48
Caere Corporation, 20

Caesars World, Inc., 6
Cagle's, Inc., 20
Cahners Business Information, 43
Calavo Growers, Inc., 47
CalComp Inc., 13
Calcot Ltd., 33
Caldor Inc., 12
California Pizza Kitchen Inc., 15
Callaway Golf Company, 15; 45 (upd.)
Callon Petroleum Company, 47
CalMat Co., 19
Calpine Corporation, 36
Caltex Petroleum Corporation, 19
Calvin Klein, Inc., 22
Cambrex Corporation, 16; 44 (upd.)
Cambridge SoundWorks, Inc., 48
Cambridge Technology Partners, Inc., 36
Camelot Music, Inc., 26
Cameron & Barkley Company, 28
Campbell Soup Company, II; 7 (upd.); 26
    (upd.)
Campbell-Mithun-Esty, Inc., 16
Campo Electronics, Appliances &
    Computers, Inc., 16
Canandaigua Brands, Inc., 34 (upd.)
Canandaigua Wine Company, Inc., 13
Candela Corporation, 48
Candie's, Inc., 31
Candlewood Hotel Company, Inc., 41
Cannondale Corporation, 21
Canterbury Park Holding Corporation, 42
Cap Rock Energy Corporation, 46
Capel Incorporated, 45
Capital Cities/ABC Inc., II
Capital Holding Corporation, III
CapStar Hotel Company, 21
Caraustar Industries, Inc., 19; 44 (upd.)
Carbide/Graphite Group, Inc., The, 40
Cardinal Health, Inc., 18
Career Education Corporation, 45
Caremark International Inc., 10
Carey International, Inc., 26
Cargill, Incorporated, II; 13 (upd.); 40
    (upd.)
Carhartt, Inc., 30
Caribiner International, Inc., 24
Caribou Coffee Company, Inc., 28
Carlisle Companies Incorporated, 8
Carlson Companies, Inc., 6; 22 (upd.)
Carmichael Lynch Inc., 28
Carmike Cinemas, Inc., 14; 37 (upd.)
Carnation Company, II
Carnegie Corporation of New York, 35
Carnival Corporation, 27 (upd.)
Carnival Cruise Lines, Inc., 6
Carolina First Corporation, 31
Carolina Freight Corporation, 6
Carolina Power & Light Company, V; 23
    (upd.)
Carolina Telephone and Telegraph
    Company, 10
Carpenter Technology Corporation, 13
CARQUEST Corporation, 29
Carr-Gottstein Foods Co., 17
Carriage Services, Inc., 37
Carrier Access Corporation, 44
Carrier Corporation, 7
Carroll's Foods, Inc., 46
Carsey-Werner Company, L.L.C., The, 37
Carson Pirie Scott & Company, 15
Carson, Inc., 31
Carter Hawley Hale Stores, Inc., V
Carter Lumber Company, 45
Carter-Wallace, Inc., 8; 38 (upd.)
Carvel Corporation, 35
Cascade Natural Gas Corporation, 9
Casco Northern Bank, 14

Casey's General Stores, Inc., 19
Cash America International, Inc., 20
Castle & Cooke, Inc., II; 20 (upd.)
Casual Corner Group, Inc., 43
Catalina Lighting, Inc., 43 (upd.)
Catalina Marketing Corporation, 18
Catalytica Energy Systems, Inc., 44
Catellus Development Corporation, 24
Caterpillar Inc., III; 15 (upd.)
Catherines Stores Corporation, 15
Catholic Order of Foresters, 24
Cato Corporation, 14
Cattleman's, Inc., 20
CB Commercial Real Estate Services
    Group, Inc., 21
CBI Industries, Inc., 7
CBRL Group, Inc., 35 (upd.)
CBS Corporation, II; 6 (upd.); 28 (upd.)
CCH Inc., 14
CDI Corporation, 6
CDW Computer Centers, Inc., 16
CEC Entertainment, Inc., 31 (upd.)
Cedar Fair, L.P., 22
Celadon Group Inc., 30
Celanese Corporation, I
Celebrity, Inc., 22
Celestial Seasonings, Inc., 16
Cendant Corporation, 44 (upd.)
Centel Corporation, 6
Centennial Communications Corporation,
    39
Centerior Energy Corporation, V
Centex Corporation, 8; 29 (upd.)
Centocor Inc., 14
Central and South West Corporation, V
Central Garden & Pet Company, 23
Central Hudson Gas and Electricity
    Corporation, 6
Central Maine Power, 6
Central Newspapers, Inc., 10
Central Parking Corporation, 18
Central Soya Company, Inc., 7
Central Sprinkler Corporation, 29
Century Communications Corp., 10
Century Telephone Enterprises, Inc., 9
Century Theatres, Inc., 31
Cephalon, Inc., 45
Cerner Corporation, 16
CertainTeed Corporation, 35
Cessna Aircraft Company, 8; 27 (upd.)
Chadbourne & Parke, 36
Chadwick's of Boston, Ltd., 29
Chalone Wine Group, Ltd., The, 36
Champion Enterprises, Inc., 17
Champion Industries, Inc., 28
Champion International Corporation, IV;
    20 (upd.)
Championship Auto Racing Teams, Inc.,
    37
Chancellor Media Corporation, 24
Chaparral Steel Co., 13
Charles River Laboratories International,
    Inc., 42
Charles Schwab Corporation, The, 8; 26
    (upd.)
Charles Stark Draper Laboratory, Inc., The,
    35
Charlotte Russe Holding, Inc., 35
Charming Shoppes, Inc., 8; 38
Chart House Enterprises, Inc., 17
Chart Industries, Inc., 21
Charter Communications, Inc., 33
ChartHouse International Learning
    Corporation, 49
Chase Manhattan Corporation, The, II; 13
    (upd.)
Chateau Communities, Inc., 37
Chattem, Inc., 17

Chautauqua Airlines, Inc., 38
Checkers Drive-Up Restaurants Inc., 16
Checkpoint Systems, Inc., 39
Cheesecake Factory Inc., The, 17
Chelsea Milling Company, 29
Chemcentral Corporation, 8
Chemed Corporation, 13
Chemfab Corporation, 35
Chemi-Trol Chemical Co., 16
Chemical Banking Corporation, II; 14
    (upd.)
Chemical Waste Management, Inc., 9
Cherokee Inc., 18
Chesapeake Corporation, 8; 30 (upd.)
Chesebrough-Pond's USA, Inc., 8
Chevron Corporation, IV; 19 (upd.)
ChevronTexaco Corporation, 47 (upd.)
Cheyenne Software, Inc., 12
Chi-Chi's Inc., 13
Chiat/Day Inc. Advertising, 11
Chic by H.I.S, Inc., 20
Chicago and North Western Holdings
    Corporation, 6
Chicago Bears Football Club, Inc., 33
Chicago Board of Trade, 41
Chick-fil-A Inc., 23
Chicken of the Sea International, 24 (upd.)
Chico's FAS, Inc., 45
Children's Comprehensive Services, Inc.,
    42
Children's Place Retail Stores, Inc., The,
    37
Childtime Learning Centers, Inc., 34
Chiles Offshore Corporation, 9
CHIPS and Technologies, Inc., 9
Chiquita Brands International, Inc., 7; 21
    (upd.)
Chiron Corporation, 10; 36 (upd.)
Chisholm-Mingo Group, Inc., 41
Chock Full o' Nuts Corp., 17
Choice Hotels International Inc., 14
Chorus Line Corporation, 30
Chris-Craft Industries, Inc., 9; 31 (upd.)
Christensen Boyles Corporation, 26
Christopher & Banks Corporation, 42
Chromcraft Revington, Inc., 15
Chronicle Publishing Company, Inc., The,
    23
Chronimed Inc., 26
Chrysler Corporation, I; 11 (upd.)
CH2M Hill Ltd., 22
Chubb Corporation, The, III; 14 (upd.); 37
    (upd.)
Church & Dwight Co., Inc., 29
Churchill Downs Incorporated, 29
Cianbro Corporation, 14
Ciber, Inc., 18
CIGNA Corporation, III; 22 (upd.); 45
    (upd.)
Cincinnati Bell, Inc., 6
Cincinnati Financial Corporation, 16; 44
    (upd.)
Cincinnati Gas & Electric Company, 6
Cincinnati Milacron Inc., 12
Cincom Systems Inc., 15
Cinnabon Inc., 23
Cintas Corporation, 21
CIPSCO Inc., 6
Circle K Company, The, II; 20 (upd.)
Circon Corporation, 21
Circuit City Stores, Inc., 9; 29 (upd.)
Circus Circus Enterprises, Inc., 6
Cirrus Design Corporation, 44
Cirrus Logic, Inc., 11; 48 (upd.)
Cisco Systems, Inc., 11; 34 (upd.)
Citadel Communications Corporation, 35
Citfed Bancorp, Inc., 16

United States (*continued*)

CITGO Petroleum Corporation, IV, 31 (upd.)
Citicorp, II; 9 (upd.)
Citigroup Inc., 30 (upd.)
Citizens Financial Group, Inc., 42
Citizens Utilities Company, 7
Citrix Systems, Inc., 44
City Public Service, 6
CKE Restaurants, Inc., 19; 46 (upd.)
Claire's Stores, Inc., 17
Clarcor Inc., 17
Clark Construction Group, Inc., The, 8
Clark Equipment Company, 8
Classic Vacation Group, Inc., 46
Clayton Homes Incorporated, 13
Clear Channel Communications, Inc., 23
Cleary, Gottlieb, Steen & Hamilton, 35
Cleco Corporation, 37
Cleveland Indians Baseball Company, Inc., 37
Cleveland-Cliffs Inc., 13
Clorox Company, The, III; 22 (upd.)
Clothestime, Inc., The, 20
ClubCorp, Inc., 33
CML Group, Inc., 10
CMP Media Inc., 26
CMS Energy Corporation, V, 14
CNA Financial Corporation, III; 38 (upd.)
CNET Networks, Inc., 47
CNS, Inc., 20
Coach Leatherware, 10
Coach USA, Inc., 24
Coach, Inc., 45 (upd.)
Coastal Corporation, The, IV, 31 (upd.)
COBE Laboratories, Inc., 13
Coborn's, Inc., 30
Cobra Electronics Corporation, 14
Cobra Golf Inc., 16
Coca Cola Bottling Co. Consolidated, 10
Coca-Cola Company, The, I; 10 (upd.); 32 (upd.)
Coca-Cola Enterprises, Inc., 13
Coeur d'Alene Mines Corporation, 20
Cogentrix Energy, Inc., 10
Coherent, Inc., 31
Cohu, Inc., 32
Coinmach Laundry Corporation, 20
Coinstar, Inc., 44
Cold Spring Granite Company, 16
Coldwater Creek Inc., 21
Cole National Corporation, 13
Coleman Company, Inc., The, 9; 30 (upd.)
Coles Express Inc., 15
Colgate-Palmolive Company, III; 14 (upd.); 35 (upd.)
Collectors Universe, Inc., 48
Collins & Aikman Corporation, 13; 41 (upd.)
Collins Industries, Inc., 33
Colorado MEDtech, Inc., 48
Colt Industries Inc., I
Colt's Manufacturing Company, Inc., 12
Columbia Gas System, Inc., The, V; 16 (upd.)
Columbia Pictures Entertainment, Inc., II
Columbia Sportswear Company, 19; 41 (upd.)
Columbia TriStar Motion Pictures Companies, 12 (upd.)
Columbia/HCA Healthcare Corporation, 15
Columbus McKinnon Corporation, 37
Comair Holdings Inc., 13; 34 (upd.)
Comcast Corporation, 7; 24 (upd.)
Comdial Corporation, 21
Comdisco, Inc., 9
Comerica Incorporated, 40

COMFORCE Corporation, 40
Commerce Clearing House, Inc., 7
Commercial Credit Company, 8
Commercial Federal Corporation, 12
Commercial Financial Services, Inc., 26
Commercial Metals Company, 15; 42 (upd.)
Commodore International Ltd., 7
Commonwealth Edison Company, V
Commonwealth Energy System, 14
Commonwealth Telephone Enterprises, Inc., 25
Community Psychiatric Centers, 15
Compaq Computer Corporation, III; 6 (upd.); 26 (upd.)
CompDent Corporation, 22
CompHealth Inc., 25
Complete Business Solutions, Inc., 31
Comprehensive Care Corporation, 15
CompuAdd Computer Corporation, 11
CompuCom Systems, Inc., 10
CompUSA, Inc., 10; 35 (upd.)
CompuServe Interactive Services, Inc., 10; 27 (upd.)
Computer Associates International, Inc., 6; 49 (upd.)
Computer Data Systems, Inc., 14
Computer Learning Centers, Inc., 26
Computer Sciences Corporation, 6
Computerland Corp., 13
Computervision Corporation, 10
Compuware Corporation, 10; 30 (upd.)
Comsat Corporation, 23
Comshare Inc., 23
Comstock Resources, Inc., 47
Comverse Technology, Inc., 15; 43 (upd.)
ConAgra Foods, Inc., II; 12 (upd.); 42 (upd.)
Conair Corp., 17
Concepts Direct, Inc., 39
Concord Camera Corporation, 41
Concord Fabrics, Inc., 16
Condé Nast Publications Inc., The, 13
Cone Mills Corporation, 8
Conexant Systems, Inc., 36
Congoleum Corp., 18
Connecticut Light and Power Co., 13
Connecticut Mutual Life Insurance Company, III
Connell Company, The, 29
Conner Peripherals, Inc., 6
Conoco Inc., IV; 16 (upd.)
Conseco, Inc., 10; 33 (upd.)
Conso International Corporation, 29
Consolidated Delivery & Logistics, Inc., 24
Consolidated Edison Company of New York, Inc., V
Consolidated Edison, Inc., 45 (upd.)
Consolidated Freightways Corporation, V; 21 (upd.); 48 (upd.)
Consolidated Natural Gas Company, V; 19 (upd.)
Consolidated Papers, Inc., 8; 36 (upd.)
Consolidated Products Inc., 14
Consolidated Rail Corporation, V
Consumers Power Co., 14
Consumers Union, 26
Consumers Water Company, 14
Container Store, The, 36
ContiGroup Companies, Inc., 43 (upd.)
Continental Airlines, Inc., I; 21 (upd.)
Continental Bank Corporation, II
Continental Cablevision, Inc., 7
Continental Can Co., Inc., 15
Continental Corporation, The, III
Continental General Tire Corp., 23
Continental Grain Company, 10; 13 (upd.)
Continental Group Company, I

Continental Medical Systems, Inc., 10
Control Data Corporation, III
Control Data Systems, Inc., 10
Converse Inc., 9; 31 (upd.)
Cooker Restaurant Corporation, The, 20
Cooper Cameron Corporation, 20 (upd.)
Cooper Companies, Inc., The, 39
Cooper Industries, Inc., II; 44 (upd.)
Cooper Tire & Rubber Company, 8; 23 (upd.)
Coopers & Lybrand, 9
Copart Inc., 23
Copley Press, Inc., The, 23
Copps Corporation, The, 32
Corbis Corporation, 31
Cordis Corporation, 19; 46 (upd.)
CoreStates Financial Corp, 17
Corinthian Colleges, Inc., 39
Corning Inc., III; 44 (upd.)
Corporate Express, Inc., 22; 47 (upd.)
Corporate Software Inc., 9
Corporation for Public Broadcasting, 14
Correctional Services Corporation, 30
Corrections Corporation of America, 23
Corrpro Companies, Inc., 20
CORT Business Services Corporation, 26
Cosmair, Inc., 8
Cosmetic Center, Inc., The, 22
Cost Plus, Inc., 27
Costco Wholesale Corporation, V; 43 (upd.)
Cotter & Company, V
Cotton Incorporated, 46
Coty, Inc., 36
Coudert Brothers, 30
Countrywide Credit Industries, Inc., 16
County Seat Stores Inc., 9
Courier Corporation, 41
Covance Inc., 30
Covington & Burling, 40
Cowles Media Company, 23
Cox Enterprises, Inc., IV; 22 (upd.)
CPC International Inc., II
CPI Corp., 38
Cracker Barrel Old Country Store, Inc., 10
Craftmade International, Inc., 44
Crain Communications, Inc., 12; 35 (upd.)
Cramer, Berkowitz & Co., 34
Crane & Co., Inc., 26
Crane Co., 8; 30 (upd.)
Crate and Barrel, 9
Cravath, Swaine & Moore, 43
Cray Research, Inc., III; 16 (upd.)
Creative Artists Agency LLC, 38
Credit Acceptance Corporation, 18
Crompton & Knowles, 9
Crompton Corporation, 36 (upd.)
Croscill, Inc., 42
Crowley Maritime Corporation, 6; 28 (upd.)
Crowley, Milner & Company, 19
Crown Books Corporation, 21
Crown Central Petroleum Corporation, 7
Crown Crafts, Inc., 16
Crown Equipment Corporation, 15
Crown Media Holdings, Inc., 45
Crown Vantage Inc., 29
Crown, Cork & Seal Company, Inc., I; 13; 32 (upd.)
CRSS Inc., 6
Cruise America Inc., 21
CryoLife, Inc., 46
Crystal Brands, Inc., 9
CS First Boston Inc., II
CSK Auto Corporation, 38
CSS Industries, Inc., 35
CSX Corporation, V; 22 (upd.)
CTB International Corporation, 43 (upd.)

CTG, Inc., 11
CTS Corporation, 39
Cubic Corporation, 19
CUC International Inc., 16
Cuisinart Corporation, 24
Culbro Corporation, 15
Cullen/Frost Bankers, Inc., 25
Culligan Water Technologies, Inc., 12; 38 (upd.)
Culp, Inc., 29
Cumberland Farms, Inc., 17
Cumberland Packing Corporation, 26
Cummins Engine Company, Inc., I; 12 (upd.); 40 (upd.)
Cumulus Media Inc., 37
Cunard Line Ltd., 23
Current, Inc., 37
Curtice-Burns Foods, Inc., 7; 21 (upd.)
Curtiss-Wright Corporation, 10; 35 (upd.)
Custom Chrome, Inc., 16
Cutter & Buck Inc., 27
CVS Corporation, 45 (upd.)
Cybermedia, Inc., 25
Cybex International, Inc., 49
Cygne Designs, Inc., 25
Cypress Semiconductor Corporation, 20; 48 (upd.)
Cyprus Amax Minerals Company, 21
Cyprus Minerals Company, 7
Cyrk Inc., 19
Cytec Industries Inc., 27
Czarnikow-Rionda Company, Inc., 32
D&K Wholesale Drug, Inc., 14
D'Agostino Supermarkets Inc., 19
D'Arcy Masius Benton & Bowles, Inc., VI; 32 (upd.)
D.G. Yuengling & Son, Inc., 38
Daffy's Inc., 26
Dain Rauscher Corporation, 35 (upd.)
Dairy Mart Convenience Stores, Inc., 7; 25 (upd.)
Daisytek International Corporation, 18
Daktronics, Inc., 32
Dal-Tile International Inc., 22
Dale Carnegie Training, Inc., 28
Dallas Cowboys Football Club, Ltd., 33
Dallas Semiconductor Corporation, 13; 31 (upd.)
Damark International, Inc., 18
Dames & Moore, Inc., 25
Dan River Inc., 35
Dana Corporation, I; 10 (upd.)
Danaher Corporation, 7
Daniel Industries, Inc., 16
Dannon Co., Inc., 14
Danskin, Inc., 12
Darden Restaurants, Inc., 16; 44 (upd.)
Darigold, Inc., 9
Dart Group Corporation, 16
Data Broadcasting Corporation, 31
Data General Corporation, 8
Datapoint Corporation, 11
Datascope Corporation, 39
Datek Online Holdings Corp., 32
Dauphin Deposit Corporation, 14
Dave & Buster's, Inc., 33
Davey Tree Expert Company, The, 11
David and Lucile Packard Foundation, The, 41
David J. Joseph Company, The, 14
David's Bridal, Inc., 33
Davis Polk & Wardwell, 36
DAW Technologies, Inc., 25
Dawn Food Products, Inc., 17
Day & Zimmermann Inc., 9; 31 (upd.)
Day Runner, Inc., 14; 41 (upd.)
Dayton Hudson Corporation, V; 18 (upd.)
DC Comics Inc., 25

DDB Needham Worldwide, 14
Dean & DeLuca, Inc., 36
Dean Foods Company, 7; 21 (upd.)
Dean Witter, Discover & Co., 12
Death Row Records, 27
Deb Shops, Inc., 16
Debevoise & Plimpton, 39
Dechert, 43
Deckers Outdoor Corporation, 22
Decora Industries, Inc., 31
DeCrane Aircraft Holdings Inc., 36
DeepTech International Inc., 21
Deere & Company, III; 21 (upd.); 42 (upd.)
Defiance, Inc., 22
DeKalb Genetics Corporation, 17
Del Laboratories, Inc., 28
Del Monte Foods Company, 7; 23 (upd.)
Del Webb Corporation, 14
Delaware North Companies Incorporated, 7
dELiA*s Inc., 29
Dell Computer Corporation, 9; 31 (upd.)
Deloitte Touche Tohmatsu International, 9; 29 (upd.)
Delphi Automotive Systems Corporation, 45
Delta Air Lines, Inc., I; 6 (upd.); 39 (upd.)
Delta and Pine Land Company, 33
Delta Woodside Industries, Inc., 8; 30 (upd.)
Deltic Timber Corporation, 46
Deluxe Corporation, 7; 22 (upd.)
DeMoulas / Market Basket Inc., 23
DenAmerica Corporation, 29
Denison International plc, 46
Dentsply International Inc., 10
DEP Corporation, 20
Department VVI, Inc., 14; 34 (upd.)
Deposit Guaranty Corporation, 17
DePuy Inc., 30; 37 (upd.)
Designer Holdings Ltd., 20
Destec Energy, Inc., 12
Detroit Diesel Corporation, 10
Detroit Edison Company, The, V
Detroit Pistons Basketball Company, The, 41
Detroit Tigers Baseball Club, Inc., 46
Deutsch, Inc., 42
DeVry Incorporated, 29
Dewey Ballantine LLP, 48
Dexter Corporation, The, I; 12 (upd.)
DH Technology, Inc., 18
DHL Worldwide Express, 6; 24 (upd.)
Di Giorgio Corp., 12
Dial Corp., The, 8; 23 (upd.)
Dial-A-Mattress Operating Corporation, 46
Dialogic Corporation, 18
Diamond Shamrock, Inc., IV
Dibrell Brothers, Incorporated, 12
dick clark productions, inc., 16
Diebold, Incorporated, 7; 22 (upd.)
Diedrich Coffee, Inc., 40
Digex, Inc., 46
Digi International Inc., 9
Digital Equipment Corporation, III; 6 (upd.)
Dillard Department Stores, Inc., V; 16 (upd.)
Dillard Paper Company, 11
Dillingham Construction Corporation, I; 44 (upd.)
Dillon Companies Inc., 12
Dime Savings Bank of New York, F.S.B., 9
DIMON Inc., 27
Dionex Corporation, 46
Direct Focus, Inc., 47
DIRECTV, Inc., 38

Discount Auto Parts, Inc., 18
Discount Drug Mart, Inc., 14
Discovery Communications, Inc., 42
Dixie Group, Inc., The, 20
Dixon Industries, Inc., 26
Dixon Ticonderoga Company, 12
DMI Furniture, Inc., 46
Do it Best Corporation, 30
Documentum, Inc., 46
Dolby Laboratories Inc., 20
Dole Food Company, Inc., 9; 31 (upd.)
Dollar Thrifty Automotive Group, Inc., 25
Dollar Tree Stores, Inc., 23
Dominion Homes, Inc., 19
Dominion Resources, Inc., V
Domino Sugar Corporation, 26
Domino's Pizza, Inc., 7; 21 (upd.)
Don Massey Cadillac, Inc., 37
Donaldson Company, Inc., 16; 49 (upd.)
Donaldson, Lufkin & Jenrette, Inc., 22
Donna Karan Company, 15
Donnelly Corporation, 12; 35 (upd.)
Donnkenny, Inc., 17
Dorsey & Whitney LLP, 47
Doskocil Companies, Inc., 12
DoubleClick Inc., 46
Doubletree Corporation, 21
Douglas & Lomason Company, 16
Dover Corporation, III; 28 (upd.)
Dover Downs Entertainment, Inc., 43
Dover Publications Inc., 34
Dow Chemical Company, The, I; 8 (upd.)
Dow Jones & Company, Inc., IV; 19 (upd.); 47 (upd.)
Dow Jones Telerate, Inc., 10
DPL Inc., 6
DQE, Inc., 6
Dr Pepper/Seven Up, Inc., 9; 32 (upd.)
Drackett Professional Products, 12
Drake Beam Morin, Inc., 44
DreamWorks SKG, 43
Drees Company, Inc., The, 41
Dress Barn, Inc., The, 24
Dresser Industries, Inc., III
Drew Industries Inc., 28
Drexel Burnham Lambert Incorporated, II
Drexel Heritage Furnishings Inc., 12
Dreyer's Grand Ice Cream, Inc., 17
Drug Emporium, Inc., 12
Drypers Corporation, 18
DSC Communications Corporation, 12
DTE Energy Company, 20 (upd.)
Duane Reade Holding Corp., 21
Duck Head Apparel Company, Inc., 42
Duckwall-ALCO Stores, Inc., 24
Ducommun Incorporated, 30
Duke Energy Corporation, V; 27 (upd.)
Dun & Bradstreet Corporation, The, IV; 19 (upd.)
Dun & Bradstreet Software Services Inc., 11
Duplex Products Inc., 17
Duracell International Inc., 9
Durametallic, 21
Duriron Company Inc., 17
Duty Free International, Inc., 11
Dyersburg Corporation, 21
Dynatech Corporation, 13
DynCorp, 45
Dynegy Inc., 49 (upd.)
E! Entertainment Television Inc., 17
E*Trade Group, Inc., 20
E. & J. Gallo Winery, I; 7 (upd.); 28 (upd.)
E.I. du Pont de Nemours & Company, I; 8 (upd.); 26 (upd.)
E.piphany, Inc., 49
E.W. Scripps Company, The, IV; 7 (upd.); 28 (upd.)

United States (*continued*)

Eagle Hardware & Garden, Inc., 16
Eagle-Picher Industries, Inc., 8; 23 (upd.)
Earl Scheib, Inc., 32
Earthgrains Company, The, 36
EarthLink, Inc., 36
Eastern Airlines, I
Eastern Company, The, 48
Eastern Enterprises, 6
Eastman Chemical Company, 14; 38 (upd.)
Eastman Kodak Company, III; 7 (upd.); 36
   (upd.)
Eateries, Inc., 33
Eaton Corporation, I; 10 (upd.)
Eaton Vance Corporation, 18
eBay Inc., 32
EBSCO Industries, Inc., 17; 40 (upd.)
ECC International Corp., 42
Echlin Inc., I; 11 (upd.)
EchoStar Communications Corporation, 35
Eckerd Corporation, 9; 32 (upd.)
Ecolab, Inc., I; 13 (upd.); 34 (upd.)
Ecology and Environment, Inc., 39
Eddie Bauer, Inc., 9; 36 (upd.)
Edelbrock Corporation, 37
Edison Brothers Stores, Inc., 9
Edison Schools Inc., 37
Edmark Corporation, 14; 41 (upd.)
EDO Corporation, 46
Education Management Corporation, 35
Educational Broadcasting Corporation, 48
Educational Testing Service, 12
Edw. C. Levy Co., 42
Edward J. DeBartolo Corporation, The, 8
Edward Jones, 30
Edwards Theatres Circuit, Inc., 31
EG&G Incorporated, 8; 29 (upd.)
Egghead Inc., 9
Egghead.com, Inc., 31 (upd.)
84 Lumber Company, 9; 39 (upd.)
800-JR Cigar, Inc., 27
Einstein/Noah Bagel Corporation, 29
Ekco Group, Inc., 16
El Camino Resources International, Inc., 11
El Chico Restaurants, Inc., 19
El Paso Electric Company, 21
El Paso Natural Gas Company, 12
Elano Corporation, 14
Elder-Beerman Stores Corporation, 10
Electric Lightwave, Inc., 37
Electromagnetic Sciences Inc., 21
Electronic Arts Inc., 10
Electronic Data Systems Corporation, III;
   28 (upd.)
Electronics for Imaging, Inc., 15; 43 (upd.)
Eli Lilly and Company, I; 11 (upd.); 47
   (upd.)
Elizabeth Arden, Inc., 8; 40 (upd.)
Eljer Industries, Inc., 24
Ellerbe Becket, 41
Ellett Brothers, Inc., 17
Elmer's Restaurants, Inc., 42
Elsinore Corporation, 48
Embers America Restaurants, 30
EMC Corporation, 12; 46 (upd.)
Emerson, 46 (upd.)
Emerson Electric Co., II
Emerson Radio Corp., 30
Emery Worldwide Airlines, Inc., 6; 25
   (upd.)
Emge Packing Co., Inc., 11
Emmis Communications Corporation, 47
Empi, Inc., 26
Empire Blue Cross and Blue Shield, III
Employee Solutions, Inc., 18
ENCAD, Incorporated, 25
Encompass Services Corporation, 33

Encore Computer Corporation, 13
Encyclopaedia Britannica, Inc., 7; 39 (upd.)
Energen Corporation, 21
Energizer Holdings, Inc., 32
Enesco Corporation, 11
Engelhard Corporation, IV; 21 (upd.)
Engle Homes, Inc., 46
Engraph, Inc., 12
Ennis Business Forms, Inc., 21
Enquirer/Star Group, Inc., 10
Enrich International, Inc., 33
Enron Corporation, V; 19; 46 (upd.)
Ensearch Corporation, V
Entergy Corporation, V; 45 (upd.)
Enterprise Rent-A-Car Company, 6
Entravision Communications Corporation,
   41
Envirodyne Industries, Inc., 17
Environmental Industries, Inc., 31
Enzo Biochem, Inc., 41
Equifax Inc., 6; 28 (upd.)
Equitable Life Assurance Society of the
   United States, III
Equitable Resources, Inc., 6
Equity Marketing, Inc., 26
Equity Residential, 49
Equus Computer Systems, Inc., 49
Erie Indemnity Company, 35
ERLY Industries Inc., 17
Ernst & Young, 9; 29 (upd.)
Escalade, Incorporated, 19
Eskimo Pie Corporation, 21
Esprit de Corp., 8; 29 (upd.)
ESS Technology, Inc., 22
Essef Corporation, 18
Esselte Pendaflex Corporation, 11
Essence Communications, Inc., 24
Estée Lauder Companies Inc., The, 9; 30
   (upd.)
Esterline Technologies Corp., 15
Ethan Allen Interiors, Inc., 12; 39 (upd.)
Ethicon, Inc., 23
Ethyl Corporation, I; 10 (upd.)
EToys, Inc., 37
Eureka Company, The, 12
Euromarket Designs Inc., 31 (upd.)
Evans & Sutherland Computer Corporation,
   19
Evans, Inc., 30
Everex Systems, Inc., 16
Everlast Worldwide Inc., 47
Exabyte Corporation, 12; 40 (upd.)
Exar Corp., 14
EXCEL Communications Inc., 18
Executive Jet, Inc., 36
Executone Information Systems, Inc., 13
Exelon Corporation, 48 (upd.)
Exide Electronics Group, Inc., 20
Expeditors International of Washington
   Inc., 17
Experian Information Solutions Inc., 45
Express Scripts Inc., 17; 44 (upd.)
Extended Stay America, Inc., 41
Exxon Corporation, IV; 7 (upd.); 32 (upd.)
EZCORP Inc., 43
E-Systems, Inc., 9
E-Z Serve Corporation, 17
Fab Industries, Inc., 27
Fabri-Centers of America Inc., 16
Fair Grounds Corporation, 44
Fair, Isaac and Company, 18
Fairchild Aircraft, Inc., 9
Fairfield Communities, Inc., 36
Falcon Products, Inc., 33
Fallon McElligott Inc., 22
Family Dollar Stores, Inc., 13
Family Golf Centers, Inc., 29
Famous Dave's of America, Inc., 40

Fannie Mae, 45 (upd.)
Fansteel Inc., 19
FAO Schwarz, 46
Farah Incorporated, 24
Farley Northwest Industries, Inc., I
Farm Family Holdings, Inc., 39
Farm Journal Corporation, 42
Farmers Insurance Group of Companies, 25
Farmland Foods, Inc., 7
Farmland Industries, Inc., 48
Farrar, Straus and Giroux Inc., 15
Fastenal Company, 14; 42 (upd.)
Fay's Inc., 17
Fazoli's Systems, Inc., 27
Featherlite Inc., 28
Fedders Corporation, 18; 43 (upd.)
Federal Express Corporation, V
Federal National Mortgage Association, II
Federal Paper Board Company, Inc., 8
Federal Prison Industries, Inc., 34
Federal Signal Corp., 10
Federal-Mogul Corporation, I; 10 (upd.);
   26 (upd.)
Federated Department Stores Inc., 9; 31
   (upd.)
FedEx Corporation, 18 (upd.); 42 (upd.)
Feld Entertainment, Inc., 32 (upd.)
Fellowes Manufacturing Company, 28
Fender Musical Instruments Company, 16;
   43 (upd.)
Fenwick & West LLP, 34
Ferolito, Vultaggio & Sons, 27
Ferrellgas Partners, L.P., 35
Ferro Corporation, 8
FHP International Corporation, 6
FiberMark, Inc., 37
Fibreboard Corporation, 16
Fidelity Investments Inc., II; 14 (upd.)
Fieldale Farms Corporation, 23
Fieldcrest Cannon, Inc., 9; 31 (upd.)
Fifth Third Bancorp, 13; 31 (upd.)
Figgie International Inc., 7
FINA, Inc., 7
Fingerhut Companies, Inc., 9; 36 (upd.)
Finish Line, Inc., The, 29
FinishMaster, Inc., 24
Finlay Enterprises, Inc., 16
Firearms Training Systems, Inc., 27
Fireman's Fund Insurance Company, III
First Albany Companies Inc., 37
First Alert, Inc., 28
First Aviation Services Inc., 49
First Bank System Inc., 12
First Brands Corporation, 8
First Chicago Corporation, II
First Commerce Bancshares, Inc., 15
First Commerce Corporation, 11
First Data Corporation, 30 (upd.)
First Empire State Corporation, 11
First Executive Corporation, III
First Fidelity Bank, N.A., New Jersey, 9
First Financial Management Corporation,
   11
First Hawaiian, Inc., 11
First Interstate Bancorp, II
First Mississippi Corporation, 8
First Nationwide Bank, 14
First of America Bank Corporation, 8
First Security Corporation, 11
First Team Sports, Inc., 22
First Tennessee National Corporation, 11;
   48 (upd.)
First Union Corporation, 10
First USA, Inc., 11
First Virginia Banks, Inc., 11
First Years Inc., The, 46
Firstar Corporation, 11; 33 (upd.)
Fiserv Inc., 11; 33 (upd.)

Fisher Companies, Inc., 15
Fisher Controls International, Inc., 13
Fisher Scientific International Inc., 24
Fisher-Price Inc., 12; 32 (upd.)
Flagstar Companies, Inc., 10
Fleer Corporation, 15
Fleet Financial Group, Inc., 9
FleetBoston Financial Corporation, 36 (upd.)
Fleetwood Enterprises, Inc., III; 22 (upd.)
Fleming Companies, Inc., II; 17 (upd.)
Flexsteel Industries Inc., 15; 41 (upd.)
FlightSafety International, Inc., 9; 29 (upd.)
Flint Ink Corporation, 13; 41 (upd.)
Florida Crystals Inc., 35
Florida Gaming Corporation, 47
Florida Progress Corporation, V; 23 (upd.)
Florida Rock Industries, Inc., 46
Florida's Natural Growers, 45
Florists' Transworld Delivery, Inc., 28
Florsheim Shoe Group Inc., 9; 31 (upd.)
Flour City International, Inc., 44
Flowers Industries, Inc., 12; 35 (upd.)
Flowserve Corporation, 33
Fluke Corporation, 15
Fluor Corporation, I; 8 (upd.); 34 (upd.)
Flying J Inc., 19
FMC Corporation, I; 11 (upd.)
FMR Corp., 8; 32 (upd.)
Foamex International Inc., 17
Foley & Lardner, 28
Follett Corporation, 12; 39 (upd.)
Food Lion, Inc., II; 15 (upd.)
Foodarama Supermarkets, Inc., 28
FoodBrands America, Inc., 23
Foodmaker, Inc., 14
Foote, Cone & Belding Communications, Inc., I
Footstar, Incorporated, 24
Forbes Inc., 30
Ford Foundation, The, 34
Ford Motor Company, I; 11 (upd.); 36 (upd.)
Ford Motor Company, S.A. de C.V., 20
FORE Systems, Inc., 25
Forest City Enterprises, Inc., 16
Forest Laboratories, Inc., 11
Forest Oil Corporation, 19
Forever Living Products International Inc., 17
Formica Corporation, 13
Forstmann Little & Co., 38
Fort Howard Corporation, 8
Fort James Corporation, 22 (upd.)
Fortune Brands, Inc., 29 (upd.)
Fortunoff Fine Jewelry and Silverware Inc., 26
Fossil, Inc., 17
Foster Poultry Farms, 32
Foster Wheeler Corporation, 6; 23 (upd.)
Foundation Health Corporation, 12
Fountain Powerboats Industries, Inc., 28
Fourth Financial Corporation, 11
Fox Entertainment Group, Inc., 43
Fox Family Worldwide, Inc., 24
Foxboro Company, 13
FoxMeyer Health Corporation, 16
FPL Group, Inc., V; 49 (upd.)
Frank J. Zamboni & Co., Inc., 34
Frank Russell Company, 46
Frank's Nursery & Crafts, Inc., 12
Frankel & Co., 39
Franklin Covey Company, 37 (upd.)
Franklin Electric Company, Inc., 43
Franklin Electronic Publishers, Inc., 23
Franklin Quest Co., 11
Franklin Resources, Inc., 9
Fred Meyer, Inc., V; 20 (upd.)

Fred W. Albrecht Grocery Co., The, 13
Fred's, Inc., 23
Frederick Atkins Inc., 16
Frederick's of Hollywood Inc., 16
Freedom Communications, Inc., 36
Freeport-McMoRan Inc., IV; 7 (upd.)
French Fragrances, Inc., 22
Fresh America Corporation, 20
Fresh Choice, Inc., 20
Fresh Foods, Inc., 29
Fretter, Inc., 10
Fried, Frank, Harris, Shriver & Jacobson, 35
Friedman's Inc., 29
Friendly Ice Cream Corp., 30
Frigidaire Home Products, 22
Frisch's Restaurants, Inc., 35
Frito-Lay Company, 32
Fritz Companies, Inc., 12
Frontier Airlines, Inc., 22
Frontier Corp., 16
Frozen Food Express Industries, Inc., 20
Fruehauf Corporation, I
Fruit of the Loom, Inc., 8; 25 (upd.)
Frymaster Corporation, 27
FSI International, Inc., 17
FTP Software, Inc., 20
Fubu, 29
Fujitsu-ICL Systems Inc., 11
Fulbright & Jaworski L.L.P., 47
Funco, Inc., 20
Fuqua Enterprises, Inc., 17
Fuqua Industries, Inc., I
Furniture Brands International, Inc., 39 (upd.)
Furon Company, 28
Furr's Supermarkets, Inc., 28
Future Now, Inc., 12
G&K Services, Inc., 16
G-III Apparel Group, Ltd., 22
G. Heileman Brewing Company Inc., I
G.A.F., I
G.D. Searle & Company, I; 12 (upd.); 34 (upd.)
G.I. Joe's, Inc., 30
G.S. Blodgett Corporation, 15
Gabelli Asset Management Inc., 30
Gables Residential Trust, 49
Gadzooks, Inc., 18
GAF Corporation, 22 (upd.)
Gage Marketing Group, 26
Gaiam, Inc., 41
Gainsco, Inc., 22
Galey & Lord, Inc., 20
Gallup Organization, The, 37
Galyan's Trading Company, Inc., 47
Gambrinus Company, The, 40
Gander Mountain, Inc., 20
Gannett Co., Inc., IV; 7 (upd.); 30 (upd.)
Gantos, Inc., 17
Gap, Inc., The, V; 18 (upd.)
Garan, Inc., 16
Garden Fresh Restaurant Corporation, 31
Garden Ridge Corporation, 27
Gardenburger, Inc., 33
Gardner Denver, Inc., 49
Gart Sports Company, 24
Gartner Group, Inc., 21
Gates Corporation, The, 9
Gateway, Inc., 10; 27 (upd.)
GATX Corporation, 6; 25 (upd.)
Gaylord Container Corporation, 8
Gaylord Entertainment Company, 11; 36 (upd.)
GC Companies, Inc., 25
GE Aircraft Engines, 9
GE Capital Aviation Services, 36
Geerlings & Wade, Inc., 45

Geffen Records Inc., 26
Gehl Company, 19
GEICO Corporation, 10; 40 (upd.)
GenCorp Inc., 8; 9
Genentech, Inc., I; 8 (upd.); 32 (upd.)
General Bearing Corporation, 45
General Binding Corporation, 10
General Cable Corporation, 40
General Chemical Group Inc., The, 37
General Cinema Corporation, I
General DataComm Industries, Inc., 14
General Dynamics Corporation, I; 10 (upd.); 40 (upd.)
General Electric Company, II; 12 (upd.); 34 (upd.)
General Host Corporation, 12
General Housewares Corporation, 16
General Instrument Corporation, 10
General Mills, Inc., II; 10 (upd.); 36 (upd.)
General Motors Corporation, I; 10 (upd.); 36 (upd.)
General Nutrition Companies, Inc., 11; 29 (upd.)
General Public Utilities Corporation, V
General Re Corporation, III; 24 (upd.)
General Signal Corporation, 9
General Tire, Inc., 8
Genesco Inc., 17
Genesee & Wyoming Inc., 27
Genesis Health Ventures, Inc., 18
Genetics Institute, Inc., 8
Geneva Steel, 7
Genmar Holdings, Inc., 45
Genovese Drug Stores, Inc., 18
GenRad, Inc., 24
Gentex Corporation, 26
Genuardi's Family Markets, Inc., 35
Genuine Parts Company, 9; 45 (upd.)
Genzyme Corporation, 13; 38 (upd.)
Geon Company, The, 11
George A. Hormel and Company, II
Georgia Gulf Corporation, 9
Georgia-Pacific Corporation, IV; 9 (upd.); 47 (upd.)
Geotek Communications Inc., 21
Gerald Stevens, Inc., 37
Gerber Products Company, 7; 21 (upd.)
Gerber Scientific, Inc., 12
German American Bancorp, 41
Getty Images, Inc., 31
Ghirardelli Chocolate Company, 30
Giant Cement Holding, Inc., 23
Giant Food Inc., II; 22 (upd.)
Giant Industries, Inc., 19
Gibraltar Steel Corporation, 37
Gibson Greetings, Inc., 12
Gibson Guitar Corp., 16
Gibson, Dunn & Crutcher LLP, 36
Giddings & Lewis, Inc., 10
Gilbane, Inc., 34
Gillett Holdings, Inc., 7
Gillette Company, The, III; 20 (upd.)
Girl Scouts of the USA, 35
Gitano Group, Inc., The, 8
Glacier Bancorp, Inc., 35
Glacier Water Services, Inc., 47
Gleason Corporation, 24
Glidden Company, The, 8
Global Crossing Ltd., 32
Global Industries, Ltd., 37
Global Marine Inc., 9
Global Outdoors, Inc., 49
GlobalSantaFe Corporation, 48 (upd.)
GM Hughes Electronics Corporation, II
Godfather's Pizza Incorporated, 25
Gold Kist Inc., 17; 26 (upd.)
Golden Belt Manufacturing Co., 16

United States (*continued*)

Golden Books Family Entertainment, Inc., 28
Golden Corral Corporation, 10
Golden Enterprises, Inc., 26
Golden State Foods Corporation, 32
Golden State Vintners, Inc., 33
Golden West Financial Corporation, 47
Goldman, Sachs & Co., II; 20 (upd.)
Golub Corporation, The, 26
Gonnella Baking Company, 40
Good Guys, Inc., The, 10; 30 (upd.)
Good Humor-Breyers Ice Cream Company, 14
Goodman Holding Company, 42
GoodMark Foods, Inc., 26
Goodrich Corporation, 46 (upd.)
GoodTimes Entertainment Ltd., 48
Goodwill Industries International, Inc., 16
Goody Products, Inc., 12
Goody's Family Clothing, Inc., 20
Goodyear Tire & Rubber Company, The, V; 20 (upd.)
Gordon Food Service Inc., 8; 39 (upd.)
Gorman-Rupp Company, The, 18
Gorton's, 13
Goss Holdings, Inc., 43
Gottschalks, Inc., 18
Gould Electronics, Inc., 14
Goulds Pumps Inc., 24
Goya Foods Inc., 22
GPU, Inc., 27 (upd.)
Graco Inc., 19
GranCare, Inc., 14
Grand Casinos, Inc., 20
Grand Union Company, The, 7; 28 (upd.)
Granite Broadcasting Corporation, 42
Granite Rock Company, 26
Granite State Bankshares, Inc., 37
Graphic Industries Inc., 25
Gray Communications Systems, Inc., 24
Great American Management and Investment, Inc., 8
Great Atlantic & Pacific Tea Company, Inc., The, II; 16 (upd.)
Great Harvest Bread Company, 44
Great Lakes Bancorp, 8
Great Lakes Chemical Corporation, I; 14 (upd.)
Great Western Financial Corporation, 10
Grede Foundries, Inc., 38
Green Bay Packers, Inc., The, 32
Green Mountain Coffee, Inc., 31
Green Tree Financial Corporation, 11
Greenbrier Companies, The, 19
GreenPoint Financial Corp., 28
Greenwood Mills, Inc., 14
Greif Bros. Corporation, 15
Grey Advertising, Inc., 6
Grey Wolf, Inc., 43
Greyhound Lines, Inc., I; 32 (upd.)
Griffin Land & Nurseries, Inc., 43
Griffon Corporation, 34
Grinnell Corp., 13
Grist Mill Company, 15
Gristede's Sloan's, Inc., 31
Grolier Incorporated, 16; 43 (upd.)
Grossman's Inc., 13
Ground Round, Inc., 21
Group Health Cooperative, 41
Grow Biz International, Inc., 18
Grow Group Inc., 12
Grubb & Ellis Company, 21
Grumman Corporation, I; 11 (upd.)
Gruntal & Co., L.L.C., 20
Gryphon Holdings, Inc., 21
GSD&M Advertising, 44

GT Bicycles, 26
GT Interactive Software, 31
GTE Corporation, V; 15 (upd.)
Guangzhou Pearl River Piano Group Ltd., 49
Guccio Gucci, S.p.A., 15
Guess, Inc., 15
Guest Supply, Inc., 18
Guilford Mills Inc., 8; 40 (upd.)
Guitar Center, Inc., 29
Gulf & Western Inc., I
Gulf Island Fabrication, Inc., 44
Gulf States Utilities Company, 6
GulfMark Offshore, Inc., 49
Gulfstream Aerospace Corporation, 7; 28 (upd.)
Gunlocke Company, The, 23
Guthy-Renker Corporation, 32
Gwathmey Siegel & Associates Architects LLC, 26
Gymboree Corporation, 15
H & R Block, Incorporated, 9; 29 (upd.)
H.B. Fuller Company, 8; 32 (upd.)
H.D. Vest, Inc., 46
H.E. Butt Grocery Company, 13; 32 (upd.)
H.F. Ahmanson & Company, II; 10 (upd.)
H.J. Heinz Company, II; 11 (upd.); 36 (upd.)
Ha-Lo Industries, Inc., 27
Habersham Bancorp, 25
Habitat for Humanity International, 36
Hach Co., 18
Hadco Corporation, 24
Haemonetics Corporation, 20
Haggar Corporation, 19
Haggen Inc., 38
Hahn Automotive Warehouse, Inc., 24
Hain Celestial Group, Inc., The, 27; 43 (upd.)
HAL Inc., 9
Half Price Books, Records, Magazines Inc., 37
Halliburton Company, III; 25 (upd.)
Hallmark Cards, Inc., IV; 16 (upd.); 40 (upd.)
Hamilton Beach/Proctor-Silex Inc., 17
Hammacher Schlemmer & Company, 21
Hampton Industries, Inc., 20
Hancock Fabrics, Inc., 18
Hancock Holding Company, 15
Handleman Company, 15
Handspring Inc., 49
Handy & Harman, 23
Hanger Orthopedic Group, Inc., 41
Hanna Andersson Corp., 49
Hanna-Barbera Cartoons Inc., 23
Hannaford Bros. Co., 12
Hanover Direct, Inc., 36
Hanover Foods Corporation, 35
Hansen Natural Corporation, 31
Happy Kids Inc., 30
Harbert Corporation, 14
Harbison-Walker Refractories Company, 24
Harcourt Brace and Co., 12
Harcourt Brace Jovanovich, Inc., IV
Harcourt General, Inc., 20 (upd.)
Hard Rock Cafe International, Inc., 12; 32 (upd.)
Harding Lawson Associates Group, Inc., 16
Hardinge Inc., 25
Harley-Davidson Inc., 7; 25 (upd.)
Harleysville Group Inc., 37
Harman International Industries Inc., 15
Harmon Industries, Inc., 25
Harmonic Inc., 43
Harnischfeger Industries, Inc., 8; 38 (upd.)
Harold's Stores, Inc., 22
Harper Group Inc., 17

HarperCollins Publishers, 15
Harpo Entertainment Group, 28
Harrah's Entertainment, Inc., 16; 43 (upd.)
Harris Corporation, II; 20 (upd.)
Harris Interactive Inc., 41
Harris Teeter Inc., 23
Harry Winston Inc., 45
Harry's Farmers Market Inc., 23
Harsco Corporation, 8
Harte-Hanks Communications, Inc., 17
Hartmarx Corporation, 8; 32 (upd.)
Hartz Mountain Corporation, The, 12; 46 (upd.)
Harveys Casino Resorts, 27
Harza Engineering Company, 14
Hasbro, Inc., III; 16 (upd.); 43 (upd.)
Hastings Entertainment, Inc., 29
Hauser, Inc., 46
Haverty Furniture Companies, Inc., 31
Hawaiian Airlines, Inc., 22 (upd.)
Hawaiian Electric Industries, Inc., 9
Hawkins Chemical, Inc., 16
Haworth Inc., 8; 39 (upd.)
Hayes Corporation, 24
Hayes Lemmerz International, Inc., 27
Hazelden Foundation, 28
HCA - The Healthcare Company, 35 (upd.)
HDR Inc., 48
Headway Corporate Resources, Inc., 40
Health Care & Retirement Corporation, 22
Health O Meter Products Inc., 14
Health Risk Management, Inc., 24
Health Systems International, Inc., 11
HealthSouth Corporation, 33 (upd.)
HealthSouth Rehabilitation Corporation, 14
Healthtex, Inc., 17
Hearst Corporation, The, IV; 19 (upd.); 46 (upd.)
Heartland Express, Inc., 18
Hechinger Company, 12
Hecla Mining Company, 20
Heekin Can Inc., 13
HEICO Corporation, 30
Heidrick & Struggles International, Inc., 28
Heilig-Meyers Company, 14; 40 (upd.)
Helen of Troy Corporation, 18
Helene Curtis Industries, Inc., 8; 28 (upd.)
Heller, Ehrman, White & McAuliffe, 41
Helmerich & Payne, Inc., 18
Helmsley Enterprises, Inc., 9; 39 (upd.)
Helzberg Diamonds, 40
Henkel Manco Inc., 22
Henley Group, Inc., The, III
Henry Modell & Company Inc., 32
Henry Schein, Inc., 31
Herbalife International, Inc., 17; 41 (upd.)
Hercules Inc., I; 22 (upd.)
Herley Industries, Inc., 33
Herman Goelitz, Inc., 28
Herman Miller, Inc., 8
Hershey Foods Corporation, II; 15 (upd.)
Hertz Corporation, The, 9; 33 (upd.)
Heska Corporation, 39
Heublein, Inc., I
Hewlett-Packard Company, III; 6 (upd.); 28 (upd.)
Hexcel Corporation, 28
Hibbett Sporting Goods, Inc., 26
Hibernia Corporation, 37
Hickory Farms, Inc., 17
Highmark Inc., 27
Hildebrandt International, 29
Hill's Pet Nutrition, Inc., 27
Hillenbrand Industries, Inc., 10
Hillhaven Corporation, The, 14
Hills Stores Company, 13
Hilton Hotels Corporation, III; 19 (upd.)
Hines Horticulture, Inc., 49

Hispanic Broadcasting Corporation, 35
Hitchiner Manufacturing Co., Inc., 23
HMI Industries, Inc., 17
HOB Entertainment, Inc., 37
Hoechst Celanese Corporation, 13
Hoenig Group Inc., 41
Hogan & Hartson L.L.P., 44
Holberg Industries, Inc., 36
Holiday Inns, Inc., III
Holiday RV Superstores, Incorporated, 26
Holland Burgerville USA, 44
Hollinger International Inc., 24
Holly Corporation, 12
Hollywood Casino Corporation, 21
Hollywood Entertainment Corporation, 25
Hollywood Park, Inc., 20
Holme Roberts & Owen LLP, 28
Holnam Inc., 8; 39 (upd.)
Holophane Corporation, 19
Holson Burnes Group, Inc., 14
Holt's Cigar Holdings, Inc., 42
Home Box Office Inc., 7; 23 (upd.)
Home Depot, Inc., The, V; 18 (upd.)
Home Insurance Company, The, III
Home Properties of New York, Inc., 42
Home Shopping Network, Inc., V; 25 (upd.)
HomeBase, Inc., 33 (upd.)
Homestake Mining Company, 12; 38 (upd.)
Hometown Auto Retailers, Inc., 44
HON INDUSTRIES Inc., 13
Honda Motor Company Limited, I; 10 (upd.); 29 (upd.)
Honeywell Inc., II; 12 (upd.)
Hooper Holmes, Inc., 22
Hooters of America, Inc., 18
Hoover Company, The, 12; 40 (upd.)
Hops Restaurant Bar and Brewery, 46
Horace Mann Educators Corporation, 22
Horizon Organic Holding Corporation, 37
Hormel Foods Corporation, 18 (upd.)
Horton Homes, Inc., 25
Hospital Corporation of America, III
Hospitality Franchise Systems, Inc., 11
Hospitality Worldwide Services, Inc., 26
Hot Topic, Inc., 33
Houghton Mifflin Company, 10; 36 (upd.)
House of Fabrics, Inc., 21
Household International, Inc., II; 21 (upd.)
Houston Industries Incorporated, V
Hovnanian Enterprises, Inc., 29
Howard Hughes Medical Institute, 39
Howard Johnson International, Inc., 17
Howmet Corp., 12
Hub Group, Inc., 38
Hubbard Broadcasting Inc., 24
Hubbell Incorporated, 9; 31 (upd.)
Hudson Foods Inc., 13
Hudson River Bancorp, Inc., 41
Huffy Corporation, 7; 30 (upd.)
Hughes Electronics Corporation, 25
Hughes Hubbard & Reed LLP, 44
Hughes Markets, Inc., 22
Hughes Supply, Inc., 14
Hulman & Company, 44
Humana Inc., III; 24 (upd.)
Hungry Howie's Pizza and Subs, Inc., 25
Hunt Consolidated, Inc., 27 (upd.)
Hunt Manufacturing Company, 12
Hunt Oil Company, 7
Hunt-Wesson, Inc., 17
Hunter Fan Company, 13
Huntington Bancshares Inc., 11
Hunton & Williams, 35
Huntsman Chemical Corporation, 8
Hutchinson Technology Incorporated, 18
Hvide Marine Incorporated, 22
Hy-Vee, Inc., 36

Hyatt Corporation, III; 16 (upd.)
Hyde Athletic Industries, Inc., 17
Hydril Company, 46
Hypercom Corporation, 27
Hyperion Software Corporation, 22
Hyster Company, 17
I.C. Isaacs & Company, 31
Iams Company, 26
IBERIABANK Corporation, 37
IBP, Inc., II; 21 (upd.)
IC Industries, Inc., I
ICF Kaiser International, Inc., 28
Icon Health & Fitness, Inc., 38
Idaho Power Company, 12
IDB Communications Group, Inc., 11
Identix Inc., 44
IDEXX Laboratories, Inc., 23
IDG Books Worldwide, Inc., 27
IDT Corporation, 34
IEC Electronics Corp., 42
Igloo Products Corp., 21
IHOP Corporation, 17
Il Fornaio (America) Corporation, 27
Ilitch Holdings Inc., 37
Illinois Bell Telephone Company, 14
Illinois Central Corporation, 11
Illinois Power Company, 6
Illinois Tool Works Inc., III; 22 (upd.)
Imation Corporation, 20
IMC Fertilizer Group, Inc., 8
IMCO Recycling, Incorporated, 32
Immunex Corporation, 14
Imo Industries Inc., 7; 27 (upd.)
IMPATH Inc., 45
Imperial Holly Corporation, 12
Imperial Sugar Company, 32 (upd.)
In Focus Systems, Inc., 22
In-N-Out Burger, 19
InaCom Corporation, 13
Indiana Bell Telephone Company, Incorporated, 14
Indiana Energy, Inc., 27
Indianapolis Motor Speedway Corporation, 46
Industrial Services of America, Inc., 46
Infinity Broadcasting Corporation, 11; 48 (upd.)
Information Access Company, 17
Information Builders, Inc., 22
Information Holdings Inc., 47
Information Resources, Inc., 10
Informix Corporation, 10; 30 (upd.)
Ingalls Shipbuilding, Inc., 12
Ingersoll-Rand Company, III; 15 (upd.)
Ingles Markets, Inc., 20
Ingram Industries, Inc., 11; 49 (upd.)
Inktomi Corporation, 45
Inland Container Corporation, 8
Inland Steel Industries, Inc., IV; 19 (upd.)
Inserra Supermarkets, 25
Insight Enterprises, Inc., 18
Insilco Corporation, 16
Inso Corporation, 26
Instinet Corporation, 34
Insurance Auto Auctions, Inc., 23
Integrity Inc., 44
Intel Corporation, II; 10 (upd.); 36 (upd.)
IntelliCorp, Inc., 45
Intelligent Electronics, Inc., 6
Inter Parfums Inc., 35
Inter-Regional Financial Group, Inc., 15
Interco Incorporated, III
Interep National Radio Sales Inc., 35
Interface, Inc., 8; 29 (upd.)
Intergraph Corporation, 6; 24 (upd.)
Interlake Corporation, The, 8
Intermet Corporation, 32
Intermountain Health Care, Inc., 27

International Brotherhood of Teamsters, 37
International Business Machines Corporation, III; 6 (upd.); 30 (upd.)
International Controls Corporation, 10
International Creative Management, Inc., 43
International Dairy Queen, Inc., 10; 39 (upd.)
International Data Group, Inc., 7; 25 (upd.)
International Family Entertainment Inc., 13
International Flavors & Fragrances Inc., 9; 38 (upd.)
International Game Technology, 10; 41 (upd.)
International Lease Finance Corporation, 48
International Management Group, 18
International Multifoods Corporation, 7; 25 (upd.)
International Paper Company, IV; 15 (upd.); 47 (upd.)
International Rectifier Corporation, 31
International Shipholding Corporation, Inc., 27
International Speedway Corporation, 19
International Telephone & Telegraph Corporation, I; 11 (upd.)
International Total Services, Inc., 37
Interpublic Group of Companies, Inc., The, I; 22 (upd.)
Interscope Music Group, 31
Interstate Bakeries Corporation, 12; 38 (upd.)
Intimate Brands, Inc., 24
Intuit Inc., 14; 33 (upd.)
Invacare Corporation, 11; 47 (upd.)
Iomega Corporation, 21
IPALCO Enterprises, Inc., 6
Iron Mountain, Inc., 33
Irvin Feld & Kenneth Feld Productions, Inc., 15
Island ECN, Inc., The, 48
Isle of Capri Casinos, Inc., 41
Ispat Inland Inc., 40 (upd.)
Itel Corporation, 9
Items International Airwalk Inc., 17
ITT Educational Services, Inc., 33
ITT Sheraton Corporation, III
IVAX Corporation, 11
IVC Industries, Inc., 45
iVillage Inc., 46
Iwerks Entertainment, Inc., 34
IXC Communications, Inc., 29
J & J Snack Foods Corporation, 24
J&R Electronics Inc., 26
J. Baker, Inc., 31
J. Crew Group Inc., 12; 34 (upd.)
J. D'Addario & Company, Inc., 48
J. Jill Group, Inc., The, 35
J.A. Jones, Inc., 16
J.B. Hunt Transport Services Inc., 12
J.C. Penney Company, Inc., V; 18 (upd.); 43 (upd.)
J.D. Edwards & Company, 14
J.D. Power and Associates, 32
J.I. Case Company, 10
J.M. Smucker Company, The, 11
J.P. Morgan & Co. Incorporated, II; 30 (upd.)
J.P. Morgan Chase & Co., 38 (upd.)
J.R. Simplot Company, 16
Jabil Circuit, Inc., 36
Jack Henry and Associates, Inc., 17
Jack Schwartz Shoes, Inc., 18
Jackpot Enterprises Inc., 21
Jackson Hewitt, Inc., 48
Jackson National Life Insurance Company, 8

United States (*continued*)

Jaco Electronics, Inc., 30
Jacob Leinenkugel Brewing Company, 28
Jacobs Engineering Group Inc., 6; 26 (upd.)
Jacobson Stores Inc., 21
Jacor Communications, Inc., 23
Jacuzzi Inc., 23
Jalate Inc., 25
Jamba Juice Company, 47
James River Corporation of Virginia, IV
Jason Incorporated, 23
Jay Jacobs, Inc., 15
Jayco Inc., 13
Jazzercise, Inc., 45
JB Oxford Holdings, Inc., 32
JDS Uniphase Corporation, 34
Jefferies Group, Inc., 25
Jefferson-Pilot Corporation, 11; 29 (upd.)
Jeld-Wen, Inc., 45
Jennifer Convertibles, Inc., 31
Jenny Craig, Inc., 10; 29 (upd.)
Jerry's Famous Deli Inc., 24
Jervis B. Webb Company, 24
JetBlue Airways Corporation, 44
Jetro Cash & Carry Enterprises Inc., 38
JG Industries, Inc., 15
Jillian's Entertainment Holdings, Inc., 40
Jim Beam Brands Co., 14
Jim Henson Company, The, 23
Jitney-Jungle Stores of America, Inc., 27
JMB Realty Corporation, IV
Jockey International, Inc., 12; 34 (upd.)
John B. Sanfilippo & Son, Inc., 14
John D. and Catherine T. MacArthur Foundation, The, 34
John H. Harland Company, 17
John Hancock Financial Services, Inc., III; 42 (upd.)
John Nuveen Company, The, 21
John Paul Mitchell Systems, 24
John Q. Hammons Hotels, Inc., 24
John W. Danforth Company, 48
John Wiley & Sons, Inc., 17
Johnny Rockets Group, Inc., 31
Johnson & Higgins, 14
Johnson & Johnson, III; 8 (upd.); 36 (upd.)
Johnson Controls, Inc., III; 26 (upd.)
Johnson Publishing Company, Inc., 28
Johnson Worldwide Associates, Inc., 28
Johnston Industries, Inc., 15
Johnstown America Industries, Inc., 23
Jones Apparel Group, Inc., 11; 39 (upd.)
Jones, Day, Reavis & Pogue, 33
Jones Intercable, Inc., 21
Jones Lang LaSalle Incorporated, 49
Jones Medical Industries, Inc., 24
Jordache Enterprises, Inc., 23
Jordan Industries, Inc., 36
Jos. A. Bank Clothiers, Inc., 31
Joseph T. Ryerson & Son, Inc., 15
Jostens, Inc., 7; 25 (upd.)
Journal Register Company, 29
JPI, 49
JPS Textile Group, Inc., 28
Juniper Networks, Inc., 43
Juno Lighting, Inc., 30
Juno Online Services, Inc., 38
Just Born, Inc., 32
Just For Feet, Inc., 19
Justin Industries, Inc., 19
JWP Inc., 9
JWT Group Inc., I
K & B Inc., 12
K & G Men's Center, Inc., 21
K-Swiss, Inc., 33
K-tel International, Inc., 21

Kaiser Aluminum & Chemical Corporation, IV
Kal Kan Foods, Inc., 22
Kaman Corporation, 12; 42 (upd.)
Kampgrounds of America, Inc. 33
Kansas City Power & Light Company, 6
Kansas City Southern Industries, Inc., 6; 26 (upd.)
Kaplan, Inc., 42
Karl Kani Infinity, Inc., 49
Kash n' Karry Food Stores, Inc., 20
Kasper A.S.L., Ltd., 40
Katy Industries, Inc., I
Katz Communications, Inc., 6
Katz Media Group, Inc., 35
Kaufman and Broad Home Corporation, 8
Kay-Bee Toy Stores, 15
Kaydon Corporation, 18
KB Home, 45 (upd.)
KB Toys, 35 (upd.)
Keebler Foods Company, 36
Keithley Instruments Inc., 16
Kelley Drye & Warren LLP, 40
Kellogg Company, II; 13 (upd.)
Kellwood Company, 8
Kelly Services Inc., 6; 26 (upd.)
Kelly-Springfield Tire Company, The, 8
Kelsey-Hayes Group of Companies, 7; 27 (upd.)
Kemet Corp., 14
Kemper Corporation, III; 15 (upd.)
Kendall International, Inc., 11
Kendall-Jackson Winery, Ltd., 28
Kenetech Corporation, 11
Kenneth Cole Productions, Inc., 25
Kent Electronics Corporation, 17
Kentucky Electric Steel, Inc., 31
Kentucky Utilities Company, 6
Kerr Group Inc., 24
Kerr-McGee Corporation, IV; 22 (upd.)
Ketchum Communications Inc., 6
Kettle Foods Inc., 48
Kewaunee Scientific Corporation, 25
Key Tronic Corporation, 14
KeyCorp, 8
Keyes Fibre Company, 9
KeySpan Energy Co., 27
Keystone International, Inc., 11
KFC Corporation, 7; 21 (upd.)
Kidde, Inc., I
Kikkoman Corporation, 47 (upd.)
Kimball International, Inc., 12; 48 (upd.)
Kimberly-Clark Corporation, III; 16 (upd.); 43 (upd.)
Kimco Realty Corporation, 11
Kinder Morgan, Inc., 45
KinderCare Learning Centers, Inc., 13
Kinetic Concepts, Inc. (KCI), 20
King & Spalding, 23
King Arthur Flour Company, The, 31
King Kullen Grocery Co., Inc., 15
King Ranch, Inc., 14
King World Productions, Inc., 9; 30 (upd.)
Kingston Technology Corporation, 20
Kinko's, Inc., 16; 43 (upd.)
Kinney Shoe Corp., 14
Kirby Corporation, 18
Kit Manufacturing Co., 18
Kitchell Corporation, 14
KitchenAid, 8
Kitty Hawk, Inc., 22
Kiwi International Airlines Inc., 20
KLA-Tencor Corporation, 11; 45 (upd.)
Kmart Corporation, V; 18 (upd.); 47 (upd.)
Knape & Vogt Manufacturing Company, 17
Knight-Ridder, Inc., IV; 15 (upd.)
Knoll Group Inc., 14

Knott's Berry Farm, 18
KnowledgeWare Inc., 9; 31 (upd.)
Koala Corporation, 44
Koch Enterprises, Inc., 29
Koch Industries, Inc., IV; 20 (upd.)
Kohl's Corporation, 9; 30 (upd.)
Kohlberg Kravis Roberts & Co., 24
Kohler Company, 7; 32 (upd.)
Koll Company, The, 8
Kollmorgen Corporation, 18
Komag, Inc., 11
Koo Koo Roo, Inc., 25
Koppers Industries, Inc., I; 26 (upd.)
Korn/Ferry International, 34
Koss Corporation, 38
Kraft Foods Inc., 45 (upd.)
Kraft General Foods Inc., II; 7 (upd.)
Kraus-Anderson, Incorporated, 36
Krause Publications, Inc., 35
Krause's Furniture, Inc., 27
Krispy Kreme Doughnut Corporation, 21
Kroger Company, The, II; 15 (upd.)
Kronos, Inc., 18
Krystal Company, The, 33
K2 Inc., 16
KU Energy Corporation, 11
Kuhlman Corporation, 20
Kulicke and Soffa Industries, Inc., 33
Kushner-Locke Company, The, 25
L-3 Communications Holdings, Inc., 48
L. Luria & Son, Inc., 19
L.A. Gear, Inc., 8; 32 (upd.)
L.A. T Sportswear, Inc., 26
L.B. Foster Company, 33
L.L. Bean, Inc., 10; 38 (upd.)
L.L. Knickerbocker Co., Inc., The, 25
L.S. Starrett Co., 13
La Choy Food Products Inc., 25
La Madeleine French Bakery & Café, 33
La Quinta Companies, The, 11; 42 (upd.)
La-Z-Boy Chair Company, 14
LaBarge Inc., 41
LabOne, Inc., 48
Labor Ready, Inc., 29
Laboratory Corporation of America Holdings, 42 (upd.)
LaBranche & Co. Inc., 37
Laclede Steel Company, 15
LaCrosse Footwear, Inc., 18
LADD Furniture, Inc., 12
Ladish Co., Inc., 30
Lafarge Corporation, 28
Lakeland Industries, Inc., 45
Lam Research Corporation, 11; 31 (upd.)
Lamar Advertising Company, 27
Lamaur Corporation, The, 41
Lamb Weston, Inc., 23
Lamonts Apparel, Inc., 15
Lamson & Sessions Co., 13
Lancaster Colony Corporation, 8
Lance, Inc., 14; 41 (upd.)
Lancer Corporation, 21
Land O'Lakes, Inc., II; 21 (upd.)
Landmark Communications, Inc., 12
Landry's Seafood Restaurants, Inc., 15
Lands' End, Inc., 9; 29 (upd.)
Lane Co., The, 12
Larry Flynt Publishing Inc., 31
Larry H. Miller Group, 29
Lason, Inc., 31
Latham & Watkins, 33
Lattice Semiconductor Corp., 16
Lawson Software, 38
Lawter International Inc., 14
Layne Christensen Company, 19
Lazare Kaplan International Inc., 21
LCI International, Inc., 16
LDDS-Metro Communications, Inc., 8

Lear Seating Corporation, 16
Lear Siegler, Inc., I
Learjet Inc., 8; 27 (upd.)
Learning Company Inc., The, 24
Learning Tree International Inc., 24
LeaRonal, Inc., 23
Leaseway Transportation Corp., 12
LeBoeuf, Lamb, Greene & MacRae,
L.L.P., 29
Lechmere Inc., 10
Lechters, Inc., 11; 39 (upd.)
LeCroy Corporation, 41
Lee Apparel Company, Inc., 8
Lee Enterprises, Incorporated, 11
Leeann Chin, Inc., 30
Lefrak Organization Inc., 26
Legal Aid Society, The, 48
Legent Corporation, 10
Legg Mason, Inc., 33
Leggett & Platt, Inc., 11; 48 (upd.)
Lehigh Portland Cement Company, 23
Leiner Health Products Inc., 34
Lennar Corporation, 11
Lennox International Inc., 8; 28 (upd.)
Lenox, Inc., 12
LensCrafters Inc., 23
Leo Burnett Company Inc., I; 20 (upd.)
Leprino Foods Company, 28
Lesco Inc., 19
Leslie Fay Companies, Inc., The, 8; 39
(upd.)
Leslie's Poolmart, Inc., 18
Leucadia National Corporation, 11
Lever Brothers Company, 9
Levi Strauss & Co., V; 16 (upd.)
Levitz Furniture Inc., 15
Levy Restaurants L.P., 26
Lewis Galoob Toys Inc., 16
LEXIS-NEXIS Group, 33
Lexmark International, Inc., 18
LG&E Energy Corporation, 6
Libbey Inc., 49
Liberty Corporation, The, 22
Liberty Livewire Corporation, 42
Life Technologies, Inc., 17
Lifetime Hoan Corporation, 27
Ligand Pharmaceuticals Incorporated, 47
Lillian Vernon Corporation, 12; 35 (upd.)
Limited, Inc., The, V; 20 (upd.)
LIN Broadcasting Corp., 9
Lincare Holdings Inc., 43
Lincoln Electric Co., 13
Lincoln National Corporation, III; 25
(upd.)
Lincoln Property Company, 8
Lincoln Snacks Company, 24
Lincoln Telephone & Telegraph Company,
14
Lindal Cedar Homes, Inc., 29
Lindsay Manufacturing Co., 20
Linear Technology, Inc., 16
Linens 'n Things, Inc., 24
Lintas: Worldwide, 14
Lionel L.L.C., 16
Liqui-Box Corporation, 16
Lithia Motors, Inc., 41
Littelfuse, Inc., 26
Little Caesar Enterprises, Inc., 7; 24 (upd.)
Little Tikes Co., 13
Litton Industries, Inc., I; 11 (upd.)
LIVE Entertainment Inc., 20
Liz Claiborne, Inc., 8; 25 (upd.)
Lockheed Corporation, I; 11 (upd.)
Lockheed Martin Corporation, 15 (upd.)
Loctite Corporation, 8; 30 (upd.)
LodgeNet Entertainment Corporation, 28
Loehmann's Inc., 24
Loews Corporation, I; 12 (upd.); 36 (upd.)

Logan's Roadhouse, Inc., 29
Logicon Inc., 20
LoJack Corporation, 48
London Fog Industries, Inc., 29
Long Island Bancorp, Inc., 16
Long Island Lighting Company, V
Long John Silver's Restaurants Inc., 13
Longaberger Company, The, 12; 44 (upd.)
Longs Drug Stores Corporation, V; 25
(upd.)
Longview Fibre Company, 8; 37 (upd.)
Loral Corporation, 8; 9
Lost Arrow Inc., 22
LOT$OFF Corporation, 24
Lotus Development Corporation, 6; 25
(upd.)
Louisiana Land and Exploration Company,
The, 7
Louisiana-Pacific Corporation, IV; 31
(upd.)
Lowe's Companies, Inc., V; 21 (upd.)
Lowrance Electronics, Inc., 18
LSI Logic Corporation, 13
LTV Corporation, The, I; 24 (upd.)
Lubrizol Corporation, I; 30 (upd.)
Luby's, Inc., 17; 42 (upd.)
Lucasfilm Ltd., 12
Lucent Technologies Inc., 34
Lucille Farms, Inc., 45
Lucky Stores, Inc., 27
Lukens Inc., 14
Lunar Corporation, 29
Lund Food Holdings, Inc., 22
Lund International Holdings, Inc., 40
Lutheran Brotherhood, 31
Lynch Corporation, 43
Lyondell Chemical Company, IV; 45
(upd.)
M&F Worldwide Corp., 38
M.A. Hanna Company, 8
M.H. Meyerson & Co., Inc., 46
Mac Frugal's Bargains - Closeouts Inc., 17
Mac-Gray Corporation, 44
MacAndrews & Forbes Holdings Inc., 28
MacDermid Incorporated, 32
Mack Trucks, Inc., I; 22 (upd.)
Mack-Cali Realty Corporation, 42
Mackay Envelope Corporation, 45
Mackie Designs Inc., 33
Macmillan, Inc., 7
MacNeal-Schwendler Corporation, The, 25
Madison Gas and Electric Company, 39
Magma Copper Company, 7
Magma Power Company, 11
MagneTek, Inc., 15; 41 (upd.)
MAI Systems Corporation, 11
Maidenform Worldwide Inc., 20
Mail Boxes Etc., 18; 41 (upd.)
Mail-Well, Inc., 28
Maine Central Railroad Company, 16
Major Automotive Companies, Inc., The,
45
Malcolm Pirnie, Inc., 42
Malden Mills Industries, Inc., 16
Mallinckrodt Group Inc., 19
Malt-O-Meal Company, 22
Management and Training Corporation, 28
Mandalay Resort Group, 32 (upd.)
Manitowoc Company, Inc., 18
Mannatech Inc., 33
Manor Care, Inc., 6; 25 (upd.)
Manpower, Inc., 9; 30 (upd.)
Manufactured Home Communities, Inc., 22
Manufacturers Hanover Corporation, II
Manville Corporation, III; 7 (upd.)
MAPCO Inc., IV
March of Dimes, 31
marchFIRST, Inc., 34

Marcus Corporation, The, 21
Marie Callender's Restaurant & Bakery,
Inc., 28
MarineMax, Inc., 30
Marion Laboratories, Inc., I
Marisa Christina, Inc., 15
Maritz Inc., 38
Mark IV Industries, Inc., 7; 28 (upd.)
Marks Brothers Jewelers, Inc., 24
Marmon Group, The, IV; 16 (upd.)
Marquette Electronics, Inc., 13
Marriott International, Inc., III; 21 (upd.)
Mars, Incorporated, 7; 40 (upd.)
Marsh & McLennan Companies, Inc., III;
45 (upd.)
Marsh Supermarkets, Inc., 17
Marshalls Incorporated, 13
Martha Stewart Living Omnimedia, L.L.C.,
24
Martin Industries, Inc., 44
Martin Marietta Corporation, I
Marvel Entertainment Group, Inc., 10
Marvin Lumber & Cedar Company, 22
Mary Kay Corporation, 9; 30 (upd.)
Masco Corporation, III; 20 (upd.); 39
(upd.)
Mashantucket Pequot Gaming Enterprise
Inc., 35
Masland Corporation, 17
Massachusetts Mutual Life Insurance
Company, III
MasTec, Inc., 19
Master Lock Company, 45
MasterCard International, Inc., 9
Matria Healthcare, Inc., 17
Mattel, Inc., 7; 25 (upd.)
Matthews International Corporation, 29
Maui Land & Pineapple Company, Inc., 29
Max & Erma's Restaurants Inc., 19
Maxco Inc., 17
Maxicare Health Plans, Inc., III; 25 (upd.)
Maxim Group, The, 25
Maxim Integrated Products, Inc., 16
MAXIMUS, Inc., 43
Maxtor Corporation, 10
Maxus Energy Corporation, 7
Maxwell Shoe Company, Inc., 30
MAXXAM Inc., 8
Maxxim Medical Inc., 12
May Department Stores Company, The, V;
19 (upd.); 46 (upd.)
Mayer, Brown, Rowe & Maw, 47
Mayflower Group Inc., 6
Mayo Foundation, 9; 34 (upd.)
Mayor's Jewelers, Inc., 41
Maytag Corporation, III; 22 (upd.)
Mazel Stores, Inc., 29
MBC Holding Company, 40
MBNA Corporation, 12; 33 (upd.)
MCA Inc., II
McCarthy Building Companies, Inc., 48
McCaw Cellular Communications, Inc., 6
McClatchy Newspapers, Inc., 23
McCormick & Company, Incorporated, 7;
27 (upd.)
McDermott International, Inc., III; 37
(upd.)
McDonald's Corporation, II; 7 (upd.); 26
(upd.)
McDonnell Douglas Corporation, I; 11
(upd.)
McGraw-Hill Companies, Inc., The, IV; 18
(upd.)
MCI WorldCom, Inc., V; 27 (upd.)
McIlhenny Company, 20
McKee Foods Corporation, 7; 27 (upd.)
McKesson Corporation, I; 12; 47 (upd.)
McKinsey & Company, Inc., 9

United States (*continued*)

McLane Company, Inc., 13
McLeodUSA Incorporated, 32
MCN Corporation, 6
MCSi, Inc., 41
MDU Resources Group, Inc., 7; 42 (upd.)
Mead Corporation, The, IV; 19 (upd.)
Mead Data Central, Inc., 10
Meade Instruments Corporation, 41
Meadowcraft, Inc., 29
Mecklermedia Corporation, 24
Medco Containment Services Inc., 9
Media Arts Group, Inc., 42
Media General, Inc., 7; 38 (upd.)
MedImmune, Inc., 35
Meditrust, 11
Medtronic, Inc., 8; 30 (upd.)
Medusa Corporation, 24
Megafoods Stores Inc., 13
Meier & Frank Co., 23
Meijer Incorporated, 7; 27 (upd.)
Mel Farr Automotive Group, 20
Melaleuca Inc., 31
Melamine Chemicals, Inc., 27
Mellon Bank Corporation, II
Mellon Financial Corporation, 44 (upd.)
Mellon-Stuart Company, I
Melville Corporation, V
Melvin Simon and Associates, Inc., 8
Men's Wearhouse, Inc., The, 17; 48 (upd.)
Menard, Inc., 34
Menasha Corporation, 8
Mentholatum Company Inc., The, 32
Mentor Corporation, 26
Mentor Graphics Corporation, 11
Mercantile Bankshares Corp., 11
Mercantile Stores Company, Inc., V; 19 (upd.)
Merck & Co., Inc., I; 11 (upd.); 34 (upd.)
Mercury Air Group, Inc., 20
Mercury General Corporation, 25
Meredith Corporation, 11; 29 (upd.)
Meridian Bancorp, Inc., 11
Meridian Gold, Incorporated, 47
Merillat Industries Inc., 13
Merisel, Inc., 12
Merit Medical Systems, Inc., 29
Meritage Corporation, 26
Merix Corporation, 36
Merrell Dow, Inc., I; 9 (upd.)
Merrill Corporation, 18; 47 (upd.)
Merrill Lynch & Co., Inc., II; 13 (upd.); 40 (upd.)
Merry-Go-Round Enterprises, Inc., 8
Mervyn's California, 10; 39 (upd.)
Mesa Air Group, Inc., 11; 32 (upd.)
Mesaba Holdings, Inc., 28
Mestek Inc., 10
Metatec International, Inc., 47
Meteor Industries Inc., 33
Methode Electronics, Inc., 13
Metro Information Services, Inc., 36
Metro-Goldwyn-Mayer Inc., 25 (upd.)
Metrocall, Inc., 41
Metromedia Co., 7; 14
Metropolitan Baseball Club Inc., 39
Metropolitan Financial Corporation, 13
Metropolitan Life Insurance Company, III
Metropolitan Opera Association, Inc., 40
Metropolitan Transportation Authority, 35
Mexican Restaurants, Inc., 41
MFS Communications Company, Inc., 11
MGM Grand Inc., 17
MGM/UA Communications Company, II
Michael Anthony Jewelers, Inc., 24
Michael Baker Corp., 14
Michael Foods, Inc., 25

Michaels Stores, Inc., 17
Michigan Bell Telephone Co., 14
Michigan National Corporation, 11
Micro Warehouse, Inc., 16
MicroAge, Inc., 16
Microdot Inc., 8
Micron Technology, Inc., 11; 29 (upd.)
Micros Systems, Inc., 18
Microsoft Corporation, 6; 27 (upd.)
Mid-America Dairymen, Inc., 7
Midas International Corporation, 10
Middleby Corporation, The, 22
Middlesex Water Company, 45
Midway Airlines Corporation, 33
Midway Games, Inc., 25
Midwest Express Holdings, Inc., 35
Midwest Grain Products, Inc., 49
Midwest Resources Inc., 6
Mikasa, Inc., 28
Mike-Sell's Inc., 15
Mikohn Gaming Corporation, 39
Milbank, Tweed, Hadley & McCloy, 27
Miles Laboratories, I
Millennium Pharmaceuticals, Inc., 47
Miller Brewing Company, I; 12 (upd.)
Miller Industries, Inc., 26
Milliken & Co., V; 17 (upd.)
Millipore Corporation, 25
Milnot Company, 46
Milton Bradley Company, 21
Milwaukee Brewers Baseball Club, 37
Mine Safety Appliances Company, 31
Miner Group International, The, 22
Minerals Technologies Inc., 11
Minnesota Mining & Manufacturing Company (3M), I; 8 (upd.); 26 (upd.)
Minnesota Power, Inc., 11; 34 (upd.)
Minntech Corporation, 22
Minute Maid Company, The, 28
Minuteman International Inc., 46
Minyard Food Stores, Inc., 33
Mirage Resorts, Incorporated, 6; 28 (upd.)
Mississippi Chemical Corporation, 39
Mitchell Energy and Development Corporation, 7
MITRE Corporation, 26
Mity Enterprises, Inc., 38
Mobil Corporation, IV; 7 (upd.); 21 (upd.)
Mobile Telecommunications Technologies Corp., 18
Modine Manufacturing Company, 8
Moen Incorporated, 12
Mohawk Industries, Inc., 19
Mohegan Tribal Gaming Authority, 37
Molex Incorporated, 11
Monaco Coach Corporation, 31
Monadnock Paper Mills, Inc., 21
Monfort, Inc., 13
Monro Muffler Brake, Inc., 24
Monsanto Company, I; 9 (upd.); 29 (upd.)
Montana Power Company, The, 11; 44 (upd.)
Montgomery Ward & Co., Incorporated, V; 20 (upd.)
Moog Inc., 13
Moore Medical Corp., 17
Moore-Handley, Inc., 39
Moran Towing Corporation, Inc., 15
Morgan Group, Inc., The, 46
Morgan Stanley Dean Witter & Company, 33 (upd.)
Morgan Stanley Group Inc., II; 16 (upd.)
Morgan, Lewis & Bockius LLP, 29
Morris Communications Corporation, 36
Morris Travel Services L.L.C., 26
Morrison Knudsen Corporation, 7; 28 (upd.)
Morrison Restaurants Inc., 11

Morse Shoe Inc., 13
Morton International Inc., 9 (upd.)
Morton Thiokol, Inc., I
Morton's Restaurant Group, Inc., 30
Mosinee Paper Corporation, 15
Mossimo, Inc., 27
Motel 6 Corporation, 13
Mothers Work, Inc., 18
Motley Fool, Inc., The, 40
Moto Photo, Inc., 45
Motor Cargo Industries, Inc., 35
Motorcar Parts & Accessories, Inc., 47
Motorola, Inc., II; 11 (upd.); 34 (upd.)
Motown Records Company L.P., 26
Mountain States Mortgage Centers, Inc., 29
Movado Group, Inc., 28
Movie Gallery, Inc., 31
Movie Star Inc., 17
MPS Group, Inc., 49
Mr. Coffee, Inc., 15
Mr. Gasket Inc., 15
Mrs. Baird's Bakeries, 29
Mrs. Fields' Original Cookies, Inc., 27
Mt. Olive Pickle Company, Inc., 44
MTS Inc., 37
Mueller Industries, Inc., 7
Multimedia Games, Inc., 41
Multimedia, Inc., 11
Murdock Madaus Schwabe, 26
Murphy Family Farms Inc., 22
Murphy Oil Corporation, 7; 32 (upd.)
Musicland Stores Corporation, 9; 38 (upd.)
Mutual Benefit Life Insurance Company, The, III
Mutual Life Insurance Company of New York, The, III
Muzak, Inc., 18
Mycogen Corporation, 21
Myers Industries, Inc., 19
Mylan Laboratories Inc., I; 20 (upd.)
Nabisco Foods Group, II; 7 (upd.)
Nabors Industries, Inc., 9
NACCO Industries, Inc., 7
Nalco Chemical Corporation, I; 12 (upd.)
Nantucket Allserve, Inc., 22
Nash Finch Company, 8; 23 (upd.)
Nashua Corporation, 8
Nathan's Famous, Inc., 29
National Amusements Inc., 28
National Association for Stock Car Auto Racing, 32
National Association of Securities Dealers, Inc., 10
National Audubon Society, 26
National Auto Credit, Inc., 16
National Beverage Corp., 26
National Broadcasting Company, Inc., II; 6 (upd.); 28 (upd.)
National Can Corporation, I
National Car Rental System, Inc., 10
National City Corp., 15
National Convenience Stores Incorporated, 7
National Discount Brokers Group, Inc., 28
National Distillers and Chemical Corporation, I
National Educational Music Co. Ltd., 47
National Envelope Corporation, 32
National Football League, 29
National Fuel Gas Company, 6
National Geographic Society, 9; 30 (upd.)
National Grape Cooperative Association, Inc., 20
National Gypsum Company, 10
National Health Laboratories Incorporated, 11
National Hockey League, 35
National Home Centers, Inc., 44

National Instruments Corporation, 22
National Intergroup, Inc., V
National Media Corporation, 27
National Medical Enterprises, Inc., III
National Patent Development Corporation, 13
National Picture & Frame Company, 24
National Presto Industries, Inc., 16; 43 (upd.)
National Public Radio, Inc., 19; 47 (upd.)
National R.V. Holdings, Inc., 32
National Railroad Passenger Corporation, 22
National Record Mart, Inc., 29
National Rifle Association of America, 37
National Sanitary Supply Co., 16
National Semiconductor Corporation, II; VI, 26 (upd.)
National Service Industries, Inc., 11
National Standard Co., 13
National Starch and Chemical Company, 49
National Steel Corporation, 12
National TechTeam, Inc., 41
National Wine & Spirits, Inc., 49
NationsBank Corporation, 10
Natrol, Inc., 49
Natural Alternatives International, Inc., 49
Natural Wonders Inc., 14
Nature Conservancy, The, 28
Nature's Sunshine Products, Inc., 15
Nautica Enterprises, Inc., 18; 44 (upd.)
Navarre Corporation, 24
Navigant International, Inc., 47
Navistar International Corporation, I; 10 (upd.)
Navy Exchange Service Command, 31
Navy Federal Credit Union, 33
NBD Bancorp, Inc., 11
NBTY, Inc., 31
NCH Corporation, 8
NCNB Corporation, II
NCO Group, Inc., 42
NCR Corporation, III; 6 (upd.); 30 (upd.)
Nebraska Public Power District, 29
Neff Corp., 32
Neiman Marcus Co., 12
Neiman Marcus Group, Inc., The, 49 (upd.)
NERCO, Inc., 7
Netscape Communications Corporation, 15; 35 (upd.)
Network Associates, Inc., 25
Neutrogena Corporation, 17
Nevada Bell Telephone Company, 14
Nevada Power Company, 11
New Balance Athletic Shoe, Inc., 25
New Brunswick Scientific Co., Inc., 45
New Dana Perfumes Company, 37
New Line Cinema, Inc., 47
New Piper Aircraft, Inc., The, 44
New Plan Realty Trust, 11
New Street Capital Inc., 8
New Times, Inc., 45
New UK Business Services, Inc., 18
New UK Confectionery Co., 15
New UK Electric System, V
New UK Mutual Life Insurance Company, III
New Valley Corporation, 17
New World Restaurant Group, Inc., 44
New York Daily News, 32
New York Life Insurance Company, III; 45 (upd.)
New York Restaurant Group, Inc., 32
New York State Electric and Gas, 6
New York Stock Exchange, Inc., 9; 39 (upd.)

New York Times Company, The, IV; 19 (upd.)
Newcor, Inc., 40
Newell Co., 9
Newhall Land and Farming Company, 14
Newman's Own, Inc., 37
Newmont Mining Corporation, 7
Newport News Shipbuilding Inc., 13; 38 (upd.)
News America Publishing Inc., 12
Nextel Communications, Inc., 10; 27 (upd.)
NFO Worldwide, Inc., 24
NGC Corporation, 18
Niagara Corporation, 28
Niagara Mohawk Holdings Inc., V; 45 (upd.)
Nichols Research Corporation, 18
Nicklaus Companies, 45
NICOR Inc., 6
NIKE, Inc., V; 8 (upd.); 36 (upd.)
Nikken Global Inc., 32
Nimbus CD International, Inc., 20
Nine West Group, Inc., 11; 39 (upd.)
99¢ Only Stores, 25
NIPSCO Industries, Inc., 6
NL Industries, Inc., 10
Nobel Learning Communities, Inc., 37
Noble Affiliates, Inc., 11
Noble Roman's Inc., 14
Noland Company, 35
Nolo.com, Inc., 49
Noodle Kidoodle, 16
NordicTrack, 22
Nordson Corporation, 11; 48 (upd.)
Nordstrom, Inc., V; 18 (upd.)
Norelco Consumer Products Co., 26
Norfolk Southern Corporation, V; 29 (upd.)
Norm Thompson Outfitters, Inc., 47
Norrell Corporation, 25
Norstan, Inc., 16
Nortek, Inc., 34
North Face, Inc., The, 18
North Fork Bancorporation, Inc., 46
North Star Steel Company, 18
Northeast Utilities, V; 48 (upd.)
Northern States Power Company, V; 20 (upd.)
Northern Trust Company, 9
Northland Cranberries, Inc., 38
Northrop Corporation, I; 11 (upd.)
Northrop Grumman Corporation, 45 (upd.)
Northwest Airlines Corporation, I; 6 (upd.); 26 (upd.)
Northwest Natural Gas Company, 45
NorthWestern Corporation, 37
Northwestern Mutual Life Insurance Company, III; 45 (upd.)
Norton Company, 8
Norton McNaughton, Inc., 27
Norwood Promotional Products, Inc., 26
NovaCare, Inc., 11
Novell, Inc., 6; 23 (upd.)
Novellus Systems, Inc., 18
NPC International, Inc., 40
Nu Skin Enterprises, Inc., 27
Nu-kote Holding, Inc., 18
Nucor Corporation, 7; 21 (upd.)
Nutraceutical International Corporation, 37
NutraSweet Company, 8
Nutrition for Life International Inc., 22
NVR L.P., 8
NYMAGIC, Inc., 41
NYNEX Corporation, V
O'Charley's Inc., 19
O'Melveny & Myers, 37
O'Reilly Automotive, Inc., 26
O'Sullivan Industries Holdings, Inc., 34
Oak Industries Inc., 21

Oak Technology, Inc., 22
Oakley, Inc., 18; 49 (upd.)
Oakwood Homes Corporation, 15
Occidental Petroleum Corporation, IV; 25 (upd.)
Ocean Spray Cranberries, Inc., 7; 25 (upd.)
Octel Communications Corp., 14
Octel Messaging, 41 (upd.)
Odetics Inc., 14
Odwalla, Inc., 31
OEC Medical Systems, Inc., 27
Office Depot Incorporated, 8; 23 (upd.)
OfficeMax, Inc., 15; 43 (upd.)
Offshore Logistics, Inc., 37
Ogden Corporation, I; 6
Ogilvy Group, Inc., The, I
Oglebay Norton Company, 17
Oglethorpe Power Corporation, 6
Ohio Art Company, The, 14
Ohio Bell Telephone Company, 14
Ohio Casualty Corp., 11
Ohio Edison Company, V
Oil-Dri Corporation of America, 20
Oklahoma Gas and Electric Company, 6
Old America Stores, Inc., 17
Old Kent Financial Corp., 11
Old National Bancorp, 15
Old Republic International Corp., 11
Old Spaghetti Factory International Inc., 24
Olin Corporation, I; 13 (upd.)
Olsten Corporation, 6; 29 (upd.)
OM Group, Inc., 17
Omni Hotels Corp., 12
Omnicare, Inc., 49
Omnicom Group, I; 22 (upd.)
OmniSource Corporation, 14
On Assignment, Inc., 20
One Price Clothing Stores, Inc., 20
1-800-FLOWERS, Inc., 26
Oneida Ltd., 7; 31 (upd.)
ONEOK Inc., 7
Opinion Research Corporation, 46
Opsware Inc., 49
Option Care Inc., 48
Opus Group, 34
Oracle Corporation, 6; 24 (upd.)
Orbital Sciences Corporation, 22
Orchard Supply Hardware Stores Corporation, 17
Ore-Ida Foods Incorporated, 13
Oregon Chai, Inc., 49
Oregon Metallurgical Corporation, 20
Oregon Steel Mills, Inc., 14
Orion Pictures Corporation, 6
Orthodontic Centers of America, Inc., 35
Orvis Company, Inc., The, 28
Oryx Energy Company, 7
Oscar Mayer Foods Corp., 12
OshKosh B'Gosh, Inc., 9; 42 (upd.)
Oshkosh Truck Corporation, 7
Oshman's Sporting Goods, Inc., 17
Osmonics, Inc., 18
Otis Elevator Company, Inc., 13; 39 (upd.)
Otis Spunkmeyer, Inc., 28
OTR Express, Inc., 25
Ottaway Newspapers, Inc., 15
Otter Tail Power Company, 18
Outback Steakhouse, Inc., 12; 34 (upd.)
Outboard Marine Corporation, III; 20 (upd.)
Outdoor Systems, Inc., 25
Outlook Group Corporation, 37
Overnite Transportation Co., 14
Overseas Shipholding Group, Inc., 11
Owens & Minor, Inc., 16
Owens Corning Corporation, III; 20 (upd.)
Owens-Illinois, Inc., I; 26 (upd.)
Owosso Corporation, 29

United States (*continued*)

Oxford Health Plans, Inc., 16
Oxford Industries, Inc., 8
P&C Foods Inc., 8
P & F Industries, Inc., 45
P.C. Richard & Son Corp., 23
P.F. Chang's China Bistro, Inc., 37
P.H. Glatfelter Company, 8; 30 (upd.)
Paccar Inc., I; 26 (upd.)
Pacer Technology, 40
Pacific Enterprises, V
Pacific Gas and Electric Company, V
Pacific Sunwear of California, Inc., 28
Pacific Telecom, Inc., 6
Pacific Telesis Group, V
PacifiCare Health Systems, Inc., 11
PacifiCorp, V; 26 (upd.)
Packaging Corporation of America, 12
Packard Bell Electronics, Inc., 13
Paging Network Inc., 11
PaineWebber Group Inc., II; 22 (upd.)
Pall Corporation, 9
Palm Harbor Homes, Inc., 39
Palm, Inc., 36
Palomar Medical Technologies, Inc., 22
Pamida Holdings Corporation, 15
Pampered Chef, Ltd., The, 18
Pan American World Airways, Inc., I; 12
  (upd.)
Pan-American Life Insurance Company, 48
Panamerican Beverages, Inc., 47
PanAmSat Corporation, 46
Panavision Inc., 24
Pancho's Mexican Buffet, Inc., 46
Panda Management Company, Inc., 35
Panera Bread Company, 44
Panhandle Eastern Corporation, V
Pantry, Inc., The, 36
Papa John's International, Inc., 15
Papetti's Hygrade Egg Products, Inc., 39
Paradise Music & Entertainment, Inc., 42
Parametric Technology Corp., 16
Paramount Pictures Corporation, II
Paris Corporation, 22
Parisian, Inc., 14
Park Corp., 22
Park-Ohio Industries Inc., 17
Parker Drilling Company, 28
Parker-Hannifin Corporation, III; 24 (upd.)
Parsons Brinckerhoff, Inc., 34
Parsons Corporation, The, 8
Pathmark Stores, Inc., 23
Patina Oil & Gas Corporation, 24
Patrick Industries, Inc., 30
Patterson Dental Co., 19
Paul Harris Stores, Inc., 18
Paul Revere Corporation, The, 12
Paul, Hastings, Janofsky & Walker LLP,
  27
Paul, Weiss, Rifkind, Wharton & Garrison,
  47
Paxson Communications Corporation, 33
Pay 'N Pak Stores, Inc., 9
Paychex, Inc., 15; 46 (upd.)
Payless Cashways, Inc., 11; 44 (upd.)
Payless ShoeSource, Inc., 18
PC Connection, Inc., 37
PDS Gaming Corporation, 44
Peabody Coal Company, 10
Peabody Energy Corporation, 45 (upd.)
Peabody Holding Company, Inc., IV
Peak Technologies Group, Inc., The, 14
Peapod, Inc., 30
Pearle Vision, Inc., 13
Peavey Electronics Corporation, 16
PECO Energy Company, 11
Pediatric Services of America, Inc., 31

Peebles Inc., 16; 43 (upd.)
Peet's Coffee & Tea, Inc., 38
Pella Corporation, 12; 39 (upd.)
Pendleton Woolen Mills, Inc., 42
Penn Engineering & Manufacturing Corp.,
  28
Penn National Gaming, Inc., 33
Penn Traffic Company, 13
Pennsylvania Blue Shield, III
Pennsylvania Power & Light Company, V
Pennwalt Corporation, I
Pennzoil Company, IV; 20 (upd.)
Penske Corporation, V; 19 (upd.)
Pentair, Inc., 7; 26 (upd.)
Pentech International, Inc., 29
Penton Media, Inc., 27
People Express Airlines, Inc., I
Peoples Energy Corporation, 6
PeopleSoft Inc., 14; 33 (upd.)
Pep Boys—Manny, Moe & Jack, The, 11;
  36 (upd.)
Pepper Hamilton LLP, 43
Pepsi Bottling Group, Inc., The, 40
Pepsico, Inc., I; 10 (upd.); 38 (upd.)
Perdue Farms Inc., 7; 23 (upd.)
Performance Food Group Company, 31
Perini Corporation, 8
Perkin-Elmer Corporation, The, 7
Perkins Family Restaurants, L.P., 22
Perot Systems Corporation, 29
Perrigo Company, 12
Perry Ellis International, Inc., 41
Pet Incorporated, 7
Petco Animal Supplies, Inc., 29
Pete's Brewing Company, 22
Peter Kiewit Sons' Inc., 8
Petersen Publishing Company, 21
Petrie Stores Corporation, 8
Petroleum Helicopters, Inc., 35
Petrolite Corporation, 15
PETsMART, Inc., 14; 41 (upd.)
Pew Charitable Trusts, The, 35
Pez Candy, Inc., 38
Pfizer Inc., I; 9 (upd.); 38 (upd.)
PG&E Corporation, 26 (upd.)
Phar-Mor Inc., 12
Pharmacia & Upjohn Inc., I; 25 (upd.)
Phat Fashions LLC, 49
Phelps Dodge Corporation, IV; 28 (upd.)
PHH Corporation, V
Philadelphia Eagles, 37
Philadelphia Electric Company, V
Philadelphia Suburban Corporation, 39
Philip Morris Companies Inc., V; 18
  (upd.); 44 (upd.)
Philips Electronics North America Corp.,
  13
Phillips Petroleum Company, IV; 40 (upd.)
Phillips, de Pury & Luxembourg, 49
Phillips-Van Heusen Corporation, 24
PHP Healthcare Corporation, 22
PhyCor, Inc., 36
Physician Sales & Service, Inc., 14
Physio-Control International Corp., 18
Piccadilly Cafeterias, Inc., 19
PictureTel Corp., 10; 27 (upd.)
Piedmont Natural Gas Company, Inc., 27
Pier 1 Imports, Inc., 12; 34 (upd.)
Pierce Leahy Corporation, 24
Piercing Pagoda, Inc., 29
Piggly Wiggly Southern, Inc., 13
Pilgrim's Pride Corporation, 7; 23 (upd.)
Pillowtex Corporation, 19; 41 (upd.)
Pillsbury Company, II; 13 (upd.)
Pillsbury Madison & Sutro LLP, 29
Pilot Corporation, 49
Pinkerton's Inc., 9
Pinnacle West Capital Corporation, 6

Pioneer Hi-Bred International, Inc., 9; 41
  (upd.)
Pioneer-Standard Electronics Inc., 19
Piper Jaffray Companies Inc., 22
Pitney Bowes Inc., III; 19; 47 (upd.)
Pittston Company, The, IV; 19 (upd.)
Pittway Corporation, 9; 33 (upd.)
Pixar Animation Studios, 34
Pizza Hut Inc., 7; 21 (upd.)
Pizza Inn, Inc., 46
Planet Hollywood International, Inc., 18;
  41 (upd.)
Platinum Entertainment, Inc., 35
PLATINUM Technology, Inc., 14
Plato Learning, Inc., 44
Play by Play Toys & Novelties, Inc., 26
Playboy Enterprises, Inc., 18
PlayCore, Inc., 27
Players International, Inc., 22
Playskool, Inc., 25
Playtex Products, Inc., 15
Pleasant Company, 27
Plexus Corporation, 35
Plum Creek Timber Company, Inc., 43
Pluma, Inc., 27
Ply Gem Industries Inc., 12
PMI Group, Inc., The, 49
PMT Services, Inc., 24
PNC Bank Corp., II; 13 (upd.)
PNC Financial Services Group Inc., The,
  46 (upd.)
Pogo Producing Company, 39
Polaris Industries Inc., 12; 35 (upd.)
Polaroid Corporation, III; 7 (upd.); 28
  (upd.)
Policy Management Systems Corporation,
  11
Polk Audio, Inc., 34
Polo/Ralph Lauren Corporation, 12
PolyGram N.V., 23
Pomeroy Computer Resources, Inc., 33
Ponderosa Steakhouse, 15
Poore Brothers, Inc., 44
Pope and Talbot, Inc., 12
Popular, Inc., 41
Port Authority of New York and New
  Jersey, The, 48
Portal Software, Inc., 47
Portland General Corporation, 6
Post Properties, Inc., 26
Potlatch Corporation, 8; 34 (upd.)
Potomac Electric Power Company, 6
Potter & Brumfield Inc., 11
Powell's Books, Inc., 40
PowerBar Inc., 44
Powerhouse Technologies, Inc., 27
PPG Industries, Inc., III; 22 (upd.)
PPL Corporation, 41 (upd.)
PR Newswire, 35
Prairie Farms Dairy, Inc., 47
Pratt & Whitney, 9
Praxair, Inc., 11; 48 (upd.)
Pre-Paid Legal Services, Inc., 20
Precision Castparts Corp., 15
Premark International, Inc., III
Premcor Inc., 37
Premier Industrial Corporation, 9
Premier Parks, Inc., 27
Premium Standard Farms, Inc., 30
PremiumWear, Inc., 30
Preserver Group, Inc., 44
President Casinos, Inc., 22
Presstek, Inc., 33
Preston Corporation, 6
Price Communications Corporation, 42
Price Company, The, V
Price Waterhouse, 9
PriceCostco, Inc., 14

PricewaterhouseCoopers, 29 (upd.)
Primark Corp., 13
Primedex Health Systems, Inc., 25
Primedia Inc., 22
Primerica Corporation, I
Prince Sports Group, Inc., 15
Princess Cruise Lines, 22
Princeton Review, Inc., The, 42
Principal Mutual Life Insurance Company, III
Printrak, A Motorola Company, 44
Printronix, Inc., 18
Procter & Gamble Company, The, III; 8 (upd.); 26 (upd.)
Prodigy Communications Corporation, 34
Professional Golfers' Association of America, The, 41
Proffitt's, Inc., 19
Progress Software Corporation, 15
Progressive Corporation, The, 11; 29 (upd.)
Promus Companies, Inc., 9
Proskauer Rose LLP, 47
Protection One, Inc., 32
Providence Journal Company, The, 28
Provident Life and Accident Insurance Company of America, III
Prudential Insurance Company of America, The, III; 30 (upd.)
PSI Resources, 6
Pubco Corporation, 17
Public Service Company of Colorado, 6
Public Service Company of New Hampshire, 21
Public Service Company of New Mexico, 6
Public Service Enterprise Group Inc., V; 44 (upd.)
Publishers Clearing House, 23
Publishers Group, Inc., 35
Publix Supermarkets Inc., 7; 31 (upd.)
Pueblo Xtra International, Inc., 47
Puget Sound Power and Light Company, 6
Pulaski Furniture Corporation, 33
Pulitzer Publishing Company, 15
Pulte Corporation, 8
Pulte Homes, Inc., 42 (upd.)
Pumpkin Masters, Inc., 48
Purina Mills, Inc., 32
Puritan-Bennett Corporation, 13
Purolator Products Company, 21
Putt-Putt Golf Courses of America, Inc., 23
PW Eagle, Inc., 48
Pyramid Breweries Inc., 33
Quad/Graphics, Inc., 19
Quaker Fabric Corp., 19
Quaker Oats Company, The, II; 12 (upd.); 34 (upd.)
Quaker State Corporation, 7; 21 (upd.)
QUALCOMM Incorporated, 20; 47 (upd.)
Quality Chekd Dairies, Inc., 48
Quality Dining, Inc., 18
Quality Food Centers, Inc., 17
Quanex Corporation, 13
Quantum Chemical Corporation, 8
Quantum Corporation, 10
Quark, Inc., 36
Quest Diagnostics Inc., 26
Questar Corporation, 6; 26 (upd.)
Quick & Reilly Group, Inc., The, 20
Quiksilver, Inc., 18
QuikTrip Corporation, 36
Quill Corporation, 28
Quintiles Transnational Corporation, 21
Quixote Corporation, 15
Quizno's Corporation, The, 42
QVC Network Inc., 9
Qwest Communications International, Inc., 37
R.B. Pamplin Corp., 45

R.C. Bigelow, Inc., 49
R.G. Barry Corporation, 17; 44 (upd.)
R.H. Macy & Co., Inc., V; 8 (upd.); 30 (upd.)
R.J. Reynolds Tobacco Holdings, Inc., 30 (upd.)
R.L. Polk & Co., 10
R.P. Scherer, I
R.R. Donnelley & Sons Company, IV; 9 (upd.); 38 (upd.)
Racal-Datacom Inc., 11
Racing Champions Corporation, 37
Radian Group Inc., 42
Radio Flyer Inc., 34
RadioShack Corporation, 36 (upd.)
Radius Inc., 16
Rag Shops, Inc., 30
RailTex, Inc., 20
Rainforest Cafe, Inc., 25
Rainier Brewing Company, 23
Raley's Inc., 14
Rally's Hamburgers, Inc., 25
Ralphs Grocery Company, 35
Ralston Purina Company, II; 13 (upd.)
Ramsay Youth Services, Inc., 41
Rand McNally & Company, 28
Randall's Food Markets, Inc., 40
Random House, Inc., 13; 31 (upd.)
Range Resources Corporation, 45
Rapala-Normark Group, Ltd., 30
Rare Hospitality International Inc., 19
Raven Industries, Inc., 33
Rawlings Sporting Goods Co., Inc., 24
Raychem Corporation, 8
Rayonier Inc., 24
Rayovac Corporation, 13; 39 (upd.)
Raytheon Aircraft Holdings Inc., 46
Raytheon Company, II; 11 (upd.); 38 (upd.)
Razorfish, Inc., 37
RCA Corporation, II
RCM Technologies, Inc., 34
RDO Equipment Company, 33
Read-Rite Corp., 10
Reader's Digest Association, Inc., The, IV; 17 (upd.)
Reckson Associates Realty Corp., 47
Recoton Corp., 15
Recovery Engineering, Inc., 25
Recreational Equipment, Inc., 18
Recycled Paper Greetings, Inc., 21
Red Apple Group, Inc., 23
Red Hat, Inc., 45
Red Roof Inns, Inc., 18
Red Wing Shoe Company, Inc., 9; 30 (upd.)
Redhook Ale Brewery, Inc., 31
Reebok International Ltd., V; 9 (upd.); 26 (upd.)
Reeds Jewelers, Inc., 22
Regal-Beloit Corporation, 18
Regis Corporation, 18
Reichhold Chemicals, Inc., 10
Reliance Electric Company, 9
Reliance Group Holdings, Inc., III
Reliance Steel & Aluminum Co., 19
Reliant Energy Inc., 44 (upd.)
RemedyTemp, Inc., 20
Remington Arms Company, Inc., 12; 40 (upd.)
Remington Products Company, L.L.C., 42
Renaissance Learning Systems, Inc., 39
Reno Air Inc., 23
Rent-A-Center, Inc., 45
Rent-Way, Inc., 33
Rental Service Corporation, 28
Rentrak Corporation, 35

Republic Engineered Steels, Inc., 7; 26 (upd.)
Republic Industries, Inc., 26
Republic New York Corporation, 11
Res-Care, Inc., 29
Resorts International, Inc., 12
Resource America, Inc., 42
Response Oncology, Inc., 27
Restaurants Unlimited, Inc., 13
Restoration Hardware, Inc., 30
Revco D.S., Inc., V
Revell-Monogram Inc., 16
Revere Ware Corporation, 22
Revlon Inc., III; 17 (upd.)
REX Stores Corp., 10
Rexel, Inc., 15
Rexnord Corporation, 21
Reynolds Metals Company, IV; 19 (upd.)
RF Micro Devices, Inc., 43
Rhino Entertainment Company, 18
Rhodes Inc., 23
Rica Foods, Inc., 41
Rich Products Corporation, 7; 38 (upd.)
Richardson Electronics, Ltd., 17
Richfood Holdings, Inc., 7
Richton International Corporation, 39
Riddell Sports Inc., 22
Ride, Inc., 22
Riese Organization, The, 38
Riggs National Corporation, 13
Right Management Consultants, Inc., 42
Riklis Family Corp., 9
Riser Foods, Inc., 9
Rite Aid Corporation, V; 19 (upd.)
Ritz Camera Centers, 34
Ritz-Carlton Hotel Company L.L.C., 9; 29 (upd.)
Rival Company, The, 19
River Oaks Furniture, Inc., 43
Riverwood International Corporation, 11; 48 (upd.)
Riviana Foods Inc., 27
RJR Nabisco Holdings Corp., V
RMH Teleservices, Inc., 42
Roadhouse Grill, Inc., 22
Roadmaster Industries, Inc., 16
Roadway Express, Inc., V; 25 (upd.)
Roanoke Electric Steel Corporation, 45
Robbins & Myers Inc., 15
Roberds Inc., 19
Robert Half International Inc., 18
Robert Mondavi Corporation, 15
Robert Wood Johnson Foundation, 35
Roberts Pharmaceutical Corporation, 16
Robertson-Ceco Corporation, 19
Roche Bioscience, 11; 14 (upd.)
Rochester Gas and Electric Corporation, 6
Rochester Telephone Corporation, 6
Rock Bottom Restaurants, Inc., 25
Rock of Ages Corporation, 37
Rock-Tenn Company, 13
Rockefeller Foundation, The, 34
Rockford Corporation, 43
RockShox, Inc., 26
Rockwell Automation, 43 (upd.)
Rockwell International Corporation, I; 11 (upd.)
Rocky Shoes & Boots, Inc., 26
Rodale Press, Inc., 23
Rodale, Inc., 47 (upd.)
Rohm and Haas Company, I; 26 (upd.)
ROHN Industries, Inc., 22
Rohr Incorporated, 9
Roll International Corporation, 37
Rollerblade, Inc., 15; 34 (upd.)
Rollins, Inc., 11
Rolls-Royce Allison, 29 (upd.)
Ronco, Inc., 15

United States (*continued*)

Rooms To Go Inc., 28
Rooney Brothers Co., 25
Roper Industries Inc., 15
Ropes & Gray, 40
Rorer Group, I
Rose's Stores, Inc., 13
Rosemount Inc., 15
Rosenbluth International Inc., 14
Ross Stores, Inc., 17; 43 (upd.)
Rotary International, 31
Roto-Rooter Corp., 15
Rottlund Company, Inc., The, 28
Rouge Steel Company, 8
Roundy's Inc., 14
Rouse Company, The, 15
Rowan Companies, Inc., 43
Roy F. Weston, Inc., 33
Royal Appliance Manufacturing Company, 15
Royal Caribbean Cruises Ltd., 22
Royal Crown Company, Inc., 23
RPM, Inc., 8; 36 (upd.)
RSA Security Inc., 46
Rubbermaid Incorporated, III; 20 (upd.)
Rubio's Restaurants, Inc., 35
Ruby Tuesday, Inc., 18
Rural Cellular Corporation, 43
Rural/Metro Corporation, 28
Rush Communications, 33
Russ Berrie and Company, Inc., 12
Russell Corporation, 8; 30 (upd.)
Russell Reynolds Associates Inc., 38
Russell Stover Candies Inc., 12
Rust International Inc., 11
Ruth's Chris Steak House, 28
Ryan's Family Steak Houses, Inc., 15
Ryder System, Inc., V; 24 (upd.)
Ryerson Tull, Inc., 40 (upd.)
Ryland Group, Inc., The, 8; 37 (upd.)
S&C Electric Company, 15
S&K Famous Brands, Inc., 23
S-K-I Limited, 15
S.C. Johnson & Son, Inc., III; 28 (upd.)
Saatchi & Saatchi, 42 (upd.)
Sabratek Corporation, 29
SABRE Group Holdings, Inc., 26
SAFECO Corporaton, III
Safeguard Scientifics, Inc., 10
Safelite Glass Corp., 19
Safeskin Corporation, 18
Safety 1st, Inc., 24
Safety-Kleen Corp., 8
Safeway Inc., II; 24 (upd.)
Saga Communications, Inc., 27
St. Joe Company, The, 31
St. Joe Paper Company, 8
St. John Knits, Inc., 14
St. Jude Medical, Inc., 11; 43 (upd.)
St. Louis Music, Inc., 48
St. Paul Bank for Cooperatives, 8
St. Paul Companies, Inc., The, III; 22 (upd.)
Saks Holdings, Inc., 24
Saks Inc., 41 (upd.)
Salant Corporation, 12
Salomon Inc., II; 13 (upd.)
Salt River Project, 19
Salton, Inc., 30
Salvation Army USA, The, 32
Sam Ash Music Corporation, 30
Sam's Club, 40
Samsonite Corporation, 13; 43 (upd.)
Samuels Jewelers Incorporated, 30
San Diego Gas & Electric Company, V
Sanderson Farms, Inc., 15
Sandia National Laboratories, 49

Santa Barbara Restaurant Group, Inc., 37
Santa Cruz Operation, Inc., The, 38
Santa Fe Gaming Corporation, 19
Santa Fe International Corporation, 38
Santa Fe Pacific Corporation, V
Sara Lee Corporation, II; 15 (upd.)
SAS Institute Inc., 10
Saturn Corporation, 7; 21 (upd.)
Saucony Inc., 35
Sauder Woodworking Company, 12; 35 (upd.)
Savannah Foods & Industries, Inc., 7
Sawtek Inc., 43 (upd.)
Sbarro, Inc., 16
SBC Communications Inc., 32 (upd.)
SBS Technologies, Inc., 25
SCANA Corporation, 6
ScanSource, Inc., 29
SCB Computer Technology, Inc., 29
SCEcorp, V
Schawk, Inc., 24
Schering-Plough Corporation, I; 14 (upd.); 49 (upd.)
Schlotzsky's, Inc., 36
Schlumberger Limited, III; 17 (upd.)
Schmitt Music Company, 40
Schneider National, Inc., 36
Schneiderman's Furniture Inc., 28
Schnitzer Steel Industries, Inc., 19
Scholastic Corporation, 10; 29 (upd.)
Schottenstein Stores Corp., 14
Schuff Steel Company, 26
Schultz Sav-O Stores, Inc., 21; 31 (upd.)
Schwan's Sales Enterprises, Inc., 7; 26 (upd.)
Schwinn Cycle and Fitness L.P., 19
SCI Systems, Inc., 9
Science Applications International Corporation, 15
Scientific-Atlanta, Inc., 6; 45 (upd.)
Score Board, Inc., The, 19
Scotsman Industries, Inc., 20
Scott Fetzer Company, 12
Scott Paper Company, IV; 31 (upd.)
Scotts Company, The, 22
Scotty's, Inc., 22
Scovill Fasteners Inc., 24
SCP Pool Corporation, 39
Seaboard Corporation, 36
Seagate Technology, Inc., 8; 34 (upd.)
Seagull Energy Corporation, 11
Sealed Air Corporation, 14
Sealed Power Corporation, I
Sealright Co., Inc., 17
Sealy Inc., 12
Seaman Furniture Company, Inc., 32
Sears, Roebuck and Co., V; 18 (upd.)
Seattle FilmWorks, Inc., 20
Seattle First National Bank Inc., 8
Seattle Times Company, 15
Seaway Food Town, Inc., 15
Sebastiani Vineyards, Inc., 28
Second Harvest, 29
Security Capital Corporation, 17
Security Pacific Corporation, II
SED International Holdings, Inc., 43
See's Candies, Inc., 30
Sega of America, Inc., 10
Segway LLC, 48
Seigle's Home and Building Centers, Inc., 41
Seitel, Inc., 47
Select Comfort Corporation, 34
Selmer Company, Inc., The, 19
SEMCO Energy, Inc., 44
Seminis, Inc., 29
Semitool, Inc., 18
Sempra Energy, 25 (upd.)

Semtech Corporation, 32
Seneca Foods Corporation, 17
Sensormatic Electronics Corp., 11
Sensory Science Corporation, 37
Sepracor Inc., 45
Sequa Corp., 13
Serta, Inc., 28
Service America Corp., 7
Service Corporation International, 6
Service Merchandise Company, Inc., V; 19 (upd.)
ServiceMaster Inc., 6; 23 (upd.)
7-11, Inc., 32 (upd.)
Sevenson Environmental Services, Inc., 42
SFX Entertainment, Inc., 36
SGI, 29 (upd.)
Shakespeare Company, 22
Shaklee Corporation, 12; 39 (upd.)
Shared Medical Systems Corporation, 14
Sharper Image Corporation, The, 10
Shaw Industries, Inc., 9; 40 (upd.)
Shawmut National Corporation, 13
Shearman & Sterling, 32
Shearson Lehman Brothers Holdings Inc., II; 9 (upd.)
Shelby Williams Industries, Inc., 14
Sheldahl Inc., 23
Shell Oil Company, IV; 14 (upd.); 41 (upd.)
Sheller-Globe Corporation, I
Shells Seafood Restaurants, Inc., 43
Sherwin-Williams Company, The, III; 13 (upd.)
Shoe Carnival Inc., 14
Shoney's, Inc., 7; 23 (upd.)
ShopKo Stores Inc., 21
Shorewood Packaging Corporation, 28
ShowBiz Pizza Time, Inc., 13
Showboat, Inc., 19
Shubert Organization Inc., 24
Sidley Austin Brown & Wood, 40
Siebel Systems, Inc., 38
Siebert Financial Corp., 32
Sierra Club, The, 28
Sierra Health Services, Inc., 15
Sierra On-Line, Inc., 15; 41 (upd.)
Sierra Pacific Industries, 22
SIFCO Industries, Inc., 41
Sigma-Aldrich Corporation, I; 36 (upd.)
Signet Banking Corporation, 11
Sikorsky Aircraft Corporation, 24
Silicon Graphics Incorporated, 9
SilverPlatter Information Inc., 23
Silverstein Properties, Inc., 47
Simmons Company, 47
Simon & Schuster Inc., IV; 19 (upd.)
Simon Property Group, Inc., 27
Simon Transportation Services Inc., 27
Simplex Technologies Inc., 21
Simpson Investment Company, 17
Simpson Thacher & Bartlett, 39
Simula, Inc., 41
Sinclair Broadcast Group, Inc., 25
Sir Speedy, Inc., 16
Six Flags Theme Parks, Inc., 17
Skadden, Arps, Slate, Meagher & Flom, 18
Skechers USA Inc., 31
Skidmore, Owings & Merrill, 13
Skyline Corporation, 30
SkyMall, Inc., 26
SkyWest, Inc., 25
SL Green Realty Corporation, 44
Sleepy's Inc., 32
SLI, Inc., 48
Slim-Fast Nutritional Foods International, Inc., 18
SLM Holding Corp., 25 (upd.)
Smart & Final, Inc., 16

SmartForce PLC, 43
Smead Manufacturing Co., 17
Smith & Wesson Corporation, 30
Smith Barney Inc., 15
Smith Corona Corp., 13
Smith International, Inc., 15
Smith's Food & Drug Centers, Inc., 8
Smithfield Foods, Inc., 7; 43 (upd.)
SmithKline Beckman Corporation, I
Smithsonian Institution, 27
Smithway Motor Xpress Corporation, 39
Smurfit-Stone Container Corporation, 26 (upd.)
Snap-On, Incorporated, 7; 27 (upd.)
Snapple Beverage Corporation, 11
Snell & Wilmer L.L.P., 28
Society Corporation, 9
Soft Sheen Products, Inc., 31
Solectron Corporation, 12; 48 (upd.)
Solo Serve Corporation, 28
Sonat, Inc., 6
Sonesta International Hotels Corporation, 44
Sonic Corp., 14; 37 (upd.)
Sonoco Products Company, 8
Soros Fund Management LLC, 28
Sorrento, Inc., 24
SOS Staffing Services, 25
Sotheby's Holdings, Inc., 11; 29 (upd.)
Sound Advice, Inc., 41
South Jersey Industries, Inc., 42
Southdown, Inc., 14
Southern Company, The, V; 38 (upd.)
Southern Indiana Gas and Electric Company, 13
Southern New UK Telecommunications Corporation, 6
Southern Pacific Transportation Company, V
Southern States Cooperative Incorporated, 36
Southern Union Company, 27
Southland Corporation, The, II; 7 (upd.)
Southtrust Corporation, 11
Southwest Airlines Co., 6; 24 (upd.)
Southwest Gas Corporation, 19
Southwest Water Company, 47
Southwestern Bell Corporation, V
Southwestern Electric Power Co., 21
Southwestern Public Service Company, 6
Southwire Company, Inc., 8; 23 (upd.)
Spacehab, Inc., 37
Spaghetti Warehouse, Inc., 25
Spangler Candy Company, 44
Spanish Broadcasting System, Inc., 41
Spartan Motors Inc., 14
Spartan Stores Inc., 8
Spartech Corporation, 19
Sparton Corporation, 18
Spec's Music, Inc., 19
Specialty Coatings Inc., 8
Specialty Equipment Companies, Inc., 25
SpeeDee Oil Change and Tune-Up, 25
Speedway Motorsports, Inc., 32
Speizman Industries, Inc., 44
Spelling Entertainment, 14; 35 (upd.)
Spencer Stuart and Associates, Inc., 14
Spiegel, Inc., 10; 27 (upd.)
Spirit Airlines, Inc., 31
Sport Chalet, Inc., 16
Sport Supply Group, Inc., 23
Sportmart, Inc., 15
Sports & Recreation, Inc., 17
Sports Authority, Inc., The, 16; 43 (upd.)
Sports Club Company, The, 25
Sportsman's Guide, Inc., The, 36
Springs Industries, Inc., V; 19 (upd.)
Sprint Communications Company, L.P., 9

Sprint Corporation, 46 (upd.)
SPS Technologies, Inc., 30
SPX Corporation, 10; 47 (upd.)
Squibb Corporation, I
Stage Stores, Inc., 24
Stanadyne Automotive Corporation, 37
Standard Commercial Corporation, 13
Standard Federal Bank, 9
Standard Microsystems Corporation, 11
Standard Motor Products, Inc., 40
Standard Register Co., 15
Standex International Corporation, 17; 44 (upd.)
Stanhome Inc., 15
Stanley Furniture Company, Inc., 34
Stanley Works, The, III; 20 (upd.)
Staples, Inc., 10
Star Banc Corporation, 11
Starbucks Corporation, 13; 34 (upd.)
Starcraft Corporation, 30
Starrett Corporation, 21
Starter Corp., 12
State Farm Mutual Automobile Insurance Company, III
State Street Boston Corporation, 8
Staten Island Bancorp, Inc., 39
Station Casinos Inc., 25
Steak n Shake Company, The, 41
Stearns, Inc., 43
Steelcase, Inc., 7; 27 (upd.)
Stein Mart Inc., 19
Steinway Musical Properties, Inc., 19
Stepan Company, 30
Stericycle Inc., 33
STERIS Corporation, 29
Sterling Chemicals, Inc., 16
Sterling Drug, Inc., I
Sterling Electronics Corp., 18
Sterling Software, Inc., 11
Stevedoring Services of America Inc., 28
Steven Madden, Ltd., 37
Stewart & Stevenson Services Inc., 11
Stewart Enterprises, Inc., 20
Stewart's Beverages, 39
Stillwater Mining Company, 47
Stock Yards Packing Co., Inc., 37
Stone & Webster, Inc., 13
Stone Container Corporation, IV
Stone Manufacturing Company, 14; 43 (upd.)
Stop & Shop Companies, Inc., The, II; 24 (upd.)
Storage Technology Corporation, 6
Storage USA, Inc., 21
Stouffer Corp., 8
StrataCom, Inc., 16
Stratus Computer, Inc., 10
Stride Rite Corporation, The, 8; 37 (upd.)
Stroh Brewery Company, The, I; 18 (upd.)
Stroock & Stroock & Lavan LLP, 40
Strouds, Inc., 33
Stryker Corporation, 11; 29 (upd.)
Stuart Entertainment Inc., 16
Student Loan Marketing Association, II
Stuller Settings, Inc., 35
Sturm, Ruger & Company, Inc., 19
Sub-Zero Freezer Co., Inc., 31
Suburban Propane Partners, L.P., 30
Subway, 32
Successories, Inc., 30
Sudbury Inc., 16
Suiza Foods Corporation, 26
Sullivan & Cromwell, 26
Summit Bancorporation, The, 14
Summit Family Restaurants, Inc. 19
Sun Communities Inc., 46
Sun Company, Inc., IV
Sun Country Airlines, 30

Sun Distributors L.P., 12
Sun Healthcare Group Inc., 25
Sun Microsystems, Inc., 7; 30 (upd.)
Sun Sportswear, Inc., 17
Sun Television & Appliances Inc., 10
Sun-Diamond Growers of California, 7
SunAmerica Inc., 11
Sunbeam-Oster Co., Inc., 9
Sunburst Hospitality Corporation, 26
Sundstrand Corporation, 7; 21 (upd.)
Sundt Corp., 24
SunGard Data Systems Inc., 11
Sunglass Hut International, Inc., 21
Sunkist Growers, Inc., 26
Sunoco, Inc., 28 (upd.)
Sunrider Corporation, The, 26
Sunrise Medical Inc., 11
SunTrust Banks Inc., 23
Super Food Services, Inc., 15
Super Valu Stores, Inc., II
Supercuts Inc., 26
Superior Industries International, Inc., 8
Superior Uniform Group, Inc., 30
Supermarkets General Holdings Corporation, II
Supervalu Inc., 18 (upd.)
Suprema Specialties, Inc., 27
Supreme International Corporation, 27
Susquehanna Pfaltzgraff Company, 8
Sutter Home Winery Inc., 16
Sverdrup Corporation, 14
Swank Inc., 17
Sweetheart Cup Company, Inc., 36
Swift Transportation Co., Inc., 42
Swinerton Inc., 43
Swisher International Group Inc., 23
Sybase, Inc., 10; 27 (upd.)
Sybron International Corp., 14
Sycamore Networks, Inc., 45
Sykes Enterprises, Inc., 45
Sylvan Learning Systems, Inc., 35
Sylvan, Inc., 22
Symantec Corporation, 10
Symbol Technologies, Inc., 15
Syms Corporation, 29
Synopsis, Inc., 11
SynOptics Communications, Inc., 10
Synovus Financial Corp., 12
Syntex Corporation, I
SyQuest Technology, Inc., 18
Syratech Corp., 14
SYSCO Corporation, II; 24 (upd.)
System Software Associates, Inc., 10
Systems & Computer Technology Corp., 19
T-Netix, Inc., 46
T. Rowe Price Associates, Inc., 11; 34 (upd.)
TAB Products Co., 17
Taco Bell Corp., 7; 21 (upd.)
Taco Cabana, Inc., 23
Taco John's International Inc., 15
Take-Two Interactive Software, Inc., 46
Talbots, Inc., The, 11; 31 (upd.)
Talley Industries, Inc., 16
Tambrands Inc., 8
Tandem Computers, Inc., 6
Tandy Corporation, II; 12 (upd.)
Tandycrafts, Inc., 31
Tanger Factory Outlet Centers, Inc., 49
Target Stores, 10; 27 (upd.)
Tarragon Realty Investors, Inc., 45
Tasty Baking Company, 14; 35 (upd.)
Tattered Cover Book Store, 43
Taylor Corporation, 36
Taylor Guitars, 48
Taylor Made Golf Co., 23
Taylor Publishing Company, 12; 36 (upd.)

United States (*continued*)

TBWA Advertising, Inc., 6
TBWA\Chiat\Day, 43 (upd.)
TCBY Enterprises Inc., 17
TCF Financial Corporation, 47
Teachers Insurance and Annuity
    Association-College Retirement Equities
    Fund, III; 45 (upd.)
TearDrop Golf Company, 32
Tech Data Corporation, 10
Tech-Sym Corporation, 18; 44 (upd.)
Technitrol, Inc., 29
TECO Energy, Inc., 6
Tecumseh Products Company, 8
Tejon Ranch Company, 35
Tektronix, Inc., 8
Tele-Communications, Inc., II
Teledyne, Inc., I; 10 (upd.)
Telephone and Data Systems, Inc., 9
Tellabs, Inc., 11; 40 (upd.)
Telxon Corporation, 10
Temple-Inland Inc., IV; 31 (upd.)
TenFold Corporation, 35
Tennant Company, 13; 33 (upd.)
Tenneco Inc., I; 10 (upd.)
Teradyne, Inc., 11
Terex Corporation, 7; 40 (upd.)
Terlato Wine Group, The, 48
Terra Industries, Inc., 13
Tesoro Petroleum Corporation, 7; 45 (upd.)
Tetra Tech, Inc., 29
Texaco Inc., IV; 14 (upd.); 41 (upd.)
Texas Air Corporation, I
Texas Industries, Inc., 8
Texas Instruments Inc., II; 11 (upd.); 46
    (upd.)
Texas Pacific Group Inc., 36
Texas Utilities Company, V; 25 (upd.)
Textron Inc., I , 34 (upd.)
Textron Lycoming Turbine Engine, 9
Thermadyne Holding Corporation, 19
Thermo BioAnalysis Corp., 25
Thermo Electron Corporation, 7
Thermo Fibertek, Inc., 24
Thermo Instrument Systems Inc., 11
Thermo King Corporation, 13
Thermos Company, 16
Thiokol Corporation, 9; 22 (upd.)
Thomas & Betts Corp., 11
Thomas Cook Travel Inc., 9; 33 (upd.)
Thomas H. Lee Co., 24
Thomas Industries Inc., 29
Thomas J. Lipton Company, 14
Thomas Nelson, Inc., 14; 38 (upd.)
Thomas Publishing Company, 26
Thomaston Mills, Inc., 27
Thomasville Furniture Industries, Inc., 12
Thor Industries, Inc., 39
Thorn Apple Valley, Inc., 7; 22 (upd.)
Thousand Trails, Inc., 33
THQ, Inc., 39
3Com Corporation, 11; 34 (upd.)
3DO Company, The, 43
Thrifty PayLess, Inc., 12
Ticketmaster Group, Inc., 13; 37 (upd.)
Tidewater Inc., 11; 37 (upd.)
Tiffany & Co., 14
TIG Holdings, Inc., 26
Tillotson Corp., 15
Timberland Company, The, 13
Timberline Software Corporation, 15
Time Warner Inc., IV; 7 (upd.)
Times Mirror Company, The, IV; 17 (upd.)
Timex Corporation, 7; 25 (upd.)
Timken Company, The, 8; 42 (upd.)
Tishman Speyer Properties, L.P., 47
Titan Corporation, The, 36

Titanium Metals Corporation, 21
TJ International, Inc., 19
TJX Companies, Inc., The, V; 19 (upd.)
TLC Beatrice International Holdings, Inc.,
    22
TMP Worldwide Inc., 30
TNT Freightways Corporation, 14
Today's Man, Inc., 20
Todd Shipyards Corporation, 14
Todd-AO Corporation, The, 33
Todhunter International, Inc., 27
Tokheim Corporation, 21
Toll Brothers Inc., 15
Tollgrade Communications, Inc., 44
Tom Brown, Inc., 37
Tom Doherty Associates Inc., 25
Tom's of Maine, Inc., 45
Tombstone Pizza Corporation, 13
Tone Brothers, Inc., 21
Tonka Corporation, 25
Tootsie Roll Industries Inc., 12
Topps Company, Inc., The, 13; 34 (upd.)
Tops Appliance City, Inc., 17
Torchmark Corporation, 9; 33 (upd.)
Toro Company, The, 7; 26 (upd.)
Torrington Company, The, 13
Tosco Corporation, 7
Total Entertainment Restaurant
    Corporation, 46
Total System Services, Inc., 18
Totem Resources Corporation, 9
Tower Air, Inc., 28
Tower Automotive, Inc., 24
Towers Perrin, 32
Town & Country Corporation, 19
Town Sports International, Inc., 46
Toy Biz, Inc., 18
Toymax International, Inc., 29
Toys 'R'' Us, Inc., V; 18 (upd.)
Tracor Inc., 17
Trader Joe's Co., 13
Trailer Bridge, Inc., 41
Trammell Crow Company, 8
Trans World Airlines, Inc., I; 12 (upd.); 35
    (upd.)
Trans World Entertainment Corporation, 24
Transaction Systems Architects, Inc., 29
Transamerica Corporation, I; 13 (upd.)
Transamerica–An AEGON Company, 41
    (upd.)
Transatlantic Holdings, Inc., 11
Transco Energy Company, V
Transmedia Network Inc., 20
TransMontaigne Inc., 28
Transocean Sedco Forex Inc., 45
Transport Corporation of America, Inc., 49
Tranzonic Companies, The, 37
Travel Ports of America, Inc., 17
Travelers Corporation, The, III
Travelocity.com, Inc., 46
Travis Boats & Motors, Inc., 37
TRC Companies, Inc., 32
Treadco, Inc., 19
Treasure Chest Advertising Company, Inc.,
    32
Tree of Life, Inc., 29
Trek Bicycle Corporation, 16
Trend-Lines, Inc., 22
Trendwest Resorts, Inc., 33
Tri Valley Growers, 32
Triarc Companies, Inc., 8; 34 (upd.)
Tribune Company, IV; 22 (upd.)
Trico Products Corporation, 15
Trigen Energy Corporation, 42
TriMas Corp., 11
Trimble Navigation Limited, 40
Trinity Industries, Incorporated, 7
TRINOVA Corporation, III

Triple Five Group Ltd., 49
Triton Energy Corporation, 11
Triumph Group, Inc., 31
TRM Copy Centers Corporation, 18
Tropicana Products, Inc., 28
True North Communications Inc., 23
Trump Organization, 23
TruServ Corporation, 24
TRW Inc., I; 11 (upd.); 14 (upd.)
TTX Company, 6
Tucson Electric Power Company, 6
Tuesday Morning Corporation, 18
Tultex Corporation, 13
Tumbleweed, Inc., 33
Tupperware Corporation, 28
Turner Broadcasting System, Inc., II; 6
    (upd.)
Turner Corporation, The, 8; 23 (upd.)
Turtle Wax, Inc., 15
Tuscarora Inc., 29
TV Guide, Inc., 43 (upd.)
TVI, Inc., 15
TW Services, Inc., II
Tweeter Home Entertainment Group, Inc.,
    30
Twentieth Century Fox Film Corporation,
    II; 25 (upd.)
24/7 Real Media, Inc., 49
Twin Disc, Inc., 21
Twinlab Corporation, 34
Ty Inc., 33
Tyco Toys, Inc., 12
Tyler Corporation, 23
Tyson Foods, Incorporated, II; 14 (upd.)
U S West, Inc., V; 25 (upd.)
U.S. Aggregates, Inc., 42
U.S. Bancorp, 14; 36 (upd.)
U.S. Borax, Inc., 42
U.S. Can Corporation, 30
U.S. Cellular Corporation, 31 (upd.)
U.S. Delivery Systems, Inc., 22
U.S. Foodservice, 26
U.S. Healthcare, Inc., 6
U.S. Home Corporation, 8
U.S. News and World Report Inc., 30
U.S. Office Products Company, 25
U.S. Robotics Inc., 9
U.S. Satellite Broadcasting Company, Inc.,
    20
U.S. Timberlands Company, L.P., 42
U.S. Trust Corp., 17
UAL Corporation, 34 (upd.)
UGI Corporation, 12
Ugly Duckling Corporation, 22
UICI, 33
Ukrop's Super Market's, Inc., 39
Ultimate Electronics, Inc., 18
Ultra Pac, Inc., 24
Ultrak Inc., 24
Ultramar Diamond Shamrock Corporation,
    31 (upd.)
Uncle Ben's Inc., 22
Underwriters Laboratories, Inc., 30
Uni-Marts, Inc., 17
Unicom Corporation, 29 (upd.)
Unifi, Inc., 12
UniFirst Corporation, 21
Union Bank of California, 16
Union Camp Corporation, IV
Union Carbide Corporation, I; 9 (upd.)
Union Electric Company, V
Union Pacific Corporation, V; 28 (upd.)
Union Texas Petroleum Holdings, Inc., 9
Unique Casual Restaurants, Inc., 27
Unison HealthCare Corporation, 25
Unisys Corporation, III; 6 (upd.); 36 (upd.)
United Airlines, I; 6 (upd.)
United Auto Group, Inc., 26

United Brands Company, II
United Defense, L.P., 30
United Dominion Industries Limited, 8; 16 (upd.)
United Foods, Inc., 21
United HealthCare Corporation, 9
United Illuminating Company, The, 21
United Industrial Corporation, 37
United Jewish Communities, 33
United Merchants & Manufacturers, Inc., 13
United Natural Foods, Inc., 32
United Parcel Service of America Inc., V; 17 (upd.)
United Press International, Inc., 25
United Rentals, Inc., 34
United Retail Group Inc., 33
United States Cellular Corporation, 9
United States Filter Corporation, 20
United States Postal Service, 14; 34 (upd.)
United States Shoe Corporation, The, V
United States Surgical Corporation, 10; 34 (upd.)
United Stationers Inc., 14
United Technologies Automotive Inc., 15
United Technologies Corporation, I; 10 (upd.); 34 (upd.)
United Telecommunications, Inc., V
United Video Satellite Group, 18
United Water Resources, Inc., 40
United Way of America, 36
Unitil Corporation, 37
Unitog Co., 19
Unitrin Inc., 16
Univar Corporation, 9
Universal Corporation, V; 48 (upd.)
Universal Electronics Inc., 39
Universal Foods Corporation, 7
Universal Forest Products Inc., 10
Universal Health Services, Inc., 6
Universal International, Inc., 25
Universal Studios, Inc., 33
Univision Communications Inc., 24
Uno Restaurant Corporation, 18
Unocal Corporation, IV; 24 (upd.)
UNUM Corp., 13
Upjohn Company, The, I; 8 (upd.)
Urban Outfitters, Inc., 14
URS Corporation, 45
US Airways Group, Inc., 28 (upd.)
USA Interactive, Inc., 47 (upd.)
USA Truck, Inc., 42
USAA, 10
USAir Group, Inc., I; 6 (upd.)
USANA, Inc., 29
USF&G Corporation, III
USG Corporation, III; 26 (upd.)
UST Inc., 9
USX Corporation, IV; 7 (upd.)
Utah Medical Products, Inc., 36
Utah Power and Light Company, 27
UtiliCorp United Inc., 6
UUNET, 38
Vail Resorts, Inc., 11; 43 (upd.)
Valassis Communications, Inc., 8; 37 (upd.)
Valero Energy Corporation, 7
Valhi, Inc., 19
Vallen Corporation, 45
Valley Media Inc., 35
Valmont Industries, Inc., 19
Valspar Corporation, The, 8; 32 (upd.)
Value City Department Stores, Inc., 38
Value Line, Inc., 16
Value Merchants Inc., 13
ValueClick, Inc., 49
ValueVision International, Inc., 22
Van Camp Seafood Company, Inc., 7

Vanguard Group, Inc., The, 14; 34 (upd.)
Vans, Inc., 16; 47 (upd.)
Varco International, Inc., 42
Vari-Lite International, Inc., 35
Varian Associates Inc., 12
Varian, Inc., 48 (upd.)
Varlen Corporation, 16
Varsity Spirit Corp., 15
Vastar Resources, Inc., 24
VECO International, Inc., 7
Vector Group Ltd., 35 (upd.)
Veeco Instruments Inc., 32
Veit Companies, 43
Velocity Express Corporation, 49
Venator Group Inc., 35 (upd.)
Vencor, Inc., 16
Venetian Casino Resort, LLC, 47
Venture Stores Inc., 12
Verbatim Corporation, 14
VeriFone, Inc., 18
VeriSign, Inc., 47
Veritas Software Corporation, 45
Verizon Communications, 43 (upd.)
Vermeer Manufacturing Company, 17
Vermont Teddy Bear Co., Inc., The, 36
VF Corporation, V; 17 (upd.)
Viacom Inc., 7; 23 (upd.)
Viasoft Inc., 27
Viatech Continental Can Company, Inc., 25 (upd.)
Vicon Industries, Inc., 44
VICORP Restaurants, Inc., 12; 48 (upd.)
Vienna Sausage Manufacturing Co., 14
Viking Office Products, Inc., 10
Village Super Market, Inc., 7
Village Voice Media, Inc., 38
Vinson & Elkins L.L.P., 30
Vintage Petroleum, Inc., 42
Virco Manufacturing Corporation, 17
Visa International, 9; 26 (upd.)
Vishay Intertechnology, Inc., 21
Vista Chemical Company, I
Vistana, Inc., 22
VISX, Incorporated, 30
Vitalink Pharmacy Services, Inc., 15
Vitesse Semiconductor Corporation, 32
Vitro Corp., 10
Vivra, Inc., 18
Vlasic Foods International Inc., 25
VLSI Technology, Inc., 16
Volt Information Sciences Inc., 26
Vons Companies, Incorporated, The, 7; 28 (upd.)
Vornado Realty Trust, 20
Vought Aircraft Industries, Inc., 49
Vulcan Materials Company, 7
W. Atlee Burpee & Co., 27
W.H. Brady Co., 17
W.L. Gore & Associates, Inc., 14
W.P. Carey & Co. LLC, 49
W.R. Berkley Corp., 15
W.R. Grace & Company, I
W.W. Grainger, Inc., V; 26 (upd.)
W.W. Norton & Company, Inc., 28
Waban Inc., 13
Wabash National Corp., 13
Wabtec Corporation, 40
Wachovia Bank of Georgia, N.A., 16
Wachovia Bank of South Carolina, N.A., 16
Wachovia Corporation, 12; 46 (upd.)
Wachtell, Lipton, Rosen & Katz, 47
Wackenhut Corporation, The, 14
Waddell & Reed, Inc., 22
Waffle House Inc., 14
Waggener Edstrom, 42
Wakefern Food Corporation, 33

Wal-Mart Stores, Inc., V; 8 (upd.); 26 (upd.)
Walbridge Aldinger Co., 38
Walbro Corporation, 13
Waldbaum, Inc., 19
Walden Book Company Inc., 17
Walgreen Co., V; 20 (upd.)
Walker Manufacturing Company, 19
Wall Drug Store, Inc., 40
Wall Street Deli, Inc., 33
Wallace Computer Services, Inc., 36
Walt Disney Company, The, II; 6 (upd.); 30 (upd.)
Walter Industries, Inc., II; 22 (upd.)
Walton Monroe Mills, Inc., 8
Wang Laboratories, Inc., III; 6 (upd.)
Warnaco Group Inc., The, 12; 46 (upd.)
Warner Communications Inc., II
Warner-Lambert Co., I; 10 (upd.)
Washington Companies, The, 33
Washington Federal, Inc., 17
Washington Football, Inc., 35
Washington Gas Light Company, 19
Washington Mutual, Inc., 17
Washington National Corporation, 12
Washington Natural Gas Company, 9
Washington Post Company, The, IV; 20 (upd.)
Washington Scientific Industries, Inc., 17
Washington Water Power Company, 6
Waste Connections, Inc., 46
Waste Holdings, Inc., 41
Waste Management, Inc., V
Water Pik Technologies, Inc., 34
Waterhouse Investor Services, Inc., 18
Waters Corporation, 43
Watkins-Johnson Company, 15
Watson Pharmaceuticals Inc., 16
Watson Wyatt Worldwide, 42
Watts Industries, Inc., 19
Waverly, Inc., 16
Wawa Inc., 17
Waxman Industries, Inc., 9
WD-40 Company, 18
Weatherford International, Inc., 39
Weber-Stephen Products Co., 40
Wegmans Food Markets, Inc., 9; 41 (upd.)
Weider Nutrition International, Inc., 29
Weight Watchers International Inc., 12; 33 (upd.)
Weiner's Stores, Inc., 33
Weirton Steel Corporation, IV; 26 (upd.)
Weis Markets, Inc., 15
Weitz Company, Inc., The, 42
Welbilt Corp., 19
Wellman, Inc., 8
WellPoint Health Networks Inc., 25
Wells Fargo & Company, II; 12 (upd.); 38 (upd.)
Wells Rich Greene BDDP, 6
Wells' Dairy, Inc., 36
Wells-Gardner Electronics Corporation, 43
Wendy's International, Inc., 8; 23 (upd.); 47 (upd.)
Wenner Media, Inc., 32
Werner Enterprises, Inc., 26
West Bend Co., 14
West Coast Entertainment Corporation, 29
West Corporation, 42
West Group, 34 (upd.)
West Marine, Inc., 17
West One Bancorp, 11
West Pharmaceutical Services, Inc., 42
West Point-Pepperell, Inc., 8
West Publishing Co., 7
Westaff Inc., 33
Westamerica Bancorporation, 17
Western Atlas Inc., 12

United States (*continued*)

Western Beef, Inc., 22
Western Company of North America, 15
Western Digital Corp., 25
Western Gas Resources, Inc., 45
Western Publishing Group, Inc., 13
Western Resources, Inc., 12
Western Wireless Corporation, 36
Westin Hotels and Resorts Worldwide, 9; 29 (upd.)
Westinghouse Electric Corporation, II; 12 (upd.)
Westmoreland Coal Company, 7
WestPoint Stevens Inc., 16
Westvaco Corporation, IV; 19 (upd.)
Westwood One, Inc., 23
Wet Seal, Inc., The, 18
Wetterau Incorporated, II
Weyco Group, Incorporated, 32
Weyerhaeuser Company, IV; 9 (upd.); 28 (upd.)
Wheaton Industries, 8
Wheelabrator Technologies, Inc., 6
Wheeling-Pittsburgh Corp., 7
Wherehouse Entertainment Incorporated, 11
Whirlpool Corporation, III; 12 (upd.)
White & Case LLP, 35
White Castle System, Inc., 12; 36 (upd.)
White Consolidated Industries Inc., 13
White Rose, Inc., 24
Whitman Corporation, 10 (upd.)
Whitman Education Group, Inc., 41
Whitney Holding Corporation, 21
Whittaker Corporation, I; 48 (upd.)
Whole Foods Market, Inc., 20
Wickes Inc., V; 25 (upd.)
Wild Oats Markets, Inc., 19; 41 (upd.)
Wildlife Conservation Society, 31
Willamette Industries, Inc., IV; 31 (upd.)
William Morris Agency, Inc., 23
Williams & Connolly LLP, 47
Williams Communications Group, Inc., 34
Williams Companies, Inc., The, IV; 31 (upd.)
Williams-Sonoma, Inc., 17; 44 (upd.)
Williamson-Dickie Manufacturing Company, 14; 45 (upd.)
Wilmington Trust Corporation, 25
Wilson Sonsini Goodrich & Rosati, 34
Wilson Sporting Goods Company, 24
Wilsons The Leather Experts Inc., 21
Wind River Systems, Inc., 37
Windmere Corporation, 16
Wine Group, Inc., The, 39
Winn-Dixie Stores, Inc., II; 21 (upd.)
Winnebago Industries Inc., 7; 27 (upd.)
WinsLoew Furniture, Inc., 21
Winston & Strawn, 35
Wisconsin Bell, Inc., 14
Wisconsin Central Transportation Corporation, 24
Wisconsin Dairies, 7
Wisconsin Energy Corporation, 6
Wisconsin Public Service Corporation, 9
Witco Corporation, I; 16 (upd.)
Wizards of the Coast Inc., 24
WLR Foods, Inc., 21
Wm. Wrigley Jr. Company, 7
WMS Industries, Inc., 15
WMX Technologies Inc., 17
Wolfgang Puck Food Company, Inc., The, 26
Wolohan Lumber Co., 19
Wolverine Tube Inc., 23
Wolverine World Wide Inc., 16
Wood-Mode, Inc., 23

Woodward Governor Company, 13; 49 (upd.)
Woolworth Corporation, V; 20 (upd.)
WordPerfect Corporation, 10
Working Assets Funding Service, 43
World Bank Group, 33
World Book, Inc., 12
World Color Press Inc., 12
World Duty Free Americas, Inc., 29 (upd.)
World Fuel Services Corporation, 47
World Wrestling Federation Entertainment, Inc., 32
World's Finest Chocolate Inc., 39
WorldCorp, Inc., 10
Worldwide Restaurant Concepts, Inc., 47
Worthington Foods, Inc., 14
Worthington Industries, Inc., 7; 21 (upd.)
WPL Holdings, Inc., 6
WTD Industries, Inc., 20
Wyant Corporation, 30
Wyle Electronics, 14
Wyman-Gordon Company, 14
Wynn's International, Inc., 33
Wyse Technology, Inc., 15
X-Rite, Inc., 48
Xerox Corporation, III; 6 (upd.); 26 (upd.)
Xilinx, Inc., 16
Yahoo! Inc., 27
Yankee Candle Company, Inc., The, 37
YankeeNets LLC, 35
Yellow Corporation, 14; 45 (upd.)
Yellow Freight System, Inc. of Delaware, V
YES! Entertainment Corporation, 26
YMCA of the USA, 31
YOCREAM International, Inc., 47
York International Corp., 13
York Research Corporation, 35
Young & Rubicam, Inc., I; 22 (upd.)
Young Broadcasting Inc., 40
Young Innovations, Inc., 44
Young's Market Company, LLC, 32
Younkers, Inc., 19
Youth Services International, Inc., 21
Yucaipa Cos., 17
YWCA of the United States, 45
Zale Corporation, 16; 40 (upd.)
Zany Brainy, Inc., 31
Zapata Corporation, 25
Zebra Technologies Corporation, 14
Zenith Data Systems, Inc., 10
Zenith Electronics Corporation, II; 13 (upd.); 34 (upd.)
Zero Corporation, 17
Ziebart International Corporation, 30
Ziegler Companies, Inc., The, 24
Ziff Communications Company, 12
Ziff Davis Media Inc., 36 (upd.)
Zila, Inc., 46
Zilog, Inc., 15
Zimmer Holdings, Inc., 45
Zion's Cooperative Mercantile Institution, 33
Zions Bancorporation, 12
Zippo Manufacturing Company, 18
Zoltek Companies, Inc., 37
Zondervan Publishing House, 24
Zoom Telephonics, Inc., 18
Zygo Corporation, 42
Zytec Corporation, 19

Venezuela

Cerveceria Polar, I
Petróleos de Venezuela S.A., IV

Wales

Hyder plc, 34

Iceland Group plc, 33
Kwik Save Group plc, 11

Zambia

Zambia Industrial and Mining Corporation Ltd., IV

NOTES ON CONTRIBUTORS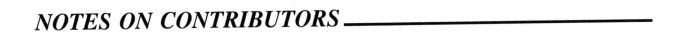

Notes on Contributors

BAXTER, Melissa Rigney. Indiana-based freelance writer.

BIANCO, David P. Freelance writer.

BROWN, Susan Windisch. Freelance writer and editor.

BRYNILDSSEN, Shawna. Freelance writer and editor based in Bloomington, Indiana.

COHEN, M. L. Novelist and freelance writer living in Paris.

COVELL, Jeffrey L. Freelance writer and corporate history contractor.

CULLIGAN, Susan B. Minnesota-based freelance writer.

DINGER, Ed. Freelance writer and editor based in Brooklyn, New York.

HEER-FORSBERG, Mary. Freelance writer in the Minneapolis area.

INGRAM, Frederick C. South Carolina-based business writer who has contributed to *GSA Business, Appalachian Trailway News,* the *Encyclopedia of Business,* the *Encyclopedia of Global Industries,* the *Encyclopedia of Consumer Brands,* and other regional and trade publications.

LORENZ, Sarah Ruth. Minnesota-based freelance writer.

MALLETT, Daryl F. Freelance writer, editor, actor; founder and owner of Angel Enterprises, Jacob's Ladder Books, and Dustbunny Productions.

MEYER, Steve. Freelance writer living in Missoula, Montana.

ROTHBURD, Carrie. Freelance writer and editor specializing in corporate profiles, academic texts, and academic journal articles.

SALAMIE, David E. Part-owner of InfoWorks Development Group, a reference publication development and editorial services company.

TRADII, Mary. Freelance writer based in Denver, Colorado.

UHLE, Frank. Ann Arbor-based freelance writer; movie projectionist, disc jockey, and staff member of *Psychotronic Video* magazine.

WALDEN, David M. Freelance writer and historian in Salt Lake City; adjunct history instructor at Salt Lake City Community College.

WOODWARD, A. Freelance writer.